SCOTT®

CATALOGUE TABS

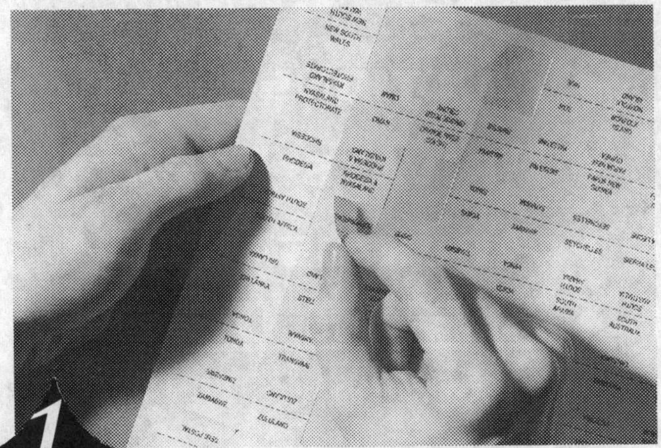

1 Select and peel tab off sheet.

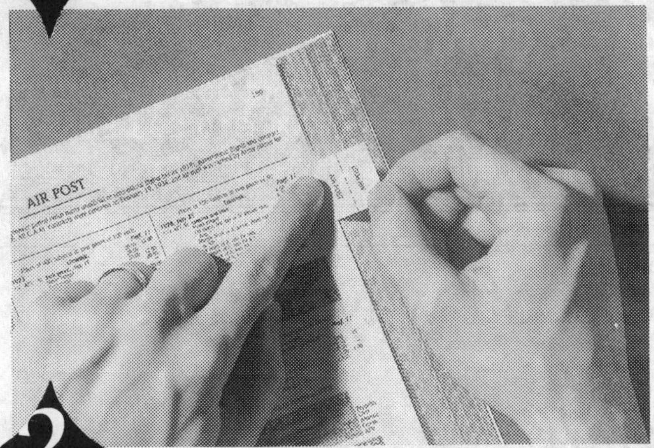

2 Affix a portion of the tab to the appropriate page. Fold tab in half at the dotted line.

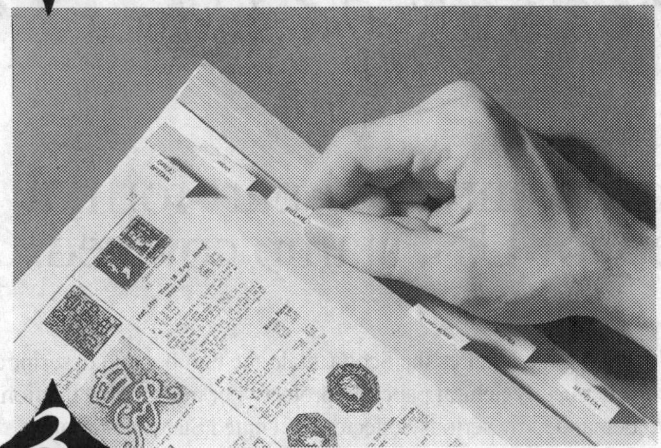

3 Use tabs to reference catalogue listings. Blank tabs also included.

Scott Catalogue Tabs make looking up listings as easy as 1-2-3!

Tabs are sold for each volume of the catalogue, plus the Specialized and the Classic.

Item No.		Price
CLGT1A	Volume 1A	$2.95
CLGT1B	Volume 1B	$2.95
CLGT2	Volume 2	$2.95
CLGT3	Volume 3	$2.95
CLGT4	Volume 4	$2.95
CLGT5	Volume 5	$2.95
CLGT6	U.S. Specialized	$2.95
CLGTC	Classic	$2.95

FOR PRODUCT AND ORDERING INFORMATION CALL

1-800-572-6885

Available from your favorite dealer or direct from:

Scott Publishing Co.
P.O. Box 828
Sidney OH 45365

1996
Standard Postage Stamp Catalogue

ONE HUNDRED AND FIFTY-SECOND EDITION IN SIX VOLUMES

VOLUME 1A

UNITED STATES
and Affiliated Territories
UNITED NATIONS
CANADA
& BRITISH AMERICA

VICE PRESIDENT/PUBLISHER	Stuart J. Morrissey
EDITOR	James E. Kloetzel
ASSOCIATE EDITOR	William W. Cummings
VALUING EDITOR	Martin J. Frankevicz
NEW ISSUES EDITOR	David C. Akin
COMPUTER CONTROL COORDINATOR	Denise Oder
VALUING ANALYST	Jose R. Capote
EDITORIAL ASSISTANTS	Judith E. Bertrand, Beth Brown
CONTRIBUTING EDITOR	Joyce Nelson
ART/PRODUCTION DIRECTOR	Janine C. S. Apple
PRODUCTION COORDINATOR	Nancy S. Martin
PRODUCTION ARTIST	Cinda McAlexander
MARKETING/SALES DIRECTOR	William Fay
ADVERTISING	David Lodge
CIRCULATION/PRODUCT PROMOTION MANAGER	Tim Wagner

Scott Publishing Co.

911 Vandemark Road, Sidney, OH 45365

A division of AMOS PRESS, INC., publishers of *Linn's Stamp News, Coin World, Cars & Parts* magazine, *Moneycard Collector* and *The Sidney Daily News.*

Table of Contents

See Volume 1B for the British Commonwealth of Nations other than British America.

See Volumes 2, 3, 4 and 5 for nations of Africa, Asia, Europe, Latin America and their affiliated territories.

Copyright Notice

Trademark Notice

ISBN 0-89487-208-7

Library of Congress Card No. 2-3301

Scott Publishing Co.

SCOTT

911 VANDEMARK ROAD, SIDNEY, OHIO 45365 513-498-0802

Dear Catalogue User:

At the beginning of each year, we get together and ask ourselves a very basic question. Why should someone buy the next edition of the Scott Catalogue? After all, in many cases a catalogue user just spent $198 for the previous edition.

What have we changed, added or improved to earn your purchase of the 1996 catalogue?

There are indeed many, many changes and improvements. So numerous I'm almost not sure where to begin. In the past I've used an imaginary snappy reporter or energetic talk show host to ask a few questions. At a recent stamp show a wag collector asked if I was going to have a man from outer space do the honors this year. Not necessary. This time I'll just ask myself the questions.

However, before I get carried away, let me remind you that Volume 1 has split. Volume 1A contains United States, United Nations and British Commonwealth Countries of North and South America and the Caribbean. The balance of British Commonwealth countries can be found in Volume 1B.

There is a special section, in this volume only, called "The Scott Annual." It contains a selection of the best articles that have appeared over the last few years in *Scott Stamp Monthly* and other publications. We've chosen World War II as a theme, although not all the pieces are related to the war.

Tell us something out of the ordinary.

I'll tell you, but you won't believe it until you read it. ***And I dare you to read it.*** I'm talking about the complete, revised and re-written catalogue introduction.

The new introduction is a pleasure to read and includes updated information on printing methods, separation methods and tagging.

Let's get down to the nitty gritty. Where are U.S. values in 1A headed?

United States is up, some of it way up and many stamps are modestly up.

There are extensive changes since the *U.S. Specialized*. For example, the 1847 10-cent black, Scott 2, increases $50 in used condition to $1,050. The change follows a $100 increase that appeared in the 1995 *U.S. Specialized*.

Some other early issues show modest value gains, especially in the used column. The 1875 re-issues of the 1869 pictorial definitives, Scott 123-133a, almost all move up in used condition. Strong upward movement is seen in the used values of the 1894 First Bureau issue, Scott 246-263.

Many 1908-20 Washington-Franklin issues show value increases in unused condition, and some of the Kansas and Nebraska issues of 1929 show gains, also in unused condition.

Large increases are to be noted in the earlier postal stationery cut squares. This is true not only in the more expensive items, but also in some of the lower-valued issues. The 1860 10¢ green cut square, Scott U32, jumps to $1,200 unused, from $1,100 in the 1995 Specialized and $1,000 in the 1995 Volume 1.

Duck stamps continue to show strength, especially the unused $3 values from 1959-71. The most dramatic increase is seen for the 1959 $3 Labrador Retriever and Mallard stamp, Scott RW26, which moves to $80 unused, from $65.

In United Nations, the 1955 10th Anniversary souvenir sheet, Scott 38, stands at $110 unused. There are many other changes in U.N. values, both up and down, but all are of a modest amount.

And what about values for British Commonwealth countries in Volume 1A?

In Canada, a number of classics record value changes. Scott 3, the 1851 12p Victoria, falls to $27,500 used, from $30,000. However, the 1855 10p Cartier, Scott 7, jumps to $4,500 unused from $4,000.

The 1951 Fishing $1, Scott 302, slips to $47.50 unused and $10 used, from $52.50 unused and $11.50 used. The 1963 $1 Export, Scott 411, slides to $12 unused and $1.40 used, from $15 unused and $1.65 used. The 1975 and 1976 $1 and $2 sets for the Montreal Olympics, Scott 656-657 and 687-688, drop sharply. However, some of the perforation varieties of the 1987-91 definitives show significant increases.

In Bermuda, a number of early stamps show strong increases and decreases. Scott 1, the 1865 dull rose 1p Victoria with Crown and CC watermark, rises to $37.50 unused, from $30. Scott 28 and 29, the 1/2p and 1p values of the 1902-03 Dry Dock set, each push up to $6.75 unused, from $4.75. However, the 1-pound George V, Scott 54, sags to $350 unused and used from $400 unused and used. Most stamps from 1985-87 show sharp increases.

Many changes are found in Cayman Islands and Montserrat. Most changes in the Caymans affect items issued from 1959-83 and virtually all are decreases. In Montserrat, decreases are recorded for many sets of the 1970s and 1980s.

Have you provided any new information to enlighten collectors on the relationship between value and condition for 19th-Century U.S. stamps?

Comprehensive listings for stamps in never-hinged condition now begin with the 1890-93 Bank Note definitives, Scott 219-229. An important informational note concerning values for stamps in never-hinged condition has been added at this point explaining that the premium for never hinged as a percentage of value will be larger for stamps in very fine, extremely fine or superb grades, and smaller for poor to fine examples. This note, which is expanded upon in the catalogue, should be helpful to both collectors and dealers, not only in understanding Scott valuing, but as an aid in valuing stamps that fall outside of the Scott fine-very fine valuing guideline.

Are you saving U.S. editorial revisions for the Specialized Catalogue?

No. Here are just a few examples of U.S. editorial changes:

A new minor number variety of the 5¢ New York Postmaster Provisional on blue paper has been added. This stamp, with an "RHM" signature, appears as Scott 9X2a.

Number changes affect booklet and coil issues from the 1990s between Scott 2594 and 2608. Complete catalogue number changes may be found at the end of the Volume 1A listings.

A footnote has been included with the listing of the 1923 1¢ green rotary issue, Scott 596, clearly indicating that the source of this stamp is sheet waste rather than coil waste.

And what about editorial improvements in British Commonwealth countries in Volume 1A?

More values for stamps in never-hinged condition have been added to listings found before breakpoints for never-hinged stamps in Barbados, British Honduras, Canada, Montserrat, St. Kitts-Nevis and the Virgin Islands. The added listings for never-hinged stamps now start in Canada with the 1912-25 George V set; in Montserrat with the 1932 Tercentenary set; in Barbados, British Honduras and Virgin Islands with the 1935 Silver Jubilees; and in St. Kitts-Nevis with the 1937 Coronation set.

A note has been added stating that values for Canada Scott 14-20 are for copies with perforations touching the design. A note in Dominica has been added stating that all copies of Scott 14 may have pin marks as a result of the surcharging process.

Anything else?

Ryukyu Islands have moved to Volume 1A from Volume 5. Ryukyu Islands were under U.S. administration from the end of World War II until 1972 when the Islands reverted to Japan. The Ryukyu Island listings can be found in this volume following Puerto Rico.

Stuart Morrissey

Stuart Morrissey/Publisher

Acknowledgments

Our appreciation and gratitude go to the following individuals and organizations who have assisted us in preparing information included in the 1996 Scott Catalogues. Some helpers prefer anonymity. These individuals have generously shared their stamp knowledge with others through the medium of the Scott Catalogue.

Those who follow provided information that is in addition to the hundreds of dealer price lists and advertisements and scores of auction catalogues and realizations which were used in producing the Catalogue Values. It is from those noted here that we have been able to obtain information on items not normally seen in published lists and advertisements. Support from these people of course goes beyond data leading to Catalogue Values, for they also are key to editorial changes.

George F. Ackermann
A. R. Allison
B. J. Ammel
Mike Armus
Don Bakos
Jules K. Beck
Vladimir Berrio-Lemm
Kenneth R. Berry
John Birkinbine II
John R. Boker, Jr.
George W. Brett
Roger Brody
William C. Brooks VI
Randall Brooksbank
Michael Bryne
A. Bryan Camarda
Nathan Carlin
Dr. Herman J. Cestero, Jr.
E. J. Chamberlin
Richard A. Champagne
Andrew Cronin
William T. Crowe
Thomas De Luca
Dan Demetriade
Brian Dias
Harry Dober
Rich Drews
Bob Dumaine
William S. Dunn
Harry A. Eisenstein
J. A. Farrington
Leon Finik
Henry Fisher
William Fletcher
Joseph E. Foley
Marvin Frey
Richard Friedberg
D. Scott Gallagher
Eugene A. Garrett
Peter Georgiadis
Brian M. Green
Henry Hahn
Erich E. Hamm
Dr. James B. Helme
Clifford O. Herrick
Lee H. Hill, Jr.
Dr. Eugene Holmok
Rollin C. Huggins, Jr.
W. Wilson Hulme II
Clyde Jennings
Jack Jonza
Henry Karen
Stanford M. Katz
Dr. James Kerr
William Langs
Ken Lawrence
Pedro Llach
David MacDonnell
Robert L. Markovits
F. Brian Marshall
Clyde R. Maxwell
Timothy M. McRee
Dr. Hector Mena
Giorgio Migliavacca
Jack Molesworth
William E. Mooz
Gary M. Morris
Peter Mosiondz, Jr.
Bruce M. Moyer
Jack Nalbandian
James Natale
Robert Odenweller
Victor Ostolaza
Sheldon Paris
John E. Pearson
Vernon Pickering
Stanley M. Piller
Jon Rose
Richard H. Salz
Byron Sandfield
Jacques C. Schiff, Jr.
F. Burton Sellers
Richard Simchak
Dr. Hubert Skinner
Richard Stambaugh
R. J. Thoden
Scott Trepel
Ming W. Tsang
James O. Vadeboncoeur
William R. Wallace
Jerome S. Wagshal
Daniel C. Warren
Richard A. Washburn
Stephen S. Washburne
Giana Wayman
Larry S. Weiss
Nelson A. L. Weller
Ernest C. Wilkins
Greg Winston
Clarke Yarbrough
Val Zabijaka
Nathan Zankel

American Air Mail Society
Stephen Reinhard, PO Box 110,
Mineola, NY 11501

American Philatelic Society
PO Box 8000, State College, PA 16803

American Revenue Association
Bruce Miller, Suite 332,
701 South First Ave.,
Arcadia, CA 91006

American Stamp Dealers' Association
3 School St., Glen Cove, NY 11542

American Topical Association
PO Box 630, Johnstown, PA 15907

Booklet Collectors Club
James Natale, PO Box 2461,
Cinnaminson, NJ 08077-5461

Bureau Issues Association
George V.H. Godin, PO Box 23707,
Belleville, IL 62223

Confederate Stamp Alliance
Richard L. Calhoun,
1749 W. Golf Rd., Suite 366,
Mt. Prospect, IL 60056

Errors, Freaks, and Oddities Collectors Club
Jim McDevitt, 1903 Village Road West,
Norwood, MA 02062-2516

International Society of Worldwide Stamp Collectors
Carol Cervenka, Route 1 Box 69A,
Caddo Mills, TX 75135

Junior Philatelists of America
Sally Horn, PO Box 850,
Boalsburg, PA 16827-0850

No-Value-Identified Collectors Club
Albert Sauvanet, Le Clos Royal B,
Boulevard des Pas Enchantes,
44230 St. Sebastien-sur-Loire, France

Plate Number Coil Collectors Club
Joann Lenz, 37211 Alper Drive,
Sterling Heights, MI 48312-2203

Precancel Stamp Society
1750 Skippack Pk. #1603,
Center Square, PA 19422

Royal Philatelic Society
D. J. Springbett, 41 Devonshire Place,
London, U.K. W1N 1PE

Royal Philatelic Society of Canada
PO Box 929, Station Q,
Toronto ON, CANADA M4T 2P1

United Postal Stationery Society
Joann Thomas, PO Box 48,
Redlands, CA 92373

US Philatelic Classics Society
Patricia S. Walker, Briarwood,
Lisbon, MD 21765

US Possessions Philatelic Society
Charles A. Richmond, PO Box 26724,
Busch Finance Station,
Columbus, OH 43226

Society for the New Republics of the Former USSR (Armenia, etc.)
Michael Padwee, 163 Joralemon St.,
PO Box 1520,
Brooklyn, NY 11201-1520

American Belgian Philatelic Society
Kenneth L. Costilow,
621 Virginius Dr.,
Virginia Beach, VA 23452-4417

Belize Philatelic Study Circle
Charles R. Gambill, 730 Collingswood,
Corpus Christi, TX 78412

Bermuda Collectors Society
Thomas J. McMahon, 86 Nash Road,
Purdys, NY 10578

Brazil Philatelic Association
Kurt Ottenheimer,
462 West Walnut St.,
Long Beach, NY 11561

British Caribbean Philatelic Study Group
Gale J. Raymond, PO Box 35695,
Houston, TX 77235

British North America Philatelic Society
Jerome C. Jarnick, 108 Duncan Drive,
Troy, MI 48098

Burma Philatelic Study Circle
A. Meech, 7208 91st Ave.,
Edmonton, AB, CANADA T6B 0R8

Canal Zone Study Group
Richard H. Salz, 60 27th Ave.,
San Francisco, CA 94121

China Stamp Society
Paul H. Gault, 140 West 18th Ave.,
Columbus, OH 43210

COPAPHIL (Colombia & Panama)
PO Box 2245, El Cajon, CA 92021

Society of Costa Rica Collectors
Dr. Hector Mena, PO Box 14831,
Baton Rouge, LA 70808

Croatian Philatelic Society (Croatia and other Balkan areas)
Eck Spahich, 1512 Lancelot Rd.,
Borger, TX 79007

Cuban Philatelic Society of America
PO Box 450207,
Miami, FL 33245-0207

Society for Czechoslovak Philately
Robert T. Cossaboom, PO Box 332,
Scott AFB, IL 62225

Ethiopian Philatelic Society
Huguette Gagnon, PO Box 8110-45,
Blaine, WA 98230

Falkland Islands Philatelic Study Group
James Driscoll, PO Box 172,
South Dennis, NJ 08245

France & Colonies Philatelic Society
Walter Parshall, 103 Spruce St.,
Bloomfield, NJ 07003

Germany Philatelic Society
PO Box 779,
Arnold, MD 21012-4779

GDR Study Group of German Philatelic Society
Ken Lawrence, PO Box 8040,
State College, PA 16803-8040

Great Britain Collectors Club
Frank J. Koch, PO Box 309,
Batavia, OH 45103-0309

Hellenic Philatelic Society of America (Greece & related areas)
Dr. Nicholas Asimakopulos,
541 Cedar Hill Ave., Wyckoff, NJ 07481

International Society of Guatemala Collectors
Mrs. Mae Vignola, 105 22nd Ave.,
San Francisco, CA 94116

Haiti Philatelic Society
Dwight Bishop, 16434 Shamhart Dr.,
Granada Hills, CA 91344

Hong Kong Stamp Society
Dr. An-Min Chung, 120 Deerfield Rd.,
Broomall, PA 19008

Hong Kong Collectors Club
Nikolai Lau, 6021 Yonge Street #888,
North York, ON, CANADA M2M 3W2

Hungary Philatelic Society
Thomas Phillips, PO Box 1162,
Samp Mortar Sta., Fairfield, CT 06432

India Study Circle
John Warren, PO Box 70775,
Washington, DC 20024

Society of Indochina Philatelists
Paul Blake, 1466 Hamilton Way,
San Jose, CA 95125

Iran Philatelic Circle
A. John Ultee, 816 Gwynne Ave.,
Waynesboro, VA 22980

Eire Philatelic Association (Ireland)
Michael J. Conway, 74 Woodside Circle,
Fairfield, CT 06430

Society of Israel Philatelists
Howard D. Chapman,
28650 Settlers Lane,
Pepper Pike, OH 44124

Italy and Colonies Study Circle
David F. Emery, PO Box 86,
Philipsburg, NJ 08865

International Society for Japanese Philately
Kenneth Kamholz, PO Box 1283,
Haddonfield, NJ 08033

Korea Stamp Society
William A. Matthews, PO Box 15306,
Columbus, OH 43215

Latin American Philatelic Society
Piet Steen, PO Box 6420,
Hinton, AB, CANADA T7V 1X7

Liberian Philatelic Society
William Thomas Lockard, PO Box 267,
Wellston, OH 45692

Plebiscite-Memel-Saar Study Group
Clay Wallace, 158 Arapaho Circle,
San Ramon, CA 94583

Mexico-Elmhurst Philatelic Society International
William E. Shelton, PO Box 39838,
San Antonio, TX 78218

Nepal & Tibet Philatelic Study Group
Roger D. Skinner,
1020 Covington Road,
Los Altos, CA 94022

American Society of Netherlands Philately
Jan Enthoven,
W6428 Riverview Drive,
Onalaska, WI 54650

Nicaragua Study Group
Clyde R. Maxwell, Airport Plaza,
2041 Business Center Drive,
Suite 101, Irvine, CA 92715

Society of Australasian Specialists/Oceania
Henry Bateman, PO Box 4862,
Monroe, LA 71211

Orange Free State Study Circle
J. R. Stroud, 28 Oxford St.,
Burnham-on-sea,
Somerset, U.K. TA8 1LQ

International Philippine Philatelic Society
Eugene A. Garrett, 446 Stratford Ave.,
Elmhurst, IL 60126-4123

American Society of Polar Philatelists (Antarctic areas)
S.H. Jacobson, PO Box 945,
Skokie, IL 60077

Pitcairn Islands Study Group
Nelson A.L. Weller,
2940 Wesleyan Lane,
Winston-Salem, NC 27106

Polonus Philatelic Society (Poland)
864 N. Ashland Ave.,
Chicago, IL 60622

International Society for Portuguese Philately
Michael Bryne, Adirondack Stamps,
PO Box 13100,
Mexico Beach, FL 32410

Rhodesian Study Circle
William R. Wallace, PO Box 16381,
San Francisco, CA 94116

Romanian Chapter of Croatian Philatelic Society
Dan Demetriade, PO Box 10182,
Detroit, MI 48210

Rossica Society of Russian Philately
Gary Combs, 8241 Chalet Ct.,
Millersville, MD 21108

Canadian Society of Russian Philately
Andrew Cronin,
PO Box 5722, Station A,
Toronto, ON, CANADA M5W 1P2

Ryukyu Philatelic Specialist Society
Carmine J. DiVincenzo, PO Box 381,
Clayton, CA 94517-0381

St. Helena, Ascension & Tristan Society
Dr. Russell V. Skavaril,
222 East Torrance Road,
Columbus, OH 43214-3834

Associated Collectors of El Salvador
Jeff Brasor, 7365 NW 68th Way,
Pompano Beach, FL 33067-3918

Sarawak Specialists' Society
Art Bunce, PO Box 2516,
Escondido, CA 92033

Arabian Philatelic Association
ARAMCO Box 1929,
Dhahran 31311, SAUDI ARABIA

Scandinavia Collectors Club
Robert W. Lang, PO Box 125,
Newark, DE 19715-0125

Philatelic Society for Greater Southern Africa
William C. Brooks VI, PO Box 2698,
San Bernardino, CA 92406-2698

Slovakia Stamp Society
Jack Benchik, PO Box 555,
Notre Dame, IN 46556

American Helvetia Philatelic Society (Switzerland, Liechtenstein)
Richard T. Hall, PO Box 666,
Manhattan Beach, CA 90267-0666

Society for Thai Philately
H.R. Blakeney, PO Box 25644,
Oklahoma City, OK 73125

Tonga/Tin Can Mail Study Circle
Paul Stanton, PO Box 700257,
Plymouth, MI 48170

Turkey and Ottoman Philatelic Society
Gary F. Paiste, 4249 Berritt St.,
Fairfax, VA 22030

Tuvalu & Kiribati Philatelic Society
Frank Caprio, PO Box 218071,
Nashville, TN 37221

Ukrainian Philatelic & Numismatic Society
Val Zabijaka, PO Box 3711,
Silver Spring, MD 20918

United Nations Philatelists
Helen Benedict,
408 S. Orange Grove Blvd.,
Pasadena, CA 91105

Vatican Philatelic Society
Louis Padavan, PO Box 127,
Remsenburg, NY 11960

Yugoslavia Study Group
Michael Lenard, 1514 North 3rd Ave.,
Wausau, WI 54401

Catalogue Information

Catalogue Value

The Scott Catalogue value is a retail value; that is, an amount you could expect to pay for a stamp in a grade of Fine to Very Fine with no faults. Any exceptions to the grade valued will be noted in the text. The value listed for any given stamp is a reference that reflects recent actual dealer selling prices for that item.

Dealer retail price lists, public auction results, published prices in advertising and individual solicitation of retail prices from dealers, collectors and specialty organizations have been used in establishing the values found in this catalogue. Scott Publishing Co. values stamps, but Scott is not a company engaged in the business of buying and selling stamps as a dealer.

Use this catalogue as a guide for buying and selling. The actual price you pay for a stamp may be higher or lower than the catalogue value because of many different factors, including the amount of personal service a dealer offers, or increased or decreased interest in the country or topic represented by a stamp or set. An item may occasionally be offered at a lower price as a "loss leader," or as part of a special sale. You also may obtain an item inexpensively at public auction because of little interest at that time or as part of a large lot.

Copies of stamps that are of a lesser grade than Fine to Very Fine, or those with condition problems, trade at lower prices than those given in this catalogue. Stamps of exceptional quality in both grade and condition often command higher prices than those listed.

Values for pre-1900 unused issues are for stamps with at least most of their original gum. Later issues are assumed to have full original gum. From breakpoints in most countries' listings, stamps are valued as never hinged, due to the wide availability of stamps in that condition. These notations are prominently placed in the listings and in the counrty information preceding the listings. Some countries also feature listings with dual values for hinged and never-hinged stamps.

Grade

A stamp's grade and condition are crucial to its value. The accompanying illustrations show examples of Fine-Very Fine stamps from different time periods, along with examples of stamps in Fine and Very Fine grades as points of reference.

FINE stamps have designs that are noticeably off center on two sides. Imperforate stamps may have small margins, and earlier issues may show the design touching one edge of the stamp. For perforated stamps, perfs may barely clear the design on one side. Used stamps may have heavier than usual cancellations.

FINE-VERY FINE stamps may be somewhat off center on one side, or slightly off center on two sides. Imperforate stamps will have two margins of at least normal size, and the design will not touch any edge. For perforated stamps, the perfs are well clear of the design, but are still noticeably off center. *However, early issues of a country may be printed in such a way that the design naturally is very close to the edges.* Used stamps will not have a cancellation that detracts from the design. This is the grade used to establish Scott Catalogue values.

VERY FINE stamps may be slightly off center on one side, but the design will be well clear of the edge. The stamp will present a nice, balanced appearance. Imperforate stamps will have three normal-sized margins. Used stamps will have light or otherwise neat cancellations.

Condition

Grade addresses only centering and (for used stamps) cancellation. *Condition* refers to factors other than grade that affect a stamp's desirability.

Factors that can increase the value of a stamp include exceptionally wide margins, particularly fresh color, the presence of selvage, and plate or die varieties. Unusual cancels on used stamps (particularly those of the 19th century) can greatly enhance their value as well.

Factors other that faults that decrease the value of a stamp include loss of original gum, regumming, a hinge remnant or foreign object adhering to the gum, natural inclusions, straight edges, and markings or notations applied by collectors or dealers.

Faults include missing pieces, tears, pin or other holes, surface scuffs, thin spots, creases, toning, short or pulled perforations, clipped perforations, oxidation or other forms of color changelings, soiling, stains, and such man-made changes as reperforations or the chemical removal or lightening of a cancellation.

Scott Publishing Co. recognizes that there is no formally enforced grading scheme for postage stamps, and that the final price you pay or obtain for a stamp will be determined by individual agreement at the time of transaction.

Catalogue Listing Policy

It is the intent of Scott Publishing Co. to list all postage stamps of the world in the *Scott Standard Postage Stamp Catalogue.* The only strict criteria for listing is that stamps be decreed legal for postage by the issuing country. Whether the primary intent of issuing a given stamp or set was for sale to postal patrons or to stamp collectors is not part of our listing criteria. Scott's role is to provide basic comprehensive postage stamp information. It is up to each stamp collector to choose which items to include in a collection.

It is Scott's objective to seek reasons why a stamp should be listed, rather than why it should not. Nevertheless, there are certain types of items that will not be listed. These include the following:

1. Unissued items that are not officially distributed or released by the issuing postal authority. Even if such a stamp is "accidentally" distributed to the philatelic or even postal market, it remains unissued. If such items are officially issued at a later date by the country, they will be listed. Unissued items consist of those that have been printed and then held from sale for reasons such as change in government, errors found on stamps or something deemed objectionable about a stamp subject or design.

2. Stamps "issued" by non-existent postal entities or fantasy countries, such as Nagaland, Occusi-Ambeno, Staffa, Sedang, Torres Straits and others.

3. Semi-official or unofficial items not required for postage. Examples include items issued by private agencies for their own express services. When such items are required for delivery, or are valid as prepayment of postage, they are listed.

4. Local stamps issued for local use only. Postage stamps issued by governments specifically for "domestic" use, such as Haiti Scott 219-228, or the United States non-denominated stamps, are not considered to be locals, since they are valid for postage throughout the country of origin.

5. Items not valid for postal use. For example, a few countries have issued souvenir sheets that are not valid for postage. This area also includes a number of worldwide charity labels (some denominated) that do not pay postage.

6. Intentional varieties, such as imperforate stamps that look like their perforated counterparts and are issued in very small quantities. These are often controlled issues intended for speculation.

7. Items distributed by the issuing government only to a limited group, such as a stamp club or a single stamp dealer, and later brought to market at inflated prices. These items normally will be included in a footnote.

The fact that a stamp has been used successfully as postage, even on international mail, is not in itself sufficient proof that it was legitimately issued. Numerous examples of so-called stamps from non-existent countries are known to have been used to post letters that have successfully passed through the international mail system.

There are certain items that are subject to interpretation. When a stamp falls outside our specifications, it may be listed along with a cautionary footnote.

A number of factors are considered in our approach to analyzing how a stamp is listed. The following list of factors is presented to share with you, the catalogue user, the complexity of the listing process.

Additional printings — "Additional printings" of a previously issued stamp may range from an item that is totally different to cases where it is impossible to differentiate from the original. At least a minor number (a small-letter suffix) is assigned if there is a distinct change in stamp shade, noticeably redrawn design, or a significantly different perforation measurement. A major number (numeral or numeral and capital-letter combination) is assigned if the editors feel the "additional printing" is sufficiently different from the original that it constitutes a different issue.

Commemoratives — Where practical, commemoratives with the same theme are placed in a set. For example, the U.S. Civil War Centenniel set of 1961-65 and the Constitution Bicentennial series of 1989-90 appear as sets. Countries such as Japan and Korea issue such material on a regular basis, with an announced, or at least predictable, number of stamps known in advance. Occasionally, however, stamp sets that were released over a period of years have been separated. Appropriately placed footnotes will guide you to each set's continuation.

Definitive sets — Blocks of numbers generally have been reserved for definitive sets, based on previous experience with any given country. If a few more stamps were issued in a set than originally expected, they often have been inserted into the original set with a capital-letter suffix, such as U.S. Scott 1059A. If it appears that many more stamps than the originally allotted block will be released before the set is completed, a new block of numbers will be reserved, with the original one being closed off. In some cases, such as the British Machin Head series or the U.S. Transportation and Great Americans series, several blocks of numbers exist. Appropriately placed footnotes will guide you to each set's continuation.

New country — Membership in the Universal Postal Union is not a consideration for listing status or order of placement within the catalogue. The index will tell you in what volume or page number the listings begin.

"No release date" items — The amount of information available for any given stamp issue varies greatly from country to country and even from time to time. Extremely comprehensive information about new stamps is available from some countries well before the stamps are released. By contrast some countries do not provide information about stamps or release dates. Most countries, however, fall between these extremes. A country may provide denominations or subjects of stamps from upcoming issues that are not issued as planned. Sometimes, philatelic agencies, those private firms hired to represent countries, add these later-issued items to sets well after the formal release date. This time period can range from weeks to years. If these items were officially released by the country, they will be added to the appropriate spot in the set. In many cases, the specific release date of a stamp or set of stamps may never be known.

Overprints — The color of an overprint is always noted if it is other than black. Where more than one color of ink has been used on overprints of a single set, the color used is noted. Early overprint and surcharge illustrations were altered to prevent their use by forgers.

Se-tenants — Connected stamps of differing features (se-tenants) will be listed in the format most commonly collected. This includes pairs, blocks or larger multiples. Se-tenant units are not always symmetrical. An example is Australia Scott 508, which is a block of seven stamps. If the stamps are primarily collected as a unit, the major number may be assigned to the multiple, with minors going to each component stamp. In cases where continuous-design or other unit se-tenants will receive significant postal use, each stamp is given a major Scott number listing. This includes issues from the United States, Canada, Germany and Great Britain, for example.

Understanding the Listings

On the following page is an enlarged "typical" listing from this catalogue. Below are detailed explanations of each of the highlighted parts of the listing.

1 **Scott number** — Scott catalogue numbers are used to identify specific items when buying, selling or trading stamps. Each listed postage stamp from every country has a unique Scott catalogue number. Therefore, Germany Scott 99, for example, can only refer to a single stamp. Although the Scott catalogue usually lists stamps in chronological order by date of issue, there are exceptions. When a country has issued a set of stamps over a period of time, those stamps within the set are kept together without regard to date of issue. This follows the normal collecting approach of keeping stamps in their natural sets.

When a country issues a set of stamps over a period of time, a group of consecutive catalogue numbers is reserved for the stamps in that set, as issued. If that group of numbers proves to be too few, capital-letter suffixes, such as "A" or "B," may be added to existing numbers to create enough catalogue numbers to cover all items in the set. A capital-letter suffix indicates a major Scott catalogue number listing. Scott uses a suffix letter only once. Therefore, a catalogue number listing with a capital-letter prefix will not also be found with the same letter (lower case) used as a minor-letter listing. If there is a Scott 16A in a set, for example, there will not also be a Scott 16a.

Suffix letters are not cumulative. A minor variety of Scott 16A would be Scott 16b, not Scott 16Ab. Any exceptions, such as Great Britain Scott 358cp, are clearly indicated.

There are times when a reserved block of Scott catalogue numbers is too large for a set, leaving some numbers unused. Such gaps in the numbering sequence also occur when the catalogue editors move an item's listing elsewhere or have removed it entirely from the catalogue. Scott does not attempt to account for every possible number, but rather attempts to assure that each stamp is assigned its own number.

Scott numbers designating regular postage normally are only numerals. Scott numbers for other types of stamps, such as air post, semi-postal, postal tax, postage due, occupation and others have a prefix consisting of one or more capital letters or a combination of numerals and capital letters.

2 **Illustration number** — Illustration or design-type numbers are used to identify each catalogue illustration. For most sets, the lowest face-value stamp is shown. It then serves as an example of the basic design approach for other stamps not illustrated. Where more than one stamp use the same illustration number, but have differences in design, the design paragraph or the description line clearly indicates the design on each stamp not illustrated. Where there are both vertical and horizontal designs in a set, a single illustration may be used, with the exceptions noted in the design paragraph or description line.

When an illustration is followed by a lower-case letter in parentheses, such as "A2(b)," the trailing letter indicates which overprint or surcharge illustration applies.

Illustrations normally are 75 percent of the original size of the stamp. An effort has been made to note all illustrations not illustrated at that percentage. Virtually all souvenir sheet illustrations are reduced even more. Overprints and surcharges are shown at 100 percent of their original size, unless otherwise noted. In some cases, the illustration will be placed above the set, between listings or omitted completely. Overprint and surcharge illustrations are not placed in this catalogue for purposes of expertizing stamps.

3 **Paper color** — The color of a stamp's paper is noted in italic type when the paper used is not white.

4 **Listing styles** — There are two principal types of catalogue listings: major and minor.

Major listings are in a larger type style than minor listings. The catalogue number is a numeral that can be found with or without a capital-letter suffix, and with or without a prefix.

Minor listings are in a smaller type style and have a small-letter suffix or (if the listing immediately follows that of the major number) may show only the letter. These listings identify a variety of the major item. Examples include perforation, color, watermark or printing method differences, multiples (some souvenir sheets, booklet panes and se-tenant combinations), and singles of multiples.

Examples of major number listings include 16, 28A, B97, C13A, 10N5, and 10N6A. Examples of minor numbers are 16a and C13b.

5 **Basic information about a stamp or set** — Introducing each stamp issue is a small section (usually a line listing) of basic information about a stamp or set. This section normally includes the date of issue, method of printing, perforation, watermark and, sometimes, some additional information of note. *Printing method, perforation and watermark apply to the following sets until a change is noted.* Stamps created by overprinting or surcharging previous issues are assumed to have the same perforation, watermark and printing method as the original. Dates of issue are as precise as Scott is able to confirm and often reflect the dates on first-day covers, rather than the actual date of release.

6 **Denomination** — This normally refers to the face value of the stamp; that is, the cost of the unused stamp at the post office at the time of issue. When a denomination is shown in parentheses, it does not appear on the stamp. This includes the non-denominated stamps of the United States, Brazil and Great Britain, for example.

7 **Color or other description** — This area provides information to solidify identification of a stamp. In many recent cases, a description of the stamp design appears in this space, rather than a listing of colors.

8 **Year of issue** — In stamp sets that have been released in a period that spans more than a year, the number shown in parentheses is the year that stamp first appeared. Stamps without a date appeared during the first year of the issue. Dates are not always given for minor varieties.

9 **Value unused and Value used** — The Scott catalogue values are based on stamps that are in a grade of Fine-Very Fine unless stated otherwise. Unused values refer to items that have not seen postal, revenue or any other duty for which they were intended. Pre-1900 unused stamps that were issued with gum must have at least most of their original gum. Later issues are assumed to have full original gum. From breakpoints specified in most countries' listings, stamps are valued as never hinged. Stamps issued without gum are noted. Modern issues with PVA or other synthetic adhesives may appear ungummed. Self-adhesive stamps are valued as appearing undisturbed on their original backing paper. For a more detailed explanation of these values, please see the "Catalogue Value," "Condition" and "Understanding Valuing Notations" elsewhere in this introduction.

In some cases, where used stamps are more valuable than unused stamps, the value is for an example with a contemporaneous cancel, rather than a modern cancel or a smudge or other unclear marking. For those stamps that were released for postal and fiscal purposes, the used value represents a postally used stamp. Stamps with revenue cancels generally sell for less.

10 **Changes in basic set information** — Bold type is used to show any changes in the basic data given for a set of stamps. This includes perforation differences from one stamp to the next or a different paper, printing method or watermark.

11 **Total value of a set** — The total value of sets of five or more stamps issued after 1900 are shown. The set line also notes the range of Scott numbers and total number of stamps included in the grouping. *Set value* is the term used to indicate the value of a stamp set when its combined total is less than the sum of the individual stamps. This happens when some of the stamps in a set have the minimum catalogue value.

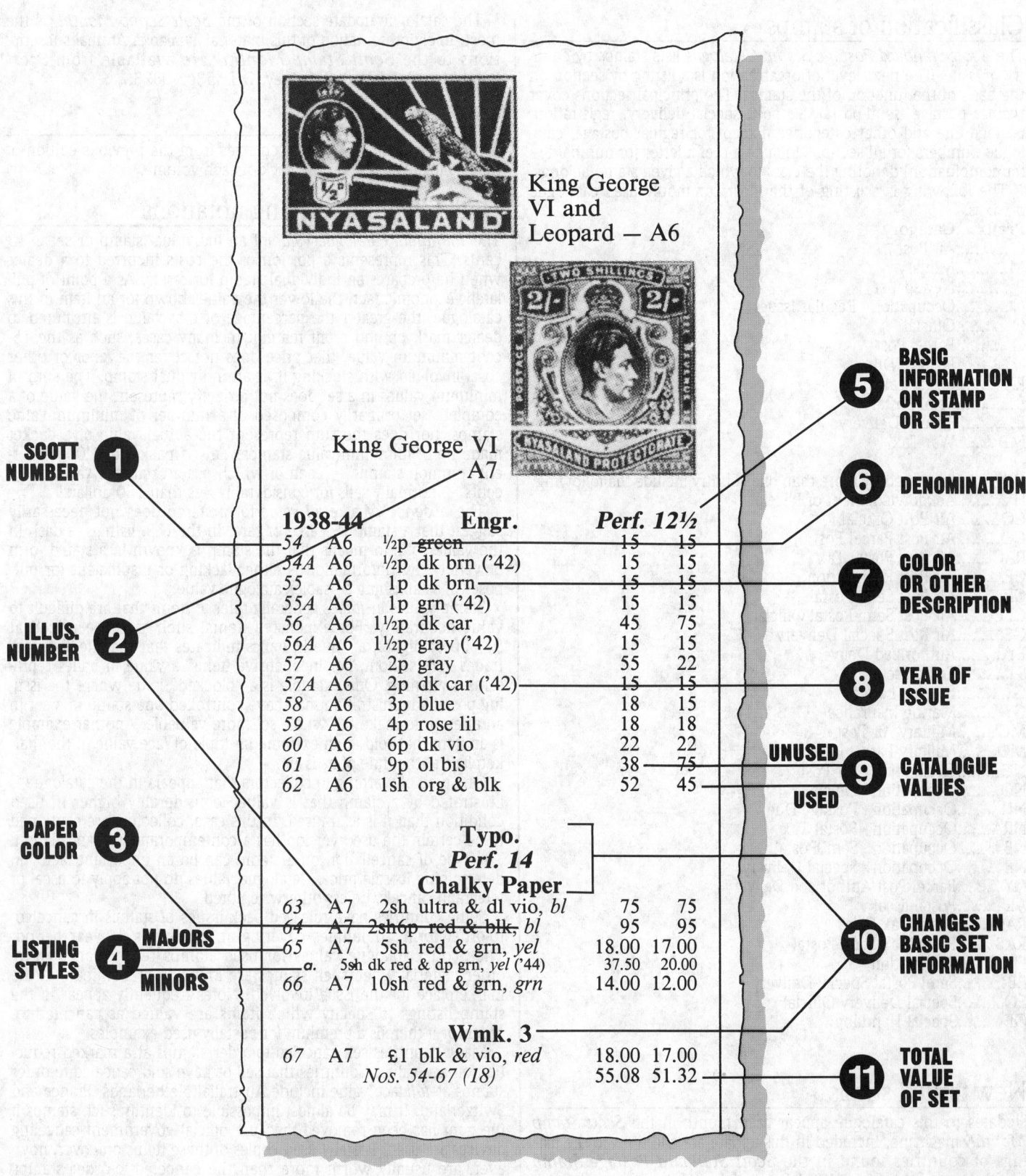

King George VI and Leopard — A6

King George VI A7

1938-44		**Engr.**		***Perf. 12½***	
54	A6	½p	green	15	15
54A	A6	½p	dk brn ('42)	15	15
55	A6	1p	dk brn	15	15
55A	A6	1p	grn ('42)	15	15
56	A6	1½p	dk car	45	75
56A	A6	1½p	gray ('42)	15	15
57	A6	2p	gray	55	22
57A	A6	2p	dk car ('42)	15	15
58	A6	3p	blue	18	15
59	A6	4p	rose lil	18	18
60	A6	6p	dk vio	22	22
61	A6	9p	ol bis	38	75
62	A6	1sh	org & blk	52	45
		Typo.			
		Perf. 14			
		Chalky Paper			
63	A7	2sh	ultra & dl vio, *bl*	75	75
64	A7	2sh6p	red & blk, *bl*	95	95
65	A7	5sh	red & grn, *yel*	18.00	17.00
a.		5sh	dk red & dp grn, *yel* ('44)	37.50	20.00
66	A7	10sh	red & grn, *grn*	14.00	12.00
		Wmk. 3			
67	A7	£1	blk & vio, *red*	18.00	17.00
		Nos. 54-67 (18)		55.08	51.32

1 SCOTT NUMBER

2 ILLUS. NUMBER

3 PAPER COLOR

4 LISTING STYLES — MAJORS — MINORS

5 BASIC INFORMATION ON STAMP OR SET

6 DENOMINATION

7 COLOR OR OTHER DESCRIPTION

8 YEAR OF ISSUE

9 CATALOGUE VALUES — UNUSED — USED

10 CHANGES IN BASIC SET INFORMATION

11 TOTAL VALUE OF SET

Special Notices

Classification of stamps

The *Scott Standard Postage Stamp Catalogue* lists stamps by country of issue. The next level of organization is a listing by section on the basis of the function of the stamps. The principal sections cover regular postage, semi-postal, air post, special delivery, registration, postage due and other categories. Except for regular postage, catalogue numbers for all sections include a prefix letter (or number-letter combination) denoting the class to which a given stamp belongs.

The following is a listing of the most commonly used catalogue prefixes.

Prefix....Category
C ....Air Post
M...........Military
P............Newspaper
N ....Occupation - Regular Issues
O ....Official
Q...........Parcel Post
J.............Postage Due
RA ....Postal Tax
B............Semi-Postal
E............Special Delivery
MR ....War Tax

Other prefixes used by more than one country include the following:
H ....Acknowledgment of Receipt
CO.........Air Post Official
CQ.........Air Post Parcel Post
RAC.......Air Post Postal Tax
CF..........Air Post Registration
CB ....Air Post Semi-Postal
CBO.......Air Post Semi-Postal Official
CE ....Air Post Special Delivery
EY..........Authorized Delivery
S............Franchise
G ....Insured Letter
GY ....Marine Insurance
MC ....Military Air Post
MQ........Military Parcel Post
NC.........Occupation - Air Post
NO.........Occupation - Official
NJ ....Occupation - Postage Due
NRA.......Occupation - Postal Tax
NB ....Occupation - Semi-Postal
NE ....Occupation - Special Delivery
QY ....Parcel Post Authorized Delivery
AR ....Postal-fiscal
RAJ ....Postal Tax Due
RAB ....Postal Tax Semi-Postal
F............Registration
EB..........Semi-Postal Special Delivery
EO ....Special Delivery Official
QE ....Special Handling

New issue listings

Updates to this catalogue appear each month in the *Scott Stamp Monthly* magazine. Included in this update are additions to the listings of countries found in the *Scott Standard Postage Stamp Catalogue* and the *Specialized Catalogue of United States Stamps*, as well as corrections and updates to current editions of this catalogue.

From time to time there will be changes in the final listings of stamps from the *Scott Stamp Monthly* to the next edition of the catalogue. This occurs as more information about certain stamps or sets becomes available.

The catalogue update section of the *Scott Stamp Monthly* is the most timely presentation of this material available. Annual subscriptions to the *Scott Stamp Monthly* are available from Scott Publishing Co., Box 828, Sidney, OH 45365-0828.

Number changes

A listing of catalogue number changes from the previous edition of the catalogue appears at the back of each volume.

Understanding valuing notations

The *minimum catalogue value* of an individual stamp or set is 15 cents. This represents a portion of the costs incurred to a dealer when he prepares an individual stamp for resale. As a point of philatelic-economic fact, the lower the value shown for an item in this catalogue, the greater the percentage of that value is attributed to dealer mark up and profit margin. In many cases, such as the 15-cent minimum value, that price does not cover the labor or other costs involved with stocking it as an individual stamp. The sum of minimum values in a set does not properly represent the value of a complete set primarily composed of a number of minimum-value stamps, nor does the sum represent the actual value of a packet made up of minimum-value stamps. Thus a packet of 1,000 different common stamps — each of which has a catalogue value of 15 cents — normally sells for considerably less than 150 dollars!

The *absence of a retail value* for a stamp does not necessarily suggest that a stamp is scarce or rare. In the U.S. listings, a dash in the value column means that the stamp is known in a stated form or variety, but information is either lacking or insufficient for purposes of establishing a usable catalogue value.

Stamp values in *italics* generally refer to items that are difficult to value accurately. For expensive items, such as those priced at $1,000 or higher, a value in italics indicates that the affected item trades very seldom. For inexpensive items, a value in italics represents a warning. One example is a "blocked" issue where the issuing postal administration may have controlled one stamp in a set in an attempt to make the whole set more valuable. Another example is an item that sold at an extreme multiple of face value in the marketplace at the time of its issue.

One type of warning to collectors that appears in the catalogue is illustrated by a stamp that is valued considerably higher in used condition than it is as unused. In this case, collectors are cautioned to be certain the used version has a contemporaneous cancellation. The type of cancellation on a stamp can be an important factor in determining its sale price. Catalogue values do not apply to fiscal or telegraph cancels, unless otherwise noted.

Some countries have released back issues of stamps in canceled-to-order form, sometimes covering at much as a 10-year period. The Scott Catalogue values for used stamps reflect canceled-to-order material when such stamps are found to predominate in the marketplace for the issue involved. Notes frequently appear in the stamp listings to specify which items are valued as canceled-to-order, or if there is a premium for postally used examples.

Many countries sell canceled-to-order stamps at a marked reduction of face value. Countries that sell or have sold canceled-to-order stamps at *full* face value include Australia, Netherlands, France and Switzerland. It may be almost impossible to identify such stamps if the gum has been removed, because official government canceling devices are used. Postally used copies of these items on cover, however, are usually worth more than the canceled-to-order stamps with original gum.

Abbreviations

Scott Publishing Co. uses a consistent set of abbreviations throughout this catalogue to conserve space, while still providing necessary information.

COLOR ABBREVIATIONS

amb.....amber	crim.....crimson	ol.........olive
anil......aniline	cr.........cream	olvn.....olivine
ap........apple	dk........dark	org.......orange
aqua.....aquamarine	dl.........dull	pck......peacock
az........azure	dp........deep	pnksh...pinkish
bis.......bister	db........drab	Prus.....Prussian
bl.........blue	emer....emerald	pur.......purple
bld.......blood	gldn.....golden	redsh....reddish
blk.......black	grysh....grayish	res.......reseda
bril.......brilliant	grn.......green	ros.......rosine
brn.......brown	grnsh...greenish	ryl........royal
brnsh....brownish	hel........heliotrope	sal........salmon
brnz.....bronze	hn........henna	saph.....sapphire
brt........bright	ind.......indigo	scar......scarlet
brnt......burnt	int........intense	sep.......sepia
car.......carmine	lav.......lavender	sien......sienna
cer.......cerise	lem......lemon	sil.........silver
chlky....chalky	lil.........lilac	sl..........slate
cham....chamois	lt..........light	stl.........steel
chnt.....chestnut	mag.....magenta	turq.....turquoise
choc.....chocolate	man.....manila	ultra.....ultramarine
chr.......chrome	mar......maroon	Ven......Venetian
cit........citron	mv.......mauve	ver.......vermilion
cl.........claret	multi....multicolored	vio.......violet
cob......cobalt	mlky....milky	yel.......yellow
cop......copper	myr......myrtle	yelsh....yellowish

When no color is given for an overprint or surcharge, black is the color used. Abbreviations for colors used for overprints and surcharges include: "(B)" or "(Blk)," black; "(Bl)," blue; "(R)," red; and "(G)," green.

Additional abbreviations in this catalogue are shown below:

Adm. ....Administration
AFL ....American Federation of Labor
Anniv. ....Anniversary
APS ....American Philatelic Society
Assoc. ....Association
ASSR. ....Autonomous Soviet Socialist Republic
b......................Born
BEP ....Bureau of Engraving and Printing
Bicent. ....Bicentennial
Bklt.................Booklet
Brit. ....British
btwn...............Between
Bur. ....Bureau
c. or ca...........Circa
Cat. ....Catalogue
Cent. ....Centennial, century, centenary
CIO ....Congress of Industrial Organizations
Conf. ....Conference
Cong...............Congress
Cpl. ....Corporal
CTO ....Canceled to order
d......................Died
Dbl. ....Double
EKU................Earliest known use
Engr................Engraved
Exhib..............Exhibition
Expo...............Exposition
Fed. ....Federation
GB..................Great Britain
Gen. ....General
GPO ....General post office
Horiz. ....Horizontal
Imperf.............Imperforate
Impt. ....Imprint
Intl. ....International
Invtd...............Inverted
L......................Left
Lieut., lt. ....Lieutenant
Litho...............Lithographed
LL....................Lower left
LR ....Lower right
mm.................Millimeter
Ms...................Manuscript
Natl. ....National
No. ....Number
NY..................New York
NYC................New York City
Ovpt. ....Overprint
Ovptd. ....Overprinted
P......................Plate number
Perf.................Perforated, perforation
Phil. ....Philatelic
Photo..............Photogravure
PO ....Post office
Pr. ....Pair
P.R. ....Puerto Rico
Prec................Precancel, precanceled
Pres. ....President
PTT ....Post, Telephone and Telegraph
Rio..................Rio de Janeiro
Sgt...................Sergeant
Soc. ....Society
Souv. ....Souvenir
SSR.................Soviet Socialist Republic, see ASSR
St.....................Saint, street
Surch...............Surcharge
Typo. ....Typographed
UL...................Upper left
Unwmkd.........Unwatermarked
UPU ....Universal Postal Union
UR...................Upper Right
US ....United States
USPOD ....United States Post Office Department
USSR ....Union of Soviet Socialist Republics
Vert. ....Vertical
VP ....Vice president
Wmk. ....Watermark
Wmkd. ....Watermarked
WWI ....World War I
WWII ....World War II

Examination

Scott Publishing Co. will not comment upon the genuineness, grade or condition of stamps, because of the time and responsibility involved. Rather, there are several expertizing groups that undertake this work for both collectors and dealers. Neither will Scott Publishing Co. appraise or identify philatelic material. The company cannot take responsibility for unsolicited stamps or covers sent by individuals.

How to order from your dealer

When ordering stamps from a dealer, it is not necessary to write the full description of a stamp as listed in this catalogue. All you need is the name of the country, the Scott catalogue number and whether the desired item is unused or used. For example, "Japan Scott 422 unused" is sufficient to identify the unused stamp of Japan listed as "422 A206 5y brown."

Basic Stamp Information

A stamp collector's knowledge of the combined elements that make a given stamp issue unique determines his or her ability to identify stamps. These elements include paper, watermark, method of separation, printing, design and gum. On the following pages each of these important areas is briefly described.

Paper

Paper is an organic material composed of a compacted weave of cellulose fibers and generally formed into sheets. Paper used to print stamps may be manufactured in sheets, or it may have been part of a large roll (called a web) before being cut to size. The fibers most often used to create paper on which stamps are printed include bark, wood, straw and certain grasses. In many cases, linen or cotton rags have been added for greater strength and durability. Grinding, bleaching, cooking and rinsing these raw fibers reduces them to a slushy pulp, referred to by paper makers as "stuff." Sizing and, sometimes, coloring matter is added to the pulp to make different types of finished paper.

After the stuff is prepared, it is poured onto sieve-like frames that allow the water to run off, while retaining the matted pulp. As fibers fall onto the screen and are held by gravity, they form a natural weave that will later hold the paper together. If the screen has metal bits that are formed into letters or images attached, it leaves slightly thinned areas on the paper. These are called watermarks.

When the stuff is almost dry, it is passed under pressure through smooth or engraved rollers - dandy rolls - or placed between cloth in a press to be flattened and dried.

Stamp paper falls broadly into two types: wove and laid. The nature of the surface of the frame onto which the pulp is first deposited causes the differences in appearance between the two. If the surface is smooth and even, the paper will be of fairly uniform texture throughout. This is known as *wove paper.* Early papermaking machines poured the pulp onto a continuously circulating web of felt, but modern machines feed the pulp onto a cloth-like screen made of closely interwoven fine wires. This paper, when held to a light, will show little dots or points very close together. The proper name for this is "wire wove," but the type is still considered wove. Any U.S. or British stamp printed after 1880 will serve as an example of wire wove paper.

Closely spaced parallel wires, with cross wires at wider intervals, make up the frames used for what is known as *laid paper.* A greater thickness of the pulp will settle between the wires. The paper, when held to a light, will show alternate light and dark lines. The spacing and the thickness of the lines may vary, but on any one sheet of paper they are all alike. See Russia Scott 31-38 for examples of laid paper.

Batonne, from the French word meaning "a staff," is a term used if the lines in the paper are spaced quite far apart, like the printed ruling on a writing tablet. Batonne paper may be either wove or laid. If laid, fine laid lines can be seen between the batons. The laid lines, which are a form of watermark, may be geometrical figures such as squares, diamonds, rectangles or wavy lines.

Quadrille is the term used when the lines in the paper form little squares. *Oblong quadrille* is the term used when rectangles, rather than squares, are formed. See Mexico-Guadalajara Scott 35-37 for examples of oblong quadrille paper.

Paper also is classified as thick or thin, hard or soft, and by color if dye is added during manufacture. Such colors may include yellowish, greenish, bluish and reddish.

Brief explanations of other types of paper used for printing stamps, as well as examples, follow.

Pelure — Pelure paper is a very thin, hard and often brittle paper that is sometimes bluish or grayish in appearance. See Serbia Scott 169-170.

Native — This is a term applied to handmade papers used to produce some of the early stamps of the Indian states. Stamps printed on native paper may be expected to display various natural inclusions that are normal and do not negatively affect value. Japanese paper, originally made of mulberry fibers and rice flour, is part of this group. See Japan Scott 1-18.

Manila — This type of paper is often used to make stamped envelopes and wrappers. It is a coarse-textured stock, usually smooth on one side and rough on the other. A variety of colors of manila paper exist, but the most common range is yellowish-brown.

Silk — Introduced by the British in 1847 as a safeguard against counterfeiting, silk paper contains bits of colored silk thread scattered throughout. The density of these fibers varies greatly and can include as few as one fiber per stamp or hundreds. U.S. revenue Scott R152 is a good example of an easy-to-identify silk paper stamp.

Silk-thread paper has uninterrupted threads of colored silk arranged so that one or more threads run through the stamp or postal stationery. See Great Britain Scott 5-6 and Switzerland Scott 14-19.

Granite — Filled with minute cloth or colored paper fibers of various colors and lengths, granite paper should not be confused with either type of silk paper. Austria Scott 172-175 and a number of Swiss stamps are examples of granite paper.

Chalky — A chalk-like substance coats the surface of chalky paper to discourage the cleaning and reuse of canceled stamps, as well as to provide a smoother, more acceptable printing surface. Because the designs of stamps printed on chalky paper are imprinted on what is often a water-soluble coating, any attempt to remove a cancellation will destroy the stamp. *Do not soak these stamps in any fluid.* To remove a stamp printed on chalky paper from an envelope, wet the paper from underneath the stamp until the gum dissolves enough to release the stamp from the paper. See St. Kitts-Nevis Scott 89-90 for examples of stamps printed on this type of chalky paper.

India — Another name for this paper, originally introduced from China about 1750, is "China Paper." It is a thin, opaque paper often used for plate and die proofs by many countries.

Double — In philately, the term double paper has two distinct meanings. The first is a two-ply paper, usually a combination of a thick and a thin sheet, joined during manufacture. This type was used experimentally as a means to discourage the reuse of stamps.

The design is printed on the thin paper. Any attempt to remove a cancellation would destroy the design. U.S. Scott 158 and other Banknote-era stamps exist on this form of double paper.

The second type of double paper occurs on a rotary press, when the end of one paper roll, or web, is affixed to the next roll to save time feeding the paper through the press. Stamp designs are printed over the joined paper and, if overlooked by inspectors, may get into post office stocks.

Goldbeater's Skin — This type of paper was used for the 1866 issue of Prussia, and was a tough, translucent paper. The design was printed in reverse on the back of the stamp, and the gum applied over the printing. It is impossible to remove stamps printed on this type of paper from the paper to which they are affixed without destroying the design.

Ribbed — Ribbed paper has an uneven, corrugated surface made by passing the paper through ridged rollers. This type exists on some copies of U.S. Scott 156-165.

Various other substances, or substrates, have been used for stamp manufacture, including wood, aluminum, copper, silver and gold foil, plastic, and silk and cotton fabrics.

Wove Laid Granite

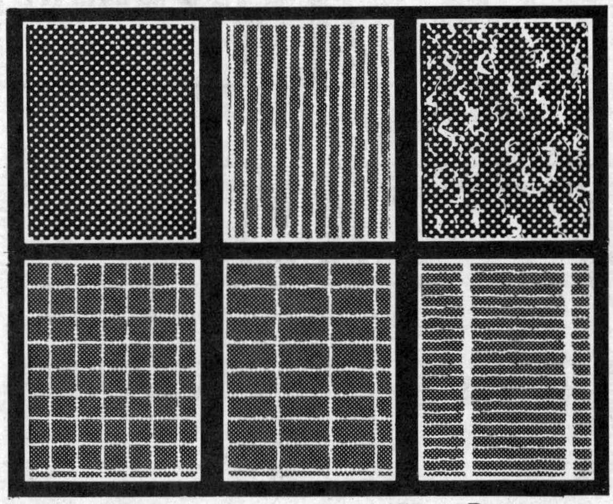

Quadrille Oblong Quadrille Batonne

Watermarks

Watermarks are an integral part of some papers. They are formed in the process of paper manufacture. Watermarks consist of small designs, formed of wire or cut from metal and soldered to the surface of the mold or, sometimes, on the dandy roll. The designs may be in the form of crowns, stars, anchors, letters or other characters or symbols. These pieces of metal - known in the paper-making industry as "bits" - impress a design into the paper. The design sometimes may be seen by holding the stamp to the light. Some are more easily seen with a watermark detector. This important tool is a small black tray into which a stamp is placed face down and dampened with a fast-evaporating watermark detection fluid that brings up the watermark image in the form of dark lines against a lighter background. These dark lines are the thinner areas of the paper known as the watermark. Some watermarks are extremely difficult to locate, due to either a faint impression, watermark location or the color of the stamp. There also are electric watermark detectors that come with plastic filter disks of various colors. The disks neutralize the color of the stamp, permitting the watermark to be seen more easily.

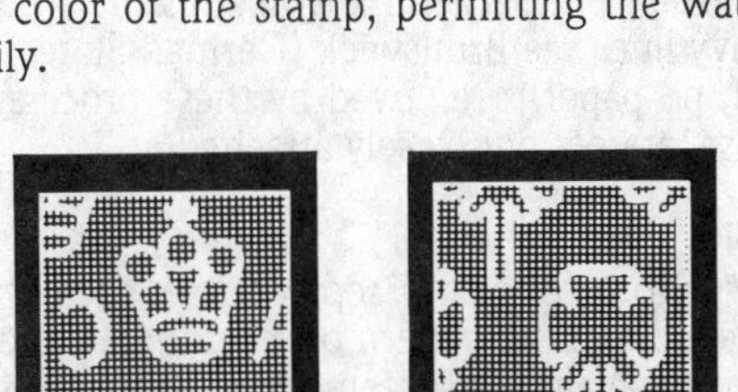

Multiple watermarks of Crown Agents and Burma

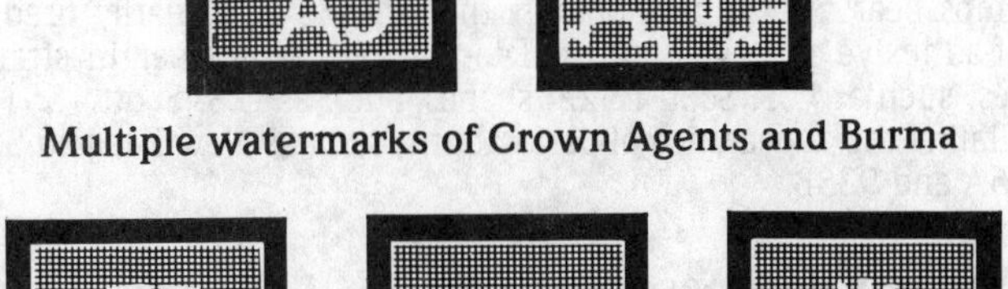

Watermarks of Uruguay, Vatican City and Jamaica

WARNING: Some inks used in the photogravure process dissolve in watermark fluids (Please see the section on Soluble Printing Inks). Also, see "chalky paper."

Watermarks may be found normal, reversed, inverted, reversed and inverted, sideways or diagonal, as seen from the back of the stamp. The relationship of watermark to stamp design depends on the position of the printing plates or how paper is fed through the press. On machine-made paper, watermarks normally are read from right to left. The design is repeated closely throughout the sheet in a "multiple-watermark design." In a "sheet watermark," the design appears only once on the sheet, but extends over many stamps. Individual stamps may carry only a small fraction or none of the watermark.

"Marginal watermarks" occur in the margins of sheets or panes of stamps. They occur on the outside border of paper (ostensibly outside the area where stamps are to be printed). A large row of letters may spell the name of the country or the manufacturer of the paper. Careless press feeding may cause parts of these letters to show on stamps of the outer row of a pane.

Soluble Printing Inks

WARNING: Most stamp colors are permanent; that is, they are not seriously affected by short-term exposure to light or water. Many colors, especially of modern inks, fade from excessive exposure to light. There are stamps printed with inks that dissolve easily in water or in fluids used to detect watermarks. Use of these inks was intentional to prevent the removal of cancellations. Water affects all aniline inks, those on so-called safety paper and some photogravure printings - all such inks are known as *fugitive colors. Removal from paper of such stamps requires care and alternatives to traditional soaking.*

Separation

"Separation" is the general term used to describe methods used to separate stamps. The three standard forms currently in use are perforating, rouletting and die-cutting. These methods are done during the stamp production process, after printing. Sometimes these methods are done on-press or sometimes as a separate step. The earliest issues, such as the 1840 Penny Black of Great Britain (Scott 1), did not have any means provided for separation. It was expected the stamps would be cut apart with scissors or folded and torn. These are examples of imperforate stamps. Many stamps were first issued in imperforate formats and were later issued with perforations. Therefore, care must be observed in buying single imperforate stamps to be certain they were issued imperforate and are not perforated copies that have been altered by having the perforations trimmed away. Stamps issued imperforate usually are valued as singles. However, imperforate varieties of normally perforated stamps should be collected in pairs or larger pieces as indisputable evidence of their imperforate character.

PERFORATION

The chief style of separation of stamps, and the one that is in almost universal use today, is perforating. By this process, paper between the stamps is cut away in a line of holes, usually round, leaving little bridges of paper between the stamps to hold them together. Some types of perforation, such as hyphen-hole perfs, can be confused with roulettes, but a close visual inspection reveals that paper has been removed. The little perforation bridges, which project from the stamp when it is torn from the pane, are called the teeth of the perforation.

As the size of the perforation is sometimes the only way to differentiate between two otherwise identical stamps, it is necessary to be able to accurately measure and describe them. This is done with a perforation gauge, usually a ruler-like device that has dots or graduated lines to show how many perforations may be counted in the space of two centimeters. Two centimeters is the space universally adopted in which to measure perforations.

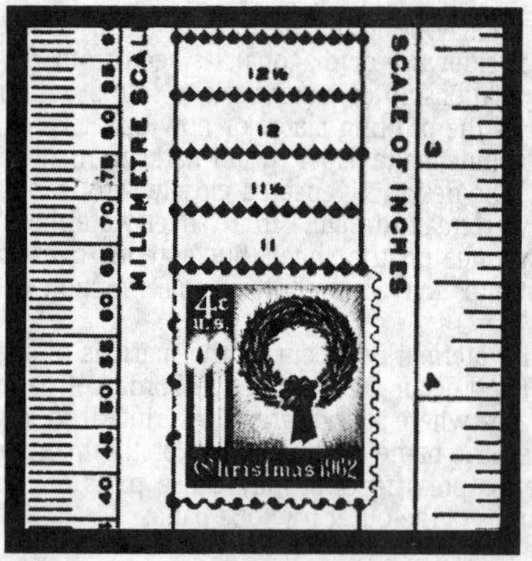

Perforation gauge

To measure a stamp, run it along the gauge until the dots on it fit exactly into the perforations of the stamp. If you are using a graduated-line perforation gauge, simply slide the stamp along the surface until the lines on the gauge perfectly project from the center of the bridges or holes. The number to the side of the line of dots or lines that fit the stamp's perforation is the measurement. For example, an "11" means that 11 perforations fit between two centimeters. The description of the stamp therefore is "perf. 11." If the gauge of the perforations on the top and bottom of a stamp differs from that on the sides, the result is what is known as *compound perforations.* In measuring compound perforations, the gauge at top and bottom is always given first, then the sides. Thus, a stamp that measures 11 at top and bottom and 10 1/2 at the sides is "perf. 11 x 10 1/2." See U.S. Scott 632-642 for examples of compound perforations.

Stamps also are known with perforations different on three or all four sides. Descriptions of such items are clockwise, beginning with the top of the stamp.

A perforation with small holes and teeth close together is a "fine perforation." One with large holes and teeth far apart is a "coarse perforation." Holes that are jagged, rather than clean-cut, are "rough perforations." *Blind perforations* are the slight impressions left by the perforating pins if they fail to puncture the paper. Multiples of stamps showing blind perforations may command a slight premium over normally perforated stamps.

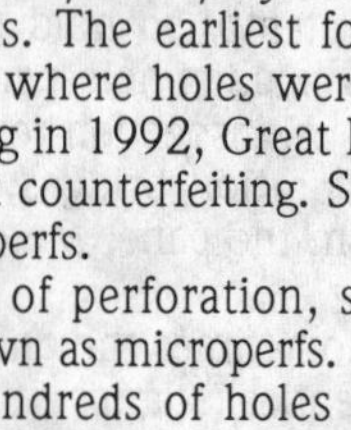

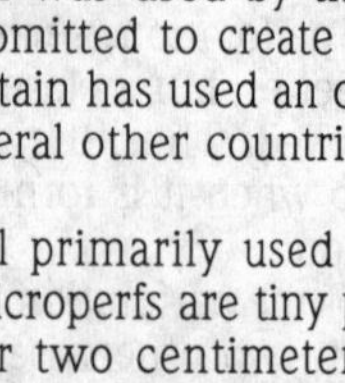

The term *syncopated perfs* describes intentional irregularities in the perforations. The earliest form was used by the Netherlands from 1925-33, where holes were omitted to create distinctive patterns. Beginning in 1992, Great Britain has used an oval perforation to help prevent counterfeiting. Several other countries have started using the oval perfs.

A new type of perforation, still primarily used for postal stationery, is known as microperfs. Microperfs are tiny perforations (in some cases hundreds of holes per two centimeters) that allows items to be intentionally separated very easily, while not accidentally breaking apart as easily as standard perforations. These are not currently measured or differentiated by size, as are standard perforations.

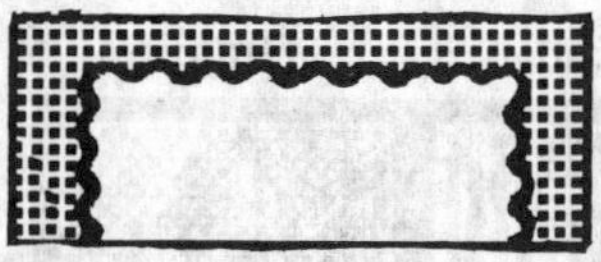

perce en arc

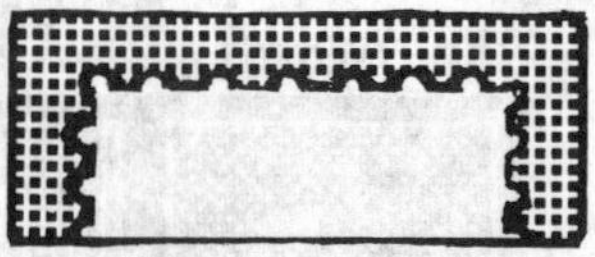

perce en lignes

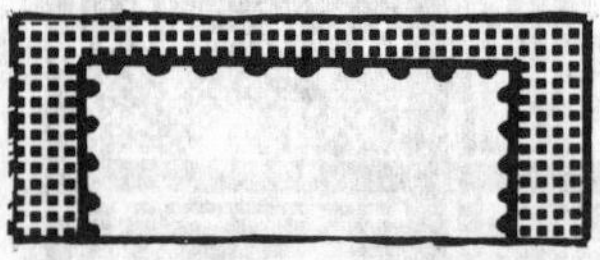

perce en points

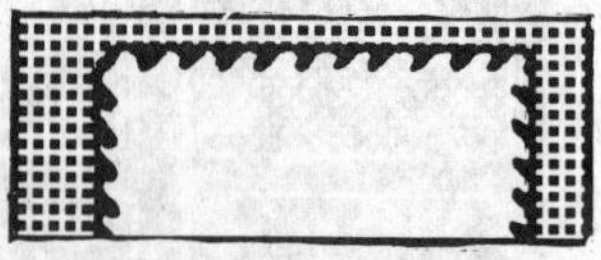

oblique roulette

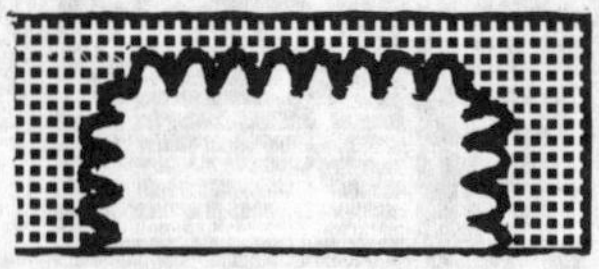

perce en scie

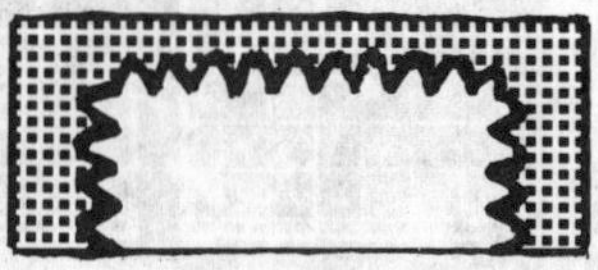

perce serpentin

ROULETTING

In rouletting, the stamp paper is cut partly or wholly through, with no paper removed. In perforating, some paper is removed. Rouletting derives its name from the French roulette, a spur-like wheel. As the wheel is rolled over the paper, each point makes a small cut. The number of cuts made in a two-centimeter space determines the gauge of the roulette, just as the number of perforations in two centimeters determines the gauge of the perforation.

The shape and arrangement of the teeth on the wheels varies. Various roulette types generally carry French names:

Perce en lignes - rouletted in lines. The paper receives short, straight cuts in lines. This is the most common type of rouletting. See Mexico Scott 500.

Perce en points - pin-rouletted. This differs from a small perforation because no paper is removed, although round, equidistant holes are pricked through the paper. See Mexico Scott 242-256.

Perce en arc and *perce en scie* - pierced in an arc or saw-toothed designs, forming half circles or small triangles. See Hanover (German States) Scott 25-29.

Perce en serpentin - serpentine roulettes. The cuts form a serpentine or wavy line. See Brunswick (German States) Scott 13-18.

Once again, no paper is removed by these processes, leaving the stamps easily separated, but closely attached.

DIE-CUTTING

The third major form of stamp separation is die-cutting. This is a method where a die in the pattern of separation is created that later cuts the stamp paper in a stroke motion. Although some standard stamps bear die-cut perforations, this process is primarily used for self-adhesive postage stamps. Die-cutting can appear in straight lines, such as U.S. Scott 2522, shapes, such as U.S. Scott 1551, or imitating the appearance of perforations, such as New Zealand Scott 935A and 935B.

Printing Processes

ENGRAVING (Intaglio, Line-engraving, Etching)

Master die - The initial operation in the process of line engraving is making the master die. The die is a small, flat block of softened steel upon which the stamp design is recess engraved in reverse.

Master die

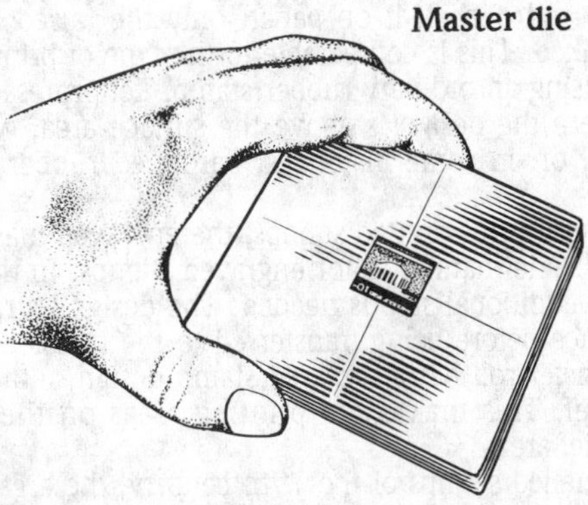

Photographic reduction of the original art is made to the appropriate size. It then serves as a tracing guide for the initial outline of the design. The engraver lightly traces the design on the steel with his graver, then slowly works the design until it is completed. At various points during the engraving process, the engraver hand-inks the die and makes an impression to check his progress. These are known as progressive die proofs. After completion of the engraving, the die is hardened to withstand the stress and pressures of later transfer operations.

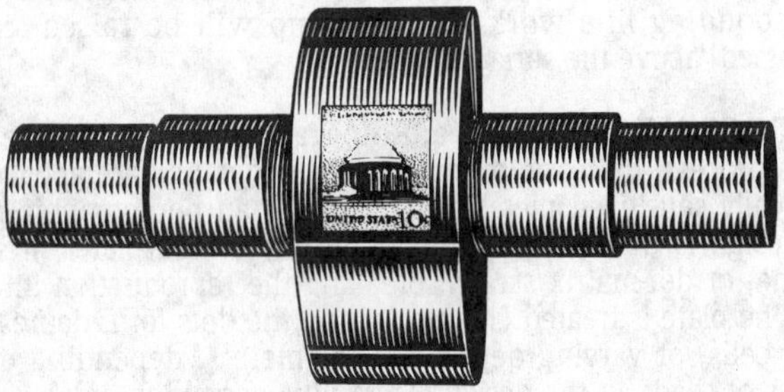

Transfer roll

Transfer roll — Next is production of the transfer roll that, as the name implies, is the medium used to transfer the subject from the master die to the printing plate. A blank roll of soft steel, mounted on a mandrel, is placed under the bearers of the transfer press to allow it to roll freely on its axis. The hardened die is placed on the bed of the press and the face of the transfer roll is applied to the die, under pressure. The bed or the roll is then rocked back and forth under increasing pressure, until the soft steel of the roll is forced into every engraved line of the die. The resulting impression on the roll is known as a "relief" or a "relief transfer." The engraved image is now positive in appearance and stands out from the steel. After the required number of reliefs are "rocked in," the soft steel transfer roll is hardened.

Different flaws may occur during the relief process. A defective relief may occur during the rocking in process because of a minute piece of foreign material lodging on the die, or some other cause. Imperfections in the steel of the transfer roll may result in a breaking away of parts of the design. This is known as a relief break, which will show up on finished stamps as small, unprinted areas. If a damaged relief remains in use, it will transfer a repeating defect to the plate. Deliberate alterations of reliefs sometimes occur. "Altered reliefs" designate these changed conditions.

Plate — The final step in pre-printing production is the making of the printing plate. A flat piece of soft steel replaces the die on the bed of the transfer press. One of the reliefs on the transfer roll is positioned over this soft steel. Position, or layout, dots determine the correct position on the plate. The dots have been lightly marked on the plate in advance. After the correct position of the relief is determined, the design is rocked in by following the same method used in making the transfer roll. The difference is that this time the image is being transferred from the transfer roll, rather than to it. Once the design is entered on the plate, it appears in reverse and is recessed. There are as many transfers entered on the plate as there are subjects printed on the sheet of stamps. It is during this process that double and shifted transfers occur, as well as re-entries. These are the result of improperly entered images that have not been properly burnished out prior to rocking in a new image.

Modern siderography processes, such as those used by the U.S. Bureau of Engraving and Printing, involve an automated form of rocking designs in on preformed cylindrical printing sleeves. The same process also allows for easier removal and re-entry of worn images right on the sleeve.

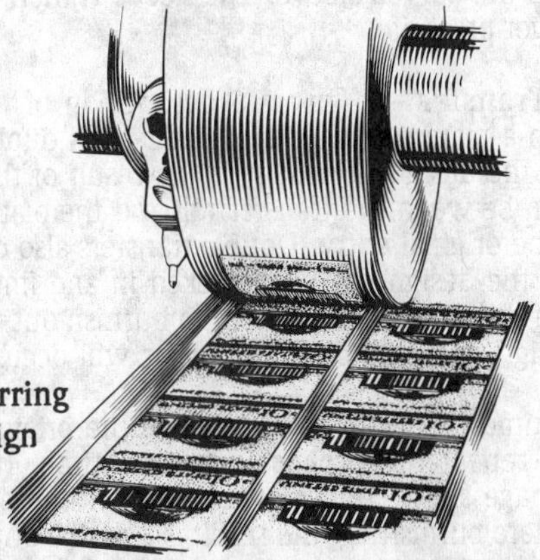

Transferring the design to the plate

Following the entering of the required transfers on the plate, the position dots, layout dots and lines, scratches and other markings generally are burnished out. Added at this time by the siderographer are any required *guide lines, plate numbers* or other *marginal markings.* The plate is then hand-inked and a proof impression is taken. This is known as a plate proof. If the impression is approved, the plate is machined for fitting onto the press, is hardened and sent to the plate vault ready for use.

On press, the plate is inked and the surface is automatically wiped clean, leaving ink only in the recessed lines. Paper is then forced under pressure into the engraved recessed lines, thereby receiving the ink. Thus, the ink lines on engraved stamps are slightly raised, and slight depressions (debossing) occur on the back of the stamp. Prior to the advent of modern high-speed presses and more advanced ink formulations, paper had to be dampened before receiving the ink. This sometimes led to uneven shrinkage by the time the stamps were perforated, resulting in improperly perforated stamps, or misperfs. Newer presses use drier paper, thus both *wet* and *dry printings* exist on some stamps.

Rotary Press — Until 1914, only flat plates were used to print engraved stamps. Rotary press printing was introduced in 1914, and slowly spread. Some countries still use flat-plate printing.

After approval of the plate proof, older *rotary press plates* require additional machining. They are curved to fit the press cylinder. "Gripper slots" are cut into the back of each plate to receive the "grippers," which hold the plate securely on the press. The plate is then hardened. Stamps printed from these bent rotary press plates are longer or wider than the same stamps printed from flat-plate presses. The stretching of the plate during the curving process is what causes this distortion.

Re-entry — To execute a re-entry on a flat plate, the transfer roll is re-applied to the plate, often at some time after its first use on the press. Worn-out designs can be resharpened by carefully burnishing out the original image and re-entering it from the transfer roll. If the original impression has not been sufficiently removed and the transfer roll is not precisely in line with the remaining impression, the resulting double transfer will make the re-entry obvious. If the registration is true, a re-entry may be difficult or impossible to distinguish. Sometimes a stamp printed from a successful re-entry is identified by having a much sharper and clearer impression than its neighbors. With the advent of rotary presses, post-press re-entries were not possible. After a plate was curved for the rotary press, it was impossible to make a re-entry. This is because the plate had already been bent once (with the design distorted).

However, with the introduction of the previously mentioned modern-style siderography machines, entries are made to the preformed cylindrical printing sleeve. Such sleeves are dechromed and softened. This allows individual images to be burnished out and reentered on the curved sleeve. The sleeve is then rechromed, resulting in longer press life.

Double Transfer — This is a description of the condition of a transfer on a plate that shows evidence of a duplication of all, or a portion of the design. It usually is the result of the changing of the registration between the transfer roll and the plate during the rocking in of the original entry. Double transfers also occur when only a portion of the design has been rocked in and improper positioning is noted. If the worker elected not to burnish out the partial or completed design, a strong double transfer will occur for part or all of the design.

It sometimes is necessary to remove the original transfer from a plate and repeat the process a second time. If the finished reworked image shows traces of the original impression, attributable to incomplete burnishing, the result is a partial double transfer.

With the modern automatic machines mentioned previously, double transfers are all but impossible to create. Those partially doubled images on stamps printed from such sleeves are more than likely re-entries, rather than true double transfers.

Re-engraved — Alterations to a stamp design are sometimes necessary after some stamps have been printed. In some cases, either the original die or the actual printing plate may have its "temper" drawn (softened), and the design will be re-cut. The resulting impressions from such a re-engraved die or plate may differ slightly from the original issue, and are known as "re-engraved." If the alteration was made to the master die, all future printings will be consistently different from the original. If alterations were made to the printing plate, each altered stamp on the plate will be slightly different from each other, allowing specialists to reconstruct a complete printing plate.

Dropped Transfers — If an impression from the transfer roll has not been properly placed, a dropped transfer may occur. The final stamp image will appear obviously out of line with its neighbors.

Short Transfer — Sometimes a transfer roll is not rocked its entire length when entering a transfer onto a plate. As a result, the finished transfer on the plate fails to show the complete design, and the finished stamp will have an incomplete design printed. This is known as a "short transfer." U.S. Scott No. 8 is a good example of a short transfer.

TYPOGRAPHY (Letterpress, Surface Printing, Flexography, Dry Offset, High Etch)

Although the word "Typography" is obsolete as a term describing a printing method, it was the accepted term throughout the first century of postage stamps. Therefore, appropriate Scott listings in this catalogue refer to typographed stamps. The current term for this form of printing, however, is "letterpress."

As it relates to the production of postage stamps, letterpress printing is the reverse of engraving. Rather than having recessed areas trap the ink and deposit it on paper, only the raised areas of the design are inked. This is comparable to the type of printing seen by inking and using an ordinary rubber stamp. Letterpress includes all printing where the design is above the surface area, whether it is wood, metal or, in some instances, hardened rubber or polymer plastic.

For most letterpress-printed stamps, the engraved master is made in much the same manner as for engraved stamps. In this instance, however, an additional step is needed. The design is transferred to another surface before being transferred to the transfer roll. In this way, the transfer roll has a recessed stamp design, rather than one done in relief. This makes the printing areas on the final plate raised, or relief areas.

For less-detailed stamps of the 19th century, the area on the die not used as a printing surface was cut away, leaving the surface area raised. The original die was then reproduced by stereotyping or electrotyping. The resulting electrotypes were assembled in the required number and format of the desired sheet of stamps. The plate used in printing the stamps was an electroplate of these assembled electrotypes.

Once the final letterpress plates are created, ink is applied to the raised surface and the pressure of the press transfers the ink impression to the paper. In contrast to engraving, the fine lines of letterpress are impressed on the surface of the stamp, leaving a debossed surface. When viewed from the back (as on a typewritten page), the corresponding line work on the stamp will be raised slightly (embossed) above the surface.

PHOTOGRAVURE (Gravure, Rotogravure, Heliogravure)

In this process, the basic principles of photography are applied to a chemically sensitized metal plate, rather than photographic paper. The design is transferred photographically to the plate through a halftone, or dot-matrix screen, breaking the reproduction into tiny dots. The plate is treated chemically and the dots form depressions, called cells, of varying depths and diameters, depending on the degrees of shade in the design. Then, like engraving, ink is applied to the plate and the surface is wiped clean. This leaves ink in the tiny cells that is lifted out and deposited on the paper when it is pressed against the plate.

Gravure is most often used for multicolored stamps, generally using the three primary colors (red, yellow and blue) and black. By varying the dot matrix pattern and density of these colors, virtually any color can be reproduced. A typical full-color gravure stamp will be created from four printing cylinders (one for each color). The original multicolored image will have been photographically separated into its component colors.

For examples of the first photogravure stamps printed (1914), see Bavaria Scott 94-114.

LITHOGRAPHY (Offset Lithography, Stone Lithography, Dilitho, Planography, Collotype)

The principle that oil and water do not mix is the basis for lithography. The stamp design is drawn by hand or transferred from engraving to the surface of a lithographic stone or metal plate in a greasy (oily) substance. This oily substance holds the ink, which will later be transferred to the paper. The stone (or plate) is wet with an acid fluid, causing it to repel the printing ink in all areas not covered by the greasy substance.

Transfer paper is used to transfer the design from the original stone or plate. A series of duplicate transfers are grouped and, in turn, transferred to the final printing plate.

Photolithography — The application of photographic processes to lithography. This process allows greater flexibility of design, related to use of halftone screens combined with line work. Unlike photogravure or engraving, this process can allow large, solid areas to be printed.

Offset — A refinement of the lithographic process. A rubber-covered blanket cylinder takes the impression from the inked lithographic plate. From the "blanket" the impression is *offset* or transferred to the paper. Greater flexibility and speed are the principal reasons offset printing has largely displaced lithography. The term "lithography" covers both processes, and results are almost identical.

EMBOSSED (Relief) Printing

Embossing, not considered one of the four main printing types, is a method in which the design first is sunk into the metal of the die. Printing is done against a yielding platen, such as leather or linoleum. The platen is forced into the depression of the die, thus forming the design on the paper in relief. This process is often used for metallic inks.

Embossing may be done without color (see Sardinia Scott 4-6); with color printed around the embossed area (see Great Britain Scott 5 and most U.S. envelopes); and with color in exact registration with the embossed subject (see Canada Scott 656-657).

COMBINATION PRINTINGS

Sometimes two or even three printing methods are combined in producing stamps. In these cases, such as Austria Scott 933, the stamp's dual printing technique can be determined by studying the individual characteristics of each printing type (intaglio and offset). A few stamps, such as Singapore Scott 684-684A, combine as many as three of the four major printing types (offset, intaglio and letterpress). When this is done it often indicates the incorporation of security devices against counterfeiting.

INK COLORS

Inks or colored papers used in stamp printing often are of mineral origin, although there are numerous examples of organic-based pigments. As a general rule, organic-based pigments are far more subject to varieties and change than those of mineral-based origin.

The appearance of any given color on a stamp may be affected by many aspects, including printing variations, light, color of paper, aging and chemical alterations.

Numerous printing variations may be observed. Heavier pressure or inking will cause a more intense color, while slight interruptions in the ink feed or lighter impressions will cause a lighter appearance. Stamps printed in the same color by water-based and solvent-based inks can differ significantly in appearance. This affects several stamps in the U.S. Prominent Americans series. Hand-mixed ink formulas (primarily from the 19th century) produced under different conditions (humidity and temperature) account for notable color variations in early printings of the same stamp (see U.S. Scott 248-250, 279B, for example). Different sources of pigment can also result in significant differences in color.

Light exposure and aging are closely related in the way they affect stamp color. Both eventually break down the ink and fade colors, so that a carefully kept stamp may differ significantly in color from an identical copy that has been exposed to light. If stamps are exposed to light either intentionally or accidentally, their colors can be faded or completely changed in some cases.

Papers of different quality and consistency used for the same stamp printing may affect color appearance. Most pelure papers, for example, show a richer color when compared with wove or laid papers. See Russia Scott 181a, for an example of this effect.

The very nature of the printing processes can cause a variety of differences in shades or hues of the same stamp. Some of these shades are scarcer than others, and are of particular interest to the advanced collector.

Luminescence

All forms of tagged stamps fall under the general category of luminescence. Within this broad category is fluorescence, dealing with forms of tagging visible under longwave ultraviolet light, and phosphorescence, which deals with tagging visible only under shortwave light. Phosphorescence leaves an afterglow and fluorescence does not. These treated stamps show up in a range of different colors when exposed to UV light. The differing wavelengths of the light activates the tagging material, making it glow in various colors that usually serve different mail processing purposes.

Intentional tagging is a post-World War II phenomenon, brought about by the increased literacy rate and rapidly growing mail volume. It was one of several answers to the problem of the need for more automated mail processes. Early tagged stamps served the purpose of triggering machines to separate different types of mail. A natural outgrowth was to also use the signal to trigger machines that faced all envelopes the same way and canceled them.

Tagged stamps come many different ways and in different forms. Some tagged stamps have luminescent shapes or images imprinted on them as a form of security device. Others have blocks (United States), stripes, frames (South Africa and Canada), overall coatings (United States), bars (Great Britain and Canada) and many other types. Some types of tagging are even mixed in with the pigmented printing ink (Australia Scott 366, Netherlands Scott 478 and U.S. Scott 1359 and 2443). Each form of tagging has a different purpose, some to give different machines different types of signals, and others as adaptive forms of technological growth.

The means of applying taggant to stamps differs as much as the intended purposes for the stamps. The most common form of tagging is a coating applied to the surface of the printed stamp. Since the taggant ink is frequently invisible except under UV light, it does not interfere with the appearance of the stamp. Another common application is the use of phosphored papers. In this case the paper itself either has a coating of taggant applied before the stamp is printed or has taggant applied during the papermaking process, incorporating it into the fibers. This is currently in use in the United States. A similar form is the application of a fluorescent coating either to the finished paper or during the papermaking process. This type of tagging has been extensively used by Australia and Germany.

Many countries now use tagging in various forms to either expedite mail handling or to serve as a printing security device against counterfeiting. Following the introduction of tagged stamps for public use in 1959 by Great Britain, other countries have steadily joined the parade. Among those are Germany (1961); Canada and Denmark (1962); United States, Australia, France and Switzerland (1963); Belgium and Japan (1966); Sweden and Norway (1967); Italy (1968); and Russia (1969). Since then, many other countries have begun using forms of tagging, including Brazil, China, Czechoslovakia, Hong Kong, Guatemala, Indonesia, Israel, Lithuania, Luxembourg, Netherlands, Penrhyn Islands, Portugal, St. Vincent, Singapore, South Africa, Spain and Sweden to name a few.

In some cases, including United States, Canada, Great Britain and Switzerland, stamps were released both with and without tagging. Many of these were released during each country's experimental period. Tagged and untagged versions are listed for the aforementioned countries and are noted in some other countries' listings. For at least a few stamps, the experimentally tagged version is worth far more than its untagged counterpart, such as the 1963 experimental tagged version of France Scott 1024.

In some cases luminescent varieties of stamps were inadvertently created. Several Russian stamps, for example, sport highly fluorescent ink that was not intended as a form of tagging. Older stamps, such as early U.S. postage dues, can be positively identified by the use of UV light, since the organic ink used has become slightly fluorescent over time. Other stamps, such as Austria Scott 70a-82a (varnish bars) and Obock Scott 46-64 (printed quadrille lines), have become fluorescent over time.

Various fluorescent substances have been added to paper to make it appear brighter. These optical brightners, as they are known, greatly affect the appearance of the stamp under UV light. The brightest of these is known as Hi-Brite paper. These paper varieties are beyond the scope of the Scott Catalogue.

Shortwave UV light also is used extensively in expertizing, since each form of paper has its own fluorescent characteristics that are impossible to perfectly match. It is therefore a simple matter to detect filled thins, added perforation teeth and other alterations that involve the addition of paper. UV light also is used to examine stamps that have had cancels chemically removed and for other purposes as well.

Gum

The gum on the back of a stamp may be shiny, dull, smooth, rough, dark, white, colored or tinted. It may be obvious or virtually impossible to distinguish, as on Canada Scott 453 or Rwanda Scott 287-294. Most stamp gumming adhesives use gum arabic or dextrine as a base. Certain polymers such as polyvinyl alcohol (PVA) have been used extensively since World War II. The PVA gum used by security printers Harrison and Sons since 1968 is dull-surfaced, slightly yellowish and almost invisible.

The *Scott Standard Postage Stamp Catalogue* does not list items by types of gum. The *Scott Specialized Catalogue of United States Stamps* does differentiate among some types of gum for certain issues.

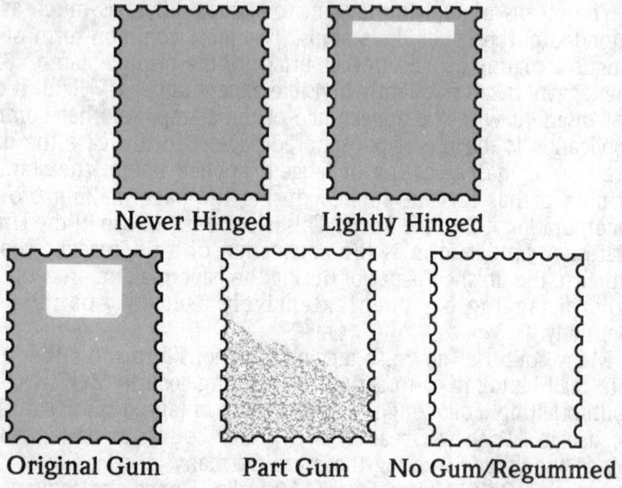

For purposes of determining the condition of an unused stamp, Scott Publishing Co. presents the following definitions (with accompanying illustrations): **Never Hinged (NH)** - Full original gum with no hinge mark or other blemish or disturbance. The presence of an expertizer's mark does not disqualify a stamp from this designation; **Lightly Hinged (LH)** - Full original gum with a light disturbance of the gum from the removal of a peelable hinge; **Original Gum (OG)** - Hinging and other disturbances should affect 20 percent or less of the original gum. **Part Gum (PG)** - Between 20 and 80 percent of the original gum remains. The stamp may have hinge remnants; **No Gum (NG) or Regummed (RE)** - A stamp with no gum or less than 20 percent of the original gum. A regummed stamp is considered the same as a stamp with none of its original gum for purposes of grading.

Reprints of stamps may have gum differing from the original issues. In addition, some countries have used different gum formulas for different seasons. These adhesives have different properties that may become more apparent over time.

Many stamps have been issued without gum, and the catalogue will note this fact. See United States Scott PR33-PR56. Sometimes, gum may have been removed to preserve the stamp. Germany Scott B68, for example, has a highly acidic gum that eventually destroys the stamps. This item is valued in the catalogue with gum removed.

Reprints and Reissues

These are impressions of stamps (usually obsolete) made from the original plates or stones. If they are valid for postage and reproduce obsolete issues (such as U.S.Scott 2875), the stamps are *reissues.* If they are from current issues, they are designated as *second, third,* etc., *printing.* If designated for a particular purpose, they are *special printings.*

Scott will list those reissues and reprints that are valid for postage if they differ significantly from the original printing.

When reprints are not valid for postage, but are made from original dies and plates by authorized persons, they are *official reprints. Private reprints* are made from original plates and dies by private hands. *Official reproductions* or imitations are made from new dies and plates by government authorization.

The U.S. government made official imitations of its first postage stamps in 1875. Produced were copies of the first two stamps (listed as Scott 3-4), reprints of the demonetized pre-1861 issues and reissues of the 1861 stamps, the 1869 stamps and the then-current 1875 denominations. An example of a private reprint is that of the New Haven, Conn., postmaster's provisional.

Most reprints differ slightly from the original stamp in some characteristic, such as gum, paper, perforation, color or watermark. Sometimes the details are followed so meticulously that only a student of that specific stamp is able to distinguish the reprint from the original.

Remainders and Canceled to Order

Some countries sell their stock of old stamps when a new issue replaces them. To avoid postal use, the *remainders* usually are canceled with a punch hole, a heavy line or bar, or a more-or-less regular-looking cancellation. The most famous merchant of remainders was Nicholas F. Seebeck. In the 1880s and 1890s, he arranged printing contracts between the Hamilton Bank Note Co., of which he was a director, and several Central and South American countries. The contracts provided that the plates and all remainders of the yearly issues became the property of Hamilton. Seebeck saw to it that ample stock remained. The "Seebecks," both remainders and reprints, were standard packet fillers for decades.

Some countries also issue stamps *canceled-to-order (CTO),* either in sheets with original gum or stuck onto pieces of paper or envelopes and canceled. Such CTO items generally are worth less than postally used stamps. In cases where the CTO material is far more prevalent in the marketplace than postally used examples, the catalogue value relates to the CTO examples, with postally used examples noted as premium items. Most CTOs can be detected by the presence of gum. However, as the CTO practice goes back at least to 1885, the gum inevitably has been soaked off some stamps so they could pass as postally used. The normally applied postmarks usually differ slightly from standard postmarks, and specialists are able to tell the difference. When applied individually to envelopes by philatelically minded persons, CTO material is known as *favor canceled* and generally sells at large discounts.

Cinderellas and Facsimiles

Cinderella is a catch-all term used by stamp collectors to describe phantoms, fantasies, bogus items, municipal issues, exhibition seals, local revenues, transportation stamps, labels, poster stamps and many other types of items. Some cinderella collectors include in their collections local postage issues, telegraph stamps, essays and proofs, forgeries and counterfeits.

A *fantasy* is an adhesive created for a nonexistent stamp-issuing authority. Fantasy items range from imaginary countries (Occusi-Ambeno, Kingdom of Sedang, Principality of Trinidad or Torres Straits), to non-existent locals (Winans City Post), or nonexistent transportation lines (McRobish & Co.'s Acapulco-San Francisco Line).

On the other hand, if the entity exists and could have issued stamps (but did not) or was known to have issued other stamps, the items are considered *bogus* stamps. These would include the Mormon postage stamps of Utah, S. Allan Taylor's Guatemala and Paraguay inventions, the propaganda issues for the South Moluccas and the adhesives of the Page & Keyes local post of Boston.

Phantoms is another term for both fantasy and bogus issues.

Facsimiles are copies or imitations made to represent original stamps, but which do not pretend to be originals. A catalogue illustration is such a facsimile. Illustrations from the Moens catalogue of the last century were occasionally colored and passed off as stamps. Since the beginning of stamp collecting, facsimiles have been made for collectors as space fillers or for reference. They often carry the word "facsimile," "falsch" (German), "sanko" or "mozo" (Japanese), or "faux" (French) overprinted on the face or stamped on the back. Unfortunately, over the years a number of these items have had fake cancels applied over the facsimile notation and have been passed off as genuine.

Forgeries and Counterfeits

Forgeries and counterfeits have been with philately virtually from the beginning of stamp production. Over time, the terminology for the two has been used interchangeably. Although both forgeries and counterfeits are reproductions of stamps, the purposes behind their creation differ considerably.

Among specialists there is an increasing movement to more specifically define such items. Although there is no universally accepted terminology, we feel the following definitions most closely mirror the items and their purposes as they are currently defined.

Forgeries (also often referred to as *Counterfeits*) are reproductions of genuine stamps that have been created to defraud collectors. Such spurious items first appeared on the market around 1860, and most old-time collections contain one or more. Many are crude and easily spotted, but some can deceive experts.

An important supplier of these early philatelic forgeries was the Hamburg printer Gebruder Spiro. Many others with reputations in this craft included S. Allan Taylor, George Hussey, James Chute, George Forune, Benjamin & Sarpy, Julius Goldner, E. Oneglia and L.H. Mercier. Among the noted 20th-century forgers were Francois Fournier, Jean Sperati and the prolific Raoul DeThuin.

Forgeries may be complete replications, or they may be genuine stamps altered to resemble a scarcer (and more valuable) type. Most forgeries, particularly those of rare stamps, are worth only a small fraction of the value of a genuine example, but a few types, created by some of the most notable forgers, such as Sperati, can be worth as much or more than the genuine. Fraudulently produced copies are known of most classic rarities and many medium-priced stamps.

In addition to rare stamps, large numbers of common 19th- and early 20th-century stamps were forged to supply stamps to the early packet trade. Many can still be easily found. Few new philatelic forgeries have appeared in recent decades. Successful imitation of well-engraved work is virtually impossible. It has proven far easier to produce a fake by altering a genuine stamp than to duplicate a stamp completely.

Counterfeit (also often referred to as *Postal Counterfeit* or *Postal Forgery*) is the term generally applied to reproductions of stamps that have been created to defraud the government of revenue. Such items usually are created at the time a stamp is current and, in some cases, are hard to detect. Because most counterfeits are seized when the perpetrator is captured, postal counterfeits, particularly used on cover, are usually worth much more than a genuine example to specialists. The first postal counterfeit was of Spain's 4-cuarto carmine of 1854 (the real one is Scott 25). Apparently, the counterfeiters were not satisfied with their first version, which is now very scarce, and they soon created an engraved counterfeit, which is common. Postal counterfeits quickly followed in Austria, Naples, Sardinia and the Roman States. They have since been created in many other countries as well, including the United States.

An infamous counterfeit to defraud the government is the 1-shilling Great Britain "Stock Exchange" forgery of 1872, used on telegraph forms at the exchange that year. The stamp escaped detection until a stamp dealer noticed it in 1898.

Fakes

Fakes are genuine stamps altered in some way to make them more desirable. One student of this part of stamp collecting has estimated that by the 1950s more than 30,000 varieties of fakes were known. That number has grown greatly since then. The widespread existence of fakes makes it important for stamp collectors to study their philatelic holdings and use relevant literature. Likewise, collectors should buy from reputable dealers who guarantee their stamps and make full and prompt refunds should a purchased item be declared faked or altered by some mutually agreed-upon authority. Because fakes always have some genuine characteristics, it is not always possible to obtain unanimous agreement among experts regarding specific items. These students may change their opinions as philatelic knowledge increases. More than 80 percent of all fakes on the philatelic market today are regummed, reperforated (or perforated for the first time), or bear forged overprints, surcharges or cancellations.

Stamps can be chemically treated to alter or eliminate colors. For example, a pale rose stamp can be re-colored to resemble a blue shade of high market value. In other cases, treated stamps can be made to resemble missing color varieties. Designs may be changed by painting, or a stroke or a dot added or bleached out to turn an ordinary variety into a seemingly scarcer stamp. Part of a stamp can be bleached and reprinted in a different version, achieving an inverted center or frame. Margins can be added or repairs done so deceptively that the stamps move from the "repaired" into the "fake" category.

Fakers have not left the backs of the stamps untouched either. They may create false watermarks, add fake grills or press out genuine grills. A thin India paper proof may be glued onto a thicker backing to create the appearance an issued stamp, or a proof printed on cardboard may be shaved down and perforated to resemble a stamp. Silk threads are impressed into paper and stamps have been split so that a rare paper variety is added to an otherwise inexpensive stamp. The most common treatment to the back of a stamp, however, is regumming.

Some in the business of faking stamps have openly advertised fool-proof application of "original gum" to stamps that lack it, although most publications now ban such ads from their pages. It is believed that very few early stamps have survived without being hinged. The large number of never-hinged examples of such earlier material offered for sale thus suggests the widespread extent of regumming activity. Regumming also may be used to hide repairs or thin spots. Dipping the stamp into watermark fluid, or examining it under longwave ultraviolet light often will reveal these flaws.

Fakers also tamper with separations. Ingenious ways to add margins are known. Perforated wide-margin stamps may be falsely represented as imperforate when trimmed. Reperforating is commonly done to create scarce coil or perforation varieties, and to eliminate the naturally occurring straight-edge stamps found in sheet margin positions of many earlier issues. Custom has made straight-edged stamps less desirable. Fakers have obliged by perforating straight-edged stamps so that many are now uncommon, if not rare.

Another fertile field for the faker is that of overprints, surcharges and cancellations. The forging of rare surcharges or overprints began in the 1880s or 1890s. These forgeries are sometimes difficult to detect, but experts have identified almost all. Occasionally, overprints or cancellations are removed to create non-overprinted stamps or seemingly unused items. This is most commonly done by removing a manuscript cancel to make a stamp resemble an unused example. "SPECIMEN" overprints may be removed by scraping and repainting to create non-overprinted varieties. Fakers use inexpensive revenues or pen-canceled stamps to generate unused stamps for further faking by adding other markings. The quartz lamp or UV lamp and a high-powered magnifying glass help to easily detect removed cancellations.

The bigger problem, however, is the addition of overprints, surcharges or cancellations - many with such precision that they are very difficult to ascertain. Plating of the stamps or the overprint can be an important method of detection.

Fake postmarks may range from many spurious fancy cancellations to a host of markings applied to transatlantic covers, to adding normally appearing postmarks to definitives of some countries with stamps that are valued far higher used than unused. With the increased popularity of cover collecting, and the widespread interest in postal history, a fertile new field for fakers has come about. Some have tried to create entire covers. Others specialize in adding stamps, tied by fake cancellations, to genuine stampless covers, or replacing less expensive or damaged stamps with more valuable ones. Detailed study of postal rates in effect at the time a cover in question was mailed, including the analysis of each handstamp used during the period, ink analysis and similar techniques, usually will unmask the fraud.

Restoration and Repairs

Scott Publishing Co. bases its catalogue values on stamps that are free of defects and otherwise meet the standards set forth earlier in this introduction. Most stamp collectors desire to have the finest copy of an item possible. Even within given grading categories there are variances. This leads to a controversial practice that is not defined in any universal manner: stamp *restoration.*

There are broad differences of opinion about what is permissible when it comes to restoration. Carefully applying a soft eraser to a stamp or cover to remove light soiling is one form of restoration, as is washing a stamp in mild soap and water to clean it. These are fairly accepted forms of restoration. More severe forms of restoration include pressing out creases or removing stains caused by tape. To what degree each of these is acceptable is dependent upon the individual situation. Further along the spectrum is the freshening of a stamp's color by removing oxide build-up or the effects of wax paper left next to stamps shipped to the tropics.

At some point in this spectrum the concept of *repair* replaces that of restoration. Repairs include filling thin spots, mending tears by reweaving or adding a missing perforation tooth. Regumming stamps may have been acceptable as a restoration or repair technique many decades ago, but today it is considered a form of fakery.

Restored stamps may or may not sell at a discount, and it is possible that the value of individual restored items may be enhanced over that of their pre-restoration state. Specific situations dictate the resultant value of such an item. Repaired stamps sell at substantial discounts from the value of sound stamps.

When the purchaser of an item has any reason to suspect that an item has been repaired, and the detection of such a repair is beyond his own ability, he should seek expert advice. There are services that specialize in giving such advice.

Terminology

Booklets — Many countries have issued stamps in small booklets for the convenience of users. This idea continues to become increasingly popular in many countries. Booklets have been issued in many sizes and forms, often with advertising on the covers, the panes of stamps or on the interleaving.

The panes used in booklets may be printed from special plates or made from regular sheets. All panes from booklets issued by the United States and many from those of other countries contain stamps that are straight edged on the sides, but perforated between. Others are distinguished by orientation of watermark or other identifying features. Any stamp-like unit in the pane, either printed or blank, that is not a postage stamp is considered to be a *label* in the catalogue listings.

Scott lists and values booklet panes only. Complete booklets are listed and valued in only a few cases, such as Grenada Scott 1055 and some forms of British prestige booklets. Individual booklet panes are listed only when they are not fashioned from existing sheet stamps and, therefore, are identifiable from their sheet stamp counterparts.

Panes usually do not have a used value assigned to them because there is little market activity for used booklet panes, even though many exist used and there is some demand for them.

Cancellations — The marks or obliterations put on stamps by postal authorities to show that they have performed service and to prevent their reuse are known as cancellations. If the marking is made with a pen, it is considered a "pen cancel." When the location of the post office appears in the marking, it is a "town cancellation." A "postmark" is technically any postal marking, but in practice the term generally is applied to a town cancellation with a date. When calling attention to a cause or celebration, the marking is known as a "slogan cancellation." Many other types and styles of cancellations exist, such as duplex, numerals, targets, fancy and others. See also "precancels," below.

Coil Stamps — These are stamps that are issued in rolls for use in dispensers, affixing and vending machines. Those coils of the United States, Canada, Sweden and some other countries are perforated horizontally or vertically only, with the outer edges imperforate. Coil stamps of some countries, such as Great Britain and Germany, are perforated on all four sides and may in some cases be distinguished from their sheet stamp counterparts by watermarks, counting numbers on the reverse or other means.

Covers — Entire envelopes, with or without adhesive postage stamps, that have passed through the mail and bear postal or other markings of philatelic interest are known as covers. Before the introduction of envelopes in about 1840, people folded letters and wrote the address on the outside. Some people covered their letters with an extra sheet of paper on the outside for the address, producing the term "cover." Used airletter sheets, stamped envelopes and other items of postal stationery also are considered covers.

Errors — Stamps that have some major, consistent unintentional deviation from the normal are considered errors. Errors include, but are not limited to, missing or wrong colors, wrong paper, wrong watermarks, inverted centers or frames on multicolor printing, inverted or missing surcharges or overprints, double impressions, missing perforations and others. Factually wrong or misspelled information, if it appears on all examples of a stamp, are not considered errors in the true sense of the word. They are errors of design. Inconsistent or randomly appearing items, such as misperfs or color shifts, are classified as freaks.

Overprints and Surcharges — Overprinting involves applying wording or design elements over an already existing stamp. Overprints can be used to alter the place of use (such as "Canal Zone" on U.S. stamps), to adapt them for a special purpose ("Porto" on Denmark's 1913-20 regular issues for use as postage due stamps, Scott J1-J7) or to commemorate a special occasion (United States Scott 647-648).

A *surcharge* is a form of overprint that changes or restates the face value of a stamp or piece of postal stationery.

Surcharges and overprints may be handstamped, typeset or, occasionally, lithographed or engraved. A few hand-written overprints and surcharges are known.

Precancels — Stamps that are canceled before they are placed in the mail are known as precancels. Precanceling usually is done to expedite the handling of large mailings and generally allow the affected mail pieces to skip certain phases of mail handling.

In the United States, precancellations generally identified the point of origin; that is, the city and state. This information appeared across the face of the stamp, usually centered between parallel lines. More recently, bureau precancels retained the parallel lines, but the city and state designations were dropped. Recent coils have a service inscription that is present on the original printing plate. These show the mail service paid for by the stamp. Since these stamps are not intended to receive further cancellations when used as intended, they are considered precancels. Such items often do not have parallel lines as part of the precancellation.

In France, the abbreviation *Affranchts* in a semicircle together with the word *Postes* is the general form of precancel in use. Belgian precancellations usually appear in a box in which the name of the city appears. Netherlands precancels have the name of the city enclosed between concentric circles, sometimes called a "lifesaver." Precancellations of other countries usually follow these patterns, but may be any arrangement of bars, boxes and city names.

Precancels are listed in the Scott catalogues only if the precancel changes the denomination (Belgium Scott 477-478); if the precanceled stamp is different from the non-precanceled version (such as untagged U.S. precancels); or if the stamp exists only precanceled (France Scott 1096-1099, U.S. Scott 2265).

Proofs and Essays — Proofs are impressions taken from an approved die, plate or stone in which the design and color are the same as the stamp issued to the public. Trial color proofs are impressions taken from approved dies, plates or stones in colors that vary from the final version. An essay is the impression of a design that differs in some way from the issued stamp. "Progressive die proofs" generally are considered to be essays.

Provisionals — These are stamps that are issued on short notice and intended for temporary use pending the arrival of regular issues. They usually are issued to meet such contingencies as changes in government or currency, shortage of necessary postage values or military occupation.

During the 1840s, postmasters in certain American cities issued stamps that were valid only at specific post offices. In 1861, postmasters of the Confederate States also issued stamps with limited validity. Both of these examples are known as "postmaster's provisionals."

Se-tenant — This term refers to an unsevered pair, strip or block of stamps that differ in design, denomination or overprint.

Unless the se-tenant item has a continuous design (see U.S. Scott 1451a, 1694a) the stamps do not have to be in the same order as shown in the catalogue (see U.S. Scott 2158a).

Specimens — The Universal Postal Union required member nations to send samples of all stamps they released into service to the International Bureau in Switzerland. Member nations of the UPU received these specimens as samples of what stamps were valid for postage. Many are overprinted, handstamped or initial-perforated "Specimen," "Canceled" or "Muestra." Some are marked with bars across the denominations (China-Taiwan), punched holes (Czechoslovakia) or back inscriptions (Mongolia).

Stamps distributed to government officials or for publicity purposes, and stamps submitted by private security printers for official approval, also may receive such defacements.

The previously described defacement markings prevent postal use, and all such items generally are known as "specimens."

Tete Beche — This term describes a pair of stamps in which one is upside down in relation to the other. Some of these are the result of intentional sheet arrangements, such as Morocco Scott B10-B11. Others occurred when one or more electrotypes accidentally were placed upside down on the plate, such as Colombia Scott 57a. Separation of the tete-beche stamps, of course, destroys the tete beche variety.

Currency Conversion

Country	Dollar	Pound	S Franc	Guilder	Yen	Lira	HK Dollar	D-Mark	Fr Franc	Cdn Dollar	Aust Dollar
Australia	1.330	2.132	1.04	0.7768	0.0136	0.0008	0.1721	0.8710	0.2533	0.9796	....
Canada	1.3578	2.1767	1.0616	0.7930	0.0139	0.0009	0.1757	0.889	0.2585	....	1.0208
France	5.2516	8.4187	4.1060	3.0670	0.0538	0.0034	0.6795	3.4389	....	3.8677	3.9483
Germany	1.5271	2.4481	1.1940	0.8918	0.0156	0.0010	0.1976	....	0.2908	1.1247	1.1481
Hong Kong	7.729	12.39	6.0426	4.5135	0.0791	0.0049	....	5.0609	1.4716	5.6919	5.8105
Italy	1565.75	2510.02	1224.20	914.41	16.034	....	202.59	1025.31	298.15	1153.15	1177.17
Japan	97.65	156.54	76.349	57.029	....	0.0624	12.635	63.945	18.594	71.918	73.416
Netherlands	1.712	2.745	1.339	....	0.0175	0.0011	0.2216	1.1213	0.3261	1.2611	1.2873
Switzerland	1.279	2.05	....	0.7469	0.0131	0.0008	0.1655	0.8375	0.2435	0.9420	0.9616
U.K.	0.6238	....	0.4877	0.3643	0.0064	0.0004	0.0807	0.4085	0.1188	0.4594	0.4690
U.S.	....	1.603	0.7819	0.5840	0.0102	0.0006	0.1294	0.6548	0.1904	0.7365	0.7518

Country	Currency	U.S. $ Equiv.
Anguilla	East Caribbean dollar	.3703
Antigua	East Caribbean dollar	.3703
Bahamas	dollar	1.00
Barbados	dollar	.4972
Barbuda	East Caribbean dollar	.3703
Belize	dollar	.5000
Bermuda	dollar	1.00
British Antarctic Territory	British pound	1.6034
Canada	dollar	.7365
Cayman Islands	dollar	1.113
Dominica	East Caribbean dollar	.3703
Falkland Islands	pound	1.6034
Grenada	East Caribbean dollar	.3703
Grenada Grenadines	East Caribbean dollar	.3703
Guyana	dollar	.0070
Jamaica	dollar	.0308
Marshall Islands	U.S. dollar	1.00
Micronesia	U.S. dollar	1.00
Montserrat	East Caribbean dollar	.3703
Nevis	East Caribbean dollar	.3703
Palau	U.S. dollar	1.00
St. Kitts	East Caribbean dollar	.3703
St. Lucia	East Caribbean dollar	.3703
St. Vincent	East Caribbean dollar	.3703
St. Vincent Grenadines	East Caribbean dollar	.3703
South Georgia	pound	1.6034
Trinidad & Tobago	dollar	.1777
Turks & Caicos Islands	U.S. dollar	1.00
United Nations-New York	U.S. dollar	1.00
United Nations-Geneva	Swiss franc	.7818
United Nations-Vienna	Austria shilling	.0903
United States	dollar	1.00
Virgin Islands	U.S. dollar	1.00

*Source: **Wall Street Journal** Nov. 14, 1994. Figures reflect values as of Nov. 11, 1994.*

UNITED STATES

GOVT. — Republic
AREA — 3,615,211 sq. mi.
POP. — 226,545,805 (1980)
CAPITAL — Washington, DC

In addition to the 50 States and the District of Columbia, the Republic includes Guam, the Commonwealth of Puerto Rico, the Virgin Islands, American Samoa, Wake, Midway, and a number of small islands in the Pacific Ocean, all of which use stamps of the United States.

100 Cents = 1 Dollar

Catalogue values for unused stamps in this country are for Never Hinged items, beginning with Scott 772 in the regular postage section, Scott C19 in the air post section, Scott E17 in the special delivery section, Scott FA1 in the certified mail section, Scott O127 in officials section, Scott J88 in the postage due section, Scott R733 in the revenues section, Scott RW1 in the hunting permit stamps section.

Watermarks

Wmk. 190- "USPS" in Single-lined Capitals

Wmk. 191- Double-lined "USPS" in Capitals

Wmk. 190PI - PIPS, used in the Philippines
Wmk. 191PI - PIPS, used in the Philippines
Wmk. 191C - US-C, used for Cuba
Wmk. 191R - USIR

PROVISIONAL ISSUES BY POSTMASTERS

Values for Envelopes are for entires.

Alexandria, Va.

A1

Type I - 40 asterisks in circle.
Type II - 39 asterisks in circle.

1846 **Typeset** *Imperf.*

1X1 A1 5c black, *buff,* Type I —
a. 5c black, *buff,* Type II *75,000.*
1X2 A1 5c black, *blue,* Type I, on cover —

All known copies of Nos. 1X1-1X2 are cut to shape.

Annapolis, Md.

ENVELOPE

E1

1846

2XU1 E1 5c carmine red *210,000.*

Handstamped impressions of the circular design with "2" in blue or red exist on envelopes and letter sheets. Values: blue $2,500, red $3,500.

A letter sheet exists with circular design and "5" handstamped in red. Values: blue $3,500, red $5,000.

A similar circular design in blue was used as a postmark.

Baltimore, Md.

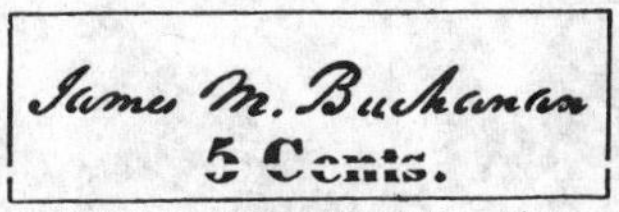

Signature of Postmaster — A1

1845 **Engr.** *Imperf.*

3X1 A1 5c black *5,000.*
3X2 A1 10c black, on cover *50,000.*
3X3 A1 5c black, *bluish* *25,000.* *5,000.*
3X4 A1 10c black, *bluish* *60,000.*

Nos. 3X1-3X4 were printed from a plate of 12 (2x6) containing nine 5c and three 10c.

ENVELOPES

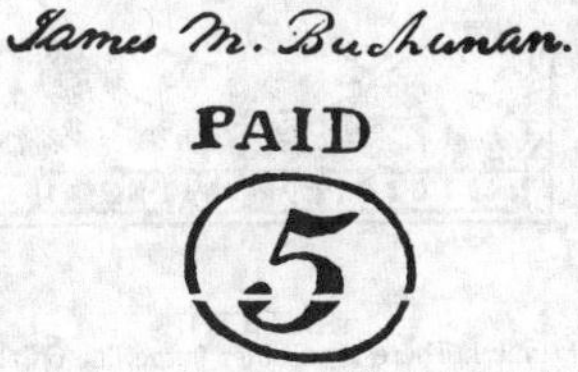

E1

The color given is that of the "PAID 5" and oval. "James M. Buchanan" is handstamped in black, blue or red. The paper is manila, buff, white, salmon or grayish.

1845 **Handstamped**
Various Papers

3XU1 E1 5c blue *5,000.*
3XU2 E1 5c red *10,000.*
3XU3 E1 10c blue *17,500.*
3XU4 E1 10c red *20,000.*

On the formerly listed "5+5" envelopes, the second "5" in oval is believed not to be part of the basic prepaid marking.

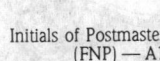

Boscawen, N. H.

A1

1846(?) **Typeset** *Imperf.*

4X1 A1 5c dull blue, *yellowish,* on cover *175,000.*

Brattleboro, Vt.

Initials of Postmaster (FNP) — A1

Plate of 10 (5x2).

1846 **Engr.** *Imperf.*

5X1 A1 5c black, *buff* *7,500.*

Lockport, N. Y.

A1

Handstamped, "5" in Black Ms

1846

6X1 A1 5c red, *buff,* on cover *150,000.*

Millbury, Mass.

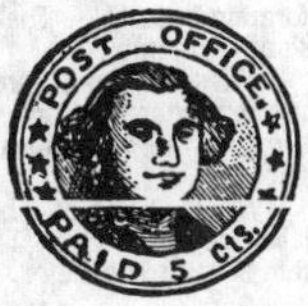

George Washington — A1

Printed from a Woodcut

1846 *Imperf.*

7X1 A1 5c blue, *bluish* *130,000.* *25,000.*

New Haven, Conn.

ENVELOPES

E1

1845 **Handstamped**
Signed in Blue, Black, Magenta or Red

8XU1 E1 5c red (Bl or M) *75,000.*
8XU2 E1 5c red, *light bluish* (Bk) *100,000.*
8XU3 E1 5c dull blue, *buff* (Bl) *75,000.*
8XU4 E1 5c dull blue (Bl) *75,000.*

Values of Nos. 8XU1-8XU4 are a guide to value. They are based on auction realizations and retail sales and take condition into consideration. All New Haven envelopes are of almost equal rarity. An entire of No. 8XU2 is the finest example known. The other envelopes are valued according to condition as much as rarity.

Reprints were made at various times between 1871 and 1932. They differ in shade and paper from the originals.

New York, N. Y.

George Washington — A1

Plate of 40 (5x8). Nos. 9X1-9X3 valued without gum.

1845 **Engr.** *Imperf.*
Bluish Wove Paper

9X1 A1 5c blk, signed ACM, connected 600. 375.
a. Signed ACM, AC connected 1,000. 425.
b. Signed A.C.M. *2,500.* 500.
c. Signed MMJr *7,500.*
d. Signed RHM *12,500.* *2,750.*
e. Without signature 1,750. 550.

These stamps were usually initialed "ACM" in magenta ink, as a control, before being sold or passed through the mails.

A plate of 9 (3x3) was made from which proofs were printed in black on white and deep blue papers; also in blue, green, brown and red on white bond paper.

1847 **Engr.** *Imperf.*
Blue Wove Paper

9X2 A1 5c blk, signed ACM, connected *6,000.* 2,750.
a. Signed RHM —
d. Without signature *10,000.* 5,000.

On the listing example of No. 9X2a the "R" is illegible and does not match those of the other "RHM" signatures.

1847 **Engr.** *Imperf.*
Gray Wove Paper

9X3 A1 5c blk, signed ACM, connected 5,000. 1,500.
a. Signed RHM *4,000.*
b. Without signature *5,000.*

Providence, R.I.

A1

A2

1846 **Engr.** *Imperf.*

10X1 A1 5c gray black 200. *1,500.*
10X2 A2 10c gray black 1,000. —
a. Se-tenant with 5c 1,400.

Plate of 12 (3x4) contains 11-5c and 1-10c.

Reprints were made in 1898. Each stamp bears one of the following letters on the back: B. O. G. E. R. T. D. U. R. B. I. N. Value of 5c, $50; 10c, $125; sheet, $725.

Reprint singles or sheets without back print sell for more.

St. Louis, Mo.

Missouri Coat of Arms
A1 A2 A3

1845-46 **Engr.** *Imperf.*
Greenish Wove Paper

11X1 A1 5c black *5,000.* *2,750.*
11X2 A2 10c black *4,500.* *2,500.*
11X3 A3 20c black *20,000.*

Three varieties of 5c, 3 of 10c, 2 of 20c.

1846
Gray Lilac Paper

11X4 A1 5c black — *4,250.*
11X5 A2 10c black *4,500.* *2,200.*
11X6 A3 20c black *13,500.*

One variety of 5c, 3 of 10c, 2 of 20c.

1847
Pelure Paper

11X7 A1 5c black *bluish* — *6,250.*
11X8 A2 10c black, *bluish* *6,250.*
a. Impression of 5c on back —

Three varieties of 5c, 3 of 10c.
Used values are for pencanceled copies.

Tuscumbia, Ala.

ENVELOPE

E1

1861 **Handstamped**
12XU1 E1 3c dull red, *buff* *16,000.*

See Confederate States Nos. 84XU1-84XU6.

GENERAL ISSUES
All Issues from 1847 to 1894 are Unwatermarked.

Benjamin Franklin A1

George Washington A2

1847, July 1 **Engr.** ***Imperf.***

1	A1	5c red brown, *bluish*	4,500.	425.
a.		5c dark brown, *bluish*	4,500.	450.
b.		5c orange brown, *bluish*	5,000.	525.
c.		5c red orange, *bluish*	*10,000.*	*4,000.*
d.		Double impression		
		Pen cancel		225.

The only known double impression shows part of the design doubled.

2	A2	10c black, *bluish*	*20,000.*	1,050.
a.		Diagonal half used as 5c on cover		*10,000.*
b.		Vertical half used as 5c on cover		*35,000.*
c.		Horizontal half used as 5c on cover		—
		Pen cancel		450.

Reproductions. The letters R. W. H. & E. at the bottom of each stamp are less distinct on the reproductions than on the originals.

5c. On the originals the left side of the white shirt frill touches the oval on a level with the top of the "F" of "Five." On the reproductions it touches the oval about on a level with the top of the figure "5."

10c. On the reproductions, line of coat at left points to right tip of "X" and line of coat at right points to center of "S" of CENTS. On the originals, line of coat points to "T" of TEN and between "T" and "S" of CENTS. On the reproductions the eyes have a sleepy look, the line of the mouth is straighter, and in the curl of hair near the left cheek is a strong black dot, while the originals have only a faint one.

See No. 948. See Special Printings following No. 211 for the reproductions of Nos. 1-2.

Franklin — A5

ONE CENT

Type I. Has complete curved lines outside the labels with "U.S. Postage" and "One Cent." The scrolls below the lower label are turned under, forming little balls. The ornaments at top are substantially complete.

Values for type I are for stamps showing the marked characteristics plainly. Copies of type I showing the balls indistinctly sell for much lower prices.

Type Ib. Same as I but balls below the bottom label are not so clear. The plumelike scrolls at bottom are not complete.

A6

Type Ia. Same as I at bottom but top ornaments and outer line at top are partly cut away.

Type Ic. Same as Ia, but bottom right plume and ball ornament incomplete. Bottom left plume complete or nearly complete.

A7

Type II. The little balls of the bottom scrolls and the bottoms of the lower plume ornaments are missing. The side ornaments are complete.

A8

Type III. The top and bottom curved lines outside the labels are broken in the middle. The side ornaments are complete.

Type IIIa. Similar to type III with the outer line broken at top or bottom but not both.

A9

Type IV. Similar to type II, but with the curved lines outside the labels recut at top or bottom or both.

Washington — A10

THREE CENTS

Type I. There is an outer frame line on all four sides.

Thomas Jefferson — A11

FIVE CENTS

Type I. There are projections on all four sides.

Washington — A12

TEN CENTS

Type I. The "shells" at the lower corners are practically complete. The outer line below the label is very nearly complete. The outer lines are broken above the middle of the top label and the "X" in each upper corner.

A13

Type II. The design is complete at the top. The outer line at the bottom is broken in the middle. The shells are partly cut away.

A14

Type III. The outer lines are broken above the top label and the "X" numerals. The outer line at the bottom and the shells are partly cut away, as in Type II.

A15

Type IV. The outer lines have been recut at top or bottom or both.

Types I, II, III and IV have complete ornaments at the sides of the stamps and three pearls at each outer edge of the bottom panel.

Washington — A16

In Nos. 5-17, the 1c, 3c, and 12c have very small margins between the stamps. The 5c and 10c have moderate size margins. The values of these stamps take the margin size into consideration.

Values for No. 5A, 6b and 19b are for the less distinct positions. Best examples sell for more.

Values for No. 16 are for outer line recut at top. Other recuts sell for more.

1851-57 ***Imperf.***

5	A5	1c blue, I	*175,000.*	*17,500.*

Values for No. 5 are for copies with margins touching or slightly cutting into the design.

5A	A5	1c blue, Ib	*9,000.*	*4,000.*
6	A6	1c blue, Ia ('57)	*22,500.*	*6,000.*
b.		Type Ic	*5,000.*	*1,200.*
7	A7	1c blue, II	575.	115.
8	A8	1c blue, III	*7,000.*	1,600.

Values for type III are for at least a 2mm break in each outer line. Examples of type III with wide breaks in outer lines command higher prices; those with small breaks sell for less.

8A	A8	1c blue, IIIa	*2,500.*	650.

Stamps of type IIIa with bottom line broken command higher prices than those with top line broken. See note after No. 8 on width of break of outer lines.

9	A9	1c blue, IV ('52)	425.	90.
a.		Printed on both sides, reverse inverted		—
10	A10	3c org brown, I	1,600.	45.
a.		Printed on both sides		—
11	A10	3c dull red, I	130.	7.
c.		Vertical half used as 1c on cover		*5,000.*

d.	Diagonal half used as 1c on cover		*5,000.*
e.	Double impression		*5,000.*
12 A11	5c red brown, I ('56)	*11,000.*	875.
13 A12	10c green, I ('55)	*9,500.*	575.
14 A13	10c green, II ('55)	2,200.	190.
15 A14	10c green, III ('55)	2,200.	190.
16 A15	10c green, IV ('55)	*12,500.*	1,200.
17 A16	12c black	2,800.	225.
a.	Diagonal half used as 6c on cover		*2,250.*
b.	Vertical half used as 6c on cover		*8,500.*
c.	Printed on both sides		*10,000.*

Same Designs as 1851-56 Issues

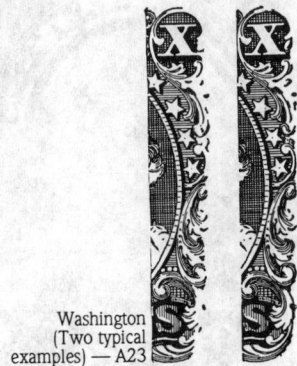

Franklin — A20

ONE CENT

Type V. Similar to type III of 1851-56 but with side ornaments partly cut away.

Washington — A21

THREE CENTS

Type II. The outer frame line has been removed at top and bottom. The side frame lines were recut so as to be continuous from the top to the bottom of the plate.

Type IIa. The side frame lines extend only to the top and bottom of the stamp design.

Jefferson — A22

FIVE CENTS

Type II. The projections at top and bottom are partly cut away.

Washington (Two typical examples) — A23

TEN CENTS

Type V. The side ornaments are slightly cut away. Usually only one pearl remains at each end of the lower label but some copies show two or three pearls at the right side. At the bottom the outer line is complete and the shells nearly so. The outer lines at top are complete except over the right "X."

Washington A17

Franklin A18

Washington — A19

TWELVE CENTS

Plate I. Outer frame lines complete.

Plate III. Outer frame lines noticeably uneven or broken, sometimes partly missing.

Nos. 18-39 have small or very small margins. The values represent stamps with perforations touching or just cutting the design on one or more sides.

1857-61 ***Perf. 15½***

18 A5	1c blue, type I ('61)	800.	325.
19 A6	1c blue, type Ia	*11,500.*	*3,250.*
b.	Type Ic	*1,600.*	*800.*
20 A7	1c blue, type II	500.	160.
21 A8	1c blue, type III	5,000.	1,100.
22 A8	1c blue, type IIIa	850.	300.
b.	Horiz. pair, imperf. btwn.		*5,000.*

One pair of No. 22b has been reported. Beware of pairs with blind perforations.

23 A9	1c blue, type IV	3,000.	375.
24 A20	1c blue, type V	120.	25.
b.	Laid paper		—
25 A10	3c rose, type I	1,050.	35.
b.	Vert. pair, imperf. horiz.		*10,000.*
26 A21	3c dull red, type II	40.	3.
a.	3c dull red, type IIa	125.	25.
b.	Horiz. pair, imperf. vert., type II	*4,000.*	—
c.	Vert. pair, imperf. horiz., type II		—
d.	Horizontal pair, imperf. between, type II		—
e.	Dbl. impression, type II		*2,500.*
27 A11	5c brick red, type I ('58)	*9,000.*	625.
28 A11	5c red brown, type I	1,500.	275.
b.	5c bright red brown	1,850.	400.
28A A11	5c Indian red, type I ('58)	*12,500.*	1,800.
29 A11	5c brown, type I ('59)	950.	200.
30 A22	5c org brown, type II ('61)	775.	1,050.
30A A22	5c brown, type II ('60)	650.	185.
b.	Printed on both sides	*3,750.*	*4,000.*
31 A12	10c green, type I	8,000.	500.
32 A13	10c green, type II	2,800.	190.
33 A14	10c green, type III	2,800.	190.
34 A15	10c green, type IV	*17,500.*	1,400.
35 A23	10c green, type V ('59)	200.	50.
36 A16	12c black, plate I	400.	105.
a.	Diagonal half used as 6c on cover (I)		*17,500.*
b.	12c black, plate III ('59)	350.	100.
c.	Horizontal pair, imperf. between (I)		*12,500.*
37 A17	24c gray lilac ('60)	700.	210.
a.	24c gray	675.	200.
38 A18	30c orange ('60)	850.	300.
39 A19	90c blue ('60)	1,250.	*5,000.*
	Pen cancel		1,100.

See Special Printings following No. 211 for the 1875 reprints of the 1857-1860 issue. See Die and Plate proofs in the Scott's United States Specialized Catalogue for imperfs. of the 12c, 24c, 30c, 90c.

Genuine cancellations on the 90c are rare.

Washington — A27a

The paper of former Nos. 55-62 (Nos. 63E11e, 65-E15h, 67-E9e, 69-E6e, 72-E6h, Essay section, Nos. 70eTC, 71bTC, Trial Color Proof section, Scott's U.S. Specialized) is thin and semitransparent. That of the postage issues is thicker and more opaque, except Nos. 62B, 70c and 70d.

1861

62B A27a	10c dark green	*4,500.*	450.

Franklin — A24

1c. A dash has been added under the tip of the ornament at right of the numeral in upper left corner.

Washington — A25

3c. Ornaments at corners have been enlarged and end in a small ball.

Jefferson — A26

5c. A leaflet has been added to the foliated ornaments at each corner.

Washington — A27

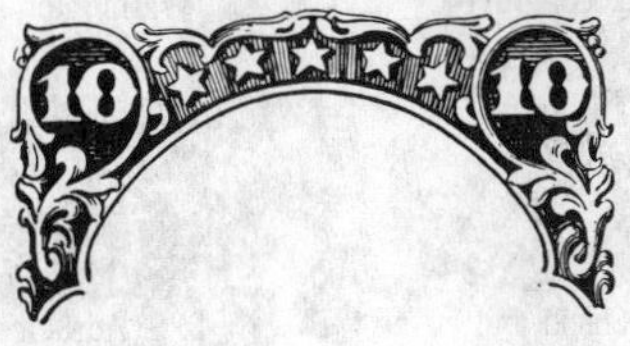

10c. A heavy curved line has been cut below the stars and an outer line added to the ornaments above them.

Washington — A28

12c. Ovals and scrolls have been added to the corners.

Washington A29

Franklin A30

Washington — A31

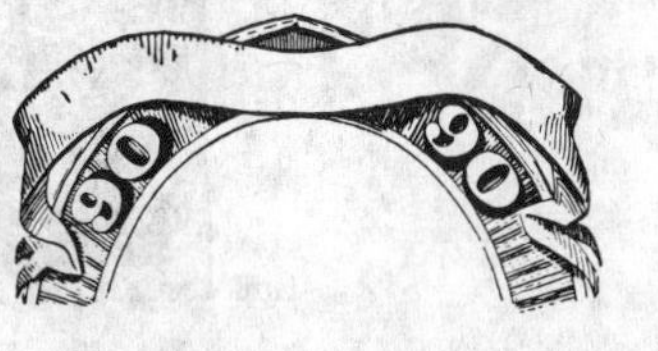

90c. Parallel lines form an angle above the ribbon with "U. S. Postage"; between these lines a row of dashes has been added and a point of color to the apex of the lower pair.

1861-62 ***Perf. 12***

63 A24	1c blue	150.00	15.00
a.	1c ultramarine	400.00	125.00
b.	1c dark blue	350.00	40.00
c.	Laid paper	—	—
d.	Vert. pair, imperf. horiz.		—
e.	Printed on both sides	—	*2,500.*
64 A25	3c pink	4,500.	450.00
a.	3c pigeon blood pink	*10,000.*	*2,500.*
b.	3c rose pink	300.00	90.00
65 A25	3c rose	90.00	1.00
b.	Laid paper		—
d.	Vert. pair, imperf. horiz.	*3,500.*	*750.00*
e.	Printed on both sides	*1,650.*	*1,000.*
f.	Double impression		*6,000.*

The 3c lake can be found in the Special Printings section, the imperfs. of the 3c rose and 3c lake in the Scott's U.S. Specialized Catalogue Die and Plate Proofs section.

67 A26	5c buff	*9,000.*	425.00
a.	5c brown yellow	*9,000.*	425.00
b.	5c olive yellow	*9,000.*	425.00

Values for Nos. 67, 67a, 67b reflect the normal small margins.

68 A27	10c yellow green	300.00	30.00
a.	10c dark green	325.00	32.50
b.	Vert. pair, imperf. horiz.		*3,500.*
69 A28	12c black	550.00	60.00
70 A29	24c red lilac ('62)	850.00	90.00
a.	24c brown lilac	750.00	80.00
b.	24c steel blue	5,000.	300.00
c.	24c violet, thin paper	7,000.	650.00
d.	24c pale gray violet, thin paper	1,400.	350.00
71 A30	30c orange	650.00	72.50
a.	Printed on both sides		—

Values for No. 71 are for copies with small margins, especially at sides. Large margined examples sell for much more.

72 A31	90c blue	1,450.	250.00
a.	90c pale blue	1,450.	250.00
b.	90c dark blue	1,600.	300.00

Nos. 70c, 70d are on a thinner, harder and more transparent paper than Nos. 70, 70a, 70b, or the later Nos. 78, 78a, 78b and 78c.

Designs as 1861 Issue

Andrew Jackson A32

Abraham Lincoln A33

1861-66 *Perf. 12*

73	A32	2c black ('63)	175.00	22.50
a.		Vert. or diag. half used as 1c as part of 3c rate on cover		*1,250.*
b.		Diagonal half used alone as 1c on cover		*3,000.*
c.		Horiz. half used as 1c as part of 3c rate on cover		—
d.		Laid paper	—	—
e.		Printed on both sides		*5,000.*

The 3c scarlet can be found under No. 74 in the Scott's U.S. Specialized Catalogue Trial Color Proofs section.

75	A26	5c red brown ('62)	2,000.	250.00
76	A26	5c brown ('63)	500.00	72.50
a.		5c dark brown	600.00	90.00
b.		Laid paper		—
77	A33	15c black ('66)	700.00	75.00
78	A29	24c lilac ('63)	425.00	60.00
a.		24c grayish lilac	425.00	60.00
b.		24c gray	425.00	60.00
c.		24c blackish violet	*17,500.*	*1,100.*
d.		Printed on both sides		*3,500.*

Values for Nos. 75, 76, 76a reflect the normal small margins.

Grill

Same as 1861-66 Issues
Embossed with grills of various sizes

Grill with Points Up

Grills A and C were made by a roller covered with ridges shaped like an inverted V. Pressing the ridges into the stamp paper forced the paper into the pyramidal pits between the ridges, causing irregular breaks in the paper.

Grill B was made by a roller with raised bosses.

A. Grill covering the entire stamp

1867 *Perf. 12*

79	A25	3c rose	2,250.	575.
b.		Printed on both sides		—
80	A26	5c brown	—	—
a.		5c dark brown		*50,000.*
81	A30	30c orange		—

An essay which is often mistaken for No. 79 (#79-E15) shows the points of the grill as small squares faintly impressed in the paper, but not cutting through it. On No. 79 the grill breaks through the paper. Copies free from defects are rare.

Six copies of Nos. 80, 80a, and eight copies of No. 81 are known. All are more or less faulty and/or off-center. Values range from $15,000 to $50,000 depending on condition and appearance.

Nos. 79, 79b, are valued for fine - very fine centering but with minor perforation faults.

The imperf. of the 3c rose can be found in the Scott's U.S. Specialized Catalogue Die and Plate Proofs section.

B. Grill about 18x15mm (22 by 18 points)

82	A25	3c rose		*95,000.*

The four known copies of No. 82 are fine.

C. Grill about 13x16mm (16 to 17 by 18 to 21 points)

83	A25	3c rose	3,000.	600.

The grilled area on each of four C grills in the sheet may total about 18x15mm when a normal C grill adjoins a fainter grill extending to the right or left edge of the stamp. This is caused by a partial erasure on the grill roller when it was changed to produce C grills instead of the all-over A grill.

The imperf. can be found in the Scott's U.S. Specialized Catalogue Die and Plate Proofs section.

Grill with Points Down

The grills were produced by rollers with the surface covered by pyramidal bosses. On the Z grill the tips of the pyramids are very short horizontal ridges. On the D, E and F grills the ridges are vertical.

D. Grill about 12x14mm (15 by 17 to 18 points)

84	A32	2c black	9,500.	1,500.

No. 84 is valued in the grade of fine.

85	A25	3c rose	3,000.	475.

Z. Grill about 11x14mm (13 to 14 by 17 to 18 points)

85A	A24	1c blue		—
85B	A32	2c black	3,000.	400.
85C	A25	3c rose	5,000.	1,200.
85D	A27	10c green		*45,000.*
85E	A28	12c black	4,000.	600.00
85F	A33	15c black		*100,000.*

Two copies of No. 85A are known. One is contained in the New York Public Library collection. Five copies of No. 85D and two copies of No. 85F are known.

E. Grill about 11x13mm (14 by 15 to 17 points)

86	A24	1c blue	1,100.	275.
a.		1c dull blue	1,100.	275.
87	A32	2c black	500.	70.
a.		Half used as 1c on cover, diagonal or vert.		*2,000.*
88	A25	3c rose	375.	10.
a.		3c lake red	425.	12.50
89	A27	10c green	2,000.	200.
90	A28	12c black	2,250.	200.
91	A33	15c black	4,250.	450.

F. Grill about 9x13mm (11 to 12 by 15 to 17 points)

92	A24	1c blue	525.00	110.00
a.		1c pale blue	500.00	100.00
93	A32	2c black	200.00	25.00
a.		Vert. or diag. half used as 1c as part of 3c rate on cover		*1,250.*
c.		Horiz. or diagonal half used alone as 1c on cover		*2,500.*
94	A25	3c red	175.00	2.50
a.		3c rose	175.00	2.50
c.		Vert. pair, imperf. horiz.	*1,000.*	
d.		Printed on both sides	*1,100.*	

The imperf. 3c can be found in the Scott's U.S. Specialized Catalogue Die and Plate Proofs section.

95	A26	5c brown	1,500.	300.
a.		5c dark brown	1,750.	325.

Values for Nos. 95, 95a reflect the normal small margins.

96	A27	10c yellow green	1,200.	110.00
a.		10c dark green	1,200.	110.00
97	A28	12c black	1,500.	125.00
98	A33	15c black	1,500.	185.00
99	A29	24c gray lilac	2,000.	450.00
100	A30	30c orange	2,750.	425.00

Values for No. 100 are for copies with small margins, especially at sides. Large margined examples sell for much more.

101	A31	90c blue	5,000.	800.

Some authorities believe that more than one size of grill probably existed on one of the grill rolls.

See Special Printings following No. 211 for the 1875 re-issues of the 1861-66 issues.

The reprints can be distinguished from the 1861-66 issues by the shades and the paper which is hard and very white instead of yellowish. The gum is white and crackly.

Franklin A34

Post Horse and Rider A35

Locomotive A36

Washington A37

Shield and Eagle A38

S. S. Adriatic A39

Landing of Columbus — A40

FIFTEEN CENTS

Type I. Picture unframed.

A40a

Type II. Picture framed.

Type III. Same as type I but without fringe of brown shading lines around central vignette.

"The Declaration of Independence" A41

Shield, Eagle and Flags A42

Lincoln — A43

G. Grill measuring 9 1/2x9mm (12 by 11 to 11 1/2 points)

1869 *Perf. 12*

112	A34	1c buff	275.00	65.00
b.		Without grill	*850.00*	
113	A35	2c brown	225.00	25.00
b.		Without grill	*750.00*	
c.		Half used as 1c on cover, diagonal, vert. or horiz.		*3,000.*
d.		Printed on both sides		—
114	A36	3c ultramarine	175.00	7.00
a.		Without grill	*600.00*	
b.		Vertical one third used as 1c on cover		—
c.		Vertical two thirds used as 2c on cover		*4,000.*
d.		Double impression		*3,500.*
115	A37	6c ultramarine	950.00	100.00
b.		Vertical half used as 3c on cover		—

No. 115 is the most difficult value in this issue to find well-centered. Such examples sell for much more.

116	A38	10c yellow	1,000.	90.
117	A39	12c green	950.	100.
118	A40	15c brn & blue, Type I	2,750.	400.
a.		Without grill	*4,000.*	
119	A40a	15c brn & blue, Type II	1,100.	150.
b.		Center inverted	*220,000.*	*16,000.*
c.		Center dbl., one invtd.		—
120	A41	24c green & vio	3,000.	475.
a.		Without grill	*5,500.*	
b.		Center inverted	*220,000.*	*18,000.*
121	A42	30c blue & car	3,000.	300.
a.		Without grill	*4,250.*	
b.		Flags inverted	*165,000.*	*55,000.*
122	A43	90c car & black	5,000.	1,200.
a.		Without grill	*8,500.*	

Values of varieties of Nos. 112-122 without grill are for copies with full original gum.

Most copies of Nos. 119b, 120b are faulty. Values are for fine centered copies without faults.

See Special Printings following No. 211 for the 1875, 1880 re-issues of the 1869 issue.

Printed by the National Bank Note Company

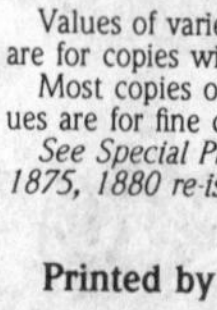

Franklin — A44

A44

Jackson — A45

A45

Washington — A46

A46

Lincoln — A47

A47

Edwin M. Stanton — A48

A48

Jefferson — A49

A49

Henry Clay — A50

A50

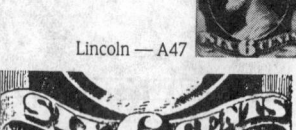

Daniel Webster — A51

A51

Gen. Winfield Scott A52

Alexander Hamilton A53

Commodore O. H. Perry — A54

Two varieties of grill are known on this issue.

H. Grill about 10x12mm (11 to 13 by 14 to 16 points) On all values, 1c to 90c
I. Grill about 8½x10mm (10 to 11 by 10 to 13 points) On 1, 2, 3, 6, 7c

On the 1870-71 stamps the grill impressions are usually faint or incomplete. This is especially true of the H grill, which often shows only a few points.

Values for 1c - 7c are for stamps showing well defined grills.

White Wove Paper

1870-71 *Perf. 12*

134	A44	1c ultramarine	900.00	65.00
135	A45	2c red brown	525.00	40.00
a.		Diagonal half used as 1c on cover		—
136	A46	3c green	400.00	11.00

The imperf. 3c can be found in the Scott's U.S. Specialized Catalogue Die and Plate Proofs section.

137	A47	6c carmine	2,100.	300.
138	A48	7c vermilion ('71)	1,500.	275.
139	A49	10c brown	2,000.	475.
140	A50	12c dull violet	*13,000.*	2,100.
141	A51	15c orange	3,000.	750.
142	A52	24c purple	—	*9,000.*
143	A53	30c black	6,000.	1,000.
144	A54	90c carmine	8,000.	900.

Without Grill
White Wove Paper

1870-71 *Perf. 12*

145	A44	1c ultramarine	225.00	8.00
146	A45	2c red brown	160.00	5.00
a.		Half used as 1c on cover, diagonal or vert.		—
c.		Double impression		—
147	A46	3c green	175.00	60
a.		Printed on both sides		*1,500.*
b.		Double impression		*1,000.*

The imperf. 3c can be found in the Scott's U.S. Specialized Catalogue Die and Plate Proofs section.

148	A47	6c carmine	325.00	12.50
a.		Vert. half used as 3c on cover		—
b.		Double impression		*1,250.*
149	A48	7c vermilion ('71)	425.00	55.00
150	A49	10c brown	325.00	12.50
151	A50	12c dull violet	750.00	80.00
152	A51	15c bright orange	725.00	90.00
a.		Double impression		—
153	A52	24c purple	775.00	85.00
154	A53	30c black	1,600.	110.00
155	A54	90c carmine	1,800.	200.00

Printed by the Continental Bank Note Co.

Designs of the 1870-71 Issue with secret marks on the values from 1c to 15c as described and illustrated below.

Franklin — A44a

1c. In pearl at left of numeral "1" is a small cresent.

Jackson — A45a

2c. Under the scroll at the left of "U. S." there is a small diagonal line. This mark seldom shows clearly. The stamp, No. 157, can be distinguished by its color.

Washington — A46a

3c. The under part of the upper tail of the left ribbon is heavily shaded.

Lincoln — A47a

6c. The first four vertical lines of the shading in the lower part of the left ribbon have been strengthened.

Stanton — A48a

7c. Two small semi-circles are drawn around the ends of the lines which outline the ball in the lower right hand corner.

Jefferson — A49a

10c. There is a small semi-circle in the scroll at the right end of the upper label.

Clay — A50a

12c. The balls of the figure "2" are crescent shaped.

Webster — A51a

15c. In the lower part of the triangle in the upper left corner two lines have been made heavier forming a "V." This mark can be found on some of the Continental and American (1879) printings, but not all stamps show it.

Secret marks were added to the dies of the 24c, 30c and 90c but new plates were not made from them. The various printings of these stamps can be distinguished only by the shades and paper.

White Wove Paper, thin to thick
Without Grill*

1873 *Perf. 12*

156	A44a	1c ultramarine	120.00	1.75
e.		With grill	*1,400.*	
f.		Imperf., pair	—	*500.00*
157	A45a	2c brown	250.00	10.00
c.		With grill	*1,100.*	*600.00*
d.		Double impression		—
e.		Vertical half used as 1c on cover		—
158	A46a	3c green	75.00	15
e.		With grill	*175.00*	
h.		Horiz. pair, imperf. vert.		—
i.		Horiz. pair, imperf. btwn.		*1,300.*
j.		Double impression		*1,250.*
k.		Printed on both sides		—

The imperf. 3c, with and without grill, can be found in the Scott's U.S. Specialized Catalogue Die and Plate Proofs section.

159	A47a	6c dull pink	275.00	10.00
b.		With grill	*1,000.*	
160	A48a	7c orange ver	600.00	57.50
a.		With grill	*1,500.*	
161	A49a	10c brown	350.00	11.50
c.		With grill	*2,000.*	
d.		Horiz. pair, imperf. btwn.		*2,500.*
162	A50a	12c black violet	950.00	70.00
a.		With grill	*3,000.*	
163	A51a	15c yellow orange	875.00	67.50
a.		With grill	*3,000.*	
164	A52	24c purple		—
165	A53	30c gray black	950.00	65.00
c.		With grill	*3,000.*	
166	A54	90c rose carmine	1,800.	200.00

The Philtelic Foundation has certified as genuine a 24c on vertically ribbed paper. Specialists believe that only Continental used ribbed paper.

* All values except 24c, 90c exist with experimental (J) grill, about 7x9½mm.

See Special Printings following No. 211 for the 1875 special printing of the 1873 issue.

These can be distinguished from the 1873 issue by the shades, also by the paper, which is very white instead of yellowish.

Zachary Taylor — A55

Yellowish Wove Paper

1875, June 21 *Perf. 12*

178	A45a	2c vermilion	225.00	5.00
b.		Half used as 1c on cover		—
c.		With grill	*325.00*	

The imperf. 2c can be found in the Scott's U.S. Specialized Catalogue Die and Plate Proofs section.

179	A55	5c blue	275.00	10.00
c.		With grill	625.00	

Almost all of the stamps of the Continental Bank Note Co. printing including the Department stamps and some of the Newspaper stamps may be found upon a paper which shows more or less of the characteristics of a ribbed paper.

See Special Printings section for the 1875 special printing of the 1875 issue.

Printed by the American Bank Note Company

Same as 1870-75 Issues
Soft Porous Paper
Varying from Thin to Thick

1879 *Perf. 12*

182	A44a	1c dark ultra	175.00	1.25
183	A45a	2c vermilion	80.00	1.25
a.		Double impression	—	*500.00*
184	A46a	3c green	60.00	15
b.		Double impression		—

The imperf. 3c can be found in the Scott's U.S. Specialized Catalogue Die and Plate Proofs section.

185	A55	5c blue	325.00	8.00
186	A47a	6c pink	600.00	15.00
187	A49	10c brown (without secret mark)	1,000.	15.00
188	A49a	10c brown (with secret mark)	750.00	16.00
189	A51a	15c red orange	225.00	15.00
190	A53	30c full black	650.00	35.00
191	A54	90c carmine	1,400.	155.00

The ABN Co. used many Continental plates to print the postage, Departmental and Newspaper stamps. Therefore, stamps bearing the Continental imprint were not always its product.

The ABN Co. also used the National 90c plate and possibly the 30c plate.

Early printings of No. 188 were from Continental plates 302 and 303 which contained the normal secret mark of 1873. After those plates were re-entered by the ABN Co. in 1880, pairs or multiple pieces contained combinations of normal, hairline or missing marks. The pairs or other multiples usually found contain at least one hairline mark which tended to disappear as the plate wore.

ABN Co. plates 377 and 378 were made in 1881 from the National transfer roll of 1870. No. 187 from those plates has no secret mark.

Perf 12 Trial/color Proofs on gummed stamp paper exist, as a 15c without speciman overprint.

The ABN Co. used many Continental plates to print the postage, Departmental and Newspaper stamps. Therefore, stamps bearing the Continental imprint were not always its product. The imperf. 90c can be found in the Scott's U.S. Specialized Catalogue Die and Plate Proofs section.

See Special Printings following No. 211 for the 1880 special printing of the 1879 issue.

James A. Garfield — A56

1882, Apr. 10 *Perf. 12*

205	A56	5c yellow brown	135.00	4.50

See Special Printings following No. 211 for the 1882 special printing.

Designs of 1873 Re-engraved

Franklin — A44b

1c. The vertical lines in the upper part of the stamp have been so deepened that the background often appears to be solid. Lines of shading have been added to the upper arabesques.

Washington — A46b

3c. The shading at the sides of the central oval appears only about one-half the previous width. A short horizontal dash has been cut about 1mm below the "TS" of "CENTS."

Lincoln — A47b

6c. On the original stamps four vertical lines can be counted from the edge of the panel to the outside of the stamp. On the re-engraved stamps there are but three lines in the same place.

Jefferson — A49b

10c. On the original stamps there are five vertical lines between the left side of the oval and the edge of the shield. There are only four lines on the re-engraved stamps. In the lower part of the latter, also, the horizontal lines of the background have been strengthened.

1881-82 *Perf. 12*

206	A44b	1c gray blue	40.00	40
207	A46b	3c blue green	45.00	15
c.		Double impression		—

208	A47b	6c rose ('82)	275.00	45.00
a.		6c brown red	225.00	65.00
209	A49b	10c brown ('82)	95.00	2.50
b.		10c black brown	200.00	20.00
c.		Double impression		—

Speciman stamps without overprint exist in a brown shade that differs from No. 209 and in green. The unoverprinted brown speciman is cheaper than No. 209.

Washington
A57

Jackson
A58

1883, Oct. 1 ***Perf. 12***

210	A57	2c red brown	37.50	15
211	A58	4c blue green	160.00	8.00

Imperfs. can be found in the Scott's U.S. Specialized Catalogue Die and Plate Proofs section.
Special Printings of 1883 follow.

The Special Printings section includes major Scott number stamps which were not issued primarily for postal purposes. These include the reproductions, reprints, reissues and special printings produced for the Post Office Department between 1875 and 1885.

REPRODUCTIONS

Actually, official imitations made from new plates by order of the Post Office Department.

A3

A4

1875 ***Imperf.***

Bluish Paper Without Gum

3	A3	5c red brown	700.
4	A4	10c black	900.

Reproductions. The letters R. W. H. & E. at the bottom of each stamp are less distinct on the reproductions than on the originals.

5c. On the originals the left side of the white shirt frill touches the oval on a level with the top of the "F" of "Five." On the reproductions it touches the oval about on a level with the top of the figure "5."

10c. On the reproductions, line of coat at left points to right tip of "X" and line of coat at right points to center of "S" of CENTS. On the originals, line of coat points to "T" of TEN and between "T" and "S" of CENTS. On the reproductions the eyes have a sleepy look, the line of the mouth is straighter, and in the curl of hair near the left cheek is a strong black dot, while the originals have only a faint one.

REPRINTS OF 1857-60 ISSUE

White Paper
Without Gum

1875 ***Perf. 12***

40	A5	1c bright blue	*450.*
41	A10	3c scarlet	*1,800.*
42	A22	5c orange brown	*800.*
43	A12	10c blue green	*1,750.*
44	A16	12c greenish blk	*2,000.*
45	A17	24c black violet	*2,000.*
46	A18	30c yellow orange	*2,000.*
47	A19	90c deep blue	*3,250.*

Nos. 41-46 are valued in the grade of fine. Exist imperf., value, set $25,000.

Re-issue of 1861-66 Issues
Without Grill
Hard White Paper
White Crackly Gum

1875 ***Perf. 12***

102	A24	1c blue	*500.*	*800.*
103	A32	2c black	*2,000.*	*4,000.*
104	A25	3c brown red	*2,250.*	*4,250.*
105	A26	5c brown	*1,750.*	*2,250.*
106	A27	10c green	*2,000.*	*3,750.*
107	A28	12c black	*2,750.*	*4,500.*
108	A33	15c black	*2,750.*	*4,750.*
109	A29	24c deep violet	*3,250.*	*6,000.*
110	A30	30c brownish org	*3,500.*	*6,000.*
111	A31	90c blue	*4,750.*	*20,000.*

These stamps can be distinguished from the 1861-66 issues by the shades and the paper which is hard and very white instead of yellowish. The gum is white and crackly.

Re-issues of the 1869 Issue
Without Grill
Hard White Paper

1875 ***Perf. 12***

123	A34	1c buff	325.	250.
124	A35	2c brown	375.	350.
125	A36	3c blue	3,000.	*10,000.*

Used value for No. 125 is for an attractive copy with minimal faults.

126	A37	6c blue	850.	600.
127	A38	10c yellow	1,400.	1,300.
128	A39	12c green	1,500.	1,300.
129	A40	15c brown & blue, type III	1,300.	750.
a.		Imperf. horiz., single	1,600.	—

Type III is same as type I but without fringe of brown shading lines around central vignette.

130	A41	24c green & violet	1,250.	950.
131	A42	30c blue & carmine	1,750.	1,600.
132	A43	90c carmine & black	4,000.	*4,500.*

1880

Soft Porous Paper

133	A34	1c buff	200.	160.
a.		1c brown orange	175.	140.

No. 133 was issued with gum, No. 133a without gum.

Special Printing of the 1873 Issue

Hard, White Wove Paper
Without Gum

1875 ***Perf. 12***

167	A44a	1c ultramarine	*8,000.*	
168	A45a	2c dark brown	*3,500.*	
169	A46a	3c blue green	*9,500.*	—
170	A47a	6c dull rose	*8,500.*	
171	A48a	7c redsh vermilion	*2,000.*	
172	A49a	10c pale brown	*8,250.*	
173	A50a	12c dark violet	*3,000.*	
174	A51a	15c bright orange	*8,250.*	
175	A52	24c dull purple	*1,850.*	—
176	A53	30c greenish black	*6,000.*	
177	A54	90c violet carmine	*7,500.*	

Although perforated, these stamps were usually cut apart with scissors. As a result, the perforations are often much mutilated and the design is frequently damaged.

These can be distinguished from the 1873 issue by the shades, also by the paper, which is very white instead of yellowish.

These and the subsequent issues listed under this heading are special printings of stamps then in current use which, together with the reprints and reissues, were made for sale to collectors. They were available for postage.

Special Printing of the 1875 Issue

Hard, White Wove Paper
Without Gum

1875

180	A45a	2c carmine ver	*22,500.*
181	A55	5c bright blue	*35,000.*

Special Printing of the 1879 Issue

Soft Porous Paper
Without Gum

1880 ***Perf. 12***

192	A44a	1c dark ultra	*10,000.*
193	A45a	2c black brown	*6,000.*
194	A46a	3c blue green	*15,000.*
195	A47a	6c dull rose	*11,000.*
196	A48a	7c scar vermilion	*2,250.*
197	A49a	10c deep brown	*10,000.*
198	A50a	12c black purple	*3,500.*
199	A51a	15c orange	*11,000.*
200	A52	24c dark violet	*3,500.*
201	A53	30c grnsh black	*8,500.*
202	A54	90c dull carmine	*9,000.*
203	A45a	2c scar vermilion	*18,000.*
204	A55	5c deep blue	*30,000.*

No. 197 was printed from Continental plate 302 (or 303) after plate was re-entered, therefore stamp may show normal, hairline or missing secret mark.

Special Printing

Soft Porous Paper
Without Gum

1882

205C	A56	5c gray brown	*18,000.*

Special Printing

Soft Porous Paper

1883-85

211B	A57	2c pale red brown	500.	—
c.		Horiz. pair, imperf. btwn.	*2,000.*	
211D	A58	4c deep blue green	*15,000.*	

No. 211D is without gum.

Franklin — A59

1887 ***Perf. 12***

212	A59	1c ultramarine	65.00	75
213	A57	2c green	25.00	15
b.		Printed on both sides		—
214	A46b	3c vermilion	50.00	37.50

Imperf. 1c, 2c can be found in the Scott's U.S. Specialized Catalogue Die and Plate Proofs section.

1888 ***Perf. 12***

215	A58	4c carmine	160.00	11.00
216	A56	5c indigo	160.00	6.50
217	A53	30c orange brown	375.00	75.00
218	A54	90c purple	850.00	150.00

Imperfs. can be found in the Scott's U.S. Specialized Catalogue Die and Plate Proofs section.

IMPORTANT INFORMATION REGARDING VALUES FOR NEVER-HINGED STAMPS

Collectors should be aware that the values given for never-hinged stamps from No. 219 on are for stamps in the grade of fine-very fine. The never-hinged premium as a percentage of value will be larger for stamps in very fine, extremely fine, or superb grades, and the premium will be less for poor to fine examples. This is particularly true of the issues of the late-19th and early-20th centuries. For example, in the grade of fine-very fine, an unused stamp may be valued at $100 hinged and $130 never hinged. The never-hinged premium is thus 30%. But in a grade of very fine, this same stamp will not only sell for more hinged, but the never-hinged premium will increase, perhaps to 50% or more over the higher very fine value. In a grade of extremely fine or superb, a hinged copy will sell for much more than a fine-very fine copy, and additionally the never hinged premium will be higher, perhaps as high as 100%-200%.

Franklin — A60

Washington — A61

Jackson — A62

Lincoln — A63

Grant — A64

Garfield — A65

William T. Sherman — A66

Daniel Webster — A67

Henry Clay — A68

Jefferson — A69

Perry — A70

1890-93 ***Perf. 12***

219	A60	1c dull blue	20.00	15
		Never hinged	27.50	
219D	A61	2c lake	160.00	45
		Never hinged	210.00	
220	A61	2c carmine	15.00	15
		Never hinged	20.00	
a.		Cap on left "2"	35.00	1.00
		Never hinged	47.50	
c.		Cap on both "2's"	150.00	10.00
		Never hinged	200.00	
221	A62	3c purple	55.00	4.50
		Never hinged	72.50	
222	A63	4c dark brown	60.00	1.50
		Never hinged	77.50	
223	A64	5c chocolate	55.00	1.50
		Never hinged	72.50	
224	A65	6c brown red	60.00	15.00
		Never hinged	77.50	
225	A66	8c lilac ('93)	45.00	8.50
		Never hinged	60.00	
226	A67	10c green	120.00	1.75
		Never hinged	160.00	
227	A68	15c indigo	160.00	15.00
		Never hinged	210.00	
228	A69	30c black	250.00	20.00
		Never hinged	325.00	
229	A70	90c orange	400.00	95.00
		Never hinged	525.00	
		Nos. 219-229 (12)	1,400.	163.50

The "cap on right 2" variety is due to imperfect inking, not a plate defect.

Imperfs. can be found in the Scott's U.S. Specialized Catalogue Die and Plate Proofs section.

Columbian Exposition Issue

Columbus in Sight of Land — A71

Landing of Columbus — A72

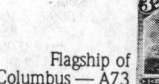

Flagship of Columbus — A73

Fleet of Columbus — A74

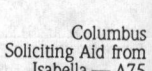

Columbus Soliciting Aid from Isabella — A75

Columbus Welcomed at Barcelona — A76

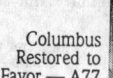

Columbus Restored to Favor — A77

Columbus Presenting Natives — A78

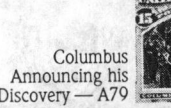

Columbus Announcing his Discovery — A79

Columbus at La Rábida — A80

Recall of Columbus — A81

Isabella Pledging her Jewels — A82

Columbus in Chains — A83

Columbus Describing his Third Voyage — A84

Isabella and Columbus — A85

Columbus — A86

1893				***Perf. 12***
230	A71	1c deep blue	21.00	25
		Never hinged	30.00	
231	A72	2c brown violet	19.00	15
		Never hinged	27.50	
232	A73	3c green	50.00	12.50
		Never hinged	70.00	
233	A74	4c ultra	70.00	5.50
		Never hinged	100.00	
a.		4c blue (error)	*15,000.*	*4,000.*
		Never hinged	—	
234	A75	5c chocolate	75.00	6.50
		Never hinged	105.00	
235	A76	6c purple	70.00	18.00
		Never hinged	100.00	
a.		6c red violet	70.00	18.00
		Never hinged	100.00	
236	A77	8c magenta	60.00	8.00
		Never hinged	85.00	
237	A78	10c black brown	115.00	5.50
		Never hinged	160.00	
238	A79	15c dark green	190.00	50.00
		Never hinged	260.00	
239	A80	30c orange brown	260.00	70.00
		Never hinged	375.00	
240	A81	50c slate blue	450.00	120.00
		Never hinged	625.00	
241	A82	$1 salmon	1,350.	525.00
		Never hinged	1,900.	
242	A83	$2 brown red	1,400.	450.00
		Never hinged	1,950.	
243	A84	$3 yellow green	2,000.	800.00
		Never hinged	2,900.	
a.		$3 olive green	2,000.	800.00
		Never hinged	2,900.	
244	A85	$4 crimson lake	2,600.	1,000.
		Never hinged	3,600.	
a.		$4 rose carmine	2,600.	1,000.
		Never hinged	3,600.	
245	A86	$5 black	3,000.	1,200.
		Never hinged	4,250.	

World's Columbian Expo., Chicago, May 1-Oct. 30, 1893.

Nos. 230-245 are known imperf., but were not regularly issued. (See Scott's U. S. Specialized Catalogue Die and Plate Proofs for the 2c.)

Condition is extremely important in evaluating Nos. 230-245. Values are for stamps free from faults and with the design well clear of the perforations. Stamps of superior quality command substantial premiums.

Never-Hinged Stamps

For valuing never-hinged stamps in grades other than fine-very fine, see note after No. 218.

Bureau Issues

Starting in 1894, the Bureau of Engraving and Printing at Washington has produced most U.S. postage stamps. Until 1965 Bureau-printed stamps were engraved except Nos. 525-536, which are offset. The combination of lithography and engraving (see No. 1253) was first used in 1964, and photogravure (see No. 1426) in 1971.

Franklin A87

Washington A88

Jackson A89

Lincoln A90

Grant A91

Garfield A92

Sherman A93

Webster A94

Clay A95

Jefferson A96

Perry A97

James Madison A98

John Marshall — A99

TWO CENTS

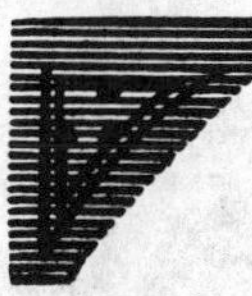
Type I

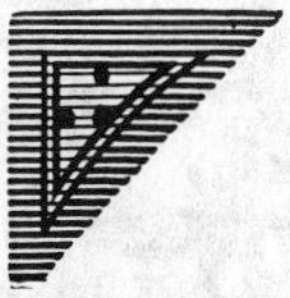
Type II

Type I. The horizontal lines of the ground work run across the triangle and are of the same thickness within it as without.

Type II. The horizontal lines cross the triangle but are thinner within it than without.

Type III

Type III. The horizontal lines do not cross the double frame lines of the triangle. The lines within the triangle are thin, as in type II.

ONE DOLLAR

Type I

Type I. The circles enclosing "$1" are broken where they meet the curved line below "One Dollar." The 15 left vert. rows of impressions from plate 76 are Type I, the balance Type II.

Type II

Type II. The circles are complete.

1894		**Unwmk.**		***Perf. 12***
246	A87	1c ultramarine	17.00	2.50
		Never hinged	25.00	
247	A87	1c blue	42.50	1.05
		Never hinged	60.00	
248	A88	2c pink, Type I	15.00	1.80
		Never hinged	21.00	
249	A88	2c carmine lake, Type I	82.50	1.20
		Never hinged	115.00	
250	A88	2c car, Type I	16.00	30
		Never hinged	22.50	
a.		Vert. pair, imperf. horiz.	*1,500.*	
b.		Horiz. pair, imperf. btwn.	*1,500.*	
251	A88	2c car, Type II	135.00	1.80
		Never hinged	190.00	
252	A88	2c car, Type III	75.00	2.50
		Never hinged	105.00	
a.		Horiz. pair, imperf. vert.	*1,350.*	
b.		Horiz. pair, imperf. btwn.	*1,500.*	
253	A89	3c purple	60.00	5.25
		Never hinged	85.00	
254	A90	4c dark brown	75.00	2.50
		Never hinged	105.00	
255	A91	5c chocolate	52.50	3.00
		Never hinged	72.50	
c.		Vert. pair, imperf. horiz.	*1,350.*	
256	A92	6c dull brown	95.00	15.00
		Never hinged	135.00	
a.		Vert. pair, imperf. horiz.	*850.00*	
257	A93	8c vio brn ('95)	85.00	9.75
		Never hinged	120.00	
258	A94	10c dark green	140.00	6.50
		Never hinged	200.00	
259	A95	15c dark blue	200.00	37.50
260	A96	50c orange	300.00	75.00
		Never hinged	280.00	
261	A97	$1 black, Type I	675.00	200.00
		Never hinged	950.00	
261A	A97	$1 black, Type II	1,650.	450.00
		Never hinged	2,300.	
262	A98	$2 bright blue	2,300.	600.00
		Never hinged	3,100.	
263	A99	$5 dark green	3,500.	1,000.
		Never hinged	4,750.	

Note on condition and valuing after No. 245 also applies to Nos. 246-263.

For imperfs. and the 2c pink, vert. pair, imperf. horiz., see Scott's U. S. Specialized Catalogue Die and Plate Proofs.

Same as 1894 Issue

1895		**Wmk. 191**		***Perf. 12***
264	A87	1c blue	4.00	16
		Never hinged	5.25	
265	A88	2c car, Type I	22.50	45
		Never hinged	30.00	
266	A88	2c car, Type II	22.50	1.90
		Never hinged	30.00	
267	A88	2c car, Type III	3.25	16
		Never hinged	4.25	

The three left vertical rows from plate 170 are Type II, the balance being Type III.

268	A89	3c purple	25.00	70
		Never hinged	32.50	
269	A90	4c dark brown	27.50	80
		Never hinged	35.00	
270	A91	5c chocolate	25.00	1.30
		Never hinged	32.50	
271	A92	6c dull brown	55.00	2.75
		Never hinged	72.50	
a.		Wmkd. USIR	*2,250.*	350.00
272	A93	8c violet brown	40.00	70
		Never hinged	52.50	
a.		Wmkd. USIR	1,750.	110.00
273	A94	10c dark green	50.00	90
		Never hinged	65.00	
274	A95	15c dark blue	140.00	6.00
		Never hinged	180.00	
275	A96	50c orange	200.00	16.00
		Never hinged	260.00	
a.		50c red orange	225.00	17.50
		Never hinged	290.00	
276	A97	$1 blk, Type I	500.00	50.00
		Never hinged	650.00	
276A	A97	$1 blk, Type II	1,050.	105.00
		Never hinged	1,375.	
277	A98	$2 bright blue	850.00	250.00
		Never hinged	1,100.	
a.		$2 dark blue	825.00	260.00
		Never hinged	1,075.	
278	A99	$5 dark green	1,750.	325.00
		Never hinged	2,275.	

For imperfs. and the 1c horiz. pair, imperf. vert., see Scott's U. S. Specialized Catalogue Die and Plate Proofs.

For "I.R." overprints see Nos. R155-R158.

TEN CENTS

Type I

Type I. Tips of foliate ornaments do not impinge on white curved line below "TEN CENTS."

Type II

Type II. Tips of ornaments break curved line below "E" of "TEN" and "T" of "CENTS."

1898		**Wmk. 191**		***Perf. 12***
279	A87	1c deep green	6.50	15
		Never hinged	8.50	
279B	A88	2c red, Type III	6.50	15
		Never hinged	8.50	
c.		2c rose carmine, Type III	185.00	25.00
		Never hinged	240.00	
d.		2c orange red, Type III	6.50	15
		Never hinged	8.50	
e.		Booklet pane of 6	300.00	—
e.		Never hinged	375.00	
f.		2c deep red, Type III	12.50	80
		Never hinged	16.00	
280	A90	4c rose brown	22.50	50
		Never hinged	30.00	
a.		4c lilac brown	22.50	50
		Never hinged	30.00	
b.		4c orange brown	20.00	50
		Never hinged	26.00	
281	A91	5c dark blue	25.00	45
		Never hinged	32.50	
282	A92	6c lake	32.50	1.60
		Never hinged	42.50	
a.		6c purple lake	40.00	1.80
		Never hinged	52.50	
282C	A94	10c brown, Type I	140.00	1.35
		Never hinged	180.00	
283	A94	10c org brown, Type II	85.00	1.10
		Never hinged	110.00	
284	A95	15c olive green	120.00	5.00
		Never hinged	160.00	
		Nos. 279-284 (8)	438.00	10.30

For "I.R." overprints see Nos. R153-R154.

Trans-Mississippi Exposition Issue

Marquette on the Mississippi A100

Farming in the West — A101

Indian Hunting Buffalo — A102

Frémont on the Rocky Mountains A103

Troops Guarding Wagon Train — A104

Hardships of Emigration A105

Western Mining Prospector A106

Western Cattle in Storm — A107

Mississippi River Bridge — A108

1898, June 17 Wmk. 191 *Perf. 12*

285	A100	1c dk yel green	22.50	4.00
		Never hinged	29.00	
286	A101	2c copper red	20.00	1.00
		Never hinged	26.00	
287	A102	4c orange	115.00	16.00
		Never hinged	150.00	
288	A103	5c dull blue	100.00	14.00
		Never hinged	130.00	
289	A104	8c violet brown	150.00	30.00
		Never hinged	200.00	
a.		Vert. pair, imperf. horiz.	*13,500.*	
290	A105	10c gray violet	135.00	18.00
		Never hinged	175.00	
291	A106	50c sage green	450.00	150.00
		Never hinged	600.00	
292	A107	$1 black	1,050.	400.00
		Never hinged	1,375.	
293	A108	$2 orange brown	1,700.	700.00
		Never hinged	2,200.	
		Nos. 285-293 (9)	3,742.	1,333.

Trans-Mississippi Exposition, Omaha, Neb., June 1 to Nov. 1, 1898.

Note on condition and pricing after No. 245 also applies to Nos. 285-293.

For "I.R." overprints see #R158A-R158B.

Never-Hinged Stamps
For valuing never-hinged stamps in grades other than fine-very fine, see note after No. 218.

Pan-American Exposition Issue

Fast Lake Navigation — A109

"Empire State" Express — A110

Electric Automobile A111

Bridge at Niagara Falls A112

Canal Locks at Sault Ste. Marie — A113

Fast Ocean Navigation — A114

1901, May 1 Wmk. 191 *Perf. 12*

294	A109	1c green & black	16.00	2.50
		Never hinged	21.00	
a.		Center inverted	*10,000.*	*5,500.*
295	A110	2c car & black	15.00	75
		Never hinged	20.00	
a.		Center inverted	*32,500.*	*13,500.*
296	A111	4c dp red brn & black	75.00	12.50
		Never hinged	100.00	
a.		Center inverted	*12,500.*	
297	A112	5c ultra & black	90.00	11.00
		Never hinged	120.00	
298	A113	8c brn vio & black	100.00	45.00
		Never hinged	130.00	
299	A114	10c yel brn & black	160.00	20.00
		Never hinged	210.00	
		Nos. 294-299 (6)	456.00	91.75

Buffalo, NY, May 1-Nov. 1, 1901.

No. 296a was a special printing.

Note on condition and pricing after No. 245 also applies to Nos. 294-299.

Almost all unused copies of Nos. 295a and 296a have partial or disturbed gum. Values are for examples with full original gum that is slightly disturbed.

Franklin A115

Washington A116

Jackson A117

Grant A118

Lincoln A119

Garfield A120

Martha Washington A121

Webster A122

Benjamin Harrison A123

Clay A124

Jefferson A125

David G. Farragut A126

Madison A127

Marshall A128

1902-03 Wmk. 191 *Perf. 12*

300	A115	1c blue grn ('03)	6.50	15
		Never hinged	8.50	
b.		Booklet pane of 6	450.00	—
		Never hinged	575.00	
301	A116	2c carmine ('03)	8.50	15
		Never hinged	11.00	
c.		Booklet pane of 6	375.00	—
		Never hinged	475.00	
302	A117	3c brt violet ('03)	35.00	2.00
		Never hinged	45.00	
303	A118	4c brown ('03)	37.50	90
		Never hinged	50.00	
304	A119	5c blue ('03)	40.00	1.10
		Never hinged	52.50	
305	A120	6c claret ('03)	45.00	2.00
		Never hinged	60.00	
306	A121	8c vio black	30.00	1.50
		Never hinged	40.00	
307	A122	10c pale red brn ('03)	37.50	70
		Never hinged	50.00	
308	A123	13c purple black	30.00	5.00
		Never hinged	40.00	
309	A124	15c olive green ('03)	110.00	3.75
		Never hinged	145.00	
310	A125	50c orange ('03)	300.00	17.50
		Never hinged	400.00	
311	A126	$1 black ('03)	575.00	45.00
		Never hinged	750.00	
312	A127	$2 dark blue ('03)	850.00	140.00
		Never hinged	1,100.	
313	A128	$5 dark green ('03)	2,250.	550.00
		Never hinged	2,900.	
		Nos. 300-313 (14)	4,355.	769.75

For listings of designs A127 and A128 with Perf. 10, see Nos. 479 and 480.

1906-08 *Imperf.*

314	A115	1c blue green	20.00	15.00
		Never hinged	30.00	
314A	A118	4c brown ('08)	*22,500.*	*16,000.*
315	A119	5c blue ('08)	300.00	*400.00*
		Never hinged	450.00	

No. 314A was issued imperforate but all copies were privately perforated with large oblong perforations at the sides (Schermack type III).

Beware of copies of No. 304 with perforations removed.

Nos. 314 & 315 are valued in the grade of very fine. Used copies must have contemporaneous cancels.

Coil Stamps

Imperforate stamps are being fraudulently perforated to resemble coil stamps and part perforate varieties.

1908 *Perf. 12 Horizontally*

316	A115	1c blue green, pair	*75,000.*	—
317	A119	5c blue, pair	*9,000.*	—

Perf. 12 Vertically

318	A115	1c blue green, pair	*5,500.*	—

Coil stamps for use in vending and affixing machines are perforated on two sides only, either horizontally or vertically. They were first issued in 1908, using perf. 12. This was changed to 8½ in 1910, and to 10 in 1914.

Imperforate sheets of certain denominations were sold to the vending machine companies which applied a variety of private perforations and separations.

Several values of the 1902 and later issues are found on an apparently coarse ribbed paper. This is caused by worn blankets on the printing press and is not a true paper variety.

Washington — A129

Type I Type II

Type I. Leaf next to left "2" penetrates the border.

Type II. Strong line forming border left of leaf.

1903, Nov. 12 Wmk. 191 *Perf. 12*

319	A129	2c carmine (I)	4.00	15
		Never hinged	5.00	
a.		2c lake (I)	—	—
b.		2c carmine rose (I)	6.00	20
		Never hinged	7.50	
c.		2c scarlet (I)	4.00	15
		Never hinged	5.00	
d.		Vert. pair, imperf. horiz.	*2,000.*	
e.		Vert. pair, imperf. btwn.	*950.00*	
f.		2c lake (II)	5.00	20
		Never hinged	6.25	
g.		Booklet pane of 6, car (I)	75.00	*125.00*
		Never hinged	95.00	
h.		As "g" (II)	135.00	
		Never hinged	170.00	
i.		2c carmine (II)	17.50	—
		Never hinged	22.50	
j.		2c carmine rose (II)	12.00	50
		Never hinged	15.00	
k.		2c scarlet (II)	10.00	30
		Never hinged	12.50	
m.		As "g," lake (I)	—	
n.		As "g," car rose (I)	100.00	
		Never hinged	125.00	
p.		As "g," scarlet (I)	110.00	*125.00*
		Never hinged	140.00	
q.		As "g," lake (II)	130.00	
		Never hinged	165.00	

1906, Oct. 2 *Imperf.*

320	A129	2c carmine (I)	17.50	11.00
		Never hinged	25.00	
a.		2c lake (II)	50.00	40.00
		Never hinged	70.00	
b.		2c scarlet (I)	16.00	12.00
		Never hinged	22.50	
c.		2c carmine rose (I)	60.00	40.00
		Never hinged	85.00	
d.		2c carmine (II)	60.00	
		Never hinged	85.00	
e.		2c scarlet (II)	60.00	
		Never hinged	85.00	
f.		2c carmine rose (II)	75.00	
		Never hinged	105.00	

Nos. 320-320f are valued in the grade of very fine.

Coil Stamps

1908 *Perf. 12 Horizontally*

321	A129	2c carmine, pair	*95,000.*	—

Five authenticated unused pairs are known. The used value is for a single on cover, of which 2 authenticated examples are known, both used from Indianapolis in 1908. Numerous counterfeits exist.

Perf. 12 Vertically

322	A129	2c carmine, pair	*6,500.*	*5,000.*

Louisiana Purchase Exposition Issue

Robert R. Livingston A130

Thomas Jefferson A131

James Monroe — A132

William McKinley A133

Map of Louisiana Purchase — A134

1904, Apr. 30 Wmk. 191 *Perf. 12*

323 A130 1c green 20.00 3.00
Never hinged 26.00
324 A131 2c carmine 17.00 1.00
Never hinged 22.50
a. Vert. pair, imperf. horiz. *6,750.*
325 A132 3c violet 65.00 24.00
Never hinged 85.00
326 A133 5c dark blue 70.00 15.00
Never hinged 90.00
327 A134 10c red brown 130.00 21.00
Never hinged 170.00
Nos. 323-327 (5) 302.00 64.00

Louisiana Purchase Expo., St. Louis, Mo., Apr. 30 to Dec. 1, 1904.
Note on condition and pricing after No. 245 also applies to Nos. 323-327.

Jamestown Exposition Issue

Captain John Smith A135

Founding of Jamestown A136

Pocahontas — A137

1907 Wmk. 191 *Perf. 12*

328 A135 1c green 13.00 2.00
Never hinged 17.00
329 A136 2c carmine 17.00 1.75
Never hinged 22.50
330 A137 5c blue 72.50 16.00
Never hinged 95.00

Jamestown Expo., Hampton Roads, Va., Apr. 26 to Dec. 1.
Values are for fine centered copies.

Franklin A138

Washington A139

Washington — A140

There are several types of some of the 2c and 3c stamps of this and succeeding issues. These types are described under the dates when they first appeared. The differences between the types are usually minute and difficult to distinguish.
Illustrations of Types I-VII of the 2c (A140) and Types I-IV of the 3c (A140) are reproduced by permission of H. L. Lindquist.

TYPE I

TYPE I

THREE CENTS
Type I. The top line of the toga rope is weak and the rope shading lines are thin. The fifth line from the left is missing.
The line between the lips is thin.
Used on both flat plate and rotary press printings.

1908-09 Wmk. 191 *Perf. 12*

331 A138 1c green 5.00 15
Never hinged 7.00
a. Booklet pane of 6 130.00 *90.00*
Never hinged 175.00
332 A139 2c carmine 4.50 15
Never hinged 6.25
a. Booklet pane of 6 115.00 *90.00*
Never hinged 140.00
333 A140 3c deep violet, Type I 22.50 1.75
Never hinged 32.50
334 A140 4c orange brown 28.00 55
Never hinged 40.00
335 A140 5c blue 35.00 1.50
Never hinged 50.00
336 A140 6c red orange 45.00 3.50
Never hinged 62.50
337 A140 8c olive green 32.50 1.75
Never hinged 45.00
338 A140 10c yellow ('09) 50.00 1.00
Never hinged 70.00
339 A140 13c blue green ('09) 30.00 14.00
Never hinged 42.50
340 A140 15c pale ultra ('09) 45.00 3.75
Never hinged 62.50
341 A140 50c violet ('09) 200.00 10.00
Never hinged 280.00
342 A140 $1 vio brown ('09) 360.00 50.00
Never hinged 500.00
Nos. 331-342 (12) 857.50 88.10

For listings of China Clay papers see Scott's U.S. Specialized Catalogue.
For listing of other perforated stamps of designs A138, A139 and A140 see

#357-366	Bluish Paper	
#374-382, 405-407	Single line wmk.	Perf. 12
#424-430	Single line wmk.	Perf. 10
#461	Single line wmk.	Perf. 11
#462-469	Unwmkd.	Perf. 10
#498-507	Unwmkd.	Perf. 11
#519	Double line wmk.	Perf. 11
#525-530, 536	Offset printing	
#538-546	Rotary press printing	

Imperf

343 A138 1c green 6.00 4.00
Never hinged 8.50
344 A139 2c carmine 7.50 2.50
Never hinged 10.50
345 A140 3c dp violet, Type I 14.00 17.50
Never hinged 20.00
346 A140 4c org brown ('09) 24.00 17.50
Never hinged 35.00
347 A140 5c blue ('09) 42.50 30.00
Never hinged 60.00
Nos. 343-347 (5) 94.00 71.50

Nos. 343-347 are valued in the grade of very fine.
For listings of other imperforate stamps of designs A138, A139 and A140 see

#383 & 384, 408 & 409, 459	Single line wmk.
#481-485	Unwmkd.
#531-535	Offset printing

Coil Stamps

1908-10 *Perf. 12 Horizontally*

348 A138 1c green 21.00 10.00
Never hinged 30.00
349 A139 2c carmine ('09) 37.50 6.00
Never hinged 52.50
350 A140 4c orange brown ('10) 85.00 60.00
Never hinged 120.00
351 A140 5c blue ('09) 95.00 90.00
Never hinged 135.00

1909 *Perf. 12 Vertically*

352 A138 1c green 40.00 25.00
Never hinged 55.00
353 A139 2c carmine 40.00 6.00
Never hinged 55.00
354 A140 4c orange brown 100.00 45.00
Never hinged 140.00
355 A140 5c blue 110.00 65.00
Never hinged 150.00
356 A140 10c yellow 1,750. 750.00
Never hinged 2,200.

Beware of copies of No. 338 with horiz. perforations removed.
For listings of other coil stamps of designs A138, A139 and A140 see

#385-396, 410-413, 441-458	Single line wmk.
#486-496	Unwmkd.

Bluish Paper

This was made with 35 per cent rag stock instead of all wood pulp. The grayish blue color goes through the paper showing clearly on the back as well as on the face.

1909 *Perf. 12*

357 A138 1c green 80.00 65.00
Never hinged 105.00
358 A139 2c carmine 75.00 55.00
Never hinged 100.00
359 A140 3c dp violet, Type I 1,600. *1,300.*
Never hinged 2,000.
360 A140 4c orange brown *15,000.*
361 A140 5c blue 3,750. *3,500.*
Never hinged 4,700.
362 A140 6c red orange 1,150. 900.00
Never hinged 1,450.
363 A140 8c olive green *16,000.*
364 A140 10c yellow 1,350. 1,000.
Never hinged 1,700.
365 A140 13c blue green 2,500. *1,400.*
Never hinged 3,150.
366 A140 15c pale ultra 1,150. 900.00
Never hinged 1,450.

Nos. 360, 363 not regularly issued.

Lincoln Memorial Issue

Lincoln — A141

1909, Feb. 12 Wmk. 191 *Perf. 12*

367 A141 2c carmine 4.25 1.40
Never hinged 5.75

Imperf

368 A141 2c carmine 20.00 16.00
Never hinged 27.50

No. 368 is valued in the grade of very fine.

Bluish Paper

1909 *Perf. 12*

369 A141 2c carmine 170.00 175.00
Never hinged 225.00

Birth of Abraham Lincoln, 100th anniv.

Alaska-Yukon Pacific Exposition Issue

William H. Seward — A142

1909, June 1 Wmk. 191 *Perf. 12*

370 A142 2c carmine 7.50 1.25
Never hinged 10.00

1909 *Imperf.*

371 A142 2c carmine 27.50 20.00
Never hinged 35.00

Seattle, Wash., June 1 to Oct. 16.
No. 371 is valued in the grade of very fine.

Hudson-Fulton Celebration Issue

"Half Moon" and Steamship A143

1909, Sept. 25 Wmk. 191 *Perf. 12*

372 A143 2c carmine 11.00 3.25
Never hinged 15.00

Imperf

373 A143 2c carmine 32.50 22.50
Never hinged 42.50

Tercentenary of the discovery of the Hudson River and Centenary of Robert Fulton's steamship.

No. 373 is valued in the grade of very fine.

Designs of 1908-09 Issue

1910-11 Wmk. 190 *Perf. 12*

374 A138 1c green 5.00 15
Never hinged 6.50
a. Booklet pane of 6 90.00 *75.00*
Never hinged 115.00
375 A139 2c carmine 5.00 15
Never hinged 6.50
a. Booklet pane of 6 75.00 *60.00*
Never hinged 100.00
376 A140 3c dp vio, Type I ('11) 12.00 1.00
Never hinged 16.00
377 A140 4c brown ('11) 20.00 30
Never hinged 26.00
378 A140 5c blue ('11) 20.00 30
Never hinged 30.00
379 A140 6c red orange ('11) 25.00 40
Never hinged 32.50
380 A140 8c olive green ('11) 75.00 8.50
Never hinged 100.00
381 A140 10c yellow ('11) 70.00 2.50
Never hinged 95.00
382 A140 15c pale ultra ('11) 190.00 11.50
Never hinged 275.00
Nos. 374-382 (9) 422.00 24.80

1910 *Imperf.*

383 A138 1c green 2.25 2.00
Never hinged 3.25
384 A139 2c carmine 3.50 2.50
Never hinged 5.00

Nos. 383-384 are valued in the grade of very fine.

Coil Stamps

1910 *Perf. 12 Horizontally*

385 A138 1c green 20.00 10.00
Never hinged 27.50
386 A139 2c carmine 35.00 12.50
Never hinged 50.00

1910-11 *Perf. 12 Vertically*

387 A138 1c green 80.00 30.00
Never hinged 110.00
388 A139 2c carmine 550.00 200.00
Never hinged 775.00
389 A140 3c dp vio, Type I ('11) *15,000.* *8,500.*

Stamps sold as No. 388 sometimes are fraudulently perforated copies of No. 384 or trimmed copies of No. 375.

1910 *Perf. 8½ Horizontally*

390 A138 1c green 3.25 4.00
Never hinged 4.50
391 A139 2c carmine 22.50 6.75
Never hinged 30.00

1910-13 *Perf. 8½ Vertically*

392 A138 1c green 12.50 14.00
Never hinged 17.50
393 A139 2c carmine 25.00 5.50
Never hinged 35.00
394 A140 3c dp vio, Type I ('11) 35.00 40.00
Never hinged 47.50
395 A140 4c brown ('12) 35.00 35.00
Never hinged 47.50
396 A140 5c blue ('13) 35.00 35.00
Never hinged 47.50

Panama-Pacific Exposition Issue

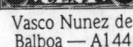

Vasco Nunez de Balboa — A144

Pedro Miguel Locks, Panama Canal — A145

Golden Gate — A146

Discovery of San Francisco Bay — A147

1913 Wmk. 190 *Perf. 12*

397 A144 1c green 12.50 85
Never hinged 17.50
398 A145 2c carmine 14.00 30
Never hinged 20.00
399 A146 5c blue 55.00 6.50
Never hinged 75.00
400 A147 10c orange yellow 100.00 14.00
Never hinged 135.00
400A A147 10c orange 185.00 10.50
Never hinged 250.00

1914-15 *Perf. 10*

401 A144 1c green 17.50 4.00
Never hinged 25.00

402 A145 2c carmine ('15) 60.00 1.00
Never hinged 80.00
403 A146 5c blue ('15) 130.00 11.00
Never hinged 175.00
404 A147 10c orange ('15) 825.00 42.50
Never hinged 1,075.

San Francisco, Cal., Feb. 20 to Dec. 4.

TYPE I

TYPE I

TWO CENTS

Type I. There is one shading line in the first curve of the ribbon above the left "2" and one in the second curve of the ribbon above the right "2."

The button of the toga has a faint outline.

The top line of the toga rope, from the button to the front of the throat, is also very faint.

The shading lines at the face terminate in front of the ear with little or no joining, to form a lock of hair.

Used on both flat and rotary press printings.

1912-14 Wmk. 190 ***Perf. 12***

405 A140 1c green 4.00 15
Never hinged 5.50
a. Vert. pair, imperf. horiz. *650.00* —
b. Booklet pane of 6 50.00 *25.00*
Never hinged 67.50
406 A140 2c carmine, Type I 3.75 15
Never hinged 5.00
a. Booklet pane of 6 50.00 *40.00*
Never hinged 67.50
b. Double impression —
407 A140 7c black ('14) 65.00 8.00
Never hinged 90.00

1912 ***Imperf.***

408 A140 1c green 1.00 50
Never hinged 1.40
409 A140 2c carmine, Type I 1.10 50
Never hinged 1.50

Nos. 408-409 are valued in the grade of very fine.

Coil Stamps

1912 ***Perf. 8½ Horizontally***

410 A140 1c green 5.00 3.00
Never hinged 6.75
411 A140 2c carmine, Type I 6.75 2.50
Never hinged 9.00

Perf. 8½ Vertically

412 A140 1c green 16.00 3.75
Never hinged 22.50
413 A140 2c carmine, Type I 27.50 75
Never hinged 37.50

Franklin — A148

1912-14 Wmk. 190 ***Perf. 12***

414 A148 8c pale olive green 30.00 85
Never hinged 42.50
415 A148 9c salmon red ('14) 37.50 9.50
Never hinged 52.50
416 A148 10c orange yellow 32.50 25
Never hinged 45.00
417 A148 12c claret brown ('14) 32.50 3.00
Never hinged 45.00
418 A148 15c gray 60.00 2.00
Never hinged 85.00
419 A148 20c ultra ('14) 140.00 9.00
Never hinged 200.00
420 A148 30c orange red ('14) 100.00 10.00
Never hinged 140.00
421 A148 50c violet ('14) 350.00 10.00
Never hinged 500.00

No. 421 almost always has an offset of the frame lines on the back under the gum. No. 422 does not have this offset.

1912, Feb. 12 Wmk. 191 ***Perf. 12***

422 A148 50c violet 190.00 9.50
Never hinged 275.00
423 A148 $1 violet brown 425.00 40.00
Never hinged 600.00

Other stamps of type A148:

#431-440	Single line wmk.	Perf. 10
#460	Double line wmk.	Perf. 10
#470-478	Unwmkd.	Perf. 10
#508-518	Unwmkd.	Perf. 11

1914-15 Wmk. 190 ***Perf. 10***

424 A140 1c green 1.60 15
Never hinged 2.25
a. Perf. 12x10 *600.00* *500.00*
b. Perf. 10x12 *250.00*
c. Vert. pair, imperf. horiz. *425.00* *250.00*
d. Booklet pane of 6 3.00 *75*
Never hinged 4.00
e. Vert. pair, imperf. btwn. & at top —
425 A140 2c rose red, Type I 1.50 15
Never hinged 2.10
c. Perf. 10x12 —
d. Perf. 12x10 — *600.00*
e. Booklet pane of 6 12.50 *3.00*
Never hinged 17.50
426 A140 3c deep violet, Type I 10.00 90
Never hinged 14.00
427 A140 4c brown 26.00 30
Never hinged 35.00
428 A140 5c blue 25.00 30
Never hinged 33.50
a. Perf. 12x10 *2,000.*
429 A140 6c red orange 35.00 90
Never hinged 50.00
430 A140 7c black 65.00 2.50
Never hinged 90.00
431 A148 8c pale olive green 27.50 1.10
Never hinged 37.50
432 A148 9c salmon red 37.50 5.00
Never hinged 52.50
433 A148 10c orange yellow 35.00 20
Never hinged 50.00
434 A148 11c dark green ('15) 17.50 5.50
Never hinged 24.00
435 A148 12c claret brown 18.00 2.75
Never hinged 25.00
a. 12c copper red 19.00 2.75
Never hinged 27.50
437 A148 15c gray 95.00 4.50
Never hinged 130.00
438 A148 20c ultra 165.00 2.50
Never hinged 225.00
439 A148 30c orange red 225.00 10.00
Never hinged 300.00
440 A148 50c violet ('15) 500.00 10.00
Never hinged 700.00
Nos. 424-440 (16) 1,284. 46.75

Coil Stamps

1914 ***Perf. 10 Horizontally***

441 A140 1c green 60 80
Never hinged 80
442 A140 2c carmine, Type I 6.50 4.50
Never hinged 8.75

1914 ***Perf. 10 Vertically***

443 A140 1c green 17.50 4.00
Never hinged 23.50
444 A140 2c carmine, Type I 22.50 1.00
Never hinged 30.00
445 A140 3c violet, Type I 190.00 100.00
Never hinged 260.00
446 A140 4c brown 100.00 30.00
Never hinged 135.00
447 A140 5c blue 35.00 20.00
Never hinged 47.50

No. 443 represents stamps from coils. Part of a sheet of No. 424 is also known perf. vert. and imperf. horiz.

TYPE II

TYPE II

TWO CENTS

Type II. Shading lines in ribbons as on type I.

The toga button, rope, and shading lines are heavy.

The shading lines of the face at the lock of hair end in a strong vertical curved line.

Used on rotary press printings only.

TYPE III

TYPE III

TWO CENTS

Type III. Two lines of shading in the curves of the ribbons.

Other characteristics similar to type II.

Used on rotary press printings only.

Fraudulently altered copies of Type III (Nos. 455, 488, 492 and 540) have had one line of shading scraped off to make them resemble Type II (Nos. 454, 487, 491 and 539).

Coil Stamps

Rotary Press Printing

1915-16 ***Perf. 10 Horizontally***

448 A140 1c green 4.50 2.50
Never hinged 6.25
449 A140 2c red, Type I 1,900. 300.00
Never hinged 2,600.
450 A140 2c car, Type III ('16) 8.00 2.25
Never hinged 11.00

1914-16 ***Perf. 10 Vertically***

452 A140 1c green 8.00 1.40
Never hinged 11.00
453 A140 2c carmine rose, Type I 95.00 3.25
Never hinged 130.00
454 A140 2c red, Type II 77.50 7.50
Never hinged 105.00
455 A140 2c carmine, Type III 7.50 75
Never hinged 10.00
456 A140 3c violet, Type I ('16) 210.00 75.00
Never hinged 285.00
457 A140 4c brown ('16) 20.00 15.00
Never hinged 27.50
458 A140 5c blue ('16) 25.00 15.00
Never hinged 32.50

1914, June 30 ***Imperf.***

459 A140 2c car, Type I 300.00 *750.00*
Never hinged 400.00

No. 459 is a horizontal coil.

The Rotary Press stamps are printed from plates that are curved to fit around a cylinder. This curvature produces stamps that are slightly larger, either horizontally or vertically, than those printed from flat plates. Stamps from flat plates measure about 18½-19mm wide by 22mm high. When the impressions are placed sideways on the curved plates the stamps are 19½-20mm wide; when they are placed vertically the stamps are 23mm high.

No. 459 is valued in the grade of very fine. The used value is for a copy with a contemporaneous cancel.

Flat Plate Printings

1915, Feb. 8 Wmk. 191 ***Perf. 10***

460 A148 $1 violet black 700.00 55.00
Never hinged 975.00

1915, June 17 Wmk. 190 ***Perf. 11***

461 A140 2c pale carmine red, Type I 80.00 *175.00*
Never hinged 110.00

Fraudulently perforated copies of No. 409 are offered as No. 461.

Unwatermarked

From 1916 onward all postage stamps except Nos. 519 and 832b are on unwatermarked paper.

1916-17 Unwmk. ***Perf. 10***

462 A140 1c green 5.00 15
Never hinged 6.75
a. Booklet pane of 6 7.50 *1.00*
Never hinged 10.50
463 A140 2c carmine, Type I 3.50 15
Never hinged 4.75
a. Booklet pane of 6 62.50 *20.00*
Never hinged 85.00
464 A140 3c violet, Type I 57.50 8.00
Never hinged 80.00
465 A140 4c orange brown 35.00 1.00
Never hinged 47.50
466 A140 5c blue 60.00 1.00
Never hinged 82.50
467 A140 5c car (error in plate of 2c, '17) 475.00 525.00
Never hinged 650.00
468 A140 6c red orange 75.00 5.00
Never hinged 105.00
469 A140 7c black 95.00 7.50
Never hinged 130.00
470 A148 8c olive green 45.00 3.75
Never hinged 60.00
471 A148 9c salmon red 45.00 9.50
Never hinged 60.00
472 A148 10c orange yel 85.00 75
Never hinged 115.00
473 A148 11c dark green 27.50 11.00
Never hinged 37.50
474 A148 12c claret brown 42.50 3.50
Never hinged 57.50
475 A148 15c gray 150.00 7.00
Never hinged 200.00
476 A148 20c lt ultra 210.00 7.50
Never hinged 290.00
476A A148 30c orange red *3,500.* —
Never hinged *4,500.*
477 A148 50c lt violet ('17) 900.00 40.00
Never hinged 1,250.
478 A148 $1 violet black 650.00 11.00
Never hinged 900.00

No. 476A is valued in the grade of fine.

Types of 1903 Issue

1917, Mar. 22 ***Perf. 10***

479 A127 $2 dark blue 290.00 30.00
Never hinged 425.00
480 A128 $5 light green 225.00 32.50
Never hinged 325.00

TYPE IA

TYPE Ia

TWO CENTS

Type Ia. Design characteristics similar to type I except that all lines of design are stronger.

The toga button, toga rope and rope shading lines are heavy. The latter characteristics are those of type II, which, however, occur only on impressions from rotary plates.

Used only on flat plates 10208 and 10209.

TYPE II

TYPE II

THREE CENTS

Type II. The top line of the toga rope is strong and the rope shading lines are heavy and complete.

The line between the lips is heavy.

Used on both flat plate and rotary press printings.

1916-17 ***Imperf.***

481 A140 1c green 80 45
Never hinged 1.10
482 A140 2c carmine, Type I 1.35 1.00
Never hinged 1.85
482A A140 2c dp rose, Type Ia *7,500.*

No. 482A was issued imperforate but all copies were privately perforated with large oblong perforations at the sides (Schermack type III).

No. 500 exists with imperforate top sheet margin. Copies have been altered by trimming perforations. Some also have faked Schermack perfs.

483 A140 3c violet, Type I ('17) 12.50 6.50
Never hinged 17.50

484	A140 3c violet, Type II	9.00	3.00
	Never hinged	12.00	
485	A140 5c car (error in plate of 2c) ('17)		*9,000.*

Nos. 481-482, 483-485 are valued in the grade of very fine. No. 485 is valued never hinged.

Coil Stamps

Rotary Press Printing

1916-19 ***Perf. 10 Horizontally***

486	A140 1c green ('18)	70	20
	Never hinged	95	
487	A140 2c car, Type II	12.50	2.50
	Never hinged	17.50	
488	A140 2c car, Type III ('19)	2.25	1.35
	Never hinged	3.00	
489	A140 3c violet, Type I ('17)	4.25	1.00
	Never hinged	5.75	

1916-22 ***Perf. 10 Vertically***

490	A140 1c green	45	15
	Never hinged	60	
491	A140 2c car, Type II	1,500.	450.00
	Never hinged	2,100.	
492	A140 2c car, Type III	6.75	15
	Never hinged	9.25	
493	A140 3c vio, Type I ('17)	14.00	2.00
	Never hinged	20.00	
494	A140 3c vio, Type II ('18)	8.00	1.00
	Never hinged	11.00	
495	A140 4c org brown ('17)	8.00	3.00
	Never hinged	11.00	
496	A140 5c blue ('19)	3.00	90
	Never hinged	4.00	
497	A148 10c orange yel ('22)	16.00	9.00
	Never hinged	22.50	

See note above #448 regarding #487, 491.

Blind Perfs.

Listings of imperforate-between varieties are for examples which show no trace of "blind perfs.," traces of impressions from the perforating pins which do not cut into the paper.

Types of 1912-14 Issue

1917-19 Flat Plate Printings ***Perf. 11***

498	A140 1c green	30	15
	Never hinged	40	
a.	Vert. pair, imperf. horiz.	175.00	
b.	Horiz. pair, imperf. btwn.	75.00	
c.	Vert. pair, imperf. btwn.	*450.00*	—
d.	Double impression	175.00	
e.	Booklet pane of 6	1.60	*35*
	Never hinged	2.25	
f.	Booklet pane of 30	*750.00*	
	Never hinged	*850.00*	
499	A140 2c rose, Type I	35	15
	Never hinged	50	
a.	Vert. pair, imperf. horiz.	150.00	
b.	Horiz. pair, imperf. vert.	200.00	*100.00*
c.	Vert. pair, imperf. btwn.	*500.00*	*225.00*
e.	Booklet pane of 6	2.75	*50*
	Never hinged	3.75	
f.	Booklet pane of 30	*15,000.*	
g.	Double impression	150.00	—
500	A140 2c deep rose, Type Ia	200.00	150.00
	Never hinged	275.00	
501	A140 3c lt violet, Type I	8.50	15
	Never hinged	12.00	
b.	Booklet pane of 6	50.00	*15.00*
	Never hinged	65.00	
c.	Vert. pair, imperf. horiz.	300.00	
d.	Double impression	200.00	
502	A140 3c dk violet, Type II	11.50	15
	Never hinged	16.00	
b.	Booklet pane of 6	35.00	*10.00*
	Never hinged	45.00	
c.	Vert. pair, imperf. horiz.	250.00	125.00
d.	Double impression	200.00	
503	A140 4c brown	7.75	15
	Never hinged	11.00	
b.	Double impression	—	
504	A140 5c blue	7.00	15
	Never hinged	9.50	
a.	Horiz. pair, imperf. btwn.	*2,500.*	—
505	A140 5c rose (error in plate of 2c)	350.00	400.00
	Never hinged	500.00	
506	A140 6c red orange	10.50	20
	Never hinged	14.50	
507	A140 7c black	22.50	85
	Never hinged	30.00	
508	A148 8c olive bister	9.50	40
	Never hinged	13.50	
b.	Vert. pair, imperf. btwn.	—	
509	A148 9c salmon red	11.50	1.40
	Never hinged	16.00	
510	A148 10c orange yellow	13.50	15
	Never hinged	18.50	
511	A148 11c lt green	7.50	2.00
	Never hinged	10.00	
512	A148 12c claret brown	7.50	30
	Never hinged	10.00	
a.	12c brown carmine	8.00	35
	Never hinged	10.75	
513	A148 13c apple green ('19)	9.00	4.75
	Never hinged	12.50	
514	A148 15c gray	30.00	80
	Never hinged	40.00	
515	A148 20c light ultra	40.00	20
	Never hinged	55.00	
b.	Vert. pair, imperf. btwn.	*325.00*	
c.	Double impression	*400.00*	
516	A148 30c orange red	32.50	60
	Never hinged	42.50	
b.	Double impression		—

The only reported copy shows part of the design doubled.

517	A148 50c red violet	60.00	45
	Never hinged	85.00	
b.	Vert. pair, imperf. btwn. & at bottom	*1,750.*	*1,000.*
518	A148 $1 violet brown	45.00	1.20
	Never hinged	65.00	
b.	$1 deep brown	*1,250.*	*600.00*
	Nos. 498-504,506-518 (20)	*534.40*	*164.20*

Beware of pairs with blind perforations inside the design of the top stamp that are offered as No. 515b.

Type of 1908-09 Issue

1917, Oct. 10 Wmk. 191 ***Perf. 11***

519	A139 2c carmine	250.00	*450.00*
	Never hinged	325.00	

Fraudulently perforated copies of No. 344 are offered as No. 519.

The used value is for a stamp with a contemporaneous cancel.

Franklin — A149

1918, Aug. 19 Unwmk. ***Perf. 11***

523	A149 $2 orange red & blk	600.00	200.00
	Never hinged	750.00	
524	A149 $5 dp grn & black	200.00	30.00
	Never hinged	275.00	

See No. 547 for $2 carmine & black.

Types of 1912-14 Issue

TYPE IV

TWO CENTS

Type IV. Top line of toga rope is broken. Shading lines in toga button are so arranged that the curving of the first and last form a "D (reversed) ID."

Line of color in left "2" is very thin and usually broken.

Used on offset printings only.

TYPE V

TWO CENTS

Type V. Top line of toga is complete.

Five vertical shading lines in toga button.

Line of color in left "2" is very thin and usually broken.

Shading dots on the nose and lip are as indicated on the diagram.

Used on offset printings only.

TYPE Va

TWO CENTS

Type Va. Characteristics same as type V, except in shading dots of nose. Third row from bottom has 4 dots instead of 6. Overall height of type Va is 1/3mm less than type V.

Used on offset printings only.

TYPE VI

TWO CENTS

Type VI. General characteristics same as type V, except that line of color in left "2" is very heavy.

Used on offset printings only.

TYPE VII

TWO CENTS

Type VII. Line of color in left "2" is invariably continuous, clearly defined, and heavier than in type V or Va, but not as heavy as in type VI.

Additional vertical row of dots has been added to the upper lip.

Numerous additional dots have been added to hair on top of head.

Used on offset printings only.

TYPE III

THREE CENTS

Type III. The top line of the toga rope is strong but the fifth shading line is missing as in type I.

Center shading line of the toga button consists of two dashes with a central dot.

The "P" and "O" of "POSTAGE" are separated by a line of color.

The frame line at the bottom of the vignette is complete.

Used on offset printings only.

TYPE IV

THREE CENTS

Type IV. Shading lines of toga rope are complete.

Second and fourth shading lines in toga button are broken in the middle and the third line is continuous with a dot in the center.

"P" and "O" of "POSTAGE" are joined.

Frame line at bottom of vignette is broken.

Used on offset printings only.

1918-20 Offset Printing ***Perf. 11***

525	A140 1c gray green	1.50	35
	Never hinged	2.25	
a.	1c dark green	1.65	75
	Never hinged	2.45	
c.	Horiz. pair, imperf. btwn.	100.00	
d.	Double impression	15.00	15.00
526	A140 2c car, Type IV ('20)	21.00	2.75
	Never hinged	30.00	
527	A140 2c car, Type V	15.00	60
	Never hinged	22.50	
a.	Double impression	55.00	10.00
b.	Vert. pair, imperf. horiz.	*600.00*	
c.	Horiz. pair, imperf. vert.	*1,000.*	—
528	A140 2c car, Type Va	6.25	15
	Never hinged	8.75	
c.	Double impression	25.00	
g.	Vert. pair, imperf. btwn.	*1,000.*	
528A	A140 2c car, Type VI	45.00	1.00
	Never hinged	65.00	
d.	Double impression	150.00	—
f.	Vert. pair, imperf. horiz.	—	
h.	Vert. pair, imperf. btwn.	*1,000.*	
528B	A140 2c car, Type VII	15.00	30
	Never hinged	21.00	
e.	Double impression	55.00	
529	A140 3c vio, Type III	2.25	15
	Never hinged	3.25	
a.	Double impression	30.00	—
b.	Printed on both sides	*350.00*	
530	A140 3c pur, Type IV	1.00	15
	Never hinged	1.40	
a.	Double impression	20.00	6.00
b.	Printed on both sides	250.00	
	Nos. 525-530 (8)	107.00	5.45

1918-20 ***Imperf.***

531	A140 1c green ('19)	7.00	7.00
	Never hinged	10.00	
532	A140 2c car rose, Type IV ('20)	37.50	25.00
	Never hinged	50.00	
533	A140 2c car, Type V	175.00	75.00
	Never hinged	235.00	
534	A140 2c car, Type Va	9.00	6.00
	Never hinged	12.50	
534A	A140 2c car, Type VI	32.50	20.00
	Never hinged	45.00	

534B A140 2c car, Type VII 1,250. 700.00
Never hinged 1,700.
535 A140 3c vio, Type IV 7.00 4.50
Never hinged 10.00
a. Double impression 100.00 —

Nos. 531-535 are valued in the grade of very fine.

1919, Aug. 15 ***Perf. 12½***
536 A140 1c gray green 12.00 14.00
Never hinged 16.50
a. Horiz. pair, imperf. vert. *500.00*

Victory Issue

"Victory" and Flags of the Allies — A150

Flat Plate Printing

1919, Mar. 3 **Engr.** ***Perf. 11***
537 A150 3c violet 7.75 2.75
Never hinged 11.00
a. 3c deep red violet *350.00* *100.00*
Never hinged *475.00*
b. 3c light reddish violet 7.75 2.75
Never hinged 11.00
c. 3c red violet 32.50 7.50
Never hinged 45.00

Victory of Allies in World War I.

Rotary Press Printings

1919 ***Perf. 11x10***

Size: 19½ to 20mm wide by 22 to 22¼mm high

538 A140 1c green 7.75 6.00
Never hinged 11.00
a. Vert. pair, imperf. horiz. 50.00 *100.00*
539 A140 2c carmine rose, Type II 3,000. *3,000.*
Never hinged 4,000.
540 A140 2c carmine rose, Type III 7.75 6.00
Never hinged 11.00
a. Vert. pair, imperf. horiz. 50.00 *100.00*
b. Horiz. pair, imperf. vert. *550.00*
541 A140 3c vio, Type II 27.50 20.00
Never hinged 37.50

The part perforate varieties of Nos. 538a and 540a were issued in sheets and may be had in blocks; similar part perforate varieties, Nos. 490 and 492, are from coils and are found only in strips.
See note over No. 448 regarding No. 539.
No. 539 is valued in the grade of fine.

Size: 19mm by 22½-22¾mm

1920, May 26 ***Perf. 10x11***
542 A140 1c green 9.00 65
Never hinged 12.50

Size: 19x22½mm

1921 ***Perf. 10***
543 A140 1c green 35 15
Never hinged 50
a. Horiz. pair, imperf. btwn. *550.00*

Size: 19x22½mm

1922 ***Perf. 11***
544 A140 1c green *12,500.* *3,000.*

No. 544 is valued in the grade of fine.

Size: 19½-20mm by 22mm

1921 ***Perf. 11***
545 A140 1c green 110.00 110.00
Never hinged 155.00
546 A140 2c car rose, Type III 70.00 *110.00*
Never hinged 100.00

Flat Plate Printing

1920, Nov. 1 ***Perf. 11***
547 A149 $2 carmine & black 175.00 32.50
Never hinged 250.00

Pilgrim Tercentenary Issue

"Mayflower" A151

Landing of the Pilgrims A152

Signing of the Compact — A153

1920, Dec. 21 ***Perf. 11***
548 A151 1c green 3.75 1.65
Never hinged 5.25
549 A152 2c carmine rose 5.50 1.25
Never hinged 7.50
550 A153 5c deep blue 37.50 10.00
Never hinged 50.00

Tercentenary of the landing of the Pilgrims at Plymouth, Mass.

Nathan Hale A154

Franklin A155

Harding A156

Washington A157

Lincoln A158

Martha Washington A159

Theodore Roosevelt A160

Garfield A161

McKinley A162

Grant A163

Jefferson A164

Monroe A165

Rutherford B. Hayes A166

Grover Cleveland A167

American Indian A168

Statue of Liberty A169

Golden Gate — A170

Niagara Falls — A171

Buffalo A172

Arlington Amphitheater A173

Lincoln Memorial A174

US Capitol A175

Head of Freedom Statue, Capitol Dome — A176

1922-25 ***Perf. 11***
551 A154 ½c olive brn ('25) 15 15
Never hinged 16
552 A155 1c dp green ('23) 1.35 15
Never hinged 1.90
a. Booket pane of 6 5.00 *50*
Never hinged 7.50
553 A156 1½c yel brn ('25) 2.25 15
Never hinged 3.35
554 A157 2c carmine ('23) 1.25 15
Never hinged 1.75
a. Horiz. pair, imperf. vert. 200.00
b. Vert. pair, imperf. horiz. *500.00*
c. Booklet pane of 6 6.00 *1.00*
Never hinged 9.00
555 A158 3c violet ('23) 15.00 85
Never hinged 24.00
556 A159 4c yel brn ('23) 15.00 20
Never hinged 24.00
a. Vert. pair, imperf. horiz. —
557 A160 5c dark blue 15.00 15
Never hinged 24.00
a. Imperf., pair *1,500.*
b. Horiz. pair, imperf. vert. —
558 A161 6c red orange 30.00 75
Never hinged 42.50
559 A162 7c black ('23) 7.00 45
Never hinged 10.00
560 A163 8c ol grn ('23) 37.50 35
Never hinged 60.00
561 A164 9c rose ('23) 12.00 90
Never hinged 19.00
562 A165 10c orange ('23) 16.00 15
Never hinged 25.00
a. Vert. pair, imperf. horiz. *1,250.*
b. Imperf., pair *1,250.*
563 A166 11c light blue 1.25 25
Never hinged 1.85
d. Imperf., pair —
564 A167 12c brn vio ('23) 5.50 15
Never hinged 8.00
a. Horiz. pair, imperf. vert. *1,000.*
565 A168 14c blue ('23) 3.50 65
Never hinged 5.25
566 A169 15c gray 19.00 15
Never hinged 27.50
567 A170 20c car rose ('23) 19.00 15
Never hinged 27.50
a. Horiz. pair, imperf. vert. *1,500.*
568 A171 25c yellow green 17.00 38
Never hinged 26.00
b. Vert. pair, imperf. horiz. *850.00*
569 A172 30c olive brn ('23) 30.00 30
Never hinged 45.00
570 A173 50c lilac 50.00 15
Never hinged 80.00
571 A174 $1 vio black ('23) 42.50 35
Never hinged 60.00
572 A175 $2 dp blue ('23) 90.00 8.00
Never hinged 125.00
573 A176 $5 car & bl ('23) 150.00 12.50
Never hinged 200.00
Nos. 551-573 (23) 580.25 27.43

For listings of other perforated stamps of designs A154 to A176 see

#578-579	Perf. 11x10
#581-591	Perf. 10
#594-595	Perf. 11
#632-642, 653, 692-696	Perf. 11x10½
#697-701	Perf. 10½x11

This series includes Nos. 622-623 (perf. 11).

1923-25 ***Imperf.***
575 A155 1c green 7.00 4.00
Never hinged 10.00
576 A156 1½c yel brn ('25) 1.50 1.50
Never hinged 2.25
577 A157 2c carmine 1.50 1.25
Never hinged 2.25

The 1½c A156 rotary press imperforate is listed as No. 631.
#575-577 are valued in the grade of very fine.

Rotary Press Printings

Perf. 11x10

578 A155 1c green 70.00 110.00
Never hinged 100.00
579 A157 2c carmine 60.00 100.00
Never hinged 90.00

Nos. 578-579 were made from coil waste of Nos. 597, 599 and measure approximately 19¾x22¼mm.

1923-26 ***Perf. 10***
581 A155 1c green 7.00 55
Never hinged 11.00
582 A156 1½c brown ('25) 3.50 45
Never hinged 5.50
583 A157 2c carmine ('24) 1.75 15
Never hinged 2.75
a. Booklet pane of 6 75.00 *25.00*
Never hinged 95.00
584 A158 3c violet ('25) 19.00 1.75
Never hinged 30.00
585 A159 4c yel brn ('25) 11.50 30
Never hinged 18.00
586 A160 5c blue ('25) 12.00 18
Never hinged 18.50
a. Horiz. pair, imperf. btwn. —
587 A161 6c red org ('25) 5.50 25
Never hinged 8.50
588 A162 7c black ('26) 8.00 4.25
Never hinged 12.50
589 A163 8c ol grn ('26) 17.50 2.75
Never hinged 27.50
590 A164 9c rose ('26) 3.75 1.90
Never hinged 6.00
591 A165 10c orange ('25) 47.50 15
Never hinged 70.00
Nos. 581-591 (11) 137.00 12.68

Perf. 11

594 A155 1c green *16,000.* 4,250.
595 A157 2c carmine 225. 250.
Never hinged 300.

Nos. 594-595 were made from coil waste of Nos. 597 and 599, and measure approximately 19¾x22¼mm.
No. 594 unused is valued without gum; perforations may touch one side.

Perf. 11

596 A155 1c green *27,500.*

No. 596 was made from rotary press sheet waste and measures approximately 19¼x22½mm. A majority of the copies carry the Bureau precancel "Kansas City, Mo." No. 596 is valued precanceled and in the grade of fine. Non-precanceled copies sell for more.

ROTARY PRESS DOUBLE PAPER

The web of paper used on rotary presses must be continuous, therefore any break in the paper must be lapped and pasted, causing the "double paper" varieties. These are no longer listed since they may occur on any rotary press stamp.

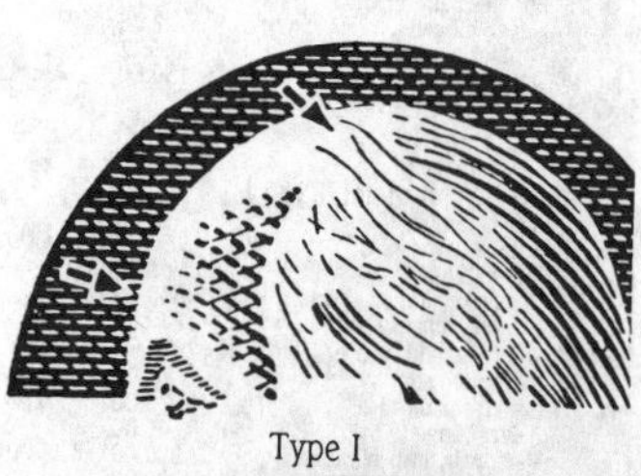

Type I

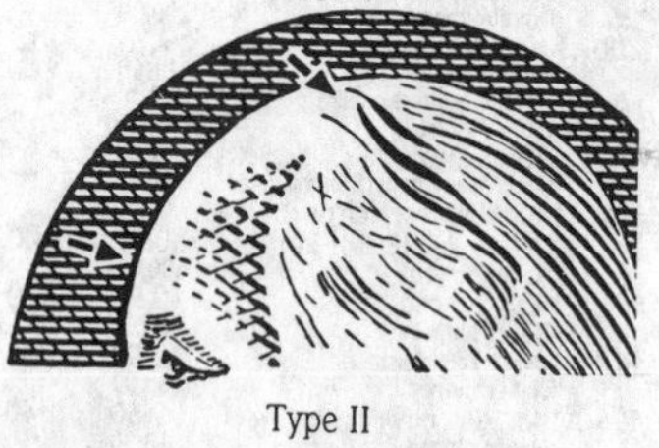

Type II

Type I

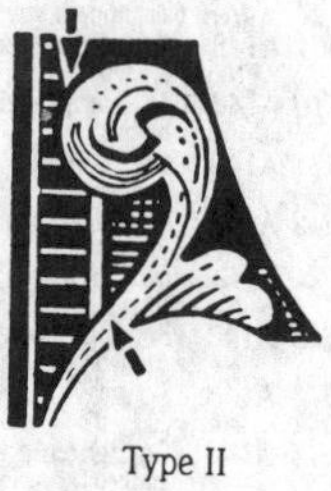

Type II

Type I. No heavy hair lines at top center of head. Outline of left acanthus scroll generally faint at top and toward base at left side.

Type II. The heavy hair lines at top center of head; two being outstanding in the white area. Outline of left acanthus scroll very strong and clearly defined at top (under left edge of lettered panel) and at lower curve (above and to left of numeral oval). Type II is found only on Nos. 599A and 634A.

Coil Stamps

Rotary Press Printing

1923-29 ***Perf. 10 Vertically***

597 A155 1c green 25 15
Never hinged 35
598 A156 1½c brown ('25) 75 15
Never hinged 1.05
599 A157 2c car, Type I ('23) 30 15
Never hinged 40
599A A157 2c car, Type II ('29) 105.00 9.50
Never hinged 140.00
600 A158 3c violet ('24) 5.50 15
Never hinged 7.50
601 A159 4c yellow brown 3.25 30
Never hinged 4.25
602 A160 5c dk bl ('24) 1.30 15
Never hinged 1.80
603 A165 10c orange ('24) 3.00 15
Never hinged 4.00

Perf. 10 Horizontally

604 A155 1c yellow green 25 15
Never hinged 35
605 A156 1½c yel brn ('25) 25 15
Never hinged 35
606 A157 2c carmine 25 15
Never hinged 35
Nos. 597-599,600-606 (10) 15.10
Set value 1.12

Harding Memorial Issue

Warren G. Harding — A177

Flat Plate Printing
(19¼x22¼mm)

1923, Sept. 1 ***Perf. 11***

610 A177 2c black 55 15
Never hinged 75
a. Horiz. pair, imperf. vert. *1,100.*

1923, Nov. 15 ***Imperf.***

611 A177 2c black 6.50 4.25
Never hinged 8.50

No. 611 is valued in the grade of very fine.

Rotary Press Printing
(19¼x22½mm)

1923, Sept. 12 ***Perf. 10***

612 A177 2c black 14.00 1.50
Never hinged 20.00

1923 ***Perf. 11***

613 A177 2c black *15,000.*

Tribute to President Warren G. Harding, who died August 2, 1923.
Nos. 610a, 613 valued in the grade of fine.

Huguenot-Walloon Tercentenary Issue

"New Netherland" A178

Landing at Fort Orange — A179

Monument to Jan Ribault at Mayport, Fla. — A180

Flat Plate Printings

1924, May 1 ***Perf. 11***

614 A178 1c dark green 2.75 3.00
Never hinged 3.75
615 A179 2c carmine rose 5.50 2.00
Never hinged 7.50
616 A180 5c dark blue 27.50 12.50
Never hinged 37.50

Tercentenary of the settling of the Walloons and in honor of the Huguenots.

Lexington-Concord Issue

Washington at Cambridge A181

"Birth of Liberty," by Henry Sandham A182

The Minute Man, by Daniel Chester French A183

1925, Apr. 4 ***Perf. 11***

617 A181 1c deep green 2.50 2.25
Never hinged 3.75
618 A182 2c carmine rose 5.00 3.75
Never hinged 7.50
619 A183 5c dark blue 24.00 12.50
Never hinged 32.50

150th anniv. of the Battle of Lexington-Concord.

Norse-American Issue

Sloop "Restaurationen" A184

Viking Ship A185

1925, May 18 ***Perf. 11***

620 A184 2c carmine & black 3.75 2.75
Never hinged 5.25
621 A185 5c dk blue & black 14.00 10.50
Never hinged 20.00

100th anniv. of the arrival in NY on Oct. 9, 1825, of the sloop "Restaurationen" with the first group of immigrants from Norway to the US.

Benjamin Harrison A186

Woodrow Wilson A187

1925-26 ***Perf. 11***

622 A186 13c green ('26) 12.00 40
Never hinged 16.00
623 A187 17c black 13.00 20
Never hinged 18.00

Sesquicentennial Exposition Issue

Liberty Bell — A188

1926, May 10 ***Perf. 11***

627 A188 2c carmine rose 2.75 40
Never hinged 3.75

150th anniv. of the Declaration of Independence, Philadelphia, June 1-Dec. 1.

Statue of John Ericsson A189

Alexander Hamilton's Battery A190

Ericsson Memorial Issue

1926, May 29 ***Perf. 11***

628 A189 5c gray lilac 5.50 2.75
Never hinged 7.75

John Ericsson, builder of the "Monitor".

Battle of White Plains Issue

1926, Oct. 18 ***Perf. 11***

629 A190 2c carmine rose 1.75 1.50
Never hinged 2.50
a. Vertical pair, imperf. btwn. —

Battle of White Plains, NY, 150th anniv.

International Philatelic Exhibition

Souvenir Sheet

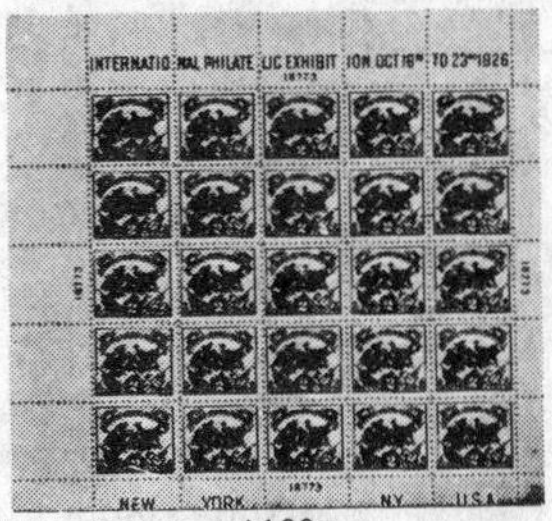

A190a

1926, Oct. 18 ***Perf. 11***

630 A190a 2c carmine rose, sheet of 25 350.00 375.00
Never hinged 450.00

Intl. Phil. Exhib. in NYC, Oct. 16-23. Size: 158-160¼x136-146½mm.

Condition Valued:

Centering: Overall centering will average F-VF, but individual stamps may be better or worse.

Perforations: No folds along rows of perforations.

Gum: There may be some light gum bends but no gum creases.

Hinging: There may be hinge marks in the selvage and on up to two or three stamps, but no heavy hinging or hinge remnants (except in the ungummed portion of the wide selvage).

Margins: Top panes should have about ½ inch bottom margin and 1 inch top margin.

Bottom panes should have about ½ inch top margin and just under ¾ inch bottom margin. Both will have one wide side (usually 1½ inches plus) and one narrow (½ inch) side margin. The wide margin corner will have a small diagonal notch on top panes.

Types of 1922-26

Rotary Press Printings

1926, Aug. 27 ***Imperf.***

631 A156 1½c yellow brown 1.75 1.60
Never hinged 2.25

No. 631 is valued in the grade of very fine.

1926-34 ***Perf. 11x10½***

632 A155 1c green ('27) 15 15
Never hinged 15
a. Booklet pane of 6 4.50 *25*
Never hinged 5.50
b. Vert. pair, imperf. btwn. 200.00 *125.00*
633 A156 1½c yel brown ('27) 1.60 15
Never hinged 2.10
634 A157 2c car, Type I 15 15
Never hinged 15
b. 2c carmine lake —
c. Horiz. pair, imperf. btwn. *2,000.*
d. Booklet pane of 6 1.40 *15*
Never hinged 1.90
634A A157 2c car, Type II ('28) 300.00 12.50
Never hinged 400.00
635 A158 3c violet ('27) 35 15
Never hinged 45
a. 3c bright violet ('34) 25 15
Never hinged 32
636 A159 4c yel brown ('27) 2.00 15
Never hinged 2.75
637 A160 5c dk bl ('27) 1.90 15
Never hinged 2.60
638 A161 6c red orange ('27) 2.00 15
Never hinged 2.75
639 A162 7c black ('27) 2.00 15
Never hinged 2.75
a. Vert. pair, imperf. btwn. 150.00 80.00
640 A163 8c ol grn ('27) 2.00 15
Never hinged 2.75
641 A164 9c orange red ('31) 2.00 15
Never hinged 2.75
642 A165 10c orange ('27) 3.25 15
Never hinged 4.35
Nos. 632-634,635-642 (11) 17.40
Set value 60

The 1½c, 2c, 4c, 5c, 6c, 8c imperf. (dry print) are printer's waste.
For ½c, 11c-50c see Nos. 653, 692-701.

Vermont Sesquicentennial Issue

Green Mountain Boy — A191

Flat Plate Printing

1927, Aug. 3 ***Perf. 11***

643 A191 2c carmine rose 1.25 75
Never hinged 1.70

Battle of Bennington, Vt., and independence of the State of Vermont, 150th anniv.

Surrender of Gen. John Burgoyne A192

Washington at Prayer A193

Burgoyne Campaign Issue

1927, Aug. 3 ***Perf. 11***

644 A192 2c carmine rose 3.00 1.90
Never hinged 4.00

Battles of Bennington, Oriskany, Fort Stanwix and Saratoga.

Valley Forge Issue

1928, May 26 ***Perf. 11***

645 A193 2c carmine rose 90 35
Never hinged 1.20

150th anniv. of Washington's encampment at Valley Forge, Pa.

Battle of Monmouth Issue

No. 634 Overprinted **MOLLY PITCHER**

Rotary Press Printing

1928, Oct. 20 ***Perf. 11x10½***

646 A157 2c carmine 95 95
Never hinged 1.25

The normal space between a vertical pair of the overprints is 18mm, but pairs are known with the space measuring 28mm.

150th anniv. of the Battle of Monmouth, NJ, and as a memorial to Molly Pitcher, the heroine of the battle.

Hawaii Sesquicentennial Issue

Nos. 634 and 637 Overprinted **HAWAII 1778 - 1928**

Rotary Press Printing

1928, Aug. 13 ***Perf. 11x10½***

647 A157 2c carmine 3.75 3.75
Never hinged 5.00
648 A160 5c dark blue 11.00 11.00
Never hinged 15.00

150th anniv. of the discovery of the Hawaiian Islands by Captain Cook.

These stamps were on sale at post offices in the Hawaiian Islands and at the Postal Agency in Washington, DC They were not on sale at post offices in the Continental US, though they were valid for postage there.

Normally the overprints were placed 18mm apart vertically, but pairs exist with a space of 28mm between the overprints.

Aeronautics Conference Issue

Wright Airplane A194

Globe and Airplane A195

Flat Plate Printing

1928, Dec. 12 ***Perf. 11***

649 A194 2c carmine rose		1.00	75
Never hinged		1.35	
650 A195 5c blue		4.50	3.00
Never hinged		6.00	

Intl. Civil Aeronautics Conf. at Washington, DC, Dec. 12-14, 1928, and of the 25th anniv. of the 1st airplane flight by the Wright brothers, Dec. 17, 1903.

George Rogers Clark Issue

Surrender of Fort Sackville A196

1929, Feb. 25 ***Perf. 11***

651 A196 2c carmine & black	55	40
Never hinged	75	

150th anniv. of the surrender of Fort Sackville, the present site of Vincennes, Ind., to George Rogers Clark.

Type of 1925

Rotary Press Printing

1929, May 25 ***Perf. 11x10½***

653 A154 ½c olive brown	15	15
Never hinged	15	

Edison's First Lamp A197

Maj. Gen. John Sullivan A198

Electric Light Jubilee Issue

1929 Flat Plate Printing ***Perf. 11***

654 A197 2c carmine rose	60	60
Never hinged	80	

Rotary Press Printing

Perf. 11x10½

655 A197 2c carmine rose	55	15
Never hinged	75	

Coil Stamp (Rotary Press)

Perf. 10 Vertically

656 A197 2c carmine rose	12.50	1.25
Never hinged	17.50	

50th anniv. of invention of the incandescent lamp by Thomas Alva Edison, Oct. 21, 1879. Issued: No. 654, June 5. Nos. 655-656, June 11.

Sullivan Expedition Issue

Flat Plate Printing

1929, June 17 ***Perf. 11***

657 A198 2c carmine rose	60	50
Never hinged	80	

150th anniv. of the Sullivan Expedition in NY State during the Revolutionary War.

Regular Issue of 1926-27 Overprinted **Kans.**

Rotary Press Printing

1929 ***Perf. 11x10½***

658 A155 1c green	1.50	1.35
Never hinged	2.00	
a. Vert. pair, one without ovpt.	*300.00*	
659 A156 1½c brown	2.50	1.90
Never hinged	3.00	
a. Vert. pair, one without ovpt.	*325.00*	
660 A157 2c carmine	2.75	75
Never hinged	3.75	
661 A158 3c violet	13.00	10.00
Never hinged	17.00	
a. Vert. pair, one without ovpt.	*400.00*	
662 A159 4c yellow brown	13.00	6.00
Never hinged	17.00	
a. Vert. pair, one without ovpt.	*400.00*	
663 A160 5c deep blue	9.00	6.50
Never hinged	12.00	
664 A161 6c red orange	20.00	12.00
Never hinged	26.00	
665 A162 7c black	19.00	18.00
Never hinged	25.00	
a. Vert. pair, one without ovpt.	*400.00*	
666 A163 8c olive green	65.00	50.00
Never hinged	85.00	
667 A164 9c light rose	10.00	7.50
Never hinged	13.00	
668 A165 10c orange yel	16.00	8.00
Never hinged	21.00	
Nos. 658-668 (11)	171.75	122.00

See note following No. 679.

Overprinted **Nebr.**

669 A155 1c green	2.25	1.50
Never hinged	3.00	
a. Vert. pair, one without ovpt.	*275.00*	
670 A156 1½c brown	2.00	1.65
Never hinged	2.75	
671 A157 2c carmine	2.00	85
Never hinged	2.75	
672 A158 3c violet	8.50	7.50
Never hinged	11.50	
a. Vert. pair, one without ovpt.	*400.00*	
673 A159 4c yellow brown	13.00	9.50
Never hinged	17.50	
674 A160 5c deep blue	11.00	9.50
Never hinged	15.00	
675 A161 6c red orange	27.50	15.00
Never hinged	35.00	
676 A162 7c black	15.00	11.50
Never hinged	20.00	
677 A163 8c olive green	21.00	16.00
Never hinged	27.50	
678 A164 9c light rose	24.00	18.00
Never hinged	30.00	
a. Vert. pair, one without ovpt.	*600.00*	
679 A165 10c orange yel	75.00	14.00
Never hinged	100.00	
Nos. 669-679 (11)	201.25	105.00

Nos. 658-660, 669-673, 677 and 678 are known with the overprints on vertical pairs spaced 32mm apart instead of the normal 22mm.

Important: Nos. 658-679 with original gum have either one horizontal gum breaker ridge per stamp or portions of two at the extreme top and bottom of the stamps, 21mm apart. Multiple complete gum breaker ridges indicate a fake overprint. Absence of the gum breaker ridges indicates either regumming or regumming and a fake overprint.

Gen. Anthony Wayne Memorial — A199

Lock No. 5, Monongahela River — A200

Battle of Fallen Timbers Issue

Flat Plate Printing

1929, Sept. 14 ***Perf. 11***

680 A199 2c carmine rose	65	65
Never hinged	85	

General Anthony Wayne memorial and the 135th anniv. of the Battle of Fallen Timbers, Ohio.

Ohio River Canalization Issue

1929, Oct. 19 ***Perf. 11***

681 A200 2c carmine rose	50	50
Never hinged	65	

Completion of the Ohio River Canalization Project between Cairo, Ill. and Pittsburgh.

Massachusetts Bay Colony Issue

Mass. Bay Colony Seal — A201

1930, Apr. 8 ***Perf. 11***

682 A201 2c carmine rose	50	38
Never hinged	65	

300th anniv. of the founding of the Massachusetts Bay Colony.

Carolina-Charleston Issue

Gov. Joseph West and Chief Shadoo, a Kiowa — A202

1930, Apr. 10 ***Perf. 11***

683 A202 2c carmine rose	1.00	90
Never hinged	1.35	

260th anniv. of the founding of the Province of Carolina, and the 250th anniv. of the City of Charleston, SC.

Warren G. Harding — A203

William H. Taft — A204

Type of 1922-26 Issue

Rotary Press Printing

1930 ***Perf. 11x10½***

684 A203 1½c brown	25	15
Never hinged	32	
685 A204 4c brown	75	15
Never hinged	1.00	
Set value		15

Coil Stamps

Perf. 10 Vertically

686 A203 1½c brown	1.50	15
Never hinged	2.00	
687 A204 4c brown	2.75	38
Never hinged	3.50	
Set value		45

Braddock's Field Issue

Statue of Col. George Washington — A205

Flat Plate Printing

1930, July 9 ***Perf. 11***

688 A205 2c carmine rose	85	75
Never hinged	1.10	

175th anniv. of the Battle of Braddock's Field, otherwise the Battle of Monongahela.

General von Steuben — A206

General Casimir Pulaski — A207

Von Steuben Issue

1930, Sept. 17 ***Perf. 11***

689 A206 2c carmine rose	45	45
Never hinged	60	
a. Imperf., pair	*2,500.*	
Never hinged	*3,250.*	

Gen. Baron Friedrich Wilhelm von Steuben (1730-1794), German soldier who served with distinction in American Revolution.

Pulaski Issue

1931, Jan. 16 ***Perf. 11***

690 A207 2c carmine rose	20	15
Never hinged	26	

150th anniv. (in 1929) of the death of Gen. Count Casimir Pulaski (1748-1779), Polish patriot and hero of American Revolution.

Types of 1922-26

Rotary Press Printing

1931 ***Perf. 11x10½***

692 A166 11c light blue	2.00	15
Never hinged	2.85	
693 A167 12c brown violet	4.00	15
Never hinged	6.00	
694 A186 13c yellow green	1.75	15
Never hinged	2.50	
695 A168 14c dark blue	2.75	22
Never hinged	3.75	
696 A169 15c gray	6.50	15
Never hinged	9.00	

Perf. 10½x11

697 A187 17c black	3.50	15
Never hinged	5.00	
698 A170 20c carmine rose	7.75	15
Never hinged	11.00	
699 A171 25c blue green	7.25	15
Never hinged	10.50	
700 A172 30c brown	11.50	15
Never hinged	16.50	
701 A173 50c lilac	35.00	15
Never hinged	50.00	
Nos. 692-701 (10)	82.00	
Set value		95

"The Greatest Mother" A208

Count de Rochambeau, Washington, Count de Grasse A209

Red Cross Issue

Flat Plate Printing

1931, May 21 ***Perf. 11***

702 A208 2c black & red	16	15
Never hinged	20	

50th anniv. of the founding of the American Red Cross Society.

Yorktown Issue

1931, Oct. 19 ***Perf. 11***

703 A209 2c carmine rose & black	35	25
Never hinged	48	
a. 2c lake & black	4.00	65
Never hinged	5.50	
b. 2c dark lake & black	*375.00*	
Never hinged	*525.00*	
c. Horiz. pair, imperf. vert.	*4,000.*	
Never hinged	*5,000.*	

Surrender of Yorktown, sesquicentennial.

Washington Bicentennial Issue

Various Portraits of George Washington

A210

A211

A212

A213

A214

A215

A216

A217

A218

A219

A220

A221

Rotary Press Printings

1932, Jan. 1 *Perf. 11x10½*
704 A210 ½c olive brown 15 15
Never hinged 15
705 A211 1c green 15 15
Never hinged 15
706 A212 1½c brown 32 15
Never hinged 40
707 A213 2c carmine rose 15 15
Never hinged 15
708 A214 3c deep violet 40 15
Never hinged 50
709 A215 4c light brown 22 15
Never hinged 28
710 A216 5c blue 1.40 15
Never hinged 1.75
711 A217 6c red orange 2.75 15
Never hinged 3.50
712 A218 7c black 22 15
Never hinged 28
713 A219 8c olive bister 2.50 50
Never hinged 3.10
714 A220 9c pale red 2.00 15
Never hinged 2.50
715 A221 10c orange yellow 8.50 15
Never hinged 10.50
Nos. 704-715 (12) 18.76
Set value 1.38

200th anniv. of the birth of Washington.

Ski Jumper
A222

Boy and Girl Planting Tree
A223

Olympic Winter Games Issue
Flat Plate Printing

1932, Jan. 25 *Perf. 11*
716 A222 2c carmine rose 35 16
Never hinged 45

Olympic Winter Games, Lake Placid, NY, Feb. 4-13.

Arbor Day Issue
Rotary Press Printing

1932, Apr. 22 *Perf. 11x10½*
717 A223 2c carmine rose 15 15
Never hinged 16

60th anniv. of the 1st observance of Arbor Day in Nebr., April, 1872, and the birth centenary of Julius Sterling Morton, who conceived the plan and the name "Arbor Day," while a member of the Nebr. State Board of Agriculture.

10th Olympic Games Issue

Runner at Starting Mark
A224

Myron's Discobolus
A225

1932, June 15 *Perf. 11x10½*
718 A224 3c violet 1.25 15
Never hinged 1.55
719 A225 5c blue 2.00 20
Never hinged 2.50
Set value 28

Los Angeles, Cal., July 30-Aug. 14.

Washington — A226

1932, June 16 *Perf. 11x10½*
720 A226 3c deep violet 15 15
Never hinged 16
b. Booklet pane of 6 27.50 *5.00*
Never hinged 35.00
c. Vert. pair, imperf. btwn. 300.00 *250.00*

Coil Stamps
Rotary Press Printing

1932, June 24 *Perf. 10 Vertically*
721 A226 3c deep violet 2.25 15
Never hinged 2.75

1932, Oct. 12 *Perf. 10 Horizontally*
722 A226 3c deep violet 1.25 30
Never hinged 1.55

Garfield Type of 1922-26 Issue

1932, Aug. 18 *Perf. 10 Vertically*
723 A161 6c deep orange 8.50 25
Never hinged 10.50

William Penn
A227

Daniel Webster
A228

William Penn Issue
Flat Plate Printing

1932, Oct. 24 *Perf. 11*
724 A227 3c violet 25 15
Never hinged 32
a. Vert. pair, imperf. horiz. —

250th anniv. of the arrival in America of William Penn (1644-1718), English Quaker and founder of Pennsylvania.

Daniel Webster Issue

1932, Oct. 24 *Perf. 11*
725 A228 3c violet 30 24
Never hinged 38

Daniel Webster (1782-1852), statesman.

Georgia Bicentennial Issue

Gen. James Edward Oglethorpe — A229

1933, Feb. 12 *Perf. 11*
726 A229 3c violet 25 18
Never hinged 32

200th anniv. of the founding of the Colony of Georgia and James Edward Oglethorpe, who landed from England, Feb. 12th, 1733, and personally supervised the establishing of the colony.

Peace of 1783 Issue

Washington's Headquarters, Newburgh, NY — A230

Rotary Press Printing

1933, Apr. 19 *Perf. 10½x11*
727 A230 3c violet 15 15
Never hinged 15

150th anniv. of the Proclamation of Peace between the US and Great Britain at the end of the Revolutionary War.
See No. 752.

Century of Progress Issue

Restoration of Fort Dearborn
A231

Federal Building at Chicago, 1933
A232

1933, May 25 *Perf. 10½x11*
728 A231 1c yellow green 15 15
Never hinged 15
729 A232 3c violet 15 15
Never hinged 16
Set value 20 15

"Century of Progress" Intl. Phil. Exhib., Chicago, 1933 and 100th anniv. of the incorporation of Chicago as a city.

American Philatelic Society Issue
Souvenir Sheets
Without Gum
Flat Plate Printing

1933, Aug. 25 *Imperf.*
730 Sheet of 25 24.00 24.00
a. A231 1c deep yellow green 65 35
731 Sheet of 25 22.50 22.50
a. A232 3c deep violet 50 35

Sheet measures 134x120mm.
See Nos. 766-767.

National Recovery Act Issue

Group of Workers — A233

Rotary Press Printing

1933, Aug. 15 *Perf. 10½x11*
732 A233 3c violet 15 15
Never hinged 16

Issued to direct attention to and arouse support of the Nation for the NRA.

Byrd Antarctic Issue

World Map on van der Grinten's Projection — A234

Flat Plate Printing

1933, Oct. 9 *Perf. 11*
733 A234 3c dark blue 40 48
Never hinged 50

Second Antarctic expedition of Rear Admiral Richard E. Byrd.
In addition to the 3 cents postage, letters sent by the ships of the expedition to be canceled in Little America were subject to a service charge of 50 cents each.
See Nos. 735, 753.

Kosciuszko Issue

Statue of Gen. Tadeusz Kosciuszko — A235

1933, Oct. 13 *Perf. 11*
734 A235 5c blue 50 22
Never hinged 62
a. Horiz. pair, imperf. vert. *2,000.*
Never hinged *2,500.*

Gen. Tadeusz Kosciuszko (1746-1807), Polish soldier and statesman who served in American Revolution. 150th anniv. of grant of American citizenship.

National Stamp Exhibition Issue
Souvenir Sheet
Without Gum

1934, Feb. 10 *Imperf.*
735 Sheet of 6 12.50 10.00
a. A234 3c dark blue 2.00 1.65

Sheet measures 87x93mm. See #768.

Maryland Tercentenary Issue

"The Ark" and "The Dove" — A236

1934, Mar. 23 *Perf. 11*
736 A236 3c carmine rose 15 15
Never hinged 16

300th anniv. of the founding of Maryland.

Mothers of America Issue

Adaptation of Whistler's Portrait of his Mother
A237

Rotary Press Printing

1934, May 2 *Perf. 11x10½*
737 A237 3c deep violet 15 15
Never hinged 16

Flat Plate Printing
Perf. 11

738 A237 3c deep violet 15 15
Never hinged 18
Set value 21 16

Mother's Day. See No. 754.

Wisconsin Tercentenary Issue

Nicolet's Landing
A238

1934, July 7 *Perf. 11*
739 A238 3c deep violet 15 15
Never hinged 16
a. Vert. pair, imperf. horiz. 250.00 *325.00*
Never hinged 325.00
b. Horiz. pair, imperf. vert. 325.00 *400.00*
Never hinged

Tercentenary of the arrival of French explorer Jean Nicolet at Green Bay, Wis.
See No. 755.

National Parks Issue

El Capitan, Yosemite (California)
A239

Old Faithful, Yellowstone (Wyoming)
A243

Grand Canyon (Arizona)
A240

Mt. Rainier and Mirror Lake (Washington)
A241

Mesa Verde (Colorado)
A242

Crater Lake (Oregon) A244

Great Head, Acadia Park (Maine) A245

Great White Throne, Zion Park (Utah) A246

Great Smoky Mts. (North Carolina) A248

Mt. Rockwell (Mt. Sinopah) and Two Medicine Lake, Glacier Natl. Park (Montana) A247

1934 Flat Plate Printing *Perf. 11*

740 A239 1c green	15	15
Never hinged	15	
a. Vert. pair, imperf. horiz., with gum	*450.00*	
Never hinged	*550.00*	
741 A240 2c red	15	15
Never hinged	15	
a. Vert. pair, imperf. horiz., with gum	*300.00*	
Never hinged	*375.00*	
b. Horiz. pair, imperf. vert., with gum	*300.00*	
Never hinged	*375.00*	
742 A241 3c deep violet	15	15
Never hinged	16	
a. Vert. pair, imperf. horiz., with gum	*350.00*	
Never hinged	*435.00*	
743 A242 4c brown	35	32
Never hinged	45	
a. Vert. pair, imperf. horiz., with gum	*500.00*	
Never hinged	*625.00*	
744 A243 5c blue	60	55
Never hinged	75	
a. Horiz. pair, imperf. vert., with gum	*400.00*	
Never hinged	*500.00*	
745 A244 6c dark blue	1.00	75
Never hinged	1.35	
746 A245 7c black	55	65
Never hinged	70	
a. Horiz. pair, imperf. vert., with gum	*550.00*	
Never hinged	*685.00*	
747 A246 8c sage green	1.40	1.65
Never hinged	1.85	
748 A247 9c red orange	1.50	55
Never hinged	1.90	
749 A248 10c gray black	2.75	90
Never hinged	3.75	
Nos. 740-749 (10)	8.60	5.82

National Parks Year.
See Nos. 750-751, 756-765, 769-770.

American Philatelic Society Issue

Souvenir Sheet

1934, Aug. 28 *Imperf.*

750 Sheet of 6	27.50	25.00
Never hinged	34.00	
a. A241 3c deep violet	3.25	3.00
Never hinged	4.00	

Sheet measures 99x97mm. See #770.

Trans-Mississippi Philatelic Exposition Issue

Souvenir Sheet

1934, Oct. 10 *Imperf.*

751 Sheet of 6	12.00	12.00
Never hinged	15.00	
a. A239 1c green	1.35	1.50
Never hinged	1.75	

Sheet measures 94x99mm. See #769.

Special Printing (Nos. 752-771)

"Issued for a limited time in full sheets as printed, and in blocks thereof, to meet the requirements of collectors and others who may be interested."—From Postal Bulletin, No. 16614.

Issuance of the following 20 stamps in complete sheets resulted from the protest of collectors and others at the practice of presenting, to certain government officials, complete sheets of unsevered panes, imperforate (except Nos. 752 and 753) and generally ungummed.

Without Gum.

Note. In 1940 the P.O. Department offered to and did gum full sheets of Nos. 754 to 771 sent in by owners.

Type of Peace Issue
Issued in sheets of 400

Rotary Press Printing

1935, Mar. 15 *Perf. 10½x11*

752 A230 3c violet	15	15

Type of Byrd Issue
Issued in sheets of 200
Flat Plate Printing
Perf. 11

753 A234 3c dark blue	40	40

No. 753 is similar to No. 733. Positive identification is by pairs or blocks showing a guide line between stamps. These lines are found only on No. 753.

Type of Mothers of America Issue
Issued in sheets of 200
Imperf

754 A237 3c deep violet	50	50

Type of Wisconsin Issue
Issued in sheets of 200
Imperf

755 A238 3c deep violet	50	50

Types of National Parks Issue
Issued in sheets of 200
Imperf

756 A239 1c green	20	20
757 A240 2c red	22	22
758 A241 3c deep violet	45	40
759 A242 4c brown	90	90
760 A243 5c blue	1.40	1.25
761 A244 6c dark blue	2.25	2.00
762 A245 7c black	1.40	1.25
763 A246 8c sage green	1.50	1.40
764 A247 9c red orange	1.75	1.50
765 A248 10c gray black	3.50	3.00
Nos. 756-765 (10)	13.57	12.12

Souvenir Sheets
Type of Century of Progress Issue
Issued in sheets of 9 panes of 25 stamps each

Note. Single items from these sheets are identical with other varieties, 766 & 730, 766a & 730a, 767 & 731, 767a & 731a, 768 & 735, 768a & 735a, 769 & 756, 770 & 758. Positive identification is by blocks or pairs showing wide gutters between stamps. These wide gutters occur only on Nos. 766 to 770 and measure, horizontally, 13mm on Nos. 766-767; 16mm on No. 768, and 23mm on Nos. 769-770.

Imperf

766 Pane of 25	24.00	24.00
a. A231 1c yellow green	65	35
767 Pane of 25	22.50	22.50
a. A232 3c violet	50	35

National Exhibition Issue
Type of Byrd Issue
Issued in sheets of 25 panes of 6 stamps each
Imperf

768 Pane of 6	18.00	12.50
a. A234 3c dark blue	2.50	2.00

Types of National Parks Issue
Issued in sheets of 20 panes of 6 stamps each
Imperf

769 Pane of 6	12.00	9.00
a. A239 1c green	1.75	1.50
770 Pane of 6	27.50	22.50
a. A241 3c deep violet	3.00	3.00

Type of Air Post Special Delivery
Issued in sheets of 200
Imperf

771 APSD1 16c dark blue	2.00	2.00

Catalogue values for unused stamps in this section, from this point to the end of the section, are for Never Hinged items.

Connecticut Tercentenary Issue

Charter Oak — A249

Rotary Press Printing

1935, Apr. 26 *Perf. 11x10½*

772 A249 3c violet	15	15

300th anniv. of the settlement of Conn.
See No. 778a.

California-Pacific Exposition Issue

View of San Diego Exposition A250

1935, May 29 *Perf. 11x10½*

773 A250 3c purple	15	15

California-Pacific Expo., San Diego.
See No. 778b.

Boulder Dam Issue

Boulder Dam — A251

Flat Plate Printing

1935, Sept. 30 *Perf. 11*

774 A251 3c purple	15	15

Dedication of Boulder Dam.

Michigan Centenary Issue

Michigan State Seal — A252

Rotary Press Printing

1935, Nov. 1 *Perf. 11x10½*

775 A252 3c purple	15	15

Advance celebration of Michigan statehood centenary. Michigan was admitted to Union Jan. 26, 1837.
See No. 778c.

Texas Centennial Issue

Sam Houston, Stephen F. Austin and the Alamo — A253

1936, Mar. 2 *Perf. 11x10½*

776 A253 3c purple	15	15

Centennial of Texas independence.
See No. 778d.

Rhode Island Tercentenary Issue

Statue of Roger Williams — A254

1936, May 4 *Perf. 10½x11*

777 A254 3c purple	15	15

Settlement of Rhode Island, 1636.

Third International Philatelic Exhibition Issue

Souvenir Sheet

A254a

Flat Plate Printing

1936, May 9 *Imperf.*

778 A254a Sheet of 4	1.75	1.75
a. A249 3c violet	40	30
b. A250 3c violet	40	30
c. A252 3c violet	40	30
d. A253 3c violet	40	30

Sheet measures 98x66mm.

Arkansas Centennial Issue

Arkansas Post, Old and New State Houses A255

Rotary Press Printing

1936, June 15 *Perf. 11x10½*

782 A255 3c purple	15	15

Centennial of Arkansas statehood.

Map of Oregon Territory A256

Susan B. Anthony A257

Oregon Territory Issue

1936, July 14 *Perf. 11x10½*

783 A256 3c purple	15	15

Centenary of Oregon Territory opening.

Susan B. Anthony Issue

1936, Aug. 26 *Perf. 11x10½*

784 A257 3c dark violet	15	15

Susan Brownell Anthony (1820-1906), woman suffrage advocate, honored on 16th anniv. of ratification of 19th Amendment granting American women the right to vote.

Army Issue

George Washington, Nathanael Greene and Mount Vernon — A258

Andrew Jackson, Winfield Scott and the Hermitage
A259

Generals Sherman, Grant and Sheridan
A260

Generals Robert E. Lee, "Stonewall" Jackson and Stratford Hall — A261

US Military Academy, West Point — A262

1936-37	*Perf. 11x10½*		
785 A258	1c green	15	15
786 A259	2c carmine ('37)	15	15
787 A260	3c purple ('37)	15	15
788 A261	4c gray ('37)	30	15
789 A262	5c ultra ('37)	60	15
	Nos. 785-789 (5)	1.35	
	Set value		42

Issued in honor of the United States Army.

Navy Issue

John Paul Jones and John Barry — A263

Stephen Decatur and Thomas MacDonough
A264

Admirals David G. Farragut and David D. Porter — A265

Admirals William T. Sampson, George Dewey and Winfield S. Schley — A266

Seal of US Naval Academy and Naval Cadets — A267

1936-37	*Perf. 11x10½*		
790 A263	1c green	15	15
791 A264	2c carmine ('37)	15	15
792 A265	3c purple ('37)	15	15
793 A266	4c gray ('37)	30	15
794 A267	5c ultra ('37)	60	15
	Nos. 790-794 (5)	1.35	
	Set value		45

Issued in honor of the United States Navy.

Northwest Ordinance Sesquicentennial Issue

Manasseh Cutler, Rufus Putnam and Map of Northwest Territory
A268

1937, July 13 *Perf. 11x10½*
795 A268 3c red violet 15 15

150th anniv. of the adoption of the Ordinance of 1787 and the creation of the Northwest Territory.

Virginia Dare Issue

Virginia Dare and Parents — A269

Flat Plate Printing

1937, Aug. 18 *Perf. 11*
796 A269 5c gray blue 20 18

350th anniv. of the birth of Virginia Dare and the settlement at Roanoke Island. Virginia was the first child born in America of English parents (Aug. 18, 1587).

Society of Philatelic Americans
Souvenir Sheet

A269a

1937, Aug. 26 *Imperf.*
797 A269a 10c blue green 60 40

Sheet measures 67x78mm.

Constitution Sesquicentennial Issue

Signing of the Constitution
A270

Rotary Press Printing

1937, Sept. 17 *Perf. 11x10½*
798 A270 3c bright red violet 15 15

Sesquicentennial of the Signing of the Constitution, Sept. 17, 1787.

Territorial Issues
Hawaii

Statue of Kamehameha I, Honolulu — A271

1937, Oct. 18 *Perf. 10½x11*
799 A271 3c violet 15 15

Alaska

Landscape with Mt. McKinley
A272

1937, Nov. 12 *Perf. 11x10½*
800 A272 3c violet 15 15

Puerto Rico

La Fortaleza, San Juan — A273

1937, Nov. 25 *Perf. 11x10½*
801 A273 3c bright violet 15 15

Virgin Islands

Charlotte Amalie — A274

1937, Dec. 15 *Perf. 11x10½*
802 A274 3c light violet 15 15

Presidential Issue

Benjamin Franklin
A275

George Washington
A276

Martha Washington
A277

John Adams
A278

Thomas Jefferson
A279

James Madison
A280

White House
A281

James Monroe
A282

John Q. Adams
A283

Andrew Jackson
A284

Martin Van Buren
A285

William H. Harrison
A286

John Tyler
A287

James K. Polk
A288

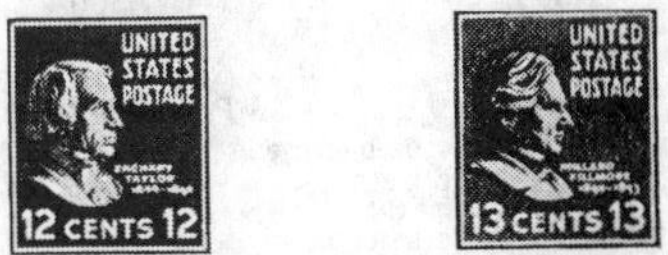

Zachary Taylor
A289

Millard Fillmore
A290

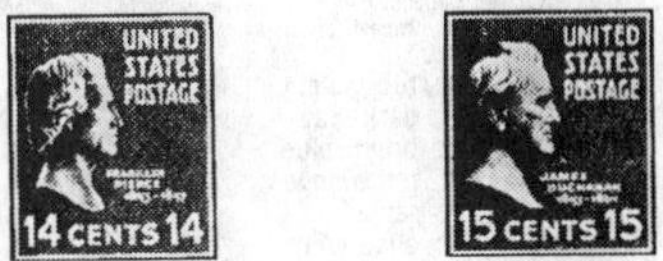

Franklin Pierce
A291

James Buchanan
A292

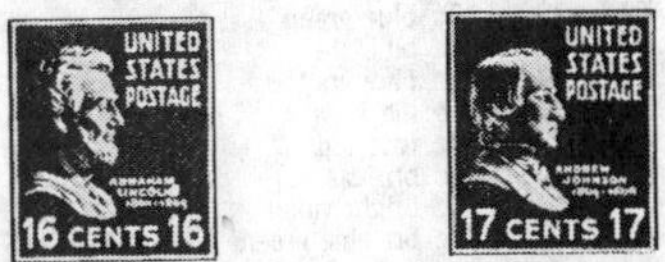

Abraham Lincoln
A293

Andrew Johnson
A294

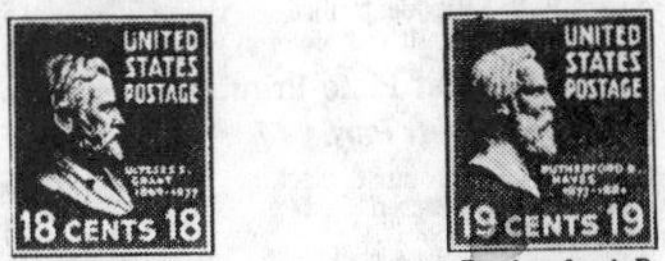

Ulysses S. Grant
A295

Rutherford B. Hayes
A296

James A. Garfield
A297

Chester A. Arthur
A298

Grover Cleveland
A299

Benjamin Harrison
A300

William McKinley
A301

Theodore Roosevelt
A302

William Howard Taft
A303

Woodrow Wilson
A304

Warren G. Harding
A305

Calvin Coolidge
A306

1938-54 *Perf. 11x10½*

803 A275	½c deep orange	15	15
804 A276	1c green	15	15
b.	Booklet pane of 6	1.50	*20*
805 A277	1½c bister brown	15	15
b.	Horiz. pair, imperf. btwn.	150.00	25.00
806 A278	2c rose carmine	15	15
b.	Booklet pane of 6	3.50	*50*
807 A279	3c deep violet	15	15
a.	Booklet pane of 6	7.00	*50*
b.	Horiz. pair, imperf. btwn.	650.00	—
c.	Imperf., pair	*2,500.*	
808 A280	4c red violet	60	15
809 A281	4½c dark gray	15	15
810 A282	5c bright blue	20	15
811 A283	6c red orange	20	15
812 A284	7c sepia	25	15
813 A285	8c olive green	28	15
814 A286	9c rose pink	32	15
815 A287	10c brown red	25	15
816 A288	11c ultra	65	15
817 A289	12c bright violet	90	15
818 A290	13c blue green	1.25	15
819 A291	14c blue	90	15
820 A292	15c blue gray	38	15
821 A293	16c black	90	25
822 A294	17c rose red	85	15
823 A295	18c brn car	1.50	15
824 A296	19c bright violet	1.25	35
825 A297	20c brt blue green	70	15
826 A298	21c dull blue	1.25	15
827 A299	22c vermilion	1.00	40
828 A300	24c gray black	3.50	18
829 A301	25c deep red lilac	60	15
830 A302	30c deep ultra	4.25	15
831 A303	50c lt red violet	6.00	15

Flat Plate Printing

Perf. 11

832 A304	$1 pur & black	7.00	15
a.	Vert. pair, imperf. horiz.	*1,500.*	
b.	Wmkd. USIR ('51)	300.00	70.00
c.	$1 red violet & black ('54)	6.00	15
d.	As "c," vert. pair, imperf. horiz.	*1,100.*	
e.	Vert. pair, imperf. btwn.	*2,500.*	
f.	As "c," vert. pair, imperf. btwn.	*7,000.*	
833 A305	$2 yel grn & blk	21.00	3.75
834 A306	$5 car & black	95.00	3.00
a.	$5 red brown & black	*2,250.*	*1,500.*
	Nos. 803-834 (32)	151.88	
	Set value		9.50

No. 832c is printed on thick white paper with smooth, colorless gum.

No. 834 can be chemically altered to resemble No. 834a. No. 834a should be purchased only with competent expert certification.

See Nos. 839-851.

Constitution Ratification Issue

Old Court House, Williamsburg, Va. — A307

Rotary Press Printing

1938, June 21 *Perf. 11x10½*
835 A307 3c deep violet 22 15

150th anniv. of the ratification of the US Constitution.

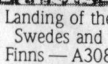

Landing of the Swedes and Finns — A308

Statue Symbolizing Colonization of the West — A309

Swedish-Finnish Tercentenary Issue

Flat Plate Printing

1938, June 27 *Perf. 11*
836 A308 3c red violet 15 15

Tercentenary of the founding of the Swedish and Finnish settlement at Wilmington, Del.

Northwest Territory Issue

Rotary Press Printing

1938, July 15 *Perf. 11x10½*
837 A309 3c bright violet 15 15

Sesquicentennial of the settlement of the Northwest Territory.

Iowa Territory Centennial Issue

Old Capitol, Iowa City — A310

1938, Aug. 24 *Perf. 11x10½*
838 A310 3c violet 15 15

Centenary of Iowa Territory.

Presidential Types of 1938
Coil Stamps

Rotary Press Printing

1939 *Perf. 10 Vertically*

839 A276	1c green	20	15
840 A277	1½c bister brown	24	15
841 A278	2c rose carmine	24	15
842 A279	3c deep violet	42	15
843 A280	4c red violet	6.00	35
844 A281	4½c dark gray	50	35
845 A282	5c bright blue	4.50	30
846 A283	6c red orange	80	15
847 A287	10c brown red	10.00	40

Perf. 10 Horizontally

848 A276	1c green	55	15
849 A277	1½c bister brown	1.10	30
850 A278	2c rose carmine	2.00	40
851 A279	3c deep violet	1.75	35
	Nos. 839-851 (13)	28.30	3.35

"Tower of the Sun"
A311

Trylon and Perisphere
A312

Golden Gate International Exposition Issue

Rotary Press Printing

1939, Feb. 18 *Perf. 10½x11*
852 A311 3c bright purple 15 15

Golden Gate Intl. Expo., San Francisco.

New York World's Fair Issue

1939, Apr. 1 *Perf. 10½x11*
853 A312 3c deep purple 15 15

Washington Inauguration Issue

George Washington Taking Oath of Office — A313

Flat Plate Printing

1939, Apr. 30 *Perf. 11*
854 A313 3c bright red violet 40 15

Sesquicentennial of the inauguration of George Washington as 1st president.

Baseball Centennial Issue

Sand-lot Baseball Game — A314

Rotary Press Printing

1939, June 12 *Perf. 11x10½*
855 A314 3c violet 1.25 15

Centennial of baseball.

Panama Canal Issue

Theodore Roosevelt, Gen. George W. Goethals and Gaillard Cut — A315

Flat Plate Printing

1939, Aug. 15 *Perf. 11*
856 A315 3c deep red violet 18 15

25th anniv. of the Panama Canal opening.

Printing Tercentenary Issue

Stephen Daye Press — A316

Rotary Press Printing

1939, Sept. 25 *Perf. 10½x11*
857 A316 3c violet 15 15

300th anniv. of printing in Colonial America.

50th Anniversary of Statehood Issue.

Map of North and South Dakota, Montana and Washington
A317

1939, Nov. 2 *Perf. 11x10½*
858 A317 3c rose violet 15 15

50th anniv. of admission to Statehood of North Dakota, South Dakota, Montana and Washington.

Famous Americans Issues

Authors

Washington Irving
A318

James Fenimore Cooper
A319

Ralph Waldo Emerson
A320

Louisa May Alcott
A321

Samuel L. Clemens (Mark Twain) — A322

1940 *Perf. 10½x11*

859 A318	1c bright blue green	15	15
860 A319	2c rose carmine	15	15
861 A320	3c bright red violet	15	15
862 A321	5c ultra	28	20
863 A322	10c dark brown	1.50	1.35
	Nos. 859-863 (5)	2.23	2.00

Poets

Henry W. Longfellow
A323

John Greenleaf Whittier
A324

James Russell Lowell
A325

Walt Whitman
A326

James Whitcomb Riley — A327

1940 *Perf. 10½x11*

864 A323	1c bright blue green	15	15
865 A324	2c rose carmine	15	15
866 A325	3c bright red violet	15	15
867 A326	5c ultra	32	18
868 A327	10c dark brown	1.65	1.40
	Nos. 864-868 (5)	2.42	2.03

Educators

Horace Mann
A328

Mark Hopkins
A329

Charles W. Eliot
A330

Frances E. Willard
A331

Booker T. Washington — A332

1940 *Perf. 10½x11*

869 A328	1c bright blue green	15	15
870 A329	2c rose carmine	15	15
871 A330	3c bright red violet	15	15
872 A331	5c ultra	38	25
873 A332	10c dark brown	1.10	1.25
	Nos. 869-873 (5)	1.93	1.95

Scientists

John James Audubon
A333

Dr. Crawford W. Long
A334

Luther Burbank A335

Dr. Walter Reed A336

Jane Addams — A337

1940 *Perf. 10½x11*

874 A333	1c bright blue green	15	15
875 A334	2c rose carmine	15	15
876 A335	3c bright red violet	15	15
877 A336	5c ultra	25	15
878 A337	10c dark brown	1.00	95
	Nos. 874-878 (5)	1.70	
	Set value		1.28

Composers

Stephen Collins Foster — A338

John Philip Sousa — A339

Victor Herbert A340

Edward MacDowell A341

Ethelbert Nevin — A342

1940 *Perf. 10½x11*

879 A338	1c bright blue green	15	15
880 A339	2c rose carmine	15	15
881 A340	3c bright red violet	15	15
882 A341	5c ultra	40	22
883 A342	10c dark brown	3.50	1.35
	Nos. 879-883 (5)	4.35	2.02

Artists

Gilbert Charles Stuart A343

James A. McNeill Whistler A344

Augustus Saint-Gaudens A345

Daniel Chester French A346

Frederic Remington — A347

1940 *Perf. 10½x11*

884 A343	1c bright blue green	15	15
885 A344	2c rose carmine	15	15
886 A345	3c bright red violet	15	15
887 A346	5c ultra	48	22
888 A347	10c dark brown	1.75	1.40
	Nos. 884-888 (5)	2.68	2.07

Inventors

Eli Whitney A348

Samuel F. B. Morse A349

Cyrus Hall McCormick A350

Elias Howe A351

Alexander Graham Bell — A352

1940 *Perf. 10½x11*

889 A348	1c brt blue green	15	15
890 A349	2c rose carmine	15	15
891 A350	3c bright red violet	25	15
892 A351	5c ultra	1.00	32
893 A352	10c dark brown	10.00	2.25
	Nos. 889-893 (5)	11.55	3.02
	Nos. 859-893 (35)	26.86	14.64

Pony Express Issue

Pony Express Rider — A353

1940, Apr. 3 *Perf. 11x10½*

894 A353 3c henna brown 25 15

80th anniv. of the Pony Express.

Pan American Union Issue

The Three Graces from Botticelli's "Spring" — A354

1940, Apr. 14 *Perf. 10½x11*

895 A354 3c light violet 20 15

Pan American Union founding, 50th anniv.

Idaho Statehood Issue

Idaho Capitol, Boise — A355

1940, July 3 *Perf. 11x10½*

896 A355 3c bright violet 15 15

Idaho statehood, 50th anniv.

Wyoming Statehood Issue

Wyoming State Seal — A356

1940, July 10 *Perf. 10½x11*

897 A356 3c brown violet 15 15

Wyoming statehood, 50th anniv.

Coronado Expedition Issue

"Coronado and His Captains" Painted by Gerald Cassidy A357

1940, Sept. 7 *Perf. 11x10½*

898 A357 3c violet 15 15

400th anniv. of the Coronado Expedition.

National Defense Issue

Statue of Liberty — A358

90-millimeter Anti-aircraft Gun — A359

Torch of Enlightenment — A360

1940, Oct. 16 *Perf. 11x10½*

899 A358	1c bright blue green	15	15
a.	Vert. pair, imperf. btwn.	*500.00*	—
b.	Horiz. pair, imperf. btwn.	40.00	—
900 A359	2c rose carmine	15	15
a.	Horiz. pair, imperf. btwn.	40.00	—
901 A360	3c bright violet	15	15
a.	Horiz. pair, imperf. btwn.	30.00	—
	Set value	20	15

Thirteenth Amendment Issue

"Emancipation," Statue of Lincoln and Slave, by Thomas Ball — A361

1940, Oct. 20 *Perf. 10½x11*

902 A361 3c deep violet 16 15

75th anniv. of the 13th Amendment to the Constitution.

Vermont Statehood Issue

Vermont Capitol, Montpelier A362

1941, Mar. 4 *Perf. 11x10½*

903 A362 3c light violet 15 15

Vermont statehood, 150th anniv.

Kentucky Statehood Issue

Daniel Boone and Three Frontiersmen, from Mural by Gilbert White — A363

1942, June 1 *Perf. 11x10½*

904 A363 3c violet 15 15

Kentucky statehood, 150th anniv.

American Eagle A364

Lincoln, Sun Yat-sen and Map A365

Win the War Issue

1942, July 4 *Perf. 11x10½*

905 A364	3c violet	15	15
b.	3c purple	—	—

Chinese Resistance Issue

1942, July 7 *Perf. 11x10½*

906 A365 5c bright blue 22 16

Five years' resistance of the Chinese people to Japanese aggression.

Allegory of Victory A366

Liberty Holding Torch of Freedom and Enlightenment A367

Allied Nations Issue

1943, Jan. 14 *Perf. 11x10½*

907 A366 2c rose carmine 15 15

Four Freedoms Issue

1943, Feb. 12 *Perf. 11x10½*

908 A367 1c bright blue green 15 15

Overrun Countries Issue

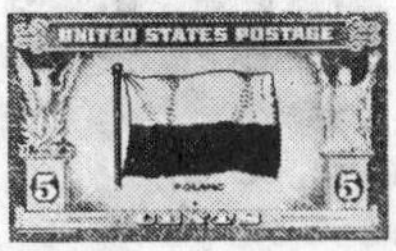
Flag of Poland — A368

Frames Engraved, Centers Indirect Letterpress

Rotary Press Printing

1943-44 **Unwmk.** *Perf. 12*

909 A368	5c Poland	16	15
910 A368	5c Czechoslovakia	16	15
911 A368	5c Norway	15	15
912 A368	5c Luxembourg	15	15
913 A368	5c Netherlands	15	15
914 A368	5c Belgium	15	15
915 A368	5c France	15	15
916 A368	5c Greece	35	25
917 A368	5c Yugoslavia	25	15
918 A368	5c Albania	18	15
919 A368	5c Austria	18	15
920 A368	5c Denmark	18	15
921 A368	5c Korea ('44)	15	15
	Nos. 909-921 (13)	2.36	
	Set value		1.50

Transcontinental Railroad Issue

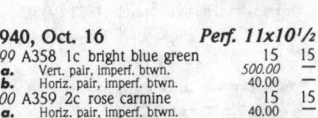

"Golden Spike Ceremony" Painting by John McQuarrie A369

Engraved; Rotary Press Printing

1944, May 10 *Perf. 11x10½*
922 A369 3c violet 20 15

75th anniv. of the completion of the first transcontinental railroad.

Steamship Issue

"Savannah" A370

1944, May 22 *Perf. 11x10½*
923 A370 3c violet 15 15

125th anniv. of the first steamship to cross the Atlantic Ocean.

Telegraph Issue

Telegraph Wires and the First Transmitted Words "What Hath God Wrought" A371

1944, May 24 *Perf. 11x10½*
924 A371 3c bright red violet 15 15

100th anniv. of the 1st message transmitted by telegraph.

Philippines Issue

View of Corregidor A372

1944, Sept. 27 *Perf. 11x10½*
925 A372 3c deep violet 15 15

Final resistance of the US and Philippine defenders on Corregidor.

Motion Pictures, 50th Anniv.

Motion Picture Showing for the Armed Forces in South Pacific — A373

1944, Oct. 31 *Perf. 11x10½*
926 A373 3c deep violet 15 15

Florida Statehood Centenary

Old Florida Seal, St. Augustine Gates and State Capitol — A374

1945, Mar. 3 *Perf. 11x10½*
927 A374 3c bright red violet 15 15

United Nations Conference Issue

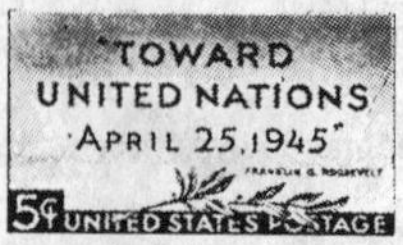

A375

1945, Apr. 25 *Perf. 11x10½*
928 A375 5c ultramarine 15 15

United Nations conference, San Francisco.

Iwo Jima (Marines) Issue

Marines Raising the Flag on Mt. Suribachi, Iwo Jima — A376

1945, July 11 *Perf. 10½x11*
929 A376 3c yellow green 15 15

Achievements of the US Marines in WWII.

Franklin D. Roosevelt Issue

Roosevelt and Hyde Park Home — A377

Roosevelt and "Little White House," Warm Springs, Georgia A378

Roosevelt and White House — A379

Roosevelt, Globe and Four Freedoms A380

1945-46 *Perf. 11x10½*

930	A377	1c blue green		15	15
931	A378	2c carmine rose		15	15
932	A379	3c purple		15	15
933	A380	5c bright blue ('46)		15	15
		Set value		26	20

Franklin Delano Roosevelt (1882-1945).

Army Issue

US Troops Passing Arch of Triumph, Paris — A381

1945, Sept. 28 *Perf. 11x10½*
934 A381 3c olive 15 15

Achievements of the US Army in WWII.

Navy Issue

US Sailors — A382

1945, Oct. 27 *Perf. 11x10½*
935 A382 3c blue 15 15

Achievements of the US Navy in WWII.

Footnotes near stamp listings often refer to other stamps of the same design.

Coast Guard Issue

Coast Guard Landing Craft and Supply Ship — A383

1945, Nov. 10 *Perf. 11x10½*
936 A383 3c bright blue green 15 15

Achievements of the US Coast Guard in WWII.

Alfred E. Smith A384

US and Texas State Flags A385

Alfred E. Smith Issue

1945, Nov. 26 *Perf. 11x10½*
937 A384 3c purple 15 15

Smith (1873-1944), governor of NY.

Texas Statehood Centenary

1945, Dec. 29 *Perf. 11x10½*
938 A385 3c dark blue 15 15

Liberty Ship Unloading Cargo A386

Honorable Discharge Emblem A387

Merchant Marine Issue

1946, Feb. 26 *Perf. 11x10½*
939 A386 3c blue green 15 15

Achievements of the US Merchant Marine in WWII.

Veterans of World War II Issue

1946, May 9 *Perf. 11x10½*
940 A387 3c dark violet 15 15

Issued to honor all veterans of WWII.

Tennessee Statehood, 150th Anniv.

Andrew Jackson, John Sevier and Tennessee Capitol — A388

1946, June 1 *Perf. 11x10½*
941 A388 3c dark violet 15 15

Iowa Statehood Centenary

Iowa State Flag and Map — A389

1946, Aug. 3 *Perf. 11x10½*
942 A389 3c deep blue 15 15

Smithsonian Institution Issue

Smithsonian Institution A390

1946, Aug. 10 *Perf. 11x10½*
943 A390 3c violet brown 15 15

Centenary of the establishment of the Smithsonian Institution, Washington, DC.

Kearny Expedition Issue

"Capture of Santa Fe" by Kenneth M. Chapman A391

1946, Oct. 16 *Perf. 11x10½*
944 A391 3c brown violet 15 15

Centenary of the entry of General Stephen Watts Kearny into Santa Fe.

Thomas Alva Edison Issue

Thomas A. Edison, Birth Centenary — A392

1947, Feb. 11 *Perf. 10½x11*
945 A392 3c bright red violet 15 15

Joseph Pulitzer Birth Centenary

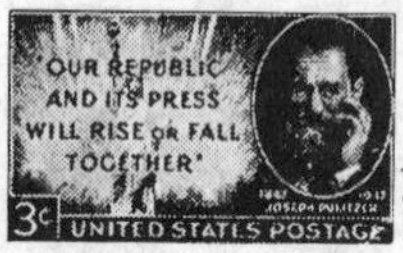

Joseph Pulitzer and Statue of Liberty — A393

1947, Apr. 10 *Perf. 11x10½*
946 A393 3c purple 15 15

US Postage Stamp Centenary

Washington and Franklin, Early and Modern Mail-carrying Vehicles A394

1947, May 17 *Perf. 11x10½*
947 A394 3c deep blue 15 15

Centenary International Philatelic Exhibition (CIPEX)

Souvenir Sheet

A395

Flat Plate Printing

1947, May 19 *Imperf.*

948	A395	Sheet of 2	60	45
a.		A1 5c blue	25	20
b.		A2 10c brown orange	30	25

Sheet size varies: 96-98x66-68mm

Doctors Issue

"The Doctor," by Sir Luke Fildes — A396

Rotary Press Printing

1947, June 9 *Perf. 11x10½*

949 A396 3c brown violet 15 15

Issued to honor the physicians of America.

Utah Settlement Centenary

Pioneers Entering the Valley of Great Salt Lake — A397

1947, July 24 *Perf. 11x10½*

950 A397 3c dark violet 15 15

US Frigate Constitution Issue

Naval Architect's Drawing of Frigate Constitution A398

1947, Oct. 21 *Perf. 11x10½*

951 A398 3c blue green 15 15

150th anniv. of the launching of the US Frigate Constitution ("Old Ironsides").

Everglades National Park Issue

Great White Heron and Map of Florida — A399

1947, Dec. 5 *Perf. 10½x11*

952 A399 3c bright green 15 15

Dedication of Everglades Natl. Park, Florida, Dec. 6, 1947.

Dr. George Washington Carver Issue

Dr. George Washington Carver — A400

1948, Jan. 5 *Perf. 10½x11*

953 A400 3c bright red violet 15 15

5th anniv. of the death of Dr. George Washington Carver, scientist.

California Gold Centennial Issue

Sutter's Mill, Coloma, California A401

1948, Jan. 24 *Perf. 11x10½*

954 A401 3c dark violet 15 15

Discovery of gold in California, centenary.

Mississippi Territory, 150th Anniv.

Map, Seal and Gov. Winthrop Sargent — A402

1948, Apr. 7 *Perf. 11x10½*

955 A402 3c brown violet 15 15

Four Chaplains Issue

Four Chaplains and Sinking S. S. Dorchester A403

1948, May 28 *Perf. 11x10½*

956 A403 3c gray black 15 15

Honoring George L. Fox, Clark V. Poling, John P. Washington and Alexander D. Goode, the four chaplains who sacrificed their lives in the sinking of the SS Dorchester, Feb. 3, 1943.

Wisconsin Statehood Centenary

Map on Scroll and State Capitol A404

1948, May 29 *Perf. 11x10½*

957 A404 3c dark violet 15 15

Swedish Pioneer Issue

Swedish Pioneer with Covered Wagon Moving Westward A405

1948, June 4 *Perf. 11x10½*

958 A405 5c deep blue 15 15

Centenary of the coming of the Swedish pioneers to the Middle West.

Progress of Women Issue

Elizabeth Stanton, Carrie C. Catt and Lucretia Mott — A406

1948, July 19 *Perf. 11x10½*

959 A406 3c dark violet 15 15

Century of progress of American women.

William Allen White Issue

William Allen White, Editor and Author — A407

1948, July 31 *Perf. 10½x11*

960 A407 3c bright red violet 15 15

US-Canada Friendship Centenary

Niagara Railway Suspension Bridge — A408

1948, Aug. 2 *Perf. 11x10½*

961 A408 3c blue 15 15

Francis Scott Key Issue

Key and American Flags of 1814 and 1948 — A409

1948, Aug. 9 *Perf. 11x10½*

962 A409 3c rose pink 15 15

Francis Scott Key (1779-1843), Maryland lawyer and author of "The Star-Spangled Banner" (1813).

Salute to Youth Issue

Girl and Boy Carrying Books — A410

1948, Aug. 11 *Perf. 11x10½*

963 A410 3c deep blue 15 15

Youth of America and "Youth Month," Sept. 1948.

Oregon Territory Issue

John McLoughlin, Jason Lee and Wagon on Oregon Trail — A411

1948, Aug. 14 *Perf. 11x10½*

964 A411 3c brown red 15 15

Centenary of the establishment of Ore. Terr.

Chief Justice Harlan Fiske Stone — A412

Observatory, Palomar Mt., Cal. — A413

Harlan Fiske Stone Issue

1948, Aug. 25 *Perf. 10½x11*

965 A412 3c bright red violet 15 15

Palomar Mountain Observatory Issue

1948, Aug. 30 *Perf. 10½x11*

966 A413 3c blue 15 15

a. Vert. pair, imperf btwn. *550.00*

Clara Barton, 1821-1912

Founder of the American Red Cross (1882) — A414

1948, Sept. 7 *Perf. 11x10½*

967 A414 3c rose pink 15 15

Poultry Industry Issue

Light Brahma Rooster — A415

1948, Sept. 9 *Perf. 11x10½*

968 A415 3c sepia 15 15

Centenary of the establishment of the American poultry industry.

Gold Star Mothers Issue

Star and Palm Frond — A416

1948, Sept. 21 *Perf. 10½x11*

969 A416 3c orange yellow 15 15

Honoring mothers of deceased members of the US armed forces.

Fort Kearny Issue

Fort Kearny and Pioneer Group — A417

1948, Sept. 22 *Perf. 11x10½*

970 A417 3c violet 15 15

Cent. of the establishment of Fort Kearny, Nebr.

Volunteer Firemen Issue

Peter Stuyvesant; Early and Modern Fire Engines A418

1948, Oct. 4 *Perf. 11x10½*

971 A418 3c bright rose carmine 15 15

300th anniv. of the organization of the 1st volunteer firemen in America by Peter Stuyvesant (1592-1672), Dutch colonial gov. of New Netherland.

Indian Centennial Issue

Map of Indian Territory and Seals of Five Tribes A419

1948, Oct. 15 *Perf. 11x10½*

972 A419 3c dark brown 15 15

Cent. of the arrival in Indian Territory, later Okla., of the Five Civilized Indian Tribes.

Rough Riders Issue

Statue of Capt. William O. (Bucky) O'Neill A420

1948, Oct. 27 *Perf. 11x10½*

973 A420 3c violet brown 15 15

50th anniv. of the organization of the Rough Riders of the Spanish-American War.

Low and Girl Scout Emblem — A421

Will Rogers — A422

Juliette Low Issue

1948, Oct. 29 *Perf. 11x10½*

974 A421 3c blue green 15 15

Juliette Gordon Low (1860-1927), organizer of the Girl Scouts of America.

Will Rogers Issue

1948, Nov. 4 *Perf. 10½x11*
975 A422 3c bright red violet 15 15

Will Rogers, 1879-1935, humorist and political commentator.

Fort Bliss and Rocket A423

Moina Michael and Poppy Plant A424

Fort Bliss Centennial Issue

1948, Nov. 5 *Perf. 10½x11*
976 A423 3c henna brown 15 15

Centenary of Fort Bliss, Texas.

Moina Michael Issue

1948, Nov. 9 *Perf. 11x10½*
977 A424 3c rose pink 15 15

Michael (1870-1944), educator who originated (1918) Flanders Field Poppy Day idea as memorial to war dead.

Gettysburg Address Issue

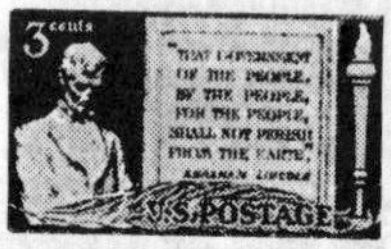

Lincoln and Quotation from Gettysburg Address A425

1948, Nov. 19 *Perf. 11x10½*
978 A425 3c bright blue 15 15

85th anniv. of Abraham Lincoln's address at Gettysburg, Pa.

Torch and American Turners' Emblem A426

Joel Chandler Harris A427

American Turners Issue

1948, Nov. 20 *Perf. 10½x11*
979 A426 3c carmine 15 15

Centenary of the formation of the American Turners Society.

Joel Chandler Harris Issue

1948, Dec. 9 *Perf. 10½x11*
980 A427 3c bright red violet 15 15

Harris (1848-1908), editor and author.

Minnesota Territory Issue

Pioneer and Red River Oxcart — A428

1949, Mar. 3 *Perf. 11x10½*
981 A428 3c blue green 15 15

Cent. of the establishment of Minn. Terr.

Washington and Lee University Issue

George Washington, Robert E. Lee and University Building A429

1949, Apr. 12 *Perf. 11x10½*
982 A429 3c ultramarine 15 15

200th anniv. of the founding of Washington and Lee Univ.

Puerto Rico Election Issue

Puerto Rican Farmer Holding Cogwheel and Ballot Box — A430

1949, Apr. 27 *Perf. 11x10½*
983 A430 3c green 15 15

1st gubernatorial election in the Territory of P.R., Nov. 2, 1948.

Annapolis Tercentenary Issue

Stoddert's 1718 Map of Regions about Annapolis, Redrawn A431

1949, May 23 *Perf. 11x10½*
984 A431 3c aquamarine 15 15

300th anniv. of the founding of Annapolis, Md.

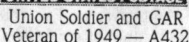

Union Soldier and GAR Veteran of 1949 — A432

Edgar Allan Poe — A433

GAR Issue

1949, Aug. 29 *Perf. 11x10½*
985 A432 3c bright rose carmine 15 15

Final encampment of the Grand Army of the Republic, Indianapolis, Aug. 28 to Sept. 1.

Edgar Allan Poe Issue

1949, Oct. 7 *Perf. 10½x11*
986 A433 3c bright red violet 15 15

Poe (1809-1849), writer and poet.

Coin, Symbolizing Fields of Banking Service A434

Samuel Gompers A435

Bankers Issue

1950, Jan. 3 *Perf. 11x10½*
987 A434 3c yellow green 15 15

75th anniv. of the formation of the American Bankers Assoc.

Samuel Gompers Issue

1950, Jan. 27 *Perf. 10½x11*
988 A435 3c bright red violet 15 15

Gompers (1850-1924), labor leader.

National Capital Sesquicentennial Issue

Statue of Freedom on Capitol Dome A436

Executive Mansion A437

Supreme Court Building — A438

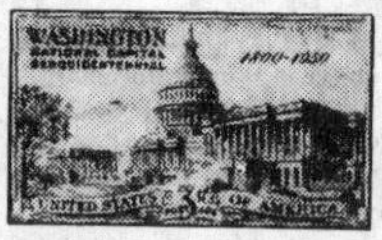

United States Capitol — A439

1950 *Perf. 10½x11, 11x10½*
989 A436 3c bright blue 15 15
990 A437 3c deep green 15 15
991 A438 3c light violet 15 15
992 A439 3c bright red violet 15 15
Set value 28 20

150th anniv. of the establishment of the National Capital, Washington, DC. Issue dates: Apr. 20, June 12, Aug. 2 and Nov. 22.

Railroad Engineers Issue

"Casey" Jones and Locomotives of 1900 and 1950 A440

1950, Apr. 29 *Perf. 11x10½*
993 A440 3c violet brown 15 15

Kansas City, Missouri, Issue

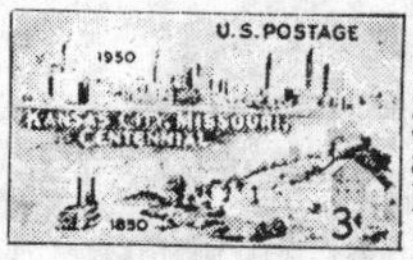

Kansas City Skyline, 1950 and Westport Landing, 1850 — A441

1950, June 3 *Perf. 11x10½*
994 A441 3c violet 15 15

Cent. of the incorporation of Kansas City, Mo.

Boy Scouts Issue

Three Boys, Statue of Liberty and Scout Badge — A442

1950, June 30 *Perf. 11x10½*
995 A442 3c sepia 15 15

Honoring the BSA on the occasion of the 2nd Natl. Jamboree, held at Valley Forge, Pa.

Indiana Territory Issue

Gov. William Henry Harrison and First Indiana Capitol, Vincennes A443

1950, July 4 *Perf. 11x10½*
996 A443 3c bright blue 15 15

150th anniv. of the establishment of Ind. Terr.

California Statehood Centenary

Gold Miner, Pioneers and S.S. *Oregon* A444

1950, Sept. 9 *Perf. 11x10½*
997 A444 3c yellow orange 15 15

United Confederate Veterans Final Reunion Issue

Confederate Soldier and United Confederate Veteran — A445

1951, May 30 *Perf. 11x10½*
998 A445 3c gray 15 15

Final reunion of the United Confederate Veterans, Norfolk, Va, May 30, 1951.

Nevada Settlement Centennial

Carson Valley, c. 1851 A446

1951, July 14 *Perf. 11x10½*
999 A446 3c light olive green 15 15

Landing of Cadillac Issue

Detroit Skyline and Cadillac Landing A447

1951, July 24 *Perf. 11x10½*
1000 A447 3c blue 15 15

250th anniv. of the landing of Antoine de la Mothe Cadillac at Detroit.

Colorado Statehood Issue

Colorado Capitol and Mount of the Holy Cross — A448

1951, Aug. 1 *Perf. 11x10½*
1001 A448 3c blue violet 15 15

Colorado statehood, 75th anniv. Design includes columbine and statue, "The Bronco Buster", by A. Phimister Proctor.

American Chemical Society Issue

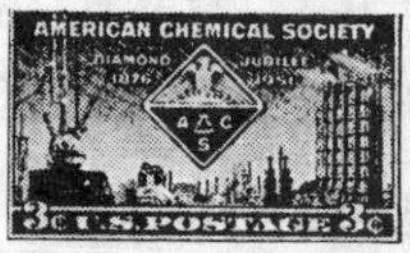

A. C. S. Emblem and Symbols of Chemistry A449

1951, Sept. 4 *Perf. 11x10½*
1002 A449 3c violet brown 15 15

American Chemical Soc., 75th anniv.

Rotary International, 50th Anniv.

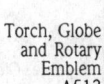

Torch, Globe and Rotary Emblem A513

1955, Feb. 23 *Perf. 11x10½*
1066 A513 8c deep blue 16 15

Armed Forces Reserve Issue

Marine, Coast Guard, Army, Navy, and Air Force Personnel A514

1955, May 21 *Perf. 11x10½*
1067 A514 3c purple 15 15

New Hampshire Issue

Great Stone Face — A515

1955, June 21 *Perf. 10½x11*
1068 A515 3c green 15 15

Honor NH on the occasion of the sesquicentennial of the discovery of the "Old Man of the Mountains."

Soo Locks Opening, Centenary

Map of Great Lakes and Two Steamers A516

1955, June 28 *Perf. 11x10½*
1069 A516 3c blue 15 15

Atoms for Peace Policy

Atomic Energy Encircling the Hemispheres A517

1955, July 28 *Perf. 11x10½*
1070 A517 3c deep blue 15 15

Fort Ticonderoga Bicentenary

Map of the Fort, Ethan Allen and Artillery A518

1955, Sept. 18 *Perf. 11x10½*
1071 A518 3c light brown 15 15

Andrew W. Mellon Issue

Andrew W. Mellon — A519

1955, Dec. 20 *Perf. 10½x11*
1072 A519 3c rose carmine 15 15

Mellon, US Sec. of the Treasury (1921-32), financier and art collector.

Benjamin Franklin Issue

"Franklin Taking Electricity from the Sky," by Benjamin West — A520

1956, Jan. 17 *Perf. 10½x11*
1073 A520 3c bright carmine 15 15

250th anniv. of the birth of Franklin.

Booker T. Washington Issue

Log Cabin — A521

1956, Apr. 5 *Perf. 11x10½*
1074 A521 3c deep blue 15 15

Washington (1856-1915), black educator.

Fifth Intl. Phil. Exhib. Issues

Souvenir Sheet

A522

Flat Plate Printing

1956, Apr. 28 *Imperf.*

1075	A522 Sheet of 2	2.25	2.00
a.	A482 3c deep violet	90	80
b.	A488 8c dk vio bl & carmine	1.25	1.00

No. 1075 measures 108x73mm; Nos. 1075a and 1075b measure 24x28mm.

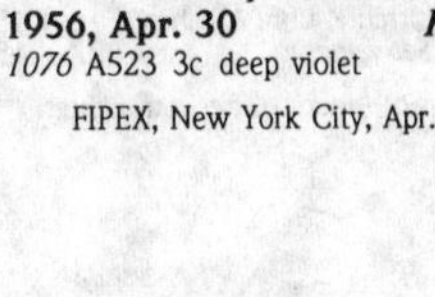

New York Coliseum and Columbus Monument A523

Rotary Press Printing

1956, Apr. 30 *Perf. 11x10½*
1076 A523 3c deep violet 15 15

FIPEX, New York City, Apr. 28-May 6.

Wildlife Conservation Issue

Wild Turkey A524

Pronghorn Antelope A525

King Salmon — A526

1956 *Perf. 11x10½*

1077	A524 3c rose lake	15	15
1078	A525 3c brown	15	15
1079	A526 3c blue green	15	15
	Set value	18	15

Emphasizing the importance of Wildlife conservation in America.
Issued May 5, June 22 and Nov. 9.
See Nos. 1098, 1392.

Pure Food and Drug Laws, 50th Anniv.

Harvey W. Wiley — A527

1956, June 27 *Perf. 10½x11*
1080 A527 3c dark blue green 15 15

Wheatland Issue

President Buchanan's Home, "Wheatland," Lancaster, PA — A528

1956, Aug. 5 *Perf. 11x10½*
1081 A528 3c black brown 15 15

Labor Day Issue

Mosaic, AFL-CIO Headquarters — A529

1956, Sept. 3 *Perf. 10½x11*
1082 A529 3c deep blue 15 15

Nassau Hall Issue

Nassau Hall, Princeton, NJ — A530

1956, Sept. 22 *Perf. 11x10½*
1083 A530 3c black, *orange* 15 15

200th anniv. of Nassau Hall, Princeton University.

Devils Tower Issue

Devils Tower — A531

1956, Sept. 24 *Perf. 10½x11*
1084 A531 3c violet 15 15

50th anniv. of the Federal law providing for protection of American natural antiquities. Devils Tower Natl. Monument, Wyoming, is an outstanding example.

Children's Issue

Children of the World A532

1956, Dec. 15 *Perf. 11x10½*
1085 A532 3c dark blue 15 15

Promoting friendship among the world's children.

Alexander Hamilton Issue

Alexander Hamilton (1757-1804) and Federal Hall — A533

1957, Jan. 11 *Perf. 11x10½*
1086 A533 3c rose red 15 15

Polio Issue

Allegory — A534

1957, Jan. 15 *Perf. 10½x11*
1087 A534 3c red lilac 15 15

Honoring "those who helped fight polio," and 20th anniv. of the Natl. Foundation for Infantile Paralysis and the March of Dimes.

Coast and Geodetic Survey Issue

Flag of Coast and Geodetic Survey and Ships at Sea — A535

1957, Feb. 11 *Perf. 11x10½*
1088 A535 3c dark blue 15 15

150th anniv. of the establishment of the Coast and Geodetic Survey.

Architects Issue

Corinthian Capital and Mushroom Type Head and Shaft — A536

1957, Feb. 23 *Perf. 11x10½*
1089 A536 3c red lilac 15 15

Centenary of the American Institute of Architects.

Steel Industry Centenary

American Eagle and Pouring Ladle — A537

1957, May 22 *Perf. 10½x11*
1090 A537 3c bright ultra 15 15

International Naval Review Issue

Aircraft Carrier and Jamestown Festival Emblem A538

1957, June 10 *Perf. 11x10½*
1091 A538 3c blue green 15 15

Intl. Naval Review and Jamestown Festival.

Oklahoma Statehood, 50th Anniv.

Map of Oklahoma, Arrow and Atom Diagram A539

1957, June 14 *Perf. 11x10½*
1092 A539 3c dark blue 15 15

School Teachers Issue

Teacher and Pupils — A540

1957, July 1 *Perf. 11x10½*
1093 A540 3c rose lake 15 15

Honoring the school teachers of America.

Flag Issue

"Old Glory" (48 Stars) — A541

Giori Press Printing

1957, July 4 *Perf. 11*
1094 A541 4c dk blue & dp carmine 15 15

Shipbuilding Issue

"Virginia of Sagadahock" and Seal of Maine — A542

Rotary Press Printing

1957, Aug. 15 *Perf. 10½x11*
1095 A542 3c deep violet 15 15

350th anniv. of shipbuilding in America.

Champion of Liberty Issue

Ramon Magsaysay, (1907-1957), Philippines President — A543

Giori Press Printing

1957, Aug. 31 *Perf. 11*
1096 A543 8c carmine, ultra & ocher 16 15

Marquis de Lafayette A544

Whooping Cranes A545

Lafayette Bicentenary Issue

Rotary Press Printing

1957, Sept. 6 *Perf. 10½x11*
1097 A544 3c rose lake 15 15

Bicentenary of the birth of Lafayette.

Wildlife Conservation Issue

Giori Press Printing

1957, Nov. 22 *Perf. 11*
1098 A545 3c blue, ocher & green 15 15

Emphasizing the importance of Wildlife Conservation in America.

Bible, Hat and Quill Pen — A546

"Bountiful Earth" — A547

Religious Freedom Issue

Rotary Press Printing

1957, Dec. 27 *Perf. 10½x11*
1099 A546 3c black 15 15

Flushing Remonstrance, 300th anniv.

Gardening-Horticulture Issue

1958, Mar. 15
1100 A547 3c green 15 15

Garden clubs of America and cent. of the birth of Liberty Hyde Bailey, horticulturist.

Brussels Fair Issue

US Pavilion at Brussels A551

Rotary Press Printing

1958, Apr. 17 *Perf. 11x10½*
1104 A551 3c deep claret 15 15

Opening of the Universal and Intl. Exhib., Brussels, Apr. 17.

James Monroe Issue

James Monroe, by Gilbert Stuart — A552

1958, Apr. 28 *Perf. 11x10½*
1105 A552 3c purple 15 15

Monroe (1758-1831), 5th pres. of the US.

Minnesota Statehood Centenary

Minnesota Lakes and Pines — A553

1958, May 11 **Rotary Press Printing**
1106 A553 3c green 15 15

Geophysical Year (IGY, 1957-58)

Solar Disc and Hands from Michelangelo's "Creation of Adam" — A554

Giori Press Printing

1958, May 31 *Perf. 11*
1107 A554 3c black & red orange 15 15

Gunston Hall Issue

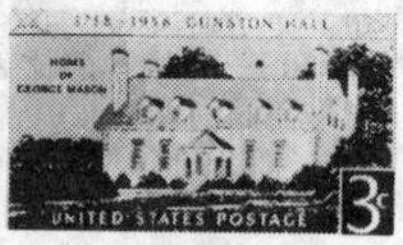

Gunston Hall, Virginia A555

Rotary Press Printing

1958, June 12 *Perf. 11x10½*
1108 A555 3c light green 15 15

Bicent. of Gunston Hall and honoring George Mason, author of the Constitution of Va. and the Va. Bill of Rights.

Mackinac Bridge A556

Simon Bolivar A557

Mackinac Bridge Issue

1958, June 25 *Perf. 10½x11*
1109 A556 3c bright greenish blue 15 15

Dedication of Mackinac Bridge, Mich.

Champion of Liberty Issue

Rotary Press Printing

1958, July 24 *Perf. 10½x11*
1110 A557 4c olive bister 15 15

Giori Press Printing

Perf. 11

1111 A557 8c carmine, ultra & ocher 16 15
Set value 22 15

Simon Bolivar, So. American freedom fighter.

Atlantic Cable Centennial Issue

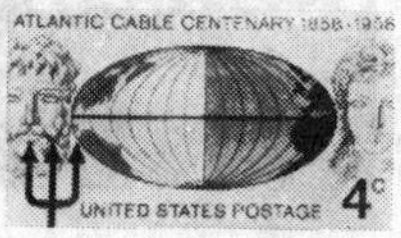

Neptune, Globe and Mermaid A558

Rotary Press Printing

1958, Aug. 15 *Perf. 11x10½*
1112 A558 4c reddish purple 15 15

Centenary of the Atlantic Cable, linking the Eastern and Western hemispheres.

Lincoln Sesquicentennial Issue

Lincoln, by George Healy A559

Lincoln, by Gutzon Borglum A560

Abraham Lincoln and Stephen A. Douglas Debating A561

Lincoln, by Daniel Chester French — A562

1958-59 *Perf. 10½x11, 11x10½*

1113 A559 1c green ('59) 15 15
1114 A560 3c purple ('59) 15 15
1115 A561 4c sepia 15 15
1116 A562 4c dark blue ('59) 15 15
Set value 27 20

No. 1114 also for the founding of Cooper Union cent., NYC. No. 1115 also for the Lincoln-Douglas debates, cent.

Issue dates: Nos. 1113, 1114, 1116, Feb. 12, Feb. 27 and May 30. No. 1115, Aug. 27.

Lajos Kossuth, (1802-1892) A563

Early Press and Hand Holding Quill A564

Champion of Liberty Issue

Rotary Press Printing

1958, Sept. 19 *Perf. 10½x11*
1117 A563 4c green 15 15

Giori Press Printing

Perf. 11

1118 A563 8c carmine, ultra & ocher 16 15
Set value 24 15

Kossuth, Hungarian freedom fighter.

Freedom of Press Issue

Rotary Press Printing

1958, Sept. 22 *Perf. 10½x11*
1119 A564 4c black 15 15

Honoring journalism and freedom of the press in connection with the 50th anniv. of the 1st School of Journalism at the Univ. of Mo.

Overland Mail Centenary

Mail Coach and Map of Southwest US — A565

1958, Oct. 10 *Perf. 11x10½*
1120 A565 4c crimson rose 15 15

Noah Webster A566

Forest Scene A567

Noah Webster Issue

1958, Oct. 16 *Perf. 10½x11*
1121 A566 4c dark carmine rose 15 15

Webster (1758-1843), lexicographer.

Forest Conservation Issue

Giori Press Printing

1958, Oct. 27 *Perf. 11*
1122 A567 4c green, yel & brown 15 15

Publicizing forest conservation and the protection of natural resources and honoring Theodore Roosevelt, a leading forest conservationist, on the cent. of his birth.

Fort Duquesne Issue

Occupation of Fort Duquesne A568

Rotary Press Printing

1958, Nov. 25 *Perf. 11x10½*
1123 A568 4c blue 15 15

Bicentennial of Fort Duquesne (Fort Pitt).

Oregon Statehood Centenary

Covered Wagon and Mt. Hood — A569

1959, Feb. 14 *Perf. 11x10½*
1124 A569 4c blue green 15 15

José de San Martin — A570

NATO Emblem — A571

Champion of Liberty Issue

Rotary Press Printing

1959, Feb. 25 *Perf. 10½x11*
1125 A570 4c blue 15 15
a. Horiz. pair, imperf. btwn. *1,100.*

Giori Press Printing

Perf. 11

1126 A570 8c car, ultra & ocher 16 15
Set value 24 15

San Martin, South American soldier and statesman.

NATO Issue

Rotary Press Printing

1959, Apr. 1 *Perf. 10½x11*
1127 A571 4c blue 15 15

North Atlantic Treaty Organ., 10th anniv.

Arctic Explorations Issue

North Pole, Dog Sled and "Nautilus" A572

1959, Apr. 6 *Perf. 11x10½*
1128 A572 4c brt greenish blue 15 15

Conquest of the Arctic by land by Rear Admiral Robert Edwin Peary in 1909 and by sea by the submarine "Nautilus" in 1958.

World Peace Through World Trade Issue

Globe and Laurel — A573

1959, Apr. 20 *Perf. 11x10½*
1129 A573 8c rose lake 16 15

Issued in conjunction with the 17th Cong. of the Intl. Chamber of Commerce, Washington, DC, Apr. 19-25.

Silver Centennial Issue

Henry Comstock at Mount Davidson Site — A574

1959, June 8 *Perf. 11x10½*
1130 A574 4c black 15 15

Cent. of the discovery of silver at the Comstock Lode, Nev.

St. Lawrence Seaway Issue

Great Lakes, Maple Leaf and Eagle Emblems A575

Giori Press Printing

1959, June 26 *Perf. 11*
1131 A575 4c red & dark blue 15 15

Opening of the St. Lawrence Seaway, June 26, 1959. See Canada No. 387.

49-Star Flag Issue

US Flag, 1959 — A576

1959, July 4 *Perf. 11*
1132 A576 4c ocher, dk blue & dp car 15 15

Soil Conservation Issue

Modern Farm — A577

1959, Aug. 26
1133 A577 4c blue, green & ocher 15 15

Tribute to farmers and ranchers who use soil and water conservation measures.

Petroleum Industry Issue

Oil Derrick — A578

Rotary Press Printing

1959, Aug. 27 *Perf. 10½x11*
1134 A578 4c brown 15 15

Cent. of the completion of the nation's 1st oil well at Titusville, Pa.

Dental Health Issue

Children A579

1959, Sept. 14 *Perf. 11x10½*
1135 A579 4c green 15 15

Publicizing dental health and cent. of the American Dental Assoc.

Ernst Reuter A580

Dr. Ephraim McDowell A581

Champion of Liberty Issue

Rotary Press Printing

1959, Sept. 29 *Perf. 10½x11*
1136 A580 4c gray 15 15

Giori Press Printing

Perf. 11

1137 A580 8c carmine, ultra & ocher 16 15
Set value 24 15

Ernst Reuter, mayor of Berlin 1948-53.

Dr. Ephraim McDowell Issue

Rotary Press Printing

1959, Dec. 3 *Perf. 10½x11*
1138 A581 4c rose lake 15 15
a. Vert. pair, imperf. btwn. *400.00*
b. Vert. pair, imperf. horiz. *275.00*

Honoring McDowell on the 150th anniv. of the 1st successful ovarian operation performed in the US.

American Credo Issue

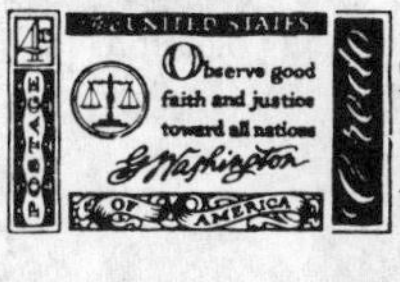

Quotation from Washington's Farewell Address, 1796 — A582

Benjamin Franklin Quotation A583

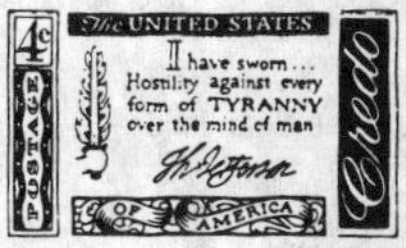

Thomas Jefferson Quotation A584

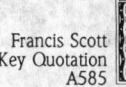

Francis Scott Key Quotation A585

Abraham Lincoln Quotation A586

Patrick Henry Quotation A587

Giori Press Printing

1960-61 *Perf. 11*
1139 A582 4c dk violet blue & car 15 15
1140 A583 4c olive bister & green 15 15
1141 A584 4c gray & vermilion 15 15
1142 A585 4c carmine & dark blue 15 15
1143 A586 4c magenta & green 15 15
1144 A587 4c green & brown ('61) 15 15
Set value 57 30

Re-emphasizing the ideals upon which America was founded and honoring those great Americans who wrote or uttered the credos.

Issue dates: Jan. 20, Mar. 31, May 18, Sept. 14, Nov. 19, and Jan. 11.

Boy Scout Jubilee Issue

Boy Scout Giving Scout Sign — A588

Giori Press Printing

1960, Feb. 8 *Perf. 11*
1145 A588 4c red, dk blue & dk bis 15 15

50th anniv. of the BSA.

Olympic Rings and Snowflake A589

Thomas G. Masaryk A590

Olympic Winter Games Issue

Rotary Press Printing

1960, Feb. 18 *Perf. 10½x11*
1146 A589 4c dull blue 15 15

Opening of the 8th Olympic Winter Games, Squaw Valley, Feb. 18-29.

Champion of Liberty Issue

Rotary Press Printing

1960, Mar. 7 *Perf. 10½x11*
1147 A590 4c blue 15 15
a. Vert. pair, imperf. btwn. *3,250.*

Giori Press Printing

Perf. 11

1148 A590 8c carmine, ultra & ocher 16 15
- *a.* Horiz. pair, imperf. btwn.
- *Set value* 24 15

Masaryk, founder and pres. of Czechoslovakia (1918-35), on the 110th anniv. of his birth.

World Refugee Year Issue

Refugee Family Walking Toward New Life — A591

Rotary Press Printing

1960, Apr. 7 ***Perf. 11x10½***

1149 A591 4c gray black 15 15

WRY, July 1, 1959 - June 30, 1960.

Water Conservation Issue

Water, from Watershed to Consumer A592

Giori Press Printing

1960, Apr. 18 ***Perf. 11***

1150 A592 4c dk blue, brn org & green 15 15

Stressing the importance of water conservation, and 7th Watershed Cong., Washington, DC.

SEATO Issue

SEATO Emblem — A593

Rotary Press Printing

1960, May 31 ***Perf. 10½x11***

1151 A593 4c blue 15 15
- *a.* Vert. pair, imperf. btwn. *150.00*

South-East Asia Treaty Org. and the SEATO Conf., Washington, DC, May 31-June 3.

American Woman Issue

Mother and Daughter A594

1960, June 2 ***Perf. 11x10½***

1152 A594 4c deep violet 15 15

A tribute to American women and their accomplishments in civic affairs, education, arts and industry.

50-Star Flag Issue

US Flag, 1960 — A595

Giori Press Printing

1960, July 4 ***Perf. 11***

1153 A595 4c dark blue & red 15 15

Pony Express Centennial Issue

Pony Express Rider — A596

Rotary Press Printing

1960, July 19 ***Perf. 11x10½***

1154 A596 4c sepia 15 15

Man in Wheelchair Operating Drill Press — A597

5th World Forestry Congress Seal — A598

Employ the Handicapped Issue

1960, Aug. 28 ***Perf. 10½x11***

1155 A597 4c dark blue 15 15

Promoting employment of the physically handicapped and publicizing the 8th World Cong. of the Intl. Soc. for the Welfare of Cripples, NYC.

World Forestry Congress Issue

1960, Aug. 29

1156 A598 4c green 15 15

5th World Forestry Cong., Seattle, Wash., Aug. 29-Sept. 10.

Mexican Independence Issue

Independence Bell — A599

Giori Press Printing

1960, Sept. 16 ***Perf. 11***

1157 A599 4c green & rose red 15 15

150th anniv. of Mexican independence. See Mexico No. 910.

US-Japan Treaty Issue

Washington Monument and Cherry Blossoms — A600

1960, Sept. 28 ***Perf. 11***

1158 A600 4c blue & pink 15 15

Cent. of the US-Japan Treaty of Amity and Commerce.

Ignacy Jan Paderewski A601

Robert A. Taft A602

Champion of Liberty Issue

Rotary Press Printing

1960, Oct. 8 ***Perf. 10½x11***

1159 A601 4c blue 15 15

Giori Press Printing

Perf. 11

1160 A601 8c carmine, ultra & ocher 16 15
- *Set value* 24 15

Paderewski (1866-1941), Polish statesman and musician.

Senator Taft Memorial Issue

Rotary Press Printing

1960, Oct. 10 ***Perf. 10½x11***

1161 A602 4c dull violet 15 15

Senator Taft (1889-1953), of Ohio.

Wheels of Freedom Issue

Globe and Steering Wheel with Tractor, Car and Truck — A603

1960, Oct. 15 ***Perf. 11x10½***

1162 A603 4c dark blue 15 15

Honoring the automotive industry and in connection with the National Automobile Show, Detroit, Oct. 15-23.

Boys' Clubs of America Issue

Profile of a Boy — A604

Giori Press Printing

1960, Oct. 18 ***Perf. 11***

1163 A604 4c indigo, slate & rose red 15 15

Cent. of the Boys' Clubs of America movement.

Automated Post Office Issue

Architect's Sketch of New Post Office, Providence, RI — A605

1960, Oct. 20 ***Perf. 11***

1164 A605 4c dk blue & carmine 15 15

Opening of the 1st automated PO in the US.

Baron Gustaf Emil Mannerheim A606

Camp Fire Girls Emblem A607

Champion of Liberty Issue

Rotary Press Printing

1960, Oct. 26 ***Perf. 10½x11***

1165 A606 4c blue 15 15

Giori Press Printing

Perf. 11

1166 A606 8c car, ultra & ocher 16 15
- *Set value* 24 15

Mannerheim (1867-1951), marshal and pres. of Finland.

Camp Fire Girls Issue

Giori Press Printing

1960, Nov. 1 ***Perf. 11***

1167 A607 4c dk blue & brt red 15 15

50th anniv. of the Camp Fire Girls' movement and with their Golden Jubilee Convention celebration.

Giuseppe Garibaldi (1807-1882) A608

Walter F. George (1878-1957) A609

Champion of Liberty Issue

Rotary Press Printing

1960, Nov. 2 ***Perf. 10½x11***

1168 A608 4c green 15 15

Giori Press Printing

Perf. 11

1169 A608 8c carmine, ultra & ocher 16 15
- *Set value* 24 15

Garibaldi, Italian patriot and freedom fighter.

Senator George Memorial Issue

Rotary Press Printing

1960, Nov. 5 ***Perf. 10½x11***

1170 A609 4c dull violet 15 15

Senator Walter F. George of Georgia.

Andrew Carnegie A610

John Foster Dulles A611

Andrew Carnegie Issue

1960, Nov. 25

1171 A610 4c deep claret 15 15

Carnegie (1835-1919), industrialist and philanthropist.

John Foster Dulles Memorial Issue

1960, Dec. 6 ***Perf. 10½x11***

1172 A611 4c dull violet 15 15

John Foster Dulles (1888-1959), Sec. of State (1953-1959).

Echo I -- Communications for Peace Issue

Radio Waves Connecting Echo I and Earth — A612

1960, Dec. 15 ***Perf. 11x10½***

1173 A612 4c deep violet 18 15

World's 1st communications satellite, Echo I, placed in orbit by NASA, Aug. 12, 1960.

Champion of Liberty Issue

Mahatma Gandhi — A613

John Muir Issue

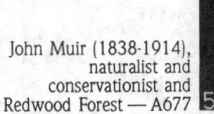

John Muir (1838-1914), naturalist and conservationist and Redwood Forest — A677

Giori Press Printing

1964, Apr. 29 *Perf. 11*

1245 A677 5c brn, grn, yel grn & ol 15 15

Kennedy Memorial Issue

Pres. John F. Kennedy (1917-63) and Eternal Flame — A678

Rotary Press Printing

1964, May 29 *Perf. 11x10½*

1246 A678 5c blue gray 15 15

New Jersey Tercentenary Issue

Philip Carteret Landing at Elizabethtown, and Map of New Jersey — A679

1964, June 15 *Perf. 10½x11*

1247 A679 5c bright ultra 15 15

300th anniv. of English colonization of NJ. The design is from a mural by Howard Pyle in the Essex County Courthouse, Newark.

Nevada Statehood Centenary

Virginia City and Map of Nevada — A680

Giori Press Printing

1964, July 22 *Perf. 11*

1248 A680 5c red, yellow & blue 15 15

Flag
A681

William Shakespeare
A682

Register and Vote Issue

Giori Press Printing

1964, Aug. 1 *Perf. 11*

1249 A681 5c dark blue & red 15 15

Campaign to draw more voters to the polls.

Shakespeare Issue

Rotary Press Printing

1964, Aug. 14 *Perf. 10½x11*

1250 A682 5c black brown, *tan* 15 15

400th anniv. of the birth of Shakespeare (1564-1616).

Doctors Mayo Issue

Drs. William and Charles Mayo — A683

1964, Sept. 11 *Perf. 10½x11*

1251 A683 5c green 15 15

William (1861-1939) and his brother, Charles (1865-1939), surgeons who founded the Mayo Foundation for Medical Education and Research in affiliation with the Univ. of Minn. at Rochester. From a sculpture by James Earle Fraser.

American Music Issue

Lute, Horn, Laurel, Oak and Music Score — A684

Giori Press Printing

1964, Oct. 15 *Perf. 11*

Gray Paper with Blue Threads

1252 A684 5c red, black & blue 15 15
 a. Blue omitted *1,250.*

50th anniv. of the founding of ASCAP (American Soc. of Composers, Authors and Publishers).

Beware of copies offered as No. 1252a which have traces of blue.

Homemakers Issue

Farm Scene Sampler — A685

Lithographed, Engraved (Giori)

1964, Oct. 26 *Perf. 11*

1253 A685 5c multicolored 15 15

Honoring American women as homemakers and 50th anniv. of the passage of the Smith-Lever Act. By providing economic experts under an extension service of the US Dept. of Agriculture, this legislation helped to improve homelife.

Christmas Issue

Holly
A686

Mistletoe
A687

Poinsettia
A688

Sprig of Conifer
A689

Giori Press Printing

1964, Nov. 9 *Perf. 11*

1254	A686 5c green, car & black	30	15
a.	Tagged	75	50
1255	A687 5c car, green & black	30	15
a.	Tagged	75	50
1256	A688 5c car, green & black	30	15
a.	Tagged	75	50
1257	A689 5c black, green & car	30	15
a.	Tagged	75	50
b.	Block of 4, #1254-1257	1.25	1.25
c.	Block of 4, #1254a-1257a	3.25	2.00
	Set value		20

Tagged stamps issued Nov. 10.

Verrazano-Narrows Bridge Issue

Verrazano-Narrows Bridge and Map of NY Bay — A690

Rotary Press Printing

1964, Nov. 21 *Perf. 10½x11*

1258 A690 5c blue green 15 15

Opening of the Verrazano-Narrows Bridge connecting Staten Island and Brooklyn, NY.

Fine Arts Issue

Abstract Design by Stuart Davis — A691

Giori Press Printing

1964, Dec. 2 *Perf. 11*

1259 A691 5c ultra, blk & dull red 15 15

Amateur Radio Issue

Radio Waves and Dial — A692

Rotary Press Printing

1964, Dec. 15 *Perf. 10½x11*

1260 A692 5c red lilac 15 15

Honoring radio amateurs on the 50th anniv. of the American Radio Relay League.

Battle of New Orleans Issue

General Andrew Jackson and Sesquicentennial Medal — A693

Giori Press Printing

1965, Jan. 8 *Perf. 11*

1261 A693 5c dp car, violet blue & gray 15 15

Battle of New Orleans, Chalmette Plantation, Jan. 8-18, 1815, which established 150 years of peace and friendship between the US and Great Britain.

Discus Thrower
A694

Microscope and Stethoscope
A695

Physical Fitness-Sokol Issue

1965, Feb. 15 *Perf. 11*

1262 A694 5c maroon & black 15 15

Importance of physical fitness and cent. of the founding of the Sokol (athletic) org. in America.

Crusade Against Cancer Issue

1965, Apr. 1 *Perf. 11*

1263 A695 5c blk, pur & red org 15 15

"Crusade Against Cancer" and stressing the importance of early diagnosis.

Churchill Memorial Issue

Winston Churchill — A696

Rotary Press Printing

1965, May 13 *Perf. 10½x11*

1264 A696 5c black 15 15

Sir Winston Spencer Churchill (1874-1965), British statesman and WWII leader.

Magna Carta Issue

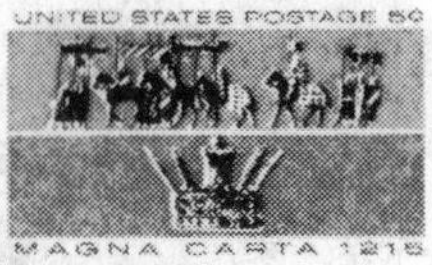

Procession of Barons and King John's Crown A697

Giori Press Printing

1965, June 15 *Perf. 11*

1265 A697 5c blk, yel ocher & red lilac 15 15

750th anniv. of the Magna Carta, the basis of English and American common law.

International Cooperation Year Issue

ICY Emblem A698

1965, June 26 *Perf. 11*

1266 A698 5c dull blue & black 15 15

ICY, 1965, and 20th anniv. of the UN.

A699

Dante — A700

Salvation Army Issue

1965, July 2 *Perf. 11*

1267 A699 5c red, black & dark blue 15 15

Cent. of the founding of the Salvation Army in London by William Booth.

Dante Alighieri Issue

Rotary Press Printing

1965, July 17 *Perf. 10½x11*

1268 A700 5c maroon, *tan* 15 15

Dante Alighieri (1265-1321), Italian poet. Design after a 16th cent. painting.

Herbert Hoover Issue

Pres. Herbert Clark Hoover (1874-1964) — A701

1965, Aug. 10 *Perf. 10½x11*

1269 A701 5c rose red 15 15

Robert Fulton Issue

Robert Fulton and Clermont A702

Giori Press Printing

1965, Aug. 19 *Perf. 11*

1270 A702 5c black & blue 15 15

Fulton (1765-1815), inventor of the 1st commercial steamship.

Settlement of Florida Issue

Spanish Explorer, Royal Flag of Spain and Ships — A703

1965, Aug. 28 **Giori Press Printing**

1271 A703 5c red, yel & blk 15 15
  a. Yellow omitted *475.00*

400th anniv. of the settlement of Fla., and the 1st permanent European settlement in the continental US, St. Augustine, Fla.

See Spain No. 1312.

Traffic Safety Issue

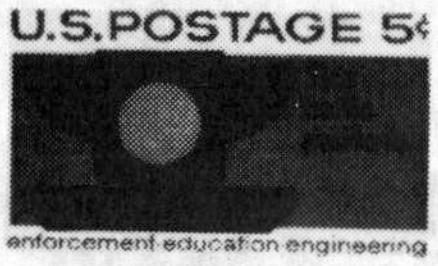

Traffic Signal A704

1965, Sept. 3 *Perf. 11*

1272 A704 5c emerald, black & red 15 15

Traffic safety and the prevention of traffic accidents.

John Singleton Copley Issue

Elizabeth Clarke Copley — A705

1965, Sept. 17

1273 A705 5c black, brown & olive 15 15

Copley (1738-1815), painter. The portrait of the artist's daughter is from the oil painting "The Copley Family," which hangs in the Natl. Gallery of Art, Washington, DC.

International Telecommunication Union Centenary

Gall Projection World Map and Radio Sine Wave — A706

1965, Oct. 6 *Perf. 11*

1274 A706 11c black, car & bister 35 16

Adlai E. Stevenson A707

Angel with Trumpet, 1840 Weather Vane A708

Adlai E. Stevenson Issue

1965, Oct. 23 **Litho., Engr. (Giori)**

1275 A707 5c pale blue, blk, car & vio blue 15 15

Stevenson (1900-65), gov. of Ill., US ambassador to the UN.

Christmas Issue
Giori Press Printing

1965, Nov. 2 *Perf. 11*

1276 A708 5c car, dk ol grn & bis 15 15
  a. Tagged 75 25

Prominent Americans Issue

Thomas Jefferson A710

Albert Gallatin A711

Frank Lloyd Wright and Guggenheim Museum, New York A712

Francis Parkman A713

Lincoln A714

Washington A715

Washington (Redrawn) A715a

Franklin D. Roosevelt A716

Albert Einstein A717

Andrew Jackson A718

Henry Ford, 1909 Model T A718a

John F. Kennedy A719

Oliver Wendell Holmes A720

George Catlett Marshall A721

Frederick Douglass A722

John Dewey A723

Thomas Paine — A724

Lucy Stone — A725

Eugene O'Neill A726

John Bassett Moore A727

Perf. 11x10½, 10½x11

1965-78 **Rotary Press Printing**

1278 A710 1c green, tagged 15 15
  a. Booklet pane of 8 1.00 *25*
  b. Bklt. pane of 4 + 2 labels 75 *20*
  c. Untagged (Bureau precanceled) 15
1279 A711 1¼c lt green 15 15
1280 A712 2c dk blue gray, tagged 15 15
  a. Booklet pane of 5 + label 1.20 *40*
  b. Untagged (Bureau precanceled) 15
  c. Booklet pane of 6 1.00 *35*
1281 A713 3c vio, tagged 15 15
  a. Untagged (Bureau precanceled) 15
1282 A714 4c black 15 15
  a. Tagged 15 15
1283 A715 5c blue 15 15
  a. Tagged 15 15
1283B A715a 5c blue, tagged 15 15
  d. Untagged (Bureau precanceled) 15
1284 A716 6c gray brown 15 15
  a. Tagged 15 15
  b. Booklet pane of 8 1.50 *50*
  c. Booklet pane of 5 + label 1.25 *50*
1285 A717 8c violet 20 15
  a. Tagged 16 15
1286 A718 10c lilac, tagged 20 15
  b. Untagged (Bureau precanceled) 20
1286A A718a 12c black, tagged 25 15
  c. Untagged (Bureau precanceled) 25
1287 A719 13c brn, tagged 25 15
  a. Untagged (Bureau precanceled) 25
1288 A720 15c rose claret, tagged 30 15
  a. Untagged (Bureau precanceled) 30
  d. Type II 55 15

Type II: necktie does not touch coat at bottom.

Perf. 10

1288B A720 15c dk rose cl (from bklt. pane) 28 15
  c. Booklet pane of 8 2.25 *1.25*
  e. As "c," vert. imperf. btwn. —

Perf. 11x10½, 10½x11

1289 A721 20c deep olive 42 15
  a. Tagged 40 15
1290 A722 25c rose lake 55 15
  a. Tagged 45 15
  b. 25c maroon —
1291 A723 30c red lilac 58 15
  a. Tagged 52 15
1292 A724 40c blue black 85 15
  a. Tagged 65 15
1293 A725 50c rose magenta 90 15
  a. Tagged 80 15
1294 A726 $1 dull purple 2.25 15
  a. Tagged 1.65 15
1295 A727 $5 gray black 12.50 2.25
  a. Tagged 8.00 2.00
  Nos. 1278-1295 (21) 20.73
  Set value 3.00

On No. 1283B the highlights and shadows have been softened.

No. 1288B issued in booklets only. All stamps have one or two straight edges.

Issue dates (without tagging)—1965: 4c, Nov. 19.

1966: 5c, Feb. 22; 6c, Jan. 29; 8c, Mar. 14; $5, Dec. 3.

1967: 1¼c, Jan. 30; 20c, Oct. 24; 25c, Feb. 14; $1, Oct. 16.

1968: 30c, Oct. 21; 40c, Jan. 29; 50c, Aug. 13.

Dates for tagged: 1965: 4c, Dec. 1.

1966: 2c, June 8; 5c, Feb. 23; 6c, Dec. 29; 8c, July 6.

1967: 3c, Sept. 16; No. 1283B, Nov. 17; No. 1284b, Dec. 28; 10c, Mar. 15; 13c, May 29.

1968: 1c & No. 1284c, Jan. 12; No. 1280a, Jan. 8; 12c, July 30; 15c, Mar. 8.

1973: 20c, 25c, 30c, 40c, 50c, $1, $5, Apr. 3.

1978: No. 1288B, June 14.

Franklin D. Roosevelt — A727a

Coil Stamps

Rotary Press Printing

1966-81 **Tagged** ***Perf. 10 Horiz.***

1297 A713 3c violet 15 15
  a. Imperf., pair *30.00*
  b. Untagged (Bureau precanceled) 15
  c. As "b," imperf. pair 6.00
1298 A716 6c gray brn 15 15
  a. Imperf., pair *2,000.*

Perf. 10 Vertically

1299 A710 1c green 15 15
  a. Untagged (Bureau precanceled) 15
  b. Imperf., pair *30.00* —
1303 A714 4c black 15 15
  a. Untagged (Bureau precanceled) 15
  b. Imperf., pair *800.00*
1304 A715 5c blue 15 15
  a. Untagged (Bureau precanceled) 15
  b. Imperf., pair *150.00*
  e. As "a," imperf. pair *450.00*

No. 1304b is valued in the grade of fine.

1304C A715a 5c blue 15 15
  d. Imperf., pair 1,250.
1305 A727a 6c gray brn 15 15
  a. Imperf., pair *70.00*
  b. Untagged (Bureau precanceled) 20
1305E A720 15c rose claret 25 15
  f. Untagged (Bureau precanceled) 30
  g. Imperf., pair *25.00*
  h. Pair, imperf. between *200.00*
  i. Type II 35 15
  j. Imperf., pair, type II *70.00*
1305C A726 $1 dull pur 1.75 20
  d. Imperf., pair *2,250.*
  Nos. 1297-1305C (9) 3.05
  Set value 60

Issued dates: 1c, Jan. 12, 1968. 3c, Nov. 4, 1975. 4c, May 28, 1966. No. 1304, Sept. 8, 1966. 6c, No. 1298, Dec. 28, 1967; No. 1305, Feb. 28, 1968. $1, Jan. 12, 1973. 15c, June 14, 1978.

See Nos. 1393-1395, 1397-1402 for more Prominent Americans.

Migratory Bird Treaty Issue

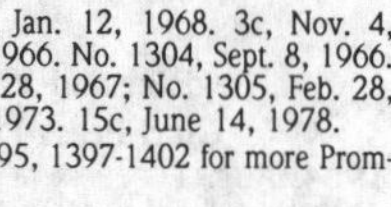

Migratory Birds over Canada-US Border — A728

Giori Press Printing

1966, Mar. 16 ***Perf. 11***

1306 A728 5c blk, crim & dk blue 15 15

50th anniv. of the Migratory Bird Treaty between the US and Canada.

Humane Treatment of Animals Issue

Mongrel A729

Lithographed, Engraved (Giori)

1966, Apr. 9 ***Perf. 11***

1307 A729 5c org brown & black 15 15

Humane treatment of all animals and cent. of the ASPCA.

Indiana Statehood Sesquicentennial

Sesquicentennial Seal; Map of Indiana with 19 Stars and Old Capitol at Corydon — A730

1966, Apr. 16 **Giori Press Printing**

1308 A730 5c yel, ocher & vio blue 15 15

American Circus Issue

Clown — A731

1966, May 2 ***Perf. 11***

1309 A731 5c multicolored 20 15

Honoring the American circus on the cent. of the birth of John Ringling.

Sixth Intl. Phil. Exhib. Issues

Stamped Cover — A732

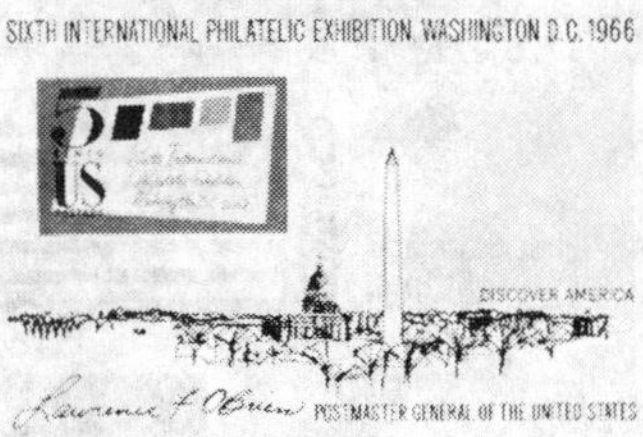

A733

Lithographed, Engraved (Giori)

1966, May ***Perf. 11***

1310 A732 5c multicolored 15 15

Souvenir Sheet

Imperf

1311 A733 5c multicolored 15 15

Set value 25 17

SIPEX, Washington, DC, May 21-30.
No. 1311 measures 108x74mm.
Issue dates: #1310, 21st. #1311, 23rd.

"Freedom" Checking "Tyranny" A734

Polish Eagle and Cross A735

Bill of Rights, 175th Anniv.

Giori Press Printing

1966, July 1 ***Perf. 11***

1312 A734 5c carmine, dk & lt blue 15 15

Polish Millennium Issue

Rotary Press Printing

1966, July 30 ***Perf. 10½x11***

1313 A735 5c red 15 15

1000th anniv. of the adoption of Christianity in Poland.

Tagging Extended

During 1966 experimental use of tagged stamps was extended to the Cincinnati Postal Region covering offices in Indiana, Kentucky and Ohio. To supply these offices about 12 percent of the following nine issues (Nos. 1314-1322) were tagged.

National Park Service Issue

National Park Service Emblem — A736

Lithographed, Engraved (Giori)

1966, Aug. 25 ***Perf. 11***

1314 A736 5c yel, black & green 15 15
a. Tagged 30 25

50th anniv. of the Natl. Park Service of the Interior Dept. The design "Parkscape U.S.A." identifies Natl. Park Service facilities. No. 1314a was issued Aug. 26.

Marine Corps Reserve Issue

Combat Marine, 1966; Frogman; WW II Flier; WW I "Devil Dog" and Marine, 1775 — A737

Lithographed, Engraved (Giori)

1966, Aug. 29 ***Perf. 11***

1315 A737 5c black, bister, red & ultra 15 15
a. Tagged 30 20
b. Black & bister (engr.) omitted —

50th anniv. of the founding of the US Marine Corps Reserve.

General Federation of Women's Clubs

Women of 1890 and 1966 — A738

Giori Press Printing

1966, Sept. 12 ***Perf. 11***

1316 A738 5c black, pink & blue 15 15
a. Tagged 30 20

75 years of service by the Gen. Fed. of Women's Clubs. No. 1316a was issued Sept. 13.

American Folklore Issue

Johnny Appleseed — A739

1966, Sept. 24 ***Perf. 11***

1317 A739 5c green, red & black 15 15
a. Tagged 30 20

Johnny Appleseed, (John Chapman, 1774-1845), who wandered over 100,000 square miles planting apple trees, and who gave away and sold seedlings to Midwest pioneers. No. 1317a issued Sept. 26.

Beautification of America Issue

Jefferson Memorial, Tidal Basin and Cherry Blossoms A740

1966, Oct. 5 ***Perf. 11***

1318 A740 5c emerald, pink & black 15 15
a. Tagged 30 20

Pres. Johnson's "Plant for a more beautiful America" campaign.

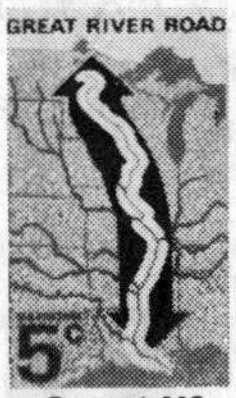

Central US Map With Great River Road A741

Statue of Liberty and "Old Glory" A742

Great River Road Issue

Lithographed, Engraved (Giori)

1966, Oct. 21 ***Perf. 11***

1319 A741 5c ver, yellow, blue & green 15 15
a. Tagged 30 20

5,600-mile Great River Road connecting New Orleans with Kenora, Ontario, following the Mississippi most of the way. No. 1319a issued Oct. 22.

Savings Bond-Servicemen Issue

1966, Oct. 26

1320 A742 5c red, dk & lt blue, black 15 15
a. Tagged 30 20
b. Red, dark blue & black omitted *4,250.*
c. Dark blue (engr.) omitted *8,000.*

25th anniv. of US Savings Bonds, and to honor American servicemen. No. 1320a issued Oct. 27.

Christmas Issue

Madonna and Child, by Hans Memling — A743

Lithographed, Engraved (Giori)

1966, Nov. 1 ***Perf. 11***

1321 A743 5c multicolored 15 15
a. Tagged 30 20

The design is from "Madonna and Child with Angels," by the Flemish artist Hans Memling (c. 1430-1494), National Gallery of Art, Washington, DC. No. 1321a was issued Nov. 2. See No. 1336.

Mary Cassatt Issue

"The Boating Party" — A744

Giori Press Printing

1966, Nov. 17 ***Perf. 11***

1322 A744 5c multicolored 15 15
a. Tagged 30 25

Cassatt (1844-1926), painter. The original painting is in the Natl. Gallery of Art, Washington, DC.

National Grange Issue

Grange Poster, 1870 — A745

1967, Apr. 17 **Tagged** ***Perf. 11***

1323 A745 5c multicolored 15 15

Cent. of the founding of the National Grange, American farmers' organization.

Phosphor Tagging

From No. 1323 onward, all postage issues are tagged, unless otherwise noted.

Tagging Omitted

Inadvertent omissions of tagging occurred on Nos. 1238, 1278, 1281, 1298 and 1305. In addition most tagged issues from 1967 on exist with tagging unintentionally omitted.

Canada Centenary Issue

Canadian Landscape A746

Giori Press Printing

1967, May 25 ***Perf. 11***

1324 A746 5c multicolored 15 15

Cent. of Canada's emergence as a nation.

Erie Canal Issue

Stern of Early Canal Boat — A747

Lithographed, Engraved (Giori)

1967, July 4 ***Perf. 11***

1325 A747 5c multicolored 15 15

150th anniv. of the Erie Canal ground-breaking ceremony. The canal links Lake Erie and NYC.

"Peace"—Lions Issue

Peace Dove — A748

Giori Press Printing

1967, July 5 ***Perf. 11***

Gray Paper with Blue Threads

1326 A748 5c blue, red & black 15 15

Publicizing the Search for Peace. This was the theme of an essay contest for young men and women sponsored by Lions Intl. on its 50th anniv.

Henry David Thoreau Issue

Henry David Thoreau (1817-1862), Writer — A749

1967, July 12
1327 A749 5c red, black & green 15 15

Nebraska Statehood Centenary

Hereford Steer and Corn — A750

Lithographed, Engraved (Giori)
1967, July 29 *Perf. 11*
1328 A750 5c dk red brn, lem & yel 15 15

Voice of America Issue

Radio Transmission Tower and Waves — A751

1967, Aug. 1 **Giori Press Printing**
1329 A751 5c red, blue, black & car 15 15

25th anniv. of the radio branch of the US Information Agency (USIA).

American Folklore Issue

Davy Crockett (1786-1836) and Scrub Pines — A752

Lithographed, Engraved (Giori)
1967, Aug. 17 *Perf. 11*
1330 A752 5c green, black & yellow 15 15
a. Vert. pair, imperf. btwn. *6,000.*
b. Green (engr.) omitted —
c. Black & green (engr.) omitted —
d. Yellow & green (litho.) omitted —

Crockett, frontiersman and congressman, died in defense of the Alamo.

A foldover on one pane created one each of Nos. 1330b-1330d. Part of the colors appear on the back of the selvage or stamps.

Space Accomplishments Issue

Space-Walking Astronaut — A753

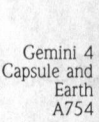

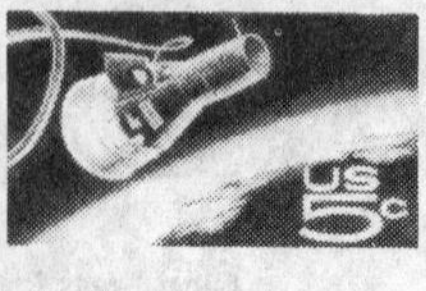

Gemini 4 Capsule and Earth A754

Lithographed, Engraved (Giori)
1967, Sept. 29 *Perf. 11*
1331 A753 5c multicolored 65 15
a. Pair, #1331-1332 1.50 1.50
1332 A754 5c multicolored 65 15

US accomplishments in space.

View of Model City — A755

Finnish Coat of Arms — A756

Urban Planning Issue

Lithographed, Engraved (Giori)
1967, Oct. 2 *Perf. 11*
1333 A755 5c dk & lt blue, black 15 15

Importance of Urban Planning and the Intl. Conf. of the American Inst. of Planners, Washington, DC, Oct. 1-6.

Finnish Independence, 50th Anniv.

Engraved (Giori)
1967, Oct. 6 *Perf. 11*
1334 A756 5c blue 15 15

Thomas Eakins Issue

"The Biglin Brothers Racing" (Sculling on Schuylkill River, Philadelphia) A757

1967, Nov. 2 **Photo.** *Perf. 12*
1335 A757 5c gold & multi 15 15

Eakins (1844-1916), painter and sculptor. The painting is in the Natl. Gallery of Art, Washington, DC.

Christmas Issue

Madonna and Child, by Hans Memling — A758

Lithographed, Engraved (Giori)
1967, Nov. 6 *Perf. 11*
1336 A758 5c multicolored 15 15

See note after No. 1321.

Magnolia — A759

Flag and White House — A760

Mississippi Statehood, 150th Anniv.

Giori Press Printing
1967, Dec. 11 *Perf. 11*
1337 A759 5c brt grnsh blue, green & red brown 15 15

Flag Issue

Giori Press Printing
1968-71 *Perf. 11*

Size: 19x22mm
1338 A760 6c dk blue, red & green 15 15
k. Vert. pair, imperf. btwn. *500.00*

Vert. pairs have been offered as imperf. horiz. Some have had the gum washed off to remove blind perfs.

Coil Stamp

Multicolor Huck Press
Perf. 10 Vert.
Size: 18¼x21mm
1338A A760 6c dk blue, red & green ('69) 15 15
b. Imperf., pair *450.00*

Multicolor Huck Press
Perf. 11x10½
Size: 18¼x21mm
1338D A760 6c dk blue, red & green ('70) 15 15
e. Horiz. pair, imperf. btwn. *175.00*
1338F A760 8c multi ('71) 15 15
i. Vert. pair, imperf. *50.00*
j. Horiz. pair, imperf. btwn. *50.00*
p. Slate green omitted *450.00*

Issued: #1338, Jan. 24, 1968; #1338A, May 30, 1969; #1338D, Aug. 7, 1970; 8c, May 10, 1971.

Coil Stamp

1971, May 10 ***Perf. 10 Vert.***
Size: 18¼x21mm
1338G A760 8c multi ('71) 20 15
h. Imperf., pair *55.00*
Set value, #1338-1338G 25

Farm House and Fields of Ripening Grain A761

Map of North and South America A762

Illinois Statehood, 150th Anniv.

Lithographed, Engraved (Giori)
1968, Feb. 12 *Perf. 11*
1339 A761 6c multicolored 15 15

HemisFair '68 Issue

1968, Mar. 30 *Perf. 11*
1340 A762 6c blue, rose red & white 15 15
a. White omitted *1,400.*

HemisFair '68 exhib. at San Antonio, Tex., Apr. 6-Oct. 6, for the 250th anniv. of San Antonio.

Airlift Issue

Eagle Holding Pennant A763

Lithographed, Engraved (Giori)
1968, Apr. 4 **Untagged** *Perf. 11*
1341 A763 $1 sep, dk blue, ocher & brn red 2.50 1.25

Issued to pay for airlift of parcels from and to US ports to servicemen overseas and in Alaska, Hawaii and P.R. Valid for all regular postage.

On Apr. 26, 1969, the POD ruled that henceforth No. 1341 "may be used toward paying the postage or fees for special services on airmail articles."

"Youth"—Elks Issue

Girls and Boys — A764

Lithographed, Engraved (Giori)
1968, May 1 *Perf. 11*
1342 A764 6c ultra & orange red 15 15

Support Our Youth program, and honoring the Benevolent and Protective Order of Elks, which extended its youth service program in observance of its centennial year.

Policeman and Small Boy — A765

Eagle Weather Vane — A766

Law and Order Issue

Giori Press Printing
1968, May 17 *Perf. 11*
1343 A765 6c chlky blue, blk & red 15 15

The police as protector and friend and respect for law and order.

Register and Vote Issue

Lithographed, Engraved (Giori)
1968, June 27 *Perf. 11*
1344 A766 6c blk, yel & org 15 15

Campaign to draw more voters to the polls. The weather vane is from an old house in the Russian Hill section of San Francisco.

Historic Flag Series

Ft. Moultrie, 1776 — A767

Ft. McHenry, 1795-1818 A768

Washington's Cruisers, 1775 — A769

Bennington, 1777 — A770

Rhode Island, 1775 — A771

First Stars and Stripes, 1777 — A772

Bunker Hill, 1775 A773

Grand Union, 1776 — A774

Philadelphia Light Horse, 1775 A775

First Navy Jack, 1775 — A776

Engraved (Giori) (#1345-1348, 1350): Engr. & Litho. (#1349, 1351-1354)

1968, July 4 *Perf. 11*

1345 A767 6c dark blue	50	25
1346 A768 6c dk blue & red	35	25
1347 A769 6c dk blue & ol green	30	25
1348 A770 6c dk blue & red	30	25
1349 A771 6c dk blue, yel & red	30	25
1350 A772 6c dk blue & red	30	25
1351 A773 6c dk bl, ol grn & red	30	25
1352 A774 6c dk blue & red	30	25
1353 A775 6c dk blue, yel & red	30	25
1354 A776 6c dk blue, red & yel	30	25
a. Strip of 10, Nos. 1345-1354	3.25	3.25

Flags carried by American colonists and by citizens of the new United States. The flag sequence on the upper panes is as listed. On the lower panes the sequence is reversed with the Navy Jack in the 1st row and the Fort Moultrie flag in the 10th.

Walt Disney Issue

Disney and Children of the World — A777

1968, Sept. 11 **Photo.** *Perf. 12*

1355 A777 6c multicolored	16	15
a. Ocher (Walt Disney, 6c, etc.) omitted	*700.*	—
b. Vert. pair, imperf. horiz.	*750.*	
c. Imperf., pair	*675.*	
d. Black omitted	*2,000.*	
e. Horiz. pair, imperf. btwn.	*4,750.*	
f. Blue omitted	*2,100.*	

Disney (1901-1966), cartoonist, film producer, creator of Mickey Mouse.

Father Marquette Issue

Father Marquette and Louis Jolliet Exploring the Mississippi A778

Giori Press Printing

1968, Sept. 20 *Perf. 11*

1356 A778 6c black, apple green & org brn	15	15

Father Jacques Marquette (1637-1675). French Jesuit missionary, who with Louis Jolliet explored the Mississippi and its tributaries.

American Folklore Issue

Daniel Boone (1734-1820)

Pennsylvania Rifle, Powder Horn, Tomahawk Pipe and Knife — A779

Lithographed, Engraved (Giori)

1968, Sept. 26 *Perf. 11*

1357 A779 6c yel, dp yel, mar & blk	15	15

Daniel Boone, frontiersman and trapper.

Arkansas River Navigation Issue

Ship's Wheel, Power Transmission Tower and Barge — A780

1968, Oct. 1 *Perf. 11*

1358 A780 6c brt bl, dk bl & blk	15	15

Opening of the Arkansas River to commercial navigation.

Leif Erikson Issue

Leif Erikson, by Stirling Calder — A781

1968, Oct. 9 **Litho., Engr.** *Perf. 11*

1359 A781 6c lt gray brn & blk brn	15	15

Erikson, 11th cent. Norse explorer, was the 1st European to set foot on the American continent, at a place he called Vinland. The statue by an American sculptor is in Reykjavik, Iceland.

The light gray brown ink carries the tagging element.

Cherokee Strip Issue

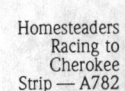

Homesteaders Racing to Cherokee Strip — A782

Rotary Press Printing

1968, Oct. 15 *Perf. 11x10½*

1360 A782 6c brown	15	15

75th anniv. of the opening of the Cherokee Strip to settlers, Sept. 16, 1893.

John Trumbull Issue

Detail from "The Battle of Bunker's Hill" — A783

Lithographed, Engraved

1968, Oct. 18 *Perf. 11*

1361 A783 6c multicolored	15	15

Trumbull (1756-1843), painter. The stamp shows Lt. Thomas Grosvenor and his attendant, Peter Salem. The painting is at Yale Univ., New Haven, CT.

Waterfowl Conservation Issue

Wood Ducks — A784

Lithographed, Engraved (Giori)

1968, Oct. 24 *Perf. 11*

1362 A784 6c black & multi	15	15
a. Vert. pair, imperf. btwn.	*550.*	
b. Red & dark blue omitted	*1,000.*	

Gabriel, from van Eyck's Annunciation A785

Chief Joseph, by Cyrenius Hall A786

Christmas Issue

Engraved (Multicolor Huck)

1968, Nov. 1 **Tagged** *Perf. 11*

1363 A785 6c multicolored	15	15
a. Untagged	15	15
b. Imperf., pair, tagged	*250.00*	
c. Light yellow omitted	*100.00*	
d. Imperf., pair, untagged	*325.00*	

"The Annunciation" by the 15th cent. Flemish artist Jan van Eyck is in the Natl. Gallery of Art, Washington, DC. No. 1363a was issued Nov. 2.

Luminescence

No. 1364 and all following postage stamps are tagged, unless otherwise noted.

American Indian Issue

Lithographed, Engraved (Giori)

1968, Nov. 4 *Perf. 11*

1364 A786 6c black & multi	16	15

Honoring American Indians and the opening of the Natl. Portrait Gallery, Oct. 5, 1968. Chief Joseph (Indian name Thunder Traveling over the Mountains) a leader of the Nez Percé tribe, was born c. 1840 in eastern Oregon and died at the Colesville Reservation in Washington in 1904.

Beautification of America Issue

Capitol, Azaleas and Tulips A787

Washington Monument, Potomac River and Daffodils A788

Poppies and Lupines along Highway A789

Blooming Crabapples along Street A790

Lithographed, Engraved (Giori)

1969, Jan. 16 *Perf. 11*

1365 A787 6c multicolored	45	15
1366 A788 6c multicolored	45	15
1367 A789 6c multicolored	45	15
1368 A790 6c multicolored	45	15
a. Block of 4, #1365-1368	2.00	2.00
Set value		48

Natural Beauty Campaign for more beautiful cities, parks, highways and streets.

Eagle from Great Seal of US A791

July Fourth, by Grandma Moses A792

American Legion, 50th Anniv.

Lithographed, Engraved (Giori)

1969, Mar. 15 *Perf. 11*

1369 A791 6c red, blue & black	15	15

American Folklore Issue

Grandma Moses

Lithographed, Engraved (Giori)

1969, May 1 *Perf. 11*

1370 A792 6c multicolored	15	15
a. Horiz. pair, imperf. btwn.	*225.00*	
b. Black and Prus blue omitted	*900.00*	

Grandma Moses (Anna Mary Robertson Moses, 1860-1961), primitive painter of American life.

Beware of pairs with blind perfs. being offered as No. 1370a. No. 1370b often comes with mottled or disturbed gum. Such stamps sell for about two-thirds as much as copies with perfect gum.

Apollo 8 Issue

Moon Surface and Earth — A793

Giori Press Printing

1969, May 5 *Perf. 11*

1371 A793 6c black, blue & ocher	15	15

Apollo 8 mission, which put the 1st men into orbit around the moon, Dec. 21-27, 1968.

Imperfs. exist. from printer's waste.

William Christopher Handy Issue

W. C. Handy (1873-1958), Jazz Musician and Composer A794

Lithographed, Engraved (Giori)

1969, May 17 *Perf. 11*

1372 A794 6c multicolored	15	15

California Settlement, 200th Anniv.

Carmel Mission Belfry — A795

1969, July 16 *Perf. 11*

1373 A795 6c multicolored	15	15

John Wesley Powell Issue

Powell Exploring Colorado River — A796

1969, Aug. 1 *Perf. 11*

1374 A796 6c multicolored	15	15

Powell (1834-1902), geologist and explorer of the Green and Colorado Rivers, 1869-1875.

Alabama Statehood, 150th Anniv.

Camellia and Yellow-shafted Flicker — A797

1969, Aug. 2 *Perf. 11*

1375 A797 6c multicolored	15	15

Botanical Congress Issue

Douglas Fir (Northwest) A798

Lady's-slipper (Northeast) A799

Ocotillo (Southwest) A800

Franklinia (Southeast) A801

Lithographed, Engraved (Giori)

1969, Aug. 23 *Perf. 11*

1376 A798 6c multicolored	75	15
1377 A799 6c multicolored	75	15
1378 A800 6c multicolored	75	15
1379 A801 6c multicolored	75	15
a. Block of 4, #1376-1379	3.25	3.25

11th Intl. Botanical Cong., Seattle, Wash., Aug. 24-Sept. 2.

Dartmouth College Case Issue

Daniel Webster and Dartmouth Hall — A802

Rotary Press Printing

1969, Sept. 22 *Perf. $10^1/_2$x11*

1380 A802 6c green	15	15

Sesquicentennial of the Dartmouth College case, argued by Daniel Webster before the Supreme Court, which reasserted the sanctity of contracts.

Professional Baseball Centenary

Batter — A803

Lithographed, Engraved (Giori)

1969, Sept. 24 *Perf. 11*

1381 A803 6c yel, red, black & green	65	15
a. Black (1869-1969, United States, 6c, Professional Baseball) omitted	1,100.	

Intercollegiate Football Centenary

Football Player and Coach — A804

1969, Sept. 26 *Perf. 11*

1382 A804 6c red & green	15	15

Dwight D. Eisenhower Issue

Dwight D. Eisenhower — A805

Giori Press Printing

1969, Oct. 14 *Perf. 11*

1383 A805 6c blue, black & red	15	15

Gen. Eisenhower, 34th Pres. (1890-1969).

Christmas Issue

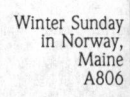

Winter Sunday in Norway, Maine A806

Engraved (Multicolor Huck)

1969, Nov. 3 *Perf. 11x$10^1/_2$*

1384 A806 6c dk green & multi	15	15
Precanceled	50	15
b. Imperf., pair	1,100.	
c. Light green omitted	25.00	
d. Lt grn, red & yel omitted	1,000.	—
e. Yellow omitted	—	
g. Red & yellow omitted	—	

The precancel value applies to the experimental precancel printed in four cities with the names between lines $4^1/_2$mm apart: in black or green "ATLANTA, GA" and in green only "BALTIMORE, MD," "MEMPHIS, TN" and "NEW HAVEN, CT." They were sold freely to the public and could be used on any class of mail at all post offices during the experimental program and thereafter.

Most examples of No. 1384c show orange where the offset green was. Value is for this variety. Copies without orange sell for a premium.

Cured Child A807

"Old Models" A808

Hope for Crippled Issue

Lithographed, Engraved (Giori)

1969, Nov. 20 *Perf. 11*

1385 A807 6c multicolored	15	15

Issued to encourage the rehabilitation of crippled children and adults, and to honor the Natl. Soc. for Crippled Children and Adults (Easter Seal Soc.) on its 50th anniv.

William M. Harnett Issue

1969, Dec. 3 *Perf. 11*

1386 A808 6c multicolored	15	15

Harnett (1848-1892), painter. The painting is in the Museum of Fine Arts, Boston.

Natural History Issue

American Bald Eagle — A809

African Elephant Herd — A810

Tlingit Chief in Haida Ceremonial Canoe — A811

Brontosaurus, Stegosaurus and Allosaurus from Jurassic Period — A812

Lithographed, Engraved (Giori)

1970, May 6 *Perf. 11*

1387 A809 6c multicolored	15	15
1388 A810 6c multicolored	15	15
1389 A811 6c multicolored	15	15
1390 A812 6c multicolored	15	15
a. Block of 4, #1387-1390	50	50
Set value	48	36

1969-1970 celebration of the cent. of the American Museum of Natural History in NYC. The design of No. 1390 is a detail from a mural by Rudolph Zallinger in Yale's Peabody Museum.

Maine Statehood Issue

Lighthouse at Two Lights, Maine — A813

Lithographed, Engraved (Giori)

1970, July 9 *Perf. 11*

1391 A813 6c black & multi	15	15

Sesquicentennial of Maine statehood. The painting by Edward Hopper (1882-1967) hangs in the Metropolitan Museum of Art, NYC.

Wildlife Conservation Issue

American Buffalo A814

Rotary Press Printing

1970, July 20 *Perf. $10^1/_2$x11*

1392 A814 6c black, *light brown*	15	15

Regular Issue

Dwight David Eisenhower

A815 Dot between "R" and "U"

A815a No dot between "R" and "U"

Benjamin Franklin A816

USPS Emblem A817

Fiorello H. LaGuardia A817a

Ernest Taylor Pyle A818

Dr. Elizabeth Blackwell A818a

Amadeo P. Giannini A818b

Rotary (6c, 7c, 14c, 16c, 18c, 21c, #1395); Giori (#1394); Photo. (#1396)

Perf. 11x$10^1/_2$, $10^1/_2$x11; 11 (#1394)

1970-74

1393 A815 6c dark blue gray	15	15
a. Booklet pane of 8	1.25	*50*
b. Booklet pane of 5 + label	1.25	*50*
c. Untagged (Bureau precanceled)		15
1393D A816 7c brt blue ('72)	15	15
e. Untagged (Bureau precanceled)		15
1394 A815a 8c blk, red & bl gray ('71)	16	15
1395 A815 8c dp claret ('71)	20	15
a. Booklet pane of 8	1.80	*1.25*
b. Booklet pane of 6	1.25	*75*
c. Booklet pane of 4 + 2 labels ('72)	1.65	*50*
d. Booklet pane of 7 + label ('72)	1.75	*1.00*
1396 A817 8c multi ('71)	15	15
1397 A817a 14c gray brn ('72)	25	15
a. Untagged (Bureau precanceled)		25
1398 A818 16c brown ('71)	28	15
a. Untagged (Bureau precanceled)		35
1399 A818a 18c violet ('74)	32	15
1400 A818b 21c green ('73)	32	15
Nos. 1393-1400 (9)	1.98	
Set value		47

No. 1395 was issued in booklets only. All stamps have one or two straight edges.

Issue dates: 6c, Aug. 6, 1970; 7c, Oct. 20, 1972; Nos. 1394-1395, May 10, 1971; No. 1396, July 1, 1971; 14c, Apr. 24, 1972; 16c, May 7, 1971; 18c, Jan. 23, 1974; 21c, June 27, 1973.

Coil Stamps

1970-71 Rotary Press *Perf. 10 Vert.*

1401 A815 6c dark blue gray	15	15
a. Untagged (Bureau precanceled)		15
b. Imperf., pair	1,500.	
1402 A815 8c deep claret	15	15
a. Imperf., pair	45.00	
b. Untagged (Bureau precanceled)		15
c. Pair, imperf. btwn.	6,250.	
Set value		15

Issue dates: 6c, Aug. 6; 8c, May 10, 1971.

Edgar Lee Masters Issue

Edgar Lee Masters (1869-1950), Poet — A819

Lithographed, Engraved (Giori)

1970, Aug. 22 *Perf. 11*
1405 A819 6c black & olive bister 15 15

Woman Suffrage Issue

Suffragettes, 1920, and Woman Voter, 1970 — A820

Giori Press Printing

1970, Aug. 26 *Perf. 11*
1406 A820 6c blue 15 15

50th anniv. of the 19th Amendment, which gave women the vote.

South Carolina Issue

Symbols of South Carolina A821

Lithographed, Engraved (Giori)

1970, Sept. 12 *Perf. 11*
1407 A821 6c bister, black & red 15 15

300th anniv. of the founding of Charles Town (Charleston), the 1st permanent settlement of SC. Against a background of pine wood the line drawings of the design represent the economic and historic development of SC: the spire of St. Phillip's Church, Capitol, state flag, a ship, 17th cent. man and woman, a Fort Sumter cannon, barrels, cotton, tobacco and yellow jessamine.

Stone Mountain Memorial Issue

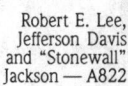

Robert E. Lee, Jefferson Davis and "Stonewall" Jackson — A822

Giori Press Printing

1970, Sept. 19 *Perf. 11*
1408 A822 6c gray 15 15

Dedication of the Stone Mountain Confederate Memorial, GA, May 9, 1970.

Fort Snelling Issue

Fort Snelling, Keelboat and Tepees — A823

Lithographed, Engraved (Giori)

1970, Oct. 17 *Perf. 11*
1409 A823 6c yellow & multi 15 15

150th anniv. of Fort Snelling, MN, which was an important outpost for the opening of the Northwest.

Anti-Pollution Issue

Globe and Wheat — A824

Globe and City — A825

Globe and Bluegill — A826

Globe and Seagull — A827

1970, Oct. 28 Photo. *Perf. 11x10½*
1410 A824 6c multicolored 25 15
1411 A825 6c multicolored 25 15
1412 A826 6c multicolored 25 15
1413 A827 6c multicolored 25 15
a. Block of 4, #1410-1413 1.25 1.25

Issued to focus attention on the mounting problems of pollution.

Christmas Issue

Nativity, by Lorenzo Lotto (1480-1556) A828

Tin and Cast-iron Locomotive A829

Toy Horse on Wheels — A830

Mechanical Tricycle A831

Doll Carriage A832

1970, Nov. 5 Photo. *Perf. 10½x11*
1414 A828 6c multicolored 15 15
a. Precanceled 15 15
b. Black omitted *650.00*
c. As "a," blue omitted *1,500.*

Perf. 11x10½

1415 A829 6c multicolored 40 15
a. Precanceled 90 15
b. Black omitted *2,500.*
1416 A830 6c multicolored 40 15
a. Precanceled 90 15
b. Black omitted *2,500.*
c. Imperf., pair (#1416, 1418) *4,000.*
1417 A831 6c multicolored 40 15
a. Precanceled 90 15
b. Black omitted *2,500.*
1418 A832 6c multicolored 40 15
a. Precanceled 90 15
b. Block of 4, #1415-1418 1.75 1.25
c. As "b," precanceled 3.75 3.50
d. Black omitted *2,500.*
Set value, #1414-1418 45

Nos. 1415-1418 are antique Christmas toys.

The precanceled stamps, Nos. 1414a-1418a, were furnished to 68 cities. The plates include two straight (No. 1414a) or two wavy (Nos. 1415a-1418a) black lines that make up the precancellation. Unused values are for copies with gum and used values are for copies with an additional cancellation or without gum.

United Nations, 25th Anniv.

"UN" and UN Emblem A833

Lithographed, Engraved (Giori)

1970, Nov. 20 *Perf. 11*
1419 A833 6c black, ver & ultra 15 15

Landing of the Pilgrims Issue

Mayflower and Pilgrims — A834

Lithographed, Engraved (Giori)

1970, Nov. 21 *Perf. 11*
1420 A834 6c black, org, yel, brn, mag & blue 15 15
a. Orange & yellow omitted *850.00*

Mayflower landing, 350th anniv.

Disabled Veterans and Servicemen Issue

A835

A836

Lithographed, Engraved (Giori)

1970, Nov. 24 *Perf. 11*
1421 A835 6c multicolored 15 15
a. Pair, #1421-1422 25 25

Engr.

1422 A836 6c dk blue, black & red 15 15
Set value 24 15

50th anniv. of the Disabled Veterans of America Organization (No. 1421); honoring the contribution of servicemen, particularly those who were prisoners of war or missing in action (No. 1422).

Ewe and Lamb A837

Douglas MacArthur A838

American Wool Industry Issue

Lithographed, Engraved (Giori)

1971, Jan. 19 *Perf. 11*
1423 A837 6c multicolored 15 15

450th anniv. of the introduction of sheep to the No. American continent and the beginning of the American wool industry.

Gen. Douglas MacArthur Issue

1971, Jan. 26 Giori Press Printing
1424 A838 6c black, red & dk blue 15 15

MacArthur (1880-1964), Chief of Staff, Supreme Commander for the Allied Powers in the Pacific Area during WW II and Supreme Commander in Japan after the war.

Blood Donor Issue

"Giving Blood Saves Lives" — A839

1971, Mar. 12 *Perf. 11*
1425 A839 6c light blue, scar & indigo 15 15

Salute to blood donors and spur to participation in the blood donor program.

Missouri Sesquicentennial Issue

"Independence and the Opening of the West," Detail, by Thomas Hart Benton — A840

1971, May 8 Photo. *Perf. 11x10½*
1426 A840 8c multicolored 15 15

The stamp design shows a Pawnee facing a hunter-trapper and a group of settlers.

Wildlife Conservation Issue

Trout A841

Alligator — A842

Polar Bear and Cubs A843

California Condor — A844

Lithographed, Engraved (Giori)

1971, June 12 *Perf. 11*
1427 A841 8c multicolored 16 15
1428 A842 8c multicolored 16 15
1429 A843 8c multicolored 16 15
1430 A844 8c multicolored 16 15
a. Block of 4, #1427-1430 65 65
b. As "a," lt grn & dk grn omitted from #1427-1428 *3,500.*
c. As "a," red omitted from #1427, 1429-1430 *9,000.*
Set value 32

Antarctic Treaty Issue

Map of Antarctica A845

1971, June 23 Giori Press Printing
1431 A845 8c red & dark blue 15 15

10th anniv. of the Antarctic Treaty pledging peaceful uses of and scientific cooperation in Antarctica.

American Revolution Bicentennial

Bicentennial Commission Emblem — A846

Lithographed, Engraved (Giori)

1971, July 4 *Perf. 11*

1432 A846 8c red, blue, gray & black 16 15
a. Gray & black omitted *650.00*
b. Gray ("U.S. Postage 8c") omitted *1,100.*

John Sloan Issue

The Wake of the Ferry — A847

1971, Aug. 2 *Perf. 11*

1433 A847 8c multicolored 15 15

Sloan (1871-1951), painter.

Space Achievement Decade Issue

Earth, Sun, Landing Craft on Moon A848

Lunar Rover and Astronauts A849

Lithographed, Engraved (Giori)

1971, Aug. 2 *Perf. 11*

1434 A848 8c blk, bl, yel & red 15 15
a. Pair, #1434-1435 30 25
b. As "a," blue & red (litho.) omitted *1,500.*
1435 A849 8c blk, bl, yel & red 15 15
Set value 20

A decade of space achievements. Apollo 15 moon exploration mission July 26-Aug. 7.

Emily Elizabeth Dickinson A850

Sentry Box, Morro Castle, San Juan A851

Emily Dickinson Issue

Lithographed, Engraved (Giori)

1971, Aug. 28 *Perf. 11*

1436 A850 8c multi, *greenish* 15 15
a. Black & olive (engr.) omitted *850.*
b. Pale rose omitted *7,500.*
c. Red omitted —

Dickinson (1830-1886), poet.

San Juan, PR, 450th Anniv.

1971, Sept. 12

1437 A851 8c multicolored 15 15

Young Woman Drug Addict — A852

Hands Reaching for CARE — A853

Prevent Drug Abuse Issue

1971, Oct. 5 Photo. *Perf. 10½x11*

1438 A852 8c bl, dp bl & blk 15 15

Drug Abuse Prevention Week, Oct. 3-9.

CARE Issue

1971, Oct. 27

1439 A853 8c multicolored 15 15
a. Black omitted *4,500.*

25th anniv. of CARE, a US-Canadian Cooperative for American Relief Everywhere.

Historic Preservation Issue

Decatur House, Washington, DC — A854

Whaling Ship Charles W. Morgan, Mystic, Conn. — A855

Cable Car, San Francisco — A856

San Xavier del Bac Mission, Tucson, Ariz. — A857

Lithographed, Engraved (Giori)

1971, Oct. 29 Buff Paper *Perf. 11*

1440 A854 8c blk brn & ocher 16 15
1441 A855 8c blk brn & ocher 16 15
1442 A856 8c blk brn & ocher 16 15
1443 A857 8c blk brn & ocher 16 15
a. Block of 4, #1440-1443 65 65
b. As "a," black brown omitted *2,400.*
c. As "a," ocher omitted —
Set value 48

Christmas Issue

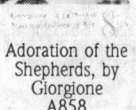

Adoration of the Shepherds, by Giorgione A858

Partridge in a Pear Tree, by Jamie Wyeth A859

1971, Nov. 10 Photo. *Perf. 10½x11*

1444 A858 8c gold & multi 15 15
a. Gold omitted *500.00*
1445 A859 8c multicolored 15 15
Set value 15

Sidney Lanier (1842-1881) A860

Peace Corps Poster, by David Battle A861

Sidney Lanier Issue

Giori Press Printing

1972, Feb. 3 *Perf. 11*

1446 A860 8c black, brown & lt blue 15 15

Lanier, poet, musician, lawyer, educator.

Peace Corps Issue

1972, Feb. 11 Photo. *Perf. 10½x11*

1447 A861 8c dk blue, light blue & red 15 15

National Parks Centennial Issue

Hulk of Ship A862 — Cape Hatteras Lighthouse A863

Laughing Gulls on Driftwood A864 — Laughing Gulls and Dune A865

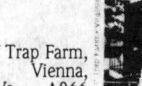

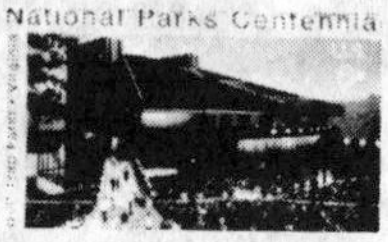

Wolf Trap Farm, Vienna, Va. — A866

Old Faithful, Yellowstone — A867

Mt. McKinley, Alaska — A868

Lithographed, Engraved (Giori)

1972 *Perf. 11*

1448 A862 2c black & multi 15 15
1449 A863 2c black & multi 15 15
1450 A864 2c black & multi 15 15
1451 A865 2c black & multi 15 15
a. Block of 4, #1448-1451 20 20
b. As "a," black (litho.) omitted *2,250.*
1452 A866 6c black & multi 15 15
1453 A867 8c blk, blue, brn & multi 15 15
1454 A868 15c black & multi 30 18
Set value 77 50

Cent. of Yellowstone Natl. Park, the 1st Natl. Park, and of the Natl. Park System. The four 2c stamps were issued for Cape Hatteras, NC, Natl. Seashore.

Issue dates: 2c, Apr. 5; 6c, June 26; 8c, Mar. 1; 15c, July 28.

See No. C84.

Family Planning Issue

Family — A869

1972, Mar. 18

1455 A869 8c black & multi 15 15
a. Yellow omitted —
b. Dark brown & olive omitted —
c. Dark brown omitted —

American Bicentennial

Colonial American Craftsmen

Glassmaker A870

Silversmith A871

Wigmaker A872

Hatter — A873

1972, July 4 Engr. *Perf. 11x10½*

Dull Yellow Paper

1456 A870 8c deep brown 16 15
1457 A871 8c deep brown 16 15
1458 A872 8c deep brown 16 15
1459 A873 8c deep brown 16 15
a. Block of 4, #1456-1459 65 65
Set value 32

Olympic Games Issue

Bicycling and Olympic Rings — A874

Bobsledding A875

Running A876

1972, Aug. 17 Photo. *Perf. 11x10½*

1460 A874 6c multicolored 15 15
1461 A875 8c multicolored 15 15
1462 A876 15c multicolored 28 18
Set value 30

11th Winter Olympic Games, Sapporo, Japan, Feb. 3-13, and 20th Summer Olympic Games, Munich, Germany, Aug. 26-Sept. 11.

See No. C85.

Parent Teacher Association, 75th Anniv.

Blackboard
A877

1972, Sept. 15 Photo. *Perf. 11x10½*
1463 A877 8c yellow & black 15 15

Wildlife Conservation Issue

Fur Seals
A878

Cardinal — A879

Brown
Pelican
A880

Bighorn
Sheep
A881

Lithographed, Engraved
1972, Sept. 20 *Perf. 11*
1464 A878 8c multicolored 16 15
1465 A879 8c multicolored 16 15
1466 A880 8c multicolored 16 15
1467 A881 8c multicolored 16 15
a. Block of 4, #1464-1467 65 65
b. As "a," brown omitted *3,750.*
c. As "a," green & blue omitted —
d. As "a," red & brown omitted *4,250.*
Set value 32

Mail Order Issue

Rural Post
Office
Store — A882

1972, Sept. 27 Photo. *Perf. 11x10½*
1468 A882 8c multicolored 15 15

Cent. of mail order business, originated by Aaron Montgomery Ward, Chicago.

Osteopathic Medicine Issue

Man's Quest for
Health — A883

1972, Oct. 9 Photo. *Perf. 10½x11*
1469 A883 8c yel, org & dk brn 15 15

75th anniv. of the American Osteopathic Assoc., founded by Dr. Andrew T. Still.

American Folklore Issue

Tom Sawyer, by Norman Rockwell — A884

Lithographed, Engraved (Giori)
1972, Oct. 13 *Perf. 11*
1470 A884 8c black & multi 15 15
a. Horiz. pair, imperf. btwn. *4,500.*
b. Red & black (engr.) omitted *2,000.*
c. Yellow & tan (litho.) omitted *2,200.*

Tom Sawyer, hero of "The Adventures of Tom Sawyer," by Mark Twain.

Angel from
"Mary, Queen
of Heaven"
A885

Santa Claus
A886

1972, Nov. 9 Photo. *Perf. 10½x11*
1471 A885 8c multicolored 15 15
a. Pink omitted *200.*
b. Black omitted *4,000.*
1472 A886 8c multicolored 15 15
Set value 15

Design of No. 1471 shows detail from a painting by the Master of the St. Lucy Legend.

Pharmacy Issue

Mortar and Pestle, Bowl of Hygeia, 19th Century Medicine Bottles
A887

Lithographed, Engraved (Giori)
1972, Nov. 10 *Perf. 11*
1473 A887 8c black & multi 15 15
a. Blue & orange omitted *900.*
b. Blue omitted *2,250.*
c. Orange omitted *2,000.*

Honoring American druggists, and 120th anniv. of the American Pharmaceutical Assoc.

Stamp Collecting Issue

US No. 1
Under
Magnifying
Glass
A888

1972, Nov. 17 *Perf. 11*
1474 A888 8c dark blue green, black & brown 15 15
a. Black (litho.) omitted *900.00*

Love Issue

"Love," by
Robert Indiana
A889

1973, Jan. 26 Photo. *Perf. 11x10½*
1475 A889 8c red, emer & vio blue 15 15

American Bicentennial
Communications in Colonial Times

Printer and
Patriots
Examining
Pamphlet
A890

Posting a
Broadside
A891

Postrider
A892

Drummer
A893

1973 Giori Press Printing *Perf. 11*
1476 A890 8c ultra, grnsh blk & red 15 15
1477 A891 8c black, ver & ultra 15 15

Lithographed, Engraved (Giori)
1478 A892 8c multicolored 15 15
1479 A893 8c multicolored 15 15
Set value 20

Issue dates: No. 1476, Feb. 16; No. 1477, Apr. 13; No. 1478, June 22; No. 1479, Sept. 28.

Boston Tea Party

British
Merchantman
A894

British Three-
master
A895

Boats and Ship's
Hull — A896

Boat and
Dock — A897

Lithographed, Engraved (Giori)
1973, July 4 *Perf. 11*
1480 A894 8c black & multi 15 15
1481 A895 8c black & multi 15 15
1482 A896 8c black & multi 15 15
1483 A897 8c black & multi 15 15
a. Block of 4, #1480-1483 60 45
b. As "a," black (engr.) omitted *1,750.*
c. As "a," black (litho.) omitted *1,650.*
Set value 40

American Arts Issue

Gershwin,
Sportin' Life,
Porgy and
Bess — A898

Robinson
Jeffers, Man
and Children
of Carmel
with Burro
A899

Henry Ossawa
Tanner, Palette
and Rainbow
A900

Willa Cather,
Pioneer Family
and Covered
Wagon
A901

1973 Photo. *Perf. 11*
1484 A898 8c dp green & multi 15 15
a. Vert. pair, imperf. horiz. *250.00*
1485 A899 8c Prus blue & multi 15 15
a. Vert. pair, imperf. horiz. *250.00*
1486 A900 8c yel brown & multi 15 15
1487 A901 8c dp brown & multi 15 15
a. Vert. pair, imperf. horiz. *300.00*
Set value 20

Honoring: No. 1484, George Gershwin (1899-1937), composer. No. 1485, Robinson Jeffers (1887-1962), poet. No. 1486, Henry Ossawa Tanner (1859-1937), black painter (portrait by Thomas Eakins). No. 1487, Willa Sibert Cather (1873-1947), novelist.

Issue dates: No. 1484, Feb. 28; No. 1485, Aug. 13; No. 1486, Sept. 10; No. 1487, Sept. 20.

Copernicus Issue

Nicolaus Copernicus
(1473-1543), Polish
Astronomer — A902

Lithographed, Engraved (Giori)
1973, Apr. 23 *Perf. 11*
1488 A902 8c black & orange 15 15
a. Orange omitted *900.*
b. Black (engraved) omitted *1,500.*

The orange color can be chemically removed.

Postal Service Employees' Issue

Stamp
Counter — A903

Mail
Collection — A904

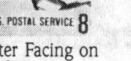

Letter Facing on Conveyor Belt — A905

Parcel Post Sorting — A906

Mail Canceling — A907

Manual Letter Routing — A908

Electronic Letter Routing — A909

Loading Mail on Truck — A910

Mailman — A911

Rural Mail Delivery — A912

1973, Apr. 30 Photo. *Perf. 10½x11*

1489 A903 8c multicolored 15 15
1490 A904 8c multicolored 15 15
1491 A905 8c multicolored 15 15
1492 A906 8c multicolored 15 15
1493 A907 8c multicolored 15 15
1494 A908 8c multicolored 15 15
1495 A909 8c multicolored 15 15
1496 A910 8c multicolored 15 15
1497 A911 8c multicolored 15 15
1498 A912 8c multicolored 15 15
a. Strip of 10, Nos. 1489-1498 1.50 1.00
Set value 1.00

A tribute to USPS employees. Emerald inscription on back, printed beneath gum in water-soluble ink, includes the USPS emblem, "People Serving You" and a statement, differing for each of the 10 stamps, about some aspect of postal service.

Each stamp in top or bottom row has a tab with blue inscription enumerating various jobs in postal service.

Harry S Truman Issue

Harry S Truman, 33rd President (1884-1972) A913

Giori Press Printing

1973, May 8 *Perf. 11*

1499 A913 8c car rose, black & blue 15 15

Electronics Progress Issue

Marconi's Spark Coil and Gap — A914

Transistors and Printed Circuit Board A915

Microphone, Speaker, Vacuum Tube, TV Camera Tube — A916

Lithographed, Engraved (Giori)

1973, July 10 *Perf. 11*

1500 A914 6c lilac & multi 15 15
1501 A915 8c tan & multi 15 15
a. Black (inscriptions & "U.S. 8c") omitted *650.*
b. Tan (background) & lilac omitted *1,500.*
1502 A916 15c gray green & multi 28 15
a. Black (inscriptions & "U.S. 15c") omitted *1,500.*
Set value 30

No. 1501b hinged is ½ unhinged value.
See No. C86.

Lyndon B. Johnson Issue

Lyndon B. Johnson (1908-1973), 36th President — A917

1973, Aug. 27 Photo. *Perf. 11*

1503 A917 8c black & multi 15 15
a. Horiz. pair, imperf. vert. *300.00*

Rural America Issue

Angus and Longhorn Cattle A918

Chautauqua Tent and Buggies A919

Wheat Fields and Train — A920

Lithographed, Engraved (Giori)

1973-74 *Perf. 11*

1504 A918 8c multicolored 15 15
a. Green & red brown omitted *1,000.*
b. Vert. pair, imperf. between —
1505 A919 10c multicolored 18 15
1506 A920 10c multicolored 18 15
a. Black & blue (engr.) omitted *750.*
Set value 15

Cent. of introduction of Aberdeen Angus cattle to US (No. 1504); of Chautauqua Institution (No. 1505); of introduction of hard winter wheat into Kansas by Mennonite immigrants (No. 1506).

Issue dates: No. 1504, Oct. 5, 1973. No. 1505, Aug. 6, 1974. No. 1506, Aug. 16, 1974.

Christmas Issue

Small Cowper Madonna, by Raphael A921

Christmas Tree in Needlepoint A922

1973, Nov. 7 Photo. *Perf. 10½x11*

1507 A921 8c tan & multi 15 15
1508 A922 8c green & multi 15 15
a. Vert. pair, imperf. btwn. *400.00*
Set value 15

50-Star and 13-Star Flags — A923

Jefferson Memorial and Signature — A924

Mail Transport — A925

Liberty Bell — A926

Multicolor Huck Press

1973-74 Tagged *Perf. 11x10½*

1509 A923 10c red & blue 18 15
a. Horiz. pair, imperf. btwn. *50.* —
b. Blue omitted *160.*
c. Vert. pair, imperf. *1,150.*
d. Horiz. pair, imperf. vert. —

Rotary Press Printing

1510 A924 10c blue 18 15
a. Untagged (Bureau precanceled) 18
b. Booklet pane of 5 + label 1.50 *30*
c. Booklet pane of 8 1.65 *30*
d. Booklet pane of 6 ('74) 5.25 *30*
e. Vert. pair, imperf. horiz. *350.00*
f. Vert. pair, imperf. btwn. —
1511 A925 10c multi, photo 22 15
a. Yellow omitted *50.00*
Set value 15

The yellow can be chemically removed.

Coil Stamps

Perf. 10 Vert.

Rotary Press Printing

1518 A926 6.3c brick red 15 15
a. Untagged (Bureau precanceled) 15
b. Imperf., pair *175.00*
c. As "a," imperf. pair *100.00*

Multicolor Huck Press

1519 A923 10c red & blue 20 15
a. Imperf., pair 30.00

Rotary Press Printing

1520 A924 10c blue 25 15
a. Untagged (Bureau precanceled) 25
b. Imperf., pair *40.00*
Set value 17

Issue dates: Nos. 1509, 1519, Dec. 8, 1973; Nos. 1510, 1520, Dec. 14, 1973; No. 1511, Jan. 4, 1974; No. 1518, Oct. 1, 1974.

Veterans of Foreign Wars Issue

V.F.W. Emblem A928

Giori Press Printing

1974, Mar. 11 *Perf. 11*

1525 A928 10c red & dark blue 16 15

75th anniv. of Veterans of Spanish American and other Foreign Wars.

Robert Frost Issue

Robert Frost (1874-1963), Poet — A929

Rotary Press Printing

1974, Mar. 26 *Perf. 10½x11*

1526 A929 10c black 16 15

EXPO '74 Issue

"Cosmic Jumper" A930

1974, Apr. 18 Photo. *Perf. 11*

1527 A930 10c multicolored 16 15

EXPO '74, Spokane, Wash., May 4-Nov. 4. Theme, "Preserve the Environment."

Horse Racing Issue

Horses Rounding Turn — A931

1974, May 4 Photo. *Perf. 11x10½*

1528 A931 10c yellow & multi 16 15
a. Blue ("Horse Racing") omitted *900.00*
b. Red ("U.S. postage 10 cents") omitted —

Beware of stamps offered as No. 1528b that have traces of red.

Skylab Issue

Skylab — A932

Lithographed, Engraved (Giori)

1974, May 14 *Perf. 11*

1529 A932 10c multicolored 18 15
a. Vert. pair, imperf. btwn. —

1st anniv. of the launching of Skylab and to honor all who participated in the Skylab projects.

Centenary of UPU Issue

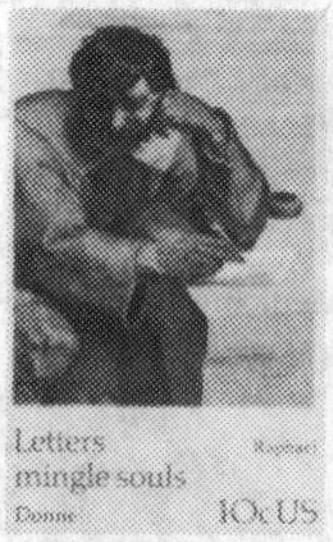

Michelangelo, from "School of Athens," by Raphael — A933

"Five Feminine Virtues," by Hokusai — A934

Old Time Letter Rack, by Peto — A935

Mlle. La Vergne, by Jean Liotard — A936

Lady Writing Letter, by Gerard Terborch — A937

Inkwell and Quill, by Jean Chardin — A938

Mrs. John Douglas, by Thomas Gainsborough A939

Don Antonio Noreiga, by Francisco de Goya A940

1974, June 6 Photo. *Perf. 11*

1530 A933	10c multicolored		20	15
1531 A934	10c multicolored		20	15
1532 A935	10c multicolored		20	15
1533 A936	10c multicolored		20	15
1534 A937	10c multicolored		20	15
1535 A938	10c multicolored		20	15
1536 A939	10c multicolored		20	15
1537 A940	10c multicolored		20	15
a.	Block or strip of 8, #1530-1537		1.60	1.50
b.	As "a" (block), imperf. vert.		*7,500.*	

Mineral Heritage Issue

Petrified Wood A941

Tourmaline — A942

Amethyst A943

Rhodochrosite — A944

Lithographed, Engraved (Giori)

1974, June 13 *Perf. 11*

1538 A941	10c lt blue & multi		16	15
a.	Light blue & yellow omitted		—	
1539 A942	10c lt blue & multi		16	15
a.	Light blue omitted		—	
b.	Black & purple omitted		—	
1540 A943	10c lt blue & multi		16	15
a.	Light blue & yellow omitted		—	
1541 A944	10c lt blue & multi		16	15
a.	Block or strip of 4, #1538-1541		75	80
b.	As "a," lt bl & yel omitted		*2,000.*	
c.	Light blue omitted		—	
d.	Black & red omitted		—	
	Set value			40

Kentucky Settlement Issue

Fort Harrod — A945

Lithographed, Engraved (Giori)

1974, June 15 *Perf. 11*

1542 A945	10c green & multi		16	15
a.	Dull black (litho.) omitted		*700.*	
b.	Green (engr. & litho.), black (engr. & litho.), blue omitted		*3,250.*	
c.	Green (engr.) omitted		—	
d.	Grn (engr.), blk (litho.) omitted		—	

American Bicentennial

First Continental Congress

Carpenters' Hall — A946

A947

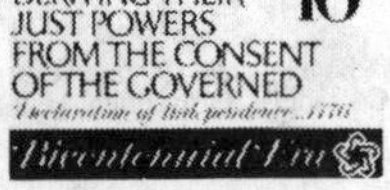

A948

Independence Hall — A949

Giori Press Printing

1974, July 4 *Perf. 11*

1543 A946	10c dark blue & red		18	15
1544 A947	10c gray, dk blue & red		18	15
1545 A948	10c gray, dk blue & red		18	15
1546 A949	10c red & dark blue		18	15
a.	Block of 4, #1543-1546		75	75
	Set value			40

Energy Conservation Issue

Molecules and Drops of Gasoline and Oil — A950

Lithographed, Engraved (Giori)

1974, Sept. 23 *Perf. 11*

1547 A950	10c multicolored		18	15
a.	Blue & orange omitted		*800.00*	
b.	Orange & green omitted		*800.00*	
c.	Green omitted		*900.00*	

To publicize the importance of conserving all forms of energy.

American Folklore Issue

Legend of Sleepy Hollow

Headless Horseman Pursuing Ichabod Crane A951

Lithographed, Engraved (Giori)

1974, Oct. 10 *Perf. 11*

1548 A951	10c dk blue, black, org & yel		16	15

Legend of Sleepy Hollow, by Washington Irving.

Retarded Children Issue

Retarded Child — A952

Giori Press Printing

1974, Oct. 12 *Perf. 11*

1549 A952	10c brn red & dk brn		16	15

Natl. Assoc. of Retarded Citizens.

Christmas Issue

Angel, from Perussis Altarpiece, 1480 — A953

"The Road-Winter," by Currier and Ives — A954

Dove Weather Vane, Mount Vernon A955

1974 Photo. *Perf. 10½x11*

1550 A953	10c multicolored		16	15

Perf. 11x10½

1551 A954	10c multicolored		16	15
a.	Buff omitted		25.00	

No. 1551a is difficult to identify. Competent expertization is necessary.

Imperf., Paper Backing Rouletted

Self-adhesive

Inscribed "Precanceled"

Untagged

1552 A955	10c multicolored		16	15
	Set value			18

Issued: #1550-1551, Oct. 23; #1552, Nov. 15.

Unused value of No. 1552 is for copy on rouletted paper backing as issued. Used value is for copy on piece, with or without postmark. Most copies are becoming discolored, probably from the adhesive. Unused and used values are for discolored copies.

Die cutting includes crossed slashes through dove, applied to prevent removal and re-use of stamp. The stamp will separate into layers if soaked.

American Arts Issue

Benjamin West, Self-portrait A956

Paul Laurence Dunbar A957

D. W. Griffith and Projector A958

1975 Photo. *Perf. 10½x11*

1553 A956	10c multicolored		18	15

Perf. 11

1554 A957	10c multicolored		18	15
a.	Imperf., pair		*1,250.*	

Litho., Engr. (Giori)

1555 A958	10c multicolored		16	15
a.	Brown (engr.) omitted		*750.*	
	Set value			15

Honoring: West (1738-1820), painter (#1553). Dunbar (1872-1906), poet (#1554). David Lewelyn Wark Griffith (1875-1948), motion picture producer (#1555).

Issue dates: No. 1553, Feb. 10. No. 1554, May 1. No. 1555, May 27.

Space Issue

Pioneer 10 Passing Jupiter A959

Mariner 10, Venus and Mercury A960

Lithographed, Engraved (Giori)

1975 *Perf. 11*

1556 A959	10c vio blue, yel & red		16	15
a.	Red (litho.) omitted		*1,400.*	
b.	Blue (engr.) omitted		*800.*	

Imperfs. exist from printer's waste.

1557 A960	10c blk, red, ultra & bis		16	15
a.	Red omitted		*600.*	
b.	Ultra & bister omitted		*1,800.*	
	Set value			15

US unmanned accomplishments in space. Pioneer 10 passed within 81,000 miles of Jupiter, Dec. 3, 1973. Mariner 10 explored Venus and Mercury in 1974, and Mercury again in Mar. 1975.

Issue dates: #1556, Feb. 28; #1557, Apr. 4.

Collective Bargaining Issue

"Labor and Management" A961

1975, Mar. 13 Photo. *Perf. 11*

1558 A961 10c multicolored 18 15

Collective Bargaining Law, enacted 1935 with Wagner Act. Imperfs. are printers waste.

American Bicentennial

Contributors to the Cause

Sybil Ludington A962

Salem Poor — A963

Haym Salomon A964

Peter Francisco A965

1975, Mar. 25 Photo. *Perf. 11x10½*

1559 A962 8c multicolored 15 15
- ***a.*** Back inscription omitted 275.00

1560 A963 10c multicolored 18 15
- ***a.*** Back inscription omitted 225.00

1561 A964 10c multicolored 18 15
- ***a.*** Back inscription omitted 275.00
- ***b.*** Red omitted 225.00

1562 A965 18c multicolored 35 20

Set value 43

Ludington, age 16, rallied militia Apr. 26, 1777. Poor, black freeman, fought in Battle of Bunker Hill. Salomon, Jewish immigrant, raised money to finance Revolutionary War. Francisco, Portuguese-French immigrant, joined Continental Army at 15.

Emerald inscription on back, printed beneath gum in water-soluble ink, gives thumbnail sketch of portrayed contributor.

Lexington-Concord Battle, 200th Anniv.

"Birth of Liberty," by Henry Sandham A966

1975, Apr. 19 Photo. *Perf. 11*

1563 A966 10c multicolored 18 15
- ***a.*** Vert. pair, imperf. horiz. 400.00

Battle of Bunker Hill, 200th Anniv.

Battle of Bunker Hill, by John Trumbull — A967

1975, June 17 *Perf. 11*

1564 A967 10c multicolored 18 15

Military Uniforms

Soldier with Flintlock Musket, Uniform Button — A968

Sailor with Grappling Hook, First Navy Jack, 1775 — A969

Marine with Musket, Full-rigged Ship — A970

Militiaman with Musket, Powder Horn — A971

1975, July 4 *Perf. 11*

1565 A968 10c multicolored 18 15

1566 A969 10c multicolored 18 15

1567 A970 10c multicolored 18 15

1568 A971 10c multicolored 18 15
- ***a.*** Block of 4, #1565-1568 75 75

Set value 32

Bicentenary of US Military Services.

Apollo Soyuz Space Issue

Apollo and Soyuz After Docking and Earth — A972

Spacecraft Before Docking, Earth and Project Emblem — A973

1975, July 15 Photo. *Perf. 11*

1569 A972 10c multicolored 18 15
- ***a.*** Pair, #1569-1570 36 25
- ***b.*** As "a," vert. pair, imperf. horiz. 2,000.

1570 A973 10c multicolored 18 15

Set value 20

Apollo Soyuz space test project (Russo-American cooperation); launching, July 15; link-up, July 17. See Russia Nos. 4339-4340.

International Women's Year Issue

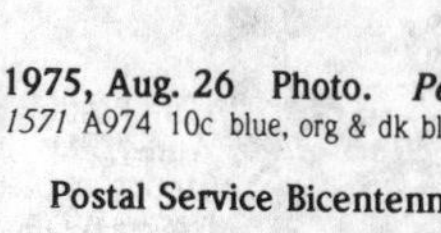

Worldwide Equality for Women A974

1975, Aug. 26 Photo. *Perf. 11x10½*

1571 A974 10c blue, org & dk blue 16 15

Postal Service Bicentennial Issue

Stagecoach and Trailer Truck A975

Old and New Locomotives A976

Early Mail Plane and Jet — A977

Satellite for Transmission of Mailgrams A978

1975, Sept. 3 Photo. *Perf. 11x10½*

1572 A975 10c multicolored 18 15

1573 A976 10c multicolored 18 15

1574 A977 10c multicolored 18 15

1575 A978 10c multicolored 18 15
- ***a.*** Block of 4, #1572-1575 75 80
- ***b.*** As "a," red ("10c") omitted —

Set value 32

World Peace Through Law Issue

Law Book, Olive Branch and Globe A979

Giori Press Printing

1975, Sept. 29 *Perf. 11*

1576 A979 10c green, Prus blue & rose brown 18 15
- ***a.*** Horiz. pair, imperf. vert.

A prelude to 7th World Conf. of the World Peace Through Law Center at Washington, DC, Oct. 12-17.

Banking and Commerce Issue

Engine Turning, Indian Head Penny and Morgan Silver Dollar A980

Seated Liberty Quarter, $20 Gold (Double Eagle), Engine Turning A981

Lithographed, Engraved (Giori)

1975, Oct. 6 *Perf. 11*

1577 A980 10c multicolored 18 15
- ***a.*** Pair, #1577-1578 36 20
- ***b.*** As "a," brown & blue (litho.) omitted 1,400.
- ***c.*** As "a," brown, blue & yellow (litho.) omitted 2,500.

1578 A981 10c multicolored 18 15

Set value 16

Banking and commerce in the US and for the Centennial Convention of the American Bankers Association.

Christmas Issue

Madonna, by Domenico Ghirlandaio A982

Christmas Card, by Louis Prang, 1878 A983

1975, Oct. 14 Photo. *Perf. 11*

1579 A982 (10c) multicolored 18 15
- ***a.*** Imperf., pair 110.00

1580 A983 (10c) multicolored 18 15
- ***a.*** Imperf., pair 120.00
- ***b.*** Perf. 10½x11 60 15

Set value 15

Americana Issue

Inkwell and Quill — A984

Speaker's Stand — A985

Early Ballot Box — A987

Books, Bookmark, Eyeglasses — A988

Dome of Capitol — A994

Contemplation of Justice — A995

Early American Printing Press — A996

Torch — A997

Liberty Bell — A998

Eagle and Shield — A999

Fort McHenry Flag — A1001

Head, Statue of Liberty — A1002

Old North Church, Boston — A1003

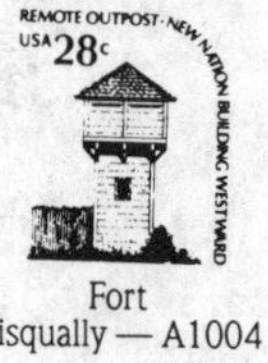

Fort Nisqually — A1004

Sandy Hook Lighthouse, NJ — A1005

Morris Township School No. 2, Devils Lake, ND — A1006

Iron "Betty" Lamp, 17th-18th Cent. — A1007

Rush Lamp and Candle Holder — A1008

Kerosene Table Lamp — A1009

Railroad Conductor's Lantern, c. 1850 — A1010

1975-81 Engr. *Perf. 11x10½*

1581 A984 1c dk blue, *grnsh* 15 15
a. Untagged (Bureau precanceled) 15
1582 A985 2c red brown, *grnsh* 15 15
a. Untagged (Bureau precanceled) 15
b. Cream paper ('81) 15 15
1584 A987 3c olive, *grnsh* 15 15
a. Untagged (Bureau precanceled) 15
1585 A988 4c rose mag, *cr* 15 15
a. Untagged (Bureau precanceled) 1.25

Size: 17½x20½mm

1590 A994 9c slate green 50 20
a. Perf. 10 20.00 12.50

Size: 18½x22½mm

1591 A994 9c slate green, *gray* 16 15
a. Untagged (Bureau precanceled) 18
1592 A995 10c violet, *gray* 18 15
a. Untagged (Bureau precanceled) 25
1593 A996 11c orange, *gray* 20 15
1594 A997 12c brown red, *beige* 22 15
1595 A998 13c brown 25 15
a. Booklet pane of 6 1.90 *50*
b. Booklet pane of 7 + label 1.75 *50*
c. Booklet pane of 8 2.00 *50*
d. Booklet pane of 5 + label ('76) 1.40 *50*
e. Vert. pair, imperf btwn. —

Photo.
Perf. 11

1596 A999 13c multi 22 15
a. Imperf., pair *50.00* —
b. Yellow omitted *200.00*

Engr.

1597 A1001 15c gray, dk blue & red 28 15
a. Vert. pair, imperf. *17.50*
b. Gray omitted *500.00*
c. Vert. strip of 3, imperf. btwn. & at top or bottom —

Perf. 11x10½

1598 A1001 15c gray, dk blue & red 35 15
a. Booklet pane of 8 3.50 *60*
1599 A1002 16c blue 34 15
1603 A1003 24c red, *blue* 45 15
1604 A1004 28c brown, *blue* 55 15
1605 A1005 29c blue, *blue* 55 15
1606 A1006 30c green, *blue* 55 15

Engr. & Litho.
Perf. 11

1608 A1007 50c tan, black & org 85 15
a. Black omitted *300.00*
b. Vert. pair, imperf. horiz. —

Beware of copies offered as No. 1608b that have blind perfs.

1610 A1008 $1 tan, brn, org & yel 1.75 20
a. Brown (engraved) omitted *300.*
b. Tan, orange & yel omitted *350.*
c. Brown inverted *15,000.*
1611 A1009 $2 tan, dk grn, org & yel 3.25 75
1612 A1010 $5 tan, red brn, yel & org 7.50 1.75
Nos. 1581-1612 (22) 18.75
Set value 3.40

Nos. 1590, 1590a, 1595, 1598 issued in booklets only. All stamps have one or two straight edges.

Years of issue: #1591, 1595-1596, 11c, 24c, 1975. #1590, 1c-4c, 10c, 1977. #1597-1598, 16c, 28c, 29c, $2, 1978. 30c-$1, $5, 1979. 12c, 1981.

Guitar A1011

Saxhorns A1012

Drum A1013

Piano A1014

Coil Stamps
Engr.
Perf. 10 Vertically

1613 A1011 3.1c brown, *yel* 15 15
a. Untagged (Bureau precanceled) 50
b. Imperf., pair *1,350.*
1614 A1012 7.7c brown, *brt yel* 20 15
a. Untagged (Bureau precanceled) 35
b. As "a," imperf., pair *1,400.*
1615 A1013 7.9c carmine, *yel* 20 15
a. Untagged (Bureau precanceled) 20
b. Imperf., pair *600.00*
1615C A1014 8.4c dk blue, *yel* 22 15
d. Untagged (Bureau precanceled) 30
e. As "d," pair, imperf. btwn. 50.00
f. As "d," imperf., pair 15.00
1616 A994 9c sl green, *gray* 20 15
a. Imperf., pair *125.00*
b. Untagged (Bureau precanceled) 35
c. As "b," imperf., pair *650.00*
1617 A995 10c violet, *gray* 20 15
a. Untagged (Bureau precanceled) 25
b. Imperf., pair *70.00*
1618 A998 13c brown 25 15
a. Untagged (Bureau precanceled) 45
b. Imperf., pair 25.00
g. Pair, imperf. between —
h. As "a," imperf., pair —
1618C A1001 15c gray, dk blue & red 40 15
d. Imperf., pair 20.00
e. Pair, imperf. between *150.00*
f. Gray omitted *40.00*
1619 A1002 16c blue 32 15
a. Huck press printing 50 15
Nos. 1613-1619 (9) 2.14
Set value 54

The 15c was printed on two different presses. Huck press printings have white background without bluish tinge, are a fraction of a millimeter smaller and have block instead of overall tagging. Cottrell press printings show a joint line.

Years of issue: 9c, 13c, 1975. 7.7c, 7.9c, 1976. 10c, 1977. 8.4c, 15c, 16c, 1978. 3.1c, 1979.

See Nos. 1811, 1813, 1816.

13-Star Flag, Independence Hall A1015

Flag over Capitol A1016

Multicolor Huck Press

1975-77 *Perf. 11x10½*

1622 A1015 13c dark blue & red 24 15
a. Horiz. pair, imperf. btwn. 50.
b. Vert. pair, imperf. *1,250.*
c. Perf. 11 ('81) 65 15
d. As "c," vert. pair, imperf. *150.*
e. Horiz. pair, imperf. vert. —

No. 1622 has overall tagging and nearly vertical multiple gum ridges. No. 1622c has block tagging and flat gum.

1623 A1016 13c blue & red ('77) 22 15
a. Booklet pane of 8 (1 #1590 and 7 #1623) 2.25 *60*
b. Perf. 10 1.00 1.00
c. Booklet pane of 8 (1 #1590a + 7 #1623b) 30.00 —
d. Se-tenant pair, #1590 & 1623 75 —
e. Se-tenant pair, #1590a & 1623b 22.50 —

Coil Stamp
Perf. 10 Vertically

1625 A1015 13c dark blue & red 25 15
a. Imperf., pair 22.50
Set value 15

Nos. 1623 and 1623b issued in booklets only. All stamps have one or two straight edges.

American Bicentennial -- Spirit of '76

Drummer Boy A1019

Old Drummer A1020

Fifer — A1021

Designed after painting "The Spirit of '76," by Archibald M. Willard.

1976, Jan. 1 Photo. *Perf. 11*

1629 A1019 13c multicolored 20 15
1630 A1020 13c multicolored 20 15
1631 A1021 13c multicolored 20 15
a. Strip of 3, #1629-1631 60 60
b. As "a," imperf. *1,450.*
c. Vert. pair, imperf. *750.*
Set value 24

Interphil Issue

"Interphil 76" A1022

Lithographed, Engraved (Giori)

1976, Jan. 17 *Perf. 11*

1632 A1022 13c dk blue, red & ultra 20 15

Interphil 76 Intl. Phil. Exhib., Philadelphia, Pa., May 29-June 6.

State Flags A1023-A1072

1976, Feb. 23 Photo. *Perf. 11*

1633 A1023 13c Delaware 25 20
1634 A1024 13c Pennsylvania 25 20
1635 A1025 13c New Jersey 25 20
1636 A1026 13c Georgia 25 20
1637 A1027 13c Connecticut 25 20
1638 A1028 13c Massachusetts 25 20
1639 A1029 13c Maryland 25 20
1640 A1030 13c South Carolina 25 20
1641 A1031 13c New Hampshire 25 20
1642 A1032 13c Virginia 25 20
1643 A1033 13c New York 25 20
1644 A1034 13c North Carolina 25 20
1645 A1035 13c Rhode Island 25 20
1646 A1036 13c Vermont 25 20
1647 A1037 13c Kentucky 25 20
1648 A1038 13c Tennessee 25 20
1649 A1039 13c Ohio 25 20
1650 A1040 13c Louisiana 25 20
1651 A1041 13c Indiana 25 20
1652 A1042 13c Mississippi 25 20
1653 A1043 13c Illinois 25 20
1654 A1044 13c Alabama 25 20
1655 A1045 13c Maine 25 20
1656 A1046 13c Missouri 25 20
1657 A1047 13c Arkansas 25 20
1658 A1048 13c Michigan 25 20
1659 A1049 13c Florida 25 20
1660 A1050 13c Texas 25 20
1661 A1051 13c Iowa 25 20
1662 A1052 13c Wisconsin 25 20
1663 A1053 13c California 25 20
1664 A1054 13c Minnesota 25 20
1665 A1055 13c Oregon 25 20
1666 A1056 13c Kansas 25 20
1667 A1057 13c West Virginia 25 20
1668 A1058 13c Nevada 25 20
1669 A1059 13c Nebraska 25 20
1670 A1060 13c Colorado 25 20
1671 A1061 13c North Dakota 25 20
1672 A1062 13c South Dakota 25 20
1673 A1063 13c Montana 25 20
1674 A1064 13c Washington 25 20
1675 A1065 13c Idaho 25 20
1676 A1066 13c Wyoming 25 20
1677 A1067 13c Utah 25 20
1678 A1068 13c Oklahoma 25 20
1679 A1069 13c New Mexico 25 20
1680 A1070 13c Arizona 25 20
1681 A1071 13c Alaska 25 20
1682 A1072 13c Hawaii 25 20
a. Pane of 50 13.00 —

Telephone Centenary Issue

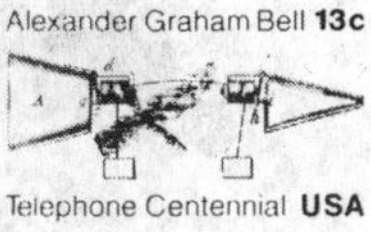

Bell's Telephone Patent Application A1073

Engraved (Giori)

1976, Mar. 10 *Perf. 11*

1683 A1073 13c blk, pur & red, *tan* 22 15

1st telephone call by Alexander Graham Bell, Mar. 10, 1876.

Commercial Aviation Issue

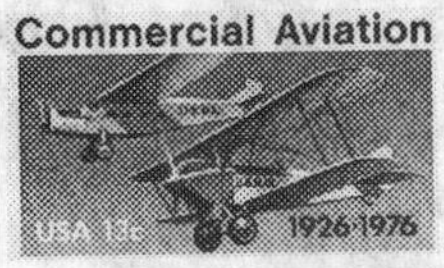

Ford-Pullman Monoplane and Laird Swallow Biplane A1074

1976, Mar. 19 Photo. *Perf. 11*

1684 A1074 13c blue & multi 22 15

50th anniv. of 1st contract airmail flights: Dearborn, MI to Cleveland, OH, Feb. 15, 1926; and Pasco, WA to Elko, NV, Apr. 6, 1926.

Chemistry Issue

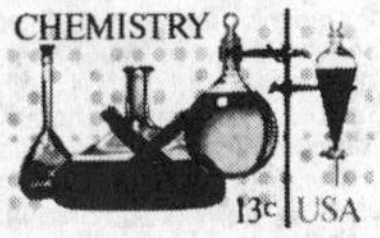

Various Flasks, Separatory Funnel, Computer Tape — A1075

1976, Apr. 6 Photo. *Perf. 11*

1685 A1075 13c multicolored 20 15

Honoring American chemists, cent. of the American Chemical Society.

Surrender of Cornwallis at Yorktown, by John Trumbull
A1076

USA 13c
The Surrender of Lord Cornwallis at Yorktown
From a Painting by John Trumbull

Declaration of Independence, by John Trumbull
A1077

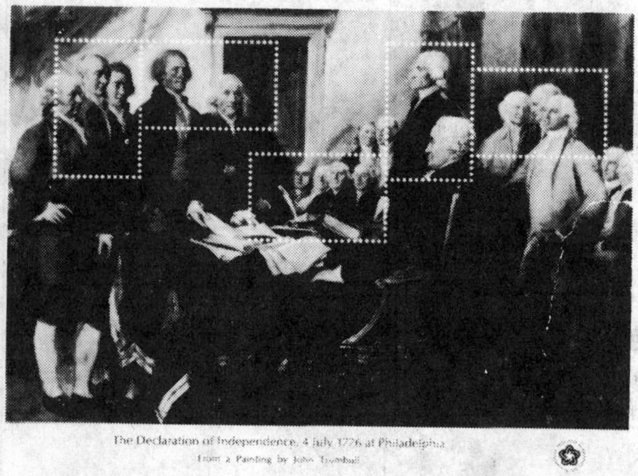

The Declaration of Independence, 4 July 1776 at Philadelphia
From a Painting by John Trumbull

Washington Crossing the Delaware, by Emanuel Leutze/Eastman Johnson
A1078

USA 31c
Washington Reviewing His Ragged Army at Valley Forge
From a Painting by William T. Trego

Washington Reviewing Army at Valley Forge, by William T. Trego
A1079

Designs, from Left to Right, No. 1686: a, Two British officers. b, Gen. Benjamin Lincoln. c, George Washington. d, John Trumbull, Col. Cobb, von Steuben, Lafayette, Thomas Nelson. Alexander Hamilton, John Laurens, Walter Stewart, all vert.

No. 1687: a, John Adams, Roger Sherman, Robert R. Livingston. b, Jefferson, Franklin. c, Thomas Nelson, Jr., Francis Lewis, John Witherspoon, Samuel Huntington. d, John Hancock, Charles Thomson. e, George Read, John Dickinson, Edward Rutledge (a, d, vert., b, c, e, horiz.).

No. 1688: a, Boatsman. b, Washington. c, Flag bearer. d, Men in boat. e, Men on shore (a, d, horiz., b, c, e, vert.).

No. 1689: a, Two officers. b, Washington. c, Officer, black horse. d, Officer, white horse. e, Three soldiers (a, c, e, horiz., b, d, vert.).

1976, May 29 — Litho. — *Perf. 11*

1686	A1076	Sheet of 5	3.25	—
	a.-e.	13c multi, any single	45	40
	f.	USA 13c omitted on "b," "c" & "d," imperf., untagged	—	*2,000.*
	g.	USA 13c omitted on "a" & "e"	*450.*	—
	h.	Imperf., untagged		*2,000.*
	i.	USA 13c omitted on "b," "c" & "d"	*450.*	
	j.	USA 13c double on "b"	—	
	k.	USA 13c omitted on "c" & "d"	—	
	l.	USA 13c omitted on "e"	*500.*	
	m.	USA 13c omitted, imperf., untagged	—	—
1687	A1077	Sheet of 5	4.25	—
	a.-e.	18c multi, any single	55	55
	f.	Design & marginal inscriptions omitted	*3,000.*	
	g.	USA 18c omitted on "a" & "c"	*800.*	
	h.	USA 18c omitted on "b," "d" & "e"	*500.*	
	i.	USA 18c omitted on "d"	*500.*	*500.*
	j.	Black omitted in design	*1,750.*	
	k.	USA 18c omitted, imperf., untagged	*3,000.*	
	m.	USA 18c omitted on "b" & "e"	*500.*	
	n.	USA 18c omitted on "b" & "d"	—	
1688	A1078	Sheet of 5	5.25	—
	a.-e.	24c multi, any single	70	70
	f.	USA 24c omitted, imperf., untagged	*3,250.*	
	g.	USA 24c omitted on "d" & "e"	—	*450.*
	h.	Design & marginal inscriptions omitted	*3,250.*	
	i.	USA 24c omitted on "a," "b" & "c"	*500.*	—
	j.	Imperf., untagged	*2,750.*	
	k.	USA 24c of "d" & "e" inverted	—	
1689	A1079	Sheet of 5	6.25	—
	a.-e.	31c multi, any single	85	85
	f.	USA 31c omitted, imperf., untagged	*2,750.*	
	g.	USA 31c omitted on "a" & "c"	—	
	h.	USA 31c omitted on "b," "d" & "e"	—	—
	i.	USA 31c omitted on "e"	*500.*	
	j.	Black omitted in design	*1,500.*	
	k.	Imperf., untagged		*2,250.*
	l.	USA 31c omitted on "b" & "d"	—	
	m.	USA 31c omitted on "a" "c" & "e"	—	
	n.	As "m," imperf., untagged	—	
	p.	As "h," imperf., untagged		*2,500.*
	q.	As "g," imperf., untagged	*2,750.*	
	r.	USA 31c omitted on "d" & "e"	—	
		Nos. 1686-1689 (4)	19.00	

Nos. 1688-1689 exist with inverted perforations.

Issued in connection with Interphil 76 Intl. Phil. Exhib., Philadelphia, Pa., May 29-June 6. Size of sheets: 203x152mm; stamps: 25x39½mm, 39½x25mm.

Benjamin Franklin Issue

Franklin and Map of North America, 1776 — A1080

Lithographed, Engraved (Giori)

1976, June 1 — *Perf. 11*

1690	A1080	13c ultra & multi	20	15
	a.	Light blue omitted	*300.00*	

American Bicentennial; Franklin (1706-1790), deputy postmaster general for the colonies (1753-1774) and statesman.

See Canada No. 691

American Bicentennial Issue

Declaration of Independence, by John Trumbull
A1081 A1082 A1083 A1084

1976, July 4 — Photo. — *Perf. 11*

1691	A1081	13c multicolored	20	15
1692	A1082	13c multicolored	20	15
1693	A1083	13c multicolored	20	15
1694	A1084	13c multicolored	20	15
	a.	Strip of 4, #1691-1694	85	75
		Set value		32

Olympic Games Issue

Diving A1085 — Skiing A1086

Running A1087 — Skating A1088

1976, July 16	Photo.	Perf. 11	
1695 A1085 13c multicolored		28	15
1696 A1086 13c multicolored		28	15
1697 A1087 13c multicolored		28	15
1698 A1088 13c multicolored		28	15
a. Block of 4, #1695-1698		1.15	85
b. As "a," imperf.		*750.00*	
Set value			32

12th Winter Olympic Games, Innsbruck, Austria, Feb. 4-15, and 21st Summer Olympic Games, Montreal, Canada, July 17-Aug. 1.

Clara Maass Issue

Clara Maass, Newark German Hospital Pin — A1089

1976, Aug. 18	Photo.	Perf. 11	
1699 A1089 13c multicolored		20	15
a. Horiz. pair, imperf. vert.		*400.00*	

Clara Maass (1876-1901), volunteer in fight against yellow fever, birth centenary.

Adolph S. Ochs Issue

Adolph S. Ochs (1858-1935), Publisher of the NY Times, 1896-1935 A1090

Giori Press Printing

1976, Sept. 18		Perf. 11	
1700 A1090 13c black & gray		20	15

Christmas Issue

Nativity, by John Singleton Copley A1091

"Winter Pastime," by Nathaniel Currier A1092

1976, Oct. 27	Photo.	Perf. 11	
1701 A1091 13c multicolored		20	15
a. Imperf., pair		*100.00*	
1702 A1092 13c multicolored		22	15
a. Imperf., pair		*110.00*	
1703 A1092 13c multicolored		22	15
a. Imperf., pair		*125.00*	
b. Vert. pair, imperf. btwn.		—	
Set value			15

No. 1702 has overall tagging. Lettering at base is black and usually ½mm below design. As a rule, no "snowflaking" in sky or pond. Pane of 50 has margins on 4 sides with slogans.

No. 1703 has block tagging the size of printed area. Lettering at base is gray black and usually ¾mm below design. "Snowflaking" generally in sky and pond. Pane has margin only at right or left, and no slogans. Copies are known with various amounts of red missing.

American Bicentennial Issue

Washington at Princeton

Washington, Nassau Hall, Hessians, 13-Star Flag, by Charles Willson Peale — A1093

1977, Jan. 3	Photo.	Perf. 11	
1704 A1093 13c multicolored		22	15
a. Horiz. pair, imperf. vert.		*500.00*	

Washington's victory at Princeton over Lord Cornwallis, bicentennial.

Sound Recording Issue

Tin Foil Phonograph A1094

Lithographed, Engraved (Giori)

1977, Mar. 23		Perf. 11	
1705 A1094 13c black & multi		22	15

Centenary of invention of the phonograph by Thomas Alva Edison, and development of sophisticated recording industry.

American Folk Art Issue

Pueblo Pottery

Zia Pot — A1095

San Ildefonso Pot — A1096

Hopi Pot — A1097

Acoma Pot — A1098

1977, Apr. 13	Photo.	Perf. 11	
1706 A1095 13c multicolored		22	15
1707 A1096 13c multicolored		22	15
1708 A1097 13c multicolored		22	15
1709 A1098 13c multicolored		22	15
a. Block or strip of 4		90	60
b. As "a," imperf. vert.		*2,250.*	
Set value			32

Pueblo art, 1880-1920, from museums in NM, AZ and CO.

Lindbergh Flight Issue

Spirit of St. Louis A1099

1977, May 20	Photo.	Perf. 11	
1710 A1099 13c multicolored		22	15
a. Imperf., pair		*1,150.*	

Charles A. Lindbergh's solo transatlantic flight from NY to Paris, 50th anniv.

Colorado Statehood Issue

Columbine and Rocky Mountains — A1100

1977, May 21	Photo.	Perf. 11	
1711 A1100 13c multicolored		22	15
a. Horiz. pair, imperf. btwn.		*500.00*	
b. Horiz. pair, imperf. vert.		*900.00*	

Colorado became a state in 1876.

Butterfly Issue

Swallowtail A1101

Checkerspot A1102

Dogface A1103

Orange Tip — A1104

1977, June 6	Photo.	Perf. 11	
1712 A1101 13c tan & multi		22	15
1713 A1102 13c tan & multi		22	15
1714 A1103 13c tan & multi		22	15
1715 A1104 13c tan & multi		22	15
a. Block of 4, #1712-1715		90	60
b. As "a," imperf. horiz.		*15,000.*	
Set value			32

American Bicentennial Issues

Lafayette

Marquis de Lafayette — A1105

1977, June 13	Engr.	Perf. 11	
1716 A1105 13c blue, black & red		22	15

200th anniv. of Lafayette's landing on the coast of SC, north of Charleston.

Skilled Hands for Independence

Seamstress A1106

Blacksmith A1107

Wheelwright A1108

Leatherworker A1109

1977, July 4	Photo.	Perf. 11	
1717 A1106 13c multicolored		22	15
1718 A1107 13c multicolored		22	15
1719 A1108 13c multicolored		22	15
1720 A1109 13c multicolored		22	15
a. Block of 4, #1717-1720		90	80
Set value			32

Peace Bridge Issue

Peace Bridge and Dove — A1110

1977, Aug. 4	Engr.	Perf. 11x10½	
1721 A1110 13c blue		22	15

50th anniv. of the Peace Bridge, connecting Buffalo, NY with Fort Erie, Ontario.

American Bicentennial Issue

Battle of Oriskany

Herkimer at Oriskany, by Frederick Yohn A1111

1977, Aug. 6	Photo.	Perf. 11	
1722 A1111 13c multicolored		22	15

200th anniv. of Battle of Oriskany, American Militia led by Brig. Gen. Nicholas Herkimer (1728-1777).

Energy Issue

Energy Conservation
A1112

Energy Development
A1113

1977, Oct. 20 Photo. *Perf. 11*

1723 A1112 13c multicolored 22 15
a. Pair, #1723-1724 45 40
1724 A1113 13c multicolored 22 15
Set value 16

Conservation and development of nation's energy resources.

Alta California Issue

Farm Houses A1114

Litho. & Engraved (Giori)

1977, Sept. 9 *Perf. 11*

1725 A1114 13c black & multi 22 15

El Pueblo de San José de Guadalupe, 1st civil settlement in Alta California, 200th anniv.

American Bicentennial Issue

Articles of Confederation

Members of Continental Congress in Conference A1115

Engraved (Giori)

1977, Sept. 30 *Perf. 11*

1726 A1115 13c red & brn, *cream* 22 15

200th anniv. of drafting the Articles of Confederation, York Town, Pa.

Talking Picture, 50th Anniv. Issue

Movie Projector and Phonograph A1116

Litho. & Engraved (Giori)

1977, Oct. 6 *Perf. 11*

1727 A1116 13c multicolored 22 15

American Bicentennial Issue

Surrender at Saratoga

Surrender of Burgoyne, by John Trumbull A1117

1977, Oct. 7 Photo. *Perf. 11*

1728 A1117 13c multicolored 22 15

200th anniv. of Gen. John Burgoyne's surrender at Saratoga.

Christmas Issue

Washington at Valley Forge A1118

Rural Mailbox A1119

1977, Oct. 21 Photo. *Perf. 11*

1729 A1118 13c multicolored 22 15
a. Imperf., pair 75.00
1730 A1119 13c multicolored 22 15
a. Imperf., pair 300.00
Set value 15

Carl Sandburg Issue

Carl Sandburg, by William A. Smith, 1952 — A1120

Engraved (Giori)

1978, Jan. 6 *Perf. 11*

1731 A1120 13c black & brown 22 15

Sandburg (1878-1967), poet, biographer and collector of American folk songs.

Captain Cook Issue

Capt. Cook, by Nathaniel Dance, 1776 A1121

"Resolution" and "Discovery," by John Webber A1122

Giori Press Printing

1978, Jan. 20 *Perf. 11*

1732 A1121 13c dark blue 22 15
a. Pair, #1732-1733 50 30
b. As "a," imperf. between 4,500.
1733 A1122 13c green 22 15
a. Vert. pair, imperf. horiz. —
Set value 16

Capt. James Cook, 200th anniv. of his arrival in Hawaii, at Waimea, Kauai, Jan. 20, 1778, and of his anchorage in Cook Inlet, near Anchorage, Alaska, June 1, 1778. Nos. 1732-1733 issued in panes of 50, containing 25 each of Nos. 1732-1733 including 5 No. 1732a. Design of No. 1733 is after etching "A View of Karakekooa in Owyhee."

Indian Head Penny, 1877 A1123

Eagle A1124

Roses — A1126

Engraved (Giori)

1978, Jan. 11 *Perf. 11*

1734 A1123 13c brown & blue green, *bister* 24 15
a. Horiz. pair, imperf. vert. 300.00

1978, May 22 Photo. *Perf. 11*

1735 A1124 (15c) orange 24 15
a. Imperf., pair 75.00
b. Vert. pair, imperf. horiz. 500.00

Engr. *Perf. 11x10½*

1736 A1124 (15c) orange 25 15
a. Booklet pane of 8 2.25 60

See No. 1743

1978, July 11 Engr. *Perf. 10*

1737 A1126 15c multicolored 25 15
a. Booklet pane of 8 2.25 60
b. As "a," imperf. —
Set value, #1734-1737 24

Nos. 1736, 1737 issued in booklets only. All stamps have 1 or 2 straight edges.

Robertson Windmill, Williamsburg A1127

Old Windmill, Portsmouth A1128

Cape Cod Windmill, Eastham — A1129

Dutch Mill, Batavia — A1130

Southwestern Windmill — A1131

1980, Feb. 7 Engr. *Perf. 11*

Booklet Stamps

1738 A1127 15c sepia, *yellow* 30 15
1739 A1128 15c sepia, *yellow* 30 15
1740 A1129 15c sepia, *yellow* 30 15
1741 A1130 15c sepia, *yellow* 30 15
1742 A1131 15c sepia, *yellow* 30 15
a. Bklt. pane, 2 each #1738-1742 3.50 60
b. Strip of 5, #1738-1742 1.50 —
Nos. 1738-1742 (5) 1.50
Set value 25

Coil Stamp

1978, May 22 Engr. *Perf. 10 Vert.*

1743 A1124 (15c) orange 25 15
a. Imperf., pair 90.00

No. 1743a is valued in the grade of fine.

Black Heritage Issue

Harriet Tubman (1820-1913), Cart Carrying Slaves — A1133

1978, Feb. 1 Photo. *Perf. 10½x11*

1744 A1133 13c multicolored 22 15

Tubman, born a slave, helped more than 300 slaves escape to freedom.

American Folk Art Issue

American Quilts, Basket Design

A1134 A1135

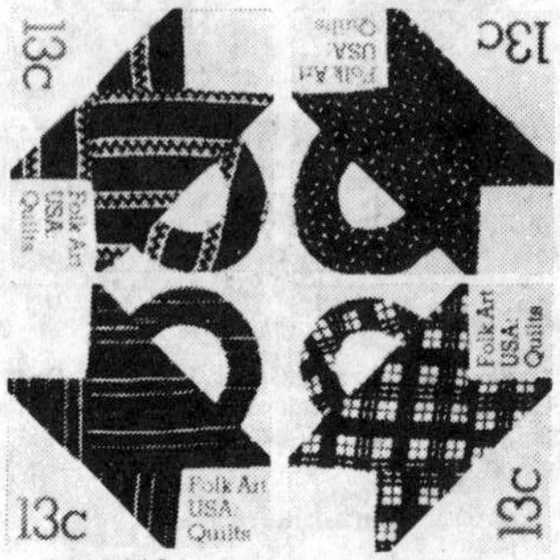

A1136 A1137

1978, Mar. 8 Photo. *Perf. 11*

1745 A1134 13c multicolored 22 15
1746 A1135 13c multicolored 22 15
1747 A1136 13c multicolored 22 15
1748 A1137 13c multicolored 22 15
a. Block of 4, #1745-1748 90 60

American Dance Issue

Ballet A1138

Theater A1139

Folk Dance A1140

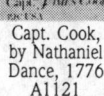

Modern Dance A1141

1978, Apr. 26 Photo. *Perf. 11*

1749 A1138 13c multicolored 22 15
1750 A1139 13c multicolored 22 15
1751 A1140 13c multicolored 22 15
1752 A1141 13c multicolored 22 15
a. Block of 4, #1749-1752 90 60
Set value 32

American Bicentennial Issue

French Alliance

Louis XVI and Franklin, Porcelain Sculpture by C. G. Sauvage — A1142

Giori Press Printing

1978, May 4 *Perf. 11*

1753 A1142 13c blue, black & red 22 15

Bicent. of French Alliance, signed in Paris, Feb. 6, 1778, and ratified by Continental Cong., May 4.

Early Cancer Detection Issue

Dr. George Papanicolaou (1883-1962), his Signature and Microscope — A1143

1978, May 18 Engr. *Perf. 10¹/₂x11*

1754 A1143 13c brown 24 15

Papanicolaou, developer of Pap Test, early cancer detection in women.

Performing Arts Issues

Jimmie Rodgers and Locomotive A1144

George M. Cohan, "Yankee Doodle Dandy" and Stars A1145

1978 Photo. *Perf. 11*

1755 A1144 13c multicolored 24 15
1756 A1145 15c multicolored 26 15
Set value 15

Rodgers (1897-1933), the "Singing Brakeman, Father of Country Music," and Cohan (1878-1942), actor and playwright.

Issue dates: #1755, May 24; #1756, July 3.

CAPEX Issue

Wildlife from Canadian-US Border — A1146

Litho. & Engr. (Giori)

1978, June 10 *Perf. 11*

1757 A1146 Block of 8 1.65 1.65
a. 13c Cardinal 20 15
b. 13c Mallard 20 15
c. 13c Canada goose 20 15
d. 13c Blue jay 20 15
e. 13c Moose 20 15
f. 13c Chipmunk 20 15
g. 13c Red fox 20 15
h. 13c Raccoon 20 15
i. Yellow, green, red, brown, blue, black (litho.) omitted *5,000.*

CAPEX, Canadian Intl. Phil. Exhib., Toronto, Ont., June 9-18.

Photography Issue

Photographic Equipment A1147

1978, June 26 Photo. *Perf. 11*

1758 A1147 15c multicolored 26 15

Viking Missions to Mars Issue

Viking 1 Lander Scooping Up Soil on Mars A1148

1978, July 20 Litho. & Engr.

1759 A1148 15c multicolored 26 15

2nd anniv. of landing of Viking 1 on Mars.

American Owls Issue

Great Gray Owl A1149

Saw-whet Owl A1150

Barred Owl A1151

Great Horned Owl A1152

1978, Aug. 26 Engr. *Perf. 11*

1760 A1149 15c multicolored 26 15
1761 A1150 15c multicolored 26 15
1762 A1151 15c multicolored 26 15
1763 A1152 15c multicolored 26 15
a. Block of 4, #1760-1763 1.05 85
Set value 32

American Trees Issue

Giant Sequoia A1153

White Pine A1154

White Oak — A1155

Gray Birch A1156

1978, Oct. 9 Photo. *Perf. 11*

1764 A1153 15c multicolored 26 15
1765 A1154 15c multicolored 26 15
1766 A1155 15c multicolored 26 15
1767 A1156 15c multicolored 26 15
a. Block of 4, #1764-1767 1.05 85
b. As "a," imperf. horiz. *12,500.*
Set value 32

Christmas Issue

Madonna and Child with Cherubim, by Andrea della Robbia — A1157

Child on Hobby-horse and Christmas Trees — A1158

1978, Oct. 18 Photo. *Perf. 11*

1768 A1157 15c blue & multi 26 15
a. Imperf., pair *90.00*
1769 A1158 15c red & multi 26 15
a. Imperf., pair *100.00*
b. Vert. pair, imperf. horiz. *1,750.*
Set value 15

Value for #1768a is for an uncreased pair.

Robert F. Kennedy Issue

Robert F. Kennedy (1925-68), US Attorney General — A1159

1979, Jan. 12 Engr. *Perf. 11*

1770 A1159 15c blue 26 15

Black Heritage Issue

Dr. Martin Luther King, Jr. (1929-68), and Civil Rights Marchers — A1160

1979, Jan. 13 Photo. *Perf. 11*

1771 A1160 15c multicolored 26 15
a. Imperf., pair

Civil rights leader.

Year of the Child Issue

Children A1161

1979, Feb. 15 Engr. *Perf. 11*

1772 A1161 15c orange red 26 15

International Year of the Child.

John Steinbeck A1162

Albert Einstein A1163

John Steinbeck Issue

1979, Feb. 27 Engr. *Perf. 10¹/₂x11*

1773 A1162 15c dark blue 26 15

John Ernst Steinbeck (1902-68), novelist.

Albert Einstein Issue

1979, Mar. 4 Engr. *Perf. 10¹/₂x11*

1774 A1163 15c chocolate 28 15

Einstein (1879-1955), theoretical physicist.

American Folk Art Issue

Pennsylvania Toleware

Coffeepot A1164

Tea Caddy A1165

Sugar Bowl A1166

Coffeepot A1167

1979, Apr. 19 Photo. *Perf. 11*

1775 A1164 15c multicolored 28 15
1776 A1165 15c multicolored 28 15
1777 A1166 15c multicolored 28 15

1778 A1167 15c multicolored 28 15
a. Block of 4, #1775-1778 1.15 85
b. As "a," imperf. horiz. *4,250.*
Set value 32

American Architecture Issue

Virginia Rotunda, by Thomas Jefferson A1168

Baltimore Cathedral, by Benjamin Latrobe A1169

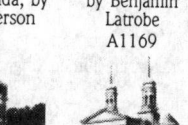

Boston State House, by Charles Bulfinch A1170

Philadelphia Exchange, by William Strickland A1171

1979, June 4 Engr. *Perf. 11*
1779 A1168 15c black & brick red 28 15
1780 A1169 15c black & brick red 28 15
1781 A1170 15c black & brick red 28 15
1782 A1171 15c black & brick red 28 15
a. Block of 4, #1779-1782 1.15 85
Set value 32

Endangered Flora Issue

Persistent Trillium A1172

Hawaiian Wild Broadbean A1173

Contra Costa Wallflower A1174

Antioch Dunes Evening Primrose A1175

1979, June 7 Photo. *Perf. 11*
1783 A1172 15c multicolored 28 15
1784 A1173 15c multicolored 28 15
1785 A1174 15c multicolored 28 15
1786 A1175 15c multicolored 28 15
a. Block of 4, #1783-1786 1.15 85
b. As "a," imperf. *600.00*
Set value 32

Seeing Eye Dogs Issue

German Shepherd Leading Man — A1176

1979, June 15
1787 A1176 15c multicolored 28 15
a. Imperf., pair *400.00*

Special Olympics Issue

Child Holding Winner's Medal — A1177

1979, Aug. 9 *Perf. 11*
1788 A1177 15c multicolored 28 15

Special Olympics for special children, Brockport, NY, Aug. 8-13.

John Paul Jones Issue

John Paul Jones, by Charles Willson Peale — A1178

1979, Sept. 23 Photo. *Perf. 11x12*
1789 A1178 15c multicolored 28 15
a. Perf. 11 30 15
b. Perf. 12 *2,000.* *1,000.*
c. Vert. pair, imperf. horiz. *200.*
d. As "a," vert. pair, imperf horiz. *150.*

John Paul Jones (1747-1792), Naval Commander, American Revolution.
Imperfs., perf. or imperf. gutter pairs and blocks exist from printer's waste.

Olympic Games Issue

Decathlon, Javelin A1179

Running A1180

Swimming, Women's A1181

Rowing — A1182

Equestrian A1183

1979 Photo. *Perf. 11*
1790 A1179 10c multicolored 20 20
1791 A1180 15c multicolored 28 15
1792 A1181 15c multicolored 28 15
1793 A1182 15c multicolored 28 15
1794 A1183 15c multicolored 28 15
a. Block of 4, #1791-1794 1.15 85
b. As "a," imperf. *1,400.*
Set value 52

22nd Summer Olympic Games, Moscow, July 19-Aug. 3, 1980.
Issue dates: 10c, Sept. 5; 15c, Sept. 28.

Winter Olympic Games Issue

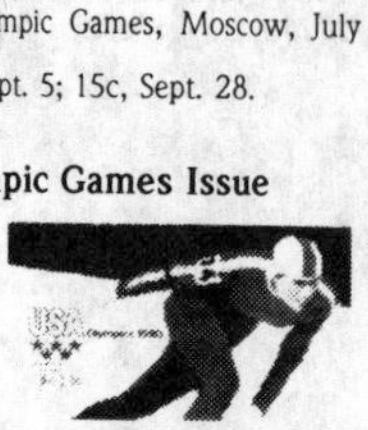

Speed Skating — A1184

Downhill Skiing — A1185

Ski Jump — A1186

Hockey Goaltender A1187

1980, Feb. 1 Photo. *Perf. 11x10½*
1795 A1184 15c multicolored 32 15
a. Perf. 11 1.05 —
1796 A1185 15c multicolored 32 15
a. Perf. 11 1.05 —
1797 A1186 15c multicolored 32 15
a. Perf. 11 1.05 —
1798 A1187 15c multicolored 32 15
a. Perf. 11 1.05 —
b. Block of 4, #1795-1798 1.30 1.00
c. Block of 4, #1795a-1798a 4.25 —
Set value 32

13th Winter Olympic Games, Lake Placid, NY, Feb. 12-24.

Christmas Issue

Virgin and Child, by Gerard David — A1188

Santa Claus, Christmas Tree Ornament — A1189

1979, Oct. 18 Photo. *Perf. 11*
1799 A1188 15c multicolored 28 15
a. Imperf., pair *100.*
b. Vert. pair, imperf. horiz. *700.*
c. Vert. pair, imperf. btwn. 2,250.
1800 A1189 15c multicolored 28 15
a. Green & yellow omitted *500.*
b. Green, yellow & tan omitted *650.*
Set value 15

Nos. 1800a, 1800b always have the remaining colors misaligned,
No. 1800b is valued in the grade of fine.

Performing Arts Issue

Will Rogers (1879-1935), Actor and Humorist — A1190

1979, Nov. 4 Photo. *Perf. 11*
1801 A1190 15c multicolored 28 15
a. Imperf., pair *225.00*

Viet Nam Veterans Issue

Ribbon for Viet Nam Service Medal A1191

1979, Nov. 11 Photo. *Perf. 11*
1802 A1191 15c multicolored 28 15

A tribute to veterans of the Viet Nam War.

Performing Arts Issue

W.C. Fields (1880-1946), actor and comedian — A1192

1980, Jan. 29 Photo. *Perf. 11*
1803 A1192 15c multicolored 28 15
a. Imperf., pair —

Black Heritage

Benjamin Banneker (1731-1806), Astronomer and Mathematician, Transverse — A1193

1980, Feb. 15 Photo. *Perf. 11*
1804 A1193 15c multicolored 28 15
a. Horiz. pair, imperf. vert. *800.00*

Imperf. printer's waste has been fraudulently perforated to simulate No. 1804a. Legitimate examples of No. 1804a do not have colors misregistered.

Letter Writing

Letters Preserve Memories A1194

P.S. Write Soon A1195

Letters Lift Spirits A1196

Letters Shape Opinions A1197

1980, Feb. 25
1805 A1194 15c multicolored 28 15
1806 A1195 15c claret & multi 28 15
1807 A1196 15c multicolored 28 15
1808 A1195 15c green & multi 28 15
1809 A1197 15c multicolored 28 15
1810 A1195 15c red & multi 28 15
a. Vert. strip of 6 #1805-1810 1.75 1.50
Nos. 1805-1810 (6) 1.68
Set value 48

Natl. Letter Writing Week, Feb. 24-Mar. 1.

Americana Type

Weaver Violins — A1199

Coil Stamps

1980-81 Engr. *Perf. 10 Vert.*
1811 A984 1c dk blue, *grnsh* 15 15
a. Imperf., pair *175.00*

1813 A1199 3.5c purple, *yel* 15 15
a. Untagged (Bureau precanceled, lines only) 15
b. Imperf., pair *225.00*
1816 A997 12c brown red, *beige* ('81) 24 15
a. Untagged (Bureau precanceled) 25
b. Imperf., pair *175.00*
Set value 36 15

A1207

1981, Mar. 15 Photo. *Perf. 11x10½*
1818 A1207 (18c) violet 32 15

Engr. *Perf. 10*
Booklet Stamp
1819 A1207 (18c) violet 40 15
a. Booklet pane of 8 3.50 *1.50*

Coil Stamp
Perf. 10 Vert.
1820 A1207 (18c) violet 40 15
a. Imperf., pair *125.00*
Set value 15

Frances Perkins

Frances Perkins (1882-1965), Sec. of Labor, 1933-45 (1st Woman Cabinet Member) — A1208

1980, Apr. 10 *Perf. 10½x11*
1821 A1208 15c Prus blue 28 15

Dolley Madison

Dolley Madison (1768-1849), First Lady, 1809-1817 — A1209

1980, May 20 *Perf. 11*
1822 A1209 15c red brown & sepia 28 15

Emily Bissell

Emily Bissell (1861-1948), Social Worker; Introduced Christmas seals in US — A1210

1980, May 31
1823 A1210 15c black & red 28 15
a. Vert. pair, imperf. horiz. *350.00*

Helen Keller

Helen Keller and Anne Sullivan — A1211

Litho. & Engr.
1980, June 27 *Perf. 11*
1824 A1211 15c multicolored 28 15

Keller (1880-1968), blind and deaf writer and lecturer taught by Sullivan (1867-1936).

Veterans Admin-istration Emblem A1212

Gen. Bernardo de Galvez A1213

Veterans Administration

1980, July 21 Photo.
1825 A1212 15c car & vio bl 28 15
a. Horiz. pair, imperf. vert. *450.00*

General Bernardo de Galvez

1980, July 23 Engr. *Perf. 11*
1826 A1213 15c multicolored 28 15
a. Red, brn & bl (engr.) omitted *800.00*
b. Red, brn, bl (engr.), bl & yel (litho.) omitted *1,400.*

Galvez (1746-1786), helped defeat British in Battle of Mobile, 1780.

Coral Reefs

Brain Coral, Beaugregory Fish A1214

Elkhorn Coral, Porkfish A1215

Chalice Coral, Moorish Idol Fish A1216

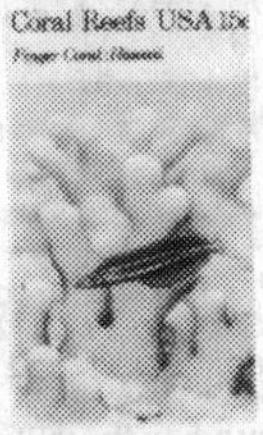

Finger Coral, Sabertooth Blenny Fish A1217

1980, Aug. 26 Photo. *Perf. 11*
1827 A1214 15c multicolored 26 15
1828 A1215 15c multicolored 26 15
1829 A1216 15c multicolored 26 15
1830 A1217 15c multicolored 26 15
a. Block of 4, #1827-1830 1.05 85
b. As "a," imperf. *1,250.*
c. As "a," vert. imperf. btwn. —
d. As "a," imperf. vert. *3,000.*
Set value 32

American Bald Eagle A1218

Edith Wharton A1219

Organized Labor

1980, Sept. 1 Photo. *Perf. 11*
1831 A1218 15c multicolored 28 15
a. Imperf., pair *375.00*

Edith Wharton

1980, Sept. 5 Engr. *Perf. 10½x11*
1832 A1219 15c purple 28 15

Edith Wharton (1862-1937), writer.

American Education

"Homage to the Square: Glow," by Josef Albers — A1220

1980, Sept. 12 Photo. *Perf. 11*
1833 A1220 15c multicolored 28 15
a. Horiz. pair, imperf. btwn. *250.00*

American Folk Art

Pacific Northwest Indian Masks

Heiltsuk, Bella Bella Tribe A1221

Chilkat Tlingit Tribe A1222

Tlingit Tribe A1223

Bella Coola Tribe A1224

1980, Sept. 25
1834 A1221 15c multicolored 30 15
1835 A1222 15c multicolored 30 15
1836 A1223 15c multicolored 30 15
1837 A1224 15c multicolored 30 15
a. Block of 4, #1834-1837 1.25 85
Set value 32

American Architecture

Smithsonian Institution, by James Renwick A1225

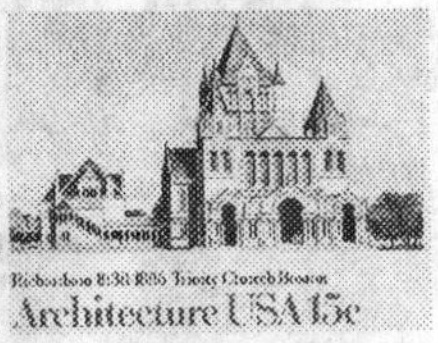

Trinity Church, Boston, by Henry Hobson Richardson A1226

Pennsylvania Academy of Fine Arts, by Frank Furness A1227

Lyndhurst, Tarrytown, NY, by Alexander Jackson Davis A1228

1980, Oct. 9 Engr. *Perf. 11*
1838 A1225 15c black & brick red 30 15
1839 A1226 15c black & brick red 30 15
1840 A1227 15c black & brick red 30 15
1841 A1228 15c black & brick red 30 15
a. Block of 4, #1838-1841 1.25 85
Set value 32

Christmas

Madonna and Child A1229

Wreath, Toys on Windowsill A1230

1980, Oct. 31 Photo. *Perf. 11*
1842 A1229 15c multicolored 28 15
a. Imperf., pair *80.00*
1843 A1230 15c multicolored 28 15
a. Imperf., pair *80.00*
b. Buff omitted 25.00
Set value 15

No. 1843b is difficult to identify and should have a competent certificate.

Great Americans

A1231

A1232

A1233

A1234

A1235

A1236

A1237

A1238

A1239

A1240

A1241

A1242

A1243

A1244

A1245

A1246

A1247

A1248

A1249

A1250

A1251

A1252

A1253

A1254

A1255

A1256

Perf. 11x10½, 11 (1, 6-11, 14, #1862, 22, 30, 39, 40, 50c)

1980-85 **Engr.**

1844 A1231 1c black	15	15
a. Imperf. pair	*350.*	
b. Vert. pair, imperf. btwn.	—	
d. Vert. pair, imperf. horiz.	—	
1845 A1232 2c brown black	15	15
1846 A1233 3c olive green	15	15
1847 A1234 4c violet	15	15
1848 A1235 5c henna brown	15	15
1849 A1236 6c orange ver	15	15
a. Vert. pair, imperf. btwn. and at bottom	*2,300.*	
1850 A1237 7c brt carmine	15	15
1851 A1238 8c olive black	15	15
1852 A1239 9c dark green	16	15
1853 A1240 10c Prus blue	18	15
a. Vert. pair, imperf. btwn. & at bottom	1,100.	
b. Horiz. pair, imperf. btwn.	*2,250.*	

Completely imperforate tagged or untagged stamps are from printer's waste.

1854 A1241 11c dark blue	20	15
1855 A1242 13c lt maroon	24	15
1856 A1243 14c slate green	25	15
a. Vert. pair, imperf. horiz.	*150.*	
b. Horiz. pair, imperf. btwn.	8.50	
c. Vert. pair, imperf. btwn.	*1,750.*	
1857 A1244 17c green	32	15
1858 A1245 18c dark blue	32	15
1859 A1246 19c brown	35	15
1860 A1247 20c claret	40	15
1861 A1248 20c green	38	15
1862 A1249 20c black	38	15
1863 A1250 22c dk chalky blue	40	15
a. Vert. pair, imperf. horiz.	*2,500.*	
b. Vert. pair, imperf. btwn.	—	
c. Horiz. pair, imperf. btwn.	*2,250.*	
1864 A1251 30c olive gray	55	15
1865 A1252 35c gray	65	15
1866 A1253 37c blue	70	15
1867 A1254 39c rose lilac	70	15
a. Vert. pair, imperf. horiz.	*600.*	
b. Vert. pair, imperf. btwn.	*1,750.*	
1868 A1255 40c dark green	70	15
1869 A1256 50c brown	90	15
Nos. 1844-1869 (26)	8.98	
Set value		1.50

Years of issue: 19c, 1980. 17c, 18c, 35c, 1981. No. 1860, 2c, 13c, 37c, 1982. No. 1861, 1c, 3c-5c, 1983. No. 1862, 10c, 30c, 40c, 1984. 6c-9c, 11c, 14c, 22c, 39c, 50c, 1985.

Everett Dirksen

Everett Dirksen (1896-1969), Senate Minority Leader, 1960-69 — A1261

1981, Jan. 4 ***Perf. 11***

1874 A1261 15c gray	28	15

Black Heritage

Whitney Moore Young (1921-1971), Civil Rights Leader — A1262

1981, Jan. 30 **Photo.** ***Perf. 11***

1875 A1262 15c multicolored	28	15

Flowers

A1263 A1264

A1265 A1266

1981, Apr. 23 ***Perf. 11***

1876 A1263 18c multicolored	35	15
1877 A1264 18c multicolored	35	15
1878 A1265 18c multicolored	35	15
1879 A1266 18c multicolored	35	15
a. Block of 4, #1876-1879	1.40	85
Set value		32

A1267-A1276

1981, May 14 **Engr.** ***Perf. 11***

Booklet Stamps

1880 A1267 18c Bighorn	35	15
1881 A1268 18c Puma	35	15
1882 A1269 18c Harbor seal	35	15
1883 A1270 18c Bison	35	15
1884 A1271 18c Brown bear	35	15
1885 A1272 18c Polar bear	35	15
1886 A1273 18c Elk (wapiti)	35	15
1887 A1274 18c Moose	35	15
1888 A1275 18c White-tailed deer	35	15
1889 A1276 18c Pronghorn	35	15
a. Bklt. pane of 10, #1880-1889	8.00	—
Set value		50

See No. 1949.

A1277

A1278

A1279

A1280

Multicolor Huck Press

1981, Apr. 24 ***Perf. 11***

1890 A1277 18c multicolored	32	15
a. Imperf., pair	100.00	
b. Vert. pair, imperf. horiz.	—	

Coil Stamp

Perf. 10 Vert.

1891 A1278 18c multicolored	36	15
a. Imperf., pair	20.00	

Beware of pairs offered as imperf. between that have faint blind perfs.

Booklet Stamps

Perf. 11

1892 A1279 6c multicolored	55	15
1893 A1280 18c multicolored	32	15
a. Booklet pane of 8 (2 #1892, 6 #1893)	3.00	—
b. As "a," vert. imperf. btwn.	*80.00*	
c. Pair, #1892, 1893	90	—
Set value, #1890-1893		25

Bureau Precanceled Coils

Starting with No. 1895e, Bureau precanceled coil stamps are valued unused as well as used. The coils issued with dull finish gum may be difficult to distinguish. When used normally these stamps do not receive any postal markings so that used stamps with an additional post-cancellation of any kind are worth considerably less than the values shown here.

A1281

1981, Dec. 17 ***Perf. 11***

1894 A1281 20c blk, dk blue & red	35	15
a. Vert. pair, imperf.	40.00	
b. Vert. pair, imperf. horiz.	*650.00*	
c. Dark blue omitted	*90.00*	
d. Black omitted	*300.00*	

Coil Stamp

Perf. 10 Vertical

1895 A1281 20c blk, dk blue & red	35	15
a. Imperf., pair	10.00	
b. Black omitted	50.00	
c. Dark blue omitted	—	
d. Pair, imperf. btwn.	*1,000.*	
e. Untagged (Bureau precanceled)	50	50

Booklet Stamp

Perf. 11x10½

1896 A1281 20c blk, dk blue & red	35	15
a. Booklet pane of 6	2.50	—
b. Booklet pane of 10	4.25	—
Set value, #1894-1896		15

Transportation Coils

A1282

A1283

A1284

A1285

A1286

A1287

A1288

A1289

A1290

A1291

A1292

A1293

A1294

A1295

1981-84 **Engr.** ***Perf. 10 Vert.***

1897 A1282 1c violet	15	15
b. Imperf., pair	*700.00*	
1897A A1283 2c black	15	15
e. Imperf., pair	*50.00*	

For similar designs to the 1c and 2c, see Nos. 2225-2226.

1898 A1284 3c dk green	15	15
1898A A1285 4c redsh brown	15	15
b. Untagged (Bureau precanceled)	15	15
c. As "b," imperf., pair	*700.00*	
d. No. 1898A, imperf., pair	*850.00*	—
1899 A1286 5c gray green	15	15
a. Imperf., pair	—	
1900 A1287 5.2c carmine	15	15
a. Untagged (Bureau precanceled)	15	15
1901 A1288 5.9c blue	18	15
a. Untagged (Bureau precanceled, lines only)	18	18
b. As "a," imperf., pair	*200.00*	
1902 A1289 7.4c brown	18	15
a. Untagged (Bureau precanceled)	20	20
1903 A1290 9.3c car rose	25	15
a. Untagged (Bureau precanceled, lines only)	22	22
b. As "a," imperf., pair	*125.00*	
1904 A1291 10.9c purple	24	15
a. Untagged (Bureau precanceled, lines only)	24	24
b. As "a," imperf., pair	*150.00*	
1905 A1292 11c red	24	15
a. Untagged	24	15
1906 A1293 17c ultra	32	15
a. Untagged (Bureau precanceled, Presorted First Class)	35	35
b. Imperf., pair	*165.00*	
c. As "a," imperf., pair	*650.00*	
1907 A1294 18c dark brown	34	15
a. Imperf., pair	*120.00*	

1908 A1295 20c vermilion 32 15
a. Imperf., pair 110.00
Nos. 1897-1908 (14) 2.97
Set value 75

Years of issue: 9.3c, 17c-20c, 1981. 2c, 4c, 5.9c, 10.9c, 1982. 1c, 3c, 5c, 5.2c, 1983. 7.4, 11c, 1984.

See Nos. 2123-2136, 2225-2231, 2252-2266, 2451-2468.

A1296

Perf. 10 Vert. on 1 or 2 Sides

1983, Aug. 12 **Photo.**
1909 A1296 $9.35 multi 22.50 14.00
a. Booklet pane of 3 62.50 —

A1297

A1298

American Red Cross Centennial

1981, May 1 ***Perf. 10½x11***
1910 A1297 18c multicolored 32 15

Savings & Loan Sesquicentennial

1981, May 8 ***Perf. 11***
1911 A1298 18c multicolored 32 15

Space Achievement

A1299

A1300
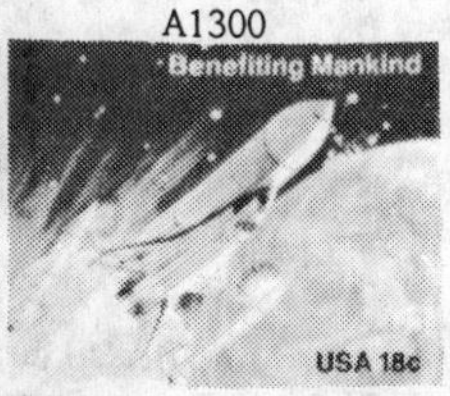

A1303

A1304

A1301
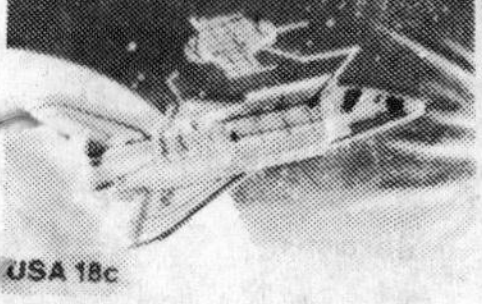

A1302

A1305

A1306

1981, May 21 ***Perf. 11***
1912 A1299 18c multicolored 32 15
1913 A1300 18c multicolored 32 15
1914 A1301 18c multicolored 32 15
1915 A1302 18c multicolored 32 15
1916 A1303 18c multicolored 32 15
1917 A1304 18c multicolored 32 15
1918 A1305 18c multicolored 32 15
1919 A1306 18c multicolored 32 15
a. Block of 8, #1912-1919 3.00 2.75
b. As "a," imperf. 9,000.
Set value 80

Professional Management

Joseph Wharton A1307

1981, June 18
1920 A1307 18c blue & black 32 15

Preservation of Wildlife Habitats

A1308 A1309

A1310 A1311

1981, June 26
1921 A1308 18c multicolored 35 15
1922 A1309 18c multicolored 35 15
1923 A1310 18c multicolored 35 15
1924 A1311 18c multicolored 35 15
a. Block of 4, #1921-1924 1.40 1.00
Set value 32

International Year of the Disabled

Man Looking through Microscope A1312

1981, June 29 **Photo.** ***Perf. 11***
1925 A1312 18c multicolored 32 15
a. Vert. pair, imperf. horiz. 2,750.

Edna St. Vincent Millay, 1892-1950

A1313

Litho. & Engr.

1981, July 10 ***Perf. 11***
1926 A1313 18c multicolored 32 15
a. Black (engr., inscriptions) omitted 425.00 —

Alcoholism

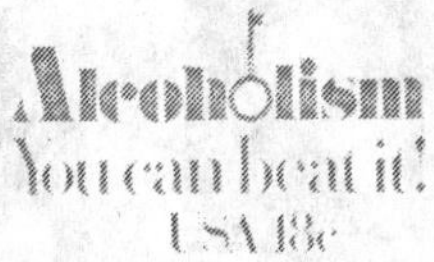

A1314

1981, Aug. 19 **Engr.** ***Perf. 11***
1927 A1314 18c blue & black 42 15
a. Imperf., pair 400.
b. Vert. pair, imperf. horiz. 1,250.

American Architecture

New York University Library by Sanford White A1315

Biltmore House by Richard Morris Hunt A1316

Palace of the Arts by Bernard Maybeck A1317

National Farmer's Bank by Louis Sullivan A1318

1981, Aug. 28 **Engr.** ***Perf. 11***
1928 A1315 18c black & red 42 15
1929 A1316 18c black & red 42 15
1930 A1317 18c black & red 42 15
1931 A1318 18c black & red 42 15
a. Block of 4, #1928-1931 1.75 1.00
Set value 32

Athletes

Mildred Didrikson Zaharias A1319

Robert Tyre Jones A1320

1981, Sept. 22 **Engr.** ***Perf. 10½x11***
1932 A1319 18c purple 32 15
1933 A1320 18c green 32 15
Set value 15

Frederic Remington, 1861-1909

Coming Through the Rye — A1321

1981, Oct. 9 ***Perf. 11***
1934 A1321 18c gray, green & brown 32 15
a. Vert. pair, imperf. btwn. 275.00
b. Brown omitted 550.00

James Hoban, 1762?-1831

Irish-American Architect of White House A1322

1981, Oct. 13 **Photo.** ***Perf. 11***
1935 A1322 18c multicolored 32 16
1936 A1322 20c multicolored 35 15
Set value 20

See Ireland No. 504.

American Bicentennial

Battle of Yorktown A1323

Battle of Virginia Capes A1324

Litho. & Engr.

1981, Oct. 16 ***Perf. 11***
1937 A1323 18c multicolored 35 15
1938 A1324 18c multicolored 35 15
a. Pair, #1937-1938 90 15
b. As "a," black (engr., inscriptions) omitted 450.00
Set value 15

Christmas

Madonna and Child, Botticelli A1325

Felt Bear on Sled A1326

1981, Oct. 28 **Photo.** ***Perf. 11***
1939 A1325 (20c) multicolored 38 15
a. Imperf., pair 125.
b. Vert. pair, imperf. horiz. 1,650.
1940 A1326 (20c) multicolored 38 15
a. Imperf., pair 275.
b. Vert. pair, imperf. horiz. —
Set value 15

John Hanson, 1721-1783

First President of Continental Congress — A1327

1981, Nov. 5 **Photo.** ***Perf. 11***
1941 A1327 20c multicolored 38 15

Desert Plants

Barrel Cactus — A1328

Saguaro — A1331

Agave
A1329

Beavertail Cactus — A1330

1981, Dec. 11 Litho. & Engr.

1942 A1328 20c multicolored 35 15
1943 A1329 20c multicolored 35 15
1944 A1330 20c multicolored 35 15
1945 A1331 20c multicolored 35 15
- **a.** Block of 4, #1942-1945 1.50 15
- **b.** As "a," deep brown omitted *7,500.*
- **c.** No. 1945 imperf., vert. pair *5,250.*

Set value 24

A1332

A1333

A1334

1981, Oct. 11 Photo. *Perf. 11x10½*

1946 A1332 (20c) brown 38 15

Coil Stamp

Perf. 10 Vert.

1947 A1332 (20c) brown 60 15
- **a.** Imperf., pair *1,750.*

Booklet Stamp

Perf. 11x10½

1948 A1333 (20c) brown 38 15
- **a.** Booklet pane of 10 4.50 —

Set value 15

1982, Jan. 8 Engr. *Perf. 11*

1949 A1334 20c dk blue (from bklt. pane) 50 15
- **a.** Booklet pane of 10 5.00 —
- **b.** As "a," vert. imperf. btwn. *100.00*
- **c.** Type II 50 15
- **d.** As "c," booklet pane of 10 10.00 —

No. 1949 is 18¾mm wide and has overall tagging. No. 1949c is 18½mm wide and has block tagging.

See No. 1880.

Franklin Delano Roosevelt

A1335

1982, Jan. 30 Engr. *Perf. 11*

1950 A1335 20c blue 38 15

A1336

1982, Feb. 1 Photo. *Perf. 11x10½*

1951 A1336 20c multicolored 38 15
- **a.** Perf. 11 48 15
- **b.** Imperf., pair *275.00*
- **c.** Blue omitted *175.00*

No. 1951c is valued in the grade of fine.

> *The values of stamps in very fine to superb condition are greater than catalogue value.*

A1337

A1338-A1387

George Washington

1982, Feb. 22 Photo. *Perf. 11*

1952 A1337 20c multicolored 38 15

State Birds & Flowers

1982, Apr. 14 Photo. *Perf. 10½x11*

1953 A1338 20c Alabama 48 25
1954 A1339 20c Alaska 48 25
1955 A1340 20c Arizona 48 25
1956 A1341 20c Arkansas 48 25
1957 A1342 20c California 48 25
1958 A1343 20c Colorado 48 25
1959 A1344 20c Connecticut 48 25
1960 A1345 20c Delaware 48 25
1961 A1346 20c Florida 48 25
1962 A1347 20c Georgia 48 25
1963 A1348 20c Hawaii 48 25
1964 A1349 20c Idaho 48 25
1965 A1350 20c Illinois 48 25
1966 A1351 20c Indiana 48 25
1967 A1352 20c Iowa 48 25
1968 A1353 20c Kansas 48 25
1969 A1354 20c Kentucky 48 25
1970 A1355 20c Louisiana 48 25
1971 A1356 20c Maine 48 25
1972 A1357 20c Maryland 48 25
1973 A1358 20c Massachusetts 48 25
1974 A1359 20c Michigan 48 25
1975 A1360 20c Minnesota 48 25
1976 A1361 20c Mississippi 48 25
1977 A1362 20c Missouri 48 25
1978 A1363 20c Montana 48 25
1979 A1364 20c Nebraska 48 25
1980 A1365 20c Nevada 48 25
1981 A1366 20c New Hampshire 48 25
1982 A1367 20c New Jersey 48 25
1983 A1368 20c New Mexico 48 25
1984 A1369 20c New York 48 25
1985 A1370 20c North Carolina 48 25
1986 A1371 20c North Dakota 48 25
1987 A1372 20c Ohio 48 25
1988 A1373 20c Oklahoma 48 25
1989 A1374 20c Oregon 48 25
1990 A1375 20c Pennsylvania 48 25
1991 A1376 20c Rhode Island 48 25
1992 A1377 20c South Carolina 48 25
1993 A1378 20c South Dakota 48 25
1994 A1379 20c Tennessee 48 25
1995 A1380 20c Texas 48 25
1996 A1381 20c Utah 48 25
1997 A1382 20c Vermont 48 25
1998 A1383 20c Virginia 48 25
1999 A1384 20c Washington 48 25
2000 A1385 20c West Virginia 48 25
2001 A1386 20c Wisconsin 48 25
2002 A1387 20c Wyoming 48 25
- **a.** #1953a-2002a, any single, perf. 11 50 30
- **b.** Pane of 50, perf. 10½x11 24.00 —
- **c.** Pane of 50, perf. 11 25.00 —
- **d.** Pane of 50, imperf. —

US-Netherlands

200th Anniv. of Diplomatic Recognition by the Netherlands
A1388

1982, Apr. 20 Photo. *Perf. 11*

2003 A1388 20c ver, brt blue & gray black 38 15
- **a.** Imperf., pair *325.00*

See Netherlands Nos. 640-641.

Library of Congress

A1389

1982, Apr. 21 Engr. *Perf. 11*

2004 A1389 20c red & black 38 15

Consumer Education

A1390

Coil Stamp

1982, Apr. 27 Engr. *Perf. 10 Vert.*

2005 A1390 20c sky blue 75 15
- **a.** Imperf., pair *100.00*

Knoxville World's Fair

A1391

A1392

A1393

A1394

1982, Apr. 29 Photo. *Perf. 11*

2006 A1391 20c multicolored 40 15
2007 A1392 20c multicolored 40 15
2008 A1393 20c multicolored 40 15
2009 A1394 20c multicolored 40 15
- **a.** Block of 4, #2006-2009 1.75 1.00

Set value 32

American Author, 1832-1899

Frontispiece from "Ragged Dick" — A1395

1982, Apr. 30 Engr. *Perf. 11*

2010 A1395 20c red & black, *tan* 38 15

Aging Together

A1396

1982, May 21 *Perf. 11*

2011 A1396 20c brown 38 15

Performing Arts

Actors John, Ethel & Lionel Barrymore — A1397

1982, June 8 Photo. *Perf. 11*

2012 A1397 20c multicolored 38 15

Dr. Mary E. Walker, 1832-1919

A1398

1982, June 10 Photo. *Perf. 11*

2013 A1398 20c multicolored 38 15

International Peace Garden

A1399

1982, June 30 Photo. *Perf. 11*

2014 A1399 20c multicolored 38 15
- **a.** Blk & grn (engr.) omitted *200.00*

A1400

A1401

America's Libraries

1982, July 13 Engr. *Perf. 11*

2015 A1400 20c red & black 38 15
- **a.** Vert. pair, imperf. horiz. *300.00*

Jackie Robinson, 1919-1972

1982, Aug. 2 Photo. *Perf. 10½x11*

2016 A1401 20c multicolored 1.00 15

Touro Synagogue

A1402

Photogravure, Engraved

1982, Aug. 22 *Perf. 11*

2017 A1402 20c multicolored 38 15
- **a.** Imperf., pair *1,250.*

Wolf Trap Farm Park

A1403

1982, Sept. 1 Photo. *Perf. 11*

2018 A1403 20c multicolored 38 15

American Architecture

Fallingwater, Mill Run, Pa., by Frank Lloyd Wright
A1404

Illinois Institute of Technology by Ludwig Mies van der Rohe
A1405

Gropius House, Lincoln, Mass., by Walter Gropius
A1406

Dulles Airport, by Eero Saarinen
A1407

1982, Sept. 30 **Engr.** ***Perf. 11***
2019 A1404 20c black & brown 38 15
2020 A1405 20c black & brown 38 15
2021 A1406 20c black & brown 38 15
2022 A1407 20c black & brown 38 15
a. Block of 4, #2019-2022 1.60 1.00
Set value 32

St. Francis of Assisi, 1182-1226

A1408

1982, Oct. 7 **Photo.** ***Perf. 11***
2023 A1408 20c multicolored 38 15

Ponce de Leon, 1527-1591

A1409

1982, Oct. 12 **Photo.** ***Perf. 11***
2024 A1409 20c multicolored 38 15
a. Imperf., pair 600.00
b. Vert. pair, Imperf. btwn. and at top —

Christmas

A1410

A1411

A1412

A1413

A1414

A1415

1982, Nov. 3 **Photo.** ***Perf. 11***
2025 A1410 13c multicolored 26 15
a. Imperf., pair 650.00

1982, Oct. 28
2026 A1411 20c multicolored 38 15
a. Imperf., pair 150.00
b. Horiz. pair, imperf. vert. —
c. Vert. pair, imperf. horiz. —
2027 A1412 20c multicolored 50 15
2028 A1413 20c multicolored 50 15
2029 A1414 20c multicolored 50 15
2030 A1415 20c multicolored 50 15
a. Block of 4, #2027-2030 2.00 1.00
b. As "a," imperf. 3,000.
c. As "a," imperf. horiz. —
Set value, #2025-2030 30

Science & Industry

A1416

Litho. & Engr.
1983, Jan. 19 ***Perf. 11***
2031 A1416 20c multicolored 38 15
a. Black (engr.) omitted 1,400.

Balloons

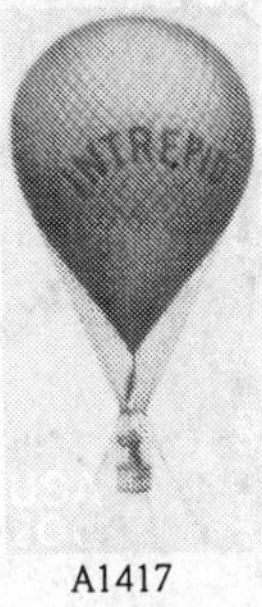

A1417

A1420

A1418

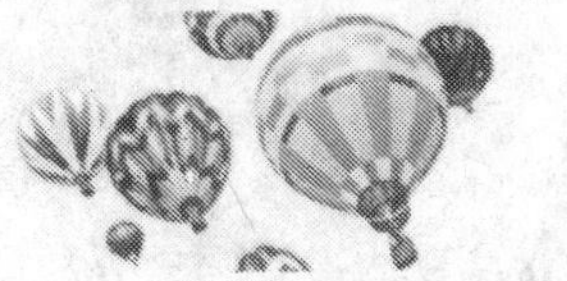

A1419

1983, Mar. 31 **Photo.** ***Perf. 11***
2032 A1417 20c multicolored 38 15
2033 A1418 20c multicolored 38 15
2034 A1419 20c multicolored 38 15
2035 A1420 20c multicolored 38 15
a. Block of 4, #2032-2035 1.65 1.00
b. As "a," imperf. —
Set value 32

US-Sweden

A1421

1983, Mar. 24 **Engr.** ***Perf. 11***
2036 A1421 20c multicolored 38 15

Civilian Conservation Corps

A1422

1983, Apr. 5 **Photo.** ***Perf. 11***
2037 A1422 20c multicolored 38 15
a. Imperf., pair 2,500.

Joseph Priestley, 1733-1804

A1423

1983, Apr. 13 **Photo.** ***Perf. 11***
2038 A1423 20c multicolored 38 15

Voluntarism

A1424

1983, Apr. 20 **Engr.** ***Perf. 11***
2039 A1424 20c red & black 40 15
a. Imperf., pair 800.00

US-Germany

Concord, 1683
A1425

1983, Apr. 29 ***Perf. 11***
2040 A1425 20c brown 38 15

Brooklyn Bridge

A1426

1983, May 17 **Engr.** ***Perf. 11***
2041 A1426 20c blue 38 15

T.V.A.

A1427

Photo. & Engr.
1983, May 18 ***Perf. 11***
2042 A1427 20c multicolored 40 15

Physical Fitness

A1428

1983, May 14 **Photo.** ***Perf. 11***
2043 A1428 20c multicolored 38 15

Scott Joplin, 1868-1917

A1429

1983, June 9 **Photo.**
2044 A1429 20c multicolored 40 15
a. Imperf., pair 500.00

Medal of Honor

A1430

1983, June 7 **Litho. & Engr.** ***Perf. 11***
2045 A1430 20c multicolored 40 15
a. Red omitted 250.00

A1431

A1432

George Herman Ruth, 1895-1948

1983, July 6 **Engr.** ***Perf. $10^1/_2$x11***
2046 A1431 20c blue 1.00 15

Nathaniel Hawthorne, 1804-1864

1983, July 8 **Photo.** ***Perf. 11***
2047 A1432 20c multicolored 40 15

1984 Los Angeles Olympics

A1433

A1434

A1435

A1436

1983, July 28 **Photo.** ***Perf. 11***

2048	A1433	13c	multicolored	35	15
2049	A1434	13c	multicolored	35	15
2050	A1435	13c	multicolored	35	15
2051	A1436	13c	multicolored	35	15
a.			Block of 4, #2048-2051	1.50	1.00
			Set value		20

Signing of Treaty of Paris

John Adams, Franklin, John Jay, David Hartley A1437

1983, Sept. 2 **Photo.** ***Perf. 11***

2052	A1437	20c	multicolored	38	15

Civil Service

A1438

1983, Sept. 9 **Photo. & Engr.**

2053	A1438	20c	buff, blue & red	40	15

Metropolitan Opera

A1439

1983, Sept. 14 **Litho. & Engr.**

2054	A1439	20c	yellow & maroon	38	15

American Inventors

A1440

A1441

A1442

A1443

1983, Sept. 21 **Litho. & Engr**

2055	A1440	20c	multicolored	45	15
2056	A1441	20c	multicolored	45	15
2057	A1442	20c	multicolored	45	15
2058	A1443	20c	multicolored	45	15
a.			Block of 4, #2055-2058	1.90	1.00
b.			As "a," black omitted	*425.00*	
			Set value		32

Streetcars

A1444

A1445

A1446

A1447

1983, Oct. 8 **Photo. & Engr.**

2059	A1444	20c	multicolored	40	15
2060	A1445	20c	multicolored	40	15
2061	A1446	20c	multicolored	40	15
2062	A1447	20c	multicolored	40	15
a.			Block of 4, #2059-2062	1.70	1.00
b.			As "a," black omitted	*475.00*	
c.			As "a," black omitted on #2059, 2061	—	
			Set value		32

Christmas

A1448

A1449

1983, Oct. 28 **Photo.** ***Perf. 11***

2063	A1448	20c	multicolored	38	15
2064	A1449	20c	multicolored	38	15
a.			Imperf., pair	*175.00*	
			Set value		15

A1450

Caribou and Alaska Pipeline — A1451

Martin Luther, 1483-1546

1983, Nov. 11 **Photo.** ***Perf. 11***

2065	A1450	20c	multicolored	38	15

25th Anniv. of Alaska Statehood

1984, Jan. 3 **Photo.** ***Perf. 11***

2066	A1451	20c	multicolored	38	15

Winter Olympic Games

Ice Dancing A1452

Downhill Skiing A1453

Cross-country Skiing A1454

Hockey A1455

1984, Jan. 6 ***Perf. $10^1/_2$x11***

2067	A1452	20c	multicolored	42	15
2068	A1453	20c	multicolored	42	15
2069	A1454	20c	multicolored	42	15
2070	A1455	20c	multicolored	42	15
a.			Block of 4, #2067-2070	1.70	1.00
			Set value		32

14th Winter Olympic Games, Sarajevo, Yugoslavia, Feb. 8-19.

A1456

A1457

Federal Deposit Insurance Corp., 50th Anniv.

1984, Jan. 12 ***Perf. 11***

2071	A1456	20c	multicolored	38	15

Love

1984, Jan. 31 **Photo. & Engr.**

2072	A1457	20c	multicolored	40	15
a.			Horiz. pair, imperf. vert.	*175.00*	

Carter G. Woodson (1875-1950), Writer — A1458

A1459

Black Heritage Issue

1984, Feb. 1 **Photo.**

2073	A1458	20c	multicolored	40	15
a.			Horiz. pair, imperf. vert.	*1,500.*	

Soil and Water Conservation

1984, Feb. 6

2074	A1459	20c	multicolored	38	15

50th Anniv. of Credit Union Act

Dollar Sign, Coin — A1460

1984, Feb. 10 **Photo.** ***Perf. 11***

2075	A1460	20c	multicolored	38	15

Orchids

A1461

A1462

A1463

A1464

1984, Mar. 5

2076	A1461	20c	Wild pink	42	15
2077	A1462	20c	Yellow lady's-slipper	42	15
2078	A1463	20c	Spreading pogonia	42	15
2079	A1464	20c	Pacific calypso	42	15
a.			Block of 4, #2076-2079	1.80	1.00
			Set value		32

25th Anniv. of Hawaii Statehood

Eastern Polynesian Canoe, Golden Plover, Mauna Loa Volcano A1465

1984, Mar. 12 **Photo.** ***Perf. 11***

2080	A1465	20c	multicolored	40	15

National Archives

Abraham Lincoln, George Washington — A1466

1984, Apr. 16 Photo. *Perf. 11*

2081 A1466 20c multicolored 40 15

1984 Los Angeles Olympics

Diving A1467 Long Jump A1468

Wrestling A1469 Kayak A1470

1984, May 4 *Perf. 11*

2082 A1467 20c multicolored 60 15
2083 A1468 20c multicolored 60 15
2084 A1469 20c multicolored 60 15
2085 A1470 20c multicolored 60 15
a. Block of 4, #2082-2085 2.40 1.00
Set value 32

New Orleans World Exposition

River Wildlife A1471

1984, May 11 *Perf. 11*

2086 A1471 20c multicolored 38 15

Health Research

Lab Equipment A1472

1984, May 17 *Perf. 11*

2087 A1472 20c multicolored 40 15

Actor Douglas Fairbanks (1883-1939) — A1473

A1474

Performing Arts

1984, May 23 Photo. & Engr.

2088 A1473 20c multicolored 38 15

Jim Thorpe, 1888-1953

1984, May 24 Engr. *Perf. 11*

2089 A1474 20c dark brown 40 15

Performing Arts

Tenor John McCormack (1884-1945) — A1475

1984, June 6 Photo. *Perf. 11*

2090 A1475 20c multicolored 40 15

25th Anniv. of St. Lawrence Seaway

Aerial View of Seaway, Freighters A1476

1984, June 26 Photo. *Perf. 11*

2091 A1476 20c multicolored 40 15

50th Anniv. of Waterfowl Preservation Act

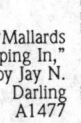

"Mallards Dropping In," by Jay N. Darling A1477

1984, July 2 Engr. *Perf. 11*

2092 A1477 20c blue 50 15
a. Horiz. pair, imperf. vert. 400.00

See No. RW1.

A1478

Author — A1479

Roanoke Voyages

1984, July 13 Photo. *Perf. 11*

2093 A1478 20c multicolored 38 15

Herman Melville (1819-1891)

1984, Aug. 1 Engr. *Perf. 11*

2094 A1479 20c sage green 38 15

Horace Moses (1862-1947)

Junior Achievement Founder — A1480

1984, Aug. 6 Engr.

2095 A1480 20c orange & dk brown 45 15

Smokey the Bear — A1481

Clemente, Puerto Rican Flag — A1482

1984, Aug. 13 Litho. & Engr.

2096 A1481 20c multicolored 38 15
a. Horiz. pair, imperf. btwn. 300.
b. Vert. pair, imperf. btwn. 250.
c. Block of 4, imperf. btwn. vert. and horiz. 4,500.
d. Horiz. pair, imperf. vert. —

Roberto Clemente (1934-1972)

1984, Aug. 17 Photo. *Perf. 11*

2097 A1482 20c multicolored 1.00 15
a. Horiz. pair, imperf. vert. 1,800.

Dogs

Beagle, Boston Terrier A1483

Chesapeake Bay Retriever, Cocker Spaniel A1484

Alaskan Malamute, Collie A1485

Black & Tan Coonhound, American Foxhound A1486

1984, Sept. 7 Photo. *Perf. 11*

2098 A1483 20c multicolored 40 15
2099 A1484 20c multicolored 40 15
2100 A1485 20c multicolored 40 15
2101 A1486 20c multicolored 40 15
a. Block of 4, #2098-2101 1.75 1.00
Set value 32

Crime Prevention

McGruff, The Crime Dog — A1487

1984, Sept. 26 Photo. *Perf. 11*

2102 A1487 20c multicolored 38 15

Hispanic Americans

A1488

1984, Oct. 31 Photo. *Perf. 11*

2103 A1488 20c multicolored 38 15
a. Vert. pair, imperf. horiz. 1,750.

Family Unity

A1489

1984, Oct. 1 Photo. & Engr.

2104 A1489 20c multicolored 40 15
a. Horiz. pair, imperf. vert. 550.00
c. Vert. pair, imperf. btwn. and at bottom —

Eleanor Roosevelt

A1490

1984, Oct. 11 Engr. *Perf. 11*

2105 A1490 20c deep blue 38 15

Nation of Readers

Lincoln, Son Tad — A1491

1984, Oct. 16 Engr. *Perf. 11*

2106 A1491 20c brown & maroon 38 15

Christmas

Madonna and Child by Fra Filippo Lippi — A1492

Santa Claus — A1493

1984, Oct. 30 Photo. *Perf. 11*

2107 A1492 20c multicolored 40 15
2108 A1493 20c multicolored 40 15
a. Horiz. pair, imperf. vert. 950.00
Set value 15

No. 2108a is valued in the grade of fine.

Vietnam Veterans Memorial

Memorial Wall — A1494

1984, Nov. 10 **Engr.** ***Perf. 10½***

2109 A1494 20c multicolored 40 15

Performing Arts

Composer Jerome Kern (1885-1945) — A1495

1985, Jan. 23 **Photo.** ***Perf. 11***

2110 A1495 22c multicolored 40 15

A1496

A1497

1985, Feb. 1 **Photo.** ***Perf. 11***

2111	A1496 (22c) green	60	15
a.	Vert. pair, imperf.	*50.*	
b.	Vert. pair, imperf. horiz.	*1,350.*	

Coil Stamp

Perf. 10 Vert.

2112	A1496 (22c) green	60	15
a.	Imperf., pair	50.00	

Booklet Stamp

Perf. 11

2113	A1497 (22c) green	80	15
a.	Booklet pane of 10	8.00	
b.	As "a," imperf. btwn. horiz.	—	
	Set value		15

A1498

Flag over Capitol Dome A1499

1985, Mar. 29 **Engr.** ***Perf. 11***

2114 A1498 22c blue, red & black 40 15

Coil Stamp

Perf. 10 Vert.

2115	A1498 22c blue, red & black	40	15
a.	Imperf., pair	10.00	
b.	Inscribed "T" at bottom ('87)	48	15
c.	Black field of stars	—	—

Booklet Stamp

Perf. 10 Horiz. on 1 or 2 Sides

2116	A1499 22c blue, red & black	48	15
a.	Booklet pane of 5	2.50	—
	Set value		15

Seashells

Frilled Dogwinkle A1500

Reticulated Helmet A1501

New England Neptune A1502

Calico Scallop A1503

Lightning Whelk — A1504

1985, Apr. 4 **Engr.** ***Perf. 10***

2117	A1500 22c black & brown	40	15
2118	A1501 22c multicolored	40	15
2119	A1502 22c black & brown	40	15
2120	A1503 22c black & violet	40	15
2121	A1504 22c multicolored	40	15
a.	Booklet pane of 10	4.00	—
b.	As "a," violet omitted	*850.00*	
c.	As "a," vert. imperf. btwn.	*600.00*	
d.	As "a," imperf.		—
e.	Strip of 5, Nos. 2117-2121	2.00	—
	Set value		25

Issued in booklets only.

Eagle and Half Moon A1505

Type I. Washed out, dull appearance most evident in the black of the body of the eagle, and the red in the background between the eagle's shoulder and the moon. "$10.75" appears slotchy or grainy (P# 11111).

Type II. Brighter, more intense colors most evident in the black on the eagle's body, and red in the background. "$10.75" appears smoother, brighter, and less grainy (P# 22222).

Perf. 10 Vert. on 1 or 2 Sides

1985, Apr. 29 **Photo.**

2122	A1505 $10.75 multi	17.00	7.00
a.	Booklet pane of 3	52.50	—
b.	Type II	17.00	—
c.	As "b," booklet pane of 3	52.50	—

Issued in booklets only.

Transportation Coils

A1506

A1507

A1508

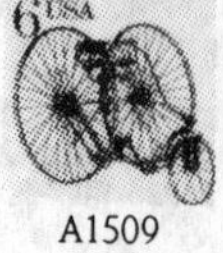

A1509

A1510

A1511

A1512

A1513

A1514

A1515

A1516

A1517

A1518

A1519

1985-87 **Engr.** ***Perf. 10 Vert.***

2123	A1506 3.4c dk bluish green	15	15
a.	Untagged (Bureau precanceled)	15	15
2124	A1507 4.9c brn blk	15	15
a.	Untagged (Bureau precanceled)	16	16
2125	A1508 5.5c deep mag	15	15
a.	Untagged (Bureau precanceled)	15	15
2126	A1509 6c red brown	15	15
a.	Untagged (Bureau precanceled)	15	15
b.	As "a," imperf., pair	200.00	
2127	A1510 7.1c lake	15	15
a.	Untagged (Bureau precanceled)	15	15
2128	A1511 8.3c green	18	15
a.	Untagged (Bureau precanceled)	18	18

For similar stamp see No. 2231.

2129	A1512 8.5c dk Prus green	16	15
a.	Untagged (Bureau precanceled)	16	16
2130	A1513 10.1c slate blue	22	15
a.	Untagged (Bureau precanceled)	22	22
b.	As "a," imperf., pair	15.00	
2131	A1514 11c dk green	22	15
2132	A1515 12c dark blue	24	15
a.	Untagged (Bureau precanceled)	24	24
b.	Type II, untagged (Bureau precanceled)	24	24

Type II has "Stanley Steamer 1909" ½mm shorter (17½mm) than No. 2132 (18mm).

2133	A1516 12.5c olive green	25	15
a.	Untagged (Bureau precanceled)	25	25
b.	As "a," imperf., pair	50.00	
2134	A1517 14c sky blue	28	15
a.	Imperf., pair	100.00	
b.	Type II	28	15

Type II design is ¼mm narrower (17¼mm) than No. 2134 (17½mm) and has block tagging. No. 2134 has overall tagging.

2135	A1518 17c sky blue	30	15
a.	Imperf., pair	*500.00*	
2136	A1519 25c org brown	45	15
a.	Imperf., pair	10.00	
b.	Pair, imperf. between	—	
	Nos. 2123-2136 (14)	3.05	
	Set value		70

Years of issue: 3.4c, 4.9c, 6c, 8.3c, 10.1c-14c, 1985. 5.5c, 17c, 25c, 1986. 7.1c, 8.5c, 1987.

See Nos. 1897-1908, 2225-2231, 2252-2266, 2451-2468.

Black Heritage Issue

Mary McLeod Bethune (1875-1955), Educator — A1520

1985, Mar. 5 **Photo.** ***Perf. 11***

2137 A1520 22c multicolored 40 15

Duck Decoys

Broadbill A1521

Mallard A1522

Canvasback A1523

Redhead A1524

1985, Mar. 22 **Photo.** ***Perf. 11***

2138	A1521 22c multicolored	60	15
2139	A1522 22c multicolored	60	15
2140	A1523 22c multicolored	60	15
2141	A1524 22c multicolored	60	15
a.	Block of 4, #2138-2141	2.50	1.00
	Set value		32

Winter Special Olympics

Ice Skater, Emblem, Skier A1525

1985, Mar. 25 **Photo.** ***Perf. 11***

2142	A1525 22c multicolored	40	15
a.	Vert. pair, imperf. horiz.	*650.00*	

Love

A1526

1985, Apr. 17 **Photo.**

2143	A1526 22c multicolored	40	15
a.	Imperf., pair	*1,750.*	

Rural Electrification Administration

Electrified Farm A1527

1985, May 11 Photo. & Engr.
2144 A1527 22c multicolored 45 15

AMERIPEX '86

US No. 134 — A1528

1985, May 25 Litho. & Engr.
2145 A1528 22c multicolored 40 15
a. Red, black & blue omitted *200.*
b. Red & black omitted *1,250.*
c. Red omitted —

US First Lady

Abigail Adams (1744-1818) — A1529

1985, June 14 Litho. *Perf. 11*
2146 A1529 22c multicolored 40 15
a. Imperf., pair *275.00*

Architect, Sculptor

Frederic Auguste Bartholdi (1834-1904), Statue of Liberty A1530

1985, July 18 Litho. & Engr.
2147 A1530 22c multicolored 40 15
a. Black (engr.) omitted

Examples exist with most, but not all, of the engraved black omitted. Expertization of No. 2147a is recommended.

George Washington, Washington Monument A1532

Envelopes A1533

COIL STAMPS

1985 Photo. *Perf. 10 Vert.*
2149 A1532 18c multicolored 32 15
a. Untagged (Bureau precanceled) 35 35
b. Imperf., pair *950.00*
c. As "a," imperf., pair *750.00*
2150 A1533 21.1c multicolored 40 15
a. Untagged (Bureau precanceled) 38 38
Set value 16

Issue dates: 18c, Nov. 6. 21.1c, Oct. 22.
Precancellations on Nos. 2149a ("PRESORTED FIRST CLASS"), 2150a ("ZIP+4") do not have lines.

Korean War Veterans

American Troops Marching A1535

1985, July 26 Engr. *Perf. 11*
2152 A1535 22c gray grn & rose red 40 15

Social Security Act, 50th Anniv.

Men, Women, Children, Corinthian Columns A1536

1985, Aug. 14 Photo. *Perf. 11*
2153 A1536 22c deep blue & lt blue 40 15

World War I Veterans

The Battle of Marne, France, by Harvey Dunn A1537

1985, Aug. 26 Engr. *Perf. 11*
2154 A1537 22c gray grn & rose red 40 15

Horses

Quarter Horse A1538

Morgan A1539

Saddlebred A1540

Appaloosa A1541

1985, Sept. 25 Photo. *Perf. 11*
2155 A1538 22c multicolored 85 15
2156 A1539 22c multicolored 85 15
2157 A1540 22c multicolored 85 15
2158 A1541 22c multicolored 85 15
a. Block of 4, #2155-2158 4.00 1.00
Set value 32

Public Education in America

Quill Pen, Apple, Spectacles, Penmanship Quiz — A1542

1985, Oct. 1 Photo. *Perf. 11*
2159 A1542 22c multicolored 42 15

International Youth Year

YMCA Youth Camping, Cent. A1543

Boy Scouts, 75th Anniv. A1544

Big Brothers/Big Sisters Fed., 40th Anniv. A1545

Camp Fire, Inc., 75th Anniv. A1546

1985, Oct. 7 Photo. *Perf. 11*
2160 A1543 22c multicolored 48 15
2161 A1544 22c multicolored 48 15
2162 A1545 22c multicolored 48 15
2163 A1546 22c multicolored 48 15
a. Block of 4, #2160-2163 2.00 1.00
Set value 32

Help End Hunger

Youths and the Elderly Suffering from Malnutrition A1547

1985, Oct. 15 Photo.
2164 A1547 22c multicolored 42 15

Christmas

Genoa Madonna, Enameled Terra-Cotta by Luca Della Robbia (1400-1482) — A1548

Poinsettia Plants A1549

1985, Oct. 30 Photo.
2165 A1548 22c multicolored 40 15
a. Imperf., pair *100.00*
2166 A1549 22c multicolored 40 15
a. Imperf., pair *130.00*
Set value 15

Arkansas Statehood, 150th Anniv.

Old State House, Little Rock A1550

1986, Jan. 3 Photo. *Perf. 11*
2167 A1550 22c multicolored 40 15
a. Vert. pair, imperf. horiz.

Great Americans

A1551

A1552

A1553

A1554

A1555

A1556

A1559

A1560

A1561

A1562

A1562a

A1563

A1565

A1566

A1567

A1567a

A1567b

A1568

A1569

A1571

A1573

A1574

A1575

A1576

A1577

A1577a

A1578

A1579

Perf. 11, 11½x11 (#2184B), 11.1x11 (#2179B)

1986-93 **Engr.**

2168	A1551	1c	brnsh ver	15	15
2169	A1552	2c	bright blue	15	15
2170	A1553	3c	bright blue	15	15
2171	A1554	4c	blue violet	15	15
a.			Untagged	15	15
2172	A1555	5c	dk ol grn	15	15
2173	A1556	5c	carmine	15	15
a.			Untagged	15	15
2176	A1559	10c	lake	18	15
2177	A1560	14c	crimson	25	15
2178	A1561	15c	claret	28	15
2179	A1562	17c	dull bl grn	30	15
2179B	A1562a	20c	red brown	40	15
2180	A1563	21c	blue vio	38	15
2182	A1565	23c	purple	42	15
2183	A1566	25c	blue	45	15
a.			Booklet pane of 10 ('88)	4.50	—
2184	A1567	28c	myr grn	50	15
2184A	A1567a	29c	blue	50	15
2184B	A1567b	29c	indigo	50	15
2185	A1568	35c	black	65	15
2186	A1569	40c	dark blue	70	15
2188	A1571	45c	brt blue	80	15
2190	A1573	52c	purple	90	15
2191	A1574	56c	scarlet	90	15
2192	A1575	65c	dark blue	1.20	18
2193	A1576	75c	dp mag	1.30	20
2194	A1577	$1	dk Prus grn	2.50	50
2194A	A1577a	$1	deep blue	1.75	50
2195	A1578	$2	brt violet	3.25	50
2196	A1579	$5	copper red	7.50	1.00
			Nos. 2168-2196 (28)	26.51	
			Set value		3.75

Booklet Stamp

Perf. 10 on 2 or 3 sides

2197	A1566	25c	blue ('88)	45	15
a.			Booklet pane of 6	2.75	—

Years of issue: Nos. 2172, 2194, 1c, 3c, 4c, 17c, 25c, 56c, $2, 1986. 2c, 10c, 14c, $5, 1987. 15c, 21c, 23c, 45c, 65c, 1988. 28c, No. 2194A, 1989. No. 2173, 40c, 1990. 35c, 52c, 1991. 29c, 75c, 1992. No. 2184B, 1993. 20c, 10/24/94.

This is an expanding set. Numbers will change if necessary.

Stamp Collecting

Handstamped Cover, No. 213, Philatelic Memorabilia A1581

Boy Examining Stamp Collection A1582

No. 836 Under Magnifying Glass, Sweden Nos. 268, 271 — A1583

1986 Presidents Miniature Sheet — A1584

Perf. 10 Vert. on 1 or 2 Sides

1986, Jan. 23 **Litho. & Engr.**

Booklet Stamps

2198	A1581	22c	multicolored	45	15
2199	A1582	22c	multicolored	45	15
2200	A1583	22c	multicolored	45	15
2201	A1584	22c	multicolored	45	15
a.			Bklt. pane of 4, #2198-2201	2.00	—
b.			As "a," black omitted on #2198, 2201	50.00	
c.			As "a," blue (litho.) omitted on #2198-2200	*2,500.*	
d.			As "a," buff (litho.) omitted	—	
			Set value		20

See Sweden Nos. 1585-1588.

A1585

A1586

Love

1986, Jan. 30 **Photo.** ***Perf. 11***

2202	A1585	22c	Puppy	40	15

Black Heritage Issue

1986, Feb. 4 **Photo.** ***Perf. 11***

2203	A1586	22c	multicolored	40	15

Sojourner Truth (c. 1797-1883), abolitionist.

Republic of Texas, 150th Anniv.

Texas State Flag and Silver Spur — A1587

1986, Mar. 2 **Photo.**

2204	A1587	22c	dk bl, dk red & grysh blk	42	15
a.			Horiz. pair, imperf. vert.	*1,250.*	
b.			Dark red omitted	*2,750.*	

Fish

Muskellunge — A1588

Atlantic Cod A1589

Largemouth Bass A1590

Bluefin Tuna A1591

Catfish A1592

Perf. 10 Horiz. on 1 or 2 Sides

1986, Mar. 21 **Photo.**

2205	A1588	22c	multicolored	50	15
2206	A1589	22c	multicolored	50	15
2207	A1590	22c	multicolored	50	15
2208	A1591	22c	multicolored	50	15
2209	A1592	22c	multicolored	50	15
a.			Bklt. pane of 5, #2205-2209	3.25	—
			Set value		25

Issued in booklets only.

Public Hospitals

A1593

1986, Apr. 11 **Photo.** ***Perf. 11***

2210	A1593	22c	multicolored	40	15
a.			Vert. pair, imperf. horiz.	*300.*	
b.			Horiz. pair, imperf. vert.	*1,350.*	

Performing Arts

Edward Kennedy "Duke" Ellington (1899-1974), Jazz Composer — A1594

1986, Apr. 29 **Photo.** ***Perf. 11***

2211	A1594	22c	multicolored	40	15
a.			Vert. pair, imperf. horiz.	*1,000.*	—

Miniature Sheets

35 Presidents — A1599

No. 2216: a, Washington. b, John Adams. c, Jefferson. d, Madison. e, Monroe. f, John Quincy Adams. g, Jackson. h, Van Buren. i, Harrison.

No. 2217; a, Tyler. b, Polk. c, Taylor. d, Fillmore. e, Pierce. f, Buchanan. g, Lincoln. h, Andrew Johnson. i, Grant.

No. 2218: a, Hayes. b, Garfield. c, Arthur. d, Cleveland. e, Harrison. f, McKinley. g, Theodore Roosevelt. h, Taft. i, Wilson.

No. 2219: a, Harding. b, Coolidge. c, Hoover. d, Franklin Delano Roosevelt. e, White House. f, Truman. g, Eisenhower. h, Kennedy. i, Lyndon B. Johnson.

1986, May 22 **Litho. & Engr.**

2216	Sheet of 9	3.50	—
a.-i.	A1599 22c any single	38	20
j.	Blue omitted	*3,500.*	
k.	Black inscription omitted	*2,000.*	
l.	Imperf.	*10,500.*	
2217	Sheet of 9	3.50	—
a.-i.	A1599 22c any single	38	20
j.	Black inscription omitted	*3,750.*	
2218	Sheet of 9	3.50	—
a.-i.	A1599 22c any single	38	20
j.	Brown omitted	—	
k.	Black inscription omitted	*3,000.*	
2219	Sheet of 9	3.50	—
a.-i.	A1599 22c any single	38	20
j.	Blackish blue (engr.) inscription omitted on a.-b., d.-e., g.-h.	—	
	Nos. 2216-2219 (4)	14.00	

Issued at AMERIPEX '86 Intl. Phil. Exhib., Chicago, IL, May 22-June 1.

Arctic Explorers

Elisha Kent Kane A1600

Adolphus W. Greely A1601

Vilhjalmur Stefansson A1602

Robert E. Peary and Matthew Alexander Henson A1603

1986, May 28 **Photo.** ***Perf. 11***

2220	A1600	22c	multicolored	50	15
2221	A1601	22c	multicolored	50	15
2222	A1602	22c	multicolored	50	15
2223	A1603	22c	multicolored	50	15
a.			Block of 4, #2220-2223	2.25	1.00
b.			As "a," black (engr.) omitted	*9,500.*	
			Set value		32

Statue of Liberty, Cent. — A1604

1986, July 4 **Engr.** ***Perf. 11***
2224 A1604 22c scarlet & dark blue 40 15

See France No. 2014.

Transportation Coils

Types of 1982-85 and

A1604a

A1604b

1986-87 **Engr.** ***Perf. 10 Vert.***
2225 A1604a 1c violet 15 15
a. Untagged 15 15
b. Imperf., pair —
2226 A1604b 2c black ('87) 15 15
a. Untagged 15 15
2228 A1285 4c reddish brown 15 15
b. Imperf., pair *300.00*
2231 A1511 8.3c grn (Bureau precancel) 16 16
Set value 34 30

Issue dates: 1c, Nov. 26. 2c, Mar. 6. Earliest known usage of 4c, Aug. 15, 1986. 8.3c, Aug. 29.

On No. 2228 "Stagecoach 1890s" is 17½mm long, on No. 1898A 19½mm long. On No. 2231 "Ambulance 1860s" is 18mm long.

No. 2226 inscribed "2 USA;" No. 1897A inscribed "USA 2c."

Navajo Art

A1605 A1606

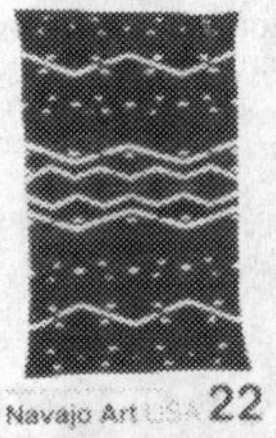

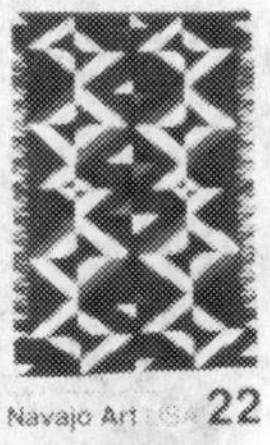

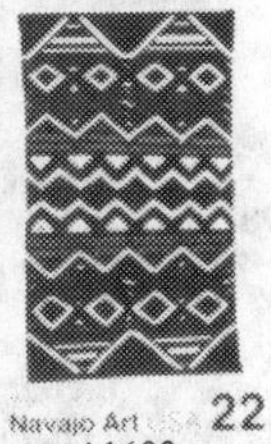

A1607 A1608

Blankets in the Museum of the American Indian and Lowe Art Museum.

1986, Sept. 4 **Litho. & Engr.** ***Perf. 11***
2235 A1605 22c multicolored 40 15
2236 A1606 22c multicolored 40 15
2237 A1607 22c multicolored 40 15
2238 A1608 22c multicolored 40 15
a. Block of 4, #2235-2238 1.65 1.00
b. As "a," blk (engr.) omitted *350.00*
Set value 32

Literary Arts

T. S. Eliot (1888-1965), Poet — A1609

1986, Sept. 26 **Engr.** ***Perf. 11***
2239 A1609 22c copper red 40 15

Woodcarved Figurines

Highlander Figure A1610 Ship Figurehead A1611

Nautical Figure A1612 Cigar Store Figure A1613

1986, Oct. 1 **Photo.** ***Perf. 11***
2240 A1610 22c multicolored 42 15
2241 A1611 22c multicolored 42 15
2242 A1612 22c multicolored 42 15
2243 A1613 22c multicolored 42 15
a. Block of 4, #2240-2243 1.75 1.00
b. As "a," imperf. vert. *1,500.*
Set value 32

Christmas

Madonna, by Perugino (c. 1450-1523) A1614

Village Scene A1615

1986, Oct. 24 ***Perf. 11***
2244 A1614 22c multicolored 40 15
2245 A1615 22c multicolored 40 15
Set value 15

Michigan Statehood Sesquicent.

White Pine — A1616

1987, Jan. 26 **Photo.** ***Perf. 11***
2246 A1616 22c multicolored 40 15

Pan American Games, Indianapolis, August 7-25

Runner in Full Stride A1617

1987, Jan. 29 ***Perf. 11***
2247 A1617 22c multicolored 40 15
a. Silver omitted *1,500.*

No. 2247a is valued in the grade of fine.

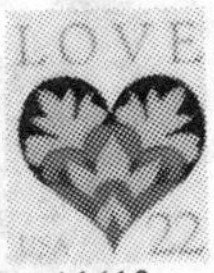

A1618

A1619

Love

1987, Jan. 30 **Photo.** ***Perf. 11½x11***
2248 A1618 22c multicolored 40 15

Black Heritage

1987, Feb. 20 **Photo.** ***Perf. 11***
2249 A1619 22c multicolored 40 15

Jean Baptiste Pointe du Sable (c. 1750-1818), pioneer trader, founder of Chicago

A1620

A1621

Performing Arts

Enrico Caruso (1873-1921), Opera Tenor

1987, Feb. 27 ***Perf. 11***
2250 A1620 22c multicolored 40 15
a. Black (engr.) omitted *4,000.*

Girl Scouts, 75th Anniv.

Litho. & Engr.

1987, Mar. 12 ***Perf. 11***
2251 A1621 22c 14 Achievement Badges 40 15
a. All litho. colors omitted —

Expertization of No. 2251a by competent authorities is recommended.

Transportation Coils

A1622

A1623

A1624

A1625

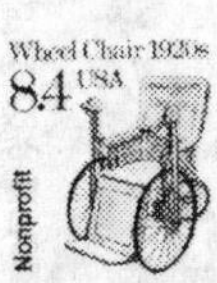

A1626

A1627

A1628

A1629

A1630

A1631

A1632

A1633

A1634

A1635

A1636

1987-88 **Engr.** ***Perf. 10 Vert.***
2252 A1622 3c claret 15 15
a. Untagged 15 15
2253 A1623 5c black 15 15
2254 A1624 5.3c blk (Bureau precancel in scarlet) 15 15
2255 A1625 7.6c brn (Bureau precancel in scarlet) 15 15
2256 A1626 8.4c dp clar (Bureau precancel in red) 15 15
a. Imperf., pair *750.00*
2257 A1627 10c sky blue 18 15
2258 A1628 13c blk (Bureau precancel in red) 22 22
2259 A1629 13.2c slate grn (Bureau precancel in red) 22 22
a. Imperf., pair *100.00*
2260 A1630 15c violet 24 15
c. Imperf., pair —
2261 A1631 16.7c rose (Bureau precancel in black) 28 28
a. Imperf., pair *150.00*

All known copies of No. 2261a are miscut top to bottom.

2262 A1632 17.5c dark violet 30 15
a. Untagged (Bureau precancel) 30 30
b. Imperf., pair *1,750.*
2263 A1633 20c blue vio 35 15
a. Imperf., pair *75.00*
2264 A1634 20.5c rose (Bureau precancel in black) 38 38
2265 A1635 21c olive grn (Bureau precancel in red) 38 38
a. Imperf., pair *65.00*
2266 A1636 24.1c deep ultra (Bureau precancel) 42 42
Set value 2.55

The 5.3c, 7.6c, 8.4c, 13c, 13.2c, 16.7c, 20.5c, 21c and 24.1c are only available precanceled and are untagged.

Years of issue: 5c, 10c, 17.5c, 1987. Others, 1988.

See Nos. 1897-1908, 2123-2136, 2225-2231, 2451-2468.

Special Occasions

A1637

A1638

A1639

A1640

A1641

A1642

A1643

A1644

Perf. 10 on 1, 2, or 3 sides

1987, Apr. 20 **Photo.**

Booklet Stamps

2267 A1637 22c	multicolored	55	15
2268 A1638 22c	multicolored	55	15
2269 A1639 22c	multicolored	55	15
2270 A1640 22c	multicolored	55	15
2271 A1641 22c	multicolored	55	15
2272 A1642 22c	multicolored	55	15
2273 A1643 22c	multicolored	55	15
2274 A1644 22c	multicolored	55	15
a.	Bklt. pane of 10, #2268-2271, 2273-2274, 2 each #2267, 2272	6.75	—
	Set value		80

United Way Centenary

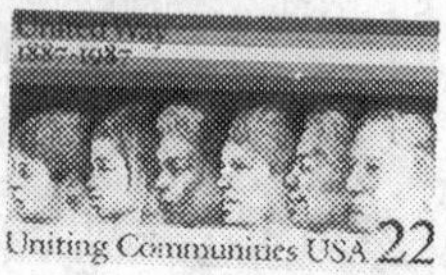

Six Profiles A1645

Litho. & Engr.

1987, Apr. 28 *Perf. 11*

2275 A1645 22c	multicolored	40	15

A1646

A1647

A1648

A1649

Pheasant A1649a

Grosbeak A1649b

Owl A1649c

Honeybee A1649d

Photo., Engr. (No. 2280), Litho. & Engr. (No. 2281)

1987-88 *Perf. 11*

2276 A1646	22c multicolored	40	15
a.	Booklet pane of 20	8.50	—
2277 A1647	(25c) multi ('88)	45	15
2278 A1648	25c multi ('88)	40	15
	Set value		15

Coil Stamps

Perf. 10 Vertical

2279 A1647	(25c) multi ('88)	45	15
a.	Imperf., pair	*100.00*	
2280 A1649	25c Green trees ('88)	45	15
a.	Imperf., pair	*15.00*	
b.	Black trees	*100.00*	—
d.	Pair, imperf. btwn.	*800.00*	
2281 A1649d	25c multi ('88)	45	15
a.	Imperf., pair	*45.00*	
b.	Black (engr.) omitted	*60.00*	
c.	Black (litho.) omitted	*400.00*	
d.	Pair, imperf. between	*900.00*	
e.	Yellow (litho.) omitted	—	
	Set value		15

Beware of copies with traces of the litho. black that are offered as No. 2281c. Vertical pairs or blocks of No. 2281 and imperfs. with the engr. black missing are from printers waste.

Booklet Stamps

Perf. 10 on 2 or 3 Sides, 11 on 2 or 3 sides (#2283)

2282 A1647	(25c) multi ('88)	50	15
a.	Booklet pane of 10	6.50	—

Vert. pairs, imperf between, are printer's waste. Other "varieties" probably exist.

2283 A1649a	25c multi ('88)	50	15
a.	Booklet pane of 10	6.00	—
b.	25c multi, red removed from sky	5.00	15
c.	As "b," booklet pane of 10	*65.00*	—
d.	As "a," horiz. imperf. between	—	

Imperfs. are printer's waste.

2284 A1649b	25c multi ('88)	45	15
2285 A1649c	25c multi ('88)	45	15
b.	Bklt. pane of 10, 5 each Nos. 2284-2285	4.50	—
d.	Pair, Nos. 2284-2285	1.00	—
2285A A1648	25c multi ('88)	45	15
c.	Booklet pane of 6	2.75	—
	Set value		30

Issue dates: No. 2276, May 9; Nos. 2277, 2279, 2282, Mar. 22; No. 2278, May 6; No. 2280, May 20; No. 2281, Sept. 2; No. 2283, Apr. 29; Nos. 2284-2285, May 28. Nos. 2285A, July 5.

American Wildlife — A1650-A1699

1987, June 13 **Photo.** *Perf. 11*

2286 A1650 22c	Barn swallow	85	15
2287 A1651 22c	Monarch butterfly	85	15
2288 A1652 22c	Bighorn sheep	85	15
2289 A1653 22c	Broad-tailed hummingbird	85	15
2290 A1654 22c	Cottontail	85	15
2291 A1655 22c	Osprey	85	15
2292 A1656 22c	Mountain lion	85	15
2293 A1657 22c	Luna moth	85	15
2294 A1658 22c	Mule deer	85	15
2295 A1659 22c	Gray squirrel	85	15
2296 A1660 22c	Armadillo	85	15
2297 A1661 22c	Eastern chipmunk	85	15
2298 A1662 22c	Moose	85	15
2299 A1663 22c	Black bear	85	15
2300 A1664 22c	Tiger swallowtail	85	15
2301 A1665 22c	Bobwhite	85	15
2302 A1666 22c	Ringtail	85	15
2303 A1667 22c	Red-winged blackbird	85	15
2304 A1668 22c	American lobster	85	15
2305 A1669 22c	Black-tailed jack rabbit	85	15
2306 A1670 22c	Scarlet tanager	85	15
2307 A1671 22c	Woodchuck	85	15
2308 A1672 22c	Roseate spoonbill	85	15
2309 A1673 22c	Bald eagle	85	15
2310 A1674 22c	Alaskan brown bear	85	15
2311 A1675 22c	Iiwi	85	15
2312 A1676 22c	Badger	85	15
2313 A1677 22c	Pronghorn	85	15
2314 A1678 22c	River otter	85	15
2315 A1679 22c	Ladybug	85	15
2316 A1680 22c	Beaver	85	15
2317 A1681 22c	White-tailed deer	85	15
2318 A1682 22c	Blue jay	85	15
2319 A1683 22c	Pika	85	15
2320 A1684 22c	Bison	85	15
2321 A1685 22c	Snowy egret	85	15
2322 A1686 22c	Gray wolf	85	15
2323 A1687 22c	Mountain goat	85	15
2324 A1688 22c	Deer mouse	85	15
2325 A1689 22c	Black-tailed prairie dog	85	15
2326 A1690 22c	Box turtle	85	15
2327 A1691 22c	Wolverine	85	15
2328 A1692 22c	American elk	85	15
2329 A1693 22c	California sea lion	85	15
2330 A1694 22c	Mockingbird	85	15
2331 A1695 22c	Raccoon	85	15
2332 A1696 22c	Bobcat	85	15
2333 A1697 22c	Black-footed ferret	85	15
2334 A1698 22c	Canada goose	85	15
2335 A1699 22c	Red fox	85	15
a.	Pane of 50, #2286-2335	47.50	
	2286b-2335b, any single, red omitted	—	

Ratification of the Constitution

A1700

A1701

A1702

A1703

A1704

A1705

A1706

A1707

A1708

A1709

A1710

A1711

A1712

Litho. & Engr., Photo. (#2337, 2343-2344, 2347)

1987-90 *Perf. 11*

2336 A1700 22c	multi	40	15
2337 A1701 22c	multi	42	15
2338 A1702 22c	multi	42	15
a.	Black (engr.) omitted	*5,250.*	
2339 A1703 22c	multi ('88)	40	15
2340 A1704 22c	multi ('88)	40	15
2341 A1705 22c	dk blue & dk red ('88)	40	15
2342 A1706 22c	multi ('88)	40	15
2343 A1707 25c	multi ('88)	45	15
a.	Strip of 3, vert. imperf. btwn.	—	
2344 A1708 25c	multi ('88)	45	15
2345 A1709 25c	multi ('88)	45	15
2346 A1710 25c	multi ('88)	45	15
2347 A1711 25c	multi ('89)	45	15
2348 A1712 25c	multi ('90)	45	15
	Nos. 2336-2348 (13)	5.54	
	Set value		65

Issue dates: No. 2336, July 4. No. 2337, Aug. 26. No. 2238, Sept. 11. No. 2339, Jan. 6. No. 2340, Jan. 9. No. 2341, Feb. 6. No. 2342, Feb. 15. No. 2343, May 23; No. 2344, June 21; No. 2345, June 25. No. 2346, July 26. No. 2347, Aug. 22; No. 2348, May 29.

US-Morocco Diplomatic Relations Bicentennial

Arabesque, Dar Batha Palace, Fez — A1713

Litho. & Engr.

1987, July 18 *Perf. 11*

2349 A1713 22c	scar & blk	40	15
a.	Black (engr.) omitted	*350.00*	

See Morocco No. 642.

Literary Arts

William Cuthbert Faulkner (1897-1962), Novelist — A1714

1987, Aug. 3 **Engr.** *Perf. 11*

2350 A1714 22c	bright green	40	15

Imperfs. are from printer's waste.

Folk Art Issue

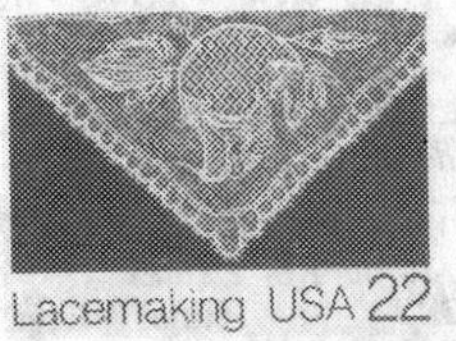

A1715

A1716

A1717

A1718

Litho. & Engr.

1987, Aug. 14 *Perf. 11*

2351 A1715 22c ultra & white	42	15
2352 A1716 22c ultra & white	42	15
2353 A1717 22c ultra & white	42	15
2354 A1718 22c ultra & white	42	15
a. Block of 4, #2351-2354	1.75	1.00
b. As "a," white omitted	*1,100.*	
Set value		32

Drafting of the Constitution Bicentennial

A1719

A1720

A1721

A1722

A1723

Perf. 10 Horiz. on 1 or 2 Sides

1987, Aug. 28 **Photo.**

Booklet Stamps

2355 A1719 22c multicolored	50	15
a. Grayish grn (background) omitted	—	
2356 A1720 22c multicolored	50	15
a. Grayish grn (background) omitted	—	
2357 A1721 22c multicolored	50	15
a. Grayish grn (background) omitted	—	
2358 A1722 22c multicolored	50	15
a. Grayish grn (background) omitted	—	
2359 A1723 22c multicolored	50	15
a. Bklt. pane of 5, #2355-2359	2.75	—
b. Grayish grn (background) omitted	—	
Set value		50

A1724

A1725

Signing of the Constitution

Litho. & Engr.

1987, Sept. 17 *Perf. 11*

2360 A1724 22c multicolored	*40*	15

Certified Public Accounting

1987, Sept. 21 **Litho. & Engr.**

2361 A1725 22c multicolored	1.90	15
a. Black (engr.) omitted	*700.00*	

Locomotives

Stourbridge Lion, 1829 A1726

Best Friend of Charleston A1727

John Bull, 1831 A1728

Brother Johnathan, 1832 A1729

Gowan & Marx, 1839 A1730

Perf. 10 Horiz. on 1 or 2 Sides

1987, Oct. 1

Booklet Stamps

2362 A1726 22c multicolored	55	15
2363 A1727 22c multicolored	55	15
2364 A1728 22c multicolored	55	15
2365 A1729 22c multicolored	55	15
a. Red omitted	—	
2366 A1730 22c multicolored	55	15
a. Bklt. pane of 5, #2362-2366	2.75	—
b. As "a," blk omitted on #2366	—	
Set value		50

Christmas

Moroni Madonna A1731

Christmas Ornaments A1732

1987, Oct. 23 **Photo.** *Perf. 11*

2367 A1731 22c multicolored	40	15
2368 A1732 22c multicolored	40	15
Set value		15

1988 Winter Olympics, Calgary

Skiing — A1733

1988, Jan. 10 **Photo.** *Perf. 11*

2369 A1733 22c multicolored	40	15

Australia Bicentennial

Caricature of Australian Koala and American Bald Eagle — A1734

1988, Jan. 10 **Photo.** *Perf. 11*

2370 A1734 22c multicolored	40	15

See Australia No. 1052.

Black Heritage

James Weldon Johnson, 1871-1938, Author, Lyricist — A1735

1988, Feb. 2 **Photo.** *Perf. 11*

2371 A1735 22c multicolored	40	15

Siamese, Exotic Shorthair A1736

Abyssinian, Himalayan A1737

Maine Coon, Burmese A1738

American Shorthair, Persian A1739

1988, Feb. 5 *Perf. 11*

2372 A1736 22c multicolored	42	15
2373 A1737 22c multicolored	42	15
2374 A1738 22c multicolored	42	15
2375 A1739 22c multicolored	42	15
a. Block of 4, #2372-2375	1.90	1.00
Set value		32

American Sports Issues

A1740

A1741

1988, Mar. 9 **Litho. & Engr.**

2376 A1740 22c multicolored	40	15

Knute Kenneth Rockne (1888-1931), Notre Dame football coach.

1988, June 13 **Photo.** *Perf. 11*

2377 A1741 25c multicolored	45	15

Francis Ouimet (1893-1967), 1st amateur golfer to win the US Open Championship.

Love Issue

Rose — A1742

A1743

1988 **Photo.** *Perf. 11*

2378 A1742 25c multicolored	45	15
a. Imperf., pair	—	
2379 A1743 45c multicolored	65	20
Set value		25

Issue dates: 25c, July 4; 45c, Aug. 8.

1988 Summer Olympics, Seoul

A1744

1988, Aug. 19 **Photo.** *Perf. 11*

2380 A1744 25c multicolored	45	15

Classic Automobiles

1928 Locomobile — A1745

1929 Pierce-Arrow A1746

1931 Cord A1747

1932 Packard A1748

1935 Duesenberg — A1749

Perf. 10 Horiz. on 1 or 2 Sides

1988, Aug. 25 **Litho. & Engr.**

Booklet Stamps

2381 A1745	25c multicolored		50	15
2382 A1746	25c multicolored		50	15
2383 A1747	25c multicolored		50	15
2384 A1748	25c multicolored		50	15
2385 A1749	25c multicolored		50	15
a.	Bklt. pane of 5, #2381-2385		3.50	—
	Set value			50

Antarctic Explorers

Nathaniel Palmer (1799-1877) A1750

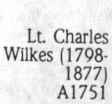

Lt. Charles Wilkes (1798-1877) A1751

Richard E. Byrd (1888-1957) A1752

Lincoln Ellsworth (1880-1951) A1753

1988, Sept. 14 **Photo.** ***Perf. 11***

2386 A1750	25c multicolored	55	15
2387 A1751	25c multicolored	55	15
2388 A1752	25c multicolored	55	15
2389 A1753	25c multicolored	55	15
a.	Block of 4, #2386-2389	2.50	1.00
b.	Black (engr.) omitted	*1,500.*	
c.	As "a," imperf. horiz.	*3,000.*	
	Set value		32

Folk Art Issue

Carousel Animals

Deer — A1754

Horse — A1755

Camel — A1756

Goat — A1757

1988, Oct. 1 **Litho. & Engr.** ***Perf. 11***

2390 A1754	25c multicolored	60	15
2391 A1755	25c multicolored	60	15
2392 A1756	25c multicolored	60	15
2393 A1757	25c multicolored	60	15
a.	Block of 4, #2390-2393	2.50	1.00
	Set value		32

Express Mail Rate

Eagle in Flight — A1758

1988, Oct. 4 **Litho. & Engr.** ***Perf. 11***

2394 A1758	$8.75 multi	13.50	8.00

Special Occasions

Happy Birthday — A1759

Best Wishes — A1760

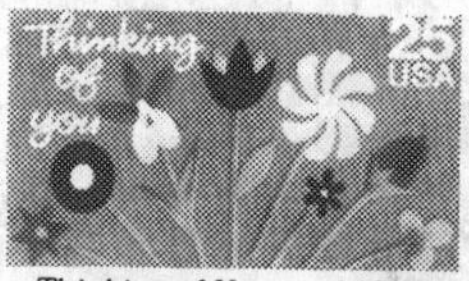

Thinking of You — A1761

Love You — A1762

Perf. 11 on 2 or 3 sides

1988, Oct. 22 **Photo.**

Booklet Stamps

2395 A1759	25c multicolored	45	15
2396 A1760	25c multicolored	45	15
a.	Bklt. pane of 6, 3 #2395 + 3 #2396 with gutter btwn.	3.00	—
2397 A1761	25c multicolored	45	15
2398 A1762	25c multicolored	45	15
a.	Bklt. pane of 6, 3 #2397 + 3 #2398 with gutter btwn.	3.00	—
b.	As "a," imperf. horiz.	—	
	Set value		40

Madonna and Child, by Botticelli A1763

One-horse Open Sleigh and Village Scene A1764

Litho. & Engr., Photo. (No. 2400)

1988, Oct. 20 ***Perf. 11½***

2399 A1763	25c multicolored	45	15
a.	Gold omitted	30.00	
2400 A1764	25c multicolored	45	15
	Set value		15

Montana Statehood Centennial

C.M. Russell and Friends, by Charles M. Russell (1865-1926) A1765

1989, Jan. 15 **Litho. & Engr.** ***Perf. 11***

2401 A1765	25c multicolored	45	15

Black Heritage Issues

Asa Philip Randolph (1889-1979), Labor and Civil Rights Leader — A1766

1989, Feb. 3 **Photo.** ***Perf. 11***

2402 A1766	25c multicolored	45	15

North Dakota Statehood Centennial

A1767

1989, Feb. 21 ***Perf. 11***

2403 A1767	25c multicolored	45	15

Washington Statehood Centennial

A1768

1989, Feb. 22 ***Perf. 11***

2404 A1768	25c multicolored	45	15

Steamboats

Experiment, 1788-1790 — A1769

Phoenix, 1809 — A1770

New Orleans, 1812 — A1771

Washington, 1816 — A1772

Walk in the Water, 1818 — A1773

Perf. 10 on 1 or 2 sides

1989, Mar. 3 **Litho. & Engr.**

Booklet Stamps

2405 A1769	25c multicolored	45	15
2406 A1770	25c multicolored	45	15
2407 A1771	25c multicolored	45	15
2408 A1772	25c multicolored	45	15
2409 A1773	25c multicolored	45	15
a.	Bklt. pane of 5, #2405-2409	2.25	—
	Set value		50

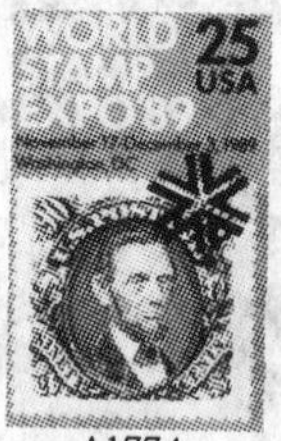

A1774

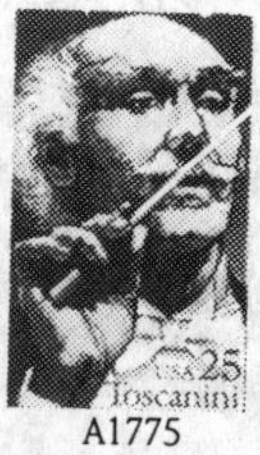

A1775

World Stamp Expo '89

Nov. 17-Dec. 3, Washington, DC

Litho. & Engr.

1989, Mar. 16 ***Perf. 11***

2410 A1774	25c No. 122	45	15

Performing Arts

Arturo Toscanini (1867-1975), Italian Conductor

1989, Mar. 25 **Photo.** ***Perf. 11***

2411 A1775	25c multicolored	45	15

Constitution Bicentennial

House of Representatives A1776

Senate A1777

Executive Branch — A1778

Supreme Court — A1779

1989-90 **Litho. & Engr.** ***Perf. 11***

2412 A1776	25c multicolored	45	15
2413 A1777	25c multicolored	45	15
2414 A1778	25c multicolored	45	15
2415 A1779	25c multicolored	45	15
	Set value		20

Issue dates: #2412, Apr. 4; #2413, Apr. 6; #2414, Apr. 16. #2415, Feb. 2, 1990.

South Dakota State Centenary

State Flower, Pioneer Woman and Sod House on Grasslands A1780

1989, May 3 **Photo.** ***Perf. 11***

2416 A1780	25c multicolored	45	15

American Sports

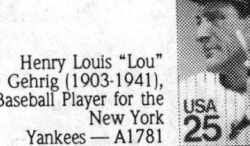

Henry Louis "Lou" Gehrig (1903-1941), Baseball Player for the New York Yankees — A1781

1989, June 10 **Photo.** *Perf. 11*
2417 A1781 25c multicolored 48 15

Literary Arts

Ernest Hemingway (1899-1961), Nobel Prize-winner for Literature, 1954 — A1782

1989, July 17 **Photo.** *Perf. 11*
2418 A1782 25c multicolored 45 15

Moon Landing, 20th Anniv.

A1783

Perf. 11x11½
1989, July 20 **Litho. & Engr.**
2419 A1783 $2.40 multicolored 4.00 2.00
a. Black (engr.) omitted *3,000.*
b. Imperf., pair *1,000.*
c. Black (litho.) omitted —

Natl. Assoc. of Letter Carriers, Cent.

Letter Carriers A1784

1989, Aug. 30 **Photo.** *Perf. 11*
2420 A1784 25c multicolored 45 15

Constitution Bicentennial

Bill of Rights — A1785

Litho. & Engr.
1989, Sept. 25 *Perf. 11*
2421 A1785 25c multicolored 45 15
a. Black (engr.) omitted *275.00*

Prehistoric Animals

Tyrannosaurus Rex — A1786

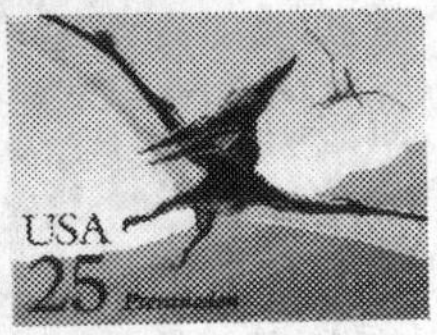

Pteranodon A1787

Stegosaurus A1788

Brontosaurus A1789

1989, Oct. 1 **Litho. & Engr.** *Perf. 11*
2422 A1786 25c multicolored 45 15
2423 A1787 25c multicolored 45 15
2424 A1788 25c multicolored 45 15
2425 A1789 25c multicolored 45 15
a. Block of 4, #2422-2425 2.00 1.00
b. As "a," black (engr.) omitted *1,100.*
Set value 32

The correct name for "Brontosaurus" is "Apatosaurus."
No. 2425b is valued in the grade of fine.

America Issue

A1790

Emblem of the Postal Union of the Americas and Spain (UPAE) and Southwestern Wood-carved Ritual Figure, Mogollon Culture, Mimbres Period, a Forerunner of the Hopi Indian Kachina Doll, A.D. 1150-1350.

1989, Oct. 12 **Photo.** *Perf. 11*
2426 A1790 25c multicolored 45 15

Discovery of America, 500th anniv. (in 1992). See No. C121.

Christmas

Madonna and Child, by Caracci A1791

Sleigh Full of Presents A1792

Litho. & Engr.
1989, Oct. 19 *Perf. 11½*
2427 A1791 25c multicolored 45 15
a. Booklet pane of 10 4.50 —
b. Red (litho.) omitted —

Photo.
Perf. 11
2428 A1792 25c multicolored 45 15
a. Vert. pair, imperf. horiz. *2,000.*

Booklet Stamp
Perf. 11½ on 2 or 3 sides
2429 A1792 25c multicolored 45 15
a. Booklet pane of 10 4.50 —
b. As "a," horiz. imperf. btwn. —
c. As "a," red omitted —
Set value 15

Marked differences exist between Nos. 2428 and 2429: The runners on the sleigh in No. 2429 are twice as thick as those in No. 2428; in No. 2429 the package to the rear of the sleigh has an identically colored bow, whereas the same package in No. 2428 has a bow of different color; and the board running underneath the sleigh on No. 2429 is pink, whereas it is the same color as the sleigh on No. 2428.

Eagle and Shield — A1793

1989, Nov. 10 **Photo.** *Die Cut*
Self-Adhesive
2431 A1793 25c multicolored 50 20
a. Booklet pane of 18 9.00
b. Vert. pair, no die cutting between *850.00*

Issued unfolded in panes of 18; peelable paper backing is booklet cover. Sold for $5.
Also available in strips of 18 with stamps spaced for use in affixing machines to service first day covers. Sold for $5.
Sold in 15 test cities and through the philatelic agency only.

Souvenir Sheet

World Stamp Expo, Washington, DC, Nov. 17-Dec. 3 — A1794

1989, Nov. 17 **Litho. & Engr.** *Imperf.*
2433 A1794 Sheet of 4 12.00 9.00
a. 90c like No. 122 2.00 1.75
b. 90c like No. 132TC (blue frame, brown center) 2.00 1.75
c. 90c like No. 132TC (green frame, blue center) 2.00 1.75
d. 90c like No. 132TC (scarlet frame, blue center) 2.00 1.75

Traditional Mail Delivery

Stagecoach, c. 1850 — A1795

Paddlewheel Steamer — A1796

Biplane A1797

Depot-hack Type Automobile A1798

Litho. & Engr.
1989, Nov. 19 *Perf. 11*
2434 A1795 25c multicolored 45 15
2435 A1796 25c multicolored 45 15
2436 A1797 25c multicolored 45 15
2437 A1798 25c multicolored 45 15
a. Block of 4, #2434-2437 2.00 2.00
b. As "a," dark blue (engr.) omitted *1,000.*
Set value 32

1989, Nov. 28 *Imperf.*
2438 Sheet of 4 4.00 1.75
a. A1795 25c multicolored 60 25
b. A1796 25c multicolored 60 25
c. A1797 25c multicolored 60 25
d. A1798 25c multicolored 60 25
e. Dark blue & gray (engr.) omitted —

20th Universal Postal Union Congress.

Idaho State Centenary

Mountain Bluebird, Sawtooth Mountains — A1799

1990, Jan. 6 **Photo.** *Perf. 11*
2439 A1799 25c multicolored 45 15

Love Issue

A1800

1990, Jan. 18 **Photo.** *Perf. 12½x13*
2440 A1800 25c brt bl, dk pink & emer grn 45 15
a. Imperf., pair *850.00*

Booklet Stamp
Perf. 11½ on 2 or 3 sides
2441 A1800 25c ultra, brt pink & dk grn 45 15
a. Booklet pane of 10 4.50 —
b. As "a," bright pink omitted *2,250.*
c. As "b," single stamp *275.*
Set value 15

No. 2441c may be obtained from booklet panes containing both normal and color-omitted stamps.

Black Heritage

Ida B. Wells (1862-1931), Journalist — A1801

1990, Feb. 1 **Photo.** *Perf. 11*
2442 A1801 25c multicolored 45 15

Beach Umbrella — A1802

1990, Feb. 3 **Photo.** *Perf. 11½x11*
Booklet Stamp
2443 A1802 15c multicolored 28 15
a. Booklet pane of 10 2.80 —
b. As "a," blue omitted *1,500.*

Wyoming State Centenary

High Mountain Meadows, by Conrad Schwiering A1803

1990, Feb. 23 Litho. & Engr. *Perf. 11*

2444 A1803 25c multicolored 45 15
a. Black (engr.) omitted 2,000. —

Classic Films

The Wizard of Oz — A1804 *Gone With the Wind* — A1805

Beau Geste A1806 *Stagecoach* A1807

1990, Mar. 23 Photo. *Perf. 11*

2445 A1804 25c multicolored 70 15
2446 A1805 25c multicolored 70 15
2447 A1806 25c multicolored 70 15
2448 A1807 25c multicolored 70 15
a. Block of 4, #2445-2448 3.25 1.00
Set value 32

Literary Arts Series

Marianne Craig Moore (1887-1972), Poet — A1808

1990, Apr. 18 Photo. *Perf. 11*

2449 A1808 25c multicolored 45 15

TRANSPORTATION ISSUE

A1810

A1811

A1812

A1816

A1823

A1827

Engr., Photo. (#2452B, 2454)
1990-94 Coil Stamps *Perf. 10 Vert.*

2451 A1810 4c claret 15 15
a. Imperf., pair 675.00
b. Untagged 15 15
2452 A1811 5c red 15 15
a. Untagged 15 15
c. Imperf., pair 1,000.
2452B A1811 5c carmine 15 15
2453 A1812 5c brn (Bureau precancel in gray) 15 15
a. Imperf., pair 500.00
2454 A1812 5c red (Bureau precancel in gray) 15 15
2457 A1816 10c grn (Bureau precancel in gray) 18 18
a. Imperf., pair 500.00
2458 A1816 10c grn (Bureau precancel in black) 20 20
2464 A1823 23c dark blue 42 15
a. Imperf., pair 175.00
2468 A1827 $1 blue & scar 1.75 50
a. Imperf., pair —
Nos. 2451-2468 (9) 3.30
Set value 1.00

Issued: $1, 4/20. #2452, 8/31. 4c, 1/25/91. #2453, 2457, 5/25/91. #2454, 10/22/91. 23c, 4/12/91. #2452B, 12/8/92. #2458, 5/25/94.

This is an expanding set. Numbers will change if necessary.

Some pairs of No. 2468 appear to be imperf but have some blind perfs on the gum. Beware of copies with the gum removed.

Lighthouses

Admiralty Head, WA — A1829

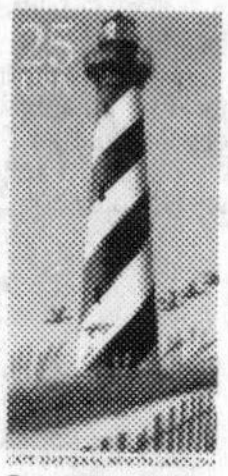

Cape Hatteras, NC — A1830

West Quoddy Head, ME — A1831

American Shoals, FL — A1832

Sandy Hook, NJ — A1833

Perf. 10 Vert. on 1 or 2 Sides
1990, Apr. 26 Litho. & Engr.
Booklet Stamps

2470 A1829 25c multicolored 45 15
2471 A1830 25c multicolored 45 15
2472 A1831 25c multicolored 45 15
2473 A1832 25c multicolored 45 15
2474 A1833 25c multicolored 45 15
a. Bklt. pane of 5, #2470-2474 2.50 —
b. As "a," white (USA 25) omitted 75.00
Set value 40

Flag

A1834

1990, May 18 Photo. *Die Cut*
Self-adhesive

2475 A1834 25c dk red & dk bl 50 25
a. Pane of 12 6.00

Sold only in panes of 12; peelable plastic backing inscribed in light ultramarine. Available for a test period of six months at 22 First National Bank automatic teller machines in Seattle.

Flora and Fauna Series

Bobcat A1835

Red Squirrel A1837

A1838

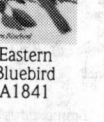

Pine Cone A1839

American Kestrel A1840

Eastern Bluebird A1841

Fawn A1846

Cardinal A1848

Pumpkinseed Sunfish A1850

Wood Duck A1852

African Violets A1853

1990, June 1 Litho. & Engr. *Perf. 11*

2476 A1835 $2 multicolored 3.00 1.25
a. Black (engr.) omitted 350.00

This is an expanding set. Numbers will change.

1993 Photo. *Die Cut*
Booklet Stamps
Self-Adhesive

2478 A1837 29c multicolored 50 15
a. Booklet pane of 18 9.00
2479 A1838 29c red, green & black 50 15
a. Booklet pane of 18 9.00

Engr.

2480 A1839 29c multicolored 50 15
a. Booklet pane of 18 9.00

Issue dates: No. 2478, June 25. No. 2479, Aug. 19. No. 2480, Nov. 5.

Perf. 11, 11½x11 (19c)
1991-92 Litho.

2481 A1840 1c multicolored 15 15
2482 A1841 3c multicolored 15 15

Photo.

2487 A1846 19c multicolored 35 15
b. Red omitted
2489 A1848 30c multicolored 50 15

Litho. & Engr.

2491 A1850 45c multicolored 78 15
a. Black (engr.) omitted 500.00 —
Nos. 2481-2491 (5) 1.93
Set value 40

Issue dates: 19c, Mar. 11. 1c, 3c, 30c, June 22. 45c, Dec. 2, 1992.

Booklet Stamps
Perf. 10 on 2 or 3 Sides
1991-93 Photo.

2493 A1852 29c black & multi 50 15
a. Booklet pane of 10 5.00
b. As "a," horiz. imperf. btwn. —

Perf. 11 on 2 or 3 Sides

2494 A1852 29c red & multi 50 15
a. Booklet pane of 10 5.00

Perf. 10x11 on 2 or 3 Sides

2495 A1853 29c multicolored 50 15
a. Booklet pane of 10 5.00 —

Issue dates: Nos. 2493-2494, Apr. 12. No. 2495, Oct. 8, 1993.

Olympians

Jesse Owens, 1936 A1855

Ray Ewry, 1900-08 A1856

Hazel Wightman, 1924 A1857

Eddie Eagan, 1920, 1932 A1858

Helene Madison, 1932 A1859

1990, July 6 Photo. *Perf. 11*

2496 A1855 25c multicolored 45 15
2497 A1856 25c multicolored 45 15
2498 A1857 25c multicolored 45 15
2499 A1858 25c multicolored 45 15
2500 A1859 25c multicolored 45 15
a. Strip of 5, #2496-2500 2.50 —
Set value 40

Indian Headdresses

Assiniboin A1860

Cheyenne A1861

Comanche
A1862

Flathead
A1863

Shoshone
A1864

Perf. 11 on 2 or 3 sides
1990, Aug. 17 **Litho. & Engr.**
Booklet Stamps

2501 A1860 25c multicolored 45 15
2502 A1861 25c multicolored 45 15
2503 A1862 25c multicolored 45 15
2504 A1863 25c multicolored 45 15
2505 A1864 25c multicolored 45 15
a. Bklt. pane, 2 each #2501-2505 4.75 —
b. As "a," black (engr.) omitted —
c. Strip of 5, #2501-2505 2.25 —
d. As "a," horiz. imperf. btwn. —
Set value 40

Micronesia, Marshall Islands

Canoe and Flag of the Federated States of Micronesia
A1865

Stick Chart, Canoe and Flag of the Republic of the Marshall Islands
A1866

1990, Sept. 28 *Perf. 11*
2506 A1865 25c multicolored 45 15
2507 A1866 25c multicolored 45 15
a. Pair, #2506-2507 1.00 16
b. As "a," black (engr.) omitted 3,500.
Set value 15

See Micronesia Nos. 124-126 and Marshall Islands No. 381.

Sea Creatures

Killer Whales
A1867

Northern Sea Lions
A1868

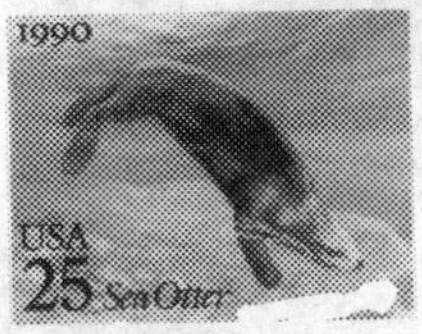

Sea Otter
A1869

Common Dolphin
A1870

1990, Oct. 3 **Litho. & Engr.** *Perf. 11*
2508 A1867 25c multicolored 45 15
2509 A1868 25c multicolored 45 15
2510 A1869 25c multicolored 45 15
2511 A1870 25c multicolored 45 15
a. Block of 4, #2508-2511 2.00 —
b. As "a," blk (engr.) omitted 1,000.
Set value 32

See Russia Nos. 5933-5936.

America Issue

Grand Canyon
A1871

1990, Oct. 12 **Photo.** *Perf. 11*
2512 A1871 25c multicolored 45 15

Dwight David Eisenhower

A1872

1990, Oct. 13 **Photo.** *Perf. 11*
2513 A1872 25c multicolored 45 15
a. Imperf., pair 2,000.

Christmas

Madonna and Child by Antonello da Messina — A1873

Christmas Tree — A1874

Litho. & Engr.
1990, Oct. 18 *Perf. 11½*
2514 A1873 25c multicolored 45 15
a. Booklet pane of 10 4.50

Photo.
Perf. 11
2515 A1874 25c multicolored 45 15
a. Vert. pair, imperf horiz. 1,100.

Perf. 11½x11 on 2 or 3 Sides
2516 A1874 25c multicolored 45 15
a. Booklet pane of 10 4.50 —
Set value 15

Marked differences exist between Nos. 2515 and 2516. The background red on No. 2515 is even while that on No. 2516 is splotchy. The bands across the tree and "GREETINGS" are blue green on No. 2515 and yellow green on No. 2516.

A1875

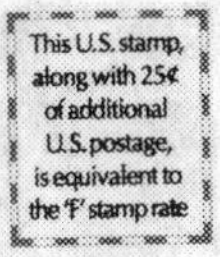

A1876

A1877

1991, Jan. 22 **Photo.** *Perf. 13*
2517 A1875 (29c) yel, blk, red & yel grn 50 15
a. Imperf., pair 750.00
b. Horiz. pair, imperf. vert. —

Coil Stamp
Perf. 10 Vert.
2518 A1875 (29c) yel, blk, dull red & dk yel grn 50 15
a. Imperf., pair 40.00

Booklet Stamps
Perf. 11 on 2 or 3 Sides
2519 A1875 (29c) yel, blk, dull red & dk grn 50 15
a. Booklet pane of 10 5.50 —
2520 A1875 (29c) pale yel, blk, red & brt grn 50 15
a. Booklet pane of 10 6.25 —
b. As "a," imperf horiz.

No. 2519 has bullseye perforations that measure approximately 11.2. No. 2520 has less pronounced black lines in the leaf, which is a much brighter green than on No. 2519.

Litho.
Perf. 11
2521 A1876 (4c) bister & car 15 15
a. Vert. pair, imperf. horiz. 150.00

Photo.
Imperf., Die Cut
Self-Adhesive
2522 A1877 (29c) blk, dk blue & red 50 25
a. Pane of 12 6.00

No. 2522 sold only in panes of 12; peelable plastic backing inscribed in light ultramarine. Available during a test period at 22 First National Bank automatic teller machines in Seattle.

Flag Over Mt. Rushmore
A1878

Flower
A1879

1991, Mar. 29 **Engr.** *Perf. 10 Vert.*
Coil Stamps
2523 A1878 29c bl, red & claret 50 15
b. Imperf., pair 20.00
c. Blue, red & brown 5.00 —

Photo.
2523A A1878 29c blue, red & brown 50 15

On No. 2523A, USA and 29 are not outlined in white and appear farther from edge of design.
Issue dates: #2523, Mar. 29. #2523A, July 4.

1991-92 **Photo.** *Perf. 11*
2524 A1879 29c dull yel, blk, red & pale yel grn 50 15
a. Perf. 13 50 15

Coil Stamps
Roulette 10 Vert.
2525 A1879 29c pale yel, blk, red & yel grn 50 15

Perf. 10 Vert.
2526 A1879 29c pale yel, blk, red & yel grn 50 15

Perf. 11 on 2 or 3 Sides
Booklet Stamp
2527 A1879 29c pale yel, blk, red & brt grn 50 15
a. Booklet pane of 10 5.00 —
b. As "a," vert. imperf between —
c. As "a," imperf horiz. —

Flower on No. 2524 has grainy appearance, inscriptions look rougher.
Issue dates: #2524, 2527, Apr. 5. #2525, Aug. 16. #2526, Mar. 3, 1992.

Flag, Olympic Rings — A1880

Perf. 11 on 2 or 3 Sides
1991, Apr. 21 **Photo.**
Booklet Stamp
2528 A1880 29c multicolored 50 15
a. Booklet pane of 10 5.00 —
b. As "a," horiz. imperf. between —

Fishing Boat — A1881

Balloon — A1882

1991, Aug. 8 **Photo.** *Perf. 10 Vert.*
Coil Stamp
2529 A1881 19c multicolored 35 15
a. Type II ('93) 35 15
b. As "a," untagged ('93) 35 15

Design of Type II stamps is created by a finer dot pattern. The vertical sides of "1" are smooth on Type II and jagged on Type I stamps.

Fishing Boat Type of 1991
1994, June 25 **Photo.** *Perf. 9.8 Vert.*
Coil Stamp
2529C A1881 19c multicolored 50 15

No. 2529C has one loop of rope tying boat to piling, numerals and USA are taller and thinner.

Perf. 10 on 2 or 3 Sides
1991, May 17 **Photo.**
Booklet Stamp
2530 A1882 19c multicolored 35 15
a. Booklet pane of 10 3.50 —

Flags on Parade — A1883

Liberty Torch — A1884

1991, May 30 **Photo.** *Perf. 11*
2531 A1883 29c multicolored 50 15

1991, June 25 **Photo.** *Die Cut*
Self-Adhesive
2531A A1884 29c blk, gold & grn 58 25
b. Pane of 18 10.50

Sold only in panes of 18; peelable paper backing inscribed in light blue.

Switzerland, 700th Anniv.

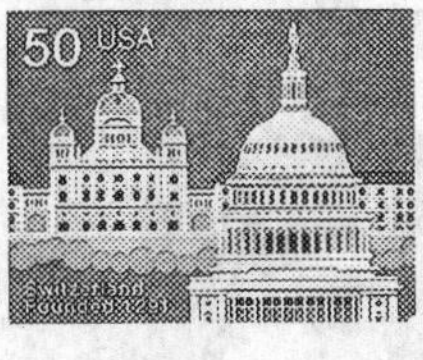

A1887

1991, Feb. 22 **Photo.** *Perf. 11*
2532 A1887 50c multicolored 1.00 25
a. Vert. pair, imperf horiz. 1,250.

Imperfs exist from printers' waste.
See Switzerland No. 888.

A1888

A1889

Vermont Statehood Bicentennial

1991, Mar. 1 *Perf. 11*

2533 A1888 29c multicolored 50 15

Savings Bonds, 50th Anniv.

1991, Apr. 30 Photo. *Perf. 11*

2534 A1889 29c multicolored 50 15

Love

A1890

A1891

1991, May 9 Photo. *Perf. 12½x13*

2535 A1890 29c multicolored 50 15
a. Perf. 11 58 15
b. Imperf., pair —

Perf. 11 on 2 or 3 Sides

Booklet Stamp

2536 A1890 29c multicolored 50 15
a. Booklet pane of 10 5.00 —

"29" is closer to edge of design on No. 2536 than on No. 2535.

Perf. 11

2537 A1891 52c multicolored 90 20

Literary Arts Series

William Saroyan A1892

1991, May 22 Photo. *Perf. 11*

2538 A1892 29c multicolored 50 15

See Russia No. 6002.

Eagle, Olympic Rings — A1893

1991, Sept. 29 Photo. *Perf. 11*

2539 A1893 $1 gold & multi 1.75 50

A1894

A1895

A1896

1991 Litho. & Engr. *Perf. 11*

2540 A1894 $2.90 Priority 5.00 2.50
2541 A1895 $9.95 Domestic express 15.00 7.50
2542 A1896 $14 Intl. express 22.50 10.00

Issue dates: $2.90, July 7. $9.95, June 16. $14, Aug. 31.

Priority Mail Rate

Futuristic Space Shuttle A1897

Perf. 11x10½

1993, June 3 Litho. & Engr.

2543 A1897 $2.90 multicolored 5.00 —

Fishing Flies

Royal Wulff A1899

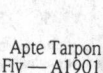

Jock Scott A1900

Apte Tarpon Fly — A1901

Lefty's Deceiver A1902

Muddler Minnow A1903

Perf. 11 Horiz. on 1 or 2 Sides

1991, May 31 Photo.

Booklet Stamps

2545 A1899 29c multicolored 50 15
2546 A1900 29c multicolored 50 15
2547 A1901 29c multicolored 50 15
2548 A1902 29c multicolored 50 15
2549 A1903 29c multicolored 50 15
a. Bklt. pane of 5, #2545-2549 2.50 —
Set value 50

Horiz. pairs, imperf. vert., exist from printers' waste.

A1904

A1905

Performing Arts

Cole Porter (1891-1964), Composer

1991, June 8 Photo. *Perf. 11*

2550 A1904 29c multicolored 50 15
a. Vert. pair, imperf. horiz. *600.00*

Operations Desert Shield & Desert Storm

1991, July 2 Photo. *Perf. 11*

2551 A1905 29c Southwest Asia service medal 50 15
a. Vert. pair, imperf horiz. *2,500.*

Perf. 11 on 1 or 2 Sides

Booklet Stamp

2552 A1905 29c multicolored 50 15
a. Booklet pane of 5 2.50 —

No. 2552 is 20½mm wide stamp. Inscriptions are shorter than on No. 2551.

Summer Olympics

Pole Vault A1907

Discus A1908

Women's Sprints A1909

Javelin A1910

Women's Hurdles A1911

1991, July 12 Photo. *Perf. 11*

2553 A1907 29c multicolored 50 15
2554 A1908 29c multicolored 50 15
2555 A1909 29c multicolored 50 15
2556 A1910 29c multicolored 50 15
2557 A1911 29c multicolored 50 15
a. Strip of #2553-2557 2.50 —
Set value 50

Numismatics

1858 Flying Eagle Cent, 1907 Standing Liberty Double Eagle, Series 1875 $1 Note, Series 1902 $10 National Currency Note — A1912

Litho. & Engr.

1991, Aug. 13 *Perf. 11*

2558 A1912 29c multicolored 50 15

World War II

A1913

Designs and events of 1941: a, Military vehicles (Burma Road, 717-mile lifeline to China). b, Recruits (America's 1st peacetime draft). c, Shipments for allies (US supports allies with Lend-Lease Act). d, Roosevelt, Churchill (Atlantic Charter sets war aims of allies). e, Tank (America becomes the "arsenal of democracy"). f, Sinking of Destroyer Reuben James, Oct. 31. g, Gas mask, helmet (Civil defense mobilizes Americans at home). h, Liberty Ship, sea gull (1st Liberty ship delivered Dec. 30). i, Sinking ships (Japanese bomb Pearl Harbor, Dec. 7). j, Congress in session (US declares war on Japan, Dec. 8). Central label is the size of 15 stamps and shows world map, extent of Axis control.

Illustration reduced.

1991, Sept. 3 Litho. & Engr. *Perf. 11*

2559 A1913 Block of 10 5.25 —
a.-j. 29c any single 52 29
k. Black (engr.) omitted *10,000.*

Basketball, 100th Anniversary

Basketball, Hoop, Players' Arms — A1914

1991, Aug. 28 Photo. *Perf. 11*

2560 A1914 29c multicolored 50 15

District of Columbia Bicentennial

Capitol Building from Pennsylvania Avenue, Circa 1903 A1915

1991, Sept. 7 Litho. & Engr. *Perf. 11*

2561 A1915 29c multicolored 50 15
a. Black (engr.) omitted *150.00*

Comedians

Stan Laurel and Oliver Hardy A1916

Edgar Bergen and Charlie McCarthy A1917

Jack Benny A1918

Fanny Brice A1919

Bud Abbott and Lou Costello A1920

Perf. 11 on 2 or 3 Sides

1991, Aug. 29 **Litho. & Engr.**

Booklet Stamps

2562 A1916 29c multicolored 50 15
2563 A1917 29c multicolored 50 15
2564 A1918 29c multicolored 50 15
2565 A1919 29c multicolored 50 15
2566 A1920 29c multicolored 50 15
a. Bklt. pane, 2 each #2562-2566 5.50 —
b. As "a," scarlet & bright violet (engr.) omitted *750.00*
c. Strip of 5, #2562-2566 2.50 —
Set value 50

Black Heritage

Jan E. Matzeliger (1852-1889), Inventor — A1921

1991, Sept. 15 **Photo.** ***Perf. 11***
2567 A1921 29c multicolored 50 15
a. Horiz. pair, imperf. vert. *1,250.*
b. Vert. pair, imperf. horiz. *1,750.*

Space Exploration

Mercury, Mariner 10 A1922

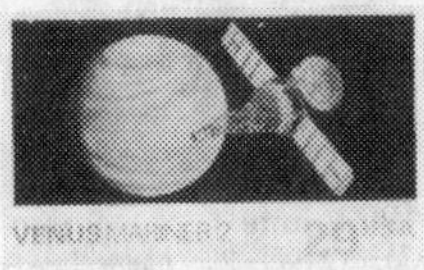
Venus, Mariner 2 A1923

Earth, Landsat A1924

Moon, Lunar Orbiter A1925

Mars, Viking Orbiter A1926

Jupiter, Pioneer 11 A1927

Saturn, Voyager 2 A1928

Uranus, Voyager 2 A1929

Neptune, Voyager 2 A1930

Pluto A1931

Perf. 11 on 2 or 3 Sides

1991, Oct. 1 **Photo.**

Booklet Stamps

2568 A1922 29c multicolored 50 15
2569 A1923 29c multicolored 50 15
2570 A1924 29c multicolored 50 15
2571 A1925 29c multicolored 50 15
2572 A1926 29c multicolored 50 15
2573 A1927 29c multicolored 50 15
2574 A1928 29c multicolored 50 15
2575 A1929 29c multicolored 50 15
2576 A1930 29c multicolored 50 15
2577 A1931 29c multicolored 50 15
a. Bklt. pane of 10, #2568-2577 5.50 —
Set value 80

Christmas

Madonna and Child by Antoniazzo Romano A1933

Santa Claus in Chimney A1934

Santa Checking List — A1935

Santa with Present — A1936

Santa at Fireplace — A1937

Santa and Sleigh — A1938

1991, Oct. 17 **Litho. & Engr.** ***Perf. 11***
2578 A1933 (29c) multicolored 50 15
a. Booklet pane of 10 5.80 —
b. As "a," single, red & black (engr.) omitted *3,000.*

Photo.

2579 A1934 (29c) multicolored 50 15
a. Horiz. pair, imperf. vert. *450.00*
b. Vert. pair, imperf. horiz. *625.00*

Booklet Stamps

Size: 25x18½mm

Perf. 11 on 2 or 3 Sides

2580 A1934 (29c) Type I 50 15
2581 A1934 (29c) Type II 50 15
a. Pair, #2580, 2581 1.00 25
b. Bklt. pane, 2 each #2580, 2581 2.00 —
2582 A1935 (29c) multicolored 50 15
a. Booklet pane of 4 2.00 —
2583 A1936 (29c) multicolored 50 15
a. Booklet pane of 4 2.00 —
2584 A1937 (29c) multicolored 50 15
a. Booklet pane of 4 2.00 —
2585 A1938 (29c) multicolored 50 15
a. Booklet pane of 4 2.00 —
Nos. 2578-2585 (8) 4.00
Set value 40

The extreme left brick in top row of chimney is missing from Type II, No. 2581.

Surrender of Gen. John François Burgoyne

A1942

1994, May 5 **Engr.** ***Perf. 11.5***
2590 A1942 $1 blue 2.00 50

Washington and Jackson

A1944

1994, Aug. 19 **Engr.** ***Perf. 11.5***
2592 A1944 $5 slate green 10.00 —

Pledge of Allegiance — A1946

Eagle and Shield — A1947

A1950

Statue of Liberty — A1951

Perf. 10 on 2 or 3 sides

1992-93 **Photo.**

Booklet Stamps

2593 A1946 29c black & multi 50 15
a. Booklet pane of 10 5.00 —

Perf. 11x10 on 2 or 3 Sides

2594 A1946 29c red & multi 50 15
a. Booklet pane of 10 5.00 —

Denomination is red on #2594 and black on #2593.

Issue dates: #2593, Sept. 8. #2594, 1993.

1992-94 **Litho. & Engr.** ***Die Cut***

Self-Adhesive

2595 A1947 29c brown & multi 50 25
a. Pane of 17 + label 9.50
b. Pair, no die cutting —
c. Brown (engr.) omitted —

Photo.

2596 A1947 29c green & multi 50 25
a. Pane of 17 + label 9.50
2597 A1947 29c red & multi 50 25
a. Pane of 17 + label 9.50
2598 A1950 29c red, cream & blue 50 15
a. Booklet pane of 18 9.00
2599 A1951 29c multicolored 50 15
a. Booklet pane of 18 9.00

Plate No. and inscription reads down on No. 2595a and up on Nos. 2596a-2597a. Design is sharper and more finely detailed on Nos. 2595, 2597.

Issued unfolded in panes of 17 + label; peelable paper backing is booklet cover. Sold for $5.

Issue dates: No. 2598, Feb. 4, 1994; No. 2599, June 24, 1994; others. Sept. 25, 1992.

A1956

A1957

A1959

A1960

Flag Over White House — A1961

1991-93 **Photo.** ***Perf. 10 Vert.***

Coil Stamps

2602 A1956 (10c) multicolored 20 15
a. Imperf. pair —
2603 A1957 (10c) orange yel & multi 20 20
a. Imperf. pair *30.00*
2604 A1957 (10c) gold & multi 20 20
2605 A1959 23c multi (Bureau precancel in blue) 40 40
2606 A1960 23c multi (Bureau Precanceled) 40 40
2607 A1960 23c multi (Bureau precanceled) 40 40
c. Imperf. pair *125.00*
2608 A1960 23c vio blue, red & blk 40 40

"23" is 7mm long on No. 2607. "First Class" is 8½mm long on No. 2608.

Engr.

2609 A1961 29c blue & red 50 15
a. Imperf., pair *20.00*
b. Pair, imperf between *100.00*

Issue dates: #2602, Dec. 13. #2603-2604, May 29, 1993. #2605, Sept. 27. #2606, July 21, 1992. #2607, Oct. 9, 1992. #2608, May 14, 1993. 29c, Apr. 23, 1992.

Winter Olympics

Hockey A1963

Figure Skating A1964

Speed Skating A1965

Skiing
A1966

Bobsledding
A1967

1992, Jan. 11 Photo. *Perf. 11*

2611 A1963 29c multicolored	50	15
2612 A1964 29c multicolored	50	15
2613 A1965 29c multicolored	50	15
2614 A1966 29c multicolored	50	15
2615 A1967 29c multicolored	50	15
a. Strip of 5, #2611-2615	2.50	—
Set value		40

A1968

A1969

World Columbian Stamp Expo

1992, Jan. 24 Litho. & Engr.

2616 A1968 29c Detail from #129	50	15

Black Heritage

1992, Jan. 31 Litho. & Engr. *Perf. 11*

2617 A1969 29c multicolored	50	15

W.E.B. Du Bois (1868-1963), writer and civil rights leader.

Love

A1970

1992, Feb. 6 Photo. *Perf. 11*

2618 A1970 29c multicolored	50	15
a. Horiz. pair, imperf vert.	*900.00*	

Olympic Baseball

A1971

1992, Apr. 3 Photo. *Perf. 11*

2619 A1971 29c multicolored	50	15

Voyages of Columbus

Seeking Queen Isabella's Support
A1972

Crossing the Atlantic
A1973

Approaching Land
A1974

Coming Ashore
A1975

1992, Apr. 24 Litho. & Engr. *Perf. 11*

2620 A1972 29c multicolored	50	15
2621 A1973 29c multicolored	50	15
2622 A1974 29c multicolored	50	15
2623 A1975 29c multicolored	50	15
a. Block of 4, #2620-2623	2.00	1.00
Set value		32

See Italy Nos. 1877-1880.

Voyages of Columbus
Souvenir Sheets

A1976

A1977

A1978

A1979

A1980

A1981

Illustrations reduced.

Margins on Nos. 2624-2628 are lithographed. Nos. 2624a-2628c, 2629 are similar in design to Nos. 230-245 but are dated 1492-1992.

Litho. & Engr.

1992, May 22 *Perf. 10½*

2624 A1976 Sheet of 3	1.60	—
a. A71 1c deep blue	15	15
b. A74 4c ultramarine	15	15
c. A82 $1 salmon	1.50	1.00
2625 A1977 Sheet of 3	6.25	—
a. A72 2c brown violet	15	15
b. A73 3c green	15	15
c. A85 $4 crimson lake	6.00	4.00
2626 A1978 Sheet of 3	1.25	—
a. A75 5c chocolate	15	15
b. A80 30c orange brown	45	30
c. A81 50c slate blue	75	50
2627 A1979 Sheet of 3	4.75	—
a. A76 6c purple	15	15
b. A77 8c magenta	15	15
c. A84 $3 yellow green	4.50	3.00
2628 A1980 Sheet of 3	3.50	—
a. A78 10c black brown	15	15
b. A79 15c dark green	22	15
c. A83 $2 brown red	3.00	2.00
2629 A1981 $5 Sheet of 1 Type A86	7.75	—
Nos. 2624-2629 (6)	25.10	

See Italy Nos. 1883-1888, Portugal Nos. 1918-1923 and Spain Nos. 2677-2682.

New York Stock Exchange Bicentennial

A1982

1992, May 17 Litho. & Engr. *Perf. 11*

2630 A1982 29c green, red & black	50	15

Space Accomplishments

Cosmonaut, US Space Shuttle — A1983

Astronaut, Russian Space Station — A1984

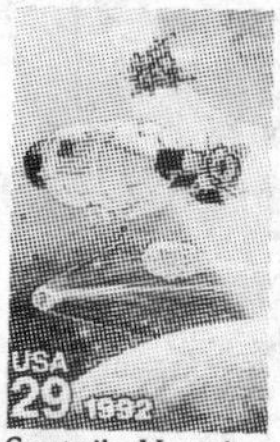

Sputnik, Vostok, Apollo Command & Lunar Modules
A1985

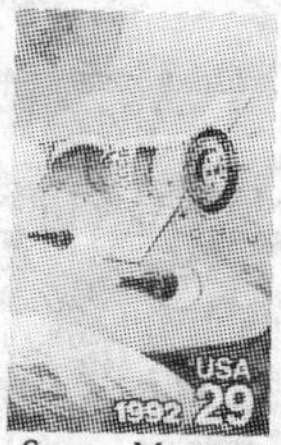

Soyuz, Mercury and Gemini Spacecraft
A1986

1992, May 29 Photo. *Perf. 11*

2631 A1983 29c multicolored	50	15
2632 A1984 29c multicolored	50	15
2633 A1985 29c multicolored	50	15
2634 A1986 29c multicolored	50	15
a. Block of 4, #2631-2634	2.00	1.00
Set value		32

See Russia Nos. 6080-6083.

Alaska Highway, 50th Anniversary

A1987

1992, May 30 Litho. & Engr. *Perf. 11*

2635 A1987 29c multicolored	50	15
a. Black (engr.) omitted	700.00	

All known examples of No. 2635a have poor to fine centering. It is valued in the grade of fine.

Kentucky Statehood Bicentennial

A1988

1992, June 1 Photo. *Perf. 11*

2636 A1988 29c multicolored	50	15

Summer Olympics

Soccer
A1989

Gymnastics
A1990

Volleyball A1991

Boxing A1992

Swimming A1993

1992, June 11 **Photo.** ***Perf. 11***

2637 A1989 29c multicolored 50 15
2638 A1990 29c multicolored 50 15
2639 A1991 29c multicolored 50 15
2640 A1992 29c multicolored 50 15
2641 A1993 29c multicolored 50 15
a. Strip of 5, #2637-2641 2.50 —
Set value 40

Hummingbirds

Ruby-throated A1994

Broad-billed A1995

Costa's A1996

Rufous A1997

Calliope — A1998

Perf. 11 on 1 or 2 sides
1992, June 15 **Photo.**

Booklet Stamps

2642 A1994 29c multicolored 50 15
2643 A1995 29c multicolored 50 15
2644 A1996 29c multicolored 50 15
2645 A1997 29c multicolored 50 15
2646 A1998 29c multicolored 50 15
a. Bklt. pane of 5, #2642-2646 2.50 —
Set value 40

Wildflowers

A1999-A2048

1992, July 24 **Litho.** ***Perf. 11***

2647 A1999 29c Indian paintbrush 50 15
2648 A2000 29c Fragrant water lily 50 15
2649 A2001 29c Meadow beauty 50 15
2650 A2002 29c Jack-in-the-pulpit 50 15
2651 A2003 29c California poppy 50 15
2652 A2004 29c Large-flowered trillium 50 15
2653 A2005 29c Tickseed 50 15
2654 A2006 29c Shooting star 50 15
2655 A2007 29c Stream violet 50 15
2656 A2008 29c Bluets 50 15
2657 A2009 29c Herb Robert 50 15
2658 A2010 29c Marsh marigold 50 15
2659 A2011 29c Sweet white violet 50 15
2660 A2012 29c Claret cup cactus 50 15
2661 A2013 29c White mountain avens 50 15
2662 A2014 29c Sessile bellwort 50 15
2663 A2015 29c Blue flag 50 15
2664 A2016 29c Harlequin lupine 50 15
2665 A2017 29c Twinflower 50 15
2666 A2018 29c Common sunflower 50 15
2667 A2019 29c Sego lily 50 15
2668 A2020 29c Virginia bluebells 50 15
2669 A2021 29c Ohi'a lehua 50 15
2670 A2022 29c Rosebud orchid 50 15
2671 A2023 29c Showy evening primrose 50 15
2672 A2024 29c Fringed gentian 50 15
2673 A2025 29c Yellow lady's slipper 50 15
2674 A2026 29c Passionflower 50 15
2675 A2027 29c Bunchberry 50 15
2676 A2028 29c Pasqueflower 50 15
2677 A2029 29c Round-lobed hepatica 50 15
2678 A2030 29c Wild columbine 50 15
2679 A2031 29c Fireweed 50 15
2680 A2032 29c Indian pond lily 50 15
2681 A2033 29c Turk's cap lily 50 15
2682 A2034 29c Dutchman's breeches 50 15
2683 A2035 29c Trumpet honeysuckle 50 15
2684 A2036 29c Jacob's ladder 50 15
2685 A2037 29c Plains prickly pear 50 15
2686 A2038 29c Moss campion 50 15
2687 A2039 29c Bearberry 50 15
2688 A2040 29c Mexican hat 50 15
2689 A2041 29c Harebell 50 15
2690 A2042 29c Desert five spot 50 15
2691 A2043 29c Smooth Solomon's seal 50 15
2692 A2044 29c Red maids 50 15
2693 A2045 29c Yellow skunk cabbage 50 15
2694 A2046 29c Rue anemone 50 15
2695 A2047 29c Standing cypress 50 15
2696 A2048 29c Wild flax 50 15
a. Pane of 50, #2647-2696 25.00 —

World War II

A2049

Designs and events of 1942: a, B-25's take off to raid Tokyo, Apr. 18. b, Ration coupons (food and other commodities rationed). c, Divebomber and deck crewman (US wins Battle of the Coral Sea, May). d, Prisoners of war (Corregidor falls to Japanese, May 6). e, Dutch Harbor buildings on fire (Japan invades Aleutian Islands, June). f, Headphones, coded message (Allies decipher secret enemy codes). g, Yorktown lost, US wins at Midway. h, Woman with drill (millions of women join war effort). i, Marines land on Guadalcanal, Aug. 7. j, Tank in desert (Allies land in North Africa, Nov.).

Central label is the size of 15 stamps and shows world map, extent of axis control.

Illustration reduced.

Litho. & Engr.
1992, Aug. 17 ***Perf. 11***

2697 A2049 Block of 10 5.25 2.90
a.-j. 29c any single 52 29
k. Red (litho.) omitted *10,000.*

Dorothy Parker — A2050

A2051

Literary Arts Series

1992, Aug. 22 **Photo.** ***Perf. 11***

2698 A2050 29c multicolored 50 15

1992, Aug. 31 **Photo.** ***Perf. 11***

2699 A2051 29c multicolored 50 15

Dr. Theodore von Karman (1881-1963), rocket scientist.

Minerals

Azurite — A2052

Copper — A2053

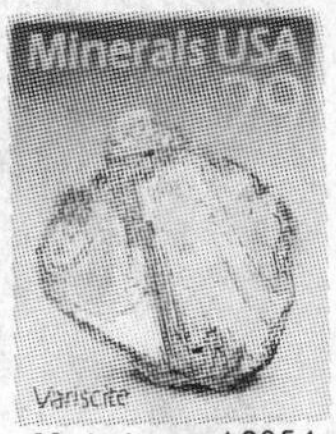

Variscite — A2054

Wulfenite — A2055

Litho. & Engr.
1992, Sept. 17 ***Perf. 11***

2700 A2052 29c multicolored 50 15
2701 A2053 29c multicolored 50 15
2702 A2054 29c multicolored 50 15
2703 A2055 29c multicolored 50 15
a. Block or strip of 4, #2700-2703 2.00 1.10
b. As "a," silver (litho.) omitted *8,000.*
Set value 32

Juan Rodriguez Cabrillo

Cabrillo (d. 1543), Ship, Map of San Diego Bay Area — A2056

Litho. & Engr.
1992, Sept. 28 ***Perf. 11***

2704 A2056 29c multicolored 50 15

Wild Animals

Giraffe A2057

Giant Panda A2058

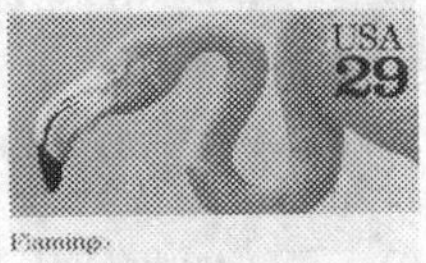

Flamingo A2059

King Penguins A2060

White Bengal Tiger A2061

Perf. 11 Horiz. on 1 or 2 sides
1992, Oct. 1 **Photo.**

Booklet Stamps

2705 A2057 29c multicolored 50 15
2706 A2058 29c multicolored 50 15
2707 A2059 29c multicolored 50 15
2708 A2060 29c multicolored 50 15
2709 A2061 29c multicolored 50 15
a. Booklet pane of 5, #2705-2709 2.50 —
b. As "a," imperforate
Set value 40

Christmas

Madonna and Child, by Giovanni Bellini — A2062

A2063

A2064

A2065

A2066

1992 **Litho. & Engr.** ***Perf. 11½x11***

2710 A2062 29c multicolored 50 15
a. Booklet pane of 10 5.00 —

Litho.

2711 A2063 29c multicolored 50 15
2712 A2064 29c multicolored 50 15
2713 A2065 29c multicolored 50 15
2714 A2066 29c multicolored 50 15
a. Block of 4, #2711-2714 2.00
Set value 40

Booklet Stamps

Photo.

Perf. 11 on 2 or 3 Sides

2715 A2063 29c multicolored 50 15
2716 A2064 29c multicolored 50 15
2717 A2065 29c multicolored 50 15
2718 A2066 29c multicolored 50 15
a. Bklt. pane of 4, #2715-2718 2.00 —
b. As "a," imperf horiz. —
Set value 40

Self-Adhesive

Die Cut

2719 A2064 29c multicolored 58 15
a. Booklet pane of 18 10.50

Issue dates: Nos. 2710-2718, Oct. 22. No. 2719, Oct. 28.

"Greetings" is 27mm long on Nos. 2711-2714, 25mm long on Nos. 2715-2718 and 21½mm long on No. 2719. Nos. 2715-2719 differ in color from Nos. 2711-2714.

New Year

A2067

1992, Dec. 30 Litho. & Engr. ***Perf. 11***

2720	A2067	29c	multicolored	50	15

American Music Series

Elvis Presley A2068

Oklahoma! A2069

Hank Williams A2070

Elvis Presley A2071

Bill Haley A2072

Clyde McPhatter A2073

Ritchie Valens A2074

Otis Redding A2075

Buddy Holly A2076

Dinah Washington A2077

1993, Jan. 8 Photo. ***Perf. 11***

2721	A2068	29c	multicolored	50	15

1993, Mar. 30 Photo. ***Perf. 10***

2722	A2069	29c	multicolored	50	15

1993

2723	A2070	29c	multicolored	50	15
a.			Perf. 11.2x11.4	20.00	*3.00*
2724	A2071	29c	multicolored	50	15
2725	A2072	29c	multicolored	50	15
2726	A2073	29c	multicolored	50	15
2727	A2074	29c	multicolored	50	15
2728	A2075	29c	multicolored	50	15
2729	A2076	29c	multicolored	50	15
2730	A2077	29c	multicolored	50	15
a.			Vertical strip of 7, #2724-2730	3.50	—
			Set value, #2724-2730		56

Booklet Stamps

Perf. 11 Horiz.

2731	A2071	29c	multicolored	50	15
2732	A2072	29c	multicolored	50	15
2733	A2073	29c	multicolored	50	15
2734	A2074	29c	multicolored	50	15
2735	A2075	29c	multicolored	50	15
2736	A2076	29c	multicolored	50	15
2737	A2077	29c	multicolored	50	15
a.			Booklet pane, 2 #2731, 1 each #2732-2737	4.00	—
b.			Booklet pane of 4, #2731, 2735-2737 + tab	2.00	—
			Set value		56

Issue dates: No. 2723, June 9. Others, June 16.

See Nos. 2769, 2771, 2775 and designs A2112-A2117.

Space Fantasy

A2086

A2087

A2088

A2089

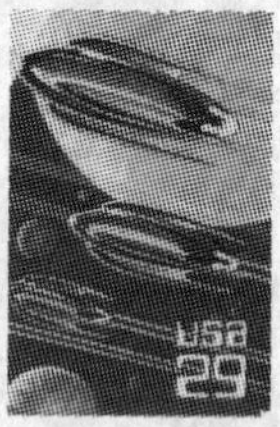

A2090

Perf. 11 Vert. on 1 or 2 Sides

1993, Jan. 25 Photo.

Booklet Stamps

2741	A2086	29c	multicolored	50	15
2742	A2087	29c	multicolored	50	15
2743	A2088	29c	multicolored	50	15
2744	A2089	29c	multicolored	50	15
2745	A2090	29c	multicolored	50	15
a.			Bklt. pane of 5, #2741-2745	2.50	—
			Set value		40

Black Heritage

Percy Lavon Julian (1899-1975), Chemist — A2091

1993, Jan. 29 Litho. & Engr. ***Perf. 11***

2746	A2091	29c	multicolored	50	15

Oregon Trail

A2092

1993, Feb. 12 Litho. & Engr. ***Perf. 11***

2747	A2092	29c	multicolored	50	15

World University Games

A2093

1993, Feb. 25 Photo. ***Perf. 11***

2748	A2093	29c	multicolored	50	15

Grace Kelly (1929-1982)

Actress, Princess of Monaco — A2094

1993, Mar. 24 Engr. ***Perf. 11***

2749	A2094	29c	blue	50	15

See Monaco No. 1851.

Circus

Clown — A2095

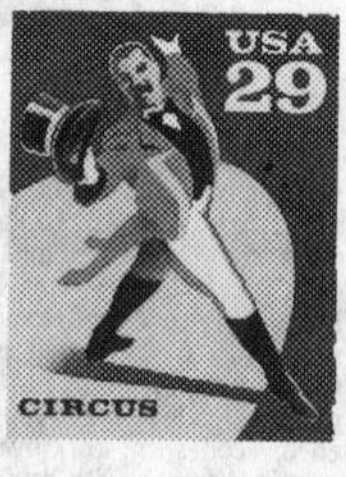

Ringmaster A2096

Trapeze Artist — A2097

Elephant A2098

1993, Apr. 6 Litho. ***Perf. 11***

2750	A2095	29c	multicolored	50	15
2751	A2096	29c	multicolored	50	15
2752	A2097	29c	multicolored	50	15
2753	A2098	29c	multicolored	50	15
a.			Block of 4, #2750-2753	2.00	1.10
			Set value		32

Cherokee Strip Land Run, Centennial

A2099

1993, Apr. 17 Litho. & Engr. ***Perf. 11***

2754	A2099	29c	multicolored	50	15

Dean Acheson (1893-1971)

Secretary of State — A2100

1993, Apr. 21 Engr. ***Perf. 11***

2755	A2100	29c	greenish gray	50	15

Sporting Horses

Steeplechase A2101

Thoroughbred Racing A2102

Harness Racing A2103

Polo
A2104

Perf. 11x11½

1993, May 1 **Litho. & Engr.**

2756	A2101 29c multicolored		50	15
2757	A2102 29c multicolored		50	15
2758	A2103 29c multicolored		50	15
2759	A2104 29c multicolored		50	15
a.	Block of 4, #2756-2759		2.00	1.10
b.	As "a," black (engr.) omitted		*2,000.*	
	Set value			32

Garden Flowers

Hyacinth
A2105

Daffodil
A2106

Tulip — A2107

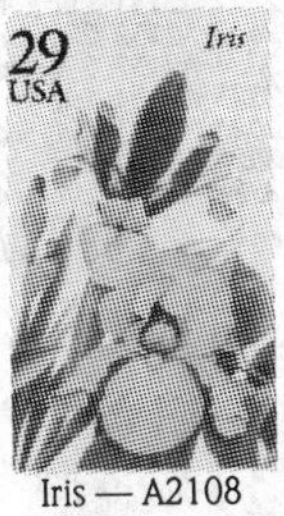

Iris — A2108

Lilac — A2109

Litho. & Engr.

1993, May 15 ***Perf. 11 Vert.***

2760	A2105 29c multicolored	50	15
2761	A2106 29c multicolored	50	15
2762	A2107 29c multicolored	50	15
2763	A2108 29c multicolored	50	15
2764	A2109 29c multicolored	50	15
a.	Booklet pane of 5, #2760-2764	2.50	—
b.	As "a," black (engr.) omitted	*475.00*	
c.	As "a," imperf	*3,000.*	
	Set value		40

World War II

A2110

Designs and events of 1943: a, Destroyers (Allied forces battle German U-boats). b, Military medics treat the wounded. c, Amphibious landing craft on beach (Sicily attacked by Allied forces, July). d, B-24s hit Ploesti refineries, August. e, V-mail delivers letters from home. f, PT boat (Italy invaded by Allies, Sept.). g, Nos. WS7, WS8, savings bonds (Bonds and stamps help war effort). h, "Willie and Joe" keep spirits high. i, Banner in window (Gold Stars mark World War II losses). j, Marines assault Tarawa, Nov.

Central label is the size of 15 stamps and shows world map with extent of Axis control and Allied operations.

Illustration reduced.

1993, May 31 **Litho. & Engr.** ***Perf. 11***

2765	A2110 Block of 10 + label	5.80	3.00
a.-j.	29c any single	58	30

Joe Louis (1914-1981)

A2111

1993, June 22 **Litho. & Engr.** ***Perf. 11***

2766	A2111 29c multicolored	50	15

American Music Series

Oklahoma! Type and

Show Boat — A2112

Porgy & Bess — A2113

My Fair Lady — A2114

Perf. 11 Horiz. on 1 or 2 Sides

1993, July 14 **Photo.**

Booklet Stamps

2767	A2112 29c multicolored	50	15
2768	A2113 29c multicolored	50	15
2769	A2069 29c multicolored	50	15
2770	A2114 29c multicolored	50	15
a.	Booklet pane of 4, #2767-2770	2.00	—

No. 2769 has smaller design size, brighter colors and shorter inscription than No. 2722, as well as a frameline around the design and other subtle design differences.

Hank Williams Type and

Patsy Cline
A2115

The Carter Family
A2116

Bob Wills
A2117

1993, Sept. 25 **Photo.** ***Perf. 10***

2771	A2070 29c multicolored	50	15
2772	A2115 29c multicolored	50	15
2773	A2116 29c multicolored	50	15
2774	A2117 29c multicolored	50	15
a.	Block or horiz. strip of 4, #2771-2774	2.00	1.10
	Set value		32

Booklet Stamps

Perf. 11 Horiz.

With Black Frameline

2775	A2070 29c multicolored	50	15
2776	A2116 29c multicolored	50	15
2777	A2115 29c multicolored	50	15
2778	A2117 29c multicolored	50	15
a.	Booklet pane of 4, #2775-2778	2.00	—
	Set value		32

Inscription at left measures 27mm on No. 2771, 27½mm on No. 2723 and 22mm on No. 2775. No. 2773 shows only two tuning keys on guitar, while No. 2771 shows those two and parts of two others.

National Postal Museum

Independence Hall, Benjamin Franklin, Printing Press, Colonial Post Rider
A2118

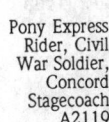

Pony Express Rider, Civil War Soldier, Concord Stagecoach
A2119

JN-4H Biplane, Charles Lindbergh, Railway Mail Car, 1931 Model A Ford Mail Truck
A2120

California Gold Rush Miner's Letter, Nos. 39, 295, C3a, C13, Barcode and Circular Date Stamp
A2121

1993, July 30 **Litho. & Engr.** ***Perf. 11***

2779	A2118 29c multicolored	50	15
2780	A2119 29c multicolored	50	15
2781	A2120 29c multicolored	50	15
2782	A2121 29c multicolored	50	15
a.	Block or strip of 4, #2779-2782	2.00	1.10

American Sign Language

A2122

A2123

Designs:

1993, Sept. 20 **Photo.** ***Perf. 11½***

2783	A2122 29c multicolored	50	15
2784	A2123 29c multicolored	50	15
a.	Pair, #2783-2784	1.00	20

Classic Books

A2124

A2125

A2126

A2127

Designs: No. 2785, Rebecca of Sunnybrook Farm, by Kate Douglas Wiggin. No. 2786, Little House on the Prairie, by Laura Ingalls Wilder. No. 2787, The Adventures of Huckleberry Finn, by Mark Twain. No. 2788, Little Women, by Louisa May Alcott.

1993, Oct. 23 **Litho. & Engr.** ***Perf. 11***

2785	A2124 29c multicolored	50	15
2786	A2125 29c multicolored	50	15
2787	A2126 29c multicolored	50	15
2788	A2127 29c multicolored	50	15
a.	Block or horiz. strip of 4, #2785-2788	2.00	1.10
	Set value		32

Christmas

Madonna and Child in a Landscape, by Giovanni Battista Cima — A2128

Jack-in-the-Box
A2129

Red-Nosed Reindeer
A2130

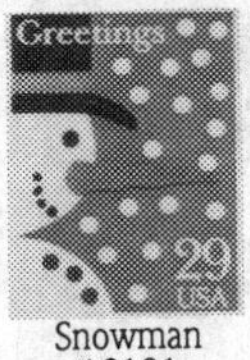

Snowman
A2131

Toy Soldier Blowing Horn
A2132

1993, Oct. 21 **Litho. & Engr.** ***Perf. 11***

2789	A2128 29c multicolored	50	15

Booklet Stamp

Size: 18x25mm

Perf. 11½x11 on 2 or 3 Sides

2790	A2128 29c multicolored	50	15
a.	Booklet pane of 4	2.00	—

No. 2790 has darker colors and smaller inscriptions than No. 2789.

1993 **Photo.** ***Perf. 11½***

2791	A2129 29c multicolored	50	15
2792	A2130 29c multicolored	50	15
2793	A2131 29c multicolored	50	15
2794	A2132 29c multicolored	50	15
a.	Block or strip of 4, #2791-2794	2.00	1.10

Booklet Stamps
Size: 18x21mm
Perf. 11x10 on 2 or 3 Sides

2795 A2132 29c multicolored 50 15
2796 A2131 29c multicolored 50 15
2797 A2130 29c multicolored 50 15
2798 A2129 29c multicolored 50 15
a. Booklet pane, 3 each #2795-2796, 2 each #2797-2798 5.00 —
b. Booklet pane, 3 each #2797-2798, 2 each #2795-2796 5.00 —

Self-Adhesive
Size: 19½x26½mm
Die Cut

2799 A2131 29c multicolored 50 15
2800 A2132 29c multicolored 50 15
2801 A2129 29c multicolored 50 15
2802 A2130 29c multicolored 50 15
a. Booklet pane, 3 each #2799-2802 6.00

Size: 17x20mm

2803 A2131 29c multicolored 50 15
a. Booklet pane of 18 9.00
Set value 1.05

Issue dates: Nos. 2791-2798, Oct. 21. Nos. 2799-2803, Oct. 28.

Snowman on Nos. 2793, 2799 has three buttons and seven snowflakes beneath nose (placement differs on both stamps). No. 2796 has two buttons and five snowflakes beneath nose. No. 2803 has two orange buttons and four snowflakes beneath nose.

Mariana Islands

A2133

1993, Nov. 4 Litho. & Engr. ***Perf. 11***
2804 A2133 29c multicolored 50 15

Columbus' Landing in Puerto Rico, 500th Anniv.

A2134

1993, Nov. 19 Photo. ***Perf. 11.2***
2805 A2134 29c multicolored 50 15

AIDS Awareness

A2135

1993, Dec. 1 Photo. ***Perf. 11.2***
2806 A2135 29c black & red 50 15
a. Perf. 11 vert. on 1 or 2 sides 50 15
b. As "a," booklet pane of 5 2.50 —

Winter Olympics

Slalom — A2136

Luge — A2137

Ice Dancing A2138

Cross-Country Skiing A2139

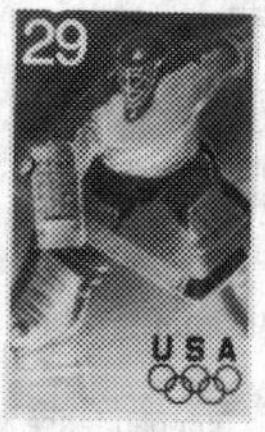

Ice Hockey — A2140

1994, Jan. 6 Litho. ***Perf. 11.2***
2807 A2136 29c multicolored 50 15
2808 A2137 29c multicolored 50 15
2809 A2138 29c multicolored 50 15
2810 A2139 29c multicolored 50 15
2811 A2140 29c multicolored 50 15
a. Strip of 5, #2807-2811 2.50 —
Set value 40

Edward R. Murrow, Journalist (1908-65)

A2141

1994, Jan. 21 Engr. ***Perf. 11.2***
2812 A2141 29c brown 50 15

Love

A2142

A2143

A2144

1994 Litho. & Engr. ***Die Cut***
2813 A2142 29c multicolored 50 15
a. Booklet pane of 18 9.00

Photo.
Perf. 10.9x11.1
2814 A2143 29c multicolored 50 15
a. Booklet pane of 10 5.00 —

Litho. & Engr.
Perf. 11.1
2814C A2143 29c multicolored 50 15

Photo. & Engr.
Perf. 11.2
2815 A2144 52c multicolored 1.00 20

Size of No. 2814C is 20x28mm. No. 2814 is 18x24½mm.

Issued: No. 2813, Jan. 27. Nos. 2814-2815, Feb. 14. No. 2814C, June 24.

Nos. 2813-2814 were issued in booklets only.

Black Heritage

Dr. Allison Davis (1902-83), Social Anthropologist, Educator — A2145

1994, Feb. 1 Engr. ***Perf. 11.2***
2816 A2145 29c red brown & brown 50 15

Chinese New Year

Year of the Dog — A2146

1994, Feb. 5 Photo. ***Perf. 11.2***
2817 A2146 29c multicolored 50 15

Buffalo Soldiers

A2147

Perf. 11.5x11.2
1994, Apr. 22 Litho. & Engr.
2818 A2147 29c multicolored 50 15

Silent Screen Stars

Rudolph Valentino (1895-1926) A2148

Clara Bow (1905-65) A2149

Charlie Chaplin (1889-1977) A2150

Lon Chaney (1883-1930) A2151

John Gilbert (1895-1936) A2152

Zasu Pitts (1898-1963) A2153

Harold Lloyd (1894-1971) A2154

Keystone Cops A2155

Theda Bara (1885-1955) A2156

Buster Keaton (1895-1966) A2157

Litho. & Engr.
1994, Apr. 27 ***Perf. 11.2***
2819 A2148 29c red, blk & brt vio 50 15
2820 A2149 29c red, blk & brt vio 50 15
2821 A2150 29c red, blk & brt vio 50 15
2822 A2151 29c red, blk & brt vio 50 15
2823 A2152 29c red, blk & brt vio 50 15
2824 A2153 29c red, blk & brt vio 50 15
2825 A2154 29c red, blk & brt vio 50 15
2826 A2155 29c red, blk & brt vio 50 15
2827 A2156 29c red, blk & brt vio 50 15
2828 A2157 29c red, blk & brt vio 50 15
a. Block of 10, #2819-2828 5.00 —
b. As "a," black (litho.) omitted —
c. As "a," black (litho.) and red & brt vio (engr.) omitted —
Set value 80

Garden Flowers

Lily — A2158

Zinnia — A2159

Gladiola A2160

Marigold A2161

Rose — A2162

Perf. 10.9 Vert.
1994, Apr. 28 Litho. & Engr.
Booklet Stamps
2829 A2158 29c multicolored 50 15
2830 A2159 29c multicolored 50 15
2831 A2160 29c multicolored 50 15
2832 A2161 29c multicolored 50 15
2833 A2162 29c multicolored 50 15
a. Booklet pane of 5, #2829-2833 2.50 —
Set value 40

1994 World Cup Soccer Championships

A2163

A2164

A2165

Design: 40c, Soccer player, diff.

1994, May 26 Photo. *Perf. 11.1*

2834	A2163	29c multicolored		50	15
2835	A2163	40c multicolored		80	18
2836	A2164	50c multicolored		1.00	20

Souvenir Sheet

2837	A2165	Sheet of 3, #a.-c.	2.50	—

Nos. 2834-2836 are printed on phosphor-coated paper, while Nos. 2837a (29c), 2837b (40c), 2837c (50c) are block tagged. No. 2837c has a portion of the yellow map in the LR corner.

World War II

A2166

Designs and events of 1944: a, Allied forces retake New Guinea. b, P-51s escort B-17s on bombing raids. c, Troops running from landing craft (Allies in Normandy, D-Day, June 6). d, Airborne units spearhead attacks. e, Officer at periscope (Submarines shorten war in Pacific). f, Parade (Allies free Rome, June 4; Paris, Aug. 25). g, Soldier firing flamethrower (US troops clear Saipan bunkers). h, Red Ball Express speeds vital supplies. i, Battleship firing main battery (Battle for Leyte Gulf, Oct. 23-26). j, Soldiers in snow (Bastogne and Battle of the Bulge, Dec.).

Central label is size of 15 stamps and shows world map with extent of Axis control and Allied operations.

Illustration reduced.

Litho. & Engr.

1994, June 6 *Perf. 10.9*

2838	A2166	Block of 10 + label	5.80	3.00
a.-j.		29c any single	58	30

Norman Rockwell

A2167

A2168

Perf. 10.9x11.1

1994, July 1 Litho. & Engr.

2839	A2167	29c multicolored	50	15

Souvenir Sheet

Litho.

2840	A2168	Sheet of 4	4.00	—
a.		50c Freedom from Want	1.00	65
b.		50c Freedom from Fear	1.00	65
c.		50c Freedom of Speech	1.00	65
d.		50c Freedom of Worship	1.00	65

Moon Landing, 25th Anniv.

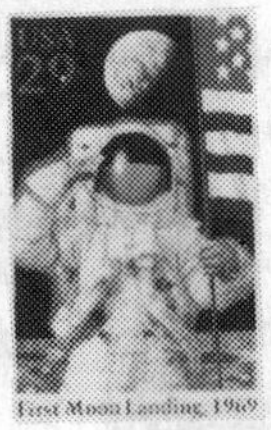

A2169

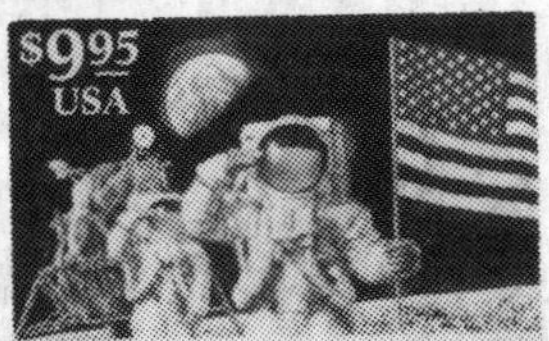

A2170

1994, July 20 Litho. *Perf. 11.2x11.1*

Miniature Sheet

2841	A2169	29c Sheet of 12	7.50	—
a.		Single stamp	60	60

Litho. & Engr.

Perf. 10.7x11.1

2842	A2170	$9.95 multicolored	17.50	7.50

Locomotives

Hudson's General A2171

McQueen's Jupiter A2172

Eddy's No. 242 — A2173

Ely's No. 10 — A2174

Buchanan's No. 999 — A2175

1994, July 28 Photo. *Perf. 11 Horiz.*

Booklet Stamps

2843	A2171	29c multicolored	50	15
2844	A2172	29c multicolored	50	15
2845	A2173	29c multicolored	50	15
2846	A2174	29c multicolored	50	15
2847	A2175	29c multicolored	50	15
a.		Booklet pane of 5, #2843-2847	2.50	—

George Meany, Labor Leader (1894-1980)

A2176

1994, Aug. 16 Engr. *Perf. 11.1x11*

2848	A2176	29c blue	50	15

American Music Series

Al Jolson (1886-1950) A2177

Bing Crosby (1904-77) A2178

Ethel Waters (1896-1977) A2179

Nat "King" Cole (1919-65) A2180

Ethel Merman (1908-84) A2181

Bessie Smith (1894-1937) A2182

Muddy Waters (1915-83) A2183

Billie Holiday (1915-59) A2184

Robert Johnson (1911-38) A2185

Jimmy Rushing (1902-72) A2186

"Ma" Rainey (1886-1939) A2187

Mildred Bailey (1907-51) A2188

Howlin' Wolf (1910-76) A2189

1994 Photo. *Perf. 10.1x10.2*

2849	A2177	29c multicolored	50	15
2850	A2178	29c multicolored	50	15
2851	A2179	29c multicolored	50	15
2852	A2180	29c multicolored	50	15
2853	A2181	29c multicolored	50	15
a.		Vert. strip of 5, #2849-2853	2.50	—
		Set value, #2849-2853		40

Perf. 11x10.8

Litho.

2854	A2182	29c multicolored	50	15
2855	A2183	29c multicolored	50	15
2856	A2184	29c multicolored	50	15
2857	A2185	29c multicolored	50	15
2858	A2186	29c multicolored	50	15
2859	A2187	29c multicolored	50	15
2860	A2188	29c multicolored	50	15
2861	A2189	29c multicolored	50	15
a.		Block of 9, #2854-2861 + 1 additional stamp	4.50	—
		Set value, #2854-2861		64

Issued: Nos. 2849-2853, 9/1/94. Nos. 2854-2861, 9/17/94.

Literary Arts Series

James Thurber (1894-1961) — A2190

Litho. & Engr.

1994, Sept. 10 *Perf. 11*

2862	A2190	29c multicolored	50	15

Wonders Of The Sea

Diver, Motorboat
A2191

Diver, Ship
A2192

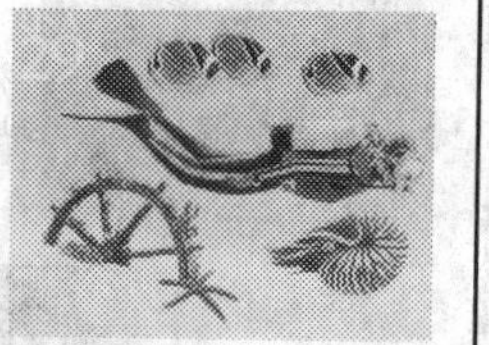

Diver, Ship's Wheel
A2193

Diver, Coral
A2194

1994, Oct. 3 Litho. *Perf. 11x10.9*

2863 A2191 29c multicolored	50	15
2864 A2192 29c multicolored	50	15
2865 A2193 29c multicolored	50	15
2866 A2194 29c multicolored	50	15
a. Block of 4, #2963-2966	2.00	1.10
b. As "a," imperf	—	
Set value		32

Cranes

Black-Necked
A2195

Whooping — A2196

Litho. & Engr.

1994, Oct. 9 *Perf. 10.8x11*

2867 A2195 29c multicolored	50	15
2868 A2196 29c multicolored	50	15
a. Pair, #2867-2868	1.00	20
b. Black and magenta (engr.) omitted	—	
Set value		15

See People's Republic of China Nos. 2528-2529.

Legends Of The West

Miniature Sheet

A2197

g. Bill Pickett (1870-1932) (Revised)

Designs: a, Home on the Range. b, Buffalo Bill Cody (1846-1917). c, Jim Bridger (1804-81). d, Annie Oakley (1860-1926). e, Native American Culture. f, Chief Joseph (c. 1840-1904). h, Bat Masterson (1853-1921). i, John C. Fremont (1813-90). j, Wyatt Earp (1848-1929). k, Nellie Cashman (c. 1849-1925). l, Charles Goodnight (1826-1929). m, Geronimo (1823-1909). n, Kit Carson (1809-68). o, Wild Bill Hickok (1837-76). p, Western Wildlife. q, Jim Beckwourth (c. 1798-1866). r, Bill Tilghman (1854-1924). s, Sacagawea (c. 1787-1812). t, Overland Mail.

1994, Oct. 18 Photo. *Perf. 10.1x10*

2869 A2197 Sheet of 20	12.00	—
a.-t. 29c any single	60	15

Legends Of The West (Recalled)

Miniature Sheet

g. Bill Picket (Recalled)

Nos. 2870b-2870d, 2870f-2870o, 2870q-2870s have a frameline around the vignette that is half the width of the frameline on similar stamps in No. 2869. Other design differences may exist.

1994 Photo. *Perf. 10.1x10*

2870 A2197 29c Sheet of 20	—	—

150,000 sheets were sold via selected orders canceled Oct. 1, 1994. The sheets were mailed December and January.

Christmas

Madonna and Child, by Elisabetta Sirani
A2200

Stocking
A2201

Santa Claus
A2202

Cardinal in Snow
A2203

Litho. & Engr.

1994, Oct. 20 *Perf. 11.1*

2871 A2200 29c multicolored	50	15
a. Perf. 9.8x10.8	50	15
b. As "a," booklet pane of 10	5.00	—
c. As "a," imperf	—	

Litho.

2872 A2201 29c multicolored	50	15
a. Booklet pane of 20	10.00	—

Booklet Stamps

Photo. *Die Cut*

Self-Adhesive

2873 A2202 29c multicolored	50	15
a. Booklet pane of 12	6.00	
2874 A2203 29c multicolored	50	15
a. Booklet pane of 18	9.00	
Set value, #2871-2874		40

Bureau Of Engraving & Printing

Souvenir Sheet

A2204

1994, Nov. 3 Litho. & Engr. *Perf. 11*

2875 A2204 $2 Sheet of 4	15.00	—
a. Single stamp	3.00	1.25

CHINESE NEW YEAR

Year of the Boar — A2205

1994, Dec. 30 Photo. *Perf. 11.2x11.1*

2876 A2205 29c multicolored	50	15

A2206

A2207

A2208

A2208a

A2209

1994, Dec. 13 Litho. *Perf. 11x10.8*

Untagged

2877 A2206 (3c) tan, bright blue & red	15	15
Perf. 10.8x10.9		
2878 A2206 (3c) tan, dark blue & red	15	15

Inscriptions on #2877 are in a thin typeface. Those on #2878 are in heavy, bold type.

PHOTOGRAVURE

Perf. 11.2x11.1

Tagged

2879 A2207 (20c) black "G," yellow & multi	40	15
Perf. 11x10.9		
2880 A2207 (20c) red "G," yellow & multi	40	15
Perf. 11.2x11.1		
2881 A2208 (32c) black "G" & multi	60	15
a. Booklet pane of 10	6.00	—
Perf. 11x10.9		
2882 A2208 (32c) red "G" & multi	60	15

Distance on #2882 from bottom of red G to top of flag immediately above is 13¾mm. Illustration A2208a shows #2885 superimposed over #2882.

BOOKLET STAMPS

Perf. 10x9.9 on 2 or 3 Sides

2883 A2208 (32c) black "G" & multi	60	15
a. Booklet pane of 10	6.00	—
Perf. 10.9 on 2 or 3 Sides		
2884 A2208 (32c) blue "G" & multi	60	15
a. Booklet pane of 10	6.00	—
Perf. 11x10.9 on 2 or 3 Sides		
2885 A2208a (32c) red "G" & multi	60	15
a. Booklet pane of 10	6.00	—

Distance on #2885 from bottom of red G to top of flag immediately above is 13½mm. See note below #2882.

A2208b

A2208c

Self-Adhesive ***Die Cut***

2886	A2208b	(32c) gray, blue, light blue, red & black	60	15
a.		Booklet pane of 18	11.00	

No. 2886 is printed on pre-phosphored paper and has only a small number of blue shading dots in the white stripes immediately below the flag's blue field.

2887	A2208c	(32c) black, blue & red	60	15
a.		Booklet pane of 18	11.00	

No. 2887 has noticeable blue shading in the white stripes immediately below the blue field and has overall tagging.

COIL STAMPS

Perf. 9.8 Vert.

2888	A2209	(25c) black "G"	50	15
2889	A2208	(32c) black "G"	60	15
2890	A2208	(32c) blue "G"	60	15
2891	A2208	(32c) red "G"	60	15

Rouletted 9.8 Vert.

2892	A2208	(32c) red "G"	60	15

A non-profit coil issued with this set has not been seen prior to processing of final pages for printing.

United States new issues through the March 1995 issue of the *Scott Stamp Monthly* appear here. If you want to keep current, a Business Reply Mail card is included at the back of this Catalogue for new subscribers.

Subject Index of Regular and Air Post Issues

AIR POST STAMPS

For prepayment of postage on all mailable matter sent by airmail.

Curtiss Jenny — AP1

Engraved (Flat Plate Printing)

1918	**Unwmk.**	***Perf. 11***	
C1 AP1 6c orange		55.00	25.00
Never hinged		75.00	
C2 AP1 16c green		80.00	27.50
Never hinged		110.00	
C3 AP1 24c car rose & blue		75.00	32.50
Never hinged		110.00	
a. Center inverted		*135,000.*	

Wooden Propeller and Radiator AP2

Emblem of Air Service AP3

De Havilland Biplane — AP4

1923		
C4 AP2 8c dark green	20.00	12.00
Never hinged	29.00	
C5 AP3 16c dark blue	75.00	25.00
Never hinged	105.00	
C6 AP4 24c carmine	75.00	22.50
Never hinged	110.00	

Map of US and Two Mail Planes AP5

1926-27		
C7 AP5 10c dark blue	2.25	25
Never hinged	3.25	
C8 AP5 15c olive brown	2.75	1.90
Never hinged	3.50	
C9 AP5 20c yellow green ('27)	7.00	1.50
Never hinged	10.00	

Lindbergh's Airplane "Spirit of St. Louis" — AP6

1927, June 18		
C10 AP6 10c dark blue	6.00	1.75
Never hinged	8.50	
a. Booklet pane of 3	75.00	*50.00*
Never hinged	87.50	

Singles from No. C10a are imperf. at sides or imperf. at sides and bottom.

Nos. C1-C10 were available for ordinary postage.

Beacon on Rocky Mountains AP7

1928, July 25	***Perf. 11***	
C11 AP7 5c carmine & blue	4.50	40
Never hinged	6.25	
a. Vertical pair, imperf. btwn.	*5,500.*	

Winged Globe AP8

1930, Feb. 10	***Perf. 11***	
Size: 46½x19mm		
C12 AP8 5c violet	8.00	25
Never hinged	11.50	
a. Horiz. pair, imperf. btwn.	*4,500.*	

See Nos. C16-C17, C19.

Graf Zeppelin Issue

Zeppelin over Atlantic Ocean AP9

Zeppelin between Continents — AP10

Zeppelin Passing Globe AP11

1930, Apr. 19	***Perf. 11***	
C13 AP9 65c green	260.00	150.00
Never hinged	350.00	
C14 AP10 $1.30 brown	500.00	350.00
Never hinged	675.00	
C15 AP11 $2.60 blue	800.00	500.00
Never hinged	1,100.	

Issued for use on mail carried on first Europe-Pan-America round-trip flight of Graf Zeppelin, May, 1930.

Type of 1930 Issue

Rotary Press Printing

1931-32	***Perf. 10½x11***	
Size: 47½x19mm		
C16 AP8 5c violet	4.75	35
Never hinged	6.00	
C17 AP8 8c olive bister ('32)	1.90	20
Never hinged	2.50	

Century of Progress Issue

Airship "Graf Zeppelin" AP12

Flat Plate Printing

1933, Oct. 2	***Perf. 11***	
C18 AP12 50c green	80.00	65.00
Never hinged	105.00	

Flight of the "Graf Zeppelin" in Oct. 1933, to Miami, Akron and Chicago, and from the last city to Europe.

Catalogue values for unused stamps in this section, from this point to the end of the section, are for Never Hinged items.

Type of 1930 Issue

Rotary Press Printing

1934, June 30	***Perf. 10½x11***	
C19 AP8 6c dull orange	2.25	15

Transpacific Issues

The "China Clipper" over the Pacific — AP13

Flat Plate Printing

1935, Nov. 22	***Perf. 11***	
C20 AP13 25c blue	1.10	75

Issued to pay postage on mail carried on the Transpacific air post service inaugurated Nov. 22, 1935.

The "China Clipper" over the Pacific AP14

1937, Feb. 15	***Perf. 11***	
C21 AP14 20c green	8.00	1.40
C22 AP14 50c carmine	7.50	4.00

Eagle Holding Shield, Olive Branch and Arrows — AP15

1938, May 14	***Perf. 11***	
C23 AP15 6c dk blue & carmine	40	15
a. Vert. pair, imperf. horiz.	375.00	
b. Horiz. pair, imperf. vert	*10,000.*	

Transatlantic Issue

Winged Globe AP16

1939, May 16	***Perf. 11***	
C24 AP16 30c dull blue	8.00	1.00

Twin-Motored Transport Plane — AP17

Rotary Press Printing

1941-44	***Perf. 11x10½***	
C25 AP17 6c carmine	15	15
a. Booklet pane of 3 ('43)	3.50	*1.00*
b. Horiz. pair, imperf. between	*1,500.*	
C26 AP17 8c olive green ('44)	16	15
C27 AP17 10c violet	1.10	20
C28 AP17 15c brown carmine	2.25	35
C29 AP17 20c bright green	1.75	30
C30 AP17 30c blue	2.00	30
C31 AP17 50c orange	9.50	2.75
Nos. C25-C31 (7)	16.91	4.20

Singles from No. C25a are imperf. at sides or imperf. at sides and bottom.

DC-4 Skymaster AP18

1946, Sept. 25	***Perf. 11x10½***	
C32 AP18 5c carmine	15	15

DC-4 Skymaster — AP19

1947, Mar. 26	***Perf. 10½x11***	
C33 AP19 5c carmine	15	15

See Nos. C37, C39, C41.

Pan American Union Building, Washington, DC — AP20

Statue of Liberty and New York Skyline AP21

Plane over San Francisco-Oakland Bay Bridge — AP22

1947	***Perf. 11x10½***	
C34 AP20 10c black	25	15
C35 AP21 15c brt blue green	35	15
a. Horiz. pair, imperf. between	*1,750.*	
C36 AP22 25c blue	85	15
Set value		23

Coil Stamp

1948, Jan. 15	***Perf. 10 Horiz.***	
C37 AP19 5c carmine	80	75

New York City Issue

Map of Five Boroughs, Circular Band and Planes — AP23

1948, July 31	***Perf. 11x10½***	
C38 AP23 5c bright carmine	15	15

50th anniv. of the consolidation of the 5 boroughs of NYC.

Type of 1947

1949, Jan. 18	***Perf. 10½x11***	
C39 AP19 6c carmine	15	15
a. Booklet pane of 6	9.50	*4.00*

Alexandria Bicentennial Issue

Home of John Carlyle, Alexandria Seal and Gadsby's Tavern — AP24

Rotary Press Printing

1949, May 11	***Perf. 11x10½***	
C40 AP24 6c carmine	15	15

Founding of Alexandria, Va, 200th anniv.

Type of 1947

Coil Stamp

1949, Aug. 25	***Perf. 10 Horiz.***	
C41 AP19 6c carmine	2.75	15

Universal Postal Union Issue

Post Office Department Building AP25

Globe and Doves Carrying Messages AP26

Boeing Stratocruiser and Globe — AP27

1949	**Unwmk.**	***Perf. 11x10½***	
C42 AP25 10c violet		20	18
C43 AP26 15c ultramarine		30	25
C44 AP27 25c rose carmine		50	40

75th anniv. of the UPU.

Wright Brothers Issue

Wilbur and Orville Wright and their Plane — AP28

1949, Dec. 17 *Perf. 11x10½*
C45 AP28 6c magenta 15 15

46th anniv. of the Wright Brothers' 1st flight, Dec. 17, 1903.

Diamond Head, Honolulu, Hawaii — AP29

1952, Mar. 26 *Perf. 11x10½*
C46 AP29 80c brt red violet 5.50 1.00

First Plane and Modern Plane AP30

Eagle in Flight AP31

Powered Flight Issue

1953, May 29 *Perf. 11x10½*
C47 AP30 6c carmine 15 15

50th anniversary of powered flight.

For Domestic Post Cards

1954, Sept. 3 *Perf. 11x10½*
C48 AP31 4c bright blue 15 15

See No. C50.

Air Force Issue

B-52 Stratofortress and F-104 Starfighters AP32

Rotary Press Printing

1957, Aug. 1 *Perf. 11x10½*
C49 AP32 6c blue 15 15

50th anniv. of US Air Force.

Flying Eagle Type of 1954
For Domestic Post Cards

1958, July 31 *Perf. 11x10½*
C50 AP31 5c rose red 15 15

Silhouette of Jet Airliner — AP33

1958, July 31 *Perf. 10½x11*
C51 AP33 7c blue 15 15
a. Booklet pane of 6 11.00 *6.00*

Coil Stamp

Perf. 10 Horizontally

C52 AP33 7c blue 2.25 15
Set value 15

See Nos. C60-C61.

Alaska Statehood Issue

Big Dipper, North Star and Map of Alaska — AP34

Rotary Press Printing

1959, Jan. 3 *Perf. 11x10½*
C53 AP34 7c dark blue 15 15

Alaska's admission to statehood.

Balloon Jupiter Issue

Balloon and Crowd — AP35

Giori Press Printing

1959, Aug. 17 *Perf. 11*
C54 AP35 7c dark blue & red 15 15

Cent. of the carrying of mail by the balloon Jupiter from Lafayette to Crawfordsville, Ind.

Hawaii Statehood Issue

Alii Warrior, Map of Hawaii and Star of Statehood AP36

Rotary Press Printing

1959, Aug. 21 *Perf. 11x10½*
C55 AP36 7c rose red 15 15

Hawaii's admission to statehood.

Pan American Games Issue

Runner Holding Torch — AP37

Giori Press Printing

1959, Aug. 27 *Perf. 11*
C56 AP37 10c violet blue & brt red 24 24

3rd Pan American Games, Chicago, Aug. 27-Sept. 7.

Liberty Bell — AP38

Statue of Liberty — AP39

Abraham Lincoln — AP40

Giori Press Printing

1959-66 *Perf. 11*
C57 AP38 10c blk & grn ('60) 1.25 70
C58 AP39 15c black & orange 35 15
C59 AP40 25c blk & mar ('60) 45 15
a. Tagged ('66) 45 30

Set value 82

Luminescence

See note following No. 1053. "Tagged" varieties of untagged airmail stamps start with No. C59a and end with No. C67a.

Airmail stamps starting with No. C69 are tagged unless otherwise noted.

Type of 1958

Rotary Press Printing

1960, Aug. 12 *Perf. 10½x11*
C60 AP33 7c carmine 15 15
a. Booklet pane of 6 15.00 *7.00*

Type of 1958
Coil Stamp

1960, Oct. 22 *Perf. 10 Horiz.*
C61 AP33 7c carmine 4.00 25

Type of 1959-60 and

Statue of Liberty — AP41

Giori Press Printing

1961-67 *Perf. 11*
C62 AP38 13c black & red 40 15
a. Tagged ('67) 75 50
C63 AP41 15c black & orange 30 15
a. Tagged ('67) 32 20
b. As "a," horiz. pair, imperf. vert. *15,000.*
Set value 16

No. C63 has a gutter between the two parts of the design; No. C58 has none.

Jet Airliner Over Capitol — AP42

Rotary Press Printing

1962, Dec. 5 *Perf. 10½x11*
C64 AP42 8c carmine 15 15
a. Tagged ('63) 15 15
b. Booklet pane 5 + label 6.75 *2.50*
c. As "b," tagged ('64) 1.65 *50*

Three different messages are found on the label in No. C64b, and one on No. C64c.

Coil Stamp

Perf. 10 Horizontally

C65 AP42 8c carmine 40 15
a. Tagged ('65) 35 15
Set value 15

The 1st luminescent tagged US issue was No. C64a issued Aug. 1, 1963, at Dayton, OH. Initial experiments there used tagged stamps and an automated facer-canceler to extract airmail as an aid to dispatch.

Montgomery Blair — AP43

Bald Eagle — AP44

Montgomery Blair Issue

Giori Press Printing

1963, May 3 **Unwmk.** *Perf. 11*
C66 AP43 15c car, dp claret & blue 60 55

Blair (1813-1883), Postmaster Gen. (1861-64), who called the 1st Intl. Postal Conf., Paris, 1863, forerunner of the UPU.

For Domestic Post Cards

Rotary Press Printing

1963, July 12 *Perf. 11x10½*
C67 AP44 6c red 15 15
a. Tagged ('67) 3.00 1.50

Amelia Earhart Issue

Amelia Earhart and Lockheed Electra — AP45

Giori Press Printing

1963, July 24 *Perf. 11*
C68 AP45 8c carmine & maroon 20 15

Earhart (1898-1937), 1st woman to fly across the Atlantic.

Dr. Robert H. Goddard Issue

Robert H. Goddard, Atlas Rocket and Launching Tower, Cape Kennedy AP46

1964, Oct. 5 **Unwmk.** **Tagged**
C69 AP46 8c blue, red & bister 40 15

Goddard (1882-1945), physicist and pioneer rocket researcher.

Tlingit Totem, Southern Alaska AP47

"Columbia Jays," by Audubon AP48

Alaska Purchase Issue

Giori Press Printing

1967, Mar. 30 *Perf. 11*
C70 AP47 8c brown 24 15

Cent. of the Alaska Purchase. The Tlingit totem is from the Alaska State Museum, Juneau.

1967, Apr. 26 *Perf. 11*
C71 AP48 20c multicolored 80 15

See note after No. 1241.

50-Star Runway — AP49

Rotary Press Printing

1968, Jan. 5 **Unwmk.** *Perf. 11x10½*
C72 AP49 10c carmine 18 15
b. Booklet pane of 8 2.00 75
c. Booklet pane of 5 + label 3.75 75

Coil Stamp

Perf. 10 Vertically

C73 AP49 10c carmine 30 15
a. Imperf., pair *600.00*
Set value 15

The $1 Air Lift stamp is listed as No. 1341.

Air Mail Service Issue

Curtiss Jenny — AP50

Lithographed, Engraved (Giori)

1968, May 15 *Perf. 11*

C74 AP50 10c blue, black & red 25 15
  a. Red (tail stripe) omitted —

50th anniv. of regularly scheduled US air mail service.

USA and Jet — AP51

1968, Nov. 22 *Perf. 11*

C75 AP51 20c red, blue & black 35 15

See No. C81.

Moon Landing Issue

First Man on the Moon — AP52

Litho. & Engr. (Giori)

1969, Sept. 9 *Perf. 11*

C76 AP52 10c multicolored 20 15
  a. Rose red (litho.) omitted *500.00* —

Man's 1st landing on the moon, July 20, 1969. US astronauts Neil A. Armstrong and Col. Edwin E. Aldrin, Jr., with Lieut. Col. Michael Collins piloting Apollo 11.

On No. C76a, the litho. rose red is missing from the entire vignette—the dots on top of the yellow areas as well as the flag shoulder patch.

Silhouette of Delta Wing Plane — AP53

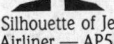

Silhouette of Jet Airliner — AP54

Winged Airmail Envelope — AP55

Statue of Liberty AP56

Design: 21c, "USA" and jet (as C75).

Rotary Press Printing

1971-73 *Perf. 10½x11*

C77 AP53 9c red 18 15

Perf. 11x10½

C78 AP54 11c carmine 18 15
  a. Booklet pane of 4 + 2 labels 1.10 *75*
  b. Untagged (Bureau precanceled) 30
C79 AP55 13c carmine ('73) 22 15
  a. Booklet pane of 5 + label ('73) 1.25 *75*
  b. Untagged (Bureau precanceled) 28

Giori Press Printing

Perf. 11

C80 AP56 17c bluish black, red & dark green 32 15

Litho. & Engr. (Giori)

Perf. 11

C81 AP51 21c red, blue & black 35 15
  Set value 47

Issue dates: 9c, May 15; 11c, May 7; 17c, July 13; 21c, May 21, 1971; 13c, Nov. 16, 1973.

The 9c was for use on domestic post cards.

No. C78b is precanceled "WASHINGTON D.C." (or "DC") and No. C79b "WASHINGTON DC" for the use of Congressmen and the public.

Coil Stamps

Rotary Press Printing

1971-73 ***Perf. 10 Vertically***

C82 AP54 11c carmine 25 15
  a. Imperf., pair *250.00*
C83 AP55 13c carmine ('73) 26 15
  a. Imperf., pair 80.00
  Set value 16

Issue dates: 11c, May 7; 13c, Dec. 27.

National Parks Centennial Issue

Kii Statue and Temple, City of Refuge, Hawaii — AP57

Litho. & Engr. (Giori)

1972, May 3 *Perf. 11*

C84 AP57 11c orange & multi 20 15
  a. Blue & green (litho) omitted *1,100.*

Cent. of the Natl. Parks system. No. C84 shows view of the City of Refuge Natl. Historical Park at Honaunau.

Olympic Games Issue

Skiing and Olympic Rings — AP58

Photogravure (Andreotti)

1972, Aug. 17 *Perf. 11x10½*

C85 AP58 11c multicolored 18 15

11th Winter Olympic Games, Sapporo, Japan, Feb. 3-13, and 20th Summer Olympic Games, Munich, Germany, Aug. 26-Sept. 11.

Electronics Progress Issue

De Forest Audions AP59

Litho. & Engr. (Giori)

1973, July 10 *Perf. 11*

C86 AP59 11c rose lilac & multi 22 15
  a. Vermilion & olive (litho.) omitted *1,400.*

Statue of Liberty AP60

Mt. Rushmore National Memorial AP61

1974 Giori Press Printing *Perf. 11*

C87 AP60 18c car, black & ultra 35 25
C88 AP61 26c ultra, black & car 48 15

Issue dates: 18c, Jan. 11; 26c, Jan. 2.

Plane and Globes — AP62

Plane, Globes and Flag — AP63

Giori Press Printing

1976, Jan. 2 *Perf. 11*

C89 AP62 25c ultra, red & black 45 15
C90 AP63 31c ultra, red & black 52 15
  Set value 24

Wright Brothers Issue

Orville and Wilbur Wright, Flyer A — AP64

Wright Brothers, Flyer A and Shed — AP65

Litho. & Engr.

1978, Sept. 23 *Perf. 11*

C91 AP64 31c ultra & multi 60 30
C92 AP65 31c ultra & multi 60 30
  a. Vert. pair, #C91-C92 1.20 85
  b. As "a," ultramarine & black (engr.) omitted *800.00*
  c. As "a," black (engr.) omitted —
  d. As "a," black, yellow, magenta, blue & brown (litho.) omitted *2,250.*

75th anniv. of 1st powered flight, Kill Devil Hill, NC, Dec. 17, 1903.

Octave Chanute Issue

Chanute and Biplane Hangglider AP66

Biplane Hanggliders and Chanute AP67

Litho. & Engr.

1979, Mar. 29 *Perf. 11*

C93 AP66 21c ultra & multi 70 32
C94 AP67 21c ultra & multi 70 32
  a. Vert. pair, #C93-C94 1.40 95
  b. As "a," ultramarine & black (engr.) omitted *4,500.*

Octave Chanute (1832-1910), civil engineer and aviation pioneer.

Wiley Post Issue

Wiley Post and "Winnie Mae" — AP68

NR-105 W, Post in Pressurized Suit, Portrait — AP69

Litho. & Engr.

1979, Nov. 20 *Perf. 11*

C95 AP68 25c ultra & multi 1.10 35
C96 AP69 25c ultra & multi 1.10 35
  a. Vert. pair, #C95-C96 2.25 95

Post (1899-1935), 1st man to fly around the world alone and high-altitude flying pioneer.

Olympic Games Issue

High Jump — AP70

1979, Nov. 1 **Photo.** *Perf. 11*

C97 AP70 31c multicolored 65 30

22nd Olympic Games, Moscow, July 19-Aug. 3, 1980.

Philip Mazzei (1730-1816), Italian-born Political Writer — AP71

1980, Oct. 13 **Photo.** *Perf. 11*

C98 AP71 40c multicolored 60 15
  a. Perf. 10½x11 3.00 —
  b. Imperf., pair *3,500.*
  c. Horiz. pair, imperf. vert. —

Blanche Stuart Scott (1886-1970) AP72

Glenn Curtiss (1878-1930) AP73

1980, Dec. 30

C99 AP72 28c multicolored 55 15
C100 AP73 35c multicolored 60 15

Scott, 1st woman pilot, and Curtiss, aviation pioneer and aircraft designer.

1984 Olympic Games

AP81

1983, June 17 *Perf. 11*

C101 AP81 28c Gymnast 60 28
C102 AP81 28c Hurdler 60 28
C103 AP81 28c Basketball 60 28
C104 AP81 28c Soccer 60 28
  a. Block of 4, #C101-C104 2.50 1.75
  b. As "a," imperf. vert. —

Nos. C101-C104 are vertical.

1983, Apr. 8

C105 AP81 40c Shot put 90 40
  a. Perf. 11x10½ 1.00 45
C106 AP81 40c Gymnast 90 40
  a. Perf. 11x10½ 1.00 45
C107 AP81 40c Swimmer 90 40
  a. Perf. 11x10½ 1.00 45
C108 AP81 40c Weightlifting 90 40
  a. Block of 4, #C105-C108 3.60 2.00
  b. As "a," imperf. *1,350.*
  c. Perf. 11x10½ 1.00 45
  d. As "a," perf. 11x10½ 4.25 —

1983, Nov. 4

C109 AP81 35c Women's fencing 90 35
C110 AP81 35c Cycling 90 35
C111 AP81 35c Women's volleyball 90 35
C112 AP81 35c Pole vaulting 90 35
  a. Block of 4, #C109-C112 3.60 1.85

Alfred V. Verville AP86

Lawrence and Elmer Sperry AP87

1985, Feb. 13 **Photo.**
C113 AP86 33c multicolored 60 20
a. Imperf., pair *800.00*
C114 AP87 39c multicolored 70 20
a. Imperf., pair *1,250.*

Alfred V. Verville (1890-1970), aircraft designer, Lawrence Sperry (1892-1931), designer and pilot, and Elmer Sperry (1860-1930), inventor.

Transpacific Airmail AP88

1985, Feb. 15 **Photo.**
C115 AP88 44c multicolored 80 20
a. Imperf., pair *800.00*

Fr. Junipero Serra (1713-84)
California Missionary

Outline Map of Southern California, Portrait, San Gabriel Mission AP89

1985, Aug. 22 **Photo.** ***Perf. 11***
C116 AP89 44c multicolored 80 20
a. Imperf., pair *1,500.*

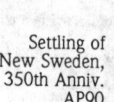

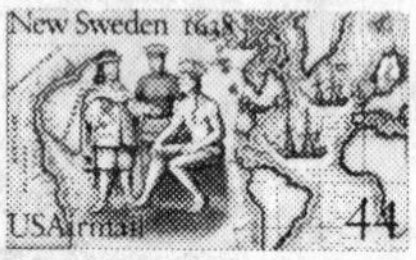
Settling of New Sweden, 350th Anniv. AP90

Design: 17th Cent. European settler negotiating with two American Indians, map of New Sweden, the Swedish ships *Kalmar Nyckel* and *Fogel Grip,* based on an 18th cent. illustration from a Swedish book about the Colonies.

1988, Mar. 29 **Litho. & Engr.**
C117 AP90 44c multicolored 1.00 20

See Finland No. 768 and Sweden No. 1672.

Samuel Pierpont Langley (1834-1906)
Astronomer, Aviation Pioneer and Inventor

Langley and Unmanned Aerodrome No. 5 — AP91

1988, May 14 **Litho. & Engr.** ***Perf. 11***
C118 AP91 45c multicolored 80 20

Igor Sikorsky (1889-1972)
Aeronautic Engineer

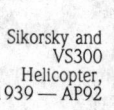

Sikorsky and VS300 Helicopter, 1939 — AP92

1988, June 23 **Photo.** ***Perf. 11***
C119 AP92 36c multicolored 65 20

French Revolution, Bicent.

Liberty, Equality and Fraternity — AP93

Perf. 11½x11
1989, July 14 **Litho. & Engr.**
C120 AP93 45c multicolored 80 22

America Issue

UPAE Emblem and Southeastern Figure, *Key Marco Cat,* Calusa Culture, Pre-Columbian Mississippian Period, A.D. 700-1450 — AP94

1989, Oct. 12 **Photo.** ***Perf. 11***
C121 AP94 45c multicolored 80 22

Discovery of America, 500th anniv. (in 1992).

Futuristic Mail Delivery

Spacecraft AP95
Air-suspended Hover Car AP96

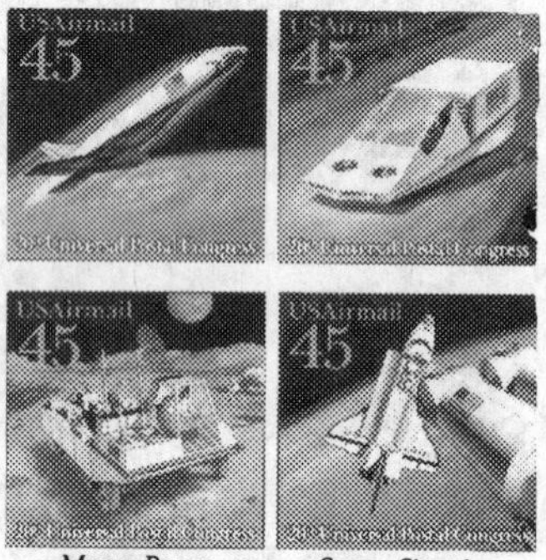
Moon Rover AP97
Space Shuttle AP98

1989, Nov. 27 ***Perf. 11***
C122 AP95 45c multicolored 90 30
C123 AP96 45c multicolored 90 30
C124 AP97 45c multicolored 90 30
C125 AP98 45c multicolored 90 30
a. Block of 4, Nos. C122-C125 3.60 2.25
b. As "a," light blue (engr.) omitted *1,000.*

1989, Nov. 24 **Litho. & Engr.** ***Imperf.***
C126 Sheet of 4 4.25 3.25
a. AP95 45c multicolored 90 50
b. AP96 45c multicolored 90 50
c. AP97 45c multicolored 90 50
d. AP98 45c multicolored 90 50

World Stamp Expo '89, 20th UPU Congress. See Russia No. 5837.

America Issue

Tropical Coast AP99

1990, Oct. 12 **Photo.** ***Perf. 11***
C127 AP99 45c multicolored 80 20

Harriet Quimby, Bleriot Aircraft AP100

1991, Apr. 27 **Photo.** ***Perf. 11***
C128 AP100 50c multicolored 90 24
a. Vert. pair, imperf. horiz. 2,000.
b. Perf. 11.2 ('93) 90 24

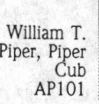

William T. Piper, Piper Cub AP101

1991, May 17
C129 AP101 40c multicolored 80 22

See No. C132.

Antarctic Treaty, 30th Anniv. AP102

1991, June 21 **Photo.** ***Perf. 11***
C130 AP102 50c multicolored 90 24

America Issue

First Americans Crossed Over From Asia — AP103

1991, Oct. 12 **Photo.** ***Perf. 11***
C131 AP103 50c multicolored 90 24

Piper Type of 1991
1993 **Photo.** ***Perf. 11***
C132 AP101 40c multicolored 80 22

Piper's hair touches top edge of design. Bullseye perf. 11.2.

AIR POST SPECIAL DELIVERY STAMPS

To provide for the payment of both the postage and the special delivery fee in one stamp.

Great Seal of United States — APSD1

Flat Plate Printing
1934 **Unwmk.** ***Perf. 11***
CE1 APSD1 16c dark blue 55 65
Never hinged 70

For imperforate variety see No. 771.

1936
CE2 APSD1 16c red & blue 30 20
Never hinged 40
a. Horiz. pair, imperf. vert. *4,000.*

SPECIAL DELIVERY STAMPS

When affixed to any letter or article of mailable matter, secure immediate delivery, between 7 A. M. and midnight, at any post office.

Messenger Running SD1

Flat Plate Printing
1885 **Unwmk.** ***Perf. 12***
E1 SD1 10c blue 200.00 30.00
Never hinged 300.00

Messenger Running SD2

1888
E2 SD2 10c blue 185.00 9.00
Never hinged 275.00

1893
E3 SD2 10c orange 120.00 15.00
Never hinged 180.00

Messenger Running SD3

Line under "Ten Cents"

1894
E4 SD3 10c blue 500.00 15.00
Never hinged 750.00

1895 **Wmk. 191**
E5 SD3 10c blue 100.00 2.00
Never hinged 150.00
b. Printed on both sides —

Messenger on Bicycle SD4

1902
E6 SD4 10c ultramarine 65.00 2.50
Never hinged 95.00

Helmet of Mercury and Olive Branch — SD5

1908
E7 SD5 10c green 40.00 25.00
Never hinged 60.00

1911 **Wmk. 190** ***Perf. 12***
E8 SD4 10c ultramarine 65.00 3.50
Never hinged 95.00
b. 10c violet blue 65.00 3.50
Never hinged 95.00

1914 ***Perf. 10***
E9 SD4 10c ultramarine 115.00 4.00
Never hinged 155.00

1916 **Unwmk.** ***Perf. 10***
E10 SD4 10c pale ultra 210.00 20.00
Never hinged 290.00

1917 ***Perf. 11***
E11 SD4 10c ultramarine 10.00 25
Never hinged 14.00
b. 10c gray violet 10.00 25
Never hinged 14.00
c. 10c blue 30.00 60
Never hinged 45.00

Postman and Motorcycle SD6

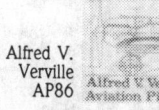

Post Office Truck — SD7

1922-25

E12 SD6 10c gray violet 20.00 15
Never hinged 27.50
a. 10c deep ultramarine 27.50 20
Never hinged 35.00
E13 SD6 15c deep orange ('25) 16.00 50
Never hinged 21.00
E14 SD7 20c black ('25) 1.65 85
Never hinged 2.25

No. E13 measures 36½x21½mm
No. E16 measures 36¾x22¼mm
No. E14 measures 35½x21½mm
No. E19 measures 36¼x22mm

Rotary Press Printing

1927-31 *Perf. 11x10½*

E15 SD6 10c gray violet 60 15
Never hinged 80
a. 10c red lilac 60 15
Never hinged 80
b. 10c gray lilac 60 15
Never hinged 80
c. Horiz. pair, imperf. btwn. 275.00

No. E15 measures 36½x21¾mm. Stamps from the flat plates measure 36x21½mm.

E16 SD6 15c orange ('31) 70 15
Never hinged 90
Set value 15

Catalogue values for unused stamps in this section, from this point to the end of the section, are for Never Hinged items.

1944-51

E17 SD6 13c blue 60 15
E18 SD6 17c orange yellow 2.75 1.75
E19 SD7 20c black ('51) 1.25 15

Special Delivery Letter, Hand to Hand — SD8

1954-57 *Perf. 11x10½*

E20 SD8 20c deep blue 40 15
E21 SD8 30c lake ('57) 50 15
Set value 15

Arrows — SD9

Giori Press Printing

1969-71 *Perf. 11*

E22 SD9 45c car & vio blue 1.25 15
E23 SD9 60c vio blue & car ('71) 1.10 15
Set value 22

Issue dates: 45c, Nov. 21; 60c, May 10.

REGISTRATION STAMP

Issued for the prepayment of registry fees; not usable for postage.

Eagle — RS1

Wmk. 190

1911, Dec. 1 Engr. *Perf. 12*

F1 RS1 10c ultramarine 60.00 4.00
Never hinged 85.00

CERTIFIED MAIL STAMP

For use on first-class mail for which no indemnity value is claimed, but for which proof of mailing and proof of delivery are available at less cost than registered mail.

Catalogue values for unused stamps in this section are for Never Hinged items.

Letter Carrier — CM1

Rotary Press Printing

1955, June 6 Unwmk. *Perf. 10½x11*

FA1 CM1 15c red 40 25

POSTAGE DUE STAMPS

For affixing, by a postal clerk to any piece of mailable matter, to denote the amount to be collected from the addressee because of insufficient prepayment of postage.

Unused Values for Nos. J1-J14 are for stamps with full original gum.

D1

D2

Printed by the American Bank Note Company

1879 Unwmk. Engraved *Perf. 12*

J1 D1 1c brown 30.00 5.00
J2 D1 2c brown 200.00 4.00
J3 D1 3c brown 25.00 2.50
J4 D1 5c brown 325.00 30.00
J5 D1 10c brown 350.00 15.00
a. Imperf., pair *1,600.*
J6 D1 30c brown 175.00 35.00
J7 D1 50c brown 225.00 40.00

Special Printing

1879

J8 D1 1c deep brown *6,250.*
J9 D1 2c deep brown *4,250.*
J10 D1 3c deep brown *3,900.*
J11 D1 5c deep brown *3,250.*
J12 D1 10c deep brown *2,250.*
J13 D1 30c deep brown *2,250.*
J14 D1 50c deep brown *2,400.*

1884

J15 D1 1c red brown 30.00 2.50
J16 D1 2c red brown 40.00 2.50
J17 D1 3c red brown 525.00 100.00
J18 D1 5c red brown 250.00 15.00
J19 D1 10c red brown 250.00 12.50
J20 D1 30c red brown 110.00 30.00
J21 D1 50c red brown 1,000. 125.00

1891

J22 D1 1c bright claret 14.00 50
J23 D1 2c bright claret 15.00 45
J24 D1 3c bright claret 32.50 5.00
J25 D1 5c bright claret 40.00 5.00
J26 D1 10c bright claret 75.00 11.00
J27 D1 30c bright claret 250.00 90.00
J28 D1 50c bright claret 275.00 90.00
Nos. J22-J28 (7) 701.50 201.95

See Die and Plate Proofs in Scott's U.S. Specialized for imperfs. on stamp paper.

Printed by the Bureau of Engraving and Printing

1894

J29 D2 1c vermilion 800. 200.
Never hinged 1,150.
J30 D2 2c vermilion 325. 60.
Never hinged 525.

1894

J31 D2 1c deep claret 22.50 3.00
Never hinged 32.50
b. Vert. pair, imperf. horiz.
J32 D2 2c deep claret 22.50 1.75
Never hinged 32.50
J33 D2 3c deep claret 90.00 20.00
Never hinged 125.00
J34 D2 5c deep claret 140.00 22.50
Never hinged 200.00
J35 D2 10c deep claret 140.00 17.50
Never hinged 200.00
J36 D2 30c deep claret 250.00 60.00
Never hinged 350.00
a. 30c carmine 250.00 75.00
Never hinged 350.00
b. 30c pale rose 210.00 55.00
Never hinged 325.00
J37 D2 50c deep claret 550.00 150.00
Never hinged 750.00
a. 50c pale rose 500.00 135.00
Never hinged 700.00

Shades are numerous in the 1894 and later issues.

See Die and Plate Proofs in Scott's U.S. Specialized for 1c imperf. on stamp paper.

1895 Wmk. 191

J38 D2 1c deep claret 5.00 30
Never hinged 9.00
J39 D2 2c deep claret 5.00 20
Never hinged 9.00
J40 D2 3c deep claret 35.00 1.00
Never hinged 55.00
J41 D2 5c deep claret 37.50 1.00
Never hinged 60.00
J42 D2 10c deep claret 40.00 2.00
Never hinged 62.50
J43 D2 30c deep claret 350.00 32.50
Never hinged 500.00
J44 D2 50c deep claret 210.00 25.00
Never hinged 300.00
Nos. J38-J44 (7) 682.50 62.00

1910-12 Wmk. 190

J45 D2 1c deep claret 20.00 2.00
Never hinged 30.00
a. 1c rose carmine 17.50 1.75
Never hinged 27.50
J46 D2 2c deep claret 20.00 30
Never hinged 30.00
a. 2c rose carmine 17.50 30
Never hinged 27.50
J47 D2 3c deep claret 375.00 20.00
Never hinged 525.00
J48 D2 5c deep claret 60.00 3.50
Never hinged 90.00
a. 5c rose carmine — —
J49 D2 10c deep claret 75.00 7.50
Never hinged 110.00
a. 10c rose carmine — —
J50 D2 50c deep claret ('12) 625.00 75.00
Never hinged 850.00

1914 *Perf. 10*

J52 D2 1c carmine lake 40.00 7.50
Never hinged 60.00
a. 1c dull rose 40.00 7.50
Never hinged 60.00
J53 D2 2c carmine lake 32.50 20
Never hinged 47.50
a. 2c dull rose 32.50 20
Never hinged 47.50
b. 2c vermilion 32.50 20
Never hinged 47.50
J54 D2 3c carmine lake 500.00 25.00
Never hinged 675.00
a. 3c dull rose 500.00 25.00
Never hinged 675.00
J55 D2 5c carmine lake 25.00 1.50
Never hinged 37.50
a. 5c dull rose 25.00 1.50
Never hinged 37.50
J56 D2 10c carmine lake 40.00 1.00
Never hinged 60.00
a. 10c dull rose 40.00 1.00
Never hinged 60.00
J57 D2 30c carmine lake 145.00 12.00
Never hinged 210.00
J58 D2 50c carmine lake *6,500.* 400.00
Never hinged 8,250.

1916 Unwmk. *Perf. 10*

J59 D2 1c rose 1,250. 200.00
Never hinged 1,800.
J60 D2 2c rose 95.00 12.50
Never hinged 140.00

1917 *Perf. 11*

J61 D2 1c carmine rose 1.75 15
Never hinged 2.75
a. 1c rose red 1.75 15
Never hinged 2.75
b. 1c deep claret 1.75 15
Never hinged 2.75
J62 D2 2c carmine rose 1.50 15
Never hinged 2.25
a. 2c rose red 1.50 15
Never hinged 2.25
b. 2c deep claret 1.50 15
Never hinged 2.25
J63 D2 3c carmine rose 8.50 15
Never hinged 12.50
a. 3c rose red 8.50 15
Never hinged 12.50
b. 3c deep claret 8.50 25
Never hinged 12.50
J64 D2 5c carmine 8.50 15
Never hinged 12.50
a. 5c rose red 8.50 15
Never hinged 12.50
b. 5c deep claret 8.50 15
Never hinged 12.50
J65 D2 10c carmine rose 12.50 20
Never hinged 18.50
a. 10c rose red 12.50 15
Never hinged 18.50
b. 10c deep claret 12.50 15
Never hinged 18.50
J66 D2 30c carmine rose 65.00 40
Never hinged 100.00
a. 30c deep claret 65.00 40
Never hinged 100.00
J67 D2 50c carmine rose 80.00 15
Never hinged 120.00
a. 50c rose red 80.00 15
Never hinged 120.00
b. 50c deep claret 80.00 15
Never hinged 120.00
Set value 1.00

1925

J68 D2 ½c dull red 70 15
Never hinged 95

D3

D4

1930 *Perf. 11*

J69 D3 ½c carmine 3.75 1.00
Never hinged 5.00
J70 D3 1c carmine 2.60 15
Never hinged 3.50
J71 D3 2c carmine 3.25 15
Never hinged 4.50
J72 D3 3c carmine 16.00 1.00
Never hinged 22.50
J73 D3 5c carmine 15.00 1.50
Never hinged 20.00
J74 D3 10c carmine 32.50 50
Never hinged 45.00
J75 D3 30c carmine 90.00 1.00
Never hinged 120.00
J76 D3 50c carmine 110.00 30
Never hinged 150.00
J77 D4 $1 carmine 27.50 15
Never hinged 35.00
a. $1 scarlet 22.50 15
Never hinged 30.00
J78 D4 $5 carmine 35.00 15
Never hinged 45.00
a. $5 scarlet 30.00 15
Never hinged 37.50

Rotary Press Printing

1931-56 *Perf. 11x10½*

J79 D3 ½c dull carmine 75 15
Never hinged 95
J80 D3 1c dull carmine 15 15
Never hinged 20
J81 D3 2c dull carmine 15 15
Never hinged 20
J82 D3 3c dull carmine 25 15
Never hinged 32
J83 D3 5c dull carmine 35 15
Never hinged 45
J84 D3 10c dull carmine 1.10 15
Never hinged 1.40
J85 D3 30c dull carmine 8.00 15
Never hinged 9.50
J86 D3 50c dull carmine 9.50 15
Never hinged 11.50

J79a D3 ½c scarlet 75 15
Never hinged 95
J80a D3 1c scarlet 15 15
Never hinged 22
J81a D3 2c scarlet 15 15
Never hinged 25
J82a D3 3c scarlet 25 15
Never hinged 32
J83a D3 5c scarlet 35 15
Never hinged 45
J84a D3 10c scarlet 1.10 15
Never hinged 1.40
J85a D3 30c scarlet 8.00 15
Never hinged 9.50
J86a D3 50c scarlet 9.50 15
Never hinged 11.50

Perf. 10½x11

J87 D4 $1 scarlet ('56) 35.00 20
Never hinged 45.00
Nos. J79-J87 (17) 75.50
Set value 65
Nos. J79a-J86a (8) 20.25
Set value 45

Catalogue values for unused stamps in this section, from this point to the end of the section, are for Never Hinged items.

D5

Denominations added by rubber plates in an operation similar to precanceling.

Rotary Press Printing
Perf. 11x10½

1959, June 19 **Unwmk.**

Denomination in Black

J88 D5 ½c carmine rose 1.25 85
J89 D5 1c carmine rose 15 15
a. "1 CENT" omitted *300.00*
b. Pair, one without "1 CENT" *450.00*
J90 D5 2c carmine rose 15 15
J91 D5 3c carmine rose 15 15
a. Pair, one without "3 CENTS" *750.00*
J92 D5 4c carmine rose 15 15
J93 D5 5c carmine rose 15 15
a. Pair, one without "5 CENTS" —
J94 D5 6c carmine rose 15 15
a. Pair, one without "6 CENTS" *800.00*
J95 D5 7c carmine rose 15 15
J96 D5 8c carmine rose 16 15
a. Pair, one without "8 CENTS" *750.00*
J97 D5 10c carmine rose 20 15
J98 D5 30c carmine rose 55 15
J99 D5 50c carmine rose 90 15

Straight Numeral Outlined in Black

J100 D5 $1 carmine rose 1.50 15
J101 D5 $5 carmine rose 8.00 15
Nos. J88-J101 (14) 13.61
Set value 1.60

All single copies with value omitted are catalogued as No. J89a.

1978-85

Denomination in Black

J102 D5 11c carmine rose 25 15
J103 D5 13c carmine rose 25 15
J104 D5 17c carmine rose ('85) 40 15
Set value 15

Issue dates: Jan. 2, 1978, June 10, 1985.

UNITED STATES OFFICES IN CHINA

Issued for sale by the postal agency at Shanghai, at their surcharged value in local currency. Valid to the amount of their original values for the prepayment of postage on mail dispatched from the US postal agency at Shanghai to addresses in the US.

Nos. 498-499, 502-504, 506-510, 512, 514-518 Surcharged

SHANGHAI
2¢
CHINA

1919 **Unwmk.** *Perf. 11*

K1 A140 2c on 1c green 17.50 20.00
Never hinged 27.50
K2 A140 4c on 2c rose, type I 17.50 20.00
Never hinged 27.50
K3 A140 6c on 3c vio, type II 32.50 45.00
Never hinged 50.00
K4 A140 8c on 4c brown 40.00 45.00
Never hinged 60.00
K5 A140 10c on 5c blue 45.00 52.50
Never hinged 67.50
K6 A140 12c on 6c red org 55.00 67.50
Never hinged 80.00
K7 A140 14c on 7c black 60.00 80.00
Never hinged 85.00
K8 A148 16c on 8c ol bis 45.00 50.00
Never hinged 67.50
a. 16c on 8c olive green 40.00 42.50
Never hinged 60.00
K9 A148 18c on 9c sal red 45.00 55.00
Never hinged 67.50
K10 A148 20c on 10c org yellow 40.00 47.50
Never hinged 60.00
K11 A148 24c on 12c brn carmine 47.50 60.00
Never hinged 70.00
a. 24c on 12c claret brown 67.50 90.00
Never hinged 100.00
K12 A148 30c on 15c gray 57.50 100.00
Never hinged 85.00
K13 A148 40c on 20c deep ultra 85.00 150.00
Never hinged 125.00
K14 A148 60c on 30c org red 80.00 125.00
Never hinged 115.00
K15 A148 $1 on 50c lt vio 300.00 400.00
Never hinged 500.00
K16 A148 $2 on $1 vio brown 275.00 325.00
Never hinged 400.00
a. Double surcharge *3,000.* *3,250.*
Nos. K1-K16 (16) 1,242. 1,642.

Nos. 498 and 528B Surcharged

SHANGHAI
2 Cts.
CHINA

1922, July 3

K17 A140 2c on 1c green 85.00 85.00
Never hinged 120.00
K18 A140 4c on 2c carmine, type VII 75.00 75.00
Never hinged 105.00

OFFICIAL STAMPS

The franking privilege having been abolished, as of July 1, 1873, these stamps were provided for each of the departments of Government for the prepayment of postage on official matter.

These stamps were supplanted on May 1, 1879, by penalty envelopes and on July 5, 1884, were declared obsolete.

Designs, except Post Office, resemble those illustrated but are not identical. Each bears the name of Department. Portraits are as follows: 1c, Franklin; 2c, Jackson; 3c, Washington; 6c, Lincoln; 7c, Stanton; 10c, Jefferson; 12c, Clay; 15c, Webster; 24c, Scott; 30c, Hamilton; 90c, Perry.

Practically all Official stamps of the 1870's exist imperf.

Grade, condition and original gum are very important in valuing No. O1-O120, unused.

Printed by the Continental Bank Note Co.

Thin Hard Paper

O1

1873 **Unwmk.** **Engr.** *Perf. 12*

Dept. of Agriculture

O1 O1 1c yellow 90.00 75.00
O2 O1 2c yellow 70.00 27.50
O3 O1 3c yellow 65.00 5.00
O4 O1 6c yellow 75.00 20.00
O5 O1 10c yellow 150.00 90.00
O6 O1 12c yellow 200.00 105.00
O7 O1 15c yellow 150.00 95.00
O8 O1 24c yellow 175.00 85.00
O9 O1 30c yellow 225.00 130.00

Special printings overprinted "SPECIMEN" follow No. O120.

Executive Dept.

O10 O1 1c carmine 350.00 190.00
O11 O1 2c carmine 225.00 110.00
O12 O1 3c carmine 275.00 100.00
a. 3c violet rose 275.00 100.00
O13 O1 6c carmine 400.00 275.00
O14 O1 10c carmine 375.00 225.00

Special printings overprinted "SPECIMEN" follow No. O120.

Dept. of the Interior

O15 O1 1c vermilion 20.00 5.00
O16 O1 2c vermilion 17.50 3.00
O17 O1 3c vermilion 27.50 3.00
O18 O1 6c vermilion 20.00 3.00
O19 O1 10c vermilion 19.00 5.00
O20 O1 12c vermilion 30.00 4.00
O21 O1 15c vermilion 50.00 9.00
O22 O1 24c vermilion 37.50 7.50
O23 O1 30c vermilion 50.00 7.50
O24 O1 90c vermilion 110.00 20.00

Special printings overprinted "SPECIMEN" follow No. O120.

Dept. of Justice

O25 O1 1c purple 60.00 45.00
O26 O1 2c purple 95.00 42.50
O27 O1 3c purple 95.00 9.00
O28 O1 6c purple 90.00 15.00
O29 O1 10c purple 100.00 32.50
O30 O1 12c purple 75.00 20.00
O31 O1 15c purple 165.00 70.00
O32 O1 24c purple 450.00 160.00
O33 O1 30c purple 400.00 100.00
O34 O1 90c purple 600.00 225.00

Special printings overprinted "SPECIMEN" follow No. O120.

Navy Dept.

O35 O1 1c ultramarine 45.00 15.00
a. 1c dull blue 52.50 17.50
O36 O1 2c ultramarine 32.50 9.00
a. 2c dull blue 42.50 9.00
O37 O1 3c ultramarine 37.50 5.00
a. 3c dull blue 42.50 7.00
O38 O1 6c ultramarine 32.50 7.50
a. 6c dull blue 42.50 7.50
O39 O1 7c ultramarine 225.00 80.00
a. 7c dull blue 250.00 80.00
O40 O1 10c ultramarine 45.00 17.50
a. 10c dull blue 50.00 17.50
O41 O1 12c ultramarine 57.50 12.50
O42 O1 15c ultramarine 95.00 25.00
O43 O1 24c ultramarine 95.00 32.50
a. 24c dull blue 110.00 —
O44 O1 30c ultramarine 85.00 15.00
O45 O1 90c ultramarine 425.00 90.00
a. Double impression *3,750.*

Special printings overprinted "SPECIMEN" follow No. O120.

O6

Post Office Dept.

O47 O6 1c black 7.25 3.00
O48 O6 2c black 7.00 2.50
a. Double impression 300.00
O49 O6 3c black 2.50 55
a. Printed on both sides *3,000.*
O50 O6 6c black 8.00 1.40
a. Diagonal half used as 3c on cover *3,000.*
O51 O6 10c black 40.00 17.50
O52 O6 12c black 22.50 5.00
O53 O6 15c black 25.00 7.50
O54 O6 24c black 32.50 9.00
O55 O6 30c black 32.50 7.50
O56 O6 90c black 47.50 7.50

Stamps of the POD are often on paper with a gray surface. This is due to insufficient wiping of the plates during printing.

Special printings overprinted "SPECIMEN" follow No. O120.

Seward — O8

Dept. of State

O57 O1 1c dark green 60.00 22.50
O58 O1 2c dark green 125.00 30.00
O59 O1 3c bright green 50.00 11.00
O60 O1 6c bright green 47.50 11.00
O61 O1 7c dark green 90.00 22.50
O62 O1 10c dark green 75.00 15.00
O63 O1 12c dark green 110.00 45.00
O64 O1 15c dark green 125.00 32.50
O65 O1 24c dark green 250.00 75.00
O66 O1 30c dark green 250.00 60.00
O67 O1 90c dark green 500.00 150.00
O68 O8 $2 green & black 550.00 425.00
O69 O8 $5 green & black 4,500. 2,000.
O70 O8 $10 green & black 3,000. 1,500.
O71 O8 $20 green & black 2,250. 850.00

Special printings overprinted "SPECIMEN" follow No. O120.

Treasury Dept.

O72 O1 1c brown 22.50 2.25
O73 O1 2c brown 25.00 2.25
O74 O1 3c brown 16.00 90
O75 O1 6c brown 22.50 2.00
O76 O1 7c brown 57.50 12.50
O77 O1 10c brown 57.50 4.00
O78 O1 12c brown 57.50 3.00
O79 O1 15c brown 50.00 4.00
O80 O1 24c brown 250.00 32.50
O81 O1 30c brown 82.50 5.00
O82 O1 90c brown 87.50 5.00

Special printings overprinted "SPECIMEN" follow No. O120.

War Dept.

O83 O1 1c rose 82.50 4.00
O84 O1 2c rose 75.00 5.00
O85 O1 3c rose 72.50 1.25
O86 O1 6c rose 250.00 3.00
O87 O1 7c rose 75.00 45.00
O88 O1 10c rose 22.50 5.00
O89 O1 12c rose 75.00 3.00
O90 O1 15c rose 20.00 3.50
O91 O1 24c rose 20.00 3.50
O92 O1 30c rose 22.50 3.00
O93 O1 90c rose 50.00 15.00

Special printings overprinted "SPECIMEN" follow No. O120.

Printed by the American Bank Note Co.

1879 **Soft Porous Paper**

Dept. of Agriculture

O94 O1 1c yel, no gum 1,600.
O95 O1 3c yellow 175.00 40.00

Dept. of the Interior

O96 O1 1c vermilion 120.00 95.00
O97 O1 2c vermilion 2.50 1.00
O98 O1 3c vermilion 2.00 60
O99 O1 6c vermilion 3.00 2.50
O100 O1 10c vermilion 37.50 30.00
O101 O1 12c vermilion 70.00 45.00
O102 O1 15c vermilion 160.00 75.00
O103 O1 24c vermilion 2,100. —

Dept. of Justice

O106 O1 3c bluish purple 50.00 30.00
O107 O1 6c bluish purple 110.00 95.00

Post Office Dept.

O108 O6 3c black 7.50 2.50

Treasury Dept.

O109 O1 3c brown 27.50 3.00
O110 O1 6c brown 50.00 17.50
O111 O1 10c brown 70.00 20.00
O112 O1 30c brown 800.00 140.00
O113 O1 90c brown 825.00 140.00

War Dept.

O114 O1 1c rose red 2.00 1.50
O115 O1 2c rose red 3.00 1.50
O116 O1 3c rose red 3.00 75
a. Imperf., pair *900.00*
b. Double impression 750.00
O117 O1 6c rose red 2.50 80
O118 O1 10c rose red 20.00 17.50
O119 O1 12c rose red 15.00 5.00
O120 O1 30c rose red 47.50 40.00

SPECIAL PRINTINGS

Special printings of Official stamps were made in 1875 at the time the other Reprints, Re-issues and Special Printings were printed. They are ungummed.

Although perforated, these stamps were sometimes (but not always) cut apart with scissors. As a result the perforations may be mutilated and the design damaged.

All values exist imperforate.

Overprinted in Block Letters **SPECIMEN**

1875 *Perf. 12*

Thin, hard white paper

Type D

AGRICULTURE

Carmine Overprint

O1S D 1c yellow 8.50
a. "Sepcimen" error 475.00
b. Small dotted "i" in "Specimen" 250.00
c. Ribbed paper 15.00
O2S D 2c yellow 17.50
a. "Sepcimen" error 525.00
O3S D 3c yellow 50.00
a. "Sepcimen" error 2,250.
O4S D 6c yellow 87.50
a. "Sepcimen" error 3,500.
O5S D 10c yellow 87.50
a. "Sepcimen" error 2,250.
O6S D 12c yellow 80.00
a. "Sepcimen" error 2,250.
O7S D 15c yellow 80.00
a. "Sepcimen" error 2,250.
O8S D 24c yellow 80.00
a. "Sepcimen" error 2,250.
O9S D 30c yellow 80.00
a. "Sepcimen" error 2,250.

EXECUTIVE

Blue Overprint

O10S D 1c carmine 8.50
a. Small dotted "i" in "Specimen" 200.00
b. Ribbed paper 15.00
O11S D 2c carmine 17.50
O12S D 3c carmine 17.50
O13S D 6c carmine 17.50
O14S D 10c carmine 17.50

INTERIOR

Blue Overprint

O15S D 1c vermilion 15.00
O16S D 2c vermilion 25.00
a. "Sepcimen" error 2,750.
O17S D 3c vermilion 350.00
O18S D 6c vermilion 325.00
O19S D 10c vermilion 325.00
O20S D 12c vermilion 350.00
O21S D 15c vermilion 350.00
O22S D 24c vermilion 350.00
O23S D 30c vermilion 350.00
O24S D 90c vermilion 350.00

JUSTICE

Blue Overprint

O25S D 1c purple 8.50
a. "Sepcimen" error 450.00
b. Small dotted "i" in "Specimen" 150.00
c. Ribbed paper 15.00
O26S D 2c purple 17.50
a. "Sepcimen" error 750.00

O27S D 3c purple 150.00
a. "Sepcimen" error 3,000.
O28S D 6c purple 150.00
O29S D 10c purple 145.00
O30S D 12c purple 145.00
a. "Sepcimen" error 3,500.
O31S D 15c purple 175.00
a. "Sepcimen" error 3,500.
O32S D 24c purple 190.00
a. "Sepcimen" error 3,500.
O33S D 30c purple 190.00
a. "Sepcimen" error 3,500.
O34S D 90c purple 190.00

NAVY

Carmine Overprint

O35S D 1c ultramarine 11.00
a. "Sepcimen" error 375.00
b. Broken "i" in "Specimen" —
O36S D 2c ultramarine 22.50
a. "Sepcimen" error 475.00
b. Broken "i" in "Specimen" —
O37S D 3c ultramarine 190.00
O38S D 6c ultramarine 225.00
O39S D 7c ultramarine 85.00
a. "Sepcimen" error 1,200.
O40S D 10c ultramarine 225.00
a. "Sepcimen" error 3,500.
O41S D 12c ultramarine 200.00
a. "Sepcimen" error 2,750.
O42S D 15c ultramarine 200.00
a. "Sepcimen" error 3,500.
O43S D 24c ultramarine 200.00
a. "Sepcimen" error 3,500.
O44S D 30c ultramarine 200.00
a. "Sepcimen" error 3,500.
O45S D 90c ultramarine 200.00

The existence is Nos. O35Sb and O36Sb has been questioned.

POST OFFICE

Carmine Overprint

O47S D 1c black 15.00
a. "Sepcimen" error 450.00
b. Inverted overprint 500.00
O48S D 2c black 45.00
a. "Sepcimen" error 1,200.
O49S D 3c black 260.00
a. "Sepcimen" error —
O50S D 6c black 260.00
O51S D 10c black 180.00
a. "Sepcimen" error 3,500.
O52S D 12c black 260.00
O53S D 15c black 280.00
a. "Sepcimen" error 3,500.
O54S D 24c black 260.00
a. "Sepcimen" error 3,500.
O55S D 30c black 275.00
O56S D 90c black 275.00
a. "Sepcimen" error 3,500.

The existence of No. O49Sa has been questioned.

STATE

Carmine Overprint

O57S D 1c bluish green 8.50
a. "Sepcimen" error 275.00
b. Small dotted "i" in "Specimen" 225.00
c. Ribbed paper 15.00
O58S D 2c bluish green 17.50
a. "Sepcimen" error 375.00
O59S D 3c bluish green 30.00
a. "Sepcimen" error 1,200.
O60S D 6c bluish green 60.00
a. "Sepcimen" error 1,500.
O61S D 7c bluish green 30.00
a. "Sepcimen" error 1,200.
O62S D 10c bluish green 110.00
a. "Sepcimen" error 5,750.
O63S D 12c bluish green 120.00
a. "Sepcimen" error 2,750.
O64S D 15c bluish green 120.00
O65S D 24c bluish green 120.00
a. "Sepcimen" error 2,750.
O66S D 30c bluish green 120.00
a. "Sepcimen" error 2,750.
O67S D 90c bluish green 120.00
a. "Sepcimen" error 2,750.
O68S D $2 green & black 4,750.
O69S D $5 green & black 6,750.
O70S D $10 green & black 9,000.
O71S D $20 green & black 10,000.

TREASURY

Blue Overprint

O72S D 1c dark brown 17.50
O73S D 2c dark brown 85.00
O74S D 3c dark brown 260.00
O75S D 6c dark brown 300.00
O76S D 7c dark brown 175.00
O77S D 10c dark brown 260.00
O78S D 12c dark brown 275.00
O79S D 15c dark brown 275.00
O80S D 24c dark brown 260.00
O81S D 30c dark brown 375.00
O82S D 90c dark brown 375.00

WAR

Blue Overprint

O83S D 1c deep rose 11.00
a. "Sepcimen" error 375.00
O84S D 2c deep rose 22.50
a. "Sepcimen" error 675.00
O85S D 3c deep rose 220.00
a. "Sepcimen" error 3,500.
O86S D 6c deep rose 260.00
a. "Sepcimen" error 3,500.
O87S D 7c deep rose 45.00
a. "Sepcimen" error 1,250.
O88S D 10c deep rose 210.00
a. "Sepcimen" error 3,500.
O89S D 12c deep rose 260.00
a. "Sepcimen" error 3,500.
O90S D 15c deep rose 260.00
a. "Sepcimen" error 3,500.
O91S D 24c deep rose 260.00
a. "Sepcimen" error 3,500.
O92S D 30c deep rose 260.00
a. "Sepcimen" error 3,500.
O93S D 90c deep rose 260.00
a. "Sepcimen" error 3,500.

SOFT POROUS PAPER

EXECUTIVE

Blue Overprint

O10xS D 1c violet rose 27.50

NAVY

Carmine Overprint

O35xS D 1c gray blue 32.50
a. Double overprint 600.00

STATE

O57xS D 1c yellow green 120.00

Official Postal Savings Mail

These stamps were used to prepay postage on official correspondence of the Postal Savings Division of the POD. Discontinued Sept. 23, 1914.

O11

1911 **Wmk. 191**

O121 O11 2c black 9.00 1.10
Never hinged 14.00
O122 O11 50c dark green 110.00 25.00
Never hinged 165.00
O123 O11 $1 ultra 100.00 7.00
Never hinged 150.00

Wmk. 190

O124 O11 1c dark violet 5.50 1.00
Never hinged 7.50
O125 O11 2c black 30.00 3.50
Never hinged 45.00
O126 O11 10c carmine 10.00 1.00
Never hinged 15.00

Catalogue values for unused stamps in this section, from this point to the end of the section, are for Never Hinged items.

Catalogue values for used stamps are for regularly used copies, not copies removed from first day covers.

Official Mail

O12

O13

Type O13 has frame line completely around blue design.

1983-85 ***Perf. 11***

O127 O12 1c red, bl & blk 15 15
O128 O12 4c red, bl & blk 15 25
O129 O12 13c red, bl & blk 26 75
O129A O12 14c red, bl & blk ('85) 28 50
O130 O12 17c red, bl & blk 34 40
O132 O12 $1 red, bl & blk 1.75 1.00
O133 O12 $5 red, bl & blk 9.00 5.00
Nos. O127-O133 (7) 11.93 8.05

Coil Stamps

Perf. 10 Vert.

O135 O12 20c red, bl & blk 2.00 *2.00*
a. Imperf., pair *2,000.*
O136 O12 22c red, bl & blk ('85) 60 *2.00*

No. O129A does not have a "c" after the "14."

Inscribed: Postal Card Rate D

1985, Feb. 4 ***Perf. 11***

O138 O12 (14c) red, bl & blk 3.50 *5.00*

Coil Stamps

Inscribed: No. O139, Domestic Letter Rate D. No. O140, Domestic Mail E.

1985-88 ***Perf. 10 Vert.***

O138A O13 15c red, bl & blk 30 50
O138B O13 20c red, bl & blk 40 30
O139 O12 (22c) red, bl & blk 4.50 *3.00*
O140 O13 (25c) red, bl & blk 50 *2.00*
O141 O13 25c red, bl & blk 50 50
a. Imperf., pair *2,000.* —
Nos. O138A-O141 (5) 6.20 6.30

Issue dates: 1985; E, Mar. 22. 1988; 15c, June 11; 20c, May 19; 25c, June 11.
See Nos. O143, O145-O151.

1989, July 5 **Litho.** ***Perf. 11***

O143 O13 1c red, blue & black 15 15

O14

1991, Jan. 22 **Litho.** ***Perf. 10 Vert.***

Coil Stamp

O144 O14 (29c) red, blue & black 58 35

Official Type of 1985

1991-93 **Litho.** ***Perf. 10 Vert.***

Coil Stamp

O145 O13 29c red, blue & black 58 25

Perf. 11

O146 O13 4c red, blue & black 15 30
O146A O13 10c red, blue & black 20 30
O147 O13 19c red, blue & black 38 50
O148 O13 23c red, blue & black 46 30
O151 O13 $1 red, blue & black 2.00 75

Nos. O146A, O151 have a line of microscopic printing below eagle. Nos. O147 and O148 have blue background made up of crosshatched lines, thicker lettering and thinner numerals.

Issue dates: No. O146, Apr. 6. Nos. O145, O147, O148, May 24. 10c, Oct. 19, 1993. No. O151, Sept. 1993.

COIL STAMP

1994, Dec. 13 **Litho.** ***Perf. 9.8 Vert.***

Inscribed: No. O152, For U.S. addresses only.

O152 O14 (32c) red, blue & black 65 —

NEWSPAPER STAMPS

For the prepayment of postage on bulk shipments of newspapers and periodicals. From 1875 on, the stamps were affixed to memorandums of mailing, canceled and retained by the post office. Discontinued on July 1, 1898.

Washington N1

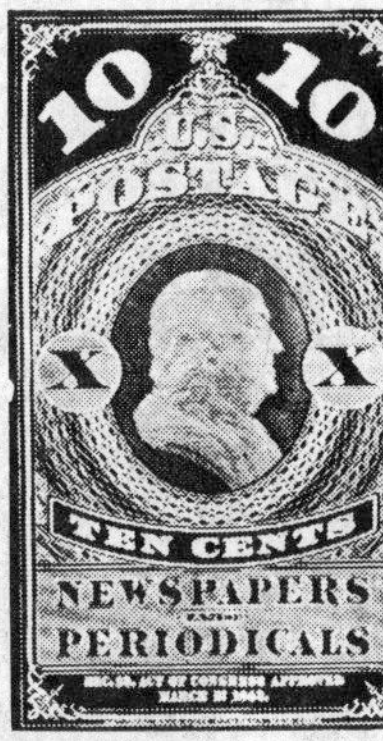

Franklin N2

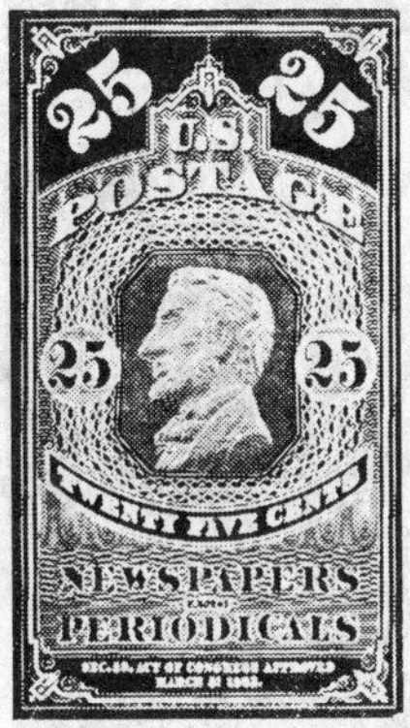

Lincoln — N3

Printed by the National Bank Note Co.

Thin Hard Paper, No Gum

1865 **Unwmk.** **Typo.** ***Perf. 12***

Size: 51x95mm

Colored Border

PR1 N1 5c dark blue 200.00 —
a. 5c light blue 225.00 —
PR2 N2 10c blue green 90.00 —
a. 10c green 90.00 —
b. Pelure paper 110.00 —
PR3 N3 25c orange red 125.00 —
a. 25c carmine red 150.00 —
b. Pelure paper 125.00

White Border

Yellowish Paper

PR4 N1 5c light blue 55.00 30.00
a. 5c dark blue 55.00 30.00
b. Pelure paper 55.00 —

Reprints of 1875 & 1880 follow No. PR89.

Statue of Freedom — N4

"Justice" — N5

Ceres — N6

"Victory" — N7

Clio — N8

Minerva — N9

Vesta — N10

"Peace" — N11

"Commerce" N12

Hebe N13

Indian Maiden — N14

Printed by the Continental Bank Note Co.

Engraved Thin Hard Paper

1875 **Size: 24x35mm**

PR9	N4	2c	black	17.50	11.00
PR10	N4	3c	black	20.00	14.50
PR11	N4	4c	black	18.00	12.50
PR12	N4	6c	black	22.50	17.00
PR13	N4	8c	black	30.00	22.50
PR14	N4	9c	black	65.00	50.00
PR15	N4	10c	black	30.00	20.00
PR16	N5	12c	rose	70.00	40.00
PR17	N5	24c	rose	87.50	45.00
PR18	N5	36c	rose	100.00	50.00
PR19	N5	48c	rose	175.00	85.00
PR20	N5	60c	rose	87.50	45.00
PR21	N5	72c	rose	215.00	110.00
PR22	N5	84c	rose	325.00	135.00
PR23	N5	96c	rose	175.00	100.00
PR24	N6	$1.92	dark brn	240.00	125.00
PR25	N7	$3	vermilion	325.00	135.00
PR26	N8	$6	ultra	525.00	185.00
PR27	N9	$9	yellow	700.00	250.00
PR28	N10	$12	blue grn	800.00	350.00
PR29	N11	$24	dk gray vio	800.00	325.00
PR30	N12	$36	brn rose	875.00	450.00
PR31	N13	$48	red brn	1,150.	500.00
PR32	N14	$60	violet	1,150.	500.00

Special printings of 1875 & 1883 follow No. PR89.

Printed by the American Bank Note Co.

1879

Soft Porous Paper

PR57	N4	2c	black	7.00	4.50
PR58	N4	3c	black	9.00	5.00
PR59	N4	4c	black	8.00	5.00
PR60	N4	6c	black	17.50	11.00
PR61	N4	8c	black	17.50	11.00
PR62	N4	10c	black	17.50	11.00
PR63	N5	12c	red	65.00	25.00
PR64	N5	24c	red	65.00	22.50
PR65	N5	36c	red	190.00	95.00
PR66	N5	48c	red	150.00	60.00
PR67	N5	60c	red	120.00	60.00
a.			Imperf., pair	*600.00*	
PR68	N5	72c	red	240.00	115.00
PR69	N5	84c	red	185.00	85.00
PR70	N5	96c	red	130.00	60.00
PR71	N6	$1.92	pale brn	90.00	55.00
PR72	N7	$3	red ver	90.00	55.00
PR73	N8	$6	blue	150.00	90.00
PR74	N9	$9	orange	110.00	60.00
PR75	N10	$12	yel green	160.00	85.00
PR76	N11	$24	dk violet	200.00	110.00
PR77	N12	$36	indian red	250.00	135.00
PR78	N13	$48	yel brown	325.00	165.00
PR79	N14	$60	purple	325.00	165.00

See Scott's U.S. Specialized Catalogue Die and Plate Proof section for other imperforates.

1885

PR81	N4	1c	black	8.50	5.00
PR82	N5	12c	carmine	30.00	12.50
PR83	N5	24c	carmine	32.50	15.00
PR84	N5	36c	carmine	47.50	17.50
PR85	N5	48c	carmine	65.00	30.00
PR86	N5	60c	carmine	90.00	40.00
PR87	N5	72c	carmine	100.00	45.00
PR88	N5	84c	carmine	210.00	110.00
PR89	N5	96c	carmine	150.00	85.00

See Scott's U.S. Specialized Catalogue Die and Plate Proof section for imperforates.

Reprints of 1865 Issue Printed by the National Bank Note Co.

Hard White Paper, Without Gum

1875

PR5	N1	5c dull blue	65.	
a.		Printed on both sides	—	
PR6	N2	10c dk bluish green	70.	
a.		Printed on both sides	*1,750.*	
PR7	N3	25c dark carmine	80.	

The 5c has white border, 10c and 25c have colored borders.

Printed by the American Bank Note Co.

Soft Porous Paper

1880

White Border

PR8	N1	5c dark blue	130.

Special Printing of the 1875 Issue Hard White Paper Without Gum

PR33	N4	2c	gray black	110.
PR34	N4	3c	gray black	115.
PR35	N4	4c	gray black	120.
PR36	N4	6c	gray black	150.
PR37	N4	8c	gray black	175.
PR38	N4	9c	gray black	200.
PR39	N4	10c	gray black	250.
PR40	N5	12c	pale rose	300.
PR41	N5	24c	pale rose	425.
PR42	N5	36c	pale rose	500.
PR43	N5	48c	pale rose	600.
PR44	N5	60c	pale rose	675.
PR45	N5	72c	pale rose	825.
PR46	N5	84c	pale rose	850.
PR47	N5	96c	pale rose	1,500.
PR48	N6	$1.92	dk brown	*3,500.*
PR49	N7	$3	vermilion	*7,000.*
PR50	N8	$6	ultra	*8,500.*
PR51	N9	$9	yellow	*20,000.*
PR52	N10	$12	blue green	*18,500.*
PR53	N11	$24	dk gray violet	—
PR54	N12	$36	brown rose	—
PR55	N13	$48	red brown	—
PR56	N14	$60	violet	—

Nos. PR33 to PR56 exist imperf. but were not regularly issued. (See Scott's US Specialized Catalogue.)

Special Printing of the 1879 Issue

1881

PR80	N4	2c intense black	250.

Printed by the Bureau of Engraving and Printing

1894 **Soft Wove Paper**

PR90	N4	1c intense black	65.00	
PR91	N4	2c intense black	65.00	
PR92	N4	4c intense black	85.00	
PR93	N4	6c intense black	1,000.	
PR94	N4	10c intense black	140.00	
PR95	N5	12c pink	550.00	—
PR96	N5	24c pink	575.00	
PR97	N5	36c pink	*3,500.*	
PR98	N5	60c pink	*3,500.*	—
PR99	N5	96c pink	*4,000.*	
PR100	N7	$3 scarlet	*5,500.*	
PR101	N8	$6 pale blue	*7,500.*	—

Statue of Freedom N15

"Justice" N16

"Victory" — N17

Clio — N18

Vesta — N19

"Peace" — N20

"Commerce" N21

Indian Maiden N22

1895 **Unwmk.**

Sizes: 1c to 50c, 21x34mm, $2 to $100, 24x35mm

PR102	N15	1c black	30.00	7.50
		Never hinged	47.50	
PR103	N15	2c black	30.00	7.50
		Never hinged	47.50	
PR104	N15	5c black	40.00	12.50
		Never hinged	60.00	
PR105	N15	10c black	85.00	32.50
		Never hinged	130.00	
PR106	N16	25c carmine	115.00	35.00
		Never hinged	175.00	
PR107	N16	50c carmine	250.00	95.00
		Never hinged	400.00	
PR108	N17	$2 scarlet	300.00	65.00
		Never hinged	475.00	
PR109	N18	$5 ultra	425.00	150.00
		Never hinged	650.00	
PR110	N19	$10 green	400.00	165.00
		Never hinged	625.00	
PR111	N20	$20 slate	675.00	300.00
		Never hinged	1,000.	
PR112	N21	$50 dull rose	700.00	300.00
		Never hinged	1,050.	
PR113	N22	$100 purple	775.00	350.00
		Never hinged	1,150.	

1895-97 **Wmk. 191**

PR114	N15	1c black ('96)	3.50	3.00
		Never hinged	5.75	
PR115	N15	2c black	4.00	3.50
		Never hinged	6.50	
PR116	N15	5c black ('96)	6.00	5.00
		Never hinged	9.75	
PR117	N15	10c black	4.00	3.50
		Never hinged	6.50	
PR118	N16	25c carmine	8.00	8.00
		Never hinged	13.00	
PR119	N16	50c carmine	10.00	12.50
		Never hinged	16.00	
PR120	N17	$2 scar ('97)	12.00	15.00
		Never hinged	19.00	
PR121	N18	$5 dk blue ('96)	20.00	25.00
		Never hinged	32.50	
a.		$5 light blue	100.00	45.00
		Never hinged	150.00	
PR122	N19	$10 green ('96)	18.00	25.00
		Never hinged	28.50	
PR123	N20	$20 slate ('96)	20.00	27.50
		Never hinged	32.50	
PR124	N21	$50 dl rose ('97)	27.50	30.00
		Never hinged	42.50	
PR125	N22	$100 purple ('96)	32.50	37.50
		Never hinged	50.00	
		Nos. PR114-PR125 (12)	165.50	195.50

In 1899 the Government sold 26,989 sets of these stamps, but, as the stock of the high values was not sufficient to make up the required number, the $5, $10, $20, $50 and $100 were reprinted. These are virtually indistinguishable from earlier printings.

For overprints see Nos. R159-R160.

PARCEL POST STAMPS

Issued for the prepayment of postage on parcel post packages only.

Post Office Clerk — PP1

City Carrier — PP2

Railway Postal Clerk — PP3

Rural Carrier — PP4

Mail Train — PP5

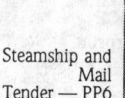

Steamship and Mail Tender — PP6

Automobile Service — PP7

Airplane Carrying Mail — PP8

Manufacturing PP9

Dairying PP10

Harvesting PP11

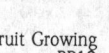

Fruit Growing PP12

1913 **Engr.** **Wmk. 190** ***Perf. 12***

Q1	PP1	1c carmine rose	2.50	85
		Never hinged	3.50	
Q2	PP2	2c carmine rose	3.00	60
		Never hinged	4.25	
Q3	PP3	3c carmine	6.50	4.50
		Never hinged	9.00	
Q4	PP4	4c carmine rose	17.50	1.90
		Never hinged	25.00	
Q5	PP5	5c carmine rose	15.00	1.25
		Never hinged	21.00	
Q6	PP6	10c carmine rose	25.00	1.75
		Never hinged	35.00	
Q7	PP7	15c carmine rose	40.00	7.75
		Never hinged	55.00	
Q8	PP8	20c carmine rose	80.00	15.00
		Never hinged	110.00	
Q9	PP9	25c carmine rose	37.50	4.00
		Never hinged	52.50	

Q10 PP10 50c carmine rose 150.00 27.50
Never hinged 210.00
Q11 PP11 75c carmine rose 45.00 22.50
Never hinged 62.50
Q12 PP12 $1 carmine rose 240.00 17.00
Never hinged 335.00
Nos. Q1-Q12 (12) 662.00 104.60

SPECIAL HANDLING STAMPS

For use on parcel post packages to secure the same expeditious handling accorded to first class mail matter.

PP13

1925-29 Unwmk. Engr. *Perf. 11*

QE1 PP13 10c yel grn ('28) 1.00 80
Never hinged 1.35
QE2 PP13 15c yel grn ('28) 1.10 70
Never hinged 1.50
QE3 PP13 20c yel grn ('28) 1.75 1.00
Never hinged 2.35
QE4 PP13 25c yel grn ('29) 15.00 5.50
Never hinged 20.00
a. 25c deep green ('25) 25.00 4.50
Never hinged 35.00

PARCEL POST POSTAGE DUE STAMPS

For affixing by a postal clerk, to any parcel post package, to denote the amount to be collected from the addressee because of insufficient prepayment of postage.

PPD1

1913 Engr. Wmk. 190 *Perf. 12*

JQ1 PPD1 1c dark green 6.00 2.75
Never hinged 8.00
JQ2 PPD1 2c dark green 50.00 13.00
Never hinged 70.00
JQ3 PPD1 5c dark green 8.00 3.50
Never hinged 10.50
JQ4 PPD1 10c dark green 110.00 30.00
Never hinged 145.00
JQ5 PPD1 25c dark green 55.00 3.25
Never hinged 75.00
Nos. JQ1-JQ5 (5) 229.00 52.50

COMPUTER VENDED POSTAGE

CVP1

CVP2

1989, Aug. 23 Tagged *Guillotined*
Self-Adhesive
Washington, DC, Machine 82
Any Date Other Than 1st Day

1 CVP1 25c **1st Class** 6.00 —
a. 1st day dated, serial #12501-15500 4.50 —
b. 1st day dated, serial #00001-12500 4.50 —
c. 1st day dated, serial over #27500 — —
2 CVP1 $1 **3rd Class** — —
a. 1st day dated, serial #24501-27500 — —
b. 1st day dated, serial over #27500 — —
3 CVP2 $1.69 **Parcel Post** — —
a. 1st day dated, serial #21501-24500 — —
b. 1st day dated, serial over #27500 — —
4 CVP1 $2.40 **Priority Mail** — —
a. 1st day dated, serial #18501-21500 — —
b. Priority Mail ($2.74), with bar code (CVP2) 100.00
c. 1st day dated, serial over #27500 — —
5 CVP1 $8.75 **Express Mail** — —
a. 1st day dated, serial #15501-18500 — —
b. 1st day dated, serial over #27500 — —
Nos. 1a-5a (5) 82.50 —

Washington, DC, Machine 83
Any Date Other Than 1st Day

6 CVP1 25c **1st Class** 6.00 —
a. 1st day dated, serial #12501-15500 4.50 —
b. 1st day dated, serial #00001-12500 4.50 —
c. 1st day dated, serial over #27500 — —
7 CVP1 $1 **3rd Class** — —
a. 1st day dated, serial #24501-27500 — —
b. 1st day dated, serial over #27500 — —
8 CVP2 $1.69 **Parcel Post** — —
a. 1st day dated, serial #21501-24500 — —
b. 1st day dated, serial over #27500 — —
9 CVP1 $2.40 **Priority Mail** — —
a. 1st day dated, serial #18501-21500 — —
b. 1st day dated, serial over #27500 — —
c. Priority Mail ($2.74), with bar code (CVP2) 100.00
10 CVP1 $8.75 **Express Mail** — —
a. 1st day dated, serial #15501-18500 — —
b. 1st day dated, serial over #27500 — —
Nos. 6a-10a (5) 57.50 —

1989, Sept. 1
Kensington, MD, Machine 82
Any Date Other Than 1st Day

11 CVP1 25c **1st Class** 6.00 —
a. 1st day dated, serial #12501-15500 4.50 —
b. 1st day dated, serial #00001-12500 4.50 —
c. 1st day dated, serial over #27500 — —
12 CVP1 $1 **3rd Class** — —
a. 1st day dated, serial #24501-27500 — —
b. 1st day dated, serial over #27500 — —
13 CVP2 $1.69 **Parcel Post** — —
a. 1st day dated, serial #21501-24500 — —
b. 1st day dated, serial over #27500 — —
14 CVP1 $2.40 **Priority Mail** — —
a. 1st day dated, serial #18501-21500 — —
b. 1st day dated, serial over #27500 — —
c. Priority Mail ($2.74), with bar code (CVP2) 100.00
15 CVP1 $8.75 **Express Mail** — —
a. 1st day dated, serial #15501-18500 — —
b. 1st day dated, serial over #27500 — —
Nos. 11a-15a (5) 57.50 —
Nos. 1b, 11b (2) 9.00 —

Kensington, MD, Machine 83
Any Date Other Than 1st Day

16 CVP1 25c **1st Class** 6.00 —
a. 1st day dated, serial #12501-15500 4.50 —
b. 1st day dated, serial #00001-12500 4.50 —
c. 1st day dated, serial over #27500 — —
17 CVP1 $1 **3rd Class** — —
a. 1st day dated, serial #24501-27500 — —
b. 1st day dated, serial over #27500 — —
18 CVP2 $1.69 **Parcel Post** — —
a. 1st day dated, serial #21501-24500 — —
b. 1st day dated, serial over #27500 — —
19 CVP1 $2.40 **Priority Mail** — —
a. 1st day dated, serial #18501-21500 — —
b. 1st day dated, serial over #27500 — —
c. Priority Mail ($2.74), with bar code (CVP2) 100.00 —
20 CVP1 $8.75 **Express Mail** — —
a. 1st day dated, serial #15501-18500 — —
b. 1st day dated, serial over #27500 — —
Nos. 16a-20a (5) 57.50 —
Nos. 6b, 16b (2) 9.00 —

1989, Nov.
Washington, DC, Machine 11

21 CVP1 25c **1st Class** *150.00*
a. 1st Class, with bar code (CVP2) —

Stamps in CVP1 design, probably certified 1st class, with $1.10 denominations exist.

22 CVP1 $1 **3rd Class** *500.00*
23 CVP2 $1.69 **Parcel Post** *500.00*
24 CVP1 $2.40 **Priority Mail** *500.00*
a. Priority Mail ($2.74), with bar code (CVP2) —
25 CVP1 $8.75 **Express Mail** *500.00*

Washington, DC, Machine 12

26 CVP1 25c **1st Class** *150.00*

A $1.10 certified 1st Class stamp, dated Nov. 20, exists on cover.

27 CVP1 $1 **3rd Class** —

A $1.40 Third Class stamp of type CVP2, dated Dec. 1 is known on a Dec. 2 cover.

28 CVP2 $1.69 **Parcel Post** —
29 CVP1 $2.40 **Priority Mail** —
a. Priority Mail ($2.74), with bar code (CVP2) —
30 CVP1 $8.75 **Express Mail** —

An $8.50 Express Mail stamp, dated Dec. 2, exists on cover.

CVP3

1992, Aug. 20 Engr. *Perf. 10 Horiz.*
Coil Stamp

31 CVP3 29c red & blue 60 —
b. Type II ('94) 60 —

No. 31 was available in all denominations from 1c to $99.99. The listing is for the first class rate. Other denominations, se-tenant combinations, or "errors" will not be listed.

Type II denomination has large san-serif numerals preceded by an asterisk measuring 2mm across. No. 31 has small numerals with serifs preceded by an asterisk 1 ½mm across.

CVP4

1994, Feb. 19 Photo. *Perf. 9.9 Vert.*
Coil Stamp

32 CVP4 29c red & blue 60 25

No. 32 was available in all denominations from 19c to $99.99. The listing is for the first class rate at time of issue. Other denominations, se-tenant combinations, or "errors" will not be listed.

CARRIERS' STAMPS

OFFICIAL ISSUES

Issued by the US Government to facilitate payment of fees for delivering and collecting letters.

Franklin
OC1

Eagle
OC2

1851 Unwmk. Engr. *Imperf.*

LO1 OC1 (1c) dull blue, *rose* *2,750.* *3,500.*
LO2 OC2 1c blue 15. *30.*

1875

REPRINT
Without Gum

LO3 OC1 (1c) blue, *rose*, imperf. 40.

SPECIAL PRINTING

LO4 OC1 (1c) blue, perf. 12 *2,500.*

REPRINT

LO5 OC2 1c blue, imperf. 20.

SPECIAL PRINTING

LO6 OC2 1c blue, perf. 12 175.

Reprints of the Franklin Carrier are printed in dark blue, instead of the dull blue or deep blue of the originals. The reprints of the Eagle carrier are on hard white paper, ungummed and sometimes perforated, and also on a coarse wove paper. Originals are on yellowish paper with brown gum.

SEMI-OFFICIAL ISSUES

Issued by officials or employees of the US Government for the purpose of securing or indicating payment of carriers' fees.

Baltimore, Md.

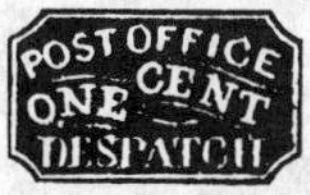

C1

1850-55 Typo. *Imperf.*

1LB1 C1 1c red, *bluish* 100. 100.
1LB2 C1 1c blue, *bluish* 125. 90.
a. Bluish laid paper — —
1LB3 C1 1c blue 75. 50.
a. Laid paper 150. 100.
1LB4 C1 1c green — 600.
1LB5 C1 1c red 350. 275.

Ten varieties.

C2

C3

1856 Typo.

1LB6 C2 1c blue 90. 60.
1LB7 C2 1c red 90. 60.

Shades exist of Nos. 1LB6-1LB7.

1857

1LB8 C3 1c black 40. 30.
a. "SENT" 45. 35.
b. Short rays 45. 35.
1LB9 C3 1c red 60. 45.
a. "SENT" 75. 50.
b. Short rays 75. 50.

Ten varieties of C3.

BOSTON, MASS.

C6

C7

1849-50 Typeset

3LB1 C6 1c blue 150. 75.
3LB2 C7 1c blue (shades), *slate* 125. 65.

CHARLESTON, S. C.

C8

C10

1849 Typo.

4LB1 C8 2c black, *brn rose* *2,500.* *2,500.*
4LB2 C8 2c black, *yellow* *2,500.*

1854 Typeset

4LB3 C10 2c black *1,000.*

C11

1849-50 — **Typeset**

4LB5 C11 2c black, *bluish, pelure* — *400.* 300.
4LB7 C11 2c black, *yellow* — *400.* 400.

Several varieties of C11.

C13

C14

C15

1851-58 — **Typeset**

4LB8 C13 2c blk, *bluish* — 175. 100.
a. Period after "Paid" — 350. 150.
b. "Cens" — *700.*
c. "Conours" and "Bents" — —
4LB9 C13 2c blk, *bluish, pelure* — *375.* *425.*
4LB11 C14 (2c) blk, *bluish* — — *250.*
4LB12 C14 (2c) blk, *bluish, pelure* — — *250.*
4LB13 C15 (2c) blk, *bluish* ('58) — 250. 125.
a. Comma after "PAID" — 600.
b. No period after "Post" — 800.

Several varieties of C13.

C16

C17

1851-58 — **Typeset**

4LB14 C16 2c black, *bluish* — *400.* *450.*
4LB15 C17 2c black, *bluish* — *500.* *500.*

Several varieties of each.

C18

1858 — **Typeset**

4LB16 C18 2c black, *bluish* — *2,000.*

Several varieties.

Same as C19, but Inscribed "Beckmann's City Post"

1860

4LB17 C19 2c black — —

One copy exists, on cover.

C19

C20

1859 — **Typeset**

4LB18 C19 2c black, *bluish* — *2,500.*
4LB19 C20 2c black, *bluish* — *2,500.* —
4LB20 C20 2c black, *pink* — *150.* —
4LB21 C20 2c black, *yellow* — 125.

The Scott Catalogue value is a retail price; that is, what you could expect to pay for the stamp in a grade of Fine-Very Fine. The value listed reflects recent actual dealer selling prices.

CINCINNATI, OHIO

C20a

1854 — **Litho.** — **Wove Paper**

9LB1 C20a 2c brown — *1,500.* 1,500.

CLEVELAND, OHIO

C20b

C20c

1854 — **Wove Paper** — **Litho.**

10LB1 C20b blue — *1,000.* *1,000.*

Vertically Laid Paper

10LB2 C20c 2c black, *bluish* — — *3,750.*

LOUISVILLE, KY.

C21

C22

1857-58 — **Litho.**

5LB1 C21 (2c) bluish green — *75.*
5LB2 C22 (2c) blue ('58) — 150. 150.
5LB3 C22 (2c) black ('58) — *600.* *1,750.*

NEW YORK, N.Y.

C23

1842 — **Engr.**

6LB1 C23 3c black, *grayish* — *1,250.*

Used copies are Carriers' stamps only when canceled with the regular government cancellation "U.S." in octagonal frame (see illustration), "U.S.CITY DESPATCH POST," or New York circular postmark. When canceled "FREE" in frame they were used as local stamps (see No. 40L1 in Scott's Specialized Catalogue of United States Stamps).

C24

1842-45 — **Engr.**

Unsurfaced Paper, Colored Through

6LB2 C24 3c black, *rosy buff* — *600.*
6LB3 C24 3c blk, *light blue* — *400.* 400.
6LB4 C24 3c black, *green* — *2,000.*

Some authorities consider No. 6LB2 to be an essay, and No. 6LB4 to be a color changeling.

Glazed Paper, Surface Colored

6LB5 C24 3c black, *blue green (shades)* — 125. 100.
a. Double impression — *500.*
b. 3c, black, *blue* — 400. *125.*
c. As "b," double impression — *750.*
d. 3c, black, *green* — 650. *600.*
e. As "d," double impression — —

No. 6LB5 Surcharged in Red — C25

1846

6LB7 C25 2c on 3c, on cover — —

The City Despatch 2c red is listed in Scott's United States Specialized Catalogue as a Local stamp.

C27

1849-50 — **Typo.**

6LB9 C27 1c black, *rose* — 60. 50.
6LB10 C27 1c black, *yellow* — 60. 60.
6LB11 C27 1c black, *buff* — 60. 50.
a. Pair, one stamp sideways — *1,000.*

PHILADELPHIA, PA.

C28

C29

1849-50 — **Typeset**

7LB1 C28 1c blk, *rose* (with letters L.P.) — 175.
7LB2 C28 1c black, *rose* (with letter S) — *500.*
7LB3 C28 1c blk, *rose* (with letter H) — 175.
7LB4 C28 1c blk, *rose* (with letters L.S.) — 175.
7LB5 C28 1c black, *rose* (with letters J.J.) — *2,000.*
7LB6 C29 1c black, *rose* — 150. 125.
7LB7 C29 1c black, *blue*, glazed — *600.*
7LB8 C29 1c blk, *ver*, glazed — *500.*
7LB9 C29 1c blk, *yel*, glazed — *2,000.*

Several varieties of each.

Nos. 7LB1-7LB9 normally received no cancellation.

The 1c black on buff (unglazed), type C29, is believed to be a color changeling.

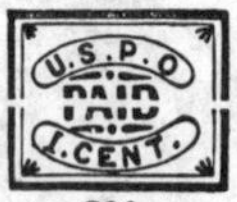

C30

C31

C32

1850-52 — **Litho.**

7LB11 C30 1c gold, *black, glazed* — 100. 75.
7LB12 C30 1c blue — 200. 150.
7LB13 C30 1c black — — *500.*

25 varieties of C30.

Handstamped

7LB14 C31 1c blue, *buff* — *2,500.*
7LB16 C31 1c black — *1,650.*

1856(?)

7LB18 C32 1c black — *900.* *1,400.*

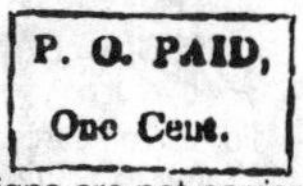

Labels in these designs are not carrier stamps.

ST. LOUIS, MO.

C36

(Actual size) — C37

Several varieties.

1849 — **Litho.**

8LB1 C36 2c black — *4,000.* *5,000.*

1857 — **Litho.**

8LB2 C37 2c blue — *5,000.*

Carrier stamps Nos. 9LB1, 10LB1-10LB2 are listed following No. 4LB21.

STAMPED ENVELOPES AND WRAPPERS

VALUES

Values are for cut squares in a grade of very fine. Very fine cut squares will have the design well centered within moderately large margins. Precanceled cut squares must include the entire precancellation. Values for unused entires are for those without printed or manuscript address. Values for letter sheets are for folded entires. Unfolded copies sell for more. A "full corner" includes back and side flaps and commands a premium. (Entire envelopes and wrappers are listed in Scott's U.S. Specialized Catalogue.)

Wrappers are listed with envelopes of corresponding designs, and indicated by prefix letter "W" instead of "U."

Envelopes with the stamp printed by error in colorless embossing from an uninked die, are "albinos." They are worth more than normal, inked impressions. Albinos of earlier issues, canceled while current, are scarce.

The papers of these issues vary greatly in texture, and in color from yellowish to bluish white and from amber to dark buff.

"+" Some authorities claim that Nos. U37, U48, U49, U110, U124, U125, U130, U133A, U137A, U137B, U137C, W138, U145, U162, U178A, U185, U220, U285, U286, U298, U299, UO3, UO32, UO38, UO45 and UO45A (each with "+" before number) were not regularly issued and are not known to have been used.

Washington
U1 U2

U1 -- "THREE" in short label with curved ends; 13mm wide at top.
U2 -- "THREE" in short label with straight ends; 15½mm wide at top.

U3 U4

U3 -- "THREE" in short label with octagon ends.
U4 -- "THREE" in wide label with straight ends; 20mm wide at top.

U5 U6

U5 -- "THREE" in medium wide label with curved ends; 14½mm wide at top.

U7 U8

U7 -- "TEN" in short label; 15⅓mm wide at top.
U8 -- "TEN" in wide label 20mm wide at top.

1853-55 On Diagonally Laid Paper

U1	U1	3c red	200.00	20.00
U2	U1	3c red, *buff*	75.00	10.00
U3	U2	3c red	800.00	35.00
U4	U2	3c red, *buff*	225.00	20.00
U5	U3	3c red ('54)	4,000.	375.00
U6	U3	3c red, *buff* ('54)	200.00	42.50
U7	U4	3c red	600.00	85.00
U8	U4	3c red, *buff*	1,250.	100.00
U9	U5	3c red ('54)	20.00	2.75
U10	U5	3c red, *buff* ('54)	15.00	2.75
U11	U6	6c red	150.00	65.00
U12	U6	6c red, *buff*	100.00	55.00
U13	U6	6c green	185.00	100.00
U14	U6	6c green, *buff*	185.00	80.00
U15	U7	10c green ('55)	150.00	70.00
U16	U7	10c green, *buff* ('55)	65.00	45.00
a.		10c pale green, *buff*	65.00	45.00
U17	U8	10c green ('55)	200.00	100.00
a.		10c pale green	175.00	100.00
U18	U8	10c green, *buff* ('55)	100.00	60.00
a.		10c pale green, *buff*	90.00	50.00

Nos. U9, U10, U11, U12, U13, U14, U17 and U18 have been reprinted on white and buff papers, vertically laid. The originals are on diagonally laid paper. Value of 8 reprints, $225.

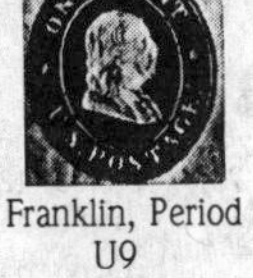

Franklin, Period after "POSTAGE."
U9 U10

U10--Bust touches inner frame-line at front and back.

No period after "POSTAGE"
U11

Washington
U12

Envelopes are on diagonally laid paper. Wrappers on vertically or horizontally laid paper.

1860-61

U19	U9	1c blue, *buff*	27.50	12.50
W20	U9	1c blue, *buff* ('61)	60.00	45.00
W21	U9	1c blue, *man* ('61)	40.00	40.00
W22	U9	1c blue, *org* ('61)	1,750.	
U23	U10	1c blue, *org*	450.00	350.00
U24	U11	1c blue, *buff*	200.00	90.00
W25	U11	1c blue, *man* ('61)	3,250.	2,100.
U26	U12	3c red	25.00	12.50
U27	U12	3c red, *buff*	17.50	12.50
U28	U12+9	3c + 1c red & blue	325.00	225.00
U29	U12+9	3c + 1c red & blue, *buff*	250.00	200.00
U30	U12	6c red	2,250.	1,250.
U31	U12	6c red, *buff*	1,750.	900.00
U32	U12	10c green	1,200.	350.00
U33	U12	10c green, *buff*	1,100.	250.00

Nos. U26, U27, U30 to U33 have been reprinted on the same papers as the reprints of the 1853-55 issue. Value for set of six, $260.

U13 U14

Washington
U15 U16

Envelopes are on diagonally laid paper.

1861

U34	U13	3c pink	17.50	5.00
U35	U13	3c pink, *buff*	15.00	5.00
U36	U13	3c pink, *bl* (letter sheet)	70.00	50.00
+U37	U13	3c pink, *org*	*2,500.*	
U38	U14	6c pink	100.00	80.00
U39	U14	6c pink, *buff*	60.00	55.00
U40	U15	10c yellow green	30.00	30.00
a.		10c blue green	30.00	27.50
U41	U15	10c yel green, *buff*	27.50	27.50
a.		10c blue green, *buff*	27.50	27.50
U42	U16	12c red & brown, *buff*	170.00	150.00
a.		12c lake & brown, *buff*	*800.00*	
U43	U16	20c red & bl, *buff*	165.00	140.00
U44	U16	24c red & green, *buff*	180.00	140.00
a.		24c lake & green, *sal*	185.00	175.00
U45	U16	40c black & red, *buff*	275.00	275.00

Nos. U38 and U39 have been reprinted on the same papers as the reprints of the 1853-55 issue and are not known entire. Value of two reprints, $60.

Jackson — U17 Jackson — U18

"U.S. POSTAGE" above

U17--The downstroke and tail of the "2" unite near the point.

U18--The downstroke and tail of the "2" touch but do not merge.

Jackson — U19 Jackson — U20

"U.S. POST" above

U19--Stamp measures 24 to 25mm in width.

U20--Stamp measures 25½ to 26¼mm in width.

Envelopes are on diagonally laid paper. Wrappers on vertically or horizontally laid paper.

1863-64

U46	U17	2c black, *buff*	32.50	15.00
W47	U17	2c black, *dk man*	45.00	35.00
+U48	U18	2c black, *buff*	1,850.	
+U49	U18	2c black, *orange*	1,050.	
U50	U19	2c blk, *buff* ('64)	9.00	8.50
W51	U19	2c blk, *buff* ('64)	160.00	150.00
U52	U19	2c blk, *org* ('64)	10.00	7.50
W53	U19	2c black, *dk man* ('64)	32.50	20.00
U54	U20	2c blk, *buff* ('64)	11.00	9.00
W55	U20	2c blk, *buff* ('64)	75.00	50.00
U56	U20	2c blk, *org* ('64)	10.00	7.00
W57	U20	2c blk, *lt man* ('64)	11.00	10.00

Washington
U21

Washington
U22

1864-65

U58	U21	3c pink	6.50	1.50
U59	U21	3c pink, *buff*	4.50	1.00
U60	U21	3c brown ('65)	40.00	20.00
U61	U21	3c brn, *buff* ('65)	35.00	20.00
U62	U21	6c pink	60.00	25.00
U63	U21	6c pink, *buff*	27.50	24.00
U64	U21	6c purple ('65)	42.50	20.00
U65	U21	6c pur, *buff* ('65)	40.00	17.50
U66	U22	9c lem, *buff* ('65)	350.00	200.00
U67	U22	9c org, *buff* ('65)	90.00	72.50
a.		9c orange yellow, *buff*	90.00	75.00
U68	U22	12c brn, *buff* ('65)	350.00	195.00
U69	U22	12c red brn, *buff* ('65)	85.00	50.00
U70	U22	18c red, *buff* ('65)	85.00	80.00
U71	U22	24c bl, *buff* ('65)	90.00	72.50
U72	U22	30c grn, *buff* ('65)	60.00	50.00
a.		30c yellow green, *buff*	55.00	65.00
U73	U22	40c rose, *buff* ('65)	80.00	*200.00*

Reay Issue

The engravings in this issue are finely executed.

Franklin — U23 Jackson — U24

U23--Bust points to the end of the "N" of "ONE".

U24--Bust narrow at back. Small, thick figures of value.

Washington — U25 Lincoln — U26

U25--Queue projects below bust.

U26--Neck very long at the back.

Stanton — U27 Jefferson — U28

U27--Bust pointed at the back, figures "7" are normal.

U28--Queue forms straight line with the bust.

Clay — U29 Webster — U30

U29--Ear partly concealed by hair, mouth large, chin prominent.

U30--Has side whiskers.

Scott — U31 Hamilton — U32

U31--Straggling locks of hair at top of head; ornaments around the inner oval end in squares.

U32--Back of bust very narrow, chin almost straight; labels containing figures of value are exactly parallel.

Perry — U33

U33--Front of bust very narrow and pointed; inner lines of shields project very slightly beyond the oval.

1870-71

U74	U23	1c blue	27.50	22.50
a.		1c ultramarine	50.00	26.00
U75	U23	1c blue, *amber*	27.50	22.50
a.		1c ultramarine, *amb*	45.00	25.00
U76	U23	1c blue, *org*	16.00	10.00
W77	U23	1c blue, *man*	40.00	25.00
U78	U24	2c brown	35.00	12.50
U79	U24	2c brown, *amb*	14.00	7.50
U80	U24	2c brown, *org*	8.00	5.00
W81	U24	2c brown, *man*	22.50	15.00
U82	U25	3c green	6.00	75
U83	U25	3c green, *amb*	4.75	1.75
U84	U25	3c green, *cream*	7.50	3.00
U85	U26	6c dark red	16.00	12.50
a.		6c vermilion	12.50	12.50
U86	U26	6c dk red, *amb*	21.00	12.50
a.		6c vermilion, *amber*	21.00	12.50
U87	U26	6c dk red, *cr*	25.00	12.50
a.		6c vermilion, *cream*	22.50	12.50
U88	U27	7c ver, *amb* ('71)	42.50	*165.00*
U89	U28	10c olive black	425.00	375.00
U90	U28	10c ol blk, *amb*	425.00	375.00
U91	U28	10c brown	45.00	65.00
U92	U28	10c brn, *amb*	65.00	45.00
a.		10c dark brown, *amb*	60.00	55.00
U93	U29	12c plum	105.00	70.00
U94	U29	12c plum, *amb*	105.00	90.00
U95	U29	12c plum, *cr*	210.00	200.00
U96	U30	15c red orange	60.00	60.00
a.		15c orange	60.00	
U97	U30	15c red org, *amb*	135.00	165.00
a.		15c orange, *amber*	140.00	
U98	U30	15c red org, *cr*	225.00	200.00
a.		15c orange, *cream*	225.00	
U99	U31	24c purple	110.00	100.00
U100	U31	24c pur, *amb*	175.00	250.00
U101	U31	24c pur, *cream*	175.00	250.00
U102	U32	30c black	70.00	80.00
U103	U32	30c blk, *amb*	175.00	200.00
U104	U32	30c blk, *cream*	200.00	325.00
U105	U33	90c carmine	130.00	185.00
U106	U33	90c car, *amb*	310.00	325.00
U107	U33	90c car, *cream*	350.00	525.00

Plimpton Issue

The profiles in this issue are inferior to the fine engraving of the Reay issue.

U34

U35

U34--Bust forms an angle at the back near the frame. Lettering poorly executed. Distinct circle in "O" of "POSTAGE."

U35--Lower part of bust points to the end of the "E" in "ONE." Head inclined downward.

U36

U37

U36--Bust narrow at back. Thin figures of value. The head of the "P" in "POSTAGE" is very narrow. The bust at front is broad and ends in sharp corners.

U37--Bust broad. Figures of value in long ovals.

U38

U39

U38--Similar to die 2 but the figure "2" at the left touches the oval.

U39--Similar to die 2 but the "O" of "TWO" has the center netted instead of plain. The "G" of "POSTAGE" and the "C" of "CENTS" have diagonal crossline.

U40

U41

U40--Bust broad; numerals in ovals short and thick.

U41--Similar to die 5 but the ovals containing the numerals are much heavier. A diagonal line runs from the upper part of the "U" to the white frame-line.

U42

U43

U42--Similar to die 5 but the middle stroke of "N" in "CENTS" is as thin as the vertical strokes.

U43--Bottom of bust cut almost semi-circularly.

U44

U45

U44--Thin lettering, long thin figures of value.

U45--Thick lettering, well-formed figures of value, queue does not project below bust.

U46

U46--Top of head egg-shaped; knot of queue well marked and projects triangularly.

Taylor — U47

Die 1

Die 2

Die 1--Figures of value with thick curved tops.

Die 2--Figures of value with long, thin tops.

U48

U49

U48--Neck very short at the back.

U49--Figures of value turned up at the ends.

U50

U51

U50--Very large head.

U51--Knot of queue stands out prominently.

U52

U53

U52--Ear prominent, chin receding.

U53--No side whiskers, forelock projects above head.

U54

U55

U54--Hair does not project; ornaments around the inner oval end in points.

U55--Back of bust rather broad, chin slopes considerably; labels containing figures of value are not exactly parallel.

U56

U56--Front of bust sloping; inner lines of shields project considerably into the inner oval.

1874-86

	U34		
U108	1c dark blue	90.00	50.00
a.	1c light blue		
U109	1c dk blue, *amb*	110.00	65.00
+U110	1c dk blue, *cr*	675.00	
U111	1c dk blue, *org*	17.50	15.00
a.	1c light blue, *org*	20.00	11.00
W112	1c dk blue, *man*	45.00	32.50
	U35		
U113	1c light blue	1.25	75
a.	1c dark blue	7.00	5.00
U114	1c lt blue, *amb*	3.75	3.00
a.	1c dark blue, *amb*	15.00	10.00
U115	1c blue, *cr*	4.00	4.00
a.	1c dark blue, *cr*	16.00	5.00
U116	1c lt blue, *org*	50	40
a.	1c dark blue, *org*	3.00	2.50
U117	1c lt bl, *bl* ('80)	5.00	4.00
U118	1c light blue, *fawn* ('79)	5.00	4.00
U119	1c lt blue, *man* ('86)	5.00	3.00
W120	1c lt blue, *man*	1.25	1.00
a.	1c dark blue, *man*	5.00	4.00
U121	1c lt blue, *amb man* ('86)	10.00	8.50
	U36		
U122	2c brown	90.00	35.00
U123	2c brown, *amb*	50.00	37.50
+U124	2c brown, *cr*	700.00	
+U125	2c brown, *org*	*8,000.*	
W126	2c brown, *man*	95.00	50.00
W127	2c ver, *man*	1,100.	250.00
	U37		
U128	2c brown	40.00	27.50
U129	2c brown, *amb*	65.00	37.50
+U130	2c brown, *cr*	*20,000.*	
W131	2c brown, *man*	14.00	13.50
	U38		
U132	2c brown	55.00	20.00
U133	2c brown, *amb*	175.00	50.00
+U133A	2c brown, *cr*	—	
	U39		
U134	2c brown	550.00	110.00
U135	2c brown, *amb*	375.00	100.00
U136	2c brown, *org*	42.50	25.00
W137	2c brown, *man*	50.00	32.50
+U137A	2c vermilion	*18,500.*	
+U137B	2c ver, *amb*	*18,500.*	
+U137C	2c ver, *org*	*18,500.*	
+W138	2c ver, *man*	*6,500.*	
	U40		
U139	2c brown ('75)	40.00	30.00
U140	2c brown, *amb* ('75)	70.00	50.00
W141	2c brown, *man* ('75)	35.00	22.50
U142	2c ver ('75)	5.50	2.25
a.	2c pink	8.50	6.00
U143	2c ver, *amber* ('75)	5.50	2.25
U144	2c ver, *cr* ('75)	11.00	5.00
+U145	2c ver, *org* ('75)	*8,250.*	
U146	2c ver, *bl* ('80)	125.00	27.50
U147	2c ver, *fawn* ('75)	6.00	4.00
W148	2c ver, *man* ('75)	3.00	3.00
	U41		
U149	2c ver ('78)	45.00	25.00
a.	2c pink	45.00	25.00
U150	2c ver, *amber* ('78)	20.00	13.00
U151	2c ver, *bl* ('80)	10.00	7.00
a.	2c pink, *blue*	8.50	7.00
U152	2c ver, *fawn* ('78)	9.00	3.75
	U42		
U153	2c ver ('76)	50.00	20.00
U154	2c ver, *amb* ('76)	275.00	75.00
W155	2c ver, *man* ('76)	17.50	8.00
	U43		
U156	2c ver ('81)	550.00	100.00
U157	2c ver, *amb* ('81)	*15,000.*	*15,000.*
W158	2c ver, *man* ('81)	75.00	50.00
	U44		
U159	3c green	20.00	5.00
U160	3c green, *amb*	25.00	9.00
U161	3c green, *cr*	32.50	11.00
+U162	3c green, *blue*	—	
	U45		
U163	3c green	1.00	25
U164	3c green, *amb*	1.25	50
U165	3c green, *cr*	7.00	6.00
U166	3c green, *blue*	7.50	4.00
U167	3c green, *fawn* ('75)	4.00	2.50
	U46		
U168	3c green ('81)	475.00	40.00
U169	3c green, *amb* ('81)	200.00	90.00
U170	3c grn, *bl* ('81)	*7,500.*	*1,600.*
U171	3c green, *fawn* ('81)	*25,000.*	*1,500.*
	U47		
U172	5c blue, die 1 ('75)	9.00	7.00
U173	5c blue, die 1, *amb* ('75)	9.50	7.50
U174	5c blue, die 1, *cr* ('75)	85.00	37.50
U175	5c blue, die 1, *bl* ('75)	20.00	12.50
U176	5c blue, die 1, *fawn* ('75)	105.00	50.00
U177	5c blue, die 2 ('75)	6.50	5.25
U178	5c blue, die 2, *amb* ('75)	6.50	5.75
+U178A	5c blue, die 2, *cr* ('76)	*3,000.*	
U179	5c blue, die 2, *blue* ('75)	11.00	7.00
U180	5c blue, die 2, *fawn* ('75)	95.00	42.50
	U48		
U181	6c red	5.00	5.00
a.	6c vermilion	5.00	4.75
U182	6c red, *amber*	9.00	5.00
a.	6c vermilion, *amber*	9.00	5.00
U183	6c red, *cream*	15.00	9.00
a.	6c vermilion, *cream*	17.50	9.00
U184	6c red, *fawn* ('75)	16.00	9.00
	U49		
+U185	7c vermilion	*1,400.*	
U186	7c ver, *amber*	90.00	52.50
	U50		
U187	10c brown	27.50	15.00
U188	10c brown, *amb*	55.00	22.50
	U51		
U189	10c choc ('75)	5.00	3.00
a.	10c bister brown	6.00	3.50
b.	10c yellow ocher	1,250.	
U190	10c choc, *amb* ('75)	6.50	5.50
a.	10c bister brown, *amb*	6.50	5.50
b.	10c yellow ocher, *amb*	1,050.	
U191	10c brn, *oriental buff* ('86)	8.50	6.50
U192	10c brn, *bl* ('86)	11.00	6.50
a.	10c gray black, *blue*	10.00	6.50
b.	10c red brown, *blue*	10.00	6.50
U193	10c brown, *man* ('86)	12.00	7.50
a.	10c red brown, *man*	10.00	7.50
U194	10c brown, *amb man* ('86)	14.00	6.00
a.	10c red brown, *amber manila*	16.00	6.25
	U52		
U195	12c plum	160.00	72.50
U196	12c plum, *amb*	155.00	130.00
U197	12c plum, *cream*	180.00	140.00
	U53		
U198	15c orange	37.50	27.50
U199	15c orange, *amb*	115.00	85.00
U200	15c org, *cream*	325.00	325.00
	U54		
U201	24c purple	140.00	100.00
U202	24c purple, *amb*	140.00	100.00
U203	24c pur, *cream*	140.00	100.00
	U55		
U204	30c black	60.00	25.00
U205	30c black, *amb*	65.00	50.00
U206	30c black, *cream*	375.00	365.00
U207	30c blk, *oriental buff* ('86)	90.00	70.00
U208	30c blk, *bl* ('86)	95.00	70.00
U209	30c black, *man* ('86)	85.00	70.00
U210	30c black, *amb man* ('86)	110.00	70.00
	U56		
U211	90c carmine ('75)	110.00	70.00
U212	90c car, *amb* ('75)	140.00	185.00
U213	90c car, *cr* ('75)	1,250.	
U214	90c car, *oriental buff* ('86)	195.00	225.00
U215	90c car, *bl* ('86)	165.00	200.00

U216	90c car, *man* ('86)	115.00	200.00
U217	90c car, *amb man* ('86)	100.00	165.00

See Nos. U336-U347.

United States Centennial Issue

Single line under "POSTAGE" — U57

Double line under "POSTAGE" — U58

1876

U218	U57 3c red	50.00	22.50
U219	U57 3c green	45.00	12.75
+*U220*	U58 3c red	*22,500.*	
U221	U58 3c green	50.00	16.00

Cent. of the US, and the World's Fair at Philadelphia.
See No. U582.

Garfield — U59

Washington — U60

1882-86

U222	U59 5c brown	3.25	2.00
U223	U59 5c brown, *amb*	3.75	2.25
U224	U59 5c brn, *oriental buff* ('86)	95.00	60.00
U225	U59 5c brown, *blue*	45.00	32.50
U226	U59 5c brown, *fawn*	200.00	

1883, Oct.

U227	U60 2c red	3.25	1.50
a.	2c brown (error), entire	*3,000.*	
U228	U60 2c red, *amber*	4.25	1.75
U229	U60 2c red, *blue*	6.00	4.00
U230	U60 2c red, *fawn*	6.00	3.00

Wavy lines fine and clear — U61

Wavy lines thick and blurred — U62

Four Wavy Lines in Oval

1883, Nov.

U231	U61 2c red	2.75	1.25
U232	U61 2c red, *amber*	4.00	2.00
U233	U61 2c red, *blue*	6.50	4.00
U234	U61 2c red, *fawn*	4.50	2.50
W235	U61 2c red, *manila*	10.00	3.50

1884, June

U236	U62 2c red	6.00	3.00
U237	U62 2c red, *amber*	10.00	7.00
U238	U62 2c red, *blue*	15.00	7.00
U239	U62 2c red, *fawn*	10.00	6.50

See Nos. U260-W269.

3 1/2 links over left "2" — U63

2 links below right "2" — U64

Round "O" in "TWO" — U65

U240	U63 2c red	55.00	30.00
U241	U63 2c red, *amber*	650.00	275.00
U242	U63 2c red, *fawn*		*6,500.*
U243	U64 2c red	70.00	40.00
U244	U64 2c red, *amber*	125.00	60.00
U245	U64 2c red, *blue*	280.00	100.00
U246	U64 2c red, *fawn*	280.00	100.00
U247	U65 2c red	1,150.	275.00
U248	U65 2c red, *amber*	2,250.	750.00
U249	U65 2c red, *fawn*	575.00	325.00

See Nos. U270-U276.

Jackson — U66

Die 1-- Numeral at left is 2 3/4mm wide

Die 2-- Numeral at left is 3 1/4mm wide

1883-86

U250	U66 4c grn, die 1	3.00	2.50
U251	U66 4c grn, die 1, *amb*	3.50	2.50
U252	U66 4c grn, die 1, *oriental buff* ('86)	6.00	6.00
U253	U66 4c grn, die 1, *bl* ('86)	6.50	5.00
U254	U66 4c grn, die 1, *man* ('86)	7.00	5.00
U255	U66 4c grn, die 1, *amb man* ('86)	15.00	8.00
U256	U66 4c grn, die 2	4.00	4.00
U257	U66 4c grn, die 2, *amb*	9.00	5.00
U258	U66 4c grn, die 2, *man* ('86)	8.50	5.00
U259	U66 4c grn, die 2, *amb man* ('86)	7.75	5.00

1884, May

U260	U61 2c brown	11.00	4.00
U261	U61 2c brn, *amber*	10.00	5.00
U262	U61 2c brn, *blue*	11.50	8.00
U263	U61 2c brn, *fawn*	10.00	7.50
W264	U61 2c brn, *manila*	12.00	8.00

1884, June **Retouched Die**

U265	U62 2c brown	13.00	4.00
U266	U62 2c brn, *amber*	55.00	35.00
U267	U62 2c brn, *blue*	12.00	5.00
U268	U62 2c brn, *fawn*	11.00	8.00
W269	U62 2c brn, *manila*	20.00	12.50

2 Links Below Right "2"

U270	U64 2c brown	80.00	32.50
U271	U64 2c brn, *amber*	190.00	80.00
U272	U64 2c brn, *fawn*	*2,250.*	900.00

Round "O" in "Two"

U273	U65 2c brown	150.00	65.00
U274	U65 2c brn, *amber*	175.00	65.00
U275	U65 2c brn, *blue*		*5,000.*
U276	U65 2c brn, *fawn*	800.00	600.00

Washington
U67 U68

U67--Extremity of bust below the queue forms a point.

U68--Extremity of bust is rounded.

Similar to U61
Two wavy lines in oval

1884-86

U277	U67 2c brown	35	15
a.	2c brown lake	20.00	17.50
U278	U67 2c brn, *amber*	60	40
a.	2c brown lake, *amber*	30.00	11.00
U279	U67 2c brn, *oriental buff* ('86)	2.50	1.50
U280	U67 2c brn, *blue*	2.00	1.25
U281	U67 2c brn, *fawn*	2.50	1.50
U282	U67 2c brn, *man* ('86)	8.50	3.00
W283	U67 2c brn, *man*	4.75	4.50
U284	U67 2c brn, *amb man* ('86)	5.00	5.00
+*U285*	U67 2c red	500.00	
+*U286*	U67 2c red, *blue*	210.00	
W287	U67 2c red, *man*	100.00	
U288	U68 2c brown	150.00	30.00
U289	U68 2c brn, *amb*	14.00	10.00
U290	U68 2c brn, *blue*	700.00	120.00
U291	U68 2c brn, *fawn*	19.00	16.00
W292	U68 2c brn, *man*	19.00	15.00

Grant — US1

1886 **Letter Sheet**

U293	US1 2c green, entire	20.00	14.00

See Scott's U.S. Specialized Catalogue.

Franklin
U69

Washington
U70

U70--Bust points between 3rd and 4th notches of inner oval; "G" of "POSTAGE" has no bar.

U71

U72

U71--Bust points between second and third notches of inner oval; "G" of "POSTAGE" has a bar; ear is indicated by one heavy line; one vertical line at corner of mouth.

U72--Frame same as die 2; upper part of head more rounded; ear indicated by two curved lines with two locks of hair in front; two vertical lines at corner of mouth.

Jackson — U73

Grant — U74

U75

U74--There is a space between the beard and the collar of the coat. A button is on the collar.

U75--The collar touches the beard and there is no button.

1887-94

U294	U69 1c blue	50	20
U295	U69 1c dk bl ('94)	6.50	2.50
U296	U69 1c bl, *amb* ('94)	2.50	1.25
U297	U69 1c dk blue, *amb* ('94)	40.00	20.00
+*U298*	U69 1c bl, *oriental buff* ('94)	*2,500.*	
+*U299*	U69 1c bl, *bl* ('94)	*4,500.*	
U300	U69 1c bl, *man* ('94)	60	30
W301	U69 1c bl, *man* ('94)	40	25
U302	U69 1c dk blue, *man* ('94)	19.00	8.00
U303	U69 1c dk blue, *man* ('94)	11.00	9.00
U304	U69 1c bl, *amb man*	4.00	3.25
U305	U70 2c green	9.00	7.50
U306	U70 2c grn, *amb*	20.00	11.00
U307	U70 2c grn, *oriental buff*	65.00	25.00
U308	U70 2c grn, *blue*	*2,750.*	675.00
U309	U70 2c grn, *man*	2,500.	450.00
U310	U70 2c grn, *amb man*	1,800.	525.00
U311	U71 2c green	25	15
U312	U71 2c grn, *amb*	40	15
U313	U71 2c grn, *oriental buff*	50	20
U314	U71 2c grn, *blue*	50	20
U315	U71 2c grn, *man*	1.50	45
W316	U71 2c grn, *man*	2.50	2.00
U317	U71 2c grn, *amb man*	2.00	1.50
U318	U72 2c green	100.00	11.50
U319	U72 2c grn, *amb*	145.00	19.00
U320	U72 2c grn, *oriental buff*	155.00	37.50
U321	U72 2c grn, *blue*	175.00	55.00
U322	U72 2c grn, *man*	145.00	60.00
U323	U72 2c grn, *amb man*	325.00	72.50
U324	U73 4c carmine	1.45	1.10
a.	4c lake	1.75	1.25
b.	4c scarlet ('94)	1.90	1.25
U325	U73 4c car, *amb*	2.00	1.75
a.	4c lake, *amber*	2.50	2.00
b.	4c scarlet, *amber* ('94)	2.50	2.75
U326	U73 4c car, *oriental buff*	5.00	2.50
a.	4c lake, *oriental buff*	6.00	3.00
U327	U73 4c car, *blue*	4.00	3.50
a.	4c lake, *blue*	4.00	3.50
U328	U73 4c car, *man*	5.75	5.00
a.	4c lake, *manila*	6.50	5.50
b.	4c pink, *manila*	6.75	4.00
U329	U73 4c car, *amb man*	4.00	2.50
a.	4c lake, *amb manila*	4.50	3.00
b.	4c pink, *amb manila*	5.00	3.50
U330	U74 5c blue	3.00	2.50
U331	U74 5c bl, *amber*	3.75	1.75
U332	U74 5c bl, *oriental buff*	4.00	3.00
U333	U74 5c bl, *blue*	5.00	4.00
U334	U75 5c blue ('94)	9.00	4.50
U335	U75 5c bl, *amb* ('94)	9.00	5.00
U336	U55 30c red brn	35.00	37.50
a.	30c yellow brown	45.00	45.00
b.	30c chocolate	45.00	47.50
U337	U55 30c red brn, *amb*	40.00	50.00
a.	30c yel brown, *amber*	42.50	42.50
b.	30c choc, *amber*	42.50	42.50
U338	U55 30c red brn, *oriental buff*	35.00	40.00
a.	30c yel brn, *oriental buff*	32.50	40.00
U339	U55 30c red brn, *bl*	35.00	40.00
a.	30c yellow brown, *blue*	32.50	40.00
U340	U55 30c red brn, *manila*	40.00	40.00
a.	30c brown, *manila*	37.50	35.00
U341	U55 30c red brown, *amb man*	45.00	25.00
a.	30c yel brn, *amb man*	45.00	25.00
U342	U56 90c purple	60.00	65.00
U343	U56 90c pur, *amb*	70.00	70.00
U344	U56 90c pur, *oriental buff*	70.00	75.00
U345	U56 90c pur, *blue*	70.00	80.00
U346	U56 90c pur, *man*	75.00	80.00
U347	U56 90c pur, *amb manila*	80.00	80.00

Columbian Exposition Issue

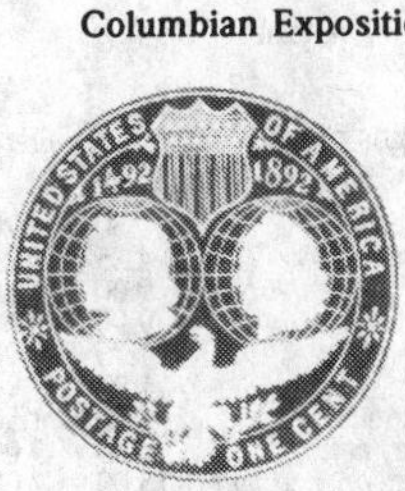
Columbus and Liberty — U76

1893

U348	U76 1c deep blue	2.00	1.00
U349	U76 2c violet	1.75	50
a.	2c dark slate (error)	*1,750.*	
U350	U76 5c chocolate	8.50	7.50
a.	5c slate brown (error)	700.00	700.00
U351	U76 10c slate brown	30.00	25.00

Franklin
U77

Washington
U78

U78- Bust points to first notch of inner oval and is only slightly concave below.

U79

U80

U79--Bust points to middle of second notch of inner oval and is quite hollow below. Queue has ribbon around it.

U80--Same as die 2 but hair flowing and no ribbon around queue.

Lincoln — U81

Pointed but not draped.

U82

U83

U82--Bust broad and draped.

U83--Head larger, inner oval has no notches.

Grant — U84

Similar to designs of 1887-95 but smaller

1899

U352	U77 1c green	50	20
U353	U77 1c grn, *amb*	4.25	1.25
U354	U77 1c grn, *oriental buff*	9.00	2.50
U355	U77 1c grn, *bl*	9.00	6.00
U356	U77 1c grn, *man*	1.75	90
W357	U77 1c grn, *man*	1.90	90
U358	U78 2c carmine	2.50	1.50
U359	U78 2c car, *amb*	16.00	9.00
U360	U78 2c car, *oriental buff*	15.00	7.00
U361	U78 2c car, *blue*	55.00	27.50
U362	U79 2c carmine	25	20
a.	2c dark lake	25.00	30.00
U363	U79 2c car, *amb*	1.00	15
U364	U79 2c car, *oriental buff*	90	15
U365	U79 2c car, *blue*	1.10	50
W366	U79 2c car, *man*	4.50	2.50
U367	U80 2c carmine	4.00	1.75
U368	U80 2c car, *amber*	7.50	6.25
U369	U80 2c car, *oriental buff*	20.00	11.00
U370	U80 2c car, *blue*	10.00	8.00
U371	U81 4c brown	15.00	10.00
U372	U81 4c brn, *amb*	15.00	11.00
U373	U82 4c brown	*5,500.*	300.00
U374	U83 4c brown	9.00	7.00
U375	U83 4c brn, *amb*	32.50	15.00
W376	U83 4c brn, *man*	14.00	7.50
U377	U84 5c blue	8.75	8.50
U378	U84 5c blue, *amb*	12.00	9.50

Franklin
U85

Washington
U86

U86--One short and two long vertical lines at right of "CENTS."

Grant — U87

Lincoln — U88

1903

U379	U85 1c green	45	15
U380	U85 1c green, *amb*	11.00	2.00
U381	U85 1c grn, *oriental buff*	11.00	2.50
U382	U85 1c green, *blue*	12.50	2.50
U383	U85 1c grn, *manila*	2.50	90
W384	U85 1c grn, *manila*	1.00	40
U385	U86 2c carmine	30	15
U386	U86 2c carmine, *amb*	1.50	20
U387	U86 2c car, *oriental buff*	1.50	30
U388	U86 2c carmine, *blue*	1.00	50
W389	U86 2c car, *manila*	14.00	8.50
U390	U87 4c chocolate	18.00	11.00
U391	U87 4c choc, *amber*	17.50	10.00
W392	U87 4c choc, *manila*	16.00	11.50
U393	U88 5c blue	16.00	9.50
U394	U88 5c blue, *amber*	16.00	11.00

U89

The three lines at the right of "CENTS" and at the left of "TWO" are usually all short; the lettering is heavier and the ends of the ribbons slightly changed.

1904 **Re-cut Die**

U395	U89 2c carmine	40	20
U396	U89 2c car, *amber*	6.50	75
U397	U89 2c car, *oriental buff*	5.00	1.00
U398	U89 2c carmine, *blue*	3.00	90
W399	U89 2c car, *manila*	11.00	8.00

Franklin — U90

Die 1

Die 2

Die 3

Die 4

Die 1. Wide "D" in "UNITED."
Die 2. Narrow "D" in "UNITED."
Die 3. Wide "S-S" in "STATES" (1910).
Die 4. Sharp angle at back of bust, "N" and "E" of "ONE" are parallel (1912).

1907-16 **Die 1**

U400	U90 1c green	25	15
a.	Die 2	75	25
b.	Die 3	75	35
c.	Die 4	65	30
U401	U90 1c green, *amber*	70	40
a.	Die 2	85	70
b.	Die 3	95	75
c.	Die 4	80	65
U402	U90 1c grn, *oriental buff*	4.00	1.00
a.	Die 2	5.00	1.50
b.	Die 3	6.00	1.50
c.	Die 4	4.25	1.50
U403	U90 1c green, *blue*	4.00	1.50
a.	Die 2	4.00	1.50
b.	Die 3	4.00	3.00
c.	Die 4	3.50	1.25
U404	U90 1c grn, *manila*	2.75	1.90
a.	Die 3	3.50	3.00
W405	U90 1c grn, *manila*	40	25
a.	Die 2	40.00	25.00
b.	Die 3	5.00	3.00
c.	Die 4	40.00	

Die 1, Washington — U91

Die 2

Die 3

Die 4

Die 5

Die 6

Die 7

Die 8

Die 1. Oval "O" in "TWO" and "C" in "CENTS," front of bust broad.

Die 2. Similar to 1 but hair in two distinct locks at top of head.

Die 3. Round "O" in "TWO" and "C" in "CENTS," coarse lettering.

Die 4. Similar to 3 but lettering fine and clear, hair lines clearly embossed. Inner oval thin and clear.

Die 5. All "S's" wide (1910).

Die 6. Similar to 1 but front of bust narrow (1913).

Die 7. Similar to 6 but upper corner of front of bust cut away (1916).

Die 8. Similar to 7 but lower stroke of "S" in "CENTS" is a straight line. Hair as in Die 2 (1916).

Die I

U406	U91 2c brown red	70	15
a.	Die 2	27.50	6.25
b.	Die 3	50	16
U407	U91 2c brn red, *amb*	4.00	2.00
a.	Die 2	100.00	45.00
b.	Die 3	2.75	1.00
U408	U91 2c brown red, *oriental buff*	6.50	1.50
a.	Die 2	125.00	55.00
b.	Die 3	6.00	2.50
U409	U91 2c brn red, *blue*	4.00	1.75
a.	Die 2	125.00	100.00
b.	Die 3	4.00	1.50
W410	U91 2c brn red, *man*	35.00	25.00
U411	U91 2c carmine	20	15
a.	Die 2	40	16
b.	Die 3	65	35
c.	Die 4	35	16
d.	Die 5	45	30
e.	Die 6	35	20
f.	Die 7	12.50	10.00
g.	Die 8	13.00	10.00
h.	Die 1, with added impression of 1c grn (#U400), entire	325.00	
i.	Die 1, with added impression of 4c blk (#U416a), entire	300.00	
U412	U91 2c carmine, *amb*	20	15
a.	Die 2	40	20
b.	Die 3	1.25	45
c.	Die 4	35	25
d.	Die 5	55	35
e.	Die 6	50	35
f.	Die 7	11.00	8.00
U413	U91 2c car, *oriental buff*	40	20
a.	Die 2	50	45
b.	Die 3	6.00	3.00
c.	Die 4	35	16
d.	Die 5	2.75	1.25
e.	Die 6	50	35
f.	Die 7	35.00	17.50
g.	Die 8	11.00	8.50
U414	U91 2c carmine, *blue*	40	16
a.	Die 2	40	35
b.	Die 3	75	60
c.	Die 4	40	25
d.	Die 5	50	30
e.	Die 6	45	30
f.	Die 7	12.50	7.50
g.	Die 8	12.50	7.50
W415	U91 2c car, *manila*	4.00	2.00
a.	Die 2	4.00	1.10
b.	Die 5	4.00	2.25
c.	Die 7	40.00	35.00

"F" 1mm from left "4" — Die 1

"F" 1¾mm from left "4" — Die 2

U416	U90 4c black, die 2	3.50	2.25
a.	Die 1	4.25	3.00
U417	U90 4c black, *amb*, die 2	5.00	2.50
a.	Die 1	5.00	2.50

Die 1-Tall "F" in "FIVE"

Die 2-Short "F" in "FIVE"

U418	U91 5c blue, die 2	6.00	2.25
a.	Die 1	6.00	2.25
b.	5c blue, *buff*, die 2 (error)	*1,000.*	
c.	5c blue, *blue*, die 2 (error)	*1,000.*	
d.	5c blue, *blue*, die 1 (error)	*1,100.*	
U419	U91 5c blue, *amber*, die 2	12.00	11.00
a.	Die 1	12.00	11.00

Franklin — U92

Die 1

Die 2

Die 3

Die 4

Die 5

(The 1c and 4c dies are the same except for figures of value.)

Die 1. UNITED nearer inner circle than outer circle.

Die 2. Large U; large NT closely spaced.

Die 3. Knob of hair at back of neck. Large NT widely spaced.

Die 4. UNITED nearer outer circle than inner circle.

Die 5. Narrow oval C, (also O and G).

1916-32 **Die 1**

U420	U92 1c green	15	15
a.	Die 2	90.00	55.00
b.	Die 3	30	15
c.	Die 4	40	40
d.	Die 5	40	35
U421	U92 1c grn, *amber*	35	30
a.	Die 2	300.00	175.00
b.	Die 3	1.00	65
c.	Die 4	1.15	85
d.	Die 5	90	55
U422	U92 1c grn, *oriental buff*	1.75	90
a.	Die 4	3.75	1.25
U423	U92 1c green, *blue*	40	35
a.	Die 3	75	45
b.	Die 4	1.25	65
c.	Die 5	65	35
U424	U92 1c grn, (unglazed) *manila*	6.00	4.00
W425	U92 1c grn, (unglazed) *manila*	20	15
a.	Die 3	140.00	125.00
U426	U92 1c grn, (glazed) *brown* ('20)	30.00	15.00
W427	U92 1c grn, (glazed) *brown* ('20)	55.00	
U428	U92 1c grn, (unglazed) *brown* ('20)	7.50	7.50

Die 1, Washington — U93

Die 2

Die 3

Die 4

Die 5

Die 6

Die 7

Die 8

Die 9

(The 1½c, 2c, 3c, 5c, and 6c are the same except for figures of value.)

Die 1. Letters broad. Numerals vertical. Large head (9¼mm) from tip of nose to back of neck. E closer to inner circle than N of cents.

Die 2. Similar to 1; but U far from left circle.

Die 3. Similar to 2; but all inner circles very thin (Rejected Die).

Die 4. Similar to 1; but C very close to left circle.

Die 5. Small head (8¾mm) from tip of nose to back of neck. T and S of CENTS close at bottom.

Die 6. Similar to 5; but T and S of CENTS far apart at bottom. Left numeral slopes to right.

Die 7. Large head. Both numerals slope to right. Clean cut lettering. All letters T have short top strokes.

Die 8. Similar to 7; but all letters T have long top strokes.

Die 9. Narrow oval C (also O and G).

Die 1

U429	U93 2c carmine	15	15
a.	Die 2	9.00	6.00
b.	Die 3	30.00	25.00
c.	Die 4	9.00	7.50
d.	Die 5	50	35
e.	Die 6	60	30
f.	Die 7	65	25
g.	Die 8	45	20
h.	Die 9	40	20
i.	2c grn, error, die 1, entire	8,000.	
j.	2c car, die 1 with added impression of 1c grn (#U420), die 1, entire	700.00	
k.	Die 1, with added impression of 4c blk (#U416a), entire	700.00	
l.	Die 1, with added impression of 1c grn (#U400), die 1, entire	500.00	
U430	U93 2c car, *amber*	25	15
a.	Die 2	9.25	7.50
b.	Die 4	20.00	10.00
c.	Die 5	1.10	35
d.	Die 6	95	40
e.	Die 7	70	35
f.	Die 8	60	30
g.	Die 9	50	20
U431	U93 2c car, *oriental buff*	2.00	65
a.	Die 2	100.00	40.00
b.	Die 4	30.00	30.00
c.	Die 5	2.75	1.75
d.	Die 6	3.00	2.00
e.	Die 7	2.75	1.75
U432	U93 2c carmine, *blue*	20	15
b.	Die 2	25.00	20.00
c.	Die 3	100.00	90.00
d.	Die 4	25.00	25.00
e.	Die 5	80	30
f.	Die 6	85	40
g.	Die 7	75	35
h.	Die 8	60	25
i.	Die 9	90	30
U432A	U93 2c car, *manila*, die 7, entire	*25,000.*	
W433	U93 2c car, *manila*	20	16
W434	U93 2c car, (glazed) *brn* ('20)	70.00	50.00
W435	U93 2c car, (unglazed) *brn* ('20)	75.00	50.00
U436	U93 3c dk violet	50	16
a.	3c purple ('32), die 1	30	15
b.	3c dark violet, die 5	1.65	75
c.	3c dark violet, die 6	2.00	1.40
d.	3c dark violet, die 7	1.40	95
e.	3c purple ('32), die 7	60	30
f.	3c purple ('32), die 9	35	16
g.	3c carmine (error), die 1	30.00	27.50
h.	3c carmine (error), die 5	30.00	27.50
i.	3c dk vio, die 1, with added impression of 1c grn (#U420), die 1, entire	600.00	
j.	3c dk vio, die 1, with added impression of 2c car (#U429), die 1, entire	700.00	—
U437	U93 3c dk violet, *amb*	3.00	1.25
a.	3c purple ('32), die 1	30	15
b.	3c dark vio, die 5	4.50	2.50
c.	3c dark vio, die 6	4.50	2.50
d.	3c dark vio, die 7	3.75	2.25
e.	3c purple ('32), die 7	60	15
f.	3c purple ('32), die 9	50	15
g.	3c carmine (error), die 5	350.00	250.00
h.	3c black (error), die 1	165.00	—
U438	U93 3c dk vio, *oriental buff*	20.00	1.50
a.	Die 5	20.00	1.00
b.	Die 6	30.00	1.65
c.	Die 7	30.00	3.50
U439	U93 3c dk violet, *bl*	6.00	2.00
a.	3c purple ('32), die 1	25	16
b.	3c dark violet, die 5	6.50	4.00
c.	3c dark violet, die 6	6.00	4.25
d.	3c dark violet, die 7	8.50	5.50
e.	3c purple ('32), die 7	55	25
f.	3c purple ('32), die 9	50	20
g.	3c carmine (error), die 5	275.00	275.00
U440	U92 4c black	1.00	60
a.	4c black with added impression of 2c car (#U429), die 1, entire	250.00	
U441	U92 4c black, *amb*	2.50	75
U442	U92 4c black, *bl* ('21)	2.75	75
U443	U93 5c blue	2.75	2.25
U444	U93 5c blue, *amber*	3.00	1.40
U445	U93 5c bl, *blue* ('21)	3.50	2.75

See Nos. U481-U485, U529-U531.

Listings of double or triple surcharges of 1920-25 are for specimens with the surcharges directly or partly upon the stamp.

Surcharged Type 1

1920-21

U446	U93 2c on 3c dk vio (U436)	10.00	9.50
a.	Die 5	10.00	9.50

Surcharged Type 2

Rose Surcharge

U447	U93 2c on 3c dk vio (U436)	6.00	5.50
b.	Die 6	9.00	8.50

Black Surcharge

U447A	U93 2c on 2c car (U429)	—	
U447C	U93 2c on 2c car, *amb* (U430)	—	
U448	U93 2c on 3c dk vio (U436)	2.00	1.75
U449	U93 2c on 3c dk vio, *amb* (U437)	5.00	5.00
U450	U93 2c on 3c dk vio, *oriental buff* (U438)	14.00	12.50
U451	U93 2c on 3c dk vio, *blue* (U439)	11.00	10.00

Surcharged Type 3

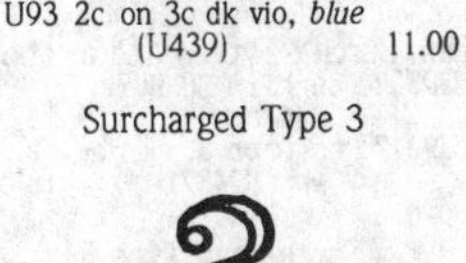

Bars 2mm apart

U451A	U90 2c on 1c grn (U400)	1,750.	
U452	U92 2c on 1c grn (U420)	950.00	
a.	Dbl. surch., Type 3	1,000.	
U453	U91 2c on 2c car (U411)	1,050.	
a.	Die 4	1,000.	
U453B	U91 2c on 2c car, *bl* (U414e)	900.00	
U453C	U91 2c on 2c car, *oriental buff* (U413e)	900.00	625.00
d.	Die 1	800.00	
U454	U93 2c on 2c car (U429)	77.50	
U455	U93 2c on 2c car, *amb* (U430)	1,250.	
U456	U93 2c on 2c car, *oriental buff* (U431)	150.00	
a.	Dbl. surch., Type 3	225.00	
U457	U93 2c on 2c car, *bl* (U432)	175.00	

U458 U93 2c on 3c dk vio (U436) 45 35
a. Double surcharge 14.00 7.50
b. Triple surcharge 35.00
c. Dbl. surch., one in mag 65.00
d. Dbl. surch., Types 2 & 3 100.00
U459 U93 2c on 3c dk vio, *amb* (U437) 2.50 1.00
a. Dbl. surch., Type 3 18.00
b. Dbl. surch., Types 2 & 3 80.00
U460 U93 2c on 3c dk vio, *oriental buff* (U438) 2.50 1.00
a. Double surcharge 12.50
b. Triple surcharge 27.50
U461 U93 2c on 3c dk vio, *bl* (U439) 4.00 1.00
a. Double surcharge 15.00
U462 U87 2c on 4c choc (U390) 350.00 160.00
U463 U87 2c on 4c choc, *amb* (U391) 350.00 100.00
U463A U90 2c on 4c blk (U416) 1,000. 375.00
U464 U93 2c on 5c bl (U443) 1,000.

Surcharged Type 4

Similar to Type 3, but bars 1½mm apart.

U465 U92 2c on 1c grn (U420) 1,000.
U466 U91 2c on 2c car (U411e) *3,000.*
U466A U93 2c on 2c car (U429) 225.00
c. Die 5 350.00
U466B U93 2c on 2c car, *amb* (U430) 1,750.
U467 U45 2c on 3c grn (U163) 225.00
U468 U93 2c on 3c dk vio (U436) 60 45
a. Double surcharge 15.00
b. Triple surcharge 20.00
c. Inverted surcharge 75.00
d. Dbl. surch., Types 2 & 4 75.00
e. 2c on 3c car (error) (U436h) 450.00
U469 U93 2c on 3c dk vio, *amb* (U437) 3.00 1.90
a. Dbl. surch., Types 2 & 4 60.00
U470 U93 2c on 3c dk vio, *oriental buff* (U438) 4.25 2.50
a. Double surcharge, Type 4 18.50
b. Dbl. surch., Types 2 & 4 60.00
U471 U93 2c on 3c dk vio, *bl* (U439) 3.00 1.00
a. Double surcharge, Type 4 18.50
b. Dbl. surch., Types 2 & 4 150.00
U472 U87 2c on 4c choc (U390) 11.00 8.00
a. Double surcharge 37.50
U473 U87 2c on 4c choc, *amb* (U391) 12.50 9.00

Dbl. Surch., Type 4 and as above

U474 U93 2c on 1c on 3c dk vio (U436) 185.00
U475 U93 2c on 1c on 3c dk vio, *amb* (U437) 185.00

Surcharged Type 5

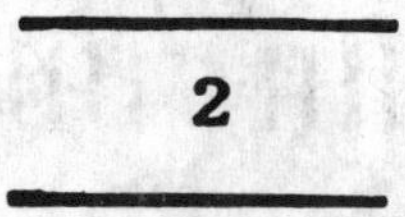

U476 U93 2c on 3c dk vio, *amb* (U437) 100.00
a. Double surcharge —

Surcharged Type 6

U477 U93 2c on 3c dk vio (U436) 95.00
U478 U93 2c on 3c dk vio, *amb* (U437) 190.00

Handstamped Surcharge in Black or Violet—Type 7

U479 U93 2c on 3c dk vio (Bk) (U436) 275.00
U480 U93 2c on 3c dk vio (V) (U436d) 1,400.

Type of 1916-32 Issue

1925-34

U481 U93 1½c brown, die 1 15 15
a. Die 8 60 25
b. 1½c pur, die 1 (error) ('34) 90.00
U482 U93 1½c brown, die 1, *amber* 90 40
a. Die 8 1.40 75
U483 U93 1½c brn, die 1, *bl* 1.50 95
a. Die 8 1.75 1.25
U484 U93 1½c brown, die 1, *manila* 6.00 3.00
W485 U93 1½c brown, die 1, *manila* 75 15
a. With added impression of No. W433 120.00

Surcharged Type 8

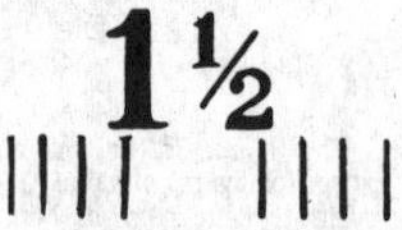

1925

U486 U71 1½c on 2c grn (U311) 675.00
U487 U71 1½c on 2c grn, *amb* (U312) 750.00
U488 U77 1½c on 1c grn (U352) 500.00
U489 U77 1½c on 1c grn, *amb* (U353) 80.00 60.00
U490 U90 1½c on 1c grn (U400) 3.75 3.50
a. Die 2 12.00 9.00
b. Die 4 6.00 2.50
U491 U90 1½c on 1c grn, *amb* (U401) 7.50 2.50
a. Die 2 75.00 65.00
b. Die 4 4.25 2.25
U492 U90 1½c on 1c grn, *oriental buff* (U402a) 200.00 80.00
a. Die 4 200.00 80.00
U493 U90 1½c on 1c grn, *bl* (U403c) 75.00 52.50
a. Die 2 75.00 52.50
U494 U90 1½c on 1c grn, *man* (U404) 190.00 72.50
U495 U92 1½c on 1c grn (U420) 50 25
a. Die 3 1.50 60
b. Die 4 1.65 75
c. Double surcharge 4.00 1.90
U496 U92 1½c on 1c grn, *amb* (U421) 13.50 12.50
U497 U92 1½c on 1c grn, *oriental buff* (U422) 3.00 1.90
U498 U92 1½c on 1c grn, *bl* (U423) 1.00 75
U499 U92 1½c on 1c grn, *man* (U424) 10.00 6.00
U500 U92 1½c on 1c grn, *brn* (unglazed) (U428) 55.00 30.00
U501 U93 1½c on 1c grn, *brn* (glazed) (U426) 55.00 25.00
U502 U93 1½c on 2c car (U429) 225.00 —
U503 U93 1½c on 2c car, *oriental buff* (U431) 250.00 —
a. Double surcharge —
U504 U93 1½c on 2c car, *bl* (U432) 250.00 —

On Envelopes of 1925

U505 U93 1½c on 1½c brn (U481) 400.00
a. Die 8 400.00
U506 U93 1½c on 1½c brn, *bl* (U483) 325.00

The paper of No. U500 is not glazed and appears to be the same as that used for wrappers of 1920.

Surcharged Type 9

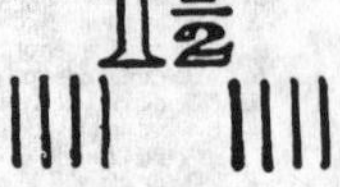

Black Surcharge

U507 U69 1½c on 1c bl (U294) 1,050.
U508 U77 1½c on 1c grn, *amb* (U353) 50.00
U508A U85 1½c on 1c grn (U379) 1,500.
U509 U85 1½c on 1c grn, *amb* (U380) 12.00 10.00
a. Double surcharge 25.00
U509B U85 1½c on 1c grn, *oriental buff* (U381) 50.00 40.00
U510 U90 1½c on 1c grn (U400) 1.75 1.25
a. Double surcharge 7.50
b. Die 2 6.00 4.00
c. Die 3 16.00 8.00
d. Die 4 3.00 1.25
U511 U90 1½c on 1c grn, *amb* (U401) 150.00 72.50
U512 U90 1½c on 1c grn, *oriental buff* (U402) 6.00 4.00
a. Die 4 17.00 14.00
U513 U90 1½c on 1c grn, *bl* (U403) 5.00 2.50
a. Die 4 5.00 4.00
U514 U90 1½c on 1c grn, *man* (U404) 22.50 9.00
a. Die 3 50.00 37.50
U515 U92 1½c on 1c grn (U420) 30 20
a. Double surcharge 6.00
b. Inverted surcharge 9.00
c. Triple surcharge 11.00
U516 U92 1½c on 1c grn, *amb* (U421) 40.00 25.00
U517 U92 1½c on 1c grn, *oriental buff* (U422) 4.25 1.25
U518 U92 1½c on 1c grn, *bl* (U423) 4.25 1.25
a. Double surcharge 9.00
U519 U92 1½c on 1c grn, *man* (U424) 20.00 10.00
a. Double surcharge 27.50
U520 U93 1½c on 2c car (U429) 225.00 —

Magenta Surcharge

U521 U92 1½c on 1c grn (U420) 4.25 3.50
a. Double surcharge 25.00

Sesquicentennial Exposition Issue

Liberty Bell — U94

Die 1. The center bar of "E" of "POSTAGE" is shorter than top bar.
Die 2. The center bar of "E" of "POSTAGE" is of same length as top bar.

1926

U522 U94 2c carmine, die 1 1.00 50
a. Die 2 6.00 4.00

See note below No. 627.

Washington Bicentennial Issue

Mount Vernon — U95

2 cent:
Die 1. "S" of "POSTAGE" normal.
Die 2. "S" of "POSTAGE" raised.

1932

U523 U95 1c olive green 1.10 1.00
U524 U95 1½c chocolate 2.00 1.50
U525 U95 2c car, die 1 40 16
a. Die 2 70.00 16.00
b. Die 1, *blue*, entire (error) *27,500.*
U526 U95 3c violet 2.00 35
U527 U95 4c black 18.00 15.00
U528 U95 5c dark blue 4.00 3.25
Nos. U523-U528 (6) 27.50 21.26

Bicen. of the birth of Washington.

1932 **Die 7**

U529 U93 6c orange 5.00 2.75
U530 U93 6c orange, *amber* 10.00 7.50
U531 U93 6c orange, *blue* 10.00 8.50

Franklin — U96

Washington — U97

Die 1

Die 2

Die 3

Die 1. Short (3½mm) and thick "1" in thick circle.
Die 2. Tall (4½mm) and thin "1" in thin circle; upper and lower bars of E in ONE long and 1mm from circle.
Die 3. As in Die 2, but E normal and 1½mm from circle.

1950

U532 U96 1c green, die 1 5.00 1.75
a. Die 2 6.00 3.00
b. Die 3 6.00 3.00
Die 3, precanceled 60

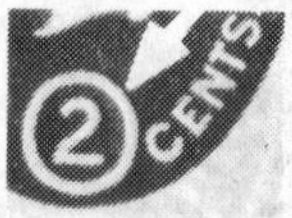

Die 1

Die 2

Die 3

Die 4

Die 1. Thick "2" in circle; toe of "2" is an acute angle.
Die 2. Thin "2" in thin circle; toe of "2" is almost right angle; line through stand of "E" in POSTAGE goes considerably below tip of chin; "N" of UNITED is tall; "O" of TWO is high.
Die 3. Thin "2" in thin circle; toe of "2" is almost right angle; short UN in UNITED: thin crossbar in A of STATES.
Die 4. Tall UN in UNITED; thick crossbar in A of STATES; otherwise like Die 3.

U533 U97 2c carmine, die 3 70 25
a. Die 1 75 30
b. Die 2 1.40 85
c. Die 4 1.40 60

Die 1

Die 2

Die 3

Die 4 Die 5

Die 1. Thick and tall (4 1/2mm) "3" in thick circle; long top bars and short stems in T's of STATES.

Die 2. Thin and tall (4 1/2mm) "3" in medium circle; short top bars and long stems in T's of STATES.

Die 3. Thin and short (4mm) "3" in thin circle; lettering wider than Dies 1 and 2; line from left stand of N to stand of E is distinctly below tip of chin.

Die 4. Figure and letters as in Die 3. Line hits tip of chin; short N in UNITED and thin crossbar in A of STATES.

Die 5. Figure, letter and chin line as in Die 4; but tall N in UNITED and thick crossbar in A of STATES.

U534 U97 3c dk violet, die 4 40 16
- *a.* Die 1 2.00 70
- *b.* Die 2 75 50
- *c.* Die 3 50 25
- *d.* Die 5 80 45

Washington — U98

1952

U535 U98 1 1/2c brown 4.50 3.50
- Precanceled 50

Die 1 Die 2

Die 3

Die 1. Head high in oval (2mm below T of STATES). Circle near (1mm) bottom of colored oval.

Die 2. Head low in oval (3mm). Circle 1 1/2mm from edge of oval. Right leg of A of POSTAGE shorter than left. Short leg on P.

Die 3. Head centered in oval (2 1/2mm). Circle as in Die 2. Legs of A of POSTAGE about equal. Long leg on P.

1958

U536 U96 4c red violet, die 1 75 16
- *a.* Die 2 1.00 16
- *b.* Die 3 1.00 16

Nos. U429, U429f, U429h, U533, U533a-U533c Surcharged in Red at Left of Stamp - b

1958

U537 U93 2c + 2c car, die 1 3.00 1.50
- *a.* 2c + 2c carmine, die 7 10.00 7.00
- *b.* 2c + 2c carmine, die 9 5.00 5.00

U538 U97 2c + 2c car, die 1 75 20
- *a.* 2c + 2c carmine, die 2 1.00 —
- *b.* 2c + 2c carmine, die 3 80 25
- *c.* 2c + 2c carmine, die 4 80 —

Nos. U436a, U436e-U436f, U534a-U534d Surcharged in Green at Left of Stamp - a

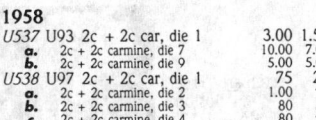

U539 U93 3c + 1c pur, die 1 14.00 10.00
- *a.* 3c + 1c purple, die 7 11.00 9.00
- *b.* 3c + 1c purple, die 9 30.00 15.00

U540 U97 3c + 1c dk violet, die 3 50 15
- *a.* 3c + 1c dk violet, die 2, entire *1,000.* —
- *b.* 3c + 1c dark violet, die 4 75 15
- *c.* 3c + 1c dark violet, die 5 75 15

See No. U545.

Franklin U99

Washington U100

Die 1 Die 2

Dies of 1 1/4c

Die 1. The "4" is 3mm high. Upper leaf in left cluster 2mm from "U."

Die 2. The "4" is 3 1/2mm high. Leaf clusters are larger. Upper leaf at left is 1mm from "U."

1960

U541 U99 1 1/4c turquoise, die 1 70 50
- Die 1, precanceled 15
- *a.* Die 2, precanceled 2.00

U542 U100 2 1/2c dull blue 80 50
- Precanceled 15

Precanceled Cut Squares

Precanceled envelopes do not normally receive another cancellation. Since the lack of a cancellation makes it impossible to distinguish between cut squares from used and unused envelopes, they are valued here as used only.

Pony Express Centennial Issue

Pony Express Rider U101

Envelope White Outside, Blue Inside

1960, July 19

U543 U101 4c brown 60 30

Abraham Lincoln — U102

Die 1 Die 2

Die 3

Die 1. Center bar of E of POSTAGE is above the middle. Center bar of E of STATES slants slightly upward. Nose sharper, more pointed. No offset ink specks inside envelope on back of die impression.

Die 2. Center bar of E in POSTAGE in middle. P of POSTAGE has short stem. Ink specks on back of die impression.

Die 3. FI of FIVE closer than Die 1 or 2. Second T of STATES seems taller than ES. Ink specks on back of die impression.

1962, Nov. 19

U544 U102 5c dark blue, die 2 80 20
- *a.* Die 1 85 25
- *b.* Die 3 90 35
- *c.* Die 2 with albino impression of 4c (#U536) 50.00 —
- *d.* Die 3 with albino impression of 4c (#U536) 70.00 —

No. U536 Surcharged Type "a" in Green at Left of Stamp

Two types of surcharge "a":

Type I. "U.S. POSTAGE" 18 1/2mm high. Serifs on cross of T both diagonal. Two lines of shading in C of CENT.

Type II. "U.S. POSTAGE" 17 1/2mm high. Right serif on cross of T is vertical. Three shading lines in C.

1962, Nov.

U545 U96 4c + 1c red vio, Type I 1.30 50
- *a.* Type II 1.00 50

New York World's Fair (1964-65)

Globe with Satellite Orbit U103

1964, Apr. 22

U546 U103 5c carmine rose 60 40

Liberty Bell — U104

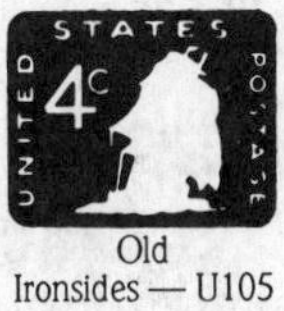

Old Ironsides — U105

Eagle — U106

Head of Statue of Liberty — U107

1965-69 **Tagged (6c)**

U547 U104 1 1/4c brown 15
U548 U104 1 4/10c brown ('68) 15
U548A U104 1 6/10c orange ('69) 15
U549 U105 4c bright blue 75 15
U550 U106 5c bright purple 75 15
- *a.* Tagged ('67) 1.00 15

U551 U107 6c lt green ('68) 70 15
- *Set value* 55

Issue dates: 5c, Jan. 5; 1 1/4c, Jan. 6; 6c, Jan. 4; 1 4/10c, Mar. 26; 1 6/10c, June 16.

No. U550a has a luminescent panel 9x29mm at left of stamp. It glows yellow green under ultraviolet light.

Nos. U549-U550 Surcharged Types "b" and "a" in Red or Green at Left of Stamp

1968, Feb. 5

U552 U105 4c + 2c brt blue (R) 3.75 2.00
U553 U106 5c + 1c brt purple (G) 3.50 2.25
- *a.* Tagged 3.50 2.50

Tagging

Envelopes from No. U554 onward are tagged, with the tagging element in the ink unless otherwise noted.

Herman Melville Issue

Moby Dick — U108

1970, Mar. 7

U554 U108 6c light blue 50 15

Herman Melville (1819-91), writer, and the whaling industry.

Youth Conference Issue

Youth Conference Emblem U109

1971, Feb. 24

U555 U109 6c light blue 75 15

White House Conference on Youth, Estes Park, Colo., Apr. 18-22.

Bell Type of 1965-69 and

Eagle — U110

1971 **Untagged (1 7/10c)**

U556 U104 1 7/10c deep lilac 15
U557 U110 8c bright ultra 40 15
- *Set value* 15

Issue dates: 1 7/10c, May 10; 8c, May 6.

Nos. U551 and U555 Surcharged in Green at Left of Stamp

1971, May 16

U561 U107 6c + (2c) light green 1.00 30
U562 U109 6c + (2c) light blue 2.00 1.50

Buying Sets

It is often less expensive to purchase complete sets than individual stamps that make up the set. Set values are provided for many such sets.

Bowling Issue

Bowling Ball and Pin — U111

1971, Aug. 21
U563 U111 8c rose red 50 15

Salute to bowling and 7th World Tournament of the Intl. Bowling Fed., Milwaukee, WI.

Aging Conference Issue

Conference Symbol — U112

1971, Nov. 5
U564 U112 8c light blue 50 15

White House Conference on Aging, Washington, DC, Nov. 28-Dec. 2, 1971.

International Transportation Exhibition Issue

Transportation Exhibition Emblem U113

Illustration 2/5 actual size.

1972, May 2
U565 U113 8c ultra & rose red 50 15

US Intl. Transportation Exhib., Dulles Intl. Airport, Washington, May 27-June 4.

No. U557 Surcharged Type "b" in Ultramarine at Left of Stamp

1973, Dec. 1
U566 U110 8c + 2c bright ultra 40 15

Liberty Bell — U114

1973, Dec. 5
U567 U114 10c emerald 40 15

"Volunteer Yourself" — U115

1974, Aug. 23 **Untagged**
U568 U115 1 8/10c blue green 15

US Tennis Centenary Issue

Tennis Racquet — U116

1974, Aug. 31
U569 U116 10c yel, brt blue & lt grn 30 16

Bicentennial Era Issue

The Seafaring Tradition--Compass Rose — U118

The American Homemaker--Quilt Pattern — U119

The American Farmer--Sheaf of Wheat U120

The American Doctor — U121

The American Craftsman--Tools, c. 1750 — U122

Designs (in brown on left side of envelope): 10c, Norwegian sloop Restaurationen. No. U572, Spinning wheel. No. U573, Plow. No. U574, Colonial era medical instruments and bottle. No. U575, Shaker rocking chair.

Light Brown Diagonally Laid Paper

1975-76
U571 U118 10c brown & blue 30 15
a. Brown ("10c/USA") omitted, entire 125.00
U572 U119 13c brn & bl grn 35 15
a. Brown ("13c/USA") omitted, entire 125.00
U573 U120 13c brn & brt grn 35 15
a. Brown ("13c/USA") omitted, entire 125.00
U574 U121 13c brown & orange 35 15
U575 U122 13c brown & car 35 15
a. Brown ("13c/USA") omitted, entire 125.00

Issue dates: 10c, Oct. 13, 1975. No. U572, Feb. 2, 1976. No. U573, Mar. 15, 1976. No. 574, June 30, 1976. No. U575, Aug. 6, 1976.

Liberty Tree, Boston, 1646 — U123

1975, Nov. 8
U576 U123 13c orange brown 30 15

Precanceled Cut Squares
See note following No. U542.

Star and Pinweel — U124

U125

U126

Eagle — U127

"Uncle Sam" — U128

1976-78
U577 U124 2c red, untagged ('76) 15
U578 U125 2.1c yel grn, untagged ('77) 15
U579 U126 2.7c grn, untagged ('78) 15
U580 U127 (15c) orange ('78) 35 15
U581 U128 15c red ('78) 35 15
Set value 45

Issue dates; 2c, Sept. 10. 2.1c June 3. 2.7c, July 5. A, May 22. 15c, June 3.

Bicentennial Issue

Centennial Envelope, 1876 — U129

1976, Oct. 15
U582 U129 13c emerald 35 15

See Nos. U218-U221.

Golf Issue

Golf Club in Motion and Golf Ball — U130

1977, Apr. 7
U583 U130 13c blk, bl & yel green 45 20
a. Black omitted, entire —
b. Black & blue omitted, entire —

Energy Issue

Energy Conservation U131

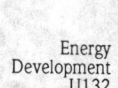

Energy Development U132

1977, Oct. 20
U584 U131 13c blk, red & yel 40 15
a. Red & yel omitted, entire —
b. Yellow omitted, entire —
c. Black omitted, entire —
d. Black & red omitted, entire 300.00
U585 U132 13c blk, red & yel 40 15

Nos. U584-U585 have a luminescent panel at left of stamp.

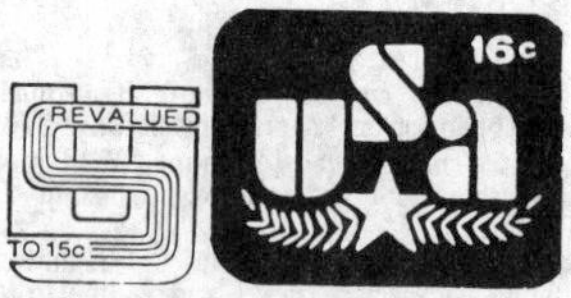

Olive Branch and Star — U133

1978, July 28
U586 U133 15c on 16c blue 35 15
a. Surcharge omitted, entire 125.00 —
b. Surcharge on #U581, entire — —

Auto Racing Issue

Indianapolis 500 Racing Car — U134

1978, Sept. 2
U587 U134 15c red, blue & black 35 15
a. Black omitted, entire 125.00
b. Black & blue omitted, entire —
c. Red omitted, entire —
d. Red & blue omitted, entire —

No. U576 Surcharged at left of Stamp Like No. U586

1978, Nov. 28 **Embossed**
U588 U123 15c on 13c org brown 35 15

Precanceled Cut Squares
See note following No. U542.

U135

Weaver Violins — U136

U137

Eagle — U138

Star — U139

Eagle
U140

1979-82 Untagged (3.1c, 3.5c, 5.9c)

U589 U135	3.1c ultramarine		15
U590 U136	3.5c purple		15
U591 U137	5.9c brown		15
U592 U138	(18c) violet	45	18
U593 U139	18c dark blue	45	18
U594 U140	(20c) brown	45	15
	Set value		77

Issue dates: 3.1c, May 18; 3.5c, June 23; 5.9c, Feb. 17, 1982. #U592, Mar. 15, 1981; #U593, Apr. 2, 1981; #U594, Oct. 11, 1981.

Veterinary Medicine Issue

Seal of
Veterinarians
U141

Design on left side of envelope shows 5 animals and a bird in brown and "Veterinary Medicine" in gray.

1979, July 24

U595 U141	15c brown & gray	35	15
a.	Gray omitted, untagged, entire	—	

Olympic Games Issue

U142

Design (multicolored on left side of envelope) shows two soccer players with ball.

1979, Dec. 10

U596 U142	15c red, green & black	60	15
a.	Red & green omitted, untagged, entire	225.00	
b.	Blk omitted, untagged, entire	225.00	
c.	Black & green omitted, entire	225.00	
d.	Red omitted, untagged, entire	—	

22nd Olympic Games, Moscow, July 19-Aug. 3, 1980.

Bicycling Issue

Highwheeler Bicycle — U143

Design (on left side of envelope) shows racing bicycle.

1980, May 16

U597 U143	15c bl & rose claret	40	15
a.	Blue ("15c USA") omitted	100.00	

America's Cup Yacht Races Issue

Racing
Yacht — U144

1980, Sept. 15

U598 U144	15c light blue	40	15

Italian
Honeybee
and Orange
Blossoms
U145

Bee & Petals Colorless Embossed

1980, Oct. 10

U599 U145	15c multicolored	35	15
a.	Brown ("USA 15c") omitted, entire	125.00	

U146

Design: Hand and braille colorless embossed

1981, Oct. 11

U600 U146	18c blue & red	45	18
a.	Blue omitted, untagged, entire	—	

Capitol
Dome — U147

1981, Nov. 13

U601 U147	20c deep magenta	45	15

U148

Illustration reduced.

1982, June 15

U602 U148	20c dk blue, blk & mag	45	15
a.	Dark blue omitted, entire	—	
b.	Dark blue & magenta omitted, entire	—	

U149

1982, Aug. 6

U603 U149	20c purple & black	45	15

U150

1983, Mar. 21 Untagged

U604 U150	5.2c orange		15

U151

1983, Aug. 3

U605 U151	20c red, blue & black	45	15
a.	Red omitted, entire	—	
b.	Blue omitted, entire	—	
c.	Red & black omitted, entire	—	
d.	Blue & black omitted, entire	—	

U152

Design shows storefronts at lower left.
Stamp and design continue on back of envelope.

1984, May 7 Photo.

U606 U152	20c multicolored	50	15

U153

1985, Feb. 1 Embossed

U607 U153	(22c) deep green	55	15

Bison
U154

1985, Feb. 25 Embossed

U608 U154	22c violet brown	55	15
a.	Untagged, precanceled with 3 blue lines		15

Frigate U.S.S.
Constitution, "Old
Ironsides" — U155

1985, May 3 Embossed Untagged

U609 U155	6c green blue		15

Mayflower — U156

Precanceled

1986, Dec. 4 Embossed

Untagged

U610 U156	8.5c black & gray		15

Stars — U157

1988, Mar. 26 Embossed & Typo.

U611 U157	25c dk bl & dk red	60	15
a.	Dark red ("25") omitted, entire	85.00	—

Sea Gulls, Frigate USS
Constellation — U158

Embossed & Typo.

1988, Apr. 12 Untagged

U612 U158	8.4c black & brt blue	—	15
a.	Black omitted, entire		

Snowflake — U159

"Holiday Greetings!" inscribed at lower left.

1988, Sept. 8 Typo.

U613 U159	25c dark red & green	50	25

Stars and "*Philatelic Mail*" Continuous
in Dark Red Below Vignette — U160

1989, Mar. 10 Typo.

U614 U160	25c dk red & dp bl	50	25

"USA" and Stars — U161

1989, July 10 Typo. Unwmk.
U615 U161 25c dk red & dp bl 50 25

Love — U162

Litho. & Typo.
1989, Sept. 25 Unwmk.
U616 U162 25c dark red & blue 50 25

Shuttle Docking at Space Station — U163

1989, Dec. 3 Typo. Unwmk.
U617 U163 25c ultramarine 60 28
a. Ultramarine omitted, entire —

A hologram, visible through the die cut window to the right of "USA 25," is affixed to the inside of the envelope. Available only in No. 9 size. No. 9 envelopes are 225mm by 100mm.
See No. U625.

Vince Lombardi Trophy, Football Players — U164

1990, Sept. 9 Litho. Unwmk.
U618 U164 25c vermilion 50 25

A hologram, visible through the die cut window to the right of "USA 25," is affixed to the inside of the envelope.

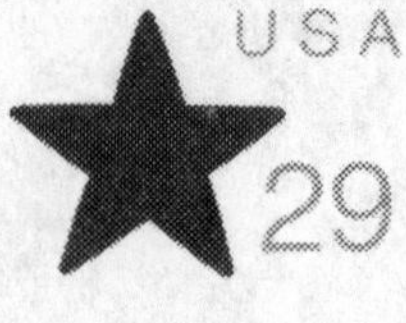

Star — U165

Has embossed bars above and below the design.

1991, Jan. 24 Embossed & Typo.
U619 U165 29c ultra & rose 58 29
a. Ultramarine omitted, entire —
b. Rose omitted, entire —

Precanceled Cut Squares
See note following No. U542.

Birds — U166

Stamp and design continue on back of envelope.

Precanceled

1991, May 3 Typo. Wmk.
U620 U166 11.1c blue & red 20

Love — U167

1991, May 9 Litho.
U621 U167 29c lt blue, maroon & brt rose 58 29
a. Bright rose omitted, entire —

Creating a Brighter World
Magazine Industry, 250th Anniv. — U168

Photo. & Typo.
1991, Oct. 7 Unwmk.
U622 U168 29c multicolored 58 29

The photogravure vignette, visible through the die cut window to the right of "USA 29," is affixed to the inside of the envelope. Available only in No. 10 size.

Star
U169

Stamp and design continue on back of envelope.

1991, July 20 Typo.
U623 U169 29c ultra & rose 58 29

Lined with a blue design to provide security for enclosures.

Country Geese
U170

1991, Nov. 8 Litho. & Typo. Wmk.
U624 U170 29c blue gray & yellow 58 58

Space Shuttle Type of 1989

1992, Jan. 21 Typo. Unwmk.
U625 U163 29c yellow green 58 29

A hologram, visible through the die cut window to the right of "USA 29," is affixed to the inside of the envelope. Available only in No. 10 size.
See No. U617a for envelopes with hologram only.

U171

Typo. & Litho.
1992, Apr. 10 Unwmk. *Die Cut*
U626 U171 29c multicolored 58 29

The lithographed vignette, visible through the die cut window to the right of "USA 29," is affixed to the inside of the envelope.

Hillebrandia — U172

Illustration reduced.

1992, Apr. 22
U627 U172 29c multicolored 58 29

The lithographed vignette, visible through the die cut window to the right of "29 USA," is affixed to the inside of the envelope.

U173

Typo. & Embossed
1992, May 19 Precanceled
U628 U173 19.8c red & blue 38

Disabled Americans

U174

1992, July 22 Typo. Unwmk.
U629 U174 29c red & blue 58 29

U175

Illustration reduced.

Typo. & Litho.
1993, Oct. 2 Unwmk. *Die Cut*
U630 U175 29c multicolored 60 30

The lithographed vignette, visible through the die cut window to the right of "USA 29," is affixed to the inside of the envelope.

U176

Typo. & Embossed
1994, Sept. 17 Unwmk.
U631 U176 29c brown & black 60 30

AIR POST STAMPED ENVELOPES AND AIR LETTER SHEETS

UC1

UC2

UC1--Vertical rudder is not semi-circular but slopes down to the left. The tail of the plane projects into the G of POSTAGE.

UC2--Vertical rudder is semi-circular. The tail of the plane touches but does not project into the G of POSTAGE.

6c: Same as UC2 except 3 types of numeral.
Die 2a- Numeral "6" 6½mm wide.
Die 2b- Numeral "6" 6mm wide.
Die 2c- Numeral "6" 5½mm wide.
Die 3- Vertical rudder leans forward. S closer to O than to T of POSTAGE. E of POSTAGE has short center bar.

1929-44 Embossed
UC1 UC1 5c blue 3.50 2.00
UC2 UC2 5c blue 11.00 5.00
UC3 UC2 6c org, die 2a ('34) 1.45 40
a. No. UC3 with added impression of 3c pur (#U436a), entire without border *3,000.*
UC4 UC2 6c org, die 2b ('42) 2.75 2.00
UC5 UC2 6c org, die 2c ('44) 75 30
UC6 UC2 6c org, die 3 ('42) 1.00 35
a. 6c org, *blue* (error), entire *3,500.* *2,400.*
UC7 UC2 8c olive green ('32) 13.00 3.50

Surcharged in black on envelopes indicated by numbers in brackets.

1945
UC8 U93 6c on 2c (U429) 1.25 65
a. 6c on 1c grn, error, (U420) *1,750.*
b. 6c on 3c purple, error, (U436a) *1,750.*
c. 6c on 3c purple, error, *amb* (U437a) *3,000.*
d. 6c on 3c vio, error, (U526) *3,000.*
UC9 U95 6c on 2c (U525) 75.00 40.00

Nos. UC8a-UC8d are known only entire.

Surcharged in Black on 6c Orange Air Post Envelopes without borders

1946
UC10 UC2 5c on 6c, die 2a 2.75 1.50
a. Double surcharge 60.00

UC11 UC2 5c on 6c, die 2b 9.00 5.50
UC12 UC2 5c on 6c, die 2c 75 50
a. Double surcharge 60.00 60.00
UC13 UC2 5c on 6c, die 3 80 60
a. Double surcharge 60.00

The 6c borderless envelopes and the revalued envelopes were issued primarily for use to and from members of the armed forces.
The 5c rate came into effect Oct. 1, 1946.

DC-4 Skymaster UC3

Die 1. The end of the wing at the right is a smooth curve. The juncture of the front end of the plane and the engine forms an acute angle. The first T of STATES and the E's of UNITED STATES lean to the left.
Die 2. The end of the wing at the right is a straight line. The juncture of the front end of the plane and the engine is wide open. The first T of STATES and the E's of UNITED STATES lean to the right.

1946 **Embossed**
UC14 UC3 5c carmine, die 1 75 20
UC15 UC3 5c carmine, die 2 85 25

See Nos. UC18, UC26.

DC-4 Skymaster — UC4

Letter Sheet for Foreign Postage

"Air Letter" on face, 2-line inscription on back.

1947, Apr. 29 **Typo.**
UC16 UC4 10c brt red, *pale bl*, entire 7.50 6.00
a. "Air Letter" on face, 4-line inscription on back ('51), entire 16.00 14.00
b. As "a," 10c chocolate, *pale bl*, entire 400.00
c. "Air Letter" and "Aerogramme" on face, 4-line inscription on back ('53), entire 45.00 12.50
d. "Air Letter" and "Aerogramme" on face, 3-line inscription on back ('55), entire 8.00 8.00

Washington and Franklin, Early and Modern Mail-carrying Vehicles — UC5

Embossed, Rotary Press Printing
1947, May 21
UC17 UC5 5c car, (22¼mm high) 40 25
a. Flat plate (21¾mm high) 50 30

Cent. of the 1st postage stamps issued by the US Government.

Type of 1946

Type I- 6's lean to right.
Type II- 6's upright.

1950, Sept. 22
UC18 UC3 6c carmine, Type I 35 15
a. Type II 75 25

Several other types differ slightly from the two listed.

Nos. UC14, UC15, UC18 Surcharged in Red at Left of Stamp

REVALUED 6¢ P. O. DEPT.

1951
UC19 UC3 6c on 5c car, die 1 85 50
UC20 UC3 6c on 5c car, die 2 80 50
a. 6c on 6c car, error, entire 1,500.
b. 6c on 5c, double surcharge 250.00 —

Nos. UC14, UC15 and UC17 Surcharged in Red at Left of Stamp

REVALUED 6¢ P. O. DEPT.

1952
UC21 UC3 6c on 5c, die 1 26.00 17.50
UC22 UC3 6c on 5c, die 2 3.50 2.50
a. Double surcharge 75.00
UC23 UC5 6c on 5c, entire 1,400.

The 6c on 4c black (No. U440) is believed to be a favor printing.

Eagle in Flight — UC6

1956, May 2 **Embossed**
UC25 UC6 6c red 75 50

FIPEX, NYC, Apr. 28-May 6. Two types exist, differing mainly in the clouds at top.

Skymaster Type of 1946

1958, July 31
UC26 UC3 7c blue 65 50

Nos. UC3-UC5, UC18 and UC25 Surcharged in Green at Left of Stamp

1958
UC27 UC2 6c + 1c, die 2a 225.00 225.00
UC28 UC2 6c + 1c, die 2b 65.00 75.00
UC29 UC2 6c + 1c, die 2c 37.50 50.00
UC30 UC3 6c + 1c, type I 1.00 50
a. Type II 1.00 50
UC31 UC6 6c + 1c 1.00 50

Jet Airliner — UC7

Letter Sheet for Foreign Postage.

Two types:
Type I- Back inscription in 3 lines.
Type II- Back inscription in 2 lines.

1958-59 **Typo.**
UC32 UC7 10c bl & red, *bl*, II ('59), entire 6.00 5.00
a. Type I ('58), entire 10.00 5.00
b. Red omitted, II, entire —
c. Blue omitted, II, entire —

Silhouette of Jet Airliner — UC8

1958, Nov. 21 **Embossed**
UC33 UC8 7c blue 60 25

1960, Aug. 18
UC34 UC8 7c carmine 60 25

Jet Plane and Globe — UC9

Letter Sheet for Foreign Postage

1961, Nov. 16 **Typo.**
UC35 UC9 11c red & bl, *bl*, entire 2.75 1.50
a. Red omitted, entire 875.00
b. Blue omitted, entire 875.00

UC10

UC11

1962, Nov. 17 **Embossed**
UC36 UC10 8c red 55 15

1965, Jan. 7
UC37 UC11 8c red 35 15
a. Tagged ('67) 1.25 30

No. UC37a has a luminescent panel ⅜x1 inches at left of stamp. It glows orange red under ultraviolet light.

Pres. John F. Kennedy and Jet Plane — UC12

Letter Sheets for Foreign Postage

1965-67 **Typo.**
UC38 UC12 11c red & dk bl, *blue*, entire 3.25 1.50
UC39 UC12 13c red & dk bl, *blue*, entire 3.00 1.50
a. Red omitted 500.00
b. Dark blue omitted 500.00

Issue dates: 11c, May 29, 1965. 13c, May 29, 1967.

UC13

1968, Jan. 8 **Tagged** **Embossed**
UC40 UC13 10c red 50 15

No. UC37 Surcharged in Red at Left of Stamp

1968, Feb. 5
UC41 UC11 8c + 2c red 65 15

Tagging
Envelopes and Letter Sheets from No. UC42 onward are tagged unless otherwise noted.

Globes and Flock of Birds UC14

Letter Sheet for Foreign Postage

1968, Dec. 3 **Photo.**
UC42 UC14 13c gray, brn, org & black, *blue*, entire 7.50 4.00
a. Orange omitted, entire —
b. Brown omitted, entire 400.00
c. Black omitted, entire —

Intl. Human Rights Year, and 20th anniv. of the UN Declaration of Human Rights.

UC15

1971, May 6 **Embossed**
UC43 UC15 11c red & blue 50 15

Birds in Flight and "usa" — UC16

Letter Sheet for Foreign Postage
"postage 15c" in Gray

1971, May 28 **Photo.**
UC44 UC16 15c gray, red, white & blue, *blue*, entire 1.50 1.10
a. "AEROGRAMME" added, entire 1.50 1.10

Folding instructions (2 steps) in capitals on No. UC44; (4 steps) in upper and lower case on No. UC44a. No. UC44a issued Dec. 13.
See No. UC46.

No. UC40 Surcharged in Green at Left of Stamp

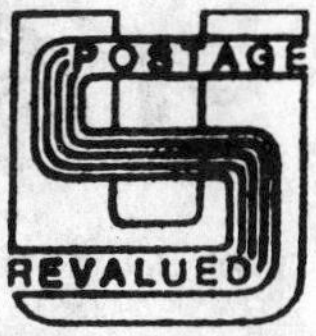

1971, June 28 **Embossed**
UC45 UC13 10c + (1c) red 1.50 20

Letter Sheet for Foreign Postage
"usa" Type of 1971

Design: Three balloons and cloud at left in address section; no birds beside stamp.

"postage 15c" in Blue

1973, Feb. 10 **Photo.**
UC46 UC16 15c red, white & bl, *blue*, entire 75 40

Hot Air Ballooning World Championships, Albuquerque, NM, Feb. 10-17. Folding instructions as on No. UC44a, with "INTERNATIONAL HOT AIR BALLOONING" added to inscription.

Bird in Flight — UC17

1973, Dec. 1 **Embossed**
UC47 UC17 13c rose red 30 15

Beginning with No. UC48 all letter sheets are for Foreign Postage unless noted otherwise.

UC18

1974, Jan. 4 **Photo.**
UC48 UC18 18c red & blue, *blue*, entire 90 30
a. Red omitted, entire —

UC19

Design: "NATO" and NATO emblem in multicolor at left in address section.

1974, Apr. 4 **Photo.**

UC49 UC19 18c red & blue, *blue*, entire 90 40

25th anniv. of NATO.

UC20

1976, Jan. 16 **Photo.**

UC50 UC20 22c red & blue, *blue*, entire 90 40

UC21

1978, Nov. 3 **Photo.**

UC51 UC21 22c bl, *bl*, entire 70 25

UC22

Design (multicolored in bottom left corner) shows discus thrower.

1979, Dec. 5 **Photo.**

UC52 UC22 22c red, blk & grn, *bluish*, entire 1.50 22

22nd Olympic Games, Moscow, July 19-Aug. 3, 1980.

UC23

Design shows Statue of Liberty at lower left. Inscribed "Tour the United States," folding area shows tourist attractions.

1980-81 **Photo.**

UC53 UC23 30c bl, red & brn, *bl*, entire 65 30

a. Red ("30c") omitted, entire *75.00*

UC54 UC23 30c yel, magenta, bl & blk, *bl*, entire ('81) 65 30

Issue dates: Dec. 29. Sept. 21, 1981.

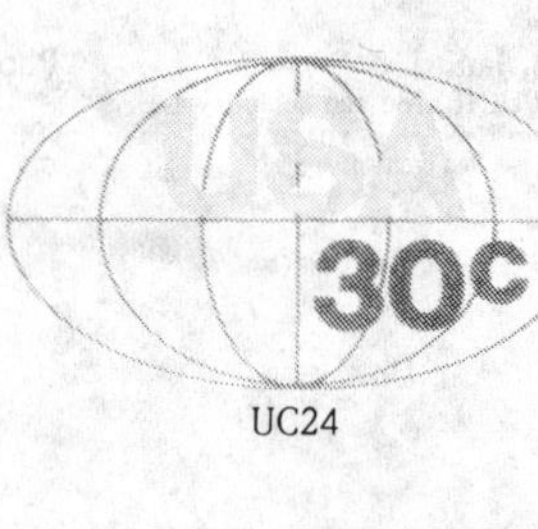

UC24

"Made in USA . . . world's best buys."

1982, Sept. 16 **Photo.**

UC55 UC24 30c multi, *bl*, entire 65 30

World Communications Year Issue

World Map Showing Locations of Satellite Tracking Stations — UC25

1983, Jan. 7 **Photo.**

UC56 UC25 30c multi, *bl*, entire 65 30

1984 Olympics

UC26

1983, Oct. 14 **Photo.**

UC57 UC26 30c multi, *bl*, entire 65 30

UC27

Design: Satellite over Earth at lower left, with Landsat photographs on folding area. Inscribed: Landsat views the Earth.

1985, Feb. 14 **Photo.**

UC58 UC27 36c multi, *bl*, entire 72 36

National Tourism Week

Urban Skyline UC28

1985, May 21 **Photo.**

UC59 UC28 36c multi, *bl*, entire 72 36

a. Black omitted, entire —

Mark Twain (1835-1910) and Halley's Comet

Comet Tail Viewed from Space — UC29

1985, Dec. 4 **Photo.**

UC60 UC29 36c multi, entire 72 36

UC30

1988, May 9 **Litho.**

UC61 UC30 39c multi, entire 78 40

Montgomery Blair and Pres. Lincoln — UC31

Design: Mail bags and text at lower left. Globe, locomotive, bust of Blair, UPU emblem and text contained on reverse folding area.

1989, Nov. 20 **Litho.**

UC62 UC31 39c multi, entire 78 40

UC32

1991, May 17 **Litho.**

UC63 UC32 45c gray, red & blue, *blue*, entire 90 45

a. White paper, entire 90 45

POSTAL CARDS
"R.F." CONTROL OVERPRINT
STAMPED ENVELOPES
are listed in Scott's Specialized Catalogue of United States Stamps.
NEWSPAPER WRAPPERS
Included in listings of Stamped Envelopes with prefix "W" instead of "U"
LETTER SHEETS Included with Stamped Envelopes

OFFICIAL STAMPED ENVELOPES

Post Office Department

"2" 9mm high — UO1

"3" 9mm high — UO2

"6" 9½mm high — UO3

1873

UO1	UO1	2c black, *lemon*	12.00	6.50
UO2	UO2	3c black, *lemon*	6.50	4.50
+*UO3*	UO2	3c black	*6,750.*	
UO4	UO3	6c black, *lemon*	14.00	10.00

"2" 9¼mm high — UO4

"3" 9¼mm high — UO5

"6" 10½mm high — UO6

1874-79

UO5	UO4	2c black, *lemon*	5.00	4.00
UO6	UO4	2c black	60.00	32.50
UO7	UO5	3c black, *lemon*	2.75	65
UO8	UO5	3c black	900.00	850.00
UO9	UO5	3c black, *amber*	40.00	35.00
UO10	UO5	3c black, *blue*	*15,000.*	
UO11	UO5	3c blue, *blue*	*14,000.*	
UO12	UO6	6c black, *lemon*	5.00	4.75
UO13	UO6	6c black	675.00	

Postal Service

UO7

1877

UO14	UO7	black	5.00	3.00
UO15	UO7	black, *amber*	35.00	22.50
UO16	UO7	blue, *amber*	35.00	22.50
UO17	UO7	blue, *blue*	6.00	6.00

War Department

Franklin — UO8

Jackson — UO9

UO8--Bust points to the end of "N" of "ONE".

UO9--Bust narrow at the back.

Washington UO10

Lincoln UO11

UO10--Queue projects below the bust.

UO11--Neck very long at the back

Jefferson — UO12

Clay — UO13

UO12--Queue forms straight line with bust.

UO13--Ear partly concealed by hair, mouth large, chin prominent.

Webster — UO14

Scott — UO15

UO14--Has side whiskers.

Hamilton — UO16

Back of bust very narrow, chin almost straight; the labels containing the letters "U S" are exactly parallel.

1873

Reay Issue

UO18	UO8	1c dark red	475.00	300.00
UO19	UO9	2c dark red	750.00	425.00
UO20	UO10	3c dark red	50.00	35.00
UO21	UO10	3c dark red, *amb*	*12,000.*	
UO22	UO10	3c dark red, *cr*	425.00	225.00
UO23	UO11	6c dark red	210.00	85.00
UO24	UO11	6c dark red, *cr*	1,500.	425.00
UO25	UO12	10c dark red	2,750.	350.00
UO26	UO13	12c dark red	100.00	45.00
UO27	UO14	15c dark red	100.00	50.00
UO28	UO15	24c dark red	110.00	45.00
UO29	UO16	30c dark red	400.00	150.00
UO30	UO8	1c vermilion	135.00	
WO31	UO8	1c ver, *man*	12.50	10.00
+UO32	UO9	2c vermilion	275.00	
WO33	UO9	2c ver, *man*	200.00	
UO34	UO10	3c vermilion	70.00	35.00
UO35	UO10	3c ver, *amb*	80.00	
UO36	UO10	3c ver, *cr*	15.00	10.00
UO37	UO11	6c vermilion	70.00	
+UO38	UO11	6c ver, *cr*	325.00	
UO39	UO12	10c vermilion	200.00	
UO40	UO13	12c vermilion	135.00	
UO41	UO14	15c vermilion	210.00	
UO42	UO15	24c vermilion	375.00	
UO43	UO16	30c vermilion	375.00	

UO17

UO18

UO17--Bottom serif on "S" is thick and short, bust at bottom below hair forms sharp point.

UO18--Bottom serif on "S" is thick and short front part of bust is rounded.

UO19

UO20

UO19--Bottom serif on "S" is short, queue does not project below bust.

UO20--Neck very short at the back.

UO21

UO22

UO21--Knot of queue stands out prominently.

UO22--Ear prominent, chin receding.

UO23

UO24

UO23--Has no side whiskers, forelock projects above head.

UO24--Back of bust rather broad; chin slopes considerably; the labels containing letters "U S" are not exactly parallel.

1875

Plimpton Issue

UO44	UO17	1c red	110.00	75.00
+UO45	UO17	1c red, *amb*	750.00	
+UO45A	UO17	1c red, *org*	*17,500.*	
WO46	UO17	1c red, *man*	3.50	2.50
UO47	UO18	2c red	85.00	
UO48	UO18	2c red, *amb*	25.00	12.50
UO49	UO18	2c red, *org*	40.00	11.00
WO50	UO18	2c red, *man*	70.00	40.00
UO51	UO19	3c red	11.00	8.00
UO52	UO19	3c red, *amb*	12.00	8.00
UO53	UO19	3c red, *cr*	5.50	3.50
UO54	UO19	3c red, *bl*	3.25	2.50
UO55	UO19	3c red, *fawn*	4.00	2.50
UO56	UO20	6c red	35.00	25.00
UO57	UO20	6c red, *amb*	65.00	35.00
UO58	UO20	6c red, *cr*	175.00	80.00
UO59	UO21	10c red	150.00	75.00
UO60	UO21	10c red, *amb*	1,100.	
UO61	UO22	12c red	40.00	35.00
UO62	UO22	12c red, *amb*	625.00	
UO63	UO22	12c red, *cr*	600.00	
UO64	UO23	15c red	160.00	120.00
UO65	UO23	15c red, *amb*	700.00	
UO66	UO23	15c red, *cr*	650.00	
UO67	UO24	30c red	160.00	120.00
UO68	UO24	30c red, *amb*	900.00	
UO69	UO24	30c red, *cr*	900.00	

POSTAL SAVINGS STAMPED ENVELOPES

UO25

1911

UO70	UO25	1c green	57.50	17.50
UO71	UO25	1c grn, *oriental buff*	175.00	60.00
UO72	UO25	2c carmine	9.00	3.50
a.		2c car, *manila* (error)	*1,800.*	

Used Values

Catalogue values for regularly used entires. Those with first day cancels generally sell for much less.

OFFICIAL MAIL

UO26

1983, Jan. 12

UO73 UO26 20c blue, entire 1.00 *30.00*

UO27

1985, Feb. 26

UO74 UO27 22c blue, entire 65 *5.00*

UO28

1987, Mar. 2 **Typo.**

UO75 UO28 22c blue, entire 65 *20.00*

Used exclusively to mail US Savings Bonds.

UO29

1988, Mar. 22 **Typo.**

UO76 UO29 (25c) blk & bl, entire 65 *20.00*

Used exclusively to mail US Saving Bonds.

UO30

1988, Apr. 11 **Embossed & Typo.**

UO77 UO30 25c blk & blue, entire 65 *5.00*

UO31

1988, Apr. 11 **Typo.**

UO78 UO31 25c black & blue, entire 65 *25.00*

Used exclusively to mail US Saving Bonds.

1990, Mar. 17 **Typo.**

UO79 UO31 45c blk & bl, entire 1.25 *40.00*
UO80 UO31 65c blk & bl, entire 1.50 *50.00*

UO32

Type UO32: sharp impression, stars and "E Pluribus Unum" are clear and distinct. Official is 14½mm long, USA is 17mm long.

1990, Aug. 10 **Typo.**

UO81 UO32 45c blk & bl, entire 1.25 *40.00*
UO82 UO32 65c blk & bl, entire 1.50 *50.00*

Used exclusively to mail US passports.

UO33

1991, Jan. 22 **Typo.** **Wmk.**

UO83 UO33 (29c) blk & bl, entire 1.00 *20.00*

Used exclusively to mail US Saving Bonds.

UO34

1991, Apr. 6 **Typo. & Embossed**

UO84 UO34 29c black & blue, entire 70 *1.00*

UO35

1991, Apr. 17 **Typo.** **Wmk.**

UO85 UO35 29c blk & bl, entire 70 *20.00*

Used exclusively to mail US Saving Bonds.

Consular Service, Bicent. — UO36

1992, July 10 **Litho.** **Unwmk.**

UO86 UO36 52c blue & red, entire 1.15 *40.00*
UO87 UO36 75c blue & red, entire 1.60 *50.00*

Used exclusively to mail US passports.

OFFICIAL WRAPPERS

Included in listings of Official Stamped Envelopes with prefix letters "WO" instead of "UO"

REVENUE STAMPS

Nos. R1-R102 were used to pay taxes on documents and proprietary articles including playing cards. Until Dec. 25, 1862, the law stated that a revenue stamp could be used only for payment of the tax upon the particular instrument or article specified on its face. After that date stamps, except the Proprietary, could be used indiscriminately.

General Issue

First Issue. Head of Washington in Oval. Various Frames as Illustrated.

Old Paper

Perf. 12

Nos. R1b to R42b, part perforate, occur perforated sometimes at sides only and sometimes at top and bottom only. The higher values, part perforate, are perforated at sides only. Imperforate and part perforate revenues often bring much more in pairs or blocks than as single copies.

The experimental silk paper is a variety of the old paper and has only a very few minute fragments of fiber.

Some of the stamps were in use eight years and were printed several times. Many color variations occurred, particularly when unstable pigments were used and the color was intended to be purple or violet, such as the 4c Proprietary, 30c and $2.50 stamps. Before 1868 dull colors predominate on these and the early red stamps. In later printings of the 4c Proprietary, 30c and $2.50 stamps, red predominates in the mixture, and on the dollar values the red is brighter. The early $1.90 stamp is dull purple, imperf. or perforated. In a later printing, perforated only, the purple is darker.

R1

R2

R3

R4

R5

1862-71 **Engr.**

R1 R1 1c Express, red 1.00
a. Imperf. 50.00
b. Part perf. 30.00
d. Silk paper 75.00
R2 R1 1c Playing Cards, red 100.00
a. Imperf. 900.00
b. Part perf. 550.00
R3 R1 1c Proprietary, red 35
a. Imperf. 600.00
b. Part perf. 100.00
d. Silk paper 11.00
R4 R1 1c Telegraph, red 8.00
a. Imperf. 300.00
R5 R2 2c Bank Check, blue 15
a. Imperf. 75
b. Part perf. 90
e. Vertical pair, imperf. between, old paper *400.00*
R6 R2 2c Bank Check, orange 15
b. Part perf. 50.00
d. Silk paper 175.00
e. Old paper, *green* 350.00
R7 R2 2c Certificate, blue 21.00
a. Imperf. 10.00
R8 R2 2c Certificate, orange 22.50
R9 R2 2c Express, blue 25
a. Imperf. 10.00
b. Part perf. 15.00

R10 R2 2c Express, orange 6.00
b. Part perf. —
d. Silk paper 45.00
R11 R2 2c Playing Cards, blue 3.00
b. Part perf. 115.00
R12 R2 2c Playing Cards, orange 27.50
R13 R2 2c Proprietary, blue 35
a. Imperf. *300.00*
b. Part perf. 100.00
d. Silk paper 32.50
e. Ultramarine 150.00
R14 R2 2c Proprietary, orange 30.00
R15 R2 2c U.S. Int. Rev., orange ('64) 15
d. Silk paper 25
e. Old paper, *green* 450.00
R16 R3 3c For. Exch., green 2.50
b. Part perf. 190.00
d. Silk paper 32.50
R17 R3 3c Playing Cards, green ('63) 100.00
a. Imperf. *8,000.*
R18 R3 3c Proprietary, green 1.75
b. Part perf. 200.00
d. Silk paper 22.50
e. Printed on both sides, old paper *1,600.*
R19 R3 3c Telegraph, green 2.25
a. Imperf. 45.00
b. Part perf. 16.00
R20 R3 4c Inland Exch., brown ('63) 1.50
d. Silk paper 35.00
R21 R3 4c Playing Cards, slate ('63) 375.00
R22 R3 4c Proprietary, purple 4.00
a. Imperf. —
b. Part perf. 175.00
d. Silk paper 45.00

Many shade and color variations of No. R22. See foreword, "Revenue Stamps."

R23 R3 5c Agreement, red 20
d. Silk paper 1.00
R24 R3 5c Certificate, red 15
a. Imperf. 2.00
b. Part perf. 8.00
d. Silk paper 30
R25 R3 5c Express, red 25
a. Imperf. 3.50
b. Part perf. 4.00
R26 R3 5c Foreign Exchange, red 25
b. Part perf. —
d. Silk paper 150.00
R27 R3 5c Inland Exch., red 15
a. Imperf. 3.50
b. Part perf. 2.50
d. Silk paper 10.00
R28 R3 5c Playing Cards, red ('63) 12.00
R29 R3 5c Proprietary, red ('64) 17.50
d. Silk paper 70.00
R30 R3 6c Inland Exch., org ('63) 1.10
d. Silk paper 42.50
R31 R3 6c Proprietary, orange ('71) *1,750.*

Nearly all copies of No. R31 are faulty or repaired and poorly centered.

The Catalogue value is for a fine centered copy with minor faults which do not detract from its appearance.

R32 R3 10c Bill of Lading, blue 85
a. Imperf. 40.00
b. Part perf. 150.00
R33 R3 10c Certificate, blue 20
a. Imperf. 90.00
b. Part perf. 140.00
d. Silk paper 4.00
R34 R3 10c Contract, blue 20
b. Part perf. 110.00
d. Silk paper 2.00
e. Ultramarine, part perf. 300.00
f. Ultramarine, old paper 65
R35 R3 10c For. Exch., blue 6.00
e. ultra, old paper 7.50
R36 R3 10c Inland Exch., blue 15
a. Imperf. 125.00
b. Part perf. 3.00
d. Silk paper 25.00
R37 R3 10c Power of Attorney, blue 25
a. Imperf. 375.00
b. Part perf. 17.00
R38 R3 10c Proprietary, blue ('64) 13.00
R39 R3 15c For. Exch., brown ('63) 12.00
R40 R3 15c Inland Exch., brown 1.00
a. Imperf. 25.00
b. Part perf. 10.00
R41 R3 20c For. Exch., red 30.00
a. Imperf. 40.00

R42 R3 20c Inland Exch., red 30
a. Imperf. 12.00
b. Part perf. 14.00
d. Silk paper —
R43 R4 25c Bond, red 1.75
a. Imperf. 115.00
b. Part perf. 4.00
R44 R4 25c Certificate, red 15
a. Imperf. 7.00
b. Part perf. 5.00
d. Silk paper 2.50
e. Printed on both sides, old paper *1,750.*
f. Impression of No. R48 on back, old paper —
R45 R4 25c Entry of Goods, red 40
a. Imperf. 15.00
b. Part perf. 45.00
d. Silk paper 17.50
R46 R4 25c Insurance, red 20
a. Imperf. 8.00
b. Part perf. 8.00
d. Silk paper 4.00
R47 R4 25c Life Insurance, red 5.00
a. Imperf. 30.00
b. Part perf. 130.00
R48 R4 25c Power of Attorney, red 25
a. Imperf. 5.00
b. Part perf. 17.50
R49 R4 25c Protest, red 6.00
a. Imperf. 20.00
b. Part perf. 175.00
R50 R4 25c Warehouse Receipt, red 21.00
a. Imperf. 35.00
b. Part perf. 150.00
R51 R4 30c For. Exch., lilac 35.00
a. Imperf. 60.00
b. Part perf. 650.00
d. Silk paper —
R52 R4 30c Inland Exch., lilac 2.25
a. Imperf. 40.00
b. Part perf. 50.00

Many shade and color variations of Nos. R51-R52. See foreword, "Revenue Stamps."

R53 R4 40c Inland Exch., brown 2.25
a. Imperf. 450.00
b. Part perf. 4.50
R54 R5 50c Conveyance, blue 15
a. Imperf. 10.00
b. Part perf. 1.00
d. Silk paper 2.75
e. Ultramarine, old paper 25
f. Ultramarine, silk paper —
R55 R5 50c Entry of Goods, blue 20
b. Part perf. 8.00
d. Silk paper 22.50
R56 R5 50c For. Exch., blue 4.50
a. Imperf. 35.00
b. Part perf. 30.00
R57 R5 50c Lease, blue 6.50
a. Imperf. 20.00
b. Part perf. 50.00
R58 R5 50c Life Insurance, blue 60
a. Imperf. 25.00
b. Part perf. 40.00
R59 R5 50c Mortgage, blue 30
a. Imperf. 10.00
b. Part perf. 1.75
d. Silk paper —
R60 R5 50c Original Process, blue 25
a. Imperf. 2.50
b. Part perf. —
d. Silk paper 1.50
R61 R5 50c Passage Ticket, blue 50
a. Imperf. 60.00
b. Part perf. 100.00
R62 R5 50c Probate of Will, blue 15.00
a. Imperf. 30.00
b. Part perf. 45.00
R63 R5 50c Surety Bond, blue 15
a. Imperf. 120.00
b. Part perf. 2.00
e. Ultramarine, old paper 70
R64 R5 60c Inland Exch., org 5.00
a. Imperf. 75.00
b. Part perf. 40.00
d. Silk paper 27.50
R65 R5 70c For. Exch., green 5.00
a. Imperf. 300.00
b. Part perf. 80.00
d. Silk paper 32.50
e. Vert. pair, imperf. btwn., old paper —

R6

R7

R8

R9

R10

(Illustration sideways)
R11

Old Paper

R66 R6 $1 Conveyance, red 3.00
a. Imperf. 10.00
b. Part perf. 275.00
d. Silk paper 65.00
R67 R6 $1 Entry of Goods, red 1.25
a. Imperf. 25.00
d. Silk paper 40.00
R68 R6 $1 For. Exch., red 50
a. Imperf. 45.00
d. Silk paper 27.50
R69 R6 $1 Inland Exch., red 35
a. Imperf. 10.00
b. Part perf. 225.00
d. Silk paper 2.00
R70 R6 $1 Lease, red 1.50
a. Imperf. 30.00
R71 R6 $1 Life Insurance, red 4.50
a. Imperf. 125.00
R72 R6 $1 Manifest, red 21.00
a. Imperf. 35.00
R73 R6 $1 Mortgage, red 125.00
a. Imperf. 15.00
R74 R6 $1 Passage Ticket, red 150.00
a. Imperf. 175.00
R75 R6 $1 Power of Attorney, red 1.50
a. Imperf. 60.00
R76 R6 $1 Probate of Will, red 27.50
a. Imperf. 55.00
R77 R7 $1.30 For. Exch., orange ('63) 45.00
a. Imperf. *2,500.*
R78 R7 $1.50 Inland Exch., blue 2.75
a. Imperf. 20.00
R79 R7 $1.60 For. Exch., green ('63) 85.00
a. Imperf. 750.00
R80 R7 $1.90 For. Exch., purple ('63) 60.00
a. Imperf. *3,000.*
d. Silk paper —

Many shade and color variations of No. R80. See foreword, "Revenue Stamps."

R81 R8 $2 Conveyance, red 1.50
a. Imperf. 85.00
b. Part perf. 900.00
d. Silk paper 20.00

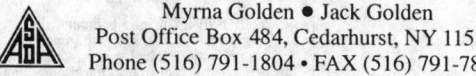

R82 R8 $2 Mortgage, red 2.50
a. Imperf. 75.00
d. Silk paper 45.00
R83 R8 $2 Probate of Will, red ('63) 45.00
a. Imperf. 2,750.
R84 R8 $2.50 Inland Exch., pur ('63) 3.00
a. Imperf. 1,100.
d. Silk paper 15.00
R85 R8 $3 Charter Party, green 3.00
a. Imperf. 90.00
d. Silk paper 65.00
e. Printed on both sides 2,000.
g. Impression of #RS208 on back 4,000.
R86 R8 $3 Manifest, green 20.00
a. Imperf. 85.00
R87 R8 $3.50 Inland Exch., blue ('63) 37.50
a. Imperf. 1,500.

Many shade and color variations of the $2.50. See foreword, "Revenue Stamps." The $3.50 has stars in upper corners.

R88 R9 $5 Charter Party, red 4.50
a. Imperf. 200.00
d. Silk paper 50.00
R89 R9 $5 Conveyance, red 4.50
a. Imperf. 30.00
d. Silk paper 45.00
R90 R9 $5 Manifest, red 70.00
a. Imperf. 90.00
R91 R9 $5 Mortgage, red 14.00
a. Imperf. 80.00
R92 R9 $5 Probate of Will, red 16.00
a. Imperf. 375.00
R93 R9 $10 Charter Party, green 20.00
a. Imperf. 450.00
R94 R9 $10 Conveyance, green 50.00
a. Imperf. 70.00
R95 R9 $10 Mortgage, green 20.00
a. Imperf. 300.00
R96 R9 $10 Probate of Will, green 20.00
a. Imperf. 900.00
R97 R10 $15 Mortgage, blue 100.00
a. Imperf. 850.00
e. Ultramarine, old paper 165.00
R98 R10 $20 Conveyance, org 45.00
a. Imperf. 75.00
d. Silk paper 80.00
R99 R10 $20 Probate of Will, orange 800.00
a. Imperf. 900.00
R100 R10 $25 Mortgage, red ('63) 80.00
a. Imperf. 825.00
d. Silk paper 140.00
e. Horiz. pair, imperf. btwn., old paper 1,100.
R101 R10 $50 U.S. Int. Rev., green ('63) 65.00
a. Imperf. 150.00
R102 R11 $200 U.S. Int. Rev., green & orange red ('64) 500.00
a. Imperf. 1,100.

DOCUMENTARY STAMPS

Second Issue

After release of the First Issue revenue stamps, the Bureau of Internal Revenue received many reports of fraudulent cleaning and re-use. The Bureau ordered a Second Issue with new designs and colors, using a patented "chameleon" paper which is usually slightly violet or pinkish, with silk fibers.

R12

R12a

R13a

R13

R13b

Head of Washington in Black within Octagon. Various Frames and Numeral Arrangements.

1871 *Perf. 12*
R103 R12 1c blue & black 30.00
a. Inverted center 850.00
R104 R12 2c blue & black 90
a. Inverted center 3,500.
R105 R12a 3c blue & black 12.00
R106 R12a 4c blue & black 45.00
R107 R12a 5c blue & black 90
a. Inverted center 1,500.
R108 R12a 6c blue & black 75.00
R109 R12a 10c blue & black 50
a. Inverted center 1,500.
R110 R12a 15c blue & black 20.00
R111 R12a 20c blue & black 4.00
a. Inverted center 7,500.

Head of Washington in Black within Circle

Various Frames

R112 R13 25c blue & black 45
a. Inverted center 9,500.
b. Sewing machine perf. 90.00
c. Perf. 8 250.00
R113 R13 30c blue & black 50.00
R114 R13 40c blue & black 30.00
R115 R13a 50c blue & black 45
a. Sewing machine perf. 75.00
b. Inverted center 750.00
Inverted center, punch cancellation 200.00
R116 R13a 60c blue & black 75.00
R117 R13a 70c blue & black 25.00
a. Inverted center 2,500.
R118 R13b $1 blue & black 2.25
a. Inverted center 4,000.
Invtd. center, punch cancel 700.
R119 R13b $1.30 blue & black 225.00
R120 R13b $1.50 blue & black 10.00
a. Sewing machine perf. 400.00
R121 R13b $1.60 blue & black 275.00
R122 R13b $1.90 blue & black 125.00
R123 R13b $2 blue & black 10.00
R124 R13b $2.50 blue & black 18.00
R125 R13b $3 blue & black 17.50
R126 R13b $3.50 blue & black 110.00
R127 R13b $5 blue & black 15.00
a. Inverted center 2,000.
Invtd. center, punch cancel 600.
R128 R13b $10 blue & black 80.00
R129 R13b $20 blue & black 275.00
R130 R13b $25 blue & black 275.00
R131 R13b $50 blue & black 325.00
R132 R13b $200 red, blue & blk 4,500.
R133 R13b $500 red org, grn & blk 12,500.

Fraudulently produced inverted centers exist, some excellently made.

Third Issue

Violet "Chameleon" Paper with Silk Fibers. Various Frames and Numeral Arrangements.

1871-72 *Perf. 12*
R134 R12 1c claret & blk ('72) 25.00
R135 R12 2c orange & blk 15
a. 2c vermilion & black (error) 500.00
b. Inverted center 250.00
c. Imperf., pair —
R136 R12a 4c brown & blk ('72) 27.50
R137 R12a 5c orange & black 20
a. Inverted center 3,000.
R138 R12a 6c orange & blk ('72) 30.00
R139 R12a 15c brown & blk ('72) 6.50
a. Inverted center 7,500.
R140 R13 30c orange & blk ('72) 9.50
a. Inverted center 2,000.
R141 R13 40c brown & blk ('72) 25.00
R142 R13 60c orange & blk ('72) 45.00
R143 R13 70c green & blk ('72) 30.00
R144 R13b $1 green & blk ('72) 1.10
a. Inverted center 5,000.
R145 R13b $2 ver & black ('72) 18.00
R146 R13b $2.50 claret & blk ('72) 30.00
a. Inverted center 13,500.
R147 R13b $3 green & blk ('72) 30.00
R148 R13b $5 ver & black ('72) 17.50
R149 R13b $10 green & blk ('72) 60.00
R150 R13b $20 orange & blk ('72) 425.00
a. $20 vermilion & black (error) 550.00

1874 *Perf. 12*
R151 R12 2c orange & black, *green* 15
a. Inverted center 325.00

Liberty — R14

1875-78
R152 R14 2c blue, *blue*, silk paper 15
b. Wmk. 191R ('78) 15
c. Wmk. 191R, rouletted 30.00
d. Vert. pair, imperf. horiz. 175.00
e. As "b," imperf., pair 350.00

The rouletted stamps probably were introduced in 1881.

Nos. 279, 267 or 279B, 272-274
Overprinted in Red or Blue

I. R. (a) I. R. (b)

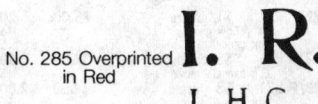

1898 **Wmk. 191** *Perf. 12*
R153 A87(a) 1c green (R) 2.00 2.00
R154 A87(b) 1c green (R) 15 15
a. Overprint inverted 15.00 17.50
b. Overprint on back instead of face, inverted —
c. Pair, one without ovpt. —
R155 A88(b) 2c carmine (Bl) 15 15
a. Overprint inverted 1.50 1.75
b. Pair, one without ovpt. 750.00
c. Overprinted on back instead of face, inverted —

Handstamped Type "b"

R156 A93 8c vio brn 3,750.
R157 A94 10c dark green 3,750.
R158 A95 15c dark blue 4,500.

Nos. R156-R158 were emergency provisionals, privately prepared, not officially issued.

Privately Prepared Provisionals

No. 285 Overprinted in Red
I. R.
L. H. C.

1898 **Wmk. 191** *Perf. 12*
R158A A100 1c dk yel grn 7,500. 7,000.

Same Overprinted "I.R./P.I.D. & Son" in Red

R158B A100 1c dk yel grn — 10,000.

Nos. R158A-R158B were overprinted with federal government permission by the Purvis Printing Co. upon order of Capt. L.H. Chapman of the Chapman Steamboat Line. Both the Chapman line and P.I. Daprix & Son operated freight-carrying steamboats on the Erie Canal. The Chapman Line touched at Syracuse, Utica, Little Falls and Fort Plain; the Daprix boat ran between Utica and Rome. 250 of each stamp were overprinted.

Dr. Kilmer & Co. provisional overprints are listed in Scott's Specialized Catalogue of United States Stamps under Private Die Medicine Stamps, Nos. RS307-RS315.

Newspaper Stamp No. PR121 Surcharged Vertically in Red

INT. REV.
$5.
DOCUMENTARY.

1898 **Wmk. 191** *Perf. 12*

Reading Down

R159 N18 $5 on $5 dk blue 200.00 150.00

Reading Up

R160 N18 $5 on $5 dk blue 100.00 65.00

Battleship
R15

Inscribed: "Series of 1898" and "Documentary."

1898 **Wmk. 191R** *Rouletted 5½*
R161 R15 ½c orange 2.00 5.50
R162 R15 ½c dark gray 25 15
a. Vert. pair, imperf. horiz. 50.00
R163 R15 1c pale blue 15 15
a. Vert. pair, imperf. horiz. 7.50
b. Imperf., pair —
R164 R15 2c carmine rose 25 25
a. Vert. pair, imperf. horiz. 40.00
b. Imperf., pair 140.00
c. Horiz. pair, imperf. vert. —
R165 R15 3c dark blue 1.00 15
R166 R15 4c pale rose 60 15
a. Vert. pair, imperf. horiz. 75.00
R167 R15 5c lilac 20 15
a. Pair, imperf. horiz. or vert. 140.00 100.00
b. Horiz. pair, imperf. btwn. 250.00
R168 R15 10c dark brown 90 15
a. Vert. pair, imperf. horiz. 20.00 20.00
b. Horiz. pair, imperf. vert. —
R169 R15 25c purple brown 90 15
R170 R15 40c blue lilac 70.00 50
Cut cancellation 30
R171 R15 50c slate violet 7.50 15
a. Imperf., pair 300.00
R172 R15 80c bister 40.00 25
Cut cancellation 15

No. R167b may not be genuine.

Hyphen Hole Perf. 7

R163p 1c 25 15
R164p 2c 30 15
R165p 3c 7.50 50
R166p 4c 2.50 90
R167p 5c 2.50 15
b. Horiz. pair, imperf. btwn. —
R168p 10c 1.50 15
R169p 25c 2.50 25
R170p 40c 100.00 20.00
R171p 50c 12.50 25
b. Horiz. pair, imperf. btwn. — 250.00
R172p 80c 110.00 25.00

Commerce — R16

1898 *Rouletted 5½*
R173 R16 $1 dark green 6.50 15
a. Vert. pair, imperf. horiz. —
b. Horiz. pair, imperf. vert. — 300.00
p. Hyphen hole perf. 7 11.00 65
R174 R16 $3 dark brown 12.50 75
Cut cancellation 25
a. Horiz. pair, imperf. vert. 450.00
p. Hyphen hole perf. 7 12.50 2.00
R175 R16 $5 orange red 17.50 1.25
Cut cancellation 18
R176 R16 $10 black 50.00 2.50
Cut cancellation 50
a. Horiz. pair, imperf. vert. —
R177 R16 $30 red 160.00 90.00
Cut cancellation 40.00
R178 R16 $50 gray brown 75.00 5.00
Cut cancellation 2.00

There are 2 styles of rouletting for the 1898 proprietary and documentary stamps, an ordinary roulette 5½ and one where small rectangles of the paper are cut out, called hyphen hole perf. 7. Except for Nos. R161, R162 and R175-R178, all the stamps of the two series exist with both roulettes.

See Nos. R182-R183.

John Marshall — R17

Set Values
A 15-cent minimum now applies to individual stamps and sets. Where the 15-cent minimum per stamp would increase the value of a set beyond retail, there is a "Set Value" notation giving the retail value of the set.

Alexander Hamilton
R18

James Madison
R19

Inscribed "Series of 1898"

1899 Without Gum *Imperf.*

R179 R17 $100 yel brn & black 100.00 30.00
Cut cancellation 20.00
R180 R18 $500 car lake & black 600.00 450.00
Cut cancellation 225.00
R181 R19 $1000 grn & blk 600.00 300.00
Cut cancellation 110.00

See Nos. R224-R227, R246-R252, R282-R286.

Type of 1898

1900 ***Hyphen-Hole Perf. 7***

R182 R16 $1 carmine 10.00 35
Cut cancellation 15
R183 R16 $3 lake 95.00 45.00
Cut cancellation 7.00

Surcharged in Black

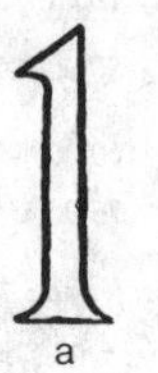

a

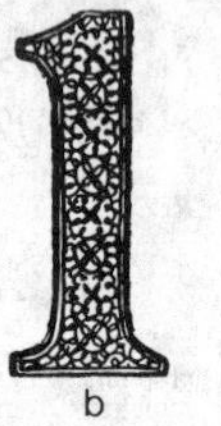

b

Surcharged type "a"

1900

R184 R16 $1 gray 7.50 15
Cut cancellation 15
a. Horiz. pair, imperf. vert. —
b. Surcharge omitted 125.00
As "b", cut cancellation 80.00
R185 R16 $2 gray 5.00 15
Cut cancellation 15
R186 R16 $3 gray 45.00 7.00
Cut cancellation 2.00
R187 R16 $5 gray 27.50 6.00
Cut cancellation 1.00
R188 R16 $10 gray 50.00 15.00
Cut cancellation 3.00
R189 R16 $50 gray 550.00 350.00
Cut cancellation 70.00

Surcharged type "b"

1902

R190 R16 $1 green 12.50 3.50
Cut cancellation 20
a. Inverted surcharge *175.00*
R191 R16 $2 green 10.00 1.25
Cut cancellation 20
a. Surcharged as #R185 75.00 75.00
b. Surch. as #R185, in vio *1,300.* —
c. Double surcharge *100.00*
R192 R16 $5 green 100.00 25.00
Cut cancellation 4.00
a. Surcharge omitted 125.00
b. Pair, one without surch. *325.00*
R193 R16 $10 green 250.00 125.00
Cut cancellation 45.00
R194 R16 $50 green 950.00 800.00
Cut cancellation 225.00

Warning: If Nos. R190-R194 are soaked, the center part of the surcharged numeral may wash off. Before surcharging, a square of soluble varnish was applied to the middle of some stamps.

R20

Liberty — R21

Inscribed "Series of 1914"
Offset Printing

1914 Wmk. 190 *Perf. 10*

R195 R20 ½c rose 6.00 3.00
R196 R20 1c rose 1.25 15
R197 R20 2c rose 1.75 15
R198 R20 3c rose 37.50 25.00
R199 R20 4c rose 10.00 1.75
R200 R20 5c rose 3.25 20
R201 R20 10c rose 2.75 15
R202 R20 25c rose 21.00 45
R203 R20 40c rose 12.50 75
R204 R20 50c rose 5.00 15
R205 R20 80c rose 70.00 8.00
Nos. R195-R205 (11) 171.00 39.75

Wmk. 191R

R206 R20 ½c rose 1.25 40
R207 R20 1c rose 15 15
R208 R20 2c rose 15 15
R209 R20 3c rose 1.25 20
R210 R20 4c rose 2.75 40
R211 R20 5c rose 1.50 25
R212 R20 10c rose 50 15
R213 R20 25c rose 4.50 1.00
R214 R20 40c rose 50.00 10.00
Cut cancellation 45
R215 R20 50c rose 10.00 25
R216 R20 80c rose 75.00 15.00
Cut cancellation 1.00
Nos. R206-R216 (11) 147.05 27.95

Engr.

R217 R21 $1 green 25.00 20
a. $1 yellow green — 15
Cut cancellation 15
R218 R21 $2 carmine 37.50 50
Cut cancellation 15
R219 R21 $3 purple 47.50 2.00
Cut cancellation 20
R220 R21 $5 blue 40.00 2.75
Cut cancellation 50
R221 R21 $10 orange 90.00 4.50
Cut cancellation 75
R222 R21 $30 vermilion 175.00 10.00
Cut cancellation 2.00
R223 R21 $50 violet 1,000. 750.00
Cut cancellation 300.00

See #R240-R245, R257-R259, R276-R281.

Portrait Types of 1899 Inscribed "Series of 1915" (#R224), or "Series of 1914"

1914-15 Without Gum *Perf. 12*

R224 R19 $60 brn *(Lincoln)* — 100.00
Cut cancellation 45.00
R225 R17 $100 grn *(Washington)* — 40.00
Cut cancellation 15.00
R226 R18 $500 blue — 450.00
Cut cancellation 200.00
R227 R19 $1000 orange — 350.00
Cut cancellation 150.00

The stamps of types R17, R18 and R19 in this and subsequent issues are issued in vert. strips of 4 which are imperf. at the top, bottom and right side; therefore, single copies are always imperf. on 1 or 2 sides.

R22

Offset Printing

1917 Wmk. 191R *Perf. 11*

Size: 21x18mm

R228 R22 1c carmine rose 15 15
R229 R22 2c carmine rose 15 15
R230 R22 3c carmine rose 1.00 35
R231 R22 4c carmine rose 40 15
R232 R22 5c carmine rose 20 15
R233 R22 8c carmine rose 1.50 30
R234 R22 10c carmine rose 25 15
R235 R22 20c carmine rose 50 15
R236 R22 25c carmine rose 90 15
R237 R22 40c carmine rose 1.25 40
R238 R22 50c carmine rose 1.75 15
R239 R22 80c carmine rose 4.50 15
Nos. R228-R239 (12) 12.55
Set value 1.30

Type of 1914 without "Series 1914"

1917-33 Engr. Size: 18½x27½mm

R240 R21 $1 yellow green 6.00 15
a. $1 green 6.00 15
R241 R21 $2 rose 10.00 15
R242 R21 $3 violet 30.00 70
Cut cancellation 15
R243 R21 $4 yellow brown ('33) 20.00 1.75
Cut cancellation 15
R244 R21 $5 dark blue 12.50 25
Cut cancellation 15
R245 R21 $10 orange 25.00 90
Cut cancellation 15

Portrait Types of 1899-1915 without "Series of" and Date

Portraits: $30, Grant. $100, Washington.

1917 Without Gum *Perf. 12*

R246 R17 $30 dp org, grn numerals 40.00 10.00
Cut cancellation 1.00
a. Imperf., pair *750.00*
b. Numerals in blue 65.00 1.75
As "b," cut cancellation 1.00
R247 R19 $60 brown 50.00 7.00
Cut cancellation 80
R248 R17 $100 green 30.00 1.00
Cut cancellation 35
R249 R18 $500 blue, red numerals 200.00 35.00
Cut cancellation 10.00
a. Numerals in orange — 50.00
R250 R19 $1000 orange 110.00 12.50
Cut cancellation 4.00
a. Imperf., pair *900.00*

See note after No. R227.

1928-29 Offset Printing *Perf. 10*

R251 R22 1c carmine rose 2.00 1.50
R252 R22 2c carmine rose 60 20
R253 R22 4c carmine rose 5.50 3.75
R254 R22 5c carmine rose 1.25 50
R255 R22 10c carmine rose 1.75 1.25
R256 R22 20c carmine rose 5.50 4.50
Nos. R251-R256 (6) 16.60 11.70

Engr.

R257 R21 $1 green 85.00 30.00
Cut cancellation 5.00
R258 R21 $2 rose 32.50 2.50
R259 R21 $10 orange 110.00 40.00
Cut cancellation 25.00

1929 Offset Printing *Perf. 11x10*

R260 R22 2c carmine rose 2.75 2.25
R261 R22 5c carmine rose 2.00 1.75
R262 R22 10c carmine rose 7.50 6.50
R263 R22 20c carmine rose 15.00 8.00

Used values for Nos. R264-R734 are for copies which are neither cut nor perforated with initials. Copies with cut cancellations or perforated initials are valued in Scott's U. S. Specialized Catalogue.

Types of 1917-33 Overprinted in Black **SERIES 1940**

1940 Offset Printing *Perf. 11*

R264 R22 1c rose pink 2.50 2.25
R265 R22 2c rose pink 2.50 1.75
R266 R22 3c rose pink 7.50 4.00
R267 R22 4c rose pink 3.00 55
R268 R22 5c rose pink 3.50 90
R269 R22 8c rose pink 12.50 12.50
R270 R22 10c rose pink 1.50 45
R271 R22 20c rose pink 2.00 60
R272 R22 25c rose pink 4.50 1.00
R273 R22 40c rose pink 4.50 65
R274 R22 50c rose pink 5.00 50
R275 R22 80c rose pink 7.50 90
Nos. R264-R275 (12) 56.50 26.05

Engr.

R276 R21 $1 green 27.50 55
R277 R21 $2 rose 27.50 1.00
R278 R21 $3 violet 40.00 20.00
R279 R21 $4 yellow brown 70.00 25.00
R280 R21 $5 dark blue 35.00 10.00
R281 R21 $10 orange 90.00 25.00

Types of 1917 Handstamped in Green Like Nos. R264-R281

Without Gum *Perf. 12*

R282 R17 $30 vermilion 450.
R283 R19 $60 brown 650.
a. As #R285a, cut cancel —
R284 R17 $100 green 950.
R285 R18 $500 blue 1,350.
a. With black 2-line handstamp in larger type *1,750.*
b. Blue handstamp, double transfer —
R286 R19 $1000 orange 650.

Alexander Hamilton — R23

Levi Woodbury — R24

Thomas Corwin — R25

Portraits: 2c, Oliver Wolcott, Jr. 3c, Samuel Dexter. 4c, Albert Gallatin. 5c, George Washington Campbell. 8c, Alexander Dallas. 10c, William H. Crawford. 20c, Richard Rush. 25c, Samuel D. Ingham. 40c, Louis McLane. 50c, William J. Duane. 80c, Roger B. Taney. $2, Thomas Ewing. $3, Walter Forward. $4, John Canfield Spencer. $5, George M. Bibb. $10, Robert J. Walker. $20, William M. Meredith. $50, James Guthrie. $60, Howell Cobb. $100, P. F. Thomas. $500, John Adams Dix. $1,000, Salmon P. Chase.

Overprinted in Black Like Nos. R264-R281

1940 Size: 19x22mm *Perf. 11*

Various Portraits

R288 R23 1c carmine 3.75 3.00
R289 R23 2c carmine 4.00 2.75
R290 R23 3c carmine 15.00 9.00
R291 R23 4c carmine 35.00 20.00
R292 R23 5c carmine 3.00 60
R293 R23 8c carmine 55.00 45.00
R294 R23 10c carmine 2.50 45
R295 R23 20c carmine 3.25 2.50
R296 R23 25c carmine 2.50 50
R297 R23 40c carmine 35.00 18.00
R298 R23 50c carmine 4.00 40
R299 R23 80c carmine 75.00 60.00
Nos. R288-R299 (12) 238.00 162.20

Size: 21¼x36¼mm

R300 R24 $1 carmine 30.00 50
R301 R24 $2 carmine 35.00 75
R302 R24 $3 carmine 110.00 75.00
R303 R24 $4 carmine 60.00 30.00
R304 R24 $5 carmine 35.00 1.50
R305 R24 $10 carmine 65.00 5.00
R305A R24 $20 carmine *1,500.* 550.00
b. Imperf., pair 750.00

Size: 28½x42mm

Various Frame Designs

Perf. 12

Without Gum

R306 R25 $30 carmine 100.00 37.50
R306A R25 $50 carmine — 1,250.
R307 R25 $60 carmine 225.00 40.00
a. Vert. pair, imperf. between *1,450.*
R308 R25 $100 carmine 150.00 55.00
R309 R25 $500 carmine — 1,000.
R310 R25 $1000 carmine — 400.00

The $30 to $1,000 denominations in this and following similar issues, and the $2,500, $5,000 and $10,000 stamps of 1952-58 have straight edges on one or two sides. They were issued without gum through No. R723.

Overprinted in Black "SERIES 1941"

1941 Size: 19x22mm *Perf. 11*

R311 R23 1c carmine 3.00 2.25
R312 R23 2c carmine 3.00 90
R313 R23 3c carmine 7.50 3.50
R314 R23 4c carmine 5.00 1.25
R315 R23 5c carmine 1.00 25
R316 R23 8c carmine 14.00 7.50
R317 R23 10c carmine 1.25 15
R318 R23 20c carmine 3.00 45
R319 R23 25c carmine 1.75 20
R320 R23 40c carmine 10.00 2.50
R321 R23 50c carmine 2.50 15
R322 R23 80c carmine 40.00 9.00
Nos. R311-R322 (12) 92.00 28.10

Size: 21¼x36¼mm

R323 R24 $1 carmine 7.50 25
R324 R24 $2 carmine 9.00 35
R325 R24 $3 carmine 15.00 2.50
R326 R24 $4 carmine 25.00 15.00
R327 R24 $5 carmine 30.00 60
R328 R24 $10 carmine 45.00 3.00
R329 R24 $20 carmine 500.00 175.00

Size: 28½x42mm

Perf. 12

Without Gum

R330	R25	$30 carmine	50.00	22.50
R331	R25	$50 carmine	175.00	150.00
R332	R25	$60 carmine	—	42.50
R333	R25	$100 carmine	—	17.50
R334	R25	$500 carmine	—	200.00
R335	R25	$1000 carmine	—	100.00

Overprinted in Black "SERIES 1942"

1942 Size: 19x22mm *Perf. 11*

R336	R23	1c carmine	48	42
R337	R23	2c carmine	42	42
R338	R23	3c carmine	70	60
R339	R23	4c carmine	1.20	90
R340	R23	5c carmine	42	16
R341	R23	8c carmine	5.50	4.25
R342	R23	10c carmine	1.20	25
R343	R23	20c carmine	1.20	42
R344	R23	25c carmine	2.10	42
R345	R23	40c carmine	4.75	1.20
R346	R23	50c carmine	3.00	16
R347	R23	80c carmine	14.50	8.50
		Nos. R336-R347 (12)	35.47	17.70

Size: 21½x36¼mm

R348	R24	$1 carmine	6.50	25
R349	R24	$2 carmine	7.50	25
R350	R24	$3 carmine	11.00	2.00
R351	R24	$4 carmine	18.00	3.75
R352	R24	$5 carmine	21.00	90
R353	R24	$10 carmine	45.00	2.50
R354	R24	$20 carmine	85.00	25.00

Size: 28½x42mm

Perf. 12

Without Gum

R355	R25	$30 carmine	40.00	20.00
R356	R25	$50 carmine	275.00	175.00
R357	R25	$60 carmine	550.00	450.00
R358	R25	$100 carmine	150.00	100.00
R359	R25	$500 carmine	—	200.00
R360	R25	$1000 carmine	—	100.00

Overprinted in Black "SERIES 1943"

1943 Size: 19x22mm *Perf. 11*

R361	R23	1c carmine	60	50
R362	R23	2c carmine	45	35
R363	R23	3c carmine	2.50	2.50
R364	R23	4c carmine	1.00	1.00
R365	R23	5c carmine	50	30
R366	R23	8c carmine	4.00	3.00
R367	R23	10c carmine	60	25
R368	R23	20c carmine	1.75	60
R369	R23	25c carmine	1.50	25
R370	R23	40c carmine	5.00	2.00
R371	R23	50c carmine	1.25	15
R372	R23	80c carmine	10.00	5.50
		Nos. R361-R372 (12)	29.15	16.40

Size: 21½x36¼mm

R373	R24	$1 carmine	4.00	35
R374	R24	$2 carmine	8.00	25
R375	R24	$3 carmine	12.50	2.00
R376	R24	$4 carmine	15.00	3.00
R377	R24	$5 carmine	20.00	50
R378	R24	$10 carmine	35.00	3.00
R379	R24	$20 carmine	75.00	17.50

Size: 28½x42mm

Perf. 12

Without Gum

R380	R25	$30 carmine	30.00	18.00
R381	R25	$50 carmine	60.00	25.00
R382	R25	$60 carmine	—	65.00
R383	R25	$100 carmine	—	10.00
R384	R25	$500 carmine	—	160.00
R385	R25	$1000 carmine	—	150.00

Overprinted in Black "Series 1944"

1944 Size: 19x22mm *Perf. 11*

R386	R23	1c carmine	40	35
R387	R23	2c carmine	40	35
R388	R23	3c carmine	40	35
R389	R23	4c carmine	55	50
R390	R23	5c carmine	30	15
R391	R23	8c carmine	1.75	1.25
R392	R23	10c carmine	40	15
R393	R23	20c carmine	75	20
R394	R23	25c carmine	1.40	15
R395	R23	40c carmine	2.75	60
R396	R23	50c carmine	3.00	15
R397	R23	80c carmine	10.00	4.00
		Nos. R386-R397 (12)	22.10	8.20

Size: 21½x36¼mm

R398	R24	$1 carmine	4.50	20
R399	R24	$2 carmine	6.50	25
R400	R24	$3 carmine	10.00	1.50
R401	R24	$4 carmine	13.50	10.00
R402	R24	$5 carmine	16.00	25
R403	R24	$10 carmine	30.00	1.25
R404	R24	$20 carmine	65.00	15.00

Size: 28½x42mm

Perf. 12

Without Gum

R405	R25	$30 carmine	50.00	20.00
R406	R25	$50 carmine	20.00	10.00
R407	R25	$60 carmine	90.00	40.00
R408	R25	$100 carmine	—	8.00
R409	R25	$500 carmine	—	950.00
R410	R25	$1000 carmine	—	165.00

Overprinted in Black "Series 1945"

1945 Size: 19x22mm *Perf. 11*

R411	R23	1c carmine	20	20
R412	R23	2c carmine	25	20
R413	R23	3c carmine	50	45
R414	R23	4c carmine	30	30
R415	R23	5c carmine	25	15
R416	R23	8c carmine	4.25	2.00
R417	R23	10c carmine	80	15
R418	R23	20c carmine	4.50	1.00
R419	R23	25c carmine	1.10	30
R420	R23	40c carmine	4.75	1.00
R421	R23	50c carmine	2.75	20
R422	R23	80c carmine	16.00	8.00
		Nos. R411-R422 (12)	35.65	13.95

Size: 21½x36¼mm

R423	R24	$1 carmine	5.00	15
R424	R24	$2 carmine	6.50	25
R425	R24	$3 carmine	11.00	2.25
R426	R24	$4 carmine	16.00	3.00
R427	R24	$5 carmine	16.00	40
R428	R24	$10 carmine	35.00	1.25
R429	R24	$20 carmine	65.00	11.00

Size: 28½x42mm

Without Gum

Perf. 12

R430	R25	$30 carmine	60.00	20.00
R431	R25	$50 carmine	65.00	25.00
R432	R25	$60 carmine	100.00	32.50
R433	R25	$100 carmine	—	12.00
R434	R25	$500 carmine	200.00	150.00
R435	R25	$1000 carmine	100.00	82.50

Overprinted in Black "Series 1946"

1946 Wmk. 191R *Perf. 11*

Size: 19x22mm

R436	R23	1c carmine	20	25
R437	R23	2c carmine	35	30
R438	R23	3c carmine	35	30
R439	R23	4c carmine	60	50
R440	R23	5c carmine	30	15
R441	R23	8c carmine	1.25	1.10
R442	R23	10c carmine	70	15
R443	R23	20c carmine	1.25	40
R444	R23	25c carmine	4.00	20
R445	R23	40c carmine	2.50	75
R446	R23	50c carmine	3.00	20
R447	R23	80c carmine	8.00	4.00
		Nos. R436-R447 (12)	22.50	8.30

Size: 21½x36¼mm

R448	R24	$1 carmine	5.00	20
R449	R24	$2 carmine	7.50	20
R450	R24	$3 carmine	11.00	5.00
R451	R24	$4 carmine	15.00	10.00
R452	R24	$5 carmine	15.00	45
R453	R24	$10 carmine	30.00	1.50
R454	R24	$20 carmine	65.00	10.00

Size: 28½x42mm

Without Gum

Perf. 12

R455	R25	$30 carmine	40.00	12.00
R456	R25	$50 carmine	20.00	9.00
R457	R25	$60 carmine	40.00	16.00
R458	R25	$100 carmine	—	10.00
R459	R25	$500 carmine	—	90.00
R460	R25	$1000 carmine	—	100.00

Overprinted in Black "Series 1947"

1947 Wmk. 191R *Perf. 11*

Size: 19x22mm

R461	R23	1c carmine	65	50
R462	R23	2c carmine	55	50
R463	R23	3c carmine	55	50
R464	R23	4c carmine	70	60
R465	R23	5c carmine	35	30
R466	R23	8c carmine	1.20	70
R467	R23	10c carmine	1.10	25
R468	R23	20c carmine	1.80	50
R469	R23	25c carmine	2.40	60
R470	R23	40c carmine	3.75	90
R471	R23	50c carmine	3.00	25
R472	R23	80c carmine	7.25	6.00
		Nos. R461-R472 (12)	23.30	11.60

Size: 21½x36¼mm

R473	R24	$1 carmine	4.50	25
R474	R24	$2 carmine	7.00	50
R475	R24	$3 carmine	7.50	5.00
R476	R24	$4 carmine	9.00	4.50
R477	R24	$5 carmine	12.50	50
R478	R24	$10 carmine	30.00	2.00
R479	R24	$20 carmine	50.00	10.00

Size: 28½x42mm

Perf. 12

Without Gum

R480	R25	$30 carmine	60.00	17.50
R481	R25	$50 carmine	30.00	12.00
R482	R25	$60 carmine	—	30.00
R483	R25	$100 carmine	30.00	10.00
R484	R25	$500 carmine	—	150.00
R485	R25	$1000 carmine	—	80.00

Overprinted in Black "Series 1948"

1948 Wmk. 191R *Perf. 11*

Size: 19x22mm

R486	R23	1c carmine	25	25
R487	R23	2c carmine	35	30
R488	R23	3c carmine	45	35
R489	R23	4c carmine	40	30
R490	R23	5c carmine	35	15
R491	R23	8c carmine	75	35
R492	R23	10c carmine	60	15
R493	R23	20c carmine	1.75	30
R494	R23	25c carmine	1.50	20
R495	R23	40c carmine	4.50	1.50
R496	R23	50c carmine	2.25	15
R497	R23	80c carmine	5.00	4.50
		Nos. R486-R497 (12)	18.15	8.50

Size: 21½x36¼mm

R498	R24	$1 carmine	4.75	20
R499	R24	$2 carmine	8.00	20
R500	R24	$3 carmine	10.00	2.50
R501	R24	$4 carmine	15.00	2.50
R502	R24	$5 carmine	14.00	50
R503	R24	$10 carmine	27.50	1.00
a.		Pair, one dated "1946"		—
R504	R24	$20 carmine	60.00	8.50

Size: 28½x42mm

Perf. 12

Without Gum

R505	R25	$30 carmine	40.00	20.00
R506	R25	$50 carmine	40.00	15.00
a.		Vert. pair, imperf. btwn.	—	
R507	R25	$60 carmine	50.00	22.50
a.		Vert. pair, imperf. btwn.	*1,100*	
R508	R25	$100 carmine	—	10.00
a.		Vert. pair, imperf. btwn.	*850.00*	
R509	R25	$500 carmine	125.00	100.00
R510	R25	$1000 carmine	80.00	60.00

Overprinted in Black "Series 1949"

1949 Wmk. 191R *Perf. 11*

Size: 19x22mm

R511	R23	1c carmine	25	25
R512	R23	2c carmine	55	35
R513	R23	3c carmine	42	35
R514	R23	4c carmine	60	48
R515	R23	5c carmine	35	20
R516	R23	8c carmine	70	60
R517	R23	10c carmine	42	25
R518	R23	20c carmine	1.30	60
R519	R23	25c carmine	1.80	70
R520	R23	40c carmine	4.25	2.10
R521	R23	50c carmine	3.50	30
R522	R23	80c carmine	7.25	4.75
		Nos. R511-R522 (12)	21.39	10.93

Size: 21½x36¼mm

R523	R24	$1 carmine	5.00	40
R524	R24	$2 carmine	7.00	2.00
R525	R24	$3 carmine	11.00	6.00
R526	R24	$4 carmine	12.50	6.00
R527	R24	$5 carmine	12.50	2.25
R528	R24	$10 carmine	27.50	2.50
R529	R24	$20 carmine	65.00	7.50

Size: 28½x42mm

Perf. 12

Without Gum

R530	R25	$30 carmine	50.00	22.50
R531	R25	$50 carmine	—	35.00
R532	R25	$60 carmine	—	35.00
R533	R25	$100 carmine	—	15.00
R534	R25	$500 carmine	—	180.00
R535	R25	$1000 carmine	—	110.00

Overprinted in Black "Series 1950"

1950 Wmk. 191R *Perf. 11*

Size: 19x22mm

R536	R23	1c carmine	20	15
R537	R23	2c carmine	30	25
R538	R23	3c carmine	35	30
R539	R23	4c carmine	50	40
R540	R23	5c carmine	30	15
R541	R23	8c carmine	1.25	65
R542	R23	10c carmine	60	20
R543	R23	20c carmine	1.00	35
R544	R23	25c carmine	1.50	35
R545	R23	40c carmine	3.25	1.75
R546	R23	50c carmine	4.00	20
R547	R23	80c carmine	5.00	4.00
		Nos. R536-R547 (12)	18.25	8.75

Size: 21½x36¼mm

R548	R24	$1 carmine	4.50	20
R549	R24	$2 carmine	6.00	2.00
R550	R24	$3 carmine	8.00	4.00
R551	R24	$4 carmine	11.00	5.00
R552	R24	$5 carmine	12.50	75
R553	R24	$10 carmine	30.00	7.50
R554	R24	$20 carmine	65.00	8.00

Size: 28½x42mm

Perf. 12

Without Gum

R555	R25	$30 carmine	—	40.00
R556	R25	$50 carmine	—	14.00
a.		Vert. pair, imperf. horiz.		—
R557	R25	$60 carmine	—	45.00
R558	R25	$100 carmine	—	17.50
R559	R25	$500 carmine	—	100.00
R560	R25	$1000 carmine	—	75.00

Overprinted in Black "Series 1951"

1951 Wmk. 191R *Perf. 11*

Size: 19x22mm

R561	R23	1c carmine	15	15
R562	R23	2c carmine	30	25
R563	R23	3c carmine	25	25
R564	R23	4c carmine	30	25
R565	R23	5c carmine	30	20
R566	R23	8c carmine	1.00	35
R567	R23	10c carmine	55	20
R568	R23	20c carmine	1.25	45
R569	R23	25c carmine	1.25	40
R570	R23	40c carmine	3.00	1.25
R571	R23	50c carmine	2.50	35
R572	R23	80c carmine	4.00	2.50
		Nos. R561-R572 (12)	14.85	6.60

Size: 21½x36¼mm

R573	R24	$1 carmine	4.50	20
R574	R24	$2 carmine	6.00	50
R575	R24	$3 carmine	9.50	3.50
R576	R24	$4 carmine	12.50	5.00
R577	R24	$5 carmine	11.00	60
R578	R24	$10 carmine	27.50	2.25
R579	R24	$20 carmine	60.00	7.50

Size: 28½x42mm

Perf. 12

Without Gum

R580	R25	$30 carmine	—	10.00
a.		Imperf., pair		*750.00*
R581	R25	$50 carmine	—	12.50
R582	R25	$60 carmine	—	35.00
R583	R25	$100 carmine	—	12.50
R584	R25	$500 carmine	125.00	82.50
R585	R25	$1000 carmine	—	90.00

Overprinted in Black "Series 1952"

Designs: 55c, $1.10, $1.65, $2.20, $2.75, $3.30, L. J. Gage; $2500, William Windom; $5000, C. J. Folger; $10,000, W. Q. Gresham.

1952 Wmk. 191R *Perf. 11*

Size: 19x22mm

R586	R23	1c carmine	20	15
R587	R23	2c carmine	35	25
R588	R23	3c carmine	30	25
R589	R23	4c carmine	30	25
R590	R23	5c carmine	25	15
R591	R23	8c carmine	65	45
R592	R23	10c carmine	40	20
R593	R23	20c carmine	1.00	35
R594	R23	25c carmine	1.50	40
R595	R23	40c carmine	3.00	1.00
R596	R23	50c carmine	2.75	20
R597	R23	55c carmine	13.50	10.00
R598	R23	80c carmine	7.00	3.00
		Nos. R586-R598 (13)	31.20	16.65

Size: 21½x36¼mm

R599	R24	$1 carmine	4.00	1.50
R600	R24	$1.10 carmine	27.50	20.00
R601	R24	$1.65 carmine	100.00	40.00
R602	R24	$2 carmine	6.00	65
R603	R24	$2.20 carmine	75.00	55.00
R604	R24	$2.75 carmine	95.00	50.00
R605	R24	$3 carmine	15.00	4.00
a.		Horiz. pair, imperf. btwn.	*500.00*	
R606	R24	$3.30 carmine	75.00	50.00
R607	R24	$4 carmine	12.50	4.00
R608	R24	$5 carmine	12.00	1.25
R609	R24	$10 carmine	27.50	1.25
R610	R24	$20 carmine	45.00	9.00

Size: 28½x42mm

Perf. 12

Without Gum

R611	R25	$30 carmine	—	18.00
R612	R25	$50 carmine	—	12.00
R613	R25	$60 carmine	—	45.00
R614	R25	$100 carmine	—	8.00
R615	R25	$500 carmine	—	100.00
R616	R25	$1000 carmine	—	30.00
R617	R25	$2500 carmine	—	150.00
R618	R25	$5000 carmine	—	1,100.
R619	R25	$10,000 carmine	—	650.00

Overprinted in Black "Series 1953"

1953 Wmk. 191R *Perf. 11*

Size: 19x22mm

R620	R23	1c carmine	20	15
R621	R23	2c carmine	20	15
R622	R23	3c carmine	25	20
R623	R23	4c carmine	35	25
R624	R23	5c carmine	20	15
R625	R23	8c carmine	75	35
R626	R23	10c carmine	40	20
R627	R23	20c carmine	75	40
R628	R23	25c carmine	1.00	50
R629	R23	40c carmine	1.75	1.00
R630	R23	50c carmine	2.50	20
R631	R23	55c carmine	3.50	2.00
a.		Horiz. pair, imperf. vert.	*350.00*	
R632	R23	80c carmine	4.00	2.00
		Nos. R620-R632 (13)	15.85	7.55

Size: 21½x36¼mm

R633	R24	$1 carmine	3.50	25
R634	R24	$1.10 carmine	5.00	2.25
a.		Horiz. pair, imperf. vert.	*500.00*	
b.		Imperf., pair	*550.00*	
R635	R24	$1.65 carmine	6.00	4.00
R636	R24	$2 carmine	5.00	65
R637	R24	$2.20 carmine	8.50	6.00

R638	R24	$2.75 carmine	12.00	7.00
R639	R24	$3 carmine	7.00	3.00
R640	R24	$3.30 carmine	17.50	8.00
R641	R24	$4 carmine	12.50	7.50
R642	R24	$5 carmine	12.50	1.00
R643	R24	$10 carmine	25.00	1.75
R644	R24	$20 carmine	50.00	18.00

Size: 28 1/2x42mm

Perf. 12

Without Gum

R645	R25	$30 carmine	—	12.00
R646	R25	$50 carmine	—	25.00
R647	R25	$60 carmine	—	125.00
R648	R25	$100 carmine	35.00	12.00
R649	R25	$500 carmine	250.00	115.00
R650	R25	$1000 carmine	125.00	57.50
R651	R25	$2500 carmine	475.00	475.00
R652	R25	$5000 carmine	—	1,250.
R653	R25	$10,000 carmine	—	*1,000.*

Types of 1940 without Overprint

1954 Wmk. 191R *Perf. 11*

Size: 19x22mm

R654	R23	1c carmine	15	15
a.		Horiz. pair, imperf. vert.	—	
R655	R23	2c carmine	15	15
R656	R23	3c carmine	15	15
R657	R23	4c carmine	15	15
R658	R23	5c carmine	15	15
R659	R23	8c carmine	25	20
R660	R23	10c carmine	25	20
R661	R23	20c carmine	50	30
R662	R23	25c carmine	60	35
R663	R23	40c carmine	1.25	60
R664	R23	50c carmine	1.65	20
a.		Horiz. pair, imperf. vert	275.00	
R665	R23	55c carmine	1.50	1.25
R666	R23	80c carmine	2.25	1.75
		Nos. R654-R666 (13)	9.00	5.60

Size: 21 1/2x36 1/4mm

R667	R24	$1 carmine	1.75	30
R668	R24	$1.10 carmine	3.25	2.50
R669	R24	$1.65 carmine	90.00	55.00
R670	R24	$2 carmine	1.75	25
R671	R24	$2.20 carmine	4.50	3.75
R672	R24	$2.75 carmine	100.00	50.00
R673	R24	$3 carmine	3.00	2.00
R674	R24	$3.30 carmine	6.50	5.00
R675	R24	$4 carmine	4.00	3.50
R676	R24	$5 carmine	7.50	45
R677	R24	$10 carmine	15.00	1.25
R678	R24	$20 carmine	20.00	5.25

Overprinted in Black "Series 1954"

Perf. 12

Size: 28 1/2x42mm

Without Gum

R679	R25	$30 carmine	—	12.00
R680	R25	$50 carmine	—	15.00
R681	R25	$60 carmine	—	20.00
R682	R25	$100 carmine	—	7.00
R683	R25	$500 carmine	—	75.00
R684	R25	$1000 carmine	150.00	55.00
R685	R25	$2500 carmine	—	175.00
R686	R25	$5000 carmine	—	725.00
R687	R25	$10,000 carmine	—	500.00

Overprinted in Black "Series 1955"

Without Gum

1955 Wmk. 191R *Perf. 12*

Size: 28 1/2x42mm

R688	R25	$30 carmine	—	11.50
R689	R25	$50 carmine	—	13.50
R690	R25	$60 carmine	—	24.00
R691	R25	$100 carmine	—	7.00
R692	R25	$500 carmine	—	125.00
R693	R25	$1000 carmine	—	35.00
R694	R25	$2500 carmine	—	125.00
R695	R25	$5000 carmine	*800.00*	700.00
R696	R25	$10,000 carmine	—	500.00

Overprinted in Black "Series 1956"

Without Gum

1956 Size: 28 1/2x42mm

R697	R25	$30 carmine	—	13.50
R698	R25	$50 carmine	—	17.00
R699	R25	$60 carmine	—	32.50
R700	R25	$100 carmine	—	12.50
R701	R25	$500 carmine	—	75.00
R702	R25	$1000 carmine	—	55.00
R703	R25	$2500 carmine	—	250.00
R704	R25	$5000 carmine	—	1,250.
R705	R25	$10,000 carmine	—	450.00

Overprinted in Black "Series 1957"

Without Gum

1957 Size: 28 1/2x42mm

R706	R25	$30 carmine	—	27.50
R707	R25	$50 carmine	—	24.00
R708	R25	$60 carmine	—	125.00
R709	R25	$100 carmine	—	12.50
R710	R25	$500 carmine	175.00	85.00
R711	R25	$1000 carmine	—	80.00
R712	R25	$2500 carmine	—	525.00
R713	R25	$5000 carmine	—	600.00
R714	R25	$10,000 carmine	—	450.00

Overprinted in Black "Series 1958"

Without Gum

1958 Size: 28 1/2x42mm

R715	R25	$30 carmine	75.00	20.00
R716	R25	$50 carmine	60.00	20.00
R717	R25	$60 carmine	—	25.00
R718	R25	$100 carmine	50.00	10.00
R719	R25	$500 carmine	125.00	55.00
R720	R25	$1000 carmine	—	67.50
R721	R25	$2500 carmine	—	600.00
R722	R25	$5000 carmine	—	1,350.
R723	R25	$10,000 carmine	—	650.00

Documentary Stamps and Type of 1940

Without Overprint

With Gum

1958 Size: 28 1/2x42mm

R724	R25	$30 carmine	35.00	7.00
a.		Vert. pair, imperf. horiz.	—	
R725	R25	$50 carmine	37.50	7.00
a.		Vert. pair, imperf. horiz.		—
R726	R25	$60 carmine	—	20.00
R727	R25	$100 carmine	17.50	4.75
R728	R25	$500 carmine	80.00	25.00
R729	R25	$1000 carmine	50.00	20.00
a.		Vert. pair, imperf. horiz.		*600.00*
R730	R25	$2500 carmine	—	140.00
R731	R25	$5000 carmine	—	150.00
R732	R25	$10,000 carmine	—	125.00

Catalogue values for unused stamps in this section, from this point to the end of the section, are for Never Hinged items.

Internal Revenue Building, Washington, DC — R26

Giori Press Printing

1962, July 1 Unwmk. *Perf. 11*

R733	R26	10c vio bl & brt grn	1.10	35

Centenary of Internal Revenue Service.

"Established 1862" Removed

1963

R734	R26	10c vio blue & brt green	4.00	35

Documentary revenue stamps were no longer required after Dec. 31, 1967.

PROPRIETARY STAMPS

Stamps for use on proprietary articles were included in the first general issue of 1862-71. They are Nos. R3, R13, R14, R18, R22, R29, R31 and R38.

Washington — RB1

Various Frames and Sizes

Violet or Green Paper with Silk Threads

1871-74 Engr. *Perf. 12*

a. left column = Violet Paper (1871)

b. right column = Green Paper (1874)

RB1	RB1	1c green & blk	4.00	6.00
c.		Imperf.	100.00	
d.		Inverted center	*2,500.*	
RB2	RB1	2c green & blk	4.50	13.00
c.		Invtd. center, *violet*	*40,000.*	
d.		Invtd. center, *green*		8,500.
RB3	RB1	3c green & blk	12.00	35.00
c.		Sewing machine perf.	200.00	
d.		Inverted center	*15,000.*	
RB4	RB1	4c green & blk	7.00	12.50
c.		Inverted center	*22,500.*	
RB5	RB1	5c green & blk	120.00	125.00
c.		Inverted center	*80,000.*	
RB6	RB1	6c green & blk	30.00	75.00
RB7	RB1	10c green & blk ('73)	150.00	40.00
RB8	RB1	50c green & blk ('73)	500.00	900.00
RB9	RB1	$1 green & blk ('73)	*1,000.*	*3,750.*
RB10	RB1	$5 green & blk ('73)	*3,000.*	*27,500.*

Washington — RB2

Various Frames and Sizes

Green Paper

Wmk. 191R, Unwmkd. (Silk Paper)

1875-81

b. left column = Perf.

c. right column = Rouletted 6

RB11	RB2	1c green	35	55.00
a.		Silk paper	1.50	
d.		Vert. pair, imperf btwn.		*250.00*
RB12	RB2	2c brown	1.25	70.00
a.		Silk paper	2.00	
RB13	RB2	3c orange	2.25	60.00
a.		Silk paper	9.00	
d.		Horiz. pair, imperf. btwn.		—
RB14	RB2	4c red brown	4.00	
a.		Silk paper	4.50	
RB15	RB2	4c red	3.50	100.00
RB16	RB2	5c black	75.00	*1,200.*
a.		Silk paper	90.00	
RB17	RB2	6c violet blue	14.00	200.00
a.		Silk paper	20.00	
RB18	RB2	6c violet	22.50	
RB19	RB2	10c blue ('81)	250.00	

Many fraudulent roulettes exist.

Battleship — RB3

Rouletted 5 1/2

1898 Wmk. 191R Engr.

RB20	RB3	1/8c yellow green	15	15
a.		Vert. pair, imperf. horiz.	*250.00*	
RB21	RB3	1/4c brown	15	15
a.		1/4c red brown	15	15
b.		1/4c yellow brown	15	15
c.		1/4c orange brown	15	15
d.		1/4c bister	15	15
e.		Vert. pair, imperf. horiz.	—	—
f.		Printed on both sides	—	
RB22	RB3	3/8c deep orange	15	15
a.		Horiz. pair, imperf. vert.	9.00	
b.		Vert. pair, imperf. horiz.	—	
RB23	RB3	5/8c deep ultra	15	15
a.		Vert. pair, imperf. horiz.	50.00	
b.		Horiz. pair, imperf. btwn.	*250.00*	
RB24	RB3	1c dark green	50	16
a.		Vert. pair, imperf. horiz.	*250.00*	
RB25	RB3	1 1/4c violet	15	15
a.		1 1/4c brown violet	15	15
b.		Vert. pair, imperf. btwn.	*250.00*	
RB26	RB3	1 7/8c dull blue	4.50	1.00
RB27	RB3	2c vio brown	35	18
a.		Horiz. pair, imperf. vert.	25.00	
RB28	RB3	2 1/2c lake	1.50	15
a.		Vert. pair, imperf. horiz.	90.00	
RB29	RB3	3 3/4c olive gray	20.00	5.00
RB30	RB3	4c purple	4.50	75
RB31	RB3	5c brown org	4.50	75
a.		Vert. pair, imperf. horiz.	—	*275.00*
b.		Horiz. pair, imperf. vert.	—	*350.00*
		Nos. RB20-RB31 (12)	36.60	8.74

Hyphen Hole Perf. 7

RB20p		1/8c	15	15
RB21p		1/4c	15	15
g.		1/4c yellow brown	15	15
h.		1/4c orange brown	15	15
RB22p		3/8c	25	16
RB23p		5/8c	25	16
RB24p		1c	25.00	15.00
RB25p		1 1/4c	20	15
c.		1 1/4c brown violet	20	15
RB26p		1 7/8c	15.00	6.00
RB27p		2c	2.00	25
RB28p		2 1/2c	1.00	20
RB29p		3 3/4c	35.00	10.00
RB30p		4c	35.00	10.00
RB31p		5c	35.00	6.00

See note following No. R178.

RB4

RB5

Offset Printing

1914 Wmk. 190 *Perf. 10*

RB32	RB4	1/8c black	20	16
RB33	RB4	1/4c black	1.50	1.00
RB34	RB4	3/8c black	20	16
RB35	RB4	5/8c black	3.00	1.75
RB36	RB4	1 1/4c black	2.00	80
RB37	RB4	1 7/8c black	30.00	15.00
RB38	RB4	2 1/2c black	5.00	2.50
RB39	RB4	3 1/8c black	70.00	50.00
RB40	RB4	3 3/4c black	30.00	19.00
RB41	RB4	4c black	45.00	24.00
RB42	RB4	4 3/8c black	*1,100.*	—
RB43	RB4	5c black	100.00	65.00
		Nos. RB32-RB41,RB43 (11)	286.90	179.37

Wmk. 191R

RB44	RB4	1/8c black	16	15
RB45	RB4	1/4c black	16	15
RB46	RB4	3/8c black	60	30
RB47	RB4	1/2c black	3.00	2.75
RB48	RB4	5/8c black	16	15
RB49	RB4	1c black	4.25	4.00
RB50	RB4	1 1/4c black	35	25
RB51	RB4	1 1/2c black	3.00	2.25
RB52	RB4	1 7/8c black	1.00	60
RB53	RB4	2c black	5.00	4.00
RB54	RB4	2 1/2c black	1.25	1.00
RB55	RB4	3c black	3.50	2.75
RB56	RB4	3 1/8c black	4.50	3.00
RB57	RB4	3 3/4c black	10.00	7.50
RB58	RB4	4c black	30	20
RB59	RB4	4 3/8c black	12.50	7.50
RB60	RB4	5c black	2.75	2.50
RB61	RB4	6c black	50.00	37.50
RB62	RB4	8c black	15.00	11.00
RB63	RB4	10c black	10.00	7.00
RB64	RB4	20c black	20.00	15.00
		Nos. RB44-RB64 (21)	147.48	109.55

1919 *Perf. 11*

RB65	RB5	1c dark blue	15	15
RB66	RB5	2c dark blue	15	15
RB67	RB5	3c dark blue	1.00	60
RB68	RB5	4c dark blue	1.00	50
RB69	RB5	5c dark blue	1.25	60
RB70	RB5	8c dark blue	12.50	9.00
RB71	RB5	10c dark blue	4.00	2.00
RB72	RB5	20c dark blue	6.00	3.00
RB73	RB5	40c dark blue	40.00	10.00
		Nos. RB65-RB73 (9)	66.05	26.00

FUTURE DELIVERY STAMPS

Issued to facilitate the collection of a tax upon each sale, agreement of sale or agreement to sell any products or merchandise at any exchange or board of trade, or other similar place for future delivery.

FUTURE

Documentary Stamps Nos. R228 to R250 Overprinted in Black or Red

DELIVERY

Offset Printing

1918-34 Wmk. 191R *Perf. 11*

Overprint Horizontal (Lines 8mm apart)

RC1	R22	2c car rose	2.00	15
RC2	R22	3c car rose ('34)	25.00	22.50
		Cut cancellation		12.50
RC3	R22	4c car rose	3.25	15
RC3A	R22	5c car rose ('33)	50.00	5.00
RC4	R22	10c car rose	7.50	15
a.		Double overprint	—	5.00
b.		"FUTURE" omitted	—	*200.00*
c.		"DELIVERY FUTURE"		35.00
RC5	R22	20c car rose	9.00	15
a.		Double overprint		20.00
RC6	R22	25c car rose	25.00	40
		Cut cancellation		15
RC7	R22	40c car rose	27.50	75
		Cut cancellation		15
RC8	R22	50c car rose	5.00	15
a.		"DELIVERY" omitted	—	*100.00*
RC9	R22	80c car rose	50.00	9.00
		Cut cancellation		1.00
a.		Double overprint		25.00
		Cut cancellation		6.00
		Nos. RC1-RC9 (10)	204.25	38.40

Overprint Vertical, Reading Up (Lines 2mm apart)

Engr.

RC10	R21	$1 green (R)	20.00	25
		Cut cancellation		15
a.		Overprint reading down		*275.00*
b.		Black overprint		—
		Cut cancellation		125.00
RC11	R21	$2 rose	25.00	25
		Cut cancellation		15
RC12	R21	$3 violet (R)	60.00	2.00
		Cut cancellation		15
a.		Overprint reading down	—	50.00
RC13	R21	$5 dark blue (R)	40.00	35
		Cut cancellation		15
RC14	R21	$10 orange	60.00	60
		Cut cancellation		16
a.		"DELIVERY FUTURE"		*100.00*
RC15	R21	$20 olive bis	110.00	3.75
		Cut cancellation		50
		Nos. RC10-RC15 (6)	315.00	7.20

Perf. 12
Overprint Horizontal
(Lines 11 1/2mm apart)
Without Gum

RC16 R17 $30 ver, green numerals 60.00 3.00
Cut cancellation 1.25
a. Numerals in blue 55.00 3.00
Cut cancellation 1.50
b. As "a," imperf. *100.00*
RC17 R19 $50 olive green 40.00 1.00
Cut cancellation 40
a. $50 olive bister 40.00 1.00
Cut cancellation 40
RC18 R19 $60 brown 60.00 2.00
Cut cancellation 75
a. Vert. pair, imperf. horiz. *400.00*
RC19 R17 $100 yel green ('34) 70.00 25.00
Cut cancellation 6.75
RC20 R18 $500 blue, red numerals (R) 60.00 10.00
Cut cancellation 4.50
a. Numerals in orange — 50.00
Cut cancellation 11.00
RC21 R19 $1000 orange 60.00 5.00
Cut cancellation 1.50
a. Vert. pair, imperf. horiz. *500.00*
Nos. RC16-RC21 (6) 46.00

See note after No. R227.

1923-24 Offset Printing *Perf. 11*
Overprint Horiz.
(Lines 2mm apart)

RC22 R22 1c carmine rose 1.00 16
RC23 R22 80c carmine rose 55.00 1.75
Cut cancellation 25

FUTURE

Documentary Stamps of 1917 Overprinted in Red or Black

DELIVERY

1925-34 Engr.

RC25 R21 $1 green (R) 15.00 60
Cut cancellation 15
RC26 R21 $10 orange (Bk) ('34) — 15.00
Cut cancellation 10.00

Overprinted like Nos. RC1-RC9

1928-29 Offset Printing *Perf. 10*

RC27 R22 10c carmine rose *1,250.*
RC28 R22 20c carmine rose *1,250.*

STOCK TRANSFER STAMPS

Issued to facilitate the collection of a tax on all sales or agreements to sell, or memoranda of sales or delivery of, or transfers of legal title to shares or certificates of stock.

STOCK

Documentary Stamps Nos. R228 to R259 Overprinted in Black or Red

TRANSFER

Offset Printing
1918-29 Wmk. 191R *Perf. 11*
Overprint Horiz. (Lines 8mm apart)

RD1 R22 1c car rose 85 15
a. Double overprint — —
RD2 R22 2c car rose 20 15
a. Double overprint — 5.00
Cut cancellation 2.50
RD3 R22 4c car rose 20 15
a. Double overprint — 4.00
Cut cancellation 2.00
b. "STOCK" omitted 10.00
d. Overprint lines 10mm apart — —
RD4 R22 5c car rose 25 15
RD5 R22 10c car rose 25 15
a. Double overprint — 5.00
Cut cancellation 2.50
b. "STOCK" omitted — —
RD6 R22 20c car rose 50 15
a. Double overprint — 6.00
b. "STOCK" double — —
RD7 R22 25c car rose 1.50 20
Cut cancellation 15
RD8 R22 40c car rose ('22) 1.25 15
RD9 R22 50c car rose 65 15
a. Double overprint — —
RD10 R22 80c car rose 2.50 30
Cut cancellation 15
Nos. RD1-RD10 (10) 8.15
Set value 90

Overprint Vertical, Reading Up
(Lines 2mm apart)
Engr.

RD11 R21 $1 green (R) 45.00 12.50
Cut cancellation 2.00
a. Ovpt. reading down 100.00 16.00
Cut cancellation 6.00
RD12 R21 $1 green (Bk) 1.75 25
a. Pair, one without ovpt. — *150.00*
b. Ovptd. on back instead of face, inverted — *100.00*
c. Ovpt. reading down — 6.00
d. $1 yellow green 2.50 15
RD13 R21 $2 rose 1.75 15
a. Ovpt. reading down 10.00
Cut cancellation 1.50
b. Vert. pair, imperf. horiz. *500.00*
RD14 R21 $3 violet (R) 12.50 4.00
Cut cancellation 20
RD15 R21 $4 yel brn 6.00 15
Cut cancellation 15
RD16 R21 $5 dk blue (R) 4.00 15
Cut cancellation 15
a. Ovpt. reading down 20.00 1.00
Cut cancellation 16
RD17 R21 $10 orange 12.50 30
Cut cancellation 15
RD18 R21 $20 ol bis ('21) 65.00 18.00
Cut cancellation 3.00
Nos. RD11-RD18 (8) 148.50 35.50

1918 Without Gum *Perf. 12*
Overprint Horizontal (Lines 11 1/2mm apart)

RD19 R17 $30 ver, green numerals 15.00 4.00
Cut cancellation 1.00
a. Numerals in blue 50.00
RD20 R19 $50 olive green, *(Cleveland)* 90.00 50.00
Cut cancellation 17.00
RD21 R19 $60 brown 100.00 17.50
Cut cancellation 8.50
RD22 R17 $100 green 20.00 5.00
Cut cancellation 2.00
RD23 R18 $500 blue (R) 275.00 100.00
Cut cancellation 60.00
a. Numerals in orange 125.00
RD24 R19 $1000 orange 150.00 65.00
Cut cancellation 22.50

See note after No. R227.

1928-32 Offset Printing *Perf. 10*
Overprint Horiz. (Lines 8mm apart)

RD25 R22 2c carmine rose 2.00 25
RD26 R22 4c carmine rose 2.00 25
RD27 R22 10c carmine rose 2.00 25
a. Inverted overprint *1,000.*
RD28 R22 20c carmine rose 2.50 25
RD29 R22 50c carmine rose 3.00 25

Overprint Vertical, Reading Up (Lines 2mm apart)
Engr.

RD30 R21 $1 green 20.00 20
a. $1 yellow green — —
RD31 R21 $2 car rose 20.00 15
a. Pair, one without overprint *150.00 170.00*
RD32 R21 $10 orange 20.00 35
Cut cancellation 15
Nos. RD25-RD32 (8) 71.50

STOCK

Overprinted Horiz. in Black

TRANSFER

1920-28 Offset Printing *Perf. 11*

RD33 R22 2c carmine rose 5.00 60
RD34 R22 10c carmine rose 1.00 30
b. Inverted overprint *1,500.*
RD35 R22 20c carmine rose 75 20
d. Inverted overprint (perf. initials) —

RD36 R22 50c carmine rose 2.50 20

Engr.

RD37 R21 $1 green 27.50 7.50
Cut cancellation 25
RD38 R21 $2 rose 25.00 7.50
Cut cancellation 25
Nos. RD33-RD38 (6) 61.75 16.30

Shifted overprints on the 10c, 20c and 50c result in "TRANSFER STOCK," "TRANSFER" omitted, "STOCK" omitted, pairs, one without overprint and other varieties.

Perf. 10
Offset Printing

RD39 R22 2c carmine rose 4.00 50
RD40 R22 10c carmine rose 1.00 50
RD41 R22 20c carmine rose 1.75 25

Used values for Nos. RD42-RD372 are for copies which are neither cut nor perforated with initials. Copies with cut cancellations or perforated initials are valued in Scott's U.S. Specialized Catalogue.

SERIES 1940

Documentary Stamps of 1917-33 Overprinted in Black

STOCK
TRANSFER

1940 *Perf. 11*

RD42 R22 1c rose pink 2.50 45
a. "Series 1940" inverted — 225.00
RD43 R22 2c rose pink 2.00 50
RD45 R22 4c rose pink 2.00 20
RD46 R22 5c rose pink 2.50 20
RD48 R22 10c rose pink 2.25 20
RD49 R22 20c rose pink 6.00 20
RD50 R22 25c rose pink 6.00 60
RD51 R22 40c rose pink 3.50 75
RD52 R22 50c rose pink 4.00 25
RD53 R22 80c rose pink 70.00 40.00
Nos. RD42-RD53 (10) 100.75 43.35

Engr.

RD54 R21 $1 green 15.00 35
RD55 R21 $2 rose 15.00 60
RD56 R21 $3 violet 100.00 9.00
RD57 R21 $4 yel brown 25.00 1.00
RD58 R21 $5 dark blue 30.00 90
RD59 R21 $10 orange 75.00 6.00
RD60 R21 $20 olive bister 200.00 60.00
Nos. RD54-RD60 (7) 69.25

Stock Transfer Stamps of 1918 Handstamped in Blue "Series 1940"

1940 Without Gum *Perf. 12*

RD61 R17 $30 vermilion 425.00
RD62 R19 $50 olive green 650.00
a. Dbl. ovpt. (perf. initials canc.) *350.00*
RD63 R19 $60 brown 900.00
RD64 R17 $100 green 500.00
RD65 R18 $500 blue 1,750.
RD66 R19 $1000 orange 2,000.

Alexander Hamilton
ST1

Levi Woodbury
ST2

Thomas Corwin — ST3

Portraits (see R23-R25): 2c, Wolcott. 4c, Gallatin. 5c, Campbell. 10c, Crawford. 20c, Rush. 25c, Ingham. 40c, McLane. 50c, Duane. 80c, Taney. $2, Ewing. $3, Forward. $4, Spencer. $5, Bibb. $10, Walker. $20, Meredith. $50, Guthrie. $60, Cobb. $100, Thomas. $500, Dix. $1,000, Chase.

SERIES 1940

Overprinted in Black

1940 Wmk. 191R *Perf. 11*
Various Portraits
Size: 19x22mm

RD67 ST1 1c brt green 6.50 2.50
RD68 ST1 2c brt green 3.75 1.25
RD70 ST1 4c brt green 7.00 3.50
RD71 ST1 5c brt green 4.00 1.25
a. Without overprint (cut canc.) *250.00*
RD73 ST1 10c brt green 6.00 1.50
RD74 ST1 20c brt green 7.50 1.75
RD75 ST1 25c brt green 20.00 7.00
RD76 ST1 40c brt green 40.00 27.50
RD77 ST1 50c brt green 6.00 1.50
RD78 ST1 80c brt green 55.00 40.00
Nos. RD67-RD78 (10) 155.75 87.75

Size: 21 1/2x36 1/4mm

RD79 ST2 $1 brt green 20.00 3.00
a. Without overprint (perf. initials canc.) *225.00*
RD80 ST2 $2 brt green 25.00 6.00
RD81 ST2 $3 brt green 40.00 8.00
RD82 ST2 $4 brt green 200.00 175.00
RD83 ST2 $5 brt green 40.00 10.00
RD84 ST2 $10 brt green 100.00 30.00
RD85 ST2 $20 brt green 350.00 50.00

Perf. 12
Without Gum
Size: 28 1/2x42mm
Various Frame Designs

RD86 ST3 $30 brt green — 110.00
RD87 ST3 $50 brt green 275.00 165.00
RD88 ST3 $60 brt green — 250.00
RD89 ST3 $100 brt green — 150.00
RD90 ST3 $500 brt green — 750.00
RD91 ST3 $1000 brt green — 650.00

Overprinted in Black "Series 1941" SERIES 1941

1941 Size: 19x22mm *Perf. 11*

RD92 ST1 1c brt green 65 50
RD93 ST1 2c brt green 45 25
RD95 ST1 4c brt green 40 20
RD96 ST1 5c brt green 35 15
RD98 ST1 10c brt green 60 15
RD99 ST1 20c brt green 1.50 25
RD100 ST1 25c brt green 1.50 40
RD101 ST1 40c brt green 2.00 75
RD102 ST1 50c brt green 3.00 35
RD103 ST1 80c brt green 15.00 6.00
Nos. RD92-RD103 (10) 25.45 9.00

Size: 21 1/2x36 1/4mm

RD104 ST2 $1 brt green 8.00 20
RD105 ST2 $2 brt green 9.00 25
RD106 ST2 $3 brt green 15.00 1.50
RD107 ST2 $4 brt green 25.00 6.00
RD108 ST2 $5 brt green 27.50 60
RD109 ST2 $10 brt green 60.00 3.75
RD110 ST2 $20 brt green 110.00 45.00
Nos. RD104-RD110 (7) 254.50 57.30

Perf. 12
Without Gum
Size: 28 1/2x42mm

RD111 ST3 $30 brt green 125.00 100.00
RD112 ST3 $50 brt green 200.00 120.00
RD113 ST3 $60 brt green 400.00 150.00
RD114 ST3 $100 brt green — 60.00
RD115 ST3 $500 brt green 800.00 575.00
RD116 ST3 $1000 brt green — 700.00

Overprinted in Black "Series 1942"

1942 Size: 19x22mm *Perf. 11*

RD117 ST1 1c brt green 50 30
RD118 ST1 2c brt green 40 35
RD119 ST1 4c brt green 3.00 1.00
RD120 ST1 5c brt green 40 15
a. Ovpt. inverted (cut cancel) *225.00*
RD121 ST1 10c brt green 1.50 15
RD122 ST1 20c brt green 1.75 15
RD123 ST1 25c brt green 1.75 15
RD124 ST1 40c brt green 3.25 35
RD125 ST1 50c brt green 4.00 20
RD126 ST1 80c brt green 12.50 5.00
Nos. RD117-RD126 (10) 29.05 7.80

Size: 21 1/2x36 1/4mm

RD127 ST2 $1 brt green 9.00 35
RD128 ST2 $2 brt green 12.50 35
RD129 ST2 $3 brt green 17.50 1.00
RD130 ST2 $4 brt green 27.50 17.50
RD131 ST2 $5 brt green 20.00 35
a. Double overprint (perf. initials cancel) —
RD132 ST2 $10 brt green 47.50 6.00
RD133 ST2 $20 brt green 110.00 27.50
Nos. RD127-RD133 (7) 244.00 53.05

Perf. 12
Without Gum
Size: 28 1/2x42mm

RD134 ST3 $30 brt green 80.00 40.00
RD135 ST3 $50 brt green 130.00 80.00
RD136 ST3 $60 brt green — 100.00
RD137 ST3 $100 brt green — 70.00
RD138 ST3 $500 brt green — —
RD139 ST3 $1000 brt green — 350.00

Overprinted in Black "Series 1943"

1943 Size: 19x22mm *Perf. 11*

RD140 ST1 1c brt green 40 25
RD141 ST1 2c brt green 50 40
RD142 ST1 4c brt green 1.75 20
RD143 ST1 5c brt green 50 15
RD144 ST1 10c brt green 75 15
RD145 ST1 20c brt green 1.50 15
RD146 ST1 25c brt green 3.00 25
RD147 ST1 40c brt green 3.00 25
RD148 ST1 50c brt green 3.00 20
RD149 ST1 80c brt green 10.00 4.00
Nos. RD140-RD149 (10) 24.40 6.00

Size: 21 1/2x36 1/4mm

RD150 ST2 $1 brt green 8.00 15
RD151 ST2 $2 brt green 10.00 35
RD152 ST2 $3 brt green 12.50 1.00
RD153 ST2 $4 brt green 25.00 14.00
RD154 ST2 $5 brt green 40.00 35
RD155 ST2 $10 brt green 50.00 4.00
RD156 ST2 $20 brt green 90.00 30.00
Nos. RD150-RD156 (7) 235.50 49.85

Perf. 12
Without Gum
Size: 28 1/2x42mm

RD157	ST3	$30 brt green	175.00	90.00
RD158	ST3	$50 brt green	250.00	100.00
RD159	ST3	$60 brt green	—	250.00
RD160	ST3	$100 brt green	—	45.00
RD161	ST3	$500 brt green	—	350.00
RD162	ST3	$1000 brt green	—	225.00

Overprinted in Black "Series 1944"

Portraits: $2,500, William Windom. $5,000, C. J. Folger. $10,000, Walter Q. Gresham.

1944 Wmk. 191R *Perf. 11*
Size: 19x22mm

RD163	ST1	1c brt green	65	60
RD164	ST1	2c brt green	45	20
RD165	ST1	4c brt green	60	25
RD166	ST1	5c brt green	50	15
RD167	ST1	10c brt green	50	15
RD168	ST1	20c brt green	1.00	20
RD169	ST1	25c brt green	1.75	30
RD170	ST1	40c brt green	7.00	5.00
RD171	ST1	50c brt green	3.75	20
RD172	ST1	80c brt green	5.50	4.50
		Nos. RD163-RD172 (10)	21.70	11.55

Size: 21 1/2x36 1/4mm

RD173	ST2	$1 brt green	5.50	40
RD174	ST2	$2 brt green	20.00	60
RD175	ST2	$3 brt green	15.00	1.25
RD176	ST2	$4 brt green	20.00	5.00
RD177	ST2	$5 brt green	17.50	90
RD178	ST2	$10 brt green	40.00	4.50
RD179	ST2	$20 brt green	85.00	7.00
		Nos. RD173-RD179 (7)	203.00	19.65

Perf. 12
Without Gum
Size: 28 1/2x42mm
Bright Green

RD180	ST3	$30	100.00	50.00
RD181	ST3	$50	75.00	45.00
RD182	ST3	$60	140.00	90.00
RD183	ST3	$100	—	45.00
RD184	ST3	$500	—	400.00
RD185	ST3	$1000 (cut canc.)	—	225.00
RD185A	ST3	$2500	—	—
RD185B	ST3	$5000	—	—
RD185C	ST3	$10,000	—	—
		(cut cancel)		*1,250.*

Overprinted in Black "Series 1945"

1945 Wmk. 191R *Perf. 11*
Size: 19x22mm

RD186	ST1	1c brt green	15	15
RD187	ST1	2c brt green	25	20
RD188	ST1	4c brt green	25	20
RD189	ST1	5c brt green	25	15
RD190	ST1	10c brt green	50	35
RD191	ST1	20c brt green	1.00	30
RD192	ST1	25c brt green	1.50	35
RD193	ST1	40c brt green	2.25	20
RD194	ST1	50c brt green	2.75	25
RD195	ST1	80c brt green	4.50	2.50
		Nos. RD186-RD195 (10)	13.40	4.65

Size: 21 1/2x36 1/4mm

RD196	ST2	$1 brt green	10.00	25
RD197	ST2	$2 brt green	12.50	45
RD198	ST2	$3 brt green	20.00	60
RD199	ST2	$4 brt green	20.00	2.50
RD200	ST2	$5 brt green	15.00	50
RD201	ST2	$10 brt green	35.00	6.00
RD202	ST2	$20 brt green	55.00	7.50

Perf. 12
Without Gum
Size: 28 1/2x42mm
Bright green

RD203	ST3	$30	60.00	40.00
RD204	ST3	$50	40.00	16.00
RD205	ST3	$60	150.00	100.00
RD206	ST3	$100	—	22.50
RD207	ST3	$500	—	375.00
RD208	ST3	$1000	—	450.00
RD208A	ST3	$2500	—	—
RD208B	ST3	$5000	—	—
RD208C	ST3	$10,000 cut canc.	—	*1,500.*

Overprinted in Black "Series 1946"

1946 Wmk. 191R *Perf. 11*
Size: 19x22mm

RD209	ST1	1c brt green	20	15
a.		Pair, one dated "1945"	*475.00*	
RD210	ST1	2c brt green	35	15
RD211	ST1	4c brt green	30	15
RD212	ST1	5c brt green	35	15
RD213	ST1	10c brt green	50	15
RD214	ST1	20c brt green	1.25	20
RD215	ST1	25c brt green	1.10	25
RD216	ST1	40c brt green	2.50	60
RD217	ST1	50c brt green	3.00	20
RD218	ST1	80c brt green	6.00	5.00
		Nos. RD209-RD218 (10)	15.55	7.00

Size: 21 1/2x36 1/4mm

RD219	ST2	$1 brt green	5.00	50
RD220	ST2	$2 brt green	6.00	50
RD221	ST2	$3 brt green	11.00	1.25
RD222	ST2	$4 brt green	12.50	5.00
RD223	ST2	$5 brt green	17.50	1.00
RD224	ST2	$10 brt green	40.00	2.50
RD225	ST2	$20 brt green	60.00	30.00
		Nos. RD219-RD225 (7)	152.00	40.75

Perf. 12
Without Gum
Size: 28 1/2x42mm

RD226	ST3	$30 brt grn	65.00	25.00
RD227	ST3	$50 brt grn	50.00	30.00
RD228	ST3	$60 brt grn	110.00	75.00
RD229	ST3	$100 brt grn	70.00	30.00
RD230	ST3	$500 brt grn	—	150.00
RD231	ST3	$1000 brt grn	—	125.00
RD232	ST3	$2500 brt grn	—	—
RD233	ST3	$5000 brt grn	—	—
RD234	ST3	$10,000 brt grn	—	—
		(cut cancel)		*2,000.*

Overprinted in Black "Series 1947"

1947 Wmk. 191R *Perf. 11*
Size: 19x22mm

RD235	ST1	1c brt green	65	55
RD236	ST1	2c brt green	60	50
RD237	ST1	4c brt green	50	40
RD238	ST1	5c brt green	45	35
RD239	ST1	10c brt green	60	50
RD240	ST1	20c brt green	90	50
RD241	ST1	25c brt green	1.25	50
RD242	ST1	40c brt green	1.75	75
RD243	ST1	50c brt green	2.50	30
RD244	ST1	80c brt green	10.00	8.00
		Nos. RD235-RD244 (10)	19.20	12.35

Size: 21 1/2x36 1/4mm

RD245	ST2	$1 brt green	5.00	50
RD246	ST2	$2 brt green	8.50	75
RD247	ST2	$3 brt green	14.00	1.50
RD248	ST2	$4 brt green	22.50	6.00
RD249	ST2	$5 brt green	17.50	1.50
RD250	ST2	$10 brt green	35.00	5.00
RD251	ST2	$20 brt green	65.00	25.00
		Nos. RD245-RD251 (7)	167.50	40.25

Perf. 12
Without Gum
Size: 28 1/2x42mm

RD252	ST3	$30 brt grn	55.00	30.00
RD253	ST3	$50 brt grn	110.00	75.00
RD254	ST3	$60 brt grn	135.00	100.00
RD255	ST3	$100 brt grn	—	25.00
RD256	ST3	$500 brt grn	—	225.00
RD257	ST3	$1000 brt grn	—	75.00
RD258	ST3	$2500 brt grn (cut canc.)	—	*275.00*
RD259	ST3	$5000 brt grn (cut canc.)	—	*275.00*
RD260	ST3	$10,000 brt grn (cut canc.)	—	50.00
a.		Horiz. pair, imperf. vert. (cut canc.)		—

Overprinted in Black "Series 1948"

1948 Wmk. 191R *Perf. 11*
Size: 19x22mm

RD261	ST1	1c brt green	25	25
RD262	ST1	2c brt green	25	25
RD263	ST1	4c brt green	30	30
RD264	ST1	5c brt green	25	24
RD265	ST1	10c brt green	30	25
RD266	ST1	20c brt green	1.10	35
RD267	ST1	25c brt green	1.10	40
RD268	ST1	40c brt green	1.50	75
RD269	ST1	50c brt green	3.00	30
RD270	ST1	80c brt green	9.00	6.00
		Nos. RD261-RD270 (10)	17.05	9.09

Size: 21 1/2x36 1/4mm

RD271	ST2	$1 brt green	6.00	40
RD272	ST2	$2 brt green	9.00	60
RD273	ST2	$3 brt green	11.00	3.75
RD274	ST2	$4 brt green	14.00	9.00
RD275	ST2	$5 brt green	20.00	2.50
RD276	ST2	$10 brt green	35.00	4.50
RD277	ST2	$20 brt green	65.00	18.00
		Nos. RD271-RD277 (7)	160.00	38.75

Perf. 12
Without Gum
Size: 28 1/2x42mm

RD278	ST3	$30 brt grn	55.00	35.00
RD279	ST3	$50 brt grn	45.00	35.00
RD280	ST3	$60 brt grn	100.00	80.00
RD281	ST3	$100 brt grn	—	15.00
RD282	ST3	$500 brt grn	—	190.00
RD283	ST3	$1000 brt grn	—	90.00
RD284	ST3	$2500 brt grn	275.00	250.00
RD285	ST3	$5000 brt grn	—	250.00
RD286	ST3	$10,000 brt grn (cut canc.)	—	50.00

Overprinted in Black "Series 1949"

1949 Wmk. 191R *Perf. 11*
Size: 19x22mm

RD287	ST1	1c brt green	48	42
RD288	ST1	2c brt green	48	42
RD289	ST1	4c brt green	60	48
RD290	ST1	5c brt green	60	48
RD291	ST1	10c brt green	1.10	60
RD292	ST1	20c brt green	1.75	48
RD293	ST1	25c brt green	2.40	85
RD294	ST1	40c brt green	4.75	1.50
RD295	ST1	50c brt green	3.50	25
RD296	ST1	80c brt green	11.00	6.50
		Nos. RD287-RD296 (10)	26.66	11.98

Size: 21 1/2x36 1/4mm

RD297	ST2	$1 brt green	7.50	65
RD298	ST2	$2 brt green	10.00	90
RD299	ST2	$3 brt green	22.50	4.50
RD300	ST2	$4 brt green	20.00	7.50
RD301	ST2	$5 brt green	30.00	2.00
RD302	ST2	$10 brt green	40.00	4.00
RD303	ST2	$20 brt green	90.00	15.00
		Nos. RD297-RD303 (7)	220.00	34.55

Perf. 12
Without Gum
Size: 28 1/2x42mm

RD304	ST3	$30 brt grn	—	35.00
RD305	ST3	$50 brt grn	125.00	50.00
RD306	ST3	$60 brt grn	150.00	125.00
RD307	ST3	$100 brt grn	—	50.00
RD308	ST3	$500 brt grn	—	200.00
RD309	ST3	$1000 brt grn	—	80.00
RD310	ST3	$2500 brt grn (cut canc.)	—	*325.00*
RD311	ST3	$5000 brt grn (cut canc.)	—	*275.00*
RD312	ST3	$10,000 brt grn (cut canc.)	—	25.00
a.		Pair, one without ovpt. (cut cancel)		—

Overprinted in Black "Series 1950"

1950 Wmk. 191R *Perf. 11*
Size: 19x22mm

RD313	ST1	1c brt green	40	35
RD314	ST1	2c brt green	40	30
RD315	ST1	4c brt green	40	35
RD316	ST1	5c brt green	40	20
RD317	ST1	10c brt green	1.75	30
RD318	ST1	20c brt green	2.00	50
RD319	ST1	25c brt green	3.00	60
RD320	ST1	40c brt green	3.50	90
RD321	ST1	50c brt green	5.50	35
RD322	ST1	80c brt green	7.00	5.00
		Nos. RD313-RD322 (10)	24.35	8.85

Size: 21 1/2x36 1/4mm

RD323	ST2	$1 brt green	7.00	40
RD324	ST2	$2 brt green	12.50	75
RD325	ST2	$3 brt green	20.00	4.00
RD326	ST2	$4 brt green	27.50	7.50
RD327	ST2	$5 brt green	25.00	1.75
RD328	ST2	$10 brt green	60.00	5.00
RD329	ST2	$20 brt green	75.00	20.00
		Nos. RD323-RD329 (7)	227.00	39.40

Perf. 12
Without Gum
Size: 28 1/2x42mm

RD330	ST3	$30 brt grn	75.00	40.00
RD331	ST3	$50 brt grn	70.00	65.00
RD332	ST3	$60 brt grn	—	100.00
RD333	ST3	$100 brt grn	—	35.00
RD334	ST3	$500 brt grn	—	150.00
RD335	ST3	$1000 brt grn	—	75.00
RD336	ST3	$2500 brt grn	—	900.00
RD337	ST3	$5000 brt grn	—	500.00
RD338	ST3	$10,000 brt grn (cut canc.)	—	50.00

Overprinted in Black "Series 1951"

1951 Wmk. 191R *Perf. 11*
Size: 19x22mm

RD339	ST1	1c brt green	75	35
RD340	ST1	2c brt green	75	30
RD341	ST1	4c brt green	1.00	50
RD342	ST1	5c brt green	80	35
RD343	ST1	10c brt green	1.00	30
RD344	ST1	20c brt green	2.75	90
RD345	ST1	25c brt green	3.00	90
RD346	ST1	40c brt green	10.00	8.00
RD347	ST1	50c brt green	5.50	90
RD348	ST1	80c brt green	12.00	10.00
		Nos. RD339-RD348 (10)	37.55	22.50

Size: 21 1/2x36 1/4mm

RD349	ST2	$1 brt green	12.50	80
RD350	ST2	$2 brt green	17.50	1.25
RD351	ST2	$3 brt green	25.00	10.00
RD352	ST2	$4 brt green	30.00	12.00
RD353	ST2	$5 brt green	37.50	2.50
RD354	ST2	$10 brt green	65.00	8.50
RD355	ST2	$20 brt green	100.00	15.00
		Nos. RD349-RD355 (7)	287.50	50.05

Perf. 12
Without Gum
Size: 28 1/2x42mm

RD356	ST3	$30 brt grn	—	40.00
RD357	ST3	$50 brt grn	—	45.00
RD358	ST3	$60 brt grn	—	*400.00*
RD359	ST3	$100 brt grn	—	45.00
RD360	ST3	$500 brt grn	—	125.00
RD361	ST3	$1000 brt grn	—	70.00
RD362	ST3	$2500 brt grn	—	*850.00*
RD363	ST3	$5000 brt grn	—	*850.00*
RD364	ST3	$10,000 brt grn	—	100.00

Overprinted in Black "Series 1952"

1952 Wmk. 191R *Perf. 11*
Size: 19x22mm

RD365	ST1	1c brt green	25.00	12.00
RD366	ST1	10c brt green	25.00	11.00
RD367	ST1	20c brt green	300.00	—
RD368	ST1	25c brt green	400.00	—
RD369	ST1	40c brt green	60.00	15.00

Size: 21 1/2x36 1/4mm

RD370	ST2	$4 brt green	650.	350.
RD371	ST2	$10 brt green	1,800.	—
RD372	ST2	$20 brt green	2,500.	—

Stock Transfer stamps were discontinued in 1952.

See the Scott United States Specialized Catalogue for other categories of Revenue stamps.

HUNTING PERMIT STAMPS

The receipts of the sales of these "Migratory Bird Hunting" stamps help to maintain waterfowl life in the United States.

Catalogue values for unused stamps in this section are for Never Hinged items. Unused stamps with part or no gum sell for substantially less than the unused never hinged values.

Department of Agriculture

Various Designs
Inscribed "U. S. Department of Agriculture"

Engraved; Flat Plate Printing

1934 Unwmk. *Perf. 11*
"Void after June 30, 1935"

RW1	HP1	$1 blue	475.00	90.00
a.		Imperf., pair		—
b.		Vert. pair, imperf. horiz.		—

Used copies are unsigned.

1935 "Void after June 30, 1936"
RW2 $1 *Canvasback Ducks Taking to Flight* 425.00 110.00

1936 "Void after June 30, 1937"
RW3 $1 *Canada Geese in Flight* 225.00 55.00

1937 "Void after June 30, 1938"
RW4 $1 *Scaup Ducks Taking to Flight* 190.00 35.00

1938 "Void after June 30, 1939"
RW5 $1 *Pintail Drake and Duck Alighting* 190.00 35.00

Department of the Interior

Green-Winged Teal — HP2

Various Designs
Inscribed: "U. S. Department of the Interior"

1939 "Void after June 30, 1940"
RW6 HP2 $1 chocolate 125.00 25.00

1940 "Void after June 30, 1941"
RW7 $1 *Black Mallards* 125.00 25.00

1941 "Void after June 30, 1942"
RW8 $1 *Family of Ruddy Ducks* 125.00 25.00

1942 "Void after June 30, 1943"
RW9 $1 *Baldpates* 125.00 25.00

1943 "Void after June 30, 1944"
RW10 $1 *Wood Ducks* 55.00 20.00

1944 "Void after June 30, 1945"
RW11 $1 *White-fronted Geese* 50.00 20.00

1945 "Void after June 30, 1946"
RW12 $1 *Shoveller Ducks in Flight* 37.50 15.00

1946 "Void after June 30, 1947"
RW13 $1 *Redhead Ducks* 32.50 10.00
a. $1 bright rose pink

Some specialists believe No. RW13a to be a color changeling.

1947 "Void after June 30, 1948"
RW14 $1 *Snow Geese* 32.50 10.00

1948 "Void after June 30, 1949"
RW15 $1 *Bufflehead Ducks in Flight* 35.00 10.00

Goldeneye Ducks HP3

1949 "Void after June 30, 1950"
RW16 HP3 $2 bright green 45.00 8.00

1950 "Void after June 30, 1951"
RW17 $2 *Trumpeter Swans in Flight* 47.50 8.00

1951 "Void after June 30, 1952"
RW18 $2 *Gadwall Ducks* 47.50 5.00

1952 "Void after June 30, 1953"
RW19 $2 *Harlequin Ducks* 50.00 5.00

1953 "Void after June 30, 1954"
RW20 $2 *Blue-winged Teal* 50.00 5.00

1954 "Void after June 30, 1955"
RW21 $2 *Ring-necked Ducks* 50.00 5.00

1955 "Void after June 30, 1956"
RW22 $2 *Blue Geese* 50.00 5.00

1956 "Void after June 30, 1957"
RW23 $2 *American Merganser* 50.00 5.00

1957 "Void after June 30, 1958"
RW24 $2 *American Eider* 50.00 5.00

1958 "Void after June 30, 1959"
RW25 $2 *Canada Geese* 50.00 5.00

Labrador Retriever Carrying Mallard Drake HP4

1959 Giori Press Printing
"Void after June 30, 1960"
RW26 HP4 $3 blue, ocher & blk 80.00 5.00

Redhead Ducks HP5

1960 "Void after June 30, 1961"
RW27 HP5 $3 red brn, dk bl & bister 65.00 5.00

1961 "Void after June 30, 1962"
RW28 $3 *Mallard Hen and Ducklings* 70.00 5.00

Pintail Drakes Coming in for Landing HP6

1962 "Void after June 30, 1963"
RW29 HP6 $3 dk bl, dk red brn & black 80.00 6.00

1963 "Void after June 30, 1964"
RW30 $3 *Pair of Brant landing* 80.00 6.00

1964 "Void after June 30, 1965"
RW31 $3 *Hawaiian Nene Geese* 80.00 6.00

1965 "Void after June 30, 1966"
RW32 $3 *3 Canvasback Drakes* 75.00 6.00

Whistling Swans HP7

1966 "Void after June 30, 1967"
RW33 HP7 $3 ultra, sl grn & blk 75.00 6.00

1967 "Void after June 30, 1968"
RW34 $3 *Old Squaw Ducks* 75.00 6.00

1968 "Void after June 30, 1969"
RW35 $3 *Hooded Mergansers* 55.00 6.00

White-winged Scoters — HP8

1969 "Void after June 30, 1970"
RW36 HP8 $3 gray, brn, indigo & brn red 55.00 5.00

1970 Litho. & Engr.
"Void after June 30, 1971"
RW37 $3 *Ross' Geese* 50.00 5.00

1971 "Void after June 30, 1972"
RW38 $3 *3 Cinnamon Teal* 35.00 5.00

1972 "Void after June 30, 1973"
RW39 $5 *Emperor Geese* 20.00 5.00

1973 "Void after June 30, 1974"
RW40 $5 *Steller's Eiders* 17.00 5.00

1974 "Void after June 30, 1975"
RW41 $5 *Wood Ducks* 16.00 5.00

1975 "Void after June 30, 1976"
RW42 $5 *Weathered canvasback duck decoy and flying ducks* 12.50 5.00

1976 Engr.
"Void after June 30, 1977"
RW43 $5 *Family of Canada Geese* 10.00 5.00

1977 Engr. & Litho.
"Void after June 30, 1978"
RW44 $5 *Ross' Geese, pair* 11.00 5.00

Hooded Merganser HP9

1978 **"Void after June 30, 1979"**
RW45 HP9 $5 multicolored 10.00 5.00

1979 **"Void after June 30, 1980"**
RW46 $7.50 *Green-winged teal* 12.00 5.00

1980 **"Void after June 30, 1981"**
RW47 $7.50 *Mallards* 12.00 5.00

1981 **"Void after June 30, 1982"**
RW48 $7.50 *Ruddy Ducks* 12.00 5.00

1982 **"Void after June 30, 1983"**
RW49 $7.50 *Canvasbacks* 12.00 5.00

1983 **"Void after June 30, 1984"**
RW50 $7.50 *Pintails* 12.00 5.00

1984 **"Void after June 30, 1985"**
RW51 $7.50 *Widgeons* 12.00 5.00

1985 **"Void after June 30, 1986"**
RW52 $7.50 *Cinnamon Teal* 12.00 5.00

1986 **"Void after June 30, 1987"**
RW53 $7.50 *Fulvous Whistling Duck* 10.00 5.00
a. Black omitted *3,250.*

1987 ***Perf. 11½x11***
"Void after June 30, 1988"
RW54 $10 *Redheads* 14.00 7.50

1988 **"Void after June 30, 1989"**
RW55 $10 *Snow Goose* 14.00 7.50

1989 **"Void after June 30, 1990"**
RW56 $12.50 *Lesser Scaups* 17.50 7.50

1990 **"Void after June 30, 1991"**
RW57 $12.50 *Black Bellied Whistling Duck* 17.50 7.50
a. Back printing omitted *850.00*

The back printing is on top of the gum so beware of copies with gum removed. Used examples of No. RW57a cannot exist.

King Eiders HP10

1991 **"Void after June 30, 1992"**
RW58 HP10 $15 multicolored 20.00 7.50
a. Black (engr.) omitted —

1992 **"Void after June 30, 1993"**
RW59 $15 *Spectacled Eider* 20.00 7.50

1993 **"Void after June 30, 1994"**
RW60 $15 *Canvasbacks* 20.00 7.50
a. Black (engr.) omitted —

1994 ***Perf. 11.2x11.1***
RW61 $15 *Red-breasted mergansers* 20.00 —

CONFEDERATE STATES

PROVISIONAL ISSUES

These stamps and envelopes were issued by individual postmasters generally during the interim between June 1, 1861, when the use of U.S. stamps stopped in the Confederacy, and Oct. 16, 1861, when the 1st Confederate Government stamps were issued. They were occasionally issued at later periods, especially in Texas, when regular issues of Government stamps were unavailable.

Canceling stamps of the post offices were often used to produce envelopes, some of which were supplied in advance by private citizens. These envelopes and other stationery therefore may be found in a wide variety of papers, colors, sizes and shapes, including patriotic and semi-official types. It is often difficult to determine whether the impression made by the canceling stamp indicates provisional usage or merely postage paid at the time the letter was deposited in the post office. Occasionally the same mark was used for both purposes.

The *press-printed* provisional envelopes are in a different category. They were produced in quantity, using envelopes procured in advance by the postmaster, such as those of Charleston, Lynchburg, Memphis, etc. *The press-printed envelopes are listed and valued on all known papers.*

The handstamped provisional envelopes are listed and valued according to type and variety of handstamp, but not according to paper. Many exist on such a variety of papers that they defy accurate, complete listing. The value of a handstamped provisional envelope is determined *primarily* by the clarity of the markings and its overall condition and attractiveness, rather than the type of paper. *All handstamped provisional envelopes, when used, should also show the postmark of the town of issue.*

Most handstamps are impressed at top right, although they exist from some towns in other positions.

Illustrations in this section are reduced in size.

XU numbers are envelope entires.

E1

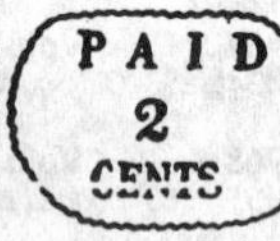

E1a

Aberdeen, Miss.

Handstamped
1XU1 E1 5c black *2,500.*
1XU2 E1 10c (ms.) on 5c black —

Abingdon, Va.

Handstamped
2XU1 E1a 2c black *11,000.*
2XU2 E1a 5c black 1,100.
2XU3 E1a 10c black — *3,500.*

No. 2XU1 is unique.

Albany, Ga.

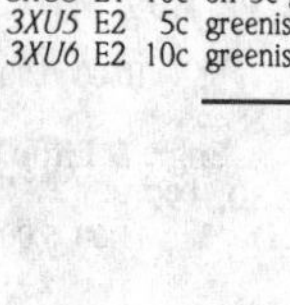

E1

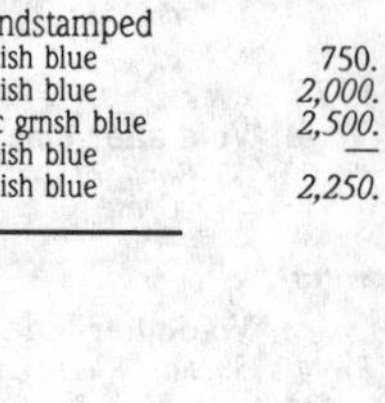

E2

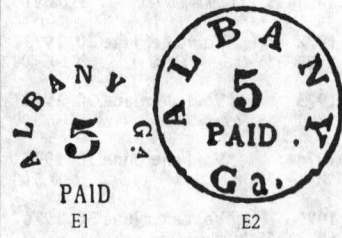

Handstamped
3XU1 E1 5c greenish blue 750.
3XU2 E1 10c greenish blue *2,000.*
3XU3 E1 10c on 5c grnsh blue *2,500.*
3XU5 E2 5c greenish blue —
3XU6 E2 10c greenish blue *2,250.*

E1

Two varieties — A1

Anderson Court House, S.C.

Handstamped
4XU1 E1 5c black 1,500.
4XU2 E1 10c (ms.) black *2,500.*

Athens, Ga.

Typo.
5X1 A1 5c purple (shades) 750. 800.
a. Vertical tete beche pair *4,000.*
5X2 A1 5c red — 3,000.

Atlanta, Ga.

E1

E2

E3

Handstamped
6XU1 E1 5c red 3,500.
6XU2 E1 5c black 150. 550.
6XU3 E1 10c on 5c black 1,500.
6XU4 E2 2c black *2,500.*
6XU5 E2 5c black 700.
6XU6 E2 10c black 650.
6XU7 E2 10c on 5c black 2,500.
6XU8 E3 5c black 3,500.
6XU9 E3 10c black ("10" upright) 2,750.

Augusta, Ga.

E1

Handstamped
7XU1 E1 5c black

Provisional status questioned.

E1

E1a

Austin, Miss.

Typo.
8XU1 E1 5c red, *amber* *20,000.*

No. 8XU1 is unique.

Austin, Texas

Handstamped
9XU1 E1a 10c black 1,500.

Autaugaville, Ala.

E1

E2

Handstamped
10XU1 E1 5c black *8,000.*
10XU2 E2 5c black *11,000.*

Baton Rouge, La.

A1

A2

A3

A4

Typeset
Ten varieties each of A1, A2 and A3
11X1 A1 2c green *5,000.* *3,500.*
a. "McCcrmick" *8,000.* *7,500.*
11X2 A2 5c green & car 1,100. 700.
a. "McCcrmick" — *2,000.*
11X3 A3 5c green & car *3,000.* *1,750.*
a. "McCcrmick" *3,250.*
11X4 A4 10c blue *6,000.*

Beaumont, Tex.

A1

A2

Typeset
Several varieties of A1
12X1 A1 10c black, *yellow* — *4,500.*
12X2 A1 10c black, *pink* — *4,000.*
12X3 A2 10c black, *yellow*, on cover *90,000.*

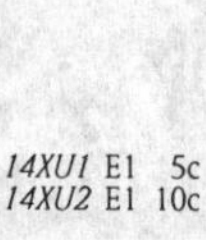

A1

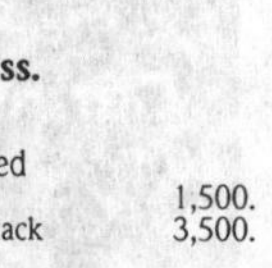

E1

Bridgeville, Ala.

Handstamped
13X1 A1 5c black & red *20,000.*

Canton, Miss.

Handstamped
14XU1 E1 5c black 1,500.
14XU2 E1 10c (ms.) on 5c black 3,500.

Carolina City, N.C.

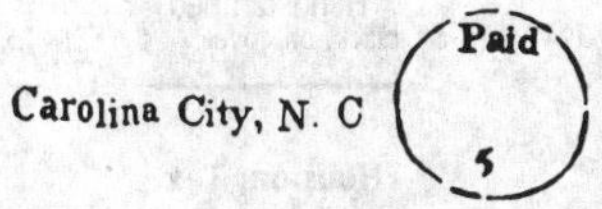

E1

Handstamped

118XU1 E1 5c black *3,500.*

Chapel Hill, N.C.

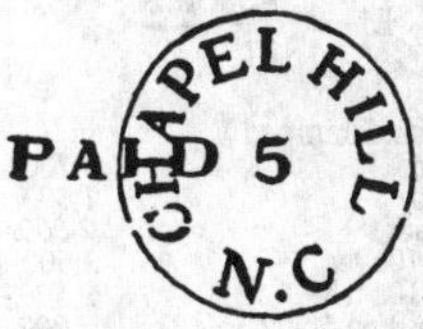

E1

Handstamped

15XU1 E1 5c black 2,500.

Charleston, S.C.

A1

E1

E2

Litho.

16X1	A1	5c blue		550.	450.

Typographed from Woodcut

16XU1	E1	5c blue		300.	1,250.
16XU2	E1	5c blue, *amber*		300.	1,250.
16XU3	E1	5c blue, *orange*		300.	1,250.
16XU4	E1	5c blue, *buff*		300.	1,250.
16XU5	E1	5c blue, *blue*		300.	1,250.
16XU6	E2	10c blue, *orange*			—

Handstamped

16XU7 E2 10c black *3,000.*

There is only one copy of No. 16XU7. It is a cut-out, not an entire. It may not have been mailed from Charleston and may not have paid postage.

Chattanooga, Tenn.

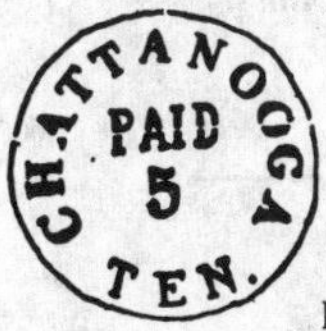

E1

Handstamped

17XU2 E1 5c black 1,600.

17XU3 E1 5c on 2c black *3,250.*

Christiansburg, Va.

E1

Typeset. Impressed at top right.

99XU1	E1	5c black, *blue*	*2,000.*
99XU2	E1	5c blue	*1,400.*
99XU3	E1	5c black, *orange*	*2,000.*
99XU4	E1	5c green, on US envelope #U27	*4,500.*
99XU5	E1	10c blue	*3,500.*

Colaparchee, Ga.

E1

Control

Handstamped

119XU1 E1 5c black *3,500.*

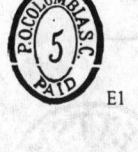

Columbia, S.C.

E1

E2

Handstamped

18XU1	E1	5c blue	135.	750.
18XU2	E1	5c black	235.	750.
18XU3	E1	10c on 5c blue		*3,000.*
18XU4	E2	5c blue (seal on front)		1,500.
a.		Seal on back		750.
18XU5	E2	10c blue (seal on back)		*2,000.*

Circular Seal similar to E2, 27mm diameter

18XU6 E2 5c blue (seal on back) *2,500.*

E1

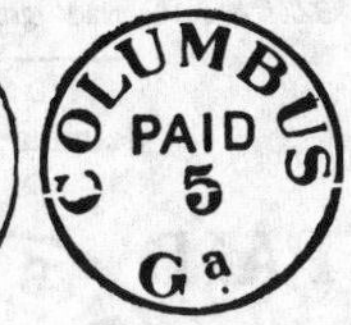

E1a

Columbia, Tenn.

Handstamped

113XU1 E1 5c red *3,500.*

Columbus, Ga.

19XU1	E1a	5c blue	800.
19XU2	E1a	10c red	*2,000.*

E1

E1a

Courtland, Ala.

Handstamped from Woodcut

103XU1	E1	5c black	—
103XU2	E1	5c red	*10,000.*

Provisional status of No. 103XU1 questioned.

Dalton, Ga.

Handstamped

20XU1	E1a	5c black	500.
20XU2	E1a	10c black	700.
20XU3	E1a	10c (ms.) on 5c black	1,500.

Danville, Va.

A1

Design measures 60x37mm — E1

E2

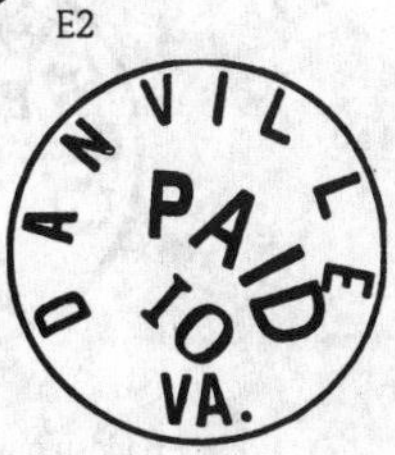

E3

Wove Paper

Typeset

21X1	A1	5c red	*5,500.*
		Cut to shape	*4,000.*

Laid Paper

21X2 A1 5c red *6,500.*

Two types: "SOUTHERN" in straight or curved line.

Typo.

21XU1	E1	5c black	*5,500.*
21XU2	E1	5c black, *amber*	*5,500.*
21XU3	E1	5c black, *dark buff*	*5,250.*

Handstamped

21XU4	E2	10c black	*2,000.*
21XU5	E2	10c blue	
21XU6	E3	10c black	*2,750.*

The existence of No. 21XU5 is doubtful.

Demopolis, Ala.

E1

Handstamped. Signature in ms.

22XU1	E1	5c black ("Jno. Y. Hall")	*2,000.*
22XU2	E1	5c black ("J. Y. Hall")	*2,000.*
22XU3	E1	5c (ms.) black ("J. Y. Hall")	*2,500.*

Eatonton, Ga.

E1

Handstamped

23XU1	E1	5c black	*3,000.*
23XU2	E1	5c + 5c black	*1,250.*

Emory, Va.

A1

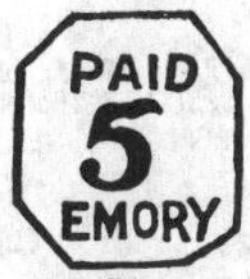

E1

E2

Handstamped on sheet margins of US 1857 1c stamps

***Perf.* 15 on Three Sides**

24X1 A1 5c blue — *3,500.*

No. 24X1 exists with "5" above or below "PAID."

Handstamped

24XU1	E1	5c blue	*2,000.*
24XU2	E2	10c blue	*3,000.*

E1

E1a

Fincastle, Va.

Typeset

104XU1 E1 10c black *20,000.*

No. 104XU1 is unique.

Forsyth, Ga.

Handstamped

120XU1 E1a 10c black *1,350.*

E1

A1

Franklin, N.C.

Typo.

25XU1 E1 5c blue, *buff* *30,000.*

No. 25XU1 is unique.

Fredericksburg, Va.

Typeset. Ten varieties.
Thin Bluish Paper
26X1 A1 5c blue, *bluish* 200. 600.
26X2 A1 10c red (shades), *bluish* 750.

Gainesville, Ala.

E1

E2

Handstamped
27XU1 E1 5c black 2,400.
27XU2 E2 10c black 5,000.

Galveston, Tex.

E1

E2

Handstamped
98XU1 E1 5c black 500. 900.
98XU2 E1 10c black 1,350.
98XU3 E2 10c black 550. 2,400.
98XU4 E2 20c black 3,500.

Georgetown, S.C.

E1

Control

Handstamped
28XU1 E1 5c black 600.

Goliad, Tex.

A1

A2

Typeset
Several varieties of A1 and A2
29X1 A1 5c black 5,000.
29X2 A1 5c black, *gray* 4,500.
29X3 A1 5c black, *rose* 5,000.
29X4 A1 10c black — 5,000.
29X5 A1 10c black, *rose* 5,000.

Type A1 stamps bear ms. control: "Clarke P.M."

29X6 A2 5c black, *gray* 5,000.
a. "Goilad" 5,500.
29X7 A2 10c black, *gray* 5,000.
a. "Goilad" 5,500.
29X8 A2 5c black, *dark blue* 6,000.
29X9 A2 10c black, *dark blue* 6,500.

Gonzales, Tex.

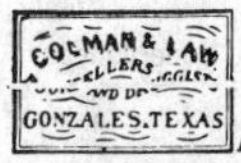

A1

30X1 A1 (5c) gold, *dark blue* 7,500.

No. 30X1 must bear double circle town cancel as validating control. All items of type A1 without this control are book labels.

Greensboro, Ala.

E1

E2

Handstamped
31XU1 E1 5c black 1,500.
31XU2 E1 10c black 2,750.
31XU3 E2 10c black 2,750.

Greensboro, N.C.

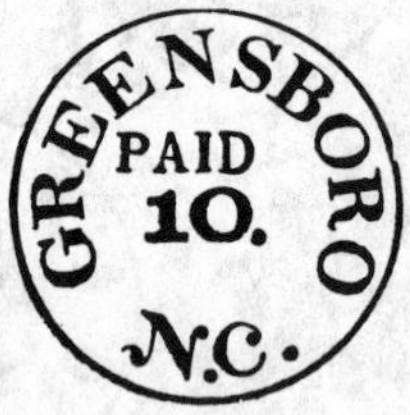

E1

Handstamped
32XU1 E1 10c red 1,000.

Greenville, Ala.

A1

A2

Typeset
Type I - "Greenville, Ala." in Roman.
Type II - "Greenville, Ala." in script.

33X1 A1 5c red & blue, Type I 4,500.
a. Type II 4,500.
33X2 A2 10c red & blue 5,000.

Greenville Court House, S.C.

E1

Control

Handstamped. Several Types.
34XU1 E1 5c black 1,800.
34XU2 E1 10c black 2,000.
34XU3 E1 20c (ms.) on 10c black 3,000.

Envelopes usually bear the black circle control on the back.

Greenwood Depot, Va.

A1

"PAID" Handstamped; value and signature ms.
Laid Paper
35X1 A1 10c black, *gray blue* 4,500. —

Griffin, Ga.

E1

Handstamped
102XU1 E1 5c black 1,750.

A1

A1a

Grove Hill, Ala.

Typo.
36X1 A1 5c black 75,000.

Hallettsville, Tex.

Handstamped
Ruled Letter Paper
37X1 A1a 10c black, *gray blue* 15,000.

Hamburgh, S.C.

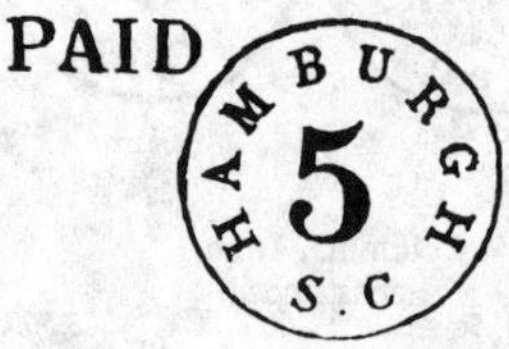

E1

Handstamped
112XU1 E1 5c black 2,000.

A1

A1a

Helena, Tex.

Typeset
Several varieties
38X1 A1 5c black, *buff* 7,500. 6,000.
38X2 A1 10c black, *gray* 5,000.

Hillsboro, N.C.

Handstamped
39X1 A1a 5c black, on cover 15,000.

Houston, Tex.

E1

Handstamped
40XU1 E1 5c red 700.
40XU2 E1 10c red 1,500.
40XU3 E1 10c black 2,000.
40XU4 E1 5c + 10c red 2,500.
40XU5 E1 10c + 10c red 2,500.
40XU6 E1 10c (ms.) on 5c red 3,000.

Huntsville, Tex.

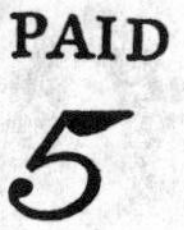

E1

Control

Handstamped
92XU1 E1 5c black 2,500.

No. 92XU1 exists with "5" outside or within control circle.

A1

E1

Independence, Tex.

Handstamped
41X1 A1 10c black, *buff* 3,250.
41X2 A1 10c black, *dull rose* 3,500.
41X3 A1 10c black, *buff* (small "10", "Pd" in ms.) 4,000.

No. 41X3 is known only cut to shape.

Iuka, Miss.

Typeset
42XU1 E1 5c black 1,600.

E1

E1a

Jackson, Miss.

Handstamped
43XU1 E1 5c black 500.
43XU2 E1 10c black 2,000.
43XU3 E1 10c on 5c black 2,750.
43XU4 E1 10c on 5c blue 2,750.

The 5c also exists on a lettersheet.

Jacksonville, Ala.

Handstamped

110XU1 E1a 5c black — 1,500.

A1

E1

Jetersville, Va.

Typeset ("5"); ms. ("AHA.")

Laid Paper

44X1 A1 5c black, vert. pair on cover 16,000.

Jonesboro, Tenn.

Handstamped

45XU1 E1 5c black *3,750.*
45XU2 E1 5c dark blue *3,250.*

Kingston, Ga.

E1

E2

E4

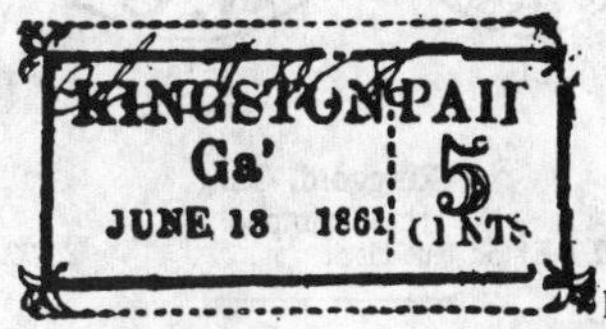

E3

Typo. (E1-E3); Handstamped (E4)

46XU1 E1 5c black 2,000.
46XU2 E2 5c black — 2,250.
a. No "C" or "S" at sides of numeral —
46XU3 E2 5c black, *amber* *2,750.*
46XU4 E3 5c black —
46XU5 E4 5c black 2,000.

Knoxville, Tenn.

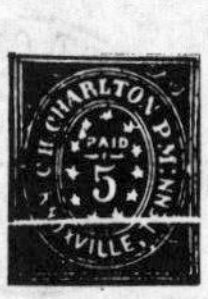

A1

Grayish White Laid Paper

47X1 A1 5c brick red *1,000.* 750.
47X2 A1 5c carmine *1,500.* 1,250.
47X3 A1 10c green —

The 5c has been reprinted in red, brown and chocolate on white and bluish wove and laid paper.

E1

E2

Typo.

47XU1 E1 5c blue 500. 1,500.
47XU2 E1 5c blue, *orange* 500. 1,500.
47XU3 E1 10c red (cut to shape) *1,800.*
47XU4 E1 10c red, *orange* (cut to shape) *1,800.*

Handstamped

47XU5 E2 5c black 500. 1,500.
47XU6 E2 10c on 5c black *3,500.*

Type E2 exists with "5" above or below "PAID."

La Grange, Tex.

E1

Handstamped

48XU1 E1 5c black — 2,000.
48XU2 E1 10c black 2,500.

Lake City, Fla.

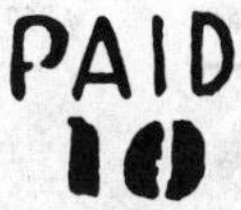

E1

Control

Handstamped

96XU1 E1 10c black *2,000.*

Envelopes have black circle control mark, or printed name of E.R. Ives, postmaster, on face or back.

Laurens Court House, S.C.

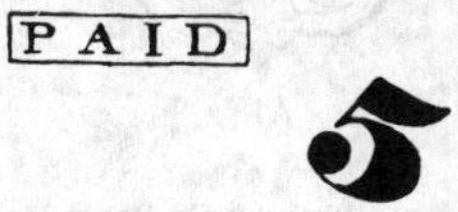

E1

Handstamped

116XU1 E1 5c black —

Lenoir, N.C.

A1

E1

Handstamped from Woodcut

Paper has ruled lines in orange

49X1 A1 5c blue *3,250.* *2,750.*

Handstamped

49XU1 A1 5c black *3,500.*
49XU2 A1 10c (5c + 5c) blue *3,500.*
49XU3 E1 5c blue *2,500.*
49XU4 E1 5c black

The existence of No. 49XU4 has been questioned.

Lexington, Miss.

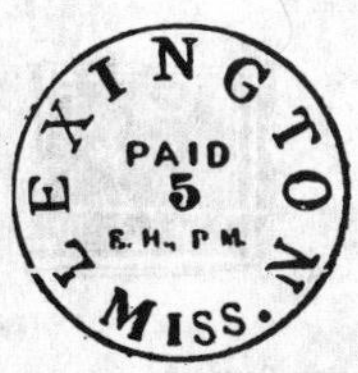

E1

Handstamped

50XU1 E1 5c black *5,000.*
50XU2 E1 10c black *5,000.*

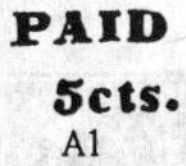

A1

A1a

Liberty, Va.

Typeset. Laid Paper

74X1 A1 5c black —

A cover with Salem, Va., postmark is known.

Limestone Springs, S.C.

Handstamped

121X1 A1a 5c black, on cover 4,000.

Stamps are round, square or rectangular. Covers are not postmarked.

Livingston, Ala.

A1

Litho.

51X1 A1 5c blue *7,000.*

Lynchburg, Va.

A1

E1

Stereotype from Woodcut

52X1 A1 5c blue (shades) 500. 850.

Typo.

52XU1 E1 5c black *1,500.*
52XU2 E1 5c black, *amber* 650. *1,500.*
52XU3 E1 5c black, *buff* *1,500.*
52XU4 E1 5c black, *brown* 900. *1,500.*

Macon, Ga.

A1

A2

A3

A4

E1

Typeset. Wove Paper.

Several varieties of each. Ten of A2.

53X1 A1 5c blk, *lt blue green* (shades) 700. 500.
53X3 A2 5c black, *yellow* 2,250. 650.
53X4 A3 5c blk, *yel* (shades) 2,250. 1,000.
a. Vertical tete beche pair *12,000.*
53X5 A4 2c black, *gray green* *6,500.*

Laid Paper

53X6 A2 5c black, *yellow* *3,000.* *3,500.*
53X7 A3 5c black, *yellow* *6,000.*
53X8 A1 5c blk, *lt blue green* 1,750. *2,000.*

Handstamped

Two types of "PAID" and "5"

53XU1 E1 5c black 250. 500.

Marietta, Ga.

E1

E2

Handstamped

Two types of "PAID" and numerals

54XU1 E1 5c black 300.
54XU2 E1 10c on 5c black 1,500.
54XU3 E1 10c black
54XU4 E2 5c black *2,000.*

The existence of No. 54XU3 is questioned.

Marion, Va.

A1

Handstamped Numeral within Typeset Frame

Wove Paper

55X1 A1 5c black *5,000.*
55X2 A1 10c black *16,500.* *8,000.*

Bluish Laid Paper

55X3 A1 5c black —

The 2c, 3c, 15c and 20c are believed to be bogus.

Memphis, Tenn.

A1

A2

Stereotype from Woodcut

56X1 A1 2c blue (shades) 65. *800.*
56X2 A2 5c red (shades) 140. 175.
a. Tete beche pair 1,500.
b. Pair, one sideways 750.
c. Pelure paper — —

Typo.

56XU1 A2 5c red 2,500.
56XU2 A2 5c red, *amber* 2,500.
56XU3 A2 5c red, *orange* 2,250.

Micanopy, Fla.

E1

Handstamped
105XU1 E1 5c black 11,500.

Milledgeville, Ga.

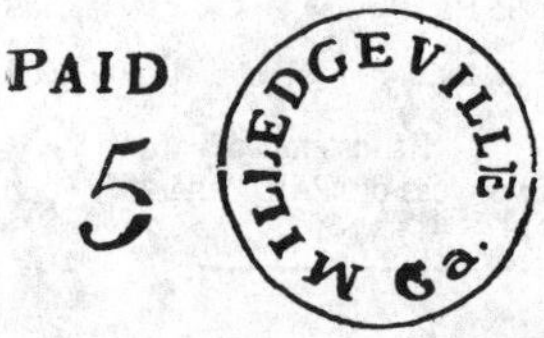

E1

E2

E3

Handstamped
57XU1 E1 5c black 250.
57XU2 E1 5c blue 800.
57XU3 E1 10c on 5c black 1,000.
57XU4 E2 10c black 225. 1,000.
57XU5 E3 10c black 750.

Mobile, Ala.

A1

Litho.
58X1 A1 2c black 1,250. 850.
58X2 A1 5c blue 225. 140.

Montgomery, Ala.

E1

E2

E3

Handstamped
59XU1 E1 5c red 800.
59XU2 E1 5c blue 400. 900.
59XU3 E1 10c red 800.
59XU4 E1 10c blue 900.
59XU5 E1 10c black 800.
59XU6 E1 10c on 5c red 2,500.

The 10c design is larger than the 5c.

59XU7 E2 2c red 2,500.
59XU7A E2 2c blue 3,500.
59XU8 E2 5c black 2,250.
59XU9 E3 10c black 2,500.
59XU10 E3 10c red 1,500.

Mt. Lebanon, La.

A1

Woodcut, Design Reversed
60X1 A1 5c red brown 100,000.

No. 60X1 is unique.

Nashville, Tenn.

A1

A2

E1

Typeset (5 varieties of 3c)
61X1 A1 3c carmine 150.

No. 61X1 was not placed in use.

Stereotype from Woodcut
Gray Blue Ribbed Paper
61X2 A2 5c carmine (shades) 700. 400.
a. Vertical tete beche pair 2,000.
61X3 A2 5c brick red 700. 375.
61X4 A2 5c gray (shades) 700. 500.
61X5 A2 5c violet brown 600. 375.
a. Vertical tete beche pair 3,500. 2,500.
61X6 A2 10c green 3,000. 3,000.

Handstamped
61XU1 E1 5c blue 750.
61XU2 E1 5c + 10c blue 2,400.

New Orleans, La.

A1

A2

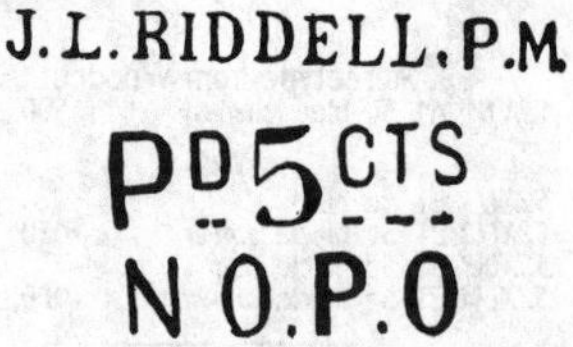

E1

Stereotype from Woodcut
62X1 A1 2c blue 100. 400.
a. Printed on both sides —
62X2 A1 2c red (shades) 100. 800.
62X3 A2 5c brown, *white* 200. 125.
a. Printed on both sides 1,250.
b. 5c ocher 550. 400.
62X4 A2 5c red brown, *bluish* 225. 95.
a. Printed on both sides 1,250.
62X5 A2 5c yellow brown, *off-white* 90. 180.
62X6 A2 5c red — 7,500.
62X7 A2 5c red, *bluish* 10,000.

Handstamped
62XU1 E1 5c black 3,250.
62XU2 E1 10c black 5,000.

"J L. RIDDELL, P.M." omitted

62XU3 E1 2c black 7,500.

A1

A1a

New Smyrna, Fla.

Handstamped
63X1 A1 10c ("01") on 5c black 45,000.

No. 63X1 is unique.

Oakway, S.C.

Handstamped
115X1 A1a 5c black, on cover — —

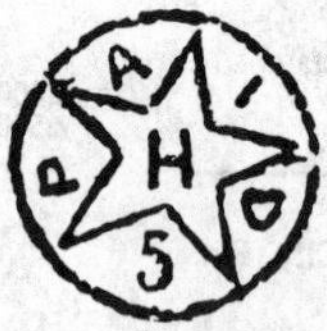

E1

A1

Pensacola, Fla.

Handstamped
106XU1 E1 5c black 3,750.
106XU2 E1 10c (ms.) on 5c black 4,250.

Petersburg, Va.

Typeset (10 varieties)
65X1 A1 5c red (shades) 1,000. 450.

A1

A1a

Pittsylvania Court House, Va.

Typeset
Wove Paper
66X1 A1 5c red 6,000. 5,000.
Octagonally cut 3,000.

Laid Paper
66X2 A1 5c red 6,500.
Octagonally cut 5,500.

Pleasant Shade, Va.

Typeset (5 varieties)
67X1 A1a 5c blue 2,500. 5,000.

A1

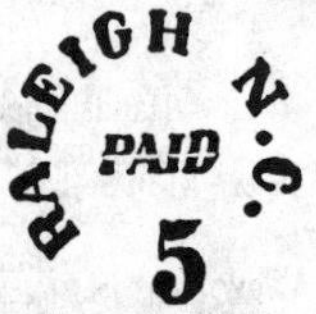

E1

Port Lavaca, Tex.

Typeset
107X1 A1 10c black 25,000.

No. 107X1 is unique.

Raleigh, N.C.

Handstamped
68XU1 E1 5c red 350.
68XU2 E1 5c blue 2,250.

A1

E1

Rheatown, Tenn.

Typeset. Three varieties.
69X1 A1 5c red 2,000. 2,750.
Pen canceled 2,000.

Richmond, Tex.

Handstamped
70XU1 E1 5c red 1,500.
70XU2 E1 10c red 1,000.
70XU3 E1 10c on 5c red 5,000.
70XU4 E1 15c (ms.) on 10c red 5,000.

E1

E1a

Ringgold, Ga.

Handstamped
71XU1 E1 5c blue black 2,500.

Rutherfordton, N.C.

Handstamped; "Paid 5cts" in ms.
72X1 E1a 5c black, cut round 25,000.

No. 72X1 is on cover, uncanceled and possibly unique.

Salem, N.C.

"Paid 5" in Ms.
E1

"Paid 5"
Handstamped
E2

Handstamped
73XU1 E1 5c black 900.
73XU2 E1 10c black 1,500.
73XU3 E2 5c black 1,000.
73XU4 E2 10c on 5c black 2,800.

Reprints exist on various papers. They either lack the "Paid" and value or have them counterfeited.

Market value for a particular scarce stamp may remain relatively low if few collectors want it.

Salisbury, N.C.

E1

Typo.
Impressed at top left

75XU1 E1 5c black, *greenish* — *5,000.*

One example known with part of envelope torn away, leaving part of design missing. Illustration E1 partly suppositional.

San Antonio, Tex.

E1

E2

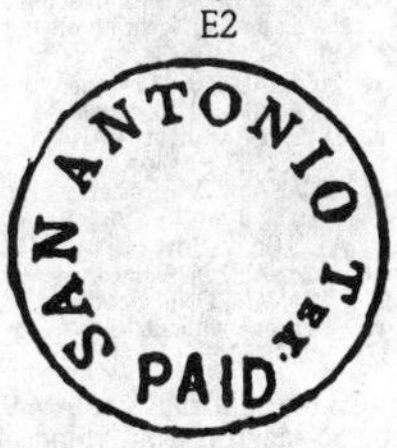

Control

Handstamped

76XU1 E1 10c black — 275. *2,000.*
76XU2 E2 10c black — *2,500.*

Black circle control mark is on front or back.

Savannah, Ga.

E1

Control

E2

Handstamped

101XU1 E1 5c black — 225.
101XU2 E2 5c black — 450.
101XU3 E1 10c black — 600.
101XU4 E2 10c black — 600.
101XU5 E1 10c on 5c black — 1,500.
101XU6 E2 20c on 5c black — 2,000.

Envelope must bear octagonal control mark. One example is known of No. 101XU6.

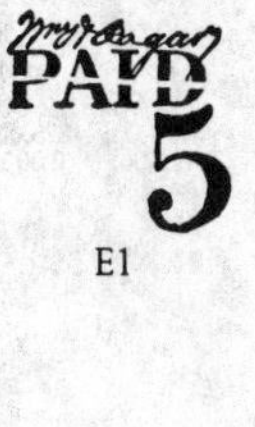

E1

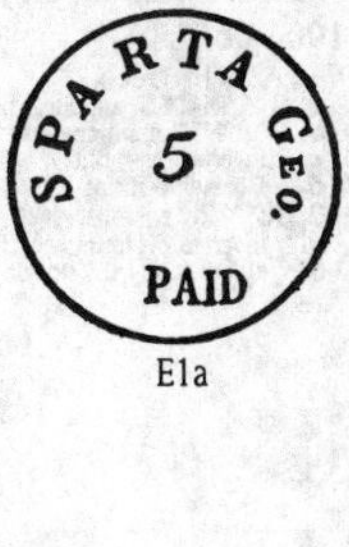

E1a

Selma, Ala.

Handstamped; Signature in ms.

77XU1 E1 5c black — *1,000.*
77XU2 E1 10c black — *2,500.*
77XU3 E1 10c on 5c black — *3,000.*

Sparta, Ga.

Handstamped

93XU1 E1a 5c red — — 1,000.
93XU2 E1a 10c red — *2,250.*

Spartanburg, S.C.

A1

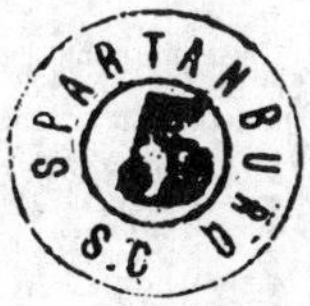

A2

Handstamped on Ruled or Plain Wove Paper

78X1 A1 5c black — *3,500.*
a. "5" omitted — —
78X2 A2 5c black, *bluish* — *4,000.*
78X3 A2 5c black, *brown* — *4,000.*

Most examples of Nos. 78X1-78X3 are cut round. Cut square examples are worth much more.

Statesville, N.C.

E1

Handstamped

79XU1 E1 5c black — 135. *450.*
79XU2 E1 10c on 5c black — *2,000.*

Sumter, S.C.

E1

Handstamped

80XU1 E1 5c black — 150.
80XU2 E1 10c black — 150.
80XU3 E1 10c on 5c black — *800.*
80XU4 E1 2c (ms.) on 10c black — *1,100.*

Used examples of Nos. 80XU1-80XU2 are indistinguishable from handstamped "Paid" covers.

E1

A1

Talbotton, Ga.

Handstamped

94XU1 E1 5c black — 750.
94XU2 E1 10c black — 500.
94XU3 E1 10c on 5c black — *2,000.*

Tellico Plains, Tenn.

Typeset — **Laid Paper**

81X1 A1 5c red — 1,000.
81X2 A1 10c red — 2,000.

Thomasville, Ga.

E1

Control

E2

Handstamped

82XU1 E1 5c black — 500.
82XU2 E2 5c black — 900.

Tullahoma, Tenn.

E1

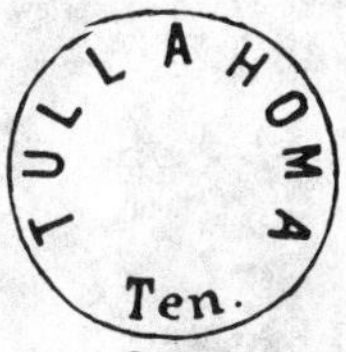

Control

Handstamped

111XU1 E1 10c black — *2,000.*

E1

E1a

Tuscaloosa, Ala.

Handstamped

83XU1 E1 5c black — 250.
83XU2 E1 10c black — 250.

Used examples of Nos. 83XU1-83XU2 are indistinguishable from handstamped "Paid" covers.

Tuscumbia, Ala.

Handstamped

84XU1 E1a 5c black — 2,250.
84XU2 E1a 5c red — 3,000.
84XU3 E1a 10c black — 3,500.

See US Postmasters' Provisional No. 12XU1.

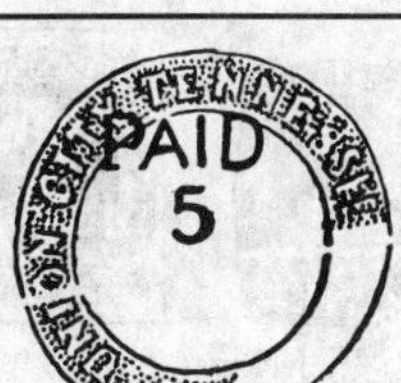

E1

Union City, Tenn.

The use of E1 to produce provisional envelopes is doubtful.

A1

A1a

Uniontown, Ala.

Typeset in settings of four (2x2)
Four varieties of each value
Laid Paper

86X1 A1 2c dk blue, *gray blue* — *9,500.* —
86X2 A1 2c dark blue — *5,500.*
86X3 A1 5c green, *gray blue* — *2,750. 2,000.*
86X4 A1 5c green — *2,750. 2,000.*
86X5 A1 10c red, *gray blue* — *10,000. 7,500.*

Unionville, S.C.

Handstamped
Wove Paper with Blue Ruled Lines

87X1 A1a 5c black, *grayish* — *17,500.*

Valdosta, Ga.

E1

Control

Handstamped

100XU1 E1 10c black — *2,000.*

The black control is usually on back of envelope.

A1

E1

Victoria, Tex.

Typeset

88X1 A1 5c red brown, *green* — *4,000.*
88X2 A1 10c red brown, *green* — *5,000. 4,500.*

Pelure Paper

88X3 A1 10c red brown, *green* ("10" in bold face type) — *6,250. 6,250.*

Walterborough, S.C.

Typeset

108XU1 E1 10c black, *buff* — *3,750.*
108XU2 E1 10c carmine — *2,500.*

Warrenton, Ga.

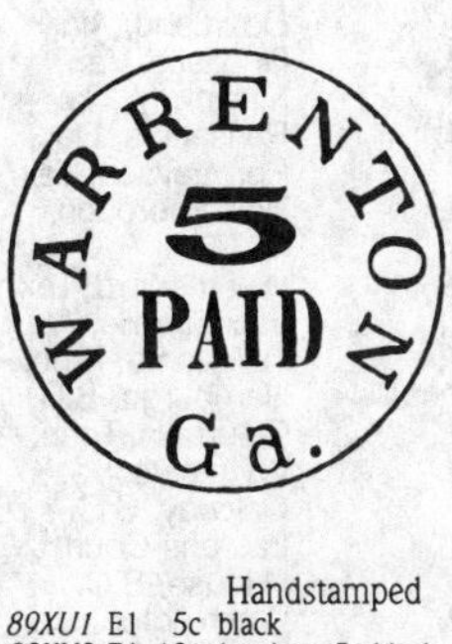

E1

Handstamped

89XU1 E1 5c black — 1,250.
89XU2 E1 10c (ms.) on 5c black — 650.

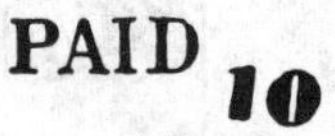

E1

E1a

Washington, Ga.

Handstamped

117XU1 E1 10c black *2,000.*

Weatherford, Tex.

Woodcut with "PAID" inserted in type.

Handstamped

109XU1 E1a 5c black *2,000.*
109XU2 E1a 5c + 5c black *12,500.*

Winnsborough, S.C.

E1

Control

Handstamped

97XU1 E1 5c black *1,500.*
97XU2 E1 10c black *2,000.*

Envelopes must bear black circle control on front or back.

Wytheville, Va.

E1

Control

Handstamped

114XU1 E1 5c black 900.

For later additions, listed out of numerical sequence, see:

No. 74X1, Liberty, Va.
No. 92XU1, Huntsville, Tex.
No. 93XU1, Sparta, Ga.
No. 94XU1, Talbotton, Ga.
No. 96XU1, Lake City, Fla.
No. 97XU1, Winnsborough, S.C.
No. 98XU1, Galveston, Tex.
No. 99XU1, Christiansburg, Va.
No. 100XU1, Valdosta, Ga.
No. 101XU1, Savannah, Ga.
No. 102XU1, Griffin, Ga.
No. 103XU1, Courtland, Ala.
No. 104XU1, Fincastle, Va.
No. 105XU1, Micanopy, Fla.
No. 106XU1, Pensacola, Fla.
No. 107X1, Port Lavaca, Tex.
No. 108XU1, Walterborough, S.C.
No. 109XU1, Weatherford, Tex.
No. 110XU1, Jacksonville, Ala.
No. 111XU1, Tullahoma, Tenn.
No. 112XU1, Hamburgh, S.C.
No. 113XU1, Columbia, Tenn.
No. 114XU1, Wytheville, Va.
No. 115X1, Oakway, S.C.
No. 116XU1, Laurens Court House, S.C.
No. 117XU1, Washington, Ga.
No. 118XU1, Carolina City, N.C.
No. 119XU1, Colaparchee, Ga.
No. 120XU1, Forsyth, Ga.
No. 121XU1, Limestone Springs, S.C.

GENERAL ISSUES

Jefferson Davis
A1

Thomas Jefferson
A2

1861 Unwmk. Litho. *Imperf.*

1 A1	5c green	130.00	100.00
a.	5c light green	140.00	100.00
b.	5c dark green	150.00	125.00
c.	5c olive green	175.00	120.00
2 A2	10c blue	175.00	125.00
a.	10c light blue	150.00	125.00
b.	10c dark blue	275.00	150.00
c.	10c indigo	*1,000.*	*1,000.*
d.	Printed on both sides	—	—
e.	10c greenish blue	275.00	225.00

The earliest printings of No. 2 were made by Hoyer & Ludwig, the later ones by J. T. Paterson & Co. Stamps of the later printings usually have a small colored dash below the lowest point of the upper left spandrel.

See Nos. 4-5.

Andrew Jackson — A3

Jefferson Davis — A4

1862

3 A3	2c green	400.00	550.00
a.	2c bright yellow green	*1,250.*	—
4 A1	5c blue	90.00	70.00
a.	5c dark blue	125.00	110.00
b.	5c light milky blue	140.00	120.00
5 A2	10c rose	750.00	325.00
a.	10c carmine	*2,000.*	1,000.

Typo.

6 A4	5c lt blue (London print)	8.00	17.50
7 A4	5c blue (local print)	10.00	11.00
a.	5c deep blue	11.00	17.50
b.	Printed on both sides	*2,500.*	1,250.

No. 6 has fine, clear impression. No. 7 has coarser impression and the color is duller and often blurred.

Both 2c and 10c stamps, types A4 and A10, were privately printed in various colors.

Andrew Jackson — A5

1863 Engr.

8 A5	2c brown red	40.00	*225.00*
a.	2c pale red	40.00	*225.00*

Jefferson Davis
A6 A6a

Thick or Thin Paper

9 A6	10c blue	500.00	400.00
a.	10c milky blue	500.00	400.00
b.	10c gray blue	600.00	500.00
10 A6a	10c blue (with frame line)	2,250.	1,100.
a.	10c milky blue	2,250.	1,100.
b.	10c greenish blue	2,750.	1,250.
c.	10c dark blue	2,750.	1,250.

Values of Nos. 10, 10a, 10b and 10c are for copies showing parts of lines on at least three sides.

A7

A8

There are many slight differences between A7 and A8, the most noticeable being the additional line outside the ornaments at the corners of A8.

11 A7	10c blue	7.00	10.00
a.	10c milky blue	20.00	25.00
b.	10c dark blue	15.00	20.00
c.	10c greenish blue	8.00	10.00
d.	10c green	40.00	55.00
e.	Perforated	150.00	175.00
12 A8	10c blue	8.00	11.00
a.	10c milky blue	20.00	25.00
b.	10c light blue	8.00	11.00
c.	10c greenish blue	20.00	35.00
d.	10c dark blue	8.00	15.00
e.	10c green	60.00	80.00
f.	Perforated	175.00	200.00

The paper of Nos. 11 and 12 varies from thin hard to thick soft. The so-called laid paper is probably due to thick streaky gum.

George Washington
A9

John C. Calhoun
A10

13 A9	20c green	25.00	*250.00*
a.	20c yellow green	40.00	*300.00*
b.	20c dark green	50.00	*350.00*
c.	Diagonal half used as 10c on cover		*2,250.*
d.	Horiz. half used as 10c on cover		*2,500.*

1862 Typo.

14 A10	1c orange	60.00
a.	1c deep orange	80.00

The 1c was never put in use.

CANAL ZONE

LOCATION — A strip of land 10 miles wide, extending through the Republic of Panama, between the Atlantic and Pacific Oceans.

GOVT. — From 1904-79 a US Government Reservation; from 1979 under control of the Republic of Panama.

AREA — 552.8 sq. mi.

POP. — 41,800 (est. 1976)

The Canal Zone, site of the Panama Canal, was leased in perpetuity to the US for a cash payment of $10,000,000 and a yearly rental. Treaties between the two countries provided for transfer of control of this area to Panama in 1979, including the postal service.

100 Centavos = 1 Peso
100 Centesimos = 1 Balboa
100 Cents = 1 Dollar

Catalogue values for unused stamps in this country are for Never Hinged items, beginning with Scott 118 in the regular postage section and Scott C6 in the air post section.

Watermarks

Wmk. 190- "USPS" in Single-lined Capitals

Wmk. 191- Double-lined "USPS" in Capitals

Map of Panama — A1

Violet to Violet-blue Handstamp, "CANAL ZONE," on Panama Nos. 72, 72c, 78 and 79

1904 Unwmk. *Perf. 12*

1 A1	2c rose, both "PANAMA" up or down	450.00	375.00
a.	"CANAL ZONE" inverted	750.00	750.00
b.	"CANAL ZONE" double	2,000.	2,000.
c.	"CANAL ZONE" double, both inverted	*15,000.*	
d.	"PANAMA" reading down and up	550.00	550.00
e.	As "d," "CANAL ZONE" inverted	6,500.	6,500.
f.	Vert. pair, "Panama" reading up on top 2c, down on other	2,000.	2,000.
2 A1	5c blue	200.00	175.00
a.	"CANAL ZONE" inverted	500.00	500.00
b.	"CANAL ZONE" double	2,250.	1,500.
c.	Pair, one without "CANAL ZONE"	5,000.	5,000.
d.	"CANAL ZONE" diagonal, running down to right	600.00	600.00
3 A1	10c yellow	400.00	275.00
a.	"CANAL ZONE" inverted	550.00	550.00
b.	"CANAL ZONE" double		*12,500.*
c.	Pair, one without "CANAL ZONE"	*6,000.*	*5,000.*

On the 2c stamp "PANAMA" is about 13mm; on the 5c and 10c about 15mm.

Varieties of "PANAMA" overprint exist on the 2c with inverted "V" for "A", accent on "A", inverted "N", etc.

Counterfeit "CANAL ZONE" overprints exist.

US Nos. 300, 319, 304, 306 and 307 Overprinted in Black

CANAL ZONE
PANAMA

1904 Wmk. 191

4 A115	1c blue green	27.50	20.00
5 A129	2c carmine	25.00	22.50
a.	2c scarlet	27.50	22.50
6 A119	5c blue	100.00	60.00
7 A121	8c violet black	160.00	75.00
8 A122	10c pale red brown	150.00	80.00
	Nos. 4-8 (5)	462.50	257.50

A2

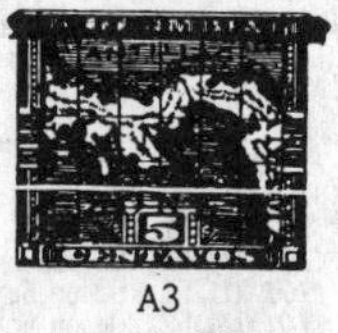

A3

CANAL
ZONE
Regular Type

CANAL
ZONE
Antique Type

Black Overprint on Stamps of Panama

1904-06 Unwmk.

9 A2	1c green	2.25	1.75
a.	"CANAL" in antique type	100.00	100.00
b.	"ZONE" in antique type	70.00	70.00
c.	Inverted overprint	—	*2,250.*
d.	Double overprint	*1,250.*	*1,000.*
10 A2	2c rose	3.50	2.00
a.	Inverted overprint	275.00	275.00
b.	"L" of "CANAL" sideways	2,500.	2,000.

Overprinted "CANAL ZONE" Black, "PANAMA" and Bar in Red on Panama Nos. 77-79 "PANAMA" 15mm long

11 A3 2c rose 6.50 4.50
a. "ZONE" in antique type 175.00 175.00
b. "PANAMA" inverted, bar at bottom 400.00 400.00
12 A3 5c blue 7.00 3.50
a. "CANAL" in antique type 75.00 75.00
b. "ZONE" in antique type 75.00 75.00
c. "CANAL ZONE" double 500.00 500.00
d. "PANAMA" ovpt. dbl. 950.00 750.00
e. "PANAMA" inverted, bar at bottom 800.00 1,000.
13 A3 10c yellow 17.50 11.00
a. "CANAL" in antique type 225.00 225.00
b. "ZONE" in antique type 175.00 175.00
c. "PANAMA" ovpt. dbl. 600.00 600.00
d. "PANAMA" overprint in red brown 25.00 25.00

With Additional Surcharge in Red on Panama No. 81

8 cts

14 A3 8c on 50c bis brn 25.00 18.00
a. "ZONE" in antique type 1,000. 900.00
b. "CANAL ZONE" invtd. 350.00 325.00
c. Rose brown overprint 37.50 37.50
d. As "c," "CANAL" in antique type 2,250.
e. As "c," "ZONE" in antique type 2,250.
f. As "c," "8 cts" double *850.00*
g. As "c," "8" omitted *4,250.*

Panama No. 74 Overprinted "CANAL ZONE" in Regular Type in Black and Surch. Like No. 14 in Red. Both "PANAMA" Reading Up. "PANAMA" 13mm long.

1905

15 A3 8c on 50c bis brn 2,400. *3,250.*
a. "PANAMA" reading down and up 6,500. —

On No. 15 with original gum the gum is always disturbed.

Panama Nos. 19 and 21 Surcharged in Black:

a

b
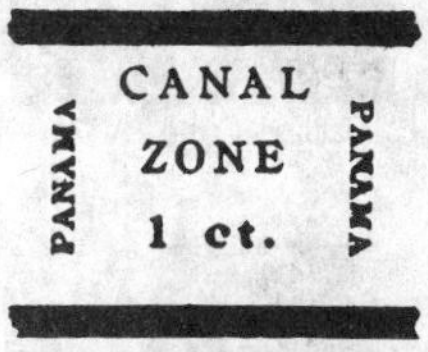

c
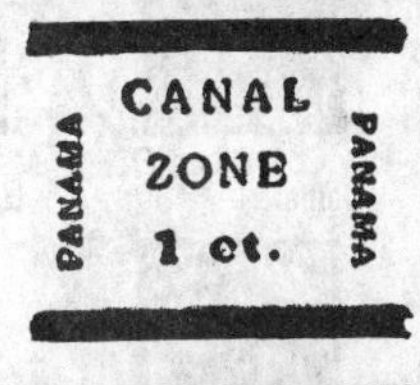

d

e
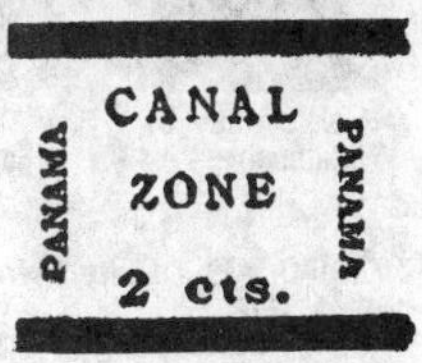

f

There were 3 printings of each denomination differing mainly in the relative position of the various parts of the surcharges. Varieties occur with invtd. "V" for the 3rd "A" in "PANAMA", "CA" spaced, "ZO" spaced, "2c" spaced, accents in various positions, and with bars shifted so that 2 bars appear on top or bottom of the stamp (either with or without the corresponding bar on top or bottom) and sometimes with only 1 bar at top or bottom.

1906

16 A4 1c on 20c vio, type a 1.75 1.50
a. Surcharge type b 1.75 1.50
b. Surcharge type c 1.50 1.50
17 A4 2c on 1p lake, type d 2.50 2.50
a. Surcharge type e 2.50 2.50
b. Surcharge type f 17.50 17.50

Panama No. 74 Overprinted "CANAL ZONE" in Regular Type in Black and Surcharged in Red

8 cts. b — **8 cts** c

Both "PANAMA" reading up

1905-06

18 A3 (b) 8c on 50c bis brn 50.00 50.00
a. "ZONE" in antique type 200.00 200.00
b. "PANAMA" down & up 175.00 175.00
19 A3 (c) 8c on 50c bis brn ('06) 45.00 40.00
a. "CANAL" in antique type 200.00 200.00
b. "ZONE" in antique type 200.00 200.00
c. "8 cts." double *1,100.* *1,100.*
d. "PANAMA" down & up 100.00 100.00

On Nos. 18-19 with original gum the gum is usually disturbed.

Panama No. 81 Overprinted "CANAL ZONE" in Regular Type in Black and Surcharged in Red Type "c" plus Period. "PANAMA" reading up and down

20 A3 8c on 50c bis brn 40.00 35.00
a. "CANAL" in antique type 200.00 200.00
b. "ZONE" in antique type 200.00 200.00
c. "8 cts" omitted 750.00 750.00
d. "8 cts" double *1,500.*

Numerous minor varieties of all these surcharges exist. Nos. 14, 18, 19 and 20 exist without CANAL ZONE overprint but were not regularly issued.

Vasco Nunez de Balboa — A5

Francisco Hernandez de Cordoba — A6

Justo Arosemena A7

Manuel J. Hurtado A8

Jose de Obaldia — A9

Stamps of Panama Ovptd. in Black

1906-07

Overprint Reading Up

21 A6 2c red & black 25.00 22.50
a. "Canal" only *4,000.*

Overprint Reading Down

22 A5 1c green & black 2.00 1.00
a. Horiz. pair, imperf. btwn. 1,200. 1,200.
b. Vert. pair, imperf. btwn. *1,750.* *1,750.*
c. Vert. pair, imperf. horiz. *1,750.* *1,750.*
d. Invtd. ovpt., reading up 450.00 450.00
e. Double overprint 275.00 275.00
f. Dbl. ovpt., one reading up 1,350. 1,350.
g. Inverted center and ovpt. reading up *3,250.* *2,750.*
23 A6 2c red & black 3.00 1.25
a. Horiz. pair, imperf. btwn. 1,350. 1,350.
b. Vertical pair, one without overprint 1,750. 1,750.
c. Double overprint 450.00 450.00
d. Dbl. ovpt., one diagonal 750.00 750.00
e. Pair, Nos. 23, 23d 1,750.
f. 2c carmine red & black 5.00 2.75
g. As "f," inverted center and overprint reading up *5,000.*
h. As "d," one "ZONE CANAL" *4,000.*
i. "CANAL" double *3,250.*
24 A7 5c ultra & black 6.00 2.00
c. Double overprint 400.00 250.00
d. "CANAL" only *3,500.*
e. "ZONE CANAL" *4,500.*
25 A8 8c purple & black 18.00 7.50
a. Horizontal pair, imperf. between and at left margin 1,350. —
26 A9 10c violet & black 18.00 7.50
a. Dbl. ovpt., one reading up *3,250.*
b. Overprint reading up *3,500.*
Nos. 22-26 (5) 47.00 19.25

Nos. 22 to 25 occur with "CA" spaced.

Cordoba A11

Arosemena A12

Hurtado — A13

Jose de Obaldia — A14

Overprint Reading Down

1909

27 A11 2c vermilion & black 12.00 6.50
a. Horiz. pair, one without ovpt. *2,600.*
b. Vert. pair, one without ovpt. *2,750.*
28 A12 5c deep blue & black 40.00 10.00
29 A13 8c violet & black 35.00 12.50
30 A14 10c violet & black 35.00 14.00
a. Horiz. pair, one without ovpt. *2,400.*
b. Vert. pair, one without ovpt. *2,600.*

Nos. 27 to 30 occur with "CA" spaced. See Nos. 32-35, 39-41, 47-48, 53-54, 56-57.

Vasco Nunez de Balboa — A15

CANAL ZONE
Type I

Smaller Black Overprint, Reading Up

Type I Overprint: "C" with serifs both top and bottom. "L" "Z" and "E" with slanting serif.

Illustrations of Types I to V are considerably enlarged and do not show actual spacing between lines of overprint.

1909-10

31 A15 1c dk green & blk 3.50 1.50
a. Inverted center and overprint reading down *12,500.*
c. Bklt. pane of 6 handmade, perf. margins 550.00
32 A11 2c vermilion & blk 4.25 1.50
a. Vert. pair, imperf. horiz 1,000. 1,000.
c. Bklt. pane of 6, handmade, perf. margins 800.00
d. Double overprint —
33 A12 5c dp blue & blk 12.50 3.50
a. Double overprint 300.00 300.00
34 A13 8c violet & blk ('10) 10.00 5.00
a. Vert. pair, one without ovpt. *1,500.*
35 A14 10c violet & black 50.00 18.00
Nos. 31-35 (5) 80.25 29.50

See Nos. 38, 46, 52, 55.

A16

A17

Black Surcharge

1911

36 A16 10c on 13c gray 5.50 2.00
a. "10 cts." inverted 300.00 250.00
b. "10 cts." omitted 250.00 —

1914

37 A17 10c gray 50.00 11.00

Type II: "C" with serif at top only. "L" and "E" with vertical serifs. Inner oval of "O" tilts to left

CANAL ZONE

1912-16

38 A15 1c green & blk ('13) 10.00 2.75
a. Vert. pair, one without ovpt. 1,500. 1,500.
b. Booklet pane of 6 550.00
c. As "b," handmade, perf. margins 900.00
39 A11 2c vermilion & blk 8.00 1.25
a. Horiz. pair, one without ovpt. 1,500.
b. "CANAL" only 1,100.
c. Booklet pane of 6 600.00
d. Overprint reading down 175.00
e. As "d," inverted center 850.00 850.00
f. As "e," booklet pane of 6 handmade, perf. margins *6,500.*
g. As "c," handmade, perf. margins 1,100.
40 A12 5c dp blue & blk 19.00 3.00
a. With portrait of 2c *7,000.*
41 A14 10c violet & blk ('16) 45.00 8.00

Map of Panama Canal — A18

Balboa Takes Possession of the Pacific Ocean — A19

Gatun Lock — A20

Culebra Cut — A21

Blue Overprint, Type II

1915

42 A18 1c dark green & black 8.00 6.00
43 A19 2c carmine & black 9.00 4.00
44 A20 5c blue & black 10.00 5.50
45 A21 10c orange & black 20.00 10.00

Type III: Similar to Type I but letters appear thinner, particularly the lower bar of "L," "Z" and "E." Impressions are often light, rough and irregular

CANAL ZONE

1915-20

46	A15	1c green & black	150.00	95.00
a.		Overprint reading down	350.00	
b.		Double overprint	275.00	
c.		"ZONE" double	*4,250.*	
d.		Dbl. ovpt., one "ZONE CANAL"	1,750.	
47	A11	2c orange ver & blk	2,400.	90.00
48	A12	5c dp blue & black	550.00	130.00

S.S. "Panama" in Culebra Cut — A22

S.S. "Panama" in Culebra Cut — A23

S.S. "Cristobal" in Gatun Locks — A24

Blue Overprint, Type II

1917

49	A22	12c purple & black	15.00	5.00
50	A23	15c brt blue & black	50.00	20.00
51	A24	24c yel brown & black	45.00	12.50

Type IV: "C" thick at bottom, "E" with center bar same length as top and bottom bars

CANAL ZONE

Black Overprint, Reading Up

1918-20

52	A15	1c green & black	30.00	10.00
a.		Overprint reading down	150.00	—
b.		Booklet pane of 6	750.00	
c.		Bklt. pane of 6, left vert. row of 3 without ovpt.	*5,000.*	
d.		Bklt. pane of 6, right vert. row of 3 with dbl. ovpt.	*7,500.*	
e.		Horiz. bklt. pair, one without overprint	*1,000.*	
f.		Horiz. bklt. pair, right stamp with dbl. overprint	*1,750.*	
53	A11	2c vermilion & blk	110.00	6.00
a.		Overprint reading down	150.00	150.00
b.		Horizontal pair, right stamp without overprint	1,500.	
c.		Booklet pane of 6	800.00	
d.		Bklt. pane of 6, left vert. row of 3 without ovpt.	*5,000.*	
e.		Horiz. bklt. pair, left stamp without overprint	*1,250.*	*4,500.*
54	A12	5c dp blue & black ('20)	200.00	30.00

Normal spacing between words of overprint on Nos. 52 and 53 is 9¼mm. On No. 54 and the booklet printings of Nos. 52 and 53, the normal spacing is 9mm. Minor spacing varieties are known. No. 53e used is unique and is on cover.

Type V: Smaller block type 1¾mm high. "A" with flat top

CANAL ZONE

Black Overprint, Reading Up

1920-21

55	A15	1c lt green & black	20.00	3.00
a.		Overprint reading down	200.00	175.00
b.		Pair, one without overprint	1,100.	
c.		"CANAL" double	*1,500.*	
d.		"ZONE" only	*2,750.*	
e.		Booklet pane of 6	*2,750.*	
56	A11	2c orange ver & blk	8.00	2.00
a.		Double overprint	500.00	
b.		Double overprint, one reading down	500.00	
c.		Horiz. pair, one without overprint	1,250.	
d.		Vertical pair, one without overprint	1,500.	
e.		"CANAL" double	1,000.	
f.		"ZONE" double	1,000.	
g.		Booklet pane of 6	700.00	
57	A12	5c dp blue & black	250.00	40.00
a.		Horiz. pair, one without overprint	*3,000.*	

Drydock at Balboa — A25

Ship in Pedro Miguel Locks — A26

Black Overprint, Type V

1920

58	A25	50c orange & black	250.00	150.00
59	A26	1b dk violet & blk	140.00	60.00

Jose Vallarino A27

The "Land Gate" A28

Bolivar's Tribute — A29

Municipal Building in 1821 and 1921 — A30

Statue of Balboa — A31

Tomas Herrera — A32

Jose de Fabrega — A33

Black or Red Overprint, Type V

1921

60	A27	1c green	3.50	1.25
a.		"CANAL" double	*2,250.*	
b.		Booklet pane of 6	*825.00*	
61	A28	2c carmine	2.75	1.40
a.		Overprint reading down	200.00	200.00
b.		Double overprint	900.00	
c.		Vertical pair, one without overprint	*3,500.*	
d.		"CANAL" double	*1,900.*	
f.		Booklet pane of 6	*1,750.*	
62	A29	5c blue (R)	10.00	4.00
a.		Overprint reading down (R)	60.00	
63	A30	10c violet	15.00	6.50
a.		Overprint reading down	100.00	
64	A31	15c light blue	50.00	16.00
65	A32	24c black brown	67.50	20.00
66	A33	50c black	135.00	90.00
		Nos. 60-66 (7)	283.75	139.15

Experts question the status of the 5c blue with a small type V overprint in red or black.

Type III Ovpt. in Black, Reading Up

1924

67	A27	1c green	500.	200.
a.		"ZONE CANAL" reading down	750.	
b.		"ZONE" reading down	*1,750.*	

Coat of Arms — A34

Black Overprint

1924

68	A34	1c dark green	10.00	4.00
69	A34	2c carmine	7.50	2.50

The 5c to 1b values were prepared but never issued. See listing in Scott's U.S. Specialized Catalogue.

US Nos. 551-554, 557, 562, 564-566, and 569-571 Overprinted in Red or Black

Type A

CANAL

ZONE

Letters "A" with Flat Tops

1924-25 Flat Plate Printing ***Perf. 11***

70	A154	½c olive brown (R)	1.00	65
71	A155	1c deep green	1.25	80
a.		Inverted overprint	500.00	500.00
b.		"ZONE" inverted	350.00	325.00
c.		"CANAL" only	1,750.	
d.		"ZONE CANAL"	450.00	
e.		Booklet pane of 6	125.00	
72	A156	1½c yellow brown	1.75	1.50
73	A157	2c carmine	7.00	1.50
a.		Booklet pane of 6	200.00	
74	A160	5c dark blue	17.50	8.00
75	A165	10c orange	40.00	20.00
76	A167	12c brown violet	32.50	30.00
a.		"ZONE" inverted	*3,000.*	*2,500.*
77	A168	14c dark blue	27.50	20.00
78	A169	15c gray	47.50	32.50
79	A172	30c olive brown	30.00	20.00
80	A173	50c lilac	65.00	40.00
81	A174	$1 violet brown	235.00	80.00
		Nos. 70-81 (12)	506.00	254.95

The space between the two lines of the overprint, on both type A and B, varies on some settings.

US Nos. 554, 555, 557, 562, 564-567, 569-571 and 623 Overprinted in Black or Red

Type B

CANAL

ZONE

Letters "A" with Sharp Pointed Tops

1925-26

84	A157	2c carmine	27.50	7.00
a.		"CANAL" ONLY	1,250.	
b.		"ZONE CANAL"	250.00	
c.		Horiz. pair, one without overprint	*3,500.*	
d.		Booklet pane of 6	200.00	
85	A158	3c violet	3.75	3.00
a.		"ZONE ZONE"	500.00	500.00
86	A160	5c dark blue	3.75	2.00
a.		"ZONE ZONE"	950.00	
b.		"CANAL" inverted	950.00	
c.		Inverted overprint	500.00	
d.		Pair, one without overprint	*3,250.*	
e.		"ZONE CANAL"	325.00	
f.		"ZONE" only	*2,000.*	
g.		Pair, one without ovpt., other ovpt. invtd.	*2,250.*	
h.		"CANAL" only	*2,250.*	
87	A165	10c orange	32.50	10.00
a.		"ZONE ZONE"	*3,000.*	
88	A167	12c brown violet	22.50	11.00
a.		"ZONE ZONE"	*5,000.*	
89	A168	14c dark blue	19.00	15.00
90	A169	15c gray	6.00	3.75
a.		"ZONE ZONE"	*5,500.*	
91	A187	17c black (R)	3.75	3.00
a.		"ZONE" only	800.00	
b.		"CANAL" only	1,700.	
c.		"ZONE CANAL"	200.00	
92	A170	20c carmine rose	6.50	3.00
a.		"CANAL" inverted	*3,500.*	
b.		"ZONE" inverted	*3,850.*	
c.		"ZONE CANAL"	*3,500.*	
93	A172	30c olive brown	4.50	3.75
94	A173	50c lilac	250.00	165.00
95	A174	$1 violet brown	125.00	60.00
		Nos. 84-95 (12)	504.75	286.50

Overprint Type B on US Sesquicentennial Stamp No. 627

1926

96	A188	2c carmine rose	4.00	3.50

On this stamp there is a space of 5mm between the two words of the overprint.

Overprint Type B on US Nos. 583, 584 and 591

1927 Rotary Press Printings ***Perf. 10***

97	A157	2c carmine	40.00	10.00
a.		Pair, one without overprint	*3,000.*	
b.		Booklet pane of 6	650.00	
c.		"CANAL" only	*1,750.*	
d.		"ZONE" only	*2,750.*	
98	A158	3c violet	7.50	4.00
99	A165	10c orange	13.00	6.50

Overprint Type B on US Nos. 632, 634, 635, 637 and 642

Rotary Press Printings

1927-31 ***Perf. 11x10½***

100	A155	1c green	2.00	1.25
a.		Pair, one without overprint	*3,000.*	
101	A157	2c carmine	2.25	80
a.		Booklet pane of 6	175.00	
102	A158	3c violet	3.75	2.50
a.		Booklet pane of 6, handmade, perf. margins	*5,000.*	
103	A160	5c dark blue	20.00	9.00
104	A165	10c orange	17.00	9.00
		Nos. 100-104 (5)	45.00	22.55

Wet and Dry Printings

Canal Zone stamps printed by both the "wet" and "dry" process are Nos. 105, 108-109, 111-114, 117, 138-140, C21-C24, C26, J25, J27. Starting with Nos. 147 and C27, the Bureau of Engraving and Printing used the "dry" method exclusively. See note following US No. 1029.

Maj. Gen. William Crawford Gorgas — A35

Maj. Gen. George Washington Goethals — A36

Gaillard Cut — A37

Maj. Gen. Harry Foote Hodges — A38

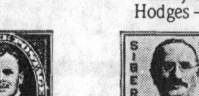

Lt. Col. David D. Gaillard — A39

Maj. Gen. William L. Sibert — A40

Jackson Smith — A41

Rear Adm. Harry H. Rousseau — A42

Col. Sydney B. Williamson — A43

J.C.S. Blackburn — A44

1928-40 Flat Plate Printing ***Perf. 11***

105	A35	1c green	15	15
106	A36	2c carmine	16	15
a.		Booklet pane of 6	17.50	*20.00*
107	A37	5c blue ('29)	1.00	40
108	A38	10c orange ('32)	20	16
109	A39	12c violet brown ('29)	75	60
110	A40	14c blue ('37)	85	85
111	A41	15c gray ('32)	40	35
112	A42	20c olive brown ('32)	60	20

113 A43 30c brown black ('40) 80 70
114 A44 50c lilac ('29) 1.50 65
Nos. 105-114 (10) 6.41 4.21

For surcharges see Nos. J21-J24. For overprints see Nos. O1-O8.

United States Nos. 720 and 695 Overprinted type B

Rotary Press Printing

1933 ***Perf. 11x10½***

115 A226 3c deep violet 2.75 25
b. "CANAL" only *2,600.*
c. Bklt. pane of 6, handmade, perf. margins 275.00
116 A168 14c dark blue 4.50 3.50
a. "ZONE CANAL" *1,500.*

Gen. George Washington Goethals — A45

Flat Plate Printing

1934, Aug. 15 ***Perf. 11***

117 A45 3c deep violet 15 15
a. Booklet pane of 6 55.00 *32.50*
b. As "a," handmade, perf. margins 225.00 —

20th anniv. of the Panama Canal opening. See No. 153.

Catalogue values for unused stamps in this section, from this point to the end of the section, are for Never Hinged items.

US Nos. 803 and 805 Overprinted in Black

CANAL ZONE

Rotary Press Printing

1939 ***Perf. 11x10½***

118 A275 ½c deep orange 15 15
119 A277 1½c bister brown 15 15
Set value 24 24

Panama Canal Anniversary Issue

Balboa-Before A46

Balboa-After A47

Gaillard Cut-Before A48

Gaillard Cut-After A49

Bas Obispo-Before A50

Bas Obispo-After A51

Gatun Locks-Before A52

Gatun Locks-After A53

Canal Channel-Before — A54

Canal Channel-After A55

Gamboa-Before — A56

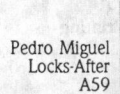

Gamboa-After A57

Pedro Miguel Locks-Before A58

Pedro Miguel Locks-After A59

Gatun Spillway-Before — A60

Gatun Spillway-After A61

Flat Plate Printing

1939, Aug. 15 ***Perf. 11***

120	A46	1c yellow green	55	30
121	A47	2c rose carmine	55	35
122	A48	3c purple	55	15
123	A49	5c dark blue	1.25	1.00
124	A50	6c red orange	2.50	2.00
125	A51	7c black	2.25	2.00
126	A52	8c green	4.00	2.75
127	A53	10c ultramarine	3.25	3.00
128	A54	11c blue green	7.50	7.50
129	A55	12c brown carmine	7.00	6.00
130	A56	14c dark violet	7.25	7.00
131	A57	15c olive green	9.75	4.00
132	A58	18c rose pink	9.00	7.50
133	A59	20c brown	11.50	6.00
134	A60	25c orange	16.50	13.00
135	A61	50c violet brown	20.00	4.00
		Nos. 120-135 (16)	103.40	66.55

25th anniv. of the Panama Canal.

Maj. Gen. George W. Davis — A62

Gov. Charles E. Magoon — A63

Theodore Roosevelt — A64

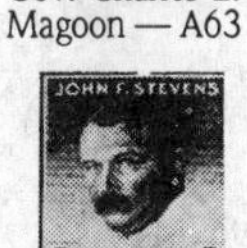

John F. Stevens — A65

John F. Wallace — A66

1946-49 **Size: 19x22mm** ***Perf. 11***

136	A62	½c bright red ('48)	35	16
137	A63	1½c chocolate ('48)	35	16
138	A64	2c rose carmine ('49)	15	15
139	A65	5c deep blue	40	15
140	A66	25c yellow green ('48)	1.00	65
		Nos. 136-140 (5)	2.25	1.27

See #155, 162, 164. For overprint see #O9.

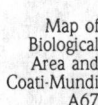

Map of Biological Area and Coati-Mundi A67

1948, Apr. 17 ***Perf. 11***

141 A67 10c black 1.25 1.00

25th anniv. of the establishment of the Canal Zone Biological Area on Barro Colorado Is.

"Forty-niners" Arriving at Chagres — A68

Journey by "Bungo" to Las Cruces — A69

Las Cruces Trail to Panama — A70

Departure for San Francisco — A71

1949, June 1 ***Perf. 11***

142	A68	3c blue	50	25
143	A69	6c violet	65	30
144	A70	12c bright green	1.00	70
145	A71	18c deep red lilac	2.00	1.50

Centenary of the California Gold Rush.

Workers in Culebra Cut — A72

Early Railroad Scene — A73

1951, Aug. 15

146 A72 10c carmine 2.50 1.65

Contribution of West Indian laborers in the construction of the Canal.

1955, Jan. 28 ***Perf. 11***

147 A73 3c violet 75 50

Cent. of the completion of the Panama Railroad and the 1st transcontinental railroad trip in Americas.

Gorgas Hospital and Ancon Hill — A74

1957, Nov. 17

148 A74 3c black, *blue green* 50 35

75th anniv. of Gorgas Hospital. Printed on two shades of blue green paper.

S.S. Ancon — A75

1958, Aug. 30 **Engr.** **Unwmk.**

149 A75 4c greenish blue 45 30

Roosevelt Medal and Map — A76

1958, Nov. 15 ***Perf. 11***

150 A76 4c brown 50 30

Theodore Roosevelt (1858-1919).

Boy Scout Badge — A77

Administration Building — A78

Giori Press Printing

1960, Feb. 8 ***Perf. 11***

151 A77 4c dk blue, red & bister 50 40

Boy Scouts of America, 50th anniv.

1960, Nov. 1 **Engr.** ***Perf. 11***

152 A78 4c rose lilac 16 15

Types of 1934, 1960 and 1946 Coil Stamps

1960-62 ***Perf. 10 Vert.***

153 A45 3c deep violet 16 15

Perf. 10 Horizontally

154 A78 4c deep rose lilac 20 15

Perf. 10 Vertically

155 A65 5c deep blue 30 20
Set value 44

Issue dates: 3c, 4c, 1960. 5c, Feb. 10, 1962.

Girl Scout Badge and Camp at Gatun Lake — A79

Giori Press Printing

1962, Mar. 12 ***Perf. 11***

156 A79 4c blue, dk green & bister 40 30

50th anniv. of Girl Scouts.

Thatcher Ferry Bridge and Map of Western Hemisphere A80

1962, Oct. 12

157 A80 4c black & silver 30 25
a. Silver (bridge) omitted *7,000.*

Opening of the Thatcher Ferry Bridge, spanning the Panama Canal.

Canal Zone stamps can be mounted in the Scott U.S. Possessions album.

Goethals Memorial, Balboa — A81

Fort San Lorenzo — A82

Giori Press Printing

1968-71 *Perf. 11*

158 A81	6c green & ultra	30	30
159 A82	8c multicolored	35	16

Issued: 6c, Mar. 15, 1968; 8c, July 14, 1971.

Portrait Type of 1928-48
Coil Stamps

1975, Feb. 14 **Engr.** ***Perf. 10 Vert.***

160 A35	1c green	15	15
161 A38	10c orange	70	35
162 A66	25c yellow green	2.75	2.75

Dredge Cascadas A83

Giori Press Printing

1976, Feb. 23 *Perf. 11*

163 A83	13c multicolored	35	20
a.	Booklet pane of 4	3.00	—

Stevens Type of 1946
Rotary Press Printing

1977 ***Perf. 11x10½***
Size: 19x22½mm

164 A65	5c deep blue	50	35

Towing Locomotive, Ship in Lock — A84

1978, Oct. 25 **Engr.** *Perf. 11*

165 A84	15c dp green & blue green	35	20

AIR POST STAMPS

AIR MAIL

Nos. 105-106 Surcharged in Dark Blue

25 CENTS 25

Type I- Flag of "5" pointing up **15**

Type II- Flag of "5" curved **15**

Flat Plat Printing

1929 **Unwmk.** *Perf. 11*

C1	A35	15c on 1c green, I	7.00	4.50
C2	A35	15c on 1c green, II	95.00	85.00
C3	A36	25c on 2c carmine	3.00	1.75

AIR MAIL

Nos. 114 and 106 Surcharged

10c

1929, Dec. 31

C4	A44	10c on 50c lilac	7.00	6.50
C5	A36	20c on 2c carmine	5.00	1.50
a.		Dropped "2" in surcharge	90.00	75.00

Catalogue values for unused stamps in this section, from this point to the end of the section, are for Never Hinged items.

Gaillard Cut — AP1

1931-49 **Engr.**

C6	AP1	4c red violet ('49)	70	55
C7	AP1	5c yellow green	60	35
C8	AP1	6c yellow brown ('46)	75	35
C9	AP1	10c orange	1.00	35
C10	AP1	15c blue	1.25	30
C11	AP1	20c red violet	2.00	30
C12	AP1	30c rose lake ('41)	3.50	1.00
C13	AP1	40c yellow	3.50	1.10
C14	AP1	$1 black	8.25	1.40
		Nos. C6-C14 (9)	21.55	5.70

For overprints see Nos. CO1-CO14.

Douglas Plane over Sosa Hill — AP2

Planes and Map of Central America — AP3

Pan American Clipper and Scene near Fort Amador — AP4

Pan American Clipper at Cristobal Harbor — AP5

Pan American Clipper over Gaillard Cut — AP6

Pan American Clipper Landing — AP7

1939, July 15

C15	AP2	5c greenish black	3.75	2.25
C16	AP3	10c dull violet	2.75	1.60
C17	AP4	15c light brown	4.00	1.25
C18	AP5	25c blue	11.00	7.00
C19	AP6	30c rose carmine	9.75	6.00
C20	AP7	$1 green	32.50	20.00
		Nos. C15-C20 (6)	63.75	38.10

10th anniv. of Air Mail service and the 25th anniv. of the opening of the Panama Canal.

Globe and Wing — AP8

1951, July 16 **Unwmk.** *Perf. 11*

C21	AP8	4c red violet	80	35
C22	AP8	6c brown	65	28
C23	AP8	10c red orange	1.10	45
C24	AP8	21c blue	7.50	4.00
C25	AP8	31c cerise	8.00	3.75
a.		Horiz. pair, imperf. vert.	900.00	—
C26	AP8	80c gray black	4.75	1.25
		Nos. C21-C26 (6)	22.80	10.08

1958, Aug. 16

C27	AP8	5c yellow green	1.00	65
C28	AP8	7c olive	1.00	52
C29	AP8	15c brown violet	4.00	2.00
C30	AP8	25c orange yellow	9.00	2.75
C31	AP8	35c dark blue	7.00	2.75
		Nos. C27-C31 (5)	22.00	8.67
		Nos. C21-C31 (11)	44.80	18.75

See No. C34.

Emblem of US Army Caribbean School — AP9

Giori Press Printing

1961, Nov. 21 *Perf. 11*

C32	AP9	15c red & dk blue	1.50	1.00

Malaria Eradication Emblem and Mosquito AP10

1962, Sept. 24 **Unwmk.** *Perf. 11*

C33	AP10	7c yellow & black	50	50

WHO drive to eradicate malaria.

Type of 1951
Rotary Press Printing

1963, Jan. 7 ***Perf. 10½x11***

C34	AP8	8c carmine	60	30

Alliance Emblem AP11

Giori Press Printing

1963, Aug. 17 **Unwmk.** *Perf. 11*

C35	AP11	15c gray, green & dark ultra	1.10	85

2nd anniv. of the Alliance for Progress, which aims to stimulate economic growth and raise living standards in Latin America.

Jet over Cristobal AP12

Designs: 8c, Gatun Locks. 15c, Madden Dam. 20c, Gaillard Cut. 30c, Miraflores Locks. 80c, Balboa.

1964, Aug. 15 *Perf. 11*

C36	AP12	6c green & black	40	35
C37	AP12	8c rose red & black	45	35
C38	AP12	15c blue & black	1.25	50
C39	AP12	20c rose lilac & blk	2.00	1.00
C40	AP12	30c redsh brown & blk	2.25	2.00
C41	AP12	80c ol bister & black	4.25	2.50
		Nos. C36-C41 (6)	10.60	6.70

50th anniv. of the Panama Canal.

Seal and Jet Plane — AP13

1965, July 15 **Unwmk.** *Perf. 11*

C42	AP13	6c green & black	35	20
C43	AP13	8c rose red & black	40	15
C44	AP13	15c blue & black	45	20
C45	AP13	20c lilac & black	55	30
C46	AP13	30c redsh brn & blk	90	30
C47	AP13	80c bister & black	2.50	65
		Nos. C42-C47 (6)	5.15	1.80

1968-76

C48	AP13	10c dull orange & blk	30	15
a.		Booklet pane of 4 ('70)	4.25	—
C49	AP13	11c gray olive & blk	30	18
a.		Booklet pane of 4	3.50	—
C50	AP13	13c emerald & black	1.10	30
a.		Booklet pane of 4	6.00	—
C51	AP13	22c violet & black	1.00	70
C52	AP13	25c pale yel green & blk	65	70
C53	AP13	35c salmon & black	1.00	80
		Nos. C48-C53 (6)	4.35	2.83

The 10c and 25c were issued Mar. 15, 1968; 11c, Sept. 24, 1971; 13c, Feb. 11, 1974; 22c, 35c, May 10, 1976.

AIR POST OFFICIAL STAMPS

Officials and Air Post Officials were sold to the public only with a Balboa Heights, Canal Zone wavy line parcel post cancel while current. After being withdrawn from use, unused copies (except for Nos. O3, O8, CO8-CO12) were sold at face value for three months beginning Jan. 2, 1952.

Used values are for the CTO copies, postally used copies being worth more.

Nos. C7, C9-C14 Overprinted in Black **OFFICIAL PANAMA CANAL**

Two Types of Overprint

1941-42 **Unwmk.** *Perf. 11*
"PANAMA CANAL" 19-20mm

CO1	AP1	5c yellow green	5.00	1.50
CO2	AP1	10c orange	8.00	2.00
CO3	AP1	15c blue	9.75	1.75
CO4	AP1	20c red violet	11.00	3.75
CO5	AP1	30c rose lake ('42)	15.00	5.00
CO6	AP1	40c yellow	15.00	7.00
CO7	AP1	$1 black	18.00	10.00
		Nos. CO1-CO7 (7)	81.75	31.00

Overprint varieties occur on Nos. CO1-CO7 and CO14: "O" over "N" of "PANAMA" (entire 3rd row). "O" broken at top (pos. 31). "O" over 2nd "A" of "PANAMA" (pos. 45). 1st "F" of "OFFICIAL" over 2nd "A" of "PANAMA" (pos. 50).

1941
"PANAMA CANAL" 17mm long

CO8	AP1	5c light green	—	150.00
CO9	AP1	10c orange	—	250.00
CO10	AP1	20c red violet	—	165.00
CO11	AP1	30c rose lake	—	60.00
CO12	AP1	40c yellow	—	180.00
		Nos. CO8-CO12 (5)		805.00

Same Overprint on No. C8

1947, Nov.
"PANAMA CANAL" 19-20mm long

CO14	AP1	6c yellow brown	11.00	4.50
a.		Inverted overprint		*2,500.*

POSTAGE DUE STAMPS

Postage Due Stamps of the US Nos. J45a, J46a and J49a Overprinted in Black **CANAL ZONE**

1914, Mar. **Wmk. 190** *Perf. 12*

J1	D2	1c rose carmine	70.00	15.00
J2	D2	2c rose carmine	210.00	45.00
J3	D2	10c rose carmine	750.00	40.00

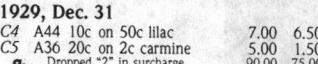

Castle Gate (See footnote) — D1

Statue of Columbus D2

Pedro J. Sosa D3

Blue Overprint, Type II, on Postage Due Stamps of Panama

1915 **Unwmk.**

J4 D1 1c olive brown 10.00 4.25
J5 D2 2c olive brown 190.00 15.00
J6 D3 10c olive brown 45.00 10.00

The 1c was intended to show a gate of San Lorenzo Castle, Chagres. By error the stamp actually shows the main gate of San Geronimo Castle, Portobelo.

Experts believe that the 1c with overprint type V, reading up or down, is bogus.

Surcharged in Red

CANAL 2 ZONE

J7 D1 1c on 1c olive brn 90.00 13.00
J8 D2 2c on 2c olive brn 22.50 7.00
J9 D3 10c on 10c olive brn 20.00 4.50

Columbus Statue — D4

Capitol, Panama City — D5

Carmine Surcharge

1919

J10 D4 2c on 2c olive brown 27.50 11.00
J11 D5 4c on 4c olive brown 32.50 14.00
a. "ZONE" omitted *7,000.*
b. "4" omitted *7,000.*

US Postage Due Stamps Nos. J61, J62b and J65b Overprinted in Black

CANAL

Type A

ZONE

Letters "A" with Flat Tops

1924 *Perf. 11*

J12 D2 1c carmine rose 100.00 22.50
J13 D2 2c deep claret 60.00 9.00
J14 D2 10c deep claret 250.00 50.00

US Postage Stamps Nos. 552, 554 and 562 Overprinted Type A and additional Overprint in Red or Blue

POSTAGE DUE

1925

J15 A155 1c deep green 90.00 13.00
J16 A157 2c carmine (Bl) 22.50 7.00
J17 A165 10c orange 50.00 11.00
a. "POSTAGE DUE" double 450.00
b. "E" of "POSTAGE" missing 400.00
c. As "a" and "b" *3,250.*

"CANAL ZONE" Type B Overprinted on US Nos. J61, J62, J65, J65a

Letters "A" with Sharp Pointed Tops

1925

J18 D2 1c carmine rose 8.00 3.00
a. "ZONE ZONE" 1,250.
J19 D2 2c carmine rose 15.00 4.00
a. "ZONE ZONE" 1,500.
J20 D2 10c carmine rose 130.00 20.00
a. Pair, one without overprint *1,750.*
b. 10c rose red 200.00 70.00
c. As "b," double overprint 400.00

No. 107 Surcharged in Black

POSTAGE DUE

10

1929-30

J21 A37 1c on 5c blue 4.50 1.75
a. "POSTAGE DUE" omitted *5,000.*
J22 A37 2c on 5c blue 7.50 2.50
J23 A37 5c on 5c blue 7.50 2.75
J24 A37 10c on 5c blue 7.50 2.75

On No. J23 the horizontal bars in the lower corners of the surcharge are omitted.

Canal Zone Seal — D6

1932-41

J25 D6 1c claret 15 15
J26 D6 2c claret 15 20
J27 D6 5c claret 35 20
J28 D6 10c claret 1.40 1.50
J29 D6 15c claret ('41) 1.10 1.00
Nos. J25-J29 (5) 3.15 3.05

The 1c and 5c are found in both "wet" and "dry" printings. (See note after US No. 1029.) The dry printings are in red violet.

OFFICIAL STAMPS

See note at beginning of Air Post Official Stamps.

Regular Issues of 1928-34 Overprinted in Black:

OFFICIAL PANAMA CANAL
Type 1

OFFICIAL PANAMA CANAL
Type 2

Type 1 - "PANAMA" 10mm long.
Type 1A - "PANAMA" 9mm long.

1941 **Unwmk.** *Perf. 11*

O1 A35 1c yellow green (1) 2.00 35
O2 A45 3c deep violet (1) 3.75 70
O3 A37 5c blue (2) — 30.00
O4 A38 10c orange (1) 6.50 1.75
O5 A41 15c gray (1) 11.00 2.00
O6 A42 20c olive brown (1) 13.00 2.50
O7 A44 50c lilac (1) 35.00 5.00
O8 A44 50c rose lilac (1A) 600.00

Same Overprint on No. 139

1947

O9 A65 5c deep blue (1) 8.00 3.00

CUBA

LOCATION — The largest island of the West Indies; south of Florida.
GOVT. — socialist; under US military governor 1899-1902 and US provisional governor 1906-1909.
AREA — 44,206 sq. mi.
POP. — 9,710,000 (1981)
CAPITAL — Havana

Formerly a Spanish possession, Cuba's attempts to gain freedom led to US intervention in 1898. Under Treaty of Paris of that year, Spain relinquished the island to US trust. In 1902, a republic was established and Cuban Congress took over government from US military authorities.

100 Cents = 1 Dollar

Watermark

Wmk. 191- Double-lined "USPS" in Capitals

King Alfonso XIII
A19 N2

United States Administration
Puerto Principe Issue

Issues of Cuba of 1898 and 1896 Surcharged:

HABILITADO 1 cent. — a
HABILITADO 1 cents. — b
HABILITADO 2 cents. — c
HABILITADO 2 cents. — d
HABILITADO 3 cents. — e
HABILITADO 3 cents. — f
HABILITADO 5 cents. — g
HABILITADO 5 cents. — h
HABILITADO 5 cents. — i
HABILITADO 5 cents. — j
HABILITADO 3 cents. — k
HABILITADO 3 cents. — l
HABILITADO 10 cents. — m

Types a, c, d, e, f, g and h are 17½mm high, the others are 19½mm high.

Black Surcharge on #156-158, 160

1898-99

176 (a) 1c on 1m org brn 45. 30.
177 (b) 1c on 1m org brn 45. 35.
a. Broken figure "1" 75. 65.
b. Inverted surcharge 200.
d. As "a," inverted *250.*
178 (c) 2c on 2m org brn 22.50 18.
a. Inverted surcharge 250. 50.
179 (d) 2c on 2m org brn 40. 35.
a. Inverted surcharge 350. 100.
179B (k) 3c on 1m org brn 300. 175.
c. Double surcharge 1,500. 750.
179D (l) 3c on 1m org brn *1,500.* *675.*
e. Double surcharge — —
179F (e) 3c on 2m org brn *1,500.*

Value for No. 179F is for copies with minor faults.

179G (f) 3c on 2m org brn — *2,000.*

Value for No. 179G is for copies with minor faults.

180 (e) 3c on 3m org brown 27.50 30.
a. Inverted surcharge 100.
181 (f) 3c on 3m org brown 75. 75.
a. Inverted surcharge *200.*
182 (g) 5c on 1m org brown 700. 200.
a. Inverted surcharge *500.*
183 (h) 5c on 1m org brown *1,300.* *500.*
a. Inverted surcharge *700.*
184 (g) 5c on 2m org brown 750. 250.
185 (h) 5c on 2m org brown 1,500. 500.
186 (g) 5c on 3m org brown 165.
a. Inverted surcharge 700.
187 (h) 5c on 3m org brown 400.
a. Inverted surcharge 1,000.
188 (g) 5c on 5m org brown 70. 60.
a. Inverted surcharge 400. 200.
b. Double surcharge — —
189 (h) 5c on 5m org brown 350. 250.
a. Inverted surcharge 400.
b. Double surcharge — —

Values for Nos. 188, 189 are for the 1st printing. The 2nd printing was surcharged using a shiny ink.

189C (i) 5c on 5m org brown *7,500.*

Black Surcharge on No. P25

190 (g) 5c on ½m blue grn 250. 75.
a. Inverted surcharge 500. 150.
b. Pair, one without surch. 500.

Value for No. 190b is for pair with unsurcharged copy at right. Exists with unsurcharged stamp at left.

191 (h) 5c on ½m blue grn 300. 90.
a. Inverted surcharge 200.
192 (i) 5c on ½m blue grn 550. 200.
a. Dbl. surch., one diagonal *8,500.*
193 (j) 5c on ½m blue grn 700. 300.

Red Surcharge on No. 161

196 (k) 3c on 1c black violet 60. 35.
a. Inverted surcharge 300.
197 (l) 3c on 1c black violet 125. 55.
a. Inverted surcharge 300.
198 (i) 5c on 1c black violet 20. 25.
a. Inverted surcharge 125.
b. Vert. surch., reading up *3,500.*
c. Double surcharge *400.* *600.*
d. Double invtd. surcharge —

No. 198b exists reading down.

199 (j) 5c on 1c black vio 50. 50.
a. Inverted surcharge 250.
b. Vertical surcharge *2,000.*
c. Double surcharge 1,000. 600.
200 (m) 10c on 1c black vio 20. *50.*
a. Broken figure "1" 40. *100.*

Black Surcharge on Nos. P26-P30

201 (k) 3c on 1m blue green 350. 350.
a. Inverted surcharge 450.
b. "EENTS" 550. 450.
c. As "b," inverted 850.
202 (l) 3c on 1m blue green 500. 400.
a. Inverted surcharge 850.
203 (k) 3c on 2m blue green 850. 350.
a. "EENTS" 1,250. 450.
b. Inverted surcharge 850.
c. As "a," inverted 950.
204 (l) 3c on 2m blue green 1,250. 600.
a. Inverted surcharge 750.
205 (k) 3c on 3m blue green 900. 350.
a. Inverted surcharge 500.
b. "EENTS" 1,250. 450.
c. As "b," inverted 700.
206 (l) 3c on 3m blue green 1,200. 550.
a. Inverted surcharge 700.
211 (i) 5c on 1m blue green 1,800.
a. "EENTS" — 2,500.
212 (j) 5c on 1m blue green 2,500.
213 (i) 5c on 2m blue green 1,800.
a. "EENTS" — 1,900.
214 (j) 5c on 2m blue green 1,900.
215 (i) 5c on 3m blue green 500.
a. "EENTS" 1,000.
216 (j) 5c on 3m blue green — 1,000.
217 (i) 5c on 4m blue green *2,500.* 900.
a. "EENTS" *3,000.* 1,500.
b. Inverted surcharge *2,000.*
c. As "a," inverted 2,000.
218 (j) 5c on 4m blue green *1,500.*
a. Inverted surcharge *2,000.*
219 (i) 5c on 8m blue green *2,500.* 1,250.
a. Inverted surcharge 1,500.
b. "EENTS" — 1,800.
c. As "b," inverted 2,500.
220 (j) 5c on 8m blue green 2,000.
a. Inverted surcharge 2,500.

CUBA

US Nos. 279, 267, 279B, 268, 281, 282C and 283 Surcharged in Black

1 c.
de PESO.

1899 Wmk. 191 *Perf. 12*

221 A87 1c on 1c yellow green 4.50 30
222 A88 2c on 2c car 5.00 35
a. 2c on 2c red 5.50 25
c. Inverted surcharge *3,500. 3,500.*
223 A88 2½c on 2c carmine 3.00 40
a. 2½c on 2c red 3.50 1.40
224 A89 3c on 3c purple 8.50 1.50
a. "CUB.A" 25.00 25.00
225 A91 5c on 5c blue 8.50 1.75
226 A94 10c on 10c brn, type I 16.00 5.50
b. "CUBA" omitted *4,000. 4,000.*
226A A94 10c on 10c brn, type II *5,000.*
Nos. 221-226 (6) 45.50 9.80

The 2½c was sold and used as a 2c stamp.
Excellent counterfeits of this and the preceding issue exist, especially inverted and double surcharges.

Issues of the Republic under US Military Rule

Statue of Columbus A20

Royal Palms A21

"Cuba" — A22

Ocean Liner — A23

Cane Field — A24

Wmk. U S-C (191C)
1899 Engr. *Perf. 12*

227 A20 1c yellow green 3.50 15
228 A21 2c carmine 3.50 15
a. 2c scarlet 3.50 15
b. Booklet pane of 6 *2,000.*
229 A22 3c purple 3.50 16
230 A23 5c blue 3.50 20
231 A24 10c brown 11.00 50
Nos. 227-231 (5) 25.00 1.16

Unwatermarked stamps of designs A20-A24 were re-engraved and issued by the Cuban Republic. See Volume 2 for details of the re-engraving.

SPECIAL DELIVERY STAMPS

United States Administration

US No. E5 Surcharged in Red

CUBA.
10c.
de PESO

1899 Wmk. 191 *Perf. 12*

E1 SD3 10c on 10c blue 110.00 75.00
a. No period after "CUBA" 350.00 300.00

Issues of the Republic under US Military Rule

Special Delivery Messenger SD2

Inscribed: "Immediata"

1899 Wmk. 191C Engr.

E2 SD2 10c orange 42.50 12.50

POSTAGE DUE STAMPS

United States Administration

Postage Due Stamps of the US Nos. J38, J39, J41 and J42 Surcharged in Black Like Nos. 221-226A

1899 Wmk. 191 *Perf. 12*

J1 D2 1c on 1c dp claret 30.00 3.50
J2 D2 2c on 2c dp claret 27.00 3.50
a. Inverted surcharge *2,000.*
J3 5c on 5c dp claret 30.00 3.50
J4 D2 10c on 10c dp claret 24.00 1.50

DANISH WEST INDIES

LOCATION — Group of islands in the West Indies, lying east of Puerto Rico
GOVT. — Danish colony
AREA — 132 sq. mi.
POP. — 27,086 (1911)
CAPITAL — Charlotte Amalie

The US bought these islands in 1917 and they became the US Virgin Islands, using US stamps and currency.

100 Cents = 1 Dollar
100 Bit = 1 Franc (1905)

Watermarks

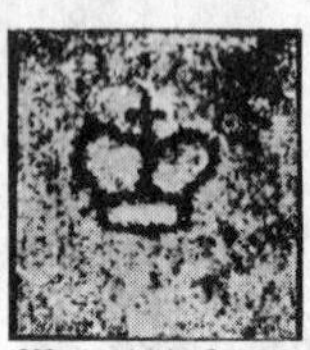
Wmk. 111- Small Crown

Wmk. 112- Crown

Wmk. 113- Crown

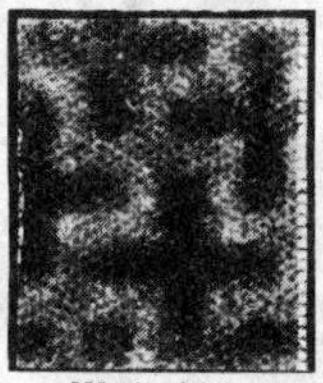
Wmk. 114- Multiple Crosses

Coat of Arms — A1

Yellowish Paper
Yellow Wavy-line Burelage, UL to LR

1856 Wmk. 111 Typo. ***Imperf.***

1 A1 3c dk car, brown gum 150.00 185.00
a. 3c dark carmine, yellow gum 160.00 200.00
b. 3c carmine, white gum *3,000. 3,000.*

Reprint: 1981, carmine, back-printed across two stamps ("Reprint by Dansk Post og Telegrafmuseum 1978"), value, pair, $10.

White Paper
Yellow Wavy-line Burelage, UR to LL

1866

2 A1 3c rose 40.00 40.00

No. 2 reprints unwatermarked: 1930 carmine, value $100. 1942 rose carmine, back-printed across each row ("Nytryk 1942 G. A. Hagemann Danmark og Dansk Vestindiens Friemaerker Bind 2"), value $50.

1872 *Perf. 12½*

3 A1 3c rose 75.00 125.00

1873

Without Burelage

4 A1 4c dull blue 100.00 250.00
a. Imperf., pair 600.00 —
b. Horiz. pair, imperf. vert. 500.00 —

#4 reprints, unwatermarked, imperf.: 1930, ultramarine, value $100. 1942, blue back-printed like 1942 reprint of #2, value $50.

A2

Normal Frame

Inverted Frame

The arabesques in the corners have a main stem and a branch. When the frame is in normal position, in the upper left corner the branch leaves the main stem half way between two little leaflets. In the lower right corner the branch starts at the foot of the second leaflet. When the frame is inverted the corner designs are, of course, transposed.

White Wove Paper, Varying from Thin to Thick

1874-79 Wmk. 112 ***Perf. 14x13½***

5 A2 1c green & brn red 13.00 10.00
a. 1c grn & rose lilac, thin paper 75.00 75.00
b. 1c grn & red violet, medium paper 40.00 40.00
c. 1c green & violet, thick paper 13.00 10.00
e. Inverted frame 13.00 10.00
6 A2 3c blue & carmine 15.00 10.00
d. Imperf., pair 300.00
e. Inverted frame 15.00 10.00
7 A2 4c brn & dull blue 12.00 15.00
b. 4c brown & ultramarine 250.00 200.00
c. Diagonal half used as 2c on cover 100.00
d. Inverted frame *1,500. 1,500.*
8 A2 5c green & gray ('76) 20.00 15.00
b. Inverted frame 20.00 15.00
9 A2 7c lilac & orange 20.00 *35.00*
a. 7c lilac & yellow 40.00 50.00
b. Inverted frame 30.00 60.00
10 A2 10c blue & brn ('76) 20.00 10.00
b. "cent.s" 25.00 15.00
c. Inverted frame 20.00 10.00
11 A2 12c red lilac & yel green ('77) 22.50 40.00
a. 12c lilac & deep green 75.00 75.00
12 A2 14c lilac & green 350.00 500.00
a. Inverted frame *2,000. 2,500.*
13 A2 50c violet, thin paper ('79) 60.00 75.00
a. 50c gray violet, thick porous paper 100.00 150.00

The central element in the fan-shaped scrollwork at the outside of the lower left corner of Nos. 5a and 7b looks like an elongated diamond.
See Nos. 16-20. For surcharges see Nos. 14-15, 23-28, 40.

Nos. 9 and 13 Surcharged in Black

1 CENT

10
CENTS
1895

1887-95

14 A2 1c on 7c lilac & org 50.00 90.00
a. 1c on 7c lilac & yellow 75.00 125.00
b. Double surcharge 200.00 300.00
c. Inverted frame 65.00 90.00
15 A2 10c on 50c violet, thin paper ('95) 20.00 50.00

Type of 1873

1896-1901 *Perf. 13*

16 A2 1c green & red vio ('98) 8.00 8.00
a. Normal frame 200.00 300.00
17 A2 3c blue & lake ('98) 8.00 8.00
a. Normal frame 225.00 250.00
18 A2 4c bister & dull blue ('01) 9.00 9.00
a. Diagonal half used as 2c on cover 25.00
b. Inverted frame 35.00 30.00
19 A2 5c green & gray 35.00 20.00
a. Normal frame 600.00 900.00
20 A2 10c blue & brown ('01) 55.00 75.00
a. Inverted frame 900.00 1,300.
b. "cent.s" 60.00 95.00
Nos. 16-20 (5) 115.00 120.00

Arms — A5

1900

21 A5 1c light green 2.00 2.00
22 A5 5c light blue 8.00 12.00

See Nos. 29-30. For surcharges see Nos. 41-42.

Nos. 6, 17, 20 Surcharged:

2
CENTS
1902
c

8
Cents
1902
d

Surcharge "c" in Black

1902 *Perf. 14x13½*

23 A2 2c on 3c blue & car 500.00 400.00
a. "2" in date with straight tail 525.00 450.00
b. Normal frame *2,500.* —

Perf. 13

24 A2 2c on 3c blue & lake 8.00 12.50
a. "2" in date with straight tail 15.00 20.00
b. Dated "1901" 325.00 400.00
c. Normal frame 150.00 175.00
d. Dark green surcharge 1,250.
e. As "d" & "a" 1,500.
f. As "d" & "c" *6,000.*
25 A2 8c on 10c blue & brn 15.00 20.00
a. "2" with straight tail 15.00 22.50
b. On No. 20b 15.00 25.00
c. Inverted frame 250.00 300.00

Only one copy of No. 24f can exist.

Surcharge "d" in Black

27 A2 2c on 3c blue & lake 8.00 17.00
a. Normal frame 200.00 300.00
28 A2 8c on 10c blue & brn 7.00 7.00
a. On No. 20b 9.00 9.00
b. Inverted frame 200.00 250.00

1903 Wmk. 113

29 A5 2c carmine 8.00 10.00
30 A5 8c brown 16.00 20.00

King Christian IX — A8

St. Thomas Harbor — A9

1905 Typo. *Perf. 13*

31 A8 5b green 3.00 2.00
32 A8 10b red 4.00 2.00
33 A8 20b green & blue 8.00 8.00
34 A8 25b ultramarine 7.00 7.00
35 A8 40b red & gray 8.00 8.00
36 A8 50b yellow & gray 7.00 9.00

Frame Typo., Center Engr.
Wmk. Two Crowns (113)
Perf. 12

37 A9 1fr green & blue 13.00 *22.50*
38 A9 2fr org red & brown 30.00 *50.00*
39 A9 5fr yellow & brown 65.00 *150.00*
Nos. 37-39 (9) 145.00

Favor cancels exist on #37-39. Value 25% less.

Nos. 18, 22, 30 Surcharged in Black

5
BIT
1905

1905 Wmk. 112 *Perf. 13*

40 A2 5b on 4c bis & dull blue 9.00 *15.00*
a. Inverted frame 30.00 *45.00*
41 A5 5b on 5c light blue 8.00 *14.00*

Wmk. 113

42 A5 5b on 8c brown 8.00 *15.00*

Favor cancels exist on #40-42. Value 25% less.

Frederik VIII — A10

Christian X — A11

Frame Typo., Center Engr.

1907-08 Wmk. 113 *Perf. 13*

43 A10 5b green 1.50 1.00
44 A10 10b red 1.50 1.00
45 A10 15b violet & brown 3.50 3.50
46 A10 20b green & blue 30.00 14.00
47 A10 25b blue & dk blue 1.50 1.00
48 A10 30b claret & slate 40.00 35.00
49 A10 40b ver & gray 4.00 4.00
50 A10 50b yellow & brown 4.00 5.00
Nos. 43-50 (8) 86.00 64.50

1915 Wmk. 114 *Perf. 14x14½*

51 A11 5b yellow green 2.00 *5.00*
52 A11 10b red 2.00 *35.00*
53 A11 15b lilac & red brown 2.00 *35.00*
54 A11 20b green & blue 2.00 *35.00*
55 A11 25b blue & dark blue 2.00 *5.00*
56 A11 30b claret & black 2.00 *35.00*
57 A11 40b orange & black 2.00 *35.00*
58 A11 50b yellow & brown 2.00 *35.00*
Nos. 51-58 (8) 16.00

Forged and favor cancellations exist.

POSTAGE DUE STAMPS

Royal Cipher, "Christian 9 Rex" — D1

1902 Unwmk. Litho. *Perf. 11½*

J1 D1 1c dark blue 5.00 10.00
J2 D1 4c dark blue 6.00 15.00
J3 D1 6c dark blue 25.00 45.00
J4 D1 10c dark blue 15.00 20.00

There are five types of each value. On the 4c they may be distinguished by differences in the figures "4"; on the other values the differences are minute.

Used values of Nos. J1-J4 are for canceled copies. Uncanceled examples without gum have probably been used. Value 60% of unused.

Counterfeits of Nos. J1-J4 exist.

D2

1905-13 *Perf. 13*

J5 D2 5b red & gray 4.00 *5.00*
J6 D2 20b red & gray 8.00 *12.50*
J7 D2 30b red & gray 7.00 *12.50*
J8 D2 50b red & gray 9.00 *9.00*
a. Perf. 14x14½ ('13) 35.00 *110.00*
b. Perf. 11½ 500.00

All values of this issue are known imperforate, but were not regularly issued.

Used values of Nos. J5-J8 are for canceled copies. Uncanceled examples without gum have probably been used. Value 60% of unused.

Counterfeits of Nos. J5-J8 exist.

Danish West Indies stamps were replaced by those of the US in 1917, after the US bought the islands.

GUAM

LOCATION — One of the Mariana Islands in the Pacific Ocean, about 1450 miles east of the Philippines
GOVT. — United States Possession
AREA — 206 sq. mi.
POP. — 9,000 (est. 1899)
CAPITAL — Agaña

Formerly a Spanish possession, Guam was ceded to the United States in 1898 following the Spanish-American War. Stamps overprinted "Guam" were superseded by the regular postage stamps of the United States in 1901.

100 Cents = 1 Dollar

US Nos. 279, 267, 268, 280a, 281, 282, 272, 282C, 283, 284, 275, 275a, 276 and 276A
Overprinted in Black (1c-50c) or Red ($1)

GUAM

1899 Wmk. 191 *Perf. 12*

1 A87 1c deep green 14.00 *17.50*
2 A88 2c red 12.50 *17.50*
a. 2c rose carmine 15.00 *20.00*
3 A89 3c purple 100.00 *125.00*
4 A90 4c lilac brown 100.00 *125.00*
5 A91 5c blue 20.00 *35.00*
6 A92 6c lake 100.00 *150.00*
7 A93 8c violet brown 100.00 *150.00*
8 A94 10c brown, type I 37.50 *45.00*
9 A94 10c brown, type II *3,500.* —
10 A95 15c olive green 125.00 *125.00*
11 A96 50c orange 250.00 *325.00*
a. 50c red orange 425.00 —
12 A97 $1 black, type I 300.00 *375.00*
13 A97 $1 black, type II *3,000.*
Nos. 1-8,10-12 (11) 1,159. 1,490.

SPECIAL DELIVERY STAMP

United States No. E5 Overprinted in Red **GUAM**

1899 Wmk. 191 *Perf. 12*

E1 SD3 10c blue 125.00 *150.00*

Guam Guard Mail stamps of 1930 are listed in Scott's Specialized United States Catalogue.

HAWAII

LOCATION — Group of 20 islands in the Pacific Ocean, about 2,000 miles southwest of San Francisco.
GOVT. — Former Kingdom and Republic
AREA — 6,435 sq. mi.
POP. — 150,000 (est. 1899)
CAPITAL — Honolulu

Until 1893 an independent kingdom, from 1893 to 1898 a republic, the Hawaiian Islands were annexed to the US in 1898 at the request of the inhabitants. The Territory of Hawaii achieved statehood in 1959.

100 Cents = 1 Dollar

Values for Nos. 1-4 are for examples with minor damage that has been skillfully repaired.

A1

A2

A3

Pelure Paper

1851-52 Unwmk. Typeset *Imperf.*

1 A1 2c blue *500,000.* *175,000.*
2 A1 5c blue *45,000.* *25,000.*
3 A2 13c blue *22,500.* *12,500.*
4 A3 13c blue *45,000.* *27,500.*

Two varieties of each.

King Kamehameha III
A4 A5

Thick White Wove Paper

1853 Engr.

5 A4 5c blue 850. 650.
6 A5 13c dark red 450. 400.

See #8-9. See Special Printings section, #10-11.

A6

1857

7 A6 5c on 13c dark red *6,500.* *6,000.*

1857

Thin White Wove Paper

8 A4 5c blue 400. 375.
a. Double impression —

1861

Thin Bluish Wove Paper

9 A4 5c blue 180. 125.

For Re-issues and Reprints of Types A4-A5 see Special Printings section.

A7

A8

A9

1859-62 Typeset

12 A7 1c lt blue, *bluish white* *6,000.* *4,000.*
a. "1 Ce" omitted —
b. "nt" omitted — —
13 A7 2c lt blue, *bluish white* *6,000.* *2,500.*
a. 2c dark blue, *grayish white* *6,000.* *2,500.*
b. Comma after "Cents" —
c. No period after "Leta" — —
14 A7 2c blk, *grnsh blue* ('62) *6,000.* *2,000.*
a. "2-Cents." —

1863

15 A7 1c black, *grayish* 400. *575.*
a. Tete beche pair *4,000.*
b. "NTER" —
16 A7 2c black, *grayish* 550. 500.
a. "2" at top of rectangle *2,250.* *3,000.*
b. Printed on both sides — 3,000.
c. "NTER" 550. 500.
d. 2c black, *grayish white* —
e. Period omitted after "Cents" —
f. Overlapping double impressions —
g. "TAGE." —
17 A7 2c dk blue, *bluish* *4,500.* *4,000.*
a. "ISL" — —
18 A7 2c black, *blue gray* *1,500.* *2,000.*

1864-65

19 A7 1c black 375. *700.*
20 A7 2c black 475. *750.*
21 A8 5c blue, *blue* ('65) 550. 400.
a. Tete beche pair *4,500.*
b. 5c black, *grayish white* —
22 A9 5c blue, *blue* ('65) 400. *500.*
a. Tete beche pair *7,000.*
b. 5c blue, *grayish white* —

1864 Laid Paper

23 A7 1c black 225. *850.*
a. HA instead of HAWAIIAN *2,500.*
b. Tete beche pair *6,000.*
24 A7 2c black 200. *850.*
a. "NTER" *2,100.*
b. "S" of "POSTAGE" omitted *700.*
c. Tete beche pair *3,500.*

A10

1865 Wove Paper

25 A10 1c dark blue 175.
26 A10 2c dark blue 175.

Nos. 12 to 26 were typeset and were printed in settings of ten, each stamp differing from the others.

King Kamehameha IV — A11

1861-63 Litho.

Horizontally Laid Paper

27 A11 2c pale rose 175. 110.
a. 2c carmine rose ('63) 1,000. 1,500.

Vertically Laid Paper

28 A11 2c pale rose 175. 110.
a. 2c carmine rose ('63) 150. 175.

For Re-issues and Reprints of Type A11 see Special Printings section.

Princess Victoria Kamamalu — A12

King Kamehameha IV — A13

King Kamehameha V
A14 A15

Mataio Kekuanaoa — A16

1864-86 Wove Paper Engr. *Perf. 12*

30 A12 1c purple ('71) 7.50 6.00
a. 1c violet 10.00 7.50
31 A13 2c rose vermilion 11.00 7.00
a. 2c vermilion ('86) 11.00 7.00
b. Half used as 1c on cover —
32 A14 5c blue ('66) 100.00 19.00
33 A15 6c yellow green ('71) 17.50 6.00
a. 6c bluish green ('79) 17.50 6.00

34	A16	18c dull rose ('71)	85.00	35.00
		Without gum	17.50	
		Nos. 30-34 (5)	221.00	73.00

No. 32 has traces of rectangular frame lines surrounding the design. Nos. 39 and 52C have no such frame lines.

For overprints see #53, 58-60, 65, 66C, 71.

King David Kalakaua
A17

Prince William Pitt Leleiohoku
A18

1875

35	A17	2c brown	6.00	2.25
36	A18	12c black	40.00	20.00

See Nos. 38, 43, 46. For overprints see Nos. 56, 62-63, 66, 69.

Princess Likelike — A19

King David Kalakaua — A20

Queen Kapiolani — A21

Statue of King Kamehameha I — A22

King William Lunalilo
A23

Queen Emma Kaleleonalani
A24

1882

37	A19	1c blue	4.00	*7.50*
38	A17	2c lilac rose	90.00	30.00
39	A14	5c ultramarine	12.00	2.50
a.		Vert. pair, imperf. horiz.	*4,500.*	*4,500.*
40	A20	10c black	22.50	15.00
41	A21	15c red brown	47.50	22.50
		Nos. 37-41 (5)	176.00	77.50

1883-86

42	A19	1c green	2.25	1.50
43	A17	2c rose ('86)	3.50	75
a.		2c dull red	40.00	15.00
44	A20	10c red brown ('84)	22.50	7.00
45	A20	10c vermilion	25.00	12.50
46	A18	12c red lilac	65.00	30.00
47	A22	25c dark violet	100.00	50.00
48	A23	50c red	135.00	75.00
49	A24	$1 rose red	200.00	125.00
		Maltese cross cancellation		45.00
		Nos. 42-49 (8)	553.25	301.75

Other fiscal cancellations exist on No. 49. For overprints see Nos. 54-55, 57, 61-61B, 64, 67-68, 70, 72-73.

For Reproduction and Reprint of the 2c see Special Printings section.

Queen Liliuokalani — A25

1890-91 *Perf. 12*

52	A25	2c dull violet ('91)	4.00	1.25
a.		Vert. pair, imperf. horiz.	*3,750.*	
52C	A14	5c deep indigo	100.00	100.00

Stamps of 1864-91 Overprinted in Red

Provisional GOVT. 1893

1893

53	A12	1c purple	5.00	7.00
a.		"189" instead of "1893"	300.00	
b.		No period after "GOVT"	*150.00*	*150.00*
54	A19	1c blue	4.00	*6.50*
b.		No period after "GOVT"	*100.00*	*100.00*
55	A19	1c green	1.50	*3.00*
a.		Pair, one without ovpt.	*5,500.*	
b.		Double overprint	600.00	400.00
56	A17	2c brown	7.50	*15.00*
a.		No period after "GOVT"	*200.00*	—
57	A25	2c dull violet	1.50	1.25
a.		Inverted overprint	*1,650.*	*1,650.*
b.		Double overprint	500.00	300.00
c.		"18 3" instead of "1893"	*300.00*	*250.00*
58	A14	5c deep indigo	9.00	*20.00*
a.		No period after "GOVT"	*175.00*	*200.00*
59	A14	5c ultra	5.00	2.50
a.		Inverted overprint	1,000.	900.00
b.		Double overprint	*2,500.*	
60	A15	6c green	10.00	*20.00*
61	A20	10c black	7.00	*10.00*
61B	A20	10c red brown	*12,500.*	*17,500.*
62	A18	12c black	7.50	*14.00*
b.		Double overprint	*2,000.*	
63	A18	12c red lilac	125.00	*175.00*
64	A22	25c dark violet	20.00	*35.00*
a.		No period after "GOVT"	*200.00*	*250.00*
		Nos. 53-61,62-64 (12)	203.00	*309.25*

Overprinted in Black

65	A13	2c vermilion	*50.00*	*55.00*
a.		No period after "GOVT"	*225.00*	*225.00*
66	A17	2c rose	1.25	*2.25*
a.		Double overprint	2,500.	
b.		No period after "GOVT"	50.00	60.00
66C	A15	6c green	*12,500.*	*17,500.*
67	A20	10c vermilion	11.00	*25.00*
68	A20	10c red brown	6.00	*10.00*
69	A18	12c red lilac	250.00	*400.00*
70	A21	15c red brown	17.50	*30.00*
a.		Double overprint	*2,000.*	
71	A16	18c dull rose	22.50	*35.00*
a.		Double overprint	*300.00*	
b.		Pair, one without ovpt.	*1,750.*	
c.		No period after "GOVT"	*300.00*	*300.00*
d.		"18 3" instead of "1893"	*350.00*	*350.00*
72	A23	50c red	55.00	*90.00*
b.		No period after "GOVT"	*275.00*	—
73	A24	$1 rose red	100.00	*160.00*
a.		No period after "GOVT"	*325.00*	—
		Nos. 65-66,67-73 (9)	513.25	*807.25*

Coat of Arms — A26

View of Honolulu — A27

Statue of Kamehameha I — A28

Stars and Palms — A29

S. S. "Arawa" — A30

Pres. Sanford Ballard Dole — A31

Statue of King Kamehameha I — A32

1894

74	A26	1c yellow	1.85	1.25
75	A27	2c brown	2.00	60
76	A28	5c rose lake	3.75	1.50
77	A29	10c yellow green	5.00	4.50
78	A30	12c blue	10.00	*15.00*
79	A31	25c deep blue	10.00	*15.00*
		Nos. 74-79 (6)	32.60	*37.85*

1899

80	A26	1c dark green	1.50	1.25
81	A27	2c rose	1.35	1.00
a.		2c salmon	1.50	1.25
b.		Vert. pair, imperf. horiz.	*3,000.*	
82	A32	5c blue	5.00	3.00

OFFICIAL STAMPS

Lorrin Andrews Thurston — O1

1896 Unwmk. Engr. *Perf. 12*

O1	O1	2c green	35.00	17.50
O2	O1	5c black brown	35.00	17.50
O3	O1	6c deep ultra	35.00	17.50
O4	O1	10c bright rose	35.00	17.50
O5	O1	12c orange	35.00	17.50
O6	O1	25c gray violet	35.00	17.50
		Nos. O1-O6 (6)	210.00	105.00

Used values for Nos. O1-O6 are for copies canceled to order "FOREIGN OFFICE/HONOLULU H.I." in double circle without date.

The stamps of Hawaii were replaced by those of the United States.

SPECIAL PRINTINGS

Re-issues

1868

Ordinary White Wove Paper

10	A4	5c blue	25.00
11	A5	13c dull rose	250.00

Reprints:

5c. Originals have two small dots near the left side of the square in the upper right corner. These dots are missing in the reprints.

13c. The bottom of the 3 of 13 in the upper left corner is flattened in the originals and rounded in the reprints. The "t" of "Cts" on the left side is as tall as the "C" in the reprints, but shorter in the originals.

On August 19, 1892, the remaining supply of reprints was overprinted in black "REPRINT." The reprints (both with and without overprint) were sold at face value. See Scott's U.S. Specialized Catalogue.

1869 Engr. Thin Wove Paper

29	A11	2c red	45.00	—

No. 29 was sold only at the Honolulu post office, at first without overprint and later with overprint "CANCELLED."

See note following No. 51.

Reproduction and Reprint

Yellowish Wove Paper

1886-89 ***Imperf.***

50	A11	2c orange vermilion	150.00
51	A11	2c carmine ('89)	25.00

In 1885 the Postmaster General wished to have on sale complete sets of Hawaii's stamps as far back as type A11, but was unable to find either the stone from which Nos. 27 and 28, or the plate from which No. 29 was printed. He therefore sent a copy of No. 29 to the American Bank Note Co., with an order to engrave a new plate and print 10,000 stamps, of which 5000 were overprinted "Specimen" in blue.

The original No. 29 was printed in sheet of 15 (5x3), but the plate of these "Official Imitations" was made up of 50 stamps (10x5). Later, in 1887, the original die for No. 29 was discovered, and after retouching, a new plate was made and 37,500 stamps were printed. These, like the originals, were printed in sheets of 15. They were delivered during 1889 and 1890. In 1892 all remaining unsold in the Post Office were overprinted "Reprint."

No. 29 is red in color, and printed on very thin white wove paper. No. 50 is orange vermilion in color, on medium, white to buff paper. In No. 50 the vertical line on the left side of the portrait touches the horizontal line over the label "Elua Keneta", while in the other two varieties, Nos. 29 and 51, it does not touch the horizontal line by half a millimeter. In No. 51 there are three parallel lines on the left side of the King's nose, while in No. 29 and No. 50 there are are no such lines. No. 51 is carmine in color and printed on thick, yellowish to buff wove paper.

It is claimed that both Nos. 50 and 51 were available for postage, although not made to fill a postal requirement.

MARSHALL ISLANDS

LOCATION — Two chains of islands in the West Pacific Ocean, about 2,500 miles southeast of Tokyo
GOVT. — Republic
AREA — 70 sq. mi.
POP. — 31,042 (1980)
CAPITAL — Dalap-Uliga-Darrit

A German possession from 1885 to 1914, stamps numbered 1-27 are listed in Volume 4 of this catalogue. Seized by Japan in 1914, the islands were taken by the US in WW II and they became part of the US Trust Territory of the Pacific in 1947. By agreement with the USPS, the islands began issuing their own stamps in 1984, with the USPS continuing to carry the mail to and from the islands.

On Oct. 21, 1986 Marshall Islands became a Federation as a Sovereign State in Compact of Free Association with the US.

100 Cents = 1 Dollar

Catalogue values for all unused stamps in this country are for Never Hinged items.

Two unauthorized issues appeared in 1979. The 1st a set of five for the "Establishment of Government, May 1, 1979," consists of 8c, 15c, 21c, 31c and 75c labels. The 75c is about the size of a postcard. The 2nd a set of four se-tenant blocks of four 10c labels for the Intl. Year of the Child. This set also exists imperf. and with specimen overprints.

Inauguration of Postal Service — A5

1984, May 2 Litho. *Perf. 14x13½*

31	A5	20c Outrigger canoe	50	50
32	A5	20c Fishnet	50	50
33	A5	20c Navigational stick chart	50	50
34	A5	20c Islet	50	50
a.		Block of 4, #31-34	2.00	2.00

Mili Atoll, Astrolabe — A6

Maps and Navigational Instruments.

1984-85 Litho. *Perf. 15x14*

35	A6	1c shown	15	15
36	A6	3c Likiep, Azimuth compass	15	15
37	A6	5c Ebon, 16th cent. compass	15	15
38	A6	10c Jaluit, anchor buoys	20	20
39	A6	13c Ailinginae, Nocturnal	26	26
a.		Booklet pane of 10	*7.00*	—
40	A6	14c Wotho Atoll, navigational stick chart	28	28
a.		Booklet pane of 10	*7.00*	—
41	A6	20c Kwajalein and Ebeye, stick chart	40	40
a.		Booklet pane of 10	*9.00*	—
b.		Bklt. pane, 5 each 13c, 20c	*8.00*	—
42	A6	22c Eniwetok, 18th cent. lodestone storage case	44	44
a.		Booklet pane of 10	*9.00*	—
b.		Bklt. pane, 5 each 14c, 22c	*8.00*	—

43	A6	28c Ailinglaplap, printed compass	56	56
44	A6	30c Majuro, navigational stick-chart	60	60
45	A6	33c Namu, stick chart	66	66
46	A6	37c Rongelap, quadrant	74	74
47	A6	39c Taka, map compass, 16th cent. sea chart	78	78
48	A6	44c Ujelang, chronograph	88	88
49	A6	50c Maloelap and Aur, nocturlabe	1.00	1.00
49A	A6	$1 Arno, 16th cent. sector compass	2.00	2.00
		Nos. 35-49A (16)	9.25	9.25

Issue dates: 1c, 3c, 10c, 30c and $1, June 12. 13c, 20c, 28c and 37c. Dec. 19, 1984. 14c, 22c, 33c, 39c, 44c and 50c, June 5, 1985.

See Nos. 107-109.

No. 7 — A7

1984, June 19 *Perf. 14½x15*

50	A7	40c shown	75	75
51	A7	40c No. 13	75	75
52	A7	40c No. 4	75	75
53	A7	40c No. 25	75	75
a.		Block of 4, #50-53	3.00	3.00

Philatelic Salon, 19th UPU Congress, Hamburg, June 19-26.

Ausipex '84 A8

Dolphins.

1984, Sept. 5 **Litho.** *Perf. 14*

54	A8	20c Common	45	45
55	A8	20c Risso's	45	45
56	A8	20c Spotter	45	45
57	A8	20c Bottlenose	45	45
a.		Block of 4, #54-57	1.80	1.80

Christmas — A9

Illustration reduced.

1984, Nov. 7 **Litho.** *Perf. 14*

58	Strip of 4	2.25	2.25
a.-d.	A9 20c any single	45	45
e.	Sheet of 16	10.00	

Printed in sheets of 16; background shows text from Marshallese New Testament, giving each stamp on the sheet a different background.

Marshall Islands Constitution, 5th Anniv. — A10

1984, Dec. 19 **Litho.** *Perf. 14*

59	A10	20c Traditional chief	45	45
60	A10	20c Amata Kabua	45	45
61	A10	20c Chester Nimitz	45	45
62	A10	20c Trygve Lie	45	45
a.		Block of 4, #59-62	1.80	1.80

Audubon Bicentenary A11

1985, Feb. 15 **Litho.** *Perf. 14*

63	A11	22c Forked-tailed Petrel	65	65
64	A11	22c Pectoral Sandpiper	65	65
a.		Pair, #63-64	1.30	1.30

See Nos. C1-C2.

Sea Shells — A12

1985, Apr. 17 **Litho.** *Perf. 14*

65	A12	22c Cymatium lotorium	50	50
66	A12	22c Chicoreus cornucervi	50	50
67	A12	22c Strombus aurisdanae	50	50
68	A12	22c Turbo marmoratus	50	50
69	A12	22c Chicoreus palmarosae	50	50
a.		Strip of 5, #65-69	2.50	2.50
		Nos. 65-69 (5)	2.50	2.50

See Nos. 119-123, 152-156, 216-220.

Decade for Women A13

1985, June 5 **Litho.** *Perf. 14*

70	A13	22c Native drum	50	50
71	A13	22c Palm branches	50	50
72	A13	22c Pounding stone	50	50
73	A13	22c Ak bird	50	50
a.		Block of 4, #70-73	2.00	2.00

Reef and Lagoon Fish A14

1985, July 15 **Litho.** *Perf. 14*

74	A14	22c Acanthurus dussumieri	50	50
75	A14	22c Adioryx caudimaculatus	50	50
76	A14	22c Ostracion meleacaris	50	50
77	A14	22c Chaetodon ephippium	50	50
a.		Block of 4, #74-77	2.00	2.00

Intl. Youth Year A15

IYY and Alele Nautical Museum emblems and: No. 78, Marshallese youths and Peace Corps volunteers playing basketball. No. 79, Legend teller reciting local history, girl listening to recording. No. 80, Islander explaining navigational stick charts. No. 81, Jabwa stick dance.

1985, Aug. 31 **Litho.** *Perf. 14*

78	A15	22c multicolored	50	50
79	A15	22c multicolored	50	50
80	A15	22c multicolored	50	50
81	A15	22c multicolored	50	50
a.		Block of 4, #78-81	2.00	2.00

1856 American Board of Commissions Stock Certificate for Foreign Missions — A16

Missionary ship Morning Star I: 22c, Launch, Jothan Stetson Shipyard, Chelsea, MA, Aug. 7, 1857. 33c, First voyage, Honolulu to the Marshalls, 1857. 44c, Marshall islanders pulling Morning Star I into Ebon Lagoon, 1857.

1985, Oct. 21 **Litho.** *Perf. 14*

82	A16	14c multicolored	25	25
83	A16	22c multicolored	45	45
84	A16	33c multicolored	65	65
85	A16	44c multicolored	90	90

Christmas.

US Space Shuttle, Astro Telescope, Halley's Comet — A17

Comet tail and research spacecraft: No. 87, Planet A Space Probe, Japan. No. 88, Giotto spacecraft, European Space Agency. No. 89, INTERCOSMOS Project Vega spacecraft, Russia, France, etc. No. 90, US naval tracking ship, NASA observational aircraft, cameo portrait of Edmond Halley (1656-1742), astronomer. Se-tenant in continuous design.

1985, Nov. 21

86	A17	22c multicolored	1.10	1.10
87	A17	22c multicolored	1.10	1.10
88	A17	22c multicolored	1.10	1.10
89	A17	22c multicolored	1.10	1.10
90	A17	22c multicolored	1.10	1.10
a.		Strip of 5, #86-90	5.50	5.50
		Nos. 86-90 (5)	5.50	5.50

Medicinal Plants A18

1985, Dec. 31 **Litho.** *Perf. 14*

91	A18	22c Sida fallax	50	50
92	A18	22c Scaevola frutescens	50	50
93	A18	22c Guettarda speciosa	50	50
94	A18	22c Cassytha filiformis	50	50
a.		Block of 4, #91-94	2.00	2.00

Maps Type of 1984

1986-87 *Perf. 15x14, 14 ($10)*

107	A6	$2 Wotje and Erikub, terrestrial globe, 1571	5.00	5.00
108	A6	$5 Bikini, Stick chart	11.00	11.00

Size: 31x31mm

109	A6	$10 Stick chart of the atolls	17.50	17.50

Issue dates: $2, $5, Mar 7, 1986. $10, Mar. 31, 1987.

Marine Invertebrates — A19

1986, Mar. 31 **Litho.** *Perf. 14½x14*

110	A19	14c Triton's trumpet	35	35
111	A19	14c Giant clam	35	35
112	A19	14c Small giant clam	35	35
113	A19	14c Coconut crab	35	35
a.		Block of 4, #110-113	1.40	1.40

Souvenir Sheet

AMERIPEX '86, Chicago, May 22-June 1 — A20

1986, May 22 **Litho.** *Perf. 14*

114	A20	$1 Douglas C-54 Globester	3.25	3.25

1st Around-the-world scheduled flight, 40th anniv. No. 114 has multicolored margin continuing the design and picturing US Air Transport Command Base, Kwajalein Atoll and souvenir card.

See Nos. C3-C6.

Operation Crossroads, Atomic Bomb Tests, 40th Anniv. A21

Designs: No. 115, King Juda, Bikinians sailing tibinal canoe. No. 116, USS Sumner, amphibious DUKW, advance landing. No. 117, Evacuating Bikinians. No. 118, Land reclamation, 1986.

1986, July 1 **Litho.** *Perf. 14*

115	A21	22c multicolored	50	50
116	A21	22c multicolored	50	50
117	A21	22c multicolored	50	50
118	A21	22c multicolored	50	50
a.		Block of 4, #115-118	2.00	2.00

See No. C7.

Seashells Type of 1985

1986, Aug. 1 Litho. *Perf. 14*

119	A12 22c Ramose murex	50	50
120	A12 22c Orange spider	50	50
121	A12 22c Red-mouth frog shell	50	50
122	A12 22c Laciniate conch	50	50
123	A12 22c Giant frog shell	50	50
a.	Strip of 5, #119-123	2.50	2.50
	Nos. 119-123 (5)	2.50	2.50

Game Fish A22

1986, Sept. 10 Litho.

124	A22 22c Blue marlin	55	55
125	A22 22c Wahoo	55	55
126	A22 22c Dolphin fish	55	55
127	A22 22c Yellowfin tuna	55	55
a.	Block of 4, #124-127	2.20	2.20

Christmas, Intl. Peace Year — A23

1986, Oct. 28 Litho. *Perf. 14*

128	A23 22c United Nations UR	70	70
129	A23 22c United Nations UL	70	70
130	A23 22c United Nations LR	70	70
131	A23 22c United Nations LL	70	70
a.	Block of 4, #128-131	2.80	2.80

See No. C8.

US Whaling Ships — A24

1987, Feb. 20 Litho. *Perf. 14*

132	A24 22c James Arnold, 1854	50	50
133	A24 22c General Scott, 1859	50	50
134	A24 22c Charles W. Morgan, 1865	50	50
135	A24 22c Lucretia, 1884	50	50
a.	Block of 4, #132-135	2.00	2.00

Historic and Military Flights A25

Designs: No. 136, Charles Lindbergh commemorative medal, Spirit of St. Louis crossing the Atlantic, 1927. No. 137, Lindbergh flying in the Battle of the Marshalls, 1944. No. 138, William Bridgeman flying in the Battle of Kwajalein, 1944. No. 139, Bridgeman testing the Douglas Skyrocket, 1951. No. 140, John Glenn flying in the Battle of the Marshalls. No. 141, Glenn, the first American to orbit the Earth, 1962.

1987, Mar. 12 Litho. *Perf. 14½*

136	A25 33c multicolored	70	70
137	A25 33c multicolored	70	70
a.	Pair, #136-137	1.40	1.40
138	A25 39c multicolored	75	75
139	A25 39c multicolored	75	75
a.	Pair, #138-139	1.50	1.50
140	A25 44c multicolored	80	80
141	A25 44c multicolored	80	80
a.	Pair, #140-141	1.60	1.60
	Nos. 136-141 (6)	4.50	4.50

Souvenir Sheet

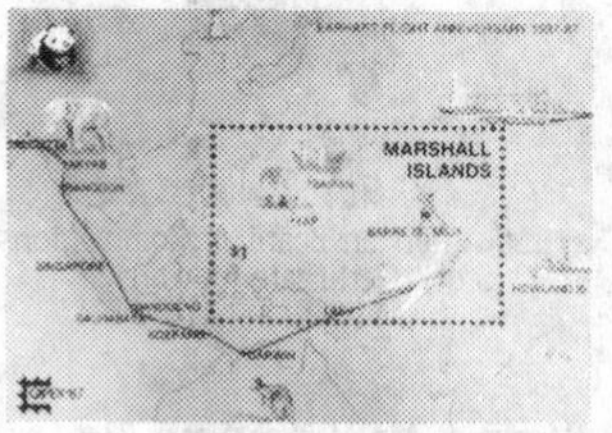

CAPEX '87 — A26

1987, June 15 Litho. *Perf. 14*

142	A26 $1 Map of flight	2.75	2.75

Amelia Earhart (1897-1937), American aviator who died during attempted round-the-world flight, 50th anniv. No. 142 has multicolored margin picturing Earhart's flight pattern from Calcutta, India, to the crash site near Barre Is., Marshall Is.

US Constitution Bicentennial — A27

Excerpts from the Marshall Islands and US Constitutions.

1987, July 16 Litho. *Perf. 14*

143	A27 14c We,... Marshall	35	35
144	A27 14c National seals	35	35
145	A27 14c We,... United States	35	35
a.	Triptych, #143-145	1.05	1.05
146	A27 22c All we have...	45	45
147	A27 22c Flags	45	45
148	A27 22c to establish...	45	45
a.	Triptych, #146-148	1.35	1.35
149	A27 44c With this Constitution...	90	90
150	A27 44c Stick chart, Liberty Bell	90	90
151	A27 44c to promote...	90	90
a.	Triptych, #149-151	2.70	2.70
	Nos. 143-151 (9)	5.10	5.10

Triptychs printed in continuous designs.

Seashells Type of 1985

1987, Sept. 1 Litho. *Perf. 14*

152	A12 22c Magnificent cone	50	50
153	A12 22c Partridge tun	50	50
154	A12 22c Scorpion spider conch	50	50
155	A12 22c Hairy triton	50	50
156	A12 22c Chiragra spider conch	50	50
a.	Strip of 5, #152-156	2.50	2.50
	Nos. 152-156 (5)	2.50	2.50

Copra Industry A28

Contest-winning crayon drawings by Amram Enox; design contest sponsored by the Tobular Copra Processing Co.

1987, Dec. 10 Litho. *Perf. 14*

157	A28 44c Planting coconut	75	75
158	A28 44c Making copra	75	75
159	A28 44c Bottling coconut oil	75	75
a.	Triptych, #157-159	2.25	2.25

Biblical Verses A29

1987, Dec. 10

160	A29 14c Matthew 2:1	30	30
161	A29 22c Luke 2:14	45	45
162	A29 33c Psalms 33:3	70	70
163	A29 44c Pslams 150:5	90	90

Christmas.

Marine Birds — A30

1988, Jan. 27

164	A30 44c Pacific reef herons	85	85
165	A30 44c Bar-tailed godwit	85	85
166	A30 44c Masked booby	85	85
167	A30 44c Northern shoveler	85	85
a.	Block of 4, #164-167	3.50	3.50

Fish — A31

Perf. 14½x14, 14 (#187)

1988-89 Litho.

168	A31 1c Damselfish	15	15
169	A31 3c Blackface butterflyfish	15	15
170	A31 14c Hawkfish	25	25
a.	Booklet pane of 10	3.00	—
171	A31 15c Balloonfish	25	25
a.	Booklet pane of 10	2.50	—
172	A31 17c Trunk fish	30	30
173	A31 22c Lyretail wrasse	35	35
a.	Booklet pane of 10	4.00	—
b.	Bklt. pane of 10 (5 each 14c, 22c)	4.00	—
174	A31 25c Parrotfish	40	40
a.	Booklet pane of 10	4.00	—
b.	Bklt. pane of 10 (5 each 15c, 25c)	4.00	—
175	A31 33c White-spotted boxfish	60	60
176	A31 36c Spotted boxfish	65	65
177	A31 39c Surgeonfish	70	70
178	A31 44c Long-snouted butterflyfish	75	75
179	A31 45c Trumpetfish	70	70
180	A31 56c Sharp-nosed puffer	1.00	1.00
181	A31 $1 Seahorse	1.75	1.75
182	A31 $2 Ghost pipefish	3.50	3.50
183	A31 $5 Big-spotted triggerfish	8.75	8.75
184	A31 $10 Blue jack ('89)	15.00	15.00
	Nos. 168-184 (17)	35.25	35.25

Issue dates: Nos. 170a, 173a, 173b, Mar. 31, 1988. 15c, 25c, 36c, 45c, July 19. 171a, 174a, 174b, Dec. 15. $10, Mar. 31, 1989. Others, Mar. 17, 1988.

A32

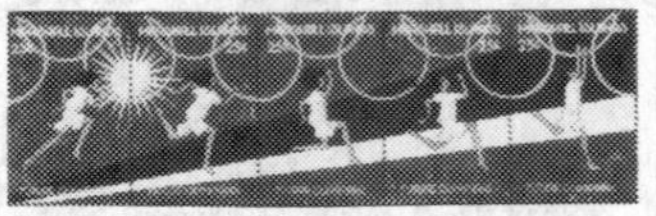

1988 Summer Olympics, Seoul — A33

Athletes in motion: 15c, Javelin thrower (Nos. 188a-188e as shown). 25c, Runner (Nos. 189a-189e as shown). Illustrations reduced.

1988, June 30 Litho. *Perf. 14*

188	Strip of 5	1.75	1.75
a.-e.	A32 15c any single	30	30
189	Strip of 5	2.25	2.25
a.-e.	A33 25c any single	45	45

Souvenir Sheet

Pacific Voyages of Robert Louis Stevenson — A34

Stick chart of the Marshalls and: a, *Casco* sailing through the Golden Gate. b, At the Needles of Ua-Pu, Marquesas. c, *Equator* departing from Honolulu and Kaiulani, an Hawaiian princess. d, Chief's canoe, Majuro Lagoon. e, Bronze medallion, 1887, by Augustus St. Gaudens in the Tate Gallery, London. f, Outrigger canoe and S.S. *Janet Nicoll* in Majuro Lagoon. g, View of Apemama, Gilbert Is. h, Samoan outrigger canoe, Apia Harbor. i, Stevenson riding horse Jack at his estate, Vallima, Samoa.

1988, July 19 Litho. *Perf. 14*

190	Sheet of 9	4.50	4.50
a.-i.	A34 25c any single	50	50

Robert Louis Stevenson (1850-1894), Scottish novelist, poet and essayist.

Colonial Ships and Flags — A35

Designs: No. 191, Galleon *Santa Maria de La Victoria*, 1526, and Spanish "Ragged Cross" ensign in use from 1516 to 1785. No. 192, Transport ships *Charlotte* and *Scarborough*, 1788, and British red ensign, 1707-1800. No. 193, Schooner *Flying Fish*, sloop-of-war *Peacock*, 1841, and U.S. flag, 1837-1845. No. 194, Steamer *Planet*, 1909, and German flag, 1867-1919.

1988, Sept. 2 Litho. *Perf. 14*

191	A35 25c multicolored	55	55
192	A35 25c multicolored	55	55
193	A35 25c multicolored	55	55
194	A35 25c multicolored	55	55
a.	Block of 4, #191-194	2.20	2.20

A36

A37

Christmas: No. 195, Santa Claus riding in sleigh. No. 196, Reindeer, hut and palm trees. No. 197, Reindeer and palm trees. No. 198, Reindeer, palm tree, fish. No. 199, Reindeer and outrigger canoe.

1988, Nov. 7 Litho. *Perf. 14*

195	A36 25c multicolored	50	50
196	A36 25c multicolored	50	50
197	A36 25c multicolored	50	50
198	A36 25c multicolored	50	50
199	A36 25c multicolored	50	50
a.	Strip of 5, #195-199	2.50	2.50
	Nos. 195-199 (5)	2.50	2.50

No. 199a has a continuous design.

1988, Nov. 22 Litho. *Perf. 14*

200	A37 25c Nuclear threat diminished	60	60
201	A37 25c Signing the Test Ban Treaty	60	60
202	A37 25c Portrait	60	60
203	A37 25c US-USSR Hotline	60	60
204	A37 25c Peace Corps enactment	60	60
a.	Strip of 5, #200-204	3.00	3.00
	Nos. 200-204 (5)	3.00	3.00

Tribute to John F. Kennedy. No. 204a has a continuous design.

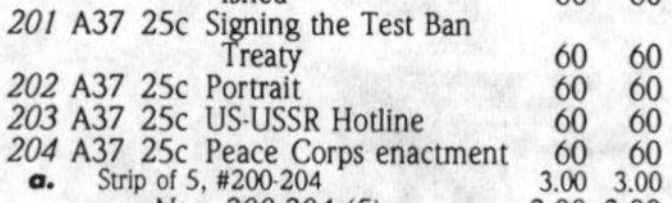

US Space Shuttle Program and Kwajalein — A38

Designs: No. 205, Launch of *Prime* from Vandenberg Air Force Base downrange to the Kwajalein Missile Range. No. 206, *Prime* X023A/SV-5D lifting body reentering atmosphere. No. 207, Parachute landing and craft recovery off Kwajalein Is. No. 208, Shuttle over island.

1988, Dec. 23 Litho. *Perf. 14*

205 A38 25c multicolored 60 60
206 A38 25c multicolored 60 60
207 A38 25c multicolored 60 60
208 A38 25c multicolored 60 60
a. Strip of 4, #205-208 2.40 2.40

NASA 30th anniv. and 25th anniv. of the Project PRIME wind tunnel tests.
See No. C21.

Links to Japan A39

Designs: No. 209, Typhoon Monument, Majuro, 1918. No. 210, Seaplane base and railway depot, Djarrej Islet, c. 1940. No. 211, Fishing boats. No. 212, Japanese honeymooners scuba diving, 1988.

1989, Jan. 19 Litho. *Perf. 14*

209 A39 45c multicolored 85 85
210 A39 45c multicolored 85 85
211 A39 45c multicolored 85 85
212 A39 45c multicolored 85 85
a. Block of 4, #209-212 3.40 3.40

Links to Alaska A40

Paintings by Claire Fejes.

1989, Mar. 31 Litho. *Perf. 14*

213 A40 45c Island Woman 90 90
214 A40 45c Kotzebue, Alaska 90 90
215 A40 45c Marshallese Madonna 90 90
a. Strip of 3, #213-215 2.70 2.70

Printed in sheets of 9.

Seashell Type of 1985

1989, May 15 Litho. *Perf. 14*

216 A12 25c Pontifical miter 60 60
217 A12 25c Tapestry turban 60 60
218 A12 25c Flame-mouthed helmet 60 60
219 A12 25c Prickly Pacific drupe 60 60
220 A12 25c Blood-mouthed conch 60 60
a. Strip of 5, #216-220 3.00 3.00
Nos. 216-220 (5) 3.00 3.00

Souvenir Sheet

In Praise of Sovereigns, 1940, by Sanko Inoue — A41

1989, May 15 Litho. *Perf. 14*

221 A41 $1 multicolored 2.00 2.00

Hirohito (1901-89) and enthronement of Akihito as emperor of Japan.

Migrant Birds A42

1989, June 27 Litho. *Perf. 14*

222 A42 45c Wandering tattler 85 85
223 A42 45c Ruddy turnstone 85 85
224 A42 45c Pacific golden plover 85 85
225 A42 45c Sanderling 85 85
a. Block of 4, #222-225 3.40 3.40

Postal History A43

PHILEXFRANCE '89 — A44

Designs: No. 226, Missionary ship *Morning Star V*, 1905, and Marshall Isls. #15 canceled. No. 227, Marshall Isls. #15-16 on registered letter, 1906. No. 228, *Prinz Eitel Friedrich*, 1914, and German sea post cancel. No. 229, Cruiser squadron led by SMS *Scharnhorst*, 1914, and German sea post cancel.

No. 230: a, SMS *Bussard* and German sea post cancel and Germany #32. b, US Type A924 and Marshall Isls. #34a on FDC. c, LST 119 FPO, 1944, US Navy cancel and pair of US #853. d, Mail boat, 1936, cancel and Japan #222. e, Majuro PO f, Marshall Isls. cancel, 1951, and four US #803.

No. 231, Germany #32 and Marshall Isls. cancel, 1889.

1989, July 7

226 A43 45c multicolored 85 85
227 A43 45c multicolored 85 85
228 A43 45c multicolored 85 85
229 A43 45c multicolored 85 85
a. Block of 4, #226-229 3.40 3.40

Souvenir Sheets

230 Sheet of 6 10.00 3.00
a.-f. A44 25c any single 1.25 1.25
231 A43 $1 multicolored 10.00 3.00

Nos. 230b and 230e are printed in a continuous design.

1st Moon Landing, 20th Anniv. A45

Apollo 11: No. 232, Liftoff. No. 233, Neil Armstrong. No. 234, Lunar module *Eagle*. No. 235, Michael Collins. No. 236, Raising the American flag on the Moon. No. 237, Buzz Aldrin. $1, 1st step on the Moon and "We came in peace for all mankind."

1989, Aug. 1 Litho. *Perf. 13½*

Booklet Stamps

232 A45 25c multicolored 1.25 1.25
233 A45 25c multicolored 1.25 1.25
234 A45 25c multicolored 1.25 1.25
235 A45 25c multicolored 1.25 1.25
236 A45 25c multicolored 1.25 1.25
237 A45 25c multicolored 1.25 1.25

Size: 75x32mm

238 A45 $1 multicolored 5.00 5.00
a. Booklet pane of 7, #232-238 13.00 —

Decorative inscribed selvage separates No. 238 from Nos. 232-237 and surrounds it like a souvenir sheet margin. Selvage around Nos. 232-237 is plain.

World War II

A46

A47

Anniversaries and events, 1939: No. 239, Invasion of Poland. No. 240, Sinking of HMS *Royal Oak*. No. 241, Invasion of Finland.

Battle of the River Plate: No. 242, HMS *Exeter*,. No. 243, HMS *Ajax*,. No. 244, *Admiral Graf Spee*,. No. 245, HMNZS *Achilles*,.

1989 Litho. *Perf. 13½*

239 A46 25c W1 (1-1) 45 45
240 A46 45c W2 (1-1) 75 75
241 A46 45c W3 (1-1) 75 75
242 A46 45c W4 (4-1) 75 75
243 A46 45c W4 (4-2) 75 75
244 A46 45c W4 (4-3) 75 75
245 A46 45c W4 (4-4) 75 75
a. Block of 4, #242-245 3.00 3.00

Issue dates: No. 239, Sept. 1. No. 240, Oct. 13. No. 241, Nov. 30; No. 245a, Dec. 13.

1990

1940: No. 246, Invasion of Denmark. No. 247, Invasion of Norway. No. 248, Katyn Forest Massacre. No. 249, Bombing of Rotterdam. No. 250, Invasion of Belgium. No. 251, Winston Churchill becomes prime minister of England. No. 252, Evacuation of the British Expeditionary Force at Dunkirk. No. 253, Evacuation at Dunkirk. No. 254, Occupation of Paris.

246 A46 25c W5 (2-1) 50 50
247 A46 25c W5 (2-2) 50 50
a. Pair, #246-247 1.00 1.00
248 A47 25c W6 (1-1) 50 50
249 A46 25c W8 (2-1) 50 50
250 A46 25c W8 (2-2) 50 50
a. Pair, #249-250 1.00 1.00
251 A46 45c W7 (1-1) 90 90
252 A46 45c W9 (2-1) 90 90
253 A46 45c W9 (2-2) 90 90
254 A47 45c W10 (1-1) 90 90

Issue dates: Nos. 246-247, Apr. 9. No. 248, Apr. 16. Nos. 249-251, May 10. Nos. 252-253, June 4. No. 254, June 14.

1990

Designs: No. 255, Battle of Mers-el-Kebir, 1940. No. 256, Battles for the Burma Road, 1940-45.

US Destroyers for British bases: No. 257, HMS Georgetown (ex-USS Maddox). No. 258, HMS Banff (ex-USCGC Saranac). No. 259, HMS Buxton (ex-USS Edwards). No. 260, HMS Rockingham (ex-USS Swasey).

Battle of Britain: No. 261, Supermarine Spitfire Mark IA. No. 262, Hawker Hurricane Mark I. No. 263, Messerschmitt Bf109E. No. 264, Junkers JU87B-2. No. 265, Tripartite Pact Signed 1940.

255 A46 25c W11 (1-1) 50 50
256 A47 25c W12 (1-1) 50 50
257 A46 45c W13 (4-1) 90 90
258 A46 45c W13 (4-2) 90 90
259 A46 45c W13 (4-3) 90 90
260 A46 45c W13 (4-4) 90 90
a. Block of 4, #257-260 3.60 3.60
261 A46 45c W14 (4-1) 90 90
262 A46 45c W14 (4-2) 90 90
263 A46 45c W14 (4-3) 90 90
264 A46 45c W14 (4-4) 90 90
a. Block of 4, #261-264 3.60 3.60
265 A46 45c W15 90 90

Issue dates: No. 255, July 3. No. 256, July 18. No. 260a, Sept. 9. No. 264a, Sept. 15. No. 265, Sept. 27.

1990-91

Designs: No. 266, Roosevelt elected to third term, 1940. Battle of Taranto: No. 267, HMS Illustrious. No. 268, Fairey Swordfish. No. 269, RM Andrea Doria. No. 270, RM Conte di Cavour.

Roosevelt's Four Freedoms Speech: No. 271, Freedom of Speech. No. 272, Freedom from Want. No. 273, Freedom of Worship. No. 274, Freedom From Fear. No. 275, Battle of Beda Fomm, Feb. 5-7, 1941.

Germany Invades the Balkans: No. 276, Invasion of Greece. No. 277, Invasion of Yugoslavia.

Sinking of the Bismarck: No. 278, HMS Prince of Wales. No. 279, HMS Hood. No. 280, Bismarck. No. 281, Fairey Swordfish. No. 282, German Invasion of Russia, 1941.

266 A47 25c W16 50 50
267 A46 25c W17 (4-1) 50 50
268 A46 25c W17 (4-2) 50 50
269 A46 25c W17 (4-3) 50 50
270 A46 25c W17 (4-4) 50 50
a. Block of 4, #266-270 2.00 2.00
271 A46 30c W18 (4-1) 60 60
272 A46 30c W18 (4-2) 60 60
273 A46 30c W18 (4-3) 60 60
274 A46 30c W18 (4-4) 60 60
a. Block of 4, #271-274 2.40 2.40
275 A46 30c Tanks, W19 60 60
276 A47 29c W20 (2-1) 58 58
277 A47 29c W20 (2-2) 58 58
a. Pair, #276-277 1.16 1.16
278 A46 50c W21 (4-1) 1.00 1.00
279 A46 50c W21 (4-2) 1.00 1.00
280 A46 50c W21 (4-3) 1.00 1.00
281 A46 50c W21 (4-4) 1.00 1.00
a. Block of 4, #278-281 4.00 4.00
282 A46 30c Tanks, W22 60 60

Issue dates: No. 266, Nov. 5. No. 270a, Nov. 11. No. 274a, Jan. 6, 1991. No. 275, Feb. 5, 1991. Nos. 276-277, Apr. 6, 1991. Nos. 278-281, May 27, 1991. No. 282, June 22, 1991.

1991

1941 - Declaration of the Atlantic Charter: No. 283, Pres. Roosevelt and USS Augusta. No. 284, Churchill and HMS Prince of Wales. No. 285, Siege of Moscow.

Sinking of USS Reuben James: No. 286, Reuben James hit by torpedo. No. 287, German U-562 submarine.

Japanese attack on Pearl Harbor: No. 288, American warplanes. No. 289, Japanese warplanes. No. 290, USS Arizona. No. 291, Japanese aircraft carrier Akagi.

283 A47 29c W23 (2-1) 58 58
284 A47 29c W23 (2-2) 58 58
a. Pair, #283-284 1.16 1.16
285 A46 29c W24 58 58
286 A46 30c W25 (2-1) 60 60
287 A46 30c W25 (2-1) 60 60
a. Pair, #286-287 1.20 1.20
288 A47 50c W26 (4-1) 1.00 1.00
289 A47 50c W26 (4-2) 1.00 1.00
200 A47 50c W26 (4-3) 1.00 1.00
291 A47 50c W26 (4-4) 1.00 1.00
a. Block of 4, #288-291 4.00 4.00

Issue dates: No. 284a, Aug. 14. No. 285, Oct. 2. No. 287a, Oct. 31. No. 291a, Dec. 7.

1991-92

1941-42: No. 292, Japanese capture Guam. No. 293, Fall of Singapore.

First combat of the Flying Tigers: No. 294, Curtiss Tomahawk. No. 295, Mitsubishi Ki-21 on fire.

No. 296, Fall of Wake Island.

No. 297, Roosevelt and Churchill at Arcadia Conference. No. 298, Japanese tank entering Manila. No. 299, Japanese take Rabaul. No. 300, Battle of the Java Sea. No. 301, Rangoon falls to Japanese. No. 302, Japanese land on New Guinea. No. 303, MacArthur evacuated from Corregidor. No. 304, Raid on Saint-Nazaire. No. 305, Surrender of Bataan / Death March. No. 306, Doolittle Raid on Tokyo. No. 307, Fall of Corregidor.

292 A47 29c W27 58 58
293 A46 29c W28 58 58
294 A46 50c W29 (2-1) 1.00 1.00
295 A46 50c W29 (2-2) 1.00 1.00
a. Pair, #294-295 2.00 2.00
296 A46 29c W30 58 58
297 A46 29c W31 58 58
298 A46 50c W32 1.00 1.00
299 A46 29c W33 58 58
300 A46 29c W34 58 58
301 A47 50c W35 1.00 1.00
302 A46 29c W36 58 58
303 A46 29c W37 58 58
304 A46 29c W38 58 58
305 A47 29c W39 58 58
306 A47 50c W40 1.00 1.00
307 A46 29c W41 58 58

Issue dates: Nos. 292-293, Dec. 10, 1991. No. 295a, Dec. 20, 1991. No. 296, Dec. 23, 1991. No. 297, Jan. 1, 1992. No. 298, Jan. 2, 1992. No. 299, Jan. 23, 1992. No. 300, Feb. 15, 1992. Nos. 301-302, Mar. 8, 1992. No. 303, Mar. 11, 1992. No. 304, Mar. 27, 1992. No. 305, Apr. 9, 1992. No. 306, Apr. 18, 1992. No. 307, May 6, 1992.

1992

1942 - Battle of the Coral Sea: No. 308, USS Lexington. No. 309, Japanese Mitsubishi A6M2 Zeros. No. 310, Douglas SBD Dauntless dive bombers. No. 311, Japanese carrier Shoho.

Battle of Midway: No. 312, Japanese aircraft carrier Akagi. No. 313, US Douglas SBD Dauntless dive bombers. No. 314, USS Yorktown. No. 315, Nakajima B5N2 Kate torpedo planes.

No. 316, Village of Lidice destroyed. No. 317, Fall of Sevastopol.

Convoy PQ17 destroyed: No. 318, British merchant ship in convoy. No. 319, German U-boats.

No. 320, Marines land on Guadalcanal. No. 323, Battle of Stalingrad. No. 324, Battle of Eastern Solomons.

No. 321, Battle of Savo Island. No. 322, Dieppe Raid. No. 325, Battle of Cape Esperance. No. 326, Battle of El Alamein.

Battle of Barents Sea: No. 327, HMS Sheffield. No. 328, Admiral Hipper.

308	A46	50c	W42 (4-1)	1.00	1.00
309	A46	50c	W42 (4-2)	1.00	1.00
310	A46	50c	W42 (4-3)	1.00	1.00
311	A46	50c	W42 (4-4)	1.00	1.00
a.			Block of 4, #308-311	4.00	4.00
312	A46	50c	W43 (4-1)	1.00	1.00
313	A46	50c	W43 (4-3)	1.00	1.00
314	A46	50c	W43 (4-2)	1.00	1.00
315	A46	50c	W43 (4-4)	1.00	1.00
a.			Block of 4, #312-315	4.00	4.00
316	A46	29c	W44	58	58
317	A47	29c	W45	58	58
318	A46	29c	W46 (2-1)	58	58
319	A46	29c	W46 (2-2)	58	58
a.			Pair, #318-319	1.16	1.16
320	A46	29c	W47	58	58
321	A47	29c	W48	58	58
322	A46	29c	W49	58	58
323	A47	50c	W50	1.00	1.00
324	A46	29c	W51	58	58
325	A46	50c	W52	1.00	1.00
326	A46	29c	W53	58	58
327	A46	29c	W54 (2-1)	58	58
328	A46	29c	W54 (2-2)	58	58
a.			Pair, #327-328	1.16	1.16

Issue dates: #311a, May 8, 1992. #315a, June 4. #316, June 9, 1992. #317, July 4. #318-319, July 5. #320, Aug. 7. #321, Aug. 9. #322-323, Aug. 19. #324, Aug. 24. #325, Oct. 11. #326, Oct. 23. #327-328, Dec. 31.

Vertical pairs, Nos. 312-313 and Nos. 314-315 have continuous designs.

No. 310 incorrectly identifies Douglas TBD torpedo bombers.

1993 Litho. *Perf. 13½*

1943 - No. 328, Casablanca Conf. No. 330, Liberation of Kharkov.

Battle of Bismarck Sea: No. 331, Japanese A6M Zeroes, destroyer Arashio. No. 332, US P38 Lightnings, Australian Beaufighter. No. 333, Japanese destroyer Shirayuki. No. 334, US A-20 Havoc, B-25 Mitchell.

No. 335, Interception of Admiral Yamamoto.

Battle of Kursk: No. 336, German Tiger I. No. 337, Soviet T-34.

329	A46	29c	W55	58	58
330	A46	29c	W56	58	58
331	A46	50c	W57 (4-1)	1.00	1.00
332	A46	50c	W57 (4-2)	1.00	1.00
333	A46	50c	W57 (4-3)	1.00	1.00
334	A46	50c	W57 (4-4)	1.00	1.00
a.			Block of 4, #331-334	4.00	4.00
335	A46	50c	W58	1.00	1.00
336	A46	29c	W59 (2-1)	58	58
337	A46	29c	W59 (2-2)	58	58
a.			Pair, #336-337	1.16	1.16
			Nos. 239-337 (99)	73.43	73.43

Issue dates: No. 329, Jan. 14. No. 330, Feb. 16. Nos. 331-334, Mar. 3. No. 335, Apr. 18. Nos. 336-337, July 5. See Nos. 467-478.

Christmas A57

Angels playing musical instruments.

1989, Oct. 25 *Perf. 13½*

341	A57	25c	Horn	85	85
342	A57	25c	Singing carol	85	85
343	A57	25c	Lute	85	85
344	A57	25c	Lyre	85	85
a.			Block of 4, #341-344	3.40	3.40

Marshall Islands stamps can be mounted in the Scott U.S. Trust Territories album.

Miniature Sheet

Milestones in Space Exploration — A58

Designs: a, Robert Goddard and 1st liquid fuel rocket launch, 1926. b, *Sputnik*, 1st man-made satellite, 1957. c, 1st American satellite, 1958. d, Yuri Gagarin, 1st man in space, 1961. e, John Glenn, 1st American to orbit Earth, 1962. f, Valentina Tereshkova, 1st woman in space, 1963. g, Aleksei Leonov, 1st space walk, 1965. h, Edward White, 1st American to walk in space, 1965. i, Gemini-Titan 6A, 1st rendezvous in space, 1965. j, 1st Soft landing on the Moon, 1966. k, Gemini 8, 1st docking in space, 1966. l, 1st Probe of Venus, 1967. m, Apollo 8, 1st manned orbit of the Moon, 1968. n, Apollo 11, 1st man on the Moon, 1969. o, Soyuz 11, 1st space station crew, 1971. p, Apollo 15, 1st manned lunar vehicle, 1971. q, *Skylab 2*, 1st American manned space station, 1973. r, 1st Flyby of Jupiter, 1973. s, Apollo-Soyuz, 1st joint space flight, 1975. t, 1st Landing on Mars, 1976. u, 1st Flyby of Saturn, 1979. v, *Columbia*, 1st space shuttle flight, 1981. w, 1st Probe beyond the solar system, 1983. x, 1st Untethered space walk, 1984. y, Launch of space shuttle *Discovery*, 1988.

1989, Nov. 24 Litho. *Perf. 13½*

345		Sheet of 25	30.00	30.00
a.-y.	A58	45c any single	1.00	1.00

No. 345 contains World Stamp Expo '89 emblem on selvage.

Birds

A59 A59a

1990-92 Litho. *Perf. 13½*

346	A59	1c	Black noddy	15	15
347	A59	5c	Red-tailed tropic bird	15	15
348	A59	10c	Sanderling	20	20
349	A59	12c	Black-naped tern	24	24
350	A59	15c	Wandering tattler	30	30
351	A59	20c	Bristle-thighed curlew	40	40
352	A59	23c	Northern shoveler	46	46
353	A59	25c	Brown noddy	50	50
354	A59	27c	Sooty tern	54	54
355	A59	29c	Wedge-tailed shearwater	58	58
356	A59a	29c	Northern pintail	1.00	1.00
357	A59	30c	Pacific golden plover	60	60
358	A59	35c	Brown booby	70	70
359	A59	36c	Red footed booby	72	72
360	A59	40c	White tern	80	80
361	A59	50c	Great frigate bird	1.00	1.00
a.			Min. sheet of 4 (#347, 350, 353, 361)	1.90	1.90
362	A59	52c	Great crested tern	1.04	1.04
363	A59	65c	Lesser sand plover	1.30	1.30
364	A59	75c	Little tern	1.50	1.50
365	A59	$1	Pacific reef heron	2.00	2.00
365A	A59	$2	Masked booby	4.00	4.00
			Nos. 346-365A (21)	18.18	18.18

No. 361a for ESSEN '90, Germany Apr. 19-22.

Issue dates: 5c, 15c, 25c, 50c, Mar. 8. 30c, 36c, 40c, $1, Oct. 11. No. 361a, Apr. 19. No. 355, 20c, 52c, Feb. 22, 1991. 27c, Mar. 8, 1991. 1c, 12c, 35c, $2, Nov. 6, 1991. No. 356, Feb. 3, 1992. 10c, 23c, 65c, 75c, Apr. 24, 1992.

See Nos. 430-433.

Children's Games A60

1990, Mar. 15

366	A60	25c	Lodidean	75	75
367	A60	25c	Lejonjon	75	75
368	A60	25c	Etobobo	75	75
369	A60	25c	Didmakol	75	75
a.			Block of 4, #366-369	3.00	3.00

Penny Black, 150th Anniv. — A61

Designs: No. 370, Penny Black, 1840. No. 371, Essay by James Chalmers. No. 372, Essay by Robert Sievier. No. 373, Essay by Charles Whiting. No. 374, Essay by George Dickinson. No. 375, Medal engraved by William Wyon to celebrate Queen Victoria's first visit to London. $1, Engraver Charles Heath, engraving for master die.

1990, Apr. 6 Booklet Stamps

370	A61	25c	multicolored	1.00	1.00
371	A61	25c	multicolored	1.00	1.00
372	A61	25c	multicolored	1.00	1.00
373	A61	25c	multicolored	1.00	1.00
374	A61	25c	multicolored	1.00	1.00
375	A61	25c	multicolored	1.00	1.00

Size: 73x31mm

376	A61	$1	multicolored	4.00	4.00
a.			Booklet pane of 7, #370-376	9.00	—

Decorative inscribed selvage picturing part of a Penny Black proof sheet separates No. 376 from Nos. 370-375 in pane and surrounds it like a souvenir sheet margin. Selvage around Nos. 370-375 is plain.

Endangered Wildlife — A62

Sea Turtles: No. 377, Pacific green turtle hatchlings entering ocean. No. 378, Pacific great turtle under water. No. 379, Hawksbill hatchling, eggs. No. 380, Hawksbill turtle in water.

1990, May 3

377	A62	25c	multicolored	75	75
378	A62	25c	multicolored	75	75
379	A62	25c	multicolored	75	75
380	A62	25c	multicolored	75	75
a.			Block of 4, #377-380	3.00	3.00

Stick Chart, Canoe and Flag of the Republic of the Marshall Islands — A63

1990, Sept. 28 *Perf. 11x10½*

381	A63	25c	multicolored	60	60

See US No. 2507, Micronesia Nos. 124-126.

German Reunification — A64

1990, Oct. 3 *Perf. 13½*

382	A64	45c	multicolored	1.25	1.25

Christmas A65

1990, Oct. 25 Litho. *Perf. 13½*

383	A65	25c	Canoe, stick chart	75	75
384	A65	25c	Missionary preaching	75	75
385	A65	25c	Sailors dancing	75	75
386	A65	25c	Youths dancing	75	75
a.			Block of 4, #383-386	3.00	3.00

Breadfruit — A66

1990, Dec. 15 Litho. *Perf. 12x12½*

387	A66	25c	Harvesting	75	75
388	A66	25c	Peeling, slicing	75	75
389	A66	25c	Preserving	75	75
390	A66	25c	Kneading dough	75	75
a.			Block of 4, #387-390	3.00	3.00

US Space Shuttle Flights, 10th Anniv. A67

1991, Apr. 12 Litho. *Perf. 13½*

391	A67	50c	747 ferry	1.00	1.00
392	A67	50c	Orbital release of LDEF	1.00	1.00
393	A67	50c	Lift-off	1.00	1.00
394	A67	50c	Landing	1.00	1.00
a.			Block of 4, #391-394	4.00	4.00

Flowers — A68

1991, June 10 Litho. *Perf. 13½*

395	A68	52c	Ixora carolinensis	1.00	1.00
396	A68	52c	Clerodendrum inerme	1.00	1.00
397	A68	52c	Messerchmidia argentea	1.00	1.00
398	A68	52c	Vigna marina	1.00	1.00
a.			Miniature sheet of 4, #395-398	4.00	4.00

Phila Nippon '91 (No. 398a). Stamps from miniature sheets inscribed C53A.

Operation Desert Storm — A69

1991, July 4 Litho. *Perf. 13½*

399	A69 29c multicolored	58	58

Birds A70

1991, July 16 Booklet Stamps

400	A70 29c Red-footed booby	58	58
401	A70 29c Great frigate bird (7-2)	58	58
402	A70 29c Brown booby	58	58
403	A70 29c White tern	58	58
404	A70 29c Great frigate bird (7-5)	58	58
405	A70 29c Black noddy	58	58

Size: 75x33mm

406	A70 $1 White-tailed tropic bird	2.00	2.00
a.	Booklet pane of 7, #400-406	5.50	—

Decorative selvage separates No. 406 from Nos. 400-405 and surrounds it like a souvenir sheet margin.

Aircraft of Air Marshall Islands — A71

1991, Sept. 10 Litho. *Perf. 13½*

407	A71 12c Dornier 228	20	20
408	A71 29c Douglas DC-8	50	50
409	A71 50c Hawker Siddeley 748	85	85
410	A71 50c Saab 2000	85	85

Admission to United Nations A72

1991, Sept. 24 Litho. *Perf. 11x10½*

411	A72 29c multicolored	65	65

Christmas — A73

1991, Oct. 25 *Perf. 13½*

412	A73 30c multicolored	75	75

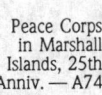

Peace Corps in Marshall Islands, 25th Anniv. — A74

1991, Nov. 26 Litho. *Perf. 11x10½*

413	A74 29c multicolored	58	58

Ships — A75

Designs: No. 414, Bulk cargo carrier, Emlain. No. 415, Tanker, CSK Valiant. No. 416, Patrol boat, Ionmeto. No. 417, Freighter, Micro Pilot.

1992, Feb. 15 Litho. *Perf. 11x10½*

414	A75 29c multicolored	45	45
415	A75 29c multicolored	45	45
416	A75 29c multicolored	45	45
417	A75 29c multicolored	45	45
a.	Strip of 4, #414-417	2.00	2.00

Voyages of Discovery A76

Designs: No. 418, Traditional tipnol. No. 419, Reconstructed Santa Maria. No. 420, Constellation Argo Navis. No. 421, Marshallese sailor, tipnol. No. 422, Columbus, Santa Maria. No. 423, Astronaunt, Argo Navis. $1, Columbus, sailor, and astronaunt.

1992, May 23 Litho. *Perf. 13½*

Booklet Stamps

418	A76 50c multicolored	1.00	1.00
419	A76 50c multicolored	1.00	1.00
420	A76 50c multicolored	1.00	1.00
421	A76 50c multicolored	1.00	1.00
422	A76 50c multicolored	1.00	1.00
423	A76 50c multicolored	1.00	1.00

Size: 75x32mm

424	A76 $1 multicolored	2.00	2.00
a.	Booklet pane of 7, #418-424	8.00	—

Decorative selvage separates No. 424 from Nos. 418-423 and surrounds it like a souvenir sheet margin.

Traditional Handicrafts — A77

1992, Sept. 9 Litho. *Perf. 13½*

425	A77 29c Basket weaving	58	58
426	A77 29c Canoe models	58	58
427	A77 29c Wood carving	58	58
428	A77 29c Fan making	58	58
a.	Strip of 4, #425-428	2.32	2.32

Christmas A78

1992, Oct. 29 Litho. *Perf. 11x10½*

429	A78 29c multicolored	58	58

Bird Type of 1990

1992, Nov. 10 Litho. *Perf. 13½*

430	A59 9c Whimbrel	18	18
431	A59 22c Greater scaup	44	44
432	A59 28c Sharp-tailed sandpiper	56	56
433	A59 45c Common teal	90	90

Reef Life — A79

1993, May 26 Litho. *Perf. 13½*

434	A79 50c Butterflyfish	1.00	1.00
435	A79 50c Soldierfish	1.00	1.00
436	A79 50c Damselfish	1.00	1.00
437	A79 50c Filefish	1.00	1.00
438	A79 50c Hawkfish	1.00	1.00
439	A79 50c Surgeonfish	1.00	1.00

Size: 75x33mm

440	A79 $1 Parrotfish	2.00	2.00
a.	Booklet pane of 7, #434-440	8.00	—

Decorative selvage separates No. 440 from Nos. 434-439 and surrounds it like a souvenir sheet margin.

Ships — A80

Marshallese Sailing Vessels — A81

Designs: 10c, Spanish galleon San Jeronimo. 15c, British merchant ship Britannia. 19c, Island transport Micro Palm. 20c, Dutch ship Eendracht. 23c, Frigate HMS Cornwallis. 24c, US naval schooner Dolphin. 29c, Missionary packet Morning Star. 30c, Russian brig Rurick. 35c, German warship SMS Nautilus. 40c, British brig Nautilus. 45c, Japanese warships Nagara, Isuzu. 50c, Aircraft carrier USS Lexington CV-16. 52c, HMS Serpent. 55c, Whaling ship Potomac. 75c, British transport Scarborough. $1, Walap, Eniwetok. $2, Walap, Jaluit. $2.90, Marshall Islands fishing vessels. $5, Tipnol, Ailuk. $10, Racing canoes.

1993-94 Litho. *Perf. 11x10½*

443	A80	10c multicolored	20	20
444	A80	15c multicolored	30	30
445	A80	20c multicolored	40	40
446	A80	19c multicolored	38	38
447	A80	23c multicolored	45	45
448	A80	24c multicolored	48	48
452	A80	29c multicolored	58	58
453	A80	30c multicolored	60	60
454	A80	35c multicolored	70	70
455	A80	40c multicolored	80	80
455A	A80	45c multicolored	90	90
456	A80	50c multicolored	1.00	1.00
457	A80	52c multicolored	1.10	1.10
457A	A80	55c multicolored	1.10	1.10
458	A80	75c multicolored	1.50	1.50

Perf. 13½

460	A81	$1 multicolored	2.00	2.00
462	A81	$2 multicolored	4.00	4.00
462A	A80	$2.90 multicolored	5.75	5.75
463	A81	$5 multicolored	10.00	10.00
463A	A81	$10 multicolored	20.00	20.00
		Nos. 443-463A (20)	52.24	52.24

Souvenir Sheet

Stamp Size: 46x26mm

464	A81	Sheet of 4, #a.-d.	3.50	3.50

Inscription reads "Hong Kong '94 Stamp Exhibition" in Chinese on Nos. 464a, 464d, and in English on Nos. 464b-464c.

Issued: 15c, 24c, 29c, 50c, 6/24. 10c, 23c, 52c, 75c, 10/14. $1, 5/29. $2, 8/26. 10c, 30c, 35c, $2.90, 4/19, 1994. $5, 3/15/94. $10, 8/18/94. 20c, 40c, 45c, 55c, 9/23/94. No. 464, Feb. 18, 1994.

This is an expanding set. Numbers may change.

World War II Type of 1989

1943 - Invasion of Sicily: No. 467, Gen. George S. Patton, Jr. No. 468, Gen. Bernard L. Montgomery. No. 469, Americans landing at at Licata. No. 470, British landing south of Syracuse.

Allied bomber raids on Schweinfurt: No. 471, B-17F Flying Fortresses and Bf-109 fighter. No. 472, Liberation of Smolensk. No. 473, Landings at Bougainville. No. 474, Invasion of Tarawa, 1943. No. 475, Teheran Conference, 1943.

Battle of North Cape: No. 476, HMS Duke of York. No. 477, Scharnhorst.

No. 478, Gen. Dwight D. Eisenhower, SHAEF Commander. No. 479, Invasion of Anzio, 1944. No. 480, Siege of Leningrad lifted, 1944. No. 481, US liberates Marshall Islands, 1944. No. 482, Japanese defeated at Truk, 1944. No. 483, Big Week, US bombing of Germany, 1944.

1993-94 Litho. *Perf. 13½*

467	A46 52c W60 (4-1)	1.05	1.05
468	A46 52c W60 (4-2)	1.05	1.05
469	A46 52c W60 (4-3)	1.05	1.05
470	A46 52c W60 (4-4)	1.05	1.05
a.	Block of 4, #467-470	4.20	4.20
471	A46 50c W61	1.00	1.00
472	A47 29c W62	58	58
473	A46 29c W63	58	58
474	A46 50c W64	1.00	1.00
475	A47 52c W65	1.10	1.10
476	A46 29c W66 (2-1)	60	60
477	A46 29c W66 (2-2)	60	60
a.	Pair, #476-477	1.20	1.20
478	A46 29c W67	60	60
479	A46 50c W68	1.00	1.00
480	A46 52c W69	1.10	1.10
481	A46 29c W70	60	60
482	A47 29c W71	60	60
483	A46 52c W72	1.10	1.10
	Nos. 467-483 (17)	14.66	14.66

Issued: Nos. 467-470, July 10. No. 471, Aug. 17. No. 472, Sept. 25. No. 473, Nov. 1. No. 474, Nov. 20. No. 475, Dec. 1. Nos. 476-477, Dec. 26. No. 478, Jan. 16, 1994. No. 479, Jan. 22, 1994. No. 480, Jan. 27, 1994. No. 481, Feb. 4, 1994. No. 482, Feb. 17, 1994. No. 483, Feb. 20, 1994.

1994 Litho. *Perf. 13½*

Designs: No. 484, Lt. Gen. Mark Clark, Rome falls to the Allies, 1944.

D-Day-Allied landings in Normandy, 1944: No. 485, Horsa gliders. No. 486, US P-51B Mustangs, British Hurricanes. No. 487, German gun defenses. No. 488, Allied amphibious landing.

No. 489, V-1 flying bombs strike England, 1944. No. 490, US Marines land on Saipan.

First Battle of the Philippine Sea, 1944: No. 491, Grumman F6F-3 Hellcat.

No. 492, US liberates Guam, 1944. No. 493, Warsaw uprising, 1944. No. 494, Liberation of Paris, 1944. No. 495, US Marines land on Peliliu, 1944. No. 496, MacArthur returns to the Philippines, 1944. No. 497, Battle of Leyte Gulf, 1944.

German battleship Tirpitz sunk, 1944: No. 498, Avro Lancaster. No. 499, Tirpitz.

484	A47 50c W73	1.00	1.00
485	A46 75c W74 (4-1)	1.50	1.50
486	A46 75c W74 (4-2)	1.50	1.50
487	A46 75c W74 (4-3)	1.50	1.50
488	A46 75c W74 (4-4)	1.50	1.50
a.	Block of 4, #485-488	6.00	6.00
489	A46 50c W75	1.00	1.00
490	A46 29c W76	60	60
491	A46 50c W77	1.00	1.00
492	A46 29c W78	60	60
493	A46 50c W79	1.00	1.00
494	A46 50c W80	1.00	1.00
495	A46 29c W81	60	60
496	A46 52c W82	1.00	1.00
497	A46 52c multicolored	1.00	1.00
498	A46 50c W84 (2-1)	1.00	1.00
499	A46 50c W84 (2-2)	1.00	1.00
a.	Pair, #498-499	2.00	2.00
	Nos. 484-499 (16)	16.80	16.80

Issued: No. 484, 6/4/94. Nos. 485-488, 6/6/94. No. 489, 6/13/94. No. 490, 6/15/94. No. 491, 6/19/94. No. 492, 7/21/94. No. 493, 8/1/94. No. 494, 8/25/94. No. 495, 9/15/94. No. 496, 10/20/94. No. 497, 10/24/94. Nos. 498-499, 11/12/94.

Souvenir Sheet

Designs: No. 562a, like #303. No. 562b, like #496.

Imperf

562	Sheet of 2	2.00	2.00
a.-b.	A46 50c any single	1.00	1.00

Issued: No. 562, 10/20/94.

Dedication of Capitol Building Complex A82

Designs: No. 567, Capitol building. No. 568, Nitijela (parliament) building. No. 569, Natl. seal, vert. No. 570, Flag over complex, vert.

1993, Aug. 11 Litho. *Perf. 11x10½*

567	A82 29c multi (4-1)	58	58
568	A82 29c multi (4-2)	58	58

Perf. 10½x11

569	A82 29c multi (4-3)	58	58
570	A82 29c multi (4-4)	58	58

The lack of a value for a listed item does not necessarily indicate rarity.

Souvenir Sheet

Christening of Mobil Super Tanker Eagle — A83

1993, Aug. 25 ***Perf. 13½***
571 A83 50c multicolored 1.00 1.00

Marshallese Life in 1800's — A84

1993, Sept. 15 Litho. ***Perf. 13½***

572 A84 29c Woman, breadfruit (4-1)	58	58
573 A84 29c Canoes, warrior (4-2)	58	58
574 A84 29c Young chief (4-3)	58	58
575 A84 29c Drummer, dancers (4-4)	58	58
a. Block of 4, #572-575	2.35	2.35

Christmas A85

1993, Oct. 25 Litho. ***Perf. 13½***
576 A85 29c multicolored 60 60

Souvenir Sheet

Constitution, 15th Anniv. — A86

1994, May 1 Litho. ***Perf. 13½***
577 A86 $2.90 multicolored 5.75 5.75

Souvenir Sheet

Marshall Islands Postal Service, 10th Anniv. — A87

1994, May 2
578 A87 29c multicolored 60 60

1994 World Cup Soccer Championships, US — A88

Design: No. 580, Soccer players, diff.

1994, June 17 Litho. ***Perf. 13½***

579 A88 50c red & multi (2-1)	1.00	1.00
580 A88 50c blue & multi (2-2)	1.00	1.00
a. Pair, #579-580	2.00	2.00

No. 580a has a continuous design.

Miniature Sheet

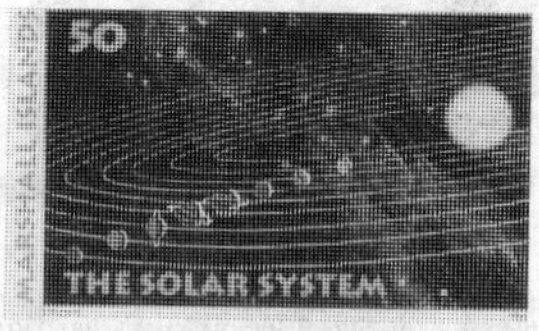

Solar System — A89

Mythological characters, symbols: a, Solar system. b, Sun. c, Moon. d, Mercury. e, Venus. f, Earth. g, Mars. h, Jupiter. i, Saturn. j, Uranus. k, Neptune. l, Pluto.

1994, July 20 Litho. ***Perf. 13½***
582 A89 50c Sheet of 12, #a.-l. 12.00 12.00

First Manned Moon Landing, 25th Anniv. — A90

Designs: No. 583, First step onto Moon's surface. No. 584, Planting US flag on Moon. No. 585, Astronaut's salute to America, flag. No. 586, Astronaut stepping onto Moon, John F. Kennedy.

1994, July 20

583 A90 75c multi (4-1)	1.50	1.50
584 A90 75c multi (4-2)	1.50	1.50
585 A90 75c multi (4-3)	1.50	1.50
586 A90 75c multi (4-4)	1.50	1.50
a. Block of 4, #583-586	6.00	6.00
b. Souvenir sheet of 4, #583-586	6.00	6.00

Souvenir Sheet

Butterflies A91

1994, Aug. 16 Litho. ***Perf. 13½***

587 A91 Sheet of 3	3.75	3.75
a. 29c Meadow argus	58	58
b. 52c Brown awl	1.10	1.10
c. $1 Great eggfly	2.00	2.00

PHILAKOREA '94.

Christmas — A92

1994, Oct. 28 Litho. ***Perf. 13½***
588 A92 29c multicolored 60 60

AIR POST STAMPS

Audubon Type of 1985

1985, Feb. 15 Litho. ***Perf. 14***

C1 A11 44c Booby Gannet, vert.	88	88
C2 A11 44c Esquimaux Curlew, vert.	88	88
a. Pair, #C1-C2	1.80	1.80

AMERIPEX Type of 1986

Designs: No. C3, Consolidated PBY-5A Catalin Amphibian. No. C4, Grumman SA-16 Albatross. No. C5, McDonnell Douglas DC-6B Super Cloudmaster. No. C6, Boeing &27-100.

1986, May 22 Litho. ***Perf. 14***

C3 A20 44c multicolored	95	95
C4 A20 44c multicolored	95	95
C5 A20 44c multicolored	95	95
C6 A20 44c multicolored	95	95
a. Block of 4, #C3-C6	3.80	3.80

Operation Crossroads Type of 1986
Souvenir Sheet

1986, July 1 Litho. ***Perf. 14***
C7 A21 44c USS Saratoga *4.50 4.50*

Statue of Liberty Cent., Intl. Peace Year — AP1

1986, Oct. 28 Litho.
C8 AP1 44c multicolored 95 95

Natl. Girl Scout Movement, 20th Anniv. — AP2

1986, Dec. 8 Litho.

C9 AP2 44c Community service	85	85
C10 AP2 44c Salute	85	85
C11 AP2 44c Health care	85	85
C12 AP2 44c Learning skills	85	85
a. Block of 4, #C9-C12	3.40	3.40

Girl Scout Movement in the US, 75th anniv. (1912-1987).

Marine Birds — AP3

1987, Jan. 12 Litho. ***Perf. 14***

C13 AP3 44c Wedge-tailed shearwater	85	85
C14 AP3 44c Red-footed booby	85	85
C15 AP3 44c Red-tailed tropicbird	85	85
C16 AP3 44c Great frigatebird	85	85
a. Block of 4, #C13-C16	3.40	3.40

CAPEX '87 — AP4

Last flight of Amelia Earhart: No. C17, Take-off at Lae, New Guinea, July 2, 1937. No. C18, USCG Itasca cutter at Howland Is. No. C19, Purported crash landing of the Electra at Mili Atoll. No. C20, Recovery of the Electra by the Koshu, a Japanese survey ship.

1987, June 15 Litho. ***Perf. 14***

C17 AP4 44c multicolored	85	85
C18 AP4 44c multicolored	85	85
C19 AP4 44c multicolored	85	85
C20 AP4 44c multicolored	85	85
a. Block of 4, #C17-C20	3.40	3.40

Space Shuttle Type of 1988

1988, Dec. 23 Litho. ***Perf. 14***
C21 A38 45c Astronaut, shuttle over Rongelap 90 90

Aircraft — AP5

1989, Apr. 24 Litho. ***Perf. 14x14½***

C22 AP5 12c Dornier Do228	25	25
a. Booklet pane of 10	3.00	—
C23 AP5 36c Boeing 737	75	75
a. Booklet pane of 10	8.00	—
C24 AP5 39c Hawker Siddeley 748	90	90
a. Booklet pane of 10	9.00	—
C25 AP5 45c Boeing 727	1.00	1.00
a. Booklet pane of 10	10.00	—
b. Bklt. pane, 5 each 36c, 45c	8.75	—

MICRONESIA, FEDERATED STATES OF

LOCATION — A group of over 600 islands in the West Pacific Ocean, north of the Equator.
GOVT. — Republic
AREA — 271 sq. miles
POP. — 73,755 (1980)
CAPITAL — Palikir

These islands, also known as the Caroline Islands, were bought by Germany from Spain in 1899. Caroline Islands stamps issued as a German territory are listed in Vol. 2 of this Catalogue. Seized by Japan in 1914, they were taken by the US in WWII and became part of the US Trust Territory of the Pacific in 1947. By agreement with the USPS, the islands began issuing their own stamps in 1984, with the USPS continuing to carry the mail to and from the islands.

On Nov. 3, 1986 Micronesia became a Federation as a Sovereign State in Compact of Free Association with the US.

100 Cents = 1 Dollar

Catalogue values for all unused stamps in this country are for Never Hinged items.

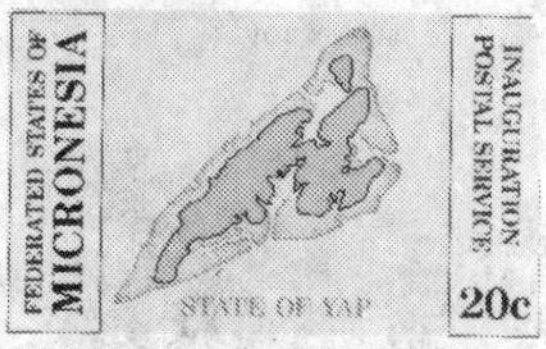

Postal Service Inauguration — A1

1984, July 12 Litho. *Perf. 14*

1	A1	20c Yap	50	50
2	A1	20c Truk	50	50
3	A1	20c Pohnpei	50	50
4	A1	20c Kosrae	50	50
a.		Block of 4, #1-4	2.00	2.00

For surcharges see Nos. 48-51.

Fernandez de Quiros — A2

Men's House, Yap — A3

Designs: 1c, 19c, Pedro Fernandez de Quiros, Spanish explorer, first discovered Pohnpei, 1595. 2c, 20c, Louis Duperrey, French explorer. 3c, 30c, Fyedor Lutke, Russian explorer. 4c, 37c, Dumont d'Urville. 10c, Sleeping Lady, Kosrae. 13c, Liduduhriap Waterfall, Pohnpei. 17c, Tonachau Peak, Truk. 50c, Devil mask, Truk. $1, Sokeh's Rock, Pohnpei. $2, Canoes, Kosrae. $5, Stone money, Yap.

1984, July 12 *Perf. 13½x13*

5	A2	1c Prussian blue	15	15
6	A2	2c deep claret	15	15
7	A2	3c dark blue	15	15
8	A2	4c green	15	15
9	A3	5c yellow brown	15	15
10	A3	10c dark violet	16	16
11	A3	13c dark blue	20	20
12	A3	17c brown lake	25	25
13	A2	19c dark violet	28	28
14	A2	20c olive green	30	30
15	A2	30c rose lake	45	45
16	A2	37c deep violet	55	55
17	A3	50c brown	75	75
18	A3	$1 olive	1.50	1.50
19	A3	$2 Prussian blue	3.00	3.00
20	A3	$5 brown lake	7.00	7.00
		Nos. 5-20 (16)	15.19	15.19

See #33, 36, 38. For surcharges see #48-51.

Ausipex '84 A4

1984, Sept. 21 Litho. *Perf. 13½*

21	A4	20c Truk Post Office	48	48

See Nos. C4-C6.

Christmas A5

Child's drawing.

1984, Dec. 20

22	A5	20c Child in manger	90	90

See Nos. C7-C9.

Ships — A6

1985, Aug. 19

23	A6	22c U.S.S. Jamestown	60	60

See Nos. C10-C12.

Christmas A7

1985, Oct. 15 Litho. *Perf. 13½*

24	A7	22c Lelu Protestant Church, Kosrae	60	60

See Nos. C13-C14.

Audubon Birth Bicentenary — A8

1985, Oct. 30 *Perf. 14½*

25	A8	22c Noddy tern	75	75
26	A8	22c Turnstone	75	75
27	A8	22c Golden plover	75	75
28	A8	22c Black-bellied plover	75	75
a.		Block of 4, #25-28	3.00	3.00

See No. C15.

Types of 1984 and

Birds — A9

Tall Ship Senyavin A10

Natl. Seal A11

Perf. 13½ (A8a), 13½x13

1985-88 Litho.

31	A9	3c Long-billed white-eye	15	15
32	A9	14c Truk monarch	28	28
33	A3	15c Liduduhriap Waterfall, Pohnpei	30	30
a.		Booklet pane of 10	3.00	—
34	A10	22c bright blue green	35	35
35	A9	22c Pohnpei mountain starling	44	44
36	A3	25c Tonachau Peak, Truk	50	50
a.		Booklet pane of 10	5.00	—
b.		Booklet pane, 5 15c + 5 25c	4.00	—
37	A10	36c ultramarine	72	72
38	A3	45c Sleeping Lady, Kosrae	90	90
39	A11	$10 bright ultra	15.00	15.00
		Nos. 31-39,C34-C36 (12)	21.64	21.64

Issue dates: $10, Oct. 15. No. 34, Apr. 14, 1986. 3c, 14c, No. 35, Aug. 1, 1988. 15c, 25c, 36c, 45c, Sept. 1, 1988.

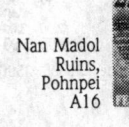

Nan Madol Ruins, Pohnpei A16

1985, Dec. Litho. *Perf. 13½*

45	A16	22c Land of the Sacred Masonry	60	60

See Nos. C16-C18.

Intl. Peace Year — A17

1986, May 16

46	A17	22c multicolored	60	60

Nos. 1-4 Surcharged

1986, May 19 Litho. *Perf. 14*

48	A1	22c on 20c No. 1	45	45
49	A1	22c on 20c No. 2	45	45
50	A1	22c on 20c No. 3	45	45
51	A1	22c on 20c No. 4	45	45
a.		Block of 4, #48-51	1.90	1.90

AMERIPEX '86 — A18

Bully Hayes (1829-1877), Buccaneer.

1986, May 22 *Perf. 13½*

52	A18	22c At ship's helm	65	65
		Nos. 52,C21-C24 (5)	5.20	5.20

First Passport A19

1986, Nov. 4 Litho. *Perf. 13½*

53	A19	22c multicolored	65	65

Christmas — A20

Virgin and child paintings: 5c, Italy, 18th cent. 22c, Germany, 19th cent.

1986, Oct. 15 Litho. *Perf. 14½*

54	A20	5c multicolored	25	25
55	A20	22c multicolored	75	75

See Nos. C26-C27.

Anniversaries and Events — A21

1987, June 13 Litho. *Perf. 14½*

56	A21	22c Intl. Year of Shelter for the Homeless	65	65

Souvenir Sheet

57	A21	$1 CAPEX '87	3.00	3.00

See Nos. C28-C30.

Christmas A22

Design: 22c, Archangel Gabriel appearing before Mary.

1987, Nov. 16 Litho. *Perf. 14½*

58	A22	22c multicolored	60	60

See Nos. C31-C33.

Colonial Eras — A23

1988, July 20 Litho. *Perf. 13x13½*

59	A23	22c German	60	60
60	A23	22c Spanish	60	60
61	A23	22c Japanese	60	60
62	A23	22c US Trust Territory	60	60
a.		Block of 4, #59-62	2.40	2.40
		Nos. 59-62,C37-C38 (6)	4.30	4.30

Printed se-tenant in sheets of 28 plus 4 center labels picturing flags of Spain (UL), Germany (UR), Japan (LL) and the US (LR).

1988 Summer Olympics, Seoul — A24

1988, Sept. 1 Litho. *Perf. 14*

63	A24	25c Running	55	55
64	A24	25c Women's hurdles	55	55
a.		Pair, #63-64	1.10	1.10
65	A24	45c Basketball	90	90
66	A24	45c Women's volleyball	90	90
a.		Pair, #65-66	1.80	1.80

Christmas A25

Children decorating tree: No. 67, Two girls, UL of tree. No. 68, Boy, girl, dove, UR of tree. No. 69, Boy, girl, LL of tree. No. 70, Boy, girl, LR of tree. Se-tenant in a continuous design.

1988, Oct. 28 Litho. *Perf. 14*

67	A25	25c multicolored	45	45
68	A25	25c multicolored	45	45
69	A25	25c multicolored	45	45
70	A25	25c multicolored	45	45
a.		Block of 4, #67-70	2.00	2.00

Miniature Sheet

Truk Lagoon State Monument — A26

Designs: a, Sun and stars angelfish. b, School of fish. c, 3 divers. d, Goldenjack. e, Blacktip reef shark. f, 2 schools of fish. g, Squirrelfish. h, Batfish. i, Moorish idols. j, Barracudas. k, Spot banded butterflyfish. l, Three-spotted damselfish. m, Foxface. n, Lionfish. o, Diver. p, Coral. q, Butterflyfish. r, Bivalve, fish, coral.

1988, Dec. 19 Litho. *Perf. 14*

71		Sheet of 18	7.50	7.50
a.-r.	A26	25c any single	40	40

Mwarmwarms — A27

1989, Mar. 31 Litho. *Perf. 14*

72	A27 45c Plumeria	70	70
73	A27 45c Hibiscus	70	70
74	A27 45c Jasmine	70	70
75	A27 45c Bougainvillea	70	70
a.	Block of 4, #72-75	3.00	3.00

Souvenir Sheet

Pheasant and Chrysanthemum, 1830s, by Hiroshige (1797-1858) — A28

1989, May 15 Litho. *Perf. 14½*

76	A28 $1 multicolored	1.65	1.65

Hirohito (1901-1989), emperor of Japan.

Sharks — A29

1989, July 7

77	A29 25c Whale	40	40
78	A29 25c Hammerhead	40	40
a.	Pair, #77-78	80	80
79	A29 45c Tiger, vert.	75	75
80	A29 45c Great white, vert.	75	75
a.	Pair, #79-80	1.50	1.50

Miniature Sheet

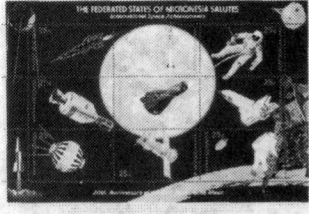

First Moon Landing, 20th Anniv. — A30

Space achievements: a, X-15 rocket plane, 1959. b, *Explorer 1* launched into orbit, 1958. c, Ed White, 1st American to walk in space, Gemini 4 mission, 1965. d, Apollo 18 command module, 1975. e. Gemini 4 capsule. f, Space shuttle *Challenger,* 1983-86. g, *San Marco 2,* satellite engineered by Italy. h, Soyuz 19 spacecraft, 1975. i, *Columbia* command module and Neil Armstrong taking man's first step onto the Moon during the Apollo 11 mission, 1969.

1989, July 20 Litho. *Perf. 14*

81	A30 Sheet of 9	4.00	4.00
a.-i.	25c any single	38	38

Earth and Lunar Module, by William Hanson, 1st Art Transported to the Moon — A31

1989, July 20 *Perf. 13½x14*

82	A31 $2.40 multicolored	3.50	3.50

First Moon landing, 20th anniv.

Seashells — A32

1989, Sept. 26 *Perf. 14*

83	A32 1c Horse's hoof	15	15
84	A32 3c Rare spotted cowrie	15	15
85	A32 15c Commercial trochus	22	22
a.	Booklet pane of 10	2.75	—
87	A32 20c General cone	30	30
88	A32 25c Triton's trumpet	38	38
a.	Booklet pane of 10	4.75	—
b.	Booklet pane, 5 each 15c, 25c	3.75	—
90	A32 30c Laciniated conch	45	45
91	A32 36c Red-mouthed olive	55	55
93	A32 45c Map cowrie	70	70
95	A32 50c Textile cone	75	75
100	A32 $1 Orange spider conch	1.75	1.75
101	A32 $2 Golden cowrie	3.50	3.50
102	A32 $5 Episcopal miter	9.00	9.00
	Nos. 83-102 (12)	17.90	17.90

Booklet panes issued Sept. 14, 1990.

This is an expanding set. Numbers will change if necessary.

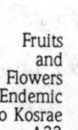

Miniature Sheet

Fruits and Flowers Endemic to Kosrae A33

Designs: a, Orange. b, Lime. c, Tangerine. d, Mango. e, Coconut. f, Breadfruit. g, Sugar cane. h, Thatched dwelling. i, Banana. j, Girl, boy. k, Pineapple picker. l, Taro. m, Hibiscus. n, Ylang ylang. o, White ginger. p, Plumeria. q, Royal poinciana. r, Yellow allamanda.

1989, Nov. 18 Litho. *Perf. 14*

103	Sheet of 18	9.50	9.50
a.-r.	A33 25c any single	50	50

Margin inscribed for World Stamp Expo '89.

Christmas A34

1989, Dec. 14 Litho. *Perf. 14½*

104	A34 25c Heralding angel	40	40
105	A34 45c Three wise men	80	80

World Wildlife Fund A35

Micronesian kingfishers and pigeons.

1990, Feb. 19 Litho. *Perf. 14*

106	A35 10c Kingfisher (juvenile)	20	20
107	A35 15c Kingfisher (adult)	30	30
108	A35 20c Pigeon	40	40
109	A35 25c Pigeon, diff.	50	50

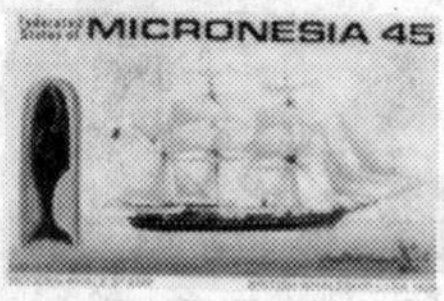

Stamp World London '90 — A36

Exhibition emblem, artifacts and whaling vessels: No. 110, Wooden whale stamp, *Lyra,* 1826. No. 111, Harpoons, *Prudent,* 1827. No. 112, Scrimshaw (whale), *Rhone,* 1851. No. 113, Scrimshaw on whale tooth, *Sussex,* 1843. $1, Whalers at kill.

1990, May 3 Litho. *Perf. 14*

110	A36 45c multicolored	70	70
111	A36 45c multicolored	70	70
112	A36 45c multicolored	70	70
113	A36 45c multicolored	70	70
a.	Block of 4, #110-113	2.80	2.80

Souvenir Sheet

114	A36 $1 multicolored	1.65	1.65

Souvenir Sheet

Penny Black, 150th Anniv. — A37

1990, May 6 *Perf. 14*

115	A37 $1 Great Britain No. 1	1.65	1.65

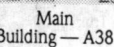

Main Building — A38

Fr. Hugh Costigan, School Founder — A39

Designs: No. 117, Fr. Costigan, students. No. 119, Fr. Costigan, Isaphu Samuel Hadley. No. 120, New York City Police Badge.

1990, July 31 Litho. *Perf. 14*

116	A38 25c multicolored	40	40
117	A38 25c multicolored	40	40
118	A39 25c multicolored	40	40
119	A38 25c multicolored	40	40
120	A38 25c multicolored	40	40
a.	Strip of 5, #116-120	2.00	2.00
	Nos. 116-120 (5)	2.00	2.00

Pohnpei Agriculture and Trade School, 25th anniversary. Printed in sheets of 15.

Souvenir Sheet

Expo '90, Intl. Garden and Greenery Exposition, Osaka, Japan — A40

1990, July 31 Litho. *Perf. 14*

121	A40 $1 multicolored	1.80	1.80

Loading Mail, Pohnpei Airport, 1990 A41

Pacifica Emblem and: 45c, Japanese mail boat, Truk Lagoon, 1940.

1990, Aug. 24

122	A41 25c multicolored	55	55
123	A41 45c multicolored	1.00	1.00

Canoe, Flag of Federated States of Micronesia A42

Designs: No. 124, Stick chart, canoe, flag of Marshall Islands. No. 125, Frigate bird, eagle, USS Constitution, flag of US.

1990, Sept. 28 *Perf. 13½*

124	A42 25c multicolored	55	55
125	A42 25c multicolored	55	55
126	A42 25c multicolored	55	55
a.	Strip of 3, #124-126	1.65	1.65

Compact of Free Association with the US. Printed in sheets of 15. See US No. 2506, Marshall Islands No. 381.

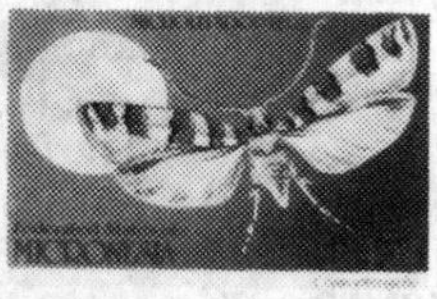

Moths A43

1990, Nov. 10 Litho. *Perf. 14*

127	A43 45c Gracillariidae	75	75
128	A43 45c Yponomeatidae	75	75
129	A43 45c shown	75	75
130	A43 45c Cosmopterigidae, diff.	75	75
a.	Block of 4, #127-130	3.00	3.00

Miniature Sheet

Christmas A44

Designs: a, Cherub. b, Star of Bethlehem. c, Cherub blowing horn. d, Goats. e, Nativity scene. f, Children, outrigger canoe. g, Messenger blowing a conch shell. h, Family walking. i, People carrying bundles.

1990, Nov. 19 Litho. *Perf. 14*

131	Sheet of 9	3.50	3.50
a.-i.	A44 25c any single	40	40

Souvenir Sheets

New Capital of Micronesia — A45

1991, Jan. 15 Litho. *Perf. 14x13½*

132 Sheet of 2 1.40 1.40
a. A45 25c Executive Branch 50 50
b. A45 45c Legislative, Judicial Branches 90 90
133 A45 $1 New Capitol 2.00 2.00

Turtles — A46

1991, Mar. 14 Litho. *Perf. 14*

134 A46 29c Hawksbill on beach 70 70
135 A46 29c Green 70 70
a. Pair, #134-135 1.40 1.40
136 A46 50c Hawksbill 1.15 1.15
137 A46 50c Leatherback 1.15 1.15
a. Pair, #136-137 2.30 2.30

Operation Desert Storm A47

1991, July 30 Litho. *Perf. 14*

138 A47 29c Battleship Missouri 60 60
139 A47 29c Multiple launch rocket system 60 60
140 A47 29c F-14 Tomcat 60 60
141 A47 29c E-3 Sentry (AWACS) 60 60
a. Block of 4, #138-141 2.40 2.40

Size: 51x38mm

142 A47 $2.90 Frigatebird, flag 5.80 5.80
a. Souvenir sheet of 1 5.80 5.80
Nos. 138-142 (5) 8.20 8.20

Miniature Sheets

Phila Nippon '91 — A48

Ukiyo-e prints by Paul Jacoulet (1902-1960): No. 143a, Evening Flowers, Toloas, Truk, 1941. b, The Chief's Daughter, Mogomog, 1953. c, Yagourouh and Mio, Yap, 1938. No. 144a, Yap Beauty and Orchids, 1934. b, The Yellow-eyed Boys, Ohlol, 1940. c, Violet Flowers, Tomil, 1937. $1, First Love, Yap, 1937, horiz.

1991, Sept. Litho. *Perf. 14*

143 Sheet of 3 1.25 1.25
a.-c. A48 29c any single 40 40
144 Sheet of 3 2.25 2.25
a.-c. A48 50c any single 75 75

Souvenir Sheet

145 A48 $1 multicolored 1.65 1.65

Christmas — A49

Handicraft scenes: 29c, Nativity. 40c, Adoration of the Magi. 50c, Adoration of the Shepherds.

1991, Oct. 30 *Perf. 14x13½*

146 A49 29c multicolored 45 45
147 A49 40c multicolored 60 60
148 A49 50c multicolored 75 75

Pohnpei Rain Forest A50

Designs: a, Pohnpei fruit bat. b, Purple capped fruit-dove. c, Micronesian kingfisher. d. Birdnest fern. e, Island swiftlet. f, Long-billed white-eye. g, Brown noddy. h, Pohnpei lory. i, Pohnpei flycatcher. j, Caroline ground-dove. k, White-tailed tropicbird. l, Micronesian honeyeater. m, Ixora. n, Pohnpei fantail. o, Gray white-eye. p, Blue-faced parrotfinch. q, Cicadabird. r, Green skink.

1991, Nov. 18

149 Sheet of 18 10.00 10.00
a.-r. A50 29c any single 48 48

Peace Corps — A51

Designs: a, Learning crop planting techniques. b, Education. c, John F. Kennedy. d, Public health nurses. e, Recreation.

1992, Apr. 10 Litho. *Perf. 14*

150 A51 29c Strip of 5, #a.-e. 2.25 2.25

Printed in sheets of 15.

Discovery of America, 500th Anniv. — A52

Designs: a, Queen Isabella I. b, Santa Maria. c, Columbus.

1992, May 23 Litho. *Perf. 13½*

151 A52 29c Strip of 3, #a.-c. 3.00 3.00

Admission to the UN, First Anniv. — A53

1992, Sept. 24 *Perf. 11x10½*

152 A53 29c multicolored 58 58
153 A53 50c multicolored 1.00 1.00
a. Souvenir sheet of 2, #152-153 1.58 1.58

Christmas A54

1992, Dec. 4 *Perf. 13½*

154 A54 29c multicolored 58 58

Pioneers of Flight A55

Designs: a, Andrei N. Tupolev. b, John A. Macready. c, Edward V. Rickenbacker. d, Manfred von Richtofen. e, Hugh M. Trenchard. f, Glenn H. Curtiss. g, Charles E. Kingsford-Smith. h, Igor I. Sikorsky.

1993, Apr. 12

155 A55 29c Block of 8, #a.-h. 4.65 4.65

See Nos. 178, 191, 200.

Fish — A56

Designs: 10c, Bigscale soldierfish. 19c, Bennett's butterflyfish. 20c, Peacock grouper. 22c, Great barracuda. 25c, Coral grouper. 29c, Regal angelfish. 30c, Bleeker's parrotfish. 35c, Picassofish. 40c, Mandarinfish. 45c, Bluebanded surgeonfish. 50c, Orange-striped triggerfish. 52c, Palette surgeonfish. 75c, Oriental sweetlips. $1, Zebra moray. $2, Foxface rabbitfish. $2.90, Orangespine unicornfish.

1993-94 Litho. *Perf. 13½*

157 A56 10c multicolored 20 20
159 A56 19c multicolored 38 38
159A A56 20c multicolored 40 40
160 A56 22c multicolored 44 44
160A A56 25c multicolored 50 50
161 A56 29c multicolored 58 58
162 A56 30c multicolored 60 60
162A A56 35c multicolored 70 70
163 A56 40c multicolored 80 80
163A A56 45c multicolored 90 90
164 A56 50c multicolored 1.00 1.00
164A A56 52c multicolored 1.10 1.10
164B A56 75c multicolored 1.50 1.50
165 A56 $1 multicolored 2.00 2.00
165A A56 $2 multicolored 4.00 4.00
166 A56 $2.90 multicolored 6.00 6.00
Nos. 157-166 (16) 21.10 21.10

Issued: 19c, 29c, 50c, $1, 5/14. 22c, 30c, 40c, 45c, 8/26. 10c, 20c, 35c, $2.90, 5/20/94. 25c, 52c, 75c, $2, 8/5/94.

This is an expanding set. Numbers may change.

A57

A59

Sailing Ships: a, Great Republic. b, Benjamin F. Packard. c, Stag Hound. d, Herald of the Morning. e, Rainbow. f, Flying Cloud. g, Lightning. h, Sea Witch. i, Columbia. j, New World. k, Young America. l, Courier.

1993, May 21 Litho. *Perf. 13½*

168 A57 29c Sheet of 12, #a.-l. 7.00 7.00

1993, July 4 Litho. *Perf. 13½*

172 A59 29c multicolored 58 58

Thomas Jefferson, 250th anniv. of birth.

Pacific Canoes — A60

1993, July 21 Litho. *Perf. 13½*

173 A60 29c Yap 58 58
174 A60 29c Kosrae 58 58
175 A60 29c Pohnpei 58 58
176 A60 29c Chuuk 58 58
a. Block of 4, #173-176 2.35 2.35

Local Leaders — A61

Designs: a, Ambilos Iehsi, (1935-81), educator. b, Andrew Roboman (1905-92), Yap chief. c, Joab N. Sigrah (1932-88), first vice-speaker of Congress. d, Petrus Mailo (1902-71), Chuuk leader.

1993, Sept. 16 Litho. *Perf. 13½*

177 A61 29c Strip of 4, #a.-d. 2.35 2.35

Pioneers of Flight Type of 1993

Designs: a, Hugh L. Dryden. b, Theodore von Karman. c, Otto Lilienthal. d, Thomas O.M. Sopwith. e, Lawrence B. Sperry. f, Alberto Santos-Dumont. g, Orville Wright. h, Wilbur Wright.

1993, Sept. 25 Litho. *Perf. 13½*

178 A55 50c Block of 8, #a.-h. 8.00 8.00

Tourist Attractions, Pohnpei — A62

1993, Oct. 5

179 A62 29c Kepirohi Falls 58 58
180 A62 50c Spanish Wall 1.00 1.00

Souvenir Sheet

181 A62 $1 Sokehs Rock 2.00 2.00

No. 181 contains one 80x50mm stamp.

See Nos. 187-189.

Butterflies — A63

Christmas — A64

Designs: No. 182a, Great eggfly female (typical). No. 182b, Great eggfly female (local variant). No. 183a, Monarch. No. 183b, Great eggfly male.

1993, Oct. 20 Litho. *Perf. 13½*

182 A63 29c Pair, #a.-b. 1.25 1.25
183 A63 50c Pair, #a.-b. 2.00 2.00

See No. 190.

1993, Nov. 11

184 A64 29c We Three Kings 60 60
185 A64 50c Silent Night, Holy Night 1.00 1.00

Miniature Sheet

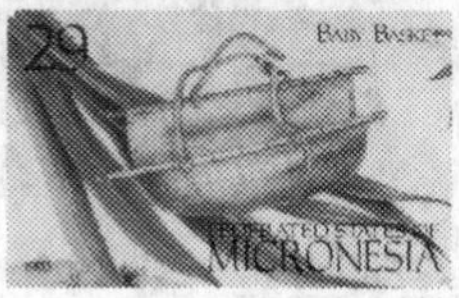

Yap Culture A65

Designs: a, Baby basket. b, Bamboo raft. c, Baskets, handbag. d, Fruit bat. e, Forest. f, Outrigger canoe. g, Dioscorea yams. h, Mangroves. i, Manta ray. j, Cyrtosperma taro. k, Fish weir. l, Seagrass, fish. m, Taro bowl. n, Thatched house. o, Coral reef. p, Lavalava. q, Dance. r, Stone money.

1993, Dec. 15 Litho. *Perf. 13½x14*

186 A65 29c Sheet of 18, #a.-r. 11.00 11.00

Tourist Attractions Type of 1993

Sites on Kosrae: 29c, Sleeping Lady Mountain. 40c, Walung. 50c, Lelu Ruins.

1994, Feb. 11 Litho. *Perf. 13½*

187 A62 29c multicolored 60 60
188 A62 40c multicolored 80 80
189 A62 50c multicolored 1.00 1.00

Butterfly Type of 1993 with Added Inscription
Souvenir Sheet

Designs: a, 29c, like No. 182a. b, 29c, like No. 182b. c, 50c, like No. 183a. d, 50c, like No. 183b.

1994, Feb. 18

190 A63 Sheet of 4, #a.-d. 3.25 3.25

Inscription reads "Hong Kong '94 Stamp Exhibition" in Chinese on Nos. 190a, 190d, and in English on Nos. 190b-190c.
Inscriptions on Nos. 190a-190d are in black.

Pioneers of Flight Type of 1993

Designs: a, Edwin E. Aldrin, Jr. b, Neil A. Armstrong. c, Michael Collins. d, Wernher von Braun. e, Octave Chanute. f, T. Claude Ryan. g, Frank Whittle. h, Waldo D. Waterman.

1994, Mar. 4 Litho. *Perf. 13½*

191 A55 29c Block of 8, #a.-h. 4.75 4.75

1994 Micronesian Games A66

Designs: a, Spearfishing. b, Basketball. c, Coconut husking. d, Tree climbing.

1994, Mar. 26 *Perf. 13½x14*

192 A66 29c Block of 4, #a.-d. 2.50 2.50

Native Costumes — A67

Designs: a, Pohnpei. b, Kosrae. c, Chuuk. d, Yap.

1994, Mar. 31 *Perf. 13½*

193 A67 29c Block of 4, #a.-d. 2.50 2.50

Constitution, 15th Anniv. — A68

1994, May 10 Litho. *Perf. 11x10½*

194 A68 29c multicolored 60 60

Flowers — A69

Designs: a, Fagraea berteriana. b, Pangium edule. c, Pittosporum ferrugineum. d, Sonneratia caseolaris.

1994, June 6 Litho. *Perf. 13½*

195 A69 29c Strip of 4, #a.-d. 2.50 2.50

1994 World Cup Soccer Championships, US — A70

Design: No. 197, Soccer players, diff.

1994, June 17 Litho. *Perf. 13½*

196 A70 50c red & multi 1.00 1.00
197 A70 50c blue & multi 1.00 1.00
a. Pair, #196-197 2.00 2.00

No. 197a has a continuous design.

Micronesian Postal Service, 10th Anniv. — A71

Stamps: a, #39, 45, 54 (c), 159, 189, 192 (b). b, #58 (d), 151, 161 (d), 176a, 183a (d). c, #4a, 137a, 184 (a), C12 (d), C39, C41. d, #161 (b), 183a (b), 183b, 193, C12, C40, C42.

1994, July 12 Litho. *Perf. 13½*

198 A71 29c Block of 4, #a.-d. 2.50 2.50

No. 198 is a continuous design.

Souvenir Sheet

PHILAKOREA '94 — A72

Dinosaurs: a, 29c, Iguanodons (b). b, 52c, Coelurosaurs (c). c, $1, Camarasaurus.

1994, Aug. 16 Litho. *Perf. 13½*

199 A72 Sheet of 3, #a.-c. 3.75 3.75

Pioneers of Flight Type of 1993

Designs: a, William A. Bishop. b, Karel J. Bossart. c, Marcel Dassault. d, Geoffrey de Havilland. e, Yuri A. Gagarin. f, Alan B. Shepard, Jr. g, John H. Towers. h, Hermann J. Oberth.

1994, Sept. 20 Litho. *Perf. 13½*

200 A55 50c Block of 8, #a.-h. 8.00 8.00

Migratory Birds — A73

Designs: a, Oriental cuckoo. b, Long-tailed cuckoo. c, Short-eared owl. d, Dollarbird.

1994, Oct. 20 Litho. *Perf. 13½*

201 A73 29c Block of 4, #a.-d. 2.50 2.50

Christmas A74

1994, Nov. 2

202 A74 29c Doves 60 60
203 A74 50c Angels 1.00 1.00

AIR POST STAMPS

Boeing 727, 1968 — AP1

1984, July 12 Litho. *Perf. 13½*

C1 AP1 28c shown 55 55
C2 AP1 35c SA-16 Albatross, 1960 70 70
C3 AP1 40c PBY-5A Catalina, 1951 80 80

Ausipex Type of 1984

Ausipex '84 emblem and: 28c, Caroline Islands No. 4. 35c, No. 7. 40c, No. 19.

1984, Sept. 21 Litho. *Perf. 13½*

C4 A4 28c multicolored 70 70
C5 A4 35c multicolored 90 90
C6 A4 40c multicolored 1.20 1.20

Christmas Type

Children's drawings.

1984, Dec. 20

C7 A5 28c Illustrated Christmas text 1.00 1.00
C8 A5 35c Decorated palm tree 1.25 1.25
C9 A5 40c Feast preparation 1.50 1.50

Ships Type

1985, Aug. 19

C10 A6 33c L'Astrolabe 70 70
C11 A6 39c La Coquille 1.00 1.00
C12 A6 44c Shenandoah 1.25 1.25

Christmas Type

1985, Oct. 15 Litho. *Perf. 13½*

C13 A7 33c Dublon Protestant Church 70 70
C14 A7 44c Pohnpei Catholic Church 90 90

Audubon Type

1985, Oct. 31 *Perf. 14½*

C15 A8 44c Sooty tern 1.20 1.20

Ruins Type

1985, Dec. Litho. *Perf. 13½*

C16 A16 33c Nan Tauas inner courtyard 70 70
C17 A16 39c Outer wall 80 80
C18 A16 44c Tomb 90 90

Halley's Comet AP2

1986, May 16

C19 AP2 44c dk bl, bl & blk 1.25 1.25

Return of Nauruans from Truk, 40th Anniv. AP3

1986, May 16

C20 AP3 44c Ship in port 1.25 1.25

AMERIPEX '86 Type

Bully Hayes (1829-1877), buccanneer.

1986, May 22

C21 A18 33c Forging Hawaiian stamp 75 75
C22 A18 39c Sinking of the Leonora, Kosrae 90 90
C23 A18 44c Hayes escapes capture 1.00 1.00
C24 A18 75c Biography, by Louis Becke 1.90 1.90

Souvenir Sheet

C25 A18 $1 Hayes ransoming chief 4.00 4.00

Christmas Type

Virgin and child paintings: 33c, Austria, 19th cent. 44c, Italy, 18th cent., diff.

1986, Oct. 15 Litho. *Perf. 14½*

C26 A20 33c multicolored 1.00 1.00
C27 A20 44c multicolored 1.40 1.40

Anniversaries and Events Type

1987, June 13 Litho. *Perf. 14½*

C28 A21 33c US currency, bicent. 80 80
C29 A21 39c 1st American in orbit, 25th anniv. 1.25 1.25
C30 A21 44c US Constitution, bicent. 1.40 1.40

Christmas Type

1987, Nov. 16 Litho. *Perf. 14½*

C31 A22 33c Holy Family 80 80
C32 A22 39c Shepherds 90 90
C33 A22 44c Three Wise Men 1.00 1.00

Bird Type

1988, Aug. 1 Litho. *Perf. 13½*

C34 A9 33c Great truk white-eye 55 55
C35 A9 44c Blue-faced parrotfinch 70 70
C36 A9 $1 Yap monarch 1.75 1.75

Colonial Era Type

1988, July 20 *Perf. 13x13½*

C37 A23 44c Traditional skills (boat-building) 95 95
C38 A23 44c Modern Micronesia (tourism) 95 95
a. Pair, #C37-C38 1.90 1.90

Printed se-tenant in sheets of 28 plus 4 center labels picturing flags of Kosrae (UL), Truk (UR), Pohnpei (LL) and Yap ((LR).

Flags of the Federated States of Micronesia AP4

1989, Jan. 19 Litho. *Perf. 13x13¹/₂*

C39 AP4 45c Pohnpei 90 90
C40 AP4 45c Truk 90 90
C41 AP4 45c Kosrae 90 90
C42 AP4 45c Yap 90 90
a. Block of 4, #C39-C42 3.60 3.60

This issue exists with 44c denominations but was not issued.

Aircraft Serving Micronesia — AP5

1990, July 16 Litho. *Perf. 14*

C43 AP5 22c shown 45 45
C44 AP5 36c multi, diff. 72 72
C45 AP5 39c multi, diff. 80 80
C46 AP5 45c multi, diff. 90 90

1992, Mar. 27

C47 AP5 40c Propeller plane, outrigger canoe 75 75
C48 AP5 50c Passenger jet, sailboat 90 90
Nos. C43-C48 (6) 4.52 4.52

Souvenir Sheet

First Manned Moon Landing, 25th Anniv. — AP6

Illustration reduced.

1994, July 20 Litho. *Perf. 13¹/₂*

C49 AP6 $2.90 US #C76 6.00 6.00

PALAU

LOCATION — Group of 100 islands in the West Pacific Ocean about 1,000 miles southeast of Manila
GOVT. — U.S. Trust Territory
AREA — 179 sq. mi.
POP. — 16,000 (est. 1983)
CAPITAL — Koror (Headquarters)

Palau, the western section of the Caroline Islands (Micronesia), is part of the US Trust Territory of the Pacific, established in 1947. By agreement with the USPS, the republic began issuing its own stamps in 1984, with the USPS continuing to carry the mail to and from the islands.

On Jan. 10, 1986 Palau became a Federation as a Sovereign State in Compact of Free Association with the US.

100 Cents = 1 Dollar

Catalogue values for all unused stamps in this country are for Never Hinged items.

Inauguration of Postal Service A1

1983, Mar. 10 Litho. *Perf. 14*

1 A1 20c Constitution preamble 50 50
2 A1 20c Hunters 50 50
3 A1 20c Fish 50 50
4 A1 20c Preamble, diff. 50 50
a. Block of 4, #1-4 2.00 2.00

Palau Fruit Dove — A2

1983, May 16 *Perf. 15*

5 A2 20c shown 40 40
6 A2 20c Palau morningbird 40 40
7 A2 20c Giant white-eye 40 40
8 A2 20c Palau fantail 40 40
a. Block of 4, #5-8 1.65 1.65

Sea Fan — A3

1983-84 Litho. *Perf. 13¹/₂x14*

9 A3 1c shown 15 15
10 A3 3c Map cowrie 15 15
11 A3 5c Jellyfish 15 15
12 A3 10c Hawksbill turtle 16 16
13 A3 13c Giant Clam 20 20
a. Booklet pane of 10 9.00 —
b. Bklt. pane of 10 (5 #13, 5 #14) 9.00 —
14 A3 20c Parrotfish 35 35
b. Booklet pane of 10 10.00 —
15 A3 28c Chambered Nautilus 45 45
16 A3 30c Dappled sea cucumber 50 50
17 A3 37c Sea Urchin 55 55
18 A3 50c Starfish 85 85
19 A3 $1 Squid 1.60 1.60

Perf. 15x14

20 A3 $2 Dugong 5.00 5.00
21 A3 $5 Pink sponge 11.00 11.00
Nos. 9-21 (13) 21.11 21.11

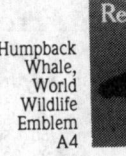

See Nos. 75-85.

Humpback Whale, World Wildlife Emblem A4

1983, Sept. 21 *Perf. 14*

24 A4 20c shown 40 40
25 A4 20c Blue whale 40 40
26 A4 20c Fin whale 40 40
27 A4 20c Great sperm whale 40 40
a. Block of 4, #24-27 1.60 1.60

Christmas 1983 — A5

Paintings by Charlie Gibbons, 1971.

1983, Oct. Litho. *Perf. 14¹/₂*

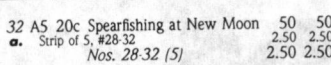

28 A5 20c First Child ceremony 50 50
29 A5 20c Spearfishing from Red Canoe 50 50
30 A5 20c Traditional feast at the Bai 50 50
31 A5 20c Taro gardening 50 50
32 A5 20c Spearfishing at New Moon 50 50
a. Strip of 5, #28-32 2.50 2.50
Nos. 28-32 (5) 2.50 2.50

A6

Capt. Wilson's Voyage, Bicentennial — A7

1983, Dec. 14 *Perf. 14x15*

33 A6 20c Capt. Henry Wilson 50 50
34 A7 20c Approaching Pelew 50 50
35 A7 20c Englishman's Camp on Ulong 50 50
36 A6 20c Prince Lee Boo 50 50
37 A6 20c King Abba Thulle 50 50
38 A7 20c Mooring in Koror 50 50
39 A7 20c Village scene of Pelew Islands 50 50
40 A6 20c Ludee 50 50
a. Block or strip of 8, #33-40 4.00 4.00
Nos. 33-40 (8) 4.00 4.00

Local Seashells — A8

Shell paintings (dorsal and ventral) by Deborah Dudley Max.

1984, Mar. 15 Litho. *Perf. 14*

41 A8 20c Triton trumpet, d. 40 40
42 A8 20c Horned helmet, d. 40 40
43 A8 20c Giant clam, d. 40 40
44 A8 20c Laciniate conch, d. 40 40
45 A8 20c Royal cloak scallop, d. 40 40
46 A8 20c Triton trumpet, v. 40 40
47 A8 20c Horned helmet, v. 40 40
48 A8 20c Giant clam, v. 40 40
49 A8 20c Laciniate conch, v. 40 40
50 A8 20c Royal cloak scallop, v. 40 40
a. Block of 10, #41-50 4.00 4.00
Nos. 41-50 (10) 4.00 4.00

Explorer Ships — A9

1984, June 19 Litho. *Perf. 14*

51 A9 40c Oroolong, 1783 95 95
52 A9 40c Duff, 1797 95 95
53 A9 40c Peiho, 1908 95 95
54 A9 40c Albatross, 1885 95 95
a. Block of 4, #51-54 3.80 3.80

UPU Congress.

Ausipex '84 A10

Fishing Methods.

1984, Sept. 6 Litho. *Perf. 14*

55 A10 20c Throw spear fishing 45 45
56 A10 20c Kite fishing 45 45
57 A10 20c Underwater spear fishing 45 45
58 A10 20c Net fishing 45 45
a. Block of 4, #55-58 1.90 1.90

Christmas Flowers — A11

1984, Nov. 28 Litho. *Perf. 14*

59 A11 20c Mountain Apple 45 45
60 A11 20c Beach Morning Glory 45 45
61 A11 20c Turmeric 45 45
62 A11 20c Plumeria 45 45
a. Block of 4, #59-62 1.90 1.90

Audubon Bicentenary A12

1985, Feb. 6 Litho. *Perf. 14*

63 A12 22c Shearwater chick 60 60
64 A12 22c Shearwater's head 60 60
65 A12 22c Shearwater in flight 60 60
66 A12 22c Swimming 60 60
a. Block of 4, #63-66 2.40 2.40

See No. C5.

Canoes and Rafts A13

1985, Mar. 27 Litho.

67 A13 22c Cargo canoe 50 50
68 A13 22c War canoe 50 50
69 A13 22c Bamboo raft 50 50
70 A13 22c Racing/sailing canoe 50 50
a. Block of 4, #67-70 2.00 2.00

Marine Life Type of 1983

1985, June 11 Litho. *Perf. 14¹/₂x14*

75 A3 14c Trumpet triton 20 20
a. Booklet pane of 10 6.00 —
76 A3 22c Bumphead parrotfish 35 35
a. Booklet pane of 10 10.00 —
b. Booklet pane, 5 14c, 5 22c 9.00 —
77 A3 25c Soft coral, damsel fish 40 40
79 A3 33c Sea anemone, clownfish 55 55
80 A3 39c Green sea turtle 65 65
81 A3 44c Pacific sailfish 70 70

Perf. 15x14

85 A3 $10 Spinner dolphins 15.00 15.00
Nos. 75-85 (7) 17.85 17.85

This is an expanding set. Numbers will change if necessary.

A14

A15

IYY emblem and children of all nationalities joined in a circle.

1985, July 15 Litho. *Perf. 14*

86 A14 44c multicolored 75 75
87 A14 44c multicolored 75 75
88 A14 44c multicolored 75 75
89 A14 44c multicolored 75 75
a. Block of 4, #86-89 3.00 3.00

No. 89a has a continuous design.

1985, Oct. 21 Litho. *Perf. 14*

Christmas: Island mothers and children.

90 A15 14c multicolored 40 40
91 A15 22c multicolored 55 55
92 A15 33c multicolored 85 85
93 A15 44c multicolored 1.15 1.15

Souvenir Sheet

Pan American Airways Martin M-130 China Clipper A16

1985, Nov. 21 Litho. *Perf. 14*

94 A16 $1 multicolored 2.75 2.75

1st Trans-Pacific Mail Flight, Nov. 22, 1935. See Nos. C10-C13.

Return of Halley's Comet A17

Fictitious local sightings.

1985, Dec. 21 Litho. *Perf. 14*

95 A17 44c Kaeb canoe, 1758 85 85
96 A17 44c U.S.S. Vincennes, 1835 85 85
97 A17 44c S.M.S. Scharnhorst, 1910 85 85
98 A17 44c Yacht, 1986 85 85
a. Block of 4, #95-98 3.40 3.40

Songbirds — A18

1986, Feb. 24 Litho. *Perf. 14*

99 A18 44c Mangrove flycatcher 90 90
100 A18 44c Cardinal honeyeater 90 90
101 A18 44c Blue-faced parrotfinch 90 90
102 A18 44c Dusky and bridled white-eyes 90 90
a. Block of 4, #99-102 3.60 3.60

World of Sea and Reef — A19

1986, May 22 Litho. *Perf. 15x14*

103 Sheet of 40 37.50
a. A19 14c any single 25 25

AMERIPEX '86, Chicago, May 22-June 1

Palau stamps can be mounted in the Scott U.S. Trust Territories album.

Seashells — A20

1986, Aug. 1 Litho. *Perf. 14*

104 A20 22c Commercial trochus 55 55
105 A20 22c Marble cone 55 55
106 A20 22c Fluted giant clam 55 55
107 A20 22c Bullmouth helmet 55 55
108 A20 22c Golden cowrie 55 55
a. Strip of 5, #104-108 2.75 2.75
Nos. 104-108 (5) 2.75 2.75

See Nos. 150-154, 191-195, 212-216.

Intl. Peace Year A21

1986, Sept. 19 Litho.

109 A21 22c Soldier's helmet 55 55
110 A21 22c Plane wreckage 55 55
111 A21 22c Woman playing guitar 55 55
112 A21 22c Airai vista 55 55
a. Block of 4, #109-112 2.20 2.20
Nos. 109-112,C17 (5) 3.10 3.10

Reptiles A22

1986, Oct. 28 Litho. *Perf. 14*

113 A22 22c Gecko 50 50
114 A22 22c Emerald tree skink 50 50
115 A22 22c Estuarine crocodile 50 50
116 A22 22c Leatherback turtle 50 50
a. Block of 4, Nos. 113-116 2.00 2.00

Christmas — A23

Butterflies — A23a

Joy to the World, carol by Isaac Watts and Handel: No. 117, Girl playing guitar, boys, goat. No. 118, Girl carrying bouquet, boys singing. No. 119, Palauan mother and child. No. 120, Children, baskets of fruit. No. 121, Girl, fairy tern. Nos. 117-121 printed in a continuous design.

1986, Nov. 26 Litho.

117 A23 22c multicolored 35 35
118 A23 22c multicolored 35 35
119 A23 22c multicolored 35 35
120 A23 22c multicolored 35 35
121 A23 22c multicolored 35 35
a. Strip of 5, #117-121 1.75 1.75

1987, Jan. 5 Litho. *Perf. 14*

121B A23a 44c Tangadik, soursop 85 85
121C A23a 44c Dira amartal, sweet orange 85 85
121D A23a 44c Ilhuochel, swamp cabbage 85 85
121E A23a 44c Bauosech, fig 85 85
f. Block of 4, #121B-121E 3.40 3.40

See Nos. 183-186.

Fruit Bats — A24

1987, Feb. 23 Litho.

122 A24 44c In flight 90 90
123 A24 44c Hanging 90 90
124 A24 44c Eating 90 90
125 A24 44c Head 90 90
a. Block of 4, #122-125 3.60 3.60

Indigenous Flowers — A25

1987-88 Litho. *Perf. 14*

126 A25 1c Ixora casei 15 15
127 A25 3c Lumnitzera littorea 15 15
128 A25 5c Sonneratia alba 15 15
129 A25 10c Tristellateria australasiae 16 16
130 A25 14c Bikkia palauensis 20 20
a. Booklet pane of 10 3.00 —
131 A25 15c Limnophila aromatica ('88) 22 22
a. Booklet pane of 10 ('88) 2.25 —
132 A25 22c Bruguiera gymnorhiza 35 35
a. Booklet pane of 10 4.00 —
b. Booklet pane, 5 each 14c, 22c 4.00 —
133 A25 25c Fagraea ksid ('88) 40 40
a. Booklet pane of 10 ('88) 4.00 —
b. Booklet pane, 5 each 15c, 25c ('88) 4.00 —
134 A25 36c Ophiorrhiza palauensis ('88) 55 55
135 A25 39c Cerbera manghas 60 60
136 A25 44c Sandera indica 70 70
137 A25 45c Maesa canfieldiae ('88) 72 72
138 A25 50c Dolichandrone spathacea 85 85
139 A25 $1 Barringtonia racemosa 1.60 1.60
140 A25 $2 Nepenthes mirabilis 3.25 3.25
141 A25 $5 Dendrobium palawense 8.00 8.00

Size: 49x28mm

142 A25 $10 Bouquet ('88) 15.00 15.00
Nos. 126-142 (17) 33.05 33.05

Issue dates: Mar. 12. $10, Mar. 17. 15c, 25c, 36c, 45c, July 1. Nos. 131a, 133a-133b, July 5.

CAPEX '87 A26

1987, June 15 Litho. *Perf. 14*

146 A26 22c Babeldaob Is. 50 50
147 A26 22c Floating Garden Isls. 50 50
148 A26 22c Rock Is. 50 50
149 A26 22c Koror 50 50
a. Block of 4, #146-149 2.00 2.00

Seashells Type of 1986

1987, Aug. 25 Litho. *Perf. 14*

150 A20 22c Black-striped triton 55 55
151 A20 22c Tapestry turban 55 55
152 A20 22c Adusta murex 55 55
153 A20 22c Little fox miter 55 55
154 A20 22c Cardinal miter 55 55
a. Strip of 5, #150-154 2.75 2.75
Nos. 150-154 (5) 2.75 2.75

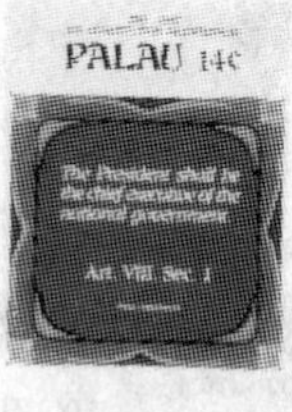

US Constitution Bicentennial — A27

Excerpts from Articles of the Palau and US Constitutions and Seals.

1987, Sept. 17 Litho. *Perf. 14*

155 A27 14c Art. VIII, Sec. 1, Palau 20 20
156 A27 14c Presidential seals 20 20
157 A27 14c Art. II, Sec. 1, US 20 20
a. Triptych + label, #155-157 60 60
158 A27 22c Art. IX, Sec. 1, Palau 35 35
159 A27 22c Legislative seals 35 35
160 A27 22c Art. I, Sec. 1, US 35 35
a. Triptych + label, #158-160 1.05 1.05
161 A27 44c Art X, Sec. 1, Palau 70 70
162 A27 44c Supreme Court seals 70 70
163 A27 44c Art. III, Sec. 1, US 70 70
a. Triptych + label, #161-163 2.10 2.10
Nos. 155-163 (9) 3.75 3.75

Triptychs printed se-tenant with inscribed label picturing national flags.

Japanese Links to Palau — A28

Japanese stamps, period cancellations and installations: 14c, No. 257 and 1937 Datsun sedan used as mobile post office, near Ngerchelechuus Mountain. 22c, No. 347 and phosphate mine at Angaur. 33c, No. B1 and Japan Airways DC-2 over stone monuments at Badrulchau. 44c, No. 201 and Japanese post office, Koror. $1, Aviator's Grave, Japanese Cemetary, Peleliu, vert.

1987, Oct. 16 Litho. *Perf. 14x13½*

164 A28 14c multicolored 30 30
165 A28 22c multicolored 45 45
166 A28 33c multicolored 70 70
167 A28 44c multicolored 85 85

Souvenir Sheet

Perf. 13½x14

168 A28 $1 multicolored 2.30 2.30

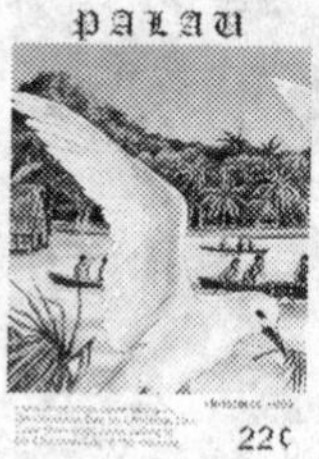

Christmas — A30

Symbiotic Marine Species — A31

Verses from carol "I Saw Three Ships," Biblical characters, landscape and Palauans in outrigger canoes.

1987, Nov. 24 Litho. *Perf. 14*

173 A30 22c I saw... 55 55
174 A30 22c And what was... 55 55
175 A30 22c 'Twas Joseph... 55 55
176 A30 22c Saint Michael... 55 55
177 A30 22c And all the bells... 55 55
a. Strip of 5, #173-177 2.75 2.75
Nos. 173-177 (5) 2.75 2.75

1987, Dec. 15

Designs: No. 178, Snapping shrimp, goby. No. 179, Mauve vase sponge, sponge crab. No. 180, Pope's damselfish, cleaner wrasse. No. 181, Clown anemone fish, sea anemone. No. 182, Four-color nudibranch, banded coral shrimp.

178 A31 22c multicolored 55 55
179 A31 22c multicolored 55 55
180 A31 22c multicolored 55 55
181 A31 22c multicolored 55 55
182 A31 22c multicolored 55 55
a. Strip of 5, #178-182 2.75 2.75

Butterflies and Flowers Type of 1987

Designs: No. 183, Dannaus plexippus, Tournefotia argentia. No. 184, Papilio machaon, Citrus reticulata. No. 185, Captopsilia, Crataeva speciosa. No. 186, Colias philodice, Crataeva speciosa.

1988, Jan. 25

183 A23a 44c multicolored 85 85
184 A23a 44c multicolored 85 85
185 A23a 44c multicolored 85 85
186 A23a 44c multicolored 85 85
a. Block of 4, #183-186 3.40 3.40

Ground-dwelling Birds — A32

1988, Feb. 29 Litho. *Perf. 14*

187 A32 44c Whimbrel		85	85
188 A32 44c Yellow bittern		85	85
189 A32 44c Rufous night-heron		85	85
190 A32 44c Banded rail		85	85
a. Block of 4, #187-190		3.40	3.40

Seashells Type of 1986

1988, May 11 Litho. *Perf. 14*

191 A20 25c Striped engina	55	55
192 A20 25c Ivory cone	55	55
193 A20 25c Plaited miter	55	55
194 A20 25c Episcopal miter	55	55
195 A20 25c Isabelle cowrie	55	55
a. Strip of 5, #191-195	2.75	2.75
Nos. 191-195 (5)	2.75	2.75

Souvenir Sheet

Postal Independence, 5th Anniv. — A33

FINLANDIA '88: a, Kaep (pre-European outrigger sailboat). b, Spanish colonial cruiser. c, German colonial cruiser SMS Cormoran, c. 1885. d, Japanese mailbox, WWII machine gun, Koror Museum. e, US Trust Territory ship, Malakal Harbor. f, Koror post office.

1988, June 8 Litho. *Perf. 14*

196 Sheet of 6	3.00	3.00
a.-f. A33 25c multicolored	50	50

Souvenir Sheet

US Possessions Phil. Soc., 10th Anniv. — A34

PRAGA '88: a, "Collect Palau Stamps," original artwork for No. 196f and head of a man. b, Soc. emblem. c, Nos. 1-4. d, China Clipper original artwork and covers. e, Man and boy studying covers. f, Girl at show cancel booth.

1988, Aug. 26 Litho. *Perf. 14*

197 A34 Sheet of 6	4.80	4.80
a.-f. 45c any single	80	80

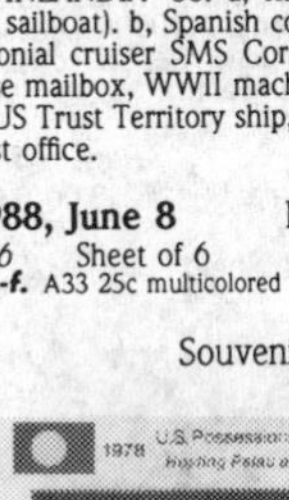

Christmas — A35

Hark! The Herald Angels Sing: No. 198, Angels playing the violin, singing and sitting. No. 199, 3 angels and 3 children. No. 200, Nativity. No. 201, 2 angels, birds. No. 202, 3 children and 2 angels playing horns. Se-tenant in a continuous design.

1988, Nov. 7 Litho. *Perf. 14*

198 A35 25c multicolored	50	50
199 A35 25c multicolored	50	50
200 A35 25c multicolored	50	50
201 A35 25c multicolored	50	50
202 A35 25c multicolored	50	50
a. Strip of 5, #199-202	2.50	2.50
Nos. 198-202 (5)	2.50	2.50

Miniature Sheet

Chambered Nautilus — A36

Designs: a, Fossil and cross section. b, Palauan *bai* symbols for the nautilus. c, Specimens trapped for scientific study. d, *Nautilus belauensis, pompilius, macromphalus, stenomphalus* and *scrobiculatus*. e, Release of a tagged nautilus.

1988, Dec. 23 Litho. *Perf. 14*

203 A36 Sheet of 5	2.75	2.75
a.-e. 25c multicolored	55	55

Endangered Birds of Palau — A37

1989, Feb. 9 Litho. *Perf. 14*

204 A37 45c Nicobar pigeon	85	85
205 A37 45c Ground dove	85	85
206 A37 45c Micronesian megapode	85	85
207 A37 45c Owl	85	85
a. Block of 4, #204-207	3.40	3.40

Exotic Mushrooms — A38

1989, Mar. 16 Litho. *Perf. 14*

208 A38 45c Gilled auricularia	85	85
209 A38 45c Rock mushroom	85	85
210 A38 45c Polyporous	85	85
211 A38 45c Veiled stinkhorn	85	85
a. Block of 4, #208-211	3.40	3.40

Seashell Type of 1986

1989, Apr. 12 Litho. *Perf. 14x14½*

212 A20 25c Robin redbreast triton	55	55
213 A20 25c Hebrew cone	55	55
214 A20 25c Tadpole triton	55	55
215 A20 25c Lettered cone	55	55
216 A20 25c Rugose miter	55	55
a. Strip of 5, #212-216	2.75	2.75
Nos. 212-216 (5)	2.75	2.75

Souvenir Sheet

A Little Bird, Amidst Chrysanthemums, 1830s, by Hiroshige (1797-1858) — A39

1989, May 17 Litho. *Perf. 14*

217 A39 $1 multicolored	2.00	2.00

Hirohito (1901-1989) and enthronement of Akihito as emperor of Japan.

Miniature Sheet

First Moon Landing, 20th Anniv. — A40

Apollo 11 mission: a, Third stage jettison. b, Lunar spacecraft. c, Module transposition *(Eagle)*. d, *Columbia* module transposition (command module). e, *Columbia* module transposition (service module). f, Third stage burn. g, Vehicle entering orbit, Moon. h, *Columbia* and *Eagle*. i, *Eagle* on the Moon. j, *Eagle* in space. k, Three birds, Saturn V third stage, lunar spacecraft and escape tower. l, Astronaut's protective visor, pure oxygen system. m, Astronaut, American flag. n, Footsteps on lunar plain Sea of Tranquillity, pure oxygen system. o, Armstrong descending from *Eagle*. p, Mobile launch tower, Saturn V second stage. q, Space suit remote control unit and oxygen hoses. r, *Eagle* lift-off from Moon. s, Armstrong's first step on the Moon. t, Armstrong descending ladder, module transposition *(Eagle* and *Columbia)*. u, Launch tower, spectators and Saturn V engines achieving thrust. v, Spectators, clouds of backwash. w, Parachute splashdown, U.S. Navy recovery ship and helicopter. x, Command module reentry. y, Jettison of service module prior to reentry.

1989, July 20 Litho. *Perf. 14*

218 A40 Sheet of 25	10.00	10.00
a.-y. 25c any single	40	40

Buzz Aldrin Photographed on the Moon by Neil Armstrong A41

1989, July 20 *Perf. 13½x14*

219 A41 $2.40 multicolored	4.00	4.00

First Moon landing 20th anniv.

Literacy — A42

Imaginary characters and children reading: a, Youth astronaut. b, Boy riding dolphin. c, Cheshire cat in palm tree. d, Mother Goose. e, New York Yankee at bat. f, Girl reading. g, Boy reading. h, Mother reading to child. i, Girl holding flower and listening to story. j, Boy dressed in baseball uniform. Printed se-tenant in a continuous design.

1989, Oct. 13 Litho. *Perf. 14*

220 Block of 10	4.00	4.00
a.-j. A42 25c any single	40	40

No. 220 printed in sheets containing two blocks of ten with strip of 5 labels between. Inscribed labels contain book, butterflies and "Give Them / Books / Give Them / Wings."

Miniature Sheet

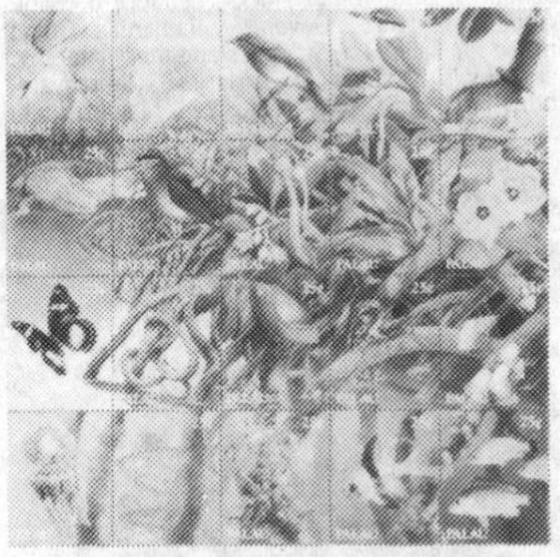

Stilt Mangrove Fauna — A43

World Stamp Expo '89: a, Bridled tern. b, Sulphur butterfly. c, Mangrove flycatcher. d, Collared kingfisher. e, Fruit bat. f, Estuarine crocodile. g, Rufous night-heron. h, Stilt mangrove. i, Bird's nest fern. j, Beach hibiscus tree. k, Common eggfly. l, Dog-faced watersnake. m, Jingle shell. n, Palau bark cricket. o, Periwinkle, mangrove oyster. p, Jellyfish. q, Striped mullet. r, Mussels, sea anemones, algae. s, Cardinalfish. t, Snapper.

1989, Nov. 20 Litho. *Perf. 14½*

221 A43 Block of 20	7.75	7.75
a.-t. 25c any single	40	40

Christmas — A44

Soft Coral — A45

Whence Comes this Rush of Wings? a carol: No. 222, Dusky tern, Audubon's shearwater, angels, island. No. 223, Fruit pigeon, angel. No. 224, Madonna and Child, ground pigeons, fairy terns, rails, sandpipers. No. 225, Angel, blue-headed green finch, red flycatcher, honeyeater. No. 226, Angel, black-headed gulls. Printed se-tenant in a continuous design.

1989, Dec. 18 Litho. *Perf. 14*

222 A44 25c multicolored 50 50
223 A44 25c multicolored 50 50
224 A44 25c multicolored 50 50
225 A44 25c multicolored 50 50
226 A44 25c multicolored 50 50
a. Strip of 5, #222-226 2.50 2.50
Nos. 222-226 (5) 2.50 2.50

1990, Jan. 3

227 A45 25c Pink coral 50 50
228 A45 25c Pink & violet coral 50 50
229 A45 25c Yellow coral 50 50
230 A45 25c Red coral 50 50
a. Block of 4, #227-230 2.00 2.00

Birds of the Forest A46

1990, Mar. 16

231 A46 45c Siberian rubythroat 80 80
232 A46 45c Palau bush-warbler 80 80
233 A46 45c Micronesian starling 80 80
234 A46 45c Cicadabird 80 80
a. Block of 4, #231-234 3.20 3.20

Miniature Sheet

State Visit of Prince Lee Boo of Palau to England, 1784 A47

Prince Lee Boo, Capt. Henry Wilson and: a, HMS *Victory* docked at Portsmouth. b, St. James's Palace, London. c, Rotherhithe Docks, London. d, Capt. Wilson's residence, Devon. e, Lunardi's Grand English Air Balloon. f, St. Paul's and the Thames. g, Lee Boo's tomb, St. Mary's Churchyard, Rotherhithe. h, St. Mary's Church. i, Memorial tablet, St. Mary's Church.

1990, May 6 Litho. *Perf. 14*

235 Sheet of 9 3.50 3.50
a.-i. A47 25c any single 38 38

Stamp World London '90.

Souvenir Sheet

Penny Black, 150th Anniv. — A48

1990, May 6

236 A48 $1 Great Britain #1 1.75 1.75

Orchids — A49

1990, June 7 *Perf. 14*

237 A49 45c *Corymborkis veratrifolia* 70 70
238 A49 45c *Malaxis setipes* 70 70
239 A49 45c *Dipodium freycinetianum* 70 70
240 A49 45c *Bulbophyllum micronesiacum* 70 70
241 A49 45c *Vanda teres* and *hookeriana* 70 70
a. Strip of 5, #237-241 3.50 3.50
Nos. 237-241 (5) 3.50 3.50

Butterflies and Flowers A50

1990, July 6 Litho. *Perf. 14*

242 A50 45c Wedelia strigulosa 70 70
243 A50 45c Erthrina variegata 70 70
244 A50 45c Clerodendrum inerme 70 70
245 A50 45c Vigna marina 70 70
a. Block of 4, #242-245 2.80 2.80

Miniature Sheet

Fairy Tern, Lesser Golden Plover, Sanderling A51

Lagoon life: b, Bidekill fisherman. c, Sailing yacht, insular halfbeaks. d, Palauan kaeps. e, White-tailed tropicbird. f, Spotted eagle ray. g, Great barracuda. h, Reef needlefish. i, Reef blacktip shark. j, Hawksbill turtle. k, Octopus. l, Batfish. m, Lionfish. n, Snowflake moray. o, Porcupine fish, sixfeeler threadfins. p, Blue sea star, regal angelfish, cleaner wrasse. q, Clown triggerfish. r, Spotted garden eel and orange fish. s, Blue-lined sea bream, bluegreen chromis, sapphire damselfish. t, Orangespine unicornfish, white-tipped soldierfish. u, Slatepencil sea urchin, leopard sea cucumber. v, Partridge tun shell. w, Mandarinfish. x, Tiger cowrie. y, Feather starfish, orange-fin anemonefish.

1990, Aug. 10 Litho. *Perf. 15x14½*

246 A51 25c Sheet of 25, #a.-y. 10.50 10.50

Nos. 246a-246y inscribed on reverse.

Pacifica — A52

1990, Aug. 24 Litho. *Perf. 14*

247 A52 45c Mailship, 1890 1.00 1.00
248 A52 45c US #803 on cover, forklift, plane 1.00 1.00
a. Pair, #247-248 2.00 2.00

Christmas — A53

Here We Come A-Caroling: No. 250, Girl with music, poinsettias, doves. No. 251, Boys playing guitar, flute. No. 252, Family. No. 253, Three girls singing.

1990, Nov. 28

249 A53 25c multicolored 40 40
250 A53 25c multicolored 40 40
251 A53 25c multicolored 40 40
252 A53 25c multicolored 40 40
253 A53 25c multicolored 40 40
a. Strip of 5, #249-253 2.00 2.00
Nos. 249-253 (5) 2.00 2.00

US Forces in Palau, 1944 A54

Designs: No. 254, B-24s over Peleliu. No. 255, LCI launching rockets. No. 256, First Marine Division launching offensive. No. 257, Soldier, children. No. 258, USS *Peleliu*.

1990, Dec. 7

254 A54 45c multicolored 75 75
255 A54 45c multicolored 75 75
256 A54 45c multicolored 75 75
257 A54 45c multicolored 75 75
a. Block of 4, #254-257 3.00 3.00

Souvenir Sheet

Perf. 14x13½

258 A54 $1 multicolored 1.75 1.75

No. 258 contains one 51x38mm stamp.
See No. 339 for No. 258 with added inscription.

Coral — A55

1991, Mar. 4 Litho. *Perf. 14*

259 A55 30c Staghorn 60 60
260 A55 30c Velvet Leather 60 60
261 A55 30c Van Gogh's Cypress 60 60
262 A55 30c Violet Lace 60 60
a. Block of 4, #259-262 2.40 2.40

Miniature Sheet

Angaur, The Phosphate Island A56

Designs: a, Virgin Mary Statue, Nkulangelul Point. b, Angaur kaep, German colonial postmark. c, Swordfish, Caroline Islands No. 13. d, Phosphate mine locomotive. e, Copra ship off Lighthouse Hill. f, Dolphins. g, Estuarine crocodile. h, Workers cycling to phosphate plant. i, Ship loading phosphate. j, Hammerhead shark, German overseer. k, Marshall Islands No. 15. l, SMS *Scharnhorst*. m, SMS *Emden*. n, Crab-eating macaque monkey. o, Great sperm whale. p, HMAS *Sydney*.

1991, Mar. 14

263 A56 30c Sheet of 16, #a.-p. 7.50 7.50

Nos. 263b-263c, 263f-263g, 263j-263k, 263n-263o printed in continuous design showing map of island.

Birds — A57

Perf. 14½x15, 13x13½

1991-92 Litho.

264 A57 1c Palau bush-warbler 15 15
266 A57 4c Common moorhen 15 15
267 A57 6c Banded rail 15 15
270 A57 19c Palau fantail 38 38
270A A57 20c Mangrove flycatcher 40 40
271 A57 23c Purple swamphen 46 46
272 A57 29c Palau fruit dove 58 58
274 A57 35c Great crested tern 70 70
275 A57 40c Pacific reef heron 80 80
276 A57 45c Micronesian pigeon 90 90
277 A57 50c Great frigatebird 1.00 1.00
278 A57 52c Little pied cormorant 1.05 1.05
280 A57 75c Jungle night jar 1.50 1.50
281 A57 95c Cattle egret 1.90 1.90
283 A57 $1.34 Great sulphur-crested cockatoo 2.68 2.68
285 A57 $2 Blue-faced parrotfinch 4.00 4.00
286 A57 $5 Eclectus parrot 10.00 10.00

Size: 52x30mm

287 A57 $10 Palau bush warbler 20.00 20.00
Nos. 264-287 (18) 46.80 46.80

The 1c, 6c, 20c, 52c, 75c, $10 are perf. 14½x15.

Issue dates: 1c, 6c, 20c, 52c, 75c, $5, Apr. 6, 1992. $10, Sept. 10, 1992. Others, Apr. 18, 1991.

This is an expanding set. Numbers may change.

Miniature Sheet

Christianity in Palau, Cent. — A58

Designs: a, Pope Leo XIII, 1891. b, Ibedul Ilengelekei, High Chief of Koror, 1871-1911. c, Fr. Marino de la Hoz, Br. Emilio Villar, Fr. Elias Fernandez. d, Fr. Edwin G. McManus (1908-1969), compiler of Palauan-English dictionary. e, Sacred Heart Church, Koror. f, Pope John Paul II.

1991, Apr. 28 *Perf. 14½*

288 A58 29c Sheet of 6, #a.-f. 3.00 3.00

Miniature Sheet

Marine Life A59

Designs: a, Pacific white-sided dolphin. b, Common dolphin. c, Rough-toothed dolphin. d, Bottlenose dolphin. e, Harbor porpoise. f, Killer whale. g, Spinner dolphin, yellowfin tuna. h, Dall's porpoise. i, Finless porpoise. j, Map of Palau, dolphin. k, Dusky dolphin. l, Southern right-whale dolphin. m, Striped dolphin. n, Fraser's dolphin. o, Peale's dolphin. p, Spectacled porpoise. q, Spotted dolphin. r, Hourglass dolphin. s, Risso's dolphin. t, Hector's dolphin.

1991, May 24 Litho. *Perf. 14*

289 A59 29c Sheet of 20, #a.-t. 11.00 11.00

Miniature Sheet

Operations Desert Shield / Desert Storm A60

Designs: a, F-4G Wild Weasel fighter. b, F-117A Stealth fighter. c, AH-64A Apache helicopter. d, TOW missle launcher on M998 HMMWV. e, Pres. Bush. f, M2 Bradley fighting vehicle. g, Aircraft carrier USS Ranger. h, Corvette fast patrol boat. i, Battleship Wisconsin.

1991, July 2 Litho. *Perf. 14*

290 A60 20c Sheet of 9, #a.-i. 3.50 3.50

Size: 38x51mm

291 A60 $2.90 Fairy tern, yellow ribbon 4.25 4.25

Souvenir Sheet

292 A60 $2.90 like #291 4.25 4.25

No. 291 has a white border around design. No. 292 printed in continuous design.

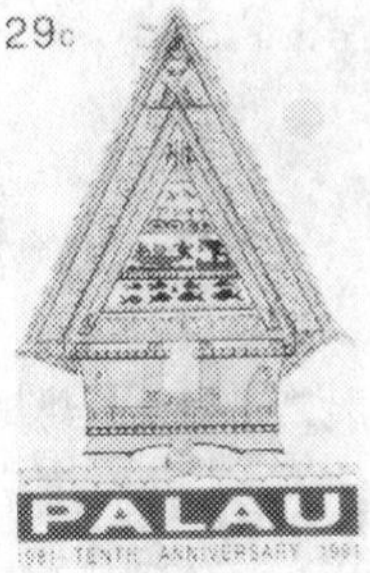

Republic of Palau, 10th Anniv. — A61

Designs: a, Palauan bai. b, Palauan bai interior, denomination UL. c, Same, denomination UR. d, Demi-god Chedechuul. e, Spider, denomination at UL. f, Money bird facing right. g, Money bird facing left. h, Spider, denomination at UR.

1991, July 9 ***Perf. 14½***

293 A61 29c Sheet of 8, #a.-h. 4.00 4.00

See No. C21.

Miniature Sheet

Giant Clams A62

Designs: a, Tridacna squamosa, Hippopus hippopus, Hippopus porcellanus, and Tridacna derasa. b, Tridacna gigas. c, Hatchery and tank culture. d, Diver, bottom-based clam nursery. e, Micronesian Mariculture Demonstration Center.

1991, Sept. 17 **Litho.** ***Perf. 14***

294 A62 50c Sheet of 5, #a.-e. 4.00 4.00

No. 294e is 109x17mm and imperf on 3 sides, perf 14 at top.

Miniature Sheet

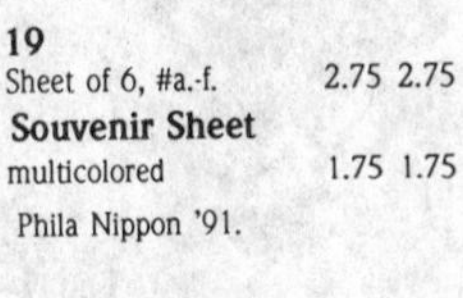

Japanese Heritage in Palau A63

Designs: No. 295a, Marine research. b, Traditional arts, carving story boards. c, Agricultural training. d, Archaeological research. e, Training in architecture and building. f, Air transportation. $1, Map, cancel from Japanese post office at Parao.

1991, Nov. 19

295 A63 29c Sheet of 6, #a.-f. 2.75 2.75

Souvenir Sheet

296 A63 $1 multicolored 1.75 1.75

Phila Nippon '91.

Miniature Sheet

Peace Corps in Palau, 25th Anniv. A64

Children's drawings: No. 297a, Flag, doves, children, and islands. b, Airplane, people being greeted. c, Red Cross instruction. d, Fishing industry. e, Agricultural training. f, Classroom instruction.

1991, Dec. 6 **Litho.** ***Perf. 13½***

297 A64 29c Sheet of 6, #a.-f. 3.00 3.00

Christmas — A65

Silent Night: No. 298a, Silent night, holy night. b, All is calm, all is bright. c, Round yon virgin, mother and Child. d, Holy Infant, so tender and mild. e, Sleep in heavenly peace.

1991, Nov. 14 ***Perf. 14***

298 A65 29c Strip of 5, #a.-e. 2.25 2.25

Miniature Sheet

World War II in the Pacific — A66

Designs: No. 299a, Pearl Harbor attack begins. b, Battleship Nevada gets under way. c, USS Shaw explodes. d, Japanese aircraft carrier Akagi sunk. e, USS Wasp sunk off Guadalcanal. f, Battle of the Philippine Sea. g, US landing craft approach Saipan. h, US 1st Cavalry on Leyte. i, Battle of Bloody Nose Ridge, Peleliu. j, US troops land on Iwo Jima.

1991, Dec. 6 ***Perf. 14½x15***

299 A66 29c Sheet of 10, #a.-j. 4.25 4.25

See No. 311.

A67 A68

Butterflies: a, Troides criton. b, Alcides zodiaca. c, Papillio poboroi. d, Vindula arsinoe.

1992, Jan. 20 **Litho.** ***Perf. 14***

300 A67 50c Block of 4, #a.-d. 3.00 3.00

1992, Mar. 11

Shells: a, Common hairy triton. b, Eglantine cowrie. c, Sulcate swamp cerith. d, Black-spined murex. e, Black-mouth moon.

301 A68 29c Strip of 5, #a.-e. 2.50 2.50

Miniature Sheet

Age of Discovery — A69

Designs: a, Columbus. b, Magellan. c, Drake. d, Wind as shown on old maps.

Maps and: e, Compass rose. f, Dolphin, Drake's ship Golden Hinde. g, Corn, Santa Maria. h, Fish. i, Betel palm, cloves and black pepper. j, Victoria, shearwater and great crested tern. k, White-tailed tropicbird, bicolor parrotfish, pineapple and potatoes. l, Compass. m, Sea monster. n, Paddles and astrolabe. o, Parallel ruler, dividers and Inca gold treasures. p, Back staff.

Portraits: q, Wind, diff. r, Vespucci. s, Pizarro. t, Balboa.

1992, May 25 **Litho.** ***Perf. 14***

302 A69 29c Sheet of 20, #a.-t. 11.60 11.60

Miniature Sheet

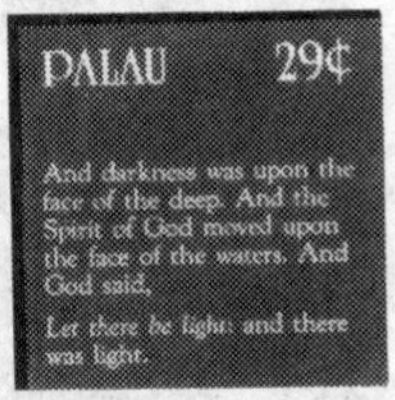

Biblical Creation of the World — A70

Designs: a, "And darkness was..." b, Sun's rays. c, Water, sun's rays. d, "...and it was good." e, "Let there be a..." f, Land forming. g, Water and land. h, "...and it was so." i, "Let the waters..." j, Tree branches. k, Shoreline. l, Shoreline, flowers, tree. m, "Let there be lights..." n, Comet, moon. o, Mountains. p, Sun, hillside. q, "Let the waters..." r, Birds. s, Fish, killer whale. t, Fish. u, "Let the earth..." v, Woman, man. w, Animals. x, "...and it was very good."

1992, June 5 ***Perf. 14½***

303 A70 29c Sheet of 24, #a.-x. 14.00 14.00

Nos. 303a-303d, 303e-303h, 303i-303l, 303m-303p, 303q-303t, 303u-303x are blocks of 4.

Souvenir Sheets

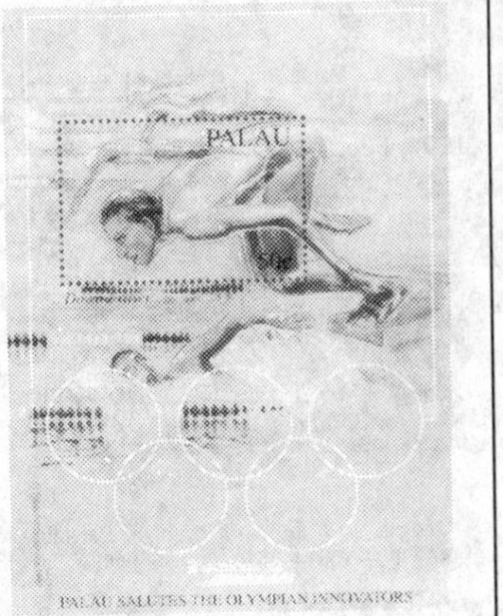

1992 Summer Olympics, Barcelona — A71

1992, July 10 ***Perf. 14***

304 A71 50c	Dawn Fraser	1.00 1.00
305 A71 50c	Olga Korbut	1.00 1.00
306 A71 50c	Bob Beamon	1.00 1.00
307 A71 50c	Carl Lewis	1.00 1.00
308 A71 50c	Dick Fosbury	1.00 1.00
309 A71 50c	Greg Louganis	1.00 1.00

Miniature Sheet

Elvis Presley A72

Various portraits.

1992, Aug. 17 ***Perf. 13½x14***

310 A72 29c Sheet of 9, #a.-i. 5.25 5.25

World War II in the Pacific Type Miniature Sheet

Aircraft: No. 311a, Grumman TBF Avenger, US Navy. b, Curtiss P-40C, Chinese Air Force "Flying Tigers." c, Mitsubishi A6M Zero-Sen, Japan. d, Hawker Hurricane, Royal Air Force. e, Consolidated PBY Catalina, Royal Netherlands Indies Air Force. f, Curtiss Hawk 75, Netherlands Indies. g, Boeing B-17E, US Army Air Force. h, Brewster Buffalo, Royal Australian Air Force. i, Supermarine Walrus, Royal Navy. j, Curtiss P-40E, Royal New Zealand Air Force.

1992, Sept. 10 **Litho.** ***Perf. 14½x15***

311 A66 50c Sheet of 10, #a.-j. 10.00 10.00

Christmas — A73

The Friendly Beasts carol depicting animals in Nativity Scene: No. 312a, "Thus Every Beast." b, "By Some Good Spell." c, "In The Stable Dark Was Glad to Tell." d, "Of The Gift He Gave Emanuel." e, "The Gift He Gave Emanuel."

1992, Oct. 1 **Litho.** ***Perf. 14***

312 A73 29c Strip of 5, #a.-e. 2.65 2.65

Fauna A74

Designs: a, Dugong. b, Masked booby. c, Macaque. d, New Guinean crocodile.

1993, July 9 **Litho.** ***Perf. 14***

313 A74 50c Block of 4, #a.-d. 3.75 3.75

Seafood A75

Designs: a, Giant crab. b, Scarlet shrimp. c, Smooth nylon shrimp. d, Armed nylon shrimp.

1993, July 22

314 A75 29c Block of 4, #a.-d. 2.15 2.15

Sharks A76

Designs: a, Oceanic whitetip. b, Great hammerhead. c, Leopard. d, Reef black-tip.

1993, Aug. 11 **Litho.** ***Perf. 14½***

315 A76 50c Block of 4, #a.-d. 4.00 4.00

Miniature Sheet

World War II in the Pacific — A77

Actions in 1943: a, US takes Guadalcanal, Feb. b, Hospital ship Tranquility supports action. c, New Guineans join Allies in battle. d, US landings in New Georgia, June. e, USS California participates in every naval landing. f, Dauntless dive bombers over Wake Island, Oct. 6. g, US flamethrowers on Tarawa, Nov. h, US landings on Makin, Nov. i, B-

25s bomb Simpson Harbor, Rabaul, Oct. 23. j, B-24s over Kwajalein, Dec. 8.

1993, Sept. 23 Litho. ***Perf. 14½x15***
316 A77 29c Sheet of 10, #a.-j. + label 5.75 5.75

See Nos. 325-326.

Christmas — A78

Christmas carol, "We Wish You a Merry Christmas," with Palauan customs: a, Girl, goat. b, Goats, children holding leis, prow of canoe. c, Santa Claus. d, Children singing. e, Family with fruit, fish.

1993, Oct. 22 Litho. ***Perf. 14***
317 A78 29c Strip of 5, #a.-e. 3.50 3.50

Miniature Sheet

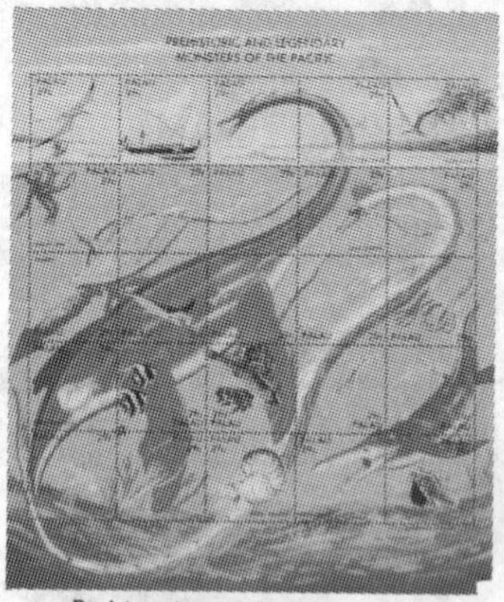

Prehistoric and Legendary Sea Creatures — A79

Illustration reduced.

1993, Nov. 26 Litho. ***Perf. 14***
318 A79 29c Sheet of 25, #a.-y. 15.00 15.00

Miniature Sheet

Intl. Year of Indigenous People — A80

Paintings, by Charlie Gibbons: No. 319a, After Child-birth Ceremony. b, Village in Early Palau.
Storyboard carving, by Ngiraibuuch: $2.90, Quarrying of Stone Money, vert.

1993, Dec. 8 ***Perf. 14x13½***
319 A80 29c Sheet of 2 each, a.-b. 2.50 2.50

Souvenir Sheet
Perf. 13½x14

320 A80 $2.90 multicolored 5.75 5.75

Miniature Sheet

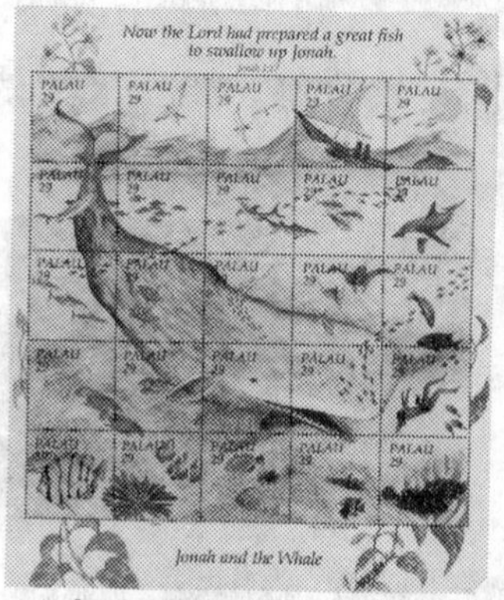

Jonah and the Whale — A81

Illustration reduced.

1993, Dec. 28 Litho. ***Perf. 14***
321 A81 29c Sheet of 25, #a.-y. 15.00 15.00

Hong Kong '94 A82

Rays: a, Manta (b). b, Spotted eagle (a). c, Coachwhip (d). d, Black spotted.

1994, Feb. 18 Litho. ***Perf. 14***
322 A82 40c Block of 4, #a.-d. 3.00 3.00

Estuarine Crocodile A83

Designs: a, With mouth open. b, Hatchling. c, Crawling on river bottom. d, Swimming.

1994, Mar. 14
323 A83 20c Block of 4, #a.-d. 1.75 1.75

World Wildlife Fund.

Large Seabirds — A84

Designs: a, Red-footed booby. b, Great frigatebird. c, Brown booby. d, Little pied cormorant.

1994, Apr. 22 Litho. ***Perf. 14***
324 A84 50c Block of 4, #a.-d. 4.00 4.00

World War II Type of 1993
Miniature Sheets

Action in the Pacific, 1944: No. 325a, US Marines capture Kwajalien, Feb. 1-7. b, Japanese enemy base at Truk destroyed, Feb. 17-18. c, SS-284 Tullibee participates in Operation Desecrate, March. d, US troops take Saipan, June 15-July 9. e, Great Marianas Turkey Shoot, June 19-20. f, Guam liberated, July-Aug. g, US troops take Peleliu, Sept. 15-Oct. 14. h, Angaur secured in fighting, Sept. 17-22. i, Gen. Douglas MacArthur returns to Philippines, Oct. 20. j, US Army Memorial, Palau, Nov. 27.

D-Day, Allied Invasion of Normandy, June 6, 1944: 326a, C-47 transport aircraft dropping Allied paratroopers. b, Allied warships attack beach fortifications. c, Commandos attack from landing craft. d, Tanks land. e, Sherman flail tank beats path through minefields. f, Allied aircraft attack enemy reinforcements. g, Gliders deliver troops behind enemy lines. h, Pegasus Bridge, first French house liberated. i, Allied forces move inland to form bridgehead. j, View of beach at end of D-Day.

1994, May ***Perf. 14½***

Sheets of 10

325 A77 29c #a.-j. + label 5.75 5.75
326 A77 50c #a.-j. + label 10.00 10.00

Pierre de Coubertin (1863-1937) — A85

Winter Olympic medalists: No. 328, Anne-Marie Moser, vert. No. 329, James Craig. No. 330, Katarina Witt. No. 331, Eric Heiden, vert. No. 332, Nancy Kerrigan. $2, Dan Jansen.

1994, July 20 Litho. ***Perf. 14***
327 A85 29c multicolored 60 60

Souvenir Sheets

328	A85	50c	multicolored	1.00	1.00
329	A85	50c	multicolored	1.00	1.00
330	A85	$1	multicolored	2.00	2.00
331	A85	$1	multicolored	2.00	2.00
332	A85	$1	multicolored	2.00	2.00
333	A85	$2	multicolored	4.00	4.00

Intl. Olympic Committee, cent.

Miniature Sheets of 8

PHILAKOREA '94 — A86

Wildlife carrying letters: No. 334a, Sailfin goby. b, Sharpnose puffer. c, Lightning butterflyfish. d, Clown anemonefish. e, Parrotfish. f, Batfish. g, Clown triggerfish. h, twinspot wrasse.

No. 335a, Palau fruit bat. b, Crocodile. c, Dugong. d, Banded sea snake. e, Bottle-nosed dophin. f, Hawksbill turtle. g, Octopus. h, Manta ray.

No. 336a, Palau fantail. b, Banded crake. c, Island swiftlet. d, Micronesian kingfisher. e. Red-footed booby. f, Great frigatebird. g, Palau owl. h, Palau fruit dove.

1994, Aug. 16 Litho. ***Perf. 14***
334 A86 29c #a.-h. 4.75 4.75
335 A86 40c #a.-h. 6.50 6.50
336 A86 50c #a.-h. 8.00 8.00

No. 336 is airmail.

Miniature Sheet of 20

First Manned Moon Landing, 25th Anniv. — A87

Various scenes from Apollo moon missions.

1994
337 A87 29c #a.-t. 12.00 12.00

Independence Day — A88

Designs: No. 338b, Natl. seal. c, Pres. Kuniwo Nakamura, Palau, US Pres. Clinton. d, Palau, US flags. e, Musical notes of natl. anthem.

1994, Oct. 1 ***Perf. 14***
338 A88 29c Strip of 5, #a.-e. 3.00 3.00

No. 338c is 57x42mm.

No. 258 with added text
"50th ANNIVERSARY / INVASION OF PELELIU / SEPTEMBER 15, 1944"

1994 Litho. ***Perf. 14X13½***
339 A54 $1 multicolored 2.00 2.00

Miniature Sheet of 9

Disney Characters Visit Palau — A89

Designs: No. 340a, Mickey, Minnie arriving. b, Goofy finding way to hotel. c, Donald enjoying beach. d, Minnie, Daisy learning the Ngloik. e, Minnie, Mickey sailing to Natural Bridge. f, Scrooge finding money in Babeldaob jungle. g, Goofy, Napoleon Wrasse. h, Minnie, Clam Garden. i, Grandma Duck weaving basket.

No. 341, Mickey exploring underwater shipwreck. No. 342, Donald visiting Airai Bai on Babeldaob. No. 343, Pluto, Mickey in boat, vert.

1994, Oct. 14 ***Perf. 13½x14***
340 A89 29c #a.-i. 5.25 5.25

Souvenir Sheets

341-342 A89 $1 each 2.00 2.00

Perf. 14x13½

343 A89 $2.90 multicolored 5.75 5.75

Miniature Sheet of 12

Intl. Year of the Family — A90

Story of Tebruchel: a, With mother as infant. b, Father. c, As young man. d, Wife-to-be. e, Bringing home fish. f, Pregnant wife. g, Elderly mother. h, Elderly father. i, With first born. j, Wife seated. k, Caring for mother. l, Father, wife and baby.

1994 Litho. ***Perf. 14***
344 A90 20c #a.-l. 4.75 4.75

SEMI-POSTAL STAMPS

Olympic Sports SP1

1988, Aug. 8 Litho. *Perf. 14*

B1 SP1 25c +5c Baseball glove, player 50 50
B2 SP1 25c +5c Running shoe, athlete 50 50
a. Pair, #B1-B2 1.00 1.00
B3 SP1 45c +5c Goggles, swimmer 1.00 1.00
B4 SP1 45c +5c Gold medal, diver 1.00 1.00
a. Pair, #B3-B4 2.00 2.00

AIR POST STAMPS

White-tailed Tropicbird AP1

1984, June 12 Litho. *Perf. 14*

C1 AP1 40c shown 75 75
C2 AP1 40c Fairy tern 75 75
C3 AP1 40c Black noddy 75 75
C4 AP1 40c Black-naped tern 75 75
a. Block of 4, #C1-C4 3.00 3.00

Audubon Type of 1985

1985, Feb. 6 Litho. *Perf. 14*

C5 A12 44c Audubon's Shearwater 70 70

Palau-Germany Political, Economic & Cultural Exchange Cent. — AP2

Germany Nos. 40, 65, Caroline Islands Nos. 19, 13 and: No. C6, German flag-raising at Palau, 1885. No. C7, Early German trading post in Angaur. No. C8, Abai architecture recorded by Prof. & Frau Kramer, 1908-1910. No. C9, S.M.S. Cormoran.

1985, Sept. 19 Litho. *Perf. 14x13½*

C6 AP2 44c multicolored 90 90
C7 AP2 44c multicolored 90 90
C8 AP2 44c multicolored 90 90
C9 AP2 44c multicolored 90 90
a. Block of 4, #C6-C9 3.60 3.60

Trans-Pacific Airmail Anniv. Type of 1985

Aircraft: No. C10, 1951 Trans-Ocean Airways PBY-5A Catalina Amphibian. No. C11, 1968 Air Micronesia DC-6B Super Cloudmaster. No. C12, 1960 Trust Territory Airline SA-16 Albatross. No. C13, 1967 Pan American Douglas DC-4.

1985, Nov. 21 Litho. *Perf. 14*

C10 A16 44c multicolored 80 80
C11 A16 44c multicolored 80 80
C12 A16 44c multicolored 80 80
C13 A16 44c multicolored 80 80
a. Block of 4, #C10-C13 3.20 3.20

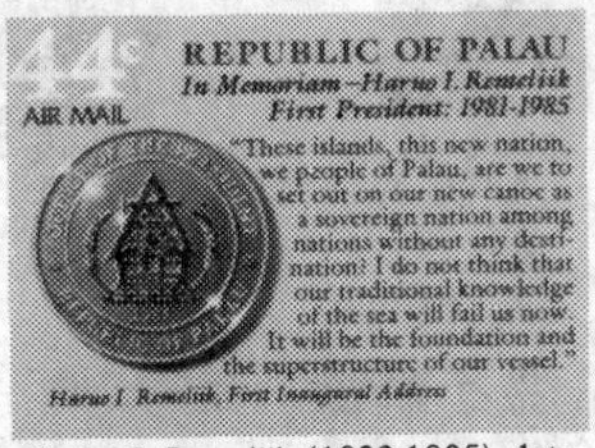

Haruo I. Remeliik (1933-1985), 1st President — AP3

Designs: No. C14, Presidential seal, excerpt from 1st inaugural address. No. C15, War canoe, address excerpt, diff. No. C16, Remeliik, US Pres. Reagan, excerpt from Reagan's speech, Pacific Basin Conference, Guam, 1984.

1986, June 30 Litho. *Perf. 14*

C14 AP3 44c multicolored 1.00 1.00
C15 AP3 44c multicolored 1.00 1.00
C16 AP3 44c multicolored 1.00 1.00
a. Strip of 3, #C14-C16 3.00 3.00

Intl. Peace Year, Statue of Liberty Cent. — AP4

1986, Sept. 19 Litho.

C17 AP4 44c multicolored 90 90

Aircraft — AP5

1989, May 17 Litho. *Perf. 14x14½*

C18 AP5 36c Cessna 207 Skywagon 70 70
a. Booklet pane of 10 7.00 —
C19 AP5 39c Embraer EMB-110 Bandeirante 80 80
a. Booklet pane of 10 8.00 —
C20 AP5 45c Boeing 727 90 90
a. Booklet pane of 10 9.00 —
b. Booklet pane, 5 each 36c, 45c 8.00 —

Palauan Bai Type

1991, July 9 Litho. *Die Cut*

Self-Adhesive

C21 A61 50c like #293a 1.10 1.10

PHILIPPINES

LOCATION — Group of 7,100 islands and islets in the Malay Archipelago, north of Borneo, in the North Pacific Ocean
GOVT. — US Admin., 1898-1946
AREA — 115,748 sq. mi.
POP. — 16,971,100 (est. 1941)
CAPITAL — Quezon City

The islands were ceded to the US by Spain in 1898. On Nov. 15, 1935, they were given their independence, subject to a transition period which ended July 4, 1946. On that date the Commonwealth became the "Republic of the Philippines."

100 Cents = 1 Dollar (1899)
100 Centavos = 1 Peso (1906)

Watermarks

Wmk. 191PI- Double-lined PIPS

Wmk. 190PI- Single-lined PIPS

Wmk. 257- Curved Wavy Lines

Issued under US Administration

Issues of the US Overprinted in Black

PHILIPPINES

On No. 260

1899-1900 Unwmk. *Perf. 12*

212 A96 50c orange 375.00 225.00

On Nos. 279, 279d, 267, 268, 281, 282C, 283, 284, 275 and 275a

Wmk. 191

213 A87 1c yellow green 2.50 50
a. Inverted overprint —
214 A88 2c orange red, type III 90 50
a. 2c carmine, type III 1.50 75
b. Booklet pane of 6 ('00) 300.00 90.00
215 A89 3c purple 5.00 1.00
216 A91 5c blue 4.50 75
a. Inverted overprint 3,750.
217 A94 10c brown, type I 17.50 3.50
217A A94 10c org brown, type II 200.00 25.00
218 A95 15c olive green 30.00 7.00
219 A96 50c orange 110.00 30.00
a. 50c red orange 225.00
Nos. 213-219 (8) 370.40 68.25

On Nos. 280b, 282 and 272

1901

220 A90 4c orange brown 17.50 4.00
221 A92 6c lake 22.50 6.00
222 A93 8c violet brown 22.50 6.00

On Nos. 276, 276A, 277a and 278

Red Overprint

223 A97 $1 black, type I 425.00 240.00
223A A97 $1 black, type II 2,250. 675.00
224 A98 $2 dark blue 475.00 250.00
225 A99 $5 dark green 850.00 650.00

On Nos. 300-313 and shades

Black Overprint

1903-04

226 A115 1c blue green 3.50 25
227 A116 2c carmine 6.00 90
228 A117 3c bright violet 60.00 11.00
229 A118 4c brown ('04) 60.00 17.50
a. 4c orange brown 60.00 15.00
230 A119 5c blue 9.00 75
231 A120 6c brownish lake ('04) 65.00 15.00
232 A121 8c vio blk ('04) 40.00 10.00
233 A122 10c pale red brown ('04) 20.00 1.75
a. 10c red brown 25.00 2.50
b. Pair, one without ovpt. 1,350.
234 A123 13c purple black 25.00 12.50
a. 13c brown violet 25.00 12.50
235 A124 15c olive green 50.00 10.00
236 A125 50c orange 115.00 30.00
Nos. 226-236 (11) 453.50 109.65

Red Overprint

237 A126 $1 black 450.00 250.00
238 A127 $2 dk blue ('04) 750.00 750.00
239 A128 $5 dk green ('04) 1,000. 900.00

On Nos. 319, 319c in Black

1904

240 A129 2c carmine 5.00 2.00
a. Booklet pane of 6 1,000.
b. 2c scarlet 5.75 2.50

Jose Rizal — A40

Arms of Manila — A41

Designs: 4c, McKinley. 6c, Magellan. 8c, Miguel Lopez de Legaspi. 10c, Gen. Henry W. Lawton. 12c, Lincoln. 16c, Adm. William T. Sampson. 20c, Washington. 26c, Francisco Carriedo. 30c, Franklin.

Each Inscribed "Philippine Islands/United States of America"

1906, Sept. 8 Engr. Wmk. 191PI

241 A40 2c deep green 20 15
a. 2c yellow green ('10) 35 15
b. Booklet pane of 6 325.00
242 A40 4c carmine 25 15
a. 4c carmine lake ('10) 50 15
b. Booklet pane of 6 450.00
243 A40 6c violet 1.00 15
244 A40 8c brown 2.00 50
245 A40 10c blue 1.50 15
246 A40 12c brown lake 4.00 1.50
247 A40 16c violet black 3.00 16
248 A40 20c orange brown 3.25 25
249 A40 26c violet brown 5.00 1.65
250 A40 30c olive green 4.00 1.10
251 A41 1p orange 22.50 5.50
252 A41 2p black 27.50 1.00
253 A41 4p dark blue 85.00 12.00
254 A41 10p dark green 175.00 55.00
Nos. 241-254 (14) 334.20 79.26

Change of Colors

1909-13 *Perf. 12*

255 A40 12c red orange 7.00 2.00
256 A40 16c olive green 2.75 50
257 A40 20c yellow 6.00 1.00
258 A40 26c blue green 1.25 55
259 A40 30c ultramarine 8.00 2.50
260 A41 1p pale violet 24.00 4.00
260A A41 2p vio brown ('13) 65.00 2.00
Nos. 255-260A (7) 114.00 12.55

1911 Wmk. 190PI *Perf. 12*

261 A40 2c green 50 15
a. Booklet pane of 6 375.00
262 A40 4c carmine lake 2.00 15
a. 4c carmine — —
b. Booklet pane of 6 375.00
263 A40 6c deep violet 1.50 15
264 A40 8c brown 6.50 35
265 A40 10c blue 2.50 15
266 A40 12c orange 2.00 35
267 A40 16c olive green 2.00 15
268 A40 20c yellow 1.65 15
a. 20c orange 1.65 15
269 A40 26c blue green 2.25 20
270 A40 30c ultramarine 2.75 35
271 A41 1p pale violet 17.50 40
272 A41 2p violet brown 22.50 60
273 A41 4p deep blue 475.00 60.00
274 A41 10p deep green 175.00 20.00
Nos. 261-274 (14) 713.65 83.15

1914

275 A40 30c gray 8.00 32

1914-23 *Perf. 10*

276 A40 2c green 1.25 15
a. Booklet pane of 6 375.00
277 A40 4c carmine 1.25 15
a. Booklet pane of 6 375.00
278 A40 6c light violet 30.00 7.50
a. 6c deep violet 35.00 4.50
279 A40 8c brown 32.50 8.25
280 A40 10c dark blue 20.00 16
281 A40 16c olive green 60.00 3.50
282 A40 20c orange 17.50 65
283 A40 30c gray 45.00 2.25
284 A41 1p pale violet 95.00 2.50
Nos. 276-284 (9) 302.50 25.11

1918-26 *Perf. 11*

285 A40 2c green 17.50 3.50
a. Booklet pane of 6 500.00
286 A40 4c carmine 22.50 2.00
a. Booklet pane of 6 1,000.
287 A40 6c deep violet 32.50 1.40
287A A40 8c light brown 175.00 25.00
288 A40 10c dark blue 45.00 1.25
289 A40 16c olive green 80.00 5.50
289A A40 20c orange 50.00 6.50
289C A40 30c gray 47.50 10.00
289D A41 1p pale violet 60.00 11.00
Nos. 285-289D (9) 530.00 66.15

1917-25 Unwmk. *Perf. 11*

290 A40 2c yellow green 15 15
a. 2c dark green 15 15
b. Vert. pair, imperf. horiz. 1,500.
c. Horiz. pair, imperf. btwn. 1,500. —
d. Vert. pair, imperf. btwn. 1,750.
e. Booklet pane of 6 20.00
291 A40 4c carmine 15 15
a. 4c light rose 16 15
b. Booklet pane of 6 15.00 —
292 A40 6c deep violet 25 15
a. 6c lilac 28 15
b. 6c red violet 28 15
c. Booklet pane of 6 450.00 —
293 A40 8c yellow brown 16 15
a. 8c orange brown 16 15
294 A40 10c deep blue 16 15
295 A40 12c red orange 25 15
296 A40 16c light olive green 40.00 16
a. 16c olive bister 40.00 35
297 A40 20c orange yellow 20 15
298 A40 26c green 35 42
a. 26c blue green 45 25
299 A40 30c gray 40 15
300 A41 1p pale violet 27.50 85
a. 1p red lilac 27.50 85
b. 1p pale rose lilac 27.50 90
301 A41 2p violet brown 25.00 60
302 A41 4p blue 22.50 35
a. 4p dark blue 22.50 35
Nos. 290-302 (13) 117.07
Set value 2.85

1923-26

Design: 16c, Adm. George Dewey.

303 A40 16c olive bister 75 15
a. 16c olive green 1.10 16
304 A41 10p deep green ('26) 50.00 4.00

See Nos. 326-353. For surcharges see Nos. 368-369, 450. For overprints see Nos. C1-C28, C36-C46, C54-C57, O5-O14.

Legislative Palace — A42

1926, Dec. 20 Unwmk. *Perf. 12*

319	A42	2c green & black	40	25
a.		Horiz. pair, imperf. btwn.	*275.00*	
b.		Vert. pair, imperf. between	*500.00*	
320	A42	4c car & black	40	32
a.		Horiz. pair, imperf. btwn.	*275.00*	
b.		Vert. pair, imperf. between	*500.00*	
321	A42	16c ol grn & black	75	65
a.		Horiz. pair, imperf. btwn.	*350.00*	
b.		Vert. pair, imperf. between	*550.00*	
c.		Double impression of center	*575.00*	
322	A42	18c lt brn & black	1.00	60
a.		Double impression of center	*575.00*	
b.		Vert. pair, imperf. between	*550.00*	
323	A42	20c orange & black	1.40	1.00
a.		20c orange & brown	*500.00*	—
b.		Imperf., pair	*450.00*	*450.00*
c.		As "a," imperf., pair	*850.00*	
d.		Vert. pair, imperf. between	*550.00*	
324	A42	24c gray & black	1.00	65
a.		Vert. pair, imperf. between	*550.00*	
325	A42	1p rose lilac & blk	60.00	27.50
a.		Vert. pair, imperf. between	*625.00*	
		Nos. 319-325 (7)	64.95	30.97

Opening of the Legislative Palace.
For overprints see Nos. O1-O4.

Coil Stamp
Rizal Type of 1906

1928 *Perf. 11 Vertically*

326	A40	2c green	6.50	15.00

Types of 1906-23

1925-31 Unwmk. *Imperf.*

340	A40	2c yel grn ('31)	15	15
a.		green ('25)	25	15
341	A40	4c car rose ('31)	15	15
a.		carmine ('25)	38	20
342	A40	6c violet ('31)	1.00	1.00
a.		deep violet ('25)	8.00	4.00
343	A40	8c brown ('31)	90	90
a.		yellow brown ('25)	6.00	3.00
344	A40	10c blue ('31)	1.00	1.00
a.		deep blue ('25)	10.00	5.00
345	A40	12c dp orange ('31)	1.50	1.50
a.		red orange ('25)	10.00	5.00
346	A40	16c olive green *(Dewey)* ('31)	1.10	1.10
a.		bister green ('25)	8.50	4.00
347	A40	20c orange yel ('31)	1.10	1.10
a.		yellow ('25)	8.50	4.00
348	A40	26c green ('31)	1.10	1.10
a.		blue green ('25)	10.00	5.00
349	A40	30c light gray ('31)	1.25	1.25
a.		gray ('25)	10.00	5.00
350	A41	1p lt violet ('31)	4.00	4.00
a.		violet ('25)	60.00	30.00
351	A41	2p brn vio ('31)	10.00	10.00
a.		violet brown ('25)	100.00	50.00
352	A41	4p blue ('31)	30.00	30.00
a.		deep blue ('25)	600.00	300.00
353	A41	10p green ('31)	90.00	90.00
a.		deep green ('25)	800.00	500.00
		Nos. 340-353 (14)	143.25	143.25

Mount Mayon, Luzon — A43

Post Office, Manila — A44

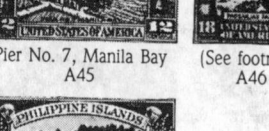

Pier No. 7, Manila Bay A45

(See footnote) A46

Rice Planting — A47

Rice Terraces — A48

Baguio Zigzag — A49

1932, May 3 *Perf. 11*

354	A43	2c yellow green	45	20
355	A44	4c rose carmine	35	22
356	A45	12c orange	50	50
357	A46	18c red orange	17.50	8.25
358	A47	20c yellow	65	55
359	A48	24c deep violet	1.00	65
360	A49	32c olive brown	1.00	70
		Nos. 354-360 (7)	21.45	11.07

The 18c vignette was intended to show Pagsanjan Falls in Laguna, central Luzon, and is so labeled. Through error the stamp pictures Vernal Falls in Yosemite Natl. Park, CA.

For overprints see Nos. C29-C35, C47-C51, C63.

Nos. 302, 302a Surcharged in Orange or Red

1932

368	A41	1p on 4p blue (O)	1.65	35
a.		1p on 4p dark blue (O)	2.25	1.00
369	A41	2p on 4p dark blue (R)	3.00	65
a.		2p on 4p blue (R)	3.00	65

Baseball — A50

Tennis — A51

Basketball — A52

1934, Apr. 14 Typo. *Perf. 11½*

380	A50	2c yellow brown	*2.00*	*1.00*
381	A51	6c ultramarine	25	20
a.		Vert. pair, imperf. between	*1,400.*	
382	A52	16c violet brown	60	60
a.		Vert. pair, imperf. horiz.	*1,400.*	

Tenth Far Eastern Championship Games.

Jose Rizal — A53

Woman and Carabao — A54

La Filipina — A55

Pearl Fishing — A56

Fort Santiago — A57

Salt Spring — A58

Magellan's Landing, 1521 A59

"Juan de la Cruz" A60

Rice Terraces — A61

"Blood Compact," 1565 — A62

Barasoain Church, Malolos — A63

Battle of Manila Bay, 1898 — A64

Montalban Gorge — A65

George Washington — A66

1935, Feb. 15 Engr. *Perf. 11*

383	A53	2c rose	15	15
384	A54	4c yellow green	15	15
385	A55	6c dark brown	15	15
386	A56	8c violet	15	15
387	A57	10c rose carmine	16	15
388	A58	12c black	15	15
389	A59	16c dark blue	15	15
390	A60	20c light olive green	16	15
391	A61	26c indigo	22	22
392	A62	30c orange red	22	22
393	A63	1p red orange & black	1.65	1.25
394	A64	2p bister brn & black	3.50	1.25
395	A65	4p blue & black	3.50	2.50
396	A66	5p green & black	7.50	1.50
		Nos. 383-396 (14)	17.81	8.14

For overprints see Nos. 411-424, 433-446, 463-466, 468, 472-474, 478-484, 485-494, C52-C53, O15-O36, O38, O40-O43, N2-N3, NO6. For surcharges see Nos. 449, N4-N9, N28, NO2-NO5.

Commonwealth Issues

The Temples of Human Progress A67

1935, Nov. 15

397	A67	2c carmine rose	15	15
398	A67	6c deep violet	16	15
399	A67	16c blue	20	15
400	A67	36c yellow green	35	30
401	A67	50c brown	55	55
		Nos. 397-401 (5)	1.41	1.30

Inauguration of the Philippine Commonwealth, Nov. 15th, 1935.

Jose Rizal — A68

President Manuel L. Quezon — A69

1936, June 19 *Perf. 12*

402	A68	2c yellow brown	15	15
403	A68	6c slate blue	15	15
a.		Horiz. pair, imperf. vert.	*1,350.*	
404	A68	36c red brown	50	45
		Set value		59

75th anniv. of the birth of Jose Rizal.

1936, Nov. 15 *Perf. 11*

408	A69	2c orange brown	15	15
409	A69	6c yellow green	15	15
410	A69	12c ultramarine	15	15
		Set value	27	24

1st anniv. of the Commonwealth.
For overprints see Nos. 467, 475.

Nos. 383-396 Overprinted in Black

COMMON-
WEALTH
a

COMMONWEALTH
b

1936-37 *Perf. 11*

411	A53 (a)	2c rose	15	15
a.		Booklet pane of 6	2.50	*65*
412	A54 (b)	4c yel grn ('37)	50	
413	A55 (a)	6c dark brown	20	15
414	A56 (b)	8c violet ('37)	22	20
415	A57 (b)	10c rose carmine	16	15
a.		"COMMONWEALT"		—
416	A58 (b)	12c black ('37)	16	15
417	A59 (b)	16c dark blue	16	15
418	A60 (a)	20c lt ol grn ('37)	60	35
419	A61 (b)	26c indigo ('37)	42	30
420	A62 (b)	30c orange red	28	15
421	A63 (b)	1p red org & black	65	16
422	A64 (b)	2p bister brn & black ('37)	4.50	2.50
423	A65 (b)	4p blue & blk ('37)	15.00	2.50
424	A66 (b)	5p green & black ('37)	1.50	1.25
		Nos. 411-424 (14)	24.50	

Map of Philippines A70

Arms of Manila A71

1937, Feb. 3

425	A70	2c yellow green	15	15
426	A70	6c light brown	15	15
427	A70	12c sapphire	15	15
428	A70	20c deep orange	22	15
429	A70	36c deep violet	40	35
430	A70	50c carmine	45	28
		Nos. 425-430 (6)	1.52	
		Set value		88

33rd Eucharistic Congress.

1937, Aug. 27 *Perf. 11*

431	A71	10p gray	4.25	2.00
432	A71	20p henna brown	2.25	1.40

For overprints see Nos. 495-496. For surcharges see Nos. 451, C58.

Nos. 383-396 Overprinted in Black

COMMON-
WEALTH
a

COMMONWEALTH
b

1938-40 *Perf. 11*

433	A53 (a)	2c rose ('39)		15	15
a.		Booklet pane of 6		3.50	65
b.		"WEALTH COMMON-"		3,500.	—
c.		Hyphen omitted		—	—
434	A54 (b)	4c yel grn ('40)		40	—
435	A55 (a)	6c dk brn ('39)		15	15
a.		6c golden brown		15	15
436	A56 (b)	8c violet ('39)		15	15
a.		"COMMONWEALT"		65.00	
437	A57 (b)	10c rose car ('39)		15	15
438	A58 (b)	12c black ('40)		15	15
439	A59 (b)	16c dark blue		15	15
440	A60 (a)	20c lt ol grn ('39)		15	15
441	A61 (b)	26c indigo ('40)		20	20
442	A62 (b)	30c org red ('39)		1.40	70
443	A63 (b)	1p red org & blk		40	16
444	A64 (b)	2p bis brn & blk		2.75	75
445	A65 (b)	4p bl & blk ('40)		80.00	65.00
446	A66 (b)	5p grn & blk ('40)		4.50	2.75
		Nos. 433-446 (14)		90.70	

Overprint "b" measures 18 1/2x1 3/4mm. No. 433b occurs in booklet pane, No. 433a, position 5; all copies are straight-edged, left and bottom.

Stamps of 1917-37 Surcharged in Red, Violet or Black

FIRST FOREIGN TRADE WEEK 2 CENTAVOS MAY 21-27,1939

FIRST FOREIGN TRADE WEEK 50CENTAVOS50

MAY 21-27, 1939 6CENTAVOS6

FIRST FOREIGN TRADE WEEK MAY 21-27,1939

1939, July 5

449	A54	2c on 4c yel green (R)	15	15
450	A40	6c on 26c blue grn (V)	15	15
a.		6c on 26c green	65	30
451	A71	50c on 20p henna brn (Bk)	1.00	1.00

Foreign Trade Week.

Triumphal Arch — A72

Malacanan Palace — A73

1939, Nov. 15 *Perf. 11*

452	A72	2c yellow green	15	15
453	A72	6c carmine	15	15
454	A72	12c bright blue	16	15
		Set value	33	17

For overprints see Nos. 469, 476.

1939, Nov. 15

455	A73	2c green	15	15
456	A73	6c orange	15	15
457	A73	12c carmine	16	15
		Set value	33	17

#452-457 for 4th anniv. of the Commonwealth. For overprint see No. 470.

Quezon Taking Oath of Office — A74

Jose Rizal — A75

1940, Feb. 8

458	A74	2c dark orange	15	15
459	A74	6c dark green	15	15
460	A74	12c purple	25	15
		Set value		23

4th anniversary of Commonwealth. For overprints see Nos. 471, 477.

Rotary Press Printing

1941, Apr. 14 *Perf. 11x10 1/2*

Size: 19x22 1/2mm

461	A75	2c apple green	15	15

Flat Plate Printing

1941-43 *Perf. 11*

Size: 18 3/4x22mm

462	A75	2c apple green ('43)	15	15
a.		2c pale apple green	16	15
b.		Bklt. pane of 6 (apple green, '43)	1.25	1.00
c.		Bklt. pane of 6 (pale apple green)	2.50	2.25

No. 462 was issued only in booklet panes and all copies have straight edges.

Further printings were made in 1942 and 1943 in different shades from the first supply of stamps sent to the islands.

For type A75 overprinted see Nos. 464, O37, O39, N1, NO1.

Philippine Stamps of 1935-41, Handstamped in Violet

VICTORY

1944 *Perf. 11, 11x10 1/2*

463	A53	2c (#411)	*260.00*	*95.00*
a.		Booklet pane of 6	*2,000.*	
463B	A53	2c (#433)	*1,200.*	*1,200.*
464	A75	2c (#461)	2.50	2.25
465	A54	4c (#384)	*25.00*	*25.00*
466	A55	6c (#385)	*1,500.*	*1,350.*
467	A69	6c (#409)	*110.00*	*85.00*
468	A55	6c (#413)	*650.00*	*600.00*
469	A72	6c (#453)	*135.00*	*110.00*
470	A73	6c (#456)	*600.00*	*550.00*
471	A74	6c (#459)	*160.00*	*150.00*
472	A56	8c (#436)	15.00	20.00
473	A57	10c (#415)	*110.00*	*75.00*
474	A57	10c (#437)	*135.00*	*110.00*
475	A69	12c (#410)	*400.00*	*175.00*
476	A72	12c (#454)	*3,500.*	*2,000.*
477	A74	12c (#460)	*190.00*	*135.00*
478	A59	16c (#389)	*700.00*	
479	A59	16c (#417)	*450.00*	*325.00*
480	A59	16c (#439)	*160.00*	*100.00*
481	A60	20c (#440)	27.50	27.50
482	A62	30c (#420)	*225.00*	*160.00*
483	A62	30c (#442)	*325.00*	*250.00*
484	A63	1p (#443)	*5,500.*	*4,000.*

Types of 1935-37 Overprinted

VICTORY

VICTORY

COMMON-
WEALTH
a

COMMONWEALTH
b

1945 *Perf. 11*

485	A53 (a)	2c rose	15	15
486	A54 (b)	4c yellow green	15	15
487	A55 (a)	6c golden brown	15	15
488	A56 (b)	8c violet	15	15
489	A57 (b)	10c rose carmine	15	15
490	A58 (b)	12c black	20	15
491	A59 (b)	16c dark blue	25	15
492	A60 (a)	20c lt olive green	30	15
493	A62 (b)	30c orange red	40	35
494	A63 (b)	1p red org & black	1.10	25

Nos. 431-432 Overprinted in Black VICTORY

495	A71	10p gray	40.00	13.50
496	A71	20p henna brown	35.00	15.00
		Nos. 485-496 (12)	78.00	30.30

Jose Rizal — A76

Rotary Press Printing

1946, May 28 *Perf. 11x10 1/2*

497	A76	2c sepia	15	15

For overprints see No. 503 (Philippines, Vol. 4) and No. O44.

Succeeding issues, released by the Philippine Republic on and after July 4, 1946, are listed in Vol. 4.

AIR POST STAMPS

Madrid-Manila Flight Issue

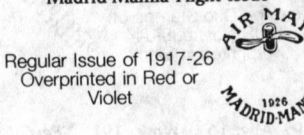

Regular Issue of 1917-26 Overprinted in Red or Violet

1926, May 13 **Unwmk.** *Perf. 11*

C1	A40	2c green (R)	5.50	2.50
C2	A40	4c carmine	7.25	3.00
a.		Inverted overprint	*1,600.*	—
C3	A40	6c lilac (R)	35.00	10.00
C4	A40	8c org brown	35.00	10.00
C5	A40	10c deep blue (R)	35.00	10.00
C6	A40	12c red orange	35.00	17.50
C7	A40	16c lt olive green *(Sampson)*	*1,500.*	*1,350.*
C8	A40	16c ol bister *(Sampson)* (R)	*2,650.*	*2,250.*
C9	A40	16c olive green *(Dewey)*	40.00	17.50
C10	A40	20c orange yellow	40.00	17.50
C11	A40	26c blue green	40.00	20.00
C12	A40	30c gray	40.00	20.00
C13	A41	2p vio brown (R)	350.00	200.00
C14	A41	4p dark blue (R)	525.00	375.00
C15	A41	10p deep green	800.00	500.00

Same Overprint on No. 269

Wmk. 190PI

Perf. 12

C16	A40	26c blue green	*2,250.*	

Same Overprint on No. 284

Perf. 10

C17	A41	1p pale violet	135.00	85.00

Flight of Spanish aviators Gallarza and Loriga from Madrid to Manila.

London-Orient Flight Issue

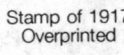

Regular Issue of 1917-25 Overprinted in Red

1928, Nov. 9 **Unwmk.** *Perf. 11*

C18	A40	2c green	40	25
C19	A40	4c carmine	40	35
C20	A40	6c violet	1.50	1.25
C21	A40	8c orange brown	1.65	1.50
C22	A40	10c deep blue	1.65	1.50
C23	A40	12c red orange	2.25	2.00
C24	A40	16c ol green *(Dewey)*	1.75	1.40
C25	A40	20c orange yellow	2.25	2.00
C26	A40	26c blue green	6.50	5.00
C27	A40	30c gray	6.50	5.00

Same Overprint on No. 271

Wmk. 190PI

Perf. 12

C28	A41	1p pale violet	35.00	22.50
		Nos. C18-C28 (11)	59.85	42.75

Flight from London to Manila.

Nos. 354-360 Overprinted

1932, Sept. 27 **Unwmk.** *Perf. 11*

C29	A43	2c yellow green	30	30
C30	A44	4c rose carmine	30	30
C31	A45	12c orange	50	50
C32	A46	18c red orange	3.00	3.00
C33	A47	20c yellow	1.50	1.50
C34	A48	24c deep violet	1.50	1.50
C35	A49	32c olive brown	1.50	1.50
		Nos. C29-C35 (7)	8.60	8.60

Visit of Capt. Wolfgang von Gronau on his round-the-world flight.

Regular Issue of 1917-25 Overprinted

F.REIN MADRID-MANILA FLIGHT-1933

1933, Apr. 11

C36	A40	2c green	30	30
C37	A40	4c carmine	35	35
C38	A40	6c deep violet	75	75
C39	A40	8c orange brown	2.00	1.40
C40	A40	10c dark blue	1.50	90
C41	A40	12c orange	1.50	90
C42	A40	16c ol green *(Dewey)*	1.50	90
C43	A40	20c yellow	1.50	1.00
C44	A40	26c green	2.00	1.40
a.		26c blue green	2.50	1.65
C45	A40	30c gray	2.25	1.50
		Nos. C36-C45 (10)	13.65	9.40

Flight from Madrid to Manila of aviator Fernando Rein y Loring.

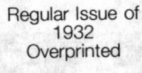

Stamp of 1917 Overprinted

1933, May 26 **Unwmk.** *Perf. 11*

C46	A40	2c green	45	40

Regular Issue of 1932 Overprinted

C47	A44	4c rose carmine	15	15
C48	A45	12c orange	25	15
C49	A47	20c yellow	25	16
C50	A48	24c deep violet	30	20
C51	A49	32c olive brown	40	30
		Nos. C46-C51 (6)	1.80	1.36

Nos. 387 and 392 Overprinted in Gold

1935, Dec. 2

C52	A57	10c rose carmine	25	20
C53	A62	30c orange red	40	35

China Clipper flight from Manila to San Francisco, Dec. 2-5, 1935.

Regular Issue of 1917-25 Surcharged in Various Colors

MANILA-MADRID ARNACAL FLIGHT-1936 2CENTAVOS2

1936, Sept. 6 *Perf. 11*

C54	A40	2c on 4c carmine (Bl)	15	15
C55	A40	6c on 12c red org (V)	15	15
C56	A40	16c on 26c blue green (Bk)	20	20
a.		16c on 26c green (Bk)	1.00	65
		Set value	35	35

Manila-Madrid flight by aviators Antonio Arnaiz and Juan Calvo.

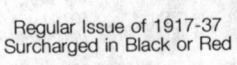

Regular Issue of 1917-37 Surcharged in Black or Red

FIRST AIR MAIL EXHIBITION Feb 17 to 19,1939 8CENTAVOS8

1939, Feb. 17

C57	A40	8c on 26c blue green	60	38
a.		8c on 26c green	1.40	50
C58	A71	1p on 10p gray (R)	2.50	2.00

1st Air Mail Exhib., Feb. 17-19, 1939.

Moro Vinta and Clipper — AP1

1941, June 30

C59 AP1 8c carmine 1.00 60
C60 AP1 20c ultramarine 1.20 45
C61 AP1 60c blue green 1.75 75
C62 AP1 1p sepia 70 42

For overprint see No. NO7. For surcharges see Nos. N10-N11, N35-N36.

No. C47 Handstamped in Violet **VICTORY**

1944, Dec. 3 Unwmk. *Perf. 11*
C63 A44 4c rose carmine *1,500. 1,500.*

SPECIAL DELIVERY STAMPS

US No. E5 Overprinted in Red **PHILIPPINES**

1901, Oct. 15 Wmk. 191 *Perf. 12*
E1 SD3 10c dark blue 90.00 80.00

Special Delivery Messenger SD2

1906 Engr. Wmk. 191PI
E2 SD2 20c ultramarine 25.00 6.50
b. 20c pale ultramarine 25.00 6.50

See Nos. E3-E6. For overprints see Nos. E7-E10, EO1.

Special Printing

Ovptd. in Red as #E1 on US #E6

1907
E2A SD4 10c ultramarine *2,000.*

1911 Wmk. 190PI
E3 SD2 20c deep ultramarine 16.00 1.40

1916 *Perf. 10*
E4 SD2 20c deep ultra 150.00 40.00

1919 Unwmk. *Perf. 11*
E5 SD2 20c ultramarine 50 20
a. 20c pale blue 65 16
b. 20c dull violet 50 16

Type of 1906 Issue

1925-31 *Imperf.*
E6 SD2 20c dull violet ('31) 17.50 *16.00*

Type of 1919 Overprinted in Black **COMMONWEALTH**

1939 *Perf. 11*
E7 SD2 20c blue violet 25 20

Nos. E5b and E7, Handstamped in Violet **VICTORY**

1944 *Perf. 11*
E8 SD2 20c (On #E5b) *500.00 375.00*
E9 SD2 20c (On #E7) *160.00 140.00*

Type SD2 Overprinted "VICTORY" As No. 486

1945
E10 SD2 20c blue violet 55 55
a. "IC" close together 2.75 2.75

SPECIAL DELIVERY OFFICIAL STAMP

Type of 1906 Issue Overprinted **O.B.**

1931 Unwmk. *Perf. 11*
EO1 SD2 20c dull violet 55 40
a. No period after "B" 16.50 14.00
b. Double overprint —

POSTAGE DUE STAMPS

Postage Due Stamps of the US Nos. J38-J44 Overprinted in Black **PHILIPPINES**

1899, Aug. 16 Wmk. 191 *Perf. 12*
J1 D2 1c deep claret 4.50 1.00
J2 D2 2c deep claret 4.50 90
J3 D2 5c deep claret 12.50 1.90
J4 D2 10c deep claret 15.00 3.50
J5 D2 50c deep claret 150.00 75.00

No. J1 was used to pay regular postage Sept. 5-19, 1902.

1901, Aug. 31
J6 D2 3c deep claret 15.00 5.00
J7 D2 30c deep claret 175.00 75.00
Nos. J1-J7 (7) 376.50 162.30

Post Office Clerk — D3

Unwmk.

1928, Aug. 21 Engr. *Perf. 11*
J8 D3 4c brown red 15 15
J9 D3 6c brown red 15 15
J10 D3 8c brown red 15 15
J11 D3 10c brown red 15 15
J12 D3 12c brown red 15 15
J13 D3 16c brown red 16 16
J14 D3 20c brown red 15 15
Set value 88 88

For overprints see Nos. O16-O22, NJ1. For surcharge see No. J15.

No. J8 Surcharged in Blue **3 CVOS. 3**

1937
J15 D3 3c on 4c brown red 16 15

Nos. J8 to J14 Handstamped in Violet **VICTORY**

1944
J16 D3 4c brown red *100.00* —
J17 D3 6c brown red *65.00* —
J18 D3 8c brown red *70.00* —
J19 D3 10c brown red *65.00* —
J20 D3 12c brown red *65.00* —
J21 D3 16c brown red *70.00* —
J22 D3 20c brown red *70.00* —

OFFICIAL STAMPS

Official Handstamped Overprints

"Officers purchasing stamps for government business may, if they so desire, overprint them with the letters "O.B." either in writing with black ink or by rubber stamps but in such a manner as not to obliterate the stamp that postmasters will be unable to determine whether the stamps have been previously used." C. M. Cotterman, Director of Posts, Dec. 26, 1905.

Beginning with Jan. 1, 1906, all branches of the Insular Government used postage stamps to prepay postage instead of franking them as before. Some officials used manuscript, some utilized typewriting machines, some made press-printed overprints, but by far the larger number provided themselves with rubber stamps. The majority of these read "O.B." but other forms were: "OFFICIAL BUSINESS" or "OFFICIAL MAIL" in 2 lines, with variations on many of these.

These "O.B." overprints are known on US 1899-1901 stamps; on 1903-06 stamps in red and blue; on 1906 stamps in red, blue, black, yellow and green.

"O.B." overprints were also made on the centavo and peso stamps of the Philippines, per order of May 25, 1907.

Beginning in 1926 the stamps were overprinted and issued by the Government, but some post offices continued to handstamp "O.B."

Regular Issue of 1926 Overprinted in Red **OFFICIAL**

1926, Dec. 20 Unwmk. *Perf. 12*
O1 A42 2c green & black 2.00 90
O2 A42 4c carmine & black 2.00 1.10
a. Vertical pair, imperf. between 750.00
O3 A42 18c lt brown & black 6.50 4.00
O4 A42 20c orange & black 6.00 1.40

Opening of the Legislative Palace.

Regular Issue of 1917-26 Overprinted **O. B.**

1931 *Perf. 11*
O5 A40 2c green 15 15
a. No period after "B" 15.00 5.00
b. No period after "O" —
O6 A40 4c carmine 15 15
a. No period after "B" 15.00 5.00
O7 A40 6c deep violet 15 15
O8 A40 8c yellow brn 15 15
O9 A40 10c deep blue 25 15
O10 A40 12c red orange 16 15
a. No period after "B" 30.00
O11 A40 16c lt ol green *(Dewey)* 16 15
a. 16c olive bister 1.00 20
O12 A40 20c orange yellow 20 15
a. No period after "B" 20.00 15.00
O13 A40 26c green 30 30
a. 26c blue green 80 65
O14 A40 30c gray 25 22
Nos. O5-O14 (10) 1.92
Set value 1.25

Same Overprint on Nos. 383-392

1935
O15 A53 2c rose 15 15
a. No period after "B" 15.00 5.00
O16 A54 4c yellow green 15 15
a. No period after "B" 15.00 10.00
O17 A55 6c dark brown 15 15
a. No period after "B" 20.00 20.00
O18 A56 8c violet 15 15
O19 A57 10c rose carmine 16 15
O20 A58 12c black 16 15
O21 A59 16c dark blue 16 15
O22 A60 20c lt olive green 16 15
O23 A61 26c indigo 25 22
O24 A62 30c orange red 30 25
Set value 1.44 1.00

Same Overprint on Nos. 411 and 418

1937-38 *Perf. 11*
O25 A53 2c rose 15 15
a. No period after "B" 4.25 2.25
O26 A60 20c lt olive green ('38) 65 50
Set value 70 55

Nos. 383-392 Overprinted in Black:

O. B.

COMMON-WEALTH
O. B.
a b

1938-40
O27 A53 (a) 2c rose 15 15
a. Hyphen omitted 20.00 20.00
b. No period after "B" 25.00 25.00
O28 A54 (b) 4c yellow green 15 15
O29 A55 (a) 6c dark brown 15 15
O30 A56 (b) 8c violet 15 15
O31 A57 (b) 10c rose carmine 15 15
a. No period after "O" 30.00 30.00
O32 A58 (b) 12c black 15 15
O33 A59 (b) 16c dark blue 16 15
O34 A60 (a) 20c lt ol green ('40) 22 22
O35 A61 (b) 26c indigo 30 30
O36 A62 (b) 30c orange red 25 25
Set value 1.50 1.25

No. 461 Overprinted in Black **O. B.**

Perf. 11x10½

1941, Apr. 14 Unwmk.
O37 A75 2c apple green 15 15

Official Stamps Handstamped in Violet **VICTORY**

1944 *Perf. 11, 11x10½*
O38 A53 2c #O27 *160.00 110.00*
O39 A75 2c #O37 5.00 3.00
O40 A54 4c #O16 *30.00 20.00*
O40A A55 6c #O29 *3,500.* —
O41 A57 10c #O31 *110.00*
a. No period after "O" —
O42 A60 20c #O22 *5,000.*
O43 A60 20c #O26 *1,400.*

No. 497 Overprinted Like No. O37 in Black

Perf. 11x10½

1946, June 19 Unwmk.
O44 A76 2c sepia 15 15

OCCUPATION STAMPS

Issued under Japanese Occupation

Nos. 461, 438 and 439 Overprinted with Bars in Black

1942-43 Unwmk. *Perf. 11x10½, 11*
N1 A75 2c apple green 15 15
a. Pair, one without overprint —
N2 A58 12c black ('43) 15 15
N3 A59 16c dark blue 4.00 3.00

Nos. 435, 442, 443 and 423 Surcharged in Black

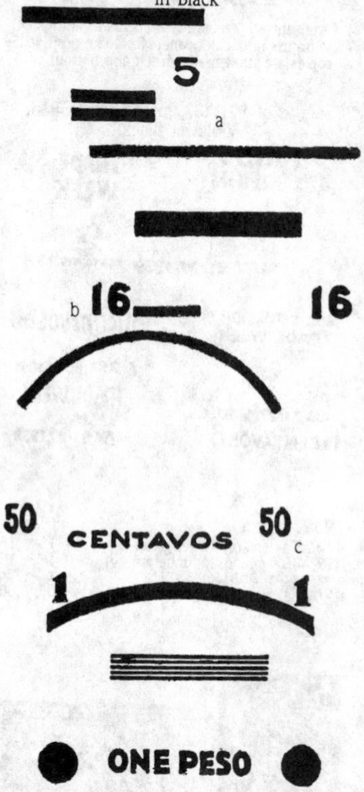

Perf. 11
N4 A55 5c on 6c golden brn 15 15
a. Top bar shorter, thinner 20 20
b. 5c on 6c dark brown 20 20
c. As "b" and "a" 20 20
N5 A62 16c on 30c orange red ('43) 25 25
N6 A63 50c on 1p red org & black ('43) 60 60
a. Double surcharge *300.00*
N7 A65 1p on 4p blue & black ('43) 90.00 90.00

On Nos. N4 and N4b, the top bar measures 1½x22½mm. On Nos. N4a and N4c, the top bar measures 1x21mm and the "5" is smaller and thinner.

No. 384 Surcharged in Black

CONGRATULATIONS
FALL OF
BATAAN AND
CORREGIDOR
1942

2

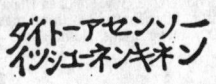

1942, May 18
N8 A54 2c on 4c yellow green 6.00 6.00

Japan's capture of Bataan and Corregidor. The American-Filipino forces finally surrendered May 7, 1942.

No. 384 Surcharged in Black

ダイトーアセンソー
イッシューネンキネン

12-8-1942 5

1942, Dec. 8
N9 A54 5c on 4c yellow green 50 50

1st anniv. of the "Greater East Asia War".

Nos. C59 and C62 Surcharged in Black

ヒトー ギヨー セイフ
イッシューオン キネン
1-23-43
2

1943, Jan. 23
N10 AP1 2(c) on 8c carmine 25 25
N11 AP1 5c on 1p sepia 50 50

1st anniv. of the Philippine Executive Commission.

Nipa Hut — OS1

Rice Planting — OS2

Mt. Mayon and Mt. Fuji — OS3

Moro Vinta — OS4

Engr., Typo. (2, 6, 25c)

1943-44 Wmk. 257 *Perf. 13*

N12 OS1	1c	deep orange	15	15
N13 OS2	2c	bright green	15	15
N14 OS1	4c	slate green	15	15
N15 OS3	5c	orange brown	15	15
N16 OS2	6c	red	15	15
N17 OS3	10c	blue green	15	15
N18 OS4	12c	steel blue	1.00	1.00
N19 OS4	16c	dark brown	15	15
N20 OS1	20c	rose violet	1.25	1.25
N21 OS3	21c	violet	15	15
N22 OS2	25c	pale brown	15	15
N23 OS3	1p	deep carmine	75	75
N24 OS4	2p	dull violet	5.00	5.00
N25 OS4	5p	dark olive	8.50	8.50
		Nos. N12-N25 (14)	17.85	17.85

For surcharges see Nos. NB5-NB7.

Map of Manila Bay Showing Bataan and Corregidor
OS5

1943, May 7 Photo. Unwmk.

N26 OS5 2c carmine red	15	15
N27 OS5 5c bright green	25	25
Set value	34	34

Fall of Bataan and Corregidor, 1st anniv.

No. 440 Surcharged in Black

Limbagan
1593 - 1943

12 12

1943, June 20 Engr. *Perf. 11*
N28 A60 12c on 20c lt olive green 20 20
a. Double surcharge

350th anniv. of the printing press in the Philippines. "Limbagan" is Tagalog for "printing press."

Rizal Monument, Filipina and Philippine Flag — OS6

1943, Oct. 14 Photo. *Perf. 12*

N29 OS6 5c light blue	15	15
a. Imperf.	15	15
N30 OS6 12c orange	15	15
a. Imperf.	15	15
N31 OS6 17c rose pink	16	16
a. Imperf.	15	15
Set value	29	29
Set value, imperf.	35	35

"Independence of the Philippines." Japan granted "independence" Oct. 14, 1943, when the puppet republic was founded.

The imperforate stamps were issued without gum.

Jose Rizal — OS7

Rev. Jose Burgos — OS8

Apolinario Mabini — OS9

1944, Feb. 17 Litho. *Perf. 12*

N32 OS7 5c blue	16	16
a. Imperf.	16	16
N33 OS8 12c carmine	15	15
a. Imperf.	15	15
N34 OS9 17c deep orange	15	15
a. Imperf.	15	15
Set value	33	33
Set value, imperf.	33	33

Nos. C60 and C61 Surcharged in Black

REPÚBLIKA
NG PILIPINAS
5-7-44
5

1944, May 7 *Perf. 11*

N35 AP1 5c on 20c ultra	35	35
N36 AP1 12c on 60c blue green	80	80

Fall of Bataan and Corregidor, 2nd anniv.

Jose P. Laurel — OS10

Without Gum

1945, Jan. 12 Litho. *Imperf.*

N37 OS10 5c dull violet brown	15	15
N38 OS10 7c blue green	15	15
N39 OS10 20c chalky blue	15	15
Set value	22	18

1st anniv. of the puppet Philippine Republic (Oct. 14, 1944). "S" stands for "sentimos."

OCCUPATION SEMI-POSTAL STAMPS

Woman, Farming and Cannery — OSP1

Unwmk.

1942, Nov. 12 Litho. *Perf. 12*

NB1 OSP1 2c + 1c pale violet	15	15
NB2 OSP1 5c + 1c brt green	15	15
NB3 OSP1 16c + 2c orange	10.00	8.00

Campaign to produce and conserve food. The surtax aided the Red Cross.

Souvenir Sheet

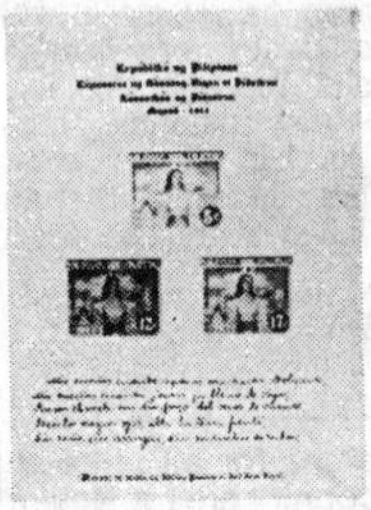
OSP2

Without Gum

1943, Oct. 14 *Imperf.*
NB4 OSP2 Sheet of 3 40.00 *4.00*

"Independence of the Philippines."

No. NB4 contains Nos. N29a-N31a. Lower inscription from Rizal's "Last Farewell." Sold for 2.50p.

Nos. N18, N20 and N21 Surcharged in Black

BAHÂ
1943
+21

1943, Dec. 8 Wmk. 257 *Perf. 13*

NB5 OS4 12c + 21c steel blue	15	15
NB6 OS1 20c + 36c rose violet	15	15
NB7 OS3 21c + 40c violet	15	15
Set value	28	28

The surtax was for the benefit of victims of a Luzon flood. "Baha" is Tagalog for "flood."

Souvenir Sheet

OSP3

Without Gum

1944, Feb. 9 Unwmk. Litho. *Imperf.*
NB8 OSP3 Sheet of 3 2.50 *2.50*

No. NB8 contains Nos. N32a-N34a.

Sheet sold for 1p, surtax going to a fund for the care of heroes' monuments.

OCCUPATION POSTAGE DUE STAMP

No. J15 Ovptd. with Bar in Blue

1942, Oct. 14 Unwmk. *Perf. 11*
NJ1 D3 3c on 4c brown red 25.00 10.00

On copies of No. J15, two lines were drawn in India ink with a ruling pen across "United States of America" by employees of the Short Paid Section of the Manila Post Office to make a provisional 3c postage due stamp which was used from Sept. 1, 1942, (when the letter rate was raised from 2c to 5c) until Oct. 14 when No. NJ1 went on sale.

OCCUPATION OFFICIAL STAMPS

Nos. 461, 413, 435, 435a and 442 Overprinted or Surcharged in Black with Bars and

公用
(K.P.)

1943-44 Unwmk. *Perf. 11x10½, 11*

NO1 A75 2c apple green	15	15
a. Double overprint	*500.00*	
NO2 A55 5c on 6c dk brown (#413, '44)	30.00	30.00
NO3 A55 5c on 6c gldn brn (No. 435a)	15	15
a. Narrower spacing btwn. bars	15	15
b. 5c on 6c dark brown (#435)	15	15
c. As "b," narrower spacing between bars	15	15
NO4 A62 16c on 30c orange red	30	30
a. Wider spacing between bars	30	30

On Nos. NO3 and NO3b, the bar deleting "United States of America" is 9¾-10mm above the bar deleting "Common-." On Nos. NO3a and NO3c, the spacing is 8-8½mm.

On No. NO4 the center bar is 19mm long, 3½mm below the top bar and 6mm above the Japanese characters. On No. NO4a, the center bar is 20½mm long, 9mm below the top bar and 1mm above the Japanese characters.

"K. P." (Kagamitang Pampamahalaan) is Tagalog for "Official Business."

Nos. 435 and 435a Surcharged in Black

5
REPUBLIKA NG
PILIPINAS
(K. P.)

1944 *Perf. 11*
NO5 A55 5c on 6c golden brown 15 15
a. 5c on 6c dark brown 15 15

Nos. 034 and C62 Overprinted in Black

Pilipinas
REPUBLIKA

a

K.P.

REPUBLIKA NG PILIPINAS

b **(K. P.)**

NO6	A60 (a)	20c lt olive green	22	22
NO7	AP1 (b)	1p sepia	65	65

PUERTO RICO

(Porto Rico)

LOCATION — Large island in the West Indies, east of Hispaniola
GOVT. — Former Spanish possession
AREA — 3,435 sq. mi.
POP. — 953,243 (1899)
CAPITAL — San Juan

The island was ceded to the US by the Treaty of 1898.

Spanish issues of 1855-73 used in both Puerto Rico and Cuba are listed as Cuba Nos. 1-4, 9-14, 18-21, 32-34, 35A-37, 39-41, 43-45, 47-49, 51-53, 55-57.

Spanish issues of 1873-1898 for Puerto Rico only are listed in Vol. 4 of this Catalogue.

100 Cents = 1 Dollar (1898)

Issued under US Administration
Ponce Issue

A11

1898 Unwmk. *Imperf.*

200	A11	5c violet, *yellowish*	*6,500.*	

The only way No. 200 is known used is handstamped on envelopes. Both unused stamps and used envelopes have a violet control mark.

Counterfeits exist of Nos. 200-201.

Coamo Issue

A12

1898 Unwmk. *Imperf.*

201	A12	5c black	600.00	*1,000.*

There are ten varieties in the setting (see the Scott United States Specialized Catalogue). The stamps bear the control mark "F. Santiago" in violet.

US Nos. 279, 267, 281, 272 and 282C Overprinted in Black at 36 degree angle

PORTO RICO

1899 Wmk. 191 *Perf. 12*

210	A87	1c yellow green	4.50	1.25
a.		Ovpt. at 25 degree angle	6.50	2.00
211	A88	2c car, type III	3.75	1.00
a.		Ovpt. at 25 degree angle	5.00	2.00
212	A91	5c blue	8.00	2.25
213	A93	8c violet brown	25.00	15.00
a.		Ovpt. at 25 degree angle	30.00	16.00
c.		"PORTO RIC"	100.00	100.00
214	A94	10c brown, type I	15.00	5.00
		Nos. 210-214 (5)	56.25	24.50

Misspellings of the overprint, actually broken letters (PORTO RICU, PORTU RICO, FORTO RICO), are found on 1c, 2c, 8c and 10c.

US Nos. 279 and 267 Overprinted Diagonally in Black

PUERTO RICO

1900

215	A87	1c yellow green	5.00	1.25
216	A88	2c red	4.00	1.00
a.		2c orange red	4.50	1.00
b.		Inverted overprint		8,250.

POSTAGE DUE STAMPS

US Nos. J38, J39, J42 Overprinted like Nos. 210-214

1899 Wmk. 191 *Perf. 12*

J1	D2	1c deep claret	20.00	5.00
a.		Overprint at 25 degree angle	20.00	7.00
J2	D2	2c deep claret	10.00	5.50
a.		Overprint at 25 degree angle	14.00	6.50
J3	D2	10c deep claret	135.00	50.00
a.		Overprint at 25 degree angle	150.00	75.00

Stamps of Puerto Rico were replaced by those of the US.

RYUKYU ISLANDS

LOCATION — Chain of 63 islands between Japan and Formosa, separating the East China Sea from the Pacific Ocean
GOVT. — Semi-autonomous under United States administration
AREA — 848 sq. mi.
POP. — 945,465 (1970)
CAPITAL — Naha, Okinawa

The Ryukyus were part of Japan until American forces occupied them in 1945. The islands reverted to Japan May 15, 1972.

Before the general issue of 1948, a number of provisional stamps were used. These included a mimeographed-handstamped adhesive for Kume Island, and various current stamps of Japan handstamped with chops by the postmasters of Okinawa, Amami, Miyako and Yaeyama. Although authorized by American authorities, these provisionals were local in nature, so are omitted in the listings that follow. They are listed in Scott's United States Specialized Catalogue.

100 Sen = 1 Yen
100 Cents = 1 Dollar (1958)

Catalogue values for all unused stamps in this country are for Never Hinged items.

Watermark

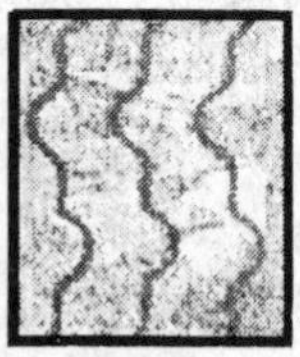

Wmk. 257

Cycad — A1

Lily — A2

Sailing Ship — A3

Farmer — A4

Wmk. 257

1949, July 18 Typo. *Perf. 13*

Second Printing

1	A1	5s magenta	1.40	1.50
2	A2	10s yellow green	3.75	3.75
3	A1	20s yellow green	2.50	2.50
4	A3	30s vermilion	1.40	1.50
5	A2	40s magenta	1.40	1.50
6	A3	50s ultra	3.00	3.25
7	A4	1y ultra	3.50	3.50
		Nos. 1-7 (7)	16.95	17.50

First Printing

1a	A1	5s magenta	2.25	4.00
2a	A2	10s yellow green	1.40	2.50
3a	A1	20s yellow green	1.40	2.50
4a	A3	30s vermilion	2.25	3.50
5a	A2	40s magenta	45.00	45.00
6a	A3	50s ultramarine	2.25	4.00
7a	A4	1y ultramarine	400.00	225.00
		Nos. 1a-7a (7)	454.55	286.50

First printing: thick yellow gum, dull colors, rough perforations, grayish paper. Second printing: white gum, sharp colors, cleancut perforations, white paper.

Roof Tiles — A5

Ryukyu University — A6

Designs: 1y, Ryukyu girl. 2y, Shuri Castle. 3y, Guardian dragon. 4y, Two women. 5y, Sea shells.

Perf. 13x13½

1950, Jan. 21 Unwmk. Photo.

8	A5	50s dk car rose	22	20
a.		White paper	50	50
9	A5	1y deep blue	2.50	2.00
10	A5	2y rose violet	9.50	6.75
11	A5	3y car rose	19.00	7.50
12	A5	4y grnsh gray	12.50	6.00
13	A5	5y blue green	5.00	4.00
		Nos. 8-13 (6)	48.72	26.45

No. 8a is on whiter paper with colorless gum. Issued Sept. 6, 1958. No. 8 is on toned paper with yellowish gum.

For surcharges see Nos. 16-17.

1951, Feb. 12 *Perf. 13½x13*

14	A6	3y red brown	40.00	16.00

Opening of Ryukyu University, Feb. 12.

Pine Tree — A7

1951, Feb. 19 *Perf. 13*

15	A7	3y dark green	37.50	16.00

Reforestation Week, Feb. 18-24.

Nos. 8 and 10 Surcharged in Black

改 訂
*
10 圓

Three types of 10y surcharge:
I - Narrow-spaced rules, "10" normal spacing.
II - Wide-spaced rules, "10" normal spacing.
III - Rules and "10" both wide-spaced.

1952 *Perf. 13x13½*

16	A5	10y on 50s, type II	9.00	9.00
a.		Type I	26.00	26.00
b.		Type III	35.00	35.00
17	A5	100y on 2y rose vio	1,500.	1,100.

There are two types of surcharge on No. 17.

Dove, Bean Sprout and Map — A8

Madanbashi Bridge — A9

1952, Apr. 1 *Perf. 13½x13*

18	A8	3y deep plum	90.00	30.00

Establishment of the Government of the Ryukyu Islands (GRI), Apr. 1, 1952.

1952-53

Designs: 2y, Main Hall, Shuri Castle. 3y, Shurei Gate. 6y, Stone Gate, Sogenji temple, Naha. 10y, Benzaiten-do temple. 30y, Sonohan Utaki (altar) at Shuri Castle. 50y, Tamaudum (royal mausoleum), Shuri. 100y, Stone Bridge, Hosho Pond.

19	A9	1y red	16	16
20	A9	2y green	20	20
21	A9	3y aqua	25	25
22	A9	6y blue	1.25	1.25
23	A9	10y crimson rose	2.00	90
24	A9	30y olive green	7.75	6.25
a.		30y light olive green ('58)	27.50	
25	A9	50y rose violet	12.00	8.25
26	A9	100y claret	16.00	6.25
		Nos. 19-26 (8)	39.61	23.51

Issue dates: 1y, 2y and 3y, Nov. 20, 1952. Others, Jan. 20, 1953.

Reception at Shuri Castle — A10

Perry and American Fleet A11

Perf. 13½x13, 13x13½

1953, May 26

27	A10	3y deep magenta	10.50	6.00
28	A11	6y dull blue	90	90

Centenary of the arrival of Commodore Matthew Calbraith Perry at Naha, Okinawa.

Chofu Ota and Pencil-shaped Matrix — A12

Shigo Toma and Pen — A13

1953, Oct. 1 *Perf. 13½x13*

29	A12	4y yellow brown	9.00	4.50

3rd Newspaper Week.

1954, Oct. 1

30	A13	4y blue	10.00	4.50

4th Newspaper Week.

Ryukyu Pottery A14

Noguni Shrine and Sweet Potato Plant A15

Designs: 15y, Lacquerware. 20y, Textile design.

1954-55 Photo. *Perf. 13*

31	A14	4y brown	1.00	60
32	A14	15y vermilion	2.50	2.00
33	A14	20y yellow orange	2.00	2.00

Issue dates: June 25, 1954, June 20, 1955.
For surcharges see Nos. C19, C21, C23.

1955, Nov. 26

34 A15 4y blue 9.50 5.00

350th anniv. of the introduction of the sweet potato to the Ryukyu Islands.

Stylized Trees — A16

Willow Dance — A17

1956, Feb. 18 Unwmk.

35 A16 4y bluish green 8.75 5.00

Arbor Week, Feb. 18-24.

1956, May 1 *Perf. 13*

Design: 8y, Straw hat dance. 14y, Dancer in warrior costume with fan.

36	A17	5y rose lilac	90	60
37	A17	8y violet blue	2.00	1.65
38	A17	14y redsh brown	2.50	2.00

For surcharges see Nos. C20, C22.

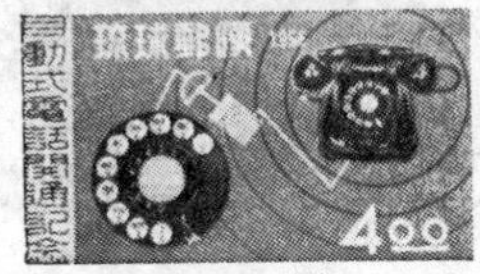

Telephone A18

1956, June 8

39 A18 4y violet blue 12.50 6.50

Establishment of dial telephone system.

Garland of Pine, Bamboo and Plum — A19

Map of Okinawa and Pencil Rocket — A20

1956, Dec. 1 *Perf. 13½x13*

40 A19 2y multicolored 2.00 1.00

New Year, 1957.

1957, Oct. 1 Photo. *Perf. 13½x13*

41 A20 4y deep violet blue 75 75

7th annual Newspaper Week, Oct. 1-7.

Phoenix — A21

1957, Dec. 1 Unwmk. *Perf. 13*

42 A21 2y multicolored 25 25

New Year, 1958.

Ryukyu Stamps — A22

1958, July 1 *Perf. 13½*

43 A22 4y multicolored 80 80

10th anniversary of first Ryukyu stamps.

Yen Symbol and Dollar Sign — A23

1958, Sept. 16 Typo. *Perf. 11*
Without Gum

44	A23	½c orange	80	80
a.		Imperf., pair	*950.00*	
b.		Horiz. pair, imperf. btwn.	80.00	
c.		Vert. pair, imperf. btwn.	100.00	
d.		Vert. strip of 4, imperf. btwn.	500.00	
45	A23	1c yellow green	1.25	1.25
a.		Horiz. pair, imperf. btwn.	120.00	
b.		Vert. pair, imperf. btwn.	90.00	
c.		Vert. strip of 3, imperf. btwn.	350.00	
d.		Vert. strip of 4, imperf. btwn.	500.00	
46	A23	2c dark blue	1.90	1.90
a.		Horiz. pair, imperf. btwn.	150.00	
b.		Vert. pair, imperf. btwn.	*1,200.*	
c.		Horiz. strip of 3, imperf. btwn.	250.00	
d.		Horiz. strip of 4, imperf. btwn.	350.00	
47	A23	3c deep carmine	1.50	1.25
a.		Horiz. pair, imperf. btwn.	120.00	
b.		Vert. pair, imperf. btwn.	90.00	
c.		Vert. strip of 3, imperf. btwn.	250.00	
d.		Vert. strip of 4, imperf. btwn.	450.00	
48	A23	4c bright green	1.90	1.90
a.		Horiz. pair, imperf. btwn.	*500.00*	
b.		Vert. pair, imperf. btwn.	150.00	
49	A23	5c orange	3.50	3.25
a.		Horiz. pair, imperf. btwn.	125.00	
b.		Vert. pair, imperf. btwn.	*750.00*	
50	A23	10c aqua	4.75	4.25
a.		Horiz. pair, imperf. btwn.	200.00	
b.		Vert. pair, imperf. btwn.	150.00	
c.		Vert. strip of 3, imperf. btwn.	450.00	
51	A23	25c brt vio blue	7.00	6.00
a.		Gummed paper ('61)	9.50	6.00
b.		Horiz. pair, imperf. btwn.	*1,400.*	
c.		Vert. pair, imperf. btwn.	*1,000.*	
d.		Vert. strip of 3, imperf. btwn.	500.00	
52	A23	50c gray	*14.00*	9.25
a.		Gummed paper ('61)	10.00	9.25
b.		Horiz. pair, imperf. btwn.	*1,200.*	
53	A23	$1 rose lilac	11.00	5.00
a.		Horiz. pair, imperf. btwn.	350.00	
b.		Vert. pair, imperf. btwn.	*1,200.*	
		Nos. 44-53 (10)	47.60	34.85

Printed locally. Perforation, paper and shade varieties exist.

Nos. 51a, 52a are on off-white paper and perf 10.3.

Gate of Courtesy — A24

1958, Oct. 15 Photo. *Perf. 13½*

54 A24 3c multicolored 1.25 1.00

Restoration of Shureimon, Gate of Courtesy, on road leading to Shuri City.
Counterfeits exist.

Lion Dance A25

Trees and Mountains A26

1958, Dec. 10 Unwmk. *Perf. 13½*

55 A25 1½c multicolored 20 20

New Year, 1959.

1959, Apr. 30 Litho. *Perf. 13½x13*

56 A26 3c bl, yel grn, grn & red 60 55

"Make the Ryukyus Green" movement.

Yonaguni Moth A27

1959, July 23 Photo. *Perf. 13*

57 A27 3c multicolored 1.10 90

Meeting of the Japanese Biological Education Society in Okinawa.

Hibiscus A28

Toy (Yakaji) A29

Designs: 3c, Fish (Moorish idol). 8c, Sea shell (Phalium bandatum). 13c, Butterfly (Kallima Inachus Eucerca), denomination at left, butterfly going up. 17c, Jellyfish (Dactylometra pacifera Goette).

Inscribed 琉球郵便

1959, Aug. 10 *Perf. 13x13½*

58	A28	½c multicolored	20	20
59	A28	3c multicolored	75	38
60	A28	8c lt ultra, blk & ocher	9.50	5.25
61	A28	13c lt bl, gray & org	2.50	1.75
62	A28	17c vio bl, red & yel	17.00	7.50
		Nos. 58-62 (5)	29.95	15.08

Four-character inscription measures 10x2mm on ½c; 12x3mm on 3c, 8c; 8½x2mm on 13c, 17c. See Nos. 76-80.

1959, Dec. 1 Litho.

63 A29 1½c gold & multi 55 38

New Year, 1960.

University Badge A30

1960, May 22 Photo. *Perf. 13*

64 A30 3c multicolored 95 48

Opening of Ryukyu University, 10th anniv.

Dancer — A31

Designs: Various Ryukyu Dances.

1960, Nov. 1 Photo. *Perf. 13*

Dark Gray Background

65	A31	1c yellow, red & vio	1.00	80
66	A31	2 1/2c crimson, bl & yel	2.00	65
67	A31	5c dk bl, yel & red	65	75
68	A31	10c dk bl, yel & car	65	65

See Nos. 81-87, 220.

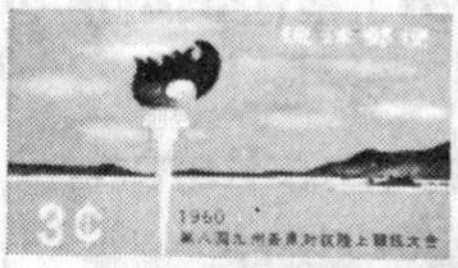

Torch and Nago Bay — A32

Runners at Starting Line — A33

1960, Nov. 8

72	A32	3c lt bl, grn & red	5.25	2.25
73	A33	8c orange & slate grn	75	75

8th Kyushu Inter-Prefectural Athletic Meet, Nago, Northern Okinawa, Nov. 6-7.

Little Egret and Rising Sun — A34

1960, Dec. 1 Unwmk. *Perf. 13*

74	A34	3c redsh brown	5.50	2.50

National census.

Okinawa Bull Fight — A35

1960, Dec. 10 *Perf. 13 1/2*

75	A35	1 1/2c bis, dk bl & red brn	1.75	65

New Year, 1961.

Type of 1959 With Japanese Inscription Redrawn:

琉 球 郵 便

1960-61 Photo. *Perf. 13x13 1/2*

76	A28	1/2c multi ('61)	35	35
77	A28	3c multi ('61)	75	25
78	A28	8c lt ultra, blk & ocher	75	60
79	A28	13c blue, brn & red	90	80
80	A28	17c vio bl, red & yel	11.00	4.25
		Nos. 76-80 (5)	13.75	6.25

Size of Japanese inscription on Nos. 78-80 is 10 1/2x11 1/2mm. On No. 79 the denomination is at right, butterfly going down.

Issue dates: 8c-17c, July 1. 3c, Aug. 23. 1/2c, Oct.

Dancer Type of 1960 with "RYUKYUS" Added

1961-64 *Perf. 13*

81	A31	1c multi	15	15
82	A31	2 1/2c multi ('62)	18	15
83	A31	5c multi ('62)	22	24
84	A31	10c multi ('62)	45	38
84A	A31	20c multi ('64)	2.50	1.40
85	A31	25c multi ('62)	85	90
86	A31	50c multi	2.25	1.40
87	A31	$1 multi	4.75	22
		Nos. 81-87 (8)	11.35	4.84

Issue dates: 50c, $1, Sept. 1. 1c, Dec. 5. 25c, Feb. 1. 2 1/2c, 5c, 10c, June 20. 20c, Jan. 20.

Pine Tree — A36

1961, May 1 Photo. *Perf. 13*

88	A36	3c yellow grn & red	1.50	1.25

"Make the Ryukyus Green" movement.

Naha, Steamer and Sailboat A37

1961, May 20

89	A37	3c aqua	2.10	1.10

40th anniversary of Naha.

White Silver Temple — A38

Books and Bird — A39

1961, Oct. 1 Typo. *Perf. 11*

90	A38	3c red brown	1.75	1.50
a.		Horiz. pair, imperf. between	*450.00*	
b.		Vert. pair, imperf. between	*550.00*	

Merger of townships Takamine, Kanegushiku and Miwa with Itoman.

1961, Nov. 12 Litho. *Perf. 13*

91	A39	3c multicolored	1.10	90

Issued for Book Week.

Rising Sun and Eagles — A40

Symbolic Steps, Trees and Government Building — A41

1961, Dec. 10 Photo. *Perf. 13 1/2*

92	A40	1 1/2c gold, ver & blk	2.00	1.50

New Year, 1962.

1962, Apr. 1 Unwmk. *Perf. 13 1/2*

Design: 3c, Government Building.

93	A41	1 1/2c multicolored	42	45
94	A41	3c brt grn, red & gray	70	55

10th anniv. of the Government of the Ryukyu Islands (GRI).

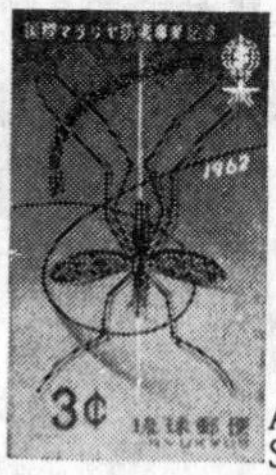

Anopheles Hyrcanus Sinensis — A42

Design: 8c, Malaria eradication emblem and Shurei gate.

1962, Apr. 7 *Perf. 13 1/2x13*

95	A42	3c multicolored	45	48
96	A42	8c multicolored	90	60

WHO drive to eradicate malaria.

Dolls and Toys — A43

Linden or Sea Hibiscus — A44

1962, May 5 Litho. *Perf. 13 1/2*

97	A43	3c red, blk, bl & buff	1.10	65

Issued for Children's Day.

1962, June 1 Photo.

Flowers: 3c, Indian coral tree. 8c, Iju (Schima liukiuensis Nakai). 13c, Touch-me-not (garden balsam). 17c, Shell flower (Alpinia speciosa).

98	A44	1/2c multicolored	15	15
99	A44	3c multicolored	35	15
100	A44	8c multicolored	40	40
101	A44	13c multicolored	52	52
102	A44	17c multicolored	75	75
		Nos. 98-102 (5)	2.17	1.97

See #107, 114 for 1 1/2c and 15c flower stamps.
For surcharge see No. 190.

Earthenware A45

1962, July 5 *Perf. 13 1/2x13*

103	A45	3c multicolored	3.25	2.50

Issued for Philatelic Week.

Japanese Fencing (Kendo) A46

1962, July 25 *Perf. 13*

104	A46	3c multicolored	4.00	3.00

All-Japan Kendo Meeting, Okinawa, July 25.

Rabbit Playing near Water, Bingata Cloth Design — A47

Young Man and Woman, Stone Relief — A48

1962, Dec. 10 *Perf. 13x13½*

105 A47 1½c gold & multi 1.00 80

New Year, 1963.

1963, Jan. 15 Photo. *Perf. 13½*

106 A48 3c gold, blk & bl 90 65

Issued for Adult Day.

Gooseneck Cactus A49

Trees and Wooded Hills A50

1963, Apr. 5 *Perf. 13x13½*

107 A49 1½c dk bl, grn, yel & pink 15 15

1963, Mar. 25 *Perf. 13½x13*

108 A50 3c ultra, grn & red brn 90 80

"Make the Ryukyus Green" movement.

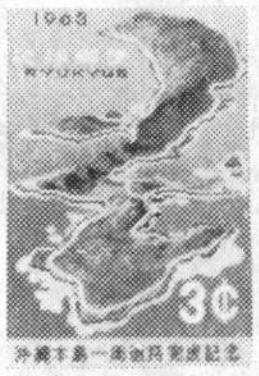

Map of Okinawa A51

Hawks over Islands A52

1963, Apr. 30 Unwmk. *Perf. 13½*

109 A51 3c multicolored 1.25 1.00

Opening of the Round Road on Okinawa.

1963, May 10 Photo.

110 A52 3c multicolored 1.10 95

Issued for Bird Day, May 10.

Shioya Bridge — A53

1963, June 5

111 A53 3c multicolored 1.10 95

Opening of Shioya Bridge over Shioya Bay.

Tsuikin-wan Lacquerware Bowl — A54

1963, July 1 Unwmk. *Perf. 13½*

112 A54 3c multicolored 3.00 2.50

Issued for Philatelic Week.

Map of Far East and JCI Emblem — A55

1963, Sept. 16 Photo. *Perf. 13½*

113 A55 3c multicolored 70 48

Meeting of the Intl. Junior Chamber of Commerce (JCI), Naha, Okinawa, Sept. 16-19.

Mamaomoto A56

Site of Nakagusuku Castle A57

1963, Oct. 15 *Perf. 13x13½*

114 A56 15c multicolored 1.00 60

1963, Nov. 1 *Perf. 13½x13*

115 A57 3c multicolored 70 42

Protection of national cultural treasures.

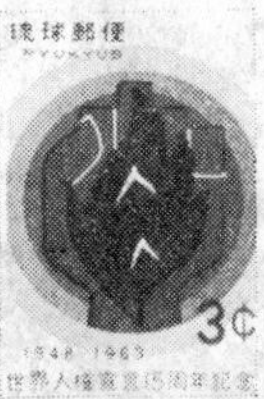

Flame — A58

Dragon (Bingata Pattern) — A59

1963, Dec. 10 *Perf. 13½*

116 A58 3c red, dk bl & yel 70 42

15th anniversary of the Universal Declaration of Human Rights.

1963, Dec. 10 Photo.

117 A59 1½c multicolored 40 25

New Year, 1964.

Carnation A60

Pineapples and Sugar Cane A61

1964, May 10 *Perf. 13½*

118 A60 3c bl, yel, blk & car 40 35

Issued for Mother's Day.

1964, June 1

119 A61 3c multicolored 40 35

Agricultural census.

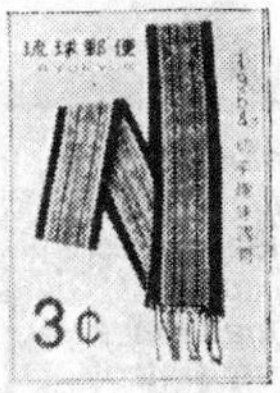

Minsah Obi (Sash Woven of Kapok) — A62

1964, July 1 Unwmk. *Perf. 13½*

120 A62 3c dp bl, rose pink & ocher 55 42
a. 3c dp bl, dp car & ocher 70 60

Issued for Philatelic Week.

Girl Scout and Emblem — A63

1964, Aug. 31 Photo.

121 A63 3c multicolored 40 30

10th anniversary of Ryukyuan Girl Scouts.

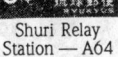

Shuri Relay Station — A64

Parabolic Antenna and Map — A65

1964, Sept. 1 Unwmk. *Perf. 13½*
Black Overprint

122 A64 3c deep green 65 65
a. Figure "1" inverted 22.50 22.50
123 A65 8c ultra 1.25 1.25

Opening of the Ryukyu Islands-Japan microwave system carrying telephone and telegraph messages between the Ryukyus and Japan. Nos. 122-123 not issued without overprint.

Gate of Courtesy, Olympic Torch and Emblem — A66

1964, Sept. 7 Photo. *Perf. 13½x13*

124 A66 3c ultra, yel & red 20 15

Relaying of the Olympic torch on Okinawa en route to Tokyo.

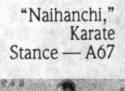

"Naihanchi," Karate Stance — A67

"Makiwara," Strengthening Hands and Feet — A68

"Kumite," Simulated Combat — A69

1964-65 Photo. *Perf. 13½*

125 A67 3c dull claret, yel & blk 48 30
126 A68 3c yellow & multi ('65) 38 30
127 A69 3c gray, red & blk ('65) 38 30

Karate, Ryukyuan self-defense sport.

Issue dates: No. 125, Oct. 5. No. 126, Feb. 5. No. 127, June 5.

Miyara Dunchi — A70

Snake and Iris (Bingata) — A71

1964, Nov. 1 *Perf. 13½*

128 A70 3c multicolored 22 18

Protection of national cultural treasures. Miyara Dunchi was built as a residence by Miyara-pechin Toen in 1819.

1964, Dec. 10 Photo.

129 A71 1½c multicolored 25 20

New Year, 1965.

Boy Scouts — A72

1965, Feb. 6 *Perf. 13½*

130 A72 3c lt blue & multi 42 28

10th anniversary of Ryukyuan Boy Scouts.

Main Stadium, Onoyama A73

1965, July 1 *Perf. 13x13½*

131 A73 3c multicolored 20 18

Inauguration of the main stadium of the Onoyama athletic facilities.

Samisen of King Shoko — A74

1965, July 1 Photo. *Perf. 13½*

132 A74 3c buff & multi 42 30

Issued for Philatelic Week.

Kin Power Plant — A75

ICY Emblem, Ryukyu Map — A76

1965, July 1

133 A75 3c green & multi 20 18

Completion of Kin power plant.

1965, Aug. 24 Photo. *Perf. 13½*

134 A76 3c multicolored 18 15

UN, 20th anniv.; Intl. Cooperation Year, 1964-65.

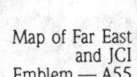

Naha City Hall — A77

1965, Sept. 18 Unwmk. ***Perf. 13½***
135 A77 3c blue & multi 18 15

Completion of Naha City Hall.

Chinese Box Turtle A78

Horse (Bingata) A79

Turtles: No. 137, Hawksbill turtle (denomination at top, country name at bottom). No. 138, Asian terrapin (denomination and country name on top).

1965-66 Photo. ***Perf. 13½***
136 A78 3c gldn brn & multi 30 30
137 A78 3c black, yel & brn 30 30
138 A78 3c gray & multi 30 30

Issue dates: No. 136, Oct. 20, 1965. No. 137, Jan. 20, 1966. No. 138, Apr. 20, 1966.

1965, Dec. 10 Photo. ***Perf. 13½***
139 A79 1½c multicolored 15 15
a. Gold omitted *1,200. 1,200.*

New Year, 1966.

Noguchi's Okinawa Woodpecker A80

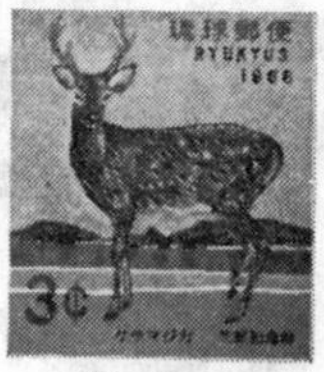
Sika Deer A81

1966 Photo. ***Perf. 13½***
140 A80 3c shown 20 20
141 A81 3c shown 24 24
142 A81 3c Dugong 24 24

Nature conservation.
Issue dates: No. 140, Feb. 15. No. 141, Mar. 15. No. 142, Apr. 20.

Ryukyu Bungalow Swallow — A82

1966, May 10 Photo. ***Perf. 13½***
143 A82 3c sky blue, blk & brn 15 15

4th Bird Week, May 10-16.

Lilies and Ruins A83

1966, June 23 ***Perf. 13x13½***
144 A83 3c multicolored 15 15

Memorial Day, commemorating the end of the Battle of Okinawa, June 23, 1945.

University of the Ryukyus A84

1966, July 1
145 A84 3c multicolored 15 15

Transfer of the University of the Ryukyus from US authority to the Ryukyu Government.

Lacquerware, 18th Century — A85

Tile-Roofed House and UNESCO Emblem — A86

1966, Aug. 1 ***Perf. 13½***
146 A85 3c gray & multi 15 15

Issued for Philatelic Week.

1966, Sept. 20 Photo. ***Perf. 13½***
147 A86 3c multicolored 15 15

UNESCO, 20th anniv.

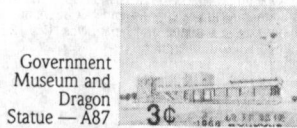

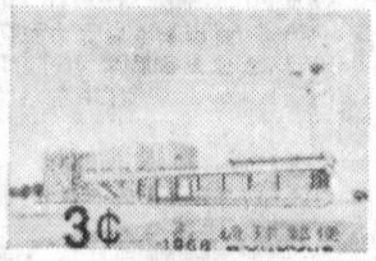
Government Museum and Dragon Statue — A87

1966, Oct. 6
148 A87 3c multicolored 15 15

Completion of the GRI (Government of the Ryukyu Islands) Museum, Shuri.

Tomb of Nakasone-Tuimya Genga, Ruler of Miyako — A88

1966, Nov. 1 Photo. ***Perf. 13½***
149 A88 3c multicolored 15 15

Protection of national cultural treasures.

Ram in Iris Wreath (Bingata) A89

Clown Fish A90

1966, Dec. 10 Photo. ***Perf. 13½***
150 A89 1½c dk blue & multi 15 15

New Year, 1967.

1966-67

Fish: No. 152, Young boxfish (white numeral at lower left). No. 153, Forceps fish (pale buff numeral at lower right). No. 154, Spotted triggerfish (orange numeral). No. 155, Saddleback butterflyfish (carmine numeral, lower left).

151 A90 3c org red & multi 18 15
152 A90 3c org yel & multi ('67) 18 15
153 A90 3c multi ('67) 25 22
154 A90 3c multi ('67) 25 22
155 A90 3c multi ('67) 28 22
Nos. 151-155 (5) 1.14 96

Issue dates: #151, Dec. 20. #152, Jan. 10. #153, Apr. 10. #154, May 25. #155, June 10.

Tsuboya Urn — A91

Episcopal Miter — A92

1967, Apr. 20
156 A91 3c yellow & multi 20 16

Issued for Philatelic Week.

1967-68 Photo. ***Perf. 13½***

Seashells: No. 158, Venus comb murex. No. 159, Chiragra spider. No. 160, Green turban. No. 161, Euprotomus bulla.

157 A92 3c lt green & multi 18 15
158 A92 3c grnsh bl & multi 18 15
159 A92 3c emerald & multi 22 18
160 A92 3c lt blue & multi 22 18
161 A92 3c brt blue & multi 40 28
Nos. 157-161 (5) 1.20 94

Issue dates: 1967, No. 157, July 20; No. 158, Aug. 30. 1968, No. 159, Jan. 18; No. 160, Feb. 20; No. 161, June 5.

Red-tiled Roofs and ITY Emblem — A93

1967, Sept. 11 Photo. ***Perf. 13½***
162 A93 3c multicolored 18 18

International Tourist Year.

Mobile TB Clinic — A94

1967, Oct. 13 Photo. ***Perf. 13½***
163 A94 3c lilac & multi 18 18

Anti-Tuberculosis Society, 15th anniv.

Hojo Bridge, Enkaku Temple, 1498 — A95

1967, Nov. 1
164 A95 3c blue grn & multi 18 18

Protection of national cultural treasures.

15-Cent Minimum Value
The minimum catalogue value is 15 cents. Separating se-tenant pieces into individual stamps does not increase the value of the stamps since demand for the separated stamps may be small.

Monkey (Bingata) — A96

TV Tower and Map — A97

1967, Dec. 11 Photo. ***Perf. 13½***
165 A96 1½c silver & multi 18 18

New Year 1968.

1967, Dec. 22
166 A97 3c multicolored 18 18

Opening of Miyako and Yaeyama television stations.

Dr. Kijin Nakachi and Helper — A98

Pill Box (Inro) — A99

1968, Mar. 15 Photo. ***Perf. 13½***
167 A98 3c multicolored 18 18

120th anniv. of the first vaccination in the Ryukyu Islands, performed by Dr. Kijin Nakachi.

1968, Apr. 18
168 A99 3c gray & multi 45 42

Philatelic Week.

Young Man, Library, Book and Map of Ryukyu Islands — A100

1968, May 13
169 A100 3c multicolored 25 22

10th International Library Week.

Mailmen's Uniforms and Stamp of 1948 A101

1968, July 1 Photo. ***Perf. 13x13½***
170 A101 3c multicolored 25 22

1st Ryukyuan postage stamps, 20th anniv.

Main Gate, Enkaku Temple — A102

Photo. & Engr.
1968, July 15 ***Perf. 13½***
171 A102 3c multicolored 25 22

Restoration of the main gate of the Enkaku Temple, built 1492-1495, and destroyed during WWII.

Old Man's Dance — A103

1968, Sept. 15 Photo. *Perf. 13½*

172 A103 3c gold & multi		25	22

Issued for Old People's Day.

Mictyris Longicarpus A104

Crabs: No. 174, Uca dubia stimpson. No. 175, Baptozius vinosus. No. 176, Cardisoma carnifex. No. 177, Ocypode ceratophthalma pallas.

1968-69 Photo. *Perf. 13½*

173 A104 3c blue, ocher & blk	30	25
174 A104 3c lt bl grn & multi	35	25
175 A104 3c lt green & multi	35	25
176 A104 3c lt ultra & multi	45	30
177 A104 3c lt ultra & multi	45	30
Nos. 173-177 (5)	1.90	1.35

Issue dates: #173, Oct. 10. #174, Feb. 5, 1969. #175, Mar. 5, 1969. #176, May 15, 1969; #177, June 2, 1969.

Saraswati Pavilion — A105

1968, Nov. 1 Photo. *Perf. 13½*

178 A105 3c multicolored	24	18

Restoration of the Saraswati Pavilion (in front of Enkaku Temple), destroyed during WWII.

Tennis Player A106

Cock and Iris (Bingata) A107

1968, Nov. 3 Photo. *Perf. 13½*

179 A106 3c green & multi	40	30

35th All-Japan East-West Men's Soft-ball Tennis Tournament, Naha City, Nov. 23-24.

1968, Dec. 10

180 A107 1½c orange & multi	15	15

New Year, 1969.

Boxer — A108

Ink Slab Screen — A109

1969, Jan. 3

181 A108 3c gray & multi	25	22

20th All-Japan Amateur Boxing Championships, University of the Ryukyus, Jan. 3-5.

1969, Apr. 17 Photo. *Perf. 13½*

182 A109 3c salmon, indigo & red	25	18

Philatelic Week.

Box Antennas and Map of Radio Link A110

Gate of Courtesy and Emblems A111

1969, July 1 Photo. *Perf. 13½*

183 A110 3c multicolored	15	15

Opening of the UHF (radio) circuit system between Okinawa and the outlying Miyako-Yaeyama Islands.

1969, Aug. 1 Photo. *Perf. 13½*

184 A111 3c Prus bl, gold & ver	15	15

22nd All-Japan Formative Education Study Conference, Naha, Aug. 1-3.

Tug of War Festival A112

Hari Boat Race A113

Izaiho Ceremony, Kudaka Island A114

Mortardrum Dance — A115

Sea God Dance A116

1969-70 Photo. *Perf. 13*

185 A112 3c multi	28	22
186 A113 3c multi	35	22
187 A114 3c multi	35	22
188 A115 3c multi ('70)	50	35
189 A116 3c multi ('70)	50	35
Nos. 185-189 (5)	1.98	1.36

Folklore. Issue dates: #185, Aug. 1; #186, Sept. 5; #187, Oct. 3; #188, Jan. 20; #189, Feb. 27.

No. 99 Surcharged 改訂 ½¢

1969, Oct. 15 Photo. *Perf. 13½*

190 A44 ½c on 3c multi	40	40

Nakamura-ke Farm House, Built 1713-51 A117

1969, Nov. 1 Photo. *Perf. 13½*

191 A117 3c multicolored	15	15

Protection of national cultural treasures.

Statue of Kyuzo Toyama, Maps of Hawaiian and Ryukyu Islands — A118

1969, Dec. 5 Photo. *Perf. 13½*

192 A118 3c lt ultra & multi	22	20
a. Without overprint	*2,500.*	
b. Wide-spaced bars	*725.00*	

Ryukyu-Hawaii emigration led by Kyuzo Toyama, 70th anniversary.

The overprint - "1969" at lower left and bars across "1970" at upper right - was applied before No. 192 was issued.

Dog and Flowers (Bingata) A119

Sake Flask Made from Coconut A120

1969, Dec. 10

193 A119 1½c pink & multi	15	15

New Year, 1970.

1970, Apr. 15 Photo. *Perf. 13½*

194 A120 3c multicolored	22	20

Philatelic Week.

Classic Opera Issue

"The Bell" (Shushin Kaneiri) — A121

Child and Kidnapper (Chunusudu) A122

Robe of Feathers (Mekarushi) A123

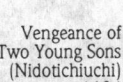

Vengeance of Two Young Sons (Nidotichiuchi) A124

The Virgin and the Dragon (Kokonomaki) A125

1970 Photo. *Perf. 13½*

195 A121 3c dull bl & multi	40	38
196 A122 3c lt blue & multi	40	38
197 A123 3c bluish grn & multi	40	38
198 A124 3c dull bl grn & multi	40	38
199 A125 3c multicolored	40	38
Nos. 195-199 (5)	2.00	1.90
195a-199a, 5 sheets of 4	17.50	17.50

Issue dates: #195, Apr. 28. #196, May 29. #197, June 30. #198, July 30. #199, Aug. 25.

Underwater Observatory and Tropical Fish — A126

1970, May 22

200 A126 3c blue grn & multi	28	25

Completion of the underwater observatory at Busena-Misaki, Nago.

Noboru Jahana (1865-1908), Politician A127

Map of Okinawa and People A128

Portraits: No. 202, Saion Gushichan Bunjaku (1682-1761), statesman. No. 203, Choho Giwan (1823-1876), regent and poet.

1970-71 Engr. *Perf. 13½*

201 A127 3c rose claret	48	30
202 A127 3c dull blue green	75	55
203 A127 3c black	48	30

Issue dates: No. 201, Sept. 25, 1970. No. 202, Dec. 22, 1970. No. 203, Jan. 22, 1971.

1970, Oct. 1 Photo.

204 A128 3c red & multi	18	15

Oct. 1, 1970 census.

Great Cycad of Une — A129

1970, Nov. 2 Photo. *Perf. 13½*

205 A129 3c gold & multi	22	20

Protection of national treasures.

Japanese Flag, Diet and Map of Ryukyus
A130

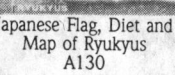

Wild Boar and Cherry Blossoms (Bingata)
A131

1970, Nov. 15 **Photo.** ***Perf. 13½***

206 A130 3c ultra & multi 70 50

Citizens' participation in national administration according to Japanese law of Apr. 24, 1970.

1970, Dec. 10

207 A131 1½c multicolored 15 15

New Year, 1971.

Low Hand Loom (Jibata) — A132

Farmer Wearing Palm Bark Raincoat and Kuba Leaf Hat — A133

Fisherman's Wooden Box and Scoop — A134

Designs: No. 209, Woman running a filature (reel). No. 211, Woman hulling rice with cylindrical "Shiri-ushi."

1971 **Photo.** ***Perf. 13½***

208	A132	3c lt blue & multi	28	22
209	A132	3c pale grn & multi	28	22
210	A133	3c lt blue & multi	35	24
211	A132	3c yellow & multi	40	30
212	A134	3c gray & multi	35	24
		Nos. 208-212 (5)	1.66	1.22

Issue dates: #208, Feb. 16; #209, Mar. 16; #210, Apr. 30; #211, May 20; #212, June 15.

Water Carrier (Taku) — A135

1971, Apr. 15 **Photo.** ***Perf. 13½***

213 A135 3c blue grn & multi 35 25

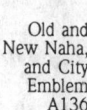

Philatelic Week.

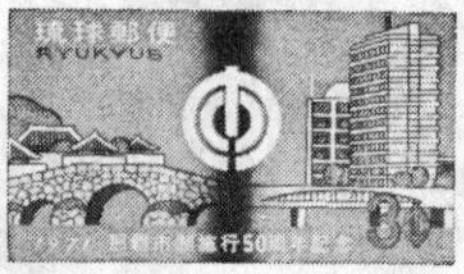

Old and New Naha, and City Emblem
A136

1971, May 20 ***Perf. 13***

214 A136 3c ultra & multi 22 20

50th anniversary of Naha as a municipality.

Caesalpinia Pulcherrima — A137

Design: 2c, Madder (Sandanka).

1971 **Photo.** ***Perf. 13***

215 A137 2c gray & multi 15 15
216 A137 3c gray & multi 16 15

Issue dates: 2c, Sept. 30; 3c, May 10.

View from Mabuni Hill — A138

Mt. Arashi from Haneji Sea — A139

Yabuchi Island from Yakena Port — A140

1971-72

217	A138	3c green & multi	20	15
218	A139	3c blue & multi	20	15
219	A140	4c multi ('72)	25	15

Government parks. Issue dates: No. 217, July 30; No. 218, Aug. 30, 1971; No. 219, Jan. 20, 1972.

Dancer — A141

Deva King, Torinji Temple — A142

1971, Nov. 1 **Photo.** ***Perf. 13***

220 A141 4c Prus bl & multi 15 15

1971, Dec. 1

221 A142 4c dp blue & multi 18 18

Protection of national cultural treasures.

Rat and Chrysanthemums
A143

Student Nurse
A144

1971, Dec. 10

222 A143 2c brown org & multi 15 15

New Year 1972.

1971, Dec. 24

223 A144 4c lilac & multi 20 15

Nurses' training, 25th anniversary.

Birds on Seashore
A145

Sun over Islands
A147

Coral Reef — A146

1972 **Photo.** ***Perf. 13***

224	A145	5c brt blue & multi	35	24
225	A146	5c gray & multi	35	24
226	A147	5c ocher & multi	35	24

Issue dates: No. 224, Apr. 14; No. 225, Mar. 30; No. 226, Mar. 21.

Dove, US and Japanese Flags — A148

1972, Apr. 17 **Photo.** ***Perf. 13***

227 A148 5c brt blue & multi 55 38

Ratification of the Reversion Agreement with US under which the Ryukyu Islands were returned to Japan.

Antique Sake Pot (Yushibin) — A149

1972, Apr. 20

228 A149 5c ultra & multi 40 25

Philatelic Week.

Ryukyu stamps were replaced by those of Japan after May 15, 1972.

AIR POST STAMPS

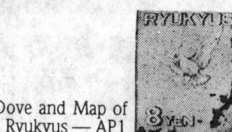

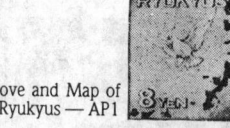

Dove and Map of Ryukyus — AP1

Perf. 13x13½

1950, Feb. 15 **Unwmk.** **Photo.**

C1	AP1	8y bright blue	85.00	50.00
C2	AP1	12y green	27.50	20.00
C3	AP1	16y rose carmine	15.00	15.00

Heavenly Maiden
AP2

1951-54

C4	AP2	13y blue	1.75	1.50
C5	AP2	18y green	2.50	2.25
C6	AP2	30y cerise	3.75	1.25
C7	AP2	40y red violet	6.00	5.50
C8	AP2	50y yellow orange	7.50	6.25
		Nos. C4-C8 (5)	21.50	16.75

Issue dates: Oct. 1, 1951, Aug. 16, 1954.

Heavenly Maiden Playing Flute — AP3

1957, Aug. 1 **Engr.** ***Perf. 13½***

C9	AP3	15y blue green	6.25	3.50
C10	AP3	20y rose carmine	8.00	5.25
C11	AP3	35y yellow green	12.00	6.00
C12	AP3	45y reddish brown	13.00	7.75
C13	AP3	60y gray	15.00	9.50
		Nos. C9-C13 (5)	54.25	32.00

Same Surcharged in Brown Red or Light Ultramarine

改訂 9¢

1959, Dec. 20

C14	AP3	9c on 15y (BrR)	2.25	1.50
a.		Inverted surcharge	*850.00*	
C15	AP3	14c on 20y (LU)	2.75	2.25
C16	AP3	19c on 35y (BrR)	5.25	3.75
C17	AP3	27c on 45y (LU)	10.00	5.50
C18	AP3	35c on 60y (BrR)	11.00	7.00
		Nos. C14-C18 (5)	31.25	20.00

改訂

Nos. 31-33, 36 and 38 Surcharged in Black, Brown, Red, Blue or Green

9¢

1960, Aug. 3 **Photo.** ***Perf. 13***

C19	A14	9c on 4y	2.25	1.40
a.		Inverted surcharge	*12,000.*	*15,000.*
C20	A17	14c on 5y (Br)	2.25	1.40
C21	A14	19c on 15y (R)	1.75	1.00
C22	A17	27c on 14y (Bl)	5.00	2.75
C23	A14	35c on 20y (G)	4.50	3.75
		Nos. C19-C23 (5)	15.75	10.30

Wind God — AP4

Designs: 9c, Heavenly Maiden (as on AP2). 14c, Heavenly Maiden (as on AP3). 27c, Wind God at right. 35c, Heavenly Maiden over treetops.

1961, Sept. 21 **Photo.** ***Perf. 13½***

C24	AP4	9c multicolored	35	20
C25	AP4	14c multicolored	55	70
C26	AP4	19c multicolored	60	70
C27	AP4	27c multicolored	2.25	60
C28	AP4	35c multicolored	1.50	1.10
		Nos. C24-C28 (5)	5.25	3.30

Jet over Gate of Courtesy — AP5

Jet Plane — AP6

1963, Aug. 28 ***Perf. 13x13½***

C29 AP5 5½c multicolored 22 22
C30 AP6 7c multicolored 22 22

SPECIAL DELIVERY STAMP

Dragon and Map of Ryukyus — SD1

Perf. 13x13½

1950, Feb. 15 **Unwmk.** **Photo.**

E1 SD1 5y bright blue 22.50 16.00

UNITED NATIONS

LOCATION — Headquarters in New York City

United Nations stamps are used on UN official mail sent from UN Headquarters, NY, or from the UN Offices in Geneva, Switzerland, and Vienna, Austria to points throughout the world. They may be used on private correspondence sent through the UN post offices, and are valid only at the individual UN post offices.

UN mail is carried by the US, Swiss and Austrian postal systems.

The UN stamps issued for use in Geneva and Vienna are listed in separate sections at the end of the NY issues. They are denominated in centimes and francs, and are valid only in Geneva or Vienna. The UN stamps issued for use in New York, denominated in cents and dollars, are valid only in New York.

Letters bearing Nos. 170-174 provide an exception as they were carried by the Canadian postal system.

See Switzerland Nos. 7O1-7O39 in Volume 5 for stamps issued by the Swiss Government for official use of the UN European Office in Geneva.

The 1962 UN Temporary Executive Authority (UNTEA) overprints on stamps of Netherlands New Guinea are listed under West Irian in Volume 5.

Catalogue values for all unused stamps in this country are for Never Hinged items.

Stamps are inscribed in English, French or Spanish or are multi-lingual.

Watermark

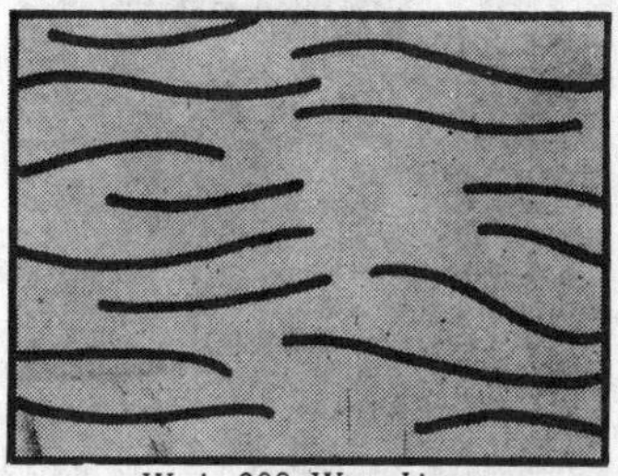

Wmk. 309- Wavy Lines

Peoples of the World — A1

UN Headquarters Building — A2

"Peace, Justice, Security" — A3

UN Flag — A4

UN Children's Fund — A5

World Unity — A6

Perf. 13x12½, 12½x13, 12½x13½ (2c, 5c)

1951 Unwmk. Engr. & Photo.

1	A1	1c	magenta	15	15
2	A2	1½c	blue green	15	15
3	A3	2c	purple	15	15
4	A4	3c	magenta & blue	15	15
5	A5	5c	blue	15	15
6	A1	10c	chocolate	15	15
7	A4	15c	violet & blue	22	20
8	A6	20c	dark brown	42	40
9	A4	25c	ol gray & blue	40	35
10	A2	50c	indigo	3.75	2.00
11	A3	$1	red	1.75	1.00
			Nos. 1-11 (11)	7.44	4.85

See Offices in Geneva Nos. 4, 14.

Veteran's War Memorial Building, San Francisco A7

1952, Oct. 24 Engr. *Perf. 12*

12	A7	5c	blue	20	16

7th anniv. of the signing of the UN charter.

Globe and Encircled Flame — A8

1952, Dec. 10 *Perf. 13½x14*

13	A8	3c	deep green	15	15
14	A8	5c	blue	35	16
			Set value		25

Fourth anniv. of the adoption of the Universal Declaration of Human Rights.

Refugee Family — A9

1953, Apr. 24 *Perf. 12½x13*

15	A9	3c	dk red brn & rose brn	15	15
16	A9	5c	indigo & blue	50	25

"Protection for Refugees."

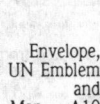

Envelope, UN Emblem and Map — A10

1953, June 12 Unwmk. *Perf. 13*

17	A10	3c	black brown	20	15
18	A10	5c	dark blue	95	40

Issued to honor the UPU.

Gearwheels and UN Emblem — A11

1953, Oct. 24 *Perf. 13x12½*

19	A11	3c	dark gray	16	15
20	A11	5c	dark green	50	30

UN activities in the field of technical assistance.

Hands Reaching Toward Flame — A12

Ear of Wheat — A13

1953, Dec. 10 *Perf. 12½x13*

21	A12	3c	bright blue	25	15
22	A12	5c	rose red	1.65	30

Human Rights Day.

1954, Feb. 11

23	A13	3c	dark green & yellow	50	15
24	A13	8c	indigo & yellow	1.00	60

Issued to honor the FAO.

UN Emblem and Anvil — A14

1954, May 10 *Perf. 12½x13*

25	A14	3c	brown	20	15
26	A14	8c	magenta	1.50	50

Honoring the ILO.

UN European Office, Geneva A15

1954, Oct. 25 *Perf. 14*

27	A15	3c	dark blue violet	2.50	75
28	A15	8c	red	35	20

UN Day.

Mother and Child — A16

1954, Dec. 10 *Perf. 14*

29	A16	3c	red orange	9.00	1.50
30	A16	8c	olive green	20	20

Human Rights Day.

Symbol of Flight — A17

1955, Feb. 9 *Perf. 13½x14*

31	A17	3c	blue	2.25	50
32	A17	8c	rose carmine	75	90

International Civil Aviation Organization.

UNESCO Emblem A18

1955, May 11 *Perf. 13½x14*

33	A18	3c	lilac rose	40	20
34	A18	8c	light blue	25	16

Honoring the UN Educational, Scientific and Cultural Organization.

UN Charter A19

1955, Oct. 24 *Perf. 13½x14*

35	A19	3c	deep plum	2.00	40
36	A19	4c	dull green	85	15
37	A19	8c	bluish black	20	16

10th anniv. of the UN.

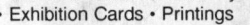

Souvenir Sheet

Wmk. 309 ***Imperf.***

38	Sheet of 3	110.00	35.00
a.	A19 3c deep plum	10.00	5.00
b.	A19 4c dull green	10.00	5.00
c.	A19 8c bluish black	10.00	5.00

Two printings were made of No. 38. The first may be distinguished by the broken line of background shading on the 8c. It leaves a small white spot below the left leg of the "n" of "Unies." For the 2nd printing, the broken line was retouched, eliminating the white spot.

Hand Holding Torch — A20

1955, Dec. 9 Unwmk. ***Perf. 14x13½***

39	A20	3c ultra	15	15
40	A20	8c green	30	25

Human Rights Day, Dec. 10.

Symbols of Telecommunication — A21

1956, Feb. 17 ***Perf. 14***

41	A21	3c turquoise blue	40	16
42	A21	8c deep carmine	75	45

Honoring the ITU.

Globe and Caduceus — A22

1956, Apr. 6 ***Perf. 14***

43	A22	3c bright greenish blue	15	15
44	A22	8c golden brown	45	25

Honoring the World Health Organization.

General Assembly A23

1956, Oct. 24 ***Perf. 14***

45	A23	3c dark blue	15	15
46	A23	8c gray olive	15	15
		Set value	17	15

UN Day, Oct. 24.

Flame and Globe — A24

1956, Dec. 10 ***Perf. 14***

47	A24	3c plum	15	15
48	A24	8c dark blue	15	15
		Set value	17	15

Human Rights Day.

Weather Balloon — A25

1957, Jan. 28 ***Perf. 14***

49	A25	3c violet blue	15	15
50	A25	8c dark carmine rose	15	15
		Set value	17	15

Honoring the World Meteorological Organization.

Badge of UN Emergency Force — A26

UN Emblem and Globe — A27

1957, Apr. 8 ***Perf. 14x12½***

51	A26	3c light blue	15	15
52	A26	8c rose carmine	15	15
		Set value	17	15

UN Emergency Force.

Re-engraved

1957, Apr.-May

53	A26	3c blue	15	15
54	A26	8c rose carmine	20	15
		Set value	24	18

On Nos. 53-54 the background within and around the circles is shaded lightly, giving a halo effect. The letters are more distinct with a line around each letter.

1957, Oct. 24 Engr. ***Perf. 12½x13***

55	A27	3c orange brown	15	15
56	A27	8c dark blue green	15	15
		Set value	17	15

Honoring the Security Council.

Flaming Torch — A28

1957, Dec. 10 ***Perf. 14***

57	A28	3c red brown	15	15
58	A28	8c black	15	15
		Set value	17	15

Human Rights Day.

Atom and UN Emblem A29

Central Hall, Westminster A30

1958, Feb. 10 ***Perf. 12***

59	A29	3c olive	15	15
60	A29	8c blue	15	15
		Set value	17	15

Honoring the International Atomic Energy Agency.

1958, Apr. 14 ***Perf. 12***

61	A30	3c violet blue	15	15
62	A30	8c rose claret	15	15
		Set value	17	15

Central Hall, Westminster, London, was the site of the first session of the UN General Assembly 1946.

UN Seal A31

Gearwheels A32

1958 ***Perf. 13½x14***

63	A31	4c red orange	15	15

Perf. 13x14

64	A31	8c bright blue	15	15
		Set value	18	16

Issue dates: 4c, Oct. 24; 8c, June 2.

1958, Oct. 24 Engr. ***Perf. 12***

65	A32	4c dark blue green	15	15
66	A32	8c vermilion	15	15
		Set value	18	16

Honoring the Economic and Social Council.

Hands Upholding Globe — A33

1958, Dec. 10 **Unwmk.**

67	A33	4c yellow green	15	15
68	A33	8c red brown	15	15
		Set value	25	16

Human Rights Day and the 10th anniv. of the signing of the Universal Declaration of Human Rights.

New York City Building, Flushing Meadows A34

1959, Mar. 30 ***Perf. 12***

69	A34	4c light lilac rose	15	15
70	A34	8c aqua	15	15
		Set value	18	16

Site of many General Assembly meetings, 1946-50.

UN Emblems and Symbols of Agriculture, Industry and Trade — A35

Figure Adapted from Rodin's "Age of Bronze" — A36

1959, May 18 ***Perf. 12***

71	A35	4c blue	20	15
72	A35	8c red orange	30	15
		Set value		17

Honoring the UN Economic Commission for Europe.

1959, Oct. 23 Engr. ***Perf. 12***

73	A36	4c bright red	15	15
74	A36	8c dark olive green	20	15
		Set value	25	16

Honor the Trusteeship Council.

World Refugee Year Emblem — A37

1959, Dec. 10 **Unwmk.**

75	A37	4c olive & red	15	15
76	A37	8c olive & brt greenish blue	15	15
		Set value	18	15

World Refugee Year, July 1, 1959-June 30, 1960.

Chaillot Palace, Paris — A38

1960, Feb. 29 ***Perf. 14***

77	A38	4c rose lilac & blue	15	15
78	A38	8c dull green & brown	20	15
		Set value	25	16

Chaillot Palace in Paris was the site of General Assembly meetings in 1948 and 1951.

Map of Far East and Steel Beam — A39

1960, Apr. 11 Photo. ***Perf. 13x13½***

79	A39	4c dp cl, bl grn & dl yel	15	15
80	A39	8c ol green, blue & rose	20	15
		Set value	25	16

Honoring the Economic Commission for Asia and the Far East (ECAFE).

Tree, FAO and UN Emblems — A40

1960, Aug. 29 ***Perf. 13½***

81	A40	4c green, dk blue & org	15	15
a.		Imperf., pair	—	
82	A40	8c yel green, black & org	15	15
		Set value	18	16

5th World Forestry Congress, Seattle, Wash., Aug. 29-Sept. 10.

UN Headquarters and Preamble to UN Charter — A41

1960, Oct. 24 Engr. ***Perf. 11***

83	A41	4c blue	15	15
84	A41	8c gray	15	15
		Set value	18	15

Souvenir Sheet
Imperf

85	Sheet of 2	1.00	30
a.	A41 4c blue	25	15
b.	A41 8c gray	25	15

15th anniv. of the UN.

Block and Tackle — A42

Scales of Justice — A43

1960, Dec. 9 Photo. *Perf. 13½x13*

86	A42 4c multicolored	15	15
87	A42 8c multicolored	15	15
a.	Imperf., pair	—	
	Set value	18	16

Honoring the International Bank for Reconstruction and Development.
No. 86 exists imperf.

1961, Feb. 13 Unwmk.

88	A43 4c yel, org brn & blk	15	15
89	A43 8c yellow, green & black	15	15
	Set value	18	16

Honoring the International Court of Justice. The design was taken from Raphael's "Stanze."
Nos. 88-89 exist imperf.

Seal of International Monetary Fund — A44

1961, Apr. 17 *Perf. 13x13½*

90	A44 4c bright bluish green	15	15
91	A44 7c fawn & yellow	15	15
	Set value	18	16

Honoring the International Monetary Fund.
No. 90 exists imperf.

Abstract Group of Flags — A45

1961, June 5 *Perf. 11½*

92	A45 30c multicolored	35	16

See Offices in Geneva No. 10.

Cogwheel and Map of Latin America — A46

1961, Sept. 18 *Perf. 13½*

93	A46 4c blue, red & citron	15	15
94	A46 11c green, lilac & org ver	30	20

Honoring the Economic Commission for Latin America.

Africa House, Addis Ababa, and Map — A47

1961, Oct. 24 Photo. *Perf. 11½*

95	A47 4c ultra, org, yel & brown	15	15
96	A47 11c emer, org, yel & brown	25	15
	Set value		18

Honoring the Economic Commission for Africa.

Mother Bird Feeding Young and UNICEF Seal — A48

1961, Dec. 4 Unwmk. *Perf. 11½*

97	A48 3c brown, gold, org & yel	15	15
98	A48 4c brown, gold, bl & emer	15	15
99	A48 13c deep green, gold, purple & pink	20	20
	Set value	35	30

15th anniv. of the UN Children's Fund.

Family and Symbolic Buildings A49

1962, Feb. 28 Photo. *Perf. 14½x14*
Central design multicolored

100	A49 4c bright blue	15	15
a.	Black omitted	—	
b.	Yellow omitted	—	
c.	Brown omitted	—	
101	A49 7c orange brown	15	15
a.	Red omitted	—	
	Set value	25	16

UN program for housing and urban development.

"The World Against Malaria" — A50

1962, Mar. 30 *Perf. 14x14½*
Word frame in gray

102	A50 4c org, yel, green & black	15	15
103	A50 11c green, yel, brn & indigo	22	15
	Set value	30	18

Honoring the WHO and to call attention to the international campaign to eradicate malaria from the world.

"Peace" — A51

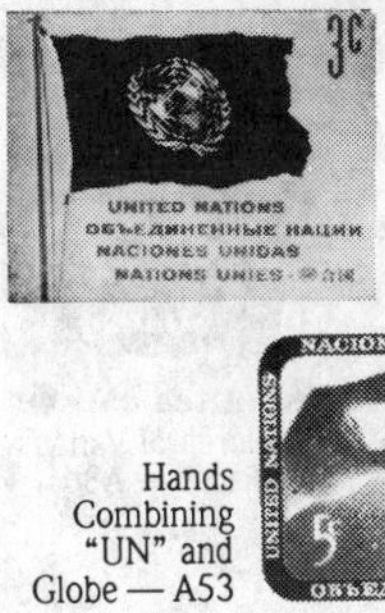

UN Flag — A52

Hands Combining "UN" and Globe — A53

UN Emblem over Globe — A54

Photogravure; Engraved (5c)

1962, May 25 *Perf. 14x14½*

104	A51 1c ver, blue, black & gray	15	15
105	A52 3c lt green, Prus blue, yel & gray	15	15

Perf. 12
Size: 36½x23½mm

106	A53 5c dark carmine rose	15	15

Perf. 12½

107	A54 11c dk & lt blue & gold	18	16
	Set value	60	35

See #167 and UN Offices in Geneva #2, 6.

Flag at Half-mast and UN Headquarters A55

World Map Showing Congo A56

1962, Sept. 17 Unwmk. *Perf. 11½*

108	A55 5c black, lt blue & blue	16	15
109	A55 15c black, gray ol & blue	25	16

1st anniv. of the death of Dag Hammarskjold, Secretary General of the UN 1953-61, in memory of those who died in the service of the UN.

1962, Oct. 24

110	A56 4c olive, org, black & yel	15	15
111	A56 11c bl grn, org, blk & yel	30	20

UN Operation in the Congo.

Globe in Universe and Palm Frond — A57

1962, Dec. 3 Engr. *Perf. 14x13½*

112	A57 4c violet blue	15	15
113	A57 11c rose claret	16	15
	Set value	30	17

Honoring the Committee on Peaceful Uses of Outer Space.

Development Decade Emblem — A58

Perf. 11½

1963, Feb. 4 Unwmk. Photo.

114	A58 5c pale grn, mar, dk blue & Prus blue	15	15
115	A58 11c yel, mar, dk blue & Prus blue	20	15
	Set value	30	16

UN Development Decade and the UN Conference on the Application of Science and Technology for the Benefit of the Less Developed Areas, Geneva, Feb. 4-20.

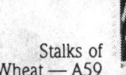

Stalks of Wheat — A59

1963, Mar. 22 *Perf. 11½*

116	A59 5c ver, green & yellow	15	15
117	A59 11c ver, dp claret & yel	25	15
	Set value	30	16

"Freedom from Hunger" campaign of the FAO.

Bridge over Map of New Guinea — A60

1963, Oct. 1 Unwmk. *Perf. 11½*

118	A60 25c blue, green & gray	45	20

1st anniv. of the UN Temporary Executive Authority (UNTEA) in West New Guinea (West Irian).

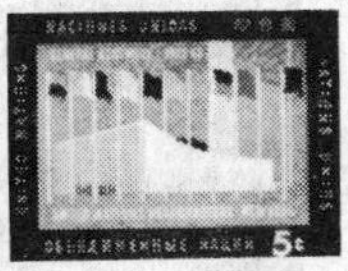

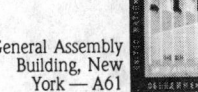

General Assembly Building, New York — A61

1963, Nov. 4 Photo. *Perf. 13*

119	A61 5c violet blue & multi	15	15
120	A61 11c green & multi	18	15
	Set value	26	16

Since Oct. 1955 all sessions of the General Assembly have been held in the General Assembly Hall, UN Headquarters, N.Y.

Flame — A62

1963, Dec. 10 *Perf. 13*

121	A62 5c green, gold, red & yel	16	15
122	A62 11c car, gold, blue & yel	20	15
	Set value	26	16

15th anniv. of the signing of the Universal Declaration of Human Rights.

Ships at Sea and IMCO Emblem — A63

1964, Jan. 13 *Perf. 11½*

123	A63 5c blue, ol, ocher & yel	15	15
124	A63 11c bl, dk grn, emer & yel	18	15
	Set value	26	16

Honoring the Intergovernmental Maritime Consultative Organization.

Map of the World — A64

UN Emblem — A65

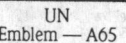

Three Men United Before Globe — A66

Stylized Globe and Weather Vane — A67

1964-71 Unwmk. Photo. *Perf. 14*

125 A64 2c lt bl, dk blue, org & yel green 15 15
a. Perf. 13x13½ ('71) 16 15

Perf. 11½

126 A65 7c dk bl, org brn & blk 16 15
127 A66 10c blue grn, ol grn & blk 16 15
128 A67 50c multicolored 75 40
Set value 95 63

Dates of issue: 2c, 7c, 10c, May 29; 50c, Mar. 6, 1964. See UN Offices in Geneva Nos. 3, 12.

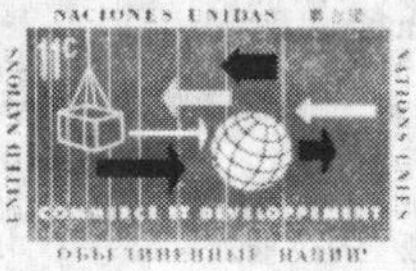

Arrows Showing Global Flow of Trade — A68

1964, June 15 *Perf. 13*

129 A68 5c black, red & yellow 15 15
130 A68 11c black, olive & yellow 18 15
Set value 26 16

UN Conference on Trade and Development, Geneva, Mar. 23-June 15.

Poppy Capsule and Hands — A69

1964, Sept. 21 Engr. *Perf. 12*

131 A69 5c rose red & black 15 15
132 A69 11c emerald & black 20 15
Set value 30 16

International efforts and achievements in the control of narcotics.

Padlocked Atomic Blast — A70

"Education for Progress" — A71

Photogravure and Engraved

1964, Oct. 23 *Perf. 11x11½*

133 A70 5c dark red & dk brown 15 15

Signing of the nuclear test ban treaty pledging an end to nuclear explosions in the atmosphere, outer space and under water.

1964, Dec. 7 Photo. *Perf. 12½*

134 A71 4c multicolored 15 15
135 A71 5c multicolored 15 15
136 A71 11c multicolored 16 15
Set value 30 20

UNESCO world campaign for universal literacy and for free compulsory primary education.

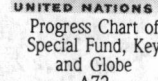

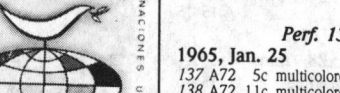

Progress Chart of Special Fund, Key and Globe A72

Leaves and View of Cyprus A73

Perf. 13½x13

1965, Jan. 25 Unwmk.

137 A72 5c multicolored 15 15
138 A72 11c multicolored 16 15
a. Black omitted (UN emblem on key) —
Set value 24 15

Special Fund Program, which aims to speed economic growth and social advancement in low-income countries.

1965, Mar. 4 Photo. *Perf. 11½*

139 A73 5c org, olive & black 15 15
140 A73 11c yel grn, blue grn & blk 16 15
Set value 24 15

UN Peace-keeping Force on Cyprus.

"From Semaphore to Satellite" — A74

1965, May 17 Unwmk. *Perf. 11½*

141 A74 5c multicolored 15 15
142 A74 11c multicolored 16 15
Set value 24 15

Cent. of the ITU.

ICY Emblem — A75

1965, June 26 Engr. *Perf. 14x13½*

143 A75 5c dark blue 15 15
144 A75 15c lilac rose 24 15
Set value 15

Souvenir Sheet

145 A75 Sheet of 2, #143-144 35 20

20th anniv. of the UN and Intl. Cooperation Year.

"Peace" — A76

Opening Words, UN Charter — A77

UN Headquarters and Emblem — A78

UN Emblem — A79

UN Emblem — A80

1965-66 Photo. *Perf. 13½*

146 A76 1c ver, bl, blk & gray 15 15

Perf. 14

147 A77 15c ol bis, dull yel, blk & dp claret 24 15

Perf. 12

148 A78 20c dk bl, bl, red & yel 30 16
a. Yellow omitted —

Lithographed and Embossed

Perf. 14

149 A79 25c lt bl & dk blue 40 20

Photo.

Perf. 11½

150 A80 $1 aqua & sapphire 1.75 75
Nos. 146-150 (5) 2.84 1.41

Issue dates: 1c, 25c, Sept. 20, 1965. 15c, 20c, Oct. 25, 1965. $1, Mar. 25, 1966.
See UN Offices in Geneva Nos. 5, 9 and 11.

Fields and People A81

Globe and Flags of UN Members A82

1965, Nov. 29 Photo. *Perf. 12*

151 A81 4c multicolored 15 15
152 A81 5c multicolored 15 15
153 A81 11c multicolored 16 15
Set value 30 20

Emphasize the importance of the world's population growth and its problems and to call attention to population trends and developments.

1966, Jan. 31 Photo. *Perf. 11½*

154 A82 5c multicolored 15 15
155 A82 15c multicolored 20 15
Set value 28 17

World Federation of UN Associations.

WHO Headquarters, Geneva — A83

1966, May 26 Photo. *Perf. 12½x12*

Granite Paper

156 A83 5c multicolored 20 15
157 A83 11c multicolored 30 15
Set value 15

WHO Headquarters, Geneva.

Coffee — A84

1966, Sept. 19 *Perf. 13½x13*

158 A84 5c multicolored 15 15
159 A84 11c multicolored 16 15
Set value 24 15

International Coffee Agreement of 1962.

UN Observer — A85

Children of Various Races — A86

1966, Oct. 24 Photo. *Perf. 11½*

Granite Paper

160 A85 15c multicolored 22 15

Peace Keeping UN Observers.

1966, Nov. 28 Litho. *Perf. 13x13½*

Designs: 5c, Children riding locomotive and tender. 11c, Children in open railroad car playing medical team.

161 A86 4c pink & multi 15 15
162 A86 5c pale green & multi 15 15
a. Yellow omitted — —
163 A86 11c ultra & multi 16 15
a. Imperf., pair —
b. Dark blue omitted —
Set value 30 20

20th anniv. of UNICEF.

Hand Rolling up Sleeve and Chart Showing Progress — A87

1967, Jan. 23 Photo. *Perf. 12½*

164 A87 5c multicolored 15 15
165 A87 11c multicolored 16 15
Set value 24 16

UN Development Program.

Type of 1962 and

UN Headquarters, New York and World Map — A88

1967 Photo. *Perf. 11½*

166 A88 1½c ultra, blk, org & ocher 15 15

Size: 33x23mm

167 A53 5c red brn, brn & org yel 15 15
Set value 15 15

Issue dates: 1½c, Mar. 17; 5c, Jan. 23. See UN Offices in Geneva No. 1.

Fireworks — A89

1967, Mar. 17 *Perf. 14x14½*

168 A89 5c dark blue & multi 15 15
169 A89 11c brown lake & multi 16 15
Set value 24 16

Honoring all nations which gained independence since 1945.

"Peace" A90

UN Pavilion, EXPO '67 A91

Litho. & Engr.; Litho. (8c)

1967, Apr. 28 *Perf. 11*

170 A90 4c shown 15 15
171 A90 5c Justice 15 15
172 A91 8c shown 15 15

173 A90 10c Fraternity 16 16
174 A90 15c Truth 20 20
Set value 66 66

Montreal World's Fair, EXPO '67, Apr. 28-Oct. 27. Under special agreement with the Canadian Government Nos. 170-174 were valid for postage only on mail posted at the UN pavilion during the fair. The denominations are expressed in Canadian currency.

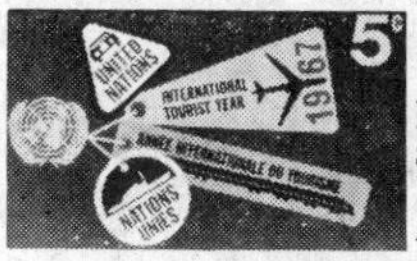

Luggage Tags and UN Emblem A92

Unwmk.

1967, June 19 **Litho.** ***Perf. 14***
175 A92 5c multicolored 15 15
176 A92 15c multicolored 22 15
Set value 30 17

International Tourist Year, 1967.

Quotation from Isaiah 2:4 — A93

1967, Oct. 24 **Photo.**
177 A93 6c multicolored 15 15
178 A93 13c multicolored 18 15
Set value 27 17

UN General Assembly's resolutions on general and complete disarmament and for suspension of nuclear and thermonuclear tests.

Art at UN Issue
Miniature Sheet

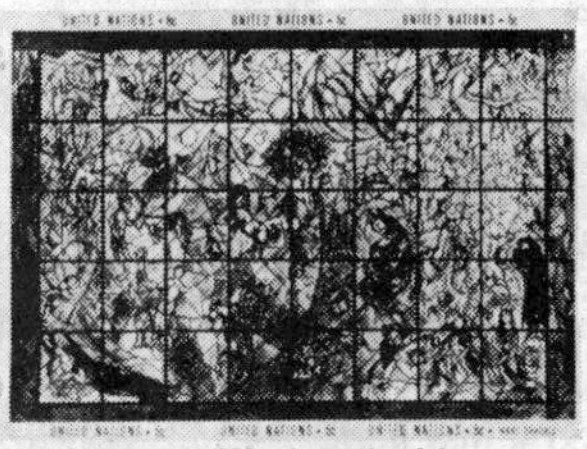
Memorial Window, by Marc Chagall — A94

"The Kiss of Peace" by Marc Chagall — A95

1967, Nov. 17 **Litho.** ***Rouletted 9***
179 A94 Sheet of 6 38 20
a. 6c multi, 41x46mm 15 15
b. 6c multi, 24x46mm 15 15
c. 6c multi, 41x33½mm 15 15
d. 6c multi, 36x33½mm 15 15
e. 6c multi, 29x33½mm 15 15
f. 6c multi, 41½x47mm 15 15

Perf. 12½x13½
180 A95 6c multicolored 15 15

No. 179 is divisible into six 6c stamps, each rouletted on 3 sides, imperf. on fourth side. Size: 124x80mm. On Nos. 179a-179c, "United Nations. 6c" appears at top; on Nos. 179d-179f, at bottom. No. 179f includes name "Marc Chagall."

Globe and Major UN Organs — A96

1968, Jan. 16 **Photo.** ***Perf. 11½***
181 A96 6c multicolored 15 15
182 A96 13c multicolored 15 15
Set value 24 17

Honoring the UN Secretariat.

Statue by Henrik Starcke A97

Factories and Chart A98

Art at UN Issue

1968, Mar. 1 **Photo.** ***Perf. 11½***
183 A97 6c blue & multi 15 15
184 A97 75c rose lake & multi 1.10 35

The 6c is part of the "Art at UN" series. The 75c belongs to the definitive series. The 6c exists imperforate.

The Starcke statue represents mankind's search for freedom and happiness.

See UN Offices in Geneva No. 13.

1968, Apr. 18 **Litho.** ***Perf. 12***
185 A98 6c multicolored 15 15
186 A98 13c multicolored 18 15
Set value 27 17

UN Industrial Development Organization.

UN Headquarters — A99

1968, May 31 **Litho.** ***Perf. 13½***
187 A99 6c multicolored 15 15

Radarscope and Globes A100

1968, Sept. 19 **Photo.** ***Perf. 13x13½***
188 A100 6c green & multi 15 15
189 A100 20c lilac & multi 30 20
Set value 39 26

World Weather Watch, a new weather system directed by the World Meterological Organization.

Human Rights Flame — A101

Books and UN Emblem — A102

Photogravure; Foil Embossed

1968, Nov. 22 ***Perf. 12½***
190 A101 6c brt bl, dp ultra & gold 15 15
191 A101 13c rose red, dk red & gold 20 15
Set value 29 18

International Human Rights Year.

1969, Feb. 10 **Litho.** ***Perf. 13½***
192 A102 6c yel green & multi 15 15
193 A102 13c bluish lilac & multi 16 15
Set value 25 18

UN Institute for Training and Research (UNITAR).

UN Building, Santiago, Chile — A103

1969, Mar. 14 **Litho.** ***Perf. 14***
194 A103 6c lt blue, vio bl & lt grn 15 15
195 A103 15c pink, cr & red brown 18 16
Set value 27 22

The UN Building in Santiago, Chile is the seat of the UN Economic Commission for Latin America and of the Latin American Institute for Economic and Social Planning.

"UN" and UN Emblem A104

UN Emblem and Scales of Justice A105

1969, Mar. 14 **Photo.** ***Perf. 13½***
196 A104 13c brt blue, black & gold 16 15

See UN Offices in Geneva No. 7.

1969, Apr. 21 **Photo.** ***Perf. 11½***
Granite Paper
197 A105 6c brt green, ultra & gold 15 15
198 A105 13c crim, lilac & gold 16 15
Set value 25 18

20th anniv. session of the UN Intl. Law Commission.

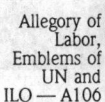

Allegory of Labor, Emblems of UN and ILO — A106

1969, June 5 **Photo.** ***Perf. 13***
199 A106 6c blue, dp bl, yel & gold 15 15
200 A106 20c org ver, mag, yel & gold 24 20
Set value 33 26

"Labor and Development" and the 50th anniv. of the ILO.

Art at UN Issue

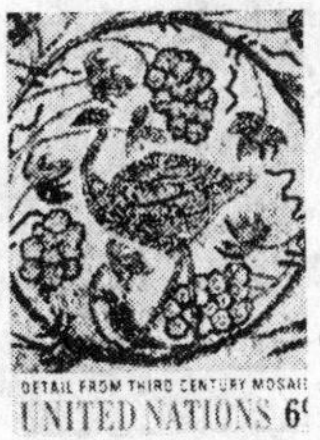

Ostrich, Tunisian Mosaic, 3rd Century — A107

Design: 13c, Pheasant.

1969, Nov. 21 **Photo.** ***Perf. 14***
201 A107 6c blue & multi 15 15
202 A107 13c red & multi 16 15
Set value 25 18

Art at UN Issue

Peace Bell, Gift of Japanese — A108

1970, Mar. 13 **Photo.** ***Perf. 13½x13***
203 A108 6c vio blue & multi 15 15
204 A108 25c claret & multi 28 25
Set value 37 31

Mekong River, Power Lines and Map of Delta — A109

1970, Mar. 13 ***Perf. 14***
205 A109 6c dk blue & multi 15 15
206 A109 13c dp plum & multi 16 15
Set value 25 18

Lower Mekong Basin, Viet Nam, Development project under UN auspices.

"Fight Cancer" — A110

1970, May 22 **Litho.** ***Perf. 14***
207 A110 6c blue & black 15 15
208 A110 13c olive & black 16 15
Set value 25 18

Fight against cancer in connection with the 10th Intl. Cancer Congress of the International Union Against Cancer, Houston, Texas, May 22-29.

UN Emblem and Olive Branch A111

UN Emblem A112

1970, June 26 **Photo.** ***Perf. 11½***
209 A111 6c red, gold, dk & lt blue 15 15
210 A111 13c dk bl, gold, grn & red 16 15

Perf. 12½
211 A112 25c dk blue, gold & lt blue 35 25
Set value 43

Souvenir Sheet
Imperf
212 Sheet of 3 50 30
a. A111 6c multicolored 15 15
b. A111 13c multicolored 16 15
c. A112 25c multicolored 30 20

25th anniv. of the UN.

Scales, Olive Branch, Progress Symbol A113

Sea Bed, Fish, Underwater Research A114

1970, Nov. 20 **Photo.** ***Perf. 13½***
213 A113 6c gold & multi 16 15
214 A113 13c silver & multi 20 15
Set value 27 18

Issued to publicize "Peace, Justice and Progress" in connection with the 25th anniv. of the UN.

Photogravure and Engraved

1971, Jan. 25 ***Perf. 13***
215 A114 6c blue & multi 15 15

Peaceful uses of the sea bed. See Offices in Geneva No. 15.

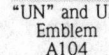

Refugees, Sculpture by Kaare K. Nygaard — A115

Wheat and Globe — A116

1971, Mar. 12 Litho. *Perf. 13x12½*

216 A115 6c brown, ocher & black 15 15
217 A115 13c ultra, grnsh blue & blk 16 15
Set value 30 18

International support for refugees. See Offices in Geneva No. 16.

1971, Apr. 13 Photo. *Perf. 14*

218 A116 13c brn red, gold & green 18 15

Publicizing the UN World Food Program. See Offices in Geneva No. 17.

UPU Headquarters, Bern — A117

1971, May 28 Photo. *Perf. 11½*

219 A117 20c brown org & multi 25 20

Opening of new UPU Headquarters, Bern. See Offices in Geneva No. 18.

"Eliminate Racial Discrimination" — A118

A119

1971, Sept. 21 Photo. *Perf. 13½*

220 A118 8c yel green & multi 15 15
221 A119 13c blue & multi 18 15
Set value 30 20

International Year Against Racial Discrimination. See Offices in Geneva Nos. 19-20.

UN Headquarters, New York — A120

UN Emblem and Symbolic Flags A121

1971, Oct. 22 *Perf. 13½; 13 (60c)*

222 A120 8c vio blue & multi 15 15
223 A121 60c ultra & multi 75 60

Maia by Pablo Picasso — A122

1971, Nov. 19 Photo. *Perf. 11½*

224 A122 8c olive & multi 15 15
225 A122 21c ultra & multi 26 20
Set value 28

UN International School. See Offices in Geneva No. 21.

Letter Changing Hands A123

1972, Jan. 5 Litho. *Perf. 14*

226 A123 95c blue & multi 1.75 35

"No More Nuclear Weapons" A124

1972, Feb. 14 Photo. *Perf. 13½x14*

227 A124 8c dull rose, blk, bl & gray 15 15

To promote non-proliferation of nuclear weapons. See Offices in Geneva No. 23.

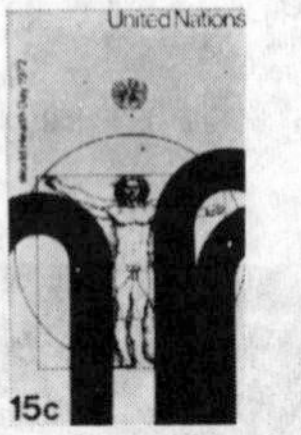

Proportions of Man (c. 1509), by Leonardo da Vinci A125

"Human Environment" A126

Lithographed and Engraved

1972, Apr. 7 *Perf. 13x13½*

228 A125 15c black & multi 30 16

World Health Day, Apr. 7. See Offices in Geneva No. 24.

Lithographed and Embossed

1972, June 5 *Perf. 12½x14*

229 A126 8c multicolored 15 15
230 A126 15c multicolored 22 16
Set value 24

UN Conference on Human Environment, Stockholm, June 5-16, 1972.
See Offices in Geneva Nos. 25-26.

"Europe" and UN Emblem A127

The Five Continents, by José Maria Sert A128

1972, Sept. 11 Litho. *Perf. 13x13½*

231 A127 21c yel brown & multi 50 20

Economic Commission for Europe, 25th anniv. See Offices in Geneva No. 27.

Art at UN Issue

1972, Nov. 17 Photo. *Perf. 12x12½*

232 A128 8c gold, brn & gldn brn 15 15
233 A128 15c gold, brn & blue grn 30 16
Set value 24

See Offices in Geneva Nos. 28-29.

Olive Branch and Broken Sword — A129

1973, Mar. 9 Litho. *Perf. 13½x13*

234 A129 8c blue & multi 20 15
235 A129 15c lilac rose & multi 40 16
Set value 24

Disarmament Decade, 1970-79.
Nos. 234-235 exist imperf. See Offices in Geneva Nos. 30-31.

Poppy Capsule and Skull — A130

Honeycomb — A131

1973, Apr. 13 Photo. *Perf. 13½*

236 A130 8c multicolored 16 15
237 A130 15c multicolored 40 40

Fight against drug abuse. See Offices in Geneva No. 32.

1973, May 25 Photo. *Perf. 14*

238 A131 8c ol bister & multi 25 15
239 A131 21c gray blue & multi 50 20
Set value 28

5th anniv. of the UN Volunteer Program. See UN Offices in Geneva No. 33.

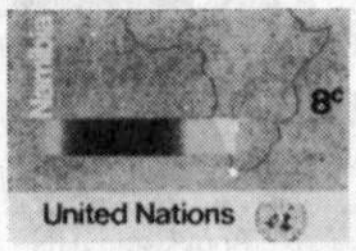

Map of Africa with Namibia — A132

1973, Oct. 1 Photo. *Perf. 13½*

240 A132 8c emerald & multi 15 15
241 A132 15c brt rose & multi 32 20
Set value 28

To publicize Namibia (South-West Africa), for which the UN General Assembly ended the mandate of South Africa and established the UN Council for Namibia to administer the territory until independence. See Offices in Geneva No. 34.

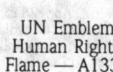

UN Emblem, Human Rights Flame — A133

1973, Nov. 16 Photo. *Perf. 13½*

242 A133 8c dp carmine & multi 15 15
243 A133 21c blue green & multi 32 20
Set value 28

25th anniv. of the adoption and proclamation of the Universal Declaration of Human Rights. See Offices in Geneva Nos. 35-36.

ILO Headquarters, Geneva — A134

1974, Jan. 11 Photo. *Perf. 14*

244 A134 10c ultra & multi 16 15
245 A134 21c blue green & multi 32 20

New Headquarters of Intl. Labor Organization. See Offices in Geneva Nos. 37-38.

Post Horn Encircling Globe — A135

1974, Mar. 22 Photo. *Perf. 14*

246 A135 10c multicolored 25 15

Centenary of UPU. See Offices in Geneva Nos. 39-40.

Art at UN Issue

Peace Mural, by Candido Portinari — A136

1974, May 6 Photo. *Perf. 14*

247 A136 10c gold & multi 20 15
248 A136 18c ultra & multi 45 18
Set value 28

See Offices in Geneva Nos. 41-42.

Dove and UN Emblem A137

UN Headquarters A138

Globe, UN Emblem, Flags — A139

1974, June 10 Photo. *Perf. 14*

249 A137 2c dk bl & lt blue 15 15
250 A138 10c multicolored 16 15
251 A139 18c multicolored 28 16
Set value 48 31

Children of the World — A140

Law of the Sea — A141

1974, Oct. 18 Photo. *Perf. 14*

252 A140 10c lt blue & multi	20	15
253 A140 18c lilac & multi	40	18
Set value		28

World Population Year. See Offices in Geneva Nos. 43-44.

1974, Nov. 22 Photo. *Perf. 14*

254 A141 10c green & multi	16	15
255 A141 26c multicolored	35	25

UN General Assembly declared the sea bed common heritage of mankind, exempt from arms race. See Offices in Geneva No. 45.

Satellite and Globe — A142

1975, Mar. 14 Litho. *Perf. 13*

256 A142 10c multicolored	16	15
257 A142 26c multicolored	35	25

Peaceful uses of outer space (meteorology, industry, fishing, communications).
See Offices in Geneva Nos. 46-47.

Equality Between Men and Women — A143

1975, May 9 Litho. *Perf. 15*

258 A143 10c multicolored	20	15
259 A143 18c multicolored	40	18
Set value		28

International Women's Year 1975. See Offices in Geneva Nos. 48-49.

UN Flag and "XXX" — A144

1975, June 26 Litho. *Perf. 13*

260 A144 10c multicolored	15	15
261 A144 26c purple & multi	50	25

Souvenir Sheet

Imperf

262 Sheet of 2	65	20
a. A144 10c olive bister & multi	16	15
b. A144 26c purple & multi	40	15

30th anniv. of the UN. See Offices in Geneva Nos. 50-52.

Hand Reaching up over Map of Africa and Namibia — A145

Wild Rose Growing from Barbed Wire — A146

1975, Sept. 22 Photo. *Perf. 13½*

263 A145 10c multicolored	20	15
264 A145 18c multicolored	35	18
Set value		28

"Namibia—United Nations direct responsibility." See note after No. 241. See Offices in Geneva Nos. 53-54.

1975, Nov. 21 Engr. *Perf. 12½*

265 A146 13c ultramarine	30	15
266 A146 26c rose carmine	55	25

UN Peace-keeping Operations. See Offices in Geneva Nos. 55-56.

Symbolic Flags Forming Dove A147

UN Emblem A149

People of All Races A148

UN Flag — A150

Dove and Rainbow — A151

Perf. 13x13½, 13½x13, 14 (9c)

1976 Litho.; Photo. (9c)

267 A147 3c multicolored	15	15
268 A148 4c multicolored	15	15
269 A149 9c multicolored	15	15
270 A150 30c blue, emer & black	45	30
271 A151 50c multicolored	75	50
Nos. 267-271 (5)	1.65	
Set value		95

Issue dates: 9c, Nov. 19. Others, Jan. 9. See Offices in Vienna No. 8.

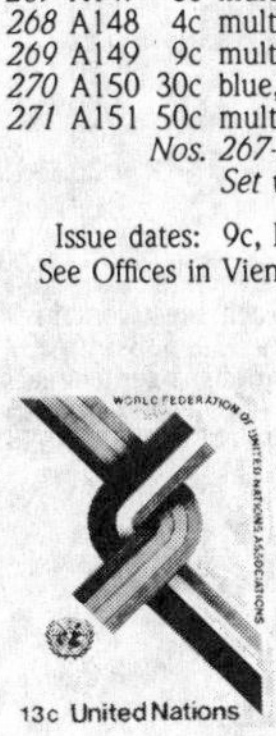

Interlocking Bands — A152

1976, Mar. 12 Photo. *Perf. 14*

272 A152 13c blue, green & black	16	15
273 A152 26c green & multi	35	25

World Federation of UN Association. See Offices in Geneva No. 57.

Cargo, Globe and Graph — A153

Houses Around Globe — A154

1976, Apr. 23 Photo. *Perf. 11½*

274 A153 13c multicolored	16	15
275 A153 31c multicolored	40	30

UN Conference on Trade and Development (UNCTAD), Nairobi, Kenya, May 1976. See Offices in Geneva No. 58.

1976, May 28 Photo. *Perf. 14*

276 A154 13c multicolored	18	15
277 A154 25c green & multi	40	25

Habitat, UN Conference on Human Settlements, Vancouver, Canada, May 31-June 11. See Offices in Geneva Nos. 59-60.

Magnifying Glass, Sheet of Stamps, UN Emblem — A155

Grain — A156

1976, Oct. 8 Photo. *Perf. 11½*

278 A155 13c blue & multi	20	16
279 A155 31c green & multi	3.00	50

UN Postal Administration, 25th anniv. Sheets of 20. See Offices in Geneva #61-62.

1976, Nov. 19 Litho. *Perf. 14½*

280 A156 13c multicolored	40	15

World Food Council. See Offices in Geneva No. 63.

WIPO Headquarters, Geneva A157

1977, Mar. 11 Photo. *Perf. 14*

281 A157 13c citron & multi	18	15
282 A157 31c brt green & multi	45	30

World Intellectual Property Organization. See Geneva No. 64.

Drops of Water Falling into Funnel — A158

1977, Apr. 22 Photo. *Perf. 13½x13*

283 A158 13c yellow & multi	16	15
284 A158 25c salmon & multi	45	25

UN Water Conf., Mar del Plata, Argentina, Mar. 14-25. See Offices in Geneva #65-66.

Burning Fuse Severed — A159

1977, May 27 Photo. *Perf. 14*

285 A159 13c purple & multi	18	15
286 A159 31c dk blue & multi	45	30

UN Security Council. See Geneva #67-68.

"Combat Racism" A160

1977, Sept. 19 Litho. *Perf. 13½x13*

287 A160 13c black & yellow	20	15
288 A160 25c black & vermilion	50	25

Fight against racial discrimination. See Geneva Nos. 69-70.

Atom, Grain, Fruit and Factory — A161

1977, Nov. 18 Photo.

289 A161 13c yellow bister & multi	18	15
290 A161 18c dull green & multi	28	18

Peaceful uses of atomic energy. See Geneva Nos. 71-72.

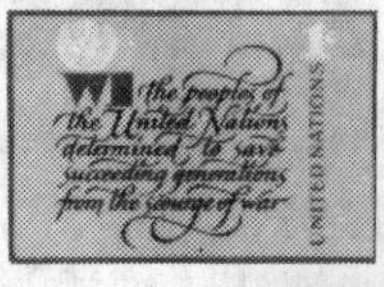

Opening Words of UN Charter — A162

"Live Together in Peace" — A163

People of the World — A164

1978, Jan. 27 Litho. *Perf. 14½*

291 A162 1c gold, brown & red	15	15
292 A163 25c multicolored	35	25
293 A164 $1 multicolored	1.25	1.10

See Offices in Geneva No. 73.

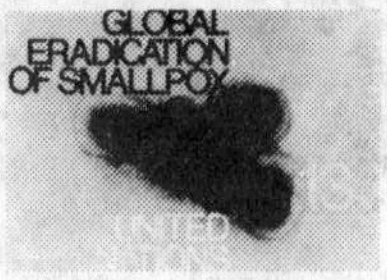

Smallpox Virus — A165

1978, Mar. 31 Photo. *Perf. 12x11½*

294 A165 13c rose & black	16	15
295 A165 31c blue & black	45	30

Global eradication of smallpox. See Offices in Geneva Nos. 74-75.

Open Handcuff
A166

Multicolored Bands and Clouds
A167

1978, May 5 Photo. *Perf. 12*

296 A166 13c multicolored	18	15
297 A166 18c multicolored	28	18

Liberation, justice and cooperation for Namibia. See Offices in Geneva No. 76.

1978, June 12 Photo. *Perf. 14*

298 A167 13c multicolored	20	15
299 A167 25c multicolored	50	25

International Civil Aviation Organization for "Safety in the Air." See Offices in Geneva #77-78.

General Assembly
A168

1978, Sept. 15 Photo. *Perf. 13½*

300 A168 13c multicolored	18	15
301 A168 18c multicolored	28	18

See Offices in Geneva Nos. 79-80.

Hemispheres as Cogwheels
A169

1978, Nov. 17 Photo. *Perf. 14*

302 A169 13c multicolored	20	15
303 A169 31c multicolored	60	30

Technical Cooperation Among Developing Countries Conf., Buenos Aires, Argentina, Sept. 1978. See Offices in Geneva No. 81.

Hand Holding Olive Branch — A170

Tree of Various Races — A171

Globe, Dove with Olive Branch — A172

Birds and Globe — A173

1979, Jan. 19 Photo. *Perf. 14*

304 A170 5c multicolored	15	15
305 A171 14c multicolored	20	15
306 A172 15c multicolored	28	16
307 A173 20c multicolored	30	20
Set value		55

UNDRO Against Fire and Water — A174

1979, Mar. 9 Photo. *Perf. 14*

308 A174 15c multicolored	30	16
309 A174 20c multicolored	45	20

Office of the UN Disaster Relief Coordinator. See Offices in Geneva Nos. 82-83.

Child and ICY Emblem — A175

1979, May 4 Photo. *Perf. 14*

310 A175 15c multicolored	20	16
311 A175 31c multicolored	60	30

International Year of the Child. See Offices in Geneva Nos. 84-85.

Map of Namibia, Olive Branch — A176

Scales and Sword of Justice — A177

1979, Oct. 5 Litho. *Perf. 13½*

312 A176 15c multicolored	20	15
313 A176 31c multicolored	38	30

For a free and independent Namibia. See Offices in Geneva No. 86.

1979, Nov. 9 Litho. *Perf. 13x13½*

314 A177 15c multicolored	20	16
315 A177 20c multicolored	45	20

Intl. Court of Justice, The Hague, Netherlands. See Offices in Geneva Nos. 87-88.

Graph of Economic Trends — A178

Key — A179

1980, Jan. 11 *Perf. 15x14½*

316 A178 15c multicolored	22	16
317 A179 31c multicolored	45	30

New International Economic Order. See Offices in Geneva No. 89; Vienna No. 7.

Women's Year Emblems
A180

1980, Mar. 7 Litho. *Perf. 14½x15*

318 A180 15c multicolored	22	16
319 A180 20c multicolored	30	20

UN Decade for Women. See Offices in Geneva Nos. 90-91; Vienna Nos. 9-10.

UN Emblem and "UN" on Helmet
A181

Arrows and UN Emblem
A182

1980, May 16 Litho. *Perf. 14x13*

320 A181 15c black & brt blue	22	16
321 A182 31c multicolored	45	30

UN Peace-keeping Operations. See Offices in Geneva No. 92; Vienna No. 11.

"35" and Flags — A183

Globe and Laurel — A184

1980, June 26 Litho. *Perf. 13*

322 A183 15c multicolored	20	16
323 A184 31c multicolored	42	30

Souvenir Sheet

Imperf

324 Sheet of 2	45	16
a. A183 15c multicolored	15	
b. A184 31c multicolored	28	

35th anniv. of the UN. See Offices in Geneva Nos. 93-95; Vienna Nos. 12-14.

Flag of Turkey
A185

1980, Sept. 26 Litho. *Perf. 12*

325 A185 15c shown	20	15
326 A185 15c Luxembourg	20	15
327 A185 15c Fiji	20	15
328 A185 15c Viet Nam	20	15
a. Se-tenant block of 4	1.25	
329 A185 15c Guinea	20	15
330 A185 15c Surinam	20	15
331 A185 15c Bangladesh	20	15
332 A185 15c Mali	20	15
a. Se-tenant block of 4	1.25	
333 A185 15c Yugoslavia	20	15
334 A185 15c France	20	15
335 A185 15c Venezuela	20	15
336 A185 15c El Salvador	20	15
a. Se-tenant block of 4	1.25	
337 A185 15c Madagascar	20	15
338 A185 15c Cameroon	20	15
339 A185 15c Rwanda	20	15
340 A185 15c Hungary	20	15
a. Se-tenant block of 4	1.25	
Nos. 325-340 (16)	3.20	
Set value		1.60

Issued in 4 sheets of 16. Each sheet contains 4 blocks of 4 (Nos. 325-328, 329-332, 333-336, 337-340). A se-tenant block of 4 designs centers each sheet. See Nos. 350-365, 374-389, 399-414, 425-440, 450-465, 477-492, 499-514, 528-543, 554-569.

Symbolic Flowers
A186

Symbols of Progress
A187

1980, Nov. 21 Litho. *Perf. 13½x13*

341 A186 15c multicolored	28	20
342 A187 20c multicolored	38	30

Economic and Social Council (ECOSOC). See Offices in Geneva Nos. 96-97; Vienna Nos. 15-16.

Inalienable Rights of the Palestinian People
A188

1981, Jan. 30 Photo.

343 A188 15c multicolored	32	15

See Offices in Geneva #98; Vienna #17.

Interlocking Puzzle Pieces — A189

Stylized Person — A190

1981, Mar. 6 Photo.

344 A189 20c multicolored	35	30
345 A190 35c multicolored	50	50

Intl. Year of the Disabled. See Offices in Geneva Nos. 99-100; Vienna Nos. 18-19.

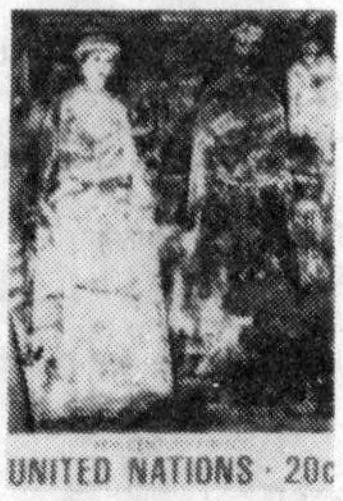

Divislava and Sebastocrator Kaloyan, Bulgarian Mural, 1259, Boyana Church, Sofia — A191

1981, Apr. 15 Photo. *Perf. 11½*

Granite Paper

346 A191 20c multicolored	30	30
347 A191 31c multicolored	50	45

See Offices in Geneva #101; Vienna #20.

Solar Energy — A192

Conference Emblem — A193

1981, May 29 Litho. *Perf. 13*

348 A192 20c multicolored	40	30
349 A193 40c multicolored	65	50

Conference on New and Renewable Sources of Energy, Nairobi, Aug. 10-21. See Offices in Geneva No. 102; Vienna No. 21.

Flag Type of 1980

1981, Sept. 25 **Litho.**

350 A185 20c Djibouti	25	15
351 A185 20c Sri Lanka	25	15
352 A185 20c Bolivia	25	15
353 A185 20c Equatorial Guinea	25	15
a. Se-tenant block of 4	1.50	
354 A185 20c Malta	25	15
355 A185 20c Czechoslovakia	25	15
356 A185 20c Thailand	25	15
357 A185 20c Trinidad & Tobago	25	15
a. Se-tenant block of 4	1.50	
358 A185 20c Ukrainian SSR	25	15
359 A185 20c Kuwait	25	15
360 A185 20c Sudan	25	15
361 A185 20c Egypt	25	15
a. Se-tenant block of 4	1.50	
362 A185 20c US	25	15
363 A185 20c Singapore	25	15
364 A185 20c Panama	25	15
365 A185 20c Costa Rica	25	15
a. Se-tenant block of 4	1.50	
Nos. 350-365 (16)	4.00	2.40

See note after No. 340.

Seedling and Tree Cross Section — A194

"10" and Symbols of Progress — A195

1981, Nov. 13 **Litho.**

366 A194 18c multicolored	35	30
367 A195 28c multicolored	65	45

UN Volunteers Program, 10th anniv. See Offices in Geneva #103-104; Vienna #22-23.

Respect for Human Rights — A196

Independence of Colonial Countries and People — A197

Second Disarmament Decade — A198

1982, Jan. 22 *Perf. 11½x12*

368 A196 17c multicolored	28	15
369 A197 28c multicolored	45	25
370 A198 40c multicolored	75	40

10th Anniv. of UN Environment Program
A199 A200

1982, Mar. 19 **Litho.** *Perf. 13½x13*

371 A199 20c multicolored	30	16
372 A200 40c multicolored	85	20

UN Emblem and Olive Branch in Outer Space — A201

1982, June 11 **Litho.** *Perf. 13 x 13½*

373 A201 20c multicolored	65	20

Exploration and Peaceful Uses of Outer Space. See Offices in Geneva Nos. 109-110; Vienna No. 27.

Flag Type of 1980

1982, Sept. 24 **Litho.** *Perf. 12*

374 A185 20c Austria	28	25
375 A185 20c Malaysia	28	25
376 A185 20c Seychelles	28	25
377 A185 20c Ireland	28	25
a. Se-tenant block of 4	2.00	
378 A185 20c Mozambique	28	25
379 A185 20c Albania	28	25
380 A185 20c Dominica	28	25
381 A185 20c Solomon Islands	28	25
a. Se-tenant block of 4	2.00	
382 A185 20c Philippines	28	25
383 A185 20c Swaziland	28	25
384 A185 20c Nicaragua	28	25
385 A185 20c Burma	28	25
a. Se-tenant block of 4	2.00	
386 A185 20c Cape Verde	28	25
387 A185 20c Guyana	28	25
388 A185 20c Belgium	28	25
389 A185 20c Nigeria	28	25
a. Se-tenant block of 4	2.00	
Nos. 374-389 (16)	4.48	4.00

See note after No. 340.

Conservation and Protection of Nature — A202

1982, Nov. 19 **Photo.** *Perf. 14*

390 A202 20c Leaf	42	30
391 A202 28c Butterfly	60	45

See Offices in Geneva Nos. 111-112; Vienna Nos. 28-29.

A203

World Communications Year — A204

1983, Jan. 28 **Litho.** *Perf. 13*

392 A203 20c multicolored	35	20
393 A204 40c multicolored	75	40

See Offices in Geneva #113; Vienna #30.

Safety at Sea
A205 A206

1983, Mar. 18 **Litho.** *Perf. 14½*

394 A205 20c multicolored	38	20
395 A206 37c multicolored	75	38

See Offices in Geneva #114-115; Vienna #31-32.

World Food Program A207

1983, Apr. 22 **Engr.** *Perf. 13½*

396 A207 20c rose lake	50	20

See Offices in Geneva #116; Vienna #33-34.

Trade and Development
A208 A209

1983, June 6 **Litho.** *Perf. 14*

397 A208 20c multicolored	40	16
398 A209 28c multicolored	85	25

See Offices in Geneva Nos. 117-118; Vienna Nos. 35-36.

Flag Type of 1980

1983, Sept. 23 **Photo.** *Perf. 12*

399 A185 20c Great Britain	38	20
400 A185 20c Barbados	38	20
401 A185 20c Nepal	38	20
402 A185 20c Israel	38	20
a. Se-tenant block of 4	2.25	
403 A185 20c Malawi	38	20
404 A185 20c Byelorussian SSR	38	20
405 A185 20c Jamaica	38	20
406 A185 20c Kenya	38	20
a. Se-tenant block of 4	2.25	
407 A185 20c People's Republic of China	38	20
408 A185 20c Peru	38	20
409 A185 20c Bulgaria	38	20
410 A185 20c Canada	38	20
a. Se-tenant block of 4	2.25	
411 A185 20c Somalia	38	20
412 A185 20c Senegal	38	20
413 A185 20c Brazil	38	20
414 A185 20c Sweden	38	20
a. Se-tenant block of 4	2.25	
Nos. 399-414 (16)	6.08	3.20

See note after No. 340.

35th Anniv. of the Universal Declaration of Human Rights
A210 A211

Photogravure and Engraved

1983, Dec. 9 *Perf. 13½*

415 A210 20c Window Right	50	20
416 A211 40c Peace Treaty with Nature	1.00	40

See Offices in Geneva #119-120, Vienna #37-38.

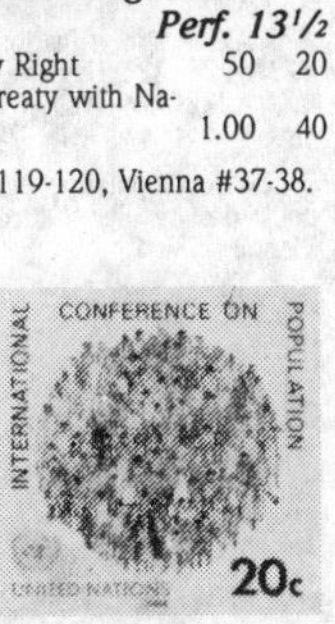

Intl. Population Conference A212

1984, Feb. 3 **Litho.** *Perf. 14*

417 A212 20c multicolored	35	20
418 A212 40c multicolored	90	40

See Offices in Geneva #121; Vienna #39.

Tractor Plowing A213

Rice Paddy A214

1984, Mar. 15 **Litho.** *Perf. 14½*

419 A213 20c multicolored	55	20
420 A214 40c multicolored	1.25	40

World Food Day, Oct. 16. See Offices in Geneva Nos. 122-123; Vienna Nos. 40-41.

Grand Canyon A215

Ancient City of Polonnaruwa, Sri Lanka — A216

1984, Apr. 18 **Litho.** *Perf. 14*

421 A215 20c multicolored	45	20
422 A216 50c multicolored	1.10	50

World Heritage (protection of world cultural and natural sites). See #601-602; Offices in Geneva #124-125, 211-212; Vienna #42-43, 125-126.

A217 A218

1984, May 29 **Photo.** *Perf. 11½*

423 A217 20c multicolored	45	20
424 A218 50c multicolored	1.00	50

Future for Refugees. See Offices in Geneva Nos. 126-127; Vienna Nos. 44-45.

Flag Type of 1980

1984, Sept. 21 **Photo.** *Perf. 12*

425 A185 20c Burundi	70	20
426 A185 20c Pakistan	70	20
427 A185 20c Benin	70	20
428 A185 20c Italy	70	20
a. Se-tenant block of 4	3.75	
429 A185 20c Tanzania	70	20
430 A185 20c United Arab Emirates	70	20
431 A185 20c Ecuador	70	20
432 A185 20c Bahamas	70	20
a. Se-tenant block of 4	3.75	
433 A185 20c Poland	70	20
434 A185 20c Papua New Guinea	70	20
435 A185 20c Uruguay	70	20
436 A185 20c Chile	70	20
a. Se-tenant block of 4	3.75	
437 A185 20c Paraguay	70	20
438 A185 20c Bhutan	70	20
439 A185 20c Central African Republic	70	20
440 A185 20c Australia	70	20
a. Se-tenant block of 4	3.75	
Nos. 425-440 (16)	11.20	3.20

Issued in 4 sheets of 16. Each sheet contains 4 blocks of 4 (Nos. 425-428, 429-432, 433-436, 437-440). A se-tenant block of 4 designs centers each sheet.

Intl. Youth Year — A219

ILO Turin Center — A220

1984, Nov. 15 Litho. *Perf. 13½*

441 A219 20c multicolored 40 20
442 A219 35c multicolored 1.00 35

See Offices in Geneva #128; Vienna #46-47.

1985, Feb. 1 Engr.

443 A220 23c Turin Center emblem 60 24

See Offices in Geneva #129-130; Vienna #48.

UN University A221

1985, Mar. 15 Photo. *Perf. 13½*

444 A221 50c multicolored 1.00 50

See Offices in Geneva #131-132; Vienna #49.

Peoples of the World — A222

Painting UN Emblem — A223

1985, May 10 Litho. *Perf. 14*

445 A222 22c multicolored 42 22
446 A223 $3 multicolored 4.00 1.00

See Offices in Geneva #133-134; Vienna #50-51.

The Corner A224

Alvaro Raking Hay A225

Oil paintings (details) by American artist Andrew Wyeth.

1985, June 26 Photo. *Perf. 12x11½*

447 A224 22c multicolored 60 22
448 A225 45c multicolored 1.00 45

Souvenir Sheet

Imperf

449 Sheet of 2 2.00 50
a. A224 22c multicolored 50 —
b. A225 45c multicolored 1.00 —

40th anniv. of the UN. No. 449 has multicolored margin with inscription and UN emblem. Size: 75x83mm. See Offices in Geneva Nos. 135-137; Vienna Nos. 52-54.

Flag Type of 1980

1985, Sept. 20 Photo. *Perf. 12*

450 A185 22c Grenada 65 20
451 A185 22c Federal Republic of Germany 65 20
452 A185 22c Saudi Arabia 65 20
453 A185 22c Mexico 65 20
a. Se-tenant block of 4 4.00
454 A185 22c Uganda 65 20
455 A185 22c St. Thomas & Prince 65 20
456 A185 22c USSR 65 20
457 A185 22c India 65 20
a. Se-tenant block of 4 4.00
458 A185 22c Liberia 65 20
459 A185 22c Mauritius 65 20
460 A185 22c Chad 65 20
461 A185 22c Dominican Republic 65 20
a. Se-tenant block of 4 4.00
462 A185 22c Sultanate of Oman 65 20
463 A185 22c Ghana 65 20
464 A185 22c Sierra Leone 65 20
465 A185 22c Finland 65 20
a. Se-tenant block of 4 4.00
Nos. 450-465 (16) 10.40 3.20

See note after No. 340.

UNICEF Child Survival Campaign — A226

Photoravure and Engraved

1985, Nov. 22 *Perf. 13½*

466 A226 22c Asian child 45 22
467 A226 33c Breastfeeding 75 32

See Offices in Geneva #138-139; Vienna #55-56.

Abstract Painting by Wosene Kosrof — A227

1986, Jan. 31 Photo. *Perf. 11½*

468 A227 22c multicolored 60 16

Africa in Crisis, campaign against hunger. See Offices in Geneva #140; Vienna #57.

Water Resources A228

1986, Mar. 14 Photo. *Perf. 13½*

469 A228 22c Dam 1.50 45
470 A228 22c Irrigation 1.50 45
471 A228 22c Hygiene 1.50 45
472 A228 22c Well 1.50 45
a. Block of 4, #469-472 7.00 1.80

UN Development program. No. 472a has continuous design. See Offices in Geneva #141-144; Vienna #58-61.

Human Rights Stamp of 1954 — A229

Stamp collecting: 44c, Engraver.

1986, May 22 Engr. *Perf. 12½*

473 A229 22c dk violet & brt blue 50 22
474 A229 44c brown & emer green 1.10 44

See Offices in Geneva #146-147; Vienna #62-63.

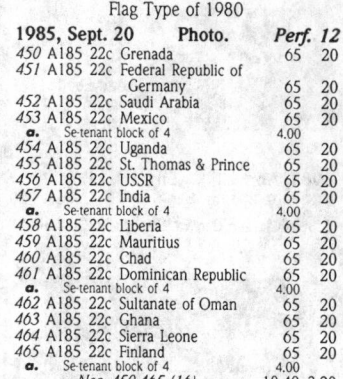

Birds Nest in Tree — A230

Peace in Seven Languages A231

Photo. & Embossed

1986, June 20 *Perf. 13½*

475 A230 22c multicolored 60 22
476 A231 33c multicolored 1.10 35

Intl. Peace Year. See Offices in Geneva Nos. 148-149; Vienna Nos. 64-65.

Flag Type of 1980

1986, Sept. 19 Photo. *Perf. 12*

477 A185 22c New Zealand 70 20
478 A185 22c Lao PDR 70 20
479 A185 22c Burkina Faso 70 20
480 A185 22c Gambia 70 20
a. Se-tenant block of 4 3.75
481 A185 22c Maldives 70 20
482 A185 22c Ethiopia 70 20
483 A185 22c Jordan 70 20
484 A185 22c Zambia 70 20
a. Se-tenant block of 4 3.75
485 A185 22c Iceland 70 20
486 A185 22c Antigua & Barbuda 70 20
487 A185 22c Angola 70 20
488 A185 22c Botswana 70 20
a. Se-tenant block of 4 3.75
489 A185 22c Romania 70 20
490 A185 22c Togo 70 20
491 A185 22c Mauritania 70 20
492 A185 22c Colombia 70 20
a. Se-tenant block of 4 3.75
Nos. 477-492 (16) 11.20 3.20

See note after No. 340.

Souvenir Sheet

World Federation of UN Associations, 40th Anniv. — A232

Designs: 22c, Mother Earth, by Edna Hibel, US. 33c, Watercolor by Salvador Dali (b. 1904), Spain. 39c, New Dawn, by Dong Kingman, US. 44c, Watercolor by Chaim Gross, US.

1986, Nov. 14 Litho. *Perf. 13x13½*

493 Sheet of 4 4.25 1.65
a. A232 22c multicolored 50 —
b. A232 33c multicolored 75 —
c. A232 39c multicolored 85 —
d. A232 44c multicolored 1.00 —

See Offices in Geneva #150; Vienna #66.

Trygve Halvdan Lie (1896-1968), 1st Secretary-General A233

Photogravure and Engraved

1987, Jan. 30 *Perf. 13½*

494 A233 22c multicolored 1.00 22

See Offices in Geneva #151; Vienna #67.

Intl. Year of Shelter for the Homeless A234

Perf. 13½x12½

1987, Mar. 13 Litho.

495 A234 22c Surveying, blueprint 50 22
496 A234 44c Cutting lumber 1.00 44

See Offices in Geneva #154-155; Vienna #68-69.

Fight Drug Abuse A235

1987, June 12 Litho. *Perf. 14½x15*

497 A235 22c Construction 55 22
498 A235 33c Education 85 35

See Offices in Geneva #156-157; Vienna #70-71.

Flag Type of 1980

1987, Sept. 18 Photo. *Perf. 12*

499 A185 22c Comoros 65 20
500 A185 22c Yemen PDR 65 20
501 A185 22c Mongolia 65 20
502 A185 22c Vanuatu 65 20
a. Se-tenant block of 4 2.75
503 A185 22c Japan 65 20
504 A185 22c Gabon 65 20
505 A185 22c Zimbabwe 65 20
506 A185 22c Iraq 65 20
a. Se-tenant block of 4 2.75
507 A185 22c Argentina 65 20
508 A185 22c Congo 65 20
509 A185 22c Niger 65 20
510 A185 22c St. Lucia 65 20
a. Se-tenant block of 4 2.75
511 A185 22c Bahrain 65 20
512 A185 22c Haiti 65 20
513 A185 22c Afghanistan 65 20
514 A185 22c Greece 65 20
a. Se-tenant block of 4 2.75
Nos. 499-514 (16) 10.40 3.20

See note after No. 340.

UN Day — A236

Designs: Multinational people in various occupations.

1987, Oct. 23 Litho. *Perf. 14½x15*

515 A236 22c multicolored 60 22
516 A236 39c multicolored 1.00 40

See Offices in Geneva Nos. 158-159; Vienna Nos. 74-75.

Immunize Every Child — A237

1987, Nov. 20 Litho. *Perf. 15x14½*

517 A237 22c Measles 65 22
518 A237 44c Tetanus 1.40 45

See Offices in Geneva Nos. 160-161; Vienna Nos. 76-77.

Intl. Fund for Agricultural Development (IFAD) — A238

1988, Jan. 29 Litho. *Perf. 13½*
519 A238 22c Fishing 50 32
520 A238 33c Farming 1.10 35

See Offices in Geneva Nos. 162-163; Vienna Nos. 78-79.

A239

1988, Jan. 29 Photo. *Perf. 13½x14*
521 A239 3c multicolored ('88) 15 15

Survival of the Forests A240

1988, Mar. 18 Litho. *Perf. 14x15*
522 A240 25c multicolored *2.75* 75
523 A240 44c multicolored *4.00* 2.25
a. Pair, #522-523 *7.50* 3.00

No. 523a has continuous design. See Offices in Geneva Nos. 165-166; Vienna Nos. 80-81.

Intl. Volunteer Day — A241

1988, May 6 *Perf. 13x14, 14x13*
524 A241 25c Education, vert. 60 25
525 A241 50c Vocational training 1.35 50

See Offices in Geneva Nos. 167-168; Vienna Nos. 82-83.

Health in Sports A242

Perf. 13½x13, 13x13½
1988, June 17 Litho.
526 A242 25c Cycling, vert. 85 38
527 A242 38c Marathon 1.50 58

See Offices in Geneva Nos. 169-170; Vienna Nos. 84-85.

Flag Type of 1980

1988, Sept. 16 Photo. *Perf. 12*
528 A185 25c Spain 60 25
529 A185 25c St. Vincent & Grenadines 60 25
530 A185 25c Ivory Coast 60 25
531 A185 25c Lebanon 60 25
a. Se-tenant block of 4 3.00
532 A185 25c Yemen (Arab Republic) 60 25
533 A185 25c Cuba 60 25
534 A185 25c Denmark 60 25
535 A185 25c Libya 60 25
a. Se-tenant block of 4 3.00
536 A185 25c Qatar 60 25
537 A185 25c Zaire 60 25
538 A185 25c Norway 60 25
539 A185 25c German Democratic Republic 60 25
a. Se-tenant block of 4 3.00
540 A185 25c Iran 60 25
541 A185 25c Tunisia 60 25
542 A185 25c Samoa 60 25
543 A185 25c Belize 60 25
a. Se-tenant block of 4 3.00
Nos. 528-543 (16) 9.60 4.00

See note after No. 340.

Universal Declaration of Human Rights, 40th Anniv. — A243

1988, Dec. 9 Photo. & Engr.
544 A243 25c multicolored 50 25

Souvenir Sheet

545 A243 $1 multicolored 1.75 1.00

See Offices in Geneva Nos. 171-172; Vienna Nos. 86-87.

World Bank — A244

1989, Jan. 27 Litho. *Perf. 13x14*
546 A244 25c Energy and nature 90 25
547 A244 45c Agriculture 1.70 45

See Offices in Geneva Nos. 173-174; Vienna Nos. 88-89.

UN Peace-Keeping Force, 1988 Nobel Peace Prize Winner — A245

1989, Mar. 17 Litho. *Perf. 14x13½*
548 A245 25c multicolored 1.25 25

See Offices in Geneva #175, Vienna #90.

Aerial Photograph of New York Headquarters — A246

1989, Mar. 17 *Perf. 14½x14*
549 A246 45c multicolored 90 45

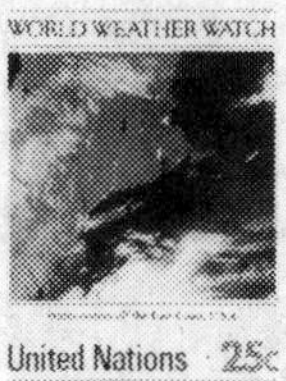

World Weather Watch, 25th Anniv. (in 1988) — A247

Satellite photographs: 25c, Storm system off the East Coast, US. 36c, Typhoon Abby in the North-West Pacific.

1989, Apr. 21 Litho. *Perf. 13x14*
550 A247 25c multicolored 1.00 25
551 A247 36c multicolored 2.00 36

See Offices in Geneva Nos. 176-177; Vienna Nos. 91-92.

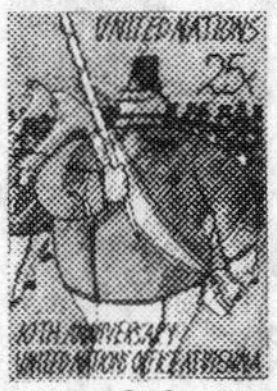

A248

A249

Photo. & Engr., Photo.

1989, Aug. 23 *Perf. 14*
552 A248 25c multicolored 3.00 25
553 A249 90c multicolored 2.00 60

Offices in Vienna, 10th anniv. See Offices in Geneva Nos. 178-179; Vienna Nos. 93-94.

Flag Type of 1980

1989, Sept. 22 Photo. *Perf. 12*
554 A185 25c Indonesia 70 25
555 A185 25c Lesotho 70 25
556 A185 25c Guatemala 70 25
557 A185 25c Netherlands 70 25
a. Se-tenant block of 4 3.25
558 A185 25c South Africa 70 25
559 A185 25c Portugal 70 25
560 A185 25c Morocco 70 25
561 A185 25c Syrian Arab Republic 70 25
a. Se-tenant block of 4 3.25
562 A185 25c Honduras 70 25
563 A185 25c Kampuchea 70 25
564 A185 25c Guinea-Bissau 70 25
565 A185 25c Cyprus 70 25
a. Se-tenant block of 4 3.25
566 A185 25c Algeria 70 25
567 A185 25c Brunei 70 25
568 A185 25c St. Kitts and Nevis 70 25
569 A185 25c United Nations 70 25
a. Se-tenant block of 4 3.25
Nos. 554-569 (16) 11.20 4.00

See note after No. 340.

Declaration of Human Rights, 40th Anniv. (in 1988) — A250

Paintings: 25c, *The Table of Universal Brotherhood,* by Jose Clemente Orozco. 45c, *Study for Composition II,* by Vassily Kandinsky.

1989, Nov. 17 Litho. *Perf. 13½*
570 A250 25c multicolored 60 25
571 A250 45c multicolored 1.10 45

Printed in sheets of 12+12 se-tenant labels containing Articles 1 (25c) or 2 (45c) inscribed in English, French or German.

See Nos. 582-583, 599-600, 616-617, 627-628; Offices in Geneva Nos. 180-181, 193-194, 209-210, 224-225, 234-235; Vienna Nos. 95-96, 108-109, 123-124, 139-140, 150-151.

Intl. Trade Center — A251

1990, Feb. 2 Litho. *Perf. 14½x15*
572 A251 25c multicolored 1.50 25

See Offices in Geneva #182; Vienna #97.

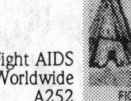

Fight AIDS Worldwide A252

Perf. 13½x12½
1990, Mar. 16 Litho.
573 A252 25c shown 75 25
574 A252 40c Shadow over crowd 1.75 40

See Offices in Geneva Nos. 184-185; Vienna Nos. 99-100.

Medicinal Plants — A253

1990, May 4 Photo. *Perf. 11½*
Granite Paper
575 A253 25c *Catharanthus roseus* 60 25
576 A253 90c *Panax quinquefolium* 2.25 90

See Offices in Geneva Nos. 186-187; Vienna Nos. 101-102.

United Nations, 45th Anniv. A254

1990, June 26 Litho. *Perf. 14½x13*
577 A254 25c shown 1.00 25
578 A254 45c "45," emblem 2.75 45

Souvenir Sheet

579 Sheet of 2, #577-578 3.25 1.20

See Offices in Geneva Nos. 188-189; Vienna Nos. 103-104.

Crime Prevention — A255

1990, Sept. 13 Photo. *Perf. 14*
580 A255 25c Crimes of youth 1.00 25
581 A255 36c Organized crime 2.50 36

See Offices in Geneva Nos. 191-192; Vienna Nos. 106-107.

Human Rights Type of 1989

Artwork: 25c, Fragment from the sarcophagus of Plotinus, c. 270 A.D. 45c, Combined Chambers of the High Court of Appeal by Charles Paul Renouard.

1990, Nov. 16 Litho. *Perf. 13½*
582 A250 25c black, gray & tan 50 25
583 A250 45c black & brown 90 45

See Offices in Geneva Nos. 193-194; Vienna Nos. 108-109.

Printed in sheets of 12+12 se-tenant labels containing Articles 7 (25c) or 8 (45c) inscribed in English, French or German.

Economic Commission for Europe A256

1991, Mar. 15 Litho. *Perf. 14*

584	A256 30c Two storks	1.00	30
585	A256 30c Woodpecker, ibex	1.00	30
586	A256 30c Capercaille, plover	1.00	30
587	A256 30c Falcon, marmot	1.00	30
a.	Block of 4, #584-587	5.00	1.20

Namibian Independence A257

1991, May 10 Litho. *Perf. 14*

588	A257 30c Dunes, Namib Desert	75	30
589	A257 50c Savanna	1.75	50

See Offices in Geneva Nos. 199-200; Vienna Nos. 114-115.

A258

The Golden Rule by Norman Rockwell — A259

1991, Sept. 11 Litho. *Perf. 13½*

590 A258 30c multicolored 75 30

Photo.

Perf. 12x11½

591 A259 50c multicolored 1.25 50

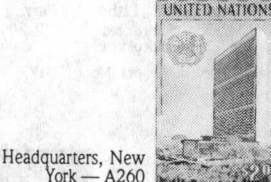

UN Headquarters, New York — A260

1991, May 10 Engr. *Perf. 13½*

592 A260 $2 dark blue 3.00 2.00

Rights of the Child A261

1991, June 14 Litho. *Perf. 14½*

593	A261 30c Children, globe	75	30
594	A261 70c Houses, rainbow	2.00	70

See Offices in Geneva Nos. 203-204; Vienna Nos. 117-118.

Banning of Chemical Weapons A262

Design: 90c, Hand holding back chemical drums.

1991, Sept. 11 Litho. *Perf. 13½*

595	A262 30c multicolored	1.00	30
596	A262 90c multicolored	2.75	90

See Offices in Geneva Nos. 205-206; Vienna Nos. 119-120.

UN Postal Administration, 40th Anniv. — A263

1991, Oct. 24 Litho. *Perf. 14x15*

597	A263 30c No. 1	1.00	30
598	A263 40c No. 3	1.50	40

See Offices in Geneva Nos. 207-208; Vienna Nos. 121-122.

Human Rights Type of 1989

Artwork: 30c, The Last of England, by Ford Madox Brown. 50c, The Emigration to the East, by Tito Salas.

1991, Nov. 20 Litho. *Perf. 13½*

599	A250 30c multicolored	90	30
600	A250 50c multicolored	1.50	50

See Offices in Geneva Nos. 209-210; Vienna Nos. 123-124.

Printed in sheets of 12+12 se-tenant labels containing Articles 13 (30c) or 14 (50c) inscribed in English, French or German.

World Heritage Type of 1984

Designs: 30c, Uluru Natl. Park, Australia. 50c, The Great Wall of China.

1992, Jan. 24 Litho. *Perf. 13*

Size: 35x28mm

601	A215 30c multicolored	85	30
602	A215 50c multicolored	1.40	50

See Offices in Geneva Nos. 211-212; Vienna Nos. 125-126.

Clean Oceans A264

1992, Mar. 13 Litho. *Perf. 14*

603	A264 29c Ocean surface	75	30
604	A264 29c Ocean bottom	75	30
a.	Pair, #603-604	1.50	60

Printed in sheets of 12 containing 6 #604a.

Earth Summit A265

Designs: No. 605, Globe at LR. No. 606, Globe at LL. No. 607, Globe at UR. No. 608, Globe at UL.

1992, May 22 Photo. *Perf. 11½*

605	A265 29c multicolored	60	30
606	A265 29c multicolored	60	30
607	A265 29c multicolored	60	30
608	A265 29c multicolored	60	30
a.	Block of 4, #605-608	2.40	1.20

See Offices in Geneva Nos. 216-219, Vienna Nos. 129-132.

Mission to Planet Earth — A266

Designs: No. 609, Satellites over city, sailboats, fishing boat. No. 610, Satellite over coast, passenger liner, dolphins, whale, volcano.

1992, Sept. 4 Photo. *Rouletted 8*

Granite Paper

609	A266 29c multicolored	2.25	30
610	A266 29c multicolored	2.25	30
a.	Pair, #609-610	6.50	60

See Offices in Geneva Nos. 220-221, Vienna Nos. 133-134.

Science and Technology for Development A267

Design: 50c, Animal, man drinking.

1992, Oct. 2 Litho. *Perf. 14*

611	A267 29c multicolored	58	30
612	A267 50c multicolored	1.00	50

See Offices in Geneva Nos. 222-223, Vienna Nos. 135-136.

UN University Building, Tokyo A268

UN Headquarters A269

Design: 40c, UN University Building, Tokyo, diff.

Perf. 14, 13½x13 (29c)

1992, Oct. 2 Litho.

613	A268 4c multicolored	20	15
614	A269 29c multicolored	75	30
615	A268 40c multicolored	1.10	40

Human Rights Type of 1989

Artwork: 29c, Lady Writing a Letter With her Maid, by Vermeer. 50c, The Meeting, by Ester Almqvist.

1992, Nov. 20 Litho. *Perf. 13½*

616	A250 29c multicolored	70	30
617	A250 50c multicolored	1.25	50

See Offices in Geneva Nos. 224-225; Vienna Nos. 139-140.

Printed in sheets of 12+12 se-tenant labels containing Articles 19 (29c) and 20 (50c) inscribed in English, French or German.

Aging With Dignity — A270

Designs: 29c, Elderly couple, family. 52c, Old man, physician, woman holding fruit basket.

1993, Feb. 5 Litho. *Perf. 13*

618	A270 29c multicolored	70	30
619	A270 52c multicolored	1.25	52

See Offices in Geneva Nos. 226-227; Vienna Nos. 141-142.

Endangered Species A271

Designs: No. 620, Hairy-nosed wombat. No. 621, Whooping crane. No. 622, Giant clam. No. 623, Giant sable antelope.

1993, Mar. 3 Litho. *Perf. 13x12½*

620	A271 29c multicolored	70	30
621	A271 29c multicolored	70	30
622	A271 29c multicolored	70	30
623	A271 29c multicolored	70	30
a.	Block of 4, #620-623	3.00	1.20

See Nos. 639-642, Offices in Geneva Nos. 228-231, 246-249; Vienna Nos. 143-146, 162-165.

Human Rights Type of 1989

Artwork: 29c, Shocking Corn, by Thomas Hart Benton. 35c, The Library, by Jacob Lawrence.

1993, June 11 Litho. *Perf. 13½*

627	A250 29c multicolored	90	30
628	A250 35c multicolored	1.15	35

See Offices in Geneva Nos. 234-235; Vienna Nos. 150-151.

Printed in sheets of 12 + 12 se-tenant labels containing Articles 25 (29c) and 26 (35c) inscribed in English, French or German.

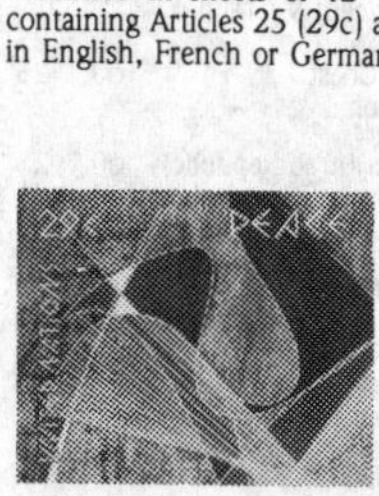

Intl. Peace Day — A274

Denomination at: No. 629, UL. No. 630, UR. No. 631, LL. No. 632, LR.

Rouletted 12½

1993, Sept. 21 Litho. & Engr.

629 A274 29c blue & multi 65 30
630 A274 29c blue & multi 65 30
631 A274 29c blue & multi 65 30
632 A274 29c blue & multi 65 30
a. Block of 4, #629-632 2.75 1.25

See Offices in Geneva Nos. 236-239; Vienna Nos. 152-155.

Environment-Climate — A275

Designs: No. 633, Chameleon. No. 634, Palm trees, top of funnel cloud. No. 635, Bottom of funnel cloud, deer, antelope. No. 636, Bird of paradise.

1993, Oct. 29 Litho. *Perf. 14½*

633 A275 29c multicolored 65 30
634 A275 29c multicolored 65 30
635 A275 29c multicolored 65 30
636 A275 29c multicolored 65 30
a. Strip of 4, #633-636 2.75 1.25

See Offices in Geneva Nos. 240-243; Vienna Nos. 156-159.

Intl. Year of the Family — A276

Designs: 29c, Mother holding child, two children, woman. 45c, People tending crops.

1994, Feb. 4 Litho. *Perf. 13.1*

637 A276 29c green & multi 60 30
638 A276 45c blue & multi 90 45

See Offices in Geneva Nos. 244-245; Vienna Nos. 160-161.

Endangered Species Type of 1993

Designs: No. 639, Chimpanzee. No. 640, St. Lucia Amazon. No. 641, American crocodile. No. 642, Dama gazelle.

1994, Mar. 18 Litho. *Perf. 12.7*

639 A271 29c multicolored 60 30
640 A271 29c multicolored 60 30
641 A271 29c multicolored 60 30
642 A271 29c multicolored 60 30
a. Block of 4, #639-642 2.50 1.25

See Offices in Geneva Nos. 246-249; Vienna Nos. 162-165.

Protection for Refugees — A277

1994, Apr. 29 Litho. *Perf. 14.3x14.8*

643 A277 50c multicolored 1.00 50

See Offices in Geneva No. 250; Vienna No. 166.

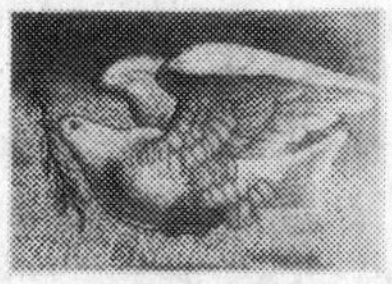

Dove of Peace — A278

Sleeping Child, by Stanislaw Wyspianski A279

Mourning Owl, by Vanessa Isitt A280

1994, Apr. 29 Litho. *Perf. 12.9*

644 A278 10c multicolored 20 15
645 A279 19c multicolored 38 18

Engr.

Perf. 13.1

646 A280 $1 red brown 2.00 1.00

Intl. Decade for Natural Disaster Reduction A281

Earth viewed from space, outline map of: No. 647, North America. No. 648, Eurasia. No. 649, South America, No. 650, Australia and South Asia.

1994, May 27 Litho. *Perf. 13.9x14.2*

647 A281 29c multicolored 60 30
648 A281 29c multicolored 60 30
649 A281 29c multicolored 60 30
650 A281 29c multicolored 60 30
a. Block of 4, #647-650 2.50 1.25

See Offices in Geneva Nos. 251-254; Vienna Nos. 170-173.

Population and Development — A282

Designs: 29c, Children playing. 52c, Family with house, car, other possessions.

1994, Sept. 1 Litho. *Perf. 13.2x13.6*

651 A282 29c multicolored 60 30
652 A282 52c multicolored 1.00 50

See Offices in Geneva Nos. 258-259; Vienna Nos. 174-175.

UNCTAD, 30th Anniv. — A283

1994, Oct. 28

653 A283 29c multicolored 60 30
654 A283 50c multi, diff. 1.00 50

See Offices in Geneva Nos. 260-261; Vienna Nos. 176-177.

AIR POST STAMPS

Plane and Gull — AP1

Swallows and UN Emblem AP2

Unwmk.

1951, Dec. 14 Engr. *Perf. 14*

C1 AP1 6c henna brown 15 15
C2 AP1 10c bright blue green 16 16
C3 AP2 15c deep ultra 28 20
C4 AP2 25c gray black 1.10 30

The 6c, 15c and 25c exist imperforate.

Airplane Wing and Globe — AP3

1957, May 27 *Perf. 12½x14*

C5 AP3 4c maroon 15 15

1959, Feb. 9 *Perf. 12½x13½*

C6 AP3 5c rose red 15 15

UN Flag and Plane — AP4

1959, Feb. 9 *Perf. 13½x14*

C7 AP4 7c ultramarine 15 15

Outer Space — AP5

UN Emblem — AP6

"Flight Across Globe" — AP8

Bird of Laurel Leaves — AP7

Jet Plane and Envelope — AP9

1963-64 Photo. *Perf. 11½*

C8 AP5 6c blk, blue & yel grn 15 15
C9 AP6 8c yel, ol green & red 15 15

Perf. 12½x12

C10 AP7 13c ultra, aqua, gray & car 18 16

Perf. 11½x12, 12x11½

C11 AP8 15c vio, buff, gray & pale green ('64) 35 20
a. Gray omitted —
C12 AP9 25c yel, org, gray, blue & red ('64) 65 30
Nos. C8-C12 (5) 1.48 96

Dates of issue: 6c, 8c, 13c, June 17, 1963; 15c, 25c, May 1. See Offices in Geneva #8.

Jet Plane and UN Emblem — AP10

1968, Apr. 18 Litho. *Perf. 13*

C13 AP10 20c multicolored 30 25

Wings, Envelopes and UN Emblem — AP11

1969, Apr. 21 Litho.

C14 AP11 10c org ver, org, yel & black 20 16

UN Emblem and Stylized Wing — AP12

Birds in Flight — AP13

Clouds AP14

"UN" and Plane — AP15

Lithograved and Engraved

1972, May 1 *Perf. 13x13½*

C15 AP12 9c lt blue, dark red & vio blue 15 15

Photo. *Perf. 14x13½*

C16 AP13 11c blue & multi 16 15

Perf. 13½x14

C17 AP14 17c yel, red & orange 22 18

Perf. 13

C18 AP15 21c silver & multi 28 22
Set value 60

Globe and Jet — AP16

Pathways Radiating from UN Emblem AP17

Bird in Flight, UN Headquarters AP18

Perf. 13, 12½x13 (18c)

1974, Sept. 16 **Litho.**

C19 AP16 13c multicolored 15 15
C20 AP17 18c multicolored 25 20
C21 AP18 26c blue & multi 35 30

Winged Airmail Letter — AP19

Symbolic Globe and Plane — AP20

1977, June 27 **Photo.** ***Perf. 14***

C22 AP19 25c grnsh blue & multi 32 25
C23 AP20 31c magenta 38 30

OFFICES IN GENEVA, SWITZERLAND

For use only on mail posted at the Palais des Nations (UN European Office), Geneva. Inscribed in French unless otherwise stated.

100 Centimes = 1 Franc

Types of UN Issues 1961-69 and

UN European Office, Geneva — G1

Designs: 5c, UN Headquarters, New York, and world map. 10c, UN flag. 20c, Three men united before globe. 50c, Opening words of UN Charter. 60c, UN emblem over globe. 70c, "UN" and UN emblem. 75c, "Flight Across Globe." 80c, UN Headquarters and emblem. 90c, Abstract group of flags. 1fr, UN Emblem. 2fr, Stylized globe and weather vane. 3fr, Statue by Henrik Starcke. 10fr, "Peace, Justice, Security."

Perf. 13 (5c, 70c, 90c); Perf. 12½x12 (10c); Perf. 11½ (20c-60c, 3fr); Perf. 11½x12 (75c); Perf. 13½x14 (80c); Perf. 14 (1fr); Perf. 12x11½ (2fr); Perf. 12 (10fr)

Photogravure; Lithographed & Embossed (1fr); Engraved (10fr)

1969-70 **Unwmk.**

1 A88 5c purple & multi 15 15
a. Green omitted —
2 A52 10c salmon & multi 15 15
3 A66 20c black & multi 15 15
4 G1 30c dk blue & multi 16 16
5 A77 50c ultra & multi 18 18
6 A54 60c dk brown, sal & gold 22 22
7 A104 70c red, black & gold 25 25
8 AP8 75c car rose & multi 30 30
9 A78 80c blue grn, red & yel 30 30
10 A45 90c blue & multi 30 30
11 A79 1fr lt & dk green 35 35
12 A67 2fr blue & multi 70 70
13 A97 3fr olive & multi 1.10 1.10
14 A3 10fr deep blue 3.50 3.50
Nos. 1-14 (14) 7.81 7.81

The 20c, 80c and 90c are inscribed in French. The 75c and 10fr carry French inscription at top, English at bottom.

Issue dates: 60c and 10fr, Apr. 17, 1970; 70c, 80c, 90c, 2fr, Sept. 22, 1970. Others, Oct. 4, 1969.

Sea Bed Type

Photogravure and Engraved

1971, Jan. 25 ***Perf. 13***

15 A114 30c green & multi 30 20

Refugee Type

1971, Mar. 12 **Litho.** ***Perf. 13x12½***

16 A115 50c dp car, dp org & black 38 30

Food Program Type

1971, Apr. 13 **Photo.** ***Perf. 14***

17 A116 50c dk purple, gold & grn 38 30

UPU Headquarters Type

1971, May 28 **Photo.** ***Perf. 11½***

18 A117 75c green & multi 30 40

Eliminate Discrimination Types

1971, Sept. 21 **Photo.** ***Perf. 13½***

19 A118 30c blue & multi 20 20
20 A119 50c multicolored 30 30

Picasso Type

1971, Nov. 19 **Photo.** ***Perf. 11½***

21 A122 1.10fr carmine & multi 45 50

Palais des Nations, Geneva G2

1972, Jan. 5 **Photo.** ***Perf. 11½***

22 G2 40c olive & multi 28 25

Nuclear Weapons Type

1972, Feb. 14 **Photo.** ***Perf. 13½x14***

23 A124 40c yel green, blk, rose & gray 25 45

World Health Day Type

Lithographed and Engraved

1972, Apr. 7 ***Perf. 13x13½***

24 A125 80c black & multi 40 50

Environment Type

Lithographed and Embossed

1972, June 5 ***Perf. 12½x14***

25 A126 40c multicolored 35 30
26 A126 80c multicolored 75 70

ECE Type

1972, Sept. 11 **Litho.** ***Perf. 13x13½***

27 A127 1.10fr red & multi 1.00 90

Art at UN Type

1972, Nov. 17 **Photo.** ***Perf. 12x12½***

28 A128 40c gold, brown & red 38 35
29 A128 80c gold, brown & olive 70 70

Disarmament Type

1973, Mar. 9 **Litho.** ***Perf. 13½x13***

30 A129 60c violet & multi 40 35
31 A129 1.10fr olive & multi 85 75

Nos. 30-31 exist imperf.

Drug Abuse Type

1973, Apr. 13 **Photo.** ***Perf. 13½***

32 A130 60c blue & multi 45 40

Volunteers Type

1973, May 25 **Photo.** ***Perf. 14***

33 A131 80c multicolored 45 70

Namibia Type

1973, Oct. 1 **Photo.** ***Perf. 13½***

34 A132 60c red & multi 55 45

Human Rights Type

1973, Nov. 16 **Photo.** ***Perf. 13½***

35 A133 40c ultra & multi 30 30
36 A133 80c olive & multi 60 60

ILO Headquarters Type

1974, Jan. 11 **Photo.** ***Perf. 14***

37 A134 60c violet & multi 50 45
38 A134 80c brown & multi 85 60

UPU Type

1974, Mar. 22 **Photo.** ***Perf. 14***

39 A135 30c multicolored 20 20
40 A135 60c multicolored 38 38

Art at UN Type

1974, May 6 **Photo.** ***Perf. 14***

41 A136 60c dark red & multi 38 38
42 A136 1fr green & multi 70 70

WPY Type

1974, Oct. 18 **Photo.** ***Perf. 14***

43 A140 60c brt green & multi 45 45
44 A140 80c brown & multi 55 55

Law of the Sea Type

1974, Nov. 22 **Photo.** ***Perf. 14***

45 A141 1.30fr blue & multi 1.00 95

Outer Space Type

1975, Mar. 14 **Litho.** ***Perf. 13***

46 A142 60c multicolored 35 35
47 A142 90c multicolored 55 55

IWY Type

1975, May 9 **Litho.** ***Perf. 15***

48 A143 60c multicolored 45 40
49 A143 90c multicolored 65 55

30th Anniv. Type

1975, June 26 **Litho.** ***Perf. 13***

50 A144 60c green & multi 42 40
51 A144 90c violet & multi 65 60

Souvenir Sheet

Imperf

52 Sheet of 2 1.00 1.00
a. A144 60c green & multi 35 35
b. A144 90c violet & multi 55 55

Namibia Type

1975, Sept. 22 **Photo.** ***Perf. 13½***

53 A145 50c multicolored 30 30
54 A145 1.30fr multicolored 1.00 70

Peace-keeping Operations Type

1975, Nov. 21 **Engr.** ***Perf. 12½***

55 A146 60c greenish blue 42 42
56 A146 70c bright violet 75 50

WFUNA Type

1976, Mar. 12 **Photo.** ***Perf. 14***

57 A152 90c multicolored 85 65

UNCTAD Type

1976, Apr. 23 **Photo.** ***Perf. 11½***

58 A153 1.10fr multicolored 80 80

Habitat Type

1976, May 28 **Photo.** ***Perf. 14***

59 A154 40c multicolored 28 28
60 A154 1.50fr violet & multi 1.00 1.00

UN Emblem, Post Horn and Rainbow — G3

1976, Oct. 8 **Photo.** ***Perf. 11½***

61 G3 80c tan & multi 90 90
62 G3 1.10fr lt green & multi 2.50 2.50

Sheets of 20.

Food Council Type

1976, Nov. 19 **Litho.** ***Perf. 14½***

63 A156 70c multicolored 55 55

WIPO Type

1977, Mar. 11 **Photo.** ***Perf. 14***

64 A157 80c red & multi 55 55

Drop of Water and Globe — G4

1977, Apr. 22 **Photo.** ***Perf. 13½x13***

65 G4 80c ultra & multi 75 50
66 G4 1.10fr dark car & multi 1.00 75

UN Water Conference, Mar del Plata, Argentina, Mar. 14-25.

Hands Protecting UN Emblem — G5

1977, May 24 **Photo.** ***Perf. 14***

67 G5 80c blue & multi 65 50
68 G5 1.10fr emerald & multi 1.00 75

UN Security Council.

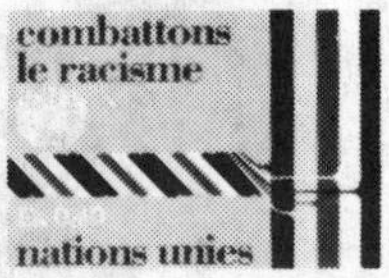

Colors of Five Races Spun into One Firm Rope — G6

1977, Sept. 19 **Litho.** ***Perf. 13***

69 G6 40c multicolored 30 30
70 G6 1.10fr multicolored 85 85

Fight against racial discrimination.

Atomic Energy Turning Partly into Olive Branch — G7

1977, Nov. 18 **Photo.**

71 G7 80c dark car & multi 50 50
72 G7 1.10fr Prus blue & multi 75 75

Peaceful uses of atomic energy.

"Tree" of Doves — G8

1978, Jan. 27 **Litho.** ***Perf. 14½***

73 G8 35c multicolored 25 20

Globes with Smallpox Distribution G9

1978, Mar. 31 **Photo.** ***Perf. 12x11½***

74 G9 80c yellow & multi 50 50
75 G9 1.10fr lt green & multi 75 75

Global eradication of smallpox.

Namibia Type

1978, May 5 **Photo.** ***Perf. 12***

76 A166 80c multicolored 1.20 60

Jets and Flight Patterns — G10

1978, June 12 **Photo.** ***Perf. 14***

77 G10 70c multicolored 60 48
78 G10 80c multicolored 1.00 52

International Civil Aviation Organization for "Safety in the Air."

General Assembly, Flags and Globe G11

1978, Sept. 15 Photo. *Perf. 13½*

79 G11	70c multicolored	60	55
80 G11	1.10fr multicolored	1.00	60

Technical Cooperation Type

1978, Nov. 17 Photo. *Perf. 14*

81 A169	80c multicolored	50	20

Seismograph Recording Earthquake G12

1979, Mar. 9 Photo. *Perf. 14*

82 G12	80c multicolored	60	60
83 G12	1.50fr multicolored	1.10	1.10

Office of the UN Disaster Relief Coordinator (UNDRO).

Children and Rainbow — G13

1979, May 4 Photo. *Perf. 14*

84 G13	80c multicolored	52	52
85 G13	1.10fr multicolored	90	90

International Year of the Child.

Namibia Type

1979, Oct. 5 Litho. *Perf. 13½*

86 A176	1.10fr multicolored	70	45

International Court of Justice, Scales — G14

1979, Nov. 9 Litho. *Perf. 13x13½*

87 G14	80c multicolored	48	48
88 G14	1.10fr multicolored	75	75

International Court of Justice, The Hague, Netherlands.

Economic Order Type

1980, Jan. 11 *Perf. 15x14½*

89 A179	80c multicolored	50	50

Women's Year Emblem G15

1980, Mar. 7 Litho. *Perf. 14½x15*

90 G15	40c multicolored	50	30
91 G15	70c multicolored	1.00	55

UN Decade for Women.

Peace-keeping Operations Type

1980, May 16 Litho. *Perf. 14x13*

92 A181	1.10fr blue & green	70	70

35th Anniv. Type and

Dove and "35" — G16

1980, June 26 Litho. *Perf. 13*

93 G16	40c multicolored	28	28
94 A183	70c multicolored	52	52

Souvenir Sheet

Imperf

95	Sheet of 2	60	80
a.	G16 40c multicolored	20	—
b.	A183 70c multicolored	40	—

35th anniv. of the UN.

ECOSOC Type and

Family Climbing Line Graph — G17

1980, Nov. 21 Litho. *Perf. 13½x13*

96 A186	40c multicolored	26	26
97 G17	70c multicolored	48	48

Palestinian Rights Type

1981, Jan. 30 Photo.

98 A188	80c multicolored	60	60

Disabled Type of UN, Vienna

1981, Mar. 6 Photo.

99 A190	40c multicolored	26	26
100 V4	1.50fr multicolored	1.00	1.00

Art Type

1981, Apr. 15 Photo. *Perf. 11½*

101 A191	80c multicolored	60	60

Energy Type

1981, May 29 Litho. *Perf. 13*

102 A192	1.10fr multicolored	75	85

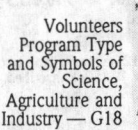

Volunteers Program Type and Symbols of Science, Agriculture and Industry — G18

1981, Nov. 13 Litho. *Perf. 13½x13*

103 A194	40c multicolored	35	30
104 G18	70c multicolored	60	55

Fight Against Apartheid — G19

Flower of Flags — G20

1982, Jan. 22 Photo. *Perf. 11½x12*

105 G19	30c multicolored	20	15
106 G20	1fr multicolored	70	35

Human Environment — G21

1982, Mar. 19 Litho. *Perf. 13½x13*

107 G21	40c multicolored	30	15
108 A199	1.20fr multicolored	95	30

Outer Space Type and

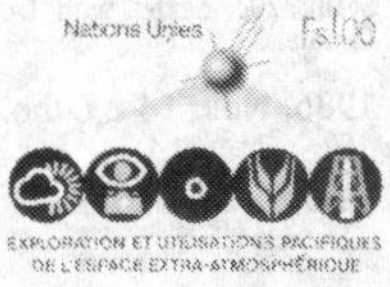

Satellite Applications of Space Technology G22

1982, June 11 Litho. *Perf. 13x13½*

109 A201	80c multicolored	60	15
110 G22	1fr multicolored	75	30

Conservation and Protection of Nature

1982, Nov. 19 Photo. *Perf. 14*

111 A202	40c Bird	30	15
112 A202	1.50fr Reptile	85	50

World Communications Year Type

1983, Jan. 28 Litho. *Perf. 13*

113 A204	1.20fr multicolored	1.10	1.00

Safety at Sea Type and

Life Preserver and Radar — G23

1983, Mar. 18 Litho. *Perf. 14½*

114 A205	40c multicolored	35	35
115 G23	80c multicolored	65	65

World Food Program Type

1983, Apr. 22 Engr. *Perf. 13½*

116 A207	1.50fr blue	1.00	50

Type of UN and

G24

1983, June 6 Litho. *Perf. 14*

117 A208	80c multicolored	50	65
118 G24	1.10fr multicolored	85	85

35th Anniv. of the Universal Declaration of Human Rights

G25 G26

Perf. 13½

1983, Dec. 9 Photo. Engr.

119 G25	40c Homo Humus Humanitas	45	38
120 G26	1.20fr Right to Create	1.25	70

Intl. Population Conference Type

1984, Feb. 3 Litho. *Perf. 14*

121 A212	1.20fr multicolored	1.00	70

Fishing G27

Women Farm Workers, Africa G28

1984, Mar. 15 Litho. *Perf. 14½*

122 G27	50c multicolored	55	25
123 G28	80c multicolored	95	40

World Food Day.

Valletta, Malta — G29

Los Glaciares Natl. Park, Argentina G30

1984, Apr. 18 Litho. *Perf. 14*

124 G29	50c multicolored	70	25
125 G30	70c multicolored	1.00	35

World Heritage. See Nos. 211-212.

G31

G32

1984, May 29 Photo. *Perf. 11½*

126 G31	35c multicolored	32	18
127 G32	1.50fr multicolored	1.50	75

Refugees.

International Youth Year — G33

1984, Nov. 15 Litho. *Perf. 13½*

128 G33	1.20fr multicolored	1.40	45

ILO Type of UN and

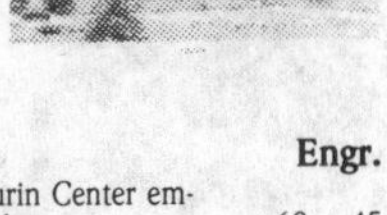

Turin Center — G34

1985, Feb. 1 Engr.

129 A220	80c Turin Center emblem	60	45
130 G34	1.20fr U Thant Pavilion	90	70

UN University Type

1985, Mar. 15 Photo. *Perf. 13½*

131 A221	50c Farmer, discussion group	60	28
132 A221	80c As above	90	45

Postman — G35

Doves — G36

1985, May 10 Litho. *Perf. 14*

133 G35 20c multicolored 24 15
134 G36 1.20fr multicolored 1.40 50

40th Anniv. Type

1985, June 26 Photo. *Perf. 12x11½*

135 A224 50c multicolored 65 20
136 A225 70c multicolored 95 28

Souvenir Sheet

Imperf

137 Sheet of 2 2.00 1.25
a. A224 50c multicolored 70 —
b. A225 70c multicolored 1.00 —

UNICEF Child Survival Campaign

Photo. & Engr.

1985, Nov. 22 *Perf. 13½*

138 A226 50c Three girls *95* 20
139 A226 1.20fr Infant drinking *2.00* 50

Africa in Crisis Type

Abstract painting by Alemayehou Gabremedhin.

1986, Jan. 31 Photo. *Perf. 11½*

140 A227 1.40fr Mother, hungry children 2.00 60

UN Development Program Type

1986, Mar. 14 Photo. *Perf. 13½*

141 A228 35c Erosion control 1.25 16
142 A228 35c Logging 1.25 16
143 A228 35c Lumber transport 1.25 16
144 A228 35c Nursery 1.25 16
a. Block of 4, #141-144 8.00 65

No. 144a has a continuous design.

Doves and Sun — G37

1986, Mar. 14 Litho. *Perf. 15x14½*

145 G37 5c multicolored 15 15

UN Stamp Collecting Type

Designs: 50c, UN Human Rights stamp. 80c, UN stamps.

1986, May 22 Engr. *Perf. 12½*

146 A229 50c dk green & hn brn 70 25
147 A229 80c dk green & yel org 1.10 42

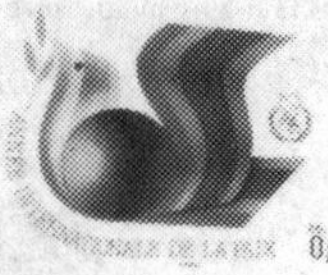

Flags and Globe as Dove — G38

Peace in French — G39

Photo. & Embossed

1986, June 20 *Perf. 13½*

148 G38 45c multicolored 60 25
149 G39 1.40fr multicolored 1.75 80

Intl. Peace Year.

WFUNA Anniv. Type

Souvenir Sheet

Designs: 35c, Abstract by Benigno Gomez, Honduras. 45c, Abstract by Alexander Calder (1898-1976), US. 50c, Abstract by Joan Miro (b. 1893), Spain. 70c, Sextet with Dove, by Ole Hamann, Denmark.

1986, Nov. 14 Litho. *Perf. 13x13½*

150 Sheet of 4 4.25 2.00
a. A232 35c multicolored 55 —
b. A232 45c multicolored 75 —
c. A232 50c multicolored 95 —
d. A232 70c multicolored 1.25 —

Trygve Lie Type

Photo. & Engr.

1987, Jan. 30 *Perf. 13½*

151 A233 1.40fr multicolored 1.90 90

Sheaf of Colored Bands, by Georges Mathieu — G40

Armillary Sphere, Palais des Nations — G41

Photo., Photo. & Engr. (No. 153)

Perf. 11½x12, 13½ (No. 153)

1987, Jan. 30

152 G40 90c multicolored 95 60
153 G41 1.40fr multicolored 1.50 90

Perf. 13½x12½

1987, Mar. 13 Litho.

154 A234 50c Construction 70 35
155 A234 90c Finishing interior 1.20 60

Fight Drug Abuse Type

1987, June 12 Litho. *Perf. 14½*

156 A235 80c Mother and child 1.00 55
157 A235 1.20fr Workers in rice paddy 1.50 80

UN Day Type

Designs: Multinational people in various occupations.

1987, Oct. 23 Litho. *Perf. 14½x15*

158 A236 35c multicolored 65 25
159 A236 50c multicolored 1.00 35

Immunize Every Child Type

1987, Nov. 20 Litho. *Perf. 15x14½*

160 A237 90c Whooping cough 1.25 60
161 A237 1.70fr Tuberculosis 2.50 1.15

IFAD Type

1988, Jan. 29 Litho. *Perf. 13½*

162 A238 35c Flocks 45 25
163 A238 1.40fr Fruit 1.75 1.10

G42

1988, Jan. 29 Photo. *Perf. 14*

164 G42 50c multicolored 65 40

Survival of the Forests Type

1988, Mar. 18 Litho. *Perf. 14x15*

165 A240 50c Pine forest *2.00* 50
166 A240 1.10fr as 50c *5.50* 1.50
a. Pair, #165-166 *7.50* 2.00

No. 166a has a continuous design.

Intl. Volunteer Day Type

Perf. 13x14, 14x13

1988, May 6 Litho.

167 A241 80c Agriculture, vert. 95 60
168 A241 90c Veterinary medicine 1.00 68

Health in Sports Type

Perf. 13½x13, 13x13½

1988, June 17 Litho.

169 A242 50c Soccer, vert. 75 35
170 A242 1.40fr Swimming 1.75 1.00

Human Rights Declaration Anniv. Type

1988, Dec. 9 Photo. & Engr. *Perf. 12*

171 A243 90c multicolored 1.10 60

Souvenir Sheet

172 A243 2fr multicolored 2.50 1.00

World Bank Type

1989, Jan. 27 Litho. *Perf. 13x14*

173 A244 80c Telecommunications 1.00 58
174 A244 1.40fr Industry 2.25 1.00

Peace-Keeping Force Type

1989, Mar. 17 Litho. *Perf. 14x13½*

175 A245 90c multicolored 1.35 60

World Weather Watch Anniv. Type

Satellite photographs: 90c, Europe under the influence of Arctic air. 1.10fr, Surface temperatures of sea, ice and land surrounding the Kattegat between Denmark and Sweden.

1989, Apr. 21 Litho. *Perf. 13x14*

176 A247 90c multicolored 1.50 60
177 A247 1.10fr multicolored 2.25 72

G43

G44

Photo. & Engr., Photo.

1989, Aug. 23 *Perf. 14*

178 G43 50c multicolored 85 30
179 G44 2fr multicolored 3.25 75

Offices in Vienna, 10th anniv.

Human Rights Type of 1989

Paintings and sculpture: 35c, *Young Mother Sewing,* by Mary Cassatt. 80c, *The Unknown Slave,* sculpture by Albert Mangones.

1989, Nov. 17 Litho. *Perf. 13½*

180 A250 35c multicolored 50 20
181 A250 80c multicolored 1.50 48

Printed in sheets of 12+12 se-tenant labels containing Articles 3 (35c) or 4 (80c) inscribed in French, German or English.

Intl. Trade Center Type

1990, Feb. 2 Litho. *Perf. 14½x15*

182 A251 1.50fr multicolored 2.50 82

G45

1990, Feb. 2 Photo. *Perf. 14x13½*

183 G45 5fr multicolored 5.25 3.25

G46

Fight AIDS Worldwide G46a

Perf. 13½x12½

1990, Mar. 16 Litho.

184 G46 50c multicolored 1.00 32
185 G46a 80c multicolored 1.75 50

Medicinal Plants Type

1990, May 4 Photo. *Perf. 11½*

Granite Paper

186 A253 90c *Plumeria rubra* 1.10 60
187 A253 1.40fr *Cinchona officinalis* 2.25 90

UN 45th Anniv. Type

"45," emblem and: 90c, Symbols of clean environment, transportation and industry. 1.10fr, Dove in silhouette.

1990, June 26 Litho. *Perf. 14½x13*

188 A254 90c multicolored 1.50 60
189 A254 1.10fr multicolored 2.25 75

Souvenir Sheet

190 A254 Sheet of 2, #188-189 3.75 2.65

Crime Prevention Type

1990, Sept. 13 Photo. *Perf. 14*

191 A255 50c Official corruption 1.00 36
192 A255 2fr Environmental crime 2.85 1.45

Human Rights Type of 1989

Paintings: 35c, The Prison Courtyard by Vincent Van Gogh. 90c, Katho's Son Redeems the Evil Doer From Execution by Albrecht Durer.

1990, Nov. 16 Litho. *Perf. 13½*

193 A250 35c multicolored 50 25
194 A250 90c black & brown 1.30 65

Printed in sheets of 12+12 se-tenant labels containing Articles 9 (35c) or 10 (90c) inscribed in French, German or English.

Economic Commission for Europe Type

1991, Mar. 15 Litho. *Perf. 14*

195 A256 90c Owl, gull 1.00 60
196 A256 90c Bittern, otter 1.00 60
197 A256 90c Swan, lizard 1.00 60
198 A256 90c Great crested grebe 1.00 60
a. Block of 4, #195-198 5.50 2.40

Namibian Independence Type

1991, May 10 Litho. *Perf. 14*

199 A257 70c Mountains 90 48
200 A257 90c Baobab tree 2.00 60

Ballots Filling Ballot Box — G47

UN Emblem — G48

1991, May 10 Litho. *Perf. 15x14½*

201 G47 80c multicolored 1.25 55
202 G48 1.50fr multicolored 2.50 1.00

G49

Rights of the Child — G50

Litho.

Perf. 14½

Perf. 15x14½

1991, June 14

203 G49 80c Hands holding infant 1.25 55
204 G50 1.10fr Children, flowers 2.00 75

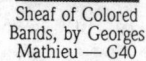

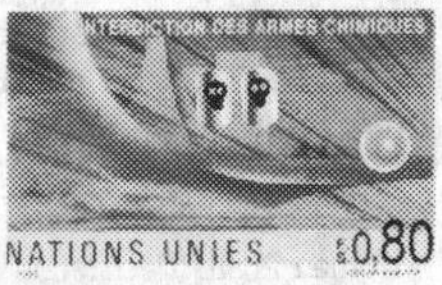

G51

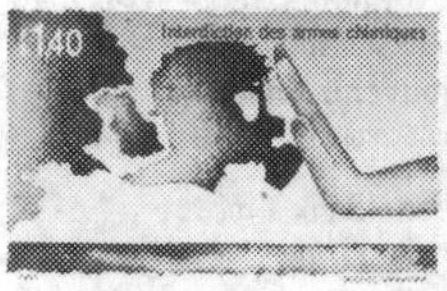

Banning of Chemical Weapons G52

1991, Sept. 11 Litho. *Perf. 13½*

205 G51 80c multicolored 1.25 52
206 G52 1.40fr multicolored 2.25 92

UN Postal Administration, 40th Anniv. Type

1991, Oct. 24 Litho. *Perf. 14x15*

207 A263 50c UN NY #7 1.00 35
208 A263 1.60fr UN NY #10 2.85 1.10

Human Rights Type of 1989

Artwork: 50c, Early Morning in Ro...1925, by Paul Klee. 90c, The Marriage of Giovanni Arnolfini and Fiovanna Cenami, by Jan Van Eyck.

1991, Nov. 20 Litho. *Perf. 13½*

209 A250 50c multicolored 85 35
210 A250 90c multicolored 1.50 62

Printed in sheets of 12+12 se-tenant labels containing Articles 15 (50c) and 16 (90c) inscribed in French, German or English.

World Heritage Type of 1984

Designs: 50c, Sagarmatha Natl. Park, Nepal. 1.10fr, Stonehenge, United Kingdom.

1992, Jan. 24 Litho. *Perf. 13*
Size: 35x28mm

211 G29 50c multicolored 1.25 35
212 G29 1.10fr multicolored 2.75 78

G53

1992, Jan. 24 *Perf. 15x14½*

213 G53 3fr multicolored 3.50 2.15

Clean Oceans Type

1992, Mar. 13 Litho. *Perf. 14*

214 A264 80c Ocean surface, diff. 1.05 52
215 A264 80c Ocean bottom, diff. 1.05 52
a. Pair, #214-215 2.50 1.05

Printed in sheets of 12 containing 6 #215a.

Earth Summit Type

Designs: No. 216, Rainbow. No. 217, Faces shaped as clouds. No. 218, Two sailboats. No. 219, Woman with parasol, sailboat, flowers.

1992, May 22 Photo. *Perf. 11½*

216 A265 75c multicolored 1.00 50
217 A265 75c multicolored 1.00 50
218 A265 75c multicolored 1.00 50
219 A265 75c multicolored 1.00 50
a. Block of 4, #216-219 4.00 2.00

Mission to Planet Earth Type

Designs: No. 220, Space station. No. 221, Probes near Jupiter.

1992, Sept. 4 Photo. *Rouletted 8*
Granite Paper

220 A266 1.10fr multicolored 2.00 85
221 A266 1.10fr multicolored 2.00 85
a. Pair, #220-221 4.50 1.70

Science and Technology Type

Designs: 90c, Doctor, nurse. 1.60fr, Graduate seated before computer.

1992, Oct. 2 Litho. *Perf. 14*

222 A267 90c multicolored 1.30 65
223 A267 1.60fr multicolored 2.30 1.15

Human Rights Type of 1989

Artwork: 50c, The Oath of the Tennis Court, by Jacques Louis David. 90c, Rocking Chair I, by Henry Moore.

1992, Nov. 20 Litho. *Perf. 13½*

224 A250 50c multicolored 90 35
225 A250 90c multicolored 1.60 62

Printed in sheets of 12+12 se-tenant labels containing Articles 21 (50c) and 22 (90c) inscribed in French, German or English.

Aging With Dignity Type

Designs: 50c, Older man coaching soccer. 1.50fr, Older man working at computer terminal.

1993, Feb. 5 Litho. *Perf. 13*

226 A270 50c multicolored 75 32
227 A270 1.50fr multicolored 2.25 98

Endangered Species Type

Designs: No. 228, Pongidae (gorilla). No. 229, Falco peregrinus (peregrine falcon). No. 230, Trichechus inunguis (Amazonian manatee). No. 231, Panthera uncia (snow leopard).

1993, Mar. 3 Litho. *Perf. 13x12½*

228 A271 80c multicolored 1.30 52
229 A271 80c multicolored 1.30 52
230 A271 80c multicolored 1.30 52
231 A271 80c multicolored 1.30 52
a. Block of 4, #228-231 5.20 2.10

Human Rights Type of 1989

Artwork: 50c, Three Musicians, by Pablo Picasso. 90c, Voice of Space, by Rene Magritte.

1993, June 11 Litho. *Perf. 13½*

234 A250 50c multicolored 70 35
235 A250 90c multicolored 1.20 60

Printed in sheets of 12 + 12 se-tenant labels containing Article 27 (50c) and 28 (90c) inscribed in French, German or English.

Intl. Peace Day Type

Denomination at: No. 236, UL. No. 237, UR. No. 238, LL. No. 239, LR.

Rouletted 12½
1993, Sept. 21 Litho. & Engr.

236 A274 60c purple & multi 85 40
237 A274 60c purple & multi 85 40
238 A274 60c purple & multi 85 40
239 A274 60c purple & multi 85 40
a. Block of 4, #236-239 3.50 1.60

Environment-Climate Type

Designs: No. 240, Polar bears. No. 241, Whale sounding. No. 242, Elephant seal. No. 243, Penguins.

1993, Oct. 29 Litho. *Perf. 14½*

240 A275 1.10fr multicolored 1.50 75
241 A275 1.10fr multicolored 1.50 75
242 A275 1.10fr multicolored 1.50 75
243 A275 1.10fr multicolored 1.50 75
a. Strip of 4, #240-243 6.00 3.00

Intl. Year of the Family Type of 1993

Designs: 80c, Parents teaching child to walk. 1fr, Two women and child picking plants.

1994, Feb. 4 Litho. *Perf. 13.1*

244 A276 80c rose violet & multi 1.10 55
245 A276 1fr brown & multi 1.40 70

Endangered Species Type of 1993

Designs: No. 246, Mexican prairie dog. No. 247, Jabiru. No. 248, Blue whale. No. 249, Golden lion tamarin.

1994, Mar. 18 Litho. *Perf. 12.7*

246 A271 80c multicolored 1.10 55
247 A271 80c multicolored 1.10 55
248 A271 80c multicolored 1.10 55
249 A271 80c multicolored 1.10 55
a. Block of 4, #246-249 4.50 2.25

Protection for Refugees Type of 1994

Design: 1.20fr, Hand lifting figure over chasm.

1994, Apr. 29 Litho. *Perf. 14.3x14.8*

250 A277 1.20fr multicolored 1.75 90

Intl. Decade for Natural Disaster Reduction Type of 1994

Earth seen from space, outline map of: No. 251, North America. No. 252, Eurasia. No. 253, South America. No. 254, Australia and South Pacific region.

1994, May 27 Litho. *Perf. 13.9x14.2*

251 A281 60c multicolored 85 42
252 A281 60c multicolored 85 42
253 A281 60c multicolored 85 42
254 A281 60c multicolored 85 42
a. Block of 4, #251-254 3.40 1.70

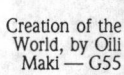

Palais des Nations, Geneva G54

Creation of the World, by Oili Maki — G55

1994, Sept. 1 Litho. *Perf. 14.3x14.6*

255 G54 60c multicolored 95 48
256 G55 80c multicolored 1.25 65
257 G54 1.80fr multi, diff. 2.75 1.40

Population and Development Type of 1994

Designs: 60c, People shopping at open-air market. 80c, People on vacation crossing bridge.

1994, Sept. 1 Litho. *Perf. 13.2x13.6*

258 A282 60c multicolored 95 48
259 A282 80c multicolored 1.25 65

UNCTAD Type of 1994

1994, Oct. 28

260 A283 80c multi, diff. 1.25 65
261 A283 1fr multi, diff. 1.65 85

OFFICES IN VIENNA, AUSTRIA

For use only on mail posted at the Vienna International Center for the UN and the International Atomic Energy Agency.

100 Groschen = 1 Schilling

Type of Geneva 1978, UN Types of 1961-72 and

Donaupark, Vienna — V1

Aerial View — V2

Perf. 11½
1979, Aug. 24 Photo. Unwmk.
Granite Paper

1 G8 50g multicolored 15 15
2 A52 1s multicolored 15 15
3 V1 4s multicolored 20 20
4 AP13 5s multicolored 25 25
5 V2 6s multicolored 35 30
6 A45 10s multicolored 50 45
Nos. 1-6 (6) 1.60 1.50

No. 6 has no frame.

Economic Order Type

1980, Jan. 11 Litho. *Perf. 15x14½*

7 A178 4s multicolored 1.00 50

Dove Type

1980, Jan. 11 Litho. *Perf. 13x13½*

8 A147 2.50s multicolored 30 16

Women's Year Emblem on World Map — V3

1980, Mar. 7 Litho. *Perf. 14½x15*

9 V3 4s lt green & dk green 40 15
10 V3 6s bister brown 60 25

UN Decade for Women.

Peace-keeping Operations Type

1980, May 16 Litho. *Perf. 14x13*

11 A182 6s multicolored 85 50

35th Anniv. Types of Geneva and UN

1980, June 26 Litho. *Perf. 13*

12 G16 4s multicolored 35 16
13 A184 6s multicolored 60 20

Souvenir Sheet
Imperf

14 Sheet of 2 75 70
a. G14 4s multicolored 25 —
b. A184 6s multicolored 45 —

35th anniv. of the UN.

ECOSOC Types of UN and Geneva

1980, Nov. 21 Litho. *Perf. 13½x13*

15 A187 4s multicolored 32 16
16 G17 6s multicolored 52 20

Palestinian Rights Type

1981, Jan. 30 Photo.

17 A188 4s multicolored 50 25

Disabled Type of UN and

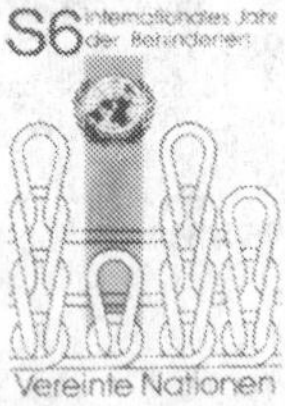

Interlocking Stitches — V4

1981, Mar. 6 Photo.

18 A189 4s multicolored 30 16
19 V4 6s multicolored 45 20

Art Type

1981, Apr. 15 Photo. *Perf. 11½*

20 A191 6s multicolored 50 25

Energy Type

1981, May 29 Litho. *Perf. 13*

21 A193 7.50s multicolored 70 35

Volunteers Program Types of UN and Geneva

1981, Nov. 13 Litho. *Perf. 13½x13*

22 A195 5s multicolored 42 20
23 G18 7s multicolored 55 30

"For a Better World" — V5

1982, Jan. 22 Photo. *Perf. 11½x12*

24 V5 3s multicolored 35 20

Human Environment Types of UN and Geneva

1982, Mar. 19 Litho. *Perf. 13½x13*

25 A200 5s multicolored 65 40
26 G21 7s multicolored 1.25 55

Outer Space Type of Geneva

1982, June 11 Litho. *Perf. 13x13½*

27 G22 5s multicolored 75 40

Conservation and Protection of Nature Type

1982, Nov. 19 Photo. *Perf. 14*

28	A202	5s Fish	52	40
29	A202	7s Animal	70	60

World Communications Year Type

1983, Jan. 28 Litho. *Perf. 13*

30	A203	4s multicolored	52	20

Safety at Sea Types of Geneva and UN

1983, Mar. 18 Litho. *Perf. 14½*

31	G23	4s multicolored	45	20
32	A206	6s multicolored	65	35

World Food Program Type

1983, Apr. 22 Engr. *Perf. 13½*

33	A207	5s green	55	16
34	A207	7s brown	75	25

Trade and Development Types of Geneva and UN

1983, June 6 Litho. *Perf. 14*

35	G24	4s multicolored	35	16
36	A209	8.50s multicolored	75	25

35th Anniv. of the Universal Declaration of Human Rights
V6 V7

Photogravure and Engraved

1983, Dec. 9 *Perf. 13½*

37	V6	5s The Second Skin	60	50
38	V7	7s Right to Think	90	70

Intl. Population Conference Type

1984, Feb. 3 Litho. *Perf. 14*

39	A212	7s multicolored	50	20

Field Irrigation V8

Pest Control V9

1984, Mar. 15 Litho. *Perf. 14½*

40	V8	4.50s multicolored	70	25
41	V9	6s multicolored	90	40

World Food Day.

Serengeti Park, Tanzania — V10

Ancient City of Shiban, People's Democratic Rep. of Yemen — V11

1984, Apr. 18 Litho. *Perf. 14*

42	V10	3.50s multicolored	35	25
43	V11	15s multicolored	1.50	90

World Heritage. See Nos. 125-126.

V12

V13

1984, May 29 Photo. *Perf. 11½*

44	V12	4.50s multicolored	70	25
45	V13	8.50s multicolored	1.40	50

Refugees.

International Youth Year — V14

1984, Nov. 15 Litho. *Perf. 13½*

46	V14	3.50s multicolored	60	20
47	V14	6.50s multicolored	1.10	40

ILO Type of Geneva

1985, Feb. 1 Engr. *Perf. 13½*

48	G34	7.50s U Thant Pavilion	1.25	45

UN University Type

1985, Mar. 15 Photo. *Perf. 13½*

49	A221	8.50s Rural scene, scientist	1.00	50

Ship of Peace — V15

Sharing Umbrella — V16

1985, May 10 Litho. *Perf. 14*

50	V15	4.50s multicolored	40	25
51	V16	15s multicolored	2.00	90

40th Anniv. Type

1985, June 26 Photo. *Perf. 12x11½*

52	A224	6.50s multicolored	60	35
53	A225	8.50s multicolored	1.00	48

Souvenir Sheet

Imperf

54		Sheet of 2	2.25	2.25
a.	A224	6.50s multicolored	80	—
b.	A225	8.50s multicolored	1.25	—

UNICEF Child Survival Campaign

Photogravure and Engraved

1985, Nov. 22 *Perf. 13½*

55	A226	4s Spoonfeeding children	85	20
56	A226	6s Mother hugging infant	1.40	30

Africa in Crisis Type

Abstract painting by Tesfaye Tessema.

1986, Jan. 31 Photo. *Perf. 11½*

57	A227	8s multicolored	1.00	45

UN Development Program Type

1986, Mar. 14 Photo. *Perf. 13½*

58	A228	4.50s Developing corp strains	2.00	22
59	A228	4.50s Animal husbandry	2.00	22
60	A228	4.50s Technical instruction	2.00	22
61	A228	4.50s Nutrition education	2.00	22
a.		Block of 4, #58-61	10.00	90

No. 61a has a continuous design.

UN Stamp Collecting Type

Designs: 3.50s, UN stamps. 6.50s, Engraver.

1986, May 22 Engr. *Perf. 12½*

62	A229	3.50s dk ultra & dk brown	50	16
63	A229	6.50s int blue & brt rose	1.00	25

Olive Branch, Rainbow, Earth — V17

Photogravure and Embossed

1986, June 20 *Perf. 13½*

64	V17	5s shown	75	32
65	V17	6s Doves, UN emblem	95	40

Intl. Peace Year.

WFUNA Anniv. Type
Souvenir Sheet

Designs: 4c, White Stallion, by Elisabeth von Janota-Bzowski, Germany. 5s, Surrealistic landscape by Ernst Fuchs, Austria. 6s, Geometric abstract by Victor Vasarely (b. 1908), France. 7s, Mythological abstract by Wolfgang Hutter (b. 1928), Austria.

1986, Nov. 14 Litho. *Perf. 13x13½*

66		Sheet of 4	4.25	3.00
a.	A232	4s multicolored	75	30
b.	A232	5s multicolored	85	35
c.	A232	6s multicolored	1.00	42
d.	A232	7s multicolored	1.25	50

Trygve Lie Type

Photogravure and Engraved

1987, Jan. 30 *Perf. 13½*

67	A233	8s multicolored	1.10	60

Shelter for the Homeless Type

Perf. 13½x12½

1987, Mar. 13 Litho.

68	A234	4s Family, homes	65	16
69	A234	9.50s Entering home	1.75	50

Fight Drug Abuse Type

1987, June 12 Litho. *Perf. 14½x15*

70	A235	5s Soccer players	75	40
71	A235	8s Family	1.25	65

Donaupark, Vienna — V18

Peace Embracing the Earth — V19

1987, June 12 *Perf. 14½x15*

72	V18	2s multicolored	30	16
73	V19	17s multicolored	1.75	1.40

UN Day Type

1987, Oct. 23 Litho. *Perf. 14½x15*

74	A236	5s multicolored	1.25	40
75	A236	6s multicolored	2.00	48

Immunize Every Child Type

1987, Nov. 20 *Perf. 15x14½*

76	A237	4s Polio	85	32
77	A237	9.50s Diphtheria	2.00	75

IFAD Type

1988, Jan. 29 Litho. *Perf. 13½*

78	A238	4s Grains	65	35
79	A238	6s Vegetables	90	50

Survival of the Forests Type

Deciduous forest in fall.

1988, Mar. 18 Litho. *Perf. 14x15*

80	A240	4s multicolored	*3.00*	1.00
81	A240	5s multicolored	*4.50*	2.00
a.		Pair, #80-81	*10.00*	4.00

No. 81a has a continuous design.

Intl. Volunteer Day Type

Perf. 13x14, 14x13

1988, May 6 Litho.

82	A241	6s Medical care, vert.	85	30
83	A241	7.50s Construction	1.10	45

Health in Sports Type

Perf. 13½x13, 13x13½

1988, June 17 Litho.

84	A242	6s Skiing, vert.	1.00	68
85	A242	8s Tennis	1.50	90

Human Rights Declaration Anniv. Type

1988, Dec. 9 Photo. & Engr. *Perf. 12*

86	A243	5s multicolored	90	52

Souvenir Sheet

87	A243	11s multicolored	1.50	1.90

World Bank Type

1989, Jan. 27 Litho. *Perf. 13x14*

88	A244	5.50s Transportation	1.10	62
89	A244	8s Health care, education	2.00	90

Peace-Keeping Force Type

1989, Mar. 17 Litho. *Perf. 14x13½*

90	A245	6s multicolored	1.35	65

World Weather Watch Anniv. Type

Designs: 4s, Helical cloud formation over Italy, the eastern Alps and parts of Yugoslavia. 9.50s, Rainfall in Tokyo, Japan.

1989, Apr. 21 Litho. *Perf. 13x14*

91	A247	4s multicolored	1.25	42
92	A247	9.50s multicolored	2.75	1.00

V20

V21

Photo. & Engr., Photo.

1989, Aug. 23 *Perf. 14*

93	V20	5s multicolored	4.00	48
94	V21	7.50s multicolored	1.00	70

Offices in Vienna, 10th anniv.

Human Rights Type

Paintings: 4s, *The Prisoners*, by Kathe Kollwitz. 6s, *Justice*, by Raphael.

1989, Nov. 17 Litho. *Perf. 13½*

95	A250	4s multicolored	80	30
96	A250	6s multicolored	1.20	20

Printed in sheets of 12+12 se-tenant labels containing Articles 5 (4s) or 6 (6s) inscribed in German, English or French.

Intl. Trade Center Type

1990, Feb. 2 Litho. *Perf. 14½x15*

97	A251	12s multicolored	1.90	1.25

Painting by Kurt Regschek V22

1990, Feb. 2 Litho. *Perf. 13x13½*

98	V22	1.50s multicolored	30	16

Fight AIDS Worldwide V23

Perf. 13½x12½

1990, Mar. 16 Litho.

99	V23	5s "AIDS"	1.00	55
100	V23	11s Stylized figures, ink blot	2.50	1.15

Medicinal Plants Type

1990, May 4 Photo. *Perf. 11½*

Granite Paper

101 A253	4.50s *Bixa orellana*	1.00	50
102 A253	9.50s *Momordica charantia*	2.50	1.10

UN 45th Anniv. Type

"45" and emblem.

1990, June 26 Litho. *Perf. 14½x13*

103 A254	7s multicolored	1.25	70
104 A254	9s multi, diff.	2.25	1.00

Souvenir Sheet

105 A254	Sheet of 2, #103-104	4.00	2.65

Crime Prevention Type

1990, Sept. 13 Photo. *Perf. 14*

106 A255	6s Domestic violence	1.25	65
107 A255	8s Crime against cultural heritage	2.35	90

Human Rights Type of 1989

Paintings: 4.50s, Before the Judge by Sandor Bihari. 7s, Young Man Greeted by a Woman Writing a Poem by Suzuki Harunobu.

1990, Nov. 16 Litho. *Perf. 13½*

108 A250	4.50s multicolored	90	38
109 A250	7s multicolored	2.25	60

Printed in sheets of 12+12 se-tenant labels containing Articles 11 (4.50s) or 12 (7s) inscribed in German, English or French.

Economic Commission for Europe Type

1991, Mar. 15 Litho. *Perf. 14*

110 A256	5s Weasel, hoopoe	1.00	55
111 A256	5s Warbler, swans	1.00	55
112 A256	5s Badgers, squirrel	1.00	55
113 A256	5s Fish	1.00	55
a.	Block of 4, #110-113	4.75	2.25

Namibian Independence Type

1991, May 10 Litho. *Perf. 14*

114 A257	6s Mountain, clouds	1.00	50
115 A257	9.50s Dune, Namib Desert	2.50	75

V24

1991, May 10 Litho. *Perf. 15x14½*

116 V24	20s multicolored	3.25	1.65

V25

Rights of the Child — V26

1991, June 14 Litho. *Perf. 14½*

117 V25	7s Stick drawings	1.40	58
118 V26	9s Child, clock, fruit	1.90	75

V27

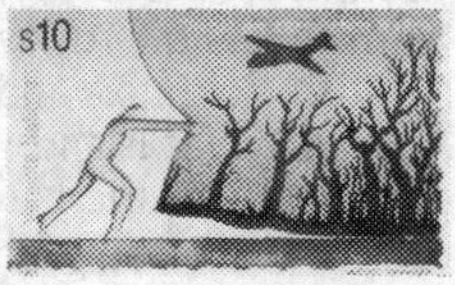

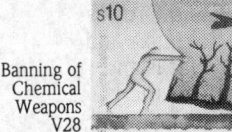

Banning of Chemical Weapons V28

1991, Sept. 11 Litho. *Perf. 13½*

119 V27	5s multicolored	1.00	40
120 V28	10s multicolored	2.00	80

UN Postal Administration, 40th Anniv. Type

1991, Oct. 24 Litho. *Perf. 14x15*

121 A263	5s UN NY No. 8	1.00	40
122 A263	8s UN NY No. 5	2.35	62

Human Rights Type of 1989

Artwork: 4.50s, Pre-columbian Mexican pottery, c. 600 A.D. 7s, Windows, 1912, by Robert Delaunay.

1991, Nov. 20 Litho. *Perf. 13½*

123 A250	4.50s black & brown	1.00	32
124 A250	7s multicolored	1.85	62

Printed in sheets of 12+12 se-tenant labels containing Articles 17 (4.50s) and 18 (7s) inscribed in German, English or French.

World Heritage Type of 1984

Designs: 5s, Iguacu Natl. Park, Brazil. 9s, Abu Simbel, Egypt.

1992, Jan. 24 Litho. *Perf. 13*

Size: 35x28mm

125 V10	5s multicolored	1.25	45
126 V10	9s multicolored	2.00	80

Clean Oceans Type

1992, Mar. 13 Litho. *Perf. 14*

127 A264	7s Ocean surface, diff.	1.20	60
128 A264	7s Ocean bottom, diff.	1.20	60
a.	Pair, #127-128	2.40	1.20

Printed in sheets of 12 containing 6 #128a.

Earth Summit Type

1992, May 22 Photo. *Perf. 11½*

129 A265	5.50s Man in space	95	48
130 A265	5.50s Sun	95	48
131 A265	5.50s Man fishing	95	48
132 A265	5.50s Sailboat	95	48
a.	Block of 4, #129-132	5.50	2.00

Mission to Planet Earth Type

Designs: No. 133, Satellite, person's mouth. No. 134, Satellite, person's ear.

1992, Sept. 4 Photo. *Rouletted 8*

Granite Paper

133 A266	10s multicolored	2.00	1.00
134 A266	10s multicolored	2.00	1.00
a.	Pair, #133-134	5.50	2.00

Science and Technology Type

Designs: 5.50s, Woman emerging from computer screen. 7s, Green thumb growing flowers.

1992, Oct. 2 Litho. *Perf. 14*

135 A267	5.50s multicolored	1.25	50
136 A267	7s multicolored	2.25	65

V29

Intl. Center, Vienna — V30

1992, Oct. 2 Litho. *Perf. 13x13½*

137 V29	5.50s multicolored	1.00	50

Perf. 13½x13

138 V30	7s multicolored	1.30	65

Human Rights Type of 1989

Artwork: 6s, Les Constructeurs, by Fernand Leger. 10s, Sunday Afternoon on the Island of La Grande Jatte, by Georges Seurat.

1992, Nov. 20 Litho. *Perf. 13½*

139 A250	6s multicolored	1.05	58
140 A250	10s multicolored	1.80	90

Printed in sheets of 12+12 se-tenant labels containing Articles 23 (6s) and 24 (10s) inscribed in German, English or French.

Aging With Dignity Type

Designs: 5.50s, Elderly couple, family working in garden. 7s, Older woman teaching.

1993, Feb. 5 Litho. *Perf. 13*

141 A270	5.50s multicolored	95	48
142 A270	7s multicolored	1.20	60

Endangered Species Type

Designs: No. 143, Equus grevyi (Grevy's zebra). No. 144, Spheniscus humboldti (Humboldt's penguins). No. 145, Varanus griseus (desert monitor). No. 146, Canis lupus (gray wolf).

1993, Mar. 3 Litho. *Perf. 13x12½*

143 A271	7s multicolored	1.25	60
144 A271	7s multicolored	1.25	60
145 A271	7s multicolored	1.25	60
146 A271	7s multicolored	1.25	60
a.	Block of 4, #143-146	5.00	2.40

Human Rights Type of 1989

Artwork: 5s, Lower Austrian Peasants' Wedding, by Ferdinand G. Waldmuller. 6s, Outback, by Sally Morgan.

1993, June 11 Litho. *Perf. 13½*

150 A250	5s multicolored	90	45
151 A250	6s multicolored	1.10	52

Printed in sheets of 12 + 12 se-tenant labels containing Article 29 (5s) and 30 (6s) inscribed in German, English or French.

Intl. Peace Day Type

Denomination at: No. 152, UL. No. 153, UR. No. 154, LL. No. 155, LR.

Rouletted 12½

1993, Sept. 21 Litho. & Engr.

152 A274	5.50s green & multi	95	48
153 A274	5.50s green & multi	95	48
154 A274	5.50s green & multi	95	48
155 A274	5.50s green & multi	95	48
a.	Block of 4, #152-155	4.00	2.00

Environment-Climate Type

Designs: No. 156, Monkeys. No. 157, Bluebird, industrial pollution, volcano. No. 158, Volcano, nuclear power plant, tree stumps. No. 159, Cactus, tree stumps, owl.

1993, Oct. 29 Litho. *Perf. 14½*

156 A275	7s multicolored	1.50	60
157 A275	7s multicolored	1.50	60
158 A275	7s multicolored	1.50	60
159 A275	7s multicolored	1.50	60
a.	Strip of 4, #156-159	6.00	2.50

Intl. Year of the Family Type of 1993

Designs: 5.50s, Adults, children holding hands. 8s, Two adults, child planting crops.

1994, Feb. 4 Litho. *Perf. 13.1*

160 A276	5.50s blue green & multi	90	45
161 A276	8s red & multi	1.25	60

Endangered Species Type of 1993

Designs: No. 162, Ocelot. No. 163, White-breasted silver-eye. No. 164, Mediterranean monk seal. No. 165, Asian elephant.

1994, Mar. 18 Litho. *Perf. 12.7*

162 A271	7s multicolored	1.40	70
163 A271	7s multicolored	1.40	70
164 A271	7s multicolored	1.40	70
165 A271	7s multicolored	1.40	70
a.	Block of 4, #162-165	5.75	3.00

Protection for Refugees Type of 1994

Design: 12s, Protective hands surround group of refugees.

1994, Apr. 29 Litho. *Perf. 14.3x14.8*

166 A277	12s multicolored	2.00	1.00

V32

V33

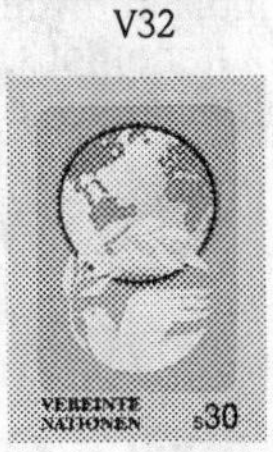

V34

1994, Apr. 29 Litho. *Perf. 12.9*

167 V32	50g multicolored	15	15
168 V33	4s multicolored	68	32
169 V34	30s multicolored	5.00	2.50

Intl. Decade for Natural Disaster Reduction Type of 1994

Earth seen from space, outline map of: No. 170, North America. No. 171, Eurasia. No. 172, South America. No. 173, Australia and South Asia.

1994, May 27 Litho. *Perf. 13.9x14.2*

170 A281	6s multicolored	1.00	50
171 A281	6s multicolored	1.00	50
172 A281	6s multicolored	1.00	50
173 A281	6s multicolored	1.00	50
a.	Block of 4, #170-173	4.00	2.00

Population and Development Type of 1994

Designs: 5.50s, Women teaching, running machine tool, coming home to family. 7s, Family on tropical island.

1994, Sept. 1 Litho. *Perf. 13.2x13.6*

174 A282	5.50s multicolored	1.00	50
175 A282	7s multicolored	1.25	65

UNCTAD Type of 1994

1994, Oct. 28

176 A283	6s multi, diff.	1.10	55
177 A283	7s multi, diff.	1.25	65

United Nations Offices in Geneva stamps can be mounted in the Scott U.N. Singles and Postal Stationery album.

United Nations Offices in Vienna stamps can be mounted in the Scott U.N. Singles and Postal Stationery album.

British Commonwealth of Nations

Dominions, Colonies, Territories, Offices and Independent Members

Comprising stamps of the British Commonwealth and associated nations.

A strict observance of technicalities would bar some or all of the stamps listed under Burma, Ireland, Kuwait, Nepal, New Republic, Orange Free State, Samoa, South Africa, South-West Africa, Stellaland, Sudan, Swaziland, the two Transvaal Republics and others but these are included for the convenience of collectors.

1. Great Britain

Great Britain: Including England, Scotland, Wales and Northern Ireland.

2. The Dominions, Present and Past

AUSTRALIA

The Commonwealth of Australia was proclaimed on January 1, 1901. It consists of six former colonies as follows:

New South Wales
Queensland
South Australia
Victoria
Tasmania
Western Australia

Territories belonging to, or administered by Australia: Australian Antarctic Territory, Christmas Island, Cocos (Keeling) Islands, Nauru, New Guinea, Norfolk Island, Papua New Guinea.

CANADA

The Dominion of Canada was created by the British North America Act in 1867. The following provinces were former separate colonies and issued postage stamps:

British Columbia and Vancouver Island
New Brunswick
Newfoundland
Nova Scotia
Prince Edward Island

FIJI

The colony of Fiji became an independent nation with dominion status on Oct. 10, 1970.

GHANA

This state came into existence Mar. 6, 1957, with dominion status. It consists of the former colony of the Gold Coast and the Trusteeship Territory of Togoland. Ghana became a republic July 1, 1960.

INDIA

The Republic of India was inaugurated on January 26, 1950. It succeeded the Dominion of India which was proclaimed August 15, 1947, when the former Empire of India was divided into Pakistan and the Union of India. The Republic is composed of about 40 predominantly Hindu states of three classes: governor's provinces, chief commissioner's provinces and princely states. India also has various territories, such as the Andaman and Nicobar Islands.

The old Empire of India was a federation of British India and the native states. The more important princely states were autonomous. Of the more than 700 Indian states, these 43 are familiar names to philatelists because of their postage stamps.

CONVENTION STATES

Chamba
Faridkot
Gwalior
Jhind
Nabha
Patiala

NATIVE FEUDATORY STATES

Alwar
Bahawalpur
Bamra
Barwani
Bhopal
Bhor
Bijawar
Bundi
Bussahir
Charkhari
Cochin
Dhar
Duttia
Faridkot (1879-85)
Hyderabad
Idar
Indore
Jaipur
Jammu
Jammu and Kashmir
Jasdan
Jhalawar
Jhind (1875-76)
Kashmir
Kishangarh
Las Bela
Morvi
Nandgaon
Nowanuggur
Orchha
Poonch
Rajpeepla
Sirmur
Soruth
Travancore
Wadhwan

NEW ZEALAND

Became a dominion on September 26, 1907. The following islands and territories are, or have been, administered by New Zealand:

Aitutaki
Cook Islands (Rarotonga)
Niue
Penrhyn
Ross Dependency
Samoa (Western Samoa)
Tokelau Islands

PAKISTAN

The Republic of Pakistan was proclaimed March 23, 1956. It succeeded the Dominion which was proclaimed August 15, 1947. It is made up of all or part of several Moslem provinces and various districts of the former Empire of India, including Bahawalpur and Las Bela. Pakistan withdrew from the Commonwealth in 1972.

SOUTH AFRICA

Under the terms of the South African Act (1909) the self-governing colonies of Cape of Good Hope, Natal, Orange River Colony and Transvaal united on May 31, 1910, to form the Union of South Africa. It became an independent republic May 3, 1961.

Under the terms of the Treaty of Versailles, South-West Africa, formerly German South-West Africa, was mandated to the Union of South Africa.

SRI LANKA (CEYLON)

The Dominion of Ceylon was proclaimed February 4, 1948. The island had been a Crown Colony from 1802 until then. On May 22, 1972, Ceylon became the Republic of Sri Lanka.

3. Colonies, Past and Present; Controlled Territory and Independent Members of the Commonwealth

Aden
Aitutaki
Antigua
Ascension
Bahamas
Bahrain
Bangladesh
Barbados
Barbuda
Basutoland
Batum
Bechuanaland
Bechuanaland Prot.
Belize
Bermuda
Botswana
British Antarctic Territory
British Central Africa
British Columbia and Vancouver Island
British East Africa
British Guiana

British Honduras
British Indian Ocean Territory
British New Guinea
British Solomon Islands
British Somaliland
Brunei
Burma
Bushire
Cameroons
Cape of Good Hope
Cayman Islands
Christmas Island
Cocos (Keeling) Islands
Cook Islands
Crete,
British Administration
Cyprus
Dominica
East Africa & Uganda
Protectorates
Egypt (see Vol. III)
Falkland Islands
Fiji
Gambia
German East Africa
Gibraltar
Gilbert Islands
Gilbert & Ellice Islands
Gold Coast
Grenada
Griqualand West
Guernsey
Guyana
Heligoland
Hong Kong
Indian Native States
(see India)
Ionian Islands
Jamaica
Jersey
Kenya
Kenya, Uganda & Tanzania
Kuwait
Labuan
Lagos
Leeward Islands
Lesotho
Madagascar
Malawi
Malaya
Federated Malay States
Johore
Kedah
Kelantan
Malacca
Negri Sembilan
Pahang
Penang
Perak
Perlis
Selangor
Singapore
Sungei Ujong
Trengganu
Malaysia
Maldive Islands
Malta
Man, Isle of
Mauritius
Mesopotamia
Montserrat
Muscat
Namibia
Natal
Nauru
Nevis
New Britain
New Brunswick
Newfoundland
New Guinea
New Hebrides
New Republic
New South Wales
Niger Coast Protectorate
Nigeria
Niue
Norfolk Island
North Borneo
Northern Nigeria
Northern Rhodesia
North West Pacific Islands
Nova Scotia
Nyasaland Protectorate
Oman
Orange River Colony
Palestine
Papua New Guinea
Penrhyn Island
Pitcairn Islands
Prince Edward Island
Queensland
Rhodesia
Rhodesia & Nyasaland
Ross Dependency
Sabah
St. Christopher
St. Helena
St. Kitts
St. Kitts-Nevis-Anguilla
St. Lucia
St. Vincent
Samoa
Sarawak
Seychelles
Sierra Leone
Solomon Islands
Somaliland Protectorate
South Arabia
South Australia
South Georgia
Southern Nigeria
Southern Rhodesia
South-West Africa
Stellaland
Straits Settlements
Sudan
Swaziland
Tanganyika
Tanzania
Tasmania
Tobago
Togo
Tokelau Islands
Tonga
Transvaal
Trinidad
Trinidad and Tobago
Tristan da Cunha
Trucial States
Turks and Caicos
Turks Islands
Tuvalu
Uganda
United Arab Emirates
Victoria
Virgin Islands
Western Australia
Zambia
Zanzibar
Zululand

POST OFFICES IN FOREIGN COUNTRIES

Africa
East Africa Forces
Middle East Forces
Bangkok
China
Morocco
Turkish Empire

Common Design Types

Pictured in this section are issues where one illustration has been used for a number of countries in the Catalogue. Not included in this section are overprinted stamps or those issues which are illustrated in each country.

BRITISH COMMONWEALTH OF NATIONS

The listings follow established trade practices when these issues are offered as units by dealers. The Peace issue, for example, includes only one stamp from the Indian state of Hyderabad. The U.P.U. issue includes the Egypt set. Pairs are included for those issues with bilingual designs se-tenant.

Silver Jubilee Issue

Windsor Castle and King George V
CD301

25th anniversary of the reign of King George V.

1935

Antigua 77-80
Ascension 33-36
Bahamas 92-95
Barbados 186-189
Basutoland 11-14
Bechuanaland Protectorate 117-120
Bermuda 100-103
British Guiana 223-226
British Honduras 108-111
Cayman Islands 81-84
Ceylon 260-263
Cyprus 136-139
Dominica 90-93
Falkland Islands 77-80
Fiji 110-113
Gambia 125-128
Gibraltar 100-103
Gilbert & Ellice Islands 33-36
Gold Coast 108-111
Grenada 124-127
Hong Kong 147-150
Jamaica 109-112
Kenya, Uganda, Tanganyika 42-45
Leeward Islands 96-99
Malta 184-187
Mauritius 204-207
Montserrat 85-88
Newfoundland 226-229
Nigeria 34-37
Northern Rhodesia 18-21
Nyasaland Protectorate 47-50
St. Helena 111-114
St. Kitts-Nevis 72-75
St. Lucia 91-94
St. Vincent 134-137
Seychelles 118-121
Sierra Leone 166-169
Solomon Islands 60-63
Somaliland Protectorate 77-80
Straits Settlements 213-216
Swaziland 20-23
Trinidad & Tobago 43-46
Turks & Caicos Islands 71-74
Virgin Islands 69-72

The following have different designs but are included in the omnibus set:

Great Britain 226-229
Offices in Morocco 67-70, 226-229, 422-425, 508-510
Australia 152-154
Canada 211-216
Cook Islands 98-100
India 142-148
Nauru 31-34
New Guinea 46-47
New Zealand 199-201
Niue 67-69
Papua 114-117
Samoa 163-165
South Africa 68-71
Southern Rhodesia 33-36
South-West Africa 121-124
249 stamps, Never Hinged $925.

Coronation Issue

Queen Elizabeth and King George VI
CD302

1937

Aden 13-15
Antigua 81-83
Ascension 37-39
Bahamas 97-99
Barbados 190-192
Basutoland 15-17
Bechuanaland Protectorate 121-123
Bermuda 115-117
British Guiana 227-229
British Honduras 112-114
Cayman Islands 97-99
Ceylon 275-277
Cyprus 140-142
Dominica 94-96
Falkland Islands 81-83
Fiji 114-116
Gambia 129-131
Gibraltar 104-106
Gilbert & Ellice Islands 37-39
Gold Coast 112-114
Grenada 128-130
Hong Kong 151-153
Jamaica 113-115
Kenya, Uganda, Tanganyika 60-62
Leeward Islands 100-102
Malta 188-190
Mauritius 208-210
Montserrat 89-91
Newfoundland 230-232
Nigeria 50-52
Northern Rhodesia 22-24
Nyasaland Protectorate 51-53
St. Helena 115-117
St. Kitts-Nevis 76-78
St. Lucia 107-109
St. Vincent 138-140
Seychelles 122-124
Sierra Leone 170-172
Solomon Islands 64-66
Somaliland Protectorate 81-83
Straits Settlements 235-237
Swaziland 24-26
Trinidad & Tobago 47-49
Turks & Caicos Islands 75-77
Virgin Islands 73-75

The following have different designs but are included in the omnibus set:

Great Britain 234
Offices in Morocco 82, 439, 514
Canada 237
Cook Islands 109-111
Nauru 35-38
Newfoundland 233-243
New Guinea 48-51
New Zealand 223-225
Niue 70-72
Papua 118-121
South Africa 74-78
Southern Rhodesia 38-41
South-West Africa 125-132
202 stamps, Never Hinged $65.

Peace Issue

King George VI and
Parliament Buildings, London – CD303

Return to peace at the close of World War II.

1945-46

Aden 28-29
Antigua 96-97
Ascension 50-51
Bahamas 130-131
Barbados 207-208
Bermuda 131-132
British Guiana 242-243
British Honduras 127-128
Cayman Islands 112-113
Ceylon 293-294
Cyprus 156-157
Dominica 112-113
Falkland Islands 97-98
Falkland Islands Dep. 1L9-1L10
Fiji 137-138
Gambia 144-145
Gibraltar 119-120
Gilbert & Ellice Islands 52-53
Gold Coast 128-129
Grenada 143-144
Jamaica 136-137
Kenya, Uganda, Tanganyika 90-91
Leeward Islands 116-117
Malta 206-207
Mauritius 223-224
Montserrat 104-105
Nigeria 71-72
Northern Rhodesia 46-47
Nyasaland Protectorate 82-83
Pitcairn Island 9-10
St. Helena 128-129
St. Kitts-Nevis 91-92
St. Lucia 127-128
St. Vincent 152-153
Seychelles 149-150
Sierra Leone 186-187
Solomon Islands 80-81
Somaliland Protectorate 108-109
Trinidad & Tobago 62-63
Turks & Caicos Islands 90-91
Virgin Islands 88-89

The following have different designs but are included in the omnibus set:

Great Britain 264-265
Offices in Morocco 523-524
Aden
Kathiri State of Seiyun 12-13
Qu'aiti State of Shihr and Mukalla 12-13
Australia 200-202
Basutoland 29-31
Bechuanaland Protectorate 137-139
Burma 66-69
Cook Islands 127-130
Hong Kong 174-175
India 195-198
Hyderabad 51
New Zealand 247-257
Niue 90-93
Pakistan-Bahawalpur O16
Samoa 191-194
South Africa 100-102
Southern Rhodesia 67-70
South-West Africa 153-155
Swaziland 38-40
Zanzibar 222-223
164 stamps, Never Hinged $35.

Silver Wedding Issue

King George VI and Queen Elizabeth
CD304 CD305

1948-49

Aden 30-31
Kathiri State of Seiyun 14-15
Qu'aiti State of Shihr and Mukalla 14-15
Antigua 98-99
Ascension 52-53
Bahamas 148-149
Barbados 210-211
Basutoland 39-40
Bechuanaland Protectorate 147-148
Bermuda 133-134
British Guiana 244-245
British Honduras 129-130
Cayman Islands 116-117
Cyprus 158-159
Dominica 114-115
Falkland Islands 99-100
Falkland Islands Dep. 1L11-1L12
Fiji 139-140
Gambia 146-147
Gibraltar 121-122
Gilbert & Ellice Islands 54-55
Gold Coast 142-143
Grenada 145-146
Hong Kong 178-179
Jamaica 138-139
Kenya, Uganda, Tanganyika 92-93
Leeward Islands 118-119
Malaya
Johore 128-129
Kedah 55-56
Kelantan 44-45
Malacca 1-2
Negri Sembilan 36-37
Pahang 44-45
Penang 1-2
Perak 99-100
Perlis 1-2
Selangor 74-75
Trengganu 47-48
Malta 223-224
Mauritius 229-230
Montserrat 106-107
Nigeria 73-74
North Borneo 238-239
Northern Rhodesia 48-49
Nyasaland Protectorate 85-86
Pitcairn Island 11-12
St. Helena 130-131
St. Kitts-Nevis 93-94
St. Lucia 129-130
St. Vincent 154-155
Sarawak 174-175
Seychelles 151-152
Sierra Leone 188-189
Singapore 21-22
Solomon Islands 82-83
Somaliland Protectorate 110-111
Swaziland 48-49
Trinidad & Tobago 64-65
Turks & Caicos Islands 92-93
Virgin Islands 90-91
Zanzibar 224-225

The following have different designs but are included in the omnibus set:

Great Britain 267-268
Offices in Morocco 93-94, 525-526
Bahrain 62-63
Kuwait 82-83
Oman 25-26
South Africa 106
South-West Africa 159
138 stamps, Never Hinged $1,100.

U.P.U. Issue

Mercury and Symbols of Communications – CD306

Plane, Ship and Hemispheres – CD307

Mercury Scattering Letters over Globe
CD308

U.P.U. Monument, Bern – CD309

Universal Postal Union, 75th anniversary.

1949

Aden ... 32-35
Kathiri State of Seiyun ... 16-19
Qu'aiti State of Shihr and Mukalla ... 16-19
Antigua ... 100-103
Ascension ... 57-60
Bahamas ... 150-153
Barbados ... 212-215
Basutoland ... 41-44
Bechuanaland Protectorate ... 149-152
Bermuda ... 138-141
British Guiana ... 246-249
British Honduras ... 137-140
Brunei ... 79-82
Cayman Islands ... 118-121
Cyprus ... 160-163
Dominica ... 116-119
Falkland Islands ... 103-106
Falkland Islands Dep. ... 1L14-1L17
Fiji ... 141-144
Gambia ... 148-151
Gibraltar ... 123-126
Gilbert & Ellice Islands ... 56-59
Gold Coast ... 144-147
Grenada ... 147-150
Hong Kong ... 180-183
Jamaica ... 142-145
Kenya, Uganda, Tanganyika ... 94-97
Leeward Islands ... 126-129
Malaya
Johore ... 151-154
Kedah ... 57-60
Kelantan ... 46-49
Malacca ... 18-21
Negri Sembilan ... 59-62
Pahang ... 46-49
Penang ... 23-26
Perak ... 101-104
Perlis ... 3-6
Selangor ... 76-79
Trengganu ... 49-52
Malta ... 225-228
Mauritius ... 231-234
Montserrat ... 108-111
New Hebrides ... 62-65
Nigeria ... 75-78
North Borneo ... 240-243
Northern Rhodesia ... 50-53
Nyasaland Protectorate ... 87-90
Pitcairn Islands ... 13-16
St. Helena ... 132-135
St. Kitts-Nevis ... 95-98
St. Lucia ... 131-134
St. Vincent ... 170-173
Sarawak ... 176-179
Seychelles ... 153-156
Sierra Leone ... 190-193
Singapore ... 23-26
Solomon Islands ... 84-87
Somaliland Protectorate ... 112-115
Southern Rhodesia ... 71-72
Swaziland ... 50-53
Tonga ... 87-90
Trinidad & Tobago ... 66-69
Turks & Caicos Islands ... 101-104
Virgin Islands ... 92-95
Zanzibar ... 226-229

The following have different designs but are included in the omnibus set:

Great Britain ... 276-279
Offices in Morocco ... 546-549
Australia ... 223
Bahrain ... 68-71
Burma ... 116-121
Ceylon ... 304-306
Egypt ... 281-283
India ... 223-226
Kuwait ... 89-92
Oman ... 31-34
Pakistan-Bahawalpur ... 26-29, O25-O28
South Africa ... 109-111
South-West Africa ... 160-162
315 stamps, Never Hinged $250.

University Issue

Arms of University College CD310

Alice, Princess of Athlone CD311

1948 opening of University College of the West Indies at Jamaica.

1951

Antigua ... 104-105
Barbados ... 228-229
British Guiana ... 250-251
British Honduras ... 141-142
Dominica ... 120-121
Grenada ... 164-165
Jamaica ... 146-147
Leeward Islands ... 130-131
Montserrat ... 112-113
St. Kitts-Nevis ... 105-106
St. Lucia ... 149-150
St. Vincent ... 174-175
Trinidad & Tobago ... 70-71
Virgin Islands ... 96-97
28 stamps

Coronation Issue

Queen Elizabeth II CD312

1953

Aden ... 47
Kathiri State of Seiyun ... 28
Qu'aiti State of Shihr and Mukalla ... 28
Antigua ... 106
Ascension ... 61
Bahamas ... 157
Barbados ... 234
Basutoland ... 45
Bechuanaland Protectorate ... 153
Bermuda ... 142
British Guiana ... 252
British Honduras ... 143
Cayman Islands ... 150
Cyprus ... 167
Dominica ... 141
Falkland Islands ... 121
Falkland Islands Dependencies ... 1L18
Fiji ... 145
Gambia ... 152
Gibraltar ... 131
Gilbert & Ellice Islands ... 60
Gold Coast ... 160
Grenada ... 170
Hong Kong ... 184
Jamaica ... 153
Kenya, Uganda, Tanganyika ... 101
Leeward Islands ... 132
Malaya
Johore ... 155
Kedah ... 82
Kelantan ... 71
Malacca ... 27
Negri Sembilan ... 63
Pahang ... 71
Penang ... 27
Perak ... 126
Perlis ... 28
Selangor ... 101
Trengganu ... 74
Malta ... 241
Mauritius ... 250
Montserrat ... 127
New Hebrides ... 77
Nigeria ... 79
North Borneo ... 260
Northern Rhodesia ... 60
Nyasaland Protectorate ... 96
Pitcairn ... 19
St. Helena ... 139
St. Kitts-Nevis ... 119
St. Lucia ... 156
St. Vincent ... 185
Sarawak ... 196
Seychelles ... 172
Sierra Leone ... 194
Singapore ... 27
Solomon Islands ... 88
Somaliland Protectorate ... 127
Swaziland ... 54
Trinidad & Tobago ... 84
Tristan da Cunha ... 13
Turks & Caicos Islands ... 118
Virgin Islands ... 114

The following have different designs but are included in the omnibus set:

Great Britain ... 313-316
Offices in Morocco ... 579-582
Australia ... 259-261
Bahrain ... 92-95
Canada ... 330
Ceylon ... 317
Cook Islands ... 145-146
Kuwait ... 113-116
New Zealand ... 280-284
Niue ... 104-105
Oman ... 52-55
Samoa ... 214-215
South Africa ... 192
Southern Rhodesia ... 80
South-West Africa ... 244-248
Tokelau Islands ... 4
106 stamps, Never Hinged $60.

Royal Visit 1953

Separate designs for each country for the visit of Queen Elizabeth II and the Duke of Edinburgh.

1953

Aden ... 62
Australia ... 267-269
Bermuda ... 163
Ceylon ... 318
Fiji ... 146
Gibraltar ... 146
Jamaica ... 154
Kenya, Uganda, Tanganyika ... 102
Malta ... 242
New Zealand ... 286-287
13 stamps

West Indies Federation

Map of the Caribbean – CD313

Federation of the West Indies, April 22, 1958.

1958

Antigua ... 122-124
Barbados ... 248-250
Dominica ... 161-163
Grenada ... 184-186
Jamaica ... 175-177
Montserrat ... 143-145
St. Kitts-Nevis ... 136-138
St. Lucia ... 170-172
St. Vincent ... 198-200
Trinidad & Tobago ... 86-88
30 stamps

Freedom from Hunger Issue

Protein Food CD314

United Nations Food and Agricultural Organization's "Freedom from Hunger" campaign.

1963

Aden ... 65
Antigua ... 133
Ascension ... 89
Bahamas ... 180
Basutoland ... 83
Bechuanaland Protectorate ... 194
Bermuda ... 192
British Guiana ... 271
British Honduras ... 179
Brunei ... 100
Cayman Islands ... 168
Dominica ... 181
Falkland Islands ... 146
Fiji ... 198
Gambia ... 172
Gibraltar ... 161
Gilbert & Ellice Islands ... 76
Grenada ... 190
Hong Kong ... 218
Malta ... 291
Mauritius ... 270
Montserrat ... 150
New Hebrides ... 93
North Borneo ... 296
Pitcairn ... 35
St. Helena ... 173
St. Lucia ... 179
St. Vincent ... 201
Sarawak ... 212
Seychelles ... 213
Solomon Islands ... 109
Swaziland ... 108
Tonga ... 127
Tristan da Cunha ... 68
Turks & Caicos Islands ... 138
Virgin Islands ... 140
Zanzibar ... 280
37 stamps

Red Cross Centenary Issue

Red Cross and Elizabeth II – CD315

Centenary of the International Red Cross.

1963

Antigua ... 134-135
Ascension ... 90-91
Bahamas ... 183-184
Basutoland ... 84-85
Bechuanaland Protectorate ... 195-196
Bermuda ... 193-194
British Guiana ... 272-273
British Honduras ... 180-181
Cayman Islands ... 169-170
Dominica ... 182-183
Falkland Islands ... 147-148
Fiji ... 203-204
Gambia ... 173-174
Gibraltar ... 162-163
Gilbert & Ellice Islands ... 77-78
Grenada ... 191-192
Hong Kong ... 219-220
Jamaica ... 203-204
Malta ... 292-293
Mauritius ... 271-272
Montserrat ... 151-152
New Hebrides ... 94-95
Pitcairn Islands ... 36-37
St. Helena ... 174-175
St. Kitts-Nevis ... 143-144
St. Lucia ... 180-181
St. Vincent ... 202-203
Seychelles ... 214-215
Solomon Islands ... 110-111
South Arabia ... 1-2
Swaziland ... 109-110
Tonga ... 134-135
Tristan da Cunha ... 69-70
Turks & Caicos Islands ... 139-140
Virgin Islands ... 141-142
70 stamps

Shakespeare Issue

Shakespeare Memorial Theatre, Stratford-on-Avon – CD316

400th anniversary of the birth of William Shakespeare.

1964

Antigua ... 151
Bahamas ... 201
Bechuanaland Protectorate ... 197
Cayman Islands ... 171

Dominica 184
Falkland Islands 149
Gambia 192
Gibraltar 164
Montserrat 153
St. Lucia 196
Turks & Caicos Islands 141
Virgin Islands 143
12 stamps

ITU ISSUE

ITU Emblem CD317

Centenary of the International Telecommunication Union.

1965
Antigua 153-154
Ascension 92-93
Bahamas 219-220
Barbados 265-266
Basutoland 101-102
Bechuanaland Protectorate 202-203
Bermuda 196-197
British Guiana 293-294
British Honduras 187-188
Brunei 116-117
Cayman Islands 172-173
Dominica 185-186
Falkland Islands 154-155
Fiji 211-212
Gibraltar 167-168
Gilbert & Ellice Islands 87-88
Grenada 205-206
Hong Kong 221-222
Mauritius 291-292
Montserrat 157-158
New Hebrides 108-109
Pitcairn Islands 52-53
St. Helena 180-181
St. Kitts-Nevis 163-164
St. Lucia 197-198
St. Vincent 224-225
Seychelles 218-219
Solomon Islands 126-127
Swaziland 115-116
Tristan da Cunha 85-86
Turks & Caicos Islands 142-143
Virgin Islands 159-160
64 stamps

Intl. Cooperation Year Issue

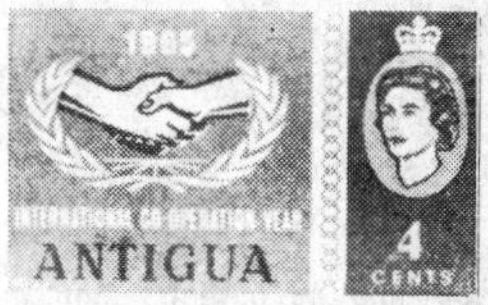

ICY Emblem – CD318

International Cooperation Year, 1965.

1965
Antigua 155-156
Ascension 94-95
Bahamas 222-223
Basutoland 103-104
Bechuanaland Protectorate 204-205
Bermuda 199-200
British Guiana 295-296
British Honduras 189-190
Brunei 118-119
Cayman Islands 174-175
Dominica 187-188
Falkland Islands 156-157
Fiji 213-214
Gibraltar 169-170
Gilbert & Ellice Islands 104-105
Grenada 207-208
Hong Kong 223-224
Mauritius 293-294
Montserrat 176-177
New Hebrides 110-111
Pitcairn Islands 54-55
St. Helena 182-183
St. Kitts-Nevis 165-166
St. Lucia 199-200
Seychelles 220-221
Solomon Islands 143-144
South Arabia 17-18
Swaziland 117-118
Tristan da Cunha 87-88
Turks & Caicos Islands 144-145
Virgin Islands 161-162
62 stamps

Churchill Memorial Issue

Winston Churchill and St. Paul's, London, During Air Attack – CD319

Sir Winston Leonard Spencer Churchill (1874-1965), statesman and World War II leader.

1966
Antigua 157-160
Ascension 96-99
Bahamas 224-227
Barbados 281-284
Basutoland 105-108
Bechuanaland Protectorate 206-209
Bermuda 201-204
British Antarctic Territory 16-19
British Honduras 191-194
Brunei 120-123
Cayman Islands 176-179
Dominica 189-192
Falkland Islands 158-161
Fiji 215-218
Gibraltar 171-174
Gilbert & Ellice Islands 106-109
Grenada 209-212
Hong Kong 225-228
Mauritius 295-298
Montserrat 178-181
New Hebrides 112-115
Pitcairn Islands 56-59
St. Helena 184-187
St. Kitts-Nevis 167-170
St. Lucia 201-204
St. Vincent 241-244
Seychelles 222-225
Solomon Islands 145-148
South Arabia 19-22
Swaziland 119-122
Tristan da Cunha 89-92
Turks & Caicos Islands 146-149
Virgin Islands 163-166
132 stamps

Royal Visit Issue, 1966

Queen Elizabeth II and Prince Philip CD320

Visit to the Caribbean, Feb. 4 - March 6, 1966.

1966
Antigua 161-162
Bahamas 228-229
Barbados 285-286
British Guiana 299-300
Cayman Islands 180-181
Dominica 193-194
Grenada 213-214
Montserrat 182-183
St. Kitts-Nevis 171-172
St. Lucia 205-206
St. Vincent 245-246
Turks & Caicos Islands 150-151
Virgin Islands 167-168
26 stamps

World Cup Soccer Issue

Soccer Player and Jules Rimet Cup CD321

World Cup Soccer Championship, Wembley, England, July 11-30.

1966
Antigua 163-164
Ascension 100-101
Bahamas 245-246
Bermuda 205-206
Brunei 124-125
Cayman Islands 182-183
Dominica 195-196
Fiji 219-220
Gibraltar 175-176
Gilbert & Ellice Islands 125-126
Grenada 230-231
New Hebrides 116-117
Pitcairn Islands 60-61
St. Helena 188-189
St. Kitts-Nevis 173-174
St. Lucia 207-208
Seychelles 226-227
Solomon Islands 167-168
South Arabia 23-24
Tristan da Cunha 93-94
40 stamps

WHO Headquarters Issue

World Health Organization Headquarters, Geneva – CD322

1966
Antigua 165-166
Ascension 102-103
Bahamas 247-248
Brunei 126-127
Cayman Islands 184-185
Dominica 197-198
Fiji 224-225
Gibraltar 180-181
Gilbert & Ellice Islands 127-128
Grenada 232-233
Hong Kong 229-230
Montserrat 184-185
New Hebrides 118-119
Pitcairn Islands 62-63
St. Helena 190-191
St. Kitts-Nevis 177-178
St. Lucia 209-210
St. Vincent 247-248
Seychelles 228-229
Solomon Islands 169-170
South Arabia 25-26
Tristan da Cunha 99-100
44 stamps

UNESCO Anniversary Issue

"Education" – CD323

Designs: "Science" (Wheat ears and flask enclosing globe). "Culture" (lyre and columns).

20th anniversary of the United Nations Educational, Scientific and Cultural Organization.

1966-67
Antigua 183-185
Ascension 108-110
Bahamas 249-251
Barbados 287-289
Bermuda 207-209
Brunei 128-130
Cayman Islands 186-188
Dominica 199-201
Gibraltar 183-185
Gilbert & Ellice Islands 129-131
Grenada 234-236
Hong Kong 231-233
Mauritius 299-301
Montserrat 186-188
New Hebrides 120-122
Pitcairn Islands 64-66
St. Helena 192-194
St. Kitts-Nevis 179-181
St. Lucia 211-213
St. Vincent 249-251
Seychelles 230-232
Solomon Islands 171-173
South Arabia 27-29
Swaziland 123-125
Tristan da Cunha 101-103
Turks & Caicos Islands 155-157
Virgin Islands 176-178
81 stamps

Silver Wedding Issue, 1972

Queen Elizabeth II and Prince Philip CD324

Designs: borders differ for each country.

1972
Anguilla 161-162
Antigua 295-296
Ascension 164-165
Bahamas 344-345
Bermuda 296-297
British Antarctic Territory 43-44
British Honduras 306-307
British Indian Ocean Territory 48-49
Brunei 186-187
Cayman Islands 304-305
Dominica 352-353
Falkland Islands 223-224
Fiji 328-329
Gibraltar 292-293
Gilbert & Ellice Islands 206-207
Grenada 466-467
Hong Kong 271-272
Montserrat 286-287
New Hebrides 169-170
Pitcairn Islands 127-128
St. Helena 271-272
St. Kitts-Nevis 257-258
St. Lucia 328-329
St.Vincent 344-345
Seychelles 309-310
Solomon Islands 248-249
South Georgia 35-36
Tristan da Cunha 178-179
Turks & Caicos Islands 257-258
Virgin Islands 241-242
60 stamps

Princess Anne's Wedding Issue

Princess Anne and Mark Phillips CD325

Wedding of Princess Anne and Mark Phillips, Nov. 14, 1973.

1973
Anguilla 179-180
Ascension 177-178
Belize 325-326

Bermuda 302-303
British Antarctic Territory 60-61
Cayman Islands 320-321
Falkland Islands 225-226
Gibraltar 305-306
Gilbert & Ellice Islands 216-217
Hong Kong 289-290
Montserrat 300-301
Pitcairn Island 135-136
St. Helena 277-278
St. Kitts-Nevis 274-275
St. Lucia 349-350
St. Vincent 358-359
St. Vincent Grenadines 1-2
Seychelles 311-312
Solomon Islands 259-260
South Georgia 37-38
Tristan da Cunha 189-190
Turks & Caicos Islands 286-287
Virgin Islands 260-261
44 stamps

Elizabeth II Coronation Anniversary Issue

Lion of England
CD326

Queen Elizabeth II
CD327

Green Turtle
CD328

Designs: Royal and local beasts in heraldic form and simulated stonework. Portrait of Elizabeth II by Peter Grugeon.

25th anniversary of coronation of Queen Elizabeth II.

1978

Ascension 229
Barbados 474
Belize 397
British Antarctic Territory 71
Cayman Islands 404
Christmas Island 87
Falkland Islands 275
Fiji 384
Gambia 380
Gilbert Islands 312
Mauritius 464
New Hebrides 258
St. Helena 317
St. Kitts-Nevis 354
Samoa 472
Solomon Islands 368
South Georgia 51
Swaziland 302
Tristan da Cunha 238
Virgin Islands 337
20 sheets

Queen Mother Elizabeth's 80th Birthday

CD330

Designs: Photographs of Queen Mother Elizabeth. Falkland Islands issued in sheets of 50; others in sheets of 9.

1980

Ascension 261
Bermuda 401
Cayman Islands 443
Falkland Islands 305
Gambia 412
Gibraltar 393
Hong Kong 364
Pitcairn Islands 193
St. Helena 341
Samoa 532
Solomon Islands 426
Tristan da Cunha 277
12 stamps

Royal Wedding Issue, 1981

Prince Charles and Lady Diana – CD331

Wedding of Charles, Prince of Wales, and Lady Diana Spencer, St. Paul's Cathedral, London, July 29, 1981.

1981

Antigua 623-625
Ascension 294-296
Barbados 547-549
Barbuda 497-499
Bermuda 412-414
Brunei 268-270
Cayman Islands 471-473
Dominica 701-703
Falkland Islands 324-326
Falkland Islands Dep. 1L59-1L61
Fiji 442-444
Gambia 426-428
Ghana 759-761
Grenada 1051-1053
Grenada Grenadines 440-443
Hong Kong 373-375
Jamaica 500-503
Lesotho 335-337
Maldive Islands 906-908
Mauritius 520-522
Norfolk Island 280-282
Pitcairn Islands 206-208
St. Helena 353-355
St. Lucia 543-545
Samoa 558-560
Sierra Leone 509-517
Solomon Islands 450-452
Swaziland 382-384
Tristan da Cunha 294-296
Turks & Caicos Islands 486-488
Caicos Island 8-10
Uganda 314-316
Vanuatu 308-310
Virgin Islands 406-408

Princess Diana

CD332 CD333

Designs: Photographs and portrait of Princess Diana, wedding or honeymoon photographs, royal residences, arms of issuing country. Portrait photograph by Clive Friend. Souvenir sheet margins show family tree, various people related to the princess. 21st birthday of Princess Diana of Wales, July 1.

1982

Antigua 663-666
Ascension 313-316
Bahamas 510-513
Barbados 585-588
Barbuda 544-546
British Antarctic Territory 92-95
Cayman Islands 486-489
Dominica 773-776
Falkland Islands 348-351
Falkland Islands Dep. 1L72-1L75
Fiji 470-473
Gambia 447-450
Grenada 1101A-1105
Grenada Grenadines 485-491
Lesotho 372-375
Maldive Islands 952-955
Mauritius 548-551
Pitcairn Islands 213-216
St. Helena 372-375
St. Lucia 591-594
Sierra Leone 531-534
Solomon Islands 471-474
Swaziland 406-409
Tristan da Cunha 310-313
Turks and Caicos Islands 530A-534
Virgin Islands 430-433

250th anniv. of first edition of Lloyd's List (shipping news publication) and of Lloyd's marine insurance.

CD335

Designs: First page of early edition of the list; historical ships, modern transportation or harbor scenes.

1984

Ascension 351-354
Bahamas 555-558
Barbados 627-630
Cayes of Belize 10-13
Cayman Islands 522-525
Falkland Islands 404-407
Fiji 509-512
Gambia 519-522
Mauritius 587-590
Nauru 280-283
St. Helena 412-415
Samoa 624-627
Seychelles 538-541
Solomon Islands 521-524
Vanuatu 368-371
Virgin Islands 466-469

Queen Mother 85th Birthday

On Holiday with the Duke of York, Balmoral, 1924 – CD336

Designs: Photographs tracing the life of the Queen Mother, Elizabeth. The high value in each set pictures the same photograph taken of the Queen Mother holding the infant Prince Henry.

1985

Ascension 372-376
Bahamas 580-584
Barbados 660-664
Bermuda 469-473
Falkland Islands 420-424
Falkland Islands Dep. 1L92-1L96
Fiji 531-535
Hong Kong 447-450
Jamaica 599-603
Mauritius 604-608
Norfolk Island 364-368
Pitcairn Islands 253-257
St. Helena 428-432
Samoa 649-653
Seychelles 567-571
Solomon Islands 543-547
Swaziland 476-480
Tristan da Cunha 372-376
Vanuatu 392-396
Zil Elwannyen Sesel 101-105

Queen Elizabeth II, 60th Birthday

CD337

1986, April 21

Ascension 389-393
Bahamas 592-596
Barbados 675-679
Bermuda 499-503
Cayman Islands 555-559
Falkland Islands 441-445
Fiji 544-548
Hong Kong 465-469
Jamaica 620-624
Kiribati 470-474
Mauritius 629-633
Papua New Guinea 640-644
Pitcairn Islands 270-274
St. Helena 451-455
Samoa 670-674
Seychelles 592-596
Solomon Islands 562-566
South Georgia 101-105
Swaziland 490-494
Tristan da Cunha 388-392
Vanuatu 414-418
Zambia 343-347
Zil Elwannyen Sesel 114-118

Royal Wedding

Marriage of Prince Andrew and Sarah Ferguson – CD338

1986, July 23

Ascension 399-400
Bahamas 602-603
Barbados 687-688
Cayman Islands 560-561
Jamaica 629-630
Pitcairn Islands 275-276
St. Helena 460-461
St. Kitts 181-182
Seychelles 602-603
Solomon Islands 567-568
Tristan da Cunha 397-398
Zambia 348-349
Zil Elwannyen Sesel 119-120

Queen Elizabeth II, 60th Birthday

Queen Elizabeth II Inspecting Guard, 1946 – CD339

Designs: Photographs tracing the life of Queen Elizabeth II.

1986

Anguilla 674-677
Antigua 925-928
Barbuda 783-786

Dominica	950-953
Gambia	611-614
Grenada	1371-1374
Grenada Grenadines	749-752
Lesotho	531-534
Maldive Islands	1172-1175
Sierra Leone	760-763
Uganda	495-498

Royal Wedding Issue, 1986

Engagement of Prince Andrew and Sarah Ferguson – CD340

Designs: Photographs of Prince Andrew and Sarah Ferguson during courtship, engagement and marriage.

1986

Antigua	939-942
Barbuda	809-812
Dominica	970-973
Gambia	635-638
Grenada	1385-1388
Grenada Grenadines	758-761
Lesotho	545-548
Maldive Islands	1181-1184
Sierra Leone	769-772
Uganda	510-513

Lloyds of London, 300th Anniv.

CD341

Designs: 17th century aspects of Lloyds, representations of each country's individual connections with Lloyds and publicized disasters insured by the organization.

1986

Ascension	454-457
Bahamas	655-658
Barbados	731-734
Bermuda	541-544
Falkland Islands	481-484
Liberia	1101-1104
Malawi	534-537
Nevis	571-574
St. Helena	501-504
St. Lucia	923-926
Seychelles	649-652
Solomon Islands	627-630
South Georgia	131-134
Trinidad & Tobago	484-487
Tristan da Cunha	439-442
Vanuatu	485-488
Zil Elwannyen Sesel	146-149

Moon Landing, 20th Anniv.

CD342

Designs: Equipment, crew photographs, spacecraft, official emblems and report profiles created for the Apollo Missions. Two stamps in each set are square in format rather than like the stamp shown; see individual country listings for more information.

1989

Ascension Is.	468-472
Bahamas	674-678
Belize	916-920
Kiribati	517-521
Liberia	1125-1129
Nevis	586-590
St. Kitts	248-252
Samoa	760-764
Seychelles	676-680
Solomon Islands	643-647
Vanuatu	507-511
Zil Elwannyen Sesel	154-158

Queen Mother, 90th Birthday

CD343

CD344

Designs: Portraits of Queen Elizabeth, the Queen Mother. See individual country listings for more information.

1990

Ascension Is.	491-492
Bahamas	698-699
Barbados	782-783
British Antarctic Territory	170-171
British Indian Ocean Territory	106-107
Cayman Islands	622-623
Falkland Islands	524-525
Kenya	527-528
Kiribati	555-556
Liberia	1145-1146
Pitcairn Islands	336-337
St. Helena	532-533
St. Lucia	969-970
Seychelles	710-711
Solomon Islands	671-672
South Georgia	143-144
Swaziland	565-566
Tristan da Cunha	480-481
Zil Elwannyen Sesel	171-172

Queen Elizabeth II, 65th Birthday, and Prince Philip, 70th Birthday

CD345 CD346

Designs: Portraits of Queen Elizabeth II and Prince Philip differ for each country. Printed in sheets of 10 + 5 labels (3 different) between. Stamps alternate, producing 5 different triptychs.

1991

Ascension Is.	505-506
Bahamas	730-731
Belize	969-970
Bermuda	617-618
Kiribati	571-572
Mauritius	733-734
Pitcairn Islands	348-349
St. Helena	554-555
St. Kitts	318-319
Samoa	790-791
Seychelles	723-724
Solomon Islands	688-689
South Georgia	149-150
Swaziland	586-587
Vanuatu	540-541
Zil Elwannyen Sesel	177-178

Royal Family Birthday, Anniversary

CD347

Queen Elizabeth II, 65th birthday, Charles and Diana, 10th wedding anniversary: Various photographs of Queen Elizabeth II, Prince Philip, Prince Charles, Princess Diana and their sons William and Henry.

1991

Antigua	1446-1455
Barbuda	1229-1238
Dominica	1328-1337
Gambia	1080-1089
Grenada	2006-2015
Grenada Grenadines	1331-1340
Guyana	2440-2451
Lesotho	871-875
Maldive Islands	1533-1542
Nevis	666-675
St. Vincent	1485-1494
St. Vincent Grenadines	769-778
Sierra Leone	1387-1396
Turks & Caicos Islands	913-922
Uganda	918-927

Queen Elizabeth II's Accession to the Throne 40th Anniversary

CD348

CD349

Various photographs of Queen Elizabeth II with local Scenes.

1992 - CD348

Antigua	1513-1518
Barbuda	1306-1309
Dominica	1414-1419
Gambia	1172-1177
Grenada	2047-2052
Grenada Grenadines	1368-1373
Lesotho	881-885
Maldive Islands	1637-1642
Nevis	702-707
St. Vincent	1582-1587
St. Vincent Grenadines	829-834
Sierra Leone	1482-1487
Turks and Caicos Islands	978-987
Uganda	990-995
Virgin Islands	742-746

1992 - CD349

Ascension Islands	531-535
Bahamas	744-748
Bermuda	623-627
British Indian Ocean Territory	119-123
Cayman Islands	648-652
Falkland Islands	549-553
Gibraltar	605-609
Hong Kong	619-623
Kenya	563-567
Kiribati	582-586
Pitcairn Islands	362-366
St. Helena	570-574
St. Kitts	332-336
Samoa	805-809
Seychelles	734-738
Soloman Islands	708-712
South Georgia	157-161
Tristan da Cunha	508-512
Vanuatu	555-559
Zambia	561-565
Zil Elwannyen Sesel	183-187

Royal Air Force, 75th Anniversary

CD350

1993

Ascension	557-561
Bahamas	771-775
Barbados	842-846
Belize	1003-1008
Bermuda	648-651
British Indian Ocean Territory	136-140
Falkland Is.	573-577
Fiji	687-691
St. Kitts	351-355

ANGUILLA

LOCATION — In the West Indies southeast of Puerto Rico
GOVT. — British territory
AREA — 60 sq. mi.
POP. — 6,500 (est. 1980)
CAPITAL — The Valley

Anguilla separated unilaterally from the Associated State of St. Kitts-Nevis-Anguilla in 1967, formalized in 1980 following direct United Kingdom intervention some years before. A British Commissioner exercises executive authority.

100 Cents = 1 Dollar

Catalogue values for all unused stamps in this country are for Never Hinged items.

St. Kitts-Nevis Nos. 145-160 Overprinted

[redacted]

Independent Anguilla
On Type A14

[redacted]

Independent Anguilla
On Type A15

Wmk. 314

1967, Sept. 4 Photo. *Perf. 14*

1	A14	½c blue & dk brn	12.50	12.50
2	A15	1c multicolored	8.50	6.50
3	A14	2c multicolored	10.00	5.00
4	A14	3c multicolored	12.00	9.00
5	A15	4c multicolored	12.50	8.00
6	A15	5c multicolored	50.00	22.50
7	A15	6c multicolored	20.00	10.00
8	A15	10c multicolored	12.50	9.00
9	A14	15c multicolored	27.50	9.50
10	A15	20c multicolored	45.00	15.00
11	A14	25c multicolored	37.50	17.50
12	A15	50c multicolored	*1,100.*	*300.00*
13	A14	60c multicolored	*3,750.*	*1,100.*
14	A14	$1 multicolored	*1,250.*	*275.00*
15	A15	$2.50 multicolored	*1,000.*	*225.00*
16	A14	$5 multicolored	*950.00*	*225.00*
		Nos. 1-16 (16)	*8,298.*	*2,249.*

Counterfeit overprints exist.

Mahogany Tree, The Quarter — A1

Designs: 2c, Sombrero Lighthouse. 3c, St. Mary's Church. 4c, Valley Police Station. 5c, Old Plantation House, Mt. Fortune. 6c, Valley Post Office. 10c, Methodist Church, West End. 15c, Wall-Blake Airport. 20c, Plane over Sandy Ground. 25c, Island Harbor. 40c, Map of Anguilla. 60c, Hermit crab and starfish. $1, Hibiscus. $2.50, Coconut harvest. $5, Spiny lobster.

Perf. 12½x13

1967-68 Litho. Unwmk.

17	A1	1c orange & multi	15	15
18	A1	2c gray green & blk	15	15
19	A1	3c emerald & blk	15	15
20	A1	4c brt blue & blk	15	15
21	A1	5c lt blue & multi	15	15
22	A1	6c ver & black	15	15
23	A1	10c multicolored	15	15
24	A1	15c multicolored	18	18
25	A1	20c multicolored	24	24
26	A1	25c multicolored	30	30
27	A1	40c blue & multi	48	48
28	A1	60c yellow & multi	70	70
29	A1	$1 lt green & multi	1.40	1.40
30	A1	$2.50 multicolored	3.50	3.50
31	A1	$5 multicolored	6.50	6.50
		Nos. 17-31 (15)	14.35	14.35

Issue dates: 1c, 5c, 10c, 20c, 25c, 40c, Nov. 27, 1967; 3c, 4c, 15c, 60c, $1, $5, Feb. 10, 1968; 2c, 6c, $2.50, Mar. 21, 1968.

For overprints, see Nos. 53-67, 78-82.

Sailboats A2

Designs: 15c, Boat building. 25c, Schooner Warspite. 40c, Yacht Atlantic Star.

1968, May 11 *Perf. 14*

32	A2	10c rose & multi	32	32
33	A2	15c olive & multi	55	55
34	A2	25c lilac rose & multi	80	80
35	A2	40c dull blue & multi	1.40	1.40

Purple-throated Carib — A3

Girl Guide Badge — A4

Anguillan Birds: 15c, Bananaquit. 25c, Black-necked stilt, horiz. 40c, Royal tern, horiz.

1968, July 8

36	A3	10c dull yel & multi	40	28
37	A3	15c yel green & multi	55	42
38	A3	25c multicolored	1.65	95
39	A3	40c multicolored	1.90	1.65

Perf. 13x13½, 13½x13

1968, Oct. 14

Designs: 10c, Girl Guide badge, horiz. 25c, Badge and Headquarters, horiz. 40c, Merit Badges.

40	A4	10c lt green & multi	20	20
41	A4	15c lt blue & multi	30	30
42	A4	25c multicolored	60	60
43	A4	40c multicolored	85	85

Anguillan Girl Guides, 35th anniversary.

Three Kings — A5

Christmas: 10c, Three Kings seeing Star, vert. 15c, Holy Family, vert. 40c, Shepherds seeing Star. 50c, Holy Family and donkey.

1968, Nov. 18

44	A5	1c lilac rose & black	15	15
45	A5	10c blue & black	16	16
46	A5	15c brown & black	35	35
47	A5	40c brt ultra & black	90	90
48	A5	50c green & black	1.25	1.25
		Nos. 44-48 (5)	2.81	2.81

Bagging Salt — A6

Salt Industry: 15c, Packing salt. 40c, Salt pond. 50c, Loading salt.

1969, Jan. 4 *Perf. 13*

49	A6	10c red & multi	15	15
50	A6	15c lt blue & multi	22	22
51	A6	40c emerald & multi	60	60
52	A6	50c purple & multi	70	70

Nos. 17-31 Overprinted: "INDEPENDENCE/JANUARY, 1969"

1969, Jan. 9 *Perf. 12½x13*

53	A1	1c orange & multi	15	15
54	A1	2c gray green & blk	15	15
55	A1	3c emerald & blk	15	15
56	A1	4c brt blue & blk	15	15
57	A1	5c lt blue & multi	15	15
58	A1	6c vermilion & blk	15	15
59	A1	10c multicolored	16	16
60	A1	15c multicolored	22	22
61	A1	20c multicolored	28	28
62	A1	25c multicolored	35	35
63	A1	40c blue & multi	50	50
64	A1	60c yellow & multi	70	70
65	A1	$1 lt green & multi	1.25	1.25
66	A1	$2.50 multicolored	3.00	3.00
67	A1	$5 multicolored	6.25	6.25
		Nos. 53-67 (15)	13.61	13.61

Crucifixion, School of Quentin Massys — A7

Easter: 40c, The Last Supper, ascribed to Roberti.

1969, Mar. 31 Litho. *Perf. 13½*

68	A7	25c multicolored	40	40
69	A7	40c multicolored	70	70

Amaryllis A8

1969, June 10 *Perf. 14*

70	A8	10c shown	20	20
71	A8	15c Bougainvillea	35	35
72	A8	40c Hibiscus	80	80
73	A8	50c Cattleya orchid	1.10	1.10

Turban and Star Shells — A9

Sea Shells: 15c, Spiny oysters. 40c, Scotch, royal and smooth bonnets. 50c, Triton trumpet.

1969, Sept. 22

74	A9	10c multicolored	38	38
75	A9	15c multicolored	55	55
76	A9	40c multicolored	1.25	1.25
77	A9	50c multicolored	1.65	1.65

Nos. 17, 25-28 Overprinted "CHRISTMAS 1969" and Various Christmas Designs

1969, Oct. 27 *Perf. 12½x13*

78	A1	1c orange & multi	15	15
79	A1	20c multicolored	50	35
80	A1	25c multicolored	70	60
81	A1	40c blue & multi	1.25	1.10
82	A1	60c yellow & multi	3.00	2.00
		Nos. 78-82 (5)	5.60	4.20

Red Goatfish A10

Designs: 15c, Blue-striped grunts. 40c, Mutton grouper. 50c, Banded butterfly-fish.

1969, Dec. 1 *Perf. 14*

83	A10	10c multicolored	28	28
84	A10	15c multicolored	40	40
85	A10	40c multicolored	1.40	1.40
86	A10	50c multicolored	1.65	1.65

Morning Glory — A11

1970, Feb. 23

87	A11	10c shown	25	25
88	A11	15c Blue petrea	40	40
89	A11	40c Hibiscus	1.40	1.40
90	A11	50c Flamboyant	1.75	1.75

The Way to Calvary, by Tiepolo — A12

Easter: 20c, Crucifixion, by Masaccio, vert. 40c, Descent from the Cross, by Rosso Fiorentino, vert. 60c, Jesus Carrying the Cross, by Murillo.

1970, Mar. 26 *Perf. 13½*

91	A12	10c multicolored	15	15
92	A12	20c multicolored	28	28
93	A12	40c multicolored	60	60
94	A12	60c multicolored	90	90

Anguilla Map, Scout Badge A13

Designs: 15c, Cub Scouts practicing first aid. 40c, Monkey bridge. 50c, Scout Headquarters, The Valley, and Lord Baden-Powell.

1970, Aug. 10 *Perf. 13*

95	A13	10c multicolored	25	25
96	A13	15c multicolored	40	40
97	A13	40c multicolored	1.00	1.00
98	A13	50c multicolored	1.25	1.25

Anguilla Boy Scouts, 40th anniversary.

Boat Building A14

Designs: 2c, Road construction. 3c, Blowing Point dock. 4c, Radio announcer. 5c, Cottage Hospital extension. 6c, Valley secondary school. 10c, Hotel extension. 15c, Sandy Ground. 20c, Supermarket and movie house. 25c, Bananas and mangoes. 40c, Wall-Blake airport. 60c, Sandy Ground jetty. $1, Administration building. $2.50, Cow and calf. $5, Sandy Hill Bay.

1970, Nov. 23 Litho. *Perf. 14*

99	A14	1c multicolored	15	15
100	A14	2c multicolored	15	15
101	A14	3c multicolored	15	15
102	A14	4c multicolored	15	15
103	A14	5c multicolored	15	15
104	A14	6c multicolored	15	15
105	A14	10c multicolored	20	20
106	A14	15c multicolored	28	28
107	A14	20c multicolored	32	32
108	A14	25c multicolored	38	38
109	A14	40c multicolored	65	65
110	A14	60c multicolored	1.00	1.00
111	A14	$1 multicolored	1.60	1.60

112	A14	$2.50	multicolored	4.00	4.00
113	A14	$5	multicolored	8.00	8.00
			Nos. 99-113 (15)	17.33	17.33

Adoration of the Shepherds, by Guido Reni — A15

Christmas: 20c, Virgin and Child, by Benozzo Gozzoli. 25c, Nativity, by Botticelli. 40c, Santa Margherita Madonna, by Mazzola. 50c, Adoration of the Kings, by Tiepolo.

1970, Dec. 11 *Perf. 13½*

114	A15	1c	multicolored	15	15
115	A15	20c	multicolored	35	35
116	A15	25c	multicolored	40	40
117	A15	40c	multicolored	60	60
118	A15	50c	multicolored	65	65
			Nos. 114-118 (5)	2.15	2.15

Angels Weeping over the Dead Christ, by Guercino — A16

Easter: 10c, Ecce Homo, by Correggio, vert. 15c, Christ Appearing to St. Peter, by Carracci, vert. 50c, The Supper at Emmaus, by Caravaggio.

1971, Mar. 29

119	A16	10c	pink & multi	18	18
120	A16	15c	lt blue & multi	30	30
121	A16	40c	yel green & multi	75	75
122	A16	50c	violet & multi	90	90

Hypolimnas Misippus A17

Butterflies: 15c, Junonia lavinia. 40c, Agraulis vanillae. 50c, Danaus plexippus.

1971, June 21 *Perf. 14x14½*

123	A17	10c	multicolored	70	70
124	A17	15c	multicolored	90	90
125	A17	40c	multicolored	1.75	1.75
126	A17	50c	multicolored	2.25	2.25

Magnanime and Aimable in Battle — A18

Ships: 15c, HMS Duke and Agamemnon against Glorieux. 25c, HMS Formidable and Namur against Ville de Paris. 40c, HMS Canada. 50c, HMS St. Albans and wreck of Hector.

1971, Aug. 30 **Litho.** *Perf. 14*

127	A18	10c	multicolored	35	35
128	A18	15c	multicolored	60	60
129	A18	25c	multicolored	1.25	1.25
130	A18	40c	multicolored	2.00	2.00
131	A18	50c	multicolored	2.75	2.75
a.			Strip of 5, #127-131	7.25	7.25

West Indies sea battles.

Ansidei Madonna, by Raphael — A19

Christmas: 25c, Mystic Nativity, by Botticelli. 40c, Virgin and Child, School of Seville, inscribed Murillo. 50c, Madonna of the Iris, ascribed to Dürer.

1971, Nov. 29 *Perf. 14x13½*

132	A19	20c	green & multi	40	40
133	A19	25c	blue & multi	55	55
134	A19	40c	lilac rose & multi	90	90
135	A19	50c	violet & multi	1.10	1.10

Map of Anguilla and St. Maarten, by Jefferys, 1775 — A20

Jesus Buffeted, Stained-glass Window — A21

Maps of Anguilla by: 15c, Samuel Fahlberg, 1814. 40c, Thomas Jefferys, 1775, horiz. 50c, Capt. E. Barnett, 1847, horiz.

Perf. 14x13½, 13½x14

1972, Jan. 24

136	A20	10c	lt blue & multi	22	22
137	A20	15c	lt green & multi	35	35
138	A20	40c	lt green & multi	90	90
139	A20	50c	lt ultra & multi	1.10	1.10

1972, Mar. 14 *Perf. 14x13½*

Easter (19th cent. Stained-glass Windows, Bray Church): 15c, Jesus Carrying the Cross. 25c, Crucifixion. 40c, Descent from the Cross. 50c, Burial.

140	A21	10c	multicolored	20	20
141	A21	15c	multicolored	32	32
142	A21	25c	multicolored	45	45
143	A21	40c	multicolored	90	90
144	A21	50c	multicolored	1.00	1.00
a.			Strip of 5, #140-144	3.00	3.00

Spear Fishing A22

Sandy Ground A23

1972-75 *Perf. 13½*

145	A22	1c	shown	15	15
146	A23	2c	Loblolly tree, vert.	15	15
147	A23	3c	shown	15	15
148	A23	4c	Ferry, Blowing Point, vert.	15	15
149	A23	5c	Agriculture	15	15
150	A23	6c	St. Mary's Church, vert.	15	15
151	A23	10c	St. Gerard's Church	16	16
152	A22	15c	Cottage Hospital	25	25
153	A23	20c	Public Library	28	28
154	A23	25c	Sunset, Blowing Point	40	40
155	A22	40c	Boat building	60	60
156	A22	60c	Hibiscus	1.00	1.00
157	A23	$1	Man-o-war bird	1.90	1.90
158	A23	$2.50	Frangipani	4.50	4.50
159	A23	$5	Brown pelican	9.00	9.00
160	A22	$10	Green-back turtle	22.50	22.50
			Nos. 145-160 (16)	41.49	41.49

Issue dates: $10, May 20, 1975; others Oct. 30, 1972.

For overprints, see Nos. 229-246.

Common Design Types are pictured beginning on page 176.

Silver Wedding Issue, 1972
Common Design Type

Design: Queen Elizabeth II, Prince Philip, schooner and dolphin.

Perf. 14x14½

1972, Nov. 20 **Photo.** **Wmk. 314**

161	CD324	25c	olive & multi	1.75	1.75
162	CD324	40c	maroon & multi	2.00	2.00

Flight into Egypt — A24

Perf. 13½

1972, Dec. 4 **Litho.** **Unwmk.**

163	A24	1c	shown	15	15
164	A24	20c	Star of Bethlehem	35	35
165	A24	25c	Nativity	40	40
166	A24	40c	Three Kings	70	70
167	A24	50c	Adoration of the Kings	1.00	1.00
a.			Vert. strip of 4, #164-167	2.75	2.75
			Nos. 163-167 (5)	2.60	2.60

Christmas.

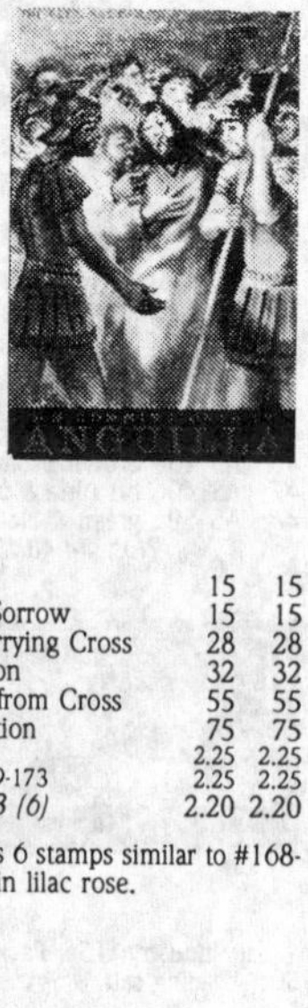
Betrayal of Jesus — A25

1973, Mar. 26

168	A25	1c	shown	15	15
169	A25	10c	Man of Sorrow	15	15
170	A25	20c	Jesus Carrying Cross	28	28
171	A25	25c	Crucifixion	32	32
172	A25	40c	Descent from Cross	55	55
173	A25	50c	Resurrection	75	75
a.			Souvenir sheet of 6	2.25	2.25
b.			Vert. strip of 5, #169-173	2.25	2.25
			Nos. 168-173 (6)	2.20	2.20

Easter. #173a contains 6 stamps similar to #168-173 with bottom panel in lilac rose.

Santa Maria A26

1973, Sept. 10

174	A26	1c	shown	15	15
175	A26	20c	Old West Indies map	55	55
176	A26	40c	Map of voyages	1.40	1.40
177	A26	70c	Sighting land	2.25	2.25
178	A26	$1.20	Columbus landing	4.75	4.75
a.			Souvenir sheet of 5, #174-178	10.00	10.00
b.			Horiz. strip of 4, #175-178	9.00	9.00
			Nos. 174-178 (5)	9.10	9.10

Discovery of West Indies by Columbus.

Princess Anne's Wedding Issue
Common Design Type

1973, Nov. 14 **Wmk. 314** *Perf. 13½*

179	CD325	60c	blue grn & multi	45	45
180	CD325	$1.20	lilac & multi	90	90

Wedding of Princess Anne and Capt. Mark Phillips, Nov. 14, 1973.

Adoration of the Shepherds, by Guido Reni — A27

Paintings: 10c, Virgin and Child, by Filippino Lippi. 20c, Nativity, by Meester Van de Brunswijkse Diptiek. 25c, Madonna of the Meadow, by Bellini. 40c, Virgin and Child, by Cima. 50c, Adoration of the Kings, by Geertgen Tot Sint Jans.

1973, Dec. 2 **Unwmk.**

181	A27	1c	multicolored	15	15
182	A27	10c	multicolored	18	18
183	A27	20c	multicolored	30	30
184	A27	25c	multicolored	35	35
185	A27	40c	multicolored	60	60
186	A27	50c	multicolored	80	80
a.			Souvenir sheet of 6, #181-186	2.50	2.50
b.			Horiz. strip of 5, #182-186	2.50	2.50
			Nos. 181-186 (6)	2.38	2.38

Christmas.

Crucifixion, by Raphael — A28

Easter (Details from Crucifixion by Raphael): 15c, Virgin Mary and St. John. 20c, The Two Marys. 25c, Left Angel. 40c, Right Angel. $1, Christ on the Cross.

1974, Mar. 30

187	A28	1c	lilac & multi	15	15
188	A28	15c	gray & multi	18	18
189	A28	20c	salmon & multi	25	25
190	A28	25c	yel green & multi	30	30
191	A28	40c	orange & multi	42	42
192	A28	$1	lt blue & multi	1.10	1.10
a.			Souvenir sheet of 6, #187-192	2.50	2.50
b.			Vert. strip of 5, #188-192	2.50	2.50
			Nos. 187-192 (6)	2.40	2.40

Churchill Making Victory Sign — A29

Designs: 20c, Roosevelt, Churchill, American and British flags. 25c, Churchill broadcasting during the war. 40c, Blenheim Palace. 60c, Churchill Statue and Parliament. $1.20, Chartwell.

1974, June 24

193	A29	1c multicolored	15	15
194	A29	20c multicolored	22	22
195	A29	25c multicolored	28	28
196	A29	40c multicolored	42	42
197	A29	60c multicolored	65	65
198	A29	$1.20 multicolored	1.40	1.40
a.		Souvenir sheet of 6, #193-198	3.50	3.50
b.		Horiz. strip of 5, #194-198	3.25	3.25
		Nos. 193-198 (6)	3.12	3.12

Sir Winston Spencer Churchill (1874-1965).

UPU Emblem, Map of Anguilla — A30

1974, Aug. 27

199	A30	1c black & ultra	15	15
200	A30	20c black & orange	18	18
201	A30	25c black & yellow	20	20
202	A30	40c black & brt lilac	42	42
203	A30	60c black & lt green	60	60
204	A30	$1.20 black & blue	1.00	1.00
a.		Souvenir sheet of 6	3.00	3.00
b.		Horiz. strip of 5, #200-204	2.50	2.50
		Nos. 199-204 (6)	2.55	2.55

UPU, centenary. No. 204a contains one each of Nos. 199-204 with second row (40c, 60c, $1.20) perf. 15 at bottom.

Fishermen Seeing Star — A31

Christmas: 20c, Nativity. 25c, King offering gift. 40c, Star over map of Anguilla. 60c, Family looking at star. $1.20, Two angels with star and "Peace."

1974, Dec. 16 Litho. *Perf. 14½*

205	A31	1c brt blue & multi	15	15
206	A31	20c dull grn & multi	18	18
207	A31	25c gray & multi	20	20
208	A31	40c car & multi	42	42
209	A31	60c dp blue & multi	60	60
210	A31	$1.20 ultra & multi	1.00	1.00
a.		Souvenir sheet of 6, #205-210	3.00	3.00
b.		Horiz. strip of 5, #206-210	2.50	2.50
		Nos. 205-210 (6)	2.55	2.55

Virgin Mary, St. John, Mary Magdalene — A32

Paintings from Isenheim Altar, by Matthias Grunewald: 10c, Crucifixion. 15c, John the Baptist. 20c, St. Sebastian and Angels. $1, Burial of Christ, horiz. $1.50, St. Anthony, the Hermit.

1975, Mar. 25 *Perf. 13½*

211	A32	1c multicolored	15	15
212	A32	10c multicolored	15	15
213	A32	15c multicolored	15	15
214	A32	20c multicolored	18	18
215	A32	$1 multicolored	75	75
216	A32	$1.50 multicolored	1.25	1.25
a.		Souvenir sheet of 6	2.75	2.75
b.		Horiz. strip of 5, #212-216	2.50	2.50
		Nos. 211-216 (6)	2.63	2.63

Easter. No. 216a contains 6 stamps similar to Nos. 211-216 with simulated perforations.

Statue of Liberty, N.Y. Skyline A33

Designs: 10c, Capitol, Washington, D.C. 15c, Congress voting independence. 20c, Washington, map and his battles. $1, Boston Tea Party. $1.50, Bicentennial emblem, historic U.S. flags.

1975, Nov. 10

217	A33	1c multicolored	15	15
218	A33	10c multicolored	15	15
219	A33	15c multicolored	15	15
220	A33	20c multicolored	22	22
221	A33	$1 multicolored	1.00	1.00
222	A33	$1.50 multicolored	1.50	1.50
a.		Souvenir sheet of 6	3.50	3.50
b.		Horiz. strip of 5, #218-222	3.25	3.25
		Nos. 217-222 (6)	3.17	3.17

American Bicentennial. No. 222a contains one each of Nos. 217-222 with second row (20c, $1, $1.50) perf. 15 at bottom.

Virgin and Child with St. John, by Raphael — A34

Paintings, Virgin and Child by: 10c, Cima. 15c, Dolci. 20c, Durer. $1, Bellini. $1.50, Botticelli.

1975, Dec. 8 *Perf. 14x13½*

223	A34	1c ultra & multi	15	15
224	A34	10c Prus blue & multi	15	15
225	A34	15c plum & multi	15	15
226	A34	20c car rose & multi	20	20
227	A34	$1 brt grn & multi	1.00	1.00
228	A34	$1.50 blue grn & multi	1.40	1.40
a.		Souvenir sheet of 6, #223-228	3.25	3.25
b.		Horiz. strip of 5, #224-228	3.25	3.25
		Nos. 223-228 (6)	3.05	3.05

Christmas.

Nos. 145-146, 148, 150-160 Overprinted "NEW CONSTITUTION 1976"

1976 Litho. *Perf. 13½*

229	A22	1c #145	15	15
230	A22	2c on 1c #145	15	15
231	A23	2c #146	70	70
232	A22	3c on 40c #155	15	15
233	A23	4c #148	15	15
234	A22	5c on 40c #155	15	15
235	A23	6c #150	15	15
236	A23	10c on 20c #153	15	15
237	A23	10c #151	90	90
238	A22	15c #152	15	15
239	A23	20c #153	20	20
240	A23	25c #154	25	25
241	A22	40c #155	35	35
242	A22	60c #156	55	55
243	A23	$1 #157	90	90
244	A23	$2.50 #158	2.25	2.25
245	A23	$5 #159	4.50	4.50
246	A22	$10 #160	10.50	10.50
		Nos. 229-246 (18)	22.30	22.30

Flowering Trees — A35

1976, Feb. 16 *Perf. 13½x14*

247	A35	1c Almond	15	15
248	A35	10c Clusia rosea	15	15
249	A35	15c Calabash	20	20
250	A35	20c Cordia	22	22
251	A35	$1 Papaya	1.00	1.00
252	A35	$1.50 Flamboyant	1.40	1.40
a.		Souvenir sheet of 6, #247-252	3.25	3.25
b.		Horiz. strip of 5, #248-252	3.25	3.25
		Nos. 247-252 (6)	3.12	3.12

The Three Marys — A36

Designs: 10c, Crucifixion. 15c, Two soldiers. 20c, Annunciation. $1, Altar tapestry, 1470, Monastery of Rheinau, Switzerland, horiz. $1.50, "Noli me Tangere" (Jesus and Mary Magdalene). Designs of vertical stamps show details from tapestry shown on $1 stamp.

1976, Apr. 5 *Perf. 14x13½, 13½x14*

253	A36	1c multicolored	15	15
254	A36	10c multicolored	15	15
255	A36	15c multicolored	18	18
256	A36	20c multicolored	20	20
257	A36	$1 multicolored	90	90
258	A36	$1.50 multicolored	1.25	1.25
a.		Souvenir sheet of 6	2.75	2.75
b.		Horiz. strip of 5, #254-258	2.75	2.75
		Nos. 253-258 (6)	2.83	2.83

Easter. No. 258a contains 6 stamps similar to Nos. 253-258 with simulated perforations.

Le Desius and La Vaillante Approaching Anguilla — A37

Sailing Ships: 3c, Sailboat leaving Anguilla for Antigua to get help. 15c, HMS Lapwing in battle with frigate Le Desius and brig La Vaillante. 25c, La Vaillante aground off St. Maarten. $1, Lapwing. $1.50, Le Desius burning.

1976, Nov. 8 Litho. *Perf. 13½x14*

259	A37	1c multicolored	15	15
260	A37	3c multicolored	15	15
261	A37	15c multicolored	20	20
262	A37	25c multicolored	35	35
263	A37	$1 multicolored	1.40	1.40
264	A37	$1.50 multicolored	2.25	2.25
a.		Souvenir sheet of 6, #259-264	6.50	6.50
b.		Strip of 5, #260-264	4.50	4.50
		Nos. 259-264 (6)	4.50	4.50

Bicentenary of Battle of Anguilla between French and British ships.

Christmas Carnival — A38

Children's Paintings: 3c, 3 children dreaming of Christmas gifts. 15c, Caroling. 25c, Candlelight procession. $1, Going to Church on Christmas Eve. $1.50, Airport, coming home for Christmas.

1976, Nov. 22

265	A38	1c multicolored	15	15
266	A38	3c multicolored	15	15
267	A38	15c multicolored	18	15
268	A38	25c multicolored	22	18
269	A38	$1 multicolored	90	80
270	A38	$1.50 multicolored	1.25	90
a.		Souvenir sheet of 6, #265-270	2.75	2.00
b.		Strip of 5, #266-270	2.75	2.25
		Nos. 265-270 (6)	2.85	2.33

Christmas. For overprints and surcharges, see Nos. 305-310a.

Prince Charles and HMS Minerva, 1973 — A39

Designs: 40c, Prince Philip landing at Road Bay, 1964. $1.20, Hommage to Queen at Coronation. $2.50, Coronation regalia and map of Anguilla.

1977, Feb. 9

271	A39	25c multicolored	18	18
272	A39	40c multicolored	30	30
273	A39	$1.20 multicolored	90	90
274	A39	$2.50 multicolored	1.75	1.75
a.		Souvenir sheet of 4, #271-274	3.50	3.50

25th anniv. of reign of Queen Elizabeth II.

Yellow-crowned Night Heron — A40

Designs: 2c, Great barracuda. 3c, Queen conch. 4c, Spanish bayonet (Yucca). 5c, Trunkfish. 6c, Cable and telegraph building. 10c, American sparrow hawk. 15c, Ground orchids. 20c, Parlorfish. 22c, Lobster fishing boat. 35c, Boat race. 50c Sea bean (flowers). $1, Sandy Island with palms. $2.50, Manchineel (fruit). $5, Ground lizard. $10, Red-billed tropic bird.

1977-78 Litho. *Perf. 13½x14*

275	A40	1c multicolored	15	15
276	A40	2c multicolored	15	15
277	A40	3c multicolored	15	15
278	A40	4c multicolored	15	15
279	A40	5c multicolored	15	15
280	A40	6c multicolored	15	15
281	A40	10c multicolored	15	15
282	A40	15c multicolored	15	15
283	A40	20c multicolored	20	20
284	A40	22c multicolored	22	22
285	A40	35c multicolored	35	35
286	A40	50c multicolored	50	50
287	A40	$1 multicolored	1.00	1.00
288	A40	$2.50 multicolored	2.50	2.50
289	A40	$5 multicolored	5.00	5.00
290	A40	$10 multicolored	10.00	10.00
		Nos. 275-290 (16)	20.97	20.97

Issue dates: Nos. 275-280, 290 Apr. 18, 1977. Others Feb. 20, 1978.

For overprints and surcharges, see Nos. 319-324, 337-342, 387-390, 402-404, 407-415, 417-423.

Crucifixion, by Quentin Massys — A41

Easter (Paintings): 3c, Betrayal of Christ, by Ugolino. 22c, Way to Calvary, by Ugolino. 30c, The Deposition, by Ugolino. $1, Resurrection, by Ugolino. $1.50, Crucifixion, by Andrea del Castagno.

1977, Apr. 25

291	A41	1c multicolored	15	15
292	A41	3c multicolored	15	15
293	A41	22c multicolored	18	18
294	A41	30c multicolored	22	22
295	A41	$1 multicolored	90	90
296	A41	$1.50 multicolored	1.25	1.25
a.		Souvenir sheet of 6, #291-296	2.50	2.50
b.		Strip of 5, #292-296	2.75	2.75
		Nos. 291-296 (6)	2.85	2.85

Nos. 271-274, 274b Overprinted: "ROYAL VISIT/TO WEST INDIES"

1977, Oct. 26 Litho. *Perf. 13½x14*

297 A39	25c multicolored	18	18
298 A39	40c multicolored	28	28
299 A39	$1.20 multicolored	75	75
300 A39	$2.50 multicolored	1.50	1.50
a.	Souvenir sheet of 4	3.00	3.00

Visit of Queen Elizabeth II to West Indies.

Suzanne Fourment in Velvet Hat, by Rubens — A42

Rubens Paintings: 40c, Helena Fourment with her Children. $1.20, Rubens with his wife. $2.50, Marchesa Brigida Spinola-Doria.

1977, Nov. 1 *Perf. 14x13½*

301 A42	25c black & multi	18	18
302 A42	40c black & multi	25	25
303 A42	$1.20 multicolored	90	90
304 A42	$2.50 black & multi	1.75	1.75
a.	Souvenir sheet of 4, #301-304	3.25	3.25

Peter Paul Rubens, 400th birth anniv. Nos. 301-304 printed in sheets of 5 stamps and blue label with Rubens' portrait.

Nos. 265-270b Overprinted 1977 and Surcharged

1977, Nov. 7 *Perf. 13½x14*

305 A38	1c multicolored	15	15
306 A38	5c on 3c multi	15	15
307 A38	12c on 15c multi	15	15
308 A38	18c on 25c multi	15	15
309 A38	$1 multicolored	65	65
310 A38	$2.50 on $1.50 multi	1.75	1.75
a.	Souvenir sheet of 6, #305-310	3.25	1.75
b.	Strip of 5, #306-310	3.00	3.00

Christmas. Stamps and souvenir sheets have "1976" and old denomination obliterated with variously shaped rectangles.

Nos. 301-304a Ovptd. in Gold: "EASTER 1978"

1978, Mar. 6 *Perf. 14x13½*

311 A42	25c black & multi	18	18
312 A42	40c black & multi	28	28
313 A42	$1.20 black & multi	80	80
314 A42	$2.50 black & multi	1.75	1.75
a.	Souvenir sheet of 4, #311-314	3.25	3.25

Buckingham Palace A43

Designs: 50c, Coronation procession. $1.50, Royal family on balcony. $2.50, Royal coat of arms.

1978, Apr. 6 *Perf. 14*

315 A43	22c multicolored	15	15
316 A43	50c multicolored	25	25
317 A43	$1.50 multicolored	75	75
318 A43	$2.50 multicolored	1.25	1.25
a.	Souvenir sheet of 4, #315-318	3.25	3.25

25th anniv. of coronation of Queen Elizabeth II. #315-318 each exist in a booklet pane of 2.

Nos. 284-285 and 288 Ovptd. and Surcharged: "VALLEY / SECONDARY / SCHOOL / 1953-1978"

1978, Aug. 14 Litho. *Perf. 13½x14*

319 A40	22c multicolored	35	35
320 A40	35c multicolored	50	50
321 A40	$1.50 on $2.50 multi	2.25	2.25

Valley Secondary School, 25th anniv. Surcharge on No. 321 includes heavy bar over old denomination.

Nos. 286-287, 289 Ovptd. and Surcharged: "ROAD / METHODIST / CHURCH / 1878-1978"

1978, Aug. 14

322 A40	50c multicolored	65	65
323 A40	$1 multicolored	1.30	1.30
324 A40	$1.20 on $5 multi	1.75	1.75

Road Methodist Church, centenary. Surcharge on No. 324 includes heavy bar over old denomination.

Mother and Child A44

Christmas: 12c, Christmas masquerade. 18c, Christmas dinner. 22c, Serenade. $1, Star over manger. $2.50, Family going to church.

1978, Dec. 11 Litho. *Perf. 13½*

325 A44	5c multicolored	15	15
326 A44	12c multicolored	15	15
327 A44	18c multicolored	15	15
328 A44	22c multicolored	15	15
329 A44	$1 multicolored	75	55
330 A44	$2.50 multicolored	1.75	1.50
a.	Souvenir sheet of 6, #325-330	3.00	2.25
	Nos. 325-330 (6)	3.10	2.65

Type A44 in Changed Colors with IYC Emblem and Inscription.

1979, Jan. 15 Litho. *Perf. 13½*

331 A44	5c multicolored	15	15
332 A44	12c multicolored	15	15
333 A44	18c multicolored	15	15
334 A44	22c multicolored	18	18
335 A44	$1 multicolored	85	85
336 A44	$2.50 multicolored	1.75	1.75
a.	Souvenir sheet of 4, #331-336	3.25	3.25
	Nos. 331-336 (6)	3.23	3.23

Intl. Year of the Child. For overprint, see No. 416

Nos. 275-278, 280-281 Surcharged

18 CENTS ■

1979, Feb. 8 Litho. *Perf. 13½x14*

337 A40	12c on 2c multi	*45*	*45*
338 A40	14c on 4c multi	*50*	*50*
339 A40	18c on 3c multi	*75*	*75*
340 A40	25c on 6c multi	*1.25*	*1.25*
341 A40	38c on 10c multi	*1.75*	*1.75*
342 A40	40c on 1c multi	*2.00*	*2.00*
	Nos. 337-342 (6)	*6.70*	*6.70*

Valley Methodist Church A45

Church Interiors: 12c, St. Mary's Anglican Church, The Valley. 18c, St. Gerard's Roman Catholic Church, The Valley. 22c, Road Methodist Church. $1.50, St. Augustine's Anglican Church, East End. $2.50, West End Methodist Church.

1979, Mar. 30 Litho. *Perf. 14*

343 A45	5c multicolored	15	15
344 A45	12c multicolored	15	15
345 A45	18c multicolored	15	15
346 A45	22c multicolored	15	15
347 A45	$1.50 multicolored	1.00	1.00
348 A45	$2.50 multicolored	1.60	1.60
a.	Souvenir sheet of 6	3.25	3.25
b.	Strip of 6, #343-348	3.25	3.25
	Nos. 343-348 (6)	3.20	3.20

Easter. No. 348a contains Nos. 343-348 in 2 horizontal rows of 3.

US No. C3a A46

Designs: No. 350, Cape of Good Hope #1. No. 351, Penny Black. No. 352, Germany #C36. No. 353, US #245. No. 354, Great Britain #93

1979, Apr. 23 Litho. *Perf. 14*

349 A46	1c multicolored	15	15
350 A46	1c multicolored	15	15
351 A46	22c multicolored	15	15
352 A46	35c multicolored	16	16
353 A46	$1.50 multicolored	80	80
354 A46	$2.50 multicolored	1.40	1.40
a.	Souvenir sheet of 6, #349-353	2.75	2.75
	Nos. 349-354 (6)	2.81	2.81

Sir Rowland Hill (1795-1879), originator of penny postage.

Wright's Flyer A — A47

History of Aviation: 12c, Louis Bleriot landing at Dover, 1909. 18c, Vickers Vimy, 1919. 22c, Spirit of St. Louis, 1927. $1.50, LZ127 Graf Zeppelin, 1928. $2.50, Concorde, 1979.

1979, May 21 Litho. *Perf. 14*

355 A47	5c multicolored	15	15
356 A47	12c multicolored	15	15
357 A47	18c multicolored	15	15
358 A47	22c multicolored	15	15
359 A47	$1.50 multicolored	1.00	1.00
360 A47	$2.50 multicolored	1.50	1.50
a.	Souvenir sheet of 6, #355-360	3.00	3.00
	Nos. 355-360 (6)	3.10	3.10

Map of Anguilla, Map and View of Sombrero Island A48

Map of Anguilla, Map and View of: 12c, Anguillita Island. 18c, Sandy Island. 25c, Prickly Pear Cays. $1, Dog Island. $2.50, Scrub Island.

1979 Litho. *Perf. 14*

361 A48	5c multicolored	15	15
362 A48	12c multicolored	15	15
363 A48	18c multicolored	15	15
364 A48	25c multicolored	18	18
365 A48	$1 multicolored	65	65
366 A48	$2.50 multicolored	1.75	1.75
a.	Souvenir sheet of 6, #361-366	3.00	3.00
	Nos. 361-366 (6)	3.03	3.03

Anguilla's Outer Islands.

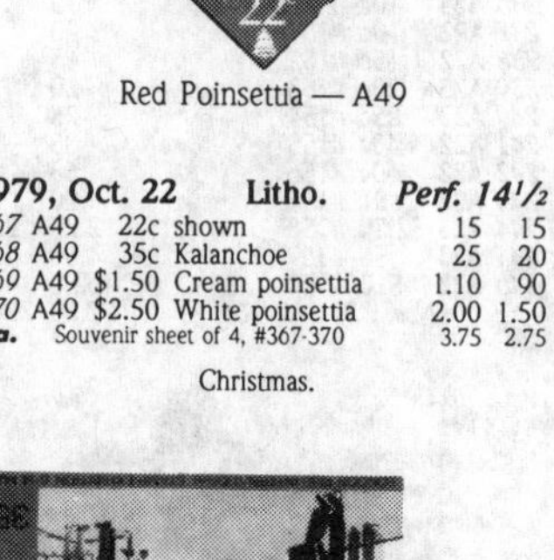
Red Poinsettia — A49

1979, Oct. 22 Litho. *Perf. 14½*

367 A49	22c shown	15	15
368 A49	35c Kalanchoe	25	20
369 A49	$1.50 Cream poinsettia	1.10	90
370 A49	$2.50 White poinsettia	2.00	1.50
a.	Souvenir sheet of 4, #367-370	3.75	2.75

Christmas.

Booths and Frames A50

Designs: 50c, Earls Court Exhibition Hall. $1.50, Penny Black, Great Britain No. 2. $2.50, Exhibition emblem.

1979, Dec. 10 Litho. *Perf. 13, 14½*

371 A50	35c multicolored	20	20
372 A50	50c multicolored	30	30
373 A50	$1.50 multicolored	1.00	1.00
374 A50	$2.50 multicolored	1.50	1.50
a.	Souvenir sheet of 4, #371-374	3.00	3.00

London 1980 Intl. Stamp Exhibition, May 6-14, 1980.

Lake Placid and Olympic Rings — A51

Olympic Rings and: 18c, Ice Hockey. 35c, Figure skating. 50c, Bobsledding. $1, Ski jump. $2.50, Luge.

1980, Jan. Litho. *Perf. 13½, 14½*

375 A51	5c multicolored	15	15
376 A51	18c multicolored	15	15
377 A51	35c multicolored	18	18
378 A51	50c multicolored	28	28
379 A51	$1 multicolored	55	55
380 A51	$2.50 multicolored	1.40	1.40
a.	Souvenir sheet of 6, #375-380	3.00	3.00
	Nos. 375-380 (6)	2.71	2.71

13th Winter Olympic Games, Lake Placid, NY, Feb. 12-24.

Salt Field A52

1980, Apr. 14 Litho. *Perf. 14*

381 A52	5c shown	15	15
382 A52	12c Tallying salt	15	15
383 A52	18c Unloading salt flats	15	15
384 A52	22c Storage pile	15	15
385 A52	$1 Bagging and grinding	60	60
386 A52	$2.50 Loading onto boats	1.40	1.40
a.	Souvenir sheet of 6, #381-386	2.50	2.50
	Set value	2.34	2.34

Salt industry.

Nos. 281, 288 Overprinted: "50th Anniversary / Scouting 1980"

1980, Apr. 16 *Perf. 13½x14*

387 A40	10c multicolored	15	15
388 A40	$2.50 multicolored	2.00	2.00

Nos. 283, 289 Overprinted: "75th Anniversary / Rotary 1980" and Rotary Emblem

1980, Apr. 16 *Perf. 13½x14*

389 A40	20c multicolored	15	15
390 A40	$5 multicolored	3.50	3.50

Rotary International, 75th anniversary.

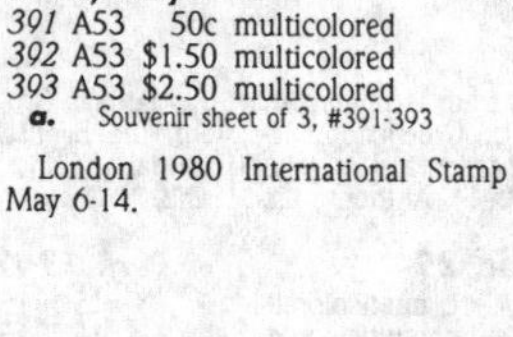
Big Ben, Great Britain #643, London 1980 Emblem A53

Designs: $1.50, Canada #756. $2.50, Statue of Liberty, US #1632.

1980, May

391 A53	50c multicolored	25	25
392 A53	$1.50 multicolored	85	85
393 A53	$2.50 multicolored	1.40	1.40
a.	Souvenir sheet of 3, #391-393	3.00	3.00

London 1980 International Stamp Exhibition, May 6-14.

Queen Mother Elizabeth, 80th Birthday — A54

1980, Aug. 4 **Litho.** ***Perf. 14***

394	A54	35c	multicolored	18	18
395	A54	50c	multicolored	30	30
396	A54	$1.50	multicolored	90	90
397	A54	$3	multicolored	1.75	1.75
a.			Souvenir sheet of 4, #394-397	3.00	3.00

Pelicans — A55

1980, Nov. 10 **Litho.** ***Perf. 14***

398	A55	5c	shown	15	15
399	A55	22c	Great gray herons	15	15
400	A55	$1.50	Swallows	1.00	1.00
401	A55	$3	Hummingbirds	2.00	2.00
a.			Souvenir sheet of 4, #398-401	3.25	3.25

Christmas. For overprints see #405-406.

Nos. 275, 278, 280-290, 334, 400-401 Overprinted: "SEPARATION 1980"

Perf. 13½x14, 14 (A55)

1980, Dec. 18 **Litho.**

402	A40	1c	#275	15	15
403	A40	2c	on 4c #278	15	15
404	A40	5c	on 15c #282	15	15
405	A55	5c	on $1.50 #400	15	15
406	A55	5c	on $3 #401	15	15
407	A40	10c	#281	15	15
408	A40	12c	on $1 #287	15	15
409	A40	14c	on $2.50 #288	15	15
410	A40	15c	#282	15	15
411	A40	18c	on $5 #289	15	15
412	A40	20c	#283	18	18
413	A40	22c	#284	20	20
414	A40	25c	on 15c #282	22	22
415	A40	35c	#285	30	30
416	A44	38c	on 22c #334	32	32
417	A40	40c	on 1c #275	35	35
418	A40	50c	#286	42	42
419	A40	$1	#287	75	75
420	A40	$2.50	#288	1.75	1.75
421	A40	$5	#289	3.50	3.50
422	A40	$10	#290	7.25	7.25
423	A40	$10	on 6c #280	7.25	7.25
			Nos. 402-423 (22)	23.99	23.99

Petition for Separation, 1825 — A56

1980, Dec. 18 ***Perf. 14***

424	A56	18c	shown	15	15
425	A56	22c	Referendum ballot, 1967	15	15
426	A56	35c	Airport blockade, 1967	25	25
427	A56	50c	Anguilla flag	35	35
428	A56	$1	Separation celebration, 1980	65	65
a.			Souvenir sheet of 5, #424-428	1.60	1.60
			Nos. 424-428 (5)	1.55	1.55

Separation from St. Kitts-Nevis.

Nelson's Dockyard, by R. Granger Barrett A57

Ship Paintings: 35c, Agamemnon, Vanguard, Elephant, Captain and Victory, by Nicholas Pocock. 50c, Victory, by Monamy Swaine. $3, Battle of Trafalgar, by Clarkson Stanfield. $5, Lord Nelson, by L.F. Abbott and Nelson's arms.

1981, Mar. 2 **Litho.** ***Perf. 14***

429	A57	22c	multicolored	15	15
430	A57	35c	multicolored	22	22
431	A57	50c	multicolored	32	32
432	A57	$3	multicolored	1.75	1.75

Souvenir Sheet

433	A57	$5	multicolored	2.75	2.75

Lord Horatio Nelson (1758-1805), 175th death anniversary (1980).

Minnie Mouse — A58

Easter: Various Disney characters in Easter outfits.

1981, Mar. 30 **Litho.** ***Perf. 13½***

434	A58	1c	multicolored	15	15
435	A58	2c	multicolored	15	15
436	A58	3c	multicolored	15	15
437	A58	5c	multicolored	15	15
438	A58	7c	multicolored	15	15
439	A58	9c	multicolored	15	15
440	A58	10c	multicolored	15	15
441	A58	$2	multicolored	1.75	1.75
442	A58	$3	multicolored	2.50	2.50
			Set value	4.65	4.65

Souvenir Sheet

443	A58	$5	multicolored	4.75	4.75

Prince Charles, Lady Diana, St. Paul's Cathedral A59

1981, June 15 **Litho.** ***Perf. 14***

444	A59	50c	shown	32	32
a.			Souvenir sheet of 2	65	65
445	A59	$2.50	Althorp	1.60	1.60
a.			Souvenir sheet of 2	3.25	3.25
446	A59	$3	Windsor Castle	2.00	2.00
a.			Souvenir sheet of 2	4.00	4.00

Souvenir Sheet

447	A59	$5	Buckingham Palace	2.50	2.50

Royal Wedding. Nos. 444a-446a contain stamps in different colors.

Boys Climbing Tree — A60

1981 **Litho.** ***Perf. 14***

448	A60	5c	shown	15	15
449	A60	10c	Boys sailing boats	15	15
450	A60	15c	Children playing instruments	15	15
451	A60	$3	Children with animals	2.25	2.25

Souvenir Sheet

452	A60	$4	Boys playing soccer, vert.	3.00	3.00

UNICEF, 35th anniv.

Issued: 5c-15c, July 31; $3-$4, Sept. 30.

"The Children were Nestled all Snug in their Beds" — A61

Christmas: Scenes from Walt Disney's The Night Before Christmas.

1981, Nov. 2 **Litho.** ***Perf. 13½***

453	A61	1c	multicolored	15	15
454	A61	2c	multicolored	15	15
455	A61	3c	multicolored	15	15
456	A61	5c	multicolored	15	15
457	A61	7c	multicolored	15	15
458	A61	10c	multicolored	15	15
459	A61	12c	multicolored	15	15
460	A61	$2	multicolored	1.75	1.75
461	A61	$3	multicolored	2.75	2.75
			Set value	4.90	4.90

Souvenir Sheet

462	A61	$5	multicolored	4.75	4.75

Red Grouper — A62

1982, Jan. 1 **Litho.** ***Perf. 14***

463	A62	1c	shown	15	15
464	A62	5c	Ferries, Blowing Point	15	15
465	A62	10c	Racing boats	15	15
466	A62	15c	Majorettes	15	15
467	A62	20c	Launching boat, Sandy Hill	20	20
468	A62	25c	Coral	25	25
469	A62	30c	Little Bay cliffs	30	30
470	A62	35c	Fountain Cave	35	35
471	A62	40c	Sandy Isld.	40	40
472	A62	45c	Landing, Sombrero	45	45
473	A62	50c	on 45c, #472	50	50
474	A62	60c	Seine fishing	60	60
475	A62	75c	Boat race, Sandy Ground	75	75
476	A62	$1	Bagging lobster, Island Harbor	1.00	1.00
477	A62	$5	Pelicans	5.00	5.00
478	A62	$7.50	Hibiscus	7.50	7.50
479	A62	$10	Queen triggerfish	10.00	10.00
			Nos. 463-479 (17)	27.90	27.90

For overprints and surcharges, see Nos. 507-510, 546A-546D, 578-582, 606-608, 640-647.

Easter — A63

Princess Diana, 21st Birthday — A64

Designs: Butterflies on flowers.

1982, Apr. 5

480	A63	10c	Zebra, anthurium	15	15
481	A63	35c	Caribbean buckeye	35	35
482	A63	75c	Monarch, allamanda	75	75
483	A63	$3	Red rim, orchid	3.00	3.00

Souvenir Sheet

484	A63	$5	Flambeau, amaryllis	3.50	3.50

1982, May 17

Designs: Portraits, 1961-1981.

485	A64	10c	1961	15	15
486	A64	30c	1968	20	20
487	A64	40c	1970	25	25
488	A64	60c	1974	40	40
489	A64	$2	1981	1.40	1.40
490	A64	$3	1981	2.00	2.00
a.			Souvenir sheet of 6, #485-490	4.50	4.50
			Nos. 485-490 (6)	4.40	4.40

Souvenir Sheet

491	A64	$5	1981	3.75	3.75

For overprints, see Nos. 639A-639G.

1982 World Cup — A65

Designs: Various Disney characters playing soccer.

1982, Aug. 3 **Litho.** ***Perf. 11***

492	A65	1c	multicolored	15	15
493	A65	3c	multicolored	15	15
494	A65	4c	multicolored	15	15
495	A65	5c	multicolored	15	15
496	A65	7c	multicolored	15	15
497	A65	9c	multicolored	15	15
498	A65	10c	multicolored	15	15
499	A65	$2.50	multicolored	2.25	2.25
500	A65	$3	multicolored	2.75	2.75
			Set value	5.50	5.50

Souvenir Sheet

Perf. 14

501	A65	$5	multicolored	5.50	5.50

Scouting Year A66

1982, July 5

502	A66	10c	Pitching tent	15	15
503	A66	35c	Marching band	30	30
504	A66	75c	Sailing	65	65
505	A66	$3	Flag bearers	2.50	2.50

Souvenir Sheet

506	A66	$5	Camping	4.00	4.00

Nos. 465, 474-475, 477 Overprinted: "COMMONWEALTH / GAMES 1982"

1982, Oct. 18 **Litho.** ***Perf. 14***

507	A62	10c	multicolored	15	15
508	A62	60c	multicolored	45	45
509	A62	75c	multicolored	55	55
510	A62	$5	multicolored	3.75	3.75

12th Commonwealth Games, Brisbane, Australia, Sept. 30-Oct. 9.

Christmas — A67

Designs: Scenes from Walt Disney's Winnie the Pooh.

1982, Nov. 29

511	A67	1c	multicolored	15	15
512	A67	2c	multicolored	15	15
513	A67	3c	multicolored	15	15
514	A67	5c	multicolored	15	15
515	A67	7c	multicolored	15	15
516	A67	10c	multicolored	15	15
517	A67	12c	multicolored	15	15

518 A67	20c	multicolored	15	15
519 A67	$5	multicolored	4.00	4.00
		Set value	4.60	4.60

Souvenir Sheet

520 A67	$5	multicolored	4.50	4.50

Commonwealth Day (Mar. 14) — A68

1983, Feb. 28 Litho. *Perf. 14*

521 A68	10c	Carnival procession	15	15
522 A68	35c	Flags	30	30
523 A68	75c	Economic cooperation	65	65
524 A68	$2.50	Salt pond	2.00	2.00

Souvenir Sheet

525 A68	$5	Map showing Commonwealth	4.00	4.00

Easter — A69

Ten Commandments.

1983, Mar. 31 Litho. *Perf. 14*

526 A69	1c	multicolored	15	15
527 A69	2c	multicolored	15	15
528 A69	3c	multicolored	15	15
529 A69	10c	multicolored	15	15
530 A69	35c	multicolored	25	25
531 A69	60c	multicolored	45	45
532 A69	75c	multicolored	55	55
533 A69	$2	multicolored	1.50	1.50
534 A69	$2.50	multicolored	1.75	1.75
535 A69	$5	multicolored	3.75	3.75
		Nos. 526-535 (10)	8.85	8.85

Souvenir Sheet

536 A69	$5	Moses Taking Tablets	4.00	4.00

Local Turtles and World Wildlife Fund Emblem A70

1983, Aug. 10 Litho. *Perf. 13½*

537 A70	10c	Leatherback	15	15
538 A70	35c	Hawksbill	35	35
539 A70	75c	Green	75	75
540 A70	$1	Loggerhead	1.00	1.00

Souvenir Sheet

541 A70	$5	Leatherback, diff.	4.00	4.00

1983, Aug. 10 Litho. *Perf. 12*

537a A70	10c	Leatherback	15	15
538a A70	35c	Hawksbill	35	35
539a A70	75c	Green	75	75
540a A70	$1	Loggerhead	1.00	1.00

Manned Flight Bicentenary — A71

1983, Aug. 22 *Perf. 14*

542 A71	10c	Montgolfiere, 1783	15	15
543 A71	60c	Blanchard & Jeffries, 1785	45	45
544 A71	$1	Giffard's airship, 1852	75	75
545 A71	$2.50	Lilienthal's glider, 1890	1.75	1.75

Souvenir Sheet

546 A71	$5	Wright Brothers' plane, 1909	3.75	3.75

Nos. 465, 471, 476-477 Overprinted: 150TH ANNIVERSARY / ABOLITION OF SLAVERY ACT

1983, Oct. 24 Litho. *Perf. 14*

546A A62	10c	Racing boats	15	15
546B A62	40c	Sandy Isld	32	32
546C A62	$1	Bagging lobster, Island Harbor	80	80
546D A62	$5	Pelicans	4.00	4.00

Jiminy Cricket — A72

Designs: Various Disney productions.

1983, Nov. 14 *Perf. 13½*

547 A72	1c	shown	15	15
548 A72	2c	Jiminy Cricket, kettle	15	15
549 A72	3c	Jiminy Cricket, toys	15	15
550 A72	4c	Mickey and Morty	15	15
551 A72	5c	Scrooge McDuck	15	15
552 A72	6c	Minnie and Goofy	15	15
553 A72	10c	Goofy and Elf	15	15
554 A72	$2	Scrooge McDuck, diff.	1.75	1.75
555 A72	$3	Disney characters	2.75	2.75
		Set value	4.80	4.80

Souvenir Sheet

556 A72	$5	Scrooge McDuck	4.50	4.50

Boys' Brigade Centenary — A73

1983, Sept. 12 Litho. *Perf. 14*

557 A73	10c	Anguilla company, banner	15	15
558 A73	$5	Marching with drummer	3.75	3.75
a.		Souvenir sheet of 2, #557-558	3.85	3.85

1984 Olympics, Los Angeles — A74

Mickey Mouse Competing in Decathlon.

1984, Feb. 20 Litho. *Perf. 14*

559 A74	1c	100-meter run	15	15
560 A74	2c	Long jump	15	15
561 A74	3c	Shot put	15	15
562 A74	4c	High jump	15	15
563 A74	5c	400-meter run	15	15
564 A74	6c	Hurdles	15	15
565 A74	10c	Discus	15	15
566 A74	$1	Pole vault	95	95
567 A74	$4	Javelin	3.75	3.75
		Set value	5.00	5.00

Souvenir Sheet

568 A74	$5	1500-meter run	5.50	5.50

1984, Apr. 24 *Perf. 12½x12*

559a A74	1c		15	15
560a A74	2c		15	15
561a A74	3c		15	15
562a A74	4c		15	15
563a A74	5c		15	15
564a A74	6c		15	15
565a A74	10c		15	15
566a A74	$1		95	95
567a A74	$4		3.75	3.75
		Set value	5.00	5.00

Souvenir Sheet

568a A74	$5	With Olympic rings emblem	5.50	5.50

Nos. 559a-567a inscribed with Olympic rings emblem. Printed in sheets of 5 plus label.

Easter — A75

Ceiling and Wall Frescoes, La Stanze della Segnatura, by Raphael (details).

1984, Apr. 19 Litho. *Perf. 13½x14*

569 A75	10c	Justice	15	15
570 A75	25c	Poetry	18	18
571 A75	35c	Philosophy	25	25
572 A75	40c	Theology	30	30
573 A75	$1	Abraham & Paul	75	75
574 A75	$2	Moses & Matthew	1.50	1.50
575 A75	$3	John & David	2.25	2.25
576 A75	$4	Peter & Adam	3.00	3.00
		Nos. 569-576 (8)	8.38	8.38

Souvenir Sheet

577 A75	$5	Astronomy	3.75	3.75

Nos. 463, 469, 477-479 Surcharged

1984 Litho. *Perf. 14*

578 A62	25c	on $7.50 #478	20	20
579 A62	35c	on 30c #469	28	28
580 A62	60c	on 1c #463	48	48
581 A62	$2.50	on $5 #477	2.00	2.00
582 A62	$2.50	on $10 #479	2.00	2.00
		Nos. 578-582 (5)	4.96	4.96

Issue dates: 25c, May 17, others, Apr. 24.

Ausipex '84 A76

Australian stamps.

1984, July 16 Litho. *Perf. 13½*

583 A76	10c	No. 2	15	15
584 A76	75c	No. 18	55	55
585 A76	$1	No. 130	80	80
586 A76	$2.50	No. 178	2.00	2.00

Souvenir Sheet

587 A76	$5	Nos. 378, 379	3.75	3.75

Slavery Abolition Sesquicentennial — A77

Abolitionists and Vignettes: 10c, Thomas Fowell Buxton, planting sugar cane. 25c, Abraham Lincoln, cotton field. 35c, Henri Christophe, armed slave revolt. 60c, Thomas Clarkson, addressing Anti-Slavery Society. 75c, William Wilberforce, Slave auction. $1, Olaudah Equiano, slave raid on Benin coast. $2.50, General Gordon, slave convoy in Sudan. $5, Granville Sharp, restraining ship captain from boarding slave.

1984, Aug. 1 *Perf. 12*

588 A77	10c	multicolored	15	15
589 A77	25c	multicolored	18	18
590 A77	35c	multicolored	25	25
591 A77	60c	multicolored	42	42
592 A77	75c	multicolored	50	50
593 A77	$1	multicolored	72	72
594 A77	$2.50	multicolored	1.75	1.75
595 A77	$5	multicolored	3.50	3.50
a.		Miniature sheet of 8, #588-595	7.75	7.75
		Nos. 588-595 (8)	7.47	7.47

For overprints, see Nos. 688-695a.

Christmas — A78

Various Disney characters and celebrations.

Perf. 14, 12½x12 ($2)

1984, Nov. 12 Litho.

596 A78	1c	multicolored	15	15
597 A78	2c	multicolored	15	15
598 A78	3c	multicolored	15	15
599 A78	4c	multicolored	15	15
600 A78	5c	multicolored	15	15
601 A78	10c	multicolored	15	15
602 A78	$1	multicolored	80	80
603 A78	$2	multicolored	1.65	1.65
604 A78	$4	multicolored	3.25	3.25
		Set value	6.00	6.00

Souvenir Sheet

605 A78	$5	multicolored	4.25	4.25

Nos. 464-465, 477 Overprinted or Surcharged: "U.P.U. CONGRESS / HAMBURG 1984"

1984, Aug. 13

606 A62	5c	#464	15	15
607 A62	20c	on 10c #465	16	16
608 A62	$5	#477	4.00	4.00

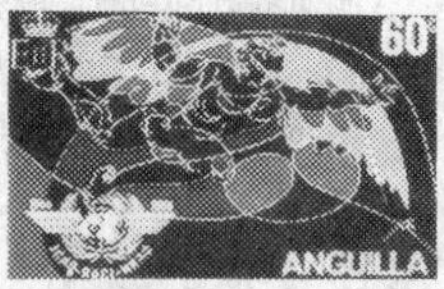

Intl. Civil Aviation Org., 40th Anniv. A79

1984, Dec. 3 Litho. *Perf. 14*

609 A79	60c	Icarus, by Hans Erni	45	45
610 A79	75c	Sun Princess, by Sadiou Diouf	55	55
611 A79	$2.50	Anniv. emblem, vert.	1.75	1.75

Souvenir Sheet

612 A79	$5	Map of the Caribbean	3.75	3.75

Audubon Birth Bicent. — A80

Queen Mother 85th Birthday — A81

Illustrations by artist and naturalist J. J. Audubon (1785-1851).

1985, Apr. 30 Litho. *Perf. 14*

613 A80	10c	Hirundo rustica	15	15
614 A80	60c	Mycteria americana	45	45
615 A80	75c	Sterna dougallii	55	55
616 A80	$5	Pandion haliaetus	3.75	3.75

Souvenir Sheets

617 A80	$4	Vireo solitarus, horiz.	3.00	3.00
618 A80	$4	Piranga ludoviciana, horiz.	3.00	3.00

1985, July 2

Photographs: 10c, Visiting the children's ward at King's College Hospital. $2, Inspecting Royal Marine Volunteer Cadets at Deal. $3, Outside Clarence House in London. $5, In an open carriage at Ascot.

619 A81	10c	multicolored	15	15
620 A81	$2	multicolored	1.50	1.50

621 A81 $3 multicolored 2.25 2.25

Souvenir Sheet

622 A81 $5 multicolored 3.75 3.75

Nos. 619-621 printed in sheetlets of 5.

Birds A82

1985-86 Litho. *Perf. 13½x14*

623 A82 5c Brown pelican 15 15
624 A82 10c Turtle dove 15 15
625 A82 15c Man-o-war 15 15
626 A82 20c Antillean crested hummingbird 15 15
627 A82 25c White-tailed tropicbird 20 20
628 A82 30c Caribbean elaenia 22 22
629 A82 35c Black-whiskered vireo 25 25
629A A82 35c Lesser Antillean bullfinch ('86) 28 28
630 A82 40c Yellow-crowned night heron 30 30
631 A82 45c Pearly-eyed thrasher 35 35
632 A82 50c Laughing bird 38 38
633 A82 65c Brown booby 48 48
634 A82 80c Gray kingbird 60 60
635 A82 $1 Audubon's shearwater 75 75
636 A82 $1.35 Roseate tern 1.00 1.00
637 A82 $2.50 Bananaquit 1.85 1.85
638 A82 $5 Belted kingfisher 3.75 3.75
639 A82 $10 Green heron 7.50 7.50
Nos. 623-639 (18) 18.51 18.51

Issue dates: 25c, 65c, $1.35, $5, July 22. 45c, 50c, 80c, $1, $10, Sept. 30. 5c-20c, 30c, No. 629, 40c, $2.50, Nov. 11. No. 629A, Mar. 10.

For overprints and surcharges, see Nos. 678-682, 713-716, 723-739, 750-753, 764-767.

Nos. 485-491 Overprinted "PRINCE HENRY / BIRTH 15.9.84."

1985, Oct. 31 Litho. *Perf. 14*

639A A64 10c multicolored 15 15
639B A64 30c multicolored 22 22
639C A64 40c multicolored 30 30
639D A64 60c multicolored 45 45
639E A64 $2 multicolored 1.50 1.50
639F A64 $3 multicolored 2.25 2.25
h. Souv. sheet of 6, #639A-639F 4.80 4.80
Nos. 639A-639F (7) 8.62 8.62

Souvenir Sheet

639G A64 $5 multicolored 3.75 3.75

Nos. 464, 469 and 477 Ovptd. with Anniversary Emblem and "GIRL GUIDES 75th ANNIVERSARY / 1910-1985"

1985, Oct. 14 Litho. *Perf. 14*

640 A62 5c multicolored 15 15
641 A62 30c multicolored 22 22
642 A62 75c multicolored 55 55
643 A62 $5 multicolored 3.75 3.75

Nos. 465 and 470 Overprinted or Surcharged with Organization Emblem and "80th ANNIVERSARY ROTARY 1985."

1985, Nov. 18

644 A62 10c multicolored 15 15
645 A62 35c on 30c multi 25 25
Set value 33 33

Nos. 476, 469 Surcharged or Ovptd. with Emblem, Text and "INTERNATIONAL YOUTH YEAR"

1985, Nov. 18

646 A62 $1 multicolored 75 75
647 A62 $5 on 30c multi 3.75 3.75

Brothers Grimm — A83

Christmas: Disney characters in Hansel and Gretel.

1985, Nov. 11 Litho. *Perf. 14*

648 A83 5c multicolored 15 15
649 A83 50c multicolored 42 42
650 A83 90c multicolored 70 70
651 A83 $4 multicolored 3.25 3.25

Souvenir Sheet

652 A83 $5 multicolored 4.50 4.50

Mark Twain (1835-1910), Author — A84

Disney characters in Huckleberry Finn.

1985, Nov. 11

653 A84 10c multicolored 15 15
654 A84 60c multicolored 65 65
654A A84 $1 multicolored 1.00 1.00
655 A84 $3 multicolored 3.25 3.25

Souvenir Sheet

656 A84 $5 multicolored 4.50 4.50

Christmas. No. 654 printed in sheets of 8.

Statue of Liberty Centennial A85

1985 Nov. 25

657 A85 10c Danmark, Denmark 15 15
658 A85 20c Eagle, USA 18 18
659 A85 60c Amerigo Vespucci, Italy 50 50
660 A85 75c Sir Winston Churchill, G.B. 60 60
661 A85 $2 Nippon Maru, Japan 1.65 1.65
662 A85 $2.50 Gorch, Germany 1.90 1.90

Souvenir Sheet

663 A85 $5 Statue of Liberty, vert. 3.75 3.75

Easter — A86

Stained glass windows.

1986, Mar. 27 Litho. *Perf. 14*

664 A86 10c multicolored 15 15
665 A86 25c multicolored 20 20
666 A86 45c multicolored 35 35
667 A86 $4 multicolored 3.00 3.00

Souvenir Sheet

668 A86 $5 multi, horiz. 4.00 4.00

A87

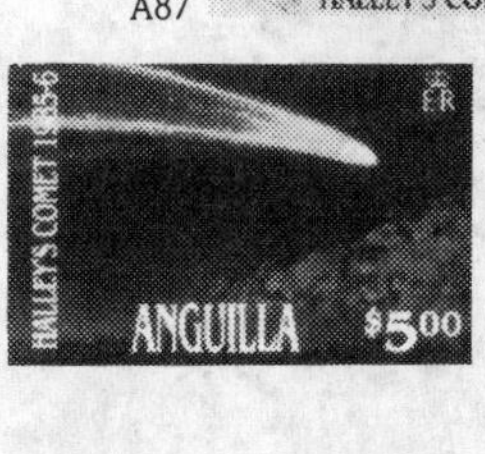

Halley's Comet A88

Designs: 5c, Johannes Hevelius (1611-1687), Mayan temple observatory. 10c, US Viking probe landing on Mars, 1976. 60c, Theatri Cosmicum (detail), 1668. $4, Sighting, 1835. $5, Comet over Anguilla.

1986, Mar. 24

669 A87 5c multicolored 15 15
670 A87 10c multicolored 15 15
671 A87 60c multicolored 45 45
672 A87 $4 multicolored 3.00 3.00

Souvenir Sheet

673 A88 $5 multicolored 3.75 3.75

Queen Elizabeth II, 60th Birthday
Common Design Type

1986, Apr. 21

674 CD339 20c Inspecting guards, 1946 15 15
675 CD339 $2 Garter Ceremony, 1985 1.50 1.50
676 CD339 $3 Trooping the color 2.25 2.25

Souvenir Sheet

677 CD339 $5 Christening, 1926 3.75 3.75

Nos. 623, 631, 635, 637 and 639 Ovptd. "AMERIPEX 1986"

1986, May 22 *Perf. 13½x14*

678 A82 5c multicolored 15 15
679 A82 45c multicolored 35 35
680 A82 $1 multicolored 75 75
681 A82 $2.50 multicolored 1.85 1.85
682 A82 $10 multicolored 7.50 7.50
Nos. 678-682 (5) 10.60 10.60

Wedding of Prince Andrew and Sarah Ferguson — A89

1986, July 23 Litho. *Perf. 14*

683 A89 10c Couple 15 15
684 A89 35c Andrew 25 25
685 A89 $2 Sarah 1.50 1.50
686 A89 $3 Couple, diff. 2.25 2.25

Souvenir Sheet

687 A89 $6 Westminster Abbey 4.50 4.50

Nos. 588-595 Ovptd. "INTERNATIONAL / YEAR OF / PEACE"

1986, Sept. 29 Litho. *Perf. 12*

688 A77 10c multicolored 15 15
689 A77 25c multicolored 20 20
690 A77 35c multicolored 28 28
691 A77 60c multicolored 48 48
692 A77 75c multicolored 60 60
693 A77 $1 multicolored 80 80
694 A77 $2.50 multicolored 1.75 1.75
695 A77 $5 multicolored 3.50 3.50
a. Miniature sheet of 8, #688-695 7.75 7.75
Nos. 688-695 (8) 7.76 7.76

Ships — A90

1986, Nov. 29 Litho. *Perf. 14*

696 A90 10c Trading Sloop 15 15
697 A90 45c Lady Rodney 35 35
698 A90 80c West Derby 65 65
699 A90 $3 Warspite 2.40 2.40

Souvenir Sheet

700 A90 $6 Boat Race Day, vert. 4.50 4.50

Christmas.

> *Anguilla stamps can be mounted in the Scott British Leeward Islands album.*

Discovery of America, 500th Anniv. (in 1992) — A91

Dragon Tree — A92

Designs: 5c, Christopher Columbus, astrolabe. 10c, Aboard ship. 35c, Santa Maria. 80c, Ferdinand, Isabella, horiz. $4, Indians. No. 707, Caribbean manatee, horiz.

1986, Dec. 22

701 A91 5c multicolored 15 15
702 A91 10c multicolored 15 15
703 A91 35c multicolored 28 28
704 A91 80c multicolored 65 65
705 A91 $4 multicolored 3.20 3.20
Nos. 701-705 (5) 4.43 4.43

Souvenir Sheets

706 A92 $5 shown 4.00 4.00
707 A92 $5 multicolored 4.00 4.00

Butterflies A93

1987, Apr. 14 Litho. *Perf. 14*

708 A93 10c Monarch 15 15
709 A93 80c White peacock 65 65
710 A93 $1 Zebra 80 80
711 A93 $2 Caribbean buckeye 1.60 1.60

Souvenir Sheet

712 A93 $6 Flambeau 4.50 4.50

Easter.

Nos. 629A, 631, 634 and 639 Ovptd. with CAPEX '87 Emblem in Red

1987, May 25 Litho. *Perf. 13½x14*

713 A82 35c on No. 629A 28 28
714 A82 45c on No. 631 35 35
715 A82 80c on No. 634 60 60
716 A82 $10 on No. 639 7.50 7.50

Separation from St. Kitts and Nevis, 20th Anniv. — A94

Designs: 10c, Old goose iron, electric iron. 35c, Old East End School, Albena Lake-Hodge Comprehensive College. 45c, Old market place, People's Market. 80c, Old ferries and modern ferry at Blowing Point. $1, Old and new cable and wireless offices. $2, Public meeting at Burrowes Park, House of Assembly.

1987, May 25 *Perf. 14*

717 A94 10c multicolored 15 15
718 A94 35c multicolored 22 22
719 A94 45c multicolored 35 35
720 A94 80c multicolored 60 60
721 A94 $1 multicolored 75 75
722 A94 $2 multicolored 1.50 1.50
a. Souvenir sheet of 6, #717-722 3.50 3.50
Nos. 717-722 (6) 3.57 3.57

Nos. 623, 625-628, 629A-639 Ovptd. "20 YEARS OF PROGRESS / 1967-1987" in Red or Surcharged in Red & Black

1987, Sept. 4 Litho. *Perf. 13½x14*

723 A82 5c No. 623 15 15
724 A82 10c on 15c No. 625 15 15
725 A82 15c No. 625 15 15
726 A82 20c No. 626 15 15

727 A82	25c	No. 627	18	18
728 A82	30c	No. 628	20	20
729 A82	35c	No. 629A	22	22
730 A82	40c	No. 630	28	28
731 A82	45c	No. 631	32	32
732 A82	50c	No. 632	35	35
733 A82	65c	No. 633	45	45
734 A82	80c	No. 634	55	55
735 A82	$1	No. 635	70	70
736 A82	$1.35	No. 636	90	90
737 A82	$2.50	No. 637	1.75	1.75
738 A82	$5	No. 638	3.50	3.50
739 A82	$10	No. 639	6.75	6.75
		Nos. 723-739 (17)	16.75	16.75

Cricket World Cup A95

Various action scenes.

1987, Oct. 5 ***Perf. 14***

740 A95	10c	multicolored	15	15
741 A95	35c	multicolored	28	28
742 A95	45c	multicolored	38	38
743 A95	$2.50	multicolored	2.00	2.00

Souvenir Sheet

744 A95	$6	multicolored	4.50	4.50

Sea Shells, Crabs A96

1987, Nov. 2

745 A96	10c	West Indian top shell	15	15
746 A96	35c	Ghost crab	28	28
747 A96	50c	Spiny Caribbean vase	42	42
748 A96	$2	Great land crab	1.60	1.60

Souvenir Sheet

749 A96	$6	Queen conch	4.75	4.75

Christmas.

Nos. 629A, 635-636 and 639 Ovptd. "40TH WEDDING ANNIVERSARY / H.M. QUEEN ELIZABETH II / H.R.H. THE DUKE OF EDINBURGH" in Scarlet

1987, Dec. 14 **Litho.** ***Perf. 13½x14***

750 A82	35c	multicolored	28	28
751 A82	$1	multicolored	75	75
752 A82	$1.35	multicolored	1.00	1.00
753 A82	$10	multicolored	7.50	7.50

Easter (Lilies) — A97

1988 Summer Olympics, Seoul — A98

1988, Mar. 28 **Litho.** ***Perf. 14***

754 A97	30c	Crinum erubescens	28	28
755 A97	45c	Hymenocallis caribaea	40	40
756 A97	$1	Crinum macowanii	88	88
757 A97	$2.50	Hemerocallis fulva	2.20	2.20

Souvenir Sheet

758 A97	$6	Lilium longiflorum	5.25	5.25

1988, July 25 **Litho.** ***Perf. 14***

759 A98	35c	4x100-Meter relay	28	28
760 A98	45c	Windsurfing	35	35
761 A98	50c	Tennis	38	38
762 A98	80c	Basketball	60	60

Souvenir Sheet

763 A98	$6	Women's 200 meters	4.50	4.50

Nos. 629A, 634-635 and 637 Ovptd. "H.R.H. PRINCESS / ALEXANDRA'S / VISIT NOVEMBER 1988"

1988, Dec. 14 **Litho.** ***Perf. 13½x14***

764 A82	35c	multicolored	28	28
765 A82	80c	multicolored	60	60
766 A82	$1	multicolored	75	75
767 A82	$2.50	multicolored	1.90	1.90

Marine Life A99

1988, Dec. 5 **Litho.** ***Perf. 14***

768 A99	35c	Common sea fan	28	28
769 A99	80c	Coral crab	60	60
770 A99	$1	Grooved brain coral	75	75
771 A99	$1.60	Old wife	1.20	1.20

Souvenir Sheet

772 A99	$6	West Indies spiny lobster	4.50	4.50

Christmas.

Lizards A100

1989, Feb. 20 **Litho.** ***Perf. 13½x14***

773 A100	45c	Wood slave	35	35
774 A100	80c	Slippery back	60	60
775 A100	$2.50	Iguana	1.75	1.75

Souvenir Sheet

776 A100	$6	Tree lizard	4.50	4.50

Easter — A101

Paintings: 35c, Christ Crowned with Thorns, by Hieronymous Bosch (c. 1450-1516. 80c, Christ Bearing the Cross, by David. $1, The Deposition, by David. $1.60, Pieta, by Rogier van der Weyden (1400-1464). $6, Crucified Christ with the Virgin Mary and Saints, by Raphael.

1989, Mar. 23 **Litho.** ***Perf. 14x13½***

777 A101	35c	multicolored	28	28
778 A101	80c	multicolored	60	60
779 A101	$1	multicolored	75	75
780 A101	$1.60	multicolored	1.20	1.20

Souvenir Sheet

781 A101	$6	multicolored	4.50	4.50

University of the West Indies, 40th Anniv. — A102

1989, Apr. 24 **Litho.** ***Perf. 14x13½***

782 A102	$5	Coat of arms	3.75	3.75

Nos. 634-636 and 638 Ovptd. "20th / ANNIVERSARY / MOON / LANDING"

1989, July 3 **Litho.** ***Perf. 13½X14***

783 A82	80c	multicolored	60	60
784 A82	$1	multicolored	75	75
785 A82	$1.35	multicolored	1.00	1.00
786 A82	$5	multicolored	3.75	3.75

Christmas — A103

Well-known and historic houses.

1989, Dec. 4 **Litho.** ***Perf. 13½x14***

787 A103	5c	Lone Star, 1930	15	15
788 A103	35c	Whitehouse, 1906	28	28
789 A103	45c	Hodges House	35	35
790 A103	80c	Warden's Place	60	60

Souvenir Sheet

791 A103	$6	Wallblake House, 1787	4.50	4.50

Fish A104

1990, Apr. 2 **Litho.** ***Perf. 13½x14***

792 A104	5c	Blear eye	15	15
793 A104	10c	Redman	15	15
794 A104	15c	Speckletail	15	15
795 A104	25c	Grunt	18	18
796 A104	30c	Amber jack	22	22
797 A104	35c	Red hind	26	26
798 A104	40c	Goatfish	30	30
799 A104	45c	Old wife	34	34
800 A104	50c	Butter fish	38	38
801 A104	65c	Shell fish	48	48
802 A104	80c	Yellowtail snapper	60	60
803 A104	$1	Katy	75	75
804 A104	$1.35	Mutton grouper	1.00	1.00
805 A104	$2.50	Doctor fish	1.85	1.85
806 A104	$5	Angelfish	3.75	3.75
807 A104	$10	Barracuda	7.50	7.50
		Nos. 792-807 (16)	18.06	18.06

Nos. 792-793, 797 exist inscribed 1992. For overprints and surcharge see #821-824, 849.

Easter — A105

1990, Apr. 2 ***Perf. 14x13½***

811 A105	35c	Last Supper	26	26
812 A105	45c	Trial	34	34
813 A105	$1.35	Calvary	1.00	1.00
814 A105	$2.50	Empty tomb	1.85	1.85

Souvenir Sheet

815 A105	$6	The Resurrection	4.50	4.50

See Nos. 834-838.

Cape of Good Hope #7 — A106

Stamps of Great Britain and exhibition emblem: 25c, #1, vert. 50c, #2, vert. $2.50, #93. $6, #1-2.

1990, Apr. 30 ***Perf. 14***

816 A106	25c	multicolored	18	18
817 A106	50c	multicolored	38	38
818 A106	$1.50	shown	1.10	1.10
819 A106	$2.50	multicolored	1.85	1.85

Souvenir Sheet

820 A106	$6	multicolored	4.50	4.50

Stamp World London '90, Penny Black 150th anniv.

Nos. 803-806 Overprinted:
a. EXPO '90
b. 1990 INTERNATIONAL / LITERACY YEAR
c. WORLD CUP FOOTBALL / CHAMPIONSHIPS 1990
d. 90TH BIRTHDAY / H.M. THE QUEEN MOTHER

1990, Sept. 24 **Litho.** ***Perf. 13½x14***

821 A104(a)	$1	Katy	75	75
822 A104(b)	$1.35	Mutton grouper	1.00	1.00
823 A104(c)	$2.50	Doctor fish	1.85	1.85
824 A104(d)	$5	Angelfish	3.75	3.75

Christmas — A107

Birds.

1990, Dec. 3 ***Perf. 14***

825 A107	10c	Laughing gull	15	15
826 A107	35c	Brown booby	26	26
827 A107	$1.50	Bridled tern	1.10	1.10
828 A107	$3.50	Brown pelican	2.65	2.65

Souvenir Sheet

829 A107	$6	Least tern	4.50	4.50

Flags A108

1991, Nov. 5 **Litho.** ***Perf. 13½x14***

830 A108	50c	Mermaid	38	38
831 A108	80c	New Anguilla official	60	60
832 A108	$1	Three dolphins	75	75
833 A108	$5	Governor's official	3.75	3.75

Nos. 811-815 Inscribed or Overprinted "1991"

1991, Apr. 30 **Litho.** ***Perf. 14x13½***

834 A105	35c	like #811	25	25
835 A105	45c	like #812	35	35
836 A105	$1.35	like #813	1.00	1.00
837 A105	$2.50	like #814	1.85	1.85

Souvenir Sheet

838 A105	$6	like #815	7.75	7.75

Easter. "1990" obliterated by black bar in souvenir sheet margin.

Christmas — A109

Perf. 14x13½, 13½x14

1991, Dec. **Litho.**

839 A109	5c	Angel, vert.	15	15
840 A109	35c	Santa, vert.	25	25
841 A109	80c	shown	60	60
842 A109	$1	Palm trees, poinsettias	75	75

Souvenir Sheet

843 A109	$5	Homes, holly	3.75	3.75

Easter A110

Designs: 35c, Church, angels holding palms, vert. 45c Church, angels singing, vert. 80c, Village. $1, People going to church, vert. $5, People at beach, sailboats.

1992 Litho. *Perf. 14*

844 A110 35c multicolored 30 30
845 A110 45c multicolored 38 38
846 A110 80c multicolored 70 70
847 A110 $1 multicolored 85 85
848 A110 $5 multicolored 4.25 4.25
Nos. 844-848 (5) 6.48 6.48

No. 796 Surcharged **$1.60**

1992, June 10 Litho. *Perf. 13½x14*

849 A104 $1.60 on 30c #796 1.40 1.40

No. 849 inscribed "1992."

Independence, 25th Anniv. — A111

1992, Aug. 10 Litho. *Perf. 14*

850 A111 80c Official seal, flag 80 80
851 A111 $1 Official seal 1.00 1.00
852 A111 $1.60 Flags, airport 1.60 1.60
853 A111 $2 First seal 2.00 2.00

Souvenir Sheet

854 A111 $10 #1, 8-11, 15-16 10.00 10.00

No. 854 contains one 85x85mm stamp.

Sailboat Racing A112

Designs: 20c, On course. 35c, Stylized boat poster. 45c, Start of race. No. 858, Blue Bird, 1971, vert. No. 859, Construction plans for Blue Bird, vert. $1, Stylized boat poster, diff. $6, Like Nos. 855 & 857.

Perf. 13½x14, 14x13½

1992, Oct. 12 Litho.

855 A112 20c multicolored 15 15
856 A112 35c multicolored 25 25
857 A112 45c multicolored 32 32
858 A112 80c multicolored 58 58
859 A112 80c multicolored 58 58
a. Pair, #858-859 1.16 1.16
860 A112 $1 multicolored 70 70
Nos. 855-860 (6) 2.58 2.58

Souvenir Sheet

861 A112 $6 multicolored 4.55 4.55

No. 861 contains one 96x31mm stamp.

Discovery of America, 500th Anniv. A113

1992, Dec. 15 Litho. *Perf. 14*

862 A113 80c Landfall 70 70
863 A113 $1 Columbus, vert. 85 85
864 A113 $2 Fleet 1.65 1.65
865 A113 $3 Pinta 2.50 2.50

Souvenir Sheet

866 A113 $6 Map of voyage, vert. 5.00 5.00

Christmas A114

Various Christmas trees and: 20c, Mucka Jumbie on stilts. 70c, Masquerading house to house. $1.05, Christmas baking, old oven style. $2.40, $5, Collecting presents.

1992, Dec. 7

867 A114 20c multicolored 16 16
868 A114 70c multicolored 60 60
869 A114 $1.05 multicolored 90 90
870 A114 $2.40 multicolored 2.05 2.05

Souvenir Sheet

871 A114 $5 Sheet of 1 + 3 labels 4.25 4.25

Labels on No. 871 are similar to Nos. 867-869, but without denomination.

Easter — A115

Children's drawings: 20c, Kite flying. 45c, Cliff top village service. 80c, Morning devotion on Sombero. $1.50, Hilltop church service. $5, Good Friday kites.

1993, Mar. 29 Litho. *Perf. 14*

872 A115 20c multicolored 16 16
873 A115 45c multicolored 38 38
874 A115 80c multicolored 65 65
875 A115 $1.50 multicolored 1.25 1.15

Souvenir Sheet

876 A115 $5 multicolored 4.25 4.25

No. 876 contains one 42x56mm stamp.

Native Industries A116

1993, June 23 Litho. *Perf. 14*

877 A116 20c Salt 16 16
878 A116 80c Tobacco 65 65
879 A116 $1 Cotton 80 80
880 A116 $2 Sugar cane 1.60 1.60

Souvenir Sheet

881 A116 $6 Fishing 4.75 4.75

Coronation of Queen Elizabeth II, 40th Anniv. — A117

Designs: 80c, Lord Great Chamberlain presents the spurs of chivalry. $1, The benediction. $2, Queen Elizabeth II, coronation photograph. $3, St. Edward's Crown. $6, Queen, Prince Philip in Gold State Coach.

1993, Aug. 16 Litho. *Perf. 14*

882 A117 80c multicolored 65 65
883 A117 $1 multicolored 80 80
884 A117 $2 multicolored 1.60 1.60
885 A117 $3 multicolored 2.40 2.40

Souvenir Sheet

886 A117 $6 multicolored 4.75 4.75

Anguilla Carnival — A118

1993, Aug. 23 Litho. *Perf. 14*

887 A118 20c Pan musician 16 16
888 A118 45c Pirates 35 35
889 A118 80c Stars 65 65
890 A118 $1 Playing mas 80 80
891 A118 $2 Masqueraders 1.60 1.60
892 A118 $3 Commandos 2.40 2.40
Nos. 887-892 (6) 5.96 5.96

Souvenir Sheet

893 A118 $5 Carnival fantasy 4.00 4.00

Christmas — A119

Mail Delivery — A120

Traditional Christmas customs: 20c, Mucka Jumbies. 35c, Serenaders. 45c, Baking. $3, Five-fingers Christmas tree. $4, Mucka Jumbies and serenaders.

1993, Dec. 7 Litho. *Perf. 14x13½*

894 A119 20c multicolored 18 18
895 A119 35c multicolored 30 30
896 A119 45c multicolored 38 38
897 A119 $3 multicolored 2.50 2.50

Souvenir Sheet

Perf. 14

898 A119 $4 multicolored 3.50 3.50

No. 898 contains one 54x42mm stamp.

1993, Feb. 11 Litho. *Perf. 14*

Designs: 20c, Traveling Branch mail van, Sandy Ground, horiz. 45c, Mail boat, Betsy R, The Forest. 80c, Old post office, horiz. $1, Mail by jeep, Island Harbor. $4, New post office, 1993, horiz.

899 A120 20c multicolored 18 18
900 A120 45c multicolored 38 38
901 A120 80c multicolored 70 70
902 A120 $1 multicolored 85 85
903 A120 $4 multicolored 3.50 3.50
Nos. 899-903 (5) 5.61 5.61

Royal Visits — A121

Easter — A122

1994, Feb. 18

904 A121 45c Princess Alexandra 38 38
905 A121 50c Princess Alice 42 42
906 A121 80c Prince Philip 70 70
907 A121 $1 Prince Charles 85 85
908 A121 $2 Queen Elizabeth II 1.65 1.65
a. Souvenir sheet of 4, #904-908 4.00 4.00
Nos. 904-908 (5) 4.00 4.00

1994 Litho. *Perf. 14x15*

Stained glass windows: 20c, Crucifixion. 45c, Empty tomb. 80c, Resurrection. $3, Risen Christ with disciples.

909 A122 20c multicolored 18 18
910 A122 45c multicolored 40 40
911 A122 80c multicolored 75 75
912 A122 $3 multicolored 2.75 2.75

ANTIGUA

LOCATION — In the West Indies, southeast of Puerto Rico
GOVT. — Independent state
AREA — 171 sq. mi.
POP. — 74,000 (est. 1981)
CAPITAL — St. John's

Antigua was one of the presidencies of the former Leeward Islands colony until becoming a Crown Colony in 1956. It became an Associated State of the United Kingdom in 1967 and an independent nation on November 1, 1981, taking the name of Antigua and Barbuda.

Antigua stamps were discontinued in 1890 and resumed in 1903. In the interim, stamps of Leeward Islands were used. Between 1903-1956, stamps of Antigua and Leeward Islands were used concurrently.

12 Pence = 1 Shilling
20 Shillings = 1 Pound
100 Cents = 1 Dollar (1951)

Catalogue values for unused stamps in this country are for Never Hinged items, beginning with Scott 96.

Watermark

Wmk. 5- Star

Queen Victoria
A1 A2

Rough Perf. 14-16

1862 Engr. Unwmk.

1 A1 6p blue green 525.00 325.00
a. Perf. 11-13 *4,250.*
b. Perf. 11-13x14-16 *2,000.*

There is a question whether Nos. 1a and 1b ever did postal duty.

Values for No. 1 are for stamps with perfs. cutting into the design. Values for No. 1b are for copies without gum.

1863-67 Wmk. 5

2 A1 1p lilac rose 80.00 15.00
a. Imperf., pair *1,750.*
3 A1 1p vermilion ('67) 60.00 15.00
a. Horiz. pair, imperf. vert. *12,000.*
4 A1 6p blue green 140.00 19.00
a. 6p yellow green *3,750.* 42.50
b. Imperf., pair *1,100.*

1872 Wmk. 1 *Perf. 12½*

5 A1 1p lake 70.00 25.00
6 A1 1p vermilion 80.00 30.00
7 A1 6p blue green 425.00 9.00

1873-79 *Perf. 14*

8 A1 1p rose 35.00 14.00
a. Half used as ½p on cover *2,000.*

Typo.

9 A2 2½p red brown ('79) 325.00 150.00

10 A2 4p blue ('79) 240.00 16.00

Engr.

11 A1 6p blue green ('76) 190.00 12.50

1882-86 Typo. Wmk. 2

12 A2 ½p green 3.00 6.00
13 A2 2½p red brown 100.00 30.00
14 A2 2½p ultra ('86) 8.50 10.00
15 A2 4p blue 225.00 20.00
16 A2 4p brown org ('86) 2.50 3.25
17 A2 1sh violet ('86) 135.00 60.00

Engr.

18 A1 1p rose ('84) 1.25 2.00
19 A1 6p deep green 47.50 62.50

No. 18 was used for a time in St. Christopher and is identified by the "A12" cancellation.

1884 Perf. 12

20 A1 1p rose red 45.00 15.00

Seal of the Colony — A3

King Edward VII — A4

1903 Typo. Wmk. 1 Perf. 14

21 A3 ½p blue grn & blk 1.00 1.35
22 A3 1p car & black 3.00 1.00
a. Bluish paper ('09) 45.00 45.00
23 A3 2p org brn & vio 5.00 10.00
24 A3 2½p ultra & black 6.75 6.00
25 A3 3p ocher & gray green 4.50 7.00
26 A3 6p black & red vio 17.00 20.00
27 A3 1sh violet & ultra 16.00 20.00
28 A3 2sh pur & gray green 22.00 25.00
29 A3 2sh6p red vio & blk 21.00 30.00
30 A4 5sh pur & gray green 62.00 80.00
Nos. 21-30 (10) 158.25 200.35

The 2½p, 1sh and 5sh exist on both ordinary and chalky paper.

1908-15 Wmk. 3

31 A3 ½p green 1.00 1.00
32 A3 1p carmine 1.00 1.00
a. 1p scarlet ('15) 1.25 1.25
33 A3 2p org brn & dull vio ('12) 3.25 5.00
34 A3 2½p ultra 4.00 5.00
35 A3 3p ocher & grn ('12) 3.75 6.00
36 A3 6p blk & red vio ('11) 8.00 12.50
37 A3 1sh vio & ultra 7.00 17.50
38 A3 2sh vio & green ('12) 45.00 57.50
Nos. 31-38 (8) 73.00 105.50

Nos. 33, 35 to 38 are on chalky paper.
For overprints, see Nos. MR1-MR3.

George V — A6

St. John's Harbor — A7

1913

41 A6 5sh violet & green 50.00 60.00

1921-29 Wmk. 4

42 A7 ½p green 50 20
43 A7 1p rose red 40 15
44 A7 1p dp violet ('23) 2.00 50
45 A7 1½p orange ('22) 3.50 5.75
46 A7 1½p rose red ('26) 1.10 1.00
47 A7 1½p fawn ('29) 1.50 1.00
48 A7 2p gray 75 40
49 A7 2½p ultra 1.00 1.00
50 A7 2½p orange ('23) 1.10 3.00

Chalky Paper

51 A7 3p violet, *yel* ('25) 2.75 4.00
52 A7 6p vio & red vio 2.25 3.25
53 A7 1sh black, *emer* ('29) 5.75 9.00
54 A7 2sh vio & ultra, *blue* ('27) 10.00 15.00
55 A7 2sh6p blk & red, *blue* ('27) 11.00 15.00
56 A7 3sh grn & vio ('22) 18.00 24.00
57 A7 4sh blk & red ('22) 32.50 35.00
Nos. 42-57 (16) 94.10 118.25

Wmk. 3

Chalky Paper

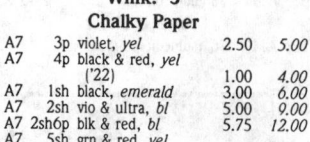

58 A7 3p violet, *yel* 2.50 5.00
59 A7 4p black & red, *yel* ('22) 1.00 4.00
60 A7 1sh black, *emerald* 3.00 6.00
61 A7 2sh vio & ultra, *bl* 5.00 9.00
62 A7 2sh6p blk & red, *bl* 5.75 12.00
63 A7 5sh grn & red, *yel* ('22) 13.00 22.50
64 A7 £1 vio & black, *red* ('22) 190.00 260.00
Nos. 58-64 (7) 220.25 318.50

Old Dockyard, English Harbour — A8

Govt. House, St. John's — A9

Nelson's "Victory," 1805 — A10

Sir Thomas Warner's Ship, 1632 — A11

Perf. 12½

1932, Jan. 27 Engr. Wmk. 4

67 A8 ½p green 80 80
68 A8 1p scarlet 80 80
69 A8 1½p lt brown 2.00 2.00
70 A9 2p gray 1.75 2.75
71 A9 2½p ultra 3.25 3.25
72 A9 3p orange 4.75 5.00
73 A10 6p violet 8.00 11.00
74 A10 1sh olive green 9.00 12.00
75 A10 2sh6p claret 37.50 47.50
76 A11 5sh red brn & black 100.00 110.00
Nos. 67-76 (10) 167.85 195.10

Tercentenary of the colony.

Silver Jubilee Issue
Common Design Type

1935, May 6 Perf. 13½x14

77 CD301 1p car & blue 80 1.10
78 CD301 1½p gray blk & ultra 1.10 1.50
79 CD301 2½p blue & brn 3.50 5.25
80 CD301 1sh brt vio & ind 8.25 13.50

Coronation Issue
Common Design Type

1937, May 12 Perf. 11x11½

81 CD302 1p carmine 20 20
82 CD302 1½p brown 22 22
83 CD302 2½p deep ultra 65 65

English Harbour — A14

Nelson's Dockyard — A15

Fort James — A16

St. John's Harbor — A17

1938-48 Engr. Perf. 12½

84 A14 ½p green 15 15
85 A15 1p red 15 15
86 A15 1½p brown violet 15 15
87 A14 2p dark gray 15 15
88 A15 2½p deep ultra 18 15
89 A16 3p orange 18 15
90 A17 6p purple 20 22
91 A17 1sh red brn & blk 45 45
92 A16 2sh6p deep claret 1.00 1.00
93 A17 5sh olive green 2.25 2.50
94 A15 10sh red vio ('48) 13.00 16.50
95 A16 £1 Prus blue ('48) 14.00 25.00
Nos. 84-95 (12) 31.86 46.57

See Nos. 107-113, 115-116, 118-121, 136-142, 144-145.
For overprint see Nos. 125-126.

Catalogue values for unused stamps in this section, from this point to the end of the section, are for Never Hinged items.

Peace Issue
Common Design Type

1946, Nov. 1 Wmk. 4 Perf. 13½x14

96 CD303 1½p brown 30 30
97 CD303 3p deep orange 38 38

Silver Wedding Issue
Common Design Types

1949, Jan. 3 Photo. Perf. 14x14½

98 CD304 2½p bright ultra 15 15

Engraved; Name Typographed
Perf. 11½x11

99 CD305 5sh dk brown olive 7.50 10.00

UPU Issue
Common Design Types
Perf. 13½, 11x11½

1949, Oct. 10 Wmk. 4
Engr.; Name Typo. on 3p and 6p

100 CD306 2½p deep ultra 25 25
101 CD307 3p orange 1.10 1.10
102 CD308 6p purple 2.25 2.25
103 CD309 1sh red brown 2.50 2.50

University Issue
Common Design Types
Perf. 14x14½

1951, Feb. 16 Engr. Wmk. 4

104 CD310 3c chocolate & blk 25 25
105 CD311 12c purple & blk 65 65

Common Design Types are pictured beginning on page 176.

Coronation Issue
Common Design Type

1953, June 2 Perf. 13½x13

106 CD312 2c dk green & blk 75 75

Types of 1938 with Portrait of Queen Elizabeth II

Martello Tower — A24

Perf. 13x13½, 13½x13

1953-56 Wmk. 4

107 A16 ½c dk red brn ('56) 15 15
108 A14 1c gray 15 15
109 A15 2c deep green 15 15
110 A15 3c yel & black 16 15
111 A14 4c rose red (shades) 16 15
112 A15 5c dull vio & blk 16 15
113 A16 6c orange 25 15
114 A24 8c deep blue 35 25
115 A17 12c violet 35 18
116 A17 24c chocolate & blk 50 22
117 A24 48c dp bl & rose lil 1.25 1.10
118 A16 60c claret 1.75 1.40
119 A17 $1.20 olive green 1.75 1.40
120 A15 $2.40 magenta 6.00 7.00
121 A16 $4.80 greenish blue 12.00 12.50
Nos. 107-121 (15) 25.13 25.10

See #143. For overprint see #125-126.

West Indies Federation
Common Design Type
Perf. 11½x11

1958, Apr. 22 Engr. Wmk. 314

122 CD313 3c green 20 18
123 CD313 6c blue 50 35
124 CD313 12c carmine rose 90 75

Nos. 110 and 115 Overprinted in Red or Black: "Commemoration Antigua Constitution 1960"

Perf. 13x13½, 13½x13

1960, Jan. 1 Wmk. 4

125 A15 3c yellow & black 22 22
126 A17 12c violet (Blk) 50 50

Constitutional reforms effective Jan. 1, 1960.

Lord Nelson and Nelson's Dockyard A26

Perf. 11½x11

1961, Nov. 14 Wmk. 314

127 A26 20c brown & lilac 50 40
128 A26 30c dk blue & green 80 60

Completion of the restoration of Lord Nelson's headquarters, English Harbour.

Stamp of 1862 and Royal Mail Steam Packet in English Harbour A27

1962, Aug. 1 Engr. Perf. 13

129 A27 3c dull green & pur 15 15
130 A27 10c dull green & ultra 20 20
131 A27 12c dull green & blk 28 28
132 A27 50c dull grn & brn org 1.40 1.40

Centenary of first Antigua postage stamp.

Freedom from Hunger Issue
Common Design Type
Perf. 14x14½

1963, June 4 Photo. Wmk. 314

133 CD314 12c green 90 90

Red Cross Centenary Issue
Common Design Type

1963, Sept. 2 Litho. Perf. 13

134 CD315 3c black & red 35 35
135 CD315 12c ultra & red 2.25 2.25

Types of 1938-53 with Portrait of Queen Elizabeth II

Perf. 13x13½, 13½x13

1963-65 Engr. Wmk. 314

136 A16 ½c brown ('65) 28 28
137 A14 1c gray ('65) 28 28
138 A15 2c deep green 16 16
139 A15 3c orange yel & blk 22 22
140 A14 4c brown red 35 35
141 A15 5c dull vio & black 35 35
142 A16 6c orange 38 38
143 A24 8c deep blue 45 45
144 A17 12c violet 85 85
145 A17 24c choc & black 1.75 1.75
Nos. 136-145 (10) 5.07 5.07

For surcharge see No. 152.

Shakespeare Issue
Common Design Type
Perf. 14x14½

1964, Apr. 23 Photo. Wmk. 314

151 CD316 12c red brown 75 75

No. 144 Surcharged with New Value and Bars

Perf. 13½x13

1965, Apr. 1 Engr. Wmk. 314

152 A17 15c on 12c violet 50 50

ITU Issue
Common Design Type
Perf. 11x11½

1965, May 17 Litho. Wmk. 314

153 CD317 2c blue & ver 15 15
154 CD317 50c orange & vio bl 2.25 2.25

Intl. Cooperation Year Issue
Common Design Type

1965, Oct. 25 *Perf. 14½*

155	CD318	4c blue grn & claret	15	15
156	CD318	15c lt vio & green	70	70

Churchill Memorial Issue
Common Design Type

1966, Jan. 24 Photo. *Perf. 14*

Design in Black, Gold and Carmine Rose

157	CD319	½c bright blue	15	15
158	CD319	4c green	25	25
159	CD319	25c brown	1.10	90
160	CD319	35c violet	1.75	1.50

Royal Visit Issue
Common Design Type

1966, Feb. 4 Litho. *Perf. 11x12*

Portraits in Black

161	CD320	6c violet blue	1.10	90
162	CD320	15c dark car rose	1.75	1.10

World Cup Soccer Issue
Common Design Type

1966, July 1 Wmk. 314 *Perf. 14*

163	CD321	6c multicolored	20	20
164	CD321	35c multicolored	80	80

WHO Headquarters Issue
Common Design Type

1966, Sept. 20 *Perf. 14*

165	CD322	2c multicolored	15	15
166	CD322	15c multicolored	75	75

Nelson's Dockyard A35

Designs: 1c, Old post office, St. John's. 2c, Health Center. 3c, Teachers' Training College. 4c, Martello Tower, Barbuda. 5c, Ruins of officers quarters, Shirley Heights. 6c, Government House, Barbuda. 10c, Princess Margaret School. 15c, Air terminal. 25c, General post office. 35c, Clarence House. 50c, Government House. 75c, Administration building. $1, Court House, St. John's. $2.50, Magistrates' Court. $5, St. John's Cathedral.

Perf. 11½x11

1966, Nov. 1 Engr. Wmk. 314

167	A35	½c green & blue	15	15
168	A35	1c purple & rose	15	15
169	A35	2c slate & org	15	15
170	A35	3c rose red & blk	15	15
171	A35	4c dull vio & brn	15	15
172	A35	5c vio bl & olive	15	15
a.		Booklet pane of 4 ('68)	40	
173	A35	6c dp org & pur	15	15
174	A35	10c brt grn & rose red	22	22
a.		Booklet pane of 4 ('68)	1.10	
175	A35	15c brn & blue	30	30
a.		Booklet pane of 4 ('68)	1.50	
176	A35	25c slate & brn	48	48
177	A35	35c dp rose & sep	70	70
178	A35	50c green & black	1.00	1.00
179	A35	75c Prus bl & vio blue	1.25	1.25
180	A35	$1 dp rose & olive	1.75	1.75
181	A35	$2.50 black & rose	4.25	4.25
182	A35	$5 ol grn & dl vio	9.00	9.00
		Nos. 167-182 (16)	20.00	20.00

For surcharge, see No. 231.

1969 *Perf. 13½*

167a	A35	½c	15	15
168a	A35	1c	15	15
169a	A35	2c	15	15
170a	A35	3c	15	15
171a	A35	4c	15	15
172b	A35	5c	15	15
173a	A35	6c	15	15
174b	A35	10c	20	20
175b	A35	15c	30	30
176a	A35	25c	48	48
177a	A35	35c	60	60
178a	A35	50c	95	95
180a	A35	$1	2.50	2.50
181a	A35	$2.50	6.25	6.25
182a	A35	$5	21.00	21.00
		Nos. 167a-182a (15)	33.33	33.33

UNESCO Anniversary Issue
Common Design Type

1966, Dec. 1 Litho. *Perf. 14*

183	CD323	4c "Education"	18	18
184	CD323	25c "Science"	50	50
185	CD323	$1 "Culture"	2.50	2.50

Independent State

Flag of Antigua, Spiny Lobster, Maps of Antigua and Barbuda A37

Designs: 15c, 35c, Flag of Antigua. 25c, Flag and Premier's Office Building.

1967, Feb. 27 Photo. *Perf. 14*

186	A37	4c multicolored	15	15
187	A37	15c multicolored	25	25
188	A37	25c multicolored	40	40
189	A37	35c multicolored	50	50

Antigua's independence, Feb. 27, 1967.

Gilbert Memorial Church, Antigua — A38

Designs: 25c, Nathaniel Gilbert's House. 35c, Map of the Caribbean and Central America.

Perf. 14x13½

1967, May 18 Photo. Wmk. 314

190	A38	4c brt red & black	15	15
191	A38	25c emerald & black	40	40
192	A38	35c ultra & black	55	55

Attainment of autonomy by the Methodist Church in the Caribbean and the Americas, and the opening of headquarters near St. John's, Antigua, May 1967.

Antiguan and British Royal Arms — A39

1967, July 21 *Perf. 14½x14*

193	A39	15c dark green & multi	20	20
194	A39	35c deep blue & multi	45	45

Granting of a new coat of arms to the State of Antigua; 300th anniv. of the Treaty of Breda.

Sailing Ship, 17th Century A40

Design: 6c, 35c, Map of Barbuda from Jan Blaeu's Atlas, 1665.

Perf. 11½x11

1967, Dec. 14 Engr. Wmk. 314

195	A40	4c dark blue	15	15
196	A40	6c deep plum	15	15
197	A40	25c green	30	30
198	A40	35c black	50	50

Resettlement of Barbuda, 300th anniv.

Dow Hill Antenna — A41

Designs: 15c, Antenna and rocket blasting off. 25c, Nose cone orbiting moon. 50c, Re-entry of space capsule.

Perf. 14½x14

1968, Mar. 29 Photo. Wmk. 314

199	A41	4c dk blue, org & black	15	15
200	A41	15c dk blue, org & black	25	25
201	A41	25c dk blue, org & black	35	35
202	A41	50c dk blue, org & black	65	65

Dedication of the Dow Hill tracking station in Antigua for the NASA Apollo project.

Beach and Sailfish A42

Designs: ½c, 50c, Limbo dancer, flames and dancing girls. 15c, Three girls on a beach and water skier. 35c, Woman scuba diver, corals and fish.

1968, July 1 Photo. *Perf. 14*

203	A42	½c red & multi	15	15
204	A42	15c sky blue & multi	25	25
205	A42	25c blue & multi	35	35
206	A42	35c brt blue & multi	45	45
207	A42	50c multicolored	75	75
		Nos. 203-207 (5)	1.95	1.95

Issued for tourist publicity.

St. John's Harbor, 1768 A43

St. John's Harbor: 15c, 1829. 25c, Map of deep-sea harbor, 1968. 35c, Dock, 1968. 2c, Like $1.

Engr. & Litho.; Engr. ($1)

1968, Oct. 31 Wmk. 314 *Perf. 13*

208	A43	2c dp car & lt blue	16	16
209	A43	15c sepia & yel grn	25	25
210	A43	25c dk blue & yel	45	45
211	A43	35c dp green & sal	50	50
212	A43	$1 black	1.75	1.75
		Nos. 208-212 (5)	3.11	3.11

Opening of St. John's deep-sea harbor.

Mace and Parliament A44

Mace and: 15c, Mace bearer. 25c, House of Representatives, interior. 50c, Antigua coat of arms and great seal.

1969, Feb. 3 Photo. *Perf. 12½*

213	A44	4c crimson & multi	15	15
214	A44	15c crimson & multi	20	20
215	A44	25c crimson & multi	30	30
216	A44	50c crimson & multi	65	65

300th anniversary of Antigua Parliament.

CARIFTA Cargo — A45

Design: 4c, 15c, Ship, plane and trucks, horiz.

Perf. 13½x13, 13x13½

1969, Apr. 14 Litho. Wmk. 314

217	A45	4c blk & brt lilac rose	15	15
218	A45	15c blk & brt grnsh blue	25	25
219	A45	25c bister & black	30	30
220	A45	35c tan & black	45	45

1st anniv. of CARIFTA (Caribbean Free Trade Area).

Map of Redonda Island A46

Design: 25c, View of Redonda from the sea and seagulls.

1969, Aug. 1 Photo. *Perf. 13x13½*

221	A46	15c ultra & multi	30	30
222	A46	25c multicolored	45	45
223	A46	50c salmon & multi	1.25	1.25

Centenary of Redonda phosphate industry.

Adoration of the Kings, by Gugliemo Marcillat A47

Christmas: 10c, 50c, Holy Family, by anonymous German artist, 15th century.

1969, Oct. 15 Litho. *Perf. 13x14*

224	A47	6c bister brn & multi	15	15
225	A47	10c fawn & multi	20	20
226	A47	35c gray olive & multi	50	50
227	A47	50c gray blue & multi	90	90

Arms of Antigua — A48

Coil Stamps

Perf. 14½x14

1970, Jan. 30 Photo. Wmk. 314

228	A48	5c bright blue	15	15
229	A48	10c bright green	20	20
230	A48	25c deep magenta	45	45

No. 176 Surcharged 20¢

1970, Jan. 2 Engr. *Perf. 11½x11*

231	A35	20c on 25c slate & brown	35	15

Sikorsky S-38 A49

Aircraft: 20c, Dornier DO-X. 35c, Hawker Siddeley 748. 50c, Douglas C-124C Globemaster II. 75c, Vickers VC 10.

1970, Feb. 16 Litho. *Perf. 14½*

232	A49	5c brt green & multi	15	15
233	A49	20c ultra & multi	35	35
234	A49	35c blue grn & multi	60	60
235	A49	50c blue & multi	90	90
236	A49	75c vio blue & multi	1.50	1.50
		Nos. 232-236 (5)	3.50	3.50

40th anniversary of air service.

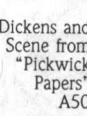

Dickens and Scene from "Pickwick Papers" A50

Charles Dickens (1812-1870), English novelist and Scene from: 5c, "Nicholas Nickleby." 35c, "Oliver Twist." $1, "David Copperfield."

Wmk. 314

1970, May 19 Litho. *Perf. 14*

237	A50	5c olive & sepia	15	15
238	A50	20c aqua & sepia	28	28
239	A50	35c violet & sepia	32	32
240	A50	$1 scarlet & sepia	1.00	1.00

Carib Indian and War Canoe — A51

Ships: 1c, Columbus and "Nina." 2c, Sir Thomas Warner's arms and sailing ship. 3c, Viscount Hood and "Barfleur." 4c, Sir George Rodney and "Formidable." 5c, Capt. Horatio Nelson and "Boreas." 6c, King William IV and "Pegasus." 10c, Blackbeard (Edward Teach) and pirate ketch. 15c, Capt. Cuthbert Collingwood and "Pelican." 20c, Admiral Nelson and "Victoria." 25c, Paddle steamer "Solent" and Steam Packet Company emblem. 35c, King George V and corvette "Canada." 50c, Cruiser "Renown" and royal badge. 75c, S.S. "Federal Maple" and maple leaf. $1, Racing yacht "Sol-Quest" and Gallant 53 class emblem. $2.50, Missile destroyer "London" and her emblem. $5, Tug "Pathfinder" and arms of Antigua.

Wmk. 314 Sideways

1970, Aug. 19 Litho. *Perf. 14*

241	A51	½c ocher & multi	15	15
242	A51	1c Prus bl & multi	15	15
243	A51	2c yel grn & multi	15	15
244	A51	3c ol bis & multi	15	15
245	A51	4c bl gray & multi	15	15
246	A51	5c fawn & multi	16	15
247	A51	6c rose lil & multi	18	15
248	A51	10c brn org & multi	22	15
249	A51	15c ultra & multi	35	22
250	A51	20c ol grn & multi	28	16
251	A51	25c olive & multi	32	20
252	A51	35c dull red brn & multi	60	35
253	A51	50c lt brn & multi	80	55
254	A51	75c beige & multi	1.10	75
255	A51	$1 Prus green & multi	1.60	1.10
256	A51	$2.50 gray & multi	4.50	2.75
257	A51	$5 yel & multi	10.50	7.00
		Nos. 241-257 (17)	21.36	14.28

1972-74 Wmk. 314 Upright

241a	A51	½c	15	15
242a	A51	1c	15	15
244a	A51	3c	15	15
245a	A51	4c	15	15
246a	A51	5c	15	15
247a	A51	6c	15	15
248a	A51	10c	20	20
249a	A51	15c	1.60	28
254a	A51	75c	3.25	1.25
255a	A51	$1	3.60	1.60
256a	A51	$2.50	6.00	*7.50*
257a	A51	$5	6.75	*10.50*
		Nos. 241a-257a (12)	22.30	*22.23*

For surcharge, see No. 368.

1975, Jan. 21 Wmk. 373

257b	A51	$5 yellow & multi	13.00	13.00

Nativity, by Albrecht Dürer — A52

Private, 4th West India Regiment, 1804 — A53

Christmas: 10c, 50c, Adoration of the Magi, by Albrecht Dürer.

Engr. & Litho.

1970, Oct. 28 *Perf. 13½x14*

258	A52	3c brt grnsh blue & blk	15	15
259	A52	10c pink & plum	20	20
260	A52	35c brick red & black	50	50
261	A52	50c lilac & violet	90	90

Perf. 14x13½

1970, Dec. 1 Litho. Wmk. 314

Military Uniforms: ½c, Drummer Boy, 4th King's Own Regiment, 1759. 20c, Grenadier Company Officer, 60th Regiment, The Royal American, 1809. 35c, Light Company Officer, 93rd Regiment, The Sutherland Highlanders, 1826-1834. 75c, Private, 3rd West India Regiment, 1851.

262	A53	½c lake & multi	15	15
263	A53	10c brn org & multi	45	45
264	A53	20c Prus grn & multi	75	75
265	A53	35c dl pur & multi	1.50	1.50
266	A53	75c dk ol grn & multi	4.00	4.00
a.		Souv. sheet of 5, #262-266 + label	10.00	10.00
		Nos. 262-266 (5)	6.85	6.85

See #274-278, 283-287, 307-311, 329-333.

Market Woman Voting — A54

Voting by: 20c, Businessman. 35c, Mother (and child). 50c, Workman.

Perf. 14½x14

1971, Feb. 1 Photo. Wmk. 314

267	A54	5c brown	15	15
268	A54	20c olive black	20	20
269	A54	35c rose magenta	35	35
270	A54	50c violet blue	60	60

Adult suffrage, 20th anniversary.

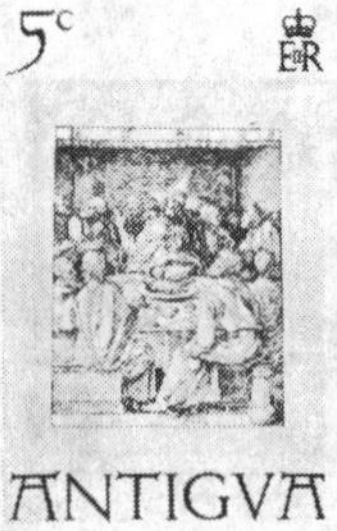

Last Supper, from The Small Passion, by Dürer — A55

Woodcuts by Albrecht Dürer: 35c, Crucifixion from Eichstaff Missal. 75c, Resurrection from The Great Passion.

Perf. 14x13½

1971, Apr. 7 Litho. Wmk. 314

271	A55	5c gray, red & black	15	15
272	A55	35c gray, violet & black	40	40
273	A55	75c gray, gold & black	90	90

Easter.

Military Uniform Type of 1970

Military Uniforms: ½c, Private, Suffolk Regiment, 1704. 10c, Grenadier, South Staffordshire, 1751. 20c, Fusilier, Royal Northumberland, 1778. 35c, Private, Northamptonshire. 1793, 75c, Private, East Yorkshire, 1805.

1971, July 12 Litho. Wmk. 314

274	A53	½c gray grn & multi	15	15
275	A53	10c bluish blk & multi	30	30
276	A53	20c dk pur & multi	50	50
277	A53	35c dk ol & multi	1.10	1.10
278	A53	75c brown & multi	2.50	2.50
a.		Souvenir sheet of 5, #274-278 + label	7.25	7.25
		Nos. 274-278 (5)	4.55	4.55

Virgin and Child, by Veronese — A56

Christmas: 5c, 50c, Adoration of the Shepherds, by Bonifazio Veronese.

1971, Oct. 4 *Perf. 14x13½*

279	A56	3c multicolored	15	15
280	A56	5c multicolored	15	15
281	A56	35c multicolored	55	55
282	A56	50c multicolored	90	90

Uniform Type of 1970

Military Uniforms: ½c, Officer, King's Own Borderers Regiment, 1815. 10c, Sergeant, Buckinghamshire Regiment, 1837. 20c, Private, South Hampshire Regiment, 1853. 35c, Officer, Royal Artillery, 1854. 75c, Private, Worcestershire Regiment, 1870.

1972, July 1

283	A53	½c ol brn & multi	15	15
284	A53	10c dp grn & multi	40	40
285	A53	20c brt vio & multi	80	80
286	A53	35c mar & multi	1.50	1.50
287	A53	75c dk vio bl & multi	3.25	3.25
a.		Souvenir sheet of 5, #283-287 + label	9.00	9.00
		Nos. 283-287 (5)	6.10	6.10

Reticulated Helmet Cowrie A57

Sea Shells: 5c, Measled cowrie. 35c, West Indian fighting conch. 50c, Hawkwing conch.

1972, Aug. 1 *Perf. 14½x14*

288	A57	3c multicolored	15	15
289	A57	5c ver & multi	35	35
290	A57	35c lt vio & multi	1.40	1.40
291	A57	50c rose red & multi	2.00	2.00

St. John's Cathedral, 1745-1843 A58

Christmas: 50c, Interior of St. John's. 75c, St. John's rebuilt.

1972, Nov. 6 Litho. *Perf. 14*

292	A58	35c org brn & multi	45	45
293	A58	50c vio & multi	85	85
294	A58	75c multicolored	1.40	1.40
a.		Souv. sheet of 3, #292-294, perf. 15	3.50	3.50

Silver Wedding Issue, 1972

Common Design Type

1972, Nov. 20 Photo. *Perf. 14x14½*

295	CD324	20c ultra & multi	30	30
296	CD324	35c steel bl & multi	50	50

Map of Antigua, Batsman Driving Ball — A60

Designs: 35c, Batsman and wicketkeeper. $1, Emblem of Rising Sun Cricket Club.

1972, Dec. 15 *Perf. 13½x14*

297	A60	5c multicolored	25	25
298	A60	35c multicolored	1.25	1.25
299	A60	$1 multicolored	3.00	3.00
a.		Souvenir sheet of 3, #297-299	5.00	5.00

Rising Sun Cricket Club, St. John's, 50th anniv.

Map of Antigua and Yacht — A61

1972, Dec. 29 *Perf. 14½*

300	A61	35c shown	35	35
301	A61	50c Racing yachts	40	40
302	A61	75c St. John's G.P.O.	70	70
303	A61	$1 Statue of Liberty	1.10	1.10
a.		Souvenir sheet of 2, #301, 303	2.50	2.50

Opening of Antigua and Barbuda Information Office in New York City.

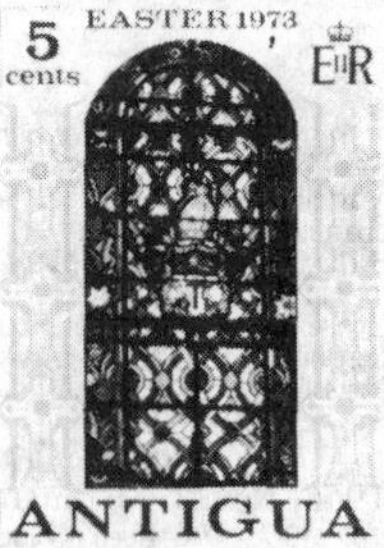

Window with Episcopal Coat of Arms — A62

Stained glass windows from Cathedral of St. John: 35c, Crucifixion. 75c, Arm of Rt. Rev. D.G. Davis, 1st bishop of Antigua.

1973, Apr. 16 Litho. *Perf. 13½*

304	A62	5c yellow & multi	15	15
305	A62	35c brt lilac & multi	40	40
306	A62	75c blue & multi	80	80

Easter.

Uniform Type of 1970

Military Uniforms: ½c, Private, Col. Zacharia Tiffin's Regiment, 1701. 10c, Private, 63rd Regiment, 1759. 20c, Officer, 35th Sussex Regiment, 1828. 35c, Private, 2nd West India Regiment, 1853. 75c, Sergeant, Princess of Wales Regiment, Hertfordshire, 1858.

Perf. 14x13½

1973, July 1 Wmk. 314

307	A53	½c dp ultra & multi	15	15
308	A53	10c rose lilac & multi	25	25
309	A53	20c gray & multi	45	45
310	A53	35c multicolored	80	80
311	A53	75c multicolored	2.00	2.00
a.		Souvenir sheet of 5	4.00	4.00
		Nos. 307-311 (5)	3.65	3.65

No. 311a contains one each of Nos. 307-311 and label with coat of arms and date.

Butterfly Costumes — A63

Designs: 20c, Carnival revelers. 35c, Costumed group. 75c, Carnival Queen.

Perf. 13½x14

1973, July 30 — Unwmk.

312	A63	5c multicolored	15	15
313	A63	20c multicolored	30	30
314	A63	35c multicolored	50	50
315	A63	75c multicolored	1.25	1.25
a.		Souvenir sheet of 4, #312-315	2.50	2.50

Carnival, July 29-Aug. 7.

Virgin of the Porridge, by David — A64

Christmas: 5c, Adoration of the Kings, by Stomer. 20c, Virgin of the Grand Duke, by Raphael. 35c, Nativity with God the Father and Holy Ghost, by Tiepolo. $1, Madonna and Child, by Murillo.

Perf. 14½

1973, Oct. 15 — Photo. — Unwmk.

316	A64	3c brt blue & multi	15	15
317	A64	5c emerald & multi	15	15
318	A64	20c gold & multi	35	35
319	A64	35c violet & multi	65	65
320	A64	$1 red & multi	1.75	1.75
a.		Souvenir sheet of 5, #316-320	3.25	3.25
		Nos. 316-320 (5)	3.05	3.05

Princess Anne and Mark Phillips A65

Design: $2, different border.

1973, Nov. 14 — Litho. — *Perf. 13½*

321	A65	35c dull ultra & multi	20	20
322	A65	$2 yel grn & multi	1.10	1.10
a.		Souvenir sheet of 2, #321-322	1.40	1.40

Wedding of Princess Anne and Capt. Mark Phillips.

Nos. 321-322 were issued in sheets of 5 plus label.

Nos. 321-322 and 322a Overprinted Vertically: "HONEYMOON / VISIT / DECEMBER 16th / 1973"

1973, Dec. 15 — Litho. — *Perf. 13½*

323	A65	35c multicolored	25	25
324	A65	$2 multicolored	1.25	1.25
a.		Souvenir sheet of 2, #323-324	1.60	1.60

Visit of Princess Anne and Mark Phillips to Antigua, Dec. 16. Same overprint in sheet margins of Nos. 323-324 and 324a.

Arms of Antigua and U.W.I. A66

Designs: 20c, Dancers. 35c, Antigua campus. 75c, Chancellor Sir Hugh Wooding.

1974, Feb. 18 — Wmk. 314

325	A66	5c multicolored	15	15
326	A66	20c multicolored	25	25
327	A66	35c multicolored	40	40
328	A66	75c multicolored	80	80

University of the West Indies, 24th anniv.

Uniform Type of 1970

Military Uniforms: ½c, Officer, 59th Foot, 1797. 10c, Gunner, Royal Artillery, 1800. 20c, Private, 1st West India Regiment, 1830. 35c, Officer, Gordon Highlanders, 1843. 75c, Private, Royal Welsh Fusiliers, 1846.

1974, May 1 — *Perf. 14x13½*

329	A53	½c dull grn & multi	15	15
330	A53	10c ocher & multi	15	15
331	A53	20c multicolored	30	30
332	A53	35c gray bl & multi	50	50
333	A53	75c dk gray & multi	1.10	1.10
a.		Souvenir sheet of 5, #329-333	2.75	2.75
		Nos. 329-333 (5)	2.20	2.20

English Mailman and Coach, Helicopter — A67

UPU, Cent.: 1c, English bellman, 1846; Orinoco mailboat, 1851; telecommunications satellite. 2c, English mailtrain guard, 1852; Swiss post passenger bus, 1906; Italian hydrofoil. 5c, Swiss messenger, 16th century; Wells Fargo coach, 1800; Concorde. 20c, German position, 1820; Japanese mailmen, 19th century; carrier pigeon. 35c, Contemporary Antiguan mailman; radar station; aquaplane. $1, Medieval French courier; American train, 1884; British Airways jet.

1974, July 15 — Litho. — *Perf. 14½*

334	A67	½c multicolored	15	15
335	A67	1c multicolored	15	15
336	A67	2c multicolored	15	15
337	A67	5c multicolored	15	15
338	A67	20c multicolored	35	30
339	A67	35c multicolored	75	55
340	A67	$1 multicolored	1.75	1.40
a.		Souvenir sheet of 7, #334-340 + label, perf. 13	3.50	3.50
		Set value	3.05	2.45

For surcharges, see Nos. 365-367.

Traditional Steel Band A68

Carnival 1974 (Steel Bands): 5c, Traditional players, vert. 35c, Modern steel band. 75c, Modern players, vert.

1974, Aug. 1, — Wmk. 314 — *Perf. 14*

341	A68	5c rose red, dk red & blk	15	15
342	A68	20c ocher, brn & blk	25	25
343	A68	35c yel grn, grn & blk	40	40
344	A68	75c dl bl, dk bl & blk	75	75
a.		Souvenir sheet of 4, #341-344	1.75	2.00

Soccer — A69

Designs: Games' emblem and soccer.

1974, Sept. 23 — Unwmk. — *Perf. 14½*

345	A69	5c multicolored	15	15
346	A69	35c multicolored	40	40
347	A69	75c multicolored	80	80
348	A69	$1 multicolored	1.10	1.10
a.		Souvenir sheet of 4	2.25	2.25

World Cup Soccer Championship, Munich, June 13-July 7. Nos. 345-348 issued in sheets of 5 plus label showing Soccer Cup. No. 348a contains one each of Nos. 345-348, perf. 13½, and 2 labels.

For overprints and surcharges, see Nos. 361-364.

Winston Churchill (1874-1965) at Harrow A70

Designs: 35c, St. Paul's during bombing and Churchill portrait. 75c, Churchill's coat of arms and catafalque. $1, Churchill during Boer war, warrant for arrest and map of his escape route.

1974, Oct. 20 — Unwmk. — *Perf. 14½*

349	A70	5c multicolored	15	15
350	A70	35c multicolored	30	30
351	A70	75c multicolored	75	75
352	A70	$1 multicolored	90	90
a.		Souvenir sheet of 4, #349-352	1.75	1.75

Virgin and Child, by Giovanni Bellini — A71

Christmas: Paintings of the Virgin and Child.

1974, Nov. 18 — Litho. — *Perf. 14½*

353	A71	½c shown	15	15
354	A71	1c Raphael	15	15
355	A71	2c Van der Weyden	15	15
356	A71	3c Giorgione	15	15
357	A71	5c Andrea Mantegna	15	15
358	A71	20c Alvise Vivarini	25	25
359	A71	35c Bartolommeo Montagna	40	40
360	A71	75c Lorenzo Costa	85	85
a.		Souvenir sheet of 4, #357-360, perf. 13½	1.60	1.60
		Set value	1.80	1.80

Nos. 346-348 Overprinted and No. 344 Surcharged and Overprinted: "EARTHQUAKE / RELIEF"

1974, Oct. 16 — Litho. — *Perf. 14½, 14*

361	A69	35c multicolored	25	20
362	A69	75c multicolored	70	60
363	A69	$1 multicolored	90	75
364	A68	$5 on 75c multi	4.50	4.00

Earthquake of Oct. 8, 1974.

Nos. 338-340 and 254a Surcharged with New Value and Two Bars

1974-75 — Wmk. 314 — *Perf. 14½*

365	A67	50c on 20c	55	55
366	A67	$2.50 on 35c	2.75	2.75
367	A67	$5 on $1	5.25	5.25

Perf. 14

368	A51	$10 on 75c	10.50	10.50

Carib War Canoe, English Harbour A72

Designs (Nelson's Dockyard): 15c, Raising ship, 1770. 35c, Lord Nelson and "Boreas." 50c, Yachts arriving for Sailing Week, 1974. $1, "Anchorage" in Old Dockyard, 1970.

1975, Mar. 17 — Unwmk. — *Perf. 14½*

369	A72	5c multicolored	15	15
370	A72	15c multicolored	32	32
371	A72	35c multicolored	60	60
372	A72	50c multicolored	90	90
373	A72	$1 multicolored	1.75	1.75
		Nos. 369-373 (5)	3.72	3.72

Souvenir Sheet

Perf. 13½

373A	A72	Sheet of 5, #369-373	4.50	4.50

Stamps in No. 373A are 43x28mm.

Lady of the Valley Church A73

Churches of Antigua: 20c, Gilbert Memorial. 35c, Grace Hill Moravian. 50c, St. Phillip's. $1, Ebenezer Methodist.

1975, May 19 — Litho. — *Perf. 14½*

374	A73	5c multicolored	15	15
375	A73	20c multicolored	18	18
376	A73	35c multicolored	32	32
377	A73	50c multicolored	52	52
378	A73	$1 multicolored	90	90
a.		Souvenir sheet of 3, #376-378, perf. 13½	2.25	2.25
		Nos. 374-378 (5)	2.07	2.07

Antigua, Senex's Atlas, 1721, and Hevelius Sextant, 1640 A74

Maps of Antigua: 20c, Jeffery's Atlas, 1775, and 18th century engraving of ship. 35c, Barbuda and Antigua, 1775 and 1975. $1, St. John's and English Harbour, 1973.

1975, July 21 — Wmk. 314

379	A74	5c multicolored	15	15
380	A74	20c multicolored	35	35
381	A74	35c multicolored	60	60
382	A74	$1 multicolored	1.75	1.75
a.		Souvenir sheet of 4, #379-382	3.00	3.00

Bugler and Sunset A75

Nordjamb 75 Emblem and: 20c, Black and white Scouts, tents and flags. 35c, Lord Baden-Powell and tents. $2, Dahomey dancers.

Unwmk.

1975, Aug. 26 — Litho. — *Perf. 14*

383	A75	15c multicolored	30	30
384	A75	20c multicolored	40	40
384	A75	35c multicolored	60	60
386	A75	$2 multicolored	2.75	2.75
a.		Souvenir sheet of 4, #383-386	4.50	4.50

Nordjamb 75, 14th Boy Scout Jamboree, Lillehammer, Norway, July 29-Aug. 7.

Eurema Elathea A76

Butterflies: 1c, Danaus plexippus. 2c, Phoebis philea. 5c, Marpesia petreus thetys. 20c, Eurema proterpia. 35c, Papilio polydamas. $2, Vanessa cardui.

1975, Oct. 30 — Litho. — *Perf. 14*

387	A76	½c multicolored	15	15
388	A76	1c multicolored	15	15
389	A76	2c multicolored	15	15
390	A76	5c multicolored	15	15
391	A76	20c multicolored	50	40
392	A76	35c multicolored	90	75
393	A76	$2 multicolored	4.50	3.50
a.		Miniature sheet of 4, #390-393	6.75	6.75
		Nos. 387-393 (7)	6.50	5.25

Virgin and Child, by Correggio — A77

Christmas: Virgin and Child paintings.

1975, Nov. 17 — Unwmk.

394	A77	½c shown	15	15
395	A77	1c El Greco	15	15
396	A77	2c Durer	15	15

397	A77	3c	Antonello	15	15
398	A77	5c	Bellini	15	15
399	A77	10c	Durer	15	15
400	A77	35c	Bellini	45	45
401	A77	$2	Durer	1.90	1.90
a.			Souvenir sheet of 4, #398-401	3.25	3.25
			Set value	2.75	2.75

West Indies Team A78

Designs: 5c, Batsman I.V.A. Richards and cup, vert. 35c, Bowler A.M.E. Roberts and cup, vert.

1975, Dec. 15 Litho. *Perf. 14*

402	A78	5c	multicolored	20	15
403	A78	35c	multicolored	90	75
404	A78	$2	multicolored	3.50	3.50

World Cricket Cup, victory of West Indies team.

Antillean Crested Hummingbird A79

Irrigation System, Diamond Estate — A80

Designs: 1c, Imperial parrot. 2c, Zenaida dove. 3c, Loggerhead kingbird. 4c, Red-necked pigeon. 5c, Rufous-throated solitaire. 6c, Orchid tree. 10c, Bougainvillea. 15c, Geiger tree. 20c, Flamboyant. 25c, Hibiscus. 35c, Flame of the Woods. 50c, Cannon at Fort James. 75c, Premier's Office. $1, Potworks Dam. $5, Government House. $10, Coolidge International Airport.

1976, Jan. 19 Litho. *Perf. 15*

405	A79	½c	multicolored	15	15
406	A79	1c	multicolored	15	15
407	A79	2c	multicolored	15	15
408	A79	3c	multicolored	15	15
409	A79	4c	multicolored	15	15
410	A79	5c	multicolored	15	15
411	A79	6c	multicolored	15	15
412	A79	10c	multicolored	15	15
413	A79	15c	multicolored	15	15
414	A79	20c	multicolored	15	15
415	A79	25c	multicolored	18	18
416	A79	35c	multicolored	26	26
417	A79	50c	multicolored	35	35
418	A79	75c	multicolored	52	52
419	A79	$1	multicolored	70	70

Perf. 13½x14

420	A80	$2.50	rose & multi	1.50	1.50
421	A80	$5	lilac & multi	3.25	3.25
422	A80	$10	multicolored	6.75	6.75
			Nos. 405-422 (18)	15.01	15.01

In 1978 Nos. 405-422 were reissued with "1978" centered below design.
For overprints, see Nos. 607-617.

Privates, Clark's Illinois Regiment — A81

Designs: 1c, Riflemen, Pennsylvania Militia. 2c, Decorated American powder horn. 5c, Water bottle of Maryland troops. 35c, "Liberty Tree" and "Rattlesnake" flags. $1, American privateer Montgomery. $2.50, Congress Flag. $5, Continental Navy sloop Ranger.

1976, Mar. 17 Litho. *Perf. 14½*

423	A81	½c	multicolored	15	15
424	A81	1c	multicolored	15	15
425	A81	2c	multicolored	15	15
426	A81	5c	multicolored	15	15
427	A81	35c	multicolored	40	40
428	A81	$1	multicolored	1.25	1.25
429	A81	$5	multicolored	5.00	5.00
			Nos. 423-429 (7)	7.25	7.25

Souvenir Sheet

Perf. 13

430	A81	$2.50	multicolored	3.75	3.75

American Bicentennial.

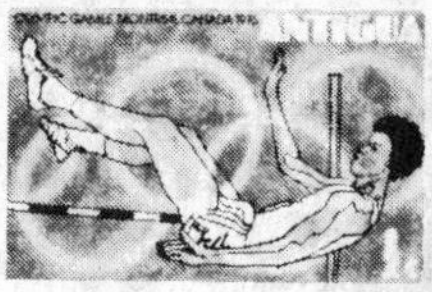

High Jump, Olympic Rings — A82

Olympic Rings and: 1c, Boxing. 2c, Pole vault. 15c, Swimming. 30c, Running. $1, Bicycling. $2, Shot put.

1976, July 12 Litho. *Perf. 14½*

431	A82	½c	yellow & multi	15	15
432	A82	1c	purple & multi	15	15
433	A82	2c	emerald & multi	15	15
434	A82	15c	brt blue & multi	15	15
435	A82	30c	olive & multi	40	40
436	A82	$1	orange & multi	1.00	1.00
437	A82	$2	red & multi	2.00	2.00
a.			Souvenir sheet of 4	3.50	3.50
			Nos. 431-437 (7)	4.00	4.00

21st Olympic Games, Montreal, Canada, July 17-Aug. 1. No. 437a contains one each of Nos. 434-437, perf. 13½.

Water Skiing A83

Water Sports: 1c, Sailfish sailing. 2c, Snorkeling. 20c, Deep-sea fishing. 50c, Scuba diving. $2, Swimming.

1976, Aug. 26 *Perf. 14*

438	A83	½c	yel grn & multi	15	15
439	A83	1c	sepia & multi	15	15
440	A83	2c	gray & multi	15	15
441	A83	20c	multicolored	15	15
442	A83	50c	brt vio & multi	40	40
443	A83	$2	lt gray & multi	1.25	1.25
a.			Souvenir sheet of 3, #441-443	2.50	2.50

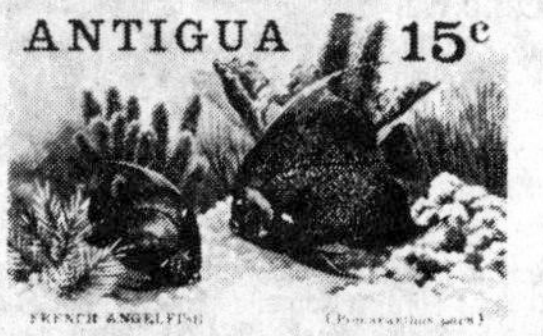

French Angelfish — A84

1976, Oct. 4 Litho. *Perf. 13½x14*

444	A84	15c	shown	20	20
445	A84	30c	Yellowfish grouper	35	35
446	A84	50c	Yellowtail snappers	65	65
447	A84	90c	Shy hamlet	1.10	1.10

The Annunciation A85

Christmas: 10c, Flight into Egypt. 15c, Three Kings. 50c, Shepherds and star. $1, Kings presenting gifts to Christ Child.

1976, Nov. 15 Litho. *Perf. 14*

448	A85	8c	multicolored	15	15
449	A85	10c	multicolored	15	15
450	A85	15c	multicolored	20	20
451	A85	50c	multicolored	50	50
452	A85	$1	multi	1.00	1.00
			Nos. 448-452 (5)	2.00	2.00

Mercury and UPU Emblem A86

Designs: 1c, Alfred Nobel, symbols of prize categories. 10c, Viking spacecraft. 50c, Vivi Richards (batsman) and Andy Roberts (bowler). $1, Alexander G. Bell, telephones, 1876 and 1976. $2, Schooner Freelance.

1976, Dec. 28 Litho. *Perf. 14*

453	A86	½c	multicolored	15	15
454	A86	1c	multicolored	15	15
455	A86	10c	multicolored	15	15
456	A86	50c	multicolored	65	65
457	A86	$1	multicolored	1.00	1.00
458	A86	$2	multicolored	1.75	1.75
a.			Souvenir sheet of 4, #455-458	4.25	4.25
			Nos. 453-458 (6)	3.85	3.85

Special 1976 Events: UN Postal Admin., 25th anniv. (½c); Nobel Prize, 75th anniv. (1c); Viking Space Mission to Mars (10c); World Cricket Cup victory (50c); Telephone cent. ($1); Operation Sail, American Bicent. ($2).

Royal Family — A87

Designs: 30c, Elizabeth II and Prince Philip touring Antigua. 50c, Queen enthroned. 90c, Queen wearing crown. $2.50, Queen and Prince Charles. $5, Queen and Prince Philip.

1977, Feb. 7 *Perf. 13½x14*

459	A87	10c	multicolored	15	15
460	A87	30c	multicolored	18	18
461	A87	50c	multicolored	30	30
462	A87	90c	multicolored	60	60
463	A87	$2.50	multicolored	1.50	1.50
			Nos. 459-463 (5)	2.73	2.73

Souvenir Sheet

464	A87	$5	multicolored	4.00	4.00

25th anniv. of the reign of Queen Elizabeth II.

Nos. 459-463 were printed in sheets of 40. Sheets of 5 plus label, perf. 12, probably were not sold by the Antigua Post Office.

A booklet of self-adhesive stamps contains one pane of six rouletted and die cut 50c stamps in design of 90c, and one pane of one die cut $5. Stamps have changed colors. Panes have marginal inscriptions.

For overprints, see Nos. 477-482.

Scouts Camping A88

Boy Scout Emblem and: 1c, Scouts on hike. 2c, Rock climbing. 10c, Cutting logs. 30c, Map and compass reading. 50c, First aid. $2, Scouts on raft.

1977, May 23 Litho. *Perf. 14*

465	A88	½c	multicolored	15	15
466	A88	1c	multicolored	15	15
467	A88	2c	multicolored	15	15
468	A88	10c	multicolored	15	15
469	A88	30c	multicolored	30	30
470	A88	50c	multicolored	50	50
471	A88	$2	multicolored	1.90	1.90
a.			Souvenir sheet of 3, #469-471	2.50	2.50
			Set value	3.00	3.00

Caribbean Boy Scout Jamboree, Jamaica.

Carnival Queen Holding Horseshoe — A89

Designs: 30c, Carnival Queen in feather costume. 50c, Butterfly costume. 90c, Carnival Queen with ornaments. $1, Carnival King and Queen.

1977, July 18 Litho. *Perf. 14*

472	A89	10c	multicolored	15	15
473	A89	30c	multicolored	18	18
474	A89	50c	multicolored	32	32
475	A89	90c	multicolored	55	55
476	A89	$1	multicolored	60	60
a.			Souvenir sheet of 4, #473-476	1.90	1.90
			Nos. 472-476 (5)	1.80	1.80

21st Summer Carnival.

Nos. 459-464 Overprinted: "ROYAL VISIT / 28th OCTOBER 1977"

Perf. 13½x14, 12

1977, Oct. 17 Litho.

477	A87	10c	multicolored	15	15
478	A87	30c	multicolored	16	16
479	A87	50c	multicolored	28	28
480	A87	90c	multicolored	50	50
481	A87	$2.50	multicolored	1.40	1.40
			Nos. 477-481 (5)	2.49	2.49

Souvenir Sheet

482	A87	$5	multicolored	3.00	3.00

Visit of Queen Elizabeth II, Oct. 28.

Virgin and Child, by Cosimo Tura — A90

Virgin and Child by: 1c, $2, Carlo Crivelli (different). 2c, 25c, Lorenzo Lotto (different). 8c, Jacopo da Pontormo. 10c, Tura.

1977, Nov. 15 Litho. *Perf. 14*

483	A90	½c	multicolored	15	15
484	A90	1c	multicolored	15	15
485	A90	2c	multicolored	15	15
486	A90	8c	multicolored	15	15
487	A90	10c	multicolored	15	15
488	A90	25c	multicolored	18	18
489	A90	$2	multicolored	1.50	1.50
a.			Souvenir sheet of 4, #486-489	2.25	2.25
			Set value	2.00	2.00

Christmas.

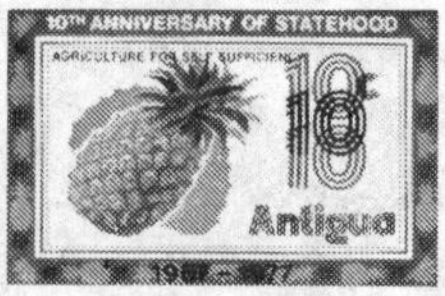

Pineapple A91

10th anniv. of Statehood: 15c, Flag of Antigua. 50c, Police band. 90c, Prime Minister V. C. Bird. $2, Coat of Arms.

1977, Dec. 28 Litho. *Perf. 13x13½*

490	A91	10c	multicolored	15	15
491	A91	15c	multicolored	15	15
492	A91	50c	multicolored	40	40
493	A91	90c	multicolored	75	75
494	A91	$2	multicolored	1.60	1.60
a.			Souv. sheet of 4, #491-494, perf. 14	2.75	2.75
			Nos. 490-494 (5)	3.05	3.05

Wright Glider III, 1902 A92

Designs: 1c, Flyer I in air, 1903. 2c, Weight and derrick launch system and Wright engine, 1903. 10c, Orville Wright, vert. 50c, Flyer III, 1905. 90c, Wilbur Wright, vert. $2, Wright Model B, 1910. $2.50, Flyer I, 1903, on ground.

1978, Mar. 28 *Perf. 14*

495 A92	½c	multicolored	15	15
496 A92	1c	multicolored	15	15
497 A92	2c	multicolored	15	15
498 A92	10c	multicolored	15	15
499 A92	50c	multicolored	35	35
500 A92	90c	multicolored	60	60
501 A92	$2	multicolored	1.40	1.40
		Set value	2.55	2.55

Souvenir Sheet

502 A92	$2.50	multicolored	2.00	2.00

75th anniv. of first powered flight by Wright brothers.

Sunfish Regatta A93

Sailing Week 1978: 50c, Fishing and work boat race. 90c, Curtain Bluff race. $2, Powerboat rally. $2.50, Guadeloupe-Antigua race.

1978, Apr. 29 **Litho.** *Perf. 14½*

503 A93	10c	multicolored	15	15
504 A93	50c	multicolored	40	40
505 A93	90c	multicolored	75	75
506 A93	$2	multicolored	1.60	1.60

Souvenir Sheet

507 A93	$2.50	multicolored	2.40	2.40

Elizabeth II and Prince Philip — A94

Designs: 30c, Coronation. 50c, State coach. 90c, Elizabth II and Archbishop. $2.50, Elizabeth II. $5, Elizabeth II, Prince Philip, Prince Charles and Princess Anne as children.

1978, June 2 **Litho.** *Perf. 14, 12*

508 A94	10c	multicolored	15	15
509 A94	30c	multicolored	16	16
510 A94	50c	multicolored	30	30
511 A94	90c	multicolored	50	50
512 A94	$2.50	multicolored	1.50	1.50
		Nos. 508-512 (5)	2.61	2.61

Souvenir Sheet

513 A94	$5	multicolored	3.00	3.00

25th anniv. of coronation of Queen Elizabeth II.

Nos. 508-512 were printed in sheets of 50 (2 panes of 25), perf. 14, and in sheets of 3 plus label, perf. 12, with frames in changed colors.

Glass Coach A95

Royal Coaches: 50c, Irish state coach. $5, Coronation coach.

1978, June 2 **Litho.** *Imperf.*

Self-adhesive

514		Souvenir booklet	6.75
a.	A95	Bklt. pane of 6 (3 each 25c and 50c)	2.00
b.	A95	Bkit. pane of 1 ($5)	4.50

25th anniversary of coronation of Queen Elizabeth II. No. 514 contains 2 booklet panes printed on peelable paper backing showing royal processions.

Soccer — A96

Purple Wreath — A97

Designs: Various soccer scenes. Stamps in souvenir sheet horizontal.

1978, Aug. 18 **Litho.** *Perf. 15*

515 A96	10c	multicolored	15	15
516 A96	15c	multicolored	15	15
517 A96	$3	multicolored	3.00	3.00

Souvenir Sheet

518		Sheet of 4	3.25	3.25
a.	A96	25c multicolored	25	25
b.	A96	30c multicolored	30	30
c.	A96	50c multicolored	50	50
d.	A96	$2 multicolored	2.00	2.00

11th World Cup Soccer Championship, Argentina, June 1-25.

1978, Oct. **Litho.** *Perf. 14*

519 A97	25c	shown	22	22
520 A97	50c	Sunflowers	45	45
521 A97	90c	Frangipani	80	80
522 A97	$2	Passionflower	1.75	1.75

Souvenir Sheet

523 A97	$2.50	Red hibiscus	2.50	2.50

St. Ildefonso Receiving Chasuble, by Rubens A98

Christmas: 25c, Flight of St. Barbara, by Rubens. $2, Holy Family, by Sebastiano del Piombo. $4, Annunciation, by Rubens.

1978, Oct. 30 **Litho.** *Perf. 14*

524 A98	8c	multicolored	15	15
525 A98	25c	multicolored	20	20
526 A98	$2	multicolored	1.90	1.90

Souvenir Sheet

527 A98	$4	multicolored	5.00	5.00

Antigua No. 2 — A99

Crucifixion, by Durer — A100

Designs: 50c, Great Britain Penny Black, 1840. $1, Woman posting letter in pillar box, and coach. $2, Mail train, ship, plane and Concorde. $2.50, Rowland Hill.

1979, Feb. 12 **Litho.** *Perf. 14*

528 A99	25c	multicolored	20	20
529 A99	50c	multicolored	40	40
530 A99	$1	multicolored	75	75
531 A99	$2	multicolored	1.65	1.65

Souvenir Sheet

532 A99	$2.50	multicolored	2.25	2.25

Sir Rowland Hill (1795-1879), originator of penny postage.

Nos. 528-531 were printed in sheets of 50 (2 panes of 25), perf. 14, and in sheets of 5 plus label, perf. 12, with frames in changed colors.

For overprints, see Nos. 571A-571D.

1979, Mar. 15

Designs (after Dürer): 10c, Deposition. $2.50, Crucifixion. $4, Man of Sorrows.

533 A100	10c	multicolored	15	15
534 A100	50c	multicolored	40	40
535 A100	$4	multicolored	3.00	3.00

Souvenir Sheet

536 A100	$2.50	multicolored	2.25	2.25

Easter.

Child Playing with Sailboat — A101

IYC emblem, child's hand holding toy: 50c, Rocket. 90c, Automobile. $2, Train. $5, Plane.

1979, Apr. 9 **Litho.** *Perf. 14*

537 A101	25c	multicolored	20	20
538 A101	50c	multicolored	40	40
539 A101	90c	multicolored	75	75
540 A101	$2	multicolored	1.65	1.65

Souvenir Sheet

541 A101	$5	multicolored	4.00	4.00

International Year of the Child.

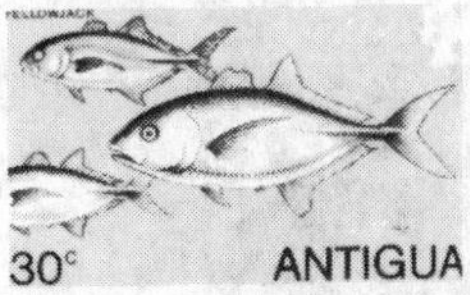

Yellowjacks A102

Sport Fish: 50c, Bluefin tunas. 90c, Sailfish. $2.50, Barracuda. $3, Wahoos.

1979, May **Litho.** *Perf. 14½*

542 A102	30c	multicolored	25	25
543 A102	50c	multicolored	40	40
544 A102	90c	multicolored	70	70
545 A102	$3	multicolored	2.25	2.25

Souvenir Sheet

546 A102	$2.50	multicolored	2.00	2.00

Capt. Cook and his Birthplace at Marton — A103

Holy Family — A104

Capt. James Cook (1728-1779) and: 50c, HMS Endeavour. 90c, Marine timekeeper. $2.50, HMS Resolution. $3, Landing at Botany Bay.

1979, July 2 **Litho.** *Perf. 14*

547 A103	25c	multicolored	20	20
548 A103	50c	multicolored	35	35
549 A103	90c	multicolored	60	60
550 A103	$3	multicolored	2.00	2.00

Souvenir Sheet

551 A103	$2.50	multicolored	2.25	2.25

1979, Oct. 1 **Litho.** *Perf. 14*

Stained-glass Windows: 25c, Flight into Egypt. 50c, Shepherd and star. $3, Angel with trumpet. $4, Three Kings offering gifts.

552 A104	8c	multicolored	15	15
553 A104	25c	multicolored	16	16
554 A104	50c	multicolored	32	32
555 A104	$4	multicolored	2.50	2.50

Souvenir Sheet

Perf. 12x12½

556 A104	$3	multicolored	2.25	2.25

Christmas.

Javelin, Olympic Rings — A105

1980, Feb. 7 **Litho.** *Perf. 14*

557 A105	10c	shown	15	15
558 A105	25c	Running	20	20
559 A105	$1	Pole vault	65	65
560 A105	$2	Hurdles	1.40	1.40

Souvenir Sheet

561 A105	$3	Boxing, horiz.	2.00	2.00

22nd Summer Olympic Games, Moscow, July 19-Aug. 3.

Disney Characters and IYC Emblem A106

Designs: Transportation scenes. ½c, 2c, 3c, 4c, 5c, $1, $2.50, horiz.

1980, Mar. 24 **Litho.** *Perf. 11*

562 A106	½c	Mickey, plane	15	15
563 A106	1c	Donald, car	15	15
564 A106	2c	Goofy driving taxi	15	15
565 A106	3c	Mickey, Minnie in sidecar	15	15
566 A106	4c	Huey, Dewey and Louie	15	15
567 A106	5c	Grandma Duck	15	15
568 A106	10c	Mickey in jeep	15	15
569 A106	$1	Chip and Dale sailing	1.00	1.00
570 A106	$4	Donald on train	4.00	4.00
		Set value	5.25	5.25

Souvenir Sheet

571 A106	$2.50	Goofy in glider	5.00	5.00

Nos. 528-531 in Changed Colors Overprinted "LONDON 1980"

1980, May 6 **Litho.** *Perf. 12*

571A A99	25c	multicolored	20	20
571B A99	50c	multicolored	35	35
571C A99	$1	multicolored	60	60
571D A99	$2	multicolored	1.40	1.40

London '80 Intl. Stamp Exhib., May 6-14.

Birth of Venus, by Botticelli A106a

Designs: 10c, David, by Donatello (vert.). 50c, Reclining Couple, sarcophagus, Cerveteri. 90c, The Garden of Earthly Delights, by Hieronymus Bosch.

$1, Portinari Altarpiece, by Hugo van der Goes. $4, Eleanora of Toledo and her Son Giovanni de Medici, by Bronzino (vert.). $5, The Holy Family, by Rembrandt.

Perf. 13½x14, 14x13½

1980, June 23 Litho.

572 A106a 10c	multicolored	15	15
573 A106a 30c	multicolored	15	15
574 A106a 50c	multicolored	25	25
575 A106a 90c	multicolored	45	45
576 A106a $1	multicolored	50	50
577 A106a $4	multicolored	2.75	2.75
	Nos. 572-577 (6)	4.25	4.25

Souvenir Sheet

Perf. 14

578 A106a $5	multicolored	3.75	3.75

Anniversary Emblem, Intl. Headquarters, Evanston, Ill. — A107

1980, July 21 Litho. *Perf. 14*

579 A107 3c	shown	20	20
580 A107 50c	Antigua club banner	35	35
581 A107 90c	Map of Antigua	60	60
582 A107 $3	Paul. P. Harris, emblem	2.00	2.00

Souvenir Sheet

583 A107 $5	Emblems, Antigua flags	3.25	3.25

Rotary International, 75th anniv.

Queen Mother Elizabeth, 80th Birthday — A108

1980, Sept. 15

584 A108 10c	multicolored	15	15
585 A108 $2.50	multicolored	1.75	1.75

Souvenir Sheet

Perf. 12

586 A108 $3	multicolored	2.00	2.00

Ringed Kingfisher — A109

1980, Nov. 3 Litho. *Perf. 14*

587 A109 10c	shown	15	15
588 A109 30c	Plain pigeon	30	30
589 A109 $1	Green-throated carib	75	75
590 A109 $2	Black-necked stilt	1.75	1.75

Souvenir Sheet

591 A109 $2.50	Roseate tern	3.50	3.50

Sleeping Beauty and the Prince — A110

Christmas: Various scenes from Walt Disney's Sleeping Beauty. $4 vert.

1980, Dec. 23 *Perf. 11, 13½x14 ($4)*

592 A110 ½c	multicolored	15	15
593 A110 1c	multicolored	15	15
594 A110 2c	multicolored	15	15
595 A110 4c	multicolored	15	15
596 A110 8c	multicolored	15	15
597 A110 10c	multicolored	15	15
598 A110 25c	multicolored	22	22
599 A110 $2	multicolored	1.75	1.75
600 A110 $2.50	multicolored	2.25	2.25
	Set value	4.50	4.50

Souvenir Sheet

601 A110 $4	multicolored	3.25	3.25

Sugar-cane Railway Diesel Locomotive No. 15 — A111

1981, Jan. 12 *Perf. 14*

602 A111 25c	shown	16	16
603 A111 50c	Narrow-gauge steam locomotive	40	40
604 A111 90c	Diesels #1, #10	75	75
605 A111 $3	Hauling sugar-cane	2.25	2.25

Souvenir Sheet

606 A111 $2.50	Sugar factory, train yard	1.90	1.90

Nos. 411-412, 414-422 Overprinted: "INDEPENDENCE 1981"

1981, Mar. 31 Litho.

607 A79 6c	multicolored	15	15
608 A79 10c	multicolored	15	15
609 A79 20c	multicolored	15	15
610 A79 25c	multicolored	20	20
611 A79 35c	multicolored	25	25
612 A79 50c	multicolored	40	40
613 A79 75c	multicolored	60	60
614 A79 $1	multicolored	75	75
615 A80 $2.50	multicolored	1.75	1.75
616 A80 $5	multicolored	3.75	3.75
617 A80 $10	multicolored	7.50	7.50
	Nos. 607-617 (11)	15.65	15.65

Pipes of Pan, by Picasso — A112

Paintings by Pablo Picasso (1881-1973): 50c, Seated Harlequin. 90c, Paulo as Harlequin. $4, Mother and Child. $5, Three Musicians.

1981, May 5 Litho. *Perf. 14*

618 A112 10c	multicolored	15	15
619 A112 50c	multicolored	32	32
620 A112 90c	multicolored	60	60
621 A112 $4	multicolored	2.50	2.50

Souvenir Sheet

Perf. 14x14½

622 A112 $5	multicolored	3.25	3.25

Royal Wedding Issue

Common Design Type

1981, June 16 Litho. *Perf. 14*

623 CD331 25c	Couple	15	15
624 CD331 50c	Glamis Castle	35	35
625 CD331 $4	Charles	2.75	2.75

Souvenir Sheet

626 CD331 $5	Glass coach	3.50	3.50
627 CD331	Booklet	9.00	
a.	Pane of 6 (2x25c, 2x$1, 2x$2), Charles	5.00	
b.	Pane of 1, $5, Couple	4.00	

No. 627 contains imperf., self-adhesive stamps.

Nos. 623-625 also printed in sheets of 5 plus label, perf. 12 in changed colors.

For surcharges, see Nos. 792, 795, 802, 805.

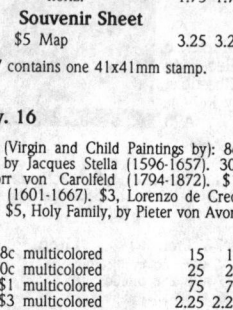

Campfire Sing — A113

1981, Oct. 28 Litho. *Perf. 15*

628 A113 10c	Irene Joshua	15	15
629 A113 50c	shown	40	40
630 A113 90c	Sailing	70	70
631 A113 $2.50	Milking cow	1.90	1.90

Souvenir Sheet

632 A113 $5	Flag raising	3.75	3.75

Girl Guides, 50th anniv.

Independence — A114

A115

1981, Nov. 1 Litho. *Perf. 15*

633 A114 10c	Arms	15	15
634 A114 50c	Flag	35	35
635 A114 90c	Prime Minister Bird	60	60
636 A114 $2.50	St. John's Cathedral, horiz.	1.75	1.75

Souvenir Sheet

637 A114 $5	Map	3.25	3.25

No. 637 contains one 41x41mm stamp.

1981, Nov. 16

Christmas (Virgin and Child Paintings by): 8c, Holy Night, by Jacques Stella (1596-1657). 30c Julius Schnorr von Carolfeld (1794-1872). $1, Alonso Cano (1601-1667). $3, Lorenzo de Credi (1459-1537). $5, Holy Family, by Pieter von Avoni (1600-1652).

638 A115 8c	multicolored	15	15
639 A115 30c	multicolored	25	25
640 A115 $1	multicolored	75	75
641 A115 $3	multicolored	2.25	2.25

Souvenir Sheet

642 A115 $5	multicolored	3.25	3.25

Intl. Year of the Disabled — A116

1981, Dec. 1 Litho. *Perf. 15*

643 A116 10c	Swimming	15	15
644 A116 50c	Discus	35	35
645 A116 90c	Archery	60	60
646 A116 $2	Baseball	1.40	1.40

Souvenir Sheet

647 A116 $4	Basketball	3.00	3.00

1982 World Cup Soccer — A117

Designs: Various soccer players.

1982, Apr. 15 Litho. *Perf. 14*

648 A117 10c	multicolored	15	15
649 A117 50c	multicolored	35	35
650 A117 90c	multicolored	60	60
651 A117 $4	multicolored	2.75	2.75

Souvenir Sheet

652 A117 $5	multicolored	3.75	3.75

Also issued in sheetlets of 5 + label in changed colors, perf. 12.

A118

A119

1982, June 17 Litho. *Perf. 14½*

653 A118 10c	A-300 Airbus	15	15
654 A118 50c	Hawker-Siddeley 748	40	40
655 A118 90c	De Havilland Twin Otter DCH6	70	70
656 A118 $2.50	Britten-Norman Islander	1.75	1.75

Souvenir Sheet

657 A118 $5	Jet, horiz.	3.50	3.50

Coolidge Intl. Airport opening.

1982, June 28 Litho. *Perf. 14½*

658 A119 10c	Cordia, vert.	15	15
659 A119 50c	Golden spotted mongoose	40	40
660 A119 90c	Corallita, vert.	70	70
661 A119 $3	Bulldog bats	2.25	2.25

Souvenir Sheet

662 A119 $5	Caribbean monk seals	3.75	3.75

Charles Darwin's death centenary.

Princess Diana Issue

Common Design Type

1982, July 1 Litho. *Perf. 14½x14*

663 CD332 90c	Greenwich Palace	60	60
664 CD332 $1	Wedding	65	65
665 CD332 $4	Diana	2.50	2.50

Souvenir Sheet

666 CD332 $5	Diana, diff.	3.75	3.75

For overprints, see Nos. 672-675. For surcharges, see Nos. 797, 799, 803, 806.

Scouting Year — A120

Designs: Independence Day celebration.

1982, July 15 *Perf. 14*

667 A120 10c	Decorating buildings	15	15
668 A120 50c	Helping woman	40	40
669 A120 90c	Princess Margaret	70	70
670 A120 $2.20	Cub Scout giving directions	1.75	1.75

Souvenir Sheet

671 A120 $5	Baden-Powell	3.75	3.75

Nos. 663-666 Overprinted: "ROYAL BABY / 21.6.82"

1982, Aug. 30 Litho. *Perf. 14½x14*

672 CD332 90c	multicolored	70	70
673 CD332 $1	multicolored	75	75
674 CD332 $4	multicolored	3.00	3.00

Souvenir Sheet

675 CD332 $5	multicolored	3.50	3.50

For surcharges, see Nos. 798, 800, 804, 807.

Roosevelt Driving by "The Little White House" A121

1982, Sept. 20 *Perf. 15*

676 A121 10c shown 15 15
677 A121 25c Washington as blacksmith 18 18
678 A121 45c Churchill, Roosevelt, Stalin 35 35
679 A121 60c Washington crossing Delaware, vert. 45 45
680 A121 $1 Roosevelt on train, vert. 75 75
681 A121 $3 Roosevelt, vert. 2.25 2.25
Nos. 676-681 (6) 4.13 4.13

Souvenir Sheets

682 A121 $4 Washington, vert. 3.00 3.00
683 A121 $4 Eleanor and Franklin 3.00 3.00

George Washington's 250th birth anniv. and Franklin D. Roosevelt's birth centenary.

Christmas — A122

Raphael Paintings.

1982, Nov. **Litho.** *Perf. 14*

684 A122 10c Annunciation 15 15
685 A122 30c Adoration of the Magi 22 22
686 A122 $1 Presentation at the Temple 75 75
687 A122 $4 Coronation of the Virgin 3.00 3.00

Souvenir Sheet

688 A122 $5 Marriage of the Virgin 3.50 3.50

500th Birth Anniv. of Raphael A123

1983, Jan. 28. **Litho.** *Perf. 14½*

689 A123 45c Galatea taking Reins of Dolphins, vert. 35 35
690 A123 50c Sea Nymphs carried by Tritons, vert. 40 40
691 A123 60c Winged Angel Steering Dolphins 45 45
692 A123 $4 Cupids Shooting Arrows 3.00 3.00

Souvenir Sheet

693 A123 $5 Galatea 3.75 3.75

A124

1983, Mar. 14 *Perf. 14*

694 A124 25c Pineapple crop 20 20
695 A124 45c Carnival 30 30
696 A124 60c Tourists, sailboat 40 40
697 A124 $3 Control Tower 2.00 2.00

Commonwealth Day.

World Communications Year — A125

1983, Apr. 5 **Litho.** *Perf. 14*

698 A125 15c TV screen, camera 15 15
699 A125 50c Police radio, car 40 40
700 A125 60c Long distance phone call 45 45
701 A125 $3 Dish antenna, planets 2.25 2.25

Souvenir Sheet

702 A125 $5 Comsat satellite 3.75 3.75

Bottlenose Dolphin A126

1983, May 9 **Litho.** *Perf. 15*

703 A126 15c shown 15 15
704 A126 50c Finback whale 35 35
705 A126 60c Bowhead whale 40 40
706 A126 $3 Spectacled porpoise 2.00 2.00

Souvenir Sheet

707 A126 $5 Unicorn whale 3.50 3.50

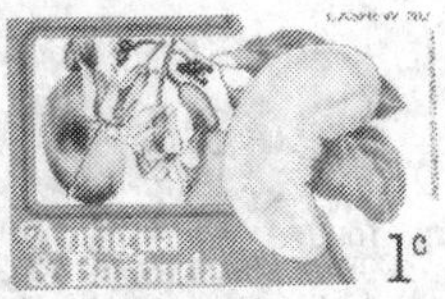

Cashew Nut — A127

1983, July 11 *Perf. 14*

708 A127 1c shown 15 15
709 A127 2c Passion fruit 15 15
710 A127 3c Mango 15 15
711 A127 5c Grapefruit 15 15
712 A127 10c Pawpaw 15 15
713 A127 15c Breadfruit 15 15
714 A127 20c Coconut 15 15
715 A127 25c Oleander 18 18
716 A127 30c Banana 22 22
717 A127 40c Pineapple 30 30
718 A127 45c Cordcia 35 35
719 A127 50c Cassia 40 40
720 A127 60c Poui 45 45
721 A127 $1 Frangipani 75 75
722 A127 $2 Flamboyant 1.50 1.50
723 A127 $2.50 Lemon 1.75 1.75
724 A127 $5 Lignum vitae 3.75 3.75
725 A127 $10 Arms 7.50 7.50
Nos. 708-725 (18) 18.20 18.20

1985 *Perf. 12½x12*

708a A127 1c 15 15
709a A127 2c 15 15
710a A127 3c 15 15
711a A127 5c 15 15
712a A127 10c 15 15
713a A127 15c 15 15
714a A127 20c 15 15
715a A127 25c 15 15
716a A127 30c 15 15
717a A127 40c 18 18
718a A127 45c 18 18
719a A127 50c 20 20
720a A127 60c 20 20
721a A127 $1 40 40
722a A127 $2 1.10 1.10
723a A127 $2.50 1.25 1.25
724a A127 $5 2.75 2.75
725a A127 $10 5.00 5.00
Nos. 708a-725a (18) 12.61 12.61

Issue dates: $2-$5, Dec. Others Mar.

Manned Flight Bicentenary A128

1983, Aug. 15 *Perf. 15*

726 A128 30c Dornier DoX 20 20
727 A128 50c Supermarine S-6B 35 35
728 A128 60c Curtiss F9C, USS Akron 40 40
729 A128 $4 Pro Juventute balloon 2.75 2.75

Souvenir Sheet

730 A128 $5 Graf Zeppelin 3.25 3.25

Christmas — A129

Raphael Paintings: 10c, 30c, $1, $4, Sybils and Angels details. $5, Vision of Ezekiel.

1983, Oct. 4 **Litho.** *Perf. 14*

731 A129 10c Angel flying with scroll 15 15
732 A129 30c Angel, diff. 30 30
733 A129 $1 Inscribing tablet 30 30
734 A129 $4 Angel showing tablet 3.25 3.25

Souvenir Sheet

735 A129 $5 multicolored 3.75 3.75

Methodist Church, Anniv. — A130

1984 Olympics, Los Angeles — A131

Designs: 15c, John Wesley founder of Methodism. 50c, Nathaniel Gilbert, Antiguan founder. 60c, St. John's Methodist Church Steeple. $3, Ebenezer Methodist Church.

1983, Nov. **Litho.** *Perf. 14*

736 A130 15c multicolored 15 15
737 A130 50c multicolored 40 40
738 A130 60c multicolored 45 45
739 A130 $3 multicolored 2.25 2.25

1984, Jan. **Litho.** *Perf. 15*

740 A131 25c Discus 18 18
741 A131 50c Gymnastics 40 40
742 A131 90c Hurdling 70 70
743 A131 $3 Bicycling 2.25 2.25

Souvenir Sheet

744 A131 $5 Volleyball, horiz. 3.75 3.75

Booker Vanguard A132

1984, June 4 **Litho.** *Perf. 15*

745 A132 45c shown 35 35
746 A132 50c Canberra 40 40
747 A132 60c Yachts 45 45
748 A132 $4 Fairwind 3.00 3.00

Souvenir Sheet

749 A132 $5 Man-of-war, vert. 3.75 3.75

Local Flowers — A133

US Presidents — A134

1984, June 25 **Litho.** *Perf. 15*

755 A133 15c multicolored 15 15
756 A133 50c multicolored 38 38
757 A133 60c multicolored 45 45
758 A133 $3 multicolored 2.25 2.25

Souvenir Sheet

759 A133 $5 multicolored 3.75 3.75

1984, July 18 **Litho.** *Perf. 14*

760 A134 10c Lincoln 15 15
761 A134 20c Truman 15 15
762 A134 30c Eisenhower 22 22
763 A134 40c Reagan 30 30
764 A134 90c Lincoln, diff. 68 68
765 A134 $1.10 Truman, diff. 85 85
766 A134 $1.50 Eisenhower, diff. 1.15 1.15
767 A134 $2 Reagan, diff. 1.50 1.50
Nos. 760-767 (8) 5.00 5.00

Slavery Abolition Sesquicentennial A135

1984, Aug. 1

768 A135 40c Moravian Mission 30 30
769 A135 50c Antigua Courthouse, 1823 38 38
770 A135 60c Sugar cane planting 45 45
771 A135 $3 Boiling House, Delaps' Estate 2.25 2.25

Souvenir Sheet

772 A135 $5 Willoughby Bay 3.75 3.75

Song Birds — A136

1984, Aug. 15 *Perf. 15*

773 A136 40c Rufous-sided towhee 30 30
774 A136 50c Parula warbler 38 38
775 A136 60c House wren 45 45
776 A136 $2 Ruby-crowned kinglet 1.50 1.50
777 A136 $3 Yellow-shafted flicker 2.25 2.25
Nos. 773-777 (5) 4.88 4.88

Souvenir Sheet

778 A136 $5 Yellow-breasted chat 3.75 3.75

AUSIPEX '84 — A137

The Blue Dancers, by Degas — A137a

1984, Sept. 21 *Perf. 15*

779 A137 $1 Grass skiing 75 75
780 A137 $5 Australian rules football 3.75 3.75

Souvenir Sheet

781 A137 $5 Boomerang 3.75 3.75

1984, Oct. **Litho.** *Perf. 15*

Paintings by Correggio: 25c, Virgin and Infant with Angels and Cherubs. 60c, The Four Saints. 90c, Saint Catherine. $3, The Campori Madonna. #790, St. John the Baptist.

Paintings by Degas: 50c, The Pink Dancers. 70c, Two Dancers. $4, Dancers at the Bar. #791, Folk Dancers.

782 A137a 15c multicolored 15 15
783 A137a 25c multicolored 20 20
784 A137a 50c multicolored 38 38
785 A137a 60c multicolored 45 45
786 A137a 70c multicolored 50 50
787 A137a 90c multicolored 68 68
788 A137a $3 multicolored 2.25 2.25
789 A137a $4 multicolored 3.00 3.00
Nos. 782-789 (8) 7.61 7.61

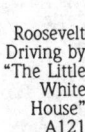

Souvenir Sheets

790 A137a $5 multicolored 3.75 3.75
791 A137a $5 multi, horiz. 3.75 3.75

Nos. 623-626, 663-666, 672-675, 694-697 Surcharged in Black or Gold

1984, June ***Perf. 14, 14½x14***

792 CD331 $2 on 25c #623 1.50 1.50
793 CD334 $2 on 25c #694 1.50 1.50
794 CD334 $2 on 45c #695 1.50 1.50
795 CD331 $2 on 50c #624 1.50 1.50
796 CD334 $2 on 60c #696 1.50 1.50
797 CD332 $2 on 90c #663 (G) 1.50 1.50
798 CD332 $2 on 90c #672 (G) 1.50 1.50
799 CD332 $2 on $1 #664 (G) 1.50 1.50
800 CD332 $2 on $1 #673 (G) 1.50 1.50
801 CD334 $2 on $3 #697 1.50 1.50
802 CD331 $2 on $4 #625 1.50 1.50
803 CD332 $2 on $4 #665 (G) 1.50 1.50
804 CD332 $2 on $4 #674 (G) 1.50 1.50
Nos. 792-804 (13) 19.50 19.50

Souvenir Sheets

805 CD331 $2 on $5 #626 1.50 1.50
806 CD332 $2 on $5 #666 1.50 1.50
807 CD332 $2 on $5 #675 1.50 1.50

Nos. 797-800, 803-804 exist with silver surcharge.

Christmas 1984 and 50th Anniv. of Donald Duck — A138

Scenes from various Donald Duck comics.

1984, Nov. **Litho.** ***Perf. 11***

808 A138 1c multicolored 15 15
809 A138 2c multicolored 15 15
810 A138 3c multicolored 15 15
811 A138 4c multicolored 15 15
812 A138 5c multicolored 15 15
813 A138 10c multicolored 15 15
814 A138 $1 multicolored 85 85
815 A138 $2 multicolored 1.65 1.65
816 A138 $5 multicolored 4.00 4.00
Nos. 808-816 (9) 7.40 7.40

Souvenir Sheets

Perf. 14

817 A138 $5 multi, horiz. 4.00 4.00
818 A138 $5 Donald on beach 4.00 4.00

20th Century Leaders A139

1984, Nov. 19 **Litho.** ***Perf. 15***

819 A139 60c John F. Kennedy (1917-1963), vert. 50 50
820 A139 60c Winston Churchill (1874-1965), vert. 50 50
821 A139 60c Mahatma Gandhi (1869-1948), vert. 50 50
822 A139 60c Mao Tse-Tung (1883-1976), vert. 50 50
823 A139 $1 Kennedy in Berlin 80 80
824 A139 $1 Churchill in Paris 80 80
825 A139 $1 Gandhi in Great Britain 80 80
826 A139 $1 Mao in Peking 80 80
Nos. 819-826 (8) 5.20 5.20

Souvenir Sheet

827 A139 $5 Flags of Great Britain, India, China, USA 3.75 3.75

Statue of Liberty Centennial A140

1985, Jan. 7

828 A140 25c Torch on display, 1885 16 16
829 A140 30c Restoration, 1984-1986, vert. 22 22
830 A140 50c Bartholdi supervising construction, 1876 35 35
831 A140 90c Statue on Liberty Island 70 70
832 A140 $1 Dedication Ceremony, 1886, vert. 75 75
833 A140 $3 Operation Sail, 1976, vert. 2.25 2.25
Nos. 828-833 (6) 4.43 4.43

Souvenir Sheet

834 A140 $5 Port of New York 3.75 3.75

Traditional Scenes A141

1985, Jan. 21

835 A141 15c Ceramics, Arawak pot shard 15 15
836 A141 50c Tatooing, body design 38 38
837 A141 60c Harvesting Manioc, god Yocahu 45 45
838 A141 $3 Caribs in battle, war club 2.25 2.25

Souvenir Sheet

839 A141 $5 Tainos worshiping 3.75 3.75

Invention of the Motorcycle, Cent. A142

1985, Mar. 7 ***Perf. 14***

840 A142 10c Triumph 2HP Jap, 1903 15 15
841 A142 30c Indian Arrow, 1949 22 22
842 A142 60c BMW R100RS, 1976 45 45
843 A142 $4 Harley Davidson Model II, 1916 3.00 3.00

Souvenir Sheet

844 A142 $5 Laverda Jota, 1975 3.75 3.75

John J. Audubon, 200th Birth Anniv. A143

1985, Mar. 25 ***Perf. 14***

845 A143 90c Horned grebe 68 68
846 A143 $1 Least petrel 75 75
847 A143 $1.50 Great blue heron 1.15 1.15
848 A143 $3 Double-crested cormorant 2.25 2.25

Souvenir Sheet

849 A143 $5 White-tailed tropic bird, vert. 3.75 3.75

See Nos.910-914.

Butterflies A144

1985, Apr. 16 ***Perf. 14***

850 A144 25c Polygrapha cyanea 16 16
851 A144 60c Leodonta dysoni 45 45
852 A144 95c Junea doraete 75 75
853 A144 $4 Prepona xenagoras 3.00 3.00

Souvenir Sheet

854 A144 $5 Caerois gerdrudtus 3.75 3.75

Cessna 172 — A145

1985, Apr. 30

855 A145 30c shown 20 20
856 A145 90c Fokker DVII 60 60
857 A145 $1.50 Spad VII 1.00 1.00
858 A145 $3 Boeing 747 1.90 1.90

Souvenir Sheet

859 A145 $5 Twin Otter, Coolidge Intl. Airport 3.75 3.75

40th anniv. of the ICAO. Nos. 855, 858-859 show the ICAO and UN emblems.

Maimonides (1135-1204), Judaic Philosopher and Physician — A146

1985, June 17 **Litho.** ***Perf. 14***

860 A146 $2 yellow green 2.00 2.00

Souvenir Sheet

861 A146 $5 deep brown 4.00 4.00

Intl. Youth Year A147

1985, July 1

862 A147 25c Agriculture 18 18
863 A147 50c Hotel management 35 35
864 A147 60c Environmental studies 50 50
865 A147 $3 Windsurfing 2.25 2.25

Souvenir Sheet

866 A147 $5 Youths, national flag 3.75 3.75

Queen Mother, 85th Birthday — A148

Designs: 90c, $1, Attending a church service. No. 867A, $1.50, Touring the London Gardens, children in a sandpit. $2.50, $3, Photograph (1979). $5, With Prince Edward at the wedding of Prince Charles and Lady Diana Spencer.

Perf. 14, 12x12½ (90c, $1, $3)

1985, July 15

866A A148 90c multi ('86) 65 65
867 A148 $1 multi 75 75
867A A148 $1 multi ('86) 75 75
868 A148 $1.50 multi 1.10 1.10
869 A148 $2.50 multi 1.85 1.85
869A A148 $3 multi ('86) 2.25 2.25
Nos. 866A-869A (6) 7.35 7.35

Souvenir Sheet

870 A148 $5 multicolored 3.75 3.75

Nos. 866A, 867A, 869A issued in sheets of 5 plus label on Jan. 13, 1986.

Antigua stamps can be mounted in the Scott British Leeward Islands album.

Marine Life — A149

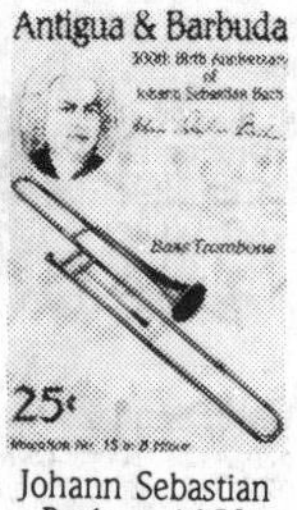

Johann Sebastian Bach — A150

1985, Aug. 1 ***Perf. 14***

871 A149 15c Fregata magnificens 15 15
872 A149 45c Diploria labyrinthiformis 40 40
873 A149 60c Oreaster reticulatus 50 50
874 A149 $3 Gymnothorax moringa 2.25 2.25

Souvenir Sheet

875 A149 $5 Acropora palmata 3.75 3.75

1985, Aug. 26 **Litho.** ***Perf. 14***

876 A150 25c Bass trombone 15 15
877 A150 50c English horn 30 30
878 A150 $1 Violino piccolo 65 65
879 A150 $3 Bass racket 1.90 1.90

Souvenir Sheet

880 A150 $5 Portrait 3.25 3.25

Girl Guides, 75th Anniv. A151

Public service and growth-oriented activities.

1985, Sept. 10

881 A151 15c Public service 15 15
882 A151 45c Guides meeting 40 40
883 A151 60c Lord and Lady Baden-Powell 50 50
884 A151 $3 Nature study 2.25 2.25

Souvenir Sheet

885 A151 $5 Barn swallow 3.75 3.75

State Visit of Elizabeth II, Oct. 24 A152

1985, Oct. 24 **Litho.** ***Perf. 14½***

886 A152 60c National flags 45 45
887 A152 $1 Elizabeth II, vert. 75 75
888 A152 $4 HMY Britannia 3.00 3.00

Souvenir Sheet

889 A152 $5 Map of Antigua 3.75 3.75

Mark Twain A153

Disney characters in Roughing It.

1985, Nov. 4 ***Perf. 14***

890 A153 25c Cowboys and Indians 22 22
891 A153 50c Canoeing 42 42
892 A153 $1.10 Pony Express 90 90
893 A153 $1.50 Buffalo hunt in Missouri 1.25 1.25
894 A153 $2 Nevada silver mine 1.75 1.75
Nos. 890-894 (5) 4.54 4.54

Souvenir Sheet

895 A153 $5 Stagecoach on Kansas plains 4.50 4.50

Jacob and Wilhelm Grimm, Fabulists and Philologists — A154

Disney characters in Spindle, Shuttle and Needle.

1985, Nov. 11

896	A154	30c multicolored	25	25
897	A154	60c multicolored	55	55
898	A154	70c multicolored	60	60
899	A154	$1 multicolored	90	90
900	A154	$3 multicolored	2.75	2.75
		Nos. 896-900 (5)	5.05	5.05

Souvenir Sheet

900A	A154	$5 multicolored	4.50	4.50

UN 40th Anniv. A155

Stamps of UN and portraits: 40c, No. 18 and Benjamin Franklin. $1, No. 391 and George Washington Carver, agricultural chemist. $3, No. 299 and Charles Lindbergh. $5, Marc Chagall, artist, vert.

1985, Nov. 18 *Perf. 13½x14*

901	A155	40c multicolored	30	30
902	A155	$1 multicolored	75	75
903	A155	$3 multicolored	2.25	2.25

Souvenir Sheet

Perf. 14x13½

904	A155	$5 multicolored	3.75	3.75

Christmas — A156

Religious paintings: 10c, Madonna and Child, by De Landi. 25c, Madonna and Child, by Bonaventura Berlinghieri (d. 1244). 60c, The Nativity, by Fra Angelico (1400-1455). $4, Presentation in the Temple, by Giovanni di Paolo Grazia (c.1403-1482). $5, The Nativity, by Antoniazzo Romano.

1985, Dec. 30 *Perf. 15*

905	A156	10c multicolored	15	15
906	A156	25c multicolored	18	18
907	A156	60c multicolored	45	45
908	A156	$4 multicolored	3.00	3.00

Souvenir Sheet

909	A156	$5 multicolored	3.75	3.75

Audubon Type of 1985

Illustrations of North American ducks.

1986, Jan. 6 *Perf. 12½x12*

910	A143	60c Mallard	45	45
911	A143	90c Dusky duck	65	65
912	A143	$1.50 Common pintail	1.10	1.10
913	A143	$3 Widgeon	2.25	2.25

Souvenir Sheet

Perf. 14

914	A143	$5 Common eider	3.75	3.75

1986 World Cup Soccer Championships, Mexico — A157

1986, Mar. 17 **Litho.** *Perf. 14*

915	A157	30c shown	22	22
916	A157	60c Heading the ball	45	45
917	A157	$1 Referee	75	75
918	A157	$4 Goal	3.00	3.00

Souvenir Sheet

919	A157	$5 Action	3.75	3.75

Nos. 916-917 vert.

For overprints, see Nos. 963-967.

A158

Halley's Comet A159

Designs: 5c, Edmond Halley, Greenwich Observatory. 10c, Me 163B Komet. German WWII fighter plane. 60c, Montezuma sighting comet, 1517. $4, Pocahontas saving Capt. John Smith's life, 1607 sighting as sign for Powhatan Indians to raid Jamestown. $5, Comet over Antigua.

1986, Mar. 24

920	A158	5c multicolored	15	15
921	A158	10c multicolored	15	15
922	A158	60c multicolored	45	45
923	A158	$4 multicolored	3.00	3.00

Souvenir Sheet

924	A159	$5 multicolored	3.75	3.75

For overprints, see Nos. 973-977.

Queen Elizabeth II, 60th Birthday

Common Design Type

1986, Apr. 21

925	CD339	60c Wedding, 1947	45	45
926	CD339	$1 Trooping the color	75	75
927	CD339	$4 Visiting Scotland	3.00	3.00

Souvenir Sheet

928	CD339	$5 Held by Queen Mary, 1927	3.75	3.75

Boats — A160

1986, May 15

929	A160	30c Tugboat	22	22
930	A160	60c Fishing boat	45	45
931	A160	$1 Sailboat 2056	75	75
932	A160	$4 Lateen-rigged sailboat	3.00	3.00

Souvenir Sheet

933	A160	$5 Boatbuilding	3.75	3.75

AMERIPEX '86 — A161

American trains.

1986, May 22 *Perf. 15*

934	A161	25c Hiawatha	20	20
935	A161	50c Grand Canyon	38	38
936	A161	$1 Powhattan Arrow	75	75
937	A161	$3 Empire State	2.25	2.25

Souvenir Sheet

938	A161	$5 Daylight	3.75	3.75

Wedding of Prince Andrew and Sarah Ferguson

Common Design Type

1986, July 23 *Perf. 14*

939	CD340	45c Couple	35	35
940	CD340	60c Prince Andrew	45	45
941	CD340	$4 Princes Andrew, Philip	3.00	3.00

Souvenir Sheet

942	CD340	$5 Couple, diff.	3.75	3.75

Conch Shells — A162

1986, Aug. 6 **Litho.** *Perf. 15*

943	A162	15c Say fly-specked cerith	15	15
944	A162	45c Gmelin smooth scotch bonnet	35	35
945	A162	60c Linne West Indian crown conch	45	45
946	A162	$3 Murex ciboney	2.25	2.25

Souvenir Sheet

947	A162	$5 Atlantic natica	3.75	3.75

Flowers A163

1986, Aug. 25 **Litho.** *Perf. 15*

948	A163	10c Water lily	15	15
949	A163	15c Queen of the night	15	15
950	A163	50c Cup of gold	38	38
951	A163	60c Beach morning glory	45	45
952	A163	70c Golden trumpet	55	55
953	A163	$1 Air plant	75	75
954	A163	$3 Purple wreath	2.25	2.25
955	A163	$4 Zephyr lily	3.00	3.00
		Nos. 948-955 (8)	7.68	7.68

Souvenir Sheets

956	A163	$4 Dozakie	3.00	3.00
957	A163	$5 Four o'clock	3.75	3.75

Fungi — A164

1986, Sept. 15

958	A164	10c Hygrocybe occidentalis scarletina	15	15
959	A164	50c Trogia buccinalis	38	38
960	A164	$1 Collybia subpruinosa	75	75
961	A164	$4 Leucocoprinus brebissonii	3.00	3.00

Souvenir Sheet

962	A164	$5 Pyrrhoglossum pyrrhum	3.75	3.75

Nos. 915-919 Ovptd. "WINNERS Argentina 3 W. Germany 2" in Gold in 2 or 3 lines

1986, Sept. 15 *Perf. 14*

963	A157	30c multicolored	22	22
964	A157	60c multicolored	45	45
965	A157	$1 multicolored	75	75
966	A157	$4 multicolored	3.00	3.00

Souvenir Sheet

967	A157	$5 multicolored	3.75	3.75

Automobile, Cent. A165

Carl Benz and classic automobiles.

1986, Oct. 20

968	A165	10c 1933 Auburn Speedster	15	15
968A	A165	15c 1986 Mercury Sable	15	15
969	A165	50c 1959 Cadillac	38	38
970	A165	60c 1950 Studebaker	45	45
970A	A165	70c 1939 Lagonda V-12	52	52
970B	A165	$1 1930 Adler Standard	75	75
970C	A165	$3 1956 DKW	2.25	2.25
971	A165	$4 1936 Mercedes 500K	3.00	3.00
		Nos. 968-971 (8)	7.65	7.65

Souvenir Sheets

972	A165	$5 1921 Mercedes Knight	3.75	3.75
972A	A165	$5 1896 Daimler	3.75	3.75

Nos. 920-924 Ovptd. with Halley's Comet Emblem in Black or Silver

1986, Oct. 22 **Litho.** *Perf. 14*

973	A158	5c multicolored	15	15
974	A158	10c multicolored	15	15
975	A158	60c multicolored	45	45
976	A158	$4 multicolored	3.00	3.00

Souvenir Sheet

977	A159	$5 multicolored (S)	3.75	3.75

Christmas — A166

Disney characters as children.

1986, Nov. 4 *Perf. 11*

978	A166	25c Mickey	20	20
979	A166	30c Mickey, Minnie	22	22
980	A166	40c Aunt Matilda, Goofy	30	30
981	A166	60c Goofy, Pluto	45	45
982	A166	70c Pluto, Donald, Daisy	55	55
983	A166	$1.50 Stringing popcorn	1.15	1.15
984	A166	$3 Grandma Duck, Minnie	2.30	2.30
985	A166	$4 Donald, Pete	3.05	3.05
		Nos. 978-985 (8)	8.22	8.22

Souvenir Sheets

Perf. 14

986	A166	$5 Playing with presents	3.80	3.80
987	A166	$5 Reindeer	3.80	3.80

Nos. 985 printed in sheets of 8.

Coat of Arms — A167

Natl. Flag — A168

1986, Nov. 25 **Litho.** *Perf. 14x14½*

988	A167	10c bright blue	15	15
989	A168	25c orange	20	20
		Set value	28	28

Marc Chagall (1887-1985), Artist — A169

Designs: No. 990, The Profile, 1957. No. 991, Portrait of the Artist's Sister, 1910. No. 992, Bride with Fan, 1911. No. 993, David in Profile, 1914. No. 994, Fiancee with Bouquet, 1977. No. 995, Self-portrait with Brushes, 1909. No. 996, The Walk, 1973. No. 997, Candles, 1938. No. 998, Fall of Icarus, 1975. No. 999, Myth of Orpheus, 1977.

1987, Mar. 30 Litho. ***Perf. 13½x14***

990	A169	10c	multicolored	15	15
991	A169	30c	multicolored	22	22
992	A169	40c	multicolored	30	30
993	A169	60c	multicolored	45	45
994	A169	90c	multicolored	70	70
995	A169	$1	multicolored	75	75
996	A169	$3	multicolored	2.25	2.25
997	A169	$4	multicolored	3.00	3.00

Size: 110x95mm

Imperf

998	A169	$5	multicolored	3.75	3.75
999	A169	$5	multicolored	3.75	3.75
			Nos. 990-999 (10)	15.32	15.32

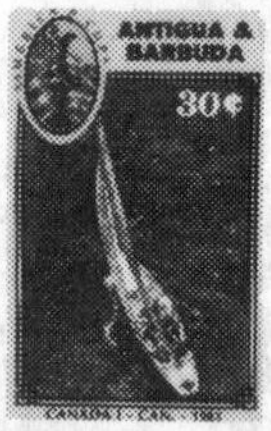

A170

America's Cup A171

1987, Feb. 5 ***Perf. 15***

1000	A170	30c	Canada I, 1981	24	24
1001	A170	60c	Gretel II, 1970	45	45
1002	A170	$1	Sceptre, 1958	75	75
1003	A170	$3	Vigilant, 1893	2.25	2.25

Souvenir Sheet

1004	A171	$5	Australia II, Liberty, 1983	3.75	3.75

Fish, World Wildlife Fund A172

Marine Birds A173

1987, Feb. 23 Litho. ***Perf. 14***

1005	A172	15c	Bridled burrfish	15	15
1006	A173	30c	Brown noddy	24	24
1007	A172	40c	Nassau grouper	32	32
1008	A173	50c	Laughing gull	40	40
1009	A172	60c	French angelfish	48	48
1010	A172	$1	Porkfish	80	80
1011	A173	$2	Royal tern	1.60	1.60
1012	A173	$3	Sooty tern	2.40	2.40
			Nos. 1005-1012 (8)	6.39	6.39

Souvenir Sheets

1013	A172	$5	Banded butterfly fish	4.00	4.00
1014	A173	$5	Brown booby	4.00	4.00

No. 1013 does not picture the WWF emblem.

For overprints, see Nos. 1137-1139A.

Statue of Liberty, Cent. A174

Photographs by Peter B. Kaplan.

1987, Apr. 20 ***Perf. 14***

1015	A174	15c	Lee Iacocca	15	15
1016	A174	30c	Statue at dusk	24	24
1017	A174	45c	Crown, head	35	35
1018	A174	50c	Iacocca, torch	40	40
1019	A174	60c	Crown observatory	48	48
1020	A174	90c	Interior restoration	70	70
1021	A174	$1	Head	80	80
1022	A174	$2	Statue at sunset	1.60	1.60
1023	A174	$3	Men on scaffold, flag	2.40	2.40
1024	A174	$5	Statue at night	4.00	4.00
			Nos. 1015-1024 (10)	11.12	11.12

Nos. 1015-1018, 1021-1022, 1024 vert.

A175

Transportation Innovations — A175a

1987, Apr. 19 ***Perf. 15***

1025	A175	10c	Spirit of Australia, 1978	15	15
1026	A175a	15c	Siemens' Electric locomotive, 1879	15	15
1027	A175	30c	USS Triton, 1960	24	24
1028	A175a	50c	Trevithick, 1801	38	38
1029	A175	60c	USS New Jersey, 1942	48	48
1030	A175a	70c	Draisine bicycle, 1818	52	52
1031	A175	90c	SS United States, 1952	68	68
1032	A175a	$1.50	Cierva C-4, 1923	1.15	1.15
1033	A175a	$2	Curtiss NC-4, 1919	1.50	1.50
1034	A175	$3	Queen Elizabeth II, 1969	2.25	2.25
			Nos. 1025-1034 (10)	7.50	7.50

Reptiles and Amphibians A176

1987, June 15 ***Perf. 14***

1035	A176	30c	Eleutherodactylus martinicensis	24	24
1036	A176	60c	Thecadactylus bapicauda	48	48
1037	A176	$1	Anolis bimaculatus leachi	75	75
1038	A176	$3	Geochelone carbonaria	2.25	2.25

Souvenir Sheet

1039	A176	$5	Ameiva griswoldi	3.75	3.75

Entertainers — A177

1987, May 11

1040	A177	15c	Grace Kelly	15	15
1041	A177	30c	Marilyn Monroe	30	30
1042	A177	45c	Orson Welles	45	45
1043	A177	50c	Judy Garland	50	50
1044	A177	60c	John Lennon	60	60
1045	A177	$1	Rock Hudson	1.00	1.00
1046	A177	$2	John Wayne	2.00	2.00
1047	A177	$3	Elvis Presley	3.00	3.00
			Nos. 1040-1047 (8)	8.00	8.00

No. 1047 Overprinted

1987, Sept. 9 Litho. ***Perf. 14***

1047A	A177	$3	multicolored	3.00	3.00

1988 Summer Olympics, Seoul A178

1987, Mar. 23

1048	A178	10c	Basketball	15	15
1049	A178	60c	Fencing	48	48
1050	A178	$1	Women's gymnastics	75	75
1051	A178	$3	Soccer	2.25	2.25

Souvenir Sheet

1052	A178	$5	Boxing glove	3.75	3.75

16th World Scout Jamboree, Australia, 1987-88 A179

1987, Nov. 2 Litho. ***Perf. 15***

1053	A179	10c	Campfire, red kangaroo	15	15
1054	A179	60c	Kayaking, blue-winged kookaburra	45	45
1055	A179	$1	Obstacle course, ring-tailed rock wallaby	75	75
1056	A179	$3	Field kitchen, koalas	2.25	2.25

Souvenir Sheet

1057	A179	$5	Flags	3.75	3.75

US Constitution Bicent. A180

Designs: 15c, Virginia House of Burgesses exercising right of freedom of speech. 45c, Connecticut state seal. 60c, Delaware state seal. $4, Gouverneur Morris (1752-1816), principal writer of the Constitution, vert. $5, Roger Sherman (1721-1793), jurist and statesman, vert.

1987, Nov. 16 Litho. ***Perf. 14***

1058	A180	15c	multicolored	15	15
1059	A180	45c	multicolored	35	35
1060	A180	60c	multicolored	48	48
1061	A180	$4	multicolored	3.00	3.00

Souvenir Sheet

1062	A180	$5	multicolored	3.80	3.80

Christmas — A181

A182

Paintings: 45c, Madonna and Child, by Bernardo Daddi (1290-1355). 60c, Joseph, detail from The Nativity, by Sano Di Pietro (1406-1481). $1, Mary, detail from Di Pietro's The Nativity. $4, Music-making Angel, by Melozzo Da Forli (1438-1494). $5, The Flight into Egypt, by Di Pietro.

1987, Dec. 1

1063	A181	45c	multicolored	32	32
1064	A181	60c	multicolored	45	45
1065	A181	$1	multicolored	75	75
1066	A181	$4	multicolored	2.95	2.95

Souvenir Sheet

1067	A181	$5	multicolored	3.80	3.80

1988, Feb. 8 Litho. ***Perf. 14***

1068	A182	25c	Wedding portrait	15	15
1069	A182	60c	Elizabeth II, c. 1970	45	45
1070	A182	$2	Christening of Charles, 1948	1.50	1.50
1071	A182	$3	Elizabeth II, c. 1980	2.25	2.25

Souvenir Sheet

1072	A182	$5	Royal family, c. 1951	3.75	3.75

40th wedding anniv. of Queen Elizabeth II and Prince Philip.

Tropical Birds A183

1988, Mar. 1

1073	A183	10c	Great blue heron, vert.	15	15
1074	A183	15c	Ringed kingfisher	15	15
1075	A183	50c	Bananaquit	38	38
1076	A183	60c	Purple gallinule	45	45
1077	A183	70c	Blue-hooded euphonia	55	55
1078	A183	$1	Caribbean parakeet, vert.	75	75
1079	A183	$3	Troupial	2.30	2.30
1080	A183	$4	Hummingbird	3.00	3.00
			Nos. 1073-1080 (8)	7.73	7.73

Souvenir Sheets

1081	A183	$5	Roseate flamingo, vert.	3.75	3.75
1082	A183	$5	Brown pelicans, vert.	3.75	3.75

Salvation Army — A184

1988, Mar. 7

1083	A184	25c	Day-care, Antigua	20	20
1084	A184	30c	Penicillin inoculation, Indonesia	22	22
1085	A184	40c	Day-care Center, Bolivia	30	30
1086	A184	45c	Rehabilitation, India	35	35
1087	A184	50c	Training the blind, Kenya	38	38
1088	A184	60c	Infant care, Ghana	45	45
1089	A184	$1	Job training, Zambia	78	78
1090	A184	$2	Food distribution, Sri Lanka	1.50	1.50
			Nos. 1083-1090 (8)	4.18	4.18

Souvenir Sheet

1091	A184	$5	General Eva Burrows	3.75	3.75

A185

Discovery of America, 500th Anniv. (in 1992)
A186

Anniv. emblem and: 10c, Fleet. 30c, View of fleet in harbor from Paino Indian village. 45c, Caravel anchored in harbor, Paino village. 60c, Columbus, 3 Indians in canoe. 90c, Indian, parrot, Columbus. $1, Columbus in longboat. $3, Spanish guard, fleet in harbor. $4, Ships under full sail. No. 1100, Stone cross given to Columbus by Queen Isabella. No. 1101, Gold exelente.

1988, Mar. 14 Litho. *Perf. 14*

1092	A185	10c multicolored	15	15
1093	A185	30c multicolored	22	22
1094	A185	45c multicolored	35	35
1095	A185	60c multicolored	45	45
1096	A185	90c multicolored	68	68
1097	A185	$1 multicolored	75	75
1098	A185	$3 multicolored	2.25	2.25
1099	A185	$4 multicolored	3.00	3.00
		Nos. 1092-1099 (8)	7.85	7.85

Souvenir Sheets

1100	A186	$5 multicolored	3.75	3.75
1101	A186	$5 multicolored	3.75	3.75

Paintings by Titian — A187

Details: 30c, Bust of Christ. 40c, Scourging of Christ. 45c, Madonna in Glory with Saints. 50c, The Averoldi Polyptych. $1, Christ Crowned with Thorns. $2, Christ Mocked. $3, Christ and Simon of Cyrene. $4, Crucifixion with Virgin and Saints. No. 1110, Ecce Homo. No. 1111, Noli Me Tangere.

1988, Apr. 11 Litho. *Perf. 13½x14*

1102	A187	30c shown	22	22
1103	A187	40c multicolored	30	30
1104	A187	45c multicolored	35	35
1105	A187	50c multicolored	38	38
1106	A187	$1 multicolored	78	78
1107	A187	$2 multicolored	1.50	1.50
1108	A187	$3 multicolored	2.25	2.25
1109	A187	$4 multicolored	3.00	3.00
		Nos. 1102-1109 (8)	8.78	8.78

Souvenir Sheets

1110	A187	$5 multicolored	3.75	3.75
1111	A187	$5 multicolored	3.75	3.75

Sailing Week
A188

1988, Apr. 18 *Perf. 15*

1112	A188	30c Canada I, 1980	22	22
1113	A188	60c Gretel II, Australia, 1970	48	48
1114	A188	$1 Sceptre, GB, 1958	78	78
1115	A188	$3 Vigilant, US, 1893	2.25	2.25

Souvenir Sheet

1116	A188	$5 Australia II, 1983	3.75	3.75

Walt Disney Animated Characters and Epcot Center, Walt Disney World — A189

1988, May 3 *Perf. 14x13½, 13½x14*

1116A	A189	1c like 25c	15	15
1116B	A189	2c like 30c	15	15
1116C	A189	3c like 40c	15	15
1116D	A189	4c like 60c	15	15
1116E	A189	5c like 70c	15	15
1116F	A189	10c like $1.50	15	15
1117	A189	25c The Living Seas	18	18
1118	A189	30c World of Motion	22	22
1119	A189	40c Spaceship Earth	30	30
1120	A189	60c Universe of Energy	45	45
1121	A189	70c Journey to Imagination	55	55
1122	A189	$1.50 The Land	1.15	1.15
1123	A189	$3 Communicore	2.25	2.25
1124	A189	$4 Horizons	3.00	3.00
		Nos. 1116A-1124 (14)	9.00	9.00

Souvenir Sheets

1125	A189	$5 Epcot Center	3.75	3.75
1126	A189	$5 The Contemporary Resort Hotel	3.75	3.75

30c, 40c, $1.50, $3 and No. 1126 are vert.

Flowering Trees
A190 A191

1988, May 16 *Perf. 14*

1127	A190	10c Jacaranda	15	15
1128	A190	30c Cordia	22	22
1129	A190	50c Orchid tree	38	38
1130	A190	90c Flamboyant	70	70
1131	A190	$1 African tulip tree	75	75
1132	A190	$2 Potato tree	1.50	1.50
1133	A190	$3 Crepe myrtle	2.25	2.25
1134	A190	$4 Pitch apple	3.00	3.00
		Nos. 1127-1134 (8)	8.95	8.95

Souvenir Sheets

1135	A191	$5 Cassia	3.75	3.75
1136	A191	$5 Chinaberry	3.75	3.75

Nos. 1011-1012, 1014 and 1013 Ovptd. in Black for Philatelic Exhibitions

a Praga '88

b INDEPENDENCE 40

c FINLANDIA 88

d OLYMPHILEX' 88

1988, May 9 Litho. *Perf. 14*

1137	A173 (a)	$2 multicolored	1.50	1.50
1138	A173 (b)	$3 multicolored	2.25	2.25

Souvenir Sheets

1139	A173 (c)	$5 multicolored	3.75	3.75
1139A	A172 (d)	$5 multicolored	3.75	3.75

1988 Summer Olympics, Seoul
A192

1988, June 10

1140	A192	40c Gymnastic rings, vert.	30	30
1141	A192	60c Weight lifting, vert.	45	45
1142	A192	$1 Water polo	75	75
1143	A192	$3 Boxing	2.25	2.25

Souvenir Sheet

1144	A192	$5 Torch-bearer, vert.	3.75	3.75

Butterflies
A193

1988-90 Litho. *Perf. 14*

1145	A193	1c Monarch	15	15
1146	A193	2c Jamaican clearwing	15	15
1147	A193	3c Yellow-barred ringlet	15	15
1148	A193	5c Cracker	15	15
1149	A193	10c Jamaican mestra	15	15
1150	A193	15c Mimic	15	15
1151	A193	20c Silver spot	15	15
1152	A193	25c Zebra	18	18
1153	A193	30c Fiery sulphur	22	22
1154	A193	40c Androgeus swallowtail	30	30
1155	A193	45c Giant brimstone	35	35
1156	A193	50c Orbed sulphur	38	38
1157	A193	60c Blue-backed skipper	45	45
1158	A193	$1 Common white skipper	75	75
1159	A193	$2 Baracoa skipper	1.50	1.50
1160	A193	$2.50 Mangrove skipper	1.90	1.90
1161	A193	$5 Silver king	3.75	3.75
1161A	A193	$10 Pygmy skipper	7.50	7.50
1162	A193	$20 Parides lycimenes	15.00	15.00
		Nos. 1145-1162 (19)	33.33	33.33

Issue dates: $20, Feb. 19, 1990. Others, Aug. 29.
This is an expanding set. Numbers will change if necessary.

John F. Kennedy
A194

1988, Nov. 22 Litho. *Perf. 14*

1162A	A194	1c like 30c	15	15
1162B	A194	2c like $4	15	15
1162C	A194	3c like $1	15	15
1162D	A194	4c like 60c	15	15
1163	A194	30c First family	22	22
1164	A194	60c Motorcade, Mexico	45	45
1165	A194	$1 Funeral procession	75	75
1166	A194	$4 Aboard PT109	3.00	3.00
		Nos. 1162A-1166 (8)	5.02	5.02

Souvenir Sheet

1167	A194	$5 Taking Oath of Office	3.75	3.75

Miniature Sheet

Christmas, Mickey Mouse 60th Anniv. — A195

Walt Disney characters: No. 1168a, Morty and Ferdie. No. 1168b, Goofy. No. 1168c, Chip-n-Dale. No. 1168d, Huey and Dewey. No. 1168e, Minnie Mouse. No. 1168f, Pluto. No. 1168g, Mickey Mouse. No. 1168h, Donald Duck and Louie. No. 1169, Goofy driving Mickey and Minnie in a horse-drawn carriage. No. 1170, Characters on roller skates, caroling.

1988, Dec. 1 *Perf. 13½x14, 14x13½*

1168	A195	Sheet of 8	6.00	6.00
a.-h.		$1 any single	75	75

Souvenir Sheets

1169	A195	$7 multicolored	5.25	5.25
1170	A195	$7 multi, horiz.	5.25	5.25

Disney Christmas Type of 1988

1988, Dec. 1 Litho. *Perf. 14*

1171	A195	10c like No. 1168e	15	15
1172	A195	25c like No. 1168f	18	18
1173	A195	30c like No. 1168g	22	22
1174	A195	70c like No. 1168h	52	52

Arawak Indian Whip Dance — A196

UPAE and discovery of America emblems and: a, Five adults. b, Eight adults. c, Seven adults. d, Three adults, three children.

1989, May 16 Litho. *Perf. 14*

1175		Strip of 4	4.50	4.50
a.-d.	A196	$1.50 any single	1.12	1.12

Souvenir Sheet

1176	A196	$6 Arawak chief	4.50	4.50

Discovery of America 500th anniv. (in 1992), pre-Columbian societies and customs.

Jet Flight, 50th Anniv.
A197

Various jet aircraft.

1989, May 29 Litho. *Perf. 14x13½*

1177	A197	10c DeHavilland Comet 4	15	15
1178	A197	30c Messerschmitt Me262	22	22
1179	A197	40c Boeing 707	30	30
1180	A197	60c Canadair F-86 Sabre	45	45
1181	A197	$1 Lockheed F-104 Starfighter	75	75
1182	A197	$2 McDonnell Douglas DC-10	1.50	1.50
1183	A197	$3 Boeing 747	2.25	2.25
1184	A197	$4 McDonnell F-4 Phantom	3.00	3.00
		Nos. 1177-1184 (8)	8.62	8.62

Souvenir Sheets

1185	A197	$7 Grumman F-14 Tomcat	5.25	5.25
1186	A197	$7 Concorde	5.25	5.25

Caribbean Cruise Ships
A198

1989, June 20 Litho. *Perf. 14*

1187	A198	25c TSS *Festivale*	18	18
1188	A198	45c M.S. *Southward*	32	32
1189	A198	50c M.S. *Sagafjord*	38	38
1190	A198	60c MTS *Daphne*	45	45
1191	A198	75c M.V. *Cunard Countess*	58	58
1192	A198	90c M.S. *Song of America*	68	68
1193	A198	$3 M.S. *Island Princess*	2.25	2.25
1194	A198	$4 S.S. *Galileo*	3.00	3.00
		Nos. 1187-1194 (8)	7.84	7.84

Souvenir Sheets

1195 A198 $6 S.S. *Norway* 4.50 4.50
1196 A198 $6 S.S. *Oceanic* 4.50 4.50

Paintings by Hiroshige — A199

Designs: 25c, *Fish Swimming by Duck Half-submerged in Stream.* 45c, *Crane and Wave.* 50c, *Sparrows and Morning Glories.* 60c, *Crested Blackbird and Flowering Cherry.* $1, *Great Knot Sitting among Water Grass.* $2, *Goose on a Bank of Water.* $3, *Black Paradise Flycatcher and Blossoms.* $4, *Sleepy Owl Perched on a Pine Branch.* No. 1205, *Bullfinch Flying Near a Clematis Branch.* No. 1206, *Titmouse on a Cherry Branch.*

1989, July 3 *Perf.* **$14x13^1/_2$**

1197 A199 25c multicolored 18 18
1198 A199 45c multicolored 35 35
1199 A199 50c multicolored 38 38
1200 A199 60c multicolored 45 45
1201 A199 $1 multicolored 75 75
1202 A199 $2 multicolored 1.50 1.50
1203 A199 $3 multicolored 2.25 2.25
1204 A199 $4 multicolored 3.00 3.00
Nos. 1197-1204 (8) 8.86 8.86

Souvenir Sheets

1205 A199 $5 multicolored 3.75 3.75
1206 A199 $5 multicolored 3.75 3.75

Hirohito (1901-1989) and enthronement of Akihito as emperor of Japan.

PHILEXFRANCE '89 — A200

Walt Disney characters, French landmarks: 1c, Helicopter over the Seine. 2c, Arc de Triomphe. 3c, Painting Notre Dame Cathedral. 4c, Entrance to the Metro. 5c, Fashion show. 10c, Follies. No. 1213, Shopping stalls on the Seine. $6, Sidewalk cafe, Left Bank. No. 1215, Hot air balloon *Ear Force One.* No. 1216, Dining.

1989, July 7 *Perf.* **$14x13^1/_2$**

1207 A200 1c multicolored 15 15
1208 A200 2c multicolored 15 15
1209 A200 3c multicolored 15 15
1210 A200 4c multicolored 15 15
1211 A200 5c multicolored 15 15
1212 A200 10c multicolored 15 15
1213 A200 $5 multicolored 3.75 3.75
1214 A200 $6 multicolored 4.50 4.50
Nos. 1207-1214 (8) 9.15 9.15

Souvenir Sheets

1215 A200 $5 multicolored 3.75 3.75
1216 A200 $5 multicolored 3.75 3.75

1990 World Cup Soccer Championships, Italy — A201

Natl. flag, various actions of a defending goalie.

1989, Aug. 21 *Perf.* **14**

1217 A201 15c multicolored 15 15
1218 A201 25c multicolored 18 18
1219 A201 $1 multicolored 75 75
1220 A201 $4 multicolored 3.00 3.00

Souvenir Sheets

1221 A201 $5 2 players, horiz. 3.75 3.75
1222 A201 $5 3 players, horiz. 3.75 3.75

For overprints see Nos. 1344-1349.

Mushrooms A202

1989, Oct. 12 **Litho.** *Perf.* **14**

1223 A202 10c Lilac fairy helmet 15 15
1224 A202 25c Rough psathyrella, vert. 18 18
1225 A202 50c Golden tops 38 38
1226 A202 60c Blue cap, vert. 45 45
1227 A202 75c Brown cap, vert. 58 58
1228 A202 $1 Green gill, vert. 75 75
1229 A202 $3 Red pinwheel 2.25 2.25
1230 A202 $4 Red chanterelle 3.00 3.00
Nos. 1223-1230 (8) 7.74 7.74

Souvenir Sheets

1231 A202 $6 Slender stalk 4.50 4.50
1232 A202 $6 Paddy straw mushroom 4.50 4.50

Nos. 1224, 1226-1228, 1231 vert.

Wildlife A203

1989, Oct. 19 **Litho.** *Perf.* **14**

1233 A203 25c Hutia 20 20
1234 A203 45c Caribbean monk seal 35 35
1235 A203 60c Mustache bat, vert. 45 45
1236 A203 $4 Manatee, vert. 3.00 3.00

Souvenir Sheet

1237 A203 $5 West Indies giant rice rat 3.75 3.75

American Philatelic Soc. Emblem, Stamps on Stamps and Walt Disney Characters Promoting Philately A204

Designs: 1c, Israel #150, printing press. 2c, Italy #1238, first day cancel. 3c, US #143L4, Pony Express recruits. 4c, Denmark #566, early radio broadcast. 5c, German Democratic Republic #702, television. 10c, Great Britain #1, stamp collector. $4, Japan #1414, integrated circuits. $6, Germany #B667, boom box. No. 1246, US #1355, C3a, and Jenny biplane over Disneyland, horiz. No. 1247, US #940, 1421 and stamps for the wounded.

1989, Nov. 2 *Perf.* **$13^1/_2x14$, $14x13^1/_2$**

1238 A204 1c multicolored 15 15
1239 A204 2c multicolored 15 15
1240 A204 3c multicolored 15 15
1241 A204 4c multicolored 15 15
1242 A204 5c multicolored 15 15
1243 A204 10c multicolored 15 15
1244 A204 $4 multicolored 3.00 3.00
1245 A204 $6 multicolored 4.50 4.50
Nos. 1238-1245 (8) 8.40 8.40

Souvenir Sheets

1246 A204 $5 multicolored 3.75 3.75
1247 A204 $5 multicolored 3.75 3.75

Locomotives and Walt Disney Characters — A205

Perf. **$14x13^1/_2$, $13^1/_2x14$**

1989, Nov. 17

1248 A205 25c John Bull, 1831 18 18
1249 A205 45c Atlantic, 1832 35 35
1250 A205 50c William Crook's, 1861 38 38
1251 A205 60c Minnetonka, 1869 45 45
1252 A205 $1 Thatcher Perkins, 1863 75 75
1253 A205 $2 Pioneer, 1848 1.50 1.50
1254 A205 $3 Peppersass, 1869 2.25 2.25
1255 A205 $4 Gimbels Flyer 3.00 3.00
Nos. 1248-1255 (8) 8.86 8.86

Souvenir Sheets

1256 A205 $6 #6100 Class S-1 & 1835 Thomas Jefferson 4.50 4.50
1257 A205 $6 Jupiter & #119 4.50 4.50

New York World's Fair, 50th anniv., and World Stamp Expo '89, Washington, DC.

1st Moon Landing, 20th Anniv. A206

1989, Nov. 24 **Litho.** *Perf.* **14**

1258 A206 10c Apollo 11 liftoff 15 15
1259 A206 45c Aldrin walking on Moon 35 35
1260 A206 $1 *Eagle* ascending from Moon 75 75
1261 A206 $4 Recovery after splashdown 3.00 3.00

Souvenir Sheet

1262 A206 $5 Armstrong 3.75 3.75

Nos. 1258-1259 and 1262, vert.

Souvenir Sheet

Smithsonian Institution, Washington, DC — A207

1989, Nov. 17 **Litho.** *Perf.* **14**

1263 A207 $4 multicolored 3.00 3.00

World Stamp Expo '89.

Christmas — A208

Religious paintings: 10c, *The Small Cowper Madonna.* 25c, *Madonna of the Goldfinch.* 30c, *The Alba Madonna.* 50c, *Bologna Altarpiece* (attendant). 60c, *Bologna Altarpiece* (heralding angel). 70c, *Bologna Altarpiece* (archangel). $4, *Bologna Altarpiece* (saint holding ledger). No. 1271, *Madonna of Foligno.* No. 1272, *The Marriage of the Virgin.* No. 1273, *Bologna Altarpiece* (Madonna and Child).

Bologna Altarpiece by Giotto. Other paintings by Raphael.

1989, Dec. 11 **Litho.** *Perf.* **14**

1264 A208 10c multicolored 15 15
1265 A208 25c multicolored 18 18
1266 A208 30c multicolored 22 22
1267 A208 50c multicolored 38 38
1268 A208 60c multicolored 45 45
1269 A208 70c multicolored 52 52
1270 A208 $4 multicolored 3.00 3.00
1271 A208 $5 multicolored 3.75 3.75
Nos. 1264-1271 (8) 8.65 8.65

Souvenir Sheets

1272 A208 $5 multicolored 3.75 3.75
1273 A208 $5 multicolored 3.75 3.75

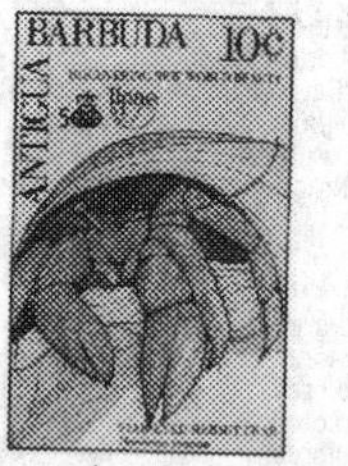

America Issue — A210

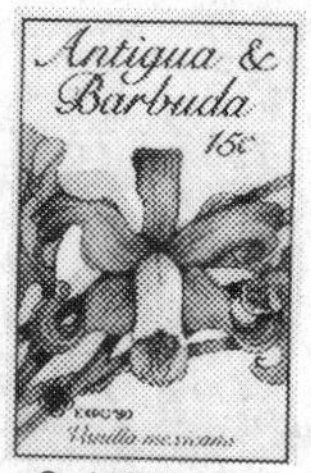

Orchids — A211

UPAE, discovery of America 500th anniv. emblems and marine life: 10c, Star-eyed hermit crab. 20c, Spiny lobster. 25c, Magnificent banded fanworm. 45c, Cannonball jellyfish. 60c, Red-spiny sea star. $2, Peppermint shrimp. $3, Coral crab. $4, Branching fire coral. No. 1283, Common sea fan. No. 1284, Portuguese man-of-war.

1990, Mar. 26 **Litho.** *Perf.* **14**

1275 A210 10c multicolored 15 15
1276 A210 20c multicolored 15 15
1277 A210 25c multicolored 18 18
1278 A210 45c multicolored 35 35
1279 A210 60c multicolored 45 45
1280 A210 $2 multicolored 1.50 1.50
1281 A210 $3 multicolored 2.25 2.25
1282 A210 $4 multicolored 3.00 3.00
Nos. 1275-1282 (8) 8.03 8.03

Souvenir Sheets

1283 A210 $5 multicolored 3.75 3.75
1284 A210 $5 multicolored 3.75 3.75

1990, Apr. 17 *Perf.* **14**

1285 A211 15c *Vanilla mexicana* 15 15
1286 A211 45c *Epidendrum ibaguense* 35 35
1287 A211 50c *Epidendrum secundum* 38 38
1288 A211 60c *Maxillaria conferta* 45 45
1289 A211 $1 *Oncidium altissimum* 75 75
1290 A211 $2 *Spiranthes lanceolata* 1.50 1.50
1291 A211 $3 *Tonopsis utricularioides* 2.25 2.25
1292 A211 $5 *Epidendrum nocturnum* 3.75 3.75
Nos. 1285-1292 (8) 9.58 9.58

Souvenir Sheets

1293 A211 $6 *Octomeria graminifolia* 4.50 4.50
1294 A211 $6 *Rodriguezia lanceolata* 4.50 4.50

EXPO '90, Osaka.

Fish A212

1990, May 21 *Perf.* **14**

1295 A212 10c Flamefish 15 15
1296 A212 15c Coney 15 15
1297 A212 50c Squirrelfish 38 38
1298 A212 60c Sergeant major 45 45
1299 A212 $1 Yellowtail snapper 75 75
1300 A212 $2 Rock beauty 1.50 1.50
1301 A212 $3 Spanish hogfish 2.25 2.25
1302 A212 $4 Striped parrotfish 3.00 3.00
Nos. 1295-1302 (8) 8.63 8.63

Souvenir sheets

1303 A212 $5 Blackbar soldierfish 3.75 3.75
1304 A212 $5 Foureye butterflyfish 3.75 3.75

Victoria and Elizabeth II — A213

1990, May 3 Litho. *Perf. 15x14*

1305 A213 45c green 35 35
1306 A213 60c bright rose 45 45
1307 A213 $5 bright ultra 3.75 3.75

Souvenir Sheet

1308 A213 $6 black 4.50 4.50

Penny Black, 150th anniv.

Royal Mail Transport A214

Designs: 50c, Steam packet *Britannia,* 1840. 75c, Railway mail car, 1892. $4, *Centaurus* seaplane, 1938. $6, Subway, 1927.

1990, May 3 *Perf. 13½*

1309 A214 50c red & deep green 38 38
1310 A214 75c red & vio brn 58 58
1311 A214 $4 red & brt ultra 3.00 3.00

Souvenir Sheet

1312 A214 $6 red & black 4.50 4.50

Stamp World London '90.

Miniature Sheet

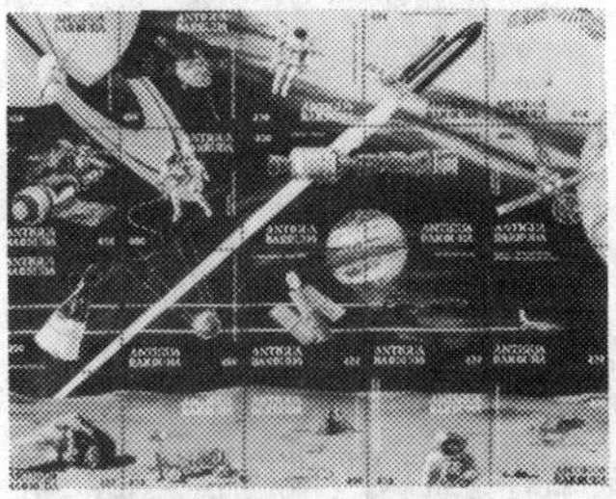

Space Achievements — A215

Designs: a, *Voyager 2* passing Saturn. b, *Pioneer 11* photographing Saturn. c, Manned maneuvering unit. d, *Columbia* space shuttle. e, Splashdown of Apollo 10 command module. f, *Skylab.* g, Ed White space walking, Gemini 4 mission. h, Apollo module, Apollo-Soyuz mission. i, Soyuz module, Apollo-Soyuz mission. j, *Mariner 1* passing Venus. k, Gemini 4 module. l, *Sputnik.* m, Hubble Space Telescope. n, X-15 rocket plane. o, Bell X-1 breaking sound barrier. p, Astronaut, Apollo 17 mission. q, American lunar rover. r, Lunar module, Apollo 14 mission. s, First men on the Moon, Apollo 11 mission. t, Lunokhod, Soviet lunar rover.

1990, June 11 Litho. *Perf. 14*

1313 A215 Sheet of 20 6.75 6.75
a.-t. 45c any single 32 32

Mickey Production Studios — A216

Walt Disney characters in Hollywood: 45c, Minnie Mouse reading script. 50c, Director Mickey Mouse, take 1 of Minnie. 60c, Make-up artist Daisy Duck. $1, Clarabelle as Cleopatra. $2, Mickey, Goofy, Donald Duck. $3, Goofy destroying set. $4, Mickey, Donald editing film. No. 1322, Mickey directs surfing film. No. 1323, Minnie, Daisy, Clarabelle in musical.

1990, Sept. 3 Litho. *Perf. 14x13½*

1314 A216 25c shown 18 18
1315 A216 45c multicolored 34 34
1316 A216 50c multicolored 38 38
1317 A216 60c multicolored 45 45
1318 A216 $1 multicolored 75 75
1319 A216 $2 multicolored 1.50 1.50
1320 A216 $3 multicolored 2.25 2.25
1321 A216 $4 multicolored 3.00 3.00
Nos. 1314-1321 (8) 8.85 8.85

Souvenir Sheets

1322 A216 $5 multicolored 3.75 3.75
1323 A216 $5 multicolored 3.75 3.75

A217

A218

1990, Aug. 27 Litho. *Perf. 14*

1324 A217 15c multicolored 15 15
1325 A217 35c multi, diff. 28 28
1326 A217 75c multi, diff. 58 58
1327 A217 $3 multi, diff. 2.25 2.25

Souvenir Sheet

1328 A217 $6 multi, diff. 4.50 4.50

Queen Mother, 90th birthday.

1990, Oct. 1 Litho. *Perf. 14*

1329 A218 50c 20-Kilometer Walk 38 38
1330 A218 75c Triple jump 55 55
1331 A218 $1 10,000 meter run 75 75
1332 A218 $5 Javelin 3.75 3.75

Souvenir Sheet

1333 A218 $6 Opening ceremony, Los Angeles, 1984 4.50 4.50

1992 Summer Olympics, Barcelona.

Intl. Literacy Year A219

Walt Disney characters in scenes from books by Charles Dickens: 15c, Huey and Dewey, Christmas Stories. 45c, Donald Duck, Bleak House. 50c, Dewey, Bad Pete, Oliver Twist. 60c, Daisy Duck, Old Curiosity Shop. $1, Little Nell. $2, Scrooge McDuck, Pickwick Papers. $3, Mickey and Minnie Mouse, Dombey and Son. $5, Minnie, Our Mutual Friend. No. 1342, Mickey and friends, David Copperfield. No. 1343, Pinocchio, Oliver Twist.

1990, Oct. 15 Litho. *Perf. 14*

1334 A219 15c multicolored 15 15
1335 A219 45c multicolored 35 35
1336 A219 50c multicolored 38 38
1337 A219 60c multicolored 45 45
1338 A219 $1 multicolored 75 75
1339 A219 $2 multicolored 1.50 1.50
1340 A219 $3 multicolored 2.25 2.25
1341 A219 $5 multicolored 3.75 3.75
Nos. 1334-1341 (8) 9.58 9.58

Souvenir Sheets

1342 A219 $6 multicolored 4.50 4.50
1343 A219 $6 multicolored 4.50 4.50

Nos. 1217-1222 Overprinted

Winners
West Germany 1
Argentina 0

1990, Nov. 11

1344 A201 15c multicolored 15 15
1345 A201 25c multicolored 18 18
1346 A201 $1 multicolored 75 75
1347 A201 $4 multicolored 3.00 3.00

Souvenir Sheets

1348 A201 $5 on #1221 3.75 3.75
1349 A201 $5 on #1222 3.75 3.75

Overprint on Nos. 1348-1349 is 32x13mm.

Birds — A220

1990, Nov. 19

1350 A220 10c Pearly-eyed thrasher 15 15
1351 A220 25c Purple-throated carib 18 18
1352 A220 50c Common yellow-throat 38 38
1353 A220 60c American kestrel 45 45
1354 A220 $1 Yellow-bellied sapsucker 75 75
1355 A220 $2 Purple gallinule 1.50 1.50
1356 A220 $3 Yellow-crowned night heron 2.25 2.25
1357 A220 $4 Blue-hooded euphonia 3.00 3.00
Nos. 1350-1357 (8) 8.66 8.66

Souvenir Sheets

1358 A220 $6 Brown pelican 4.50 4.50
1359 A220 $6 Frigate bird 4.50 4.50

Christmas — A221

Paintings: 25c, Madonna and Child with Saints by del Piombo. 30c, Virgin and Child with Angels by Grunewald, vert. 40c, Holy Family and a Shepherd by Titian. 60c, Virgin and Child by Fra Filippo Lippi, vert. $1, Jesus, St. John and Two Angels by Rubens. $2, Adoration of the Shepherds by Catena. $4, Adoration of the Magi by Giorgione. $5, Virgin and Child Adored by a Warrior by Catena. No. 1368, Allegory of the Blessings of Jacob by Rubens, vert. No. 1369, Adoration of the Magi by Fra Angelico, vert.

Perf. 14x13½, 13½x14

1990, Dec. 10 Litho.

1360 A221 25c multicolored 18 18
1361 A221 30c multicolored 22 22
1362 A221 40c multicolored 30 30
1363 A221 60c multicolored 45 45
1364 A221 $1 multicolored 75 75
1365 A221 $2 multicolored 1.50 1.50
1366 A221 $4 multicolored 3.00 3.00
1367 A221 $5 multicolored 3.75 3.75
Nos. 1360-1367 (8) 10.15 10.15

Souvenir Sheets

1368 A221 $6 multicolored 4.50 4.50
1369 A221 $6 multicolored 4.50 4.50

Peter Paul Rubens (1577-1640), Painter — A222

Entire paintings or different details from: 25c, Rape of the Daughters of Leucippus. 45c, $2, $4, Bacchanal. 50c, $1, $3, Rape of the Sabine Women. 60c, Battle of the Amazons. No. 1378, Rape of Hippodameia. No. 1379, Battle of the Amazons.

1991, Jan. 21 Litho. *Perf. 14*

1370 A222 25c multicolored 18 18
1371 A222 45c multicolored 35 35
1372 A222 50c multicolored 38 38
1373 A222 60c multicolored 45 45
1374 A222 $1 multicolored 75 75
1375 A222 $2 multicolored 1.50 1.50
1376 A222 $3 multicolored 2.25 2.25
1377 A222 $4 multicolored 3.00 3.00
Nos. 1370-1377 (8) 8.86 8.86

Souvenir Sheets

1378 A222 $6 multicolored 4.50 4.50
1379 A222 $6 multicolored 4.50 4.50

World War II Milestones A223

Designs: 10c, US troops enter Germany, Sept. 11, 1944. 15c, All axis forces surrender in North Africa, May 12, 1943. 25c, US troops invade Kwajalein, Jan. 31, 1944. 45c, Roosevelt and Churchill meet in Casablanca, Jan. 14, 1943. 50c, Marshal Badoglio signs agreement with allies, Sept. 1, 1943. $1, Mountbatten appointed Supreme Allied Commander, Southeast Asia Command, Aug. 25, 1943. $2, Major Greek tactical victory, Koritza, Nov. 22, 1940. $4, Britain and USSR sign mutual assistance pact, July 12, 1941. $5, Operation Torch, Nov. 8, 1942. No. 1389, Japanese attack on Pearl Harbor, Dec. 7, 1941. No. 1390, American bombing attack on Schweinfurt, Oct. 14, 1943.

1991, Mar. 11 Litho. *Perf. 14*

1380 A223 10c multicolored 15 15
1381 A223 15c multicolored 15 15
1382 A223 25c multicolored 18 18
1383 A223 45c multicolored 35 35
1384 A223 50c multicolored 38 38
1385 A223 $1 multicolored 75 75
1386 A223 $2 multicolored 1.50 1.50
1387 A223 $4 multicolored 3.00 3.00
1388 A223 $5 multicolored 3.75 3.75
Nos. 1380-1388 (9) 10.21 10.21

Souvenir Sheets

1389 A223 $6 multicolored 4.50 4.50
1390 A223 $6 multicolored 4.50 4.50

Cog Railways of the World A224

Designs: 25c, Prince Regent, Middleton Colliery, 1812. 30c, Snowdon Mountain Railway, Wales. 40c, 1st Railcar at Hell Gate, Manitou and Pike's Peak Railway. 60c, PNKA Rack Railway, Amberawa, Java. $1, Green Mountain Railway, Mt. Desert Island, Maine, 1883. $2, Cog locomotive, Pike's Peak, 1891. $4, Vitznau-Rigi Cog Railway, Lake Lucerne. $5, Leopoldina Railway, Brazil. No. 1399, Electric Cog Donkey Engines, Panama Canal. No. 1400, Gornergratbahn, 1st electric cog railway in Switzerland, vert.

1991, Mar. 18 Litho. *Perf. 14*

1391 A224 25c multicolored 18 18
1392 A224 30c multicolored 22 22
1393 A224 40c multicolored 30 30
1394 A224 60c multicolored 45 45
1395 A224 $1 multicolored 75 75
1396 A224 $2 multicolored 1.50 1.50
1397 A224 $4 multicolored 3.00 3.00
1398 A224 $5 multicolored 3.75 3.75
Nos. 1391-1398 (8) 10.15 10.15

Souvenir Sheets

1399 A224 $6 multicolored 4.50 4.50
1400 A224 $6 multicolored 4.50 4.50

Butterflies A225

1991, Apr. 15 Litho. *Perf. 14*

1401 A225 10c Zebra 15 15
1402 A225 35c Southern daggertail 26 26
1403 A225 50c Red anartia 38 38
1404 A225 75c Malachite 55 55
1405 A225 $1 Polydamas swallowtail 75 75
1406 A225 $2 Orion 1.50 1.50
1407 A225 $4 Mimic 3.00 3.00
1408 A225 $5 Cracker 3.75 3.75
Nos. 1401-1408 (8) 10.34 10.34

Souvenir Sheets
Caterpillars

1409	A225	$6	Monarch, vert.	4.50	4.50
1410	A225	$6	Painted lady, vert.	4.50	4.50

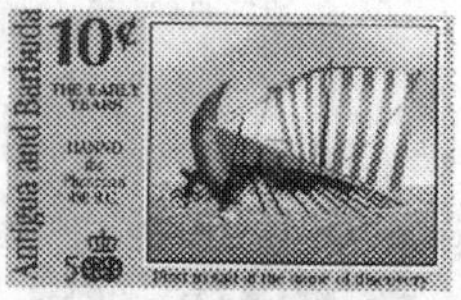

Voyages of Discovery A226

Designs: 10c, Hanno, Phoenicia, c. 450 B.C. 15c, Pytheas, Greece, 325 B.C. 45c, Eric the Red, Viking, A.D. 985. 60c, Leif Erikson, Viking, A.D. 1000. $1, Scylax, Greece, A.D. 518. $2, Marco Polo, A.D. 1259. $4, Queen Hatsheput, Egypt, 1493 B.C. $5, St. Brendan, Ireland, 500 A.D. No. 1419, Columbus, bareheaded. No. 1420, Columbus, wearing hat.

1991, Apr. 22

1411	A226	10c	multicolored	15	15
1412	A226	15c	multicolored	15	15
1413	A226	45c	multicolored	35	35
1414	A226	60c	multicolored	45	45
1415	A226	$1	multicolored	75	75
1416	A226	$2	multicolored	1.50	1.50
1417	A226	$4	multicolored	3.00	3.00
1418	A226	$5	multicolored	3.75	3.75
			Nos. 1411-1418 (8)	10.10	10.10

Souvenir Sheets

1419	A226	$6	multicolored	4.50	4.50
1420	A226	$6	multicolored	4.50	4.50

Discovery of America, 500th anniv. (in 1992).

Paintings by Vincent Van Gogh — A227

Designs: 5c, Portrait of Camille Roulin. 10c, Portrait of Armand Roulin. 15c, Young Peasant Woman with Straw Hat Sitting in the Wheat. 25c, Portrait of Adeline Ravoux. 30c, The Schoolboy (Camille Roulin). 40c, Portrait of Doctor Gachet. 50c, Portrait of a Man. 75c, Two Children. $2, Portrait of Postman Joseph Roulin. $3, The Seated Zouave. $4, L'arlesienne: Madame Ginoux with Books. No. 1432, Self Portrait, November/December 1888. No. 1433, Flowering Garden. No. 1434, Farmhouse in Provence. $6, The Bridge at Trinquetaille.

1991, May 13 *Perf. 13½*

1421	A227	5c	multicolored	15	15
1422	A227	10c	multicolored	15	15
1423	A227	15c	multicolored	15	15
1424	A227	25c	multicolored	18	18
1425	A227	30c	multicolored	22	22
1426	A227	40c	multicolored	30	30
1427	A227	50c	multicolored	38	38
1428	A227	75c	multicolored	55	55
1429	A227	$2	multicolored	1.50	1.50
1430	A227	$3	multicolored	2.25	2.25
1431	A227	$4	multicolored	3.00	3.00
1432	A227	$5	multicolored	3.75	3.75
			Nos. 1421-1432 (12)	12.58	12.58

Size: 102x76mm
Imperf

1433	A227	$5	multicolored	3.75	3.75
1434	A227	$5	multicolored	3.75	3.75
1435	A227	$6	multicolored	4.50	4.50

Phila Nippon '91 — A228

Walt Disney characters demonstrating Japanese martial arts: 10c, Mickey as champion sumo wrestler, vert. 15c, Goofy using tonfa. 45c, Ninja Donald in full field dress. 60c, Mickey using weapon in kung fu, vert. $1, Goofy tries kendo, vert. $2, Mickey, Donald demonstrating special technique of aikido. $4, Mickey flips Donald with judo throw. $5, Mickey demonstrates yabusame (target shooting from running horse), vert. No. 1444, Mickey using karate. No. 1445, Mickey demonstrating tamashiwara (powerbreaking), vert.

Perf. 13½x14, 14x13½

1991, June 29 **Litho.**

1436	A220	10c	multicolored	15	15
1437	A228	15c	multicolored	15	15
1438	A228	45c	multicolored	35	35
1439	A220	60c	multicolored	45	45
1440	A228	$1	multicolored	75	75
1441	A220	$2	multicolored	1.50	1.50
1442	A220	$4	multicolored	3.00	3.00
1443	A228	$5	multicolored	3.75	3.75
			Nos. 1436-1443 (8)	10.10	10.10

Souvenir Sheets

1444	A228	$6	multicolored	4.50	4.50
1445	A228	$6	multicolored	4.50	4.50

Royal Family Birthday, Anniversary
Common Design Type

1991, July 8 **Litho.** *Perf. 14*

1446	CD347	10c	multicolored	15	15
1447	CD347	15c	multicolored	15	15
1448	CD347	20c	multicolored	15	15
1449	CD347	40c	multicolored	30	30
1450	CD347	$1	multicolored	75	75
1451	CD347	$2	multicolored	1.50	1.50
1452	CD347	$4	multicolored	3.00	3.00
1453	CD347	$5	multicolored	3.75	3.75
			Nos. 1446-1453 (8)	9.75	9.75

Souvenir Sheets

1454	CD347	$4	Elizabeth, Philip	3.00	3.00
1455	CD347	$4	Charles, Diana, sons	3.00	3.00

10c, 40c, $1, $5, No. 1455, Charles and Diana, 10th wedding anniversary. Others, Queen Elizabeth II, 65th birthday.

Walt Disney Characters Playing Golf A229

Designs: 10c, Daisy Duck teeing off. 15c, Goofy using 3-Wood. 45c, Mickey using 3-Iron. 60c, Mickey missing ball using 6-Iron. $1, Donald trying 8-Iron to get out of pond. $2, Minnie using 9-Iron. $4, Donald digging hole with sand wedge. $5, Goofy trying new approach with putter. No. 1464, Grandma Duck using pitching wedge. No. 1465, Mickey cheering Minnie as she uses her 5-Wood, horiz.

Perf. 13½x14, 14x13½

1991, Aug. 7 **Litho.**

1456	A229	10c	multicolored	15	15
1457	A229	15c	multicolored	15	15
1458	A229	45c	multicolored	35	35
1459	A229	60c	multicolored	45	45
1460	A229	$1	multicolored	75	75
1461	A229	$2	multicolored	1.50	1.50
1462	A229	$4	multicolored	3.00	3.00
1463	A229	$5	multicolored	3.75	3.75
			Nos. 1456-1463 (8)	10.10	10.10

Souvenir Sheets

1464	A229	$6	multicolored	4.50	4.50
1465	A229	$6	multicolored	4.50	4.50

1992 Summer Olympics, Barcelona A230

Archie Comics, 50th anniv.: 10c, Moose receiving gold medal. 25c, Archie, Veronica, Mr. Lodge, polo match, horiz. 40c, Archie & Betty, fencing. 60c, Archie, women's volleyball. $1, Archie, tennis. $2, Archie, marathon race. $4, Archie, judging women's gymnastics, horiz. $5, Archie, Betty, Veronica, basketball. No. 1474, Archie, soccer. No. 1475, Archie, Betty, baseball, horiz.

Perf. 13½x14, 14x13½

1991, Aug. 19

1466	A230	10c	multicolored	15	15
1467	A230	25c	multicolored	18	18
1468	A230	40c	multicolored	30	30
1469	A230	60c	multicolored	45	45
1470	A230	$1	multicolored	75	75
1471	A230	$2	multicolored	1.50	1.50
1472	A230	$4	multicolored	3.00	3.00
1473	A230	$5	multicolored	3.75	3.75
			Nos. 1466-1473 (8)	10.08	10.08

Souvenir Sheets

1474	A230	$6	multicolored	4.50	4.50
1475	A230	$6	multicolored	4.50	4.50

Charles de Gaulle, Birth Cent. A231

Charles de Gaulle: 10c, and Pres. Kennedy, families, 1961. 15c, and Pres. Roosevelt, 1945, vert. 45c, and Chancellor Adenauer, 1962, vert. 60c, Liberation of Paris, 1944, vert. $1, Crossing the Rhine, 1945. $2, In Algiers, 1944. $4, and Pres. Eisenhower, 1960. $5, Returning from Germany, 1968, vert. No. 1484, and Churchill at Casablanca, 1943. No. 1485, and Citizens.

1991, Sept. 11 **Litho.** *Perf. 14*

1476	A231	10c	multicolored	15	15
1477	A231	15c	multicolored	15	15
1478	A231	45c	multicolored	35	35
1479	A231	60c	multicolored	45	45
1480	A231	$1	multicolored	75	75
1481	A231	$2	multicolored	1.50	1.50
1482	A231	$4	multicolored	3.00	3.00
1483	A231	$5	multicolored	3.75	3.75
			Nos. 1476-1483 (8)	10.10	10.10

Souvenir Sheets

1484	A231	$6	multicolored	4.50	4.50
1485	A231	$6	multicolored	4.50	4.50

Independence, 10th Anniv. — A232

Designs: 10c, Island maps, government building. $6, Old P. O., St. Johns, #1 & #635.

1991, Oct. 28

1486	A232	10c	multicolored	15	15

Souvenir Sheet

1487	A232	$6	multicolored	4.50	4.50

No. 1487 contains one 50x38mm stamp.

Miniature Sheet

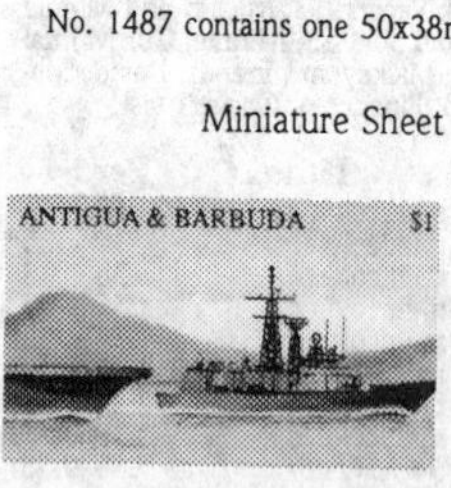

Attack on Pearl Harbor, 50th Anniv. A233

Designs: No. 1488a, Bow of Nimitz class carrier, Ticonderoga class cruiser. b, Tourist boat to Arizona Memorial. c, USS Arizona Memorial. d, Aircraft salute to missing men. e, White tern. f, Japanese Kate torpedo bombers. g, Japanese Zero fighters. h, Battleship row in flames. i, USS Nevada breaking out. j, Zeros returning to carriers.

1991, Dec. 9 *Perf. 14½x15*

1488	A233	$1	Sheet of 10, #a.-j.	7.50	7.50

Inscription for No. 1488f incorrectly describes torpedo bombers as Zekes.

3rd Antigua Methodist Cub Scout Pack, 60th Anniv. A234

Designs: $2, Lord Robert Baden-Powell, scouts, vert. $3.50, Scouts around campfire. $5, Antigua & Barbuda flag, Jamboree emblem, vert.

1991, Dec. 9 *Perf. 14*

1489	A234	75c	multicolored	58	58
1490	A234	$2	multicolored	1.50	1.50
1491	A234	$3.50	multicolored	2.65	2.65

Souvenir Sheet

1492	A234	$5	multicolored	3.75	3.75

17th World Scout Jamboree, Korea.

Wolfgang Amadeus Mozart, Death Bicent. A235

Portrait of Mozart and: $1.50, Scene from opera, Don Giovanni. $4, St. Peter's Cathedral, Salzburg.

1991, Dec. 9

1493	A235	$1.50	multicolored	1.15	1.15
1494	A235	$4	multicolored	3.00	3.00

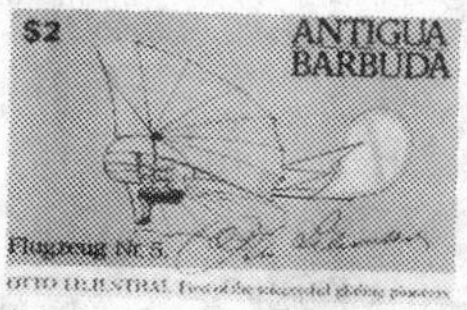

Anniversaries and Events — A236

Designs: $2, Otto Lilienthal's glider No. 5. $2.50, Locomotive cab, vert.

1991, Dec. 9 **Litho.** *Perf. 14*

1495	A236	$2	multicolored	1.50	1.50
1496	A236	$2.50	multicolored	1.90	1.90

First glider flight, cent. (No. 1495). Trans-Siberian Railway, cent. (No. 1496). Numbers have been reserved for additional values in this set.

Brandenburg Gate, Bicent. — A237

Designs: 25c, Demonstrators in autos, German flag. $2, Statue. $3, Portions of decorative frieze.

1991, Dec. 9 **Litho.** *Perf. 14*

1499	A237	25c	multicolored	18	18
1500	A237	$2	multicolored	1.50	1.50
1501	A237	$3	multicolored	2.25	2.25

Souvenir Sheet

1502	A237	$4	multicolored	3.00	3.00

Christmas A238

Paintings by Fra Angelico: 10c, The Annunciation. 30c, Nativity. 40c, Adoration of the Magi. 60c, Presentation in the Temple. $1, Circumcision. $3, Flight into Egypt. $4, Massacre of the Innocents. $5, Christ Teaching in the Temple. No. 1511, Adoration of the Magi, diff. No. 1512, Adoration of the Magi (Cook Tondo).

1991, Dec. 12 *Perf. 12*

1503	A238	10c multicolored	15	15
1504	A238	30c multicolored	22	22
1505	A238	40c multicolored	30	30
1506	A238	60c multicolored	45	45
1507	A238	$1 multicolored	75	75
1508	A238	$3 multicolored	2.25	2.25
1509	A238	$4 multicolored	3.00	3.00
1510	A238	$5 multicolored	3.75	3.75
		Nos. 1503-1510 (8)	10.87	10.87

Souvenir Sheets

1511	A238	$6 multicolored	4.50	4.50
1512	A238	$6 multicolored	4.50	4.50

Queen Elizabeth II's Accession to the Throne, 40th Anniv.

Common Design Type

Queen Elizabeth II and various island scenes.

1992, Feb. 6 **Litho.** *Perf. 14*

1513	CD348	10c multicolored	15	15
1514	CD348	30c multicolored	22	22
1515	CD348	$1 multicolored	75	75
1516	CD348	$5 multicolored	3.75	3.75

Souvenir Sheets

1517	CD348	$6 Beach	4.50	4.50
1518	CD348	$6 Flora	4.50	4.50

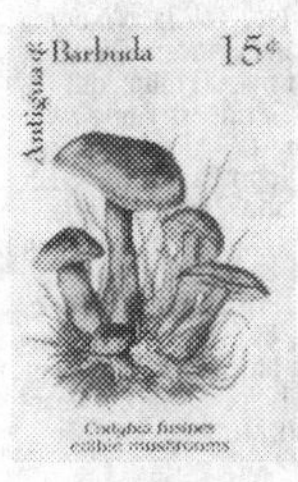

Mushrooms — A239

1992, Mar. **Litho.** *Perf. 14*

1519	A239	10c Amanita caesarea	15	15
1520	A239	15c Collybia fusipes	15	15
1521	A239	30c Boletus aereus	22	22
1522	A239	40c Laccaria amethystina	30	30
1523	A239	$1 Russula virescens	75	75
1524	A239	$2 Tricholoma auratum	1.50	1.50
1525	A239	$4 Calocybe gambosa	3.00	3.00
1526	A239	$5 Panus tigrinus	3.75	3.75
		Nos. 1519-1526 (8)	9.82	9.82

Souvenir Sheet

1527	A239	$6 Auricularia auricula	4.50	4.50
1528	A239	$6 Clavariadelphus truncatus	4.50	4.50

Issue dates: 10c, 30c, $1, $5, No. 1528, May 18. Others, Mar.

Disney Characters at Summer Olympics, Barcelona A240

Designs: 10c, Mickey presenting gold medal to mermaid for swimming. 15c, Dewey and Huey watching Louie in kayak. 30c, Uncle McScrooge, Donald yachting. 50c, Donald, horse trying water polo. $1, Big Pete weight lifting. $2, Donald, Goofy fencing. $4, Mickey, Donald playing volleyball. $5, Goofy vaulting over horse. No. 1537, Mickey playing basketball, horiz. No. 1538, Minnie Mouse on uneven parallel bars, horiz. No. 1539, Mickey, Goofy, and Donald judging Minnie's floor exercise, horiz. No. 1540, Mickey running after soccer ball.

1992, Mar. 16 *Perf. 13*

1529	A240	10c multicolored	15	15
1530	A240	15c multicolored	15	15
1531	A240	30c multicolored	22	22
1532	A240	50c multicolored	38	38
1533	A240	$1 multicolored	75	75
1534	A240	$2 multicolored	1.50	1.50
1535	A240	$4 multicolored	3.00	3.00
1536	A240	$5 multicolored	3.75	3.75
		Nos. 1529-1536 (8)	9.90	9.90

Souvenir Sheets

1537	A240	$6 multicolored	4.50	4.50
1538	A240	$6 multicolored	4.50	4.50
1539	A240	$6 multicolored	4.50	4.50
1540	A240	$6 multicolored	4.50	4.50

Dinosaurs A241

1992, Apr. 6 *Perf. 14*

1541	A241	10c Pteranodon	15	15
1542	A241	15c Brachiosaurus	15	15
1543	A241	30c Tyrannosaurus rex	22	22
1544	A241	50c Parasaurolophus	38	38
1545	A241	$1 Deinonychus	75	75
1546	A241	$2 Triceratops	1.50	1.50
1547	A241	$4 Protoceratops	3.00	3.00
1548	A241	$5 Stegosaurus	3.75	3.75
		Nos. 1541-1548 (8)	9.90	9.90

Souvenir Sheets

1549	A241	$6 Apatosaurus	4.50	4.50
1550	A241	$6 Allosaurus	4.50	4.50

Nos. 1541-1544 are vert.

Easter A242

Paintings: 10c, Supper at Emmaus, by Caravaggio. 15c, The Vision of St. Peter, by Francisco de Zurbaran. 30c, $1, Christ Driving the Money Changers from the Temple, by Tiepolo (detail on $1). 40c, Martyrdom of St. Bartholomew (detail), by Jusepe de Ribera. $2, Crucifixion (detail), by Albrecht Altdorfer. $4, $5, The Deposition (diff. detail), by Fra Angelico. No. 1559, Crucifixion, by Albrecht Altdorfer, vert. No. 1560, The Last Supper, by Vicente Juan Masip.

1992 *Perf. 14x13½*

1551	A242	10c multicolored	15	15
1552	A242	15c multicolored	15	15
1553	A242	30c multicolored	22	22
1554	A242	40c multicolored	30	30
1555	A242	$1 multicolored	75	75
1556	A242	$2 multicolored	1.50	1.50
1557	A242	$4 multicolored	3.00	3.00
1558	A242	$5 multicolored	3.75	3.75
		Nos. 1551-1558 (8)	9.82	9.82

Souvenir Sheet

Perf. 13½x14

1559	A242	$6 multicolored	4.50	4.50
1560	A242	$6 multicolored	4.50	4.50

Spanish Art — A243

Designs: 10c, The Miracle at the Well, by Alonso Cano. 15c, The Poet Luis de Gongora y Argote, by Velazquez. 30c, The Painter Francisco Goya, by Vincente Lopez Portana. 40c, Maria de Las Nieves Michaela Fourdiniere, by Luis Paret y Alcazar. $1, Charles III Eating before His Court, by Paret y Alcazar, horiz. $2, A Rain Shower in Granada, by Antonio Munoz Degrain, horiz. $4, Sarah Bernhardt, by Santiago Rusinol y Prats. $5, The Hermitage Garden, by Joaquin Mir Trinxet. No. 1569, Olympus: Battle with the Giants, by Francisco Bayeu y Subias. No. 1570, The Ascent of Monsieur Boucle's Montgolfier Balloon in the Gardens of Aranjuez, by Antonio Carnicero.

1992, May 11

1561	A243	10c multicolored	15	15
1562	A243	15c multicolored	15	15
1563	A243	30c multicolored	22	22
1564	A243	40c multicolored	30	30
1565	A243	$1 multicolored	75	75
1566	A243	$2 multicolored	1.50	1.50
1567	A243	$4 multicolored	3.00	3.00
1568	A243	$5 multicolored	3.75	3.75

Size: 120x95mm

Imperf

1569	A243	$6 multicolored	4.50	4.50
1570	A243	$6 multicolored	4.50	4.50
		Nos. 1561-1570 (10)	18.82	18.82

Granada '92.

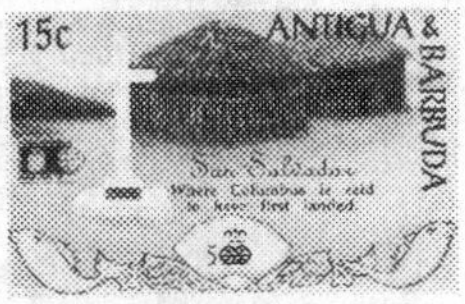

Discovery of America, 500th Anniv. — A244

Designs: 15c, San Salvador Island. 30c, Martin Alonzo Pinzon, captain of Pinta. 40c, Columbus, signature, coat of arms. $1, Pinta. $2, Nina. $4, Santa Maria. No. 1577, Sea monster. No. 1578, Map, sailing ship.

1992, May 25 **Litho.** *Perf. 14*

1571	A244	15c multicolored	15	15
1572	A244	30c multicolored	22	22
1573	A244	40c multicolored	30	30
1574	A244	$1 multicolored	75	75
1575	A244	$2 multicolored	1.50	1.50
1576	A244	$4 multicolored	3.00	3.00
		Nos. 1571-1576 (6)	5.92	5.92

Souvenir Sheets

1577	A244	$6 multicolored	4.50	4.50
1578	A244	$6 multicolored	4.50	4.50

World Columbian Stamp Expo '92, Chicago.

Hummel Figurines — A245

Wanderers: 15c, No. 1587a, Boy sitting on rock pointing to flower in cap. 30c, No. 1587b, Girl sitting on fence. 40c, No. 1587c, Boy holding binoculars. 50c, No. 1587d, Boy carrying umbrella. $1, No. 1588a, Two boys looking up at direction marker. $2, No. 1588b, Boy carrying basket on back, walking with stick. $4, No. 1588c, Two girls, goat. $5, No. 1588d, Boy carrying walking stick.

1993, Jan. 6 **Litho.** *Perf. 14*

1579	A245	15c multicolored	15	15
1580	A245	30c multicolored	22	22
1581	A245	40c multicolored	30	30
1582	A245	50c multicolored	38	38
1583	A245	$1 multicolored	75	75
1584	A245	$2 multicolored	1.50	1.50
1585	A245	$4 multicolored	3.00	3.00
1586	A245	$5 multicolored	3.75	3.75
		Nos. 1579-1586 (8)	10.05	10.05

Souvenir Sheet

1587	A245	$1.50 Sheet of 4, #a.-d.	4.50	4.50
1588	A245	$1.50 Sheet of 4, #a.-d.	4.50	4.50

Hummingbirds and Flowers — A246

Designs: 10c, Antillean crested, wild plantain. 25c, Green mango, parrot's plantain. 45c, Purple-throated carib, lobster claws. 60c, Antillean mango, coral plant. $1, Vervain, cardinal's guard. $2, Rufous breasted hermit, heliconia. $4, Blue-headed, red ginger. $5, Green-throated carib, ornamental banana. No. 1597, Bee, jungle flame. No. 1598, Western streamertails, bignonia.

1992, Aug. 10 **Litho.** *Perf. 14*

1589	A246	10c multicolored	15	15
1590	A246	25c multicolored	18	18
1591	A246	45c multicolored	35	35
1592	A246	60c multicolored	45	45
1593	A246	$1 multicolored	75	75
1594	A246	$2 multicolored	1.50	1.50
1595	A246	$4 multicolored	3.00	3.00
1596	A246	$5 multicolored	3.75	3.75
		Nos. 1589-1596 (8)	10.13	10.13

Souvenir Sheets

1597	A246	$6 multicolored	6.75	6.75
1598	A246	$6 multicolored	6.75	6.75

Genoa '92.

Discovery of America, 500th Anniv. — A247

1992 **Litho.** *Perf. 14½*

1599	A247	$1 Coming ashore	75	75
1600	A247	$2 Natives, ships	1.50	1.50

Organization of East Caribbean States.

Souvenir Sheet

Madison Square Garden, NYC — A248

1992 **Litho.** *Perf. 14*

1601	A248	$6 multicolored	5.00	5.00

Postage Stamp Mega-Event, Jacob Javits Center, New York City.

Elvis Presley (1935-1977) A249

Various pictures of Elvis Presley.

1992 *Perf. 13½x14*

1602	A249	$1 Sheet of 9, #a.-i.	7.00	7.00

Inventors and Pioneers A250

Designs: 10c, Ts'ai Lun, paper. 25c, Igor I. Sikorsky, 4-engine airplane. 30c, Alexander Graham Bell, telephone. 40c, Johannes Gutenberg, printing press. 60c, James Watt, steam engine. $1, Anton van Leeuwenhoek, microscope. $4, Louis Braille, Braille printing. $5, Galileo, telescope. No. 1607, Phonograph. No. 1608, Steamboat.

1992, Oct. 19 Litho. *Perf. 14*

1603	A250	10c	multicolored	15	15
1604	A250	25c	multicolored	18	18
1605	A250	30c	multicolored	22	22
1605A	A250	40c	multicolored	40	40
1605B	A250	60c	multicolored	45	45
1605C	A250	$1	multicolored	75	75
1605D	A250	$4	multicolored	3.00	3.00
1606	A250	$5	multicolored	3.75	3.75
	Nos. 1603-1606 (8)			8.90	8.90

Souvenir Sheet

1607	A250	$6	multicolored	4.50	4.50
1608	A250	$6	multicolored	4.50	4.50

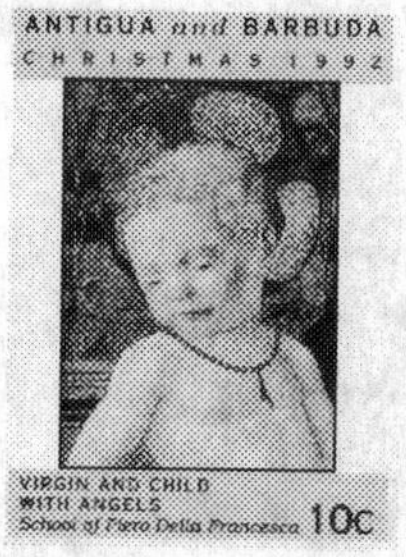

Christmas A251

Details from Paintings: 10c, Virgin and Child with Angels, by School of Piero Della Francesca. 25c, Madonna Degli Alberelli, by Giovanni Bellini. 30c, Madonna and Child with St. Anthony Abbot and St. Sigismund, by Neroccio di Landi. 40c, Madonna and the Grand Duke, by Raphael. 60c, The Nativity, by George de la Tour. $1, Holy Family, by Jacob Jordaens. $4, Madonna and Child Enthroned, by Margaritone. $5, Madonna and Child on a Curved Throne, by Byzantine artist. No. 1617, Madonna and Child, by Domenico Ghirlandaio (both names misspelled). No. 1618, The Holy Family, by Pontormo.

1992 *Perf. 13½x14*

1609	A251	10c	multicolored	15	15
1610	A251	25c	multicolored	18	18
1611	A251	30c	multicolored	22	22
1612	A251	40c	multicolored	30	30
1613	A251	60c	multicolored	45	45
1614	A251	$1	multicolored	75	75
1615	A251	$4	multicolored	3.00	3.00
1616	A251	$5	multicolored	3.75	3.75

Souvenir Sheet

1617	A251	$6	multicolored	4.50	4.50
1618	A251	$6	multicolored	4.50	4.50

A252

A253

Anniversaries and Events: 10c, Cosomonauts. 40c, Graf Zeppelin, Goodyear blimp. 45c, Right Rev. Daniel C. Davis, St. John's Cathedral. 75c, Konrad Adenauer. $1, Bus Mosbacher, Weatherly. $1.50, Rain forest. No. 1625, Felis tigris. No. 1626, Flag, emblems, plant. No. 1627, Women acting on stage. $2.25, Women carrying baskets of food on their heads. $3, Lions Club emblem, club member. No. 1630, West German, NATO flags. No. 1631, China's Long March Booster Rocket. No. 1632, Dr. Hugo Eckener. No. 1633, The Hindenburg. No. 1634, Brandenburg Gate, German flag. No. 1635, Monarch butterfly. No. 1636, Hermes Shuttle, Columbus Space Station.

1992 Litho. *Perf. 14*

1619	A252	10c	multicolored	15	15
1620	A252	40c	multicolored	30	30
1621	A253	45c	multicolored	35	35
1622	A252	75c	multicolored	58	58
1623	A252	$1	multicolored	75	75
1624	A252	$1.50	multicolored	1.15	1.15
1625	A252	$2	multicolored	1.50	1.50
1626	A253	$2	multicolored	1.50	1.50
1627	A253	$2	multicolored	1.50	1.50
1628	A252	$2.25	multicolored	1.70	1.70
1629	A252	$3	multicolored	2.25	2.25
1630	A252	$4	multicolored	3.00	3.00
1631	A252	$4	multicolored	3.00	3.00
1632	A252	$6	multicolored	4.50	4.50
	Nos. 1619-1632 (14)			22.23	22.23

Souvenir Sheets

1633	A252	$6	multicolored	4.50	4.50
1634	A252	$6	multicolored	4.50	4.50
1635	A252	$6	multicolored	4.50	4.50
1636	A252	$6	multicolored	4.50	4.50

Intl. Space Year (#1619, 1631, 1636). Count Zeppelin, 75th anniv. of death (#1620, 1632-1633). Diocese of Northeast Caribbean and Aruba District, 150th anniv. (#1621). Konrad Adenauer, 25th anniv. of death (#1622, 1630, 1634). 1962 winner of America's Cup (#1623). Earth Summit, Rio (#1624-1625, 1635). Inter-American Institute for Cooperation on Agriculture, 50th anniv. (#1626). Cultural Development, 40th anniv. (#1627). WHO Intl. Conf. on Nutrition, Rome (#1628). Lions Club, 75th anniv. (#1629).

Issue dates: Nos. 1619, 1621-1623, 1626-1631, 1634, 1636, November. Nos. 1624-1625, 1635, Dec. 14.

Euro Disney, Paris — A254

Disney characters: 10c, Golf course. 25c, Davy Crockett Campground. 30c, Cheyenne Hotel. 40c, Santa Fe Hotel. $1, New York Hotel. $2, In car, map showing location. $4, Pirates of the Caribbean. $5, Adventureland. No. 1645, Mickey Mouse on map with star, vert. No. 1646, Roof turret at entrance, Mickey Mouse in uniform. No. 1646A, Mickey Mouse, colored spots on poster, vert. No. 1646B, Mickey on poster, vert., diff.

1992-93 Litho. *Perf. 14x13½*

1637	A254	10c	multicolored	15	15
1638	A254	25c	multicolored	18	15
1639	A254	30c	multicolored	22	22
1640	A254	40c	multicolored	30	30
1641	A254	$1	multicolored	75	75
1642	A254	$2	multicolored	1.50	1.50
1643	A254	$4	multicolored	3.00	3.00
1644	A254	$5	multicolored	3.75	3.75
	Nos. 1637-1644 (8)			9.85	9.82

Souvenir Sheet

Perf. 13½x14

1645	A254	$6	multicolored	4.50	4.50
1646	A254	$6	multicolored	4.50	4.50
1646A	A254	$6	multicolored	4.50	4.50
1646B	A254	$6	multicolored	4.50	4.50

Issue dates: Nos. 1638-1639, 1642-1643, 1646-1646B, Feb. 22, 1993. Others, Dec. 1992.

Miniature Sheets

Louvre Museum, Bicent. A255

Details or entire paintings, by Peter Paul Rubens: No. 1647a, Destiny of Marie de' Medici. b, Birth of Marie de'Medici. c, Marie's Education. d, Destiny of Marie de'Medici, diff. e, Henry IV Receives the Portrait. f, The Meeting at Lyons. g, The Marriage. h, The Birth of Louis XIII.

No. 1648a, The Capture of Juliers. b, The Exchange of Princesses. c, The Happiness of the Regency. d, The Majority of Louis XIII. e, The Flight from Blois. f, The Treaty of Angouleme. g, The Peace of Angers. h, The Queen's Reconciliation with Her Son.

$6, Helene Fourment Au Carosse.

1993, Mar. 22 Litho. *Perf. 12*

1647	A255	$1	Sheet of 8, #a.-h. + label	6.00	6.00
1648	A255	$1	Sheet of 8, #a.-h. + label	6.00	6.00

Souvenir Sheet

Perf. 14½

1649	A255	$6	multicolored	4.50	4.50

No. 1649 contains one 55x88mm stamp.

Flowers — A256

1993, Mar. 15 Litho. *Perf. 14*

1650	A256	15c	Cardinal's guard	15	15
1651	A256	25c	Giant granadilla	18	18
1652	A256	30c	Spider flower	22	22
1653	A256	40c	Gold vine	30	30
1654	A256	$1	Frangipani	75	75
1655	A256	$2	Bougainvillea	1.50	1.50
1656	A256	$4	Yellow oleander	3.00	3.00
1657	A256	$5	Spicy jatropha	3.75	3.75
	Nos. 1650-1657 (8)			9.85	9.85

Souvenir Sheets

1658	A256	$6	Bird lime tree	4.50	4.50
1659	A256	$6	Fairy lily	4.50	4.50

Endangered Species — A257

Designs: No. 1660a, St. Lucia parrot. b, Cahow. c, Swallow-tailed kite. d, Everglades kite. e, Imperial parrot. f, Humpback whale. g, Puerto Rican plain pigeon. h, St. Vincent parrot. i, Puerto Rican parrot. j, Leatherback turtle. k, American crocodile. l, Hawksbill turtle.

No. 1662, West Indian manatee.

1993, Apr. 5

1660	A257	$1	Sheet of 12, #a.-l.	9.00	9.00

Souvenir Sheets

1661	A257	$6	like #1660f	4.50	4.50
1662	A257	$6	multicolored	4.50	4.50

Philatelic Publishing Personalities — A258

Portrait, stamp: No. 1663, J. Walter Scott (1842-1919), US "#C3a," Antigua #1. No. 1664, Theodore Champion, France #8, Antigua #1. No. 1665, E. Stanley Gibbons (1856-1913), cover of his first price list and catalogue, Antigua #1. No. 1666, Hugo Michel (1866-1944), Bavaria #1, Antigua #1. No. 1667, Alberto (1877-1944) and Giulio (1902-1987) Bolaffi, Sardinia #1, Great Britain #3. No. 1668, Richard Borek (1874-1947), Brunswick #24, Bavaria #1.

Front pages, Mekeel's Weekly Stamp News: No. 1669a, Jan. 7, 1890. b, Feb. 12, 1993.

1993, June 14

1663	A258	$1.50	multicolored	1.10	1.10
1664	A258	$1.50	multicolored	1.10	1.10
1665	A258	$1.50	multicolored	1.10	1.10
1666	A258	$1.50	multicolored	1.10	1.10
1667	A258	$1.50	multicolored	1.10	1.10
1668	A258	$1.50	multicolored	1.10	1.10
	Nos. 1663-1668 (6)			6.60	6.60

Souvenir Sheet

1669	A258	$3	Sheet of 2, #a.-b.	4.50	4.50

Mekeel's Weekly Stamp News, cent. (in 1891; #1669).

Miniature Sheets

Coronation of Queen Elizabeth II, 40th Anniv. — A259

Coronation: 1670a, 30c, Official photograph. b, 40c, Crown of Queen Elizabeth, the Queen Mother. c, $2, Dignataries attending ceremony. d, $4, Queen, Prince Edward.

$6, Portrait, by Denis Fildes.

First decade, 1953-1963: No. 1671a, Wedding photograph of Princess Margaret and Antony Armstrong-Jones. b, Queen opening Parliament, Prince Philip. c, Queen holding infant. d, Royal family. e, Queen Elizabeth II, formal portrait. f, Queen, Charles de Gaulle. g, Queen, Pope John XXIII. h, Queen inspecting troops.

Second decade, 1963-1973: No. 1672a, Investiture of Charles as Prince of Wales. b, Queen opening Parliament, Prince Philip, diff. c, Queen holding infant, diff. d, Queen, Prince Philip, children. e, Wearing blue robe, diadem. f, Prince Philip, Queen seated. g, Prince Charles, Queen at microphone. h, Queen conversing, model airplane.

Third decade, 1973-1983: No. 1673a, Wedding photograph of Prince Charles and Princess Diana. b, Queen opening Parliament, Prince Philip, diff. c, Princess Diana with infant. d, Princess Anne with infant. e, Portrait of Queen. f, Queen waving, Prince Philip. g, Queen, Pope John Paul II. h, Wedding portrait of Mark Phillips and Princess Anne.

Fourth decade, 1983-1993: No. 1674a, Wedding photograph of Sarah Ferguson and Prince Andrew. b, Queen opening Parliament, Prince Philip, diff. c, Princess Diana holding infant, diff. d, Sarah Ferguson, infant. e, Queen wearing blue dress. f, Queen waving from carriage, Prince Philip. g, Queen wearing military uniform. h, Queen Mother.

1993, June 2 Litho. *Perf. 13½x14*

1670	A259		Sheet, 2 each #a.-d.	10.00	10.00

Sheets of 8

1671	A259	$1	#a.-h. + label	6.00	6.00
1672	A259	$1	#a.-h. + label	6.00	6.00
1673	A259	$1	#a.-h. + label	6.00	6.00
1674	A259	$1	#a.-h. + label	6.00	6.00

Souvenir Sheet

Perf. 14

1675	A259	$6	multicolored	4.50	4.50

No. 1675 contains one 28x42mm stamp.

Wedding of Japan's Crown Prince Naruhito and Masako Owada A260

Cameo photos of couple and: 40c, Crown Prince. $3, Princess.

$6, Princess wearing white coat, vert.

1993, Aug. 16 Litho. *Perf. 14*

1676	A260	40c	multicolored	30	30
1677	A260	$3	multicolored	2.25	2.25

Souvenir Sheet

1678	A260	$6	multicolored	4.50	4.50

Picasso (1881-1973) — A261

Paintings: 30c, Cat and Bird, 1939. 40c, Fish on a Newspaper, 1957. $5, Dying Bull, 1934. $6, Woman with a Dog, 1953.

1993, Aug. 16 Litho. *Perf. 14*

1679 A261	30c multicolored	25	25
1680 A261	40c multicolored	32	32
1681 A261	$5 multicolored	4.00	4.00

Souvenir Sheet

1682 A261	$6 multicolored	4.50	4.50

Copernicus (1473-1543) — A262

Designs: 40c, Astronomical devices. $4, Photograph of supernova. $5, Copernicus.

1993, Aug. 16

1683 A262	40c multicolored	32	32
1684 A262	$4 multicolored	3.25	3.25

Souvenir Sheet

1685 A262	$5 multicolored	3.75	3.75

Willy Brandt (1913-1992), German Chancellor — A263

Designs: 30c, Helmut Schmidt, George Leber, Brandt. $4, Brandt, newspaper headlines. $6, Brandt at Warsaw Ghetto Memorial, 1970.

1993, Aug. 16

1686 A263	30c multicolored	25	25
1687 A263	$4 multicolored	3.25	3.25

Souvenir Sheet

1688 A263	$6 multicolored	4.50	4.50

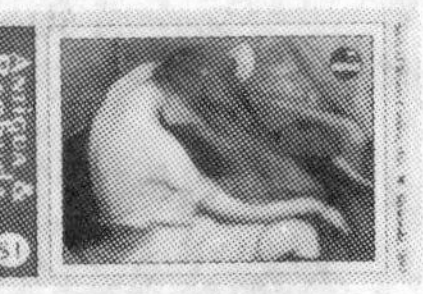

Polska '93 — A264

Paintings: $1, Study of a Woman Combing Her Hair, by Wladyslaw Slewinski, 1897. $3, Artist's Wife with Cat, by Konrad Kryzanowski, 1912. $6, General Confusion, by S. I. Witkiewicz, 1930, vert.

1993, Aug. 16

1689 A264	$1 multicolored	80	80
1690 A264	$3 multicolored	2.50	2.50

Souvenir Sheet

1691 A264	$6 multicolored	4.50	4.50

Inauguration of Pres. William J. Clinton — A265

Designs: $5, Pres. William J. Clinton, driving car. $6, Pres. William J. Clinton, inauguration ceremony, vert.

1993, Aug. 16

1692 A265	$5 multicolored	4.00	4.00

Souvenir Sheet

1693 A265	$6 multicolored	4.50	4.50

No. 1693 contains one 43x57mm stamp.

1994 Winter Olympics, Lillehammer, Norway — A266

Designs: 15c, Irina Rodnina, Alexei Ulanov, gold medalists, pairs figure skating, 1972. $5, Alberto Tomba, gold medal, giant slalom, 1988, 1992. $6, Yvonne van Gennip, Andrea Ehrig, gold, bronze medalists, speedskating, 1988.

1993, Aug. 16

1694 A266	15c multicolored	15	15
1695 A266	$5 multicolored	4.00	4.00

Souvenir Sheet

1696 A266	$6 multicolored	4.50	4.50

1994 World Cup Soccer Championships, US — A267

English soccer players: No. 1697, Gordon Banks. No. 1698, 1709, Bobby Moore. No. 1699, Peter Shilton. No. 1700, Nobby Stiles. No. 1701, Bryan Robson. No. 1702, Geoff Hurst. No. 1703, Gary Lineker. No. 1704, Bobby Charlton. No. 1705, Martin Peters. No. 1706, John Barnes. No. 1707, David Platt. No. 1708, Paul Gascoigne. No. 1710, Player holding 1990 Fair Play Winners Trophy.

1993, July 30 Litho. *Perf. 14*

1697-1708 A267	$2 Set of 12	18.00	18.00

Souvenir Sheets

1709 A267	$6 multicolored	4.50	4.50
1710 A267	$6 multicolored	4.50	4.50

Nos. 1697-1708 issued in sheets of five plus label identifying player.

Aviation Anniversaries — A268

Designs: 30c, Dr. Hugo Eckener, Dr. Wm. Beckers, zeppelin over Lake George, NY. No. 1712, Chicago Century of Progress Exhibition seen from zeppelin. No. 1713, George Washington, Blanchard's balloon, vert. No. 1714, Gloster E.28/39, first British jet plane. $4, Pres. Wilson watching take-off of first scheduled air mail plane. No. 1716, Hindenburg over Ebbets Field, Brooklyn, NY, 1937. No. 1717, Gloster Meteor in combat. No. 1718, Eckener, vert. No. 1719, Alexander Hamilton, Pres. Washington, John Jay, gondola of Blanchard's balloon. No. 1720, PBY-5.

1993, Oct. 11

1711 A268	30c multicolored	22	22
1712 A268	40c multicolored	30	30
1713 A268	40c multicolored	30	30
1714 A268	40c multicolored	30	30
1715 A268	$4 multicolored	3.00	3.00
1716 A268	$5 multicolored	3.75	3.75
1717 A268	$5 multicolored	3.75	3.75
	Nos. 1711-1717 (7)	11.62	11.62

Souvenir Sheets

1718 A268	$6 multicolored	4.50	4.50
1719 A268	$6 multicolored	4.50	4.50
1720 A268	$6 multicolored	4.50	4.50

Dr. Hugo Eckener, 125th anniv. of birth (#1711-1712, 1716, 1718). First US balloon flight, bicent. (#1713, 1715, 1719). Royal Air Force, 75th anniv. (#1714, 1717, 1720).

No. 1720 contains one 57x43mm stamp.

Mickey Mouse Movie Posters A269

Nos. 1721-1729: 10c, The Musical Farmer, 1932. 15c, Little Whirlwind, 1941. 30c, Pluto's Dream House, 1940. 40c, Gulliver Mickey, 1934. 50c, Alpine Climbers, 1936. $1, Mr. Mouse Takes a Trip, 1940. $2, The Nifty Nineties, 1941. $4, Mickey Down Under, 1948. $5, The Pointer, 1939.

Souvenir Sheets: No. 1730, $6, The Simple Things, 1953. No. 1731, $6, The Prince and the Pauper, 1990.

1993, Oct. 25 Litho. *Perf. 13½x14*

1721-1731 A269	Set of 11	21.00	21.00

St. John's Lodge #492, 150th Anniv. A270

Designs: 10c, W.K. Heath, Grand Inspector 1961-82, vert. 30c, Present Masonic Hall. 40c, 1st Masonic Hall. 60c, J.L.E. Jeffery, Grand Inspector 1953-61, vert.

1993, Aug. 16 Litho. *Perf. 14*

1732-1735 A270	Set of 4	1.10	1.10

First Ford Engine and Benz's First 4-Wheel Car, Cent. A271

Designs: 30c, Lincoln Continental. 40c, 1914 Mercedes racing car. $4, 1966 Ford GT40. $5, 1954 Mercedes Benz gull wing coupe, street version. No. 1740, Mustang emblem. No. 1741, US #1286A, Germany #471.

1993, Oct. 11 Litho. *Perf. 14*

1736-1739 A271	Set of 4	7.00	7.00

Souvenir Sheets

1740-1741 A271	$6 each	4.50	4.50

Christmas — A272

Nos. 1742-1750, Disney characters in The Nutcracker: 10c, 15c, 20c, 30c, 40c, 50c, 60c, $3, $6. 1751, Minnie and Mickey. No. 1752, Mickey, vert.

1993, Nov. 8 *Perf. 14x13½, 13½x14*

1742-1750 A272	Set of 9	8.50	8.50

Souvenir Sheets

1751-1752 A272	$6 each	4.50	4.50

Fine Art — A273

Paintings by Rembrandt: No. 1753, 15c, Hannah and Samuel. 30c, Isaac & Rebecca (The Jewish Bride). 40c, Jacob Wrestling with the Angel. $5, Moses with the Tablets of the Law.

Paintings by Matisse: No. 1754, 15c, Guitarist. 60c, Interior with a Goldfish Bowl. $1, Portrait of Mlle. Yvonne Landsberg. $4, The Toboggan, Plate XX from Jazz. No. 1761, The Blinding of Samson by the Philistines, by Rembrandt. No. 1762, The Three Sisters, by Matisse.

1993, Nov. 22 *Perf. 13½x14*

1753-1760 A273	Set of 8	9.00	9.00

Souvenir Sheets

1761-1762 A273	$6 each	4.50	4.50

A274

Hong Kong '94 A275

Stamps, fishing boats at Shau Kei Wan: No. 1763, Hong Kong #370, bow of boat. No. 1764, Stern of boat, #1300.

Museum of Qin figures, Shaanxi Province, Tomb of Qin First Emperor: No. 1765a, Inside museum. b, Cavalryman, horse. c, Warriors in battle formation. d, Painted bronze horses, chariot. e, Pekingese dog (not antiquity). f, Chin warrior figures, horses.

1994, Feb. 18 Litho. *Perf. 14*

1763 A274	40c multicolored	30	30
1764 A274	40c multicolored	30	30
a.	Pair, #1763-1764	60	60

Miniature Sheet

1765 A275	40c Sheet of 6, #a.-f.	1.75	1.75

Nos. 1763-1764 issued in sheets of 5 pairs. No. 1764a is a continuous design.

New Year 1994 (Year of the Dog) (#1765e).

Hong Kong '94 — A276

Disney characters: 10c, Mickey's "Pleasure Junk." 15c, Mandarin Minnie. 30c, Donald, Daisy journey by house boat. 50c, Mickey, Birdman of Mongkok. $1, Pluto encounters a good-luck dog. $2, Minnie, Daisy celebrate Bun Festival. $4, Goofy, the noodle maker. $5, Goofy pulls Mickey in a rickshaw.

No. 1774, Mickey celebrating New Year with Dragon Dance, horiz. No. 1775, View of Hong Kong Harbor, horiz.

1994, Feb. 18 Litho. *Perf. 13½x14*

1766-1773 A276	Set of 8	10.00	10.00

Souvenir Sheets

Perf. 14x13½

1774-1775 A276 $5 each 3.75 3.75

Miniature Sheets of 8

Sierra Club, Cent. — A277

Designs: No. 1776a, Bactrian camel, emblem UR. b, Bactrian camel, emblem UL. c, African elephant, emblem UL. d, African elephant, emblem UR. e, Leopard, blue background. f, Leopard, emblem UR. g, Leopard, emblem UL. h, Club emblem.

No. 1777a, Sumatran rhinoceros, lying on ground. b, Sumatran rhinoceros, looking straight ahead. c, Ring-tailed lemur standing. d, Ring-tailed lemur sitting on branch. e, Red-fronted brown lemur on branch. f, Red-fronted brown lemur. g, Red-fronted brown lemur, diff.

No. 1778, Sumatran rhinoceros, horiz. No. 1779, Ring-tailed lemur, horiz. No. 1780, Bactrian camel, horiz. No. 1781, African elephant, horiz.

1994, Mar. 1 Litho. *Perf. 14*

1776 A277 $1.50 #a.-h. 9.00 9.00

1777 A277 $1.50 #a.-g, #1776h 9.00 9.00

Souvenir Sheets

1778-1781 A277 $1.50 each 1.10 1.10

Miniature Sheets

New Year 1994 (Year of the Dog) A278

Small breeds of dogs: No. 1782a, West highland white terrier. b, Beagle. c, Scottish terrier. d, Pekingese. e, Dachshund. f, Yorkshire terrier. g, Pomeranian. h, Poodle. i, Shetland sheepdog. j, Pug. k, Shih tzu. l, Chihuahua.

Large breeds of dogs: No. 1783a, Mastiff. b, Border collie. c, Samoyed. d, Airedale terrier. e, English setter. f, Rough collie. g, Newfoundland. h, Weimaraner. i, English springer spaniel. j, Dalmatian. k, Boxer. l, Old English sheepdog.

No. 1784, Welsh corgi. No. 1785, Labrador retriever.

1994, Apr. 5 *Perf. 14*

1782 A278 50c Sheet of 12, #a.-l. 4.50 4.50

1783 A278 75c Sheet of 12, #a.-l. 6.75 6.75

Souvenir Sheets

1784-1785 A278 $6 each 4.50 4.50

Orchids — A279

Butterflies — A280

Designs: 10c, Spiranthes lanceolata. 20c, Ionopsis utricularioides. 30c, Tetramicra canaliculata. 50c, Oncidium picturatum. $1, Epidendrum difforme. $2, Epidendrum ciliare. $4, Epidendrum ibaguense. $5, Epidendrum nocturnum.

No. 1794, Encyclia cochleata. No. 1795, Rodriguezia lanceolata.

1994, Apr. 11 *Perf. 14*

1786-1793 A279 Set of 8 10.00 10.00

Souvenir Sheets

1794-1795 A279 $6 each 4.50 4.50

1994, June 27 *Perf. 14*

Designs: 10c, Monarch. 15c, Florida white. 30c, Little sulphur. 40c, Troglodyte. $1, Common long-tail skipper. $2, Caribbean buckeye. $4, Polydamas swallowtail. $5, Zebra.

#1804, Cloudless sulphur. #1805, Hanno blue.

1796-1803 A280 Set of 8 10.00 10.00

Souvenir Sheets

1804-1805 A280 $6 each 4.50 4.50

Miniature Sheet of 9

Marine Life — A281

Designs: No. 1806a, Bottlenose dolphin. b, Killer whale (a). c, Spinner dolphin (b). d, Ocean sunfish (a). e, Caribbean reef shark, short fin pilot whale (d, f). f, Butterfly fish. g, Moray eel. h, Trigger fish. i, Red lobster (h).

No. 1807, Blue marlin, horiz. No. 1808, Sea horse.

1994, July 21 Litho. *Perf. 14*

1806 A281 50c a.-i. 3.50 3.50

Souvenir Sheets

1807-1808 A281 $6 each 4.50 4.50

Intl. Year of the Family A282

1994, Aug. 4

1809 A282 90c multicolored 70 70

D-Day, 50th Anniv. A283

Designs: 40c, Short Sunderland attacks U-boat. $2, Lockheed P-38 Lightning attacks train. $3, B-26 Marauders of 9th Air Force.

$6, Hawker Typhoon Fighter Bombers.

1994, Aug. 4

1810-1812 A283 Set of 3 4.25 4.25

Souvenir Sheet

1813 A283 $6 multicolored 4.50 4.50

A284

Intl. Olympic Committee, Cent. — A285

Designs: 50c, Edwin Moses, US, hurdles, 1984. $1.50, Steffi Graf, Germany, tennis, 1988. $6, Johann Olav Koss, Norway, speed skating, 1994.

1994, Aug. 4

1814 A284 50c multicolored 38 38

1815 A284 $1.50 multicolored 1.10 1.10

Souvenir Sheet

1816 A285 $6 multicolored 4.50 4.50

English Touring Cricket, Cent. A286

Designs: 35c, M.A. Atherton, England, Wisden Trophy. 75c, I.V.A. Richards, Leeward Islands, vert. $1.20, R.B. Richardson, Leeward Islands, Wisden Trophy.

$3, First English team, 1895.

1994, Aug. 4

1817-1819 A286 Set of 3 1.75 1.75

Souvenir Sheet

1820 A286 $3 multicolored 2.25 2.25

Miniature Sheets of 6

First Manned Moon Landing, 25th Anniv. A287

Designs: No. 1821a, Edwin E. Aldrin, Jr. b, First footprint on Moon. c, Neil A. Armstrong. d, Aldrin descending to lunar surface. e, Aldrin deploys ALSET. f, Aldrin, US flag, Tranquility Base.

No. 1822a, Scientific research, Tranquility Base. b, Plaque on Moon. c, Eagle ascending to docking. d, Command module in lunar orbit. e, US No. C76 made from die carried to Moon. f, Pres. Nixon, Apollo 11 crew.

$6, Armstrong, Aldrin, Postmaster General Blount.

1994, Aug. 4

1821-1822 A287 $1.50 #a.-f. 6.75 6.75

Souvenir Sheet

1823 A287 $6 multicolored 4.50 4.50

A288

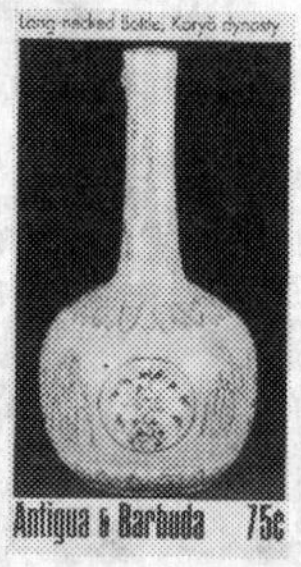

PHILAKOREA '94 — A289

Designs: 40c, Entrance bridge, Songgwangsa Temple. 90c, Song-op Folk Village, Cheju. $3, Panoramic view, Port Sogwip'o.

Ceramics, Koryo & Choson Dynasties: No. 1827a, Long-necked bottle. b, Jar. c, Jar, diff. d, Ewer in form of bamboo shoot. e, Jar, diff. f, Pear-shaped bottle. g, Porcelain jar with dragon design. h, Porcelain jar with bonsai design.

$4, Ox, ox herder, vert.

1994, Aug. 4 *Perf. 14, 13½ (#1827)*

1824-1826 A288 Set of 3 3.50 3.50

Miniature Sheet of 8

1827 A289 75c #a.-h. 6.00 6.00

Souvenir Sheet

1828 A288 $4 multicolored 3.00 3.00

Miniature Sheets of 8

Stars of Country & Western Music — A290

Designs: No. 1829a, Patsy Cline. b, Tanya Tucker. c, Dolly Parton. d, Anne Murray. e, Tammy Wynette. f, Loretta Lynn. g, Reba McEntire. h, Skeeter Davis.

No. 1830a, Travis Tritt. b, Dwight Yoakam. c, Billy Ray Cyrus. d, Alan Jackson. e, Garth Brooks. f, Vince Gill. g, Clint Black. h, Eddie Rabbit.

No. 1831a, Hank Snow. b, Gene Autry. c, Jimmie Rogers. d, Ernest Tubb. e, Eddy Arnold. f, Willie Nelson. g, Johnny Cash. h, George Jones.

No. 1832, Kitty Wells, horiz. No. 1833, Hank Williams, Sr. No. 1834, Hank Williams, Jr.

1994, Aug. 18 Litho. *Perf. 14*

1829-1831 A290 75c #a.-h, each 4.50 4.50

Souvenir Sheets

1832-1834 A290 $6 each 4.50 4.50

1994 World Cup Soccer Championships, US — A291

Designs: 15c, Hugo Sanchez, Mexico. 35c, Juergen Klinsman, Germany. 65c, Antigua player. $1.20, Cobi Jones, US. $4, Roberto Baggio, Italy. $5, Bwalya Kalusha, Zambia.

No. 1841, FIFA World Cup Trophy, vert. No. 1842, Maldive Islands player, vert.

1994, Sept. 19

1835-1840 A291 Set of 6 8.50 8.50

Souvenir Sheets

1841-1842 A291 $6 each 4.50 4.50

Order of the Caribbean Community — A292

First award recipients: 65c, Sir Shridath Ramphal, statesman, Guyana. 90c, William Demas, economist, Trinidad & Tobago. $1.20, Derek Walcott, writer, St. Lucia.

1994

1843-1845 A292 Set of 3 2.00 2.00

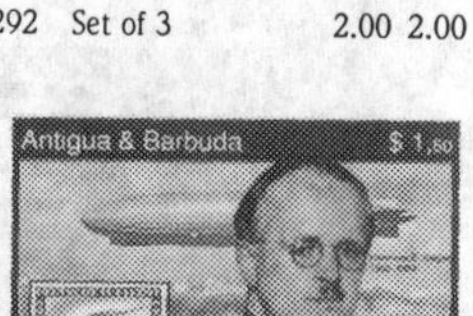

Herman E. Sieger (1902-54) A293

Design: Germany #C35, Graf Zeppelin, Sieger.

1994 Litho. *Perf. 14*

1846 A293 $1.50 multicolored 1.25 1.25

WAR TAX STAMPS

No. 31 and Type A3 Overprinted in Black or Red

WAR STAMP

1916-18 Wmk. 3 *Perf. 14*

MR1	A3	½p green	30	30
MR2	A3	½p green (R) ('17)	35	35
MR3	A3	1½p orange ('18)	40	40

BAHAMAS

LOCATION — A group of about 700 islands and 2,000 rocks in the West Indies, off the coast of Florida. Only 30 islands are inhabited.
GOVT. — Independent state in British Commonwealth
AREA — 5,353 sq. mi.
POP. — 209,505 (1980)
CAPITAL — Nassau

The principal island, on which the capital is located, is New Providence. The Bahamas obtained internal self-government on January 7, 1964, and independence on July 10, 1973.

12 Pence = 1 Shilling
20 Shillings = 1 Pound
100 Cents = 1 Dollar (1966)

Catalogue values for unused stamps in this country are for Never Hinged items, beginning with Scott 130, and Scott C1 in the air post section.

Values for Nos. 2-26 are for stamps with perforations cutting into the design.
Pen cancellations usually indicate revenue use. Such stamps sell for much less than postally canceled copies. Stamps with revenue or pen cancellations removed are often found with forged postal cancellations. Value, 50 cents to $2.50.

Queen Victoria
A1 A2

1859-60 Unwmk. Engr. *Imperf.*

1	A1	1p dull lake ('60)	40.00	600.00
a.		1p reddish lake	2,750.	1,250.
b.		1p brownish lake	2,750.	1,400.

Most unused copies of #1 are remainders, and false cancellations are plentiful. #1a and 1b are on thicker paper than #1.

1861 *Rough Perf. 14 to 16*

2	A1	1p lake	725.00	175.00
a.		Clean-cut perf. ('60)	1,000.	450.00
3	A2	4p dull rose	1,300.	450.00
a.		Imperf. between, pair		
4	A2	6p gray lilac	2,000.	400.00

1862 *Perf. 11½, 12*

5	A1	1p lake	475.00	125.00
a.		Horiz. or vert. pair, imperf. between	4,750.	
6	A2	4p dull rose	2,500.	250.00
7	A2	6p gray violet	2,750.	325.00

No. 5a was not issued in the Bahamas.
Nos. 5-7 exist with perf. 11½ or 12 compound with 11.

Perf. 13

8	A1	1p brown lake	300.00	125.00
a.		1p carmine lake	300.00	125.00
9	A2	4p rose	2,500.	225.00
10	A2	6p gray violet	3,000.	225.00
a.		6p dull violet	3,000.	225.00

Queen Victoria — A3

1863-65 Wmk. 1 *Perf. 12½*

11	A1	1p lake	45.00	40.00
a.		1p brown lake	45.00	40.00
b.		1p rose lake	45.00	40.00
12	A1	1p vermilion	40.00	40.00
13	A2	4p rose	225.00	45.00
a.		4p rose lake	250.00	67.50
b.		4p bright rose	140.00	50.00
14	A2	6p dk violet	110.00	35.00
a.		6p violet	250.00	65.00
b.		6p rose lilac	4,750.	3,750.
c.		6p lilac	300.00	65.00
15	A3	1sh green ('65)	2,000.	200.00

For surcharge see No. 26.

1863-81 *Perf. 14*

16	A1	1p vermilion	27.50	12.50
17	A1	1p car lake (anil)	1,500.	
18	A2	4p rose	350.00	35.00
a.		4p deep rose	350.00	42.50
19	A3	1sh green ('63)	5.00	5.00

1882-98 Wmk. 2

20	A1	1p vermilion	200.00	32.50
21	A2	4p rose	675.00	40.00
22	A3	1sh green	27.50	15.00
23	A3	1sh blue grn ('98)	25.00	15.00

Perf. 12

24	A1	1p vermilion	30.00	22.50
25	A2	4p rose	425.00	40.00

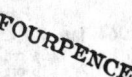

No. 14a Surcharged in Black **FOURPENCE**

1883 Wmk. 1 *Perf. 12½*

26	A2	4p on 6p violet	575.00	275.00

The surcharge, being handstamped, is found in various positions. Counterfeit overprints exist.

Queen Victoria
A5

Queen's Staircase
A6

1884-90 Typo. Wmk. 2 *Perf. 14*

27	A5	1p car rose	2.50	85
a.		1p pale rose	12.50	6.00
28	A5	2½p ultra	2.00	1.10
a.		2½p dull blue	12.50	7.50
29	A5	4p yellow	3.75	3.75
30	A5	6p violet	2.50	5.25
31	A5	5sh olive green	40.00	50.00
32	A5	£1 brown	325.00	200.00
		Revenue cancellation		45.00
		Nos. 27-32 (6)	375.75	260.95

Cleaned fiscally used copies of No. 32 are often found with postmarks of small post offices added.

1901-03 Engr. Wmk. 1

33	A6	1p carmine & blk	2.25	3.25
34	A6	5p org & blk ('03)	8.25	14.00
35	A6	2sh ultra & blk ('03)	9.50	15.00
36	A6	3sh green & blk ('03)	15.00	22.50

See Nos. 48, 58-62, 71, 78, 81-82.

Edward VII
A7

George V
A8

1902 Wmk. 2 Typo.

37	A7	1p carmine rose	1.90	80
38	A7	2½p ultra	6.00	2.25
39	A7	4p orange	5.00	8.75
40	A7	6p bister brn	6.00	7.75
41	A7	1sh gray blk & car	7.25	9.50
42	A7	5sh violet & ultra	32.50	40.00
43	A7	£1 green & blk	275.00	350.00
		Nos. 37-43 (7)	333.65	419.05

1906-11 Wmk. 3

44	A7	½p green	3.75	1.40
45	A7	1p car rose	5.00	90
46	A7	2½p ultra ('07)	14.00	17.50
47	A7	6p bister brn ('11)	42.50	55.00

1910-16 Engr.

48	A6	1p red & gray blk ('16)	1.50	1.50
a.		1p carmine & black	5.50	5.50

For overprints, see Nos. B1-B2.

1912-19 Typo.

49	A8	½p green	85	1.25
50	A8	1p car rose	1.75	35
50A	A8	2p gray ('19)	1.75	2.25
51	A8	2½p ultra	4.00	5.75
52	A8	4p orange	1.75	3.00
53	A8	6p bister brn	1.75	3.00

Chalky Paper

54	A8	1sh black & red	2.50	3.00
55	A8	5sh violet & ultra	22.50	20.00
56	A8	£1 green & blk	150.00	200.00
		Nos. 49-56 (9)	186.85	238.60

1917-19 Engr.

58	A6	3p purple, *yel*	7.75	8.50
59	A6	3p brown & blk ('19)	2.25	4.75
60	A6	5p violet & blk	2.25	6.75
61	A6	2sh ultra & black	12.50	19.00
62	A6	3sh green & black	30.00	32.50
		Nos. 58-62 (5)	54.75	71.50

Peace Commemorative Issue

King George V and Seal of Bahamas — A9

1920, Mar. 1 Engr. *Perf. 14*

65	A9	½p gray green	42	2.25
66	A9	1p deep red	1.10	90
67	A9	2p gray	2.75	4.75
68	A9	3p brown	2.75	9.50
69	A9	1sh dark green	22.50	30.00
		Nos. 65-69 (5)	29.52	47.40

Types of 1901-12

1921-34 Typo., Engr. (A6) Wmk. 4

70	A8	½p green ('24)	15	15
71	A6	1p car & black	85	85
72	A8	1p car rose	16	15
73	A8	1½p fawn ('34)	80	1.25
74	A8	2p gray ('27)	65	2.25
75	A8	2½p ultra ('22)	65	2.25
76	A8	3p violet, *yel* ('31)	5.75	11.00
77	A8	4p yellow ('24)	1.50	4.75
78	A6	5p red vio & gray blk ('29)	5.75	9.00
79	A8	6p bister brn ('22)	90	4.00
80	A8	1sh blk & red ('26)	3.00	8.25
81	A6	2sh ultra & blk ('22)	30.00	50.00
82	A6	3sh grn & blk ('24)	42.50	55.00
83	A8	5sh vio & ultra ('24)	25.00	32.50
84	A8	£1 grn & blk ('26)	140.00	225.00
		Nos. 70-84 (15)	257.66	406.40

The 3p, 1sh, 5sh and £1 are on chalky paper.

Seal of Bahamas — A10

1930, Jan. 2 Engr. *Perf. 12*

85	A10	1p red & black	1.00	2.50
86	A10	3p dp brown & blk	3.00	7.50
87	A10	5p dk vio & blk	3.50	7.50
88	A10	2sh ultra & black	22.50	35.00
89	A10	3sh dp green & blk	27.50	55.00
		Nos. 85-89 (5)	57.50	107.50

The dates on the stamps commemorate important events in the history of the colony. The 1st British occupation was in 1629. The Bahamas were ceded to Great Britain in 1729 and a treaty of peace was signed by that country, France and Spain.

Type of 1930 Issue
Without Dates at Top

1931-42

90	A10	2sh ultra & black	70	70
a.		2sh ultra & slate purple ('42)	12.00	11.00
91	A10	3sh dp green & blk	80	80
a.		3sh deep grn & slate purple ('42)	11.00	11.00

Nos. 90-91 are on thick paper with yellowish gum, Nos. 90-91 are on thin white paper with colorless gum.
For overprints, see Nos. 126-127.

Silver Jubilee Issue
Common Design Type

1935, May 6 *Perf. 13½x14*

92	CD301	1½p car & blue	45	35
93	CD301	2½p blue & brn	1.50	2.25
94	CD301	6p ol grn & lt bl	4.00	6.00
95	CD301	1sh brt vio & ind	6.50	8.00
		Set, never hinged	25.00	

Flamingos in Flight — A11

1935, May 22 *Perf. 12½*

96	A11	8p car & ultra	5.00	3.25
		Never hinged	8.50	

Coronation Issue
Common Design Type

1937, May 12 *Perf. 13½x14*

97	CD302	½p dp green	15	15
98	CD302	1½p brown	20	20
99	CD302	2½p brt ultra	60	60
		Set, never hinged	1.50	

George VI — A12

Sea Gardens, Nassau — A13

Fort Charlotte A14

Flamingos in Flight — A15

1938-46 Typo. Wmk. 4 *Perf. 14*

100	A12	½p green	15	15
101	A12	1p carmine	1.10	85
101A	A12	1p gray ('41)	15	15
102	A12	1½p red brown	15	15
103	A12	2p gray	8.75	14.00
103B	A12	2p car ('41)	18	18
c.		"TWO PENCE" double		1,750.
104	A12	2½p ultra	1.40	85
104A	A12	2½p lt violet ('43)	20	20
105	A12	3p lt violet	5.50	7.50
105A	A12	3p ultra ('43)	28	35

Engr.
Perf. 12½

106	A13	4p red org & blue	52	45
107	A14	6p blue & ol grn	35	28
108	A15	8p car & ultra	70	60

Typo.
Perf. 14

109	A12	10p yel org ('46)	48	48
110	A12	1sh black & car	85	70
112	A12	5sh pur & ultra	7.50	6.00
a.		5sh lilac & light ultra	30.00	30.00
113	A12	£1 green & blk	27.50	25.00
		Nos. 100-113 (17)	55.76	57.89
		Set, never hinged	125.00	

Nos. 110-113 printed on chalky and ordinary paper.
See Nos. 154-156. For overprints see Nos. 116-125, 128-129.

No. 104 Surcharged in Black **3d.**

1940, Nov. 28 *Perf. 14*
115 A12 3p on 2½p ultra 25 25
Never hinged 40

Stamps of 1931-42 Overprinted in Black

1492 LANDFALL OF COLUMBUS 1942

1942, Oct. 12 *Perf. 14, 12½, 12*
116 A12 ½p green 15 15
117 A12 1p gray 15 15
118 A12 1½p red brn 15 15
119 A12 2p carmine 15 15
120 A12 2½p ultra 15 15
121 A12 3p ultra 15 15
122 A13 4p red org & blue 18 16
123 A14 6p blue & ol grn 30 25
124 A15 8p car & ultra 35 30
125 A12 1sh black & car 50 40
126 A10 2sh dk ultra & blk 4.50 *9.50*
a. 2sh ultra & slate purple 7.00 *13.00*
127 A10 3sh dp grn & sl pur 2.75 *9.00*
a. 3sh deep green & black 8.50 *17.00*
128 A12 5sh lilac & ultra 3.75 *9.00*
129 A12 £1 green & black 19.00 *30.00*
Nos. 116-129 (14) 32.23 *59.51*
Set, never hinged 50.00

450th anniv. of the discovery of America by Columbus.

Nos. 125, 128-129 printed on chalky and ordinary paper.

Two printings of the basic stamps were overprinted, the first with dark gum, the second with white gum.

Catalogue values for unused stamps in this section, from this point to the end of the section, are for Never Hinged items.

Peace Issue
Common Design Type
Perf. 13½x14
1946, Nov. 11 Engr. Wmk. 4
130 CD303 1½p brown 15 15
131 CD303 3p deep blue 16 16

Infant Welfare Clinic — A16

Designs: 1p, Modern agriculture. 1½p, Sisal. 2p, Native straw work. 2½p, Modern dairying. 3p, Fishing fleet. 4p, Out island settlement. 6p, Tuna fishing. 8p, Paradise Beach. 10p, Modern hotel. 1sh, Yacht racing. 2sh, Water skiing. 3sh, Shipbuilding. 5sh, Modern transportation. 10sh, Modern salt production. £1, Parliament Building.

1948, Oct. 11 Unwmk. *Perf. 12*
132 A16 ½p orange 15 15
133 A16 1p olive green 15 15
134 A16 1½p olive bister 35 28
135 A16 2p vermilion 25 18
136 A16 2½p red brown 65 50
137 A16 3p brt ultra 45 35
138 A16 4p gray black 45 1.25
139 A16 6p emerald 65 1.25
140 A16 8p violet 65 1.10
141 A16 10p rose car 70 55
142 A16 1sh olive brn 1.25 90
143 A16 2sh claret 6.00 *8.00*
144 A16 3sh brt blue 6.00 *8.00*
145 A16 5sh purple 4.75 *7.50*
146 A16 10sh dk gray 4.75 *9.50*
147 A16 £1 red org 9.50 *14.00*
Nos. 132-147 (16) 36.70 *53.66*

300th anniv., in 1947, of the settlement of the colony.

Silver Wedding Issue
Common Design Type
Perf. 14x14½
1948, Dec. 1 Wmk. 4 Photo.
148 CD304 1½p red brown 16 15

Engr.; Name Typo.
Perf. 11½x11
149 CD305 £1 gray green 35.00 *40.00*

UPU Issue
Common Design Types
Engr.; Name Typo. on #151 & 152
1949, Oct. 10 *Perf. 13½, 11x11½*
150 CD306 2½p violet 25 25
151 CD307 3p indigo 50 50
152 CD308 6p blue gray 1.00 1.00
153 CD309 1sh rose car 1.65 1.65

George VI Type of 1938
Perf. 13½x14
1951-52 Wmk. 4 Typo.
154 A12 ½p claret ('52) 20 20
a. Wmk. 4a (error) *1,250.*
155 A12 2p green 40 40
156 A12 3p rose red ('52) 80 *3.00*

Coronation Issue
Common Design Type
1953, June 3 Engr. *Perf. 13½x13*
157 CD312 6p blue & black 60 60

Infant Welfare Clinic — A17

Designs: 1p, Modern Agriculture. 1½p, Out island settlement. 2p, Native strawwork. 3p, Fishing fleet. 4p, Water skiing. 5p, Modern dairying. 6p, Modern transportation. 8p, Paradise Beach. 10p, Modern hotels. 1sh, Yacht racing. 2sh, Sisal. 2sh6p, Shipbuilding. 5sh, Tuna fishing. 10sh, Modern salt production. £1, Parliament Building.

1954, Jan. 1 *Perf. 11x11½*
158 A17 ½p red org & blk 15 15
159 A17 1p org brn & ol grn 15 15
a. Booklet pane of 4 52
160 A17 1½p black & blue 15 15
a. Booklet pane of 4 70
161 A17 2p dk grn & brn org 15 15
a. Booklet pane of 4 70
162 A17 3p dp car & blk 18 15
163 A17 4p lil rose & bl green 28 25
a. Booklet pane of 4 1.75
164 A17 5p dp ultra & brn 65 *1.75*
165 A17 6p blk & aqua 42 25
a. Booklet pane of 4 2.25
166 A17 8p rose vio & blk 48 25
a. Booklet pane of 4 2.50
167 A17 10p ultra & blk 55 35
168 A17 1sh ol brn & ultra 65 52
169 A17 2sh blk & brn org 1.10 75
170 A17 2sh6p dp bl & blk 2.50 1.10
171 A17 5sh dp org & emer 5.00 2.50
172 A17 10sh grnsh blk & black 7.00 5.00
173 A17 £1 vio & grnsh black 15.00 11.00
Nos. 158-173 (16) 34.41 24.47

See No. 203. For types overprinted or surcharged, see Nos. 181-182, 185-200, 202.

Queen Elizabeth II — A18

Wmk. 314
1959, June 10 Engr. *Perf. 13*
174 A18 1p dk red & black 15 15
175 A18 2p green & black 15 15
176 A18 6p blue & black 28 28
177 A18 10p brown & black 55 55

Cent. of the 1st postage stamp of Bahamas.

Christ Church Cathedral, Nassau — A19

Perf. 14x13
1962, Jan. 30 Photo. Unwmk.
178 A19 8p shown 60 60
179 A19 10p Public library 60 60

Centenary of the city of Nassau.

Freedom from Hunger Issue
Common Design Type
Perf. 14x14½
1963, June 4 Wmk. 314
180 CD314 8p sepia 1.25 1.10
a. "8d" and "BAHAMAS" omitted 750.00

Nos. 166-167 Overprinted: "BAHAMAS TALKS/ 1962"
Perf. 11x11½
1963, July 15 Engr. Wmk. 4
181 A17 8p rose vio & black 1.00 85
182 A17 10p ultra & black 1.75 1.65

Meeting of Pres. Kennedy and Prime Minister Harold Macmillan, Dec. 1962.

Red Cross Centenary Issue
Common Design Type
Wmk. 314
1963, Sept. 2 Litho. *Perf. 13*
183 CD315 1p black & red 18 15
184 CD315 10p ultra & red 2.00 1.40

Type of 1954 Overprinted: "NEW CONSTITUTION/ 1964"

Designs as Before

Perf. 11x11½
1964, Jan. 7 Engr. Wmk. 314
185 A17 ½p red org & blk 15 15
186 A17 1p org brn & ol green 15 15
187 A17 1½p black & blue 15 15
188 A17 2p dk grn & brn org 15 15
189 A17 3p dp car & blk 15 15
190 A17 4p lil rose & bl green 16 15
191 A17 5p dp ultra & brn 22 18
192 A17 6p blk & aqua 25 20
193 A17 8p rose vio & blk 35 28
194 A17 10p ultra & black 45 32
195 A17 1sh ol brn & ultra 60 45
196 A17 2sh blk & brn org 1.25 95
197 A17 2sh6p dp bl & blk 1.50 1.25
198 A17 5sh dp org & emer 3.00 2.50
199 A17 10sh grnsh blk & black 5.50 4.75
200 A17 £1 vio & grnsh black 11.50 9.50
Nos. 185-200 (16) 25.53 21.28

Shakespeare Issue
Common Design Type
Perf. 14x14½
1964, Apr. 23 Photo. Wmk. 314
201 CD316 6p greenish blue 42 35

Type of 1954 Surcharged with Olympic Rings, New Value and Bars
Perf. 11x11½
1964, Oct. 1 Engr. Wmk. 314
202 A17 8p on 1sh ol brn & ultra 45 45

18th Olympic Games, Tokyo, Oct. 10-25.

Queen Type of 1954
1964, Oct. 6 Wmk. 314
203 A17 2p dk grn & brn org 50 50

Out Island Regatta A21

Designs: ½p, Colony badge. 1½p, Princess Margaret Hospital. 2p, High School. 3p, Flamingo. 4p, Liner "Queen Elizabeth." 6p, Island development. 8p, Yachting. 10p, Public Square, Nassau. 1sh, Sea Garden, Nassau. 2sh, Cannons at Fort Charlotte. 2sh6p, Sea plane and jetliner. 5sh, 1914 Williamson film project and 1939 underwater post office. 10sh, Conch shell. £1, Columbus' flagship.

Engr. and Litho.
1965, Jan. 7 *Perf. 13½x13*
204 A21 ½p multi, *bluish* 15 15
205 A21 1p multi 15 15
a. Booklet pane of 4 38
206 A21 1½p multi 15 15
a. Booklet pane of 4 45
207 A21 2p multi 15 15
a. Booklet pane of 4 55
208 A21 3p multi 18 15
209 A21 4p multi 22 15
a. Booklet pane of 4 1.10
210 A21 6p multi 30 15
a. Booklet pane of 4 1.25
211 A21 8p multi 38 30
a. Booklet pane of 4 1.65
212 A21 10p multi 35 15
213 A21 1sh multi, *grnsh* 55 26
214 A21 2sh multi, *grnsh* 1.10 65
215 A21 2sh6p multi 1.50 80
216 A21 5sh multi 3.00 1.60
217 A21 10sh multi 6.00 3.75
218 A21 £1 multi 12.00 7.25
Nos. 204-218 (15) 26.18 15.81

Booklet panes were issued Mar. 23, 1965.

See Nos. 252-266. For surcharges, see Nos. 221, 230-244.

ITU Issue
Common Design Type
Perf. 11x11½
1965, May 17 Litho. Wmk. 314
219 CD317 1p emerald & org 18 18
220 CD317 2sh lilac & olive 2.25 2.25

No. 211 Surcharged **9d**

Perf. 13½x13
1965, July 12 Engr. & Litho.
221 A21 9p on 8p multi 60 60

Intl. Cooperation Year Issue
Common Design Type
Perf. 14½
1965, Oct. 25 Wmk. 314 Litho.
222 CD318 ½p blue grn & claret 15 15
223 CD318 1sh lt violet & grn 85 70

Churchill Memorial Issue
Common Design Type
1966, Jan. 24 Photo. *Perf. 14*
224 CD319 ½p multicolored 15 15
225 CD319 2p multicolored 20 20
226 CD319 10p multicolored 1.00 1.00
227 CD319 1sh multicolored 1.50 1.50

Royal Visit Issue
Common Design Type Inscribed "Royal Visit / 1966"
1966, Feb. 4 Litho. *Perf. 11x12*
228 CD320 6p violet blue 65 65
229 CD320 1sh dk car rose 1.65 1.65

Nos. 204-218 Surcharged **2¢**

Perf. 13½x13
Engr. & Litho.
1966, May 25 Wmk. 314
230 A21 1c on ½p multi 15 15
231 A21 2c on 1p multi 15 15
232 A21 3c on 2p multi 15 15
233 A21 4c on 3p multi 15 15
234 A21 5c on 4p multi 15 15
a. Surch. omitted, vert. strip of 7-10 *3,000.*
235 A21 8c on 6p multi 20 22
236 A21 10c on 8p multi 24 25
237 A21 11c on 1½p multi 35 25
238 A21 12c on 10p multi 40 30
239 A21 15c on 1sh multi 48 35
240 A21 22c on 2sh multi 65 42
241 A21 50c on 2sh6p multi 1.40 1.25
242 A21 $1 on 5sh multi 2.50 2.50
243 A21 $2 on 10sh multi 5.50 5.00
244 A21 $3 on £1 multi 8.00 7.50
Nos. 230-244 (15) 20.47 18.79

The denominations are next to the bars instead of below on Nos. 232, 235-240; the length of the bars varies to cover old denomination.

No. 234a, if single, is identical with No. 209, but distinguishable if in vertical strip of 7 to 10. No. 234 was printed in sheets of 100 (10x10); No. 209 in sheets of 60 (10x6).

World Cup Soccer Issue
Common Design Type
1966, July 1 Litho. *Perf. 14*
245 CD321 8c multicolored 30 30
246 CD321 15c multicolored 60 60

WHO Headquarters Issue
Common Design Type
1966, Sept. 20 Litho. *Perf. 14*
247 CD322 11c multicolored 52 52
248 CD322 15c multicolored 70 70

UNESCO Anniversary Issue
Common Design Type
1966, Dec. 1 Litho. *Perf. 14*
249 CD323 3c "Education" 15 15
250 CD323 15c "Science" 65 65
251 CD323 $1 "Culture" 3.25 3.25

Type of 1965
Values in Cents and Dollars
Perf. 13¹/₂x13

1967, May 25 Engr. & Litho.

Designs: 1c, Colony badge. 2c, Out Island Regatta. 3c, High School. 4c, Flamingo. 5c, Liner "Oceanic." 8c, Island development. 10c, Yachting. 11c, Princess Margaret Hospital. 12c, Public Square, Nassau. 15c, Sea Garden, Nassau. 22c, Cannon at Fort Charlotte. 50c, Sea plane and jetliner. $1, 1914 Williamson film project and 1939 underwater post office. $2, Conch shell. $3, Columbus' flagship.

252	A21	1c brown & multi	15	15
253	A21	2c grn, slate & bl	15	15
254	A21	3c grn, indigo & vio	15	15
255	A21	4c ultra, blue & red	15	15
256	A21	5c pur, bl & indigo	15	15
257	A21	8c dk brn, bl & dl grn	22	16
258	A21	10c car rose, bl & pur	25	16
259	A21	11c bl, grn & rose red	35	24
260	A21	12c ol grn, bl & lt brn	40	20
261	A21	15c rose & multi	52	32
262	A21	22c rose red, brn & bl	60	40
263	A21	50c emer, ol & bl	1.40	90
264	A21	$1 sep, brn org & dk blue	2.75	1.75
265	A21	$2 green & multi	5.50	4.25
266	A21	$3 pur, bl & brn org	8.50	6.75
		Nos. 252-266 (15)	21.24	15.88

Nos. 252-266 are on toned paper. Printings on very white, untinted paper appeared between late 1969 and May, 1971. Value, set $500.

Seal of Bahamas, Queen Elizabeth II and Lord Baden-Powell A22

60th anniv. of world Scouting: 15c, Scout emblem and portraits as on 3c.

Perf. 14x13¹/₂

1967, Sept. 1 Photo. Wmk. 314

267	A22	3c multicolored	22	22
268	A22	15c multicolored	85	85

Human Rights Flame and Globe A23

Intl. Human Rights Year: 12c, Human rights flame and scales of justice. $1, Human rights flame and Seal of Bahamas.

1968, May 13 Litho. *Perf. 14*

269	A23	3c multicolored	15	15
270	A23	12c multicolored	50	50
271	A23	$1 multicolored	2.25	2.25

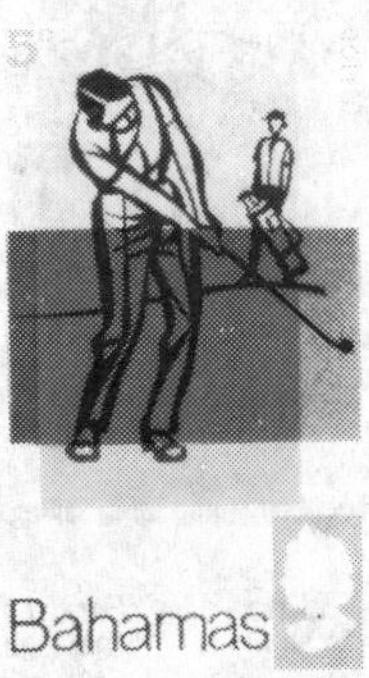
Golf — A24

Tourist Publicity: 11c, Yachting. 15c, Horse racing. 50c, Water skiing.

1968, Aug. 20 Unwmk. *Perf. 13¹/₂*

272	A24	5c multicolored	25	25
273	A24	11c multicolored	52	52
274	A24	15c multicolored	65	65
275	A24	50c multicolored	2.25	2.25

Olympic Monument and Sailboat — A25

Olympic Monument, San Salvador Island, Bahamas, and: 11c, Long jump. 50c, Running. $1, Sailing.

1968, Sept. 30 Photo. *Perf. 14¹/₂x14*

276	A25	5c multicolored	16	16
277	A25	11c multicolored	40	40
278	A25	50c multicolored	1.65	1.65
279	A25	$1 multicolored	3.50	3.50

19th Olympic Games, Mexico City, Oct. 12-27.

Legislative Building A26

Designs: 10c, Bahamas mace and Big Ben, London, vert. 12c, Local straw market, vert. 15c, Horse-drawn surrey.

Perf. 14¹/₂

1968, Nov. 1 Unwmk. Litho.

280	A26	3c brt blue & multi	15	15
281	A26	10c yel, blk & blue	38	38
282	A26	12c brt rose & multi	42	42
283	A26	15c green & multi	52	52

14th Commonwealth Parliamentary Conf., Nassau, Nov. 1-8.

$100 Coin with Queen Elizabeth II and Landing of Columbus — A27

Gold Coins with Elizabeth II on Obverse: 12c, $50 coin and Santa Maria flagship. 15c, $20 coin and Nassau Harbor Lighthouse. $1, $10 coin and Fort.

Engr. on Gold Paper

1968, Dec. 2 Unwmk. *Perf. 13¹/₂*

284	A27	3c dark red	20	20
285	A27	12c dark green	65	65
286	A27	15c lilac	75	75
287	A27	$1 black	4.50	2.50

First gold coinage in the Bahamas.

Bahamas Postal Card and Airplane Wing A28

Design: 15c, Seaplane, 1929.

Perf. 14¹/₂x14

1969, Jan. 30 Litho. Unwmk.

288	A28	12c multicolored	90	90
289	A28	15c multicolored	1.10	1.10

50th anniv. of the 1st flight from Nassau, Bahamas, to Miami, Fla., Jan. 30, 1919.

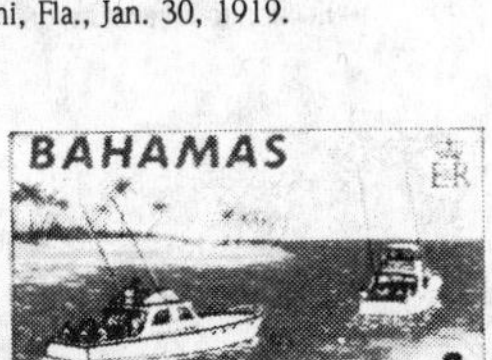
Game Fishing Boats A29

Designs: 11c, Paradise Beach. 12c, Sunfish sailboats. 15c, Parade on Rawson Square.

1969, Aug. 26 Litho. Wmk. 314

290	A29	3c multicolored	16	16
291	A29	11c multicolored	60	60
292	A29	12c multicolored	65	65
293	A29	15c multicolored	80	80
a.		Souvenir sheet of 4, #290-293	4.25	4.25

Tourist publicity.

Holy Family, by Nicolas Poussin — A30

Paintings: 3c, Adoration of the Shepherds, by Louis Le Nain. 12c, Adoration of the Kings, by Gerard David. 15c, Adoration of the Kings, by Vincenzo Foppa.

1969, Oct. 15 Photo. *Perf. 12*

294	A30	3c red & multi	15	15
295	A30	11c emerald & multi	60	60
296	A30	12c ultra & multi	70	70
297	A30	15c multicolored	90	90

Christmas.

Girl Guides, Globe and Flags — A31

Designs: 12c, Yellow elder and Brownie emblem. 15c, Ranger emblem.

1970, Feb. 23 Wmk. 314 *Perf. 14¹/₂*

298	A31	3c vio blue, yel & red	18	18
299	A31	12c dk brn, grn & yel	60	60
300	A31	15c vio bl, bluish grn & yel	80	80

60th anniversary of the Girl Guides.

Opening of UPU Headquarters, Bern — A32

1970, May 20 Litho. *Perf. 14¹/₂*

301	A32	3c ver & multi	15	15
302	A32	15c orange & multi	75	75

Bus and Globe A33

Globe and: 11c, Train. 12c, Sailboat and ship. 15c, Plane.

1970, July 14 *Perf. 13¹/₂x13*

303	A33	3c orange & multi	16	16
304	A33	11c emerald & multi	65	65
305	A33	12c multicolored	70	70
306	A33	15c blue & multi	1.00	1.00
a.		Souvenir sheet of 4, #303-306	8.00	8.00

Issued to promote good will through world-wide travel and tourism.

People, Palms and Flamingo A34

Design: 15c, Red Cross Headquarters, Nassau, and marlin.

1970, Aug. 18 *Perf. 14x14¹/₂*

307	A34	3c multicolored	15	15
308	A34	15c multicolored	80	80

Centenary of British Red Cross Society.

Nativity by G. B. Pittoni — A35

Christmas: 11c, Holy Family, by Anton Raphael Mengs. 12c, Adoration of the Shepherds, by Giorgione. 15c, Adoration of the Shepherds, School of Seville.

Perf. 12¹/₂x13

1970, Nov. 3 Litho. Wmk. 314

309	A35	3c multicolored	16	16
310	A35	11c red org & multi	55	55
311	A35	12c emerald & multi	65	65
312	A35	15c blue & multi	80	80
a.		Souv. sheet of 4, #309-312 + 3 labels	2.25	2.25

International Airport — A36

Designs: 2c, Breadfruit. 3c, Straw market. 4c, 6c, Hawksbill turtle. 5c, Grouper. 8c, Yellow elder. 10c, Bahamian sponge boat. 11c, Flamingos. 7c, 12c, Hibiscus. 15c, Bonefish. 18c, 22c, Royal poinciana. 50c, Post office, Nassau. $1, Pineapple, vert. $2, Crayfish, vert. $3, "Junkanoo" (costumed drummer), vert.

Wmk. 314 Upright (Sideways on $1, $2, $3)

1971 *Perf. 14¹/₂x14, 14x14¹/₂*

313	A36	1c blue & multi	15	15
314	A36	2c red & multi	15	15
315	A36	3c lilac & multi	15	15
316	A36	4c brown & multi	42	42
317	A36	5c dp org & multi	30	28
318	A36	6c brown & multi	15	15
319	A36	7c green & multi	30	28
320	A36	8c yel & multi	65	40
321	A36	10c red & multi	38	38
322	A36	11c red & multi	40	40
323	A36	12c green & multi	1.10	1.10
324	A36	15c gray & multi	32	32
325	A36	18c multicolored	40	40
326	A36	22c green & multi	1.40	1.40
327	A36	50c multicolored	1.65	1.40
328	A36	$1 red & multi	3.50	2.75
329	A36	$2 blue & multi	6.75	5.50
330	A36	$3 vio bl & multi	10.00	8.75
		Nos. 313-330 (18)	28.17	24.38

See Nos. 398-401, 426-443.

Wmk. 314 Sideways (Upright on $1, $2, $3)

1973

317a	A36	5c	16	16
320a	A36	8c	24	24
327a	A36	50c	1.40	1.40
328a	A36	$1	3.00	3.00
329a	A36	$2	5.50	5.50
330a	A36	$3	8.50	8.50
		Nos. 317a-330a (6)	18.80	18.80

1976 Wmk. 373

313a	A36	1c	15	15
314a	A36	2c	15	15
315a	A36	3c	15	15
317b	A36	5c	15	15
320b	A36	8c	15	15
321a	A36	10c	18	18
327b	A36	50c	1.25	1.25
328b	A36	$1	2.50	2.50

329b	A36	$2	4.75	4.75
330b	A36	$3	7.50	7.50
		Nos. 313a-330b (10)	16.93	16.93

Snowflake with Peace Signs — A37

Christmas: 11c, "Peace on Earth" with doves. 15c, Christmas wreath around old Bahamas coat of arms. 18c, Star of Bethlehem over palms.

Perf. 14x14½

1971 Photo. Wmk. 314

331	A37	3c dp lil rose, gold & org	15	15
332	A37	11c violet & gold	45	45
333	A37	15c gold embossed & multi	65	65
334	A37	18c brt bl, gold & vio bl	90	90
a.		Souv. sheet of 4, #331-334, perf. 15	2.50	2.50

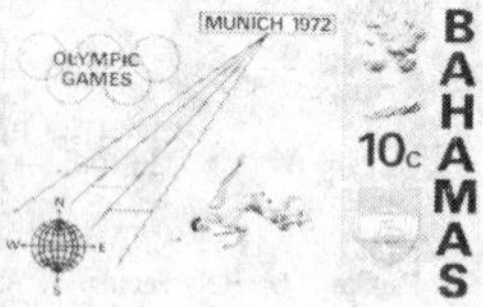

High Jump, Arms of Bahamas A38

Olympic Rings, Compass, Arms of Bahamas and: 11c, Bicycling. 15c, Running. 18c, Sailing.

1972, June 27 Litho. *Perf. 13x13½*

335	A38	10c lt violet & multi	40	40
336	A38	11c ocher & multi	48	48
337	A38	15c yel green & multi	70	70
338	A38	18c blue & multi	95	95
a.		Souvenir sheet of 4, #335-338	3.25	4.50

20th Olympic Games, Munich, Aug. 26-Sept. 10.

Shepherd and Star of Bethlehem — A39

Designs: 6c, Bells. 15c, Holly and monstrance. 20c, Poinsettia.

1972, Oct. 3 Wmk. 314 *Perf. 14*

339	A39	3c gold & multi	15	15
340	A39	6c black & multi	28	28
341	A39	15c black & multi	70	70
342	A39	20c gold & multi	95	95
a.		Souvenir sheet of 4, #339-342	2.75	3.25

Christmas. Gold on 15c is embossed.

Souvenir Sheet

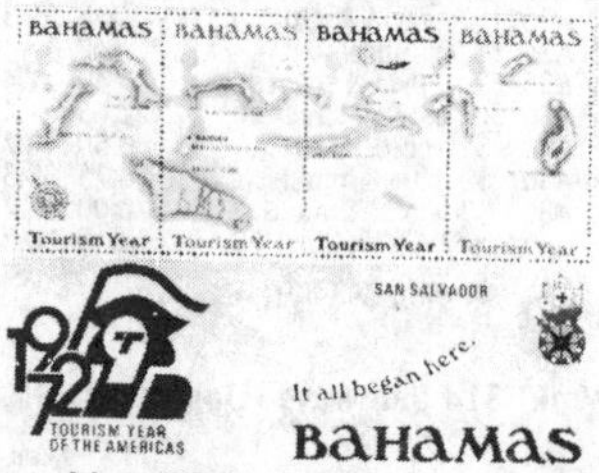

Map of Bahama Islands — A40

1972, Nov. 1 Litho. *Perf. 15*

343	A40	Sheet of 4	3.75	4.75
a.		11c blue & multi	35	35
b.		15c blue & multi	45	45
c.		18c blue & multi	52	52
d.		50c blue & multi	1.50	1.50

Tourism Year of the Americas.

Silver Wedding Issue, 1972

Common Design Type

Design: Queen Elizabeth II, Prince Philip, mace and galleon.

Perf. 14x14½

1972, Nov. 13 Photo. Wmk. 314

344	CD324	11c car rose & multi	35	35
345	CD324	18c violet & multi	55	55

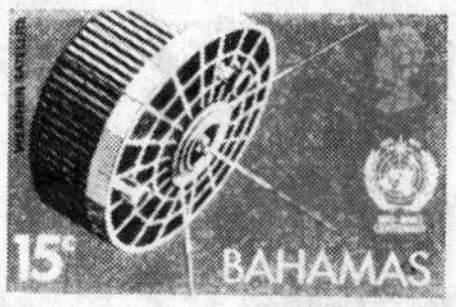

Weather Satellite, WMO Emblem A41

1973, Apr. 3 Litho. *Perf. 14*

346	A41	15c shown	65	65
347	A41	18c Weather radar	90	90

Intl. meteorological cooperation, cent.

Clarence A. Bain — A42

Virgin in Prayer, by Sassoferrato — A43

Independence: 11c, New Bahamian coat of arms. 15c, New flag and Government House. $1, Milo B. Butler, Sr.

1973 Wmk. 314 *Perf. 14½x14*

348	A42	3c lilac & multi	15	15
349	A42	11c lt blue & multi	30	30
350	A42	15c lt green & multi	45	45
351	A42	$1 yel & multi	2.25	2.25
a.		Souvenir sheet of 4, #348-351	3.50	4.50

Issue dates: Nos. 348-350, July 10, Nos. 351, 351a, Aug. 1.

1973, Oct. 16 Litho. *Perf. 14*

Christmas: 11c, Virgin and Child with St. John, by Filippino Lippi. 15c, Choir of Angels, by Marmion. 18c, The Two Trinities, by Murillo.

352	A43	3c blue & multi	18	18
353	A43	11c multicolored	60	60
354	A43	15c gray grn & multi	80	80
355	A43	18c lil rose & multi	1.10	1.10
a.		Souvenir sheet of 4, #352-355	2.75	3.75

Agriculture, Science and Medicine — A44

Design: 18c, Symbols of engineering, art, and law.

1974, Feb. 5 Litho. *Perf. 13½x14*

356	A44	15c dull grn & multi	48	48
357	A44	18 multicolored	65	65

University of the West Indies, 25th anniv.

UPU Emblem A45

Designs: 13c, UPU emblem, vert. 14c, UPU emblem. 18c, UPU monument, Bern, vert.

1974, Apr. 23 *Perf. 14*

358	A45	3c multicolored	15	15
359	A45	13c multicolored	45	45
360	A45	14c olive bis & multi	52	52
361	A45	18c multicolored	80	80
a.		Souvenir sheet of 4, #358-361	1.90	2.25

Centenary of Universal Postal Union.

Roseate Spoonbills, Trust Emblem — A46

Protected Birds (National Trust Emblem and): 14c, White-crowned pigeons. 21c, White-tailed tropic birds. 36c, Bahamian parrot.

1974, Sept. 10 Litho. *Perf. 14*

362	A46	13c multicolored	95	70
363	A46	14c multicolored	95	70
364	A46	21c multicolored	1.40	1.10
365	A46	36c multicolored	2.50	1.75
a.		Souvenir sheet of 4, #362-365	7.50	8.50

Bahamas National Trust, 15th anniv.

Holy Family, by Jacques de Stella A47

Christmas: 10c, Virgin and Child, by Girolamo Romanino. 12c, Virgin and Child with St. John and St. Catherine, by Andrea Previtali. 21c, Virgin and Child with Angels, by Previtali.

1974, Oct. 29 Wmk. 314 *Perf. 13*

366	A47	8c black & multi	40	40
367	A47	10c green & multi	48	48
368	A47	12c red & multi	60	60
369	A47	21c ultra & multi	1.00	1.00
a.		Souvenir sheet of 4, #366-369	2.50	2.50

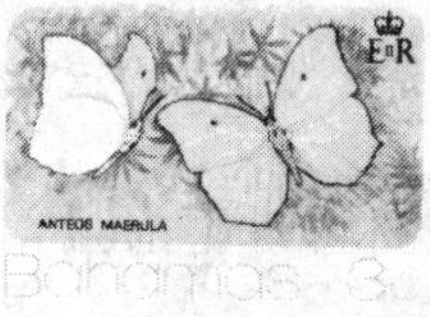

Anteos Maerula A48

1975, Feb. 4 Litho. *Perf. 14x13½*

370	A48	3c shown	28	24
371	A48	14c Eurema nicippe	1.00	70
372	A48	18c Papilio andraemon	1.25	1.00
373	A48	21c Euptoieta hegesia	1.50	1.40
a.		Souvenir sheet of 4, #370-373	6.00	5.00

Sheep Raising A49

Designs: 14c, Electric reel fishing, vert. 18c, Growing food. 21c, Crude oil refinery, vert.

1975, May 27 Litho. *Perf. 14*

374	A49	3c dull grn & multi	15	15
375	A49	14c green & multi	50	50
376	A49	18c brown & multi	65	65
377	A49	21c vio bl & multi	75	75
a.		Souvenir sheet of 4, #374-377	2.25	2.25

Economic diversification.

Rowena Rand, Staff and Chrismon — A50

Plant and IWY Emblem — A51

1975, July 22 Litho. *Perf. 14*

378	A50	14c multicolored	60	60
379	A51	18c multicolored	80	80

International Women's Year.

Adoration of the Shepherds, by Perugino — A52

Christmas: 8c, 18c, Adoration of the Kings, by Ghirlandaio. 21c, like 3c.

1975, Dec. 2 Litho. *Perf. 13½*

380	A52	3c dk green & multi	15	15
381	A52	8c dk violet & multi	30	30
382	A52	18c purple & multi	70	70
383	A52	21c maroon & multi	85	85
a.		Souvenir sheet of 4, #380-383	2.25	2.25

Telephones, 1876 and 1976 — A53

Designs: 16c, Radio-telephone link, Deleporte, Nassau (radar). 21c, Alexander Graham Bell. 25c, Communications satellite.

1976, Mar. 23 Litho. *Perf. 14*

384	A53	3c multicolored	15	15
385	A53	16c multicolored	40	40
386	A53	21c multicolored	52	52
387	A53	25c multicolored	65	65

Centenary of first telephone call by Alexander Graham Bell, Mar. 10, 1876.

Bicycling and Olympic Rings — A54

Olympic Rings and: 16c, Long jump. 25c, Sailing. 40c, Boxing.

1976, July 13 Litho. *Perf. 14*

388	A54	8c magenta & blue	24	24
389	A54	16c orange & brn	42	42
390	A54	25c magenta & blue	60	60
391	A54	40c orange & brn	1.10	1.10
a.		Souvenir sheet of 4, #388-391	2.75	2.75

21st Olympic Games, Montreal, Canada, July 17-Aug. 1.

John Murray, Earl of Dunmore A55

Design: 16c, Map of US and Bahamas.

1976, June 1 Wmk. 373 *Perf. 14*

392 A55 16c multicolored	52	52
393 A55 $1 multicolored	2.50	2.50
a. Souvenir sheet of 4, #393	10.00	10.00

American Bicentennial.

Virgin and Child, Filippo Lippi — A56

Christmas: 21c, Adoration of the Shepherds, School of Seville. 25c, Adoration of the Kings, by Vincenzo Foppa. 40c, Virgin and Child, by Vivarini.

1976, Oct. 19 Litho. *Perf. 14½x14*

394 A56 3c brt blue & multi	15	15
395 A56 21c dp org & multi	60	60
396 A56 25c emerald & multi	75	75
397 A56 40c red lilac & multi	1.10	1.10
a. Souvenir sheet of 4, #394-397	2.75	2.75

Type of 1971

Designs: 16c, Hibiscus. 21c, Breadfruit. 25c, Hawksbill turtle. 40c, Bahamian sponge boat.

1976, Nov. 2 Litho. Wmk. 373

398 A36 16c emerald & multi	35	35
399 A36 21c vermilion & multi	38	38
400 A36 25c brown & multi	52	52
401 A36 40c vermilion & multi	70	70

Elizabeth II Seated under Gold Canopy — A57

Designs: 16c, Coronation. 21c, Taking and signing of oath. 40c, Queen holding orb and scepter.

1977, Feb. 7 *Perf. 12*

402 A57 8c silver & multi	20	20
403 A57 16c silver & multi	35	35
404 A57 21c silver & multi	48	48
405 A57 40c silver & multi	1.00	1.00
a. Souvenir sheet of 4, #402-405	3.00	3.50

Reign of Queen Elizabeth II, 25th anniv.

Featherduster — A58

Marine Life: 8c, Porkfish. 16c, Elkhorn coral. 21c, Soft coral and sponge.

1977, May 24 Litho. *Perf. 13½*

406 A58 3c multicolored	18	18
407 A58 8c multicolored	32	32
408 A58 16c multicolored	80	80
409 A58 21c multicolored	1.00	1.00
a. Souvenir sheet of 4, #406-409, perf. 14½	2.50	3.00

Campfire and Shower A59

1977, Sept. 27 Litho. Wmk. 373

410 A59 16c shown	42	42
411 A59 21c Boating	52	52

6th Caribbean Jamboree, Kingston, Jamaica, Aug. 5-14.

Nos. 402-405a Overprinted: "Royal Visit / October 1977"

1977, Oct. 19 Litho. *Perf. 12*

412 A57 8c silver & multi	16	16
413 A57 16c silver & multi	32	32
414 A57 21c silver & multi	38	38
415 A57 40c silver & multi	80	80
a. Souvenir sheet of 4	2.25	2.75

Caribbean visit of Queen Elizabeth II, Oct. 19-20.

Virgin and Child — A60

Nassau Public Library — A61

Crèche Figurines: 16c, Three Kings. 21c, Adoration of the Kings. 25c, Three Kings.

1977, Oct. 25 Litho. *Perf. 13½*

416 A60 3c gold & multi	15	15
417 A60 16c gold & multi	38	38
418 A60 21c gold & multi	48	48
419 A60 25c gold & multi	60	60
a. Souvenir sheet of 4, #416-419, perf. 14½	1.90	1.90

Christmas.

1978, Mar. 28 Litho. *Perf. 14½x14*

Architectural Heritage: 8c, St. Matthew's Church. 16c, Government House. 18c, The Hermitage, Cat Island.

420 A61 3c black & yel green	15	15
421 A61 8c black & lt blue	18	18
422 A61 16c black & lilac rose	32	32
423 A61 18c black & salmon	35	35
a. Souvenir sheet of 4, #420-423	1.10	1.10

Scepter, St. Edward's Crown, Orb — A62

Perf. 14x13½

1978, June 27 Litho. Wmk. 373

424 A62 16c shown	28	28
425 A62 $1 Elizabeth II	1.65	1.65
a. Souvenir sheet of 2, #424-425	2.25	2.25

Coronation of Queen Elizabeth II, 25th anniv.

Type of 1971

Designs as before and: 16c, Hibiscus. 25c, Hawksbill turtle.

Perf. 14½x14, 14x14½

1978, June Unwmk.

426 A36 1c blue & multi	15	15
430 A36 5c dp org & multi	15	15
436 A36 16c brt grn & multi	38	38
439 A36 25c brown & multi	60	60
440 A36 50c lemon & multi	1.10	1.10
441 A36 $1 lemon & multi	2.50	2.50
442 A36 $2 blue & multi	4.75	4.75
443 A36 $3 vio bl & multi	7.25	7.25
Nos. 426-443 (8)	16.88	16.88

Angels and Palms — A63

Christmas: 5c, Coat of arms within wreath, and sailing ships.

Perf. 14x14½

1978, Nov. 14 Litho. Wmk. 373

444 A63 5c car, pink & gold	15	15
445 A63 21c ultra, dk bl & gold	32	32
a. Souvenir sheet of 2, #444-445	*2.50*	*2.50*

Baby Walking, IYC Emblem — A64

IYC Emblem and: 16c, Children playing leapfrog. 21c, Girl skipping rope. 25c, Building blocks with "IYC" and emblem.

Perf. 13½x13

1979, May 15 Litho. Wmk. 373

446 A64 5c multicolored	15	15
447 A64 16c multicolored	25	25
448 A64 21c multicolored	35	35
449 A64 25c multicolored	40	40
a. Souvenir sheet of 4, #446-449, perf. 14	1.10	1.10

International Year of the Child.

Rowland Hill and Penny Black — A65

Designs: 21c, Stamp printing press, 1840, and Bahamas No. 7. 25c, Great Britain No. 27 with 1850's Nassau cancellation, and Great Britain No. 29. 40c, Early mailboat and Bahamas No. 1.

1979, Aug. 14 *Perf. 13½x14*

450 A65 10c multicolored	16	16
451 A65 21c multicolored	35	35
452 A65 25c multicolored	40	40
453 A65 40c multicolored	65	65
a. Souvenir sheet of 4, #450-453	1.65	1.65

Sir Rowland Hill (1795-1879), originator of penny postage.

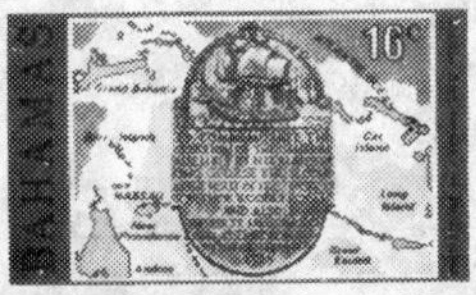

Commonwealth Plaque over Map of Bahamas — A66

Designs: 21c, Parliament buildings. 25c, Legislative chamber. $1, Senate chamber.

1979, Sept. 27 Litho. *Perf. 13½*

454 A66 16c multicolored	25	25
455 A66 21c multicolored	35	35
456 A66 25c multicolored	40	40
457 A66 $1 multicolored	1.65	1.65
a. Souvenir sheet of 4, #454-457	2.75	2.75

Parliament of Bahamas, 250th anniv.

Headdress — A67

Christmas: Goombay Carnival costumes.

1979, Nov. 6 Litho. *Perf. 13*

458 A67 5c multicolored	15	15
459 A67 10c multicolored	15	15
460 A67 16c multicolored	22	22
461 A67 21c multicolored	32	32
462 A67 25c multicolored	38	38
463 A67 40c multicolored	60	60
a. Souvenir sheet of 6	1.90	1.90
Nos. 458-463 (6)	1.82	1.82

No. 463a contains Nos. 458-463, perf. 13½.

Columbus' Landing, 1492 — A68

1980, July 9 Litho. *Perf. 15*

464 A68 1c shown	15	15
465 A68 3c Blackbeard	15	15
466 A68 5c Articles, 1647, Eleuthera map	15	15
467 A68 10c Ceremonial mace	20	20
468 A68 12c Col. Andrew Deveaux	24	24
469 A68 15c Slave trading, Vendue House	28	28
470 A68 16c Shipwreck salvage, 19th cent.	30	30
471 A68 18c Blockade runner, 1860s	32	32
472 A68 21c Bootlegging, 1919-1929	40	40
473 A68 25c Pineapple cultivation	24	24
474 A68 40c Sponge clipping	75	75
475 A68 50c Victoria & Colonial Hotels	1.00	1.00
476 A68 $1 Modern agriculture	2.00	2.00
477 A68 $2 Ship, jet	3.70	3.70
478 A68 $3 Central Bank, Arms	5.75	5.75
479 A68 $5 Prince Charles, Prime Minister Pindling	9.50	9.50
Nos. 464-479 (16)	25.13	25.13

For overprints and surcharges see Nos. 496-499, 532-535.

1985, Nov. 6 Wmk. 384

464a A68 1c	15	15
465a A68 3c	15	15
467a A68 10c	20	20
473a A68 25c	48	48

Virgin and Child, Straw Figures — A69

1980, Oct. 28 Litho. *Perf. 14½*

480 A69 5c shown	15	15
481 A69 21c Three kings	35	35
482 A69 25c Angel	40	40
483 A69 $1 Christmas tree	1.65	1.65
a. Souvenir sheet of 4, #480-483	2.50	2.50

Christmas.

Man with Crutch, Sun Rays A70

1981, Feb. 10 Litho. *Perf. 14½*

484 A70 5c shown 15 15
485 A70 $1 Man in wheelchair 1.65 1.65
a. Souvenir sheet of 2, #484-485 1.75 1.75

International Year of the Disabled.

Grand Bahama Tracking Station A71

Satellite Views: 20c, Bahamas, vert. 25c, Eleuthera. 50c, Andros and New Providence, vert.

Perf. 13½
1981, Apr. 21 Litho. Wmk. 373

486 A71 10c multi 18 18
487 A71 20c multi 35 35
488 A71 25c multi 45 45
489 A71 50c multi 90 90
a. Souvenir sheet of 4, #486-489 2.00 2.75

Prince Charles and Lady Diana — A72

Perf. 14½
1981, July 22 Litho. Wmk. 373

490 A72 30c shown 52 52
491 A72 $2 Charles, Prime Minister 3.50 3.50
a. Souvenir sheet of 2, #490-491 5.00 5.75

Royal wedding.

Bahama Ducks — A73

Wmk. 373
1981, Aug. 25 Litho. *Perf. 14*

492 A73 5c shown 15 15
493 A73 20c Reddish egrets 50 50
494 A73 25c Brown boobies 65 65
495 A73 $1 West Indian tree ducks 2.50 2.50
a. Souvenir sheet of 4, #492-495 4.00 4.00

See Nos. 514-517.

Nos. 466-467, 473, 475 Overprinted: "COMMONWEALTH FINANCE MINISTERS' MEETING 21-23 SEPTEMBER 1981"

1981, Sept. Litho. *Perf. 15*

496 A68 5c multicolored 15 15
497 A68 10c multicolored 16 16
498 A68 25c multicolored 42 42
499 A68 50c multicolored 85 85

World Food Day — A74

Perf. 13x13½
1981, Oct. 16 Wmk. 373

500 A74 5c Chickens 18 18
501 A74 20c Sheep 40 40
502 A74 30c Lobster 60 60
503 A74 50c Pigs 1.00 1.00
a. Souvenir sheet of 4, #500-503 2.25 2.75

Bahamas stamps can be mounted in the Scott British North and West Caribbean album.

Christmas — A75

Wmk. 373
1981, Nov. 23 Litho. *Perf. 14*

504 Sheet of 9 4.25 4.25
a. A75 5c Father Christmas 15 15
b. A75 5c shown 15 15
c. A75 5c St. Nicholas, Holland 15 15
d. A75 25c Lussibruden, Sweden 35 35
e. A75 25c Mother and child 35 35
f. A75 25c King Wenceslas, Czechoslovakia 35 35
g. A75 30c Mother and child 42 42
h. A75 30c Mother and child standing 42 42
i. A75 $1 Christkindl angel, Germany 1.50 1.50

TB Bacillus Centenary A76

1982, Feb. 3 Litho. *Perf. 14*

505 A76 5c Koch 15 15
506 A76 16c X-ray 30 30
507 A76 21c Microscopes 42 42
508 A76 $1 Mantoux test 1.90 1.90
a. Souvenir sheet of 4, #505-508, perf. 14½ 3.50 4.00

Flamingoes — A77

Designs: a, Females. b, Males. c, Nesting. d, Juvenile birds. e, Immature birds. No. 509 in continuous design.

Wmk. 373
1982, Apr. 28 Litho. *Perf. 14*

509 Strip of 5, multicolored 4.00 4.00
a.-e. A77 25c any single 80 80

Princess Diana Issue
Common Design Type

1982, July 1 Litho. *Perf. 14*

510 CD333 16c Arms 25 25
511 CD333 25c Diana 38 38
512 CD333 40c Wedding 60 60
513 CD333 $1 Portrait 1.50 1.50

Bird Type of 1981
Wmk. 373
1982, Aug. 18 Litho. *Perf. 14*

514 A73 10c Bat 18 18
515 A73 16c Hutia 28 28
516 A73 21c Racoon 35 35
517 A73 $1 Dolphins 1.75 1.75
a. Souvenir sheet of 4, #514-517 3.25 3.25

28th Commonwealth Parliamentary Conference — A78

Perf. 14x13½
1982, Oct. 16 Litho. Wmk. 373

518 A78 5c Plaque 15 15
519 A78 25c Assoc. arms 50 50
520 A78 40c Natl. arms 80 80
521 A78 50c House of Assembly 1.00 1.00

Christmas A79

Designs: 5c, Wesley Methodist Church, Baillou Hill Road. 12c, Centerville Seventh Day Adventist Church. 15c, Church of God of Prophecy, East Street. 21c, Bethel Baptist Church, Meeting Street. 25c, St. Francis Xavier Catholic Church, West Hill Street. $1, Holy Cross Anglican Church, Highbury Park.

1982, Nov. 3 *Perf. 14*

522 A79 5c multicolored 15 15
523 A79 12c multicolored 24 24
524 A79 15c multicolored 28 28
525 A79 21c multicolored 40 40
526 A79 25c multicolored 48 48
527 A79 $1 multicolored 1.90 1.90
Nos. 522-527 (6) 3.45 3.45

CD334

1983, Mar. 14 Litho.

528 CD334 5c Lynden O. Pindling 15 15
529 CD334 25c Flags 40 40
530 CD334 35c Map 55 55
531 CD334 $1 Ocean liner 1.65 1.65

Commonwealth Day.

Nos. 469-472 Surcharged

1983, Apr. 5 Litho. *Perf. 15*

532 A68 20c on 15c multi 35 35
533 A68 31c on 21c multi 55 55
534 A68 35c on 16c multi 65 65
535 A68 80c on 18c multi 1.50 1.50

30th Anniv. of Customs Cooperation Council A81

10th Anniv. of Independence A82

Perf. 14x13½
1983, May 31 Wmk. 373

536 A81 31c Officers, ship 52 52
537 A81 $1 Officers, jet 1.65 1.65

1983, July 6 Litho. *Perf. 14*

538 A82 $1 Flag raising 1.50 1.50
a. Souvenir sheet, perf. 12 1.50 1.50

Local Butterflies A83

1983, Aug. 24 *Perf. 14½x14*

539 A83 5c Carters skipper 18 18
540 A83 25c Giant southern white 90 90
541 A83 31c Large orange sulphur 1.10 1.10
542 A83 50c Flambeau 1.75 1.75
a. Souvenir sheet of 4 4.25 4.25

No. 542a contains Nos. 539-542, perf. 14 and perf. 14½x14.

American Loyalists Arrival Bicentenary A84

Paintings by Alton Lowe.

1983, Sept. 28 *Perf. 14*

543 A84 5c Loyalist Dreams 15 15
544 A84 31c New Plymouth, Abaco 55 55
545 A84 35c New Plymouth Hotel 60 60
546 A84 50c Island Hope 90 90
a. Souvenir sheet of 4, #543-546 2.25 2.25

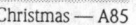

Christmas — A85

125th Anniv. of Bahamas Stamps — A86

Children's designs: 5c, Christmas Bells, by Monica Pinder. 20c, The Flamingo by Cory Bullard. 25c, The Yellow Hibiscus with Christmas Candle by Monique A. Bailey. 31c, Santa goes a Sailing by Sabrina Seiler, horiz. 35c, Silhouette scene with palm trees by James Blake. 50c, Silhouette scene with Pelicans, by Erik Russell, horiz.

1983, Nov. 1 *Perf. 14*

547 A85 5c multicolored 15 15
548 A85 20c multicolored 32 32
549 A85 25c multicolored 42 42
550 A85 31c multicolored 50 50
551 A85 35c multicolored 60 60
552 A85 50c multicolored 80 80
Nos. 547-552 (6) 2.79 2.79

1984, Feb. 22 Litho. *Perf. 14*

553 A86 5c No. 3 15 15
554 A86 $1 No. 1 1.65 1.65

Lloyd's List Issue
Common Design Type
Perf. 14½
1984, Apr. 25 Litho. Wmk. 373

555 CD335 5c Trent 15 15
556 CD335 31c Orinoco 55 55
557 CD335 35c Nassau Harbor 60 60
558 CD335 50c Container ship Oropesa 85 85

1984 Summer Olympics A87

1984, June 20 Litho. *Perf. 14x14½*

559 A87 5c Running 15 15
560 A87 25c Discus 42 42
561 A87 31c Boxing 52 52
562 A87 $1 Basketball 1.65 1.65
a. Souvenir sheet of 4, #559-562 2.75 2.75

Flags of Bahamas and Caribbean Community — A88

Wmk. 373

1984, July 4 Litho. *Perf. 14*

563 A88 50c multicolored		90	90

Conference of Heads of Government of Caribbean Community, 5th Meeting.

Allen's Cay Iguana — A89

1984, Aug. 15 *Perf. 14*

564 A89 5c shown	15	15
565 A89 25c Curly-tailed lizard	60	60
566 A89 35c Greenhouse frog	80	80
567 A89 50c Atlantic green turtle	1.00	1.00
a. Souvenir sheet of 4, #564-567	3.00	3.00

25th Anniv. of Natl. Trust — A90

Christmas — A91

Wildlife: a, Calliphlox evelynae. b, Megaceryle alcyon, Eleutherodactylus planirostris. c, Phoenicopterus ruber, Himantopus himantopus, Phoebus sennae. d, Urbanus proteus, Chelonia mydas. e, Pandion haliaetus. Continuous design.

1984, Aug. 15 Litho. *Perf. 14*

568 Strip of 5	4.75	4.75
a.-e. A90 31c any single	95	95

1984, Nov. 7 Litho. *Perf. 13½x13*

Madonna and Child Paintings.

569 A91 5c Titian	15	15
570 A91 31c Anais Colin	55	55
571 A91 35c Elena Caula	60	60
a. Souvenir sheet of 3, #569-571	1.40	1.40

Girl Guides, 75th Anniv., Intl. Youth Year — A92

1985, Feb. 22 Litho. *Perf. 14*

572 A92 5c Brownies	15	15
573 A92 25c Camping	40	40
574 A92 31c Girl Guides	50	50
575 A92 35c Rangers	55	55
a. Souvenir sheet of 4, #572-575	1.65	1.65

Audubon Birth Bicentenary A93

Wmk. 373

1985, Apr. 24 Litho. *Perf. 14*

576 A93 5c Killdeer	15	15
577 A93 31c Mourning dove, vert.	65	65
578 A93 35c Mourning doves, diff., vert.	70	70
579 A93 $1 Killdeers, diff.	2.00	2.00

Queen Mother 85th Birthday

Common Design Type

Perf. 14½x14

1985, June 7 Litho. Wmk. 384

580 CD336 5c Portrait, 1927	15	15
581 CD336 25c At christening of Peter Phillips	42	42
582 CD336 35c Portrait, 1985	60	60
583 CD336 50c Holding Prince Henry	85	85

Souvenir Sheet

584 CD336 $1.25 In a pony and trap	2.00	2.00

UN and UN Food and Agriculture Org., 40th Annivs. A94

Wmk. 373

1985, Aug. 26 Litho. *Perf. 14*

585 A94 25c Wheat, emblems	42	42

Commonwealth Heads of Government Meeting, 1985 — A95

1985, Oct. 16 Wmk. 373 *Perf. 14½*

586 A95 31c Queen Elizabeth II	48	48
587 A95 35c Flag, Commonwealth emblem	55	55

Christmas A96

Paintings by Alton Roland Lowe: 5c, Grandma's Christmas Bouquet. 25c, Junkanoo Romeo and Juliet, vert. 31c, Bunce Girl, vert. 35c, Home for Christmas.

1985, Nov. 5 *Perf. 13*

588 A96 5c multicolored	15	15
589 A96 25c multicolored	48	48
590 A96 31c multicolored	62	62
591 A96 35c multicolored	65	65
a. Souvenir sheet of 4, #588-591, perf. 14	1.90	1.90

Queen Elizabeth II 60th Birthday

Common Design Type

Designs: 10c, Age 1, 1927. 25c, Coronation, Westminster Abbey, 1953. 35c, Giving speech, royal visit, Bahamas. 40c, At Djakova, Yugoslavia, state visit, 1972. $1, Visiting Crown Agents, 1983.

1986, Apr. 21 Wmk. 384 *Perf. 14½*

592 CD337 10c scar, blk & sil	16	16
593 CD337 25c ultra & multi	40	40
594 CD337 35c green & multi	55	55
595 CD337 40c violet & multi	65	65
596 CD337 $1 rose vio & multi	1.65	1.65
Nos. 592-596 (5)	3.41	3.41

AMERIPEX '86 — A97

1986, May 19 *Perf. 14*

597 A97 5c Nos. 464, 471	15	15
598 A97 25c Nos. 288-289	45	45
599 A97 31c No. 392	55	55
600 A97 50c No. 489a	90	90
601 A97 $1 Statue of Liberty, vert.	1.75	1.75
a. Souvenir sheet of one	1.75	1.75
Nos. 597-601 (5)	3.80	3.80

Statue of Liberty, cent.

Royal Wedding Issue, 1986

Common Design Type

Designs: 10c, Formal engagement. $1, Andrew in dress uniform.

1986, July 23 *Perf. 14½x14*

602 CD338 10c multicolored	16	16
603 CD338 $1 multicolored	1.65	1.65

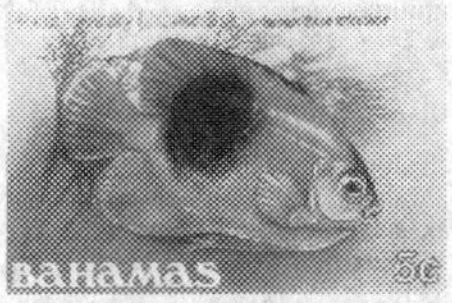

Fish — A98

1986-87 Wmk. 384 *Perf. 14*

604 A98 5c Rock beauty	15	15
605 A98 10c Stoplight parrotfish	15	15
606 A98 15c Jacknife fish	22	22
607 A98 20c Flamefish	28	28
608 A98 25c Swissguard basslet	35	35
609 A98 30c Spotfin butterflyfish	42	42
610 A98 35c Queen triggerfish	52	52
611 A98 40c Four-eyed butterflyfish	55	55
612 A98 45c Fairy basslet	65	65
613 A98 50c Queen angelfish	70	70
614 A98 60c Blue chromis	85	85
615 A98 $1 Spanish hogfish	1.40	1.40
616 A98 $2 Harlequin bass	2.75	2.75
617 A98 $3 Blackbar soldierfish	4.50	4.50
618 A98 $5 Pygmy angelfish	7.25	7.25
618A A99 $10 Red hind ('87)	16.00	16.00
Nos. 604-618A (16)	36.74	36.74

No. 604 exists inscribed "1989," Nos. 605, 608, 611-613, 615, 617-618 "1990."

Issue dates: $10, Jan. 2, others, Aug. 5.

1987, June 25 Wmk. 373

604a 5c	15	15
605a 10c	15	15
606a 15c	22	22
611a 40c	55	55
612a 45c	65	65
613a 50c	70	70
614a 60c	85	85
615a $1	1.40	1.40
616a $2	2.75	2.75
Nos. 604a-616a (9)	7.42	7.42

Nos. 604a-616a dated 1987.

Christ Church Cathedral — A99

Perf. 14½

1986, Sept. 16 Litho. Wmk. 373

619 A99 10c View, 19th cent.	16	16
620 A99 40c View, 1986	65	65
a. Souvenir sheet of 2, #619-620	85	85

City of Nassau, Diocese of Nassau and the Bahamas and Christ Church, 125th anniv.

Christmas, Intl. Peace Year — A100

Wmk. 384

1986, Nov. 4 Litho. *Perf. 14*

621 A100 10c Nativity	16	16
622 A100 40c Flight to Egypt	65	65
623 A100 45c Children praying	75	75
624 A100 50c Exchanging gifts	80	80
a. Souvenir sheet of 4, #621-624	2.50	2.50

Pirates of the Caribbean — A101

Map of the Bahamas — A102

Perf. 14½

1987, June 2 Litho. Wmk. 373

625 A101 10c Anne Bonney	22	22
626 A101 40c Blackbeard (d. 1718)	90	90
627 A101 45c Capt. Edward England	1.00	1.00
628 A101 50c Capt. Woodes Rogers (c. 1679-1732)	1.25	1.25

Souvenir Sheet

629 A102 $1.25 shown	2.75	2.75

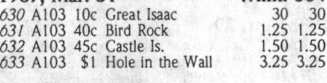

Paintings of Lighthouses by Alton Roland Lowe — A103

1987, Mar. 31 Wmk. 384

630 A103 10c Great Isaac	30	30
631 A103 40c Bird Rock	1.25	1.25
632 A103 45c Castle Is.	1.50	1.50
633 A103 $1 Hole in the Wall	3.25	3.25

Tourist Transportation A104

Ships: No. 634a, Cruise ship, sailboat. b, Cruise ships, tugboat, speedboat. c, Pleasure boat leaving harbor, sailboat. d, Pleasure boat docked, sailboats. e, Sailboats.

Aircraft: No. 635a, Bahamasair plane. b, Bahamasair and Pan Am aircraft. c, Aircraft, radar tower. d, Control tower, aircraft. e, Helicopter, planes.

1987, Aug. 26 Wmk. 373 *Perf. 14*

634 Strip of 5	3.75	3.75
a.-e. A104 40c any single	75	75
635 Strip of 5	3.75	3.75
a.-e. A104 40c any single	75	75

Orchids Painted by Alton Roland Lowe — A105

1987, Oct. 20 Wmk. 384 *Perf. 14½*

636 A105 10c Cattleyopis lindenii	16	16
637 A105 40c Encyclia lucayana	65	65
638 A105 45c Encyclia hodgeana	75	75
639 A105 50c Encyclia lleidae	80	80
a. Souvenir sheet of 4, #636-639	2.50	2.50

Christmas.

Discovery of America, 500th Anniv. (in 1992) — A106

Designs: 10c, Ferdinand and Isabella. 40c, Columbus before the Talavera Committee. 45c, Lucayan village. 50c, Lucayan potters. $1.50, Map, c. 1500.

Perf. 14x14½

1988, Feb. 23 Litho. Wmk. 373

640 A106 10c multicolored 16 16
641 A106 40c multicolored 65 65
642 A106 45c multicolored 75 75
643 A106 50c multicolored 80 80

Souvenir Sheet

644 A106 $1.50 multicolored 3.00 3.00

See Nos. 663-667, 725-729, 749-753, 762.

World Wildlife Fund — A107

Whistling ducks, Dendrocygna arborea.

1988, Apr. 29 *Perf. 14½*

645 A107 5c Ducks in flight 18 15
646 A107 10c Among marine plants 16 16
647 A107 20c Adults, ducklings 32 32
648 A107 45c Wading 75 75

Abolition of Slavery, 150th Anniv. A108

1988, Aug. 9 *Perf. 14*

649 A108 10c African hut 20 20
650 A108 40c Basket weavers in hut, Grantstown 80 80

1988 Summer Olympics, Seoul A109

Games emblem and details of painting by James Martin: 10c, Olympic flame, high jump, hammer throw, basketball and gymnastics. 40c, Swimming, boxing, weight lifting, fencing and running. 45c, Gymnastics, shot put and javelin. $1, Running, cycling and gymnastics.

Wmk. 384

1988, Aug. 30 Litho. *Perf. 14*

651 A109 10c multicolored 20 20
652 A109 40c multicolored 80 80
653 A109 45c multicolored 90 90
654 A109 $1 multicolored 2.00 2.00
a. Souvenir sheet of 4, #651-654 4.00 4.00

Lloyds of London, 300th Anniv.

Common Design Type

Designs: 10c, Lloyds List No. 560, 1740. 40c, Freeport Harbor, horiz. 45c, Space shuttle over the Bahamas, horiz. $1, Supply ship Yarmouth Castle on fire.

1988, Oct. 4 Wmk. 373

655 CD341 10c multicolored 20 20
656 CD341 40c multicolored 80 80
657 CD341 45c multicolored 90 90
658 CD341 $1 multicolored 2.00 2.00

Christmas Carols — A110

Designs: 10c, O' Little Town of Bethlehem. 40c, Little Donkey. 45c, Silent Night. 50c, Hark! The Herald Angels Sing.

1988, Nov. 21 Wmk. 384 *Perf. 14½*

659 A110 10c multicolored 20 20
660 A110 40c multicolored 80 80
661 A110 45c multicolored 90 90
662 A110 50c multicolored 1.00 1.00
a. Souvenir sheet of 4, #659-662 2.90 2.90

Discovery of America Type of 1988

Design: 10c, Columbus as chartmaker. 40c, Development of the caravel. 45c, Navigational tools. 50c, Arawak artifacts. $1.50, Caravel under construction, an illumination from the Nuremburg Chronicles, 15th cent.

Perf. 14½x14

1989, Jan. 25 Litho. Wmk. 373

663 A106 10c multicolored 20 20
664 A106 40c multicolored 80 80
665 A106 45c multicolored 90 90
666 A106 50c multicolored 1.00 1.00

Souvenir Sheet

667 A106 $1.50 multicolored 3.00 3.00

Hummingbirds A111

Perf. 14½

1989, Mar. 29 Litho. Wmk. 384

668 A111 10c Cuban emerald 20 20
669 A111 40c Ruby-throated 80 80
670 A111 45c Bahama woodstar 90 90
671 A111 50c Rufous 1.00 1.00

Intl. Red Cross and Red Crescent Organizations, 125th Annivs. A112

1989, May 31 *Perf. 14x14½*

672 A112 10c Water safety 20 20
673 A112 $1 Dunant, Battle of Solferino 2.00 2.00

Moon Landing, 20th Anniv.

Common Design Type

Apollo 8: 10c, Apollo Communications System, Grand Bahama Is. 40c, James Lovell Jr., William Anders and Frank Borman. 45c, Mission emblem. $1, The Rising Earth (photograph). $2, Astronaut practicing lunar surface activities at Manned Spacecraft Center, Houston, in training for Apollo 11 mission.

1989, July 20 *Perf. 14x13½*

Size of Nos. 674-675: 29x29mm

674 CD342 10c multicolored 20 20
675 CD342 40c multicolored 80 80
676 CD342 45c multicolored 90 90
677 CD342 $1 multicolored 2.00 2.00

Souvenir Sheet

678 CD342 $2 multicolored 4.00 4.00

Christmas — A113

Designs: 10c, Church of the Nativity, Bethlehem. 40c, Basilica of the Annunciation, Nazareth. 45c, By the Sea of Galilee, Tabgha. $1, Church of the Holy Sepulcher, Jerusalem.

Perf. 14½x14

1989, Oct. 16 Wmk. 373

679 A113 10c multicolored 20 20
680 A113 40c multicolored 80 80
681 A113 45c multicolored 90 90
682 A113 $1 multicolored 2.00 2.00
a. Souvenir sheet of 4, #679-682 4.00 4.00

World Stamp Expo '89 A114

Expo emblem and: 10c, Earth, #359. 40c, UPU Headquarters, #301. 45c, US Capitol, #601. $1, Passenger jet, #150. $2, Washington, DC, on map.

1989, Nov. 17 Wmk. 384 *Perf. 14*

683 A114 10c multicolored 20 20
684 A114 40c multicolored 80 80
685 A114 45c multicolored 90 90
686 A114 $1 multicolored 2.00 2.00

Souvenir Sheet

Perf. 14½x14

687 A114 $2 multicolored 4.00 4.00

No. 687 contains one 31x38mm stamp.

Discovery of America Type of 1988

Designs: 10c, Caravel launch. 40c, Provisioning ships. 45c, Shortening sails. 50c, Lucayan fishermen. $1.50, Columbus's fleet departing from Cadiz.

Perf. 14½x14

1990, Jan. 24 Litho. Wmk. 373

688 A106 10c multicolored 20 20
689 A106 40c multicolored 80 80
690 A106 45c multicolored 90 90
691 A106 50c multicolored 1.00 1.00

Souvenir Sheet

692 A106 $1.50 multicolored 3.00 3.00

Organization of American States, Cent. — A115

1990, Mar. 14 Wmk. 384 *Perf. 14*

693 A115 40c multicolored 80 80

Souvenir Sheet

Stamp World London '90 — A116

Aircraft: a, Spitfire I. b, Hurricane IIc.

1990, May 3 Wmk. 384

694 A116 Sheet of 2 4.00 4.00
a.-b. $1 any single 2.00 2.00

For surcharge see No. B3.

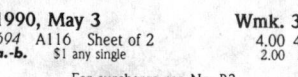

Intl. Literacy Year A117

Designs: 10c, Teacher helping student. 40c, Children reading to each other. 50c, Children reading aloud.

1990, June 27 Wmk. 384 *Perf. 14*

695 A117 10c multicolored 20 20
696 A117 40c multicolored 80 80
697 A117 50c multicolored 1.00 1.00

Queen Mother, 90th Birthday

Common Design Types

1990, Aug. 4 *Perf. 14x15*

698 CD343 40c Portrait, c. 1938 80 80

Perf. 14½

699 CD344 $1.50 At garden party, 1938 3.00 3.00

Bahamian Parrot — A118

1990, Sept. 26 Wmk. 373 *Perf. 14*

700 A118 10c shown 20 20
701 A118 40c In flight 80 80
702 A118 45c Head 90 90
703 A118 50c On branch 1.00 1.00

Souvenir Sheet

704 A118 $1.50 On branch, diff. 3.00 3.00

Christmas — A119

Birds — A120

Perf. 13½

1990, Nov. 5 Litho. Wmk. 373

705 A119 10c Angel appears to Mary 20 20
706 A119 40c Nativity 80 80
707 A119 45c Angel appears to shepherds 90 90
708 A119 $1 Three kings 2.00 2.00
a. Souvenir sheet of 4, #705-708 3.90 3.90

Wmk. 384

1991, Feb. 4 Litho. *Perf. 14*

709 A120 5c Green heron 15 15
710 A120 10c Turkey vulture 20 20
711 A120 15c Osprey 30 30
712 A120 20c Clapper rail 40 40
713 A120 25c Royal tern 50 50
714 A120 30c Key West quail dove 60 60
715 A120 40c Smooth-billed ani 80 80
716 A120 45c Burrowing owl 90 90
717 A120 50c Hairy woodpecker 1.00 1.00
718 A120 55c Mangrove cuckoo 1.10 1.10
719 A120 60c Bahama mockingbird 1.20 1.20
720 A120 70c Red-winged blackbird 1.40 1.40
721 A120 $1 Thick-billed vireo 2.00 2.00
722 A120 $2 Bahama yellowthroat 4.00 4.00
723 A120 $5 Stripe-headed tanager 10.00 10.00

724 A120 $10 Greater Antillean bullfinch 20.00 20.00
Nos. 709-724 (16) 44.55 44.55

Nos. 710, 713, 718, 723 exist inscribed 1993.
Issued: $10, July 1. Others, Feb. 4.

Discovery of America Type of 1988

Designs: 15c, Columbus practices celestial navigation. 40c, The fleet in rough seas. 55c, Natives on the beach. 60c, Map of voyage. $1.50, Pinta's crew sights land.

Perf. 14½x14

1991, Apr. 9 Litho. Wmk. 384

725 A106 15c multicolored 30 30
726 A106 40c multicolored 80 80
727 A106 55c multicolored 1.10 1.10
728 A106 60c multicolored 1.20 1.20

Souvenir Sheet

729 A106 $1.50 multicolored 3.00 3.00

Elizabeth & Philip, Birthdays
Common Design Types
Perf. 14½

1991, June 17 Litho. Wmk. 384

730 CD346 15c multicolored 30 30
731 CD345 $1 multicolored 2.00 2.00
a. Pair, #730-731 + label 2.30 2.30

Hurricane Awareness A121

Designs: 15c, Weather radar image of Hurricane Hugo. 40c, Anatomy of hurricane rotating around eye. 55c, Flooding caused by Hurricane David. 60c, Lockheed WP-3D Orion.

1991, Aug. 28 ***Perf. 14***

732 A121 15c multicolored 30 30
733 A121 40c multicolored 80 80
734 A121 55c multicolored 1.10 1.10
735 A121 60c multicolored 1.20 1.20

Christmas A122

Designs: 15c, The Annunciation. 55c, Mary and Joseph traveling to Bethlehem. 60c, Angel appearing to shepherds. $1, Adoration of the Magi.

1991, Oct. 28 Wmk. 373 ***Perf. 14***

736 A122 15c multicolored 30 30
737 A122 55c multicolored 1.10 1.10
738 A122 60c multicolored 1.20 1.20
739 A122 $1 multicolored 2.00 2.00
a. Souvenir sheet of 4, #736-739 4.60 4.60

Majority Rule, 25th Anniv. A123

Designs: 15c, First Progressive Liberal Party cabinet. 40c, Signing of Independence Constitution. 55c, Handing over constitutional instrument, vert. 60c, First Bahamian Governor-General, Sir Milo Butler, vert.

Wmk. 373

1992, Jan. 10 Litho. ***Perf. 14***

740 A123 15c multicolored 28 28
741 A123 40c multicolored 75 75
742 A123 55c multicolored 1.00 1.00
743 A123 60c multicolored 1.10 1.10

Queen Elizabeth II's Accession to the Throne, 40th Anniv.
Common Design Type
Wmk. 373

1992, Feb. 6 Litho. ***Perf. 14***

744 CD349 15c multicolored 28 28
745 CD349 40c multicolored 75 75
746 CD349 55c multicolored 1.00 1.00
747 CD349 60c multicolored 1.10 1.10
748 CD349 $1 multicolored 1.85 1.85
Nos. 744-748 (5) 4.98 4.98

Discovery of America Type of 1988

Designs: 15c, Lucayans first sight of fleet. 40c, Approaching Bahamas coastline. 55c, Lucayans about to meet Columbus. 60c, Columbus gives thanks for safe arrival. $1.50, Monument to Columbus' landing.

Perf. 14½x14

1992, Mar. 17 Litho. Wmk. 384

749 A106 15c multicolored 28 28
750 A106 40c multicolored 75 75
751 A106 55c multicolored 1.00 1.00
752 A106 60c multicolored 1.10 1.10

Souvenir Sheet

753 A106 $1.50 multicolored 2.75 2.75

Templeton, Galbraith and Hansberger Ltd. Building — A124

Perf. 14½

1992, Apr. 22 Litho. Wmk. 384

754 A124 55c multicolored 1.00 1.00

Templeton Prize for Progress in Religion, 20th Anniv.

1992 Summer Olympics, Barcelona — A125

Perf. 14½x14

1992, June 2 Wmk. 373

755 A125 15c Pole vault 28 28
756 A125 40c Javelin 75 75
757 A125 55c Hurdling 1.00 1.00
758 A125 60c Basketball 1.15 1.15

Souvenir Sheet

759 A125 $2 Sailing 3.75 3.75

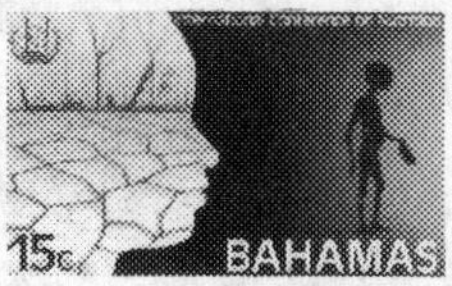

Intl. Conference on Nutrition A126

Designs: 15c, Drought-affected earth, starving child. 55c, Hand holding plant, stalks of grain.

Perf. 14½x13

1992, Aug. 11 Litho. Wmk. 373

760 A126 15c multicolored 28 28
761 A126 55c multicolored 1.00 1.00

Discovery of America Type of 1988
Souvenir Sheet
Perf. 14x13½

1992, Oct. 12 Litho. Wmk. 384

762 A106 $2 Coming ashore 3.75 3.75

Christmas — A127

1992, Nov. 2 Wmk. 373 ***Perf. 14***

763 A127 15c The Annunciation 28 28
764 A127 55c Nativity Scene 1.00 1.00
765 A127 60c Angel, shepherds 1.10 1.10
766 A127 70c The Magi 1.30 1.30
a. Souvenir sheet of 4, #763-766 3.75 3.75

The Contract, Farm Labor Program, 50th Anniv. — A128

Bahamian, American flags and: 15c, Silhouette of worker's head. 55c, Onions. 60c, Citrus fruits. 70c, Apples.

Perf. 14x14½

1993, Mar. 16 Litho. Wmk. 384

767 A128 15c multicolored 28 28
768 A128 55c multicolored 1.00 1.00
769 A128 60c multicolored 1.10 1.10
770 A128 70c multicolored 1.30 1.30

Royal Air Force, 75th Anniv.
Common Design Type

Designs: 15c, Westland Wapiti. 40c, Gloster Gladiator. 55c, DeHavilland Vampire. 70c, English Electric Lightning.

No. 775a, Avro Shackleton. b, Fairey Battle. c, Douglas Boston. d, DeHavilland DH9a.

Wmk. 373

1993, Apr. 1 Litho. ***Perf. 14***

771 CD350 15c multicolored 26 26
772 CD350 40c multicolored 70 70
773 CD350 55c multicolored 95 95
774 CD350 70c multicolored 1.25 1.25

Souvenir Sheet

775 CD350 60c Sheet of 4, #a.-d. 4.50 4.50

Coronation of Queen Elizabeth II, 40th Anniv. — A129

Perf. 13½

1993, June 2 Litho. Wmk. 373

776 A129 15c Nos. 424-425 28 28
777 A129 55c No. 157 1.00 1.00
778 A129 60c Nos. 402-403 1.10 1.10
779 A129 70c Nos. 404-405 1.30 1.30

A130

A131

Natl. symbols: 15c, Lignum vitae. 55c, Yellow elder. 60c, Blue marlin. 70c, Flamingo.

1993, July 8 Litho. ***Perf. 14***

780 A130 15c multicolored 28 28
781 A130 55c multicolored 1.00 1.00
782 A130 60c multicolored 1.10 1.10
783 A130 70c multicolored 1.30 1.30

Independence, 20th anniv.

1993, Sept. 8 Litho. ***Perf. 14***

Wildflowers.

784 A131 15c Cordia 30 30
785 A131 55c Seaside morning glory 1.10 1.10
786 A131 60c Poinciana 1.25 1.25
787 A131 70c Spider lily 1.40 1.40

Christmas A132

1993, Nov. 1 Litho. ***Perf. 14***

788 A132 15c Angel, Mary 28 28
789 A132 55c Shepherds, angel 1.00 1.00
790 A132 60c Holy family 1.10 1.10
791 A132 70c Three wise men 1.25 1.25

Souvenir Sheet

792 A132 $1 Madonna and Child 1.90 1.90

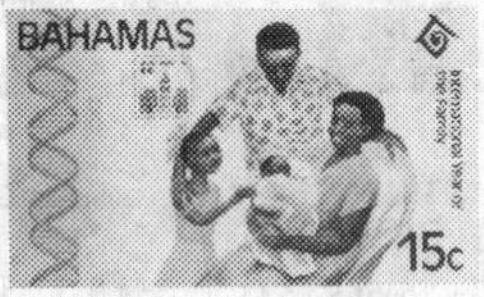

Intl. Year of the Family A133

Perf. 13½

1994, Feb. 18 Litho. Wmk. 384

793 A133 15c shown 28 28
794 A133 55c Children studying 1.00 1.00
795 A133 60c Son, father fishing 1.10 1.10
796 A133 70c Children, grandmother 1.25 1.25

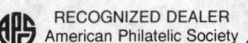

Hong Kong '94.

Royal Visit — A134

Designs: 15c, Bahamas, United Kingdom flags. 55c, Royal Yacht Britannia. 60c, Queen Elizabeth II. 70c, Prince Philip, Queen.

Perf. 14x13½

1994, Mar. 7 **Wmk. 373**

797 A134 15c multicolored 28 28
798 A134 55c multicolored 1.00 1.00
799 A134 60c multicolored 1.10 1.10
800 A134 70c multicolored 1.25 1.25

Natl. Family Island Regatta, 40th Anniv. A135

Designs: 15c, 55c, 60c, 70c, Various sailing boats at sea. $2, Beached yacht, vert.

Wmk. 373

1994, Apr. 27 **Litho.** ***Perf. 14***

801 A135 15c multicolored 28 28
802 A135 55c multicolored 1.00 1.00
803 A135 60c multicolored 1.10 1.10
804 A135 70c multicolored 1.25 1.25

Souvenir Sheet

805 A135 $2 multicolored 3.75 3.75

Intl. Olympic Committee, Cent. — A136

Flag, Olympic rings, and: 15c, Nos. 276-279, horiz. 55c, Nos. 388-391. 60c, Nos. 559-562, horiz. 70c, Nos. 755-758.

Wmk. 373

1994, May 31 **Litho.** ***Perf. 14***

806 A136 15c multicolored 28 28
807 A136 55c multicolored 1.00 1.00
808 A136 60c multicolored 1.10 1.10
809 A136 70c multicolored 1.25 1.25

Souvenir Sheet

First Recipients of the Order of the Caribbean Community — A137

Illustration reduced.

Perf. 13x14

1994, July 5 **Litho.** **Wmk. 373**

810 A137 $2 multicolored 4.00 4.00

A138

A139

Butterfly, flower: 15c, Canna skipper, canna. 55c, Cloudless sulphur, cassia. 60c, White peacock, passion flower. 70c, Devillier's swallowtail, calico flower.

1994, Aug. 16 **Litho.** ***Perf. 14***

811 A138 15c multicolored 30 30
812 A138 55c multicolored 1.10 1.10
813 A138 60c multicolored 1.25 1.25
814 A138 70c multicolored 1.40 1.40
Nos. 811-814 (4) 4.05 4.05

1994, Sept. 13 ***Perf. 13½x14***

Marine Life: a, Cuban hogfish, Spanish hogfish. b, Tomate, squirrelfish. c, French angelfish. d, Queen angelfish. e, Rock beauty.

815 A139 40c Strip of 5, #a.-e. 4.00 4.00

A number has been reserved for a souvenir sheet with this set.

Christmas A140

Wmk. 384

1994, Oct. 31 **Litho.** ***Perf. 14***

817 A140 15c Angel 30 30
818 A140 55c Holy family 1.10 1.10
819 A140 60c Shepherds 1.25 1.25
820 A140 70c Magi 1.40 1.40
Nos. 817-820 (4) 4.05 4.05

Souvenir Sheet

821 A140 $2 Christ Child, vert. 3.75 3.75

SEMI-POSTAL STAMPS

No. 48 Overprinted in Red — **1.1.17.**

1917, May 18 **Wmk. 3** ***Perf. 14***

B1 A6 1p car & black 42 42

Type of 1911 Overprinted in Red — **WAR CHARITY 3.6.18.**

1919, Jan. 1

B2 A6 1p red & black 45 45
a. Double overprint 2,000.

This stamp was originally scheduled for release in 1918.

Souvenir Sheet

No. 694 Surcharged — **HURRICANE RELIEF +$1**

Wmk. 384

1992, Nov. 16 **Litho.** ***Perf. 14***

B3 A116 Sheet of 2, #a.-b. 8.00 8.00

AIR POST STAMPS

Catalogue values for all unused stamps in this section are for Never Hinged items.

Manned Flight Bicentenary AP1

Airplanes.

Wmk. 373

1983, Oct. 13 **Litho.** ***Perf. 14***

C1 AP1 10c Consolidated Catalina 18 18
a. Without emblem ('85) 18 18
b. Without emblem, wmk. 384 ('86) 18 18
C2 AP1 25c Avro Tudor IV 42 42
a. Without emblem ('85) 45 45
b. Without emblem, wmk. 384 ('86) 45 45
C3 AP1 31c Avro Lancastrian 55 55
a. Without emblem ('85) 55 55
C4 AP1 35c Consolidated Commodore 60 60
a. Without emblem ('85) 65 65

Aircraft AP2

1987, July 7

C5 AP2 15c Bahamasair Boeing 737 25 25
C6 AP2 40c Eastern Boeing 757 65 65
C7 AP2 45c Pan Am Airbus A300 B4 75 75
C8 AP2 50c British Airways Boeing 747 85 85

SPECIAL DELIVERY STAMPS

No. 34 Overprinted — **SPECIAL DELIVERY**

1916 **Wmk. 1** ***Perf. 14***

E1 A6 5p orange & black 7.00 7.00
a. Double overprint 1,100. 1,100.
b. Inverted overprint 1,500. 1,500.
c. Double ovpt., one invtd. 1,900. 1,900.
d. Pair, one without overprint 12,000. 12,000.

The No. E1 overprint exists in two types. Type I (illustrated) is much scarcer. Type II shows "SPECIAL" farther right, so that the letter "I" is slightly right of the vertical line of the "E" below it.

Type of Regular Issue of 1903 Overprinted — **SPECIAL DELIVERY**

1917, July 2 **Wmk. 3**

E2 A6 5p orange & black 90 1.25

No. 60 Overprinted in Red — **SPECIAL DELIVERY**

1918

E3 A6 5p violet & black 65 1.25

WAR TAX STAMPS

Stamps of 1912-18 Overprinted — **WAR TAX**

1918, Feb. 21 **Wmk. 3** ***Perf. 14***

MR1 A8 ½p green 3.00 4.00
a. Double overprint 1,000. 1,000.
b. Inverted overprint 1,000. 1,000.
MR2 A8 1p car rose 80 1.10
a. Double overprint 1,000. 1,000.
b. Inverted overprint 1,000. 1,000.
MR3 A6 3p brown, *yel* 3.75 4.75
a. Inverted overprint *1,100.* *1,100.*
b. Double overprint 1,000. 1,000.
MR4 A8 1sh black & red 75.00 100.00
a. Double overprint 2,750. 2,500.

Same Overprint on No. 48a

1918, July 10

MR5 A6 1p car & black 3.50 6.00
a. Double overprint 1,200.
b. Double ovpt., one invtd. 1,000.
c. Inverted overprint *1,100.* *1,100.*

Nos. 49-50, 54 Overprinted in Black or Red — **WAR TAX**

MR6 A8 ½p green 20 20
MR7 A8 1p car rose 20 20
a. Watermarked sideways 850.00
MR8 A8 1sh black & red (R) 1.25 2.00

Nos. 58-59 Overprinted — **WAR TAX**

1918-19

MR9 A6 3p brown, *yel* 1.00 *3.50*
MR10 A6 3p brown & blk ('19) 1.00 *3.50*

Nos. 49-50, 54 Overprinted in Red or Black — **WAR TAX**

1919, July 14

MR11 A8 ½p green (R) 32 55
MR12 A8 1p car rose 32 55
MR13 A8 1sh black & red (R) 3.00 *10.50*

No. 59 Overprinted — **WAR TAX**

MR14 A6 3p brown & black 90 1.50

BARBADOS

LOCATION — A West Indies island east of the Windwards
GOVT. — Independent state in the British Commonwealth
AREA — 166 sq. mi.
POP. — 270,500 (1981)
CAPITAL — Bridgetown

The British colony of Barbados became an independent state on November 30, 1966.

4 Farthings = 1 Penny
12 Pence = 1 Shilling
20 Shillings = 1 Pound
100 Cents = 1 Dollar (1950)

Catalogue values for unused stamps in this country are for Never Hinged items, beginning with Scott 207 in the regular postage section, Scott B2 in the semi-postal section and Scott J1 in the postage due section.

Watermarks

Wmk. 5- Small Star

Wmk. 6- Large Star

Britannia
A1 A2

1852-55 Unwmk. Engr. *Imperf.*
Blued Paper
1 A1 (½p) deep green 90.00 150.00
a. (½p) yellow green *7,500.* 700.00
2 A1 (1p) dark blue 16.00 45.00
a. (1p) blue 16.00 110.00
3 A1 (2p) slate blue 10.00
a. (2p) grayish slate 200.00
b. Vert. half (#3a) used as 1p on cover 6,500.
4 A1 (4p) brown red ('55) 30.00 110.00

No. 3 was not placed in use. No. 3a was used only when bisected.

1855-58
White Paper
5 A1 (½p) deep green ('58) 75.00 100.00
a. (½p) yellow green ('57) 400.00 75.00
6 A1 (1p) blue 17.50 30.00
a. (1p) pale blue 30.00 30.00

It is believed that the (4p) brownish red on white paper exists only as No. 17b.

1859
8 A2 6p rose red 500.00 90.00
9 A2 1sh black 125.00 40.00
Pin-perf. 14
10 A1 (½p) pale yel grn 2,250. 250.00
11 A1 (1p) blue 2,250. 100.00
Pin-perf. 12½
12 A1 (½p) pale yel grn 5,500. 400.00
12A A1 (1p) blue *15,000.* 1,250.

1861 *Clean-Cut Perf. 14 to 16*
13 A1 (½p) dark blue grn 40.00 9.00
14 A1 (1p) blue 550.00 16.00
a. (1p) pale blue 550.00 16.00
b. Half used as ½p on cover 3,250.
Rough Perf. 14 to 16
15 A1 (½p) green 6.50 6.00
a. (½p) blue green 45.00 45.00
b. Imperf., pair 400.00
16 A1 (1p) blue 11.00 3.25
a. Diagonal half used as ½p on cover *1,250.*
b. Imperf., pair 600.00
17 A1 (4p) rose red 35.00 15.00
a. (4p) brown red 90.00 12.00
b. As "a," imperf., pair 750.00
c. (4p) rose red, imperf., pair 675.00
18 A1 (4p) vermilion 140.00 50.00
a. Imperf., pair 600.00
19 A2 6p rose red 150.00 9.00
20 A2 6p orange ver 27.50 7.50
a. 6p vermilion 27.50 7.50
b. Imperf., pair 400.00 *800.00*
21 A2 1sh black 20.00 6.00
a. Horiz. pair, imperf. btwn. *5,500.*
b. 1sh blue (error) *15,000.*

No. 21b was never placed in use. All copies are pen-marked (some have been removed) and have clipped perfs on one or more sides.

Perf. 11 to 13
22 A1 (½p) deep green *6,000.*
23 A1 (1p) blue *2,250.*

Nos. 22 and 23 were never placed in use.

1871 Wmk. 6 *Rough Perf. 14 to 16*
24 A1 (½p) yellow green 60.00 10.00
a. Imperf., pair 625.00
25 A1 (1p) blue 1,100. 15.00
a. Imperf., pair *1,300.*
26 A1 (4p) dull red 550.00 37.50
27 A2 6p vermilion 500.00 35.00
28 A2 1sh black 190.00 15.00

1871 Wmk. 5
29 A1 (1p) blue 60.00 3.00
30 A1 (4p) rose red 500.00 14.00
31 A2 6p vermilion 325.00 17.50
32 A2 1sh black 110.00 9.00
Clean-Cut Perf. 14½ to 16
33 A1 (1p) blue 175.00 2.50
a. Diagonal half used as ½p on cover *1,000.*
34 A2 6p vermilion 500.00 25.00
35 A2 1sh black 75.00 7.50
Perf. 11 to 13x14½ to 16
36 A1 (½p) blue green 200.00 15.00
37 A1 (4p) vermilion 375.00 45.00

1873 *Perf. 14*
38 A2 3p claret 325.00 55.00

Wmk. 6
Clean-Cut Perf. 14½ to 16
39 A1 (½p) blue green 150.00 15.00
40 A1 (4p) rose red 600.00 110.00
41 A2 6p vermilion 525.00 55.00
a. Imperf., pair 80.00 *1,500.*
b. Horiz. pair, imperf. btwn. *4,000.*
42 A2 1sh black 75.00 11.00
a. Imperf.

Britannia — A3

1873 Wmk. 5 *Perf. 15½x15*
43 A3 5sh dull rose 800.00 200.00

For surcharged bisects see Nos. 57-59.

1874 Wmk. 6 *Perf. 14*
44 A2 ½p blue green 10.00 5.50
45 A2 1p blue 60.00 2.50
Clean-Cut Perf. 14½ to 16
45A A2 1p blue *12,500.*

1875 Wmk. 1 *Perf. 12½*
46 A2 ½p yellow green 10.00 2.50
47 A2 4p scarlet 140.00 9.00
48 A2 6p orange 650.00 50.00
49 A2 1sh purple 350.00 16.00

1875-78 *Perf. 14*
50 A2 ½p yel green ('76) 5.00 1.50
51 A2 1p ultramarine 15.00 50
a. 1p gray blue 16.00 50
b. Half used as ½p on cover 1,000.
c. Watermarked sideways 1,750.
52 A2 3p violet ('78) 65.00 10.00
53 A2 4p rose red 70.00 4.00
a. 4p scarlet 100.00 5.00
b. As "a," perf. 14x12½ *4,000.*
54 A2 4p lake 300.00 4.00
55 A2 6p chrome yel 75.00 3.25
a. 6p yellow 275.00 12.50
56 A2 1sh purple ('76) 90.00 4.50
a. 1sh violet 2,000. 45.00
b. 1sh dull mauve 250.00 4.00
c. Half used as 6p on cover *4,750.*

Nos. 48, 49, 55 and 56 have the watermark sideways.
No. 53b was never placed in use. Value is for copy with perfs touching design and part original gum.

A4 A5

Large Surcharge, ("1" 7mm High, "D" 2¾mm High)

1878 Wmk. 5 *Perf. 15½x15*
Slanting Serif
57 A4 1p on half of 5sh *3,500.* 400.00
a. Unsevered pair *15,000.* *2,000.*
b. Unsevered horiz. pairs, #57 + 58, imperf. between 4,750.
Straight Serif
58 A4 1p on half of 5sh *4,000.* *800.00*
a. Unsevered pair *4,250.*
Small Surcharge, ("1" 6mm, "D" 2½mm High)
59 A5 1p on half of 5sh *5,000.* *1,100.*
a. Unsevered pair *12,500.* *3,500.*

On Nos. 57, 58 and 59 the surcharge is found reading upwards or downwards.
The perforation, which divides the stamp into halves, measures 11½ to 13.
The old denominatiom has been cut off the bottom of the stamps.

Queen Victoria — A6

1882-85 Typo. Wmk. 2 *Perf. 14*
60 A6 ½p green 1.50 45
61 A6 1p carmine rose 1.50 40
a. 1p rose 5.50 75
b. Half used as ½p on cover 375.00
62 A6 2½p dull blue 13.00 50
a. 2½p ultramarine 13.00 75
63 A6 3p magenta 1.75 1.75
a. 3p lilac 27.50 18.75
64 A6 4p slate 160.00 1.25
65 A6 4p brown ('85) 1.25 75
66 A6 6p olive gray 8.50 8.50
67 A6 1sh org brown 7.00 4.50
68 A6 5sh bister 110.00 125.00
Nos. 60-68 (9) 304.50 143.10

No. 65 Surcharged in Black HALF-PENNY

1892
69 A6 ½p on 4p brown 90 1.00
a. Without hyphen 4.00 4.00
b. Double surcharge
c. Double surch., red & black 450.00 1,200.
d. As "c," without hyphen 1,400. 1,400.

Badge of Colony
A8 A9

1892-1903 Wmk. 2
70 A8 1f sl & car ('96) 25 15
71 A8 ½p green 35 15
72 A8 1p carmine rose 35 15
73 A8 2p sl & org ('99) 3.25 1.50
74 A8 2½p ultramarine 2.50 30
75 A8 5p olive brn 4.00 2.50
76 A8 6p vio & car 4.00 2.50
77 A8 8p org & ultra 1.50 *6.25*
78 A8 10p bl grn & car 3.00 4.00
79 A8 2sh6p slate & org 12.50 14.00
80 A8 2sh6p pur & grn ('03) 50.00 *60.00*
Nos. 70-80 (11) 81.70 *87.54*

See Nos. 90-101. For surcharge, see No B1.

Victoria Jubilee Issue

1897 Wmk. 1
81 A9 1f gray & car 25 25
82 A9 ½p gray green 60 30
83 A9 1p carmine rose 1.25 35
84 A9 2½p ultra 5.00 75
85 A9 5p dk olive brn 8.25 8.25
86 A9 6p vio & car 9.25 9.25
87 A9 8p org & ultra 8.25 9.25
88 A9 10p bl grn & car 16.50 16.50
89 A9 2sh6p slate & org 17.00 17.00
Nos. 81-89 (9) 66.35 61.90
Bluish Paper
81a A9 1f gray & car 18.00 *19.00*
82a A9 ½p gray green 18.00 *19.00*
83a A9 1p carmine rose 27.50 *30.00*
84a A9 2½p ultra 30.00 *32.50*
85a A9 5p dk olive brn 175.00 *190.00*
86a A9 6p vio & car 72.50 *75.00*
87a A9 8p org & ultra 60.00 *65.00*
88a A9 10p bl grn & car 95.00 *100.00*
89a A9 2sh6p slate & org *72.50* *75.00*
Nos. 81a-89a (9) 568.50 *605.50*

Badge Type of 1892-1903

1904-10 Wmk. 3
90 A8 1f gray & car 50 40
91 A8 1f brown ('09) 25 18
92 A8 ½p green 65 15
93 A8 1p carmine rose 1.50 20
94 A8 1p carmine ('09) 2.50 15
95 A8 2p gray ('09) 3.50 2.50
96 A8 2½p ultramarine 2.25 40
97 A8 6p vio & car 15.00 9.00
98 A8 6p dl vio & vio ('10) 4.25 4.25
99 A8 8p org & ultra 17.50 20.00
100 A8 1sh blk, *grn* ('10) 6.50 7.50
101 A8 2sh6p pur & green 27.50 *35.00*
Nos. 90-101 (12) 81.90 *79.73*

Nelson Centenary Issue

Lord Nelson Monument — A10

1906 Engr. Wmk. 1
102 A10 1f gray & black 85 60
103 A10 ½p green & black 2.00 40
104 A10 1p car & black 85 28
105 A10 2p org & black 4.00 4.25
106 A10 2½p ultra & black 5.00 4.00
107 A10 6p lilac & black 14.00 14.00
108 A10 1sh rose & black 14.00 14.00
Nos. 102-108 (7) 40.70 37.53

See Nos. 110-112.

The "Olive Blossom" — A11

1906, Aug. 15 Wmk. 3
109 A11 1p blk, green & blue 6.50 1.25

Tercentenary of the 1st British landing.

Nelson Type of 1906

1907, July 6 Wmk. 3
110 A10 1f gray & black 1.40 1.40
111 A10 2p org & black 10.00 11.00
112 A10 2½p ultra & black 10.00 11.00
a. 2½p indigo & black 850.00 *1,200.*

A12 A13

King George V — A14

1912 Typo.
116 A12 ¼p brown 22 15
117 A12 ½p green 50 16
a. Booklet pane of 6
118 A12 1p carmine 85 15
a. 1p scarlet 2.25 40
b. Booklet pane of 6
119 A12 2p gray 2.25 *6.50*
120 A12 2½p ultramarine 1.40 50
121 A13 3p violet, *yel* 1.50 *3.50*
122 A13 4p blk & scar, *yel* 1.40 *4.25*
123 A13 6p vio & red vio 2.25 2.50
124 A14 1sh black, *green* 5.00 7.00
125 A14 2sh vio & ultra, *bl* 22.50 30.00
126 A14 3sh grn & violet 27.50 35.00
Nos. 116-126 (11) 65.37 89.71

Seal of the Colony — A15

1916-18 Engr.
127 A15 ¼p brown 15 15
128 A15 ½p green 16 15
129 A15 1p red 50 15
130 A15 2p gray 3.50 *7.25*
131 A15 2½p ultramarine 85 65
132 A15 3p violet, *yel* 2.25 1.90
133 A15 4p red, *yel* 60 1.75
134 A15 4p red & black ('18) 85 1.25
135 A15 6p claret 85 1.10
136 A15 1sh black, *green* 2.75 3.50
137 A15 2sh violet, *blue* 10.00 8.50
138 A15 3sh dark violet 27.50 *55.00*
139 A15 3sh dk vio & grn ('18) 14.00 20.00
a. 3sh bright violet & green ('18) 120.00 130.00
Nos. 127-139 (13) 63.96 101.35

Nos. 134 and 139 are from a re-engraved die. The central medallion is not surrounded by a line and there are various other small alterations.

Victory Issue

Victory
A16 A17

1920, Sept. 9 **Wmk. 3**
140 A16 ¼p bister & black 20 18
141 A16 ½p yel green & blk 40 30
a. Booklet pane of 2
142 A16 1p org red & blk 65 22
a. Booklet pane of 2
143 A16 2p gray & black 1.40 *4.00*
144 A16 2½p ultra & dk bl 1.40 2.00
145 A16 3p red lilac & blk 85 *1.50*
146 A16 4p gray grn & blk 1.10 *3.50*
147 A16 6p orange & blk 1.50 *3.50*
148 A17 1sh yel green & blk 4.25 *8.00*
149 A17 2sh brown & blk 8.25 *12.00*
150 A17 3sh orange & blk 13.50 *16.00*

1921, Aug. 22 **Wmk. 4**
151 A16 1p orange red & blk 5.50 28
Nos. 140-151 (12) 39.00 *51.48*

A18

A19

1921-24 **Wmk. 4**
152 A18 ¼p brown 15 15
153 A18 ½p green 35 18
154 A18 1p carmine 16 15
155 A18 2p gray 55 30
156 A18 2½p ultramarine 30 45
158 A18 6p claret 55 55
159 A18 1sh blk, *emer* ('24) 20.00 21.00
160 A18 2sh dk vio, *blue* 13.00 15.00
161 A18 3sh dark violet 13.00 15.00

Wmk. 3
162 A18 3p violet, *yel* 35 65
163 A18 4p red, *yel* 65 1.40
164 A18 1sh black, *green* 3.25 *5.50*
Nos. 152-164 (12) 52.31 60.33

1925-35 **Wmk. 4** ***Perf. 14***
165 A19 ¼p brown 15 15
166 A19 ½p green 15 15
a. Perf. 13½x12½ ('32) 16 15
b. Booklet pane of 10
167 A19 1p carmine 15 15
a. Perf. 13½x12½ ('32) 25 15
b. Booklet pane of 10
168 A19 1½p org, perf. 13½x12½ ('32) 65 15
a. Booklet pane of 6
b. Perf. 14 1.30 55
169 A19 2p gray 20 30
170 A19 2½p ultramarine 45 15
a. Perf. 13½x12½ ('32) 2.25 40
171 A19 3p vio brn, *yel* 35 25
172 A19 3p red brn, *yel* ('35) 6.00 6.00
173 A19 4p red, *yel* 45 40
174 A19 6p claret 80 80
175 A19 1sh blk, *emerald* 1.25 1.00
a. Perf. 13½x12½ ('32) 3.50 3.25
176 A19 1sh brn blk, *yel grn* ('32) 4.25 4.25
177 A19 2sh violet, *bl* 2.00 2.00
178 A19 2sh6p car, *blue* ('32) 11.00 13.00
179 A19 3sh dark violet 3.75 3.75
Nos. 165-179 (15) 31.60 32.50

Charles I and George V — A20

1927, Feb. 17 ***Perf. 12½***
180 A20 1p carmine lake 75 60

Tercentenary of the settlement of Barbados.

Silver Jubilee Issue
Common Design Type

1935, May 6 ***Perf. 11x12***
186 CD301 1p car & dk bl 18 18
187 CD301 1½p blk & ultra 35 28
188 CD301 2½p ultra & brn 85 85
189 CD301 1sh brn vio & ind 4.00 4.00
Set, never hinged 14.00

Coronation Issue
Common Design Type

1937, May 14 ***Perf. 13½x14***
190 CD302 1p carmine 15 15
191 CD302 1½p brown 20 20
192 CD302 2½p bright ultra 40 40
Set, never hinged 1.00

A21

1938-47 ***Perf. 13-14 & Compound***
193 A21 ½p green 40 15
b. Perf. 14 22.50 1.40
c. Booklet pane of 10
193A A21 ½p bister ('42) 15 15
194 A21 1p carmine 1.75 15
b. Perf. 13½x13 50.00 1.40
c. Booklet pane of 10
194A A21 1p green ('42) 15 15
d. Perf. 13½x13 28 15
195 A21 1½p red orange 15 15
c. Perf. 14 60 15
d. Booklet pane of 6
195A A21 2p rose lake ('41) 1.10 22
195B A21 2p bright rose red ('43) 20 15
e. Perf. 14 15 15
196 A21 2½p ultramarine 20 15
197 A21 3p brown 20 16
b. Perf. 14 28 16
197A A21 3p deep bl ('47) 16 15
198 A21 4p black 16 15
a. Perf. 14 30 30
199 A21 6p violet 20 16
199A A21 8p red vio ('46) 65 65
200 A21 1sh brn olive 50 20
a. 1sh olive green 2.75 1.40
201 A21 2sh6p brown vio 1.75 65
201A A21 5sh indigo ('41) 2.75 1.40
Nos. 193-201A (16) 10.47
Set, never hinged 22.50
Set value 4.20

For surcharge, see No. 209.

Kings Charles I, George VI Assembly Chamber and Mace
A22

Perf. 13½x14
1939, June 27 **Engr.** **Wmk. 4**
202 A22 ½p deep green 18 15
203 A22 1p scarlet 20 15
204 A22 1½p deep orange 35 25
205 A22 2½p ultramarine 60 60
206 A22 3p yellow brown 65 65
Nos. 202-206 (5) 1.98 1.80
Set, never hinged 5.00

Tercentenary of the General Assembly.

Catalogue values for unused stamps in this section, from this point to the end of the section, are for Never Hinged items.

Peace Issue
Common Design Type

1946, Sept. 18
207 CD303 1½p deep orange 15 15
208 CD303 3p brown 15 15

Nos. 195e, 195B, Surcharged in Black **ONE PENNY**

1947, Apr. 21 ***Perf. 14***
209 A21 1p on 2p brt rose red 55 55
a. Double surcharge
b. Perf. 13½x13 65 65

Silver Wedding Issue
Common Design Types

Perf. 14x14½
1948, Nov. 24 **Photo.** **Wmk. 4**
210 CD304 1½p orange 15 15

Engraved; Name Typographed
Perf. 11½x11
211 CD305 5sh dark blue 8.00 8.00

UPU Issue
Common Design Types

1949, Oct. 10 ***Perf. 13½, 11x11½***
212 CD306 1½p red orange 32 35
213 CD307 3p indigo 55 55
214 CD308 4p gray 1.00 1.00
215 CD309 1sh olive 1.40 1.40

Dover Fort — A23

Admiral Nelson Statue — A24

Designs: 2c, Sugar cane breeding. 3c, Public buildings. 6c, Casting net. 8c, Intercolonial schooner. 12c, Flying Fish. 24c, Old Main Guard Garrison. 48c, Cathedral. 60c, Careenage. $1.20, Map. $2.40, Great Seal, 1660.

Perf. 11x11½ (A23), 13x13½ (A24)
1950, May 1 **Engr.** **Wmk. 4**
216 A23 1c slate 15 15
217 A23 2c emerald 15 15
218 A23 3c slate & brown 15 15
219 A24 4c carmine 20 20
220 A23 6c blue 22 18
221 A23 8c choc & blue 38 25
222 A23 12c olive & aqua 75 45
223 A23 24c gray & red 90 65
224 A24 48c violet 2.50 1.75
225 A23 60c brn car & bl grn 1.50 1.90
226 A24 $1.20 olive & car 5.50 3.25
227 A23 $2.40 gray 13.00 8.00
Nos. 216-227 (12) 25.40 17.08

University Issue
Common Design Types

1951, Feb. 16 ***Perf. 14x14½***
228 CD310 3c turq bl & choc 15 15
229 CD311 12c ol brn & turq bl 75 75

Stamp of 1852 — A25

Perf. 13½
1952, Apr. 15 **Wmk. 4** **Engr.**
230 A25 3c slate bl & dp grn 15 15
231 A25 4c rose pink & bl 25 25
232 A25 12c emer & slate bl 40 40
233 A25 24c gray blk & red brn 65 65

Centenary of Barbados postage stamps.

Coronation Issue
Common Design Type

1953, June 4 ***Perf. 13½x13***
234 CD312 4c red orange & black 15 15

Harbor Police — A26

Designs as in 1950 with portrait of Queen Elizabeth II. $2.40, Great Seal, 1660 ("E II R").

Perf. 11x11½ (horiz.), 13x13½ (vert.)
1953-57 **Engr.**
235 A23 1c slate ('53) 15 15
236 A23 2c grnsh blue & deep org 15 15
237 A23 3c emerald & blk 15 15
238 A24 4c orange & gray 15 15
239 A26 5c dp car & dp bl 16 15
240 A23 6c red brown 20 15
241 A23 8c brt blue & blk 28 15
242 A23 12c brn ol & aqua 38 15
243 A23 24c gray & red ('56) 55 20
244 A24 48c violet ('56) 1.75 1.10
245 A23 60c brown car & blue grn ('56) 3.00 1.75
246 A24 $1.20 ol & car ('56) 5.25 3.25
247 A23 $2.40 gray ('57) 11.00 6.25
Nos. 235-247 (13) 23.17 13.75

See Nos. 257-264.

West Indies Federation
Common Design Type

Perf. 11½x11
1958, Apr. 23 **Wmk. 314**
248 CD313 3c green 15 15
249 CD313 6c blue 40 40
250 CD313 12c carmine rose 50 50

Deep Water Harbor, Bridgetown
A27

1961, May 6 **Engr.** ***Perf. 11x11½***
251 A27 4c orange & black 15 15
252 A27 8c ultra & black 28 28
253 A27 24c black & pink 65 65

Opening of the Deep Water Harbor at Bridgetown.

Scout Emblem and Map of Barbados — A28

Perf. 11½x11
1962, Mar. 9 **Wmk. 314**
254 A28 4c orange & black 15 15
255 A28 12c gray & blue 30 30
256 A28 $1.20 greenish gray & carmine rose 2.00 2.00

50th anniv. of the founding of the Boy Scouts of Barbados.

Queen Types of 1953-57
Perf. 11x11½, 13x13½
1964-65 **Engr.** **Wmk. 314**
257 A23 1c slate 25 25
258 A24 4c orange & gray 35 35
259 A23 8c brt bl & blk ('65) 48 42
260 A23 12c brn ol & aqua ('65) 60
261 A23 24c gray & red 60 48
262 A24 48c violet 2.50 2.50
263 A23 60c brn car & bl grn 3.50 3.50
264 A23 $2.40 gray ('65) 5.50 5.50
Nos. 257-264 (8) 13.78

The 12c was never put on sale in Barbados.

ITU Issue
Common Design Type

Perf. 11x11½
1965, May 17 **Litho.** **Wmk. 314**
265 CD317 2c lilac & ver 15 15
266 CD317 48c yellow & gray 1.50 1.50

Sea Horse — A29

Designs: 1c, Deep sea coral. 2c, Lobster. 4c, Sea urchin. 5c, Staghorn coral. 6c, Butterflyfish. 8c, File shell. 12c, Balloonfish. 15c, Angelfish. 25c, Brain coral. 35c, Brittle star. 50c, Flyingfish. $1, Queen conch shell. $2.50, Fiddler crab.

Wmk. 314 Upright

1965, July 15 Photo. *Perf. 14x13½*

267 A29 1c dk blue, pink & black 15 15
268 A29 2c car rose, sepia & orange 15 15
269 A29 3c org, brn & sep ("Hippocampus") 15 15
270 A29 4c ol grn & dk bl 15 15
a. Imperf., pair 450.00
271 A29 5c lil, brn & pink 15 15
272 A29 6c greenish bl, yel & blk 15 15
273 A29 8c ultra, orange, red & black 25 18
274 A29 12c rose lil, yel & blk 40 25
275 A29 15c red, yel & blk 75 50
276 A29 25c yel brn & ultra 1.10 80
277 A29 35c grn, rose brn & blk 1.75 1.00
278 A29 50c yel grn & ultra 2.75 1.65
279 A29 $1 gray & multi 5.50 4.00
280 A29 $2.50 lt bl & multi 12.00 10.00
Nos. 267-280 (14) 25.40 19.28

1966-69 Wmk. 314 Sideways

Design: $5, "Dolphin" (coryphaena hippurus).

267a A29 1c 15 15
268a A29 2c ('67) 15 15
269A A29 3c ("Hippocampus") ('67) 18 15
270b A29 4c 15 15
271a A29 5c 15 15
272a A29 6c ('67) 20 15
273a A29 8c ('67) 25 20
274a A29 12c ('67) 35 20
275a A29 15c 50 35
276a A29 25c 60 55
277a A29 35c 85 60
278a A29 50c 1.25 1.10
279a A29 $1 2.50 1.90
280a A29 $2.50 6.25 6.00
280B A29 $5 dk ol & multi ('69) 12.50 12.50
Nos. 267a-280B (15) 26.03 24.30

For surcharge, see No. 327.

Churchill Memorial Issue
Common Design Type

1966, Jan. 24 Wmk. 314 *Perf. 14*

281 CD319 1c multicolored 15 15
282 CD319 4c multicolored 20 20
283 CD319 25c multicolored 1.00 1.00
284 CD319 35c multicolored 1.40 1.40

Royal Visit Issue
Common Design Type

1966, Feb. 4 Litho. *Perf. 11x12*

285 CD320 3c violet blue 20 20
286 CD320 35c dark car rose 1.75 1.75

UNESCO Anniversary Issue
Common Design Type

1967, Jan. 6 Litho. *Perf. 14*

287 CD323 4c "Education" 15 15
288 CD323 12c "Science" 55 55
289 CD323 25c "Culture" 1.40 1.40

Arms of Barbados — A30

Policeman and Anchor Monument — A31

Designs: 25c, Hilton Hotel, horiz. 35c, Garfield Sobers, captain of Barbados and West Indies Cricket Team. 50c, Pine Hill Dairy, horiz.

1966, Dec. 2 Unwmk. Photo.

290 A30 4c multicolored 15 15
291 A30 25c multicolored 35 35
292 A30 35c multicolored 50 50
293 A30 50c multicolored 75 75

Barbados' independence, Nov. 30, 1966.

1967, Oct. 16 Litho. *Perf. 13½x14*

Designs: 25c, Policeman with telescope. 35c, Police motor launch, horiz. 50c, Policemen at Harbor Gate.

294 A31 4c multicolored 15 15
295 A31 25c multicolored 32 32
296 A31 35c multicolored 50 50
297 A31 50c multicolored 80 80

Centenary of Bridgetown Harbor Police.
For surcharge, see No. 322.

Independence Arch — A32

1st Anniv. of Independence: 4c, Sir Winston Scott, Governor-General, vert. 35c, Treasury Building. 50c, Parliament Building.

Perf. 14½x14, 14x14½

1967, Dec. 4 Photo. Unwmk.

298 A32 4c multicolored 15 15
299 A32 25c multicolored 26 26
300 A32 35c multicolored 38 38
301 A32 50c multicolored 60 60

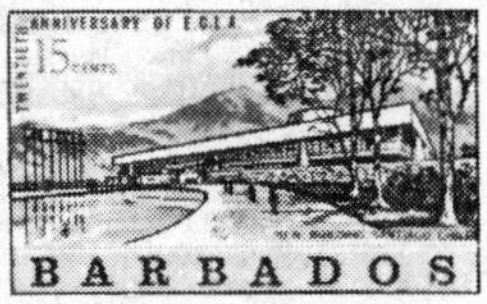

UN Building, Santiago, Chile A33

1968, Feb. 27 *Perf. 14½x14*

302 A33 15c multicolored 20 20

20th anniv. of the UN Economic Commission for Latin America.

Radar Antenna on Top of Old Sugar Mill, Sugar Cane — A34

Designs: 25c, Caribbean Meteorological Institute, Barbados, horiz. 50c, HARP gun used in High Altitude Research Program, at Paragon in Christ Church, Barbados.

Perf. 14x14½, 14½x14

1968, June 4 Photo. Unwmk.

303 A34 3c violet & multi 15 15
304 A34 25c ver & multi 30 30
305 A34 50c orange & multi 70 70

World Meteorological Day.

Girl Scout at Campfire, Lady Baden-Powell and Queen Elizabeth II — A35

Lady Baden-Powell, Queen Elizabeth II and: 25c, Pax Hill Headquarters. 35c, Girl Scout badge.

Perf. 14x14½

1968, Aug. 29 Photo. Unwmk.

306 A35 3c dp ultra, blk & gold 15 15
307 A35 25c bluish green, black & gold 35 35
308 A35 35c org yel, blk & gold 70 70

Barbados Girl Scouts' 50th anniv.

Human Rights Flame and Escape to Freedom A36

Designs: 4c, Human Rights flame, hands, and broken chain. 25c, Human Rights flame, family and broken chain.

Perf. 11x11½

1968, Dec. 10 Litho. Unwmk.

309 A36 4c violet, gray grn & red brown 15 15
310 A36 25c org, blk & blue 38 38
311 A36 35c greenish blue, blue, blk & org 55 55

International Human Rights Year.

In the Paddock A37

Horse Racing: 25c, "They're off!" 35c, On the flat. 50c, The Finish.

1969, Mar. 15 Litho. *Perf. 14½*

312 A37 4c multicolored 15 15
313 A37 25c multicolored 24 24
314 A37 35c multicolored 32 32
315 A37 50c multicolored 55 55
a. Souvenir sheet of 4, #312-315 2.50 3.00

Map of Caribbean — A38

Design: 12c, 50c, "Strength in Unity," horiz.

Perf. 14x14½, 14½x14

1969, May 6 Photo. Wmk. 314

316 A38 5c brown & multi 15 15
317 A38 12c ultra & multi 18 18
318 A38 25c green & multi 28 28
319 A38 50c magenta & multi 65 65

1st anniv. of CARIFTA (Caribbean Free Trade Area).

ILO Emblem A39

Perf. 14x13

1969, Aug. 5 Litho. Unwmk.

320 A39 4c bl grn, brt grn & blk 15 15
321 A39 25c red brn, brt mag & red 38 38

50th anniv. of the ILO.

No. 294 Surcharged ONE CENT

1969, Aug. 30 *Perf. 13½x14*

322 A31 1c on 4c multicolored 35 35

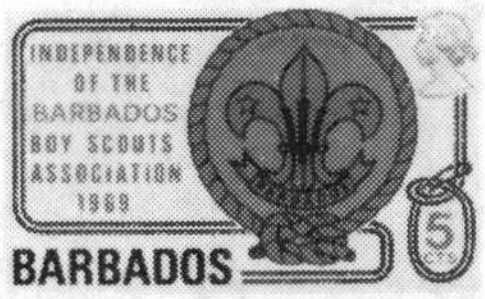

Barbados Boy Scout Emblem A40

Designs: 25c, Sea Scouts rowing in Bridgetown harbor. 35c, Campfire. 50c, Various Scouts in front of National Headquarters and Training Center, Hazelwood.

Perf. 13½x13

1969, Dec. 16 Litho. Unwmk.

323 A40 5c multicolored 15 15
324 A40 25c multicolored 50 50
325 A40 35c multicolored 65 65
326 A40 50c multicolored 1.00 1.00
a. Souvenir sheet of 4, #323-326 10.00 12.00

Attainment of independence by the Barbados Boy Scout Assoc.

No. 271a Surcharged 4 X

Wmk. 314 Sideways

1970, Mar. 11 Photo. *Perf. 14x13½*

327 A29 4c on 5c multicolored 18 18

This locally applied surcharge exists in several variations: double, triple, on back, in pair with one missing, etc.

Lion at Gun Hill — A41

Barbados Museum A42

Designs: 2c, Trafalgar Fountain. 3c, Montefiore Drinking Fountain. 4c, St. James' Monument. 5c, St. Ann's Fort. 6c, Old Sugar Mill, Morgan Lewis. 8c, Cenotaph. 10c, South Point Lighthouse. 15c, Sharon Moravian Church. 25c, George Washington House. 35c, St. Nicholas Abbey. 50c, Bowmanston Pumping Station. $1, Queen Elizabeth Hospital. $2.50, Modern sugar factory. $5, Seawell International Airport.

Wmk. 314 Upright (A41), Sideways (A42)

Perf. 12½x13, 13x12½

1970, May 4 Photo.

328 A41 1c blue grn & multi 15 15
329 A41 2c crimson & multi 15 15
330 A41 3c blue & multi 15 15
331 A41 4c yellow & multi 15 15
332 A41 5c dp org & multi 15 15
333 A41 6c dull yel & multi 15 15
334 A41 8c dp blue & multi 15 15
335 A41 10c red & multi 16 16
336 A42 12c ultra & multi 20 20
337 A42 15c yellow & multi 22 20
338 A42 25c orange & multi 40 40
339 A42 35c pink & multi 60 60
340 A42 50c bl grn & multi 65 65
341 A42 $1 emerald & multi 1.40 1.40
342 A42 $2.50 ver & multi 3.50 3.50
343 A42 $5 yellow & multi 6.50 6.50
Nos. 328-343 (16) 14.68 14.66

Nos. 328-332, 334-343 were reissued in 1971 on glazed paper.

Wmk. 314 Sideways (A41), Upright (A42)

1972-74

331a A41 4c 15 15
332a A41 5c 15 15
333a A41 6c 15 15
334a A41 8c 15 15
335a A41 10c ('74) 25 25
336a A42 12c 25 25
337a A42 15c 32 32
338a A42 25c 55 55
339a A42 35c 85 85
340a A42 50c 1.25 1.25
341a A42 $1 2.50 2.50

No.	Type	Description	Unused	Used
342a	A42	$2.50 ('73)	6.50	6.50
343a	A42	$5 ('73)	13.00	13.00
		Nos. 331a-343a (13)	26.07	26.07

For surcharge, see No. 391.

Primary Education, UN and Education Year Emblems A43

Designs (UN and Education Year Emblems and): 5c, Secondary education (student with microscope). 25c, Technical education (men working with power drill). 50c, University building.

1970, June 26 Litho. *Perf. 14*

No.	Type	Description	Unused	Used
344	A43	4c multicolored	15	15
345	A43	5c multicolored	15	15
346	A43	25c multicolored	35	35
347	A43	50c multicolored	75	75

UN, 25th anniv., and Intl. Education Year.

Minnie Root A44

Flowers: 1c, Barbados Easter lily, vert. 10c, Eyelash orchid. 25c, Pride of Barbados, vert. 35c, Christmas hope.

1970, Aug. 24 Litho. Wmk. 314

Flowers in Natural Colors

No.	Type	Description	Unused	Used
348	A44	1c green	15	15
349	A44	5c deep magenta	15	15
350	A44	10c dark blue	28	22
351	A44	25c brt orange brown	70	55
352	A44	35c blue	1.10	90
a.		Souvenir sheet of 5	3.00	2.25
		Nos. 348-352 (5)	2.38	1.97

No. 352a contains 5 imperf. stamps similar to Nos. 348-352 with simulated perforations.

Christ Carrying Cross — A45

Easter: 10c, 50c, Resurrection, by Benjamin West, St. George's Anglican Church. 35c like 4c, Window from St. Margaret's Anglican Church, St. John.

1971, Apr. 7 Wmk. 314 *Perf. 14*

No.	Type	Description	Unused	Used
353	A45	4c purple & multi	15	15
354	A45	10c silver & multi	15	15
355	A45	35c brt blue & multi	52	52
356	A45	50c gold & multi	80	80

Sailfish Craft — A46

Tourism: 5c, Tennis. 12c, Horseback riding. 25c, Water-skiing. 50c, Scuba diving.

1971, Aug. 17 *Perf. 14x14½*

No.	Type	Description	Unused	Used
357	A46	1c multicolored	15	15
358	A46	5c multicolored	15	15
359	A46	12c multicolored	20	20
360	A46	25c multicolored	50	50
361	A46	50c multicolored	1.00	1.00
		Nos. 357-361 (5)	2.00	2.00

Samuel Jackman Prescod — A47

1971, Sept. 26 *Perf. 14*

No.	Type	Description	Unused	Used
362	A47	3c orange & multi	15	15
363	A47	35c ultra & multi	65	65

Samuel Jackman Prescod (1806-1871), 1st black member of Barbados Assembly.

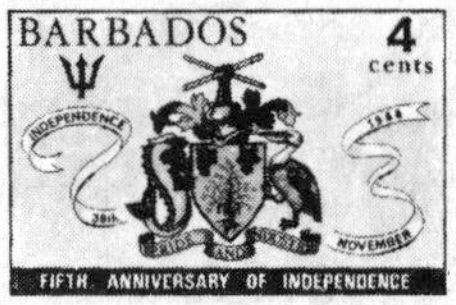

Coat of Arms — A48

Designs: 15c, 50c, Flag and map of Barbados.

1971, Nov. 23

No.	Type	Description	Unused	Used
364	A48	4c light blue & multi	15	15
365	A48	15c multicolored	28	28
366	A48	25c yel green & multi	45	45
367	A48	50c blue & multi	90	90

5th anniv. of independence.

Telegraphy, 1872 and 1972 A49

Designs: 10c, "Stanley Angwin" off St. Lawrence Coast. 35c, Earth station and Intelsat 4. 50c, Mt. Misery tropospheric scatter station.

1972, Mar. 28 Litho. *Perf. 14*

No.	Type	Description	Unused	Used
368	A49	4c purple & multi	15	15
369	A49	10c emerald & multi	26	26
370	A49	35c red & multi	55	55
371	A49	50c orange & multi	85	85

Centenary of telecommunications to and from Barbados.

Lord Baden-Powell, Charles W. Springer, George B. Burton — A50

Designs: 5c, Map of Barbados and Combermere School, vert. 25c, Photograph of 1922 troop. 50c, Flags of various Boy Scout troops.

1972, Aug. 1

No.	Type	Description	Unused	Used
372	A50	5c ultra & multi	15	15
373	A50	15c ultra & multi	40	40
374	A50	25c ultra & multi	60	60
375	A50	50c ultra & multi	1.10	1.10

60th anniv. of Barbados Boy Scouts and 4th Caribbean Jamboree.

Bookmobile, Open Book — A51

Intl. Book Year: 15c, Visual aids truck. 25c, Central Library, Bridgetown. $1, Codrington College.

1972, Oct. 31 Litho. Wmk. 314

No.	Type	Description	Unused	Used
376	A51	4c brt pink & multi	15	15
377	A51	15c dull org & multi	25	25
378	A51	25c buff & multi	42	42
379	A51	$1 lt violet & multi	1.90	1.90

Pottery Wheels A52

Barbados pottery industry: 15c, Kiln. 25c, Finished pottery, Chalky Mount. $1, Pottery on sale at market.

1973, Mar. 1 Wmk. 314 *Perf. 14*

No.	Type	Description	Unused	Used
380	A52	5c dull red & multi	15	15
381	A52	15c olive grn & multi	22	22
382	A52	25c gray & multi	35	35
383	A52	$1 yellow & multi	1.40	1.40

First Flight in Barbados, Wright Box Kite, 1911 A53

Aircraft: 15c, First flight to Barbados, De Havilland biplane, 1928. 25c, Passenger plane, 1939. 50c, Vickers VC-10 over control tower, 1973.

1973, July 25 *Perf. 12½x12*

No.	Type	Description	Unused	Used
384	A53	5c blue & multi	15	15
385	A53	15c vio blue & multi	40	40
386	A53	25c multicolored	65	65
387	A53	50c blue & multi	1.40	1.40

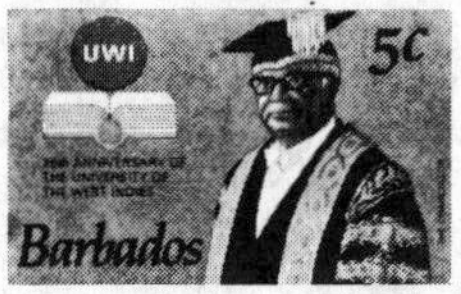

Chancellor Sir Hugh Wooding A54

Designs: 25c, Sherlock Hall, Cave Hill Campus. 35c, Cave Hill Campus.

1973, Dec. 11 *Perf. 13x14*

No.	Type	Description	Unused	Used
388	A54	5c dp orange & multi	15	15
389	A54	25c red brown & multi	40	40
390	A54	35c multicolored	60	60

25th anniv. of the Univ. of the West Indies.

No. 338a Surcharged **4c.**

1974, Apr. 30 Photo. *Perf. 13x12½*

No.	Type	Description	Unused	Used
391	A42	4c on 25c multi	15	15
a.		"4c." omitted	20.00	

Old Sailboat A55

Designs: 25c, Rowboat. 50c, Motor-powered fishing boat. $1, Trawler "Calamar."

1974, June 11 Wmk. 314 *Perf. 14*

No.	Type	Description	Unused	Used
392	A55	15c blue & multi	24	24
393	A55	35c multicolored	48	48
394	A55	50c vio blue & multi	70	70
395	A55	$1 blue & multi	1.40	1.40
a.		Souvenir sheet of 4, #392-395	3.00	*3.75*

Fishing boats of Barbados.

Fire Orchid — A56

Orchids. 1c, 20c, 25c, $2.50, $5 horizontal.

Wmk. 314 Sideways; Upright (1c, 20c, 25c, $1, $10)

1974-77 Photo. *Perf. 14*

No.	Type	Description	Unused	Used
396	A56	1c Cattleya gaskelliana alba	15	15
397	A56	2c shown	15	15
398	A56	3c Rose Marie	15	15
399	A56	4c Fiery red orchid	15	15
400	A56	5c Schomburgkia humboltii	15	15
401	A56	8c Dancing dolls	15	15
402	A56	10c Spider orchids	18	15
403	A56	12c Dendrobium aggregatum	20	18
404	A56	15c Lady slippers	30	25
404C	A56	20c Spathoglottis	35	30
405	A56	25c Eyelash	50	40
406	A56	35c Bletia patula	55	45
406B	A56	45c Sunset Glow	75	60
407	A56	50c Sunset Glow	75	60
		Perf. 14½x14, 14x14½		
408	A56	$1 Ascocenda red gem	1.40	1.10
409	A56	$2.50 Brassolaeliocattleya nugget	3.25	2.75
410	A56	$5 Caularthron bicornutum	6.50	5.50
411	A56	$10 Moon orchid	12.50	11.00
		Nos. 396-411 (18)	28.13	24.18

Issue dates: 20c, 45c, May 3, 1977. Others, Sept. 16, 1974.

For surcharge see No. B2.

Wmk. 314 Upright; Sideways (1c, 25c, $1)

1976 *Perf. 14*

No.	Type	Description	Unused	Used
396a	A56	1c multicolored	15	15
397a	A56	2c multicolored	15	15
398a	A56	3c multicolored	20	15
399a	A56	4c multicolored	25	20
402a	A56	10c multicolored	45	40
404a	A56	15c multicolored	80	70
405a	A56	25c multicolored	1.00	90
406a	A56	35c multicolored	1.50	1.25
		Perf. 14½x14		
408a	A56	$1 multicolored	4.00	3.50
		Nos. 396a-408a (9)	8.50	7.40

1975 Wmk. 373 *Perf. 14*

No.	Type	Description	Unused	Used
396b	A56	1c multicolored	15	15
397b	A56	2c multicolored	15	15
398b	A56	3c multicolored	15	15
399b	A56	4c multicolored	25	22
400b	A56	5c multicolored	15	15
402b	A56	10c multicolored	20	18
403b	A56	12c multicolored	25	22
404b	A56	15c multicolored	50	45
406c	A56	45c multicolored	1.10	90
		Perf. 14½x14, 14x14½		
408b	A56	$1 multicolored	2.00	1.90
409b	A56	$2.50 multicolored	5.00	4.50
410b	A56	$5 multicolored	10.00	9.50
411b	A56	$10 multicolored	18.00	18.00
		Nos. 396b-411b (13)	37.90	36.47

UPU Emblem, Barbados No. 64 A57

Cent. of the UPU: 35c, Letters encircling globe. 50c, Barbados coat of arms. $1, Map of Barbados, sailing ship and jet.

1974, Oct. 9 Litho. *Perf. 14½*

No.	Type	Description	Unused	Used
412	A57	8c brt rose, org & gray	15	15
413	A57	35c red, blk, & ocher	45	45
414	A57	50c vio blue, bl & sil	65	65
415	A57	$1 ultra, blk & brn	1.25	1.25
a.		Souvenir sheet of 4, #412-415	3.00	3.00

Yacht Britannia off Barbados A58

Royal Visit, Feb. 1975: 35c, $1, Palms and sunset.

1975, Feb. 18

416	A58	8c	brown & multi	15	15
417	A58	25c	blue & multi	38	38
418	A58	35c	purple & multi	60	60
419	A58	$1	violet & multi	1.65	1.65

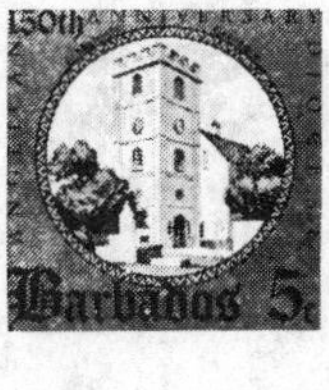

St. Michael's Cathedral — A59

Designs: 15c, Bishop Coleridge. 50c, All Saint's Church. $1, St. Michael, stained glass window, St. Michael's Cathedral.

Wmk. 314

1975, July 29 Litho. *Perf. 14*

420	A59	5c	blue & multi	15	15
421	A59	15c	lilac & multi	18	18
422	A59	50c	green & multi	55	55
423	A59	$1	multicolored	1.00	1.00
a.			Souvenir sheet of 4, #420-423	2.25	*2.75*

Anglican Diocese in Barbados, sesquicentennial.

Pony Float A60

Designs: 25c, Stiltsman (band and masqueraders). 35c, Maypole dancing. 50c, Cuban dancers.

1975, Nov. 18 Litho. Wmk. 373

424	A60	8c	yellow & multi	15	15
425	A60	25c	buff & multi	32	32
426	A60	35c	ultra & multi	40	40
427	A60	50c	orange & multi	65	65
a.			Souvenir sheet of 4, #424-427	1.75	1.75

Crop-over (harvest) festival.

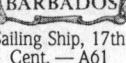

Sailing Ship, 17th Cent. — A61

Coat of Arms — A62

350th Anniv. of 1st Settlement: 10c, Bearded fig tree and fruit. 25c, Ogilvy's 17th cent. map. $1, Capt. John Powell.

1975, Dec. 17 Wmk. 373 *Perf. 13½*

428	A61	4c	lt blue & multi	15	15
429	A61	10c	lt blue & multi	22	16
430	A61	25c	yellow & multi	55	50
431	A61	$1	dk red & multi	1.90	1.65
a.			Souvenir sheet of 4, #428-431	3.00	2.75

Coil Stamps

1975, Dec. Unwmk. *Perf. 15x14*

432	A62	5c	light blue	15	15
433	A62	25c	violet	25	25
			Set value	32	32

Map of West Indies, Bats, Wicket and Ball — A63

Prudential Cup — A64

1976, July 7 Litho. *Perf. 14*

438	A63	25c	lt blue & multi	85	50
439	A64	45c	lilac rose & black	1.10	1.00

World Cricket Cup, won by West Indies Team, 1975.

Map of South Carolina settled by Barbadians — A65

American Bicentennial: 25c, George Washington and map of Bridge Town area. 50c, Declaration of Independence. $1, Masonic emblem and Prince Hall, founder and Grand Master of African Grand Lodge, Boston, 1790-1807.

1976, Aug. 17 Wmk. 373 *Perf. 13½*

440	A65	15c	multicolored	20	20
441	A65	25c	multicolored	35	35
442	A65	50c	multicolored	65	65
443	A65	$1	multicolored	1.40	1.40

Mailman with Bicycle A66

PO Act, 125th anniv.: 35c, Mailman on motor scooter. 50c, Cover with Barbados No. 2. $1, Mail truck.

1976, Oct. 19 Litho. *Perf. 14*

444	A66	8c	rose red, blk & bis	15	15
445	A66	35c	multicolored	40	40
446	A66	50c	vio blue & multi	60	60
447	A66	$1	red & multi	1.10	1.10

Coast Guard Vessels A67

Designs: 15c, Bank note, reverse, showing Barbados Parliament. 25c, National anthem by Van Roland Edwards (music) and Irvine Burgie (lyrics). $1, Independence Day parade.

1976, Nov. 30 *Perf. 13x13½*

448	A67	5c	multicolored	15	15
449	A67	15c	multicolored	16	16
450	A67	25c	yel, brown & blk	25	25
451	A67	$1	multicolored	1.00	1.00
a.			Souvenir sheet of 4, #448-451	2.00	2.00

10th anniv. of independence.

Queen Knighting Garfield Sobers, 1957 Visit — A68

Designs: 50c, Queen arriving at Westminster Abbey. $1, Queen leaving coach.

1977, Feb. 7 *Perf. 14x13½*

452	A68	15c	silver & multi	20	20
453	A68	50c	silver & multi	60	60
454	A68	$1	silver & multi	1.25	1.25

25th anniv. of the reign of Queen Elizabeth II. See Nos. 467-469.

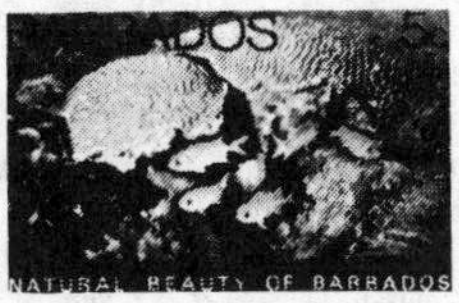

Underwater Park — A69

Beauty of Barbados: 35c, Royal palms, vert. 50c, Underwater caves. $1, Stalagmite in Harrison's Cave, vert.

1977, May 3 Wmk. 373 *Perf. 14*

455	A69	5c	multicolored	15	15
456	A69	35c	multicolored	50	50
457	A69	50c	multicolored	65	65
458	A69	$1	multicolored	1.40	1.40
a.			Souvenir sheet of 4, #455-458	2.75	2.75

House of Commons Maces — A70

Charles I Handing Charter to Carlisle — A71

Designs: 25c, Speaker's chair. 50c, Senate Chamber. $1, Sam Lord's Castle, horiz.

1977, Aug. 2 Litho. *Perf. 13½*

459	A70	10c	red brown & yel	15	15
460	A70	25c	slate grn & org	30	30
461	A70	50c	dk green, grn & yel	60	60
462	A70	$1	dk & lt blue & org	1.10	1.10

13th Regional Conference of Commonwealth Parliamentary Association.

Perf. 13½x13, 13x13½

1977, Oct. 11 Litho. Wmk. 373

Designs: 12c, Charter scroll. 45c, Charles I and Earl of Carlisle, horiz. $1, Map of Barbados, by Richard Ligon, 1657, horiz.

463	A71	12c	buff & multi	15	15
464	A71	25c	buff & multi	30	30
465	A71	45c	buff & multi	55	55
466	A71	$1	buff & multi	1.10	1.10

350th anniv. of charter granting Barbados to the Earl of Carlisle.

Silver Jubilee Type, 1977, Inscribed: "ROYAL VISIT"

1977, Oct. 31 Unwmk. *Roulette 5*

Self-adhesive

467	A68	15c	silver & multi	20	20
468	A68	50c	silver & multi	60	60
469	A68	$1	silver & multi	1.10	1.10

Caribbean visit of Queen Elizabeth II. Printed on peelable paper backing inscribed in ultramarine multiple rows: "SILVER JUBILEE ROYAL VISIT BARBADOS". Printed with die-cut label inscribed in black "BEND & PEEL" attached at left of stamp. Sheets of 50 stamps and 50 labels.

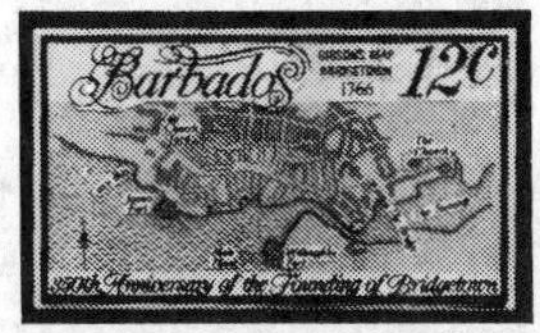

Gibson's Map of Bridgetown, 1766 — A72

Designs: 25c, Bridgetown, engraving by S. Copens, 1695. 45c, Trafalgar Square, Bridgetown, drawing by J. M. Carter, 1835. $1, The Bridges, 1978.

Perf. 14½

1978, Mar. 1 Litho. Wmk. 373

470	A72	12c	gold & multi	15	15
471	A72	25c	gold & multi	25	25
472	A72	45c	gold & multi	45	45
473	A72	$1	gold & multi	85	85

350th anniv. of founding of Bridgetown.

Elizabeth II Coronation Anniv. Issue

Souvenir Sheet

Common Design Types

1978, Apr. 21 Unwmk. *Perf. 15*

474	Sheet of 6	3.00	3.00
a.	CD326 50c Griffin of Edward III	50	50
b.	CD327 50c Elizabeth II	50	50
c.	CD328 50c Pelican	50	50

No. 474 contains 2 se-tenant strips of Nos. 474a-474c, separated by horizontal gutter with commemorative and descriptive inscriptions and showing central part of coronation with coach.

Freak Bridge Hand A73

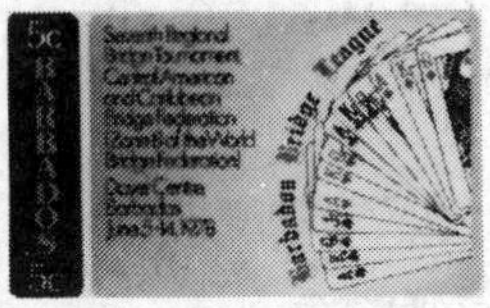

Designs: 10c, World Bridge Fed. emblem. 45c, Central American and Caribbean Bridge Fed. emblem. $1, Map of Caribbean and cards.

Perf. 14½

1978, June 6 Litho. Wmk. 373

475	A73	5c	multicolored	15	15
476	A73	10c	multicolored	15	15
477	A73	45c	multicolored	50	50
478	A73	$1	multicolored	1.00	1.00
a.			Souvenir sheet of 4, #475-478	1.50	1.50

7th Regional Bridge Tournament, Dover Centre, Barbados, June 5-14.

Girl Guides' Camp — A74

Designs: 28c, Girl Guides helping children and handicapped. 50c, Badge with "60," vert. $1, Badge with initials, vert.

1978, Aug. 1 Litho. *Perf. 13½*

479	A74	12c	multicolored	15	15
480	A74	28c	multicolored	28	28
481	A74	50c	multicolored	50	50
482	A74	$1	multicolored	1.00	1.00

Girl Guides of Barbados, 60th anniv.

Garment Industry A75

Industries of Barbados: 28c, Cooper, vert. 45c, Blacksmith, vert. 50c, Wrought iron industry.

1978, Nov. 14 Litho. *Perf. 14*

483	A75	12c multicolored	15	15
484	A75	28c multicolored	28	28
485	A75	45c multicolored	42	42
486	A75	50c multicolored	50	50

Early Mail Steamer A76

Ships: 25c, Q.E.II in Deep Water Harbour. 50c, Ra II (raft) nearing Barbados. $1, Early mail steamer.

1979, Feb. 8 Litho. *Perf. 13x13½*

487	A76	12c multicolored	15	15
488	A76	25c multicolored	28	28
489	A76	50c multicolored	50	50
490	A76	$1 multicolored	1.00	1.00

Barbados No. 235 A77

Designs: 28c, Barbados No. 430, vert. 45c, Penny Black and Maltese postmark, vert. 50c, Barbados No. 21b.

Wmk. 373

1979, May 8 Litho. *Perf. 14*

491	A77	12c multicolored	15	15
492	A77	28c multicolored	20	20
493	A77	45c multicolored	30	30

Souvenir Sheet

494	A77	50c multicolored	40	40

Sir Rowland Hill (1795-1879), originator of penny postage.

Birds — A78

Launcher Transported through Barbados — A79

1979-81 Photo. Wmk. 373 *Perf. 14*

495	A78	1c Grass canaries	15	15
496	A78	2c Rain birds	15	15
497	A78	5c Sparrows	15	15
498	A78	8c Frigate birds	15	15
499	A78	10c Cattle egrets	15	15
500	A78	12c Green gaulins	15	15
501	A78	20c Hummingbirds	16	15
502	A78	25c Ground doves	20	16
503	A78	28c Blackbirds	22	20
504	A78	35c Green-throated caribs	28	24
505	A78	45c Wood doves	35	30
506	A78	50c Ramiers	40	35
506A	A78	55c Black-breasted plover ('81)	50	38
507	A78	70c Yellow breasts	50	45
508	A78	$1 Pee whistlers	80	65
509	A78	$2.50 Christmas birds	2.00	1.60
510	A78	$5 Kingfishers	4.00	3.50
511	A78	$10 Red-seal coot	8.50	6.50
		Nos. 495-511 (18)	18.81	15.38

Issue dates: 55c, Sept. 1; others, Aug. 7.
See #570-572. For surcharges see #563-565.

1979, Oct. 9 Photo.

Designs: 10c, Gun on landing craft, Foul Bay, horiz. 20c, Firing of 16-inch launcher by day. 28c, Bath Earth Station and Intelsat IV-A, horiz. 45c, Intelsat over Caribbean, horiz. 50c, Intelsat IV-A over Atlantic, and globe. $1, Lunar landing module, horiz.

512	A79	10c multicolored	15	15
513	A79	12c multicolored	15	15
514	A79	20c multicolored	15	15
515	A79	28c multicolored	20	20
516	A79	45c multicolored	30	30
517	A79	50c multicolored	35	35
		Nos. 512-517 (6)	1.30	1.30

Souvenir Sheet

518	A79	$1 multicolored	85	85

Space exploration. No. 518 commemorates 10th anniversary of first moon landing.

Family, IYC Emblem — A80

IYC Emblem and: 28c, Children holding hands and map of Barbados. 45c, Boy and teacher. 50c, Children playing. $1, Boy and girl flying kite.

1979, Nov. 27 Litho. *Perf. 14*

519	A80	12c multicolored	15	15
520	A80	28c multicolored	20	20
521	A80	45c multicolored	30	30
522	A80	50c multicolored	35	35
523	A80	$1 multicolored	65	65
		Nos. 519-523 (5)	1.65	1.65

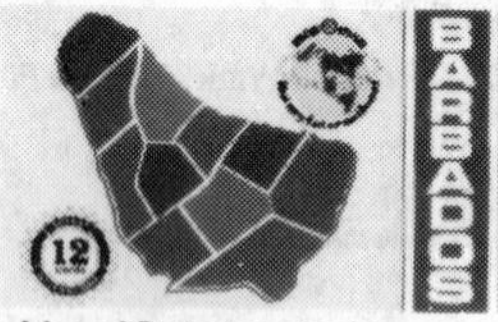

Map of Barbados, Anniversary Emblem — A81

Rotary Intl., 75th Anniv.: 28c, Map of district 404. 50c, 75th anniv. emblem. $1, Paul P. Harris, founder.

1980, Feb. 19 Litho. *Perf. 13½*

524	A81	12c multicolored	15	15
525	A81	28c multicolored	20	20
526	A81	50c multicolored	35	35
527	A81	$1 multicolored	65	65

Regiment Volunteer, Artillery Company, 1909 — A82

Perf. 14½

1980, Apr. 8 Litho. Wmk. 373

528	A82	12c shown	15	15
529	A82	35c Drum major	22	22
530	A82	50c Sovereign's, regimental flags	35	35
531	A82	$1 Women's corps	65	65

Barbados Regiment, 75th anniv.

Souvenir Sheets

Early Mailman, London 1980 Emblem — A83

The vignette is a different color for each stamp.

Wmk. 373

1980, May 6 Litho. *Perf. 14*

532	Sheet of 6	1.10	1.10
a.-f.	A83 28c any single	20	20
533	Sheet of 6	2.25	2.25
a.-f.	A83 50c any single	35	35

London 80 Intl. Stamp Exhib., May 6-14.

Underwater Scenes — A84

1980, Sept. 30 Litho. *Perf. 13½*

534	A84	12c multicolored	15	15
535	A84	28c multicolored	24	24
536	A84	50c multicolored	42	42
537	A84	$1 multicolored	75	75
a.		Souvenir sheet of 4, #534-537	1.50	1.50

Bathsheba Railroad Station A85

1981, Jan. 13 Litho. *Perf. 14½*

538	A85	12c shown	15	15
539	A85	28c Cab stand, The Green	20	20
540	A85	45c Mule-drawn tram	30	30
541	A85	70c Horse-drawn bus	50	50
542	A85	$1 Fairchild St. railroad station	65	65
		Nos. 538-542 (5)	1.80	1.80

Visually Handicapped Girl at Typewriter — A86

1981, May 19 Litho. *Perf. 14*

543	A86	10c shown	15	15
544	A86	25c Sign language alphabet, vert.	16	16
545	A86	45c Blind people crossing street, vert.	30	30
546	A86	$2.50 Baseball game	1.65	1.65

International Year of the Disabled.

Royal Wedding Issue

Common Design Type

Perf. 13½

1981, July 22 Litho. Wmk. 373

547	CD331	28c Bouquet	20	20
548	CD331	50c Charles	35	35
549	CD331	$2.50 Couple	1.65	1.65

4th Caribbean Arts Festival (CARIFESTA), July 19-Aug. 3 — A87

1981, Aug. 11 Litho. *Perf. 14½*

550	A87	15c Landship maneuver	15	15
551	A87	20c Yoruba dancer	15	15
552	A87	40c Tuk band	30	30
553	A87	55c Frank Collymore (sculpture)	40	40
554	A87	$1 Barbados Harbor (painting)	75	75
		Nos. 550-554 (5)	1.75	1.75

Hurricane Gladys, View from Apollo A88

1981, Sept. 29 Litho. *Perf. 14*

555	A88	35c Satellite view over Barbados	30	30
556	A88	50c shown	42	42
557	A88	60c Police watch	50	50
558	A88	$1 Spotter plane	85	85

Harrison's Cave — A89

Perf. 14x14½

1981, Dec. 1 Litho. Wmk. 373

559	A89	10c Twin Falls	15	15
560	A89	20c Rotunda Room Stream	15	15
561	A89	55c Rotunda Room formation	35	35
562	A89	$2.50 Cascade Pool	1.65	1.65

Nos. 503, 505, 507 Surcharged

1982, Feb. 1 Photo. *Perf. 14*

563	A78	15c on 28c multi	15	15
564	A78	40c on 45c multi	40	40
565	A78	60c on 70c multi	60	60

Black Belly Sheep A90

1982, Feb. 9 Litho.

566	A90	40c Ram	40	40
567	A90	50c Ewe	50	50
568	A90	60c Ewe, lambs	60	60
569	A90	$1 Pair, map	1.00	1.00

Bird Type of 1979

Wmk. 373

1982, Mar. 1 Photo. *Perf. 14*

570	A78	15c like #503	15	15
571	A78	40c like #506	40	40
572	A78	60c like #507	60	60

Early Marine Transport A91

1982, Apr. 6 Litho. *Perf. 14½*

577	A91	20c Lighter	20	20
578	A91	35c Rowboat	35	35
579	A91	55c Speightstown schooner	55	55
580	A91	$2.50 Inter-colonial schooner	2.50	2.50

Visit of Pres. Ronald Reagan A92

1982, Apr. 8 Litho. *Perf. 14*

581 A92 20c Barbados Flag, arms 22 18
582 A92 20c US Flag, arms 22 18
583 A92 55c like #581 55 48
584 A92 55c like #582 55 48

Stamps of same denomination printed in sheets of 8 with gutter showing Pres. Reagan and Prime Minister Tom Adams.

Princess Diana Issue

Common Design Type

1982, July 1 Litho. *Perf. 14½*

585 CD333 20c Arms 15 15
586 CD333 60c Diana 45 45
587 CD333 $1.20 Wedding 90 90
588 CD333 $2.50 Portrait 1.75 1.75

Scouting Year — A93

Washington's 250th Birth Anniv. — A94

1982, Sept. 7 Wmk. 373 *Perf. 14*

589 A93 15c Helping woman 16 16
590 A93 40c Sign, emblem, flag, horiz. 45 45
591 A93 55c Religious service, horiz. 55 55
592 A93 $1 Flags 1.00 1.00

Souvenir Sheet

593 A93 $1.50 Laws 1.65 1.65

1982, Nov. 2 *Perf. 13½x13*

594 A94 10c Arms 15 15
595 A94 55c Washington's house, Barbados 55 55
596 A94 60c Taking command 60 60
597 A94 $2.50 Taking oath 2.50 2.50

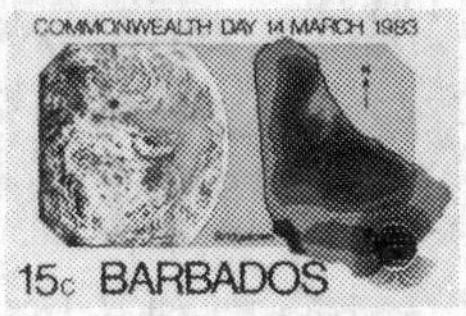

A95

1983, Mar. 14 Litho. *Perf. 14*

598 A95 15c Map, globe 15 15
599 A95 40c Beach 40 40
600 A95 60c Sugar cane harvest 60 60
601 A95 $1 Cricket game 1.00 1.00

Commonwealth day.

Gulf Fritillary A96

Perf. 13½x13

1983, Feb. 8 Litho. Wmk. 373

602 A96 20c shown 20 20
603 A96 40c Monarch 40 40
604 A96 55c Mimic 55 55
605 A96 $2.50 Hanno Blue 2.50 2.50

Manned Flight Bicentenary A97

1983, June 14 Litho. *Perf. 14*

606 A97 20c US Navy dirigible 20 20
607 A97 40c Douglas DC-3 40 40
608 A97 55c Vickers Viscount 55 55
609 A97 $1 Lockheed TriStar 1.00 1.00

Nash 600, 1941 A98

1983, Aug. 9 Litho. *Perf. 14*

610 A98 25c shown 25 25
611 A98 45c Dodge, 1938 45 45
612 A98 75c Ford Model AA, 1930 75 75
613 A98 $2.50 Dodge Four, 1918 2.50 2.50

A99

A100

1983, Aug. 30 Litho. *Perf. 14*

614 A99 20c Players 20 20
615 A99 65c Emblem, map 65 65
616 A99 $1 Cup 1.00 1.00

World Cup Table Tennis Championship.

1983, Nov. 1 *Perf. 14*

Christmas: 10c, 25c, Angel with lute, painting details. $2, The Virgin and Child, by Masaccio.

617 A100 10c multicolored 15 15
618 A100 25c multicolored 25 25

Souvenir Sheet

619 A100 $2 multicolored 2.00 2.00

Barbados Museum, Golden Jubilee A101

Museum Paintings: 45c, by Richard Day. 75c, St. Ann's Garrison in Barbados by W.S. Hedges. $2.50, Needham's Point, Carlisle Bay.

1983, Nov. 1 *Perf. 14*

620 A101 45c multicolored 45 45
621 A101 75c multicolored 75 75
622 A101 $2.50 multicolored 2.50 2.50

1984 Olympics, Los Angeles A102

1984, Apr. 3 Litho. *Perf. 14*

623 A102 50c Track & field 50 50
624 A102 65c Shooting 65 65
625 A102 75c Sailing 75 75
626 A102 $1 Bicycling 1.00 1.00
a. Souvenir sheet of 4, #623-626 3.00 3.00

Lloyd's List Issue

Common Design Type

1984, Apr. 25 Litho. *Perf. 14½*

627 CD335 45c World map 45 45
628 CD335 50c Bridgetown Harbor 50 50
629 CD335 75c Philosopher 75 75
630 CD335 $1 Sea Princess 1.00 1.00

Souvenir Sheet

1984 UPU Congress A103

1984, June 6 Litho. *Perf. 13½*

631 A103 $2 #213, UPU emblem 2.00 2.00

World Chess Fed., 60th Anniv. — A104

1984, Aug. 8 *Perf. 14x14½*

632 A104 25c Junior match 30 30
633 A104 45c Knights 52 52
634 A104 65c Queens 75 75
635 A104 $2 Rooks 2.25 2.25

Christmas — A105

1984, Oct. 24 Litho. *Perf. 14*

636 A105 50c Poinsettia 50 50
637 A105 65c Snow-on-the-mountain 65 65
638 A105 75c Christmas candle 75 75
639 A105 $1 Christmas hope 1.00 1.00

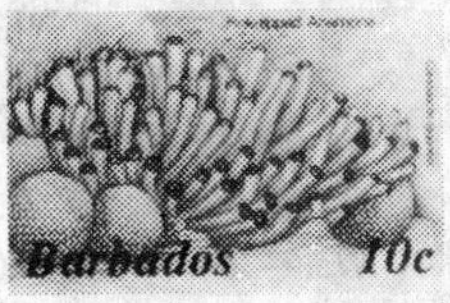

Marine Life A106

1985 Litho. Wmk. 373 *Perf. 14*

640 A106 1c Bristle worm 15 15
641 A106 2c Spotted trunk fish 15 15
642 A106 5c Coney fish 15 15
643 A106 10c Pink-tipped anemone 15 15
645 A106 20c Christmas tree worm 30 30
646 A106 25c Hermit crab 35 35
648 A106 35c Animal flower 50 50
649 A106 40c Vase sponge 60 60
650 A106 45c Spotted moray 65 65
651 A106 50c Ghost crab 75 75
653 A106 65c Flaming tongue snail 95 95
654 A106 75c Sergeant major fish 1.10 1.10
656 A106 $1 Caribbean warty anemone 1.50 1.50
657 A106 $2.50 Green turtle 3.75 3.75
658 A106 $5 Rock beauty 7.25 7.25
659 A106 $10 Elkhorn coral 15.00 15.00
Nos. 640-659 (16) 33.30 33.30

Issue dates: 10c, 20c, 25c, 50c, $2.50 and $5, Feb. 26; 5c, 35c, 40c, 65c and $10, Apr. 9; 1c, 2c, 45c, 75c and $1, May 7.
Exist inscribed "1987," etc.

1986 (?) Wmk. 384

640a A106 1c 15 15
641a A106 2c 15 15
642a A106 5c 15 15
643a A106 10c 15 15
645a A106 20c 30 30
646a A106 25c 35 35
648a A106 35c 45 45
649a A106 40c 60 60
650a A106 45c 65 65
651a A106 50c 75 75
653a A106 65c 95 95
654a A106 75c 1.10 1.10
656a A106 $1 1.50 1.50
657a A106 $2.50 3.75 3.75
658a A106 $5 7.25 7.25
659a A106 $10 15.00 15.00
Nos. 640a-659a (16) 33.25 33.25

Some inscribed "1986." Also exist with "1987," "1988," and with no date.

Queen Mother 85th Birthday

Common Design Type

Perf. 14½x14

1985, June 7 Litho. Wmk. 384

660 CD336 25c At Buckingham Palace, 1930 25 25
661 CD336 65c With Lady Diana, 1981 65 65
662 CD336 75c At the docks 75 75
663 CD336 $1 Holding Prince Henry 1.00 1.00

Souvenir Sheet

664 CD336 $2 Opening the Garden Center, Syon House 2.00 2.00

Audubon Birth Bicentenary A107

Illustrations of North American bird species. Nos. 666-668 vert.

Wmk. 373

1985, Aug. 6 Litho. *Perf. 14*

665 A107 45c Falco peregrinus 60 60
666 A107 65c Dendroica discolor 90 90
667 A107 75c Ardea herodias 1.10 1.10
668 A107 $1 Dendroica petechia 1.40 1.40

Satellite Orbiting Earth A108

1985, Sept. 10

669 A108 75c multicolored 75 75

INTELSAT, Intl. Telecommunications Satellite Consortium, 20th anniv.

Royal Barbados Police, 150th Anniv. — A109

1985, Nov. 19

670 A109 25c Traffic Dept. 25 25
671 A109 50c Police Band 50 50
672 A109 65c Dog Force 65 65
673 A109 $1 Mounted Police 1.00 1.00

Souvenir Sheet

674 A109 $2 Band on parade, horiz. 2.00 2.00

Queen Elizabeth II 60th Birthday

Common Design Type

Designs: 25c, Age 2. 50c, Senate House opening, University College of the West Indies, Jamaica, 1953. 65c, With Prince Philip, Caribbean Tour, 1985. 75c, Banquet, state visit to Sao Paulo, Brazil, 1968. $2, Visiting Crown Agents, 1983.

Perf. 14x14½

1986, Apr. 21 Litho. Wmk. 384

675 CD337 25c scar, blk & sil 22 22
676 CD337 50c ultra & multi 45 45
677 CD337 65c green & multi 60 60
678 CD337 75c violet & multi 70 70
679 CD337 $2 rose vio & multi 1.90 1.90
Nos. 675-679 (5) 3.87 3.87

EXPO '86, Vancouver
A110

1986, May 2 *Perf. 14*

680 A110 50c Trans-Canada North Star 50 50
681 A110 $2.50 Lady Nelson 2.50 2.50

AMERIPEX '86
A111

1986, May 22 **Wmk. 373**

682 A111 45c No. 441 45 45
683 A111 50c No. 442 50 50
684 A111 65c No. 558 65 65
685 A111 $1 Nos. 583-584 1.00 1.00

Souvenir Sheet

686 A111 $2 Statue of Liberty, NY Harbor 2.00 2.00

Statue of Liberty, cent.

Royal Wedding Issue, 1986
Common Design Type

Designs: 45c, Informal portrait. $1, Andrew in navy uniform.

Perf. 14¹/₂x14
1986, July 23 Litho. Wmk. 384

687 CD338 45c multicolored 45 45
688 CD338 $1 multicolored 1.00 1.00

Electrification of Barbados, 75th Anniv. — A112

Designs: 10c, Transporting utility poles, 1923. 25c, Heathfield ladder, 1935, vert. 65c, Transport fleet, 1941. $2, Bucket truck, 1986, vert.

Wmk. 384
1986, Sept. 16 Litho. *Perf. 14*

689 A112 10c multicolored 15 15
690 A112 25c multicolored 25 25
691 A112 65c multicolored 65 65
692 A112 $2 multicolored 2.00 2.00

Christmas — A113

Church windows and flowers.

1986, Oct. 28 **Wmk. 373**

693 A113 25c Alpinia purpurata 25 25
694 A113 50c Anthurium andraeanum 50 50
695 A113 75c Heliconia rostrata 75 75
696 A113 $2 Heliconia psittacorum 2.00 2.00

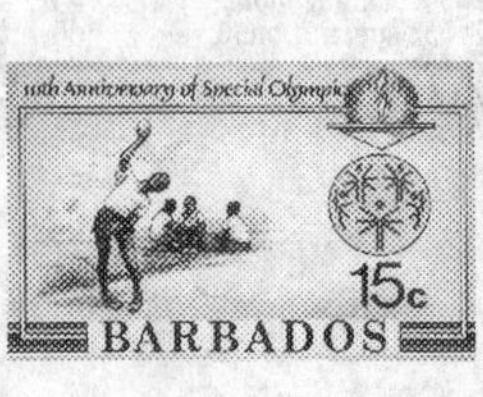

Natl. Special Olympics, 10th Anniv.
A114

1987, Mar. 27 Wmk. 373 *Perf. 14*

697 A114 15c Shot put 15 15
698 A114 45c Wheelchair race 45 45
699 A114 65c Girl's long jump 65 65
700 A114 $2 Emblem, creed 2.00 2.00

CAPEX '87 — A115

1987, June 12

701 A115 25c Barn swallow 35 35
702 A115 50c Yellow warbler 75 75
703 A115 65c Audubon's shearwater 90 90
704 A115 75c Black-whiskered vireo 1.10 1.10
705 A115 $1 Scarlet tanager 1.50 1.50
Nos. 701-705 (5) 4.60 4.60

Natl. Scouting Movement, 75th Anniv. — A116

1987, July 24 *Perf. 14x14¹/₂*

706 A116 10c Scout sign 15 15
707 A116 25c Campfire 25 25
708 A116 65c Merit badges, etc. 65 65
709 A116 $2 Marching band 2.00 2.00

Bridgetown Synagogue Restoration
A117

1987, Oct. 6 Wmk. 384 *Perf. 14¹/₂*

710 A117 50c Exterior 65 65
711 A117 65c Interior 85 85
712 A117 75c Ten Commandments, vert. 1.00 1.00
713 A117 $1 Marble laver, vert. 1.40 1.40

Natl. Independence, 21st Anniv. — A118

E.W. Barrow (1920-87), Father of Independence
A119

Designs: 25c, Coat of arms and seal of the colony. 45c, Natl. flag and the Union Jack. 65c, Silver dollar and penny. $2, Old and new regimental flags and Queen Elizabeth's colors.

1987, Nov. 24 Litho. *Perf. 14¹/₂*

714 A118 25c multicolored 25 25
715 A118 45c multicolored 45 45
716 A118 65c multicolored 65 65
717 A118 $2 multicolored 2.00 2.00

Souvenir Sheet

718 A119 $1.50 multicolored 1.50 1.50

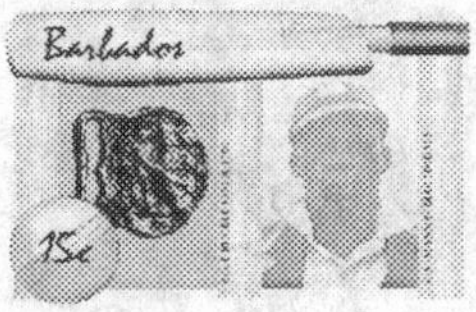

Cricket
A120

Bat, wicket posts, ball, 18th cent. belt buckle and batters: 15c, E.A. "Manny" Martindale. 45c, George Challenor. 50c, Herman C. Griffith. 75c, Harold Austin. $2, Frank Worrell.

1988 Litho. Wmk. 373 *Perf. 14*

719 A120 15c multicolored 15 15
720 A120 45c multicolored 45 45
720A A120 50c multicolored 50 50
721 A120 75c multicolored 75 75
722 A120 $2 multicolored 2.00 2.00
Nos. 719-722 (5) 3.85 3.85

Issue dates: No. 720A: July 11. Others, June 6.

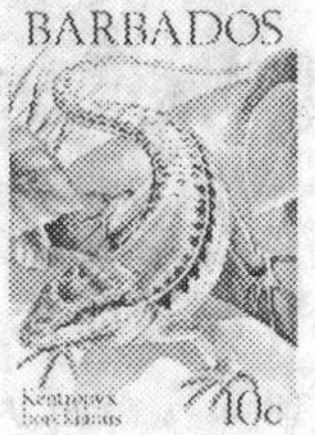

Lizards — A121

1988 Summer Olympics, Seoul — A122

1988, June 13

723 A121 10c Kentropyx borckianus 15 15
724 A121 50c Hemidactylus mabouia 60 60
725 A121 65c Anolis extremus 75 75
726 A121 $2 Gymnophthalmus underwoodii 2.25 2.25

Perf. 14¹/₂
1988, Aug. 2 Litho. Wmk. 373

727 A122 25c Cycling 25 25
728 A122 45c Running 45 45
729 A122 75c Swimming 75 75
730 A122 $2 Yachting 2.00 2.00
a. Souvenir sheet of 4, #727-730 3.50 3.50

Lloyds of London, 300th Anniv.
Common Design Type

Designs: 40c, Royal Exchange, 1774. 50c, Sugar mill (windmill), horiz. 65c, Container ship Author, horiz. $2, Sinking of the Titanic, 1912.

1988, Oct. 18 Litho. *Perf. 14*

731 CD341 40c multicolored 40 40
732 CD341 50c multicolored 50 50
733 CD341 65c multicolored 65 65
734 CD341 $2 multicolored 2.00 2.00

Harry Bayley Observatory, 25th Anniv.
A123

Designs: 25c, Observatory, crescent Moon, Venus and Harry Bayley. 65c, Observatory and constellations. 75c, Andromeda Galaxy and telescope. $2, Orion Constellation.

1988, Nov. 28 Wmk. 384 *Perf. 14¹/₂*

735 A123 25c multicolored 25 25
736 A123 65c multicolored 65 65
737 A123 75c multicolored 75 75
738 A123 $2 multicolored 2.00 2.00

Commercial Aviation, 50th Anniv. — A124

Designs: 25c, Caribbean Airline Liat BAe748. 65c, Pan American DC-8. 75c, Two British Airways Concordes, Grantley Adams Intl. Airport. $2, Two Caribbean Air Cargo Boeing 707-351c.

1989, Mar. 20 Litho. *Perf. 14*

739 A124 25c multicolored 25 25
740 A124 65c multicolored 65 65
741 A124 75c multicolored 75 75
742 A124 $2 multicolored 2.00 2.00

Parliament, 350th Anniv. — A125

1989, July 19 Litho. *Perf. 13¹/₂*

743 A125 25c Assembly chamber 25 25
744 A125 50c The Speaker 50 50
745 A125 75c Parliament, c. 1882 75 75
746 A125 $2.50 Queen in Parliament 2.50 2.50

Parliament, 350th anniv. See No. 752.

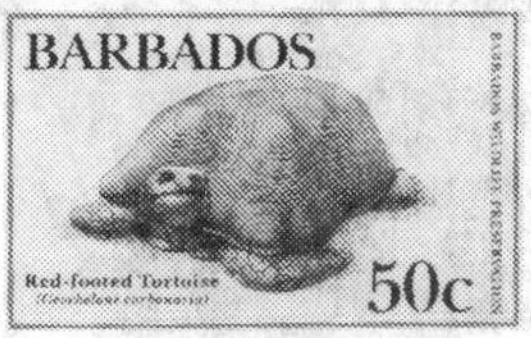

Wildlife Preservation — A126

1989, Aug. 1 *Perf. 14x13¹/₂*

747 A126 10c Wild hare, vert. 15 15
748 A126 50c Red-footed tortoise 50 50
749 A126 65c Green monkey, vert. 65 65
750 A126 $2 Toad 2.00 2.00

Souvenir Sheet

751 A126 $1 Mongoose, vert. 1.00 1.00

Parliament Anniv. Type of 1989
Souvenir Sheet

1989, Oct. 9 Wmk. 373 *Perf. 13¹/₂*

752 A125 $1 The Mace 1.00 1.00

35th Commonwealth Parliamentary Conf.

Wild Plants — A127

World Stamp Expo '89, Washington, DC — A128

1989-92 Wmk. 373 *Perf. 14¹/₂*

753 A127 2c Bread'n cheese 15 15
754 A127 5c Scarlet cordia 15 15
755 A127 10c Columnar cactus 15 15
756 A127 20c Spiderlily 20 20
757 A127 25c Rock balsam 25 25
758 A127 30c Hollyhock 30 30
758A A127 35c Red sage 35 35
759 A127 45c Yellow shakshak 45 45
760 A127 50c Whitewood 50 50
761 A127 55c Bluebell 55 55
762 A127 65c Prickly sage 65 65

763	A127	70c Seaside samphire	70	70
764	A127	80c Flat-hand dildo	80	80
764A	A127	90c Herringbone	90	90
765	A127	$1.10 Lent tree	1.10	1.10
766	A127	$2.50 Rodwood	2.50	2.50
767	A127	$5 Cowitch	5.00	5.00
768	A127	$10 Maypole	10.00	10.00
		Nos. 753-768 (18)	24.70	24.70

Issue dates: 35c, 90c, June 9, 1992 (inscribed 1991). Others, Nov. 1.

Nos. 754-756, 763, 765 exist inscribed "1991."

For overprints see Nos. 788-790.

1990 Litho. Wmk. 384

753a	A127	2c	15	15
754a	A127	5c	15	15
755a	A127	10c	15	15
756a	A127	20c	18	18
757a	A127	25c	22	22
759a	A127	45c	40	40
760a	A127	50c	45	45
762a	A127	65c	58	58
766a	A127	$2.50	2.25	2.25
767a	A127	$5	4.50	4.50
768a	A127	$10	9.00	9.00
		Nos. 753a-768a (11)	18.03	18.03

Inscribed 1990.

1989, Nov. 17 Wmk. 384 *Perf. 14*

Water sports.

769	A128	25c Water skiing	25	25
770	A128	50c Yachting	50	50
771	A128	65c Scuba diving	65	65
772	A128	$2.50 Surfing	2.50	2.50

Horse Racing A129

Wmk. 373

1990, May 3 Litho. *Perf. 14*

773	A129	25c Bugler, jockeys	25	25
774	A129	45c Parade ring	45	45
775	A129	75c In the straight	75	75
776	A129	$2 Winner, vert.	2.00	2.00

Barbados No. 2 — A130

Stamps on stamps: No. 778, Barbados #61. 65c, Barbados #73. $2.50, Barbados #121. No. 781a, Great Britain #1. No. 781b, Barbados #108.

1990, May 3

777	A130	25c shown	25	25
778	A130	50c multicolored	50	50
779	A130	65c multicolored	65	65
780	A130	$2.50 multicolored	2.50	2.50

Souvenir Sheet

781		Sheet of 2	1.00	1.00
a.-b.	A130	50c any single	50	50

Stamp World London '90.

Queen Mother, 90th Birthday

Common Design Types

1990, Aug. 8 Wmk. 384 *Perf. 14x15*

782	CD343	75c At age 23	75	75

Perf. 14½

783	CD344	$2.50 Engagement portrait, 1923	2.50	2.50

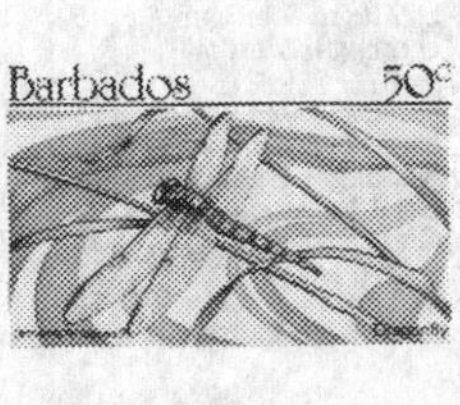

Insects A131

Wmk. 373

1990, Oct. 16 Litho. *Perf. 14*

784	A131	50c Dragonfly	50	50
785	A131	65c Black hardback beetle	65	65
786	A131	75c Green grasshopper	75	75
787	A131	$2 God-horse	2.00	2.00

Nos. 757, 764 and 766 Overprinted

VISIT OF
HRH THE
PRINCESS ROYAL
OCTOBER 1990

1990, Nov. 21 *Perf. 14½*

788	A127	25c on No. 757	25	25
789	A127	80c on No. 764	80	80
790	A127	$2.50 on No. 766	2.50	2.50

Christmas — A132

1990, Dec. 4 *Perf. 14*

791	A132	20c Christmas star	20	20
792	A132	50c Nativity scene	50	50
793	A132	$1 Stained glass window	1.00	1.00
794	A132	$2 Angel	2.00	2.00

Yellow Warbler A133

1991, Mar. 4

795	A133	10c shown	15	15
796	A133	20c Male, female, nest	20	20
797	A133	45c Female, chicks	45	45
798	A133	$1 Male, fledgling	1.00	1.00

World Wildlife Fund.

Fishing A134

Perf. 13½x14, 14x13½

1991, June 18 Litho. Wmk. 373

799	A134	5c Daily catch, vert.	15	15
800	A134	50c Line fishing	50	50
801	A134	75c Cleaning fish	75	75
802	A134	$2.50 Game fishing, vert.	2.50	2.50

Freemasonry in Barbados, 250th Anniv. — A135

Designs: 25c, Masonic Building, Bridgetown. 65c, Compass and square. 75c, Royal arch jewel. $2.50, Columns, apron and centenary badge.

1991, Sept. 17 *Perf. 14*

803	A135	25c multicolored	25	25
804	A135	65c multicolored	65	65
805	A135	75c multicolored	75	75
806	A135	$2.50 multicolored	2.50	2.50

Butterflies A136

1991, Nov. 15 Wmk. 384

807	A136	20c Polydamus swallowtail	20	20
808	A136	50c Long-tailed skipper, vert.	50	50
809	A136	65c Cloudless sulphur	65	65
810	A136	$2.50 Caribbean buckeye, vert.	2.50	2.50

Souvenir Sheet

811	A136	$4 Painted lady	4.00	4.00

Phila Nippon '91.

Independence, 25th Anniv. — A137

Governor-General Dame Nita Barrow and: 10c, Students in classroom. 25c, Barbados Workers Union headquarters. 65c, Building industry. 75c, Agriculture. $1, Inoculations given at health clinic. $2.50, Gordon Greenidge, Desmond Haynes, cricket players (no portrait).

1991, Nov. 20 Wmk. 373

812	A137	10c multicolored	15	15
813	A137	25c multicolored	25	25
814	A137	65c multicolored	65	65
815	A137	75c multicolored	75	75
816	A137	$1 multicolored	1.00	1.00
		Nos. 812-816 (5)	2.80	2.80

Souvenir Sheet

817	A137	$2.50 multi, vert.	2.40	2.50

Easter — A138

Wmk. 384

1992, Apr. 7 Litho. *Perf. 14*

818	A138	35c Christ carrying cross	35	35
819	A138	70c Christ on cross	70	70
820	A138	90c Christ taken down from cross	90	90
821	A138	$3 Christ risen	3.00	3.00

Flowering Trees A139

Perf. 14x13½

1992, June 9 Litho. Wmk. 373

822	A139	10c Cannon ball	15	15
823	A139	30c Golden shower	30	30
824	A139	80c Frangipani	80	80
825	A139	$1.10 Flamboyant	1.10	1.10

Orchids A140

Designs: 55c, Epidendrum "Costa Rica." 65c, Cattleya guttaca. 70c, Laeliacattleya "Splashing Around." $1.40, Phalaenopsis "Kathy Saegert."

1992, Sept. 8 *Perf. 13½x14*

826	A140	55c multicolored	55	55
827	A140	65c multicolored	65	65
828	A140	70c multicolored	70	70
829	A140	$1.40 multicolored	1.40	1.40

For overprints see Nos. 838-841.

Transport and Tourism A141

Designs: 5c, Mini Moke, Gun Hill Signal Station, St. George. 35c, Tour bus, Bathsheba Beach, St. Joseph. 90c, BWIA McDonnell Douglas MD 83, Grantley Adams Airport. $2, Cruise ship Festivale, deep water harbor, Bridgetown.

Perf. 14½

1992, Dec. 15 Litho. Wmk. 373

830	A141	5c multicolored	15	15
831	A141	35c multicolored	35	35
832	A141	90c multicolored	90	90
833	A141	$2 multicolored	2.00	2.00

Cacti and Succulents — A142

Wmk. 373

1993, Feb. 9 Litho. *Perf. 14*

834	A142	10c Barbados gooseberry	15	15
835	A142	35c Night-blooming cereus	35	35
836	A142	$1.40 Aloe	1.40	1.40
837	A142	$2 Scrunchineel	2.00	2.00

Nos. 826-829 Ovptd. "WORLD ORCHID CONFERENCE 1993" on 2 or 4 lines

Perf. 13½x14

1993, Apr. 1 Litho. Wmk. 373

838	A140	55c on #826 multi	55	55
839	A140	65c on #827 multi	65	65
840	A140	70c on #828 multi	70	70
841	A140	$1.40 on #829 multi	1.40	1.40

Royal Air Force, 75th Anniv.

Common Design Type

Designs: 10c, Hawker Hunter. 30c, Handley Page Victor. 70c, Hawker Typhoon. $3, Hawker Hurricane.

No. 846a, Armstrong Whitworth Siskin 3a. b, Supermarine S.6B. c, Supermarine Walrus. d, Hawker Hart.

1993, Apr. 1 *Perf. 14*

842	CD350	10c multicolored	15	15
843	CD350	30c multicolored	30	30
844	CD350	70c multicolored	70	70
845	CD350	$3 multicolored	3.00	3.00

Souvenir Sheet

846	CD350	50c Sheet of 4, #a.-d.	2.00	2.00

Cannon A143

Designs: 5c, 18-pounder Culverin, 1625, Denmark Fort. 45c, 6-pounder Commonwealth gun, 1649-1660, St. Ann's Fort. $1, 9-pounder Demi-culverin, 1691, The Main Guard. $2.50, 32-pounder Demi-cannon, 1693-94, Charles Fort.

Wmk. 373

1993, June 8 Litho. *Perf. 13*

847 A143	5c	multicolored	15	15
848 A143	45c	multicolored	45	45
849 A143	$1	multicolored	1.00	1.00
850 A143	$2.50	multicolored	2.50	2.50

Barbados Museum, 60th Anniv. — A144

Designs: 10c, Shell box, carved figure. 75c, Map, print of three people. 90c, Silver cup, print of soldier. $1.10, Map.

Wmk. 373

1993, Sept. 14 Litho. *Perf. 14*

851 A144	10c	multicolored	15	15
852 A144	75c	multicolored	75	75
853 A144	90c	multicolored	90	90
854 A144	$1.10	multicolored	1.10	1.10

A145

A146

Prehistoric Aquatic Reptiles: a, Plesiosaurus. b, Ichthyosaurus. c, Elasmosaurus. d, Mosasaurus. e, Archelon. Continuous design.

Wmk. 373

1993, Oct. 28 Litho. *Perf. 13*

855 A145	90c	Strip of 5, #a.-e.	4.50	4.50

Wmk. 384

1994, Jan. 11 Litho. *Perf. 14*

856 A146	10c	Cricket	15	15
857 A146	35c	Motor racing	35	35
858 A146	50c	Golf	48	48
859 A146	70c	Run Barbados 10k	70	70
860 A146	$1.40	Swimming	1.40	1.40
		Nos. 856-860 (5)	3.08	3.08

Sports & tourism.

Migratory Birds A147

Wmk. 373

1994, Feb. 18 Litho. *Perf. 14*

861 A147	10c	Whimbrel	15	15
862 A147	35c	American golden plover	35	35
863 A147	70c	Ruddy turnstone	70	70
864 A147	$3	Tricolored heron	3.00	3.00

Hong Kong '94.

1st UN Conference of Small Island Developing States — A148

1994, Apr. 25 *Perf. 14x14¹/₂*

865 A148	10c	Bathsheba	15	15
866 A148	65c	Pico Tenneriffe	65	65
867 A148	90c	Ragged Point Lighthouse	90	90
868 A148	$2.50	Consett Bay	2.50	2.50

Order of the Carribbean Community — A149

First award recipients: No. 869, Sir Shridath Ramphal, statesman, Guyana. No. 870, Derek Walcott, writer, Nobel Laureate, St. Lucia. No. 871, William Demas, economist, Trinidad and Tobago.

Wmk. 373

1994, July 4 Litho. *Perf. 14*

869 A149	70c	multicolored	70	70
870 A149	70c	multicolored	70	70
871 A149	70c	multicolored	70	70

Ships A150

Designs: 5c, Dutch Flyut, 1695. 10c, Geestport, 1994. 25c, HMS Victory, 1805. 30c, Royal Viking Queen, 1994. 35c, HMS Barbados, 1945. 45c, Faraday, 1924. 50c, USCG Hamilton, 1974. 65c, HMCS Saguenay, 1939. 70c, Inanda, 1928. 80c, HMS Rodney, 1944. 90c, USS John F. Kennedy, 1982. $1.10, William & John, 1627. $5, USCG Champlain, 1931. $10, Artist, 1877.

Wmk. 373

1994, Aug. 16 Litho. *Perf. 14*

872 A150	5c	multicolored	15	15
873 A150	10c	multicolored	15	15
874 A150	25c	multicolored	25	25
875 A150	30c	multicolored	30	30
876 A150	35c	multicolored	35	35
877 A150	45c	multicolored	45	45
878 A150	50c	multicolored	50	50
879 A150	65c	multicolored	65	65
880 A150	70c	multicolored	70	70
881 A150	80c	multicolored	80	80
882 A150	90c	multicolored	90	90
883 A150	$1.10	multicolored	1.10	1.10
884 A150	$5	multicolored	5.00	5.00
885 A150	$10	multicolored	10.00	10.00
		Nos. 872-885 (14)	21.30	21.30

SEMI-POSTAL STAMPS

No. 73 Surcharged in Red

Kingston Relief Fund. 1d.

Wmk. 2

1907, Jan. 25 Typo. *Perf. 14*

B1 A8	1p on 2p sl & org		1.75	2.50
a.	No period after 1d		15.00	17.50
b.	Inverted surcharge		1.75	2.50
c.	Inverted surcharge, no period after 1d		15.00	17.50
d.	Double surcharge		750.00	
e.	Dbl. surch., both invtd.		750.00	

Catalogue values for unused stamps in this section, from this point to the end of the section, are for Never Hinged items.

No. 406 Surcharged

28c + 4c
ST. VINCENT
RELIEF
FUND

1979, May 29 Photo. Wmk. 314

B2 A56	28c + 4c on 35c multi		30	30

The surtax was for victims of the eruption of Mt. Soufrière.

POSTAGE DUE STAMPS

Catalogue values for unused stamps in this section are for Never Hinged items.

D1

D2

1934-47 Typo. Wmk. 4 *Perf. 14*

J1 D1	¹/₂p	green ('35)	60	70
J2 D1	1p	black	1.10	40
J3 D1	3p	dk car rose ('47)	17.50	22.50

A 2nd die of the 1p was introduced in 1947.

1950

J4 D1	1c	green	18	18
J5 D1	2c	black	40	40
J6 D1	6c	carmine rose	1.50	1.75

Values are for 1953 chalky paper printing.

Wmk. 4a (error)

J4a D1	1c	green	57.50	
J5a D1	2c	black	65.00	
J6a D1	6c	carmine rose	75.00	

1965-74 Wmk. 314 *Perf. 14*

J7 D1	1c	green	30	30
J8 D1	2c	black	35	35
J9 D1	6c	carmine rose	65	65
a.		Watermarked sideways ('74)	2.25	2.25

Perf. 13¹/₂x14

1976, May 12 Litho. Wmk. 373

Designs: Each stamp shows different stylized flower in background.

J10 D2	1c	brt pink & mag	15	15
J11 D2	2c	lt & dk vio blue	15	15
J12 D2	5c	yellow & brown	15	15
J13 D2	10c	lilac & purple	15	15
J14 D2	25c	yel green & dk grn	22	22
J15 D2	$1	rose & red	90	90
		Set value	1.35	1.35

1985, July *Perf. 15x14*

J10a D2	1c		15	15
J11a D2	2c		15	15
J12a D2	5c		15	15
J13a D2	10c		15	15
J14a D2	25c		22	22
		Set value	43	43

WAR TAX STAMP

No. 118 Overprinted **WAR TAX**

1917 Wmk. 3 *Perf. 14*

MR1 A12	1p	carmine	15	15
a.		Imperf., pair	*4,000.*	

BARBUDA

LOCATION — Northernmost of the Leeward Islands, West Indies

GOVT. — Dependency of Antigua

AREA — 63 sq. mi.

POP. — 1,000 (estimated)

See Antigua.

12 Pence = 1 Shilling

Catalogue values for unused stamps in this country are for Never Hinged items, beginning with Scott 12 in the regular postage section, and Scott B1 in the semi-postal section.

Watermark

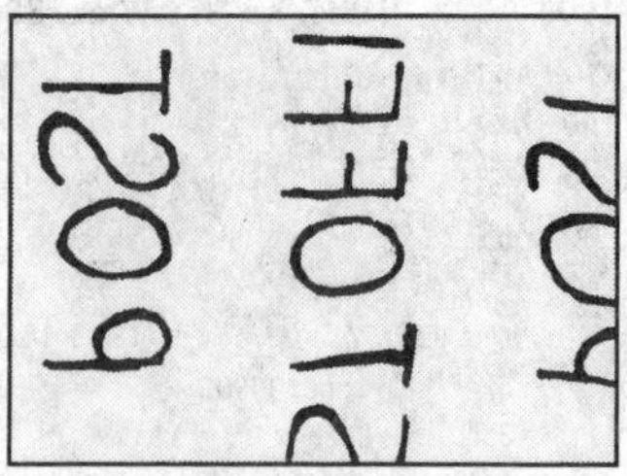

Wmk. 380- "POST OFFICE"

Leeward Islands Stamps and Types of 1912-22 Overprinted in Black or Red

BARBUDA

Die II

For description of dies I and II see back of this section of the Catalogue.

1922, July 13 Wmk. 4 *Perf. 14*

1 A5	¹/₂p	green	1.40	*1.50*
2 A5	1p	rose red	1.40	*1.50*
3 A5	2p	gray	1.50	*1.90*
4 A5	2¹/₂p	ultramarine	1.50	*1.90*
5 A5	6p	vio & red vio	3.75	*3.75*
6 A5	2sh	vio & ultra, *bl*	15.00	*18.00*
7 A5	3sh	grn & violet	30.00	*35.00*
8 A5	4sh	blk & scar (R)	30.00	*35.00*

Wmk. 3

9 A5	3p	violet, *yel*	1.40	*1.90*
10 A5	1sh	blk, *emer* (R)	3.00	*3.75*
11 A5	5sh	grn & red, *yel*	92.50	*110.00*
		Nos. 1-11 (11)	181.45	*214.20*

Catalogue values for unused stamps in this section, from this point to the end of the section, are for Never Hinged items.

Map — B1

Fish — B2

1968-70 Litho. Unwmk. *Perf. 14*

12 B1	¹/₂c	blk, salmon pink & red brn	15	15
13 B1	1c	blk, org & brt org	15	15
14 B1	2c	blk, brt pink & brt rose	15	15
15 B1	3c	blk, yel & org yel	15	15
16 B1	4c	blk, lt grn & brt grn	15	15
17 B1	5c	blk, bl grn & brt bl grn	15	15
18 B1	6c	blk, lt lil & red lil	15	15
19 B1	10c	blk, lt bl & dk bl	15	15
20 B1	15c	blk, dl grn & grn	16	16
21 B2	20c	Great barracuda	22	22
22 B2	25c	Great amberjack	26	26
23 B2	35c	French angelfish	38	38
24 B2	50c	Porkfish	52	52
25 B2	75c	Striped parrotfish	80	80

26 B2 $1 Longspine squirrelfish 1.10 1.10
27 B2 $2.50 Catalufa 2.75 2.75
28 B2 $5 Blue chromis 5.50 5.50
Nos. 12-28 (17) 12.89 12.89

Issue dates: ½c-15c, Nov. 19. 20c, July 22, 1970. 25c-75c, Feb. 5, 1969. Others, Mar. 6, 1969.
For surcharge see No. 80.

1968 Summer Olympics, Mexico City — B3

Designs: 25c, Running, Aztec calendar stone. 35c, High jumping, Aztec statue. 75c, Yachting, Aztec lion mask. $1, Soccer, Aztec carved stone.

1968, Dec. 20
29 B3 25c multicolored 25 25
30 B3 35c multicolored 35 35
31 B3 75c multicolored 75 75

Souvenir Sheet
32 B3 $1 multicolored 2.75 2.75

The Ascension, by Orcagna — B4

1969, Mar. 24
33 B4 25c blue & black 15 15
34 B4 35c dp carmine & blk 16 16
35 B4 75c violet & black 32 32

Easter.

3rd Caribbean Boy Scout Jamboree B5

1969, Aug. 7
36 B5 25c Flag ceremony 45 45
37 B5 35c Campfire 65 65
38 B5 75c Rowing 1.40 1.40

The Sistine Madonna, by Raphael — B6

1969, Oct. 20
39 B6 ½c multicolored 15 15
40 B6 25c multicolored 18 18
41 B6 35c multicolored 25 25
42 B6 75c multicolored 55 55
Set value 1.00 1.00

Christmas.

English Monarchs — B7

1970-71 *Perf. 14½x14*
43 B7 35c William I 26 26
44 B7 35c William II 26 26
45 B7 35c Henry I 26 26
46 B7 35c Stephen 26 26
47 B7 35c Henry II 26 26
48 B7 35c Richard I 26 26
49 B7 35c John 26 26
50 B7 35c Henry III 26 26
51 B7 35c Edward I 26 26
52 B7 35c Edward II 26 26
53 B7 35c Edward III 26 26
54 B7 35c Richard II 26 26
55 B7 35c Henry IV 26 26
56 B7 35c Henry V 26 26
57 B7 35c Henry VI 26 26
58 B7 35c Edward IV 26 26
59 B7 35c Edward V 26 26
60 B7 35c Richard III 26 26
61 B7 35c Henry VII 26 26
62 B7 35c Henry VIII 26 26
63 B7 35c Edward VI 26 26
64 B7 35c Lady Jane Grey 26 26
65 B7 35c Mary I 26 26
66 B7 35c Elizabeth I 26 26
67 B7 35c James I 26 26
68 B7 35c Charles I 26 26
69 B7 35c Charles II 26 26
70 B7 35c James II 26 26
71 B7 35c William III 26 26
72 B7 35c Mary II 26 26
73 B7 35c Anne 26 26
74 B7 35c George I 26 26
75 B7 35c George II 26 26
76 B7 35c George III 26 26
77 B7 35c George IV 26 26
78 B7 35c William IV 26 26
79 B7 35c Victoria 26 26
Nos. 43-79 (37) 9.62 9.62

Issue dates: 1970, No. 43, Feb. 16; No. 44, Mar. 2; No. 45, Mar. 16; No. 46, Apr. 4; No. 47, Apr. 15; No. 48, May 1; No. 49, May 15; No. 50, June 1; No. 51, June 15; No. 52, July 1; No. 53, July 15; No. 54, Aug. 1; No. 55, Aug. 15; No. 56, Sept. 1; No. 57, Sept. 15; No. 58, Oct. 1; No. 59, Oct. 15; No. 60, Nov. 2; No. 61, Nov. 16; No. 62, Dec. 1; No. 63, Dec. 15.
1971; No. 64, Jan. 2; No. 65, Jan. 15; No. 66, Feb. 1; No. 67, Feb. 15; No. 68, Mar. 1; No. 69, Mar. 15; No. 70, Apr. 1; No. 71, Apr. 15; No. 72, May 1; No. 73, May 15; No. 74, June 1; No. 75, June 15; No. 76, July 1; No. 77, July 15; No. 78, Aug. 2; No. 79, Aug. 16.
See Nos. 626-631 for other Monarchs.

No. 12 Surcharged

20c

1970, Feb. 26 *Perf. 14*
80 B1 20c on 1/2c multicolored 15 15

Easter — B8

1970, Mar. 16
81 B8 25c Carrying Cross 15 15
82 B8 35c Descent from cross 18 18
83 B8 75c Crucifixion 35 35
a. Strip of 3, #81-83 70 70

Charles Dickens B9

1970, July 10
84 B9 20c Oliver Twist 15 15
85 B9 75c Old Curiosity Shop 55 55

Christmas B10

Designs: 20c, Madonna of the Meadow, by Giovanni Bellini. 50c, Madonna, Child and Angels from Wilton Diptych. 75c, Nativity, by Piero della Francesca.

1970, Oct. 15
86 B10 20c multicolored 15 15
87 B10 50c multicolored 26 26
88 B10 75c multicolored 42 42

British Red Cross, Cent. B11

1970, Dec. 21
89 B11 20c Patient in wheelchair, vert. 22 22
90 B11 35c shown 38 38
91 B11 75c Child care 80 80

Easter — B12

Details from the Mond Crucifixion, by Raphael.

1971, Apr. 7
92 B12 35c Angel 22 22
93 B12 50c Crucifixion 30 30
94 B12 75c Angel, diff. 48 48
a. Strip of 3, #92-94 1.00 1.00

Martello Tower B13

1971, May 10
95 B13 20c shown 15 15
96 B13 25c Sailboats 15 15
97 B13 50c Hotel bungalows 30 30
98 B13 75c Government House, mystery stone 45 45

Christmas — B14

Paintings: ½c, The Granduca Madonna, by Raphael. 35c, The Ansidei Madonna, by Raphael. 50c, The Virgin and Child, by Botticelli. 75c, The Madonna of the Trees, by Bellini.

1971, Oct. 4
99 B14 ½c multicolored 15 15
100 B14 35c multicolored 25 25
101 B14 50c multicolored 38 38
102 B14 75c multicolored 60 60
Set value 1.25 1.25

A set of four stamps for Durer (20c, 35c, 50c, 75c) was not authorized.

All stamps are types of Antigua or overprinted on stamps of Antigua unless otherwise specified. Many of the "BARBUDA" overprints are vertical.

Nos. 321-322 Ovptd. "BARBUDA"

1973, Nov. 14 *Perf. 13½*
103 A65 35c multicolored 1.50 1.50
104 A65 $2 multicolored 8.00 8.00

Nos. 313-315a Ovptd. in Red "BARBUDA"

1973, Nov. 26 *Perf. 13½x14*
105 A63 20c multicolored 24 24
106 A63 35c multicolored 40 40
107 A63 75c multicolored 85 85

Souvenir Sheet
108 Sheet of 4, #105-107, 108a 4.00 4.00
a. A63 5c multicolored

Carnival, 1973.

Nos. 307, 309, 311, 311a Ovptd. "BARBUDA"

Perf. 14x13½

1973, Nov. 26 **Wmk. 314**
109 A53 ½c multicolored 15 15
110 A53 20c multicolored 20 20
111 A53 75c multicolored 80 80

Souvenir Sheet
112 Sheet of 5, #109-111, 112a-112b + label 3.50 3.50
a. A53 10c multicolored
b. A53 35c multicolored

Nos. 241a, 242-243, 244a, 245-248, 249a, 250-254, 255a, 256, 256a, 257 Ovptd. "BARBUDA"

Wmk. 314 Sideways, Upright

1973-74 *Perf. 14*
113 A51 ½c multicolored 15 15
114 A51 1c multicolored 15 15
115 A51 2c multicolored 15 15
116 A51 3c multicolored 15 15
117 A51 4c multicolored 15 15
118 A51 5c multicolored 15 15
119 A51 6c multicolored 15 15
120 A51 10c multicolored 18 18
121 A51 15c multicolored 28 28
122 A51 20c multicolored 38 38
123 A51 25c multicolored 45 45
124 A51 35c multicolored 65 65
125 A51 50c multicolored 95 95
126 A51 75c multicolored 1.40 1.40
127 A51 $1 multicolored 1.90 1.90
128 A51 $2.50 multicolored 4.75 4.75
a. Wmk. upright 9.25 9.25
129 A51 $5 multicolored 9.25 9.25
Nos. 113-129 (17) 21.24 21.24

Issue dates: ½c, 3c, 15c, $1, $2.50, Feb. 18, 1974. Others, Nov. 26.

Nos. 316-320a Ovptd. in Silver or Red "BARBUDA"

Perf. 14½

1973, Dec. 11 **Photo.** **Unwmk.**
130 A64 3c multicolored 15 15
131 A64 5c multicolored 15 15
132 A64 20c multicolored 30 30
133 A64 35c multicolored (R) 55 55
134 A64 $1 multicolored (R) 1.50 1.50
Nos. 130-134 (5) 2.65 2.65

Souvenir Sheet

135 Sheet of 5 + label 9.00 9.00
a. A64 35c multicolored (S)
b. A64 $1 multicolored (S)

No. 135 contains Nos. 130-132, 135a-135b.

Nos. 323-324a Ovptd. "BARBUDA"

1973, Dec. 16 Litho. *Perf. 13½*

136 A65 35c multicolored 32 32
137 A65 $2 multicolored 1.75 1.75
a. Souvenir sheet of 2, #136-137 2.50 2.50

Nos. 325-328 Ovptd. "BARBUDA"

1974, Feb. 18 Wmk. 314

138 A66 5c multicolored 15 15
139 A66 20c multicolored 18 18
140 A66 35c multicolored 32 32
141 A66 75c multicolored 70 70

Nos. 329-333 Ovptd. "BARBUDA"

1974, May 1 *Perf. 14x13½*

142 A53 ½c multicolored 15 15
143 A53 10c multicolored 15 15
144 A53 20c multicolored 30 30
145 A53 35c multicolored 52 52
146 A53 75c multicolored 1.10 1.10
Nos. 142-146 (5) 2.22 2.22

No. 333a exists with overprint.

Nos. 334-340 Ovptd. Type "a" or "b" and No. 340 "BARBUDA" in Red

BARBUDA
15 SEPT.
1874 G.P.U.
a

BARBUDA
13 JULY 1922
b

1974, July 15 Unwmk. *Perf. 14½*
Se-tenant Pairs Overprinted Type "a" on Left Stamp, Type "b" on Right Stamp

148 A67 ½c multicolored 15 15
149 A67 1c multicolored 15 15
150 A67 2c multicolored 15 15
151 A67 5c multicolored 40 40
152 A67 20c multicolored 1.50 1.50
153 A67 35c multicolored 2.75 2.75
154 A67 $1 multicolored 7.50 7.50
Nos. 148-154 (7) 12.60 12.60

Souvenir Sheet
Perf. 13

155 Sheet of 7 + label 10.00 10.00
a. A67 ½c multicolored 15 15
b. A67 1c multicolored 15 15
c. A67 2c multicolored 15 15
d. A67 5c multicolored 30 30
e. A67 20c multicolored 1.25 1.25
f. A67 35c multicolored 2.00 2.00
g. A67 $1 multicolored 6.00 6.00

UPU, cent.

Nos. 341-344a Ovptd. "BARBUDA"

1974, Aug. 14 Wmk. 314 *Perf. 14*

156 A68 5c multicolored 15 15
157 A68 20c multicolored 18 18
158 A68 35c multicolored 32 32
159 A68 75c multicolored 65 65
a. Souvenir sheet of 4, #156-159 1.25 1.25

Nos. 345-348a Ovptd. "BARBUDA" and

World Cup Soccer Championships — B16

Various soccer plays.

1974, Sept. 2 Unwmk. *Perf. 15, 14*

160 A69 5c multicolored 15 15
161 A69 35c multicolored 30 30
162 B16 35c multicolored 16 16
163 A69 75c multicolored 65 65
164 A69 $1 multicolored 85 85
a. Souv. sheet of 4, #160-161, 163-164 + 2 labels, perf. 13½ 2.25 2.25
165 B16 $1.20 multicolored 55 55
166 B16 $2.50 multicolored 1.25 1.25
a. Souv. sheet of 3, #162, 165-166 3.00 3.00
Nos. 160-166 (7) 3.91 3.91

UPU, Cent. — B17

1974, Sept. 30 *Perf. 14x13½*

167 B17 35c Ship letter, 1833 15 15
168 B17 $1.20 #1, 2 on FDC 48 48
169 B17 $2.50 Airplane, map 1.00 1.00
a. Souvenir sheet of 3, #167-169 4.00 4.00

Greater Amberjack B18

1974-75 *Perf. 14x14½, 14½x14*

170 B18 ½c Oleander, rose bay 15 15
171 B18 1c Blue petrea 15 15
172 B18 2c Poinsettia 15 15
173 B18 3c Cassia tree 15 15
174 B18 4c shown 15 15
175 B18 5c Holy Trinity School 15 15
176 B18 6c Snorkeling 15 15
177 B18 10c Pilgrim Holiness Church 15 15
178 B18 15c New Cottage Hospital 15 15
179 B18 20c Post Office & Treasury 16 16
180 B18 25c Island jetty & boats 20 20
181 B18 35c Martello Tower 28 28

Size: 39x25mm
Perf. 14

182 B18 50c Warden's House 40 40
183 B18 75c Inter-island air service 60 60
184 B18 $1 Tortoise 80 80

Size: 45x29mm
Perf. 13½x14

185 B18 $2.50 Spiny lobster 2.00 2.00
186 B18 $5 Frigate birds 4.00 4.00
a. Perf. 14x15

Size: 34x47mm

187 B18 $10 Hibiscus 8.00 8.00
Nos. 170-187 (18) 17.79 17.79

Nos. 170-173, 180, 187 vert. Issue dates: 4c, 5c, 6c, 10c, 15c, 20c, 25c, 35c, 75c, Oct. 15, 1974, ½c, 1c, 2c, 3c, 50c, $1, $2.50, No. 186, Jan. 6, 1975, No. 186a, July 24, 1975, $10, Sept. 19, 1975.
For overprints see Nos. 213-214.

Nos. 349-352a Ovptd. "BARBUDA" in Red and

Winston Churchill, Birth Cent. — B19

1974 *Perf. 14½, 13½x14*

188 A70 5c multicolored 15 15
189 B19 5c Making broadcast 15 15
190 A70 35c multicolored 70 70
191 B19 35c Portrait 28 28
192 A70 75c multicolored 1.50 1.50
193 B19 75c Painting 60 60
194 A70 $1 multicolored 2.00 2.00
a. Souv. sheet of 4, #188, 190, 192, 194 8.50 8.50
195 B19 $1 Victory sign 80 80
a. Souv. sheet of 4, #189, 191, 193, 195 3.50 3.50
Nos. 188-195 (8) 6.18 6.18

Issue dates: Nos. 188, 190, 192, 194, Oct. 15, others, Nov. 20. For overprints see Nos. 213-214.

Nos. 353-360a Ovptd. "BARBUDA"

1974, Nov. 25 *Perf. 14½*

196 A71 ½c multicolored 15 15
197 A71 1c multicolored 15 15
198 A71 2c multicolored 15 15
199 A71 3c multicolored 15 15
200 A71 5c multicolored 15 15
201 A71 20c multicolored 20 20
202 A71 35c multicolored 38 38
203 A71 75c multicolored 80 80
a. Souv. sheet of 4, #200-203, perf. 13½ 1.40 1.40
Set value 1.50 1.50

Nos. 369-373a Ovptd. "BARBUDA"

1975, Mar. 17

204 A72 5c multicolored 15 15
205 A72 15c multicolored 28 28
206 A72 35c multicolored 65 65
207 A72 50c multicolored 90 90
208 A72 $1 multicolored 1.75 1.75
a. Souv. sheet of 5, #204-208 + label, perf. 13½x14 4.50 4.50
Nos. 204-208 (5) 3.73 3.73

Stamps from No. 208a are 43x28mm.

Battle of the Saints B20

1975, May 30 *Perf. 13½x14*

209 B20 35c shown 1.25 1.25
210 B20 50c Two ships 1.75 1.75
211 B20 75c Ships firing 2.75 2.75
212 B20 95c Sailors abandoning ship 3.25 3.25

Barbuda No. 186a Ovptd.

a

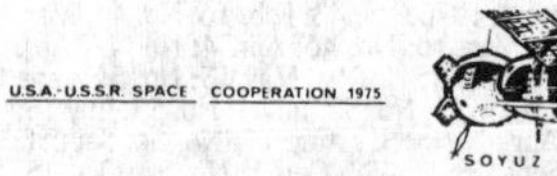

b

1975, July 2 *Perf. 14x15*

213 B18 (a) $5 multicolored
214 B18 (b) $5 multicolored

Overprint "a" is in 1st and 3rd vertical rows, "b" 2nd and 4th. The 5th row has no overprint. This can be collected se-tenant either as Nos. 213, 214 or 213, 214 and 186a.

Military Uniforms — B21

Designs: 35c, Officer of 65th Foot, 1763. 50c, Grenadier, 27th Foot, 1701-1710. 75c, Officer of 21st Foot, 1793-1796. 95c, Officer, Royal Regiment of Artillery, 1800.

1975, Sept. 17 *Perf. 14*

215 B21 35c multicolored 70 70
216 B21 50c multicolored 1.00 1.00
217 B21 75c multicolored 1.50 1.50
218 B21 95c multicolored 1.90 1.90

Barbuda Nos. 189, 191, 193, 195 Ovptd. "30th ANNIVERSARY / UNITED NATIONS / 1945 - 1975"

1975, Oct. 24 *Perf. 13½x14*

219 B19 5c multicolored 15 15
220 B19 35c multicolored 15 15
221 B19 75c multicolored 25 25
222 B19 $1 multicolored 60 60

Nos. 394-401a Ovptd. "BARBUDA"

1975, Nov. 17 *Perf. 14*

223 A77 ½c multicolored 15 15
224 A77 1c multicolored 15 15
225 A77 2c multicolored 15 15
226 A77 3c multicolored 15 15
227 A77 5c multicolored 15 15
228 A77 10c multicolored 15 15
229 A77 35c multicolored 20 20
230 A77 $2 multicolored 1.25 1.25
a. Souvenir sheet of 4, #227-230 2.50 2.50
Set value 1.55 1.55

Nos. 402-404 Ovptd. "BARBUDA"

1975, Dec. 15 *Perf. 14*

231 A78 5c multicolored 15 15
232 A78 35c multicolored 85 85
233 A78 $2 multicolored 5.00 5.00

American Revolution, Bicent. — B22

Details from Surrender of Cornwallis at Yorktown, by Trumbull: No. 234a, British officers. b, Gen. Benjamin Lincoln. c, Washington, Allied officers.
The Battle of Princeton: No. 235a, Infantry. b, Battle. c, Cannon fire.
Surrender of Burgoyne at Saratoga by Trumbull: No. 236a, Mounted officer. b, Washington, Burgoyne. c, American officers.
Signing the Declaration of Independence, by Trumbull: No. 237a, Delegates to Continental Congress. b, Adams, Sherman, Livingston, Jefferson and Franklin. c, Hancock, Thomson, Read, Dickinson, and Rutledge. Strips of 3 have continuous designs.

1976, Mar. 8 *Perf. 13½x13*

234 B22 15c Strip of 3, #a.-c. 32 32
235 B22 35c Strip of 3, #a.-c. 75 75
d. Souvenir sheet, #234-235 1.65 1.65
236 B22 $1 Strip of 3, #a.-c. 2.25 2.25
237 B22 $2 Strip of 3, #a.-c. 4.25 4.25
d. Souvenir sheet, #236-237 10.00 10.00

See Nos. 244-247.

Birds B23

1976, June 30 *Perf. 13½x14*

238 B23 35c Bananaquits 1.40 1.40
239 B23 50c Blue-hooded euphonia 2.00 2.00
240 B23 75c Royal tern 3.00 3.00
241 B23 95c Killdeer 3.75 3.75
242 B23 $1.25 Glossy cowbird 5.00 5.00
243 B23 $2 Purple gallinule 8.25 8.25
Nos. 238-243 (6) 23.40 23.40

Barbuda #234-237 With Inscription Added at Top Across the Three Stamps in Blue
"H.M. Queen Elizabeth" "Royal Visit 6th July 1976" "H.R.H. Duke of Edinburgh"

1976, Aug. 12 *Perf. 13½x14*
Size: 38x31mm

244 B22 15c Strip of 3, #a.-c. 30 30
245 B22 35c Strip of 3, #a.-c. 70 70
d. Souvenir sheet of 2, #244-245 1.10 1.10
246 B22 $1 Strip of 3, #a.-c. 2.00 2.00
247 B22 $2 Strip of 3, #a.-c. 4.00 4.00
d. Souvenir sheet, #246-247 7.00 7.00

Nos. 244-247 are perforated on outside edges; imperf. vertically within.

Nos. 448-452 Ovptd. "BARBUDA"

1976, Dec. 2 *Perf. 14*

248 A85 8c multicolored 15 15
249 A85 10c multicolored 15 15
250 A85 15c multicolored 15 15
251 A85 50c multicolored 32 32
252 A85 $1 multicolored 65 65
Set value 1.20 1.20

Nos. 431-437 Ovptd. "BARBUDA"

1976, Dec. 28 *Perf. 15*

253 A82 ½c yellow & multi 15 15
254 A82 1c purple & multi 15 15
255 A82 2c emerald & multi 15 15
256 A82 15c brt blue & multi 15 15

257 A82 30c olive & multi 20 20
258 A82 $1 orange & multi 65 65
259 A82 $2 red & multi 1.25 1.25
a. Souv. sheet of 4, #256-259, perf. 13½ 3.50 3.50
Set value 2.25 2.25

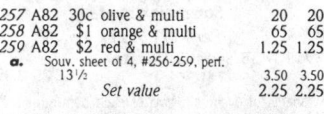

Telephone, Cent. — B24

1977, Jan. 31 ***Perf. 14***
260 B24 75c shown 30 30
261 B24 $1.25 Satellite dish, television 45 45
262 B24 $2 Satellites in earth orbit 75 75
a. Souv. sheet of 3, #260-262, perf. 15 3.50 3.50

Coronation of Queen Elizabeth II, 25th Anniv. — B25

Designs: Nos. 263a, St. Margaret's Church, Westminster. b, Westminster Abbey entrance. c, Westminster Abbey.

Nos. 264a, Riders on horseback. b, Coronation coach. c, Team of horses. Strips of 3 have continuous designs.

1977, Feb. 7 ***Perf. 13½x13***
263 B25 75c Strip of 3, #a.-c. 85 85
264 B25 $1.25 Strip of 3, #a.-c. 1.35 1.35

Souvenir Sheet
265 B25 Sheet of 6 2.25 2.25

Nos. 263a-264c se-tenant with labels. No. 265 contains Nos. 263a-264c with silver borders.

Nos. 405-422 Ovptd. "BARBUDA"

1977, Apr. 4 ***Perf. 15***
266 A79 ½c multicolored 15 15
267 A79 1c multicolored 15 15
268 A79 2c multicolored 15 15
269 A79 3c multicolored 15 15
270 A79 4c multicolored 15 15
271 A79 5c multicolored 15 15
272 A79 6c multicolored 15 15
273 A79 10c multicolored 15 15
274 A79 15c multicolored 15 15
275 A79 20c multicolored 15 15
276 A79 25c multicolored 18 18
277 A79 35c multicolored 28 28
278 A79 50c multicolored 38 38
279 A79 75c multicolored 52 52
280 A79 $1 multicolored 70 70

Perf. 13½x14
281 A80 $2.50 multicolored 1.75 1.75
282 A80 $5 multicolored 3.50 3.50
283 A80 $10 multicolored 7.25 7.25
Nos. 266-283 (18) 16.06 16.06

For overprints see Nos. 506-516.

Nos. 459-464 Ovptd. "BARBUDA"

1977, Apr. 4 ***Perf. 13½x14, 12***
284 A87 10c multicolored 15 15
285 A87 30c multicolored 28 28
286 A87 50c multicolored 45 45
287 A87 90c multicolored 85 85
288 A87 $2.50 multicolored 2.25 2.25
Nos. 284-288 (5) 3.98 3.98

Souvenir Sheet
289 A87 $5 multicolored 4.50 4.50

A booklet of self-adhesive stamps contains one pane of six rouletted and die cut 50c stamps in design of 90c (silver overprint), and one pane of one die cut $5 (gold overprint) in changed colors. Panes have marginal inscriptions.

For overprints see Nos. 312-317.

Nos. 465-471a Ovptd. "BARBUDA"

1977, June 13 ***Perf. 14***
290 A88 ½c multicolored 15 15
291 A88 1c multicolored 15 15
292 A88 2c multicolored 15 15
293 A88 10c multicolored 15 15
294 A88 30c multicolroed 45 45
295 A88 50c multicolored 75 75
296 A88 $2 multicolored 3.00 3.00
a. Souvenir sheet of 3, #294-296 5.00 5.00
Nos. 290-296 (7) 4.80 4.80

Overprint is slightly smaller on No. 296a.

Nos. 472-476a Ovptd. "BARBUDA"

1977, Aug. 12
297 A89 10c multicolored 15 15
298 A89 30c multicolored 22 22
299 A89 50c multicolored 38 38
300 A89 90c multicolored 65 65
301 A89 $1 multicolored 75 75
a. Souvenir sheet of 4, #298-301 2.50 2.50
Nos. 297-301 (5) 2.15 2.15

Royal Visit B26

1977, Oct. 27 ***Perf. 14½***
302 B26 50c Royal yacht Britannia 24 24
303 B26 $1.50 Jubliee emblem 65 65
304 B26 $2.50 Flags 1.10 1.10
a. Souvenir sheet of 3, #302-304 3.00 3.00

Nos. 483-489 Ovptd. "BARBUDA"

1977, Nov. 15 ***Perf. 14***
305 A90 ½c multicolored 15 15
306 A90 1c multicolored 15 15
307 A90 2c multicolored 15 15
308 A90 8c multicolored 15 15
309 A90 10c multicolored 15 15
310 A90 25c multicolored 20 20
311 A90 $2 multicolored 1.65 1.65
a. Souvenir sheet of 4, #308-311 2.50 2.50
Set value 2.00 2.00

Nos. 477-482 Ovptd. "BARBUDA" in Black

1977, Dec. 20 ***Perf. 12***
312 A87 10c multicolored 15 15
313 A87 30c multicolored 18 18
314 A87 50c multicolored 28 28
315 A87 90c multicolored 52 52
316 A87 $2.50 multicolored 1.50 1.50
Nos. 312-316 (5) 2.63 2.63

Nos. 312-316 exist with blue overprint.

1977, Nov. 28 ***Perf. 13½x14***
312a A87 10c multicolored 15 15
313a A87 30c multicolored 28 28
314a A87 50c multicolored 38 38
315a A87 90c multicolored 70 70
316a A87 $2.50 multicolored 2.00 2.00
Nos. 312a-316a (5) 3.51 3.51

Souvenir Sheet
317 A87 $5 multicolored 3.75 3.75

Overprint of Nos. 312a-316a differs from that on Nos. 312-316.

Anniversaries — B27

First navigable airships, 75th anniv: No. 318a, Zeppelin LZ1. b, German Naval airship L31. c, Graf Zeppelin. d, Gondola on military airship.

Soviet space program, 20th anniv: No. 319a, Sputnik, 1957. b, Vostok rocket, 1961. c, Voskhod rocket, 1964. d, Space walk, 1965.

Lindbergh's Atlantic crossing, 50th anniv: No. 320a, Fueling for flight. b, New York take-off. c, Spirit of St. Louis. d, Welcome in England.

Coronation of Queen Elizabeth II, 25th anniv: No. 321a, Lion of England. b, Unicorn of Scotland. c, Yale of Beaufort. d, Falcon of Plantagenets.

Rubens, 400th birth anniv: No. 322a, Two lions. b, Daniel in the Lion's Den. c, Two lions lying down. d, Lion at Daniel's feet. Block of 4 has continuous design.

1977, Dec. 29 ***Perf. 14½x14***
318 B27 75c Block of 4, #a.-d. 2.25 2.25
319 B27 95c Block of 4, #a.-d. 3.00 3.00
320 B27 $1.25 Block of 4, #a.-d. 3.75 3.75
321 B27 $2 Block of 4, #a.-d. 6.00 6.00
322 B27 $5 Block of 4, #a.-d. 15.00 15.00
e. Min. sheet, #318-322 + 4 labels 30.00 30.00
Nos. 318-322 (5) 30.00 30.00

Nos. 490-494a Ovptd. "BARBUDA"

1978, Feb. 15 ***Perf. 13x13½***
323 A91 10c multicolored 15 15
324 A91 15c multicolored 15 15
325 A91 50c multicolored 28 28
326 A91 90c multicolored 52 52
327 A91 $2 multicolored 1.10 1.10
a. Souv. sheet of 4, #324-327, perf. 14 2.25 2.25
Set value 2.00 2.00

Pieta, by Michelangelo — B28

Works by Michelangelo: 95c, Holy Family. $1.25, Libyan Sibyl. $2, The Flood.

1978, Mar. 23 ***Perf. 13½x14***
328 B28 75c multicolored 38 38
329 B28 95c multicolored 50 50
330 B28 $1.25 multicolored 65 65
331 B28 $2 multicolored 1.00 1.00
a. Souvenir sheet of 4, #328-331 3.00 3.00

Nos. 495-502 Ovptd. "BARBUDA"

1978, Mar. 23 ***Perf. 14***
332 A92 ½c multicolored 15 15
333 A92 1c multicolored 15 15
334 A92 2c multicolored 15 15
335 A92 10c multicolored 15 15
336 A92 50c multicolored 35 35
337 A92 90c multicolored 60 60
338 A92 $2 multicolored 1.40 1.40
Set value 2.45 2.45

Souvenir Sheet
339 A92 $2.50 multicolored 1.75 1.75

Nos. 503-507 Ovptd. "BARBUDA"

1978, May 22 ***Perf. 14½***
340 A93 10c multicolored 15 15
341 A93 50c multicolored 40 40
342 A93 90c multicolored 75 75
343 A93 $2 multicolored 1.65 1.65

Souvenir Sheet
344 A93 $2.50 multicolored 2.00 2.00

Coronation of Queen Elizabeth II, 25th Anniv. — B29

Crowns: No. 345a, St. Edward's. b, Imperial State. No. 346a, Queen Mary's. b, Queen Mother's. No. 347a, Queen Consort's. b, Queen Victoria's.

1978, June 2 ***Perf. 15***
Miniature Sheets of Two Each Plus Two Labels
345 B29 75c Sheet of 4 1.30 1.30
346 B29 $1.50 Sheet of 4 2.50 2.50
347 B29 $2.50 Sheet of 4 4.50 4.50

Souvenir Sheet
Perf. 14½
348 B29 Sheet of 6, #345a-347b 4.00 4.00

Nos. 508-514 Ovptd. in Black or Deep Rose Lilac "BARBUDA"

1978 ***Perf. 14***
349 A94 10c multicolored 15 15
350 A94 30c multicolored 18 18
351 A94 50c multicolored 28 28
352 A94 90c multicolored 52 52
353 A94 $2.50 multicolored 1.50 1.50
Nos. 349-353 (5) 2.63 2.63

Souvenir Sheet
354 A94 $5 multicolored 3.00 3.00

Self-adhesive
355 Souvenir booklet
a. A95 Bklt. pane, 3 each 25c and 50c, die cut, rouletted (DRL)
b. A95 $5 Bklt. pane of 1, die cut

Issue dates: #349-354. June 2, #355, Oct. 12.

Nos. 515-518 Ovptd. "BARBUDA"

1978, Sept. 12 ***Perf. 15***
356 A96 10c multicolored 15 15
357 A96 15c multicolored 15 15
358 A96 $3 multicolored 2.25 2.25

Souvenir Sheet
359 Sheet of 4 2.50 2.50
a. A96 25c multicolored 18 18
b. A96 30c multicolored 22 22
c. A96 50c multicolored 38 38
d. A96 $2 multicolored 1.50 1.50

Nos. 519-523 Ovptd. "BARBUDA"

1978, Nov. 20 ***Perf. 14***
360 A97 25c multicolored 26 26
361 A97 50c multicolored 52 52
362 A97 90c multicolored 95 95
363 A97 $2 multicolored 2.25 2.25

Souvenir Sheet
364 A97 $2.50 multicolored 3.00 3.00

Flora and Fauna B30

1978, Nov. 20 ***Perf. 15***
365 B30 25c Blackbar soldierfish 50 50
366 B30 50c Painted lady 1.00 1.00
367 B30 75c Dwarf poinciana 1.50 1.50
368 B30 95c Zebra butterfly 1.90 1.90
369 B30 $1.25 Bougainvillea 2.50 2.50
Nos. 365-369 (5) 7.40 7.40

Nos. 524-527 Ovptd. in Silver "BARBUDA"

1978, Nov. 20 ***Perf. 14***
370 A98 8c multicolored 15 15
371 A98 25c multicolored 18 18
372 A98 $2 multicolored 1.50 1.50

Souvenir Sheet
373 A98 $4 multicolored 3.25 3.25

Events and Annivs. B31

Designs: 75c, 1978 World Cup Soccer Championships, vert. 95c, Wright Brothers 1st powered flight, 75th anniv. $1.25, First Trans-Atlantic balloon flight, Aug. 1978. $2, Coronation of Elizabeth II, 25th anniv., vert.

1978, Dec. 20 ***Perf. 14***
374 B31 75c multicolored 50 50
375 B31 95c multicolored 65 65
376 B31 $1.25 multicolored 80 80
377 B31 $2 multicolored 1.40 1.40
a. Souv. sheet of 4, #374-377, imperf. 4.50 4.50

No. 377a has simulated perfs.

Nos. 528-532 Ovptd. in Bright Blue "BARBUDA" and

Sir Rowland Hill, Death Cent. B32

1979, Apr. 4
378 A99 25c multicolored 16 16
379 A99 50c multicolored 35 35
380 B32 75c Sir Rowland Hill, vert. 42 42
381 B32 95c Mail coach, 1840 52 52
382 A99 $1 multicolored 65 65
383 B32 $1.25 London's first pillar box, 1855 70 70
384 B32 $2 St. Martin's Post Office, London, vert. 1.10 1.10
a. Souvenir sheet of 4, #380-381, 383-384, imperf. 2.75 2.75
385 A99 $2 multicolored 1.40 1.40
Nos. 378-385 (8) 5.30 5.30

Souvenir Sheet
386 A99 $2.50 multicolored 2.00 2.00

No. 384a has simulated perfs.

For overprints see Nos. 423-426.

Nos. 533-536 Ovptd. "BARBUDA"

1979, Apr. 16

387	A100	10c multicolored	15	15
388	A100	50c multicolored	35	35
389	A100	$4 multicolored	2.50	2.50

Souvenir Sheet

390	A100	$2.50 multicolored	1.90	1.90

Intl. Civil Aviation Organization, 30th Anniv. — B33

1979, May 24 *Perf. 13½x14*

391	B33	75c Passengers leaving 747	50	50
392	B33	95c Air traffic controllers	65	65
393	B33	$1.25 Plane on runway	85	85
a.		Block of 3, #391-393 + label	2.00	2.00

Nos. 537-541 Ovptd. "BARBUDA"

1979, May 24 *Perf. 14*

394	A101	25c multicolored	18	18
395	A101	50c multicolored	38	38
396	A101	90c multicolored	65	65
397	A101	$2 multicolored	1.40	1.40

Souvenir Sheet

398	A101	$5 multicolored	3.50	3.50

Nos. 542-546 Ovptd. "BARBUDA"

1979, Aug. 1 *Perf. 14½*

399	A102	30c multicolored	24	24
400	A102	50c multicolored	42	42
401	A102	90c multicolored	70	70
402	A102	$3 multicolored	2.50	2.50

Souvenir Sheet

403	A102	$2.50 multicolored	2.50	2.50

Nos. 547-551 Ovptd. "BARBUDA"

1979, Aug. 1 *Perf. 14*

404	A103	25c multicolored	16	16
405	A103	50c multicolored	38	38
406	A103	90c multicolored	65	65
407	A103	$3 multicolored	2.25	2.25

Souvenir Sheet

408	A103	$2.50 multicolored	2.00	2.00

Intl. Year of the Child — B34

Details of the Christ Child from various paintings by Durer: 25c, 1512. 50c, 1516. 75c, 1526. $1.25, 1502.

1979, Sept. 24 *Perf. 14x13½*

409	B34	25c multicolored	18	18
410	B34	50c multicolored	38	38
411	B34	75c multicolored	58	58
412	B34	$1.25 multicolored	90	90
a.		Souvenir sheet of 4, #409-412	2.25	2.25

Nos. 552-556 Ovptd. "BARBUDA"

1979, Nov. 21 *Perf. 14*

413	A104	8c multicolored	15	15
414	A104	25c multicolored	15	15
415	A104	50c multicolored	30	30
416	A104	$4 multicolored	2.50	2.50

Souvenir Sheet

Perf. 12x12½

417	A104	$3 multicolored	2.25	2.25

Nos. 557-561 Ovptd. "BARBUDA"

1980, Mar. 18

418	A105	10c multicolored	15	15
419	A105	25c multicolroed	15	15
420	A105	$1 multicolored	52	52
421	A105	$2 multicolored	1.00	1.00

Souvenir Sheet

422	A105	$3 multicolored	2.00	2.00

Nos. 571A-571D Overprinted "BARBUDA" in Dark Blue

1980, May 6 *Perf. 12*

423	A99	25c multicolored	18	18
424	A99	50c multicolored	42	42
425	A99	$1 multicolored	75	75
426	A99	$2 multicolored	1.65	1.65

First Moon Landing, 10th Anniv. — B35

1980, May 21 *Perf. 13½x14*

427	B35	75c Crew badge	45	45
428	B35	95c Plaque left on moon	60	60
429	B35	$1.25 Lunar, command modules	75	75
430	B35	$2 Lunar module	1.25	1.25
a.		Souvenir sheet of 4, #427-430	3.25	3.25

American Widgeon B36

1980, June 16 *Perf. 14½x14*

431	B36	1c shown	15	15
432	B36	2c Snowy plover	15	15
433	B36	4c Rose-breasted grosbeak	15	15
434	B36	6c Mangrove cuckoo	15	15
435	B36	10c Adelaide's warbler	15	15
436	B36	15c Scaly-breasted thrasher	15	15
437	B36	20c Yellow-crowned night heron	15	15
438	B36	25c Bridled quail dove	15	15
439	B36	35c Carib grackle	22	22
440	B36	50c Northern pintail	32	32
441	B36	75c Black-whiskered vireo	48	48
442	B36	$1 Blue-winged teal	65	65

Perf. 14x14½

443	B36	$1.50 Green-throated carib	1.00	1.00
444	B36	$2 Red-necked pigeon	1.40	1.40
445	B36	$2.50 Stolid flycatcher	1.65	1.65
446	B36	$5 Yellow-bellied sapsucker	3.25	3.25
447	B36	$7.50 Caribbean elaenia	4.75	4.75
448	B36	$10 Great egret	6.50	6.50
		Nos. 431-448 (18)	21.42	21.42

Nos. 443-448 vert.

Nos. 572-578 Ovptd. "BARBUDA"

Perf. 13½x14, 14x13½

1980, July 29

449	A106a	10c multicolored	15	15
450	A106a	30c multicolored	20	20
451	A106a	50c multicolored	35	35
452	A106a	90c multicolored	60	60
453	A106a	$1 multicolored	60	60
454	A106a	$4 multicolored	2.50	2.50
		Nos. 449-454 (6)	4.40	4.40

Souvenir Sheet

Perf. 14

455	A106a	$5 multicolored	3.00	3.00

Nos. 579-583 Ovptd. "BARBUDA"

1980, Sept. 8 *Perf. 14*

456	A107	30c multicolored	20	20
457	A107	50c multicolored	35	35
458	A107	90c multicolored	60	60
459	A107	$3 multicolored	2.00	2.00

Souvenir Sheet

460	A107	$5 multicolored	3.50	3.50

Nos. 584-586 Optd. "BARBUDA"

1980, Oct. 6

461	A108	10c multicolored	15	15
462	A108	$2.50 multicolored	2.50	2.50

Souvenir Sheet

Perf. 12

463	A108	$3 multicolored	2.75	2.75

Nos. 587-591 Ovptd. "BARBUDA"

1980, Dec. 8 *Perf. 14*

464	A109	10c multicolored	16	16
465	A109	30c multicolored	45	45
466	A109	$1 multicolored	1.50	1.50
467	A109	$2 multicolored	3.00	3.00

Souvenir Sheet

468	A109	$2.50 multicolored	3.25	3.25

Nos. 602-606 Ovptd. "BARBUDA"

1981, Jan. 26

469	A111	25c multicolored	22	22
470	A111	50c multicolored	45	45
471	A111	90c multicolored	80	80
472	A111	$3 multicolored	2.75	2.75

Souvenir Sheet

473	A111	$2.50 multicolored	2.50	2.50

Famous Women — B37

1981, Mar. 9 *Perf. 14x13½*

474	B37	50c Florence Nightingale	28	28
475	B37	90c Marie Curie	48	48
476	B37	$1 Amy Johnson	55	55
477	B37	$4 Eleanor Roosevelt	2.25	2.25

Walt Disney Characters at Sea — B38

1981, May 15 *Perf. 13½x14*

478	B38	10c Goofy	16	16
479	B38	20c Donald Duck	32	32
480	B38	25c Mickey Mouse	42	42
481	B38	30c Goofy fishing	50	50
482	B38	35c Goofy sailing	60	60
483	B38	40c Mickey fishing	65	65
484	B38	75c Donald Duck boating	1.25	1.25
485	B38	$1 Minnie Mouse	1.75	1.75
486	B38	$2 Chip 'n Dale	3.50	3.50
		Nos. 478-486 (9)	9.15	9.15

Souvenir Sheet

487	B38	$2.50 Donald Duck, diff.	8.00	8.00

Nos. 618-622 Ovptd. "BARBUDA"

1981, June 9 *Perf. 14*

488	A112	10c multicolored	15	15
489	A112	50c multicolored	35	35
490	A112	90c multicolored	60	60
491	A112	$4 multicolored	2.75	2.75

Souvenir Sheet

Perf. 14x14½

492	A112	$5 multicolored	3.50	3.50

Miniature Sheets

Royal Wedding — B39

Designs: $1, Buckingham Palace. $1.50, Caernarvon Castle. $4, Highgrove House.

1981, July 27 *Perf. 11x11½*

493	B39	Sheet of 6	8.00	8.00
494	B39	Sheet of 6	8.00	8.00
495	B39	Sheet of 6	8.00	8.00

Souvenir Sheet

Perf. 11½x11

496	B39	$5 St. Paul's Cathedral, vert.	2.25	2.25

Sheets of 6 contain two of each denomination. Stamps of same denomination have continuous design. For surcharges see Nos. 592-594.

Nos. 623-627 Ovptd. in Black or Silver "BARBUDA"

1981, Aug. 14 *Perf. 14*

497	CD331	25c multicolored	15	15
498	CD331	50c multicolored	30	30
499	CD331	$4 multicolored	2.00	2.00

Souvenir Sheet

500	CD331	$5 multicolored	3.50	3.50

Self-adhesive

501	CD331	Booklet	15.00	15.00
a.		Pane of 6 (2x25c, 2x$1, 2x$2), Charles, die cut, rouletted (S)	8.00	8.00
b.		Pane of 1, $5 Couple, die cut (S)	6.50	6.50

Issued: #497-500, Aug. 24; #501, Oct. 12.
For surcharge see No. B1.

Intl. Year of the Disabled B40

1981, Sept. 14 *Perf. 14*

502	B40	50c Travel	35	35
503	B40	90c Braille, sign language	65	65
504	B40	$1 Helping hands	70	70
505	B40	$4 Mobility aids	2.75	2.75

Nos. 607-617 Ovptd. "BARBUDA"

1981, Nov. 1 *Perf. 15*

506	A79	6c multicolored	15	15
507	A79	10c multicolored	15	15
508	A79	20c multicolored	15	15
509	A79	25c multicolored	18	18
510	A79	35c multicolored	28	28
511	A79	50c multicolored	38	38
512	A79	75c multicolored	60	60
513	A79	$1 multicolored	75	75

Perf. 13½x14

514	A80	$2.50 multicolored	1.90	1.90
515	A80	$5 multicolored	3.75	3.75
516	A80	$10 multicolored	7.50	7.50
		Nos. 506-516 (11)	15.79	15.79

Nos. 628-632 Ovptd. "BARBUDA"

1981, Dec. 14 *Perf. 15*

517	A113	10c multicolored	15	15
518	A113	50c multicolored	48	48
519	A113	90c multicolored	90	90
520	A113	$2.50 multicolored	2.50	2.50

Souvenir Sheet

521	A113	$5 multicolored	4.00	4.00

Nos. 643-647 Ovptd. "BARBUDA"

1981, Dec. 14

522	A116	10c multicolored	15	15
523	A116	50c multicolored	55	55
524	A116	90c multicolored	1.00	1.00
525	A116	$2 multicolored	2.25	2.25

Souvenir Sheet

526	A116	$4 multicolored	3.00	3.00

Nos. 638-642 Ovptd. in Black or Silver "BARBUDA"

1981, Dec. 22

527	A115	8c multi	15	15
528	A115	30c multi	20	20
529	A115	$1 multi (S)	65	65
530	A115	$3 multi	2.00	2.00

Souvenir Sheet

531	A115	$5 multi	3.50	3.50

Birth of Prince William — B41

Various portraits.

1982, June 21 Wmk. 380 *Perf. 14*

532 B41 $1 buff & multi 60 60
533 B41 $2.50 lt pink & multi 1.50 1.50
534 B41 $5 lt lilac & multi 3.00 3.00

Souvenir Sheet

535 B41 $5 Couple 4.00 4.00

See Nos. 540-543.

The overprint on stamps of Antigua, from here on, read "BARBUDA MAIL" in one or two lines.

#672-675 Ovptd. in Black or Silver

Perf. 14¹/₂x14

1982, Oct. 12 Unwmk.

536 CD332 90c multi 65 65
537 CD332 $1 multi (S) 75 75
538 CD332 $4 multi (S) 3.00 3.00

Souvenir Sheet

539 CD332 $5 multi 3.50 3.50

Barbuda Nos. 532-535 Inscribed "Twenty First Birthday Greetings to H.R.H. The Princess of Wales"

Various portraits.

Perf. 14x14¹/₂

1982, July 1 Wmk. 380

540 B41 $1 lt grn & multi 60 60
541 B41 $2.50 pale sal & multi 1.50 1.50
542 B41 $5 lt bl & multi 3.00 3.00

Souvenir Sheet

543 B41 $4 Couple 3.50 3.50

#663-666 Ovptd. in Black or Silver

Perf. 14¹/₂x14

1982, Aug. 30 Unwmk.

544 CD332 90c multi 75 75
545 CD332 $1 multi (S) 85 85
546 CD332 $4 multi 3.25 3.25

Souvenir Sheet

547 CD332 $5 multi 4.50 4.50

Nos. 676-683 Overprinted

1982, Dec. 6 *Perf. 15*

551 A121 10c multicolored 15 15
552 A121 25c multicolored 22 22
553 A121 45c multicolored 40 40
554 A121 60c multicolored 55 55
555 A121 $1 multicolored 90 90
556 A121 $3 multicolored 2.75 2.75
Nos. 551-556 (6) 4.97 4.97

Souvenir Sheets

557 A121 $4 on #682 3.25 3.25
558 A121 $4 on #683 3.25 3.25

Nos. 684-688 Overprinted

1982, Dec. 6 *Perf. 14*

559 A122 10c multicolored 15 15
560 A122 30c multicolored 22 22
561 A122 $1 multicolored 75 75
562 A122 $4 multicolored 3.00 3.00

Souvenir Sheet

563 A122 $5 multicolored 3.75 3.75

Nos. 689-693 Overprinted

1983, Mar. 14 *Perf. 14¹/₂*

564 A123 45c multicolored 32 32
565 A123 50c multicolored 38 38
566 A123 60c multicolored 45 45
567 A123 $4 multicolored 3.00 3.00

Souvenir Sheet

568 A123 $5 multicolored 3.75 3.75

Nos. 694-697 Overprinted

1983, Mar. 14 *Perf. 14*

569 CD334 25c multicolored 22 22
570 CD334 45c multicolored 42 42
571 CD334 60c multicolored 55 55
572 CD334 $3 multicolored 2.75 2.75

Nos. 698-702 Overprinted

1983, Apr. 12

573 A125 15c multicolored 15 15
574 A125 50c multicolored 48 48
575 A125 60c multicolored 55 55
576 A125 $3 multicolored 3.00 3.00

Souvenir Sheet

577 A125 $5 multicolored 4.00 4.00

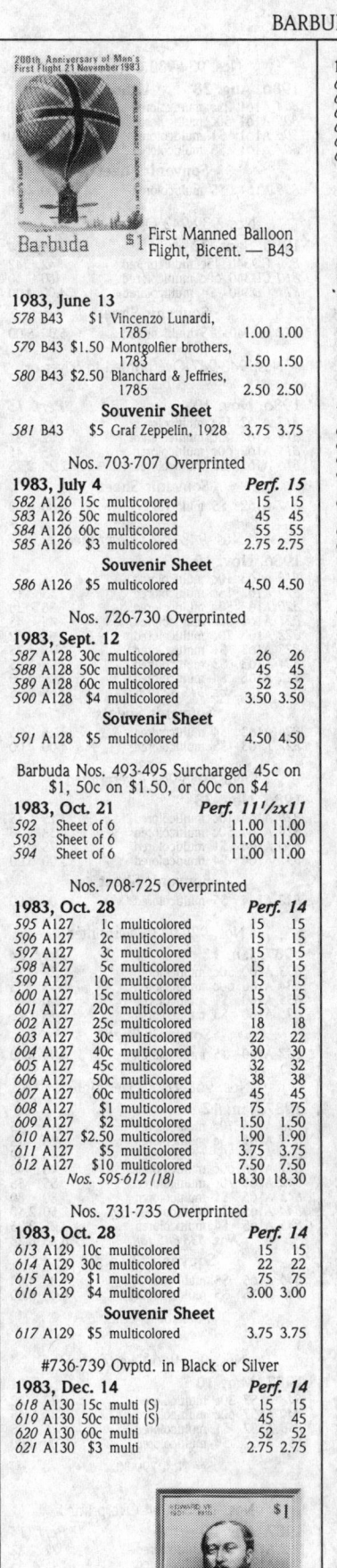

First Manned Balloon Flight, Bicent. — B43

1983, June 13

578 B43 $1 Vincenzo Lunardi, 1785 1.00 1.00
579 B43 $1.50 Montgolfier brothers, 1783 1.50 1.50
580 B43 $2.50 Blanchard & Jeffries, 1785 2.50 2.50

Souvenir Sheet

581 B43 $5 Graf Zeppelin, 1928 3.75 3.75

Nos. 703-707 Overprinted

1983, July 4 *Perf. 15*

582 A126 15c multicolored 15 15
583 A126 50c multicolored 45 45
584 A126 60c multicolored 55 55
585 A126 $3 multicolored 2.75 2.75

Souvenir Sheet

586 A126 $5 multicolored 4.50 4.50

Nos. 726-730 Overprinted

1983, Sept. 12

587 A128 30c multicolored 26 26
588 A128 50c multicolored 45 45
589 A128 60c multicolored 52 52
590 A128 $4 multicolored 3.50 3.50

Souvenir Sheet

591 A128 $5 multicolored 4.50 4.50

Barbuda Nos. 493-495 Surcharged 45c on $1, 50c on $1.50, or 60c on $4

1983, Oct. 21 *Perf. 11¹/₂x11*

592 Sheet of 6 11.00 11.00
593 Sheet of 6 11.00 11.00
594 Sheet of 6 11.00 11.00

Nos. 708-725 Overprinted

1983, Oct. 28 *Perf. 14*

595 A127 1c multicolored 15 15
596 A127 2c multicolored 15 15
597 A127 3c multicolored 15 15
598 A127 5c multicolored 15 15
599 A127 10c multicolored 15 15
600 A127 15c multicolored 15 15
601 A127 20c multicolored 15 15
602 A127 25c multicolored 18 18
603 A127 30c multicolored 22 22
604 A127 40c multicolored 30 30
605 A127 45c multicolored 32 32
606 A127 50c multicolored 38 38
607 A127 60c multicolored 45 45
608 A127 $1 multicolored 75 75
609 A127 $2 multicolored 1.50 1.50
610 A127 $2.50 multicolored 1.90 1.90
611 A127 $5 multicolored 3.75 3.75
612 A127 $10 multicolored 7.50 7.50
Nos. 595-612 (18) 18.30 18.30

Nos. 731-735 Overprinted

1983, Oct. 28 *Perf. 14*

613 A129 10c multicolored 15 15
614 A129 30c multicolored 22 22
615 A129 $1 multicolored 75 75
616 A129 $4 multicolored 3.00 3.00

Souvenir Sheet

617 A129 $5 multicolored 3.75 3.75

#736-739 Ovptd. in Black or Silver

1983, Dec. 14 *Perf. 14*

618 A130 15c multi (S) 15 15
619 A130 50c multi (S) 45 45
620 A130 60c multi 52 52
621 A130 $3 multi 2.75 2.75

Members of Royal Family — B44

1984, Feb. 14 *Perf. 14¹/₂x14*

622 B44 $1 Edward VII 1.00 1.00
623 B44 $1 George V 1.00 1.00
624 B44 $1 George VI 1.00 1.00
625 B44 $1 Elizabeth II 1.00 1.00
626 B44 $1 Prince Charles 1.00 1.00
627 B44 $1 Prince William 1.00 1.00
Nos. 622-627 (6) 6.00 6.00

Nos. 740-744 Overprinted and

1984 Summer Olympics, Los Angeles B45

1984 *Perf. 15, 13¹/₂ (B45)*

628 A131 25c multicolored 20 20
629 A131 50c multicolored 40 40
630 A131 90c multicolored 45 45
631 B45 $1.50 Olympic Stadium, Athens 1.10 1.10
632 B45 $2.50 Olympic Stadium, Los Angeles 1.90 1.90
633 A131 $3 multicolored 2.50 2.50
634 B45 $5 Torch bearer 4.00 4.00
a. Souv. sheet of 1, perf. 15 4.00 4.00
Nos. 628-634 (7) 10.55 10.55

Souvenir Sheet

635 A131 $5 multicolored 4.00 4.00

Issue dates: A131, Apr. 26, B45, July 27.

Nos. 755-759 Overprinted

1984, July 12 *Perf. 15*

636 A133 15c multicolored 15 15
637 A133 50c multicolored 45 45
638 A133 60c multicolored 55 55
639 A133 $3 multicolored 2.75 2.75

Souvenir Sheet

640 A133 $5 multicolored 4.25 4.25

Nos. 745-749 Overprinted

1984, July 12

641 A132 45c multicolored 38 38
642 A132 50c multicolored 42 42
643 A132 60c multicolored 52 52
644 A132 $4 multicolored 3.50 3.50

Souvenir Sheet

645 A132 $5 multicolored 4.50 4.50

#760-767 Ovptd. in Black or Silver

1984, Oct. 1 *Perf. 14*

646 A134 10c multicolored (S) 15 15
647 A134 20c multicolored 16 16
648 A134 30c multicolored 24 24
649 A134 40c multicolored 32 32
650 A134 90c multicolored (S) 70 70
651 A134 $1.10 multicolored (S) 90 90
652 A134 $1.50 multicolored (S) 1.25 1.25
653 A134 $2 multicolored 1.65 1.65
Nos. 646-653 (8) 5.37 5.37

Nos. 768-772 Overprinted

1984, Oct. 1

654 A135 40c multicolored 35 35
655 A135 50c multicolored 45 45
656 A135 60c multicolored 52 52
657 A135 $3 multicolored 2.75 2.75

Souvenir Sheet

658 A135 $5 multicolored 4.25 4.25

Nos. 773-778 Overprinted

1984, Nov. 21 *Perf. 15*

659 A136 40c multicolored 35 35
660 A136 50c multicolored 45 45
661 A136 60c multicolored 55 55
662 A136 $2 multicolored 1.90 1.90
663 A136 $3 multicolored 2.75 2.75
Nos. 659-663 (5) 6.00 6.00

Souvenir Sheet

664 A136 $5 multicolored 4.75 4.75

Nos. 782-791 Overprinted in Silver

1984 *Perf. 15*

665 A137a 15c multicolored 15 15
666 A137a 25c multicolored 20 20
667 A137a 50c multicolored 40 40
668 A137a 60c multicolored 48 48
669 A137a 70c multicolored 55 55
670 A137a 90c multicolored 75 75
671 A137a $3 multicolored 2.50 2.50
672 A137a $4 multicolored 3.25 3.25
Nos. 665-672 (8) 8.28 8.28

Souvenir Sheets

673 A137a $5 #790 4.50 4.50
674 A137a $5 #791, horiz. 4.50 4.50

Issue dates: Correggio, Nov. 21. Degas, Nov. 30.

Nos. 779-781 Overprinted

1984, Nov. 30

675 A137 $1 multicolored 80 80
676 A137 $5 multicolored 4.00 4.00

Souvenir Sheet

677 A137 $5 multicolored 4.50 4.50

Nos. 819-827 Overprinted

1985, Feb. 18

678 A139 60c multicolored 45 45
679 A139 60c multicolored 45 45
680 A139 60c multicolored 45 45
681 A139 60c multicolored 45 45
682 A139 $1 multicolored 75 75
683 A139 $1 multicolored 75 75
684 A139 $1 multicolored 75 75
685 A139 $1 multicolored 75 75
Nos. 678-685 (8) 4.80 4.80

Souvenir Sheet

686 A139 $5 multicolored 4.50 4.50

Queen Mother (Lady Elizabeth Bowes-Lyon), 1907 — B46

1985, Feb. 26 *Perf. 14x14¹/₂*

687 B46 15c shown 15 15
688 B46 45c Duchess of York, 1926 35 35
689 B46 50c Coronation, 1937 40 40
690 B46 60c Queen Mother 48 48
691 B46 90c Wearing tiara 70 70
692 B46 $2 Wearing blue hat 1.65 1.65
693 B46 $3 With children 2.50 2.50
Nos. 687-693 (7) 6.23 6.23

For overprints see Nos. 724-728, 733, 735.

Nos. 828-834 Overprinted

1985, May 10 *Perf. 15*

694 A140 25c multicolored 20 20
695 A140 30c multicolored 24 24
696 A140 50c multicolored 40 40
697 A140 90c multicolored 70 70
698 A140 $1 multicolored 80 80
699 A140 $3 multicolored 2.50 2.50
Nos. 694-699 (6) 4.84 4.84

Souvenir Sheet

700 A140 $5 multicolored 4.00 4.00

Audubon, Birth Bicentenary — B47

1985, Apr. 4 *Perf. 14*

701 B47 45c Roseate tern 40 40
702 B47 50c Mangrove cuckoo 45 45
703 B47 60c Yellow-crowned night heron 55 55
704 B47 $5 Brown pelican 4.50 4.50

Nos. 845-849, 910-913 Ovptd. in Black or Silver

1985-86 *Perf. 15, 12¹/₂x12*

705 A143 60c on #910 (S) 48 48
706 A143 90c on #845 70 70
707 A143 90c on #911 (S) 70 70
708 A143 $1 on #846 80 80
709 A143 $1.50 on #847 1.25 1.25
710 A143 $1.50 on #912 1.25 1.25
711 A143 $3 on #848 2.50 2.50
712 A143 $3 on #913 2.50 2.50
Nos. 705-712 (8) 10.18 10.18

Souvenir Sheet

713 A143 $5 on #849 4.50 4.50

Issue dates: Nos. 706, 708-709, 711, 713, July 18, 1985. Others, Dec. 1986.

Nos. 850-854 Overprinted

1985, July 18 *Perf. 14*

714 A144 25c multicolored 22 22
715 A144 60c multicolored 52 52
716 A144 95c multicolored 80 80

717 A144 $4 multicolored 3.50 3.50

Souvenir Sheet

718 A144 $5 multicolored 4.50 4.50

Nos. 840-844 Overprinted

1985, Aug. 2

719 A142 10c multicolored 15 15
720 A142 30c multicolored 28 28
721 A142 60c multicolored 52 52
722 A142 $4 multicolored 3.75 3.75

Souvenir Sheet

723 A142 $5 multicolored 4.50 4.50

Barbuda Nos. 687-693 Ovptd. "4TH AUG 1900-1985" and Antigua Nos. 866A-870 Ovptd. "BARBUDA / MAIL" in Silver or Black

Perf. 14, 12x12½ (#729, 731, 736)

1985-86

724 B46 15c multi 15 15
725 B46 45c multi 35 35
726 B46 50c multi 40 40
727 B46 60c multi 48 48
728 B46 90c multi 70 70
729 A148 90c multi 70 70
730 A148 $1 multi (S) 80 80
731 A148 $1 like #730 80 80
732 A148 $1.50 multi (S) 1.20 1.20
733 B46 $2 multi 1.65 1.65
734 A148 $2.50 multi 2.00 2.00
735 B46 $3 multi 2.50 2.50
736 A148 $3 multi 2.50 2.50
Nos. 724-736 (13) 14.23 14.23

Souvenir Sheet

737 A148 $5 multi 4.50 4.50

Queen Mother's 85th birthday.
Issue dates: 15c, 45c, 50c, 60c, No. 728, $2, No. 735, Aug. 2. No. 730, $1.50, $2.50, Nov. 8. Others, Dec. 1986. Nos. 729, 731, 736 issued in sheets of 5 plus label.

Nos. 835-839 Overprinted

1985, Aug. 30 ***Perf. 15***

738 A141 15c multicolored 15 15
739 A141 50c multicolored 40 40
740 A141 60c multicolored 45 45
741 A141 $3 multicolored 2.50 2.50

Souvenir Sheet

742 A141 $5 multicolored 4.00 4.00

Nos. 855-859 Overprinted

1985, Aug. 30 ***Perf. 14***

743 A145 30c multicolored 24 24
744 A145 90c multicolored 70 70
745 A145 $1.50 multicolored 1.25 1.25
746 A145 $3 multicolored 2.50 2.50

Souvenir Sheet

747 A145 $5 multicolored 4.25 4.25

Nos. 860-861 Overprinted

1985, Nov. 25 ***Perf. 14***

748 A146 $2 yellow green 1.65 1.65

Souvenir Sheet

749 A146 $5 deep brown 4.00 4.00

#871-875 Ovptd. in Black or Silver

1985, Nov. 25

750 A149 15c multi (S) 15 15
751 A149 45c multi 40 40
752 A149 60c multi 55 55
753 A149 $3 multi(S) 3.00 3.00

Souvenir Sheet

754 A149 $5 multi 4.50 4.50

Nos. 862-866 Overprinted

1986, Feb. 17

755 A147 25c multicolored 20 20
756 A147 50c multicolored 40 40
757 A147 60c multicolored 48 48
758 A147 $3 multicolored 2.50 2.50

Souvenir Sheet

759 A147 $5 multicolored 4.00 4.00

Nos. 886-889 Overprinted

1986, Feb. 17 ***Perf. 14½***

760 A152 60c multicolored 48 48
761 A152 $1 multicolored 80 80
762 A152 $4 multicolored 3.25 3.25

Souvenir Sheet

763 A152 $5 multicolored 4.00 4.00

Nos. 876-880 Overprinted

1986, Mar. 10 ***Perf. 14***

764 A150 25c multicolored 20 20
765 A150 50c multicolored 40 40
766 A150 $1 multicolored 80 80
767 A140 $3 multicolored 2.50 2.50

Souvenir Sheet

768 A150 $5 multicolored 4.00 4.00

Nos. 881-885 Overprinted

1986, Mar. 10 ***Perf. 14***

769 A151 15c multicolored 15 15
770 A151 45c multicolored 35 35
771 A151 60c multicolored 48 48
772 A151 $3 multicolored 2.50 2.50

Souvenir Sheet

773 A151 $5 multicolored 4.00 4.00

Nos. 905-909 Overprinted

1986, Apr. 4 ***Perf. 15***

774 A156 10c multicolored 15 15
775 A156 25c multicolored 20 20
776 A156 60c multicolored 48 48
777 A156 $4 multicolored 3.25 3.25

Souvenir Sheet

778 A156 $5 multicolored 4.00 4.00

B48

1986, Apr. 21

779 B48 $1 Shaking hands 80 80
780 B48 $2 Talking with woman 1.65 1.65
781 B48 $2.50 With officer 2.00 2.00

Souvenir Sheet

Perf. 13½x14

782 B48 $5 Portraits 4.00 4.00

No. 782 contains one 34x27mm stamp.

Nos. 925-928 Overprinted in Silver or Black

1986, Aug. 12

783 CD339 60c multi 48 48
784 CD339 $1 multi 80 80
785 CD339 $4 multi 3.25 3.25

Souvenir Sheet

786 CD339 $5 multi (Bk) 4.00 4.00

Nos. 920-924 Overprinted and

Halley's Comet B49

1986 ***Perf. 14, 15 (B49)***

787 A158 5c multicolored 15 15
788 A158 10c multicolored 15 15
789 A158 60c multicolored 48 48
790 B49 $1 shown 80 80
791 B49 $2.50 Early telescope, dish antenna, vert. 2.00 2.00
792 A158 $4 multicolored 3.25 3.25
793 B49 $5 World map, comet 4.00 4.00

Souvenir Sheet

794 A159 $5 multicolored 4.00 4.00

Issue dates: Nos. 790-791, 793, July 10, others, Sept. 22.

Nos. 901-904 Overprinted

1986, Aug. 12 ***Perf. 13½x14***

795 A156 40c multicolored 32 32
796 A156 $1 multicolored 80 80
797 A156 $3 multicolored 2.50 2.50

Souvenir Sheet

Perf. 14x13½

798 A156 $5 multicolored 4.00 4.00

Nos. 915-919 Overprinted

1986, Aug. 28 ***Perf. 14***

799 A157 30c multicolored 24 24
800 A157 60c multicolored 48 48
801 A157 $1 multicolored 80 80
802 A157 $4 multicolored 3.25 3.25

Souvenir Sheet

803 A157 $5 multicolored 4.00 4.00

See Nos. 848-851.

Nos. 934-938 Overprinted

1986, Aug. 28 Litho. ***Perf. 15***

804 A161 25c multicolored 20 20
805 A161 50c multicolored 40 40
806 A161 $1 multicolored 80 80
807 A161 $3 multicolored 2.50 2.50

Souvenir Sheet

808 A161 $5 multicolored 4.00 4.00

Nos. 939-942 Ovptd. in Silver

1986, Sept. 22 ***Perf. 14***

809 CD340 45c multicolored 42 42
810 CD340 60c multicolored 60 60
811 CD340 $4 multicolored 4.00 4.00

Souvenir Sheet

812 CD340 $5 multicolored 5.00 5.00

Nos. 943-947 Overprinted in Silver or Black

1986, Nov. 10 ***Perf. 15***

813 A162 15c multicolored 15 15
814 A162 45c multicolored 32 32
815 A162 60c multicolored 45 45
816 A162 $3 multicolored 2.25 2.25

Souvenir Sheet

817 A162 $5 multi (Bk) 4.00 4.00

Nos. 948-957 Overprinted

1986, Nov. 10

818 A163 10c multicolored 15 15
819 A163 15c multicolored 15 15
820 A163 50c multicolored 38 38
821 A163 60c multicolored 45 45
822 A163 70c multicolored 52 52
823 A163 $1 multicolored 75 75
824 A163 $3 multicolored 2.25 2.25
825 A163 $4 multicolored 3.00 3.00
Nos. 818-825 (8) 7.65 7.65

Souvenir Sheets

826 A163 $4 multicolored 3.25 3.25
827 A163 $5 multicolored 4.00 4.00

Nos. 958-962 Overprinted

1986, Nov. 28

828 A164 10c multicolored 15 15
829 A164 50c multicolored 38 38
830 A164 $1 multicolored 75 75
831 A164 $4 multicolored 3.00 3.00

Souvenir Sheet

832 A164 $5 multicolored 4.00 4.00

Nos. 929-933 Overprinted

1987, Jan. 12 ***Perf. 14***

833 A160 30c multicolored 28 28
834 A160 60c multicolored 55 55
835 A160 $1 multicolored 90 90
836 A160 $3 multicolored 2.75 2.75

Souvenir Sheet

837 A160 $5 multicolored 4.00 4.00

Nos. 968-972A Overprinted

1987, Jan. 12

838 A165 10c multicolored 15 15
839 A165 15c multicolored 15 15
840 A165 50c multicolored 40 40
841 A165 60c multicolored 48 48
842 A165 70c multicolored 55 55
843 A165 $1 multicolored 80 80
844 A165 $3 multicolored 2.50 2.50
845 A165 $4 multicolored 3.25 3.25
Nos. 838-845 (8) 8.28 8.28

Souvenir Sheets

846 A165 $5 multi (#972) 4.00 4.00
847 A165 $5 multi (#972A) 4.00 4.00

Automobile, cent.

Nos. 963-966 Overprinted

1987, Mar. 10

848 A157 30c multicolored 22 22
849 A157 60c multicolored 45 45
850 A157 $1 multicolored 75 75
851 A157 $4 multicolored 3.00 3.00

See Nos. 799-802.

Nos. 1000-1004 Overprinted

1987, Apr. 23 ***Perf. 15***

852 A170 30c multicolored 22 22
853 A170 60c multicolored 45 45
854 A170 $1 multicolored 2.25 2.25
855 A170 $3 multicolored 75 75

Souvenir Sheet

856 A171 $5 multicolored 5.00 5.00

Nos. 1005-1014 Overprinted

1987, July 1 ***Perf. 14***

857 A172 15c multicolored 15 15
858 A173 30c multicolored 22 22
859 A172 40c multicolored 30 30
860 A173 50c multicolored 38 38
861 A172 60c multicolored 45 45
862 A172 $1 multicolored 75 75
863 A173 $2 multicolored 1.50 1.50
864 A173 $3 multicolored 2.25 2.25
Nos. 857-864 (8) 6.00 6.00

Souvenir Sheets

865 A172 $5 multicolored 4.00 4.00
866 A173 $5 multicolored 4.00 4.00

Nos. 1025-1034 Overprinted

1987, July 28 ***Perf. 15***

867 A175 10c multicolored 15 15
868 A175 15c multicolored 15 15
869 A175 30c multicolored 24 24
870 A175 50c multicolored 40 40
871 A175 60c multicolored 48 48
872 A175 70c multicolored 55 55
873 A175 90c multicolored 70 70
874 A175 $1.50 multicolored 1.20 1.20
875 A175 $2 multicolored 1.65 1.65
876 A175 $3 multicolored 2.25 2.25
Nos. 867-876 (10) 7.77 7.77

Marine Life B50

1987, July 28

877 B50 5c Shore crab 15 15
878 B50 10c Sea cucumber 15 15
879 B50 15c Stop light parrotfish 15 15
880 B50 25c Banded coral shrimp 18 18
881 B50 35c Spotted drum 26 26
882 B50 60c Thorny star-fish 45 45
883 B50 75c Atlantic trumpet triton 55 55
884 B50 90c Feather-star, yellow beaker sponge 65 65
885 B50 $1 Blue gorgonian, vert. 75 75
886 B50 $1.25 Slender filefish, vert. 90 90
887 B50 $5 Barred hamlet, vert. 3.75 3.75
888 B50 $7.50 Fairy basslet, vert. 5.50 5.50
889 B50 $10 Fire coral, butterfly fish, vert. 7.50 7.50
Nos. 877-889 (13) 20.94 20.94

For surcharges see Nos. 1133-1134.

#1048-1052 Ovptd. in Silver or Black

1987, Oct. 12 ***Perf. 14***

890 A178 10c multicolored 15 15
891 A178 60c multicolored 48 48
892 A178 $1 multicolored 80 80
893 A178 $3 multicolored 2.25 2.25

Souvenir Sheet

894 A178 $5 multi (Bk) 4.00 4.00

1988 Summer Olympics, Seoul.

#990-999 Ovptd. in Black or Silver

1987, Oct. 12 ***Perf. 13½x14***

895 A169 10c multicolored 15 15
896 A169 30c multicolored 24 24
897 A169 40c multicolored 32 32
898 A169 60c multicolored 48 48
899 A169 90c multicolored 70 70
900 A169 $1 multi (S) 80 80
901 A169 $3 multicolored 2.25 2.25
902 A169 $4 multicolored 3.00 3.00
Nos. 895-902 (8) 7.94 7.94

Size: 110x95mm

Imperf

903 A169 $5 multicolored 4.00 4.00
904 A169 $5 multi (S) 4.00 4.00

#1015-1024 Ovptd. in Silver or Black

1987, Nov. 5 ***Perf. 14***

905 A174 15c multi 15 15
906 A174 30c multi 24 24
907 A174 45c multi 35 35
908 A174 50c multi (Bk) 40 40
909 A174 60c multi 48 48
910 A174 90c multi 70 70
911 A174 $1 multi 80 80
912 A174 $2 multi 1.65 1.65
913 A174 $3 multi (Bk) 2.25 2.25
914 A174 $5 multi 4.00 4.00
Nos. 905-914 (10) 11.02 11.02

#1040-1047 Ovptd. in Black or Silver

1987, Nov. 5

915 A177 15c multicolored 15 15
916 A177 30c multicolored 28 28
917 A177 45c multicolored 42 42
918 A177 50c multicolored 48 48
919 A177 60c multicolored 55 55

920 A177 $1 multicolored 95 95
921 A177 $2 multicolored 2.00 2.00
922 A177 $3 multicolored (S) 2.75 2.75
Nos. 915-922 (8) 7.58 7.58

Nos. 1035-1039 Overprinted

1987, Dec. 8
923 A176 30c multicolored 24 24
924 A176 60c multicolored 48 48
925 A176 $1 multicolored 80 80
926 A176 $3 multicolored 2.25 2.25

Souvenir Sheet
927 A176 $5 multicolored 4.00 4.00

Nos. 1063-1067 Overprinted

1988, Jan. 12
928 A181 45c multicolored 32 32
929 A181 60c multicolored 45 45
930 A181 $1 multicolored 75 75
931 A181 $4 multicolored 3.00 3.00

Souvenir Sheet
932 A181 $5 multicolored 4.00 4.00

Nos. 1083-1091 Overprinted

1988, Mar. 25
933 A184 25c multicolored 20 20
934 A184 30c multicolored 24 24
935 A184 40c multicolored 32 32
936 A184 45c multicolored 35 35
937 A184 50c multicolored 40 40
938 A184 60c multicolored 48 48
939 A184 $1 multicolored 80 80
940 A184 $2 multicolored 1.65 1.65
Nos. 933-940 (8) 4.44 4.44

Souvenir Sheet
941 A184 $5 multicolored 4.00 4.00

Nos. 1058-1062 Ovptd. in Silver

1988, May 6
942 A180 15c multicolored 15 15
943 A180 45c multicolored 35 35
944 A180 60c multicolored 48 48
945 A180 $4 multicolored 3.25 3.25

Souvenir Sheet
946 A180 $5 multicolored 4.00 4.00

Nos. 1068-1072 Overprinted

1988, July 4
947 A182 25c multicolored 20 20
948 A182 60c multicolored 48 48
949 A182 $2 multicolored 1.65 1.65
950 A182 $3 multicolored 2.25 2.25

Souvenir Sheet
951 A182 $5 multicolored 4.00 4.00

Nos. 1073-1082 Overprinted

1988, July 4
952 A183 10c multicolored 15 15
953 A183 15c multicolored 15 15
954 A183 50c multicolored 40 40
955 A183 60c multicolored 48 48
956 A183 70c multicolored 55 55
957 A183 $1 multicolored 80 80
958 A183 $3 multicolored 2.25 2.25
959 A183 $4 multicolored 3.25 3.25
Nos. 952-959 (8) 8.03 8.03

Souvenir Sheets
960 A183 $5 multi (#1081) 4.00 4.00
961 A183 $5 multi (#1082) 4.00 4.00

Nos. 1092-1101 Overprinted

1988, July 25
962 A185 10c multicolored 15 15
963 A185 30c multicolored 25 25
964 A185 45c multicolored 38 38
965 A185 60c multicolored 50 50
966 A185 90c multicolored 75 75
967 A185 $1 multicolored 85 85
968 A185 $3 multicolored 2.50 2.50
969 A185 $4 multicolored 3.50 3.50
Nos. 962-969 (8) 8.88 8.88

Souvenir Sheets
970 A185 $5 multi (#1100) 4.00 4.00
971 A185 $5 multi (#1101) 4.00 4.00

Nos. 1102-1111 Overprinted

1988, July 25 ***Perf. 13½x14***
972 A187 30c multicolored 24 24
973 A187 40c multicolored 32 32
974 A187 45c multicolored 35 35
975 A187 50c multicolored 40 40
976 A187 $1 multicolored 80 80
977 A187 $2 multicolored 1.65 1.65
978 A187 $3 multicolored 2.25 2.25
979 A187 $4 multicolored 3.25 3.25
Nos. 972-979 (8) 9.26 9.26

Souvenir Sheets
980 A187 $5 multi (#1110) 4.00 4.00
981 A187 $5 multi (#1111) 4.00 4.00

Nos. 1053-1057 Overprinted

1988, Aug. 25 ***Perf. 15***
982 A179 10c multicolored 15 15
983 A179 60c multicolored 45 45
984 A179 $1 multicolored 75 75
985 A179 $3 multicolored 2.25 2.25

Souvenir Sheet
986 A179 $5 multicolored 4.00 4.00

Nos. 1112-1116 Overprinted

1988, Aug. 25
987 A188 30c multicolored 24 24
988 A188 60c multicolored 48 48
989 A188 $1 multicolored 80 80
990 A188 $3 multicolored 2.25 2.25

Souvenir Sheet
991 A188 $5 multicolored 4.00 4.00

Nos. 1127-1136 Overprinted

1988, Sept. 16 ***Perf. 14***
992 A190 10c multicolored 15 15
993 A190 30c multicolored 22 22
994 A190 50c multicolored 38 38
995 A190 90c multicolored 65 65
996 A190 $1 multicolored 75 75
997 A190 $2 multicolored 1.65 1.65
998 A190 $3 multicolored 2.25 2.25
999 A190 $4 multicolored 3.00 3.00
Nos. 992-999 (8) 9.05 9.05

Souvenir Sheets
1000 A191 $5 multi (#1135) 4.00 4.00
1001 A191 $5 multi (#1136) 4.00 4.00

Nos. 1140-1144 Overprinted

1988, Sept. 16
1002 A192 40c multicolored 32 32
1003 A192 60c multicolored 48 48
1004 A192 $1 multicolored 80 80
1005 A192 $3 multicolored 2.25 2.25

Souvenir Sheet
1006 A192 $5 multicolored 4.00 4.00

Nos. 1145-1162 Overprinted

1988-90
1007 A193 1c multicolored 15 15
1008 A193 2c multicolored 15 15
1009 A193 3c multicolored 15 15
1010 A193 5c multicolored 15 15
1011 A193 10c multicolored 15 15
1012 A193 15c multicolored 15 15
1013 A193 20c multicolored 16 16
1014 A193 25c multicolored 20 20
1015 A193 30c multicolored 24 24
1016 A193 40c multicolored 32 32
1017 A193 45c multicolored 35 35
1018 A193 50c multicolored 40 40
1019 A193 60c multicolored 48 48
1020 A193 $1 multicolored 80 80
1021 A193 $2 multicolored 1.65 1.65
1022 A193 $2.50 multicolored 2.00 2.00
1023 A193 $5 multicolored 4.00 4.00
1024 A193 $10 multicolored 8.00 8.00
1025 A193 $20 multi ('90) 16.00 16.00
Nos. 1007-1025 (19) 35.50 35.50

Issue dates: $20, May 4, others Dec. 8.

Nos. 1162A-1167 Overprinted

1989, Apr. 28
1026 A194 1c multicolored 15 15
1027 A194 2c multicolored 15 15
1028 A194 3c multicolored 15 15
1029 A194 4c multicolored 15 15
1030 A194 30c multicolored 24 24
1031 A194 60c multicolored 48 48
1032 A194 $1 multicolored 80 80
1033 A194 $4 multicolored 3.25 3.25
Nos. 1026-1033 (8) 5.37 5.37

Souvenir Sheet
1034 A194 $5 multicolored 4.00 4.00

Nos. 1175-1176 Overprinted

1989, May 24
1035 A196 $1.50 Strip of 4, #a.-d. 4.75 4.75

Souvenir Sheet
1036 A196 $6 multicolored 4.75 4.75

Nos. 1177-1186 Overprinted

1989, May 29
1037 A197 10c multicolored 15 15
1038 A197 30c multicolored 35 35
1039 A197 40c multicolored 48 48
1040 A197 60c multicolored 70 70
1041 A197 $1 multicolored 1.20 1.20
1042 A197 $2 multicolored 2.25 2.25
1043 A197 $3 multicolored 3.50 3.50
1044 A197 $4 multicolored 4.75 4.75
Nos. 1037-1044 (8) 13.38 13.38

Souvenir Sheets
1045 A197 $7 multi (#1185) 5.50 5.50
1046 A197 $7 multi (#1186) 5.50 5.50

Nos. 1187-1196 Overprinted

1989, Sept. 18
1047 A198 25c multicolored 18 18
1048 A198 45c multicolored 32 32
1049 A198 50c multicolored 38 38
1050 A198 60c multicolored 45 45
1051 A198 75c multicolored 55 55
1052 A198 90c multicolored 65 65
1053 A198 $3 multicolored 2.25 2.25
1054 A198 $4 multicolored 3.00 3.00
Nos. 1047-1054 (8) 7.78 7.78

Souvenir Sheets
1055 A198 $6 multi (#1195) 4.50 4.50
1056 A198 $6 multi (#1196) 4.50 4.50

Nos. 1197-1206 Overprinted

1989, Dec. 14 ***Perf. 14x13½***
1057 A199 25c multicolored 18 18
1058 A199 45c multicolored 32 32
1059 A199 50c multicolored 38 38
1060 A199 60c multicolored 45 45
1061 A199 $1 multicolored 75 75
1062 A199 $2 multicolored 1.50 1.50
1063 A199 $3 multicolored 2.25 2.25
1064 A199 $4 multicolored 3.00 3.00
Nos. 1057-1064 (8) 8.83 8.83

Souvenir Sheets
1065 A199 $5 multi (#1205) 3.75 3.75
1066 A199 $5 multi (#1206) 3.75 3.75

Nos. 1217-1222 Overprinted

1989, Dec. 20 ***Perf. 14***
1067 A201 15c multicolored 15 15
1068 A201 25c multicolored 18 18
1069 A201 $1 multicolored 75 75
1070 A201 $4 multicolored 3.00 3.00

Souvenir Sheets
1071 A201 $5 multi (#1221) 3.75 3.75
1072 A201 $5 multi (#1222) 3.75 3.75

Nos. 1264-1273 Overprinted

1989, Dec. 20
1073 A208 10c multicolored 15 15
1074 A208 25c multicolored 18 18
1075 A208 30c multicolored 22 22
1076 A208 50c multicolored 38 38
1077 A208 60c multicolored 45 45
1078 A208 70c multicolored 52 52
1079 A208 $4 multicolored 3.00 3.00
1080 A208 $5 multicolored 3.75 3.75
Nos. 1073-1080 (8) 8.65 8.65

Souvenir Sheets
1081 A208 $5 multi (#1272) 3.75 3.75
1082 A208 $5 multi (#1273) 3.75 3.75

Nos. 1223-1232 Overprinted

1990, Feb. 21
1083 A202 10c multicolored 15 15
1084 A202 25c multicolored 18 18
1085 A202 50c multicolored 38 38
1086 A202 60c multicolored 45 45
1087 A202 75c multicolored 55 55
1088 A202 $1 multicolored 75 75
1089 A202 $3 multicolored 2.25 2.25
1090 A202 $4 multicolored 3.00 3.00
Nos. 1083-1090 (8) 7.71 7.71

Souvenir Sheets
1091 A202 $6 multi (#1231) 4.50 4.50
1092 A202 $6 multi (#1232) 4.50 4.50

Nos. 1233-1237 Overprinted

1990, Mar. 30
1093 A203 25c multicolored 18 18
1094 A203 45c multicolored 32 32
1095 A203 60c multicolored 45 45
1096 A203 $4 multicolored 3.00 3.00

Souvenir Sheet
1097 A203 $5 multicolored 3.75 3.75

Nos. 1258-1262 Overprinted

1990, Mar. 30
1098 A206 10c multicolored 15 15
1099 A206 45c multicolored 32 32
1100 A206 $1 multicolored 75 75
1101 A206 $4 multicolored 3.00 3.00

Souvenir Sheet
1102 A206 $5 multicolored 3.75 3.75

Nos. 1275-1284 Overprinted

1990, June 6
1103 A210 10c multicolored 15 15
1104 A210 20c multicolored 15 15
1105 A210 25c multicolored 18 18
1106 A210 45c multicolored 32 32
1107 A210 60c multicolored 45 45
1108 A210 $2 multicolored 1.50 1.50
1109 A210 $3 multicolored 2.25 2.25
1110 A210 $4 multicolored 3.00 3.00
Nos. 1103-1110 (8) 8.00 8.00

Souvenir Sheets
1111 A210 $5 multi (#1283) 3.75 3.75
1112 A210 $5 multi (#1284) 3.75 3.75

Nos. 1285-1294 Overprinted

1990, July 12
1113 A211 15c multicolored 15 15
1114 A211 45c multicolored 32 32
1115 A211 50c multicolored 38 38
1116 A211 60c multicolored 45 45
1117 A211 $1 multicolored 75 75
1118 A211 $2 multicolored 1.50 1.50
1119 A211 $3 multicolored 2.25 2.25
1120 A211 $5 multicolored 3.75 3.75
Nos. 1113-1120 (8) 9.55 9.55

Souvenir Sheets
1121 A211 $6 multi (#1293) 4.50 4.50
1122 A211 $6 multi (#1294) 4.50 4.50

Nos. 1295-1304 Overprinted

1990, Aug. 14
1123 A212 10c multicolored 15 15
1124 A212 15c multicolored 15 15
1125 A212 50c multicolored 38 38
1126 A212 60c multicolored 45 45
1127 A212 $1 multicolored 75 75
1128 A212 $2 multicolored 1.50 1.50
1129 A212 $3 multicolored 2.25 2.25
1130 A212 $4 multicolored 3.00 3.00
Nos. 1123-1130 (8) 8.63 8.63

Souvenir Sheets
1131 A212 $5 multi (#1303) 3.75 3.75
1132 A212 $5 multi (#1304) 3.75 3.75

Barbuda Nos. 888-889 Surcharged "1st Anniversary / Hurricane Hugo / 16th September, 1989-1990"

1990, Sept. 17 ***Perf. 15***
1133 A50 $5 on $7.50 3.75 3.75
1134 A50 $7.50 on $10 5.50 5.50

Nos. 1324-1328 Overprinted

1990, Oct. 12 ***Perf. 14***
1135 A217 15c multicolored 15 15
1136 A217 35c multicolored 28 28
1137 A217 75c multicolored 55 55
1138 A217 $3 multicolored 2.25 2.25

Souvenir Sheet
1139 A217 $6 multicolored 4.50 4.50

No. 1313 Ovptd. in Silver
Miniature Sheet

1990, Dec. 14
1140 A215 45c Sheet of 20, #a.-t. 6.75 6.75

Nos. 1360-1369 Overprinted
Perf. 14x13½, 13½x14

1990, Dec. 14
1141 A221 25c multicolored 18 18
1142 A221 30c multicolored 22 22
1143 A221 40c multicolored 30 30
1144 A221 60c multicolored 45 45
1145 A221 $1 multicolored 75 75
1146 A221 $2 multicolored 1.50 1.50
1147 A221 $4 multicolored 3.00 3.00
1148 A221 $5 multicolored 3.75 3.75
Nos. 1141-1148 (8) 10.15 10.15

Souvenir Sheets
1149 A221 $6 multi (#1368) 4.50 4.50
1150 A221 $6 multi (#1369) 4.50 4.50

Nos. 1305-1308 Overprinted

1991, Feb. 4 ***Perf. 15x14***
1151 A213 45c green 35 35
1152 A213 60c bright rose 45 45
1153 A213 $5 bright ultra 3.75 3.75

Souvenir Sheet
1154 A213 $6 black 4.50 4.50

Nos. 1309-1312 Overprinted

1991, Feb. 4 ***Perf. 13½***
1155 A214 50c red & deep grn 38 38
1156 A214 75c red & vio brn 55 55
1157 A214 $4 red & brt ultra 3.00 3.00

Souvenir Sheet
1158 A214 $6 red & black 4.50 4.50

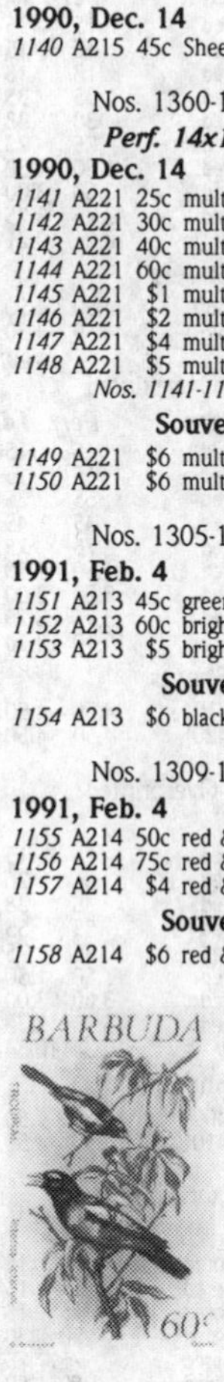

Birds — B52

1991, Mar. 25 Litho. *Perf. 14*

1164 B52 60c Troupial 45 45
1168 B52 $2 Christmas bird 1.50 1.50
1169 B52 $4 Rose-breasted grosbeak 3.00 3.00
1171 B52 $7 Stolid flycatcher 5.25 5.25

This is an expanding set. Numbers will change.

Nos. 1329-1333 Overprinted

1991, Apr. 23 Litho. *Perf. 14*

1173 A218 50c multicolored 38 38
1174 A218 75c multicolored 55 55
1175 A218 $1 multicolored 75 75
1176 A218 $5 multicolored 3.75 3.75

Souvenir Sheet

1177 A218 $6 multicolored 4.50 4.50

Nos. 1350-1359 Overprinted

1991, Apr. 23

1178 A220 10c multicolored 15 15
1179 A220 25c multicolored 18 18
1180 A220 50c multicolored 38 38
1181 A220 60c multicolored 45 45
1182 A220 $1 multicolored 75 75
1183 A220 $2 multicolored 1.50 1.50
1184 A220 $3 multicolored 2.25 2.25
1185 A220 $4 multicolored 3.00 3.00
Nos. 1178-1185 (8) 8.66 8.66

Souvenir Sheets

1186 A220 $6 multi (#1358) 4.50 4.50
1187 A220 $6 multi (#1359) 4.50 4.50

Nos. 1370-1379 Overprinted

1991, June 21 *Perf. 14x13½*

1188 A222 25c multicolored 18 18
1189 A222 45c multicolored 35 35
1190 A222 50c multicolored 38 38
1191 A222 60c multicolored 45 45
1192 A222 $1 multicolored 75 75
1193 A222 $2 multicolored 1.50 1.50
1194 A222 $3 multicolored 2.25 2.25
1195 A222 $4 multicolored 3.00 3.00
Nos. 1188-1195 (8) 8.86 8.86

Souvenir Sheets

1196 A222 $6 multi (#1378) 4.50 4.50
1197 A222 $6 multi (#1379) 4.50 4.50

Nos. 1380-1390 Overprinted

1991, July 25 Litho. *Perf. 14*

1198 A223 10c multicolored 15 15
1199 A223 15c multicolored 15 15
1200 A223 25c multicolored 18 18
1201 A223 45c multicolored 35 35
1202 A223 50c multicolored 38 38
1203 A223 $1 multicolored 75 75
1204 A223 $2 multicolored 1.50 1.50
1205 A223 $4 multicolored 3.00 3.00
1206 A223 $5 multicolored 3.75 3.75
Nos. 1198-1206 (9) 10.21 10.21

Souvenir Sheets

1207 A223 $6 multi (#1389) 4.50 4.50
1208 A223 $6 multi (#1390) 4.50 4.50

Nos. 1411-1420 Overprinted

1991, Aug. 26 Litho. *Perf. 14*

1209 A226 10c multicolored 15 15
1210 A226 15c multicolored 15 15
1211 A226 45c multicolored 35 35
1212 A226 60c multicolored 45 45
1213 A226 $1 multicolored 75 75
1214 A226 $2 multicolored 1.50 1.50
1215 A226 $4 multicolored 3.00 3.00
1216 A226 $5 multicolored 3.75 3.75
Nos. 1209-1216 (8) 10.10 10.10

Souvenir Sheets

1217 A226 $6 multi (#1419) 4.50 4.50
1218 A226 $6 multi (#1420) 4.50 4.50

Nos. 1401-1410 Overprinted

1991, Oct. 18

1219 A225 10c multicolored 15 15
1220 A225 35c multicolored 26 26
1221 A225 50c multicolored 38 38
1222 A225 75c multicolored 55 55
1223 A225 $1 multicolored 75 75
1224 A225 $2 multicolored 1.50 1.50
1225 A225 $4 multicolored 3.00 3.00
1226 A225 $5 multicolored 3.75 3.75
Nos. 1219-1226 (8) 10.34 10.34

Souvenir Sheets

1227 A225 $6 multi (#1409) 4.50 4.50
1228 A225 $6 multi (#1410) 4.50 4.50

Nos. 1446-1455 Overprinted

1991, Nov. 18

1229 CD347 10c multicolored 15 15
1230 CD347 15c multicolored 15 15
1231 CD347 20c multicolored 15 15
1232 CD347 40c multicolored 30 30
1233 CD347 $1 multicolored 75 75
1234 CD347 $2 multicolored 1.50 1.50
1235 CD347 $4 multicolored 3.00 3.00
1236 CD347 $5 multicolored 3.75 3.75
Nos. 1229-1236 (8) 9.75 9.75

Souvenir Sheets

1237 CD347 $4 multi (#1454) 3.00 3.00
1238 CD347 $4 multi (#1455) 3.00 3.00

Nos. 1503-1510 Overprinted

1991, Dec. 24 *Perf. 12*

1239 A238 10c multicolored 15 15
1240 A238 30c multicolored 22 22
1241 A238 40c multicolored 30 30
1242 A238 60c multicolored 45 45
1243 A238 $1 multicolored 75 75
1244 A238 $3 multicolored 2.25 2.25
1245 A238 $4 multicolored 3.00 3.00
1246 A238 $5 multicolored 3.75 3.75
Nos. 1239-1246 (8) 10.87 10.87

Nos. 1421-1435 Overprinted

1992, Feb. 20 *Perf. 13½*

1249 A227 5c multicolored 15 15
1250 A227 10c multicolored 15 15
1251 A227 15c multicolored 15 15
1252 A227 25c multicolored 18 18
1253 A227 30c multicolored 22 22
1254 A227 40c multicolored 30 30
1255 A227 50c multicolored 38 38
1256 A227 75c multicolored 55 55
1257 A227 $2 multicolored 1.50 1.50
1258 A227 $3 multicolored 2.25 2.25
1259 A227 $4 multicolored 3.00 3.00
1260 A227 $5 multicolored 3.75 3.75
Nos. 1249-1260 (12) 12.58 12.58

Size: 102x76mm

Imperf

1261 A227 $5 multi (#1433) 3.75 3.75
1262 A227 $5 multi (#1434) 3.75 3.75
1263 A227 $6 multi 4.50 4.50

Nos. 1476-1483 Overprinted

1992, Apr. 7 Litho. *Perf. 14*

1264 A231 10c multi 15 15
1265 A231 15c multi, vert. 15 15
1266 A231 45c multi, vert. 35 35
1267 A231 60c multi, vert. 45 45
1268 A231 $1 multi 75 75
1269 A231 $2 multi 1.50 1.50
1270 A231 $4 multi 3.00 3.00
1271 A231 $5 multi, vert. 3.75 3.75
Nos. 1264-1271 (8) 10.10 10.10

Nos. 1484-1485 Overprinted

1992, Apr. 7 Litho. *Perf. 14*

Souvenir Sheets

1272 A231 $6 multi (#1484) 5.00 5.00
1273 A231 $6 multi (#1485) 5.00 5.00

Nos. 1551-1560 Overprinted

1992, Apr. 16 Litho. *Perf. 14x13½*

1274 A242 10c multicolored 15 15
1275 A242 15c multicolored 15 15
1276 A242 30c multicolored 25 25
1277 A242 40c multicolored 35 35
1278 A242 $1 multicolored 85 85
1279 A242 $2 multicolored 1.65 1.65
1280 A242 $4 multicolored 3.30 3.30
1281 A242 $5 multicolored 4.15 4.15
Nos. 1274-1281 (8) 10.85 10.85

Souvenir Sheets

1282 A242 $6 multi (#1559) 5.00 5.00
1283 A242 $6 multi (#1560) 5.00 5.00

Nos. 1489-1492 Overprinted

1992, June 19 Litho. *Perf. 14*

1284 A234 75c multi 55 55
1285 A234 $2 multi, vert. 1.50 1.50
1286 A234 $3.50 multi 2.65 2.65

Souvenir Sheet

1287 A234 $5 multi, vert. 4.25 4.25

Nos. 1493-1494 Overprinted

1992, June 19

1288 A235 $1.50 multi 1.10 1.10
1289 A235 $4 multi 3.00 3.00

Nos. 1495-1496 Overprinted

1992, June 19

1290 A236 $2 multi 1.50 1.50
1291 A236 $2.50 multi, vert. 1.90 1.90

Nos. 1499-1502 Overprinted

1992, June 19

1292 A237 25c multi 18 18
1293 A237 $2 multi 1.50 1.50
1294 A237 $3 multi 2.25 2.25
1295 A237 $4 multi 3.50 3.50

Nos. 1571-1578 Overprinted

1992, Oct. 12 Litho. *Perf. 14*

1296 A244 15c multicolored 15 15
1297 A244 30c multicolored 22 22
1298 A244 40c multicolored 30 30
1299 A244 $1 multicolored 75 75
1300 A244 $2 multicolored 1.50 1.50
1301 A244 $4 multicolored 3.00 3.00
Nos. 1296-1301 (6) 5.92 5.92

Souvenir Sheets

1302 A244 $6 multicolored 4.50 4.50
1303 A244 $6 multicolored 4.50 4.50

Nos. 1599-1600 Overprinted

1992, Oct. 12 *Perf. 14½*

1304 A247 $1 multicolored 75 75
1305 A247 $2 multicolored 1.50 1.50

Nos. 1513-1518 Overprinted

1992, Nov. 3 *Perf. 14*

1306 CD348 10c multicolored 15 15
1307 CD348 30c multicolored 22 22
1308 CD348 $1 multicolored 75 75
1309 CD348 $5 multicolored 3.75 3.75

Souvenir Sheets

1310 CD348 $6 multi (#1517) 4.50 4.50
1311 CD348 $6 multi (#1518) 4.50 4.50

Nos. 1541-1550 Ovptd. "BARBUDA / MAIL"

1992, Dec. 8

1312 A241 10c multicolored 15 15
1313 A241 15c multicolored 15 15
1314 A241 30c multicolored 22 22
1315 A241 50c multicolored 38 38
1316 A241 $1 multicolored 75 75
1317 A241 $2 multicolored 1.50 1.50
1318 A241 $4 multicolored 3.00 3.00
1319 A241 $5 multicolored 3.75 3.75
Nos. 1312-1319 (8) 9.90 9.90

Souvenir Sheets

1320 A241 $6 multi (#1549) 5.50 5.50
1321 A241 $6 multi (#1550) 5.50 5.50

Nos. 1608-1617 Ovptd. "BARBUDA MAIL"

1992, Dec. 8 Litho. *Perf. 13½x14*

1322 A251 10c multicolored 15 15
1323 A251 25c multicolored 18 18
1324 A251 30c multicolored 22 22
1325 A251 40c multicolored 30 30
1326 A251 60c multicolored 45 45
1327 A251 $1 multicolored 75 75
1328 A251 $4 multicolored 3.00 3.00
1329 A251 $5 multicolored 3.75 3.75
Nos. 1322-1329 (8) 8.80 8.80

Souvenir Sheets

1330 A251 $6 multi (#1616) 5.50 5.50
1331 A251 $6 multi (#1617) 5.50 5.50

No. 1601 Ovptd. "BARBUDA MAIL"

1992 Litho. *Perf. 14*

Souvenir Sheet

1332 A248 $6 multicolored 4.50 4.50

Nos. 1519-1528 Ovptd.

1993, Jan. 25 Litho. *Perf. 14*

1333 A239 10c multicolored 15 15
1334 A239 15c multicolored 15 15
1335 A239 30c multicolored 28 28
1336 A239 40c multicolored 35 35
1337 A239 $1 multicolored 90 90
1338 A239 $2 multicolored 1.80 1.80
1339 A239 $4 multicolored 3.50 3.50
1340 A239 $5 multicolored 4.50 4.50
Nos. 1332-1339 (8) 11.63 11.63

Souvenir Sheets

1341 A239 $6 multi (#1527) 5.50 5.50
1342 A239 $6 multi (#1528) 5.50 5.50

Nos. 1561-1570 Ovptd.

1993, Mar. 22 Litho. *Perf. 13*

1343 A243 10c multicolored 15 15
1344 A243 15c multicolored 15 15
1345 A243 30c multicolored 22 22
1346 A243 40c multicolored 30 30
1347 A243 $1 multicolored 75 75
1348 A243 $2 multicolored 1.50 1.50
1349 A243 $4 multicolored 3.00 3.00
1350 A243 $5 multicolored 3.75 3.75
Nos. 1343-1350 (8) 9.82 9.82

Imperf

Size: 120x95mm

1351 A243 $6 multi (#1569) 5.50 5.50
1352 A243 $6 multi (#1570) 5.50 5.50

Nos. 1589-1598 Ovptd.

1993, May 10 Litho. *Perf. 14*

1353 A246 10c multicolored 15 15
1354 A246 25c multicolored 18 18
1355 A246 45c multicolored 35 35
1356 A246 60c multicolored 45 45
1357 A246 $1 multicolored 75 75
1358 A246 $2 multicolored 1.50 1.50
1359 A246 $4 multicolored 3.00 3.00
1360 A246 $5 multicolored 3.75 3.75
Nos. 1353-1360 (8) 10.13 10.13

Souvenir Sheets

1361 A246 $6 multi (#1597) 5.50 5.50
1362 A246 $6 multi (#1598) 5.50 5.50

Nos. 1603-1608 Ovptd.

1993, June 29 Litho. *Perf. 14*

1363 A250 10c multicolored 15 15
1364 A250 25c multicolored 22 22
1365 A250 30c multicolored 28 28
1366 A250 40c multicolored 35 35
1367 A250 60c multicolored 55 55
1368 A250 $1 multicolored 90 90
1369 A250 $4 multicolored 3.60 3.60
1370 A250 $5 multicolored 4.50 4.50
Nos. 1363-1370 (8) 10.55 10.55

Souvenir Sheets

1371 A250 $6 multi (#1607) 5.50 5.50
1372 A250 $6 multi (#1608) 5.50 5.50

Nos. 1619-1632 Ovptd.

1993, Aug. 16 Litho. *Perf. 14*

1373 A252 10c multicolored 15 15
1374 A252 40c multicolored 30 30
1375 A253 45c multicolored 35 35
1376 A252 75c multicolored 58 58
1377 A252 $1 multicolored 75 75
1378 A252 $1.50 multicolored 1.15 1.15
1379 A252 $2 multicolored 1.50 1.50
1380 A253 $2 multi (#1626) 1.50 1.50
1381 A253 $2 multi (#1627) 1.50 1.50
1382 A252 $2.25 multicolored 1.70 1.70
1383 A252 $3 multicolored 2.25 2.25
1384 A252 $4 multi (#1630) 3.00 3.00
1385 A252 $4 multi (#1631) 3.00 3.00
1386 A252 $6 multicolored 4.50 4.50
Nos. 1373-1386 (14) 22.23 22.23

Numbers have been reserved for four souvenir sheets in this set.

Nos. 1650-1657 Ovptd.

1993, Sept. 21 Litho. *Perf. 14*

1391 A256 15c multicolored 15 15
1392 A256 25c multicolored 18 18
1393 A256 30c multicolored 22 22
1394 A256 40c multicolored 30 30
1395 A256 $1 multicolored 75 75
1396 A256 $2 multicolored 1.50 1.50
1397 A256 $4 multicolored 3.00 3.00
1398 A256 $5 multicolored 3.75 3.75
Nos. 1391-1398 (8) 9.85 9.85

Numbers have been reserved for two souvenir sheets with this set.

No. 1660 Ovptd.

1993, Nov. 11 Litho. *Perf. 14*

1401 A257 $1 Sheet of 12, #a.-l. 9.00 9.00

Numbers have been reserved for two souvenir sheets in this set.

Nos. 1697-1710 Ovptd.

1994, Mar. 3 Litho. *Perf. 14*

1404-1415 A267 $2 Set of 12 18.00 18.00

Souvenir Sheets

1416-1417 A267 $6 each 4.50 4.50

Nos. 1676-1678 Ovptd.

1994, Apr. 21 Litho. *Perf. 14*

1418 A260 40c multicolored 30 30
1419 A260 $3 multicolored 2.25 2.25

Souvenir Sheet

1420 A260 $6 multicolored 4.50 4.50

Nos. 1679-1682 Ovptd.

1994, Apr. 21

1421-1423 A261 Set of 3 4.50 4.50

Souvenir Sheet

1424 A261 $6 multicolored 4.50 4.50

Nos. 1683-1685 Ovptd.

1994, Apr. 21

1425 A262 40c multicolored 32 32
1426 A262 $4 multicolored 3.25 3.25

Souvenir Sheet

1427 A262 $5 multicolored 3.75 3.75

Nos. 1686-1688 Ovptd.

1994, Apr. 21

1428 A263 30c multicolored 25 25
1429 A263 $4 multicolored 3.25 3.25

Souvenir Sheet

1430 A263 $6 multicolored 4.50 4.50

Nos. 1692-1693 Ovptd.

1994, Apr. 21

1431 A265 $5 multicolored 4.00 4.00

Souvenir Sheet

1432 A265 $6 multicolored 4.50 4.50

Nos. 1694-1696 Ovptd.

1994, Apr. 21

1433 A266 15c multicolored 15 15

1434 A266 $5 multicolored 4.00 4.00

Souvenir Sheet

1435 A266 $6 multicolored 4.50 4.50

Nos. 1732-1735 Ovptd.

1994, Apr. 21

1436-1439 A270 Set of 4 1.10 1.10

Nos. 1711-1720 Ovptd.

1994, June 15

1440-1446 A268 Set of 7 12.00 12.00

Souvenir Sheets

1447-1449 A268 $6 each 4.50 4.50

Nos. 1736-1741 Ovptd.

1994, June 15

1450-1453 A271 30c Set of 4 7.25 7.25

Souvenir Sheets

1454-1455 A271 $6 each 4.50 4.50

Nos. 1689-1691 Ovptd.

1994, Sept. 21 Litho. *Perf. 14*

1456 A264 $1 multicolored 75 75
1457 A264 $3 multicolored 2.25 2.25

Souvenir Sheet

1458 A264 $6 multicolored 4.50 4.50

Nos. 1786-1795 Ovptd.

1994, Sept. 21 Litho. *Perf. 14*

1459-1466 A279 Set of 8 10.00 10.00

Souvenir Sheets

1467-1468 A279 $6 each 4.50 4.50

SEMI-POSTAL STAMP

Catalogue values for unused stamps in this section are for Never Hinged items.

Barbuda No. 501 Crudely Surcharged

S. Atlantic Fund + 50c

1982, June 28

Self-Adhesive

B1 CD331 Booklet 16.00

BELIZE

LOCATION — Central America bordering on Caribbean Sea to east, Mexico to north, Guatemala to west
GOVT. — Independent state
AREA — 8,867 sq. mi.
POP. — 152,000 (1982 est.)
CAPITAL — Belmopan

Belize was known as British Honduras until 1973. The former British colony achieved independence in September 1981.

100 Cents = 1 Dollar

Catalogue values for all unused stamps in this country are for Never Hinged items.

Fish-Animal Type of British Honduras Regular Issue 1968-72 Overprinted in Black on Silver Panel

☼BELIZE☼

Wmk. 314 (½c, 5c, $5), Unwmkd.

1973, June 1 Litho. *Perf. 13x12½*

312 A37 ½c multi (#235) 15 15
313 A37 1c multi (#214) 15 15
314 A37 2c multi (#215) 15 15
315 A37 3c multi (#216) 15 15
316 A37 4c multi (#217) 15 15
317 A37 5c multi (#238) 15 15
318 A37 10c multi (#219) 16 16
319 A37 15c multi (#220) 25 25
320 A37 25c multi (#221) 40 40
321 A37 50c multi (#222) 65 65
322 A37 $1 multi (#223) 1.20 *1.60*
323 A37 $2 multi (#224) 2.50 *3.25*
324 A37 $5 multi (#240) 6.50 *8.75*
Nos. 312-324 (13) 12.56 *15.96*

Princess Anne's Wedding Issue

Common Design Type

1973, Nov. 14 Wmk. 314 *Perf. 14*

325 CD325 26c blue grn & multi 25 25
326 CD325 50c ocher & multi 50 50

Crana — A50

1974, Jan. 1 Litho. *Perf. 13½*

327 A50 ½c shown 15 15
328 A50 1c Jewfish 15 15
329 A50 2c White-lipped peccary 15 15
330 A50 3c Grouper 15 15
331 A50 4c Collared anteater 15 15
332 A50 5c Bonefish 15 15
333 A50 10c Paca 16 16
334 A50 15c Dolphinfish 22 22
335 A50 25c Kinkajou 38 38
336 A50 50c Muttonfish 80 80
337 A50 $1 Tayra 1.50 1.50
338 A50 $2 Great barracudas 3.00 3.00
339 A50 $5 Mountain lion 7.75 7.75
Nos. 327-339 (13) 14.71 14.71

Stag, Mayan Pottery A51

Designs: Mayan pottery decorations.

1974, May 1 *Perf. 14½*

340 A51 3c shown 15 15
341 A51 6c Fire snake 15 15
342 A51 16c Mouse 18 18
343 A51 26c Eagle 30 30
344 A51 50c Parrot 65 65
Nos. 340-344 (5) 1.43 1.43

Parides Arcas A52

Designs: Butterflies of Belize.

Wmk. 314 Sideways

1974-77 *Perf. 14*

345 A52 ½c shown 15 15
346 A52 1c Thecla regalis 15 15
347 A52 2c Colobura dirce 15 15
348 A52 3c Catonephele numilia 15 15
349 A52 4c Battus belus 15 15
350 A52 5c Callicore patelina 20 20
351 A52 10c Callicore astala 35 35

Perf. 14x15; 14 (26, 35c)

352 A52 15c Nessaea aglaura 50 50
a. Watermark upright ('75) 40 40
353 A52 16c Prepona pseudojoiceyi 25 25
354 A52 25c Papilio thoas 65 65
a. Watermark upright ('77) 45 45
355 A52 26c Hamadryas arethusa 4.00 *7.50*
356 A52 50c Thecla bathildis 1.25 1.25
a. Watermark upright ('77) 60 60
357 A52 $1 Caligo uranus 1.20 1.20
358 A52 $2 Heliconius sapho 2.40 2.40
359 A52 $5 Eurytides philolaus 7.50 7.50
a. Watermark upright ('75) 6.00 6.00
360 A52 $10 Philaethria dido 12.00 12.00
Nos. 345-360 (16) 31.05 34.55

Issue dates: No. 355A, July 25, 1977; No. 360, Jan. 2, 1975; others Sept. 2, 1974.
For surcharges, see Nos. 380, 386. For overprint, see No. 395.

1975-78 Wmk. 373

345a A52 ½c multicolored 15 15
347a A52 2c multi ('77) 15 15
348a A52 3c multi ('77) 18 18
349a A52 4c multi ('77) 25 25
350a A52 5c multi ('77) 32 32
351a A52 10c multicolored 65 65
352b A52 15c multi ('77) 90 90
354b A52 25c multi ('78) 1.25 1.25
355A A52 35c Parides arcas ('77) 2.00 2.00
Nos. 345a-355A (9) 5.85 5.85

For overprints and surcharges see Nos. 395-396, 424, 426-427.

Churchill and Coronation Coach of Queen Elizabeth II — A53

Design: $1, Churchill and Williamsburg, Va. Liberty Bell.

Wmk. 373

1974, Nov. 30 Litho. *Perf. 14*

363 A53 50c multicolored 32 32
364 A53 $1 multicolored 70 70

Sir Winston Churchill (1874-1965).

Mayan Urn — A54

Designs: Various Mayan vessels.

1975, June 2 Wmk. 314 *Perf. 14*

365 A54 3c lt green & multi 15 15
366 A54 6c lt blue & multi 15 15
367 A54 16c dull yel & multi 22 22
368 A54 26c lilac & multi 35 35
369 A54 50c lt brown & multi 75 75
Nos. 365-369 (5) 1.62 1.62

Musicians A55

Christmas: 26c, Nativity (Thatched hut and children). 50c, Drummers, vert. $1, Map of Belize, star, fleeing family, vert.

Perf. 14x14½, 14½x14

1975, Nov. 17 Litho. Wmk. 314

370 A55 6c multicolored 15 15
371 A55 26c multicolored 20 20
372 A55 50c multicolored 35 35
373 A55 $1 multicolored 75 75

William Wrigley, Jr., Sapodilla Tree A56

Bicentennial Emblem and: 35c, Charles Lindbergh and "Spirit of St. Louis." $1, John Lloyd Stephens and Mayan temple.

1976, Mar. 29 Wmk. 373 *Perf. 14½*

374 A56 10c multicolored 15 15
375 A56 35c multicolored 32 32
376 A56 $1 multicolored 90 90

American Bicentennial.

Bicycling A57

Perf. 14½

1976, July 17 Litho. Wmk. 373

377 A57 35c shown 40 40
378 A57 45c Running 50 50
379 A57 $1 Shooting 1.10 1.10

21st Olympic Games, Montreal, Canada, July 17-Aug. 1.

No. 355 Surcharged with New Value and Bar

Wmk. 314

1976, Aug. 30 Litho. *Perf. 14*

380 A52 20c on 26c multi 50 50

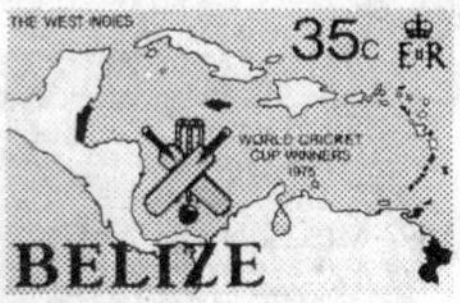

Map of West Indies, Bats, Wicket and Ball — A57a

Prudential Cup — A57b

Unwmk.

1976, Oct. 18 Litho. *Perf. 14*

381 A57a 35c lt blue & multi 60 60
382 A57b $1 lilac rose & blk 1.65 1.65

World Cricket Cup, won by West Indies Team, 1975.

Royal Visit, 1975 A58

Designs: 35c, Rose window and Queen's head. $2, Queen surrounded by bishops.

1977, Feb. 7 Litho. *Perf. 13½x14*

383 A58 10c multicolored 15 15
384 A58 35c multicolored 32 32
385 A58 $2 multicolored 1.50 1.50

25th anniv. of the reign of Elizabeth II.

No. 352 Surcharged with New Value and Bar

1977 Wmk. 314 *Perf. 14*

386 A52 5c on 15c multi 30 30

The first setting has the "5c" close to the the right edge of the block (varies). The second, and more common, setting has about 7mm from the right edge to the "5c."

Red-capped Manakin — A59

Designs: Birds of Belize.

Perf. 14½

1977, Sept. 3 Litho. Wmk. 373

387 A59 8c shown 30 15
388 A59 10c Hooded oriole 35 18
389 A59 25c Blue-crowned motmot 90 45
390 A59 35c Slaty-breasted tinamou 1.00 60
391 A59 45c Ocellated turkey 1.50 75

392 A59 $1 White hawk 3.00 1.75
a. Souvenir sheet of 6, #387-392 8.50 4.25
Nos. 387-392 (6) 7.05 3.88

See Nos. 398-403, 416-421, 500-501. For overprints and surcharges see No. 502.

Medical Laboratory A60

Design: $1, Mobile medical unit and children receiving treatment.

1977, Dec. 2 *Perf. 13½*
393 A60 35c multicolored 38 38
394 A60 $1 multicolored 1.00 1.00
a. Souvenir sheet of 2, #393-394 1.40 1.40

Pan American Health Org., 75th anniv.

Nos. 351 and 355A Overprinted in Gold: "BELIZE DEFENCE FORCE / 1ST JANUARY 1978"

Wmk. 314, 373
1978, Feb. 15 Litho. *Perf. 14*
395 A52 10c multicolored 15 15
396 A52 35c multicolored 35 35

Elizabeth II Coronation Anniversary Issue

Common Design Types
Souvenir Sheet

1978, Apr. 21 Unwmk. *Perf. 15*
397 Sheet of 6 1.90 1.90
a. CD326 75c White lion of Mortimer 30 30
b. CD327 75c Elizabeth II 30 30
c. CD328 75c Jaguar (Maya god) 30 30

No. 397 contains 2 se-tenant strips of Nos. 397a-397c, separated by horizontal gutter with commemorative and descriptive inscriptions and showing central part of coronation procession with coach.

Bird Type of 1977
Perf. 14½

1978, July 31 Litho. Wmk. 373
398 A59 10c White-crowned parrot 25 18
399 A59 25c Crimson-collared tanager 55 42
400 A59 35c Citreoline trogon 60 50
401 A59 45c Sungrebe 75 60
402 A59 50c Muscovy duck 80 65
403 A59 $1 King vulture 1.50 1.25
a. Souvenir sheet of 6, #398-403 6.50 4.00
Nos. 398-403 (6) 4.45 3.60

Russelia Sarmentosa — A61

Wild Flowers and Ferns: 15c, Lygodium polymorphum. 35c, Heliconia aurantiaca. 45c, Adiantum tetraphyllum. 50c, Angelonia ciliaris. $1, Thelypteris obliterata.

1978, Oct. 16 Litho. *Perf. 14x13½*
404 A61 10c multicolored 15 15
405 A61 15c multicolored 22 22
406 A61 35c multicolored 40 40
407 A61 45c multicolored 50 50
408 A61 50c multicolored 55 55
409 A61 $1 multicolored 1.10 1.10
Nos. 404-409 (6) 2.92 2.92

Christmas.

Internal Airmail Service, 1937 A62

Mail Service: 10c, MV Heron, 1949. 35c, Dugout canoe on river, 1920. 45c, Stann Creek railroad, 1910. 50c, Mounted courier, 1882. $2, RMS Eagle, 1856, and "paid" cancel.

Perf. 13½x14
1979, Jan. 15 Litho. Wmk. 373
410 A62 5c multicolored 15 15
411 A62 10c multicolored 15 15
412 A62 35c multicolored 30 30
413 A62 45c multicolored 40 40
414 A62 50c multicolored 42 42
415 A62 $2 multicolored 1.75 1.75
Nos. 410-415 (6) 3.17 3.17

Centenary of membership in UPU.

Bird Type of 1977

1979, Apr. 16 Unwmk. *Perf. 14½*
416 A59 10c Boat-billed heron 25 25
417 A59 25c Gray-necked wood rail 70 60
418 A59 35c Lineated woodpecker 85 85
419 A59 45c Blue gray tanager 1.10 1.10
420 A59 50c Laughing falcon 1.25 1.20
421 A59 $1 Long-tailed hermit 2.50 2.50
a. Souvenir sheet of 6, #416-421 7.25 7.00
Nos. 416-421 (6) 6.65 6.50

Nos. 477, 354b, 595, 355A, 599, 651 Surcharged with New Value and Bar

1979-83 Litho. *Perf. 14*
422 A67 10c on 15c multi 65 65
423 A67 10c on 15c multi 65 65
424 A52 10c on 25c multi 65 65
424A A67 10c on 35c multi
b. Round obliterator
425 A76 10c on 35c multi
426 A52 15c on 35c multi
427 A52 15c on 35c multi 32 32
428 A76 $1.25 on $2 multi 2.00 2.00
429 A81 $1.25 on $2 multi 2.00 2.00

No. 422 has a square the width of the "10c" obliterating the old value. No. 423 has a rectangle that is wider than the "10c."
No. 424A has a square obliterator.
No. 426 has "15c" at top of stamp, No. 427 has "15c" at right of rectangle. Type differs.
No. 429 has rectangular obliterator with new value at top of stamp.
Many errors exist from printer's waste.
Issue dates: #426, Mar. 1979. #427, June, 1979. #424, Mar. 31, 1980. #422, Aug. 22, 1981. #423, Jan. 28, 1983. #425, Apr. 15, 1983. #428-429, June 9, 1983.

Used Stamps
Most used stamps from No. 430-679 exist CTO. Most of these appeared on the market after the contract was canceled and were not authorized. The cancellations are printed and the paper differs from the issued stamps. Postally used copies are valued the same as unused. CTO's are of minimal value.

Queen Elizabeth II, 25th Anniv. of Coronation — A63

Designs: 25c, No. 439, Paslow Bldg., #397c. 50c, Parliament, London, #397a. 75c, Coronation coach. $1, Queen on horseback, vert. $2, Prince of Wales, vert. $3, Queen and Prince Philip, vert. $4, Queen Elizabeth II, portrait, vert. No. 437, St. Edward's Crown, vert. No. 438a, $5, Princess Anne on horseback, Montreal Olympics, vert. No. 438b, $10, Queen, Montreal Olympics, vert.

Unwmk.
1979, May 31 Litho. *Perf. 14*
430 A63 25c multicolored 22
431 A63 50c multicolored 45
432 A63 75c multicolored 70
433 A63 $1 multicolored 90
434 A63 $2 multicolored 1.75
435 A63 $3 multicolored 2.75
436 A63 $4 multicolored 3.75
437 A63 $5 multicolored 4.50
Nos. 430-437 (8) 15.02

Souvenir Sheets
438 A63 Sheet of 2, #a.-b. 12.00
439 A63 $15 multicolored 12.00

Powered Flight, 75th Anniv. — A64

1979, July 30
440 A64 4c Safety, 1909
441 A64 25c Boeing 707
442 A64 50c Concorde
443 A64 75c Handley Page W8b, 1922
444 A64 $1 AVRO F, 1912
445 A64 $1.50 Cody, 1910
446 A64 $2 Triplane Roe II, 1909
447 A64 $3 Santos-Dumont, 1906
448 A64 $4 Wright Brothers Flyer, 1903

Souvenir Sheets
Perf. 14½
449 Sheet of 2
a. A64 $5 Dunne D.5, 1910
b. A64 $5 Great Britain #581
450 A64 $10 Belize Airways Jet

Sir Rowland Hill, death cent., "75th anniv." of ICAO.

1980 Summer Olympics, Moscow — A65

1979, Oct. 10 *Perf. 14*
451 A65 25c Handball 22
452 A65 50c Weight lifting 45
453 A65 75c Track 70
454 A65 $1 Soccer 90
455 A65 $2 Sailing 1.75
456 A65 $3 Swimming 2.75
457 A65 $4 Boxing 3.75
458 A65 $5 Cycling 4.50
Nos. 451-458 (8) 15.02

Souvenir Sheets
Perf. 14½
459 Sheet of 2 12.00
a. A65 $5 Track, diff. 4.00
b. A65 $10 Boxing, diff. 8.00
460 A65 $15 Cycling, diff. 12.00

1980 Winter Olympics, Lake Placid — A66

1979, Dec. 4 *Perf. 14*
461 A66 25c Torch 20
462 A66 50c Slalom skiing 42
463 A66 75c Figure skating 65
464 A66 $1 Downhill skiing 85
465 A66 $2 Speed skating 1.75
466 A66 $3 Cross country skiing 2.50
467 A66 $4 Biathlon 3.50
468 A66 $5 Olympic medals 4.25
Nos. 461-468 (8) 14.12

Souvenir Sheets
Perf. 14½
469 Sheet of 2 12.00
a. A66 $5 Torch bearers 4.00
b. A66 $10 Medals, diff. 8.00
470 A66 $15 Torch, diff. 12.00

See Nos. 503-512.

Cypraea Zebra A67

1980, Jan. 7 Litho. *Perf. 14*
471 A67 1c shown 15 15
472 A67 2c Macrocallista maculata 15 15
473 A67 3c Arca zebra, vert. 15 15
474 A67 4c Chama macerophylla, vert. 15 15
475 A67 5c Latirus cariniferus 15 15
476 A67 10c Conus spurius, vert. 15 15
477 A67 15c Murex cabritii, vert. 18 15
478 A67 20c Atrina rigida 25 15
479 A67 25c Chlamys imbricata, vert. 30 15
480 A67 35c Conus granulatus 42 15
481 A67 45c Tellina radiata, vert. 55 15
482 A67 50c Leucozonia nassa 60 18
483 A67 85c Tripterotyphis triangularis 1.05 28
484 A67 $1 Strombus gigas, vert. 1.25 35
485 A67 $2 Strombus gallus, vert. 2.50 70
486 A67 $5 Fasciolaria tulipa 6.25 1.75
487 A67 $10 Arene cruentata 12.50 3.50
Nos. 471-487 (17) 26.75 8.41

Souvenir Sheets
488 A67 Sheet of 2, 85c, $5 7.50 7.50
489 A67 Sheet of 2, $2, $10 15.00 17.50

Stamps in Nos. 488-489 have different color border and are of a slightly different size than the sheet stamps.
The 10c, 50c, 85c, $1 exist dated 1981.
For overprints and surcharges see Nos. 422-423, 424A, 572-589, 592-593.

Intl. Year of the Child — A68

Various children. No. 498a, Three children. No. 498b, Madonna and Child by Durer. No. 499, Children before Christmas tree.

1980, Mar. 15 Litho. *Perf. 14*
490 A68 25c multicolored 16
491 A68 50c multicolored 35
492 A68 75c multicolored 50
493 A68 $1 multicolored 65
494 A68 $1.50 multicolored 1.00
495 A68 $2 multicolored 1.40
496 A68 $3 multicolored 2.00
497 A68 $4 multicolored 2.75
Nos. 490-497 (8) 8.81

Souvenir Sheets
Perf. 13½
498 A68 $5 Sheet of 2, #a.-b. 6.00
499 A68 $10 multicolored 6.00

No. 498 contains two 35x54mm stamps. No. 499 contains one 73x110mm stamp.

Bird Type of 1977
Souvenir Sheets

1980, June 16 Unwmk. *Perf. 13½*
500 Sheet of 6 5.50 4.50
a. A59 10c Jabiru 20 15
b. A59 25c Barred antshrike 50 35
c. A59 35c Royal flycatcher 65 50
d. A59 45c White-necked puffbird 75 65
e. A59 50c Ornate hawk-eagle 85 75
f. A59 $1 Golden-masked tanager 1.90 1.50
g. Sheet of 12 11.00 9.00
501 Sheet of 2 8.00 8.00
a. A59 $2 Jabiru 3.00 3.00
b. A59 $3 Golden-masked tanager 4.50 4.50

No. 500g contains 2 each Nos. 500a-500f with gutter between; inscribed "Protection of Environment" and "Wildlife Protection."

No. 500 Overprinted or Surcharged with Exhibition Emblem

1980, Oct. 3 Litho. *Perf. 13½*
502 Sheet of 6 4.00 4.00
a. A59 10c multicolored 20 20
b. A59 25c multicolored 50 50
c. A59 35c multicolored 65 65
d. A59 40c on 45c multi 85 85
e. A59 40c on 50c multi 85 85
f. A59 40c on $1 multi 85 85

ESPAMER '80 Stamp Exhibition, Madrid, Spain, Oct. 3-12.

1980 Winter Olympics, Lake Placid — A69

Events and winning country: 25c, Men's speed skating, US. 50c, Ice hockey, US. 75c, No. 512, Men's figure skating, Great Britain. $1, Alpine skiing, Austria. $1.50, Women's giant slalom, Germany. $2, Women's speed skating, Netherlands. $3, Cross country skiing, Sweden. $5, Men's giant slalom, Sweden. Nos. 511a ($5), 511b ($10), Speed skating, US.

1980, Aug. 20 Litho. *Perf. 14*
503 A69 25c multicolored 24
504 A69 50c multicolored 48
505 A69 75c multicolored 75
506 A69 $1 multicolored 95
507 A69 $1.50 multicolored 1.50
508 A69 $2 multicolored 1.90
509 A69 $3 multicolored 3.00
510 A69 $5 multicolored 4.75
Nos. 503-510 (8) 13.57

Souvenir Sheets
Perf. 14½
511 A69 Sheet of 2, #a.-b. 9.50
512 A69 $10 multicolored 9.50

Nos. 503-510 issued with se-tenant label.

Intl. Year of the Child — A70

Nos. 513-521: Scenes from Sleeping Beauty. $8, Detail from Paumgartner Family Altarpiece by Albrecht Durer.

1980, Nov. 24 *Perf. 14*
513 A70 35c multicolored 30
514 A70 40c multicolored 35
515 A70 50c multicolored 42
516 A70 75c multicolored 65
517 A70 $1 multicolored 85
518 A70 $1.50 multicolored 1.25
519 A70 $3 multicolored 2.50
520 A70 $4 multicolored 3.50
Nos. 513-520 (8) 9.82

Souvenir Sheets
Perf. 14½
521 Sheet of 2 9.50
a. A70 $5 Marriage 4.25
b. A70 $5 Couple on horseback 4.25
522 A70 $8 multicolored 7.50

Nos. 513-520 issued with se-tenent label.

Queen Mother Elizabeth, 80th Birthday A71

1980, Dec. 12
523 A71 $1 multicolored 1.00 1.00

Souvenir Sheet
Perf. 14½
524 A71 $5 multicolored

No. 524 contains one 46x31mm stamp.
No. 523 issued in sheet of 6.

Christmas — A72

1980, Dec. 30 Litho. *Perf. 14*
525 A72 25c Annunciation 20
526 A72 50c Bethlehem 42
527 A72 75c Holy Family 65
528 A72 $1 Nativity 85
529 A72 $1.50 Flight into Egypt 1.25
530 A72 $2 Shepards 1.65
531 A72 $3 With angel 2.50
532 A72 $4 Adoration 3.25
Nos. 525-532 (8) 10.77

Souvenir Sheets
Perf. 14½
533 A72 $5 Nativity 5.00
534 A72 $10 Madonna & Child 10.00

Nos. 526-532 issued in sheets of 20 + 10 labels. The 2nd and 5th vertical rows consist of labels.

Nos. 529, 532, 534 Surcharged $2 WIPA 1981

1981, May 22
535 A72 $1 on $1.50 multi
536 A72 $2 on $4 multi

Souvenir Sheet
Perf. 14½
537 A72 $2 on $10 multi

Location of overprint and surcharge varies.

Intl. Rotary Club — A73

Designs: 25c, Paul P. Harris, founder. 50c, No. 546, Rotary, project emblem. $1, No. 545b, 75th anniv. emblem. $1.50 Diploma, horiz. $2, No. 545a, Project Hippocrates. $3, 75th anniv. project emblems, horiz. No. 544, Hands reach out, horiz.

1981, May 26 *Perf. 14*
538 A73 25c multicolored 24
539 A73 50c multicolored 48
540 A73 $1 multicolored 95
541 A73 $1.50 multicolored 1.40
542 A73 $2 multicolored 1.90
543 A73 $3 multicolored 2.75
544 A73 $5 multicolored 4.75
Nos. 538-544 (7) 12.47

Souvenir Sheets
Perf. 14½
545 Sheet of 2 18.00
a. A73 $5 multicolored 5.75
b. A73 $10 multicolored 12.00
546 A73 $10 multicolored 12.00

Originally scheduled to be issued Mar. 30, the set was postponed and issued without a 75c stamp. Supposedly some of the 75c were sold to the public.

For overprints and surcharges see Nos. 563-571, 590-591.

Royal Wedding of Prince Charles and Lady Diana — A74

1981, July 16 *Perf. 13½x14*
548 A74 50c Coat of Arms 55
549 A74 $1 Prince Charles 1.10
550 A74 $1.50 Couple 1.65

Size: 25x43mm
Perf. 13½
551 A74 50c like No. 548 55
552 A74 $1 like No. 549 1.10
553 A74 $1.50 like No. 550 1.65
Nos. 548-553 (6) 6.60

Miniature Sheet
Perf. 14½
554 Sheet of 3, #554a-554c 6.75
a. A74 $3 like No. 550 2.25
b. A74 $3 like No. 548 2.25
c. A74 $3 like No. 549 2.25

Nos. 551-553 issued in sheets of 6 + 3 labels. No. 554 contains three 35x50mm stamps.

For overprints see Nos. 659-665.

1984 Olympics — A75

1981, Sept. 14 *Perf. 14*
555 A75 85c Track 75
556 A75 $1 Cycling 90
557 A75 $1.50 Boxing 1.40
558 A75 $2 Emblems 1.90
559 A75 $3 Baron Coubertin 2.75
560 A75 $5 Torch, emblems 4.50
Nos. 555-560 (6) 12.20

Souvenir Sheets
Perf. 13½
561 Sheet of 2 8.25
a. A75 $5 like No. 559 2.75
b. A75 $10 like No. 560 5.50

Perf. 14½
562 A75 $15 like No. 558 8.25

No. 561 contains two 35x54mm stamps. No. 562 contains one 46x68mm stamp.

Nos. 561-562 exist with gold inscription.

Nos. 538-546 Overprinted in Black or Gold **INDEPENDENCE 21 SEPT.,1981**

1981, Sept. 21 *Perf. 14*
563 A73 25c multicolored (G)
564 A73 50c multicolored
565 A73 $1 multicolored
566 A73 $1.50 multicolored
567 A73 $2 multicolored (G)
568 A73 $3 multicolored
569 A73 $5 multicolored

Souvenir Sheets
Perf. 14½
570 A73 Sheet of 2, #570a-570b (G)
571 A73 $10 multicolored

Size of overprint varies.

Nos. 471-483, 485-489 Overprinted *Independence 21 Sept.,1981*

1981, Sept. 21
572 A67 1c multicolored
573 A67 2c multicolored
574 A67 3c multicolored
575 A67 4c multicolored
576 A67 5c multicolored
577 A67 10c multicolored
578 A67 15c multicolored
579 A67 20c multicolored
580 A67 25c multicolored
581 A67 35c multicolored
582 A67 45c multicolored
583 A67 50c multicolored
584 A67 85c multicolored
585 A67 $2 multicolored
586 A67 $5 multicolored
587 A67 $10 multicolored

Souvenir Sheets
588 A67 Sheet of 2, #488
589 A67 Sheet of 2, #489

Size and style of overprint varies, italic on horiz. stamps, upright on vert. stamps and upright capitals on souvenir sheets.

The 10c is dated 1981. Less than 16 sheets dated 1980 were also overprinted.

Nos. 541, 545 Surcharged

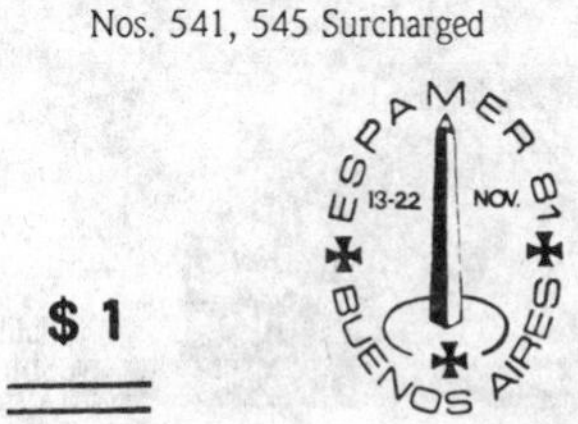

1981, Nov. 13 *Perf. 14*
590 A73 $1 on $1.50 multi

Souvenir Sheet
Perf. 14½
591 Sheet of 2
a. A73 $1 on $5 multicolored
b. A73 $1 on $10 multicolored

Espamer '81.

Nos. 488, 489 Surcharged in Red

1981, Nov. 14 *Perf. 14½*
Souvenir Sheets
592 Sheet of 2
a. A67 $1 on 85c
b. A67 $1 on $5
593 Sheet of 2
a. A67 $1 on $2
b. A67 $1 on $10

Independence — A76

1981-82 *Perf. 14*
594 A76 10c Flag
595 A76 35c Map, vert.
596 A76 50c Black orchid, vert.
597 A76 85c Tapir
598 A76 $1 Mahogany tree, vert.
599 A76 $2 Keel-billed toucan

Souvenir Sheet

Perf. 14½

600 A76 $5 like 10c

Issue dates: 50c-$2, Dec. 18. 10c, 35c, $5, Feb. 10, 1982.
For surcharges see Nos. 425, 428, 616.

1982 World Cup Soccer Championships, Spain — A77

1981, Dec. 28 *Perf. 14*
601 A77 10c Uruguay '30, '50
602 A77 25c Italy '34, '38
603 A77 50c Germany '54, '74
604 A77 $1 Brazil '58, '62, '70
605 A77 $1.50 Argentina '78
606 A77 $2 England '66

Souvenir Sheets

Perf. 14½

607 A77 $2 Emblem
608 A77 $3 Player

No. 608 contains one 46x78mm stamp.
For surcharge see No. 617.

Sailing Ships A78

1982, Mar. 15 *Perf. 14*
609 A78 10c Man of war, 19th cent.
610 A78 25c Madagascar, 1837
611 A78 35c Whitby, 1838
612 A78 50c China, 1838
613 A78 85c Swiftsure, 1850
614 A78 $2 Windsor Castle, 1857

Souvenir Sheet

Perf. 14½

615 A78 $5 19th cent. ships

Nos. 599 and 606 Surcharged

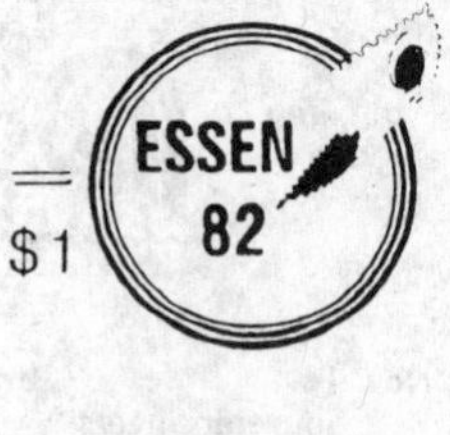

1982, Apr. 28
616 A76 $1 on $2 multi
617 A77 $1 on $2 multi

Essen '82 Philatelic Exhibition.

Values quoted in this catalogue are for stamps graded Fine-Very Fine and with no faults. An illustrated guide to grade is provided in the "Catalogue Information" section of the Introduction.

Princess of Wales, 21st Birthday — A79

Various portraits.

1982, May 20 *Perf. 13½x14*
618 A79 50c multicolored 65
619 A79 $1 multicolored 1.40
620 A79 $1.50 multicolored 2.00

Size: 25x42mm

Perf. 13½

621 A79 50c like No. 618 70
622 A79 $1 like No. 619 1.40
623 A79 $1.50 like No. 620 2.25
Nos. 618-623 (6) 8.40

Souvenir Sheet

Stamp Size: 31x47mm

Perf. 14½

624 A79 $3 Sheet of 3, #a.-c. like #618-620 8.50

Nos. 618-620 also exist with gold borders, size: 30x45mm.

BIRTH OF H.R.H.

Overprinted in Silver

PRINCE
WILLIAM ARTHUR
PHILIP LOUIS
21ST JUNE 1982

1982, Oct. 21 *Perf. 13½x14*
628 A79 50c multicolored 48
629 A79 $1 multicolored 95
630 A79 $1.50 multicolored 1.40

Size: 25x42mm

Perf. 13½

631 A79 50c multicolored 48
632 A79 $1 multicolored 95
633 A79 $1.50 multicolored 1.40
Nos. 628-633 (6) 5.66

Souvenir Sheet

Perf. 14½

634 A79 $3 Sheet of 3, #a.-c. 10.50

Size of overprint varies. The overprint exists on the gold bordered stamps. No. 634 exists with a second type of overprint.

Boy Scouts A80

1982, Aug. 31 *Perf. 14*
638 A80 10c Building camp fire 15
639 A80 25c Bird watching 22
640 A80 35c Playing guitar 30
641 A80 50c Hiking 42
642 A80 85c Flag, scouts 75
643 A80 $2 Salute 1.75
Nos. 638-643 (6) 3.59

Souvenir Sheets

Perf. 14½

644 A80 $2 Scout holding flag, vert. 2.00
645 A80 $3 Lord Baden Powell, vert. 3.00

Scouting, 75th anniv. and Lord Baden Powell, 125th birth anniv.
For overprints see Nos. 653-658.

Marine Life — A81

1982, Sept. 20 *Perf. 14*
646 A81 10c Gorgonia ventalina
647 A81 35c Carpilius corallinus
648 A81 50c Plexaura flexuosa
649 A81 85c Condylactis gigantea
650 A81 $1 Stenopus hispidus
651 A81 $2 Abudefduf saxatilis

Souvenir Sheet

Perf. 14½

652 A81 $5 Scyllarides aequinoctialis

For surcharge see No. 429.

Nos. 638-643 Ovptd. in Gold:
BELGICA 82
INT. YEAR OF THE CHILD
SIR ROWLAND HILL 1795 1879
Picasso CENTENARY OF BIRTH
and Emblems

1982, Oct. 1 *Perf. 14*
653 A80 10c Building camp fire
654 A80 25c Bird watching
655 A80 35c Playing guitar
656 A80 50c Hiking
657 A80 85c Flag, scouts
658 A80 $2 Salute

Overprint is different on Nos. 654-655.
Sheets include labels with native Christmas themes.

Nos. 548-554 Overprinted in Gold Similar to Nos. 628-637

1982, Oct. 25 *Perf. 13½x14*
659 A74 50c Coat of Arms 1.40
660 A74 $1 Prince Charles 2.75
661 A74 $1.50 Couple 4.25

Size: 25x43mm

Perf. 13½

662 A74 50c like No. 659 1.40
663 A74 $1 like No. 660 2.75
664 A74 $1.50 like No. 661 4.25
Nos. 659-664 (6) 16.80

Miniature Sheet

Perf. 14½

665 Sheet of 3, #665a-665c 14.00
a. A74 $3 like No. 661 3.50
b. A74 $3 like No. 659 3.50
c. A74 $3 like No. 660 3.50

Nos. 662-664 issued in sheets of 6 plus 3 labels. No. 665 contains three 35x50mm stamps. Size and style of overprint varies.

Visit by Pope John Paul II — A82

1983, Mar. 7 *Perf. 13½*
666 A82 50c Belize Cathedral 1.90

Souvenir Sheet

Perf. 14½

667 A82 $2.50 Pope John Paul II 4.75

No. 667 contains one 30x47mm stamp.
No. 666 issued in sheet of 6.

Commonwealth Day — A83

1983, Mar. 14 *Perf. 13½*
668 A83 35c Map, vert. 42
669 A83 50c Maya Stella 60
670 A83 85c Supreme Court Bldg. 1.00
671 A83 $2 University Center 2.50

Issued in miniature sheets of 4. Other formats are suspect.

First Manned Flight, Bicent. — A84

1983, May 16 *Perf. 14*
672 A84 10c Flying boat, 1670 15
673 A84 25c Flying machine, 1709 16
674 A84 50c Airship Guyton de Morveau 30
675 A84 85c Dirigible 52
676 A84 $1 Clement Bayard 60
677 A84 $1.50 Great Britain R-34 95
Nos. 672-677 (6) 2.68

Souvenir Sheets

Perf. 14½

678 A84 $3 Nassau Balloon 1.65
679 A84 $3 Montgolfier Brothers balloon, vert. 1.65

"Errors"

Many "errors" exist of Nos. 680-898. These unauthorized varieties were printed without the knowledge of the Belize postal service. There may be large quantities of them.

Mayan Monuments — A85

1983, Nov. 14 Litho. *Perf. 13½x14*
680 A85 10c Altun Ha 15 15
681 A85 15c Xunantunich 20 20
682 A85 75c Cerros 1.00 1.00
683 A85 $2 Lamanai 2.50 2.50

Souvenir Sheet

684 A85 $3 Xunantunich, diff. 5.00 5.00

World Communications Year — A86

1983, Nov. 28 *Perf. 14*
685 A86 10c Belmopan Earth Station 15 15
686 A86 15c Telstar 2 15 15
687 A86 75c UPU monument 75 75
688 A86 $2 Mail boat 2.00 2.00

Jaguar, World Wildlife Fund Emblem A87

1983, Dec. 9
689 A87 5c Sitting 15 15
690 A87 10c Standing 15 15
691 A87 85c Swimming 1.10 1.10
692 A87 $1 Walking 1.40 1.40

Souvenir Sheet

693 A87 $3 Sitting in tree 3.25 3.25

No. 693 contains one stamp 45x28mm.

Christmas — A88

Scenes from mass celebrated by Pope John Paul II during visit, Mar.

1983, Dec. 22

694	A88	10c multicolored	15	15
695	A88	15c multicolored	15	15
696	A88	75c multicolored	75	75
697	A88	$2 multicolored	2.00	2.00

Souvenir Sheet

698	A88	$3 multicolored	3.25	3.25

Foureye Butterflyfish A89

1984, Feb. 27 *Perf. 15*

699	A89	1c shown	15	15
700	A89	2c Cushion star	15	15
701	A89	3c Flower coral	15	15
702	A89	4c Fairy basslets	15	15
703	A89	5c Spanish hogfish	15	15
704	A89	6c Star-eyed hermit crab	15	15
705	A89	10c Sea fans, fire sponge	15	15
706	A89	15c Blueheads	15	15
707	A89	25c Blue-striped grunt	25	25
708	A89	50c Coral crab	50	50
709	A89	60c Tube sponge	60	60
710	A89	75c Brain coral	75	75
711	A89	$1 Yellow-tail snapper	1.00	1.00
712	A89	$2 Common lettuce slug	2.00	2.00
713	A89	$5 Yellow damselfish	5.00	5.00
714	A89	$10 Rock beauty	10.00	10.00
		Nos. 699-714 (16)	21.30	21.30

For overprints and surcharge see Nos. 715-716, 762A-762C, 922.

The 50c, 60c, 75c, $1 exist inscribed "1986."

1988, July *Perf. 13½*

705a	A89	10c	15	15
706a	A89	15c	15	15
707a	A89	25c	25	25
708a	A89	50c	48	48
709a	A89	60c	58	58
711a	A89	$1	95	95
		Nos. 705a-711a (6)	2.56	2.56

Nos. 705, 708 Overprinted: "VISIT OF THE LORD / ARCHBISHOP OF CANTERBURY / 8th-11th MARCH 1984"

1984, Mar. 8

715	A89	10c multicolored	15	15
716	A89	50c multicolored	60	60

1984 Summer Olympics — A90

1984, Apr. 30 *Perf. 13½x14*

717	A90	25c Shooting	24	24
718	A90	75c Boxing	75	75
719	A90	$1 Running	1.10	1.10
720	A90	$2 Bicycling	1.90	1.90

Souvenir Sheet

721	A90	$3 Discus	3.00	3.00

1984 Summer Olympics A91

1984, Apr. 30 Litho. *Perf. 14½*

Booklet Stamps

722	A91	5c Running	15	15
a.		Booklet pane of 4	30	
723	A91	20c Javelin	25	25
a.		Booklet pane of 4	1.10	
724	A91	25c Shot put	35	35
a.		Booklet pane of 4	1.50	
725	A91	$2 Torch	2.50	2.50
a.		Booklet pane of 4	10.50	

Ausipex '84 — A92

1984, Sept. 26 Litho. *Perf. 15*

726	A92	15c Br. Honduras #3	15	15
727	A92	30c Bath-Bristol mail coach, 1784	30	30
728	A92	65c Penny Black, Rowland Hill	65	65
729	A92	75c Railroad Pier, Commerce Bight	75	75

Perf. 14

730	A92	$2 Royal Exhibition Bldgs.	2.00	2.00
		Nos. 726-730 (5)	3.85	3.85

Souvenir Sheet

731	A92	$3 Australia #132, Br. Hond. #3	3.00	3.00

House of Tudor, 500th Anniv. — A93

White-fronted Parrot — A94

1984, Oct. 15 *Perf. 14*

732	A93	50c Queen Victoria	50	50
733	A93	50c Prince Albert	50	50
a.		Sheet of 4, 2 each, #732-733	2.00	
734	A93	75c King George VI	75	75
735	A93	75c Queen Elizabeth	75	75
a.		Sheet of 4, 2 each, #734-735	3.00	
736	A93	$1 Prince Charles	1.00	1.00
737	A93	$1 Princess Diana	1.00	1.00
a.		Sheet of 4, 2 each, #736-737	4.00	
		Nos. 732-737 (6)	4.50	4.50

Souvenir Sheet

738		Sheet of 2	3.00	3.00
a.	A93	$1.50 Prince Philip	1.50	1.50
b.	A93	$1.50 Queen Elizabeth II	1.50	1.50

1984, Nov. 1 *Perf. 11*

Parrots: b, White-capped. c, Red-lored. d, Mealy. b, d, horiz.

739		Block of 4	4.00	4.00
a.-d.	A94	$1 any single	1.00	1.00

Miniature Sheet

Perf. 14

740	A94	$3 Scarlet macaw	3.00	3.00

No. 740 contains one 48x32mm stamp.

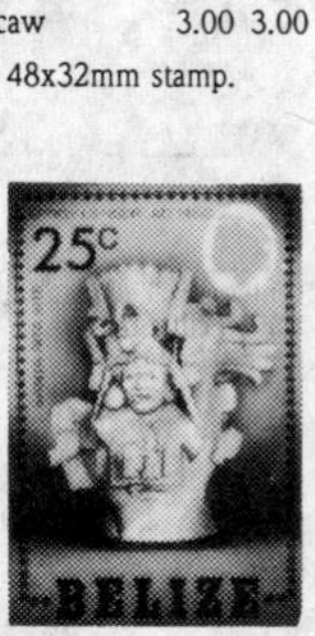

Mayan Artifacts — A95

1984, Nov. 30 *Perf. 15*

741	A95	25c Incense holder, 1450	25	25
742	A95	75c Cylindrical vase, 675	75	75
743	A95	$1 Tripod vase, 500	1.00	1.00
744	A95	$2 Kinich Ahau (sun god)	2.00	2.00

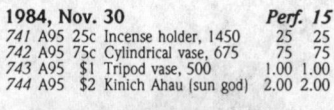

Girl Guides 75th Anniv., Intl. Youth Year A96

1985, Mar. 15 Litho. *Perf. 15*

745	A96	25c Gov.-Gen. Gordon	25	25
746	A96	50c Camping	50	50
747	A96	90c Map reading	90	90
748	A96	$1.25 Students in laboratory	1.25	1.25
749	A96	$2 Lady Baden-Powell	2.00	2.00
		Nos. 745-749 (5)	4.90	4.90

Each stamp shows the scouting and IYY emblems.

For overprints see Nos. 777-781.

Audubon Birth Bicentenary A97

Illustrations by Audubon. 10c, 25c, 75c, $1, $5 vert.

1985, May 30-1988 Litho. *Perf. 14*

750	A97	10c White-tailed kite	15	15
751	A97	15c Cuvier's kinglet	15	15
752	A97	25c Painted bunting	25	25
752A	A97	60c like #752 ('88)		
753	A97	75c Belted kingfisher	75	75
754	A97	$1 Northern cardinal	1.00	1.00
755	A97	$3 Long-billed curlew	3.00	3.00

Souvenir Sheet

Perf. 13½x14

756	A97	$5 Portrait of Audubon, 1826, by John Syme	5.00	5.00

No. 756 contains one 38x51mm stamp.

Queen Mother, 85th Birthday A98

Designs: 10c, The Queen Consort and Princess Elizabeth, 1928. 15c, Queen Mother, Elizabeth. 75c, Queen Mother waving a greeting. No. 760, Royal family photograph, christening of Prince Henry. $2, Holding the infant Prince Henry. No. 762, Queen Mother, diff.

1985, June 20

757	A98	10c shown	15	15
758	A98	15c multicolored	15	15
759	A98	75c multicolored	75	75
760	A98	$5 multicolored	5.00	5.00

Souvenir Sheets

761	A98	$2 multicolored	2.00	2.00
762	A98	$5 multicolored	5.00	5.00

Nos. 761-762 contain one 38x51mm stamp.

For overprints see Nos. 771-776.

Nos. 705-706, 708 Ovptd.: INAUGURATION OF NEW GOVERNMENT 21st. DECEMBER 1984

1985, June 24 *Perf. 15*

762A	A89	10c multicolored	30	30
762B	A89	15c multicolored	45	45
762C	A89	50c multicolored	1.25	1.25

Miniature Sheet

Commonwealth Stamp Omnibus, 50th Anniv. — A99

British Honduras Nos. 111-112, 127, 129, 143, 194, 307 and Belize Nos. 326, 385 and 397b on: a, George V and Queen Mary in an open carriage. b, George VI and Queen Consort Elizabeth crowned. c, Civilians celebrating the end of WWII. d, George VI and Queen Consort at mass service. e, Elizabeth II wearing robes of state and the imperial crown. f, Winston Churchill, WWII fighter planes. g, Bridal photograph of Elizabeth II and Prince Philip. h, Bridal photograph of Princess Anne and Capt. Mark Phillips. i, Elizabeth II. j, Imperial crown.

1985, July 25 *Perf. 14½x14*

763		Sheet of 10	5.00	5.00
a.-j.	A99	50c any single	50	50

Souvenir Sheet

Perf. 14

764	A99	$5 Elizabeth II coronation photograph	5.00	5.00

No. 764 contains one 38x51mm stamp.

For overprints see Nos. 796-797.

British Post Office, 350th Anniv. A100

1985, Aug. 1 *Perf. 15*

765	A100	10c Postboy, letters	15	15
766	A100	15c Packet, privateer	15	15
767	A100	25c Duke of Marlborough	25	25
768	A100	75c Diana	75	75
769	A100	$1 Falmouth P.O. packet	1.00	1.00
770	A100	$3 S. S. Conway	3.00	3.00
		Nos. 765-770 (6)	5.30	5.30

Nos. 757-762 Ovptd. in Silver "COMMONWEALTH SUMMIT / CONFERENCE, BAHAMAS / 16th-22nd OCTOBER 1985"

1985, Sept. 5 Litho. *Perf. 15*

771	A98	10c multicolored	15	15
772	A98	15c multicolored	15	15
773	A98	75c multicolored	75	75
774	A98	$5 multicolored	5.00	5.00

Souvenir Sheets

775	A98	$2 multicolored	2.00	2.00
776	A98	$5 multicolored	5.00	5.00

Nos. 745-749 Ovptd. "80th ANNIVERSARY OF / ROTARY INTERNATIONAL"

1985, Sept. 25 *Perf. 15*

777	A96	25c multicolored	25	25
778	A96	50c multicolored	50	50
779	A96	90c multicolored	90	90
780	A96	$1.25 multicolored	1.25	1.25
781	A96	$2 multicolored	2.00	2.00
		Nos. 777-781 (5)	4.90	4.90

Royal Visit — A101

1985, Oct. 9 *Perf. 15x14½*

782	A101	25c Royal and natl. flags	25	25
783	A101	75c Elizabeth II	75	75

Size: 81x38mm

784	A101	$4 Britannia	4.00	4.00
a.		Strip of 3, #782-784	5.00	

Souvenir Sheet

Perf. 13½x14

785 A101 $5 Elizabeth II, diff. 5.00 5.00

No. 785 contains one 38x51mm stamp.

Disneyland, 30th Anniv. A102

Characters from "It's a Small World."

1985, Nov. 1 ***Perf. 11***

786 A102 1c Royal Canadian Mounted Police 15 15
787 A102 2c American Indian 15 15
788 A102 3c Inca of the Andes 15 15
789 A102 4c Africa 15 15
790 A102 5c Far East 15 15
791 A102 6c Belize 15 15
792 A102 50c Balkans 50 50
793 A102 $1.50 Saudi Arabia 1.50 1.50
794 A102 $3 Japan 3.00 3.00
Set value 5.25 5.25

Souvenir Sheet

Perf. 14

795 A102 $4 Montage 4.00 4.00

Christmas.

Nos. 763-764 Ovptd. "PRE 'WORLD CUP FOOTBALL' / MEXICO 1986"

1985, Dec. 20 ***Perf. 14½x14***

796 Sheet of 10 5.00 5.00
a.-j. A99 50c, any single 50 50

Souvenir Sheet

797 A99 $5 multicolored 5.00 5.00

Women in Folk Costumes — A103

1986, Jan. 15 ***Perf. 15***

798 A103 5c India 15 15
799 A103 10c Maya 15 15
800 A103 15c Garifuna 15 15
801 A103 25c Creole 25 25
802 A103 50c China 50 50
803 A103 75c Lebanon 75 75
804 A103 $1 Europe 1.00 1.00
805 A103 $2 South America 2.00 2.00
Nos. 798-805 (8) 4.95 4.95

Souvenir Sheet

Perf. 14

806 A103 $5 Maya, So. America 5.00 5.00

No. 806 contains one 38x51mm stamp.

Miniature Sheet

A104

Easter — A105

Papal arms, crucifix and: a, Pius X. b, Benedict XV. c, Pius XI. d, Pius XII. e, John XXIII. f, Paul VI. g, John Paul I. h, John Paul II. No. 573, John Paul II saying mass in Belize.

1986, Apr. 15 **Litho.** ***Perf. 11***

807 Sheet of 8 + label 4.00 4.00
a.-h. A104 50c, any single 50 50

Souvenir Sheet

Perf. 14

808 A105 $4 multi 4.00 4.00

No. 807 contains center label picturing the Vatican, and papal crest.

A106

Queen Elizabeth II, 60th Birthday A107

1986, Apr. 21 ***Perf. 14***

809 Strip of 3 1.50 1.50
a. A106 25c Age 2 25 25
b. A106 50c Coronation 50 50
c. A106 75c Riding horse 75 75
810 A106 $3 Wearing crown jewels 3.00 3.00

Souvenir Sheet

811 A107 $4 Portrait 4.00 4.00

A108

Halley's Comet A109

1986, Apr. 30

812 Strip of 3 75 75
a. A108 10c Planet-A probe 15 15
b. A108 15c Sighting, 1910 15 15
c. A108 50c Giotto probe 50 50
813 Strip of 3 3.75 3.75
a. A108 75c Weather bureau 75 75
b. A108 $1 US space telescope, shuttle 1.00 1.00
c. A108 $2 Edmond Halley 2.00 2.00

Souvenir Sheet

814 A109 $4 Computer graphics 4.00 4.00

Miniature Sheet

A110

US Presidents A111

1986, May ***Perf. 11***

815 Sheet of 6 + 3 labels 4.60 4.60
a. A110 10c George Washington 15 15
b. A110 20c John Adams 20 20
c. A110 30c Thomas Jefferson 30 30
d. A110 50c James Madison 50 50
e. A110 $1.50 James Monroe 1.50 1.50
f. A110 $2 John Quincy Adams 2.00 2.00

Souvenir Sheet

Perf. 14

816 A111 $4 Washington 4.00 4.00

No. 815 contains 3 center labels picturing the great seal of the US.

Issue dates: #815, May 5. #816, May 7.

A112

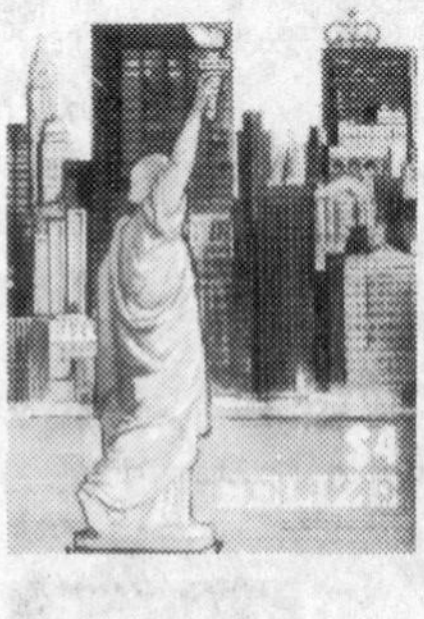

Statue of Liberty, Cent. — A113

Designs: 25c, Bartholdi, statue. 50c, Statue, US centennial celebration, Philadelphia, 1876. 75c, Statue close-up, flags, 1886 unveiling. $3, Flags, statue close-up. $4, Statue, New York City skyline.

1986, May 15 ***Perf. 14***

817 Strip of 3 4.00 4.00
a. A112 25c multicolored 25 25
b. A112 75c multicolored 75 75
c. A112 $3 multicolored 3.00 3.00
818 A112 50c multicolored 50 50

Souvenir Sheet

819 A113 $4 multicolored 4.00 4.00

A114

AMERIPEX '86, Chicago, May 22-June 1 — A115

1986, May 22

820 Strip of 3 75 75
a. A114 10c British Honduras No. 3 15 15
b. A114 15c Stamp of 1981 15 15
c. A114 50c US No. C3a 50 50
821 Strip of 3 3.75 3.75
a. A114 75c USS Constitution 75 75
b. A114 $1 Liberty Bell 1.00 1.00
c. A114 $2 White House 2.00 2.00

Souvenir Sheet

822 A115 $4 Capitol Building 4.00 4.00

For overprints, see Nos. 835-837.

1986 World Cup Soccer Championships, Mexico — A116

Designs: 25c, England vs. Brazil. 50c, Mexican player, Mayan statues. 75c, Belize players. $3, Aztec calendar stone, Mexico. $4, Flags composing soccer balls.

1986, June 16 **Litho.** ***Perf. 11***

823 A116 25c multicolored 25 25
824 A116 50c multicolored 50 50
825 A116 75c multicolored 75 75
826 A116 $3 multicolored 3.00 3.00

Souvenir Sheet

Perf. 14

827 A116 $4 multicolored 4.00 4.00

Nos. 823-826 printed in sheets of 8 plus label picturing Azteca Stadium, 2 each value per sheet.

Nos. 823-827 Overprinted "ARGENTINA - /WINNERS 1986"

1986, Aug. 15

828 A116 25c multicolored 25 25
829 A116 50c multicolored 50 50
830 A116 75c multicolored 75 75
831 A116 $3 multicolored 3.00 3.00

Souvenir Sheet

832 A116 $4 multicolored 4.00 4.00

Wedding of Prince Andrew and Sarah Ferguson

A117 A118

1986, July 23 *Perf. 14x14½*

833	Strip of 3	4.00	4.00
a.	A117 25c Sarah	25	25
b.	A117 75c Andrew	75	75
c.	A117 $3 Couple	3.00	3.00

Souvenir Sheet

Perf. 14½

834	Sheet of 2	4.00	4.00
a.	A118 $1 Sarah, diff.	1.00	1.00
b.	A118 $3 Andrew, diff.	3.00	3.00

Size of No. 833c: 92x41mm.

Nos. 820-822 Ovptd. with STOCKHOLMIA '86 Emblems

1986, Aug. 28 **Litho.** ***Perf. 14***

835	Strip of 3	75	75
a.	A114 10c multi	15	15
b.	A114 15c multi	15	15
c.	A114 50c multi	50	50
836	Strip of 3	3.75	3.75
a.	A114 75c multi	75	75
b.	A114 $1 multi	1.00	1.00
c.	A114 $2 multi	2.00	2.00

Souvenir Sheet

837 A115 $4 multi 4.00 4.00

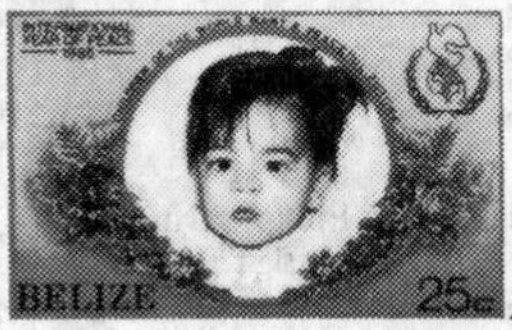
A119

Intl. Peace Year — A120

Children.

1986, Oct. 3 **Litho.** ***Perf. 14***

838 A119	25c	Infant	25	25
839 A119	50c	Caucasians	50	50
840 A119	75c	Oriental	75	75
841 A119	$3	Indian, caucasian	3.00	3.00

Souvenir Sheet

842 A120 $4 shown 4.00 4.00

Nos. 838-841 printed se-tenant in sheets of 8 (2 each) plus center label.

Fungi — A121

Toucans — A122

1986, Oct. 30 ***Perf. 14***

843 A121	5c	Amanita lilloi	15	15
844 A122	10c	Keel-billed toucan	15	15
845 A121	20c	Boletellus cubensis	20	20
846 A122	25c	Collared aracari	25	25
847 A121	75c	Psilocybe caerulescens	75	75
848 A122	$1	Emerald toucanet	1.00	1.00
849 A122	$1.25	Crimson-rumped toucan	1.25	1.25
850 A121	$2	Russula puiggarii	2.00	2.00
		Nos. 843-850 (8)	5.75	5.75

Stamps of the same design printed in sheets of 8 plus center label picturing Audubon Society emblem.

Christmas A123

Disney characters.

1986, Nov. 14 ***Perf. 11***

851	Sheet of 9	4.75	4.75
a.	A123 2c Jose Carioca	15	15
b.	A123 3c Carioca, Panchito, Donald	15	15
c.	A123 4c Daisy	15	15
d.	A123 5c Mickey, Minnie	15	15
e.	A123 6c Carioca playing music	15	15
f.	A123 50c Panchito, Donald	50	50
g.	A123 65c Donald, Carioca	65	65
h.	A123 $1.35 Donald	1.35	1.35
i.	A123 $2 Goofy	2.00	2.00

Souvenir Sheet

Perf. 14

852 A123 $4 Donald 4.00 4.00

A124

Marriage of Queen Elizabeth II and the Duke of Edinburgh, 40th Anniv. — A125

1987, Oct. 7 **Litho.** ***Perf. 15***

853 A124	25c	Elizabeth, 1947	25	25
854 A124	75c	Couple, c. 1980	75	75
855 A124	$1	Elizabeth, 1986	1.00	1.00
856 A124	$4	Wearing robes of Order of the Garter	4.00	4.00

Souvenir Sheet

Perf. 14

857 A125 $6 shown 6.00 6.00

A126

America's Cup 1986-87 — A127

Yachts that competed in the 1987 finals.

1987, Oct. 21 ***Perf. 15***

858 A126	25c	America II	25	25
859 A126	75c	Stars and Stripes	75	75
860 A126	$1	Australia II	1.00	1.00
861 A126	$4	White Crusader	4.00	4.00

Souvenir Sheet

Perf. 14

862 A127 $6 Australia II sails 6.00 6.00

A128

Woodcarvings by Sir George Gabb (b. 1928) — A129

1987, Nov. 4 ***Perf. 15***

863 A128	25c	Mother and Child	20	20
864 A128	75c	Standing Form	60	60
865 A128	$1	Love-Doves	80	80
866 A128	$4	Depiction of Music	3.25	3.25

Souvenir Sheet

Perf. 14

867 A129 $6 African Heritage 4.50 4.50

A130

Indigenous Primates — A131

1987, Nov. 11 ***Perf. 15***

868 A130	25c	Black spider monkey	25	25
869 A130	75c	Male black howler	75	75
870 A130	$1	Spider monkeys	1.00	1.00
871 A130	$4	Howler monkeys	4.00	4.00

Souvenir Sheet

Perf. 14

872 A131 $6 Black spider, diff. 6.00 6.00

Natl. Girl Guides Movement, 50th Anniv. A132

Lady Olave Baden-Powell, Founder — A133

1987, Nov. 25 ***Perf. 15***

873 A132	25c	Flag-bearers	25	25
874 A132	75c	Camping	75	75
875 A132	$1	On parade, camp	1.00	1.00
876 A132	$4	Olave Baden-Powell	4.00	4.00

Souvenir Sheet

Perf. 14

877 A133 $6 Lady Olave, diff. 6.00 6.00

Intl. Year of Shelter for the Homeless A134

1987, Dec. 3 ***Perf. 15***

878 A134	25c	Tent dwellings	25	25
879 A134	75c	Urban slum	75	75
880 A134	$1	Tents, diff.	1.00	1.00
881 A134	$4	Construction	4.00	4.00

Orchids A135 1c

Designs: Illustrations from Reichenbachia, published by Henry F. Sander in 1886.

1987, Dec. 16 Litho. *Perf. 14*

882	A135	1c Laelia euspatha	15	15
883	A135	2c Cattleya citrina	15	15
884	A135	3c Masdevallia bachousiana	15	15
885	A135	4c Cypripedium tautzianum	15	15
886	A135	5c Trichopilia suavis alba	15	15
887	A135	6c Odontoglossum hebraicum	15	15
888	A135	7c Cattleya trianaei schroederiana	15	15
889	A135	10c Saccolabium giganteum	15	15
890	A135	30c Cattleya warscewiczii	30	30
891	A135	50c Chysis bractescens	50	50
892	A135	70c Cattleya rochellensis	70	70
893	A135	$1 Laelia elegans schilleriana	1.00	1.00
894	A135	$1.50 Laelia anceps percivaliana	1.50	1.50
895	A135	$3 Laelia gouldiana	3.00	3.00
		Nos. 882-895 (14)	8.20	8.20

Miniature Sheets

896	A135	$3 Odontoglossum roezlii	3.00	3.00
897	A135	$5 Cattleya dowiana aurea	5.00	5.00

Nos. 882-887 and 889-894 printed in blocks of six. Sheets of 14 contain 2 blocks of Nos. 882-887 plus 2 No. 888 and center label or 2 blocks of Nos. 889-894 plus center strip containing 2 No. 895 and center label. Center labels picture various illustrations from Reichenbachia.

Nos. 896, 897 contain one 44x51mm stamp.

Miniature Sheet

Easter — A136

Stations of the Cross (in sequential order): a, Jesus condemned to death. b, Carries the cross. c, Falls the first time. d, Meets his mother, Mary. e, Cyrenean takes up the cross. f, Veronica wipes Jesus's face. g, Falls the second time. h, Consoles the women of Jerusalem. i, Falls the third time. j, Stripped of his robes. k, Nailed to the cross. l, Dies. m, Taken down from the cross. n, Laid in the sepulcher.

1988, Mar. 21 *Perf. 14*

898	Sheet of 14 + label	5.60	5.60
a.-n.	A136 40c, any single	40	40

1988 Summer Olympics, Seoul — A137

1988, Aug. 15 Litho. *Perf. 14*

899	A137	10c Basketball	15	15
900	A137	25c Volleyball	25	25
901	A137	60c Table tennis	60	60
902	A137	75c Diving	75	75
903	A137	$1 Judo	1.00	1.00
904	A137	$2 Field hockey	2.00	2.00
		Nos. 899-904 (6)	4.75	4.75

Souvenir Sheet

905	A137	$3 Women's gymnastics	3.00	3.00

Intl. Red Cross, 125th Anniv. A138

1988, Nov. 18 Litho. *Perf. 14*

906	A138	60c Travelling nurse, 1912	60	60
907	A138	75c Hospital ship, ambulance boat, 1937	75	75
908	A138	$1 Ambulance, 1956	1.00	1.00
909	A138	$2 Ambulance plane, 1940	2.00	2.00

Indigenous Small Animals A139

1989 Litho. Wmk. 384 *Perf. 14*

910	A139	10c Gibnut (agouti)	15	15

Unwmk.

911	A139	25c Four-eyed opossum, vert.	25	25
a.		Wmk. 384	25	25
912	A139	50c Ant bear	50	50
913	A139	60c like 10c	60	60
914	A139	75c Antelope	75	75
915	A139	$2 Peccary	2.00	2.00
		Nos. 910-915 (6)	4.25	4.25

Issued: 10c, July 23; No. 911a, Dec. 6; others, Feb. 24.

Moon Landing, 20th Anniv.

Common Design Type

Apollo 9: 25c, Command service and lunar modules docked in space. 50c, Command service module. 75c, Mission emblem. $1, First manned lunar module in space. $5, Apollo 11 command service module.

Perf. 14x13½

1989, July 20 Wmk. 384

Size of Nos. 680-681: 29x29mm

916	CD342	25c multi	25	25
917	CD342	50c multi	50	50
918	CD342	75c multi	75	75
919	CD342	$1 multi	1.00	1.00

Souvenir Sheet

920	CD342	$5 multi	5.00	5.00

No. 920 Overprinted

WORLD STAMP EXPO '89™
United States Postal Service
Nov. 17 — 20 and
Nov. 24 — Dec. 3, 1989
Washington Convention Center
Washington, DC

1989, Nov. 17 *Perf. 14x13½*

921	CD342	$5 multicolored	5.00	5.00

World Stamp Expo '89.

No. 704 Surcharged

5c

1989, Nov. 15 *Perf. 15*

922	A89	5c on 6c multi		

Christmas — A140

A141

Old churches.

Wmk. 384

1989, Dec. 13 Litho. *Perf. 14*

927	A140	10c Wesley	15	15
928	A140	25c Baptist	25	25
929	A140	60c St. John's Cathedral	60	60
930	A140	75c St. Andrew's Presbyterian	75	75
931	A140	$1 Holy Redeemer Cathedral	1.00	1.00
		Nos. 927-931 (5)	2.75	2.75

Wmk. 373

1990, Mar. 1 Litho. *Perf. 14*

Birds and Butterfies: 5c, *Piranga leucoptera, Catonephele numilia* female. 10c, *Ramphastos sulfuratus, Nessaea aglaura.* 15c, *Fregata magnificens, Eurytides philolaus.* 25c, *Jabiru mycteria, Heliconius sapho.* 30c, *Ardea herodias, Colobura dirce.* 50c, *Icterus galbula, Hamadryas arethusia.* 60c, *Ara macao, Thecla regalis.* 75c, *Cyanerpes cyaneus, Callicore patelina.* $1, *Pulsatrix perspicillata, Caligo uranus.* $2, *Cyanocorax yncas, Philaethria dido.* $5, *Cathartes aura, Battus belus.* $10, *Pandion haliaetus, Papilio thoas.*

932	A141	5c multicolored	15	15
933	A141	10c multicolored	15	15
934	A141	15c multicolored	15	15
935	A141	25c multicolored	25	25
936	A141	30c multicolored	30	30
937	A141	50c multicolored	50	50
938	A141	60c multicolored	60	60
939	A141	75c multicolored	75	75
940	A141	$1 multicolored	1.00	1.00
941	A141	$2 multicolored	2.00	2.00
942	A141	$5 multicolored	5.00	5.00
943	A141	$10 multicolored	10.00	10.00
		Nos. 932-943 (12)	20.85	20.85

The 10c exists inscribed "1993."

For overprint see No. 940.

No. 940 Overprinted in Gold: "FIRST DOLLAR / COIN / 1990"

1990, Mar. 1

944	A141	$1 multicolored	1.00	1.00

Turtles A142

Wmk. 373

1990, Aug. 8 Litho. *Perf. 14*

945	A142	10c Green	15	15
946	A142	25c Hawksbill	25	25
947	A142	60c Loggerhead	60	60
948	A142	75c Loggerhead, diff.	75	75
949	A142	$1 Bocatora	1.00	1.00
950	A142	$2 Hicatee	2.00	2.00
		Nos. 945-950 (6)	4.75	4.75

Battle of Britain, 50th Anniv. A143

Aircraft.

1990, Sept. 15 Wmk. 384 *Perf. 13½*

951	A143	10c Fairey Battle	15	15
952	A143	25c Bristol Beaufort	25	25
953	A143	60c Bristol Blenheim	60	60
954	A143	75c Armstrong-Whitworth Whitley	75	75
955	A143	$1 Vickers-Armstrong Wellington	1.00	1.00
956	A143	$2 Handley-Page Hampden	2.00	2.00
		Nos. 951-956 (6)	4.75	4.75

Orchids — A144

1990, Nov. 1 Wmk. 384 *Perf. 14*

957	A144	25c Cattleya bowringiana	25	25
958	A144	50c Rhyncholaelia digbyana	50	50
959	A144	60c Sobralia macrantha	60	60
960	A144	75c Chysis bractescens	75	75
961	A144	$1 Vanilla planifolia	1.00	1.00
962	A144	$2 Epidendrum polyanthum	2.00	2.00
		Nos. 957-962 (6)	5.10	5.10

Christmas.

Indigenous Fauna A145

1991, Apr. 10

963	A145	25c Iguana	25	25
964	A145	50c Crocodile	50	50
965	A145	60c Manatee	60	60
966	A145	75c Boa constrictor	75	75
967	A145	$1 Tapir	1.00	1.00
968	A145	$2 Jaguar	2.00	2.00
		Nos. 963-968 (6)	5.10	5.10

Elizabeth & Philip, Birthdays

Common Design Types

1991, June 17 *Perf. 14½*

969	CD345	$1 multicolored	1.00	1.00
970	CD346	$1 multicolored	1.00	1.00
a.		Pair, #969-970 + label	2.00	2.00

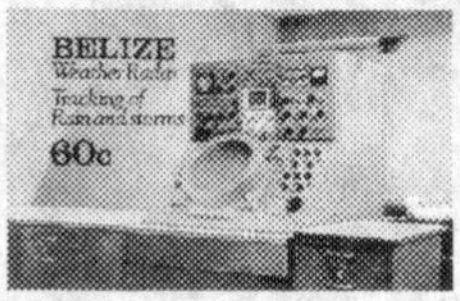

Hurricanes A146

1991, July 31 Wmk. 373 *Perf. 14*

971	A146	60c Weather radar	60	60
972	A146	75c Weather observation station	75	75
973	A146	$1 Scene after hurricane	1.00	1.00
974	A146	$2 Hurricane Gilbert	2.00	2.00

Independence, 10th Anniv. — A147

Famous Men: 25c, Thomas V. Ramos (1887-1955). 60c, Sir Isaiah Morter (1860-1924). 75c, Antonio Soberanis (1897-1975). $1, Santiago Ricalde (1920-1975).

1991, Sept. 4 Wmk. 384

975	A147	25c multicolored	28	28
976	A147	60c multicolored	65	65
977	A147	75c multicolored	80	80
978	A147	$1 multicolored	1.10	1.10

Folktales A148

Christmas.

Wmk. 373

1991, Nov. 6 Litho. *Perf. 14*

979	A148	25c Anansi	28	28
980	A148	50c Jack-O-Lantern	55	55
981	A148	60c Tata Duende, vert.	65	65
982	A148	75c Xtabai	80	80
983	A148	$1 Warrie Massa, vert.	1.10	1.10
984	A148	$2 Old Heg	2.20	2.20
		Nos. 979-984 (6)	5.58	5.58

See Nos. 999-1002.

Orchids — A149

Easter: 25c, Gongora quinquenervis. 50c, Oncidium sphacelatum. 60c, Encyclia bractescens. 75c, Epidendrum ciliare. $1, Psygmorchis pusilla. $2, Galeandra batemanii.

1992, Apr. 1

985	A149	25c	multicolored	28	28
986	A149	50c	multicolored	55	55
987	A149	60c	multicolored	65	65
988	A149	75c	multicolored	80	80
989	A149	$1	multicolored	1.10	1.10
990	A149	$2	multicolored	2.20	2.20
			Nos. 985-990 (6)	5.58	5.58

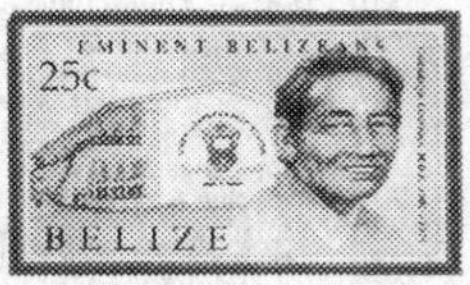

Famous Belizeans A150

Designs: 25c, Gwendolyn Lizarraga, MBE (1901-75). 60c, Rafael Fonseca, CMG, OBE (1921-78). 75c, Vivian Seay, MBE (1881-1971). $1, Samuel A. Haynes (1898-1971).

1992, Aug. 26 *Perf. 13x12¹/₂*

991	A150	25c	multicolored	28	28
992	A150	60c	multicolored	65	65
993	A150	75c	multicolored	80	80
994	A150	$1	multicolored	1.10	1.10

See Nos. 1013-1016.

Discovery of America, 500th Anniv. — A151

Mayan ruins, modern buildings: 25c, Xunantunich, National Assembly. 60c, Altun Ha, Supreme Court Building. 75c, Santa Rita, Tower Hill Sugar Factory. $5, Lamanai, The Citrus Company.

Perf. 13¹/₂x14

1992, Oct. 1 Litho. Wmk. 384

995	A151	25c	multicolored	28	28
996	A151	60c	multicolored	65	65
997	A151	75c	multicolored	80	80
998	A151	$5	multicolored	5.50	5.50

Folklore Type of 1991

Christmas.

Perf. 13x12¹/₂

1992, Nov. 16 Litho. Wmk. 373

999	A148	25c	Hashishi Pampi	25	25
1000	A148	60c	Cadejo	62	62
1001	A148	$1	La Sucia, vert.	1.05	1.05
1002	A148	$5	Sisimito	5.00	5.00

Royal Air Force, 75th Anniv.

Common Design Type

Designs: 25c, Aerospatiale Puma. 50c, British Aerospace Harrier. 60c, DeHavilland Mosquito. 75c, Avro Lancaster. $1, Consolidated Liberator. $3, Short Stirling.

Wmk. 373

1993, Apr. 1 Litho. *Perf. 14*

1003	CD350	25c	multicolored	25	25
1004	CD350	50c	multicolored	52	52
1005	CD350	60c	multicolored	65	65
1006	CD350	75c	multicolored	80	80
1007	CD350	$1	multicolored	1.05	1.05
1008	CD350	$3	multicolored	3.15	3.15
			Nos. 1003-1008 (6)	6.42	6.42

1993 World Orchid Conference, Glasgow — A152

Perf. 14¹/₂x14

1993, Apr. 24 Litho. Wmk. 384

1009	A152	25c	Lycaste aromatica	28	28
1010	A152	60c	Sobralia decora	65	65
1011	A152	$1	Maxillaria alba	1.10	1.10
1012	A152	$2	Brassavola nodosa	2.20	2.20

Famous Belizeans Type of 1992

Designs: 25c, Herbert Watkin Beaumont (1880-1978). 60c, Dr. Selvyn Walford Young (1899-1977). 75c, Cleopatra White (1898-1987). $1, Dr. Karl Heusner (1872-1960).

Wmk. 384

1993, Aug. 11 Litho. *Perf. 14*

1013	A150	25c	multicolored	28	28
1014	A150	60c	multicolored	65	65
1015	A150	75c	multicolored	85	65
1016	A150	$1	multicolored	1.10	1.10

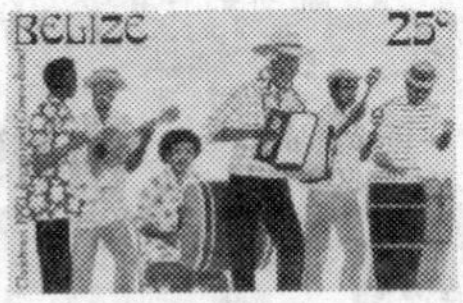

Christmas A153

Wmk. 373

1993, Nov. 3 Litho. *Perf. 14*

1017	A153	25c	Boom and chime band	28	28
1018	A153	60c	John Canoe dance	65	65
1019	A153	75c	Cortez dance	80	80
1020	A153	$2	Maya Musical Group	2.25	2.25

No. 940 Ovptd. with Hong Kong '94 Emblem

Wmk. 373

1994, Feb. 18 Litho. *Perf. 14*

1021	A141	$1	multicolored	1.10	1.10

Royal Visit — A154

Designs: 25c, Belize, United Kingdom Flags. 60c, Queen Elizabeth II wearing hat. 75c, Queen. $1, Queen, Prince Philip.

Perf. 14¹/₂x14

1994, Feb. 24 Litho. Wmk. 373

1022	A154	25c	multicolored	28	28
1023	A154	60c	multicolored	65	65
1024	A154	75c	multicolored	80	80
1025	A154	$1	multicolored	1.10	1.10

Bats A155

Wmk. 384

1994, May 30 Litho. *Perf. 14*

1026	A155	25c	Insect feeder	25	25
1027	A155	60c	Fruit feeder	60	60
1028	A155	75c	Fish feeder	75	75
1029	A155	$2	Common vampire	2.00	2.00

SEMI-POSTAL STAMPS

World Cup Soccer Championship — SP1

Designs: 20c+10c, 30c+15c, Scotland vs. New Zealand (diff.). 40c+20c, Kuwait vs. France. 60c+30c, Italy vs. Brazil. No. B5, France vs. Northern Ireland. $1.50+75c, Austria vs. Chile. No. B7, Italy vs. Germany, vert. $2+$1, England vs. France, vert.

1982, Dec. 10 Litho. *Perf. 14*

B1	SP1	20c	+10c multi
B2	SP1	30c	+15c multi
B3	SP1	40c	+20c multi
B4	SP1	60c	+30c multi
B5	SP1	$1	+50c multi
B6	SP1	$1.50	+75c multi

Souvenir Sheets

Perf. 14¹/₂

B7	SP1	$1	+50c multi
B8	SP1	$2	+$1 multi

Nos. B7-B8 each contain one 50x70mm stamp.

POSTAGE DUE STAMPS

Numeral — D2

Designs: Each denomination has different border.

1976, July 1 Litho. Wmk. 373

J6	D2	1c	green & red	15	15
J7	D2	2c	violet & rose lil	15	15
J8	D2	5c	ocher & brt grn	15	15
J9	D2	15c	brown org & yel grn	32	32
J10	D2	25c	slate grn & org	50	50
			Set value	1.00	1.00

CAYES OF BELIZE

Catalogue values for all unused stamps in this country are for Never Hinged items.

Spiny Lobster A1

Perf. 14¹/₂x14, 14x14¹/₂

1984, May 30 Litho. Unwmk.

1	A1	1c	shown	15	15
2	A1	2c	Blue crab	15	15
3	A1	5c	Red-footed booby	15	15
4	A1	10c	Brown pelican	15	15
5	A1	15c	White-tailed deer	15	15
6	A1	25c	Lighthouse, English Caye	25	25
7	A1	75c	Spanish galleon, Santa Yaga, c. 1750	75	75
8	A1	$3	Map of Ambergris Caye, vert.	3.00	3.00
9	A1	$5	Jetty, windsurfers	5.00	5.00
			Nos. 1-9 (9)	9.75	9.75

The $1 stamp was not issued. Eighteen sheets of 40 were sold for postage by accident.

Lloyd's List Issue

Common Design Type

1984, June 6 *Perf. 14¹/₂x14*

10	CD335	25c	Queen Elizabeth 2	25	25
11	CD335	75c	Lutine Bell	75	75
12	CD335	$1	Loss of the Fishburn	1.00	1.00
13	CD335	$2	Trafalgar Sword	2.00	2.00

1984 Summer Olympics, Los Angeles — A2

1984, Oct. 5 *Perf. 15*

14	A2	10c	Yachting	15	15
15	A2	15c	Windsurfing	15	15
16	A2	75c	Swimming	75	75
17	A2	$2	Kayaking	2.00	2.00

No. 17 inscribed Canoeing.

First Cayes Stamps, 90th Anniv. A3

1984, Nov. 5

18	A3	10c	1895 cover	15	15
19	A3	15c	Sydney Cuthbert	15	15
20	A3	75c	Cuthbert's steam yacht	75	75
21	A3	$2	British Honduras #133	2.00	2.00

Audubon Birth Bicentenary A4

Illustrations by Audubon.

1985, May 20 *Perf. 14*

22	A4	25c	Blue-winged teal	25	25
23	A4	75c	Semipalmated sandpiper	75	75
24	A4	$1	Yellow-crowned night heron, vert.	1.00	1.00
25	A4	$3	Common gallinule	3.00	3.00

Shipwrecks — A5

Designs: a, Oxford, c. 1675. b, Santa Yaga, 1780. c, No. 27, Comet, 1822. d, Yeldham, 1800.

1985, June 5 *Perf. 15*

26	A5	$1	Strip of 4+label, #a.-d.	4.00	4.00

Souvenir Sheet

Perf. 13¹/₂x14

27	A5	$5	multicolored	5.00	5.00

No. 27 contains one 38x51mm stamp. No. 26 has continuous design.

BERMUDA

LOCATION — A group of about 150 small islands of which only 20 are inhabited, lying in the Atlantic Ocean about 580 miles southeast of Cape Hatteras.
GOVT. — British Crown Colony
AREA — 20.5 sq. mi.
POP. — 54,893 (1980)
CAPITAL — Hamilton

Bermuda achieved internal self-government in 1968.

4 Farthings = 1 Penny
12 Pence = 1 Shilling
20 Shillings = 1 Pound
100 Cents = 1 Dollar (1970)

Catalogue values for unused stamps in this country are for Never Hinged items, beginning with Scott 131.

POSTMASTER STAMPS

PM1

1848-54 Unwmk. *Imperf.*

X1	PM1 1p blk, *bluish* (1848, 1849)	*125,000.*
X2	PM1 1p red, *bluish* (1854, 1856)	*125,000.*
X3	PM1 1p red (1853)	*160,000.*

PM2

1860

X4	PM2 (1p) red, *yellowish*	*100,000.*

Same inscribed "HAMILTON"

1861

X5	PM2 (1p) red, *bluish*	*125,000.*

Nos. X1-X3 were produced and used by Postmaster William B. Perot of Hamilton. No. X4 is attributed to Postmaster James H. Thies of St. George's.

GENERAL ISSUES

Values for Nos. 1, 1a, 2-15 are for stamps with perforations touching the frame line.

Queen Victoria
A1 A2

A3

A4

A5

1865-74 Typo. Wmk. 1 *Perf. 14*

1	A1	1p dull rose	37.50	2.00
a.		1p rose red	50.00	4.00
b.		Imperf.	*19,000.*	*10,000.*
2	A2	2p blue ('66)	55.00	10.00
3	A3	3p buff ('73)	350.00	35.00
4	A4	6p brown lilac	800.00	100.00
5	A4	6p lilac ('74)	16.00	16.00
6	A5	1sh green	125.00	27.50

See Nos. 7-9, 19-21, 23, 25. For surcharges, see Nos. 10-15.

1882-1903 *Perf. 14x12½*

7	A3	3p buff	140.00	35.00
8	A4	6p violet ('03)	14.50	16.00
9	A5	1sh green ('94)	22.50	*50.00*
a.		Vert. strip of 3, perf. all around & imperf. btwn.	*12,500.*	

Handstamped Diagonally **THREE PENCE**

1874 *Perf. 14*

10	A5	3p on 1sh green	1,300.	925.00

Handstamped Diagonally ***THREE PENCE***

11	A1	3p on 1p rose	*11,000.*	
12	A5	3p on 1sh green	1,750.	800.00
a.		"P" with top like "R"	2,250.	1,000.

No. 11 is stated to be an essay, but a few copies are known used. Nos. 10-12 are found with double or partly double surcharges.

Surcharged in Black **One Penny.**

1875

13	A2	1p on 2p blue	425.00	300.00
a.		Without period	*10,000.*	*6,750.*
14	A3	1p on 3p buff	375.00	225.00
15	A5	1p on 1sh green	350.00	250.00
a.		Inverted surcharge		
b.		Without period		

A6

A7

1880 Wmk. 1

16	A6	½p brown	1.50	2.75
17	A7	4p orange	5.50	2.50

See Nos. 18, 24.

A8

A9

1883-1904 Wmk. 2

18	A6	½p green ('92)	60	60
19	A1	1p aniline car ('89)	1.75	25
a.		1p dull rose	60.00	3.00
b.		1p rose red	40.00	1.75
c.		1p carmine rose ('86)	15.00	65
20	A2	2p blue ('86)	25.00	2.25
21	A2	2p aniline pur ('93)	8.00	3.50
a.		2p brown purple ('98)	3.00	2.50
22	A8	2½p ultra ('84)	6.00	38
23	A3	3p gray ('86)	9.25	3.50
24	A7	4p brown org ('04)	19.00	40.00
25	A5	1sh ol bis ('93)	14.00	12.00
a.		1sh yellow brown	14.00	13.00
		Nos. 18-25 (8)	83.60	62.48

Black Surcharge

1901

26	A9	1f on 1sh gray	15	15

Dry Dock — A10

1902-03

28	A10	½p gray grn & blk ('03)	6.75	2.75
29	A10	1p car rose & brown	6.75	38
30	A10	3p ol grn & violet	2.00	4.00

1906-10 Wmk. 3

31	A10	¼p pur & brn ('08)	65	1.00
32	A10	½p gray grn & blk	3.75	2.25
33	A10	½p green ('09)	3.75	2.00
34	A10	1p car rose & brn	3.50	28
35	A10	1p carmine ('08)	2.50	32
36	A10	2p orange & gray	3.50	3.50
37	A10	2½p blue & brown	8.75	14.00
38	A10	2½p ultra ('10)	14.00	10.00
39	A10	4p vio brn & blue ('09)	3.50	8.25
		Nos. 31-39 (9)	43.90	41.60

Caravel
A11

King George V
A12

1910-20 Engr. *Perf. 14*

40	A11	¼p brown	45	*1.25*
41	A11	½p yel green	90	25
a.		½p dark green	3.00	1.40
42	A11	1p rose red (I)	7.00	15
a.		1p carmine (I)	25.00	2.75
43	A11	2p gray	2.00	*3.75*
44	A11	2½p ultra (I)	2.25	60
45	A11	3p violet, *yel*	1.40	*3.25*
46	A11	4p red, *yellow*	2.75	*4.50*
47	A11	6p claret	8.00	*10.00*
48	A11	1sh blk, *green*	4.00	*5.75*
a.		1sh black, *olive*	3.75	*5.75*

Typographed
Chalky Paper

49	A12	2sh ultra & dl vio, *bl* ('20)	7.25	*20.00*
50	A12	2sh6p red & blk, *bl*	18.00	*27.50*
51	A12	4sh car & black ('20)	35.00	*55.00*
52	A12	5sh red & grn, *yellow*	45.00	*62.50*
53	A12	10sh red & grn, *green*	130.00	*65.00*
54	A12	£1 black & vio, *red*	350.00	*350.00*
		Nos. 40-54 (15)	614.00	*609.50*

Types I of 1p and 2½p are illustrated above Nos. 81-97.

The 1p was printed from two plates, the 2nd of which, #42a, exists only in carmine on opaque paper with a bluish tinge. Compare #MR1 (as #42) and MR2 (as #42a).

Revenue cancellations are found on Nos. 52-54. See Nos. 81-97.

Seal of the Colony and King George V — A13

1920-21 Wmk. 3 Ordinary Paper

55	A13	¼p brown	35	*2.00*
56	A13	½p green	65	*3.00*
57	A13	2p gray	5.75	*10.00*

Chalky Paper

58	A13	3p vio & dl vio, *yellow*	4.50	*10.00*
59	A13	4p red & blk, *yellow*	5.75	*11.00*
60	A13	1sh blk, *gray grn*	11.00	*18.00*

Ordinary Paper

Wmk. 4

67	A13	1p	rose red	65	60
68	A13	2½p	ultra	4.50	*9.00*

Chalky Paper

69	A13	6p	red vio & dl vio	9.50	*21.00*
			Nos. 55-60,67-69 (9)	42.65	*84.60*

Issued: 6p, Jan. 19, 1921; others, Nov. 11, 1920.

King George V — A14

1921, May 12 **Engr.**

71	A14	¼p	brown	38	*1.00*
72	A14	½p	green	2.75	*3.50*
73	A14	1p	carmine	2.00	80

Wmk. 3

74	A14	2p	gray	5.00	*7.50*
75	A14	2½p	ultra	4.50	3.00
76	A14	3p	vio, *orange*	3.50	*8.00*
77	A14	4p	scarlet, *org*	5.00	*8.00*
78	A14	6p	claret	6.00	*18.00*
79	A14	1sh	blk, *green*	16.00	*22.50*
			Nos. 71-79 (9)	45.13	*72.30*

Tercentenary of "Local Representative Institutions" (Nos. 55-79).

Types of 1910-20 Issue

Types of 1p: **1d** (I) **1d** (II) **1d** (III)

Types of 2½p: **2½d** (I) **2½d** (II)

1922-34 **Wmk. 4**

81	A11	¼p	brown ('28)	15	*50*
82	A11	½p	green	15	15
83	A11	1p	car, III ('28)	5.00	25
a.			1p carmine, II ('26)	7.50	50
b.			1p carmine, I	6.00	35
84	A11	1½p	red brown ('34)	2.00	35
85	A11	2p	gray ('23)	1.00	1.00
86	A11	2½p	ap grn ('23)	1.00	1.00
87	A11	2½p	ultra, II ('32)	2.00	32
a.			2½p ultra, I ('26)	1.75	32
88	A11	3p	ultra ('24)	12.00	*17.00*
89	A11	3p	vio, *yellow* ('26)	45	45
90	A11	4p	red, *yellow* ('24)	1.00	*85*
91	A11	6p	claret ('24)	95	95
92	A11	1sh	blk, *emer* ('27)	3.50	3.25
93	A11	1sh	brn blk, *yel grn* ('34)	20.00	*30.00*

Chalky Paper

94	A12	2sh	ultra & vio, *bl* ('27)	20.00	30.00
a.			2sh bl & dp vio, *dp bl* ('31)	25.00	35.00
95	A12	2sh 6p	red & blk, *bl* ('27)	35.00	37.50
a.			2sh6p pale org ver & blk, *gray bl* ('30)	2,250.	2,250.
b.			2sh6p dp ver & blk, *deep blue* ('31)	40.00	45.00
96	A12	10sh	red & grn, *emer* ('24)	150.00	*190.00*
a.			10sh dp red & pale grn, *dp emer* ('31)	150.00	*190.00*
97	A12	12sh 6p	ocher & gray blk ('32)	275.00	350.00
			Nos. 81-97 (17)	529.20	*663.57*

Revenue cancellations are found on Nos. 94-97.

The 12sh6p with "Revenue" on both sides, was used postally from Feb. 1 to Apr., 1937. Copies with postal cancels in that time period are valued at three times No. 97.

Silver Jubilee Issue

Common Design Type

1935, May 6 ***Perf. 11x12***

100	CD301	1p	car & dk bl	15	15
101	CD301	1½p	blk & ultra	48	48
102	CD301	2½p	ultra & brn	1.50	1.50
103	CD301	1sh	brn vio & ind	6.25	10.00
			Set, never hinged	14.00	

Hamilton Harbor — A15

Yacht "Lucie" — A17

South Shore — A16

Grape Bay — A18

Typical Cottage A19

Scene at Par-la-Ville A20

1936-40 ***Perf. 12***

105	A15	½p	blue green	15	15
106	A16	1p	car & black	22	15
107	A16	1½p	choc & black	25	25
108	A17	2p	lt bl & blk	1.90	1.90
109	A17	2p	brn blk & turq bl ('38)	18.00	9.00
109A	A17	2p	red & ultra ('40)	22	18
110	A18	2½p	dk bl & lt bl	45	45
111	A19	3p	car & black	1.90	1.90
112	A20	6p	vio & rose lake	22	18
113	A18	1sh	deep green	4.50	5.00
114	A15	1sh6p	brown	40	40
			Nos. 105-114 (11)	28.21	19.56
			Set, never hinged	39.00	

No. 108, blue border and black center.
No. 109, black border, blue center.

Coronation Issue

Common Design Type

1937, May 14 ***Perf. 13½x14***

115	CD302	1p	carmine	15	15
116	CD302	1½p	brown	16	16
117	CD302	2½p	bright ultra	45	45
			Set, never hinged	1.50	

Hamilton Harbor — A21

Grape Bay — A22

St. David's Lighthouse A23

King George VI A25

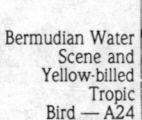

Bermudian Water Scene and Yellow-billed Tropic Bird — A24

1938-51 **Wmk. 4** ***Perf. 12***

118	A21	1p	red & black ('40)	15	15
a.			1p rose red & black	11.50	1.10
119	A21	1½p	vio brn & blue	15	15
a.			1½p dl vio brn & bl ('43)	15	15
120	A22	2½p	blue & lt bl	2.00	1.10
120A	A22	2½p	ol brn & lt bl ('41)	28	25
b.			2½p dk ol blk & pale blue ('43)	28	25
121	A23	3p	car & blk	4.25	3.00
121A	A23	3p	dp ultra & blk ('42)	28	20
c.			3p brt ultra & blk ('41)	35	16
121D	A24	7½p	yel grn, bl & blk ('41)	1.10	1.10
122	A22	1sh	green	85	55

Typo.

Perf. 13

123	A25	2sh	ultra & red vio, *bl* ('50)	5.50	3.75
a.			2sh ultra & vio, *bl*, perf. 14	5.25	4.00
b.			2sh ultra & dl vio, *bl* (mottled paper), perf. 14 ('42)	5.00	4.75
124	A25	2sh 6p	red & blk, *bl*	8.00	2.75
a.			Perf. 14	8.00	3.00
125	A25	5sh	red & grn, *yel*	8.00	4.75
a.			Perf. 14	10.00	6.50
126	A25	10sh	red & grn, *grn* ('51)	21.00	14.00
a.			10sh brn lake & grn, *grn*, perf. 14	175.00	225.00
b.			10sh red & grn, *grn*, perf. 14 ('39)	40.00	40.00
127	A25	12sh 6p	org & gray blk	55.00	50.00
a.			12sh6p orange & gray, perf. 14	42.50	35.00
b.			12sh6p yellow & gray, perf. 14 ('47)	500.00	525.00
c.			12sh6p brown orange & gray, perf. 14	300.00	300.00

Wmk. 3

128	A25	£1	blk & vio, *red* ('51)	42.50	30.00
a.			£1 blk & pur, *red*, perf. 14	100.00	100.00
b.			£1 blk & dk vio, *salmon*, perf. 14 ('42)	40.00	25.00
			Nos. 118-128 (14)	149.06	111.75
			Set, never hinged	220.00	

No. 127b is the so-called "lemon yellow" shade.

Revenue cancellations are found on Nos. 123-128. Copies with removed revenue cancellations and forged postmarks are abundant.

HALF PENNY

X X

No. 118a Surcharged in Black

1940, Dec. 20 **Wmk. 4** ***Perf. 12***

129	A21	½p	on 1p rose red & blk	30	30
			Never hinged	50	

Catalogue values for unused stamps in this section, from this point to the end of the section, are for Never Hinged items.

Peace Issue

Common Design Type

Perf. 13½x14

1946, Nov. 6 **Engr.** **Wmk. 4**

131	CD303	1½p	brown	18	18
132	CD303	3p	deep blue	30	30

Silver Wedding Issue

Common Design Types

1948, Dec. 1 **Photo.** ***Perf. 14x14½***

133	CD304	1½p	red brown	15	15

Engr.; Name Typo.

Perf. 11½x11

134	CD305	£1	rose carmine	52.50	32.50

Postmaster Stamp of 1848 — A26

1949, Apr. 11 Engr. *Perf. 13x13½*

135	A26	2½p	dk brown & dp bl	18	18
136	A26	3p	dp blue & black	22	22
137	A26	6p	green & rose vio	45	45

No. 137 shows a different floral arrangement. Bermuda's first postage stamp, cent.

UPU Issue
Common Design Types
Perf. 13½, 11x11½

1949, Oct. 10 Engr.; Name Typo.

138	CD306	2½p	slate	55	55
139	CD307	3p	indigo	70	70
140	CD308	6p	rose violet	1.10	1.10
141	CD309	1sh	blue green	2.25	2.25

Coronation Issue
Common Design Type

1953, June 4 Engr. *Perf. 13½x13*

142	CD312	1½p	dk blue & blk	38	22

A27

Easter Lilies — A28

Designs: 1p, 4p, Perot stamp. 2p, Racing dinghy. 2½p, Sir George Somers and "Sea Venture." 3p, 1sh3p, Map. 4½p, 9p, "Sea Venture," boat, hog coin and Perot stamp. 6p, 8p, Yellow-billed tropic bird. 1sh, Hog coins. 2sh, Arms of St. George. 2sh6p, Warwick Fort. 5sh, Hog coin. 10sh, Earliest hog coin. £1, Arms of Bermuda.

1953-58 *Perf. 13½x13, 13x13½*

143	A27	½p	olive green	15	15
144	A27	1p	rose red & blk	15	15
145	A28	1½p	dull green	15	15
146	A27	2p	red & ultra	15	15
147	A27	2½p	carmine rose	18	15
148	A27	3p	vio *(Sandy's)*	48	26
149	A27	3p	violet *(Sandys)* ('57)	25	18
150	A27	4p	dp ultra & blk	18	18
151	A27	4½p	green	60	60
152	A27	6p	dk bluish grn & blk	35	22
153	A27	8p	red & blk ('55)	95	35
154	A27	9p	violet ('58)	2.00	95
155	A27	1sh	orange	40	22
156	A27	1sh3p	blue *(Sandy's)*	95	28
157	A27	1sh3p	blue *(Sandys)* ('57)	65	35
158	A27	2sh	yellow brown	2.00	65
159	A28	2sh6p	scarlet	2.00	1.25
160	A27	5sh	dp car rose	4.75	2.00
161	A27	10sh	deep ultra	8.50	4.50

Engr. and Typo.

162	A27	£1	dp ol grn & multi	20.00	12.50
			Nos. 143-162 (20)	44.84	25.24

For overprints, see Nos. 164-167.

Type of 1953 Inscribed "ROYAL VISIT 1953"

Design: 6p, Yellow-billed tropic bird.

1953, Nov. 26 Engr.

163	A27	6p	dk bluish grn & blk	42	38

Visit of Queen Elizabeth II and the Duke of Edinburgh, 1953.

Nos. 148 and 156 Overprinted in Violet Blue or Red

Three Power Talks
December, 1953

1953, Dec. 8 *Perf. 13½x13*

164	A27	3p	violet	18	18
165	A27	1sh3p	blue (R)	48	42

Three Power Conference, Tucker's Town, December 1953.

Nos. 153 and 156 Overprinted in Black or Red

50TH ANNIVERSARY
U S — BERMUDA
OCEAN RACE 1956

1956, June 22

166	A27	8p	red & black	24	24
167	A27	1sh3p	blue (R)	38	38

Newport-Bermuda Yacht Race, 50th anniv.

Perot Post Office, Hamilton A29

Perf. 13½x13

1959, Jan. 1 Engr. Wmk. 4

168	A29	6p	lilac & black	42	32

Restoration and reopening of the post office operated at Hamilton by W. B. Perot in the mid-nineteenth century.

Arms of James I and Elizabeth II — A30

Engr. and Litho.

1959, July 29 Wmk. 314 *Perf. 13*

Coats of Arms in Blue, Yellow & Red

169	A30	1½p	dark blue	15	15
170	A30	3p	gray	26	26
171	A30	4p	rose violet	35	35
172	A30	8p	violet gray	75	75
173	A30	9p	olive green	95	95
174	A30	1sh3p	orange brown	1.50	1.50
			Nos. 169-174 (6)	3.96	3.96

350th anniv. of the shipwreck of the "Sea Venture" which resulted in the first permanent settlement of Bermuda.

The Old Rectory, St. George's, 1730 — A31

Designs: 2p, Church of St. Peter. 3p, Government House. 4p, Cathedral, Hamilton. 5p, No. 185A, H.M. Dockyard. 6p, Perot's Post Office, 1848. 8p, General Post Office, 1869. 9p, Library and Historical Society. 1sh, Christ Church, Warwick, 1719. 1sh3p, City Hall, Hamilton. 10p, No. 185, Bermuda Cottage, 1705. 2sh, Town of St. George. 2sh3p, Bermuda House, 1710. 2sh6p, Bermuda House, 18th century. 5sh, Colonial Secretariat, 1833. 10sh, Old Post Office, Somerset, 1890. £1, House of Assembly, 1815.

Wmk. 314 Upright

1962-65 Photo. *Perf. 12½*

175	A31	1p	org, lil & blk	15	15
176	A31	2p	sl, lt vio, grn & yel	15	15
	a.		Light vio omitted	*650.00*	
	b.		Green omitted		
	d.		Imperf., pair	*650.00*	
177	A31	3p	lt bl & yel brown	15	15
	a.		Yellow brown omitted	*1,250.*	
178	A31	4p	car rose & red brn	15	15
179	A31	5p	dk blue & pink	32	32
180	A31	6p	emer, lt & dk blue	18	15
181	A31	8p	grn, dp org & ultra	35	30
182	A31	9p	org brn & grnsh bl	32	28
182A	A31	10p	brt vio & bister ('65)	65	55
183	A31	1sh	multicolored	42	26
184	A31	1sh3p	sl, lem & rose car	48	26
185	A31	1sh6p	brt vio & bis	2.75	2.25
186	A31	2sh	brown & org	1.25	85
187	A31	2sh3p	brn & brt yel green	2.50	2.00
188	A31	2sh6p	grn, yel & sep	1.50	1.10
189	A31	5sh	choc & brt green	2.50	1.65
190	A31	10sh	dl grn, buff & rose car	4.00	3.50
191	A31	£1	cit, bis, blk & orange	9.50	7.75
			Nos. 175-191 (18)	27.32	21.82

See No. 252a. For surcharges, see Nos. 238, 240-244, 247, 250-254.

1966-69 Wmk. 314 Sideways

Unnamed Colors as in 1962-65 Issue

176c	A31	2p	('69)	2.50	1.65
181a	A31	8p	('67)	1.10	90
182b	A31	10p		1.40	1.10
183a	A31	1sh	('67)	1.40	1.25
185A	A31	1sh6p	indigo & rose	2.50	3.00
186a	A31	2sh	('67)	4.50	4.50
			Nos. 176c-186a (6)	13.40	12.40

For surcharges, see #239, 245-246, 248-249.

Freedom from Hunger Issue
Common Design Type

1963, June 4 *Perf. 14x14½*

192	CD314	1sh3p	sepia	2.75	2.25

Red Cross Centenary Issue
Common Design Type

Wmk. 314

1963, Sept. 2 Litho. *Perf. 13*

193	CD315	3p	black & red	50	30
194	CD315	1sh3p	ultra & red	5.50	3.00

Finn Boat — A32

Perf. 13½

1964, Sept. 28 Photo. Wmk. 314

195	A32	3p	blue, vio & red	28	28

18th Olympic Games, Tokyo, Oct. 10-25.

ITU Issue
Common Design Type
Perf. 11x11½

1965, May 17 Litho. Wmk. 314

196	CD317	3p	blue & emerald	42	30
197	CD317	2sh	yel & vio blue	3.50	3.50

Scout Badge and Royal Cipher A33

1965, July 24 Photo. *Perf. 12½*

198	A33	2sh	multicolored	85	85

50th anniversary of Scouting in Bermuda.

Intl. Cooperation Year Issue
Common Design Type

1965, Oct. 25 Litho. *Perf. 14½*

199	CD318	4p	blue grn & cl	30	30
200	CD318	2sh6p	lt violet & grn	2.25	2.25

Churchill Memorial Issue
Common Design Type

1966, Jan. 24 Photo. *Perf. 14*

Design in Black, Gold and Carmine Rose

201	CD319	3p	bright blue	30	20
202	CD319	6p	green	65	45
203	CD319	10p	brown	1.25	1.00
204	CD319	1sh3p	violet	2.50	2.00

World Cup Soccer Issue
Common Design Type

1966, July 1 Litho. *Perf. 14*

205	CD321	10p	multicolored	65	65
206	CD321	2sh6p	multicolored	1.75	1.75

UNESCO Anniversary Issue
Common Design Type

1966, Dec. 1 Litho. *Perf. 14*

207	CD323	4p	"Education"	40	40
208	CD323	1sh3p	"Science"	1.50	1.50
209	CD323	2sh	"Culture"	2.50	2.50

Post Office, Hamilton A34

Perf. 14½

1967, June 23 Photo. Wmk. 314

210	A34	3p	vio blue & multi	15	15
211	A34	1sh	orange & multi	40	40
212	A34	1sh6p	green & multi	70	70
213	A34	2sh6p	red & multi	1.10	1.10

Opening of the new GPO, Hamilton.

Cable Ship Mercury A35

Designs: 1sh, Map of Bermuda and Virgin Islands, telephone and microphone. 1sh6p, Radio tower, television set, telephone and cable. 2sh6p, Cable at sea bottom and ship.

1967, Sept. 14 Photo. Wmk. 314

214	A35	3p	multicolored	15	15
215	A35	1sh	multicolored	40	40
216	A35	1sh6p	multicolored	70	70
217	A35	2sh6p	multicolored	1.10	1.10

Completion of the Bermuda-Tortola, Virgin Islands, telephone link.

Common Design Types are pictured beginning on page 176.

Human Rights Flame, Globe and Doves A36

1968, Feb. 1 Litho. *Perf. 14x14½*

218	A36	3p	indigo, lt grn & bl	15	15
219	A36	1sh	brown, lt bl & bl	45	45
220	A36	1sh6p	black, pink & blue	75	75
221	A36	2sh6p	green, yellow & bl	95	95

International Human Rights Year.

Mace A37

Design: 1sh6p, 2sh6p, House of Assembly, Bermuda; Parliament, London, and royal cipher.

1968, July 1 Photo. *Perf. 14½*

222	A37	3p	rose red & multi	15	15
223	A37	1sh	ultra & multi	45	45
224	A37	1sh6p	yellow & multi	75	75
225	A37	2sh6p	multicolored	95	95

New constitution.

Olympic Sports and Rings — A38

1968, Sept. 24 Wmk. 314 *Perf. 12½*

226	A38	3p lilac & multi	15	15
a.		Rose brown omitted ("3d BERMUDA")		*2,000.*
227	A38	1sh multicolored	42	35
228	A38	1sh6p multicolored	60	60
229	A38	2sh6p multicolored	1.00	1.00

19th Olympic Games, Mexico City, Oct. 12-27.

Girl Guides A39

Designs: 1sh, Like 3p. 1sh6p, 2sh6p, Girl Guides and arms of Bermuda.

1969, Feb. 17 Litho. *Perf. 14*

230	A39	3p lilac & multi	15	15
231	A39	1sh green & multi	35	35
232	A39	1sh6p gray & multi	55	55
233	A39	2sh6p red & multi	1.00	1.00

Bermuda Girl Guides, 50th anniv.

Gold and Emerald Cross — A40

Design: 4p, 2sh, Different background.

1969, Sept. 29 Photo. *Perf. 14½x14*
Cross in Yellow, Brown and Emerald

234	A40	4p violet	24	24
235	A40	1sh3p green	75	75
236	A40	2sh black	1.10	1.10
237	A40	2sh6p carmine rose	1.40	1.25

Treasures salvaged off the coast of Bermuda. The cross shown is from the Tucker treasure from the 16th century Spanish galleon San Pedro.

Buildings Issue and Type of 1962-69 Surcharged with New Value and Bar in Black or Brown

1970, Feb. 6 Wmk. 314 *Perf. 12½*

238	A31	1c on 1p multi	15	15
239	A31	2c on 2p multi	15	15
a.		Watermark upright	1.25	1.25
b.		Light violet omitted	*650.00*	
c.		Pair, one without surch.	*2,000.*	
240	A31	3c on 3p multi	15	15
241	A31	4c on 4p multi (Br)	15	15
242	A31	5c on 8p multi	15	15
243	A31	6c on 6p multi	15	15
244	A31	9c on 9p multi (Br)	22	*40*
245	A31	10c on 10p multi	28	*50*
246	A31	12c on 1sh multi	32	*60*
247	A31	15c on 1sh3p multi	70	*1.10*
248	A31	18c on 1sh6p multi	70	*1.25*
249	A31	24c on 2sh multi	85	*1.50*
250	A31	30c on 2sh6p multi	1.00	*1.90*
251	A31	36c on 2sh3p multi	1.25	*2.50*
252	A31	60c on 5sh multi	2.00	*3.75*
a.		Surcharge omitted	*450.00*	
253	A31	$1.20 on 10sh multi	4.00	*7.50*
254	A31	$2.40 on £1 multi	8.00	*15.00*
		Nos. 238-254 (17)	20.22	*36.90*

Watermark upright on 1c, 3c to 9c and 36c; sideways on others. Watermark is sideways on No. 252a, upright on No. 189.

Spathiphyllum — A41

Flowers: 2c, Bottlebrush. 3c, Oleander, vert. 4c, Bermudiana. 5c, Poinsettia. 6c, Hibiscus. 9c, Cereus. 10c, Bougainvillea, vert. 12c, Jacaranda. 15c, Passion flower. 18c, Coralita. 24c, Morning glory. 30c, Tecoma. 36c, Angel's trumpet. 60c, Plumbago. $1.20, Bird of paradise. $2.40, Chalice cup.

Wmk. 314, Sideways on Horiz. Stamps
1970, July 6 *Perf. 14*

255	A41	1c lt green & multi	15	15
256	A41	2c pale bl & multi	26	15
257	A41	3c yellow & multi	16	15
258	A41	4c buff & multi	18	15
259	A41	5c pink & multi	60	26
a.		Imperf., pair	800.00	
260	A41	6c orange & multi	60	30
261	A41	9c lt green & multi	35	16
262	A41	10c pale salmon & multi	35	16
263	A41	12c pale yellow & multi	1.65	85
264	A41	15c buff & multi	1.40	70
265	A41	18c pale salmon & multi	2.50	1.10
266	A41	24c pink & multi	1.65	75
267	A41	30c plum & multi	1.65	75
268	A41	36c dark gray & multi	2.50	1.10
269	A41	60c gray & multi	3.25	1.75
270	A41	$1.20 blue & multi	7.50	3.50
271	A41	$2.40 multicolored	15.00	8.25
		Nos. 255-271 (17)	39.75	20.23

See #322-328. For overprints see #288-291.

1974-76 Wmk. 314 Upright

259b	A41	5c multicolored	1.00	1.00
260a	A41	6c multicolored	2.25	2.25
263a	A41	12c multicolored	1.65	1.65
267a	A41	30c multicolored ('76)	3.00	3.00

Issued: 30c, June 11; others, June 13.

1975-76 Wmk. 373

256a	A41	2c multicolored	1.00	1.00
260b	A41	6c multicolored	2.00	2.00

Issued: 2c, Dec. 8; 6c, June 11, 1976.

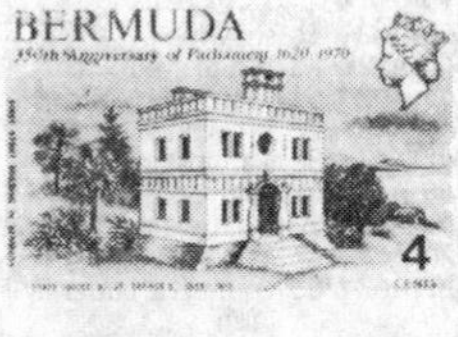

State House, St. George's, 1622-1815 A42

Designs: 15c, The Sessions House, Hamilton, 1893. 18c, First Assembly House, St. Peter's Church, St. George's. 24c, Temporary Assembly House, Hamilton, 1815-26.

1970, Oct. 12 Litho. *Perf. 14*

272	A42	4c multicolored	15	15
273	A42	15c multicolored	45	45
274	A42	18c multicolored	65	65
275	A42	24c multicolored	1.10	1.10
a.		Souvenir sheet of 4, #272-275	3.75	4.25

350th anniv. of Bermuda's Parliament.

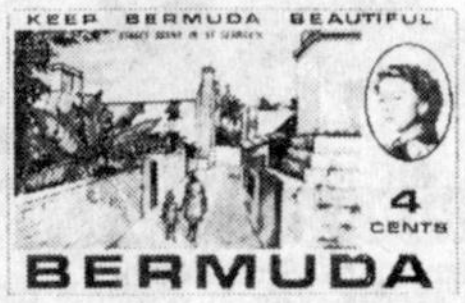

Street in St. George's A43

"Keep Bermuda Beautiful": 15c, Horseshoe Bay. 18c, Gibb's Hill Lighthouse. 24c, View of Hamilton Harbor.

1971, Feb. 8 Wmk. 314 *Perf. 14*

276	A43	4c multicolored	24	24
277	A43	15c multicolored	70	70
278	A43	18c multicolored	90	90
279	A43	24c multicolored	1.50	1.50

Building of "Deliverance" — A44

Designs: 15c, "Deliverance" and "Patience" arriving in Jamestown, Va., 1610, vert. 18c, Wreck of "Sea Venture," vert. 24c, "Deliverance" and "Patience" under sail, 1610.

1971, May 10 Litho. Wmk. 314

280	A44	4c multicolored	40	40
281	A44	15c brown & multi	1.40	1.40
282	A44	18c purple & multi	1.75	1.75
283	A44	24c blue & multi	2.50	2.50

Voyage of Sir George Somers to Jamestown, Va., from Bermuda, 1610.

Ocean View Golf Course A45

Golf Courses: 15c, Port Royal. 18c, Castle Harbour. 24c, Belmont.

1971, Nov. 1 *Perf. 13*

284	A45	4c multicolored	18	18
285	A45	15c multicolored	65	65
286	A45	18c multicolored	75	75
287	A45	24c multicolored	1.10	1.10

Golfing in Bermuda.

Nos. 258, 264-266 Overprinted: "HEATH-NIXON / DECEMBER 1971"

1971, Dec. 20 Photo. *Perf. 14*

288	A41	4c buff & multi	15	15
289	A41	15c buff & multi	42	42
290	A41	18c pale sal & multi	52	52
291	A41	24c pink & multi	70	70

Meeting of President Richard M. Nixon and Prime Minister Edward Heath of Great Britain, at Hamilton, Dec. 20-21, 1971.

Bonefish A46

1972, Aug. 7 Litho. *Perf. 13½x14*

292	A46	4c shown	26	26
293	A46	15c Wahoo	75	75
294	A46	18c Yellowfin tuna	90	90
295	A46	24c Greater amberjack	1.40	1.40

World fishing records.

Silver Wedding Issue, 1972
Common Design Type

Design: Queen Elizabeth II, Prince Philip, Admiralty oar and mace.

1972, Nov. 20 Photo. *Perf. 14x14½*

296	CD324	4c violet & multi	15	15
297	CD324	15c car rose & multi	52	52

Palmettos — A47

1973, Sept. 3 Wmk. 314 *Perf. 14*

298	A47	4c shown	25	25
299	A47	15c Olivewood	75	75
300	A47	18c Bermuda cedar	1.00	1.20
301	A47	24c Mahogany	1.25	1.25

Bermuda National Trust, and "Plant a Tree" campaign.

Princess Anne's Wedding Issue
Common Design Type

1973, Nov. 21 Litho.

302	CD325	15c lilac & multi	35	35
303	CD325	18c slate & multi	45	45

National Tennis Stadium, Pembroke, 1973 A48

Designs: 15c, Bermuda's first tennis court, Pembroke, 1873. 18c, Britain's first tennis court, Leamington Spa, 1872. 24c, First U.S. tennis club, Staten Island, 1874.

1973, Dec. 17 Wmk. 314

304	A48	4c black & multi	20	20
305	A48	15c black & multi	65	65
306	A48	18c black & multi	90	90
307	A48	24c black & multi	1.25	1.25

Centenary of tennis in Bermuda.

Rotary Emblem, Weather Vane, City Hall, Hamilton A49

Rotary Emblem and: 17c, St. Peter's Church, St. George's. 20c, Somerset Drawbridge, Somerset. 25c, Map of Bermuda on globe, 1626.

1974, June 24 *Perf. 14*

308	A49	5c emerald & multi	22	22
309	A49	17c blue & multi	75	75
310	A49	20c yel org & multi	85	85
311	A49	25c lt violet & multi	1.10	1.10

50th anniv. of Rotary Intl. in Bermuda.

Jack of Clubs and a Good Bridge Hand — A50

Bermuda Bowl and: 17c, Queen of diamonds. 20c, King of hearts. 25c, Ace of spades.

1975, Jan. 27 Litho. Wmk. 314

312	A50	5c blue & multi	24	24
313	A50	17c dull yel & multi	75	75
314	A50	20c ver & multi	80	80
315	A50	25c lilac & multi	1.10	1.10

World Bridge Championship, Bermuda, Jan. 1975.

Queen Elizabeth II and Prince Philip — A51

Perf. 14x14½

1975, Feb. 17 Photo. Wmk. 373

316	A51	17c multicolored	60	60
317	A51	20c dk blue & multi	80	80

Royal Visit, Feb. 16-18, 1975.

British Cavalier Flying Boat, 1937 A52

Designs: 17c, U.S. Navy airship "Los Angeles," 1925, flying from Lakehurst, N.J. to Hamilton, Bermuda. 20c, Constellation over Kindley Field, 1946. 25c, Boeing 747 on tarmac, 1970.

1975, Apr. 28 Litho. *Perf. 14*

318	A52	5c lt green & multi	42	42
319	A52	17c lt ultra & multi	1.25	1.25
320	A52	20c multicolored	1.75	1.75
321	A52	25c rose lil & multi	2.00	2.00
a.		Souvenir sheet of 4, #318-321	6.00	*7.50*

Airmail service to Bermuda, 50th anniv.

Flower Type of 1970

1975, June 2 Photo. Wmk. 314

322	A41	17c Passion flower	1.25	1.25
323	A41	20c Coralita	1.25	1.25
324	A41	25c Morning glory	1.25	1.25
325	A41	40c Angel's trumpet	1.25	1.25
326	A41	$1 Plumbago	2.00	2.00
327	A41	$2 Bird-of-paradise flower	3.50	3.50
328	A41	$3 Chalice cup	6.00	6.00
		Nos. 322-328 (7)	16.50	16.50

Royal Magazine Break-in A54

Designs: 17c, Sympathizers rowing towards magazine. 20c, Loading gun powder barrels onto ships. 25c, Gun powder barrels on beach.

Perf. 13x13½

1975, Oct. 27 Litho. Wmk. 373

329	A54	5c multicolored	24	24
330	A54	17c multicolored	75	75
331	A54	20c multicolored	85	85
332	A54	25c multicolored	1.25	1.25
a.		Souv. sheet of 4, #329-332, perf. 14	4.00	*5.00*

Gunpowder Plot, 1775, American War of Independence.

Bermuda Biological Station A55

Designs: 5c, Launching of bathysphere from "Ready," vert. 20c, Sailing ship Challenger, 1873. 25c, Descent of Beebe's bathysphere, 1934, and marine life, vert.

1976, Mar. 29 Litho. *Perf. 14*

333	A55	5c multicolored	28	28
334	A55	17c multicolored	70	70
335	A55	20c multicolored	85	85
336	A55	25c multicolored	1.00	1.00

Bermuda Biological Station, 50th anniv.

Christian Radich, Norway A56

Tall Ships: 12c, Juan Sebastian de Elcano, Spain. 17c, Eagle, US. 20c, Sir Winston Churchill, Great Britain. 40c, Kruzenshtern, USSR. $1, Cutty Sark (silver trophy).

1976, June 15 Litho. *Perf. 13*

337	A56	5c lt green & multi	30	30
338	A56	12c violet & multi	55	55
339	A56	17c ultra & multi	75	75
340	A56	20c blue & multi	1.00	1.00
341	A56	40c yellow & multi	1.50	1.50
342	A56	$1 sl grn & multi	4.50	4.50
		Nos. 337-342 (6)	8.60	8.60

Trans-Atlantic Cutty Sark International Tall Ships Race, Plymouth, England-New York City (Operation Sail '76).

Silver Cup Trophy and Crossed Club Flags A57

Designs: 17c, St. George's Cricket Club and emblem. 20c, Somerset Cricket Club and emblem. 25c, Cricket match.

1976, Aug. 16 Wmk. 373 *Perf. 14½*

343	A57	5c multicolored	26	26
344	A57	17c multicolored	85	85
345	A57	20c multicolored	95	95
346	A57	25c multicolored	1.40	1.40

St. George's and Somerset Cricket Club matches, 75th anniversary.

Queen's Visit to Bermuda, 1975 — A58

Designs: 20c, St. Edward's Crown. $1, Queen seated in Chair of Estate.

1977, Feb. 7 Litho. *Perf. 14x13½*

347	A58	5c silver & multi	18	18
348	A58	20c silver & multi	50	50
349	A58	$1 silver & multi	2.25	2.25

Reign of Queen Elizabeth II, 25th anniv.

Stockdale House, St. George's A59

UPU Emblem and: 15c, Perot Post Office and Perot Stamp. 17c, St. George's Post Office, c. 1860. 20c, Old GPO, Hamilton, c. 1935. 40c, New GPO, Hamilton, 1967.

1977, June 20 Litho. *Perf. 13x13½*

350	A59	5c multicolored	15	15
351	A59	15c multicolored	35	35
352	A59	17c multicolored	40	40
353	A59	20c multicolored	50	50
354	A59	40c multicolored	1.00	1.00
		Nos. 350-354 (5)	2.40	2.40

Bermuda's UPU membership, cent.

Sailing Ship, 17th Century, Approaching Castle Island — A60

Designs: 15c, King's pilot leaving 18th century naval ship at Murray's Anchorage. 17c, Pilot gigs racing to meet steamship, early 19th century. 20c, Harvest Queen, late 19th century. 40c, Pilot cutter and Queen Elizabeth II off St. David's Lighthouse.

Perf. 13½x14

1977, Sept. 26 Wmk. 373

355	A60	5c multicolored	15	15
356	A60	15c multicolored	42	42
357	A60	17c multicolored	48	48
358	A60	20c multicolored	60	60
359	A60	40c multicolored	1.25	1.25
		Nos. 355-359 (5)	2.90	2.90

Piloting in Bermuda waters.

Elizabeth II — A61

Designs: 8c, Great Seal of Elizabeth I. 50c, Great Seal of Elizabeth II.

1978, Aug. 28 Litho. *Perf. 14x13½*

360	A61	8c gold & multi	15	15
361	A61	50c gold & multi	85	85
362	A61	$1 gold & multi	1.65	1.65

25th anniv. of coronation of Elizabeth II.

White-tailed Tropicbird — A62

Perf. 14; 14x14½ (4c, 5c, $2, $3, $5)

1978-79 Photo. Wmk. 373

363	A62	3c shown	15	15
364	A62	4c White-eyed vireo	15	15
365	A62	5c Eastern bluebird	15	15
366	A62	7c Whistling tree frog	15	15
367	A62	8c Cardinal	15	15
368	A62	10c Spiny lobster	15	15
369	A62	12c Land crab	16	16
370	A62	15c Skink	20	20
371	A62	20c Four-eyed butter-flyfish	26	26
372	A62	25c Red hind	35	35
373	A62	30c Monarch butterfly	40	40
374	A62	40c Rock beauty	55	55
375	A62	50c Banded butter-flyfish	75	75
376	A62	$1 Blue angelfish	1.65	1.65
377	A62	$2 Humpback whale	3.25	3.25
378	A62	$3 Green turtle	4.75	4.75
379	A62	$5 Bermuda Petrel	8.00	8.00
		Nos. 363-379 (17)	21.22	21.22

Issued: 3c, 4c, 5c, 8c, $5, 1978. Others, 1979.
For surcharge see No. 509.

Map of Bermuda, by George Somers, 1609 — A63

Old Maps of Bermuda: 15c, by John Seller, 1685. 20c, by Herman Moll, 1729, vert. 25c, by Desbruslins, 1740. 50c, by John Speed, 1626.

1979, May 14 Litho. *Perf. 13½*

380	A63	8c multicolored	16	16
381	A63	15c multicolored	30	30
382	A63	20c multicolored	40	40
383	A63	25c multicolored	45	45
384	A63	50c multicolored	95	95
		Nos. 380-384 (5)	2.26	2.26

Bermuda Police Centenary — A64

Designs: 20c, Traffic direction, horiz. 25c, Water patrol, horiz. 50c, Motorbike and patrol car.

1979, Nov. 26 Wmk. 373 *Perf. 14*

385	A64	8c multicolored	16	16
386	A64	20c multicolored	40	40
387	A64	25c multicolored	50	50
388	A64	50c multicolored	1.00	1.00

Bermuda No. X1, Penny Black — A65

Bermuda #X1 and: 20c, Hill. 25c, "Paid 1" marking on cover. 50c, "Paid 1" marking.

1980, Feb. 25 Litho. *Perf. 13½x14*

389	A65	8c multicolored	16	16
390	A65	20c multicolored	40	40
391	A65	25c multicolored	50	50
392	A65	50c multicolored	1.00	1.00

Sir Rowland Hill (1795-1879), originator of penny postage.

Tristar-500, London 1980 Emblem — A66

1980, May 6 Litho. *Perf. 13x14*

393	A66	25c shown	35	35
394	A66	50c "Orduna," 1926	70	70
395	A66	$1 "Delta," 1856	1.50	1.50
396	A66	$2 "Lord Sidmouth," 1818	3.00	3.00

London 1980 Intl. Stamp Exhib., May 6-14.

Gina Swainson, Miss World, 1979-80, Arms of Bermuda — A67

1980, May 8 *Perf. 14*

397	A67	8c shown	15	15
398	A67	20c After crowning ceremony	35	35
399	A67	50c Welcome home party	90	90
400	A67	$1 In carriage	1.75	1.75

Queen Mother Elizabeth Birthday Issue

Common Design Type

1980, Aug. 4 Wmk. 373 *Perf. 14*

401	CD330	25c multicolored	46	46

Camden, Prime Minister's House
A68

1980, Sept. 24 Litho. *Perf. 14*

402 A68 8c View from satellite 16 16
403 A68 20c shown 40 40
404 A68 25c Princess Hotel, Hamilton 50 50
405 A68 50c Government House 1.00 1.00

Commonwealth Finance Ministers Meeting, Bermuda, Sept.

18th Century Kitchen
A69

1981, May 21 Wmk. 373 *Perf. 14*

406 A69 8c shown 15 15
407 A69 25c Gathering Easter lilies 42 42
408 A69 30c Fisherman 52 52
409 A69 40c Stone cutting, 19th cent. 70 70
410 A69 50c Onion shipping, 19th cent. 85 85
411 A69 $1 Ships, 17th cent. 1.75 1.75
Nos. 406-411 (6) 4.39 4.39

Royal Wedding Issue
Common Design Type

1981, July 22 Wmk. 373 *Perf. 14*

412 CD331 30c Bouquet 52 52
413 CD331 50c Charles 90 90
414 CD331 $1 Couple 1.75 1.75

Girl Helping Blind Man Cross Street — A70

1981, Sept. 28 Litho. *Perf. 14*

415 A70 10c shown 18 18
416 A70 25c Kayaking, Paget Island 48 48
417 A70 30c Mountain climbing, St. David's Island 55 55
418 A70 $1 Duke of Edinburgh 1.90 1.90

Duke of Edinburgh's Awards, 25th anniv.

Conus Species
A71

1982, May 13 Wmk. 373 *Perf. 14*

419 A71 10c shown 20 20
420 A71 25c Bursa finlayi 50 50
421 A71 30c Sconsia striata 60 60
422 A71 $1 Murex pterynotus lightbourni 1.90 1.90

Bermuda Regiment
A72

1982, June 17 Litho. Wmk. 373

423 A72 10c Color guard 16 16
424 A72 25c Queen's birthday parade 40 40
425 A72 30c Governor inspecting honor guard 45 45
426 A72 40c Beating the retreat 60 60
427 A72 50c Ceremonial gunners 80 80
428 A72 $1 Royal visit, 1975 1.65 1.65
Nos. 423-428 (6) 4.06 4.06

Southampton Fort — A73

1982, Nov. 18 Litho. Wmk. 373

429 A73 10c Charles Fort, vert. 20 20
430 A73 25c Pembroks Fort, vert. 50 50
431 A73 30c shown 60 60
432 A73 $1 Smiths and Pagets Forts 1.90 1.90

Arms of Sir Edwin Sandys (1561-1629) — A74

Fitted Dinghies — A75

Coats of Arms: 25c, Bermuda Company. 50c, William Herbert, 3rd Earl of Pembroke (1584-1630). $1, Sir George Somers (1554-1610).

1983, Apr. 14 Litho. *Perf. 13½*

433 A74 10c multicolored 18 18
434 A74 25c multicolored 45 45
435 A74 50c multicolored 90 90
436 A74 $1 multicolored 1.75 1.75

See Nos. 457-460, 474-477.

1983, July 21 Wmk. 373 *Perf. 14*

Old and modern boats.

437 A75 12c multicolored 22 22
438 A75 30c multicolored 55 55
439 A75 40c multicolored 70 70
440 A75 $1 multicolored 1.75 1.75

Manned Flight Bicentenary
A76

Designs: 12c, Curtiss Jenny, 1919 (first flight over Bermuda). 30c, Stinson Pilot Radio, 1930 (first completed US-Bermuda flight). 40c, Cavalier, 1937 (first scheduled passenger flight). $1, USS Los Angeles airship moored to USS Patoka, 1925.

1983, Oct. 13 Litho. *Perf. 14*

441 A76 12c multicolored 28 28
442 A76 30c multicolored 65 65
443 A76 40c multicolored 90 90
444 A76 $1 multicolored 1.75 1.75

Newspaper and Postal Services, 200th Anniv. — A77

1984, Jan. 26 Litho. *Perf. 14*

445 A77 12c Joseph Stockdale 22 22
446 A77 30c First Newspaper 55 55
447 A77 40c Stockdale's Postal Service, horiz. 70 70
448 A77 $1 "Lady Hammond," horiz. 1.75 1.75

375th Anniv. of Bermuda Settlement
A78

Designs: 12c, Thomas Gates, George Somers. 30c, Jamestown, Virginia, US. 40c, Sea Venture shipwreck. $1, Fleet leaving Plymouth, England.

1984, May 3 Litho. Wmk. 373

449 A78 12c multicolored 22 22
450 A78 30c multicolored 55 55
451 A78 40c multicolored 70 70
452 A78 $1 multicolored 1.75 1.75
a. Souv. sheet of 2, #450, 452 5.00 5.00

1984 Summer Olympics
A79

1984, July 19 Litho. *Perf. 14*

453 A79 12c Swimming, vert. 20 20
454 A79 30c Track & field 48 48
455 A79 40c Equestrian, vert. 65 65
456 A79 $1 Sailing 1.65 1.65

Arms Type of 1983

1984, Sept. 27 Litho. *Perf. 13½*

457 A74 12c Southampton 20 20
458 A74 30c Smith 60 60
459 A74 40c Devonshire 75 75
460 A74 $1 St. George 1.65 1.65

Architecture, Butter — A80

1985, Jan. 24 Litho. *Perf. 13½x13*

461 A80 12c shown 35 35
462 A80 30c Rooftops 75 75
463 A80 40c Chimneys 1.00 1.00
464 A80 $1.50 Archway 3.50 3.50

Audubon Birth Bicentenary
A81

1985, Mar. 21 Wmk. 373 *Perf. 14*

465 A81 12c Osprey, vert. 30 30
466 A81 30c Yellow-crowned night heron, vert. 75 75
467 A81 40c Great egret 1.00 1.00
468 A81 $1.50 Bluebird, vert. 3.50 3.50

Queen Mother 85th Birthday Issue
Common Design Type

Designs: 12c, Queen Consort, 1937. 30c, With grandchildren, 80th birthday. 40c, At Clarence House, 83rd birthday. $1.50, Holding Prince Henry. No. 473, In coach with Prince Charles.

Perf. 14½x14

1985, June 7 Wmk. 384

469 CD336 12c gray, bl & blk 35 35
470 CD336 30c multicolored 75 75
471 CD336 40c multicolored 1.00 1.00
472 CD336 $1.50 multicolored 3.50 3.50

Souvenir Sheet

473 CD336 $1 multicolored 4.50 4.50

Arms Type of 1983

Coats of Arms: 12c, James Hamilton, 2nd Marquess of Hamilton (1589-1625). 30c, William Paget, 4th Lord Paget (1572-1629). 40c, Robert Rich, 2nd Earl of Warwick (1587-1658). $1.50, Hamilton, 1957.

1985, Sept. 19 Litho. *Perf. 13½*

474 A74 12c multicolored 30 30
475 A74 30c multicolored 75 75
476 A74 40c multicolored 1.00 1.00
477 A74 $1.50 multicolored 3.75 3.75

Halley's Comet — A82

1985, Nov. 21 Wmk. 384 *Perf. 14½*

478 A82 15c Bermuda Archipelago 38 38
479 A82 40c Nuremberg Chronicles, 1493 1.00 1.00
480 A82 50c Peter Apian woodcut, 1532 1.25 1.25
481 A82 $1.50 Painting by Samuel Scott (c.1702-72) 3.75 3.75

Shipwrecks
A83

1986 Wmk. 384 *Perf. 14*

482 A83 3c Constellation, 1943 15 15
483 A83 5c Early Riser, 1876 15 15
484 A83 7c Madiana, 1903 15 15
485 A83 10c Curlew, 1856 16 16
486 A83 12c Warwick, 1619 18 18
487 A83 15c HMS Vixen, 1890 22 22
488 A83 20c San Pedro, 1594 30 30
489 A83 25c Alert, 1877 40 40
490 A83 40c North Carolina, 1880 60 60
491 A83 50c Mark Antonie, 1777 80 80
492 A83 60c Mary Celestia, 1864 90 90
493 A83 $1 L'Herminie, 1839 1.50 1.50
494 A83 $1.50 Caesar, 1818 2.25 2.25
495 A83 $2 Lord Amherst, 1778 3.00 3.00
496 A83 $3 Minerva, 1849 4.50 4.50
497 A83 $5 Caraquet, 1923 7.50 7.50
498 A83 $8 HMS Pallas, 1783 12.00 12.00
Nos. 482-498 (17) 34.76 34.76

Nos. 493, 495-496 exist inscribed "1989." Nos. 482, 488, "1990."

See #545-546. For surcharges see #598-600.

Inscribed "1992"

1992 Litho. Wmk. 373 *Perf. 14*

485a A83 10c 18 18
487a A83 15c 28 28
488a A83 20c 36 36
489a A83 25c 45 45
492a A83 60c 1.10 1.10
497a A83 $5 9.25 9.25
498a A83 $8 14.75 14.75
Nos. 485a-498a (7) 26.37 26.37

Queen Elizabeth II 60th Birthday
Common Design Type

Designs: 15c, Age 3. 40c, With the Earl of Rosebury, Oaks May Meeting, Epsom, 1954. 50c, With Prince Philip, state visit, 1979. 60c, At the British embassy in Paris, state visit, 1972. $1.50, Visiting Crown Agents' offices, 1983.

1986, Apr. 21 Wmk. 384 *Perf. 14½*

499 CD337 15c scar, blk & sil 24 24
500 CD337 40c ultra & multi 65 65
501 CD337 50c green & multi 80 80
502 CD337 60c violet & multi 95 95
503 CD337 $1.50 rose vio & multi 2.50 2.50
Nos. 499-503 (5) 5.14 5.14

AMERIPEX '86 — A84

1986, May 22 *Perf. 14*

504 A84 15c No. 452a 24 24
505 A84 40c No. 307 65 65
506 A84 50c No. 441 80 80
507 A84 $1 No. 339 1.65 1.65

Souvenir Sheet

508 A84 1.50 Statue of Liberty, S.S. Queen of Bermuda 4.50 4.50

Statue of Liberty, cent.

No. 378 Surcharged

Perf. 14x14½

1986, Dec. 4 Photo. Wmk. 373

509 A62 90c on $3 multi 3.00 3.00

Transport Railway, c. 1931-1947 — A85

Wmk. 373

1987, Jan. 22 Litho. *Perf. 14*

510 A85 15c Front Street, c. 1940 24 24
511 A85 40c Springfield Trestle 65 65
512 A85 50c No. 101, Bailey's Bay Sta. 80 80
513 A85 $1.50 No. 31, ship Prince David 2.50 2.50

Paintings by Winslow Homer (1836-1910) A86

1987, Apr. 30 *Perf. 14½*

514 A86 15c Bermuda Settlers, 1901 28 28
515 A86 30c Bermuda, 1900 55 55
516 A86 40c Bermuda Landscape, 1901 75 75
517 A86 50c Inland Water, 1901 95 95
518 A86 $1.50 Salt Kettle, 1899 3.00 3.00
Nos. 514-518 (5) 5.53 5.53

Booklet Stamps

519 A86 40c like 15c 65 65
520 A86 40c like 30c 65 65
521 A86 40c like No. 516 65 65
522 A86 40c like 50c 65 65
523 A86 40c like $1.50 65 65
a. Bklt. pane, 2 each #519-523 6.50

Nos. 519-523 printed in strips of 5 within pane. "ER" at lower left.

Intl. Flights Inauguration — A87

1987, June 18 *Perf. 14*

524 A87 15c Sikorsky S-42B, 1937 25 25
525 A87 40c Shorts S-23 Cavalier 70 70
526 A87 50c S-42B Bermuda Clipper 85 85
527 A87 $1.50 Cavalier, Bermuda Clipper 2.50 2.50

Bermuda Telephone Company, Cent. — A88

1987, Oct. 1 Litho. Wmk. 384

528 A88 15c Telephone poles on wagon 25 25
529 A88 40c Operators 70 70
530 A88 50c Telephones 85 85
531 A88 $1.50 Satellite, fiber optics, world 2.50 2.50

Horse-drawn Commercial Vehicles — A89

1988, Mar. 3 Litho. *Perf. 14*

532 A89 15c Mail wagon, c. 1869 28 28
533 A89 40c Open cart, c. 1823 75 75
534 A89 50c Closed cart, c. 1823 95 95
535 A89 $1.50 Two-wheel wagon, c. 1930 2.75 2.75

Old Garden Roses — A90

1988, Apr. 21 Wmk. 373

536 A90 15c Old blush 26 26
537 A90 30c Anna Olivier 52 52
538 A90 40c Rosa chinensis semperflorens, vert. 70 70
539 A90 50c Archduke Charles 90 90
540 A90 $1.50 Rosa chinensis viridiflora, vert. 2.75 2.75
Nos. 536-540 (5) 5.13 5.13

See Nos. 561-575.

Lloyds of London, 300th Anniv.

Common Design Type

Designs: 18c, Loss of the H.M.S. Lutine, 1799. 50c, Cable ship Sentinel, horiz. 60c, The Bermuda, Hamilton, 1931, horiz. $2, Valerian, lost during a hurricane, 1926.

1988, Oct. 13 Litho. Wmk. 384

541 CD341 18c multi 32 32
542 CD341 50c multi 90 90
543 CD341 60c multi 1.10 1.10
544 CD341 $2 multi 3.50 3.50

Shipwreck Type of 1986

1988 Litho. Wmk. 384 *Perf. 14*

545 A83 18c like 7c 35 35
546 A83 70c like $1.50 1.40 1.40

Issue dates: 18c, Sept. 22; 70c, Oct. 27.

Military Uniforms — A91

Designs: 18c, Devonshire Parish Militia, 1812. 50c, 71st Regiment Highlander, 1831-34. 60c, Cameron Highlander, 1942. $2, Troop of Horse, 1774.

1988, Nov. 10 Wmk. 373 *Perf. 14½*

547 A91 18c multicolored 30 30
548 A91 50c multicolored 85 85
549 A91 60c multicolored 1.00 1.00
550 A91 $2 multicolored 3.50 3.50

Ferry Service A92

1989 Litho. Wmk. 384 *Perf. 14*

551 A92 18c Corona 30 30
552 A92 50c Rowboat ferry 85 85
553 A92 60c St. George's Ferry 1.00 1.00
554 A92 $2 Laconia 3.50 3.50

Photography, Sesquicent. A93

Perf. 14x14½

1989, May 11 Litho. Wmk. 373

555 A93 18c Morgan's Is. 35 35
556 A93 30c Front Street, Hamilton (cannon in square) 60 60
557 A93 50c Front Street (seascape) 1.00 1.00
558 A93 60c Crow Lane, Hamilton Harbor 1.20 1.20
559 A93 70c Hamilton Harbor (ship-building) 1.40 1.40
560 A93 $1 Dockyard 2.00 2.00
Nos. 555-560 (6) 6.55 6.55

Old Garden Roses Type of 1988

1989, July 13 *Perf. 14*

561 A90 18c Agrippina 35 35
562 A90 30c Smith's Parish 60 60
563 A90 50c Champney's pink cluster 1.00 1.00
564 A90 60c Rosette delizy 1.20 1.20
565 A90 $1.50 Rosa bracteata 3.00 3.00
Nos. 561-565 (5) 6.15 6.15

Nos. 561-562 vert.

Old Garden Roses Type of 1988 with Royal Cipher Instead of Queen's Silhouette

1989, July 13 Booklet Stamps

566 A90 50c like No. 562 90 90
567 A90 50c like No. 540 90 90
568 A90 50c like No. 561 90 90
569 A90 50c like No. 538 90 90
570 A90 50c like No. 563 90 90
571 A90 50c like No. 536 90 90
572 A90 50c like No. 564 90 90
573 A90 50c like No. 537 90 90
574 A90 50c like No. 565 90 90
575 A90 50c like No. 539 90 90
a. Bklt. pane of 10, #566-575 9.00
Nos. 566-575 (10) 9.00 9.00

Bermuda Library, 150th Anniv. — A94

1989, Sept. 14 *Perf. 13½x14*

576 A94 18c Hamilton Main Library 30 30
577 A94 50c St. George's, The Old Rectory 85 85
578 A94 60c Springfield, Sommerset Library 1.00 1.00
579 A94 $2 Cabinet Building 3.50 3.50

Commonwealth Postal Conference — A95

1989, Nov. 3 Wmk. 384 *Perf. 14*

580 A95 18c No. 1 30 30
581 A95 50c No. 2 85 85
582 A95 60c Type A4 1.00 1.00
583 A95 $2 No. 6 3.50 3.50

For overprints see Nos. 594-597.

Fairylands, Bermuda, c. 1890, by Ross Sterling Turner — A96

Paintings: 50c, *Shinebone Alley, c. 1953,* by Ogden M. Pleissner. 60c, *Salt Kettle, 1916,* by Prosper Senate. $2, *St. George's, 1934,* by Jack Bush.

1990, Apr. 19

590 A96 18c multicolored 30 30
591 A96 50c multicolored 85 85
592 A96 60c multicolored 1.00 1.00
593 A96 $2 multicolored 3.50 3.50

Nos. 580-583 Overprinted

1990, May 3

594 A95 18c multicolored 35 35
595 A95 50c multicolored 1.00 1.00
596 A95 60c multicolored 1.20 1.20
597 A95 $2 multicolored 4.00 4.00

Stamp World London '90.

80c

Nos. 486, 491, 494 Surcharged

1990, Aug. 13

598 A83 30c on 12c No. 486 55 55
599 A83 55c on 50c No. 491 1.00 1.00
600 A83 80c on $1.50 No. 494 1.50 1.50

Nova Scotia-Bermuda Cable, Cent. — A97

1990, Oct. 18 Litho. Unwmk.

601 A97 20c Office 35 35
602 A97 55c Cableship SS Westmeath 1.00 1.00
603 A97 70c Radio station, 1928 1.25 1.25
604 A97 $2 Cableship Sir Eric Sharp 3.50 3.50

Nos. 601-602 with Added Inscription: "BUSH-MAJOR / 16 MARCH 1991"

1991, Mar. Unwmk. *Perf. 14*

605 A97 20c like #601 40 40
606 A97 55c like #602 1.10 1.10

Carriages A98

Designs: 20c, Two-seat pony cart, c. 1805. 30c, Varnished rockaway, c. 1830. 55c, Vis-a-Vis Victoria, c. 1895. 70c, Semi-formal phaeton, c. 1900. 80c, Pony runabout, c. 1905. $1, Ladies' phaeton, c. 1910.

Perf. 14x14½

1991, Mar. 21 Litho. Wmk. 373

607 A98 20c green & multi 40 40
608 A98 30c bl gray & multi 60 60
609 A98 55c dk car & multi 1.10 1.10
610 A98 70c blue & multi 1.40 1.40
611 A98 80c yel org & multi 1.60 1.60
612 A98 $1 dk gray & multi 2.00 2.00
Nos. 607-612 (6) 7.10 7.10

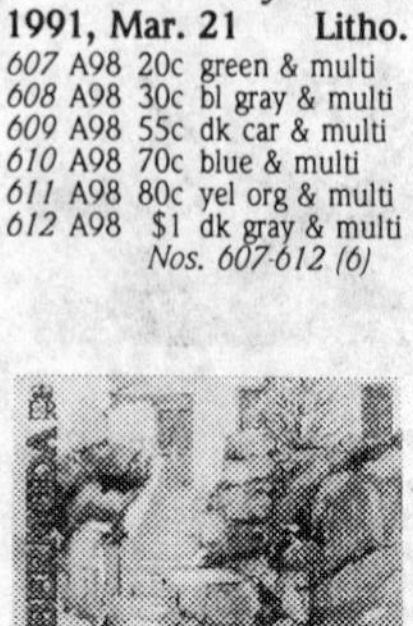

Paintings A99

Designs: 20c, Bermuda by Prosper Senat, vert. 55c, Bermuda Cottage by Frank Allison. 70c, Old Maid's Lane by Jack Bush, vert. $2, St. George's by Ogden M. Pleissner.

Perf. 14x13½

1991, May 16 Litho. Wmk. 373

613	A99	20c multicolored	40	40
614	A99	55c multicolored	1.10	1.10
615	A99	70c multicolored	1.40	1.40
616	A99	$2 multicolored	4.00	4.00

Elizabeth & Philip, Birthdays

Common Design Types

1991, June 20 Wmk. 384 *Perf. 14½*

617	CD346	55c multicolored	1.10	1.10
618	CD345	70c multicolored	1.40	1.40
a.		Pair, #617-618 + label	2.50	2.50

Bermuda in World War II A100

Designs: 20c, Floating drydock. 55c, Kindley Air Field. 70c, Trans-atlantic air route, Boeing 314. $2, Censored trans-atlantic mail.

1991, Sept. 19 Wmk. 373 *Perf. 14*

619	A100	20c multicolored	40	40
620	A100	55c multicolored	1.10	1.10
621	A100	70c multicolored	1.40	1.40
622	A100	$2 multicolored	4.00	4.00

Queen Elizabeth II's Accession to the Throne, 40th Anniv.

Common Design Type

1992, Feb. 6

623	CD349	20c multicolored	40	40
624	CD349	30c multicolored	60	60
625	CD349	55c multicolored	1.10	1.10
626	CD349	70c multicolored	1.40	1.40
627	CD349	$1 multicolored	2.00	2.00
		Nos. 623-627 (5)	5.50	5.50

Age of Exploration — A101

Artifacts: 25c, Rings, medallion. 35c, Ink wells. 60c, Gold pieces. 75c, Bishop button, crucifix. 85c, Pearl earrings and buttons. $1, 8-real coin, jug and measuring cups.

1992, July 23 *Perf. 13½*

628	A101	25c multicolored	50	50
629	A101	35c multicolored	70	70
630	A101	60c multicolored	1.20	1.20
631	A101	75c multicolored	1.50	1.50
632	A101	85c multicolored	1.70	1.70
633	A101	$1 multicolored	2.00	2.00
		Nos. 628-633 (6)	7.60	7.60

Stained Glass Windows — A102

Designs: 25c, Ship wreck. 60c, Birds in tree. 75c, St. Francis feeding bird. $2, Seashells.

1992, Sept. 24 *Perf. 14*

634	A102	25c multicolored	50	50
635	A102	60c multicolored	1.20	1.20
636	A102	75c multicolored	1.50	1.50
637	A102	$2 multicolored	4.00	4.00

7th World Congress of Kennel Clubs — A103

Perf. 13½x14, 14x13½

1992, Nov. 12 Litho. Wmk. 373

638	A103	25c German shepherd	48	48
639	A103	35c Irish setter	65	65
640	A103	60c Whippet, vert.	1.15	1.15
641	A103	75c Border terrier, vert.	1.40	1.40
642	A103	85c Pomeranian, vert.	1.60	1.60
643	A103	$1 Schipperke, vert.	1.85	1.85
		Nos. 638-643 (6)	7.13	7.13

Tourist Posters
A104 A105

1993, Feb. 25 Wmk. 373 *Perf. 14*

644	A104	25c Cyclist, carriage, ship	48	48
645	A105	60c Golf course	1.15	1.15
646	A105	75c Coastline	1.40	1.40
647	A104	$2 Dancers	3.70	3.70

Royal Air Force, 75th Anniv.

Common Design Type

Designs: 25c, Consolidated Catalina. 60c, Supermarine Spitfire. 75c, Bristol Beaufighter. $2, Handley Page Halifax.

1993, Apr. 1

648	CD350	25c multicolored	48	48
649	CD350	60c multicolored	1.15	1.15
650	CD350	75c multicolored	1.40	1.40
651	CD350	$2 multicolored	3.70	3.70

Duchesse de Brabant Rose, Bee — A106

1993, Apr. 1 Wmk. 384

Booklet Stamps

652	A106	10c green & multi	20	20
653	A106	25c violet & multi	48	48
a.		Booklet pane of 5	2.40	
654	A106	50c sepia & multi	1.00	1.00
a.		Booklet pane, 2 #652, 3 #654	3.50	
655	A106	60c vermilion & multi	1.10	1.10
a.		Booklet pane of 5	5.50	

Hamilton, Bicent. — A107

Designs: 25c, Modern skyline. 60c, Front Street, ships at left. 75c, Front Street, horse carts. $2, Hamilton Harbor, 1823.

Perf. 14½

1993, Sept. 16 Litho. Wmk. 373

656	A107	25c multicolored	48	48
657	A107	60c multicolored	1.10	1.10
658	A107	75c multicolored	1.40	1.40
659	A107	$2 multicolored	3.75	3.75

Furness Lines — A108

Designs: 25c, Furness Liv-Aboard Bermuda cruises, vert. 60c, SS Queen of Bermuda entering port. 75c, SS Queen of Bermuda, SS Ocean Monarch. $2, Starlit night aboard ship, vert.

Perf. 15x14, 14x15

1994, Jan. 20 Litho. Wmk. 373

660	A108	25c multicolored	48	48
661	A108	60c multicolored	1.10	1.10
662	A108	75c multicolored	1.40	1.40
663	A108	$2 multicolored	3.75	3.75

Royal Visit — A109

Designs: 25c, Queen Elizabeth II. 60c, Queen Elizabeth II, Duke of Edinburgh. 75c, Royal yacht Britannia.

Perf. 13½

1994, Mar. 9 Litho. Wmk. 373

664	A109	25c multicolored	48	48
665	A109	60c multicolored	1.10	1.10
666	A109	75c multicolored	1.50	1.50

Flowering Fruits A110

1994 Litho. Wmk. 373 *Perf. 14*

668	A110	5c Peach	15	15
669	A110	7c Fig	15	15
672	A110	15c Natal plum	30	30
673	A110	20c Pomegranate	38	38
683	A110	$8 Lemon	16.00	16.00
		Nos. 668-683 (5)	16.98	16.98

Issued: 5c, 7c, 15c, 20c, $8, 7/14/94. This is an expanding set. Numbers may change.

WAR TAX STAMPS

No. 42 Overprinted **WAR TAX**

1918 Wmk. 3 *Perf. 14*

MR1	A11	1p rose red	38	38

No. 42a Overprinted **WAR TAX**

1920

MR2	A11	1p carmine	38	38

BRITISH ANTARCTIC TERRITORY

LOCATION — South Atlantic Ocean between 20-80 degrees longitude and south of 60 degrees latitude

GOVT. — British territory

POP. — About 100 scientific staff at research stations.

This territory includes Graham Land (Palmer Peninsula), South Shetland Islands and South Orkney Islands. Formerly part of Falkland Islands Dependency.

12 Pence = 1 Shilling
20 Shillings = 1 Pound
100 Pence = 1 Pound (1971)

Catalogue values for all unused stamps in this country are for Never Hinged items.

M. V. Kista Dan — A1

Designs: 1p, Skiers hauling load. 1½p, Muskeg (tractor). 2p, Skiers. 2½p, Beaver seaplane. 3p, R.R.S. John Biscoe. 4p, Camp scene. 6p, H.M.S. Protector. 9p, Dog sled. 1sh, Otter ski-plane. 2sh, Huskies and aurora australis. 2sh6p, Helicopter. 5sh, Snocat (truck). 10sh, R.R.S. Shackleton. £1, Map of Antarctica.

Perf. 11x11½

1963, Feb. 1 Engr. Wmk. 314

1	A1	½p dark blue	22	16
2	A1	1p brown	16	15
3	A1	1½p plum & red	20	16
4	A1	2p rose violet	28	20
5	A1	2½p dull green	32	22
6	A1	3p Prus blue	42	35
7	A1	4p sepia	48	40
8	A1	6p dk blue & ol	85	70
9	A1	9p olive	1.00	85
10	A1	1sh steel blue	1.35	1.10
11	A1	2sh dl vio & bis	6.75	5.50
12	A1	2sh6p blue	7.50	6.25
13	A1	5sh rose red & org	14.50	14.00
14	A1	10sh grn & vio bl	35.00	32.50
15	A1	£1 black & blue	85.00	67.50
		Nos. 1-15 (15)	154.03	130.04

See No. 24. For surcharges, see Nos. 25-38.

Churchill Memorial Issue

Common Design Type

1966, Jan. 24 Photo. *Perf. 14*

16	CD319	½p bright blue	38	30
17	CD319	1p green	1.50	75
18	CD319	1sh brown	18.00	15.00
19	CD319	2sh violet	25.00	16.00

Lemaire Channel, Iceberg and Adelie Penguins A2

Designs: 6p, Weather sonde and operator. 1sh, Muskeg (tractor) pulling tent equipment. 2sh, Surveyors with theodolite.

1969, Feb. 6 Litho.

20	A2	3½p blue, vio bl & blk	1.25	1.10
21	A2	6p emer, blk & dp org	2.00	1.90
22	A2	1sh ultra, blk & ver	3.50	3.50
23	A2	2sh grnsh bl, blk & ocher	6.75	6.75

25 years of continuous scientific work in the Antarctic.

Type of 1963

Design: £1, H.M.S. Endurance and helicopter.

1969, Dec. 1 Engr. *Perf. 11x11½*

24	A1	£1 black & rose red	150.00	150.00

Common Design Types are pictured beginning on page 176.

Nos. 1-14 Surcharged in Decimal Currency; Three Bars Overprinted

1971, Feb. 15 Wmk. 314

25	A1	½p on ½p dk blue	15	15
26	A1	1p on 1p brown	20	18
27	A1	1½p on 1½p plum & red	28	25
28	A1	2p on 2p rose vio	30	30
29	A1	2½p on 2½p dl grn	35	40
30	A1	3p on 3p Prus bl	70	60

31 A1 4p on 4p sepia 1.00 95
32 A1 5p on 6p dk bl & ol 1.40 1.25
33 A1 6p on 9p olive 1.75 1.50
34 A1 7½p on 1sh steel bl 2.25 2.00
35 A1 10p on 2sh dl vio & bis 5.00 4.25
36 A1 15p on 2sh6p blue 15.00 13.00
37 A1 25p on 5sh rose red & org 30.00 25.00
38 A1 50p on 10sh grn & vio blue 65.00 62.50
Nos. 25-38 (14) 123.38 112.33

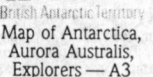

Map of Antarctica, Aurora Australis, Explorers — A3

Capt. Cook and "Resolution" — A4

Map of Antarctica, Aurora Australis and: 4p, Sea gulls. 5p, Seals. 10p, Penguins.

Litho. & Engr.

1971, June 23 ***Perf. 14x13***

39 A3 1½p multicolored 3.25 1.25
40 A3 4p multicolored 6.00 4.00
41 A3 5p multicolored 8.00 6.00
42 A3 10p multicolored 13.00 10.00

10th anniv. of the Antarctic Treaty pledging peaceful uses of and scientific cooperation in Antarctica.

Silver Wedding Issue, 1972
Common Design Type

Design: Queen Elizabeth II, Prince Philip, seals and emperor penguins.

1972, Dec. 13 Photo. ***Perf. 14x14½***

43 CD324 5p rose brn & multi 2.00 2.00
44 CD324 10p olive & multi 4.00 4.00

Perf. 14½

1975-80 Litho. Wmk. 373

Polar Explorers and their Crafts: 1p, Thaddeus von Bellingshausen and "Vostok." 1½p, James Weddell and "Jane." 2p, John Biscoe and "Tula." 2½p, J. S. C. Dumont d'Urville and "Astrolabe." 3p, James Clark Ross and "Erebus." 4p, C. A. Larsen and "Jason." 5p, Adrien de Gerlache and "Belgica." 6p, Otto Nordenskjöld and "Antarctic." 7½p, W. S. Bruce and "Scotia." 10p, Jean-Baptiste Charcot and "Pourquoi Pas?" 15p, Ernest Shackleton and "Endurance." 25p, Hubert Wilkins and airplane "San Francisco." 50p, Lincoln Ellsworth and airplane "Polar Star." £1, John Rymill and "Penola."

45 A4 ½p multi 15 15
46 A4 1p multi ('78) 15 15
47 A4 1½p multi ('78) 15 15
48 A4 2p multi ('79) 15 15
49 A4 2½p multi ('79) 18 18
50 A4 3p multi ('79) 20 20
52 A4 5p multi ('79) 32 32
55 A4 10p multi ('79) 65 65
56 A4 15p multi ('79) 1.00 1.00
57 A4 25p multi ('79) 1.60 1.60
58 A4 50p multi ('79) 3.25 3.25
59 A4 £1 multi ('78) 5.25 5.25
Nos. 45-59 (12) 13.05 13.05

Nos. 55-59 exist perf. 12, same values.

1973, Feb. 14 Wmk. 314

45a A4 ½p multi *1.75 1.75*
46a A4 1p multi *2.00 2.10*
47a A4 1½p multi *3.50 3.50*
48a A4 2p multi 24 15
49a A4 2½p multi 30 18
50a A4 3p multi 30 20
51a A4 4p multi 30 20
52a A4 5p multi 40 32
53a A4 6p multi 38 32
54a A4 7½p multi 55 52
55a A4 10p multi 1.05 55
56a A4 15p multi 1.75 1.00
57a A4 25p multi 2.00 1.50
58a A4 50p multi 4.00 3.00
59a A4 £1 multi 12.00 11.00
Nos. 45a-59a (15) *30.52 26.29*

1980 Wmk. 373 ***Perf. 12***

51 A4 4p multi 28 28
53 A4 6p multi 40 40
54 A4 7½p multi 50 50
55b A4 10p multi 65 65
56b A4 15p multi 70 70
57b A4 25p multi 1.25 1.25
58b A4 50p multi 2.50 2.50
59b A4 £1 multi 5.00 5.00
Nos. 51-59b (8) 11.28 11.28

Princess Anne's Wedding Issue
Common Design Type

1973, Nov. 14 Wmk. 314 ***Perf. 14***

60 CD325 5p ocher & multi 55 55
61 CD325 15p blue grn & multi 1.40 1.40

Wedding of Princess Anne and Capt. Mark Phillips, Nov. 14, 1973.

Churchill and Map of Churchill Peninsula A5

Design: 15p, Churchill and "Trepassey" of Operation Tabarin, 1943.

1974, Nov. 30 Litho. ***Perf. 14***

62 A5 5p multicolored 1.25 80
63 A5 15p multicolored 2.50 2.50
a. Souvenir sheet of 2, #62-63 6.75 4.50

Sir Winston Churchill (1874-1965).

Humpback Whale — A6

Wmk. 373

1977, Jan. 4 Litho. ***Perf. 14***

64 A6 2p Sperm whale 2.25 1.00
65 A6 8p Fin whale 2.75 1.50
66 A6 11p shown 5.50 3.00
67 A6 25p Blue whale 6.50 4.50

Conservation of whales.

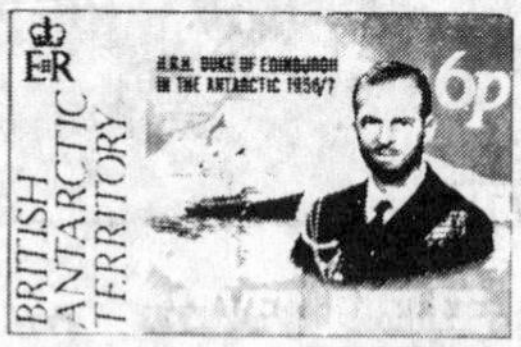

Prince Philip in Antarctica, 1956-57 — A7

Designs: 11p, Coronation oath. 33p, Queen before taking oath.

1977, Feb. 7 ***Perf. 13½x14***

68 A7 6p multicolored 40 40
69 A7 11p multicolored 65 65
70 A7 33p multicolored 2.25 2.25

25th anniv. of the reign of Elizabeth II.

Elizabeth II Coronation Anniversary Issue
Common Design Types
Souvenir Sheet

Unwmk.

1978, June 2 Litho. ***Perf. 15***

71 Sheet of 6 7.00 7.00
a. CD326 25p Black bull of Clarence 1.00 1.00
b. CD327 25p Elizabeth II 1.00 1.00
c. CD328 25p Emperor penguin 1.00 1.00

No. 71 contains 2 se-tenant strips of Nos. 71a-71c, separated by horizontal gutter with commemorative and descriptive inscriptions and showing central part of coronation procession with coach.

Macaroni Penguins — A8

Perf. 13½x14

1979, Jan. 14 Litho. Wmk. 373

72 A8 3p shown *5.75 2.00*
73 A8 8p Gentoo *1.50 1.00*
74 A8 11p Adelie *1.25 1.25*
75 A8 25p Emperor *3.25 1.50*

John Barrow, Tula, Society Emblem A9

Royal Geographical Society Sesquicentennial (Past Presidents and Expedition Scenes): 7p, Clement Markham 11p, Lord Curzon. 15p, William Goodenough. 22p, James Wordie. 30p, Raymond Priestley.

Perf. 13½

1980, Dec. 1 Litho. Wmk. 373

76 A9 3p multicolored 15 15
77 A9 7p multicolored 22 22
78 A9 11p multicolored 35 35
79 A9 15p multicolored 60 60
80 A9 22p multicolored 90 90
81 A9 30p multicolored 1.10 1.10
Nos. 76-81 (6) 3.32 3.32

20th Anniv. of Antarctic Treaty — A10

1981, Dec. 1 ***Perf. 13½x14***

82 A10 10p Map 32 32
83 A10 13p Conservation research 42 42
84 A10 25p Satellite image mapping 80 80
85 A10 26p Global geophysics 85 85

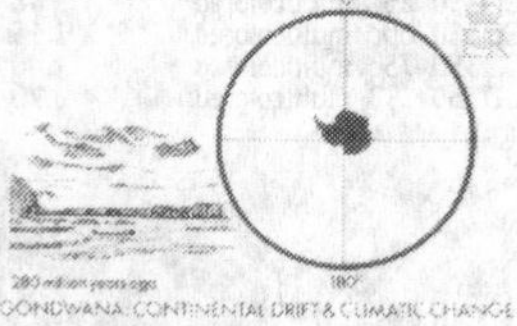

Continental Drift and Climatic Change — A11

1982, Mar. 8 Litho. ***Perf. 13½x14***

86 A11 3p Land, water 15 15
87 A11 6p Shrubs 22 22
88 A11 10p Dinosaur 38 38
89 A11 13p Volcano 50 50
90 A11 25p Trees 90 90
91 A11 26p Penguins 1.00 1.00
Nos. 86-91 (6) 3.15 3.15

Princess Diana Issue
Common Design Type

1982, July 1 Litho. ***Perf. 14½x14***

92 CD333 5p Arms 16 16
93 CD333 17p Diana, by Bryan Organ 55 55
94 CD333 37p Wedding 1.25 1.25
95 CD333 50p Portrait 1.65 1.65

10th Anniv. of Convention for Conservation of Antarctic Seals — A12

1982, Nov. Litho.

96 A12 5p shown 16 16
97 A12 10p Weddell seals 32 32
98 A12 13p Elephant seals 42 42
99 A12 17p Fur seals 55 55
100 A12 25p Ross seal 55 55
101 A12 34p Crabeater seals 1.10 1.10
Nos. 96-101 (6) 3.10 3.10

Corethron Criophilum A13

1984, Mar. 15 Litho. ***Perf. 14***

102 A13 1p shown 15 15
103 A13 2p Desmonema gaudichaudi 15 15
104 A13 3p Tomopteris carpenteri 15 15
105 A13 4p Pareuchaeta antarctica 15 15
106 A13 5p Antarctomysis maxima 16 16
107 A13 6p Antarcturus signiensis 20 20
108 A13 7p Serolis comuta 22 22
109 A13 8p Parathemisto gaudichaudii 25 25
110 A13 9p Bovallia gigantea 30 30
110A A13 10p Euphausia superba 32 32
111 A13 15p Colossendeis australis 50 50
112 A13 20p Todarodes sagittatus 65 65
113 A13 25p Notothenia neglecta 85 85
114 A13 50p Chaenocephalus aceratus 1.65 1.65
115 A13 £1 Lobodon carcinophagus 3.25 3.25
116 A13 £3 Antarctic marine food chain 8.25 *11.50*
Nos. 102-116 (16) 17.20 *20.45*

Manned Flight Bicentenary A14

1983, Dec. 17 Wmk. 373

117 A14 5p De Havilland Twin Otter 15 15
118 A14 13p De Havilland Single Otter 30 30
119 A14 17p Consolidated Canso 50 50
120 A14 50p Lockheed Vega 1.50 1.50

British-Graham Land Expedition, 1934-1937 — A15

Designs: 7p, M. Y. Penola in Stella Creek. 22p, Northern base, Winter Island. 27p, D. H. Fox Moth at southern base, Barry Island. 54p, Dog team near Ablation Point, George VI Sound.

1985, Mar. 23 Litho. ***Perf. 14½***

121 A15 7p multicolored 18 18
122 A15 22p multicolored 55 55
123 A15 27p multicolored 65 65
124 A15 54p multicolored 1.30 1.30

A16

A17

Naturalists, fauna and flora: 7p, Robert McCormick (1800-1890), Catharacta Skua Maccormicki. 22p, Sir Joseph Dalton Hooker (1817-1911), Deschampsea antarctica. 27p, Jean Rene C. Quoy (1790-1869), Lagenorhynchus cruciger. 54p, James Weddell (1787-1834), Leptonychotes weddelli.

1985, Nov. 4 Litho. ***Perf. 14½***

125 A16 7p multicolored 24 24
126 A16 22p multicolored 80 80
127 A16 27p multicolored 95 95
128 A16 54p multicolored 1.90 1.90

1986, Jan. 6 Wmk. 373 *Perf. 14*

Halley's comet.

129 A17 7p Edmond Halley 24 24
130 A17 22p Halley Station 75 75
131 A17 27p Trajectory, 1531 95 95
132 A17 54p Giotto space probe 1.75 1.75

Intl. Glaciological Society, 50th Anniv. — A18

Different snowflakes.

1986, Dec. 6 Wmk. 384 *Perf. 14½*

133 A18 10p dp blue & lt bl 30 30
134 A18 24p blue grn & lt bl grn 70 70
135 A18 29p dp rose lil & lt lil 85 85
136 A18 58p dp vio & pale vio blue 1.70 1.70

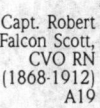

Capt. Robert Falcon Scott, CVO RN (1868-1912) A19

Designs: 24p, The Discovery at Hut Point, 1902-1904. 29p, Cape Evans Hut, 1911-1913. 58p, South Pole, 1912.

1987, Mar. 19 Litho. Wmk. 373

137 A19 10p multicolored 30 30
138 A19 24p multicolored 70 70
139 A19 29p multicolored 85 85
140 A19 58p multicolored 1.70 1.70

Intl. Geophysical Year, 30th Anniv. — A20

Commonwealth Trans-Antarctic Expedition — A21

1987, Dec. 25 Wmk. 384

141 A20 10p Emblem 32 32
142 A20 24p Port Lockroy 75 75
143 A20 29p Argentine Islands 90 90
144 A20 58p Halley Bay 1.75 1.75

1988, Mar. 19 *Perf. 14*

145 A21 10p Aurora over South Ice 32 32
146 A21 24p Otter aircraft 80 80
147 A21 29p Seismic ice-depth sounding 95 95
148 A21 58p Sno-cat over crevasse 1.90 1.90

Lichens A22

1989, Mar. 25 Wmk. 373

149 A22 10p Xanthoria elegans 32 32
150 A22 24p Usnea aurantiaco-atra 80 80
151 A22 29p Cladonia chlorophaea 95 95
152 A22 58p Umbilicaria antarctica 1.90 1.90

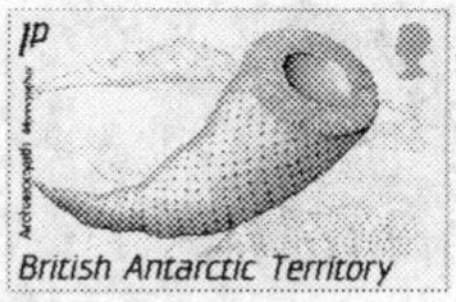

Fossils A23

1990, Apr. 2 Litho. Wmk. 384

153 A23 1p Archaeocyath 15 15
154 A23 2p Brachiopod 15 15
155 A23 3p Trilobite *(Triplagnostus)* 15 15
156 A23 4p Trilobite *(Lyriaspis)* 15 15
157 A23 5p Gymnosperm 16 16
158 A23 6p Fern 18 18
159 A23 7p Belemnite 22 22
160 A23 8p Ammonite *(Sanmartinoceras)* 25 25
161 A23 9p Bivalve *(Pinna)* 28 28
162 A23 10p Bivalve *(Aucellina)* 32 32
163 A23 20p Bivalve *(Trigonia)* 65 65
164 A23 25p Gastropod 80 80
165 A23 50p Ammonite *(Ainoceras)* 1.50 1.50
166 A23 £1 Ammonite *(Gunnarites)* 3.00 3.00
167 A23 £3 Crayfish 9.00 9.00
Nos. 153-167 (15) 16.96 16.96

Queen Mother, 90th Birthday

Common Design Types

1990, Aug. 4 Wmk. 384 *Perf. 14x15*

170 CD343 26p Wedding portrait, 1923 88 88

Perf. 14½

171 CD344 £1 Family portrait, 1940 3.40 3.40

Age of Dinosaurs A24

1991, Mar. 27 Wmk. 373 *Perf. 14*

172 A24 12p Late Cretaceous forest 46 46
173 A24 26p Hypsilophodont dinosaur 1.00 1.00
174 A24 31p Frilled shark 1.20 1.20
175 A24 62p Mosasaur, plesiosaur 2.40 2.40

Antarctic Ozone Hole — A25

1991, Mar. 30 *Perf. 14½x14*

176 A25 12p Launching weather balloon 46 46
177 A25 26p Measuring ozone 1.00 1.00
178 A25 31p Ozone hole over Antarctica 1.20 1.20
179 A25 62p Airplane, chemical studies 2.40 2.40

Antarctic Treaty, 30th Anniv. — A26

1991, June 24 *Perf. 14½*

180 A26 12p Dry valley 46 46
181 A26 26p Mapping ice sheet 1.00 1.00
182 A26 31p BIOMASS emblem 1.20 1.20
183 A26 62p Ross seal 2.40 2.40

Royal Research Ship James Clark Ross — A27

Designs: 12p, HMS Erebus and Terror in Antarctic by John W. Carmichael. 26p, Launch of RRS James Clark Ross. 62p, Scientific research.

1991, Dec. 10 *Perf. 14x14½*

184 A27 12p multicolored 46 46
185 A27 26p multicolored 1.00 1.00
186 A27 31p shown 1.20 1.20
187 A27 62p multicolored 2.40 2.40

Inscribed in Blue

200th Anniversary M. Faraday 1791-1867

1991, Dec. 24

188 A27 12p like #184 46 46
189 A27 26p like #185 1.00 1.00
190 A27 31p like #186 1.20 1.20
191 A27 62p like #187 2.40 2.40

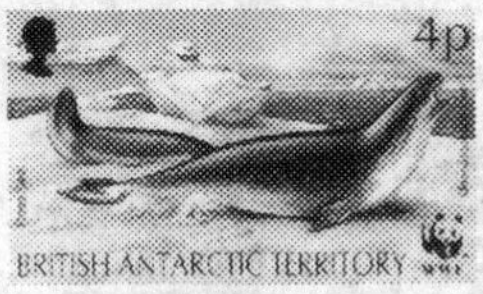

Seals and Penguins A28

1992, Oct. 20 *Perf. 13½*

192 A28 4p Ross seal 15 15
193 A28 5p Adelie penguin 18 18
194 A28 7p Weddell seal 26 26
195 A28 29p Emperor penguin 1.10 1.10
196 A28 34p Crabeater seal 1.30 1.30
197 A28 68p Chinstrap penguin 2.60 2.60
Nos. 192-197 (6) 5.59 5.59

World Wildlife Fund.

Lower Atmospheric Phenomena A29

Perf. 14x14½

1992, Dec. 22 Litho. Wmk. 373

198 A29 14p Sun pillar at Faraday 52 52
199 A29 29p Halo with iceberg 1.10 1.10
200 A29 34p Lee wave cloud 1.30 1.30
201 A29 68p Nacreous clouds 2.60 2.60

Research Ships A30

Wmk. 373

1993, Dec. 13 Litho. *Perf. 14*

202 A30 1p SS Fitzroy 15 15
203 A30 2p HMS William Scoresby 15 15
204 A30 3p SS Eagle 15 15
205 A30 4p MV Trepassey 15 15
206 A30 5p RRS John Biscoe (I) 15 15
207 A30 10p MV Norsel 28 28
208 A30 20p HMS Protector 55 55
209 A30 30p MV Oluf Sven 85 85
210 A30 50p RRS John Biscoe (II), RRS Shackleton 1.40 1.40
211 A30 £1 MV Tottan 2.75 2.75
212 A30 £3 MV Perla Dan 8.50 8.50
213 A30 £5 HMS Endurance (I) 14.00 14.00
Nos. 202-213 (12) 29.08 29.08

British Columbia and Vancouver Island stamps can be mounted in the Scott Canada Specialty and Master Canada albums.

Operation Taberin, 50th Anniv. — A31

Designs: 15p, Bransfield House and Post Office, Port Lockroy. 31p, Survey team, Hope Bay. 36p, Dog team, Hope Bay. 72p, SS Fitzroy, HMS William Scoresby at sea.

Wmk. 373

1994, Mar. 19 Litho. *Perf. 14*

214 A31 15p multicolored 42 42
215 A31 31p multicolored 90 90
216 A31 36p multicolored 1.10 1.10
217 A31 72p multicolored 2.25 2.25

Old and New Transportation — A32

Designs: 15p, Huskies. 24p, DeHavilland DHC-2 Turbo Beaver, British Antarctic Survey. 31p, Dogs, cargo being taken from aircraft. 36p, DHC-6 Twin Otter, sled team. 62p, DHC-6 in flight. 72p, DHC-6 taxiing down runway.

1994, Mar. 21

218 A32 15p multicolored 42 42
219 A32 24p multicolored 70 70
220 A32 31p multicolored 90 90
221 A32 36p multicolored 1.10 1.10
222 A32 62p multicolored 1.75 1.75
223 A32 72p multicolored 2.25 2.25
Nos. 218-223 (6) 7.12 7.12

Ovptd. with Hong Kong '94 Emblem

1994, Feb. 18

224 A32 15p on #218 42 42
225 A32 24p on #219 70 70
226 A32 31p on #220 90 90
227 A32 36p on #221 1.10 1.10
228 A32 62p on #222 1.75 1.75
229 A32 72p on #223 2.25 2.25
Nos. 224-229 (6) 7.12 7.12

BRITISH COLUMBIA & VANCOUVER IS.

LOCATION — On the northwest coast of North America
GOVT. — A former British Colony
AREA — 355,900 sq. mi.
POP. — 694,300

In 1871 the colony became a part of the Canadian Confederation and the postage stamps of Canada have since been used.

12 Pence = 1 Shilling
20 Shillings = 1 Pound
100 Cents = 1 Dollar (1865)

Values of perforated stamps (Nos. 2, 5-18) are for copies with perfs. touching.

Queen Victoria — A1

1860 Unwmk. Typo. *Imperf.*

1 A1 2½p dull rose 2,250.

No. 1 was not placed in use. It is ungummed and may be a proof or reprint.

Perf. 14

2 A1 2½p dull rose 175.00 110.00

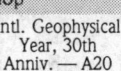

VANCOUVER ISLAND

A2

A3

1865 Wmk. 1 *Imperf.*

3	A2 5c rose	*22,500.*	*5,250.*
4	A3 10c blue	1,100.	800.00

Perf. 14

5	A2 5c rose	200.00	110.00
6	A3 10c blue	250.00	110.00

BRITISH COLUMBIA

Seal — A4

1865, Nov. 1

7	A4 3p blue	42.50	38.00

Type A4 of 1865 Surcharged in Various Colors

TWO CENTS 2c **5.CENTS.5** 5c - $1

1867-69 *Perf. 14*

8	2c on 3p brown (Bk)	42.50	42.50
9	5c on 3p brt red (Bk) ('69)	65.00	65.00
10	10c on 3p lilac rose (Bl)	550.00	
11	25c on 3p orange (V) ('69)	75.00	75.00
12	50c on 3p violet (R)	450.00	
13	$1 on 3p green (G)	550.00	

Nos. 10 and 13 were not placed in use.

1869 *Perf. 12½*

14	5c on 3p brt red (Bk)	450.00	450.00
15	10c on 3p lilac rose (Bl)	300.00	275.00
16	25c on 3p orange (V)	300.00	250.00
17	50c on 3p violet (R)	375.00	275.00
18	$1 on 3p green (G)	550.00	600.00

BRITISH GUIANA

LOCATION — On the northeast coast of South America
GOVT. — Former British Crown Colony
AREA — 83,000 sq. mi.
POP. — 628,000 (estimated 1964)
CAPITAL — Georgetown

British Guiana became the independent state of Guyana May 26, 1966.

100 Cents = 1 Dollar

Catalogue values for unused stamps in this country are for Never Hinged items, beginning with Scott 242 in the regular postage section and Scott J1 in the postage due section.

Values of early British Guiana stamps vary according to condition. Quotations for Nos. 1-16 are for fine copies. Very fine to superb specimens sell at higher prices, and inferior or poor copies sell at much reduced prices, depending on the condition of the individual specimen.

A1

1850-51 Typeset Unwmk. *Imperf.*

1	A1 2c blk, *pale rose*, cut to shape ('51)	*65,000.*	
2	A1 4c black, *orange*	*18,000.*	
a.	4c black, *yellow*	*25,000.*	
	Cut to shape	*4,000.*	
3	A1 4c blk, *yellow* (pelure)	*35,000.*	
	Cut to shape	*4,000.*	
4	A1 8c black, *green*	*12,500.*	
	Cut to shape	*2,500.*	
5	A1 12c black, *blue*	*5,250.*	
	Cut to shape	*1,900.*	
a.	12c black, *pale blue*	*10,500.*	
b.	12c black, *indigo*	*12,500.*	
c.	"1" of "12" omitted		

These stamps were initialed before use by the Deputy Postmaster General or by one of the clerks of the Colonial Postoffice at Georgetown. The following initials are found:—E. T. E. D(alton); E. D. W(ight); G. B. S(mith); H. A. K(illikelley); W. H. L(ortimer). As these stamps are type-set there are several types of each value.

Ship and Motto of Colony — A2

Seal of the Colony — A3

1852 Litho.

6	A2 1c black, *magenta*	*9,000.*	*5,000.*
7	A2 4c black, *blue*	*14,000.*	*5,000.*

Both 1c and 4c are found in two types. Copies with paper cracked or rubbed sell for much less.

Some copies are initialed E. D. W(ight).

The reprints are on thicker paper and the colors are brighter. They are perforated 12½ and imperforate. Value $15 each.

1853-59 *Imperf.*

Without Line above Value

8	A3 1c vermilion	4,000.	800.00

Copies in reddish brown probably are proofs.

Full or Partial White Line Above Value

9	A3 1c red	2,250.	550.00
10	A3 4c blue	825.00	300.00

On No. 9, "ONE CENT" varies from 11 to 13mm in width.

No. 10 Retouched; White Line above Value Removed

11	A3 4c blue	1,250.	300.00
a.	4c dark blue	1,600.	350.00

Reprints of Nos. 8 and 10 are on thin paper, perf. 12½ or imperf. The 1c is orange red, the 4c sky blue.

1860

Numerals in Corners Framed

12	A3 4c blue	3,000.	425.00

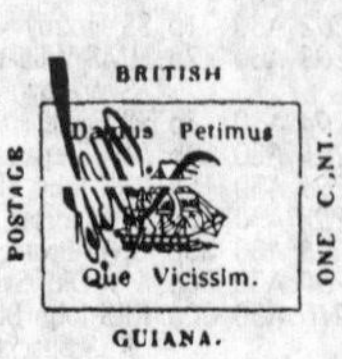

A4

1856 Typeset *Imperf.*

13	A4 1c black, *magenta*		
14	A4 4c black, *magenta*	*7,500.*	
a.	4c black, *rose carmine*	*10,500.*	
15	A4 4c black, *blue*	*45,000.*	
16	A4 4c black, *blue, paper colored through*	*60,000.*	

These stamps were initialed before being issued and the following initials are found:—E. T. E. D.; E. D. W.; W. H. L.; C. A. W. No. 13 is unique.

A5

Wide space between value and "Cents"

1860-61 Thick Paper Litho. *Perf. 12*

17	A5 1c brown red ('61)	250.00	65.00
18	A5 1c pink	900.00	165.00
19	A5 2c orange	80.00	25.00
20	A5 8c rose	225.00	35.00
21	A5 12c gray	225.00	25.00
a.	12c lilac	250.00	25.00
22	A5 24c green	750.00	55.00

All denominations of type A5 above four cents are expressed in Roman numerals.

Bisects and trisects are found on covers. These were not officially authorized.

The reprints of the 1c pink are perforated 12½; the other values have not been reprinted.

Thin Paper

1862

23	A5 1c brown	250.00	125.00
24	A5 1c black	50.00	20.00
25	A5 2c orange	40.00	15.00
26	A5 8c rose	52.50	25.00
27	A5 12c lilac	52.50	16.00
28	A5 24c green	500.00	47.50

Perf. 12½ and 13

29	A5 1c black	18.00	9.00
30	A5 2c orange	40.00	10.00
31	A5 8c rose	110.00	32.50
32	A5 12c lilac	325.00	47.50
33	A5 24c green	100.00	40.00

Perf. 10

34	A5 12c gray lilac	225.00	22.50

Imperfs. are proofs. See Nos. 44-62.

A6

A7

A8

A9

A10

A11

1862 Typeset *Rouletted*

35	A6 1c black, *rose*	1,100.	175.00
	Unsigned	140.00	
36	A7 1c black, *rose*	1,200.	300.00
	Unsigned	150.00	
37	A8 1c black, *rose*	2,250.	300.00
	Unsigned	275.00	
38	A6 2c red, *yellow*	1,100.	175.00
	Unsigned	125.00	
39	A7 2c red, *yellow*	1,500.	225.00
	Unsigned	150.00	
40	A8 2c red, *yellow*	2,500.	475.00
	Unsigned	300.00	
41	A9 4c *blue*	1,200.	250.00
	Unsigned	225.00	
42	A10 4c *blue*	2,500.	1,250.
	Unsigned	425.00	
a.	Without inner lines	1,200.	350.00
	As "a" Unsigned	200.00	
43	A11 4c *blue*	1,300.	275.00
	Unsigned	225.00	

Nos. 35-43 were typeset, there being 24 types of each value. They were initialed before use "R. M. Ac. R. G"., being the initials of Robert Mather, Acting Receiver General.

An alkali was used on the blue stamps, which, destroying the color of the paper, caused the initials to appear to be written in white.

Uninitialed stamps are remainders, few sheets having been found.

Specimens with roulette on all sides are valued higher.

Narrow space between value and "Cents"

1860 Thick Paper Litho. *Perf. 12*

44	A5 4c blue	200.00	32.50

Thin Paper

44A	A5 4c blue	35.00	17.50

Medium Paper

1863 *Perf. 12½ and 13*

45	A5 1c black	25.00	12.00
46	A5 2c orange	27.50	5.00
47	A5 4c blue	50.00	9.00
48	A5 8c rose	90.00	16.00
49	A5 12c lilac	225.00	22.50

1866 *Perf. 10*

50	A5 1c black	5.00	4.00
51	A5 2c orange	7.00	2.00
52	A5 4c blue	32.50	5.75
a.	Half used as 2c on cover		*3,500.*
53	A5 8c rose	55.00	6.00
a.	Diagonal half used as 4c on cover		
54	A5 12c lilac	65.00	10.00
a.	Third used as 4c on cover		

1875 *Perf. 15*

58	A5 1c black	27.50	5.00
59	A5 2c orange	125.00	8.00
60	A5 4c blue	175.00	55.00
61	A5 8c rose	150.00	40.00
62	A5 12c lilac	350.00	32.50

Seal of Colony
A12 A13

1863 *Perf. 12*

63	A12 24c green	90.00	6.00

Perf. 12½ to 13

64	A12 6c blue	60.00	27.50
65	A12 24c green	70.00	6.50
66	A12 48c deep red	100.00	22.50
a.	48c rose	150.00	22.50

1866 *Perf. 10*

67	A12 6c blue	65.00	10.00
a.	6c ultramarine	65.00	16.00
68	A12 24c green	110.00	5.00
69	A12 48c rose red	200.00	17.50

For surcharges, see Nos. 83-92.

1875 *Perf. 15*

70	A12 6c ultra	250.00	40.00
71	A12 24c green	300.00	17.50

1876 Typo. Wmk. 1 *Perf. 14*

72	A13 1c slate	2.50	35
a.	Perf. 14x12½		150.00
73	A13 2c orange	10.00	1.10
74	A13 4c ultra	50.00	4.75
a.	Perf. 12½	1,100.	125.00
75	A13 6c chocolate	35.00	6.50
76	A13 8c rose	50.00	1.90
77	A13 12c lilac	35.00	3.50
78	A13 24c green	35.00	5.00
79	A13 48c red brown	65.00	9.25
80	A13 96c bister	325.00	190.00
	Nos. 72-80 (9)	607.50	222.35

See Nos. 107-111. For surcharges, see Nos. 93-95, 98-101.

Stamps Surcharged by Brush-like Pen Lines

Surcharge Types:
Type a - Two horiz. lines.
Type b - Two lines, one horiz., one vert.
Type c - Three lines, two horiz., one vert.
Type d - One horiz. line.

On Nos. 75 and 67

1878 *Perf. 10, 14*

82	A13(a) (1c) on 6c choc	32.50	32.50
83	A12(b) (1c) on 6c blue	125.00	45.00
84	A13(b) (1c) on 6c choc	125.00	35.00

On Nos. O3, O8-O10

85	A13(c) (1c) on 4c ultra	70.00	45.00
a.	Type b		*2,500.*
86	A13(c) (1c) on 6c choc	110.00	45.00
87	A5(c) (2c) on 8c rose	95.00	45.00
88A	A13(b) (2c) on 8c rose	125.00	45.00

On Nos. O1, O3, O6-O7

89	A5(d)	(1c) on 1c blk	110.00	45.00
89A	A5(d)	(2c) on 8c rose		
90	A13(d)	(1c) on 1c sl	125.00	20.00
91	A13(d)	(2c) on 2c org	125.00	30.00

The provisional values of Nos. 82 to 91 were established by various official decrees. The horizontal lines crossed out the old value, "OFFICIAL," or both.

Nos. 69 and 80 Surcharged with New Values in Black

No. 92 No. 93

No. 94 No. 95

1881

92	A12	1c on 48c red	17.50	4.25
93	A13	1c on 96c bister	3.75	4.00
94	A13	2c on 96c bister	4.00	6.00
95	A13	2c on 96c bister	25.00	25.00

Unissued Official Stamps Surcharged with New Values

A24

No. 96

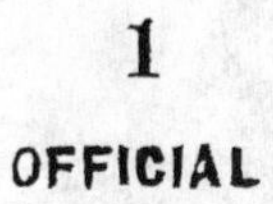

No. 97

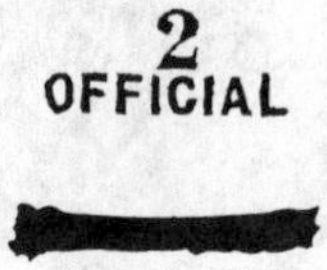

Nos. 99, 101

No. 102

1881

96	A13	1c on 12c lilac	50.00	25.00
97	A13	1c on 48c red brn	52.50	45.00
98	A24	2c on 12c lilac	110.00	110.00
99	A13	2c on 12c lilac	30.00	15.00
a.		"2" inverted		
b.		"2" double	450.00	425.00
100	A24	2c on 24c green	550.00	550.00
101	A13	2c on 24c green	42.50	32.50
a.		"2" inverted		
d.		Double surcharge	650.00	
102	A13	2c on 24c green	110.00	110.00

A27

Typeset

ONE AND TWO CENTS.
Type I - Ship with three masts.
Type II - Brig with two masts.

"SPECIMEN"
Perforated Diagonally across Stamp

1882 Unwmk. *Perf. 12*

103	A27	1c black, *lil rose*, I	30.00	17.50
a.		Without "Specimen"	50.00	50.00
104	A27	1c black, *lil rose*, II	30.00	22.50
a.		Without "Specimen"	50.00	50.00
105	A27	2c black, *yel*, I	35.00	40.00
a.		Without "Specimen"	50.00	50.00
b.		Diagonal half used as 1c on cover		
106	A27	2c black, *yel*, II	32.50	32.50
a.		Without "Specimen"	50.00	50.00

Nos. 103-106 were typeset, 12 to a sheet, and, to prevent fraud on the government, the word *"Specimen"* was perforated across them before they were issued. There were 2 settings of the 1c and 3 settings of the 2c, thus there are 24 types of the former and 36 of the latter.

Type of 1876

1882 Typo. Wmk. 2 *Perf. 14*

107	A13	1c slate	2.75	35
108	A13	2c orange	9.50	45
a.		"2 CENTS" double		
109	A13	4c ultra	35.00	7.00
110	A13	6c brown	4.75	7.75
111	A13	8c rose	50.00	1.40
		Nos. 107-111 (5)	102.00	16.95

A28

A29

4 CENTS and $4
Type I - Figure "4" is 3mm high.
Type II - Figure "4" is 3½mm high.
6 CENTS
Type I - Top of "6" is flat.
Type II - Top of "6" turns downward.

"INLAND REVENUE" Overprint and Surcharged in Black

1889

112	A28	1c lilac	1.65	70
113	A28	2c lilac	1.00	45
114	A28	3c lilac	1.00	45
115	A28	4c lilac, I	1.00	45
116	A28	4c lilac, II	20.00	14.00
117	A28	6c lilac, I	4.00	4.00
118	A28	6c lilac, II	3.00	3.00
119	A28	8c lilac	1.10	80
120	A28	10c lilac	2.00	2.00
121	A28	20c lilac	4.25	3.75
122	A28	40c lilac	7.25	5.50
123	A28	72c lilac	9.00	8.75
124	A28	$1 green	325.00	250.00
125	A28	$2 green	110.00	110.00
126	A28	$3 green	52.50	52.50
127	A28	$4 green, I	225.00	175.00
127A	A28	$4 green, II	600.00	600.00
128	A28	$5 green	125.00	125.00
		Nos. 112-128 (18)	1,492.	1,356.

For surcharges, see Nos.129, 148-151B.

No. 113 Surcharged "2" in Red

1889

129	A29	2c on 2c lilac	80	40

Inverted and double surcharges of "2" were privately made.

A30

A31

1889-1903 Typo.

130	A30	1c lilac & gray	75	22
131	A30	1c green ('90)	30	16
131A	A30	1c gray grn ('00)	1.10	15
132	A30	2c lilac & org	70	15
133	A30	2c lil & rose ('00)	2.75	15
134	A30	2c vio & blk, *red* ('01)	1.10	15
135	A30	4c lilac & ultra	2.25	1.00
a.		4c lilac & blue	7.50	1.25
136	A30	5c ultra ('91)	2.50	25
137	A30	6c lilac & mar	4.75	1.50
a.		6c lilac & brown	11.00	5.50
138	A30	6c gray blk & ultra ('02)	4.75	3.00
139	A30	8c lilac & rose	5.50	75
140	A30	8c lil & blk ('90)	2.50	1.40
141	A30	12c lilac & vio	3.50	1.00
142	A30	24c lilac & grn	3.00	1.40
143	A30	48c lilac & ver	14.00	4.25
144	A30	48c dk gray & lil brn ('01)	9.00	7.00
145	A30	60c gray grn & car ('03)	55.00	60.00
146	A30	72c lil & org brn	16.00	14.00
147	A30	96c lilac & rose	40.00	40.00
		Nos. 130-147 (19)	169.45	136.53

Stamps of the 1889-1903 issue with pen or revenue cancellation sell for a small fraction of the above quotations.
See Nos. 160-177.

Red Surcharge

1890

148	A31	1c on $1 grn & blk	55	40
a.		Double surcharge	40.00	40.00
149	A31	1c on $2 grn & blk	32	32
a.		Double surcharge	75.00	75.00
150	A31	1c on $3 grn & blk	65	65
a.		Double surcharge	55.00	55.00
151	A31	1c on $4 grn & blk, type I	1.40	1.40
a.		Double surcharge	67.50	
151B	A31	1c on $4 grn & blk, type II	8.75	8.75
c.		Double surcharge		
		Nos. 148-151B (5)	11.67	11.52

Mt. Roraima — A32

Kaieteur (Old Man's) Falls — A33

1898 Wmk. 1 Engr.

152	A32	1c car & gray blk	2.50	90
153	A33	2c blue & brn	2.50	90
a.		Horiz. pair, imperf. between	4,500.	
154	A32	5c brown & grn	10.50	4.75
155	A33	10c red & blue blk	12.00	12.00
156	A32	15c blue & red brn	10.50	12.00
		Nos. 152-156 (5)	38.00	30.55

60th anniv. of Queen Victoria's accession to the throne.

Nos. 154-156 Surcharged in Black **TWO CENTS.**

1899

157	A32	2c on 5c brn & grn	1.40	1.65
a.		Without period	27.50	27.50
158	A33	2c on 10c red & bl black	85	1.10
a.		"GENTS"	55.00	55.00
b.		Inverted surcharge	200.00	225.00
c.		Without period	22.50	22.50
159	A32	2c on 15c bl & red brown	1.40	1.40
a.		Without period	50.00	50.00
b.		Double surcharge	60.00	
c.		Inverted surcharge	300.00	300.00

There are many slight errors in the setting of this surcharge, such as: small "E" in "CENTS"; no period and narrow "C"; comma between "T" and "S"; dash between "TWO" and "CENTS"; comma between "N" and "T."

Ship Type of 1889-1903

1905-10 Wmk. 3

Chalky Paper

160	A30	1c gray green	40	15
a.		1c blue green, ordinary paper ('10)	40	15
b.		Booklet pane of 6		
161	A30	2c vio & blk, *red*	1.75	22
162	A30	4c lilac & ultra	12.00	6.75
163	A30	5c lil & blue, *bl*	7.75	1.75
164	A30	6c gray black & ultra	14.00	12.50
165	A30	12c lilac & vio	14.00	12.50
166	A30	24c lil & grn ('06)	3.50	3.50
167	A30	48c gray & vio brn	9.25	12.50
168	A30	60c gray grn & car rose	11.00	12.50
169	A30	72c lil & org brn ('07)	27.50	25.00
170	A30	96c blk & red, *yel* ('06)	22.50	*27.50*
		Nos. 160-170 (11)	123.65	*114.87*

The 2c-60c exist on ordinary paper.

A34

George V — A35

Black Overprint

171	A34	$2.40 grn & vio	165.00	*165.00*

Ship Type of 1889-1903
Ordinary Paper

TWO CENTS
Type I - Only the upper right corner of the flag touches the mast.
Type II - The entire right side of the flag touches the mast.

1907

172	A30	2c red, type I	2.25	18
b.		2c red, type II	60	15
174	A30	4c brown & vio	1.95	1.00
175	A30	5c blue	3.00	42
176	A30	6c gray & black	7.50	3.00
177	A30	12c orange & vio	3.25	3.00
		Nos. 172-177 (5)	17.95	7.60

1913-16 *Perf. 14*

178	A35	1c green	1.00	15
179	A35	2c scarlet	52	15
a.		2c carmine	38	15
180	A35	4c brn & red vio	65	20
181	A35	5c ultra	65	25
182	A35	6c gray & black	65	55
183	A35	12c org & vio	90	90

Chalky Paper

184	A35	24c dl vio & grn	1.40	1.40
185	A35	48c blk & vio brn	3.50	3.50
186	A35	60c grn & car	7.75	11.00
187	A35	72c dl vio & org brn	14.00	17.00

Surface Colored Paper

188	A35	96c blk & red, *yel*	14.00	18.00

Paper Colored Through

189	A35	96c blk & red, *yel* ('16)	10.00	12.50
		Nos. 178-189 (12)	55.02	65.60

The 72c and late printings of the 2c and 5c are from redrawn dies. The ruled lines behind the value are thin and faint, making the tablet appear lighter than before. The shading lines in other parts of the stamps are also lighter.

1921-27 Wmk. 4

191	A35	1c green	32	18
192	A35	2c rose red	65	15
193	A35	2c dp vio ('23)	55	15
194	A35	4c brn & vio	1.00	15
195	A35	6c ultra	1.10	22
196	A35	12c org & vio	1.65	80

Chalky Paper

197	A35	24c dl vio & grn	2.75	1.90
198	A35	48c blk & vio brn ('26)	6.75	2.00
199	A35	60c grn & car ('26)	7.50	*11.00*
200	A35	72c dl vio & brn org	8.00	9.00
201	A35	96c blk & red, *yel* ('27)	9.50	*12.00*
		Nos. 191-201 (11)	39.77	*37.55*

Plowing a Rice Field — A36

Indian Shooting Fish — A37

Kaieteur Falls — A38

Georgetown, Public Buildings — A39

1931, July 21 Engr. *Perf. 12½*

205	A36	1c blue green	38	38
206	A37	2c dk brown	1.00	45
207	A38	4c car rose	2.75	1.75

208 A39 6c ultra 2.25 1.90
209 A38 $1 violet 24.00 26.00
Nos. 205-209 (5) 30.38 30.48

Cent. of the union of Berbice, Demerara and Essequibo to form the Colony of British Guiana.

A40

A41

Gold Mining — A42

Shooting Logs over Falls — A44

Kaieteur Falls — A43

Stabroek Market — A45

Sugar Cane in Punts — A46

Forest Road — A47

Victoria Regia Lilies — A48

Mt. Roraima — A49

Sir Walter Raleigh and Son — A50

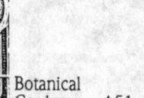

Botanical Gardens — A51

1934, Oct. 1 ***Perf. 12½***
210 A40 1c green 15 15
211 A41 2c brown 20 15
212 A42 3c carmine 15 15
b. Perf. 12½x13½ ('43) 28 15
c. Perf. 13x13½ ('49) 15 15
213 A43 4c vio black 90 15
a. Vert. pair, imperf. horiz. *8,000.*
214 A44 6c dp ultra 1.50 1.40
215 A45 12c orange 15 15
a. Perf. 13½x13 ('51) 15 15
216 A46 24c rose violet 3.00 1.25
217 A47 48c black 10.50 9.25
218 A43 50c green 12.00 15.00
219 A48 60c brown 21.00 24.00
220 A49 72c rose violet 1.25 1.00
221 A50 96c black 20.00 21.00
222 A51 $1 violet 19.00 17.00
Nos. 210-222 (13) 89.80 90.65

See Nos. 236, 238, 240.

Silver Jubilee Issue
Common Design Type

1935, May 6 ***Perf. 13½x14***
223 CD301 2c gray blk & ultra 18 18
224 CD301 6c blue & brown 85 42
225 CD301 12c indigo & grn 1.40 1.00
226 CD301 24c brt vio & ind 3.25 3.25

Coronation Issue
Common Design Type

1937, May 12 ***Perf. 13½x14***
227 CD302 2c brown 15 15
228 CD302 4c gray black 15 15
229 CD302 6c bright ultra 20 20

A52

A53

A54

A56

A55

A57

A58

Victoria Regia Lilies and Jacanas — A59

1938-52 Engr. Wmk. 4 ***Perf. 12½***
230 A52 1c green 15 15
b. Perf. 14x13 ('49) 15 15
231 A53 2c violet blk 15 15
b. Perf. 13x14 ('49) 15 15
232 A54 4c black & rose, perf. 13x14 ('52) 15 15
a. Perf. 12½ 16 15
c. Vert. pair, imperf. between *5,500.* *3,000.*
233 A55 6c deep ultra 15 15
a. Perf. 13x14 ('49) 15 15
234 A56 24c deep green 55 15
a. Wmk. upright 5.00 1.50
235 A53 36c pur, perf. 13x14 ('51) 75 15
a. Perf. 12½ 55 15
236 A47 48c orange yel 28 15
a. Perf. 14x13 ('51) 45 25
237 A57 60c brown 1.65 55
238 A50 96c brown vio 1.00 65
a. Perf. 12½x13½ ('44) 70 75
239 A58 $1 deep violet 2.00 15
a. Perf. 14x13 ('51) 200.00 375.00
240 A49 $2 rose vio, perf. 14x13 ('50) 2.25 2.25
a. Perf. 12½ ('45) 2.25 2.00
241 A59 $3 orange brn ('45) 10.00 5.75
a. Perf. 14x13 ('52) 9.50 8.00
Nos. 230-241 (12) 19.08 10.40

The watermark on No. 234 is sideways.

British Guiana stamps can be mounted in the Scott British East Caribbean album.

Catalogue values for unused stamps in this section, from this point to the end of the section, are for Never Hinged items.

Peace Issue
Common Design Type

1946, Oct. 21 ***Perf. 13½x14***
242 CD303 3c carmine 15 15
243 CD303 6c deep blue 16 16
Set value 24 24

Silver Wedding Issue
Common Design Types

1948, Dec. 20 Photo. ***Perf. 14x14½***
244 CD304 3c scarlet 15 15

Engr.
Perf. 11½x11
245 CD305 $3 org brown 10.00 *16.00*

UPU Issue
Common Design Types

Engr.; Name Typo. on 6c and 12c
Perf. 13½, 11x11½

1949, Oct. 10 **Wmk. 4**
246 CD306 4c rose carmine 35 15
247 CD307 6c indigo 55 55
248 CD308 12c orange 70 70
249 CD309 24c blue green 1.40 1.40

University Issue
Common Design Types

1951, Feb. 16 Engr. ***Perf. 14x14½***
250 CD310 3c car & black 32 22
251 CD311 6c dp ultra & black 42 42

Coronation Issue
Common Design Type

1953, June 2 ***Perf. 13½x13***
252 CD312 4c car & black 20 15

Common Design Types are pictured beginning on page 176.

G. P. O., Georgetown — A60

Indian Shooting Fish — A61

Designs: 2c, Botanical gardens. 3c, Victoria regia lilies and jacanas. 5c, Map. 6c, Rice combine. 8c, Sugar cane entering factory. 12c, Felling greenheart tree. 24c, Bauxite mining. 36c, Mt. Roraima. 48c, Kaieteur Falls. 72c, Arapaima (fish). $1, Toucan. $2, Dredging gold. $5, Coat of Arms.

Engr., Center Litho. on $1
Perf. 12½x13, 13

1954, Dec. 1 **Wmk. 4**
253 A60 1c black 15 15
254 A60 2c dark green 15 15
255 A60 3c red brn & ol 15 15
256 A61 4c violet 15 15
257 A60 5c black & red 16 15
258 A60 6c yel green 16 15
259 A60 8c ultramarine 16 15
260 A61 12c brown & black 35 15
261 A60 24c orange & black 75 18
262 A60 36c black & rose 1.10 42
263 A61 48c red brn & ultra 1.40 70
264 A61 72c emerald & rose 2.00 1.60
265 A60 $1 blk, yel, grn & sal 3.25 90
266 A60 $2 magenta 4.25 2.25
267 A61 $5 black & ultra 9.25 7.75
Nos. 253-267 (15) 23.43 15.00

See Nos. 279-287.

Clasped Hands — A62

Perf. 14½x14

1961, Oct. 23 Photo. Wmk. 314
268 A62 5c sal pink & brown 15 15
269 A62 6c lt blue grn & brown 16 16
270 A62 30c lt orange & brown 42 42

Fourth annual History and Culture Week.

Freedom from Hunger Issue
Common Design Type

1963, June 4 ***Perf. 14x14½***
271 CD314 20c lilac 48 40

Red Cross Centenary Issue
Common Design Type

Wmk. 314

1963, Sept. 2 Litho. ***Perf. 13***
272 CD315 5c black & red 15 15
273 CD315 20c ultra & red 65 65

Queen Types of 1954

Engr.; Center Litho. on $1
Perf. 12½x13, 13

1963-65 **Wmk. 314**
279 A60 3c red brn & ol ('65) 85 65
280 A60 5c blk & red ('64) 15 15
281 A61 12c brn & blk ('64) 30 15
282 A60 24c orange & black 52 15
283 A60 36c black & rose 85 15
284 A61 48c red brn & ultra 1.50 1.10
285 A61 72c emerald & rose 4.25 3.00
286 A60 $1 blk, yel, grn & sal 5.25 2.50
287 A60 $2 magenta 7.50 4.75
Nos. 279-287 (9) 21.17 12.60

Weight Lifter A63

1964, Oct. 1 Photo. ***Perf. 13x13½***
290 A63 5c orange 15 15
291 A63 8c blue 15 15
292 A63 25c carmine rose 42 42

18th Olympic Games, Tokyo, Oct. 10-25.

ITU Issue
Common Design Type

Perf. 11x11½

1965, May 17 Litho. Wmk. 314
293 CD317 5c emerald & olive 15 15
294 CD317 25c lt blue & brt pink 45 45

Intl. Cooperation Year Issue
Common Design Type

1965, Oct. 25 Wmk. 314 ***Perf. 14½***
295 CD318 5c blue grn & claret 15 15
296 CD318 25c lt vio & green 50 50

Winston Churchill and St. George's Cathedral, Georgetown A64

1966, Jan. 24 Photo. ***Perf. 14x14½***
297 A64 5c multicolored 15 15
298 A64 25c dp blue, blk & gold 60 48

Sir Winston Leonard Spencer Churchill (1874-1965), statesman and WWII leader.

Royal Visit Issue
Common Design Type

1966, Feb. 4 Litho. *Perf. 11x12*
299 CD320 3c violet blue 25 18
300 CD320 25c dark car rose 1.40 1.10

POSTAGE DUE STAMPS

Catalogue values for unused stamps in this section are for Never Hinged items.

D1

Perf. 13½x14
1940-52 Typo. Wmk. 4
J1 D1 1c green 26 26
a. Wmk. 4a (error) 40.00
J2 D1 2c black 32 32
a. Wmk. 4a (error) 35.00
J3 D1 4c ultra ('52) 80 80
a. Wmk. 4a (error) 35.00
J4 D1 12c carmine 1.65 *4.00*

The 2c and 12c are on chalky paper as well as ordinary paper.

WAR TAX STAMP

Regular Issue No. 179 Overprinted **War Tax**

1918, Jan. 4 Wmk. 3 *Perf. 14*
MR1 A35 2c scarlet 15 15

OFFICIAL STAMPS

Counterfeit overprints exist.

No. 50 Overprinted in Red **OFFICIAL**

1875 Unwmk. *Perf. 10*
O1 A5 1c black 35.00 10.00

Nos. 51, 53-54, 68 Overprinted in Black **OFFICIAL**

O2 A5 2c orange 125.00 11.00
O3 A5 8c rose 300.00 100.00
O4 A5 12c lilac 1,000. 500.00
O5 A12 24c green 600.00 225.00

For surcharges, see Nos. 87, 89, 89A, 96, 102.

Same Overprint on Nos. 72-76

1877 Wmk. 1 *Perf. 14*
O6 A13 1c slate 225.00 85.00
O7 A13 2c orange 75.00 7.50
O8 A13 4c ultramarine 100.00 35.00
O9 A13 6c chocolate 2,750. 525.00
O10 A13 8c rose 2,250. 400.00

The type A13 12c lilac, 24c green and 48c red brown overprinted "OFFICIAL" were never placed in use. A few copies of the 12c and 24c have been seen but the 48c is only known surcharged with new value for provisional use in 1881. See Nos. 97-101.

For surcharges, see Nos. 85-86, 88A, 90-91.

BRITISH HONDURAS

LOCATION — Central America bordering on Caribbean on east, Mexico on north and Guatemala on west.
GOVT. — British Crown Colony
AREA — 8,867 sq. mi.
POP. — 130,000 (est. 1972)
CAPITAL — Belmopan

Before British Honduras became a colony (subordinate to Jamaica) in 1862, it was a settlement under British influence. In 1884 it became an independent colony. In 1973 the colony changed its name to Belize. Issues of Belize are listed under that name in this volume.

12 Pence = 1 Shilling
100 Cents = 1 Dollar (1888)

Catalogue values for unused stamps in this country are for Never Hinged items, beginning with Scott 127 in the regular postage section, Scott J1 in the postage due section.

Queen Victoria — A1

1866 Unwmk. Typo. *Perf. 14*
1 A1 1p blue 37.50 37.50
a. Horiz. pair, imperf. btwn.
2 A1 6p rose 140.00 82.50
3 A1 1sh green 150.00 72.50

The 6p and 1sh were printed only in a sheet with the 1p. The 1sh is known in se-tenant gutter pairs with the 1p and the 6p.

1872 Wmk. 1 *Perf. 12½*
4 A1 1p blue 37.50 11.00
5 A1 3p brown 70.00 45.00
6 A1 6p rose 140.00 27.50
7 A1 1sh green 175.00 18.00
a. Horiz. pair, imperf. btwn. *18,000.*

For surcharges, see Nos. 18-19.

1877-79 *Perf. 14*
8 A1 1p blue 26.00 12.00
a. Horiz. strip of 3, imperf. btwn. *4,500.*
9 A1 3p brown 60.00 16.00
10 A1 4p violet ('79) 110.00 10.00
11 A1 6p rose ('78) 225.00 165.00
12 A1 1sh green 150.00 9.00

For surcharges, see Nos. 20-21, 29.

1882-87 Wmk. 2
13 A1 1p blue ('84) 22.50 18.00
14 A1 1p rose ('84) 10.50 9.00
a. Diagonal half used as ½p on cover
15 A1 4p violet 45.00 4.00
16 A1 6p yellow ('85) 225.00 150.00
17 A1 1sh gray ('87) 175.00 110.00

For surcharges, see Nos. 22-26, 28-35.

Stamps of 1872-87 Surcharged in Black **2 CENTS**

1888 Wmk. 1 *Perf. 12½*
18 A1 2c on 6p rose 95.00 95.00
19 A1 3c on 3p brown 8,000. 3,000.

Perf. 14
20 A1 2c on 6p rose 62.50 62.50
a. Diagonal half used as 1c on cover 225.00
b. Double surcharge 1,300. 1,300.
c. "2" with curved tail 725.00 725.00
21 A1 3c on 3p brown 47.50 47.50

Wmk. 2
22 A1 2c on 1p rose 6.00 *15.00*
a. Diagonal half used as 1c on cover 250.00
b. Double surcharge 800.00 800.00
c. Inverted surcharge 1,300. 1,250.
23 A1 10c on 4p violet 24.00 9.00
a. Inverted surcharge
24 A1 20c on 6p yellow 22.50 15.00
25 A1 50c on 1sh gray 250.00 425.00

No. 25 with Additional Surcharge in Red or Black **TWO**

26 A1 2c (R) on 50c on 1sh gray 25.00 *37.50*
a. "TWO" in black *8,750.* *8,500.*
b. "TWO" double (Blk + R) *8,750.* *8,000.*
c. Diagonal half used as 1c on cover 325.00

Stamps of 1872-87 Surcharged in Black c **2 CENTS**

1888-89
28 A1 2c on 1p rose 52 *85*
a. Diagonal half used as 1c on cover 110.00
29 A1 3c on 3p brown 60 *1.00*
30 A1 10c on 4p violet 2.00 *1.75*
31 A1 20c on 6p yel ('89) 5.25 *11.00*
32 A1 50c on 1sh gray 14.00 *22.50*
Nos. 28-32 (5) 22.37 *37.10*

For other examples of this surcharge see Nos. 36, 47. For overprint, see No. 51.

No. 30 with Additional Surcharge in Black or Red **6**

1891
33 A1 6c (Blk) on 10c on 4p 1.00 *3.75*
a. "6" and bar inverted *3,000.* *900.00*
b. "6" only inverted *3,000.*
34 A1 6c (R) on 10c on 4p 65 *2.50*
a. "6" and bar inverted *500.00* *500.00*
b. "6" only inverted *3,000.*

Stamps similar to No. 33 but with "SIX" instead of "6," both with and without bar, were prepared but not regularly issued.
See No. 37.

No. 29 with Additional Surcharge in Black **FIVE**

35 A1 5c on 3c on 3p brown 1.50 *3.25*
a. Double surcharge of "Five" and bar 150.00 *200.00*

Black Surcharge, Type "c"
36 A1 6c on 3p blue 75 1.40

No. 36 with Additional Surcharge like Nos. 33-34 in Red

1891
37 A1 15c (R) on 6c on 3p blue 5.00 *8.75*
a. Double surcharge

A8

A9

1891-98 Wmk. 2 *Perf. 14*
38 A8 1c green 90 1.00
39 A8 2c carmine rose 75 24
40 A8 3c brown 95 1.25
41 A8 5c ultra ('95) 10.00 90
42 A8 6c ultramarine 1.75 50
43 A8 10c vio & grn ('95) 5.25 4.75
44 A8 12c vio & green 3.50 2.50
45 A8 24c yellow & blue 3.00 3.50
46 A8 25c red brn & grn ('98) 10.00 *15.00*
Nos. 38-46 (9) 36.10 *29.64*

Numeral tablet on Nos. 43-46 has lined background with colorless value and "c".
For overprints, see Nos. 48-50.

Type of 1866 Surcharged Type "c"

1892
47 A1 1c on 1p green 22 22

Regular Issue Overprinted REVENUE in Black

1899
48 A8 5c ultramarine 1.75 2.25
a. "BEVENUE" 50.00 *65.00*
49 A8 10c lilac & green 3.50 *6.50*
a. "BEVENUE" 150.00 *200.00*
50 A8 25c red brn & grn 2.50 4.25
a. "BEVENUE" 90.00 *125.00*
51 A1 50c on 1sh gray (No. 32) 110.00 *140.00*
a. "BEVENUE" 2,750. 2,750.

The overprint is found in two lengths: 12mm (43 to the pane) and 11mm (17 to the pane). The "U" is found in both a tall, narrow type and the more common small type.

1899-1901
52 A9 5c gray blk & ultra, *bl* ('00) 1.90 60
53 A9 10c vio & grn ('01) 2.50 *3.75*
54 A9 50c grn & car rose 7.50 *12.50*
55 A9 $1 grn & car rose 11.00 *13.00*
56 A9 $2 green & ultra 26.00 *32.50*
57 A9 $5 green & black 240.00 *250.00*
Nos. 52-57 (6) 288.90 *312.35*

Numeral tablet on Nos. 53-54 has lined background with colorless value and "c".

King Edward VII — A10

1902-04 Typo. Wmk. 2
58 A10 1c gray grn & grn ('04) 6.00 *7.25*
59 A10 2c vio & blk, *red* 2.00 38
60 A10 5c gray blk & ultra, *blue* 3.00 1.00
61 A10 20c dl vio & vio ('04) 7.25 *12.00*

1904-06 Chalky Paper Wmk. 3
62 A10 1c green 30 22
63 A10 2c vio & blk, *red* 1.25 15
64 A10 5c blk & ultra, *bl* ('05) 1.25 28
65 A10 10c vio & grn ('06) 2.50 1.25
67 A10 25c vio & org ('06) 4.00 6.00
68 A10 50c grn & car rose ('06) 6.00 *13.00*
69 A10 $1 grn & car rose ('06) 12.00 *20.00*
70 A10 $2 grn & ultra ('06) 45.00 57.50
71 A10 $5 grn & blk ('06) 175.00 175.00
Nos. 62-71 (9) 247.30 273.40

The 1c and 2c exist also on ordinary paper.

1909
Ordinary Paper
72 A10 2c carmine 2.00 28
73 A10 5c ultramarine 2.25 48

1911
74 A10 25c black, *green* 8.25 *11.00*

Numeral tablet on #61, 65-68, 74 has lined background with colorless value and "c".

King George V
A11 A12

1913-17 Wmk. 3 *Perf. 14*
75 A11 1c green 35 40
76 A11 2c scarlet 65 20
a. 2c carmine 85 95
77 A11 3c orange ('17) 45 20
78 A11 5c ultra 2.25 1.25

Chalky Paper
79 A12 10c dl vio & ol grn 2.50 *4.25*
80 A12 25c blk, *gray grn* 3.75 4.25
a. 25c black, *emerald* 2.50 2.75
b. 25c blk, *bl grn, olive back* 3.25 4.25
81 A12 50c vio & ultra, *bl* 4.50 *7.00*
82 A11 $1 black & scar 6.00 9.00
83 A11 $2 grn & dull vio 22.50 *35.00*
84 A11 $5 vio & blk, *red* 200.00 *225.00*
Nos. 75-84 (10) 242.95 *286.55*

See No. 91. For overprints, see Nos. MR2-MR5.

With Moire Overprint in Violet

1915
85 A11 1c green 95 *4.00*
86 A11 2c carmine 1.10 *3.25*
87 A11 5c ultramarine 1.25 *3.25*

For overprint, see No. MR1.

Peace Commemorative Issue

Seal of Colony and George V — A13

1921, Apr. 28 Engr.
89 A13 2c carmine 2.50 1.00

Similar to A13 but without "Peace Peace"

1922 **Wmk. 4**
90 A13 4c dark gray 2.75 95

Type of 1913-17

1921 **Typo.** **Wmk. 4**
91 A11 1c green 2.00 1.65

A14

1922-33 **Typo.** **Wmk. 4**
92 A14 1c green ('29) 48 38
93 A14 2c dark brown 35 20
94 A14 2c rose red ('27) 85 70
95 A14 3c orange ('33) 95 75
96 A14 4c gray ('29) 85 20
97 A14 5c ultramarine 75 20

Chalky Paper

98 A14 10c olive grn & lil 1.25 35
99 A14 25c black, *emerald* 1.50 1.90
100 A14 50c ultra & vio, *bl* 3.25 *5.50*
101 A14 $1 scarlet & blk 6.50 *9.00*
102 A14 $2 red vio & grn 17.50 *26.00*

Wmk. 3

103 A14 25c black, *emerald* 4.25 *13.00*
104 A14 $5 blk & vio, *red* 200.00 *175.00*
Nos. 92-104 (13) 238.48 *233.18*

For surcharges, see Nos. B1-B5.

Silver Jubilee Issue
Common Design Type
Perf. 11x12

1935, May 6 **Engr.** **Wmk. 4**
108 CD301 3c black & ultra 65 65
109 CD301 4c indigo & grn 1.10 1.40
110 CD301 5c ultra & brn 2.00 2.00
111 CD301 25c brn vio & ind 4.00 *6.00*
Set, never hinged 12.00

Coronation Issue
Common Design Type

1937, May 12 ***Perf. 13¹/₂x14***
112 CD302 3c deep orange 15 15
113 CD302 4c gray black 15 15
114 CD302 5c bright ultra 18 18
Set, never hinged 1.50

Mayan Figures — A15

Chicle Tapping — A16

Cohune Palm — A17

Local Products A18

Grapefruit Industry A19

Mahogany Logs in River — A20

Sergeant's Cay — A21

Dory — A22

Chicle Industry A23

Court House, Belize — A24

Mahogany Cutting — A25

Seal of Colony — A26

1938 ***Perf. 11x11¹/₂, 11¹/₂x11***
115 A15 1c green & violet 15 15
116 A16 2c car & black 15 15
a. Perf. 12 ('47) 2.25 2.00
117 A17 3c brown & dk vio 15 15
118 A18 4c green & black 15 15
119 A19 5c slate bl & red vio 15 15
120 A20 10c brown & yel grn 22 22
121 A21 15c blue & brown 40 32
122 A22 25c green & ultra 70 45
123 A23 50c dk vio & blk 1.40 1.40
124 A24 $1 ol green & car 2.25 2.25
125 A25 $2 rose lake & ind 4.50 4.50
126 A26 $5 brn & carmine 18.00 16.00
Nos. 115-126 (12) 28.22 25.89
Set, never hinged 55.00

Issue dates: 3c-5c, Jan. 10. 1c, 2c, 10c-50c, Feb. 14. $1-$5, Feb. 28.

Catalogue values for unused stamps in this section, from this point to the end of the section, are for Never Hinged items.

Peace Issue
Common Design Type
Perf. 13¹/₂x14

1946, Sept. 9 **Engr.** **Wmk. 4**
127 CD303 3c brown 15 15
128 CD303 5c deep blue 15 15
Set value 23 23

Silver Wedding Issue
Common Design Types

1948, Oct. 1 **Photo.** ***Perf. 14x14¹/₂***
129 CD304 4c dark green 18 18

Engraved; Name Typographed
Perf. 11¹/₂x11

130 CD305 $5 light brown 22.50 *25.00*

St. George's Cay — A27

H.M.S. Merlin — A28

1949, Jan. 10 **Engr.** ***Perf. 12¹/₂***
131 A27 1c green & ultra 15 15
132 A27 3c yel brn & dp blue 18 18
133 A27 4c purple & brn ol 28 28
134 A28 5c dk blue & brown 28 28
135 A28 10c vio brn & blue grn 50 50
136 A28 15c ultra & emerald 90 90
Nos. 131-136 (6) 2.29 2.29

Battle of St. George's Cay, 150th anniv.

UPU Issue
Common Design Types
Perf. 13¹/₂, 11x11¹/₂

1949, Oct. 10 **Engr.** **Wmk. 4**
137 CD306 4c blue green 35 35
138 CD307 5c indigo 55 55
139 CD308 10c chocolate 90 90
140 CD309 25c blue 1.50 1.50

University Issue
Common Design Types

1951, Feb. 16 **Engr.** ***Perf. 14x14¹/₂***
141 CD310 3c choc & purple 32 32
142 CD311 10c choc & green 65 65

Coronation Issue
Common Design Type

1953, June 2 ***Perf. 13¹/₂x13***
143 CD312 4c dk green & black 42 42

Arms — A29

Maya — A30

Designs: 2c, Tapir. 3c, Legislative Council Chamber and mace. 4c, Pine industry. 5c, Spiny lobster. 10c, Stanley Field Airport. 15c, Mayan frieze. 25c, Blue butterfly. $1, Armadillo. $2, Hawkesworth Bridge. $5, Pine Ridge orchid.

1953-57 **Engr.** ***Perf. 13¹/₂***
144 A29 1c gray blk & green 15 15
145 A29 2c gray blk & brn, perf. 14 ('57) 15 15
a. Perf. 13¹/₂ 28 24
146 A29 3c mag & rose lil, perf. 14 ('57) 15 15
a. Perf. 13¹/₂ 15 15
147 A29 4c grn & dk brn 15 15
148 A29 5c car & ol brn, perf. 14 ('57) 22 18
a. Perf. 13¹/₂ 42 42
149 A29 10c ultra & bl gray 22 20
150 A29 15c vio & yel grn 35 35
151 A29 25c brown & ultra 80 60
152 A30 50c purple & brown 2.00 1.10
153 A29 $1 red brn & sl bl 2.75 2.50
154 A29 $2 gray & car 7.00 6.50
155 A30 $5 blue gray & pur 14.00 11.00
Nos. 144-155 (12) 27.94 23.03

Issue dates: No. 148, May 15, Nos. 145-146, Sept. 18, perf. 13¹/₂, Sept. 2.
For overprints, see Nos. 159-166.

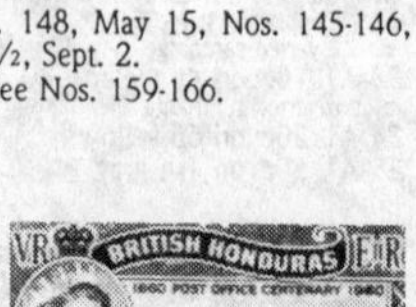

View of Belize, 1842 — A31

Designs: 10c, Public seals, 1860 and 1960. 15c, Tamarind Tree, Newtown Barracks.

Perf. 11¹/₂x11

1960, July 1 **Wmk. 314**
156 A31 2c green 15 15
157 A31 10c carmine 28 28
158 A31 15c blue 48 48

Cent. of the establishment of a local PO.

Nos. 145-146 and 149-150 Overprinted: "NEW CONSTITUTION/1960"

1961, Mar. 1 **Wmk. 4** ***Perf. 14, 13***
159 A29 2c gray black & brn 15 15
160 A29 3c mag & rose lilac 16 16
161 A29 10c ultra & blue gray 35 35
162 A29 15c violet & yel green 60 60

Nos. 144, 149, 151 and 152 Overprinted: "HURRICANE/HATTIE"

1962, Jan. 15 ***Perf. 13***
163 A29 1c gray black & green 15 15
164 A29 10c ultra & blue gray 15 15
165 A29 25c brown & ultra 32 32
166 A30 50c purple & brown 70 70

Hurricane Hattie struck Belize, Oct. 31, 1961.

Great Curassow A32

Birds: 2c, Red-legged honeycreeper. 3c, American jacana. 4c, Great kiskadee. 5c, Scarlet-rumped tanager. 10c, Scarlet macaw. 15c, Massena trogon. 25c, Redfooted booby. 50c, Keel-billed toucan. $1, Magnificent frigate bird. $2, Rufoustailed jacamar. $5, Montezuma oropendola.

Perf. 14x14¹/₂

1962, Apr. 2 **Photo.** **Wmk. 314**
Birds in Natural Colors; Black Inscriptions

167 A32 1c yellow 15 15
168 A32 2c gray 15 15
a. Green omitted *100.00*
169 A32 3c lt yel green 15 15
a. Dark grn (legs) omitted *175.00*
170 A32 4c lt gray 15 15
171 A32 5c buff 15 15
172 A32 10c beige 28 16
a. Blue omitted *150.00*
173 A32 15c pale lemon 40 25
174 A32 25c bluish gray & pink 75 45
175 A32 50c pale blue 2.50 1.65
b. Blue (beak & claw) omitted
176 A32 $1 blue 5.75 3.75
177 A32 $2 pale gray 8.00 6.50
178 A32 $5 light blue 25.00 20.00
Nos. 167-178 (12) 43.43 33.51

For overprints see Nos. 182-186, 195-199.

1967 **Wmk. 314 Sideways**
Colors as 1962 Issue

167a A32 1c 15 15
168b A32 2c 15 15
170a A32 4c 28 24
171a A32 5c 55 32
172b A32 10c 80 65
173a A32 15c 1.10 95
175a A32 50c 4.25 3.50
Nos. 167a-175a (7) 7.28 5.96

Issue dates: 1c, 4c, 5c, 50c, Feb. 16, 2c, 10c, 15c, Nov. 28.

Freedom from Hunger Issue
Common Design Type

1963, June 4 ***Perf. 14x14¹/₂***
179 CD314 22c green 85 85

Red Cross Centenary Issue
Common Design Type
Wmk. 314

1963, Sept. 2 **Litho.** ***Perf. 13***
180 CD315 4c black & red 15 15
181 CD315 22c ultra & red 1.40 1.40

Nos. 167, 169, 170, 172 and 174 Overprinted: "SELF GOVERNMENT / 1964"

1964 **Photo.** ***Perf. 14x14¹/₂***
182 A32 1c multicolored 15 15
a. Yellow omitted *125.00*
183 A32 3c multicolored 15 15
184 A32 4c multicolored 15 15
185 A32 10c multicolored 30 30
186 A32 25c multicolored 55 55
Set value 1.09 1.09

Attainment of self-government.

ITU Issue
Common Design Type
Perf. 11x11½

1965, May 17 Litho. Wmk. 314

187 CD317	2c ver & green	15	15
188 CD317	50c yel & red lilac	1.00	1.00

Intl. Cooperation Year Issue
Common Design Type

1965, Oct. 25 ***Perf. 14½***

189 CD318	1c bl grn & claret	15	15
190 CD318	22c lt violet & green	75	75

Churchill Memorial Issue
Common Design Type

1966, Jan. 24 Photo. ***Perf. 14***

Design in Black, Gold and Carmine Rose

191 CD319	1c bright blue	15	15
192 CD319	4c green	15	15
193 CD319	22c brown	65	65
194 CD319	25c violet	90	90

Bird Type of 1962 Overprinted: "DEDICATION OF SITE / NEW CAPITAL / 9th OCTOBER 1965"

Wmk. 314 Sideways

1966, July 1 ***Perf. 14x14½***

195 A32	1c multicolored	15	15
196 A32	3c multicolored	15	15
197 A32	4c multicolored	15	15
198 A32	10c multicolored	25	25
199 A32	25c multicolored	52	52
	Set value	95	95

Citrus Grove — A33

Designs: 10c, Half Moon Cay and Lighthouse Reef. 22c, Hidden Valley Falls and Mountain Pine Ridge. 25c, Xunantunich Mayan ruins in Cayo district.

Perf. 14x14½

1966, Oct. 1 Photo. Wmk. 314

200 A33	5c multicolored	15	15
201 A33	10c multicolored	22	22
202 A33	22c multicolored	48	48
203 A33	25c multicolored	65	65

1st British Honduras stamp issue, cent.

International Tourist Year — A34

1967, Dec. 4 ***Perf. 12½***

204 A34	5c Sailfish	15	15
205 A34	10c Deer	20	20
206 A34	22c Jaguar	42	42
207 A34	25c Tarpon	52	52

Schomburgkia Tibicinis — A35

Belizean Patriots' Memorial, Belize City, and Human Rights Flame — A36

Orchids: 10c, Maxillaria tenuifolia. 22c, Bletia purpurea. 25c, Sobralia macrantha.

Inscribed: "20th Anniversary of E.C.L.A."

Perf. 14½x14

1968, Apr. 16 Photo. Wmk. 314

208 A35	5c violet & multi	15	15
209 A35	10c green & multi	22	22
210 A35	22c multicolored	55	55
211 A35	25c olive & multi	70	70

20th anniv. of the Economic Commission for Latin America. See #226-229, 255-258.

Perf. 13x13½

1968, July 15 Litho. Wmk. 314

Design: 50c, Mayan motif stele, monument at new capital site and Human Rights flame.

212 A36	22c multicolored	30	30
213 A36	50c multicolored	70	70

International Human Rights Year.

Jewfish — A37

Designs: 2c, White-lipped peccary. 3c, Grouper (sea bass). 4c, Collared anteater. 5c, Bonefish. 10c, Paca. 15c, Dolphinfish. 25c, Kinkajou. 50c, Yellow-and-green-banded muttonfish. $1, Tayra. $2, Great barracudas. $5, Mountain lion.

Perf. 13x12½

1968, Oct. 15 Litho. Unwmk.

214 A37	1c yellow & multi	15	15
215 A37	2c brt yel & multi	15	15
216 A37	3c pink & multi	15	15
217 A37	4c brt grn & multi	15	15
218 A37	5c brick red & multi	15	15
219 A37	10c lilac & multi	18	15
220 A37	15c org yel & multi	26	22
221 A37	25c multicolored	45	42
222 A37	50c bl grn & multi	95	85
223 A37	$1 ocher & multi	1.90	1.75
224 A37	$2 violet & multi	3.75	3.50
225 A37	$5 ultra & multi	8.25	7.50
	Nos. 214-225 (12)	16.49	15.14

See Nos. 234-240, 327-339.
For overprints, see Nos. 251-254, 281-282.

Orchid Type of 1968
Inscribed "Orchids of Belize"

Designs: 5c, Rhyncholaetia digbyana. 10c, Cattleya bowringiana. 22c, Lycaste cochleatum. 25c, Coryanthes speciosum.

Perf. 14½x14

1969, Apr. 9 Photo. Wmk. 314

226 A35	5c Prus blue & multi	15	15
227 A35	10c ol bister & multi	30	30
228 A35	22c yel green & multi	70	70
229 A35	25c vio blue & multi	85	85

Hardwood Trees — A38

Virgin and Child, by Giovanni Bellini — A39

1969, Sept. 1 Litho. ***Perf. 14***

230 A38	5c Ziricote	15	15
231 A38	10c Rosewood	20	20
232 A38	22c Mayflower	42	42
233 A38	25c Mahogany	50	50

Timber industry of British Honduras. Issued in sheets of 9 (3x3) on simulated wood background.

Fish-Animal Type of 1968

Designs: ½c, Crana (fish). Others as before.

Wmk. 314 Sideways

1969-72 Litho. ***Perf. 13x12½***

234 A37	½c vio bl, yel & blk	18	18
235 A37	½c cit, blk & bl ('71)	15	15
236 A37	2c brt yel, blk & grn ('72)	15	15
237 A37	3c pink & multi ('72)	20	20
a.	Wmk. upright ('72)	20	20
238 A37	5c brick red & multi, wmk. upright ('72)	28	28
239 A37	10c lilac & multi ('72)	50	50
a.	Wmk. upright ('72)	50	50
240 A37	$5 ultra & multi ('70)	7.75	7.75
	Nos. 234-240 (7)	9.21	9.21

For overprints, see Nos. 251-252.

1969, Oct. 1 Litho. ***Perf. 14***

Christmas: 22c, 25c, Adoration of the Kings, by Veronese.

247 A39	5c multicolored	15	15
248 A39	15c dp orange & multi	26	26
249 A39	22c lilac rose & multi	45	45
250 A39	25c emerald & multi	60	60

Nos. 238-239 and Type of 1968 Overprinted "POPULATION/ CENSUS 1970"

Wmk. 314 Sideways

1970, Feb. 2 Photo. ***Perf. 13x12½***

251 A37	5c brick red & multi	15	15
252 A37	10c lilac & multi	20	20
253 A37	15c org yel & multi	28	28
254 A37	25c multicolored	48	48

Orchid Type of 1968
Inscribed: "Orchids of Belize"

Wmk. 314

1970, Apr. 2 Litho. ***Perf. 14***

255 A35	5c Black	15	15
256 A35	15c White butterfly	38	38
257 A35	22c Swan	60	60
258 A35	25c Butterfly	70	70

Santa Maria Tree and Wood (Calophyllum Brasiliense) — A40

Nativity, by Arthur Hughes — A41

Hardwood Trees and Woods: 15c, Nargusta (terminalia amazonia). 22c, Cedar (cedrela mexicana). 25c, Sapodilla (achras sapota).

1970, Sept. 7 ***Perf. 14***

259 A40	5c multicolored	15	15
260 A40	15c multicolored	30	30
261 A40	22c multicolored	45	45
262 A40	25c multicolored	55	55

1970, Nov. 2 ***Perf. 14***

Christmas: 5c, 15c, 50c, Mystic Nativity, by Botticelli.

263 A41	½c black & multi	15	15
264 A41	5c brown & multi	15	15
265 A41	10c multicolored	18	18
266 A41	15c slate bl & multi	28	28
267 A41	22c dk green & multi	45	45
268 A41	50c black & multi	95	95
	Nos. 263-268 (6)	2.16	2.16

Legislative Assembly House A42

Designs: 5c, View of South Side of Belize. 10c, Government Plaza, Belmopan. 22c, Magistrates' Court. 25c, Police Headquarters. 50c, New General Post Office.

1971, Jan. 30 Litho. ***Perf. 13½x14***

Size: 59x22mm

269 A42	5c multicolored	15	15
270 A42	10c multicolored	15	15

Size: 37x21½mm

271 A42	15c multicolored	25	25
272 A42	22c multicolored	38	38
273 A42	25c multicolored	45	45
274 A42	50c multicolored	85	85
	Nos. 269-274 (6)	2.23	2.23

New capital at Belmopan.

Tabebuia Chrysantha — A43

Flowers: 5c, 22c, Hymenocallis littoralis. 10c, 25c, Hippeastrum equestre. 15c, like ½c.

1971, Mar. 27 Litho. ***Perf. 14***

275 A43	½c vio blue & multi	15	15
276 A43	5c olive & multi	15	15
277 A43	10c violet & multi	22	22
278 A43	15c multicolored	32	32
279 A43	22c multicolored	48	48
280 A43	25c lt brown & multi	60	60
	Nos. 275-280 (6)	1.92	1.92

Easter.

Type of 1968 Overprinted: "RACIAL EQUALITY / YEAR—1971"

Perf. 13x12½

1971, June 14 Litho. Wmk. 314

281 A37	10c lilac & multi	15	15
282 A37	50c blue green & multi	70	70

Intl. year against racial discrimination.

Tubroos (Enterolobium Cyclocarpum) A44

Hardwood Trees of Belize: 15c, Yemeri (Vochysia hondurensis). 26c, Billyweb (Sweetia panamensis). 50c, Logwood (Haematoxylum campechiaum).

1971, Aug. 16 ***Perf. 14***

Queen's Head in Silver

283 A44	5c green, brn & blk	15	15
284 A44	15c multicolored	50	50
285 A44	26c multicolored	85	85
286 A44	50c multicolored	1.50	1.50
a.	Souvenir sheet of 4, #283-286	5.25	5.25

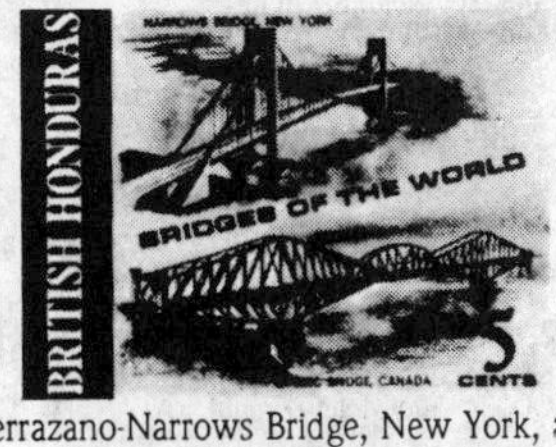

Verrazano-Narrows Bridge, New York, and Quebec Bridge, Canada — A45

Bridges of the World: ½c, Hawksworth Bridge connecting San Ignacio and Santa Helena and Belcan Bridge, Belize, Br. Honduras. 26c, London Bridge in 1871, and at Lake Havasu City, Ariz., in 1971. 50c, Belize-Mexico Bridge and Belize Swing Bridge.

1971, Sept. 23 Litho.

287 A45	½c multicolored	15	15
288 A45	5c multicolored	15	15
289 A45	26c multicolored	55	55
290 A45	50c multicolored	1.10	1.10

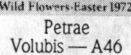

Petrae Volubis — A46

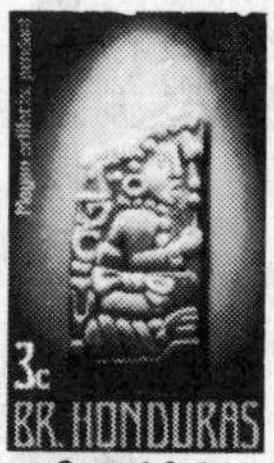

Seated Jade Figure — A47

Wild Flowers: 15c, Vochysia hondurensis. 26c, Tabebuia pentaphylla. 50c, Erythrina americana.

1972, Feb. 28

Flowers in Natural Colors; Black Inscriptions

292	A46	6c lilac & yel	15	15
293	A46	15c lt blue & pale grn	32	32
294	A46	26c pink & lt blue	60	60
295	A46	50c orange & lt grn	1.10	1.10

Easter.

Perf. 14x13½, 13½x14

1972, May 22 Unwmk.

Mayan Carved Jade, 4th-8th centuries: 6c, Dancing priest. 16c, Sun god's head (horiz.). 26c, Priest on throne and sun god's head. 50c, Figure and mask.

296	A47	3c rose red & multi	15	15
297	A47	6c vio bl & multi	15	15
298	A47	16c brn & multi	32	32
299	A47	26c ol grn & multi	52	52
300	A47	50c pur & multi	95	95
		Nos. 296-300 (5)	2.09	2.09

Black inscription with details of designs on back of stamps.

Banak (Virola Koschnyi) — A48

Hardwood Trees of Belize: 5c, Quamwood (Schizolobium parahybum). 16c, Waika chewstick (Symphonia globulifera). 26c, Mammee-apple (Mammea americana). 50c, My lady (Aspidosperma megalocarpon).

1972, Aug. 21 Wmk. 314 *Perf. 14*

Queen's Head in Gold

301	A48	3c brt pink & multi	15	15
302	A48	5c gray & multi	15	15
303	A48	16c green & multi	32	32
304	A48	26c lemon & multi	52	52
305	A48	50c lt violet & multi	1.00	1.00
		Nos. 301-305 (5)	2.14	2.14

Silver Wedding Issue, 1972

Common Design Type

Design: Queen Elizabeth II, Prince Philip and Belize orchids.

1972, Nov. 20 Photo. *Perf. 14x14½*

306	CD324	26c slate grn & multi	42	42
307	CD324	50c violet & multi	80	80

Baron Bliss Day A49

Festivals of Belize: 10c, Labor Day boat race. 26c, Carib Settlement Day dance. 50c, Pan American Day parade.

1973, Mar. 9 Litho. *Perf. 14½*

308	A49	3c dull blue & black	15	15
309	A49	10c red & multi	20	20
310	A49	26c ver & multi	45	45
311	A49	50c black & multi	85	85

See Belize for later issues inscribed "Belize."

SEMI-POSTAL STAMPS

Regular Issue of 1921-29 Surcharged in Black or Red

BELIZE
RELIEF FUND
PLUS
3 CENTS

1932 Wmk. 4 *Perf. 14*

B1	A14	1c + 1c green	1.50	*4.75*
B2	A14	2c + 2c rose red	1.50	*4.75*
B3	A14	3c + 3c orange	2.50	*6.25*
B4	A14	4c + 4c gray (R)	3.25	*9.50*
B5	A14	5c + 5c ultra	5.00	*16.00*
		Nos. B1-B5 (5)	13.75	*41.25*

The surtax was for a fund to aid sufferers from the destruction of the city of Belize by a hurricane in Sept. 1931.

POSTAGE DUE STAMPS

Catalogue values for unused stamps in this section are for Never Hinged items.

D1

1923 Typo. Wmk. 4 *Perf. 14*

J1	D1	1c black	90	*2.50*
J2	D1	2c black	1.10	*2.50*
J3	D1	4c black	3.00	*10.00*

Nos. J1-J3 were re-issued on chalky paper in 1956.

Perf. 13½x13, 13½x14

1965-72 Wmk. 314

J4	D1	2c black ('72)	50	*2.00*
J5	D1	4c black	1.25	*3.00*

WAR TAX STAMPS

Nos. 85, 75 and 77 Overprinted

WAR

1916-17 Wmk. 3 *Perf. 14*

With Moire Overprint

MR1	A11	1c green	18	18
a.		"WAR" inverted	250.00	*250.00*

Without Moire Overprint

MR2	A11	1c green ('17)	18	*18*
MR3	A11	3c orange ('17)	75	75
a.		Double overprint	450.00	*450.00*

Nos. 75 and 77 Overprinted

WAR

1918

MR4	A11	1c green	18	*18*
MR5	A11	3c orange	22	*22*

CANADA

LOCATION — Northern part of North American continent, except for Alaska
GOVT. — Self-governing dominion in the British Commonwealth of Nations
AREA — 3,851,809 sq. mi.
POP. — 24,907,100 (est. 1983)
CAPITAL — Ottawa

Included in the dominion are British Columbia, Vancouver Island, Prince Edward Island, Nova Scotia, New Brunswick and Newfoundland, all of which formerly issued stamps.

12 Pence = 1 Shilling
100 Cents = 1 Dollar (1859)

Catalogue values for unused stamps in this country are for Never Hinged items, beginning with Scott 268 in the regular postage section, Scott B1 in the semi-postal section, Scott C9 in the air post section, Scott CE3 in the air post special delivery section, Scott CO1 in the air post official section, Scott E11 in the special delivery section, Scott EO1 in the special delivery official section, Scott J15 in the postage due section, and Scott O1 in the official section.

Values of early Canada stamps vary according to condition. Quotations for Nos. 1-10 are for fine copies. Fine to very fine and better examples may be expected to sell at higher prices, and inferior or poor copies sell at reduced prices.

Province of Canada

Beaver — A1

Prince Albert — A2

Queen Victoria — A3

1851 Unwmk. Engr. *Imperf.*

Laid Paper

1	A1	3p red	10,000.	350.
2	A2	6p grayish pur	10,000.	550.
a.		Diagonal half used as 3p on cover		
3	A3	12p black	65,000.	27,500.

On some stamps the laid lines of Nos. 1-3 are practically invisible.

1852-55

Wove Paper

4	A1	3p red	1,000.	95.
a.		3p brown red ('53)	1,050.	125.
b.		Diagonal half used as 1½p on cover		*30,000.*
c.		Ribbed paper	2,000.	275.
d.		Thin paper	1,000.	150.
5	A2	6p slate gray ('55)	7,500.	425.
a.		6p brownish gray	9,000.	700.
b.		6p greenish gray	7,500.	650.
c.		Diagonal half used as 3p on cover		*15,500.*
d.		Thick hard paper (gray vio)	9,000.	775.

Re-entries of the 3p are numerous. The main re-entry is distinguishable most easily by the line through "EE" and "PEN."

Most authorities believe the 12p black does not exist on wove paper.

Jacques Cartier — A4

1855

7	A4	10p blue	4,500.	700.
a.		Thick paper	5,500.	1,000.

Queen Victoria A5 A6

1857

8	A5	½p rose	475.	265.
a.		Horizontally ribbed paper	3,000.	1,200.
b.		Vertically ribbed paper	3,750.	1,750.
9	A6	7½p green	5,000.	850.

Very Thick Soft Wove Paper

10	A2	6p reddish pur	11,000.	1,800.
a.		Half used as 3p on cover		*20,000.*

1858-59 Wove Paper *Perf. 12*

11	A5	½p rose	1,400.	425.
12	A1	3p red	2,000.	275.
13	A2	6p brown vio ('59)	5,750.	1,800.
a.		6p gray violet	5,750.	1,800.
b.		Diagonal half used as 3p on cover		

Nos. 11-13 values are for copies with perfs touching the design.

A7

A8

A9

A10

A11

A12

1859

14	A7	1c rose	190.00	22.50
a.		Imperf., pair	2,500.	
15	A8	5c vermilion	175.00	10.00
a.		Imperf., pair	6,000.	
b.		Diagonal half used as 2½c on cover		*5,500.*
16	A9	10c black brn	6,000.	1,800.
a.		Half used as 5c on cover		*7,500.*
17	A9	10c red lilac	450.00	35.00
a.		10c violet	500.00	35.00
b.		10c brown	475.00	35.00
c.		Imperf., pair	4,500.	
d.		Diagonal half used as 5c on cover		*3,500.*
18	A10	12½c yel green	225.00	22.50
a.		12½c blue green	325.00	27.50
b.		Imperf., pair	2,500.	
19	A11	17c blue	450.00	50.00
a.		17c slate blue	575.00	60.00
b.		Imperf., pair	3,000.	

No. 15b was used with a 10c for a 12½c rate.

Imperfs. are without gum.

Re-entries of the 5c are numerous. Many of them are slight and have only small premium value. The major re-entry has many lines of the design double, especially the outlines of the ovals and frame at left. Value, used, about $300.

Nos. 14-13 values are for copies with perfs touching the design.

1864

20	A12	2c rose	325.00	125.00
a.		2c deep claret rose	400.00	150.00
b.		Imperf., pair	1,750.	

Imperfs. are without gum.

Values are for copies with perfs touching the design.

The Scott editorial staff regrettably cannot accept requests to identify, authenticate, or appraise stamps and postal markings.

Dominion of Canada

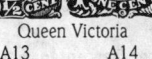

Queen Victoria
A13 A14

A15 A16

A17 A18

A19 A20

1868-76 *Perf. 12, 11½x12 (5c)*

21	A13	½c black	25.00	25.00
a.		Perf. 11½x12 ('73)	25.00	25.00
b.		Watermarked	*16,500.*	*7,000.*
c.		Thin paper	30.00	27.50
22	A14	1c brown red	225.00	32.50
a.		Watermarked	1,200.	125.00
b.		Thin paper	250.00	32.50
23	A14	1c yellow org	400.00	55.00
a.		1c deep orange	500.00	55.00
24	A15	2c green	225.00	22.50
a.		Watermarked	1,750.	150.00
b.		Thin paper	250.00	30.00
c.		Diagonal half used as 1c on cover		*3,000.*
25	A16	3c red	400.00	10.00
a.		Watermarked	2,000.	140.00
b.		Thin paper	500.00	12.00
26	A17	5c ol grn ('75)	475.00	50.00
27	A18	6c dark brown	400.00	30.00
a.		6c yellow brown	375.00	27.50
b.		Watermarked	3,250.	850.00
c.		Thin paper	550.00	45.00
d.		Diagonal half used as 3c on cover		*2,500.*
e.		Vertical half used as 3c on cover		
28	A19	12½c blue	250.00	32.50
a.		Watermarked	1,500.	125.00
b.		Thin paper	300.00	50.00
c.		Horiz. pair, imperf. vert.		
d.		Vert. pair, imperf. horiz.		
29	A20	15c gray violet	30.00	18.00
a.		Perf. 11½x12 ('74)	525.00	80.00
b.		15c red lilac	600.00	42.50
c.		Wmk. (Clutha Mills)	3,000.	500.00
d.		Imperf., pair	800.00	
e.		Thin paper	450.00	55.00
30	A20	15c gray	40.00	18.00
a.		Perf. 11½x12 ('73)	600.00	80.00
b.		15c blue gray ('75)	27.50	22.50
c.		Very thick paper (dp vio)	3,000.	800.00
d.		Script wmk., Perf. 11½x12, ('76)	6,500.	2,250.

The watermark on Nos. 21b, 22a, 24a, 25a, 27b, 28a and 29c consists of double-lined letters reading: "E. & G. BOTHWELL CLUTHA MILLS." The script watermark on No. 30d reads in full: "Alexr. Pirie & Sons."

The existence of No. 28c has been questioned.

1868 Laid Paper

31	A14	1c brown red	10,000.	1,750.
32	A15	2c green		*160,000.*
33	A16	3c bright red	9,500.	400.

Montreal and Ottawa Printings

A21 A22 A23

A24 A25

A26 A27

1870-89 Wove Paper *Perf. 12*

34	A21	½c black ('82)	4.25	4.25
a.		Imperf., pair	350.00	
b.		Pair, imperf. between	650.00	
35	A22	1c yellow	15.00	50
a.		1c orange ('70)	70.00	4.50
b.		Imperf., pair	200.00	
c.		Diagonal half used as ½c on cover		3,500.
36	A23	2c green ('72)	15.00	90
a.		Imperf., pair	250.00	
b.		Diagonal half used as 1c on cover		575.00
c.		Vertical half used as 1c on cover		
d.		2c blue green ('89)	30.00	2.50
f.		Double impression		
37	A24	3c dull red ('72)	35.00	1.25
a.		3c rose ('71)	200.00	5.00
b.		3c copper red ('70)	650.00	12.50
c.		3c orange red ('73)	32.50	90
38	A25	5c sl green ('76)	185.00	8.25
39	A26	6c yel brn ('72)	175.00	9.00
a.		Diagonal half used as 3c on cover		500.00
40	A27	10c dull rose lilac ('77)	300.00	25.00
a.		10c magenta ('80)	225.00	27.50
b.		10c deep lilac rose	225.00	27.50

Copies of Nos. 36b and 36c postmarked "Halifax" are a private speculation.

1870 *Perf. 12½*

37d	A24	3c copper red (Ottawa)	4,500.	575.

1873-79 *Perf. 11½x12*

35d	A22	1c orange	90.00	6.50
36e	A23	2c green	105.00	10.00
37e	A24	3c red	110.00	5.00
38a	A25	5c slate green	250.00	17.00
39b	A26	6c yellow brown	325.00	17.00
40c	A27	10c pale milky rose lilac ('74)	450.00	135.00

The gum on Nos. 35d-40c is always dull and usually blotchy or streaky. It is distinct from the earlier clear, smooth gum and from the bright shiny gums of the later periods.

Nos. 38 and 40 were printed at Montreal. Printings of Nos. 34 to 37, and 39 were made at Ottawa or Montreal and can be separated only by differences in paper and gum.

Ottawa Printing

A28 A29

1888-93 *Perf. 12*

41	A24	3c brt vermilion	10.50	30
a.		3c rose carmine	200.00	2.75
42	A25	5c gray	25.00	2.50
43	A26	6c red brown	25.00	4.75
a.		6c chocolate ('90)	32.50	7.25
44	A28	8c gray ('93)	25.00	2.00
a.		8c blue gray	25.00	2.00
b.		8c slate	25.00	2.00
c.		8c violet black	25.00	2.00
45	A27	10c brown red	75.00	18.00
a.		10c dull rose	80.00	18.00
b.		10c pink	80.00	22.50
46	A29	20c ver ('93)	115.00	30.00
47	A29	50c dp blue ('93)	150.00	20.00

Stamps of the 1870-93 issues are found on paper varying from very thin to thick, also occasionally on paper showing a distinctly ribbed surface.

The gum on Nos. 41-47 appears bright and shiny, often with a yellowish tint.

Imperf., Pairs

41b	A24	3c	200.00
42a	A25	5c	300.00
43b	A26	6c	350.00
44d	A28	8c	300.00
45c	A27	10c	250.00
46a	A29	20c	675.00
47a	A29	50c	675.00

Jubilee Issue

Queen Victoria, "1837" and "1897" — A30

1897, June 19 Unwmk. *Perf. 12*

50	A30	½c	black	40.00	40.00
51	A30	1c	orange	3.50	2.25
52	A30	2c	green	3.50	3.50
53	A30	3c	bright rose	2.75	85
54	A30	5c	deep blue	11.50	11.00
55	A30	6c	yellow brown	60.00	75.00
56	A30	8c	dark violet	14.00	9.50
57	A30	10c	brown violet	37.50	37.50
58	A30	15c	steel blue	70.00	60.00
59	A30	20c	vermilion	65.00	62.50
60	A30	50c	ultra	65.00	65.00
61	A30	$1	lake	400.00	475.00
62	A30	$2	dk purple	650.00	275.00
63	A30	$3	yel bister	775.00	675.00
64	A30	$4	purple	775.00	675.00
65	A30	$5	olive green	800.00	625.00
			Nos. 50-60 (11)	372.75	367.10

60th year of Queen Victoria's reign.

Roller and smudged cancels on Nos. 61-65 sell for less.

A31

A32

1897-98

66	A31	½c	black	3.00	2.75
67	A31	1c	blue green	6.50	45
68	A31	2c	purple	7.50	65
69	A31	3c	carmine ('98)	7.50	15
70	A31	5c	dk bl, *bluish*	32.50	2.75
71	A31	6c	brown	30.00	10.50
72	A31	8c	orange	45.00	5.00
73	A31	10c	brown vio ('98)	82.50	30.00
			Nos. 66-73 (8)	214.50	52.25

For surcharge, see No. 87.

Imperf., Pairs

66a	A31	½c	300.00
67a	A31	1c	300.00
68a	A31	2c	300.00
69a	A31	3c	600.00
70a	A31	5c	300.00
71a	A31	6c	600.00
72a	A31	8c	300.00
73a	A31	10c	350.00

1898-1902

TWO CENTS:
Type I - Frame of four very thin lines.
Type II - Frame of a thick line between two thin ones.

74	A32	½c	black	90	70
75	A32	1c	gray green	5.50	15
76	A32	2c	purple (I)	6.25	15
a.			Thick paper	65.00	6.00
77	A32	2c	car (I) ('99)	7.75	15
a.			2c carmine (II)	8.50	18
b.			Booklet pane of 6 (II)	650.00	*650.00*
78	A32	3c	carmine	10.50	25
79	A32	5c	blue, *bluish*	37.50	52
80	A32	6c	brown	50.00	20.00
81	A32	7c	ol yel ('02)	32.50	9.00
82	A32	8c	orange	62.50	11.00
83	A32	10c	brown vio	70.00	9.00
84	A32	20c	ol grn ('00)	150.00	42.50
			Nos. 74-84 (11)	433.40	93.42

For surcharges, see Nos. 88-88C.

Imperf., Pairs

74a	A32	½c	200.
75a	A32	1c	600.
77c	A32	2c	180.
79a	A32	5c	600.
80a	A32	6c	600.
81a	A32	7c	225.
82a	A32	8c	600.
83a	A32	10c	600.
84a	A32	20c	1,500.

Imperial Penny Postage Issue

Map of British Empire on Mercator Projection — A33

1898, Dec. 7 Engr. & Typo.

85	A33	2c	black, lav & car	11.00	5.00
a.			Imperf., pair	250.00	
86	A33	2c	black, bl & car	11.00	5.00
a.			Imperf., pair	250.00	

Imperfs. are without gum.

Nos. 69 and 78 Surcharged in Black **2 CENTS**

1899, July

87	A31	2c on 3c carmine	4.00	2.25
88	A32	2c on 3c carmine	4.50	2.00

No. 78 Surcharged in Blue or Violet

A32a

A32b

1899, Jan. 5

88B A32a 1(c) on ⅓rd of 3c (Bl)
88C A32b 2(c) on ⅔rds of 3c (V)

Nos. 88B-88C were prepared and used at Port Hood, Nova Scotia, without official authorization.

King Edward VII — A34

1903-08 Engr.

89	A34	1c	green	5.75	15
90	A34	2c	carmine	5.75	15
b.			Booklet pane of 6	725.00	*725.00*
91	A34	5c	blue, *blue*	30.00	1.75
92	A34	7c	olive bister	18.00	1.75
93	A34	10c	brown lilac	50.00	3.50
94	A34	20c	olive green	190.00	16.00
95	A34	50c	purple ('08)	225.00	35.00
			Nos. 89-95 (7)	524.50	58.30

Imperf., Pairs

89a	A34	1c	400.00	
90a	A34	2c	22.50	25.00
91a	A34	5c	625.00	
92a	A34	7c	400.00	
93a	A34	10c	700.00	

Nos. 89a, 91a, 92a, 93a are without gum.

Quebec Tercentenary Issue

Prince and Princess of Wales, 1908 — A35

Jacques Cartier and Samuel de Champlain A36

Queen Alexandra and King Edward — A37

Champlain's Home in Quebec — A38

Generals Montcalm and Wolfe — A39

View of Quebec in 1700 — A40

Champlain's Departure for the West — A41

Arrival of Cartier at Quebec — A42

1908, July 16

96	A35	½c black brown	2.00	1.75
97	A36	1c blue green	3.75	1.75
98	A37	2c carmine	5.75	55
99	A38	5c dark blue	22.00	14.00
100	A39	7c olive green	27.50	18.00
101	A40	10c dk violet	42.50	27.50
102	A41	15c red org	52.50	42.50
103	A42	20c yel brown	70.00	47.50
		Nos. 96-103 (8)	226.00	153.55

Imperf., Pairs

96a	A35	½c	350.00
97a	A36	1c	350.00
98a	A37	2c	350.00
99a	A38	5c	350.00
100a	A39	7c	350.00
101a	A40	10c	350.00
102a	A41	15c	350.00
103a	A42	20c	350.00

King George V — A43

1912-25

104	A43	1c green	3.00	15
a.		Booklet pane of 6	17.00	17.00
105	A43	1c yellow ('22)	2.50	15
a.		Booklet pane of 4 + 2 labels	32.50	32.50
b.		Booklet pane of 6	21.00	21.00
106	A43	2c carmine	3.00	15
a.		Booklet pane of 6	18.00	18.00
107	A43	2c yel green ('22)	2.25	15
a.		Thin paper ('24)	2.25	2.25
b.		Booklet pane of 4 + 2 labels	27.50	27.50
c.		Booklet pane of 6	250.00	250.00
108	A43	3c brown ('18)	3.00	15
a.		Booklet pane of 4 + 2 labels	65.00	65.00
109	A43	3c car ('23)	2.75	15
a.		Booklet pane of 4 + 2 labels	25.00	25.00
110	A43	4c ol bis ('22)	9.00	75
111	A43	5c dark blue	32.50	15
112	A43	5c violet ('22)	5.50	15
a.		Thin paper ('24)	9.00	3.25
113	A43	7c yel ocher	12.00	75
a.		7c olive bister	13.00	85
114	A43	7c red brown ('24)	6.75	3.00
115	A43	8c blue ('25)	11.50	3.25
116	A43	10c plum	50.00	38
117	A43	10c blue ('22)	15.00	55
118	A43	10c bis brn ('25)	12.00	55
119	A43	20c olive green	22.50	32
120	A43	50c blk brn ('25)	24.00	85
a.		50c black	45.00	2.00
122	A43	$1 orange ('23)	47.50	3.25
		Nos. 104-122 (18)	264.75	14.85
		Set, never hinged	475.00	

For type A43 perforated 12x8 see No. 184.
For surcharges, see Nos. 139-140.

Imperf., Pairs

110a	A43	4c	700.
112b	A43	5c	700.
114a	A43	7c	700.
115a	A43	8c	700.
118a	A43	10c	700.
119a	A43	20c	775.
120b	A43	50c	950.
122a	A43	$1	950.

Coil Stamps

1912 ***Perf. 8 Horizontally***

123	A43	1c dark green	30.00	26.00
		Never hinged	55.00	
124	A43	2c carmine	30.00	26.00
		Never hinged	55.00	

1912-24 ***Perf. 8 Vertically***

125	A43	1c green	6.00	40
		Never hinged	11.00	
126	A43	1c yellow ('23)	4.00	3.25
		Never hinged	8.00	
a.		Block of 4	25.00	25.00
127	A43	2c carmine	9.00	35
		Never hinged	14.00	
128	A43	2c green ('22)	4.00	40
		Never hinged	8.50	
a.		Block of 4	25.00	25.00
129	A43	3c brown ('18)	3.75	40
		Never hinged	8.00	
130	A43	3c carmine ('24)	27.50	3.00
		Never hinged	50.00	
a.		Block of 4	450.00	450.00
		Nos. 125-130 (6)	54.25	7.80

Nos. 126a, 128a and 130a were supplied to the Postal Agency in sheets. Nos. 126a and 128a exist on thick and thin paper. No. 130a exists on thick paper only.

1915-24 ***Perf. 12 Horizontally***

131	A43	1c dark green	3.25	4.00
		Never hinged	5.25	
132	A43	2c carmine	8.50	6.00
		Never hinged	16.00	
133	A43	2c yellow grn ('24)	40.00	42.50
		Never hinged	60.00	
134	A43	3c brown ('21)	3.25	3.50
		Never hinged	5.75	

"The Fathers of Confederation" A44

1917, Sept. 15 ***Perf. 12***

135	A44	3c brown	11.50	28
		Never hinged	22.50	
a.		Imperf., pair	300.00	

50th anniv. of the Canadian Confederation. Imperfs. are without gum.

1924 ***Imperf.***

136	A43	1c yellow	27.50	27.50
		Never hinged	40.00	
137	A43	2c green	20.00	20.00
		Never hinged	37.50	
138	A43	3c carmine	12.00	14.00
		Never hinged	18.00	

No. 109 Surcharged:

2 CENTS
a

2
CENTS
b

1926 ***Perf. 12***

139	A43(a)	2c on 3c car	32.50	35.00
		Never hinged	45.00	
a.		Pair, one without surcharge	250.00	
b.		Double surcharge	150.00	
140	A43(b)	2c on 3c car	12.50	14.00
		Never hinged	15.00	
a.		Double surcharge	150.00	
b.		Triple surcharge	150.00	

Sir John A. Macdonald A45

Sir Wilfrid Laurier A48

"The Fathers of Confederation" — A46

Parliament Building at Ottawa — A47

Map of Canada — A49

1927, June 29

141	A45	1c orange	1.25	25
		Never hinged	2.00	
142	A46	2c green	85	15
		Never hinged	1.50	

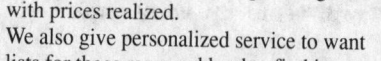

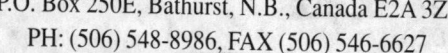

143 A47 3c brn carmine 3.75 1.75
Never hinged 6.00
144 A48 5c violet 2.50 80
Never hinged 4.00
145 A49 12c dark blue 7.50 1.65
Never hinged 12.00
Nos. 141-145 (5) 15.85 4.60

60th year of the Canadian Confederation. Nos. 141-145 exist partly perforated.

Imperf., Pairs

141a	A45	1c	75.00
142a	A46	2c	75.00
143a	A47	3c	75.00
144a	A48	5c	75.00
145a	A49	12c	75.00

Thomas d'Arcy McGee A50

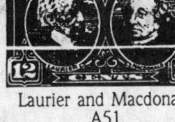

Laurier and Macdonald A51

Robert Baldwin and Sir Louis Hippolyte Lafontaine A52

1927, June 29

146 A50 5c violet 1.75 1.00
Never hinged 2.25
147 A51 12c green 4.75 2.00
Never hinged 6.00
148 A52 20c brown carmine 11.00 2.50
Never hinged 14.00

Nos. 146-148 were to have been issued in July, 1926, as a commemorative series, but were withheld and issued June 29, 1927. They exist partly perforated.

Imperf., Pairs

146a	A32	5c	80.00
147a	A32	12c	80.00
148a	A32	20c	80.00

King George V — A53

Mt. Hurd from Bell-Smith's Painting "The Ice-crowned Monarch of the Rockies" — A54

Quebec Bridge — A55

Harvesting Wheat — A56

Schooner "Bluenose" A57

Parliament Building — A58

1928-29

149 A53 1c orange 90 16
Never hinged 2.00
a. Booklet pane of 6 9.00 9.00
150 A53 2c green 50 15
Never hinged 1.00
a. Booklet pane of 6 18.00 18.00
151 A53 3c dk carmine 6.00 5.50
Never hinged 16.00
152 A53 4c bister ('29) 5.25 3.00
Never hinged 10.00
153 A53 5c dp violet 2.50 1.40
Never hinged 6.25
a. Booklet pane of 6 50.00 50.00
154 A53 8c blue 4.00 2.75
Never hinged 9.00
155 A54 10c green 4.25 45
Never hinged 9.00
156 A55 12c gray ('29) 6.00 2.75
Never hinged 14.00
157 A56 20c dk car ('29) 10.50 4.25
Never hinged 24.00
158 A57 50c dk blue ('29) 110.00 25.00
Never hinged 175.00
159 A58 $1 olive grn ('29) 125.00 30.00
Never hinged 200.00
Nos. 149-159 (11) 274.90 75.41

Nos. 149 to 159 exist partly perforated.

Imperf., Pairs

149b	A53	1c	40.00
150b	A53	2c	40.00
151a	A53	3c	47.50
152a	A53	4c	47.50
153b	A53	5c	47.50
154a	A53	8c	47.50
155a	A53	10c	75.00
156a	A53	12c	75.00
157a	A53	20c	75.00
158a	A53	50c	400.00
159a	A53	$1	400.00

Coil Stamps

1929 ***Perf. 8 Vertically***

160 A53 1c orange 11.00 10.00
Never hinged 18.00
Precanceled 3.00
161 A53 2c green 9.25 1.75
Never hinged 12.00

King George V A59

Library of Parliament A60

The Citadel at Quebec — A61

Harvesting Wheat — A62

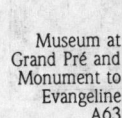

Museum at Grand Pré and Monument to Evangeline A63

Mt. Edith Cavell — A64

Two dies of 2c.
Die I - The top of the letter "P" encloses a tiny dot of color.
Die II - The top of the "P" encloses a larger spot of color than in die I. The "P" appears almost like a "D."
There are two dies of the 1c also, but differences are trivial.

1930-31 ***Perf. 11***

162 A59 1c orange 65 35
Never hinged 85
163 A59 1c deep green 90 15
Never hinged 1.40
a. Booklet pane of 4 + 2 labels 80.00 80.00
c. Booklet pane of 6 9.00 9.00
164 A59 2c dull green (I) 70 15
Never hinged 85
a. Booklet pane of 6 15.00 15.00
165 A59 2c deep red (II) 1.00 15
Never hinged 1.50
a. Die I 80 15
Never hinged 1.10
b. Booklet pane of 6 (I) 13.00 13.00
166 A59 2c dk brn (II) ('31) 70 15
Never hinged 95
a. Booklet pane of 4 + 2 labels (II) 75.00 75.00
b. Die I 2.50 2.50
Never hinged 4.25
c. Booklet pane of 6 (I) 17.50 17.50
167 A59 3c deep red ('31) 1.25 15
Never hinged 2.00
a. Booklet pane of 4 + 2 labels 17.50 17.50
168 A59 4c yel bister 4.00 2.25
Never hinged 8.50
169 A59 5c dull violet 2.50 1.90
Never hinged 4.25
170 A59 5c dull blue 1.75 15
Never hinged 2.50
171 A59 8c dark blue 8.00 3.75
Never hinged 17.00
172 A59 8c red orange 2.75 1.50
Never hinged 5.00
173 A60 10c olive green 4.00 75
Never hinged 8.50
174 A61 12c gray black 6.25 3.00
Never hinged 15.00
175 A62 20c brown red 12.00 25
Never hinged 25.00
176 A63 50c dull blue 85.00 9.50
Never hinged 165.00
177 A64 $1 dk ol green 85.00 16.00
Never hinged 165.00
Nos. 162-177 (16) 216.45 40.15

No. 169 was printed from both flat and rotary press plates.
See No. 201. For surcharge, see No. 191. For overprint, see No. 203.

Imperf., Pairs

163d	A59	1c	1,100.
173a	A60	10c	1,100.
174a	A61	12c	500.
175a	A62	20c	500.
176a	A63	50c	750.
177a	A64	$1	750.

Coil Stamps

1930-31 ***Perf. 8½ Vertically***

178 A59 1c orange 6.00 4.75
Never hinged 8.50
179 A59 1c deep green 3.50 3.50
Never hinged 5.50
180 A59 2c dull green 3.00 2.00
Never hinged 4.25
181 A59 2c deep red 7.50 1.50
Never hinged 10.00
182 A59 2c dark brown ('31) 5.25 45
Never hinged 8.50
183 A59 3c deep red ('31) 7.50 32
Never hinged 12.50
Nos. 178-183 (6) 32.75 12.52

George V Type of 1912-25

1931, June 24 ***Perf. 12x8***

184 A43 3c carmine 1.75 1.75
Never hinged 2.75

Sir Georges Etienne Cartier — A65

1931, Sept. 30 ***Perf. 11***

190 A65 10c dark green 4.75 15
Never hinged 6.00
a. Imperf., pair 250.00

Nos. 165, 165a Surcharged **3**

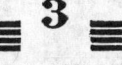

1932, June 21

191 A59 3c on 2c dp red (II) 70 15
Never hinged 1.00
a. Die I 1.50 1.00
Never hinged 2.00

King George V — A66

Edward, Prince of Wales — A67

Allegory of British Empire — A68

1932, July 12

192 A66 3c deep red 45 15
Never hinged 55
193 A67 5c dull blue 3.50 1.40
Never hinged 4.00
194 A68 13c deep green 4.00 3.25
Never hinged 5.00

Imperial Economic Conference, Ottawa.

Type of 1930 and

King George V — A69

1932, Dec. 1

195 A69 1c dark green 45 15
Never hinged 55
a. Booklet pane of 4 + 2 labels 62.50 62.50
b. Booklet pane of 6 20.00 20.00
196 A69 2c black brown 55 15
Never hinged 80
a. Booklet pane of 4 + 2 labels 62.50 62.50
b. Booklet pane of 6 15.00 15.00
197 A69 3c deep red 75 15
Never hinged 1.00
a. Booklet pane of 4 + 2 labels 20.00 20.00
198 A69 4c ocher 18.00 2.75
Never hinged 37.50
199 A69 5c dark blue 3.50 15
Never hinged 5.75
a. Horiz. pair, imperf. vert. 500.00
200 A69 8c red orange 11.00 1.75
Never hinged 20.00
201 A61 13c dull violet 17.00 1.50
Never hinged 27.50
Nos. 195-201 (7) 51.25 6.60

Type A66 has at the foot of the stamp "OTTAWA CONFERENCE 1932". This inscription does not appear on the stamps of type A69.

Imperf., Pairs

195c	A69	1c	130.00
196c	A69	2c	130.00
197b	A69	3c	130.00
198a	A69	4c	130.00
199b	A69	5c	130.00
200a	A69	8c	130.00
201a	A69	13c	400.00

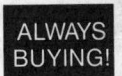

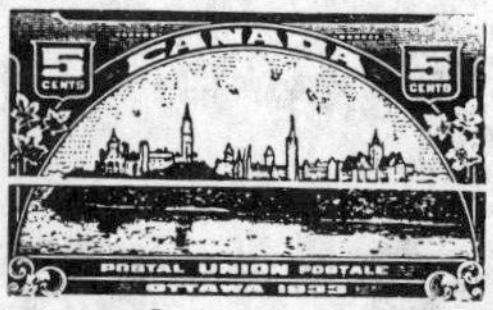
Government Buildings, Ottawa — A70

1933, May 18

202 A70 5c dark blue 5.00 2.00
Never hinged 7.00
a. Imperf., pair 375.00

Meeting of the Executive Committee of the UPU at Ottawa, May and June, 1933.

WORLD'S GRAIN EXHIBITION & CONFERENCE

No. 175 Overprinted in Blue

REGINA 1933

1933, July 24

203 A62 20c brown red 18.00 9.00
Never hinged 27.00
a. Imperf., pair 375.00

World's Grain Exhibition and Conference at Regina.

Steamship Royal William A71

1933, Aug. 17

204 A71 5c dark blue 5.00 1.75
Never hinged 7.00
a. Imperf., pair 375.00

Centenary of the linking by steam of the Dominion, then a colony, with Great Britain, the mother country. The Royal William's 1833 voyage was the first Trans-Atlantic passage under steam all the way.

George V Type of 1932
Coil Stamps

1933 *Perf. 8½ Vertically*

205 A69 1c dark green 9.00 1.50
Never hinged 12.00
206 A69 2c black brown 9.00 60
Never hinged 12.50
207 A69 3c deep red 7.00 24
Never hinged 10.00

Cartier's Arrival at Quebec — A72

1934, July 1 *Perf. 11*

208 A72 3c blue 1.90 80
Never hinged 3.25
a. Imperf., pair 375.00

Landing of Jacques Cartier, 400th anniv.

Group from Loyalists Monument, Hamilton, Ontario A73

1934, July 1

209 A73 10c olive green 11.00 6.00
Never hinged 18.00
a. Imperf., pair 700.00

Emigration of the United Empire Loyalists from the US to Canada, 150th anniv.

Seal of New Brunswick — A74

1934, Aug. 16

210 A74 2c red brown 1.10 1.10
Never hinged 1.75
a. Imperf., pair 375.00

150th anniv. of the founding of the Province of New Brunswick.

Princess Elizabeth A75

Duke of York A76

King George V and Queen Mary A77

Prince of Wales A78

Windsor Castle — A79

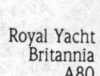

Royal Yacht Britannia A80

1935, May 4 *Perf. 12*

211 A75 1c green 28 18
Never hinged 50
212 A76 2c brown 42 15
Never hinged 90
213 A77 3c carmine 1.10 15
Never hinged 2.25
214 A78 5c blue 2.75 1.90
Never hinged 4.75
215 A79 10c green 3.00 1.65
Never hinged 5.00
216 A80 13c dark blue 4.25 3.50
Never hinged 7.25
Nos. 211-216 (6) 11.80 7.53

25th anniv. of the accession to the throne of George V.

Imperf., Pairs

211a A75 1c 90.00
212a A76 2c 90.00
213a A77 3c 90.00
214a A78 5c 90.00
215a A79 10c 90.00
216b A80 13c 90.00

King George V — A81

Royal Canadian Mounted Police — A82

Confederation Conference at Charlottetown, 1864 — A83

Niagara Falls — A84

Parliament Buildings, Victoria, B.C. — A85

Champlain Monument, Quebec — A86

1935, June 1

217 A81 1c green 16 15
Never hinged 25
a. Booklet pane of 4 + 2 labels 40.00 40.00
b. Booklet pane of 6 13.00 13.00
218 A81 2c brown 18 15
Never hinged 30
a. Booklet pane of 4 + 2 labels 40.00 40.00
b. Booklet pane of 6 10.00 10.00
219 A81 3c dark car 28 15
Never hinged 45
a. Booklet pane of 4 + 2 labels 13.00 13.00
220 A81 4c yellow 1.50 30
Never hinged 2.50
221 A81 5c blue 1.50 15
Never hinged 2.50
a. Horiz. pair, imperf. vert. 65.00
222 A81 8c dp orange 1.50 1.25
Never hinged 2.50
223 A82 10c car rose 4.25 15
Never hinged 7.00
224 A83 13c violet 4.25 45
Never hinged 7.00
225 A84 20c olive green 12.00 28
Never hinged 20.00
226 A85 50c dull violet 16.00 3.00
Never hinged 26.00
227 A86 $1 deep blue 32.50 6.00
Never hinged 52.50
Nos. 217-227 (11) 74.12 12.03

Imperf., Pairs

217c A81 1c 85.00
218c A81 2c 85.00
219b A81 3c 85.00
220a A81 4c 85.00
221b A81 5c 85.00
222a A81 8c 85.00
223a A82 10c 140.00
224a A83 13c 140.00
225a A84 20c 140.00
226a A85 50c 140.00
227a A86 $1 160.00

Coil Stamps

1935 *Perf. 8 Vertically*

228 A81 1c green 6.50 1.50
Never hinged 10.00
229 A81 2c brown 5.50 50
Never hinged 8.50
230 A81 3c dark carmine 5.50 25
Never hinged 8.50

George VI — A87

George VI and Queen Elizabeth — A88

1937 *Perf. 12*

231 A87 1c green 20 15
Never hinged 32
a. Booklet pane of 4 + 2 labels 8.50 8.50
b. Booklet pane of 6 1.00 1.00
232 A87 2c brown 30 15
Never hinged 45
a. Booklet pane of 4 + 2 labels 5.00 5.00
b. Booklet pane of 6 2.50 2.50
233 A87 3c carmine 40 15
Never hinged 52
a. Booklet pane of 4 + 2 labels 1.50 1.50
234 A87 4c yellow 1.50 15
Never hinged 2.50
235 A87 5c blue 1.65 15
Never hinged 2.25
236 A87 8c orange 1.75 45
Never hinged 2.75
Nos. 231-236 (6) 5.80
Set value 80

Imperf., Pairs

231c A87 1c 85.00
232c A87 2c 85.00
233b A87 3c 85.00
234a A87 4c 85.00
235a A87 5c 85.00
236a A87 8c 85.00

1937, May 10

237 A88 3c carmine 15 15
Never hinged 35
a. Imperf., pair 300.00

Coronation of King George VI and Queen Elizabeth.

George VI Types of 1937
Coil Stamps

1937 *Perf. 8 Vertically*

238 A87 1c green 70 50
Never hinged 1.00
239 A87 2c brown 1.10 15
Never hinged 1.50
240 A87 3c carmine 1.75 15
Never hinged 2.50
Set value 68

Memorial Chamber, Parliament Building, Ottawa — A89

Entrance to Halifax Harbor — A90

Fort Garry Gate, Winnipeg A91

Vancouver Harbor — A92

Chateau de Ramezay, Montreal A93

1938 *Perf. 12*

241 A89 10c dk carmine	2.50	15
Never hinged	4.00	
a. 10c carmine rose	4.00	15
Never hinged	7.00	
242 A90 13c deep blue	4.50	25
Never hinged	8.00	
243 A91 20c red brown	9.00	18
Never hinged	16.00	
244 A92 50c green	11.50	3.00
Never hinged	21.00	
245 A93 $1 dull violet	35.00	3.50
Never hinged	60.00	
a. Vert. pair, imperf., horiz.	1,750.	
Nos. 241-245 (5)	62.50	7.08

Imperf., Pairs

241b	A89	10c	125.00
242a	A90	13c	125.00
243a	A91	20c	125.00
244a	A92	50c	125.00
245b	A93	$1	250.00

Princess Elizabeth and Princess Margaret Rose — A94

War Memorial, Ottawa — A95

King George VI and Queen Elizabeth A96

Unwmk.

1939, May 15 **Engr.** *Perf. 12*

246 A94 1c green & black	15	15
Never hinged	18	
247 A95 2c brown & black	15	15
Never hinged	18	
248 A96 3c dk car & black	15	15
Never hinged	18	
Set value		25

Visit of George VI and Queen Elizabeth to Canada and the US.

Imperf., Pairs

246a	A94	1c	140.00
247a	A95	2c	140.00
248a	A96	3c	140.00

King George VI

A97 A98 A99

Grain Elevators A100

Farm Scene A101

Parliament Buildings A102

"Ram" Tank A103

Corvette A104

Munitions Factory — A105

Destroyer A106

1942-43 **Engr.** *Perf. 12*

249 A97 1c green	15	15
Never hinged	18	
a. Booklet pane of 4 + 2 labels	2.50	2.50
b. Booklet pane of 6	1.00	1.00
c. Booklet pane of 3	1.00	1.00
250 A98 2c brown	22	15
Never hinged	26	
a. Booklet pane of 4 + 2 labels	2.50	2.50
b. Booklet pane of 6	2.50	2.50
251 A99 3c dk carmine	22	15
Never hinged	28	
a. Booklet pane of 4 + 2 labels	1.10	1.10
252 A99 3c rose violet ('43)	20	15
Never hinged	25	
a. Booklet pane of 4 + 2 labels	1.00	1.00
b. Booklet pane of 3	1.40	1.40
c. Booklet pane of 6	2.50	2.50
253 A100 4c greenish black	80	60
Never hinged	1.00	
254 A98 4c dk car ('43)	20	15
Never hinged	25	
a. Booklet pane of 6	1.10	1.10
b. Booklet pane of 3	1.25	1.25
255 A97 5c deep blue	55	15
Never hinged	70	
256 A101 8c red brown	1.10	25
Never hinged	1.50	
257 A102 10c brown	2.25	15
Never hinged	3.00	
258 A103 13c dull green	3.00	2.00
Never hinged	4.00	
259 A103 14c dull grn ('43)	4.50	15
Never hinged	6.00	
260 A104 20c chocolate	3.75	15
Never hinged	5.00	
261 A105 50c violet	15.00	1.10
Never hinged	20.00	
262 A106 $1 deep blue	40.00	4.00
Never hinged	52.00	
Nos. 249-262 (14)	71.94	9.30

Canada's contribution to the war effort of the Allied Nations.

For overprints, see Nos. O1-O4.

Imperf., Pairs

249d	A97	1c	90.00
250c	A98	2c	90.00
251b	A99	3c	90.00
252d	A99	3c	90.00
253a	A100	4c	90.00
254c	A98	4c	90.00
255a	A97	5c	90.00
256a	A100	8c	90.00
257a	A102	10c	225.00
258a	A103	13c	225.00
259a	A103	14c	225.00
260a	A104	20c	225.00
261a	A105	50c	225.00
262a	A106	$1	350.00

Types of 1942
Coil Stamps

1942-43 ***Perf. 8 Vertically***

263 A97 1c green	50	20
Never hinged	1.00	
264 A98 2c brown	75	45
Never hinged	1.50	
265 A99 3c dark carmine	75	45
Never hinged	1.50	
266 A99 3c rose violet ('43)	1.25	15
Never hinged	2.50	
267 A98 4c dk carmine ('43)	1.75	15
Never hinged	3.50	
Nos. 263-267 (5)	5.00	1.40

See Nos. 278-281.

Catalogue values for unused stamps in this section, from this point to the end of the section, are for Never Hinged items.

Farm Scene, Ontario — A107

Great Bear Lake, Mackenzie A108

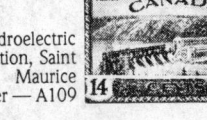

Hydroelectric Station, Saint Maurice River — A109

Combine A110

Logging, British Columbia A111

Train Ferry, Prince Edward Island — A112

1946, Sept. 16 **Engr.** *Perf. 12*

268 A107 8c red brown	1.10	30
269 A108 10c olive	1.10	15
270 A109 14c black brown	2.50	15
271 A110 20c slate black	2.50	15
272 A111 50c dk blue green	14.00	1.25
273 A112 $1 red violet	32.50	1.65
Nos. 268-273 (6)	53.70	3.65

For overprints, see Nos. O6-O10, O21-O23, O25.

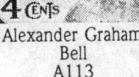

Alexander Graham Bell A113

Citizen of Canada A114

1947, Mar. 3

274 A113 4c deep blue	16	15

Birth centenary of Alexander Graham Bell.

1947, July 1

275 A114 4c deep blue	16	15

Issued on the 80th anniv. of the Canadian Confederation, to mark the advent of Canadian Citizenship.

Princess Elizabeth A115

Parliament Buildings Ottawa A116

1948, Feb. 16

276 A115 4c deep blue	16	15

Marriage of Princess Elizabeth to Lieut. Philip Mountbatten, R. N., on Nov. 20, 1947.

1948, Oct. 1

277 A116 4c gray	16	15

Centenary of Responsible Government.

George VI Types of 1942
Coil Stamps

1948 ***Perf. 9½ Vertically***

278 A97 1c green	2.75	1.25
279 A98 2c brown	9.00	5.50
280 A99 3c rose violet	5.50	1.50
281 A98 4c dark carmine	7.50	1.75

John Cabot's Ship "Matthew" A117

1949, Apr. 1 **Engr.** *Perf. 12*

282 A117 4c deep green	16	15

Entry of Newfoundland into confederation with Canada.

"Founding of Halifax, 1749" — A118

1949, June 21 **Unwmk.**

283 A118 4c purple	16	15

200th anniv. of the founding of Halifax, Nova Scotia.

A119 A120 A121

A122

A123

1949, Nov. 19

284 A119 1c green	15	15
a. Booklet pane of 3 ('50)	70	70
285 A120 2c sepia	15	15
286 A121 3c rose violet	18	15
a. Booklet pane of 3 ('50)	85	85
b. Booklet pane of 4 + 2 labels	1.10	1.10
287 A122 4c dk carmine	30	15
a. Booklet pane of 3 ('50)	6.50	6.50
b. Booklet pane of 6 ('51)	9.75	9.75
288 A123 5c deep blue	70	15
Nos. 284-288 (5)	1.48	
Set value		30

Stamps from booklet panes of 3 are imperf. on 2 or 3 sides.

"POSTES POSTAGE" Omitted

1950, Jan. 19

289 A119 1c green	15	15
290 A120 2c sepia	18	15
291 A121 3c rose violet	15	15
292 A122 4c dark carmine	16	15
293 A123 5c deep blue	80	70
Nos. 289-293 (5)	1.44	
Set value		90

See Nos. 295-300, 305-306, 309-310. For overprints, see Nos. O12-O20.

Oil Wells, Alberta — A124

1950, Mar. 1 **Engr.** *Perf. 12*

294 A124 50c dull green	11.00	90

Development of oil wells in Canada.
For overprints, see Nos. O11, O24.

Coil Stamps
Types of 1949
"POSTES POSTAGE" Omitted

1950 ***Perf. 9½ Vertically***
295 A119 1c green 25 22
296 A121 3c rose violet 50 40

With "POSTES POSTAGE"
Perf. 9½ Vertically
297 A119 1c green 25 18
298 A120 2c sepia 1.50 95
299 A121 3c rose violet 85 15
300 A122 4c dark carmine 10.00 55

See note after No. 288.

Indians Drying Skins on Stretchers A125

1950, Oct. 2 ***Perf. 12***
301 A125 10c black brown 65 15

Canada's fur resources. For overprint, see No. O26.

Fishing — A126

1951, Feb. 1 **Unwmk.**
302 A126 $1 bright ultra 47.50 10.00

Canada's fish resources. For overprint, see No. O27.

Sir Robert Laird Borden — A127

William L. Mackenzie King — A128

1951, June 25 ***Perf. 12***
303 A127 3c turquoise green 20 15
304 A128 4c rose pink 22 15
Set value 20

George VI Types of 1949

1951 ***Perf. 12***
305 A120 2c olive green 15 15
306 A122 4c orange vermilion 20 15
a. Booklet pane of 3 1.50 1.50
b. Booklet pane of 6 2.00 2.00
Set value 15

For overprints, see Nos. O28-O29.

Coil Stamps
Perf. 9½ Vertically
309 A120 2c olive green 1.00 50
310 A122 4c orange vermilion 1.65 60

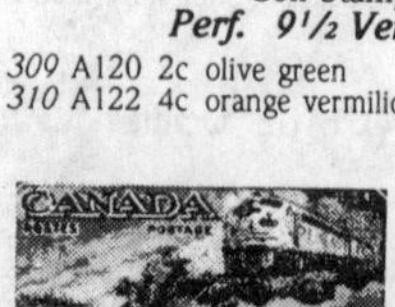

Trains of 1851 and 1951 — A129

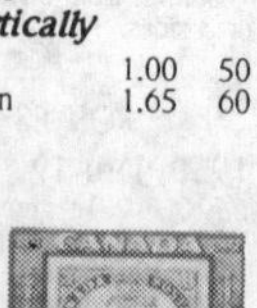

"Threepenny Beaver" of 1851 — A130

Designs: 5s, Steamships City of Toronto and Prince George. 7c, Stagecoach and Plane.

1951, Sept. 24 **Unwmk.** ***Perf. 12***
311 A129 4c dark gray 48 15
312 A129 5c purple 1.50 1.10
313 A129 7c deep blue 90 25
314 A130 15c bright red 90 22

Centenary of British North American postal administration.

Princess Elizabeth and Duke of Edinburgh A131

1951, Oct. 26 **Engr.**
315 A131 4c violet 16 15

Visit of Princess Elizabeth, Duchess of Edinburgh and the Duke of Edinburgh to Canada and the US.

Symbols of Newsprint Paper Production A132

1952, Apr. 1 **Unwmk.** ***Perf. 12***
316 A132 20c gray 1.25 15

Canada's paper production. For overprint, see No. O30.

Red Cross on Sun — A133

1952, July 26 **Engr. and Litho.**
317 A133 4c blue & red 16 15

18th Intl. Red Cross Conference, Toronto, July 1952.

Sir John J. C. Abbott A134

Alexander Mackenzie A135

1952, Nov. 3 **Engr.**
318 A134 3c rose lilac 15 15
319 A135 4c orange vermilion 18 15
Set value 15

Canada Goose — A136

1952, Nov. 3
320 A136 7c blue 35 15

For overprint, see No. O31.

Pacific Coast Indian House and Totem Pole — A137

1953, Feb. 2
321 A137 $1 gray 12.00 60

For overprint, see No. O32.

Natl. Wildlife Week — A138

Elizabeth II — A139

1953, Apr. 1
322 A138 2c Polar Bear 15 15
323 A138 3c Moose 15 15
324 A138 4c Bighorn sheep 20 15
Set value 18

1953, May 1
325 A139 1c violet brown 15 15
a. Booklet pane of 3 80 60
326 A139 2c green 15 15
327 A139 3c carmine rose 15 15
a. Booklet pane of 3 1.25 80
b. Booklet pane of 4 + 2 labels 1.40 1.40
328 A139 4c violet 22 15
a. Booklet pane of 3 1.50 1.40
b. Booklet pane of 6 1.50 1.40
329 A139 5c ultramarine 30 15
Nos. 325-329 (5) 97
Set value 25

Stamps from booklet panes of 3 are imperf. on 2 or 3 sides.
For overprints, see Nos. O33-O37.

Coronation Issue

Queen Elizabeth II — A140

1953, June 1
330 A140 4c violet 16 15

Coil Stamps

1953 ***Perf. 9½ Vertically***
331 A139 2c green 1.25 75
332 A139 3c carmine rose 1.25 75
333 A139 4c violet 3.00 1.25

See note after No. 329.

Bobbin, Cloth and Spinning Wheel — A141

1953, Nov. 2 ***Perf. 12***
334 A141 50c light green 3.50 18

For overprint, see No. O38.

Walrus A142

Beaver A143

1954, Apr. 1
335 A142 4c gray 22 15
336 A143 5c ultramarine 25 15
a. Booklet pane of 5 + label 2.00 2.00
Set value 15

National Wildlife Week, 1954.

Elizabeth II A144

Gannet A145

1954-61
337 A144 1c violet brn 15 15
a. Booklet pane of 5 + label 80 75
338 A144 2c green 15 15
a. Pane of 25 ('61) 5.00 5.00
339 A144 3c carmine rose 15 15
a. Horiz. pair, imperf. vert. *900.00*
340 A144 4c violet 15 15
a. Booklet pane of 5 + label 1.40 1.25
b. Booklet pane of 6 4.50 4.50
341 A144 5c bright blue 16 15
a. Booklet pane of 5 + label 1.50 1.25
b. Pane of 20 (5 x 4) ('61) 9.00 9.00
342 A144 6c orange 25 15
343 A145 15c gray 80 15
Set value 1.53 45

Panes of 20 and 25 are imperf. on 4 sides.
For overprints, see Nos. O40-O44.

Luminescence

The overprinting of regular stamps with vertical luminescent bands began experimentally in 1962 when Nos. 337p-341p were released at Winnipeg. The bands are of varying number, position and chemical content.

Tagged varieties of stamps which were issued both untagged and with luminescent overprint are listed with suffix letter "p".

Tagged

1962, Jan. 13
337p A144 1c violet brown 85 85
338p A144 2c green 85 85
339p A144 3c carmine rose 85 85
340p A144 4c violet 2.50 3.00
341p A144 5c bright blue 2.75 2.25
Nos. 337p-341p (5) 7.80 7.80

Coil Stamps

1954 ***Perf. 9½ Vertically***
345 A144 2c green 32 15
347 A144 4c violet 1.10 15
348 A144 5c bright blue 1.75 15

Sir John Sparrow David Thompson A146

Sir Mackenzie Bowell A147

1954, Nov. 1 ***Perf. 12***
349 A146 4c violet 20 15
350 A147 5c bright blue 20 15
Set value 16

Eskimo and Kayak — A148

1955, Feb. 21
351 A148 10c violet brown 24 15

For overprint, see No. O39.

Musk Ox — A149

Whooping Cranes — A150

1955, Apr. 4
352 A149 4c purple 24 15
353 A150 5c blue 28 15
Set value 15

National Wildlife Week, April 10-16.

Torch, Dove and Maple Leaves — A151

1955, June 1 **Unwmk.**
354 A151 5c light blue 24 15

ICAO, 10th anniversary.

Pioneer Settlers — A152

1955, June 30 ***Perf. 12***
355 A152 5c ultramarine 24 15

50th anniv. of the founding of the provinces of Alberta and Saskatchewan.

Globe and Scout Emblem A153

1955, Aug. 20 **Engr.**
356 A153 5c green & org brown 24 15

8th Boy Scout World Jamboree, Niagara-on-the-Lake, Ont.

Richard Bedford Bennett — A154

Sir Charles Tupper — A155

1955, Nov. 8
357 A154 4c violet 22 15
358 A155 5c ultramarine 22 15
Set value 16

Ice Hockey Players — A156

1956, Jan. 23
359 A156 5c ultramarine 22 15

Issued to publicize Canada's most popular winter sport.

Caribou A157

Mountain Goat A158

1956, Apr. 12
360 A157 4c deep violet 22 15
361 A158 5c ultramarine 22 15
Set value 15

National Wildlife Week, 1956.

"Paper Industry" A159

"Chemical Industry" A160

1956, June 7 **Engr.**
362 A159 20c green 90 15
363 A160 25c red 1.10 15
Set value 18

For overprint, see No. O45.

House on Fire — A161

Canada's Outdoor Recreation Facilities — A162

1956, Oct. 9 **Unwmk.** ***Perf. 12***
364 A161 5c gray & red 22 15

Issued to emphasize the needless waste caused by preventable fires.

1957, Mar. 7
365 A162 5c Fishing 30 20
366 A162 5c Swimming 30 20
367 A162 5c Hunter and dog 30 20
368 A162 5c Skiing 30 20

All four designs are printed alternating in sheet of 50, with various combinations possible.

Loon A163

David Thompson and Map of Western Canada A164

1957, Apr. 10 ***Perf. 12***
369 A163 5c black 30 15

1957, June 5 **Unwmk.**
370 A164 5c ultramarine 22 15

David Thompson (1770-1857), explorer and geographer.

Parliament Building, Ottawa — A165

Post Horn and Globe — A166

1957, Aug. 14 ***Perf. 12***
371 A165 5c dark blue 22 15
372 A166 15c dark blue 1.90 1.25

UPU, 14th Congress, Ottawa, Aug. 1957.

Miner With Pneumatic Drill — A167

Elizabeth II and Prince Philip — A168

1957, Sept. 5
373 A167 5c black 22 15

Canada's mining industry; 6th Commonwealth Mining and Metallurgical Congress, Vancouver, Sept. 8-Oct. 8.

1957, Oct. 10 **Unwmk.**
374 A168 5c black 22 15

Visit of Queen Elizabeth II and Prince Philip to Canada, Oct. 12-16.

Newspapers and Symbols of Industry A169

Micro-scope and Globe A170

1958, Jan. 22 **Engr.**
375 A169 5c black 28 15

Canadian press; the importance of a free press.

1958, Mar. 5 ***Perf. 12***
376 A170 5c blue 25 15

Intl. Geophysical Year, 1957-1958.

Miner Panning Gold — A171

1958, May 8 **Unwmk.**
377 A171 5c bluish green 22 15

Province of British Columbia, cent.

La Verendrye A172

1958, June 4 ***Perf. 12***
378 A172 5c bright ultra 22 15

Pierre Gaultier de Varenne, Sieur de la Verendrye, 18th century French explorer of Western Canada.

Champlain and View of Quebec — A173

1958, June 26
379 A173 5c dk green & bis brn 22 15

Founding of Quebec, 350th anniv.

Nurse — A174

Kerosene Lamp and Refinery — A175

1958, July 30 **Engr.**
380 A174 5c rose lilac 22 15

Importance of health, both to the individual and to the nation.

1958, Sept. 10 ***Perf. 12***
381 A175 5c olive & red 22 15

Centennial of Canada's oil industry.

Speaker's Chair and Mace — A176

1958, Oct. 2
382 A176 5c slate blue 22 15

Bicentennial of the meeting of the first House of Representatives in Canada, Halifax, Oct. 2, 1758.

"Silver Dart" and Delta Wing Planes — A177

1959, Feb. 23 ***Perf. 12***
383 A177 5c blue & black 22 15

50th anniv. of the 1st airplane flight in Canada near Baddeck, N. S., with J. A. D. McCurdy as pilot.

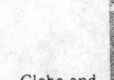

Globe and Dove — A178

1959, Apr. 2
384 A178 5c violet blue 22 15

NATO, 10th anniversary.

Woman Tending Tree A179

Elizabeth II A180

1959, May 13
385 A179 5c apple green & blk 22 15

Associated Country Women of the World.

1959, June 18
386 A180 5c dark carmine 22 15

Visit of Queen Elizabeth and Prince Philip to Canada, June 18-Aug. 1.

Great Lakes, Maple Leaf and Eagle Emblems A181

1959, June 26 **Engr.**
387 A181 5c red & blue 22 15
a. Center inverted *8,000. 6,250.*

Opening of the St. Lawrence Seaway, June 26, 1959.
See United States No. 1131.

British Lion, Fleur-de-Lis and Maple Leaves A182

1959, Sept. 10 ***Perf. 12***
388 A182 5c crim rose & dk green 22 15

Bicentenary of the Battle of the Plains of Abraham.

Girl Guide Emblem — A183

Dollard des Ormeaux and Battle Scene — A184

1960, Apr. 20 **Unwmk.**
389 A183 5c brown org & ultra 22 15

Canadian Girl Guides Assoc., 50th anniv.

1960, May 19
390 A184 5c ultra & bis brown 22 15

Battle of the Long Sault, 300th anniv.

Compass Rose, Earth Mover and Surveyor A185

Emily Pauline Johnson A186

1961, Feb. 8 **Engr.** ***Perf. 12***
391 A185 5c green & vermilion 22 15

Development of Canada's Northland.

1961, Mar. 10
392 A186 5c green & red 22 15

Emily Pauline Johnson (1861-1913), Mohawk princess and poet.

Arthur Meighen A187

Power Plant and Men Holding Blueprint A188

1961, Apr. 19
393 A187 5c ultramarine 22 15

Arthur Meighen, Prime Minister of Canada, (1920-21, 1926).

1961, June 28 **Unwmk.** ***Perf. 12***
394 A188 5c lt red brn & blue 22 15

10th anniv. of the Colombo Plan, initiated to assist underdeveloped countries by providing trained manpower and resources.

Natural Resources and Hands Holding Cogwheel — A189

1961, Oct. 12 **Engr.** ***Perf. 12***
395 A189 5c brown & blue grn 22 15

Canada's "Resources for Tomorrow Program" and to publicize the close link between industry and the country'srenewable natural resources.

Young Adults and Education Symbols — A190

1962, Feb. 28 **Unwmk.** ***Perf. 12***
396 A190 5c black & lt red brn 22 15
a. Light red brown (symbols) omitted

Issued to stimulate public awareness of the importance of education.

Scottish Settler and Lord Selkirk — A191

1962, May 3 ***Perf. 12***
397 A191 5c lt green & vio brn 22 15

150th anniv. of the Red River Settlement in Western Canada (Prairie Provinces).

Jean Talon Presenting Gifts to Young Farm Couple — A192

1962, June 13 **Unwmk.** ***Perf. 12***
398 A192 5c dark blue 22 15

Jean Talon, administrator of New France (Canada), 1665-1668.

British Columbia Legislative Building and Stamp of 1860 — A193

1962, Aug. 22 **Engr.** ***Perf. 12***
399 A193 5c black & rose 22 15

Centenary of Victoria as incorporated city.

Arms of the Provinces A194

1962, Aug. 31
400 A194 5c brown orange & black 22 15

Official opening of the Trans-Canada Highway, Rogers Pass, Glacier National Park, Sept. 4.

Queen Elizabeth II and Wheat — A195

Designs (Symbol in upper left corner): 1c, Mineral crystals. 2c, Tree. 3c, Fish. 4c, Electric high tension tower.

1962-63 **Engr.** ***Perf. 12***
401 A195 1c deep brown ('63) 15 15
a. Booklet pane of 5 + label ('63) 2.75 2.75
402 A195 2c green ('63) 15 15
a. Pane of 25 ('63) 3.75 3.75
403 A195 3c purple ('63) 15 15
404 A195 4c carmine ('63) 15 15
a. Booklet pane of 5 + label ('63) 3.50 3.50
b. Pane of 25 ('63) 5.25 5.25
405 A195 5c violet blue 18 15
a. Booklet pane of 5 + label ('63) 4.25 3.75
b. Pane of 20 ('63) 5.75 5.50
Set value 60 25

Nos. 402a, 404b, and 405b are imperf. on four sides.
For overprints, see Nos. O46-O49.

Tagged

1963
401p A195 1c deep brown 15 15
402p A195 2c green 16 15
403p A195 3c purple 25 15
404p A195 4c carmine 85 50
405p A195 5c violet blue 50 25
q. Pane of 20 35.00
Nos. 401p-405p (5) 1.91 1.20

See note after No. 343.

Coil Stamps

1963-64 ***Perf. 9½ Horiz.***
406 A195 2c green 2.75 1.40
407 A195 3c purple ('64) 2.00 1.00
408 A195 4c carmine 3.00 1.40
409 A195 5c violet blue 3.00 52

Sir Casimir Stanislaus Gzowski (1813-98), Engineer, Soldier and Educator — A196

1963, Mar. 5 **Unwmk.** ***Perf. 12***
410 A196 5c rose lilac 22 15

Export Crate and Mercator Map — A197

1963, June 14 **Unwmk.** ***Perf. 12***
411 A197 $1 rose carmine 12.00 1.40

Sir Martin Frobisher (1535-1594), Explorer and Discoverer of Frobisher Bay — A198

1963, Aug. 21 **Engr.**
412 A198 5c ultramarine 22 15

Postrider and First Land Mail Routes A199

1963, Sept. 25
413 A199 5c green & red brn 22 15

Bicentennial of the 1st regular postal service between Quebec, Three Rivers & Montreal.

Jet at Ottawa Airport — A200

Canada Geese — A201

1963-64
414 A200 7c blue ('64) 50 38
415 A201 15c deep ultra 3.00 20

See No. 436. For surcharge, see No. 430.

"Peace on Earth" — A202

1964, Apr. 8 **Engr. & Litho.**
416 A202 5c grnsh blue, Prus bl & ocher 22 15

Issued to promote world peace.

Three-Maple-Leaf Emblem (Canadian Unity) — A203

White Trillium and Arms of Ontario — A204

Design: No. 419, White garden lily and arms of Quebec. No. 420, Mayflower (trailing arbutus) and arms of Nova Scotia. No. 421, Purple violet and arms of New Brunswick. No. 422, Prairie crocus and arms of Manitoba. No. 423, Dogwood and arms of British Columbia. No. 424, Lady's slipper and arms of Prince Edward Island. No. 425, Prairie lily and arms of Saskatchewan. No. 426, Wild rose and arms of Alberta. No. 427, Pitcher plant and arms of Newfoundland. No. 428, Fireweed and arms of Yukon. No. 429, Mountain avens and arms of Northwest Territories. No. 429A, Maple leaf and arms of Canada.

1964-66 Engr. & Litho. *Perf. 12*

417	A203	5c lt blue & dk car	20	15
418	A204	5c red brn, buff & green	20	15
419	A204	5c grn, yel & org	20	15
420	A204	5c blue, pink & grn	20	15
421	A204	5c car, green & vio	20	15
422	A204	5c red brn, lil & dl grn	20	15
423	A204	5c lilac, grn & bis	20	15
424	A204	5c vio, grn & dp rose	20	15
425	A204	5c sepia, org & grn	20	15
426	A204	5c dl grn, yel & car	20	15
427	A204	5c black, grn & car	20	15
428	A204	5c dk bl, rose & grn	20	15
429	A204	5c ol, yel & green	20	15
429A	A204	5c dk blue & dp red	20	15
		Nos. 417-429A (14)	2.80	
		Set value		1.15

Issue dates: No. 417, May 14, 1964. Nos. 418-419, June 30, 1964. Nos. 420-421, Feb. 3, 1965. Nos. 422-423, Apr. 28, 1965. No. 424, July 21, 1965. Nos. 425-426, Jan. 19, 1966. No. 427, Feb. 23, 1966. Nos. 428-429, Mar. 23, 1966. No. 429A, June 30, 1966.

No. 414 Surcharged 

1964, July 15 Engr.

430 A200 8c on 7c blue 28 28
a. Pair, one without surcharge *2,000.*

Fathers of Confederation Memorial, Charlottetown A205

1964, July 29 Engr.

431 A205 5c black 22 15

Centenary of the Charlottetown, P.E.I., Conference, Sept. 1-9, 1864, which led to the creation of the Canadian nation in 1867.

Maple Leaf and Hand Holding Quill Pen — A206

1964, Sept. 9 Unwmk. *Perf. 12*

432 A206 5c dk brown & rose 20 15

Centenary of the Quebec Conference, Oct. 10-27, 1864, which led to the creation of the Canadian nation.

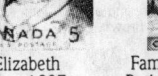

Elizabeth II — A207

Family and Star of Bethlehem — A208

1964, Oct. 5 Engr.

433 A207 5c claret 20 15

Queen Elizabeth's visit, Oct. 6-13.

1964, Oct. 14 *Perf. 12*

434 A208	3c red		15	15
a.	Pane of 25		6.25	6.25
p.	Tagged		52	25
q.	As "a," tagged		10.00	10.00
435 A208	5c blue		18	15
p.	Tagged		1.00	25
	Set value			15

Panes of 25 are imperf. on four sides.

Jet Type of 1964

1964, Nov. 18 Unwmk. *Perf. 12*

436 A200 8c blue 32 18

Maple Leaf and ICY Emblem A209

1965, Mar. 3 Engr. *Perf. 12*

437 A209 5c slate green 18 15

International Cooperation Year.

Sir Wilfred Grenfell at Wheel of Hospital Ship Strathcona II A210

1965, June 9 Engr. *Perf. 12*

438 A210 5c Prussian blue 18 15

Sir Wilfred Grenfell, author, medical missionary and founder of the Grenfell Mission, birth cent.

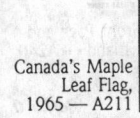

Canada's Maple Leaf Flag, 1965 — A211

1965, June 30 Unwmk.

439 A211 5c blue & red 18 15

Winston Churchill — A212

Peace Tower, Ottawa — A213

1965, Aug. 12 Litho. *Perf. 12*

440 A212 5c brown 20 15

Sir Winston Spencer Churchill (1874-1965).

1965, Sept. 8 Engr. *Perf. 12*

441 A213 5c slate green 18 15

Meeting of the Inter-Parliamentary Union, Ottawa, Sept. 8-17.

Parliament and Ottawa River — A214

1965, Sept. 8

442 A214 5c brown 18 15

Centenary of the selection of Ottawa as national capital.

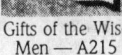

Gifts of the Wise Men — A215

Alouette II Orbiting Globe — A216

1965, Oct. 13 Engr.

443 A215	3c olive		15	15
a.	Pane of 25		5.75	5.75
p.	Tagged		20	15
q.	As "a" tagged		6.75	6.75
444 A215	5c violet blue		15	15
p.	Tagged		28	20
	Set value			15

Christmas. Panes of 25 are imperf. on four sides.

1966, Jan. 5 Unwmk. *Perf. 12*

445 A216 5c dark violet blue 18 15

Launching (in California) of the Canadian satellite Alouette II, Nov. 28, 1965, as part of the Canadian-American program of space research.

La Salle, Map of 17th Century Canada, Ship, Canoe, Spyglass and Compass — A217

1966, Apr. 13 Engr. *Perf. 12*

446 A217 5c blue green 18 15

Tercentenary of the arrival in Canada of Rene Robert Cavelier, Sieur de La Salle (1643-1687).

Traffic Signs — A218

1966, May 2

447 A218 5c black, blue & yel 18 15

Issued to publicize traffic safety.

House of Commons, Thames River and Canadian Delegates A219

1966, May 26

448 A219 5c brown 18 15

Centenary of the London Conference, Dec. 4, 1866, which resulted in the British North America Act.

Atomic Reactor, Heavy Water Atom Symbol and Microscope A220

1966, July 27 Engr. *Perf. 12*

449 A220 5c deep ultra 18 15

Peaceful uses of atomic power. The design shows a stylized view of the Douglas Point Nuclear Power Station, Lake Huron, Ontario.

Parliamen-tary Library, Ottawa — A221

Praying Hands, by Albrecht Dürer — A222

1966, Sept. 8 Engr. *Perf. 12*

450 A221 5c plum 18 15

12th General Conference of the Commonwealth Parliamentary Assoc., Ottawa, Sept. 8-Oct. 5.

1966, Oct. 12 Engr. *Perf. 12*

451 A222	3c carmine rose		15	15
a.	Pane of 25		3.25	3.25
p.	Tagged		15	15
q.	As "a," tagged		4.00	4.00
452 A222	5c orange		15	15
p.	Tagged		40	25
	Set value		24	15

Christmas. Panes of 25 are imperf. on four sides.

Canadian Flag over Globe and Centennial Emblem — A223

1967, Jan. 11 Engr. *Perf. 12*

453 A223 5c blue & red 22 15
p. Tagged 35 28

Canada's centenary as a nation.

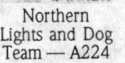

Northern Lights and Dog Team — A224

"Alaska Highway" by A. Y. Jackson — A225

Two types of 6c black:

Type I

Type II

Designs: 2c, Totem pole (Pacific Area). 3c, Combine and oil rig (Prairie Region). 4c, Ship in lock (Central Canada). 5c, Lobster traps and boat (Atlantic Provinces). 6c, Transportation means. 10c, "The Jack Pine" by Tom Thomson. 15c, "Bylot Island" by Lawren Harris. 20c, "The Ferry, Quebec" by James Wilson Morrice. 25c, "The Solemn Land" by J. E. H. MacDonald. 50c, "Summer's Stores" by John Ensor (grain elevators). $1, Oilfield near Edmonton, by H. G. Glyde.

1967-72 Engr. *Perf. 12*

454	A224	1c brown	15	15
a.		Booklet pane of 5 + label	65	65
b.		Bklt. pane (1 #454d, 4 #459 + label), perf. 10 ('68)	2.10	2.10
c.		Bklt. pane (5 #454d + 5 #457d) perf. 10 ('68)	3.75	3.75
d.		Perf. 10	25	15
e.		Perf. 12½x12	50	18
455	A224	2c green	15	15
a.		Bklt. pane (4 #455, 4 #456 with gutter btwn.)	2.50	2.50
456	A224	3c dull purple	15	15
a.		Perf. 12½x12	80	40
457	A224	4c car rose	15	15
a.		Booklet pane of 5 + label	1.75	1.75
b.		Pane of 25 (5x5)	14.00	
c.		Booklet pane of 25 + 2 labels, perf. 10 ('68)	8.00	
d.		Perf. 10	75	25
458	A224	5c blue	15	15
a.		Booklet pane of 5 + label	5.50	5.25
b.		Pane of 20	20.00	
c.		Bklt. pane of 20, perf. 10 ('68)	8.00	
d.		Perf. 10	75	25
459	A224	6c org, perf. 10 ('68)	40	15
a.		Bklt. pane of 25 + 2 labels, perf. 10 ('69)	6.75	
b.		Perf. 12½x12 ('69)	35	15
460	A224	6c black (I), perf. 12½x12 ('70)	20	15
a.		Bklt. pane of 25 + 2 labels (I), perf. 10 ('70)	13.00	13.00
b.		As "a," perf. 12½x12	17.50	
c.		Type II, perf. 12½x12	24	15
d.		As "c," booklet pane of 4	6.00	6.00
e.		As "d," perf. 10 ('70)	8.75	5.50
f.		Type II, perf. 12 ('72)	42	15
g.		Type I, perf. 10	1.40	35
h.		Type II, perf. 10	2.25	1.00
461	A225	8c violet brown	35	15
462	A225	10c olive green	35	15
463	A225	15c dull purple	70	15
464	A225	20c dark blue	70	15
465	A225	25c slate green	1.25	15
465A	A225	50c brown org	4.00	15
465B	A225	$1 carmine rose	8.50	40
		Nos. 454-465B (14)	17.20	
		Set value		1.25

Nos. 454d, 457d, 458d, 460g and 460h are from booklet panes.

See Nos. 543-544, 549-550.

Tagged

454p	A224	1c brown	20	20
ep.		Perf. 12½x12 ('71)	15	15
455p	A224	2c green	16	15
456p	A224	3c dull purple	16	15
457p	A224	4c car rose	45	25
458p	A224	5c blue	45	25
bp.		Pane of 20	40.00	40.00
459p	A224	6c org, perf. 10 ('68)	52	25
pb.		Perf. 12½x12 ('69)	52	40
460p	A224	6c black (I), perf. 12½x12 ('70)	24	15
cp.		Black (II), perf. 12½x12 ('70)	50	50
fp.		As "cp," perf. 12 ('72)	35	15
462p	A225	10c olive green ('70)	90	50
463p	A225	15c dull purple ('70)	90	50
464p	A225	20c dark blue ('70)	1.40	75
465p	A225	25c slate green ('70)	2.75	1.50
		Nos. 454p-465p (11)	8.13	4.65

See note after No. 343.

Coil Stamps

1967-70 *Perf. 9½ Horiz.*

466	A224	3c dull purple	1.75	1.25
467	A224	4c carmine rose	75	60
468	A224	5c blue	1.40	1.00

Perf. 10 Horiz.

468A	A224	6c orange ('69)	28	15
c.		Imperf., pair	175.00	
468B	A224	6c black, die II ('70)	28	15
d.		Imperf., pair	550.00	
		Nos. 466-468B (5)	4.46	3.15

Horizontal pairs or blocks of Nos. 468A and 468B may be found with a fine vertical score line between the stamps. These sell for little more than vertical pairs or strips.

EXPO '67 Emblem and Canadian Pavilion A226

1967, Apr. 28 **Engr.** *Perf. 12*
469 A226 5c blue & red 18 15

EXPO '67, Intl. Exhib., Montreal, Apr. 28-Oct. 27.

Symbolic Woman and Ballot — A227

Elizabeth II — A228

1967, May **Litho.** *Perf. 12*
470 A227 5c black & rose lilac 18 15

50th anniversary of woman suffrage.

1967, June 30 **Engr.** *Perf. 12*
471 A228 5c deep org & purple 18 15

Centennial Year visit of Queen Elizabeth II and the Duke of Edinburgh.

Runner — A229

1967, July 19 **Engr.** *Perf. 12*
472 A229 5c red 18 15

Pan-American Games, Winnipeg, Manitoba, July 22-Aug. 7.

Globe and Flash — A230

1967, Aug. 31 **Unwmk.**
473 A230 5c deep ultra 18 15

50th anniv. of the Canadian Press, news gathering and distributing service.

Georges Philias Vanier — A231

Engr. & Litho.

1967, Sept. 15 *Perf. 12*
474 A231 5c black 18 15

Georges Philias Vanier (1888-1967), Governor General of Canada, 1959-1967.

Toronto in 1967 and Citizens of 1867 — A232

1967, Sept. 28 **Engr.**
475 A232 5c sl green & sal pink 18 15

Centenary of Toronto as capital of Ontario.

Singing Children and Peace Tower, Ottawa — A233

1967, Oct. 11 **Engr.** *Perf. 12*

476	A233	3c carmine	15	15
a.		Pane of 25	2.50	2.50
p.		Tagged	15	15
q.		As "a" tagged	3.50	3.50
477	A233	5c green	15	15
p.		Tagged	25	20
		Set value	24	15

Christmas. Panes of 25 are imperf. on four sides.

Gray Jays — A234

Weather Map and Composite of Instruments — A235

1968, Feb. 15 **Litho.**
478 A234 5c green, blk & red 35 15

1968, Mar. 13 *Perf. 11*
479 A235 5c dk & lt blue, yel & red 18 15

200th anniv. of Canada's first long-term fixed point weather observations at Fort Prince of Wales, Churchill, by William Wales and Joseph Dymond.

Male Narwhal A236

1968, Apr. 10 **Litho.** *Perf. 11*
480 A236 5c multicolored 18 15

Weighing Rain Gauge, World Map and Maple Leaf — A237

1968, May 8 **Litho.** *Perf. 11*
481 A237 5c multicolored 18 15

Intl. Hydrological Decade, 1967-74.

The Nonsuch A238

Photo. & Engr.

1968, June 5 *Perf. 10*
482 A238 5c dk blue & multi 18 15

300th anniv. of the voyage of the Nonsuch which opened the way to Canada's West through the fur trade.

Contemporary and Indian Lacrosse Players — A239

1968, July 3 **Photo. & Engr.**
483 A239 5c yel, black & red 18 15

George Brown, "Globe" Front Page and Legislature, Prince Edward Island — A240

1968, Aug. 21 *Perf. 10*
484 A240 5c multicolored 18 15

George Brown (1818-1880), founder of Toronto "Globe" and political leader.

Henri Bourassa and Newspaper Page A241

Canadian Memorial, Vimy Near France A242

1968, Sept. 4 **Litho. & Engr.** *Perf. 12*
485 A241 5c ver, buff & black 18 15

Henri Bourassa (1868-1952), jounalist and statesman.

1968, Oct. 15 **Engr.** *Perf. 12*
486 A242 15c slate 1.40 1.00

50th anniv. of the Armistice which ended WWI. The stamp shows "The Defenders and the Breaking of the Sword," a detail from the memorial designed by W. S. Allward.

John McCrae and "Flanders Fields" A243

Eskimo Family, Carving A244

1968, Oct. 15 **Litho. & Engr.**
487 A243 5c multicolored 18 15

50th death anniv. of Lt. Col. John McCrae (1872-1918), author of "In Flanders Fields."

1968, Nov. **Photo.** *Perf. 12*

Eskimo soapstone carving: 6c, Mother and infant, by Munamee of Cape Dorset.

488	A244	5c brt blue & black	15	15
a.		Booklet pane of 10	2.75	
p.		Tagged	20	16
q.		As "a" tagged	5.00	
489	A244	6c dp bister & black	15	15
p.		Tagged	25	16
		Set value		15

Christmas. Issue dates: 5c, Nov. 1; 6c, Nov. 15.

Curling A245

Vincent Massey A246

1969, Jan. 15 **Photo. & Engr.** *Perf. 10*
490 A245 6c black, brt blue & car 18 15

Litho. & Engr.

1969, Feb. 20 *Perf. 12*
491 A246 6c yel olive & dk brn 18 15

Vincent Massey (1887-1967), 1st Canadian-born Governor General of Canada, 1952-59.

Return from the Harvest Field, by Aurele de Foy Suzor-Cote A247

1969, Mar. 14 **Photo.**
492 A247 50c multicolored 2.50 1.65

Aurele de Foy Suzor-Cote (1869-1937), painter.

Globe and Tools of Various Trades — A248

1969, May 21 **Engr.** *Perf. 12x12½*
493 A248 6c dk olive green 18 15

50th anniv. of the ILO.

Vickers Vimy, 1919, and Map of the Atlantic A249

1969, June 13 **Photo. and Engr.**
494 A249 15c red brn, yel grn & lt ultra 1.40 1.50

50th anniv. of the first non-stop Atlantic flight from Newfoundland to Ireland of Capt. John Alcock and Lt. Arthur Whitten Brown.

Sir William Osler — A250

Ipswich Sparrow — A251

1969, June 23 *Perf. 12½x12*
495 A250 6c dk blue & lt red brn 18 15

Osler (1849-1919), physician, professor of physiology and pathology in Canada, US and England.

1969, July 23 Litho. *Perf. 12*

Birds: 6c, White-throated sparrows, vert. 25c, Hermet thrush.

496 A251	6c multicolored		40	15
497 A251	10c ultra & multi		80	50
498 A251	25c black & multi		2.00	1.50

Map of Prince Edward Island A252

Photo. & Engr.

1969, Aug. 15 *Perf. 12x12½*

499 A252 6c ultra, org brn & black 18 15

Bicentenary of Charlottetown as capital of Prince Edward Island.

Flags of Summer and Winter Canada Games — A253

Litho. & Engr.

1969, Aug. 15 *Perf. 14*

500 A253 6c ultra, brt green & red 18 15

1st Canada Summer Games, Halifax and Dartmouth, N.S., Aug. 16-24.

Sir Isaac Brock and Memorial Queenston Heights — A254

1969, Sept. 12 Litho. and Engr.

501 A254 6c yel brown, brn & pale sal 18 15

Major General Sir Isaac Brock (1769-1812), administrator of Upper Canada and leader in the war of 1812.

Children of Various Races — A255

1969, Oct. 8 Litho. *Perf. 12*

502 A255 5c blue & multi		15	15
a.	Booklet pane of 10	3.75	
p.	Tagged	20	15
q.	As "a" tagged	4.50	
503 A255 6c red & multi		15	15
a.	Black (inscriptions & frame line) omitted	1,000.	1,000.
p.	Tagged	25	16
	Set value	24	15

Christmas.

Stephen Leacock, Comedy Mask and Mariposa View — A256

Photo. & Engr.

1969, Nov. 12 *Perf. 12x12½*

504 A256 6c multicolored 18 15

Stephen Butler Leacock (1869-1944), humorist, historian and economist.

Manitoba, Crossroads of Canada A257

1970, Jan. 27 Litho. *Perf. 12*

505 A257 6c violet blue & multi		18	15
p.	Tagged	30	20

Centenary of the province of Manitoba.

Enchanted Owl, by Kenojuak — A258

1970, Jan. 27 Engr. *Perf. 12*

506 A258 6c dark red & black 18 15

Centenary of Nortwest Territories.

Microscopic View of Inside of Leaf — A259

1970, Feb. 18 Photo. & Engr.

507 A259 6c green, lt org & blue 18 15

Canada's participation in the Intl. Biological Program, 1967-1972.

Emblems of EXPO '67 and '70 — A260

EXPO '70 Emblem and Dogwood, British Columbia A261

Designs: No. 510, EXPO '70 emblem and white garden lily, Quebec. No. 511, EXPO '70 emblem and white trillium, Ontario.

1970, Mar. 18 Litho. *Perf. 12*

508 A260 25c red emblem		1.75	1.75
p.	Tagged	2.50	2.50
509 A261 25c violet emblem		1.75	1.75
p.	Tagged	2.50	2.50
510 A261 25c green emblem		1.75	1.75
p.	Tagged	2.50	2.50
511 A261 25c blue emblem		1.75	1.75
p.	Tagged	2.50	2.50
a.	Block of 4, #508-511	8.00	8.00
b.	As "a," tagged	12.50	12.50

EXPO '70 Intl. Exhibition, Osaka, Japan, Mar. 15-Sept. 13. Nos. 508-511 printed se-tenant in sheets of 50 (5x10), with various combinations possible.

Henry Kelsey — A262

Photo. & Engr.

1970, Apr. 15 *Perf. 12x12½*

512 A262 6c multicolored 18 15

300th birth anniv. of Henry Kelsey, explorer of Canada's western plains.

"A Divided World, with Energy Focused on Unification..." A263

1970, May 13 Litho. *Perf. 11*

513 A263 10c blue		55	45
p.	Tagged	1.00	1.00
514 A263 15c lilac & dk red		70	60
p.	Tagged	1.50	1.50

25th anniversary of the United Nations.

Louis Riel — A264

Mackenzie Rock, Dean Channel — A265

1970, June 19 Photo. *Perf. 12½x12*

515 A264 6c red & brt blue 18 15

Louis Riel (1844-1885), Metis leader who became president of the Council of Assiniboin in 1870.

1970, June 25 Engr. *Perf. 12*

516 A265 6c brown 18 15

Sir Alexander Mackenzie (1764-1820), Scottish explorer who in 1793 completed the first crossing of the North American continent north of Mexico.

Sir Oliver Mowat and Parliament, Ottawa — A266

Photo. & Engr.

1970, Aug. 12 *Perf. 12x12½*

517 A266 6c red & black 18 15

Sir Oliver Mowat (1820-1903), government leader and a Father of Confederation.

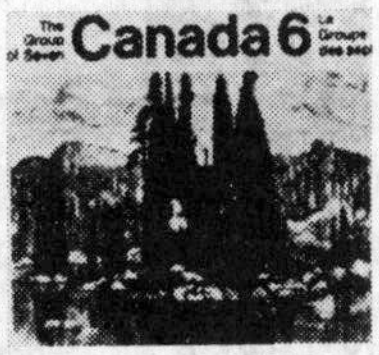

Isle of Spruce, by Arthur Lismer — A267

1970, Sept. 18 Litho. *Perf. 11*

518 A267 6c multicolored 18 15

50th anniv. of "The Group of Seven," Canadian landscape artists.

Santa Claus — A268

Christ Child — A269

Child in the Manger and Star-studded Sky — A270

Christmas: Designs by Canadian School Children.

1970, Oct. 7 Litho. *Perf. 12*

519 A268	5c Santa Claus	25	15
520 A268	5c Horse-drawn Sleigh	25	15
521 A268	5c Nativity	25	15
522 A268	5c Children Skiing	25	15
523 A268	5c Snowmen and Christmas Tree	25	15
a.	Strip of 5, #519-523	1.65	1.65
524 A269	6c Christ Child	35	15
525 A269	6c Christmas Tree and Children	35	15
526 A269	6c Toy Store	35	15
527 A269	6c Santa Claus	35	15
528 A269	6c Church	35	15
a.	Strip of 5, #524-528	1.75	1.75
529 A270	10c Christ Child	35	30
530 A270	15c Snowmobile and Trees	85	85
	Nos. 519-530 (12)	4.20	
	Set value		2.00

Tagged

519p A268	5c multicolored	40	18
520p A268	5c multicolored	40	18
521p A268	5c multicolored	40	18
522p A268	5c multicolored	40	18
523p A268	5c multicolored	40	18
b.	Strip of 5, #519p-523p	2.00	2.00
524p A269	6c multicolored	50	18
525p A269	6c multicolored	50	18
526p A269	6c multicolored	50	18
527p A269	6c multicolored	50	18
528p A269	6c multicolored	50	18
b.	Strip of 5, #524p-528p	2.50	2.50
529p A270	10c multicolored	52	45
530p A270	15c multicolored	1.10	1.10
	Nos. 519p-530p (12)	6.12	3.35

Christmas.

The sheets of 100 of both 5c and 6c contain all 5 designs, generally alternating, and arranged to permit vertical and horizontal pairs of each design in the two center vertical and horizontal rows. The center block of 4 is entirely of No. 522 (5c) and 525 (6c). The sheet may also be broken to provide 20 strips of 5, each stamp of different design.

Sir Donald Alexander Smith — A271

Big Raven, by Emily Carr — A272

1970, Nov. 4 Litho. *Perf. 12*

531 A271 6c dk grn, yel & black 18 15

Smith (1820-1914), railroad builder and Canadian High Commissioner, 1896-1914.

1971, Feb. 12 Litho. *Perf. 12*

532 A272 6c multicolored 18 15

Emily Carr (1871-1945), painter and writer.

Laboratory Equipment Used for Insulin Discovery — A273

1971, Mar. 3 Litho. *Perf. 11*

533 A273 6c multicolored 18 15

Discovery of insulin by Dr. Frederick G. Banting and Dr. Charles H. Best, 50th anniversary.

A274

1971, Mar. 24 Litho. *Perf. 11*

534 A274 6c red, org & black 18 15

Sir Ernest Rutherford (1871-1937), physicist, developer of theory of spontaneous disintegration of the atom.

Spring, Winged Maple Seed A275

Louis Joseph Papineau A276

1971 Litho. *Perf. 11*

535 A275 6c shown 22 15
a. Imperf., pair 700.00
536 A275 6c Summer 22 15
537 A275 7c Autumn 22 15
538 A275 7c Winter 22 15
Set value 20

Issue dates: No. 535, Apr. 14; No. 536, June 16; No. 537, Sept. 3; No. 538, Nov. 19.

1971, May 7 Litho. & Engr. *Perf. 12*

539 A276 6c multicolored 18 15

Louis Joseph Papineau (1786-1871), member of Legislative Assembly and leader of French Canadian Patriote party.

Map of Copper Mine River Basin — A277

1971, May 7

540 A277 6c buff, red & brown 18 15

Bicentenary of Samuel Hearne's expedition to the Copper Mine River.

Maple Leaves — A278

1971, June 1

541 A278 15c blk, red org & yel 1.10 90
p. Tagged 2.50 2.25

Inauguration of new transmitters for Radio Canada International.

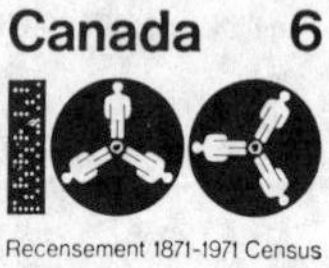

Computer Tape and Reels — A279

1971, June 1

542 A279 6c black, ultra & red 18 15

Centenary of measured progress through census.

Migrating Phosphor

Canada's "Ottawa/General" tagging of engraved stamps printed March-October, 1972, used a phosphor which migrates onto or through other stamps, booklet covers and album pages. It fluoresces yellow under ultraviolet light.

This bleeding, contaminating "OP4" phosphor can be somewhat contained in mounts or envelopes of acetate, glassine or polyethylene, but it may leak or penetrate.

The migrating phosphor is found on all copies of Nos. 560p-561p, and on some of Nos. 544p, 544q, 544r, 544s, 562p-565p and 594-598.

Transportation Means — A280

Design: 8c, Library of Parliament.

1971-72 Engr. *Perf. 12¹/₂x12*

543 A280 7c slate green 24 15
a. Booklet pane of 5 + label (#454e, #456a + 3#543) 2.75
b. Booklet pane of 20 (4 #454e, 4 #456a, 12 #543) 9.25
p. Tagged 60 22
544 A280 8c slate 15 15
a. Booklet pane of 6 (3 #454e, 1 #460c, 2 #544) 2.25
b. Booklet pane of 18 (6 #454e, 1 #460c, 11 #544) 7.50
c. Booklet pane of 10 (4 #454e, 1 #460c, 5 #544 ('72) 1.90
p. Tagged 30 16
q. As "a," tagged 2.00
r. As "b," tagged 6.50
s. As "c," tagged 2.75
Set value 15

Coil Stamps

1971 *Perf. 10 Horiz.*

549 A280 7c slate green 35 15
a. Imperf., pair 700.00
550 A280 8c slate 32 15
a. Imperf., pair 250.00
p. Tagged 30 15
Set value 18

See note below No. 468B.

Abstract "BC" A282

1971, July 20 Litho. *Perf. 12*

552 A282 7c multicolored 18 15

Centenary of British Columbia's entry into Canadian Confederation.

Indian Encampment on Lake Huron, by Kane — A283

1971, Aug. 11 *Perf. 12¹/₂*

553 A283 7c multicolored 28 15

Paul Kane (1810-1871), painter.

Snowflake A284

Pierre Laporte A285

1971, Oct. 6 Engr. *Perf. 12*

Size: 24x30mm

554 A284 6c dark blue 15 15
p. Tagged 18 15
555 A284 7c bright green 18 15
p. Tagged 24 15

Litho. and Engr.

Size: 30x30mm

556 A284 10c dp car & silver 28 30
p. Tagged 35 30
557 A284 15c lt ultra, dp car & silver 55 65
p. Tagged 75 75
Set value 1.00

Christmas.

1971, Oct. 20 Engr. *Perf. 12*

558 A285 7c black 18 15

Pierre Laporte (1921-1970), Minister of Labor, kidnapped and killed.

Figure Skating — A286

1972, Mar. 1 Litho. *Perf. 12*

559 A286 8c deep red lilac 18 15

World Figure Skating Championships, Calgary, Alberta, Mar. 6-12.

"Your Heart is your Health" A287

1972, Apr. 7 Engr. *Perf. 12x12¹/₂*

560 A287 8c red 22 15
p. Tagged 60 35

World Health Day, Apr. 7.

Frontenac, by Philippe Hébert and Fort Saint Louis, Quebec — A288

Photo. and Engr.

1972, May 17 *Perf. 12x12¹/₂*

561 A288 8c red brown & multi 18 15
p. Tagged 52 52

Tercentenary of the appointment of Louis de Buade, Count of Frontenac and Palluau (1622-1698), as Governor of New France.

Indians of Canada

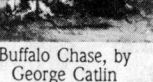

Buffalo Chase, by George Catlin A289

Thunderbird, Assiniboin Pattern A290

In Nos. 562-581, the first two and last two stamps of each annual set are printed checkerwise in same sheet of 50.

1972 Litho. *Perf. 12x12¹/₂*

562 A289 8c shown 32 15
p. Tagged 38 20
563 A289 8c Plains Indian artifacts 32 15
p. Tagged 38 20
a. Pair, #562-563 65 65
b. As "a," tagged 76 76

Perf. 12¹/₂x12

Photo. & Engr.

564 A290 8c shown 32 15
p. Tagged 38 20
565 A290 8c Ceremonial sun dance costume 32 15
p. Tagged 38 20
a. Pair, #564-565 65 65
b. As "a," tagged 76 76

Plains Indians of Canada.

Issue dates: Nos. 562-563, July 6. Nos. 564-565, Oct. 4.

Tagged (Nos. 566-581)

1973 Litho. *Perf. 12x12¹/₂*

566 A289 8c Algonkian artifacts 32 15
567 A289 8c "Micmac Indians" 32 15
a. Pair, #566-567 65 65

Perf. 12¹/₂x12

Photo. & Engr.

568 A290 8c Thunderbird and belt 32 15
569 A290 8c Algonkian man and woman 32 15
a. Pair, #568-569 65 65

Algonkian-speaking Indians of Canada (Malecite, Micmac, Montagnais, Algonquin and Ojibwa).

Issue dates: Nos. 566-567, Feb. 21, Nos. 568-569, Nov. 28.

1974 Litho. *Perf. 12x12¹/₂*

570 A289 8c Nootka Sound, house, inside 32 15
571 A289 8c Artifacts 32 15
a. Pair, #570-571 65 65

Perf. 12¹/₂x12

Photo. & Engr.

572 A290 8c Chief wearing Chilkat blanket 32 15
573 A290 8c Thunderbird from Kwakiutl house 32 15
a. Pair, #572-573 65 65

Pacific Coast Indians of Canada (Haida, Salish, Tsimshian, Chilkat and Kwakiutl).

Issue dates: Nos. 570-571, Jan. 16. Nos. 572-573, Feb. 22.

1975, Apr. 4 Litho. *Perf. 13¹/₂*

574 A289 8c Montagnais-Naskapi artifacts 30 15
575 A289 8c Dance of the Kutcha-Kutchin 30 15
a. Pair, #574-575 60 60

Perf. 12¹/₂

576 A290 8c Kutchin ceremonial costume 30 15

Litho. and Embossed

577 A290 8c Ojibwa thunderbird and Naskapi pattern 30 15
a. Pair, #576-577 60 60

Subarctic Indians.

1976, Sept. 17 Litho. *Perf. 13¹/₂*

578 A289 10c Cornhusk mask, artifacts 30 15
579 A289 10c Iroquoian Encampment, by George Heriot 30 15
a. Pair, #578-579 60 60

Perf. 12¹/₂

Litho. & Embossed

580 A290 10c Iroquoian thunderbird 30 15

Litho.

581 A290 10c Iroquoian man, woman 30 15
a. Pair, #580-581 60 60
Nos. 562-581 (20) 6.24
Set value 1.85

Iroquois (Mohawk, Cayuga, Seneca, Oneida, Onondaga and Tuscarora).

Geological Fault — A291

1972, Aug. 2 *Perf. 12*

582 A291 15c shown 1.50 1.25
p. Tagged 2.50 2.50
583 A291 15c Bird's eye view of town 1.50 1.25
p. Tagged 2.50 2.50
584 A291 15c Aerial map photography 1.50 1.25
p. Tagged 2.50 2.50
585 A291 15c Contour lines 1.50 1.25
p. Tagged 2.50 2.50
a. Block of 4, #582-585 6.00 6.00
b. As "a," tagged 10.00 10.00

Earth sciences: 24th Intl. Geological Cong. (#582); 22nd Intl. Geographical Cong. (#583); 12th Cong. of Intl. Soc. of Photogrammetry (#584); 6th Cong. of Intl. Cartographic Assoc. (#585).

Sir John A. Macdonald A292

Elizabeth II A292a

Forest, Central Canada — A293

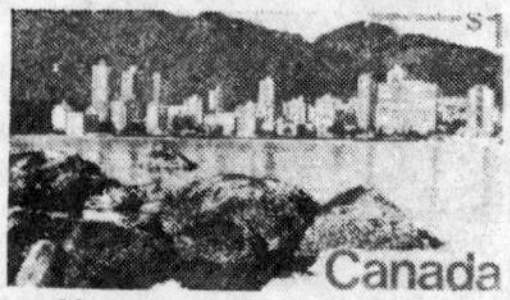

Vancouver, B.C. — A294

Designs: 2c, Sir Wilfrid Laurier. 3c, Sir Robert L. Borden. 4c, William Lyon Mackenzie King. 5c Richard Bedford Bennett. 6c, Lester B. Pearson. 7c, Louis St. Laurent. 15c, Mountain sheep, Western Canada. 20c, Grain fields, Prairie. 25c, Polar bears, North. 50c, Seashore. $2, Quebec.

1972-76 Engr. *Perf. 12x12½*
Tagged

586	A292	1c orange ('73)	15	15
a.		Booklet pane of 6 (3 #586, 1 #591, 2 #593) ('74)	55	
b.		Booklet pane of 18 (6 #586, 1 #591, 11 #593) ('75)	2.10	
c.		Booklet pane of 10 (2 #586, 4 #587, 4 #593c) ('76)	1.60	
587	A292	2c green ('73)	15	15
588	A292	3c brown ('73)	15	15
589	A292	4c black ('73)	15	15
590	A292	5c lilac ('73)	15	15
591	A292	6c dk red ('73)	15	15
592	A292	7c dk brown ('74)	15	15
593	A292a	8c ultra ('73)	15	15
b.		Perf. 13x13½ ('76)	50	15

Perf. 13x13½

593A	A292a	10c dk car ('76)	18	15
c.		Perf. 12x12½	22	15

Perf. 12½x12
Photo. & Engr.

594	A293	10c multi	18	15
595	A293	15c multi	25	15
596	A293	20c multi	35	15
597	A293	25c multi	40	15
598	A293	50c multi	80	15
599	A294	$1 multi ('73)	1.90	40

Perf. 11
Litho. & Engraved

600	A294	$1 multi	3.50	1.40
601	A294	$2 multi	3.25	1.90
		Nos. 586-601 (17)	12.01	
		Set value		4.40

No. 599 has engraved shading added in some areas.

Plates 1 and 2 of the scenic 10c differ in impression and colors. Plate 1 has distinct crosshatching of "Canada" background. On plate 2, released in 1974, this area appears solidly inked. A 1974 printing of the 50c has darker shading and a deeper tone for the dark blue areas of the photogravure impression.

Nos. 600 and 601 are untagged.

1976-77 Photo. & Engr. *Perf. 13½*

594a	A293	10c multicolored	22	15
595a	A293	15c multicolored	32	15
596a	A293	20c multicolored	50	15
597a	A293	25c multicolored	60	15
598a	A293	50c multicolored	1.65	15
599a	A294	$1 multi ('77)	2.00	25
		Nos. 594a-599a (6)	5.29	
		Set value		50

Coil Stamps

1974-76 *Perf. 10 Vert.*

604	A292a	8c ultramarine	20	15
605	A292a	10c dk carmine ('76)	28	15
		Set value		15

See note below No. 468B. No. 604 also exists in horizontal multiples without score line.

Candles A295

Candles and Fruit A296

Christmas: 8c, Like 6c. 15c, Candles, 15th century prayer book, boxes and brass vase.

1972, Nov. 1 Litho. *Perf. 12½x12*

606	A295	6c red & multi	15	15
p.		Tagged	25	25
607	A295	8c vio blue & multi	18	15
p.		Tagged	30	25

Perf. 11

608	A296	10c green & multi	40	38
p.		Tagged	60	60
609	A296	15c yel bister & multi	60	65
p.		Tagged	1.10	1.25
		Set value		1.12

"The Blacksmith's Shop," by Krieghoff A297

1972, Nov. 29 Litho. *Perf. 12½*

610	A297	8c multicolored	22	15
p.		Tagged	24	15

Cornelius Krieghoff (1815-1872), painter.

Tagged
From No. 611 onward, all stamps are tagged unless otherwise noted.

Monsignor de Laval — A298

1973, Jan. 31 Litho. *Perf. 11*

611	A298	8c silver, ultra & gold	18	15

Francois-Xavier de Montmorency-Laval de Montigny (1623-1708), 1st Bishop of Quebec and founder of many educational institutions; one of the builders of New France.

Commissioner G. A. French and Map of 1874 Trek — A299

Designs: 10c, Spectrograph. 15c, R.C.M.P. Musical Ride.

1973, Mar. 9 Litho. *Perf. 11*

612	A299	8c dk brn, org & red	16	15
613	A299	10c dk blue & multi	28	18
614	A299	15c yel grn & multi	55	40
a.		Imperf., pair	300.00	

Royal Canadian Mounted Police, cent.

Jeanne Mance A300

Joseph Howe A301

1973, Apr. 18

615	A300	8c multicolored	18	15

Jeanne Mance (1606-1673), first secular nurse in North America and founder of first hospital, the Hôtel-Dieu in Montreal settlement.

1973, May 16 Litho. *Perf. 11*

616	A301	8c gold & black	18	15

Joseph Howe (1804-1873), journalist, poet and Lieutenant-Governor of Nova Scotia.

Mist Fantasy, by James MacDonald — A302

1973, June 8 Litho. *Perf. 12½*

617	A302	15c multicolored	45	45

Centenary of the birth of James E. H. MacDonald (1873-1932), painter.

Oaks on Shore — A303

Photo. & Engr.

1973, June 22 *Perf. 12x12½*

618	A303	8c orange & red brn	18	15

Centenary of Prince Edward Island's entry into Confederation.

Scottish Settlers and "Hector" — A304

1973, July 20 Litho. *Perf. 12x12½*

619	A304	8c multicolored	18	15

Bicentenary of arrival of Scottish settlers at Pictou, N.S.

Queen Elizabeth II — A305

1973, Aug. 2 Photo. and Engr.

620	A305	8c silver & multi	18	15
621	A305	15c gold & multi	52	40

Visit to Ottawa of Elizabeth II and the Duke of Edinburgh, July 31-Aug. 4, and meeting of Commonwealth Heads of Government, Ottawa, Aug. 2-10.

Nellie McClung A306

Montreal Olympic Games A307

1973, Aug. 29 Litho. *Perf. 10½x11*

622	A306	8c multicolored	18	15

Nellie McClung (1873-1951), leader of women's suffrage movement, social reformer and writer.

1973, Sept. 20 Litho. *Perf. 12x12½*
Size: 26x44mm

623	A307	8c silver & multi	15	15
624	A307	15c gold & multi	55	30
		Set value		38

21st Olympic Games, Montreal, 1976.
See Nos. B1-B3.

Ice Skate — A308

Santa Claus — A309

1973, Nov. 7 Litho. *Perf. 12½x12*

625	A308	6c shown	15	15
626	A308	8c Dove	15	15

Perf. 10½

627	A309	10c shown	24	24
628	A309	15c Shepherd and star	50	50
		Set value		84

Christmas.

Children Diving from Dock — A310

1974, Mar. 22 Engr. *Perf. 12*

629	A310	8c shown	22	15
630	A310	8c Joggers	22	15
631	A310	8c Bicycling family	22	15
632	A310	8c Hikers	22	15
a.		Block of 4, #629-632	90	90
		Set value		40

"Keep Fit." 21st Summer Olympic Games, Montreal, 1976. When stamps are observed at an angle the Montreal Olympic Games' emblem can be seen.

Main St. and Portage Ave., Winnipeg, 1872 — A311

Perf. 12x12½

1974, May 3 Litho. & Engr.

633	A311	8c multicolored	18	15

Winnipeg's incorporation as a city, cent.

Postmaster A312

1974, June 11 Litho. *Perf. 13½x13*

634	A312	8c shown	35	20
635	A312	8c Mail collector and truck	35	20
636	A312	8c Mail handler	35	20
637	A312	8c Mail sorters	35	20
638	A312	8c Mailman	35	20
639	A312	8c Rural mail delivery	35	20
a.		Block of 6, #634-639	2.50	2.50
		Nos. 634-639 (6)	2.10	1.20

Centenary of letter carrier delivery service. Printed in sheets of 50 (5x10).

Agricultural Education — A313

1974, July 12 Litho. *Perf. 12½x12*

640	A313	8c multicolored	20	15

Ontario Agricultural College centenary.

Pedestal, Gallows Frame and Contempra Telephones A314

1974, July 26 *Perf. 12½*

641	A314	8c multicolored	20	15

Centenary of the idea for the telephone by Alexander Graham Bell while visiting Brantford, Canada.

Bicycle Wheel and Cycling Emblem
A315

Photo. & Engr.

1974, Aug. 7 *Perf. 12x12½*
642 A315 8c black, red & silver 20 15

World Cycling Championships, Montreal, Aug. 14-25.

Mennonite Settlers
A316

1974, Aug. 28 Litho. *Perf. 12x12½*
643 A316 8c multicolored 20 15

Centenary of arrival of Mennonite settlers in Manitoba.

Snowshoeing
A317

1974, Sept. 23 Engr. *Perf. 13½*
644 A317 8c shown 25 15
645 A317 8c Skiing 25 15
646 A317 8c Skating 25 15
647 A317 8c Curling 25 15
a. Block of 4, #644-647 1.00 1.00

"Keep Fit." 1976 Winter Olympic Games. When the stamps are observed at an angle the Montreal Olympic Games' emblem can be seen.

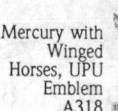

Mercury with Winged Horses, UPU Emblem
A318

Photo. & Engr.

1974, Oct. 9 *Perf. 12x12½*
648 A318 8c violet, red & blue 16 15
649 A318 15c violet, red & blue 65 50

Centenary of Universal Postal Union.

Nativity, by Jean Paul Lemieux — A319

Skaters at Hull, by Henri Masson — A320

Christmas (Paintings): 10c, The Ice Cone, Montmorency Falls, by Robert C. Todd. 15c, Village in the Laurentian Mountains, by Clarence A. Gagnon.

1974, Nov. 1 Litho. *Perf. 13½*
650 A319 6c multicolored 15 15
651 A320 8c multicolored 15 15
652 A319 10c multicolored 30 18
653 A319 15c multicolored 50 35
Set value 63

Marconi and St. John's, Newfoundland, from Signal Hill — A321

1974, Nov. 15 Litho. *Perf. 13*
654 A321 8c multicolored 18 15

Guglielmo Marconi (1874-1937), Italian electrical engineer and inventor.

Merritt and Welland Canal — A322

Perf. 13x13½

1974, Nov. 29 Litho. & Engr.
655 A322 8c multicolored 18 15

Sesquicentennial of the start of construction of the Welland Canal between Lakes Ontario and Erie, a project conceived and supervised by William Hamilton Merritt (1793-1862). Portrait by Robert Whale.

The Sprinter
A323

The Plunger
A324

Designs: Sculptures by Robert Tait McKenzie, M.D. (1867-1938), and Montreal Olympic Games' emblem.

Perf. 12½x12, 12x12½

1975, Mar. 14 Litho.; Embossed
656 A323 $1 multicolored 2.00 1.65
657 A324 $2 multicolored 4.25 3.25

21st Olympic Games, Montreal, July 17-Aug. 1, 1976.

Anne of Green Gables
A325

Maria Chapdelaine
A326

1975, May 15 Litho. *Perf. 13*
658 A325 8c blue & multi 18 15
659 A326 8c brown & multi 18 15
a. Pair, #658-659 36 35
Set value 16

Birth centenary of Lucy Maud Montgomery (1874-1942), writer and author of "Anne of Green Gables"; Louis Hémon (1880-1913), writer and author of "Maria Chapdelaine." Nos. 658-659 printed checkerwise.

Marguerite Bourgeoys — A327

Alphonse Desjardins — A328

1975, May 30 Litho. *Perf. 12½x12*
660 A327 8c red & multi 18 15
661 A328 8c red & multi 18 15
Set value 16

Marguerite Bourgeoys (1620-1700), founder of the Congrégation de Notre-Dame, Montreal, first girls' school in New France; Alphonse Desjardins (1854-1920), journalist, founder of first credit union in North America.

Samuel Dwight Chown — A329

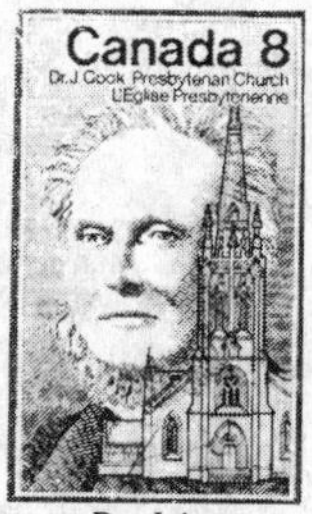

Dr. John Cook — A330

Photo. & Engr.

1975, May 30 *Perf. 12x12½*
662 A329 8c dk brown, yel & buff 18 15
663 A330 8c dk brown, yel & buff 18 15
a. Pair, #662-663 60 60
Set value 16

Chown (1853-1933), Methodist minister, leader of temperance movement, founder of United Church. Cook (1805-92), 1st Moderator of the United Presbyterian Church in Canada.
Nos. 662-663 printed checkerwise.

Pole Vaulting — A331

Hurdling — A332

Design: 25c, Marathon running and Montreal Olympic Games' emblem.

1975, June 11 Litho. *Perf. 12x12½*
664 A331 20c dk blue & multi 55 50
665 A331 25c maroon & multi 65 55
666 A332 50c multicolored 1.25 1.00

21st Olympic Games, Montreal, July 17-Aug. 1, 1976.

"Untamed" (Wild Horse Race) — A333

1975, July 3 *Perf. 12x12½*
667 A333 8c gray & multi 18 15

Centenary of the founding of Calgary.

Female Symbol
A334

"Justice," by Walter S. Allward
A335

Photo. & Engr.

1975, July 14 *Perf. 13*
668 A334 8c dp yel, gray & black 18 15

International Women's Year.

1975, Sept. 2 Litho. *Perf. 12½*
669 A335 8c multicolored 18 15

Supreme Court of Canada, centenary.

"Wm. D. Lawrence"
A336

Photo. & Engr.

1975, Sept. 24 *Perf. 13*
670 A336 8c shown 35 28
671 A336 8c "Beaver" 35 28
672 A336 8c "Neptune" 35 28
673 A336 8c "Quadra" 35 28
a. Block of 4, #670-673 1.40 1.40

Coastal ships.

Santa Claus — A337

Child — A338

Trees — A339

Designs by Canadian School Children: "What Christmas Means to Me."

1975, Oct. 22 Litho. *Perf. 13½*
674 A337 6c shown 15 15
675 A337 6c Skater 15 15
a. Pair, #674-675 25 25
676 A338 8c shown 15 15
677 A338 8c Family and Christmas tree 15 15
a. Pair, #676-677 30 30
678 A338 10c Gift box 20 20
679 A339 15c shown 40 40
Nos. 674-679 (6) 1.20
Set value 88

Christmas. Stamps of same denomination printed checkerwise.

Legion Emblem and Bugle — A340

Photo. & Engr.

1975, Nov. 10 *Perf. 13*
680 A340 8c gray & multi 18 15

Royal Canadian Legion, 50th anniversary.

Olympic Torch Ignited by Satellite in Canada — A341

Communication Arts — A342

High-rise Tower, Notre Dame Church, Montreal, and Games' Emblem — A343

Snowflake, Winter Olympics' Emblem — A344

Montreal Olympic Games' Emblem and: 20c, Canadian athletes carrying Olympic flag. 25c, Women athletes receiving Olympic medals.

1976, June 18 Litho. *Perf. 13*

681	A341 8c blk & multi	15	15
682	A341 20c blk & multi	45	35
683	A341 25c blk & multi	55	55

1976 Olympic Games ceremonies.

1976, Feb. 6 Photo. *Perf. 12x12½*

Designs: 25c, Handicraft tools. 50c, Performing arts.

684	A342 20c gray & multi	75	35
685	A342 25c ocher & multi	85	42
686	A342 50c blue & multi	1.40	65

Olympic Fine Arts and Cultural Program.

Photo. & Engr.

1976, Mar. 12 *Perf. 13*

Design: $2, Olympic Stadium, Velodrome, flags and emblem.

687	A343 $1 silver & multi	2.25	1.75
688	A343 $2 gold & multi	4.50	3.50

Nos. 681-688 were issued in commemoration of, or in connection with the 21st Olympic Games, Montreal, July 17-Aug. 1. Nos. 687-688 were issued in panes of 8.

Photo. and Embossed

1976, Feb. 6 *Perf. 12½*

689	A344 20c multicolored	80	40

12th Winter Olympic Games, Innsbruck, Austria, Feb. 4-15.

Flower Growing from City — A345

1976, May 12 Litho. *Perf. 12x12½*

690	A345 20c multicolored	42	40

Habitat, UN Conference on Human Settlements, Vancouver, May 31-June 11.

Franklin and Map of North America, 1776 — A346

1976, June 1 Litho. & Engr. *Perf. 13*

691	A346 10c multicolored	22	15

American Bicentennial; Benjamin Franklin (1706-1790), deputy postmaster general for the colonies (1753-1774).

See US No. 1690.

Color Parade, Memorial Arch — A347

Wing Parade, Mackenzie Building — A348

1976, June 1 Litho. *Perf. 12*

692	A347 8c red & multi	15	15
693	A348 8c red & multi	15	15
a.	Pair, #692-693	30	30
	Set value		16

Royal Military College, Kingston, Ont., centenary.

Archer in Wheelchair A349

1976, Aug. 3 Litho. *Perf. 12x12½*

694	A349 20c green & multi	45	42

Olympiad for the Physically Disabled (25th Stoke Mandeville Games), Toronto, Aug. 3-11.

The Cremation of Sam McGee — A350

The Outlander — A351

1976, Aug. 17 *Perf. 13½*

695	A350 8c multicolored	15	15
696	A351 8c multicolored	15	15
a.	Pair, #695-698	30	30
	Set value		16

Robert W. Service (1874-1958), author of poem "The Cremation of Sam McGee"; Germaine Guevremont, author of "Le Survenant" (The Outlander).

Nativity, St. Michael's, Toronto — A352

Nativity, Stained-glass windows: 10c, St. Jude, London, Ontario. 20c, Designed and owned by Yvonne Williams.

1976, Nov. 3 Litho. *Perf. 13½*

697	A352 8c multicolored	15	15
698	A352 10c multicolored	15	15
699	A352 20c multicolored	40	60
	Set value		70

Christmas.

Inland Vessals A353

Litho. & Engr.

1976, Nov. 19 *Perf. 12*

700	A353 10c Northcote	28	22
701	A353 10c Passport	28	22
702	A353 10c Chicora	28	22
703	A353 10c Athabasca	28	22
a.	Block of 4, #700-703	1.10	1.10

Elizabeth II — A354

Litho. and Typo.

1977, Feb. 4 *Perf. 12½x12*

704	A354 25c silver & multi	55	40

25th anniv. of the reign of Elizabeth II.

Bottle Gentian — A355

Elizabeth II — A356

Parliament, Ottawa A357

Trembling Aspen A358

Main Street, Prairie Town — A359

Fundy National Park A359a

Designs: 2c, Western columbine. 3c, Canada lily. 4c, Hepatica. 5c, Shooting star. 10c, Franklin's lady's-slipper. No. 712, Jewelweed. No. 715, Parliament, Ottawa. No. 716, Queen Elizabeth II. 20c, Douglas fir. 25c, Maple. 30c, Red oak. 75c, Old houses, eastern City Street. 80c, Street leading to the sea, Eastern Maritime Provinces. $2 Kluane National Park.

Perf. 12x12½

1977-79 Litho. & Engr.

705	A355 1c multicolored	15	15
707	A355 2c multicolored	15	15
708	A355 3c multicolored	15	15
709	A355 4c multicolored	15	15
710	A355 5c multicolored	15	15
711	A355 10c multicolored	15	15
a.	Perf. 13 ('78)	15	15

Photo. & Engr.

Perf. 13x13½

712	A355 12c multi ('78)	35	15
713	A356 12c blue & multi	20	15
a.	Perf. 12x12½	35	15

Engraved

Perf. 13

714	A357 12c blue	18	15
715	A357 14c red ('78)	18	15

Photo. & Engr.

Perf. 13x13½

716	A356 14c red & black ('78)	18	15
a.	Perf. 12x12½	20	15
b.	As "a," booklet pane of 25 + 2 labels ('78)	7.50	
c.	Red omitted	*000.00*	

Perf. 13½

717	A358 15c multi	35	15
718	A358 20c multi	24	15
719	A358 25c multi	40	15
720	A358 30c multi ('78)	45	15
721	A358 35c multi ('79)	45	20
723	A359 50c multi ('78)	90	15
723A	A359 50c multi, litho. & engr. ('78)	75	15
724	A359 75c multi ('78)	1.10	22
725	A359 80c multi ('78)	1.10	24

Lithographed and Engraved

Perf. 13

726	A359a $1 multi ('79)	1.25	45
a.	Untagged	1.40	60
727	A359a $2 multi ('79)	2.75	1.10
	Nos. 705-727 (22)	11.73	
	Set value		3.40

On No. 723A license plate on yellow car reads "1978." See Nos. 781-806, 931, 934-937, 1084.

Coil Stamps

1977-78 Engr. *Perf. 10 Vert.*

729	A357 12c blue	20	15
a.	Imperf., pair	100.00	
730	A357 14c red ('78)	22	15
a.	Imperf., pair	100.00	
	Set value		16

See note below No. 468B.

Eastern Cougar A360

1977, Mar. 30 Litho. *Perf. 12½*

732	A360 12c multicolored	20	15

Wildlife protection.

April in Algonquin Park, by Thomson — A361

Design: No. 734, Autumn Birches, by Tom Thomson.

1977, May 26 Litho. *Perf. 12*

733	A361 12c black & multi	20	15
734	A361 12c ocher & multi	20	15
a.	Pair, #733-734	40	40
	Set value		20

Tom Thomson (1877-1917), landscape painter, birth centenary. Nos. 733-734 printed checkerwise.

Names of Governors General and Standard A362

1977, June 30 *Perf. 12½*

735	A362 12c vio blue & multi	20	15

Honoring Canadian-born Governors General: Vincent Massey, Georges Philias Vanier, Daniel Roland Michener and Jules Léger.

Order of Canada A363

1977, June 30 Litho. & Embossed

736	A363	12c multicolored	20	15

Order of Canada, 10th anniversary.

Peace Bridge, Canadian, US and UN Flags A364

1977, Aug. 4 Litho. *Perf. 12½*

737	A364	12c blue & multi	20	15

50th anniversary of the Peace Bridge, connecting Fort Erie, Ontario, with Buffalo, N.Y.

Joseph E. Bernier, CGS Arctic — A365

Sandford Fleming, Railroad Bridge A366

1977, Sept. 16 Engr. *Perf. 13*

738	A365	12c dark blue	20	15
739	A366	12c brown	20	15
a.		Pair, #738-739	40	40
		Set value		20

Joseph-Elzéar Bernier (1852-1934), explorer; Sandford Fleming (1827-1915), mapped route for Intercolonial Railway and designed Canada's first stamp.

Nos. 738-739 printed checkerwise.

Peace Tower, Parliament, Ottawa A367

1977, Sept. 19 Litho. *Perf. 12½*

740	A367	25c multicolored	52	50

23rd Commonwealth Parliamentary Conference, Ottawa, Sept. 19-25.

Hunters Following Star — A368

Christmas: 12c, Angelic choir in northern light. 25c, Christ Child in Ring of Glory blessing chiefs from afar. Illustrations for Canada's first Christmas carol, written by Father Brébeuf, 1649.

1977, Oct. 26 Litho. *Perf. 13½*

741	A368	10c multicolored	15	15
742	A368	12c multicolored	18	15
743	A368	25c multicolored	35	35
		Set value		50

Pinky A369

Designs: Canadian sailing ships.

Litho. and Engr.

1977, Nov. 18 *Perf. 12x12½*

744	A369	12c shown	20	15
745	A369	12c Tern schooner	20	15
746	A369	12c 5-masted schooner	20	15
747	A369	12c Mackinaw boat	20	15
a.		Block of 4, #744-747	80	80

See Nos. 776-779.

Seal Hunter, Soapstone Sculpture A370

Disguised Caribou Hunter, Print — A371

Inuit Art: No. 749, Spear fishing. No. 751, Walrus hunt. Nos. 749-751 are after stonecut prints.

1977, Nov. 18 Litho. *Perf. 12x12½*

748	A370	12c multicolored	20	15
749	A371	12c multicolored	20	15
a.		Pair, #748-749	40	40
750	A371	12c multicolored	20	15
751	A371	12c multicolored	20	15
a.		Pair, #750-751	40	40

Inuit hunting. Nos. 748-749 and Nos. 750-751 printed se-tenant checkerwise.

Peregrine Falcon A372

1978, Jan. 18 Litho. *Perf. 12½*

752	A372	12c multicolored	20	15

Endangered wildlife.

Canada No. 3, 1851 — A373

1978 Photo. & Engr. *Perf. 13½*

753	A373	12c shown	15	15
754	A373	14c No. 7	18	15
755	A373	30c No. 8	42	22
756	A373	$1.25 No. 2	1.65	65
a.		Souvenir sheet of 3	2.25	
		Set value		98

CAPEX '78, Canadian Intl. Phil. Exhib., Toronto, June 9-18 (cent. of Canada's admission to UPU).

No. 756a contains one each of Nos. 754-756 ($1.25 untagged).

Issue dates: 12c, Jan. 18. Others, June 10.

Games' Emblem A374

Stadium A375

Design: 30c, Badminton.

1978, Mar. 31 Litho. *Perf. 12½*

757	A374	14c silver & multi	24	15
758	A374	30c silver & multi	52	35

1978, Aug. 3

Designs: No. 760, Running. No. 761, Alberta Legislature building, Edmonton. No. 762, Bowls.

759	A375	14c silver & multi	20	15
760	A375	14c silver & multi	20	15
a.		Pair, #759-760	40	40
761	A375	30c silver & multi	50	35
762	A375	30c silver & multi	50	35
a.		Pair, #761-762	1.00	1.00
		Set value		86

Nos. 757-762 commemorate 11th Commonwealth Games, Edmonton, Aug. 3-12.

Stamps of same denomination printed checkerwise.

Capt. Cook, by Nathaniel Dance — A376

Nootka Sound, by John Webber — A377

1978, Apr. 26 Litho. *Perf. 13*

763	A376	14c multicolored	20	15
764	A377	14c multicolored	20	15
a.		Pair, #763-764	40	40
		Set value		20

Capt. James Cook (1728-1779), explorer of Canada's East and West Coasts and bicentenary of his anchorage near Anchorage, June 1, 1778. Nos. 763-764 printed checkerwise.

Silver Mine, Cobalt Lake A378

Stripmining, Athabasca Tar Sands A379

1978, May 19 Litho. *Perf. 12½*

765	A378	14c multicolored	20	15
766	A379	14c multicolored	20	15
a.		Pair, #765-766	40	40
		Set value		20

Development of national resources. Nos. 765-766 printed checkerwise.

Prince's Gate — A380

1978, Aug. 16 Litho. *Perf. 12½*

767	A380	14c multicolored	20	15

Canadian National Exhibition, centenary.

Mère d'Youville and Miracle of Food — A381

1978, Sept. 21 Litho. *Perf. 13x13½*

768	A381	14c multicolored	20	15

Marguerite d'Youville (1701-1771), founder of the Gray Nuns, beatified 1959.

Woman Walking, by Pitseolak A382

Migration, Soapstone by Joe Talurinili A383

Works by Eskimo Artists: No. 771, Plane over village, stonecut and stencil print by Pudlo. No. 772, Dogteam and sled, ivory sculpture by Abraham Kingmeatook.

1978, Sept. 27 *Perf. 13½*

769	A382	14c multicolored	22	15
770	A383	14c multicolored	22	15
a.		Pair, #769-770	45	45
771	A382	14c multicolored	22	15
772	A383	14c multicolored	22	15
a.		Pair, #771-772	45	45

Travels of the Inuit. Printed checkerwise.

Madonna of the Flowering Pea, Cologne School — A384

Renaissance Paintings in National Gallery of Canada: 14c, Virgin and Child, by Hans Memling. 30c, Virgin and Child, by Jacopo Di Cione.

1978, Oct. 20 Litho. *Perf. 12½*

773	A384	12c multicolored	15	15
774	A384	14c multicolored	20	15
775	A384	30c multicolored	45	28
		Set value		44

Christmas.

Sailing Ships Type of 1977

Litho. & Engr.

1978, Nov. 15 *Perf. 13*

776	A369	14c "Chief Justice Robinson," 1842	22	15
777	A369	14c "St. Roch," 1928	22	15
778	A369	14c "Northern Light," 1928	22	15
779	A369	14c "Labrador," 1954	22	15
a.		Block of 4, #776-779	90	90

Ice vessels.

Quebec Carnival — A386

1979, Feb. 1 Litho. *Perf. 13*

780	A386	14c multicolored	22	15

Flower, Queen & Parliament Types of 1977

Designs: 1c, Bottle gentian. 2c, Western columbine. 3c, Canada lily. 4c, Hepatica. 5c, Shooting star. 10c, Franklin's lady's-slipper. 15c, Canada violet. No. 789, Elizabeth II. No. 790, Parliament, Ottawa.

Photo. & Engr., Engr. (#790)

1977-83 *Perf. 13x13½*

781	A355	1c multi ('79)	15	15
a.		Perf. 12x12½ ('77)	15	15
b.		Bklt. pane, 2 #781a, 4 #713a	1.50	
782	A355	2c multi ('79)	15	15
a.		Bklt. pane, 4 #782, 3 #716a + label	1.00	
b.		Perf. 12x12½ ('78)	15	15

783 A355 3c multi ('79) 15 15
784 A355 4c multi ('79) 15 15
785 A355 5c multi ('79) 15 15
786 A355 10c multi ('79) 15 15
787 A355 15c multi ('79) 24 15
789 A356 17c green & blk ('79) 24 15
a. Perf. 12x12½ 28 15
b. Bklt. pane of 25 + 2 labels 7.50
790 A357 17c slate green ('79) 24 15
791 A356 30c multi ('82) 45 15
792 A356 32c multi ('83) 45 15
Set value 2.10 70

Nos. 781a, 782b, 789a are from booklet panes. No. 782b has one straight edge, others one or two.

Booklet Stamps
Parliament Type of 1977

1979, Mar. 28 Engr. *Perf. 12x12½*
797 A357 1c slate blue 15 15
a. Bklt. pane, 1 #797, 3 #800, 2 #789a 1.00
800 A357 5c violet brown 15 15
Set value 20 20

#797 has one straight edge, #800 has one or two.

Coil Stamp

1979, Mar. 8 Engr. *Perf. 10 Vert.*
806 A357 17c slate green 28 15
a. Imperf., pair 200.00

Endangered Wildlife A392

1979, Apr. 10 Litho. *Perf. 12½*
813 A392 17c Turtle 22 15
814 A392 35c Whale 60 35

Ribbon Around Woman's Finger — A393

Design: No. 816, String around man's finger.

1979, Apr. 10
815 A393 17c multicolored 28 15
816 A393 17c multicolored 28 15
a. Pair, #815-816 56 55
Set value 16

Use postal code. Printed checkerwise.

Fruits of the Earth, by F. P. Grove — A394

The Golden Vessel, by Emile Nelligan — A395

1979, May 3 Litho. *Perf. 13x13½*
817 A394 17c multicolored 28 15
818 A395 17c multicolored 28 15
a. Pair, #817-818 56 55
Set value 20

Frederick Philip Grove (1879-1948), teacher and writer; Emile Nelligan (1879-1941), French-Canadian poet. Nos. 817-818 printed checkerwise.

De Salaberry — A396

John By — A397

1979, May 11 *Perf. 13½*
819 A396 17c multicolored 28 15
820 A397 17c multicolored 28 15
a. Pair, #819-820 56 55
Set value 20

Charles-Michel d'Irumberry de Salaberry (1778-1829), and John By (1779-1836), Canadian colonels. Printed checkerwise.

Flag of Ontario — A398

Designs: Provincial and Territorial flags.

1979, June 15 Litho. *Perf. 13*
821 A398 17c shown 32 20
822 A398 17c Quebec 32 20
823 A398 17c Nova Scotia 32 20
824 A398 17c New Brunswick 32 20
825 A398 17c Manitoba 32 20
826 A398 17c British Columbia 32 20
827 A398 17c Prince Edward Island 32 20
828 A398 17c Saskatchewan 32 20
829 A398 17c Alberta 32 20
830 A398 17c Newfoundland 32 20
831 A398 17c Northwest Territories 32 20
832 A398 17c Yukon Territory 32 20
a. Sheet of 12, #821-832 4.00
Nos. 821-832 (12) 3.84 2.40

White Water Kayak Race — A399

1979, July 3 Litho. *Perf. 12½*
833 A399 17c multicolored 28 15

Canoe-Kayak (Slalom and Wild Water) World Championships, Jonquière and Desbiens, Quebec, June 30-July 8.

Women's Field Hockey A400

1979, Aug. 16
834 A400 17c multicolored 28 15

Women's Field Hockey Championship, Vancouver, B.C., Aug. 16-30.

Summer Tent, Print by Kiakshuk — A401

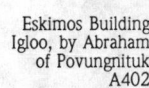

Eskimos Building Igloo, by Abraham of Povungnituk A402

Works by Eskimo Artists: No. 837, The Dance, print by Kalvak of Holman Island. No. 838, Two soapstone figures from Repulse Bay, by Madeleine Isserkut and Jean Mapsalak.

1979, Sept. 13 Litho. *Perf. 13½*
835 A401 17c multicolored 24 15
836 A402 17c multicolored 24 15
a. Pair, #835-836 50 50
837 A401 17c multicolored 24 15
838 A402 17c multicolored 24 15
a. Pair, #837-838 50 50
Set value 40

Inuit shelters and community. Printed checkerwise.

Painted Wooden Train — A403

Antique Toys: 17c, Horse, pull toy. 35c, Knitted doll (vert.).

1979, Oct. 17 Litho. *Perf. 13*
839 A403 15c multicolored 24 15
840 A403 17c multicolored 25 15
841 A403 35c multicolored 52 28
Set value 42

Christmas.

Girl Watering Tree of Life — A404

1979, Oct. 24
842 A404 17c multicolored 24 15

International Year of the Child.

Curtiss HS-2L — A405

1979, Nov. 15 Litho. *Perf. 12½*
843 A405 17c shown 28 15
844 A405 17c Canadair CL-215 28 15
a. Pair, #843-844 56 55
845 A405 35c Vichers Vedette 55 50
846 A405 35c Consolidated Canso 55 50
a. Pair, #845-846 1.10 1.10

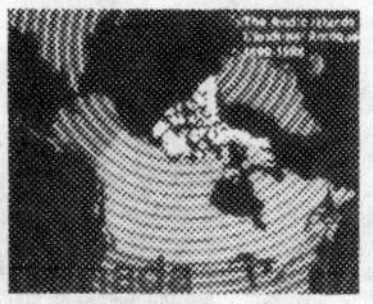
Map of Canada Showing Arctic Islands — A406

1980, Jan. 23 Litho. *Perf. 13½*
847 A406 17c multicolored 24 15

Acquisition of the Arctic Islands, centenary.

Downhill Skiing — A407

1980, Jan. 23
848 A407 35c multicolored 45 30

13th Winter Olympic Games, Lake Placid, NY, Feb. 12-24.

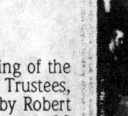

Meeting of the School Trustees, by Robert Harris — A408

Royal Canadian Academy of Arts Centenary: No. 850, Inspiration, bronze sculpture, by Louis-Philippe Hebert (1850-1917). No. 851, Parliament Buildings, by Thomas Fuller (1822-1919). No. 852, Sunrise on the Saguenay, by Lucius O'Brien (1832-99).

1980, Mar. 6 Litho.
849 A408 17c multicolored 25 15
850 A408 17c multicolored 25 15
a. Pair, #849-850 50 50
851 A408 35c multicolored 52 40
852 A408 35c multicolored 52 40
a. Pair, #851-852 1.05 1.05

Printed checkerwise.

Atlantic Whitefish A409

Endangered wildlife. No. 854, Greater prairie chicken.

1980, May 6 Litho. *Perf. 12½*
853 A409 17c multicolored 28 15
854 A409 17c multicolored 28 15
Set value 20

Garden — A410

Helping Hands — A411

1980, May 29 Litho. *Perf. 13½*
855 A410 17c multicolored 24 15

Intl. Flower Show, Montreal, May 17-Sept. 1.

Litho. & Embossed

1980, May 29 *Perf. 12½*
856 A411 17c ultra & gold 24 15

14th World Congress of Rehabilitation International, Winnipeg, June 22-27.

"O Canada" Opening Bars — A412

Composers Lavallee, Routhier, Weir — A413

1980, June 6 Litho. *Perf. 12½*
857 A412 17c multicolored 24 15
858 A413 17c multicolored 24 15
a. Pair, #857-858 50 50
Set value 20

"O Canada" centenary. Printed checkerwise in sheets of 16.

Canada stamps can be mounted in the Scott Canada Specialty and Master Canada albums.

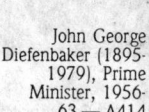

John George Diefenbaker (1895-1979), Prime Minister, 1956-63 — A414

1980, June 20 **Engr.** *Perf. 13½*

859	A414 17c dark blue		24	15

Emma Albani (1847-1930), Soprano — A415

Design: No. 861, Healey Willan (1880-1968), organist and composer. Printed checkerwise.

1980, July 4 **Litho.** *Perf. 13½*

860 A415 17c multicolored	24	15
861 A415 17c multicolored	24	15
a. Pair, #860-861	50	50
Set value		20

Ned Hanlan (1855-1908), Oarsman A416

1980, July 4 **Litho.**

862 A416 17c multicolored	24	15

Wheat Fields, Saskatchewan A417

Design: No. 864, Strip mining and town, Alberta.

1980, Aug. 27 **Litho.** *Perf. 13½*

863 A417 17c multicolored	24	15
864 A417 17c multicolored	24	15
Set value		20

75th anniversary of Saskatchewan's and Alberta's entry into Confederation.

Uraninite Molecular Structure — A418

1980, Sept. 3

865 A418 35c multicolored	48	40

Discovery of uranium in Canada, 80th anniversary.

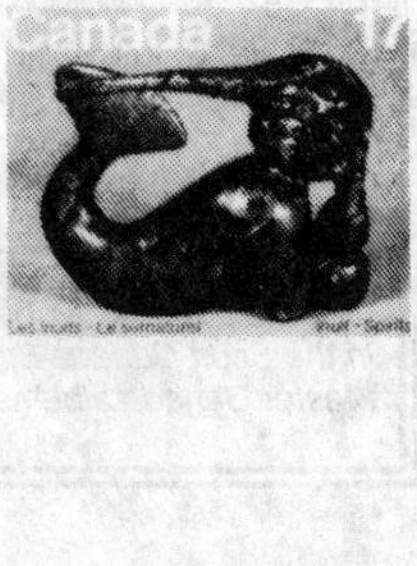

Sedna, by Ashoona Kiawak A419

Return of the Sun, Print by Kenojouak A420

Works by Eskimo Artists: No. 868, Bird Spirit, by Doris Hagiolok. No. 869, Shaman, print by Simon Tookoome.

1980, Sept. 25 **Litho.** *Perf. 13½*

866 A419 17c multicolored	25	15
867 A420 17c multicolored	25	15
a. Pair, #866-867	50	50
868 A419 35c multicolored	52	50
869 A420 35c multicolored	52	50
a. Pair, #868-869	1.05	1.00

Inuit spirits. Printed checkerwise.

Christmas Morning, by Frank Charles Hennessey — A421

Christmas (Greeting Cards, 1931): 17c, Sleigh Ride, by Joseph Sydney Hallam. 35c, McGill Cab Stand, by Kathleen Morris.

1980, Oct. 22 **Litho.** *Perf. 12½x12*

870 A421 15c multicolored	22	15
871 A421 17c multicolored	25	15
872 A421 35c multicolored	52	25
Set value		41

Avro Canada CF-100, 1950 — A422

Military Aircraft: No. 874, Avro Lancaster, 1941. No. 875, Curtiss JN-4 Canuck. No. 876, Hawker Hurricane, 1935.

1980, Nov. 10 *Perf. 13x13½*

873 A422 17c multicolored	25	15
874 A422 17c multicolored	25	15
a. Pair, #873-874	50	20
875 A422 35c multicolored	55	50
876 A422 35c multicolored	55	50
a. Pair, #875-876	1.10	1.00

Printed checkerwise.

Emmanuel-Persillier Lachapelle, Caduceus — A423

1980, Dec. 5 *Perf. 13½*

877 A423 17c multicolored	25	15

Lachapelle (1845-1918), physician, founded Notre Dame Hospital, Montreal, 1880.

Mandora, 18th Century A424

1981, Jan. 19 **Litho.** *Perf. 12½*

878 A424 17c multicolored	25	15

"The Look of Music" rare musical instrument exhibition, Vancouver, Nov. 2, 1980-Apr. 5, 1981.

Emily Stowe (1831-1903) and Toronto General Hospital A425

Designs: No. 880, Louise McKinney, (1868-1931) Alberta legislative building. No. 881, Idola Saint-Jean, (1875-1945) Quebec legislative building. No. 882, Henrietta Edwards, (1849-1931) clubwomen.

1981, Mar. 4 **Litho.** *Perf. 13x13½*

879 A425 17c multicolored	28	15
880 A425 17c multicolored	28	15
881 A425 17c multicolored	28	15
882 A425 17c multicolored	28	15
a. Block of 4, #879-882	1.15	1.10
Set value		32

Vancouver Island Marmot, by Michael Dumas A426

Endangered Wildlife: 35c, Wood bison, by Robert Bateman.

1981, Apr. 6 **Litho.**

883 A426 17c multicolored	24	15
884 A426 35c multicolored	60	60

Kateri Tekakwitha ("Lily of the Mohawks"), by Emile Brunet — A427

Brunet Sculpture: No. 886, Marie de L'Incarnation.

1981, Apr. 24 *Perf. 12½*

885 A427 17c brown & pale grn	25	15
886 A427 17c lt blue & ultra	25	15
a. Pair, #885-886	50	50
Set value		20

Beatification of Kateri Tekakwitha (1656-1680), first North American Indian saint, and Marie De L'Incarnation (1599-1672), founder of Ursuline Order.

At Baie Saint-Paul, by Marc-Aurele Fortin (1888-1970) — A428

Paintings: No. 888, Self-portrait, by Frederick H. Varley (1881-1969), vert. 35c, Untitled No. 6, by Paul-Emile Borduas (1905-1960), vert.

1981, May 22 **Litho.** *Perf. 12½*

887 A428 17c multicolored	25	15
888 A428 17c multicolored	25	15

Photo.

Perf. 13

889 A428 35c multicolored	40	35
Set value		55

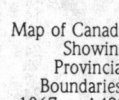

Map of Canada Showing Provincial Boundaries, 1867 — A429

1981, June 30 **Litho.** *Perf. 13½*

890 A429 17c shown	30	15
891 A429 17c 1873	30	15
892 A429 17c 1905	30	15
893 A429 17c 1949	30	15
a. Strip of 4, #890-893	1.20	1.20

Canada Day.

Frere Marie-Victorin (1885-1944) Botanist — A430

Montreal Rose — A431

Botanists: No. 895, John Macoun (1831-1920).

1981, July 22 **Litho.** *Perf. 12½*

894 A430 17c multicolored	25	15
895 A430 17c multicolored	25	15
a. Pair, #894-895	50	50
Set value		20

1981, July 22 *Perf. 13½*

896 A431 17c multicolored	25	15

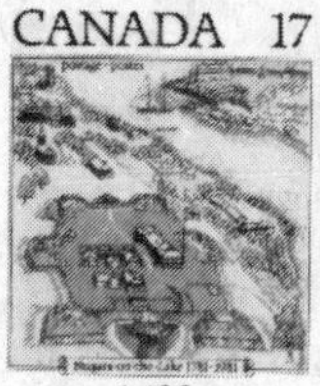

A432

A433

Photo. & Engr.

1981, July 31 *Perf. 13½*

897 A432 17c multicolored	25	15

Niagara-on-the-Lake (1st capital of Upper Canada).

1981, Aug. 14 **Litho.**

898 A433 17c multicolored	25	15

Acadian Congress centenary.

A434

A435

1981, Sept. 8

899 A434 17c multicolored	25	15

Aaron Mosher (1881-1959), Labor Congress founder.

1981, Nov. 16 **Litho.** *Perf. 13½*

900 A435 15c 1781	24	15
901 A435 15c 1881	24	15
902 A435 15c 1981	24	15
Set value		24

Christmas; bicentenary of 1st illuminated Christmas tree in Canada.

Canadair CL-41 Tutor A436

1981, Nov. 24 Litho. *Perf. 12½*

903 A436 17c shown 25 15
904 A436 17c de Havilland Tiger Moth 25 15
a. Pair, #903-904 50 30
905 A436 35c Avro Canada C-102 52 40
906 A436 35c de Havilland Canada Dash-7 52 40
a. Pair, #905-906 1.05 80

A437

1981, Dec. 29 Engr. *Perf. 13x13½*

907 A437 (30c) red 55 15

Coil Stamp

Perf. 10 Vert.

908 A437 (30c) red 85 15

See Nos. 923-924, 941-951.

CANADA '82 Intl. Philatelic Youth Exhibition, Toronto, May 20-24 — A438

1982 Litho. *Perf. 13½*

909 A438 30c No. 1 45 16
910 A438 30c No. 102 45 16
911 A438 35c No. 223 52 30
912 A438 35c No. 155 52 30
913 A438 60c No. 158 1.00 55
a. Souvenir sheet of 5, #909-913 3.25 2.00
Nos. 909-913 (5) 2.94 1.47

Issud: Nos. 909, 911, Mar. 11; others, May 20.

Jules Leger (1913-1980), 26th Governor General — A439

Terry Fox (1958-1981), Marathon of Hope — A440

1982, Apr. 2 Litho. *Perf. 13½*

914 A439 30c multicolored 42 15

1982, Apr. 13 *Perf. 12½*

915 A440 30c multicolored 42 15

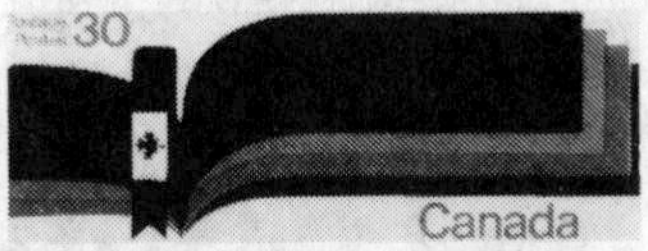

1982 Constitution — A441

1982, Apr. 16 Litho. *Perf. 12x12½*

916 A441 30c multicolored 42 15

Types of 1977-82 and

Decoy — A442

Parliament (Library) — A443

Parliament (West Block) — A444

Parliament (East Block) — A445

Elizabeth II — A446

Designs: Artifacts, 18th and 19th cent.

1982-87 Litho. *Perf. 14x13½*

917 A442 1c shown 15 15
a. Perf. 13x13½ ('85) 15 15
918 A442 2c Fishing spear 15 15
a. Perf. 13x13½ ('84) 15 15
919 A442 3c Stable lantern 15 15
a. Perf. 13x13½ ('85) 15 15
920 A442 5c Bucket 15 15
a. Perf. 13x13½ ('84) 15 15
921 A442 10c Weathercock 18 15
a. Perf. 13x13½ ('85) 20 15
922 A442 20c Ice skates 35 15

Photo. & Engr.

Perf. 13x13½

923 A437 30c lt blue, bl, & red 48 15
a. Bklt. pane of 20, perf. 12x12½ 10.00
b. Perf. 12x12½ 60 15
924 A437 32c beige, red & brn ('83) 52 15
a. Bklt. pane of 25, perf. 12x12½ 14.00
b. Perf. 12x12½ 60 15

Litho.

Perf. 13½x13

925 A443 34c multi ('85) 50 15
a. Booklet pane of 25 12.50
b. Perf. 13½x14 50 15
c. Bklt. pane of 25, perf. 13½x14 12.50

Photo. & Engr.

Perf. 13x13½

926 A446 34c lt bl & int bl ('85) 55 15

Perf. 13½x14

926A A446 36c plum ('87) *4.00 2.00*

Perf. 13½x13

926B A443 36c multi ('87) 55 15
c. Booklet pane of 10 5.50
d. Booklet pane of 25 13.75
e. Perf. 13½x14 ('87) 55 15

Perf. 12x12½, 12½x12

Litho.

Size A442: 26x20mm

927 A442 37c Wooden plow ('83) 60 20
928 A442 39c Settle-bed ('85) 60 20
929 A442 48c Cradle 70 30
930 A442 50c Sleigh ('85) 75 25
931 A359 60c Street scene, Ontario City, perf. 13½ 1.00 20
932 A442 64c Wood stove ('83) 1.00 40
933 A442 68c Spinning wheel ('85) 1.00 35

Perf. 13½

934 A359a $1 Glacier Natl. Park 1.50 40
935 A359a $1.50 Waterton Lakes Natl. Park 2.75 60
936 A359a $2 Moraine Lake, Banff Park 3.00 1.00
937 A359a $5 Point Pelee Natl. Park ('83) 8.50 2.25
Nos. 917-937 (23) 29.13 9.80

Booklet Stamps

Perf. 12x12½ (A437), 12½x12

Engr.

938 A445 1c sage green ('87) 15 15
939 A444 2c myrtle grn ('85) 15 15
a. 2c slate green ('89) 15 15
940 A437 5c deep claret 15 15
941 A445 5c dp brown ('85) 15 15
942 A444 6c henna brn ('87) 15 15
943 A437 8c dk blue ('83) 16 15
944 A437 10c dark green 25 15
945 A437 30c red 65 15
a. Bklt. pane of 4 + 2 labels (2 #940, 944, 945) 1.25
946 A437 32c brown ('83) 65 15
b. Bklt. pane of 4 + 2 labels (2 #941, 943, 946) 1.00
947 A443 34c dp sl bl ('85) 50 15
a. Bklt. pane of 6 (3 #939, 2 #941, #947) 1.30
948 A443 36c dark lil rose ('87) 55 20
a. Bklt. pane of 5 + label (2 #938, 2 #942, #948) 85
Set value 75

Coil Stamps

Engr. *Perf. 10 Vert.*

950 A437 30c red 1.00 15
951 A437 32c brown ('83) 65 15

Perf. 10 Horiz.

952 A443 34c dull red brn ('85) 50 15
953 A443 36c dark red ('87) 55 15
Set value, #950-953 52

See #1080-1083, 1186-1188, 1194-1194A.

Centenary of Salvation Army in Canada — A457

1982, June 25 Litho. *Perf. 13*

954 A457 30c multicolored 52 18

Canada Day — A458

Paintings: No. 955, The Highway near Kluana Lake, by A.Y. Jackson. No. 956, Montreal Street Scene, by Adrien Hebert. No. 957, Breakwater, by Christopher Pratt. No. 958, Along Great Slave Lake, by Rene Richard. No. 959, Tea Hill, by Molly Lamb. No. 960, Family and Rainstorm, by Alex Colville. No. 961, Brown Shadows, by Dorothy Knowles. No. 962, The Red Brick House, by David Milne. No. 963, Campus Gates, by Bruno Bobak. No. 964, Prairie Town—Early Morning, by Illingworth Kerr. No. 965, Totems at Ninstints, by Joe Plaskett. No. 966, Doc Snider's House, by Lionel LeMoine FitzGerald.

1982, June 30 *Perf. 12½x12*

955 A458 30c multicolored 45 30
956 A458 30c multicolored 45 30
957 A458 30c multicolored 45 30
958 A458 30c multicolored 45 30
959 A458 30c multicolored 45 30
960 A458 30c multicolored 45 30
961 A458 30c multicolored 45 30
962 A458 30c multicolored 45 30
963 A458 30c multicolored 45 30
964 A458 30c multicolored 45 30
965 A458 30c multicolored 45 30
966 A458 30c multicolored 45 30
a. Min. sheet of 12, #955-966 7.50
Nos. 955-966 (12) 5.40 3.60

Regina Centenary A459

1982, Aug. 3 *Perf. 13½x13*

967 A459 30c multicolored 50 18

Centenary of Royal Canadian Henley Regatta, St. Catharines, Aug. 4-8 — A460

1982, Aug. 4

968 A460 30c multicolored 50 18

Fairchild FC-2W1 A461

1982, Oct. 5 Litho. *Perf. 12½*

969 A461 30c shown 48 18
970 A461 30c De Havilland Canada Beaver 48 18
a. Pair, #969-970 1.00 1.00
971 A461 60c Noorduyn Norseman 1.00 75
972 A461 60c Fokker Super Universal 1.00 75
a. Pair, #971-972 2.00 2.00

Christmas — A462

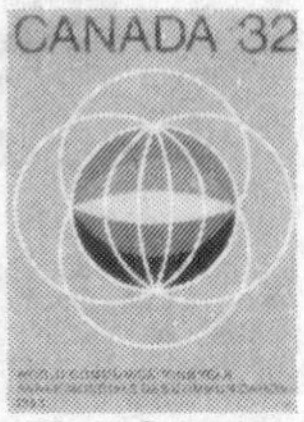

World Communications Year — A463

Designs: Creche figures.

1982, Nov. 3 *Perf. 13½*

973 A462 30c Holy Family 48 18
974 A462 35c Shepherds 60 20
975 A462 60c Three Kings 1.00 35

1983, Mar. 10 Litho. *Perf. 12x12½*

976 A463 32c multicolored 55 20

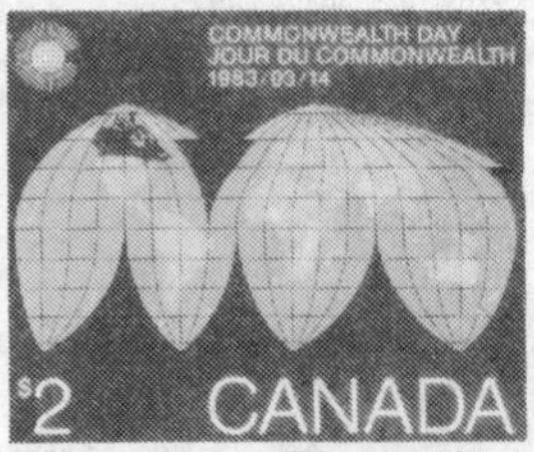

Commonwealth Day — A464

1983, Mar. 14

977 A464 $2 multicolored 3.00 1.65

Scene from Angeline de Montbrun, by Laure Conan (1845-1924), Painted by Rene Milot — A465

Design: No. 979, Sea Gulls, by Edwin John Pratt (1882-1966), woodcut by Claire Pratt.

1983, Apr. 22 Litho. *Perf. 13½*

978 A465 32c multicolored 52 20
979 A465 32c multicolored 52 20
a. Pair, #978-979 1.05 1.00

St. John Ambulance Centenary A466

1983, June 3 *Perf. 13½*

980 A466 32c Emblem 52 20

World University Games, Edmonton, July 1-11 — A467

1983, June 28 *Perf. 13½*

981	A467	32c multicolored	42	20
982	A467	64c multicolored	1.25	60

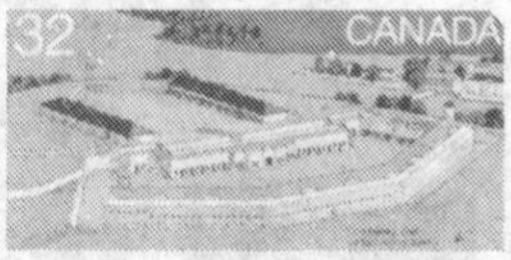

Canada Day A468

Forts: No. 983, Fort Henry, Ontario. No. 984, Fort William, Ontario. No. 985, Fort Rodd Hill, British Columbia. No. 986, Fort Wellington, Ontario. No. 987, Fort Prince of Wales, Manitoba. No. 988, Halifax Citadel, Nova Scotia. No. 989, Fort Chambly, Quebec. No. 990, Fort No. 1, Point Levis, Quebec. No. 991, Fort at Coteau-du-Lac, Quebec. No. 992, Fort Beausejour, New Brunswick. Sizes: Nos. 983, 988: 44x22mm.; Nos. 984-985, 989-990, 36x22mm.; Nos. 986-987, 991-992, 28x22mm. Nos. 983-992 issued in booklet only.

1983, June 30 *Perf. 12½x13*

Booklet Stamps

983	A468	32c multicolored	65	28
984	A468	32c multicolored	65	28
985	A468	32c multicolored	65	28
986	A468	32c multicolored	65	28
987	A468	32c multicolored	65	28
988	A468	32c multicolored	65	28
989	A468	32c multicolored	65	28
990	A468	32c multicolored	65	28
991	A468	32c multicolored	65	28
992	A468	32c multicolored	65	28
a.		Booklet pane of 10, #938-992	7.00	
		Nos. 983-992 (10)	6.50	2.80

Scouting Year — A469

1983, July 6 *Perf. 13½*

993	A469	32c multicolored	52	20

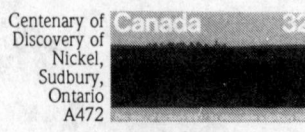

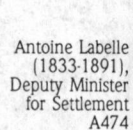

Church Council Emblem — A470

Humphrey Gilbert — A471

1983, July 22 **Litho.**

994	A470	32c tan & green	52	20

6th World Council of Churches Assembly, Vancouver, July 24-Aug. 10.

1983, Aug. 3 **Litho.**

995	A471	32c multicolored	52	20

400th anniv. of discovery of Newfoundland by Sir Humphrey Gilbert (1537-1583).

Centenary of Discovery of Nickel, Sudbury, Ontario A472

Photo. & Embossed

1983, Aug. 12 *Perf. 13*

996	A472	32c multicolored	52	20

Josiah Henson (1789-1883), Preacher A473

1983, Sept. 16 *Perf. 13x13½*

997	A473	32c multicolored	52	20

Antoine Labelle (1833-1891), Deputy Minister for Settlement A474

1983, Sept. 16 *Perf. 13½*

998	A474	32c multicolored	52	20

Locomotives A475

1983, Oct. 3 *Perf. 12½x13*

999	A475	32c Toronto 4-4-0, 1853	52	30
1000	A475	32c Dorchester 0-4-0, 1836	52	30
a.		Pair, #999-1000	1.05	60
1001	A475	37c Samson 0-6-0, 1838	60	52
1002	A475	64c Adam Brown 4-4-0, 1860	1.05	90

Dalhousie Law School Centenary A476

1983, Oct. 28 **Litho.** *Perf. 13*

1003	A476	32c Arms	52	20

Christmas A477

1983, Nov. 3 **Litho.** *Perf. 13½*

1004	A477	32c Urban church	52	20
1005	A477	37c Family going to church	60	38
1006	A477	64c Rural church	1.05	75

Army Regiment Centenaries — A478

19th Cent. Uniforms: No. 1007, Royal Canadian Regiment, British Columbia Regiment. No. 1008, Royal Winnipeg Rifles, Royal Canadian Dragoons.

1983, Nov. 10 *Perf. 13½x13*

1007	A478	32c shown	52	20
1008	A478	32c multicolored	52	20
a.		Pair, #1007-1008	1.05	1.00

50th Anniv. of Yellowknife — A479

1984, Mar. 15 **Litho.** *Perf. 13½*

1009	A479	32c Gold mine	52	20

50th Anniv. of Montreal Symphony Orchestra A480

1984, Mar. 24 **Litho.** *Perf. 12½*

1010	A480	32c multicolored	52	20

450th Anniv. of Cartier's Landing in Quebec A481

1984, Apr. 20 **Photo. & Engr.**

1011	A481	32c multicolored	60	20

See France No. 1923.

Voyage of Tall Ships, Saint-Malo, France, to Quebec City — A482

1984, May 18 **Litho.** *Perf. 12x12½*

1012	A482	32c multicolored	65	20

450th anniv. of Cartier's landing in Quebec.

A483

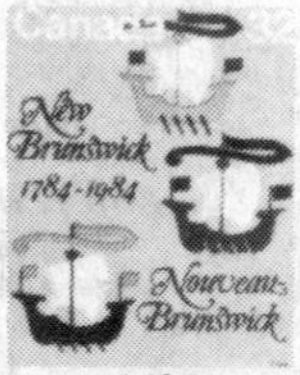

A484

1984, May 28 **Litho.** *Perf. 13*

1013	A483	32c Meritorious Service Medal	65	20

Canadian Red Cross Society, 75th anniv.

Photo. & Engr.

1984, June 18 *Perf. 13*

1014	A484	32c Galleys	65	20

New Brunswick bicentenary.

St. Lawrence Seaway, 25th Anniv. — A485

1984, June 26 **Litho.** *Perf. 13*

1015	A485	32c Seaway, Lake Superior	65	20

Canada Day — A486

Provincial Landscapes by Jean Paul Lemieux (b. 1904).

1984, June 29 *Perf. 13*

1016	A486	32c New Brunswick	65	20
1017	A486	32c British Columbia	65	20
1018	A486	32c Yukon Territory	65	20
1019	A486	32c Quebec	65	20
1020	A486	32c Manitoba	65	20
1021	A486	32c Alberta	65	20
1022	A486	32c Prince Edward Island	65	20
1023	A486	32c Saskatchewan	65	20
1024	A486	32c Nova Scotia, vert.	65	20
1025	A486	32c Northwest Territories	65	20
1026	A486	32c Newfoundland	65	20
1027	A486	32c Ontario, vert.	65	20
a.		Min. sheet of 12, #1016-1027	8.00	
		Nos. 1016-1027 (12)	7.80	2.40

Nos. 1018 and 1025 incorrectly inscribed. No. 1018 shows Northwest Territories landscape; No. 1025, Yukon Territory church.

Loyalists, British Flag (1606-1801) A487

1984, July 3

1028	A487	32c multicolored	52	20

United Empire Loyalists, American colonists who remained loyal to British throne and emigrated to Canada during American Revolution.

Roman Catholic Church in Newfoundland A488

1984, Aug. 17 **Litho.** *Perf. 13½*

1029	A488	32c St. John's Basilica	52	25

Papal Visit — A489

1984, Aug. 31 **Litho.** *Perf. 12½*

1030	A489	32c multicolored	52	25
1031	A489	64c multicolored	1.05	50

Lighthouses A490

1984, Sept. 21 **Litho.** *Perf. 12½*

1032	A490	32c Louisbourg, 1734	60	15
1033	A490	32c Fisgard, 1860	60	15
1034	A490	32c Ile Verte, 1809	60	15
1035	A490	32c Gibraltar Point, 1808	60	15
a.		Block of 4, #1032-1035	2.40	2.40

Steam Locomotives — A491

1984, Oct. 25 Litho. *Perf. 12½x13*
1036 A491 32c Scotia 60 25
1037 A491 32c Countess of Dufferin 60 25
a. Pair, #1036-1037 1.20 1.20
1038 A491 37c Grand Trunk Class E3 70 50
1039 A491 64c Canadian Pacific D10a 1.25 80
a. Souvenir sheet 3.50 1.50

No. 1039a contains Nos. 1036-1039 in changed colors.
See Nos. 1071-1074, 1118-1121.

Christmas — A492

Paintings: 32c, The Annunciation, by Jean Dallaire. 37c, The Three Kings, by Simone Mary Bouchard. 64c, Snow in Bethlehem, by David Milne.

1984, Nov. 2 Litho. *Perf. 13*
1040 A492 32c multicolored 52 25
1041 A492 37c multicolored 60 28
1042 A492 64c multicolored 1.05 50

Royal Canadian Air Force — A493

Cent. of La Presse — A494

1984, Nov. 9 Litho. *Perf. 12x12½*
1043 A493 32c Pilots 52 25

1984, Nov. 16 Litho. *Perf. 13x13½*
1044 A494 32c Treffle Berthiaume 52 25

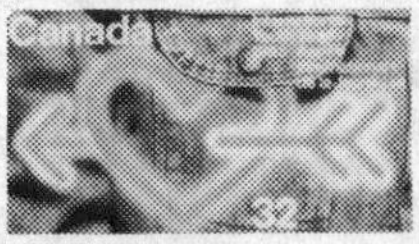

International Youth Year — A495

1985, Feb. 8 Litho. *Perf. 12½*
1045 A495 32c Heart, arrow, jeans 50 25

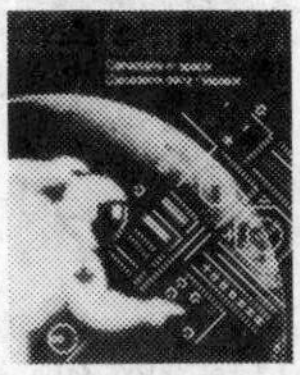

Canadians in Space — A496

1985, Mar. 15 Litho. *Perf. 13½*
1046 A496 32c Astronaut 50 25

Therese Casgrain (1896-1981), Suffragist A497

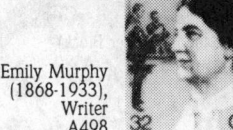

Emily Murphy (1868-1933), Writer A498

1985, Apr. 17 Litho.
1047 A497 32c multicolored 55 24
1048 A498 32c multicolored 55 24
a. Pair, #1047-1048 1.10 1.10

Gabriel Dumont (1837-1906), Metis Leader A499

1985, May 6 Litho. *Perf. 13*
1049 A499 32c multicolored 55 24

Centenary of the Northwest Rebellion.

Canada Day A500

Forts: No. 1050, Lower Ft. Garry, Manitoba. No. 1051, Ft. Anne, Nova Scotia. No. 1052, Ft. York, Ontario. No. 1053, Castle Hill, Newfoundland. No. 1054, Ft. Whoop Up, Alberta. No. 1055, Ft. Erie, Ontario. No. 1056, Ft. Walsh, Saskatchewan. No. 1057, Ft. Lennox, Quebec. No. 1058, York Redoubt, Nova Scotia. No. 1059, Ft. Frederick, Ontario. Sizes: Nos. 1050, 1055: 48x26mm. Nos. 1051-1052, 1056-1057: 40x26mm. Nos. 1053-1054, 1058-1059, 32x26mm.

1985, June 28 Litho. *Perf. 12½x13*
Booklet Stamps
1050 A500 34c multicolored 70 25
1051 A500 34c multicolored 70 25
1052 A500 34c multicolored 70 25
1053 A500 34c multicolored 70 25
1054 A500 34c multicolored 70 25
1055 A500 34c multicolored 70 25
1056 A500 34c multicolored 70 25
1057 A500 34c multicolored 70 25
1058 A500 34c multicolored 70 25
1059 A500 34c multicolored 70 25
a. Bklt. pane of 10, #1050-1059 7.25
Nos. 1050-1059 (10) 7.00 2.50

A501

A502

Design: Louis Hebert (1575-1627), 1st French Apothecary in North America.

1985, Aug. 30 Litho. *Perf. 12½*
1060 A501 34c multicolored 50 25

Intl. Pharmaceutical Federation Congress.

1985, Sept. 3 *Perf. 13½*
1061 A502 34c multicolored 50 25

Interparliamentary Union '85, Ottawa.

A503

Lighthouses — A504

1985, Sept. 12 Photo. *Perf. 13½x13*
1062 A503 34c Guide, brownie saluting 50 25

Natl. Girl Guides movement, cent.

1985, Oct. 3 Litho. *Perf. 13½*
1063 A504 34c Sisters Islets 50 30
1064 A504 34c Pelee Passage 50 30
1065 A504 34c Haut-fond Prince 50 30
1066 A504 34c Rose Blanche 50 30
a. Block of 4, #1063-1066 2.00 2.00
b. Souv. sheet of 4, #1063-1066 2.00 2.00

Santa Claus Parade — A505

Paintings by Barbara Carroll.

1985, Oct. 23 Litho. *Perf. 13½*
1067 A505 34c Santa Claus 50 25
1068 A505 39c Horse-drawn coach 60 30
1069 A505 68c Christmas tree 1.00 50

Perf. 13½ on 3 Sides
1070 A505 32c Polar float 48 24
a. Booklet pane of 10 4.80

No. 1070 printed in booklets only.

Locomotives Type of 1984

1985, Nov. 7 *Perf. 12½x13*
1071 A491 34c Grand Trunk K2 50 25
1072 A491 34c Canadian Pacific P2a 50 25
a. Pair, #1071-1072 1.00 50
1073 A491 39c Canadian Northern O10a 60 30
1074 A491 68c Canadian Govt. Railways H4D 1.00 60

1910 Gunner's Mate, World War II Officer, 1985 Woman Recruit — A507

1985, Nov. 8 *Perf. 13½x13*
1075 A507 34c multicolored 50 25

Royal Canadian Navy, 75th anniv.

Old Holton House, Sherbrooke Street, Montreal, by James Wilson Morrice (1865-1924)
CANADA 34 A508

1985, Nov. 15 *Perf. 13½*
1076 A508 34c multicolored 50 25

Montreal Museum of Fine Arts, 120th anniv.

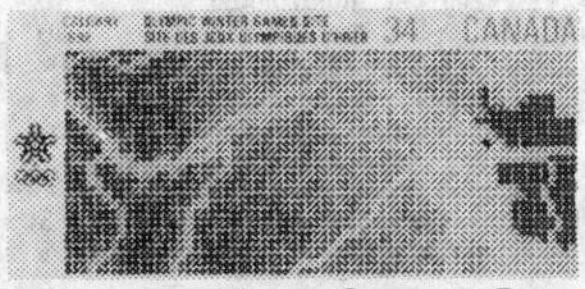

Southwestern Alberta, Computer Design Map — A509

1986, Feb. 13 Litho. *Perf. 12½x13*
1077 A509 34c multicolored 50 25

1988 Winter Olympics, Calgary, Alberta, Feb. 13-28.

EXPO '86, Vancouver, May 2-Oct. 13 — A510

1986, Mar. 7 Photo. & Engr.
1078 A510 34c Canada Pavilion 50 25
1079 A510 39c Communications 58 28

Heritage Artifacts Type of 1982

1987, May 6 Litho. *Perf. 14x13½*
1080 A442 25c Butter stamp 38 15

Size: 20x26mm
Perf. 12x12½
1081 A442 42c Linen chest 65 15
1082 A442 55c Iron kettle 85 20
1083 A442 72c Hand-drawn cart 1.10 25

Park Type of 1979
Litho. & Engr.

1986, Mar. 14 *Perf. 13½*
1084 A359a $5 La Mauricie Natl. Park 7.00 1.75

Philippe Aubert de Gaspe (1786-1871), Novelist — A511

Molly Brant (1736-1796), Iroquois Leader and Loyalist — A512

1986, Apr. 14 Litho. *Perf. 12½*
1090 A511 34c multicolored 50 25

Perf. 13½
1091 A512 34c multicolored 50 25

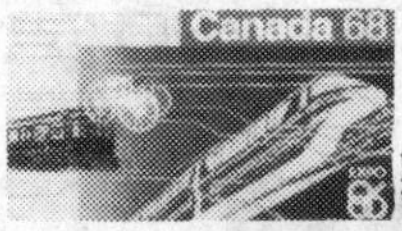

EXPO '86 — A513

Photo. & Engr.
1986, Apr. 28 *Perf. 13x13½*
1092 A513 34c Expo Center, Vancouver 50 25
1093 A513 68c Transportation 1.00 50

Canadian Forces Postal Service, 75th Anniv. — A514

1986, May 9 Litho. *Perf. 13½*
1094 A514 34c multicolored 50 25

Indigenous Birds — A515

1986, May 22
1095 A515 34c Great blue heron 60 32
1096 A515 34c Snow goose 60 32
1097 A515 34c Great horned owl 60 32
1098 A515 34c Spruce grouse 60 32
a. Block of 4, #1095-1098 2.50 2.50

19th Intl. Ornithological Congress, Ottawa, June 22-29.

Canada Day — A516

Invention blueprints.

1986, June 27 Litho.
1099 A516 34c Rotary snowplow, 1869 50 25
1100 A516 34c Canadarm, 1986 50 25
1101 A516 34c Anti-gravity flight suit, 1938 50 25
1102 A516 34c Variable pitch propeller, 1923 50 25
a. Block of 4, #1099-1102 2.00 2.00

Canadian Broadcasting Corp., 50th Anniv. A517

1986, July 23 Litho. *Perf. 12½*
1103 A517 34c Emblem, map 50 25

Exploration of Canada A518

Designs: No. 1104, Siberian Indians discover and inhabit No. America, 10,000 B.C. No. 1105, Viking settlement, A.D. 1000. No. 1106, John Cabot lands, 1498. No. 1107, Henry Hudson pioneers Hudson Strait and Bay, 1610.

1986, Aug. 29 Litho. *Perf. 12½x13*
1104 A518 34c multicolored 50 25
1105 A518 34c multicolored 50 25
1106 A518 34c multicolored 50 25
1107 A518 34c multicolored 50 25
a. Block of 4, #1104-1107 2.00 2.00
b. Souv. sheet of 4, #1104-1107 2.00 2.00

No. 1107b issued Oct. 1 for CAPEX '87.
See #1126-1129, 1199-1202, 1232-1236.

Peacemakers of the Frontier, 1870s A519

Designs: No. 1108, Crowfoot (1830-1890), Blackfoot Indian chief. No. 1109, James F. Macleod (1836-1894), asst. commissioner of Northwest Mounted Police.

1986, Sept. 5 *Perf. 13x13½*
1108 A519 34c scar, gray & ind 50 25
1109 A519 34c ind, gray & scar 50 25
a. Pair, #1108-1109 1.00 1.00

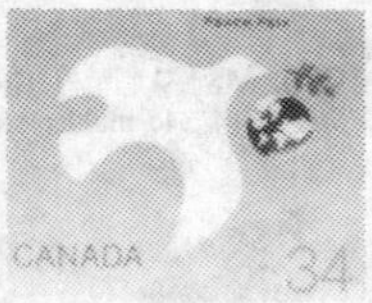
Intl. Peace Year — A520

Litho. & Embossed
1986, Sept. 16 *Perf. 13½*
1110 A520 34c multicolored 50 25

A521

Christmas — A522

1986, Oct. 15 Litho. *Perf. 13½x13*
1111 A521 34c Ice hockey 50 25
1112 A521 34c Biathlon 50 25
a. Pair, #1111-1112 1.00 1.00

1988 Calgary Winter Olympics.
See Nos. 1130-1131, 1152-1153, 1195-1198.

1986, Oct. 29 Litho. *Perf. 12½*
Angels.
1113 A522 34c multicolored 50 25
1114 A522 39c multicolored 58 30
1115 A522 68c multicolored 1.00 50

Size: 72x26mm
Perf. 12½ Horiz.
1116 A522 29c multicolored 45 22
a. Booklet pane of 10 4.50
b. Perf. 13½ horiz. 2.50

No. 1116 has bar code in at left, for use on covers with printed postal code matrix. Issued in booklets only.

John Molson (1763-1836), Entrepreneur A523

1986, Nov. 4
1117 A523 34c multicolored 50 25

Locomotives Type of 1985

Locomotives, 1925-1945.

1986, Nov. 21 *Perf. 12½x13*
1118 A506 34c CN V1a 50 25
1119 A506 34c CP T1a 50 25
a. Pair, #1118-1119 1.00 1.00
1120 A506 39c CN U2a 55 38
1121 A506 68c CP H1c 1.00 60

CAPEX '87 — A524

1987 Litho. & Engr. *Perf. 13x13½*
1122 A524 34c 1st Toronto P.O. 50 25
1123 A524 36c Nelson-Miramichi P.O. 55 28
1124 A524 42c Saint Ours P.O. 65 32
1125 A524 72c Battleford P.O. 1.10 60

Souvenir Sheet
Yellow Green Inscription
1125A Sheet of 4 3.00 3.00
b. A524 36c like #1122 55 28
c. A524 36c like #1123 55 28
d. A524 42c like #1124 65 32
e. A524 72c like #1125 1.10 60

Issue dates: 34c, Feb. 16. Others, June 12.

Exploration Type of 1986

Pioneers of New France: No. 1126, Etienne Brule (c. 1592-1633), first European to see the Great Lakes. No. 1127, Pierre Esprit Radisson (c. 1636-1710) and Medard Chouart des Groseilliers (1625-1698), British expedition to Hudson Bay, 1668. No. 1128, Louis Jolliet (1645-1700) and Fr. Jacques Marquette (1637-1675) discovering the Mississippi River, 1673. No. 1129, Recollet wilderness mission, 1615.

1987, Mar. 13 Litho. *Perf. 12½x13*
1126 A518 34c multicolored 50 25
1127 A518 34c multicolored 50 25
1128 A518 34c multicolored 50 25
1129 A518 34c multicolored 50 25
a. Block of 4, #1126-1129 2.00 2.00

Olympics Type of 1986

1987, Apr. 3 *Perf. 13½x13*
1130 A521 36c Speed skating 55 28
1131 A521 42c Bobsledding 65 32

Volunteers Week — A525

1987, Apr. 13 *Perf. 12½x13*
1132 A525 36c multicolored 55 28

Law Day — A526

1987, Apr. 15 *Perf. 14x13½*
1133 A526 36c Coat of arms 55 28

Canadian Charter of Rights and Freedoms, 5th anniv.

Engineering Institute of Canada, Cent. — A527

1987, May 19 *Perf. 12½x13*
1134 A527 36c multicolored 55 28

Canada Day — A528

Inventors and communications innovations: No. 1135, Reginald Aubrey Fessenden (1866-1932), AM radio, 1900. No. 1136, Charles Fenerty, newsprint, 1838. No. 1137, Georges-Edouard Desbarats and William Leggo, half-tone engraving, 1869. No. 1138, Frederick Newton Gisborne, No. America's first undersea cable, 1852, New Brunswick to Prince Edward Island.

1987, June 25 Litho. *Perf. 13½*
1135 A528 36c multicolored 55 28
1136 A528 36c multicolored 55 28
1137 A528 36c multicolored 55 28
1138 A528 36c multicolored 55 28
a. Block of 4, #1135-1138 2.25 2.25

Steamships A529

1987, July 20 *Perf. 13½x13*
1139 A529 36c Segwun, 1887 55 28

51x22mm
1140 A529 36c Princess Marguerite, 1948 55 28
a. Pair, #1139-1140 1.10 1.10

Shipwrecks A530

1987, Aug. 7
1141 A530 36c Hamilton & Scourge, 1813 55 28
1142 A530 36c San Juan, 1565 55 28
1143 A530 36c Breadalbane, 1853 55 28
1144 A530 36c Ericsson, 1892 55 28
a. Block of 4, #1141-1144 2.25 2.25

A531

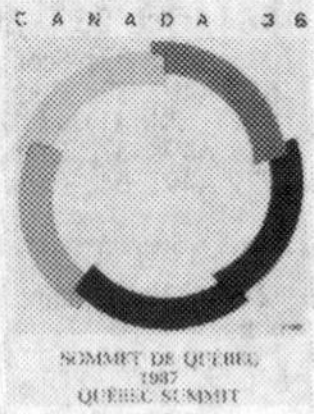
A532

1987, Sept. 1 *Perf. 13½*
1145 A531 36c multicolored 58 30

Air Canada, 50th anniv.

1987, Sept. 2 *Perf. 13x12½*
1146 A532 36c multicolored 58 30

2nd Intl. Francophone Summit, Quebec, 9/2-4.

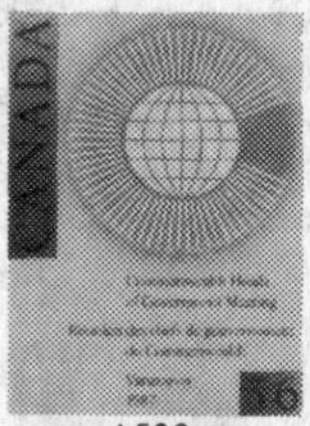
A533

Christmas — A534

1987, Oct. 13
1147 A533 36c multicolored 58 30

9th Commonwealth Meeting, Vancouver, Oct. 13-17.

1987, Nov. 2 Litho. *Perf. 13½*
1148 A534 36c Poinsettia 58 30
1149 A534 42c Holly wreath 65 32
1150 A534 72c Mistletoe, Christmas tree 1.15 58

Size: 39x25mm
1151 A534 31c Gifts, Christmas tree 48 25
a. Booklet pane of 10 4.80

No. 1151 has bar code at left, for use on covers with printed postal code matrix. Issued in booklets only.

Olympics Type of 1986

1987, Nov. 13 *Perf. 13½x13*
1152 A521 36c Cross-country skiing 58 30
1153 A521 36c Ski jumping 58 30
a. Pair, #1152-1153 1.16 1.10

75th Grey Cup, Vancouver, Nov. 29 — A535

1987, Nov. 20 *Perf. 12½*
1154 A535 36c multicolored 58 30

Types of 1982 and

Elizabeth II — A536

Mammals — A538

A537

A539

Parliament (Center Block)
A537 A539

Architecture — A540

Flag and Clouds A541

Flag A542

Natl. Flag, Deciduous Forest A543

Flag and Mountains A544

1987-91 Litho. *Perf. 13x13½*
Sizes Vary on A536, A538

1155 A538 1c Flying squirrel 15 15
1156 A538 2c Prickly porcupine 15 15
1157 A538 3c Muskrat 15 15
1158 A538 5c Varying hare 15 15
1159 A538 6c Red fox 15 15
1160 A538 10c Skunk 18 15
 a. Perf. 13x12½ 65
1161 A538 25c Beaver 42 15

Perf. 13½x13

1162 A536 37c multicolored 58 15
1163 A537 37c multicolored 58 15
 a. Bklt. pane of 10, #1163c 5.80
 b. Bklt. pane of 25, #1163c 14.50
 c. Perf. 13½x14 58 15

Perf. 13x12½

1164 A536 38c multicolored 65 15
 a. Perf. 13x13½ 65 15
 b. As "a," bklt. pane of 10+2 labels 6.50

Perf. 13x13½ on 3 or 4 Sides

1165 A539 38c multicolored 65 15
 a. Bklt. pane of 10+2 labels 6.50
 b. Bklt. pane of 25+2 labels 16.25

Perf. 13½x13

1166 A541 39c multi 68 35
 a. Booklet pane of 10 + 2 labels 6.80
 b. Booklet pane of 25 + 2 labels 17.00
 c. Perf. 12½x13 2.65

Perf. 13x13½

1167 A536 39c multi 68 35
 a. Booklet pane of 10 + 2 labels 6.80
 b. Perf. 13 2.00 35
1168 A536 40c multi 68 35
 a. Bklt. pane of 10+2 labels 6.80

Perf. 13½x13

1169 A544 40c multi 68 35
 a. Bklt. pane of 25+2 labels 17.00
 b. Bklt. pane of 10+2 labels 6.80

Perf. 12x12½

1170 A538 43c Lynx 68 22

Perf. 14½x14

1171 A538 44c Walrus 75 25
 a. Perf. 12½x13 75 25
 b. As "a," bklt. pane of 5 + label 3.75
 c. Perf. 13½x13 *20.00*
1172 A538 45c Pronghorn 80 40
 b. As "f," bklt. pane of 5 + label 4.00
 d. Perf. 13 80 40
 f. Perf. 12½x13 80 40

Perf. 13

1172A A538 46c Wolverine 80 40
 c. Perf. 12½x13 80 40
 e. As "c," bklt. pane of 5 + label 4.00
 g. Perf. 14½x14 80 40

Perf. 12x12½

1173 A538 57c Killer whale 90 30

Perf. 14½x14

1174 A538 59c Musk-ox 1.00 35
 a. Perf. 13 3.00
1175 A538 61c Timber wolf 1.05 52
 a. Perf. 13 2.00 52
1176 A538 63c Harbor porpoise 1.10 55
 a. Perf. 13 1.10 55

Perf. 12x12½

1177 A538 74c Wapiti 1.15 38

Perf. 14½x14

1178 A538 76c Grizzly bear 1.30 45
 a. Perf. 12½x13 1.30 45
 b. As "a," bklt. pane of 5 + label 6.50
 c. Perf. 13 *17.50*
1179 A538 78c Beluga 1.35 68
 a. As "c," bklt. pane of 5 6.75
 b. Perf. 13 3.00 68
 c. Perf. 12½x13 1.35 68

Perf. 13

1180 A538 80c Peary caribou 1.40 70
 a. Perf. 12½x13 1.40 70
 b. As "a," bklt. pane of 5 + label 7.00
 c. Perf. 14½x14 1.40 70

Perf. 13½
Litho. & Engr.

1181 A540 $1 Runnymede Library, Toronto 1.70 55
1182 A540 $2 McAdam Railway Station 3.40 1.25
1183 A540 $5 Bonsecours Market, Montreal 8.50 2.75
 Nos. 1155-1183 (30) 32.41 12.80

Issued: 1c, 2c, 3c, 5c, 6c, 10c, 25c, Oct. 3, 1988. 37c, Dec. 30, 1987. 38c, Dec. 29, 1988. 43c, 57c, 74c, Jan. 18, 1988. 44c, 59c, 76c, Jan. 18, 1989. $1, $2, May 5, 1989. No. 1166, Dec. 28, 1989; 45c, 61c, 78c, No. 1167, Jan. 12, 1990. $5, May 28, 1990. 40c, 46c, 63c, 80c, Dec. 28, 1990.

A later printing of No. 1182 has more intense and clearly defined green shading on the roofline and the deep orange background extends closer to the roofline.

Booklet Stamps
Perf. 13½x14 on 3 Sides
Litho.

1184 A542 1c shown 15 15
 a. Perf. 12½x13 1.75
1185 A542 5c multi 15 15

Perf. 12½x12 on 2 or 3 sides
Engr.

1186 A445 6c dark purple 15 15
1187 A443 37c dark blue 58 15
 a. Bklt. pane of 4 + 2 labels (#938, 2 #942, #1187) 85
1188 A443 38c dark blue 65 20
 a. Bklt. pane of 5 (3 #939a, #1186, #1188) 90

Perf. 13½x14 on 3 Sides
Litho.

1189 A542 39c multi 68 35
 a. Bklt. pane of 4 (#1184, 2 #1185, #1189) 95
1190 A542 40c multi 68 35
 a. Bklt. pane of 4 (2 #1184, #1185, #1190) 95

No. 1190a sold for 50c.

Issue dates: No. 1187, Feb. 3, 1988. No. 1188, Jan. 18, 1989. No. 1186, 1989. Nos. 1184-1185, 1189, Jan. 12, 1990. 1190, Dec. 28, 1990.

Self-Adhesives
Die Cut
Imperf
Booklet Stamps

1191 A543 38c multi 62 30
 a. Booklet of 12 8.25
1192 A543 39c Flag, field 72 38
 a. Booklet of 12 8.75
1193 A543 40c Flag, seacoast 68 35
 a. Booklet of 12 8.20

Issue dates: 38c, June 30, 1989. 39c, Feb. 8, 1990. 40c, Jan. 11, 1991.

Issued on peelable paper backing serving as booklet cover. Nos. 1191a, 1192a sold for $5, No. 1193a for $5.25.

Coil Stamps
Perf. 10 Horiz.
Engr.

1194 A443 37c dark blue 58 15
1194A A443 38c dark green 65 15
1194B A542 39c violet 68 35
1194C A542 40c blue gray 68 35

Issue dates: 37c, Feb. 22, 1988. 38c, Feb. 1, 1989. 39c, Feb. 8, 1990. 40c, Dec. 28, 1990.

See #1358-1360, 1360B, 1375-1376, 1388, 1394-1395.

Olympics Type of 1986

1988, Feb. 12 Litho. *Perf. 12x12½*

1195 A521 37c Alpine skiing 58 30
1196 A521 37c Curling 58 30
 a. Pair, #1195-1196 1.20 1.20
1197 A521 43c Figure skating 68 35
1198 A521 74c Luge 1.15 65

Exploration Type of 1986

18th Cent. explorers of the western territories: No. 1199, Anthony Henday, who traveled the Prairies in 1754 from the Hayes River to Red Deer, Alberta. No. 1200, George Vancouver (1757-1798), who circumnavigated Vancouver Is. and explored the Pacific Coast, 1792-94. No. 1201, Simon Fraser (1776-1862), fur trader who discovered and navigated the Fraser River. No. 1202, John Palliser (1807-1887), geographer who determined the topographical boundary between Canada and the US from Lake Superior to the Pacific Coast.

1988, Mar. 17 Litho. *Perf. 12½x13*

1199 A518 37c multicolored 60 30
1200 A518 37c multicolored 60 30
1201 A518 37c multicolored 60 30
1202 A518 37c multicolored 60 30
 a. Block of 4, #1199-1202 2.40 2.40

The Young Reader, by Ozias Leduc A546

Photo. & Engr.

1988, May 20 *Perf. 13x13½*

1203 A546 50c multicolored 85 85

Masterpieces of Canadian art. Printed in sheets of 16.

See Nos. 1241, 1271, 1310, 1419, 1466, 1516.

Wildlife and Habitat Conservation A547

1988, June 1 Litho. *Perf. 13x13½*

1204 A547 37c Duck 60 30
1205 A547 37c Moose at water hole 60 30
 a. Pair, #1204-1205 1.20 1.20

Grey Owl, born Archibald Belaney, (b. 1888), conservationist; Ducks Unlimited Canada, 50th anniv.

Science and Technology A548

Intl. Entomology Congress, Vancouver A549

Inventions: No. 1206, Kerosene, invented by Abraham Gesner (1797-1864), patented in 1854. No. 1207, Marquis wheat, developed in 1908 by Charles Saunders. No. 1208, Electron microscope, developed in 1938 at the University of Toronto by James Hillier and Albert Prebus under the supervision of Eli Burton. No. 1209, Cobalt cancer therapy, introduced by Dr. Harold Johns and Atomic Energy of Canada, Ltd., in 1951.

1988, June 17 *Perf. 12½x13*

1206 A548 37c multicolored 60 30
1207 A548 37c multicolored 60 30
1208 A548 37c multicolored 60 30
1209 A548 37c multicolored 60 30
 a. Block of 4, #1206-1209 2.40 2.40

1988, July 4 Litho. *Perf. 12*

1210 A549 37c Short-tailed swallowtail 62 40
1211 A549 37c Northern blue 62 40
1212 A549 37c Macoun's Arctic 62 40
1213 A549 37c Canadian tiger swallowtail 62 40
 a. Block of 4, #1210-1213 2.50 2.50

St. John's, Newfoundland, Cent. of Incorporation — A550

1988, July 22 *Perf. 13½x13*

1214 A550 37c Harbor entrance, skyline 62 30

Canadian 4-H Council, 75th Anniv. A551

1988, Aug. 5

1215 A551 37c Motto, farm, young scientists 62 30

Les Forges Du St. Maurice (1738-1883), Canada's 1st Industrial Complex — A552

Litho. & Engr.

1988, Aug. 19 *Perf. 13½*

1216 A552 37c multicolored 62 30

Canadian Kennel Club, Cent. — A553

1988, Aug. 26 *Perf. 12½x12*

1217 A553 37c Tahltan bear dog 62 40
1218 A553 37c Nova Scotia duck-tolling retriever 62 40
1219 A553 37c Canadian Eskimo dog 62 40
1220 A553 37c Newfoundland 62 40
 a. Block of 4, #1217-1220 2.50 2.50

A554

A555

1988, Sept. 9 Litho. *Perf. 13½x13*

1221 A554 37c multicolored 62 30

Sesquicentennial of the 1st baseball game played in Canada, June 4, 1838 at Beachville, Upper Canada.

1988, Oct. 27 Litho. *Perf. 13½*

Christmas (Icons of the Eastern Church): 32c, Nativity. 37c, Conception. 43c, Virgin and Child. 74c, Virgin and Child, diff.

1222 A555 37c multicolored 62 30
1223 A555 43c multicolored 72 40
1224 A555 74c multicolored 1.25 65

Booklet Stamp
Size: 35½x21mm
Perf. 12½x13½

1225 A555 32c multicolored		55	28
a.	Booklet pane of 10	5.50	

Millennium of Christianity in the Ukraine. No. 1225 has bar code at left; for use on covers with printed postal code matrix.

Inglis and Anglican Church A556

1988, Nov. 1 ***Perf. 12½x12***

1226 A556 37c multicolored	62	30

Charles Inglis (1734-1816), Canada's 1st Anglican bishop and founder of the Kings-Edgehill School, Nova Scotia, and the University of King's College at Halifax, bicent.

Hopkins and *Canoe Manned by Voyageurs* A557

1988, Nov. 18 ***Perf. 13½x13***

1227 A557 37c multicolored	62	30

Frances Ann Hopkins (1838-1918), painter.

The Bluenose and Capt. Walters — A558

1988, Nov. 18 ***Perf. 13½***

1228 A558 37c multicolored	62	30

Angus Walters (1882-1968), mariner.

Small Craft A559

1989, Feb. 1 Litho. ***Perf. 13½x13***

1229 A559 38c Chipewyan canoe	65	32
1230 A559 38c Haida canoe	65	32
1231 A559 38c Inuit kayak	65	32
1232 A559 38c Micmac canoe	65	32
a. Block of 4, #1229-1232	2.60	2.60

See Nos. 1266-1269, 1317-1320.

Exploration Type of 1986

Explorers of the North: No. 1233, Matonabbee (c. 1737-1782), Indian guide who led 1st overland European expedition to the Arctic Ocean. No. 1234, Relics of expedition led by Sir John Franklin (1786-1847) that proved the existence of the Northwest Passage. No. 1235, Relics of the discovery of the Alberta fossil bed by geologist Joseph Burr Tyrrell (1858-1957). No. 1236, Vilhjalmur Stefansson (1879-1962), American ethnologist who discovered the last uncharted islands in the Arctic Archipelago.

1989, Mar. 22 Litho. ***Perf. 12½x13***

1233 A518 38c multicolored	65	32
1234 A518 38c multicolored	65	32
1235 A518 38c multicolored	65	32
1236 A518 38c multicolored	65	32
a. Block of 4, #1233-1236	2.60	2.60

Photography in Canada, Sesquicentennial A560

Photographers and their work: No. 1237, William Notman (1826-1891). No. 1238, W. Hanson Boorne (1859-1945). No. 1239, Alexander Henderson (1831-1913). No. 1240, Jules-Ernest Livernois (1851-1933).

1989, June 23 Litho. ***Perf. 12½x12***

1237 A560 38c multicolored	65	32
1238 A560 38c multicolored	65	32
1239 A560 38c multicolored	65	32
1240 A560 38c multicolored	65	32
a. Block of 4, #1237-1240	2.60	2.60

Art Type of 1988

Design: Ceremonial Frontlet (headpiece) Worn by Tsimshian Indian Chiefs, Early 20th Cent.

1989, June 29 ***Perf. 12½x13***

1241 A546 50c multicolored	85	85

Masterpieces of Canadian Art and opening of the Museum of Civilization.

Poets — A562

1989, July 7 ***Perf. 13½***

1243 A562 38c Louis Frechette (1839-1908)	62	30
1244 A562 38c Archibald Lampman (1861-1899)	62	30
a. Pair, #1243-1244	1.25	1.25

Mushrooms — A563

1989, Aug. 4

1245 A563 38c *Clavulinopsis fusiformis*	62	30
1246 A563 38c *Boletus mirabilis*	62	30
1247 A563 38c *Cantharellus cinnabarinus*	62	30
1248 A563 38c *Morchella esculenta*	62	30
a. Block of 4, #1245-1248	2.50	2.50

Infantry Regiments, 75th Annivs. A564

Designs: No. 1249, Princess Patricia's Canadian Light Infantry. No. 1250, Royal 22nd Regiment.

1989, Sept. 8 Litho. & Engr. ***Perf. 13***

1249 A564 38c multicolored	65	32
1250 A564 38c multicolored	65	32
a. Pair, #1249-1250	1.30	1.30

Intl. Trade — A565

1989, Oct. 2 Litho. ***Perf. 13½x13***

1251 A565 38c multicolored	65	32

Performing Arts — A566

1989, Oct. 4 ***Perf. 13x13½***

1252 A566 38c Dancers	65	32
1253 A566 38c Musicians	65	32
1254 A566 38c Camera, director	65	32
1255 A566 38c Youth and adult entertainers	65	32
a. Block of 4, #1252-1255	2.60	2.60

Royal Winnipeg Ballet 50th anniv. (No. 1252), Vancouver Opera 30th anniv. (No. 1253), Natl. Film Board 50th anniv. (No. 1254), and Confederation Center of the Arts, Charlottetown, P.E.I., 25th anniv. (No. 1255).

Champ-de-Mars, Winter, 1892, by William Brymner (1855-1925) — A567

Winter landscapes: 38c, *Bend in the Gosselin River, Arthabaska*, c. 1906, by Marc-Aurele de Foy Suzor-Cote (1869-1937). 44c, *Snow II*, 1915, by Lawren S. Harris (1885-1970). 76c, *Ste. Agnes*, c. 1925-30, by Albert H. Robinson (1881-1956). Nos. 1256-1258 vert.

1989, Oct. 26 Litho. ***Perf. 13x13½***
Size of 44c, 76c: 25x31mm

1256 A567 38c multicolored	65	32
a. Booklet pane of 10, #1256b	6.50	
b. Perf. 13x12½	6.50	

Perf. 13½

1257 A567 44c multicolored	75	38
a. Booklet pane of 5 + label	3.75	
1258 A567 76c multicolored	1.30	65
a. Booklet pane of 5 + label	6.50	

Booklet Stamp
Size: 35x21mm
Perf. 12½x13½

1259 A567 33c shown	56	28
a. Booklet pane of 10	5.60	

Christmas. No. 1259 has bar code at left; for use on covers with printed postal code matrix.
Booklet panes separate easily.

Declaration of War, 1939 — A568

Political and military actions taken by Canada at the outbreak of World War II.

1989, Nov. 10 ***Perf. 13½***

1260 A568 38c shown	65	32
1261 A568 38c Army mobilization	65	32
1262 A568 38c Navy convoy system	65	32
1263 A568 38c Commonwealth Air Training Plan	65	32
a. Block of 4, #1260-1263	2.60	2.60

See Nos. 1298-1301, 1345-1348, 1448-1451, 1503-1506, 1537-1540.

Norman Bethune (1890-1939), Surgeon A569

Perf. 13x13½
1990, Mar. 2 Litho. & Engr.

1264 A569 39c In Canada	68	35
1265 A569 39c In China	68	35
a. Pair, #1264-1265	2.50	2.50

See People's Republic of China Nos. 2263-2264.

Small Craft Type of 1989
1990, Mar. 15 Litho. ***Perf. 13½x13***

1266 A559 39c Dory	68	35
1267 A559 39c Pointer	68	35
1268 A559 39c York boat	68	35
1269 A559 39c North canoe	68	35
a. Block of 4, #1266-1269	2.75	2.75

Multicultural Heritage of Canada A570

1990, Apr. 5 Litho. & Engr. ***Perf. 13***

1270 A570 39c multicolored	65	32

Art Type of 1988

Painting: *The West Wind*, by Tom Thomson.

1990, May 3 Litho. ***Perf. 12½x13***

1271 A546 50c multicolored	85	85

Masterpieces of Canadian Art.

Mail Trucks
A571 A572

1990, May 3 Litho. ***Perf. 13½***
Booklet Stamps

1272 A571 39c multicolored	68	35
1273 A572 39c multicolored	68	35
a. Bklt. pane of 8+printed margin (4 each #1272-1273)	5.50	
b. Bklt. pane of 9+3 labels, printed margin (5 #1272, 4 #1273)	6.25	

Dolls — A573

1990, June 8 Litho. ***Perf. 12½x12***

1274 A573 39c Native	68	35
1275 A573 39c Settler's	68	35
1276 A573 39c 4 Commercial	68	35
1277 A573 39c 5 Commercial	68	35
a. Block of 4, #1274-1277	2.75	2.75

Natl. Flag, 25th Anniv. — A574

1990, June 29 ***Perf. 13x12½***

1278 A574 39c Flag, fireworks	68	35

Printed in sheets of 16.

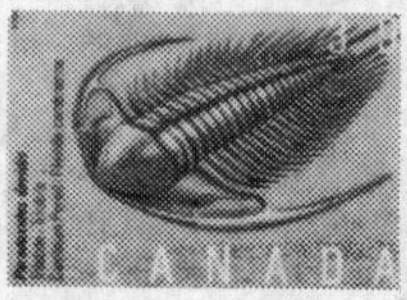

Prehistoric Life — A575

Perf. 13x13½

1990, July 12 — Litho. & Engr.

1279 A575 39c Trilobite 68 35
1280 A575 39c Sea scorpion 68 35
1281 A575 39c Fossil algae 68 35
1282 A575 39c Soft invertebrate 68 35
a. Block of 4, #1279-1282 2.75 2.75

See Nos. 1306-1309.

Canadian Forests A576

1990, Aug. 7 — Litho. — *Perf. 12½x13*

1283 A576 39c Acadian 68 35
a. Sheet of 4 2.75 2.75
1284 A576 39c Great Lakes-St. Lawrence 68 35
a. Sheet of 4 2.75 2.75
1285 A576 39c Coast 68 35
a. Sheet of 4 2.75 2.75
1286 A576 39c Boreal 68 35
a. Block of 4, #1283-1286 2.75 2.75
b. Sheet of 4 2.75 2.75

Sheets of four sold for $1 each through Petro-Canada gas stations, and for full face value through the philatelic bureau. Issue date: Sept. 7.

Weather Observations in Canada, 150th Anniv. A577

1990, Sept. 5 — Litho. — *Perf. 12½x13½*

1287 A577 39c multicolored 68 35

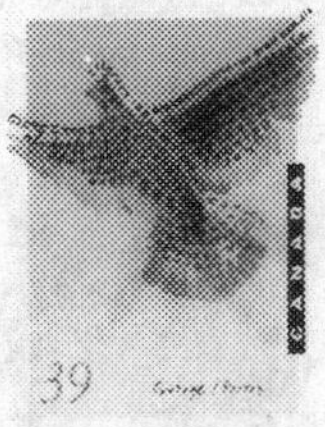

Intl. Literacy Year — A578

1990, Sept. 7 — *Perf. 13½x13*

1288 A578 39c multicolored 68 35

Legendary Creatures A579

1990, Oct. 1 — Litho. — *Perf. 12½x13½*

1289 A579 39c Sasquatch 66 32
1290 A579 39c Kraken 66 32
1291 A579 39c Werewolf 66 32
1292 A579 39c Ogopogo 66 32
a. Block of 4, #1289-1292 2.65 2.65

Agnes Campbell Macphail (1890-1954), First Woman Member of Parliament — A580

1990, Oct. 9 — Litho. — *Perf. 13x13½*

1293 A580 39c multicolored 66 32

Virgin Mary with Christ Child and St. John the Baptist by Norval Morrisseau — A581

Rebirth by Jackson Beardy A582

Indian Art: 45c, Sculpture of Mother and Child by an Inuit artist. 78c, Children of the Raven by Bill Reid.

1990, Oct. 25 — Litho. — *Perf. 13½*

1294 A581 39c multicolored 66 32
a. Booklet pane of 10 6.60
1295 A581 45c multicolored 78 40
a. Bklt. pane of 5 + label 3.90
1296 A581 78c multicolored 1.35 68
a. Bklt. pane of 5 + label 6.75

Booklet Stamp

Perf. 12½x13 on 2 or 3 Sides

1297 A582 34c multicolored 60 30
a. Booklet pane of 10 6.00

Christmas. No. 1297 has bar code at left; for use on covers with printed postal code matrix.

World War II Type of 1989

1990, Nov. 9 — *Perf. 12½x12*

1298 A568 39c Home front 66 50
1299 A568 39c Communal war efforts 66 50
1300 A568 39c Food production 66 50
1301 A568 39c Science and war 66 50
a. Block of 4, #1298-1301 2.65 2.65

A583

A584

Physicians: No. 1302, Jennie Trout (1841-1921), first licensed Canadian woman physician. No. 1303, Wilder Penfield (1891-1976), neurosurgeon. No. 1304, Sir Frederick Banting (1891-1941), discoverer of insulin. No. 1305, Harold Griffith (1894-1985), anesthesiologist.

1991, Mar. 15 — Litho. — *Perf. 13½*

1302 A583 40c multicolored 68 34
1303 A583 40c multicolored 68 34
1304 A583 40c multicolored 68 34
1305 A583 40c multicolored 68 34
a. Block of 4, #1302-1305 2.75 2.75

Prehistoric Life Type of 1990

1991, Apr. 5 — Litho. — *Perf. 12½x13½*

1306 A575 40c Microfossils 68 34
1307 A575 40c Early tree 68 34
1308 A575 40c Early fish 68 34
1309 A575 40c Land reptile 68 34
a. Block of 4, #1306-1309 2.75 2.75

Art Type of 1988

Painting: Forest, British Columbia by Emily Carr.

1991, May 7 — Litho. — *Perf. 12½x13*

1310 A546 50c multicolored 85 85

Masterpieces of Canadian Art.

1991, May 22 — Litho. — *Perf. 13x12½*

Public Gardens: #1311, Butchart Gardens, Victoria, B.C. #1312, Intl. Peace Garden, Boissevain, Manitoba. #1313, Royal Botanical Gardens, Hamilton, Ontario. #1314, Montreal Botanical Gardens. #1315, Halifax Public Gardens, Nova Scotia.

Booklet Stamps

1311 A584 40c multicolored 68 34
1312 A584 40c multicolored 68 34
1313 A584 40c multicolored 68 34
1314 A584 40c multicolored 68 34
1315 A584 40c multicolored 68 34
a. Strip of 5, #1311-1315 3.40 3.40
b. Bklt. pane, 2 each #1311-1315 6.80
Nos. 1311-1315 (5) 3.40 1.70

Canada Day — A585

Canadian Rivers — A586

1991, June 28 — *Perf. 13½x13*

1316 A585 40c multicolored 68 34

Small Craft Type of 1989

1991, July 18

1317 A559 40c Verchere rowboat 68 34
1318 A559 40c Touring kayak 68 34
1319 A559 40c Sailing dinghy 68 34
1320 A559 40c Cedar strip canoe 68 34
a. Block of 4, #1317-1320 2.75 2.75

1991, Aug. 20 — *Perf. 13x12½*

Booklet Stamps

1321 A586 40c South Nahanni 68 34
1322 A586 40c Athabasca 68 34
1323 A586 40c Boundary Waters-Voyageur Waterway 68 34
1324 A586 40c Jacques Cartier 68 34
1325 A586 40c Main 68 34
a. Strip of 5, #1321-1325 3.40 3.40
b. Bklt. pane, 2 each #1321-1325 6.80

See Nos. 1408-1412, 1485-1489, 1511-1515.

A587

A588

Paintings by William Kurelek.

1991, Aug. 29 — *Perf. 13½x13*

1326 A587 40c Leaving homeland 68 34
1327 A587 40c Winter in Canada 68 34
1328 A587 40c Clearing land 68 34
1329 A587 40c Growing wheat 68 34
a. Block of 4, #1326-1329 2.75 2.75

Arrival of Ukrainians, cent.

1991, Sept. 23 — *Perf. 13½*

1330 A588 40c Ski Patrol 68 34
1331 A588 40c Police 68 34
1332 A588 40c Fire fighters 68 34
1333 A588 40c Search & Rescue 68 34
a. Block of 4, #1330-1333 2.75 2.75

Dangerous public service occupations.

Folktales — A589

A590

1991, Oct. 1 — Litho. — *Perf. 13½x12½*

1334 A589 40c Witched Canoe 70 35
1335 A589 40c Orphan Boy 70 35
1336 A589 40c Chinook Wind 70 35
1337 A589 40c Buried Treasure 70 35
a. Block of 4, #1334-1337 2.80 2.75

1991, Oct. 16 — Litho. — *Perf. 13x12½*

1338 A590 40c multicolored 70 35
a. Bklt. pane of 10 + 2 labels 7.00

Queen's University, Kingston, Ont., sesquicentennial.

A591

Santa Claus — A592

1991, Oct. 23 — *Perf. 13½*

1339 A591 40c At fireplace 70 35
a. Booklet pane of 10 7.00
1340 A591 46c With white horse, tree 80 40
a. Bklt. pane of 5 + label 4.00
1341 A591 80c Sinterklaas, girl 1.40 70
a. Bklt. pane of 5 + label 7.00

Booklet Stamp

Perf. 12½x13 on 2 or 3 Sides

1342 A592 35c With punchbowl 62 30
a. Booklet pane of 10 6.20

Christmas. No. 1342 has bar code at left; for use on covers with printed postal code matrix.

Basketball, Cent. — A593

1991, Oct. 25 — *Perf. 13x13½*

1343 A593 40c multicolored 70 35

Souvenir Sheet

1344 Sheet of 3 2.90 2.90
a. A593 40c like #1343 70 70
b. A593 46c Player shooting, diff. 80 80
c. A593 80c Player dribbling 1.40 1.40

No. 1344a has 3-line inscription.

World War II Type of 1989

1991, Nov. 8 — *Perf. 13½*

1345 A568 40c Women's Armed Forces 70 35
1346 A568 40c War industry 70 35
1347 A568 40c Cadets and veterans 70 35
1348 A568 40c Defense of Hong Kong 70 35
a. Block or strip of 4, #1345-1348 2.80 2.75

Types of 1987-91 and

Edible Berries — A593a

Trees — A594

1991-94 — Litho. — *Perf. 13x13½*

1349 A593a 1c Blueberry 15 15
1350 A593a 2c Wild strawberry 15 15
1351 A593a 3c Black crowberry 15 15
1352 A593a 5c Rose hip 15 15
1353 A593a 6c Black raspberry 15 15
1354 A593a 10c Kinnikinnick 16 15
1355 A593a 25c Saskatoon berry 40 20

Perf. 13½x13

1358 A544 42c Flag, rolling hills 70 35
a. Booklet pane of 10 7.00
b. Bklt. pane of 50 + 2 labels 35.00
c. Bklt. pane of 25 + 2 labels 17.50

Perf. 13x13½

1359 A536 42c multi 70 35
a. Booklet pane of 10 7.00

1360 A536 43c multicolored 70 35
a. Booklet pane of 10 7.00

Perf. 13½x13

1360B A544 43c Flag, prairie 70 35
c. Booklet pane of 10 7.00
d. Bklt. pane of 25 + 2 labels 17.50
e. Perf. 14½ 70 35
f. As "e," bklt. pane of 10 7.00
g. As "e," bklt. pane of 25 + 2 labels 17.50

Perf. 13

1361 A594 48c McIntosh apple 80 40
a. Perf. 14½x14 on 3 sides 80 40
b. As "a," bklt. pane of 5 + label 4.00
1362 A594 49c Delicious apple 75 38
a. Perf. 14½x14 75 38
b. As "a," bklt. pane of 5 + 1 label 3.75
c. Booklet pane of 5 + label 3.75
1363 A594 50c Snow apple 75 38
a. Booklet pane of 5 + label 3.75
1366 A594 65c Black walnut 1.10 55
1367 A594 67c Beaked hazelnut 1.05 58
1368 A594 69c Shagbark hickory 1.00 50
1371 A594 84c Stanley plum 1.40 70
a. Perf. 14½x14 on 3 sides 1.40 70
b. As "a," bklt. pane of 5 + label 7.00
1372 A594 86c Bartlett pear 1.35 68
a. Perf. 14½x14 1.35 68
b. As "a," bklt. pane of 5 + 1 label 6.75
c. Booklet pane of 5 + label 6.75
1373 A594 88c Westcot apricot 1.25 62
a. Booklet pane of 5 + label 6.25

1991-94 Litho *Perf. 13x13½*

Size: 48x40mm

Litho. & Engr.

Perf. 14½x14

1375 A540 $1 Court House, Yorkton 1.50 75
1376 A540 $2 Provincial Normal School, Truro 3.00 1.50
Nos. 1349-1376 (22) 18.06 9.54

Self-Adhesive

Die Cut

Imperf

Booklet Stamps

1388 A543 42c Flag, mountains 75 38
a. Booklet of 12 9.00
1389 A543 43c Flag, estuary shore 68 35
a. Booklet pane of 12 8.20

Nos. 1388a, 1389a issued on peelable paper backing serving as booklet cover and sold for $5.25.

Coil Stamp

Perf. 10 Horiz.

Engr.

1394 A542 42c red 70 35
1395 A542 43c olive green 70 35

Issue dates: 1c-25c, Aug. 5, 1992. Nos. 1358-1359, 1394, 48c, 65c, 84c, Dec. 27, 1991. No. 1388, Jan. 28, 1992. Nos. 1360, 1360B, 1362, 1367, 1372, 1395, Dec. 30, 1992. No. 1389, Feb. 15, 1993. Nos. 1360e-1360g, Jan. 18, 1994. Nos. 1362c, 1372c, Jan. 7, 1994. 50c, 69c, 88c, Feb. 25, 1994. $1, $2, Feb. 21, 1994.

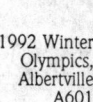

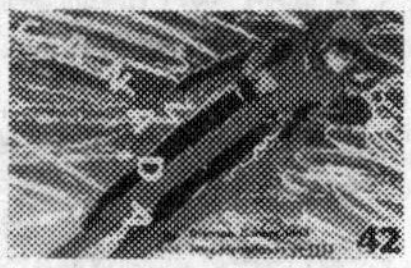

1992 Winter Olympics, Albertville A601

1992, Feb. 7 Litho. *Perf. 12½x13*

Booklet Stamps

1399 A601 42c Ski jumping 70 35
1400 A601 42c Pairs figure skating 70 35
1401 A601 42c Hockey 70 35
1402 A601 42c Bobsledding 70 35
1403 A601 42c Alpine skiing 70 35
a. Strip of 5, #1399-1403 3.50 3.50
b. Bklt. pane, 2 each #1399-1403 7.00

See Nos. 1414-1418.

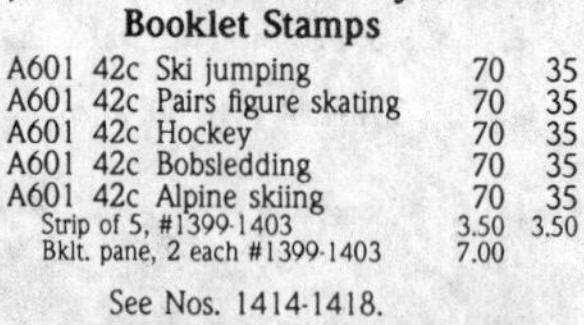

City of Montreal, 350th Anniv. — A602

Designs: No. 1404, City of Montreal, modern times. No. 1405, Early settlement of Montreal (Ville-Marie). 48c, Jacques Cartier's chart of Canada, snowshoe, ship's mast. 84c, World map, nocturnal and Aztec calendar stone.

1992, Mar. 25 *Perf. 13½*

1404 A602 42c multicolored 70 35
1405 A602 42c multicolored 70 35
a. Pair, #1404-1405 1.40 1.40
1406 A602 48c multicolored 80 40
1407 A602 84c multicolored 1.40 70
a. Sheet of 4, #1404-1407 3.60 3.60

Discovery of America, 500th anniv. (#1407).
Nos. 1404-1405 printed checkerwise. No. 1407a with engraved signatures in margin was produced in limited quantities for World Philatelic Youth Exhibition catalogue which sold for $12.

Canadian Rivers Type of 1991

1992, Apr. 22 *Perf. 12½*

Booklet Stamps

1408 A586 42c Margaree 70 35
1409 A586 42c West (Eliot) 70 35
1410 A586 42c Ottawa 70 35
1411 A586 42c Niagara 70 35
1412 A586 42c South Saskatchewan 70 35
a. Strip of 5, #1408-1412 3.50 3.50
b. Bklt. pane, 2 each #1408-1412 7.00

Nos. 1408-1412 are horiz.

Alaska Highway, 50th Anniv. — A603

1992, May 15 *Perf. 13½*

1413 A603 42c multicolored 70 35

1992 Olympic Games Type

1992, June 15 Litho. *Perf. 12½x13*

1414 A601 42c Gymnastics 70 35
1415 A601 42c Running 70 35
1416 A601 42c Diving 70 35
1417 A601 42c Cycling 70 35
1418 A601 42c Swimming 70 35
a. Strip of 5, #1414-1418 3.50 3.50
b. Bklt. pane, 2 each #1414-1418 7.00

1992 Summer Olympics, Barcelona.
Stamps in bottom row of #1418b are in different sequence than those in #1418a.

Art Type of 1988

Painting: Red Nasturtiums, by David Milne.

1992, June 29 Litho. *Perf. 12½x13*

1419 A546 50c multicolored 85 42

Masterpieces in Canadian Art.

Miniature Sheet

Canada Day A604

1992, June 29 Litho. *Perf. 12½x13*

1420 A604 42c Nova Scotia 70 35
1421 A604 42c Ontario 70 35
1422 A604 42c Prince Edward Island 70 35
1423 A604 42c New Brunswick 70 35
1424 A604 42c Quebec 70 35
1425 A604 42c Saskatchewan 70 35
1426 A604 42c Manitoba 70 35
1427 A604 42c Northwest Territories 70 35
1428 A604 42c Alberta 70 35
1429 A604 42c British Columbia 70 35
1430 A604 42c Yukon 70 35
1431 A604 42c Newfoundland 70 35
a. Sheet of 12, #1420-1431 + 13 labels 8.40 8.40

Canadian Folklore — A605

Legendary heroes: No. 1432, Jerry Potts, guide, interpreter. No. 1433, Captain William Jackman, rescuer. No. 1434, Laura Secord, patriot. No. 1435, Jos Monferrand, lumberjack.

1992, Sept. 8 Litho. *Perf. 12½*

1432 A605 42c multicolored 70 35
1433 A605 42c multicolored 70 35
1434 A605 42c multicolored 70 35
1435 A605 42c multicolored 70 35
a. Block of 4, #1432-1435 2.80 2.80

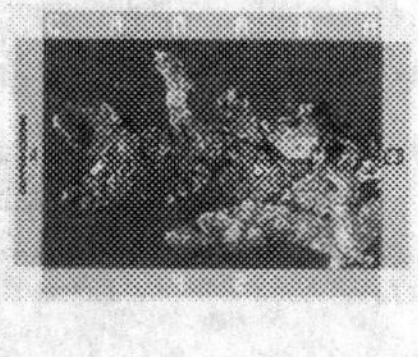

Minerals A606

1992, Sept. 21 *Perf. 12½*

1436 A606 42c Copper 70 35
1437 A606 42c Sodalite 70 35
1438 A606 42c Gold 70 35
1439 A606 42c Galena 70 35
1440 A606 42c Grossular 70 35
a. Strip of 5, #1436-1440 3.50 3.50
b. Bklt. pane, 2 each #1436-1440 7.00

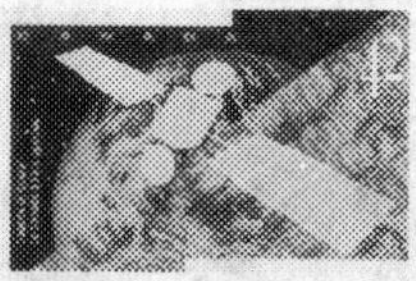

Canada in Space — A607

1992, Oct. 1 Litho. *Perf. 13*

1441 A607 42c Anik E2 satellite 70 35

Size: 32x26mm

1442 A607 42c Earth, space shuttle 70 35
a. Pair, #1441-1442 1.40 1.40

No. 1442 has a holographic image. Soaking in water may affect the hologram.

Natl. Hockey League, 75th Anniv. A608

Designs: No. 1443, Skates, stick, puck, photograph from the early years (1917-1942). No. 1444, Photograph, team emblems from the six-team years (1942-1967). No. 1445, Goalie's mask, gloves, photograph from the expansion years (1967-1992).

1992, Oct. 9 Litho. *Perf. 13x12½*

Booklet Stamps

1443 A608 42c multicolored 70 35
a. Bklt. pane of 8 + 4 labels 5.60
1444 A608 42c multicolored 70 35
a. Bklt. pane of 8 + 4 labels 5.60
1445 A608 42c multicolored 70 35
a. Bklt. pane of 9 + 3 labels 6.30

Order of Canada, 25th Anniv. — A609

Daniel Roland Michener (1900-1991), Governor General — A610

1992, Oct. 21 *Perf. 12½*

1446 A609 42c multicolored 70 35
1447 A610 42c multicolored 70 35
a. Pair, #1446-1447 1.40 1.40

Nos. 1446-1447 printed in sheets of 25 containing 16 #1446 and 9 #1447.

World War II Type of 1989

1992, Nov. 10 Litho. *Perf. 13½*

1448 A568 42c War reporting 70 35
1449 A568 42c Newfoundland air bases 70 35
1450 A568 42c Raid on Dieppe 70 35
1451 A568 42c U-boats offshore 70 35
a. Block or strip of 4, #1448-1451 2.80 2.80

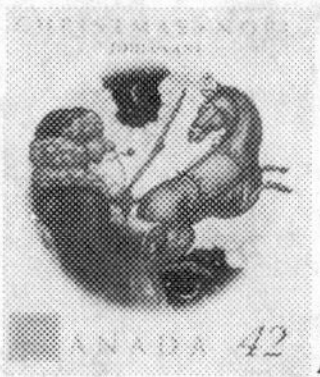

A611

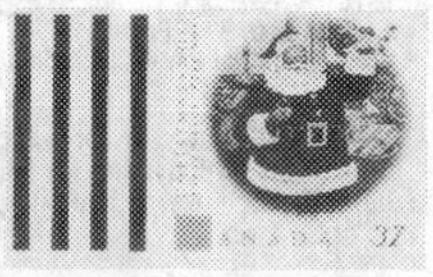

Santa Claus — A612

1992, Nov. 13 Litho. *Perf. 12½*

1452 A611 42c Jouluvana 70 35
a. Perf. 13½ 70 35
b. As "a," booklet pane of 10 7.00

Perf. 13½

1453 A611 48c La Befana 80 40
a. Booklet pane of 5 + label 4.00
1454 A611 84c Weihnachtsmann 1.40 70
a. Booklet pane of 5 + label 7.00

Booklet Stamp

Perf. 12½x13

1455 A612 37c Santa Claus 62 30
a. Booklet pane of 10 6.20

Christmas. No. 1455 has bar code at left; for use on covers with printed postal code matrix.

A613

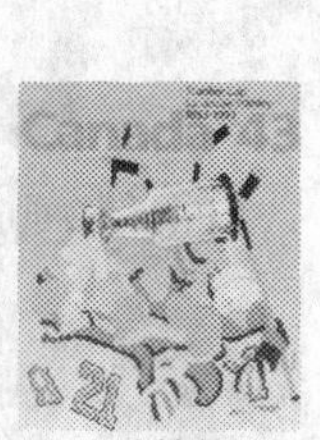

A614

Canadian Women: No. 1456, Adelaide Sophia Hoodless (1857-1910), founder of Victorian Order of Nurses. No. 1457, Marie-Josephine Gerin-Lajoie (1890-1971), founder of Notre-Dame du Bon Conseil Institute. No. 1458, Pitseolak Ashoona (c. 1904-83), Inuit graphic artist. No. 1459, Helen Alice Kinnear (1894-1970), first woman appointed King's Counsel and first federally appointed woman judge.

1993, Mar. 8 Litho. *Perf. 12½*

1456 A613 43c multicolored 68 35
1457 A613 43c multicolored 68 35
1458 A613 43c multicolored 68 35
1459 A613 43c multicolored 68 35
a. Block or strip of 4, #1456-1459 2.75 2.75

Natl. Council of Women of Canada (NCWC), and Natl. office of YWCA, cent.

1993, Apr. 16 Litho. *Perf. 13½*

1460 A614 43c multicolored 68 35

Stanley Cup, cent.

Handcrafted Textiles A615

Designs: No. 1461, Coverlet, New Bruswick. No. 1462, Pieced quilt, Ontario. No. 1463, Doukhobor bedcover, Saskatchewan. No. 1464, Kwakwaka'wakw ceremonial robe, British Columbia. No. 1465, Boutonne coverlet, Quebec.

Perf. 13x12½ on 3 Sides

1993, Apr. 30

Booklet Stamps

1461 A615 43c multicolored	68	35
1462 A615 43c multicolored	68	35
1463 A615 43c multicolored	68	35
1464 A615 43c multicolored	68	35
1465 A615 43c multicolored	68	35
a. Strip of 5, #1461-1465	3.40	3.40
b. Booklet pane, 2 each #1461-1465	6.80	

Stamps in bottom row of #1465b are in different sequence than those in #1465a.

Art Type of 1988

Painting: Drawing for The Owl, by Kenojuak Ashevak.

Perf. 12½x13½

1993, May 17 Litho.

1466 A546 86c multicolored	1.40	70

Intl. Year of Indigenous People.

Historic Canadian Pacific Railway Hotels — A616

Hotels: No. 1467, Empress, Victoria, B.C. No. 1468, Banff Springs, Banff, Alberta. No. 1469, Royal York, Toronto, Ont. No. 1470, Chateau Frontenac, Quebec. No. 1471, Algonquin, St. Andrews, N.B.

Perf. 13½ on 3 Sides

1993, June 14 Litho.

Booklet Stamps

1467 A616 43c multicolored	68	35
1468 A616 43c multicolored	68	35
1469 A616 43c multicolored	68	35
1470 A616 43c multicolored	68	35
1471 A616 43c multicolored	68	35
a. Strip of 5, #1467-1471	3.40	3.40
b. Booklet pane, 2 #1471a	6.80	

Opening of Chateau Frontenac, cent.

Miniature Sheet

Canada Day — A617

Provincial and Territorial Parks: No. 1472, Algonquin, Ontario. No. 1473, De la Gaspesie, Quebec. No. 1474, Cedar Dunes, Prince Edward Island. No. 1475, Cape St. Mary's Seabird Ecological Reserve, Newfoundland. No. 1476, Mount Robson, British Colombia. No. 1477, Writing-On-Stone, Alberta. No. 1478, Spruce Woods, Manitoba. No. 1479, Herschel Island, Yukon. No. 1480, Cypress Hills, Saskatchewan. No. 1481, The Rocks, New Brunswick, No. 1482, Blomidon, Nova Scotia. No. 1483, Katannilik, Northwest Territories.

1993, June 30 Litho. ***Perf. 13***

1472 A617 43c multicolored	68	35
1473 A617 43c multicolored	68	35
1474 A617 43c multicolored	68	35
1475 A617 43c multicolored	68	35
1476 A617 43c multicolored	68	35
1477 A617 43c multicolored	68	35
1478 A617 43c multicolored	68	35
1479 A617 43c multicolored	68	35
1480 A617 43c multicolored	68	35
1481 A617 43c multicolored	68	35
1482 A617 43c multicolored	68	35
1483 A617 43c multicolored	68	35
a. Sheet of 12, #1472-1483	8.25	8.25

Algonquin Park, centennial.

City of Toronto, Bicent. — A618

1993, Aug. 6 Litho. ***Perf. 13½x13***

1484 A618 43c multicolored	68	35

Canadian Rivers Type of 1991

1993, Aug. 10 ***Perf. 13x12½***

Booklet Stamps

1485 A586 43c Fraser	68	35
1486 A586 43c Yukon	68	35
1487 A586 43c Red	68	35
1488 A586 43c St. Lawrence	68	35
1489 A586 43c St. John	68	35
a. Strip of 5, #1485-1489	3.40	3.40
b. Bklt. pane, 2 each #1485-1489	6.80	

Miniature Sheet

Historic Automobiles A619

Designs: a, 1867 H.S. Taylor Steam Buggy. b, 1908 Russell Model L Touring Car. c, 1914 Ford Model T Open Touring Car. d, 1950 Studebaker Champion Deluxe Starlight Coupe. e, 1928 McLaughlin-Buick Model 28-496 Special Car. f, 1923-24 Gray-Dort 25-SM Luxury Sedan.

1993, Aug. 23 Litho. ***Perf. 12½x13***

1490 Sheet of 6	5.75	5.75
a.-b. A619 43c any single	70	70
c.-d. A619 49c any single	80	80
e.-f. A619 86c any single	1.40	1.40

Nos. 1490c-1490f are 43x22mm.

See No. 1527.

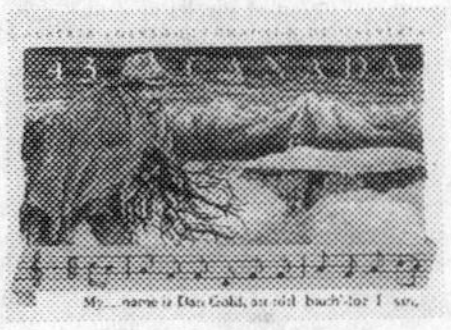

Folk Songs A620

Designs: No. 1491, The Alberta Homesteader, Alberta. No. 1492, Les Raftmans, Quebec. No. 1493, I'se the B'y That Builds the Boat, Newfoundland. No. 1494, Onkwa:ri tenhanonniahkwe, Kanien'kehaka (Mohawk).

1993, Sept. 7 Litho. ***Perf. 12½***

1491 A620 43c multicolored	68	35
1492 A620 43c multicolored	68	35
1493 A620 43c multicolored	68	35
1494 A620 43c multicolored	68	35
a. Block of 4, #1491-1494	2.75	2.75

Dinosaurs A621

1993, Oct. 1 Litho. ***Perf. 13½***

1495 A621 43c Massospondylus	70	35
1496 A621 43c Styracosaurus	70	35
1497 A621 43c Albertosaurus	70	35
1498 A621 43c Platecarpus	70	35
a. Block or strip of 4, #1495-1498	3.00	3.00

See Nos. 1529-1532.

A622

Santa Claus — A623

1993, Nov. 4 Litho. ***Perf. 13½***

1499 A622 43c Swiety Mikolaj	70	35
a. Booklet pane of 10	7.00	
1500 A622 49c Ded Moroz	80	40
a. Booklet pane of 5 + label	4.00	
1501 A622 86c Father Christmas, Australia	1.40	70
a. Booklet pane of 5 + label	7.00	

Booklet Stamp

Perf. 13

1502 A623 38c Santa Claus	60	30
a. Booklet pane of 10	6.00	

Christmas. No. 1502 has bar code at left; for use on covers with printed postal code matrix.

World War II Type of 1989

1993, Nov. 8 Litho. ***Perf. 13½***

1503 A568 43c Aid to Allies	70	35
1504 A568 43c Bomber forces	70	35
1505 A568 43c Battle of the Atlantic	70	35
1506 A568 43c Italian campaign	70	35
a. Block or strip of 4, #1503-1506	3.00	3.00

Greetings — A624

Design: No. 1508, "Canada" at right.

1994, Jan. 28 Litho. ***Die Cut***

1507 A624 43c multicolored	70	35
1508 A624 43c multicolored	70	35
a. Booklet pane, 5 each #1507-1508	7.00	

No. 1508a also contains 35 self-adhesive greetings labels in seven designs that complete the design when placed in the central circle of Nos. 1507-1508.

Jeanne Sauve (1922-93), Governor General A625

1994, Mar. 8 Litho. ***Perf. 12½x13***

1509 A625 43c + label, multi	70	35
a. Block or horiz. strip of 4 + 4 labels	3.00	1.50

No. 1509 issued se-tenant with label in sheets of 20 + 20 labels in four designs. In alternating rows, labels appear on left or right side of stamp.

T. Eaton Company, 125th Anniv. — A626

1994, Mar. 17 Litho. ***Perf. 13½x13***

1510 A626 43c multicolored	70	35
a. Booklet pane of 10 + 2 labels	7.00	

Canadian Rivers Type of 1991

1994, Apr. 22 ***Perf. 13½***

Booklet Stamps

1511 A586 43c Saguenay	65	32
1512 A586 43c French	65	32
1513 A586 43c Mackenzie	65	32
1514 A586 43c Churchill	65	32
1515 A586 43c Columbia	65	32
a. Strip of 5, #1511-1515	3.25	1.65
b. Booklet pane, 2 each #1511-1515	6.50	

Art Type of 1988

Painting: Vera, by Frederick H. Varley (1881-1969).

1994, May 6 Litho. ***Perf. 14x14½***

1516 A546 88c multicolored	1.25	65

XV Commonwealth Games, Victoria, BC — A627

1994 Litho. ***Perf. 14***

1517 A627 43c Lawn bowls	65	32
1518 A627 43c Lacrosse	65	32
a. Pair, #1517-1518	1.30	65
1519 A627 43c Wheelchair marathon	65	32
1520 A627 43c High jump	65	32
a. Pair, #1519-1520	1.30	65
1521 A627 50c Diving	75	38
1522 A627 88c Cycling	1.25	65

Issued: Nos. 1517-1518, May 20.

Souvenir Sheet

Intl. Year of the Family — A628

Designs: a, Mother and infant. b, Adults, children playing. c, Elderly woman, child. d, Adults, children in class. e, Judge, health care worker, child.

1994, June 2 Litho. *Perf. 14*

1523 Sheet of 5 3.25 3.25
a.-e. A628 43c any single 65 65

Canada Day — A629

Maple trees: a, Big leaf. b, Sugar. c, Silver. d, Striped. e, Norway. f, Manitoba. g, Black. h, Douglas. i, Mountain. j, Vine. k, Hedge. l, Red.

1994, June 30 Litho. *Perf. 13x13½*

1524 Sheet of 12 8.00 8.00
a.-l. A629 43c any single 65 32

Billy Bishop (1894-1956), Fighter Ace — A630

Design: No. 1526, Mary Travers, "La Bolduc" (1894-1941), folk singer.

1994, Aug. 12 *Perf. 13*

1525 A630 43c multicolored 65 32
1526 A630 43c multicolored 65 32
a. Pair, #1525-1526 1.30 65

Historic Vehicles Type of 1993
Miniature Sheet

Designs: a, 1942 Ford F60L-AMB military ambulance. b, 1925 REO Speed Wagon Police Wagon. c, 1927 Sicard Snow Remover/Snowblower. d, 1936 Bickle Chieftain Fire Engine. e, 1894 Ottawa Car Company Streetcar. f, 1950 Motor Coach Industries Courier 50 Skyview bus.

1994, Aug. 19 Litho. *Perf. 12½x13*

1527 Sheet of 6 5.25 5.25
a.-b. A619 43c any single 62 62
c.-d. A619 50c any single 75 75
e.-f. A619 88c any single 1.25 1.25

ICAO, 50th Anniv. A632

1994, Sept. 16 Litho. *Perf. 13*

1528 A632 43c multicolored 65 32

Dinosaur Type of 1993

Prehistoric animals: No. 1529, Coryphodon. No. 1530, Megacerops. No. 1531, Short-faced bear. No. 1532, Woolly mammoth.

1994, Sept. 26

1529 A621 43c multicolored 65 32
1530 A621 43c multicolored 65 32
1531 A621 43c multicolored 65 32
1532 A621 43c multicolored 65 32
a. Block or strip of 4, #1529-1532 2.60 1.30

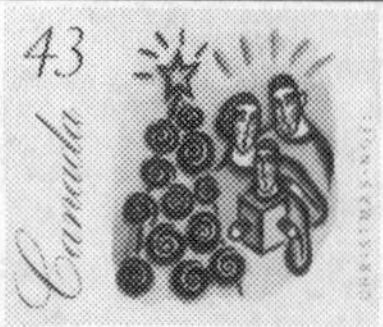

Family Singing Carols — A633

Soloist A634

1994, Nov. 3 Litho. *Perf. 13½*

1533 A633 43c multicolored 65 32
a. Booklet pane of 10 6.50
1534 A633 50c Choir, vert. 75 38
a. Booklet pane of 5 + label 3.75
1535 A633 88c Caroling, vert. 1.25 62
a. Booklet pane of 5 + label 6.25

Booklet Stamp
Perf. 13

1536 A634 38c multicolored 55 28
a. Booklet pane of 10 5.50
Nos. 1533-1536 (4) 3.20 1.60

Christmas. No. 1536 has bar code at left; for use on covers with printed postal code matrix.

World War II Type of 1989

1994, Nov. 7 Litho. *Perf. 13½*

1537 A568 43c D-Day beachhead 65 32
1538 A568 43c Artillery-Normandy 65 32
1539 A568 43c Tactical Air Forces 65 32
1540 A568 43c Walcheren and the Scheldt 65 32
a. Block or strip of 4, #1537-1540 2.75 1.30
Nos. 1537-1540 (4) 2.60 1.28

SEMI-POSTAL STAMPS

Catalogue values for unused stamps in this section are for Never Hinged items.

Olympic Type of 1973 and

SP1

SP2

1974, Apr. 17 Litho. *Perf. 12½*
Size: 20x36mm

B1 A307 8c + 2c multi 22 22
B2 A307 10c + 5c multi 35 35
B3 A307 15c + 5c multi 45 45

1975, Feb. 5 Litho. *Perf. 13*

B4 SP1 8c + 2c Swimming 22 22
B5 SP1 10c + 5c Rowing 35 35
B6 SP1 15c + 5c Sailing 45 45

1975, Aug. 6 Litho. *Perf. 13*

B7 SP2 8c + 2c Woman fencer 22 22
B8 SP2 10c + 5c Boxing 35 35
B9 SP2 15c + 5c Judo 45 45

1976, Jan. 7

B10 SP2 8c + 2c Basketball 22 22
B11 SP2 10c + 5c Vaulting 35 35
B12 SP2 20c + 5c Soccer 45 45

21st Olympic Games, Montreal, July 17-Aug. 1. The surtax was for the Canadian Olympic Committee.

AIR POST STAMPS

Allegory of Flight — AP1

Unwmk.

1928, Sept. 21 Engr. *Perf. 12*

C1 AP1 5c brown olive 4.75 1.65
Never hinged 6.50
a. Imperf., pair 175.00

No. C1 is known imperforate horizontally and imperforate vertically.
For surcharge, see No. C3.

Allegory-Air Mail Circles Globe — AP2

1930, Dec. 4 *Perf. 11*

C2 AP2 5c olive brown 20.00 13.00
Never hinged 27.50

For surcharge, see No. C4.

No. C1 Surcharged

6

1932, Feb. 22 *Perf. 12*

C3 AP1 6c on 5c brown olive 3.25 1.50
Never hinged 5.00
a. Inverted surcharge 150.00
b. Double surcharge 500.00
c. Triple surcharge 150.00
d. Pair, one without surcharge 600.00

Counterfeit surcharges exist.

No. C2 Surcharged in Dark Blue

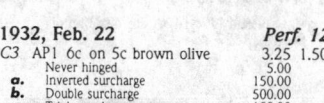

6 6
OTTAWA CONFERENCE
1932

1932, July 12 *Perf. 11*

C4 AP2 6c on 5c olive brown 7.00 6.00
Never hinged 10.00

Daedalus AP3

1935, June 1 Engr. *Perf. 12*

C5 AP3 6c red brown 1.50 80
Never hinged 2.50
a. Horiz. pair, imperf. vert. 1,750.
b. Imperf., pair 375.00

Mackenzie River Steamer and Seaplane — AP4

1938, June 15

C6 AP4 6c blue 1.65 15
Never hinged 2.50
a. Imperf., pair 375.00

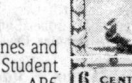

Planes and Student Flyers — AP5

1942-43

C7 AP5 6c deep blue 2.50 50
Never hinged 3.50
a. Imperf., pair 375.00
C8 AP5 7c deep blue ('43) 45 15
Never hinged 70
a. Imperf., pair 375.00
Set value 55

Canada's contribution to the war effort of the Allied Nations.

Catalogue values for unused stamps in this section, from this point to the end of the section, are for Never Hinged items.

Canada Geese in Flight — AP6

1946, Sept. 16

C9 AP6 7c deep blue 48 15
a. Booklet pane of 4 2.25 1.75

For overprints see Nos. CO1, CO2.

AIR POST SPECIAL DELIVERY STAMPS

Trans-Canada Airplane and Aerial View of a City — APSD1

1942-43 Unwmk. Engr. *Perf. 12*

CE1 APSD1 16c bright ultra 1.50 1.40
Never hinged 2.25
a. Imperf., pair 350.00
CE2 APSD1 17c brt ultra ('43) 2.25 2.00
Never hinged 3.00
a. Imperf., pair 350.00

Canada's contribution to the war effort of the Allied Nations.

Catalogue values for unused stamps in this section, from this point to the end of the section, are for Never Hinged items.

DC-4 Transatlantic Mail Plane Over Quebec — APSD2

1946, Sept. 16

CE3 APSD2 17c bright ultra 3.75 4.50

Circumflex accent on second "E" of "EXPRES."

Corrected Die

1947

CE4 APSD2 17c bright ultra 3.75 4.50

Grave accent on the 2nd "E" of "EXPRES."

AIR POST OFFICIAL STAMPS

Catalogue values for unused stamps in this section are for Never Hinged items.

No. C9 Overprinted in Black **O.H.M.S.**

1949 Unwmk. *Perf. 12*

CO1 AP6 7c deep blue 5.00 3.00
a. No period after "S" 60.00 45.00

Same Overprinted **G**

1950

CO2 AP6 7c deep blue 15.00 15.00

SPECIAL DELIVERY STAMPS

SD1

Unwmk.

1898, June 28 Engr. *Perf. 12*

E1 SD1 10c blue green 25.00 3.75
Never hinged 30.00

SD2

1922, Sept.

E2 SD2 20c carmine 27.50 4.25
Never hinged 35.00

Five Stages of Mail Transportation — SD3

1927, June

E3 SD3 20c orange 4.50 4.25
Never hinged 6.00
a. Imperf., pair 125.00

No. E3 forms part of the Confederation Commemorative issue. It is known imperforate vertically and imperforate horizontally.

SD4

1930, Sept. 2 *Perf. 11*

E4 SD4 20c henna brown 22.50 7.50
Never hinged 35.00

SD5

1933

E5 SD5 20c henna brown 22.50 8.75
Never hinged 27.50
a. Imperf., pair 300.00

Symbolical of Progress — SD6

1935, June 1 *Perf. 12*

E6 SD6 20c dark carmine 4.50 3.50
Never hinged 6.00
a. Imperf., pair 200.00

Arms of Canada SD7

1938-39

E7 SD7 10c dk green ('39) 3.00 1.40
Never hinged 4.00
a. Imperf., pair 350.00
E8 SD7 20c dark carmine 20.00 20.00
Never hinged 27.50
a. Imperf., pair 350.00

No. E8 Surcharged in Black

≡10 10≡

1939, Mar. 1

E9 SD7 10c on 20c dk car 4.25 3.50
Never hinged 5.00

Coat of Arms and Flags SD8

1942, July 1 Engr.

E10 SD8 10c green 1.50 85
Never hinged 2.00
a. Imperf., pair 400.00

Canada's contribution to the war effort of the Allied Nations.

Catalogue values for unused stamps in this section, from this point to the end of the section, are for Never Hinged items.

Arms of Canada SD9

1946, Sept. 16

E11 SD9 10c green 1.10 45

The laurel and olive branches symbolize Victory and Peace.
For overprints, see Nos. EO1, EO2.

SPECIAL DELIVERY OFFICIAL STAMPS

Catalogue values for unused stamps in this section are for Never Hinged items.

No. E11 Overprinted in Black **O.H.M.S.**

1950 Unwmk. *Perf. 12*

EO1 SD9 10c green 15.00 13.00

Same Overprinted **G**

EO2 SD9 10c green 30.00 27.50

REGISTRATION STAMPS

R1

1875-88 Unwmk. Engr. *Perf. 12*

F1 R1 2c orange 37.50 1.50
a. 2c vermilion 47.50 4.50
b. 2c rose carmine 115.00 47.50
c. As "a," imperf., pair *1,000.*
d. Perf. 12x11½ 185.00 47.50
F2 R1 5c dark green 47.50 1.75
a. 5c blue green ('88) 57.50 1.75
b. 5c yellow green 47.50 1.75
c. Imperf., pair *575.00*
d. Perf. 12x11½ 325.00 100.00
F3 R1 8c blue 200.00 150.00

POSTAGE DUE STAMPS

D1

D2

1906-28 Unwmk. Engr. *Perf. 12*

J1 D1 1c violet 4.00 1.40
a. Thin paper 4.50 2.75
b. Imperf., pair 175.00
J2 D1 2c violet 4.00 32
a. Thin paper 4.50 3.25
b. Imperf., pair 175.00
J3 D1 4c violet ('28) 18.00 5.50
J4 D1 5c violet 4.00 55
a. Thin paper 3.25 2.75
b. Imperf., pair 175.00
J5 D1 10c violet ('28) 12.50 4.00
Nos. J1-J5 (5) 42.50 11.77

In 1924 there was a printing of Nos. J1, J2 and J4 on thin semi-transparent paper.

1930-32 *Perf. 11*

J6 D2 1c dark violet 3.50 1.65
Never hinged 7.75
J7 D2 2c dark violet 2.50 42
Never hinged 5.75
J8 D2 4c dark violet 5.25 1.25
Never hinged 11.00
J9 D2 5c dark violet 5.25 2.25
Never hinged 11.00
J10 D2 10c dark vio ('32) 30.00 4.00
Never hinged 62.50
a. Vert. pair, imperf. horiz. 225.00
Nos. J6-J10 (5) 46.50 9.57

D3

D4

1933-34

J11 D3 1c dark vio ('34) 4.25 2.25
Never hinged 7.50
a. Imperf., pair 200.00
J12 D3 2c dark violet 1.75 40
Never hinged 3.75
J13 D3 4c dark violet 4.50 2.50
Never hinged 7.50
J14 D3 10c dark violet 7.75 1.90
Never hinged 16.00

Catalogue values for unused stamps in this section, from this point to the end of the section, are for Never Hinged items.

1935-65 *Perf. 12*

J15 D4 1c dark violet 15 15
a. Imperf., pair 100.00
J16 D4 2c dark violet 15 15
a. Imperf., pair 100.00
J16B D4 3c dark vio ('65) 1.75 85
J17 D4 4c dark violet 25 15
a. Imperf., pair 100.00
J18 D4 5c dark vio ('48) 35 20
J19 D4 6c dark vio ('57) 1.75 1.00
J20 D4 10c dark violet 25 15
a. Imperf., pair 100.00
Nos. J15-J20 (7) 4.65
Set value 2.30

D5

1967, Feb. 8 Litho. *Perf. 12*

Size: 20x17mm

J21 D5 1c carmine rose 15 15
J22 D5 2c carmine rose 20 20
J23 D5 3c carmine rose 22 20
J24 D5 4c carmine rose 25 25
J25 D5 5c carmine rose 1.25 1.25
J26 D5 6c carmine rose 25 25
J27 D5 10c carmine rose 25 25
Nos. J21-J27 (7) 2.57 2.55

1969-78 *Perf. 12*

Size: 20x15¾mm

J28 D5 1c car rose ('70) 45 28
a. Perf. 12½x12 ('77) 15 15
J29 D5 2c car rose ('72) 15 15
J30 D5 3c car rose ('74) 15 15
J31 D5 4c carmine rose 15 15
a. Perf. 12½x12 ('77) 15 15
J32 D5 5c car rose, perf. 12½x12 ('77) 15 15
a. Perf. 12 18.00 18.00
J33 D5 6c car rose ('72) 15 15
J34 D5 8c carmine rose 18 15
a. Perf. 12½x12 ('78) 30 15
J35 D5 10c carmine rose 15 15
a. Perf. 12½x12 ('77) 15 15
J36 D5 12c carmine rose 2.50 80
a. Perf. 12½x12 ('77) 30 15
J37 D5 16c carmine rose ('74) 25 20

Perf. 12 1/2x12

J38 D5 20c carmine rose ('77) 25 20
J39 D5 24c carmine rose ('77) 38 22
J40 D5 50c carmine rose ('77) 80 60
Nos. J28-J40 (13) 5.71
Set value 2.90

WAR TAX STAMPS

WT1

WT2

Unwmk.

1915, Mar. 25 Engr. *Perf. 12*

MR1 WT1 1c green 4.00 15
MR2 WT1 2c carmine 4.00 15
Set value 25

In 1915 postage stamps of 5, 20 and 50 cents were overprinted "WAR TAX" in two lines. These stamps were intended for fiscal use, the war tax on postal matter being 1 cent. A few of these stamps were used to pay postage.

1916

TWO DIES:
Die I - There is a colored line between two white lines below the large letter "T."
Die II - The right half of the colored line is replaced by two short diagonal lines and five small dots.

MR3 WT2 2c + 1c car (I) 4.00 15
a. 2c + 1c carmine (II) 35.00 1.65
MR4 WT2 2c + 1c brn (II) 2.75 15
a. 2c + 1c brown (I) 125.00 4.00
b. Imperf., pair (I) 90.00
c. Imperf., pair (II) 575.00
Set value 15

Perf. 12x8

MR5 WT2 2c + 1c car (I) 14.00 12.00

Coil Stamps

Perf. 8 Vertically

MR6 WT2 2c + 1c car (I) 37.50 2.50
MR7 WT2 2c + 1c brn (II) 5.50 40
a. 2c + 1c brown (I) 45.00 2.50

OFFICIAL STAMPS

With Perforated Initials O H M S
On March 28, 1939 the Treasury Board ruled that on and after June 30, 1939 all stamps used by government departments throughout the country should be perforated O H M S (On His Majesty's Service) and that "the Post Office Department is to make arrangements required to provide that all stamps sold to Government Departments are perforated with the letters O H M S." The sale of such perforated stamps was discontinued in 1948.
We do not list varieties with perforated initials.

Catalogue values for unused stamps in this section are for Never Hinged items.

Nos. 249, 250, 252 and 254 Overprinted in Black **O.H.M.S.**

1949-50 Unwmk. *Perf. 12*

O1 A97 1c green 2.75 1.75
a. No period after "S" 40.00 40.00
O2 A98 2c brown 11.00 7.25
a. No period after "S" 55.00 55.00
O3 A99 3c rose violet 2.75 1.10
O4 A98 4c dark carmine 3.00 50

Nos. 269 to 273 Overprinted in Black **O.H.M.S.**

O6 A108 10c olive 4.25 50
a. No period after "S" 45.00 42.50
O7 A109 14c black brown 4.50 2.00
a. No period after "S" 57.50 52.50
O8 A110 20c slate black 14.00 2.75
a. No period after "S" 70.00 65.00
O9 A111 50c dk bl grn 180.00 95.00
a. No period after "S" 400.00 375.00
O10 A112 $1 red violet 42.50 27.50
a. No period after "S" 1,000. 750.00
Nos. O1-O4,O6-O10 (9) 264.75 138.35

Same Overprint on No. 294

1950

O11 A124 50c dull green 25.00 14.00

Nos. 284 to 288 Overprinted in Black **O.H.M.S.**

1950

O12 A119 1c green 24 20
O13 A120 2c sepia 70 60
O14 A121 3c rose violet 90 30
O15 A122 4c dark carmine 90 15
b. No period after "S" 45.00 35.00
O15A A123 5c deep blue 1.50 1.10
c. No period after "S" 42.50 40.00
Nos. O12-O15A (5) 4.24 2.35

Stamps of 1946-50 Overprinted in Black **G G G**
a b c

1950

O16 A119(a) 1c green (#284) 28 15
O17 A120(a) 2c sepia (#285) 1.40 80
O18 A121(a) 3c rose vio (#286) 1.40 15
O19 A122(a) 4c dk car (#287) 1.40 15
O20 A123(a) 5c dp bl (#288) 1.65 85
O21 A108(b) 10c olive 2.75 45
O22 A109(b) 14c black brn 5.50 2.00
O23 A110(b) 20c slate blk 14.00 1.00
O24 A124(b) 50c dull green 7.75 5.50
O25 A112(b) $1 red violet 72.50 60.00
Nos. O16-O25 (10) 108.63 71.05

Nos. 301-302 Overprinted Type "b"

1950-51

O26 A125 10c black brown 85 15
a. Pair, one without "G" 375.00 350.00
O27 A126 $1 brt ultra ('51) 60.00 60.00

Nos. 305-306 Overprinted Type "a"

1951-52 Unwmk. *Perf. 12*

O28 A120 2c olive green 35 15
O29 A122 4c orange ver ('52) 52 15
Set value 20

No. 316 Overprinted Type "b"

1952

O30 A132 20c gray 1.65 15

Nos. 320-321 Overprinted Type "b"

1952-53

O31 A136 7c blue 2.75 65
O32 A137 $1 gray ('53) 11.50 6.50

Same Overprints on Nos. 325-329, 334

1953-61

O33 A139(a) 1c violet brown 18 15
O34 A139(a) 2c green 20 15
O35 A139(a) 3c carmine rose 20 15
O36 A139(a) 4c violet 30 15
O37 A139(a) 5c ultramarine 30 15
O38 A141(b) 50c light green 4.00 75
a. Overprinted type "c" ('61) 3.25 1.10
Nos. O33-O38 (6) 5.18
Set value 1.00

No. 351 Overprinted Type "b"

1955-62

O39 A148 10c violet brown 85 15
a. Overprinted type "c" ('62) 1.40 65

Nos. 337-338, 340-341 Overprinted Type "a"

1955-56

O40 A144 1c vio brown ('56) 18 15
O41 A144 2c green ('56) 24 15
O43 A144 4c violet ('56) 75 15
O44 A144 5c bright blue 28 15
Set value 29

No. 362 Overprinted Type "b"

1956-62

O45 A159 20c green 1.25 15
a. Overprinted type "c" ('62) 3.75 30

Nos. 401-402, 404-405 Overprinted Type "a"

1963, May 15 Engr. *Perf. 12*

O46 A195 1c deep brown 50 50
O47 A195 2c green 50 50
a. Pair, one without "G" 750.00
O48 A195 4c carmine 55 55
O49 A195 5c violet blue 32 32

CAYMAN ISLANDS

LOCATION — Three islands in the Caribbean Sea, about 200 miles northwest of Jamaica
GOVT. — British Crown Colony, formerly a dependency of Jamaica
AREA — 100 sq. mi.
POP. — 18,285 (1982)
CAPITAL — George Town, located on Grand Cayman

12 Pence = 1 Shilling
20 Shilling = 1 Pound
100 Cents = 1 Dollar (1969)

Catalogue values for unused stamps in this country are for Never Hinged items, beginning with Scott 112.

Victoria
A1

Edward VII
A2

1900 Typo. Wmk. 2 *Perf. 14*

1 A1 1/2p green 1.10 1.40
2 A1 1p carmine rose 2.25 65

1901-03

3 A2 1/2p green ('02) 2.25 3.75
4 A2 1p car rose ('03) 3.75 3.75
5 A2 2 1/2p ultramarine 4.25 5.00
6 A2 6p chocolate 12.00 15.00
7 A2 1sh brown orange 40.00 45.00
Nos. 3-7 (5) 62.25 72.50

1905 Wmk. 3

8 A2 1/2p green 1.10 2.00
9 A2 1p carmine rose 6.75 7.50
10 A2 2 1/2p ultramarine 2.50 3.00
11 A2 6p chocolate 16.00 18.50
12 A2 1sh brown orange 32.50 40.00
Nos. 8-12 (5) 58.85 71.00

For surcharge, see No. 17.

1907, Mar. 13

13 A2 4p brown & blue 17.50 21.00
14 A2 6p ol green & rose 17.50 21.00
15 A2 1sh violet & green 32.50 40.00
16 A2 5sh ver & green 150.00 175.00

Numerals of 4p, 1sh and 5sh of type A2 are in color on colorless tablet.
For surcharges, see Nos. 18-20.

Nos. 9, 16, 13 Handstamped

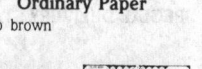

One Halfpenny.
No. 17

1/2 D
No. 18

1D
No. 19

2 1/2 D
No. 20

1907-08

17 A2 1/2p on 1p 30.00 42.50
18 A2 1/2p on 5sh 175.00 250.00
19 A2 1p on 5sh 165.00 225.00
20 A2 2 1/2p on 4p ('08) 1,400. *2,500.*

The 1p on 4p is a revenue stamp not authorized for postal use. Value about $250.
Nos. 19-20 exist with double surcharge. No. 18 exists inverted, double, double with one inverted, and in pair, one without surcharge.

A3

A4

1907-09 *Perf. 14*

21 A3 1/2p green 95 1.40
22 A3 1p carmine rose 60 90
23 A3 2 1/2p ultramarine 3.00 5.25

Chalky Paper

24 A3 3p violet, *yellow* 3.00 5.25
25 A3 4p blk & red, *yel* 40.00 42.50
26 A3 6p violet 5.25 7.75
27 A3 1sh black, *grn* 3.75 6.50
28 A3 5sh grn & red, *yel* 35.00 42.50
Nos. 21-28 (8) 91.55 112.05

Issue dates: 1/2p, 1p, Dec. 27, 1907. 2 1/2p, 3p, 4p, 5sh, Mar. 30, 1908. 6d, Oct. 2, 1908. 1sh, Apr. 5, 1909.
Forged cancellations are found on No. 28.

1908, Mar. 30 Wmk. 2

29 A3 1sh black, *green* 35.00 42.50
30 A3 10sh grn & red, *grn* 175.00 250.00

Numerals of 3p, 4p, 1sh and 5sh of type A3 are in color on plain tablet.
Forged cancellations are found on No. 30.

1908 Wmk. 3

Ordinary Paper

31 A4 1/4p brown 15 18

King George V
A5 A6

1912-20

32 A5 1/4p brown ('13) 15 15
33 A5 1/2p green 45 1.25
34 A5 1p carmine ('13) 75 85
35 A5 2p gray 42 1.50
36 A5 2 1/2p ultra ('14) 3.75 4.50

Chalky Paper

37 A5 3p vio, *yel* ('13) 1.25 2.50
38 A5 4p blk & red, *yel* ('13) 90 1.50
39 A5 6p vio & red vio ('13) 1.65 3.25
40 A5 1sh blk, *grn* ('13) 4.25 5.50
41 A5 2sh vio & ultra, *bl* 8.00 12.50
42 A5 3sh green & vio 9.50 12.50
43 A5 5sh grn & red, *yel* ('14) 27.50 35.00
44 A5 10sh grn & red, *bl grn*, olive back ('18) 67.50 87.50
a. 10sh green & red, *grn* ('13) 75.00 100.00
Nos. 32-44 (13) 126.07 168.50

The first printings of the 3p, 1sh and 10sh have a white back.
For surcharges, see Nos. MR1-MR7.

1913, Nov. 19

Surface-colored Paper

45 A5 3p violet, *yel* 1.90 3.25
46 A5 1sh black, *green* 3.25 5.50
47 A5 10sh grn & red, *grn* 70.00 82.50

Numeral of 1/4p, 2p, 3p, 4p, 1sh, 2sh, 3sh and 5sh of type A5 are in color on plain tablet.

1921-26 Wmk. 4 *Perf. 14*

50 A6 1/4p yel brown 15 16
51 A6 1/2p gray green 35 35
52 A6 1p rose red 55 85
53 A6 1 1/2p orange brn 42 85
54 A6 2p gray 1.10 2.25
55 A6 2 1/2p ultramarine 85 1.40
56 A6 3p violet, *yel* 70 1.10
57 A6 4 1/2p olive grn 1.40 3.75
58 A6 6p claret 4.25 6.75
59 A6 1sh black, *grn* 3.25 6.75
60 A6 2sh violet, *blue* 5.50 8.25
61 A6 3sh violet 14.00 19.00
62 A6 5sh green, *yel* 17.00 22.50
63 A6 10sh car, *green* 45.00 55.00
Nos. 50-63 (14) 94.52 128.96

Issue dates: 1 1/2p, Apr. 4, 1921. 1/4p, 1/2p, 1p, 2p, 2 1/2p, 6p, 2sh, 3sh, Apr. 1, 1922. 3p, 4 1/2p, June 29, 1923. 5sh, Feb. 15, 1925. 1sh, May 15, 1925. 10sh, Sept. 5, 1926.

1921-22 Wmk. 3

64 A6 3p violet, *org* 1.25 1.65
65 A6 4p red, *yel* 85 1.25
66 A6 1sh black, *green* 2.50 3.25
67 A6 5sh green, *yel* 13.00 21.00
68 A6 10sh car, *green* 52.50 65.00
Nos. 64-68 (5) 70.10 92.15

Issue dates: 4p, Apr. 1, 1922. Others, Apr. 4, 1921.

King William IV, King George V
A7

Perf. 12½

1932, Dec. 5 Wmk. 4 Engr.

69	A7	¼p brown	15	25
70	A7	½p green	25	60
71	A7	1p carmine	30	60
72	A7	1½p orange	35	30
73	A7	2p gray	50	75
74	A7	2½p ultramarine	45	50
75	A7	3p olive green	90	1.75
76	A7	6p red violet	6.25	10.00
77	A7	1sh brn & black	7.50	12.50
78	A7	2sh ultra & blk	22.50	35.00
79	A7	5sh green & blk	90.00	125.00
80	A7	10sh car & black	250.00	350.00
		Nos. 69-80 (12)	379.15	537.25

Centenary of the formation of the Cayman Islands Assembly.

Silver Jubilee Issue

Common Design Type

1935, May 6 *Perf. 13½x14*

81	CD301	½p green & black	20	22
82	CD301	2½p blue & brown	2.25	2.50
83	CD301	6p ol grn & lt bl	3.00	2.50
84	CD301	1sh brt vio & ind	3.75	3.25

King George V
A8

Catboat
A9

Red-footed Boobies
A10

Conches and Coconut Palms — A11

Hawksbill Turtles
A12

1935-36 *Perf. 12½*

85	A8	¼p brown & blk	15	15
86	A9	½p yel grn & ultra	15	15
87	A10	1p car & ultra	80	48
88	A11	1½p org & black	42	40
89	A9	2p brown vio & ultra	1.10	60
90	A12	2½p dp blue & blk	4.25	1.90
91	A8	3p ol grn & blk	2.25	1.10
92	A12	6p red vio & blk	8.50	8.00
93	A9	1sh org & ultra	4.50	5.25
94	A10	2sh black & ultra	22.50	24.00
95	A12	5sh green & blk	30.00	37.50
96	A11	10sh car & black	67.50	80.00
		Nos. 85-96 (12)	142.12	159.53

Issue dates: No. 86, 2½p, 6p, 1sh, Jan. 1, 1936. Others, May 1, 1935.

Coronation Issue

Common Design Type

1937, May 13 *Perf. 11x11½*

97	CD302	½p deep green	18	18
98	CD302	1p dark carmine	22	22
99	CD302	2½p deep ultra	55	55

Beach View, Grand Cayman
A13

Dolphin — A14

Hawksbill Turtles — A16

Map of the Islands
A15

Cayman Schooner
A17

Perf. 12½; 11½x13 or 13x11½ (A14, #111); 14 (#104, 107)

1938-43 Engr.

100	A13	¼p red orange	15	15
a.		Perf. 13½x12½ ('43)	15	15
101	A14	½p yel green	15	15
a.		Perf. 14 ('43)	15	15
102	A15	1p carmine	15	15
103	A13	1½p black	15	15
104	A16	2p dp violet ('43)	15	15
a.		Perf. 11½x13	24	24
105	A17	2½p ultra	15	15
106	A15	3p orange	15	15
107	A16	6p dk ol grn ('43)	65	45
a.		Perf. 11½x13	1.00	1.00
108	A14	1sh reddish brown	1.25	1.25
a.		Perf. 14 ('43)	1.25	1.25
109	A13	2sh green	6.00	6.00
110	A17	5sh deep rose	4.75	4.75
111	A16	10sh dark brown	9.50	8.50
a.		Perf. 14 ('43)	7.25	7.25
		Nos. 100-111 (12)	23.20	22.00

See Nos. 114-115.

Catalogue values for unused stamps in this section, from this point to the end of the section, are for Never Hinged items.

Peace Issue

Common Design Type

1946, Aug. 26 Wmk. 4 *Perf. 13½*

112	CD303	1½p black	15	15
113	CD303	3p orange	20	20

Types of 1938

1947, Aug. 25 *Perf. 12½*

114	A17	2½p orange	2.00	30
115	A15	3p ultramarine	42	42

Silver Wedding Issue

Common Design Types

1948, Nov. 29 Photo. *Perf. 14x14½*

116	CD304	½p dark green	15	15

Perf. 11½x11

Engr.; Name Typo.

117	CD305	10sh blue violet	14.00	14.00

UPU Issue

Common Design Types

Engr.; Name Typo. on #119, 120

1949, Oct. 10 *Perf. 13½, 11x11½*

118	CD306	2½p orange	40	40
119	CD307	3p indigo	65	65
120	CD308	6p olive	1.10	1.10
121	CD309	1sh red brown	2.25	2.25

Catboat — A18

Designs: ½p, Coconut grove. 1p, Green turtle. 1½p, Thatch rope industry. 2p, Caymanian seamen. 2½p, Map. 3p, Parrot fish. 6p, Bluff, Cayman Brac. 9p, Georgetown harbor. 1sh, Turtle "crawl". 2sh, Cayman schooner. 5sh, Boat-building. 10sh, Government offices.

Perf. 11½x11

1950, Oct. 2 Wmk. 4 Engr.

122	A18	¼p rose red & blue	20	20
123	A18	½p bl grn & red violet	28	28
124	A18	1p dp blue & olive	55	55
125	A18	1½p choc & bl grn	45	45
126	A18	2p rose car & vio	45	45
127	A18	2½p sepia & aqua	80	80
128	A18	3p bl & blue grn	2.25	2.25
129	A18	6p dp bl & org brn	1.90	1.90
130	A18	9p dk grn & rose red	3.25	3.25
131	A18	1sh red org & brn	3.25	3.25
132	A18	2sh red vio & vio	6.50	6.50
133	A18	5sh vio & olive	13.00	13.00
134	A18	10sh rose red & blk	19.00	19.00
		Nos. 122-134 (13)	51.88	51.88

Types of 1950 with Portrait of Queen Elizabeth II and

Lighthouse, South Sound — A20

Elizabeth II and Turtles — A21

Perf. 11½x11, 11x11½

1953-59 Engr.

135	A18	¼p rose red & bl	15	15
136	A18	½p bl grn & red violet	15	15
137	A18	1p dp bl & olive	15	15
138	A18	1½p choc & bl grn	15	15
139	A18	2p rose car & vio	15	15
140	A18	2½p black & aqua	15	15
141	A18	3p blue & bl grn	18	18
142	A20	4p dp blue & black	25	24
143	A18	6p dp bl & red brn	22	22
144	A18	9p dk green & rose red	40	38
145	A18	1sh red org & brn	85	75
146	A18	2sh red vio & vio	2.50	2.50
147	A18	5sh violet & olive	6.00	5.50
148	A18	10sh rose red & blk	9.00	10.50
149	A21	£1 bright blue	30.00	27.50
		Nos. 135-149 (15)	50.30	48.67

Issue dates: 4p, Mar. 2. 2p, 2½p, 9p, June 2, 1954. ½p, 1p, 1½p, 6p, July 7, 1954. ¼p, 3p, 1sh-10sh, Feb. 21, 1955. £1, Jan. 6, 1959.

Coronation Issue

Common Design Type

1953, June 2 *Perf. 13½x13*

150	CD312	1p brt green & black	25	25

Arms of Cayman Islands — A22

Wmk. 4

1959, July 4 Photo. *Perf. 12*

151	A22	2½p dull blue & blk	45	45
152	A22	1sh red orange & blk	45	45

Granting of a new constitution.

Cayman Parrot — A23

Catboat
A24

Designs: 1½p, Orchid. 2p, May of Islands. 2½p, Fisherman casting net. 3p, West Bay Beach. 4p, Green turtle. 6p, Cayman schooner. 9p, Angler with kingfish. 1sh, Iguana. 1sh3p, Swimming pool, Cayman Brac. 1sh9p, Girl and sailboat. 5sh, Fort George. 10sh, Coat of Arms. £1, Queen Elizabeth II.

Perf. 11x11½, 11½x11

1962, Nov. 28 Wmk. 314 Engr.

153	A23	¼p rose red & emer	15	15
154	A24	1p olive & black	15	15
155	A24	1½p purple & yel	15	15
156	A24	2p sepia & blue	15	15
157	A24	2½p green & vio	15	15
158	A24	3p car & blue	15	15
159	A24	4p pur & green	16	16
160	A24	6p sepia & green	25	25
161	A23	9p pur & vio bl	40	40
162	A24	1sh rose & sepia	60	60
163	A24	1sh3p brn org & lt grn	1.50	1.50
164	A24	1sh9p vio & bl grn	2.00	2.00
165	A24	5sh grn & dl pur	5.00	5.00
166	A23	10sh blue & olive	7.25	7.25
167	A23	£1 blk & car rose	14.00	14.00
		Revenue cancel		75
		Nos. 153-167 (15)	32.06	32.06

Freedom from Hunger Issue

Common Design Type

1963, June 4 Photo. *Perf. 14x14½*

168	CD314	1sh9p car rose	1.50	1.50

Red Cross Centenary Issue

Common Design Type

Wmk. 314

1963, Sept. 2 Litho. *Perf. 13*

169	CD315	1p black & red	15	15
170	CD315	1sh9p ultra & red	2.50	2.50

Shakespeare Issue

Common Design Type

1964, Apr. 23 Photo. *Perf. 14x14½*

171	CD316	6p deep lilac rose	28	28

ITU Issue

Common Design Type

1965, May 17 Litho. Wmk. 314

172	CD317	1p ultra & red lil	15	15
173	CD317	1sh3p rose lil & grn	1.10	1.10

Intl. Cooperation Year Issue

Common Design Type

1965, Oct. 25 Wmk. 314 *Perf. 14½*

174	CD318	1p blue grn & claret	15	15
175	CD318	1sh lt vio & green	85	85

Churchill Memorial Issue

Common Design Type

1966, Jan. 24 Photo. *Perf. 14*

Design in Black, Gold and Carmine Rose

176	CD319	¼p bright blue	15	15
177	CD319	1p green	15	15
178	CD319	1sh brown	75	75
179	CD319	1sh9p violet	1.25	1.25

Royal Visit Issue

Common Design Type

1966, Feb. 4 Litho. *Perf. 11x12*

180	CD320	1p violet blue	15	15
181	CD320	1sh9p dk car rose	1.10	1.10

World Cup Soccer Issue
Common Design Type

1966, July 1 Litho. *Perf. 14*

182	CD321	1½p multicolored	15	15
183	CD321	1sh9p multicolored	75	75

Common Design Types are pictured beginning on page 176.

WHO Headquarters Issue
Common Design Type

1966, Sept. 20 Litho. *Perf. 14*

184	CD322	2p multicolored	18	18
185	CD322	1sh3p multicolored	85	85

UNESCO Anniversary Issue
Common Design Type

1966, Dec. 1 Litho. *Perf. 14*

186	CD323	1p "Education"	15	15
187	CD323	1sh9p "Science"	90	90
188	CD323	5sh "Culture"	2.75	2.75

Telephone and Map of Caymans — A25

Perf. 14½x14

1966, Dec. 5 Litho. Wmk. 314

189	A25	4p multicolored	15	15
190	A25	9p multicolored	35	35

Linking of the Cayman telephone system with the intl. system.

BAC 1-11 Jet Liner over Schooner A26

1966, Dec. 17

191	A26	1sh blue, ol & black	25	25
192	A26	1sh9p ultra, grn & sepia	50	50

Opening of the Grand Cayman Airport jet service.

Water Skiing and ITY Emblem A27

ITY Emblem and: 6p, Skin diving. 1sh, Sport fishing. 1sh9p, Sailing.

Perf. 14½x14

1967, Dec. 1 Photo. Wmk. 314

193	A27	4p multi & gold	15	15
a.		Gold omitted	100.00	
194	A27	6p multi & gold	15	15
195	A27	1sh multi & gold	32	32
196	A27	1sh9p multi & gold	55	55

International Tourist Year.

Human Rights Flame and Freed Slaves A28

1968, June 3 Photo. Wmk. 314

197	A28	3p slate bl, grn & gold	15	15
198	A28	9p lt brn, grn & gold	24	24
199	A28	5sh ultra, grn & gold	1.25	1.25

International Human Rights Year.

Long Jump A29

Designs: 1sh3p, High jump. 2sh, Pole vault, vert.

1968, Oct. 1 Litho. *Perf. 13½*

200	A29	1sh multicolored	25	25
201	A29	1sh3p multicolored	35	35
202	A29	2sh yellow & multi	65	65

19th Olympic Games, Mexico City, Oct. 12-27.

Adoration of Shepherds, by Carel Fabritius A30

Christmas: 1p, 8p, 2sh, Adoration of the Shepherds, by Rembrandt.

Perf. 14x14½

1968, Nov. 18 Photo. Wmk. 314

203	A30	¼p brown & multi	15	15
a.		Gold omitted	190.00	
204	A30	1p violet & multi	15	15
205	A30	6p multicolored	18	18
206	A30	8p car & multi	28	28
207	A30	1sh3p multicolored	45	45
208	A30	2sh gray & multi	75	75
		Nos. 203-208 (6)	1.96	1.96

1969, Jan. 8 Unwmk.

209	A30	¼p red lilac & multi	15	15

Grand Cayman Thrush A31

Designs: 1p, Brahman cattle. 2p, Blowholes on coast. 2½p, Map of Grand Cayman. 3p, Town scene in Georgetown. 4p, Royal poinciana. 6p, Map of Cayman Brac and Little Cayman. 8p, Ships in harbor. 1sh, Basket making. 1sh3p, Beach scene. 1sh6p, Rope making. 2sh, Barracudas. 4sh, Government House. 10sh, Coat of arms, vert. £1, Queen Elizabeth II, vert.

Unwmk.

1969, June 5 Litho. *Perf. 14*

210	A31	¼p multicolored	15	15
211	A31	1p multicolored	15	15
212	A31	2p multicolored	15	15
213	A31	2½p multicolored	15	15
214	A31	3p multicolored	15	15
215	A31	4p multicolored	15	15
216	A31	6p multicolored	15	15
217	A31	8p multicolored	20	20
218	A31	1sh multicolored	30	30
219	A31	1sh3p multicolored	45	45
220	A31	1sh6p multicolored	52	52
221	A31	2sh multicolored	70	70
222	A31	4sh multicolored	1.50	1.50
223	A31	10sh multicolored	3.00	3.00
224	A31	£1 multicolored	6.25	6.25
		Nos. 210-224 (15)	13.97	13.97

See #262-276. For surcharges see #227-241.

1969, Aug. 11 Wmk. 314 Sideways

225	A31	¼p multicolored	15	15

Type of 1969 Surcharged

C-DAY
8th September 1969
¼c

1969, Sept. 8 Wmk. 314 *Perf. 14*

227	A31	¼c on ¼p multi	15	15
228	A31	1c on 1p multi	15	15
229	A31	2c on 2p multi	15	15
230	A31	3c on 4p multi	15	15
231	A31	4c on 2½p multi	15	15
232	A31	5c on 6p multi	15	15
233	A31	7c on 8p multi	15	15
234	A31	8c on 3p multi	15	15
235	A31	10c on 1s multi	22	22
236	A31	12c on 1sh3p multi	30	30
237	A31	15c on 1sh6p multi	38	38
238	A31	20c on 2sh multi	52	52
239	A31	40c on 4sh multi	1.10	1.10
240	A31	$1 on 10sh multi	3.00	3.00
241	A31	$2 on £1 multi	6.00	6.00
		Nos. 227-241 (15)	12.72	12.72

The surcharge is arranged differently on various denominations.

Madonna and Child, by Alvise Vivarini — A32

"Noli me Tangere," by Titian — A33

Christmas: 1c, 7c, 20c, The Adoration of the Kings, by Jan Gossaert.

1969, Nov. 4 Photo. *Perf. 14*

242	A32	¼c blue & multi	15	15
243	A32	¼c emer & multi	15	15
244	A32	¼c red org & multi	15	15
245	A32	¼c brt pink & multi	15	15
246	A32	1c vio blue & multi	15	15
247	A32	5c red org & multi	15	15
248	A32	7c dk green & multi	15	15
249	A32	12c emer & multi	32	32
250	A32	20c multicolored	50	50
		Set value	1.25	1.25

1970, Mar. 23 Litho. Unwmk.

251	A33	¼c dull grn & multi	15	15
252	A33	¼c dk car & multi	15	15
253	A33	¼c violet & multi	15	15
254	A33	¼c bister & multi	15	15
255	A33	10c vio blue & multi	25	25
256	A33	12c red brn & multi	28	28
257	A33	40c brn vio & multi	1.00	1.00
		Set value	1.70	1.70

Easter.

Barnaby from "Barnaby Rudge" by Dickens (1812-70), English Novelist — A34

Characters from Charles Dickens: 12c, Sairey Gamp, from "Martin Chuzzlewit." 20c, Mr. Micawber and David, from "David Copperfield." 40c, The Marchioness from "The Old Curiosity Shop."

1970, June 17 Photo. *Perf. 14½x14*

258	A34	1c ol green, yel & blk	15	15
259	A34	12c red brn, brick red & black	40	40
260	A34	20c dk ol bister, gold & black	70	70
261	A34	40c dp ultra, lt bl & blk	1.40	1.40

Type of Regular Issue 1969 Values in Cents and Dollars

Designs: ¼c, Grand Cayman thrush. 1c, Brahman cattle. 2c, Blowholes on coast. 3c, Royal poinciana. 4c, Map of Grand Cayman. 5c, Map of Cayman Brac and Little Cayman. 7c, Ships in harbor. 8c, Town scene in Georgetown. 10c, Basket making. 12c, Beach scene. 15c, Rope making. 20c, Barracudas. 40c, Government House. $1, Coat of arms, vert. $2, Queen Elizabeth II, vert.

Wmk. 314

1970, Sept. 8 Litho. *Perf. 14*

262	A31	¼c multicolored	15	15
263	A31	1c multicolored	15	15
264	A31	2c multicolored	15	15
265	A31	3c multicolored	15	15
266	A31	4c multicolored	15	15
267	A31	5c multicolored	15	15
268	A31	7c multicolored	20	20
269	A31	8c multicolored	25	25
270	A31	10c multicolored	32	32
271	A31	12c multicolored	35	35
272	A31	15c multicolored	50	50
273	A31	20c multicolored	65	65
274	A31	40c multicolored	1.40	1.40
275	A31	$1 multicolored	4.00	4.00
276	A31	$2 multicolored	7.00	7.00
		Nos. 262-276 (15)	15.57	15.57

The Three Wise Men A35

Christmas: 1c, 10c, 20c, Nativity and globe.

1970, Oct. 8 Litho. *Perf. 14*

277	A35	¼c brt grn & yel grn	15	15
278	A35	1c bl grn, yel grn & blk	15	15
279	A35	5c dp claret & org	15	15
280	A35	10c red org, yel & blk	32	32
281	A35	12c ultra & lt grnsh bl	40	40
282	A35	20c grn, yel grn & blk	65	65
		Set value		91
		Nos. 277-282 (6)	1.82	1.82

Grand Cayman Terrapin A36

Cayman Islands Turtles: 7c, Green turtle. 12c, Hawksbill turtle. 20c, Turtle farm.

1971, Jan. 28 *Perf. 14x14½*

283	A36	5c multicolored	45	45
284	A36	7c multicolored	65	65
285	A36	12c multicolored	1.25	1.25
286	A36	20c multicolored	2.00	2.00

Dendrophylax Fawcetii — A37

Adoration of the Kings, 15th Century — A38

Wild Orchids of West Indies: 2c, Schomburgkia thomsoniana. 10c, Vanilla claviculata. 40c, Oncidium variegatum.

1971, Apr. 7 Wmk. 314 *Perf. 14*

287	A37	¼c brown & multi	15	15
288	A37	2c ol green & multi	24	24
289	A37	10c gray bl & multi	1.00	1.00
290	A37	40c lt violet & multi	3.25	3.25

1971, Sept. 27 *Perf. 14*

Christmas: 1c, 15c, Nativity (detail), Paris, 14th cent. 5c, 20c, Adoration of the Kings (detail), Burgundian, 15th cent.

291	A38	¼c gold & multi	15	15
292	A38	1c gold & multi	15	15
293	A38	5c gold & multi	15	15
294	A38	12c gold & multi	38	38
295	A38	15c gold & multi	50	50
296	A38	20c gold & multi	80	80
a.		Souvenir sheet of 6, #291-296	3.00	3.00
		Nos. 291-296 (6)	2.13	2.13

Underwater Cable, Turtle and Telephone A39

1972, Jan. 10

297	A39	2c multicolored	15	15
298	A39	10c multicolored	35	35
299	A39	40c multicolored	1.65	1.65

Coaxial cable for world communications.

Courthouse — A40

Designs: 15c, 40c, Legislative Assembly Building, Georgetown.

1972, Aug. 15 *Perf. 13½x14*

300	A40	5c dp car & multi	*15*	*15*
301	A40	15c lilac rose & multi	*18*	*18*
302	A40	25c dull grn & multi	*28*	*28*
303	A40	40c dk blue & multi	*50*	*50*
a.		Souvenir sheet of 4, #300-303	2.25	2.25

New Cayman Islands government buildings.

Silver Wedding Issue, 1972

Common Design Type

Design: Queen Elizabeth II, Prince Philip, hawksbill turtle and conch.

1972, Nov. 20 Photo. *Perf. 14x14½*

304	CD324	12c vio black & multi	22	22
305	CD324	30c olive & multi	52	52

$1 Note and 1c Coin A41

Designs: 6c, $5 note and 5c coin. 15c, $10 note and 10c coin. 25c, $25 note and 25c coin.

1973, Jan. 15

306	A41	3c emerald & multi	15	15
307	A41	6c yellow & multi	15	15
308	A41	15c lilac & multi	50	50
309	A41	25c orange & multi	80	80
a.		Souvenir sheet of 4, #306-309	2.75	2.75

First Cayman Islands coinage and bank notes, May 1, 1972.

Last Supper A42

Stained Glass Windows: 10c, Christ Carrying Cross, vert. 12c, Resurrection, vert. 30c, Crucifixion.

Perf. 14½x14, 14x14½

1973, Apr. 11 **Litho.**

310	A42	10c pink & multi	22	22
311	A42	12c yel green & multi	32	32
312	A42	20c lt blue & multi	65	65
313	A42	30c yellow & multi	95	95
a.		Souvenir sheet of 4	2.50	2.50

Easter. No. 313a contains 4 stamps similar to Nos. 310-313 with simulated perforations.

Nativity — A43

White-winged Dove — A44

Christmas: 5c, 12c, 25c, Adoration of the Magi, from Breviary of Queen Isabella. 9c, 15c, Like 3c, Nativity from Sforza Book of Hours.

1973, Oct. 2 *Perf. 14½*

314	A43	3c dull green & multi	15	15
315	A43	5c dull pur & multi	15	15
316	A43	9c sepia & multi	22	22
317	A43	12c dk blue & multi	30	30
318	A43	15c dp rose & multi	40	40
319	A43	25c black & multi	60	60
		Nos. 314-319 (6)	1.82	1.82

Princess Anne's Wedding Issue

Common Design Type

1973, Nov. 14 Wmk. 314 *Perf. 14*

320	CD325	10c brt green & multi	20	20
321	CD325	30c lilac & multi	60	60

1974, Jan. 2 Litho. *Perf. 14x14½*

322	A44	3c shown	40	22
323	A44	10c Vitelline warblers	1.10	65
324	A44	12c Greater Antillean grackles	1.65	1.00
325	A44	20c West Indian red-bellied woodpecker	2.50	1.50
326	A44	30c Stripe-headed tanagers	4.00	2.25
327	A44	50c Yucatan vireos	6.50	4.00
		Nos. 322-327 (6)	16.15	9.62

See Nos. 354-359.

One-room Schoolhouse A45

Designs: 20c, New comprehensive school. 30c, Creative Arts Center, Mona, Jamaica.

1974, May 1 *Perf. 14*

328	A45	12c multicolored	24	24
329	A45	20c multicolored	50	50
330	A45	30c multicolored	70	70

25th anniv. of the University College of the West Indies.

Hermit Crab and Pirate Gold A46

Coat of Arms — A47

Elizabeth II — A48

Designs: 3c, Pirate, treasure chest and lion's paw. 4c, Spotted scorpionfish and crown. 5c, Flintlock pistol and brain coral. 6c, Blackbeard on Grand Cayman and green turtle. 8c, 9c, Jeweled pomander and porkfish. 10c, Spiny lobster and gold coins. 12c, Jeweled sword, dagger and sea fan. 15c, Cabrit's murex and jeweled necklace. 20c, Queen conch, pistol and gold cup. 25c, Hogfish and pirate chest. 40c, Gold chalice and sea whip.

Wmk. 314 Upright, Sideways (#331-332, 336, 344-345)

1974-75 Litho. *Perf. 14*

331	A46	1c multi ('75)	16	16
a.		Wmk. upright	20	20
332	A46	3c multicolored	30	30
a.		Wmk. upright	42	42
333	A46	4c multicolored	26	26
334	A46	5c multicolored	26	26
335	A46	6c multicolored	15	15
336	A46	8c multicolored	45	45
337	A46	9c multicolored	2.75	2.75
338	A46	10c multicolored	65	65
339	A46	12c multicolored	24	24
340	A46	15c multicolored	32	32
341	A46	20c multicolored	1.10	1.10
342	A46	25c multicolored	52	52
343	A46	40c multicolored	85	85
344	A47	$1 multicolored	5.25	5.25
345	A48	$2 multicolored	10.50	10.50
		Nos. 331-345 (15)	23.76	23.76

Issue dates: No. 332, Nov. 12, 8c. Dec. 16, No. 331, Sept. 29, others, Aug. 1.

1976-77 **Wmk. 373**

332b	A46	3c multicolored	18	15
333a	A46	4c multi ('77)	22	18
334a	A46	5c multi ('77)	25	20
336b	A46	8c multicolored	18	25
338b	A46	10c multicolored	25	20
341b	A46	20c multicolored	90	70
344a	A47	$1 multi ('77)	5.00	4.50
345b	A48	$2 multicolored	9.00	9.00
		Nos. 332b-345b (8)	15.98	15.18

Issue dates: 3c, 8c, 10c, 20c, $2, Sept. 3. 4c, 5c, $1, Oct. 19.

Design Smaller

Size: 40x25mm

Wmk. 373 (Sideways on 1c-40c)

1978-80

346	A46	1c multicolored	1.00	1.00
346A	A46	3c multicolored	1.10	1.10
346B	A46	5c multi ('79)	1.75	1.75
347	A46	10c multicolored	2.25	2.25
347A	A46	20c multicolored	4.50	4.50
347B	A46	40c multi ('79)	11.00	11.00
347C	A47	$1 multi ('80)	9.25	9.25
348	A48	$2 multi ('80)	10.00	10.00
		Nos. 346-348 (8)	40.85	40.85

Issue dates: 1c, 3c, Mar. 16. 10c, 20c, May 25. 5c, Dec. 11. $2, Apr. 3. $1, July 30.

Sea Captain and Ship A49

1974, Oct. 7 Wmk. 314 *Perf. 14*

349	A49	8c shown	20	20
350	A49	12c Thatch weaver	25	25
351	A49	20c Farmer	45	45
a.		Miniature sheet of 3, #349-351	1.50	1.50

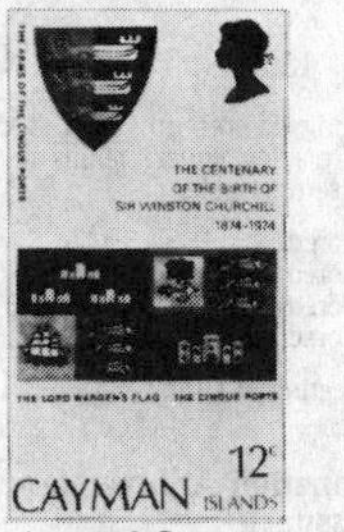

Arms of Cinque Ports and Lord Warden's Flag — A50

Churchill Coat of Arms — A51

1974, Nov. 30

352	A50	12c multicolored	28	28
353	A51	50c multicolored	1.10	1.10
a.		Souvenir sheet of 2, #352-353	1.75	1.75

Sir Winston Churchill (1874-1965).

Bird Type of 1974

Wmk. 314

1975, Jan. 1 Litho. *Perf. 14*

354	A44	3c Yellow-shafted flicker	18	18
355	A44	10c West Indian tree duck	65	65
356	A44	12c Yellow warblers	85	85
357	A44	20c White-bellied dove	1.40	1.40
358	A44	30c Magnificent frigate bird	2.00	2.00
359	A44	50c Cayman amazon	3.50	3.50
a.		Wmk. 362 (Lesotho)	400.00	
		Nos. 354-359 (6)	8.58	8.58

Ivory Crosier with Crucifixion — A52

Design: 35c, Crucifixion, ivory and gilt. Designs show heads of 14th century French pastoral staffs.

Wmk. 314

1975, Mar. 24 Litho. *Perf. 14*

360	A52	15c plum & multi	30	30
361	A52	35c gray & multi	80	80
a.		Souvenir sheet of 2, #360-361	1.40	1.40

Easter. No. 361a exists imperf.

See Nos. 366-367.

Israel Hands A53

Designs: Pirates and various scenes.

1975, July 25 **Wmk. 314**

362	A53	10c shown	38	38
363	A53	12c John Fenn	50	50
364	A53	20c Thomas Anstis	85	85
365	A53	30c Edward Low	1.25	1.25

Easter Type of 1975

Designs after ivory carved pastoral staffs showing Virgin and Child with angels, French, 14th century.

Wmk. 373

1975, Oct. 31 Litho. *Perf. 14*

366	A52	12c dk green & multi	25	25
367	A52	50c multicolored	1.00	1.00
a.		Souvenir sheet of 2, #366-367	1.75	1.75

Christmas.

Registered Letter with Nos. 1-2; Cayman Brac Government House and Sub Post Office — A54

Cayman Islands 1st postage stamps, 75th anniv.: 20c, Cayman Islands #1 and cancelation used 1890-94; 30c, #2, 20; 50c, #1-2.

1976, Mar. 12 Litho. *Perf. 13½x14*

368	A54	10c lt blue & multi	25	25
369	A54	20c pink & multi	50	50
370	A54	30c multicolored	75	75
371	A54	50c yellow & multi	1.25	1.25
a.		Souvenir sheet of 4, #368-371	3.00	3.00

Seals of Georgia, Delaware and New Hampshire — A55

Designs: 15c, Seals of South Carolina, New Jersey and Maryland. 20c, Seals of Virginia, Rhode Island and Massachusetts. 25c, Seals of New York, Connecticut and North Carolina. 30c, Seal of Pennsylvania, Liberty Bell and Great Seal of the U.S.

Wmk. 373

1976, May 29 Litho. ***Perf. 14***

372 A55	10c olive & multi	35	35
373 A55	15c blue & multi	50	50
374 A55	20c multicolored	70	70
375 A55	25c blue grn & multi	85	85
376 A55	30c red brn & multi	1.10	1.10
a.	Souvenir sheet of 5 + label	5.00	*5.00*
	Nos. 372-376 (5)	3.50	3.50

American Bicentennial. Nos. 372-376 printed in sheets of 5. No. 376a contains one each of Nos. 372-376 and corner label inscribed "USA 200."

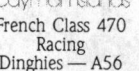

French Class 470 Racing Dinghies — A56

Queen Elizabeth II — A57

Design: 50c, One racing dinghy.

1976, Aug. 16 Litho. ***Perf. 14***

377 A56	20c multicolored	42	42
378 A56	50c multicolored	1.10	1.10

21st Olympic Games, Montreal, Canada, July 17-Aug. 1.

Perf. 14x13½, 13½x14

1977, Feb. 7 Litho. Wmk. 373

Designs: 8c, Prince Charles, 1973 visit. 50c, Preparation for anointing ceremony, horiz.

379 A57	8c multicolored	16	16
380 A57	30c multicolored	60	60
381 A57	50c multicolored	1.10	1.10

25th anniv. of the reign of Elizabeth II.

Scuba Diving A58

Designs: 10c, Divers examining underwater wreck. 20c, Fairy basslets (fish). 25c, Sergeant majors (fish).

1977, July 25 ***Perf. 13½***

382 A58	5c multicolored	18	18
383 A58	10c multicolored	32	32
384 A58	20c multicolored	65	65
385 A58	25c multicolored	80	80
a.	Souvenir sheet of 4	2.25	2.25

Tourist publicity. No. 385a contains one each of Nos. 382-385, perf. 14½.

Composia Fidelissima A59

Butterflies: 8c, Heliconius charitonius. 10c, Danaus gilippus. 15c, Agraulis vanillae. 20c, Junonia evarete. 30c, Anartia jatrophae.

1977, Dec. 2 Wmk. 373 ***Perf. 14x13***

386 A59	5c multicolored	25	25
387 A59	8c multicolored	42	42
388 A59	10c multicolored	50	50
389 A59	15c multicolored	80	80
390 A59	20c multicolored	1.00	1.00
391 A59	30c multicolored	1.65	1.65
	Nos. 386-391 (6)	4.62	4.62

Cruise Ship "Southward" A60

Designs: 5c, "Renaissance." 30c, New harbor, vert. 50c, "Daphne," vert.

1978, Jan. 23 Litho. ***Perf. 14***

392 A60	3c multicolored	15	15
393 A60	5c multicolored	15	15
394 A60	30c multicolored	65	65
395 A60	50c multicolored	1.10	1.10

New harbor and cruise ships.

Crucifixion, by Dürer — A61

Explorers, Singing Game — A62

Etchings by Dürer: 15c, Christ at Emmaus. 20c, Entry into Jerusalem. 30c, Christ washing Peter's feet.

1978, Mar. 20 Litho. ***Perf. 12***

396 A61	10c multicolored	22	22
397 A61	15c multicolored	30	30
398 A61	20c multicolored	42	42
399 A61	30c multicolored	60	60
a.	Souvenir sheet of 4, #396-399	1.65	1.65

Easter; 450th death anniv. of Albrecht Dürer (1471-1528). Nos. 396-399 issued in sheets of 6.

1978, Apr. 25 Litho. ***Perf. 14***

Designs: 10c, Girls' Brigade presenting flag. 20c, Guides studying Bible, playing guitar, tennis and volleyball. 50c, Guides setting table.

400 A62	3c multicolored	15	15
401 A62	10c multicolored	30	30
402 A62	20c multicolored	55	55
403 A62	50c multicolored	1.25	1.25

3rd Intl. Council Meeting of Girls' Brigade.

Elizabeth II Coronation Anniversary Issue

Common Design Types

Souvenir Sheet

1978, June 2 Unwmk. ***Perf. 15***

404	Sheet of 6	3.00	*3.00*
a.	CD326 30c Yale of Beaufort	50	50
b.	CD327 30c Elizabeth II	50	50
c.	CD328 30c Screech owl	50	50

No. 404 contains 2 se-tenant strips of Nos. 404a-404c, separated by horizontal gutter with commemorative and descriptive inscriptions.

A63

A63a

A63: 1c, Trumpetfish. 3c, Nassau grouper. 5c, French angelfish. 10c, Schoolmaster snappers. 20c, Banded butterflyfish. 50c, Black-bar soldierfish.

A63a: 3c, Four-eyed butterflyfish. 5c, Grey angel fish. 10c, Squirrelfish. 15c, Parrotfish. 20c, Spanish hogfish. 30c, Queen angelfish.

1978-79 Wmk. 373 Litho. ***Perf. 14***

405 A63	1c multicolored	15	15
406 A63	3c multicolored	15	15
407 A63a	3c multicolored	15	15
408 A63a	5c multicolored	15	15
409 A63	5c multicolored	15	15
412 A63a	10c multicolored	28	28
413 A63	10c multicolored	28	28
414 A63a	15c multicolored	38	38
415 A63a	20c multicolored	45	45
416 A63	20c multicolored	45	45
417 A63a	30c multicolored	75	75
418 A63	50c multicolored	1.10	1.10
	Nos. 405-418 (12)	4.44	4.44

Issue dates: type A63, Apr. 20, 1979, type A63a, Aug. 28, 1978.

Lockheed Lodestar A64

Aircraft: 5c, Consolidated PBY. 10c, Vickers Viking. 15c, BAC1-11. 20c, Piper Cheyenne, HS 125 and Bell 47. 30c, BAC1-11.

1979, Feb. 5 ***Perf. 14½***

420 A64	3c multicolored	15	15
421 A64	5c multicolored	15	15
422 A64	10c multicolored	24	24
423 A64	15c multicolored	32	32
424 A64	20c multicolored	48	48
425 A64	30c multicolored	65	65
	Nos. 420-425 (6)	1.99	1.99

Opening of Owen Roberts Airport, 25th anniv.

Rowland Hill and No. 2 — A65

Sir Rowland Hill (1795-1879), originator of penny postage, and: 10c, Great Britain No. 132. 20c, Cayman Islands No. 149. 50c, Cayman Islands No. 20.

Perf. 13½x14½

1979, Aug. 15 Litho.

426 A65	5c multicolored	15	15
427 A65	10c multicolored	22	22
428 A65	20c multicolored	45	45

Souvenir Sheet

429 A65	50c multicolored	1.00	1.00

Flight into Egypt A66

Christmas: 20c, Shepherds, Star of Bethlehem. 30c, Nativity. 40c, Three Kings, Star of Bethlehem.

1979, Nov. 20 Litho. ***Perf. 13½***

430 A66	10c multicolored	18	18
431 A66	20c multicolored	38	38
432 A66	30c multicolored	55	55
433 A66	40c multicolored	80	80

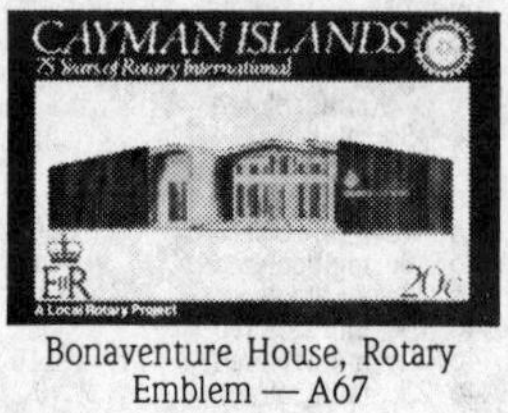

Bonaventure House, Rotary Emblem — A67

Perf. 14x13½, 13½x14

1980, Feb. 14 Litho. Wmk. 373

434 A67	20c shown	40	40
435 A67	30c Paul P. Harris, vert.	60	60
436 A67	50c Anniversary emblem, vert.	1.00	1.00

Rotary International, 75th anniversary.

Mailman, London 1980 Emblem A68

1980, May 6 Litho. ***Perf. 14***

437 A68	5c shown	15	15
438 A68	10c Cat boat	20	20
439 A68	15c Mounted mailman	28	28
440 A68	30c Mail wagon	60	60
441 A68	40c Mailman on bicycle	75	75
442 A68	$1 Mail truck	1.90	*1.90*
	Nos. 437-442 (6)	3.88	3.88

London '80 Intl. Stamp Exhib., May 6-14.

Queen Mother Elizabeth Birthday Issue

Common Design Type

1980, Aug. 4 Litho. ***Perf. 14***

443 CD330	20c multicolored	40	40

Spondylus Americanus — A69

1980, Aug. 12 ***Perf. 14½x14***

444 A69	5c shown	15	15
445 A69	10c Murex brevifrons	22	22
446 A69	30c Cymatium femorale	65	65
447 A69	50c Vasum muricatum	1.10	1.10

See Nos. 502-505, 518-521.

Lantana — A70

1980, Oct. 21 Litho. ***Perf. 14***

448 A70	5c shown	15	15
449 A70	15c Bauhinia	35	35
450 A70	30c Hibiscus	70	70
451 A70	$1 Milk and wine lily	2.25	2.25

See Nos. 478-481.

Juvenile Tarpon and Fire Sponges — A71

1980, Dec. 9 Litho. ***Perf. 13½x13***

452 A71	3c shown	15	15
453 A71	5c Mangrove root oysters	15	15
454 A71	10c Mangrove crab	20	15
455 A71	15c Lizard, crescent spot butterfly	30	20
456 A71	20c Tricolored heron	38	25
457 A71	30c Red mangrove flower	60	40
458 A71	40c Red mangrove seeds	80	55
459 A71	50c Waterhouse's leaf-nosed bat	95	65

460	A71	$1	Black-crowned night heron	1.90	1.25
461	A71	$2	Cayman Isls. arms	3.75	2.50
462	A71	$4	Queen Elizabeth II	7.75	5.50
			Nos. 452-462 (11)	16.93	11.75

Also issued inscribed 1982; 5c, 1984; 3c-$2, 1985; 5c, 10c, 1986. Other dates probably exist.

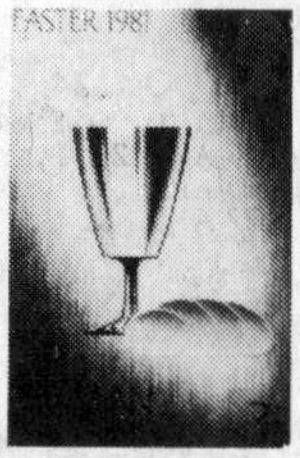

Bread and Wine — A72

1981, Mar. 17 Wmk. 373 *Perf. 14*

463	A72	3c	shown	15	15
464	A72	10c	Crown of thorns	18	18
465	A72	20c	Crucifix	35	35
466	A72	$1	Christ	1.75	1.75

Easter.

Wood Slave — A73

1981, June 16 Litho. *Perf. 13½*

467	A73	20c	shown	40	40
468	A73	30c	Cayman iguana	60	60
469	A73	40c	Lion lizard	80	80
470	A73	50c	Freshwater turtle	95	95

Royal Wedding Issue
Common Design Type

1981, July 22 Litho. *Perf. 14*

471	CD331	20c	Bouquet	38	38
472	CD331	30c	Charles	60	60
473	CD331	$1	Couple	1.90	1.90

Intl. Year of the Disabled A74

1981, Sept. 29 Litho. *Perf. 14*

474	A74	5c	Scuba divers	15	15
475	A74	15c	Old School for Handicapped	26	26
476	A74	20c	New School for Handicapped	35	35
477	A74	$1	Beach scene	1.75	1.75

Flower Type of 1980

1981, Oct. 20 Litho. *Perf. 14*

478	A70	3c	Bougainvillea	15	15
479	A70	10c	Morning glory	22	22
480	A70	20c	Wild amaryllis	45	45
481	A70	$1	Cordia	2.25	2.25

TB Bacillus Centenary A75

1982, Mar. 24 Litho. *Perf. 14½*

482	A75	15c	Koch, horizontal microscope	30	30
483	A75	30c	Koch, vert.	60	60
484	A75	40c	Microscope, vert.	75	75
485	A75	50c	Koch, diff., vert.	1.00	1.00

Princess Diana Issue
Common Design Type

1982, July 1 Litho. *Perf. 13*

486	CD333	20c	Arms	35	35
487	CD333	30c	Diana	55	55
488	CD333	40c	Wedding	75	75
489	CD333	50c	Portrait	90	90

Scouting Year A76

1982, Aug. 24 Wmk. 373 *Perf. 14*

490	A76	3c	Pitching tent	15	15
491	A76	20c	Cooking	45	45
492	A76	30c	Troop	70	70
493	A76	50c	Boating skills	1.10	1.10

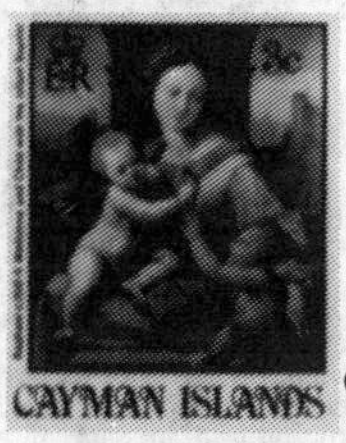

Christmas 1982 — A77

Virgin and Child Paintings by Raphael.

1982, Oct. 26 *Perf. 14½*

494	A77	3c	multicolored	15	15
495	A77	10c	multicolored	22	22
496	A77	20c	multicolored	45	45
497	A77	30c	multicolored	65	65

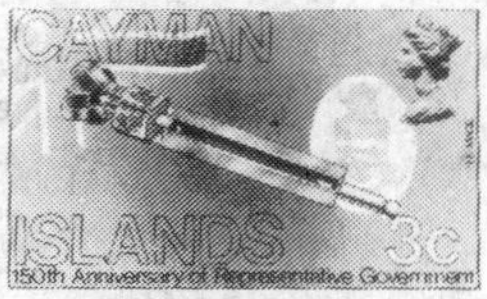

Representative Govt. Sesquicentennial — A78

1982, Nov. 9 Litho. Wmk. 373

498	A78	3c	Mace	15	15
499	A78	10c	Old Courthouse	22	22
500	A78	20c	Commonwealth Parliamentary Assoc. arms	42	42
501	A78	30c	Legislative Assembley building	65	65

Shell Type of 1980

1983, Jan. 11 Litho. *Perf. 13½*

502	A69	5c	Natica canrena	15	15
503	A69	10c	Cassis tuberosa	25	25
504	A69	20c	Strombus gallus	50	50
505	A69	$1	Cypraecassis testiculus	2.50	2.50

Visit of Queen Elizabeth II and Prince Philip A79

1983, Feb. 15 Litho. *Perf. 14*

506	A79	20c	Legislative Building, Cayman Brac	45	45
507	A79	30c	Leg. Bldg., Grand Cayman	70	70
508	A79	50c	Prince Philip	1.10	1.10
509	A79	$1	Queen Elizabeth II	2.25	2.25
a.			Souvenir sheet of 4, #506-509	4.50	4.50

CD334

1983, Mar. 14

510	CD334	3c	Globe	15	15
511	CD334	15c	Flags	32	32
512	CD334	20c	Fisherman	42	42
513	CD334	40c	Elizabeth II	85	85

Commonwealth Day.

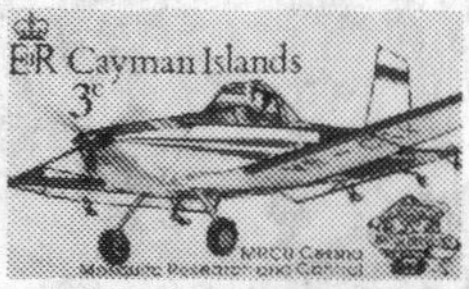

Manned Flight Bicentenary and Mosquito Research and Control Unit A81

Airplanes.

1983, Oct. 10 Litho. *Perf. 14½*

514	A81	3c	MRCU Cessna	15	15
515	A81	10c	Consolidated Catalina PBY	25	25
516	A81	20c	Boeing 727	50	50
517	A81	40c	Hawker Siddeley HS-748	1.00	1.00

Shell Type of 1980

1984, Jan. 18 *Perf. 14x14½*

518	A69	3c	Natica floridana	15	15
519	A69	10c	Conus austini	28	28
520	A69	30c	Colubrania obscura	80	80
521	A69	50c	Turbo cailletii	1.40	1.40

Lloyd's List Issue
Common Design Type

1984, May 16 Litho. *Perf. 14*

522	CD335	5c	Cruise ship	15	15
523	CD335	10c	The Old Harbor	22	22
524	CD335	25c	Ridgefield	60	60
525	CD335	50c	Goldfield	1.25	1.25

Souvenir Sheet

526	CD335	$1	Goldfield, diff.	2.50	2.50

No. 525 Overprinted: "U.P.U. CONGRESS HAMBURG 1984"

1984, June 18

527	CD335	50c	multicolored	1.25	1.25

Local Birds — A82

Perf. 14x14½

1984, Aug. 15 Litho. Wmk. 373

528	A82	5c	Snowy egret	15	15
529	A82	10c	Bananaquit	24	24
530	A82	35c	Kingfisher	85	85
531	A82	$1	Brown booby	2.50	2.50

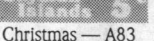

Christmas — A83

Orchids — A84

Designs: Nos. 532a-532d, evening beach scenes. Nos. 533a-533d, daytime boating and beach scenes.

1984, Oct. 17 Litho. *Perf. 14*

532		Strip of 4	50	50
a.-d.	A83 5c	Any single	15	15
533		Strip of 4	2.50	2.50
a.-d.	A83 25c	Any single	62	62

Souvenir Sheet

534	A83	$1	Bonfire, diff.	2.50	2.50

No. 534 contains one stamp 29x48mm.

1985, Mar. 13 Litho. *Perf. 14x13½*

535	A84	5c	Schomburgkia thomsoniana var.	15	15
536	A84	10c	Schomburgkia thomsoniana	20	20
537	A84	25c	Encyclia plicata	50	50
538	A84	50c	Dendrophylax fawcetti	1.00	1.00

Shipwrecks A85

Unspecified shipwrecks found in Cayman waters.

1985, May 22 *Perf. 14*

539	A85	5c	multicolored	15	15
540	A85	25c	multicolored	50	50
541	A85	35c	multicolored	70	70
542	A85	40c	multicolored	80	80

Intl. Youth Year — A86

Designs: 5c, Natl. Athletic Assoc. track competition. 15c, High school students studying in Grand Cayman Campus Library. 25c, Amateur League Competition Football. 50c, Natl. Netball Assoc. competition.

1985, Aug. 14 *Perf. 14½*

543	A86	5c	multicolored	15	15
544	A86	15c	multicolored	30	30
545	A86	25c	multicolored	50	50
546	A86	50c	multicolored	1.00	1.00

Telecommunications, 50th Anniv. — A87

Designs: 5c, Morse Code transmitter, 1935. 10c, Hand-cranked telephone, 1935. 25c, Tropospheric scatter dish, 1966. 50c, Earth dish receiver, 1979.

1985, Oct. 25 *Perf. 14*

547	A87	5c	multicolored	15	15
548	A87	10c	multicolored	20	20
549	A87	25c	multicolored	50	50
550	A87	50c	multicolored	1.00	1.00

Birds — A88

1986, Mar. 20 Litho. Wmk. 384

551	A88	10c	Magnificent frigatebird	18	18
552	A88	25c	West Indian whistling duck	50	50
553	A88	35c	La Sagra's flycatcher	85	85
554	A88	40c	Yellow-faced grassquit	1.40	1.40

Nos. 552-553 vert.

Queen Elizabeth II 60th Birthday
Common Design Type

Designs: 5c, As bridesmaid at wedding of Lady Mary Cambridge, 1931. 10c, Royal visit to Norway, 1955. 25c, Inspecting West Indian troop, royal tour, 1985. 50c, Gulf tour, 1979. $1, Visiting Crown Agents' offices, 1983.

1986, Apr. 21 *Perf. 14x14½*

555	CD337	5c	scar, blk & sil	15	15
556	CD337	10c	ultra, blk & sil	24	24
557	CD337	25c	grn & multi	60	60
558	CD337	50c	vio & multi	1.20	1.20
559	CD337	$1	rose vio & multi	2.40	2.40
			Nos. 555-559 (5)	4.59	4.59

Royal Wedding Issue, 1986
Common Design Type

Designs: 5c, Informal portrait. 50c, Andrew in uniform, helicopter.

Perf. 14½x14

1986, July 23 Litho. Wmk. 384

560 CD338	5c multicolored		15	15
561 CD338	50c multicolored		1.20	1.20

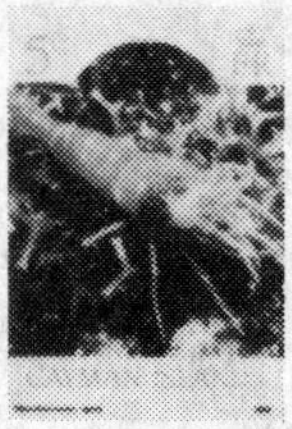

Marine Life — A89

Perf. 13½x13

1986, Sept. 15 Wmk. 373

562 A89	5c	Rhynchocinetes rigeus	15	15
563 A89	10c	Nemaster rubiginosa	16	16
564 A89	15c	Calcinus tibicen	25	25
565 A89	20c	Rhodactis sanctithomae	35	35
566 A89	25c	Spirobranchus giganteа	45	45
567 A89	35c	Diodon holacanthus	60	60
568 A89	50c	Pseudocorynactis aribbeorum	85	85
569 A89	60c	Astrophyton muricatum	1.00	1.00
570 A89	75c	Cyphoma gibbosum	1.25	1.25
571 A89	$1	Conolylactis gigantea	1.75	1.75
572 A89	$2	Malacoctenus boehlkei	3.50	3.50
573 A89	$4	Lima scabra	7.00	7.00
		Nos. 562-573 (12)	17.31	17.31

Nos. 562-565, 571-573 exist inscribed "1987," Nos. 562-564, 566, 572 "1990."

Tourism A90

Perf. 13x13½

1987, Jan. 26 Wmk. 384

574 A90	10c	Golfing	24	24
575 A90	15c	Sailing	35	35
576 A90	25c	Snorkeling	60	60
577 A90	35c	Parasailing	85	85
578 A90	$1	Fishing	2.40	2.40
		Nos. 574-578 (5)	4.44	4.44

Fruit — A91

1987, May 20 *Perf. 14½*

579 A91	5c	Akee	15	15
580 A91	25c	Breadfruit	55	55
581 A91	35c	Papaya	80	80
582 A91	$1	Soursop	2.25	2.25

Lizards A92

1987, Aug. 26 Litho. *Perf. 14*

583 A92	10c	Lion lizard	22	22
584 A92	50c	Iguana	1.10	1.10
585 A92	$1	Anole	2.25	2.25

Flowers — A93

Herons — A95

Butterflies A94

1987, Nov. 18 *Perf. 14½x14*

586 A93	5c	Poinsettia	15	15
587 A93	25c	Periwinkle	55	55
588 A93	35c	Yellow allamanda	80	80
589 A93	75c	Blood lily	1.65	1.65

1988, Mar. 29 Wmk. 384 *Perf. 14*

Designs: 5c, Hemiargus ammon erembis and Strymon martialis. 25c, Phocides pigmalion batabano. 50c, Anaea troglodyta cubana. $1, Papilio andraemon andraemon.

590 A94	5c	multicolored	15	15
591 A94	25c	multicolored	60	60
592 A94	50c	multicolored	1.20	1.20
593 A94	$1	multicolored	2.40	2.40

1988, Jan. 26 Litho. *Perf. 14*

594 A95	5c	Butorides striatus	15	15
595 A95	25c	Egretta tricolor	60	60
596 A95	50c	Nycticorax violaceus	1.20	1.20
597 A95	$1	Egretta caerulea	2.40	2.40

1988 Summer Olympics, Seoul — A96

1988, Sept. 21 *Perf. 14½*

598 A96	10c	Cycling	24	24
599 A96	50c	Natl. team, passenger jet	1.20	1.20
600 A96	$1	Yachting	2.40	2.40

Souvenir Sheet

Wmk. 373

601 A96	$1	Tennis	2.40	2.40

No. 601 commemorates the 75th anniv. of the Intl. Tennis Federation.

Visit of Princess Alexandra — A97

1988, Nov. 1 Wmk. 373 *Perf. 15*

602 A97	5c	Portrait	15	15
603 A97	$1	Seated in garden	2.40	2.40

Cayman Islands P.O., Cent. — A98

Designs: 5c, P.O., Georgetown, 1889, and Jamaica #24, canceled. 25c, S.S. Orinoco and Cayman Isls. #1. 35c, Grand Cayman G.P.O. and #442. $1, Cayman Airways mail plane and #191.

1989, Apr. 12 Wmk. 384 *Perf. 14½*

604 A98	5c	multicolored	15	15
605 A98	25c	multicolored	60	60
606 A98	35c	multicolored	85	85
607 A98	$1	multicolored	2.40	2.40

Mutiny on the Bounty — A99

Designs: a, Capt. Bligh. b, HMS Providence, two crewmen. c, HMS Assistant, transplanted breadfruit. d, Moving breadfruit on land, in longboat. e, Midshipman among casks and crates.

1989, May 24 *Perf. 14*

608	Strip of 5	6.00	6.00
a.-e.	A99 50c any single	1.20	1.20

Natl. Trust Emblem and Architecture, George Town — A100

Perf. 14½x14

1989, Oct. 18 Litho. Wmk. 373

609 A100	5c	Panton House	15	15
610 A100	10c	Town Hall	25	25
611 A100	25c	Old Courts House	60	60
612 A100	35c	Elmslie Memorial Church	85	85
613 A100	$1	Post office	2.40	2.40
		Nos. 609-613 (5)	4.25	4.25

Island Surveys A101

Maps or survey ships: 5c, Navigational instruments and George Gauld's map of 1773. 25c, Instruments and map created by surveyors aboard HMS *Vidal*, 1956. 50c, *Mutine*, 1914. $1, HMS *Vidal*.

1989, Nov. 15

614 A101	5c	multicolored	15	15
615 A101	25c	multicolored	60	60
616 A101	50c	multicolored	1.20	1.20
617 A101	$1	multicolored	2.45	2.45

Angelfish A102

1990, Apr. 25 Wmk. 384 *Perf. 14*

618 A102	10c	French	24	24
619 A102	25c	Gray	60	60
620 A102	50c	Queen	1.20	1.20
621 A102	$1	Rock beauty	2.40	2.40

Queen Mother, 90th Birthday

Common Design Types

1990, Aug. 4 Wmk. 384 *Perf. 14x15*

622 CD343	50c	King, Queen Elizabeth, 1948	1.20	1.20

Perf. 14½

623 CD344	£1	King, Queen with Churchill, 1940	2.40	2.40

Butterflies A103

1990, Oct. 24 *Perf. 14½x14*

624 A103	5c	Soldier	15	15
625 A103	25c	Pygmy blue	60	60
626 A103	35c	Cayman crescent spot	85	85
627 A103	$1	Gulf fritillary	2.40	2.40

Expo '90. International Garden and Greenery Exposition, Osaka, Japan.

Hurricane Awareness A104

Designs: 5c, Goes weather satellite. 30c, Meteorologist tracks storm. 40c, Hurricane damage. $1, Lockheed WP-3D Orion flying in hurricane's eye.

1991, Aug. 8 *Perf. 14*

628 A104	5c	multicolored	15	15
629 A104	30c	multicolored	70	70
630 A104	40c	multicolored	90	90
631 A104	$1	multicolored	2.25	2.25

Christmas A105

Local flowers and Christmas scenes: 5c, Angel's trumpet, angels with trumpets. 30c, Golden trumpet, Mary on donkey led by Joseph. 40c, Christmas flower, Adoration of the Magi. 60c, Tree of life, nativity scene.

1991, Nov. 6 Wmk. 373

632 A105	5c	multicolored	15	15
633 A105	30c	multicolored	70	70
634 A105	40c	multicolored	90	90
635 A105	60c	multicolored	1.35	1.35

Island Scenes A106

Perf. 12½x13, 13x12½

1991, Dec. 11 Litho. Wmk. 373

636 A106	5c	Coconut tree, vert.	15	15
637 A106	15c	Beach scene	35	35
638 A106	20c	Poincianas in bloom	45	45
639 A106	30c	Blowholes	65	65
640 A106	40c	Police band	90	90
641 A106	50c	Downtown scene, vert.	1.10	1.10
642 A106	60c	The Bluff, Cayman Brac	1.35	1.35
643 A106	80c	Coat of arms, vert.	1.80	1.80
644 A106	90c	View of Hell	2.00	2.00
645 A106	$1	Sportfishing	2.25	2.25
646 A106	$2	Harbor scene, vert.	4.50	4.50
647 A106	$8	Queen Elizabeth II, vert.	17.75	17.75
		Nos. 636-647 (12)	33.25	33.25

Queen Elizabeth II's Accession to the Throne, 40th Anniv.

Common Design Type

Wmk. 373, 384 (40c)

1992, Feb. 6 Litho. *Perf. 14*

648 CD349	5c	multicolored	15	15
649 CD349	20c	multicolored	45	45
650 CD349	30c	multicolored	65	65
651 CD349	40c	multicolored	90	90
652 CD349	$1	multicolored	2.25	2.25
		Nos. 648-652 (5)	4.40	4.40

1992 Summer Olympics, Barcelona
A107

1992, Aug. 5 **Wmk. 373**
653 A107 15c Cyclist 35 35
654 A107 40c Two cyclists 90 90
655 A107 60c Feet, pedals 1.35 1.35
656 A107 $1 Two cyclists, diff. 2.25 2.25

Island Heritage — A108

1992, Oct. 21
657 A108 5c Lady with donkey 15 15
658 A108 30c Making fish nets 70 70
659 A108 40c Maypole dancing 95 95
660 A108 60c Basket making 1.40 1.40
661 A108 $1 Cooking on caboose 2.35 2.35
Nos. 657-661 (5) 5.55 5.55

Rays
A109

Perf. 13½x14
1993, June 16 **Litho.** **Wmk. 373**
662 A109 5c Yellow stingray 15 15
663 A109 30c Southern stingray 70 70
664 A109 40c Spotted eagle ray 95 95
665 A109 $1 Manta ray 2.30 2.30

A110 A111

Tourism: No. 666a, Turtle, sailboats. b, Diver, coral, boats. c, Golf. d, Beach, tennis. e, Pirates, sailing ship.

No. 667a, Cruise ship, boat, sailboat. b, City street scene. c, Submarines. d, Cyclist, scooters. e, Jet planes.

Perf. 14x13½
1993, Sept. 30 **Litho.** **Wmk. 373**
666 A110 15c Strip of 5, #a.-e. 1.75 1.75
667 A110 30c Strip of 5, #a.-e. 3.50 3.50
f. Booklet pane of 10, #666-667 5.25

1993, Oct. 29 ***Perf. 14***

Various views of Grand Cayman Parrot.

668 A111 5c green & multi 15 15
669 A111 5c red & multi 15 15
670 A111 30c yellow & multi 70 70
671 A111 30c blue & multi 70 70

Christmas
A112

Christmas scenes, orchids: 5c, Manger, Ionopsis utricularioides. 40c, Shepherd, lamb, Encyclia cochleata. 60c, Magi, Vanilla pompona. $1, Virgin in prayer, Oncidium caymanense.

Perf. 13½x14
1993, Dec. 6 **Litho.** **Wmk. 384**
672 A112 5c multicolored 15 15
673 A112 40c multicolored 95 95
674 A112 60c multicolored 1.40 1.40
675 A112 $1 multicolored 2.25 2.25

Souvenir Sheet

Reef Life — A113

Designs: a, Holocanthus ciliaris. b, Bodianus pulchellus, anisotremus virginicus. c, Holocanthus tricolor, gramma loreto. d, Pomacanthus paru, chaeton striatus.

Perf. 14½x13
1994, Feb. 18 **Litho.** **Wmk. 373**
676 A113 60c Sheet of 4, #a.-d. 5.75 5.75

Hong Kong '94.

Royal Visit — A114

Designs: 5c, Cayman Islands, United Kingdom flags. 15c, Royal yacht Britannia. 30c, Queen Elizabeth II. $2, Queen, Prince Philip.

1994, Feb. 22 ***Perf. 14½***
677 A114 5c multicolored 15 15
678 A114 15c multicolored 35 35
679 A114 30c multicolored 70 70
680 A114 $2 multicolored 4.50 4.50

West Indian Whistling Duck — A115

Designs: 5c, One standing, vert. 15c, Landing in water. 20c, Four ducks, various activities. 80c, One raising wings, vert. $1, Adult, chick, vert.

Wmk. 373
1994, Apr. 21 **Litho.** ***Perf. 14***
681 A115 5c multicolored 15 15
682 A115 15c multicolored 35 35
683 A115 20c multicolored 48 48
684 A115 80c multicolored 1.90 1.90
685 A115 $1 multicolored 2.25 2.25
a. Souvenir sheet of 1 2.25 2.25
Nos. 681-685 (5) 5.13 5.13

No. 685a has a continuous design and contains Cayman Islands Natl. Trust emblem.

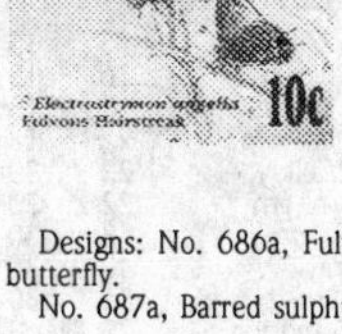

Butterflies — A116

Designs: No. 686a, Fulvous hairstreak. b, Atala butterfly.
No. 687a, Barred sulphur. b, Dorantes skipper.

Perf. 13½
1994, Aug. 16 **Litho.** **Wmk. 373**
686 A116 10c Pair, #a.-b. 50 50
687 A116 $1 Pair, #a.-b. 4.75 4.75

WAR TAX STAMPS

No. 36 Surcharged:

WAR STAMP. 1½d — a
WAR STAMP. 1½d — b

1917, Feb. 26 **Wmk. 3** ***Perf. 14***
MR1 A5(a) 1½p on 2½p 1.75 *5.00*
a. Fraction bar omitted 70.00 *110.00*
MR2 A5(b) 1½p on 2½p 65 *5.00*
a. Fraction bar omitted 52.50 *100.00*

No. 1 exists with missing period. On No. 1 the distance between "WAR STAMP" and "1½" varies.

Surcharged WAR STAMP 1½d

1917, Sept. 4
MR3 A5 1½p on 2½p ultra 500.00 *1,250.*

Surcharged WAR STAMP 1½d

1917, Sept. 4
MR4 A5 1½p on 2½p ultra 20 *50*

No. 33 Overprinted WAR STAMP

1919, Feb. 4
MR5 A5 ½p green 15 *50*

The "brownish paper" variety comes from the interleaving used for shipment from England.

Type of 1912-16 Surcharged WAR STAMP 1½d

1919, Feb. 4
MR6 A5 1½p on 2½p orange 1.40 *3.00*

No. 35 Surcharged WAR STAMP 1½d.

1920, Mar. 10
MR7 A5 1½p on 2p gray 1.50 *6.00*

The "rose-tinted paper" variety comes from the interleaving used for shipment from England.
A surcharge in red was not issued.

DOMINICA

LOCATION — The largest island of the Windward group in the West Indies. Southeast of Puerto Rico.
GOVT. — Republic in British Commonwealth
AREA — 290 sq. mi.
POP. — 74,859 (1981)
CAPITAL — Roseau

Formerly a Presidency of the Leeward Islands, Dominica became a separate colony under the governor of the Windward Islands on January 1, 1940. Dominica joined the West Indies federation April 22, 1958. In 1968, Dominica became an associate state of Britain; in 1978, an independent nation.

12 Pence = 1 Shilling
20 Shillings = 1 Pound
100 Cents = 1 Dollar (1949)

Catalogue values for unused stamps in this country are for Never Hinged items, beginning with Scott 112.

Watermark

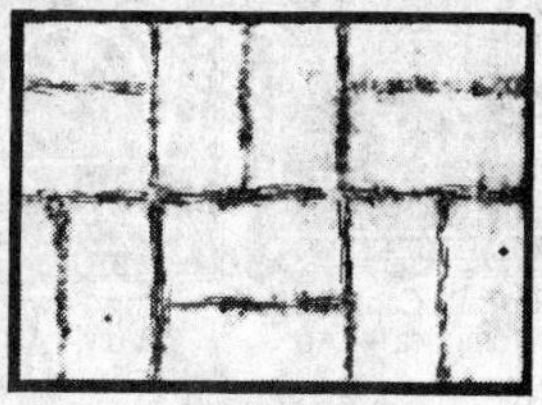

Wmk. 334- Rectangles

Queen Victoria — A1

Perf. 12½
1874, May 4 **Typo.** **Wmk. 1**
1 A1 1p violet 120.00 30.00
2 A1 6p green 350.00 70.00
3 A1 1sh dp lilac rose 200.00 45.00

During 1875-87 some issues were manuscript dated with village names. These are considered postally used.

1877-79 ***Perf. 14***
4 A1 ½p bister ('79) 8.50 *9.50*
5 A1 1p violet 4.00 1.75
a. Diagonal or vertical half used as ½p on cover 1,500.
6 A1 2½p red brn ('79) 110.00 22.50
7 A1 4p blue ('79) 85.00 7.50
8 A1 6p green 110.00 27.50
9 A1 1sh dp lilac rose 110.00 45.00

For surcharges, see Nos. 10-15.

No. 5 Bisected and Surcharged in Black or Red:

½ — a
HALF PENNY — b
1/2 — c

1882
10 A1(a) ½p on half of 1p 125.00 60.00
a. Inverted surcharge 1,000. 700.00
b. Surcharge tete beche pair 1,400. 1,400.
11 A1(b) ½p on half of 1p 30.00 32.50
a. Surcharge reading downward 30.00 32.50
b. Double surcharge 750.00
12 A1(c) ½p on half of 1p (R) 17.50 14.00
a. Inverted surcharge 900.00 775.00
b. Double surcharge 1,750.

The existence of genuine copies of No. 10b has been questioned.

Nos. 8 and 9 Surcharged in Black — Half Penny

1886
13 A1 ½p on 6p green 7.50 7.25
14 A1 1p on 6p green *17,500.* *16,000.*
15 A1 1p on 1sh 9.50 *12.50*
a. Double surcharge 5,000. 3,750.

All copies of No. 14 may have small pin marks which may have been part of the surcharging process.

1883-88 **Wmk. 2**

16	A1	½p bister ('83)	2.50	3.50
17	A1	½p green ('86)	50	1.50
18	A1	1p violet ('86)	9.00	6.00
a.		Half used as ½p on cover		1,400.
19	A1	1p car rose ('87)	1.50	1.50
a.		1p rose	6.50	6.50
b.		Vert. half used as ½p on cover		1,500.
20	A1	2½p red brn ('84)	100.00	7.00
21	A1	2½p ultra ('88)	3.50	2.00
22	A1	4p gray ('86)	2.50	1.50
23	A1	6p orange ('88)	12.50	35.00
24	A1	1sh dp lil rose ('88)	150.00	250.00
		Nos. 16-24 (9)	282.00	308.00

Roseau, Capital of Dominica — A6

King Edward VII — A7

1903 **Wmk. 1** ***Perf. 14***

25	A6	½p gray green	1.75	2.25
26	A6	1p car & black	1.75	40
27	A6	2p brn & gray grn	5.00	7.50
28	A6	2½p ultra & blk	7.50	9.00
29	A6	3p black & vio	7.50	10.00
30	A6	6p org brn & blk	11.00	15.00
31	A6	1sh gray grn & red vio	12.00	16.00
32	A6	2sh red vio & blk	15.50	20.00
33	A6	2sh6p ocher & gray grn	16.00	30.00
34	A7	5sh brown & blk	95.00	150.00
		Nos. 25-34 (10)	173.00	260.15

Nos. 25 to 29 and 31 are on both ordinary and chalky paper.

1907-20 **Wmk. 3**

Chalky Paper

35	A6	½p gray green	70	1.00
36	A6	1p car & black	1.40	40
37	A6	2p brn & gray grn	4.50	6.00
38	A6	2½p ultra & black	6.00	8.00
39	A6	3p black & vio	5.50	7.00
40	A6	3p vio, *yel* ('09)	1.50	1.50
41	A6	6p org brn & blk ('08)	50.00	50.00
42	A6	6p vio & dl vio ('09)	2.00	2.50
43	A6	1sh gray grn & red vio	12.50	13.75
44	A6	1sh blk, *green* ('10)	3.25	3.50
45	A6	2sh red vio & blk ('08)	18.75	21.25
46	A6	2sh ultra & vio, *bl* ('19)	12.50	23.75
47	A6	2sh6p ocher & gray grn ('08)	20.00	26.25
48	A6	2sh6p red & blk, *bl* ('20)	9.00	15.00
49	A7	5sh brn & blk ('08)	55.00	50.00
		Nos. 35-49 (15)	202.60	229.90

Nos. 40 and 42 are on both ordinary and chalky paper. For type surcharged, see No. 55.

1908-09 **Ordinary Paper**

50	A6	½p green	55	42
51	A6	1p scarlet	52	15
a.		1p carmine	52	15
52	A6	2p gray ('09)	2.75	2.50
53	A6	2½p ultramarine	2.25	1.50

King George V — A8

1914 **Chalky Paper** ***Perf. 14***

54	A8	5sh grn & scar, *yel*	42.50	62.50

Type of 1903 Surcharged **1½D.**

1920

55	A6	1½p on 2½p orange	1.00	75

1921 **Wmk. 4**

Ordinary Paper

56	A6	½p green	2.25	3.50
57	A6	1p rose red	1.50	2.25
58	A6	1½p orange	4.50	8.50
59	A6	2p gray	5.50	9.00
60	A6	2½p ultra	3.00	8.50
61	A6	6p vio & dl vio	4.50	15.00
62	A6	2sh ultra & vio, *bl*	21.00	50.00
63	A6	2sh6p red & blk, *bl*	26.00	55.00
		Nos. 56-63 (8)	68.25	151.75

No. 61 is on chalky paper.

Seal of Colony and George V — A9

1923-33 **Chalky Paper** **Wmk. 4**

65	A9	½p green & blk	20	15
66	A9	1p violet & blk	1.25	50
67	A9	1p scar & black	2.50	2.00
68	A9	1½p car & black	75	35
69	A9	1½p dp brn & blk	2.50	35
70	A9	2p gray & black	60	45
71	A9	2½p org & black	65	2.50
72	A9	2½p ultra & black	1.40	1.50
73	A9	3p ultra & black	65	3.75
74	A9	3p red & blk, *yel*	1.00	1.25
75	A9	4p brown & blk	1.25	4.25
76	A9	6p red vio & blk	1.40	3.25
77	A9	1sh blk, *emerald*	2.25	3.00
78	A9	2sh ultra & blk, *bl*	4.00	7.50
79	A9	2sh6p red & blk, *bl*	7.50	10.00
80	A9	3sh vio & blk, *yel*	6.25	10.00
81	A9	4sh red & blk, *emer*	7.50	14.00
82	A9	5sh grn & blk, *yel*	11.50	16.00
		Nos. 65-82 (18)	53.15	80.80

Issue years: Nos. 80, 82, 1927. Nos. 72, 74, 1928. Nos. 67, 69, 1933. Others, 1923.

1923 **Wmk. 3**

83	A9	3sh vio & blk, *yel*	7.50	12.50
84	A9	5sh grn & blk, *yel*	8.75	17.50
85	A9	£1 vio & blk, *red*	225.00	325.00

Silver Jubilee Issue

Common Design Type

Perf. 13½x14

1935, May 6 **Wmk. 4** **Engr.**

90	CD301	1p car & blue	25	25
91	CD301	1½p gray blk & ultra	75	75
92	CD301	2½p blue & brn	2.50	2.75
93	CD301	1sh brt vio & ind	4.50	5.00

Coronation Issue

Common Design Type

1937, May 12 ***Perf. 11x11½***

94	CD302	1p dark carmine	15	15
95	CD302	1½p brown	15	15
96	CD302	2½p deep ultra	20	20

Fresh-Water Lake — A10

Layou River — A11

Picking Limes — A12

Boiling Lake — A13

1938-47 **Wmk. 4** ***Perf. 12½***

97	A10	½p grn & red brn	15	15
98	A11	1p car & gray	15	15
99	A12	1½p rose vio & grn	15	15
100	A13	2p brn blk & dp rose	15	15
101	A12	2½p ultra & rose vio	15	15
102	A11	3p red brn & ol	15	15
103	A12	3½p red vio & brt ultra	15	15
104	A10	6p vio & yel grn	18	18
105	A10	7p org brn & grn	28	28
106	A13	1sh olive & vio	32	32
107	A11	2sh red vio & blk	2.00	2.00
108	A10	2sh6p scar ver & blk	1.10	1.10
109	A11	5sh dk brn & bl	1.75	1.75
110	A13	10sh dl org & blk	6.25	7.50
		Nos. 97-110 (14)	12.93	14.18

Issue dates: 3½p, 7p, 2sh, 10sh, Oct. 15, 1947, others, Aug. 15, 1938.

King George VI — A14

1940, Apr. 15 **Photo.** ***Perf. 14½x14***

111	A14	¼p brown violet	15	15

Catalogue values for unused stamps in this section, from this point to the end of the section, are for Never Hinged items.

Peace Issue

Common Design Type

1946, Oct. 14 **Engr.** ***Perf. 13½x14***

112	CD303	1p carmine	15	15
113	CD303	3½p deep blue	15	15
		Set value	18	18

Silver Wedding Issue

Common Design Types

1948, Dec. 1 **Photo.** ***Perf. 14x14½***

114	CD304	1p scarlet	15	15

Engraved; Name Typographed

Perf. 11½x11

115	CD305	10sh orange brn	11.00	13.00

UPU Issue

Common Design Types

Engr.: Name Typo. on 6c and 12c

1949, Oct. 10 ***Perf. 13½, 11x11½***

116	CD306	5c blue	18	18
117	CD307	6c chocolate	45	45
118	CD308	12c rose violet	75	75
119	CD309	24c olive	1.25	1.25

University Issue

Common Design Types

1951, Feb. 16 **Engr.** ***Perf. 14x14½***

120	CD310	3c purple & green	32	32
121	CD311	12c dp car & dk bl grn	70	70

George VI A15

Drying Cocoa A16

Picking Oranges — A17

Designs: 2c and 60c, Carib Baskets. 3c and 48c, Lime Plantation. 4c, Picking Oranges. 5c, Bananas. 6c, Botanical Gardens. 8c, Drying Vanilla Beans. 12c and $1.20, Fresh Water Lake. 14c, Layou River. 24c, Boiling Lake.

Perf. 14½x14

1951, July 1 **Photo.** **Wmk. 4**

122	A15	½c brown	15	15

Perf. 13x13½

Engr.

123	A16	1c red org & blk	15	15
124	A16	2c dp grn & red brn	16	15
125	A16	3c red vio & bl grn	16	15
126	A16	4c dk brn & brn org	22	18
127	A16	5c rose red & blk	22	20
128	A16	6c org brn & ol grn	22	20
129	A16	8c dp bl & dp grn	38	30
130	A16	12c emer & gray	40	35
131	A16	14c pur & blue	85	80
132	A16	24c rose car & red vio	75	60
133	A16	48c red org & bl grn	2.00	3.50
134	A16	60c gray & car	4.00	5.50
135	A16	$1.20 gray & emer	6.25	7.75

Perf. 13½x13

136	A17	$2.40 gray & org	14.00	16.00
		Nos. 122-136 (15)	29.91	35.98

Nos. 125, 127, 129 and 131 Overprinted in Black or Carmine **NEW CONSTITUTION 1951**

1951, Oct. 15 ***Perf. 13x13½***

137	A16	3c red vio & bl green	20	20
138	A16	5c rose red & black	25	25
139	A16	8c dp blue & dp grn (C)	35	35
140	A16	14c purple & blue (C)	50	50

Adoption of a new constitution for the Windward Islands, 1951.

Coronation Issue

Common Design Type

1953, June 2 **Engr.** ***Perf. 13½x13***

141	CD312	2c dk green & black	20	20

Types of 1951 with Portrait of Queen Elizabeth II

1954, Oct. 1 **Photo.** ***Perf. 14½x14***

142	A15	½c brown	15	15

Perf. 13x13½

Engr.

143	A16	1c red org & blk	15	15
144	A16	2c dp grn & red brn	15	15
145	A16	3c red vio & bl grn	30	28
146	A16	4c dk brn & brn org	15	15
147	A16	5c rose red & blk	38	35
148	A16	6c org brn & ol grn	15	15
149	A16	8c dp bl & dp grn	15	15
150	A16	12c emer & gray	20	18
151	A16	14c pur & bl	22	20
152	A16	24c rose car & red vio	38	28
153	A16	48c red org & bl grn	6.50	6.00
154	A16	60c gray & car	1.10	1.00
155	A16	$1.20 gray & emer	2.75	2.50

Perf. 13½x13

156	A17	$2.40 gray & org	6.50	5.50
		Nos. 142-156 (15)	19.23	17.19

Mat Making — A18

Designs: 5c, Canoe making. 10c, Bananas. 48c, like 3c.

Perf. 13x13½

1957, Oct. 15 **Wmk. 4**

157	A18	3c car rose & black	15	15
158	A18	5c brown & blue	2.00	25
159	A18	10c redsh brn & brt grn	25	20
160	A18	48c violet & brown	2.50	2.50

West Indies Federation

Common Design Type

Perf. 11½x11

1958, Apr. 22 **Wmk. 314**

161	CD313	3c green	15	15
162	CD313	6c blue	15	15
163	CD313	12c car rose	25	25
		Set value	46	46

Sailing Canoe — A19

Traditional Costume — A20

Designs: 1c, Seashore, Rosalie. 2c, 5c, Queen Elizabeth II by Annigoni. 4c, Sulphur Springs. 6c, Road making. 8c, Dugout canoe. 10c, Frog (mountain chicken). 12c, Boats and Scotts Head. 15c, Bananas. 24c, Imperial parrot. 48c, View of Goodwill. 60c, Cacao tree. $1.20, Coat of Arms. $2.40, Trafalgar Falls. $4.80, Coconut palm.

Two types of 14c:

I - Mountain light violet. Girl's eyes look straight out.

II - Mountain blue. Eyes look sideways.

Perf. 14½x14, 14x14½

1963, May 16 Photo. Wmk. 314

164	A19	1c	bl, brn & grn	15	15
165	A20	2c	ultramarine	15	15
166	A19	3c	lt ultra & blk	15	15
167	A19	4c	sl, grn & brn	15	15
168	A20	5c	magenta	15	15
169	A19	6c	lt grn, vio & buff	15	15
170	A19	8c	tan, blk & lt grn	15	15
171	A19	10c	pink & brn	15	15
172	A19	12c	bl, blk, grn & brn	15	15
173	A20	14c	multi (II)	16	16
a.			Type I	40	40
174	A19	15c	grn, yel & brn	16	16
175	A20	24c	multicolored	50	35
176	A19	48c	bl, blk & grn	85	65
177	A19	60c	blk, grn, org & brn	1.10	1.00
178	A19	$1.20	multicolored	2.25	2.25
179	A20	$2.40	grn, bl, brn & blk	4.00	4.00
180	A20	$4.80	bl, brn & grn	8.00	8.00
			Nos. 164-180 (17)	18.37	17.92

For overprints, see Nos. 211-232.

1966-67 Wmk. 314 Sideways

167a	A19	4c	('67)	15	15
169a	A19	6c		25	25
170a	A19	8c		40	40
171a	A19	10c	('67)	45	45
174a	A19	15c	('67)	75	75
			Nos. 167a-174a (5)	2.00	2.00

Freedom from Hunger Issue

Common Design Type

1963, June 4 *Perf. 14x14½*

181	CD314	15c	lilac	35	35

Red Cross Centenary Issue

Common Design Type

Wmk. 314

1963, Sept. 2 Litho. *Perf. 13*

182	CD315	5c	black & red	20	20
183	CD315	15c	ultra & red	90	90

Shakespeare Issue

Common Design Type

1964, Apr. 23 Photo. *Perf. 14x14½*

184	CD316	15c	lilac rose	30	30

ITU Issue

Common Design Type

1965, May 17 Litho. *Perf. 11x11½*

185	CD317	2c	emerald & blue	15	15
186	CD317	48c	grnsh blue & slate	90	90

Intl. Cooperation Year Issue

Common Design Type

1965, Oct. 25 *Perf. 14½*

187	CD318	1c	blue grn & claret	15	15
188	CD318	15c	lt violet & grn	35	35
			Set value	40	40

Churchill Memorial Issue

Common Design Type

1966, Jan. 24 Photo. *Perf. 14*

Design in Black, Gold and Carmine Rose

189	CD319	1c	bright blue	15	15
a.			Gold omitted	*750.00*	
190	CD319	5c	green	15	15
191	CD319	15c	brown	30	30
192	CD319	24c	violet	65	65

Royal Visit Issue

Common Design Type

1966, Feb. 4 Litho. *Perf. 11x12*

193	CD320	5c	violet blue	15	15
194	CD320	15c	dk car rose	40	40

World Cup Soccer Issue

Common Design Type

1966, July 1 Litho. *Perf. 14*

195	CD321	5c	multicolored	15	15
196	CD321	24c	multicolored	45	45

WHO Headquarters Issue

Common Design Type

1966, Sept. 20 Litho. *Perf. 14*

197	CD322	5c	multicolored	15	15
198	CD322	24c	multicolored	45	45

UNESCO Anniversary Issue

Common Design Type

1966, Dec. 1 Litho. *Perf. 14*

199	CD323	5c	"Education"	15	15
200	CD323	15c	"Science"	30	30
201	CD323	24c	"Culture"	50	50

Carib, Negro and Caucasian Children A21

Designs: 10c, Columbus' ship Santa Maria and banderol. 15c, Hands with banderol. 24c, Belaire dancers.

Perf. 14½x14

1967, Nov. 3 Photo. Wmk. 314

202	A21	5c	multicolored	15	15
203	A21	10c	multicolored	15	15
204	A21	15c	multicolored	15	15
205	A21	24c	multicolored	25	25
			Set value	55	55

Issued for National Day, Nov. 3.

Common Design Types are pictured beginning on page 176.

John F. Kennedy and Human Rights Flame A22

Human Rights Flame and: 10c, Cecil E. A. Rawle (1891-1938), Dominican crusader for human rights. 12c, Pope John XXIII. 48c, Florence Nightingle. 60c, Dr. Albert Schweitzer.

Wmk. 314 Sideways

1968, Apr. 20 Litho. *Perf. 14*

206	A22	1c	multicolored	15	15
207	A22	10c	multicolored	15	15
208	A22	12c	multicolored	15	15
209	A22	48c	multicolored	40	40
210	A22	60c	multicolored	60	60
			Set value	1.22	1.22

International Human Rights Year.

Stamps and Types of 1963-67 Overprinted in Silver or Black: "ASSOCIATED / STATEHOOD"

Perf. 14½x14, 14x14½

1968, July 8 Photo. Wmk. 314

211	A19	1c	multi	15	15
212	A20	2c	ultra	15	15
213	A19	3c	lt ultra & blk	15	15
214	A19	4c	multi	15	15
215	A20	5c	magenta	15	15
216	A19	6c	multi (B)	15	15
217	A19	8c	multi (B)	15	15
218	A19	10c	pink & brn	15	15
219	A19	12c	multi	15	15
a.			Watermark upright	15	15
220	A20	14c	multi (II)	15	15
221	A19	15c	multi	15	15
222	A20	24c	multi	20	20
223	A19	48c	multi	50	50
a.			Watermark upright	3.50	3.50
224	A19	60c	multi (B)	75	75
225	A19	$1.20	multi (B)	1.25	1.25
226	A20	$2.40	multi	2.50	2.50
227	A20	$4.80	multi	5.00	5.00
			Set value	10.50	10.50

In this set, overprint was applied to 2c, 3c, 12c, 14c, 24c, 48c, 60c, $1.20, $2.40 and $4.80 with watermark upright. A reprinting of the 1c, 4c, 6c, 8c, 10c, 12c No. 219, 15c and 48c No. 223 on paper with watermark sideways was made. Same value.

Nos. 164-166, 173 and 178 Overprinted: "NATIONAL DAY / 3 NOVEMBER 1968"

Perf. 14½x14, 14x14½

1968, Nov. 3 Photo. Wmk. 314

228	A19	1c	blue, brn & grn	15	15
229	A20	2c	ultra	15	15
230	A19	3c	lt ultra & blk	15	15
231	A20	14c	multi (I)	15	15
232	A19	$1.20	multicolored	1.00	1.00
			Set value	1.25	1.25

Basketball A23

Designs: No. 233, Three soccer players. No. 234, Soccer player and goalie. No. 235, Swimmers at start. No. 236, Divers. No. 237, Javelin thrower and hurdlers. No. 238, Hurdlers. No. 240, Three basketball players.

Perf. 11½

1968, Nov. 23 Unwmk. Litho.

233	A23	1c	brt lilac & multi	15	15
234	A23	1c	brt lilac & multi	15	15
235	A23	5c	brt grnsh bl & multi	15	15
236	A23	5c	brt grnsh bl & multi	15	15
237	A23	48c	lt olive & multi	40	40
238	A23	48c	lt olive & multi	40	40
239	A23	60c	dp org & multi	50	50
240	A23	60c	dp org & multi	50	50
			Set value	2.00	2.00

19th Olympic Games, Mexico City, Oct. 12-27. The stamps of the same denomination are printed se-tenant in sheets of 40 with continuous design across each se-tenant pair (10 rows of 2 horizontal pairs separated by vertical gutter).

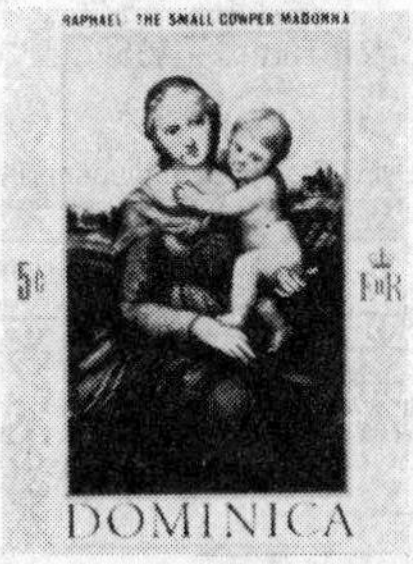

The Small Cowper Madonna, by Raphael A24

Perf. 12½x12

1968, Dec. 23 Photo. Unwmk.

241	A24	5c	multicolored	15	15

Christmas. No. 241 printed in sheets of 20. Sheets of 6 (3x2) exist containing two each of 12c, 24c, and $1.20 stamps, each picturing a different madonna painting. Value $2.50.

Venus and Adonis, by Rubens — A25

Citrus Fruit Picker — A26

Paintings: 15c, The Death of Socrates, by Louis Jacques David. 24c, Christ at Emmaus, by Velazquez. 50c, Pilate Washing his Hands, by Rembrandt.

Perf. 14½x15

1969, Jan. 30 Litho. Wmk. 314

242	A25	5c	lilac & multi	15	15
243	A25	15c	emerald & multi	15	15
244	A25	24c	lt blue & multi	20	20
245	A25	50c	crimson & multi	40	40
			Set value	76	76

20th anniv. (in 1968) of the WHO.

1969, Mar. 10 *Perf. 14½*

Designs: No. 247, Woman and child. No. 248, Hotel. No. 249, Red-necked parrots. No. 250, Calypso band. No. 251, Women dancers. No. 252, Tropical fish and coelenterates. No. 253, Diver and turtle.

246	A26	10c	multicolored	15	15
247	A26	10c	multicolored	15	15
248	A26	12c	multicolored	15	15
249	A26	12c	multicolored	15	15
250	A26	24c	multicolored	25	25
251	A26	24c	multicolored	25	25
252	A26	48c	multicolored	50	50
253	A26	48c	multicolored	50	50
			Set value	1.86	1.86

Tourist publicity. Stamps of same denomination are printed se-tenant.

Spinning, by Millet, Flags and ILO Emblem — A27

50th anniv. of the ILO (Etchings by Jean F. Millet, Flags and ILO Emblem): 30c, Threshing. 30c, Flax pulling.

1969, July Unwmk. *Perf. 13½*

254	A27	15c	multicolored	15	15
255	A27	30c	multicolored	30	30
256	A27	38c	multicolored	40	40

"Strength in Unity," Bananas and Cacao A28

"Strength in Unity" Emblem and: 8c, Map of Dominica and Hawker Siddeley 748. 12c, Map of Caribbean. 24c, Ships in harbor.

1969, July Litho.

257	A28	5c	orange & multi	15	15
258	A28	8c	gray & multi	15	15
259	A28	12c	lilac & multi	16	16
260	A28	24c	lt blue & multi	40	40
			Set value	73	73

Caribbean Free Trade Area (CARIFTA).

Gandhi at Spinning Wheel and Big Ben, London A29

Designs: 38c, Gandhi, Nehru and Fatehpur Sikri Mausoleum. $1.20, Gandhi and Taj Mahal.

1969, Oct. Litho. *Perf. 14½*

261	A29	6c	multicolored	15	15
262	A29	38c	multicolored	50	50
263	A29	$1.20	multicolored	1.75	1.75

Mohandas K. Gandhi (1869-1948), leader in India's fight for independence. "Gandhi" is misspelled "Ghandi" on Nos. 261-263.

St. Joseph — A30

Stained Glass Windows, from 17th Century French Churches: 8c, St. John. 12c, St. Peter. 60c, St. Paul.

1969, Nov. 10 Litho. *Perf. 14*

264	A30	6c	black & multi	15	15
265	A30	8c	black & multi	15	15
266	A30	12c	black & multi	15	15
267	A30	60c	black & multi	75	75
			Set value	1.05	1.05

National Day, Nov. 3. Issued in sheets of 16 (4x4) with control numbers and 4 tabs with a patriotic poem by W. O. M. Pond.

Queen Elizabeth II — A31

Purplethroated Carib (Hummingbird) A32

Designs: 2c, Poinsettia. 3c, Red-necked pigeon. 4c, Imperial parrot. 5c, Swallowtail butterfly. 6c, Brown Julia butterfly. 8c, Banana shipment. 10c, Portsmouth Harbor. 12c, Copra processing plant. 15c, Women with straw work. 25c, Timber plant. 30c, Mining pumice. 38c, Cricket, Grammar School. 50c, Roman Catholic Cathedral. 60c, Government headquarters. $1.20, Melville Hall Airport. $2.40, Coat of Arms. $4.80, Queen Elizabeth II.

Perf. 13½

1969, Nov. 26 Unwmk. Photo.

268	A31	½c silver & multi	15	15
269	A32	1c yellow & multi	15	15
270	A32	2c yellow & multi	15	15
271	A32	3c yellow & multi	15	15
272	A32	4c yellow & multi	15	15
273	A32	5c yellow & multi	15	15
274	A32	6c brown & multi	15	15
275	A32	8c brown & multi	15	15
276	A32	10c yellow & multi	15	15
277	A32	12c citron & multi	20	18
278	A32	15c blue & multi	24	22
279	A32	25c pink & multi	38	35
280	A32	30c olive & multi	50	42
281	A32	38c multicolored	65	60
282	A32	50c brown & multi	75	70

Wmk. Rectangles (334)

Perf. 14

Size: 38x26mm, 26x38mm

283	A32	60c yel & multi	1.00	85
284	A32	$1.20 yel & multi	1.90	1.75
285	A32	$2.40 gold & multi	4.50	3.75
286	A31	$4.80 gold & multi	8.75	8.00
		Nos. 268-286 (19)	20.22	18.17

Madonna and Child, by Filippino Lippi — A33

Paintings: 10c, Holy Family with Lamb, by Raphael. 15c, Virgin and Child, by Perugino. $1.20, Madonna of the Rose Hedge, by Botticelli.

Perf. 14½

1969, Dec. Unwmk. Litho.

287	A33	6c lt blue & multi	15	15
288	A33	10c multicolored	15	15
289	A33	15c lilac & multi	20	20
290	A33	$1.20 lt grn & multi	1.25	1.25
a.		Souvenir sheet of 2	1.75	1.75

Christmas. No. 290a contains 2 imperf. stamps with simulated perforations similar to Nos. 289-290.

Neil A. Armstrong, First Man on the Moon — A34

Designs: 5c, American flag and astronauts on moon. 8c, Astronauts collecting moon rocks. 30c, Landing module, moon and earth. 50c, Memorial tablet left on moon. 60c, Astronauts Armstrong, Aldrin and Collins.

1970, Feb. 2 Litho. *Perf. 12½*

291	A34	½c lilac & multi	15	15
292	A34	5c lt blue & multi	15	15
293	A34	8c orange & multi	15	15
294	A34	30c blue & multi	25	25
295	A34	50c red brn & multi	50	50
296	A34	60c rose & multi	60	60
a.		Souvenir sheet of 4	2.00	2.00
		Set value	1.50	1.50

See note after US No. C76. No. 296a contains 4 stamps similar to Nos. 293-296, but imperf. with simulated perforations.

Giant Green Turtle — A35

Designs: 24c, Flying fish. 38c, Anthurium lily. 60c, Imperial and red-necked parrots.

1970, Sept. 6 Litho. *Perf. 13½x13*

297	A35	6c lt green & multi	15	15
298	A35	24c multicolored	30	30
299	A35	38c green & multi	50	50
300	A35	60c yellow & multi	85	85
a.		Souvenir sheet of 4, #297-300	3.25	3.25

Women in 18th Century Dress A36

National Day: 8c, Carib mace and wife leader, 18th century. $1, Map and flag of Dominica.

1970, Nov. 3 Litho. *Perf. 14*

301	A36	5c yellow & multi	15	15
302	A36	8c green & multi	15	15
303	A36	$1 lt blue & multi	1.50	1.50
a.		Souv. sheet of 3, #301-303 + 3 labels	2.00	2.00

Marley's Ghost — A37

Designs (from A Christmas Carol, by Dickens): 15c, Fezziwig's Ball. 24c, Scrooge and his Nephew's Christmas Party. $1.20, The Ghost of Christmas Present.

1970, Nov. 23 Litho. *Perf. 14x14½*

304	A37	2c blue & multi	15	15
305	A37	15c multicolored	20	20
306	A37	24c red & multi	30	30
307	A37	$1.20 multicolored	1.40	1.40
a.		Souvenir sheet of 4, #304-307	3.00	3.00

Christmas; Charles Dickens (1812-1870).

Hands and Red Cross A38

Designs: 8c, The Doctor, by Sir Luke Fildes. 15c, Dominica flag and Red Cross. 50c, The Sick Child, by Edvard Munch.

1970, Dec. 28 *Perf. 14½x14*

308	A38	8c multicolored	15	15
309	A38	10c multicolored	15	15
310	A38	15c multicolored	20	20
311	A38	50c multicolored	75	75
a.		Souvenir sheet of 4, #308-311	2.50	2.50

Centenary of the British Red Cross Society.

Marigot Primary School A39

Education Year Emblem and: 8c, Goodwill Junior High School. 14c, University of the West Indies. $1, Trinity College, Cambridge, England.

1971, Mar. 1 Litho. *Perf. 13½*

312	A39	5c multicolored	15	15
313	A39	8c multicolored	15	15
314	A39	14c multicolored	20	20
315	A39	$1 multicolored	90	90
a.		Souvenir sheet of 2, #314-315	1.25	1.25

International Education Year.

Waterfall and Bird-of-Paradise Flower — A40

Tourist Publicity: 10c, Boat building. 30c, Sailboat along North Coast. 50c, Speed boat and steamer.

1971, Mar. 22 *Perf. 13½x14*

316	A40	5c multicolored	15	15
317	A40	10c multicolored	15	15
318	A40	30c multicolored	30	30
319	A40	50c multicolored	65	65
a.		Souvenir sheet of 4, #316-319	1.25	1.25
		Set value	1.10	1.10

UNICEF Emblem, Letter "D" A41

1971, June 14 Litho. *Perf. 14*

320	A41	5c multicolored	15	15
321	A41	10c multicolored	15	15
322	A41	38c multicolored	30	30
323	A41	$1.20 multicolored	90	90
a.		Souvenir sheet of 2, #321, 323	1.25	1.25

25th anniv. of UNICEF.

Boy Scout, Jamboree Emblem, Torii, Camp and Mt. Fuji — A42

Designs: 24c, British Scout and flag. 30c, Japanese Scout and flag. $1, Dominican Scout and flag.

1971, Oct. 18 Unwmk. *Perf. 11*

324	A42	20c bister & multi	25	25
325	A42	24c green & multi	32	32
326	A42	30c red lilac & multi	40	40
327	A42	$1 blue & multi	1.75	1.75
a.		Souvenir sheet of 2, #326-327	2.75	2.75

13th Boy Scout World Jamboree, Asagiri Plain, Japan, Aug. 2-10.

Boats at Portsmouth — A43

Designs: 15c, Carnival street scene. 20c, $1.20, Anthea Mondesire, Carifta Queen, vert. 50c, Rock of Atkinson, vert.

Perf. 13½x14, 14x13½

1971, Nov. 15 Litho.

328	A43	8c multicolored	15	15
329	A43	15c multicolored	15	15
330	A43	20c multicolored	20	20
331	A43	50c multicolored	50	50

Souvenir Sheet

Perf. 15

332	A43	$1.20 multicolored	1.25	1.25

National Day.

First Dominica Coin, 8 Reals, 1761 A44

Early Dominica Coins: 30c, Eleven and 3-bit pieces, 1798. 35c, Two-real coin, 1770, vert. 50c, Three "mocos" and piece of 8, 1798.

1972, Feb. 7 Litho. *Perf. 14*

333	A44	10c violet, silver & blk	15	15
334	A44	30c green, silver & blk	30	30
335	A44	35c ultra, silver & blk	60	60
336	A44	50c red, silver & blk	60	60
a.		Souvenir sheet of 2, #335-336	1.50	1.50

Margin of #336a inscribed "Christmas 1971."

Common Opossum, Environment Emblem — A45

Environment Emblem and: 35c, Agouti. 60c, Oncidium papillo (orchid). $1.20, Hibiscus.

1972, June 5

337	A45	½c yel grn & multi	15	15
338	A45	35c org brn & multi	50	50
339	A45	60c lt blue & multi	1.00	1.00
340	A45	$1.20 yellow & multi	1.90	1.90
a.		Souvenir sheet of 4, #337-340	5.00	5.00

UN Conf. on Human Environment, Stockholm, June 5-16.

100-meter Sprint, Olympic Rings — A46

Olympic Rings and: 35m, 400-meter hurdles. 58c, Hammer throw, vert. 72c, Broad jump, vert.

1972, Oct. 9 Litho. *Perf. 14*

341	A46	30c dp org & multi	30	30
342	A46	35c blue & multi	35	35
343	A46	58c lilac rose & multi	60	60
344	A46	72c yel green & multi	75	75
a.		Souv. sheet of 2, #343-344, perf. 15	2.75	2.75

20th Olympic Games, Munich, Aug. 26-Sept. 11.

General Post Office A47

1972, Nov. 1 *Perf. 13½*

345	A47	10c shown	15	15
346	A47	20c Morne Diablotin Mountain	15	15
347	A47	30c Rodney's Rock	30	30
a.		Souvenir sheet of 2, #346-347, perf. 15	85	85
		Set value	53	53

National Day.

Adoration of the Shepherds, by Caravaggio — A48

Paintings: 14c, Madonna and Child, by Rubens. 30c, Madonna and Child, with St. Anne by Orazio Gentileschi. $1, Adoration of the Kings, by Jan Mostaert. (On 8c, painting is mistakenly attributed to Boccaccino, according to Fine Arts Philatelist.)

1972, Dec. 4.

348	A48	8c gold & multi	15	15
349	A48	14c gold & multi	15	15
350	A48	30c gold & multi	30	30
351	A48	$1 gold & multi	1.00	1.00
a.		Souvenir sheet of 2	2.50	2.50

Christmas. No. 351a contains one each of Nos. 350-351 with simulated perforations.

Silver Wedding Issue, 1972

Common Design Type

Design: Queen Elizabeth II, Prince Philip, bananas, sisseron parrot.

Perf. 14x14½

1972, Nov. 13 Photo. Wmk. 314

352	CD324	5c olive & multi	15	15
353	CD324	$1 multicolored	60	60
		Set value	66	66

See note after Antigua No. 296.

Launching of Tiros Weather Satellite — A49

Designs: 1c, Nimbus satellite. 2c, Radiosonde balloon and equipment. 30c, Radarscope. 35c, General circulation of atmosphere. 50c, Picture of hurricane transmitted by satellite. $1, Computer weather map. (30c, 35c, 50c, $1, horizontal).

Perf. 14½

1973, July 16 Unwmk. Litho.

354	A49	½c black & multi	15	15
355	A49	1c black & multi	15	15
356	A49	2c black & multi	15	15
357	A49	30c black & multi	30	30
358	A49	35c black & multi	38	38
359	A49	50c black & multi	55	55
360	A49	$1 black & multi	1.10	1.10
a.		Souvenir sheet of 2, #359-360	2.50	2.50
		Nos. 354-360 (7)	2.78	2.78

Intl. meteorological cooperation, cent.

Going to the Hospital A50

WHO Emblem and: 1c, Maternity and infant care. 2c, Inoculation against smallpox. 30c, Emergency service. 35c, Waiting patients. 50c, Examination. $1, Traveling physician.

1973, Aug. 20 Unwmk. *Perf. 14½*

361	A50	½c lt blue & multi	15	15
362	A50	1c gray grn & multi	15	15
363	A50	2c yellow & multi	15	15
364	A50	30c lt vio & multi	25	25
365	A50	35c yel grn & multi	30	30
366	A50	50c multicolored	45	45
367	A50	$1 bister & multi	90	90
a.		Souvenir sheet of 2, #366-367, perf. 14x14½	2.25	2.25
		Set value	2.00	2.00

WHO, 25th anniv. #367a exists perf. 14½.

DOMINICA Cyrique Crab — A51

1973, Oct.

368	A51	½c shown	22	22
369	A51	22c Blue land crab	45	45
370	A51	25c Breadfruit	52	52
371	A51	$1.20 Sunflower	2.10	2.10
a.		Souvenir sheet of 4, #368-371	3.50	3.50

Princess Anne and Mark Phillips A52

1973, Nov. 14 *Perf. 13½*

372	A52	25c salmon & multi	15	15
373	A52	$2 blue & multi	1.20	1.20
a.		Souv. sheet of 2 (75c, $1.20)	1.75	1.75

Wedding of Princess Anne and Capt. Mark Phillips.

#372-373 were issued in sheets of 5 + label.

No. 373a contains 2 stamps of type A52: 75c in colors of the 25c, and $1.20 in colors of the $2.

Nativity, by Brueghel A53

Paintings of the Nativity by: 1c, Botticelli. 2c, Dürer. 12c, Botticelli. 22c, Rubens. 35c, Dürer. $1, Giorgione (inscribed "Giorgeone").

1973 Unwmk. *Perf. 14½x15*

374	A53	½c gray & multi	15	15
375	A53	1c gray & multi	15	15
376	A53	2c gray & multi	15	15
377	A53	12c gray & multi	15	15
378	A53	22c gray & multi	20	20
379	A53	35c gray & multi	25	25
380	A53	$1 gray & multi	75	75
a.		Souvenir sheet of 2	2.25	2.25
		Set value	1.40	1.40

Christmas. No. 380a contains one each of Nos. 379-380 in changed colors.

Carib Basket Weaving A54

Designs: 10c, Staircase of the Snake. 50c, Miss Caribbean Queen, Kathleen Telemacque, vert. 60c, Miss Carifta Queen, Esther Fadelle, vert. $1, La Jeune Etoille Dancers.

Perf. 13½x14, 14x13½

1973, Dec. 17

381	A54	5c buff & multi	15	15
382	A54	10c multicolored	15	15
383	A54	50c multicolored	30	30
384	A54	60c multicolored	40	40
385	A54	$1 multicolored	65	65
a.		Souv. sheet of 3, #381-382, 385	1.10	1.10
		Nos. 381-385 (5)	1.65	1.65

National Day.

U.W.I. Center, Dominica A55

Designs: 30c, Graduation. $1, University coat of arms.

1974, Jan. 21 Litho. *Perf. 13½x14*

386	A55	12c dp org & multi	15	15
387	A55	30c violet & multi	25	25
388	A55	$1 multicolored	85	85
a.		Souvenir sheet of 3, #386-388	1.25	1.25

University of the West Indies, 25th anniv.

Dominica No. 1 and Map of Island A56

Designs: 1c, 50c, No. 8 and post horn. 2c, $1.20, No. 9 and coat of arms. 10c, Like ½c.

1974, May 4 Litho. *Perf. 14½*

389	A56	½c brt pur & multi	15	15
390	A56	1c salmon & multi	15	15
391	A56	2c ultra & multi	15	15
392	A56	10c violet & multi	16	16
393	A56	50c yel grn & multi	50	50
394	A56	$1.20 rose & multi	1.10	1.10
a.		Souv. sheet of 3, #392-394, perf. 15	2.25	2.25
		Set value	1.85	1.85

Centenary of Dominican postage stamps.

Soccer Player and Cup, Brazilian Flag — A57

Designs: Soccer cup, various players and flags.

1974, July Litho. *Perf. 14½*

395	A57	½c shown	15	15
396	A57	1c Germany, Fed. Rep.	15	15
397	A57	2c Italy	15	15
398	A57	30c Scotland	25	25
399	A57	40c Sweden	35	35
400	A57	50c Netherlands	40	40
401	A57	$1 Yugoslavia	85	85
a.		Souvenir sheet of 2, #400-401, perf. 13½	1.50	1.50
		Set value	2.00	2.00

World Cup Soccer Championship, Munich, June 13-July 7.

Indian Hole A58

Designs: 40c, Teachers' Training College. $1, Petite Savane Co-operative Bay Oil Distillery.

1974, Nov. 1 Litho. *Perf. 13½x14*

402	A58	10c multicolored	15	15
403	A58	40c multicolored	35	35
404	A58	$1 multicolored	85	85
a.		Souvenir sheet of 3, #402-404	1.50	1.50

Churchill at Race Track — A59

Sir Winston Churchill (1874-1965): 1c, with Gen. Eisenhower. 2c, with Franklin D. Roosevelt. 20c, as First Lord of the Admiralty. 45c, painting outdoors. $2, giving "V" sign.

1974, Nov. 25 Litho. *Perf. 14½*

405	A59	½c multicolored	15	15
406	A59	1c multicolored	15	15
407	A59	2c multicolored	15	15
408	A59	20c multicolored	20	20
409	A59	45c multicolored	40	40
410	A59	$2 multicolored	1.75	1.75
a.		Souvenir sheet of 2, #409-410, perf. 13½	2.50	2.50
		Nos. 405-410 (6)	2.80	2.80

Virgin and Child, by Oronzo Tiso — A60

Paintings (Virgin and Child): 1c, by Lorenzo Costa. 2c, by unknown Master. 10c, by G. F. Romanelli. 25c, Holy Family, by G. S. da Sermoneta. 45c, Adoration of the Shepherds, by Guido Reni. $1, Adoration of the Kings, by Cristoforo Caselli.

1974, Dec. 16 Litho. *Perf. 14*

411	A60	½c multicolored	15	15
412	A60	1c multicolored	15	15
413	A60	2c multicolored	15	15
414	A60	10c multicolored	18	18
415	A60	25c multicolored	40	40
416	A60	45c multicolored	65	65
417	A60	$1 multicolored	1.50	1.50
a.		Souvenir sheet of 2, #416-417	3.25	3.25
		Nos. 411-417 (7)	3.18	3.18

Christmas.

Seamail, "Orinoco," 1851, and "Geesthaven," 1966 — A61

Cent. of UPU: $2, $2.40, Airmail, De Havilland 4, 1918, and Boeing 747, 1974.

1974, Dec. 4 Litho. *Perf. 13½*

418	A61	10c multicolored	20	20
419	A61	$2 multicolored	2.75	2.75

Souvenir Sheet

419A		Sheet of 2	3.75	3.75
b.	A61	$1.20 multicolored	1.25	1.25
c.	A61	$2.40 multicolored	2.50	2.50

Oldwife A62

1975, June 2 — Litho. — *Perf. 14½*

421	A62	½c	shown	15	15
422	A62	1c	Ocyurus chrysurus	15	15
423	A62	2c	Blue marlin	15	15
424	A62	3c	Swordfish	15	15
425	A62	20c	Great barracuda	45	30
426	A62	$2	Grouper	3.50	2.75
a.			Souvenir sheet, perf. 13½	4.00	3.25
			Nos. 421-426 (6)	4.55	3.65

Myscelia Antholia A63

Designs: Butterflies.

1975, July 28 — Litho. — *Perf. 14½*

427	A63	½c	shown	15	15
428	A63	1c	Lycorea ceres	15	15
429	A63	2c	Siderone nemesis	15	15
430	A63	6c	Battus polydamas	15	15
431	A63	30c	Anartia lytrea	65	60
432	A63	40c	Morpho peleides	80	65
433	A63	$2	Dryas julia	4.75	3.50
a.			Souvenir sheet, perf. 13½	4.25	4.25
			Nos. 427-433 (7)	6.80	5.35

Royal Mail Ship Yare — A64

Ships Tied in with Dominican History: 1c, Royal mail ship Thames. 2c, Canadian National S.S. Lady Nelson. 20c, C.N. S.S. Lady Rodney. 45c, Harrison Line M.V. Statesman. 50c, Geest Line M.V. Geestcape. $2, Geest Line M.V. Geeststar.

1975, Sept. 1 — *Perf. 14*

434	A64	½c	black & multi	15	15
435	A64	1c	black & multi	15	15
436	A64	2c	black & multi	15	15
437	A64	20c	black & multi	40	30
438	A64	45c	black & multi	75	65
439	A64	50c	black & multi	90	75
440	A64	$2	black & multi	4.50	3.00
a.			Souvenir sheet of 2, #439-440	4.50	4.00
			Nos. 434-440 (7)	7.00	5.15

IWY Emblem, Farm Women A65

Design: $2, IWY emblem, dressmaker and saleswoman.

1975, Oct. 30 — Litho. — *Perf. 14*

441	A65	10c	pink & multi	15	15
442	A65	$2	yellow & multi	2.50	2.50

International Women's Year.

Public Library A66

Designs: 5c, Miss Caribbean Queen 1975, vert. 30c, Citrus factory. $1, National Day Cup, vert.

1975, Nov. 6

443	A66	5c	multicolored	15	15
444	A66	10c	multicolored	15	15
445	A66	30c	multicolored	40	40
446	A66	$1	multicolored	1.50	1.50
a.			Souvenir sheet of 3	2.10	2.10

National Day. No. 446a contains 3 stamps similar to Nos. 444-446 with simulated perforations.

Virgin and Child, by Mantegna — A67

Christmas: Paintings of the Virgin and Child.

1975, Nov. 24

447	A67	½c	shown	15	15
448	A67	1c	Fra Filippo Lippi	15	15
449	A67	2c	Bellini	15	15
450	A67	10c	Botticelli	15	15
451	A67	25c	Bellini	30	30
452	A67	45c	Correggio	65	65
453	A67	$1	Durer	1.50	1.50
a.			Souvenir sheet of 2, #452-453	3.00	3.00
			Nos. 447-453 (7)	3.05	3.05

Hibiscus A68

Queen Elizabeth II — A69

Designs: 1c, African tulip. 2c, Castor oil tree. 3c, White cedar flower. 4c, Eggplant. 5c, Garfish. 6c, Okra. 8c, Zenaida doves. 10c, Screw pine. 20c, Mangoes. 25c, Crayfish. 30c, Manicou. 40c, Bay leaf groves. 50c, Tomatoes. $1, Lime factory. $2, Rum distillery. $5, Bay oil distillery.

1975, Dec. 8 — Litho. — *Perf. 14½*

454	A68	½c	ultra & multi	15	15
455	A68	1c	lilac & multi	15	15
456	A68	2c	orange & multi	15	15
457	A68	3c	multicolored	15	15
458	A68	4c	pink & multi	15	15
459	A68	5c	multicolored	15	15
460	A68	6c	gray & multi	15	15
461	A68	8c	multicolored	15	15
462	A68	10c	violet & multi	15	15
463	A68	20c	yellow & multi	20	16
464	A68	25c	lemon & multi	22	20
465	A68	30c	salmon & multi	26	22
466	A68	40c	multicolored	40	32
467	A68	50c	red & multi	50	40
468	A68	$1	citron & multi	1.00	75
469	A68	$2	multicolored	2.00	1.65
470	A68	$5	multicolored	5.00	4.00
			Perf. 14		
471	A69	$10	blue & multi	10.00	8.00
			Nos. 454-471 (18)	20.93	17.05

For overprints, see Nos. 584-601, 640-643.

American Infantry — A70

Rowing — A71

Designs: 1c, English three-decker, 1782. 2c, George Washington. 45c, English sailors. 75c, English ensign with regimental flag. $2, Admiral Hood. All designs have old maps in background.

1976, Apr. 12 — Litho. — *Perf. 14½*

472	A70	½c	green & multi	15	15
473	A70	1c	purple & multi	15	15
474	A70	2c	orange & multi	15	15
475	A70	45c	brown & multi	75	60
476	A70	75c	ultra & multi	1.25	1.00
477	A70	$2	red & multi	3.50	3.00
a.			Souvenir sheet of 2	6.00	4.50
			Nos. 472-477 (6)	5.95	5.05

American Bicentennial. No. 477a contains 2 stamps similar to Nos. 476-477, perf. 13.

1976, May 24 — Litho. — *Perf. 14½*

Olympic Rings and: 1c, Shot put. 2c, Swimming. 40c, Relay race. 45c, Gymnastics. 60c, Sailing. $2, Archery.

478	A71	½c	ocher & multi	15	15
479	A71	1c	ocher & multi	15	15
480	A71	2c	ocher & multi	15	15
481	A71	40c	ocher & multi	38	38
482	A71	45c	ocher & multi	40	40
483	A71	60c	ocher & multi	60	60
484	A71	$2	ocher & multi	1.75	1.75
a.			Souv. sheet of 2, #483-484, perf 13	3.50	3.50
			Nos. 478-484 (7)	3.58	3.58

21st Olympic Games, Montreal, Canada, July 17-Aug. 1.

Ringed Kingfisher A72

Birds: 1c, Mourning dove. 2c, Green heron. 15c, Broad-winged hawk. 30c, Blue-headed hummingbird. 45c, Banana-quit. $2, Imperial parrot. 15c, 30c, 45c, $2, vert.

1976, June 28

485	A72	½c	multicolored	15	15
486	A72	1c	multicolored	15	15
487	A72	2c	multicolored	15	15
488	A72	15c	multicolored	60	30
489	A72	30c	multicolored	1.10	60
490	A72	45c	multicolored	2.25	1.00
491	A72	$2	multicolored	10.00	5.00
a.			Souv. sheet of 3, #489-491, perf. 13	15.00	7.50
			Nos. 485-491 (7)	14.40	7.35

Map of West Indies, Bats, Wicket and Ball — A72a

Prudential Cup — A72b

1976, July 26 — Litho. — *Perf. 14*

492	A72a	15c	lt blue & multi	50	25
493	A72b	25c	lilac rose & black	1.00	50

World Cricket Cup, won by West Indies Team, 1975.

Viking Spacecraft — A73

Virgin and Child, by Giorgione — A74

Designs: 1c, Titan launch center, horiz. 2c, Titan 3-D and Centaur D-IT. 3c, Orbiter and landing capsule. 45c, Capsule with closed parachute. 75c, Capsule with open parachute. $1, Landing capsule descending on Mars, horiz. $2, Viking on Mars, horiz.

1976, Sept. 20 — Litho. — *Perf. 15*

494	A73	½c	multicolored	15	15
495	A73	1c	multicolored	15	15
496	A73	2c	multicolored	15	15
497	A73	3c	multicolored	15	15
498	A73	45c	multicolored	35	35
499	A73	75c	multicolored	60	60
500	A73	$1	multicolored	75	75
501	A73	$2	multicolored	1.50	1.50
a.			Souvenir sheet of 2, #500, 501, perf. 13½	2.50	2.50
			Nos. 494-501 (8)	3.80	3.80

Viking mission to Mars.

1976, Nov. 1 — Litho. — *Perf. 14*

Virgin and Child by: 1c, Bellini. 2c, Mantegna. 6c, Mantegna. 25c, Memling. 45c, 50c, Correggio. $1, $3, Raphael.

502	A74	½c	multicolored	15	15
503	A74	1c	multicolored	15	15
504	A74	2c	multicolored	15	15
505	A74	6c	multicolored	15	15
506	A74	25c	multicolored	22	22
507	A74	45c	multicolored	38	38
508	A74	$3	multicolored	2.75	2.75
			Nos. 502-508 (7)	3.95	3.95

Souvenir Sheet

509		Sheet of 2	2.00	2.00
a.	A74	50c multicolored	50	
b.	A74	$1 multicolored	1.00	

Christmas.

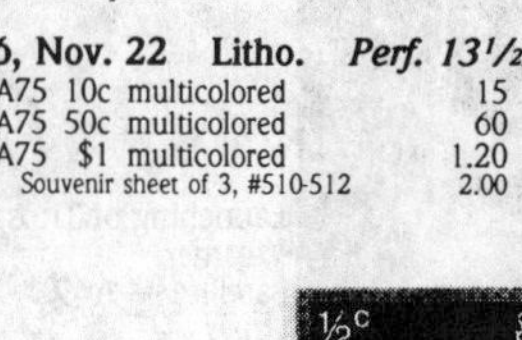

Island Craft Co-operative — A75

National Day: 50c, Banana harvest, Castle Bruce Co-operative. $1, Banana shipping plant, Bourne Farmers' Co-operative.

1976, Nov. 22 — Litho. — *Perf. 13½x14*

510	A75	10c	multicolored	15	15
511	A75	50c	multicolored	60	60
512	A75	$1	multicolored	1.20	1.20
a.			Souvenir sheet of 3, #510-512	2.00	2.00

Common Sundial — A76

Sea Shells: 1c, Flame helmet. 2c, Mouse cone. 20c, Caribbean vase. 40c, West Indian fighting conch. 50c, Short coral shell. $2, Long-spined star shell. $3, Apple murex.

1976, Dec. 20 Litho. *Perf. 14*

513	A76	½c black & multi	15	15
514	A76	1c black & multi	15	15
515	A76	2c black & multi	15	15
516	A76	20c black & multi	22	18
517	A76	40c black & multi	45	35
518	A76	50c black & multi	50	45
519	A76	$3 black & multi	3.50	2.50
		Nos. 513-519 (7)	5.12	3.93

Souvenir Sheet

520	A76	$2 black & multi	2.75	1.75

Queen Enthroned — A77

Designs: 1c, Imperial crown. 45c, Elizabeth II and Princess Anne. $2, Coronation ring. $2.50, Ampulla and spoon. $5, Royal visit to Dominica.

1977, Feb. 7 *Perf. 14*

521	A77	½c multicolored	15	15
522	A77	1c multicolored	15	15
523	A77	45c multicolored	42	42
524	A77	$2 multicolored	1.75	1.75
525	A77	$2.50 multicolored	2.25	2.25
		Nos. 521-525 (5)	4.72	4.72

Souvenir Sheet

526	A77	$5 multicolored	3.75	3.75

25th anniv. of the reign of Elizabeth II.
Nos. 521-525 were printed in sheets of 40 (4x10), perf. 14, and sheets of 5 plus label, perf. 12, in changed colors.
For overprints, see Nos. 549-554.

Joseph Haydn — A78

Designs: 1c, Fidelio, act I, scene IV. 2c, Dancer Maria Casentini. 15c, Beethoven working on Pastoral Symphony. 30c, "Wellington's Victory." 40c, Soprano Henriette Sontag. $2, Young Beethoven.

1977, Apr. 25 Litho. *Perf. 14*

527	A78	½c multicolored	15	15
528	A78	1c multicolored	15	15
529	A78	2c multicolored	15	15
530	A78	15c multicolored	15	15
531	A78	30c multicolored	30	30
532	A78	40c multicolored	38	38
533	A78	$2 multicolored	1.75	1.75
a.		Souvenir sheet of 3, #531-533	3.00	3.00
		Nos. 527-533 (7)	3.03	3.03

Ludwig van Beethoven (1770-1827), composer.

Boy Scouts on Hike — A79

Saluting Boy Scout and: 1c, First aid. 2c, Scouts setting up camp. 45c, Rock climbing. 50c, Kayaking. 75c, Map reading. $2, Campfire. $3, Sailing.

1977, Aug. 8 Litho. *Perf. 14*

534	A79	½c multicolored	15	15
535	A79	1c multicolored	15	15
536	A79	2c multicolored	15	15
537	A79	45c multicolored	40	40
538	A79	50c multicolored	42	42
539	A79	$3 multicolored	2.50	2.50
		Nos. 534-539 (6)	3.77	3.77

Souvenir Sheet

540		Sheet of 2	3.50	3.50
a.		A79 75c multicolored	90	
b.		A79 $2 multicolored	2.50	

6th Caribbean Jamboree, Kingston, Jamaica, Aug. 5-14.

Nativity A80

Christmas: 1c, Annunciation to the Shepherds. 2c, 45c, Presentation at the Temple (different). 6c, $2, $3, Flight into Egypt (different). 15c, Adoration of the Kings. 50c, Virgin and Child with Angels. ½c to 45c are illustrations from De Lisle Psalter, 14th century. 50c, $2, $3 are from other Psalters.

1977, Nov. 14 Litho. *Perf. 14*

541	A80	½c multicolored	15	15
542	A80	1c multicolored	15	15
543	A80	2c multicolored	15	15
544	A80	6c multicolored	15	15
545	A80	15c multicolored	15	15
546	A80	45c multicolored	30	30
547	A80	$3 multicolored	1.90	1.90
		Set value	2.50	2.50

Souvenir Sheet

548		Sheet of 2	2.25	2.25
a.		A80 50c multicolored	35	
b.		A80 $2 multicolored	1.25	

Nos. 521-526 Overprinted "ROYAL VISIT / W.I. 1977"

1977, Nov. 24 Litho. *Perf. 12, 14*

549	A77	½c multicolored	15	15
550	A77	1c multicolored	15	15
551	A77	45c multicolored	30	30
552	A77	$2 multicolored	1.40	1.40
553	A77	$2.50 multicolored	1.75	1.75
		Nos. 549-553 (5)	3.75	3.75

Souvenir Sheet

Perf. 14

554	A77	$5 multicolored	3.50	3.50

Caribbean visit of Queen Elizabeth II. #549-550 are perf. 12, others perf. 12 and 14.
Two types of No. 554: I. Overprinted only on stamp. II. Overprinted "W.I. 1977" on stamp and "Royal Visit W.I. 1977" on margin.

Masqueraders — A81

Designs: 1c, Sensay costume. 2c, Street musicians. 45c, Douiette band. 50c, Pappy Show wedding. $2, $2.50, Masquerade band.

1978, Jan. 9 *Perf. 14*

555	A81	½c multicolored	15	15
556	A81	1c multicolored	15	15
557	A81	2c multicolored	15	15
558	A81	45c multicolored	30	30
559	A81	50c multicolored	35	35
560	A81	$2 multicolored	1.40	1.40
		Nos. 555-560 (6)	2.50	2.50

Souvenir Sheet

561	A81	$2.50 multicolored	1.75	1.75

History of Carnival.

Lindbergh and Spirit of St. Louis — A82

Designs: 10c, Spirit of St. Louis take-off, Long Island, May 20, 1927. 15c, Lindbergh and map of route New York to Paris. 20c, Lindbergh and plane in Paris. 40c, 1st Zeppelin, trial over Lake Constance. 50c, Spirit of St. Louis. 60c, Count Zeppelin and Zeppelin LZ-2, 1906. $2, Graf Zeppelin, 1928. $3, LZ-127, 1928.

1978, Mar. 13 Litho. *Perf. 14½*

562	A82	6c multicolored	15	15
563	A82	10c multicolored	15	15
564	A82	15c multicolored	15	15
565	A82	20c multicolored	15	15
566	A82	40c multicolored	30	30
567	A82	60c multicolored	45	45
568	A82	$3 multicolored	2.25	2.25
		Nos. 562-568 (7)	3.60	3.60

Souvenir Sheet

569		Sheet of 2	2.75	2.75
a.		A82 50c multicolored	50	
b.		A82 $2 multicolored	2.00	

Charles A. Lindbergh's solo transatlantic flight from New York to Paris, 50th anniv., and flights of Graf Zeppelin.

Royal Family on Balcony — A83

Designs: 45c, Coronation. $2.50, Elizabeth II and Prince Philip. $5, Elizabeth II.

1978, June 2 Litho. *Perf. 14*

570	A83	45c multicolored	30	30
571	A83	$2 multicolored	1.40	1.40
572	A83	$2.50 multicolored	1.75	1.75

Souvenir Sheet

573	A83	$5 multicolored	3.50	3.50

Coronation of Queen Elizabeth II, 25th anniv. Nos. 570-572 were issued in sheets of 50, and in sheets of 3 stamps and label, in changed colors, perf. 12.

Wright Plane Coming out of Hangar A84

Designs: 40c, 1908 plane. 60c, Flyer I gliding. $2, Flyer I taking off. $3, Wilbur and Orville Wright and Flyer I.

1978, July 10 Litho. *Perf. 14½*

574	A84	30c multicolored	20	20
575	A84	40c multicolored	28	28
576	A84	60c multicolored	40	40
577	A84	$2 multicolored	1.50	1.50

Souvenir Sheet

578	A84	$3 multicolored	2.50	2.50

75th anniv. of first powered flight.

Two Apostles, by Rubens — A85

Rubens Paintings: 45c, Descent from the Cross. 50c, St. Ildefonso Receiving Chasuble. $2, Holy Family. $3, Assumption of the Virgin.

1978, Oct. 16 Litho. *Perf. 14*

579	A85	20c multicolored	20	20
580	A85	45c multicolored	45	45
581	A85	50c multicolored	50	50
582	A85	$3 multicolored	3.00	3.00

Souvenir Sheet

583	A85	$2 multicolored	2.25	2.25

Christmas.

Nos. 454-471 Overprinted: "INDEPENDENCE/ 3rd NOVEMBER 1978"

1978 Nov. 1 Litho. *Perf. 14½*

584	A68	½c ultra & multi	15	15
585	A68	1c lilac & multi	15	15
586	A68	2c orange & multi	15	15
587	A68	3c multicolored	15	15
588	A68	4c pink & multi	15	15
589	A68	5c multicolored	15	15
590	A68	6c gray & multi	15	15
591	A68	8c multicolored	15	15
592	A68	10c violet & multi	15	15
a.		Perf. 13½ ('79)	15	15
593	A68	20c yellow & multi	15	15
594	A68	25c lemon & multi	18	18
595	A68	30c salmon & multi	22	22
596	A68	40c multicolored	30	30
597	A68	50c red & multi	38	38
598	A68	$1 citron & multi	75	75
599	A68	$2 multicolored	1.50	1.50
600	A68	$5 multicolored	3.25	3.25

Perf. 14

601	A69	$10 blue & multi	6.75	6.75
		Nos. 584-601 (18)	14.83	14.83

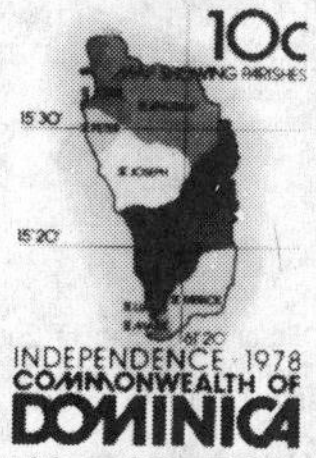

Map of Dominica with Parishes — A86

Rowland Hill — A87

Designs: 25c, Sabinea carinalis, national flower, and map. 45c, New flag and map. 50c, Coat of arms and map. $2, Prime Minister Patrick John.

1978, Nov. 1 *Perf. 14*

602	A86	10c multicolored	15	15
603	A86	25c multicolored	20	20
604	A86	45c multicolored	35	35
605	A86	50c multicolored	40	40
606	A86	$2 multicolored	1.60	1.60
		Nos. 602-606 (5)	2.70	2.70

Souvenir Sheet

607	A86	$2.50 multicolored	*8.50*	*5.75*

Dominican independence.

1979, Mar. 19

Designs: 45c, Great Britain No. 2. 50c, Dominica No. 1. $2, Maltese Cross handstamps. $5, Penny Black.

608	A87	25c multicolored	16	16
609	A87	45c multicolored	30	30
610	A87	50c multicolored	35	35
611	A87	$2 multicolored	1.40	1.40

Souvenir Sheet

612	A87	$5 multicolored	6.50	6.50

Sir Rowland Hill (1795-1879), originator of penny postage.
Nos. 608-611 printed in sheets of 5 plus label, perf. 12x12½, in changed colors.
For overprints, see Nos. 663A-663D.

Boys and Dugout Canoe A88

IYC Emblem and: 40c, Children carrying bananas. 50c, Boys playing cricket. $3, Child feeding rabbits. $5, Boy showing catch of fish.

1979, Apr. 23 Litho. *Perf. 14*

613	A88	30c multicolored	25	25
614	A88	40c multicolored	35	35
615	A88	50c multicolored	40	40
616	A88	$3 multicolored	2.50	2.50

Souvenir Sheet

617	A88	$5 multicolored	4.50	4.50

Grouper A89

Designs: 30c, Spotted dolphin. 50c, White-tailed tropic birds. 60c, Brown pelicans. $1, Pilot whale. $2, Brown booby. $3, Elkhorn coral.

1979, May 21 Litho. *Perf. 14*

618	A89	10c	multicolored	15	15
619	A89	30c	multicolored	30	30
620	A89	50c	multicolored	50	50
621	A89	60c	multicolored	60	60
622	A89	$1	multicolored	1.00	1.00
623	A89	$2	multicolored	2.00	2.00
			Nos. 618-623 (6)	4.55	4.55

Souvenir Sheet

624	A89	$3	multicolored	3.25	3.25

Wildlife protection.

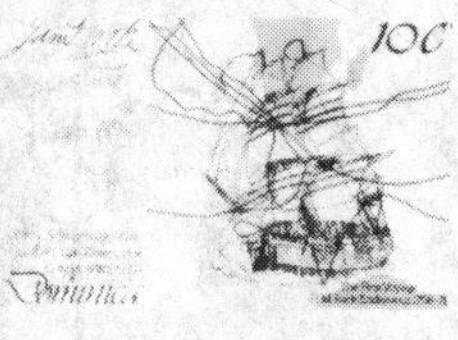

Capt. Cook, Bark Endeavour A90

Capt. Cook and: 50c, Resolution, map of 2nd voyage. 60c, Discovery, map of 3rd voyage. $2, Cook's map of New Zealand, 1770. $5, Portrait.

1979, July 16 Litho. *Perf. 14*

625	A90	10c	multicolored	15	15
626	A90	50c	multicolored	40	40
627	A90	60c	multicolored	50	50
628	A90	$2	multicolored	1.60	1.60

Souvenir Sheet

629	A90	$5	multicolored	3.75	3.75

200th death anniv. of Capt. James Cook (1728-1779).

Girl Guides Cooking A91

Girl Guides: 20c, Setting up emergency rain tent. 50c, Raising flag of independent Dominica. $2.50, Playing accordion and singing. $3, Leader and Guides of different ages.

1979, July 30

630	A91	10c	multicolored	15	15
631	A91	20c	multicolored	16	16
632	A91	50c	multicolored	40	40
633	A91	$2.50	multicolored	2.00	2.00

Souvenir Sheet

634	A91	$3	multicolored	3.00	3.00

50th anniv. of Dominican Girl Guides.

Colvillea — A92

Flowering Trees: 40c, Lignum vitae. 60c, Dwarf poinciana. $2, Fern tree. $3, Perfume tree.

1979, Sept. 3 Litho. *Perf. 14*

635	A92	20c	multicolored	20	20
636	A92	40c	multicolored	40	40
637	A92	60c	multicolored	60	60
638	A92	$2	multicolored	2.00	2.00

Souvenir Sheet

639	A92	$3	multicolored	3.50	3.50

Nos. 459, 466, 470-471 Overprinted: "HURRICANE / RELIEF"

Perf. 14½, 13½, 13½x14, 14

1979, Oct. 29 Litho.

640	A68	5c	multicolored	15	15
641	A68	40c	multicolored	40	40
642	A68	$5	multicolored	5.00	5.00
643	A68	$10	multicolored	10.00	10.00

Hurricane devastation, Aug. 29. Vertical overprint on No. 643, others horizontal.

Music Scenes A92a

1979, Nov. 2 Litho. *Perf. 11*

644	A92a	½c	Mickey Mouse	15	15
645	A92a	1c	Goofy playing guitar	15	15
646	A92a	2c	Mickey Mouse and Goofy	15	15
647	A92a	3c	Donald Duck	15	15
648	A92a	4c	Minnie Mouse	15	15
649	A92a	5c	Goofy playing accordion	15	15
650	A92a	10c	Horace Horsecollar and Dale	15	15
651	A92a	$2	Huey, Dewey, Louie	1.60	1.60
652	A92a	$2.50	Donald and Huey	2.00	2.00
			Set value	3.90	3.90

Souvenir Sheet

Perf. 13

653	A92a	$3	Mickey Mouse playing piano	2.50	2.50

Cathedral of the Assumption A93

Cathedrals: 40c, St. Patrick's, New York. 45c, St. Paul's, London, vert. 60c, St. Peter's, Rome. $2, Cologne Cathedral. $3, Notre Dame, Paris, vert.

1979, Nov. 26 Litho. *Perf. 14*

654	A93	6c	multicolored	15	15
655	A93	45c	multicolored	30	30
656	A93	60c	multicolored	40	40
657	A93	$3	multicolored	2.00	2.00

Souvenir Sheet

658			Sheet of 2	1.75	1.75
a.			A93 40c multicolored	28	28
b.			A93 $2 multicolored	1.40	1.40

Christmas.

Nurse and Patients, Rotary Emblem A94

1980, Mar. 31 Litho. *Perf. 14*

659	A94	10c	shown	15	15
660	A94	20c	Electrocardiogram machine	15	15
661	A94	40c	Mental hospital	28	28
662	A94	$2.50	Paul Harris, founder	1.75	1.75

Souvenir Sheet

663	A94	$3	Map of Africa and Europe	2.25	2.25

Rotary International, 75th anniv. Nos. 659-662 each contain quadrant of Rotary emblem.

Nos. 608-611 Overprinted "LONDON 1980"

1980, May 6 Litho. *Perf. 12*

663A	A87	25c	multicolored	50	50
663B	A87	45c	multicolored	90	90
663C	A87	50c	multicolored	1.00	1.00
663D	A87	$2	multicolored	4.00	4.00

London 80 Intl. Stamp Exhib., May 6-14.

Shot Put, Moscow '80 Emblem A95 30c

1980, May 27 Litho. *Perf. 14*

664	A95	30c	shown	20	20
665	A95	40c	Basketball	28	28
666	A95	60c	Swimming	40	40
667	A95	$2	Gymnast	1.40	1.40

Souvenir Sheet

668	A95	$3	Running	2.00	2.00

22nd Summer Olympic Games, Moscow, July 19-Aug. 3.

Embarkation for Cythera, by Watteau — A96

Paintings: 20c, Supper at Emmaus, by Caravaggio. 25c, Charles I Hunting, by Van Dyck, vert. 30c, The Maids of Honor, by Velazquez, vert. 45c, Rape of the Sabine Women, by Poussin. $1, Embarkation for Cythera, by Watteau. $3, Holy Family, by Rembrandt. $5, Girl before a Mirror, by Picasso, vert.

Perf. 14x13½, 13½x14

1980, June Litho.

669	A96	20c	multicolored	16	16
670	A96	25c	multicolored	20	20
671	A96	30c	multicolored	22	22
672	A96	45c	multicolored	35	35
673	A96	$1	multicolored	80	80
674	A96	$5	multicolored	4.00	4.00
			Nos. 669-674 (6)	5.73	5.73

Souvenir Sheet

675	A96	$3	multicolored	2.50	2.50

Queen Mother Elizabeth, 80th Birthday A97

1980, Aug. 4 *Perf. 12, 14*

676	A97	40c	multicolored	40	40
677	A97	$2.50	multicolored	2.50	2.50

Souvenir Sheet

678	A97	$3	multicolored	3.50	3.50

Tinkerbell — A98

Designs: Scenes from Disney's Peter Pan.

1980, Oct. 1 Litho. *Perf. 11*

679	A98	½c	multicolored	15	15
680	A98	1c	multicolored	15	15
681	A98	2c	multicolored	15	15
682	A98	3c	multicolored	15	15
683	A98	4c	multicolored	15	15
684	A98	5c	multicolored	15	15
685	A98	10c	multicolored	15	15
686	A98	$2	multicolored	1.60	1.60
687	A98	$2.50	multicolored	2.00	2.00
			Set value	3.90	3.90

Souvenir Sheet

688	A98	$4	multicolored	3.50	3.50

Christmas.

Douglas Bay — A99

1981, Feb. 12 Litho. *Perf. 14*

689	A99	20c	shown	15	15
690	A99	30c	Valley of Desolation	22	22
691	A99	40c	Emerald Pool, vert.	30	30
692	A99	$3	Indian River, vert.	2.25	2.25

Souvenir Sheet

693	A99	$4	Trafalgar Falls	3.00	3.00

Pluto and Fifi — A100

Design: $4, Pluto in Blue Note (1947 cartoon).

1981, Apr. 30 Litho. *Perf. 13½x14*

694	A100	$2	multicolored	2.00	2.00

Souvenir Sheet

695	A100	$4	multicolored	4.00	4.00

50th anniversary of Walt Disney's Pluto.

Forest Thrush A101

1981, Apr. 30 *Perf. 14*

696	A101	20c	shown	16	16
697	A101	30c	Stolid flycatcher	24	24
698	A101	40c	Blue-hooded euphonia	32	32
699	A101	$5	Lesser antillean peewee	4.00	4.00

Souvenir Sheet

700	A101	$3	Sisserou parrot	2.25	2.25

Royal Wedding Issue

Common Design Type

1981, June 16 Litho. *Perf. 14*

701	CD331	45c	Couple	35	35
702	CD331	60c	Windsor Castle	45	45
703	CD331	$4	Charles	3.00	3.00

Souvenir Sheet

704	CD331	$5	Helicopter	3.00	3.00

Booklet

705	CD331		11.75	
a.	Pane of 6 (3x25c, Lady Diana, 3x$2, Charles)		6.75	
b.	Pane of 1, $5, Couple		5.00	

No. 705 contains imperf., self-adhesive stamps.

Nos. 701-703 also printed in sheets of 5 plus label, perf. 12, in changed colors.

Elves Repairing Santa's Sleigh — A102

Christmas: Scenes from Walt Disney's Santa's Workshop.

1981, Nov. 2 Litho. *Perf. 14*

706	A102	½c	multicolored	15	15
707	A102	1c	multicolored	15	15
708	A102	2c	multicolored	15	15
709	A102	3c	multicolored	15	15
710	A102	4c	multicolored	15	15
711	A102	5c	multicolored	15	15
712	A102	10c	multicolored	15	15
713	A102	45c	multicolored	35	35
714	A102	$5	multicolored	3.75	3.75
			Set value	4.45	4.45

Souvenir Sheet

715	A102	$4	multicolored	4.00	4.00

Ixora A103

1981, Dec. 1 Litho. *Perf. 14*

716 A103 1c shown 15 15
717 A103 2c Flamboyant 15 15
718 A103 4c Poinsettia 15 15
719 A103 5c Sabinea carinalis 15 15
720 A103 8c Annatto roucou 15 15
721 A103 10c Passion fruit 15 15
722 A103 15c Breadfruit 15 15
723 A103 20c Allamanda butter-cup 15 15
724 A103 25c Cashew 18 18
725 A103 35c Soursop 25 25
726 A103 40c Bougainvillea 30 30
727 A103 45c Anthurium 32 32
728 A103 60c Cacao 45 45
729 A103 90c Pawpaw tree 60 60
730 A103 $1 Coconut palm 70 70
731 A103 $2 Coffee tree 1.40 1.40
732 A103 $5 Lobster claw 3.50 3.50
a. Perf. 12½x12 ('85) 2.25 2.25
733 A103 $10 Banana fig 7.00 7.00
Nos. 716-733 (18) 15.90 15.90

Nos. 721, 730, 732-733 exist dated "1984," Nos. 721-722, 728, 732 "1985."
For overprints, see Nos. 852-853.

Intl. Year of the Disabled — A104

Bathers, by Picasso — A105

1981, Dec. 22 Litho. *Perf. 14*

734 A104 45c Ramp curb 30 30
735 A104 60c Bus steps 40 40
736 A104 75c Hand-operated car 50 50
737 A104 $4 Bus lift 2.75 2.75

Souvenir Sheet

738 A104 $5 Elevator buttons 3.50 3.50

1981, Dec. 30 *Perf. 14½*

739 A105 45c Olga in Armchair 35 35
740 A105 60c shown 45 45
741 A105 75c Woman in Spanish Costume 55 55
742 A105 $4 Dog and Cock 3.00 3.00

Souvenir Sheet

743 A105 $5 Sleeping Peasants 3.75 3.75

1982 World Cup Soccer — A106

Designs: Various Disney characters playing soccer.

1982, Jan. 29 *Perf. 14*

744 A106 ½c multicolored 15 15
745 A106 1c multicolored 15 15
746 A106 2c multicolored 15 15
747 A106 3c multicolored 15 15
748 A106 4c multicolored 15 15
749 A106 5c multicolored 15 15
750 A106 10c multicolored 15 15
751 A106 60c multicolored 45 45
752 A106 $5 multicolored 3.75 3.75
Set value 4.50 4.50

Souvenir Sheet

753 A106 $4 multicolored 3.50 3.50

Golden Days, by Norman Rockwell — A107

1982, Mar. 10 Litho. *Perf. 14x13½*

754 A107 10c shown 15 15
755 A107 25c The Morning News 18 18
756 A107 45c The Marbles Champ 35 35
757 A107 $1 Speeding Along 75 75

Intl. Decade for Women (1975-85) A108

Famous Women: 10c, Elma Napier (1890-1973), first woman elected to Legislative Council in British West Indies, 1940. 45c, Margaret Mead (1901-1978), anthropologist. $1, Mabel Caudiron (1909-1968), musician and folk historian. $3, Florence Nightingale, founder of modern nursing. $4, Eleanor Roosevelt.

1982, Apr. 15 Litho. *Perf. 14*

758 A108 10c multicolored 15 15
759 A108 45c multicolored 35 35
760 A108 $1 multicolored 75 75
761 A108 $4 multicolored 3.00 3.00

Souvenir Sheet

762 A108 $3 multicolored 2.25 2.25

George Washington and Independence Hall, Philadelphia — A109

Washington or Roosevelt and: 60c, Capitol Building. 90c, The Surrender of Cornwallis, by John Trumbull. $2, Dam construction during New Deal (mural by William Gropper). $5, Washington, Roosevelt.

1982, May 1 *Perf. 14½*

763 A109 45c multicolored 35 35
764 A109 60c multicolored 45 45
765 A109 90c multicolored 70 70
766 A109 $2 multicolored 1.50 1.50

Souvenir Sheet

767 A109 $5 multicolored 4.00 4.00

George Washington's 250th birth anniv. and Franklin D. Roosevelt's birth cent.

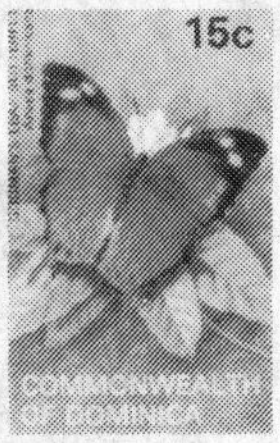

Godman's Leaf Butterfly — A110

1982, June 1 Litho. *Perf. 14*

768 A110 15c shown 15 15
769 A110 45c Zebra 45 45
770 A110 60c Mimic 60 60
771 A110 $3 Red rim 2.00 2.00

Souvenir Sheet

772 A110 $5 Southern dagger tail 3.75 3.75

Princess Diana Issue

Common Design Type

1982, July 1 Litho. *Perf. 14½x14*

773 CD332 45c Buckingham Palace 35 35
774 CD332 $2 Engagement portrait 1.50 1.50
775 CD332 $4 Wedding 3.00 3.00

Souvenir Sheet

776 CD332 $5 Diana, diff. 3.75 3.75

Also issued in sheet of 5 plus label.
For overprints, see Nos. 782-785.

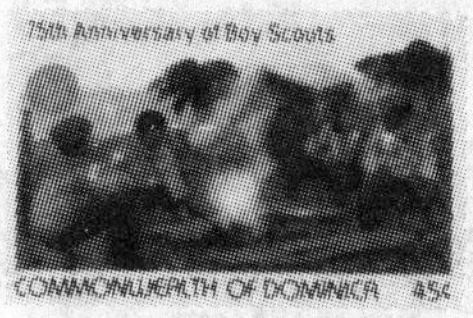

Scouting Year A111

1982, July 1 Litho. *Perf. 14*

777 A111 45c Cooking 35 35
778 A111 60c Meteorological study 45 45
779 A111 75c Sisserou parrot, cub scouts 55 55
780 A111 $3 Canoeing, Indian River 2.25 2.25

Souvenir Sheet

781 A111 $5 Flagbearer 3.75 3.75

Nos. 773-776 Overprinted: "ROYAL BABY / 21.6.82"

1982, Sept. 1 Litho. *Perf. 14½x14*

782 CD332 45c multicolored 35 35
783 CD332 $2 multicolored 1.50 1.50
784 CD332 $4 multicolored 3.00 3.00

Souvenir Sheet

785 CD332 $5 multicolored 3.75 3.75

Birth of Prince William of Wales, June 21.
Also issued in sheet of 5 plus label.

Christmas — A112

Holy Family Paintings by Raphael.

1982, Oct. 18 Litho. *Perf. 14*

786 A112 25c multicolored 18 18
787 A112 30c multicolored 22 22
788 A112 90c multicolored 70 70
789 A112 $4 multicolored 3.00 3.00

Souvenir Sheet

790 A112 $5 multicolored 3.75 3.75

Goosebeak Whale Eating Squid A113

1983, Feb. 15 Litho. *Perf. 14*

791 A113 45c shown 35 35
792 A113 60c Humpback whale 45 45
793 A113 75c Great right whale 55 55
794 A113 $3 Melonhead whale 2.25 2.25

Souvenir Sheet

795 A113 $5 Pygmy sperm whale 3.75 3.75

CD334

1983, Mar. 14

796 CD334 25c Banana industry 18 18
797 CD334 30c Road construction 22 22
798 CD334 90c Community nursing 70 70
799 CD334 $3 Basket weavers 2.25 2.25

Commonwealth Day.

World Communications Year — A114

1983, Apr. 18 Litho. *Perf. 14*

800 A114 45c Hurricane pattern, map 35 35
801 A114 60c Air-to-ship communication 45 45
802 A114 90c Columbia shuttle, dish antenna 70 70
803 A114 $2 Walkie-talkie 1.50 1.50

Souvenir Sheet

804 A114 $5 Satellite 3.75 3.75

Manned Flight Bicentenary A115

1983, July 19 Litho. *Perf. 15*

805 A115 45c Mayo Composite 35 35
806 A115 60c Macchi M-39 45 45
807 A115 90c Fairey Swordfish 70 70
808 A115 $4 Zeppelin LZ-3 3.00 3.00

Souvenir Sheet

809 A115 $5 Double Eagle II, vert. 3.75 3.75

Duesenberg SJ, 1935 A116

1983, Sept. 1 Litho. *Perf. 14*

810 A116 10c shown 15 15
811 A116 45c Studebaker Avanti, 1962 35 35
812 A116 60c Cord 812, 1936 45 45
813 A116 75c MG-TC, 1945 55 55
814 A116 90c Camaro 350-SS, 1967 70 70
815 A116 $3 Porsche 356, 1948 2.25 2.25
Nos. 810-815 (6) 4.45 4.45

Souvenir Sheet

816 A116 $5 Ferrari 312-T, 1975 3.75 3.75

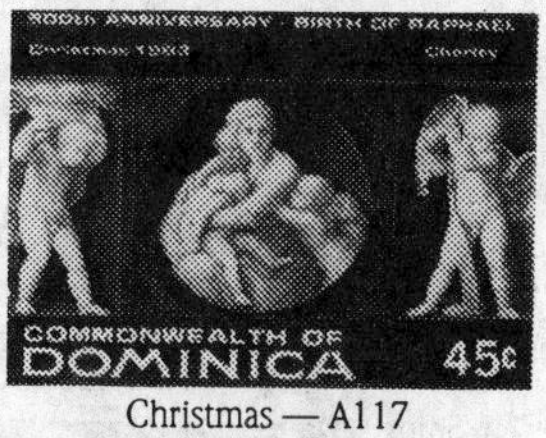

Christmas — A117

Raphael Paintings.

1983, Oct. 4 Litho. *Perf. 13½*

817 A117 45c multicolored 35 35
818 A117 60c multicolored 50 50
819 A117 90c multicolored 75 75
820 A117 $4 multicolored 3.25 3.25

Souvenir Sheet

821 A117 $5 multicolored 3.75 3.75

23rd Olympic Games, Los Angeles, July 28-Aug. 12 — A118

1984, Mar. Litho. *Perf. 14*

822 A118 30c Gymnastics 22 22
823 A118 45c Javelin 35 35
824 A118 60c Diving 52 52
825 A118 $4 Fencing 3.25 3.25

Souvenir Sheet

826 A118 $5 Equestrian 3.75 3.75

Local Birds A119

1984, May Litho.

827 A119 5c Plumbeous warbler 15 15
828 A119 45c Imperial parrot 42 42
829 A119 60c Blue-headed hummingbird 55 55
830 A119 90c Red-necked parrot 80 80

Souvenir Sheet

831 A119 $5 Roseate flamingoes 3.75 3.75

Easter — A120

Various Disney characters and Easter bunnies.

1984, Apr. 15 Litho. *Perf. 11*

832 A120 ½c multicolored 15 15
833 A120 1c multicolored 15 15
834 A120 2c multicolored 15 15
835 A120 3c multicolored 15 15
836 A120 4c multicolored 15 15
837 A120 5c multicolored 15 15
838 A120 10c multicolored 15 15
839 A120 $2 multicolored 1.60 1.60
840 A120 $4 multicolored 3.25 3.25
Set value 5.20 5.20

Souvenir Sheet

Perf. 14

841 A120 $5 multicolored 4.25 4.25

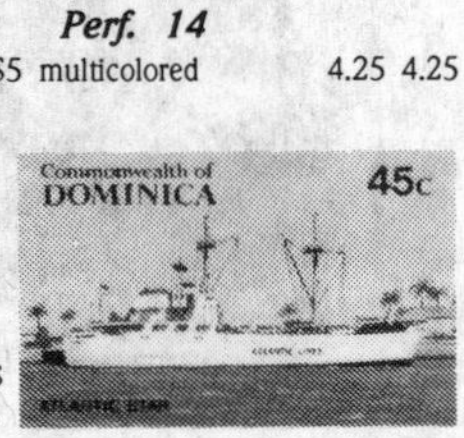

Ships A121

1984, June 14 Litho. *Perf. 14*

842 A121 45c Atlantic Star 34 34
843 A121 60c Atlantic 45 45
844 A121 90c Carib fishing pirogue 68 68
845 A121 $4 Norway 3.00 3.00

Souvenir Sheet

846 A121 $5 Santa Maria 3.75 3.75

Market value for a particular scarce stamp may remain relatively low if few collectors want it.

Local Plants — A122

Correggio & Degas — A122a

1984, Aug. 13

847 A122 45c Guzmania lingulata 34 34
848 A122 60c Pitcairnia angustifolia 45 45
849 A122 75c Tillandsia fasciculata 56 56
850 A122 $3 Aechmea smithiorum 2.25 2.25

Souvenir Sheet

851 A122 $5 Tillandsia utriculata 3.75 3.75

Ausipex Intl. Stamp Exhibition.

Nos. 721, 732 Overprinted: "19th UPU / CONGRESS HAMBURG"

1984 Litho. *Perf. 14*

852 A103 10c multicolored 15 15
853 A103 $5 multicolored 3.75 3.75

1984, Nov. Litho. *Perf. 15*

Correggio: 25c, Virgin and Child with Young St. John. 60c, Christ Bids Farewell to the Virgin Mary. 90c, Do Not Touch Me. $4, The Mystical Marriage of St. Catherine. No. 862, Adoration of the Magi. Degas, horiz.: 30c, Before the Start. 45c, On the Racecourse. $1, Jockeys at the Flagpole. $3, Racehorses at Longchamp. No. 863, Self-portrait.

854 A122a 25c multicolored 18 18
855 A122a 30c multicolored 22 22
856 A122a 45c multicolored 34 34
857 A122a 60c multicolored 45 45
858 A122a 90c multicolored 68 68
859 A122a $1 multicolored 75 75
860 A122a $3 multicolored 2.25 2.25
861 A122a $4 multicolored 3.00 3.00
Nos. 854-861 (8) 7.87 7.87

Souvenir Sheets

862 A122a $5 multicolored 3.75 3.75
863 A122a $5 multicolored 3.75 3.75

A123 A124

1984, Dec. *Perf. 14*

864 A123 30c Avro 748 22 22
865 A123 60c Twin Otter 45 45
866 A123 $1 Islander 75 75
867 A123 $3 Casa 2.25 2.25

Souvenir Sheet

868 A123 $5 Boeing 747 3.75 3.75

Intl. Civil Aviation Org., 40th anniv.

1984, Nov. Litho.

Scenes from various Donald Duck movies.

869 A124 45c multicolored 40 40
870 A124 60c multicolored 50 50
871 A124 90c multicolored 80 80
872 A124 $2 multicolored, perf. 12x12½ 1.75 1.75
873 A124 $4 multicolored 3.50 3.50
Nos. 869-873 (5) 6.95 6.95

Souvenir Sheet

Perf. 13½x14

874 A124 $5 multicolored 4.50 4.50

Christmas and 50th anniv. of Donald Duck.

Cats A125

1984, Nov. 12 Litho. *Perf. 15*

875 A125 10c Tabby 15 15
876 A125 15c Calico shorthair 15 15
877 A125 20c Siamese 15 15
878 A125 25c Manx 18 18
879 A125 45c Abyssinian 32 32
880 A125 60c Tortoise shell longhair 42 42
881 A125 $1 Rex 72 72
882 A125 $2 Persian 1.50 1.50
883 A125 $3 Himalayan 2.25 2.25
884 A125 $5 Burmese 3.50 3.50
Nos. 875-884 (10) 9.34 9.34

Souvenir Sheet

885 A125 $5 Gray Burmese, Persian, American shorthair 3.75 3.75

Girl Guides, 75th Anniv. A126

1985, Feb. 18 *Perf. 14*

886 A126 35c Lady Baden-Powell 25 25
887 A126 45c Inspecting Dominican troop 35 35
888 A126 60c With Dominican troop leaders 45 45
889 A126 $3 Lord and Lady Baden-Powell, vert. 2.25 2.25

Souvenir Sheet

890 A126 $5 Flag ceremony 3.75 3.75

John James Audubon A127

1985, Apr. 4

891 A127 45c King rails 35 35
892 A127 $1 Black-winged hawks, vert. 75 75
893 A127 $2 Broad-winged hawks, vert. 1.50 1.50
894 A127 $3 Ring-necked ducks 2.25 2.25

Souvenir Sheet

895 A127 $5 Reddish egrets, vert. 3.75 3.75

Nos. 891-894 exist vertically se-tenant with labels showing additional bird species.

See Nos. 965-969.

Duke of Edinburgh Awards, 1984 — A128

1985, Apr. 30

896 A128 45c Woman at computer terminal 35 35
897 A128 60c Medical staff, patient 45 45
898 A128 90c Runners 68 68
899 A128 $4 Family jogging 3.00 3.00

Souvenir Sheet

900 A128 $5 Duke of Edinburgh 3.75 3.75

Intl. Youth Year — A129

1985, July 8 Litho. *Perf. 14*

901 A129 45c Cricket match 30 30
902 A129 60c Environmental study, parrot 40 40
903 A129 $1 Stamp collecting 65 65
904 A129 $3 Boating, leisure 2.00 2.00

Souvenir Sheet

905 A129 $5 Youths join hands 3.25 3.25

Queen Mother, 85th Birthday — A130

Johann Sebastian Bach — A131

1985, July 15

906 A130 60c Visiting Sadlers Wells 40 40
907 A130 $1 Fishing 65 65
908 A130 $3 At Clarence House, 1984 2.00 2.00

Souvenir Sheet

909 A130 $5 Attending Windsor Castle Garter Ceremony 4.00 4.00

1985, Sept. 2

Portrait, signature, music from Explication and: 45c, Cornett 60c, Coiled trumpet. $1, Piccolo. $3, Violoncello piccolo.

910 A131 45c multicolored 30 30
911 A131 60c multicolored 40 40
912 A131 $1 multicolored 65 65
913 A131 $3 multicolored 2.50 2.50

Souvenir Sheet

914 A131 $5 Portrait 3.75 3.75

State Visit of Elizabeth II, Oct. 25 — A132

1985, Oct. 25 *Perf. 14½*

915 A132 60c Flags of U.K., Dominica 40 40
916 A132 $1 Elizabeth II, vert. 70 70
917 A132 $4 HMS Britannia 3.00 3.00

Souvenir Sheet

918 A132 $5 Map 3.75 3.75

Mark Twain A133

Disney characters in Tom Sawyer.

1985, Nov. 11 Litho. *Perf. 14*

919 A133 20c multicolored 15 15
920 A133 60c multicolored 45 45
921 A133 $1 multicolored 75 75
922 A133 $1.50 multicolored 1.50 1.50
923 A133 $2 multicolored 2.00 2.00
Nos. 919-923 (5) 4.85 4.85

Souvenir Sheet

924 A133 $5 multicolored 4.25 4.25

Christmas.

The Brothers Grimm — A134

Disney characters in Little Red Cap (Little Red Riding Hood).

1985, Nov. 11

925	A134	10c	multicolored	15	15
926	A134	45c	multicolored	38	38
927	A134	90c	multicolored	80	80
928	A134	$1	multicolored	90	90
929	A134	$3	multicolored	2.75	2.75
			Nos. 925-929 (5)	4.98	4.98

Souvenir Sheet

930	A134	$5	multicolored	4.25	4.25

Christmas.

UN, 40th Anniv. A135

Stamps of UN, famous men and events: 45c, No. 442 and Lord Baden-Powell. $2, No. 157 and Maimonides (1135-1204) Judaic scholar. $3, No. 278 and Sir Rowland Hill. $5, Apollo-Soyuz Mission, 10th anniv.

1985, Nov. 22 *Perf. 14½*

931	A135	45c	multicolored	32	32
932	A135	$2	multicolored	1.50	1.50
933	A135	$3	multicolored	2.25	2.25

Souvenir Sheet

934	A135	$5	multicolored	3.75	3.75

1986 World Cup Soccer Championships, Mexico — A136

Various soccer plays.

1986, Mar. 26 *Perf. 14*

935	A136	45c	multicolored	32	32
936	A136	60c	multicolored	45	45
937	A136	$1	multicolored	75	75
938	A136	$3	multicolored	2.25	2.25

Souvenir Sheet

939	A136	$5	multicolored	3.75	3.75

For overprints, see Nos. 974-978.

Statue of Liberty, Cent. A137

Statue and: 15c, New York police pursuing river pirates, c. 1890. 25c, Police patrol boat. 45c, Hoboken Ferry Terminal, c. 1890. $4, Holland Tunnel.

1986, Mar. 26

940	A137	15c	multicolored	15	15
941	A137	25c	multicolored	18	18
942	A137	45c	multicolored	32	32
943	A137	$4	multicolored	3.00	3.00

Souvenir Sheet

944	A137	$5	Statue, vert.	3.75	3.75

Halley's Comet A138

Designs: 5c, Jantal Mantar Observatory, Delhi, India, Nasir al Din al Tusi (1201-1274), astronomer. 10c, US Bell X-1 rocket plane breaking sound barrier. 45c, Astronomicum Caesareum, 1540, manuscript diagram of comet's trajectory, 1531. $4, Mark Twain, comet appeared at birth and death. $5, Comet.

1986, Apr. 17

945	A138	5c	multicolored	15	15
946	A138	10c	multicolored	15	15
947	A138	45c	multicolored	32	32
948	A138	$4	multicolored	3.00	3.00

Souvenir Sheet

949	A138	$5	multicolored	3.75	3.75

For overprints, see Nos. 984-988.

Queen Elizabeth II, 60th Birthday

Common Design Type

1986, Apr. 21 **Litho.** *Perf. 14*

950	CD339	2c	Wedding, 1947	15	15
951	CD339	$1	With Pope John Paul II, 1982	75	75
952	CD339	$4	Royal visit, 1971	3.00	3.00

Souvenir Sheet

953	CD339	$5	Age 10	3.75	3.75

AMERIPEX '86 — A139

Walt Disney characters involved in stamp collecting.

1986, May 22 *Perf. 11*

954	A139	25c	Mickey Mouse and Pluto	18	18
955	A139	45c	Donald Duck	32	32
956	A139	60c	Chip-n-Dale	45	45
957	A139	$4	Donald, nephews	3.00	3.00

Souvenir Sheet

Perf. 14

958	A139	$5	Uncle Scrooge	3.75	3.75

British Monarchs — A140

1986, June 9 *Perf. 14*

959	A140	10c	William I	15	15
960	A140	40c	Richard II	30	30
961	A140	50c	Henry VIII	38	38
962	A140	$1	Charles II	75	75
963	A140	$2	Queen Anne	1.50	1.50
964	A140	$4	Queen Victoria	3.00	3.00
			Nos. 959-964 (6)	6.08	6.08

Audubon Type of 1985

Perf. 12½x12, 12x12½

1986, June 18

965	A127	25c	Black-throated diver	20	20
966	A127	60c	Great blue heron	45	45
967	A127	90c	Yellow-crowned night heron	65	65
968	A127	$4	Shoveler duck	3.00	3.00

Souvenir Sheet

Perf. 14

969	A127	$5	Goose	3.75	3.75

Nos. 966-967 vert.

Royal Wedding Issue, 1986

Common Design Type

1986, July 23 *Perf. 14*

970	CD340	45c	Couple	32	32
971	CD340	60c	Prince Andrew	45	45
972	CD340	$4	Prince, aircraft	3.00	3.00

Souvenir Sheet

973	CD340	$5	Couple, diff.	3.75	3.75

Nos. 935-939 Ovptd. "WINNERS / Argentina 3 / W. Germany 2" in Gold

1986, Sept. 15 **Litho.** *Perf. 14*

974	A136	45c	multicolored	32	32
975	A136	60c	multicolored	45	45
976	A136	$1	multicolored	75	75
977	A136	$3	multicolored	2.25	2.25

Souvenir Sheet

978	A136	$5	multicolored	3.75	3.75

Paintings by Albrecht Durer
A141 A142

1986, Dec. 2 **Litho.** *Perf. 14*

979	A141	45c	Virgin in Prayer	35	35
980	A141	60c	Madonna and Child	48	48
981	A141	$1	Madonna and Child, diff.	80	80
982	A141	$3	Madonna and Child with St. Anne	2.40	2.40

Souvenir Sheet

983	A142	$5	Nativity	4.00	4.00

Nos. 945-949 Printed with Halley's Comet Logo in Black or Silver

1986, Dec. 16

984	A138	5c	multicolored	15	15
985	A138	10c	multicolored	15	15
986	A138	45c	multicolored	35	35
987	A138	$4	multicolored	3.60	3.60

Souvenir Sheet

988	A138	$5	multi (S)	4.00	4.00

Birds — A143

1987, Jan. 20 **Litho.** *Perf. 15*

989	A143	1c	Broad-winged hawk	15	15
990	A143	2c	Ruddy quail dove	15	15
991	A143	5c	Red-necked pigeon	15	15
992	A143	10c	Green heron	15	15
993	A143	15c	Common gallinule	15	15
994	A143	20c	Ringed kingfisher	16	16
995	A143	25c	Brown pelican	20	20
996	A143	35c	White-tailed tropicbird	28	28
997	A143	45c	Red-legged thrush	35	35
998	A143	60c	Purple throated carib	48	48
999	A143	90c	Magnificent frigatebird	72	72
1000	A143	$1	Trembler	80	80
1001	A143	$2	Black-capped petrel	1.60	1.60
1002	A143	$5	Barn owl	4.00	4.00
1003	A143	$10	Imperial parrot	8.00	8.00
			Nos. 989-1003 (15)	17.34	17.34

Inscribed "1989" and "Questa"

1989, Aug. 31 **Litho.** *Perf. 14*

990a	A143	2c	15	15
991a	A143	5c	15	15
992a	A143	10c	15	15
993a	A143	15c	15	15
994a	A143	20c	16	16
995a	A143	25c	20	20
996a	A143	35c	28	28
997a	A143	45c	35	35
998a	A143	60c	48	48
1000a	A143	$1	80	80
1001a	A143	$2	1.60	1.60
1002a	A143	$5	4.00	4.00
1003a	A143	$10	8.00	8.00
		Nos. 990a-1003a (13)	16.47	16.47

Inscribed "1989" and "Questa"

1990 **Litho.** *Perf. 12*

990b	A143	2c	15	15
991b	A143	5c	15	15
992b	A143	10c	15	15
993b	A143	15c	15	15
994b	A143	20c	16	16
995b	A143	25c	20	20
996b	A143	35c	28	28
997b	A143	45c	35	35
998b	A143	60c	48	48
1000b	A143	$1	80	80
1001b	A143	$2	1.60	1.60
1002b	A143	$5	4.00	4.00
1003b	A143	$10	8.00	8.00
		Nos. 990b-1003b (13)	16.47	16.47

Inscribed "1989" and "Questa"

1991 **Litho.** *Perf. 13x11½*

990c	A143	2c	15	15
991c	A143	5c	15	15
992c	A143	10c	15	15
993c	A143	15c	15	15
994c	A143	20c	16	16
995c	A143	25c	20	20
996c	A143	35c	28	28
997c	A143	45c	35	35
998c	A143	60c	48	48
1000c	A143	$1	80	80
1001c	A143	$2	1.60	1.60
1002c	A143	$5	4.00	4.00
1003c	A143	$10	8.00	8.00
		Nos. 990c-1003c (13)	16.47	16.47

Paintings by Marc Chagall (1887-1985) A144

Designs: 25c, Artist and His Model. 35c, Midsummer Night's Dream. 45c, Joseph the Shepherd. 60c, the Cellist. 90c, Woman with Pigs. $1, the Blue Circus. $3, For Vava. $4, the Rider. No. 1012, Purim. No. 1013, Firebird design for the curtain of the Stravinsky Ballet production.

1987, Mar. 2 *Perf. 14*

1004	A144	25c	multicolored	20	20
1005	A144	35c	multicolored	28	28
1006	A144	45c	multicolored	35	35
1007	A144	60c	multicolored	48	48
1008	A144	90c	multicolored	72	72
1009	A144	$1	multicolored	80	80
1010	A144	$3	multicolored	2.40	2.40
1011	A144	$4	multicolored	3.20	3.20

Size: 110x95mm

Imperf

1012	A144	$5	multicolored	4.00	4.00
1013	A144	$5	multicolored	4.00	4.00
			Nos. 1004-1013 (10)	16.43	16.43

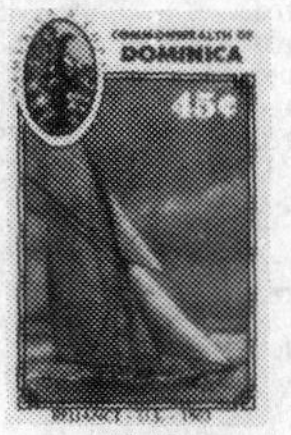

A145

Conch Shells — A147

America's Cup A146

1987, Feb. 5 *Perf. 15*

1014 A145 45c Reliance, 1903 35 35
1015 A145 60c Freedom, 1980 48 48
1016 A145 $1 Mischief, 1881 80 80
1017 A145 $3 Australia, 1977 2.40 2.40

Souvenir Sheet

1018 A146 $5 Courageous, Australia, 1977 4.00 4.00

1987, Apr. 13 **Litho.**

Designs: 35c, Morch Poulsen's triton. 45c, Swainson globe purple sea snail. 60c, Banded tulip. No. 1022, Lamarck deltoid rock shell. No. 1023, Junoia volute.

1019 A147 35c multicolored 28 28
1020 A147 45c multicolored 35 35
1021 A147 60c multicolored 48 48
1022 A147 $5 multicolored 4.00 4.00

Souvenir Sheet

1023 A147 $5 multicolored 4.00 4.00

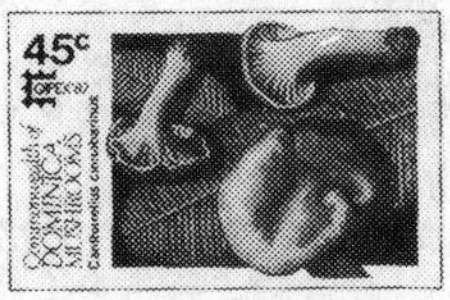

CAPEX '87 — A148

Mushrooms.

1987, June 15 **Litho.** *Perf. 14*

1024 A148 45c Cantharellus cinnabarinus 35 35
1025 A148 60c Boletellus cubenis 60 60
1026 A148 $2 Eccilia cystiophorus 2.00 2.00
1027 A148 $3 Xerocomus guadelupae 3.00 3.00

Souvenir Sheet

1028 A148 $5 Gymnopilus chrysopellus 3.75 3.75

A149

Discovery of America, 500th Anniv. (in 1992) A150

Explorations of Christopher Columbus: 10c, Discovery of Dominica. 15c, Ships greeted by Carib Indians. 45c, Claiming New World for Spain. 60c, Wrecking of the Santa Maria. 90c, Fleet setting sail. $1, Sighting land. $3, Trading with the Indians. No. 1036, First settlement. No. 1037, Arrival of Second Fleet at Dominica, Nov. 3, 1493. No. 1038, Map of exploration of the Leeward Islands.

1987, July 27 *Perf. 15*

1029 A149 10c multicolored 15 15
1030 A149 15c multicolored 15 15
1031 A149 45c multicolored 35 35
1032 A149 60c multicolored 45 45
1033 A149 90c multicolored 68 68
1034 A149 $1 multicolored 75 75
1035 A149 $3 multicolored 2.25 2.25
1036 A149 $5 multicolored 3.75 3.75
Nos. 1029-1036 (8) 8.53 8.53

Souvenir Sheets

1037 A150 $5 multicolored 3.75 3.75
1038 A150 $5 multicolored 3.75 3.75

For overprints, see Nos. 1083-1084.

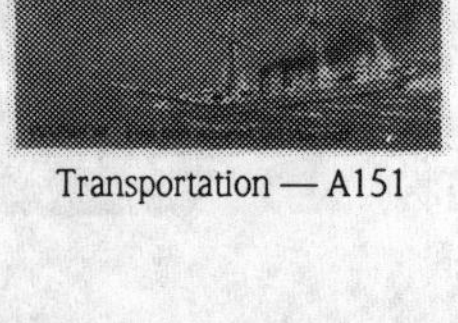

Transportation — A151

Designs: 10c, Warrior, first iron-clad warship. 15c, Maglev-MLU 001, fastest passenger train. 25c, Clipper Flying Cloud, fastest New York to San Francisco voyage, 1852. 35c, First elevated railway, New York City. 45c, Tom Thumb, first U.S. passenger train locomotive. 60c, Joshua Slocum, first solo circumnavigation of the world in a sloop. 90c, Se-Land Commerce, fastest Pacific crossing. $1, First cable car, San Francisco. $3, Orient Express. $4, The North River Steamboat of Clermont, invented by Robert Fulton, first successful commercial steamboat.

1987 **Litho.** *Perf. 14*

1039 A151 10c multicolored 15 15
1040 A151 15c multicolored 15 15
1041 A151 25c multi, vert. 18 18
1042 A151 35c multi, vert. 25 25
1043 A151 45c multicolored 32 32
1044 A151 60c multi, vert. 45 45
1045 A151 90c multi, vert. 65 65
1046 A151 $1 multicolored 72 72
1047 A151 $3 multicolored 2.15 2.15
1048 A151 $4 multicolored 2.90 2.90
Nos. 1039-1048 (10) 7.92 7.92

Issue dates: 10c, 5c, 45c, 60c, $4, Sept. 28; others Aug. 1.

For overprints, see Nos. 1081-1082.

Christmas — A152

Paintings (details): 20c, Virgin and Child with St. Anne, by Durer. 25c, The Virgin and Child, by Murillo. $2, Madonna and Child, by Vincenzo Foppa (c. 1427-1516). $4, Madonna and Child, by Paolo Veronese (1528-1588). $5, Angel of the Annunciation, anonymous.

1987, Nov. 16

1049 A152 20c multicolored 15 15
1050 A152 25c multicolored 18 18
1051 A152 $2 multicolored 1.45 1.45
1052 A152 $4 multicolored 2.90 2.90

Souvenir Sheet

1053 A152 $5 multicolored 3.60 3.60

Mickey Mouse, 60th Anniv. A153

Disney theme parks and trains: 20c, People Mover, Disney World. 25c, Horse-drawn Trolley, Disneyland. 45c, Roger E. Broggie, Disney World. 60c, Big Thunder Mountain, Disneyland. 90c, Walter E. Disney, Disneyland. $1, Monorail, Disney World. $3, Casey Jr. from Dumbo. $4, Lilly Belle, Disney World. No. 1062, Rainbow Caverns Mine Train, Disneyland, horiz. No. 1063, Toy train from movie Out of Scale, horiz.

1987, Dec. 7 **Litho.** *Perf. 14*

1054 A153 20c multicolored 15 15
1055 A153 25c multicolored 20 20
1056 A153 45c multicolored 35 35
1057 A153 60c multicolored 48 48
1058 A153 90c multicolored 65 65
1059 A153 $1 multicolored 75 75
1060 A153 $3 multicolored 2.25 2.25
1061 A153 $4 multicolored 3.00 3.00
Nos. 1054-1061 (8) 7.83 7.83

Souvenir Sheets

1062 A153 $5 multicolored 3.80 3.80
1063 A153 $5 multicolored 3.80 3.80

40th Wedding Anniv. of Queen Elizabeth II and Prince Philip — A154

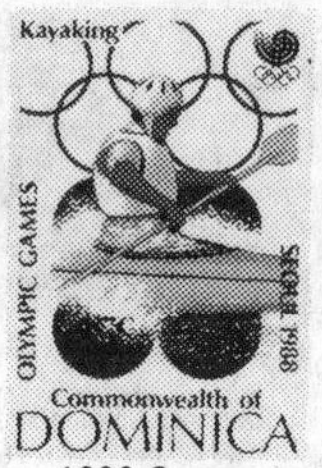

1988 Summer Olympics, Seoul — A155

1988, Feb. 15 **Litho.** *Perf. 14*

1064 A154 45c Couple, wedding party, 1947 35 35
1065 A154 60c Elizabeth, Charles, c. 1952 45 45
1066 A154 $1 Royal Family, c. 1952 78 78
1067 A154 $3 Queen with tiara, c. 1960 2.30 2.30

Souvenir Sheet

1068 A154 $5 Elizabeth, 1947 3.80 3.80

1988, Mar. 15

1069 A155 45c Kayaking 35 35
1070 A155 60c Tae kwon-do 45 45
1071 A155 $1 Diving 78 78
1072 A155 $3 Parallel bars 2.30 2.30

Souvenir Sheet

1073 A155 $5 Soccer 3.80 3.80

Reunion '88 Tourism Campaign A156

1988, Apr. 13 **Litho.** *Perf. 15*

1074 A156 10c Carib Indian, vert. 15 15
1075 A156 25c Mountainous interior 20 20
1076 A156 35c Indian River, vert. 28 28
1077 A156 60c Belaire dancer, vert. 45 45
1078 A156 90c The Boiling Lake, vert. 68 68
1079 A156 $3 Coral reef 2.25 2.25
Nos. 1074-1079 (6) 4.01 4.01

Souvenir Sheet

1080 A156 $5 Belaire dancer, diff., vert. 3.80 3.80

Independence, 10th anniv.

Nos. 1046-1047, 1037-1038 Ovptd. for Philatelic Exhibitions in Black

a FINLANDIA 88

b INDEPENDENCE 40

c OLYMPHILEX '88

d Praga '88

1988, June 1 **Litho.** *Perf. 14*

1081 A151(a) $1 multi 75 75
1082 A151(b) $3 multi 2.25 2.25

Souvenir Sheets

Perf. 15

1083 A150(c) $5 multi 3.75 3.75
1084 A150(d) $5 multi 3.75 3.75

Miniature Sheet

Rain Forest Flora and Fauna — A157

Designs: a, White-tailed tropicbirds. b, Blue-throated euphonia. c, Smooth-billed ani. d, Scaly-breasted thrasher. e, Purple-throated carib. f, Southern daggertail and Clench's hairstreak. g, Trembler. h, Imperial parrot. i, Mangrove cuckoo. j, Hercules beetle. k, Orion. l, Red-necked parrot. m, Tillandsia. n, Polystacha luteola and bananaquit. o, False chameleon. p, Iguana. q, Hypolimnas. r, Green-throated carib. s, Heliconia. t, Agouti.

1988, July 25 *Perf. 14½*

1085 Sheet of 20 7.00 7.00
a.-t. A157 45c any single 35 35

Intl. Fund for Agricultural Development (IFAD), 10th Anniv. — A158

1988, Sept. 5 **Litho.** *Perf. 14*

1086 A158 45c Hen house 35 35
1087 A158 60c Pig farm 45 45
1088 A158 90c Cattle 70 70
1089 A158 $3 Black-belly sheep 2.25 2.25

Souvenir Sheet

1090 A158 $5 Mixed crops, vert. 3.75 3.75

Entertainers — A159

1988, Sept. 8

1091 A159 10c Gary Cooper 15 15
1092 A159 35c Josephine Baker 28 28
1093 A159 45c Maurice Chevalier 35 35
1094 A159 60c James Cagney 45 45
1095 A159 $1 Clark Gable 75 75
1096 A159 $2 Louis Armstrong 1.50 1.50
1097 A159 $3 Liberace 2.25 2.25
1098 A159 $4 Spencer Tracy 3.00 3.00
Nos. 1091-1098 (8) 8.73 8.73

Souvenir Sheets

1099 A159 $5 Elvis Presley 3.75 3.75
1100 A159 $5 Humphrey Bogart 3.75 3.75

Flowering Trees and Shrubs A160

1988, Sept. 29 **Litho.** *Perf. 14*

1101 A160 15c Sapodilla 15 15
1102 A160 20c Tangerine 15 15
1103 A160 25c Avocado pear 18 18
1104 A160 45c Amherstia 35 35
1105 A160 90c Lipstick tree 68 68
1106 A160 $1 Cannonball tree 75 75
1107 A160 $3 Saman 2.25 2.25
1108 A160 $4 Pineapple 3.00 3.00
Nos. 1101-1108 (8) 7.51 7.51

Souvenir Sheets

1109 A160 $5 Lignum vitae 3.75 3.75
1110 A160 $5 Sea grape 3.75 3.75

Paintings by Titian — A161

Designs: 25c, Jacopo Strada, c. 1567. 35c, Titian's Daughter Lavinia, c. 1565. 45c, Andrea Navagero, c. 1515. 60c, Judith with Head of Holoferenes, c. 1570. $1, Emilia di Spilimbergo, c. 1560. $2, Martyrdom of St. Lawrence, c. 1548. $3, Salome With the Head of St. John the Baptist, 1560. $4, St. John the Baptist, c. 1540. No. 1119, Self-portrait, c. 1555. No. 1120, Sisyphus, 1549.

1988, Oct. 10 Litho. *Perf. 13½x14*

1111	A161	25c multicolored	18	18
1112	A161	35c multicolored	28	28
1113	A161	45c multicolored	35	35
1114	A161	60c multicolored	45	45
1115	A161	$1 multicolored	75	75
1116	A161	$2 multicolored	1.50	1.50
1117	A161	$3 multicolored	2.25	2.25
1118	A161	$4 multicolored	3.00	3.00
		Nos. 1111-1118 (8)	8.76	8.76

Souvenir Sheets

1119	A161	$5 multicolored	3.75	3.75
1120	A161	$5 multicolored	3.75	3.75

Independence, 10th Anniv. — A162

John F. Kennedy — A163

1988, Oct. 31 Litho. *Perf. 14*

1121	A162	20c Imperial parrot	15	15
1122	A162	45c No. 1, landscape	35	35
1123	A162	$2 No. 602, waterfall	1.50	1.50
1124	A162	$3 Carib wood	2.25	2.25

Souvenir Sheet

1125	A162	$5 Natl. band performing	3.75	3.75

Nos. 1122-1123 horiz.

1988, Nov. 22

1126	A163	20c With Jackie	15	15
1127	A163	25c Sailing Vicuna	20	20
1128	A163	$2 Walking in Hyannis Port	1.50	1.50
1129	A163	$4 Berlin Wall speech	3.00	3.00

Souvenir Sheet

1130	A163	$5 Portrait	3.75	3.75

Nos. 1126-1128 horiz.

Miniature Sheet

Christmas, Mickey Mouse 60th Anniv. — A164

Designs: No. 1131a, Huey, Dewey and Louie. No. 1131b, Daisy Duck. No. 1131c, Winnie-the-Pooh. No. 1131d, Goofy. No. 1131e, Donald Duck. No. 1131f, Mickey Mouse. No. 1131g, Minnie Mouse. No. 1131h, Chip-n-Dale. No. 1132, Mickey, Morty and Ferdy. No. 1133, Characters visiting shopping mall Santa.

1988, Dec. 1 *Perf. 13½x14*

1131	A164	Sheet of 8	3.60	3.60
a.-h.		60c any single	45	45

Souvenir Sheets

1132	A164	$6 multi	4.50	4.50
1133	A164	$6 multi, horiz.	4.50	4.50

UN Declaration of Human Rights, 40th Anniv. A165

Designs: $3, Flag of Sweden and Raoul Wallenberg, who helped save 100,000 Jews in Budapest from deportation to Nazi concentration camps. $5, Human Rights Flame.

1988, Dec. 12 *Perf. 14*

1134	A165	$3 multicolored	2.25	2.25

Souvenir Sheet

1135	A165	$5 multi, vert.	3.75	3.75

Coastal Game Fish A166

1988, Dec. 22 Litho. *Perf. 14*

1136	A166	10c Greater amberjack	15	15
1137	A166	15c Blue marlin	15	15
1138	A166	35c Cobia	28	28
1139	A166	45c Dolphin	35	35
1140	A166	60c Cero	45	45
1141	A166	90c Mahogany snapper	68	68
1142	A166	$3 Yellowfin tuna	2.25	2.25
1143	A166	$4 Rainbow parrotfish	3.00	3.00
		Nos. 1136-1143 (8)	7.31	7.31

Souvenir Sheets

1144	A166	$5 Manta ray	3.75	3.75
1145	A166	$5 Tarpon	3.75	3.75

Caribbean Insects and Reptiles A167

1988, Dec. 29

1146	A167	10c Leatherback turtle	15	15
1147	A167	25c Monarch butterfly	20	20
1148	A167	60c Green anole	45	45
1149	A167	$3 Praying mantis	2.25	2.25

Souvenir Sheet

1150	A167	$5 Hercules beetle	3.75	3.75

Nos. 1069-1072 Ovptd. for Olympic Winners

a. "Men's c-1,500m O. Heukrodt DDR"
b. "Women's Flyweight N.Y. Choo S. Korea"
c. "Women's Platform Y. Xu China"
d. "V. Artemov USSR"
e. "USSR defeated Brazil 3-2 on penalty kicks after a 1-1 tie"

1989, Mar. 20 Litho. *Perf. 14*

1151	A155(a)	45c multi	35	35
1152	A155(b)	60c multi	45	45
1153	A155(c)	$1 multi	78	78
1154	A155(d)	$3 multi	2.30	2.30

Souvenir Sheet

1155	A155(e)	$5 multi	3.80	3.80

Pre-Columbian Societies and Their Customs — A168

UPAE and discovery of America anniv. emblems and: 20c, Carib Indians canoeing. 35c, Bow hunting. $1, Canoe making. $3, Shield wrestling. $6, Dancing.

1989, May 8 Litho. *Perf. 14*

1156	A168	20c multicolored	15	15
1157	A168	35c multicolored	28	28
1158	A168	$1 multicolored	75	75
1159	A168	$3 multicolored	2.25	2.25

Souvenir Sheet

1160	A168	$6 multicolored	4.50	4.50

Discovery of America 500th anniv. (in 1992).

Paintings by Yokoyama Taikan (1868-1958) A169

Designs: 10c, Lao-tzu. 20c, Red Maple Leaves (panels 1-2). 45c, King Wen Learns a Lesson from His Cook. 60c, Red Maple Leaves (panels 3-4). $1, Wild Flowers. $2, Red Maple Leaves (panels 5-6). $3, Red Maple Leaves (panels 7-8). $4, The Indian Ceremony of Floating Lamps on the River. No. 1169, Innocence. No. 1170, Red Maple Leaves (4 panels).

1989, Aug. 8 Litho. *Perf. 13½x14*

1161	A169	10c multicolored	15	15
1162	A169	20c multicolored	15	15
1163	A169	45c multicolored	35	35
1164	A169	60c multicolored	45	45
1165	A169	$1 multicolored	75	75
1166	A169	$2 multicolored	1.50	1.50
1167	A169	$3 multicolored	2.25	2.25
1168	A169	$4 multicolored	3.00	3.00
		Nos. 1161-1168 (8)	8.60	8.60

Souvenir Sheets

1169	A169	$5 multicolored	3.75	3.75
1170	A169	$5 multicolored	3.75	3.75

Hirohito (1901-89) and enthronement of Akihito as emperor of Japan.

PHILEXFRANCE '89, July 7-17, Paris — A170

Designs: 10c, Map of Dominica with French place names, 1766. 35c, French coin, 1688. $1, French ship, 1720. $4, Introduction of coffee to Dominica by the French, 1772. $5, Text.

1989, July 17 Litho. *Perf. 14*

1171	A170	10c multi, vert.	15	15
1172	A170	35c shown	28	28
1173	A170	$1 multicolored	75	75
1174	A170	$4 multicolored	3.00	3.00

Souvenir Sheet

1175	A170	$5 multicolored	3.75	3.75

Butterflies A171

Designs: 10c, Homerus swallowtail. 15c, *Morpho peleides*. 25c, Julia. 35c, Gundlach's swallowtail. 60c, Monarch. $1, Gulf fritillary. $3, Red-splashed sulphur. $5, *Papilio andraemon*. No. 1184, *Heliconius doris, Adelpha cytherea, Calliona argenissa, Eurema proterpia*. No. 1185, *Adelpha iphicla, Dismorphia spio, Lucinia sida*.

1989, Sept. 11 Litho. *Perf. 14*

1176	A171	10c multicolored	15	15
1177	A171	15c multicolored	15	15
1178	A171	25c multicolored	18	18
1179	A171	35c multicolored	28	28
1180	A171	60c multicolored	45	45
1181	A171	$1 multicolored	75	75
1182	A171	$3 multicolored	2.25	2.25
1183	A171	$5 multicolored	3.75	3.75
		Nos. 1176-1183 (8)	7.96	7.96

Souvenir Sheets

1184	A171	$6 multicolored	4.50	4.50
1185	A171	$6 multicolored	4.50	4.50

Misspellings: No. 1181, "Frittillary"; No. 1182, "Sulper."

Orchids — A172

1989, Sept. 28

1186	A172	10c *Oncidium pusillum*	15	15
1187	A172	35c *Epidendrum cochleata*	28	28
1188	A172	45c *Epidendrum ciliare*	35	35
1189	A172	60c *Cyrtopodium andersonii*	45	45
1190	A172	$1 *Habenaria pauciflora*	75	75
1191	A172	$2 *Maxillaria alba*	1.50	1.50
1192	A172	$3 *Selenipedium palmifolium*	2.25	2.25
1193	A172	$4 *Brassavola cucullata*	3.00	3.00
		Nos. 1186-1193 (8)	8.73	8.73

Souvenir Sheets

1194	A172	$5 *Oncidium lanceanum*	3.75	3.75
1195	A172	$5 *Comparettia falcata*	3.75	3.75

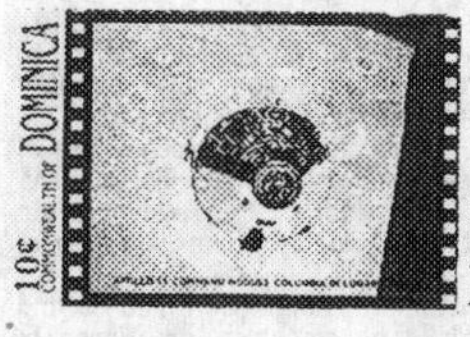

1st Moon Landing, 20th Anniv. A173

1989, Oct. 31 Litho. *Perf. 14*

1196	A173	10c *Columbia* in lunar orbit	15	15
1197	A173	60c Aldrin descending ladder	45	45
1198	A173	$2 Aldrin, Sea of Tranquility	1.50	1.50
1199	A173	$3 Flag raising	2.25	2.25

Souvenir Sheet

1200	A173	$6 Liftoff	4.50	4.50

Souvenir Sheets

A174

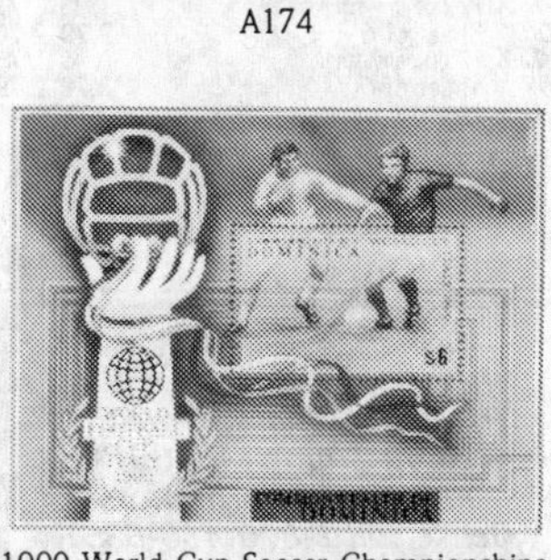

1990 World Cup Soccer Championships, Italy — A175

Past championship match scenes, flags and soccer ball: a, Brazil vs. Italy, Mexico, 1970. b, England vs. West Germany, England, 1966. c, West Germany vs. Netherlands, West Germany, 1974. d, Italy vs. West Germany, Spain, 1982.

1989, Nov. 7 *Perf. 14*

1201 A174 Sheet of 4 3.00 3.00
a.-d. $1 any single 75 75

Perf. 14

1202 A175 $6 shown 4.50 4.50

Souvenir Sheet

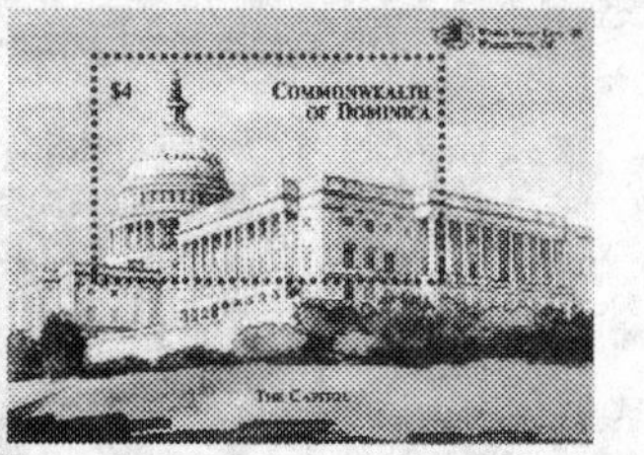

The Capitol, Washington, DC — A176

1989, Nov. 17 Litho. *Perf. 14*

1203 A176 $4 multicolored 3.00 3.00

World Stamp Expo '89.

Miniature Sheets

American Presidency, 200th Anniv. — A177

US presidents, historic events and monuments.

No. 1204: a, Washington, 1st inauguration. b, John Adams, presidential mansion, 1800. c, Jefferson, Graff House in Philadelphia, excerpt from the 1st draft of the Declaration of Independence. d, Madison, USS *Constitution* at the defeat of HMS *Guerriere*, 1812. e, Monroe, freed slaves settle Liberia, 1822. f, John Quincy Adams, opening of the Erie Canal, 1825.

No. 1205: a, Fillmore, Commodore Perry laying groundwork for US trade agreement with Japan. b, Pierce, Jefferson Davis and San Xavier del Bac mission, Tucson, AZ, Gadsden Purchase, 1853. c, Buchanan, Pony Express stamp, Buffalo Bill Cody as express rider. d, Lincoln, UPU emblem, Intl. Postal Congress, Paris, 1863. e, Andrew Johnson, polar bear, purchase of Alaska from Russia, 1867. f, Grant, 1st transcontinental railway link, Promontory Point, Utah, 1869.

No. 1206: a, Theodore Roosevelt, construction of the Panama Canal, 1904. b, Taft, Adm. Peary becomes 1st man to reach the North Pole, 1909. c, Wilson, US #C3, cancel commemorating 1st scheduled airmail service, 1918. d, Harding, airship USS *Shenandoah* at Lakehurst, NJ. e, Coolidge, Lindbergh's solo transatlantic flight, 1927. f, Mt. Rushmore, by Gutzon Borglum, 1927.

No. 1207: a, Lyndon B. Johnson, space exploration. b, Richard Nixon visiting People's Republic of China, 1971. c, Gerald Ford, tall ship in NY Harbor for Operation Sail, 1976, US bicentennial celebrations. d, Carter, Sadat of Egypt and Begin of Israel during the Camp David Accords, 1979. e, Reagan, European Space Agency emblem, flags and *Columbia* space shuttle. f, Bush, Grumman Avenger bomber he piloted during WWII.

1989, Nov. 17 *Perf. 14*

1204 Sheet of 6 2.70 2.70
a.-f. A177 60c any single 45 45
1205 Sheet of 6 2.70 2.70
a.-f. A177 60c any single 45 45
1206 Sheet of 6 2.70 2.70
a.-f. A177 60c any single 45 45
1207 Sheet of 6 2.70 2.70
a.-f. A177 60c any single 45 45

Mickey Mouse as a Hollywood Star — A178

Walt Disney characters: 20c, Reading script. 35c, Television interview. 45c, Named a star in tabloid headline. 60c, Signing autographs. $1, In dressing room, holding fans at bay. $2, Riding in limousine. $3, With Minnie in the limelight. $4, Accepting award. No. 1216, Giving interview during celebrity tennis tournament. No. 1217, Footprint impression in cement outside theater.

1989, Nov. 30 Litho. *Perf. 14x13½*

1208 A178 20c multicolored 15 15
1209 A178 35c multicolored 28 28
1210 A178 45c multicolored 35 35
1211 A178 60c multicolored 45 45
1212 A178 $1 multicolored 75 75
1213 A178 $2 multicolored 1.50 1.50
1214 A178 $3 multicolored 2.25 2.25
1215 A178 $4 multicolored 3.00 3.00
Nos. 1208-1215 (8) 8.73 8.73

Souvenir Sheets

1216 A178 $5 multicolored 3.75 3.75
1217 A178 $5 multicolored 3.75 3.75

Christmas — A179

Religious paintings by Botticelli: 20c, *Madonna in Glory with Seraphim.* 25c, *The Annunciation.* 35c, *Madonna of the Pomegranate.* 45c, *Madonna of the Rose Garden.* 60c, *Madonna of the Book.* $1, *Madonna and Child Under a Baldachin with Three Angels.* $4, *Madonna and Child with Angels.* No. 1225, *Bardi Madonna.* No. 1226, *The Mystic Nativity.* No. 1227, *The Adoration of the Magi.*

1989, Dec. 4 *Perf. 14*

1218 A179 20c multicolored 15 15
1219 A179 25c multicolored 18 18
1220 A179 35c multicolored 28 28
1221 A179 45c multicolored 35 35
1222 A179 60c multicolored 45 45
1223 A179 $1 multicolored 75 75
1224 A179 $4 multicolored 3.00 3.00
1225 A179 $5 multicolored 3.75 3.75
Nos. 1218-1225 (8) 8.91 8.91

Souvenir Sheets

1226 A179 $5 multicolored 3.75 3.75
1227 A179 $5 multicolored 3.75 3.75

Nehru — A180

Girl Guides — A181

1989, Dec. 27 Litho. *Perf. 14*

1228 A180 60c shown 45 45

Souvenir Sheet

1229 A180 $5 Parliament House, New Delhi, horiz. 3.75 3.75

Jawaharlal Nehru (1889-1964), 1st prime minister of independent India.

1989, Dec. 29

Guide movement in Dominica, 60th anniv.: 60c, Lady Baden-Powell and Agatha Robinson, former Guide leader on Dominica. $5, Dorris Stockmann, chairman of the world committee of the World Assoc. of Girl Guides and Girl Scouts, and Judith Pestaina, chief commissioner of the Dominica Girl Guides Assoc., horiz.

1230 A181 60c multicolored 45 45

Souvenir Sheet

1231 A181 $5 multi, horiz. 3.75 3.75

Miniature Sheet

Marine Life A182

Designs: a, Cocoa damselfish. b, Stinging jellyfish. c, Dolphin. d, Queen angelfish. e, French angelfish. f, Blue striped grunt. g, Pork fish. h, Hammerhead shark. i, Spadefish. j, Great barracuda. k, Stingray. l, Black grunt. m, Two-spotted butterflyfish. n, Dog snapper. o, Southern puffer. p, Four-eyed butterflyfish. q, Lane snapper. r, Green moray.

1990 Litho. *Perf. 14*

1232 Sheet of 18 6.15 6.15
a.-r. A182 45c any single 34 34

Penny Black, 150th Anniv. — A183

Stamp World London '90: 50c, Post Office accelerator, 1830. 60c, $4, No. 1239, London skyline, St. Paul's Cathedral. 90c, Railway post car, 1838. $3, Center cycle, 1883. No. 1240, Mail truck, 1899.

1990, May 3 Litho. *Perf. 13½*

1233 A183 45c green & black 34 34
1234 A183 50c blk & slate blue 38 38
1235 A183 60c dk blue & blk 45 45
1236 A183 90c black & green 68 68
1237 A183 $3 blk & dk bl vio 2.25 2.25
1238 A183 $4 dk bl vio & blk 3.00 3.00
Nos. 1233-1238 (6) 7.10 7.10

Souvenir Sheet

1239 A183 $5 beige & black 3.75 3.75
1240 A183 $5 gray & red brn 3.75 3.75

A184

A185

Birds: 10c, Blue-headed hummingbird. 20c, Black-capped petrel. 45c, Red-necked parrot. 60c, Black swift. $1, Troupial. $2, Brown noddy. $4, Lesser Antillean pewee. $5. Little blue heron. No. 1249, House wren. No. 1250, Imperial parrot.

1990, July 16 Litho. *Perf. 14*

1241 A184 10c multicolored 15 15
1242 A184 20c multicolored 16 16
1243 A184 45c multicolored 34 34
1244 A184 60c multicolored 45 45
1245 A184 $1 multicolored 75 75
1246 A184 $2 multicolored 1.50 1.50
1247 A184 $4 multicolored 3.00 3.00
1248 A184 $5 multicolored 3.75 3.75
Nos. 1241-1248 (8) 10.10 10.10

Souvenir Sheets

1249 A184 $6 multicolored 4.50 4.50
1250 A184 $6 multicolored 4.50 4.50

1990, July 19

Shells: 10c, Reticulated cowrie-helmet. 20c, West Indian chank. 35c, West Indian fighting conch. 60c, True tulip. $1, Sunrise tellin. $2, Crown cone. $3, Common dove shell. $4, Atlantic fig shell. No. 1259, Giant tun. No. 1260, King helmet.

1251 A185 10c multicolored 15 15
1252 A185 20c multicolored 16 16
1253 A185 35c multicolored 25 25
1254 A185 60c multicolored 45 45
1255 A185 $1 multicolored 75 75
1256 A185 $2 multicolored 1.50 1.50
1257 A185 $3 multicolored 2.25 2.25
1258 A185 $4 multicolored 3.00 3.00
Nos. 1251-1258 (8) 8.51 8.51

Souvenir Sheets

1259 A185 $5 multicolored 3.75 3.75
1260 A185 $5 multicolored 3.75 3.75

A186

A187

Queen Mother, 90th Birthday: various photos.

1990, Sept. 10

1261 A186 20c multicolored 15 15
1262 A186 45c multicolored 30 30
1263 A186 60c multicolored 45 45
1264 A186 $3 multicolored 2.25 2.25

Souvenir Sheet

1265 A186 $5 multicolored 3.75 3.75

1990, Nov. 5 Litho. *Perf. 14*

1266 A187 45c Men's singles, tennis 30 30
1267 A187 60c Men's foil fencing 45 45
1268 A187 $2 100m freestyle swimming 1.50 1.50
1269 A187 $3 Star class yachting 2.25 2.25

Souvenir Sheet

1270 A187 $5 Coxless pairs, rowing 3.75 3.75

1992 Summer Olympics, Barcelona.

Christmas A188

Walt Disney characters on carousel animals: 10c, Mickey, frog. 15c, Huey, Dewey & Louie, white elephant. 25c, Donald, polar bear. 45c, Goofy, goat. $1, Donald, giraffe. $2, Daisy, stork. $4, Goofy, lion. $5, Daisy, horse. No. 1279, Mickey, swan chariot, horiz. No. 1280, Mickey, Minnie & Goofy, griffin chariot.

1990, Dec. 13 *Perf. 13½x14*

1271 A188 10c multicolored 15 15
1272 A188 15c multicolored 15 15
1273 A188 25c multicolored 18 18
1274 A188 45c multicolored 30 30
1275 A188 $1 multicolored 75 75
1276 A188 $2 multicolored 1.50 1.50
1277 A188 $4 multicolored 3.00 3.00
1278 A188 $5 multicolored 3.75 3.75
Nos. 1271-1278 (8) 9.78 9.78

Souvenir Sheets

Perf. 14x13½

1279 A188 $6 multicolored 4.50 4.50
1280 A188 $6 multicolored 4.50 4.50

World Cup Soccer Championships, Italy — A189

Players and coaches from participating countries.

1990, Dec. 28 Litho. *Perf. 14*

1281	A189	15c England	15	15
1282	A189	45c Brazil	30	30
1283	A189	60c West Germany	45	45
1284	A189	$4 Austria	3.00	3.00

Souvenir Sheets

1285	A189	$6 Ireland, vert.	4.50	4.50
1286	A189	$6 USSR, vert.	4.50	4.50

Cog Trains of Switzerland A190

Designs: 10c, Glion-Roches de Naye, 1890. 35c, Electric cog rail car ascending Mt. Pilatus. 45c, Cog railway to Schynige Platte, view of Eiger, Monch and Jungfrau Mountains. 60c, Furka-Oberalp train on Bugnli Viaduct, vert. $1, 1910 Jungfraubahn Cog Railway, Jungfrau Mountain, 1910. $2, Testing Swiss rail cars built for Pike's Peak on Arth-Rigibahn, 1963. $4, Brienz-Rothorn Bahn, 1991. $5, Private 1870 Rigi-Scheideck Hotel post stamp, 1890 Arth-Rigi Railway Engine. No. 1291, Sherlock Holmes watching Brunigline train descending from Brunig Pass. No. 1292, Switzerland #738 and first passenger train to ascend Mt. Rigi, 1871.

1991, Mar. 26 Litho. *Perf. 14*

1287	A190	10c multicolored	15	15
1288	A190	35c multicolored	28	28
1289	A190	45c multicolored	35	35
1290	A190	60c multicolored	45	45
1291	A190	$1 multicolored	75	75
1292	A190	$2 multicolored	1.50	1.50
1293	A190	$4 multicolored	3.00	3.00
1294	A190	$5 multicolored	3.75	3.75
		Nos. 1287-1294 (8)	10.23	10.23

Souvenir Sheets

Perf. 13½

1295	A190	$6 multicolored	4.50	4.50
1296	A190	$6 multicolored	4.50	4.50

Nos. 1295-1296 each contain one 50x37mm stamp.

Voyages of Discovery A191

Explorer's ships: 10c, Gil Eannes, 1433-1434. 25c, Alfonso Gonclaves Baldaya, 1436. 45c, Bartolomeu Dias, 1487. 60c, Vasco da Gama, 1497-1499. $1, Vallarte the Dane. $2, Aloisio Cadamosto, 1456-1458. $4, Diogo Gomes, 1457. $5, Diogo Cao, 1482-1485.

1991, Apr. 8 Litho. *Perf. 14*

1297	A191	10c multicolored	15	15
1298	A191	25c multicolored	18	18
1299	A191	45c multicolored	30	30
1300	A191	60c multicolored	45	45
1301	A191	$1 multicolored	75	75
1302	A191	$2 multicolored	1.50	1.50
1303	A191	$4 multicolored	3.00	3.00
1304	A191	$5 multicolored	3.75	3.75
		Nos. 1297-1304 (8)	10.08	10.08

Souvenir Sheets

1305	A191	$6 Blue and yellow macaw	4.50	4.50
1306	A191	$6 Red and yellow macaw	4.50	4.50

Discovery of America, 500th anniv. (in 1992).

Japanese Costumes — A192

Walt Disney characters wearing Japanese costumes: 10c, Donald as soldier. 15c, Mickey as Kabuki actor. 25c, Mickey, Minnie in traditional wedding clothes. 45c, Daisy as Geisha girl, vert. $1, Mickey in sokutai dress of high government official, vert. $2, Goofy as mino farmer, vert. $4, Pete as shogun, vert. $5, Donald as warlord. No. 1315, Mickey, as Noh player, vert. No. 1316, Goofy as Kabubei-Jishi street performer, vert.

1991, May 22 Litho. *Perf. 14*

1307	A192	10c multicolored	15	15
1308	A192	15c multicolored	15	15
1309	A192	25c multicolored	18	18
1310	A192	45c multicolored	30	30
1311	A192	$1 multicolored	75	75
1312	A192	$2 multicolored	1.50	1.50
1313	A192	$4 multicolored	3.00	3.00
1314	A192	$5 multicolored	3.75	3.75
		Nos. 1307-1314 (8)	9.78	9.78

Souvenir Sheets

1315	A192	$6 multicolored	4.50	4.50
1316	A192	$6 multicolored	4.50	4.50

Phila Nippon '91.

Mushrooms — A193

1991, June 3 Litho. *Perf. 14*

1318	A193	10c Horn of plenty	15	15
1319	A193	15c Shaggy mane	15	15
1320	A193	45c Yellow morel	30	30
1321	A193	60c Chanterelle	45	45
1322	A193	$1 Blewit	75	75
1323	A193	$2 Slippery jack	1.50	1.50
1324	A193	$4 Emetic russula	3.00	3.00
1325	A193	$5 Honey mushroom	3.75	3.75
		Nos. 1318-1325 (8)	10.05	10.05

Souvenir Sheets

1326	A193	$6 Beefsteak polypore	4.50	4.50
1327	A193	$6 Voluminous-latex milky	4.50	4.50

Royal Family Birthday, Anniversary

Common Design Type

1991, June 17 Litho. *Perf. 14*

1328	CD347	10c multicolored	15	15
1329	CD347	15c multicolored	15	15
1330	CD347	40c multicolored	30	30
1331	CD347	60c multicolored	45	45
1332	CD347	$1 multicolored	75	75
1333	CD347	$2 multicolored	1.50	1.50
1334	CD347	$4 multicolored	3.00	3.00
1335	CD347	$5 multicolored	3.75	3.75
		Nos. 1328-1335 (8)	10.05	10.05

Souvenir Sheets

1336	CD347	$5 Elizabeth, Philip	3.75	3.75
1337	CD347	$5 Charles, Diana, sons	3.75	3.75

10c, 60c, $2, $4, No. 1336, Queen Elizabeth II, 65th birthday. Others, Charles and Diana, 10th wedding anniversary.

Vincent Van Gogh (1853-1890), Painter — A194

Paintings: 10c, Thatched Cottages. 25c, The House of Pere Eloi. 45c, The Midday Siesta. 60c, Portrait of a Young Peasant, vert. $1, Still Life: Vase with Irises Against a Yellow Background, vert. $2, Still Life Vase with Irises. $4, Blossoming Almond Tree. $5, Irises. No. 1346, A Meadow in the Mountains: Le Mas De Saint-Paul. No. 1347, Doctor Gachet's Garden in Auvers, vert.

1991, July 8 Litho. *Perf. 13½*

1338	A194	10c multicolored	15	15
1339	A194	25c multicolored	18	18
1340	A194	45c multicolored	30	30
1341	A194	60c multicolored	45	45
1342	A194	$1 multicolored	75	75
1343	A194	$2 multicolored	1.50	1.50
1344	A194	$4 multicolored	3.00	3.00
1345	A194	$5 multicolored	3.75	3.75
		Nos. 1338-1345 (8)	10.08	10.08

Size: 101x75mm

Imperf

1346	A194	$6 multicolored	4.50	4.50
1347	A194	$6 multicolored	4.50	4.50

Intl. Literacy Year — A195

Scenes from Walt Disney's "The Little Mermaid": 10c, Ariel with Flounder and Sebastian. 25c, King Triton. 45c, Sebastian drums in "Kiss De Girl" concert. 60c, Flotsam and Jetsam taunt Ariel. $1, Scuttle, Flounder and Ariel. $2, Ariel and Flounder discover a book. $4, Prince Eric, dog Max, manservant Grimsby, and crew. $5, Ursula the sea witch. No. 1356, Ariel transformed into human being. No. 1357, Ariel and Prince Eric dancing in town, vert.

1991, Aug. 6 *Perf. 14*

1348	A195	10c multicolored	15	15
1349	A195	25c multicolored	18	18
1350	A195	45c multicolored	30	30
1351	A195	60c multicolored	45	45
1352	A195	$1 multicolored	75	75
1353	A195	$2 multicolored	1.50	1.50
1354	A195	$4 multicolored	3.00	3.00
1355	A195	$5 multicolored	3.75	3.75
		Nos. 1348-1355 (8)	10.08	10.08

Souvenir Sheets

1356	A195	$6 multicolored	4.50	4.50
1357	A195	$6 multicolored	4.50	4.50

World Landmarks A196

Designs: 10c, Empire State Building, US, vert. 25c, Kremlin, USSR. 45c, Buckingham Palace, United Kingdom. 60c, Eiffel Tower, France, vert. $1, Taj Mahal, India. $2, Sydney Opera House, Australia. $4, Colosseum, Italy. $5, Pyramids, Egypt. No. 1366, Galileo demonstrating laws of physics from Tower of Pisa, Italy. No. 1367, Great Wall of China and Emperor Shi Huang Ti.

1991, Aug. 12 Litho. *Perf. 14*

1358	A196	10c multicolored	15	15
1359	A196	25c multicolored	18	18
1360	A196	45c multicolored	30	30
1361	A196	60c multicolored	45	45
1362	A196	$1 multicolored	75	75
1363	A196	$2 multicolored	1.50	1.50
1364	A196	$4 multicolored	3.00	3.00
1365	A196	$5 multicolored	3.75	3.75
		Nos. 1358-1365 (8)	10.08	10.08

Souvenir Sheets

1366	A196	$6 multicolored	4.50	4.50
1367	A196	$6 multicolored	4.50	4.50

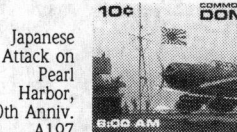

Japanese Attack on Pearl Harbor, 50th Anniv. A197

Designs: 10c, 6:00am, First wave of Japanese planes leave carrier Akagi. 15c, 6:40am, Destroyer Ward and PBY attack midget submarine. 45c, 7:00am, Second wave of Japanese planes leave carriers. 60c, 7:48am, Japanese Zeros attack on Kaneohe Air Station. $1, 8:30am, Destroyers Breeze, Medusa and Curtiss sink midget submarine. $2, 8:45am, Damaged battleship Nevada sorties. $4, 8:10am, Battleship Arizona explodes, killing 1,177 men. $5, 9:45am, Japanese attack ends. No. 1376, 8:00am, Japanese fighters and bombers attack Hickam Air Base. No. 1377, 7:55am, Pearl Harbor attack begins.

1991, Sept. 2

1368	A197	10c multicolored	15	15
1369	A197	15c multicolored	15	15
1370	A197	45c multicolored	30	30
1371	A197	60c multicolored	45	45
1372	A197	$1 multicolored	75	75
1373	A197	$2 multicolored	1.50	1.50
1374	A197	$4 multicolored	3.00	3.00
1375	A197	$5 multicolored	3.75	3.75
		Nos. 1368-1375 (8)	10.05	10.05

Souvenir Sheets

1376	A197	$6 multicolored	4.50	4.50
1377	A197	$6 multicolored	4.50	4.50

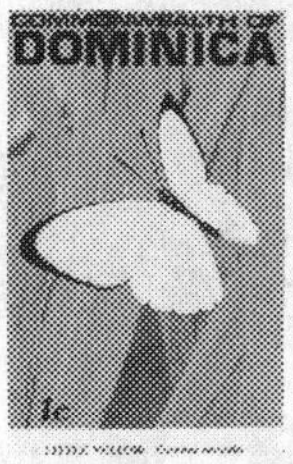

Butterflies — A198

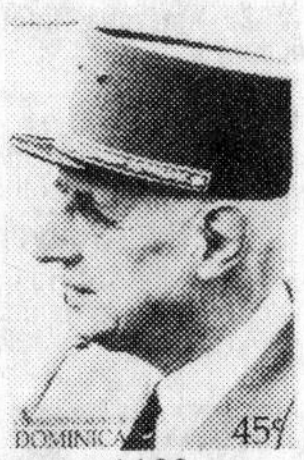

A199

1991-92 *Perf. 13½x14*

1378	A198	1c Little yellow	15	15
1379	A198	2c Gulf fritillary	15	15
1380	A198	5c Monarch	15	15
1381	A198	10c Red rim	15	15
1382	A198	15c Flambeau	15	15
1383	A198	20c Large orange sulphur	15	15
1384	A198	25c Caribbean buckeye	18	18
1385	A198	35c Polydamas swallowtail	28	28
1386	A198	45c Cassius blue	30	30
1386A	A198	55c Great southern white	42	42
1387	A198	60c Godman's leaf	45	45
1387A	A198	65c Hanno blue	48	48
1388	A198	90c Mimic	70	70
1389	A198	$1 Long-tailed skipper	75	75
1389A	A198	$1.20 Orion	90	90
1390	A198	$2 Cloudless sulphur	1.50	1.50
1391	A198	$5 Painted lady	3.75	3.75

Perf. 13½x13

1391A	A198	$10 Southern dag-gertail	7.50	7.50

Perf. 13½x14

1391B	A198	$20 White peacock	15.00	15.00
		Nos. 1379-1391B (18)	32.96	32.96

Issue dates: 55c, 66c, $1.20, 1992; others, Oct. 14, 1991.

1991, Nov. 1

1392	A199	45c shown	30	30

Souvenir Sheet

1393	A199	$5 blk & bl, horiz.	3.75	3.75

Charles de Gaulle, birth cent.

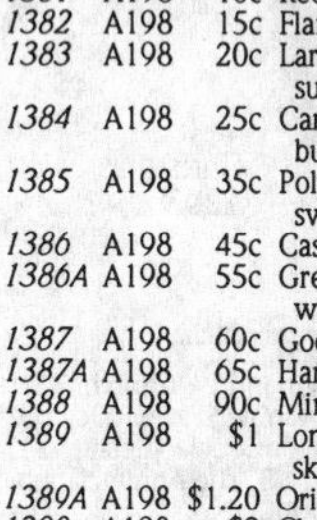

Creole Week — A200

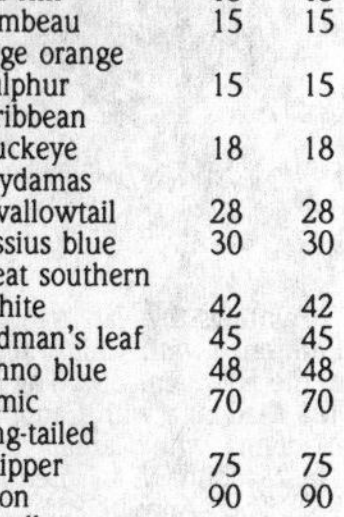

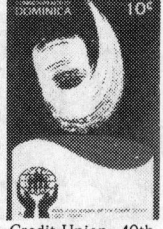

Credit Union, 40th Anniv. — A201

Designs: 45c, Man in 18th cent. costume. 60c, Accordion player. $1, Dancers. $5, Stick fight c. 1785.

1991, Nov. 1 ***Perf. 14***

1394 A200 45c multicolored	30	30
1395 A200 60c multicolored	45	45
1396 A200 $1 multicolored	75	75

Souvenir Sheet

1397 A200 $5 multicolored	3.75	3.75

1991, Nov. 1

1398 A201 10c black	15	15
1399 A201 60c Emblem, founder, horiz.	45	45

Year of the Environment and Shelter — A202

Designs: 15c, Keep the beaches clean. 60c, No. 1402, Amazona imperalis. No. 1403, Lagoon outlet.

1991, Nov. 18

1400 A202 15c multicolored	15	15
1401 A202 60c multicolored	45	45

Souvenir Sheets

1402 A202 $5 multicolored	3.75	3.75
1403 A202 $5 multicolored	3.75	3.75

Christmas A203

Paintings by Jan van Eyck: 10c, The Virgin Enthroned with Child (detail). 20c, The Madonna at the Fountain. 35c, The Virgin in a Church. 45c, The Madonna with Canon van der Paele. 60c, The Madonna with Canon van der Paele (detail). $1, The Madonna in an Interior. $3, The Annunciation. $5, The Annunciation, diff. No. 1412, The Madonna with Chancellor Rolin. No. 1413, Virgin and Child with Saints and Donor.

1991, Dec. 2 ***Perf. 12***

1404 A203 10c multicolored	15	15
1405 A203 20c multicolored	15	15
1406 A203 35c multicolored	28	28
1407 A203 45c multicolored	30	30
1408 A203 60c multicolored	45	45
1409 A203 $1 multicolored	75	75
1410 A203 $3 multicolored	2.25	2.25
1411 A203 $5 multicolored	3.75	3.75
Nos. 1404-1411 (8)	8.08	8.08

Souvenir Sheets

Perf. 14x14½

1412 A203 $6 multicolored	4.50	4.50
1413 A203 $6 multicolored	4.50	4.50

Queen Elizabeth II's Accession to the Throne, 40th Anniv.

Common Design Type

1992, Feb. 6 Litho. ***Perf. 14***

1414 CD348 10c multicolored	15	15
1415 CD348 15c multicolored	15	15
1416 CD348 $1 multicolored	75	75
1417 CD348 $5 multicolored	3.75	3.75

Souvenir Sheets

1418 CD348 $6 River scene	4.50	4.50
1419 CD348 $6 Seaside village	4.50	4.50

Botantical Gardens, Cent. — A204

Designs: 10c, Cricket match. 15c, Scenic entrance. 45c, Traveller's tree. 60c, Bamboo house. $1, Old pavilion. $2, Ficus benjamina. $4, Cricket ground. $5, Thirty-five steps. No. 1428, Fountain. No. 1429, Cricket masters.

1992, Mar. 30 Litho. ***Perf. 14***

1420 A204 10c multicolored	15	15
1421 A204 15c multicolored	15	15
1422 A204 45c multicolored	30	30
1423 A204 60c multicolored	45	45
1424 A204 $1 multicolored	75	75
1425 A204 $2 multicolored	1.50	1.50
1426 A204 $4 multicolored	3.00	3.00
1427 A204 $5 multicolored	3.75	3.75
Nos. 1420-1427 (8)	10.05	10.05

Souvenir Sheets

1428 A204 $6 multicolored	4.50	4.50
1429 A204 $6 multicolored	4.50	4.50

Spanish Art — A205

Paintings or details from paintings by Velazquez: 10c, Pope Innocent X. 15c, 45c The Forge of Vulcan (different details). 60c, Queen Mariana of Austria. $1, Pablo de Valladolid. $2, Sebastian de Morra. $3, Felipe IV (detail). $4, Felipe IV. No. 1438, Surrender of Breda. No. 1439, The Drunkards.

1992, May 4 ***Perf. 13***

1430 A205 10c multicolored	15	15
1431 A205 15c multicolored	15	15
1432 A205 45c multicolored	40	40
1433 A205 60c multicolored	45	45
1434 A205 $1 multicolored	75	75
1435 A205 $2 multicolored	1.50	1.50
1436 A205 $3 multicolored	2.25	2.25
1437 A205 $4 multicolored	3.00	3.00

Size: 120x95mm

Imperf

1438 A205 $6 multicolored	4.50	4.50
1439 A205 $6 multicolored	4.50	4.50

Granada '92.

Easter A206

Paintings: 10c, The Supper at Emmaus, studio of Gerrit Van Honthorst. 15c, Christ before Caiaphas, by Van Honthorst, vert. 45c, The Taking of Christ, by Valentin de Boulogne. 60c, Pilate Washing his Hands, by Mattia Preti, vert. $1, The Last Supper (detail), by Master of the Reredos of The Chapel of the Church of S. Francisco D'Evora. $2, The Three Marys at the Tomb (detail), by Adolphe William Bouguereau, vert. $3, Denial of St. Peter, by Hendrik Terbrugghen. $5, Doubting Thomas, by Bernardo Strozzi, vert. No. 1448, The Crucifixion (detail), by Mathias Grunewald, vert. No. 1449, The Resurrection (detail), by Caravaggio, vert.

1992 ***Perf. 14***

1440 A206 10c multicolored	15	15
1441 A206 15c multicolored	15	15
1442 A206 45c multicolored	30	30
1443 A206 60c multicolored	45	45
1444 A206 $1 multicolored	75	75
1445 A206 $2 multicolored	1.50	1.50
1446 A206 $3 multicolored	2.25	2.25
1447 A206 $5 multicolored	3.75	3.75
Nos. 1440-1447 (8)	9.30	9.30

Souvenir Sheets

1448 A206 $6 multicolored	4.50	4.50
1449 A206 $6 multicolored	4.50	4.50

Columbus and New World Flora and Fauna — A207

1992, May 18

1450 A207 10c Hercules beetle	15	15
1451 A207 25c Crapaud frog	18	18
1452 A207 75c Parrot	55	55
1453 A207 $2 Anole	1.50	1.50
1454 A207 $4 Royal gramma	3.00	3.00
1455 A207 $5 Hibiscus	3.75	3.75
Nos. 1450-1455 (6)	9.13	9.13

Souvenir Sheets

1456 A207 $6 Giant katydid	4.50	4.50
1457 A207 $6 Columbus' fleet	4.50	4.50

Nos. 1456-1457 are horiz.

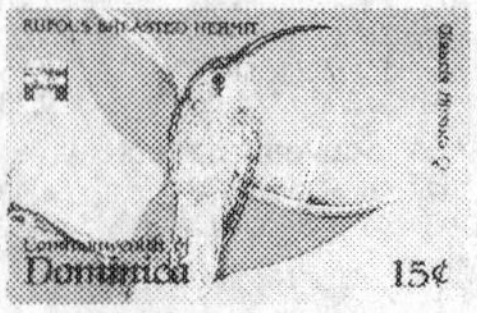

Hummingbirds — A208

Designs: 10c, Purple throated carib. 15c, Rufous breasted hermit. 45c, Puerto Rican emerald. 60c, Antillean mango. $1, Green throated carib. $2, Blue headed. $4, Eastern streamertail. $5, Antillean crested. No. 1466, Green mango. No. 1467, Vervain hummingbird.

1992, May 28

1458 A208 10c multicolored	15	15
1459 A208 15c multicolored	15	15
1460 A208 45c multicolored	30	30
1461 A208 60c multicolored	45	45
1462 A208 $1 multicolored	75	75
1463 A208 $2 multicolored	1.50	1.50
1464 A208 $4 multicolored	3.00	3.00
1465 A208 $5 multicolored	3.75	3.75
Nos. 1458-1465 (8)	10.05	10.05

Souvenir Sheets

1466 A208 $6 multicolored	4.50	4.50
1467 A208 $6 multicolored	4.50	4.50

Genoa '92.

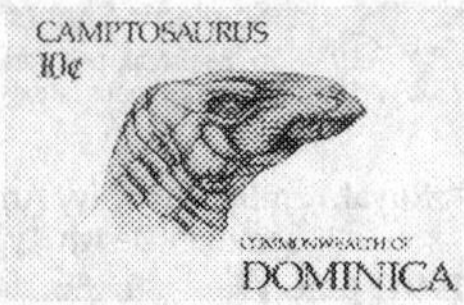

Dinosaurs A209

1992, June 23 Litho. ***Perf. 14***

1468 A209 10c Camptosaurus	15	15
1469 A209 15c Edmontosaurus	15	15
1470 A209 25c Corythosaurus	18	18
1471 A209 60c Stegosaurus	45	45
1472 A209 $1 Torosaurus	75	75
1473 A209 $3 Euoplocephalus	2.25	2.25
1474 A209 $4 Tyrannosaurus	3.00	3.00
1475 A209 $5 Parasaur- olophus	3.80	3.80
Nos. 1468-1475 (8)	10.73	10.73

Souvenir Sheets

1476 A209 $6 like #1472	4.50	4.50
1477 A209 $6 like #1470	4.50	4.50

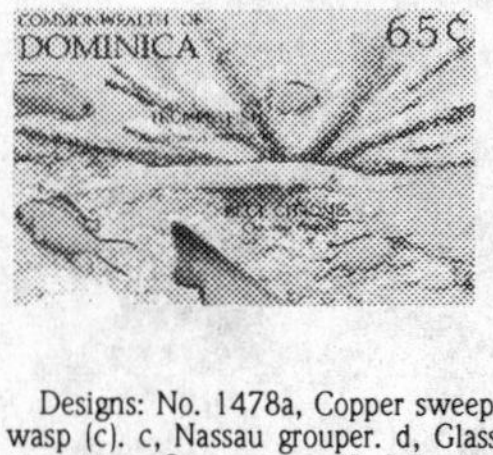

Marine Life A210

Designs: No. 1478a, Copper sweeper (b). b, Sea wasp (c). c, Nassau grouper. d, Glasseye snapper, margate. e, Green moray (f). f, Reef squid. g, Octopus. h, Porkfish (g, i). i, Reef squirrelfish (h). j, Coral crab, flower coral. k, Red coral shrimp, sea star, pillar coral (l, n). l, Cubbyu, brain coral (o). m, Basket starfish, thick finger coral. n, Belted cardinal fish, boulder coral (k, m). o, Fire worm, crenelated fire coral.

No. 1479a, Trumpetfish, blue chromis. b, Queen triggerfish. c, Hawksbill turtle. d, Sergeant major, rock beauty. e, Sharksucker. f, Lemon shark. g, Spotted trunkfish, bluehead. h, Blue tang, yellowtail damselfish. i, Queen angelfish, banded butterflyfish. j, Spotted seahorse, flower coral. k, Stoplight parrotfish, pillar coral. l, Smallmouth grunt, brain coral. m, Flamingo tongue, thick finger coral. n, Arrow crab, boulder coral. o, Sharknose goby, crenelated fire coral.

No. 1480, Harlequin bass. No. 1481, Flamefish.

1992, July 20 Litho. ***Perf. 14***

1478 A210 65c Sheet of 15, #a.-o.	7.30	7.30
1479 A210 65c Sheet of 15, #a.-o.	7.30	7.30

Souvenir Sheets

1480 A210 $6 multicolored	4.50	4.50
1481 A210 $6 multicolored	4.50	4.50

A211

A212

1992, Aug. 10 Litho. ***Perf. 14***

1482 A211 10c Archery	15	15
1483 A211 15c Two-man canoeing	15	15
1484 A211 25c 110-meter hurdles	18	18
1485 A211 60c Men's high jump	45	45
1486 A211 $1 Greco-Roman wrestling	75	75
1487 A211 $2 Men's rings	1.50	1.50
1488 A211 $4 Men's parallel bars	3.00	3.00
1489 A211 $5 Equestrian	3.75	3.75
Nos. 1482-1489 (8)	9.93	9.93

Souvenir Sheets

1490 A211 $6 Field hockey	4.50	4.50
1491 A211 $6 Women's platform diving	4.50	4.50

1992 Summer Olympics, Barcelona.

1992 Litho. ***Perf. 14½***

1492 A212 $1 Coming ashore	75	75
1493 A212 $2 Natives, ships	1.50	1.50

Discovery of America, 500th anniv. Organization of East Caribbean States.

Walt Disney's Goofy, 60th Anniv. — A213

Scenes from Disney cartoon films: 10c, Two Weeks Vacation, 1952. 15c, Aquamania, 1961. 25c, Goofy Gymnastics, 1949. 45c, How to Ride a Horse, 1941. $1, Foul Hunting, 1947. $2, For Whom the Bulls Toil, 1953. $4, Tennis Racquet, 1949. $5, Double Dribble, 1946. No. 1502, Aquamania, 1961, vert. No. 1503, The Goofy Sports Story, 1956, vert.

1992, Nov. 11 Litho. ***Perf. 14x13½***

1494 A213 10c multicolored	15	15
1495 A213 15c multicolored	15	15
1496 A213 25c multicolored	18	18
1497 A213 45c multicolored	35	35
1498 A213 $1 multicolored	75	75
1499 A213 $2 multicolored	1.50	1.50
1500 A213 $4 multicolored	3.00	3.00
1501 A213 $5 multicolored	3.75	3.75
Nos. 1494-1501 (8)	9.83	9.83

Souvenir Sheets

Perf. 13½x14

1502 A213 $6 multicolored	4.50	4.50
1503 A213 $6 multicolored	4.50	4.50

Model Trains A214

Designs: 15c, Brass Reno 4-4-0, HO scale, c. 1963. 25c, Union Pacific Golden Classic, G gauge, 1992. 55c, LMS 3rd class brake coach, OO scale, 1970s. 65c, Brass Wabash 2-6-0, HO scale, c. 1958. 75c, Pennsylvania RR T-1 duplex, O gauge, 1991. $1, Streamline engine 2-6-0, O gauge, post World War II. $3, Japanese National Railways class C62, HO scale, c. 1960. $5, Tinplate friction-drive floor trains, 1960s. No. 1512, First "toy" train in Japan, 1854. No. 1513, Stephenson's Rocket, 1:26 scale, c. 1972, vert.

1992, Nov. 11 *Perf. 14*

1504	A214	15c multicolored	15	15
1505	A214	25c multicolored	15	15
1506	A214	55c multicolored	42	42
1507	A214	65c multicolored	48	48
1508	A214	75c multicolored	58	58
1509	A214	$1 multicolored	75	75
1510	A214	$3 multicolored	2.25	2.25
1511	A214	$5 multicolored	3.75	3.75
		Nos. 1504-1511 (8)	8.53	8.53

Souvenir Sheets

Perf. 13

1512	A214	$6 multicolored	4.50	4.50
1513	A214	$6 multicolored	4.50	4.50

No. 1512 contains one 52x40mm stamp, No. 1513 one 39x51mm stamp.

Hummel Figurines — A215

Angel: 20c, Playing violin. 25c, Playing horn. 55c, Playing mandolin. 65c, Seated, playing trumpet. 90c, On cloud with lantern. $1, Holding candle. $1.20, Flying. $6, On cloud with candle.

1992, Nov. 2 *Perf. 14*

1514	A215	20c multicolored	15	15
1515	A215	25c multicolored	18	18
1516	A215	55c multicolored	42	42
1517	A215	65c multicolored	48	48
a.		Sheet of 4, #1514-1517	1.25	1.25
1518	A215	90c multicolored	65	65
1519	A215	$1 multicolored	75	75
1520	A215	$1.20 multicolored	90	90
1521	A215	$6 multicolored	4.50	4.50
a.		Sheet of 4, #1518-1521	6.80	6.80
		Nos. 1514-1521 (8)	8.03	8.03

Anniversaries and Events
A216 A217

Designs: 25c, Graf Zeppelin, 1929. No. 1523, Elderly man, plant. No. 1524, Elderly man on bicycle. No. 1525, Elderly man helping boy bait hook. No. 1526, Konrad Adenauer. No. 1527, Space shuttle. No. 1528, Wolfgang Amadeus Mozart. No. 1529, Snowy egret. No. 1530, Sir Thomas Lipton, Shamrock V, 1930. $2, Men pulling fishing net toward beach. $3, Helen Keller. No. 1533, Earth Resources Satellite. No. 1534, Map of Germany, 1949. No. 1535, Eland. $5, Count Ferdinand von Zeppelin. No. 1537, Cologne Cathedral, Germany. No. 1538, Scene from the Magic Flute. No. 1539, MIR Space Station. No. 1540, Engine of Graf Zeppelin. No. 1541, Rhinoceros hornbill.

1992 Litho. *Perf. 14*

1522	A216	25c multicolored	18	18
1523	A216	45c multicolored	35	35
1524	A216	45c multicolored	35	35
1525	A216	45c multicolored	35	35
1526	A216	90c multicolored	65	65
1527	A216	90c multicolored	65	65
1528	A217	$1.20 multicolored	90	90
1529	A216	$1.20 multicolored	90	90
1530	A216	$1.20 multicolored	90	90
1531	A216	$2 multicolored	1.50	1.50
1532	A216	$3 multicolored	2.25	2.25
1533	A216	$4 multicolored	3.00	3.00
1534	A216	$4 multicolored	3.00	3.00
1535	A216	$4 multicolored	3.00	3.00
1536	A216	$5 multicolored	3.75	3.75
		Nos. 1522-1536 (15)	21.73	21.73

Souvenir Sheets

1537	A216	$6 multicolored	4.50	4.50
1538	A217	$6 multicolored	4.50	4.50
1539	A216	$6 multicolored	4.50	4.50
1540	A216	$6 multicolored	4.50	4.50
1541	A216	$6 multicolored	4.50	4.50

Konrad Adenauer, 25th anniv. of death (#1526, 1534, 1537). Intl. Space Year (#1527, 1533, 1539). Mozart, 200th anniv. of death (in 1991) (#1528, 1538). Count Zeppelin, 75th anniv. of death (#1522, 1536, 1540). Intl. Day of the Elderly (#1523-1525). UN Earth Summit, Rio (#1529, 1535, 1541). America's Cup yacht race (#1530). WHO Intl. Conference on Nutrition, Rome (#1531). Lions Intl., 75th anniv. (#1532).

Issue dates: Nos. 1528, 1539, Oct. Nos. 1523-1527, 1533-1534, 1537-1538, Nov. Nos. 1522, 1529, 1535-1536, 1540-1541, Dec. 1992.

Miniature Sheet

Louvre Museum, Bicent. A218

Details or entire paintings by Titian: a-b, Madonna and Child with St. Catherine and a Rabbit (diff. details). c, A Woman at Her Toilet. d-e, The Supper at Emmaus (diff. details). f, The Pastoral Concert. g-h, An Allegory, Perhaps of Marriage (diff. details).

Painting by Hieronymus Bosch: $6, The Ship of Fools.

1993, Mar. 24 Litho. *Perf. 12*

1542	A218	$1 Sheet of 8, #a.-h. + label	6.00	6.00

Souvenir Sheet

Perf. 14½

1543	A218	$6 multicolored	4.50	4.50

No. 1543 contains one 55x88mm stamp.

Elvis Presley, 15th Anniv. of Death (in 1992) — A219

Designs: a, Portrait. b, With guitar. c, Holding microphone.

1993, Feb. *Perf. 14*

1544	A219	$1 Strip of 3, #a.-c.	2.25	2.25

Miniature Sheet

Birds of Dominica — A220

Designs: a, Plumbeous warbler. b, Black swift. c, Blue-hooded euphonia. d, Rufous-throated solitaire. e, Ringed kingfisher. f, Blue-headed hummingbird. g, Bananaquit. h, Trembler. i, Forest thrush. j, Purple-throated carib. k, Ruddy quail dove. l, Least bittern.

No. 1546, Imperial parrot. No. 1547, Red-necked parrot (Amazona arausiaca).

1993, Apr. 30

1545	A220	90c Sheet of 12, #a.-l.	8.25	8.25

Souvenir Sheet

1546	A220	$6 multicolored	4.50	4.50
1547	A220	$6 multicolored	4.50	4.50

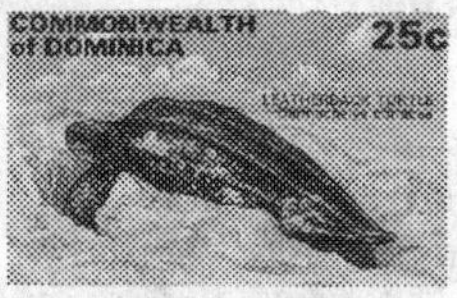

Turtles A221

Designs: 25c, Leatherback laying eggs. 55c, Hawksbill. 65c, Atlantic Ridley. 90c, Green turtle laying eggs. $1, Green turtle at sea. $2, Hawksbill, diff. $4, Loggerhead. $5, Leatherback at sea. No. 1556, Green turtle hatchling. No. 1557, Head of hawksbill.

1993, May 26 Litho. *Perf. 14*

1548	A221	25c multicolored	18	18
1549	A221	55c multicolored	42	42
1550	A221	65c multicolored	48	48
1551	A221	90c multicolored	68	68
1552	A221	$1 multicolored	75	75
1553	A221	$2 multicolored	1.50	1.50
1554	A221	$4 multicolored	3.00	3.00
1555	A221	$5 multicolored	3.75	3.75
		Nos. 1548-1555 (8)	10.76	10.76

Souvenir Sheets

1556	A221	$6 multicolored	4.50	4.50
1557	A221	$6 multicolored	4.50	4.50

Automobiles — A222

Designs: 90c, 1928 Model A Ford. $1.20, Mercedes-Benz winning Swiss Grand Prix, 1936. $4, Mercedes-Benz winning German Grand Prix, 1935. $5, 1915 Model T Ford.

No. 1562a, 1993 Mercedes-Benz coupe/roadster. b, 1893 Benz Viktoria.

No. 1563, Ford GT-40.

1993, May Litho. *Perf. 14*

1558	A222	90c multicolored	68	68
1559	A222	$1.20 multicolored	90	90
1560	A222	$4 multicolored	3.00	3.00
1561	A222	$5 multicolored	3.75	3.75

Souvenir Sheets

1562	A222	$3 Sheet of 2, #a.-b.	4.50	4.50
1563	A222	$6 multicolored	4.50	4.50

No. 1563 contains one 57x42mm stamp.

First Ford gasoline engine, cent. (#1558, 1561, 1563). Benz's first four-wheeled vehicle, cent. (#1559-1560, 1562).

Dominica Grammar School, Cent. A223

Designs: 25c, School crest. 30c, V. A. A. Archer, first West Indian headmaster. 65c, Hubert A. Charles, first Dominican headmaster. 90c, Present school building.

1993, May

1564	A223	25c multicolored	20	20
1565	A223	30c multicolored	22	22
1566	A223	65c multicolored	48	48
1567	A223	90c multicolored	68	68

Aviation Anniversaries — A224

Designs: 25c, New York ticker tape parade, 1928. 55c, BAC Lightning F2. 65c, Graf Zeppelin over Sphinx, pyramids, 1929. $1, Boeing 314 flying boat. $2, Astronaut stepping onto moon. $4, Viktoria Louise over Kiel harbor, 1912. $5, Supermarine Spitfire, vert. No. 1575, Royal Air Force Crest, vert. No. 1576, Hugo Eckener in airship cockpit, vert. No. 1577, Jean-Pierre Blanchard's hot air balloon, 1793, vert.

1993, May 28 Litho. *Perf. 14*

1568	A224	25c multicolored	18	18
1569	A224	55c multicolored	42	42
1570	A224	65c multicolored	48	48
1571	A224	$1 multicolored	75	75
1572	A224	$2 multicolored	1.50	1.50
1573	A224	$4 multicolored	3.00	3.00
1574	A224	$5 multicolored	3.75	3.75
		Nos. 1568-1574 (7)	10.08	10.08

Souvenir Sheets

1575	A224	$6 multicolored	4.50	4.50
1576	A224	$6 multicolored	4.50	4.50
1577	A224	$6 multicolored	4.50	4.50

Zeppelin Capt. Hugo Eckener, 125th anniv. of birth (#1568, 1570, 1573, 1576). Royal Air Force, 75th anniv. (#1569, 1574-1575).

Nos. 1575-1576 each contain one 42x57mm stamp.

Miniature Sheet

Coronation of Queen Elizabeth II, 40th Anniv. — A225

Designs: No. 1578a, 20c, Official coronation photograph. b, 25c, Ceremony. c, 65c, Gold State Coach. d, $5, Queen Elizabeth II, Queen Mother.

$6, Portrait, by Norman Hutchinson, 1969.

1993, June 2 Litho. *Perf. 13½x14*

1578	A225	Sheet, 2 each #a.-d.	9.25	9.25

Souvenir Sheet

Perf. 14

1579	A225	$6 multicolored	4.50	4.50

No. 1579 contains one 28x42mm stamp.

For overprints see Nos. 1688-1689.

Wedding of Japan's Crown Prince Naruhito and Masako Owada
A226

Cameo photos of couple and: 90c, Crown Prince holding flowers. $5, Princess wearing full-length coat.

$6, Princess riding in limousine.

1993, June 14 Litho. *Perf. 14*

1580	A226	90c multicolored	68	68
1581	A226	$5 multicolored	3.75	3.75

Souvenir Sheet

1582	A226	$6 multicolored	4.50	4.50

Inauguration of Pres. William J. Clinton — A227

Designs: $5, Bill, Hillary Clinton. $6, Bill Clinton, vert.

1993, July 30 Litho. *Perf. 14*

1583 A227 $5 multicolored 3.75 3.75

Souvenir Sheet

1584 A227 $6 multicolored 4.50 4.50

Willy Brandt (1913-92), German Chancellor A228

Brandt and: 65c, Pres. Eisenhower, 1959. $5, N.K. Winston, 1964. $6, Portrait.

1993, July 30

1585 A228 65c black & brown 48 48
1586 A228 $5 black & brown 3.75 3.75

Souvenir Sheet

1587 A228 $6 black & brown 4.50 4.50

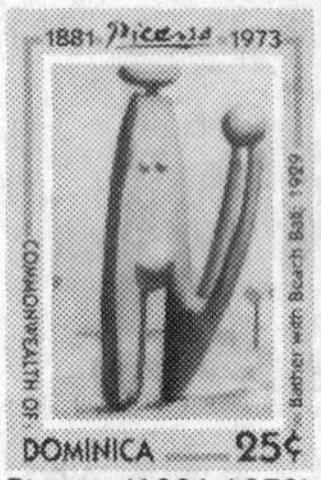

Picasso (1881-1973) A229

Polska '93 A230

Paintings: 25c, Bather with Beach Ball, 1929. 90c, Portrait of Leo Stein, 1906. $5, Portrait of Wilhelm Unde, 1910. $6, Man with a Pipe, 1915.

1993, July 30

1588 A229 25c multicolored 18 18
1589 A229 90c multicolored 70 70
1590 A229 $5 multicolored 3.75 3.75

Souvenir Sheet

1591 A229 $6 multicolored 4.50 4.50

1993, July 30

Paintings: 90c, Self-portrait, by Marian Szczyrbula, 1921. $3, Portrait of Bruno Jasienski, by Tytus Czyzewski, 1921. $6, Miser, by Tadeusz Makowski, 1973.

1592 A230 90c multicolored 70 70
1593 A230 $3 multicolored 2.25 2.25

Souvenir Sheet

1594 A230 $6 multicolored 4.50 4.50

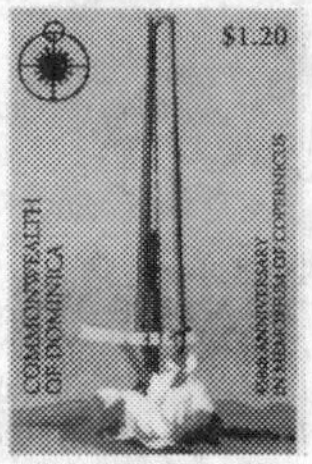

A231 A232

Designs: 90c, Monika Holzner, speedskating, 1984. $4, US hockey players, Ray Leblanc, Tim Sweeney, 1992. $6, Men's ski jump.

1993, July 30

1595 A231 90c multicolored 70 70
1596 A231 $4 multicolored 3.00 3.00

Souvenir Sheet

1597 A231 $6 multicolored 4.50 4.50

1994 Winter Olympics, Lillehammer, Norway.

1993, July 30

Designs: $1.20, Astronomer using quadrant. $3, Observatory. $5, Copernicus.

1598 A232 $1.20 multicolored 90 90
1599 A232 $3 multicolored 2.25 2.25

Souvenir Sheet

1600 A232 $5 multicolored 3.75 3.75

Copernicus (1473-1543).

Opening of New General Post Office A233

New General Post Office and: 25c, Prince Philip. 90c, Queen Elizabeth II.

1993, July 30

1601 A233 25c multicolored 18 18
1602 A233 90c multicolored 70 70

1994 World Cup Soccer Championships, US — A234

1993, Sept. 8 Litho. *Perf. 14*

1603 A234 25c Maradona, Buchwald 18 18
1604 A234 55c Gullit 42 42
1605 A234 65c Chavarria, Bliss 48 48
1606 A234 90c Maradona 70 70
1607 A234 90c Alvares 70 70
1608 A234 $1 Altobelli, Yong-hwang 75 75
1609 A234 $2 Referee, Stopyra 1.50 1.50
1610 A234 $5 Renquin, Yaremtchuk 3.75 3.75
Nos. 1603-1610 (8) 8.48 8.48

Souvenir Sheets

1611 A234 $6 Brehme 4.50 4.50
1612 A234 $6 Fabbri 4.50 4.50

Taipei '93 — A235

Chinese kites: No. 1617a, Chang E Rising up to the Moon. b, Red Phoenix and Rising Sun. c, Heavenly Judge. d, Monkey King. e, Goddess of the Luo River. f, Heavenly Maiden Scatters Flowers.

1993, Oct. 4 Litho. *Perf. 13½x14*

1613 25c Tiger Balm Gardens 18 18
1614 65c Building, Kenting Park 48 48
1615 90c Tzu-en Tower 70 70
1616 $5 Villa, Lan Tao Island 3.75 3.75

Miniature Sheet

1617 $1.65 Sheet of 6, #a.-f. 7.50 7.50

Souvenir Sheet

1618 $6 Jade Girl, Liao Dynasty 4.50 4.50

With Bangkok '93 Emblem

Puppets: No. 1623a, Thai, Rama and Sita. b, Burmese, Tha Khi Lek. c, Burmese, diff. d, Thai, Demons, Wat Phra Kaew. e, Thai, Hun Lek performing Khun Chang, Khun Phaen. f, Thai, Hun Lek performing Ramakien.

1993

1619 25c Tugu Monument, Java 18 18
1620 55c Candi Cangkuang, West Java 42 42
1621 90c Pura Taman Ayun, Mengwi 70 70
1622 $5 Stone mosaics, Ceto 3.75 3.75

Miniature Sheet

1623 $1.65 Sheet of 6, #a.-f. 7.50 7.50

Souvenir Sheet

1624 $6 Stone carving, Thailand 4.50 4.50

With Indopex '93 Emblem

Designs: 25c, Ornate Chedi, Wat Phra Boromathat Chaiya. 55c, Preserved temple ruins, Sukhothai Historical Park. 90c, Prasat Hin Phimai, Thailand. $5, Main sanctuary, Prasat Phanom Rung, Thailand.

Indonesian puppets: No. 1629a, Arjuna & Prabu Gilling Wesi. b, Loro Blonyo. c, Yogyanese puppets, Menak cycle. d, Wayang gedog, Ng Setro. e, Wayang golek, Kencana Wungu. f, Wayang gedog, Raden Damar Wulan.

$6, Sculpture of Majapahit noble, Pura Sada, Kapel.

1993, Oct. 4 Litho. *Perf. 13½x14*

1625 25c multicolored 18 18
1626 55c multicolored 42 42
1627 90c multicolored 70 70
1628 $5 multicolored 3.75 3.75

Miniature Sheet

1629 $1.65 Sheet of 6, #a.-f. 7.50 7.50

Souvenir Sheet

1630 $6 multicolored 4.50 4.50

Miniature Sheet

Willie the Operatic Whale — A236

Nos. 1631-1633, Characters and scenes from Disney's animated film Willie the Operatic Whale.

1993, Nov. 1 Litho. *Perf. 14x13½*

1631 A236 $1 Sheet of 9, #a.-i. 6.75 6.75

Souvenir Sheets

1632 A236 $6 multicolored 4.50 4.50

Perf. 13½x14

1633 A236 $6 multi, vert. 4.50 4.50

Christmas A237

Designs: 25c, 55c, 65c, 90c (No. 1637), Details or entire woodcut, The Adoration of the Magi, by Durer.

90c (No. 1638), $1, $3, $5, Details or entire painting, The Foligni Madonna, by Raphael.

Souvenir Sheets: No. 1642, $6, The Adoration of the Magi, by Durer. No. 1643, $6, The Foligni Madonna, by Raphael.

1993, Nov. 8 Litho. *Perf. 13*

1634-1643 A237 Set of 10 18.00 18.00

A238

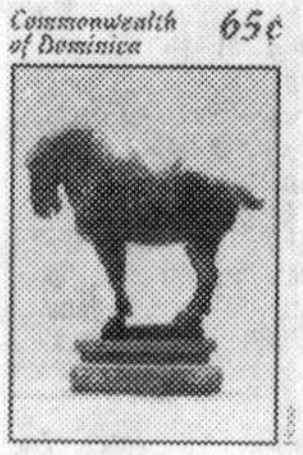

Hong Kong '94 — A239

Stamps, scene from Peak Tram: No. 1644, Hong Kong #527, city buildings, trees. No. 1645, Trees, tram, #1292.

Chinese jade: No. 1646a, Horse. b, Cup with handle. c, Vase with birthday peaches. d, Vase. e, Fu dog and puppy. f, Drinking vessel.

1994, Feb. 18 Litho. *Perf. 14*

1644 A238 65c multicolored 48 48
1645 A238 65c multicolored 48 48
a. Pair, #1644-1645 95 95

Miniature Sheet

1646 A239 65c Sheet of 6, #a.-f. 3.00 3.00

Nos. 1644-1645 issued in sheets of 5 pairs. No. 1645a is a continuous design.

New Year 1994 (Year of the Dog) (#1646e).

Insects, Butterflies, & Birds A240

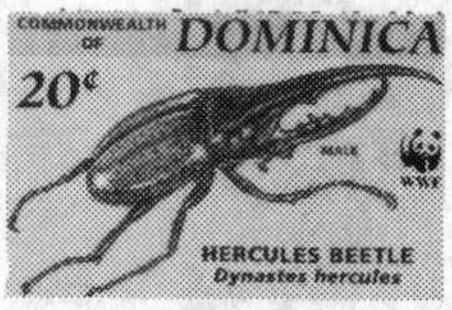

Various Hercules beetles: 20c, 25c, 65c, Male. 90c, Female.

$1, Imperial parrot. $2, Southern dagger tail. $3, The mimic. $5, Purple-throated carib.

No. 1655, Snout butterfly. No. 1656, Blue-headed hummingbird.

1994, Mar. 15 Litho. *Perf. 14*

1647-1654 A240 Set of 8 10.00 10.00
1650a Min. sheet, 3 each #1647-1650 4.50 4.50

Souvenir Sheets

1655-1656 A240 $6 each 4.50 4.50

World Wildlife Fund (#1647-1650).

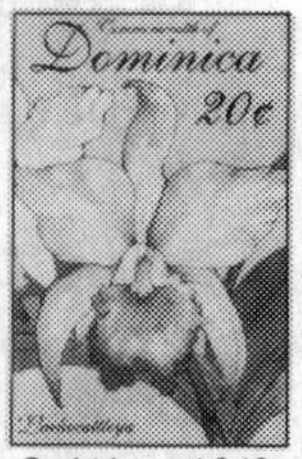

Mushrooms — A241 Orchids — A242

Designs: 20c, Russula matoubenis. 25c, Leptonia caeruleocapita. 65c, Inocybe littoralis. 90c, Russula hygrophytica. $1, Pyrrhoglossum lilaceipes. $2, Hygrocybe konradii. $3, Inopilus magnificus. $5, Boletellus cubensis.

No. 1665, Gerronema citrinum. No. 1666, Lentinus strigosus.

1994, Apr. 18

1657 A241 20c multicolored 15 15
1658 A241 25c multicolored 18 18
1659 A241 65c multicolored 48 48
1660 A241 90c multicolored 70 70
1661 A241 $1 multicolored 75 75
1662 A241 $2 multicolored 1.50 1.50
1663 A241 $3 multicolored 2.25 2.25
1664 A241 $5 multicolored 3.75 3.75
Nos. 1657-1664 (8) 9.76 9.76

Souvenir Sheets

1665 A241 $6 multicolored 4.50 4.50
1666 A241 $6 multicolored 4.50 4.50

1994, May 3

Designs: 20c, Laeliocattleya. 25c, Sophrolaeliocattleya. 65c, Odontocidium. 90c, Laeliocattleya, diff. $1, Cattleya. $2, Odontocidium, diff. $3, Epiphronitis. $4, Oncidium.
#1675, Schombocattleya. #1676, Cattleya, diff.

1667-1674 A242 Set of 8 9.00 9.00

Souvenir Sheets

1675-1676 A242 $6 each 4.50 4.50

New Year 1994 (Year of the Dog) — A243

Designs: 20c, Dachshund. 25c, Beagle. 55c, Greyhound. 90c, Jack Russell terrier. $1, Pekingese. $2, White fox terrier. $4, English toy spaniel. $5, Irish setter.
No. 1686, Welsh corgi.No. 1687, Labrador retriever.

1994, May 17

1678 A243 20c multicolored 15 15
1679 A243 25c multicolored 18 18
1680 A243 55c multicolored 40 40
1681 A243 90c multicolored 65 65
1682 A243 $1 multicolored 75 75
1683 A243 $2 multicolored 1.50 1.50
1684 A243 $4 multicolored 3.00 3.00
1685 A243 $5 multicolored 3.75 3.75
Nos. 1678-1685 (8) 10.38 10.38

Souvenir Sheets

1686 A243 $6 multicolored 4.50 4.50
1687 A243 $6 multicolored 4.50 4.50

Nos. 1578-1579 Ovptd. "ROYAL VISIT / FEBRUARY 19, 1994" in Black or Silver

1994, June 27 Litho. ***Perf. 13½x14***

1688 A225 Sheet, 2 each #a.-d. 9.25 9.25

Souvenir Sheet

1689 A225 $6 multicolored (S) 4.50 4.50

Overprint on No. 1689 appears in sheet margin.

Miniature Sheet

1994 World Cup Soccer Championships, US — A244

Designs: No. 1690a, Dos Armstrong, US. b, Dennis Bergkamp, Netherlands. c, Roberto Baggio, Italy. d, Rai, Brazil. e, Cafu, Brazil. f, Marco Van Baston, Netherlands.
No. 1691, Roberto Mancini, Italy. No. 1692, Stanford Stadium, San Francisco.

1994, July 5 ***Perf. 14***

1690 A244 $1 Sheet of 6, #a.-f. 4.50 4.50

Souvenir Sheets

1691-1692 A244 $6 each 4.50 4.50

Butterflies A245

1994, May 3 Litho. ***Perf. 14***

1693 A245 20c Florida white 15 15
1694 A245 25c Red rim 18 18
1695 A245 55c Barred sulphur 42 42
1696 A245 65c Mimic 48 48
1697 A245 $1 Large orange sulphur 75 75
1698 A245 $2 Southern dagger tail 1.50 1.50
1698A A245 $3 Dominican snout butterfly 2.25 2.25
1699 A245 $5 Caribbean buckeye 3.75 3.75

Souvenir Sheets

1700 A245 $6 Clench's hairstreak 4.50 4.50
1701 A245 $6 Painted lady 4.50 4.50

10th Caribbean Scout Jamboree — A246

Designs: 20c, Backpacking. 25c, Cooking over campfire. 55c, Making camp. 65c, Camping. $1, Scout drum unit. $2, Planting trees. $4, Sailing. $5, Scout salute.
No. 1710, Early Scout troop. No. 1711, Pres. C.A. Sorhaindo, vert.

1994, July 18 Litho. ***Perf. 14***

1702-1709 A246 Set of 8 10.50 10.50

Souvenir Sheets

1710-1711 A246 $6 each 4.50 4.50

D-Day, 50th Anniv. A247

Designs: 65c, US Waco glider brings reinforcements. $2, British Horsa gliders land more troops. $3, Glider troops take Pegasus Bridge.
$6, Hadrian glider.

1994, July 26

1712-1714 A247 Set of 3 4.25 4.25

Souvenir Sheet

1715 A247 $6 multicolored 4.50 4.50

A248

Intl. Olympic Committee, Cent. — A249

Designs: 55c, Urike Meyfath, Germany, high jump, 1984. $1.45, Dieter Baumann, Germany, 5000-meter run, 1992.
$6, Ji Hoon Chae, South Korea, 500-meter short track speed skating, 1994.

1994, July 26

1716 A248 55c multicolored 42 42
1717 A248 $1.45 multicolored 1.10 1.10

Souvenir Sheet

1718 A249 $6 multicolored 4.50 4.50

English Touring Cricket, Cent. A250

Designs: 55c, D.I. Goweer Leics, England, vert. 90c, E.C.L. Ambrose, Leeward Islands. $1, G.A. Gooch, England, vert.
$3, First English team, 1895.

1994, July 26

1719-1721 A250 Set of 3 1.90 1.90

Souvenir Sheet

1722 A250 $3 multicolored 2.25 2.25

Miniature Sheet of 6

First Manned Moon Landing, 25th Anniv. A251

Designs: No. 1723a, Apollo 14 crew. b, Apollo 14 patch. c, Apollo 14 lunar module Antares at Fra Mauro Crater. d, Apollo 15 crew. e, Apollo 15 patch. f, Apollo 15 mission, Mount Hadley from rover.
$6, 25th anniv. emblem, lunar surface.

1994, July 26

1723 A251 $1 #a.-f. 4.50 4.50

Souvenir Sheet

1724 A251 $6 multicolored 4.50 4.50

A252

PHILAKOREA '94 — A253

Designs: 65c, P'alsang-jon Hall, Korea. 90c, Popchu-sa Temple. $2, Uhwajong Pavillion, Korea.
Screen, Late Choson Dynasty showing flowers and: No. 1728a, c, e, Birds. b, g, Butterfly. d, Roosters. f, Duck. h, Pheasant. i, Cranes. j, Deer.
$4, Stylized "spirit post" guardian.

1994, July 26 ***Perf. 14, 13 (#1728)***

1725-1727 A252 Set of 3 2.75 2.75

Miniature Sheet of 10

1728 A253 55c #a.-j. 4.25 4.25

Souvenir Sheet

1729 A252 $4 multicolored 3.00 3.00

Mickey Mouse, 65th Birthday A254

Disney characters: 20c, Dippy dawg. 25c, Clarabelle Cow. 55c, Horace Horsecollar. 65c, Mortimer Mouse. $1, Joe Piper. $3, Mr. Casey. $4, Chief O'Hara. $5, Mickey and the Blot.
No. 1738, Minnie, Tanglefoot. No. 1739, Pluto, Minnie, horiz.

Perf. 13½x14, 14x13½ (#1739)

1994, Oct. 3

1730-1737 A254 Set of 8 11.00 11.00

Souvenir Sheets

1738-1739 A254 $6 each 4.50 4.50

WAR TAX STAMPS

No. 50 Surcharged in Red

WAR TAX
ONE HALFPENNY

1916 Wmk. 3 ***Perf. 14***

MR1 A6 ½p on ½p green 15 15

No. 50 Overprinted in Black

WAR TAX

1918

MR2 A6 ½p green 20 20

Nos. 50, 40 in Black or Red

WAR TAX

1918

MR3 A6 ½p green 15 *15*
MR4 A6 3p violet, *yel* (R) 15 *40*
Set value 16

Type of 1908-09 Surcharged in Red

WAR TAX
1½D.

1919

MR5 A6 1½p on 2½p orange 15 *35*

FALKLAND ISLANDS

LOCATION — A group of islands about 300 miles east of the Straits of Magellan at the southern limit of South America
GOVT. — British Crown Colony
AREA — 4,700 sq. mi.
POP. — 1,813 (1980)
CAPITAL — Stanley

Dependencies of the Falklands are South Georgia and South Sandwich. In March 1962, three other dependencies —South Shetland Islands, South Orkneys and Graham Land—became the new separate colony of British Antarctic Territory.

12 Pence = 1 Shilling
20 Shillings = 1 Pound
100 Pence = 1 Pound (1971)

Catalogue values for unused stamps in this country are for Never Hinged items, beginning with Scott 97 in the regular postage section, Scott B1 in the semi-postal section, Scott J1 in the postage due section, Scott 1L1 in Falkland Island Dependencies regular issues, Scott 1LB1 in Falkland Island Dependencies semi-postals, and Scott 2L1, 3L1, 4L1, 5L1 in the Issues for Separate Islands.

Queen Victoria — A1

1878-79 Unwmk. Engr. ***Perf. 14***

1 A1 1p claret 450.00 *800.00*
2 A1 4p dark gray ('79) 1,050. 200.00
3 A1 6p green 27.50 45.00
4 A1 1sh bister brown 27.50 45.00

1883-95 Wmk. 2

5 A1 1p brt claret ('94) 24.00 24.00
a. 1p claret 350.00 100.00
b. Horiz. pair, imperf. vert. *42,500.*
c. Diagonal half used as ½p on cover *3,250.*
6 A1 4p olive gray ('95) 12.50 25.00
a. 4p gray black 22.50 32.50

For surcharge, see No. 19E.

1886 — **Wmk. 2 Sideways**

7	A1	1p claret	40.00	27.50
a.		Diagonal half used as ½p on cover		3,250.
8	A1	4p olive gray	175.00	32.50

For surcharge, see No. 19.

1891-96 — **Wmk. 2**

9	A1	½p blue green	12.50	14.00
10	A1	½p yel green ('92)	60	1.00
11	A1	1p orange brown	21.00	25.00
a.		Diagonal half used as ½p on cover		3,250.
12	A1	1p org red ('95)	2.50	2.50
a.		1p red brown	3.50	2.50
13	A1	2p magenta ('96)	3.50	5.50
14	A1	2½p deep blue	200.00	175.00
15	A1	2½p deep ultra	3.75	3.75
a.		2½p pale ultra	55.00	30.00
16	A1	6p orange ('92)	10.00	16.00
a.		6p yellow ('96)	11.00	12.50
17	A1	9p ver ('96)	19.00	40.00
18	A1	1sh bis brn ('96)	16.00	24.00
		Nos. 9-18 (10)	288.85	306.75

Nos. 7 and 5a Surcharged in Black **½d.**

1891 — **Wmk. 2 Sideways**

19	A1	½p on half of 1p, #7	550.00	285.00
d.		Unsevered pair	1,650.	900.00

Wmk. 2

19E	A1	½p on half of 1p, #5a	450.00	150.00
f.		Unsevered pair		425.00

Genuine used bisects should be canceled with a segmented circular cork cancel. Any other cancel must be linked by date to known mail ship departures. This surcharge exists on "souvenir" bisects, including copies of No. 11, and can be found inverted, double and sideways.

A3 A4

1898 — **Wmk. 1**

20	A3	2sh6p dark blue	150.00	225.00
21	A4	5sh brown red	150.00	225.00

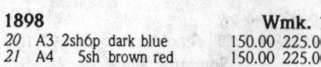

King Edward VII
A5 A6

1904-07 — **Wmk. 3** — *Perf. 14*

22	A5	½p yellow green	1.05	1.05
23	A5	1p red	2.50	42
a.		Wmk. sideways ('07)	70	1.05
24	A5	2p dull vio ('05)	5.25	12.00
25	A5	2½p ultramarine	11.50	10.00
a.		2½p deep blue	300.00	275.00
26	A5	6p orange ('05)	22.50	32.50
27	A5	1sh bis brn ('05)	22.50	26.00
28	A6	3sh gray green	90.00	95.00
29	A6	5sh dull red ('05)	125.00	125.00
		Nos. 22-29 (8)	280.30	301.97

King George V
A7 A8

1912-14

30	A7	½p yellow green	1.50	1.50
31	A7	1p red	1.75	85
32	A7	2p brown violet	2.50	4.25
33	A7	2½p deep ultra	8.00	9.00
34	A7	6p orange	8.75	10.50
35	A7	1sh bister brown	16.00	18.00
36	A8	3sh dark green	45.00	47.50
37	A8	5sh brown red	50.00	65.00
38	A8	5sh plum ('14)	50.00	65.00
39	A8	10sh red, *green*	165.00	200.00
40	A8	£1 black, *red*	300.00	425.00
		Nos. 30-40 (11)	648.50	846.60

For overprints, see Nos. MR1-MR3.

1921-29 — **Wmk. 4**

41	A7	½p yellow green	90	1.00
42	A7	1p red ('24)	90	90
43	A7	2p brown vio ('23)	2.25	2.75
44	A7	2½p dark blue	2.50	3.00
a.		2½p Prussian blue ('29)	325.00	425.00
45	A7	2½p vio, *yel* ('23)	5.00	8.75
46	A7	6p orange ('25)	5.50	10.00
47	A7	1sh bister brown	16.00	25.00
48	A8	3sh dk green ('23)	75.00	100.00
		Nos. 41-48 (8)	108.05	151.40

No. 43 Surcharged **2½D**

1928

52	A7	2½p on 2p brn vio	850.00	950.00

Beware of forged surcharges.

King George V — A9

1929-31 — *Perf. 14*

54	A9	½p green	15	18
55	A9	1p scarlet	16	16
56	A9	2p gray	40	45
57	A9	2½p blue	90	1.25
58	A9	4p deep orange	3.50	6.00
59	A9	6p brown violet	4.25	4.50
60	A9	1sh black, *green*	6.00	6.50
a.		1sh black, *emerald*	21.00	35.00
61	A9	2sh6p red, *blue*	14.00	20.00
62	A9	5sh green, *yel*	30.00	32.50
63	A9	10sh red, *green*	47.50	60.00

Wmk. 3

64	A9	£1 black, *red*	350.00	375.00
		Nos. 54-64 (11)	456.86	506.54

Issue dates: 4p, 1931, others, Sept. 2.

Romney Marsh Ram — A10

Iceberg — A11

Whaling Ship — A12

Port Louis — A13

Map of the Islands — A14

South Georgia A15

Blue Whale — A16

Government House — A17

Battle Memorial A18

King Penguin A19

Coat of Arms — A20

King George V — A21

1933, Jan. 2 — **Wmk. 4** — *Perf. 12*

65	A10	½p green & blk	70	70
66	A11	1p dl red & blk	90	70
67	A12	1½p lt bl & blk	2.00	2.25
68	A13	2p ol brn & blk	3.00	3.50
69	A14	3p dl vio & blk	5.25	6.00
70	A15	4p orange & blk	7.00	8.00
71	A16	6p gray & black	40.00	40.00
72	A17	1sh ol grn & blk	30.00	37.50
73	A18	2sh6p dp vio & blk	85.00	77.50
74	A19	5sh yellow & blk	425.00	450.00
a.		5sh yellow orange & black	900.00	1,100.
75	A20	10sh lt brn & blk	550.00	500.00
76	A21	£1 rose & black	1,200.	1,200.
		Nos. 65-76 (12)	2,348.	2,326.

Cent. of the permanent occupation of the islands as a British colony.

Silver Jubilee Issue
Common Design Type

1935, May 7 — *Perf. 11x12*

77	CD301	1p carmine & blue	45	45
78	CD301	2½p ultra & brown	90	90
79	CD301	4p indigo & grn	1.65	1.90
80	CD301	1sh brn vio & ind	3.75	4.50
		Set, never hinged	16.00	

Coronation Issue
Common Design Type

1937, May 12 — *Perf. 11x11½*

81	CD302	½p deep green	15	15
82	CD302	1p dark carmine	25	25
83	CD302	2½p deep ultra	38	38
		Set, never hinged	1.50	

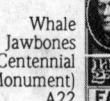

Whale Jawbones (Centennial Monument) A22

Designs: Nos. 85, 86A, Black-necked swan. Nos. 85B, 86, Battle memorial. 2½p, 3p, Flock of sheep. 4p, Upland goose. 6p, R.R.S. "Discovery II." 9p, R.R.S. "William Scoresby." 1sh, Mt. Sugar Top. 1sh3p, Turkey vultures. 2sh6p, Gentoo penguins. 5sh, Sea lions. 10sh, Deception Island. £1, Arms of Colony.

1938-46 — *Perf. 12*

84	A22	½p green & blk	15	15
85	A22	1p red & black	1.10	85
a.		1p rose carmine & black	6.00	6.00
85B	A22	1p dk vio & blk ('41)	15	15
86	A22	2p dk vio & blk	75	55

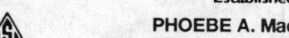

86A	A22	2p	rose car & black ('41)	20	20
87	A22	2½p	ultra & blk	65	55
87A	A22	3p	deep bl & black ('41)	35	35
88	A22	4p	rose vio & black	75	75
89	A22	6p	brown & blk	2.25	2.00
90	A22	9p	sl bl & blk	75	65
91	A22	1sh	dull blue	2.75	1.50
92	A22	1sh3p	carmine & blk ('46)	75	1.25
93	A22	2sh6p	gray black	17.50	10.00
94	A22	5sh	org brown & ultra	25.00	20.00
a.			5sh yel brown & indigo	300.00	175.00
95	A22	10sh	org & blk	27.50	20.00
96	A22	£1	dk vio & blk	55.00	40.00
			Nos. 84-96 (16)	135.60	98.95
			Set, never hinged	235.00	

Issue dates: No. 85B, No. 86A, 3p, July 14. 1sh3p, Dec. 10. Jan. 3.

See Nos. 101-102. For overprints, see Nos. 2L1-2L8, 3L1-3L8, 4L1-4L8.

Catalogue values for unused stamps in this section, from this point to the end of the section, are for Never Hinged items.

Peace Issue
Common Design Type

Perf. 13½x14

1946, Oct. 7 Engr. Wmk. 4

97	CD303	1p	purple	30	30
98	CD303	3p	deep blue	45	45

Silver Wedding Issue
Common Design Types

1948, Nov. 1 Photo. *Perf. 14x14½*

99	CD304	2½p	bright ultra	25	25

Engr.; Name Typo.

Perf. 11½x11

100	CD305	£1	purple	87.50	67.50

Types of 1938-46

Designs: 2½p, Upland geese. 6p, R.R.S. "Discovery II."

Wmk. 4

1949, June 15 Engr. *Perf. 12*

101	A22	2½p	dp blue & black	2.25	5.00
102	A22	6p	gray black	2.25	2.25

UPU Issue
Common Design Types

Engr.; Name Typo. on 3p, 1sh3p

1949, Oct. 10 *Perf. 13½, 11x11½*

103	CD306	1p	violet	50	50
104	CD307	3p	indigo	1.00	90
105	CD308	1sh3p	green	3.25	3.00
106	CD309	2sh	blue	6.75	6.00

Sheep — A35

Arms of the Colony — A36

Designs: 1p, R.M.S. Fitzroy. 2p Upland goose. 2½p, Map. 4p, Auster plane. 6p, M.S.S. John Biscoe. 9p, "Two Sisters" peaks. 1sh, Gentoo penguins. 1sh 3p, Kelp goose and gander. 2sh 6p, Sheet shearing. 5sh, Battle memorial. 10sh, Sea lion and clapmatch. £1, Hulk of "Great Britain."

Perf. 13½x13, 13x13½

1952, Jan. 2 Engr. Wmk. 4

107	A35	½p	green	50	42
108	A35	1p	red	60	50
109	A35	2p	violet	1.50	1.25
110	A35	2½p	ultra & blk	1.00	85
111	A36	3p	deep ultra	1.00	85
112	A35	4p	claret	1.25	1.10
113	A35	6p	yellow brn	3.00	95
114	A35	9p	orange yel	2.50	2.00
115	A36	1sh	black	5.00	4.00
116	A35	1sh3p	red orange	3.00	8.50
117	A36	2sh6p	olive	7.50	8.50
118	A36	5sh	red violet	8.00	6.75
119	A35	10sh	gray	15.00	27.50
120	A35	£1	black	32.50	37.50
			Nos. 107-120 (14)	82.35	100.67

Coronation Issue
Common Design Type

1953, June 4 *Perf. 13½x13*

121	CD312	1p	car & black	95	95

Types of 1952 with Portrait of Queen Elizabeth II

1955-57 *Perf. 13½x13, 13x13½*

122	A35	½p	green ('57)	35	35
123	A35	1p	red ('57)	80	40
124	A35	2p	violet ('56)	2.00	1.65
125	A35	6p	light brown	3.50	2.00
126	A35	9p	ocher ('57)	16.00	16.00
127	A36	1sh	black	10.00	8.25
			Nos. 122-127 (6)	32.65	28.65

Falkland Islands Thrush A37

Birds: 1p, Dominican gull. 2p, Gentoo penguins. 2½p, Marsh starling. 3p, Upland geese. 4p, Steamer ducks. 5½p, Rock-hopper penguin. 6p, black-browed albatross. 9p, Silver grebe. 1sh, Pied oystercatchers. 1sh3p, Yellow-billed teal. 2sh, Kelp geese, 5sh, King shag. 10sh, Guadelupe caracara. £1, Black-necked swan.

Perf. 13½x13

1960, Feb. 10 Engr. Wmk. 314

Center in Black

128	A37	½p	green	22	18
a.			Wmk. sideways ('66)	35	30
129	A37	1p	rose red	25	22
130	A37	2p	blue	35	30
131	A37	2½p	bister brn	1.10	40
132	A37	3p	olive	50	28
133	A37	4p	rose car	75	28
134	A37	5½p	violet	85	40
135	A37	6p	sepia	1.10	75
136	A37	9p	orange	1.25	80
137	A37	1sh	dull purple	1.10	80
138	A37	1sh3p	ultra	3.00	2.25
139	A37	2sh	brown car	6.25	2.50
140	A37	5sh	grnsh blue	12.50	9.25
141	A37	10sh	rose lilac	30.00	15.00
142	A37	£1	yellow org	55.00	37.50
			Nos. 128-142 (15)	114.22	70.91

Morse Key — A38

1962, Oct. 5 Photo. *Perf. 11½x11*

143	A38	6p	dp org & dk red	1.25	70
144	A38	1sh	brt ol grn & dp green	1.50	1.40
145	A38	2sh	brt ultra & violet	2.50	2.50

Falkland Islands radio station, 50th anniv.

Freedom from Hunger Issue
Common Design Type

1963, June 4 *Perf. 14x14½*

146	CD314	1sh	ultramarine	10.50	8.50

Red Cross Centenary Issue
Common Design Type

Wmk. 314

1963, Sept.2 Litho. *Perf. 13*

147	CD315	1p	black & red	1.65	1.10
148	CD315	1sh	ultra & red	12.50	10.50

Shakespeare Issue
Common Design Type

1964, Apr. 23 Photo. *Perf. 14x14½*

149	CD316	6p	black	1.10	1.10

H.M.S. Glasgow A39

Designs: 6p, H.M.S. Kent. 1sh, H.M.S. Invincible. 2sh, Falkland Islands Battle Memorial, vert.

1964, Dec. 8 Engr. *Perf. 13*

150	A39	2½p	ver & black	4.00	1.40
151	A39	6p	blue & black	1.25	90
a.			"Glasgow" vignette	15,000.	
152	A39	1sh	carmine & blk	3.00	1.75

Perf. 13x14

153	A39	2sh	dk blue & blk	5.00	3.25

Battle of the Falkland Islands between the British and German navies, 50th anniv.

ITU Issue
Common Design Type

Perf. 11x11½

1965, May 26 Litho. Wmk. 314

154	CD317	1p	blue & dl dk bl	50	40
155	CD317	2sh	lilac & dl yel	7.50	3.25

Intl. Cooperation Year Issue
Common Design Type

1965, Oct. 25 *Perf. 14½*

156	CD318	1p	blue grn & cl	75	40
157	CD318	1sh	lt violet & grn	6.00	3.50

Churchill Memorial Issue
Common Design Type

1966, Jan. 24 Photo. *Perf. 14*

Design in Black, Gold and Carmine Rose

158	CD319	½p	bright blue	18	15
159	CD319	1p	green	1.10	30
160	CD319	1sh	brown	3.25	2.25
161	CD319	2sh	violet	7.25	4.75

Human Rights Flame and Globe — A40

Perf. 14x14½

1968, July 4 Photo. Wmk. 314

162	A40	2p	brt rose & multi	20	15
163	A40	6p	brt green & multi	42	42
164	A40	1sh	orange & multi	65	65
165	A40	2sh	ultra & multi	1.25	1.25

International Human Rights Year.

Dusty Miller — A41

Falkland Islands flora: 1½p, Pig vine, horiz. 2p, Pale maiden. 3p, Dog orchard. 3½p, Sea cabbage, horiz. 4½p, Vanilla daisy. 5½p, Arrowleaf marigold, horiz. 6p, Diddle-dee, horiz. 1sh, Scurvy grass, horiz. 1sh6p, Prickly burr. 2sh, Fachine. 3sh, Lavender. 5sh, Felton's flower, horiz. £1, Yellow orchid.

1968, Oct. 9 Photo. *Perf. 14*

166	A41	½p	multicolored	15	15
167	A41	1½p	multicolored	15	15
168	A41	2p	multicolored	18	18
169	A41	3p	multicolored	30	30
170	A41	3½p	multicolored	40	40
171	A41	4½p	multicolored	55	55
172	A41	5½p	multicolored	70	70
173	A41	6p	multicolored	85	85
174	A41	1sh	multicolored	1.75	1.75
175	A41	1sh6p	multicolored	4.25	2.75
176	A41	2sh	multicolored	5.50	4.00
177	A41	3sh	multicolored	6.75	5.75
178	A41	5sh	multicolored	20.00	11.00
179	A41	£1	multicolored	11.50	11.50
			Nos. 166-179 (14)	53.03	40.03

See #210-222. For surcharges see #197-209.

Common Design Types are pictured beginning on page 176.

Beaver DHC 2 Seaplane A42

Designs: 6p, Norseman seaplane. 1sh, Auster plane. 2sh, Falkland Islands arms.

1969, Apr. 8 Litho. *Perf. 14*

180	A42	2p	multicolored	22	18
181	A42	6p	multicolored	45	50
182	A42	1sh	multicolored	80	80
183	A42	2sh	multicolored	2.25	1.65

21st anniv. of Government Air Service.

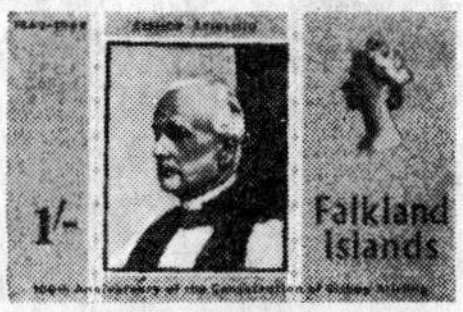

Bishop Stirling A43

Designs: 2p, Holy Trinity Church, 1869. 6p, Christ Church Cathedral, 1969. 2sh, Bishop's miter.

1969, Oct. 30 *Perf. 14*

184	A43	2p	emerald & black	18	18
185	A43	6p	red orange & black	45	45
186	A43	1sh	lilac & black	90	90
187	A43	2sh	yellow & multi	1.75	1.75

Consecration of Waite Hocking Stirling (1829-1923), as first Bishop of the Bishopric of the Falkland Islands, cent.

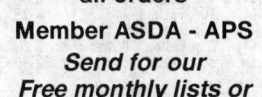

Gun Emplacement — A44

Designs: 2p, Volunteer on horseback, vert. 1sh, Volunteer in dress uniform, vert. 2sh, Defense Force badge.

Perf. 13½x13, 13x13½

1970, Apr. 30 Litho. Wmk. 314

188 A44 2p ultra & multi 65 30
189 A44 6p multicolored 1.25 75
190 A44 1sh buff & multi 2.50 1.25
191 A44 2sh yellow & multi 5.25 2.50

Falkland Islands Defense Force, 50th anniv.

The Great Britain, 1843 A45

The Great Britain in: 4p, 1845. 9p, 1876. 1sh, 1886. 2sh, 1970.

1970, Oct. 30 Litho. *Perf. 14½*

192 A45 2p lemon & multi 40 24
193 A45 4p lilac & multi 80 55
194 A45 9p bister & multi 1.50 1.25
195 A45 1sh org brn & multi 2.75 2.00
196 A45 2sh multicolored 5.25 4.25
Nos. 192-196 (5) 10.70 8.29

Nos. 166-178 Surcharged with New Value (Decimal Currency) and Bar

1971, Feb. 15 Photo. *Perf. 14*

197 A41 ½p on ½p multi 80 80
198 A41 1p on 1½p multi 20 20
199 A41 1½p on 2p multi 28 28
200 A41 2p on 3p multi 35 35
201 A41 2½p on 3½p multi 48 48
202 A41 3p on 4½p multi 55 55
203 A41 4p on 5½p multi 70 70
204 A41 5p on 6p multi 90 90
205 A41 6p on 1sh multi 1.40 1.10
206 A41 7½p on 1sh6p multi 1.75 1.40
207 A41 10p on 2sh multi 2.75 2.00
208 A41 15p on 3sh multi 5.00 3.50
209 A41 25p on 5sh multi 10.00 7.25
Nos. 197-209 (13) 25.16 19.51

Flower Type of 1968
"p" instead of "d"

Designs as before. 1p, 2½p, 4p, 5p, 6p, 25p, horizontal.

Wmk. 314, Sideways on Vert. Stamps

1972, June 1 *Perf. 14*

210 A41 ½p Dusty miller 75 75
a. Wmk. upright ('74) 4.25 6.25
b. Wmk. 373 ('75) 80 80
211 A41 1p Pig vine 25 15
212 A41 1½p Pale maiden 30 22
213 A41 2p Dog orchid 2.00 2.00
a. Wmk. upright ('74) 2.50 2.50
214 A41 2½p Sea cabbage 60 50
215 A41 3p Vanilla daisy 60 55
216 A41 4p Arrowleaf marigold 70 70
217 A41 5p Diddle-dee 85 85
218 A41 6p Scurvy grass 9.50 8.50
a. Wmk. sideways ('74) 2.00 2.00
219 A41 7½p Prickly burr 2.00 2.00
220 A41 10p Fachine 4.25 4.25
221 A41 15p Lavender 3.75 3.75
222 A41 25p Felton's flower 7.25 7.25
Nos. 210-222 (13) 32.80 31.47

No. 213 has watermark sideways.

Silver Wedding Issue, 1972

Common Design Type

Design: Queen Elizabeth II, Prince Philip, Romney Marsh sheep and giant sea lions.

1972, Nov 20 Photo. *Perf. 14x14½*

223 CD324 1p sl grn & multi 28 28
224 CD324 10p ultra & multi 1.40 1.40

Princess Anne's Wedding Issue

Common Design Type

1973, Nov. 14 Litho. *Perf. 14*

225 CD325 5p lilac & multi 25 25
226 CD325 15p citron & multi 85 85

Fur Seals — A46

Tourist Publicity: 4p, Trout fishing. 5p, Rockhopper penguins. 15p, Military starling.

1974, Mar. 6 Litho. Wmk. 314

227 A46 2p lt ultra & multi 1.90 1.10
228 A46 4p brt blue & multi 2.50 1.65
229 A46 5p yellow & multi 3.00 1.65
230 A46 15p lt ultra & multi 5.00 3.50

Early 19th Cent. Mail Coach, UPU Emblem — A47

UPU Cent.: 5p, Packet, 1841. 8p, First British mail planes, 1911. 16p, Catapult mail, 1920's.

1974, July 31 *Perf. 14*

231 A47 2p multicolored 16 16
232 A47 5p multicolored 42 42
233 A47 8p multicolored 75 75
234 A47 16p multicolored 1.50 1.50

Churchill, Parliament and Big Ben — A48

Design: 20p, Churchill and warships.

1974, Nov. 30 *Perf. 13x13½*

235 A48 16p multicolored 1.00 1.00
236 A48 20p multicolored 1.25 1.25
a. Souvenir sheet of 2, #235-236 6.00 6.00

Sir Winston Churchill (1874-1965).

HMS Exeter A49

Battleships: 6p, HMNZS Achilles. 8p, Admiral Graf Spee. 16p, HMS Ajax.

1974, Dec. 13 *Perf. 14*

237 A49 2p multicolored 1.50 85
238 A49 6p multicolored 2.50 2.00
239 A49 8p multicolored 3.00 3.00
240 A49 16p multicolored 8.00 8.00

35th anniv. of the Battle of the River Plate between British ships and the German battleship Graf Spee.

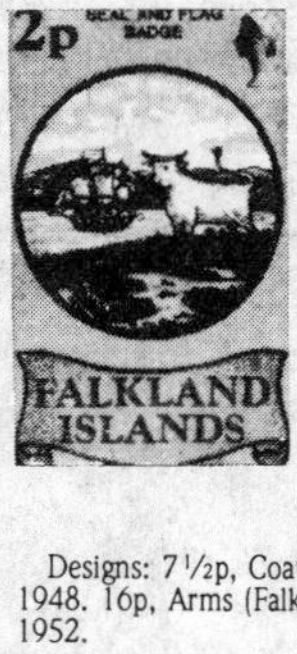

Seal and Flag Badge — A50

Designs: 7½p, Coat of arms, 1925. 10p, Arms, 1948. 16p, Arms (Falkland Islands Dependencies), 1952.

1975, Oct. 28 Litho. Wmk. 373

241 A50 2p multicolored 35 30
242 A50 7½p multicolored 1.10 1.00
243 A50 10p multicolored 1.40 1.25
244 A50 16p multicolored 2.25 2.00

Falkland Islands heraldic arms, 50th anniv.

½p-Coin and Trout A51

New Coinage: 5½p, 1p-coin and gentoo penguins, 8p, 2p-coin and upland geese. 10p, 5p-coin and black-browed albatross. 16p, 10p-coin and sea lions.

1975, Dec. 31 Litho. Wmk. 373

245 A51 2p copper & multi 22 22
246 A51 5½p copper & multi 45 45
247 A51 8p copper & multi 95 95
248 A51 10p silver & multi 1.40 1.40
249 A51 16p silver & multi 4.25 4.25
Nos. 245-249 (5) 7.27 7.27

Gathering Sheep A52

Sheep Farming: 7½p, Shearing. 10p, Dipping sheep. 20p, Motor Vessel Monsunen collecting wool.

1976, Apr. 28 Litho. *Perf. 13½*

250 A52 2p multicolored 22 16
251 A52 7½p multicolored 1.50 45
252 A52 10p multicolored 80 65
253 A52 20p multicolored 1.65 1.65

Prince Philip, 1957 Visit A53

Designs: 11p, Queen, ampulla and spoon. 33p, Queen awaiting anointment, and Knights of the Garter.

1977, Feb. 7 *Perf. 13½x14*

254 A53 6p multicolored 35 35
a. Booklet pane of 4, wmk. 314 2.50
255 A53 11p multicolored 60 60
a. Booklet pane of 4 2.75
256 A53 33p multicolored 1.50 1.50
a. Booklet pane of 4 6.25

25th anniv. of the reign of Elizabeth II.

Map of West and East Falkland with Communications Centers — A54

Telecommunications: 11p, Ship to shore communications at Fox Bay. 40p, Globe with Telex tape and telephone.

1977, Oct. 24 Litho. *Perf. 14½x14*

257 A54 3p yel brown & multi 30 25
258 A54 11p lt ultra & multi 70 60
259 A54 40p rose & multi 3.00 3.00

A.E.S., 1957-1974 A55

Designs: Mail ships.

1978, Jan. 25 Wmk. 373 *Perf. 14*

260 A55 1p shown 15 15
261 A55 2p Darwin, 1957-75 15 15
262 A55 3p Merak-N 1951-53 18 18
263 A55 4p Fitzroy, 1936-57 22 22
264 A55 5p Lafonia 1936-41 28 28
265 A55 6p Fleurus, 1924-33 35 35
266 A55 7p S.S. Falkland, 1914-34 40 40
267 A55 8p Oravia, 1900-12 45 45
268 A55 9p Memphis, 1890-97 50 50
269 A55 10p Black Hawk, 1873-80 60 60
270 A55 20p Foam, 1963-72 80 80
271 A55 25p Fairy, 1857-61 1.00 1.00
272 A55 50p Amelia, 1852-54 1.90 1.90
273 A55 £1 Nautilus, 1846-48 3.75 3.75
274 A55 £3 Hebe, 1842-46 10.50 10.50
Nos. 260-274 (15) 21.23 21.23

The 1p, 3p, 5p, 6p and 10p were also issued in booklet panes of 4.

Nos. 260-274 also issued inscribed 1982.

For overprints, see Nos. 352-353.

Elizabeth II Coronation Anniversary Issue

Souvenir Sheet

Common Design Type

1978, June 2 Unwmk. *Perf. 15*

275 Sheet of 6 6.00 6.00
a. CD326 25p Red Dragon of Wales 95 95
b. CD327 25p Elizabeth II 95 95
c. CD328 25p Hornless ram 95 95

No. 275 contains 2 se-tenant strips of Nos. 275a-275c, separated by horizontal gutter with commemorative and descriptive inscriptions.

Short Sunderland Mark III — A56

Design: 33p, Pane in flight and route Southampton to Stanley.

1978, Apr. 28 Wmk. 373 *Perf. 14*

276 A56 11p multicolored 1.75 1.75
277 A56 33p multicolored 3.00 3.00

First direct flight Southampton, England to Stanley, Falkland Islands, 26th anniv.

First Fox Bay PO and No. 1 — A57

Macrocystis Pyrifera — A58

Designs: 11p, Second Stanley Post Office and #2. 15p, New Island Post Office and #3. 22p, 1st Stanley Post Office and #4.

1978, Aug. 8 Litho. *Perf. 13½x13*

278 A57 3p multicolored 25 16
279 A57 11p multicolored 60 60
280 A57 15p multicolored 80 80
281 A57 22p multicolored 1.25 1.25

Falkland Islands postage stamps, cent.

1979, Feb. 19 Litho. *Perf. 14*

Kelp: 7p, Durvillea. 11p, Lessoniae, horiz. 15p, Callophyllis, horiz. 25p, Iridea.

282 A58	3p	multicolored	18	18
283 A58	7p	multicolored	35	35
284 A58	11p	multicolored	50	50
285 A58	15p	multicolored	65	65
286 A58	25p	multicolored	1.10	1.10
		Nos. 282-286 (5)	2.78	2.78

Britten-Norman Islander over Map — A59

Opening of Stanley Airport: 11p, Fokker F27 over map. 15p, Fokker F28 over Stanley. 25p, Cessna 172 Skyhawk, Islander and Fokkers F27, F28 aver runway.

1979, May 1 Litho. *Perf. 13½*

287 A59	3p	multicolored	22	18
288 A59	11p	multicolored	70	70
289 A59	15p	multicolored	90	90
290 A59	25p	multicolored	1.65	1.65

Rowland Hill and No. 121 A60

Sir Rowland Hill (1795-1879), originator of penny postage, and: 11p, Falkland Islands No. 1, vert. 25p, Penny Black. 33p, Falkland Islands No. 37, vert.

1979, Aug. 27 *Perf. 14*

291 A60	3p	multicolored	15	15
292 A60	11p	multicolored	42	42
293 A60	25p	multicolored	90	90

Souvenir Sheet

294 A60	33p	multicolored	1.40	1.40

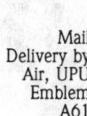

Mail Delivery by Air, UPU Emblem A61

UPU Membership Cent. (Modes of Mail Delivery): 11p, Horseback. 25p, Schooner Gwendolin.

1979, Nov. 26

295 A61	3p	multicolored	16	16
296 A61	11p	multicolored	60	60
297 A61	25p	multicolored	1.25	1.25

Commerson's Dolphin — A62

1980, Feb. 25 Wmk. 373 *Perf. 14*

298 A62	3p	Peale's porpoise, vert.	16	15
299 A62	6p	shown	28	24
300 A62	7p	Hour-glass dolphin	32	32
301 A62	11p	Spectacled porpose, vert.	48	48
302 A62	15p	Dusky dolphin	65	65
303 A62	25p	Killer whale	1.25	1.25
		Nos. 298-303 (6)	3.14	3.09

Miniature Sheet

Falkland Islands Cancel, 1878 A63

Designs: b, New Islds., 1915. c, Falklands Islds., 1901. d, Port Stanley, 1935. e, Port Stanley airmail, 1952. f, Fox Bay, 1934.

1980, May 6 Litho. *Perf. 14*

304	Sheet of 6	2.00	2.00
a.-f.	A63 11p any single	32	32

London 1980 Intl. Stamp Exhib., May 6-14.

Queen Mother Elizabeth Birthday
Common Design Type

1980, Aug. 4 Litho. *Perf. 14*

305 CD330	11p	multicolored	50	50

Striated Caracara A64

1980, Aug. 11 Wmk. 373 *Perf. 13½*

306 A64	3p	shown	16	15
307 A64	11p	Red-backed buzzard	60	60
308 A64	15p	Crested caracara	70	70
309 A64	25p	Cassin's falcon	1.40	1.40

Port Egmont, Early Settlement A65

1980, Dec. 22 Litho. *Perf. 14*

310 A65	3p	Stanley	16	15
311 A65	11p	shown	60	60
312 A65	25p	Port Louis	1.25	70
313 A65	33p	Mission House, Keppel Island	1.50	1.25

Polwarth Sheep A66

1981, Jan. 19 Litho. *Perf. 14*

314 A66	3p	shown	15	15
315 A66	11p	Frisian cow and calf	40	40
316 A66	25p	Horse	85	85
317 A66	33p	Welsh collies	1.10	1.10

Map of Falkland Islands, Bowles and Carver, 1779 — A67

1981, May 22 Litho. *Perf. 14*

318 A67	3p	shown	15	15
319 A67	10p	Hawkin's Mainland, 1773	35	32
320 A67	13p	New Isles, 1747	45	40
321 A67	15p	French & British Islands	55	45
322 A67	25p	Falklands, 1771	90	70
323 A67	26p	Falklands, 1764	90	75
		Nos. 318-323 (6)	3.30	2.77

Royal Wedding Issue
Common Design Type

1981, July 22 Litho. *Perf. 13½x13*

324 CD331	10p	Bouquet	40	40
325 CD331	13p	Charles	52	52
326 CD331	52p	Couple	1.75	1.75

Duke of Edinburgh's Awards, 25th Anniv. — A68

1981, Sept. 28 Litho. *Perf. 14*

327 A68	10p	Spinning	30	30
328 A68	13p	Camping	40	40
329 A68	15p	Kayaking	45	45
330 A68	26p	Duke of Edinburgh	80	80

The Holy Virgin, by Guido Reni (1575-1642) — A69

Rock Cod — A70

Christmas: 3p, Adoration of the Holy Child, 16th cent. Dutch. 13p, Holy Family in an Italian Landscape, 17th cent. Italian.

1981, Nov. 2 Litho. *Perf. 14*

331 A69	3p	multicolored	15	15
332 A69	13p	multicolored	52	52
333 A69	26p	multicolored	1.00	1.00

1981, Dec. 7

Designs: Shelf fish. 5p, 15p, 25p horiz.

334 A70	5p	Falkland herring	15	15
335 A70	13p	shown	42	42
336 A70	15p	Patagonian hake	50	50
337 A70	25p	Southern blue whiting	85	85
338 A70	26p	Gray-tailed skate	85	85
		Nos. 334-338 (5)	2.77	2.77

Shipwrecks A71

1982, Feb. 15 Wmk. 373 *Perf. 14½*

339 A71	5p	Lady Elizabeth, 1913	18	18
340 A71	13p	Capricorn, 1882	48	48
341 A71	15p	Jhelum, 1870	55	55
342 A71	25p	Snowsquall, 1864	80	80
343 A71	26p	St. Mary, 1890	80	80
		Nos. 339-343 (5)	2.81	2.81

Sesquicentennial of Charles Darwin's Visit — A72

1982, Apr. 19 Litho. *Perf. 14*

344 A72	5p	Darwin	15	15
345 A72	17p	Microscope	55	55
346 A72	25p	Warrah	85	85
347 A72	34p	Beagle	1.10	1.10

Princess Diana Issue
Common Design Type

1982, July 5 Wmk. 373 *Perf. 13*

348 CD333	5p	Arms	15	15
349 CD333	17p	Diana	48	48
350 CD333	37p	Wedding	1.00	1.00
351 CD333	50p	Portrait	1.40	1.40

Nos. 264, 271 Overprinted: "1st PARTICIPATION / COMMONWEALTH GAMES 1982"

1982, Oct. 7 Litho. *Perf. 14*

352 A55	5p	multicolored	18	18
353 A55	25p	multicolored	90	90

12th Commonwealth Games, Brisbane, Australia, Sept. 30-Oct. 9.

Tussock Bird — A73

1982, Dec. 6 *Perf. 15x14½*

354 A73	5p	shown	15	15
355 A73	10p	Black-chinned siskin	32	32
356 A73	13p	Grass wren	42	42
357 A73	17p	Black-throated finch	55	55
358 A73	25p	Falkland-correndera pipit	85	85
359 A73	34p	Dark-faced ground-tyrant	1.10	1.10
		Nos. 354-359 (6)	3.39	3.39

British Occupation Sesquicentennial — A74

Designs: 1p, Raising the Standard, Port Louis, 1833, vert. 2p, Chelsea pensioners and barracks, 1849. 5p, Wool trade, 1874, vert. 10p, Ship repairing trade, 1850-90. 15p, Government House, early 20th cent. 20p, Battle of the Falkland Islands, 1914, vert. 25p, Whalebone Arch centenary, 1933. 40p, Contribution to World War II effort, 1939-45, vert. 50p, Visit of Duke of Edinburgh, 1957. £1, Royal Marines, 1933, 1983, vert. £2, Queen Elizabeth II, vert.

1983, Jan. 1 Litho. *Perf. 14*

360 A74	1p	multicolored	15	15
361 A74	2p	multicolored	15	15
362 A74	5p	multicolored	15	15
363 A74	10p	multicolored	22	22
364 A74	15p	multicolored	35	35
365 A74	20p	multicolored	45	45
366 A74	25p	multicolored	60	60
367 A74	40p	multicolored	1.00	1.00
368 A74	50p	multicolored	1.25	1.25
369 A74	£1	multicolored	2.50	2.50
370 A74	£2	multicolored	5.50	5.50
		Nos. 360-370 (11)	12.32	12.32

For surcharges, see Nos. 402-403.

A75

1983, Mar. 14

371 A75	5p	No. 69	15	15
372 A75	17p	No. 65	55	55
373 A75	34p	No. 75, vert.	1.25	1.25
374 A75	50p	No. 370, vert.	1.25	1.25

Commonwealth Day.

First Anniv. of Liberation A76

1983, June 14 Wmk. 373 *Perf. 14*

375 A76	5p	Army	15	15
376 A76	13p	Merchant Navy	30	30
377 A76	17p	Royal Air Force	45	45
378 A76	50p	Royal Navy	1.25	1.25
a.		Souvenir sheet of 4, #375-378	2.50	2.50

Local Fruit
A77

1983, Oct. 10 Litho. *Perf. 14*
379 A77 5p Diddle dee 15 15
380 A77 17p Tea berries 50 50
381 A77 25p Mountain berries 75 75
382 A77 34p Native strawberries 1.00 1.00

Britten-Norman Islander — A78

1983, Nov. 14 Litho. *Perf. 14*
383 A78 5p shown 15 15
384 A78 13p DHC-2 Beaver 22 22
385 A78 17p Noorduyn Norseman 30 30
386 A78 50p Auster 85 85

Green Spider — A79

Insects and Spiders.

1984, Jan. 1 Litho. *Perf. 14*
387 A79 1p shown 15 15
388 A79 2p Ichneumon-Fly 15 15
389 A79 3p Brocade Moth 15 15
390 A79 4p Black Beetle 15 15
391 A79 5p Fritillary 15 15
392 A79 6p Green Spider, diff. 15 15
393 A79 7p Ichneumon-Fly, diff. 16 16
394 A79 8p Ochre Shoulder 18 18
395 A79 9p Clocker Weevil 20 20
396 A79 10p Hover Fly 22 22
397 A79 20p Weevil 45 45
398 A79 25p Metallic Beetle 55 55
399 A79 50p Camel Cricket 1.10 1.10
400 A79 £1 Beauchene Spider 2.25 2.25
401 A79 £3 Southern Painted Lady 6.85 6.85
Nos. 387-401 (15) 12.86 12.86

No. 388 exists inscribed "1986."

Nos. 364, 366 Surcharged

1984, Jan. 3 Litho. *Perf. 14*
402 A74 17p on 15p multi 38 38
403 A74 22p on 25p multi 48 48

Lloyd's List Issue
Common Design Type

1984, May 7 Wmk. 373 *Perf. 14½*
404 CD335 6p Wavertree 15 15
405 CD335 17p Port Stanley, 1910 38 38
406 CD335 22p Oravia 52 52
407 CD335 52p Cunard Countess 1.25 1.25

Great Grebe — A80

1984, Aug. 6 *Perf. 14½x14*
408 A80 17p shown 52 52
409 A80 22p Silver grebe 70 70
410 A80 52p Rolland's grebe 1.75 1.75

See Nos. 450-453.

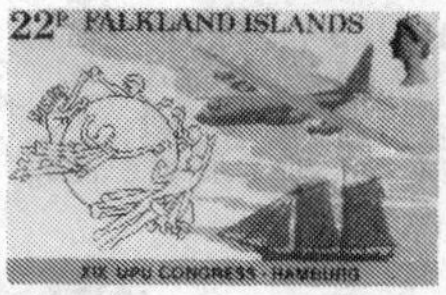

1984 UPU Congress
A81

1984, June 22 Litho. *Perf. 14*
411 A81 22p Emblem, jet, ship 60 60

Wildlife Conservation — A82

1984, Nov. 5 Litho. *Perf. 14½*
412 A82 6p Birds 16 16
413 A82 17p Plants 50 50
414 A82 22p Mammals 65 60
415 A82 52p Marine Life 1.65 1.40
a. Souvenir sheet of 4, #412-415 3.75 3.25

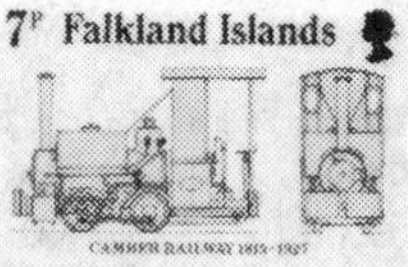

Camber Railway, 1915-1927
A83

1985, Feb. 18 Litho. *Perf. 14*
416 A83 7p multicolored 20 20
417 A83 22p multicolored 60 60
418 A83 27p multicolored 75 75

Size: 77x26mm
419 A83 54p multicolored 1.50 1.50

Queen Mother 85th Birthday
Common Design Type

Designs: 7p, Commonwealth Visitor's Reception. 22p, With Prince Charles, Mark Phillips, Princess Anne. 27p, 80th birthday celebration. 54p, Holding Prince Henry. £1, In coach with Princess Diana.

Perf. 14½x14
1985, June 7 Litho. Wmk. 384
420 CD336 7p multicolored 20 20
421 CD336 22p multicolored 60 60
422 CD336 27p multicolored 75 75
423 CD336 54p multicolored 1.50 1.50

Souvenir Sheet
424 CD336 £1 multicolored 2.75 2.75

Mount Pleasant Airport Opening
A84

1985, May 12 Litho. *Perf. 14½*
425 A84 7p Pioneer camp, docked ship 20 20
426 A84 22p Construction site 60 60
427 A84 27p Runway layout 70 70
428 A84 54p Aircraft landing 1.40 1.40

Captain J. McBride, HMS Jason, 1765 — A85

18th-19th century naval explorers: 22p, Commodore J. Byron, HMS Dolphin and Tamar, 1765. 27p, Vice-Adm. R. Fitzroy, HMS Beagle, 1831. 54p, Adm. Sir B.J. Sulivan, HMS Philomel, 1842.

1985, Sept. 23
429 A85 7p multicolored 22 22
430 A85 22p multicolored 65 65
431 A85 27p multicolored 75 75
432 A85 54p multicolored 1.65 1.65

Philibert Commerson (1727-1773), Commerson's Dolphin — A86

Naturalists, endangered species: 22p, Rene Primevere Lesson (1794-1849), kelp. 27p, Joseph Paul Gaimard (1796-1858), diving petrel. 54p, Charles Darwin (1803-1882), Calceolaria darwinii.

1985, Nov. 4 *Perf. 14½*
433 A86 7p multicolored 35 35
434 A86 22p multicolored 1.10 1.10
435 A86 27p multicolored 1.25 1.25
436 A86 54p multicolored 2.50 2.50

Seashells
A87

1986, Feb. 10 Wmk. 384 *Perf. 14½*
437 A87 7p Painted keyhole limpet 30 30
438 A87 22p Magellanic volute 1.00 1.00
439 A87 27p Falkland scallop 1.25 1.25
440 A87 54p Rough thorn drupe 2.50 2.50

Queen Elizabeth II 60th Birthday
Common Design Type

Designs: 10p, With Princess Margaret at St. Paul's, Waldenbury, 1932. 24p, Christmas broadcast from Sandringham, 1958. 29p, Order of the Thistle, St. Giles Cathedral, Edinburgh, 1962. 45p, Royal reception on the Britannia, US visit, 1976. 58p, Visiting Crown Agents' offices, 1983.

1986, Apr. 21 Litho. *Perf. 14x14½*
441 CD337 10p scar, blk & sil 30 30
442 CD337 24p ultra, blk & sil 72 72
443 CD337 29p green & multi 88 88
444 CD337 45p violet & multi 1.35 1.35
445 CD337 58p rose vio & multi 1.75 1.75
Nos. 441-445 (5) 5.00 5.00

AMERIPEX '86 — A88

SS Great Britain's arrival in the Falkland Isls., Cent.: 10p, Maiden voyage, crossing the Atlantic, 1845. 24p, Wreck in Sparrow Cove, 1937. 29p, Refloating wreck, 1970. 58p, Restored vessel, Bristol, 1986.

1986, May 22
446 A88 10p multicolored 20 20
447 A88 24p multicolored 70 70
448 A88 29p multicolored 90 90
449 A88 58p multicolored 1.75 1.75
a. Souvenir sheet of 4, #446-449 3.75 3.75

Bird Type of 1984

Rockhopper Penguins.

1986, Aug. 25 Wmk. 373 *Perf. 14½*
450 A80 10p Adult 32 32
451 A80 24p Adults swimming 75 75
452 A80 29p Adults, diff. 90 90
453 A80 58p Adult and young 1.90 1.90

Wedding of Prince Andrew and Sarah Ferguson — A90

Various photographs: 17p, Presenting Queen's Polo Cup, Windsor, 1986. 22p, Open carriage, wedding. 29p, Andrew wearing military fatigues.

1986, Nov. 10 Wmk. 384 *Perf. 14½*
454 A90 17p multicolored 50 50
455 A90 22p multicolored 65 65
456 A90 29p multicolored 85 85

Royal Engineers, 200th Anniv. — A91

1987, Feb. 9 Litho. *Perf. 14½*
457 A91 10p Surveying Sapper Hill 30 30
458 A91 24p Explosives disposal 75 75
459 A91 29p Boxer Bridge, Pt. Stanley 85 85
460 A91 58p Postal services, Stanley Airport 1.90 1.90

Seals
A92

1987, Apr. 27
461 A92 10p Southern sea lion 32 32
462 A92 24p Falkland fur seal 80 80
463 A92 29p Southern elephant seal 95 95
464 A92 58p Leopard seal 1.90 1.90

Hospitals — A93

Designs: 10p, Victorian Cottage Home, c. 1912. 24p, King Edward VII Memorial Hospital, c. 1914. 29p, Churchill Wing, 1953. 58p, Prince Andrew Wing, 1987.

1987, Dec. 8 *Perf. 14*
465 A93 10p multicolored 30 30
466 A93 24p multicolored 70 70
467 A93 29p multicolored 85 85
468 A93 58p multicolored 1.65 1.65

Fungi — A94

1987, Sept. 14 Litho. *Perf. 14½*
469 A94 10p Suillus luteus 35 35
470 A94 24p Mycena 80 80
471 A94 29p Camarophyllus adonis 1.00 1.00
472 A94 58p Gerronema schusteri 2.00 2.00

1940 Morris Truck, Fitzroy — A95

Classic automobiles: 24p, 1929 Citroen Kegresse, San Carlos. 29p, 1933 Ford 1-Ton Truck, Port Stanley. 58p, 1935 Ford Model T Saloon, Darwin.

1988, Apr. 11 Litho. *Perf. 14*

473	A95	10p	multicolored	35	35
474	A95	24p	multicolored	85	85
475	A95	29p	multicolored	1.05	1.05
476	A95	58p	multicolored	2.05	2.05

Geese A96

1988, July 25

477	A96	10p	Kelp	35	35
478	A96	24p	Upland	85	85
479	A96	29p	Ruddy-headed	1.05	1.05
480	A96	58p	Ashy-headed	2.05	2.05

Lloyds of London, 300th Anniv.

Common Design Type

Designs: 10p, Lloyd's Nelson Collection silver service. 24p, Hydroponic Gardens, horiz. 29p, Supply ship A.E.S., horiz. 58p, Wreck of the Charles Cooper near the Falklands, 1866.

1988, Nov. 14 Litho. Wmk. 373

481	CD341	10p	multicolored	35	35
482	CD341	24p	multicolored	75	75
483	CD341	29p	multicolored	95	95
484	CD341	58p	multicolored	1.90	1.90

Ships of Cape Horn A97

1989, Feb. 28

485	A97	1p	Padua	15	15
486	A97	2p	Priwall, vert.	15	15
a.			Wmk. 384	15	15
487	A97	3p	Passat	15	15
a.			Wmk. 384	15	15
488	A97	4p	Archibald Russell, vert.	15	15
489	A97	5p	Pamir, vert.	16	16
490	A97	6p	Mozart	20	20
a.			Wmk. 384	20	20
491	A97	7p	Pommern	22	22
492	A97	8p	Preussen	26	26
493	A97	9p	Fennia	28	28
a.			Wmk. 384	28	28
494	A97	10p	Cassard	35	35
495	A97	20p	Lawhill	70	70
496	A97	25p	Garthpool	80	80
497	A97	50p	Grace Harwar	1.65	1.65
498	A97	£1	Criccieth Castle	3.25	3.25
a.			Wmk. 384	3.25	3.25
499	A97	£3	Cutty Sark, vert.	10.00	10.00
500	A97	£5	Flying Cloud	17.00	17.00
			Nos. 485-500 (16)	35.47	35.47

Nos. 486a, 487a, 490a, 493a, 498a are dated "1991."

Whales A98

1989, May 15 Wmk. 384 *Perf. 14*

501	A98	10p	Southern right	35	35
502	A98	24p	Minke	82	82
503	A98	29p	Humpback	1.00	1.00
504	A98	58p	Blue	2.00	2.00

Sports Assoc. Activities A99

Children's drawings.

1989, Sept. 16

505	A99	5p	Gymkhana	16	16
506	A99	10p	Steer Riding	32	32
507	A99	17p	Sheep shearing	55	55
508	A99	24p	Dog trial	78	78
509	A99	29p	Horse racing	95	95
510	A99	45p	Sack race	1.45	1.45
			Nos. 505-510 (6)	4.21	4.21

Battles — A100

Commanders, ships and ship crests: 10p, Vice-Adm. Sturdee, HMS *Invincible*. 24p, Vice-Adm. Von Spee, SMS *Scharnhorst*. 29p, Commodore Harwood, HMS *Ajax*. 58p, Capt. Langsdorff, *Admiral Graff Spee*.

1989, Dec. 8 *Perf. 14x13½*

511	A100	10p	multicolored	32	32
512	A100	24p	multicolored	75	75
513	A100	29p	multicolored	92	92
514	A100	58p	multicolored	1.85	1.85

Battle of the Falklands, 75th anniv. (10p, 24p); Battle of the River Plate, 50th anniv. (29p, 58p).

Emblems and Presentation Spitfires, 1940 — A101

1990, May 3 Wmk. 373 *Perf. 14*

515	A101	12p	No. 92 Squadron	40	40
516	A101	26p	No. 611 Squadron	88	88
517	A101	31p	No. 92 Squadron, diff.	1.05	1.05
518	A101	62p	Spitfires scramble	2.10	2.10

Souvenir Sheet

519	A101	£1	Battle of Britain	3.35	3.35

Stamp World London '90.
For souvenir sheet similar to #519, see #530.

A102

A103

1990, Apr. 1 Wmk. 384 *Perf. 14½*

520	A102	12p	Kidney Is.	38	38
521	A102	26p	Beauchene Is.	85	85
522	A102	31p	Bird Is.	1.00	1.00
523	A102	62p	Elephant Jason Is.	2.00	2.00

Nature reserves and bird sanctuaries.

Queen Mother, 90th Birthday

Common Design Types

1990, Aug. 4 Wmk. 384 *Perf. 14x15*

524	CD343	26p	Queen Mother in Dover	88	88

Perf. 14½

525	CD344	£1	Steering the "Queen Elizabeth", 1946	3.40	3.40

Wmk. 384

1990, Oct. 3 Litho. *Perf. 14*

Black Browed Albatross

526	A103	12p	shown	42	42
527	A103	26p	Adult bird	90	90
528	A103	31p	Adult, chick	1.10	1.10
529	A103	62p	Bird in flight	2.15	2.15

Battle of Britain Type of 1990 inscribed "SECOND VISIT OF / HRH THE DUKE OF EDINBURGH"

Souvenir Sheet

1991, Mar. 7

530	A101	£1	multicolored	4.00	4.00

Orchids — A104

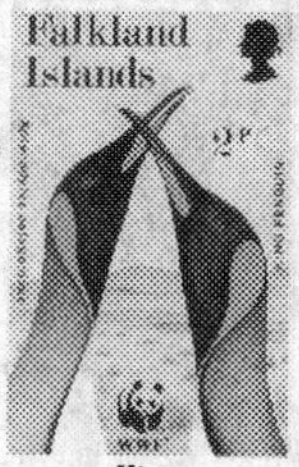

King Penguin — A105

1991, Mar. 18 Wmk. 373

531	A104	12p	Gavilea australis	42	42
532	A104	26p	Codonorchis lessonii	90	90
533	A104	31p	Chlorea gaudichaudii	1.10	1.10
534	A104	62p	Gavilea littoralis	2.15	2.15

1991, Aug. 26 Wmk. 384

535	A105	2p	Two adults crossing bills	15	15
536	A105	6p	Two adults, one brooding	20	20
537	A105	12p	Adult with two young	42	42
538	A105	20p	Adult swimming	70	70
539	A105	31p	Adult feeding young	1.10	1.10
540	A105	62p	Two adults, diff.	2.15	2.15
			Nos. 535-540 (6)	4.72	4.72

World Wildlife Fund.

Falkland Islands Bisects, Cent. A106

1991, Sept. 10 Wmk. 384 *Perf. 14½*

541	A106	12p	#9, #15	42	42
542	A106	26p	On cover	90	90
543	A106	31p	Unsevered pair	1.10	1.10
544	A106	62p	S.S. Isis	2.15	2.15

Discovery of America, 500th Anniv. (in 1992) — A107

Sailing ships: 14p, STV Eye of the Wind. 29p, STV Soren Larsen. 34p, Nina, Santa Maria, Pinta. 68p, Columbus and Santa Maria.

1991, Dec. 12 Wmk. 373 *Perf. 14*

545	A107	14p	multicolored	50	50
546	A107	29p	multicolored	1.00	1.00
547	A107	34p	multicolored	1.20	1.20
548	A107	68p	multicolored	2.40	2.40

World Columbian Stamp Expo '92, Chicago and Genoa '92 Intl. Philatelic Exhibitions.

Falkland Islands stamps can be mounted in the Scott British South Atlantic album.

Queen Elizabeth II's Accession to the Throne, 40th Anniv.

Common Design Type

1992, Feb. 6

549	CD349	7p	multicolored	25	25
550	CD349	14p	multicolored	50	50
551	CD349	29p	multicolored	1.00	1.00
552	CD349	34p	multicolored	1.20	1.20
553	CD349	68p	multicolored	2.40	2.40
			Nos. 549-553 (5)	5.35	5.35

Christ Church Cathedral, Cent. — A108

1992, Feb. 21 Wmk. 384 *Perf. 14½*

554	A108	14p	Laying foundation stone	50	50
555	A108	29p	Interior, 1920	1.00	1.00
556	A108	34p	Bishop's chair	1.20	1.20
557	A108	68p	Without tower c. 1900, horiz.	2.40	2.40

First Sighting of Falkland Islands by Capt. John Davis, 400th Anniv. A109

Designs: 22p, Capt. John Davis using backstaff. 29p, Capt. Davis working on chart. 34p, Queen Elizabeth I, Queen Elizabeth II. 68p, The Desire sights Falkland Islands.

1992, Aug. 14 Wmk. 373

558	A109	22p	multicolored	85	85
559	A109	29p	multicolored	1.15	1.15
560	A109	34p	multicolored	1.30	1.30
561	A109	68p	multicolored	2.60	2.60

Falkland Islands Defense Force and West Yorkshire Regiment — A110

Designs: 7p, Private, Falkland Islands Volunteers, 1892. 14p, Officer, Falkland Islands Defense Corps, 1914. 22p, Officer, Falkland Islands Defense Force, 1920. 29p, Private, Falkland Islands Defense Force, 1939-45. 34p, Officer, West Yorkshire Regiment, 1942. 68p, Private, West Yorkshire Regiment, 1942.

1992, Oct. 1 *Perf. 14*

562	A110	7p	multicolored	28	28
563	A110	14p	multicolored	55	55
564	A110	22p	multicolored	85	85
565	A110	29p	multicolored	1.15	1.15
566	A110	34p	multicolored	1.30	1.30
567	A110	68p	multicolored	2.60	2.60
			Nos. 562-567 (6)	6.73	6.73

Gulls and Terns — A111

Perf. 14x14½

1993, Jan. 2 Litho. Wmk. 384

568	A111	15p	South American tern	52	52
569	A111	31p	Pink breasted gull	1.05	1.05
570	A111	36p	Dolphin gull	1.25	1.25
571	A111	72p	Dominican gull	2.50	2.50

Souvenir Sheet

Visit of Liner QE II to Falkland Islands — A112

Wmk. 373

1993, Jan. 22 Litho. *Perf. 14*

572 A112	£2	multicolored	6.00	6.00

Royal Air Force, 75th Anniv.

Common Designs Type

Designs: No. 573, Lockheed Tristar. No. 574, Lockheed Hercules. No. 575, Boeing Vertol Chinook. No. 576, Avro Vulcan.

No. 577a, Hawker Siddeley Andover. b, Westland Wessex. c, Panavia Tornado F3. d, McDonnell Douglas Phantom.

Wmk. 373

1993, Apr. 3 Litho. *Perf. 14*

573 CD350	15p	multicolored	42	42
574 CD350	15p	multicolored	42	42
575 CD350	15p	multicolored	42	42
576 CD350	15p	multicolored	42	42

Souvenir Sheet

577 CD350	36p	Sheet of 4, #a.-d.	4.25	4.25

Fisheries A113

Designs: 15p, Short-finned squid. 31p, Stern haul of whiptailed hake. 36p, Fishery Patrol Vessel Falkalnds Protector. 72p, Aerial surveillance by Britten-Norman Islander.

Wmk. 384

1993, July 1 Litho. *Perf. 14*

578 A113	15p	multicolored	42	42
579 A113	31p	multicolored	86	86
580 A113	36p	multicolored	1.00	1.00
581 A113	72p	multicolored	2.00	2.00

Launch of SS Great Britain, 150th Anniv. — A114

Perf. 14x13½

1993, July 19 Litho. Wmk. 384

582 A114	8p	In drydock, Bristol	24	24
583 A114	£1	At sea	2.90	2.90

Cruise Ships and Penguins A115

Wmk. 373

1993, Oct. 1 Litho. *Perf. 14*

584 A115	16p	Explorer	45	45
585 A115	34p	Rockhopper penguins	1.00	1.00
586 A115	39p	World Discoverer	1.10	1.10
587 A115	78p	Columbus Caravelle	2.25	2.25

Pets — A116

Perf. 14x14½

1993, Dec. 1 Litho. Wmk. 384

588 A116	8p	Pony	24	24
589 A116	16p	Lamb	45	45
590 A116	34p	Puppy, kitten	1.00	1.00

Perf. 14½x14

591 A116	39p	Kitten, vert.	1.10	1.10
592 A116	78p	Collie, vert.	2.25	2.25
		Nos. 588-592 (5)	5.04	5.04

Ovptd. with Hong Kong '94 Emblem

1994, Feb. 18

593 A116	8p	on #588	24	24
594 A116	16p	on #589	45	45
595 A116	34p	on #590	1.00	1.00
596 A116	39p	on #591	1.10	1.10
597 A116	78p	on #592	2.25	2.25
		Nos. 593-597 (5)	5.04	5.04

Inshore Marine Life A117

Wmk. 384

1994, Apr. 4 Litho. *Perf. 14*

598 A117	1p	Goose barnacles, vert.	15	15
599 A117	2p	Painted shrimp	15	15
600 A117	8p	Common limpet	22	22
601 A117	9p	Mullet	25	25
602 A117	10p	Sea anemones	30	30
603 A117	20p	Rock eel	60	60
604 A117	25p	Spider crab	75	75
605 A117	50p	Lobster krill, vert.	1.50	1.50
606 A117	80p	Falkland skate	2.50	2.50
607 A117	£1	Centollon crab	3.00	3.00
608 A117	£3	Rock cod	9.00	9.00
609 A117	£5	Octopus, vert.	15.00	15.00
		Nos. 598-609 (12)	33.42	33.42

Founding of Stanley, 150th Anniv. A118

Designs: 9p, Blacksmith's shop, dockyard, Sir James Clark Ross, explorer. 17p, James Leith Mody, first colonial chaplain, home at 21 Fitzroy Road. 30p, Stanley cottage, Dr. Henry J. Hamblin, first colonial surgeon. 35p, Pioneer row, Sergeant Major Henry Felton. 40p, Government House, Governor R. C. Moody R.E. 65p, View of Stanley, Edward Stanley, 14th Earl of Derby, Secretary of State for Colonies.

Wmk. 373

1994, July 1 Litho. *Perf. 14*

610 A118	9p	multicolored	25	25
611 A118	17p	multicolored	50	50
612 A118	30p	multicolored	90	90
613 A118	35p	multicolored	1.00	1.00
614 A118	40p	multicolored	1.10	1.10
615 A118	65p	multicolored	1.90	1.90
		Nos. 610-615 (6)	5.65	5.65

SEMI-POSTAL STAMP

Catalogue values for unused stamps in this section are for Never Hinged items.

Rebuilding after Conflict with Argentina — SP1

Wmk. 373

1982, Sept. 13 Litho. *Perf. 11*

B1 SP1	£1 + £1	Battle sites	5.00	5.00

Liberation of Falkland Islands, 10th Anniv. — SP2

Designs: 14p+6p, San Carlos Cemetery. 29p+11p, 1982 War Memorial, Port Stanley. 34p+16p, South Atlantic Medal. 68p+32p, Government House, Port Stanley.

Wmk. 373

1992, June 14 Litho. *Perf. 14*

B2 SP2	14p +6p	multi	65	65
B3 SP2	29p +11p	multi	1.50	1.50
B4 SP2	34p +16p	multi	2.00	2.00
B5 SP2	68p +32p	multi	3.80	3.80
a.		Souvenir sheet of 4, #B2-B5	8.00	8.00

Surtax for Soldiers', Sailors' and Airmen's Families Association.

POSTAGE DUE STAMPS

Catalogue values for unused stamps in this section are for never hinged items.

Penguin — D1

Perf. 14½x14

1991, Jan. 7 Litho. Wmk. 373

J1 D1	1p	lilac rose & lake	15	15
J2 D1	2p	buff & brown org	15	15
J3 D1	3p	yel & orange yel	15	15
J4 D1	4p	lt bl grn & dk bl grn	16	16
J5 D1	5p	sky blue & Prus bl	20	20
J6 D1	10p	lt blue & dk blue	40	40
J7 D1	20p	lt violet & dk vio	80	80
J8 D1	50p	brt yel grn & dk yel green	1.95	1.95
		Nos. J1-J8 (8)	3.96	3.96

WAR TAX STAMPS

Regular Issue of 1912-14 **WAR STAMP** Overprinted

1918, Oct. 7 Wmk. 3 *Perf. 14*

MR1 A7	½p	yellow green	50	*3.00*
MR2 A7	1p	red	32	*2.00*
a.		Double overprint	*2,500.*	
MR3 A7	1sh	bister brown	7.50	*35.00*
a.		Pair, one without overprint	*6,000.*	

No. MR3a probably is caused by a foldover and is not constant.

FALKLAND ISLANDS DEPENDENCIES

Catalogue values for unused stamps in this section are for Never Hinged items.

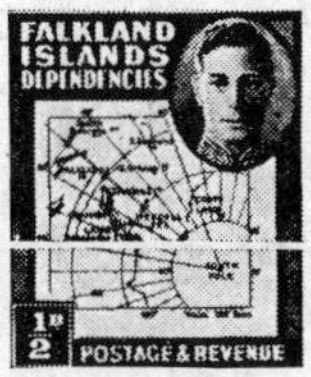

Map of Falkland Islands — A1

Engr., Center Litho. in Black

1946, Feb. 1 Wmk. 4 *Perf. 12*

1L1	A1	1/2p	yellow green	65	1.00
1L2	A1	1p	blue violet	65	1.25
1L3	A1	2p	deep carmine	65	1.25
1L4	A1	3p	ultramarine	1.25	1.25
1L5	A1	4p	deep plum	1.25	2.00
1L6	A1	6p	orange yellow	1.90	2.50
1L7	A1	9p	brown	1.90	2.50
1L8	A1	1sh	rose violet	3.75	5.00
			Nos. 1L1-1L8 (8)	12.00	16.75

Nos. 1L1-1L8 were reissued in 1948, printed on more opaque paper with the lines of the map finer and clearer. See No. 1L13.

Peace Issue

Common Design Type

1946, Oct. 4 *Perf. 13 1/2x14*

1L9	CD303	1p	purple	50	50
1L10	CD303	3p	deep blue	90	90

Silver Wedding Issue

Common Design Types

1948, Dec. 6 Photo. *Perf. 14x14 1/2*

1L11	CD304	2 1/2p	brt ultra	50	50

Perf. 11 1/2x11

Engr.

1L12	CD305	1sh	blue violet	6.00	6.00

Type of 1946

1949, Mar. 6 *Perf. 12*

Center Litho. in Black

1L13	A1	2 1/2p	deep blue	9.00	9.00

UPU Issue

Common Design Types

Engr.; Name Typo. on 2p, 3p

1949, Oct. 10 *Perf. 13 1/2, 11x11 1/2*

1L14	CD306	1p	violet	2.50	1.65
1L15	CD307	2p	dp carmine	5.00	2.00
1L16	CD308	3p	indigo	7.50	4.25
1L17	CD309	6p	red orange	12.50	8.50

Coronation Issue

Common Design Type

1953, June 4 *Perf. 13 1/2x13*

1L18	CD312	1p	purple & black	1.65	1.65

John Biscoe — A2

Trepassey A3

Ships: 1 1/2p, Wyatt Earp. 2p, Eagle. 2 1/2p, Penola. 3p, Discovery II. 4p, William Scoresby. 6p, Discovery. 9p, Endurance. 1sh, Deutschland. 2sh, Pourquoi-pas? 2sh6p, Français. 5sh, Scotia. 10sh, Antarctic. £1, Belgica.

1954, Feb. 1 Engr. *Perf. 12 1/2*

Center in Black

1L19	A2	1/2p	blue green	22	22
1L20	A3	1p	sepia	22	22
1L21	A3	1 1/2p	olive	30	30
1L22	A3	2p	rose red	45	45
1L23	A3	2 1/2p	yellow	45	45
1L24	A3	3p	ultra	55	55
1L25	A3	4p	red violet	65	65
1L26	A2	6p	rose violet	1.10	1.10
1L27	A2	9p	black	2.00	1.50
1L28	A3	1sh	org brown	2.50	2.00
1L29	A3	2sh	lilac rose	4.50	3.25
1L30	A2	2sh6p	blue gray	6.75	5.50
1L31	A2	5sh	violet	22.50	15.00
1L32	A3	10sh	brt blue	45.00	27.50
1L33	A2	£1	black	110.00	65.00
			Nos. 1L19-1L33 (15)	197.19	123.69

Nos. 1L20, 1L23-1L24, 1L26 Overprinted in Black

TRANS-ANTARCTIC
EXPEDITION 1955-1958

1956, Jan 30 Center in Black

1L34	A3	1p	sepia	16	16
1L35	A3	2 1/2p	yellow	85	85
1L36	A3	3p	ultramarine	95	95
1L37	A2	6p	rose violet	1.10	1.10

Trans-Antarctic Expedition, 1955-1958.

Map of Falkland Islands Dependencies — A4

Perf. 13 1/2

1980, May 5 Litho. Wmk. 373

1L38	A4	1p	shown	15	15
1L39	A4	2p	Shag Rocks	15	15
1L40	A4	3p	Bird and Willis Islds.	15	15
1L41	A4	4p	Gulbrandsen Lake	15	15
1L42	A4	5p	King Edward Point	15	15
1L43	A4	6p	Shackleton's Memorial Cross	15	15
1L44	A4	7p	Shackleton's grave	18	18
1L45	A4	8p	Grytviken Church	20	20
1L46	A4	9p	Coaling Hulk "Louise"	28	28
1L47	A4	10p	Clerke Rocks	25	25
1L48	A4	20p	Candlemas Island	50	50
1L49	A4	25p	Twitcher Rock, Cook Island	65	65
1L50	A4	50p	"John Biscoe"	1.25	1.25
1L51	A4	£1	"Bransfield"	2.50	2.50
1L52	A4	£3	"Endurance"	8.00	8.00
			Nos. 1L38-1L52 (15)	14.71	14.71

Nos. 1L38-1L50 issued May 3, 1094 dated "1984." Same values.

1985, Nov. 18 Wmk. 384

1L48a	A4	20p		50	50
1L49a	A4	25p		60	60
1L50a	A4	50p		1.65	1.65
1L51a	A4	£1		2.25	2.25
1L52a	A4	£3		7.25	7.25
			Nos. 1L48a-1L52a (5)	12.25	12.25

Magellanic Clubmoss — A5

1981, Feb. 5 Litho. *Perf. 14*

1L53	A5	3p	shown	15	15
1L54	A5	6p	Alpine cat's-tail	25	25
1L55	A5	7p	Greater burnet	30	30
1L56	A5	11p	Antarctic bedstraw	45	45
1L57	A5	15p	Brown rush	60	60
1L58	A5	25p	Antarctic hair grass	85	85
			Nos. 1L53-1L58 (6)	2.60	2.60

Royal Wedding Issue

Common Design Type

1981, July 22 Litho. *Perf. 14*

1L59	CD331	10p	Bouquet	40	40
1L60	CD331	13p	Charles	52	52
1L61	CD331	52p	Couple	1.25	1.25

Reindeer in Spring A6

1982, Jan. 29 Litho. *Perf. 14*

1L62	A6	5p	shown	20	20
1L63	A6	13p	Autumn	52	52
1L64	A6	25p	Winter	1.00	1.00
1L65	A6	26p	Late winter	1.00	1.00

Gamasellus Racovitzai — A7

1982, Mar. 16 Litho. *Perf. 14*

1L66	A7	5p	shown	15	15
1L67	A7	10p	Alaskozetes antarcticus	25	25
1L68	A7	13p	Cryptopygus antarcticus	32	32
1L69	A7	15p	Notiomaso australis	38	38
1L70	A7	25p	Hydromedion sparsutum	60	60
1L71	A7	26p	Parochlus steinenii	65	65
			Nos. 1L66-1L71 (6)	2.35	2.35

Princess Diana Issue

Common Design Type

1982, July 1 Litho. *Perf. 14x14 1/2*

1L72	CD333	5p	Arms	15	15
1L73	CD333	17p	Diana	55	55
a.			Perf. 14	10.00	10.00
1L74	CD333	37p	Wedding	1.25	1.25
1L75	CD333	50p	Portrait	1.65	1.65

Crustacea — A8

Perf. 14 1/2x14

1984, Mar. 23 Wmk. 373

1L76	A8	5p	Euphausia superba	15	15
1L77	A8	17p	Glyptonotus antarcticus	55	55
1L78	A8	25p	Epimeria monodon	85	85
1L79	A8	34p	Serolis pagenstecheri	1.10	1.10

Manned Flight Bicentenary — A9

1983, Dec. 23 Litho. *Perf. 14*

1L80	A9	5p	Westland Whirlwind	15	15
1L81	A9	13p	Westland Wasp	35	35
1L82	A9	17p	Saunders-Roe Walrus	48	48
1L83	A9	50p	Auster	1.50	1.50

South Sandwich Islds. Volcanoes A10

1984, Nov. 8 Wmk. 373 *Perf. 14 1/2*

1L84	A10	6p	Zavodovski Isld.	20	20
1L85	A10	17p	Mt. Michael, Saunders Isld.	55	55
1L86	A10	22p	Bellingshausen Isld.	70	70
1L87	A10	52p	Bristol Isld.	1.75	1.75

Albatrosses A11

1985, May 5 Wmk. 384 *Perf. 14 1/2*

1L88	A11	7p	Diomedea chrysostoma	24	24
1L89	A11	22p	Diomedea melanophris	75	75
1L90	A11	27p	Diomedea exulans	85	85
1L91	A11	54p	Phoebetria palpebrata	1.65	1.65

Queen Mother 85th Birthday

Common Design Type

Designs: 7p, 14th birthday celebration. 22p, With Princess Anne, Lady Sarah Armstrong-Jones, Prince Edward. 27p, Queen Mother. 54p, Holding Prince Henry. £1, On the Britannia.

1985, June 23 *Perf. 14 1/2x14*

1L92	CD336	7p	multicolored	20	20
1L93	CD336	22p	multicolored	60	60
1L94	CD336	27p	multicolored	75	75
1L95	CD336	54p	multicolored	1.50	1.50

Souvenir Sheet

1L96	CD336	£1	multicolored	2.75	2.75

Falkland Islands Naturalists Type of 1985

Naturalists, endangered species: 7p, Dumont d'Urville (1790-1842), kelp. 22p, Johann Reinhold Forster (1729-1798), king penguin. 27p, Johann Georg Adam Forster (1754-1794), tussock grass. 54p, Sir Joseph Banks (1743-1820), dove prion.

1985, Nov. 4 *Perf. 13 1/2x14*

1L97	A86	7p	multicolored	25	25
1L98	A86	22p	multicolored	75	75
1L99	A86	27p	multicolored	90	90
1L100	A86	54p	multicolored	1.90	1.90

SEMI-POSTAL STAMP

Catalogue values for unused stamps from No. 1LB1 through 5L1 are for Never Hinged items.

Rebuilding Type of Falkland Islands

Wmk. 373

1982, Sept. 13 Litho. *Perf. 11*

1LB1	SP1	£1	Map of So. Georgia	5.00	5.00

ISSUES FOR THE SEPARATE ISLANDS

Graham Land

Nos. 84, 85B, 86A, 87A, 88-91 Overprinted in Red

GRAHAM LAND

DEPENDENCY OF

1944, Feb. 12 Wmk. 4 *Perf. 12*

2L1	A22	1/2p	green & black	45	40
2L2	A22	1p	dk vio & black	50	50
2L3	A22	2p	rose car & blk	75	70
2L4	A22	3p	deep bl & blk	1.00	90
2L5	A22	4p	rose vio & blk	1.25	1.20
2L6	A22	6p	brown & black	3.25	3.00
2L7	A22	9p	slate bl & blk	2.50	2.50
2L8	A22	1sh	dull blue	2.50	2.25
			Nos. 2L1-2L8 (8)	12.20	11.45

South Georgia

SOUTH GEORGIA

DEPENDENCY OF

1944, Apr. 3 Wmk. 4 *Perf. 12*

3L1	A22	1/2p	green & black	50	40
3L2	A22	1p	dark vio & blk	55	50
3L3	A22	2p	rose car & blk	85	70
3L4	A22	3p	deep bl & blk	1.10	90
3L5	A22	4p	rose vio & blk	1.40	1.25
3L6	A22	6p	brown & black	3.50	3.00
3L7	A22	9p	slate bl & blk	2.75	2.50
3L8	A22	1sh	dull blue	2.75	2.25
			Nos. 3L1-3L8 (8)	13.40	11.50

South Orkneys

SOUTH ORKNEYS

DEPENDENCY OF

1944, Feb. 21 Wmk. 4 *Perf. 12*

4L1	A22	½p green & black	45	40
4L2	A22	1p dark vio & blk	50	50
4L3	A22	2p rose car & blk	75	70
4L4	A22	3p deep bl & blk	1.00	90
4L5	A22	4p rose vio & blk	1.25	1.25
4L6	A22	6p brown & black	3.25	3.00
4L7	A22	9p slate bl & blk	2.50	2.50
4L8	A22	1sh dull blue	2.50	2.25
		Nos. 4L1-4L8 (8)	12.20	11.50

South Shetlands

SOUTH SHETLANDS

DEPENDENCY OF

1944 Wmk. 4 *Perf. 12*

5L1	A22	½p green & black	45	40
5L2	A22	1p dark vio & blk	50	50
5L3	A22	2p rose car & blk	75	70
5L4	A22	3p deep bl & blk	1.00	90
5L5	A22	4p rose vio & blk	1.25	1.25
5L6	A22	6p brown & black	3.25	3.00
5L7	A22	9p slate bl & blk	2.50	2.50
5L8	A22	1sh dull blue	2.50	2.25
		Nos. 5L1-5L8 (8)	12.20	11.50

GRENADA

LOCATION — Windward Islands, West Indies
GOVT. — Independent nation in the British Commonwealth
AREA — 133 sq. mi.
POP. — 115,000 (est. 1981)
CAPITAL — St. George's

Grenada consists of Grenada Island and the southern Grenadines, including Carriacou. This colony was granted associated statehood with Great Britain in 1967 and became an independent state Feb. 7, 1974.

12 Pence = 1 Shilling
100 Cents = 1 Dollar (1949)

Catalogue values for unused stamps in this country are for Never Hinged items, beginning with Scott 143 in the regular postage section, Scott B1 in the semi-postal section, Scott C1 in the air post section, Scott J15 in the postage due section, and Scott O1 in the official section.

Watermarks

Wmk. 5- Small Star

Wmk. 6- Large Star

Wmk. 7- Large Star with Broad Points

Values of stamps of designs A1-A6 are for copies with perforations cutting into the design.

Queen Victoria — A1

Rough Perf. 14 to 16

1861 Engr. Unwmk.

1	A1	1p green	55.00	45.00
a.		1p blue green	2,500.	275.00
b.		Horiz. pair, imperf. btwn.		
2	A1	6p rose	600.00	70.00
b.		6p lake red, perf. 11-12	1,000.	

No. 2b was not issued. No. 2 imperf is a proof.

1863-71 Wmk. 5

3	A1	1p green ('64)	65.00	12.50
4	A1	6p rose	525.00	20.00
5	A1	6p vermilion ('71)	600.00	20.00
a.		6p dull red	3,000.	200.00
g.		Double impression		2,000.

No. 5a always has sideways watermark. Other colors sometimes have sideways watermark.

1873-78 ***Clean-Cut Perf. about 15***

5B	A1	1p deep green	55.00	27.50
c.		1p blue green ('78)	300.00	35.00
h.		Half used as ½p on cover		7,500.
5D	A1	6p vermilion ('75)	625.00	30.00
e.		6p dull red	750.00	35.00
f.		Double impression		1,750.

1873 Wmk. 6

6	A1	1p blue green	50.00	20.00
a.		Diagonal half used as ½p on cover		7,500.
7	A1	6p vermilion	600.00	30.00

1875 *Perf. 14*

7A	A1	1p yellow green	35.00	15.00
b.		Half used as ½p on cover		7,500.
c.		Perf. 15		

A2

A2a

Revenue Stamps Surcharged in Black

1875-81 *Perf. 14, 14½*

8	A2	½p purple ('81)	6.00	6.00
a.		"OSTAGE"	150.00	125.00
b.		Imperf., pair	300.00	
c.		"ALF"	*2,000.*	
d.		"PEN"		
e.		No hyphen between "HALF" and "PENNY"	150.00	100.00
f.		Double surcharge	250.00	250.00
9	A2a	2½p lake ('81)	35.00	12.50
a.		Imperf., pair	325.00	
b.		Imperf. vertically, pair	2,000.	
c.		"PENCF"	300.00	225.00
d.		No period after "PENNY"	100.00	75.00
e.		"PENOE"	150.00	
10	A2	4p blue ('81)	80.00	25.00

Revenue Stamps Surcharged in Dark Blue

11	A2	1sh purple	400.00	22.50
a.		"SHLLIING"	*4,000.*	700.00
b.		"NE SHILLING"		*2,500.*
c.		"OSTAGE"		*1,400.*
d.		Invtd. "S" in "POSTAGE"	*3,500.*	*1,000.*

See Nos. 27-35.

1881 Wmk. 7

12	A2	2½p lake	225.00	35.00
a.		2½p claret	500.00	110.00
b.		"PENCF"	550.00	190.00
c.		No period after "PENNY"	500.00	175.00
13	A2	4p blue	200.00	165.00

A3

A4

A5

A6

Revenue Stamp Overprinted "POSTAGE" in Black

1883 Wmk. 5

Denomination & Crown in 2nd Color

14	A3	½p orange & grn	1,000.	250.00
a.		Unsevered pair	*4,000.*	*1,500.*
15	A4	½p orange & grn	200.00	150.00
a.		Unsevered pair	*1,250.*	*350.00*
16	A5	1p orange & grn	*140.00*	50.00
a.		Inverted overprint	1,250.	600.00
b.		Double overprint	900.00	575.00
c.		Inverted "S" in "Postage"	500.00	475.00

"Postage" in Manuscript, Red or Black

18	A6	1p orange & grn (R)		*2,750.*
19	A6	1p orange & green		*2,000.*

On Nos. 14-19 the words "ONE PENNY" measure from 10-11¼mm in length.

On No. 15, the lower "POSTAGE" is always inverted.

It has been claimed that although Nos. 18 and 19 were used, they were not officially issued.

A8

A10

1883 Wmk. 2 *Perf. 14*

20	A8	½p green	1.10	1.10
a.		Tete beche pair	2.75	*4.50*
21	A8	1p rose	22.50	3.50
a.		Tete beche pair	175.00	175.00
22	A8	2½p ultra	5.50	.75
a.		Tete beche pair	20.00	25.00
23	A8	4p slate	3.50	3.50
a.		Tete beche pair	12.00	17.50
24	A8	6p red lilac	5.00	6.50
a.		Tete beche pair	18.00	*30.00*
25	A8	8p bister	10.00	12.00
a.		Tete beche pair	32.50	*35.00*
26	A8	1sh violet	65.00	42.50
a.		Tete beche pair	900.00	900.00
		Nos. 20-26 (7)	112.60	69.85

Stamps of types A8, A10 and D2 were printed with alternate horizontal rows inverted.

For surcharges, see Nos. 36-38.

Revenue Stamps Surcharged

d.
1
POSTAGE.

1886 Wmk. 6

27	A2	1p on 1½ org	25.00	20.00
a.		Inverted surcharge	250.00	250.00
b.		Diagonal half used as ½ on cover		1,500.
c.		Double surcharge	250.00	250.00
d.		"HALH" instead of "HALF"	250.00	250.00
28	A2	1p on 1sh org	25.00	24.00
a.		"SHILLING" instead of "SHILLING"	450.00	400.00
b.		No period after "POSTAGE"		
c.		Half used as ½p on cover		1,750.

Wmk. 5

29	A2	1p on 4p org	125.00	85.00

1887 Wmk. 2

30	A10	1p rose	25	25
a.		Tete beche pair	2.25	4.50

Revenue Stamps Surcharged:

HALF
PENNY
POSTAGE
h

4*d.*
POSTAGE
i

POSTAGE
AND
d.
1
REVENUE
k

POSTAGE
AND
REVENUE
1d.
l

1888-91 Wmk. 5 *Perf. 14½*

31	A2 (h)	½p on 2sh org ('89)	15.00	16.00
a.		Double surcharge	600.00	600.00
b.		First "S" in "SHILLINGS" inverted	350.00	350.00
32	A2 (i)	4p on 2sh org	22.50	22.50
a.		"4d" and "POSTAGE" 5mm apart	25.00	30.00
b.		"S" inverted, as in #31b	550.00	550.00
c.		As "a," inverted "S," as in #31b	500.00	500.00

"d" Vertical instead of Slanting

33	A2 (i)	4p on 2sh org	500.00	500.00
34	A2 (k)	1p on 2sh org ('90)	55.00	55.00
a.		Inverted surcharge	350.00	350.00
35	A2 (l)	1p on 2sh org ('91)	40.00	40.00
a.		Inverted surcharge	350.00	350.00
b.		No period after "d"	275.00	275.00

No. 25 Surcharged in Black:

POSTAGE
AND
REVENUE
1d.

2½d.

Wmk. 2

36	A8	1p on 8p bister	9.00	11.00
a.		Tete beche pair	90.00	*125.00*
b.		Inverted surcharge	325.00	325.00
c.		No period after "d"	375.00	375.00

"2" of "½" Upright

37	A8	2½p on 8p bister	16.00	21.00
a.		Tete beche pair	110.00	*150.00*
b.		Inverted surcharge		
c.		Double surcharge	600.00	750.00
d.		Triple surcharge		1,100.
e.		Double surcharge, one inverted	450.00	450.00

"2" of "½" Italic

38	A8	2½p on 8p bister	16.00	21.00
a.		Tete beche pair	125.00	*175.00*
b.		Tete beche pair, #37, 38	110.00	
c.		Inverted surcharge		
d.		Double surcharge	650.00	750.00
e.		Triple surcharge		1,100.
f.		Triple surch., two inverted		1,000.

Queen Victoria — A17

1895-99 Wmk. 2 Typo. *Perf. 14*

39	A17	½p lilac & green	1.25	1.60
40	A17	1p lilac & car rose	1.25	25
41	A17	2p lilac & brown	5.00	27.50
42	A17	2½p lilac & ultra	7.00	1.00
43	A17	3p lilac & orange	8.00	10.00
44	A17	6p lilac & green	4.00	5.25
45	A17	8p lilac & black	16.00	18.00
46	A17	1sh green & org	20.00	22.50
		Nos. 39-46 (8)	62.50	86.10

Numerals of ½p, 3p, 8p and 1sh of type A17 are in color on colorless tablet.

Issue dates: 1p, May, 1896. ½p, 2p, Sept. 1899. Others, Sept. 5, 1895.

Columbus' Flagship, La Concepcion
A18

King Edward VII
A19

1898, Aug. 15 Engr. Wmk. 1

47	A18	2½p ultra	10.00	10.00
a.		Bluish paper	45.00	60.00

Discovery of the island by Columbus, Aug. 15th, 1498.

1902 Wmk. 2 Typo.

48	A19	½p violet & grn	32	45
49	A19	1p vio & car rose	45	20
50	A19	2p vio & brown	2.00	4.75
51	A19	2½p vio & ultra	2.50	3.25
52	A19	3p vio & org	2.50	3.50
53	A19	6p vio & green	2.50	4.75
54	A19	1sh green & org	5.50	9.00
55	A19	2sh grn & ultra	14.00	27.50
56	A19	5sh grn & car rose	25.00	37.50
57	A19	10sh green & vio	110.00	135.00
		Nos. 48-57 (10)	164.77	225.90

Numerals of ½p, 3p, 1sh, 2sh and 10sh of type A19 are in color on colorless tablet.

1904-06 Wmk. 3 *Perf. 14*

58	A19	½p vio & green	9.00	12.00
59	A19	1p vio & car rose	4.50	2.50
60	A19	2p vio & brown	21.00	25.00
61	A19	2½p vio & ultra	21.00	25.00
62	A19	3p vio & org	3.00	4.25
63	A19	6p vio & green	4.50	6.00
64	A19	1sh green & org	5.00	9.00
65	A19	2sh grn & ultra	12.50	17.50
66	A19	5sh grn & car rose	30.00	45.00
67	A19	10sh green & vio	120.00	150.00
		Nos. 58-67 (10)	230.50	296.25

Nos. 62, 63 and 65 are on both ordinary and chalky paper.

Issue years: Nos. 58, 60-62, 64, 1905. Nos. 63, 65-67, 1906.

Seal of Colony — A20

King George V — A21

1906-11 Engr.

68	A20	½p green	70	18
69	A20	1p carmine	1.00	15
70	A20	2p yellow	1.75	4.00
71	A20	2½p blue	2.75	3.75
a.		2½p ultramarine	5.00	3.00

Typo.

Chalky Paper

Numerals white on dark ground

72	A20	3p vio, *yel* ('08)	1.75	3.25
73	A20	6p violet ('08)	6.25	9.50
74	A20	1sh blk, *grn* ('11)	1.75	3.25
75	A20	2sh vio & blue, *blue* ('08)	6.25	9.50
76	A20	5sh red & green, *yel* ('08)	20.00	35.00
		Nos. 68-76 (9)	42.20	68.58

1908 Wmk. 2

77	A20	1sh black, *green*	10.00	15.00
78	A20	10sh red & grn, *grn*	100.00	110.00

1913 Ordinary Paper Wmk. 3

79	A21	½p green	15	15
80	A21	1p scarlet	75	50
a.		1p carmine	50	50
81	A21	2p orange	20	26
82	A21	2½p ultra	1.00	1.90

Chalky Paper

83	A21	3p violet, *yel*	30	50
84	A21	6p dull vio & red vio	1.50	3.75
85	A21	1sh black, *green*	2.50	3.50
a.		1sh black, *emerald*	1.75	2.50
b.		1sh blk, *bl grn*, olive back	37.50	55.00
c.		As "a," olive back	1.75	2.50
86	A21	2sh vio & ultra, *bl*	3.25	7.75
87	A21	5sh grn & red, *yel*	7.50	14.00
88	A21	10sh grn & red, *grn*	30.00	47.50
a.		10sh grn & red, *emer*	30.00	47.50
		Nos. 79-88 (10)	47.15	79.81

1914 Surface-colored Paper

89	A21	3p violet, *yel*	50	1.50
90	A21	1sh black, *green*	1.40	3.75

1921-29 Ordinary Paper Wmk. 4

91	A21	½p green	15	15
92	A21	1p rose red	20	15
93	A21	1p brown ('22)	20	15
94	A21	1½p rose red ('22)	40	32
95	A21	2p orange	25	32
96	A21	2p gray ('26)	2.00	2.25
97	A21	2½p ultramarine	75	1.25
98	A21	2½p gray ('22)	50	3.25
99	A21	3p ultra ('22)	1.75	4.00

Chalky Paper

100	A21	3p vio, *yel* ('26)	1.25	3.25
101	A21	4p blk & red, *yel* ('26)	1.00	3.75
102	A21	5p gray vio & ol grn	65	3.25
103	A21	6p dl vio & red vio	1.90	5.00
104	A21	6p blk & red ('26)	2.00	4.00
105	A21	9p gray vio & blk	1.75	4.50
106	A21	1sh blk, *emer*	2.50	6.25
107	A21	1sh org brn ('26)	5.00	8.00
108	A21	2sh vio & ultra, *bl*	5.00	7.75
109	A21	2sh6p blk & red, *bl* ('29)	7.50	14.00
110	A21	3sh grn & vio	7.50	19.00
111	A21	5sh green & red, *yel*	10.00	25.00
112	A21	10sh green & red, *emer*	32.50	62.50
		Nos. 91-112 (22)	84.75	178.09

Grand Anse Beach — A22

Seal of the Colony — A23

View of Grand Etang — A24

View of St. George's — A25

1934, Oct. 23 Engr. *Perf. 12½*

114	A22	½p green	15	15
a.		Perf. 12½x13 ('36)	3.25	5.00
115	A23	1p blk brn & blk	22	22
a.		Perf. 13x12½	1.40	1.65
116	A24	1½p car & black	70	55
a.		Perf. 12½x13 ('36)	2.00	2.25
117	A23	2p org & black	30	35
118	A25	2½p deep blue	30	30
119	A23	3p ol grn & blk	1.40	1.50
120	A23	6p claret & blk	1.90	2.00
121	A23	1sh brown & blk	2.00	2.25
122	A23	2sh6p ultra & blk	12.00	13.00
123	A23	5sh vio & black	16.50	22.50
		Nos. 114-123 (10)	35.47	42.82

Silver Jubilee Issue

Common Design Type

1935, May 6 *Perf. 11x12*

124	CD301	½p green & blk	22	22
125	CD301	1p black & ultra	34	34
126	CD301	1½p car & blue	80	80
127	CD301	1sh brn vio & ind	3.50	3.75

Coronation Issue

Common Design Type

Perf. 11x11½

1937, May 12 Wmk. 4

128	CD302	1p dark purple	18	18
129	CD302	1½p dark carmine	30	30
130	CD302	2½p deep ultra	38	38

George VI — A26

Seal of the Colony — A28

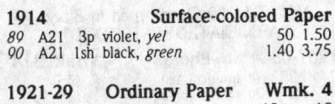

Grand Anse Beach — A27

View of Grand Etang — A29

View of St. George's — A30

Seal of the Colony — A31

1937, July 12 Photo. *Perf. 14½x14*

131	A26	¼p chestnut	15	15

1938, Mar. 16 Engr. *Perf. 12½*

132	A27	½p green	15	15
133	A28	1p blk brn & blk	15	15
134	A29	1½p scarlet & blk	15	15
135	A28	2p orange & blk	15	15
136	A30	2½p ultramarine	15	18
137	A28	3p olive grn & blk	18	18
138	A28	6p red vio & blk	22	22
139	A28	1sh org brn & blk	50	50
140	A28	2sh ultra & black	1.25	1.25
141	A28	5sh purple & blk	2.25	2.25

Perf. 14

142	A31	10sh rose car & gray blue	6.50	6.50
a.		10sh deep car & gray blue, perf. 12 ('43)	240.00	250.00
b.		Perf. 12x13	6.50	6.75
		Nos. 131-142 (12)	11.80	11.80

Perf. 12½x13½, 13½x12½

1938-42

132a	A49	½p	75	75
133a	A49	1p	15	15
134a	A49	1½p car & blk	1.75	38
135a	A49	2p	18	15
136a	A49	2½p	3,000.	275.00
137a	A49	3p	38	38
138a	A49	6p ('42)	38	35
139a	A49	1sh ('42)	50	50
140a	A49	2sh ('41)	3.00	3.00
141a	A49	5sh ('47)	4.50	4.50

Catalogue values for unused stamps in this section, from this point to the end of the section, are for Never Hinged items.

Peace Issue

Common Design Type

1946, Sept. 25 *Perf. 13½x14*

143	CD303	1½p carmine	15	15
144	CD303	3½p deep blue	15	15

Silver Wedding Issue

Common Design Types

1948, Oct. 27 Photo. *Perf. 14x14½*

145	CD304	1½p scarlet	15	15

Engr.; Name Typo.

Perf. 11½x11

146	CD305	10sh gray green	9.00	9.00

UPU Issue

Common Design Types

Engr.; Name Typo. on 6c, 12c

Perf. 13½, 11x11½

1949, Oct. 10 Wmk. 4

147	CD306	5c ultra	40	40
148	CD307	6c deep olive	50	50
149	CD308	12c red lilac	1.00	1.00
150	CD309	24c red brown	1.50	1.50

A32

A33

A34

1951, Jan. 8 Engr. *Perf. 11½*

Center in Black

151	A32	½c chestnut	18	18
152	A32	1c blue green	18	18
153	A32	2c dark brown	20	18
154	A32	3c carmine	25	18
155	A32	4c deep orange	30	25
156	A32	5c purple	50	50
157	A32	6c olive	50	45
158	A32	7c blue	50	40
159	A32	12c red violet	1.90	1.40

Perf. 11½x12½

160	A33	25c dark brown	1.75	85
161	A33	50c ultra	1.60	1.00
162	A33	$1.50 orange	7.50	6.00

Perf. 11½x13

Center in Gray Blue

163	A34	$2.50 deep carmine	9.50	7.50
		Nos. 151-163 (13)	24.86	19.07

See Nos. 180-183, 202. For overprints, see Nos. 166-169.

University Issue

Common Design Types

1951, Feb. 16 *Perf. 14x14½*

164	CD310	3c dp car & gray blk	30	30
165	CD311	6c olive & black	50	50

NEW CONSTITUTION

1951

Nos. 154-156 and 159 Overprinted in Black or Carmine

1951, Sept. 21 *Perf. 11½*

166	A32	3c carmine & black	15	15
167	A32	4c dp orange & black	20	20
168	A32	5c purple & black (C)	22	22
169	A32	12c red violet & black	35	35

Adoption of a new constitution for the Windward Islands.

Coronation Issue

Common Design Type

1953, June 3 *Perf. 13½x13*

170	CD312	3c carmine & black	20	20

Types of 1951 Inscribed "E II R" and

Queen Elizabeth II — A35

1953-59 Engr. *Perf. 11½*

Center in Black

171	A35	½c chestnut ('54)	15	15
172	A35	1c blue green	15	15
173	A35	2c dark brown	15	15
174	A35	3c carmine ('54)	15	15
175	A35	4c deep org ('54)	15	15
176	A35	5c purple ('54)	15	15
177	A35	6c olive	24	15
178	A35	7c blue ('55)	28	16
179	A35	12c red violet	28	16

Perf. 11½x12½

180	A33	25c dark brown ('55)	48	25
181	A33	50c ultra ('55)	2.25	1.00
182	A33	$1.50 orange ('55)	8.00	4.50

Perf. 11½x13

Center in Gray Blue

183	A34	$2.50 deep car ('59)	8.00	4.50
		Nos. 171-183 (13)	20.43	11.62

See Nos. 195-202.

No. 182 was locally surcharged "2" and two black horizontal lines and issued Dec. 23, 1965, for revenue use. It was used postally, though not authorized for postal use. The "2" is found in two type faces.

West Indies Federation
Common Design Type

Perf. 11½x11

1958, Apr. 22 **Wmk. 314**

184	CD313	3c green	15	15
185	CD313	6c blue	20	20
186	CD313	12c carmine rose	40	40

Victoria and Elizabeth II and Mail Truck — A36

Queens and: 8c, "La Concepcion" and Dakota plane. 25c, Steam Packet "Solent" and B.O.A.C. plane.

1961, June 1 **Photo.** ***Perf. 14½x14***

187	A36	3c gray & deep car	15	15
188	A36	8c orange & ultra	38	38
189	A36	25c blue & maroon	75	75

Centenary of first Grenada postage stamps.

Freedom from Hunger Issue
Common Design Type

1963, June 4 ***Perf. 14x14½***

190	CD314	8c green	35	35

Red Cross Centenary Issue
Common Design Type

1963, Sept. 2 **Litho.** ***Perf. 13***

191	CD315	3c black & red	15	15
192	CD315	25c ultra & red	65	65

Types of 1953-55

Perf. 11½

1963-64 **Wmk. 314** **Engr.**

Center in Black

195	A35	2c dark brown	15	15
196	A35	3c carmine	15	15
197	A35	4c dp orange	15	15
198	A35	5c purple	16	16
199	A35	6c olive	225.00	70.00
201	A35	12c red violet	35	35

Perf. 11½x12½

202	A33	25c dark brown	80	80
		Nos. 195-198,201-202 (6)	1.76	1.76

Issue dates: 6c in 1963; others, May 12, 1964.

ITU Issue
Common Design Type

1965, May 17 **Litho.** ***Perf. 11x11½***

205	CD317	2c vermilion & olive	15	15
206	CD317	50c yellow & ver	70	70

Intl. Cooperation Year Issue
Common Design Type

1965, Oct. 25 **Litho.** ***Perf. 14½***

207	CD318	1c blue grn & claret	15	15
208	CD318	25c lt violet & green	50	50
		Set value	56	56

Churchill Memorial Issue
Common Design Type

1966, Jan. 24 **Photo.** ***Perf. 14***

Design in Black, Gold and Carmine Rose

209	CD319	1c bright blue	15	15
210	CD319	3c green	15	15
211	CD319	25c brown	38	38
212	CD319	35c violet	70	70

Royal Visit Issue
Common Design Type

1966, Feb. 4 **Litho.** ***Perf. 11x12***

213	CD320	3c violet blue	15	15
214	CD320	35c dark car rose	75	75

Careenage, St. George's A37

Queen Elizabeth II — A38

Designs: 1c, Hillsborough, Carriacou. 2c, Bougainvillea. 3c, Flamboyant plant. 5c, Levera Beach. 8c, Annandale Falls. 10c, Cacao pods. 12c, Inner Harbor. 15c, Nutmeg. 25c, St. George's. 35c, Grand Anse Beach. 50c, Bananas. $1, Seal of Colony. $3, Map of Grenada.

Perf. 14½x13½, 14½ (A38)

1966, Apr. 1 **Photo.** **Wmk. 314**

215	A37	1c blue, grn & yel	15	15
216	A37	2c dk grn & dp car rose	15	15
217	A37	3c multicolored	15	15
218	A37	5c multicolored	15	15
219	A37	6c ultra, grn & car rose	15	15
220	A37	8c dp grn, ind & yel	15	15
221	A37	10c yel grn, brn & dk car	15	15
222	A37	12c multicolored	15	15
223	A37	15c multicolored	16	16
224	A37	25c dk bl, grn & car rose	32	32
225	A37	35c multicolored	50	50
226	A37	50c violet & green	70	70
227	A38	$1 brn, ultra & dull grn	1.40	1.40
228	A38	$2 multicolored	2.75	2.75
229	A38	$3 brt grnsh bl, dk bl & dl yel	4.25	4.25
		Nos. 215-229 (15)	11.28	11.28

For overprints and surcharges, see Nos. 237-261.

The overprint "Children Need Milk" and surcharges were applied in 1968 in Grenada to Nos. 227-229. The surcharges respectively are 1c+3c, 2c+3c and 3c+3c. The surcharge exists in two sizes on the $2 stamp.

World Cup Soccer Issue
Common Design Type

1966, July 1 **Litho.** ***Perf. 14***

230	CD321	5c multicolored	15	15
231	CD321	50c multicolored	60	60

WHO Headquarters Issue
Common Design Type

1966, Sept. 20 **Litho.** ***Perf. 14***

232	CD322	8c multicolored	15	15
233	CD322	25c multicolored	40	40

UNESCO Anniversary Issue
Common Design Type

1966, Dec. 1 **Litho.** ***Perf. 14***

234	CD323	2c "Education"	15	15
235	CD323	15c "Science"	22	22
236	CD323	50c "Culture"	80	80

Nos. 216-217, 220 and 224 Overprinted "ASSOCIATED STATEHOOD 1967" in Silver

Perf. 14½x13½

1967, Mar. 3 **Photo.** **Wmk. 314**

237	A37	2c dk grn & dp car rose	15	15
238	A37	3c multicolored	15	15
239	A37	8c dp grn, ind & yel	15	15
240	A37	25c dk bl, grn & car rose	38	38
		Set value	60	60

Nos. 216, 221, 223 and 227-228 Surcharged

Perf. 14½x13½, 14½ (A38)

1967, July 1 **Photo.** **Wmk. 314**

241	A37	1c on 15c multi	15	15
242	A37	2c dk grn & dp car rose	15	15
243	A37	3c on 10c multi	15	15
244	A38	$1 multicolored	80	80
245	A38	$2 multicolored	1.65	1.65
		Nos. 241-245 (5)	2.90	2.90

EXPO '67 Intl. Exhib., Montreal, Apr. 28-Oct. 27.

Nos. 215-229 Overprinted in Black: "ASSOCIATED STATEHOOD"

1967-68 **Photo.** **Wmk. 314**

246	A37	1c multicolored	15	15
247	A37	2c multicolored	15	15
248	A37	3c multicolored	15	15
249	A37	5c multicolored	15	15
250	A37	6c multicolored	15	15
251	A37	8c multicolored	15	15
252	A37	10c multicolored	15	15
253	A37	12c multicolored	15	15
254	A37	15c multicolored	15	15
255	A37	25c multicolored	22	22
256	A37	35c multicolored	30	30
257	A37	50c multicolored	50	50
258	A38	$1 multicolored	1.10	1.10
259	A38	$2 multicolored	2.25	2.25
260	A38	$3 multicolored	3.75	3.75

Overprinted and Surcharged

261	A38	$5 on $2 multi	5.00	5.00
		Nos. 246-261 (16)	14.47	14.47

Issue dates: $5, May 18, 1968. Others, Oct. 19, 1967.

Pres. John F. Kennedy A39

Pres. Kennedy and: 25c, 50c, Bird-of-paradise flower. 35c, $1, Roses.

Perf. 14½x14

1968, Jan. 13 **Unwmk.**

262	A39	1c lt blue & multi	15	15
263	A39	15c orange & multi	15	15
264	A39	25c violet & multi	18	18
265	A39	35c multicolored	25	25
266	A39	50c blue & multi	35	35
267	A39	$1 multicolored	75	75
		Nos. 262-267 (6)	1.83	1.83

50th anniv. of the birth of Pres. John F. Kennedy (1917-1963).

Bugler and Jamboree Emblem — A40

Jamboree Emblem and: 2c, 50c, Boy Scouts sitting in tent. 3c, $1, Lord Baden-Powell.

1968, Feb. 1 **Photo.** ***Perf. 13x14***

268	A40	1c orange & multi	15	15
269	A40	2c emer & multi	15	15
270	A40	3c yellow & multi	15	15
271	A40	35c multicolored	40	40
272	A40	50c blue & multi	50	50
273	A40	$1 multicolored	1.00	1.00
		Nos. 268-273 (6)	2.35	2.35

12th Boy Scout Jamboree, Farragut State Park, Idaho, Aug. 1-9, 1967.

Seascape, by Winston Churchill A41

Paintings: 12c, Pine at the shore. 15c, 35c, Houses at the shore. 50c, Churchill painting a seascape.

Perf. 14x14½

1968, Mar. 23 **Unwmk.**

274	A41	10c multicolored	15	15
275	A41	12c multicolored	16	16
276	A41	15c multicolored	20	20
277	A41	25c multicolored	32	32
278	A41	35c multicolored	45	45
279	A41	50c multicolored	75	75
		Nos. 274-279 (6)	2.03	2.03

Winston Churchill as a painter.

Edith McGuire, US, 200m. Dash, 1964 — A42

Gold Medal Winners: 2c, 50c, Arthur Wint, Jamaica, 400m run, 1948. 3c, 60c, Adhemar Ferreira da Silva, Brazil, hop, step and jump, 1952 & 1956. 10c, Like 1c.

1968, Sept. 24 **Photo.** ***Perf. 12½***

280	A42	1c ultra & multi	15	15
281	A42	2c lilac & multi	15	15
282	A42	3c green & multi	15	15
283	A42	10c red org & multi	15	15
284	A42	50c Prus blue & multi	42	42
285	A42	60c orange & multi	60	60
		Set value	1.25	1.25

19th Olympic Games, Mexico City, Oct. 12-27. Nos. 280-282 and 283-285 are printed in sheets of 9 (3 of each denomination).

For surcharges, see Nos. 310-315.

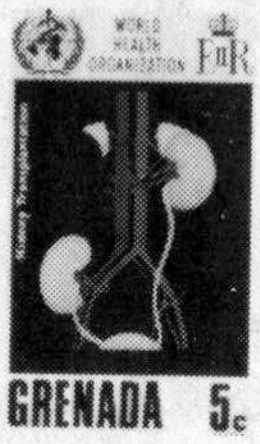

Transplant Operations — A43

Perf. 13x13½

1968, Nov. 25 **Photo.** **Unwmk.**

286	A43	5c Kidney	15	15
287	A43	25c Heart	28	28
288	A43	35c Lung	40	40
289	A43	50c Cornea	55	55

20th anniv. of WHO.

Adoration of the Magi, by Veronese A44

Paintings: 15c, Madonna and Child with St. John and St. Catherine, by Titian. 35c, Adoration of the Magi, by Botticelli. $1, "A Knight Adoring the Infant Christ" by Vincenzo di Biagio Catena.

1968, Dec. 3 ***Perf. 12½***

290	A44	5c vio blue & multi	15	15
291	A44	15c crimson & multi	16	16
292	A44	35c dk green & multi	38	38
293	A44	$1 dk blue & multi	95	95

Christmas. For overprints, see Nos. 341-344.

Hibiscus and "La Concepcion" — A45

Yacht in St. George's Harbour A45a

Designs: 2c, Bird-of-paradise flower. 3c, Bougainvillea. 5c, Rock hind (fish; horiz.). 6c, Sailfish. 8c, Red snapper, horiz. 10c, Giant toad, horiz. 12c, Yellowfoot tortoise. No. 302, Tree boa, horiz. No. 302A, Thunbergia. 25c, Mouse opossum. 35c Armadillo, horiz. 50c, Mona monkey. $1, Bananaquit (bird). $2, Brown pelican. $3, Magnificent frigate bird. $5, Bare-eyed thrush.

Perf. 14x14½, 14½x14; 14x13½ (#302A); 13½x14 (#305A)

Photo.; Litho. (#302A, 305A)

1968-71 Unwmk.

294	A45	1c dl yel & multi	15	15
295	A45	2c brt pink & multi	15	15
296	A45	3c blue & multi	15	15
297	A45	5c violet & multi	15	15
298	A45	6c emer & multi	15	15
299	A45	8c multicolored	24	15
300	A45	10c multicolored	15	15
301	A45	12c ver & multi	22	18
302	A45	15c emer & multi	80	65
302A	A45	15c gray & multi	4.00	2.50
303	A45	25c multicolored	55	42
304	A45	35c multicolored	75	60
305	A45	50c ultra & multi	1.20	85
305A	A45a	75c blue & multi	2.75	2.25
306	A45	$1 multicolored	2.00	1.75
307	A45	$2 multicolored	3.25	2.50
308	A45	$3 yel & multi	4.75	3.75
309	A45	$5 multicolored	7.50	6.50
		Nos. 294-309 (18)	28.91	23.00

Nos. 294-309 vary in size from 25x44mm to 29x46mm.

The overprint "VOTE/FEB. 28 1972" was applied to the 2c, 3c, 6c and 25c in Feb., 1972.

Issue dates: 5c, 10c, 25c, $2, Feb. 4, 1969. 3c, 8c, 35c, $5, July 1, 1969. No. 302A, 1970. 75c, Oct. 9, 1971. Others, Oct. 1978.

For surcharges, see Nos. 462-464. For overprints, see Nos. 528-541, C3-C19.

Nos. 280-285 Surcharged in Carmine

VISIT CARIFTA EXPO 69
April 5-30
5c

1969, Feb. *Perf. 12½*

310 A42	5c on 1c multi	15	15
311 A42	8c on 2c multi	15	15
312 A42	25c on 3c multi	25	25
313 A42	35c on 10c multi	40	40
314 A42	$1 on 50c multi	95	95
315 A42	$2 on 60c multi	2.00	2.00
	Nos. 310-315 (6)	3.90	3.90

Gov. Hilda Bynoe and View of St. George's A46

Designs: 15c, Premier Eric M. Gairy, fruits and St. George's. 60c, Emblems of Brussels, New York and Montreal World's Fairs.

1969, May 1 Litho. *Perf. 13x13½*

316 A46	5c multicolored	15	15
317 A46	15c multicolored	15	15
318 A46	50c multicolored	38	38
319 A46	60c multicolored	42	42

Nos. 310-319 issued to publicize CARIFTA (Caribbean Free Trade Area) Exposition, St. George's, Apr. 5-30.

Gov. Hilda Bynoe — A47

Designs: 25c, Dr. Martin Luther King, Jr. $1, Belshazzar's Feast, by Rembrandt, horiz.

Perf. 13x12½, 12½x13

1969, June 8 Photo. Unwmk.

320 A47	5c multicolored	15	15
321 A47	25c multicolored	18	18
322 A47	35c multicolored	30	30
323 A47	$1 multicolored	75	75

International Human Rights Year.

Batsman Playing Off-drive A48

Cricket: 10c, Batsman playing defensive stroke. 25c, Batsman sweeping ball. 35c, Batsman playing on-drive.

1969, Aug. 1 *Perf. 14x14½*

324 A48	3c dk blue & multi	15	15
325 A48	10c fawn & multi	50	50
326 A48	25c dp green & multi	1.00	1.00
327 A48	35c brt purple & multi	1.50	1.50

Astronaut Collecting Moon Rocks, Landing Module and Earth — A49

Designs: ½c, like $1. 1c, Apollo 11, moon and earth. 2c, Landing module "Eagle." 3c, Memorial tablet left on moon. 8c, Separation of rocket and spaceship. 25c, Take off from Cape Kennedy, vert. 35c, Apollo 11 circling the moon, vert. 50c, Splashdown, vert. ½c, 2c, 25c, 50c, $1 inscribed: "We came in peace for all mankind." 1c, 3c, 8c, 35c inscribed: "Like the moon it shall be established forever" Psalms 89:37.

Perf. 13x13½ (½c), 12½

1969, Sept. 24 Litho. Unwmk.

Size: 56x35mm

328 A49	½c multicolored	15	15

Size: 44½x28mm, 28x44½mm

329 A49	1c multicolored	15	15
330 A49	2c multicolored	15	15
331 A49	3c multicolored	15	15
332 A49	8c multicolored	15	15
333 A49	25c multicolored	22	22
334 A49	35c multicolored	42	42
335 A49	50c multicolored	60	60
336 A49	$1 multicolored	1.10	1.10
a.	Souvenir sheet of 2	1.25	1.25
	Set value	2.50	2.50

Man's first moonlanding (Apollo 11), July 20, 1969.

No. 336a contains stamps similar to Nos. 331 and 336 with simulated perforations.

For surcharge, see No. 349. For overprints, see Nos. 379-382.

Mahatma Gandhi — A50

Designs: Gandhi in various positions. 15c, 25c are vertical.

1969, Oct. 8 *Perf. 11½x12, 12x11½*

Queen's Head in Gold

337 A50	6c multicolored	15	15
338 A50	15c multicolored	35	35
339 A50	25c multicolored	65	65
340 A50	$1 multicolored	1.75	1.75
a.	Souvenir sheet of 4	3.00	3.00

Mohandas K. Gandhi (1869-1948), leader in India's fight for independence.

No. 340a contains stamps similar to Nos. 337-340 with simulated perforation.

Nos. 290-293 Overprinted in Black or Silver with Bars and "1969"

1969, Dec. 23 Photo. *Perf. 12½*

341 A44	2c on 15c multi	15	15
342 A44	5c multi (S)	15	15
343 A44	35c multi (S)	32	32
344 A44	$1 multi (S)	80	80

Christmas.

Edward Teach (Blackbeard) A51

Pirates: 25c, Anne Bonney and sailboats. 50c, Jean Lafitte and sailboats. $1, Mary Read, ships and fighting pirates.

1970, Feb. 1 Engr. *Perf. 13x13½*

345 A51	15c black	40	22
346 A51	25c emerald	65	45
347 A51	50c purple	1.50	1.00
348 A51	$1 carmine	3.50	2.00

No. 328 Surcharged

5c — Type I

5c — Type II

1970, Mar. 18 Litho. *Perf. 13x13½*

349 A49	5c on ½c multi (I)	15	15
a.	Type II	1.50	1.50

Christ, from "The Last Supper," by Andrea del Sarto — A52

Paintings: No. 351 (5c), St. John, from Last Supper by Andrea del Sarto. Nos. 352-353 (15c), Christ Crowned with Thorns, by Anthony Van Dyck. Nos. 354-355 (25c), Passion of Christ, by Hans Memling. Nos. 356-357 (60c), Christ in the Tomb, by Peter Paul Rubens. Nos. 350, 352, 354 and 356 have denomination in lower right corner; others in lower left corner. The stamps of the same denomination are printed se-tenant without separating margin, reproducing continuous picture.

1970, Apr. 13 Litho. *Perf. 11½x11*

350 A52	5c rose car & multi	15	15
351 A52	5c rose car & multi	15	15
352 A52	15c ultra & multi	15	15
353 A52	15c ultra & multi	15	15
354 A52	25c brt vio & multi	22	22
355 A52	25c brt vio & multi	22	22
356 A52	60c dull org & multi	50	50
357 A52	60c dull org & multi	50	50
a.	Souvenir sheet of 4, #354-357	1.65	1.65
	Nos. 350-357 (8)	2.04	2.04

Easter.

Girl Pushing Carriage with Kittens — A53

Designs: 15c, Girl playing with puppy and kitten. 30c, Boy fishing and cat. 60c, Children with pets.

1970, May 27 Litho. *Perf. 11*

358 A53	5c multicolored	15	15
359 A53	15c multicolored	22	22
360 A53	30c multicolored	38	38
a.	Souvenir sheet of 2	65	65
361 A53	60c multicolored	75	75
a.	Souvenir sheet of 2	1.75	1.75

William Wordsworth (1770-1850). English poet. No. 360a contains stamps similar to Nos. 358 and 360; No. 361a contains stamps similar to Nos. 359 and 361. Sheets have simulated perforations.

Indian Parliament A54

Commonwealth Parliamentary Association Emblem and: 25c, British Parliament. 50c, Canadian Parliament. 60c, Grenadian Parliament.

1970, June 15 *Perf. 14½x14*

362 A54	5c multicolored	15	15
363 A54	25c multicolored	22	22
364 A54	50c multicolored	45	45
365 A54	60c multicolored	55	55
a.	Souvenir sheet of 4, #362-365	1.50	1.50

7th Caribbean Regional Conf. of the Commonwealth Parliamentary Assoc., St. George's. June 13-20.

Sun Tower and EXPO Emblem — A55

EXPO Emblem and: 2c, Livelihood Industry pavilion, horiz. 3c, Ikenobo, Japanese floral art, vert. 10c, Adam and Eve, by Tintoretto and Italian pavilion, horiz. 25c, UN pavilion and flags reflected in pool, 50c, Peace statue of St. Francis, San Francisco pavilion, cable car and Golden Gate Bridge, $1, Toshiba-Ihi pavilion, horiz.

1970, Aug. 8 Litho. *Perf. 13½*

366 A55	1c brt blue & multi	15	15
367 A55	2c multicolored	15	15
368 A55	3c buff & multi	15	15
369 A55	10c multicolored	18	18
370 A55	25c gray & multi	35	35
371 A55	50c gray & multi	70	70
	Set value	1.40	1.40

Souvenir Sheet

372 A55	$1 gold & multi	1.40	1.40

EXPO '70 Intl. Exhib., Osaka, Japan, Mar. 15-Sept. 13.

Grenada stamps can be mounted in the Scott British Windward Islands album.

Pres. Roosevelt and Flag-Raising on Iwo Jima — A56

Designs: 5c, Marshal Georgi K. Zhukov and fall of Berlin. 15c, Winston Churchill and evacuation of Dunkirk. 25c, Charles de Gaulle and liberation of Paris. 50c, General Dwight D. Eisenhower and D-Day landing. 60c, Field Marshal Bernard Montgomery and Battle of Alamein.

1970, Sept. 3 *Perf. 11*

373	A56	1/2c multicolored	15	15
374	A56	5c multicolored	20	15
375	A56	15c multicolored	50	25
376	A56	25c multicolored	1.40	80
377	A56	50c multicolored	2.75	1.50
378	A56	60c multicolored	2.75	1.90
a.		Souv. sheet of 4 #373, 375, 377-378	6.50	4.50
		Nos. 373-378 (6)	7.75	4.75

End of World War II, 25th anniversary.

Nos. 333-336 Overprinted in Black or Silver: "PHILYMPIA / LONDON 1970"

1970, Sept. 18 *Perf. 12 1/2*

379	A49	25c multicolored	18	18
380	A49	35c multicolored	24	24
381	A49	50c multicolored	38	38
382	A49	$1 multi (S)	75	75

Philympia 1970, London philatelic exhibition, Sept. 18-26. The overprint on No. 382 is vertical, reading up.

This overprint was applied in silver to No. 336a.

UPU Headquarters, Emblem and Old Transportation — A57

UPU Headquarters, emblem and: 25c, Jet plane, ship and diesel train. 50c, Rowland Hill, vert. $1, Abraham Lincoln, vert.

1970, Oct. 17 **Litho.** *Perf. 14 1/2*

383	A57	15c orange & multi	20	20
384	A57	25c blue & multi	28	28
385	A57	50c multicolored	55	55
386	A57	$1 rose & multi	1.00	1.00
a.		Souvenir sheet of 2	2.25	2.25

Opening of the new UPU Headquarters in Bern. No. 386a contains stamps similar to Nos. 385-386.

Madonna of the Goldfinch, by Tiepolo — A58

Christmas (Paintings): No. 388, 35c, Virgin and Child with Sts. Peter and Paul, by Dirk Bouts. No. 389, $1, Virgin and Child, by Bellini. 3c, Like No. 387. 2c, 50c, Madonna of the Basket, by Correggio.

1970, Dec. 5 *Perf. 14x13 1/2*

387	A58	1/2c yel grn & multi	15	15
388	A58	1/2c pink & multi	15	15
389	A58	1/2c yellow & multi	15	15
390	A58	2c lt blue & multi	15	15
391	A58	3c dp rose & multi	15	15
392	A58	35c dk green & multi	38	35
393	A58	50c brown & multi	60	50
394	A58	$1 purple & multi	1.25	1.10
a.		Souvenir sheet of 2, #393-394	3.00	1.90
		Set value	2.45	2.15

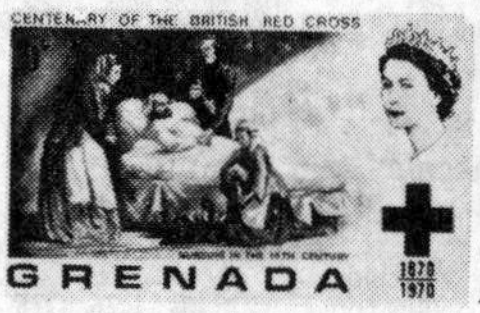

Nursing in 19th Century A59

Designs: 15c, Horse-drawn ambulance, Northern France, 1918. 25c, First aid station, 1941. 60c, Red Cross truck loaded on plane, 1970 emergency aid.

1970, Dec. 12 **Litho.** *Perf. 14 1/2x14*

395	A59	5c red & multi	15	15
396	A59	15c red & multi	18	18
397	A59	25c red & multi	35	35
398	A59	60c red & multi	95	95
a.		Souvenir sheet of 4, #395-398	2.25	2.25

Centenary of the British Red Cross Society.

John Dewey, Children Learning to Paint — A60

Designs: 10c, Jean-Jacques Rousseau and students. 50c, Moses Maimonides and biology student. $1, Bertrand Russell and boys.

1971, May 8 **Litho.** *Perf. 13 1/2*

399	A60	5c multicolored	15	15
400	A60	10c multicolored	15	15
401	A60	50c multicolored	75	75
402	A60	$1 multicolored	1.50	1.50
a.		Souvenir sheet of 2, #401-402	2.75	2.75

International Education Year.

Jennifer Hosten and Map of Grenada — A61

1971, June 1 **Litho.** *Perf. 13 1/2*

403	A61	5c vio blue & multi	15	15
404	A61	10c red lilac & multi	18	15
405	A61	15c brt rose & multi	38	18
406	A61	25c violet & multi	65	30
407	A61	35c blue & multi	90	60
408	A61	50c red & multi	1.75	1.75
a.		Souvenir sheet of 1	3.00	3.00
		Nos. 403-408 (6)	4.01	3.13

Honoring Miss Jennifer Hosten of Grenada, Miss World, 1971. No. 408a, printed on silk, contains imperf. stamp similar to No. 408.

Nos. 403-408 and 408a were overprinted "INTERPEX/1972" in Mar. 1972.

For surcharge, see No. 465. For overprints, see Nos. C23-C26.

Canadian and French Boy Scouts — A62

Boy Scouts from: 35c, West Germany and US. 50c, Australia and Japan. 75c, Grenada and Great Britain.

1971, Aug. **Litho.** *Perf. 11*

409	A62	5c multicolored	15	15
410	A62	35c multicolored	52	45
411	A62	50c multicolored	75	70
412	A62	75c multicolored	1.10	1.10
a.		Souvenir sheet of 2, #411-412	3.00	3.00

13th Boy Scout World Jamboree, Asagiri Plain, Japan, Aug. 2-10.

Napoleon, by Edouard Détaille A63

Paintings of Napoleon: 15c, Outside Madrid, by Carle Vernet. 35c, Crossing the Alps, by Jacques Louis David. $2, Portrait, by David.

1971, Sept. *Perf. 13x13 1/2*

413	A63	5c multicolored	15	15
414	A63	15c multicolored	22	22
415	A63	35c multicolored	60	60
a.		Souvenir sheet of 1	1.75	1.75
416	A63	$2 multicolored	3.00	3.00

Sesquicentennial of the death of Napoleon Bonaparte (1769-1821).

No. 415a contains stamp similar to No. 415 with simulated perforations.

Grenada No. 1 — A64

Designs: 15c, Grenada No. 2 and Queen Elizabeth II. 35c, Grenada Nos. 1 and 2. 50c, Grenada No. 1 and scroll.

1971, Nov. 6 **Litho.** *Perf. 11*

417	A64	5c dk red & multi	15	15
418	A64	15c multicolored	18	18
419	A64	35c dull org & multi	55	55
420	A64	50c dk green & multi	90	90
a.		Souvenir sheet of 2, #419-420	1.75	1.75

110th anniversary of postal service.

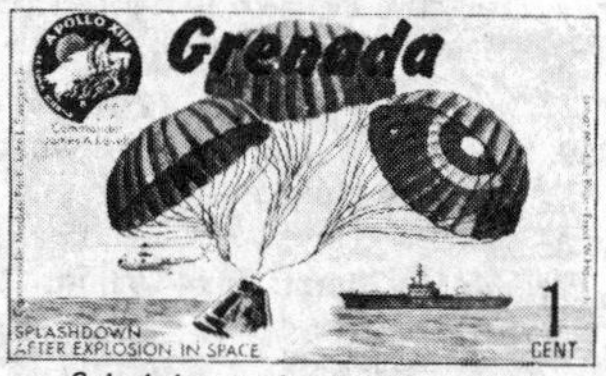

Splashdown, Apollo 13 — A65

Designs: 2c, Capsule and rafts in ocean, Apollo 13. 3c, Separation of landing module from rocket, Apollo 14. 10c, Astronauts collecting moon rocks, Apollo 14. 25c, Astronauts in moon rover, Apollo 15. 50c, $1, Rocket blast-off, Apollo 15, vert.

1971, Nov.

421	A65	1c multicolored	15	15
422	A65	2c multicolored	15	15
423	A65	3c black & multi	15	15
424	A65	10c black & multi	20	20
425	A65	25c multicolored	52	52
426	A65	$1 multicolored	2.25	2.25
		Nos. 421-426 (6)	3.42	3.42

Souvenir Sheet

427	A65	50c multicolored	2.75	2.75

US moon missions of Apollo 13, 14 and 15.

67th Regiment of Foot, 1787 — A66

Designs: 1c, 45th Regiment of Foot, 1792. 2c, 29th Regiment of Foot, 1794. 10c, 9th Regiment of Foot, 1801. 25c, 2nd Regiment of Foot, 1815. $1, 70th Regiment of Foot, 1764.

1971, Dec. *Perf. 13 1/2x14*

428	A66	1/2c red & multi	15	15
429	A66	1c red & multi	15	15
430	A66	2c red & multi	15	15
431	A66	10c red & multi	25	25
432	A66	25c red & multi	75	75
433	A66	$1 red & multi	2.75	2.75
a.		Souv. sheet of 2, #432-433, perf. 15	5.00	5.00
		Nos. 428-433 (6)	4.20	4.20

Uniforms of British units stationed in Grenada.

For surcharges, see Nos. 439, C1-C2.

Adoration of the Kings, by Memling — A67

Christmas: 25c, Madonna and Child, sculpture by Michelangelo. 35c, Madonna and Child, by Murillo. 50c, Madonna with the Apple, by Memling. $1, Adoration of the Kings, by Jan Mostaert.

1971, Dec. *Perf. 14x13 1/2*

434	A67	15c gold & multi	18	18
435	A67	25c gold & multi	32	32
436	A67	35c gold & multi	48	48
437	A67	50c gold & multi	75	75

Souvenir Sheet

438	A67	$1 gold & multi	1.75	1.75

No. 430 Surcharged with New Value, Olympic Rings and: "WINTER OLYMPICS / FEB. 3-13, 1972 / SAPPORO, JAPAN"

1972, Feb. 3 *Perf. 13 1/2x14*

439	A66	$2 on 2c red & multi	2.75	2.75
a.		Souvenir sheet of 2	3.75	3.75

11th Winter Olympic Games, Sapporo, Japan, Feb. 3-13. See Nos. C1-C2.

No. 439a is overprinted in red on No. 433a (no surcharge); margin inscribed in red: "SAPPORO 1972."

King Arthur, UNICEF Emblem A68

UNICEF Emblem and: 1c, 50c, Robin Hood. 2c, 75c, Robinson Crusoe, vert. 25c, like 1/2c. $1, Mary and her Little Lamb, vert.

1972, Mar. 4 *Perf. 14 1/2x14, 14x14 1/2*

450	A68	1/2c dp blue & multi	15	15
451	A68	1c yellow & multi	15	15
452	A68	2c dp yel & multi	15	15
453	A68	25c salmon & multi	20	20
454	A68	50c multicolored	42	42
455	A68	75c blue & multi	60	60
456	A68	$1 multicolored	85	85
a.		Souvenir sheet of 1	1.75	1.75
		Nos. 450-456 (7)	2.52	2.52

25th anniv. (in 1971) of UNICEF.

Yachting A69

Olympic rings and: 1c, 50c, Equestrian. 2c, 35c, Running, vert.

1972, Sept. 8 Litho. *Perf. 14*

457 A69 ½c multicolored	15	15
458 A69 1c lt blue & multi	15	15
459 A69 2c orange & multi	15	15
460 A69 35c yel & multi	90	90
461 A69 50c yel grn & multi	1.25	1.25
Nos. 457-461,C20-C21 (7)	3.97	3.97

20th Olympic Games, Munich, Aug. 26-Sept. 11. See No. C22.

Nos. 294-296, 403 Surcharged with New Value and Two Bars

Perf. 14x14½, 13½

1972, Oct. Photo.

462 A45 12c on 1c multi	45	45
463 A45 12c on 2c multi	45	45
464 A45 12c on 3c multi	45	45
465 A61 12c on 5c multi	45	45

Silver Wedding Issue, 1972
Common Design Type

Design: Queen Elizabeth II, Prince Philip, seal of Grenada and myristica fragrans.

Perf. 14x14½

1972, Nov. 20 Wmk. 314

466 CD324 8c olive & multi	15	15
467 CD324 $1 multicolored	95	95

Boy Scout Saluting A70

Designs: 1c, Two Scouts knotting ropes. 2c, 70c, 75c, Scouts from different nations. 3c, 60c, $1, Lord Baden-Powell.

Unwmk.

1972, Dec. 2 Litho. *Perf. 14*

468 A70 ½c yellow & multi	15	15
469 A70 1c red & multi	15	15
470 A70 2c yellow & multi	15	15
471 A70 3c brt lilac & multi	15	15
472 A70 75c lt blue & multi	1.25	1.25
473 A70 $1 multicolored	1.75	1.75
Nos. 468-473,C27-C28 (8)	4.70	4.70

Souvenir Sheet

474 Sheet of 2	2.75	2.75
a. A70 60c ocher & multi	1.25	1.25
b. A70 70c pale lilac & multi	1.50	1.50

Boy Scouts, 65th anniversary.

Virgin and Child, Crosier — A71

Christmas: 3c, 35c, 70c, The Three Kings. 5c, $1, Holy Family. 25c, 60c, Like 1c.

1972, Dec. 9 Litho. *Perf. 14x13½*

475 A71 1c blue & multi	15	15
476 A71 3c gray & multi	15	15
477 A71 5c multicolored	15	15
478 A71 25c multicolored	28	28
479 A71 35c lt blue & multi	50	50
480 A71 $1 ocher & multi	1.65	1.65
Nos. 475-480 (6)	2.88	2.88

Souvenir Sheet

Perf. 15

481 Sheet of 2	2.00	1.90
a. A71 60c blue & multi	75	75
b. A71 70c bright pink & multi	85	85

Flamingos A72

1973, Jan. 5 Litho. *Perf. 14*

482 A72 25c shown	30	30
483 A72 35c Tapir	45	45
484 A72 60c Macaws	90	90
485 A72 70c Ocelot	1.10	1.10

National Zoo of Grenada.

Class II Ocean Racing Yacht A73

1973, Jan. 26 Litho. *Perf. 13½x14*

486 A73 25c shown	35	35
487 A73 35c Boats in St. George's Harbour	48	48
488 A73 60c Yacht "Bloodhound"	85	85
489 A73 70c St. George's Harbour	95	95

Yachting off Grenada.

Sun God Helios, Equinoxes and Solstices — A74

WMO Emblem and: 1c, Poseidon and Nomad automatic storm detector. 2c, Zeus and radarscope. 3c, Goddess Iris, rainbow, weather balloon. 35c, Hermes, ATS 3 satellite. 50c, Zephyr and circulation of atmosphere. 75c, Demeter, space photograph of storm. $1, Selene, globe showing world rainfall. $2, Computer weather map (42x31mm).

1973, July 6 Litho. *Perf. 13½*

490 A74 ½c multicolored	15	15
491 A74 1c multicolored	15	15
492 A74 2c multicolored	15	15
493 A74 3c multicolored	15	15
494 A74 35c multicolored	38	38
495 A74 50c multicolored	60	60
496 A74 75c multicolored	90	90
497 A74 $1 multicolored	1.10	1.10
Nos. 490-497 (8)	3.58	3.58

Souvenir Sheet

498 A74 $2 multicolored	3.00	2.75

Intl. meteorological cooperation, cent.

Racing Class Yachts A75

1973, Aug. 3 Litho. *Perf. 13½*

499 A75 ½c shown	15	15
500 A75 1c Cruising class	15	15
501 A75 2c Open-decked sloops	15	15
502 A75 35c Sloop Mermaid	40	40
503 A75 50c St. George's Harbour	60	60
504 A75 75c Map of Carriacou	90	90
505 A75 $1 Boat building	1.25	1.25
Nos. 499-505 (7)	3.60	3.60

Souvenir Sheet

506 A75 $2 End of race	2.75	2.75

Carriacou Regatta, August 1973.

Ignaz Philipp Semmelweiss — A76

Designs: Physicians and scientists.

1973, Sept. 17 Litho. *Perf. 14½*

507 A76 ½c shown	15	15
508 A76 1c Louis Pasteur	15	15
509 A76 2c Edward Jenner	15	15
510 A76 3c Sigmund Freud	15	15
511 A76 25c Emil von Behring	35	35
512 A76 35c Carl Jung	50	50
513 A76 50c Charles Calmette	75	75
514 A76 $1 William Harvey	1.50	1.50
Nos. 507-514 (8)	3.70	3.70

Souvenir Sheet

515 A76 $2 Marie Curie	3.00	2.75

WHO, 25th anniv.

Princess Anne and Mark Phillips A77

1973, Nov. 14 Wmk. 314 *Perf. 13½*

516 A77 25c dp orange & multi	24	24
517 A77 $2 green & multi	1.75	1.75
a. Souv. sheet of 2 (75c, $1)	2.00	2.00

Wedding of Princess Anne and Capt. Mark Phillips.

Nos. 516-517 were issued only in sheets of 5 plus label. Colors of 75c and $1 are as those of 25c and $2.

Virgin and Child, by Carlo Maratti — A78

Christmas (Paintings): 1c, Virgin and Child, by Carlo Crivelli. 2c, Virgin and Child, by Verrocchio. 3c, Adoration of the Shepherds, by Roberti. 25c, Holy Family, by Federigo Baroccio. 35c, Holy Family, by Bronzino. 75c, Mystic Nativity, by Botticelli. $1, Adoration of the Kings, by Geertgen tot Sint Jans. $2, Adoration of the Kings, by Jan Mostaert (30x45mm).

1973, Nov. Unwmk. *Perf. 14½*

519 A78 ½c lt brown & multi	15	15
520 A78 1c citron & multi	15	15
521 A78 2c blue & multi	15	15
522 A78 3c green & multi	15	15
523 A78 25c multicolored	35	35
524 A78 35c multicolored	50	50
525 A78 75c vio blue & multi	1.10	1.10
526 A78 $1 multicolored	1.40	1.40
Nos. 519-526 (8)	3.95	3.95

Souvenir Sheet

Perf. 13½x14

527 A78 $2 red & multi	2.50	2.50

Nos. 294-297, 299-301, 303-304, 305A-309 Overprinted

INDEPENDENCE
7TH FEB 1974

Perf. 14x14½, 14½x14

1974, Feb. 7 Photo.

528 A45 1c multicolored	15	15
529 A45 2c multicolored	15	15
530 A45 3c multicolored	15	15
531 A45 5c multicolored	15	15
532 A45 8c multicolored	15	15
533 A45 10c multicolored	15	15
534 A45 12c multicolored	22	15
535 A45 25c multicolored	45	20
536 A45 35c multicolored	70	35

Litho.

Perf. 13½x14

537 A45a 75c multicolored	2.00	1.00

Photo.

Perf. 14x14½

538 A45 $1 multicolored	3.00	1.50
539 A45 $2 multicolored	6.50	3.25
540 A45 $3 multicolored	10.00	5.00
541 A45 $5 multicolored	30.00	15.00
Nos. 528-541 (14)	53.77	27.35

Grenada's independence, Feb. 7, 1974. Size of overprint on vertical stamps 16x5mm.; on horizontal stamps 20x6mm.

Creative Arts Theater, Jamaica Campus A79

Designs: 25c, Marryshow House, University Center. 50c, Chapel, vert. $1, $2, University coat of arms, vert.

1974, Apr. 10 Litho. *Perf. 13½*

542 A79 10c multicolored	15	15
543 A79 25c multicolored	38	38
544 A79 50c multicolored	65	65
545 A79 $1 multicolored	1.40	1.40

Souvenir Sheet

546 A79 $2 multicolored	2.50	2.50

25th anniv. of the University of the West Indies.

Prime Minister Eric M. Gairy — A80

Soccer, Flags of West Germany and Chile — A81

1974, Aug. 19 Litho. *Perf. 13½*

547 A80 3c Nutmeg and mace	15	15
548 A80 8c Map of Grenada	15	15
549 A80 25c shown	32	32
550 A80 35c Anse Beach and Flag	48	48
551 A80 $1 Coat of arms	1.50	1.50
Nos. 547-551 (5)	2.60	2.60

Souvenir Sheet

552 A80 $2 Coat of arms	2.75	2.75

Grenada's independence.

1974, Sept. 3 Litho. *Perf. 14½*

Soccer Games and Flags: 1c, East Germany and Australia. 2c, Yugoslavia and Brazil. 10c, Scotland and Zaire. 25c, Netherlands and Uruguay. 50c, Sweden and Bulgaria. 75c, Italy and Haiti. $1, Poland and Argentina. $2, Flags of participating nations, horiz.

553 A81 ½c multicolored	15	15
554 A81 1c multicolored	15	15
555 A81 2c multicolored	15	15
556 A81 10c multicolored	15	15
557 A81 25c multicolored	25	25
558 A81 50c multicolored	50	50
559 A81 75c multicolored	85	85
560 A81 $1 multicolored	1.00	1.00
Nos. 553-560 (8)	3.20	3.20

Souvenir Sheet

Perf. 13

561 A81 $2 multicolored	2.75	2.50

World Cup Soccer Championship, Munich, June 13-July 7.

19th Century US Mail Train, Concorde and UPU Emblem
A82

UPU Emblem and: 1c, Sailing ship "Caesar," 1839, and helicopter. 2c, Zeppelin, jet and early planes. 8c, Pigeon post, 1480, telephone dial. 15c, Bellman, 18th cent. and radar. 25c, German Imperial messenger, 1450, satellite. 35c, French pillar box and ocean liner. $1, German mailman, 18th cent., and futuristic mail train. $2, St. Gotthard mail coach, 1735, vert.

1974, Oct. 8 Litho. *Perf. 14½*

562	A82	½c rose & multi	15	15
563	A82	1c gray & multi	15	15
564	A82	2c dull pink & multi	15	15
565	A82	8c yellow & multi	15	15
566	A82	15c yel grn & multi	20	20
567	A82	25c dull yel & multi	35	35
568	A82	35c lilac & multi	45	45
569	A82	$1 lt blue & multi	1.25	1.25
		Nos. 562-569 (8)	2.85	2.85

Souvenir Sheet

Perf. 13

570	A82	$2 multicolored	2.50	2.50

UPU, cent.

Sir Winston Churchill
A83

Design: $2, Churchill, different portrait.

1974, Oct. 28 Litho. *Perf. 13½*

571	A83	35c multicolored	45	45
572	A83	$2 multicolored	2.50	2.50

Souvenir Sheet

573		Sheet of 2	2.50	2.50
a.		A83 75c like 35c	1.00	1.00
b.		A83 $1 like $2	1.25	1.25

Winston Churchill (1874-1965).

Virgin and Child, by Botticelli — A84

Christmas: Paintings of the Virgin and Child.

1974, Nov. 18 *Perf. 14½*

574	A84	½ shown	15	15
575	A84	1c Niccolo di Pietro	15	15
576	A84	2c Van der Weyden	15	15
577	A84	3c Bastiani	15	15
578	A84	10c Giovanni	15	15
579	A84	25c Van der Weyden	30	30
580	A84	50c Botticelli	60	60
581	A84	$1 Mantegna	1.20	1.20

Souvenir Sheet

Perf. 13½

582	A84	$2 Niccolo di Pietro	2.00	2.00

Yachts and Point Saline — A85

Designs: 1c, Grenada Yacht Club race, St. George's. 2c, Careenage taxi (boat). 3c, Large working boats. 5c, Deep Water Dock, St. George's. 6c, Cacao beans in drying trays. 8c, Nutmeg branch. 10c, River Antoine Estate rum distillery, c. 1785. 12c, Cacao branch. 15c, Fishermen landing catch at Fontenoy. 20c, Parliament Building, St. George's. 25c, Fort George cannons. 35c, Pearls Airport. 50c, General Post Office. 75c, Carib Leap, Sauteurs Bay. $1, Careenage, St. George's. $2, St. George's harbor at night. $3, Grand Anse Beach. $5, Canoe Bay and Black Bay from Point Saline Lighthouse. $10, Sugar-loaf Island from Levera Beach.

1975 Litho. *Perf. 14½*

Size: 38x25mm

583	A85	½c multicolored	15	15
584	A85	1c multicolored	15	15
585	A85	2c multicolored	15	15
586	A85	3c multicolored	15	15
587	A85	5c multicolored	15	15
588	A85	6c multicolored	15	15
589	A85	8c multicolored	15	15
590	A85	10c multicolored	15	15
591	A85	12c multicolored	15	15
592	A85	15c multicolored	15	15
593	A85	20c multicolored	15	15
594	A85	25c multicolored	20	20
595	A85	35c multicolored	25	25
596	A85	50c multicolored	38	38

Perf. 13½x14

Size: 45x28mm

597	A85	75c multicolored	60	60
598	A85	$1 multicolored	75	75
599	A85	$2 multicolored	1.50	1.50
600	A85	$3 multicolored	2.25	2.25
601	A85	$5 multicolored	3.75	3.75
602	A85	$10 multicolored	7.50	7.50
		Nos. 583-602 (20)	18.83	18.83

Issue dates: Nos. 583-596, Jan. 13; Nos. 597-601, Jan. 22; No. 602, Mar. 26.

For overprints, see Nos. 965-979.

1978 *Perf. 13*

584a	A85	1c	15	15
585a	A85	2c	15	15
586a	A85	3c	15	15
587a	A85	5c	15	15
588a	A85	6c	15	15
590a	A85	10c	15	15
592a	A85	15c	15	15
593a	A85	20c	15	15
594a	A85	25c	20	20
596a	A85	50c	38	38
		Nos. 584a-596a (10)	1.78	1.78

Sailfish
A86

Designs: Big game fish.

1975, Feb. 3 *Perf. 14½*

603	A86	½c shown	15	15
604	A86	1c Blue marlin	15	15
605	A86	2c White marlin	15	15
606	A86	10c Yellowfin tuna	15	15
607	A86	25c Wahoo	30	30
608	A86	50c Dolphin	55	55
609	A86	70c Grouper	85	85
610	A86	$1 Great barracuda	1.25	1.25
		Nos. 603-610 (8)	3.55	3.55

Souvenir Sheet

Perf. 13

611	A86	$2 Mako shark	2.75	2.75

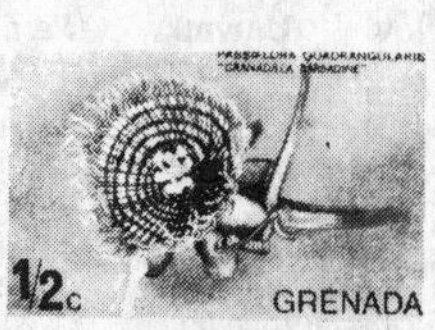

Passiflora Quadrangularis — A87

Designs: Flowers of Grenada.

1975, Feb. 26 Litho. *Perf. 14½*

612	A87	½c shown	15	15
613	A87	1c Bleeding heart	15	15
614	A87	2c Poinsettia	15	15
615	A87	3c Obroma cacao	15	15
616	A87	10c Gladioli	18	18
617	A87	25c Red head-yellow head	40	40
618	A87	50c Plumbago	75	75
619	A87	$1 Orange blossoms	1.40	1.40
		Nos. 612-619 (8)	3.33	3.33

Souvenir Sheet

Perf. 13½

620	A87	$2 Barbados gooseberry	2.75	2.75

Grenada Flag and UN Emblem — A88

Designs: 1c, UN and Grenada flags. 2c, $1, UN emblem and Grenada coat of arms. 35c, UN emblem over map of Grenada. 50c, Grenada flag in front of UN Headquarters. 75c, like ½c. $2, UN emblem and scroll.

1975, Mar. 19 *Perf. 14½*

621	A88	½c multicolored	15	15
622	A88	1c multicolored	15	15
623	A88	2c multicolored	15	15
624	A88	35c multicolored	40	40
625	A88	50c multicolored	55	55
626	A88	$2 multicolored	2.25	2.25
		Nos. 621-626 (6)	3.65	3.65

Souvenir Sheet

Perf. 13½

627		Sheet of 2	2.25	2.25
a.		A88 75c multicolored	85	85
b.		A88 $1 multicolored	1.10	1.10

Grenada's admission to the United Nations, Sept. 17, 1974.

Midnight Ride of Paul Revere — A89

Designs: 1c, Crispus Attucks at Boston Massacre. 2c, Patrick Henry. 3c, Franklin visiting Washington at the front. 5c, Lexington-Concord. 10c, John Paul Jones. No. 634, Arms of Grenada and United States. No. 635, Flags of Grenada and United States.

1975, May 6 Litho. *Perf. 14½, 13*

628	A89	½c Prus blue & multi	15	*15*
629	A89	1c buff & multi	15	*15*
630	A89	2c dp org & multi	15	*15*
631	A89	3c orange & multi	15	*15*
632	A89	5c Prus blue & multi	15	*15*
633	A89	10c ultra & multi	15	*15*
		Nos. 628-633,C29-C32 (10)	4.60	
		Set value		*1.20*

Souvenir Sheets

Perf. 13½

634	A89	$2 tan & multi	2.75	*50*
635	A89	$2 gray & multi	2.75	*50*

American Revolution Bicentennial. Size of stamps on Nos. 634-635: 47x34mm.

Nos. 628-633 issued in sheets of 40. Each denomination was also printed in sheets of 5 plus label, perf. 13.

Angel Collecting Jesus' Blood in Grail, by Bellini — A90

Easter (Paintings): 1c, Pieta, by Bellini. 2c, The Deposition, by Rogier van der Weyden. 3c, Pieta, by Bellini. 35c, Descent from the Cross, by Bellini. 75c, Jesus Rising from the Tomb, by Bellini. $1, Descent from the Cross, by Procaccini. $2, Pieta, by Botticelli.

1975, May 21

636	A90	½c multicolored	15	*15*
637	A90	1c multicolored	15	*15*
638	A90	2c multicolored	15	*15*
639	A90	3c multicolored	15	*15*
640	A90	35c multicolored	60	*15*
641	A90	75c multicolored	1.35	*25*
642	A90	$1 multicolored	1.80	*50*
		Nos. 636-642 (7)	4.35	
		Set value		*1.05*

Souvenir Sheet

Perf. 13½

643	A90	$2 multicolored	3.75	*70*

Scouts Studying Wildlife, Nordjamb 75 Emblem
A91

Nordjamb 75 Emblem and: 1c, Seamanship; Scouts in sailboat. 2c, Survival; Scouts reading map. 35c, First aid. 40c, Physical fitness; gymnastics. 75c, Mountaineering. $1, Emergency boat building. $2, Scouts singing.

1975, July 2 Litho. *Perf. 14*

644	A91	½c blue & multi	15	*15*
645	A91	1c blue & multi	15	*15*
646	A91	2c blue & multi	15	*15*
647	A91	35c blue & multi	50	*20*
648	A91	40c blue & multi	60	*20*
649	A91	75c blue & multi	1.00	*30*
650	A91	$2 blue & multi	2.75	*65*
		Nos. 644-650 (7)	5.30	
		Set value		*1.40*

Souvenir Sheet

651	A91	$1 blue & multi	1.50	*25*

Nordjamb 75, 14th Boy Scout World Jamboree, Lillehammer, Norway, July 29-Aug. 7.

Leafy Jewel Box — A92

Butterflies — A93

Designs: Sea shells.

1975, Aug. 1 Litho. *Perf. 14*

652	A92	½c shown	15	*15*
653	A92	1c Emerald nerite	15	*15*
654	A92	2c Yellow cockle	15	*15*
655	A92	25c Purple sea snail	50	*20*
656	A92	50c Turkey wing	1.00	*40*
657	A92	75c West Indian fighting conch	1.50	*1.50*
658	A92	$1 Noble wentletrap	2.00	*60*
		Nos. 652-658 (7)	5.45	3.15

Souvenir Sheet

659	A92	$2 Music volute	4.00	*90*

1975, Sept. 22 Litho. *Perf. 14*

660	A93	½c Large tiger	15	*15*
661	A93	1c Five continents	15	*15*
662	A93	2c Large striped blue	15	*15*
663	A93	35c Gonatryx	50	*22*
664	A93	45c Spear-winged cattle heart	65	*30*
665	A93	75c Risty nymula	1.10	*40*
666	A93	$2 Blue night	3.00	*75*
		Nos. 660-666 (7)	5.70	*2.12*

Souvenir Sheet

667	A93	$1 Lycrophon	3.25	*60*

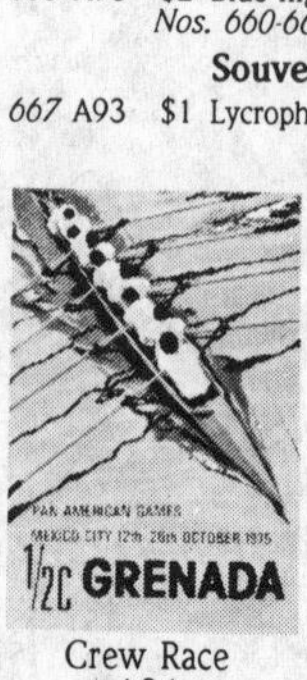

Crew Race
A94

Young Man, by Michelangelo
A95

1975, Oct. 13 Litho. *Perf. 14*

668	A94	½c shown	15	*15*
669	A94	1c Women's swimming	15	*15*
670	A94	2c Steeplechase	15	*15*
671	A94	35c Gymnastics	35	*15*

672 A94 45c Soccer 45 18
673 A94 75c Boxing 75 25
674 A94 $2 Bicycling 2.00 50
Nos. 668-674 (7) 4.00
Set value 1.20

Souvenir Sheet

675 A94 $1 Sailing 1.50 35

7th Pan-American Games, Mexico City, Oct. 13-26.

1975, Nov. 3

Works by Michelangelo (except 50c): 1/2c, David. 2c, Moses. 40c, Zachariah. 50c, St. John the Baptist (sculpture). 75c, Judith and Holofernes (detail). $1, Madonna (head from Pietà). $2, Doni Madonna (detail from Holy Family).

676 A95 1/2c black & multi 15 15
677 A95 1c black & multi 15 15
678 A95 2c black & multi 15 15
679 A95 40c black & multi 45 15
680 A95 50c black & multi 55 20
681 A95 75c black & multi 85 25
682 A95 $2 black & multi 2.25 50
Nos. 676-682 (7) 4.55
Set value 1.20

Souvenir Sheet

683 A95 $1 black & multi 1.25 30

Michelangelo Buonarroti (1475-1564), Italian painter, sculptor and architect.

Virgin and Child Paintings — A96

Bananaquit — A97

1975, Dec. 8

684 A96 1/2c Filippino Lippi 15 15
685 A96 1c Mantegna 15 15
686 A96 2c Luis de Morales 15 15
687 A96 35c G. M. Morandi 35 15
688 A96 50c Antonello da Messina 50 20
689 A96 75c Durer 75 25
690 A96 $1 Velazquez 1.00 30
Nos. 684-690 (7) 3.05
Set value 1.00

Souvenir Sheet

691 A96 $2 Bellini 3.75 60

Christmas.

1976, Jan. 20 Litho. *Perf. 14*

Designs: 1c, Orange-rumped agouti. 2c, Hawksbill turtle, horiz. 5c, Dwarf poinciana. 35c, Albacores, horiz. 40c, Cardinal's guard flower. $1, Belted kingfisher. $2, Antillean armadillo, horiz.

692 A97 1/2c multicolored 15 15
693 A97 1c multicolored 15 15
694 A97 2c multicolored 15 15
695 A97 5c multicolored 15 15
696 A97 35c multicolored 75 75
697 A97 40c multicolored 85 85
698 A97 $2 multicolored 4.25 4.25
Nos. 692-698 (7) 6.45 6.45

Souvenir Sheet

699 A97 $1 multicolored 4.25 4.25

Carnival Dancers A98

Designs: 1c, Scuba diving. 2c, Cruise ship in St. George's Harbor. 35c, Game fishing. 50c, St. George's Golf Course. 75c, Tennis. $1, Mount Rich rock carvings. $2, Sailboats.

1976, Feb. 25 Litho. *Perf. 14*

700 A98 1/2c multicolored 15 15
701 A98 1c multicolored 15 15
702 A98 2c multicolored 15 15
703 A98 35c multicolored 40 40
704 A98 50c multicolored 55 55
705 A98 75c multicolored 80 80
706 A98 $1 multicolored 1.10 1.10
Nos. 700-706 (7) 3.30 3.30

Souvenir Sheet

707 A98 $2 multicolored 2.20 2.20

Tourist publicity.

Descent from the Cross, by Master of Okolicsno — A99

Easter (Paintings): 1c, Pieta, by Correggio. 2c, Crucifixion, by van der Weyden. 3c, Burial of Christ, by Dürer. 35c, God the Father Holding Crucified Christ, by unknown master (Florence). 75c, Ascension, by Raphael. $1, Burial of Christ, by Raphael. $2, Pieta, by Crespi.

1976, Mar. 29

708 A99 1/2c multicolored 15 15
709 A99 1c multicolored 15 15
710 A99 2c multicolored 15 15
711 A99 3c multicolored 15 15
712 A99 35c multicolored 28 28
713 A99 75c multicolored 60 60
714 A99 $1 multicolored 85 85
Set value 1.90 1.90

Souvenir Sheet

715 A99 $2 multicolored 1.75 1.75

Sharpshooters, 1780 — A100

First Stars and Stripes and: 1c, Defense of Liberty Pole. 2c, Men loading muskets. 35c, 75c, Fight for Liberty. 50c, $2, Peace Treaty, 1783. $1, Drumming march on Breed's Hill. $3, Gunboat, c. 1776.

1976, Apr. 15 Litho. *Perf. 14*

716 A100 1/2c multicolored 15 15
717 A100 1c multicolored 15 15
718 A100 2c multicolored 15 15
719 A100 35c multicolored 35 35
720 A100 50c multicolored 50 50
721 A100 $1 multicolored 1.00 1.00
722 A100 $3 multicolored 2.75 2.75
Nos. 716-722 (7) 5.05 5.05

Souvenir Sheet

723 Sheet of 2 3.00 3.00
a. A100 75c multicolored 75 75
b. A100 $2 multicolored 2.00 2.00

American Bicentennial.

Girl Guide Emblems, Nature Study — A101

Volleyball — A102

Various Girl Guide Emblems and: 1c, Cooking. 2c, $2, First aid (diff.). 50c, Tenting. 75c, Home economics. $1, Drawing.

1976, June 1 Litho. *Perf. 14*

724 A101 1/2c multicolored 15 15
725 A101 1c multicolored 15 15
726 A101 2c multicolored 15 15
727 A101 50c multicolored 50 50
728 A101 75c multicolored 75 75
729 A101 $2 multicolored 2.25 2.25
Nos. 724-729 (6) 3.95 3.95

Souvenir Sheet

730 A101 $1 multicolored 2.25 2.25

Girl Guides of Grenada, 50th anniv.

1976, June 21 Litho. *Perf. 14*

Olympic Rings and: 1c, Bicycling. 2c, Rowing. 35c, Judo. 45c, Hockey. 75c, Women's gymnastics. $1, High jump. $3, Equestrian.

731 A102 1/2c multicolored 15 15
732 A102 1c multicolored 15 15
733 A102 2c multicolored 15 15
734 A102 35c multicolored 25 25
735 A102 45c multicolored 30 30
736 A102 75c multicolored 52 52
737 A102 $1 multicolored 70 70
Set value 1.90 1.90

Souvenir Sheet

738 A102 $3 multicolored 2.50 2.50

21st Olympic Games, Montreal, Canada, July 17-Aug. 1.

Moulin Rouge, by Toulouse-Lautrec A103

Paintings by Toulouse-Lautrec: 1c, Start of the Quadrille. 2c, Woman's Head. 3c, Hall at the Moulin Rouge. 40c, Man Delivering Laundry. 50c, Dancing the Bolero. $1, Lady with Boa. $2, Signor Boileau at the Cafe.

1976, July 20 Litho. *Perf. 14*

739 A103 1/2c multicolored 15 15
740 A103 1c multicolored 15 15
741 A103 2c multicolored 15 15
742 A103 3c multicolored 15 15
743 A103 40c multicolored 40 40
744 A103 50c multicolored 50 50
745 A103 $2 multicolored 2.00 2.00
Set value 3.00 3.00

Souvenir Sheet

746 A103 $1 multicolored 1.20 1.20

Henri de Toulouse-Lautrec (1864-1901), painter, 75th death anniv.

Map of West Indies, Bats, Wicket and Ball A103a

Prudential Cup — A103b

1976, July 26

747 A103a 35c lt blue & multi 70 70
748 A103b $1 lilac rose & blk 2.00 2.00

World Cricket Cup, won by West Indies Team, 1975.

Piper Apache A104

Airplanes: 1c, Beech Twin Bonanza. 2c, D.H. Twin Otter. 40c, Britten Norman Islander. 50c, D.H. Heron. $2, Hawker Siddeley Avro 748. $3, B.A.C. One-Eleven.

1976, Aug. 18

749 A104 1/2c multicolored 15 15
750 A104 1c multicolored 15 15
751 A104 2c multicolored 15 15
752 A104 40c multicolored 40 40
753 A104 50c multicolored 50 50
754 A104 $2 multicolored 2.00 2.00
Nos. 749-754 (6) 3.35 3.35

Souvenir Sheet

755 A104 $3 multicolored 3.30 3.30

Helios Mission, Assembly — A105

Designs: 1c, Helios spacecraft in space 2c, Helios assembled. 15c, Helios, system test and checkout. 45c, Viking nearing Mars, horiz. 75c, Viking on Mars. $2, Viking spacecraft assembled. $3, Helios orbiter and Viking lander.

1976, Sept. 1 Litho. *Perf. 14*

756 A105 1/2c multicolored 15 15
757 A105 1c multicolored 15 15
758 A105 2c multicolored 15 15
759 A105 15c multicolored 15 15
760 A105 45c multicolored 35 35
761 A105 75c multicolored 60 60
762 A105 $2 multicolored 1.60 1.60
Nos. 756-762 (7) 3.15 3.15

Souvenir Sheet

763 A105 $3 multicolored 2.75 2.75

Helios (solar probe) mission and Viking Mars missions.

S.S. Geestland, Geest Line Flag A106

Ships: 1c, M.V. Federal Palm, West Indies Shipping Service. 2c, H.M.S. Blake and ship's crest. 25c, M.V. Vistafjord and Norwegian-American Line flag. 75c, S.S. Canberra and P. & O. Line flag. $1, S.S. Regina and Chandris Line flag. $2, Santa Maria and Spanish flag, 1492. $5, S.S. Arandora and Blue Star Line flag.

1976, Nov. 3 Litho. *Perf. 14 1/2*

764 A106 1/2c blue & multi 15 15
765 A106 1c blue & multi 15 15
766 A106 2c blue & multi 15 15
767 A106 25c blue & multi 20 20
768 A106 75c blue & multi 55 55
769 A106 $1 blue & multi 75 75
770 A106 $5 blue & multi 3.75 3.75
Nos. 764-770 (7) 5.70 5.70

Souvenir Sheet

771 A106 $2 multicolored 2.75 2.75

Ships connected with Grenada's development.

Altarpiece of San Barnaba, by Botticelli A107

Christmas (Paintings): 1c, Annunciation, by Botticelli. 2c, Madonna with Chancellor Rolin, by Jan van Eyck. 35c, Annunciation, by Fra Filippo Lippi. 50c, Madonna of the Magnificat, by Botticelli. 75c, Madonna of the Pomegranate, by Botticelli. $2, Gipsy Madonna, by Titian. $3, Madonna with St. Cosmas and Saints, by Botticelli.

1976, Dec. 8 Litho. *Perf. 14*

772 A107 1/2c multicolored 15 15
773 A107 1c multicolored 15 15
774 A107 2c multicolored 15 15

775	A107	35c multicolored	30	30
776	A107	50c multicolored	45	45
777	A107	75c multicolored	65	65
778	A107	$3 multicolored	2.75	2.75
		Nos. 772-778 (7)	4.60	4.60

Souvenir Sheet

779	A107	$2 multicolored	2.00	2.00

Globe and Telephone Users A108

Designs: ½c, A. G. Bell, 1876 and modern telephones. 2c, Satellites around globe, world map. 18c, Videophone. 40c, Satellite and ground stations. $1, Satellite and telephone communication with ships. $2, British "Trimphone" and radar station. $5, Flags of the world surrounding globe, and telephone.

1976, Dec. 17 Litho. *Perf. 14*

780	A108	½c multicolored	15	15
781	A108	1c multicolored	15	15
782	A108	2c multicolored	15	15
783	A108	18c multicolored	18	18
784	A108	40c multicolored	40	40
785	A108	$1 multicolored	1.00	1.00
786	A108	$2 multicolored	2.00	2.00
		Nos. 780-786 (7)	4.03	4.03

Souvenir Sheet

787	A108	$5 multicolored	4.00	4.00

Centenary of first telephone conversation by Alexander Graham Bell, Mar. 10, 1876.

Coronation of Elizabeth II — A109

Designs: 1c, $1, Orb and scepter. 35c, $3, Trooping of the Guards. 50c, $2, Spoon and ampulla. 35c, (bklt.), $2.50, Elizabeth II and Prince Philip. $5, Royal visit to Grenada.

1977, Feb. 8 Litho. *Perf. 14, 12*

788	A109	½c multicolored	15	15
789	A109	1c multicolored	15	15
790	A109	35c multicolored	25	25
791	A109	$2 multicolored	1.40	1.40
792	A109	$2.50 multicolored	1.75	1.75
a.		Booklet pane of 6 (35c)	2.00	
b.		Booklet pane of 3 (50c, $1, $3)	6.00	
		Nos. 788-792 (5)	3.70	3.70

Souvenir Sheet

793	A109	$5 multicolored	3.25	3.25

Reign of Queen Elizabeth II, 25th anniv.

Nos. 792a-792b are self-adhesive, roulette x imperf. Marginal inscriptions.

Nos. 788-792 were printed in sheets of 40 (10x4), perf. 14, and sheets of 5 plus label, perf. 12, in changed colors.

For overprints, see Nos. 821-826.

Water Skiing, One-ski Slalom A110

Designs: 1c, Speedboat racing around Grand Anse. 2c, Crew racing, St. George's. 22c, Swimming, Grand Anse. 35c, Local work boat races. 75c, Water polo, careenage, St. George's. $2, Game fishing. $3, South Coast yacht race.

1977, Apr. 13 Litho. *Perf. 14*

794	A110	½c multicolored	15	15
795	A110	1c multicolored	15	15
796	A110	2c multicolored	15	15
797	A110	22c multicolored	20	20
798	A110	35c multicolored	30	30
799	A110	75c multicolored	65	65
800	A110	$2 multicolored	1.90	1.90
		Nos. 794-800 (7)	3.50	3.50

Souvenir Sheet

801	A110	$3 multicolored	3.00	3.00

1977 Easter Water Parade.

Tent, OAS Emblem A111

1977, June 14 Litho. *Perf. 14*

802	A111	35c multicolored	35	35
803	A111	$1 multicolored	1.00	1.00
804	A111	$2 multicolored	2.00	2.00

7th Regular Session, General Assembly of Organization of American States.

Scouts on Raft — A112

Designs: 1c, Tug-of-war. 2c, Boy Scout regatta. 18c, Scouts around camp fire. 40c, Field kitchen. $1, Boy Scouts and Sea Scouts. $2, Hiking and map reading. $3, Semaphore.

1977, Sept. 6 Litho. *Perf. 14*

805	A112	½c multicolored	15	15
806	A112	1c multicolored	15	15
807	A112	2c multicolored	15	15
808	A112	18c multicolored	18	18
809	A112	40c multicolored	40	40
810	A112	$1 multicolored	1.00	1.00
811	A112	$2 multicolored	2.00	2.00
		Nos. 805-811 (7)	4.03	4.03

Souvenir Sheet

812	A112	$3 multicolored	3.00	3.00

6th Caribbean Jamboree, Kingston, Jamaica, Aug. 5-14.

Annunciation to the Shepherds — A113

Ceiling Paintings, St. Martin's Church, Zillis, Switzerland, 12th Century: 1c, Joseph on his way. 2c, Virgin and Child, Flight into Egypt. 22c, Angel leading the way. 35c, King on way to Herod. 75c, Three horses. $2, Virgin and Child. $3, Adoration of the Kings.

1977, Nov. 3 Litho. *Perf. 14*

813	A113	½c multicolored	15	15
814	A113	1c multicolored	15	15
815	A113	2c multicolored	15	15
816	A113	22c multicolored	15	15
817	A113	35c multicolored	25	25
818	A113	75c multicolored	50	50
819	A113	$2 multicolored	1.40	1.40
		Nos. 813-819 (7)	2.75	2.75

Souvenir Sheet

820	A113	$3 multicolored	2.25	2.25

Christmas.

Nos. 788-793 Overprinted "Royal Visit W.I. 1977"

1977, Nov. 10 *Perf. 12, 14*

821	A109	½c multicolored	15	15
822	A109	1c multicolored	15	15
823	A109	35c multicolored	25	25
824	A109	$2 multicolored	1.40	1.40
825	A109	$2.50 multicolored	1.75	1.75
		Nos. 821-825 (5)	3.70	3.70

Souvenir Sheet

Perf. 14

826	A109	$5 multicolored	3.25	3.25

Caribbean visit of Queen Elizabeth II. Nos. 821-822 are perf. 12, others perf. 12 and 14.

Christjaan Eijkman — A114

Portraits: 1c, Winston Churchill, Literature, 1953. 2c, Woodrow Wilson, Peace, 1919. 35c, Frederic Passy, Peace 1901. $1, Albert Einstein, Physics, 1921. $2, Alfred Nobel, founder. $3, Carl Bosch, Chemistry, 1931.

1978, Jan. 25 Litho. *Perf. 14*

827	A114	½c multicolored	15	15
828	A114	1c multicolored	15	15
829	A114	2c multicolored	15	15
830	A114	35c multicolored	28	28
831	A114	$1 multicolored	75	75
832	A114	$3 multicolored	2.25	2.25
		Nos. 827-832 (6)	3.73	3.73

Souvenir Sheet

833	A114	$2 multicolored	1.50	1.50

Nobel Prize winners.

Early Zeppelin and Count Zeppelin A115

Designs: 1c, Lindbergh and Spirit of St. Louis. 2c, "Deutschland" airship. 22c, Lindbergh landing in Paris. 35c, Lindbergh in cockpit. 75c, Lindbergh and Spirit of St. Louis in flight. $1, Zeppelin over Alps. $2, Count Zeppelin and early airship. $3, Zeppelin over White House.

1978, Feb. 13 Litho. *Perf. 14*

834	A115	½c multicolored	15	15
835	A115	1c multicolored	15	15
836	A115	2c multicolored	15	15
837	A115	22c multicolored	18	18
838	A115	75c multicolored	60	60
839	A115	$1 multicolored	80	80
840	A115	$3 multicolored	2.50	2.50
		Nos. 834-840 (7)	4.53	4.53

Souvenir Sheet

841		Sheet of 2	2.25	2.25
a.	A115	35c multicolored	32	
b.	A115	$2 multicolored	1.75	

Aviation history.

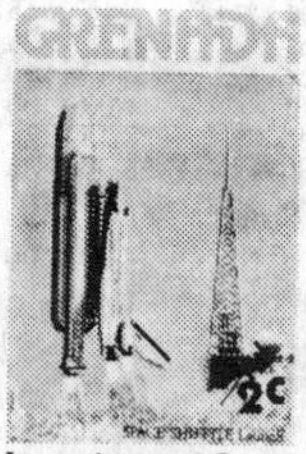

Launching of Space Shuttle — A116

Black- headed Gulls — A117

Space Shuttle: 1c, Booster separation. 2c, External tank separation. 18c, In orbit. 75c, Satellite placement. $2, Landing approach. $3, On landing pad.

1978, Feb. 28

842	A116	½c multicolored	15	15
843	A116	1c multicolored	15	15
844	A116	2c multicolored	15	15
845	A116	18c multicolored	18	18
846	A116	75c multicolored	75	75
847	A116	$2 multicolored	2.00	2.00
		Nos. 842-847 (6)	3.38	3.38

Souvenir Sheet

848	A116	$3 multicolored	3.00	3.00

US space shuttle.

Wild Birds of Grenada and Wildlife Fund Emblem: 1c, Wilson's petrels. 2c, Killdeers. 50c, White-necked jacobin and hibiscus. 75c, Blue-faced booby. $1, Broad-winged hawk. $2, Scaley-necked pigeon. $3, Scarlet ibis.

1978, Mar. 8 Litho. *Perf. 14*

849	A117	½c multicolored	15	15
850	A117	1c multicolored	15	15
851	A117	2c multicolored	15	15
852	A117	50c multicolored	45	45
853	A117	75c multicolored	70	70
854	A117	$1 multicolored	90	90
855	A117	$2 multicolored	1.75	1.75
		Nos. 849-855 (7)	4.25	4.25

Souvenir Sheet

856	A117	$3 multicolored	4.00	4.00

Marquise de Spinola, by Rubens A118

Ludwig van Beethoven A119

Paintings by Peter Paul Rubens (1577-1640): 5c, Reception of Marie de Medicis. 15c, Rubens and Helena Fourment. 25c, Ludovicus Nonnius. 45c, Helena Fourment with her Children. 75c, Child's head. $3, Suzanne Fourment in Velvet Hat.

1978, Mar. 30 Litho. *Perf. 13½x14*

857	A118	5c lt blue & multi	15	15
858	A118	15c lt blue & multi	15	15
859	A118	18c lt blue & multi	15	15
860	A118	25c lt blue & multi	20	20
861	A118	45c lt blue & multi	35	35
862	A118	75c lt blue & multi	60	60
863	A118	$3 lt blue & multi	2.50	2.50
		Nos. 857-863 (7)	4.10	4.10

Souvenir Sheet

864	A118	$5 lt blue & multi	4.00	4.00

1978, Apr. 24 *Perf. 14*

Designs: 15c, Woman violinist playing concerto. 18c, Various musical instruments. 22c, Piano. 50c, Two violins. 75c, Beethoven's piano and score. $2, Beethoven and score. $3, Beethoven and his house. (15c, 18c, 22c, 75c, $2, $3, horiz.).

865	A119	5c multicolored	15	15
866	A119	15c multicolored	15	15
867	A119	18c multicolored	15	15
868	A119	22c multicolored	18	18
869	A119	50c multicolored	38	38
870	A119	75c multicolored	55	55
871	A119	$3 multicolored	2.25	2.25
		Nos. 865-871 (7)	3.81	3.81

Souvenir Sheet

872	A119	$2 multicolored	2.25	2.25

Ludwig van Beethoven (1770-1827), composer, death sesquicentennial.

Elizabeth II with Crown, Scepter and Orb — A120

Trooping of the Colors — A121

Designs: 35c, Coronation. $2.50, St. Edward's crown. $5, Elizabeth II and Prince Philip.

1978, June 2 Litho. *Perf. 14*

873	A120	35c multicolored	25	25
874	A120	$2 multicolored	1.50	1.50
875	A120	$2.50 multicolored	1.75	1.75

Souvenir Sheet

876 A120 $5 multicolored 3.25 3.25

Litho.

Imperf

Self-adhesive

Designs: 35c, Elizabeth II at Maundy Money distribution ceremony.
$5, Elizabeth II and Prince Philip.

877 Souvenir booklet 5.00
a. A121 Bklt. pane, 3 each 25c, 35c 1.25
b. A121 Booklet pane of 1, $5 3.50

Coronation of Queen Elizabeth II, 25th anniv.
Nos. 873-875 were printed in sheets of 40 (10x4), perf. 14, and sheets of 3 plus label, perf. 12, in changed colors. Labels show royal insignia.
No. 877 contains 2 booklet panes printed on peelable paper backing showing coins.

Goalkeeper Reaching for Ball — A122

Designs: Goalkeeper reaching for ball, various stages of motion.

1978, Aug. 1 Litho. *Perf. 15*
878 A122 40c multicolored 28 28
879 A122 60c multicolored 40 40
880 A122 90c multicolored 60 60
881 A122 $2 multicolored 1.40 1.40

Souvenir Sheet

882 A122 $2.50 multicolored 2.00 2.00

11th World Cup Soccer Championship, Argentina, June 1-25.

Flying Objects, 16th Century Drawing and Flying Saucer, 1962
A123

Designs: 35c, Radar probing skies, and Mars surface. $2, Prime Minister Eric Gairy and UN General Assembly Building. $3, Flying saucer with downwards beam, and UFO photograph.

1978, Aug. 17
883 A123 5c multicolored 15 15
884 A123 35c multicolored 28 28
885 A123 $3 multicolored 2.25 2.25

Souvenir Sheet

886 A123 $2 multicolored 1.75 1.75

Proposal by Prime Minister Eric Gairy of Grenada to the UN General Assembly to study unidentified flying objects, Oct. 7, 1977.

Wright Glider and Allegory of Flight A124

Designs: 15c, Flyer I, 1903, and eagle. 18c, Flyer III and allegory of flight. 22c, Flyer III and eagle. 50c, Orville Wright, Flyer and allegory of flight. 75c, Flyer, 1908, and eagle. $2, Flyer and allegory of flight. $3, Wilbur Wright, Flyer and allegory of flight.

1978, Aug. 24 *Perf. 14*
887 A124 5c multicolored 15 15
888 A124 15c multicolored 15 15
889 A124 18c multicolored 15 15
890 A124 22c multicolored 18 18
891 A124 50c multicolored 38 38
892 A124 75c multicolored 55 55
893 A124 $3 multicolored 2.25 2.25
Nos. 887-893 (7) 3.81 3.81

Souvenir Sheet

894 A124 $2 multicolored 1.50 1.50

75th anniversary of first powered flight by Wright brothers, Dec. 17, 1903.

Hawaiian Feast in Capt. Cook's Honor A125

Capt. Cook and: 35c, Hawaiian warriors' dance. 75c, Honolulu harbor. $3, "Resolution." $4, Death scene.

1978, Dec. 5 Litho. *Perf. 14*
895 A125 18c multicolored 15 15
896 A125 35c multicolored 28 28
897 A125 75c multicolored 60 60
898 A125 $3 multicolored 2.50 2.50

Souvenir Sheet

899 A125 $4 multicolored 2.75 2.75

Bicentenary of Capt. Cook's arrival in Hawaii and 250th anniversary of his birth.

Detail from Paumgartner Altar, by Dürer — A126

Convention and Cultural Center — A127

Dürer Paintings: 60c, The Three Kings. 90c, Virgin and Child. $2, Head of the Virgin. $4, Virgin and Child.

1978, Dec. 20 Litho. *Perf. 14*
900 A126 40c multicolored 30 30
901 A126 60c multicolored 45 45
902 A126 90c multicolored 70 70
903 A126 $2 multicolored 1.50 1.50

Souvenir Sheet

904 A126 $4 multicolored 2.75 2.75

Christmas and 450th death anniv. of Albrecht Durer (1471-1528), German painter.

1979, Feb. 8 Litho. *Perf. 14*

Designs: 18c, Geodesic Dome. 22c, Rowboat race, Easter parade, St. George's. 35c, Prime Minister Eric M. Gairy. $3, Cross at Fort Frederick at night.

905 A127 5c multicolored 15 15
906 A127 18c multicolored 15 15
907 A127 22c multicolored 15 15
908 A127 35c multicolored 25 25
909 A127 $3 multicolored 2.00 2.00
Nos. 905-909 (5) 2.70 2.70

5th anniversary of independence.

Chenille Plant — A128

Birds in Flight — A129

Native Flowers: 50c, Red hibiscus. $1, Skyflower. $2, Pink pride of India. $3, Rosebay.

1979, Feb. 26
910 A128 18c multicolored 15 15
911 A128 50c multicolored 40 40
912 A128 $1 multicolored 80 80
913 A128 $3 multicolored 2.50 2.50

Souvenir Sheet

914 A128 $2 multicolored 2.00 2.00

1979, Mar. 15

Design: $2, Bird in flight and Human Rights emblem.

915 A129 15c multicolored 15 15
916 A129 $2 multicolored 1.50 1.50

Universal Declaration of Human Rights, 30th anniversary.

Children Playing Cricket — A130

IYC Emblem and: 22c, Boys playing baseball. $4, Children with model spaceship. $5, Three children.

1979, Apr. 23 Litho. *Perf. 14*
917 A130 18c multicolored 16 16
918 A130 22c multicolored 20 20
919 A130 $5 multicolored 4.75 4.75

Souvenir Sheet

920 A130 $4 multicolored 3.25 3.25

Intl. Year of the Child.

Balloon and Space Shuttle A131

Designs: 35c, Octopus holding sailors, nuclear submarine. 75c, Rocket and moon. $3, Imaginary plane and space ship. $4, Multi-propellered ship and US space shuttle.

1979, May 4
921 A131 18c multicolored 15 15
922 A131 35c multicolored 25 25
923 A131 75c multicolored 55 55
924 A131 $3 multicolored 2.25 2.25

Souvenir Sheet

925 A131 $4 multicolored 2.75 2.75

Jules Verne (1828-1905), science fiction writer.

African Mail Runner A132

Sir Rowland Hill (1795-1879), originator of penny postage, and: 40c, American Pony Express. $1, Oriental pigeon post. $3, European mail coach. $5, Tete-beche stamps with revenue surcharge, 1883.

1979, June Litho. *Perf. 14*
926 A132 20c multicolored 15 15
927 A132 40c multicolored 28 28
928 A132 $1 multicolored 65 65
929 A132 $3 multicolored 2.00 2.00

Souvenir Sheet

930 A132 $5 multicolored 3.25 3.25

Nos. 926-929 were printed in sheets of 40, perf. 14, and in sheets of 5 plus label, perf. 12, in changed colors.
For overprints, see Nos. 989A-989D.

Boys, Map of Grenada, Vaccination Gun — A133

1979, Aug. 2 Litho. *Perf. 14*
931 A133 5c multicolored 15 15
932 A133 $1 multicolored 1.50 1.50

Intl. Year of the Child, immunization of children.

Reef Shark A134

Designs: 45c, Spotted eagle ray. 50c, Manytooth conger. 60c, Golden olive shells. 70c, West Indian murex. 75c, Giant tuns. 90c, Brown boobies. $1, Magnificent frigate bird. $2.50, Sooty tern.

1979, Aug. 22 Litho. *Perf. 14*
933 A134 40c multicolored 30 30
934 A134 45c multicolored 35 35
935 A134 50c multicolored 38 38
936 A134 60c multicolored 45 45
937 A134 70c multicolored 55 55
938 A134 75c multicolored 60 60
939 A134 90c multicolored 70 70
940 A134 $1 multicolored 75 75
Nos. 933-940 (8) 4.08 4.08

Souvenir Sheet

941 A134 $2.50 multicolored 3.00 3.00

Flight into Egypt, Tapestry A135

Tapestries: 25c, Virgin and Child. 30c, Angel, vert. 40c, Infant Jesus, by Doge Marino Grimani, vert. 90c, Shepherds, vert. $1, Flight into Egypt, vert. $2, Virgin in Glory, vert. $4, Virgin and Child, by Grimani, vert.

1979, Oct. 16 Litho. *Perf. 14*
942 A135 6c multicolored 15 15
943 A135 25c multicolored 18 18
944 A135 30c multicolored 20 20
945 A135 40c multicolored 28 28
946 A135 90c multicolored 60 60
947 A135 $1 multicolored 65 65
948 A135 $2 multicolored 1.40 1.40
Nos. 942-948 (7) 3.46 3.46

Souvenir Sheet

949 A135 $4 multicolored 2.75 2.75

Christmas.

Disney Characters and IYC Emblem A135a

Designs: Sport scenes.

1979, Nov. 2 Litho. *Perf. 11*
950 A135a 1/2c Mickey Mouse, baseball 15 15
951 A135a 1c Donald, high jump 15 15
952 A135a 2c Goofy, basketball 15 15
953 A135a 3c Goofy, hurdles 15 15

954 A135a 4c Donald Duck, golf 15 15
955 A135a 5c Mickey, cricket 15 15
956 A135a 10c Mickey, soccer 15 15
957 A135a $2 Mickey, tennis 2.00 2.00
958 A135a $2.50 Minnie, equestrian 2.50 2.50
Set value 4.80 4.80

Souvenir Sheet

Perf. 13½

959 CD329 $3 Goofy in riding habit 3.00 3.00

See Nos. 1031-1032.

Hands, Paul P. Harris, Rotary Emblem — A136

Rotary Emblem and Hands Holding: 30c, Caduceus. 90c, Wheat. $2, Family. $4, Emblem.

1980, Feb. 25 Litho. *Perf. 14*

960 A136 6c multicolored 15 15
961 A136 30c multicolored 20 20
962 A136 90c multicolored 60 60
963 A136 $2 multicolored 1.40 1.40

Souvenir Sheet

964 A136 $4 multicolored 2.75 2.75

Rotary International, 75th anniversary.

Nos. 585-586, 588-591, 593-594, 596-602 Overprinted in Black: PEOPLE'S REVOLUTION / 13 MARCH 1979

1980 *Perf. 15, 13½*

965 A85 2c multicolored 15 15
966 A85 3c multicolored 15 15
967 A85 6c multicolored 15 15
968 A85 8c multicolored 15 15
969 A85 10c multicolored 15 15
970 A85 12c multicolored 15 15
971 A85 20c multicolored 15 15
972 A85 25c multicolored 16 16
973 A85 50c multicolored 35 35
974 A85 75c multicolored 50 50
975 A85 $1 multicolored 65 65
976 A85 $2 multicolored 1.40 1.40
977 A85 $3 multicolored 2.00 2.00
978 A85 $5 multicolored 3.50 3.50
979 A85 $10 multicolored 6.50 6.50
Nos. 965-979 (15) 16.11 16.11

Issue dates: 25c, Apr. 7; others, Feb. 28.

Boxing, Kremlin, Olympic Rings A137

1980, Mar. 24 *Perf. 14*

980 A137 25c shown 16 16
981 A137 40c Bicycling 28 28
982 A137 90c Equestrian 60 60
983 A137 $2 Running 1.40 1.40

Souvenir Sheet

984 A137 $4 Yachting 2.75 2.75

22nd Summer Olympic Games, Moscow, July 19-Aug. 3.

Tropical Kingbirds — A138

1980, Apr. 8

985 A138 20c shown 20 20
986 A138 40c Rufous-breasted hermits 40 40
987 A138 $1 Troupials 1.00 1.00
988 A138 $2 Ruddy quail doves 2.00 2.00

Souvenir Sheet

989 A138 $3 Prairie warblers 3.25 3.25

Nos. 926-929 Overprinted: "LONDON 1980"

1980, May 6 Litho. *Perf. 12*

989A A132 20c multicolored 15 15
989B A132 40c multicolored 28 28
989C A132 $1 multicolored 65 65
989D A132 $3 multicolored 2.00 2.00

London '80 Intl. Stamp Exhib., May 6-14.

Free School Hot Lunches A139

1980, May 19 Litho. *Perf. 14*

990 A139 10c shown 15 15
991 A139 40c Food canning 28 28
992 A139 $1 Health care 65 65
993 A139 $2 Housing projects 1.40 1.40

Souvenir Sheet

994 A139 $5 Prime Minister Bishop, vert. 3.50 3.50

People's Revolution, 1st anniv.

Jamb Statues, West Portal, Chartres Cathedral — A140

Masterpieces: 10c, Les Desmoiselles d'Avignon, by Picasso. 40c, Winged Victory of Samothrace. 50c, The Night Watch, by Rembrandt. $1, Edward VI as a Child, by Holbein, the Younger. $3, Queen Nefertiti. $4, Weier Haws, by Durer, vert.

1980, June Litho. *Perf. 14*

995 A140 8c multicolored 15 15
996 A140 10c multicolored 15 15
997 A140 40c multicolored 28 28
998 A140 50c multicolored 35 35
999 A140 $1 multicolored 65 65
1000 A140 $3 multicolored 2.00 2.00
Nos. 995-1000 (6) 3.58 3.58

Souvenir Sheet

1001 A140 $4 multicolored 2.75 2.75

Carib Canoes A141

Designs: 1c, Boat building. 2c, Small workboat. 4c, "Santa Maria." 5c, West India man barque, 1840. 6c, "Orinoco," 1851. 10c, Schooner. 12c, Trimaran. 15c, "Petite Amie," Spice Island cruising yacht. 20c, Fishing pirogue. 25c, Harbor police launch. 30c, Grand Anse speedboat. 40c, "Seimstrand." 50c, "Ariadne," 3-masted schooner. 90c, "Geestide," banana boat. $1, "Cunard Countess," cruise ship. $3, Rumrunner. $5, "Statendam." $10, Coast Guard patrol boat.

1980, Sept. 9 Litho. *Perf. 14*

1002 A141 ½c multi 15 15
1003 A141 1c multi 15 15
1004 A141 2c multi 15 15
1005 A141 4c multi 15 15
1006 A141 5c multi 15 15
1007 A141 6c multi 15 15
1008 A141 10c multi 15 15
1009 A141 12c multi 15 15
1010 A141 15c multi 15 15
1011 A141 20c multi 15 15
1012 A141 25c multi 18 18
1013 A141 30c multi 22 22
1014 A141 40c multi 30 30
1015 A141 50c multi 38 38
1016 A141 90c multi 70 70
1017 A141 $1 multi 75 75
1018 A141 $3 multi 2.25 2.25
1019 A141 $5 multi 3.75 3.75
1020 A141 $10 multi 7.50 7.50
Nos. 1002-1020 (19) 17.53 17.53

No. 1017 reprinted inscribed 1982, No. 1015, 1984.

For overprints, see Nos. O1-O10, O12-O13, O15, O17.

1982-84 *Perf. 12½x12*

1002a A141 ½c 15 15
1006a A141 5c 15 15
1008a A141 10c 15 15
1011a A141 20c 15 15
1012a A141 25c 18 18
1013a A141 30c 22 22
1014a A141 40c 30 30
1015a A141 50c ('84) 38 38
1018a A141 $3 2.25 2.25
1019a A141 $5 3.75 3.75
1020a A141 $10 ('84) 7.50 7.50
Nos. 1002a-1020a (11) 15.18 15.18

Snow White at Well A142

Christmas: Various scenes from Walt Disney's Snow White and the Seven Dwarfs.

1980, Sept. 25 Litho. *Perf. 11*

1021 A142 ½c multicolored 15 15
1022 A142 1c multicolored 15 15
1023 A142 2c multicolored 15 15
1024 A142 3c multicolored 15 15
1025 A142 4c multicolored 15 15
1026 A142 5c multicolored 15 15
1027 A142 10c multicolored 15 15
1028 A142 $2.50 multicolored 2.00 2.00
1029 A142 $3 multicolored 2.50 2.50
Set value 4.80 4.80

Souvenir Sheet

1030 A142 $4 multicolored 3.75 3.75

No. 1030 contains a vertical stamp.

Disney Type of 1980

50th anniversary of Pluto character: $2, Pluto and birthday cake. $4, Pluto.

1981, Jan. 19 Litho. *Perf. 14*

1031 A135a $2 multicolored 2.50 2.50

Souvenir Sheet

1032 A135a $4 multicolored 3.50 3.50

No. 1031 issued in sheets of 8.

Adult Education — A143

1981, Mar. 13 Litho. *Perf. 12½*

1033 A143 5c Flags of the Revolution and Grenada 15 15
1034 A143 10c shown 15 15
1035 A143 15c Food processing plant 15 15
1036 A143 25c Agriculture 18 18
1037 A143 40c Fishing boat, crawfish 30 30
1038 A143 90c Ships 70 70
1039 A143 $1 Palm trees 75 75
1040 A143 $3 Map 2.25 2.25
Nos. 1033-1040 (8) 4.63 4.63

2nd Festival of the Revolution.

Mickey Mouse and Goofy with Easter Basket — A144

Easter: Various Disney characters with Easter baskets.

1981, Apr. 7 *Perf. 11*

1041 A144 35c multi 30 30
1042 A144 40c multi 35 35
1043 A144 $2 multi 1.75 1.75
1044 A144 $2.50 multi 2.25 2.25

Souvenir Sheet

1045 A144 $4 multi 3.50 3.50

Large Heads, by Picasso — A145

Paintings by Pablo Picasso (1881-1973): 25c, Woman-Flower. 30c, Portrait of Madame. 90c, Cavalier with Pipe. $5, Woman on the Bank of the Seine.

1981, Apr. 28 *Perf. 14*

1046 A145 25c multicolored 20 20
1047 A145 30c multicolored 25 25
1048 A145 90c multicolored 70 70
1049 A145 $4 multicolored 3.25 3.25

Souvenir Sheet

1050 A145 $5 multicolored 3.50 3.50

Royal Wedding Issue

Common Design Type

1981, June 16 Litho. *Perf. 15*

1051 CD331 50c Couple 38 38
1052 CD331 $2 Holyrood House 1.50 1.50
1053 CD331 $4 Charles 3.00 3.00

Souvenir Sheet

1054 CD331 $5 Glass coach 3.75 3.75

Souvenir Booklet

1055 CD331 9.00
a. Pane of 6 (3x$1, Lady Diana, 3x$2, Charles) 6.00
b. Pane of 1, $5, Couple 3.00

No. 1055 contains imperf., self-adhesive stamps.

Sheets of 5 plus label contain 30c, 40c or $4 in changed colors, perf. 14x14½.

For overprints, see Nos. O11, O14, O16,

The Bath, by Mary Cassatt (1845-1926) — A146

Decade for Women (Paintings by Women): 40c, Mademoiselle Charlotte du Val d'Ognes, by Constance Marie Charpentier. 60c, Self-portrait, by Mary Beale. $3, Woman in White Stockings, by Suzanne Valadon. $5, The Artist Hesitating between the Arts of Music and Painting, horiz.

1981, Oct. 13 Litho. *Perf. 14*

1058 A146 15c multi 15 15
1059 A146 40c multi 30 30
1060 A146 60c multi 45 45
1061 A146 $3 multi 2.25 2.25

Souvenir Sheet

1062 A146 $5 multi 3.50 3.50

Cinderella and Prince Charming Dancing at the Ball — A147

Christmas: Scenes from Walt Disney's Cinderella.

1981, Nov. 2 Litho. *Perf. 14x13½*

1063 A147	½c multi	15	15
1064 A147	1c multi	15	15
1065 A147	2c multi	15	15
1066 A147	3c multi	15	15
1067 A147	4c multi	15	15
1068 A147	5c multi	15	15
1069 A147	10c multi	15	15
1070 A147	$2.50 multi	2.25	2.25
1071 A147	$3 multi	2.75	2.75
Nos. 1063-1071 (9)		6.05	6.05

Souvenir Sheet

1072 A147 $5 multi 4.75 4.75

Columbia Space Shuttle — A148

Designs: Views of the Columbia space shuttle.

1981, Nov. 12

1073 A148	30c multi	20	20
1074 A148	60c multi	40	40
1075 A148	70c multi	50	50
1076 A148	$3 multi	2.00	2.00

Souvenir Sheet

1077 A148 $5 multi 3.75 3.75

UPU Membership Centenary A149

1981, Dec. 10 Litho. *Perf. 15*

1078 A149	25c St. George's P.O.	16	16
1079 A149	30c No. 1	20	20
1080 A149	90c No. 384	60	60
1081 A149	$4 No. 189	2.75	2.75

Souvenir Sheet

1082 A149 $5 No. 562 3.75 3.75

Intl. Year of the Disabled (1981) — A150

1982, Feb. 4 *Perf. 14*

1083 A150	30c Artist	20	20
1084 A150	40c Computer operator	28	28
1085 A150	70c Teaching Braille	50	50
1086 A150	$3 Drummer	2.00	2.00

Souvenir Sheet

1087 A150 $4 Auto mechanic 3.00 3.00

Scouting Year — A151

1982, Feb. 19 *Perf. 15*

1088 A151	70c Gardening	50	50
1089 A151	90c Map reading	60	60
1090 A151	$1 Bee keeping	65	65
1091 A151	$4 Hospital reading	2.00	2.00

Souvenir Sheet

1092 A151 $5 Trophy presentation 3.00 3.00

Flambeaux — A152

Norman Rockwell — A153

1982, Mar. 24 Litho. *Perf. 14*

1093 A152	10c shown	15	15
1094 A152	60c Large orange sulphurs	45	45
1095 A152	$1 Red anartias	75	75
1096 A152	$3 Polydamas swallowtails	2.50	2.50

Souvenir Sheet

1097 A152 $5 Caribbean buckeyes 4.00 4.00

1982, Apr. 12 Litho. *Perf. 14x13½*

1098 A153	15c shown	15	15
1099 A153	30c Card Tricks	22	22
1100 A153	60c Pharmacist	45	45
1101 A153	70c Pals	55	55

Princess Diana Issue

Common Design Type

1982, July 1 Litho. *Perf. 14½x14*

1101A CD332	50c Kensington Palace	35	35
1102 CD332	60c like 50c	40	40
1102A CD332	$1 Couple in field	65	65
1103 CD332	$2 like $1	1.40	1.40
1103A CD332	$3 Diana in green dress	2.00	2.00
1104 CD332	$4 like $3	2.75	2.75

Souvenir Sheet

1105 CD332 $5 Diana, diff. 3.50 3.50

For overprints, see Nos. 1115A-1119.

Franklin Roosevelt Birth Centenary A154

Designs: 10c, Mary McLeod Bethune, director of Negro Affairs, 1942. 60c, Leadbelly (Huddie Ledbetter, Works Progress Administration). $1.10, Signing Fair Employment Act, 1941. $3, Farm Security Administration.

1982, July 27 Litho. *Perf. 14*

1106 A154	10c multi	15	15
1107 A154	60c multi	40	40
1108 A154	$1.10 multi	75	75
1109 A154	$3 multi	2.00	2.00

Souvenir Sheet

1110 A154 $5 multi 3.50 3.50

Easter A155

Details from Raphael's On the Way to Calvary. 70c, $1.10, $4, $5, vert.

1982, Sept. 2 *Perf. 14½*

1111 A155	40c multi	28	28
1112 A155	70c multi	40	40
1113 A155	$1.10 multi	65	65
1114 A155	$4 multi	2.75	2.75

Souvenir Sheet

1115 A155 $5 multi 3.50 3.50

Nos. 1101A-1105 Overprinted: "ROYAL BABY / 21.6.82"

1982, Sept. 27 Litho. *Perf. 14½x14*

1115A CD332	50c multi	35	35
1116 CD332	60c multi	40	40
1116A CD332	$1 multi	65	65
1117 CD332	$2 multi	1.40	1.40
1117A CD332	$3 multi	2.00	2.00
1118 CD332	$4 multi	2.75	2.75

Souvenir Sheet

1119 CD332 $5 multi 3.50 3.50

Birth of Prince William of Wales, June 21.

Orient Express A156

1982, Oct. 4

1120 A156	30c shown	20	20
1121 A156	60c Trans-Siberian Express	40	40
1122 A156	70c Fleche D'or	50	50
1123 A156	90c Flying Scotsman	60	60
1124 A156	$1 German Federal Railways	65	65
1125 A156	$3 German Natl. Railways	2.00	2.00
Nos. 1120-1125 (6)		4.35	4.35

Souvenir Sheet

1126 A156 $5 20th Century Limited, US 3.50 3.50

Christmas — A157

Designs: Scenes from Walt Disney's Robin Hood.

1982, Dec. 7 Litho. *Perf. 14*

1127 A157	½c multi	15	15
1128 A157	1c multi	15	15
1129 A157	2c multi	15	15
1130 A157	3c multi	15	15
1131 A157	4c multi	15	15
1132 A157	5c multi	15	15
1133 A157	10c multi	15	15
1134 A157	$2.50 multi	2.00	2.00
1135 A157	$3 multi	2.75	2.75
Set value		5.05	5.05

Souvenir Sheet

1136 A157 $5 multi 4.50 4.50

Italy's Victory in 1982 World Cup A158

1982, Dec. 2 *Perf. 14x13½*

1137 A158	60c Stolen ball	45	45
1138 A158	$4 Captain holding trophy	3.00	3.00

Souvenir Sheet

1139 A158 $5 Flags 3.75 3.75

Killer Whale — A159

1982, Dec. 15 *Perf. 14*

1140 A159	15c shown	15	15
1141 A159	40c Sperm whale	30	30
1142 A159	70c Blue whale	50	50
1143 A159	$3 Common dolphins	2.25	2.25

Souvenir Sheet

1144 A159 $5 Humpback whale 3.75 3.75

500th Birth Anniv. of Raphael — A160

1983, Feb. 15 Litho. *Perf. 14*

1145 A160	25c Construction of the Ark	18	18
1146 A160	30c Jacob's Vision	22	22
1147 A160	90c Joseph Interprets the Dreams	70	70
1148 A160	$4 Joseph Interprets Pharaoh's Dream	3.00	3.00

Souvenir Sheet

1149 A160 $5 Creation of the Animals 3.75 3.75

CD334

1983, Mar. 14

1150 CD334	10c Dental care	15	15
1151 CD334	70c Airport runway construction	55	55
1152 CD334	$1.10 Beach	85	85
1153 CD334	$3 Boat building	2.25	2.25

Commonwealth Day.

World Communication Year — A162

1983, Apr. 18

1154 A162	30c Ship-satellite communication	22	22
1155 A162	40c Rural telephone installation	30	30
1156 A162	$2.50 Weather map	1.75	1.75
1157 A162	$3 Airport control tower	2.25	2.25

Souvenir Sheet

1158 A162 $5 Satellite 3.75 3.75

For overprints, see Nos. 1248-1250.

Franklin Sport Sedan, 1928 A163

1983, May 4 Litho. *Perf. 15*

1159 A163 6c shown 15 15
1160 A163 10c Delage D8, 1933 15 15
1161 A163 40c Alvis, 1938 30 30
1162 A163 60c Invicta S-type Tourer, 1931 45 45
1163 A163 70c Alfa-Romeo 1750 Gran Sport, 1930 50 50
1164 A163 90c Isotta Fraschini, 1930 70 70
1165 A163 $1 Bugatti Royal Type 41, 1941 75 75
1166 A163 $2 BMV 328, 1938 1.50 1.50
1167 A163 $3 Marmon V-16, 1931 2.25 2.25
1168 A163 $4 Lincoln KB Saloon, 1932 3.00 3.00
Nos. 1159-1168 (10) 9.75 9.75

Souvenir Sheet

1169 A163 $5 Cougar XR-7, 1972 3.75 3.75

Manned Flight Bicentenary A164

1983, July 18 Litho. *Perf. 14*

1170 A164 30c Norge blimp 22 22
1171 A164 60c Gloster-VI sea plane 45 45
1172 A164 $1.10 Curtiss NC-4 80 80
1173 A164 $4 Dornier Do-18 3.00 3.00

Souvenir Sheet

1174 A164 $5 Hot air ballooning, vert. 3.75 3.75

Christmas A165

Designs: Walt Disney's It's Beginning to look a lot like Christmas.

1983, Nov. *Perf. 11*

1175 A165 ½c Morty and Patches 15 15
1176 A165 1c Ludwig von Drake 15 15
1177 A165 2c Gyro Gearloose 15 15
1178 A165 3c Pluto and Figaro 15 15
1179 A165 4c Morty and Ferdy 15 15
1180 A165 5c Mickey Mouse and Goofy 15 15
1181 A165 10c Chip'n'Dale 15 15
1182 A165 $2.50 Mickey and Minnie 1.75 1.75
1183 A165 $3 Donald and Grandma Duck 2.50 2.50
Set value 4.00 4.00

Souvenir Sheet

1184 A165 $5 Goofy 4.00 4.00

1984 Olympics — A166

Designs: Various Disney characters.

1983, Dec. 19 Litho. *Perf. 13½*

1185 A166 ½c Pommel Horse 15 15
1186 A166 1c Boxing 15 15
1187 A166 2c Archery 15 15
1188 A166 3c Uneven bars 15 15
1189 A166 4c Hurdles 15 15
1190 A166 5c Weightlifting 15 15
1191 A166 $1 Kayak 75 75
1192 A166 $2 Marathon 1.50 1.50
1193 A166 $3 Pole Vault 2.25 2.25
Nos. 1185-1193 (9) 5.40 5.40

Souvenir Sheet

1194 A166 $5 Medley Relay, vert. 4.50 4.50

Inscribed with Olympic Rings Emblem

1984 *Perf. 12½x12*

1185a A166 ½c 15 15
1186a A166 1c 15 15
1187a A166 2c 15 15
1188a A166 3c 15 15
1189a A166 4c 15 15
1190a A166 5c 15 15
1191a A166 $1 75 75
1192a A166 $2 1.50 1.50
1193a A166 $3 2.25 2.25
Nos. 1185a-1193a (9) 5.40 5.40

Souvenir Sheet

1194a A166 $5 Olympic rings emblem inscribed 4.50 4.50

Nos. 1185a-1193a printed in sheets of 5.

Banana Boat — A167

1984, July 16 Litho. *Perf. 15*

1195 A167 40c shown 30 30
1196 A167 70c Queen Elizabeth 2 50 50
1197 A167 90c Working sailboats 70 70
1198 A167 $4 Amerikanis 3.00 3.00

Souvenir Sheet

1199 A167 $5 Spanish galleon, flotilla 3.75 3.75

King William I, 1066-87 — A168

British Kings or Queens and Years of their reigns: No. 1200b, William II, 1087-1100. c, Henry I, 1100-35. d, Stephen, 1135-54. e, Henry II, 1154-89. f, Richard I, 1189-99. g, John, 1199-1216.

No. 1201a, Henry III, 1216-72. b, Edward I, 1272-1307. c, Edward II, 1307-27. d, Edward III, 1327-77. e, Richard II, 1377-99. f, Henry IV, 1399-1413. g, Henry V, 1413-22.

No. 1202a, Henry VI, 1422-61. b, Edward IV, 1461-83. c, Edward V, 1483. d, Richard III, 1483-85. e, Henry VII, 1485-1509. f, Henry VIII, 1509-47. g, Edward VI, 1547-53.

No. 1203a, Jane Grey, 1553. b, Mary I, 1553-58. c, Elizabeth I, 1558-1603. d, James I, 1603-25. e, Charles I, 1625-49. f, Charles II, 1660-85. g, James II, 1685-88.

No. 1204a, William III, 1688-1702. b, Mary II, 1688-94. c, Anne, 1702-14. d, George I, 1714-27. e, George II, 1727-60. f, George III, 1760-1820. g, George IV, 1820-30.

No. 1205a, William IV, 1830-37. b, Victoria, 1837-1901. c, Edward VII, 1901-10. d, George V, 1910-36. e, Edward VIII, 1936. f, George VI, 1936-52. g, Elizabeth II, since 1952. Size: 141x128mm.

1984, Jan. 25 Litho. *Perf. 14*

1200 Sheet of 7 + label 21.00 21.00
a.-g. A168 $4, any single 3.00 3.00
1201 Sheet of 7 + label 21.00 21.00
a.-g. A168 $4, any single 3.00 3.00
1202 Sheet of 7 + label 21.00 21.00
a.-g. A168 $4, any single 3.00 3.00
1203 Sheet of 7 + label 21.00 21.00
a.-g. A168 $4, any single 3.00 3.00
1204 Sheet of 7 + label 21.00 21.00
a.-g. A168 $4, any single 3.00 3.00
1205 Sheet of 7 + label 21.00 21.00
a.-g. A168 $4, any single 3.00 3.00

Local Flowers A169

1984, May *Perf. 15*

1206 A169 25c Lantana 18 18
1207 A169 30c Plumbago 22 22
1208 A169 90c Spider lily 70 70
1209 A169 $4 Giant alocasia 3.00 3.00

Souvenir Sheet

1210 A169 $5 Orange trumpet vine 3.75 3.75

For overprints, see Nos. 1216-1218.

Coral Reef Fish, World Wildlife Fund Emblem A170

1984, May Litho. *Perf. 14*

1211 A170 10c Blue parrot fish 15 15
1212 A170 30c Flame-back cherub fish 22 22
1213 A170 70c Painted wrasse 52 52
1214 A170 90c Straight-tailed razorfish 68 68

Souvenir Sheet

1215 A170 $5 Spanish hogfish 3.75 3.75

Nos. 1208-1210 Overprinted: "19th U.P.U CONGRESS—HAMBURG"

1984 Litho. *Perf. 15*

1216 A169 90c multi 68 68
1217 A169 $4 multi 3.00 3.00

Souvenir Sheet

1218 A169 $5 multi 3.75 3.75

AUSIPEX '84 — A171

Correggio & Degas — A171a

1984, Sept. 21 *Perf. 14*

1219 A171 $1.10 Puffing Billy 82 82
1220 A171 $4 Australia II 3.00 3.00

Souvenir Sheet

1221 A171 $5 Melbourne tram 3.75 3.75

1984, Aug. Litho. *Perf. 14*

Paintings by Correggio: 10c, The Night (detail). 30c, Virgin Adoring the Child. 90c, Mystical Marriage of St. Catherine with St. Sebastian. $4, Madonna and the Fruit Basket. No. 1230, Madonna at the Spring.

Paintings by Degas: 25c, L'Absinthe. 70c, Pouting, horiz. $1.10, The Millinery Shop. $3, The Bellelli Family. No. 1231, The Cotton Market.

1222 A171a 10c multi 15 15
1223 A171a 25c multi 20 20
1224 A171a 30c multi 22 22
1225 A171a 70c multi 52 52
1226 A171a 90c multi 68 68
1227 A171a $1.10 multi 82 82
1228 A171a $3 multi 2.25 2.25
1229 A171a $4 multi 3.00 3.00
Nos. 1222-1229 (8) 7.84 7.84

Souvenir Sheets

1230 A171a $5 multi 3.75 3.75
1231 A171a $5 multi 3.75 3.75

19th Cent. Locomotives A172

1984, Oct. *Perf. 14½*

1232 A172 30c Locomotion, 1825 22 22
1233 A172 40c Novelty, 1829 30 30
1234 A172 60c Washington Farmer, 1836 45 45
1235 A172 70c French Crampton, 1859 52 52
1236 A172 90c Dutch State, 1873 68 68
1237 A172 $1.10 Champion, 1882 82 82
1238 A172 $2 Webb Compound, 1893 1.50 1.50
1239 A172 $4 Berlin 74, 1900 3.00 3.00
Nos. 1232-1239 (8) 7.49 7.49

Souvenir Sheets

1240 A172 $5 Crampton Phoenix, 1863 3.75 3.75
1241 A172 $5 2-8-2 Mikado, 1897 3.75 3.75

Christmas and 50th Anniv. of Donald Duck — A173

Scenes from various Donald Duck movies.

Perf. 13½x14, 12 ($2)

1984, Nov. Litho.

1242 A173 45c multicolored 35 35
1243 A173 60c multicolored 52 52
1244 A173 90c multicolored 80 80
1245 A173 $2 multicolored 1.75 1.75
1246 A173 $4 multicolored 3.50 3.50
Nos. 1242-1246 (5) 6.92 6.92

Souvenir Sheet

1247 A173 $5 multicolored 4.50 4.50

Nos. 1155. 1157, and 1158 Overprinted: "OPENING OF / POINT SALINE / INT'L AIRPORT"

1984, Oct. 28 Litho. *Perf. 14½x14*

1248 A162 40c on #1155 30 30
1249 A162 $3 on #1157 2.25 2.25

Souvenir Sheet

Same Overprint in Margin in 2 Lines

1250 A162 $5 on #1158 3.75 3.75

Audubon Birth Bicentenary — A174

1985, Feb. Litho. *Perf. 14*

1251 A174 50c Clapper Rail 37 37
1252 A174 70c Hooded Warbler 52 52
1253 A174 90c Flicker 66 66
1254 A174 $4 Bohemian Waxwing 3.00 3.00

Souvenir Sheet

1255 A174 $5 Pigeon Hawk, horiz. 3.75 3.75

See Nos. 1352-1356.

Motorcycle Centenary A175

1985, Mar. 11 Litho. *Perf. 14*

1256 A175 25c Honda XL500R 12 12
1257 A175 50c Suzuki GS1100ES 28 28
1258 A175 90c Kawasaki KZ700 45 45
1259 A175 $4 BMW K100 1.75 1.75

Souvenir Sheet

1260 A175 $5 Yamaha 500CC 3.75 3.75

Girl Guides, 75th Anniv. A176

1985, Apr. 15

1261 A176 25c Nature hike 16 16
1262 A176 60c Cookout 45 45
1263 A176 90c Singing around camp-fire 65 65
1264 A176 $3 Public service 2.25 2.25

Souvenir Sheet

1265 A176 $5 Flags 3.75 3.75

Opening of Point Saline Intl. Airport, Oct. 28, 1984
A177

Inaugural flights.

1985, Apr. 30

1266 A177 70c From Barbados 60 60
1267 A177 $1 From New York 85 85
1268 A177 $4 To Miami 3.25 3.25

Souvenir Sheet

1269 A177 $5 Point Saline Intl. Airport 3.75 3.75

Intl. Civil Aviation Org., 40th Anniv.
A178

1985, May 15

1270 A178 10c McDonnell Douglas DC-8 15 15
1271 A178 50c Super Constellation 42 42
1272 A178 60c Vickers Vanguard 48 48
1273 A178 $4 DeHavilland Twin Otter 3.00 3.00

Souvenir Sheet

1274 A178 $5 Avro 748 Turboprop 3.75 3.75

Water Sports
A179

1985, June 15 *Perf. 15*

1275 A179 10c Model boat racing 15 15
1276 A179 50c Snorkeling, Sandy Island carriacou 42 42
1277 A179 $1.10 Sailing, Grand Anse Beach 90 90
1278 A179 $4 Windsurfing 3.00 3.00

Miniature Sheet

1279 A179 $5 Snorkelers, surfers, sailboats 3.75 3.75

Island Flowers — A180

1985-88 *Perf. 14*

1280 A180 ½c Strelitzia reginae 15 15
1281 A180 1c Passiflora coccinea 15 15
1282 A180 2c Nerium oleander 15 15
1283 A180 4c Ananas comosus 15 15
1284 A180 5c Anthurium andrae-anum 15 15
1285 A180 6c Bougainvillea glabra 15 15
1286 A180 10c Hibiscus rosa-sinensis 15 15
1287 A180 15c Alpinia purpurata 15 15
1288 A180 25c Euphorbia pulcherrima 15 15
1289 A180 30c Antigonon leptopus 20 20
1290 A180 40c Datura candida 30 30
1291 A180 50c Hippeastrum puniceum 35 35
1292 A180 60c Opuntia megacantha 40 40
1293 A180 70c Acalypha hispida 45 45
1293B A180 75c Cordia sebestina 60 60
1294 A180 $1 Catharan-thus roseus 68 68
1295 A180 $1.10 Ixora macro-thyrsa 75 75
1296 A180 $3 Justicia brandegeeana 2.00 2.00
1297 A180 $5 Plumbago capensis 3.25 3.25
1297A A180 $10 Lantana camara 6.50 6.50
1297B A180 $20 Jatropha in-tegerrima 13.00 13.00
Nos. 1280-1297B (21) 29.83 29.83

Issued: #1280-1293, 1294-1297, July 1. $10, Nov. 11. $20, Aug. 1, 1986. 75c, Jan. 12, 1988.

For overprints see Nos. 1357-1358, 1558-1560.

1986 *Perf. 12x12½*

1280a A180 ½c 15 15
1281a A180 1c 15 15
1282a A180 2c 15 15
1283a A180 4c 15 15
1284a A180 5c 15 15
1285a A180 6c 15 15
1286a A180 10c 15 15
1287a A180 15c 15 15
1288a A180 25c 15 15
1289a A180 30c 20 20
1290a A180 40c 30 30
1291a A180 50c 35 35
1292a A180 60c 40 40
1293a A180 70c 45 45
1294a A180 $1 68 68
1295a A180 $1.10 75 75
1296a A180 $3 2.00 2.00
1297c A180 $5 3.25 3.25
1297d A180 $10 6.50 6.50
Nos. 1280a-1297d (19) 16.23 16.23

Issue dates: Nos. 1280a-1285a, 1287a-1292a, 1294a-1296a, Mar. 10c, 70c, $5, July. $10, Dec.

Nos. 1289, 1291, 1292 and 1294 reprinted with "1987" imprint, No. 1286 with "1988" imprint.

Queen Mother, 85th Birthday
A181

Photographs: $1, At the Royal Opera, vert. $1.50, Playing pool, London Press Club. $2.50, At Epsom for the Oaks Day races, vert. $5, In open carriage with Prince Charles, Thanksgiving Day, 1980, vert.

1985, July 5

1298 A181 $1 multicolored 68 68
1299 A181 $1.50 multicolored 1.05 1.05
1300 A181 $2.50 multicolored 1.75 1.75

Souvenir Sheet

1301 A181 $5 multicolored 3.75 3.75

1986, Jan. 20 Litho. *Perf. 12x12½*

1301A A181 90c like #1298 65 65
1301B A181 $1 like #1299 75 75
1301C A181 $3 like #1300 2.25 2.25

Nos. 1301A-1301C issued in sheets of 5 plus label.

Intl. Youth Year — A182

1985, Aug. 21 *Perf. 15*

1302 A182 25c Gardening 15 15
1303 A182 50c At the beach 35 35
1304 A182 $1.10 Education 75 75
1305 A182 $3 Health care 2.00 2.00

Souvenir Sheet

1306 A182 $5 Harmonizing 3.25 3.25

4th Caribbean Cuboree, Aug. 17-23
A183

1985, Sept. 5 *Perf. 14*

1307 A183 10c Pitching tents 15 15
1308 A183 50c Swimming 42 42
1309 A183 $1 Stamp collecting 85 85
1310 A183 $4 Bird watching 3.25 3.25

Souvenir Sheet

1311 A183 $5 Grand Circle ritual 4.00 4.00

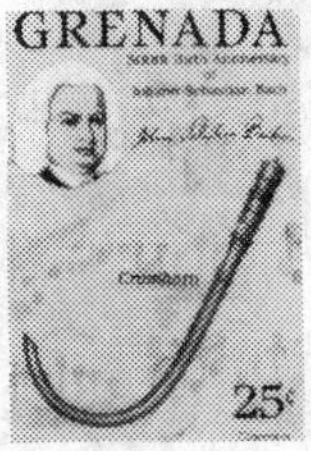

Johann Sebastian Bach — A184

Portrait, signature, music from Ciaccona and: 25c, Crumhorn. 70c, Oboe d'amore. $1, Violin. $3, Harpsichord. $5, Portrait.

1985, Sept. 19

1312 A184 25c multicolored 15 15
1313 A184 70c multicolored 45 45
1314 A184 $1 multicolored 68 68
1315 A184 $3 multicolored 2.00 2.00

Souvenir Sheet

1316 A184 $5 multicolored 3.50 3.50

The Prince & the Pauper — A185

Walt Disney characters.

1985, Oct. 30

1317 A185 25c Prince & Pauper meet 18 18
1318 A185 50c Exchange clothes 45 45
1319 A185 $1.10 Prince as the Pauper 95 95
1320 A185 $1.50 Prince rescued 1.40 1.40
1321 A185 $2 Pauper as the Prince 1.75 1.75
Nos. 1317-1321 (5) 4.73 4.73

Souvenir Sheet

1322 A185 $5 Prince & Pauper celebrate 4.25 4.25

Intl. Youth Year, Mark Twain (1835-1910), author.

Elizabeth II, Royal Visit to Spice Island
A186

1985, Oct. 31 *Perf. 14½*

1323 A186 50c Flags of Grenada, U.K. 42 42
1324 A186 $1 Elizabeth II, vert. 80 80
1325 A186 $4 HMS Britannia 3.00 3.00

Souvenir Sheet

1326 A186 $5 Map 3.75 3.75

The Brothers Grimm — A187

Disney characters in The Fisherman and His Wife.

1985, Nov. 4 Litho. *Perf. 14*

1327 A187 30c multicolored 25 25
1328 A187 60c multicolored 55 55
1329 A187 70c multicolored 60 60
1330 A187 $1 multicolored 90 90
1331 A187 $3 multicolored 2.75 2.75
Nos. 1327-1331 (5) 5.05 5.05

Souvenir Sheet

1332 A187 $5 multicolored 4.00 4.00

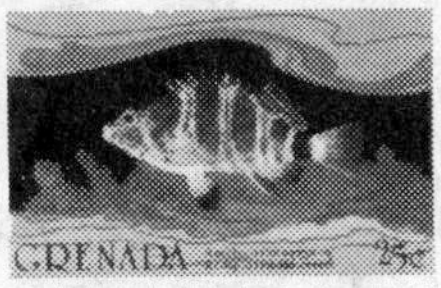

Indigenous Fish and Coral
A188

1985, Nov. 15

1333 A188 25c Red-spotted hawkfish 18 18
1334 A188 50c Spotfin butterflyfish 38 38
1335 A188 $1.10 Fire coral, orange sponge 80 80
1336 A188 $3 Pillar coral 2.25 2.25

Souvenir Sheet

1337 A188 $5 Bigeye 3.75 3.75

UN, 40th Anniv.
A189

UN stamps and famous people: 50c, No. 258, Mary McLeod Bethune (1875-1955), American educator. $2, No. 156, Maimonides (1135-1204), Judaic scholar. $2.50, No. 41, Alexander Graham Bell (1847-1922), inventor of the telephone. $5, Dag Hammarskjold (1905-1961), 2nd UN secretary general.

1985, Nov. 22 *Perf. 14½*

1338 A189 50c multicolored 38 38
1339 A189 $2 multicolored 1.50 1.50
1340 A189 $2.50 multicolored 1.75 1.75

Souvenir Sheet

1341 A189 $5 multicolored 3.75 3.75

Christmas
A190

Religious paintings: 25c, Adoration of the Shepherds, by Andre Mantegna (1431-1506). 60c, Journey of the Magi, by Sassetta (d. 1450). 90c, Madonna and Child Enthroned with Saints, by Raphael (1483-1520). $4, Nativity, by Monaco. $5, Madonna and Child Enthroned with Saints, by Agnolo Gaddi (c. 1350-1396).

1985, Dec. 23 *Perf. 15*

1342 A190 25c multicolored 18 18
1343 A190 60c multicolored 45 45
1344 A190 90c multicolored 65 65
1345 A190 $4 multicolored 3.00 3.00

Souvenir Sheet

1346 A190 $5 multicolored 3.75 3.75

Statue of Liberty, Cent.
A191

Views of New York City.

1986, Jan. 6

1347 A191 5c Columbus Circle, 1893 15 15
1348 A191 25c Circle, 1986 18 18
1349 A191 40c Central Park Mounted Police, 1895 30 30
1350 A191 $4 Mounted Police, 1986 3.00 3.00

Souvenir Sheet

1351 A191 $5 Statue of Liberty 3.75 3.75

Nos. 1347-1348, 1351 vert.

Audubon Type of 1985

1986, Jan. 20 *Perf. 12x12½*

1352 A174 50c Snowy egret 38 38
1353 A174 90c Red flamingo 65 65
1354 A174 $1.10 Barnacle goose 80 80
1355 A174 $3 Smew 2.25 2.25

Souvenir Sheet

Perf. 14

1356 A174 $5 Brant Goose, horiz. 3.75 3.75

Nos. 1291 and 1297 Overprinted "VISIT OF PRES. REAGAN 20 FEB. 1986"

1986, Feb. 20 *Perf. 14*

1357 A180 50c multicolored 38 38
1358 A180 $5 multicolored 3.75 3.75

St. George Methodist Church, Bicent. A192

1986, Feb. 24 *Perf. 15*

1359 A192 60c multicolored 45 45

Souvenir Sheet

1360 A192 $5 multicolored 3.75 3.75

Heritage Year.

1986 World Cup Soccer Championships, Mexico — A193

Various soccer plays.

1986, Mar. 6 *Perf. 14*

1361 A193 50c multicolored 38 38
1362 A193 70c multicolored 52 52
1363 A193 90c multicolored 65 65
1364 A193 $4 multicolored 3.00 3.00

Souvenir Sheet

1365 A193 $5 multicolored 3.75 3.75

For overprints, see Nos. 1399-1403.

Halley's Comet A194

Designs: 5c, Clyde Tombaugh, discovered Pluto, 1930, and Dudley Observatory. 20c, US X-24B space shuttle prototype, 1973. 40c, Medallic art, Catholic Church, 1618. $4, Lot and his daughters fleeing Sodom and Gomorrah, 1949 B.C. $5, Comet over Grand Anse Beach.

1986, Mar. 20

1366 A194 5c multicolored 15 15
1367 A194 20c multicolored 15 15
1368 A194 40c multicolored 30 30
1369 A194 $4 multicolored 3.00 3.00

Souvenir Sheet

1370 A194 $5 multicolored 3.75 3.75

For overprints, see Nos. 1416-1420.

Queen Elizabeth II, 60th Birthday

Common Design Type

Designs: 2c, Signing the log, 1951. $1.50, Presenting polo trophy, Windsor, 1965. $4, Derby Day, 1977. $5, Royal family portrait, 1939.

1986, Apr. 21 *Perf. 14*

1371 CD339 2c yel & blk 15 15
1372 CD339 $1.50 pale grn & multi 1.15 1.15
1373 CD339 $4 dl lil & multi 3.00 3.00

Souvenir Sheet

1374 CD339 $5 tan & blk 3.75 3.75

AMERIPEX '86 — A195

Walt Disney characters playing baseball.

1986, May 22 **Litho.** *Perf. 11*

1375 A195 1c Pitcher 15 15
1376 A195 2c Catcher 15 15
1377 A195 3c Strike 15 15
1378 A195 4c Force out 15 15
1379 A195 5c Fly ball 15 15
1380 A195 6c Third base 15 15
1381 A195 $2 Manager 1.50 1.50
1382 A195 $3 Error 2.25 2.25
Set value 4.00 4.00

Souvenir Sheets

Perf. 14

1383 A195 $5 Batter 3.75 3.75
1384 A195 $5 Grand slam 3.75 3.75

Royal Wedding Issue, 1986

Common Design Type

Designs: 2c, Prince Andrew and Sarah Ferguson. $1.10, Andrew. $4, Andrew in flight suit, helicopter. $5, Couple, diff.

1986, July 23 *Perf. 14*

1385 CD340 2c multicolored 15 15
1386 CD340 $1.10 multicolored 82 82
1387 CD340 $4 multicolored 3.00 3.00

Souvenir Sheet

1388 CD340 $5 multicolored 3.75 3.75

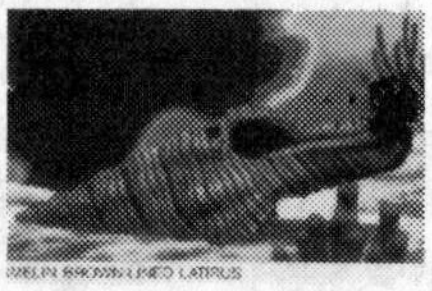

Seashells A196

Designs: 25c, Gmelin brown-lined latirus. 60c, Lamarck lamellose wentletrap. 70c, Swainson turkey wing. $4, Linne rooster-tail conch. $5, Linne angular triton.

1986, July 15 **Litho.** *Perf. 15*

1389 A196 25c multicolored 18 18
1390 A196 60c multicolored 45 45
1391 A196 70c multicolored 52 52
1392 A196 $4 multicolored 3.00 3.00

Souvenir Sheet

1393 A196 $5 multicolored 3.75 3.75

Mushrooms — A197

1986, Aug. 1 *Perf. 15*

1394 A197 10c Lepiota roselamellata 15 15
1395 A197 60c Lentinus bertieri 45 45
1396 A197 $1 Lentinus retinervis 75 75
1397 A197 $4 Eccilia cystiophorus 3.00 3.00

Souvenir Sheet

1398 A197 $5 Cystolepiota eriophora 3.75 3.75

Nos. 1361-1365 Ovptd. "WINNERS Argentina 3 / W. Germany 2" in Gold

1986, Sept. 15 **Litho.** *Perf. 14*

1399 A193 50c multicolored 38 38
1400 A193 70c multicolored 52 52
1401 A193 90c multicolored 65 65
1402 A193 $4 multicolored 3.00 3.00

Souvenir Sheet

1403 A193 $5 multicolored 3.75 3.75

Disarmament Week and Intl. Peace Year — A198

Designs: 60c, Mahatma Gandhi, rifles, dove, vert. $4, Martin Luther King, Jr., hands, olive branch.

1986, Sept. 15 *Perf. 15*

1404 A198 60c multicolored 45 45
1405 A198 $4 multicolored 3.00 3.00

Christmas — A199

Disney characters. Nos. 1406-1407, 1411-1412 vert.

1986, Nov. 3 *Perf. 11*

1406 A199 30c Mickey, hearth 28 28
1407 A199 45c Mickey, Santa 42 42
1408 A199 60c Donald, Mickey Mouse phone 55 55
1409 A199 70c Goofy, toy band 65 65
1410 A199 $1.10 Daisy, dolls 1.00 1.00
1411 A199 $2 Goofy as Santa 1.90 1.90
1412 A199 $2.50 Goofy playing piano 2.25 2.25
1413 A199 $3 Train ride 2.75 2.75
Nos. 1406-1413 (8) 9.80 9.80

Souvenir Sheets

1414 A199 $5 Donald, Goofy, Mickey 4.75 4.75
1415 A199 $5 Dewey 4.75 4.75

Nos. 1366-1370 Ovptd. with Halley's Comet Emblem

HALLEY'S COMET 1985 OFFICIAL 1986

1986, Oct. 15 **Litho.** *Perf. 14*

1416 A194 5c multicolored 15 15
1417 A194 20c multicolored 15 15
1418 A194 40c multicolored 30 30
1419 A194 $4 multicolored 3.00 3.00

Souvenir Sheet

1420 A194 $5 multicolored 3.75 3.75

Fauna and Flora A200

1986, Nov. 17 *Perf. 14*

1421 A200 10c Chicken, rooster 15 15
1422 A200 30c Fish-eating bat 24 24
1423 A200 60c Goat 48 48
1424 A200 70c Cow 58 58
1425 A200 $1 Anthurium 80 80
1426 A200 $1.10 Royal poinciana 90 90
1427 A200 $2 Frangipani 1.60 1.60
1428 A200 $4 Orchid 3.25 3.25
Nos. 1421-1428 (8) 8.00 8.00

Souvenir Sheets

1429 A200 $5 Horse 4.00 4.00
1430 A200 $5 Trees 4.00 4.00

Automobile, Cent. A202

1886 Daimler and modern automobiles.

1986, Nov. 20 *Perf. 15*

1431 A202 10c 1984 Maserati Biturbo 15 15
1432 A202 30c 1960 AC Cobra 24 24
1433 A202 60c 1963 Corvette 48 48
1434 A202 70c 1932 Duesenberg SJ7 55 55
1435 A202 90c 1957 Porsche 72 72
1436 A202 $1.10 1930 Stoewer 88 88
1437 A202 $2 1957 VW Beetle 1.60 1.60
1438 A202 $3 1963 Mercedes 600 Limo 2.40 2.40
Nos. 1431-1438 (8) 7.02 7.02

Souvenir Sheets

1439 A202 $5 1914 Stutz 4.00 4.00
1440 A202 $5 1941 Packard 4.00 4.00

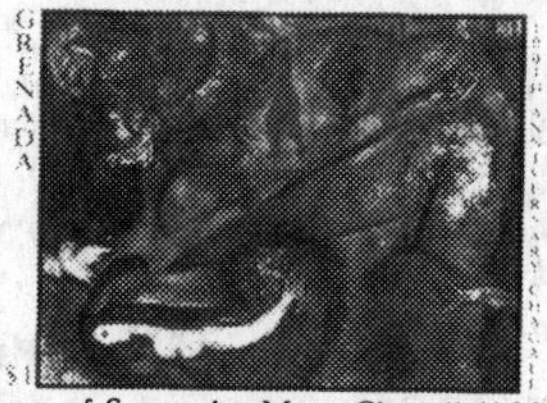

Song of Songs, by Marc Chagall (1887-1984) — A203

Paintings: No. 1441, The Rooster. No. 1442, Lovers in the Moonlight. No. 1443, Woman and Haystack. No. 1444, Snow-Covered Church. No. 1445, Peasant Life. No. 1446, Moses Receiving the Tablets. No. 1447, Vitebsk: From Mt. Zadunuv. No. 1449, Song of Songs, diff. No. 1450, The Creation of Man. No. 1451, Spring. No. 1452, Jacob's Struggle with the Angel. No. 1453, Song of Songs (wedding detail). No. 1454, The Painter to the Moon, 1917. No. 1455, Moses Striking the Rock. No. 1456, To My Betrothed, 1911. No. 1457, Sacrifice of Isaac. No. 1458, Monkey Acting as Judge Over Dispute Between Wolf and Fox, 1925. No. 1459, Song of Songs (bride riding Pegasus). No. 1460, Lovers in the Lilac, 1930. No. 1461, Song of Songs (sun, spirits). No. 1462, Jacob's Dream. No. 1463, Purim, 1916. No. 1464, Fantastic Horsecart. No. 1465, Listening to the Cock, 1944. No. 1466, Self-portrait, 1914. No. 1467, The Juggler, 1943. No. 1468, Noah and the Rainbow. No. 1469, Moses Before the Burning Bush. No. 1470, Around Her, 1945. No. 1471, The Trough, 1925. No. 1472, The Poet of Half-Past-Three. No. 1473, The Tree of Life, 1948. No. 1474, Woman with the Blue Face, 1932. No. 1475, Chrysanthemums, 1926. No. 1476, Spoonful of Milk, 1912. No. 1477, The Soldier Drinks, 1911. No. 1478, Noah's Ark. No. 1479, Flowers and Fruit. No. 1480, Adam and Eve Expelled fron Paradise. No. 1481. Return from Synagogue. No. 1482, Aleko: A Fantasy of St. Petersburg. No. 1483, The Orchard. No. 1484, Solitude. No. 1485, Paris Through the Window, 1913. No. 1486, The Wedding, 1910. No. 1487, Paradise. No. 1488, The Dream, 1939. No. 1489, Abraham and the Three Angels. No. 1490, Water Carrier Under the Moon, 1914.

1986-87

1441 A203 $1 multi 80 80
1442 A203 $1 multi 80 80
1443 A203 $1 multi 80 80
1444 A203 $1 multi 80 80
1445 A203 $1 multi 80 80
1446 A203 $1 multi 80 80
1447 A203 $1 multi 80 80
1448 A203 $1 multi 80 80
1449 A203 $1 multi 80 80
1450 A203 $1 multi 80 80
1451 A203 $1 multi 80 80
1452 A203 $1 multi 80 80
1453 A203 $1 multi ('87) 80 80
1454 A203 $1 multi ('87) 80 80
1455 A203 $1 multi ('87) 80 80
1456 A203 $1 multi ('87) 80 80
1457 A203 $1 multi ('87) 80 80
1458 A203 $1 multi ('87) 80 80
1459 A203 $1 multi ('87) 80 80
1460 A203 $1 multi ('87) 80 80
1461 A203 $1 multi ('87) 80 80
1462 A203 $1 multi ('87) 80 80
1463 A203 $1 multi ('87) 80 80
1464 A203 $1 multi ('87) 80 80
1465 A203 $1 multi ('87) 80 80
1466 A203 $1 multi ('87) 80 80
1467 A203 $1 multi ('87) 80 80
1468 A203 $1 multi ('87) 80 80
1469 A203 $1 multi ('87) 80 80
1470 A203 $1 multi ('87) 80 80
1471 A203 $1 multi ('87) 80 80
1472 A203 $1 multi ('87) 80 80
1473 A203 $1 multi ('87) 80 80
1474 A203 $1 multi ('87) 80 80
1475 A203 $1 multi ('87) 80 80
1476 A203 $1 multi ('87) 80 80
1477 A203 $1 multi ('87) 80 80
1478 A203 $1 multi ('87) 80 80
1479 A203 $1 multi ('87) 80 80
1480 A203 $1 multi ('87) 80 80

Size: 110x95mm

Imperf

1481 A203 $5 multi 4.00 4.00
1482 A203 $5 multi 4.00 4.00
1483 A203 $5 multi 4.00 4.00
1484 A203 $5 multi ('87) 4.00 4.00
1485 A203 $5 multi ('87) 4.00 4.00
1486 A203 $5 multi ('87) 4.00 4.00
1487 A203 $5 multi ('87) 4.00 4.00
1488 A203 $5 multi ('87) 4.00 4.00
1489 A203 $5 multi ('87) 4.00 4.00
1490 A203 $5 multi ('87) 4.00 4.00
Nos. 1441-1490 (50) 72.00 72.00

Nos. 1441-1446, 1450-1452 1455-1458, 1464-1467 and 1470-1479 vert.

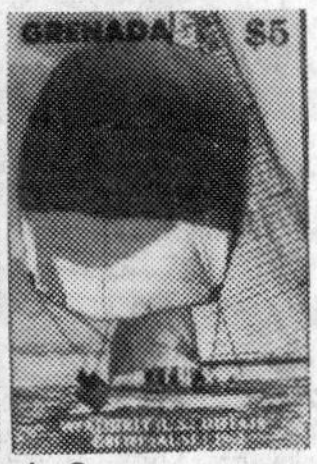

America's Cup
A204 A205

1987, Feb. 5 Litho. *Perf. 15*

1491 A204 10c Columbia, 1958 15 15
1492 A204 60c Resolute, 1920 48 48
1493 A204 $1.10 Endeavor, 1934 88 88
1494 A204 $4 Rainbow, 1934 3.25 3.25

Souvenir Sheet

1495 A205 $5 Weatherly, 1962 4.00 4.00

Virgin Mary — A206

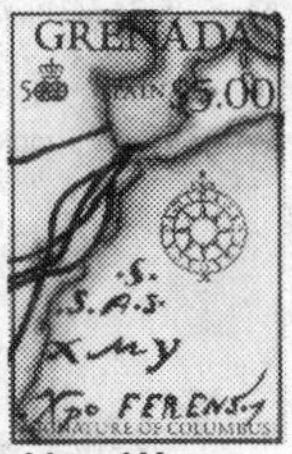

Map of Voyage, Columbus' Signature — A207

1987, Apr. 27 *Perf. 15*

1496 A206 10c shown 15 15
1497 A206 30c Nina, Pinta, Santa Maria 22 22
1498 A206 50c Columbus, map 38 38
1499 A206 60c Columbus 45 45
1500 A206 90c Isabella, Ferdinand 68 68
1501 A206 $1.10 Discovering the Antilles 82 82
1502 A206 $2 Carib Indians 1.50 1.50
a. Souv. sheet of 3, 30c, 90c, $2 2.40 2.40
1503 A206 $3 American Indians, 1493 2.25 2.25
a. Souv. sheet of 5 + label, 10c, 50c, 60c, $1.10, $3 4.00 4.00
Nos. 1496-1503 (8) 6.45 6.45

Souvenir Sheets

1504 A207 $5 shown 3.75 3.75
1505 A207 $5 Columbus, Christ child 3.75 3.75

Discovery of America 500th anniv. (in 1992). Nos. 1497, 1500 and 1502 horiz.

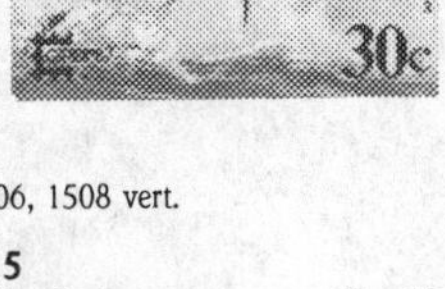

CAPEX '87 — A208

Fish. Nos. 1506, 1508 vert.

1987, June 15

1506 A208 10c Black grouper 15 15
1507 A208 30c Blue marlin 22 22
1508 A208 60c White marlin 45 45
1509 A208 70c Big-eye thresher shark 52 52
1510 A208 $1 Bonefish 75 75
1511 A208 $1.10 Wahoo 82 82
1512 A208 $2 Sailfish 1.50 1.50
1513 A208 $4 Albacore 3.00 3.00
Nos. 1506-1513 (8) 7.41 7.41

Souvenir Sheets

1514 A208 $5 Barracuda 3.75 3.75
1515 A208 $5 Yellowfin tuna, vert. 3.75 3.75

Transportation Innovations — A209

1987, May 18 *Perf. 14*

1516 A209 10c Cornu's Helicopter, 1907 15 15
1517 A209 15c The Monitor and Merrimack, 1862 15 15
1518 A209 30c LZ1 Zeppelin, c. 1900 22 22
1519 A209 50c S.S. Sirius, 1838 38 38
1520 A209 60c Trans-Siberian Railway 45 45
1521 A209 70c USS Enterprise, 1960 52 52
1522 A209 90c Blanchard's Balloon, 1785 68 68
1523 A209 $1.50 USS Holland 1, 1900 1.15 1.15
1524 A209 $2 S.S. Oceanic, 1871 1.50 1.50
1525 A209 $3 1984 Lamborghini Countach 2.25 2.25
Nos. 1516-1525 (10) 7.45 7.45

For overprints, see Nos. 1599-1602.

Statue of Liberty, Cent. A210

1987, Aug. 5

1526 A210 10c Computer structural diagrams 15 15
1527 A210 25c Fireworks around statue 20 20
1528 A210 50c Fireworks in front of statue 38 38
1529 A210 60c Statue, boats 45 45
1530 A210 70c Structural diagram, close-up 52 52
1531 A210 $1 Rear of statue, close-up 75 75
1532 A210 $1.10 Liberty and Manhattan Isls. 82 82
1533 A210 $2 Statue, boats, diff. 1.50 1.50
1534 A210 $4 Ocean liner, New York Harbor 3.00 3.00
Nos. 1526-1534 (9) 7.77 7.77

Nos. 1529, 1531-1534 vert.

Inventors and Innovators A211

Designs: 50c, Sir Isaac Newton (1642-1727), law of gravity. $1.10, Jons Jakob Berzelius (1779-1848), symbols of chemical elements. $2, Robert Boyle (1627-1691), and Boyle's Law of pressure and volume. $3, James Watt (1736-1819), and diagram of steam engine. $5, Wright Flyer, Voyager.

1987, Sept. 9

1535 A211 50c multicolored 38 38
1536 A211 $1.10 multicolored 82 82
1537 A211 $2 multicolored 1.50 1.50
1538 A211 $3 multicolored 2.25 2.25

Souvenir Sheet

1539 A211 $5 multicolored 3.75 3.75

No. 1536 inscribed with incorrect spelling of inventors name, "John Jacob Berzelius." No. 1538 inscribed with incorrect caption; James Watt and Watt engine are pictured, not Rudolf Diesel and the Diesel engine.

Miniature Sheets

Fairy Tales A212

Snow White (50th Anniv.): No. 1540a, Snow White scrubs stairs. b, Wicked Queen, looking glass. c, Snow White fleeing. d, Dwarfs, mine. e, Snow White at cottage. f, Snow White, dwarfs. g, Snow White dancing with dwarfs. h, Eating poison apple. i, Prince kissing Snow White.

Sleeping Beauty: No. 1541a, Royal family. b, Maleficent cursing infant (Aurora). c, Merryweather altering curse. d, Three good fairies. e, Briar Rose (Aurora), forest animals. f, Aurora, spinning wheel. g, Sleeping Beauty (Aurora). h, Prince Phillip battling dragon (Maleficent). i, Sleeping Beauty awakes.

Cinderella: No. 1542a, Ella (Cinderella) and father. b, Cinderella sweeping. c, Cinderella, animals in barn. d, Cinderella, stepmother, stepsisters. e, Mice. f, Fairy Godmother. g, Cinderella transformed, coach. h, i, Duke puts glass slipper on Cinderella's foot.

Pinocchio: No. 1543a, Geppetto and puppet. b, Jiminy Cricket. c, Pinocchio, J. Worthington Foulfellow and Gideon. d, Pinocchio, Master Stromboli. e, Blue Fairy rescues Pinocchio. f, Pinocchio, donkeys. g, Pinocchio riding fish. h, Pinocchio and Geppetto at sea. i, Pinocchio transformed into a boy.

Alice in Wonderland: No. 1544a, Alice, rabbit hole. b, Alice in bottle. c, Walrus and Carpenter. d, White Rabbit in pink house. e, Alice, pink butterfly. f, March Hare, Mad Hatter. g, Alice in garden. h, Queen of Hearts. i, Alice on trial.

Peter Pan: No. 1545a, Nana. b, Peter Pan. c, Peter Pan, Tinker Bell, Wendy, John and Michael Darling flying. d, In NeverNever Land. e, Peter Pan and Tiger Lily. f, Captain Hook and First Mate Smee. g, Pater Pan dueling with Captain Hook. h, Tinker Bell, pirate ship. i, Captain Hook, crocodile.

No. 1546, Snow White and Prince riding off into sunset. No. 1547, Aurora and Prince Phillip dancing. No. 1548, Cinderella and Prince Charming marry. No. 1549, Pinocchio, Jiminy Cricket and Gepetto. No. 1550, Alice, cat, mother. No. 1551, Darling children waving goodbye to Peter Pan.

1987, Sept. 9 *Perf. 14x13½*

1540 Sheet of 9 2.00
a.-i. A212 30c any single 22 22
1541 Sheet of 9 2.00
a.-i. A212 30c any single 22 22
1542 Sheet of 9 2.00
a.-i. A212 30c any single 22 22
1543 Sheet of 9 2.00
a.-i. A212 30c any single 22 22
1544 Sheet of 9 2.00
a.-i. A212 30c any single 22 22
1545 Sheet of 9 2.00
a.-i. A212 30c any single 22 22
Nos. 1540-1545 (6) 12.00

Souvenir Sheets

1546 A212 $5 multicolored 3.75 3.75
1547 A212 $5 multicolored 3.75 3.75
1548 A212 $5 multicolored 3.75 3.75
1549 A212 $5 multicolored 3.75 3.75
1550 A212 $5 multicolored 3.75 3.75
1551 A212 $5 multicolored 3.75 3.75

Souvenir Sheet

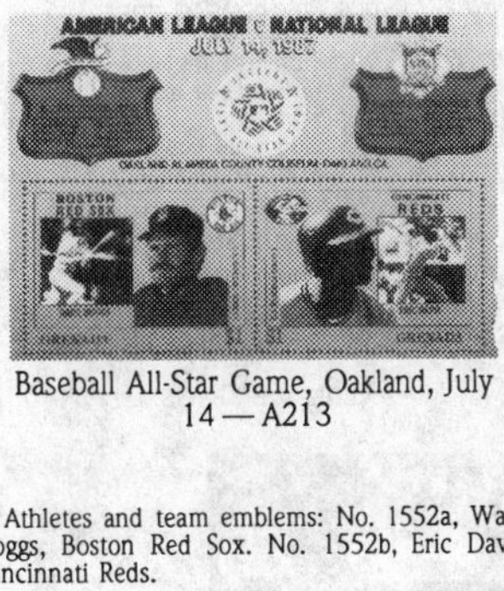

Baseball All-Star Game, Oakland, July 14 — A213

Athletes and team emblems: No. 1552a, Wade Boggs, Boston Red Sox. No. 1552b, Eric Davis, Cincinnati Reds.

1987, Nov. 2 Litho. *Perf. 14*

1552 A213 Sheet of 2 1.45 1.45
a.-b. $1 any single 72 72

Massachusetts State Crest — A214

Designs: 15c, Independence Hall, Philadelphia. 50c, Benjamin Franklin. $4, Robert Morris (1734-1806), financier of American Revolution. $5, Pres. James Madison.

1987, Nov. 2

1553 A214 15c multi, vert. 15 15
1554 A214 50c multi, vert. 35 35
1555 A214 60c shown 45 45
1556 A214 $4 multi, vert. 2.90 2.90

Souvenir Sheet

1557 A214 $5 multi, vert. 3.60 3.60

US Constitution bicent.

Nos. 1286, 1291 and 1296 Overprinted

International Social Security Association

1987, Nov. 2

1558 A180 10c multicolored 15 15
1559 A180 50c multicolored 35 35
1560 A180 $3 multicolored 2.00 2.00

HAFNIA '87 — A215

Disney animated characters in adaptation of fairy tales by Hans Christian Andersen.

1987, Nov. 16 Litho. *Perf. 14*

1561 A215 25c The Shadow 20 20
1562 A215 30c The Storks 22 22
1563 A215 50c The Emperor's New Clothes 38 38
1564 A215 60c The Tinderbox 45 45
1565 A215 70c The Shepherdess and the Chimney Sweep 55 55
1566 A215 $1.50 The Little Mermaid 1.15 1.15
1567 A215 $3 The Princess and the Pea 2.25 2.25
1568 A215 $4 The Marsh King's Daughter 3.00 3.00
Nos. 1561-1568 (8) 8.20 8.20

Souvenir Sheets

1569 A215 $5 The Flying Trunk, horiz. 3.75 3.75
1570 A215 $5 The Sandman, horiz. 3.75 3.75

Christmas — A216

Religious paintings: 15c, The Annunciation, by Fra Angelico. 30c, The Annunciation, attributed to Hubert van Eyck (c. 1370-1426). 60c, Adoration of the Magi, by Januarius Zick (1730-1797). $4, The Flight Into Egypt, by David. $5, The Circumcision, produced by artists of the Giovanni Bellini Studio, 14th cent.

1987, Dec. 15

1571	A216	15c	multicolored	15	15
1572	A216	30c	multicolored	22	22
1573	A216	60c	multicolored	45	45
1574	A216	$4	multicolored	3.00	3.00

Souvenir Sheet

1575	A216	$5	multicolored	3.75	3.75

T. Albert Marryshow (b. 1887) A217

1988, Jan. 22 Litho. *Perf. 14*

1576	A217	25c	scarlet, red brn & brn blk	20	20

40th Wedding Anniv. of Queen Elizabeth II and Prince Philip — A218

1988, Feb. 15

1577	A218	15c	Wedding portrait, 1947	15	15
1578	A218	50c	Elizabeth, Charles, Anne	38	38
1579	A218	$1	Elizabeth, Anne	75	75
1580	A218	$4	Elizabeth, c. 1980	3.00	3.00

Souvenir Sheet

1581	A218	$5	Elizabeth, 1947	3.75	3.75

Disney Animated Characters and 1988 Summer Olympics, Seoul — A219

1988, Apr. 13 Litho. *Perf. 13½x14*

1582	A219	1c	Lighting torch, Olympia	15	15
1583	A219	2c	Torch bearers	15	15
1584	A219	3c	Flag bearers	15	15
1585	A219	4c	Releasing doves	15	15
1586	A219	5c	Opening ceremony	15	15
1587	A219	10c	Olympic motto	15	15
1588	A219	$6	Tiger character trademark	3.75	3.75
1589	A219	$7	Oldest Korean p.o.	4.50	4.50
			Nos. 1582-1589 (8)	9.15	9.15

Souvenir Sheets

1590	A219	$5	Sportsmanship oath	3.50	3.50
1591	A219	$5	Closing ceremony	3.50	3.50

Boy Scouts A220

1988, May 3 Litho. *Perf. 14*

1592	A220	20c	Fishing, vert.	15	15
1593	A220	70c	Hiking	55	55
1594	A220	90c	First-aid	70	70
1595	A220	$3	Canoeing, vert.	2.25	2.25

Souvenir Sheet

1596	A220	$5	Scout holding koala, vert.	3.75	3.75

Rotary Conference, District 405, St. George, May 5-7 — A221

Rotary Intl emblem and: $2, Map of District 405 island nations (Grenada, Guyana, Surinam and French Guiana), 15th cent. Spanish galleon Santa Maria, vert. $10, Motto "Service Above Self."

1988, May 5 *Perf. 13½x14*

1597	A221	$2	multicolored	1.50	1.50

Souvenir Sheet

Perf. 14x13½

1598	A221	$10	shown	7.50	7.50

Nos. 1522-1525 Overprinted for Philatelic Exhibitions

a OLYMPHILEX '88

b INDEPENDENCE 40

c FINLANDIA 88

d Praga '88

1988, Apr. 19 Litho. *Perf. 14*

1599	A209	(a)	90c	multi	68	68
1600	A209	(b)	$1.50	multi	1.15	1.15
1601	A209	(c)	$2	multi	1.50	1.50
1602	A209	(d)	$3	multi	2.25	2.25

Birds — A222

1988, May 31

1603	A222	10c	Roseate tern	15	15
1604	A222	25c	Laughing gull	18	18
1605	A222	50c	Osprey	38	38
1606	A222	60c	Rose-breasted grosbeak	45	45
1607	A222	90c	Purple gallinule	68	68
1608	A222	$1.10	White-tailed tropicbird	82	82
1609	A222	$3	Blue-faced booby	2.25	2.25
1610	A222	$4	Northern shoveler	3.00	3.00
			Nos. 1603-1610 (8)	7.91	7.91

Souvenir Sheet

1611	A222	$5	Belted kingfisher	3.75	3.75
1612	A222	$5	Rusty-tailed flycatcher	3.75	3.75

Miniature Sheets

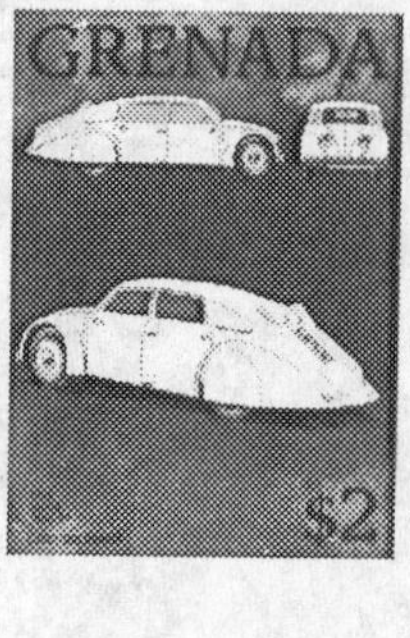

Classic Automobiles A223

Cars (US unless otherwise stated): No. 1613a, 1934 Tatra Type 77, Czechoslovakia. b, 1938 Rolls-Royce Phantom III, Britain. c, 1947 Studebaker Champion Starlight. d, 1948 Porsche Gmund, Germany. e, 1948 Tucker. f, 1931 Peerless V-16. g, 1931 Minerva AL, Belgium. h, 1933 REO Royale. i, 1933 Pierce-Arrow Silver Arrow. j, 1934 Hupmobile Aerodynamic.

No. 1614a, 1925 Vauxhall Type OE30/98, Britain. b, 1926 Wills Sainte Claire. c, 1928 Bucciali, France. d, 1929 Irving Napier Golden Arrow, Britain. e, 1930 Studebaker President. f, 1907 Thomas Flyer. g, 1908 Isotta-Fraschini Tipo J, Italy. h, 1910 Fiat 10/14HP, Italy. i, 1911 Mercer Type 35 Raceabout. j, 1917 Marmon Model 34 Cloverleaf.

No. 1615a, 1965 Peugeot 404, France. b, 1969 Ford Capri, Britain. c, 1975 Ferrari 312T, Italy. d, 1978 Lotus T-79, Britain. e, 1979 Williams-Cosworth FW07, Britain. f, 1948 H.R.G. 1500 Sports, Britain. g, 1949 Crosley Hotshot. h, 1955 Volvo PV444, Sweden. i, 1960 Maserati Tipo 61, Italy. j, 1963 Saab 96, Sweden.

1988, June 1 *Perf. 13x13½*

1613		Sheet of 10	14.50	14.50
a.-j.	A223	$2 any single	1.45	1.45
1614		Sheet of 10	14.50	14.50
a.-j.	A223	$2 any single	1.45	1.45
1615		Sheet of 10	14.50	14.50
a.-j.	A223	$2 any single	1.45	1.45

Paintings by Titian (c. 1488-1576) A224

Paintings by Titian: 10c, Lavinia Vecellio, c. 1546. 20c, Portrait of a Man, c. 1510. 25c, Andrea De Franceschi, 1532. 90c, Head of a Soldier, 1511. $1, Man With a Flute. $2, Lucrezia and Tarquinius, c. 1515. $3, Duke of Mantua with Dog, 1525. $4, La Bella Di Tiziano, 1536. No. 1624, Allegory of Alfonso D'Avalos. No. 1625, Fall of Man, 1570, horiz.

1988, June 15 *Perf. 13½x14*

1616	A224	10c	multicolored	15	15
1617	A224	20c	multicolored	15	15
1618	A224	25c	multicolored	18	18
1619	A224	90c	multicolored	68	68
1620	A224	$1	multicolored	75	75
1621	A224	$2	multicolored	1.50	1.50
1622	A224	$3	multicolored	2.25	2.25
1623	A224	$4	multicolored	3.00	3.00
			Nos. 1616-1623 (8)	8.66	8.66

Souvenir Sheets

1624	A224	$5	multicolored	3.75	3.75

Perf. 14x13½

1625	A224	$5	multicolored	3.75	3.75

Zeppelins A225

Designs: 10c, Graf Zeppelin over the Federal Building, Chicago, 1933 World's Fair, vert. 15c, LZ-1 over Lake Constance, 1900. 25c, Washington aerial balloon lifting off the aircraft carrier USS George Washington Curtis off Port Royal, South Carolina, 1862, vert. 45c, Hindenburg over a Maybach Zeppelin automobile, Friedrichshaven, 1936. 50c, Goodyear Blimp over the Statue of Liberty, 1986, vert. 60c, Hindenburg passing over the Statue of Liberty during its final flight, 1937. 90c, Experimental docking of aircraft (piloted by Ernst Udet) with the Hindenburg, 1936. $2, Hindenburg over the Olympic stadium, Berlin, 1936, vert. $3, Hindenburg over Christ of the Andes statue, Rio de Janeiro, 1937, vert. $4, Hindenburg over mail plane catapult ship Bremen, 1936. No. 1636, Zepplin over DLH base, Bathurst, Gambia, 1935. No. 1637, Graf Zeppelin over mosque, Moscow, 1930.

1988, July 1 *Perf. 14*

1626	A225	10c	multicolored	15	15
1627	A225	15c	multicolored	15	15
1628	A225	25c	multicolored	18	18
1629	A225	45c	multicolored	35	35
1630	A225	50c	multicolored	38	38
1631	A225	60c	multicolored	45	45
1632	A225	90c	multicolored	68	68
1633	A225	$2	multicolored	1.50	1.50
1634	A225	$3	multicolored	2.25	2.25
1635	A225	$4	multicolored	3.00	3.00
			Nos. 1626-1635 (10)	9.09	9.09

Souvenir Sheets

1636	A225	$5	multicolored	3.75	3.75
1637	A225	$5	multicolored	3.75	3.75

SYDPEX '88, Sydney, Australia — A226

Walt Disney characters in Australian settings: 1c, Camping in the Outback, a howling Tasmanian wolf. 2c, Offering peanuts to wallabies. 3c, With a kangaroo and joey against Ayers Rock. 4c, Riding emus, emu-wrens. 5c, Camp and wombat. 10c, Duck-billed platypuses. No. 1664, Photographing a kookaburra. $6, Koala and Mickey waving flags of Grenada, Australia and the United States, map. No. 1646, Flags and candles atop Cake in the shape of Australia. No. 1647, Mickey, Minnie Pluto and Goofy taking a break during a walkabout.

1988, Aug. 1 Litho. *Perf. 14x13½*

1638	A226	1c	multicolored	15	15
1639	A226	2c	multicolored	15	15
1640	A226	3c	multicolored	15	15
1641	A226	4c	multicolored	15	15
1642	A226	5c	multicolored	15	15
1643	A226	10c	multicolored	15	15
1644	A226	$5	multicolored	3.75	3.75
1645	A226	$6	multicolored	4.50	4.50
			Nos. 1638-1645 (8)	9.15	9.15

Souvenir Sheet

1646	A226	$5	multicolored	3.75	3.75
1647	A226	$5	multicolored	3.75	3.75

Mickey Mouse, 60th anniversary.

Intl. Fund for Agricultural Development, 10th Anniv. A227

1988, Aug. 11 Litho. *Perf. 14*

1648	A227	25c	Pineapple, vert.	20	20
1649	A227	75c	Banana, vert.	58	58
1650	A227	$3	Mace, nutmeg	2.25	2.25

Flowering Trees and Shrubs of the Caribbean A228

1988, Sept. 30 Litho.

1651	A228	15c	Lignum vitae	15	15
1652	A228	25c	Saman	18	18
1653	A228	35c	Red frangipani	25	25
1654	A228	45c	Flowering maple	32	32
1655	A228	60c	Yellow poui	42	42
1656	A228	$1	Wild chestnut	70	70
1657	A228	$3	Mountain immortelle	2.10	2.10
1658	A228	$4	Queen of flowers	2.75	2.75
			Nos. 1651-1658 (8)	6.87	6.87

Souvenir Sheets

1659	A228	$5	Flamboyant	3.50	3.50
1660	A228	$5	Orchid tree	3.50	3.50

Miniature Sheet

Christmas, Mickey Mouse 60th Anniv. — A229

Designs: a, Huey draping garland. b, Goofy stringing popcorn. c, Chip'n'Dale decorating tree. d, Santa Claus in his sleigh. e, Dewey hanging stockings. f, Louie unpacking decorations. g, Donald Duck. h, Mickey Mouse. No. 1662, Morty and Ferdie leaving milk and cookies for Santa, horiz. No. 1663, Morty and Ferdie dreaming of presents, horiz.

Illustration reduced.

Perf. 13½x14, 14x13½

1988, Dec. 1			**Litho.**	
1661	A229	Sheet of 8	6.00	6.00
a.-h.		$1 any single	75	75

Souvenir Sheets

1662	A229	$5 multicolored	3.75	3.75
1663	A229	$5 multicolored	3.75	3.75

Miniature Sheets

Major League Baseball Players — A230

No. 1664: a, Mickey Mantle. b, Roger Clemens. c, Rod Carew. d, Ryne Sandberg. e, Mike Scott. f, Tim Raines. g, Willie Mays. h, Bret Saberhagen. i, Honus Wagner.

No. 1665: a, Roberto Clemente. b, Cal Ripken, Jr. c, Bob Feller. d, George Bell. e, Mark McGwire. f, Alvin Davis. g, Pete Rose. h, Dan Quisenberry. i, Babe Ruth.

No. 1666: a, Jackie Robinson. b, Dwight Gooden. c, Brooks Robinson, Jr. d, Nolan Ryan. e, Mike Schmidt. f, Gary Gaetti. g, Nellie Fox. h, Tony Gwynn. i, Dizzy Dean.

No. 1667: a, Ernie Banks. b, National League emblem. c, Julio Franco. d, Jack Morris. e, Fernando Valenzuela. f, Lefty Grove. g, Ted Williams. h, Darryl Strawberry. i, Dale Murphy.

No. 1668: a, Johnny Bench. b, Dave Stieb. c, Reggie Jackson. d, Harold Baines. e, Wade Boggs. f, Pete O'Brien. g, Stan Musial. h, Wally Joyner. i, Grover Cleveland Alexander.

No. 1669: a, Jose Cruz. b, American League emblem. c, Al Kaline. d, Chuck Klein. e, Don Mattingly. f, Mike Witt. g, Mark Langston. h, Hubie Brooks. i, Harmon Killebrew.

No. 1670: a, George Brett. b, Joe Carter. c, Frank Robinson. d, Mel Ott. e, Benito Santiago. f, Teddy Higuera. g, Lloyd Moseby. h, Bobby Bonilla. i, Warren Spahn.

No. 1671: a, Gary Carter. b, Hank Aaron. c, Gaylord Perry. d, Ty Cobb. e, Andre Dawson. f, Charlie Hough. g, Kirby Puckett. h, Robin Yount. i, Don Drysdale.

No. 1672: a, Luis Aparicio. b, Paul Molitor. c, Lou Gehrig. d, Jeffrey Leonard. e, Eric Davis. f, Pete Incaviglia. g, Steve Rogers. h, Ozzie Smith. i, Randy Jones.

1988, Nov. 28	**Litho.**	***Perf. 14***	
1664	Sheet of 9	1.90	
a.-i.	A230 30c any single	20	20
1665	Sheet of 9	1.90	
a.-i.	A230 30c any single	20	20
1666	Sheet of 9	1.90	
a.-i.	A230 30c any single	20	20
1667	Sheet of 9	1.90	
a.-i.	A230 30c any single	20	20
1668	Sheet of 9	1.90	
a.-i.	A230 30c any single	20	20
1669	Sheet of 9	1.90	
a.-i.	A230 30c any single	20	20
1670	Sheet of 9	1.90	
a.-i.	A230 30c any single	20	20
1671	Sheet of 9	1.90	
a.-i.	A230 30c any single	20	20
1672	Sheet of 9	1.90	
a.-i.	A230 30c any single	20	20
	Nos. 1664-1672 (9)	17.10	

No. 1665 was reprinted with No. 1665g replaced by a label inscribed "U.S. Baseball Series."

Singers — A231

1988, Dec. 5		**Litho.**	***Perf. 14***	
1673	A231	10c Tina Turner	15	15
1674	A231	25c Lionel Ritchie	18	18
1675	A231	45c Whitney Houston	35	35
1676	A231	60c Joan Armatrading	45	45
1677	A231	75c Madonna	58	58
1678	A231	$1 Elton John	75	75
1679	A231	$3 Bruce Springsteen	2.25	2.25
1680	A231	$4 Bob Marley	3.00	3.00
		Nos. 1673-1680 (8)	7.71	7.71

Souvenir Sheet

1681	Sheet of 4 (2 55c,+ $1)	2.35	2.35
a.	A231 55c Yoko Minamino	42	42
b.	A231 $1 Yoko Minamino, diff.	75	75

Armatrading is misspelled "Ammertrading."

Car Type of 1988
Miniature Sheets

Locomotives.

No. 1682: a, 1889 Canada Atlantic Railway No. 2 0-6-0, Canada. b, 1875 Virginia & Truckee Railroad J.W. Bowker 2-4-0, US. c, 1872 Philadelphia & Reading Railway Ariel 2-2-2, US. d, 1867 Chicago & Rock Is. Railroad America 4-4-0, US. e, 1866 Lehigh Valley Railroad Consolidation No. 63 2-8-0, US. f, 1860 Great Western Railway Scotia 0-6-0, Canada. g, 1854 Grand Trunk Railway Birkenhead Class 4-4-0, Canada. h, 1837 Camden & Amboy Railroad Monster 0-8-0, US. i, 1834 B&O Railroad Grasshopper Class 0-4-0, US. j, 1829 B&O Railroad Tom Thumb 0-2-2, US.

No. 1683: a, 1925 United Railways of Yucatan Yucatan 4-4-0, Mexico. b, 1924 Canadian Natl. Railways Class T2 2-10-2, Canada. c, 1919 St. Louis-San Francisco Railroad USRA Light Mikado 2-8-2, US. d, 1919 Atlantic Coast Line Railroad USRA Light Pacific 4-6-2, US. e, 1913 Edaville Railroad (Bridgton & Saco River Railroad) No. 7 2-4-4-T, US. f, 1903 Denver & Rio Grande Western Railroad Mudhens Class K27 2-8-2, US. g, 1902 PRR Class E-2 No. 7002 4-4-2, US. h, 1899 PRR Class H6 2-8-0, US. i, 1893 Mohawk & Hudson Railroad De Witt Clinton 0-4-0, US. j, 1891 St. Clair Tunnel Company No. 598 0-10-0, Canada.

No. 1684: a, 1947 Chesapeake & Ohio Railroad M-1 Class No. 500 steam turbine electric, US. b, 1946 Rutland Railroad No. 93 4-8-2, US. c, 1942 PRR Class T1 4-4-4-4, US. d, 1942 Chesapeake & Ohio Railroad Class H-8 2-6-6-6, US. e, 1941 Atchison, Topeka & Santa Fe Railway EMD Model FT Bo-Bo, US. f, 1940 Gulf, Mobile & Ohio Railroad ALCO Models S-1 & S-2 Bo-Bo, US. g, 1937 New York, New Haven & Hartford Railroad Class 15 4-6-4, US. h, 1936 Seaboard Air Line Railroad Class R 2-6-6-4, US. i, 1930 Newfoundland Railway Class R-2 2-8-2, Canada. j, 1928 Canadian Natl. Railway No. 9000 2-Do-1 + 1-Do-2, Canada.

1989, Jan. 23	**Litho.**	***Perf. 13x13½***	
1682	Sheet of 10	14.50	14.50
a.-j.	A223 $2 any single	1.45	1.45
1683	Sheet of 10	14.50	14.50
a.-j.	A223 $2 any single	1.45	1.45
1684	Sheet of 10	14.50	14.50
a.-j.	A223 $2 any single	1.45	1.45

Medalists of the 1988 Summer Olympics, Seoul — A232

Designs: 10c, Jackie Joyner-Kersee, US, long jump. 25c, Steffi Graf, Federal Republic of Germany, women's singles tennis. 45c, Peter Rono, Kenya, 1500m run. 75c, Greg Barton, US, kayak singles. $1, Italy, women's team foil. $2, Kristin Otto, German Democratic Republic, women's 100m freestyle swimming. $3, Holger Behrendt, German Democratic Republic, still rings. $4, Japan, duet synchronized swimming. No. 1693, Yukio Iketani, Japan, men's floor exercise. No. 1694, West Germany, 400m relay, and (Olympic) flame over track.

1989, Apr. 6		**Litho.**	***Perf. 14***	
1685	A232	10c multicolored	15	15
1686	A232	25c multicolored	18	18
1687	A232	45c multicolored	35	35
1688	A232	75c multicolored	58	58
1689	A232	$1 multicolored	75	75
1690	A232	$2 multicolored	1.50	1.50
1691	A232	$3 multicolored	2.25	2.25
1692	A232	$4 multicolored	3.00	3.00
		Nos. 1685-1692 (8)	8.76	8.76

Sovuenir Sheets

1693	A232	$6 multicolored	4.50	4.50
1694	A232	$6 multicolored	4.50	4.50

"The Fifty-three Stations on the Tokaido" — A233

Prints by Hiroshige (1797-1858): 10c, Shinagawa on Edo Bay. 25c, Pine Trees on the Road to Totsuka. 60c, Kanagawa on Edo Bay. 75c, Crossing Banyu River to Hiratsuka. $1, Windy Shore at Odawara. $2, Snow-covered Post Station of Mishima. $3, Full Moon at Fuchu. $4, Crossing the Stream at Okitsu. No. 1703, Mt. Uzu at Okabe. No. 1704, Mountain Pass at Nissaka.

1989, May 15		**Litho.**	***Perf. 14x13½***	
1695	A233	10c multicolored	15	15
1696	A233	25c multicolored	18	18
1697	A233	60c multicolored	45	45
1698	A233	75c multicolored	58	58
1699	A233	$1 multicolored	75	75
1700	A233	$2 multicolored	1.50	1.50
1701	A233	$3 multicolored	2.25	2.25
1702	A233	$4 multicolored	3.00	3.00
		Nos. 1695-1702 (8)	8.86	8.86

Souvenir Sheets

1703	A233	$5 multicolored	3.75	3.75
1704	A233	$5 multicolored	3.75	3.75

Hirohito (1901-1989) and enthronement of Akihito as emperor of Japan.

Indigenous Birds A234

1989, June 6		**Litho.**	***Perf. 14***	
1705	A234	5c Great blue heron	15	15
1706	A234	10c Green heron	15	15
1707	A234	15c Ruddy turnstone	15	15
1708	A234	25c Blue-winged teal	18	18
1709	A234	35c Ring-necked plover	28	28
1710	A234	45c Emerald-throated hummingbird	35	35
1711	A234	50c Hairy hermit	38	38
1712	A234	60c Lesser Antillean bullfinch	45	45
1713	A234	75c Brown pelican	58	58
1714	A234	$1 Black-crowned night heron	75	75
1715	A234	$3 Sparrow hawk	2.25	2.25
1716	A234	$5 Barn swallow	3.75	3.75
1717	A234	$10 Red-billed tropicbird	7.50	7.50
1718	A234	$20 Barn owl	15.00	15.00
		Nos. 1705-1718 (14)	31.92	31.92

Nos. 1709-1718 vert.

1993		**Litho.**	***Perf. 11½x13***	
1705a	A234	5c	15	15
1706a	A234	10c	15	15
1707a	A234	15c	15	15
1708a	A234	25c	18	18

Perf. 13x11½

1709a	A234	35c	25	25
1710a	A234	45c	35	35
1711a	A234	50c	38	38
1712a	A234	60c	45	45
1713a	A234	75c	55	55
1714a	A234	$1	75	75
1715a	A234	$3	2.25	2.25
1716a	A234	$5	3.75	3.75
		Nos. 1705a-1716a (12)	9.36	9.36

1990 World Cup Soccer Championships, Italy — A235

1989, June 12			***Perf. 14***	
1719	A235	10c Scotland	15	15
1720	A235	25c England vs. Brazil	18	18
1721	A235	60c Paolo Rossi, Italy	45	45
1722	A235	75c Jairzinho of Brazil	58	58
1723	A235	$1 Swedish Striker	75	75
1724	A235	$2 Pele, Brazil	1.50	1.50
1725	A235	$3 Mario Kempes, Argentina	2.25	2.25
1726	A235	$4 Pat Jennings	3.00	3.00
		Nos. 1719-1726 (8)	8.86	8.86

Souvenir Sheets

1727	A235	$6 Argentina vs. Holland	4.50	4.50
a.		$6 1990 score ovptd. in margin	4.50	4.50
1728	A235	$6 Goalie	4.50	4.50

Issue date: No. 1727a, Nov. 30, 1990.

PHILEXFRANCE '89 — A236

19th Cent. ships and cargo: 25c, Chebeck, sugarcane. 75c, Lugger, cotton. $1, Merchantman, cocoa. $4, Ketch, coffee. $6, Vue du Fort et Ville de St. George dans l'Isle de la Grenade et du Morne, 1779.

1989, July 7			***Perf. 14***	
1729	A236	25c multicolored	20	20
1730	A236	75c multicolored	58	58
1731	A236	$1 multicolored	75	75
1732	A236	$4 multicolored	3.00	3.00

Size: 114x71mm

Imperf

1733	A236	$6 multicolored	4.50	4.50

First Moon Landing, 20th Anniv. A237

Space achievements: 15c, Alan Shepard, 1st American in space, 1961. 35c, Friendship 7, piloted by John Glenn, 1st manned orbit of the Earth, 1962. 45c, Apollo 8 mission, 1st manned orbit of the Moon, 1968. 70c, Lunar rover on Moon, 1972. $1, Apollo 11 mission emblem and Eagle lunar module on the Moon, 1969. $2, Gemini 8-Agena, 1st space docking, 1969. $3, Edward White, 1st American to walk in space, 1965. $4, Apollo 7 mission emblem. No. 1742, Simple flight plan for the Apollo 11 mission. No. 1743, Raising of the American flag on the Moon.

1989, July 20			***Perf. 14***	
1734	A237	15c multicolored	15	15
1735	A237	35c multicolored	28	28
1736	A237	45c multicolored	35	35
1737	A237	70c multicolored	52	52
1738	A237	$1 multicolored	75	75
1739	A237	$2 multicolored	1.50	1.50
1740	A237	$3 multicolored	2.25	2.25
1741	A237	$4 multicolored	3.00	3.00
		Nos. 1734-1741 (8)	8.80	8.80

Souvenir Sheets

1742	A237	$5 multicolored	3.75	3.75
1743	A237	$5 multicolored	3.75	3.75

Mushrooms
A238

YWCA, Cent.
A239

1989, Aug. 17 Litho. *Perf. 14*

1744 A238 15c *Hygrocybe occidentalis scarletina* 15 15
1745 A238 40c *Marasmius haemato- cephalus* 30 30
1746 A238 50c *Hygrocybe hypohaemacta* 38 38
1747 A238 70c *Lepiota pseudoignicolor* 52 52
1748 A238 90c *Cookeina tricholoma* 68 68
1749 A238 $1.10 *Leucopaxillus gracillimus* 82 82
1750 A238 $2.25 *Hygrocybe nigrescens* 1.70 1.70
1751 A238 $4 *Clathrus crispus* 3.00 3.00
Nos. 1744-1751 (8) 7.55 7.55

Souvenir Sheets

1752 A238 $6 *Mycena holoporphyra* 4.50 4.50
1753 A238 $6 *Xeromphalina tenuipes* 4.50 4.50

1989, Sept. 11 *Perf. 14*

1754 A239 50c shown 38 38
1755 A239 75c Emblem, horiz. 58 58

Butterflies
A240

1989, Oct. 2 *Perf. 14*

1756 A240 6c Orion 15 15
1757 A240 30c Southern daggertail 22 22
1758 A240 40c Soldier 30 30
1759 A240 60c Silver spot 45 45
1760 A240 $1.10 Gulf fritillary 82 82
1761 A240 $1.25 Monarch 95 95
1762 A240 $4 Polydamas swallowtail 3.00 3.00
1763 A240 $5 Flambeau 3.75 3.75
Nos. 1756-1763 (8) 9.64 9.64

Souvenir Sheets

1764 A240 $6 St. Christopher hairstreak 4.50 4.50
1765 A240 $6 White peacock 4.50 4.50

Discovery of America, 500th Anniv. (in 1992) — A241

Anniv. and UPAE emblems and various pre-Columbian petroglyphs.

1989, Oct. 16 Litho. *Perf. 14*

1766 A241 45c multicolored 35 35
1767 A241 60c multi, diff. 45 45
1768 A241 $1 multi, diff. 75 75
1769 A241 $4 multi, diff. 3.00 3.00

Souvenir Sheet

1770 A241 $6 multi, diff. 4.50 4.50

World Stamp Expo '89, Scenes from *Ben and Me* — A242

Walt Disney characters, story of the American Revolution: 1c, Amos leaves home. 2c, Amos meets young Benjamin Franklin. 3c, Invention of the Franklin stove. 4c, Invention of bifocals. 5c, *Pennsylvania Gazette.* 6c, Franklin at printing press. 10c, Experimenting with electricity. $5, As an American diplomat in England. No. 1779, Amos's "Document of Agreement." No. 1780, Franklin presiding over meeting of the Ben Franklin Stamp Club. No. 1781, 2nd Continental Congress, Philadelphia, 1775.

Perf. 14x13¹/₂, 13¹/₂x14

1989, Nov. 17 Litho.

1771 A242 1c multi 15 15
1772 A242 2c multi 15 15
1773 A242 3c multi 15 15
1774 A242 4c multi 15 15
1775 A242 5c multi 15 15
1776 A242 6c multi 15 15
1777 A242 10c multi 15 15
1778 A242 $5 multi 3.25 3.25
1779 A242 $6 multi 3.75 3.75
Nos. 1771-1779 (9) 8.05 8.05

Souvenir Sheets

1780 A242 $6 multi, vert. 3.75 3.75
1781 A242 $6 multi 3.75 3.75

Christmas — A243

Paintings by Rubens: 20c, *Christ in the House of Mary and Martha.* 35c, *The Circumcision.* 60c, *Trinity Adored by Duke of Mantua and Family.* $2, *Holy Family with St. Francis.* $3, *The Ildefonso Altarpiece.* $4, *Madonna and Child with Garland and Putti,* by Rubens and Jan Brueghel. No. 1788, *Adoration of the Magi.* No. 1789, *Virgin and Child Adored by Angels.*

1990, Jan. 4 Litho. *Perf. 14*

1782 A243 20c multicolored 15 15
1783 A243 35c multicolored 28 28
1784 A243 60c multicolored 45 45
1785 A243 $2 multicolored 1.50 1.50
1786 A243 $3 multicolored 2.25 2.25
1787 A243 $4 multicolored 3.00 3.00
Nos. 1782-1787 (6) 7.63 7.63

Souvenir Sheets

1788 A243 $5 multicolored 3.75 3.75
1789 A243 $5 multicolored 3.75 3.75

Anniversaries and Events (in 1989) — A244

Designs: 10c, Alexander Graham Bell, early telephone, telephone lines. 25c, George Washington, the Capitol Building. 35c, William Shakespeare, birthplace, Stratford-on-Avon. 75c, Jawaharlal Nehru, Mahatma Gandhi. $1, Hugo Eckener, Ferdinand von Zeppelin, zeppelin *Delag.* $2, Charlie Chaplin. $3, Ship in port. $4, Pres. Friedrich Ebert, Heidelberg Gate. No. 1798, Concorde jet. No. 1799, Ship, 13th century, vert.

1990, Feb. 12 Litho. *Perf. 14*

1790 A244 10c multicolored 15 15
1791 A244 25c multicolored 18 18
1792 A244 35c multicolored 28 28
1793 A244 75c multicolored 58 58
1794 A244 $1 multicolored 75 75
1795 A244 $2 multicolored 1.50 1.50
1796 A244 $3 multicolored 2.25 2.25
1797 A244 $4 multicolored 3.00 3.00
Nos. 1790-1797 (8) 8.69 8.69

Souvenir Sheets

1798 A244 $6 multicolored 4.50 4.50
1799 A244 $6 multicolored 4.50 4.50

Invention of the telephone, 1876 (10c); American presidency, 200th anniv. (25c); 425th birth anniv. of Shakespeare (35c); birth cent. of Nehru (75c); 1st passenger zeppelin, 80th anniv. ($1); birth cent. of Charlie Chaplin ($2); Hamburg, 800th anniv. ($3, No. 1799); Federal Republic of Germany, 40th anniv. ($4); and test flight of the Concorde supersonic jet, 20th anniv. (No. 1798).

Orchids — A245

America Issue — A246

1990, Mar. 6 Litho. *Perf. 14*

1800 A245 1c *Odontoglossum triumphans* 15 15
1801 A245 25c *Oncidium splendidum* 18 18
1802 A245 60c *Laelia anceps* 45 45
1803 A245 75c *Cattleya trianaei* 58 58
1804 A245 $1 *Odontoglossum rossii* 75 75
1805 A245 $2 *Brassia gireoudiana* 1.50 1.50
1806 A245 $3 *Cattleya dowiana* 2.25 2.25
1807 A245 $4 *Sobralia macrantha* 3.00 3.00
Nos. 1800-1807 (8) 8.86 8.86

Souvenir Sheets

1808 A245 $6 *Laelia rubescens* 4.50 4.50
1809 A245 $6 *Oncidium lanceanum* 4.50 4.50

EXPO '90 Intl. Garden and Greenery Exposition, Japan.

1990, Mar. 16 Litho. *Perf. 14*

Butterflies, UPAE and discovery of America 500th anniv. emblems: 15c, Southern dagger tail. 25c, Caribbean buckeye. 75c, Malachite. 90c, Orion. $1, St. Lucia mestra. $2, Red rim. $3, Flambeau. $4, Red anartia. No. 1818, Giant hairstreak. No. 1819, Orange-barred sulphur.

1810 A246 15c multicolored 15 15
1811 A246 25c multicolored 18 18
1812 A246 75c multicolored 58 58
1813 A246 90c multicolored 68 68
1814 A246 $1 multicolored 75 75
1815 A246 $2 multicolored 1.50 1.50
1816 A246 $3 multicolored 2.25 2.25
1817 A246 $4 multicolored 3.00 3.00
Nos. 1810-1817 (8) 9.09 9.09

Souvenir Sheets

1818 A246 $6 multicolored 4.50 4.50
1819 A246 $6 multicolored 4.50 4.50

Wildlife
A247

1990, Apr. 3 Litho. *Perf. 14*

1820 A247 10c Caribbean monk seal 15 15
1821 A247 15c Little brown bat 15 15
1822 A247 45c Norway rat 35 35
1823 A247 60c Old-world rabbit 45 45
1824 A247 $1 Water opossum 75 75
1825 A247 $2 White-nosed ichneumon 1.50 1.50
1826 A247 $3 Little big-eared bat 2.25 2.25
1827 A247 $4 Mouse opossums 3.00 3.00
Nos. 1820-1827 (8) 8.60 8.60

Souvenir Sheets

1828 A247 $6 Old-world rabbit. diff. 4.50 4.50
1829 A247 $6 Water opossum 4.50 4.50

No. 1826 is vert. Nos. 1828-1829 have multicolored decorative margins contininuing the designs and picturing little brown bat, prehensile-tailed porcupine and mouse opossum (No. 1828) or four-eyed opossum, West Indies manatee and Norway rat (No. 1829).

World War II
A248

Designs: 25c, Operation Battleaxe, June 15, 1941. 35c, Allied landing in southern France, Aug. 15, 1944. 45c, US invasion of Guadalcanal, Aug. 7, 1942. 50c, Allied defeat of Japanese army in New Guinea, Jan. 22, 1943. 60c, US forces secure Leyte, Dec. 11, 1944. 75c, US forces enter Cologne, Mar. 5, 1945. $1, Allied offensive to break out of Anzio, May 23, 1944. $2, Battle of the Bismarck Sea, Mar. 3, 1943. $3, US fleet under Adm. Nimitz, Dec. 17, 1941. $4, Allied landing at Salerno, Sept. 9, 1943. $6, German U-boat.

1990, Apr. 30 Litho. *Perf. 14x13¹/₂*

1830 A248 25c multicolored 18 18
1831 A248 35c multicolored 26 26
1832 A248 45c multicolored 32 32
1833 A248 50c multicolored 38 38
1834 A248 60c multicolored 45 45
1835 A248 75c multicolored 58 58
1836 A248 $1 multicolored 75 75
1837 A248 $2 multicolored 1.50 1.50
1838 A248 $3 multicolored 2.25 2.25
1839 A248 $4 multicolored 3.00 3.00
Nos. 1830-1839 (10) 9.67 9.67

Souvenir Sheet

1840 A248 $6 multicolored 4.50 4.50

Souvenir Sheet

Penny Black, 150th Anniv. — A249

1990, May 3 Litho. *Perf. 14*

1841 A249 $6 vio 4.50 4.50

Stamp World London '90.

Stamp World London '90 — A250

Walt Disney characters and British trains.

1990, June 21 *Perf. 14*

1844 A250 5c 1925 King Arthur Class 15 15
1845 A250 10c 1813 Puffing Billy 15 15
1846 A250 20c 1765 Colliery Tramwagon 15 15
1847 A250 45c 1935 No. 2509 Silver Link 32 32
1848 A250 $1 1948 No. 60149 Amadis 75 75
1849 A250 $2 1830 Liverpool 1.50 1.50
1850 A250 $4 1870 Flying Scotsman 3.00 3.00
1851 A250 $5 1972 Advanced Passenger Train 3.75 3.75
Nos. 1844-1851 (8) 9.77 9.77

Souvenir Sheets

1852 A250 $6 Stockton & Darlington Railway Opening, 1825, vert. 4.50 4.50
1853 A250 $6 1809 *Catch-Me-Who-Can* 4.50 4.50

Queen Mother, 90th Birthday — A251

1990, July 5 Litho. *Perf. 14*
1854 A251 $2 Wearing black hat 1.50 1.50
1855 A251 $2 shown 1.50 1.50
1856 A251 $2 Wearing crown 1.50 1.50

Souvenir Sheet
1857 A251 $6 Like No. 1855 4.50 4.50

1992 Summer Olympics, Barcelona — A252

Character trademark and: 10c, Men's steeplechase. 15c, Equestrian. 45c, Men's 200 meter butterfly. 50c, Field hockey. 65c, Balance beam. 75c, Flying Dutchman Class yachting. $2, Freestyle wrestling. $3, Men's diving. $4, Women's cycling. $5, Men's basketball. No. 1863, Three-day equestrian event. No. 1863A, Men's 10,000 M race.

1990, July 9
1858 A252 10c multicolored 15 15
1858A A252 15c multicolored 15 15
1859 A252 45c multicolored 35 35
1859A A252 50c multicolored 38 38
1860 A252 65c multicolored 48 48
1860A A252 75c multicolored 58 58
1861 A252 $2 multicolored 1.50 1.50
1861A A252 $3 multicolored 2.25 2.25
1862 A252 $4 multicolored 3.00 3.00
1862A A252 $5 multicolored 3.80 3.80
Nos. 1858-1862A (10) 12.64 12.64

Souvenir Sheet
1863 A252 $8 multicolored 6.00 6.00
1863A A252 $8 multicolored 6.00 6.00

Nos. 1858A, 1859A, 1860A, 1861A, 1862A, 1863A were not available until 1991.

US Airborne, 50th Anniv. A253

1990, July 3
1864 A253 75c Mass jump 58 58

Souvenir Sheets
1865 A253 $2.50 Paratrooper landing 1.90 1.90
1866 A253 $6 Paratroopers 1940, 1990 4.50 4.50

Yellow Goatfish A254

1990, Aug. 8
1867 A254 10c shown 15 15
1868 A254 25c Black margate 20 20
1869 A254 65c Bluehead wrasse 52 52
1870 A254 75c Puddingwife 60 60
1871 A254 $1 Foureye butterflyfish 80 80
1872 A254 $2 Honey damselfish 1.60 1.60
1873 A254 $3 Queen angelfish 2.40 2.40
1874 A254 $5 Cherubfish 4.00 4.00
Nos. 1867-1874 (8) 10.27 10.27

Souvenir Sheets
1875 A254 $6 Smooth trunkfish 4.75 4.75
1876 A254 $6 Sergeant major 4.75 4.75

Birds A255

1990, Sept. 10 Litho. *Perf. 14*
1877 A255 15c Tropical mockingbird 15 15
1878 A255 25c Gray kingbird 20 20
1879 A255 65c Bare-eyed thrush 52 52
1880 A255 75c Antillean crested hummingbird 60 60
1881 A255 $1 House wren 80 80
1882 A255 $2 Purple martin 1.60 1.60
1883 A255 $4 Hooded tanager 3.20 3.20
1884 A255 $5 Common ground dove 4.00 4.00
Nos. 1877-1884 (8) 11.07 11.07

Souvenir Sheets
1885 A255 $6 Fork-tailed flycatcher 4.80 4.80
1886 A255 $6 Smooth-billed ani 4.80 4.80

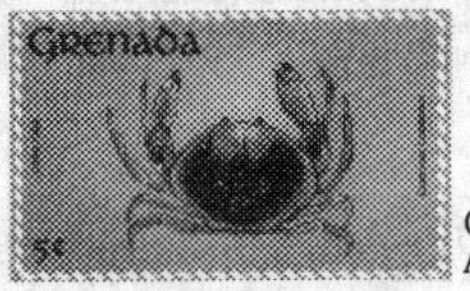
Crustaceans A256

1990, Sept. 17
1887 A256 5c Coral crab 15 15
1888 A256 10c Smoothtail spiny lobster 15 15
1889 A256 15c Flamestreaked box crab 15 15
1890 A256 25c Spotted swimming crab 20 20
1891 A256 75c Sally lightfoot rock crab 60 60
1892 A256 $1 Spotted spiny lobster 80 80
1893 A256 $3 Longarm spiny lobster 2.40 2.40
1894 A256 $20 Caribbean spiny lobster 16.00 16.00
Nos. 1887-1894 (8) 20.45 20.45

Souvenir Sheets
1895 A256 $6 Spanish lobster 4.80 4.80
1896 A256 $6 Copper lobster 4.80 4.80

World Cup Soccer Championships, Italy — A257

Players from participating countries.

1990, Sept. 24
1897 A257 10c Cameroun 15 15
1898 A257 25c Spain 20 20
1899 A257 $1 West Germany 80 80
1900 A257 $5 Scotland 4.00 4.00

Souvenir Sheets
1901 A257 $6 Uruguay 4.80 4.80
1902 A257 $6 Italy 4.80 4.80

Christmas A258

Paintings by Raphael: 10c, The Ansidei Madonna. 15c, The Sistine Madonna. $1, Madonna of the Baldacchino. $2, The Large Holy Family. $5, Madonna in the Meadow. No. 1908, Madonna of the Veil. No. 1909, Madonna of the Diadem.

1990, Dec. 31 Litho. *Perf. 14*
1903 A258 10c multicolored 15 15
1904 A258 15c multicolored 15 15
1905 A258 $1 multicolored 80 80
1906 A258 $2 multicolored 1.60 1.60
1907 A258 $5 multicolored 4.00 4.00
Nos. 1903-1907 (5) 6.70 6.70

Souvenir Sheets
1908 A258 $6 multicolored 4.80 4.80
1909 A258 $6 multicolored 4.80 4.80

Peter Paul Rubens (1577-1640), Painter — A259

Entire paintings or different details from: 5c, $1, $4, The Brazen Serpent. 10c, Garden of Love. 25c, Head of Cyrus. 75c, Tournament in Front of a Castle. $2, Judgement of Paris. $5, The Karmesse. No. 1918, The Prodigal Son. No. 1919, Anger of Neptune.

1991, Jan. 31 Litho. *Perf. 14*
1910 A259 5c multicolored 15 15
1911 A259 10c multicolored 15 15
1912 A259 25c multicolored 20 20
1913 A259 75c multicolored 60 60
1914 A259 $1 multicolored 80 80
1915 A259 $2 multicolored 1.60 1.60
1916 A259 $4 multicolored 3.20 3.20
1917 A259 $5 multicolored 4.00 4.00
Nos. 1910-1917 (8) 10.70 10.70

Souvenir Sheets
1918 A259 $6 multicolored 4.80 4.80
1919 A259 $6 multicolored 4.80 4.80

Disney Film *Fantasia,* 50th Anniv. — A260

Designs: 5c, Mickey as Sorcerer's apprentice, walking broom. 10c, Mushroom Dance Ensemble from The Nutcracker Suite. 20c, Pterodactyls from The Rite of Spring. 45c, Centaurs from The Pastoral Symphony. $1, Bacchus and Jacchus from The Pastoral Symphony. $2, Ostrich ballerina in Dance of the Hours. $4, Elephant dance from Dance of the Hours. $5, Diana, Goddess of the Moon from Dance of the Hours. No. 1928, Mickey as Sorcerer's apprentice. No. 1929, Mickey, Leopold Stokowski. $12, Mickey as Sorcerer's Apprentice, vert.

1991, Feb. 4 Litho. *Perf. 14*
1920 A260 5c multicolored 15 15
1921 A260 10c multicolored 15 15
1922 A260 20c multicolored 16 16
1923 A260 45c multicolored 35 35
1924 A260 $1 multicolored 80 80
1925 A260 $2 multicolored 1.60 1.60
1926 A260 $4 multicolored 3.20 3.20
1927 A260 $5 multicolored 4.00 4.00
Nos. 1920-1927 (8) 10.41 10.41

Souvenir Sheets
1928 A260 $6 multicolored 4.80 4.80
1929 A260 $6 multicolored 4.80 4.80
1930 A260 $12 multicolored 9.60 9.60

Butterflies A261

Designs: 5c, Adelphia iphicla. 10c, Nymphalidae claudina. 15c, Brassolidae polyxena. 20c, Zebra longwing. 25c, Marpesia corinna. 30c, Morpho hecuba. 45c, Morpho rhetenor. 50c, Dismorphia spio. 60c, Prepona omphale. 70c, Morpho anaxibia. 75c, Marpesia iole. $1, Metalmark. $2, Morpho cisseis. $3, Danaidae plexippus. $4, Morpho achilleana. $5, Calliona argenissa. No. 1947, Anteos clorinde. No. 1948, Haetera piera. No. 1949, Papilio cresphontes. No. 1950, Prepona pheridames.

1991, Apr. 8 Litho. *Perf. 14*
1931 A261 5c multicolored 15 15
1932 A261 10c multicolored 15 15
1933 A261 15c multicolored 15 15
1934 A261 20c multicolored 16 16
1935 A261 25c multicolored 20 20
1936 A261 30c multicolored 25 25
1937 A261 45c multicolored 35 35
1938 A261 50c multicolored 40 40
1939 A261 60c multicolored 48 48
1940 A261 70c multicolored 58 58
1941 A261 75c multicolored 60 60
1942 A261 $1 multicolored 80 80
1943 A261 $2 multicolored 1.60 1.60
1944 A261 $3 multicolored 2.40 2.40
1945 A261 $4 multicolored 3.20 3.20
1946 A261 $5 multicolored 4.00 4.00
Nos. 1931-1946 (16) 15.47 15.47

Souvenir Sheets
1947 A261 $6 multicolored 4.80 4.80
1948 A261 $6 multicolored 4.80 4.80
1949 A261 $6 multicolored 4.80 4.80
1950 A261 $6 multicolored 4.80 4.80

Voyages of Discovery A262

Explorer's ships: 5c, Vitus Bering, 1728-1729. 10c, Louis de Bougainville, 1766-1769. 25c, Polynesians. 50c, Alvaro de Mendana, 1567-1569. $1, Charles Darwin, 1831-1835. $2, Capt. James Cook, 1768-1771. $4, Capt. Willem Schouten, 1615-1617. $5, Abel Tasman, 1642-1644. No. 1959, Columbus' ship Santa Maria. No. 1960, Loss of Santa Maria.

1991, Apr. 29
1951 A262 5c multicolored 15 15
1952 A262 10c multicolored 15 15
1953 A262 25c multicolored 20 20
1954 A262 50c multicolored 40 40
1955 A262 $1 multicolored 80 80
1956 A262 $2 multicolored 1.60 1.60
1957 A262 $4 multicolored 3.20 3.20
1958 A262 $5 multicolored 4.00 4.00
Nos. 1951-1958 (8) 10.50 10.50

Souvenir Sheets
1959 A262 $6 multicolored 4.80 4.80
1960 A262 $6 multicolored 4.80 4.80

Discovery of America, 500th anniv. (in 1992).

PHILANIPPON '91 — A263

Walt Disney characters celebrating festivals of Japan: 5c, Daisy Duck and Minnie Mouse, Peach Fete, Festival of the Dolls. 10c, Morty and Ferdie, Tango Festival, Boys' Day Festival. 20c, Mickey, Minnie Mouse, Hoshi-Matsuri, Star Festival. 45c, Minnie, Daisy folk dancing at Bon-Odori Summer Festival. $1, Huey, Dewey and Louie wearing Eboshi headdresses at Yari-Matsuri, Spear Festival of Ohji. $2, Mickey, Goofy pulling Daisy, Minnie in Yamaboko, Gion Festival of Kyoto. $4, Minnie, Daisy preparing rice broth for Nanakusa, Festival of the Seven Plants. $5, Huey, Dewey floating straw boat at O-Bon, Festival of Lanterns. No. 1969, Goofy, Tori-No-Hichi or Rake Festival, vert. No. 1970, Minnie Mouse, Japanese New Year, vert. No. 1971, Mickey, Snow Festival, vert.

1991, May 6 Litho. *Perf. 13½x14*
1961 A263 5c multicolored 15 15
1962 A263 10c multicolored 15 15
1963 A263 20c multicolored 16 16
1964 A263 45c multicolored 35 35
1965 A263 $1 multicolored 80 80

1966 A263	$2	multicolored	1.60	1.60
1967 A263	$4	multicolored	3.20	3.20
1968 A263	$5	multicolored	4.00	4.00
Nos. 1961-1968 (8)			10.41	10.41

Souvenir Sheets

1969 A263	$6	multicolored	4.80	4.80
1970 A263	$6	multicolored	4.80	4.80
1971 A263	$6	multicolored	4.80	4.80

Paintings by Vincent Van Gogh — A264

Designs: 20c, Blossoming Almond Branch in a Glass, vert. 25c, La Mousme, Sitting, vert. 30c, Still Life with Red Cabbages and Onions. 40c, Japonaiserie: Flowering Plum Tree, vert. 45c, Japonaiserie: Bridge in Rain, vert. 60c, Still Life with Basket of Apples. 75c, Italian Woman (Agostina Segatori), vert. $1, The Painter on His Way to Work, vert. $2, Portrait of Pere Tanguy, vert. $3, Still Life with Plaster Statuette, a Rose and Two Novels, vert. $4, Still Life: Bottle, Lemons and Oranges. $5, Orchard with Blossoming Apricot Trees. No. 1984, Farmhouse in a Wheatfield. No. 1985, The "Roubine du Roi" Canal with Washerwoman, vert. No. 1986, Japonaiserie: Oiran, vert. No. 1987, The Gleize Bridge over the Viguerat Canal. No. 1988, Rocks with Oak Tree.

1991, May 13 Litho. *Perf. 13½*

1972 A264	20c	multicolored	16	16
1973 A264	25c	multicolored	20	20
1974 A264	30c	multicolored	25	25
1975 A264	40c	multicolored	32	32
1976 A264	45c	multicolored	35	35
1977 A264	60c	multicolored	48	48
1978 A264	75c	multicolored	60	60
1979 A264	$1	multicolored	80	80
1980 A264	$2	multicolored	1.60	1.60
1981 A264	$3	multicolored	2.40	2.40
1982 A264	$4	multicolored	3.20	3.20
1983 A264	$5	multicolored	4.00	4.00
Nos. 1972-1983 (12)			14.36	14.36

Size: 100x75mm, 75x100mm

Imperf

1984 A264	$6	multicolored	4.80	4.80
1985 A264	$6	multicolored	4.80	4.80
1986 A264	$6	multicolored	4.80	4.80
1987 A264	$6	multicolored	4.80	4.80
1988 A264	$6	multicolored	4.80	4.80

Mushrooms — A265

Designs: 15c, Psilocybe cubensis. 25c, Leptonia caeruleocapitata. 65c, Cystolepiota eriophora. 75c, Chlorophyllum molybdites. $1, Xerocomus hypoxanthus. $2, Volvariella cubensis. $4, Xerocomus coccolobae. $5, Pluteus chrysophlebius. No. 1997, Hygrocybe miniata. No. 1998, Psathyrella tuberculata.

1991, June 1 *Perf. 14*

1989 A265	15c	multicolored	15	15
1990 A265	25c	multicolored	20	20
1991 A265	65c	multicolored	52	52
1992 A265	75c	multicolored	60	60
1993 A265	$1	multicolored	80	80
1994 A265	$2	multicolored	1.60	1.60
1995 A265	$4	multicolored	3.20	3.20
1996 A265	$5	multicolored	4.00	4.00
Nos. 1989-1996 (8)			11.07	11.07

Souvenir Sheet

1997 A265	$6	multicolored	4.80	4.80
1998 A265	$6	multicolored	4.80	4.80

Miniature Sheets

Exploration of Mars — A266

Designs (all different): No. 1999: a, Johannes Kepler, 1571-1630. b, Galileo Galilei, 1564-1642. c, Martian canals drawn by Giovanni Schiaparelli, 1886. d, Sir William Herschel, 1738-1882. e, Mars, planets. f, Percival Lowell at telescope. g, Mariner 4. h, Mars 2. i, Mars 3.

No. 2000: a, e, Profiles of Mars. b, Olympus Mons. c, Dusty face of Mars. d, Martian moon Phobos. f, Martian moon Deimos. g, Nix Olympica. h, Terrain feature resembling human face. i, South Polar Cap.

No. 2001: a, Mars from Thobus. b, Martian dusk. c, "Voyager descent." d, Viking 2 lander on Mars. e, f, Martian landscape. g, h, i, Panorama view from Viking 2 lander.

No. 2002: a, b, Mariner 9. c, Mars. d, Polar cycle. e, Plain of Sinai. f, South pole. g, Nix Olympica. h, Martian surface. i, Outflow channel.

No. 2003, Phobos spacecraft over Mars. No. 2004, Future spacecraft. No. 2005, Future spacecraft, Mars.

1991, June 21 *Perf. 14x13½*

1999 A266	75c	Sheet of 9, #a.-i.	5.40	5.40
2000 A266	$1.25	Sheet of 9, #a.-i.	9.00	9.00
2001 A266	$2	Sheet of 9, #a.-i.	14.40	14.40
2002 A266	$7	Sheet of 9, #a.-i.	50.00	50.00

Souvenir Sheets

2003 A266	$6	multicolored	4.80	4.80
2004 A266	$6	multicolored	4.80	4.80
2005 A266	$6	multicolored	4.80	4.80

Royal Family Birthday, Anniversary

Common Design Type

1991, July 5 Litho. *Perf. 14*

2006 CD347	10c	multicolored	15	15
2007 CD347	15c	multicolored	15	15
2008 CD347	40c	multicolored	32	32
2009 CD347	50c	multicolored	40	40
2010 CD347	$1	multicolored	80	80
2011 CD347	$2	multicolored	1.60	1.60
2012 CD347	$4	multicolored	3.20	3.20
2013 CD347	$5	multicolored	4.00	4.00
Nos. 2006-2013 (8)			10.62	10.62

Souvenir Sheet

2014 CD347	$5	Philip, Elizabeth	4.00	4.00
2015 CD347	$5	Diana, sons, Charles	4.00	4.00

10c, 50c, $1, Nos. 2013, 2015, Charles and Diana, 10th Wedding anniversary. Others, Queen Elizabeth II, 65th birthday.

University of West Indies, 40th Anniv. A266a

Designs: 45c, Marryshow House, Grenada. 50c, Administrative Building, Barbados.

1991, July 19

2016 A266a	45c	multicolored	35	35
2017 A266a	50c	multicolored	40	40

Anglican High School, 75th Anniv. A267

1991, July 29

2018 A267	10c	Existing school	15	15
2019 A267	25c	New school design	20	20
		Set value	28	28

Railways of the World A269

Railways of Great Britain: No. 2020a, Stephenson's first engine, 1814. b, George Stephenson (1781-1848). c, Stephenson's Killingworth engine, 1816. d, Locomotion No. 1, 1825. e, Locomotion in Darlington, 1825. f, Opening of Stockton & Darlington Railway, 1825. g, Royal George No. 5, 1827. h, Northumbrian Rocket, 1829. i, Planet Class engine, 1830.

No. 2021a, Old Ironsides, US, 1832. b, Wilberforce, Stockton & Darlington Railway, Great Britain, 1832. c, Stephenson's Der Adler, Germany, 1835. d, Stephenson's North Star, Great Britain, 1837. e, London & Birmingham No. 1, Great Britain, 1838. f, Stephenson's 1st Austrian locomotive, 1838. g, Mud Digger, US, 1840. h, Standard Norris, US, 1840. i, Fire Fly Class, Great Britain, 1840.

No. 2022a, Lion, Liverpool and Manchester, Great Britain, 1841. b, Beuth 2-2-2, Berlin-Anhalt Railway, Germany, 1843. c, Derwent No. 25, Stockton & Darlington Railway, Great Britain, 1845. d, MKpV, WCB, Vienna, 1846. e, First railway in Hungary, Budapest to Vac, 1846. f, Stockton & Darlington, 1846. g, Stephenson's long boiler type, Paris, 1847. h, Baldwin 4-4-0, US, 1850. i, 2-4-0, Germany, 1850. No. 2023, Boiler of Locomotion No. 1. No. 2024, Liverpool & Manchester Railway, Great Britain, 1833.

1991-92 Litho. *Perf. 14*

Sheets of 9

2020 A269	75c	#a.-i.	5.40	5.40
2021 A269	$1	#a.-i.	7.20	7.20
2022 A269	$2	#a.-i.	14.50	14.50

Souvenir Sheet

2023 A269	$6	multicolored	4.80	4.80
2024 A269	$6	multicolored	4.80	4.80

Issue dates: 75c, No. 2023, Dec. 2. Others, May 7, 1992.

Miniature Sheet

Marine Life in the Sand Flats A270

Designs: No. 2025a, Barbu. b, Beaugregory. c, Porcupinefish. d, Conchfish, queen conch. e, Hermit crab. f, Bluestripe lizardfish. g, Spotfin mojarra. h, Southern stingray. i, Slippery dick, long-spined sea urchin. j, Peacock flounder. k, West Indian sea star. l, Spotted goatfish. m, West Indian sea egg, reticulated olive. n, Pearly razorfish. o, Mottled and yellowhead jawfish. $6, Shortnose batfish.

1991, Dec. 5 Litho. *Perf. 14*

2025 A270	50c	Sheet of 15, #a.-o.	6.00	6.00

Souvenir Sheet

2026 A270	$6	multicolored	4.80	4.80

Christmas A271

Details from paintings by Albrecht Durer: 10c, Adoration of the Magi. 35c, The Madonna with the Siskin. 50c, The Feast of the Rose Garlands. 75c, Madonna and Child (Virgin with the Pear). $1, The Virgin in Half-Length. $2, Madonna and Child. $4, Virgin and Child with St. Anne. $5, Virgin and Child, diff. No. 2035, Virgin with a Multitude of Animals. No. 2036, The Nativity.

1991, Dec. 9 *Perf. 12*

2027 A271	10c	multicolored	15	15
2028 A271	35c	multicolored	28	28
2029 A271	50c	multicolored	40	40
2030 A271	75c	multicolored	60	60
2031 A271	$1	multicolored	80	80
2032 A271	$2	multicolored	1.60	1.60
2033 A271	$4	multicolored	3.20	3.20
2034 A271	$5	multicolored	4.00	4.00
Nos. 2027-2034 (8)			11.03	11.03

Souvenir Sheets

Perf. 14½

2035 A271	$6	multicolored	4.80	4.80
2036 A271	$6	multicolored	4.80	4.80

Thrill Sports — A272

Walt Disney characters enjoying thrill sports.

1992, Feb. 11 Litho. *Perf. 14x13½*

2037 A272	5c	Windsurfing	15	15
2038 A272	10c	Skateboarding	15	15
2039 A272	20c	Gliding	16	16
2040 A272	45c	Stunt kite flying	35	35
2041 A272	$1	Mountain biking	75	75
2042 A272	$2	Parachuting	1.60	1.60
2043 A272	$4	Go-carting	3.20	3.20
2044 A272	$5	Water skiing	3.75	3.75
Nos. 2037-2044 (8)			10.11	10.11

Souvenir Sheets

2045 A272	$6	Roller blade hockey	4.80	4.80
2046 A272	$6	Bungee jumping	4.80	4.80
2046A A272	$6	Hang gliding	4.80	4.80
2046B A272	$6	River rafting	4.80	4.80

Queen Elizabeth II's Accession to the Throne, 40th Anniv.

Common Design Type

1992, Feb. 6 *Perf. 14*

2047 CD348	10c	multicolored	15	15
2048 CD348	50c	multicolored	40	40
2049 CD348	$1	multicolored	80	80
2050 CD348	$5	multicolored	4.00	4.00

Souvenir Sheets

2051 CD348	$6	Queen at left	4.80	4.80
2052 CD348	$6	Queen at right	4.80	4.80

Spanish Art — A273

Paintings: 10c, The Corpus Christi Procession in Seville, by Manuel Cabral y Aguado, horiz. 35c, The Mancorbo Channel, by Carlos de Haes. 50c, Countess of Vilches, by Federico de Madrazo y Kuntz. 75c, Countess of Santovenia, by Eduardo Rosales Gallina. $1, Queen Maria Isabel de Braganza, by Bernardo Lopez Piquer. $2, $4, The Presentation of Don John of Austria to Charles V (different details), by Gallina. $5, The Testament of Isabella the Catholic, by Eduardo Rosales Gallina, horiz. No. 2061, Meeting of Poets in Antonio Maria Esquivel's Studio, by Antonio Maria Esquivel y Suarez de Urbina. No. 2062, The Horse Corral in the Old Madrid Bullring, by Manuel Castellano, horiz.

1992, Apr. 30 Litho. *Perf. 13*

2053 A273	10c	multicolored	15	15
2054 A273	35c	multicolored	28	28
2055 A273	50c	multicolored	40	40
2056 A273	75c	multicolored	60	60
2057 A273	$1	multicolored	80	80
2058 A273	$2	multicolored	1.60	1.60
2059 A273	$4	multicolored	3.20	3.20
2060 A273	$5	multicolored	4.00	4.00

Size: 120x95mm

Imperf

2061 A273	$6	multicolored	4.80	4.80
2062 A273	$6	multicolored	4.80	4.80
		Nos. 2053-2062 (10)	20.63	20.63

Granada '92.

Discovery of America, 500th Anniv.
A274 A275

1992, May 7 Litho. *Perf. 14*

2063 A274	10c	Green-winged parrot	15	15
2064 A274	25c	Santa Maria	20	20
2065 A274	35c	Columbus	30	30
2066 A274	50c	Hourglass	40	40
2067 A274	75c	Queen Isabella	60	60
2068 A274	$4	Cantino map, 1502	3.20	3.20
		Nos. 2063-2068 (6)	4.85	4.85

Souvenir Sheets

2069 A274	$6	Map, ship, fish	4.80	4.80
2070 A274	$6	Map, arms, Genoa	4.80	4.80

World Columbian Stamp Expo '92, Chicago.

1992 *Perf. 14½*

2071 A275	$1	Coming ashore	80	80
2072 A275	$2	Native, ships	1.60	1.60

Organization of East Caribbean States.

Hummingbirds
A276

1992, May 28

2073 A276	10c	Ruby-throated	15	15
2074 A276	25c	Vervain	20	20
2075 A276	35c	Blue-headed	30	30
2076 A276	50c	Cuban Emerald	40	40
2077 A276	75c	Antillean Mango	60	60
2078 A276	$2	Purple-throated carib	1.60	1.60
2079 A276	$4	Puerto Rican emerald	3.20	3.20
2080 A276	$5	Green-throated carib	4.00	4.00
		Nos. 2073-2080 (8)	10.45	10.45

Souvenir Sheets

2081 A276	$6	Rufous-breasted hermit	4.80	4.80
2082 A276	$6	Antillean crested	4.80	4.80

Genoa '92.

USO, 50th Anniv. — A277

1992 Summer Olympics, Barcelona — A278

1992, June 1 *Perf. 14*

2083 A277	15c	Gracie Fields	15	15
2084 A277	25c	Jack Benny	20	20
2085 A277	35c	Jinx Falkenburg	28	28
2086 A277	50c	Frances Langford	38	38
2087 A277	75c	Joe E. Brown	60	60
2088 A277	$1	Phil Silvers	80	80
2089 A277	$2	Danny Kaye	1.50	1.50
2090 A277	$5	Frank Sinatra	4.00	4.00
		Nos. 2083-2090 (8)	7.91	7.91

Souvenir Sheets

2091 A277	$6	Anna May Wong	4.80	4.80
2092 A277	$6	Bob Hope	4.50	4.50

1992

2093 A278	10c	Badminton	15	15
2094 A278	25c	Women's long jump	20	20
2095 A278	35c	Women's 100-meter dash	28	28
2096 A278	50c	Cycling	40	40
2097 A278	75c	Decathlon (pole vault), horiz.	60	60
2098 A278	$2	Judo, horiz.	1.60	1.60
2099 A278	$4	Women's gymnastics	3.20	3.20
2100 A278	$5	Javelin	4.00	4.00
		Nos. 2093-2100 (8)	10.43	10.43

Souvenir Sheets

2101 A278	$6	Men's floor exercise	4.80	4.80
2102 A278	$6	Men's vault	4.80	4.80

Model Trains
A279

Designs: 10c, The Blue Comet, standard gauge, US, 1933. 35c, Switching locomotive, 2-inch gauge, 1906. 40c, B & O Tunnel locomotive, 2-inch gauge, 1905. 75c, Grand Canyon, standard gauge, US, 1931. $1, Lithographed tin streamliner, O gauge, 1930's. $2, Switching locomotive #237, No. 1 gauge, US, 1911. $4, Parlor car, standard gauge, US, 1928. $5, Locomotive #4687 of Improved President's Special, standard gauge, 1927. No. 2111, Engine #3239, No. 1 gauge, US, 1912. No. 2112, Ives engine #1132, 1921.

1992, Oct. 22 Litho. *Perf. 14*

2103 A279	10c	multicolored	15	15
2104 A279	35c	multicolored	28	28
2105 A279	40c	multicolored	30	30
2106 A279	75c	multicolored	58	58
2107 A279	$1	multicolored	75	75
2108 A279	$2	multicolored	1.50	1.50
2109 A279	$4	multicolored	3.00	3.00
2110 A279	$5	multicolored	3.75	3.75
		Nos. 2103-2110 (8)	10.31	10.31

Souvenir Sheet

Perf. 13

2111 A279	$6	multicolored	4.50	4.50
2112 A279	$6	multicolored	4.50	4.50

Nos. 2111-2112 contains one 51x40mm stamp.

Souvenir Sheet

Guggenheim Museum, NYC — A280

1992, Oct. 28 *Perf. 14*

2113 A280	$6	multicolored	5.25	5.25

Postage Stamp Mega Event '92, NYC.

Christmas
A281

Details or entire paintings: 10c, The Adoration of the Magi, by Fra Filippo Lippi. 15c, Madonna Adoring Child in a Wood, by Fra Filippo Lippi. 25c, Adoration of the Magi, by Botticelli. 35c, The Epiphany-Adoration of the Magi, by Hieronymus Bosch. 50c, Adoration of the Magi, by Giovanni de Paolo. 75c, The Adoration of the Magi, by Gentile da Fabriano. 90c, Adoration of the Magi, by Juan Batista Maino. $1, The Adoration of the Child, by Master of Liesborn. $2, The Adoration of the Kings, by Master of Liesborn. $3, The Adoration of the Three Wise Men, by Pedro Berruguete. $4, The Adoration of the Child, by Filippo Lippi. $5, Adoration of the Child, by Correggio. No. 2126, Adoration of the Magi, by Hans Memling. No. 2127, Adoration of the Magi, by Andrea Mantegna. No. 2128, Adoration of the Shepherds, by De La Tour.

1992, Nov. 16 Litho. *Perf. 13½x14*

2114 A281	10c	multicolored	15	15
2115 A281	15c	multicolored	15	15
2116 A281	25c	multicolored	20	20
2117 A281	35c	multicolored	28	28
2118 A281	50c	multicolored	38	38
2119 A281	75c	multicolored	58	58
2120 A281	90c	multicolored	70	70
2121 A281	$1	multicolored	75	75
2122 A281	$2	multicolored	1.50	1.50
2123 A281	$3	multicolored	2.25	2.25
2124 A281	$4	multicolored	3.00	3.00
2125 A281	$5	multicolored	3.75	3.75
		Nos. 2114-2125 (12)	13.69	13.69

Souvenir Sheet

2126 A281	$6	multicolored	4.50	4.50
2127 A281	$6	multicolored	4.50	4.50
2128 A281	$6	multicolored	4.50	4.50

Regattas of the World — A282

Yachts, races: 15c, Matador, Newport News Regatta. 25c, Awesome, Antigua Regatta. 35c, Mistress Quickly, Bermuda Regatta. 50c, Emeraude, St. Tropez Regatta. $1, Diva G, German Admirals Cup. $2, Lady Be, French Admirals Cup. $4, Midnight Sun, Admirals Cup Regatta. $5, Carat, Sardinia Cup Regatta. No. 2137, 1979 Fastnet Race, horiz. No. 2138, Grenada Regatta, horiz.

1992, Oct. Litho. *Perf. 14*

2129 A282	15c	multicolored	15	15
2130 A282	25c	multicolored	20	20
2131 A282	35c	multicolored	28	28
2132 A282	50c	multicolored	38	38
2133 A282	$1	multicolored	75	75
2134 A282	$2	multicolored	1.50	1.50
2135 A282	$4	multicolored	3.00	3.00
2136 A282	$5	multicolored	3.75	3.75
		Nos. 2129-2136 (8)	10.01	10.01

Souvenir Sheets

2137 A282	$6	multicolored	4.50	4.50
2138 A282	$6	multicolored	4.50	4.50

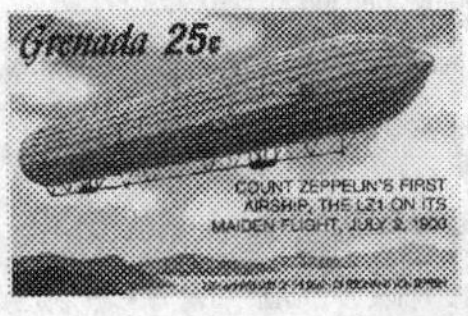

A283

Anniversaries and Events — A284

Designs: 25c, LZ1 on maiden flight, 1900. 50c, Endosat, proposed robot plane. 75c, Konrad Adenauer, factory. $1.50, Golden lion tamarin. No. 2143 Mountain gorilla. No. 2144, WHO emblem and "Heartbeat-the Rhythm of Health." $3, Wolfgang Amadeus Mozart. No. 2146, German flag, map, Adenauer. No. 2147, Voyager 2, Neptune. $5, Count Zeppelin, Graf Zeppelin. $6, Lion's Club emblem, Admiral Richard E. Byrd. No. 2150, Scene from "The Magic Flute." No. 2151, Konrad Adenauer. No. 2152, Earth Summit emblem, northern spotted owl. No. 2153, Count Zeppelin. No. 2154, Satellite rescue, vert.

1992 Litho. *Perf. 14*

2139 A283	25c	multicolored	20	20
2140 A283	50c	multicolored	38	38
2141 A283	75c	multicolored	58	58
2142 A283	$1.50	multicolored	1.15	1.15
2143 A283	$2	multicolored	1.50	1.50
2144 A283	$2	multicolored	1.50	1.50
2145 A284	$3	multicolored	2.25	2.25
2146 A283	$4	multicolored	3.00	3.00
2147 A283	$4	multicolored	3.00	3.00
2148 A283	$5	multicolored	3.75	3.75
2149 A283	$6	multicolored	4.50	4.50
		Nos. 2139-2149 (11)	21.81	21.81

Souvenir Sheets

2150 A284	$6	multicolored	4.50	4.50
2151 A283	$6	multicolored	4.50	4.50
2152 A283	$6	multicolored	4.50	4.50
2153 A283	$6	multicolored	4.50	4.50
2154 A283	$6	multicolored	4.50	4.50

Count Ferdinand von Zeppelin, 75th anniv. of death (#2139, 2148, 2153). Intl. Space Year (#2140, 2147, 2154). Konrad Adenauer, 25th anniv. of death (#2141, 2146, 2151). Earth Summit, Rio de Janeiro (#2142-2143, 2152). Mozart, bicent. of death (in 1991) (#2145, 2150). Lions Intl., 75th anniv. (#2149).

Issue dates: Nos. 2145, 2150, Oct. Nos. 2140-2141, 2144, 2146-2147, 2149, 2151, 2154, Nov. Nos. 2139, 2142-2143, 2148, 2152-2153, Dec.

Grenada Dove
A285

Entertainers
A286

1992

2155 A285	10c	multicolored	15	15

1992, Nov. 19 Litho. *Perf. 14*

Gold record award winners: No. 2156a, Cher. b, Michael Jackson. c, Elvis Presley. d, Dolly Parton. e, Johnny Mathis. f, Madonna. g, Nat King Cole. h, Janis Joplin.

No. 2157a, Frank Sinatra. b, Perry Como.

No. 2158a, Chuck Berry. b, James Brown.

Miniature Sheet

2156 A286	90c	Sheet of 8, #a.-h.	5.50	5.50

Souvenir Sheets

2157 A286	$3	Sheet of 2, #a.-b.	4.50	4.50
2158 A286	$3	Sheet of 2, #a.-b.	4.50	4.50

Care Bears Promote Conservation — A287

Designs: 75c, Bear on uncontaminated beachfront. $2, Bear with parasol, butterfly on flower, vert.

1992, Dec. 15 Litho. *Perf. 14*

2159 A287	75c	multicolored	58	58

Souvenir Sheet

2160 A287	$2	multicolored	1.50	1.50

Dogs
A288

Designs: 10c, Samoyed, St. Basil's Cathedral, Moscow. 15c, Chow chow, Ling Yin Monastery, China. 25c, Boxer, Traitor's Gate, United Kingdom. 90c, Basenji, Yamma Mosque, Niger. $1, Golden Labrador Retriever, Parliament, Ottawa, Canada.

$3, Saint Bernard, Parsenn, Switzerland. $4, Rhodesian ridgeback, Melrose House, South Africa. $5, Afghan, Mazar-i-Sharif, Afghanistan. No. 2169, Alaskan malamute, Alaska. No. 2170, Australian cattle dog, Australia.

1993, Jan. 20 Litho. *Perf. 14*

2161 A288	10c multicolored	15	15
2162 A288	15c multicolored	15	15
2163 A288	25c multicolored	20	20
2164 A288	90c multicolored	68	68
2165 A288	$1 multicolored	75	75
2166 A288	$3 multicolored	2.30	2.30
2167 A288	$4 multicolored	3.00	3.00
2168 A288	$5 multicolored	3.75	3.75
	Nos. 2161-2168 (8)	10.98	10.98

Souvenir Sheet

2169 A288	$6 multicolored	4.50	4.50
2170 A288	$6 multicolored	4.50	4.50

Miniature Sheet

Louvre Museum, Bicent. A289

Paintings by Jean-Antoine Watteau (1684-1721): a, The Faux-Pas. b, A Gentleman. c, Young Lady with Archlute. d, Young Man Dancing. e, Autumn. f, The Judgement of Paris. g-h, Pierrot (diff. details).
No. 2172, The Embarkation for Cythera, horiz.

1993, Mar. 8 Litho. *Perf. 12*

2171 A289	$1 Sheet of 8, #a.-h. + label	6.00	6.00

Souvenir Sheet

Perf. 14½

2172 A289	$6 multicolored	4.50	4.50

No. 2172 contains one 88x55mm stamp.

Moths A290

1993, Apr. 13 Litho. *Perf. 14*

2173 A290	10c Magnificant	15	15
2174 A290	35c Metzl's io	28	28
2175 A290	45c Owl	35	35
2176 A290	75c Pink-spotted hawk	58	58
2177 A290	$1 Faithful beauty	75	75
2178 A290	$2 Green geometrid	1.50	1.50
2179 A290	$4 Gaudy sphinx	3.00	3.00
2180 A290	$5 Black witch	3.75	3.75
	Nos. 2173-2180 (8)	10.36	10.36

Souvenir Sheets

2181 A290	$6 Titan hawk, vert.	4.50	4.50
2182 A290	$6 Avocado, vert.	4.50	4.50

Flowers — A291

Baha'i Shrine, Haifa, Israel — A292

1993, May 17 Litho. *Perf. 14*

2183 A291	10c Heliconia	15	15
2184 A291	35c Pansy	28	28
2185 A291	45c Water lily	35	35
2186 A291	75c Bougainvillea	58	58
2187 A291	$1 Calla lily	75	75
2188 A291	$2 California poppy	1.50	1.50
2189 A291	$4 Red ginger	3.00	3.00
2190 A291	$5 Anthurium	3.75	3.75

Souvenir Sheet

2191 A291	$6 Christmas rose, horiz.	4.50	4.50
2192 A291	$6 Moth orchids, horiz.	4.55	4.55

1993, May Litho. *Perf. 13½x14*

2193 A292	75c multicolored	58	58

Baha'i faith in Grenada, cent.

Miniature Sheet

Coronation of Queen Elizabeth II, 40th Anniv. — A293

Designs: a, 35c, Official coronation photograph. b, 70c, Queen Consort's Ivory Rod, Queen Consort's Scepter. c, $1, Elizabeth accepting scepter during ceremony. $5, Queen, family, 1960s.
$6, Portrait, by Peter George Greenham, 1965.

1993, June 2 *Perf. 13½x14*

2194 A293	Sheet, 2 each #a.-d.	10.50	10.50

Souvenir Sheet

Perf. 14

2195 A293	$6 multicolored	4.50	4.50

No. 2195 contains one 28x42mm stamp.

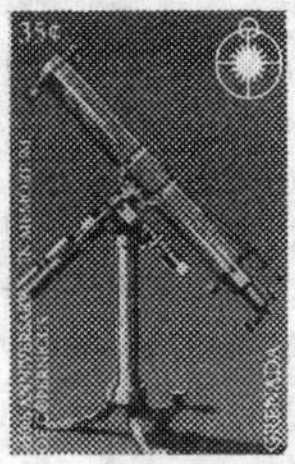

A294

Anniversaries and Events — A295

Designs: 35c, Telescope. 50c, Willy Brandt, Sen. Edward Kennedy, Mrs. Robert Kennedy, 1973. $4, Astronaut standing on moon. No. 2199, Willy Brandt, Kurt Waldheim. No. 2200, Copernicus. $6, Newspaper headline announcing Brandt's resignation.

1993, July 1 Litho. *Perf. 14*

2196 A294	35c multicolored	28	28
2197 A295	50c black & brown	38	38
2198 A294	$4 multicolored	3.00	3.00
2199 A295	$5 black & brown	3.75	3.75

Souvenir Sheets

2200 A294	$5 multicolored	3.75	3.75
2201 A295	$6 brown & black	4.50	4.50

Nicolaus Copernicus, 450th anniv. of death (#2196, 2198, 2200). Willy Brandt, 1st anniv. of death (#2197, 2199, 2201).

Grenada Carnival, 1992 A296

1993, July 1

2202 A296	35c Public Library, vert.	28	28
2203 A296	75c Dancers	58	58

Public Library, cent. (in 1992) (#2202).

Miniature Sheet

Songbirds A297

Designs: No. 2204a, 15c, Red-eyed vireo. b, 25c, Scissor-tailed flycatcher (g). c, 35c, Palmchat. d, 35c, Chaffinch. e, 45c, Yellow wagtail. f, 45c Painted bunting. g, 50c, Short-tailed pygmy flycatcher. h, 65c, Rainbow bunting. i, 75c, Red crossbill. j, 75c, Kauai akialoa. k, $1, Yellow-throated wagtail. l, $4, Barn swallow.
No. 2205, Song thrush. No. 2206, White-crested laughing thrush.

1993, July 13

2204 A297	Sheet of 12, #a.-l.	6.60	6.60

Souvenir Sheets

2205 A297	$6 multicolored	4.50	4.50
2206 A297	$6 multicolored	4.50	4.50

Miniature Sheet

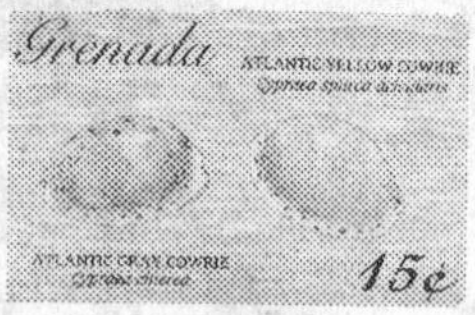

Seashells A298

Designs: No. 2207a, 15c, Atlantic gray cowrie, Atlantic yellow cowrie. b, 15c, Candy stick tellin, sunrise tellin. c, 25c, Common Atlantic vase. d, 35c, Lightning venus, royal comb venus. e, 35c, Crown cone. f, 45c, Reticulated cowrie-helmet. g, 50c, Barbados miter, variegated turret shell. h, 50c, Common egg cockle, Atlantic strawberry cockle. i, 75c, Measled cowrie. j, 75c, Rooster tail conch. k, $1, Lion's paw, Antillean scallop. l, $4, Dog-head triton.
No. 2208, Dyson's keyhole limpet. No. 2209, Virgin nerite, emerald nerite.

1993, July 19 Litho. *Perf. 14*

2207 A298	Sheet of 12, #a.-l.	7.00	7.00

Souvenir Sheets

2208 A298	$6 multicolored	4.50	4.50
2209 A298	$6 multicolored	4.50	4.50

A299

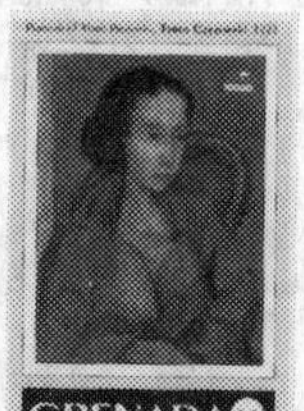

A300

Picasso (1881-1973): 25c, Woman with Loaves, 1906. 90c, Weeping Woman, 1937. $4, Woman Seated in Armchair, 1947. $6, Three Women at the Spring, 1921.

1993, July 1 Litho. *Perf. 14*

2210 A299	25c multicolored	18	18
2211 A299	90c multicolored	70	70
2212 A299	$4 multicolored	3.00	3.00

Souvenir Sheet

2213 A299	$6 multicolored	4.50	4.50

1993, July 1

1994 Winter Olympics, Lillehammer, Norway: 35c, Gaeten Boucher, speedskating gold medalist, 1984. $5, Norbert Schramm, figure skater. $6, Michela Figini, Sigrid Wolf, Karen Percy, Super G medalists, 1988, horiz.

2214 A300	35c multicolored	25	25
2215 A300	$5 multicolored	3.75	3.75

Souvenir Sheet

2216 A300	$6 multicolored	4.50	4.50

Polska '93 — A301

Paintings: $1, Portrait of Marii Prohaska, by Tytus Czyzewski, 1923. $3, Marysia et Burek a Geylan, by S.I. Wirkiewicz, 1920-21. $6, Parting, by Witold Wojtkiewicz, 1908.

1993, July 1 Litho. *Perf. 14*

2217 A301	$1 multicolored	75	75
2218 A301	$3 multicolored	2.25	2.25

Souvenir Sheet

2219 A301	$6 multicolored	4.50	4.50

Taipei '93 — A302

Designs: 35c, Fire-breathing dragon, New Year's Fair, Chongqing. 45c, Stone elephant, Spirit Way to Ming Tomb, Nanjing. $2, Marble peifang, Ming Tombs, Beijing. $4, Stone pillar, Nanjing.
Paintings by Han Meilin: No. 2224a, Ornamental cock. b, Tiger cub. c, Owl. d, Cat. e, Gorillas. f, Leopard.
No. 2225, Orangutan.

1993, Aug. 13 Litho. *Perf. 14*

2220 A302	35c multicolored	25	25
2221 A302	45c multicolored	35	35
2222 A302	$2 multicolored	1.50	1.50
2223 A302	$4 multicolored	3.00	3.00

Miniature Sheet

2224 A302	$1.50 Sheet of 6, #a.-f.	6.75	6.75

Souvenir Sheet

2225 A302	$6 multicolored	4.50	4.50

With Bangkok '93 Emblem

Designs: 35c, Nora Nair, Prasad Phra Thepidon, Wat Phra Kaew. 45c, Stucco deities, Library, Wat Phra Singh. $2, Naga snake, Chiang Mai's Temple. $4, Stucco elephants, Wat Chang Lom.
Thai sculpture: No. 2230a, Horses. b, Wheel of the Law, 7th-8th cent. c, Lanna bronze elephant, 1575. d, Kendi in form of elephant. e, Bronze duck, 14th-15th cent. f, Horseman, 14th-15th cent.
No. 2231, Elephants, horiz.

1993, Aug. 13

2226 A302	35c multicolored	25	25
2227 A302	45c multicolored	35	35
2228 A302	$2 multicolored	1.50	1.50
2229 A302	$4 multicolored	3.00	3.00

Miniature Sheet

2230 A302	$1.50 Sheet of 6, #a.-f.	6.75	6.75

Souvenir Sheet

2231 A302	$6 multicolored	4.50	4.50

With Indopex '93 Emblem

Designs: 35c, Megalithic carving, Sumba Island, Indonesia. 45c, Entrance to Gao Gaja (Elephant Cave), Bali. $2, Loving Mother Bridge, Taroko Gorge Natl. Park. $4, Kala head gateway to Balinese Temple, Northern Bali.
Indonesian sculpture: No. 2236a, Kris holder and Kris, 19th cent. b, Hanuman protecting Sita, I. Dojotan of Mas. c, Sendi of Visnu mounted on Garuda, 19th cent. d, Wahana (mini vehicle for votive fig.), 20th cent. e, Mercurial monkey warrior Hanuman, Rodja of Mas. f, Singa (polychrome lion).
No. 2237, Loris.

1993, Aug. 13 *Perf. 13½x14*

2232 A302	35c multicolored	25	25
2233 A302	45c multicolored	35	35
2234 A302	$2 multicolored	1.50	1.50
2235 A302	$4 multicolored	3.00	3.00

Miniature Sheet

2236 A302 $1.50 Sheet of 6, #a.-f. 1.10 1.10

Souvenir Sheet

2237 A302 $6 multicolored 4.50 4.50

Miniature Sheets

Italian Soccer Assoc. and Genoa Soccer Club, Cent. — A303

Players for Genoa Soccer Club: No. 2238a, Vittorio Sardelli. b, Juan Carlos Verdeal. c, Fosco Becattini. d, Julio Cesar Abadie. e, Luigi Meroni. f, Roberto Pruzzo.

No. 2239a, James K. Spensley. b, Renzo de Vecchi. c, Giovanni de Pra. d, Luigi Burlando. e, Felice Levratto. f, Guglielmo Stabile.

No. 2240, 1991 Genoa team photo, horiz. No. 2241, Genoa team emblem.

1993, Sept. 7 Litho. *Perf. 14*

2238 A303 $3 Sheet of 6, #a.-f. 13.50 13.50
2239 A303 $3 Sheet of 6, #a.-f. 13.50 13.50

Souvenir Sheets

2240 A303 $15 multicolored 11.00 11.00
2241 A303 $15 multicolored 11.00 11.00

No. 2240 contains one 48x35mm stamp. No. 2241 contains one 29x45mm stamp.

1994 World Cup Soccer Championships, US — A304

Designs: 10c, Nikolai Larionov, Russia. 25c, Andrea Carnevale, Italy. 35c, Enzo Scifo, Belgium, Soon-Ho Choi, South Korea. 45c, Gary Lineker, England. $1, Diego Maradona, Argentina. $2, Lothar Mattaeus, Germany. $4, Jan Karas, Poland, Julio Cesar Silva, Brazil. $5, Claudio Caniggia, Argentina.

Souvenir sheets: No. 2250, $6, Wlodzimierz, Poland. No. 2251, $6, Jose Basualdo, Argentina.

1993, Sept. 7 Litho. *Perf. 14*

2242-2251 A304 Set of 10 18.00 18.00

Mickey Mouse, 65th Birthday — A305

Movie clips: 25c, The Band Concert, 1935. 35c, Mickey's Circus, 1936. 50c, Magician Mickey, 1937. 75c, Moose Hunters, 1937. $1, Mickey's Amateurs, 1937. $2, Tugboat Mickey, 1940. $4, Orphan's Benefit, 1941. $5, Mickey's Christmas, 1983.

No. 2260, Mickey's Birthday Party, 1942. No. 2261, Mickey's Trailer, 1938.

1993, Nov. 11 Litho. *Perf. 14x13½*

2252-2259 A305 Set of 8 9.00 9.00

Souvenir Sheets

2260-2261 A395 $6 each 4.50 4.50

Christmas A306

Woodcuts by Durer: 10c, The Nativity. 25c, "The Annunciation." $1, "Adoration of the Magi." $5, "The Virgin Mary in the Sun."

Paintings by Leonardo Da Vinci: 35c, The Litta Madonna. 60c, Madonna and Child with St. Anne and the Infant St. John. 90c, Madonna with the Carnation. $4, The Benois Madonna.

No. 2270, The Holy Family with Three Hares, by Durer. No. 2271, Adoration of the Magi, by Da Vinci.

The 25c actually shows the Adoration of the Magi. The $1 actually shows The Virgin Mary in the Sun. The $5 actually shows The Annunciation.

1993, Nov. 22 Litho. *Perf. 13½x14*

2262-2269 A306 Set of 10 9.00 9.00

Souvenir Sheets

2270-2271 A306 $6 each 4.50 4.50

Hugo Eckener (1868-1954) — A307

Graf Zeppelin over: 35c, Vienna. 75c, Pyramids at Giza. $5, Rio de Janeiro. #2275, Flensburg.

1993, Dec. 21 *Perf. 14*

2272-2274 A307 Set of 3 4.50 4.50

Souvenir Sheet

2275 A307 $6 multicolored 4.50 4.50

Royal Air Force, 75th Anniv. A308

1993, Dec. 21

2276 A308 50c Lysander 38 38
2277 A308 $3 Hawker Typhoon 2.25 2.25

Souvenir Sheet

2278 A308 $6 Hawker Hurricane 4.50 4.50

Automotive Anniversaries — A309

Designs: 35c, 1932 Mercedes Benz 370 S Cabriolet. 45c, 1966 Ford Mustang. $3, 1930 Model A Ford Phaeton. $4, Mercedes Benz 300 SL Gullwing.

No. 2283, 1903 Ford Model A. No. 2284, 1934 Mercedes Benz 290.

1993, Dec. 21 Litho. *Perf. 14*

2279-2282 A309 Set of 4 6.00 6.00

Souvenir Sheets

2283-2284 A309 $6 each 4.50 4.50

1st Benz 4-wheel car, cent. 1st Ford engine, cent.

First Gas Balloon Flight in America, Bicent. A310

Designs: 45c, Lift-off from Philadelphia. $2, Balloon in flight, vert. $6, Blanchard's balloon in flight, diff., vert.

1993, Dec. 21 Litho. *Perf. 14*

2285-2286 A310 Set of 2 2.00 2.00

Souvenir Sheet

2287 A310 $6 multicolored 4.50 4.50

Fine Art — A311

Self-portraits, by Matisse: 15c, 1900. 45c, 1918. $2, 1906. $4, 1900, diff.

Self-portraits, by Rembrandt: 35c, 1629. 50c, 1640. 75c, 1652. $5, 1625-31.

No. 2296, The Painter in His Studio, by Matisse. No. 2297, The Sampling Officials of the Draper's Guild, by Rembrandt, horiz.

1993, Dec. 31 Litho. *Perf. 13½x14*

2288 A311 15c multicolored 15 15
2289 A311 35c multicolored 25 25
2290 A311 45c multicolored 35 35
2291 A311 50c multicolored 38 38
2292 A311 75c multicolored 55 55
2293 A311 $2 multicolored 1.50 1.50
2294 A311 $4 multicolored 3.00 3.00
2295 A311 $5 multicolored 3.75 3.75
Nos. 2288-2295 (8) 9.93 9.93

Souvenir Sheets

2296 A311 $6 multicolored 4.50 4.50

Perf. 14x13½

2297 A311 $6 multicolored 4.50 4.50

Spice Islands Billfish Tournament, 25th Anniv. — A312

Designs: 15c, Blue marlin. 25c, Sailfish with angler. 35c, Yellowfin tuna with angler. 50c, White marlin with angler. 75c, Catching a sailfish.

1993, Dec. Litho. *Perf. 14*

2302-2306 A312 Set of 5 1.50 1.50

A313

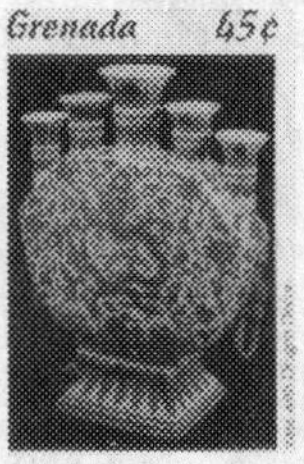

Hong Kong '94 — A314

Stamps, painting, Hong Kong Post Office-1846, by M. Bruce: No. 2307, Hong Kong #263, left detail. No. 2308, Right detail, #1597.

Porcelain ware, Qing Dynasty: No. 2309a, Vase with dragon decor. b, Hat stand. c, Gourd-shaped vase. d, Rotating vase with openwork. e, Candlestick with dogs. f, Hat stand, diff.

1994, Feb. 18 Litho. *Perf. 14*

2307 A313 40c multicolored 30 30
2308 A313 40c multicolored 30 30
a. Pair, #2307-2308 60 60

Miniature Sheet

2309 A314 45c Sheet of 6, #a.-f. 2.00 2.00

Nos. 2307-2308 issued in sheets of 5 pairs. No. 2308a is a continuous design.

New Year 1994 (Year of the Dog) (#2309e).

Independence, 10th Anniv. — A315

1994, Feb. 8 Litho. *Perf. 14*

2310 A315 35c Natl. flag, boat 25 25

Souvenir Sheet

2311 A315 $6 Map of Granada 4.50 4.50

Miniature Sheets

Dinosaurs — A316

Jurassic: No. 2312a, Germanodactylus. b, Dimorphodon. c, Ramphorhynchus. d, Apatosaurus (h). e, Pterodactylus. f, Stegosaurus. g, Brachiosaurus. h, Allosaurus (l). i, Plesiosaurus. j, Ceratosaurus. k, Compsognathus. l, Elaphosaurus.

Cretaceous: No. 2313a, Quetzalcoatlus. b, Pteranodon ingens (c). c, Tropeognathus. d, Phobetor. e, Alamosaurus (i). f, Triceratops (e). g, Tyrannosaurus rex (h). h, Tyrannosaurus rex (up close) (l). i, Lambeosaurus. j, Spinosaurus. k, Parasaurolophus (l). l, Hadrosaurus.

No. 2314, Plateosaurus, vert. No. 2315, Pteranodon ingens.

1994, Apr. 13

2312 A316 75c Sheet of 12, #a.-l. 6.75 6.75
2313 A316 75c Sheet of 12, #a.-l. 6.75 6.75

Souvenir Sheets

2314 A316 $6 multicolored 4.50 4.50
2315 A316 $6 multicolored 4.50 4.50

Mushrooms — A317

Designs: 35c, Hygrocybe acutoconica. 45c, Leucopaxillus gracillimus. 50c, Leptonia caeruleocapitata. 75c, Leucoprinus birnbaumii. $1, Marasmius atrorubens. $2, Boletellus cubensis. $4, Chlorophyllum molybdites. $5, Psilocybe cubensis.
No. 2324, Mycena pura. No. 2325, Pyrrhoglossum lilaceipes.

1994, Apr. 6

2316	A317	35c multicolored	25	25
2317	A317	45c multicolored	35	35
2318	A317	50c multicolored	38	38
2319	A317	75c multicolored	55	55
2320	A317	$1 multicolored	75	75
2321	A317	$2 multicolored	1.50	1.50
2322	A317	$4 multicolored	3.00	3.00
2323	A317	$5 multicolored	3.75	3.75
		Nos. 2316-2323 (8)	10.53	10.53

Souvenir Sheets

2324	A317	$6 multicolored	4.50	4.50
2325	A317	$6 multicolored	4.50	4.50

D-Day, 50th Anniv. A318

Designs: 40c, Sherman Dual-Drive swimming tanks. $2, Churchill "Ark" in operation. $3, Churchill "Bobbin" lays path over soft ground.
$6, Churchill "Avre."

1994, Aug. 4 Litho. *Perf. 14*

2326-2328	A318	Set of 3	4.00	4.00

Souvenir Sheet

2329	A318	$6 multicolored	4.50	4.50

Miniature Sheet of 6

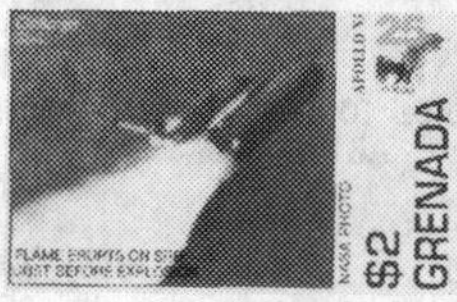

First Manned Moon Landing, 25th Anniv. A319

Tribute to crew of space shuttle Challenger: No. 2330a, Flame erupting before explosion. b, Judith A. Resnick. c, Aircraft flyover in "Missing Man" formation. d, Dick Scobee. e, Challenger 51-L patch. f, Michael J. Smith.
$6, Crew of mission 51-L.

1994, Aug. 4

2330	A319	$2 #a.-f.	5.00	5.00

Souvenir Sheet

2331	A319	$6 multicolored	4.50	4.50

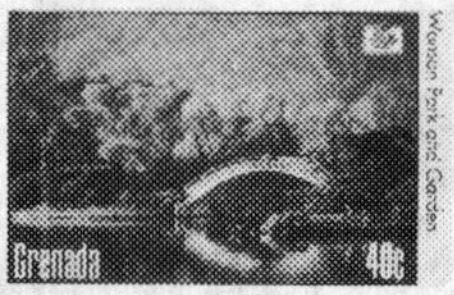

A320

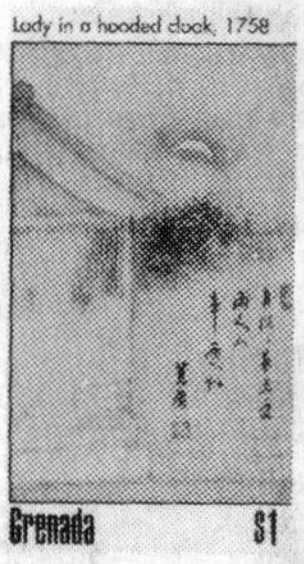

PHILAKOREA '94 — A321

Designs: 40c, Wonson Park & Garden. $1, Port of Pusan. $4, National Theatre, Seoul.
Paintings by Sin Yunbok, Late Choson Dynasty: No. 2335a-2335b, Lady in a Hooded Cloak. c-d, Kiaseng House. e-f, Amorous Youth on a Picnic. g-h, Chasing a Cat.
$6, Roof Tiling, by Kim Hongdo, vert.

1994, Aug. 4 *Perf. 14, 13½ (#2335)*

2332-2334	A320	Set of 3	4.00	4.00

Miniature Sheet of 8

2335	A321	$1 #a.-h.	6.00	6.00

Souvenir Sheet

2336	A320	$6 multicolored	4.50	4.50

A322

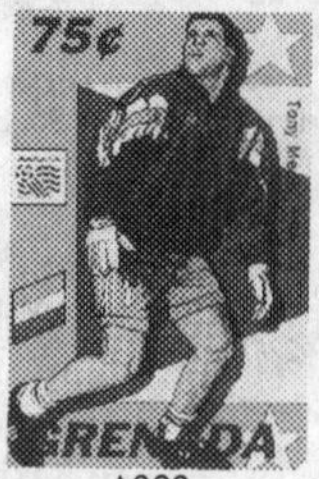

A323

Orchids: 15c, Brassavola cuculatta. 25c, Comparettia falcata. 45c, Epidendrum ciliare. 75c, Epidendrum cochleatum. $1, Ionopsis utriculariodes. $2, Oncidium ceboletta. $4, Oncidium luridium. $5, Rodriquezia secunda.
No. 2345, Ionopis utriculariodes, diff. No. 2346, Onicium luridum, diff.

1994, Aug. 7 *Perf. 14*

2337-2344	A322	Set of 8	10.00	10.00

Souvenir Sheets

2345-2346	A322	$6 each	4.50	4.50

1994, Aug. 11 *Perf. 14*

1994 World Cup Soccer Championships, US: No. 2347a, Tony Meola, US. b, Steve Mark, Grenada. c, Gianluigi Lentini, Italy. d, Belloumi, Algeria. e, Nunoz, Spain. f, Lothar Matthaus, Germany.
No. 2348, Steve Mark, diff. No. 2349, Poster from first World Cup Championships, Uruguay, 1930.

Miniature Sheet of 6

2347	A323	75c #a.-f.	3.50	3.50

Souvenir Sheet

2348-2349	A323	$6 each	4.50	4.50

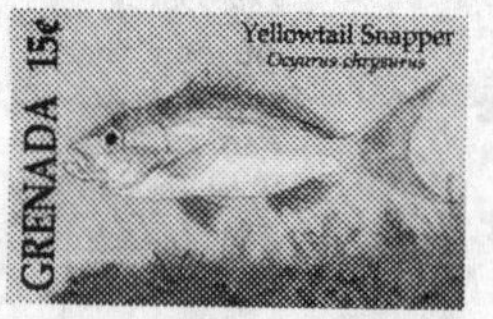

Fish A324

Designs: 15c, Yellowtail snapper. 20c, Blue tang. 25c, Porkfish, vert. 75c, Foureye butterflyfish. $1, Longsnout seahorse, vert. $2, Spotted moray eel, vert. $4, Fairy basslet. $5, Queen triggerfish, vert. #2358, Queen angelfish. #2359, Squirrelfish.

1994, Sept. 1

2350-2357	A324	Set of 8	10.00	10.00

Souvenir Sheets

2358-2359	A324	$6 each	4.50	4.50

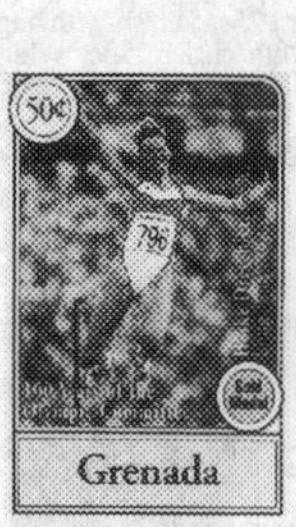

Intl. Olympic Committee, Cent.
A325 A326

Designs: 50c, Heike Dreschler, Germany, long jump, 1992. $1.50, Nadia Comaneci, Romania, Gymnastics, 1976, 1980.
$6, Dan Jansen, US, 1000-meters long track speed skating, 1994.

1994

2360	A325	50c multicolored	38	38
2361	A325	$1.50 multicolored	1.10	1.10

Souvenir Sheet

2362	A326	$6 multicolored	4.50	4.50

1994, Year of the Dog A327

Scenes from Disney's Society Dog Show: 2c, Mickey bathing Pluto. 3c, Using atomizer. 4c, Having tail "set." 5c, Putting on mascara. 10c, Having nails done. 15c, Mickey using flea powder on Pluto. 20c, On judge's stand. $4, Judge looking at Pluto. $5, Pluto in chair with first prize.
No. 2372, Pluto wearing "13," first prize ribbon. No. 2373, Little dog beside judge. No. 2374, Pluto with first prize ribbon.

1994, Sept. 22 Litho. *Perf. 14x13½*

2363-2371	A327	Set of 9	7.25	7.25

Souvenir Sheets

2372-2374	A327	$6 each	4.50	4.50

Butterflies — A328

1994, Sept. 28 *Perf. 14*

2375	A328	10c Red anartia	15	15
2376	A328	15c Ruddy daggerwing	15	15
2377	A328	25c Fiery skipper	18	18
2378	A328	35c Caribbean buckeye	28	28
2379	A328	45c Giant hairstreak	32	32
2380	A328	50c Zebra longwing	38	38
2381	A328	75c Diadem	55	55
2382	A328	$1 Blue night	75	75
2383	A328	$2 Orion	1.50	1.50
2384	A328	$3 Orange-barred sulphur	2.25	2.25
2385	A328	$4 Long-tail skipper	3.00	3.00
2386	A328	$5 Polydamas swallowtail	3.75	3.75
		Nos. 2375-2386 (12)	13.26	13.26

Intl. Year of the Family A329

1994

2387	A329	$1 multicolored	75	75

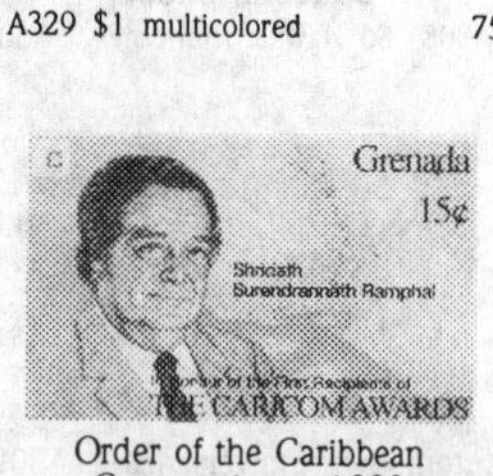

Order of the Caribbean Community — A330

First award recipients: 15c, Sir Shridath Ramphal, statesman, Guyana. 65c, William Demas, economist, Trinidad & Tobago. $2, Derek Walcott, writer, St. Lucia.

1994

2388-2390	A330	Set of 3	2.25	2.25

SEMI-POSTAL STAMPS

Catalogue values for unused stamps in this section are for Never Hinged items.

ESPANA '82 World Cup Soccer SP1

Designs: Players and Flags of Winning Countries.

Unwmk.

1981, Nov. 30 Litho. *Perf. 14*

B1	SP1	25c + 10c West Germany, 1974	35	35
B2	SP1	40c + 20c Argentina, 1978	60	60
B3	SP1	50c + 25c Brazil, 1970	75	75
B4	SP1	$1 + 50c Grt. Britain, 1966	1.50	1.50

Souvenir Sheet

B5	SP1	$5 + 50c World Cup, ESPANA '82	3.75	3.75

Nos. B1-B4 each issued in sheets of 12 with sheet background showing soccer ball.

1988 Seoul Olympics — SP2

1986, Dec. 1 Litho. *Perf. 15*

B6	SP2	10c + 5c Pole vault	15	15
B7	SP2	50c + 20c Balance beam	30	30
B8	SP2	70c + 30c Shot put	40	40
B9	SP2	$2 + $1 High jump	1.20	1.20

Souvenir Sheet

B10	SP2	$3 + $1 Swimming	1.75	1.75

Surtax for natl. Olympic team.

World Philatelic Programs SP3

Halley's Comet or Stamp Collecting emblem and: No. B11, Halley's initial work on nebulae, 1676. No. B12, Experiments at sea (tall ship, manned capsule). No. B13, Halley observes complete lunar cycle, 1720-1738. No. B14, Halley publishes Newton's Principia, 1687. No. B15, Halley charts the southern skies, 1676.

1989, Apr. 25 Litho. *Perf. 14*

B11	SP3	25c +5c multi	22	22
B12	SP3	75c +5c multi	60	60
B13	SP3	90c +5c multi	72	72
B14	SP3	$2 +5c multi	1.55	1.55

Size: 111x78mm

Imperf

B15	SP3	$5 +5c multi	3.80	3.80

AIR POST STAMPS

Catalogue values for unused stamps in this section are for Never Hinged items.

Nos. 428-429 Surcharged with New Value, Olympic Rings, "Air Mail" and: "WINTER OLYMPICS / FEB. 3-13, 1972 / SAPPORO, JAPAN"

Perf. 13½x14

1972, Feb. 3 Litho. Unwmk.

C1	A66	35c on ½c multi	40	40
C2	A66	50c on 1c multi	60	60

11th Winter Olympic Games, Sapporo, Japan, Feb. 3-13.

Nos. 294-300, 302A, 303-309 Overprinted Type "a" or Surcharged Type "b"

AIR MAIL

AIR MAIL

30c

a b

Perfs. as Before

1972, May 2 Photo.; Litho.

C3	A45	5c violet & multi	15	15
C4	A45	8c multicolored	15	15
C5	A45	10c orange & multi	15	15
C6	A45	15c gray & multi	16	16
C7	A45	25c multicolored	32	32
C8	A45	30c on 1c multi	35	35
C9	A45	35c multicolored	40	40
C10	A45	40c on 2c multi	45	45
C11	A45	45c on 3c multi	48	48
C12	A45	50c multicolored	55	55
C13	A45	60c on 5c multi	70	70
C14	A45	70c on 6c multi	80	80
C15	A45	$1 multicolored	1.10	1.10
C16	A45	$1.35 on 8c multi	1.60	1.60
C17	A45	$2 multicolored	2.25	2.25
C18	A45	$3 multicolored	3.25	3.25
C19	A45	$5 multicolored	5.50	5.50
		Nos. C3-C19 (17)	18.36	18.36

"AIR MAIL" reading down on 5c, 15c, 25c, 35c, 60c and $5.

Olympic Type of Regular Issue

Olympic Rings and: 25c, 60c, $1, Boxing. 70c, Equestrian (not inscribed air mail).

1972, Sept. 8 Litho. *Perf. 14*

C20	A69	25c blue & multi	52	52
C21	A69	$1 green & multi	85	85

Souvenir Sheet

C22	Sheet of 2	2.25	2.25
a.	A69 60c blue & multi	85	85
b.	A69 70c deep yellow & multi	1.00	1.00

Nos. 409-412 Overprinted Vertically, Reading Up "AIR MAIL"

1972, Oct. Litho. *Perf. 11*

C23	A62	5c multicolored	15	15
C24	A62	35c multicolored	50	50
C25	A62	50c multicolored	85	85
C26	A62	75c multicolored	1.50	1.50

Boy Scout Type of Regular Issue

Designs: 25c, Scout saluting. 35c, Two Scouts knotting ropes.

1972, Nov. *Perf. 14*

C27	A70	25c dp blue & multi	45	45
C28	A70	35c brn org & multi	65	65

John Hancock — AP1

Designs: 50c, Benjamin Franklin. 75c, John Adams. $1, Marquis de Lafayette.

1975, May 6 Litho. *Perf. 14½, 13*

C29	AP1	40c multicolored	55	*15*
C30	AP1	50c multicolored	65	*20*
C31	AP1	75c multicolored	1.00	*25*
C32	AP1	$1 multicolored	1.50	*30*

American Revolution Bicentennial.

Nos. C29-C32 issued in sheets of 40. Each denomination was also printed in sheets of 5 plus label, perf. 13.

POSTAGE DUE STAMPS

D1

D2

1892 Typo. Wmk. 2 *Perf. 14*

J1	D1	1p black	22.50	1.90
J2	D1	2p black	45.00	2.50
J3	D1	3p black	55.00	3.00

Black Surcharge

J4	D2	1p on 6p red lilac	50.00	2.50
a.		Tete beche pair	150.00	
b.		Double surcharge		50.00
c.		Same as "b," tete beche pair		
J5	D2	1p on 8p bister	250.00	6.75
a.		Tete beche pair	900.00	
J6	D2	2p on 6p red lilac	80.00	5.00
a.		Tete beche pair	275.00	
J7	D2	2p on 8p bister	500.00	12.00
a.		Tete beche pair	1,500.	

Nos. J4-J7 were printed with alternate horizontal rows inverted.

1906-11 Wmk. 3

J8	D1	1p black ('11)	1.50	1.50
J9	D1	2p black	3.00	2.50
J10	D1	3p black	6.00	4.00

D3

1921-22 Wmk. 4

J11	D3	1p black	45	*90*
J12	D3	1½p black	2.00	*4.00*
J13	D3	2p black	1.40	*2.75*
J14	D3	3p black	1.50	*3.00*

Issued: 1½p, Dec. 15, 1922, others, Dec. 1921.

Catalogue values for unused stamps in this section, from this point to the end of the section, are for Never Hinged items.

1952, Mar. 1

J15	D3	2c black	30	*3.00*
a.		Wmk. 4a (error)	25.00	
J16	D3	4c black	30	*3.00*
a.		Wmk. 4a (error)	25.00	
J17	D3	6c black	40	*5.00*
a.		Wmk. 4a (error)	42.50	
J18	D3	8c black	30	*5.00*
a.		Wmk. 4a (error)	50.00	

WAR TAX STAMPS

Nos. 80a, 80 Overprinted WAR TAX

1916 Wmk. 3 *Perf. 14*

MR1	A21	1p carmine	1.25	1.50
a.		1p scarlet	3.00	3.00
b.		Double overprint	225.00	
c.		Inverted overprint	225.00	

No. 80 Overprinted WAR TAX

MR2	A21	1p scarlet	15	15

OFFICIAL STAMPS

Catalogue values for unused stamps in this section are for Never Hinged items.

Nos. 1006-1018, 1020, 1051-1053 Overprinted: "P.R.G."

1982, July 15 Litho. *Perf. 14, 15*

O1	A141	5c multicolored	15	15
O2	A141	6c multicolored	15	15
O3	A141	10c multicolored	15	15
O4	A141	12c multicolored	15	15
O5	A141	15c multicolored	15	15
O6	A141	20c multicolored	16	16
O7	A141	25c multicolored	20	20
O8	A141	30c multicolored	25	25
O9	A141	40c multicolored	32	32
O10	A141	50c multicolored	40	40
O11	CD331	50c multicolored	40	40
O12	A141	90c multicolored	75	75
O13	A141	$1 multicolored	80	80
O14	CD331	$2 multicolored	1.60	1.60
O15	A141	$3 multicolored	2.50	2.50
O16	CD331	$4 multicolored	3.25	3.25
O17	A141	$10 multicolored	8.00	8.00
		Nos. O1-O17 (17)	19.38	19.38

PRG stands for People's Revolutionary Government.

GRENADA GRENADINES

LOCATION — North of Grenada
GOVT. — Part of Grenada
CAPITAL — None

Main islands are Carriacou and Ronde.

Catalogue values for all unused stamps in this country are for Never Hinged items.

All stamps are a type of Grenada unless otherwise noted or illustrated. Nos. 15-58 have the additional inscription Grenadines.

Grenada Nos. 516-517a Overprinted GRENADINES

Perf. 13½x14

1973, Dec. 23 Litho. Wmk. 314

1	A77	25c dp orange & multi	22	22
2	A77	$2 green & multi	1.75	1.75
a.		Souvenir sheet of 2 (75c, $1)	2.40	2.40

Grenada Nos. 294-297, 299-301, 303, 306-309 Overprinted GRENADINES

Perf. 14x14½, 14½x14

1974, May 29 Photo. Unwmk.

Size: 25x44mm

3	A45	1c multicolored	15	15
4	A45	2c multicolored	15	15
5	A45	3c multicolored	15	15
6	A45	5c multicolored	15	15
7	A45	8c multicolored	15	15
8	A45	10c multicolored	15	15
9	A45	12c multicolored	16	16
10	A45	25c multicolored	35	35

Size: 25x47mm

11	A45	$1 multicolored	1.40	1.40
12	A45	$2 multicolored	2.75	2.75
13	A45	$3 multicolored	4.25	4.25
14	A45	$5 multicolored	7.00	7.00
		Nos. 3-14 (12)	16.81	16.81

World Cup Soccer Type

Designs: Soccer matches and flags. ½c, West Germany-Chile. 1c, East Germany-Australia. 2c, Yugoslavia-Brazil. 10c, Scotland-Zaire. 25c, Netherlands-Uruguay. 50c, Sweden-Bulgaria. 75c, Italy-Haiti. $1, Poland-Argentina. $2, Flags of participating nations.

1974, Sept. 17 Litho. *Perf. 14½*

15	A81	½c multicolored	15	15
16	A81	1c multicolored	15	15
17	A81	2c multicolored	15	15
18	A81	10c multicolored	15	15
19	A81	25c multicolored	25	25
20	A81	50c multicolored	52	52
21	A81	75c multicolored	75	75
22	A81	$1 multicolored	1.00	1.00
		Set value	2.65	2.65

Souvenir Sheet

23	A81	$2 multicolored	2.00	2.00

UPU Centenary Type

UPU Emblem and: 8c, Mailboat *Caesar,* 1839, helicopter. 25c, German messenger, 1540, satellite. 35c, Biplanes, zeppelin, jet. No. 27, US Mail train, 19th cent., Concorde. No. 28a, Bellman, 18th cent., radar. $2, German postman, 18th cent., mail train, 1980's.

1974, Oct. 8 *Perf. 14½*

24	A82	8c multicolored	15	15
25	A82	25c multicolored	20	20
26	A82	35c multicolored	30	30
27	A82	$1 multicolored	85	85

Souvenir Sheet

Perf. 13

28	Sheet of 2	2.50	2.50
a.	A82 $1 multicolored	85	85
b.	A82 $2 multicolored	1.65	1.65

Churchill Type

Design: $2, Churchill, different portrait.

1974, Nov. 11 *Perf. 13½*

29	A83	35c multicolored	35	35
30	A83	$2 multicolored	2.00	2.00

Souvenir Sheet

31	Sheet of 2	1.90	1.90
a.	A82 75c like 35c	80	80
b.	A82 $1 like $2	1.10	1.10

Christmas Type

Paintings of the Virgin and Child.

1974, Nov. 27 *Perf. 14½*

32	A84	½c Botticelli	15	15
33	A84	1c Niccolo di Pietro	15	15
34	A84	2c Van der Weyden	15	15
35	A84	3c Bastiani	15	15
36	A84	10c Giovanni	15	15
37	A84	25c Van der Weyden, diff.	40	40
38	A84	50c Botticelli	80	80
39	A84	$1 Mantegna	1.50	1.50
		Set value	3.00	3.00

Souvenir Sheet

Perf. 13½

40	A84	$2 Niccolo di Pietro	3.00	3.00

Big Game Fish Type

1975, Feb. 17 *Perf. 14½*

41	A86	½c Sailfish	15	15
42	A86	1c Blue marlin	15	15
43	A86	2c White marlin	15	15
44	A86	10c Yellowfin tuna	15	15
45	A86	25c Wahoo	25	25
46	A86	50c Dolphin	48	48
47	A86	70c Grouper	65	65
48	A86	$1 Great barracuda	95	95
		Set value	2.50	2.50

Souvenir Sheet

Perf. 13

49	A86	$2 Mako shark	1.90	1.90

Flowers of Grenada Type

1975, Mar. 11 *Perf. 14½*

50	A87	½c Grandilla barbadine	15	15
51	A87	1c Bleeding heart	15	15
52	A87	2c Poinsettia	15	15
53	A87	3c Cocoa	15	15
54	A87	10c Gladioli	15	15
55	A87	25c Red head-yellow head	28	28
56	A87	50c Plumbago	55	55
57	A87	$1 Orange blossoms	1.10	1.10
		Set value	2.15	2.15

Souvenir Sheet

Perf. 13½

58	A87	$2 Barbados gooseberry	2.00	2.00

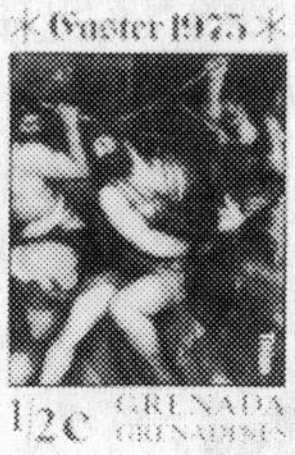

Christ Crowned with Thorns, by Titian — G1

Easter paintings of the Crucifixion by various artists.

1975, June 24 *Perf. 14½*

59	G1	½c shown	15	15
60	G1	1c Giotto	15	15
61	G1	2c Tintoretto	15	15
62	G1	3c Cranach	15	15
63	G1	35c Caravaggio	20	20
64	G1	75c Tiepolo	40	40
65	G1	$2 Velasquez	1.10	1.10
		Set value	1.75	1.75

Souvenir Sheet

Perf. 13½

66	G1	$1	Titian, diff.	1.50	1.50

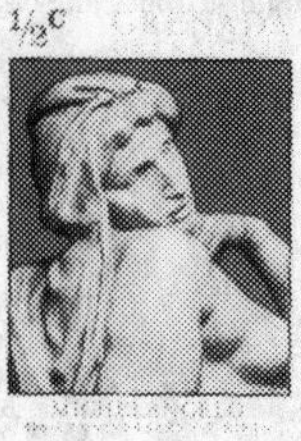

Works by Michelangelo (1475-1564) — G2

Butterflies — G3

Designs: ½c, Dawn (sculpture, detail from Medici tomb). 1c, Delphic Sibyl. 2c, Giuliano de Medici (sculpture). 40c, The Creation. 50c, Lorenzo de Medici (sculpture). 75c, Persian Sibyl. $1, The Prophet Jeremiah. $2, Head of Christ (sculpture).

1975, July 16 *Perf. 14½*

67	G2	½c	violet & multi	15	15
68	G2	1c	multicolored	15	15
69	G2	2c	green & multi	15	15
70	G2	40c	multicolored	40	40
71	G2	50c	brt red & multi	50	50
72	G2	75c	multicolored	75	75
73	G2	$2	brt blue & multi	2.00	2.00
			Nos. 67-73 (7)	4.10	4.10

Souvenir Sheet

Perf. 13½

74	G2	$1	multicolored	2.00	2.00

1975, Aug. 12 *Perf. 15*

75	G3	½c	Emperor	15	15
76	G3	1c	Queen	15	15
77	G3	2c	Tiger pierid	15	15
78	G3	35c	Cracker	60	60
79	G3	45c	Scarlet bamboo page	80	80
80	G3	75c	Apricot	1.40	1.40
81	G3	$2	Purple king shoemaker	3.50	3.50
			Nos. 75-81 (7)	6.75	6.75

Souvenir Sheet

Perf. 13½

82	G3	$1	Bamboo page	2.00	2.00

Jamboree Scenes and Badges G4

Nordjamb 75 Emblem and: ½c, Progress badge. 1c, Boating badge. 2c, Coxswain badge. 35c. Interpreter badge. 45c, Ambulance badge. 75c, Chief scout's award. $1, Venture award. $2, Queen's scout award.

1975, Aug. 22 *Perf. 15*

83	G4	½c	lemon yel & multi	15	15
84	G4	1c	vio blue & multi	15	15
85	G4	2c	green & multi	15	15
86	G4	35c	dull vio & multi	32	32
87	G4	45c	org brown & multi	40	40
88	G4	75c	brown & multi	70	70
89	G4	$2	green & multi	1.90	1.90
			Nos. 83-89 (7)	3.77	3.77

Souvenir Sheet

Perf. 13½

90	G4	$1	dull vio & multi	1.25	1.25

Nordjamb 75, 14th Boy Scout World Jamboree, Lillehammer, Norway, July 29-Aug. 7.

Surrender of Lord Cornwallis G5

Designs: 1c, Minuteman. 2c, Paul Revere's Ride. 3c, Battle of Bunker Hill. 5c, *Spirit of '76.* 45c, Backwoodsman. 75c, Boston Tea Party. No. 98, Naval engagement. No. 99, George Washington. No. 100, White House, flags.

1975, Sept. 30 *Perf. 14*

Size: 39x25mm

91	G5	½c	multicolored	15	15
92	G5	1c	multicolored	15	15
93	G5	2c	multicolored	15	15
94	G5	3c	multicolored	15	15
95	G5	5c	multicolored	15	15
96	G5	45c	multicolored	45	45
97	G5	75c	multicolored	75	75
98	G5	$2	multicolored	2.00	2.00

Size: 59x39mm

Perf. 11

99	G5	$2	multicolored, vert.	2.25	2.25
a.			Souvenir sheet of 1, imperf.	2.50	2.50
100	G4	$2	multicolored	2.25	2.25
a.			Souvenir sheet of 1, imperf.	2.50	2.50
			Nos. 91-100 (10)	8.45	8.45

American Revolution Bicentennial.

Nos. 99a, 100a have simulated perfs.

Fencing G6

1975, Oct. 27 *Perf. 15*

101	G6	½c	shown	15	15
102	G6	1c	Hurdling	15	15
103	G6	2c	Pole vault	15	15
104	G6	35c	Weightlifting	25	25
105	G6	45c	Javelin	32	32
106	G6	75c	Discus	52	52
107	G6	$2	Diving	1.40	1.40
			Set value	2.60	2.60

Souvenir Sheet

108	G6	$1	Sprinter	1.00	1.00

Pan American Games, Mexico City, Oct. 12-26, 1975.

Type of 1975

Designs: ½c, Cruising Yachts, Point Saline. 1c, Yacht Club race, St. George's. 2c, Careenage Taxi. 3c, Working boats. 5c, Deep water dock, St. George's. 6c, Cocoa beans drying. 8c, Nutmegs. 10c, Rum distillery, River Antoine Estate. 12c, Cocoa tree. 15c, Landing catch at Fontenoy. 20c, Parliament building, St. George's. 25c, Fort George cannons. 35c, Pearls airport. 50c, General Post Office. 75c, Caribs Leap, Sauteurs Bay. $1, Careenage, St. George's. $2, St. George's harbor at night. $3, Grand Anse beach. $5, Canoe and Black Bays from Point Saline lighthouse. $10, Sugar Loaf Island from Levera beach.

1975-76 *Perf. 14½*

Size: 38x25mm

109	A85	½c	multicolored	15	15
110	A85	1c	multicolored	15	15
111	A85	2c	multicolored	15	15
112	A85	3c	multicolored	15	15
113	A85	5c	multicolored	15	15
114	A85	6c	multicolored	15	15
115	A85	8c	multicolored	15	15
116	A85	10c	multicolored	15	15
117	A85	12c	multicolored	15	15
118	A85	15c	multicolored	15	15
119	A85	20c	multicolored	20	20
120	A85	25c	multicolored	25	25
121	A85	35c	multicolored	25	25
122	A85	50c	multicolored	35	35

Perf. 13½x14

Size: 45x28mm

123	A85	75c	multicolored	75	75
124	A85	$1	multicolored	1.00	1.00
125	A85	$2	multicolored	2.00	2.00
126	A85	$3	multicolored	3.00	3.00
127	A85	$5	multicolored	5.00	5.00
128	A85	$10	multicolored	10.00	10.00
			Nos. 109-128 (20)	24.30	24.30

Issue dates: Nos. 109-127, Nov. 5, 1975. No. 128, Jan. 1, 1976.

For overprints see Nos. 360-372.

Madonna and Child by Durer — G8

Christmas: Paintings showing Madonna and Child by various artists.

1975, Dec. 17 *Perf. 14*

129	G8	½c	shown	15	15
130	G8	1c	Durer, diff.	15	15
131	G8	2c	Correggio	15	15
132	G8	40c	Botticelli	22	22
133	G8	50c	Niccolo da Cremona	28	28
134	G8	75c	Correggio, diff.	40	40
135	G8	$2	Correggio, diff.	1.10	1.10
			Set value	2.05	2.05

Souvenir Sheet

136	G8	$1	Bellini	1.50	1.50

Sea Shells — G9

1976, Jan. 13

137	G9	½c	Bleeding Tooth	15	15
138	G9	1c	Wedge clam	15	15
139	G9	2c	Hawk wing conch	15	15
140	G9	3c	Distorsio clathrata	15	15
141	G9	25c	Scotch bonnet	55	55
142	G9	50c	King helmet	1.10	1.10
143	G9	75c	Queen conch	1.65	1.65
			Set value	3.40	3.40

Souvenir Sheet

144	G9	$2	Atlantic triton	3.00	3.00

Lignum Vitae G10

Designs: 1c, Cocoa thrush. 2c, Tarantula. 35c, Hooded tanager. 50c, Nyctaginaceae. 75c, Grenada dove. $1, Marine toad. $2, Blue-hooded euphonia.

1976, Feb. 4

145	G10	½c	multicolored	15	15
146	G10	1c	multicolored	15	15
147	G10	2c	multicolored	15	15
148	G10	35c	multicolored	70	70
149	G10	50c	multicolored	1.00	1.00
150	G10	75c	multicolored	1.50	1.50
151	G10	$1	multicolored	2.00	2.00
			Nos. 145-151 (7)	5.65	5.65

Souvenir Sheet

152	G10	$2	multicolored	3.75	3.75

Hooked Sailfish G11

Designs: 1c, Careened schooner, Carriacou. 2c, Annual regatta. 18c, Boat building. 22c, Workboat race. 75c, Cruising off Petit Martinique. $1, Water skiing. $2, Yacht racing.

1976, Feb. 17

153	G11	½c	multicolored	15	15
154	G11	1c	multicolored	15	15
155	G11	2c	multicolored	15	15
156	G11	18c	multicolored	15	15
157	G11	22c	multicolored	20	20
158	G11	75c	multicolored	65	65
159	G11	$1	multicolored	90	90
			Set value	1.95	1.95

Souvenir Sheet

160	G11	$2	multicolored	1.90	1.90

Making a Camp Fire G12

50th anniv. of Girl Guides of Grenada: 1c, First aid. 2c, Nature study. 50c, Cooking. $1, Drawing. $2, Playing guitar.

1976, Mar. 17

161	G12	½c	multicolored	15	15
162	G12	1c	multicolored	15	15
163	G12	2c	multicolored	15	15
164	G12	50c	multicolored	60	60
165	G12	$1	multicolored	1.25	1.25
			Set value	1.95	1.95

Souvenir Sheet

166	G12	$2	multicolored	1.90	1.90

Christ Mocked by Bosch — G13

Easter Paintings: 1c, Christ Crucified by Messina. 2c, Adoration by Durer. 3c, Lamentation of Christ by Durer. 35c, The Entombment by Van Der Weyden. $2, Blood of the Redeemer by Bellini. $3, The Deposition by Raphael.

1976, Apr. 28

167	G13	½c	multicolored	15	15
168	G13	1c	multicolored	15	15
169	G13	2c	multicolored	15	15
170	G13	3c	multicolored	15	15
171	G13	35c	multicolored	22	22
172	G13	$3	multicolored	2.00	2.00
			Nos. 167-172 (6)	2.82	2.82

Souvenir Sheet

173	G13	$2	multicolored	1.65	1.65

Frigate South Carolina G14

Designs: 1c, Schooner Lee. 2c, HMS Roebuck. 35c, Andrew Doria. 50c, Sloop Providence. $1, Flagship Alfred. $2, Frigate Confederacy. $3. Cutter Revenge.

1976, May 18

174	G14	½c	multicolored	15	15
175	G14	1c	multicolored	15	15
176	G14	2c	multicolored	15	15
177	G14	35c	multicolored	65	65
178	G14	50c	multicolored	90	90
179	G14	$1	multicolored	1.75	1.75
180	G14	$2	multicolored	3.50	3.50
			Nos. 174-180 (7)	7.25	7.25

Souvenir Sheet

181	G14	$3	multicolored	5.25	5.25

American Revolution Bicentennial.

Piper Apache G15

Designs: 1c, Beech Twin Bonanza. 2c, de Havilland Twin Otter. 40c, Britten Norman Islander. 50c, de Havilland Heron. $2, Hawker Siddeley Avro 748. $3, BAC 1-11.

1976, June 10

182	G15	½c	multicolored	15	15
183	G15	1c	multicolored	15	15
184	G15	2c	multicolored	15	15
185	G15	40c	multicolored	40	40
186	G15	50c	multicolored	50	50
187	G15	$2	multicolored	2.00	2.00
			Nos. 182-187 (6)	3.35	3.35

Souvenir Sheet

188	G15	$3	multicolored	3.00	3.00

Olympic Games, Montreal G16

1976, July 1

189	G16	½c	Cycling	15	15
190	G16	1c	Gymnastics	15	15
191	G16	2c	Hurdling	15	15
192	G16	35c	Shot put	22	22
193	G16	45c	Diving	30	30
194	G16	75c	Sprinting	50	50
195	G16	$2	Rowing	1.40	1.40
			Set value	2.35	2.35

Souvenir Sheet

196	G16	$3	Sailing	2.00	2.00

Virgin and Child by Cima — G17

Christmas: 1c, 2c, The Nativity by Romanino. 35c, Adoration of the Kings by Brueghel. 50c, Madonna and Child by Girolamo. 75c, Adoration of the Magi by Giorgione (horiz.). $2, The Adoration of the Kings by Angelico (horiz.). $3, The Holy Family by Garofalo.

1976, Oct. 19

197	G17	½c	multicolored	15	15
198	G17	1c	multicolored	15	15
199	G17	2c	multicolored	15	15
200	G17	35c	multicolored	22	22
201	G17	50c	multicolored	32	32
202	G17	75c	multicolored	50	50
203	G17	$2	multicolored	1.25	1.25
			Set value	2.30	2.30

Souvenir Sheet

204	G17	$3	multicolored	1.90	1.90

Alexander Graham Bell, First Telephone G18

Portraits of Bell and Telephone from: 1c, 1895. 2c, 1900. 35c, 1915. 75c, 1920. $1, 1929. $2, 1963. $3, 1976.

1977, Jan. 28

205	G18	½c	multicolored	15	15
206	G18	1c	multicolored	15	15
207	G18	2c	multicolored	15	15
208	G18	35c	multicolored	25	25
209	G18	75c	multicolored	55	55
210	G18	$1	multicolored	75	75
211	G18	$2	multicolored	1.50	1.50
			Set value	3.05	3.05

Souvenir Sheet

212	G18	$3	multicolored	2.50	2.50

Centenary of 1st telephone conversation, Mar. 10, 1876.

Coronation Coach — G19

Royal Visit — G20

Designs: 50c, Crown of St. Edward. No. 214, Queen entering Abbey. No. 219, Queen and Prince Charles. $4, Queen is crowned. No. 216, Mall on Coronation Night. No. 220, Queen's Flag.

Litho. and Embossed

1977, Feb. 7 ***Perf. 13½***

213	G19	35c	multicolored	20	20
214	G19	$2	multicolored	1.10	1.10
215	G19	$4	multicolored	2.25	2.25

Souvenir Sheet

Perf. 14

216	G19	$5	multicolored	3.00	3.00

Booklet Stamps

Roulette x imperf.

Self-adhesive

217	G20	35c	multicolored	20	20
a.			Booklet pane of 6	1.25	1.25
218	G20	50c	multicolored	30	30
219	G20	$2	multicolored	1.25	1.25
220	G20	$5	multicolored	3.00	3.00
a.			Bklt. pane of 3, #218, #219, #220	4.75	4.75

Reign of Queen Elizabeth II, 25th anniv.

Nos. 213-215, perf. 11, have different background colors and come from sheetlets of 3 stamps plus label.

For overprints see Nos. 237-240.

Easter — G21

Adoration of Jesus by Correggio — G22

Designs: Paintings of the Crucifixion by various artists.

1977, July 5 **Litho.** ***Perf. 14***

221	G21	½c	Fra Angelico	15	15
222	G21	1c	Fra Angelico, diff.	15	15
223	G21	2c	El Greco	15	15
224	G21	18c	El Greco, diff.	15	15
225	G21	35c	Fra Angelico, diff.	25	25
226	G21	50c	Giottino	35	35
227	G21	$2	da Messina	1.40	1.40
			Set value	2.10	2.10

Souvenir Sheet

228	G21	$3	Fra Angelico, diff.	2.00	2.00

1977, Nov. 17 ***Perf. 14***

Christmas: Paintings of the Madonna and Child by various artists.

229	G22	½c	shown	15	15
230	G22	1c	Giorgione	15	15
231	G22	2c	Morales	15	15
232	G22	18c	Raphael	15	15
233	G22	35c	Van Dyck	25	25
234	G22	50c	Filippo Lippi	35	35
235	G22	$2	Filippo Lippi, diff.	1.40	1.40
			Set value	2.10	2.10

Souvenir Sheet

236	G22	$3	Ghirlandaio	2.00	2.00

Nos. 213-216 Overprinted

ROYAL VISIT **W.I. 1977**

1977, Nov. 23 ***Perf. 13½***

237	G19	35c	multicolored	18	18
238	G19	$2	multicolored	1.25	1.25
239	G19	$4	multicolored	2.25	2.25

Souvenir Sheet

240	G19	$5	multicolored	3.00	3.00

Caribbean visit of Queen Elizabeth II.

Nos. 237-239 exist perf. 11.

Swimming and Life Saving G23

6th Caribbean Jamboree, Kingston, Jamaica, Aug. 5-14: 1c, Hiking. 2c, Ropes and Knots. 22c, Erecting Tent. 35c, Limbo dance. 75c, Cooking. $2, Pioneer bridge building. $3, Sea Scouts' race.

1977, Dec. 7 ***Perf. 14***

241	G23	½c	multicolored	15	15
242	G23	1c	multicolored	15	15
243	G23	2c	multicolored	15	15
244	G23	22c	multicolored	20	20
245	G23	35c	multicolored	30	30
246	G23	75c	multicolored	65	65
247	G23	$3	multicolored	2.75	2.75
			Nos. 241-247 (7)	4.35	4.35

Souvenir Sheet

248	G23	$2	multicolored	2.00	2.00

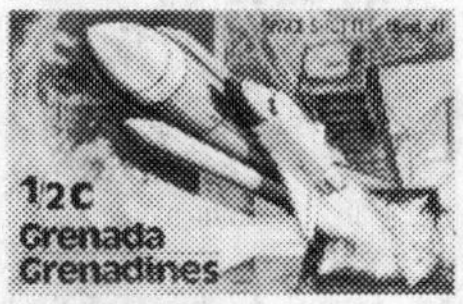

Space Shuttle Blast-off G24

Designs: 1c, Booster separation. 2c, External tank separation. 22c, Working in orbit. 50c, Reentry. $2, Towing in. $3, Landing.

1978, Feb. 3

249	G24	½c	multicolored	15	15
250	G24	1c	multicolored	15	15
251	G24	2c	multicolored	15	15
252	G24	22c	multicolored	15	15
253	G24	50c	multicolored	35	35
254	G24	$3	multicolored	2.00	2.00
			Set value	2.55	2.55

Souvenir Sheet

255	G24	$2	multicolored	1.50	1.50

US Space Shuttle.

Alfred Nobel, Medicine Medal G25

Alfred Nobel and: 1c, Physics, Chemistry Medal. 2c, Peace Medal. 22c, Nobel Institute, Oslo. 75c, Peace Prize committee. $2, Peace Medal, Nobel's will. $3, Literature Medal.

1978, Feb. 22

256	G25	½c	multicolored	15	15
257	G25	1c	multicolored	15	15
258	G25	2c	multicolored	15	15
259	G25	22c	multicolored	15	15
260	G25	75c	multicolored	50	50
261	G25	$3	multicolored	2.00	2.00
			Set value	3.10	3.10

Souvenir Sheet

262	G25	$2	multicolored	1.65	1.65

Nobel Prize awards.

Germany No. C37 — G26

Designs: 15c, France #C43. 25c, Liechtenstein #C8 specimen. 35c, Panama #257. 50c, Russia #C15. 75c, US #C10. $2, Germany #C57. $3, Spain #C56.

1978, Mar. 15

263	G26	5c	multicolored	15	15
264	G26	15c	multicolored	15	15
265	G26	25c	multicolored	15	15
266	G26	35c	multicolored	22	22
267	G26	50c	multicolored	35	35
268	G26	$3	multicolored	1.90	1.90
			Nos. 263-268 (6)	2.92	2.92

Souvenir Sheet

269			Sheet of 2	1.90	1.90
a.	G26	75c	multicolored	50	50
b.	G26	$2	multicolored	1.40	1.40

50th anniv. of Lindbergh's solo trans-Atlantic flight. 75th anniv. of 1st Zeppelin flight.

Coronation Ring G27

Designs: $2, Queen's Orb. $2.50, Imperial State Crown. $5, Queen Elizabeth II.

1978, Apr. 12 ***Perf. 14***

270	G27	50c	multicolored	30	30
271	G27	$2	multicolored	1.25	1.25
272	G27	$2.50	multicolored	1.50	1.50

Souvenir Sheet

273	G27	$5	multicolored	3.50	3.50

Nos. 270-272, perf 12, printed in sheets of 3 + label, have different background colors. Issue date, June 2, 1978.

G28

G29

Designs: 18c, Drummer, Royal Regiment of Fusiliers. 50c, Drummer, Royal Anglian Regiment. $5, Drum Major, Queen's Regiment.

1978, Apr. 12 ***Roulette x imperf.***

Booklet Stamps

Self-Adhesive

274			Souvenir booklet	5.25	5.25
a.	G28		Pane of 6 (3 ea 18c, 50c)	1.50	1.50
b.	G28		Pane of 1 ($5)	3.75	3.75

1978, May 18 ***Perf. 14***

Paintings by Rubens: 5c, Le Chapeau de Paille. 15c, Hector Killed by Achilles. 18c, Helene Fourment and Her Children. 22c, Rubens and Isabella Brandt. 35c, Ildefonso Altarpiece. $2, Self-portrait. $3, Four Negro Heads.

275	G29	5c	multicolored	15	15
276	G29	15c	multicolored	15	15
277	G29	18c	multicolored	15	15
278	G29	22c	multicolored	15	15
279	G29	35c	multicolored	24	24
280	G29	$3	multicolored	1.90	1.90
			Nos. 275-280 (6)	2.74	2.74

Souvenir Sheet

281	G29	$2	multicolored	1.40	1.40

400th birth anniv. of Rubens.

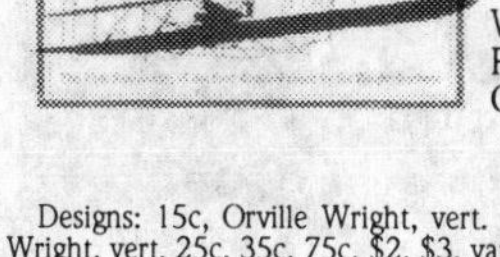

Wright Flyer G30

Designs: 15c, Orville Wright, vert. 18c, Wilbur Wright, vert. 25c, 35c, 75c, $2, $3, various Wright airplanes.

1978, Aug. 10

282 G30	5c multicolored	15	15
283 G30	15c multicolored	15	15
284 G30	18c multicolored	15	15
285 G30	25c multicolored	15	15
286 G30	35c multicolored	20	20
287 G30	75c multicolored	42	42
288 G30	$3 multicolored	1.65	1.65
	Nos. 282-288 (7)	2.87	2.87

Souvenir Sheet

289 G30	$2 multicolored	1.40	1.40

75th anniv. of first powered flight by the Wright brothers, Dec. 17, 1903.

Audubon's Shearwater — G31

Players, Soccer Ball — G32

Designs: 10c, Northern ring-necked plover. 18c, Garnet-throated hummingbird, horiz. 22c, Black-bellied tree duck, horiz. 40c, Purple martin, horiz. $1, Yellow-bellied tropic bird. $2, Long-billed curlew. $5, Snowy egret.

1978, Sept. 28

290 G31	5c multicolored	15	15
291 G31	10c multicolored	15	15
292 G31	18c multicolored	20	20
293 G31	22c multicolored	25	25
294 G31	40c multicolored	50	50
295 G31	$1 multicolored	1.10	1.10
296 G31	$2 multicolored	2.25	2.25
	Nos. 290-296 (7)	4.60	4.60

Souvenir Sheet

297 G31	$5 multicolored	5.50	5.50

1978, Nov. 2

Soccer players in action.

298 G32	15c multicolored	15	15
299 G32	35c multicolored	25	25
300 G32	50c multicolored	35	35
301 G32	$3 multicolored	2.00	2.00

Souvenir Sheet

302 G32	$2 multicolored	1.50	1.50

World Cup Soccer Championships, Argentina, June 1-25.

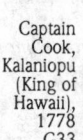

Captain Cook, Kalaniopu (King of Hawaii), 1778 G33

Designs: 22c, Cook, Hawaiian native. 50c, Cook, death scene, Feb. 14, 1779. $3, Cook and offering ceremony. $4, Cook, HMS Resolution.

1978, Dec. 13

303 G33	18c multicolored	15	15
304 G33	22c multicolored	16	16
305 G33	50c multicolored	35	35
306 G33	$3 multicolored	2.25	2.25

Souvenir Sheet

307 G33	$4 multicolored	3.00	3.00

250th birth anniv. of Captain James Cook and Bicentennial of his discovery of the Hawaiian Islands.

Durer Paintings — G34

Strelitzia Reginae — G35

Christmas: 40c, The Virgin at Prayer. 60c, Dresden Alterpiece. 90c, Madonna and Child. $2, Madonna and Child. $4, Salvator Mundi.

1978, Dec 20

308 G34	40c multicolored	25	25
309 G34	60c multicolored	40	40
310 G34	90c multicolored	60	60
311 G34	$2 multicolored	1.40	1.40

Souvenir Sheet

312 G34	$4 multicolored	2.75	2.75

1979, Feb. 15

313 G35	22c shown	15	15
314 G35	40c Euphorbia pulcherrima	25	25
315 G35	$1 Heliconia humilis	60	60
316 G35	$3 Thunbergia alata	1.90	1.90

Souvenir Sheet

317 G35	$2 Bougainvillea glabra	1.65	1.65

Children with Pig — G36

International Year of the Child: 50c, Children with donkey. $1, Children with goats. $3, Children fishing. $4, Child with coconuts.

1979, Mar. 22

318 G36	18c multicolored	15	15
319 G36	50c multicolored	30	30
320 G36	$1 multicolored	1.65	1.65
321 G36	$3 multicolored	1.90	1.90

Souvenir Sheet

322 G36	$4 multicolored	5.00	5.00

Around the World in 80 Days G37

150th birth anniv. of Jules Verne: 18c, 20,000 Leagues Under the Sea. 38c, From the Earth to the Moon. 75c, From the Earth to the Moon, diff. $3, Five Weeks in a Balloon.

1979, Apr. 20

323 G37	18c multicolored	15	15
324 G37	38c multicolored	22	22
325 G37	75c multicolored	45	45
326 G37	$3 multicolored	1.75	1.75

Souvenir Sheet

327 G37	$4 multicolored	2.50	2.50

Sir Rowland Hill, Mail Truck G38

Designs: $1, Ocean liner. $2, Mail train. $3, Concorde. $4, Sir Rowland Hill.

1979, July 30 *Perf. 14*

328 G38	15c multicolored	15	15
329 G38	$1 multicolored	60	60
330 G38	$2 multicolored	1.10	1.10
331 G38	$3 multicolored	1.75	1.75

Souvenir Sheet

332 G38	$4 multicolored	2.75	2.75

Death centenary of Sir Rowland Hill.

Nos. 328-331, perf. 12, printed in sheets of 5 + label, have different colored backgrounds.

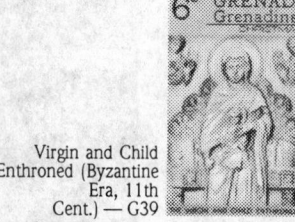

Virgin and Child Enthroned (Byzantine Era, 11th Cent.) — G39

Christmas sculptures: 25c, Presentation in the Temple by Beauneveu c. 1390. 30c, Flight to Egypt (Utrecht, c. 1510). 40c, Madonna and Child by della Quercia, 1047-48. 90c, Madonna della Mela by della Robbia, c. 1455. $1, Madonna and Child by Rossellino, 1461-66. $2, Madonna (Antwerp, 1700). $4, Virgin (Krumau, c. 1390).

1979, Oct. 23 *Perf. 14*

333 G39	6c multicolored	15	15
334 G39	25c multicolored	15	15
335 G39	30c multicolored	18	18
336 G39	40c multicolored	25	25
337 G39	90c multicolored	55	55
338 G39	$1 multicolored	65	65
339 G39	$2 multicolored	1.25	1.25
	Nos. 333-339 (7)	3.18	3.18

Souvenir Sheet

340 G39	$4 multicolored	2.50	2.50

Great Hammerhead Shark — G40

Designs: 45c, Banded butterflyfish. 50c, Permit. 60c, Threaded turban. 70c, Milk conch. 75c, Great blue heron. 90c, Colored Atlantic natica. $1, Red footed booby. $2.50, Collared plover.

1979, Nov. 9

341 G40	40c multicolored	28	28
342 G40	45c multicolored	30	30
343 G40	50c multicolored	35	35
344 G40	60c multicolored	42	42
345 G40	70c multicolored	50	50
346 G40	75c multicolored	55	55
347 G40	90c multicolored	65	65
348 G40	$1 multicolored	70	70
	Nos. 341-348 (8)	3.75	3.75

Souvenir Sheet

349 G40	$2.50 multicolored	2.25	2.25

Doctor Goofy G41

International Year of the Child: 1c, Admiral Mickey Mouse. 2c, Fireman Goofy. 3c, Nurse Minnie Mouse. 4c, Drum Major Mickey Mouse. 5c, Policeman Donald Duck. 10c, Pilot Donald Duck. $2, Mailman Goofy, horiz. $2.50 Engineer Donald Duck, horiz. $3, Fireman Mickey Mouse.

1979, Dec. 12 *Perf. 11*

350 G41	½c multicolored	15	15
351 G41	1c multicolored	15	15
352 G41	2c multicolored	15	15
353 G41	3c multicolored	15	15
354 G41	4c multicolored	15	15
355 G41	5c multicolored	15	15
356 G41	10c multicolored	15	15
357 G41	$2 multicolored	1.65	1.65
358 G41	$2.50 multicolored	2.00	2.00
	Set value	3.90	3.90

Souvenir Sheet

Perf. 13½

359 G41	$3 multicolored	7.50	7.50

Nos. 114, 117-128 Overprinted **PEOPLE'S REVOLUTION 13 MARCH 1979**

1980, Mar. 10 *Perf. 15*

360 A85	6c multicolored	15	15
361 A85	12c multicolored	15	15
362 A85	15c multicolored	15	15
363 A85	20c multicolored	15	15
364 A85	25c multicolored	16	16
365 A85	35c multicolored	22	22
366 A85	50c multicolored	35	35

Perf. 13½x14

367 A85	75c multicolored	50	50
368 A85	$1 multicolored	65	65
369 A85	$2 multicolored	1.40	1.40
370 A85	$3 multicolored	2.00	2.00
371 A85	$5 multicolored	3.25	3.25
372 A85	$10 multicolored	6.50	6.50
	Nos. 360-372 (13)	15.63	15.63

Classroom G42

Rotary International, 75th anniv.: 30c, Rotary International emblem, people. 60c, Rotary executive making contribution to physician. $3, Young patients, nurses. $4, Paul P. Harris, founder of Rotary International.

1980, Mar. 12 *Perf. 14*

373 G42	6c multicolored	15	15
374 G42	30c multicolored	20	20
375 G42	60c multicolored	42	42
376 G42	$3 multicolored	2.00	2.00

Souvenir Sheet

377 G42	$4 multicolored	2.75	2.75

Yellow-bellied Seedeater — G43

Designs: 40c, Blue-hooded euphonia. 90c, Yellow warbler. $2, Tropical mockingbird. $3, Barn owl.

1980, Apr. 14

378 G43	25c multicolored	25	25
379 G43	40c multicolored	42	42
380 G43	90c multicolored	95	95
381 G43	$2 multicolored	2.00	2.00

Souvenir Sheet

382 G43	$3 multicolored	3.00	3.00

Running G44

Designs: 40c, Soccer. 90c, Boxing. $2, Wrestling. $4, Runners in silhouette.

1980, Apr. 21

383 G44	30c multicolored	20	20
384 G44	40c multicolored	25	25
385 G44	90c multicolored	60	60
386 G44	$2 multicolored	1.25	1.25

Souvenir Sheet

387 G44	$4 multicolored	2.75	2.75

22nd Summer Olympic Games, Moscow, July 19-Aug. 3.

Nos. 328-331 Overprinted ***LONDON 1980***

1980, May 6 *Perf. 12*

388	G38	15c multicolored	15	15
389	G38	$1 multicolored	48	48
390	G38	$2 multicolored	1.00	1.00
391	G38	$3 multicolored	1.50	1.50

Issued in sheets of 5 + label.

Longspine Squirrelfish G45

Designs: 1c, Blue chromis. 2c, Foureye butterflyfish. 4c, Sergeant major. 5c, Yellowtail snapper. 6c, Mutton snapper. 10c, Cocoa damselfish. 12c, Royal gramma. 15c, Cherubfish. 20c, Blackbar soldierfish. 25c, Comb grouper. 30c, Longsnout butterflyfish. 40c, Pudding wife. 50c, Midnight parrotfish. 90c, Redspotted hawkfish. $1, Hogfish. $3, Beau gregory. $5, Rock beauty. $10, Barred hamlet.

1980, Aug. 6 *Perf. 14*

392	G45	1/2c multicolored	15	15
a.		Perf. 12, inscribed 1982		
393	G45	1c multicolored	15	15
394	G45	2c multicolored	15	15
395	G45	4c multicolored	15	15
396	G45	5c multicolored	15	15
397	G45	6c multicolored	15	15
398	G45	10c multicolored	15	15
399	G45	12c multicolored	15	15
400	G45	15c multicolored	15	15
401	G45	20c multicolored	15	15
402	G45	25c multicolored	18	18
403	G45	30c multicolored	22	22
404	G45	40c multicolored	30	30
405	G45	50c multicolored	35	35
406	G45	90c multicolored	65	65
407	G45	$1 multicolored	75	75
408	G45	$3 multicolored	2.25	2.25
409	G45	$5 multicolored	3.75	3.75
410	G45	$10 multicolored	7.25	7.25
		Nos. 392-410 (19)	17.20	17.20

No. 398 exists with 1984 date below design.

Bambi with Mother — G46

Various scenes from Walt Disney's Bambi.

1980, Oct. 7 *Perf. 11*

411	G46	1/2c multicolored	15	15
412	G46	1c multicolored	15	15
413	G46	2c multicolored	15	15
414	G46	3c multicolored	15	15
415	G46	4c multicolored	15	15
416	G46	5c multicolored	15	15
417	G46	10c multicolored	15	15
418	G46	$2.50 multicolored	2.00	2.00
419	G46	$3 multicolored	2.50	2.50
		Nos. 411-419 (9)	5.55	5.55

Souvenir Sheet

420	G46	$4 multicolored	3.75	3.75

Christmas.

The Unicorn in Captivity by Unknown 15th Cent. Artist — G47

Designs: 10c, The Fighting Temeraire by J.M.W. Turner. 25c, Sunday Afternoon on the Ile De La Grande-Jatte by Seurat. 90c, Max Schmitt in a Single Scull by Eakins. $2, The Burial of the Count of Orgaz by El Greco. $3, George Washington by Stuart. $5, Kaiser Karl the Great by Durer. Nos. 425-427 are vert.

1981, Jan. 25 *Perf. 14*

421	G47	6c multicolored	15	15
422	G47	10c multicolored	15	15
423	G47	25c multicolored	18	18
424	G47	90c multicolored	60	60
425	G47	$2 multicolored	1.40	1.40
426	G47	$3 multicolored	2.00	2.00
		Nos. 421-426 (6)	4.48	4.48

Souvenir Sheet

427	G47	$5 multicolored	3.50	3.50

Disney Type of 1979

50th anniv. of Pluto character: $2, Mickey Mouse, Pluto and birthday cake. $4, Pluto.

1981, Jan. 26

428	A135a	$2 multicolored	2.00	2.00

Souvenir Sheet

429	A135a	$4 multicolored	3.75	3.75

No. 428 issued in sheets of 8.

Chip Coloring Easter Eggs — G48

Easter: Various Disney characters coloring Easter eggs.

1981, Apr. 14 *Perf. 11*

430	G48	35c multicolored	28	28
431	G48	40c multicolored	35	35
432	G48	$2 multicolored	1.75	1.75
433	G48	$2.50 multicolored	2.25	2.25

Souvenir Sheet

Perf. 14

434	G48	$4 multicolored	3.50	3.50

Bust of a Woman — G49

Diana — G50

Paintings by Pablo Picasso (1881-1973): 40c, Woman (Study for Les Demoiselles d'Avignon). 90c, Nude with Raised Arms (The Dancer of Avignon). $4, The Dryad. $5, Les Demoiselles d'Avignon.

1981, May 5 *Perf. 14*

435	G49	6c multicolored	15	15
436	G49	40c multicolored	25	25
437	G49	90c multicolored	55	55
438	G49	$4 multicolored	2.50	2.50

Size: 103x128mm

Imperf

439	G49	$5 multicolored	3.50	3.50

Royal Wedding Issue

Common Design Type

1981, June 16 *Perf. 15*

440	CD331	40c Couple	25	25
441	CD331	$2 Balmoral Castle	1.40	1.40
442	CD331	$4 Charles	2.50	2.50

Souvenir Sheet

443	CD331	$5 Royal Coach	3.25	3.25

Sheets of 5 plus label contain 30c (like No. 440), 40c (like No. 441), or $4 in changed colors, perf 15x14 1/2.

Roulette x imperf. (#444a), Imperf. (#444b)

1981, June 16

Designs: $2, Charles. $5, Diana and Charles.

Booklet

Self-Adhesive

444	G50	Souvenir Booklet	9.50	
a.		Pane of 6 (3 each $1, $2)	6.00	
b.		Pane of 1, $5	3.50	

Royal wedding.

Amy Johnson, Pilot of 1st Britain-Australia Solo Flight by a Woman, May 1930 — G51

Decade for Women: 70c, Mme. la Baronne de Laroche, 1st qualified aviatrix, May 1910. $1.10, Ruth Nichols. $3, Amelia Earhart, 1st Atlantic solo flight by woman, May 1932. $5, Valentina Tereshkova, 1st woman in space, June 1963.

1981, Oct. 13 *Perf. 14*

445	G51	30c multicolored	22	22
446	G51	70c multicolored	50	50
447	G51	$1.10 multicolored	80	80
448	G51	$3 multicolored	2.25	2.25

Souvenir Sheet

449	G51	$5 multicolored	3.50	3.50

Lady and the Tramp — G52

Christmas. Various scenes from Walt Disney's film Lady and the Tramp.

1981, Nov. 2

450	G52	1/2c multicolored	15	15
451	G52	1c multicolored	15	15
452	G52	2c multicolored	15	15
453	G52	3c multicolored	15	15
454	G52	4c multicolored	15	15
455	G52	5c multicolored	15	15
456	G52	10c multicolored	15	15
457	G52	$2.50 multicolored	1.75	1.75
458	G52	$3 multicolored	2.25	2.25
		Nos. 450-458 (9)	5.05	5.05

Souvenir Sheet

459	G52	$5 multicolored	4.00	4.00

747 Carrying Space Shuttle G53

Designs: 40c, Re-entry. $1.10, External tank separation. $3, Touchdown. $5, Lift-off.

1981, Nov. 2 *Perf. 14 1/2*

460	G53	10c multicolored	15	15
461	G53	40c multicolored	30	30
462	G53	$1.10 multicolored	80	80
463	G53	$3 multicolored	2.25	2.25

Souvenir Sheet

464	G53	$5 multicolored	3.50	3.50

Soccer Player — G54

World Cup Soccer Championships, Spain, 1982: Soccer players in various positions.

1981, Nov. 30 *Perf. 14*

465	G54	20c multicolored	15	15
466	G54	40c multicolored	30	30
467	G54	$1 multicolored	75	75
468	G54	$2 multicolored	1.50	1.50

Souvenir Sheet

469	G54	$4 multicolored	3.50	3.50

Stagecoach, Mail Truck G55

UPU Membership Centenary: 40c, UPU Emblem. $2.50, Sailing ship, ocean liner. $4, Biplane, Concorde. $5, Steam train, high-speed trains.

1982, Jan. 13 *Perf. 15*

470	G55	30c multicolored	20	20
471	G55	40c multicolored	28	28
472	G55	$2.50 multicolored	1.65	1.65
473	G55	$4 multicolored	2.75	2.75

Souvenir Sheet

474	G55	$5 multicolored	4.00	4.00

Sprinting G56

Designs: 90c, Sea scouts sailing. $1.10, Hand crafts. $3, Animal husbandry. $5, Music around campfire.

1982, Feb. 19

475	G56	6c multicolored	15	15
476	G56	90c multicolored	65	65
477	G56	$1.10 multicolored	80	80
478	G56	$3 multicolored	2.25	2.25

Souvenir Sheet

479	G56	$5 multicolored	3.75	3.75

Boy Scouts, 75th anniv. Lord Baden-Powell, 125th birth anniv.

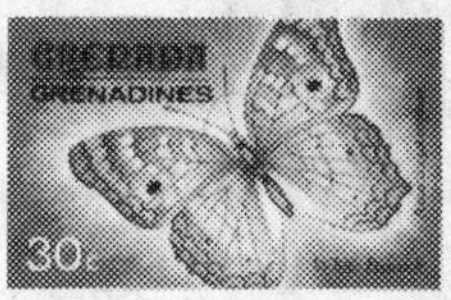

White Peacock G57

Designs: 40c, St. Vincent long-tail skipper. $1.10, Painted lady. $3, Orion. $5, Silver spot.

1982, Mar. 24 *Perf. 14*

480	G57	30c multicolored	30	30
481	G57	40c multicolored	40	40
482	G57	$1.10 multicolored	1.00	1.00
483	G57	$3 multicolored	2.75	2.75

Souvenir Sheet

484	G57	$5 multicolored	3.75	3.75

Princess Diana Issue

Common Design Type

1982, July 1 *Perf. 14 1/2x14*

485	CD332	50c Blenheim Palace	20	20
486	CD332	60c Like 50c	25	25
487	CD332	$1 Couple in field	45	45
488	CD332	$2 Like $1	85	85

489 CD332 $3 Diana 1.40 1.40
490 CD332 $4 Like $3 1.75 1.75
Nos. 485-490 (6) 4.90 4.90

Souvenir Sheet

491 CD332 $5 Diana, diff. 4.00 4.00

50c, $1, $3 issued in sheets of 5 plus label.

Overprinted **ROYAL BABY 21.6.82**

1982, Aug. 30

492 CD332 50c multicolored 30 30
493 CD332 60c multicolored 35 35
494 CD332 $1 multicolored 60 60
495 CD332 $2 multicolored 1.25 1.25
496 CD332 $3 multicolored 1.75 1.75
497 CD332 $4 multicolored 2.50 2.50
Nos. 492-497 (6) 6.75 6.75

Souvenir Sheet

498 CD332 $5 multicolored 4.00 4.00

Birth of Prince William of Wales, June 21.

Roosevelt Type of 1982

Designs: 30c, New Deal soil conservation. 40c, Roosevelt, George Washington Carver. 70c, Civilian Conservation Corps. $3, Roosevelt, Liberian Pres. Edwin Barclay. $5, Roosevelt addressing Howard University.

1982, July 27 *Perf. 14*

499 A154 30c multicolored 24 24
500 A154 40c multicolored 30 30
501 A154 70c multicolored 55 55
502 A154 $3 multicolored 2.25 2.25

Souvenir Sheet

503 A154 $5 multicolored 3.75 3.75

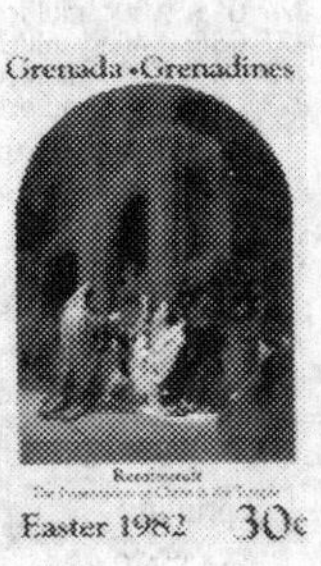

Presentation of Christ in the Temple — G58

Easter Paintings by Rembrandt: 60c, Descent from the Cross. $2, Raising of the Cross. $4, Resurrection of Christ. $5, The Risen Christ.

1982, Sept. 2 *Perf. 14½*

504 G58 30c multicolored 20 20
505 G58 60c multicolored 42 42
506 G58 $2 multicolored 1.40 1.40
507 G58 $4 multicolored 3.00 3.00

Souvenir Sheet

508 G58 $5 multicolored 3.75 3.75

G59

1982, Oct. 4 *Perf. 15*

509 G59 10c Santa Fe 15 15
510 G59 40c Mistral 30 30
511 G59 70c Rheingold 55 55
512 G59 $1 ET 403 80 80
513 G59 $1.10 Mallard 85 85
514 G59 $2 Tokaido 1.65 1.65
Nos. 509-514 (6) 4.30 4.30

Souvenir Sheet

515 G59 $5 Settebello 3.75 3.75

Soccer Players G60

Italy, World Cup Soccer Champions: $4, Soccer players, diff. $5, Map of Italy.

1982, Dec. 2 *Perf. 14*

516 G60 60c multicolored 45 45
517 G60 $4 multicolored 3.00 3.00

Souvenir Sheet

518 G60 $5 multicolored 3.25 3.25

Christmas Type of 1982

Designs: Scenes from Walt Disney's film The Rescuers.

1982, Dec. 14 *Perf. 13½*

519 A157 ½c multicolored 15 15
520 A157 1c multicolored 15 15
521 A157 2c multicolored 15 15
522 A157 3c multicolored 15 15
523 A157 4c multicolored 15 15
524 A157 5c multicolored 15 15
525 A157 10c multicolored 15 15
526 A157 $2.50 multicolored 2.00 2.00
527 A157 $3 multicolored 2.50 2.50
Nos. 519-527 (9) 5.55 5.55

Souvenir Sheet

528 A157 $5 multicolored 4.50 4.50

Whales Type of 1982

Designs: 10c, Pilot whale. 60c, Dall porpoise. $1.10, Humpback whale. $3, Bowfin whale. $5, Spotted dolphin.

1983, Jan. 10 *Perf. 14*

529 A159 10c multicolored 15 15
530 A159 60c multicolored 55 55
531 A159 $1.10 multicolored 1.00 1.00
532 A159 $3 multicolored 2.75 2.75

Souvenir Sheet

533 A159 $5 multicolored 4.50 4.50

Raphael Paintings Type

Designs: 25c, David and Goliath. 30c, David Sees Bathsheba. 90c, Triumph of David. $4, Anointing of Solomon. $5, Anointing of David.

1983, Feb. 15 *Perf. 14*

534 A160 25c multicolored 18 18
535 A160 30c multicolored 22 22
536 A160 90c multicolored 65 65
537 A160 $4 multicolored 3.00 3.00

Souvenir Sheet

538 A160 $5 multicolored 3.75 3.75

Audio and Video Communication — G61

World Communications Year: 60c, Ambulance. $1.10, Helicopters. $3, Satellite. $5, Diver, bottlenose porpoise.

1983, Apr. 7 *Perf. 14*

539 G61 30c multicolored 22 22
540 G61 60c multicolored 45 45
541 G61 $1.10 multicolored 80 80
542 G61 $3 blk, red & blue 2.25 2.25

Souvenir Sheet

543 G61 $5 multicolored 3.75 3.75

For overprints, see Nos. 629-630A.

Car Type of 1983

Designs: 10c, 1931 Chrysler Imperial Roadster. 30c, 1925 Doble Steam Car. 40c, 1965 Ford Mustang. 60c, 1930 Packard Tourer. 70c, 1913 Mercer Raceabout. 90c, 1963 Corvette Stingray. $1.10, 1935 Auburn 851 Supercharger Speedster. $2.50, 1933 Pierce Arrow Silver Arrow. $3, 1929 Duesenberg Dual Cowl Phaeton. $4, 1928 Mercedes-Benz SSK. $5, 1923 McFarlan Knickerbocker Cabriolet.

1983, May 4 *Perf. 14½*

544 A163 10c multicolored 15 15
545 A163 30c multicolored 22 22
546 A163 40c multicolored 30 30
547 A163 60c multicolored 45 45
548 A163 70c multicolored 52 52
549 A163 90c multicolored 65 65
550 A163 $1.10 multicolored 85 85
551 A163 $2.50 multicolored 1.90 1.90
552 A163 $3 multicolored 2.25 2.25
553 A163 $4 multicolored 3.25 3.25
Nos. 544-553 (10) 10.54 10.54

Souvenir Sheet

554 A163 $5 multicolored 3.75 3.75

Anniversary of Manned Flight Type

Designs: 40c, Short Solent flying boat. 70c, Curtiss R3C-2 seaplane. 90c, Hawker Nimrod biplane. $4, Montgolfier balloon. $5, Victoria Luise airship.

1983, July 18 *Perf. 14*

555 A164 40c multicolored 25 25
556 A164 70c multicolored 45 45
557 A164 90c multicolored 55 55
558 A164 $4 multicolored 2.50 2.50

Souvenir Sheet

559 A164 $5 multicolored 3.75 3.75

Christmas G62

Walt Disney characters in scenes from "Jingle Bells."

1983, Nov. 7 *Perf. 11*

560 G62 ½c multicolored 15 15
561 G62 1c multicolored 15 15
562 G62 2c multicolored 15 15
563 G62 3c multicolored 15 15
564 G62 4c multicolored 15 15
565 G62 5c multicolored 15 15
566 G62 10c multicolored 15 15
567 G62 $2.50 multicolored 2.00 2.00
568 G62 $3 multicolored 2.50 2.50
Nos. 560-568 (9) 5.55 5.55

Souvenir Sheet

Perf. 13½

569 G62 $5 multicolored 4.25 4.25

G63

G64

1984, Jan. 9 *Perf. 14*

570 G63 30c Weightlifting 22 22
571 G63 60c Gymnastics 45 45
572 G63 70c Archery 52 52
573 G63 $4 Sailing 3.00 3.00

Souvenir Sheet

574 G63 $5 Basketball 3.25 3.25

Olympic Games, Los Angeles.

1984, Apr. 9 *Perf. 15*

Designs: 15c, Frangipani. 40c, Dwarf poinciana. 70c, Walking iris. $4, Lady's slipper. $5, Brazilian glory vine.

575 G64 15c multicolored 15 15
576 G64 40c multicolored 30 30
577 G64 70c multicolored 55 55
578 G64 $4 multicolored 3.00 3.00

Souvenir Sheet

579 G64 $5 multicolored 3.50 3.50

For overprints, see Nos. 598-600.

Set Values

A 15-cent minimum now applies to individual stamps and sets. Where the 15-cent minimum per stamp would increase the value of a set beyond retail, there is a "Set Value" notation giving the retail value of the set.

Easter — G65

Walt Disney characters with Easter hats.

1984, May 1 *Perf. 11*

580 G65 ½c multicolored 15 15
581 G65 1c multicolored 15 15
582 G65 2c multicolored 15 15
583 G65 3c multicolored 15 15
584 G65 4c multicolored 15 15
585 G65 5c multicolored 15 15
586 G65 10c multicolored 16 16
587 G65 $2 multicolored 1.65 1.65
588 G65 $4 multicolored 3.25 3.25
Set value 5.20 5.20

Souvenir Sheet

589 G65 $5 multicolored 4.50 4.50

Bobolink G66

Birds: 50c, Eastern kingbird. 60c, Barn swallow. 70c, Yellow warbler. $1, Rose-breasted grosbeak. $1.10, Yellowthroat. $2, Catbird. $5, Fork-tailed flycatcher.

1984, May 21 *Perf. 14*

590 G66 40c multicolored 30 30
591 G66 50c multicolored 40 40
592 G66 60c multicolored 45 45
593 G66 70c multicolored 55 55
594 G66 $1 multicolored 80 80
595 G66 $1.10 multicolored 85 85
596 G66 $2 multicolored 1.50 1.50
Nos. 590-596 (7) 4.85 4.85

Souvenir Sheet

597 G66 $5 multicolored 4.00 4.00

Nos. 577-579 Overprinted **19TH U.P.U CONGRESS HAMBURG**

1984, June 19 *Perf. 15*

598 G64 70c multicolored 55 55
599 G64 $4 multicolored 3.25 3.25

Souvenir Sheet

600 G64 $5 multicolored 4.00 4.00

Geeststar G67

Designs: 60c, Daphne. $1.10, Schooner Southwind. $4, Oceanic. $5, Privateer.

1984, July 16 *Perf. 15*

601 G67 30c multicolored 24 24
602 G67 60c multicolored 45 45
603 G67 $1.10 multicolored 85 85
604 G67 $4 multicolored 3.25 3.25

Souvenir Sheet

605 G67 $5 multicolored 4.50 4.50

Correggio Paintings Type

Designs: 10c, The Hunt—Blowing the Horn. 30c, St. John the Evangelist, horiz. 90c, The Hunt—The Deer's Head. $4, The Virgin Crowned by Christ, horiz. $5, Martyrdom of the Four Saints.

1984, Aug. 22 *Perf. 14*

606 A171a 10c multicolored 15 15
607 A171a 30c multicolored 24 24
608 A171a 90c multicolored 70 70

609 A171a $4 multicolored 3.25 3.25

Souvenir Sheet

610 A171a $5 multicolored 4.00 4.00

The Song of the Dog — G68

Paintings by Edgar Degas: 70c, Cafe-Concert. $1.10, The Orchestra of the Opera. $3, The Dance Lesson. $5, Madame Camus at the Piano.

1984, Aug. 22

611 G68 25c multicolored 20 20
612 G68 70c multicolored 55 55
613 G68 $1.10 multicolored 85 85
614 G68 $3 multicolored 2.50 2.50

Souvenir Sheet

615 G68 $5 multicolored 4.00 4.00

150th birth anniv. of Degas.

Queen Victoria Gardens G69

Designs: $4, Ayers Rock. $5, Yarra River, Melbourne.

1984, Sept. 21

616 G69 $1.10 multicolored 85 85
617 G69 $4 multicolored 3.25 3.25

Souvenir Sheet

618 G69 $5 multicolored 4.00 4.00

AUSIPEX International Stamp Exhibition, Melbourne, Australia.

Colonel Steven's Model, 1825 G70

Locomotives: 50c, Royal George, 1827. 60c, Stourbridge Lion, 1829. 70c, Liverpool, 1830. 90c, South Carolina, 1832. $1.10, Monster, 1836. $2, Lafayette, 1837. $4, Lion, 1838.

1984, Oct. 3 *Perf. 15*

619 G70 20c multicolored 16 16
620 G70 50c multicolored 42 42
621 G70 60c multicolored 50 50
622 G70 70c multicolored 60 60
623 G70 90c multicolored 75 75
624 G70 $1.10 multicolored 90 90
625 G70 $2 multicolored 1.65 1.65
626 G70 $4 multicolored 3.50 3.50
Nos. 619-626 (8) 8.48 8.48

Souvenir Sheets

627 G70 $5 Sequin's Engine, 1829 4.25 4.25
628 G70 $5 Der Adler, 1835 4.25 4.25

Nos. 539, 541, 543 Overprinted

OPENING OF POINT SALINE INT'L AIRPORT

1984, Oct. 28 *Perf. 14*

629 G61 30c multicolored 25 25
630 G61 $1.10 multicolored 95 95

Souvenir Sheet

630A G61 $5 multicolored 4.00 4.00

Opening of the Point Saline International Airport. No. 630A is overprinted in the margin.

Christmas Type of 1984

Designs: Scenes from various Donald Duck movies.

1984, Nov. 26 *Perf. 13½x14*

631 A173 45c multicolored 38 38
632 A173 60c multicolored 50 50
633 A173 90c multicolored 75 75
634 A173 $2 multi, perf. 12 1.75 1.75
635 A173 $4 multicolored 3.50 3.50
Nos. 631-635 (5) 6.88 6.88

Souvenir Sheet

636 A173 $5 multicolored 4.50 4.50

No. 634 issued in sheets of 8.

Audubon Type of 1985

Designs: 50c, Blue-winged teal. 90c, White ibis. $1.10, Swallow-tailed kite. $3, Common Gallinule. $5, Mangrove cuckoo.

1985, Feb. 11 *Perf. 14*

637 A174 50c multicolored 42 42
638 A174 90c multicolored 75 75
639 A174 $1.10 multicolored 95 95
640 A174 $3 multicolored 2.50 2.50

Souvenir Sheet

641 A174 $5 multicolored 4.00 4.00

See Nos. 732-736.

Motorcycle Centenary — G71

Anniv. emblem and: 30c, Kawasaki 750, 1972. 60c, Honda Goldwing GL1000, 1974, horiz. 70c, Kawasaki Z650, 1976, horiz. $4, Honda CBX, 1977. $5, BMW R100RS, 1978.

1985, Mar. 11

642 G71 30c multicolored 22 22
643 G71 60c multicolored 45 45
644 G71 70c multicolored 52 52
645 G71 $4 multicolored 3.00 3.00

Souvenir Sheet

646 G71 $5 multicolored 4.25 4.25

Intl. Youth Year G72

Designs: 50c, Folding bandages (health). 70c, Diver, turtle (environment). $1.10, Sailing (leisure). $3, Boys playing chess (education). $5, Hands touching globe.

1985, Apr. 15

647 G72 50c multicolored 40 40
648 G72 70c multicolored 54 54
649 G72 $1.10 multicolored 85 85
650 G72 $3 multicolored 2.25 2.25

Souvenir Sheet

651 G72 $5 multicolored 4.00 4.00

Intl. Civil Aviation Org., 40th Anniv. G73

Designs: 5c, Lockheed Lodestar. 70c, Avro 748 Turboprop. $1.10, Boeing 727. $4, Boeing 707. $5, Pilatus Britten-Norman Islander.

1985, Apr. 30

652 G73 5c multicolored 15 15
653 G73 70c multicolored 50 50
654 G73 $1.10 multicolored 80 80
655 G73 $4 multicolored 3.00 3.00

Souvenir Sheet

656 G73 $5 multicolored 4.00 4.00

Girl Guides Type

Designs: 30c, Lady Baden-Powell, Guide leaders. 50c, Botany field trip. 70c, Making camp, vert. $4, Sailing, vert. $5, Lord and Lady Baden-Powell, vert.

1985, May 30

657 A176 30c multicolored 25 25
658 A176 50c multicolored 40 40
659 A176 70c multicolored 60 60
660 A176 $4 multicolored 3.25 3.25

Souvenir Sheet

661 A176 $5 multicolored 4.00 4.00

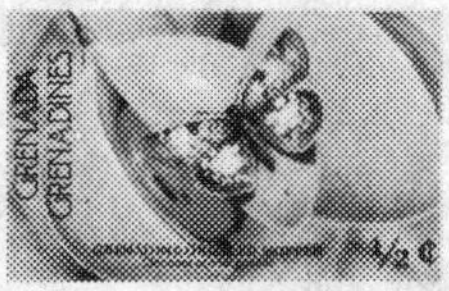

Grenadine Grizzled Skipper G74

Butterflies: 1c, Red anartia. 2c, Lesser Antillean giant hairstreak. 4c, Santa Domingo long-tail skipper. 5c, Spotted Manuel's skipper. 6c, Grenada's polydamus swallowtail. 10c, Palmira sulphur. 12c, Pupillated orange sulphur. 15c, Migrant sulphur. 20c, St. Christopher's hairstreak. 25c, St. Lucia mestra. 30c, Insular gulf fritillary. 40c, Michael's Caribbean buckeye. 60c, Frampton's flambeau. 70c, Bamboo page. $1.10, Antillean cracker. $2.50, Red crescent hairstreak. $5, Single colored Antillean white. $10, Lesser whirlabout. $20, Blue night.

1985-86 *Perf. 14*

662 G74 ½c multicolored 15 15
663 G74 1c multicolored 15 15
664 G74 2c multicolored 15 15
665 G74 4c multicolored 15 15
666 G74 5c multicolored 15 15
667 G74 6c multicolored 15 15
668 G74 10c multicolored 15 15
669 G74 12c multicolored 15 15
670 G74 15c multicolored 15 15
671 G74 20c multicolored 15 15
672 G74 25c multicolored 18 18
673 G74 30c multicolored 22 22
674 G74 40c multicolored 28 28
675 G74 60c multicolored 45 45
676 G74 70c multicolored 50 50
677 G74 $1.10 multicolored 80 80
678 G74 $2.50 multicolored 1.90 1.90
679 G74 $5 multicolored 3.50 3.50
680 G74 $10 multicolored 7.25 7.25
681 G74 $20 multicolored 15.00 15.00
Nos. 662-681 (20) 31.58 31.58

Issue dates: Nos. 662-679, June 17, 1985. No. 680, Nov. 11, 1985. No. 681, Jan. 8, 1986.

For overprints see Nos. 737-738.

1986 *Perf. 12½x12*

662a G74 ½c multicolored 15 15
663a G74 1c multicolored 15 15
664a G74 2c multicolored 15 15
665a G74 4c multicolored 15 15
666a G74 5c multicolored 15 15
667a G74 6c multicolored 15 15
668a G74 10c multicolored 15 15
669a G74 12c multicolored 15 15
670a G74 15c multicolored 15 15
671a G74 20c multicolored 15 15
672a G74 25c multicolored 18 18
673a G74 30c multicolored 22 22
674a G74 40c multicolored 28 28
675a G74 60c multicolored 45 45
676a G74 70c multicolored 50 50
677a G74 $1.10 multicolored 80 80
678a G74 $2.50 multicolored 1.90 1.90
679a G74 $5 multicolored 3.50 3.50
680a G74 $10 multicolored 7.25 7.25
681a G74 $20 multicolored 15.00 15.00
Nos. 662a-681a (20) 31.58 31.58

Issue dates: Nos. 662a-677a, 679a, 1986. Nos. 678a, 680a, Sept. 1986. No. 681a, May 1989.

Queen Mother Birthday Type

Designs: $1, Portrait. $1.50, At Ascot, horiz. $2.50, Queen Mother, Prince Charles. $5, Portrait, diff.

1985, July 3 *Perf. 14*

682 A181 $1 multicolored 80 80
683 A181 $1.50 multicolored 1.25 1.25
684 A181 $2.50 multicolored 2.00 2.00

Souvenir Sheet

685 A181 $5 multicolored 4.00 4.00

1986, Jan. 28 *Perf. 12x12½*

686 A181 70c like #682 60 60
687 A181 $1.10 like #683 75 75
688 A181 $3 like #684 2.50 2.50

Issued in sheets of 5 plus label.

Water Sports Type

Designs: 15c, Scuba diving. 70c, Playing in waterfall. 90c, Water skiing. $4, Swimming. $5, Skin diver, sailboat.

1985, July 15 *Perf. 15*

689 A179 15c multicolored 15 15
690 A179 70c multicolored 55 55
691 A179 90c multicolored 70 70
692 A179 $4 multicolored 3.00 3.00

Souvenir Sheet

693 A179 $5 multicolored 4.00 4.00

Queen Conch G75

Marine Life: 90c, Porcupine fish, fire coral. $1.10, Ghost crab. $4, West Indies spiny lobster. $5, Long-spined urchin.

1985, Aug. 1 *Perf. 14*

694 G75 60c multicolored 48 48
695 G75 90c multicolored 75 75
696 G75 $1.10 multicolored 90 90
697 G75 $4 multicolored 3.25 3.25

Souvenir Sheet

698 G75 $5 multicolored 4.00 4.00

Bach Anniversary Type

Portrait, signature, music from Invention No. 9 and: 15c, Natural trumpet. 60c, Bass viol. $1.10, Flute. $3, Double flageolet. $5, Portrait.

1985, Sept. 3 *Perf. 14*

699 A184 15c multicolored 15 15
700 A184 60c multicolored 50 50
701 A184 $1.10 multicolored 85 85
702 A184 $3 multicolored 2.50 2.50

Souvenir Sheet

703 A184 $5 multicolored 4.00 4.00

Royal Visit Type

Designs: 10c, Arms of Great Britain, Grenada. $1, Queen Elizabeth II, vert. $4, HMY Britannia. $5, Map.

1985, Nov. 4 *Perf. 14½*

704 A186 10c multicolored 15 15
705 A186 $1 multicolored 80 80
706 A186 $4 multicolored 3.25 3.25

Souvenir Sheet

707 A186 $5 multicolored 4.00 4.00

UN Anniversary Type

UN stamps and famous people: $1, #373, Neil Armstrong. $2, #221, Mahatma Gandhi. $2.50, #43, Maimonides. $5, Ralph Bunche.

1985, Nov. 22

708 A189 $1 multicolored 80 80
709 A189 $2 multicolored 1.50 1.50
710 A189 $2.50 multicolored 2.00 2.00

Souvenir Sheet

711 A189 $5 multicolored 4.00 4.00

Twain & Disney Type

Walt Disney characters in scenes from "Letters From Hawaii": 25c, Mickey, Minnie on beach. 50c, Donald Duck surfing. $1.50, Donald roasting marshmallow. $3, Mickey canoeing. $5, Mickey, cat.

1985, Nov. 27 *Perf. 14x13½*

712 A185 25c multicolored 20 20
713 A185 50c multicolored 42 42
714 A185 $1.50 multicolored 1.25 1.25
715 A185 $3 multicolored 2.50 2.50

Souvenir Sheet

716 A185 $5 multicolored 4.15 4.15

Brothers Grimm & Disney Type

Walt Disney characters in scenes from "The Elves and the Shoemaker": 30c, Mickey as shoemaker. 60c, Elves helping. 70c, Mickey, new shoes. $4, Minnie at sewing machine. $5, Minnie & Mickey.

1985, Nov. 27 *Perf. 13½x14*

717 A187 30c multicolored 25 25
718 A187 60c multicolored 50 50
719 A187 70c multicolored 55 55
720 A187 $4 multicolored 3.25 3.25

Souvenir Sheet

721 A187 $5 multicolored 4.15 4.15

Madonna and Child by Titian — G76

Christmas paintings: 70c, Madonna and Child with St. Mary and John the Baptist by Bugiardini. $1.10, Adoration of the Magi by Di Fredi. $3, Madonna and Child with Young St. John the Baptist by Bartolomeo. $5, The Annunciation by Botticelli.

1985, Dec. 23 *Perf. 15*

722 G76 50c multicolored 38 38
723 G76 70c multicolored 52 52
724 G76 $1.10 multicolored 85 85
725 G76 $3 multicolored 2.25 2.25

Souvenir Sheet

726 G76 $5 multicolored 3.75 3.75

Statue of Liberty Type of 1985

Designs: 5c, Croton Reservoir, 1875. 10c, NY Public Library, 1986. 70c, Old Boathouse, Central Park, 1894. $4, Boating, Central Park, 1986. $5, Statue of Liberty, vert.

1986, Jan. 6 *Perf. 15*

727 A191 5c multicolored 15 15
728 A191 10c multicolored 15 15
729 A191 70c multicolored 52 52
730 A191 $4 multicolored 3.00 3.00

Souvenir Sheet

731 A191 $5 multicolored 3.75 3.75

Audubon Type of 1985

Designs: 50c, Louisiana heron. 70c, Black-crowned night heron. 90c, Bittern. $4, Glossy ibis. $5, King eider.

1986, Jan. 28 *Perf. 12½x12*

732 A174 50c multicolored 38 38
733 A174 70c multicolored 52 52
734 A174 90c multicolored 70 70
735 A174 $4 multicolored 3.00 3.00

Souvenir Sheet

Perf. 14

736 A174 $5 multicolored 3.70 3.70

Nos. 732-735 issued in sheets of 5 plus label.

Nos. 676, 679 Overprinted

VISIT OF PRES. REAGAN

20 FEBRUARY 1986

1986, Feb. 20 *Perf. 14*

737 G74 70c multicolored 52 52
738 G75 $5 multicolored 3.75 3.75

World Cup Soccer Championships, Mexico — G77

Various soccer plays.

1986, Mar. 18

739 G77 10c multicolored 15 15
740 G77 70c multicolored 52 52
741 G77 $1 multicolored 75 75
742 G77 $4 multicolored 3.00 3.00

Souvenir Sheet

743 G77 $5 multicolored 3.75 3.75

For overprints, see Nos. 772-776.

Halley's Comet Type

Designs: 5c, Nicolaus Copernicus, Earl of Rossi's six foot reflector. 20c, Sputnik. 40c, Tycho Brahe's notes, sketch of comet of 1577. $4, Edmond Halley, comet of 1682. $5, Halley's comet. Captions on 40c and $4 are reversed.

1986, Mar. 26

744 A194 5c multicolored 15 15
745 A194 20c multicolored 15 15
746 A194 40c multicolored 30 30
747 A194 $4 multicolored 3.00 3.00

Souvenir Sheet

748 A194 $5 multicolored 3.75 3.75

"Tycho," on 40c, and "Nicolaus" on 5c misspelled.

For overprints, see Nos. 787-791. Compare No. 748 with No. 913.

Queen Elizabeth II, 60th Birthday

Common Design Type

Designs: 2c, At Windsor Park, 1933. $1.50, Queen Elizabeth II. $4, In Sydney, Australia, 1970. $5, Family portrait, Coronation Day, 1937.

1986, Apr. 21

749 CD339 2c yel & blk 15 15
750 CD339 $1.50 pale grn & multi 1.10 1.10
751 CD339 $4 dl lil & multi 3.00 3.00

Souvenir Sheet

752 CD339 $5 tan & blk 3.75 3.75

AMERIPEX '86 Type

Walt Disney characters visiting: 30c, Grand Canyon. 60c, Golden Gate Bridge. $1, Chicago Watertower. $3, The White House. $5, NY Harbor, Statue of Liberty.

1986, May 22 *Perf. 11*

753 A195 30c multicolored 22 22
754 A195 60c multicolored 45 45
755 A195 $1 multicolored 75 75
756 A195 $3 multicolored 2.25 2.25

Souvenir Sheet

Perf. 14

757 A195 $5 multicolored 3.75 3.75

Royal Wedding Issue, 1986

Common Design Type

Designs: 60c, Prince Andrew and Sarah Ferguson. 70c, Andrew. $4, Andrew in dress uniform, helicopter. $5, Couple, diff.

1986, July 1 *Perf. 14*

758 CD340 60c multicolored 45 45
759 CD340 70c multicolored 52 52
760 CD340 $4 multicolored 3.00 3.00

Souvenir Sheet

761 CD340 $5 multicolored 3.75 3.75

Mushrooms — G78

Seashells — G79

Designs: 15c, Hygrocybe firma. 50c, Xerocomus coccolobae. $2, Volvariella cubensis. $3, Lactarius putidus. $5, Leponia caeruleocapitata.

1986, July 15 *Perf. 15*

762 G78 15c multicolored 15 15
763 G78 50c multicolored 40 40
764 G78 $2 multicolored 1.50 1.50
765 G78 $3 multicolored 2.25 2.25

Souvenir Sheet

766 G78 $5 multicolored 3.75 3.75

1986, Aug. 1

Designs: 15c, Giant Atlantic pyram. 50c, Beau's murex. $1.10, West Indian fighting conch. $4, Alphabet coral. $5, Brown-lined paper bubble.

767 G79 15c multicolored 15 15
768 G79 50c multicolored 40 40
769 G79 $1.10 multicolored 85 85
770 G79 $4 multicolored 3.00 3.00

Souvenir Sheet

771 G79 $5 multicolored 3.75 3.75

Nos. 739-743 Overprinted in Gold: WINNERS / Argentina 3 / W.Germany 2

1986, Sept. 15 *Perf. 14*

772 G77 10c multicolored 15 15
773 G77 70c multicolored 52 52
774 G77 $1 multicolored 75 75
775 G77 $4 multicolored 3.00 3.00

Souvenir Sheet

776 G77 $5 multicolored 3.75 3.75

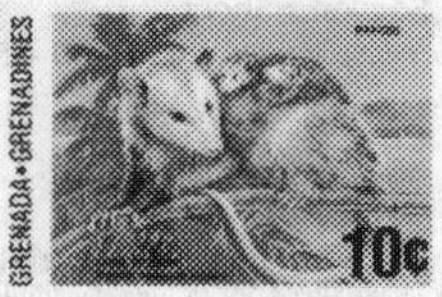

Manicou G80

Wildlife: 30c, Giant toad. 60c, Land tortoise. 70c, Murine opossum, vert. 90c, Burmese mongoose, vert. $1.10, Antillean armadillo. $2, Agouti. $3, Humpback whale.

1986, Sept. 15 *Perf. 15*

777 G80 10c multicolored 15 15
778 G80 30c multicolored 22 22
779 G80 60c multicolored 45 45
780 G80 70c multicolored 52 52
781 G80 90c multicolored 65 65
782 G80 $1.10 multicolored 85 85
783 G80 $2 multicolored 1.50 1.50
784 G80 $3 multicolored 2.25 2.25
Nos. 777-784 (8) 6.59 6.59

Souvenir Sheets

785 G80 $5 Mona monkey 3.65 3.65
786 G80 $5 Iguana 3.65 3.65

Nos. 744-748 Overprinted in Silver or Black

HALLEY'S COMET 1985 OFFICIAL 1986

1986, Oct. 15 *Perf. 14*

787 A194 5c multicolored (Bk) 15 15
788 A194 20c multicolored 15 15
789 A194 40c multicolored (Bk) 30 30
790 A194 $4 multicolored 3.00 3.00

Souvenir Sheet

791 A194 $5 multicolored 3.75 3.75

Christmas Type of 1986

1986 Nov. 3 *Perf. 11*

792 A199 25c Chip 'n' Dale 18 18
793 A199 30c Mickey Mouse 22 22
794 A199 50c Piglet, Pooh, Jose Carioca 35 35
795 A199 60c Daisy 42 42
796 A199 70c A kiss under the mistletoe 52 52
797 A199 $1.50 Huey, Dewey, and Louie 1.10 1.10
798 A199 $3 Mickey Mouse, Morty 2.25 2.25
799 A199 $4 Kittens on the keys 3.00 3.00
Nos. 792-799 (8) 8.04 8.04

Souvenir Sheets

800 A199 $5 Mickey Mouse 3.65 3.65
801 A199 $5 Bambi 3.65 3.65

Nos. 793, 795-796, 799 vert.

Automobile Centenary Type

Designs: 10c, 1984 Aston-Martin Volante. 30c, 1948 Jaguar Mk V. 60c, 1956 Nash Ambassador. 70c, 1984 Toyota Supra. 90c, 1985 Ferrari Testarossa. $1, 1955 BMW 501B. $2, 1968 Mercedes-Benz 280SL. $3, 1932 Austro-Daimler ADR8.

1986, Nov. 20 *Perf. 15*

802 A202 10c multicolored 15 15
803 A202 30c multicolored 22 22
804 A202 60c multicolored 45 45
805 A202 70c multicolored 52 52
806 A202 90c multicolored 70 70
807 A202 $1 multicolored 75 75
808 A202 $2 multicolored 1.50 1.50
809 A202 $3 multicolored 2.25 2.25
Nos. 802-809 (8) 6.54 6.54

Souvenir Sheets

810 A202 $5 1977 Morgan +8 3.75 3.75
811 A202 $5 Checker Taxi 3.75 3.75

Chagall Type

Paintings: No. 812, The Mirror. No. 813, Dancer with a Fan. No. 814, The Acrobat. No. 815, Abraham's Sacrifice. No. 816, The Fruit Seller. No. 817, The Rooster. No. 818, The Wedding. No. 819, Horsewoman. No. 820, The Aged Lion from Fables of La Fontaine. No. 821, The Fruit Basket. No. 822, The Satyr and the Wayfarer. No. 823, Self-portrait with Seven Fingers. No. 824, Fruit and Flowers. No. 825, Lovers and Flowers. No. 826, The Wedded with an Angel. No. 827, In the Cafe, 1936. No. 828, The Equestrian. No. 829, Blue Violinist, 1947. No. 830, I and the Village. No. 831, Portrait of Vava, 1955. No. 832, To Russia, Asses and Cattle, 1911. No. 833, The Accordion Player. No. 834, The Violinist, 1913. No. 835, Mother and Child, 1968. No. 836. Sunday, 1953. No. 837, Red and Black World, 1951. No. 838, Double Portrait with Wineglass, 1917. No. 839, Homage to Apollinaire. No. 840, Time is a River without Banks, 1930. No. 841, The Rue de La Paix, 1953. No. 842, Bonjour Paris. No. 843, The Blue Home, 1926, horiz. No. 844, Still-life, 1912, horiz. No. 845, Autumn Village. No. 846, Aleko: Scene I (Costume Design). No. 847, The Jew in Pink, 1914. No. 848, The Clown Musician, 1927. No. 849, War, 1943. No. 850, The Artist Angel. No. 851, Woman at Window, 1961. No. 852, Birthday, 1915. No. 853, Wheatfield on a Summer Afternoon, 1942. No. 854, The Nude Above Vitebsk. No. 855, Aleko and Zemphira by Moonlight. No. 856, The Family Dinner. No. 857, Life. No. 858, The Flying Carriage, 1913. No. 859, The Studio. No. 860, Birth. No. 861, Rain.

1986-87 *Perf. 14x13½*

812 A203 $1.10 multicolored 85 85
813 A203 $1.10 multicolored 85 85
814 A203 $1.10 multicolored 85 85
815 A203 $1.10 multicolored 85 85
816 A203 $1.10 multicolored 85 85
817 A203 $1.10 multicolored 85 85
818 A203 $1.10 multicolored 85 85
819 A203 $1.10 multicolored 85 85
820 A203 $1.10 multicolored 85 85
821 A203 $1.10 multicolored 85 85
822 A203 $1.10 multicolored 85 85
823 A203 $1.10 multicolored 85 85
824 A203 $1.10 multicolored 85 85
825 A203 $1.10 multicolored 85 85
826 A203 $1.10 multicolored 85 85
827 A203 $1.10 multicolored 85 85
828 A203 $1.10 multicolored 85 85
829 A203 $1.10 multicolored 85 85
830 A203 $1.10 multicolored 85 85
831 A203 $1.10 multicolored 85 85
832 A203 $1.10 multicolored 85 85
833 A203 $1.10 multicolored 85 85
834 A203 $1.10 multicolored 85 85
835 A203 $1.10 multicolored 85 85
836 A203 $1.10 multicolored 85 85
837 A203 $1.10 multicolored 85 85
838 A203 $1.10 multicolored 85 85
839 A203 $1.10 multicolored 85 85
840 A203 $1.10 multicolored 85 85
841 A203 $1.10 multicolored 85 85
842 A203 $1.10 multicolored 85 85
843 A203 $1.10 multicolored 85 85
844 A203 $1.10 multicolored 85 85
845 A203 $1.10 multicolored 85 85
846 A203 $1.10 multicolored 85 85
847 A203 $1.10 multicolored 85 85
848 A203 $1.10 multicolored 85 85
849 A203 $1.10 multicolored 85 85
850 A203 $1.10 multicolored 85 85
851 A203 $1.10 multicolored 85 85

Size: 110x95mm

Imperf

852 A203 $5 multicolored 3.75 3.75
853 A203 $5 multicolored 3.75 3.75
854 A203 $5 multicolored 3.75 3.75
855 A203 $5 multicolored 3.75 3.75
856 A203 $5 multicolored 3.75 3.75
857 A203 $5 multicolored 3.75 3.75
858 A203 $5 multicolored 3.75 3.75
859 A203 $5 multicolored 3.75 3.75
860 A203 $5 multicolored 3.75 3.75
861 A203 $5 multicolored 3.75 3.75
Nos. 812-861 (50) 71.50 71.50

Issue date: Nos. 824-851, 855-861, 1987.

America's Cup Type

1987, Feb. 5 *Perf. 15*

862 A204 25c Defender, 1895 18 18
863 A204 45c Caleta, 1886 32 32
864 A204 70c Azzurra, 1981 52 52
865 A204 $4 Australia II, 1983 3.00 3.00

Souvenir Sheet

866 A204 $5 Columbia, Shamrock, 1899 3.75 3.75

Discovery of America Type

1987, Apr. 27

867 A206 15c Columbus 15 15
868 A206 30c Queen Isabella 20 20
869 A206 50c Santa Maria 35 35
870 A206 60c Landing in New World 40 40
871 A206 90c Lesser Antilles 60 60
872 A206 $1 King Ferdinand 65 65
873 A206 $2 Fort of La Navidad 1.40 1.40
874 A206 $3 Galley off Hispaniola 2.00 2.00
a. Sheet of 8 6.25 6.25

Souvenir Sheets

875 A207 $5 Native Canoe 3.75 3.75
876 A207 $5 Santa Maria at anchor 3.75 3.75

Transportation Innovations Type

Designs: 10c, Saunders Roe SR-N1 Hovercraft, 1959. 15c, Bugatti Royale, 1931. 30c, Aleksei Leonov, 1st space walk, 1965. 50c, CSS Hunley, submarine, 1864. 60c, Rolls Royce Flying Bedstead,

VTOL aircraft, 1954. 70c, Jenny Lind, locomotive, 1854. 90c, Duryea, 1893. $1.50, Steam locomotive, London subway, 1863. $2, SS Great Britain, screw-driven steamship, 1843. $3, Budweiser rocket, 1979.

1987, May 18 ***Perf. 14***

877 A209 10c multicolored 15 15
878 A209 15c multicolored 15 15
879 A209 30c multicolored 22 22
880 A209 50c multicolored 40 40
881 A209 60c multicolored 45 45
882 A209 70c multicolored 52 52
883 A209 90c multicolored 70 70
884 A209 $1.50 multicolored 1.10 1.10
885 A209 $2 multicolored 1.50 1.50
886 A209 $3 multicolored 2.25 2.25
Nos. 877-886 (10) 7.44 7.44

Capex '87 Type

Fish.

1987, June 15

887 A208 6c Yellow chub 15 15
888 A208 30c Kingfish 22 22
889 A208 50c Mako shark 40 40
890 A208 60c Dolphinfish 45 45
891 A208 90c Bonito 70 70
892 A208 $1.10 Cobia 85 85
893 A208 $3 Great tarpon 2.25 2.25
894 A208 $4 Swordfish 3.00 3.00
Nos. 887-894 (8) 8.02 8.02

Souvenir Sheets

895 A208 $5 Jewfish 3.75 3.75
896 A208 $5 Amberjack 3.75 3.75

Statue of Liberty Type

Designs: 10c, Washing statue's face. 15c, Commemorative medals. 25c, Band facing right. 30c, Band facing forward. 45c, Liberty's face. 50c, Washing statue's hair, horiz. 60c, Commemorative statuettes, horiz. 70c, Boats in NY Harbor, horiz. $1, Re-opening. $1.10, Blimps, Liberty and Manhattan Islands. $2, Warship. $3, Commemorative flags.

1987, Aug. 5

897 A210 10c multicolored 15 15
898 A210 15c multicolored 15 15
899 A210 25c multicolored 18 18
900 A210 30c multicolored 22 22
901 A210 45c multicolored 35 35
902 A210 50c multicolored 40 40
903 A210 60c multicolored 42 42
904 A210 70c multicolored 52 52
905 A210 $1 multicolored 75 75
906 A210 $1.10 multicolored 85 85
907 A210 $2 multicolored 1.50 1.50
908 A210 $3 multicolored 2.25 2.25
Nos. 897-908 (12) 7.74 7.74

Inventors Type

Designs: 60c, Isaac Newton, Newton Medal. $1, Louis Daguerre, inventor of Daguerreotype. $2, Antoine Lavoisier, French chemist, apparatus. $3, Rudolf Diesel, German engineer, Diesel engine. $5, Halley's comet.

1987, Sept. 9

909 A211 60c multicolored 42 42
910 A211 $1 multicolored 75 75
911 A211 $2 multicolored 1.50 1.50
912 A211 $3 multicolored 2.25 2.25

Souvenir Sheet

913 A211 $5 multicolored 3.75 3.75

No. 913 inscribed "Great Scientific Discoveries" in margin.
No. 912 incorrectly inscribed "James Watt, Steam Engine." See Grenada No. 1538.

US Constitution Bicentennial Type

Designs: 10c, Constitutional Convention, Philadelphia. 50c, Georgia state flag. 60c, Capitol, vert. $4, Thomas Jefferson, vert. $5, Alexander Hamilton, vert.

1987, Nov. 1

914 A214 10c multicolored 15 15
915 A214 50c multicolored 40 40
916 A214 60c multicolored 42 42
917 A214 $4 multicolored 3.00 3.00

Souvenir Sheet

918 A214 $5 multicolored 3.75 3.75

Hafnia '87 Type

Walt Disney characters in adaptations of Hans Christian Andersen Fairy Tales: 25c, The Swineherd. 30c, What the Good Man Does is Always Right. 50c, Little Tuk. 60c, The World's Fairest Rose. 70c, The Garden of Paradise. $1.50, The Naughty Boy. $3, What the Moon Saw. $4, Thumbelina. No. 927, Hans Clodhopper. No. 928, Elder Tree Mother.

1987, Nov. 16

919 A215 25c multicolored 18 18
920 A215 30c multicolored 22 22
921 A215 50c multicolored 40 40
922 A215 60c multicolored 42 42
923 A215 70c multicolored 52 52
924 A215 $1.50 multicolored 1.10 1.10
925 A215 $3 multicolored 2.25 2.25
926 A215 $4 multicolored 3.00 3.00
Nos. 919-926 (8) 8.09 8.09

Souvenir Sheets

927 A215 $5 multicolored 3.75 3.75
928 A215 $5 multicolored 3.75 3.75

Christmas — G81

Paintings by El Greco: 10c, Virgin and Child with Saints Martin and Agnes. 50c, Detail from Virgin and Child with Saints Martin and Agnes. 60c, The Annunciation. $4, Holy Family with St. Anne. $5, Adoration of the Shepherds.

1987, Dec. 15

929 G81 10c multicolored 15 15
930 G81 50c multicolored 40 40
931 G81 60c multicolored 42 42
932 G81 $4 multicolored 2.25 2.25

Souvenir Sheet

933 G81 $5 multicolored 3.75 3.75

Wedding Anniv. Type

1988, Feb. 15

934 A218 20c Elizabeth, Anne 15 15
935 A218 30c Wedding portrait 22 22
936 A218 $2 Elizabeth, Charles, Anne 1.50 1.50
937 A218 $3 Elizabeth wearing tiara 2.25 2.25

Souvenir Sheet

938 A218 $5 Elizabeth in wedding gown 3.75 3.75

1988 Summer Olympics Type

Walt Disney characters in modern and ancient events.

Perf. 13½x14, 14x13½

1988, Apr. 13

939 A219 1c Rhythmic gymnastics 15 15
940 A219 2c Pankration 15 15
941 A219 3c Synchronized swimming 15 15
942 A219 4c Hoplite race 15 15
943 A219 5c Baseball 15 15
944 A219 10c Horse race 15 15
945 A219 $6 Windsurfing 4.50 4.50
946 A219 $7 Chariot race 5.25 5.25
Nos. 939-946 (8) 10.65 10.65

Souvenir Sheet

947 A219 $5 Tennis 3.75 3.75
948 A219 $5 Pentathlon 3.75 3.75

Boy Scout Type

1988, May 3 ***Perf. 14***

949 A220 50c Semaphore, vert. 40 40
950 A220 70c Canoeing, vert. 52 52
951 A220 $1 Cook-out 75 75
952 A220 $3 Campfire 2.25 2.25

Souvenir Sheet

953 A220 $5 Pitching tent 3.75 3.75

Bird Type

1988, May 31

954 A222 20c Yellow-crowned night heron 15 15
955 A222 25c Brown pelican 18 18
956 A222 45c Audubon's shearwater 35 35
957 A222 60c Red-footed booby 42 42
958 A222 70c Bridled tern 52 52
959 A222 90c Red-billed tropicbird 65 65
960 A222 $3 Blue-winged teal 2.25 2.25
961 A222 $4 Sora 3.00 3.00
Nos. 954-961 (8) 7.52 7.52

Souvenir Sheets

962 A222 $5 Little blue heron 3.75 3.75
963 A222 $5 Purple-throated carib 3.75 3.75

Titian Type

Paintings by Titian: 15c, Man with Blue Eyes, 1545. 30c, The Three Ages of Man, 1512. 60c, Don Diego Mendoza, 1545. 75c, Emperor Charles V Seated, 1548. $1, A Young Man in a Fur, 1515. $2, Tobias and the Angel, 1543. $3, Pietro Bembo, 1540. $4, Pier Luigi Farnese, 1546. No. 972, Sacred and Profane Love. No. 973, Venus and Adonis.

1988, June 15 ***Perf. 13½x14***

964 A224 15c multicolored 15 15
965 A224 30c multicolored 22 22
966 A224 60c multicolored 42 42
967 A224 75c multicolored 55 55
968 A224 $1 multicolored 75 75
969 A224 $2 multicolored 1.50 1.50
970 A224 $3 multicolored 2.25 2.25
971 A224 $4 multicolored 3.00 3.00
Nos. 964-971 (8) 8.84 8.84

Souvenir Sheet

972 A224 $5 multicolored 3.75 3.75
973 A224 $5 multicolored 3.75 3.75

Airship Type

Historic flights: 10c, Hindenburg over Rio de Janeiro, 1937. 20c, Hindenburg over NYC, 1937. 30c, US Navy airships, WWII convoy to Europe, 1944. 40c, Hindenburg docking at Lakehurst, NJ, 1937, vert. 60c, Joint flight, Hindenburg and Graf Zeppelin, 1936, vert. 70c, DC-3, Hindenburg, Los Angeles at Lakehurst, 1936. $1, Graf Zeppelin II over England, 1939, vert. $2, Deutschland, 1st passenger flight, 1912. $3, Graf Zeppelin over Dome of the Rock, Jerusalem, 1931. $4, Hindenburg Olympic flight, 1936. No. 984, Graf Zeppelin over Vatican City, 1933, vert. No. 985, Graf Zeppelin Polar flight, 1931.

1988, July 1 ***Perf. 14***

974 A225 10c multicolored 15 15
975 A225 20c multicolored 15 15
976 A225 30c multicolored 22 22
977 A225 40c multicolored 30 30
978 A225 60c multicolored 42 42
979 A225 70c multicolored 50 50
980 A225 $1 multicolored 75 75
981 A225 $2 multicolored 1.50 1.50
982 A225 $3 multicolored 2.25 2.25
983 A225 $4 multicolored 3.00 3.00
Nos. 974-983 (10) 9.24 9.24

Souvenir Sheets

984 A225 $5 multicolored 3.75 3.75
985 A225 $5 multicolored 3.75 3.75

Fairy Tales Type
Miniature Sheets

Bambi: No. 986a, Newborn Bambi, mother and forest animals. b, Bambi, Flower and Thumper. c, Bambi and opossum family hanging from tree. d, Bambi, his mother, and Faline, a female fawn. e, Foraging in a snow storm. f, Meeting his father, the Great Stag. g, Competing for Faline's attention. h, The Great Stag leading animals to safety during forest fire. i, Bambi, grown, becomes the Great Stag.

The Fox and the Hound: No. 987a, Big Mama, consoling the orphaned baby fox, Tod. b, Widow Tweed feeding Tod. c, Tod playing with Copper, the hound. d, Copper leashed. e, Copper and Chief. f, Chief barking at Tod, Copper shocked. g, Porcupine. h, Vixey, a female fox. i, Bear attacking Copper.

101 Dalmatians: No. 988a, Pongo, Perdita and their masters. b, Pongo and Perdita, courting. c, Three puppies. d, Cruella de Ville and henchmen. e, Captain the Horse, Colonel the Sheepdog and Tibbs the Cat. f, Dalmatians following Tibbs to freedom. g, Cruella racing car in pursuit. h, Dalmatians disguised in soot. i, Nanny dusting off the soot.

Dumbo: No. 989a, Stork delivering Dumbo. b, Elephant making fun of Dumbo's large ears. c, Dumbo, Mrs. Jumbo performing. d, Timothy the Mouse. e, Timothy and Dumbo. f, Crows pushing Dumbo off a cliff. g, Dumbo flying away from burning building. h, Dumbo flying with the crows. i, Dumbo and Mrs. Jumbo on train.

Lady and the Tramp: No. 990a, Darling holding Lady. b, Lady meets the Tramp. c, Lady looking in bassinet. d, Siamese cats, Lady. e, Lady, Tramp, crocodiles. f, Tramp kisses Lady. g, Lady in dog catcher's carriage. h, Lady and Tramp attacking rat. i, Trusty and Jock overturning dog catcher's carriage where Tramp is imprisoned.

The Aristocats: No. 991a, Edgar driving Madame Mornfamille's carriage. b, Dutchess and kittens. c, Edgar feeding the cats cream spiked with sleeping pills. d, Edgar transporting cats on motorcycle. e, Walter O'Malley discovers the abandoned cats. f, Three geese. g, Scat Cat and friends holding a jam session. h, Edgar attacks O'Malley with a pitch fork. i, Frau-Frau kicking Edgar.

No. 992, Faline and newborn twin fawns. No. 993, Tod and Vixey. No. 994, Pongo, Perdita and puppies. No. 995, Dumbo flying with Timothy the Mouse. No. 996, Lady and Tramp's puppies. No. 997, Walter O'Malley, Dutchess and kittens.

1988, July 25 ***Perf. 14x13½***

986 Sheet of 9 2.00 2.00
a.-i. A212 30c any single 22 22
987 Sheet of 9 2.00 2.00
a.-i. A212 30c any single 22 22
988 Sheet of 9 2.00 2.00
a.-i. A212 30c any single 22 22
989 Sheet of 9 2.00 2.00
a.-i. A212 30c any single 22 22
990 Sheet of 9 2.00 2.00
a.-i. A212 30c any single 22 22
991 Sheet of 9 2.00 2.00
a.-i. A212 30c any single 22 22
Nos. 986-991 (6) 12.00 12.00

Souvenir Sheets

992 A212 $5 multicolored 3.75 3.75
993 A212 $5 multicolored 3.75 3.75
994 A212 $5 multicolored 3.75 3.75
995 A212 $5 multicolored 3.75 3.75
996 A212 $5 multicolored 3.75 3.75
997 A212 $5 multicolored 3.75 3.75

SYDPEX '88 Type

Walt Disney characters: 1c, Conducting at Sydney Opera House. 2c, Climbing Ayers Rock. 3c, Working at a sheep station. 4c, Visiting Lone Pine Koala Sanctuary. 5c, Playing Australian football. 10c, Racing camels. No. 1004, Lawn bowling. $6, America's Cup trophy and Australia II. No. 1006, The Great Barrier Reef. No. 1007, Beach party.

1988, Aug. 1 ***Perf. 14x13½***

998 A226 1c multicolored 15 15
999 A226 2c multicolored 15 15
1000 A226 3c multicolored 15 15
1001 A226 4c multicolored 15 15
1002 A226 5c multicolored 15 15
1003 A226 10c multicolored 15 15
1004 A226 $5 multicolored 3.25 3.25
1005 A226 $6 multicolored 3.75 3.75
Set value 7.25 7.25

Souvenir Sheets

1006 A226 $5 multicolored 3.25 3.25
1007 A226 $5 multicolored 3.25 3.25

Flowering Trees Type

1988, Sept. 30 ***Perf. 14***

1008 A228 10c Potato tree, vert. 15 15
1009 A228 20c Wild cotton 15 15
1010 A228 30c Shower of gold, vert. 22 22
1011 A228 60c Napoleon's button, vert. 42 42
1012 A228 90c Geiger tree 65 65
1013 A228 $1 Fern tree 75 75
1014 A228 $2 French cashew 1.50 1.50
1015 A228 $4 Amherstia, vert. 3.00 3.00
Nos. 1008-1015 (8) 6.84 6.84

Souvenir Sheets

1016 A228 $5 African tulip tree, vert. 3.75 3.75
1017 A228 $5 Swamp immortelle 3.75 3.75

Car Type
Miniature Sheets

Designs: No. 1018a, 1925 Doble Series E, US. b, 1926 Alvis 12/50, United Kingdom. c, 1927 Sunbeam 3-liter, UK. d, 1928 Franklin Airman, US. e, 1929 Delage D8S, France. f, 1897 Mors, France. g, 1904 Peerless Green Dragon, US. h, 1909 Pope-Hartford, US. i, 1920 Daniels Submarine Speedster, US. j, 1922 McFarlan 9.3 liter, US.

No. 1019a, 1949 Frazer Nash Lemans Replica, UK. b, 1953 Pegaso Z102, Spain. No. 1019c, 1953 Siata Spyder V-8, Italy. d, 1953 Kurtis-Offenhauser, US. No. 1019e, 1954 Kaiser-Darrin, US. f, 1930 Tracta, France. g, 1932 Maybach Zeppelin, Germany. h, 1934 Railton Light Sports, UK. i, 1936 Hotchkiss, France. j, 1939 Mercedes-Benz W163, Germany.

No. 1020a, 1982 Aston Martin Vantage V8, UK. b, 1982 Porsche 956, Germany. No. 1020c, 1983 Lotus Esprit Turbo, UK. d, 1984 McLaren MP4/2, UK. e, 1985 Mercedes-Benz 190E 2-3-16, Germany. f, 1963 Ferrari 250 GT Lusso, Italy. g, 1964 Porsche 904, Germany. h, 1967 Volvo P1800, Sweden. i, 1970 McLaren-Chevrolet M8D, US. j, 1981 Jaguar XJ6, UK.

1988, Oct. 7 ***Perf. 13x13½***

1018 Sheet of 10 15.00 15.00
a.-j. A223 $2 any single 1.50 1.50
1019 Sheet of 10 15.00 15.00
a.-j. A223 $2 any single 1.50 1.50
1020 Sheet of 10 15.00 15.00
a.-j. A223 $2 any single 1.50 1.50

Christmas and Mickey Mouse 60th Anniv. Type
Miniature Sheet

"Mickey's Christmas Parade": No. 1021a, Dumbo. b, Goofy. c, Minnie Mouse. d, Morty, Ferdy and Clarabelle Cow. e, Huey, Dewey and Louie. f, Donald Duck. g, Wooden soldiers marching. h, Mickey Mouse leading parade. No. 1022, Capt. Hook on float. No. 1023, Mickey and Donald on float.

1988, Dec. 1 ***Perf. 13½x14***

1021 Sheet of 8 6.00 6.00
a.-h. A229 $1 any single 75 75

Souvenir Sheets

Perf. 14x13

1022 A229 $7 multicolored 5.25 5.25
1023 A229 $7 multicolored 5.25 5.25

Japanese Painting Type

"The Fifty-three Stations on the Tokaido" by Hiroshige (1979-1858): 15c, Crossing the Oi at Shimada by Ferry. 20c, Daimyo and Entourage at

Arai. 45c, Cargo Portage through Goyu. 75c, Snowfall at Fujigawa. $1, Horses for the Emperor at Chirifu. $2, Rainfall at Tsuchiyama. $3, At Inn of Ishibe. $4, On the Shore of Lake Biwa at Otsu. No. 1032, Pilgrimage to Atsuta Shrine at Miya. No. 1033, Fishing Village of Yokkaichi on the Mie.

1989, May 15 ***Perf. 14x13½***

1024	A233	15c multicolored	15	15
1025	A233	20c multicolored	15	15
1026	A233	45c multicolored	32	32
1027	A233	75c multicolored	55	55
1028	A233	$1 multicolored	75	75
1029	A233	$2 multicolored	1.50	1.50
1030	A233	$3 multicolored	2.25	2.25
1031	A233	$4 multicolored	3.00	3.00
		Nos. 1024-1031 (8)	8.67	8.67

Souvenir Sheets

1032	A233	$5 multicolored	3.75	3.75
1033	A233	$5 multicolored	3.75	3.75

1988 Olympic Medalists Type

Designs: 15c, Henry Maske, East Germany, boxing (165 lbs.). 50c, Andreas Schroeder, East Germany, freestyle wrestling (286 lbs.). 60c, East German team, women's gymnastics. 75c, Greg Louganis, US, men's springboard and platform diving. $1, Mitsuru Sato, Japan, freestyle wrestling (115 lbs.). $2, West German team, 4x200m freestyle relay. $3, Dieter Baumann, West Germany, 5000m race. $4, Jackie Joyner-Kersee, US, heptathlon. No. 1042, Joachim Kunz, East Germany, weight lifting (149 lbs.). No. 1043, West German equestrian team, 3-day event.

1989, Apr. 13 ***Perf. 14***

1034	A232	15c multicolored	15	15
1035	A232	50c multicolored	35	35
1036	A232	60c multicolored	42	42
1037	A232	75c multicolored	55	55
1038	A232	$1 multicolored	75	75
1039	A232	$2 multicolored	1.50	1.50
1040	A232	$3 multicolored	2.25	2.25
1041	A232	$4 multicolored	3.00	3.00
		Nos. 1034-1041 (8)	8.97	8.97

Souvenir Sheets

1042	A232	$6 multicolored	4.25	4.25
1043	A232	$6 multicolored	4.25	4.25

World Cup Soccer Championships, Italy — G82

Designs: 15c, World Cup, vert. 45c, Kaiser Franz, West Germany, vert. 75c, Like 20c, flag of Italy, 1982 champions. $1, Pele, Brazil, vert. $2, Like 20c, flag of West Germany, 1974 champions. $3, Like 20c, flag of Brazil, 1970 champions. $4, Jules Rimet Cup, vert. No. 1052, Pele, Jules Rimet Cup, vert. No. 1053, Goalie.

1989, June 12

1044	G82	15c multicolored	15	15
1045	G82	20c multicolored	15	15
1046	G82	45c multicolored	32	32
1047	G82	75c multicolored	55	55
1048	G82	$1 multicolored	1.50	1.50
1049	G82	$2 multicolored	3.00	3.00
1050	G82	$3 multicolored	2.25	2.25
1051	G82	$4 multicolored	3.00	3.00
		Nos. 1044-1051 (8)	10.92	10.92

Souvenir Sheets

1052	G82	$6 multicolored	4.25	4.25
1053	G82	$6 multicolored	4.25	4.25

Car Type of 1988
Miniature Sheets

North American locomotives: No. 1054a, Morris & Essex, Dover, 1841. No. 1054b, B&O, Memmon No. 57, 1848. No. 1054c, Camden & Amboy, John Stevens, 1849. No. 1054d, Lawrence Machine Shop, Lawrence, 1853. No. 1054e, South Carolina, James S. Corry, 1859. No. 1054f, Mine Hill & Schuylkill Haven, Flexible Beam No. 3, 1860. No. 1054g, DL&W, Montrose, 1861. No. 1054h, Central Pacific, Pequop No. 68, 1868. No. 1054i, Boston & Providence, Daniel Nason, 1863. No. 1054j, Morris & Essex, Joe Scranton, 1870.

No. 1055a, Central Railroad of New Jersey, No. 124, 1871. No. 1055b, Baldwin Steam Motor for Street Railways, 1876. No. 1055c, Lackawanna & Bloomsburg, Luzerne, 1878. No. 1055d, Central Mexicano, No. 150, 1892. No. 1055e, Denver, South Park & Pacific, Breckenridge No. 15, 1879. No. 1055f, Miles Planting & Manufacturing Co., "Daisy" Plantation locomotive, 1894. No. 1055g, Central of Georgia, Baldwin 854 No. 1136, 1895. No. 1055h, Savannah, Florida & Western, No. 111, 1900. No. 1055i, Douglas, Gilmore, & Co. No. 3, 1902. No. 1055j, Lehigh Valley Coal Co., Compressed Air locomotive No. 900, 1903.

No. 1056a, Morgan's Louisiana & Texas, McKeen Motorcar, 1908. No. 1056b, Clear Lake Lumber Co., Type B Climax, 1910. No. 1056c, Blue Jay Lumber Co., Heisler No. 10, 1912. No. 1056d, Stewartstown, Gasoline Engine No. 6, 1920's. No. 1056e, Bangor & Aroostook, Class G No. 186, 1921. No. 1056f, Hammond Lumber Co., No. 6, 1923. No. 1056g, Central Railroad of New Jersey, No. 1000, 1925. No. 1056h, Atchison, Topeka & Santa Fe, Super Chief No. 1-1A, 1935. No. 1056i, Norfolk & Western, Class Y-6, 1948. No. 1056i, Boston & Maine, Budd Railcar, 1949.

1989, June 28 ***Perf. 13x13½***

1054	Sheet of 10	15.00	15.00
a.-j.	A223 $2 any single	1.50	1.50
1055	Sheet of 10	15.00	15.00
a.-j.	A223 $2 any single	1.50	1.50
1056	Sheet of 10	15.00	15.00
a.-j.	A223 $2 any single	1.50	1.50

PHILEXFRANCE '89 — G83

Walt Disney characters in Paris.

1989, July 7 ***Perf. 14x13½, 13½x14***

1057	G83	1c Military school	15	15
1058	G83	2c Conciergerie	15	15
1059	G83	3c Hotel de Ville, vert.	15	15
1060	G83	4c Genie of the Bastille, vert.	15	15
1061	G83	5c The Opera	15	15
1062	G83	10c Gardens of Luxembourg	15	15
1063	G83	$5 Arche de la Defense, vert.	3.25	3.25
1064	G83	$6 Place Vendome, vert.	3.50	3.50
		Set value	7.00	7.00

Souvenir Sheets

1065	G83	$6 Riding moped	4.00	4.00
1066	G83	$6 Hot air ballooning	4.00	4.00

Moon Landing Anniv. Type

Apollo 11 mission, 1969: 25c, Liftoff, vert. 50c, Splashdown. 60c, Spacecraft approaching moon, vert. 75c, Buzz Aldrin conducting experiment on lunar surface. $1, Leaving Earth orbit. $2, Transport of launch vehicle to pad, vert. $3, Lunar module liftoff. $4, Eagle lands on moon, vert. No. 1075, Footprint on moon. No. 1076, Armstrong stepping onto the moon, vert.

1989, July 20 ***Perf. 14***

1067	A237	25c multicolored	18	18
1068	A237	50c multicolored	35	35
1069	A237	60c multicolored	42	42
1070	A237	75c multicolored	55	55
1071	A237	$1 multicolored	75	75
1072	A237	$2 multicolored	1.50	1.50
1073	A237	$3 multicolored	2.25	2.25
1074	A237	$4 multicolored	3.00	3.00
		Nos. 1067-1074 (8)	9.00	9.00

Souvenir Sheets

1075	A237	$5 multicolored	3.75	3.75
1076	A237	$5 multicolored	3.75	3.75

Mushroom Type

1989, Aug. 17

1078	A238	6c Collybia aurea	15	15
1079	A238	10c Podaxis pistillaris	15	15
1080	A238	20c Hygrocybe firma	15	15
1081	A238	30c Agaricus rufoaurantiacus	22	22
1082	A238	75c Leptonia howellii	55	55
1083	A238	$2 Marasmiellus purpureus	1.50	1.50
1084	A238	$3 Marasmius trinitatis	2.25	2.25
1085	A238	$4 Hygrocybe martinicensis	3.00	3.00
		Nos. 1078-1085 (8)	7.97	7.97

Souvenir Sheets

1086	A238	$6 Lentinus crinitus	4.25	4.25
1087	A238	$6 Agaricus purpurellus	4.25	4.25

Butterflies Type

1989, Oct. 2 ***Perf. 14***

1088	A239	25c Androgeus swallowtail	18	18
1089	A239	35c Cloudless sulpher	25	25
1090	A239	45c Cracker	32	32
1091	A239	50c Painted lady	35	35
1092	A239	75c Great southern white	55	55
1093	A239	90c Little sulpher	65	65
1094	A239	$2 Migrant sulpher	1.50	1.50
1095	A239	$3 Mimic	2.25	2.25
		Nos. 1088-1095 (8)	6.05	6.05

Souvenir Sheets

1096	A239	$6 Giant hairstreak	4.25	4.25
1097	A239	$6 Red anartia	4.25	4.25

World Stamp Expo Type

Scenes from Walt Disney animated films and quotes from Poor Richard's Almanack by Benjamin Franklin: 1c, "Beware of little expenses, a small leak will sink a great ship." 2c, "Trust thyself and another shall not betray thee." 3c, "A spoonful of honey will catch more flies than a gallon of vinegar." 4c, "No gain without pain." 5c, "A true friend is the best possession." 6c, "Haste makes waste." 8c, "A quiet conscience sleeps in thunder, but rest and guilt live far asunder." 10c, "The muses love the morning." $5, "An egg today is better than a hen tomorrow." No. 1107, "He that riseth late, must trot all day." No. 1108, "If you'd be belov'd, make yourself amiable." No. 1109, "In Christmas feasting pray take care; let not your table be a snare; but with the poor God's bounty share. Adieu my friends! Till the next year," vert.

1989, Nov. **Litho.** ***Perf. 14x13½***

1098	A242	1c multicolored	15	15
1099	A242	2c multicolored	15	15
1100	A242	3c multicolored	15	15
1101	A242	4c multicolored	15	15
1102	A242	5c multicolored	15	15
1103	A242	6c multicolored	15	15
1104	A242	8c multicolored	15	15
1105	A242	10c multicolored	15	15
1106	A242	$5 multicolored	3.50	3.50
1107	A242	$6 multicolored	3.75	3.75
		Set value	7.50	7.50

Souvenir Sheet

1108	A242	$6 multicolored	3.75	3.75
1109	A242	$6 multicolored	3.75	3.75

World Stamp Expo '89, Washington, D.C.

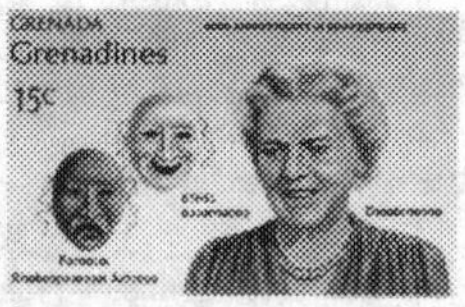

Shakespearean Actors and Theater Masks — G84

Designs: 15c, Ethel Barrymore (1879-1959). $1.10, Richard Burton (1925-1984). $2, John Barrymore (1882-1942). $3, Paul Robeson (1898-1976). $6, Bando Tamasaburo and Nakamura Kanzaburo.

1989, Oct. 9 **Litho.** ***Perf. 14***

1110	G84	15c multicolored	15	15
1111	G84	$1.10 multicolored	82	82
1112	G84	$2 multicolored	1.50	1.50
1113	G84	$3 multicolored	2.25	2.25

Souvenir Sheet

1114	G84	$6 multicolored	4.50	4.50

20th Century Musicians — G85

1989, Oct. 9

1115	G85	10c Buddy Holly	15	15
1116	G85	25c Jimi Hendrix	18	18
1117	G85	75c Mighty Sparrow	58	58
1118	G85	$4 Katsutoji Kineya	3.00	3.00

Souvenir Sheet

1119	G85	$6 Lotte Lenya, Kurt Weill	4.50	4.50

Jimi is spelled incorrectly as "Jimmy."

Discovery of America Type

1989, Oct. 16

1120	A241	15c Canoeing	15	15
1121	A241	75c Cooking	58	58
1122	A241	90c Using stone tools	68	68
1123	A241	$3 Eating	2.25	2.25

Souvenir Sheet

1124	A241	$6 Building fire	4.50	4.50

Christmas Type

Religious paintings by Rubens: 10c, The Annunciation. 15c, The Flight of the Holy Family into Egypt. 25c, The Presentation in the Temple. 45c, The Holy Family Under the Apple Tree. $2, Madonna and Child with Saints. $4, The Virgin and Child Enthroned with Saints. No. 1132, The Holy Family. No. 1132, Adoration of the Magi. No. 1133, Adoration of the Magi, diff.

1990, Jan. 4 ***Perf. 14***

1125	A243	10c multicolored	15	15
1126	A243	15c multicolored	15	15
1127	A243	25c multicolored	18	18
1128	A243	45c multicolored	35	35
1129	A243	$2 multicolored	1.50	1.50
1130	A243	$4 multicolored	3.00	3.00
1131	A243	$5 multicolored	3.75	3.75
		Nos. 1125-1131 (7)	9.08	9.08

Souvenir Sheets

1132	A243	$5 multicolored	3.75	3.75
1133	A243	$5 multicolored	3.75	3.75

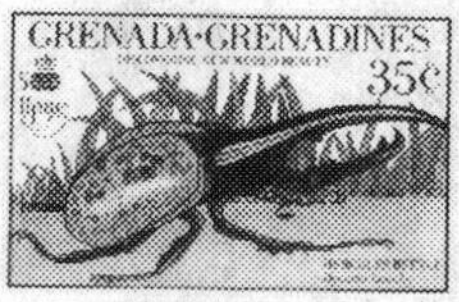

America Issue (Insects) G86

1990, Mar. 16 ***Perf. 14***

1134	G86	35c Hercules beetle	28	28
1135	G86	40c Click beetle	30	30
1136	G86	50c Harlequin beetle	38	38
1137	G86	60c Gold rim butterfly	45	45
1138	G86	$1 Red skimmer dragonfly	75	75
1139	G86	$2 Buprestid beetle	1.50	1.50
1140	G86	$3 Mimic butterfly	2.25	2.25
1141	G86	$4 Scarab beetle	3.00	3.00
		Nos. 1134-1141 (8)	8.91	8.91

Souvenir Sheets

1142	G86	$6 Canna skipper butterfly	4.50	4.50
1143	G86	$6 Monarch butterfly	4.50	4.50

Orchids — G87

1990, Mar. 6 **Litho.** ***Perf. 14***

1144	G87	15c Brassocattleya thalie	15	15
1145	G87	20c Odontocidium tigersun	15	15
1146	G87	50c Odontioda hambuhren	38	38
1147	G87	75c Paphiopedium delrosi	55	55
1148	G87	$1 Vuylstekeara yokara	75	75
1149	G87	$2 Paphiopedilum geelong	1.50	1.50
1150	G87	$3 Wilsonara tigerwood	2.25	2.25
1151	G87	$4 Cymbidium ormoulu	3.00	3.00
		Nos. 1144-1151 (8)	8.73	8.73

Souvenir Sheets

1152	G87	$6 Odontonia sappho	4.50	4.50
1153	G87	$6 Cymbidium vieux rose	4.50	4.50

EXPO '90 Intl. Garden and Greenery Exposition, Osaka, Japan.

Wildlife Type

1990, Apr. 3

1154	A247	5c West Indies giant rice rat	15	15
1155	A247	25c Agouti	18	15
1156	A247	30c Humpback whale	22	22
1157	A247	40c Pilot whale	30	30
1158	A247	$1 Spotted dolphin	75	75
1159	A247	$2 Mongoose	1.50	1.50
1160	A247	$3 Prehensile-tailed porcupine	2.25	2.25
1161	A247	$4 West Indies manatee	3.00	3.00
		Nos. 1154-1161 (8)	8.35	8.32

Souvenir Sheets

1162	A247	$6 Caribbean monk seal	4.50	4.50
1163	A247	$6 Mongoose	4.50	4.50

World War II Type

Designs: 6c, First British troops arrive in France, Sept. 6, 1939. 10c, British launch "Operation Crusader", Nov. 18, 1941. 20c, Rommel begins retreat from El Alamein, Nov. 4, 1942. 45c, US forces land on Aleutian Islands, May 11, 1943. 50c, US Marines land on Tarawa, Nov. 20, 1943. 60c, US 5th Army enters Rome, June 4, 1944. 75c, US troops reach River Seine, Aug. 19, 1944. $1, Battle of the Bulge, Dec. 16, 1944. $5, Allies launch final phase of Italian Campaign, Apr. 9, 1945. No. 1173, Atom bomb dropped on Hiroshima, Aug. 6, 1945. No. 1174, St. Paul's Catherdral during London blitz, Battle of Britain, 1940.

1990, Apr. 30

1164 A248 6c multicolored 15 15
1165 A248 10c multicolored 15 15
1166 A248 20c multicolored 15 15
1167 A248 45c multicolored 35 35
1168 A248 50c multicolored 38 38
1169 A248 60c multicolored 45 45
1170 A248 75c multicolored 55 55
1171 A248 $1 multicolored 75 75
1172 A248 $5 multicolored 3.75 3.75
1173 A248 $6 multicolored 4.50 4.50
Nos. 1164-1173 (10) 11.18 11.18

Souvenir Sheets

1174 A248 $6 multicolored 4.50 4.50

Disney Type

Disney characters portraying Shakespearian characters: 15c, Daisy Duck at Ann Hathaway's Cottage, Shottery. 30c, Minnie Mouse and a young Shakespeare walking in Stratford birthplace, vert. 50c, Minnie as Mary Arden, Shakespeare's mother in Wilmcote, vert. 60c, Mickey in front of New Place, Stratford. $1, Mickey walking in Great Garden of New Place. $2, Mickey at Guild Chapel, Scholars Lane, vert. $4, Mickey at the Royal Shakespeare Theater, Stratford, vert. $5, Ludwig von Drake instructing Shakespeare. No. 1183, Mickey at Edge Hill, Stratford, vert. No. 1184, Mickey and Minnie rowing past Holy Trinity Church, Stratford-Upon-Avon.

1990, May *Perf. 14x13½*

1175 A250 15c multicolored 15 15
1176 A250 30c multicolored 22 22
1177 A250 50c multicolored 38 38
1178 A250 60c multicolored 45 45
1179 A250 $1 multicolored 75 75
1180 A250 $2 multicolored 1.25 1.25
1181 A250 $4 multicolored 2.75 2.75
1182 A250 $5 multicolored 3.50 3.50
Nos. 1175-1182 (8) 9.45 9.45

Souvenir Sheets

Perf. 14

1183 A250 $6 multicolored 4.00 4.00
1184 A250 $6 multicolored 4.00 4.00

Penny Black Type
Souvenir Sheet

1990, May 3 Litho. *Perf. 14*

1185 A249 $6 Globe with South America 4.50 4.50

Stamp World London '90.

Queen Mother, 90th Birthday Type

1990, July 5

1186 A251 $2 Pink hat 1.50 1.50
1187 A251 $2 With Charles 1.50 1.50
1188 A251 $2 Blue outfit 1.50 1.50

Souvenir Sheet

1189 A251 $6 like #1187 4.50 4.50

Bird Type

1990, Sept. 10 Litho. *Perf. 14*

1190 A255 25c Yellow-bellied seedeater 18 18
1191 A255 45c Carib grackle 35 35
1192 A255 50c Black-whiskered vireo 38 38
1193 A255 75c Bananaquit 55 55
1194 A255 $1 Collared swift 75 75
1195 A255 $2 Yellow-bellied elaenia 1.50 1.50
1196 A255 $3 Blue-hooded euphonia 2.25 2.25
1197 A255 $5 Eared dove 3.75 3.75
Nos. 1190-1197 (8) 9.71 9.71

Souvenir Sheets

1198 A255 $6 Mangrove cuckoo 4.50 4.50
1199 A255 $6 Scaly-breasted thrasher 4.50 4.50

Crustaceans

1990, Sept. 17

1200 A256 10c Slipper lobster 15 15
1201 A256 25c Green reef crab 18 18
1202 A256 65c Caribbean lobsterette 48 48
1203 A256 75c Blind deep sea lobster 55 55
1204 A256 $1 Flattened crab 75 75
1205 A256 $2 Ridged slipper lobster 1.50 1.50
1206 A256 $3 Land crab 2.25 2.25
1207 A256 $4 Mountain crab 3.00 3.00
Nos. 1200-1207 (8) 8.86 8.86

Souvenir Sheets

1208 A256 $6 Caribbean king crab 4.50 4.50
1209 A256 $6 Purse crab 4.50 4.50

G88

G89

Players from participating countries.

1990, Sept. 24

1210 G88 15c England 15 15
1211 G88 45c Argentina 35 35
1212 G88 $2 Sweden 1.50 1.50
1213 G88 $4 South Korea 3.00 3.00

Souvenir Sheets

1214 G88 $6 Yugoslavia 4.50 4.50
1215 G88 $6 United States 4.50 4.50

World Cup Soccer Championships, Italy.

1990, Nov. 11 Litho. *Perf. 14*

1216 G89 10c Boxing 15 15
1217 G89 25c Olympic flame 18 18
1218 G89 50c Soccer 38 38
1219 G89 75c Discus 55 55
1220 G89 $1 Pole vault 75 75
1221 G89 $2 Equestrian 3-day event 1.50 1.50
1222 G89 $4 Women's basketball 3.00 3.00
1223 G89 $5 Men's gymnastics 3.75 3.75
Nos. 1216-1223 (8) 10.26 10.26

Souvenir Sheets

1224 G89 $6 Sailboarding 4.50 4.50
1225 G89 $6 Decathlon 4.50 4.50

1992 Summer Olympics, Barcelona.

Rubens Type

Entire paintings or different details from: 5c, 25c, Adam and Eve, vert. 15c, Esther before Ahasuerus. 50c, Expulsion from Eden. $1, Cain Slaying Abel, vert. $2, Lot's Flight. $4, Samson and Delilah. $5, Abraham and Melchizedek. No. 1234, The Meeting of David and Abigail. No. 1235, Daniel in the Lions Den.

1991, Jan. 31 Litho. *Perf. 14*

1226 A259 5c multicolored 15 15
1227 A259 15c multicolored 15 15
1228 A259 25c multicolored 18 18
1229 A259 50c multicolored 38 38
1230 A259 $1 multicolored 75 75
1231 A259 $2 multicolored 1.50 1.50
1232 A259 $4 multicolored 3.00 3.00
1233 A259 $5 multicolored 3.75 3.75
Nos. 1226-1233 (8) 9.86 9.86

Souvenir Sheets

1234 A259 $6 multicolored 4.50 4.50
1235 A259 $6 multicolored 4.50 4.50

Fish Type of 1990

1991, Feb. 5

1236 A254 15c Barred hamlet 15 15
1237 A254 35c Squirrelfish 25 25
1238 A254 45c Red-spotted hawkfish 35 35
1239 A254 75c Bigeye 55 55
1240 A254 $1 Spiny puffer 75 75
1241 A254 $2 Smallmouth grunt 1.50 1.50
1242 A254 $3 Harlequin bass 2.25 2.25
1243 A254 $4 Creole fish 3.00 3.00
Nos. 1236-1243 (8) 8.80 8.80

Souvenir Sheets

1244 A254 $6 Fairy basslet 4.50 4.50
1245 A254 $6 Copper sweeper 4.50 4.50

Hummel Figurines — G90

Orchids — G91

1991, Mar. 1 Litho. *Perf. 14*

1246 G90 10c Angel, star 15 15
1247 G90 15c Angel, guitar, Christ Child 15 15
1248 G90 25c Shepherd 18 18
1249 G90 50c Angel, lantern, horn 36 36
1250 G90 $1 Angel, children, Christ Child 72 72
1251 G90 $2 Angel, candle, Christ Child 1.45 1.45
1252 G90 $4 Angel with baskets 2.90 2.90
1253 G90 $5 Angels singing 3.65 3.65
Nos. 1246-1253 (8) 9.56 9.56

Souvenir Sheets

1254 Sheet of 4 2.90 2.90
a. G90 5c like No. 1247 15 15
b. G90 40c like No. 1249 28 28
c. G90 60c like No. 1250 42 42
d. G90 $3 like No. 1253 2.15 2.15
1255 Sheet of 4 5.25 5.25
a. G90 20c like No. 1246 15 15
b. G90 30c like No. 1248 22 22
c. G90 75c like No. 1251 55 55
d. G90 $6 like No. 1252 4.30 4.30

Christmas 1990.

1991-92 Litho. *Perf. 14*

Designs: 5c, Brassia maculata. 10c, Oncidium lanceanum. 15c, Broughtonia sanguinea. 25c, Diacrium bicornutum. 35c, Cattleya labiata. 45c, Epidendrum fragrans. 50c, Oncidium papilio. 75c, Neocogniauxia monophylla. $1, Epidendrum polybulbon. $2, Spiranthes speciosa. $4, Epidendrum ciliare. $5, Phais tankervilliae. $10, Brassia caudata. $20, Brassavola cordata.

1256 G91 5c multicolored 15 15
1257 G91 10c multicolored 15 15
1258 G91 15c multicolored 15 15
1259 G91 25c multicolored 18 18
1260 G91 35c multicolored 25 25
1261 G91 45c multicolored 32 32
1262 G91 50c multicolored 36 36
1263 G91 75c multicolored 55 55
1264 G91 $1 multicolored 72 72
1265 G91 $2 multicolored 1.45 1.45
1266 G91 $4 multicolored 2.90 2.90
1267 G91 $5 multicolored 3.60 3.60
1268 G91 $10 multicolored 7.20 7.20
1269 G91 $20 multicolored 15.20 15.20
Nos. 1256-1269 (14) 33.18 33.18

Issue dates: $20, June 1992. Others, Apr. 1, 1991.

Butterfly Type

Designs: 5c, Crimson-patched longwing. 10c, Morpho helena. 15c, Morpho sulkowskyi. 20c, Dynastor napoleon. 25c, Pieridae callinira. 30c, Anartia amathea. 35c, Heliconiidae dido. 45c, Papilionidae columbus. 50c, Nymphalidae praeneste. 60c, Panacea prola. 75c, Julia. $1, Papilionidae orthosilaus. $2, Pyrrhopyge cometes. $3, Papilionidae paeon. $4, Morpho cypris. $5, Choringa. No. 1286, Caligo idomenides. No. 1287, Monarch. No. 1287A, Nymphalidae amydon. No. 1287B, Papilio childrenae.

1991, Apr. 8 Litho. *Perf. 14*

1270 A261 5c multicolored 15 15
1271 A261 10c multicolored 15 15
1272 A261 15c multicolored 15 15
1273 A261 20c multicolored 15 15
1274 A261 25c multicolored 18 18
1275 A261 30c multicolored 22 22
1276 A261 35c multicolored 25 25
1277 A261 45c multicolored 32 32
1278 A261 50c multicolored 36 36
1279 A261 60c multicolored 45 45
1280 A261 75c multicolored 55 55
1281 A261 $1 multicolored 72 72
1282 A261 $2 multicolored 1.45 1.45
1283 A261 $3 multicolored 2.15 2.15
1284 A261 $4 multicolored 2.90 2.90
1285 A261 $5 multicolored 3.60 3.60
Nos. 1270-1285 (16) 13.75 13.75

Souvenir Sheets

1286 A261 $6 multicolored 4.30 4.30
1287 A261 $6 multicolored 4.30 4.30
1287A A261 $6 multicolored 4.30 4.30
1287B A261 $6 multicolored 4.30 4.30

Save Our Planet — G100

Walt Disney characters and ecology themes: 10c, Daisy and Donald, alternate forms of transportation. 15c, Goofy saving water. 25c, Donald, Daisy camping simply. 45c, Donald protecting birds. $1, Donald holding ascending balloons. $2, Minnie, Daisy using natural coolers. $4, Mickey, nephews cleaning beaches. $5, Scrooge McDuck using pedal power. No. 1288, Little Hiawatha and Iron Eyes Cody viewing destroyed forest. No. 1289, Donald, recycling. No. 1290, Minnie, Mickey planting trees.

1991, Apr. 22 Litho. *Perf. 14*

1288 G100 10c multicolored 15 15
1289 G100 15c multicolored 15 15
1290 G100 25c multicolored 18 18
1291 G100 45c multicolored 32 32
1292 G100 $1 multicolored 72 72
1293 G100 $2 multicolored 1.45 1.45
1294 G100 $4 multicolored 2.90 2.90
1295 G100 $5 multicolored 3.60 3.60
Nos. 1288-1295 (8) 9.47 9.47

Souvenir Sheets

1296 G100 $6 multicolored 4.30 4.30
1297 G100 $6 multicolored 4.30 4.30
1298 G100 $6 multicolored 4.30 4.30

Voyages of Discovery Type

Discovery of America, 500th anniv. (in 1992).: 15c, Ferdinand Magellan, 1519-1521. 20c, Sir Francis Drake, 1577-1580. 50c, Capt. James Cook, 1768-1771. 60c, Douglas World Cruiser, 1924. $1, Sputnik, 1957. $2, Yuri Gagarin, 1961. $4, John Glenn, 1962. $5, Space Shuttle, 1981. No. 1307, Columbus' fleet. No. 1308, The Pinta, vert.

1991, Apr. 29 Litho. *Perf. 14*

1299 A262 15c multicolored 15 15
1300 A262 20c multicolored 15 15
1301 A262 50c multicolored 36 36
1302 A262 60c multicolored 45 45
1303 A262 $1 multicolored 72 72
1304 A262 $2 multicolored 1.45 1.45
1305 A262 $4 multicolored 2.90 2.90
1306 A262 $5 multicolored 3.60 3.60
Nos. 1299-1306 (8) 9.78 9.78

Souvenir Sheets

1307 A262 $6 multicolored 4.30 4.30
1308 A262 $6 multicolored 4.30 4.30

Disney Phila Nippon '91 Type

Walt Disney characters demonstrating arts, crafts and industries of Japan: 15c, Minnie, silkworms. 30c, Mickey, Minnie, Morty and Ferdie photographing the Torii. 50c, Donald, Mickey, origami. 60c, Mickey, Minnie diving for pearls. $1, Minnie modeling kimono. $2, Mickey making masks. $4, Donald, Mickey making paper. $5, Minnie, Pluto, pottery. #1317, Mickey making prints, vert. #1318, Mickey arranging flowers, vert. #1319, Mickey, tea ceremony, vert. #1320, Mickey carving ivory and wood into netsukes, vert.

1991, May 6

1309 A263 15c multi 15 15
1310 A263 30c multi 22 22
1311 A263 50c multi 36 36
1312 A263 60c multi 45 45
1313 A263 $1 multi 72 72
1314 A263 $2 multi 1.45 1.45
1315 A263 $4 multi 2.90 2.90
1316 A263 $5 multi 3.60 3.60
Nos. 1309-1316 (8) 9.85 9.85

Souvenir Sheets

1317 A263 $6 multi 4.30 4.30
1318 A263 $6 multi 4.30 4.30
1319 A263 $6 multi 4.30 4.30
1320 A263 $6 multi 4.30 4.30

Mushrooms Type

1991, June 1 Litho. *Perf. 14*

1321 A265 5c Pyrrhoglossum pyrrhum 15 15
1322 A265 45c Agaricus purpurellus 32 32
1323 A265 50c Amanita craseoderma 36 36
1324 A265 90c Hygrocybe acutoconica 65 65
1325 A265 $1 Limacella guttata 72 72
1326 A265 $2 Lactarius hygrophoroides 1.45 1.45
1327 A265 $4 Boletellus cubensis 2.90 2.90
1328 A265 $5 Psilocybe caerulescens 3.60 3.60
Nos. 1321-1328 (8) 10.15 10.15

Souvenir Sheets

1329 A265 $6 Marasmius haemato- cephalus 4.30 4.30
1330 A265 $6 Lepiota spiculata 4.30 4.30

Royal Family Birthday, Anniversary
Common Design Type

1991, July 5 Litho. *Perf. 14*

1331 CD347 5c multi 15 15
1332 CD347 20c multi 15 15
1333 CD347 25c multi 18 18
1334 CD347 60c multi 45 45
1335 CD347 $1 multi 72 72
1336 CD347 $2 multi 1.45 1.45

1337 CD347 $4 multi 2.90 2.90
1338 CD347 $5 multi 3.60 3.60
Nos. 1331-1338 (8) 9.60 9.60

Souvenir Sheet

1339 CD347 $5 Elizabeth, Philip 3.60 3.60
1340 CD347 $5 Diana, Charles, with sons 3.60 3.60

5c, 60c, $1, Nos. 1338, 1340, Charles and Diana, 10th wedding anniversary. Others, Queen Elizabeth II, 65th birthday.

Van Gogh Painting Type

Designs: 5c, Two Thistles, vert. 10c, The Baby Marcelle Roulin, vert. 15c, Still Life: Basket with Six Oranges. 25c, Orchard in Blossom, vert. 45c, Portrait of Armand Roulin, vert. 50c, Wood Gatherers in the Snow (detail). 60c, Almond Tree in Blossom, vert. $1, Portrait of an Old Man, vert. $2, The Seine Bridge at Asnieres. $3, Vase with Lilacs, Daisies & Anemones, vert. $4, Self-portrait, vert. $5, Portrait of Patience Escalier, vert. No. 1353, Les Alyscamps, vert. No. 1354, Quay with Men Unloading Sand Barges. No. 1355, Sunset: Wheat Fields Near Arles.

Perf. 13½x14, 14x13½

1991, Nov. 18 **Litho.**

1341 A264 5c multicolored 15 15
1342 A264 10c multicolored 15 15
1343 A264 15c multicolored 15 15
1344 A264 25c multicolored 18 18
1345 A264 45c multicolored 32 32
1346 A264 50c multicolored 38 38
1347 A264 60c multicolored 45 45
1348 A264 $1 multicolored 75 75
1349 A264 $2 multicolored 1.45 1.45
1350 A264 $3 multicolored 2.15 2.15
1351 A264 $4 multicolored 2.90 2.90
1352 A264 $5 multicolored 3.60 3.60
Nos. 1341-1352 (12) 12.63 12.63

Size: 102x127mm, 127x102mm

Imperf

1353 A264 $6 multicolored 4.30 4.30
1354 A264 $6 multicolored 4.30 4.30
1355 A264 $6 multicolored 4.30 4.30

Marine Life Type
Miniature Sheet

Marine life of the deeper reef: No. 1356a, Sargassum triggerfish. b, Tobaccofish. c, Longsnout butterflyfish. d, Cherubfish. e, Black jack head. f, Black jack tail, masked goby. g, Spotfin hogfish. h, Fairy basslet. i, Orangeback bass. j, Candy basslet. k, Blackcap basslet. l, Longspine squirrelfish. m, Jackknife fish. n, Bigeye. o, Short Bigeye. $6, Caribbean flashlight fish.

1991, Dec. 5 **Litho.** ***Perf. 14***

1356 A270 50c Sheet of 15, #a.-o. 5.40 5.40

Souvenir Sheet

1357 A270 $6 multicolored 4.30 4.30

Christmas Art Type

Details, entire paintings or engravings by Martin Schongauer: 10c, Angel of the Annunciation. 35c, Madonna of the Rose Hedge. 50c, Madonna of the Rose Hedge, diff. 75c, Nativity. $1, Adoration of the Shepherds. $2, Nativity, diff. $4, Nativity, diff. $5, Symbol of St. Matthew. No. 1366, Nativity, diff. No. 1367, Adoration of the Shepherds.

1991, Dec. 9 ***Perf. 12***

1358 A271 10c multicolored 15 15
1359 A271 35c multicolored 25 25
1360 A271 50c multicolored 36 36
1361 A271 75c multicolored 55 55
1362 A271 $1 multicolored 72 72
1363 A271 $2 multicolored 1.45 1.45
1364 A271 $4 multicolored 2.90 2.90
1365 A271 $5 multicolored 3.60 3.60
Nos. 1358-1365 (8) 9.98 9.98

Souvenir Sheets

Perf. 14½

1366 A271 $6 multicolored 4.30 4.30
1367 A271 $6 multicolored 4.30 4.30

Queen Elizabeth II's Accession to the Throne, 40th Anniv.

Common Design Type

1992, Feb. 6 **Litho.** ***Perf. 14***

1368 CD348 60c multicolored 45 45
1369 CD348 75c multicolored 55 55
1370 CD348 $2 multicolored 1.45 1.45
1371 CD348 $4 multicolored 2.90 2.90

Souvenir Sheets

1372 CD348 $6 Queen, rural scene 4.30 4.30
1373 CD348 $6 Queen, harbor 4.30 4.30

Railways of the World Type

Steam locomotives: No. 1379a, Medoc Class, Switzerland, 1857. b, Sterling, Great Britain, 1870. c, No. 90, France, 1877. d, Standard, US, 1880. e, Vittorio Emanuel II, Italy, 1884. f, Johnson Single, Great Britain, 1887. g, No. 999, US, 1893. h, Q1 Class, Great Britain, 1896. i, Claud Hamilton, Great Britain, 1900.

No. 1380a, Class P8, Germany, 1906. b, Class P, Denmark, 1935. c, Class Ps, US, 1926. d, Class 4-4-0, Ireland, 1932. e, Class GS, US, 1937. f, Class 12, Belgium, 1938. g, Class J, US, 1941. h, PA series, US, 1946. i, Class 4E1, South Africa, 1954.

No. 1381a, Tee 4-car train, Europe, 1957. b, FL9B, US, 1960. c, Shin-Kansen 16-car train, Japan, 1964. d, Class 103.1, Germany 1970. e, RTG 4-car train set, France, 1972. f, ETR 401 Pendolino 4-car train, Italy, 1976. g, Class 370, Great Britain, 1981. h, LRC, Canada, 1982. i, Mav BZMOT 601 1B1, Hungary, 1983.

No. 1382, ETR 401 four-car train, Italy, 1976. No. 1382A, Werner von Siemens' first electric locomotive, Germany, 1879.

1992, Feb. 13 **Litho.** ***Perf. 14***

Sheets of 9

1379 A269 75c #a.-i. 5.00 5.00
1380 A269 $1 #a.-i. 6.80 6.80
1381 A269 $2 #a.-i. 13.50 13.50

Souvenir Sheets

1382 A269 $6 multicolored 4.50 4.50
1382A A269 $6 multicolored 4.50 4.50

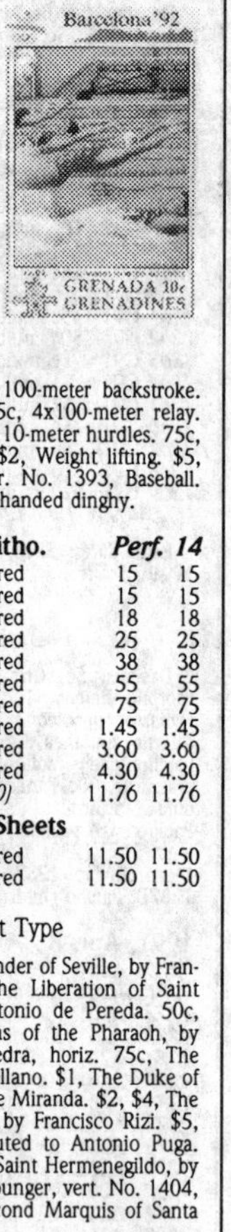

1992 Summer Olympics, Barcelona — G101

Designs: 10c, Women's 100-meter backstroke. 15c, Women's handball. 25c, 4x100-meter relay. 35c, Hammer throw. 50c, 110-meter hurdles. 75c, Pole vault. $1, Volleyball. $2, Weight lifting. $5, Stationary rings. $6, Soccer. No. 1393, Baseball. No. 1394, Finn class single-handed dinghy.

1992, Mar. 23 **Litho.** ***Perf. 14***

1383 G101 10c multicolored 15 15
1384 G101 15c multicolored 15 15
1385 G101 25c multicolored 18 18
1386 G101 35c multicolored 25 25
1387 G101 50c multicolored 38 38
1388 G101 75c multicolored 55 55
1389 G101 $1 multicolored 75 75
1390 G101 $2 multicolored 1.45 1.45
1391 G101 $5 multicolored 3.60 3.60
1392 G101 $6 multicolored 4.30 4.30
Nos. 1383-1392 (10) 11.76 11.76

Souvenir Sheets

1393 G101 $15 multicolored 11.50 11.50
1394 G101 $15 multicolored 11.50 11.50

Spanish Art Type

Paintings: 10c, The Surrender of Seville, by Francisco de Zurbaran. 35c, The Liberation of Saint Peter by an Angel, by Antonio de Pereda. 50c, Joseph Explains the Dreams of the Pharaoh, by Antonio del Castillo Saavedra, horiz. 75c, The Flower Vase, by Juan de Arellano. $1, The Duke of Pastrana, by Juan Carreno de Miranda. $2, $4, The Annunciation (diff. details), by Francisco Rizi. $5, Old Woman Seated, attributed to Antonio Puga. No. 1403, The Triumph of Saint Hermenegildo, by Francisco de Herrera, the Younger, vert. No. 1404, Relief of Genoa by the Second Marquis of Santa Cruz, by de Pereda, horiz.

1992, Apr. 30 ***Perf. 13***

1395 A273 10c multicolored 15 15
1396 A273 35c multicolored 25 25
1397 A273 50c multicolored 38 38
1398 A273 75c multicolored 55 55
1399 A273 $1 multicolored 75 75
1400 A273 $2 multicolored 1.50 1.50
1401 A273 $4 multicolored 3.00 3.00
1402 A273 $5 multicolored 3.60 3.60

Size: 95x110mm

Imperf

1403 A273 $6 multicolored 4.30 4.30
1404 A273 $6 multicolored 4.50 4.50
Nos. 1395-1404 (10) 18.98 18.98

Granada '92.

Discovery of America, 500th Anniv. G102

Designs: 10c, Don Isaac Abarbanel (1437-1508), Spanish Minister of Finance. 25c, Columbus. 35c, Crewman sighting land. 50c, King Ferdinand and Queen Isabella. 60c, Columbus and Queen Isabella. $5, Santa Maria and map. No. 1411, Portrait of Columbus. No. 1412, Columbus at first landfall.

1992, May 7 **Litho.** ***Perf. 14***

1405 G102 10c multicolored 15 15
1406 G102 25c multicolored 18 18
1407 G102 35c multicolored 25 25
1408 G102 50c multicolored 36 36
1409 G102 60c multicolored 45 45
1410 G102 $5 multicolored 3.60 3.60
Nos. 1405-1410 (6) 4.99 4.99

Souvenir Sheets

1411 G102 $6 multicolored 4.50 4.50
1412 G102 $6 multicolored 4.50 4.50

World Columbian Expo '92, Chicago.

USO Anniv. Type of 1992

1992, May 7

1413 A277 10c James Cagney 15 15
1414 A277 15c Ann Sheridan 15 15
1415 A277 35c Jerry Colonna 28 28
1416 A277 50c Spike Jones 38 38
1417 A277 75c Edgar Bergen, Charlie McCarthy 55 55
1418 A277 $1 Andrews Sisters 75 75
1419 A277 $2 Dinah Shore 1.50 1.50
1420 A277 $5 Bing Crosby 3.75 3.75
Nos. 1413-1420 (8) 7.51 7.51

Souvenir Sheets

1421 A277 $6 Marlene Dietrich 4.50 4.50
1422 A277 $6 Fred Astaire 4.50 4.50

Hummingbird Type of 1992

Designs: 5c, Blue-headed male. 10c, Rufous-breasted hermit female. 20c, Blue-headed female. 45c, Green-throated carib male. 90c, Antillean crested male. $2, Purple-throated carib male. $4, Purple-throated carib female. $5, Antillean crested female. No. 1431, Rufous-breated hermit female. No. 1432, Green-throated carib female.

1992, May 7

1423 A276 5c multicolored 15 15
1424 A276 10c multicolored 15 15
1425 A276 20c multicolored 15 15
1426 A276 45c multicolored 32 32
1427 A276 90c multicolored 65 65
1428 A276 $2 multicolored 1.50 1.50
1429 A276 $4 multicolored 3.00 3.00
1430 A276 $5 multicolored 3.75 3.75
Nos. 1423-1430 (8) 9.67 9.67

Souvenir Sheets

1431 A276 $6 multicolored 4.50 4.50
1432 A276 $6 multicolored 4.50 4.50

Genoa '92.

Discovery of America Type

1992 ***Perf. 14½***

1433 A275 $1 Coming ashore 75 75
1434 A275 $2 Natives, ships 1.50 1.50

Walt Disney's Goofy, 60th Anniv. — G103

Scenes from Disney cartoon films: 5c, Father's Day Off, 1953. 10c, Cold War, 1951. 15c, Home Made Home, 1951. 25c, Get Rich Quick, 1951. 50c, Man's Best Friend, 1952. 75c, Aquamania, 1961. 90c, Tomorrow We Diet, 1951. $1, Teachers Are People, 1952. $2, The Goofy Success Story, 1955. $3, Double Dribble, 1946. $4, Hello Aloha, 1952. $5, Father's Lion, 1952. No. 1447, Father's Weekend, 1953, vert. No. 1448, Motor Mania, 1950. No. 1449, Hold That Pose, 1950, vert.

1992, Nov. 24 **Litho.** ***Perf. 14x13½***

1435 G103 5c multicolored 15 15
1436 G103 10c multicolored 15 15
1437 G103 15c multicolored 15 15
1438 G103 25c multicolored 20 20
1439 G103 50c multicolored 38 38
1440 G103 75c multicolored 58 58
1441 G103 90c multicolored 70 70
1442 G103 $1 multicolored 75 75
1443 G103 $2 multicolored 1.50 1.50
1444 G103 $3 multicolored 2.25 2.25
1445 G103 $4 multicolored 3.00 3.00
1446 G103 $5 multicolored 3.75 3.75
Nos. 1435-1446 (12) 13.56 13.56

Souvenir Sheets

Perf. 13½x14

1447 G103 $6 multicolored 4.50 4.50
1448 G103 $6 multicolored 4.50 4.50
1449 G103 $6 multicolored 4.50 4.50

Model Trains Type of 1992

Designs: 15c, #2220 Switcher locomotive, 2-inch gauge, US, 1910. 75c, J. C. Penney Special, standard gauge, US, 1920. $1, Cast metal locomotive, O gauge, US, 1916. $5, Ives long cab locomotive of the Olympian set, standard gauge, US, 1929. No. 1458, Clockwork model, O gauge, US, 1910.

Designs: 25c, 0-4-0 Engine, Bridge Port Line, O gauge, US, 1907. 50c, First Ives Co. electric toy locomotive, O gauge, US, 1910. $2, Copper-plated cast iron locomotive & tender pull toy, US, 1900. $4, Chromium plated locomotive #4689, standard gauge, US, 1928. No. 1459, American Flyer Statesman passenger train.

1992, Oct. 22 **Litho.** ***Perf. 14***

1450 A279 15c multicolored 15 15
1451 A279 25c multicolored 20 20
1452 A279 50c multicolored 38 38
1453 A279 75c multicolored 58 58
1454 A279 $1 multicolored 75 75
1455 A279 $2 multicolored 1.50 1.50
1456 A279 $4 multicolored 3.00 3.00
1457 A279 $5 multicolored 3.75 3.75
Nos. 1450-1457 (8) 10.31 10.31

Souvenir Sheet

Perf. 13

1458 A279 $6 multicolored 4.50 4.50
1459 A279 $6 multicolored 4.50 4.50

Nos. 1458-1459 contains one 51x40mm stamp.

New York City Type
Souvenir Sheet

1992, Oct. 28 ***Perf. 14***

1460 A280 $6 Brooklyn Bridge 4.50 4.50

Postage Stamp Mega Event '92, New York City.

Christmas Type of 1992

Details or entire paintings of The Annunciation by: 5c, Robert Campin. 15c, Melchior Broederlam. 25c, The Annunciation (2 panels), by Fra Filippo Lippi. 35c, Simone Martini. 50c, Fra Filippo Lippi, detail of angel. 75c, The Annunciation (Mary), by Fra Filippo Lippi. 90c, Albert Bouts. $1, D. Di Michelino. $2, Van der Weyden. $3, Sandro Botticelli, detail of angel. $4, Botticelli, detail of Mary. $5, Bernardo Daddi, horiz. No. 1472, Rogier Van der Weyden, vert. No. 1473, Hubert Van Eyck. No. 1474, Botticelli.

Perf. 13½x14, 14x13½

1992, Nov. 16

1461 A281 5c multicolored 15 15
1462 A281 15c multicolored 15 15
1463 A281 25c multicolored 20 20
1464 A281 35c multicolored 28 28
1464A A281 50c multicolored 38 38
1465 A281 75c multicolored 58 58
1466 A281 90c multicolored 70 70
1467 A281 $1 multicolored 75 75
1468 A281 $2 multicolored 1.50 1.50
1469 A281 $3 multicolored 2.25 2.25
1470 A281 $4 multicolored 3.00 3.00
1471 A281 $5 multicolored 3.75 3.75
Nos. 1461-1471 (12) 13.69 13.69

Souvenir Sheets

1472 A281 $6 multicolored 4.50 4.50
1473 A281 $6 multicolored 4.50 4.50
1474 A281 $6 multicolored 4.50 4.50

America's Cup Yacht Race — G104

Designs: 15c, Atalanta, Mischief, 1881. 25c, Valkyrie III, Defender. 35c, Shamrock IV, Resolute. 75c, Endeavour II, Ranger, 1937. $1, Sceptre, Columbia, 1958. $2, Australia II, Liberty. $4, Stars and Stripes, Kookaburra III. $5, New Zealand, Stars and Stripes, 1988. No. 1483, America, Aurora, 1851. No. 1484, Emblems of 1992 participants.

1992, Oct. ***Perf. 14***

1475 G104 15c multicolored 15 15
1476 G104 25c multicolored 20 20
1477 G104 35c multicolored 28 28
1478 G104 75c multicolored 58 58

1479 G104 $1 multicolored 75 75
1480 G104 $2 multicolored 1.50 1.50
1481 G104 $4 multicolored 3.00 3.00
1482 G104 $5 multicolored 3.75 3.75
Nos. 1475-1482 (8) 10.21 10.21

Souvenir Sheets

1483 G104 $6 multicolored 4.50 4.50
1484 G104 $6 multicolored 4.50 4.50

Nos. 1483-1484 contains one 58x43mm stamp.

G105

Anniversaries and Events — G106

Designs: 25c, Zeppelin Viktoria Luise over Kiel Harbor. 50c, Space Shuttle Columbia. 75c, Flag, arms of Germany, Konrad Adenauer. $1.50, Giant anteater. No. 1489, Scarlet macaw, vert. No. 1490, Emblem of Intl. Conf. on Nutrition. $3, Wolfgang Amadeus Mozart. No. 1492, Berlin airlift. No. 1493, Space Shuttle Endeavour crew repairing Intelsat VI. $5, Hindenburg disaster. No. 1495, Adm. Richard E. Byrd's Ford Trimotor flying over North Pole, 1926. No. 1496, Map of Federal Republic of Germany, vert. No. 1497, Zeppelin Z.4 above clouds. No. 1498, First flight of space shuttle Endeavour. No. 1499, Scene from "The Marriage of Figaro." No. 1500, Jaguar.

1992 Litho. *Perf. 14*

1485 G105 25c multicolored 20 20
1486 G105 50c multicolored 38 38
1487 G105 75c multicolored 58 58
1488 G105 $1.50 multicolored 1.15 1.15
1489 G105 $2 multicolored 1.50 1.50
1490 G105 $2 multicolored 1.50 1.50
1491 G106 $3 multicolored 2.25 2.25
1492 G105 $4 multicolored 3.00 3.00
1493 G105 $4 multicolored 3.00 3.00
1494 G105 $5 multicolored 3.75 3.75
1495 G105 $5 multicolored 3.75 3.75
Nos. 1485-1495 (11) 21.06 21.06

Souvenir Sheets

Perf. 13½

1496 G105 $6 multicolored 4.50 4.50
1497 G105 $6 multicolored 4.50 4.50
1498 G105 $6 multicolored 4.50 4.50

Perf. 14

1499 G106 $6 multicolored 4.50 4.50
1500 G105 $6 multicolored 4.50 4.50

Count Zeppelin, 75th anniv. of death (#1485, 1494, 1497). Intl. Space Year (#1486, 1493). Konrad Adenauer, 25th anniv. of death (#1487, 1492, 1496).Earth Summit, Rio de Janeiro (#1488-1489, 1500). Intl. Conf. on Nutrition, Rome (#1490). Wolfgang Amadeus Mozart, bicent. of death (in 1991) (#1491, 1499). Intl. Lions Intl., 75th anniv. (#1495). Space Year (#1498).

Issue dates: Nos. 1491, 1499, Oct. Nos. 1485-1486, 1490, 1493-1495, 1497, Nov. Nos. 1487-1489, 1492, 1496, 1500, Dec.

No. 1496 contains one 39x50mm stamp, Nos. 1497-1498 one 50x39mm stamp, No. 1500 one 52x40mm stamp.

Miniature Sheet

Entertainers Type of 1992

Grammy award winners: No. 1501a, Leonard Bernstein. b, Ray Charles. c, Bob Dylan. d, Barbra Streisand. e, Frank Sinatra. f, Harry Belafonte. g, Aretha Franklin. h, Garth Brooks.

No. 1502a, Johnny Cash. b, Willie Nelson.

No. 1503a, Charlie Parker. b, Miles Davis.

1992, Nov. 19 *Perf. 14*

1501 A286 90c Sheet of 8, #a.-h. 5.50 5.50

Souvenir Sheets

1502 A286 $3 Sheet of 2, #a.-b. 4.50 4.50
1503 A286 $3 Sheet of 2, #a.-b. 4.50 4.50

Dogs — G107

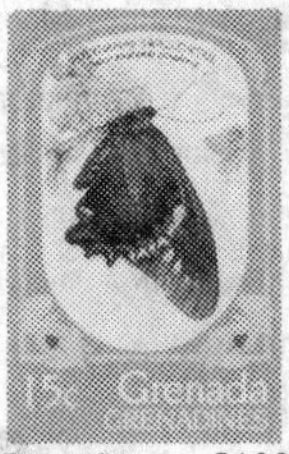

Butterflies — G108

Designs: 35c, Irish Setter, Glendalough, Ireland. 50c, Boston terrier, State House, Boston, US. 75c, Beagle, Temple to Athena, Greece. $1, Weimaraner, Nesselwang, Germany. $3, Norwegian elkhound, Urnes Stave Church, Norway. $4, Mastiff, Great Sphinx, Egypt. No. 1510, Akita, Kyoto torii, Japan. No. 1511, Saluki, Rub'al Khali, Saudi Arabia. No. 1512, Shar pei, China. No. 1513, Bulldog, United Kingdom.

1993, Jan. 20 Litho. *Perf. 14*

1504 G107 35c multicolored 28 28
1505 G107 50c multicolored 38 38
1506 G107 75c multicolored 58 58
1507 G107 $1 multicolored 75 75
1508 G107 $3 multicolored 2.25 2.25
1509 G107 $4 multicolored 3.00 3.00
1510 G107 $5 multicolored 3.75 3.75
1511 G107 $5 multicolored 3.75 3.75
Nos. 1504-1511 (8) 14.74 14.74

Souvenir Sheets

1512 G107 $6 multicolored 4.50 4.50
1513 G107 $6 multicolored 4.50 4.50

Louvre Painting Type

Miniature Sheet

Details or entire paintings: No. 1514a, The Virgin and Child with Young St. John the Baptist, by Botticelli. b, The Buffet, by Chardin. c, The Provider, by Chardin. d, Erasmus, by Durer. e, Self-Portrait, by Durer. f, Jeanne of Aragon, by Raphael. g-h, La Belle Jardiniere (diff. details), by Raphael.

$6, Charles I, King of England, Hunting, by Van Dyck.

1993, Mar. 8 Litho. *Perf. 12*

1514 A289 $1 Sheet of 8, #a.-h. + label 6.00 6.00

Souvenir Sheet

Perf. 14½

1515 A289 $6 multicolored 4.50 4.50

No. 1515 contains one 55x88mm stamp.

1993, Apr. 13 Litho. *Perf. 14*

1516 G108 15c Polydamas swallowtail 15 15
1517 G108 35c Guaraguao skipper 28 28
1518 G108 45c Giant hairstreak 35 35
1519 G108 75c Malachite 58 58
1520 G108 $1 Cloudless sulphur 75 75
1521 G108 $2 Silver spot 1.50 1.50
1522 G108 $4 St. Christopher's hairstreak 3.00 3.00
1523 G108 $5 Common long-tail skipper 3.75 3.75
Nos. 1516-1523 (8) 10.36 10.36

Souvenir Sheets

1524 G108 $6 Orion 4.50 4.50
1525 G108 $6 Zebra 4.50 4.50

Flowers Type of 1993

1993, May 17

1526 A291 35c Hibiscus 28 28
1527 A291 35c Columbine 28 28
1528 A291 45c Red ginger 35 35
1529 A291 75c Bougainvillea 58 58
1530 A291 $1 Crown imperial 75 75
1531 A291 $2 Fairy orchid 1.50 1.50
1532 A291 $4 Heliconia 3.00 3.00
1533 A291 $5 Tulip 3.75 3.75
Nos. 1526-1533 (8) 10.49 10.49

Souvenir Sheets

1534 A291 $6 Balloonflower, horiz. 5.50 5.50
1535 A291 $6 Blackberry lily, horiz. 4.50 4.50

No. 1536 will not be assigned.

Coronation of Queen Elizabeth II Type of 1993

Miniature Sheet

Designs: a, 35c, Official coronation photograph. b, 50c, Ampulla, spoon. c, $2, Queen, following coronation. d, $4, Queen, Prince Charles and his family, c. 1984.

$6, Portrait, by Pietro Annigoni, 1954.

1993, June 2 Litho. *Perf. 13½x14*

1537 A293 Sheet, 2 each #a.-d. 10.50 10.50

Souvenir Sheet

Perf. 14

1538 A293 $6 multicolored 4.50 4.50

No. 1538 contains one 28x42mm stamp.

Anniversaries and Events Types of 1993

Designs: 50c, Telescope. 75c, Willy Brandt, Lyndon Johnson, 1961. $4, Radio telescope. $5, Willy Brandt, Eleanor Hulles, 1957. No. 1543, Copernicus. No. 1544, Willy, Rut Brandt.

1993, July 1 Litho. *Perf. 14*

1539 A294 50c multicolored 38 38
1540 A295 75c multicolored 58 58
1541 A294 $4 multicolored 3.00 3.00
1542 A295 $5 multicolored 3.75 3.75

Souvenir Sheets

1543 A294 $6 multicolored 4.50 4.50
1544 A295 $6 multicolored 4.50 4.50

Copernicus, 450th death anniv. (#1539, 1541, 1543). Willy Brandt, 1st death anniv. (#1540, 1542, 1544).

Songbird Type of 1993

Miniature Sheet

Designs: No. 1545a, 15c, Painted bunting. b, 15c, White-throated sparrow. c, 25c, Common grackle. d, 25c, Royal flycatcher. e, 35c, Swallow tanager. f, 35c, Vermilion flycatcher. g, 45c, Black headed bunting. h, 50c, Rosebreasted grosbeak. i, 75c, Corn bunting. j, 75c, Rosebreasted thrush tanager. k, $1, Buff-throated saltator. l, $4, Plush-capped finch.

No. 1546, Bohemian waxwing. No. 1547, Pine grosbeak.

1993, July 13

1545 A297 Sheet of 12, #a.-l. 6.75 6.75

Souvenir Sheets

1546 A297 $6 multicolored 4.50 4.50
1547 A297 $6 multicolored 4.50 4.50

Seashell Type of 1993

Miniature Sheet

Designs: No. 1548a, 15c, Hawk wing conch. b, 15c, Music volute. c, 25c, Globe vase, deltoid rock shell. d, 35c, Spiny vase. e, 35c, Common sundial, common purple snail. f, 45c, Caribbean donax, gaudy asaphis. g, 45c, Mouse cone. h, 50c, Gold-mouthed triton. i, 75c, Tulip mussel, trigonal tivela. j, 75c, Common dove shell, chestnut latirus. k, $1, Wide-mouthed purpura. l, $4, Atlantic thorny oyster, Atlantic wing oyster.

No. 1549, Turkey wing. No. 1550, Zebra periwinkle.

1993, July 19 Litho. *Perf. 14*

1548 A298 Sheet of 12, #a.-l. 7.00 7.00

Souvenir Sheet

1549 A298 $6 multicolored 4.50 4.50
1550 A298 $6 multicolored 4.50 4.50

Picasso Type of 1993

Paintings: 15c, Painter and Model, 1928. $1, The Artist and His Model, 1963. $4, The Drawing Lession, 1925. $6, Picasso seated in front of canvas, 1956.

1993, July 1 Litho. *Perf. 14*

1551 A299 15c multi, horiz. 15 15
1552 A299 $1 multi, horiz. 75 75
1553 A299 $4 multi, horiz. 3.00 3.00

Souvenir Sheet

1554 A299 $6 multi, horiz. 4.50 4.50

Olympics Type of 1993

Design: $6, Emil Zogragski, ski jump.

1993, July 1

1555 A300 $6 multicolored 4.50 4.50

Polska '93 Type of 1993

Paintings: 75c, Gra w Gudziki, by Ludomir Slerdinski, 1928. $2, Pocalunek Mongoskiego Ksiecia, by S.I. Witkiewicz, 1915. $6, Allegory, by Jan Wydra, 1929.

1993, July 1

1556 A301 75c multi, horiz. 55 55
1557 A301 $2 multi, horiz. 1.50 1.50

Souvenir Sheet

1558 A301 $6 multicolored 4.50 4.50

Taipei '93 Type

Designs: 35c, Macao Palace, Hong Kong. 45c, Stone pixie, Ming Tomb, Nanjing. $1, Stone camels, Ming Tomb, Nanjing. $5, Stone lion and elephant, Ming Tomb, Nanjing.

Sculpture: No. 1563a, Nesting quail incense burner. b, Standing quail incense burner. c, Seated qilin incense burner. d, Pottery horse, Han Dynasty. e, Seated caparisoned elephant. f, Cow (imitation delft).

No. 1564, Sumatran tiger.

1993, Aug. 13 Litho. *Perf. 14x13½*

1559 A302 35c multi, horiz. 25 25
1560 A302 45c multi, horiz. 35 35
1561 A302 $1 multi, horiz. 75 75
1562 A302 $5 multi, horiz. 3.75 3.75

Miniature Sheet

1563 A302 $1.50 Sheet of 6, #a.-f. 6.75 6.75

Souvenir Sheet

Perf. 13½x14

1564 A302 $6 multicolored 4.50 4.50

Nos. 1563a-1563f are horiz.

With Bangkok '93 Emblem

Designs: 35c, Naga snakes, Chiang Mai's Temple, Thailand. 45c, Sri Mariamman Temple, Singapore. $1, Topiary, Hua Hin Resort, Thailand. $5, Pak Tai Temple, Cheung Chau Island.

Thai paintings: No. 1569a, Buddha's victory over Mara. b, Mythological elephant. c, Battle with Mara. d, Untitled work, by Panya Wijinthanasarn, 1984. e, Temple mural. f, Elephants in Pahcekha Buddha's Heaven.

No. 1570, Monkey.

1993 *Perf. 14x13½*

1565 A302 35c multi, horiz. 25 25
1566 A302 45c multi, horiz. 35 35
1567 A302 $1 multi, horiz. 75 75
1568 A302 $5 multi, horiz. 3.75 3.75

Miniature Sheet

1569 A302 $1.50 Sheet of 6, #a.-f. 6.75 6.75

Souvenir Sheet

Perf. 13½x14

1570 A302 $6 multicolored 4.50 4.50

Nos. 1569a-1569f are horiz.

Indopex '93 Type

Designs: 35c, Natl. Museum, Central Jakarta, Indonesia. 45c, Sacred Wheel & Deer, Monastery. $1, Ramayana relief, Panataran Temple. $5, Candi Tikus, Trawulan, East Java.

Paintings: No. 1575a, Bullock Carts, bu Batara Lubis, 1951. b, Surat Irsa II, by A.D. Pirous, 1983. c, Self-portrait with Goat, by Kartika, 1987. d, The Cow-est Cow, by Ivan Sagito, 1987. e, Rain Storm, by Sudjana Kerton, 1984. f, Story of Pucuk Flower, by Effendi, 1972.

No. 1576, Banteng cattle.

1993, Aug. 13 Litho. *Perf. 14x13½*

1571 A302 35c multicolored 25 25
1572 A302 45c multicolored 35 35
1573 A302 $1 multicolored 75 75
1574 A302 $5 multicolored 3.75 3.75

Miniature Sheet

1575 A302 $1.50 Sheet of 6, #a.-f. 6.75 6.75

Souvenir Sheet

1576 A302 $6 multicolored 4.50 4.50

Nos. 1571-1576 are horiz.

1994 World Cup Soccer Championships, US — G109

Designs: 15c, Stuart McCall, Carlos Verri. 25c, Carlos Verri, Diego Maradona. 35c, S. Schillaci, J.P. Saldana. 45c, Ruud Gullit, Mark Wright. $1, Carlos Verri, Diego Maradona. $2, Zubizarreta, Fernandez, Albert. $4, Gheorghe Hagi, Paul McGrath. $5, Alberto Gorriz, Enzo Scifo. No. 1585, Schaefer Stadium, Foxboro, MA. No. 1586, Rudi Voeller, vert.

1993, Sept. 7 Litho. *Perf. 14*

1577 G109 15c multicolored 15 15
1578 G109 25c multicolored 15 15
1579 G109 35c multicolored 15 15
1580 G109 45c multicolored 35 35
1581 G109 $1 multicolored 75 75
1582 G109 $2 multicolored 1.50 1.50
1583 G109 $4 multicolored 3.00 3.00
1584 G109 $5 multicolored 3.75 3.75
Nos. 1577-1584 (8) 9.80 9.80

Souvenir Sheets

1585 G109 $6 multicolored 4.50 4.50
1586 G109 $6 multicolored 4.50 4.50

Mickey Mouse, 65th Anniv. Type of 1993

Movie clips: 15c, Mickey's Rival, 1936. 35c, The Worm Turns, 1937. 50c, The Pointer, 1939. 75c, Society Dog Show, 1939. $1, A Gentleman's Gentleman, 1941. $2, The Little Whirlwind, 1941. $4, Mickey Down Under, 1948. $5, R'coon Dawg, 1951.
No. 1595, Mickey's Garden, 1935, vert. No. 1596, Lonesome Ghosts, 1937.

Perf. 13½x14, 14x13½

1993, Nov. 11 **Litho.**

1587 A305 15c multicolored 15 15
1588 A305 35c multicolored 28 28
1589 A305 50c multicolored 38 38
1590 A305 75c multicolored 55 55
1591 A305 $1 multicolored 75 75
1592 A305 $2 multicolored 1.50 1.50
1593 A305 $4 multicolored 3.00 3.00
1594 A305 $5 multicolored 3.75 3.75
Nos. 1587-1594 (8) 10.36 10.36

Souvenir Sheets

1595 A305 $6 multicolored 4.50 4.50
1596 A305 $6 multicolored 4.50 4.50

Christmas Type of 1993

Various details from Adoration of the Shepherds by Durer: 10c, 75c, $1, $4, No. 1605, horiz.
Various details from Oddi Altarpiece by Raphael: 25c, 35c, 50c, $5, No. 1606.

Perf. 13½x14, 14x13½ (#1605)

1993, Nov. 22 **Litho.**

1597-1604 A306 Set of 8 9.00 9.00

Souvenir Sheets

1605-1606 A306 $6 each 4.50 4.50

Eckener Type of 1993

Designs: 50c, Graf Zeppelin over Rio De Janeiro. 75c, Dr. Hugo Eckener. $5, Eckener commanding Graf Zeppelin. $6, Eckener, Pres. Herbert Hoover.

1993, Dec. 21 **Litho.** ***Perf. 14***

1607-1609 A307 Set of 3 4.75 4.75

Souvenir Sheet

1610 A307 $6 multicolored 4.50 4.50

Royal Air Force Anniv. Type of 1993

Designs: 15c, Avro Lancaster. $5, Short Sunderland. $6, Supermarine Spitfire.

1993, Dec. 21

1611 A308 15c multicolored 15 15
1612 A308 $5 multicolored 3.75 3.75

Souvenir Sheet

1613 A308 $6 multicolored 4.50 4.50

Automobile Anniv. Type of 1993

Designs: 25c, 1955 Mercedes Benz 300SLR. 45c, 1957 Ford Thunderbird. $4, 1929 Ford 150A Station Wagon. $5, Mercedes Benz 540K. No. 1618, 1929 Mercedes Benz SSK. No. 1619, 1924 Ford Model T.

1993, Dec. 21 **Litho.** ***Perf. 14***

1614 A309 25c multicolored 18 18
1615 A309 45c multicolored 35 35
1616 A309 $4 multicolored 3.00 3.00
1617 A309 $5 multicolored 3.75 3.75

Souvenir Sheets

1618 A309 $6 multicolored 4.50 4.50
1619 A309 $6 multicolored 4.50 4.50

1st Benz 4-wheel car, 1st Ford engine, cent.

First Gas Balloon Flight in America Type of 1993

Designs: 35c, Blanchard's balloon crossing Delaware River. $3, Blanchard delivering Washington's passport of introduction. $6, Balloon in flight, vert.

1993, Dec. 21 **Litho.** ***Perf. 14***

1620-1621 A310 Set of 3 2.50 2.50

Souvenir Sheet

1622 A310 $6 multicolored 4.50 4.50

Fine Art Type of 1993

Details or entire paintings by Rembrandt: 15c, Hendrickje Stoffels as Flora. 35c, Lady & Gentlemen in Black. 50c, Aristotle with Bust of Homer. $5, Christ & the Woman of Samaria.
Details or entire paintings by Matisse: 75c, Interior: Flowers and Parakeets. $1, Goldfish. $2, The Girl with Green Eyes. $3, Still Life with a Plaster Figure.
No. 1631, Anna Accused of Stealing the Kid, by Rembrandt. No. 1632, Tea in the Garden by Matisse, horiz.

Perf. 13½x14, 14x13½

1993, Dec. 31 **Litho.**

1623-1630 A311 Set of 10 10.00 10.00

Souvenir Sheets

1631-1632 A311 $6 each 4.50 4.50

Hong Kong '94 Type

Designs: No. 1633, Hong Kong #426, jet at Kai Tak Airport. No. 1634, Junk, Kwaloon Bay, #975.
Chinese jade: No. 1635a, White jade brush washer. b, Archaic jade brush washer. c, Dark green jade brush washer. d, Green jade alms bowl. e, Archaic jade dog. f, Yellow jade brush washer.

1994, Feb. 18 **Litho.** ***Perf. 14***

1633 A313 40c multicolored 30 30
1634 A313 40c multicolored 30 30
a. Pair, #1633-1634 60 60

Miniature Sheet

1635 A314 45c Sheet of 6, #a.-f. 2.00 2.00

Nos. 1633-1634 issued in sheets of of 5 pairs. No. 1634a is a continuous design. Nos. 1635a-1635f are horiz.
New Year 1994 (Year of the Dog) (#1635e).

Dinosaurs G110

Designs: 15c, Spinosaurus. 35c, Apatosaurus. 45c, Tyrannosaurus rex. 55c, Triceratops. $1, Pachycephalosaurus. $2, Pteranodon. $4, Parasaurolophus. $5, Brachiosaurus.
No. 1644, Brachiosaurus, vert. No. 1645, Tyrannosaurus, spinosaurus, vert.

1994, Apr. 13 **Litho.** ***Perf. 14***

1636 G110 15c multicolored 15 15
1637 G110 35c multicolored 25 25
1638 G110 45c multicolored 35 35
1639 G110 55c multicolored 42 42
1640 G110 $1 multicolored 75 75
1641 G110 $2 multicolored 1.50 1.50
1642 G110 $4 multicolored 3.00 3.00
1643 G110 $5 multicolored 3.75 3.75
Nos. 1636-1643 (8) 10.17 10.17

Souvenir Sheets

1644 G110 $6 multicolored 4.50 4.50
1645 G110 $6 multicolored 4.50 4.50

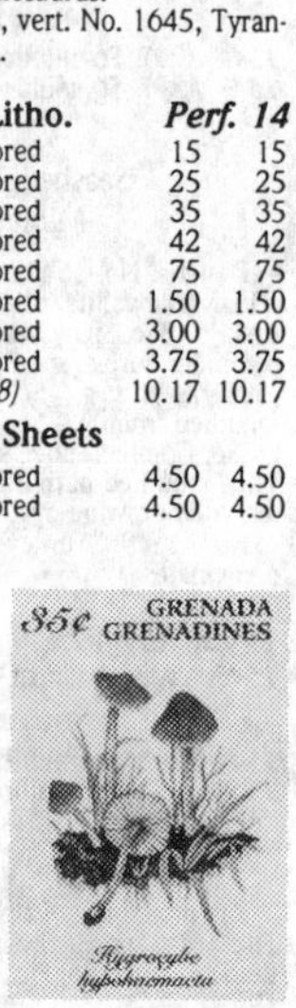

Mushrooms — G111

Designs: 35c, Hygrocybe hypohaemacta. 45c, Cantherellus cinnabarinus. 50c, Marasmius haematocephalus. 75c, Mycena pura. $1, Gymnopilus russipes. $2, Galocybe cyanocephala. $4, Pleuteus chrysophlebius. $5, Chlorophyllum molybdites.
No. 1654, Collybia fibrosipes. No. 1655, Xeromphalina tenuipes.

1994, Apr. 6

1646 G111 35c multicolored 25 25
1647 G111 45c multicolored 35 35
1648 G111 50c multicolored 38 38
1649 G111 75c multicolored 55 55
1650 G111 $1 multicolored 75 75
1651 G111 $2 multicolored 1.50 1.50
1652 G111 $4 multicolored 3.00 3.00
1653 G111 $5 multicolored 3.75 3.75
Nos. 1646-1653 (8) 10.53 10.53

Souvenir Sheets

1654 G111 $6 multicolored 4.50 4.50
1655 G111 $6 multicolored 4.50 4.50

D-Day Type of 1994

Designs: 40c, Churchill bridgelayer in action. $2, Sherman "Firefly" attacks beach. $3, Churchill Crocodile flame thrower. $6, Sherman "Crab" flail tank.

1994, Aug. 4 **Litho.** ***Perf. 14***

1656-1658 A318 Set of 3 4.00 4.00

Souvenir Sheet

1659 A318 $6 multicolored 4.50 4.50

First Manned Moon Landing, 25th Anniv. Type of 1994
Miniature Sheet of 6

Tribute to Challenger crew: No. 1660a, Slidewire escape training. b, Christa A. McAuliffe. c, Challenger 51-L on pad LC39B. d, Gregory B. Jarvis. e, Ellison S. Onizuka. f, Ronald E. McNair.
$6, Judith A. Resnick, vert.

1994, Aug. 4

1660 A319 $1.10 #a.-f. 5.00 5.00

Souvenir Sheet

1661 A319 $6 multicolored 4.50 4.50

PHILAKOREA '94 Type

Designs: 40c, Onung Tomb, Korea. $1, Stone pogoda, Mt. Nansan, Kyongju. $4, Pusan Port.
Paintings, by Sin Yunbok, late Choson Dynasty, 1758: No. 1665a-1665b, Admiring spring in the Country. c-d, Women on Dano Day. e-f, Enjoying Lotuses While Listening to Music. g-h, Women by a Crystal Stream.
$6, Blacksmith's Shop, by Kim Duksin (1754-1822).

1994, Aug. 4 ***Perf. 14, 13½ (#1665)***

1662-1664 A320 Set of 3 4.00 4.00

Miniature Sheet of 8

1665 A321 $1 #a.-h. 6.00 6.00

Souvenir Sheet

1666 A320 $6 multicolored 4.50 4.50

Orchid Type of 1994

Designs: 15c, Cattleya aurantiaca. 25c, Blettia patula. 45c, Sobralia macrantha. 75c, Encyclia belizensis. $1, Sophrolaeliocattleya. $2, Encyclia frangrans. $4, Schombocattleya. $5, Brassolaeliocattleya.
No. 1675, Brassavola nodosa. No. 1676, Ornithidium coccineum.

1994, Aug. 7 ***Perf. 14***

1667-1674 A322 Set of 8 10.00 10.00

Souvenir Sheets

1675-1676 A322 $6 each 4.50 4.50

1994 World Cup Soccer Type
Miniature Sheet of 6

Designs: No. 1677a, Steve Mark, Grenada. b, Jurgen Kohler, Germany. c, Almir, Brazil. d, Michael Windiscmann, US. e, Guiseppe Giannini, Italy. f, Rashidi Yekini, Nigeria.
No. 1678, Kemari. No. 1679, The World Cup.

1994, Aug. 11 ***Perf. 14***

1677 A323 75c #a.-f. 3.50 3.50

Souvenir Sheets

1678-1679 A323 $6 each 4.50 4.50

Disney's PHILAKOREA '94 — G112

Designs: 15c, Mickey, Unjin Miruk, Kwanch Ok Temple. 35c, Goofy, statue of Admiral Yi, Chonju. 50c, Cousin Gus, Donald. 75c, Mickey playing flute. $1, Goofy, Tolharubang Grandfather statue. $2, Mickey, Minnie, Hyang-Wonjong. $4, Mickey, Unsan Pyolshin Festival. $5, Minnie, ceremonial fan.
No. 1688, Minnie, Buk drum, vert. No. 1689, Mickey, Pugok Hawaii, vert.

1994, Aug. 16 **Litho.** ***Perf. 14x13½***

1680-1687 G112 Set of 8 10.50 10.50

Souvenir Sheets

Perf. 13½x14

1688-1689 G112 $6 each 4.50 4.50

Fish Type of 1994
Miniature Sheets of 12

Designs: No. 1690a, Yellowtail snapper (b, e). b, Caribbean reef shark (a). c, Great barracuda. d, Redtail parrotfish. e, Blue tang. f, Queen angelfish. g, Red hind (h). h, Rock beauty. i, Queen parrotfish. j, Spanish hogfish. k, Spotted moray. l, Queen triggerfish (i).
No. 1691a, Pork fish (b). b, Blue chromis (a). c, Caribbean reef shark. d, Longspine squirrelfish. e, Foureye butterflyfish. f, Blue head. g, Royal gramma. h, Sharpnose puffer. i, Longsnout seahorse. j, Blackbar soldierfish (g, k). k, Redlip blenny. l, Rainbow wrasse.
No. 1692, Rainbow wrasse, diff. No. 1693, Queen angelfish, diff.

1994, Sept. 1 ***Perf. 14***

1690-1691 A324 75c #a.-l., each 6.75 6.75

Souvenir Sheets

1692-1693 A324 $6 each 4.50 4.50

Intl. Olympic Committe Type of 1994

Designs: 50c, Silke Renk, Germany, javelin, 1992. $1.50, Mark Spitz, US, swimming, 1972.
$6, Team Japan, Nordic combined, 1994.

1994 ***Perf. 14***

1694 A325 50c multi, horiz. 38 38
1695 A325 $1.50 multi, horiz. 1.10 1.10

Souvenir Sheet

1696 A326 $6 multicolored 4.50 4.50

Intl. Year of the Family Type of 1994

1994

1697 A329 $1 Family of 5 75 75

Order of the Caribbean Community Type of 1994

Designs: 25c, Sir Shridath Ramphal, statesman, Guyana. 50c, William Demas, economist, Trinidad & Tobago. $2, Derek Walcott, writer, St. Lucia.

1994

1698-1700 A330 Set of 3 2.00 2.00

SEMI-POSTAL STAMPS

1988 Seoul Olympics Type

1986, Dec. 1 ***Perf. 15***

B1 SP2 10c +5c Cycling 15 15
B2 SP2 50c +20c Sailing 55 55
B3 SP2 70c +30c Uneven Parallel Bars 75 75
B4 SP2 $2 +$1 Dressage 2.25 2.25

Souvenir Sheet

B5 SP2 $3 +$1 Marathon 3.50 3.50

OFFICIAL STAMPS

Grenada Grenadines Nos. 396-408, 410, 440-442, 465-468 Overprinted "P.R.G."

1982, June ***Perf. 14, 15***

O1 G45 5c multicolored 15 15
O2 G45 6c multicolored 15 15
O3 G45 10c multicolored 15 15
O4 G45 12c multicolored 15 15
O5 G45 15c multicolored 15 15
O6 G45 20c multicolored 16 16
O7 G54 20c multicolored 16 16
O8 G45 25c multicolored 18 18
O9 G45 30c multicolored 24 24
O10 G45 40c multicolored 32 32
O11 CD331 40c multicolored 32 32
O12 G54 40c multicolored 32 32
O13 G45 50c multicolored 42 42
O14 G45 90c multicolored 75 75
O15 G45 $1 multicolored 85 85
O16 G54 $1 multicolored 85 85
O17 CD331 $2 multicolored 1.70 1.70
O18 G54 $2 multicolored 1.70 1.70
O19 G45 $3 multicolored 2.50 2.50
O20 CD331 $4 multicolored 3.50 3.50
O21 G45 $10 multicolored 8.50 8.50
Nos. O1-O21 (21) 23.22 23.22

Royal Wedding stamps in changed colors, perf 15x14½ were also overprinted.

GUYANA

LOCATION — Northeast coast of South America
GOVT. — Republic
AREA — 83,000 sq. mi.
POP. — 900,000 (est. 1983)
CAPITAL — Georgetown

The former Crown Colony of British Guiana became an independent member of the British Commonwealth May 26, 1966, taking the name Guyana. On February 23, 1970, Guyana became a republic, remaining a Commonwealth nation.

100 Cents = 1 Dollar

Catalogue values for all unused stamps in this country are for Never Hinged items.

Watermark

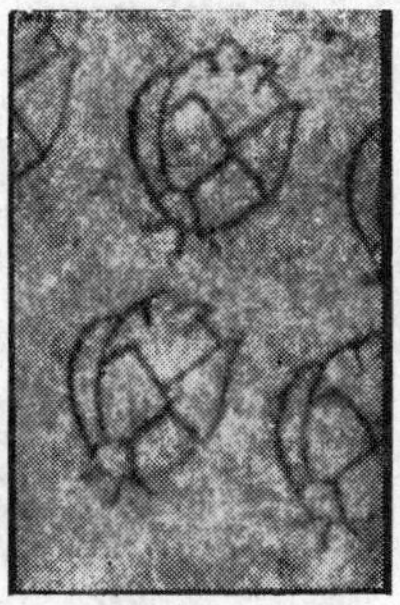

Wmk. 364-Lotus Bud Multiple

British Guiana Stamps of 1954 Overprinted

GUYANA INDEPENDENCE 1966

Perf. 12½x13, 13

1966, May 26 Wmk. 4 Engr.

1	A60	2c dk green (#254)	15	15
1A	A60	3c red brn & ol (#255)	2.50	2.50
2	A61	4c violet (#256)	15	15
3	A60	6c yel green (#258)	15	15
4	A60	8c ultra (#259)	15	15
5	A61	12c brn & blk (#260)	25	25
6	A61	$5 blk & ultra (#267)	42.50	42.50
		Nos. 1-6 (7)	45.85	45.85

Same Overprint on British Guiana Stamps and Types of 1954

Engr.; Center Litho. on $1

1966-67 Wmk. 314 Upright

7	A60	1c black ('67)	15	15
8	A60	3c red brn & ol (#279)	15	15
9	A61	4c violet ('67)	15	15
10	A60	5c blk & red (#280)	15	15
10A	A60	6c yel green ('67)	15	15
11	A60	8c ultra ('67)	15	15
12	A61	12c brn & blk (#281)	15	15
13	A60	24c org & blk (#282)	50	25
14	A60	36c blk & rose (#283)	30	25
15	A61	48c red brn & ultra (#284)	4.00	4.00
16	A61	72c emer & rose (#285)	50	42
17	A60	$1 blk & multi (#286)	65	55
18	A60	$2 mag (#287)	1.40	95
19	A61	$5 black & ultra	4.50	4.00
		Nos. 7-19 (14)	12.90	11.47

For surcharges see Nos. 543, 544A, 625-626, 1446.

1966-67 Wmk. 314 Sideways

7a	A60	1c black	15	15
9a	A61	4c violet	15	15
11a	A60	8c ultramarine	15	15
12a	A61	12c brown & black ('67)	15	15
13a	A60	24c orange & black	20	15
14a	A60	36c black & rose ('67)	28	20
15a	A61	48c red brown & ultra	40	28
16a	A61	72c emerald & rose ('67)	50	45
17a	A60	$1 black & multi ('67)	1.00	80
18a	A60	$2 magenta ('67)	2.00	1.75
19a	A61	$5 black & ultra ('67)	6.00	5.50
		Nos. 7a-19a (11)	10.98	9.73

See Nos. 32-32T and note. For surcharges see Nos. 544, 627-628, 1447.

Flag and Map of Guyana — A1

Designs: 25c, $1, Arms of Guyana.

Unwmk.

1966, May 26 Photo. *Perf. 14*

20	A1	5c violet & multi	15	15
21	A1	15c dk red brown & multi	15	15
22	A1	25c brt blue & multi	22	22
23	A1	$1 sepia & multi	80	80

Guyana's independence, May 26, 1966.

Bank of Guyana A2

1966, Oct. 11 *Perf. 13½x14*

24	A2	5c yel grn, blue, blk & gold	15	15
25	A2	25c blue, black & gold	22	22
		Set value	28	28

Establishment of the Bank of Guyana.

British Guiana No. 13 — A3

1967, Feb. 23 Litho. *Perf. 12½*

26	A3	5c multicolored	15	15
a.		Imperf., pair		
27	A3	25c multicolored	22	15
		Set value	30	15

Issued to honor the unique British Guiana 1c black on magenta stamp of 1856.

Canceled to Order

Remainders of Nos. 26-30, 33-38 and 54-67 were canceled and sold by the Post Office in 1969. Values are for these canceled to order stamps. Postally used copies do not command a significant premium.

Chateau Margot — A4

Designs: 15c, Independence Arch. 25c, Guyana Fort, Fort Island, horiz. $1, Parliament, National Assembly Hall, horiz.

Perf. 14, 14½x14, 14x14½

1967, May 26 Photo. Unwmk.

28	A4	6c multicolored	15	15
29	A4	15c multicolored	15	15
30	A4	25c multicolored	20	15
31	A4	$1 multicolored	80	80
		Set value		96

First anniversary of independence.

British Guiana Stamps and Types of 1954 Locally Overprinted

GUYANA INDEPENDENCE 1966

1967 Wmk. 4

32	A60	1c black	15	15
32A	A60	2c dark green	15	15
32B	A60	3c red brown & ol	15	15
32C	A61	4c violet	15	15
32D	A60	6c yellow green	15	15
32E	A60	8c ultramarine	15	15
32F	A61	12c brown & black	15	15
32G	A60	$2 magenta	2.50	2.50
32H	A61	$5 black & ultra	4.50	4.50
		Nos. 32-32H (9)	8.05	8.05

The 24c with Wmk. 4 also exists with this overprint. Value $100.

1967-68 Wmk. 314 Upright

32I	A60	1c black ('68)	15	15
32J	A60	2c dk green ('68)	15	15
32K	A60	3c red brown & ol	15	15
32L	A61	4c violet ('68)	15	15
32M	A60	5c black & red	35	35
32N	A60	6c yel green ('68)	20	15
32O	A60	24c orange & blk	30	25
32P	A60	36c black & rose	40	30
32Q	A61	48c red brn & ultra	60	50
32R	A61	72c emer & rose	75	75
32S	A60	$1 black & multi	1.00	1.00
32T	A60	$2 magenta	2.25	2.00
		Nos. 32I-32T (12)	6.45	5.90

The 1c, 4c, 6c, 8c and $5 with Wmk. 314 were not issued without overprint.

For surcharges see Nos. 540, 542, 543A.

"Millie," the Bilingual Macaw — A5

Wicketkeeper, Emblem of West Indies Cricket Team — A6

Christmas Issues

1967, Nov. 6 *Perf. 14½x14*

33	A5	5c olive green & multi	15	15
33A	A5	25c purple & multi	28	15
		Set value	34	15

1968, Jan. 22

34	A5	5c red & multi	15	15
35	A5	25c yel green & multi	28	15
		Set value	34	15

1968, Jan. 8 Photo. *Perf. 14*

Designs: 6c, Batsman and emblem of Marylebone Cricket Club. 25c, Bowler and emblem of West Indies Cricket Team.

36	A6	5c multicolored	15	15
37	A6	6c multicolored	15	15
38	A6	25c multicolored	35	15
a.		Strip of 3, #36-38	55	
		Set value	53	22

Visit of the Marylebone Cricket Club to the West Indies, Jan.-Feb. 1968. Printed in sheets of 9.

Pike Cichlid — A7

Marail Guan — A8

Christ of St. John of the Cross, by Salvador Dali — A9

Designs: 2c, Piranha. 3c, Cichla ocellaris (fish). 5c, Armored catfish. 6c, Two-spotted cichlid. 15c, Harpy eagle. 20c, Hoatzin. 25c, Andean cock-of-the-rock. 40c, Great kiskadee. 50c, Agouti. 60c, Peccary. $1, Paca. $2, Armadillo. $5, Ocelot.

Perf. 14x14½, 14½x14

1968, Mar. 4 Photo. Unwmk.

39	A7	1c chalky blue & multi	15	15
40	A7	2c gray & multi	15	15
41	A7	3c grnsh bl & multi	15	15
42	A7	5c ultra & multi	15	15
43	A7	6c brt olive & multi	15	15
44	A8	10c yel green & multi	15	15
45	A8	15c green & multi	15	15
46	A8	20c ap grn & multi	15	15
47	A8	25c brt green & multi	20	15
48	A8	40c pale brn & multi	32	20
49	A7	50c rose brn & multi	40	28
50	A7	60c lilac rose & multi	50	30
51	A7	$1 dp orange & multi	80	65
52	A7	$2 ocher & multi	2.00	1.50
53	A7	$5 red & multi	5.75	4.50
		Nos. 39-53 (15)	11.17	8.78

See Nos. 68-82.

For overprints & surcharges see #357, 410-413, 603, 752, 756, 761a, 1463, 1501, 1839, 2045.

1968, Mar. 25 *Perf. 14x14½*

54	A9	5c car rose & multi	15	15
55	A9	25c brt violet & multi	28	15
		Set value	34	15

Easter.

"Efficiency Year" — A10

Designs: 30c, 40c, "Savings bonds."

1968, July 22 Litho. *Perf. 14*

56	A10	6c green & multi	15	15
57	A10	25c fawn & multi	22	15
58	A10	30c multicolored	25	15
59	A10	40c multicolored	35	15
		Set value		24

Issued to promote the sale of savings bonds and to publicize Efficiency Year.

Open Koran A11

Perf. 14x13½

1968, Oct. 9 Photo. Unwmk.

60	A11	6c sal pink, gold & blk	15	15
61	A11	25c pale vio, gold & blk	22	15
62	A11	30c pale yel grn, gold & blk	25	15
63	A11	40c pale blue, gold & blk	35	15
		Set value		27

Koran's 1400th anniversary.

For overprints and surcharges see Nos. 354, 355, 441, 445, 487-488, 575, 630, 1464-1465.

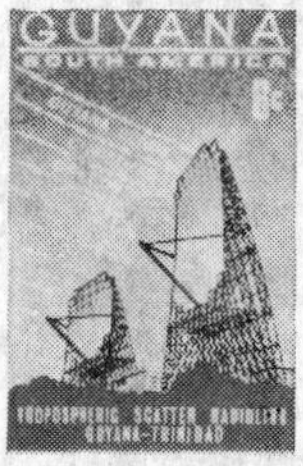

Dish Aerials, Thomas Lands, Guyana — A12

Designs: 30c, 40c, Map showing connection between Guyana and Trinidad. All stamps are inscribed: "Guyana Sends Christmas Greetings to the World."

Wmk. 364

1968, Nov. 11 Litho. *Perf. 14*

64	A12	6c blue, gray, ocher & emer	15	15
65	A12	25c brt rose lil, brn & emer	18	15
66	A12	30c blue grn & dk blue grn	25	15
67	A12	40c blue grn & red	32	15
		Set value		25

Christmas; communications link with Trinidad by the tropospheric scatter system.

Types of 1968

Designs as before.

Perf. 14x14½, 14½x14

1968 Photo. Wmk. 364

68	A7	1c chalky bl & multi	15	15
69	A7	2c gray & multi	15	15
70	A7	3c grnsh bl & multi	15	15
71	A7	5c ultra & multi	15	15
72	A7	6c brt olive & multi	15	15
73	A8	10c yel grn & multi	15	15
74	A8	15c green & multi	18	15
75	A8	20c apple grn & multi	25	15
76	A8	25c brt green & multi	32	20
77	A8	40c pale brn & multi	55	32
78	A7	50c rose brn & multi	75	45
79	A7	60c lilac rose & multi	90	65
80	A7	$1 dp org & multi	1.25	1.10
81	A7	$2 ocher & multi	2.50	2.00
82	A7	$5 red & multi	6.50	6.00
		Nos. 68-82 (15)	14.10	11.92

For overprints & surcharges see #373, 376-377, 413D, 565-566, 633, 635, 704-705, 744, 749, 752a, 757-758, 761-762, 1862-1863, 1981, O2.

Celebrants Spraying Perfumed Powder A13

Phagwah (Holi) Hindu Festival: 25c, 40c, Two celebrants spraying colored water.

1969, Feb. 26 Litho. *Perf. 13½*

83	A13	6c multicolored	15	15
84	A13	25c multicolored	18	18
85	A13	30c multicolored	22	22
86	A13	40c multicolored	30	30

The Last Supper, by Salvador Dali A14

1969, Mar. 10 Photo. *Perf. 13*

87	A14	6c dp carmine & multi	15	15
88	A14	25c green & multi	18	18
89	A14	30c org brown & multi	25	22
90	A14	40c dp violet & multi	35	30

Easter. For overprints and surcharges, see Nos. 393-394, 482-485, 572, 576, 634, 765, 772, 1407-1410, 1813, 1815-1817, 2050.

Map of Caribbean — A15

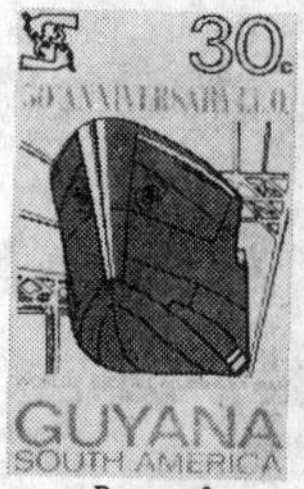

Prow of Aluminum Ship — A16

Design: 25c, "Strength in Unity," horiz.

Perf. 13½

1969, Apr. 30 Litho. Wmk. 364

91	A15	6c violet blue & multi	15	15
92	A15	25c brt rose, yel & brown	20	18
		Set value	27	24

1st anniv. of CARIFTA (Caribbean Free Trade Area).

1969, Apr. 30 *Perf. 12x11, 11x12*

50th Anniv. of the ILO: 40c, Bauxite processing plant, horiz.

93	A16	30c black, blue & silver	20	20
94	A16	40c multicolored	25	25

Flag Raising A17

Designs: 8c, 30c, Campfire.

1969, Aug. 13 Litho. *Perf. 13½x13*

95	A17	6c pale green & multi	15	15
96	A17	8c orange & multi	15	15
97	A17	25c pale brown & multi	18	18
98	A17	30c multicolored	25	25
99	A17	50c rose & multi	50	50
		Set value	1.04	1.04

60th anniv. of Scouting in Guyana; 3rd Caribbean Scout Jamboree, Georgetown, Aug. 13-22. For overprints and surcharges, see Nos. 392, 395, 397, 402, 404-405, 453.

Gandhi and Spinning Wheel A18

1969, Oct. 1 *Perf. 14½x14*

100	A18	6c olive, blk & lt brn	18	15
101	A18	15c rose lilac, blk & lt brn	60	45

Mohandas K. Gandhi (1868-1948), leader in India's fight for independence.

Mother Sally Troupe A19

City Hall, Georgetown A20

1969, Nov. 17 *Perf. 14x13½*

102	A19	5c multicolored	15	15
103	A20	6c blue & multi	15	15
104	A19	25c multicolored	20	20
105	A20	60c orange & multi	45	45
		Set value	78	78

Christmas. The 5c, 6c, and 25c exist without the "Christmas 1969" overprint.

Prime Minister Forbes Burnham and Map — A21

Descent from the Cross, by Rubens — A22

Designs: 6c, "Rural Self Help Project" (man and woman building house). 15c, University of Guyana, horiz. 25c, President's Residence, horiz.

1970, Feb. 23 Litho. *Perf. 14*

106	A21	5c bl, brn & ocher	15	15
107	A21	6c bl, blk ocher & brn	15	15
108	A21	15c apple grn & multi	15	15
109	A21	25c multicolored	20	18
		Set value	48	38

Issued for Republic Day, Feb. 23, 1970.

1970, Mar. 24 *Perf. 14x14½*

Easter: 6c, 25c, Christ on the Cross, by Rubens.

110	A22	5c blue & multi	15	15
111	A22	6c rose lilac & multi	15	15
112	A22	15c dark red & multi	20	18
113	A22	25c yellow & multi	35	30
		Set value	68	58

"Peace" and UN Emblem A23

UN 25th Anniv.: 6c, 25c, UN emblem, panning for gold and drilling for minerals.

1970, Oct. 26 *Perf. 14½x14*

114	A23	5c red & multi	15	15
115	A23	6c blue & multi	15	15
116	A23	15c multicolored	18	18
117	A23	25c brown & multi	28	28
		Set value	56	56

Mother and Child, by Philip Moore — A24

1970, Dec. 8 Litho. *Perf. 13½*

118	A24	5c violet & multi	15	15
119	A24	6c brown & multi	15	15
120	A24	15c dk green & multi	18	18
121	A24	25c maroon & multi	28	28
		Set value	56	56

Christmas.

National Cooperative Bank A25

1971, Feb. 23 Wmk. 364 *Perf. 14*

122	A25	6c red & multi	15	15
123	A25	15c yellow & multi	18	18
124	A25	25c ultra & multi	20	20
		Set value	38	38

Republic Day.

"Togetherness, Vision, Understanding" A26

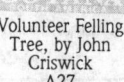

Volunteer Felling Tree, by John Criswick A27

1971, Mar. 22 *Perf. 14½x14*

125	A26	5c yel grn & multi	15	15
126	A26	6c lil rose & multi	15	15
127	A26	15c multicolored	15	15
128	A26	25c yellow & multi	20	20
		Set value	42	42

Intl. year against racial discrimination.

1971, July 19 *Perf. 14*

129	A27	5c blue & multi	15	15
130	A27	20c green & multi	20	20
131	A27	25c yellow & multi	20	20
132	A27	50c brown & multi	45	45
		Set value	82	82

1st anniv. of the Natl. Self-help Road Project.

Yellow Allamanda — A28

Flora: 1c, Pitcher plant of Mt. Roraima. 3c, Hanging heliconia. 5c, Annatto tree. 6c, Cannonball tree. 10c, Cattleya violacea. 15c, Christmas orchid. 20c, Paphinia cristata. 25c, Gongora quinquinervis. 40c, Tiger beard. 50c, Guzmania lingulata. 60c, Soldier's cap. $1, Chelonanthus uliginoides. $2, Norantea guianensis. $5, Odontadenia grandiflora.

1971-76 Litho. *Perf. 13x13½*

133	A28	1c multi ('72)	15	15
134	A28	2c lilac & multi	15	15
135	A28	3c multicolored	15	15
136	A28	5c lt bl & multi	15	15
137	A28	6c dl rose & multi	15	15
		Perf. 13½		
138	A28	10c multi ('72)	15	15
a.		Perf. 13		
139	A28	15c multi ('72)	15	15
a.		Perf. 13 ('76)	15	15
140	A28	20c multi ('72)	20	20
a.		Perf. 13		
141	A28	25c multi, 25c at center ('72)	50	50
141A	A28	25c multi, 25c right of center ('73)	25	25
b.		Perf. 13 ('76)	25	25
142	A28	40c multi ('72)	40	40
143	A28	50c multi ('73)	50	50
144	A28	60c multi ('73)	60	60
145	A28	$1 multi ('73)	1.00	1.00
146	A28	$2 multi ('73)	2.00	2.00
147	A28	$5 multi ('73)	5.00	5.00
		Nos. 133-147 (16)	11.50	11.50

No. 141 has 2 blossoms at left, 3 at right; this is reversed on No. 141A.

The overprint "REVENUE / ONLY" between rules was applied to Nos. 134-136, 141A, 142-147 in 1975. Postal use was permitted in Nov.-Dec., 1975.

See Nos. 433-434, 731-732.

For overprints and surcharges, see Nos. 192, 209, 234, 331-335, 351, 358-359, 367, 370, 372, 374-375, 379-383, 385-390, 401, 407, 422-425, 433-434, 438-440, 447, 450, 451, 457-458, 460-461, 464-466, 497-500, 545-546, 550, 563-564, 597, 602, 618, 631-632, 641-642, 666-667, 727, 747-748, 750-751, 753-754, 759-760, 803, 805, 807-808, 810-812, 847-848, 910-911, 995, 1361, 1382-1383, 1385-1386, 1391-1392, 1452, 1454, 1456-1460, 1466, 1499, 1778-1779, 1781-1784, 1837-1838, 1870-1872, 1898-1900, 2046-2049, 2225-2227, C2-C4, O1, O3-O5, O7, O13-O14, Q1-Q4, QO1.

The Lord's Prayer, by School Girl Veronica Bassoo — A29

Guyana Masker, by School Boy Michael Austin — A30

Perf. 13½x14, 14x13½

1971, Nov. 15 Litho. Wmk. 364

148	A29	5c brt grn & multi	15	15
149	A29	20c brt grn & multi	18	18
150	A30	25c multicolored	20	20
151	A30	50c multicolored	45	45

Christmas.

Guyana Dollar — A31

Handclasp and Mosque — A32

1972, Feb. 23 Litho. *Perf. 14½x14*

152	A31	5c blk, dp org & silver	15	15
153	A31	20c blk, dp lil rose & sil	20	20
154	A31	25c black, ultra & sil	22	22
155	A31	50c blk, emerald & sil	45	45

Republic Day.

1972, Apr. 3 *Perf. 14*

156	A32	5c brown & multi	15	15
157	A32	25c blue & multi	20	20
158	A32	30c green & multi	25	25
159	A32	60c yel brn & multi	50	50

Youman Nabi (Peaceful Prophet), Mohammedan festival.

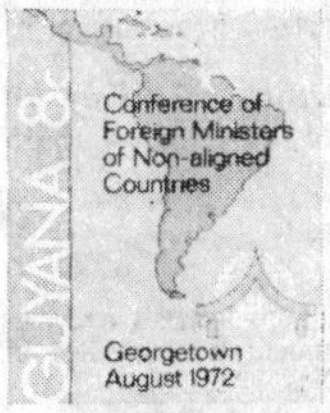

Map of South America, Emblem of Non-aligned Countries — A33

CARIFESTA '72 Emblem — A34

1972, July 20

160	A33	8c violet & multi	15	15
161	A33	25c yel grn & multi	20	20
162	A33	40c orange & multi	25	25
163	A33	50c red brn & multi	40	40

Conf. of Foreign Ministers of Nonaligned Countries, Georgetown, Aug. 7-12.

For overprints and surcharges, see Nos. 573, 611, O17.

1972, Aug. 25

164	A34	8c orange & multi	15	15
165	A34	25c orange & multi	20	20
166	A34	40c orange & multi	25	25
167	A34	50c orange & multi	40	40

Caribbean Festival of Arts (CARIFESTA), Georgetown, Aug. 25-Sept. 15.

Holy Family — A35

Umana Yana (Meeting Place of Wai Wai Chiefs) — A36

1972, Oct. 18 Litho. *Perf. 13x13½*

168	A35	8c blue & multi	15	15
169	A35	25c blue & multi	15	15
170	A35	40c blue & multi	20	20
171	A35	50c blue & multi	30	30

Christmas.

1973, Feb. 23 Litho. *Perf. 14x14½*

Designs: 25c, 40c, Bethel Chapel.

172	A36	8c brt bl & multi	15	15
173	A36	25c rose red & multi	20	20
174	A36	40c emer & multi	25	25
175	A36	50c black & multi	40	40

Republic Day.

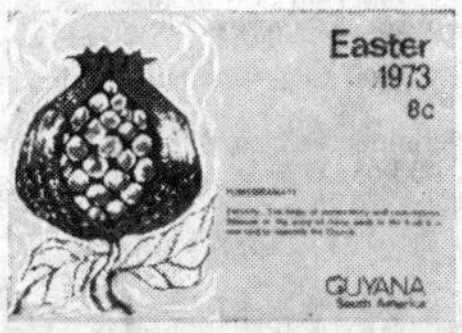

Pomegranate, Fertility and Church Symbol — A37

Map of Guyana and People Looking to the Cross — A38

1973, Apr. 19 *Perf. 14x14½, 13½*

176	A37	8c pink & multi	15	15
177	A38	25c yellow & multi	18	18
178	A38	40c ultra & multi	25	25
179	A37	50c yellow & multi	35	35

Easter.

Symbolic of Blood Donation — A39

Perf. 14x14½

1973, Oct. 1 Wmk. 364

180	A39	8c red & black	15	15
181	A39	25c red & lilac	20	20
182	A39	40c red & vio blue	32	32
183	A39	50c red & brown	40	40

Guyana Red Cross, 25th anniversary.

Steel Band, Star, Pegasus Hotel — A40

Madonna and Child, St. Philip's Anglican Church, Georgetown A41

1973, Nov. 20 Litho. *Perf. 14x14½*

184	A40	8c lilac & multi	15	15
185	A40	25c lilac & multi	18	18

Perf. 13½x14

186	A41	40c vio bl & multi	25	25
187	A41	50c vio bl & multi	38	38

Christmas.

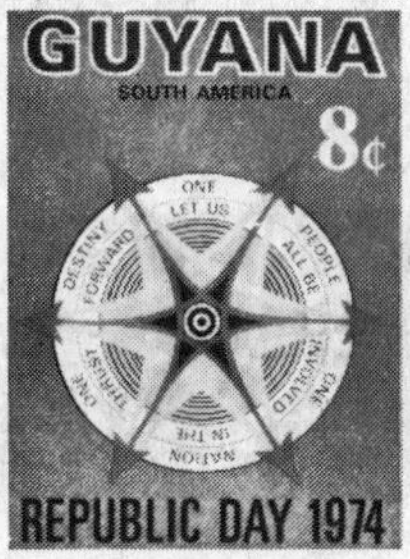

"One People, One Nation, One Destiny" A42

Designs: 25c, 50c, Wai Wai Indian.

1974, Feb. 23 Litho. *Perf. 13½*

188	A42	8c multicolored	15	15
189	A42	25c multicolored	18	18
190	A42	40c multicolored	30	30
191	A42	50c multicolored	40	40

Republic Day.

No. 137 Surcharged with New Value and 2 Bars

Perf. 13x13½

1974, Mar. 18 Wmk. 364

192	A28	8c on 6c multi	15	15

For overprints and surcharges see Nos. 424, 459, 474-478, 1453, 1500, 1780.

Crucifix Superimposed on Eddy Bow Kite — A43

Crucifix in Pre-Columbian Timehri Style — A44

1974, Apr. 8 *Perf. 13½x14*

193	A43	8c green & multi	15	15
194	A44	25c black, green & gray	18	18
195	A44	40c blk, gray & carmine	25	25
196	A43	50c gold & multi	35	35

Easter.

UPU Emblem and British Guiana Type of 1863 — A45

Mailman and UPU Emblem A46

1974, June 18 Litho. *Perf. 14, 14½*

197	A45	8c rose & multi	15	15
198	A46	25c yel green & multi	18	18
199	A45	40c blue & multi	25	25
200	A46	50c yel green & multi	35	35

Centenary of Universal Postal Union.

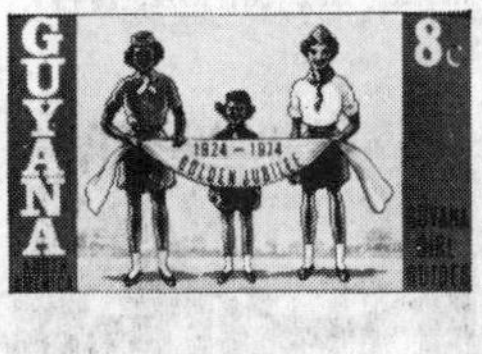

Girl Guides Holding Banner A47

Designs: 25c, 40c, Guides in camp cooking and carrying water. 50c, Like 8c.

1974, Aug. 1 *Perf. 14½*

201	A47	8c multicolored	15	15
202	A47	25c multicolored	18	18
203	A47	40c multicolored	30	30
204	A47	50c multicolored	40	40
a.		Souv. sheet of 4, #201-204	1.50	1.50

Girl Guides of Guyana, 50th anniv. For overprints see Nos. 574, 1352.

Buck Toyeau — A48

Golden Arrow of Courage — A49

Christmas (Fruit): 35c, Carambola (starfruit) and awaras. 50c, Pawpaw and tangerine. $1, Pineapple and sapodillas.

1974, Nov. 18 Litho. *Perf. 14x13½*

205	A48	8c multicolored	15	15
206	A48	35c multicolored	28	28
207	A48	50c multicolored	40	40
208	A48	$1 multicolored	75	75
a.		Souvenir sheet of 4, #205-208	1.75	1.75

For overprints and surcharges see Nos. 551, 612, 716.

No. 135 Surcharged with New Value and Two Bars

1975, Jan. 20 Litho. *Perf. 13x13½*

209	A28	8c on 3c multi	15	15

For surcharge, see No. 423.

1975, Feb. 23 *Perf. 13x13½*

Republic Day: 35c, Cacique's Crown of Honour. 50c, Cacique's Crown of Valour. $1, Order of Excellence.

210	A49	10c brown & multi	15	15
211	A49	35c brn red & multi	25	25
212	A49	50c green & multi	35	35
213	A49	$1 vio bl & multi	65	65

For overprints and surcharges see Nos. 360, 368, 398, 637, 1359.

Old Sluice Gate — A50

Modern Sluice Gate A51

1975, May 2 *Perf. 14*

214	A50	10c bister & multi	15	15
215	A51	35c brown & multi	20	20
216	A50	50c bister & multi	30	30
217	A51	$1 green & multi	60	60
a.		Souvenir sheet of 4, #214-217	1.75	1.75

Intl. Commission on Irrigation and Drainage, 25th anniv.

For overprints see Nos. 361, 592, 794-795, 1374-1375.

IWY Emblem, Symbolic Man and Woman A52

Designs: IWY emblem and petroglyph designs of men and women.

1975, July 1 Litho. Wmk. 364

218	A52	10c yel & dull grn	15	15
219	A52	35c Prus blue & pur	25	25
220	A52	50c org & dk blue	35	35
221	A52	$1 ultra & brown	65	65
a.		Souvenir sheet of 4, #218-221, perf. 14½	1.75	1.75

Intl. Women's Year. For overprints and surcharges, see Nos. 362, 399, 555.

Demand, as well as supply, determine a stamp's market value.

Freedom Monument, Georgetown A53

"GNS," Flower and Clasped Hands A54

Designs: Various views of Freedom Monument, Georgetown.

1975, Aug. 26 Litho. *Perf. 14*

222	A53	10c gray & multi	15	15
223	A53	35c yellow & multi	25	25
224	A53	50c lilac & multi	35	35
225	A53	$1 olive & multi	65	65

Namibia Day (independence for South-West Africa).

For overprints and surcharges, see Nos. 330, 582, 593, 619, 1360.

1975, Oct. 2 Wmk. 364 *Perf. 14*

"GNS" and Clasped hands: 35c, Wheel. 50c, Soccer ball. $1, Uniform cap.

226	A54	10c vio, yel & grn	15	15
227	A54	35c brt bl, org & grn	25	25
228	A54	50c lt brn, brt bl & grn	35	35
229	A54	$1 grn, vio & brt grn	65	65
a.		Souvenir sheet of 4, #226-229	1.50	1.50

Guyana National Service, 1st anniv. For surcharges see Nos. 636, 638. For overprint see No. 448.

Foresters' Building and Badge A55

Designs: 35c, Rock painting of hunter. 50c, Crossed axes and hunting horn. $1, Bow and arrow.

1975, Nov. 14 Litho. Wmk. 364

230	A55	10c red, blk & gold	15	15
231	A55	35c red, blk & gold	25	25
232	A55	50c gold & multi	35	35
233	A55	$1 gold & multi	65	65
a.		Souvenir sheet of 4, #230-233	1.50	1.50

Ancient Order of Foresters, centenary.

For overprints and surcharges, see Nos. 356, 363, 400, 422, 583.

No. 144 Surcharged  35c

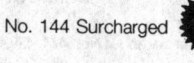

1976, Feb. 10 *Perf. 13½*

234	A28	35c on 60c multi	25	25

For overprints see Nos. 703-703b, 852.

St. John Ambulance Emblem — A56

Independence Arch, 1966 — A57

1976, Mar. 29 Litho. *Perf. 14*

235	A56	8c blk, lil rose & sil	15	15
236	A56	15c blk, orange & sil	15	15
237	A56	35c blk, emer & silver	25	25
238	A56	40c black, blue & sil	30	30

Guyana St. John Ambulance, 50th anniv. For surcharges see Nos. 715, 717, 1411.

1976, May 25 *Perf. 13½*

Stylized Designs: 15c, Victoria regia. 35c, Letter "S" for socialism. 40c, Worker with pitchfork.

239	A57	8c silver & multi	15	15
240	A57	15c silver & multi	15	15
241	A57	35c silver & multi	25	25
242	A57	40c silver & multi	30	30
a.		Souv. sheet of 4, #239-242, perf. 14	75	75

10th anniv. of independence. For surcharges see Nos. 567, 639, 1444.

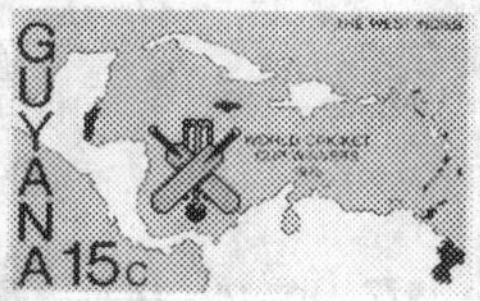

Map of West Indies, Bats, Wicket and Ball — A57a

Prudential Cup — A57b

Unwmk.

1976, Aug. 3 Litho. *Perf. 14*

243	A57a	15c light bl & multi	25	25
244	A57b	15c lilac rose & blk	25	25

World Cricket Cup, won by West Indies Team, 1975.

For overprints see Nos. 352-353. For surcharges see Nos. 653-654.

Lamp — A58

Guitar-Sitar, Benin Head — A59

Designs: 15c, Hand and flame. 35c, Flame. 40c, Lakshmi, Hindu goddess of wealth.

1976, Oct. 21 *Perf. 14*

245	A58	8c multicolored	15	15
246	A58	15c orange & multi	15	15
247	A58	35c purple & multi	35	35
248	A58	40c ultra & multi	40	40
a.		Souvenir sheet of 4, #245-248	1.25	1.25

Deepavali, Hindu Festival of Lights.

For surcharges see Nos. 719-721.

1977, Feb. 1 Litho. *Perf. 14½*

249	A59	10c gold & multi	15	15
250	A59	35c gold & multi	25	25
251	A59	50c gold & multi	40	40
252	A59	$1 gold & multi	75	75
a.		Souvenir sheet of 4, #249-252	2.00	2.00

2nd World Black and African Festival, Lagos, Nigeria, Jan. 15-Feb. 12. Nos. 249-252a were not issued without black bar.

For overprints see Nos. 364, 369, 584.

1c and 5c Coins A60

Coins (Obverse): 15c, 10c and 25c. 35c, 50c and $1. 40c, $5 and $10. $1, $50 and $100. $2, Reverse, Coat of arms.

1977, May 26 *Perf. 14*

253	A60	8c multicolored	15	15
254	A60	15c multicolored	15	15
255	A60	35c multicolored	25	25
256	A60	40c multicolored	30	30
257	A60	$1 multicolored	65	65
258	A60	$2 multicolored	1.40	1.40
		Nos. 253-258 (6)	2.90	2.90

New coinage. For overprints and surcharges see Nos. 539-541, 568, 594, O18, O20, Q5.

Hand Pump, c. 1850 A61

National Fire Prevention Week: 15c, Steam engine, c. 1860. 35c, Fire engine, c. 1930. 40c, Fire engine, 1977.

Perf. 14x14½

1977, Nov. 15 Litho. Wmk. 364

259	A61	8c multicolored	15	15
260	A61	15c multicolored	15	15
261	A61	35c multicolored	28	28
262	A61	40c multicolored	30	30
		Set value	76	76

For surcharges see Nos. 1370-1371.

Cuffy Monument — A62

Wildlife Protection — A63

Designs: 8c, 35c, Cuffy statue from monument.

1977, Dec. 7 Litho. *Perf. 14*

263	A62	8c multicolored	15	15
264	A62	15c multicolored	15	15
265	A62	35c multicolored	28	28
266	A62	40c multicolored	30	30
		Set value	76	76

Cuffy, Guyana's national hero, led a slave revolution in 1763. The monument was unveiled in 1976. For overprints see Nos. 446, 569, 613.

1978, Feb. 15 *Perf. 14*

267	A63	8c Manatee	15	15
268	A63	15c Giant sea turtle	15	15
269	A63	35c Harpy eagle	35	35
270	A63	40c Iguana	40	40

8c, 15c are horiz. For overprints and surcharges see Nos. 443, 722-723, 1416.

Parliament and Prime Minister Burnham — A64

Prime Minister and: 15c, Student and school children. 35c, Bauxite mine. 40c, Cooperative village.

1978, Apr. 27 Litho. *Perf. 13½x14*

271 A64 8c vio & black 15 15
272 A64 15c gray, blk & bl 15 15
273 A64 35c multicolored 25 25
274 A64 40c gray, blk & org 30 30
a. Souvenir sheet of 4, #271-274 75 75
Set value 71 71

Prime Minister Linden Forbes Burnham, 25th anniv. of his entry into parliament. For surcharges see Nos. 648-649.

Dr. George Giglioli, Anopheles Mosquito — A65

Agrias Claudina — A66

Designs: 30c, Institute of Applied Science and Technology, proposed for University of Guyana, horiz. 50c, Map of Guyana and National Science Research Council emblem. 60c, Commonwealth Science Council emblem, horiz.

Perf. 13½x14, 14x13½

1978, Sept. 4 Litho. Wmk. 364

275 A65 10c multicolored 15 15
276 A65 30c multicolored 15 15
277 A65 50c multicolored 25 25
278 A65 60c multicolored 30 30
Set value 76 76

For overprints see Nos. 577, 585, 590.

1978-80 *Perf. 14x13½*

Size: 22x16mm

279 A66 5c Prepona pheridamas 15 15
280 A66 10c Archonias bellona 15 15
281 A66 15c Eryphanis polyxena 15 15
282 A66 20c Helicopis cupido 15 15
283 A66 25c Nessaea batesli 18 18
283A A66 30c Nymphidium mantus ('80) 22 22
284 A66 35c Siderone galanthis 28 28
285 A66 40c Morpho rhetenor, male 30 30
286 A66 50c Hamadryas amphinone 40 40
286A A66 60c Papilio androgens ('80) 45 45

Perf. 13½x13

287 A66 $1 Agrias claudina 75 75
288 A66 $2 Morpho rhetenor, female 1.50 1.50
289 A66 $5 Morpho deidamia 3.75 3.75
289A A66 $10 Elbella patrobas, perf. 14 ('80) 7.50 7.50
Nos. 279-289A (14) 15.93 15.93

Issue dates: Nos. 279-283, 284-286, 287-289, Oct. 1, 1978. For overprints and surcharges see Nos. 391, 406, 436-436A, 481, 486, 554, 668-670, 733-743, 858, 933, 944, 998, 1373, 1418, 1455, 1786, 1812, 1814, 1832-1833, 1873, 1901, 1912-1913, 1984-1988, 2053, 2055, 2057-2059, 2082-2111, C5-C6, O14, O16.

Indian Making Stone Chip Grater — A67

UNESCO Emblem and: 30c, Arawak Cassiri jar and decorated Amerindian jar. 50c, Gate to old Dutch fort, Kykover-al. 60c, Fort Island, Dutch ruins.

1978, Dec. 27 Wmk. 364 *Perf. 14*

290 A67 10c green & multi 15 15
291 A67 30c green & multi 20 20
292 A67 50c green & multi 35 35
293 A67 60c green & multi 40 40

National and International Heritage Year. For surcharges see Nos. 604-606.

Earth Station at Dawn, Georgetown A68

Designs: 30c, Earth Station in daylight, Georgetown. 50c, Intelsat V. $3, Intelsat IVa.

1979, Feb. 7 Litho. *Perf. 14x14½*

294 A68 10c multicolored 15 15
295 A68 30c multicolored 20 20
296 A68 50c multicolored 35 35
297 A68 $3 multicolored 2.00 2.00

For surcharges see Nos. 384, 655, 714, 1376-1377, 1380, O9.

British Guyana No. 5 — A69

Designs: 30c, British Guiana No. 13 (vert.). 50c, British Guiana No. 152. $3, Printing press used for 1c Magenta (vert.).

1979, May 30 Wmk. 364 *Perf. 14*

298 A69 10c multicolored 15 15
299 A69 30c multicolored 20 20
300 A69 50c multicolored 35 35
301 A69 $3 multicolored 2.00 2.00

Sir Rowland Hill (1795-1879), originator of penny postage. For overprints and surcharges see Nos. 409, 426, 428, 449, 479, 480, 578, 586, 598, 614, O6.

"Fun with the Fowls" and IYC Emblem — A70

Children's Drawings and IYC Emblem: 10c, "Me and my sister," vert. 50c, "Two boys catching ducks." $3, "Mango season."

1979, Aug. 20 Litho. *Perf. 13½*

302 A70 10c multicolored 15 15
303 A70 30c multicolored 20 20
304 A70 50c multicolored 35 35
305 A70 $3 multicolored 2.00 2.00

Intl. Year of the Child. For overprints and surcharges see Nos. 435, 579, 587, 599, 615, 943.

H. N. Critchlow, Worker Hauling Sack — A71

Critchlow and: 30c, Baker, horiz. 50c, Flag and crowd. $3, Portrait only.

1979, Sept. 27 Litho. *Perf. 14*

306 A71 10c multicolored 15 15
307 A71 30c multicolored 20 20
308 A71 50c multicolored 35 35
309 A71 $3 multicolored 2.00 2.00

Guyana Labor Union, 60th anniversary. For surcharges see Nos. 403, 429, 718.

Cooperative Republic Centenary — A72

Wmk. 364

1980, Feb. 23 Litho. *Perf. 14*

313 A72 10c shown 15 15
314 A72 35c Demerara River Bridge 25 25
315 A72 60c Kaieteur Falls 40 40
316 A72 $3 Makanaima, American Indian 2.00 2.00

For overprints and surcharges see Nos. 365, 371, 442, 591, 600, 656.

Miniature Sheet

Snoek, London 1980 Emblem A73

London 80 Emblem and Fish; a, Snoek. b, Haimara. c, Electric eel. d, Golden rivulus. e, Pencil fish. f, Four-eyed fish. g, Pirai. h, Smoking hassar. i, Devil ray. j, Flying patwa. k, Arapaima. l, Lukanani.

1980, May 6 Wmk. 373 *Perf. 14*

317 Sheet of 12 3.00 3.00
a.-l. A73 35c multi, any stamp 25 25

London 1980 Intl. Stamp Exhib., May 6-14. For overprints and surcharges see Nos. 444, 725-726, 1414.

Children's Convalescent Home, Rotary Emblem — A74

Rotary International, 75th anniversary (Emblem and): 30c, Georgetown club emblem. 50c, District 404 emblem (hibiscus), vert. $3, Anniversary emblem, vert.

Perf. 14x14½, 14½x14

1980, June 23 Litho. Wmk. 364

318 A74 10c multicolored 15 15
319 A74 30c multicolored 30 30
320 A74 50c multicolored 50 50
321 A74 $3 multicolored 3.00 3.00

For overprints and surcharges see Nos. 552, 580, 601, C1.

Emblem and Caduceus A75

Perf. 13½

1980, Sept. 23 Litho. Wmk. 364

322 A75 10c shown 15 15
323 A75 60c Scientist, beach scene 40 40
324 A75 $3 Emblems over island 2.00 2.00

Commonwealth Caribbean Medical Research Council, 25th anniversary. For overprints and surcharges see Nos. 366, 427, 430, 494, 553.

Virola Surinamensis (Christmas 1980) — A76

1980, Nov. 1 Wmk. 373 *Perf. 14*

325 A76 10c shown 15 15
326 A76 30c Hymenaea courbaril 20 20
327 A76 50c Mora excelsa 35 35
328 A76 $3 Peltogyne venosa 2.00 2.00

For overprints and surcharges see Nos. 431, 773, 790, 792-793.

Miniature Sheet

A77

Designs: a, Tree porcupine. b, Howler monkeys. c, Squirrel monkeys. d, Two-toed sloth. e, Tapir. f, Collared peccary. g, Six-banded armadillo. h, Anteater. i, Great anteaters. j, Mouse opossums. k, Four-eyed opossum. l, Orange-rumped agouti.

1981, Mar. 2 Wmk. 364 *Perf. 14*

329 Sheet of 12 2.75 2.75
a.-l. A77 30c, any single 20 20
m. As #329g, perf. 12 20 20

For overprints see Nos. 581, 819, 1399, 1503, 1844.

From this point on there seem to be numerous sources creating stamps for Guyana. According to our information as many as 5-7 parties are active at any one time.

No. 222 Surcharged "1981 CONFERENCE"

1981, May 4

330 A53 $1.05 on 10c multi

For surcharges see Nos. 396, 620.

Nos. 135, 146-147 Surcharged "Royal Wedding / 1981" and New Value and

ROYAL
WEDDING
1981

$3.60

X X

Nos. 145 and 147 Surcharged in Blue or Black

1981 Litho. Wmk. 364 *Perf. 13½*

331 A28 60c on 3c #135
332 A28 75c on $5 #147
333 A28 $1.10 on $2 #146
334 A28 $3.60 on $5 #147 (Blk)
a. Blue overprint
335 A28 $7.20 on $1 #145 (Bl)
a. Black overprint

No. 333 is airmail. Issue dates: $3.60, $7.20, May 6. Others July 22. Diagonal overprint on No. 332. Vertical overprint on No. 333. Location of surcharge varies.

See Nos. 621, 666-667, O4, OO5. For overprints and surcharges see Nos. 378, 489-496, 547, 549, 646, 818, 867-868, O11, O3, OO3.

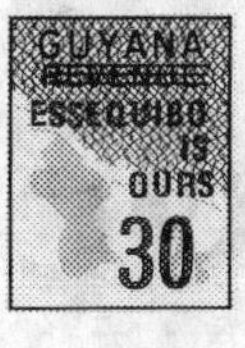

Map of Guyana — A78

1981, May 11 **Photo.** ***Perf. 13½***

336 A78 10c on 3c multi
337 A78 30c on 2c multi
338 A78 50c on 2c multi
339 A78 60c on 2c multi
340 A78 75c on 3c multi

Revenue stamps surcharged for postal use. For similar stamp, see No. 934a. For surcharge see No. 503.

Nos. J5-J8 Surcharged in Red, Black, or Brown

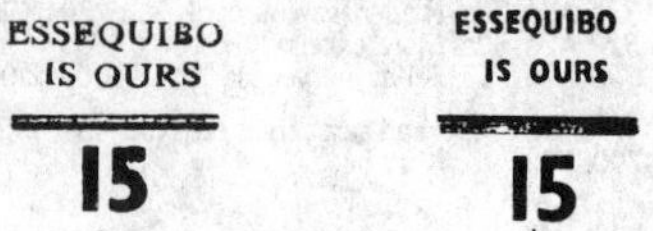

a b

1981, June 8 **Typo.** ***Perf. 13½x14***

Type "a"

341 D1 10c on 2c #J6
342 D1 15c on 12c #J8 (Blk)
343 D1 20c on 1c #J5
344 D1 45c on 2c #J6
345 D1 55c on 4c #J7
346 D1 60c on 4c #J7 (Brn)
347 D1 65c on 2c #J6
348 D1 70c on 4c #J7
349 D1 80c on 4c #J7

Type "b"

341a D1 10c on 2c #J6
342a D1 15c on 12c #J8 (Blk)
343a D1 20c on 1c #J5
344a D1 45c on 2c #J6
345a D1 55c on 4c #J7
347a D1 65c on 2c #J6
348a D1 70c on 4c #J7
349a D1 80c on 4c #J7

Pairs with types a and b exist for all values except the 60c.

Nos. 48, 61-62, 74, 139, 142-143, 145-147, 212-213, 216, 220, 231-232, 243-244, 251-252, 315-316, and 323 Overprinted in Black or Red

1981 ***Perfs. as Before***

Watermarks & Printing Methods as Before

350 A8 15c on #74
351 A28 15c on #139
 a. Red overprint
 b. On #139a, red overprint
352 A57a 15c on #243
353 A57b 15c on #244
354 A11 25c on #61 (R)
355 A11 30c on #62 (R)
356 A55 35c on #231 (R)
357 A8 40c on #48
358 A28 40c on #142
359 A28 50c on #143
360 A49 50c on #212
361 A50 50c on #216
362 A52 50c on #220
363 A55 50c on #232
364 A59 50c on #251
365 A72 60c on #315
366 A75 60c on #323
367 A28 $1 on #145
 a. Red overprint
368 A49 $1 on #213
369 A59 $1 on #252
370 A28 $2 on #146
 a. Red overprint
 b. Black ovpt. with serifs
371 A72 $3 on #316
372 A28 $5 on #147

Issue dates: Nos. 354-356, 367, June 8. Nos. 350, 357, 370, July 1. Nos. 351-353, 359-366, 368-369, 371-372, July 7. Location and size of overprint varies. Refer to second paragraph in footnote following No. 147 for Nos. 358-359.

For surcharges and overprints, see Nos. 556, 607, 659, 745, 849-850, 1362.

Nos. 68, 135-136, 145-147, 297, 333 Surcharged or Overprinted

1981 **Litho.** ***Perfs. as Before***

Watermarks & Printing Methods as Before

373 A8 15c on 1c #68
374 A28 50c on 5c #136
375 A28 75c on 5c #136
376 A8 100c on 1c #68
377 A8 110c on 1c #68
 a. Strip of 3, #373, 376-377
378 A28 $1.10 on #333
379 A28 120c on $1 #145
380 A28 140c on $1 #145
381 A28 150c on $2 #146
382 A28 210c on $5 #147
383 A28 220c on 5c #136
384 A68 220c on $3 #297
385 A28 250c on $5 #147
386 A28 280c on $5 #147
387 A28 360c on $2 #146
388 A28 375c on $5 #147
389 A28 $7.20 on 3c #135
390 A28 720c on 60c #144

Location and size of surcharge and obliterator varies. Obliterator is an "X" on Nos. 381-388, 390, two solid boxes on Nos. 379-380, and five bars on No. 389. Numeral "7" is placed before 5 make surcharge on No. 375. "Royal Wedding 1981" obliterated by three bars on No. 378.

Refer to second paragraph in footnote following No. 147 for Nos. 381, 387 and 390. Nos. 376-378 are airmail.

Issue dates: Nos. 375 & 382, June 8. Nos. 373-374, 376-388, & 390, July 1.

For overprint and surcharges see Nos. 408, 788, 859-860, 863-864, 1379, 1417.

No. 281 Overprinted "ESSEQUIBO / IS OURS"

1981, July **Litho.** ***Perf. 14x13½***

391 A66 15c on #281
 a. Ovpt. without serifs

Nos. 87, 95-96, 142, 146, 210, 218, 230, 309, 330, O15 Surcharged

1981 ***Perfs. as Before***

Watermarks & Printing Methods as Before

392 A17 55c on 6c #95
393 A14 70c on 6c #87
394 A14 100c on 6c #87
395 A17 100c on 8c #96
396 A53 100c on #330 (surcharge reading down)
 a. Surcharge reading up
397 A17 110c on 6c #95
398 A49 110c on 10c #210
399 A52 110c on 10c #218
400 A55 110c on 10c #230
401 A28 125c on $2 #146
402 A17 180c on 6c #95
403 A71 240c on $3 #309
404 A17 400c on 6c #95
405 A17 $4.40 on 6c #95
 a. Fours same size
406 A66 550c on $10 #O15
407 A28 625c on 40c #142

Issue dates: Nos. 392, 394-395, 397-399, 405, 405a, & 407, July 7. Nos. 393, 402-404, 406, Sept. 15. Refer to second paragraph in footnote following No. 147 for No. 407. For overprints and surcharges see Nos. 651-652, 996, 1858-1859, 1861, O8, O10, O12.

No. 383 Ovptd. "Espana 82"
No. 301 Surcharged "1831-1981 / Von Stephan"

Perfs. as Before

1981, July 22 **Litho.** **Wmk. 364**

408 A28 220c on #383
409 A69 330c on $3 #301

For surcharges see Nos. 616, 622.

Nos. 43, 72 Surcharged

1981 **Photo.** **Unwmk.** ***Perf. 14x14½***

410 A7 12c on 12c on 6c #43
411 A7 Pair, #a.-b.
 a. 15c on 10c on 6c #43
 b. 15c on 30c on 6c #43
412 A7 Pair, #a.-b.
 a. 15c on 50c on 6c #43
 b. 15c on 60c on 6c #43
413 A7 Strip of 3, #a.-c.
 a. 12c On 6c #43
 b. 50c On 6c #43
 c. $1 On 6c #43

Wmk. 364

413D A7 Strip of 3, #e.-g.
 e. 12c On 6c #72
 f. 50c On 6c #72
 g. $1 On 6c #72

Issue dates: Nos. 410-412, Aug. 24. No. 413-413D, Nov. 10.

Nos. 410-412 were not issued without large numeral surcharges. Obliterator is black box on Nos. 410-412, "X" on Nos. 413a & 413e. Nos. 413b-413c, 413f-g are airmail.

For overprints and surcharges see Nos. 728-728a, 914, 994, 994a, 1400-1401.

16th Anniv. of the Guyana Defense Force — A79

1981, Oct. 1 **Wmk. 364** ***Perf. 13½***

414 A79	15c on 10c Armed Ranger, 1772	15	15
415 A79	50c Private, Foot Regiment, 1825	40	40
416 A79	$1 on 30c Marine Private, 1775	75	75
417 A79	$1.10 on $3 Defense Force officers, 1966	80	80

Nos. 414, 416-417 not issued without surcharge. For overprints see Nos. 570, 588, 595, 1368-1369.

Louis Braille and Boy Reading Braille — A80

Intl. Year of the Disabled: 50c, Helen Keller and Rajkumari Singh. $1, Beethoven and Sonny Thomas. $1.10, Renoir and painting.

1981, Nov. 2 ***Perf. 13½x14***

418 A80	15c on 10c multi	15	15
419 A80	50c multi	40	40
420 A80	$1 on 60c multi	75	75
421 A80	$1.10 on $3 multi	80	80

Nos. 418, 420-421 not issued without surcharge. For overprints see #571, 589, 596.

Nos. 192, 209, 230, 298, 301, 309, 322, 324, 328, O1 Surcharged in Blue or Red

1981, Nov. 14 ***Perfs. as Before***

Watermarks & Printing Methods as Before

422 A55 110c on 10c #230
423 A28 110c on #209
424 A28 110c on #192
425 A28 110c on #O1
426 A69 110c on 10c #298 (R)
427 A75 110c on 10c #322
428 A69 110c on $3 #301 (R)
429 A71 110c on $3 #309
430 A75 110c on $3 #324
 a. Red surcharge
431 A76 110c on $3 #328
 a. Red surcharge

Nos. 423-424 were issued with two 110c surcharges of different sizes. Refer to second paragraph in footnote below No. 147 for No. 425. For overprints and surcharges see Nos. 791, 820, 855, 1000, 1364-1366.

Flower Type of 1971-76 Surcharged

1981, Nov. 24 **Photo.** ***Perf. 15x14***

Size: 20x23mm

Coil Stamps

433 A28 15c on 2c like #134
434 A28 15c on 8c Mazaruni Pride
 a. Pair, #433-434

Nos. 433-434 were not issued without surcharge. See Nos. 731-732.

No. 305 Surcharged "U.N.I.C.E.F. / 1946-1981"

Perf. 13½

1981, Nov. 14 **Litho.** **Wmk. 364**

435 A70 125c on $3 #305

For surcharge see No. 942.

No. 279 Surcharged "Nov. 81" (#436) or "Cancun 81" (#436A)

1981, Nov. 14 ***Perf. 14x13½***

436 A66 50c on 5c #279
436A A66 50c on 5c #279

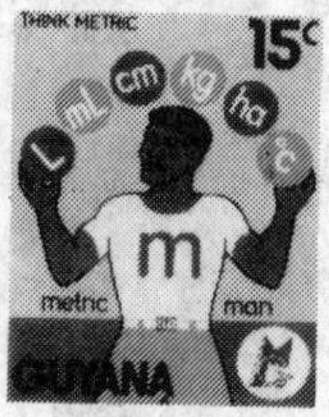

Conversion to Metric System, Jan. 2 — A81

Designs: a, Tape measure. b, Juggler. c, Man, envelope. d, Baby on scale. e, Canje Bridge. f, Liter bucket.

Perf. 14½x14

1982, Jan. 18 **Wmk. 364**

437 A81	15c Sheet of 6, #a.-f.	75	75

For surcharge see No. 557.

Nos. 61, 63, 139, 140, 141A, 144, 146-147, 259, 316-317, and 443 Ovptd. "1982" Vertically or Horizontally in Blue or Violet

1982-83 ***Perfs. as Before***

Watermarks & Printing Methods as Before

438 A28 15c on #139
 a. On #139a
439 A28 20c on #140
440 A28 25c on #141A
441 A11 25c on #61 (V)
442 A72 35c on #314
443 A63 35c on #269
444 A73 35c on block of 6, #317a-317f
445 A11 40c on #63 (V)
446 A62 40c on #266
447 A28 50c on #143
448 A54 50c on #228
449 A69 50c on #300
449A A28 60c on #144
450 A28 $2 on #146
450A A72 $3 on #316
451 A28 $5 on #147

Issue dates: Nos. 439-441, Feb. 8. Nos. 450-451, Apr. 23. No. 445-446, Apr. 27. No. 438, June 17. Nos. 443-444, Aug. 16. Nos. 447-449, Oct. 11. No. 449A, July 1, 1983. No. 450A, Nov. 3, 1983.

For other stamps overprinted "1982" only, see Nos 482-483, 555.

For overprints and surcharges see Nos. 600, 806, 809, 813-814, 851, 999, 1354, 1415.

Nos. 97, O3, O4, O9-O10 Ovptd. "POSTAGE" in Blue

1982 ***Perfs. as Before***

Watermarks and Printing Methods as Before

452 A28 15c on #O3
453 A17 25c on #97
454 A28 50c on #O4
455 A68 100c on #O9
456 A17 110c on #O10

For surcharge see No. 853. For similar overprints see Nos. 729-730. Refer to second paragraph in footnote following No. 147 for No. 454.

Nos. 133, 137, 142, and 192 Surcharged in Blue or Green

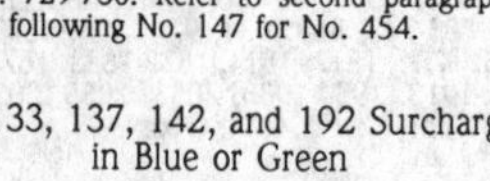

Perfs. as Before

1982 **Litho.** **Wmk. 364**

457 A28 20c on 6c #137
458 A28 20c on 6c #137 (G)
459 A28 125c on #192
460 A28 180c on #142 ovpt. "1982"
461 A28 220c on 1c #133

No. 458 has no obliterator, "20c" is 23mm long. Issue dates: Nos. 457-459, Feb. 8. No. 460, Apr. 8. No. 461, Apr. 23. Refer to second paragraph in footnote following No. 147 for No. 460. For overprints see #755, 856, 862.

Savings Campaign A81a

1982 Litho. *Perf. 14½*

462 A81a $1 Soldier & flag
463 A81a $1.10 on $5, two soldiers, flag
a. Inverted comma before "OURS"

Size of obliterator differs on Nos. 463 and 463a. Nos. 462-463a are revenue stamps ovptd. for postal use.

Issue dates: No. 462, Feb. 8. No. 463, Mar. 3. No. 463a, July 13.

Nos. 134, 136, & 192 Surcharged in Black or Green
"BADEN-POWELL / 1857-1982" (#464a, 465a, 466a)
"Scout Movement / 1907-1982" (#464b, 465b, 466b)
"1907-1982" (#464c, 465c, 466c)
"1857-1982" (#464d, 465d, 466d)
"1982" (#464e, 465e, 466e)

Perf. 13x13½

1982, Feb. 22 Litho. Wmk. 364

Sheets of 25

464 8 #a.-b., 4 #c.-d., 1 #e.
a.-e. A28 15c on 2c #134, any single
465 8 #a.-b., 4 #c.-d., 1 #e.
a.-e. A28 110c on 5c #136, any single
466 8 #a.-b., 4 #c.-d., 1 #e.
a.-e. A28 125c on #192, any single (G)

Lord Robert Baden-Powell, 125th anniv. of birth. Boy Scout Movement, 75th anniv.

For overprints and surcharges see Nos. 558, 778-784, 836-837, 1347.

Nos. 289, 299, 301 Surcharged or Overprinted in Black or Blue

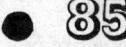

100

Geo Washington
1732... 1982

GEORGE
WASHINGTON
1732 — 1982

Perfs. as Before

1982, Feb. 15 Litho. Wmk. 364

479 A69 100c on $3 #301
480 A69 400c on 30c #299
481 A66 $5 on #289 (Bl)

For surcharges, see Nos. 617, 904-906, 937-939, O22-O29.

Nos. 88-89 Ovptd. "1982" in Blue and Nos. 87, 90 Surcharged in Blue or Red

1982, Mar. 15 Photo. *Perf. 13*

482 A14 25c on #88
483 A14 30c on #89
484 A14 45c on 6c #87
485 A14 75c on 40c #90 (R)

For overprints see Nos. 766-767.

Nos. 60, 284, 324, and 331-333 Surcharged in Black or Blue

● 85 ●

1982 *Perfs. as Before*

Watermarks & Printing Methods as Before

486 A66 20c on 35c #284
487 A11 80c on 6c #60 (Bl)
488 A11 85c on 6c #60 (Bl)
489 A28 85c on #331
490 A28 130c on #331
491 A28 160c on #333 (Bl)
a. Black surcharge
492 A28 170c on #333
493 A28 210c on #332 (Bl)
494 A75 210c on $3 #324 (Bl)
495 A28 235c on #332
a. Blue surcharge
496 A28 330c on #333

Nos. 491-491a, 492, & 496 are airmail. Obliterators differ.

Issue dates: #486, Mar. 15. Others, Apr. 27.

For surcharges see Nos. 647, 1367.

Nos. 135, 137, 144 & 145 Overprinted or Surcharged in Blue or Black "ESPANA / 1982" or "ESPANA / 1982" and "ITALY" (#499)

Perf. 13½

1982, May 15 Litho. Wmk. 364

497 A28 $1 on #145 (Blk)
498 A28 110c on 3c #135
499 A28 $2.35 on 180c on 60c #144
500 A28 250c on 6c #137

Refer to second paragraph in footnote below No. 147 for No. 499.

#499 not issued without $2.35 surcharge.

See No. 597 for stamp with one-line Espana 1982 overprint. For surcharges see #774-777.

Map Revenue Type A78 Surcharged in Black, Blue, or Red

1982-83 Photo. Wmk. 364 *Perf. 13*

501 A78 15c on 2c (Bl)
502 A78 20c on 2c (Bl)
503 A78 20c on 10c #336 (Bl)
504 A78 25c on 2c
a. Blue surcharge
b. Red surcharge
505 A78 30c on 2c (Bl)
506 A78 40c on 2c
a. Blue surcharge
507 A78 45c on 2c (Bl)
508 A78 50c on 2c (Bl)
509 A78 60c on 2c (Bl)
510 A78 75c on 2c (Bl)
511 A78 80c on 2c (Bl)
512 A78 85c on 2c (Bl)
513 A78 $1.00 on 3c
514 A78 $1.10 on 3c
515 A78 $1.20 on 3c
516 A78 $1.25 on 3c
517 A78 $1.30 on 3c
518 A78 $1.50 on 3c
519 A78 $1.60 on 3c
520 A78 $1.70 on 3c
521 A78 $1.75 on 3c
522 A78 $1.80 on 3c
523 A78 $2.00 on 3c
524 A78 $2.10 on 3c
525 A78 $2.20 on 3c
526 A78 $2.35 on 3c
527 A78 $2.40 on 3c
528 A78 $2.50 on 3c
529 A78 $3.00 on 3c
530 A78 $3.30 on 3c
531 A78 $3.75 on 3c
532 A78 $4.00 on 3c
533 A78 $4.40 on 3c
534 A78 $5.00 on 3c
535 A78 $5.50 on 3c
536 A78 $6.25 on 3c
537 A78 $15 on 2c (R)
538 A78 $20 on 2c (R)

Revenue stamps surcharged for postal use. Issue dates: Nos. 501-502 & 504-538, May 17, 1982. No. 503, Mar. 14, 1983.

For surcharge see No. 935.

British Guiana Nos. 254, 255, 279, Guyana 10A, 13, 13a, 32J, 32K, 32N Surcharged "H.R.H. / Prince William / 21st June 1982" in Blue

British Guiana stamps also have "GUYANA."

1982, July 12 *Perfs. as Before*

Watermarks & Printing Methods as Before

539 A60 50c on 2c #254
540 A60 50c on 2c #32J
541 A60 $1.10 on 3c #279
541A A60 $1.10 on 3c #255
542 A60 $1.10 on 3c #32K
543 A60 $1.25 on 6c #10A
543A A60 $1.25 on 6c #32N
544 A60 $2.20 on 24c #13a
544A A60 $2.20 on 24c #13

For surcharges see Nos. 797-800.

Nos. 133-134 Surcharged "C.A. & CARIB / Games / 1982"

Perf. 13x13½

1982, Aug. 16 Litho. Wmk. 364

545 A28 50c on 2c #134
546 A28 60c on 1c #133

Central American and Caribbean Games, Havana. For overprint see No. 816.

Nos. 331, C2 Surcharged

1982, Sept. 15

547 A28 130c on #331
548 A28 170c on #C2
549 A28 440c on #331 ovptd. "1982"
a. Without "1982"

No. 137 Surcharged "Commonwealth / GAMES / AUSTRALIA / 1982" in Blue

1982, Sept. 27

550 A28 $1.25 on 6c #137

For surcharge see No. 789.

No. 207 Ovptd. "INT. / FOOD DAY / 1982" in Dark Blue

No. 320 Ovptd. "INT. YEAR / OF THE / ELDERLY" in Dark Blue

No. 323 Ovptd. "Dr. R. KOCH / CENTENARY / TBC BACILLUS / DISCOVERY" in Dark Blue

No. 287 Ovptd. "F.D. ROOSEVELT / 1882-1982 " in Green

No. 221 Ovptd. "1982" in Blue

No. 332 Surcharged "GAC Inaug. Flight / Georgetown- / Boa Vista, Brasil" in Blue and "1982" in Blue Green

1982, Oct. 15 *Perfs. as Before*

Watermarks & Printing Methods as Before

551 A48 50c on #207
552 A74 50c on #320
553 A75 60c on #323
554 A66 $1 on #287
555 A52 $1 on #221
556 A28 200c on #332

For surcharges see Nos. 895, 902, 936, 1363.

No. 437 Surcharged "CARICOM / Heads of Gov't / Conference / July 1982"

Perf. 14½x14

1982, Jan. 18 Litho. Wmk. 364

557 Sheet of 6
a.-f. A81 50c on 15c, any single

Nos. 464 Ovptd. "CHRISTMAS / 1982" in Red

1982, Dec. 1 *Perf. 13x13½*

558 Sheet of 25, 8 #a.-b., 4 #c.-d., 1 #e.
a.-e. A28 15c on #464a-464e, any single

Nos. 134, 137 Surcharged in Black, Blue, Red, or Green

15

Perf. 13x13½

1982-83 Litho. Wmk. 364

563 A28 15c on 2c #134
a. Red surcharge
b. Blue surcharge
564 A28 20c on 6c #137 (G)
a. Black surcharge

Issue dates: No. 563, Dec. 15. No. 564, Jan. 5, 1983.

Compare No. 564a with Nos. 631-632. For surcharges, see Nos. 846, 846a, 846b.

No. 72 Surcharged

1982, Dec. 15 Photo. *Perf. 14x14½*

565 A7 50c on 6c #72
566 A7 $1.00 on 6c #72

Nos. 62, 88-89, 144, 161, 202, 217, 224-225, 232, 240, 251, 254, 257, 264, 276-278, 299-301, 303-305, 315, 319, 321, 329m, 414-416, and 418-420 Ovptd. "1983" Vertically or Horizontally

1983 *Perfs. as Before*

Watermarks & Printing Methods as Before

567 A57 15c on #240
568 A60 15c on #254
569 A62 15c on #264
570 A79 15c on 10c #414
571 A80 15c on 10c #418
572 A14 25c on #88
573 A33 25c on #161
574 A47 25c on #202
575 A11 30c on #62
576 A14 30c on #89
577 A65 30c on #276
578 A69 30c on #299
579 A70 30c on #303
580 A74 30c on #319
581 A77 30c on #329m
582 A53 50c on #224
583 A55 50c on #232
584 A59 50c on #251
585 A65 50c on #277
586 A69 50c on #300
587 A70 50c on #304
588 A79 50c on #415
589 A80 50c on #419
590 A65 60c on #278
591 A72 60c on #315
592 A51 $1 on #217
593 A53 $1 on #225
594 A60 $1 on #257
595 A79 $1 on 30c #416
596 A80 $1 on 60c #420
597 A28 180c on 60c #144
598 A69 $3 on #301
599 A70 $3 on #305
601 A74 $3 on #321
602 A28 360c on $2 #146

Issue dates: Nos. 565-571, 583, and 585-586, Feb. 1. No. 596, Mar. 7. No. 573, Mar. 11. Nos. 572, 576, Mar. 17. Nos. 582, 584, 587, 589, 592-595, 588, 598-599, 601, Apr. 1. No. 574, May 23. Nos. 575, 577-580, 590-591, July 1. No. 602, Nov. 3. No. 581, Nov. 15. No. 597, Dec. 14.

Refer to the second paragraph in footnote under No. 147 for Nos. 597 & 602. No. 597 contains unissued overprint, "ESPANA 1982."

For overprints and surcharges see Nos. 724, 901, 940, 943A.

No. O2 Ovptd. "POSTAGE" in Red

Perf. 14½x14

1983, Feb. 1 Photo. Wmk. 364

603 A7 15c on #O2

For surcharge see Nos. 746-746a.

Nos. 291-293, 356 Surcharged in Blue or Black

Wmk. 364

1983, Feb. 8 Litho. *Perf. 14*

604 A67 90c on 30c #291 (Blk)
605 A67 90c on 50c #292
606 A67 90c on 60c #293
607 A55 90c on #356

For overprints and surcharges see Nos. 763-764, 768-769, 770-771.

Flag A82

Cooperative Youth Palace — A83

1983, Feb. 19 *Perf. 14½x14*

608 A82	Pair	40	40
a.	25c Flag flying right	20	20
b.	25c Flag flying left	20	20

Perf. 13½

609 A83	$1.30 shown	1.00	1.00

Size: 43x25mm

Perf. 14½

610 A83	$6 Map	4.50	4.50

60th birthday of Pres. Linden Forbes Burnham. No. 608a inscribed for birthday; No. 608b for Burnham's 30th anniv. of election to parliament.

See Nos. 660 & 913. For overprints and surcharges see Nos. 826-835, 924-926, 1404-1406.

Nos. 160, 205, 222, 263, 298, 302, 330, 333, 408-409, 480, C4, O1 and O3 Ovptd. in Blue or Red

FIFTY CENTS

1983 Litho. *Perfs. as Before*

Watermarks & Printing Methods as Before

611 A33 50c on 8c #160 (R)
612 A48 50c on 8c #205
613 A62 50c on 8c #263
614 A69 50c on 10c #298 (R)
615 A70 50c on 10c #302
616 A69 50c on #409

617 A69 50c on #480
618 A28 50c on #O1
619 A53 $1 on #222
620 A53 $1 on #330
621 A28 $1 on #146
622 A28 $1 on #408
623 A28 $1 on #C4
624 A28 $1 on #O3

No. 621 has Royal Wedding ovpt. similar to No. 331. No. 624 also ovptd. "1982." See Nos. 648-649 for similar surcharges. For overprint see Nos. 815, 941. Issue dates: Nos. 614, 617, 619-624, Mar. 7. No. 611, Mar. 11. Others, Apr. 1.

Nos. 10A, 13a Surcharged "Commonwealth / Day / 14 March 1983" and Emblem in Blue or Black

Wmk. 314 Upright

1983, Mar. 14 Engr. ***Perf. 12½x13***

625 A60 25c on 6c #10A
626 A60 $1.20 on 6c #10A (Bl)

Wmk. 314 Sideways

627 A60 $1.30 on 24c #13a
628 A60 $2.40 on 24c #13a (Bl)

For overprints see Nos. 1823-1825.

Intl. Maritime Organization, 25th Anniv. — A84

Wmk. 3

1983, Mar. 17 Typo. ***Perf. 14***

Red Overprint on British Guiana Revenue Stamp

629 A84 $4.80 grn & blue

Nos. 60, 72, 87 & 137 Surcharged in Black or Blue

1983 ***Perfs. as Before***

Watermarks & Printing Methods as Before

630 A11 15c on 6c #60
a. Blue surcharge
631 A28 20c on 6c #137, two obliterators
632 A28 20c on 6c #137
633 A7 50c on 6c #72
634 A14 50c on 6c #87

Issue dates: Nos. 630, 632-633, May 23. Nos. 630a, 631, 634, May 2.
Surcharge on No. 632 has "c" after value. No. 564a does not.
For surcharge see No. 916.

No. 72 Surcharged in Black or Red

Perf. 14x14½

1983 Photo. Wmk. 364

635 A7 $1 on 6c #72
a. Red overprint, 4mm high

Issue dates: #635, May 2. #635a, May 23.
For surcharge see No. 916A.

Nos. 142, 147, 211, 226-227, 239 & 249 Surcharged in Blue

1983 ***Perfs. as Before***

Watermarks & Printing Methods as Before

636 A54 110c on 10c #226
637 A49 120c on 35c #211
638 A54 120c on 35c #227
639 A57 120c on 8c #239
640 A59 120c on 10c #249
641 A28 250c on 40c #142
642 A28 400c on $5 #147

Issue dates: Nos. 636, 641-642, May 2. Others, July 1. For surcharge see No. 865.

Buying Sets
It is often less expensive to purchase complete sets than individual stamps that make up the set. Set values are provided for many such sets.

Nos. 332, 495, C3 Surcharged in Red or Blue
"ITU / 1983" or (#643)
"WHO / 1983" or (#644)
"17 MAY '83 / ITU/WHO /" (#645)
"ITU/WHO / 17 MAY / 1983" (#646-647)

1983, May 17 ***Perfs. as Before***

Watermarks & Printing Methods as Before

643 A28 25c on #C3
644 A28 25c on #C3
645 A28 25c on #C3
646 A28 $4.50 on #332 (Bl)
647 A28 $4.50 on #495 (Bl)

Nos. 643-645 issued in sheets of 25 with 8 each Nos. 643-644 and 9 No. 645.

Nos. 272, 274 Surcharged in Dark Blue

Perf. 13½x14

1983, May 18 Litho. Wmk. 364

648 A64 $1 on 15c #272
649 A64 $1 on 40c #274

Surcharge on No. 648 also contains overprint "1983."

Nos. 402, 404, O8 Surcharged or Overprinted "CANADA 1983"

1983, June 15 ***Perf. 13½x13***

650 A17 $1.30 on #O8
651 A17 180c on #402
652 A17 $3.90 on #404

For surcharge see No. 1860.

Nos. 243-244 Surcharged

1983, June 22 Unwmk. ***Perf. 14***

653 A57a 60c on 15c #243
654 A57b $1.50 on 15c #244

Nos. 297, 313 Surcharged

Perfs. as Before

1983, July 1 Wmk. 364

655 A68 120c on #297
656 A72 120c on 10c #313 (R)

No. 655 has unissued surcharge, "INTERNATIONAL / SCIENCE YEAR / 375."

British Guiana No. J1 and Guyana No. J5 Surcharged "120 / GUYANA" in Dark Blue

1983, July 1 Wmk. 4 ***Perf. 13½x14***

657 D1 120c on 1c #J1

Wmk. 364

658 D1 120c on 1c #J5

No. 371 Surcharged in Red "CARICOM DAY 1983"

1983, July 1 Wmk. 364 ***Perf. 14***

659 A72 60c on $3 #371

Type A82 Without Inscription

1983, July 1 Litho. ***Perf. 14½x14***

660 A82	Pair	30	30
a.	25c, Flag flying right	15	15
b.	25c, Flag flying left	15	15

River Steamers A85

1983, July 11 Litho. ***Perf. 14***

661 A85	30c Kurupukari	18	18
662 A85	60c Makouria	36	36
663 A85	120c Powis	72	72
664 A85	130c Pomeroon	78	78
665 A85	150c Lukanani	90	90
	Nos. 661-665 (5)	2.94	2.94

No. 146 Surcharged in Dark Blue

1983, July 22 ***Perf. 13½***

666 A28 $2.30 on $1.10 on $2
667 A28 $3.20 on $1.10 on $2

Nos. 666-667 have unissued surcharge of "$1.10 / Royal Wedding / 1981" similar to No. 331.

Nos. 282-283 & 283A Overprinted as Shown or with Various Initials in Red or Blue

Mont Golfier

1783-1983

Overprints: No. 668a, BW. b, LM. c, GY 1963 / 1983. d, JW. e, CU. f. Mont Golfier / 1783-1983.
No. 669a, BGI. b, GEO. c, MIA. d, BVB. e, PBM. f, Mont Golfier / 1783-1983. g, POS. h, JFK.
No. 670a, AHL. b, BCG. c, BMJ. d, EKE. e, GEO. f, GFO. g, IBM. h, Mont Golfier / 1783-1983. i, KAI. j, KAR. k, KPG. l, KRG. m, KTO. n, LTM. o, MHA. p, MWI. q, MYM. r, NAI. s, ORJ. t, USI. u, VEG.

1983, Sept. 5 ***Perf. 14x13½***

Sheets of 25

668 A66 20c 4 each #a.-e., 5 #f
669 A66 25c 2 each #a., c.-e., g.-h., 8 #b., 5 #f.
670 A66 30c #a.-e., g.-u., 5 #f., (Bl)

Manned flight, bicentennial and Guyana Airways, 20th anniv. For ovpts. see #871, 969.

No. 234 Surcharged in Dark Blue

1983, Sept. 14 ***Perf. 13½***

703 A28 240c on #234
a. "4" with serif

Nos. 703, 703a appear in same sheet.

Nos. 68, 70 Surcharged "FAO 1983" in Red

Perf. 14x14½

1983, Sept. 15 Photo. Wmk. 364

704 A7 30c on 1c #68
705 A7 $2.60 on 3c #70

For overprints see Nos. 1497-1498.

Great Britain, Postal Use In British Guiana, 150th Anniv. — A86

Stamps: a, #20. b, #26. c, #27. d, #28.

1983, Oct. 1 Litho. ***Perf. 14***

Inscribed in Black

706 A86	25c #20	15	15
707 A86	30c #26	18	18
708 A86	60c #27	36	36
709 A86	120c #28	72	72

Inscribed in Blue

710	Block of 4	60	60
a.-d.	A86 25c, any single	15	15
711	Block of 4	72	72
a.-d.	A86 30c, any single	18	18
712	Block of 4	1.12	1.12
a.-d.	A86 45c, any single	28	28
713	Block of 4	3.60	3.60
a.	A86 120c #20	72	72
b.	A86 130c #26, Demerara	78	78
c.	A86 150c #27, Berbice	90	90
d.	A86 200c #28, Essequibo	1.20	1.20
	Nos. 706-713 (8)	7.45	7.45

Nos. 706-709 printed in sheets with bottom two rows inverted. Nos. 710-712 printed in sheets of 60. No. 713 printed in sheets with blue marginal text.
For overprints and surcharges, see Nos. 796, 903, 912, 1448, 1982.

Nos. 235 & 238 Surcharged
No. 297 Surcharged "INT. / COMMUNICATIONS / YEAR"
No. 206 Surcharged "Int. Food Day / 1983"
No. 309 Surcharged "1918-1983 / I.L.O."

1983, Oct. 15 ***Perfs. as Before***

Watermarks & Printing Methods as Before

714 A68 50c on 375c on $3 #297
715 A56 75c on 8c #235
716 A48 $1.20 on 35c #206
717 A56 $1.20 on 40c #238
718 A71 240c on $3 #309

No. 714 was not issued without 375c surcharge. For overprint see No. 821.

Nos. 245, 247-248 Surcharged

Unwmk.

1983, Nov. 1 Litho. ***Perf. 14***

719 A58 25c on 8c #245
720 A58 $1.50 on 35c #247
721 A58 $1.50 on 40c #248

Nos. 268 & 270 Surcharged

1983, Nov. 15 Wmk. 364

722 A63 60c on 15c #268
723 A63 $1.20 on 40c #270

No. 601 Ovptd. "Human Rights / Day"

1983, Dec. 1 ***Perf. 14½x14***

724 A74 $3 on #601

For surcharge, see No. 997a.

Nos. 317 and 726 Surcharged "LOS ANGELES / 1984"

1983, Dec. 6 Wmk. 373

725 Sheet of 12
a.-l. A73 55c on 125c on 35c #726a-726l, any single
726 Sheet of 12
a.-l. A73 125c on 35c #317a-317l, any single

For surcharge, see No. 1897.

No. 133 Surcharged "COMMONWEALTH / HEADS OF GOV'T / MEETING--INDIA / 1983"

Perf. 13x13½

1983, Dec. 14 Litho. Wmk. 364

727 A28 150c on 1c #133

Nos. 413a, 413e Surcharged "CHRISTMAS / 1983"

1983, Dec. 14 Photo. ***Perf. 14x14½***

Watermarks as before

728 A7 20c on #413a
a. 20c on #413e

Nos. 146, O15 Ovptd. "POSTAGE" in Blue

1984, Jan. 8 ***Perfs. as before***

729 A28 $2 on #146
730 A66 550c on $10 #O15

Refer to second paragraph in footnote following No. 147 for No. 729.

Flower Type of 1971-76 Surcharged in Blue

Perf. 15x14

1984, Jan. Photo. Unwmk.

Size: 20x23mm

Coil Stamps

731 A28 17c on 2c, like #134
732 A28 17c on 8c, Mazaruni Pride
a. Pair, #731-732

Nos. 731-732 were intended for use on 8c envelopes to increase postage rate to 25c and were not issued without surcharge.

Nos. 284, 286A Surcharged in Black or Overprinted in Dark Blue
(1) "ALL / OUR HERITAGE"
(2) "1984" 7mm long
(3) "REPUBLIC / DAY"
(4) "BERBICE"
(5) "DEMERARA"
(6) "ESSEQUIBO"
(7) "1984" 18mm long

Perf. 14x13½

1984, Feb. 24 Litho. Wmk. 364

733 A66 25c on 35c (1)
734 A66 25c on 35c (2)
735 A66 25c on 35c (3)
736 A66 25c on 35c #284
737 A66 25c on 35c (4)
738 A66 25c on 35c (5)
739 A66 25c on 35c (6)
740 A66 25c on 35c (7)
741 A66 60c on #286A (1) (DBl)
742 A66 60c on #286A (3) (DBl)
743 A66 60c on #286A (2) (DBl)

Nos. 733-740 were issued in sheets of 25, 6 #733, 4 each #734-736, 2 each #737-739, 1 #740. Nos. 741-743 were issued in sheets of 25, 8 each #741-742, 9 #743.

Nos. 49-50, 52, 73-74, 77-80, 82, 139, 141A-143, 350, 603 Surcharged or Overprinted in Black and/or Blue "Protecting Our Heritage"

1984, Mar. 5 *Perfs. as Before*
Watermarks & Printing Methods as Before

744 A8 20c on 15c #74
a. Blue surcharge (value and words)
745 A8 20c on 15c #350
746 A8 20c on 15c #603 (Bl)
a. "Protecting our Heritage" in black
747 A28 25c on #141A
a. 25c on #141b
748 A28 30c on 15c #139
749 A8 40c on #77
750 A28 50c on #143
751 A28 50c on #143 (Revenue Ovpt.)
752 A7 60c on #50
a. 60c on #79
753 A28 90c on 40c #142
754 A28 90c on 40c #142 (Revenue Ovpt.)
755 A28 180c on #460
756 A7 $2 on #52
757 A8 225c on 10c on #73
758 A7 260c on $1 #80
759 A28 320c on 40c #142
760 A28 350c on 40c #142
761 A7 390c on 50c #78
a. 390c on #49
762 A7 450c on $5 #82

Nos. 748, 753-754, 759-760 use row of "X", 6mm high, as obliterator. Nos. 744-746, 757 have new value printed vertically over old value. Nos. 758, 761-762 have new value printed horizontally over old value. Refer to second paragraph in footnote under No. 147 for Nos. 751, 754-755.

Nos. 89, 484-485, 606 Overprinted or Surcharged in Dark Blue "1984"
No. 87 Surcharged
No. 606 Surcharged "INT. / CHESS / FED. / 1924-1984" in Dark Blue (#764a, 769a, 771a)

1984 *Perfs. as Before*
Watermarks & Printing Methods as Before

763 A67 25c on #606
764 A67 25c on #606
a. Pair, #763-764
765 A14 30c on #89
766 A14 45c on 6c #484
767 A14 75c on 40c #485
768 A67 75c on #606
769 A67 75c on #606
a. Pair, #768-769
770 A67 90c on #606
771 A67 90c on #606
a. Pair, #770-771
772 A14 130c on 6c #87
773 A76 $3 on #328

Issue dates: Nos. 765-767, 772, Mar. 17. No. 773, June 15. Nos. 763-764, 768-769, 770-771, July 20.
No. 767 exists with surcharge either above old value or in center of stamp.

Nos. 497-500 Surcharged

1984, Apr. 2 **Litho.** *Perf. 13½*

774 A28 75c on #497
775 A28 75c on #498
776 A28 225c on #500
777 A28 230c on #499

Nos. 464e, 465a, 465b, 465e, 466a, 466b, 466e Surcharged Like No. 748

1984, May 2

778 A28 20c on #464e
779 A28 75c on #465e
780 A28 90c on #465a
781 A28 90c on #465b
782 A28 120c on #466a
783 A28 120c on #466e
784 A28 120c on #466b

No. C3 Surcharged "ITU DAY / 1984" (#785)
No. C3 Surcharged "WHO DAY / 1984" (#786)
Nos. C3, 386 Surcharged "ITU/WHO / DAY / 1984" (#787-788)

1984, May 17

785 A28 25c on #C3
786 A28 25c on #C3
787 A28 25c on #C3
788 A28 $4.50 on #386

The surcharge is vertical on Nos. 785-787, horizontal on No. 788.

No. 550 Surcharged

1984, June 11

789 A28 120c on #550

Nos. 325-327, 431 Surcharged in Blue or Black

Wmk. 373

1984, June 15 **Litho.** *Perf. 14*

790 A76 55c on 30c #326 (Blk)
791 A76 75c on #431
792 A76 160c on 50c #327
793 A76 260c on 10c #325

No. 214 Surcharged

1984, June 18 **Litho.** **Wmk. 364**

794 A50 55c on 110c on 10c
795 A50 90c on 110c on 10c

No. 214 surcharged 110c only was never issued.

No. 713 Ovptd. "UPU / Congress 1984 / Hamburg"

1984, June 19

796 Block of 4
a. A86 120c on #713a
b. A86 130c on #713b
c. A86 150c on #713c
d. A86 200c on #713d

Nos. 539, 541, 543-544 Surcharged in Black, Blue or Dark Green

1984, June 21 *Perfs. as Before*
Watermarks & Printing Methods as Before

797 A60 45c on #539
798 A60 60c on #541 (DkG)
a. 60c on British Guiana #255 (DkG)
799 A60 120c on #543
800 A60 200c on #544 (Bl)

Nos. 135, C2-C3 Surcharged in Blue or Black
No. C4 Overprinted "1984"

Perf. 13x13½

1984, June 30 **Litho.** **Wmk. 364**

801 A28 75c on #C2 (Blk)
802 A28 120c on #C2 (Blk)
803 A28 150c on #135
804 A28 200c on #C3
804A A28 330c on #C4

Surcharge on Nos. 801-802, 804 is like No. 748. Surcharge on No. 803 is like No. 457.

No. 135 Surcharged "CARICOM / HEADS OF GOV'T / CONFERENCE / JULY 1984"
No. 450A Surcharged "CARICOM DAY 1984"

1984, June 30 *Perfs. as Before*
Watermarks & Printing Methods as Before

805 A28 60c on 3c #135
806 A72 60c on #450A

Nos. 140-141, 141A, 329, 334, 427, 439-440, 546, 611, 718, O13 Ovptd. "1984" in Black or Blue

1984 *Perfs. as Before*
Watermarks & Printing Methods as Before

807 A28 20c on #140
a. On #140a
808 A28 20c on #140
a. On #140a
809 A28 20c on #439, 1984 omitted
810 A28 25c on #141
a. 1984 omitted
811 A28 25c on #141 (Revenue Only)
812 A28 25c on #141A
813 A28 25c on #439, 1984 omitted
814 A28 25c on #440, 1984 omitted
815 A33 50c on #611 (Bl)
816 A28 60c on #546 (Bl)
817 A28 $2 on #O13 (Bl)
818 A28 $3.60 on #334
c. As #818, fleur-de-lis omitted
d. On #334a (Bl)
e. As "d," fleur-de-lis omitted
819 Sheet of 12
a.-l. A77 30c on #329a-329l, any single
820 A71 240c on #429
821 A71 240c on #718

Overprint on Nos. 808-818 contains fleur-de-lis. Refer to second paragraph in footnote below No. 147 for Nos. 811-812, 817.
Issue dates: No. 819, Sept. 15. Nos. 820-821, Oct. 15.

Teachers' Assoc. Centenary — A87

1984, July 16 **Wmk. 364** *Perf. 14*

822 A87 25c Children dancing	15	15
823 A87 25c Torch, graduate	15	15
824 A87 25c Torch concentric circles	15	15
825 A87 25c Teachers, school	15	15
a. Block of 4	60	60

No. 609 Surcharged in Blue:
"CYCLING" (#826, 831)
"TRACK / AND / FIELD" (#827, 832)
"OLYMPIC / GAMES / 1984" (#828, 833)
"BOXING" (#829, 834)
"OLYMPIC / GAMES / 1984 / LOS ANGELES" (#830, 835)

Perf. 14½x14

1984, July 28 **Litho.** **Wmk. 364**

826 A83 25c on $1.30
827 A83 25c on $1.30
828 A83 25c on $1.30
829 A83 25c on $1.30
830 A83 25c on $1.30
831 A83 $1.20 on $1.30
832 A83 $1.20 on $1.30
833 A83 $1.20 on $1.30
834 A83 $1.20 on $1.30
835 A83 $1.20 on $1.30

Nos. 465-466 Surcharged "GIRL / GUIDES / 1924-1984" in Blue

1984, Aug. 15 *Perf. 13x13½*
Sheets of 25

836 8 #a.-b., 4 #c.-d., 1 #e.
a.-e. A28 25c on #465a-465e, any single
837 8 #a.-b., 4 #c.-d., 1 #e.
a.-e. A28 25c on #466a-466e, any single

Nos. 138-139, 234, 335, 351, 378, 380, 388, 401, 423, 438, 452, 459, 461, 563, 642, O3, O11-O12, O14 Surcharged

1984 *Perfs. as Before*
Watermarks & Printing Methods as Before

846 A28 20c on #563
a. 20c on #563a (Blk over R)
b. 20c on #563b (Blk over Bl)
847 A28 25c on #138
a. 25c on #138a
848 A28 25c on #139
849 A28 25c on #351
a. 25c on #351a
850 A28 25c on #351a
851 A28 25c on #438
a. 25c on #438a
852 A28 25c on #234
853 A28 25c on #452
854 A28 25c on #O3
855 A28 60c on #423, two obliterators
a. Single obliterator
856 A28 120c on #459
857 A28 120c on #401
858 A28 120c on #O12
859 A28 120c on #380
860 A28 130c on #378
861 A28 130c on #O11
862 A28 200c on #461
863 A28 320c on #378
864 A28 350c on #388
865 A28 390c on #642
866 A28 450c on #O14
867 A28 600c on #335
a. 600c on #335a
868 A28 600c on #335
a. 600c on #335a

Nos. 860-861 are airmail. Obliterator on Nos. 846, 856-859, 862-866 is row of "X", on Nos. 847, 850, 852 is single line, on Nos. 848-849, 851, 853-854 is fleur-de-lis, on No. 855 is a block of 6 lines, on No. 867 is 3 lines, on No. 868 is 3 lines and fleur-de-lis.

Nos. 556, 670, C4 Overprinted in Blue or Surcharged in Blue and Black

Overprints: #a-f, ICAO on #670a-670f. g, IMB/ICAO on #g. h, KCV/ICAO on #h. i, KAI/ICAO on #i. j-k, ICAO on #670j-670k. l, 1984 on #h. m, KPM/ICAO on #h. n-p, ICAO on #670l-670n. q, PMT/ICAO on #h. r-x, ICAO on #670o-670u.

Perf. 14x13½

1984, Sept. 6 **Litho.** **Wmk. 364**

871 A66 30c Sheet of 25, #a.-k., m.-x., 2 #l
895 A28 200c ICAO on #556
896 A28 200c ICAO on #C4 (Bl & Blk)

No. 896 is airmail with unissued "GAC" overprint. For surcharge see No. 1470.

Nos. J3-J4, J7-J8 Surcharged "120 / GUYANA" in Blue

Perf. 13½x14

1984, Oct. 1 **Typo.** **Wmk. 314**

897 D1 120c on 4c #J3
898 D1 120c on 12c #J4

Wmk. 364

899 D1 120c on 4c #J7
900 D1 120c on 12c #J8

Nos. 551, 571 Surcharged in Black or Blue

Perfs. as Before

1984, Oct. 15 **Wmk. 364**

901 A80 $1.50 on #571 (Bl)
902 A48 150c on 50c #551

Obliterator is "X" on No. 901. Surcharge on No. 902 places "1" before existing 50c value, obliterates "1982" and adds "1984."

Nos. 712, 479-481 Surcharged

1984, Oct. 22 *Perf. 14*

903 Block of 4
a.-d. A86 25c on 45c on #712a-712d, any single
904 A69 120c on #479
905 A69 120c on #480
906 A69 320c on #481

Nos. 135-136 Surcharged "MAHA SABHA / 1934-1984" in Blue

1984, Nov. 1 *Perf. 13x13½*

910 A28 25c on 5c #136
911 A28 $1.50 on 3c #135

No. 713 Ovptd. "Philatelic Exhibition / New York 1984" in Red

1984, Nov. 15 *Perf. 14*

912 Block of 4
a. A86 120c on No. 713a
b. A86 130c on No. 713b
c. A86 150c on No. 713c
d. A86 200c on No. 713d

Type A83 Inscribed with Olympic Rings and "OLYMPIC GAMES 1984 / LOS ANGELES"

1984, Nov. 16 *Perf. 13½*

913 A83 $1.20 multicolored	60	60

For similar stamp overprinted, see No. 923.
For surcharges see Nos. 1953-1957.

Nos. 410, 413e, 633, 635a Surcharged

1984, Nov. 24 **Photo.** *Perf. 14x14½*
Watermarks as Before

914 A7 20c on #410
915 A7 20c on #413e
916 A7 25c on #633
916A A7 60c on #635a

No. 914 has an "X" obliterating a "1" and no obliterating lines. No. 1400 has obliterating lines and small "20" in UR.

Elanoides Forficatus A88

Designs: a, Pair in tree. b, Landing on branch. c, In flight, wings up. d, In flight, wings down. e, In flight, wings outstretched.

1984, Dec. 3 *Perf. 14½*

917 A88 60c Strip of 5, #a.-e.	1.50	1.50

Inscribed "Christmas 1982."
For surcharges see Nos. 1502, 1840.

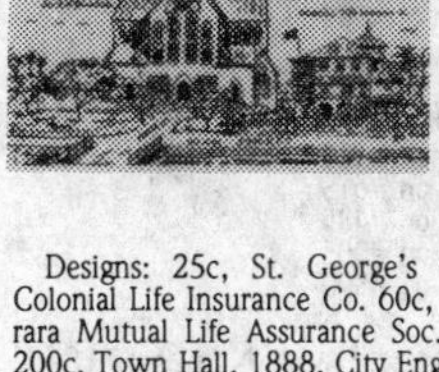

High Street Architecture A89

Designs: 25c, St. George's Cathedral, 1892, Colonial Life Insurance Co. 60c, No. 920a, Demerara Mutual Life Assurance Soc., Ltd. No. 920b, 200c, Town Hall, 1888, City Engineers Office. No. 920c, 300c, Victoria Law Courts, 1887.

1985, Feb. 8 *Perf. 14*

918 A89 25c multi	15	15
919 A89 60c multi	30	30
920 Triptych	1.80	1.80
a.-c. A89 120c, any single	60	60

921 A89 200c multi 1.00 1.00
922 A89 300c multi 1.50 1.50
Nos. 918-922 (5) 4.75 4.75

For surcharge see No. 1850.

Type A83 Ovptd. "INTERNATIONAL / YOUTH YEAR 1985"

Perf. 14½

1985, Feb. 15 Litho. Wmk. 364

923 A83 $1.20 multi

Bars obliterate Olympic Games inscription with second line spelled "LOS ANGELLES." No. 913 spells "Los Angeles" correctly.

Nos. 608, 610 Ovptd. in Red "Republic / Day / 1970-1985" or "1970 / 1985 / Republic / Day"

1985, Feb. 22 ***Perfs. as Before***

924 A82 25c on #608
925 A83 120c on $6 #610
926 A83 130c on $6 #610

Ocelot Cub Xica — A90

Macaw Nena — A90a

Perf. 12½x13

1985, Mar. 11 Wmk. 364

927 A90 25c multi 15 15
928 A90 60c multi 30 30
929 Triptych 1.80 1.80
a.-c. A90 120c, like #927-928, 930 60 60
930 A90 130c multi 65 65

Perf. 14½

931 A90a 320c shown 1.60 1.60
932 A90a 330c Cub on hind legs 1.65 1.65
Nos. 927-932 (6) 6.15 6.15

Stamps in No. 929d inscribed "1986."
No. 929, perf. 14, were from the liquidation of stock held by the printer, value 75c.
For overprints see #1903-1905, 1983, 2032.

Map Revenue Type A78 and Nos. 481, 501, 554, O6 Surcharged in Black or Blue

1985 ***Perfs as Before***

Watermarks & Printing Methods as Before

933 A69 30c on 50c on #O6 (Bl)
934 A78 55c on 2c multi
a. "ESSEQUIBO IS OURS" omitted
935 A78 55c on #501
936 A66 90c on #554 (Bl)
937 A66 225c on #481
938 A66 230c on #481 (Bl)
939 A66 260c on #481 (Bl)

Issue dates: Nos. 933-936, 938-939, Mar. 11. No. 937, Apr. 11. Obliterator on Nos. 934-935 is fleur-de-lis.

Nos. 305, 435, 587, 599, & 615 Ovptd. "INTERNATIONAL / YOUTH YEAR / 1985" in Blue

Perf. 13½

1985, Apr. 15 Litho. Wmk. 364

940 A70 50c on #587
941 A70 50c on #615
942 A70 120c on #435
943 A70 $3 on #305
943A A70 $3 on #599

No. 280 Surcharged with Names of 1860 Post Offices or Postal Agencies in Blue

Overprints: a, Airy Hall. b, Belfield / Arab. Coast. c, Belfield / E.C. Dem. d, Belladrum. e, Beterver- / wagting. f, Blairmont / Ferry. g, Boeraserie. h, Brahn. i, Bushlot. j, De / Kinderen. k, Fort / Wellington. l, Georgetown. m, Hague. n, Leguan. o, Mahaica. p, Mahaicony. q, New / Amsterdam. r, Plaisance. s, No. 6 Police / Station. t, Queenstown. u, Vertenoegen. v, Vigilance. w, Vreed-en- / Hoop. x, Wakenaam. y, Windsor / Castle.

Perf. 14x13½

1985, May 2 Litho. Wmk. 364

Sheet of 25

944 A66 25c on 10c, #a.-y.

Colonial Post Office, 125th anniv.

Nos. 670 Ovptd. "1985" or with Letters in Red

Overprints: a-f, 1985 on #670a-670f. g, I on #670g. h, T on #670h. i, U on #670i. j-k, 1985 on #670j-670k. l, W on #670h. m, H on #670h. n, O on #670h. o-p, 1985 on #670 l-670m. q, D on #670n. r, A on #670h. s, Y on #670o. t-y, 1985 on #670p-#670u.

1985, May 17

Sheet of 25

969 A66 30c #a.-y.

Nos. 413a & 413e Surcharged

1985, May 21 Photo. ***Perf. 14x14½***

Watermarks as Before

994 A7 20c on #413a
a. 20c on #413e

#994a has "20" at left and 11 obliterating lines. #1401 has "20" at right and 12 lines.

No. 135 Surcharged "CARDI / 1975-1985"

Perf. 13x13½

1985, May 29 Litho. Wmk. 364

995 A28 60c on 3c #135

Caribbean Agricultural Research Development Institute, 10th anniv.

No. 407 Surcharged

1985, June 3

996 A28 600c on #407

Nos. 288, 724, C1 Surcharged "ROTARY / INTERNATIONAL / 1905-1985" in Red

1985, June 21 ***Perfs. as Before***

Watermarks & Printing Methods as Before

997 A74 120c on #C1
998 A74 300c on #288

No. 724 with a similar surcharge is usually found on first day covers.

No. 450A Surcharged "CARICOM DAY / 1985" and No. 426 Surcharged "135th Anniversary / Cotton Reel / 1850-1985" in Red

1985, June 28 ***Perfs. as Before***

Watermarks & Printing Methods as Before

999 A72 60c on #450A
1000 A69 120c on #426

Orchids from Reichenbachia, by Sanders A91

Natl. Arms A92

1985-87 ***Perf. 14***

Wmk. 364 (#1027, 1031, 1036, 1046, 1049, 1052, 1054, 1071, 1074, 1076, 1079, 1091, 1108), Unwmkd.

Series 1

1021 A91 120c Plate No. 1 60 60
1022 A91 60c Plate No. 2 30 30
1023 A91 130c Plate No. 3 65 65
1024 A91 200c Plate No. 4 1.00 1.00
1025 A91 60c Plate No. 5 45 45
1026 A91 75c like #1025 38 38
a. Wmk. 364 ('87)
1027 A91 100c Plate No. 6 75 75
1028 A91 130c like #1027 65 65
a. Wmk. 364 ('86) 65 65
1029 A91 60c Plate No. 7 30 30
1030 A91 25c Plate No. 8 15 15
1031 A91 50c Plate No. 9 38 38
1032 A91 55c like #1031 28 28
a. Wmk. 364 ('86) 28 28
1033 A91 60c Plate No. 10 30 30
1034 A91 120c Plate No. 11 60 60
1035 A91 25c Plate No. 12 15 15
1036 A91 100c Plate No. 13 75 75
1037 A91 130c like #1036 65 65
a. Wmk. 364 ('86) 65 65
1038 A91 200c Plate No. 14 1.00 1.00
1039 A91 55c Plate No. 15 42 42
1040 A91 180c like #1039 90 90
a. Wmk. 364 ('87)

Issue dates: #1022-1024, 1028-1029, 1033, 1035, 1037, July 9. #1032, Aug. 12. #1021, 1030, 1034, 1038, Sept. 16. #1026, Feb. 26, 1986. #1040, July 24, 1986. #1025, 1027, 1031, 1036, 1039, Aug. 21, 1986.
Nos. 1021, 1034 horiz.

1041 A91 130c Plate No. 16 65 65
1042 A91 55c Plate No. 17 28 28
a. Wmk. 364 ('87)
1043 A91 80c like #1042 40 40
1044 A91 130c Plate No. 18 65 65
1045 A91 60c Plate No. 19 30 30
1046 A91 100c Plate No. 20 75 75
1047 A91 130c like #1046 65 65
a. Wmk. 364 ('86) 65 65
1048 A91 200c Plate No. 21 1.00 1.00
1049 A91 50c Plate No. 22 38 38
1050 A91 55c like #1049 28 28
a. Wmk. 364 ('86) 28 28
1051 A91 25c Plate No. 23 15 15
1052 A91 50c Plate No. 24 38 38
1053 A91 225c like #1052 1.15 1.15
a. Wmk. 364 ('86) 1.15 1.15
1054 A91 100c Plate No. 25 75 75
1055 A91 130c like #1054 65 65
a. Wmk. 364 ('86) 65 65
1056 A91 150c Plate No. 26 75 75
1057 A91 120c Plate No. 27 60 60
1058 A91 120c Plate No. 28 60 60
1059 A91 130c Plate No. 29 65 65
1060 A91 130c Plate No. 30 65 65

Issue dates: #1044-1045, 1047, 1055, 1057, 1059-1060, July 9. #1041, 1050, Aug. 12. #1048, 1051, 1058, Sept. 16. #1042, 1053, 1056, July 10, 1986. #1046, 1049, 1052, 1054, Aug. 21, 1986. #1043, Nov. 25, 1986.
Nos. 1048, 1058 horiz.

1061 A91 60c Plate No. 31 30 30
1062 A91 150c Plate No. 32 75 75
1063 A91 200c Plate No. 33 1.00 1.00
1064 A91 150c Plate No. 34 75 75
1065 A91 150c Plate No. 35 75 75
1066 A91 120c Plate No. 36 60 60
1067 A91 120c Plate No. 37 60 60
1068 A91 130c Plate No. 38 65 65
1069 A91 80c Plate No. 39 60 60
1070 A91 260c like #1069 1.30 1.30
a. Wmk. 364 ('87)
1071 A91 100c Plate No. 40 75 75
1072 A91 150c like #1071 75 75
a. Wmk. 364 ('86) 75 75
1073 A91 150c Plate No. 41 75 75
1074 A91 100c Plate No. 42 75 75
1075 A91 150c like #1075 75 75
a. Wmk. 364 ('86) 75 75
1076 A91 100c Plate No. 43 75 75
1077 A91 200c like #1076 1.00 1.00
a. Wmk. 364 ('86) 1.00 1.00
1078 A91 60c Plate No. 44 30 30
1079 A91 100c Plate No. 45 75 75
1080 A91 150c like #1079 75 75
a. Wmk. 364 ('86) 75 75

Issue dates: #1061, July 9. #1062, 1064-1066, 1068, 1073, 1078, Aug. 12. #1072, 1075, 1077, 1080, Sept. 16. #1063, 1067, 1070, July 10, 1986. #1069, 1071, 1074, 1076, 1079, Aug. 21, 1986.
Nos. 1063, 1071-1072, 1074-1077, 1079-1080 horiz.

1081 A91 120c Plate No. 46 60 60
1082 A91 60c Plate No. 47 30 30
1083 A91 150c Plate No. 48 75 75
1084 A91 50c Plate No. 49 25 25
1085 A91 55c like #1084 28 28
a. Wmk. 364 ('86) 28 28
1086 A91 60c Plate No. 50 45 45
1087 A91 320c like #1086 1.60 1.60
a. Wmk. 364 ('87)
1088 A91 25c Plate No. 51 15 15
1089 A91 25c Plate No. 52 15 15
1090 A91 30c Plate No. 53 15 15
a. Wmk. 364 ('86) 15 15
1091 A91 50c like #1090 38 38
1092 A91 45c Plate No. 54 22 22
a. Wmk. 364 ('87)
1093 A91 60c like #1092 45 45
1094 A91 50c Plate No. 55 25 25
1095 A91 60c like #1094 30 30
1096 A91 75c like #1094 38 38
a. Wmk. 364 38 38
1097 A91 120c Plate No. 56 60 60
1098 A91 60c Plate No. 57 30 30
1099 A91 120c Plate No. 58 60 60
1100 A91 25c Plate No. 59 15 15
a. Dark red flowers ('86) 15 15

Issue dates: #1082-1083, 1085, 1089, Aug. 12. #1088, Sept. 16. #1095, Oct. 7. #1087, 1092, Feb. 26, 1986. #1081, 1090, 1096-1100, July 10, 1986. #1086, 1091, 1093, Aug. 21, 1986. # 1084, Dec. 22, 1986. #1094, Jan. 16, 1987.

No. 1098 horiz.

1101 A91 75c Plate No. 60 55 55
1102 A91 225c like #1101 1.15 1.15
a. Wmk. 364 ('87)
1103 A91 25c Plate No. 61 15 15
1104 A91 150c Plate No. 62 75 75
1105 A91 25c Plate No. 63 15 15
1106 A91 50c Plate No. 64 25 25
1107 A91 55c like #1106 28 28
a. Wmk. 364 ('86) 28 28
1108 A91 50c Plate No. 65 38 38
1109 A91 100c like #1108 50 50
a. Wmk. 364 50 50
1110 A91 130c Plate No. 66 65 65
1111 A91 120c Plate No. 67 60 60
1112 A91 40c Plate No. 68 20 20
1113 A91 100c like #1112 50 50
a. Wmk. 364 ('87)
1114 A91 60c Plate No. 69 45 45
1115 A91 120c like #1114 60 60
a. Wmk. 364 ('87)
1116 A91 25c Plate No. 70 15 15
1117 A91 25c Plate No. 71 15 15
a. Wmk. 364 ('87)
1118 A91 60c like #1117 45 45
1119 A91 25c Plate No. 72 15 15
1120 A91 60c Plate No. 73 30 30

Issue dates: #1104, 1107, Aug. 12. #1103, 1105, 1116, 1119, Sept. 16. #1102, 1115, 1117, Apr. 4, 1986. #1109-1111, 1113, 1120, July 10, 1986. #1101, 1108, 1114, 1118, Aug. 21, 1986. #1112, Nov. 25, 1986.
No. 1114-1115, 1117-1118, 1120 horiz.

1121 A91 80c Plate No. 74 60 60
1122 A91 250c like #1121 1.25 1.25
a. Wmk. 364 ('87)
1123 A91 60c Plate No. 75 30 30
1124 A91 65c Plate No. 76 48 48
1125 A91 150c like #1124 75 75
a. Wmk. 364 ('87)
1126 A91 40c Plate No. 77 20 20
a. Wmk. 364 ('87)
1127 A91 45c like #1126 32 32
1128 A91 45c Plate No. 78 32 32
1129 A91 150c like #1128 75 75
a. Wmk. 364 ('87)
1130 A91 60c Plate No. 79 45 45
1131 A91 200c like #1130 1.00 1.00
a. Wmk. 364 ('87)
1132 A91 65c Plate No. 80 48 48
1133 A91 330c like #1132 1.65 1.65
a. Wmk. 364 ('87)
1134 A91 45c Plate No. 81 22 22
a. Wmk. 364 ('87)
1135 A91 55c like #1134 42 42
1136 A91 55c Plate No. 82 42 42
1137 A91 320c like #1136 1.60 1.60
a. Wmk. 364 ('87)
1138 A91 75c Plate No. 83 55 55
1139 A91 300c like #1138 1.50 1.50
a. Wmk. 364 ('87)
1140 A91 45c Plate No. 84 32 32
1141 A91 90c like #1140 45 45
a. Wmk. 364 ('87)

Issue dates: #1126, 1129, 1131, 1139, 1141, Feb. 26, 1986. #1122-1123, July 10, 1986. #1125, 1133-1134, 1137, July 24, 1986. #1121, 1124, 1127-1128, 1130, 1132, 1135-1136, 1138, 1140, Aug. 21, 1986.
No. 1123 horiz.

1142 A91 45c Plate No. 85 32 32
1143 A91 360c like #1142 1.80 1.80
a. Wmk. 364 ('87)
1144 A91 30c Plate No. 86 15 15
a. Wmk. 364 ('87)
1145 A91 40c like #1144 20 20
1146 A91 60c Plate No. 87 45 45
1147 A91 150c like #1146 75 75
a. Wmk. 364 ('87)
1148 A91 65c Plate No. 88 48 48
1149 A91 100c like #1148 50 50
a. Wmk. 364 ('87)
1150 A91 55c Plate No. 89 42 42
1151 A91 90c like #1150 45 45
a. Wmk. 364 ('87)
1152 A91 40c Plate No. 90 30 30
1153 A91 375c like #1152 1.90 1.90
a. Wmk. 364 ('87)
1154 A91 40c Plate No. 91 20 20
1155 A91 130c like #1154 65 65
a. Wmk. 364 ('87)
1156 A91 50c Plate No. 92 25 25
a. Wmk. 364 ('87)
1157 A91 75c like #1156 55 55
1158 A91 60c Plate No. 93 30 30
a. Wmk. 364 ('87)
1159 A91 80c like #1158 60 60
1160 A91 60c Plate No. 94 45 45
1161 A91 350c like #1160 1.75 1.75
a. Wmk. 364 ('87)
1162 A91 60c Plate No. 95 30 30
a. Wmk. 364 ('87)
1163 A91 75c like #1162 55 55
1164 A91 40c Plate No. 96 20 20
a. Wmk. 364 ('87)
1165 A91 65c like #1164 48 48

See note below #1341. Issue dates: #1143, 1156, 1162, Feb. 26, 1986. #1147, 1161, Apr. 4, 1986. #1144, 1153, 1155, 1158, July 10, 1986. #1149, 1151, 1164, July 24, 1986. #1142, 1146, 1148, 1150, 1152, 1157, 1159-1160, 1163, 1165, Aug. 21, 1986. #1154, Sept. 26, 1986. #1145, Oct. 23, 1986.
Some stamps printed in sheets of 25, blocks of 4 each of different stamps separated by gutter containing 2 #1337 and strip of 5 #1339. Margin contains separation marks for #1337, 1339.
Nos. 1146-1147, 1160-1161 horiz.

Nos. 1025, 1027, 1031, 1036, 1039, 1046, 1049, 1052, 1054, 1069, 1071, 1074, 1076, 1079, 1086, 1091, 1093, 1101, 1108, 1114, 1118, 1121, 1124, 1127-1128, 1130, 1132, 1135-1136, 1138, 1140, 1142, 1146, 1148, 1150, 1152, 1157, 1159-1160, 1163, 1165 sold in booklets only. Two booklets of 48 stamps each contain these numbers and previous values issued in the series.

See #1372. For overprints and surcharges see #1342-1346, 1393, 1402-1403, 1412-1413, 1494, 1511-1670F, 1731-1740, 1742-1750, 1755-1759, 1761, 1764-1773, 1785, 1845-1849, 1906-1909, 1914-1933, 1939-1941, 1943-1947, 1958-1959, 1960-1979, 2000, C7, C9-C12, E2, E4.

1986-89 Litho. Unwmk. *Perf. 14*
Series 2

1166 A91 175c Plate No. 1 62 62
1167 A91 560c like #1166 1.65 1.65
1168 A91 90c Plate No. 2 45 45
1169 A91 200c like #1168 1.00 1.00
1170 A91 50c Plate No. 3 18 18
1171 A91 90c like #1170 45 45
1172 A91 90c Plate No. 4 45 45
1173 A91 140c like #1172 50 50
1174 A91 130c Plate No. 5 48 48
1175 A91 160c like #1174 80 80
1176 A91 50c Plate No. 6 18 18
1177 A91 390c like #1176 1.95 1.95
1178 A91 30c Plate No. 7 15 15
1179 A91 40c like #1178 20 20
1180 A91 70c Plate No. 8 25 25
1181 A91 75c like #1180 38 38
1182 A91 70c Plate No. 9 25 25
1183 A91 200c like #1182 1.00 1.00
1184 A91 90c Plate No. 10 45 45
1185 A91 320c like #1184 1.60 1.60

Issue dates: #1172, 1175, 1181, 1183, Sept. 23. #1184, Oct. 23. #1177, 1185, Oct. 31. #1169, Nov. 25. #1171, 1179, Dec. 27. #1168, Jan. 5, 1987. #1167, Apr. 24, 1987. #1166, 1170, 1173-1174, 1176, 1178, 1180, 1182, Aug. 23, 1988.
Nos. 1174-1175 horiz.

1186 A91 200c Plate No. 11 72 72
1187 A91 70c Plate No. 12 25 25
1188 A91 320c like #1187 1.60 1.60
1189 A91 50c Plate No. 13 25 25
1190 A91 90c like #1189 45 45
1191 A91 30c Plate No. 14 15 15
1192 A91 120c like #1191 60 60
1193 A91 50c Plate No. 15 25 25
1194 A91 85c like #1193 42 42
1195 A91 260c Plate No. 16 52 52
1196 A91 320c like #1195 1.25 1.25
1197 A91 45c Plate No. 17 22 22
1198 A91 70c like #1197 25 25
1199 A91 85c Plate No. 18 42 42
1200 A91 320c like #1199 1.60 1.60
1201 A91 175c Plate No. 19 62 62
1202 A91 450c like #1201 1.25 1.25
1203 A91 25c Plate No. 20 15 15
1204 A91 50c like #1203 18 18
1205 A91 45c Plate No. 21 22 22

Issue dates: #1188, 1205, Sept. 23. #1190, 1197, Oct. 31. #1189, Dec. 3. #1192, 1194, 1200, 1203, Dec. 27. #1193, 1199, Jan. 5, 1987. #1202, Apr. 24, 1987. #1196, June 1, 1988. #1186-1187, 1191, 1198, 1201, 1204, Aug. 23, 1988. #1195, July 7, 1989.
Nos. 1201-1202, 1205, horiz.

1206 A91 30c Plate No. 22 15 15
1207 A91 150c like #1206 75 75
1208 A91 200c Plate No. 23 72 72
1209 A91 85c Plate No. 24 42 42
1210 A91 225c like #1209 1.15 1.15
1211 A91 140c Plate No. 25 50 50
1212 A91 230c like #1211 58 58
1213 A91 200c Plate No. 26 72 72
1214 A91 60c Plate No. 27 30 30
1215 A91 90c like #1214 45 45
1216 A91 30c Plate No. 28 15 15
1217 A91 330c like #1216 1.65 1.65
1218 A91 130c Plate No. 29 48 48
1219 A91 350c like #1218 1.75 1.75
1220 A91 30c Plate No. 30 15 15
1221 A91 875c Plate No. 31 3.50 3.50
1222 A91 50c Plate No. 32 18 18
1223 A91 130c like #1222 65 65
1224 A91 50c Plate No. 33 25 25
1225 A91 100c like #1224 72 72

Issue dates: #1219, 1220, Sept. 23. #1214, 1224, Oct. 31. #1210, Nov. 25. #1209, 1215, Dec. 15. #1207, 1217, 1223, Dec. 27. #1212, Feb. 14, 1987. #1221, June 15, 1988. #1206, 1208, 1211, 1213, 1216, 1218, 1222, 1225, Aug. 23, 1988.
Nos. 1218-1219 horiz.

1226 A91 140c Plate No. 34 50 50
1227 A91 360c like #1226 1.80 1.80
1228 A91 380c Plate No. 35 1.35 1.35
1229 A91 525c Plate No. 36 2.25 2.25
1230 A91 175c Plate No. 37 62 62
1231 A91 390c like #1230 1.25 1.25
1232 A91 130c Plate No. 38 65 65
1233 A91 140c like #1232 50 50
1234 A91 175c Plate No. 39 62 62
1235 A91 260c like #1234 75 75
1236 A91 250c Plate No. 40 90 90
1237 A91 $10 like #1236 4.25 4.25
1238 A91 140c Plate No. 41 50 50
1239 A91 180c like #1238 45 45
1240 A91 80c Plate No. 42 40 40
1241 A91 130c like #1240 48 48
1242 A91 200c Plate No. 43 52 52
1243 A91 100c Plate No. 44 72 72
1244 A91 200c like #1243 1.00 1.00
1245 A91 35c Plate No. 45 18 18
1246 A91 85c like #1245 42 42

Issue dates: #1227, 1232, 1240, Sept. 23. #1244, 1246, Oct. 31. #1245, Jan. 5, 1987. #1239, Feb. 14, 1987. #1231, 1235, Apr. 24, 1987. #1242, Sept. 29, 1987. #1237, Mar. 24, 1988. #1229, June 1, 1988. #1226, 1228, 1230, 1233-1234, 1236, 1238, 1241, 1243, Aug. 23, 1988.
Nos. 1230-1231, 1240-1241 horiz.

1247 A91 225c Plate No. 46 80 80
1248 A91 175c Plate No. 47 62 62
1249 A91 240c like #1248 70 70
1250 A91 200c Plate No. 48 52 52
1251 A91 200c Plate No. 49 52 52
1252 A91 720c like #1251 3.00 3.00
1253 A91 160c Plate No. 50 55 55
1254 A91 300c like #1253 1.50 1.50
1255 A91 175c Plate No. 51 60 60
1256 A91 500c like #1255 1.50 1.50
1257 A91 140c Plate No. 52 38 38
1258 A91 590c like #1257 1.50 1.50
1259 A91 200c Plate No. 53 52 52
1260 A91 290c like #1259 1.25 1.25
1261 A91 175c Plate No. 54 60 60
1261A A91 460c like #1261 1.40 1.40
1262 A91 120c Plate No. 55 32 32
1263 A91 75c Plate No. 56 38 38
1264 A91 100c like #1263 28 28
1265 A91 225c Plate No. 57 60 60

Issue dates: #1254, 1263, Oct. 31. #1258, Feb. 14, 1987. #1249, 1256, 1261A, Apr. 24, 1987. #1250, Sept. 29, 1987. #1252, 1260, Nov. 23, 1987. #1247-1248, Aug. 23, 1988. #1253, 1255, Nov. 3, 1988. #1251, 1257, 1259, 1261-1262, 1264-1265, Jan. 3, 1989.
Nos 1261, 1261A horiz.

1266 A91 175c Plate No. 58 48 48
1267 A91 275c like #1266 85 85
1268 A91 775c Plate No. 59 3.25 3.25
1269 A91 200c Plate No. 60 52 52
1270 A91 575c like #1269 1.50 1.50
1271 A91 255c Plate No. 61 1.00 1.00
1272 A91 280c Plate No. 62 95 95
1273 A91 700c like #1272 3.00 3.00
1274 A91 285c Plate No. 63 1.00 1.00
1275 A91 200c Plate No. 64 52 52
1276 A91 680c like #1275 2.75 2.75
1277 A91 140c Plate No. 65 38 38
1278 A91 650c like #1277 1.65 1.65
1279 A91 280c Plate No. 66 75 75
1280 A91 750c like #1279 3.00 3.00
1281 A91 280c Plate No. 67 75 75
1282 A91 $15 like #1281 6.25 6.25
1283 A91 325c Plate No. 68 85 85
1284 A91 530c Plate No. 69 2.25 2.25
1285 A91 550c Plate No. 70 2.75 2.75

Issue dates: #1278, Feb. 14, 1987. #1267, Apr. 24, 1987. #1270, 1283, Oct. 26, 1987. #1271, 1276, 1280, Nov. 23, 1987. #1282, 1284, June 1, 1988. #1268, 1273, June 15, 1988. #1285, Aug. 15, 1988. #1272, 1274, Nov. 3, 1988. #1266, 1269, 1275, 1277, 1279, 1281, Jan. 3, 1989.
No. 1266-1267, 1283, 1285 horiz.

1286 A91 670c Plate No. 71 3.25 3.25
1287 A91 300c Plate No. 72 80 80
1288 A91 $25 like #1287 6.50 6.50
1289 A91 130c Plate No. 73 26 26
1290 A91 475c like #1289 2.00 2.00
1291 A91 350c Plate No. 74 1.50 1.50
1291A A91 900c like #1291
1291B A91 600c on 900c #1291A
1292 A91 200c Plate No. 75 70 70
1293 A91 250c Plate No. 76 65 65
1294 A91 850c like #1293 3.50 3.50
1295 A91 300c Plate No. 77 80 80
1296 A91 480c like #1295 1.25 1.25
1297 A91 280c Plate No. 78 75 75
1298 A91 950c like #1298 4.00 4.00
1299 A91 250c Plate No. 79 90 90
1300 A91 800c like #1299 3.25 3.25
1301 A91 300c Plate No. 80 80 80
1302 A91 400c like #1301 1.10 1.10
1303 A91 305c Plate No. 81 82 82
1304 A91 250c Plate No. 82 65 65
1305 A91 330c like #1304 85 85

Issue dates: #1305, Feb. 14, 1987. #1288, 1296, 1302, July 22, 1987. #1291A-1291B, Oct. 9, 1987. #1294, 1300, Nov. 23, 1987. #1290, June 1, 1988. #1298, June 15, 1988. #1291, June 22, 1988. #1286, Aug. 15, 1988. #1292, 1299, Nov. 3, 1988. #1287, 1293, 1295, 1297, 1301, 1303-1304, Jan. 3, 1989. #1289, July 7, 1989.
No. 1286 horiz.

1306 A91 350c Plate No. 83 95 95
1307 A91 $20 like #1306 5.25 5.25
1308 A91 360c Plate No. 84 1.75 1.75
1309 A91 250c Plate No. 85 65 65
1310 A91 300c like #1309 75 75
1311 A91 350c Plate No. 86 95 95
1312 A91 500c like #1311 1.25 1.25
1313 A91 250c Plate No. 87 65 65
1314 A91 425c like #1313 1.05 1.05
1315 A91 250c Plate No. 88 65 65
1316 A91 440c like #1315 1.10 1.10
1317 A91 350c Plate No. 89 95 95
1318 A91 520c like #1317 1.40 1.40
1319 A91 270c Plate No. 90 1.25 1.25
1320 A91 250c Plate No. 91 65 65
1321 A91 $12 like #1320 5.00 5.00
1322 A91 200c Plate No. 92 52 52
1323 A91 200c Plate No. 93 70 70
1324 A91 300c Plate No. 94 80 80
1325 A91 600c like #1324 1.65 1.65
1326 A91 420c Plate No. 95 1.25 1.25
1327 A91 200c Plate No. 96 40 40
1328 A91 375c like #1327 1.50 1.50

Issue dates: #1310, 1314, 1316, Feb. 14, 1987. #1307, 1312, 1318, June 2, 1987. #1325, July 22, 1987. #1322, Sept. 29, 1987. #1326, Oct. 26, 1987. #1328, Nov. 23, 1987. #1321, Mar. 24, 1988. #1308, 1319, Aug. 15, 1988. #1323, Nov. 3, 1988. #1306, 1309, 1311, 1313, 1315, 1317, 1320, 1324, Jan. 3, 1989. #1327, July 7, 1989.
No. 1326, horiz.

Miniature Sheets of 4

Designs: Nos. 1329a, 1330b, 1331b, like #1303. Nos. 1329b, 1330a, 1332a, like #1265. Nos. 1329c, 1330c, 1332b, like #1247. Nos. 1330d, 1331a, 1332c, like #1262.

1329 #1262, 1329a-1329c 1.00 1.00
a.-c. A91 120c any single 24 24
1330 #a.-d. 1.20 1.20
a.-d. A91 150c any single 30 30
1331 #1247, 1265, 1331a-1331b 1.80 1.80
a.-b. A91 225c any single 45 45
1332 #1303, 1332a-1332c 2.50 2.50
a.-c. A91 305c any single 62 62
1333 4.50 4.50
a. A91 320c like #1262 95 95
b. A91 330c like #1247 95 95
c. A91 350c like #1303 1.00 1.00
d. A91 500c like #1265 1.50 1.50
1334 4.50 4.50
a. A91 320c like #1247 95 95
b. A91 330c like #1262 95 95
c. A91 350c like #1265 1.00 1.00
d. A91 500c like #1303 1.50 1.50
1335 4.50 4.50
a. A91 320c like #1303 95 95
b. A91 330c like #1265 95 95
c. A91 350c like #1262 1.00 1.00
d. A91 500c like #1247 1.50 1.50
1336 4.50 4.50
a. A91 320c like #1265 95 95
b. A91 330c like #1303 95 95
c. A91 350c like #1247 1.00 1.00
d. A91 500c like #1262 1.50 1.50

Issue dates: Nos. 1329-1332, July 7, 1989. Nos. 1333-1336, Feb. 26, 1988.

For surcharges and overprints see Nos. 1671-1727, 1776-1777, 1834-1835, 1942, 1948-1952, 1998-1999, 2031, 2033-2044, 2064, E3, E5, O40-O56.

1985-87 *Perf. 14 Vert.*

1337 A92 25c multi 15 15
1338 A92 25c multi ('87) 15 15
Set value 19 19

Perf. 14 Horiz.

1339 A92 25c multi 15 15
1340 A92 25c multi ('87) 15 15
Set value 19 19

Perf. 14

1341 A92 25c multi

Nos. 1337-1340 were cut from orchid sheet gutters. Stamps vary considerably in size.

Nos. 1338, 1340 are Nos. 1337 and 1339 redrawn to include black border.

Issue dates: Nos. 1337, 1339, 1341, July 1985. No. 1338, 1340 June 2, 1987.

See Nos. 1467-1468. For surcharges see Nos. 1777A-1777C.

Nos. 1024, 1044, 1047, 1059, 1060 Surcharged or Overprinted in Blue or Black "QUEEN MOTHER 1900-1985" on 1 or 2 Lines

1985 *Perfs. as Before*

1342 A91 130c on #1044
1343 A91 130c on #1059
1344 A91 130c on #1060

Miniature sheets of 4

1345
a.-d. A91 200c on #1024, any single
1346
a.-d. A91 200c on 130c #1047, any single (Bk)

Issued: #1342-1345, July 9; #1346, Sept. 12.

Nos. 1345a, 1346a overprinted "LADY BOWES-LYON 1900-1923". Nos. 1345b, 1346b overprinted "DUCHESS OF YORK 1923-1937". Nos. 1345c, 1346c overprinted "QUEEN ELIZABETH 1937-1952". Surcharge on No. 1346 sans serif.

For overprints see #1741, 1751-1754, 1774-1775.

Nos. 465 Surcharged in Red "INTERNATIONAL / YOUTH YEAR / 1985"

Perf. 13x13¹/₂

1985, July 18 Litho. Wmk. 364

1347 Sheet of 25, 8 #a.-b., 4 #c.-d., 1 #e.
a.-e. A28 25c on #465a-465e, any single

No. 203 Surcharged "1910-1985" and

J. J. Audubon
1785-1985

No. 443 Surcharged

240
1982

1985, July 26 *Perfs. as Before*
Watermarks & Printing Methods as Before

1352 A47 225c on #203
1354 A63 240c on #443

Girl Guides, 75th anniv. (#1352), John J. Audubon, bicentennial of birth. No. 203 surcharged only with 350c, $2.25 or surcharged with both was not issued.

Abolition of Slavery, Sesquicent. A93

Designs: 25c, Revolution leaders, 1763. 60c, Damon's execution, 1834. 130c, Demerara Uprising, 1823. 150c Den Arendt slave ship.

Unwmk.
1985, July 29 Litho. *Perf. 14*

1355 A93 25c gray & black 15 15
1356 A93 60c pink & black 28 28
1357 A93 130c blue grn & blk 60 60
1358 A93 150c lilac & blk 70 70

See Nos. 1994-1997 for changed colors.

No. 210 Surcharged "Guyana/Libya / Friendship 1985"
No. 223 Surcharged in Brown
No. 135 Surcharged "Mexico / 1986"

1985, Aug. 16 *Perfs. as Before*
Watermarks and Printing Methods as Before

1359 A49 150c on #210
1360 A53 150c on #223
1361 A28 275c on 3c #135

Refer to 2nd paragraph under No. 147 for No. 1361. See No. 1452 for 225c Mexico 1986 surcharge.

Nos. 366, 427, 430, 430a, 494, & 553 Ovptd. or Surcharged "1955-1985" Vertically or Horizontally

Perf. 13¹/₂

1985, Sept. 23 Litho. Wmk. 364

1362 A75 60c on #366
1363 A75 60c on #553
1364 A75 120c on #427
1365 A75 120c on #430
1366 A75 120c on #430a
1367 A75 120c on #494

No. 417 Surcharged "1965-1985" Vertically

1985, Sept. 30

1368 A79 25c on #417
1369 A79 225c on #417

Nos. 260 & 262 Surcharged "1985"

1985, Oct. 5 Litho. *Perf. 14x14¹/₂*

1370 A61 25c on 40c #262
1371 A61 320c on 15c #260

Orchid Type of 1985 Surcharged in Red "CRISTOBAL COLON / 1492-1992"

1985, Oct. 12 *Perf. 14*

1372 A91 350c on 120c like #1108

No. 1372 not issued without surcharge. For overprint see No. E1. For surcharge see No. 1591A.

No. 288 Overprinted "SIR WINSTON CHURCHILL / 1965-1985"

1985, Oct. 15 *Perf. 13½x13*
1373 A66 $2 on #288

No. 214 Surcharged "1950-1985"

1985, Oct. 15 *Perf. 14*
1374 A50 25c on 110c on 10c
1375 A50 200c on 110c on 10c

No. 214 with 110c surcharge only was not issued.

Nos. 295-297, 384, and O9 Overprinted or Surcharged "United / Nations / 1945-1985"

1985, Oct. 28 *Perf. 14x14½*
1376 A68 30c on #295
1377 A68 50c on #296
1378 A68 100c on #O9
1379 A68 225c on #384
1380 A68 $3 on #297

Nos. 142-144, 289A, O4-O5, O7, O15, and OO1-OO2 Ovptd. "POSTAGE"

1985, Oct. 29 *Perfs. as Before*
Watermarks and Printing Methods as Before
1381 A28 30c on #O4
1382 A28 40c on #142
1383 A28 50c on #143
1384 A28 50c on #O5
1385 A28 60c on #144
1386 A28 60c on #144 (Revenue Only)
1387 A28 60c on #O7
1388 A66 $10 on #O15
1389 A28 $15 on #OO1
1390 A28 $20 on #OO2

Refer to 2nd paragraph in footnote following #147 for #1381, 1384, 1386-1387.

Nos. 133-134 Surcharged "Deepavali / 1985"

1985, Nov. 1
1391 A28 25c on 2c #134
1392 A28 150c on 1c #133

Miniature Sheet
No. 1050 Ovptd. in Red

Overprinted: a, "Christmas 1985." b, "Happy New Year." c, "Merry Christmas." d, "Happy Holidays."

1985, Nov. 3 **Unwmk.** *Perf. 14*
1393 A91 55c Sheet of 4, #a.-d.

For surcharge, see No. 1670F.

Clive Lloyd, Cricketer
A94

Lloyd Holding Intl. Cup
A95

Designs: #a, $2.25, Lloyd playing cricket. #b, $1.30, Lloyd, bat and wicket. #c, 60c, Gloves, wicket, bat, natl. flag.

1985, Nov. 7 *Perf. 14½x14*

1394		Triptych	38	38
a.-c.		A94 25c any single	15	15

Size: 30x38mm

Perf. 14x14½

1395	A94	60c multi	28	28
1396	A94	$1.30 multi	60	60
1397	A94	$2.25 multi	1.10	1.10
1398	A95	$3.50 multi	1.75	1.75
		Nos. 1394-1398 (5)	4.11	4.11

For surcharge see No. 1504.

Miniature Sheet
No. 329 Ovptd. "1985" in Red

Wmk. 364

1985, Nov. 15 **Litho.** *Perf. 14*
1399 A77 30c Sheet of 12, #a.-l.

Nos. 410 and 413e Surcharged

1985, Dec. 23 **Photo.** *Perf. 14x14½*
Watermarks as Before
1400 A7 20c on #410
1401 A7 20c on #413e

Compare No. 1400 with No. 914 and 1401 with No. 994a.

Nos. 1075, 1077 Ovptd. "REICHENBACHIA 1886-1986" in Purple

1986, Jan. 13 **Litho.** *Perf. 14J*
1402 A91 150c on #1075
1403 A91 200c on #1077

For surcharge and overprints, see Nos. 1553, 1760, 1762-1763.

Nos. 608, 610 Surcharged "Republic Day / 1986"

Perfs. as Before

1986, Feb. 22 **Wmk. 364**
1404 A82 25c on #608
1405 A83 120c on $6 #610
1406 A83 225c on $6 #610

No. 87 Surcharged "1986"

1986, Mar. 24 **Photo.** *Perf. 13*
1407 A14 25c on 6c #87
1408 A14 50c on 6c #87
1409 A14 100c on 6c #87
1410 A14 200c on 6c #87

No. 237 Surcharged "1926 / 1986"

1986, Mar. 27 **Litho.** *Perf. 14*
1411 A56 150c on 35c #237

St. John Ambulance, 60th anniv.

Nos. 1028, 1037 Surcharged "Queen Elizabeth / 1926 1986"

1986, Apr. 21 **Unwmk.**
1412 A91 Sheet of 4
a. 130c on 130c #1028
b. 200c on 130c #1028
c. 260c on 130c #1028
d. 330c on 130c #1028
1413 A91 130c on #1037

Location of overprint on No. 1413 differs from No. 1412.
For overprints and surcharges see Nos. 1670A, 1738B.

Nos. 267, 317g-317 l, 444a-444f Surcharged "Protect the"

Wmk. 373

1986, May 3 **Litho.** *Perf. 14*
1414 A73 60c on 35c #317g-317l, block of 6, #a.-f.
1415 A73 60c on 35c #444, block of 6, #a.-f.

Wmk. 364

1416 A63 $6 on 8c #267

No. 390 Surcharged

1986, May 5 **Litho.** *Perf. 13*
1417 A28 600c on #390

No. 283A Surcharged

Overprints: a, Abary. b, Anna Regina. c, Aurora. d, Bartica Grove. e, Bel Air. f, Belle Plaine. g, Clonbrook. h, T.P.O. Dem. / Railway. i, Enmore. j, Fredericks / burg. k, Good Success. l, 1986. m, Mariabba. n, Massaruni. o, Nigg. p, No. 50. q, No. 63 / Benab. r, Philadelphia. s, Sisters. t, Skeldon. u, Suddie. v, Taymouth / Manor. w, Wales. x, Whim.

Perf. 14x13½

1986, May 15 **Litho.** **Wmk. 364**
1418 Sheet of 25, #a.-k., m.-x., 2 #l.

British Guiana No. 254 Surcharged "GUYANA / INDEPENDENCE 1966-1986"
Nos. 10A and 13a Surcharged "1986"
No. 237 Surcharged
No. 713a-713d Surcharged "INDEPENDENCE / 1966-1986"

1986, May 26 *Perfs. as Before*
Watermarks and Printing Methods as Before
1443 A60 25c on 2c British Guiana #254
1444 A57 25c on 35c #237
1445 A60 60c on 2c British Guiana #254
1446 A60 120c on 6c #10A
1447 A60 130c on 24c #13a
1448 Block of 4
a. A86 25c on 120c #713a
b. A86 25c on 130c #713b
c. A86 25c on 150c #713c
d. A86 225c on 200c #713d

No. 135 Surcharged "MEXICO / 1986" in Blue

Perf. 13x13½

1986, May 31 **Litho.** **Wmk. 364**
1452 A28 225c on 3c #135

World Cup Soccer Championships, Mexico City.

Nos. 135 and 192 Surcharged "CARICOM HEADS OF GOV'T / CONFERENCE / JULY 1986" in Blue
No. 286A Ovptd. "CARICOM / DAY 1986" in Blue

1986 *Perfs. as Before*
Watermarks and Printing Methods as Before
1453 A28 25c on #192
1454 A28 60c on 3c #135
1455 A66 60c on #286A

Issue dates: No. 1455, June 28. Nos. 1453-1454, July 1.

Nos. 133 and 137 Surcharged "INT. YEAR / OF PEACE" in Black or Blue

1986, July 14 **Litho.** *Perf. 13x13½*
1456 A28 25c on 1c #133 (Bl)
1457 A28 60c on 6c #137
1458 A28 120c on 6c #137
1459 A28 130c on 6c #137
1460 A28 150c on 6c #137

Halley's Comet — A96

Designs: a, Br. Guiana #172. b, Guyana #931.

1986, July 19 *Perf. 14*

1461	A96	320c Pair, #a.-b.	3.20	3.20
c.		Imperf.	3.00	

No. 1461 has continuous design. No. 1461 exists imperf. between. Most were overprinted.
For overprints and surcharges see Nos. 1822, 1836, 2029, E5-E6, E11, E14.

No. 43 Surcharged

1986, July 28 **Photo.** *Perf. 14x14½*
1463 A7 20c on 6c #43

Nos. 60-61 Surcharged "GUSIA / 1936-1986"

Perf. 14x13½

1986, Aug. 15 **Photo.** **Unwmk.**
1464 A11 25c on #61
1465 A11 $1.50 on 6c #60

No. 136 Surcharged "REGIONAL / PHARMACY / CONFERENCE / 1986" in Blue

Perf. 13x13½

1986, Aug. 15 **Litho.** **Wmk. 364**
1466 A28 130c on 5c #136

Nos. 1337, 1339, 1341 Inscribed "1966-1986"

Perfs. as Before

1986, Sept. 23 **Unwmk.**
1467 A92 25c on #1337
1468 A92 25c on #1339
1469 A92 25c on #1341

No. 871 Surcharged

Perf. 14x13½

1986, Oct. 1 **Litho.** **Wmk. 364**
Sheet of 25
1470 #a.-k., m.-x., 2 #l
a.-x. A66 120c any single

No. 1145 Surcharged "12th World Orchid Conference" / "TOKYO JAPAN MARCH 1987"

Unwmk.

1986, Oct. 6 **Litho.** *Perf. 14*
1494 A91 650c on 40c #1145

For overprint see No. 1851.

Orchid Type like No. 1052 Surchd. "1492-1992" and "CHRISTOPHER COLUMBUS" in Black and Red or Red

1986, Oct.
1495 A91 320c on 150c
1496 A91 320c on 150c (R)

Nos. 1495-1496 not issued without surcharge. Issue dates: No. 1495, Oct. 10. No 1496, Oct. 30.

Nos. 704 and 705 Surcharged "1986"

Perf. 14x14½

1986, Oct. 15 **Photo.** **Wmk. 364**
1497 A7 50c on #704
1498 A7 225c on #705

Nos. 134, 192 Surcharged "Deepavali /1986"

1986, Nov. 3 **Litho.** *Perf. 13x13½*
1499 A28 25c on 2c #134
1500 A28 200c on #192

No. 43 Surcharged "CHRISTMAS / 1986" in Red
No. "917" Surcharged in Red

1986, Nov. 26 *Perfs. as Before*
Watermarks and Printing Methods as Before
1501 A7 20c on 6c #43

Miniature Sheet

1502 A88 120c on 60c on #a.-e.

No. 1502 is surcharged on an unissued miniature sheet containing No. 917.

No. 329 Ovptd. "1986" in Blue

Wmk. 364

1986, Nov. 26 **Litho.** *Perf. 14*
1503 A77 30c Sheet of 12, #a.-l.

No. 1398 Surcharged in Red

1986, Dec. 1 **Litho.** *Perf. 14x14½*
1504 A95 $15 on $3.50 #1398

L.F.S. Burnham, President 1980-85
A97

1986, Dec. 13 **Litho.** *Perf. 12½x13*

1505	A97	25c Tomb	15	15
1506	A97	120c Flags, map	60	60
1507	A97	130c Government building	65	65
1508	A97	$6 Portrait, necklace, vert.	3.00	3.00

Orchid Type of 1985-87 Surcharged "GPOC / 1977 - 1987"

1987, Jan. 19 *Perf. 14*
1509 A91 225c on 25c like #1090
1510 A91 $10 on 50c like #1052

Nos. 1509-1510 not issued without surcharge. No. 1509 adds "2" to 25c value, No. 1510 uses flower as obliterator.

Stamps of Type A91 Surcharged in Black or Red

120

120 a

b

200

c

200 d

200 e

120 f

1987

g 15.oo

TWO DOLLARS h

i 225

120 j

240 k

POSTAGE l

1987-89 *Perfs. as Before*

Design A91

Series 1

(Plate Number in Parentheses)

On Nos. 1022-1039

1511 (a) 120c on 60c (2)
1512 (b) 120c on 60c (2)
1513 (a) 120c on 60c (5)
1514 (c) 200c on 60c (5)
1515 (c) 200c on 75c (5)

Obliterator invtd. in surch. on #1514-1515.

1516 (d) 200c on 60c (7)
1517 (d) 200c on 25c (8)
1518 (e) 200c on 25c (8)
1519 (a) 120c on 50c (9)
1520 (b) 120c on 50c (9)
1521 (f) 120c on 50c (9)
1522 (g) 120c on 50c (9)
1523 (a) 120c on 55c (9)
1524 (f) 120c on 55c (9)
a. 120c on 55c #1032a
1525 (g) 120c on 55c (9)
1526 (a) 120c on 60c (10)
1527 (d) 200c on 60c (10)
1528 (h) $2 on 25c (12)

Surcharge on No. 1528 lacks obliterator.

1529 (f) 120c on 55c (15)
1530 (a) 200c on 55c (15)

Issue dates: #1518, 1528, Mar. 6. 1514-1515, Mar. 17. #1516-1517, 1522, 1525, 1527, Mar. 1987. #1521, 1524, 1529, July 1987. #1511, 1513, 1519, 1523, 1526, 1530, Sept. 1987. #1512, 1520, July 1988.

On Nos. 1042-1061

1531 (b) 120c on 55c (17)
1532 (d) 200c on 55c (17)
1533 (a) 600c on 80c (17)
1534 (a) 120c on 60c (19)
1535 (d) 200c on 60c (19)
1536 (a) 120c on 50c (22)
1537 (b) 120c on 50c (22)
1538 (f) 120c on 50c (22)
1539 (c) 200c on 50c (22)
1540 (i) 225c on 50c (22)
1541 (a) 120c on 55c (22)
1542 (f) 120c on 55c (22)
1543 (c) 200c on 55c #1050a (22)
1544 (h) $2 on 25c (23)
1545 (a) 120c on 50c (24)
1546 (a) 200c on 50c (24)
1547 (d) 200c on 50c (24)
1548 (a) 120c on 60c (31)
1549 (d) 200c on 60c (31)

Issue dates: #1544, Mar. 6. #1539, 1543, Mar. 17. #1532, 1535, 1547, 1549, Mar. 1987. #1540, June 1987. #1538, 1542, July 1987. #1533-1534, 1536, 1541, 1545-1546, 1548, Sept. 1987. #1531, 1537, July 1988.

On Nos. 1069-1091

1550 (b) 120c on 80c (39)
1551 (a) 600c on 80c (39)
1552 (g) $15 on 80c (39)
1553 (i) 225c on #1402 (42)
1554 (d) 200c on 60c (44)
1555 (d) 200c on 60c (47)
1556 (a) 120c on 50c (49)
1557 (f) 120c on 50c (49)
1558 (a) 120c on 55c (49)
1559 (f) 120c on 55c (49)
a. 120c on 55c on #1085a
1560 (d) 200c on 55c (49)
a. 200c on 55c on #1085a
1561 (a) 120c on 60c (50)
1562 (b) 120c on 60c (50)
1563 (e) 200c on 25c (51)
1564 (d) 200c on 25c (52)
1565 (b) 120c on 30c (53)
a. 120c on 30c on #1090a
1566 (a) 120c on 50c (53)
1567 (d) 200c on 30c (53)
1568 (a) 200c on 50c (53)
1569 (d) 200c on 50c (53)
1570 (g) $10 on 25c (53)
1571 (g) $25 on 25c (53)

Surcharge on #1571 lacks obliterator and places a "$" in front of original denomination. #1570-1571 not issued without surcharge.

Issue dates: #1563, Mar. 6. #1552, 1554-1555, 1560, 1564, 1567, 1569-1571, Mar. 1987. #1553, June 1987. #1557, 1559, July 1987. #1551, 1556, 1558, 1561, 1566, 1568, Sept. 1987. #1550, 1562, 1565, July 1988.

On Nos. 1092-1108, 1372

1572 (b) 120c on 45c (54)
1573 (a) 120c on 60c (54)
1574 (b) 120c on 60c (54)
1575 (a) 200c on 50c (55)
1576 (i) 225c on 60c (55)
1577 (b) 120c on 60c (57)
a. New value at bottom
1578 (d) 200c on 60c (57)
1579 (b) 120c on 25c (59)
1580 (a) 120c on 75c (60)
1581 (c) 200c on 75c (60)
1582 (b) 120c on 25c (61)
1583 (b) 120c on 25c (63)
1584 (a) 120c on 50c (64)
1585 (f) 120c on 50c (64)
1586 (a) 120c on 55c (64)
1587 (f) 120c on 55c (64)
a. 120c on 55c on #1107a
1588 (g) 120c on 55c (64)
a. 120c on 55c on #1107a

Surcharge on Nos. 1522, 1525, 1588-1588a does not contain date.

1589 (a) 120c on 50c (65)
1590 (a) 200c on 50c (65)
1591 (d) 200c on 50c (65)
1591A (i) 225c on #1372 (65)

Issue dates: #1581, Mar. 17. #1578, 1588, 1591, Mar. 1987. #1576, June 1987. #1585, 1587, July 1987. #1573, 1575, 1580, 1584, 1586, 1589-1590, Sept. 1987. #1591A, Oct. 9, 1987. #1572, 1574, 1577, 1579, 1582-1583, July 1988.

On Nos. 1112-1124

1592 (b) 120c on 40c (68)
a. New value at LL
1593 (c) 200c on 40c (68)
a. Obliterator inverted
1594 (a) 225c on 40c (68)
1595 (a) 120c on 60c (69)
1596 (b) 120c on 60c (69)
1597 (b) 120c on 25c (70)
1598 (b) 120c on 25c (71)
1599 (a) 120c on 60c (71)
1600 (d) 200c on 25c (71)
1601 (d) 200c on 60c (71)
1602 (j) 120c on 25c (72)
1603 (d) 200c on 25c (72)
1604 (b) 120c on 60c (73)
1605 (d) 200c on 60c (73)
1606 (b) 120c on 80c (74)
1607 (a) 600c on 80c (74)
1608 (g) $12 on 80c (74)
1609 (b) 120c on 60c (75)
a. New value at left
1610 (d) 200c on 60c (75)
1611 (a) 225c on 65c (76)

Issue dates: #1593, Mar. 17. #1600-1601, 1603, 1605, 1608, 1610, Mar. 1987. #1594-1595, 1599, 1611, Sept. 1987. #1592, 1596-1598, 1604, 1606-1607, 1609, July 1988. #1602, Sept. 1988.

On Nos. 1126-1142

1612 (b) 120c on 40c (77)
a. New value at UL
1613 (d) 200c on 40c (77)
1614 (a) 200c on 45c (77)
1615 (d) 200c on 45c (77)
1616 (a) 200c on 45c (78)
1617 (d) 200c on 45c (78)
1618 (a) 120c on 60c (79)
1619 (b) 120c on 60c (79)
1620 (a) 225c on 65c (80)
1621 (b) 120c on 45c (81)
1622 (f) 120c on 55c (81)
1623 (d) 200c on 45c (81)
1624 (a) 200c on 55c (81)
1625 (f) 120c on 55c (82)
1626 (a) 200c on 55c (82)
1627 (a) 120c on 75c (83)
1628 (b) 120c on 90c (84)
1629 (a) 200c on 45c (84)
1630 (a) 200c on 45c (85)
1631 (d) 200c on 45c (85)

Issue dates: #1613, 1615, 1617, 1623, 1631, Mar. 1987. #1622, 1625, July 1987. #1614, 1616, 1618, 1620, 1624, 1626-1627, 1629-1630, Sept. 1987. #1612, 1619, 1621, 1628, July 1988.

On Nos. 1144-1153

1632 (b) 120c on 30c (86)
1633 (b) 120c on 40c (86)
1634 (d) 200c on 30c (86)
1635 (d) 200c on 40c (86)
1636 (a) 225c on 40c (86)
a. Inscribed "ONTOGLOSSUM"
1637 (a) 120c on 60c (87)
a. Surcharge reading up
1638 (d) 200c on 60c (87)
1639 (a) 225c on 65c (88)
1640 (f) 120c on 55c (89)
1641 (b) 120c on 90c (89)
1642 (a) 200c on 55c (89)
1643 (d) 225c on 90c (89)
1644 (a) 120c on 40c (90)
1645 (b) 120c on 40c (90)
1646 (c) 200c on 40c (90)
1647 (d) 200c on 40c (R) (90)
1648 (c) 200c on 375c (90)
a. 200c on 375c #1153a
1649 (a) 225c on 40c (90)
1650 (i) 225c on 40c (90)
1651 (k) 260c on 375c (90)

Issue dates: #1647, Feb. 9, 1987. #1646, 1648, Mar. 17, 1987. #1634-1635, 1638, 1643, Mar. 1987. #1650, June 1987. #1640, July 1987. #1636-1637, 1639, 1642, 1644, 1649, Sept. 1987. #1632-1633, 1641, 1645, July 1988. #1651, Oct. 1988.

Surcharge on #1651 is placed over original value and has no obliterator.

On Nos. 1154-1165

1652 (a) 120c on 40c (91)
1653 (b) 120c on 40c (91)
a. New value at LR
1654 (a) 225c on 40c (91)
1655 (i) 225c on 40c (91)
1656 (b) 120c on 50c (92)
1657 (a) 120c on 75c (92)
1658 (c) 200c on 50c (92)
1659 (c) 200c on 75c (92)
1660 (b) 120c on 60c (93)
1661 (b) 120c on 80c (93)
1662 (i) 225c on 60c (93)
1663 (i) 225c on 80c (93)
1664 (a) 600c on 80c (93)
1665 (a) 120c on 60c (94)
1666 (b) 120c on 60c (94)
1667 (b) 120c on 60c (95)
1668 (a) 120c on 75c (95)
1669 (b) 120c on 40c (96)
1670 (a) 225c on 65c (96)

Miniature Sheets

1670A Sheet of 4
b. (a) 600c on 130c #1413a (6)
c. (a) 600c on 200c #1413b (6)
d. (a) 600c on 260c #1413c (6)
e. (a) 600c on 330c #1413d (6)
1670F Sheet of 4
g. (i) 225c on #1393a (22)
h. (i) 225c on #1393b (22)
i. (i) 225c on #1393c (22)
j. (i) 225c on #1393d (22)

Issue dates: #1658-1659, Mar. 17, 1987. #1655, 1662-1663, June 1987. #1652, 1654, 1657, 1664-1665, 1668, 1670, Sept. 1987. #1670F, Nov. 9, 1987. #1670A, Nov. 20, 1987. #1653, 1656, 1660-1661, 1666-1667, 1669, July 1988.

For overprints see Nos. 1975, 1979.

Series 2

On Nos. 1168-1204

1671 (b) 120c on 90c (2)
1672 (b) 120c on 50c (3)
1673 (f) 120c on 50c (3)
1674 (b) 200c on 90c (4)
1675 (b) 120c on 50c (6)
1676 (f) 120c on 50c (6)
1677 (b) 120c on 30c (7)
1678 (b) 120c on 70c (8)
1679 (b) 120c on 70c (9)
a. New value at LR
1680 (b) 120c on 90c (10)
1681 (b) 120c on 70c (12)
a. New value at LL
1682 (b) 120c on 50c (13)
1683 (b) 120c on 90c (13)
1684 (b) 120c on 30c (14)
a. New value at UR
1685 (b) 120c on 50c (15)
1686 (b) 120c on 85c (15)
1687 (b) 120c on 70c (17)
1688 (b) 120c on 85c (18)
1689 (c) 200c on 85c (18)
1690 (b) 120c on 50c (20)
1691 (f) 120c on 50c (20)

Issue dates: #1689, Mar. 17, 1987. #1673, 1676, 1691, July 1987. #1671-1672, 1674-1675, 1677-1688, 1690, July 1988.

On Nos. 1205-1240

1692 (b) 120c on 45c (21)
1693 (b) 120c on 30c (22)
1694 (l) 350c on 330c #O52 (23)
1695 (b) 120c on 85c (24)
1696 (j) 120c on 140c (R) (25)
1697 (l) 250c on 225c #O46 (26)
a. New value at UL
1698 (b) 120c on 60c (27)
1699 (b) 120c on 90c (27)
1700 (b) 120c on 30c (28)
a. New value at UL
1701 (b) 120c on 30c (30)
1702 (k) 240c on 140c (30)

No. 1702 not issued without surcharge.

1703 (l) 150c on 175c #O44 (31)
1704 (b) 120c on 50c (32)
1705 (f) 120c on 50c (32)
1706 (k) 240c on 140c (34)
1707 (l) 125c on 140c #O42 (36)
1708 (k) 120c on 140c (38)
1709 (k) 120c on 140c (41)
1710 (b) 200c on 80c (42)
1711 (l) 150c on #O43 (43)

Issue dates: #1705, July 1987. #1692-1693, 1695, 1698-1701, 1704, 1710, July 1988. #1702, 1706, Oct. 1988. #1696, 1708-1709, Feb. 22,

1989. #1694, 1697, 1703, 1707, 1711, Mar. 1989.

On Nos. 1245-1314

1712 (b) 120c on 35c (45)
1713 (b) 120c on 85c (45)
1714 (j) 120c on 140c (R) (52)
1715 (k) 300c on 290c (53)
1716 (j) 120c on 175c (R) (54)
1717 (k) 170c on 175c (58)
1718 (l) 250c on #O48 (59)
1719 (j) 120c on 140c (R) (65)
1720 (k) 250c on 280c (66)
1721 (k) 250c on 280c (67)
1722 (l) 250c on 230c #O47 (68)
1723 (l) 250c on 260c #O49 (69)
a. New value at UR
1724 (l) 600c on #O54 (70)
1725 (l) $12 on #O55 (71)
1726 (l) $15 on #O56 (84)
1727 (k) 240c on 425c (87)
1728 (l) 300c on 275c #O50 (90)
1729 (l) 125c on 130c #O41 (92)
1730 (l) 350c on #O53 (95)

Issue dates: #1712-1713, July 1988. #1727, Oct. 1988. #1714, 1716, 1719, Feb. 22, 1989. #1715, 1717-1718, 1720-1726, 1728-1730, Mar. 1989.
Obliterator on Nos. 1708-1709, 1715, 1717, 1720-1721 has two thick bars.

Stamps of Type A91 Overprinted

1987 (m) 1987 (n)
1987 (o) 1987 (p)

1987 *Perfs. as Before*

Series 1

1731 (m) 120c on #1021 (1)
1732 (n) 130c on #1023 (3)
1733 (m) 130c on #1028a (6)
1734 (n) 130c on #1028 (6)
a. 130c on #1028a
1735 (m) 120c on #1034 (11)
1736 (m) 130c on #1037a (13)
1737 (n) 130c on #1037 (13)
1738 (o) 130c on #1037 (13)
a. 130c on #1037a
1738B (p) 130c on #1412 (13)
1739 (n) 200c on #1038 (14)
1740 (n) 130c on #1041 (16)
1741 (n) 130c on #1342 (18)
1742 (p) 130c on #1342 (18)
1743 (m) 130c on #1047a (20)
1744 (n) 130c on #1047 (20)
a. 130c on #1047a
1745 (m) 200c on #1048 (21)
1746 (n) 200c on #1048 (21)
1747 (m) 130c on #1055a (25)
1748 (o) 130c on #1055 (25)
a. 130c on #1055a
1749 (p) 150c on #1056 (26)
1750 (m) 120c on #1058 (28)
1751 (n) 130c on #1343 (29)
1752 (p) 130c on #1343 (29)

Issue dates: #1732, 1734, 1737-1741, 1744, 1746, 1748, 1751, Mar. #1731, 1733, 1735-1736, 1743, 1745, 1747, 1750, July. #1738B, Nov. 20. #1742, 1749, 1752, Dec.

1753 (n) 130c on #1344 (30)
1754 (p) 130c on #1344 (30)
1755 (n) 200c on #1063 (33)
1756 (m) 120c on #1067 (37)
1757 (n) 260c on #1070 (39)
1758 (m) 150c on #1072 (40)
a. 150c on #1072a, ovpt. reading up
1759 (m) 150c on #1075a (42)
1760 (m) 150c on #1402 (42)
1761 (m) 200c on #1077a (43)
1762 (m) 200c on #1403 (43)
1763 (n) 200c on #1403 (43)
1764 (m) 150c on #1080 (45)
a. 150c on #1080a ovpt. reading down
1765 (m) 120c on #1081 (46)
1766 (m) 120c on #1097 (56)
1767 (m) 120c on #1099 (58)
1768 (n) 130c on #1110 (66)
1769 (p) 130c on #1110 (66)
1770 (p) 120c on #1111 (67)
1771 (n) 250c on #1122 (74)
1772 (n) 200c on #1131 (79)
1773 (o) 130c on #1155 (91)

Miniature Sheets of 4

1774 (n) 200c on #1345 (4)
1775 (n) 200c on 130c #1346 (20)

Series 2

1776 (n) 200c on #1169 (2)
1777 (n) 200c on #1183 (9)

Issue dates: #1753, 1755, 1757, 1763, 1768, 1771-1777, Mar. #1756, 1758, 1759-1762, 1764-1767, July. #1754, 1769-1770, Dec.
See Nos. 1813-1814, 1844 for other stamps overprinted "1987" only.

Nos. 1337, 1339, 1341 Surcharged

1987, Mar. 6 ***Perfs. as Before***

1777A A92 200c on #1337
1777B A92 200c on #1339
1777C A92 200c on #1341

See note following No. 1341.

Nos. 134, 136, 139a, and 192 Surcharged "Post Office / Corp. / 1977-1987" in Blue

Perfs. as Before

1987, Feb. 17 Litho. Wmk. 364

1778 A28 25c on 2c #134
1779 A28 25c on 5c #136
1780 A28 25c on #192
1781 A28 25c on 15c #139a
1782 A28 60c on 15c #139a
1783 A28 $1.20 on 2c #134
1784 A28 $1.30 on 15c #139a

Nos. 1032, 1032a Surcharged "12th World Orchid Conference" and "TOKYO JAPAN"

1987, Mar. 12 Unwmk. ***Perf. 14***

1785 A91 650c on 55c #1032
a. 650c on 55c #1032a

No. 280 Surcharged with Names of Post Offices Operating in 1885

Overprints: a, AGRICOLA. b, BAGOTVILLE. c, BOURDA. d, BUXTON. e, CABACABURI. f, CAR- / MICHAEL STREET. g, COTTON / TREE. h, DUNOON. i, FELLOW- / SHIP. j, GROVE. k, HACKNEY. l, LEONORA. m, 1987. n, MALLALI. o, PROVI- / DENCE. p, RELIANCE. q, SPARTA. r, STEWART- / VILLE. s, TARLOGY. t, T.P.O. / BERBICE RIV. u, T.P.O. / DEM. RIV. v, T.P.O. / ESSEQ. RIV. w, T.P.O. / MASSARUNI / RIV. x, TUSCHEN / (De / VRIENDEN). y, ZORG.

Perf. 14x13½

1987, Mar. 17 Wmk. 364

1786 Sheet of 25, #a.-y.
a.-y. A66 25c on 10c, any single

British Guiana Post Office, 125th Anniv.

No. 289A Ovptd. "28 MARCH 1927 / PAA / GEO-POS"

1987, Mar. 28 ***Perf. 13½x13***

1811 A66 $10 on #289A

First Georgetown to Port-of-Spain Flight, 50th Anniv.

No. 285 Surcharged

1987, Apr. 6 ***Perf. 14x13½***

1812 A66 25c on 40c #285

Nos. 87-88, 90, 287 Surcharged or Overprinted "1987"

1987, Apr. ***Perfs. as Before***

Watermarks and Printing Methods as Before

1813 A14 25c on #88
1814 A66 $1 on #287
1815 A14 120c on 6c #87
1816 A14 320c on 6c #87
1817 A14 500c on 40c #90

Issue dates: Nos. 1813, 1815-1817, Apr. 21. No. 1814, Apr.

No. 1461 Ovptd. "CAPEX '87"

1987, June 10 Litho. ***Perf. 14***

1822 A96 320c Pair, #a.-b.
c. on #1461, imperf. between

For surcharges see Nos. 2030, E15.

Nos. 626-628 Ovptd. "1987"

Wmk. 314 Upright

1987, July 15 Engr. ***Perf. 12½x13***

1823 A60 $1.20 on #626

Wmk. 314 Sideways

1824 A60 $1.30 on #627
1825 A60 $2.40 on #628

A99

A100

Locomotives — A101

Designs: Nos. 1826a, 1827a, Alexandra 4. Nos. 1826b, 1827b, Diesel locomotive facing right. Nos. 1826c, 1827c, Steam locomotive facing right. Nos. 1826d, 1827d, Diesel locomotive No. 21 facing left.
Nos. 1829a, 1830b, Alexandra 4. Nos. 1829b, 1830a, Diesel locomotive. Nos. 1829c, 1830d, Steam locomotive facing right. Nos. 1829d, 1830c, Diesel locomotive No. 21. No. 1830e, Photograph of trains in Georgetown Station. No. 1831, Steam locomotive pulling cattle cars, map of routes from Parika to Vreedenhoop and from Georgetown to Rosignol.

1987, Aug. 3 ***Perf. 15***

1826 Block of 4 1.00 1.00
a.-d. A99 $1.20 green, any single .24 .24
1827 Block of 5 3.25 3.25
a.-d. A99 $3.20 blue, any single .65 .65
e. A100 $3.20 blue .65 .65
1828 A101 $12 shown 2.40 2.40
Nos. 1826-1828 (3) 6.65 6.65

1987, Dec. 4

1829 Block of 4 1.15 1.15
a.-d. A99 $1.20 rose lake, any single .28 .28
1830 Block of 5 3.75 3.75
a.-d. A99 $3.30 blk, any single .75 .75
e. A100 $3.30 black .75 .75
1831 A101 $10 multi 2.25 2.25
Nos. 1829-1831 (3) 7.15 7.15

Sizes: Nos. 1827e, 1830e, 84x57mm. Nos. 1828, 1831, 90x40mm.
For surcharges see Nos. E12-E13. For overprints see Nos. 1910-1911, 1935-1938, 2024-2028F, 2054, 2056.

No. 287 Ovptd. "FAIREY NICHOLL / 15 AUG 1927 / GEO-MAB" or "FAIREY NICHOLL / 8 AUG 1927 / GEO-MAZ"

1987, Aug. 7 Litho. ***Perf. 13½x13***

1832 A66 $1 "MAB" on #287
1833 A66 $1 "MAZ" on #287
a. Pair, #1832-1833

No. 1291A Surcharged "CRISTOVAO COLOMBO / 1492 - 1992" (#1834) or "CHRISTOPHE COLOMB / 1492 - 1992" (#1835)

No. 1461c Surcharged "THE PASSING OF HALLEY'S COMET: / PROPHESY OF THE ARRIVAL OF / HERNAN CORTES 1519. / V CENTENARY OF THE LANDING OF / CHRISTOPHER COLUMBUS / IN THE AMERICAS"

Unwmk.

1987, Oct. 9 Litho. ***Perf. 14***

1834 A91 950c on 900c #1291A
1835 A91 950c on 900c #1291A
a. Pair, #1834-1835

Imperf

1836 A96 $20 on 320c #1461c

Nos. 135-136 Surcharged "DEEPAVALI / 1987"

1987, Nov. 2 Litho. ***Perf. 13x13½***

1837 A28 25c on 3c #135
1838 A28 $3 on 5c #136

No. 43 Surcharged "CHRISTMAS / 1987" in Red
No. 1502 Surcharged "1987" in Blue

1987, Nov. 9 ***Perfs. as Before***

Watermarks and Printing Methods as Before

1839 A7 20c on 6c #43

Miniature Sheet

1840 A88 120c on 60c #1502

No. 329 Overprinted "1987"
No. 920 Surcharged "Protect Our Heritage '87" in Red
Nos. 1037, 1040, 1056, 1110-1111, 1494 Surcharged "PROTECT OUR HERITAGE '87"

1987, Dec. 9 ***Perfs. as Before***

Watermarks and Printing Methods as Before

1844 A77 30c Sheet of 12, #a.-l, on #329
1845 A91 120c on #1111
1846 A91 130c on #1110
1847 A91 150c on #1056
1848 A91 180c on #1040
1849 A91 320c on #1137
1850 A89 320c Triptych, #a.-c, on 120c #920
1851 A91 650c on #1494

1988 Summer Olympics, Seoul — A102

1987, Dec. 30 Litho. ***Perf. 13½x14***

1852 A102 $2 Jumping
1853 A102 $3 Discus
1854 A102 $5 Running
a. Strip of 3, #1852-1854

Souvenir Sheet

Perf. 14

1855 A102 $3.50 Olympic Rings, horiz.

Christmas 1987 — A103

Paintings: #a, The Virgin of the Rocks, by Da Vinci. #b, Virgin with Grapes, by Mignard. #c, Sacred Family, by Raphael. #d, Virgin Mary, by Lucas Cranach. No. 1857, Adoration of Three Kings, by Rubens.

1988, Jan. 7 Litho. ***Perf. 14***

1856 A103 $2 Strip of 4, #a.-d.

Souvenir Sheet

1857 A103 $10 Sheet of 1

Dated 1987.

Nos. 397, 405 and 651 Ovptd. or Surcharged "*AUSTRALIA* / 1987 JAMBOREE 1988" in Red

1988, Jan. 7 ***Perf. 13½x13***

1858 A17 $4.40 on #405
1859 A17 $10 on #397
1860 A17 $10 on #651
1861 A17 $10 on #405
a. $10 on #405a

Obliterator on Nos. 1859-1861 is red fleur-de-lis. Size and location of overprint varies.

Nos. 68 and 70 Surcharged "IFAD / For a World / Without Hunger"

Perf. 14x14½

1988, Jan. 26 Photo. Wmk. 364

1862 A68 25c on 1c #68
1863 A68 $5 on 3c #70

No. 1862 uses new denomination as obliterator and No. 1863 uses "X."

Flora and Fauna — A104

Mushrooms: No. 1864a, Corprinus comatus. b, Amanita muscaria. c, Pholiota aurivella. d, Laccaria amethstina.
Birds: No. 1865a, Starling. b, Reed warbler. c, Kingfisher. d, Goldcrest.
Cats: No. 1866a, Himalayan. b, American shorthaired. c, Maine coon. d, Abyssinian.
Cactus flowers: No. 1866e, Sulcorebutia densiseta. f, Subutia hyalacantha. g, Echinopsis. h, Lobivia polycephala.
Nos. 1866a-1866h horiz.

1988, Jan. 28 ***Perf. 14***

1864 A104 $2 Strip of 4, #a.-d.
1865 A104 $2 Strip of 4, #a.-d.

Miniature Sheet

Perf. 14x13½

1866 A104 $2 Sheet of 8, #a.-h.

Dated 1987.

Santa Maria — A105

Ships: Nos. 1867a, 1868a, Santa Maria. Nos. 1867b, 1868b, Grande Francoise. No. 1869, San Martin, horiz.

1988, Feb. 10 Litho. ***Perf. 13½x14***

1867 A105 $7 Pair, #a.-b., pale yel & multi
1868 A105 $7 Pair, #a.-b., bl & multi

Souvenir Sheet

Perf. 14

1869 A105 $7 silver & multi

Discovery of America, 500th anniv. (in 1992). Nos. 1867-1868 printed checkerwise with se-tenant labels describing ship dimensions. No. 1869 exists with gold border.

Nos. 136, 139a, and 146 Surcharged "Republic / Day / 1988" in Blue

Perfs. as Before

1988, Feb. 23 Litho. Wmk. 364

1870 A28 25c on 5c #136
1871 A28 120c on 15c #139a
1872 A28 $10 on $2 #146

No. 283A Surcharged with Names of Post Offices Operating in 1900

Overprints: a, Albouystown. b, Anns Grove. c, Amacura. d, Arakaka. e, Baramanni. f, Cuyuni. g, Hope Placer. h, HMPS. i, Kitty. j, M'M'Zorg. k, Maccaseema. l, 1988. m, Morawhanna. n, Naamryck. o, Purini. p, Potaro / Landing. q, Rockstone. r, Rosignol. s, Stanleytown. t, Santa Rosa. u, Tumatumari. v, Weldaad. w, Wismar. x, TPO Berbice / Railway.

1988, Apr. 5 ***Perf. 14x13½***

1873 Sheet of 25, #a.-k., m.-x., 2 #l.
a.-x. A66 25c on 10c, any single

British Guiana Post Office, 125th Anniv.

No. 725 Surcharged "Olympic / Games / 1988"

Perf. 14½x14

1988, May 3 Litho. Wmk. 373

1897 A73 120c Sheet of 12, #a.-l.

Nos. 136-137 and 146 Surcharged "Caricom Day / 1988"

Perf. 13x13½

1988, June 15 Litho. Wmk. 364

1898 A28 25c on 5c #136
1899 A28 $1.20 on 6c #137
1900 A28 $10 on $2 #146

No. 286A Overprinted

Overprints: a, 1988. b, WHO / 1948-1988.

1988, June 17 Litho. ***Perf. 14x13½***

1901 Sheet of 25, 24 #a., 1 #b.
a.-b. A28 60c any single

World Health Day, 40th anniv.

Nos. 929d Overprinted as Indicated
Nos. 1053a, 1063, 1131, and 1161 Overprinted "CONSERVE / WATER"

Overprints: No. 1903, "CONSERVE TREES" on ocher stamp, "CONSERVE ELECTRICITY on green stamp, "CONSERVE WATER on brown stamp. No. 1904, "CONSERVE ELECTRICITY" on ocher stamp, "CONSERVE WATER on green stamp, "CONSERVE TREES on brown stamp. No. 1905, "CONSERVE WATER" on ocher stamp, "CONSERVE TREES on green stamp, "CONSERVE ELECTRICITY on brown stamp.

1988, July 15 Litho. ***Perfs. as Before***

Watermarks as Before

1903 Triptych
a.-c. A90 120c any single
1904 Triptych
a.-c. A90 120c any single
1905 Triptych
a.-c. A90 120c any single
1906 A91 200c on #1063
1907 A91 200c on #1131
1908 A91 225c on #1053a
1909 A91 350c on #1161

Location and size of overprint varies.

Nos. 1826a and 1829a Ovptd. "BEWARE / OF ANIMALS" (a.)
Nos. 1826b and 1829b Ovptd. "BEWARE / OF CHILDREN" (b.)
Nos. 1826c and 1829c Ovptd. "DRIVE SAFELY" (c.)
Nos. 1826d and 1829d Ovptd. "DO NOT / DRINK AND DRIVE" (d.)

Unwmk.

1988, July 15 Litho. ***Perf. 15***

1910 A99 $1.20 Block of 4, #a.-d., on #1826
1911 A99 $1.20 Block of 4, #a.-d., on #1829

No. 287 Ovptd. or Surcharged

Perf. 13½x13

1988, July Litho. Wmk. 364

1912 A66 $1 "1988" on #287
1913 A66 120c on $1 #287

Nos. 1037a, 1047a, 1056-1057, 1066-1068, 1097, 1099, 1109-1109a, 1110-1111, 1113, 1115, 1122, 1125, 1129, 1147, 1149, and 1155 Ovptd. "CONSERVE / OUR RESOURCES"

1988, July ***Perf. 14***

Watermarks as Before

Design A91

Series 1

Plate Numbers in Parentheses

1914 130c on #1037a (13)
a. Overprint inverted

#1914a probably is as common as #1914.

1915 130c on #1047a (20)
1916 150c on #1056 (26)
1917 120c on #1057 (27)
1918 120c on #1066 (36)
1919 120c on #1067 (37)
1920 130c on #1068 (38)
1921 120c on #1097 (56)
1922 120c on #1099 (58)
1923 100c on #1109 (65)
a. 100c on #1109a
1924 130c on #1110 (66)
1925 120c on #1111 (67)
1926 100c on #1113 (68)
1927 120c on #1115 (69)
1928 250c on #1122 (74)
1929 150c on #1125 (76)
1930 150c on #1129 (78)
1931 150c on #1147 (87)
1932 100c on #1149 (88)
1933 130c on #1155 (91)

Nos. 1827a-1827d and 1830a-1830d Ovptd. with Red Cross

1988, Aug. 3 Litho. ***Perf. 15***

1935 A99 $3.20 Pair, #a.-b., on #1827a, 1827c
1936 A99 $3.20 Pair, #a.-b., on #1827b, 1827d
1937 A99 $3.30 Pair, #a.-b., on #1830a, 1830c
1938 A99 $3.30 Pair, #a.-b., on #1830b, 1830d

Intl. Red Cross, 125th anniv.

Nos. 1038, 1131 Ovptd. and Nos. 1147, 1175 Surcharged "1928-1988 / CRICKET / JUBILEE"

1988, Sept. 5 Litho. ***Perf. 14***

Watermarks as Before

Design A91

Plate Numbers in Parentheses

1939 200c on #1038 (14)
1940 200c on #1131 (79)
1941 800c on 150c #1147 (87)
1942 800c on 160c #1175 (5)

Nos. 1063, 1081, 1139, 1147, 1161, 1185, 1219, 1232, and 1305 Ovptd. and No. 1227 Surcharged "OLYMPIC GAMES / 1988"

1988, Sept. 16 Unwmk.

Design A91

Series 1

Plate Numbers in Parentheses

1943 A91 200c on #1063 (33)
1944 A91 120c on #1081 (46)
1945 A91 300c on #1139 (83)
1946 A91 150c on #1147 (87)
1947 A91 350c on #1161 (94)

Series 2

1948 A91 320c on #1185 (10)
1949 A91 350c on #1219 (29)
1950 A91 300c on 360c #1227 (34)
1951 A91 130c on #1232 (38)
1952 A91 330c on #1305 (82)

Overprint reads up on No. 1947.

Type A83 Ovptd. or Surcharged "OLYMPICS 1988" (a.) or "KOREA 1988" (b.)

1988 Litho. Wmk. 364 ***Perf. 13½***

1953 A83 $1.20 Pair, #a.-b.
1954 A83 130c on $1.20, pair, #a.-b.
1955 A83 150c on $1.20, pair, #a.-b.
1956 A83 200c on $1.20, pair, #a.-b.
1957 A83 350c on $1.20, pair, #a.-b.
c. Strip of 5, #1953a-1957a
d. Strip of 5, #1953b-1957b

Overprint obliterates inscription spelled "LOS ANGELLES."

No. 1087 Ovptd. and No. 1143 Surcharged "V CENTENARY OF / THE LANDING OF / CHRISTOPHER COLUMBUS / IN THE AMERICAS"

Unwmk.

1988, Oct. 12 Litho. ***Perf. 14***

1958 A91 320c on #1087
1959 A91 $15 on 360c #1143

Nos. 1027, 1036, 1040, 1046, 1054, 1062, 1070, 1071, 1074, 1076, 1079, 1102, 1104, 1133, 1137 and 1143 Surcharged "SEASON'S / GREETINGS" in Blue or Black
Nos. 1053, 1053a, 1102, 1591A and 1670F Ovptd. or Surcharged "SEASON'S / GREETINGS / 1988" in Blue

1988, Nov. 10 ***Perfs. as Before***

Watermarks and Printing Methods as Before

Design A91

Plate Numbers in Parentheses

1960 120c on 100c #1027 (6)
1961 120c on 100c #1036 (13)
1962 240c on 180c #1040 (15) (Bk)
1963 120c on 100c #1046 (20)
1964 225c on #1053 (24)
a. 225c on #1053a
1965 120c on 100c #1054 (25)
1966 150c on #1062 (32) (Bk)
1967 260c on #1070 (39) (Bk)
1968 120c on 100c #1071 (40)
1969 120c on 100c #1074 (42)
1970 120c on 100c #1076 (43)
1971 120c on 100c #1079 (45)
1972 225c on #1102 (60) (Bk)
1973 225c on #1102 (60)
1974 150c on #1104 (62) (Bk)
1975 225c on #1591A (65)
1976 330c on #1133 (80) (Bk)
1977 320c on #1137 (82) (Bk)
1978 360c on #1143 (85) (Bk)

Miniature Sheet

1979 225c on #1670F (22)

Size and location of overprint varies.

Nos. 72, 713 and 932 Surcharged or Ovptd. "CHRISTMAS / 1988" in Red or Black

1988, Nov. 16 ***Perfs. as Before***

Watermarks and Printing Methods as Before

1981 A7 20c on 6c #72
1982 A86 Block of 4 (Bk)
a. 120c on #713a
b. 120c on 130c #713b
c. 120c on 150c #713c
d. 120c on 200c #713d
1983 A90a 500c on 330c #932

Overprint reads up on No. 1983.

Nos. 288, 289, and 289A Surcharged or Ovptd. for Prevention of AIDS

Beginnning of overprint reads: Nos. 1984a, 1985e, "Get information..." Nos. 1984b, 1985a, "Get the facts..." Nos. 1984c, 1985b, "Say no to drugs..." Nos. 1984d, 1985c, $2, $5, $10, "Protect yourself..." Nos. 1984e, 1985d, "Be compassionate..."

Perf. 13½x13

1988, Dec. 1 Litho. Wmk. 364

1984 A66 120c Strip of 5, #a.-e., on #289
1985 A66 120c Strip of 5, #a.-e., on #289A
1986 A66 $2 on #288
1987 A66 $5 on #289
1988 A66 $10 on #289A

1988 Winter Olympics, Calgary — A106

Design: $3.50, Olympic rings.

1988, Dec. 1 ***Perf. 14***

1989 A106 $7 Downhill skiing

Souvenir Sheet

1990 A106 $3.50 Sheet of 1

No. 1989 exists in souvenir sheet of 1.

Abolition of Slavery Type of 1985

1988, Dec. 16 Litho. ***Perf. 14***

Designs as Before

1994 A93	25c	brown & black	15	15
1995 A93	60c	magenta & black	28	28
1996 A93	130c	green & black	60	60
1997 A93	150c	blue & black	70	70

Nos. 1087, 1167, and 1200 Surcharged "SALUTING WINNERS / OLYMPIC GAMES / 1988"

Unwmk.

1989, Jan. 3 Litho. ***Perf. 14***

1998 A91 $5.50 on 560c #1167
1999 A91 $9 on 320c #1200
2000 A91 $10.50 on 320c #1087

Miniature Sheets

Red Cross, 125th Anniv. — A108

Designs: No. 2001, Henri Dunant, vert. No. 2002, First maritime ambulance. No. 2003, Red Cross hospital ship in African War. No. 2004, Red Cross air ambulance. No. 2005, Red Cross train.

Nos. 2001-2004 printed with red cross in center of sheet. Each stamp contains part of the red cross at the: a, LR. b, LL. c, UR. d, UL.

Perf. 13½x14, 14x13½

1989, Jan. 5 Litho.

2001 A108 $2 Sheet of 4, #a.-d.
2002 A108 $2 Sheet of 4, #a.-d.
2003 A108 $2 Sheet of 4, #a.-d.
2004 A108 $2 Sheet of 4, #a.-d.

Souvenir Sheet

Perf. 14x13½

2005 A108 $7 Sheet of 1

Dated 1988.

Naval Airship LZ 92, 1916 — A110

Designs: No. 2008b, Astronaut on moon. No. 2008c, Graf Zeppelin over San Francisco Bay, 1929. No. 2008d, Testu-Brissy on horseback ascending in balloon, 1798. No. 2009, Naval Airship LZ 92, 1916, diff.

1989, Jan. 26 ***Perf. 14***

2008 A110 $2 Strip of 4, #a.-d.

Souvenir Sheet

2009 A110 $2 Sheet of 1

Nos. 2008a, 2008c, 2009, Ferdinand von Zeppelin, 150th birth anniv. in 1988. No. 2008b, 1st moon landing, 20th anniv. in 1989. Dated 1988.

Mushrooms — A111

Designs: No. 2010a, Cortinarius bolaris. No. 2010b, Cortinarius laniger. No. 2010c, Tricholoma sulphureum. No. 2010d, Lepiota cristata.

No. 2011, Sarcoscypha coccinea, vert.

1989, Feb. 1 ***Perf. 14x13½***

2010 A111 $2 Block of 4, #a.-d.

Souvenir Sheet

Perf. 13½x14

2011 A111 $5 Sheet of 1

Dated 1988.

Boy Scout Jamboree, Australia — A112

Design: $8, Scouts of different races.

1989, Feb. 10

2012 A112 $10 grn, black & yel

Souvenir Sheet

2013 A112 $8 Sheet of 1

Dated 1988. No. 2012 exists in souvenir sheet of 1.

1988 Summer Olympics, Seoul — A113

Designs: No. 2014, Florence Griffith-Joyner. No. 2015, Carl Lewis. No. 2016, Equestrian. No. 2017, Runners, horiz. No. 2018, City skyline, Olympic Rings, horiz. No. 2019, 1988 & 1992 Olympic mascots, horiz. No. 2022, Griffith-Joyner, Lewis, horiz. No. 2023, Cosmic Athlete by Dali, horiz.

1989, Feb. 15 Litho. ***Perf. 14***

2014 A113 $2 multicolored
2015 A113 $2 multicolored
2016 A113 $2 multicolored
2017 A113 $2 multicolored
2018 A113 $2 multicolored
2019 A113 $2 multicolored

Souvenir Sheets

2022 A113 $3.50 multicolored
2023 A113 $3.50 multicolored

No. 2023 exists with gold border and inscriptions. Nos. 2014-2019 inscribed 1988.

Nos. 1826, 1829 and 1831 Ovptd. "REPUBLIC DAY 1989" in Red

1989, Feb. 22 Litho. ***Perf. 15***

2024 A99 $1.20 Block of 4, #a.-d., on #1826
2025 A99 $1.20 Block of 4, #a.-d., on #1829
2026 A101 $10 on #1831

Nos. 1827a-1827d and 1830a-1830d Surcharged in Red

1989, Feb. 22

2027 A99 $5 Pair, #a.-b., on $3.20 #a., c.
2028 A99 $5 Pair, #a.-b., on $3.20 #b., d.
2028C A99 $5 Pair, #d.-e., on $3.30 #a., c.
2028F A99 $5 Pair, #g.-h., on $3.30 #b., d.

Nos. 1461, 1822 Surcharged in Red

1989, Feb. 22 Litho. ***Perf. 14***

2029 A96 $10 #a.-b. on #1461
2030 A96 $10 #a.-b. on #1822

No. 1188 Surcharged "EASTER"

1989, Mar. 22 ***Perf. 14***

2031 A91 Sheet of 4 on #1188
a. 125c on 320c #1188
b. 250c on 320c #1188
c. 300c on 320c #1188
d. 350c on 320c #1188

No. 927 Surcharged

1989, Mar. Wmk. 364 ***Perf. 14***

2032 A90 250c on 25c #927

Inscribed "1986."

No. 1197 Surcharged "RED CROSS / 1948 / 1988"

1989, Apr. Unwmk. ***Perf. 14***

2033 A91 375c on 45c #1197
2034 A91 425c on 45c #1197

Guyana Red Cross, 40th anniv.

Nos. 1252 and 1263 Surcharged "ALL FOR / HEALTH" (a.) or "HEALTH / FOR ALL" (b.)

1989, Apr. 3

2035 Pair
2036 Pair

For surcharge see No. 2052.

Nos. 1224-1225, and 1254 Overprinted or Surcharged "BOY SCOUTS / 1924 1989" (a.) or "GIRL GUIDES / 1924 1989" (b.) Nos. 1272-1273 Surcharged "LADY BADEN POWELL / 1889-1989"

1989, Apr. 11

2037 A91 250c on 100c, pair, #a.-b.
2038 A91 $2.50 on 50c, pair, #a.-b.
2039 A91 300c Pair, #a.-b.
c. Pair, #d.-e., Prussian bl ovpt.
2040 A91 $25 on 280c #1272
a. Prussian blue overprint
2041 A91 $25 on 700c #1273
a. Prussian blue overprint

Nos. 2037-2039, Boy Scouts in Guyana, 80th anniversary and Girl Guides, 65th anniversary. Nos. 2040-2041, Lady Baden Powell, birth centenary.

No. 1177 Surcharged "PHOTOGRAPHY / 1839-1989"

1989, Apr. 15

2042 A91 550c on 390c
2043 A91 650c on 390c, 2 bar obliterator
a. 6 bar obliterator

Nos. 2042-2043 printed in sheets of 4 with alternating overprints.

No. 1263 Surcharged "I.L.O. / 1919-1989"

1989, May 2

2044 A91 300c on 75c #1263

Intl. Labor Organization, 70th anniversary.

Nos. 43, 87, 134-137, 280, 285, and 286A 288, 1827, 1830, and 2035-2036 Surcharged in Black or Blue

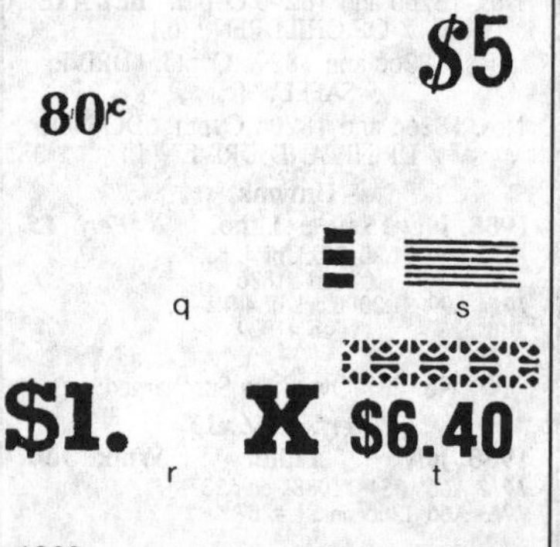

1989 ***Perfs. as Before***

Watermarks and Printing Methods as Before

2045 A7(q) 80c on 6c #43
a. A7 80c on 6c #43
2046 A28(q) $1 on 2c #134
a. A28(r) $1 on 2c #134
2047 A28(q) $2.05 on 3c #135
2048 A28(q) $2.55 on 5c #136
a. A28(r) $2.55 on 5c #136
2049 A28(q) $3.25 on 6c #137
a. A28(r) $3.25 on 6c #137
2050 A14(q) $5 on 6c #87
a. A14(s) $5 on 6c #87
2052 A91 640c Pair, #2036
2053 A66(q) $6.40 on 10c #280
a. A66 $6.40 on 10c #280
2054 Block of 5, #a.-e. on #1830
a. A99(t) $6.40 on $3.30 #a.-d.
b. A100(t) $190 on $3.30 #e.
2055 A66 $7.65 on 40c #285
2056 Block of 5, #a.-e. on #1827
a. A99(t) $7.65 on $3.20 #a.-d.
b. A100(t) $225 on $3.20 #e.
2057 A66(q) $8.90 on 60c #286A
a. A66 $8.90 on 60c #286A
2058 A66(r) $50 on $2 #288 (Bl)
2059 A66(r) $100 on $2 #288

Issue dates: #2045a, 2053-2053a, 2055, May 18. #2057, May 26. #2058-2059, June 5. #2045, 2049, 2046a, 2048a, 2049a, June 15. #2050-2050a, 2051, 2052, 2054, 2056, Aug. 16.

Nos. 2045a, 2053a, 2055, 2057a have no obliterator. New denominations are larger on Nos. 2045a, 2053a and 2057a. No. 2045a has no cent sign.

Nos. 2054b, 2056b additionally overprinted "SPECIAL DELIVERY."

No. 1244 Surcharged "CARICOM / DAY"

Unwmk.

1989, June 26 Litho. ***Perf. 14***

2064 A91 125c on 200c #1244, 2 bar obliterator
a. 125c on 200c #1244, 6 bar obliterator

No. 280 Ovptd. in Gold or Silver for Gold Medalists at 1988 Summer Olympics

Overprints read: Nos. 2082a, 2083a, "SEOUL / OLYMPICS." Nos. 2082b, 2083b, "Men's 800M / Ereng / Kenya." Nos. 2082c, 2083c, "KOREA." Nos. 2082d, 2083d, "Men's / Gymnastics / Artemov / USSR." Nos. 2082e, 2083e, "Men's / Swimming / Louganis / USA." Nos. 2082f, 2083f, "Woman's / Swimming / Otto / DDR." Nos. 2082g, 2083g, "Men's Fencing / Lamour / France." Nos. 2082h, 2083h, "Men's / Gymnastics / Lou / China." Nos. 2082i, 2083i, "Women's / Cycling / Knol / Holland." Nos. 2082j, 2083j, "Men's / Swimming / Szabo / Hungary." Nos. 2082k, 2083k, "1988." Nos. 2082l, 2083l, "Men's / Swimming / Nesty / Suriname." Nos. 2082m, 2083m, "Men's Boxing / Lewis / Canada." Nos. 2082n, 2083n, "Men's Javelin / Korjus / Finland." Nos. 2082o, 2083o, "Basketball / USA." Nos. 2082p, 2083p, "Men's / Equestrian / Klimke / W. Germany." Nos. 2082q, 2083q, "Men's Boxing / Park / Korea." Nos. 2082r, 2083r, "Women's / Marathon / Mota / Portugal." Nos. 2082s, 2083s, "Men's / Swimming / Suzuki / Japan."

Nos. 2084a, 2085a, "Men's 100M / Lewis / USA." Nos. 2084b, 2085b, "Men's / Pole Vault / Bubka / USSR." Nos. 2084c, 2085c, "Women's / 100-200m / Joyner / USA." Nos. 2084d, 2085d, "Men's Pentathlon / Martinek / Hungary." Nos. 2084e, 2085e, "Men's Wrestling / Sako / Japan." Nos. 2084f, 2085f, "Men's Judo / Saito / Japan." Nos. 2084g, 2085g, "Women's 800M / Wodars / DDR." Nos. 2084h, 2085h, "Men's Boxing / Gross / W. Germany." Nos. 2084i, 2085i, "Men's Boxing / Maske / DDR." Nos. 2084j, 2085j, "Men's Boxing / Kim / Korea." Nos. 2084k, 2085k, "Woman's / Swimming / Evans / USA." Nos. 2084l, 2085l, "Soccer / USSR." Nos. 2084m, 2085m, "Woman's / Gymnastics / Silivas / Romania." Nos. 2084n, 2085n, "Men's Boxing / Mercer / USA." Nos. 2084o, 2085o, "Men's Marathon / Bordin / Italy." Nos. 2084p, 2085p, "Women's Tennis / Graf / W. Germany."

Perf. 14x13½

1989, Apr. Litho. Wmk. 364

Sheets of 25

2082 5 #a., 3 #c., #b., d.-s.
a.-s. A66 10c on #280, any single
2083 5 #a., 3 #c., #b., d.-s. (S)
a.-s. A66 10c on #280, any single
2084 #a.-p., 5 #2082a, 3 #2082c, #2082k
a.-p. A66 10c on #280, any single
2085 #a.-p., 5 #2083a, 3 #2083c, #2083k (S)
a.-p. A66 10c on #280, any single

Nos. 280 Ovptd. in Gold or Silver for Gold Medalists at 1988 Winter Olympics

Overprints read: Nos. 2086a, 2087a, "Gold Medal / Winners." Nos. 2086b, 2087b, "Ice Hockey / USSR." Nos. 2086c, 2087c, "CALGARY / OLYMPICS." Nos. 2086d, 2087d, "Bobsled / Kipours-Kozlov / USSR." Nos. 2086e, 2087e, "Women's Skating / 1500-3000-5000M / Gennip / Netherlands." Nos. 2086f, 2087f, "Men's / Speed / Skating / 5000-10000M / Gustafson / Sweden." Nos. 2086g, 2087g, "Men's Figure / Skating / Boitano / USA." Nos. 2086h, 2087h, "Women's / 500M Skating / Blair / USA." Nos. 2086i, 2087i, "Women's / Figure Skating / Witt / DDR." Nos. 2086j, 2087j, "Men's Giant / Slalom / Tomba / Italy." Nos. 2086k, 2087k, "CANADA." Nos. 2086l, 2087l, "Men's Super / Giant Slalom / Picard / France." Nos. 2086m, 2087m, "Women's / Downhill Skiing / Kiehl / W. Germany." Nos. 2086n, 2087n, "Men's 50km Skiing Svan / Sweden." Nos. 2086o, 2087o, "Men's Nordic / Combined Skiing / Mueller-Pohl / Schwarz / W. Germany." Nos. 2086p, 2087p, "Women's / Giant Slalom / Schneider / Switzerland." Nos. 2086q, 2087q, "Women's / 5-km Skiing / Matikainen / Finland." Nos. 2086r, 2087r, "Men's Downhill / Alpine Skiing / Zurbriggen / Switzerland." Nos. 2086s, 2087s, "Men's Ski / Jumping / Nykanen / Finland."

1989, Apr.

2086 4 #a., 3 #c., #b., d.-s., #2082k
a.-s. A66 10c on #280, any single
2087 4 #a., 3 #c., #b., d.-s., #2083k (S)
a.-s. A66 10c on #280, any single

No. 281 Ovptd. in Gold or Silver in Memory of Hirohito, Emperor of Japan

Overprints read: Nos. 2088a, 2089a, "Emperor / Hirohito." Nos. 2088b, 2089b, "Showa / Era." Nos. 2088c, 2089c, "Chrysanthemum / Dynasty." Nos. 2088d, 2089d, "Emperor / of Japan." Nos. 2088e, 2089e, "1901." Nos. 2088f, 2089f, "1989." Nos. 2088g, 2089g, "Emperor / Hirohito / 1901-1989."

1989, Apr.

2088 5 #a., 4 #c.-d., 9 #b., #e.-g.
a.-g. A66 15c on #281, any single
2089 5 #a., 4 #c.-d., 9 #b., #e.-g. (S)
a.-g. A66 15c on #281, any single

No. 280 Ovptd. in Gold or Silver for Enthronment of Akihito, Emperor of Japan

Overprints reads: Nos. 2090a, 2091a, "Honoring / His / Majesty." Nos. 2090b, 2091b, "Emperor / of / Japan." Nos. 2090c, 2091c, "1989." Nos. 2090d, 2091d, "HEISI / ERA."

1989, Apr.

2090 12 #a, 8 #b., 4 #c., #d.
a.-d. A66 10c on #280, any single
2091 12 #a., 8 #b., 4 #c., #d. (S)
a.-d. A66 10c on #280, any single

Overprint is 10mm long on #2090c, 2091c.

Nos. 280-281 and 283 Ovptd. with Emblems of Scouts, Rotary Intl., and Lions Intl. in Gold, Silver, Metallic Red, Metallic Green and Black

Overprints: Nos. 2092a, 2093a, 2094a, 2095a, 2096b, 2097b, 2098b, 2099b, 2100c, 2101c, 2102c, 2103c, Scouting emblem. Nos. 2092b, 2093b, 2094b, 2095b, 2096a, 2097a, 2098a, 2099a, 2100b, 2101b, 2102b, 2103b, Rotary emblem. Nos. 2092c, 2093c, 2094c, 2095c, 2096c, 2097c, 2098c, 2099c, 2100a, 2101a, 2102a, 2103a, Lions emblem. Nos. 2092d, 2093d, 2094d, 2095d, 2096d, 2097d, 2098d, 2099d, 2100d, 2101d, 2102d, 2103d, "1989." Nos. 2092e, 2093e, 2094e, 2095e, Large scouting emblem. Nos. 2096e, 2097e, 2098e, 2099e, Large Rotary emblem. Nos. 2100e, 2101e, 2102e, 2103e, Large Lions emblem.

1989, Apr.

2092 8 #a.-b., 6 #c., 2 #d., #e.
a.-e. A66 10c on #280, any single
2093 8 #a.-b., 6 #c., 2 #d., #e. (S)
a.-e. A66 10c on #280, any single
2094 8 #a.-b., 6 #c., 2 #d., #e. (R)
a.-e. A66 10c on #280, any single
2095 8 #a.-b., 6 #c., 2 #d., #e. (Bk)
a.-e. A66 10c on #280, any single
2096 8 #a.-b., 6 #c., 2 #d., #e.
a.-e. A66 15c on #281, any single
2097 8 #a.-b., 6 #c., 2 #d., #e. (S)
a.-e. A66 15c on #281, any single
2098 8 #a.-b., 6 #c., 2 #d., #e. (R)
a.-e. A66 15c on #281, any single
2099 8 #a.-b., 6 #c., 2 #d., #e. (Gr)
a.-e. A66 15c on #281, any single
2100 8 #a.-b., 6 #c., 2 #d., #e.
a.-e. A66 25c on #283, any single
2101 8 #a.-b., 6 #c., 2 #d., #e. (S)
a.-e. A66 25c on #283, any single
2102 8 #a.-b., 6 #c., 2 #d., #e. (R)
a.-e. A66 25c on #283, any single
2103 8 #a.-b., 6 #c., 2 #d., #e. (Gr)
a.-e. A66 25c on #283, any single

"1989" overprints are 7½mm long.

No. 280 Ovptd. in Gold or Silver for Halley's Comet

Overprints read: Nos. 2104a, 2105a, "Halley's / Comet." Nos. 2104b, 2105b, "Famous / Space Event." Nos. 2104c, 2105c, "Edmund / Halley / 1656-1742." Nos. 2104d, 2105d, "1910." Nos. 2104e, 2105e, "1986."

1989, Apr.

2104 11 #a., 6 #b., 4 #c., 2 #d.-e.
a.-e. A66 10c on #280, any single
2105 11 #a., 6 #b., 4 #c., 2 #d.-e. (S)
a.-e. A66 10c on #280, any single

No. 280 Ovptd. in Gold or Silver for Space Achievements

Overprints read: Nos. 2106a, 2107a, "Sputnik I / Oct. 4, 1957." Nos. 2106b, 2107b, "Explorer I / Jan. 31, 1958." Nos. 2106c, 2107c, "Sputnik II / Laika / Spacedog / Nov. 3, 1957." Nos. 2106d, 2107d, "Alan Shepard, Jr. / Mercury III / May 5, 1961." Nos. 2106e, 2107e, "Yuri Gagarin / Vostok I / April 12, 1961." Nos. 2106f, 2107f, "John Glenn / Mercury VI / Feb. 20, 1962." Nos. 2106g, 2107g, "Vostok III / Vostok IV / Aug. 12, 1962." Nos. 2106h, 2107h, "Grissom-Young / Gemini III / March 23, 1965." Nos. 2106i, 2107i, "Luna III / Oct. 4, 1959." Nos. 2106j, 2107j, "Edward H. White II / Gemini IV / June 3, 1965." Nos. 2106k, 2107k, "V. Tereshkova / First Woman / in Space / June 16-19, 1963." Nos. 2106 l, 2107 l, "Surveyor I / June 2, 1966." Nos. 2106m, 2107m, "Space / Achievements." Nos. 2106n, 2107n, "Voskod I / First 3 Man Crew / Oct. 12-13, 1964." Nos. 2106o, 2107o, "Apollo I / Jan. 27, 1967." Nos. 2106p, 2107p, "Alexei A. Leonov / First Walk in Space / March 18-19, 1965." Nos. 2106q, 2107q, "Apollo VIII / Dec. 21-27, 1968." Nos. 2106r, 2107r, "V. Komarov / Soyuz I / April 24, 1967." Nos. 2106s, 2107s, "Apollo XI / First Man on Moon / July 20, 1969." Nos. 2106t, 2107t, "Lunokhod 1 / Dec. 10, 1970." Nos. 2106u, 2107u, "Apollo XIII / April 11-17, / 1970." Nos. 2106v, 2107v, "Soyuz XI / June 30, 1971." Nos. 2106w, 2107w, "Viking I / July 20, 1976." Nos. 2106x, 2107x, "Vega I / March 6, 1986." Nos. 2106y, 2107y, "Columbia Sts-1 / April 12-14, / 1981."

1989, Apr.

2106 #a.-y.
a.-y. A66 10c on #280, any single
2107 #a.-y. (S)
a.-y. A66 10c on #280, any single

No. 280 Ovptd. in Gold or Silver

Overprints read: Nos. 2108a, 2109a, "1969- / 1989." Nos. 2108b, 2109b, "Apollo XI." Nos. 2108c, 2109c, "First Man / on Moon." Nos. 2108d, 2109d, "USA." Nos. 2108e, 2109e, "Neil A. / Armstrong." Nos. 2108f, 2109f, "Col. Edwin E. / Aldrin, Jr." Nos. 2108g, 2109g, "Lt. Col. / Michael / Collins."

1989, Apr.

2108 5 #a, 7 #b., 4 #c., 6 #d., #e.-g.
a.-g. A66 10c on #280, any single
2109 5 #a., 7 #b., 4 #c., 6 #d., #e.-g. (S)
a.-g. A66 10c on #280, any single

Moon Landing, 20th anniv.

No. 281 Ovptd. in Gold or Silver for Space Shuttle Program

Overprints read: Nos. 2110a, 2111a, "Enterprise / Aug. 12, 1977." Nos. 2110b, 2111b, "Columbia / April 12, 1981." Nos. 2110c, 2111c, "Space / Shuttles." Nos. 2110d, 2111d, "Discovery / Aug. 30, 1984." Nos. 2110e, 2111e, "Atlantis / Oct. 3, 1985." Nos. 2110f, 2111f, "Challenger / Heroes." Nos. 2110g, 2111g, "Resnik / McAuliffe / Jarvis." Nos. 2110h, 2111h, "In Memoriam / Challenger / Jan. 28, 1986." Nos. 2110i, 2111i, "Onizuka / Smith / McNair / Scobee."

1989, Apr.

2110 4 #a.-e., 2 #f., #g.-i.
a.-i. A66 15c on #281, any single
2111 4 #a.-e., 2 #f., #g.-i. (S)
a.-i. A66 15c on #281, any single

Butterflies — A115

1989, Sept. 7			Litho.	Perf. 14	
2208	A115	80c	Stalachtis calliope	15	15
2209	A115	$2.25	Morpho rhetenor	15	15
2210	A115	$5	Agrias claudia	30	30
2211	A115	$6.40	Marpesia marcella	40	40
2212	A115	$7.65	Papilio zagreus	45	45
2213	A115	$8.90	Chorinea faunus	55	55
2214	A115	$25	Cepheuptychia cephus	1.50	1.50
2215	A115	$100	Nessaea regina	6.00	6.00
			Nos. 2208-2215 (8)	9.50	9.50

See Nos. E16-E17. For overprints see Nos. 2251-2254, 2256-2257, 2260-2261, 2283-2290, E19-E22, E24, E26-E27, E31.

Women in Space, 25th Anniv. (in 1988) — A116

Designs: $6.40, Kathryn Sullivan, 1st US woman to walk in space. $12.80, Svetlana Savitskaya, 1st Soviet woman to walk in space. $15.30, Judy Resnik & Christa McAuliffe, astronauts killed in Challenger explosion. $100, Sally Ride, 1st US woman astronaut.

1989, Nov. 8					
2216	A116	$6.40	multicolored	40	40
2217	A116	$12.80	multicolored	75	75
2218	A116	$15.30	multicolored	92	92
2219	A116	$100	multicolored	6.40	6.40

See No. E18. For overprints see Nos. 2255, 2258-2259, 2262, E23, E25, E28, E32.

1990 World Cup Soccer Championships, Italy — A117

Various soccer players.

Perf. 14x13½, 13½x14

1989, Nov. 20			
2220	A117	$2.55	shown
2221	A117	$2.55	Yellow shirt, vert.
2222	A117	$2.55	Goalie
2223	A117	$2.55	Green shirt, vert.

Souvenir Sheet

2224 A117 $20 Championships emblem, vert.

#2220-2223 exist in souvenir sheets of 1. For surcharges see Nos. 2263-2267.

No. 134-136 Surcharged "AHMADIYYA / CENTENARY / 1889-1989"

Perf. 13x13½

1989, Nov. 22		Litho.	Wmk. 364
2225	A28	80c	on 2c #134
2226	A28	$6.40	on 3c #135
2227	A28	$8.90	on 5c #136

1992 Summer Olympics, Barcelona A118

1989, Dec. 5		*Perf. 13½x14, 14x13½*	
2228	A118	$2.55	shown
2229	A118	$2.55	Boxing, horiz.
2230	A118	$2.55	Chariot racing, horiz.
2231	A118	$2.55	Javelin, horiz.
2232	A118	$2.55	Running, horiz.
2233	A118	$2.55	Wrestling

Souvenir Sheets

2234 A118 $10 Running, horiz., diff.
2235 A118 $10 Columbus Walk by Picasso

#2228-2233 exist in souvenir sheets of 1.

Christmas — A119

Paintings: No. 2236, Child Declaring in Favor of His Mother, by Titian. No. 2237, The Sacred Family, by Rubens. No. 2238, Saint Anne, the Virgin and Child, by Durer. No. 2239, Madonna Enthroned, Surrounded by Saints, by Rubens. $20, Saint Ildefonso, by Rubens.

Perf. 14x13½, 13½x14

1989, Dec. 26			
2236	A119	$2.55	multicolored
2237	A119	$2.55	multi, vert.
2238	A119	$2.55	multi, vert.
2239	A119	$2.55	multi, vert.

Souvenir Sheet

2240 A119 $20 multi, vert.

#2236-2239 exist in souvenir sheets of 1.

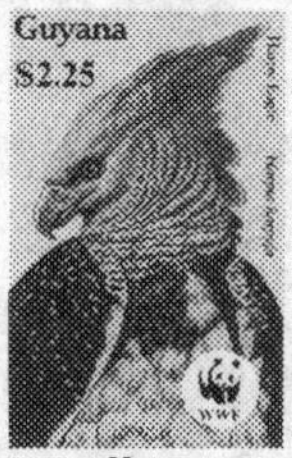

Harpy Eagle — A120

Channel-billed Toucan — A121

1990, Jan. 23			Litho.	Perf. 14	
2241	A120	$2.25	Eagle's head	15	15
2242	A120	$5	Eagle with prey	32	32
2243	A120	$8.90	Eagle facing right	58	58
2244	A121	$15	shown	1.00	1.00
2245	A121	$25	Blue & yellow macaw	1.50	1.50
2246	A120	$30	Eagle facing left	2.00	2.00
2247	A121	$50	Wattled jacana, horiz.	3.00	3.00
2248	A121	$60	Hoatzin, horiz.	4.00	4.00
			Nos. 2241-2248 (8)	12.55	12.55

Souvenir Sheets

2249	A121	$100	Great kiskadee, horiz.	6.25	6.25
2250	A121	$100	Amazon kingfisher, horiz.	6.25	6.25

Nos. 2241-2243, 2246, World Wildlife Fund.

Nos. 2208-2184 Ovptd. in Silver with Rotary Emblem and "ROTARY INTERNATIONAL 1905-1990" on 2 or 3 Lines

1990, Mar. 15			
2251	A115	80c	on #2208
2252	A115	$2.25	on #2209
2253	A115	$5	on #2210
2254	A115	$6.40	on #2211
2255	A116	$6.40	on #2216
2256	A115	$7.65	on #2212
2257	A115	$8.90	on #2213
2258	A116	$12.80	on #2217
2259	A116	$15.30	on #2218
2260	A115	$25	on #2214
2261	A115	$100	on #2215
2262	A116	$100	on #2219

Nos. 2220-2222, 2224 Surcharged "GERMANY / CHAMPION"

No. 2223 Surcharged "GERMANY / CHAMPION / ARGENTINA / SUB-CHAMPION"

1990			*Perfs. as Before*
2263	A117	$75	on #2220
2264	A117	$75	on #2221
2265	A117	$75	on #2222
2266	A117	$75	on #2223

Souvenir Sheet

2267 A117 $225 on #2224

#2263-2266 exist in souvenir sheets of 1.

Miniature Sheets

Penny Black, 150th Anniv., 500th Anniv. of Thurn & Taxis Postal Service
A122

Designs: No. 2268a, Banghy Post runner, 1832. b, Penny Black, Sir Rowland Hill. c, Dutch mail ship. d, Paddle steamer Monarch, 1830. e, Paddle steamer Hindostan, 1842. f, Mail steamer Chusan. g, Sailing ship Madagascar, 1853. h, Paddle steamer Orinoco, 1855. i, Packet Orpheus, 1835.

No. 2269a, Imperial postal messenger. b, Swiss messenger, 1499. c, River messenger, 15th century. d, Russian courier, Middle Ages. e, Oldenburg postilions, 1820. f, Indian mail coach, 1829. g, Baden mail coach postilions, 1820. h, Pony Express, 1860. i, Camel rider.

No. 2270a, Mail coach, 1840. b, Danish Ball Post, 1815. c, Australian Bush mailman, 1838. d, Japanese postmen, 1870. e, Mail cart, 1857. f, Russian mail troika. g, Wells, Fargo Overland Express. h, Phantoms of the Night, 1853. i, Cobb & Co. coach, Australia.

No. 2271a, Postilions, 1850. b, Mounted postilion, Holland. c, Paddle steamer Arctic, 1850. d, Peruvian swimming couriers. e, First London post box, 1855. f, Indian mail cart, 1870. g, Balloon post, 1870. h, Bath Mail Coach. i, Postrider, 1837.

No. 2272a, Northeastern Railway post office. b, Traveling post office, 1838. c, American Express. d, Graf Zeppelin. e, Columbia Post airplane, 1925. f, Calcutta flying boat. g, Junkers JU-52/3M mail plane. h, Douglas M2 mail plane. i, US air mail service, DH-4.

No. 2273a, First Atlantic Airways. b, Morris post office van, 1931. c, Swiss post-passenger bus. d, Westland-Sikorsky S51 helicopter mail flight. e, Union Pacific Railway. f, Boeing Model 314 flying boat, Yankee Clipper. g, Boeing 747. h, Concorde. i, Apollo 11, US #C69.

No. 2274, Mounted postilion. No. 2275, Thurn & Taxis #7. No. 2276, Thurn & Taxis #45.

1990, May 3

Sheets of 9

2268	A122	$15.30	#a.-i.	6.90	6.90
2269	A122	$15.30	#a.-i.	6.90	6.90
2270	A122	$15.30	#a.-i.	6.90	6.90
2271	A122	$17.80	#a.-i.	8.00	8.00
2272	A122	$20	#a.-i.	9.00	9.00
2273	A122	$20	#a.-i.	9.00	9.00
	Nos. 2268-2273 (6)			46.70	46.70

Souvenir Sheets

2274	A122	$150	multi	7.50	7.50
2275	A122	$150	multi	7.50	7.50
2276	A122	$150	multi	7.50	7.50

For overprint see No. 2551.

Nos. 1028, 1032, 1055, 1085, 1107 Surcharged "ROTARY / DISTRICT 405 / 9th CONFERENCE / MAY 1990 / GEORGETOWN"

Unwmk.

1990, May 8 **Litho.** ***Perf. 14***

Design A91

Plate Numbers in Parentheses

2277	80c on 55c #1032 (9)	
2278	80c on 55c #1085 (49)	
2279	80c on 55c #1107 (64)	
2280	$6.40 on 130c #1028 (6)	
2281	$6.40 on 130c #1055 (25)	
2282	$7.65 on 130c #1055 (25)	

Nos. 2208-2215 Overprinted

90th Birthday
H.M. The Queen Mother

1990, June 8 **Litho.** ***Perf. 14***

2283	A115	80c	on #2208	15	15
2284	A115	$2.25	on #2209	15	15
2285	A115	$5	on #2210	30	30
2286	A115	$6.40	on #2211	40	40
2287	A115	$7.65	on #2212	45	45
2288	A115	$8.90	on #2213	55	55
2289	A115	$25	on #2214	1.50	1.50
2290	A115	$100	on #2215	6.00	6.00
	Nos. 2283-2290 (8)			9.50	9.50

See Nos. E26-E27.

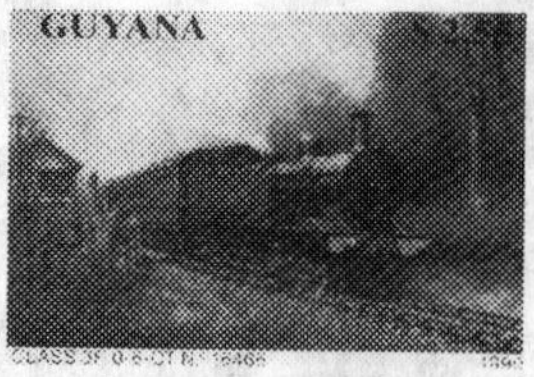

Locomotives — A123

1990, July 15 ***Perf. 14x13½***

2291	A123	$2.55	Class 3F
2292	A123	$2.55	Class A4
2293	A123	$2.55	Liner Class A34
2294	A123	$2.55	Pacific Class
2295	A123	$2.55	Grange Class

Souvenir Sheets

Perf. 13½x14, 14x13½

2296	A123	$20	Castle Class, vert.
2297	A123	$20	Southern Railway

Still Life with Guitar, by Picasso — A124

Paintings: No. 2299, Horseman, by Velazquez. No. 2300, Sunflowers, by Van Gogh, vert. No. 2301, Man Wearing Striped Shirt, by Miro, vert. No. 2302, Franz von Taxis, by Durer, vert. No. 2303, Virgin and Child, by Titian, vert. No. 2304, Presentation of Marie de Medici, by Rubens, vert.

Perf. 14x13½, 13½x14

1990, Aug. 1 **Litho.**

2298	A124	$2.55	multicolored
2299	A124	$2.55	multicolored
2300	A124	$2.55	multicolored
2301	A124	$2.55	multicolored
2302	A124	$2.55	multicolored

Souvenir Sheets

2303	A124	$20	multicolored
2304	A124	$20	multicolored

Postal System of Thurn and Taxis, 500th anniv. (#2302). Titian, 500th birth anniv. (#2303). Rubens, 350th death anniv. (#2304).

Birds — A125

Designs: 80c, Guiana partridge, horiz. $2.55, Collared trogon. $3.25, Derby aracari. $5, Black-necked aracari. $5.10, Green aracari. $5.80, Ivory-billed aracari. $6.40, Guiana toucanet. $6.50, Sulphur-breasted toucan. $7.55, Red-billed toucan. $7.65, Toco toucan. $8.25, Natterers toucanet. $8.90, Welcome trogon. $9.75, Doubtful trogon. $11.40, Banded aracari. $12.65, Golden-headed train bearer. $12.80, Rufus-breasted hermit. $13.90, Band-tail barbthroat. $15.30, White-tipped sickle bill. $17.80, Black jacobin. $19.20, Fiery topaz. $22.95, Tufted coquette. $26.70, Ecuadorian pied-tail. $30, Quetzal. $50, Green-crowned brilliant. $100, Emerald-chinned hummingbird. $190, Lazuline sabre-wing. $225, Berylline hummingbird.

1990, Sept. 12 **Litho.** ***Perf. 14***

2305	A125	80c	multi	15	15
2306	A125	$2.55	multi	15	15
2307	A125	$3.25	multi	15	15
2308	A125	$5	multi	15	15
2309	A125	$5.10	multi	15	15
2310	A125	$5.80	multi	15	15
2311	A125	$6.40	multi	16	16
2312	A125	$6.50	multi	16	16
2313	A125	$7.55	multi	18	18
2314	A125	$7.65	multi	18	18
2315	A125	$8.25	multi	20	20
2316	A125	$8.90	multi	22	22
2317	A125	$9.75	multi	24	24
2318	A125	$11.40	multi	28	28
2319	A125	$12.65	multi	32	32
2320	A125	$12.80	multi	32	32
2321	A125	$13.90	multi	35	35
2322	A125	$15.30	multi	38	38
2323	A125	$17.80	multi	45	45
2324	A125	$19.20	multi	48	48
2325	A125	$22.95	multi	58	58
2326	A125	$26.70	multi	68	68
2327	A125	$30	multi	75	75
2328	A125	$50	multi	1.25	1.25
2329	A125	$100	multi	2.50	2.50
2330	A125	$190	multi	4.75	4.75
2331	A125	$225	multi	5.65	5.65
	Nos. 2305-2331 (27)			20.98	20.98

Butterflies — A126

Designs: No. 2340a, Thecla falerina. b, Pheles heliconides. c, Echenais leucocyana. d, Heliconius xanthocles. e, Mesopthalma idotea. f, Parides aeneas. g, Heliconius numata. h, Thecla critola. i, Themone pais. j, Nymula agle. k, Adelpha cocala. l, Anaea eribotes. m, Prepona demophon. n, Selenophanes cassiope. o, Consul hippona. p, Antirrhaea avernus.

No. 2341a, Thecla telemus. b, Thyridia confusa. c, Heliconius burneyi. d, Parides lysander. e, Eunica orphise. f, Adelpha melona. g, Morpho menelaus. h, Nymula phylleus. i, Stalachtis phlegia. j, Theope barea. k, Morpho perseus. l, Lycorea ceres. m, Archonias bellona. n, Caerois chorinaeus. o, Vila azeca. p, Nessaea batesii.

No. 2342a, Heliconius silvana. b, Eunica alcmena. c, Mechanitis polymnia. d, Mesosemia ephyne. e, Thecla erema. f, Callizona acesta. g, Stalachtis phaedusa. h, Battus belus. i, Nymula phliasus. j, Parides childrenae. k, Stalachtis euterpe. l, Dysmathia portia. m, Tithorea hermias. n, Prepona pheridamas. o, Dismorphia fortunata. p, Hamadryas amphinome.

No. 2343a, Heliconius vetustus. b, Mesosemia eumene. c, Parides phosphorus. d, Polystichtis emylius. e, Xanthocleis aedesia. f, Doxocopa agathina. g, Adelpha plesaure. h, Heliconius wallacei. i, Notheme eumeus. j, Melinaea mediatrix. k, Theritas coronata. l, Dismorphia orise. m, Phycicodes ianthe. n, Morpho aega. o, Zaretis isidora. p, Pierella lena.

Nos. 2340-2341 are horiz.

1990, Sept. 26 **Litho.** ***Perf. 14***

2332	A126	80c	Melinaea idae	15	15
2333	A126	$2.55	Rhetus dysonii	15	15
2334	A126	$5	Actinote anteas	15	15
2335	A126	$6.40	Heliconius tales	16	16
2336	A126	$7.65	Thecla telemus	18	18
2337	A126	$8.90	Theope eudocia	22	22
2338	A126	$50	Heliconius vicini	1.25	1.25
2339	A126	$100	Amarynthis meneria	2.50	2.50
	Nos. 2332-2339 (8)			4.76	4.76

Miniature Sheets

Sheets of 16

2340	A126	$10	#a.-p.	4.00	4.00
2341	A126	$10	#a.-p.	4.00	4.00
2342	A126	$10	#a.-p.	4.00	4.00
2343	A126	$10	#a.-p.	4.00	4.00

Souvenir Sheets

2344	A126	$150	Heliconius aoede	3.75	3.75
2345	A126	$150	Phyciodes clio, horiz.	3.75	3.75
2346	A126	$190	Nymphidium caricae	4.75	4.75
2347	A126	$190	Thecla hemon	4.75	4.75

For surcharges see #2415-2425, 2596-2606.

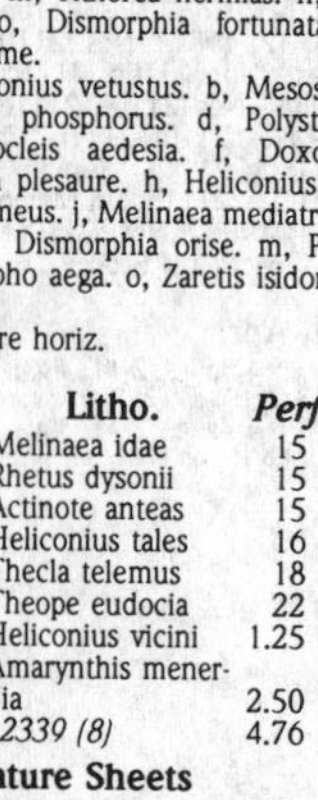

Mushrooms
A127

1990, Oct. 12

2348	A127	$2.55	Oudemanseilla mucida
2349	A127	$2.55	Pholiota squarosa
2350	A127	$2.55	Coprinus comatus
2351	A127	$2.55	Anellaria semiovaja

Souvenir Sheet

2352	A127	$20	Phallus impudicus

Sailing Ships — A128

1990, Oct. 12

2353	A128	$2.55	Brig century
2354	A128	$2.55	Dutch marine ship
2355	A128	$2.55	Galleon, 1588
2356	A128	$2.55	Warship, 16th cent.
2357	A128	$2.55	Hulk, 17th cent.

Souvenir Sheet

2358	A128	$20	Dutch ships, 16th-17th cent.

No. 2358 printed in continuous design. Discovery of America, 500th anniv. (in 1992).

Flora — A129

Orchids: $7.65, Vanilla inodora. $8.90, Epidendrum ibaguense. No. 858, Maxillaria parkeri. $15.30, Epidendrum nocturnum. $17.80, Catasetum discolor. $20, Scuticaria hadwenii. $25, Epidendrum fragrans. $100, Epistephium parviflorum.

No. 2367a, Dichea muricata. b, Octomeria erosilabia. c, Spiranthes orchiodes. d, Brassavola nodosa. e, Epidendrum rigidum. f, Brassia caudata. g, Pleurothallis diffusa. h, Aspasia variegata. i, Stenia pallida. j, Cyrtopodium punctatum. k, Cattleya deckeri. l, Cryptarrhena lunata. m, Cattleya violacea. n, Caularthron bicornutum. o, Oncidium carthagenense. p, Galeandra devoniana.

No. 2368a, Bifrenaria aurantiaca. b, Epidendrum ciliare. c, Dichaea picta. d, Scaphyglottis violacea. e, Cattleya percivaliana. f, Map of Guyana (no flower). g, Epidendrum difforme. h, Eulophia maculata. i, Spiranthes tenuis. j, Peristeria guttata. k, Pleurothallis pruinosa. l, Cleistes rosea. m, Maxillaria variabilis. n, Brassavola cucullata. o, Epidendrum moyobambae. p, Oncidium orthostates.

No. 2369a, Brassavola martiana. b, Paphinia cristata. c, Aganisia pulchella. d, Oncidium lanceanum. e, Lockhartia imbricata. f, Caularthron bilamellatum. g, Oncidium nanum. h, Pleurothallis ovalifolia. i, Galeandra dives. j, Cycnoches loddigesii. k, Ada aurantiaca. l, Catasetum barbatum. m, Palmorchis pubescens. n, Epidendrum anceps. o, Huntleya meleagris. p, Sobralia sessilis.

No. 2370a, Maxillaria camaridii. b, Vanilla pompona. c, Stanhopea grandiflora. d, Oncidium pusillum. e, Polycycnis vittata. f, Cattleya lawrenceana. g, Menadenium labiosum. h, Rodriguezia secunda. i, Mormodes buccinator. j, Otostylis brachystalix. k, Maxillaria discolor. l, Liparis elata. m, Gongora maculata. n, Koellensteinia graminea. o, Rudolfiella aurantiaca. p, Scuticaria steelei.

Flowering Trees: No. 2371a, Cochlospermum vitifolium. b, Eugenia malaccensis. c, Plumiera rubra. d, Erythrina glauca. e, Spathodea campanulata. f, Jacaranda filicifolia. g, Samanea saman. h, Cassia fistula. i, Abutilon integerrimum. j, Lagerstroemia speciosa. k, Tabebuia serratifolia. l, Guaiacum officinale. m, Solanum macranthum. n, Peltophorum roxburghii. o, Bauhinia variegata. p, Plumiera alba.

Flowering Vines: No. 2372a, Gloriosa rothschildiana. b, Pseudocalymma alliaceum. c, Callichlamys latifolia. d, Distictis riversii. e, Maurandya barclaiana. f, Beaumontia fragrans. g, Phaseolus caracalla. h, Mandevilla splendens. i, Solandra longiflora. j, Passiflora coccinea. k, Allamanda cathartica. l, Bauhinia galpini. m, Verbena maritima. n,

Mandevilla suaveolens. o, Phryganocydia corymbosa. p, Jasminum sambac.

1990, Oct. 16 Litho. *Perf. 14*

2359	A129	$7.65	multicolored	32	32
2360	A129	$8.90	multicolored	38	38
2361	A129	$12.80	multicolored	55	55
2362	A129	$15.30	multicolored	65	65
2363	A129	$17.80	multicolored	75	75
2364	A129	$20	multicolored	85	85
2365	A129	$25	multicolored	1.05	1.05
2366	A129	$100	multicolored	4.25	4.25
			Nos. 2359-2366 (8)	8.80	8.80

Miniature Sheets

Sheets of 16

2367	A129	$10	#a.-p.	7.00	7.00
2368	A129	$10	#a.-p.	7.00	7.00
2369	A129	$12.80	#a.-p.	8.50	8.50
2370	A129	$12.80	#a.-p.	8.50	8.50
2371	A129	$12.80	#a.-p.	8.50	8.50
2372	A129	$12.80	#a.-p.	8.50	8.50

Souvenir Sheets

2373	A129	$150	Coleandra devoniana	6.75	6.75
2374	A129	$150	Delonix regia	6.75	6.75
2375	A129	$150	Hexisea bidentata	6.75	6.75
2376	A129	$150	Lecythis ollaria	6.75	6.75
2377	A129	$190	Ionopsis utricularioides	8.50	8.50

Nos. 2370-2375 are horiz. For surcharges see Nos. 2593-2595.

Souvenir Sheet

Cenozoic Era Wildlife — A130

Designs: a, Palaelodus. b, Archaeotrogon. c, Vulture. d, Bradyrus tridactylus. e, Natalus stramineus bat. f, Cebidae. g, Cuvieronius. h, Phororhacos. i, Smilodectes. j, Megatherium. k, Titanotylopus. l, Teleoceras. m, Macrauchenia. n, Mylodon. o, Smilodon. p, Glyptodon. q, Protohydrocherus. r, Archaeohyrax. s, Pyrotherium. t, Platypittamys.

1990, Nov. 6

2378	A130	$12.80	Sheet of 20, #a.-t.	12.00	12.00

Miniature Sheets

Endangered Wildlife — A131

Designs: No. 2379a, Ivory-billed woodpecker. b, Cauca guan. c, Sun conure. d, Quetzal. e, Long-wattled umbrellabird. f, Banded cotinga. g, Blue-chested parakeet. h, Rufous-bellied chachalaca. i, Yellow-faced amazon. j, Toucan barbet. k, Red siskin. l, Cock-of-the-rock. m, Hyacinth macaw. n, Yellow cardinal. o, Bare-necked umbrellabird. p, Saffron toucanette. q, Red-billed curassow. r, Spectacled parrotlet. s, Lovely cotinga. t, Black-breasted gnateater.

No. 2380a, Swallow-tailed kite. b, Hoatzin. c, Ruby topaz hummingbird. d, Black vulture. e, Rufous-tailed jacamar. f, Scarlet macaw. g, Rose-breasted thrush tanager. h, Toco toucan. i, Bearded bellbird. j, Blue-crowned motmot. k, Green oropendola. l, Pompadour cotinga. m, Vermilion flycatcher. n, Blue and yellow macaw. o, White-barred piculet. p, Great razor-billed curassow. q, Ruddy quail-dove. r, Paradise tanager. s, Anhinga. t, Greater flamingo.

No. 2381a, Harpy eagle. b, Andean condor. c, Amazonian umbrellabird. d, Spider monkeys. e, Hyacinth macaw, diff. f, Red siskin, diff. g, Toucan barbet, diff. h, Three-toed sloth. i, Guanaco. j, Spectacled bear. k, White-lipped peccary. l, Maned wolf. m, Jaguar. n, Spectacled caiman. o, Giant armadillo. p, Giant anteater. q, South American river otter. r, Yapok. s, Central American river turtle. t, Cauca guan, diff.

Perf. 14x13½, 13½x14

1990, Nov. 6 Litho.

Sheets of 20

2379	A131	$12.80	#a.-t.	12.50	12.50
2380	A131	$12.80	#a.-t.	12.50	12.50
2381	A131	$12.80	#a.-t.	12.50	12.50

#2381a-2381t are horiz. #2380s incorrectly inscribed Anhigna. See #E29-E30.

Numbers have been reserved for additional values in this set.

Independence, 25th Anniv. — A132

Illustration reduced.

1991, June 25 Litho. *Imperf.*

2389	A132	$225	multicolored	10.00	10.00

Miniature Sheets

Olympic Gold Medal Winners A133

Designs: No. 2390a, Ramon Fonst. b, Lucien Gaudin. c, Ole A. Lilloe-Olsen. d, Morris Fisher. e, Ray C. Ewry. f, Hubert Van Innes. g, Alvin Kraenzlein. h, Johnny Weissmuller. i, Hans Winkler.

No. 2391a, Viktor Chukarin. b, Agnes Keleti. c, Barbel Wochel. d, Eric Heiden. e, Alvodar Gerevich. f, Guiseppe Delfino. g, Alexander Tikhonov. h, C.F. Pahud de Mortanges. i, Patricia McCormick.

No. 2392a, Nelli Kim. b, Viktor Krovopuskov. c, Viktor Sidiak. d, Nikolai Andrianov. e, Nadia Comaneci. f, Mitsuo Tsukahara. g, Yelena Novikova-Belova. h, John Naber. i, Kornelia Ender.

No. 2393a, Olga Korbut. b, Lyudmila Turischeva. c, Lasse Viren. d, George Miez. e, Roland Matthes. f, Pal Kovaks. g, Jesse Owens. h, Mark Spitz. i, Eduardo Mangiarotti.

No. 2394a, Sawao Kato. b, Rudolf Karpati. c, Jeno Fuchs. d, Emil Zatopek. e, Fanny Blankers-Koen. f, Melvin Sheppard. g, Gert Fredriksson. h, Paul Elvstrom. i, Harrison W. Dillard.

No. 2395a, Lydia Skoblikova. b, Ivar Ballangrud. c, Clas Thunberg. d, Anton Heida. e, Akinori Nakayama. f, Sixten Jernberg. g, Yevgeniy Grischin. h, Paul Radmilovic. i, Charles Daniels.

No. 2396a, Betty Cuthbert. b, Vera Caslavska. c, Galina Kulakova. d, Yukio Endo. e, Vladimir Morozov. f, Boris Shaklin. g, Don Schollander. h, Gyozo Kulscar. i, Christian D'Oriola.

No. 2397a, Al Oerter. b, Polina Astakhova. c, Takashi Ono. d, Valentin Muratov. e, Henri St. Cyr. f, Iain Murray Rose. g, Larissa Latynina. h, Carlo Pavesi. i, Dawn Fraser.

No. 2398, Paavo Nurmi, vert. No. 2399, Johannes Kolehmainen, vert. $190. Nedo Nadi, vert.

1991, Aug. 12 Litho. *Perf. 14x13½*

Sheets of 9

2390	A133	$15.30	#a.-i.	2.75	2.75
2391	A133	$17.80	#a.-i.	3.25	3.25
2392	A133	$20	#a.-i.	3.60	3.60
2393	A133	$20	#a.-i.	3.60	3.60
2394	A133	$25	#a.-i.	4.50	4.50
2395	A133	$25	#a.-i.	4.50	4.50
2396	A133	$30	#a.-i.	5.50	5.50
2397	A133	$30	#a.-i.	5.50	5.50

Souvenir Sheets

Perf. 13x13½

2398	A133	$150	multicolored	3.00	3.00
2399	A133	$150	multicolored	3.00	3.00
2400	A133	$190	multicolored	3.85	3.85

For overprints see Nos. 2552-2557.

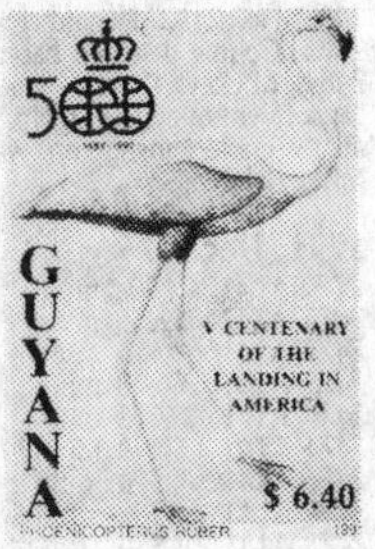

Discovery of America, 500th Anniv. (in 1992) — A134

Birds: $6.40, Phoenicopterus ruber. $7.65, Ostinops decumanus. $50, Falco peregrinus. $100, Nymphicus hollandicus. $190, Vultur feriphus. $260, Merganetta armata, horiz.

1991, Sept. 15 Litho. *Perf. 13½x14*

2401	A134	$6.40	multicolored		
2402	A134	$7.65	multicolored		
2403	A134	$50	multicolored		
2404	A134	$100	multicolored		
2405	A134	$190	multicolored		

Souvenir Sheet

Perf. 14x13½

2406	A134	$260	multicolored		

A135

Swiss Confederation, 700th Anniv. — A136

Various orchids.

Perf. 13½x14, 14x13½

1991, Sept. 30

2407	A135	$6.40	multicolored		
2408	A135	$7.65	multi, horiz.		
2409	A135	$50	multicolored		
2410	A135	$100	multicolored		
2411	A135	$190	Odontoglossum		

Souvenir Sheets

2412	A135	$360	multicolored		
2413	A135	$360	Cycnoches ventricosum		
2414	A135	$360	Miltonia hibrida, horiz.		

Nos. 2332-2339, 2343-2345 Ovptd. or Surcharged

Overprints: 80c, $2.55, Nos. 2421-2422, 2423a, 2423p, Rotary emblem and "1905-1990." $5.00, $6.40, $7.65, Nos. 2420, 2423d, 2423m, Rotary emblem and "Paul Percy Harris Founder 1868-1947" on 2 or 3 lines. Nos. 2423b, 2423l, 2423n, Boy Scout emblem and "1907-1992." Nos. 2423c, 2423i, 2423o, Lions Intl. emblem and "1917-1992." Nos. 2423e, 2423h, Red Cross emblem and "125 Years / Red Cross." Nos. 2423f-2423g, 2423j-2423k have parts of larger Rotary emblem. Nos. 2424-2425 ovptd. with service emblems in sheet margins.

1991, Oct. 29 *Perfs. as Before*

2415	A126	80c	on #2332	15	15
2416	A126	$2.55	on #2333	15	15
2417	A126	$5	on #2334	15	15
2418	A126	$6.40	on #2335	16	16
2419	A126	$7.65	on #2336	18	18
2420	A126	$100	on $8.90 #2337	2.50	2.50
2421	A126	$190	on $50 #2338	4.75	4.75
2422	A126	$225	on $100 #2339	5.60	5.60
			Nos. 2415-2422 (8)	13.64	13.64

Miniature Sheet

2423	A126		Sheet of 16	13.40	13.40
a.-l.			$10 any single	25	25
m.			$50 on $10 #2343m	1.25	1.25
n.			$75 on $10 #2343n	1.90	1.90
o.			$100 on $10 #2343o	2.50	2.50
p.			$190 on $10 #2343p	4.75	4.75

Souvenir Sheets

2424	A126	$400	on $150 #2344	10.00	10.00
2425	A126	$500	on $150 #2345	12.50	12.50

1991, Oct. 30 *Perf. 13½x14*

Designs: $6.40, Painting by Diego Giacometti. $7.65, Swiss puppets. $50, Man in top hat by Goya. $100, Stained glass window of Mary and Joseph. $190, Stained glass window of Jesus healing the sick.

No. 2431, Ship's cross-section, by Le Corbusier. No. 2432, Portrait of Giovanna Tornabuoni.

2426	A136	$6.40	multicolored		
2427	A136	$7.65	multicolored		
2428	A136	$50	multicolored		
2429	A136	$100	multicolored		
2430	A136	$190	multicolored		

Souvenir Sheets

2431	A136	$360	multicolored		
2432	A136	$360	multicolored		

Phila Nippon '91 — A137

Trains: $6.40, Class 581 12-car. $7.65, Class EF-81. $50, Class 381 9-car. $100, Kodama 8-car. $190, Shin-Kansen 16-car. No. 2438, Shin-Kansen 16-car, diff. No. 2439, Japanese locomotives in Calcutta.

1991, Nov. 16 *Perf. 14x13½*

2433	A137	$6.40	multicolored		
2434	A137	$7.65	multicolored		
2435	A137	$50	multicolored		
2436	A137	$100	multicolored		
2437	A137	$190	multicolored		

Souvenir Sheets

2438	A137	$360	multicolored		
2439	A137	$360	multicolored		

Swiss Confederation, 700th anniv., #2439.

Royal Family Birthday, Anniversary

Common Design Type

1991, Nov. Litho. *Perf. 14*

2440	CD347	$8.90	multi	20	20
2441	CD347	$12.80	multi	28	28
2442	CD347	$15.30	multi	32	32
2443	CD347	$50	multi	1.10	1.10
2444	CD347	$75	multi	1.65	1.65
2445	CD347	$100	multi	2.20	2.20
2446	CD347	$130	multi	2.85	2.85
2447	CD347	$150	multi	3.25	3.25
2448	CD347	$190	multi	4.10	4.10
2449	CD347	$200	multi	4.40	4.40
			Nos. 2440-2449 (10)	20.35	20.35

Souvenir Sheets

2450	CD347	$225	Elizabeth	4.90	4.90
2451	CD347	$225	Charles, Diana, sons	4.90	4.90

$8.90, $50, $75, $190, No. 2451, Charles and Diana, 10th wedding anniversary. $130, $150, Prince Philip, 70th birthday. Others, Queen Elizabeth II, 65th birthday.

Miniature Sheet

Japanese Attack on Pearl Harbor, 50th Anniv. A138

Designs: a, Akagi launches attack planes. b, Sakamaki's midget submarine beached. c, Mistubishi ASM Zero fighter. d, USS Arizona under attack. e, Aichi D3A1 Val dive bomber. f, USS California. g, P40 defends Pearl Harbor. h, USS Cassin and Downes hit at dry dock. i, B17 crash lands at Bellows Field. j, USS Nevada burns at Hospital Point.

1991, Dec. 7 ***Perf. 14½x15***

2452	A138	$50 Sheet of 10, #a.-j.	11.00	11.00

1992 Winter Olympics, Albertville — A139

Walt Disney characters at the Olympics: $6.40, Gus Gander playing ice hockey. $7.65, Mickey, Minnie in bobsled. $8.90, Huey, Dewey, Louie pretending to luge. $12.80, Goofy freestyle skiing. $50, Goofy ski jumping. $100, Donald, Daisy Duck speed skating. $130, Pluto cross-country skiing. $190, Mickey, Minnie ice dancing. No. 2461, Scrooge McDuck slalom skiing. No. 2462, Huey curling.

1991, Dec. 12 ***Perf. 13½x13***

2453	A139	$6.40 multi	15	15
2454	A143	$7.65 multi	16	16
2455	A139	$8.90 multi	20	20
2456	A143	$12.80 multi	28	28
2457	A143	$50 multi	1.10	1.10
2458	A139	$100 multi	2.20	2.20
2459	A139	$130 multi	2.85	2.85
2460	A143	$190 multi	4.20	4.20
		Nos. 2453-2460 (8)	11.14	11.14

Souvenir Sheets

2461	A139	$225 multi	5.00	5.00
2462	A143	$225 multi	5.00	5.00

Mushrooms — A140

Designs: $6.40, Boletus satanoides. $7.65, Russula nigricans. $50, Cortinarius glaucopus. $100, Lactarius camphoratus. $190, Cortinarius callisteus. No. 2468, Russula integra. No. 2469, Coprinus micaceus, vert.

1991, Dec. 16 **Litho.** ***Perf. 14x13½***

2463	A140	$6.40 multicolored		
2464	A140	$7.65 multicolored		
2465	A140	$50 multicolored		
2466	A140	$100 multicolored		
2467	A140	$190 multicolored		

Souvenir Sheets

Perf. 14x13½, 13½x14

2468	A140	$360 multicolored		
2469	A140	$360 multicolored		

Walt Disney Christmas Cards — A141

Designs and year of issue: 80c, Mickey, friends singing carols, 1989. $2.55, Mickey, friends riding trolley car, 1962. $5, Donald, Pluto wrapping package, 1971. $6.40, Mickey holding candle, 1948. $7.65, Mickey with Santa mask, 1947. $8.90, Pinocchio's shadow, 1939. $50, Three Little Pigs, dancing on wolf's back, 1933. $200, Mickey, mice singing carols, 1949.

No. 2478a, Conductor, Donald. b, Elephant with book. c, Goofy, centaurs. d, Snow White, dwarfs. e, Pluto, dinosaur.

No. 2479a, Mickey in sleigh. b, Three little pigs, Winnie-the-Pooh, Bambi. c, Dalmatian, bear, monkey, Lady and the Tramp. d, Alice, Goofy, Mad Hatter. e, Pinocchio, Tinker Bell, Peter Pan, Seven Dwarfs, Donald Duck. f, Pluto, 1974.

No. 2480, Mickey and friends riding in coach, 1932. No. 2481, Mickey, Pluto greeting friends, 1935. No. 2482, Donald, Jose Carioca, 1944. No. 2483, Couple dancing, baseball batter, 1945. No. 2484, Mickey, Donald, Goofy, 1946. No. 2485, Santa in chimney, 1969. No. 2486, Portrait of Winnie-the-Pooh hanging on wall, 1969. No. 2487, Mickey, 1978.

1991, Dec. 17 ***Perf. 14x13½***

2470	A141	80c multi	15	15
2471	A141	$2.55 multi	15	15
2472	A141	$5 multi	15	15
2473	A141	$6.40 multi	15	15
2474	A141	$7.65 multi	16	16
2475	A141	$8.90 multi	20	20
2476	A141	$50 multi	1.10	1.10
2477	A141	$200 multi	4.35	4.35
2478	A141	$50 Strip of 5, #a.-e.	5.50	5.50
2479	A141	$50 Strip of 5, #a.-e.	5.50	5.50
		Nos. 2470-2479 (10)	17.41	17.41

Souvenir Sheets

2480	A141	$260 multi	5.65	5.65
2481	A141	$260 multi	5.65	5.65
2482	A141	$260 multi	5.65	5.65
2483	A141	$260 multi	5.65	5.65
2484	A141	$260 multi	5.65	5.65
2485	A141	$260 multi	5.65	5.65
2486	A141	$260 multi	5.65	5.65
2487	A141	$260 multi	5.65	5.65

Nos. 2478a-2478e, 2479a-2479f, 2480-2481, 2485 and 2487 are vert.

Christmas A142

Paintings: $6.40, Madonna and Child with Angels, by Titian, horiz. $7.65, Madonna and Child with Angels, by Rubens. $50, Madonna and Child, by Raphael. $100, Madonna and Child, by Durer. $190, Madonna, by Durer. No. 2493, Madonna and Child, by Rubens, horiz. No. 2494, Madonna, by Durer, diff.

Perf. 14x13½, 13½x14

1991, Dec. 30

2488	A142	$6.40 multicolored		
2489	A142	$7.65 multicolored		
2490	A142	$50 multicolored		
2491	A142	$100 multicolored		
2492	A142	$190 multicolored		

Souvenir Sheets

2493	A142	$360 multicolored		
2494	A142	$360 multicolored		

Brandenburg Gate, Bicent. — A143

Designs: $10, Map of Berlin. $25, US Pres. George Bush, Polish Pres. Lech Walesa. $100, German Chancellor Helmut Kohl, Foreign Minister Hans-Dietrich Genscher. $190, Armored helmet.

1991, Dec. ***Perf. 14***

2495	A143	$10 multicolored	22	22
2496	A143	$25 multicolored	55	55
2497	A143	$100 multicolored	2.20	2.20

Souvenir Sheet

2498	A143	$190 multicolored	4.15	4.15

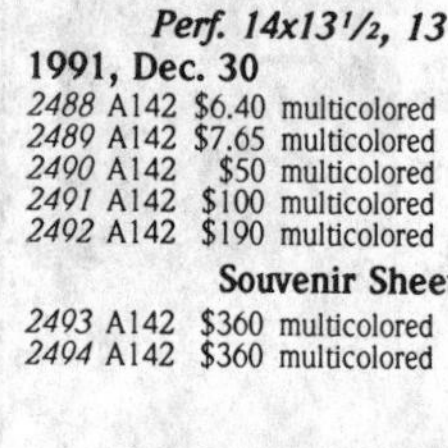

Wolfgang Amadeus Mozart, Death Bicent. A144

Portrait of Mozart and: $75, Laxenburg. $80, Death of Leopold II. $100, Mozart's birthplace, Salzburg.

1991, Dec.

2499	A144	$75 multicolored	1.65	1.65
2500	A144	$80 multicolored	1.75	1.75
2501	A144	$100 multicolored	2.15	2.15

Souvenir Sheet

2502	A144	$190 Bust of Mozart, vert.	4.15	4.15

17th World Scout Jamboree, Korea A145

Designs: $30, Scouts hiking. $40, Emblems, flag. $100, Lord Baden-Powell, vert. $190, Rocket cover with US No. 1145.

1991, Dec.

2503	A145	$25 multicolored	55	55
2504	A145	$30 multicolored	65	65
2505	A145	$40 multicolored	88	88
2506	A145	$100 multicolored	2.20	2.20

Souvenir Sheet

2507	A145	$190 multicolored	4.15	4.15

Charles de Gaulle A146

De Gaulle: $60, In Venice, 1944. $75, With Khrushchev, 1960. $80, In Algiers, 1958. $100, With Pope Paul VI, 1967.

1991, Dec.

2508	A146	$60 multicolored	1.30	1.30
2509	A146	$75 multicolored	1.65	1.65
2510	A146	$80 multicolored	1.75	1.75
2511	A146	$100 multicolored	2.20	2.20

Souvenir Sheets

2512	A146	$150 Portrait, vert.	3.25	3.25
2513	A146	$190 Portrait, diff, vert.	4.15	4.15

Anniversaries and Events — A147

Designs: No. 2515, Caroline Herschel, astronomer, Old Town Hall, Hanover. No. 2516, Map of Switzerland, woman in traditional dress. $80, Otto Lilienthal's glider No. 3. $100, Locomotive. $190, Arms of Bern and Solothurn.

1991, Dec.

2515	A147	$75 multicolored	1.65	1.65
2516	A147	$75 multicolored	1.65	1.65
2517	A147	$80 multicolored	1.75	1.75
2518	A147	$100 multicolored	2.20	2.20

Souvenir Sheet

2519	A147	$190 multicolored	4.15	4.15

Hanover, 750th anniv. (#2515), Swiss Confederation, 700th anniv. (#2516, 2519), first glider flight, cent. (#2517), Trans-Siberian Railway, cent. (#2518).

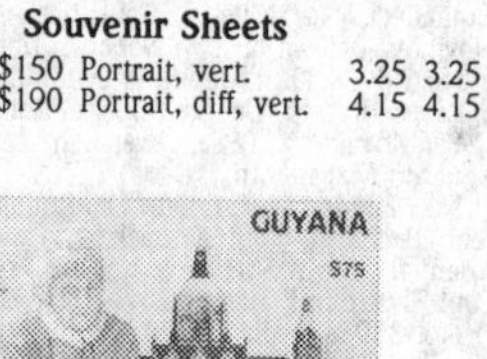

Discovery of America, 500th Anniv. A148

Designs: $6.40, Columbus lands on Trinidad. $7.65, Columbus, globe. $8.90, Ships blown off course by hurricane. $12.80, Map, hands in chains. $15.30, Land sighted. $50, Nina, Pinta. $75, Santa Maria. $100, Columbus trading with natives. $125, Superstitions and sea monsters. $130, Map, Columbus ashore. $140, Priest and natives. $150, Columbus kneeling before King Ferdinand and Queen Isabella. No. 2532, Map of New World. No. 2533, One of Columbus' ships, vert. No. 2534, Columbus.

1992, Jan. 2 ***Perf. 14***

2520	A148	$6.40 multi	15	15
2521	A148	$7.65 multi	16	16
2522	A148	$8.90 multi	20	20
2523	A148	$12.80 multi	28	28
2524	A148	$15.30 multi	34	34
2525	A148	$50 multi	1.10	1.10
2526	A148	$75 multi	1.65	1.65
2527	A148	$100 multi	2.20	2.20
2528	A148	$125 multi	2.75	2.75
2529	A148	$130 multi	2.85	2.85
2530	A148	$140 multi	3.10	3.10
2531	A148	$150 multi	3.30	3.30
		Nos. 2520-2531 (12)	18.08	18.08

Souvenir Sheets

2532	A148	$280 multi	6.15	6.15
2533	A148	$280 multi	6.15	6.15
2534	A148	$280 multi	6.15	6.15

Movie Posters — A149

Designs: $8.90, The Great K & A Train Robbery. $12.80, Cimarron. $15.30, Buzzin' Around. $25, Adventures of Captain Marvel. $30, The Mummy. $50, A Sainted Devil. $75, A Tale of Two Cities. $100, A Tugboat Romeo. $130, Thief of Bagdad. $150, Bacon Grabbers. $190, A Night at the Opera. $200, Citizen Kane. No. 2547, She Done Him Wrong. No. 2548, The Circus. No. 2549, Babe Comes Home. No. 2550, Zeppelin, horiz.

1992, Mar. 11 **Litho.** ***Perf. 14***

2535	A149	$8.90 multi	20	20
2536	A149	$12.80 multi	28	28
2537	A149	$15.30 multi	34	34
2538	A149	$25 multi	55	55
2539	A149	$30 multi	65	65
2540	A149	$50 multi	1.10	1.10
2541	A149	$75 multi	1.65	1.65
2542	A149	$100 multi	2.20	2.20
2543	A149	$130 multi	2.85	2.85
2544	A149	$150 multi	3.30	3.30
2545	A149	$190 multi	4.20	4.20
2546	A149	$200 multi	4.40	4.40
		Nos. 2535-2546 (12)	21.72	21.72

Size: 70x100mm, 100x70mm

Imperf

2547	A149	$225 multi	5.00	5.00
2548	A149	$225 multi	5.00	5.00
2549	A149	$225 multi	5.00	5.00
2550	A149	$225 multi	5.00	5.00

No. 2273 Overprinted or Surcharged with Olympic Rings and "ALBERTVILLE '92" or "XVIth Olympic Winter / Games in Albertville" (No. 2551e)

1992 ***Perfs. as Before***

2551	A122	Sheet of 9		
a.-f.		$20 on #2273a-2273f		
g.		$70 on $20 #2273g		
h.		$100 on $20 #2273h		
i.		$190 on $20 #2273i		

Nos. 2391g, 2395c, 2396c, 2398, 2400 Ovptd. "ALBERTVILLE '92" No. 2399 Ovptd. "Barcelona '92" and emblems in Sheet Margin

1992 ***Perfs. as Before***

2552	A133	$17.80 on #2391g		
2553	A133	$25 on #2395c		
2554	A133	$30 on #2396c		

Souvenir Sheets

2555	A133	$150 on #2398		
2556	A133	$150 on #2399	3.00	3.00
2557	A133	$190 on #2400		

Nos. 2552-2554 printed in sheets of 9, overprint applied to only one stamp per sheet. Overprint on Nos. 2555, 2557 applied to sheet margin.

Easter — A150

Various details from paintings by Durer: $6.40, $12.80, $50, $130, No. 2567, The Martyrdom of Ten Thousand. $7.65, $15.30, $100, $190, No. 2566, Adoration of the Trinity.

1992 Litho. *Perf. 13½x14*

2558	A150	$6.40 multi		15	15
2559	A150	$7.65 multi		16	16
2560	A150	$12.80 multi		28	28
2561	A150	$15.30 multi		34	34
2562	A150	$50 multi		1.10	1.10
2563	A150	$100 multi		2.20	2.20
2564	A150	$130 multi		2.85	2.85
2565	A150	$190 multi		4.20	4.20
	Nos. 2558-2565 (8)			11.28	11.28

Souvenir Sheets

2566	A150	$225 multi	5.00	5.00
2567	A150	$225 multi	5.00	5.00

Queen Elizabeth II's Accession to the Throne, 40th Anniv. A151

Queen Elizabeth II: $8.90, With Prince Philip. $12.80, In uniform. $100, At coronation. $130, Wearing black cape and hat. No. 2572, Coronation portrait. No. 2573, Fortieth anniv. portrait.

1992 Litho. *Perf. 14*

2568	A151	$8.90 multicolored	20	20
2569	A151	$12.80 multicolored	28	28
2570	A151	$100 multicolored	2.20	2.20
2571	A151	$130 multicolored	2.85	2.85

Souvenir Sheets

2572	A151	$225 multicolored	5.00	5.00
2573	A151	$225 multicolored	5.00	5.00

Diocese of Guyana, 150th Anniv. A152

Designs: $6.40, Holy Cross Church, Annai Bupununi. $50, St. Peter's Church. $100, St. George's Cathedral, interior, vert. $190, Map, vert. $225, Religious symbols.

1992 Litho. *Perf. 14*

2574	A152	$6.40 multicolored	15	15
2575	A152	$50 multicolored	1.00	1.00
2576	A152	$100 multicolored	2.00	2.00
2577	A152	$190 multicolored	3.75	3.75

Souvenir Sheet

2578	A152	$225 multicolored	4.50	4.50

Miniature Sheet

Horses — A153

Designs: No. 2579a, Palomino. b, Appaloosa. c, Clydesdale. d, Arab. e, Morgan. f, Friesian. g, Pinto. h, Thoroughbred. No. 2580, Lipizzaner.

1992, Aug. 10

2579	A153	$190 Sheet of 8, #a.-h.	30.00	30.00

Souvenir Sheet

2580	A153	$190 multicolored	3.75	3.75

No. 2580 contains one 58x29mm stamp.

Cats — A154

Designs: No. 2588b, Russian blue. c, Havana brown. d, Himalayan. e, Manx. f, Cornish rex. g, Black Persian. h, Scottish fold. i, Siamese.

1992, Aug. 10 *Perf. 14½x14*

2581	A154	$5 Burmese	15	15
2582	A154	$6.40 Turkish van	15	15
2583	A154	$12.80 American shorthair	25	25
2584	A154	$15.30 Egyptian	30	30
2585	A154	$50 Egyptian mau	1.00	1.00
2586	A154	$100 Japanese bob-tail	2.00	2.00
2587	A154	$130 Abyssinian	2.60	2.60
2588	A154	$225 Oriental shorthair	4.50	4.50
	Nos. 2581-2588 (8)		10.95	10.95

Miniature Sheet

Perf. 14x13½

2588A	A154	$50 Sheet of 8, #b.-i.	8.00	8.00

Souvenir Sheets

Perf. 14x14½

2589	A152	$250 Chartreuse, vert.	4.50	4.50
2590	A154	$250 Turkish angora	5.00	5.00
2591	A154	$250 Maine coon	5.00	5.00
2592	A154	$250 Chinchilla	5.00	5.00

No. 2589 has continuous design. Nos. 2590-2592 are vert. and have continous design.

Nos. 2368-2369 Surcharged on 4 stamps and Overprinted in Red "PHILA NIPPON '91 / WORLD STAMP EXHIBITION NIPPON '91" and Show Emblem in Sheet Margin

No. 2376 Surcharged in Red

1992 *Perfs. as Before*

Sheets of 12

2593 A129 #a.-d., #2368a-2368l
- ***a.*** $25 on $10 #2368m
- ***b.*** $50 on $10 #2368n
- ***c.*** $75 on $10 #2368o
- ***d.*** $130 on $10 #2368p

2594 A129 #a.-d., 2369a-2369l
- ***a.*** $25 on $12.80 #2369m
- ***b.*** $50 on $12.80 #2369n
- ***c.*** $75 on $12.80 #2369o
- ***d.*** $100 on $12.80 #2369p

Souvenir Sheet

2595 A129 $250 on $150 #2376

Nos. 2332-2340, 2346-2347 Overprinted or Surcharged

Overprints: 80c, $2.55, Nos. 2602-2603, Lions emblem and "Lions International / 1917-1992." $5, $6.40, $7.65, Nos. 2601, 2604d, 2604m, Lions emblem and "Melvin Jones Founder 1880-1961" on 2 or 3 lines. Nos. 2604a, 2604p, Lions emblem and "1917-1992." Nos. 2604b, 2604i, 2604o, Rotary emblem and "1905-1990." Nos. 2604c, 2604l, 2604n, Boy Scout emblem and "1907-1992." Nos. 2604e, 2604h, Red Cross emblem and "125 Years Red Cross." Nos. 2604f-2604g, 2604j-2604k have parts of larger Lions emblem. Nos. 2605-2606 have service organization emblems in sheet margins.

1992 *Perfs. as Before*

2596	A126	80c	on #2332
2597	A126	$2.55	on #2333
2598	A126	$5	on #2334
2599	A126	$6.40	on #2335
2600	A126	$7.65	on #2336
2601	A126	$100	on $8.90 #2337
2602	A126	$190	on $50 #2338
2603	A126	$225	on $100 #2339

Miniature Sheet

2604 Sheet of 16
- ***a.-l.*** A126 $10 any single
- ***m.*** A126 $50 on $10 #2340m
- ***n.*** A126 $75 on $10 #2340n
- ***o.*** A126 $100 on $10 #2340o
- ***p.*** A126 $190 on $10 #2340p

Souvenir Sheets

2605	A126	$400	on $190 #2346
2606	A126	$500	on $190 #2347

Elephants A155

Designs: No. 2607a, Mammoth, Oligocene Epoch. b, Stegodon, mid- Miocene Epoch. c, Mammoth, Pliocene Epoch. d, Hannibal's army crossing Alps. e, Royal elephant of the Maharaja of Mysore, India. f, Elephant pulling tree trunks, Burma. g, Tiger hunt, India. h, Elephant towing raft on River Kwai, Thailand.

$225, African elephants, Kenya.

1992, Aug. 10 Litho. *Perf. 14*

2607	A155	$50 Sheet of 8, #a.-h.	8.00	8.00

Souvenir Sheet

2608	A155	$225 multicolored	4.50	4.50

No. 2607 has continuous design.

Animals of Guyana A156

1992, Aug. 10

2609	A156	$8.90 Red howler monkey	18	18
2610	A156	$12.80 Ring-tailed coati	25	25
2611	A156	$15.30 Jaguar	30	30
2612	A156	$25 Two-toed sloth	50	50
2613	A156	$50 Giant armadillo	1.00	1.00
2614	A156	$75 Giant anteater	1.50	1.50
2615	A156	$100 Capybara	2.00	2.00
2616	A156	$130 Ocelot	2.60	2.60
	Nos. 2609-2616 (8)		8.33	8.33

Souvenir Sheets

2617	A156	$225 Wooly opossum, vert.	4.50	4.50
2618	A156	$225 Night monkey, vert.	4.50	4.50

Souvenir Sheet

Statue of Liberty, New York — A157

1992, Oct. 28

2619	A157	$325 multicolored	6.50	6.50

Postage Stamp Mega Event '92, New York City.

Miniature Sheet

Model Trains A158

Marklin toy locomotives: No. 2620a, 2-4-4-2 Crocodile locomotive, 1 gauge, 1933. b, French prototype streetcar, 1 gauge, 1933. c, British prototype Flatiron 2-4-4 tank engine, O gauge, 1913. d, German National Railways 0-6-0 switching engine, Z gauge, 1970. e, Smoking/non-smoking third class car, 1 gauge, 1909. f, American style 0-4-0 locomotive, O gauge, 1904. g, Zurich, Switzerland prototype streetcar, O gauge, 1928. h, Central London Railway Bo-Bo, 1 gauge, 1904. i, "The Great Bear" Pacific, 1 gauge, 1909.

No. 2621a, 0-4-4 American style locomotive, 2 gauge, 1907. b, German first and second class passenger car, 1 gauge, 1908. c, British Great Eastern Railway 4-4-0, 1 gauge, 1908. d, English prototype steeplecab, O gauge, 1904. e, Santa Fe Railroad diesel, 1962. f, British Great Northern 4-4-0, 3 gauge, live steam model, 1903. g, Caledonian Railway "Cardean" of Scotland, 1 gauge, 1904. h, British LNWR passenger car, 1 gauge, 1903. i, Swiss Gotthard Rwy. 0-4-0 locomotive, O gauge, 1920.

No. 2622a, British LB & SCR tank engine, O gauge, 1920. b, Central London Railway, tunnel locomotive, 1 gauge, 1904. c, "Borsig" 4-6-4 streamliner, O gauge, 1935. d, French PLM first class car, 1 gauge, 1929. e, American style 0-4-0 locomotive #1021, 1 gauge, 1904. f, "Paris-Orsay" long-nose steeplecab, 1 gauge, 1920. g, British "Cock O' The North," 1 gauge, 1936. h, Prussian State Railways P8 4-6-0 live steam model, 1 gauge, 1975. i, 1937 German "Schnell Treibwagen," O gauge, 1937.

No. 2623a, Marklin North British Railway "Atlantic," 1 gauge, 1913. b, Bing British London & Western Railway 4-4-2 "Precursor," O gauge, clockwork model, 1916. c, Marklin British Great Western "King George V," O gauge, 1937. d, Marklin passenger car, "Kaiser Train," 1 gauge, 1901. e, Bing 4-4-0 side tank engine, 1 gauge, live steam model, 1904. f, Marklin short-nose steeplecab, 1 gauge, 1912. g, Marklin "Der Adler", 1 gauge, 1935. h, Bing British Great Western Railway "County of Northampton," 1 gauge, live steam model, 1909. i, Bing British Midland Railway "Black Prince," 3 gauge, live steam model, 1908.

Bing toy locomotives: No. 2624a, Midland Railway "Deeley Type" 4-4-0, 1 gauge clockwork model, 1909. b, No. 2631, British Midland Railway 0-4-0, 3 gauge clockwork model, 1903. c, German 4-6-2 Pacific, O gauge clockwork model, 1927. d, British Great Western Railway, third class coach, O gauge, 1926. e, British London & Southwestern "M7" 0-4-4, 1 gauge clockwork model, 1909. f, "Pilot" 4-4-0 side tank engine, 3 gauge live steam model, 1901. g, British London & Northwestern Railway Webb "Cauliflower," O gauge clockwork model, 1912. h, No. 112, 4-4-0 side tank locomotive, 1 gauge live steam model, 1910. i, British Great Northern Railway, "Stirling Single," 2 gauge live steam model, 1904.

Carette toy locomotives: No. 2625a, Lithographed tin "Penny Bazaar" train, 1904. b, Winteringham 0-4-0 locomotive, O gauge, 1917. c, British Northeastern Railway, Smith Compound, 3 gauge, 1905. d, SE & CR 2-2-4 steam railcar, 1 gauge, live steam model, 1908. e, No. 776 British Great Northern Railway Stirling "Single," 3 gauge, live steam model, 1903. f, British Midland Railway 4-4-0, O gauge, clockwork model, 1911. g, London Metropolitan Railway "Westinghouse," 1 gauge, 1908. h, Clestory coach, 1 gauge, 1907. i, Steam railcar No. 1, O gauge, live steam model, 1906.

Marklin toy locomotives: No. 2626a, LMS "Precursor" 4-4-2 tank engine, O gauge clockwork model, 1923. b, American "Congressional Limited" passenger car, 1 gauge, 1908. c, Swiss prototype "Ae 3/6" locomotive, O gauge, 1934. d, German National Railways class 80, 0-6-0, 1 gauge, 1975. e, British Southern Railway third class coach, O gauge, 1926. f, "Bowen-Cooke" 4-6-2 tank engine, O gauge, 1913. g, First electric prototype model, "Two Penny Tube," London, 1 gauge clockwork model, 1901. h, "Paris-Orsay" steeplecab, 1 gauge, 1920. i, 0-2-2 Passenger engine, O gauge clockwork model, 1895.

Bing toy locomotives: No. 2627a, 2-2-0 engine and tender, 2 gauge live steam model, 1895. b, British Midland Railway "single," O gauge clockwork model, 1913. c, #524/510 reversible express passenger locomotive, 1 gauge, 1916. d, "Kaiser Train" passenger car with Gothic windows, 1 gauge, 1902. e, Tinplate model, British rural station, 1 gauge, 1915. f, British LSMR "M7" side tank locomotive, O gauge clockwork model, 1909. g, 4-4-4 "Windcutter," 1 gauge live steam model, 1912. h, British Great Central Railway "Sir Sam Fay," 1 gauge clockwork model, 1914. i, "Dunalastair" locomotive Caledonian Railway, 1 gauge clockwork model, 1910.

No. 2628, German National Railroad class 0-1 Pacific, O gauge, 1937. No. 2629, Bing 0-4-0 Contractor's locomotive, 4 gauge, 1904. No. 2630, Rack Railway "Steeplecab" locomotive, 2 gauge, 1908. No. 2631, Bing Pabst Blue Ribbon Beer refrigerator car, O gauge, 1925. No. 2632, Marklin "Commodore Vanderbilt," O gauge, 1937. No. 2633, Bing British Great Western Railway "County of Northampton," 1 gauge, live steam model, 1909. No. 2634, Marklin French Prototype PLM Pacific, 1 gauge, live steam model, 1912. No. 2635, Marklin "Mountain Etat" second series, O gauge, 1933.

1992, Nov. 19 *Perf. 14*

2620	A158	$45 Sheet of 9, #a.-i.	8.25	8.25
2621	A158	$45 Sheet of 9, #a.-i.	8.25	8.25
2622	A158	$45 Sheet of 9, #a.-i.	6.50	6.50
2623	A158	$45 Sheet of 9, #a.-i.	6.50	6.50
2624	A158	$45 Sheet of 9, #a.-i.	6.50	6.50
2625	A158	$45 Sheet of 9, #a.-i.	6.50	6.50
2626	A158	$45 Sheet of 9, #a.-i.	6.50	6.50
2627	A158	$45 Sheet of 9, #a.-i.	6.50	6.50

Souvenir Sheets

2628	A158	$350 multicolored	7.00	7.00
2629	A158	$350 multicolored	7.00	7.00

Perf. 14x13½

2630	A158	$350 multicolored	7.00	7.00

Perf. 13x13½, 13½x13

2631	A158	$350	multicolored	5.50	5.50
2632	A158	$350	multicolored	5.60	5.60
2633	A158	$350	multicolored	5.75	5.75
2634	A158	$350	multicolored	5.75	5.75
2635	A158	$350	multicolored	5.75	5.75

Genoa '92. Nos. 2628-2635 each contain one 50x39mm stamp.

While Nos. 2622-2623 & 2631 have the issue date as Nos. 2620-2621 & 2628-2630, the face value of of Nos. 2622-2623 & 2631 was lower when they were released.

Anniversaries and Events — A159

Designs: $12.80, Zeppelin over Lake Constance, 1909. No. 2638, Voyager 1, Jupiter. No. 2639, Konrad Adenauer, John F. Kennedy. No. 2640, Aeromedical airlift. No. 2641, Amazon dolphins. No. 2642, Lift-off of Voyager 1, 1977. No. 2643, Baby gorilla. No. 2644, America's Cup yacht Stars and Stripes. No. 2644A, Eye screening van, doctor with patient. $190, Adenauer, Charles de Gaulle. $225, Zeppelin preparing for takeoff. No. 2647, Count Zeppelin, vert. No. 2648 View of Earth from space, vert. No. 2649, Konrad Adenauer, vert. No. 2650, Tree frog, vert.

1993, Jan. Litho. *Perf. 14*

2637	A159	$12.80	multicolored	25	25
2638	A159	$50	multicolored	1.00	1.00
2639	A159	$50	multicolored	1.00	1.00
2640	A159	$100	multicolored	2.00	2.00
2641	A159	$100	multicolored	2.00	2.00
2642	A159	$130	multicolored	2.60	2.60
2643	A159	$130	multicolored	2.60	2.60
2644	A159	$130	multicolored	2.60	2.60
2644A	A159	$130	multicolored	2.60	2.60
2645	A159	$190	multicolored	3.80	3.80
2646	A159	$225	multicolored	4.50	4.50
		Nos. 2637-2646 (11)		24.95	24.95

Souvenir Sheets

2647	A159	$225	multicolored	4.50	4.50
2648	A159	$225	multicolored	4.50	4.50
2649	A159	$225	multicolored	4.50	4.50
2650	A159	$225	multicolored	4.50	4.50

Count Zeppelin, 75th anniv. of death (#2637, 2646-2647). Intl. Space Year (#2638, 2642, 2648). Konrad Adenauer, 25th anniv. of death (#2639, 2645, 2649). World Health Organization (#2640). Earth Summit, Rio (#2641, 2643, 2650). America's Cup Yacht Race (#2644). Lions Intl., 75th anniv. (#2644A).

Miniature Sheet

Biblical Story of David and Goliath — A160

Designs: No. 2651a, City of Jerusalem, two birds in flight. b, City, bird in flight at right. c, City, sun above. d, City, bird in flight at left. e, City with clouds above. f, Philistine army (i-k, q-r). g, Goliath. h, Goliath's arm, spear shaft (b, i, n). l, Goliath's leg (m, q-s), shield. n, David (r-t, w) with slingshot. o, Jewish soldiers with spears or swords (p-y).

1992, Dec. 29 Litho. *Perf. 14*

2651	A160	$25	Sheet of 25, #a.-y.	12.50	12.50

No. 2651 has a continuous design.

Parrots A161

1993, Mar. 10

2652	A161	80c	Hyacinth macaw	15	15
2653	A161	$6.40	Scarlet macaw	15	15
2654	A161	$7.65	Green macaw, vert.	15	15
2655	A161	$15.30	Tovi parakeet	25	25
2656	A161	$50	Blue & yellow macaw	80	80
2657	A161	$100	Military macaw, vert.	2.00	2.00
2658	A161	$130	Red & green macaw, vert.	2.60	2.60
2659	A161	$190	Severa macaw	3.00	3.00
		Nos. 2652-2659 (8)		9.10	9.10

Souvenir Sheet

2660	A161	$225	Scarlet macaw, diff.	4.50	4.50
2661	A161	$225	Green parakeet, vert.	3.75	3.75

While Nos. 2654-2656, 2659, 2661 have the same issue date as Nos. 2652-2653, 2657-2658, 2660, the value of Nos. 2654-2656, 2659, 2661 was lower when released.

Miniature Sheet

Dinosaurs A162

Designs: No. 2662a, Archaeopteryx. b, Pteranodon. c, Quetzalcoatlus. d, Protoavis. e, Dicraeosaurus. f, Moschops. g, Lystrosaurus. h, Dimetrondon. i, Staurikosaurus. j, Cacops. k, Diarthrognathus. l, Estemmenosuchus.

No. 2663a, Pteranodon. b, Cearadactylus. c, Eudimorphodon. d, Pterodactylus. e, Stauirkosaurus. f, Euoplocephalus. g, Tuojiangosaurus. h, Oviraptor. i, Protoceratops. j, Panaoplosaurus. k, Psittacosaurus. l, Corythosaurus.

No. 2664a, Sordes. b, Quetzalcoatlus. c, Archaeopteryx. d, Rhamphorynchus. e, Spinosaurus. f, Anchisaurus. g, Stegosaurus. h, Leaellynosaurus. i, Minmi. j, Heterdontosaurus. k, Lesothosaurus. l, Deninonychus.

1993 Litho. *Perf. 14*

2662	A162	$30	Sheet of 12, #a.-l.	6.00	6.00
2663	A162	$30	Sheet of 12, #a.-l.	6.00	6.00
2664	A162	$30	Sheet of 12, #a.-l.	6.00	6.00

Issue dates: No. 2662, Jan. Nos. 2663-2664, Mar. 10.

Numbers have been reserved for additional values in this set.

Miniature Sheet

Signs of the Zodiac A163

Designs: a, Aquarius. b, Pisces. c, Aries. d, Taurus. e, Gemini. f, Cancer. g, Leo. h, Virgo. i, Libra. j, Scorpio. k, Sagittarius. l, Capricorn.

1993 Litho. *Perf. 14x13½*

2665	A163	$30	Sheet of 12, #a.-l.	5.80	5.80

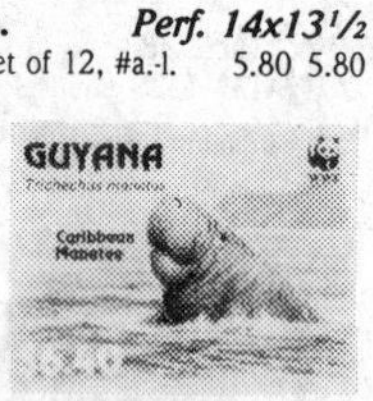

Caribbean Manatee — A164

Designs: $6.40, Adult sticking head out of water. $7.65, Adult, eating, with young. $8.90, Adult swimming underwater. $50, Adult swimming with young.

1993, Mar. 10 Litho. *Perf. 15x14½*

2666	A164	$6.40	multicolored	15	15
2667	A164	$7.65	multicolored	18	18
2668	A164	$8.90	multicolored	20	20
2669	A164	$50	multicolored	1.15	1.15

World Wildlife Federation.

Miniature Sheets

Fauna — A165

Designs: No. 2670a, Southern tamandua. b, Three-toed sloth. c, Red howler monkey. d, Four-eyed opossum. e, Black spider monkey. f, Giant otter. g, Red brocket. h, Tree porcupine. i, Tayra. j, Tapir. k, Ocelot. l, Giant armadillo.

No. 2671a, Crimson topaz hummingbird. b, Bearded bellbird (f). c, Amazonian umbrellabird. d, Paradise jacamar (h). e, Paradise tanager. f, White-tailed trogon (i-j). g, Scarlet macaw (k). h, Red fan parrot. i, Red-billed toucan. j, White plumed antbird. k, Crimson-hooded manakin. l, Guyanan cock-of-the-rock.

No. 2672, Paca. No. 2673, Tufted coquettes, horiz.

1993, Mar. 10 *Perf. 14*

2670	A165	$50	Sheet of 12, #a.-l.	10.00	10.00
2671	A165	$50	Sheet of 12, #a.-l.	10.00	10.00

Souvenir Sheets

2672	A165	$325	multicolored	5.25	5.25
2673	A165	$325	multicolored	5.25	5.25

Miniature Sheet

Coronation of Queen Elizabeth II, 40th Anniv. — A166

Designs: a, $25, Official coronation photograph. b, $50, Gems from royal collection. c, $75, Queen, Duke of Edingurgh. d, $130, Queen opening Parliament.

$325, State Portrait, by Sir James Gunn, 1954-56.

1993, June 2 Litho. *Perf. 13½x14*

2674	A166		Sheet, 2 each #a.-d.	9.00	9.00

Souvenir Sheet

Perf. 14

2675	A166	$325	multicolored	5.25	5.25

No. 2675 contains one 28x42mm stamp.

For overprints see Nos. 2793-2795.

Miniature Sheets

A167

Famous People A168

Athletes: No. 2676a, O. J. Simpson, football. b, Rohan B. Kanhai, cricket. c, Gabriela Sabatini, tennis. d, Severiano Ballesteros, golf. e, Peace dove. f, Franz Beckenbauer, soccer. g, Pele, soccer. h, Wilt Chamberlain, basketball, i, Nadia Comaneci, gymnastics.

Scientists: No. 2677a, Louis Leakey, archaeology. b, Jonas Salk, polio vaccine. c, Hideyo Noguchi, yellow fever. d, Karl Landsteiner, blood transfusions. e, Peace dove. f, Sigmund Freud, psychoanalysis. g, Louis Pasteur. h, Madame Curie, radium tubes. i, Jean Baptiste Perrin, physics.

Artists, entertainers: No. 2678a, Gabriel Marquez, writer. b, Pablo Picasso, artist. c, Cecil DeMille, film director. d, Martha Graham, dance. e, Peace dove. f, Charles Chaplin, actor. g, Paul Robeson, singer. h, Rudolph Dunbar, musician. i, Louis Armstrong, musician.

Politicians: No. 2679a, Jawaharlal Nehru. b, Dr. Eric Williams, first prime minister of Trinidad and Tobago. c, John F. Kennedy. d, Hugh Desmond Hoyte, president of Guyana. e, Peace dove over map. f, Friedrich Ebert. g, Franklin D. Roosevelt. h, Mikhail Gorbachev. i, Winston Churchill.

Humanitarians: No. 2680a, Gandhi. b, Dalai Lama. c, Michael Manley, prime minister of Jamaica. d, Javier Perez de Cuellar, former UN Secretary General. e, Peace dove, globe. f, Mother Teresa. g, Martin Luther King, Jr. h, Nelson Mandela. i, Raoul Wallenberg.

Transportation, communication: No. 2681a, DC-3 cargo plane. b, Space shuttle. c, Concorde. d, Ferdinand von Zeppelin. e, Peace dove. f, Guglielmo Marconi. g, Adrian Thompson, mountaineer. h, Bullet train, Japan. i, John von Neuman, mathematician.

1993, July 26 Litho. *Perf. 14*

2676	A167	$50	Sheet of 9, #a.-i.	7.25	7.25
2677	A167	$50	Sheet of 9, #a.-i.	7.25	7.25
2678	A167	$50	Sheet of 9, #a.-i.	7.25	7.25
2679	A168	$100	Sheet of 9, #a.-i.	14.50	14.50
2680	A168	$100	Sheet of 9, #a.-i.	14.50	14.50
2681	A168	$100	Sheet of 9, #a.-i.	14.50	14.50

Souvenir Sheet

2682	A168	$250	UN Flag, natl. flags, vert.	4.00	4.00
2683	A167	$250	Jackie Robinson, vert.	4.00	4.00
2684	A167	$250	Einstein's formula, vert.	4.00	4.00
2685	A167	$250	Elvis Presley, vert.	4.00	4.00
2686	A168	$250	Nobel Peace Prize certificate, vert.	4.00	4.00
2687	A168	$250	Apollo Moon Landing	4.00	4.00

Willy Brandt (1913-1992), German Chancellor — A169

Designs: $25, Brandt, Golda Meir, 1969. $190, Brandt at steel mill, 1969. $325, Brandt.

1993, Aug. 16 Litho. *Perf. 14*

2688	A169	$25	multicolored	40	40
2689	A169	$190	multicolored	3.00	3.00

Souvenir Sheet

2690	A169	$325	multicolored	5.25	5.25

A170

A171

Copernicus (1473-1543): $50, Armillary sphere. $190, Satellite antenna. $300, Copernicus.

1993, Aug. 16

2691	A170	$50	multicolored	80	80
2692	A170	$190	multicolored	3.00	3.00

Souvenir Sheet

2693	A170	$300	multicolored	4.75	4.75

1993, Aug. 16

1994 Winter Olympics, Lillehammer, Norway: $50, Georg Hackl, luge gold medalist, 1992. $130, Karen Magnussen, figure skater, 1972. $325, German bobsled team, 1992.

2694	A171	$50	multicolored	80	80
2695	A171	$130	multicolored	2.00	2.00

Souvenir Sheet

2696	A171	$325	multicolored	5.25	5.25

A172

World War II — A173

Designs: $6.40, Audie Murphy. $7.65, British, US forces link up in France, June 8, 1944. $8.90, Monte Cassino falls to Allies, May 18, 1944. $12.80, Battleship Yamato attacked by US in Battle of East China Sea, Apr. 7, 1945. $15.30, St. Basil's Cathedral, Moscow, Foreign Ministers Conf., Oct. 19, 1943. $50, US forces cross Rhine River, Mar. 7, 1945. $130, Gen. George S. Patton, Jr., Battle of Sicily ends, Aug. 17, 1943. $190, Battleship Tirpitz sunk, Nov. 12, 1944. $200, US Sherman tank, US forces enter Brittany after taking Normandy, Aug. 1, 1944. $100, B-29s begin bombing raids on Japan from China, June 15, 1944. $225, End of fighting in Italy, May 2, 1945.

War at Sea, 1943: No. 2708a, Adm. Yamamoto launches air offensive, Apr. 7. b, PT-109 in Blackett Strait, Aug. 1. c, USS Enterprise. d, Allied ships attack Rabaul, Oct. 12. e, US troops land at Cape Gloucester, Dec. 26. f, USS Bogue enters service, Feb. g, Wildcat fighters sink U-118. h, Battle of Atlantic reaches peak, U-boats sink 108 ships. i, Italian fleet surrenders at Malta, Sept. 10. j, Battleship Duke of York sinks Scharnhorst, Dec. 26.

War in the Air, 1943: No. 2709a, Royal Australian Air Force Beaufighter, Battle of Bismark Sea, Mar. 2-4. b, P-38 Lightening shoots down Adm. Yamamoto's plane over Bougainville, Apr. 7. c, B-24 Liberators bomb Tarawa prior to landings, Sept. 17-19. d, B-25 Mitchell of Fifth Air Force bombs Rabaul, Oct. 12. e, US Navy aircraft attack Makin, Nov. 19. f, US Army Air Force's first daylight raid over Germany, Jan. 27. g, Royal Air Force Mosquito bombers make first daylight raid on Berlin, Jan. 30. h, Allies devastate Hamburg with first firestorm, July 24-30. i, B-24 bombers raid Ploesti oil refineries in Romania, Aug. 1. j, Battle of Berlin begins, Nov. 18.

No. 2710, $325, US, Russian infantry meeting at Elbe River, Apr. 25, 1945.

1993, Oct. 18 Litho. *Perf. 14*

2697	A172	$6.40	multicolored	15	15
2698	A172	$7.65	multicolored	15	15
2699	A172	$8.90	multicolored	15	15
2700	A172	$12.80	multicolored	20	20
2701	A172	$15.30	multicolored	25	25
2702	A172	$50	multicolored	75	75
2703	A172	$100	multicolored	1.50	1.50
2704	A172	$130	multicolored	2.00	2.00
2705	A172	$190	multicolored	3.00	3.00
2706	A172	$200	multicolored	3.00	3.00
2707	A172	$225	multicolored	3.50	3.50
			Nos. 2697-2707 (11)	14.65	14.65

Miniature Sheets

Perf. 15

2708	A173	$50	Sheet of 10, #a.-j.	8.00	8.00
2709	A172	$50	Sheet of 10, #a.-j.	8.00	8.00

Nos. 2709a-2709j are 35½x22mm.

Souvenir Sheet

Perf. 14

2710	A172	$325	multicolored	5.00	5.00

1994 World Cup Soccer Championships, US — A174

Player, country: $5, Stuart Pearce, England. $6.40, Ronald Koeman, Holland. $7.65, Gianluca Vialli, Italy. $12.80, McStay, Scotland, Alemao, Brazil. $15.30, Ceulemans, Belgium, Butcher, England. $50, Dragan Stojkovic, Yugoslavia. $100, Ruud Gullit, Holland. $130, Miloslav Kadlec, Czechoslovakia. $150, Ramos, Uruguay, Berthold, Germany. $190, Baggio, Italy; Wright, England. $200, Yarentchuck, Russia, Renquin, Belgium. $225, Timofte, Romania; Aleinikov, Russia. No. 2724, Rene Higuita, Colombia. No. 2723, Salvatore Schillaci, Italy, horiz.

1993, Oct. 18 Litho. *Perf. 14*

2711	A174	$5	multicolored	15	15
2712	A174	$6.40	multicolored	15	15
2713	A174	$7.65	multicolored	15	15
2714	A174	$12.80	multicolored	20	20
2715	A174	$15.30	multicolored	25	25
2716	A174	$50	multicolored	75	75
2717	A174	$100	multicolored	1.50	1.50
2718	A174	$130	multicolored	2.00	2.00
2719	A174	$150	multicolored	2.25	2.25
2720	A174	$190	multicolored	2.75	2.75
2721	A174	$200	multicolored	3.25	3.25
2722	A174	$225	multicolored	3.50	3.50
			Nos. 2711-2722 (12)	16.90	16.90

Souvenir Sheets

2723	A174	$325	multicolored	5.25	5.25
2724	A174	$325	multicolored	5.25	5.25

Order of the Caribbean Community — A175

1993, Sept. 27 Litho. *Perf. 14*

2725	A175	$7.65	William Demas	15	15
2726	A175	$7.65	Derek Walcott	15	15
2727	A175	$7.65	Sir Shridath Ramphal	15	15
			Set value	35	35

Christmas A176

Details from Holy Family Under the Apple Tree, by Rubens: $6.40, $12.80, $130, $190.

Details from The Virgin in Glory, by Durer: $7.65, $15.30, $50, $250.

Souvenir sheets: No. 2736, $325, Holy Family Under the Apple Tree (entire). No. 2737, $325, The Virgin in Glory (entire).

1993, Dec. 1 *Perf. 13½x14*

2728-2737	A176	Set of 10	21.00	21.00

Miniature Sheets

Louvre Museum, Bicent. A177

Details or entire paintings: No. 2738, Mona Lisa, by Da Vinci.

No. 2739a, La Femme A La Puce, by Crespi. b, La Femme Hydropique, by Dou. c, Portrait of a Couple, by Ittenbach. d, Cleopatra Enthroned, by Moreau. e, La Richesse, by Vouet. f, Vieillard Et Jeune Garcon, by Ghirlandaio. g, Louis XIV, by Rigaud. h, La Buveuse, by Pieter De Hooch.

No. 2740a, Self-portrait Wearing Spectacles, by Chardin. b, L'Infante Marie-Therese, by Velasquez. c, Spring, by Arcimboldo. d, The Virgin of Sorrows, by Bouts. e, The Study, by Fragonard. f. Francis I, by Clouet. g, Le Condottiere, by Antonello Da Messina. h, La Bohemienne, by Hals.

No. 2741a, Le Femme A La Puce, entire, by Crespi. b, Self-portrait, by Rembrandt. c, Femmes D'Alger Dans Leur Appartement, by Delacroix. d, Tete De Jeune Homme, by Raphael. e, Venus and the Graces, by Botticelli. f, Nature Morte A L'Echiquier, by Lubin Baugin. g, Lady MacBeth Sleepwalking, by Fussli. h, La Tabagie, by Chardin.

Nos. 2742a-c, L'Accordee de Village (left, center, right), by Greuze. d, Self-portrait, by Melendez. e, Knight and Young Girl on Horseback, by Baldung-Grien. f, The Young Begger, by Murillo. g-h, The Pilgrims of Emmaus (left, right), by Mathieu Le Nain.

No. 2743a-b, The Virgin and the Rabbit (diff. details), by Titian. c, La Belle Jardiniere, by Raphael. d, The Lacemaker, by Vermeer. e, Jeanne D'Aragon, by Raphael. f, The Astronomer, by Vermeer. g, The Bridge at Rialto, by Canaletto. h, Sigismond Malatesta, by Piero Della Francesca.

No. 2744, Cour De Ferme, by Jan Brueghel, the Younger. No. 2745, The Bridge at Rialto, by Canaletto. No. 2746, The Coronation of Napoleon I, by David. No. 2747, Details and painting of Mona Lisa. No. 2748, The Fortune Teller, by Caravaggio. No. 2749, The Marriage at Cana, by Veronese.

1993, Dec. 6 Litho. *Perf. 13½x14*

2738	A177	$50	multicolored	80	80
a.			Sheet of 8 + label	6.50	6.50

Sheets of 8 + label

2739	A177	$50	#a.-h.	6.50	6.50
2740	A177	$50	#a.-h.	6.50	6.50
2741	A177	$50	#a.-h.	6.50	6.50
2742	A177	$50	#a.-h.	6.50	6.50
2743	A177	$50	#a.-h.	6.50	6.50

Souvenir Sheets

Perf. 12

2744	A177	$325	multicolored	5.25	5.25
2745	A177	$325	multicolored	5.25	5.25
2746	A177	$325	multicolored	5.25	5.25
2747	A177	$325	multicolored	5.25	5.25
2748	A177	$325	multicolored	5.25	5.25
2749	A177	$325	multicolored	5.25	5.25

Nos. 2744-2746 each contain one 80x47mm stamp. Nos. 2747-2749 one 80x53mm stamp.

Polska '93 — A178

Paintings: $50, $130, Pantaloons, by Tadeusz Brzozowski, 1966. $75, Fortress, by Miedzyrecz. $325, Children in the Garden, by Wladyslaw Podkowinski, 1892, horiz.

1993 *Perf. 14*

2750	A178	$50	multicolored	80	80
2751	A178	$75	multicolored	1.10	1.10
2752	A178	$130	multicolored	2.00	2.00
a.			Pair, #2750, #2752	2.80	2.80

Souvenir Sheet

2753	A178	$325	multicolored	5.25	5.25

Picasso (1881-1973) A179

Paintings: $15.30, Bather, Paris, 1909. $100, Two Nudes, 1906. $190, Nude Seated on a Rock, 1921. $325, The Rescue, 1922.

1993, Nov. Litho. *Perf. 14*

2754	A179	$15.30	multicolored	15	15
2755	A179	$100	multicolored	1.60	1.60
2756	A179	$190	multicolored	3.00	3.00

Souvenir Sheet

2756A	A179	$325	multicolored	5.25	5.25

Rebirth of Democracy, 1st Anniv. — A180

Design: Dr. Cheddie B. Jagan, President of Guyana.

1993, Dec. 17 Litho. *Perf. 13½x14*

2757	A180	$6.40	multicolored	15	15

Miniature Sheet

Aladdin — A181

Nos. 2758a-h, Various characters from Disney animated film, vert. Nos. 2759a-i, Various film scenes. Nos. 2760a-i, Various scenes from Disney animated film.

No. 2761, Genie, Jasmine, and Aladdin. No. 2762, Aladdin, the Genie, Abu, Magic Carpet. No. 2763, Aladdin as Prince Ali Ababwa. No. 2764, Aladdin, Abu, Jasmine.

1993, Dec. 20 Litho. *Perf. 14x13½*

2758	A181	$7.65	Sheet of 8, #a.-h.	1.10	1.10
2759	A181	$50	Sheet of 9, #a.-i.	7.25	7.25
2760	A181	$65	Sheet of 9, #a.-i.	9.00	9.00

Souvenir Sheets

2761	A181	$325	multicolored	5.00	5.00
2762	A181	$325	multicolored	5.00	5.00
2763	A181	$325	multicolored	5.00	5.00
2764	A181	$325	multicolored	5.00	5.00

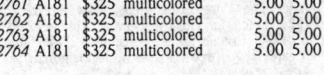

A182

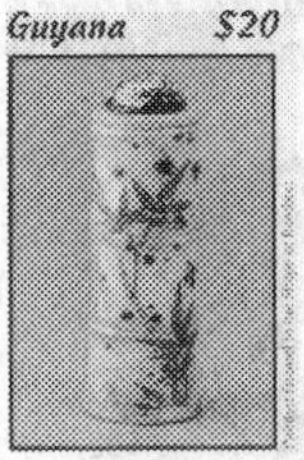

Hong Kong '94 — A183

Stamps, photograph of Happy Valley Horse Race Course: No. 2765, Hong Kong #437, scoreboard. No. 2766, Track, horses, #2545.

Snuff boxes, Qing Dynasty: No. 2767a, Painted enamel in shape of bamboo. b, Painted enamel with human figure. c, Amber with lions playing ball. d, Agate in shape of two gourds. e, Glass overlay with dog. f, Glass, foliage design.

Porcelain, Ch'ing Dynasty: No. 2768a, Covered jar with dragon. b, Rotating brush holder. c, Covered jar with horses. d, Amphora vase with bats & peaches. e, Tea caddy with Fo dogs. f, Vase with wild camellia & peaches.

1994, Feb. 18 *Perf. 14*

2765	A182	$50	multicolored	80	80
2766	A182	$50	multicolored	80	80
a.			Pair, #2765-2766	1.60	1.60

Miniature Sheets

2767	A183	$20	Sheet of 6, #a.-f.	2.00	2.00
2768	A183	$20	Sheet of 6, #a.-f.	2.00	2.00

Nos. 2765-2766 issued in sheets of 5 pairs. No. 2766a is continuous design.

New Year 1994 (Year of the Dog) (#2767e, #2768e).

Miniature Sheets of 6 and 8

Vintage Donald Duck — A184

Movie posters: No. 2769a, Donald's Better Self, 1938. b, Donald's Golf Game, 1938. c, Sea Scouts, 1939. d, Donald's Penguin, 1939. e, A Good Time for a Dime, 1941. f, Truant Officer Donald. g, Orphan's Benefit, 1941. h, Chef Donald, 1941.

No. 2770a, The Village Smithy, 1942. b, Donald's Snow Fight, 1942. c, Donald's Garden, 1942. d, Donald's Gold Mine, 1942. e, The Vanishing Private, 1942. f, Sky Trooper, 1942. g, Bellboy Donald, 1942. h, The New Spirit, 1942.

No. 2771a, Saludos Amigos, 1943. b, The Eyes Have It, 1945. c, Donald's Crime, 1945. d, Straight Shooters, 1947. e, Donald's Dilemma, 1947. f, Bootle Beetle, 1947. g, Dadddy Duck, 1948. h, Soup's On, 1948.

Story boards from Pirate Gold, horiz.: No. 2772a, Pirate ship. b, Carrying treasure chest. c, Donald Duck with map. d, Donald, souvenir shop. e, Donald following Aracuan bird. f, Angry Donald.

Movie posters: No. 2773a, Donald's Happy Birthday, 1949. b, Sea Salts, 1949. c, Honey Harvester, 1949. d, All in a Nutshell, 1949. e, The Greener Yard, 1949. f, Slide, Donald, Slide, 1949. g, Lion Around, 1950. h, Trailer Horn, 1950.

No. 2774a, Bee at the Beach, 1950. b, Out on a Limb, 1950. c, Corn Chips, 1951. d, Test Pilot Donald, 1951. e, Lucky Number, 1951. f, Out of Scale, 1951. g, Bee on Guard, 1951. h, Let's Stick Together, 1952.

No. 2775a, Trick or Treat, 1952. b, Don's Fountain of Youth, 1953. c, Rugged Bear, 1953. d, Canvas Back Duck, 1953. e, Dragon Around, 1954. f, Grin and Bear It, 1954. g, The Flying Squirrel, 1954. h, Up a Tree, 1955.

No. 2776, Studio Fan Card, Melody Time, 1948.

No. 2777, Scene from picture book of first movie, The Wise Little Hen, 1944, horiz. No. 2778, Sketch for closing scene of Timber, 1941. No. 2779, Donald Duck, horiz. No. 2780, Studio fan card, The Three Caballeros, 1945, horiz.

Perf. 14x13½, 13½x14

1993, Dec. 6 **Litho.**

2769-2771	A184	$60 each	7.75	7.75
2772	A184	$80 #a.-f.	7.50	7.50
2773-2775	A184	$80 #a.-h, each	10.00	10.00

Size: 130x104mm

Imperf

2776	A184	$500 multi	7.75	7.75

Souvenir Sheets

Perf. 14x13½, 13½x14

2777-2780	A184	$500 each	8.00	8.00

Tropical Flowers A185

Designs: No. 2781, $6.40, Cestrum parqui. No. 2782, $7.65, Brunfelsia calycina. No. 2783, $12.80, Datura rosei. No. 2784, $15.30, Ruellia macrantha. No. 2785, $50, Portlandia albiflora. No. 2786, $130, Pachystachys coccinea. No. 2787, $190, Beloperone guttata. No. 2788, $250, Ferdinandusa speciosa.

No. 2789a, Clusia grandiflora. b, Begonia haageana. c, Fuchsia simplicicaulis. d, Guaiacum officinale (a). e, Pithecoctenium cynanchoides. f, Sphaeralcea umbellata. g, Erythrina poeppigiana. h, Steriphoma paradoxa. i, Allemanda violacea (f). j, Centropogon cornutus (g). k, Passiflora quadrangularis. l, Victoria amazonica.

No. 2790a, Cobaea scandens. b, Pyrostegia venusta (c). c, Petrea kohautiana (b). d, Hippobroma longiflora (a). e, Cleome hassleriana (b, d, f, h, i). f, Verbena peruviana (c). g, Tropaeolum peregrinum. h, Plumeria rubra (g, i). i, Selenicereus grandiflorus. j, Mandevilla splendens (g). k, Pereskia aculeata. l, Ipomoea learii.

No. 2791, Columnea fendleri. No. 2792, Lophospermum erubescens.

2781-2788	A185	Set of 8	10.00	10.00
2789-2790	A185	$50 each	10.00	10.00
2791-2792	A185	$325 each	5.25	5.25

Nos. 2674-2675 Ovptd. "ROYAL VISIT FEB 19-22, 1994" in One or Two Lines

1994 **Litho.** ***Perf. 13½X14***

2793	A166	Sheet, 2 each #a.-d.	9.00	9.00

Souvenir Sheet

Perf. 14

2794	A166	$325 multicolored	5.25	5.25

Hummel Figurines — A186

Designs: $20, #2803a ($30), Girl holding basket and heart. $25, Boy holding heart. $35, #2804a ($20), Chef holding dessert. $50, #2804b ($130), Girl holding planter of mushrooms. $60, Girl holding plant, horn. No. 2800 ($130), #2803b ($6), Four girls. $190, Two girls, boy and puppy. $250, #2804c ($35), Boy holding covered dish, puppy.

1994, May 5 **Litho.** ***Perf. 14***

2795-2802	A186	Set of 8	11.50	11.50

Souvenir Sheets

2803	A186	#a.-b, #2796, 2801	4.00	4.00
2804	A186	#a.-c, #2799	4.00	4.00

Miniature Sheets

Sierra Club, Cent. A187

Various animals or scenic places: No. 2805a-2805b, American alligator. c.-d, Italian Alps. e.-f, Mono Lake.

No. 2806: a, Red kangaroo. b.-d, Whooping crane. e.-f, Alaskan brown bear. g, Bald eagle. h, Giant panda.

No. 2807, vert.: a.-b, Red kangaroo. c, American alligator. d, Alaskan brown bear. e.-f, Bald eagle. g.-h, Giant panda.

No. 2808, vert.: a.-c, Sea lion. d, Mono Lake. e, Sierra Club centennial emblem. f, Italian Alps. g.-i, Matterhorn.

1994, May 20 **Litho.** ***Perf. 14***

2805	A187	$70 Sheet of 6, #a.-f.	6.50	6.50
2806	A187	$70 Sheet of 8, #a.-h.	8.75	8.75
2807	A187	$70 Sheet of 8, #a.-h.	8.75	8.75
2808	A187	$70 Sheet of 9, #a.-i.	10.00	10.00

Miniature Sheets of 6

First Manned Moon Landing, 25th Anniv. A188

Famous men, aviation & space scenes: No. 2809a, Robert R. Gilruth, Apollo 16. b, Ernst Stuhlinger, Apollo 17. c, Christopher C. Kraft, X-30 National Aero-Space Plane. d, Rudolf Opitz, Me-163, July 24, 1943. e, Clyde W. Tombaugh, "Face on Mars." f, Hermann Oberth, Scene from "The Girl in the Moon."

No. 2810: a, Werner von Braun, Apollo 11. b, Rocco A. Petrone, Apollo 11. c, Eberhard Rees, Apollo 12. d, Charles A. Berry, Apollo 13. e, Thomas O. Paine, Apollo 14. f, A.F. Staats, Apollo 15.

No. 2811: a, Walter Dornberger, 1st A-4 launch. b, Rudolph Nebel, Surveyor 1. c, Robert H. Goddard, Apollo 7. d, Kurt Debus, Apollo 8. e, James T. Webb, Apollo 9. f, George E. Mueller, Apollo 10.

No. 2812, Frank J. Everest, Jr.

1994, July 20 **Litho.** ***Perf. 14***

2809-2811	A188	$60 #a.-f, each	5.75	5.75

Souvenir Sheet

2812	A188	$325 multicolored	5.00	5.00

A189

World War II — A190

Designs: $6, Photo reconnaissance Spitfire. $35, 226 Squadron B-25. $190, 76 Squadron P-47 Thunderbolts.

Europe and North Africa, 1944: No. 2816a Allied landings, Anzio, Jan. 22. b, RAF bombs Amiens prison, Feb. 18. c, Sevastopol falls to Red Army, May 9. d, Allies breach Gustav Line, May 19. e, D-Day, June 6. f, V-1 attacks on London begin, June 13. g, Cease fire declared for Paris, Aug. 19. h, Germany launches V-2 rockets, Sept. 8. i, German battleship Tirpitz sunk, Nov. 12. j, Siege of Bastogne lifted, Dec. 29.

D-Day: No. 2817a, Paratroops drop behind enemy lines. b, Glider-born commandos land behind enemy lines. c, USS Arkansas shells Omaha beach defenses. d, Allied aircraft attack enemy movements. e, Allied landing craft hit the beach. f, Allied troops pinned down by enemy fire. g, Commandos exit landing craft. h, Specialized Allied tanks destroy enemy mines. i, Allies break through beach defenses. j, Consolidation of position.

No. 2818, RAF Lancaster bomber.

1994, June 20 ***Perf. 14***

2813	A189	$6 multicolored	15	15
2814	A189	$35 multicolored	55	55
2815	A189	$190 multicolored	3.00	3.00

Miniature Sheets of 10

Perf. 13

2816	A190	$60 #a.-j.	9.50	9.50
2817	A190	$60 #a.-j.	9.50	9.50

Souvenir Sheet

Perf. 14

2818	A189	$325 multicolored	5.00	5.00

A191

Butterflies A192

Designs: $6, Heliconius melpomene. $20, Helicopius cupido. $25, Agrias claudina. $30, Parides coelus. $50, Heliconius hecale. $60, Morpho diana. $190, Dismorphia orise. $250, Morpho deidamia.

No. 2827: a, Anaea marthesia. b, Brassolis astyra. c, Heliconius melpomene. d, Haetera piera. e, Morpho diana dixey. f, Parides coelus. g, Catagramma pitheas. h, Nessaea obrinus. i, Automeris janus. j, Papilio torquatus. k, Eunica sophonisba. l, Ceratinia nise. m, Panacea procilla. n, Pyrrhogyra neaerea. o, Morpho deidamia. p, Dismorphia orise.

No. 2829, Eunica sophonisba. No. 2830, Anaea eribotes. No. 2831, Hamadryas velutina. No. 2832, Agrias claudina.

1994, July 5 **Litho.** ***Perf. 14***

2819-2826	A191	Set of 8	10.00	10.00

Miniature Sheet of 16

2827	A192	$50 #a.-p.	12.50	12.50

Souvenir Sheets

2829-2830	A191	$325 each	5.00	5.00
2831-2832	A192	$325 each	5.00	5.00

Nos. 2829-2830 each contain one 43x28mm stamp.

Miniature Sheets of 24

Bible Stories — A193

Story of Ruth and Naomi: Nos. 2833a-2833f: Ruth & Naomi preparing to leave Moab & return to Israel. g.-l: Ruth harvesting grain in fields of Boaz. m-r: Boaz receives a man's sandal, finalizing sale of Naomi's field. s-x: Naomi, Boaz, Ruth and Obed, who was David's grandfather.

Story of Joseph: Nos. 2834a-2834d, Jacob made Joseph a coat of many colors. e-h, Joseph's brothers take his coat and cast him into pit. i-l, Joseph is sold to the Ishmaelites. m-p, Joseph is accused by Potiphar's wife and thrown into prison. q-t, Joseph interprets Pharoah's dreams. u-x, Joseph is reunited with his brothers.

Parting of the Red Sea: Nos. 2835a-2835x, Moses leading Israelites through sea, Pharoah's army drowning.

Daniel and the Lions: No. 2836a-2836x, Daniel in lion's den surrounded by various animals, angel.

1994, Aug. 4 **Litho.** ***Perf. 14***

2833-2836	A193	$20 #a.-x, each	7.75	7.75

Nos. 2835-2836 have continuous design.

PHILAKOREA '94

A194 A195

Designs: $6, Statues of socialist ideals, Pyongyang. $25, Statue of Adm. Yi Sun-sin. $120, Sokkat'ap Pagoda, Pulguksa. $130, Village guardian, Chejudo Island.

Ten-fold screens: Nos. 2841b-2841e, Cranes. h-i, Deer. j, Deer, mushrooms, waterfall.

Nos. 2842b-2842d, Cranes. f-h, Deer. c, h, Waterfalls. i-j, Mushrooms.

No. 2843, Falled Rock, horiz. No. 2844, Westerners at Korean Court, horiz.

1994, June 20 **Litho.** ***Perf. 14***

2837-2840	A194	Set of 4	5.00	5.00

Miniature Sheets of 10

Perf. 13

2841-2842	A195	$60 each, #a.-j.	11.00	11.00

Souvenir Sheets

Perf. 14

2843-2844	A194	$325 each	5.75	5.75

Nos. 2841-2842 have continuous design.

Miniature Sheet of 8

Entertainers of Takarazuka Revue, Japan — A196

Designs: a, $60, Mira Anju. b, $60, Yuki Amami. c, $60, Maki Ichiro. d, $60, Yu Shion. e, $20, Miki Maya. f, $20, Fubuki Takane. g, $20, Seika Juze. h, $20, Saki Asaji.

1994 ***Perf. 14½***

2845	A196	#a.-h. + 4 labels	5.75	5.75

Nos. 2845a-2845d are 34x47mm.

Intl. Olympic Committee, Cent.
A197 A198

Designs: $20, Nancy Kerrigan, US, figure skating, 1994. $35, Sawao Kato, Japan, gymnastics, 1976. $130, Florence Griffith-Joyner, US, 100-, 200-meters, 1988.

$325, Mark Wasmeier, Germany, super giant & giant slalom, 1994.

1994, June 20

2846-2848 A197 Set of 3 3.00 3.00

Souvenir Sheet

2849 A198 $325 multicolored 5.25 5.25

1994 World Cup Soccer Championships, US — A199

Designs: $6, Paulo Futre, Portugal. $35, Lyndon Hooper, Canada. $60, Enzo Francescoli, Uruguay. $190, Freddy Rincon, Colombia.

No. 2854a, Paolo Maldini, Italy. b, Guyana player. c, Bwalya Kalusha, Zambia. d, Diego Maradona, Argentina. e, Andreas Brehme, Germany. f, Eric Wynalda, US.

No. 2855a, John Doyle, US. b, Eric Wynalda, US, diff. c, Thomas Dooley, US. d, Ernie Stewart, US. f, Marcelo Balboa, US. g, Coach Bora Milutinovic, US.

No. 2856, 1994 World Cup program cover. No. 2857, Oiler Watson.

1994, Aug. 8

2850-2853 A199 Set of 4 4.00 4.00

Miniature Sheets of 6

2854-2855 A199 $60 #a.-f., each 4.75 4.75

Souvenir Sheets

2856-2857 A199 $325 each 5.25 5.25

A200 A201

Birds: No. 2858a, Goshawk. b, Lapwing. c, Ornate umbrellabird. d, Slatey-headed parakeet. e, Regent bowerbird. f, Egytian goose. g, White-winged crossbill. h, Waxwing. i, Ruff. j, Hoopoe. k, Superb starling. l, Great jacamar.

No. 2859a, Peregrine falcon. b, Great spotted woodpecker. c, White-throated kingfisher. d, Peruvian cock-of-the-rock. e, Yellow-headed Amazon. f, Victoria crowned pigeon. g, Little owl. h, Pheasant. i, Goldfinch. j, Jay. k, Sulphur-brasted toucan. l, Japanese blue flycatcher.

No. 2860, Gould's violet-ear. No. 2861, Bald eagle.

1994, Sept. 15

Sheets of 12

2858-2859 A200 $35 #a.-l., each 6.75 6.75

Souvenir Sheets

2860-2861 A200 $325 each 5.25 5.25

PHILAKOREA '94.

1994

German athletes: $6, Anja Fichtel, fencing, 1988, horiz. $25, Annegret Richter, 100-meter dash, 1976. $30, Heike Henkel, high jump, 1982. $35, Armin Hary, 100-meter dash, 1960. $50, Heide Rosendahl, long jump, 1972. $60, Josef Neckermann, equestrian grand prix, 1968. $130, Heike Drechsler, long jump, 1988. $190, Ulrike Mayfarth, high jump, 1984. $250, Michael Gross, swimming, 1984, horiz.

No. 2871, Franziska van Almsick, swimming, 1992. No. 2872, Steffi Graf, tennis, 1992.

2862-2870 A201 Set of 9 12.50 12.50

Souvenir Sheets

2871-2872 A201 $325 each 5.25 5.25

1996 Summer Olympics, Atlanta.

Miniature Sheets of 9

Space Missions, First Manned Moon Landing, 25th Anniv. A202

Designs: No. 2873a, Laika, first dog in space. b, Yuri Gagarin, first man in space. c, John Glenn, first American to orbit earth. d, Edward White, first American to walk in space. e, Neil Armstrong, first to step foot onto moon. f, Luna 16. g, Luna 17. h, Skylab 1. i, 1975 Apollo-Soyuz.

Unmanned probes: No. 2874a, Mars 3, Mars. b, Mariner 10, Mercury. c, Voyager, planetary grand tour. d, Pioneer, Venus. e, Giotto, Halley's Comet. f, Megellan, Venus. g, Galileo, Jupiter. h, Ulysses, Sun. i, Cassini, Titan.

No. 2875, "Buzz" Aldrin, Neil Armstrong, Michael Collins. No. 2876, Pioneer 1, 2.

1994, Nov. 10 Litho. *Perf. 13½*

2873-2874 A202 $60 #a.-i, each 8.75 8.75

Souvenir Sheets

2875-2876 A202 $325 each 5.25 5.25

Steam Locomotives — A203

Designs: No. 2877, $25, South Eastern Railway #285, 1882. No. 2878, $25, West Point Foundry, 1830. No. 2879, $300, Mt. Washington Cog Railway, 1886. No. 2880, $300, Stroudley-Brighton, 1872.

No. 2881a, "John Bull," 1831. b, Stephenson, 1837. c, "Atlantic," 1832. d, Stourbridge Lion, 1829. e, Polonceau, 1854. f, Rogers, 1856. g, "Vulcan," 1858. h, "Namur," 1846.

No. 2882a, West Point Foundry, 1832. b, Sequin, 1830. c, Stephenson's Planet, 1830. d, Norris 4-2-0, 1840. e, Union Iron Works os San Francisco, 1867. f, Andrew Jackson, 1832. g, Herald, 1831. h, Cumberland, 1845.

No. 2883a, Pennsylvania's Class K, 1880. b, Cooke, 1885. c, John B. Turner, 1867. d, Baldwin, 1871. e, Richard Trevithick, 1804. f, John Stephens, 1825. g, John Blenkinsop, 1814. h, Pennsylvania, 1803.

$250, Est Railway, 1878. $300, "Claud Hamilton," 1840.

1994, Nov. 15 *Perf. 14*

2877-2880 A203 Set of 4 4.50 4.50

Miniature Sheets of 8 + Label

2881-2883 A203 $30 #a.-h, each 3.75 3.75

Souvenir Sheets

2884 A203 $250 multicolored 4.00 4.00
2885 A203 $300 multicolored 4.75 4.75

NUMBERS CHANGED IN 1994 EDITION

Old	New	Old	New
373	1035	530	1101
374	1089	531	1138
375	1119	532	1157
376	1051	533	1163
377	1030	534	1069
378	1103	535	1121
379	1088	536	1159
380	1116	537	1027
381	1105	538	1036
382	1100	539	1046
383	1117	540	1054
384	1090	541	1071
385	1144	542	1074
386	1126	543	1076
387	1164	544	1079
388	1092	545	1235
389	1134	546	1145
390	1156	547	1106
391	1050	548	1084
392	1032	549	1193
393	1085	550	1094
394	1107	551	1209
395	1042	552	1199
396	1029	553	1184
397	1033	554	1215
398	1022	555	1168
399	1061	556	1239
400	1045	557	1169
401	1078	558	1210
402	1082	559	1212
403	1095	560	1310
404	1098	561	1305
405	1120	562	1314
406	1123	563	1316
407	1162	564	1258
408	1158	565	1278
409	1096	583	1249
410	1026	584	1235
411	1141	585	1267
412	1151	586	1231
413	1109	587	1202
414	1113	588	1261A
415	1149	589	1256
416	1057	590	1167
417	1066	591	1312
418	1058	592	1318
419	1034	593	1307
420	1021	594	1322
421	1081	595	1250
422	1067	596	1242
423	1111	597	1283
424	1097	598	1302
425	1099	599	1326
426	1115	600	1296
427	1023	601	1270
428	1044	602	1325
429	1060	603	1288
430	1059	604	1271
431	1028	605	1260
432	1055	606	1328
433	1037	607	1276
434	1047	608	1252
435	1041	609	1280
436	1068	610	1300
437	1110	611	1294
438	1155	612	1333
439	1104	613	1334
440	1062	614	1335
441	1065	615	1336
442	1064	616	1196
443	1083	617	1291
444	1073	618	1290
445	1080	619	1229
446	1075	620	1284
447	1072	621	1273
448	1056	622	1268
449	1129	623	1221
450	1147	624	1298
451	1125	624A	1237
452	1040	624B	1321
453	1024	624C	1282
454	1038	631	1319
455	1077	632	1308
456	1048	633	1285
457	1063	634	1286
458	1131	635	1216
459	1053	636	1178
460	1102	637	1206
461	1122	638	1191
462	1070	639	1170
463	1139	640	1176
464	1087	641	1204

465	1137	642	1222
466	1133	643	1198
467	1161	644	1180
468	1143	645	1187
469	1153	646	1182
470	1220	647	1225
471	1154	648	1243
472	1205	649	1241
473	1197	650	1218
474	1224	651	1174
475	1214	652	1226
476	1181	653	1233
477	1263	654	1211
478	1240	655	1238
479	1246	656	1173
480	1172	657	1248
481	1190	658	1234
482	1232	659	1166
483	1175	660	1201
484	1183	661	1230
485	1244	662	1208
486	1254	663	1213
487	1188	664	1186
488	1185	665	1247
489	1219	666	1236
490	1227	667	1228
491	1177	668	1253
492	1203	669	1255
493	1112	670	1299
494	1179	671	1272
495	1189	672	1274
496	1043	673	1292
497	1194	674	1323
498	1171	676	1264
499	1192	677	1262
500	1223	678	1257
501	1207	679	1277
502	1200	680	1266
503	1217	681	1251
504	1152	682	1259
505	1127	683	1269
506	1228	684	1275
507	1140	685	1265
508	1142	686	1293
509	1031	687	1304
510	1049	688	1309
511	1091	689	1313
512	1052	690	1315
513	1108	691	1320
514	1039	692	1279
515	1135	693	1281
516	1136	694	1297
517	1150	695	1287
518	1025	696	1295
519	1086	697	1301
520	1093	698	1324
521	1114	699	1303
522	1118	700	1306
523	1130	701	1311
524	1146	702	1317
525	1160	703	1289
526	1124	704	1327
527	1132	705	1195
528	1148	706	1329
529	1165	707	1330
		708	1331
		709	1332

Other Issues

Old	New
330-333	414-417
334-337	418-421
338	437
339-341	608-610
342-346	661-665
347-354	706-713
355-358	822-825
359	660
360	913
361	917
362-366	918-922
367-372	927-932
566-567A	1337-1340
568-571	1355-1358
571A-571D	1994-1997
572-576	1394-1398
577-578	1461
579-582	1505-1508
625-630	1826-1831
710-715	1852-1857
716-721	1864-1869
722-723	1989-1990
727-731	2001-2005
734-735	2010-2011
736-737	2008-2009
738-749	2012-2023
750-757	2208-2215

759-767	2216-2224
768-780	2228-2240
788-797	2241-2250
798-806	2268-2276
807-813	2291-2297
814-840	2305-2331
841-848	2283-2290
849-855	2298-2304
856-874	2359-2377
875-901	2332-2358
902	2378
903-905	2379-2381
912	2389
913-923	2390-2400
940-952	2440-2452
953-970	2495-2513
971-975	2515-2519
976-992A	2470-2487
993-1006	2401-2414
1007-1020	2426-2439
1021-1037	2453-2469
1038-1044	2488-2494
1045-1075	2520-2550
1076-1085	2558-2567
1090-1102	2568-2580
1105-1106	2583-2584
1108-1109	2586-2587
1112	2589
E1	E7
E2-E3	E9-E10
E4	E8
E5-E6	E16-E17
E7	E18
E8-E10	E26-E28
E11-E12	E29-E30
O1	O46
O2-O4	O50-O52
O5-O7	O54-O56
O8-O9	O40-O41
O10	O43
O11	O45
O12	O47
O13	O53
O14	O42
O15	O44
O16-O17	O48-O49

AIR POST STAMPS

No. 321 Surcharged in Blue "HUMAN RIGHTS / DAY / 1981 / 110 AIR"

1981, Nov. 14 *Perfs. as Before*

C1 A74 110c on $3 No. 321

For surcharge see No. 997.

Nos. 133, 136 and 146 Surcharged in Red, Black or Blue "AIR / Princess / of Wales / 1961-1982"

1982, June 25 *Perfs. as Before*

Printing Methods as Before

C2 A28 110c on 5c No. 136 (R)
C3 A28 220c on 1c No. 133
C4 A28 330c on $2 No. 146 (Bl)

For surcharges see Nos. 623, 785-787, 801-802, 804, 804A, O19, O21, O30-O39.

No. 287 Surcharged in Dark Blue "UNICEF / 1946-1986 / AIR" or "UNESCO / 1946-1986 / AIR"

1986, Oct. 24 **Litho.** *Perfs. as Before*

C5 A66 120c on $1 UNICEF
C6 A66 120c on $1 UNESCO
a. Pair, #C5-C6

Nos. 1026, 1096, 1096a, 1100, 1138, 1163 Surcharged "AIR"

1987-88 **Litho.** *Perf. 14*

Design A91

Plate Numbers in Parentheses

C7 75c on 25c No. 1100 (59)
C9 75c on No. 1026 (5)
C10 75c on No. 1096 (55)
a. 75c on No. 1096a
C11 75c on No. 1138 (83)
C12 75c on No. 1163 (95)

Issue dates: No. C7, Nov. 1987. Nos. C9-C12, Aug. 1988.

SPECIAL DELIVERY STAMPS

Orchid Type of 1985 Surcharged "EXPRESS"

1986-87 **Litho.** *Perf. 14*

Plate Numbers in Parentheses

E1 A91 $12 on #1372 (65)
E2 A91 $15 on 40c #1145 (86)
E3 A91(p) $15 on #E2 (86)
E4 A91 $25 on 25c like #1090 (53)

Issue dates: $12, $25, #E2, Nov. 10. #E3, Dec. 1987. #E4 not issued without surcharge.

No. 1461c Surcharged "EXPRESS"

1986-87 **Litho.** *Imperf.*

E5 A96 $20 on 320c #1461c

No. E5 Ovptd. with Maltese Cross

1987, Mar. 3

E6 A96 $20 on No. E5

Orchid Type of 1985 Inscribed "Express"

1987-88 **Litho.** *Perf. 14*

Series 2

Plate Numbers in Parentheses

E7 A91 $15 like #1186 (11) 4.00 4.00
E8 A91 $20 like #1323 (93) 7.25 7.25
E9 A91 $25 like #1274 (63) 6.50 6.50
E10 A91 $45 like #1228 (35) 12.00 12.00

Issue dates: $45, Sept. 1. $15, Sept. 29. $25, Oct. 26. $20, May 17, 1988.

No. "1461" Surcharged "EXPRESS / FORTY DOLLARS"

1987, Nov. *Perf. 14*

E11 A96 $40 on 320c No. 1461, imperf. btwn.

A five-pointed star appears between the lines of the surcharge on #E11. See #E14.

Nos. 1827e, 1830e Surcharged in Red "SPECIAL DELIVERY"

1988, Aug. 10 *Perf. 15*

E12 A100 $40 on $3.20 #1827e
E13 A100 $45 on $3.30 #1830e

See Nos. 2054b, 2056b.

Nos. "1461," 1822c Surcharged in Red "EXPRESS / FORTY DOLLARS"

1989, Mar. *Perf. 14*

E14 A96 $40 on 320c #1461, imperf. btwn.
E15 A96 $40 on 320c #1822c, imperf. btwn.

Butterflies Type of 1989 Inscribed "EXPRESS"

Souvenir Sheets

1989, Sept. 7 **Litho.** *Perf. 14*

E16 A115 $130 Phareas coeleste 7.75 7.75
E17 A115 $190 Papilio torquatus 12.25 12.25

For overprints see Nos. E19-E22, E24, E26-E27, E31.

Women in Space Type of 1989 Inscribed "EXPRESS"

Souvenir Sheets

1989, Nov. 8

E18 A116 $190 Valentina Tereshkova 12.25 12.25

For overprints see No. E23, E25, E28, E32.

Nos. E16-E17 Ovptd. with World Stamp Expo '89 Emblem

1989, Nov. 17

E19 A115 $130 on No. E16
E20 A115 $190 on No. E17

Nos. E16-E18 Ovptd. in Sheet Margin "Stamp World London 90" and Show Emblem

1990, May 3

E21 A115 $130 on No. E16
E22 A115 $190 on No. E17
E23 A116 $190 on No. E18

Nos. E17-E18 Ovptd. in Sheet Margin with Rotary Emblem and "ROTARY / INTERNATIONAL / 1905-1990"

1990, Mar.

E24 A115 $190 on No. E17
E25 A116 $190 on No. E18

Nos. E16-E18 Ovptd. in Sheet Margin "90th BIRTHDAY / H.M. THE / QUEEN MOTHER"

1990, June 8 **Litho.** *Perf. 14*

E26 A115 $130 on No. E16 7.75 7.75
E27 A115 $190 on No. E17 12.25 12.25
E28 A116 $190 on No. E18 12.25 12.25

Endangered Wildlife Type

Souvenir Sheets

1990, Nov. 6 **Litho.** *Perf. 14*

E29 A131 $130 Harpy eagle 6.25 6.25
E30 A131 $150 Ocelot 7.25 7.25

Nos. E29-E30 each contain one 43x57mm stamp.

Nos. E16, E18 Ovptd. in Sheet Margin with "BELGICA PHILATELIC / EXPOSITION 1990" and Scout, Lions, Rotary and Show Emblems

1990, June 2

E31 A115 $130 on No. E16
E32 A116 $190 on No. E18

No. E31 has Scout and Lions emblems. No. E32 has Scout and Rotary emblems.

POSTAGE DUE STAMPS

Type of British Guiana Inscribed "Guyana"

Perf. $13^1/_2$x14

1967-68 **Wmk. 314** **Typo.**

J2 D1 2c black ('68) 60 60
J3 D1 4c ultramarine 18 18
J4 D1 12c carmine 40 40

For surcharges see Nos. 897-898.

1973 **Wmk. 364**

J5 D1 1c green 15 15
J6 D1 2c black 15 15
J7 D1 4c ultramarine 15 15
J8 D1 12c carmine 25 25
Set value 55 55

For surcharges see #341-349, 658, 899-900.

OFFICIAL STAMPS

Nos. 74, 139, 141, 143-144, 146-147, 289A, 297, 300, 333, 395, 397, 401 Surcharged in Black, Red, or Black and Red

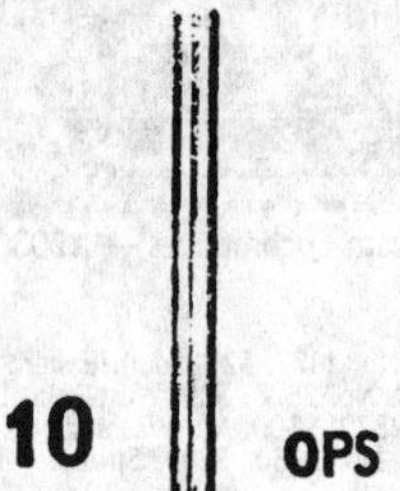

1981-82 *Perfs. as Before*

Printing Methods as Before

O1 A28 10c on 25c #141 (Bk & R)
O2 A8 15c on #74
O3 A28 15c on #139
O4 A28 30c on $2 #146 (Bk & R)
O5 A28 50c on #143 (R)
O6 A69 50c on #300
O7 A28 60c on #144 (R)
O8 A17 100c on #395
O9 A68 100c on $3 #297 (Bk & R)
O10 A17 110c on #397
O11 A28 $1.10 on #333 (R)
O12 A28 125c on #401 (R)
O13 A28 $2 on #146 (R)
O14 A28 $5 on #147 (R)
O15 A66 $10 on #289A

Issue dates: Nos. O1, O5, O7, O15, June 8. Nos. O2, O4, O9, O11-O12, July 1. No. O13, July 12, 1982. Others, July 7.

Surcharge on Nos. O3, O6, O8, O10, O13-O14 have no obliterator. No. O11 is airmail.

Refer to 2nd paragraph in footnote following #147 for #O1, O4-O5, O7 and O13.

For overprints and surcharges see No. 406, 425, 452, 454-456, 603, 618, 650, 817, 854, 861, 866, 933, 1378, 1381, 1384, 1387-1388.

Nos. 162, 256, 258, 282, 480, C2-C3 Surcharged in Blue or Black

1982 *Perfs. as Before*

Printing Methods as Before

O16 A66 20c on #282
O17 A33 40c on #162
O18 A60 40c on #256
O19 A28 110c on #C2 (Bk)
O20 A60 $2 on #258
O21 A28 220c on #C3
O22 A69 250c on #480

Issue dates: 110c, Sept. 15. Others, May 17. Nos. O19, O21 are airmail.

No. 481 Surcharged "OPS" Reading Up in Blue Violet or Blue Violet and Black

1984, Apr. 2 *Perfs. as Before*

O23 A66 150c on $5
O24 A66 200c on $5
O25 A66 225c on $5 (BV & Bk)
O25A A66 230c on $5
O26 A66 260c on $5
O27 A66 320c on $5
O28 A66 350c on $5
O29 A66 600c on $5

Nos. C2-C3 Surcharged "OPS" in Black and Blue, Black or Blue

1984, June 25 *Perfs. as Before*

O30 A28 25c on No. C2 (Bk)
O31 A28 30c on No. C2
O32 A28 45c on No. C3
O33 A28 55c on No. C2 (Bk)
O34 A28 60c on No. C3
O35 A28 75c on No. C3
O36 A28 90c on No. C3 (Bl)
O37 A28 120c on No. C3
O38 A28 130c on No. C3 (Bl)
O39 A28 330c on No. C3 (Bl)

Overprint reads up on No. O39.

Orchid Type of 1985

1987-88 **Litho.** **Unwmk.** *Perf. 14*

Series 2

Plate Numbers in Parentheses

O40 A91 120c like #1250 (48) 24 24
O41 A91 130c like #1322 (92) 25 25
O42 A91 140c like #1229 (36) 28 28
O43 A91 150c like #1242 (43) 30 30
O44 A91 175c like #1221 (31) 38 38
O45 A91 200c like #1271 (61) 40 40
O46 A91 225c like #1213 (26) 45 45
O47 A91 230c like #1283 (68) 45 45
O48 A91 250c like #1268 (59) 52 52
O49 A91 260c like #1284 (69) 55 55
O50 A91 275c like #1319 (90) 55 55
O51 A91 320c like #1292 (75) 62 62
O52 A91 330c like #1208 (23) 65 65
O53 A91 350c like #1326 (95) 70 70
O54 A91 600c like #1285 (70) 1.20 1.20
O55 A91 $12 like #1286 (71) 2.40 2.40
O56 A91 $15 like #1308 (84) 3.00 3.00
Nos. O40-O56 (17) 12.94 12.94

Nos. O47, O53-O56 horiz.

Issue dates: Nos. O42, O44, O48, O49, Oct. 5, 1988. Others, Oct. 5, 1987.

For overprints & surcharges see #1694, 1697, 1703, 1707, 1722-1726, 1728-1730.

PARCEL POST STAMPS

No. 145 Surcharged "PARCEL POST"

1981, June 8 **Litho.** *Perf. $13^1/_2$*

Q1 A28 $15 on $1 No. 145
Q2 A28 $20 on $1 No. 145

For overprints see Nos. QO1-QO2.

No. 333 Surcharged "PARCEL POST" in Blue

1983, Jan. 15

Q3 A28 $12 on No. 333

For surcharge see No. 624.

No. 146 Surcharged "Parcel Post"

1983, Sept. 14
Q4 A28 $12 on $1.10 on $2

No. Q4 has a horizontal Royal Wedding / 1981 surcharge similar to No. 331. For overprint see No. QO5.

No. 255 Surcharged in Red "TWENTY FIVE DOLLARS / PARCEL POST 25.00"

1985, Apr. 25 *Perf. 14*
Q5 A60 $25 on 35c No. 255

PARCEL POST OFFICIAL STAMPS

Nos. Q1-Q2 Overprinted "OPS" in Red

1981, June 8
QO1 A28 $15 on No. Q1
QO2 A28 $20 on No. Q2

For surcharges see Nos. 1389-1390.

No. 333 Surcharged in Blue "OPS / 1982 / Parcel Post / $12.00"

1983, Jan. 15
QO3 A28 $12 on No. 333

No. QO3 Overprinted "OPS" in Black

1983, Aug. 22
QO4 A28 $12 on No. QO3

No. Q4 Overprinted "OPS" in Blue

1983, Nov. 3
QO5 A28 $12 on No. Q4

JAMAICA

LOCATION — Caribbean Sea, about 90 miles south of Cuba
GOVT. — Independent state in the British Commonwealth
AREA — 4,411 sq. mi.
POP. — 2,230,000 (est. 1982)
CAPITAL — Kingston

Jamaica became an independent state in the British Commonwealth in August 1962. As a colony, it administered two dependencies: Cayman Islands and Turks and Caicos Islands.

12 Pence = 1 Shilling
20 Shillings = 1 Pound
100 Cents = 1 Dollar (1969)

Catalogue values for unused stamps in this country are for Never Hinged items, beginning with Scott 129 in the regular postage section and Scott B4 in the semi-postal section.

Values for Nos. 1-12 are for copies with perforations cutting into the design.

Queen Victoria
A1 A2

A3

A4

A5

A6

1860-63 Typo. Wmk. 45 *Perf. 14*
1 A1 1p blue 37.50 6.75
a. Diagonal half used as ½p on cover 850.00
2 A2 2p rose 90.00 30.00
3 A3 3p green ('63) 110.00 24.00
4 A4 4p brown org 140.00 16.00
a. 4p orange 140.00 16.00
5 A5 6p lilac 165.00 10.00
a. 6p deep lilac 550.00 30.00
6 A6 1sh brown 165.00 17.00
a. 1sh lilac brown 500.00 17.00
b. 1sh yellow brown 450.00 17.00

All except No. 3 exist imperforate.

1870-71 Wmk. 1
7 A1 1p blue 22.50 1.00
8 A2 2p rose 32.50 35
a. 2p brownish rose 75.00 35
9 A3 3p green 72.50 3.50
10 A4 4p brown org ('72) 140.00 3.50
a. 4p red orange 475.00 4.50
11 A5 6p lilac ('71) 40.00 2.75
12 A6 1sh brown ('73) 17.50 5.25

The 1p and 4p exist imperf.
See Nos. 17-23, 40, 43, 47-53.

A7

A8

A9

A10

1872, Oct. 29
13 A7 ½p claret 8.50 1.40

Exists imperf. See No. 16.

1875, Aug. 27 *Perf. 12½*
14 A8 2sh red brown 22.50 22.50
15 A9 5sh violet 70.00 92.50

Exist imperf.
See Nos. 29-30, 44, 54.

1883-90 Wmk. 2 *Perf. 14*
16 A7 ½p blue green ('85) 30 15
a. ½p gray green 30 15
17 A1 1p blue ('84) 250.00 6.75
18 A1 1p carmine ('85) 7.50 70
a. 1p rose 32.50 70
19 A2 2p rose ('84) 150.00 3.50
20 A2 2p slate ('85) 27.50 28
a. 2p gray 37.50 35
21 A3 3p ol green ('86) 1.25 70
22 A4 4p red brown 1.65 28
a. 4p orange brown 250.00 12.00
23 A5 6p orange yel ('90) 7.00 5.00
a. 6p yellow 17.50 8.50
Nos. 16-23 (8) 445.20 17.36

Nos. 18 and 20 exist imperf. Perf. 12 stamps are considered to be proofs.
For surcharge, see No. 27.

1889-91
24 A10 1p lilac & red vio 70 15
25 A10 2p green 2.75 1.75
26 A10 2½p lilac & ultra ('91) 2.75 90

No. 22a Surcharged in Black **TWO PENCE HALF-PENNY**

1890, June
27 A4 2½p on 4p org brn 22.50 7.50
b. Double surcharge 250.00 225.00
d. "PFNNY" 100.00 67.50
f. As "d," double surcharge

Three settings of surcharge.

1897
28 A6 1sh brown 4.75 3.00
29 A8 2sh red brown 26.00 14.00
30 A9 5sh violet 35.00 *45.00*

The 2sh exists imperf.

Llandovery Falls
A12

Arms of Jamaica
A13

1900, May 1 Engr. Wmk. 1
31 A12 1p red 55 15

1901, Sept. 25
32 A12 1p red & black 1.10 15
a. Pair, imperf. horiz.
b. Bluish paper 175.00 125.00

1903-04 Typo. Wmk. 2
33 A13 ½p green & black 68 15
b. "SERv ET" for "SERVIET" 32.50 37.50
34 A13 1p car & black ('04) 2.00 15
b. "SERv ET" for "SERVIET" 35.00 35.00
35 A13 2½p ultra & black 2.00 45
a. "SERv ET" for "SERVIET" 45.00 50.00
36 A13 5p yel & black ('04) 14.00 *22.50*
a. "SERv ET" for "SERVIET" 600.00 *625.00*

1905-11 Chalky Paper Wmk. 3
37 A13 ½p green & black 75 15
b. "SERv ET" for "SERVIET" 35.00 35.00
38 A13 1p car & black 8.50 15
39 A13 2½p ultra & blk ('07) 1.50 65
40 A4 4p black, *yel* ('10) 8.50 17.50
41 A13 5p yel & black ('07) 16.00 19.00
a. "SERv ET" for "SERVIET" 500.00 700.00
42 A13 6p red vio & vio ('11) 6.50 8.50
43 A6 1sh black, *green* ('10) 2.00 4.25
44 A8 2sh vio, *blue* ('10) 4.25 2.50
45 A13 5sh vio & black 26.00 22.50
Nos. 37-45 (9) 74.00 75.20

1905-11 Ordinary Paper
46 A13 2½p ultra ('10) 95 42
47 A3 3p olive green 1.15 25
48 A3 3p vio, *yel* ('10) 70 45
49 A4 4p red brn ('08) 32.50 27.50
50 A4 4p red, *yel* ('11) 1.25 2.75
51 A5 6p dull vio ('09) 2.50 6.25
52 A5 6p org yel ('09) 12.50 15.00
a. 6p orange ('06) 12.50 15.00
53 A6 1sh brown ('06) 10.00 4.00
54 A8 2sh red brn ('08) 85.00 87.50
Nos. 46-54 (9) 146.55 144.12

Nos. 48 and 51 also come on chalky paper.

A14

A15

1906
58 A14 ½p green 32 15
a. Booklet pane of 6
59 A15 1p carmine 38 15
Set value 15

For overprints, see Nos. MR1, MR4, MR7, MR10.

Edward VII
A16

George V
A17

1911, Feb. 3
60 A16 2p gray 2.00 *7.75*

1912-20
61 A17 1p scarlet ('16) 15 15
a. 1p carmine ('12) 15 15
b. Booklet pane of 6
62 A17 1½p brn org ('16) 1.40 15
a. 1½p yellow orange 3.25 95
63 A17 2p gray 45 75
64 A17 2½p ultra ('13) 25 15

Chalky Paper
65 A17 3p violet, *yel* 45 15
66 A17 4p scar & blk, *yel* ('13) 60 38
67 A17 6p red vio & dl vio 60 1.25
68 A17 1sh black, *green* 85 55
a. 1sh blk, *bl grn*, olive back ('20) 4.50 3.25
69 A17 2sh ultra & vio, *blue* ('19) 7.75 9.25
70 A17 5sh scar & green, *yel* ('19) 27.50 30.00

Surface-colored Paper
71 A17 3p violet, *yel* ('13) 45 22
72 A17 4p scar & black, *yel* ('14) 85 1.75
73 A17 1sh black, *green* ('15) 1.75 3.00
Nos. 61-73 (13) 43.05 47.75

See Nos. 101-102. For overprints, see Nos. MR2-MR3, MR5-MR6, MR8-MR9, MR11.

Exhibition Buildings of 1891 — A18

Arawak Woman Preparing Cassava — A19

World War I Contingent Embarking for Overseas Duty — A20

King's House, Spanish Town — A21

Return of Overseas Contingent, 1919 — A22

Columbus Landing in Jamaica — A23

Cathedral in Spanish Town — A24

Statue of Queen Victoria — A26

Memorial to Admiral Rodney — A27

Monument to Sir Charles Metcalfe — A28

Woodland Scene — A29

King George V — A30

1919-21 Typo. Wmk. 3 *Perf. 14*

Chalky Paper

75	A18	½p ol grn & dk grn ('20)	16	15
76	A19	1p org & car ('21)	2.00	15

Engr.

Ordinary Paper

77	A20	1½p green	16	15
78	A21	2p grn & bl ('21)	1.00	1.50
79	A22	2½p blue & dk blue ('21)	65	52
80	A23	3p blue & grn ('21)	1.00	32
81	A24	4p green & dk brown ('21)	2.00	5.00
83	A26	1sh brt org & org ('20)	2.25	2.25
a.		Frame inverted	18,500.	12,000.
		As "a," revenue cancel		2,500.
84	A27	2sh brn & bl ('20)	12.50	15.00
85	A28	3sh org & violet ('20)	19.00	30.00
86	A29	5sh ocher & blue ('21)	32.50	32.50
87	A30	10sh dk myrtle grn ('20)	65.00	110.00
		Nos. 75-87 (12)	138.22	197.54

See note after No. 100.

A 6p stamp depicting the abolition of slavery was sent to the Colony but was not issued. "Specimen" copies exist with wmk. 3 or 4. Value $1,250 each. Without "Specimen", value $20,000.

Port Royal in 1853 A31

1921-23 Typo. Wmk. 4 *Perf. 14*

Chalky Paper

88	A18	½p ol grn & dk grn ('22)	65	15
a.		Booklet pane of 4		
89	A19	1p org & car ('22)	42	15
a.		Booklet pane of 6		

Engr.

Ordinary Paper

90	A20	1½p green	1.65	15
91	A21	2p grn & blue	1.00	18
92	A22	2½p bl & dk bl	60	18
93	A23	3p bl & grn ('22)	35	15
94	A24	4p grn & dk brn	45	15
95	A31	6p bl & blk ('22)	7.50	1.25
96	A26	1sh brn org & dl org	1.25	22
97	A27	2sh brn & bl ('22)	1.65	90
98	A28	3sh org & violet	10.00	12.00
99	A29	5sh ocher & bl ('23)	12.50	12.50
a.		5sh orange & blue	16.00	13.00
100	A30	10sh dk myrtle green ('22)	45.00	45.00
		Nos. 88-100 (13)	83.02	72.98

No. 89 differs from No. 76 in having the words "Postage and Revenue" at the bottom.

On No. 79 the horizontal bar of the flag at the left has a broad white line below the colored line. On No. 92 this has been corrected and the broad white line placed above the colored line.

Watermark is sideways on #76-77, 87, 89-90.

Type of 1912-19 Issue

1921-27 Typo. Wmk. 4

101	A17	½p green ('27)	15	15
a.		Booklet pane of 6		
102	A17	6p red vio & dl vio	8.50	3.25

No. 102 is on chalky paper.

A32

Type I

Type II

Type II - Cross shading beneath "Jamaica."

1929-32 Engr. *Perf. 13½x14, 14*

103	A32	1p red, type I	22	15
a.		1p red, type II ('32)	15	15
b.		Booklet pane of 6, type II		
104	A32	1½p brown	1.75	15
105	A32	9p violet brown	3.75	1.40

The frames on Nos. 103 to 105 differ.

Coco Palms at Columbus Cove — A33

Scene near Castleton, St. Andrew — A34

Priestman's River, Portland Parish — A35

1932 *Perf. 12½*

106	A33	2p grn & gray blk	3.50	45
a.		Vertical pair, imperf. between	3,500.	
107	A34	2½p ultra & sl blue	1.65	60
a.		Vertical pair, imperf. between	4,000.	4,000.
108	A35	6p red vio & gray black	2.75	1.65

Silver Jubilee Issue

Common Design Type

1935, May 6 *Perf. 11x12*

109	CD301	1p car & blue	16	16
a.		Booklet pane of 6	150.00	
110	CD301	1½p blk & ultra	32	32
111	CD301	6p indigo & grn	2.00	2.00
112	CD301	1sh brn vio & ind	2.50	2.50

Coronation Issue

Common Design Type

1937, May 12 *Perf. 13½x14*

113	CD302	1p carmine	15	15
114	CD302	1½p gray black	15	15
115	CD302	2½p bright ultra	32	22
		Set value		38
		Set, never hinged	1.10	

King George VI — A36

Coco Palms at Columbus Cove — A37

Scene near Castleton, St. Andrew — A38

Bananas A39

Citrus Grove A40

Priestman's River, Portland Parish — A41

Kingston Harbor A42

Sugar Industry A43

Bamboo Walk — A44

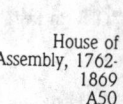

Woodland Scene — A45

King George VI — A46

1938-51 *Perf. 13½x14*

116	A36	½p dk blue grn	15	15
a.		Booklet pane of 6	6.75	
b.		Wmkd. sideways		
117	A36	1p carmine	15	15
a.		Booklet pane of 6	11.00	
118	A36	1½p brown	15	15

Perf. 12½, 13x13½, 13½x13, 12½x13

119	A37	2p grn & gray blk, perf. 12½	15	15
a.		Perf. 13x13½ ('39)	15	15
b.		Perf. 12½x13 ('51)	15	15
120	A38	2½p ultra & sl bl	1.50	1.10
121	A39	3p grn & lt ultra	15	15
122	A40	4p grn & yel brn	15	15
123	A41	6p red vio & gray blk, perf. 13½x13 ('50)	15	15
a.		Perf. 12½	15	15
124	A42	9p rose lake	28	22
125	A43	1sh dk brn & brt grn	28	15
126	A44	2sh brn & brt bl	1.10	42

Perf. 13, 14

127	A45	5sh ocher & bl, perf. 13 ('50)	2.00	1.00
a.		Bluish paper, perf. 13 ('49)	5.00	5.00
b.		Perf. 14	1.50	1.10
128	A46	10sh dk myrtle grn, perf. 14	4.00	2.75
a.		Perf. 13 ('50)	3.50	2.50
		Nos. 116-128 (13)	10.21	6.69
		Set, never hinged	20.00	

See Nos. 140, 148, 149, 152.

Catalogue values for unused stamps in this section, from this point to the end of the section, are for Never Hinged items.

Courthouse, Falmouth — A47

Kings Charles II and George VI — A48

House of Assembly, 1762-1869 A50

Institute of Jamaica — A49

Allegory of Labor and Learning — A51

Constitution and Flag of Jamaica — A52

Perf. 12½

1945, Aug. 20 Engr. Wmk. 4

129	A47	1½p brown	15	15
a.		Booklet pane of 4	27.50	
b.		Perf. 12½x13½ ('46)	15	15
130	A48	2p dp grn, perf. 12½x13½	15	15
a.		Perf. 12½	95	48
131	A49	3p bright ultra	18	16
a.		Perf. 13 ('46)	38	32
132	A50	4½p slate black	24	24
a.		Perf. 13 ('46)	42	42
133	A51	2s chocolate	80	80
134	A52	5s deep blue	1.00	1.25
135	A49	10s green	2.25	2.50
		Nos. 129-135 (7)	4.77	5.25

Granting of a new Constitution in 1944.

Peace Issue

Common Design Type

1946, Oct. 14 Wmk. 4 *Perf. 13½*

136	CD303	1½p black brown	15	15
a.		Perf. 13½x14	15	15

Perf. 13½x14

137	CD303	3p deep blue	20	20
a.		Perf. 13½	35	35

Silver Wedding Issue

Common Design Types

1948, Dec. 1 Photo. *Perf. 14x14½*

138	CD304	1½p red brown	15	15

Engr.; Name Typo.

Perf. 11½x11

139	CD305	£1 red	20.00	22.50

Type of 1938 and

Tobacco Industry A53

1949, Aug. 15 Engr. *Perf. 12½*

140	A39	3p ultra & slate blue	1.10	40
141	A53	£1 purple & brown	27.50	27.50

UPU Issue
Common Design Types
Perf. 13½, 11x11½

1949, Oct. 10 **Wmk. 4**

142	CD306	1½p red brown	28	15
143	CD307	2p dark green	38	22
144	CD308	3p indigo	75	48
145	CD309	6p rose violet	1.90	1.25

University Issue
Common Design Types

1951, Feb. 16 *Perf. 14x14½*

146	CD310	2p brown & gray blk	18	15
147	CD311	6p rose lilac & gray blk	52	35

George VI Type of 1938

1951, Oct. 25 *Perf. 13½x14*

148	A36	½p orange	15	15
a.		Booklet pane of 6	5.00	
149	A36	1p blue green	18	15
a.		Booklet pane of 6	11.00	
		Set value	23	15

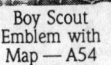

Boy Scout Emblem with Map — A54

Map and Emblem — A55

Perf. 13½x13, 13x13½

1952, Mar. 5 **Typo.** **Wmk. 4**

150	A54	2p blk, yel grn & blue	35	16
151	A55	6p blk, yel grn & dk red	60	40

1st Caribbean Boy Scout Jamboree, 1952.

Banana Type of 1938

1952, July 1 **Engr.** *Perf. 12½*

152	A39	3p rose red & green	50	40

Coronation Issue
Common Design Type

1953, June 2 *Perf. 13½x13*

153	CD312	2p dk green & black	18	15

Type of 1938 with Portrait of Queen Elizabeth II and Inscription: "ROYAL VISIT 1953"

1953, Nov. 25 *Perf. 13*

154	A37	2p green & gray black	15	15

Visit of Queen Elizabeth II and the Duke of Edinburgh, 1953.

Warship off Port Royal A56

Designs: 2½p, Old Montego Bay. 3p, Old Kingston. 6p, Proclaiming abolition of slavery.

1955, May 10 **Engr.** *Perf. 12x12½*
Center in Black

155	A56	2p olive green	15	15
156	A56	2½p light ultra	20	18
157	A56	3p deep plum	25	20
158	A56	6p rose red	32	30

300th anniv. of Jamaica's establishment as a British territory.

Palm Trees — A57

Blue Mountain Peak — A58

Arms of Jamaica — A59

Arms of Jamaica — A60

Designs: 1p, Sugar cane. 2p, Pineapple. 2½p, Bananas. 3p, Mahoe flower. 4p, Breadfruit. 5p, Ackee fruit. 6p, Streamer (hummingbird). 1sh, Royal Botanic Gardens, Hope. 1sh6p, Rafting on the Rio Grande. 2sh, Fort Charles.

1956 **Wmk. 4** *Perf. 12½*

159	A57	½p org ver & black	15	15
a.		Booklet pane of 6	32	
160	A57	1p emerald & black	15	15
a.		Booklet pane of 6	50	
161	A57	2p rose red & black	15	15
a.		Booklet pane of 6	80	
162	A57	2½p lt ultra & black	15	15
a.		Booklet pane of 6	1.65	
163	A57	3p brown & green	15	15
164	A57	4p dk blue & ol grn	15	15
165	A57	5p ol green & car	20	15
166	A57	6p carmine & black	24	15
		Perf. 13½		
167	A58	8p red org & brt ultra	24	16
168	A58	1sh blue & yel grn	32	15
169	A58	1sh6p dp cl & ultra	60	20
170	A58	2sh ol grn & ultra	2.00	40
		Perf. 11½		
171	A59	3sh blue & black	1.90	90
172	A59	5sh carmine & blk	2.75	1.25
173	A60	10sh blue grn & blk	6.50	4.00
174	A60	£1 purple & blk	12.00	6.50
		Nos. 159-174 (16)	27.65	14.76

For overprints, see Nos. 185-196. For types overprinted, see Nos. 208-216.

West Indies Federation
Common Design Type
Perf. 11½x11

1958, Apr. 22 **Engr.** **Wmk. 314**

175	CD313	2p green	15	15
176	CD313	5p blue	32	32
177	CD313	6p carmine rose	42	32

Britannia Plane over 1860 Packet Boat — A61

1sh Stamps of 1860 and 1956 — A62

Design: 6p, Victorian post cart and mail truck.

1960, Jan. 4 *Perf. 13x13½*

178	A61	2p lilac & blue	15	15
179	A61	6p ol grn & car rose	28	20
		Perf. 13		
180	A62	1sh blue, yel grn & brn	52	52

Centenary of Jamaican postal service.

Independent State

Zouave Bugler and Map of Jamaica A63

Designs: 1sh6p, Gordon House (Legislature) and hands of three races holding banner. 5sh, Map and symbols of agriculture and industry.

1962, Aug. 8 **Photo.** *Perf. 13*

181	A63	2p multicolored	15	15
182	A63	4p multicolored	15	15
a.		Yellow omitted		
183	A63	1sh6p red, black & brn	45	24
184	A63	5sh multicolored	1.65	1.65

Issue of 1956 Overprinted:

1962 INDEPENDENCE
a

1962 INDEPENDENCE 1962
b

Perf. 12½

1962, Aug. 8 **Wmk. 4** **Engr.**

185	A57(a)	½p org ver & blk	15	15
186	A57(a)	1p emer & black	15	15
187	A57(a)	2½p lt ultra & blk	15	15
188	A57(b)	3p brown & green	15	15
189	A57(b)	5p ol green & car	18	15
190	A57(b)	6p car & black	18	15
		Perf. 13½		
191	A58(b)	8p red org & brt ultra	28	18
192	A58(b)	1sh blue & yel grn	35	28
193	A58(b)	2sh ol green & ultra	1.00	65
		Perf. 11½		
194	A59(a)	3sh blue & blk	1.50	1.65
195	A60(a)	10sh bl grn & blk	4.00	4.50
196	A60(a)	£1 pur & black	7.75	9.00
		Nos. 185-196 (12)	15.84	17.16

Nos. 181-196 issued to commemorate Jamaica's independence.

"Independence" measures 17½x1½mm on #185-187; 18x1mm on #194-196.

See Nos. 208-216.

Weight Lifting, Soccer, Boxing and Cycling A64

Designs: 6p, Various water sports. 8p, Running and jumping. 2sh, Arms and runner.

Perf. 14½x14

1962, Aug. 11 **Photo.** **Wmk. 314**

197	A64	1p car & dk brown	15	15
198	A64	6p blue & brown	15	15
199	A64	8p olive & dk brown	22	16
200	A64	2sh multicolored	75	75

IX Central American and Caribbean Games, Kingston, Aug. 11-25.

A souvenir sheet containing one each of Nos. 197-200, imperf., was sold exclusively by National Sports, Ltd., at 5sh (face 3sh3p). The Jamaican Post Office sold the entire issue of this sheet to National Sports at face value, plus the printing cost. The stamps are postally valid. The sheet has marginal inscriptions and simulated perforations in ultramarine. Value $3.25.

Freedom from Hunger Issue

Man Planting Mango Tree and Produce A65

Perf. 12½

1963, June 4 **Unwmk.** **Litho.**

201	A65	1p blue & multi	15	15
202	A65	8p rose & multi	60	60

See note after CD314, Common Design section.

Red Cross Centenary Issue
Common Design Type

1963, Sept. 2 **Wmk. 314** *Perf. 13*

203	CD315	2p black & red	15	15
204	CD315	1sh6p ultra & red	60	50
		Set value		56

Carole Joan Crawford — A66

Unwmk.

1964, Feb. 14 **Photo.** *Perf. 13*

205	A66	3p multicolored	15	15
206	A66	1sh olive & multi	30	26
207	A66	1sh6p multicolored	40	40
a.		Souvenir sheet of 3	90	90

Carole Joan Crawford, Miss World, 1963.

No. 207a contains one each of Nos. 205-207 with simulated perforations. Issued May 25. Sold for 4sh.

Types of 1956 Overprinted like 1962 Independence Issue
Perf. 12½

1963-64 **Wmk. 314** **Engr.**

208	A57(a)	½p org ver & blk	15	15
209	A57(a)	1p emer & blk ('64)	15	15
210	A57(a)	2½p lt ultra & blk ('64)	22	18
211	A57(b)	3p brown & green	35	18
212	A57(b)	5p ol grn & car ('64)	65	60
		Perf. 13½		
213	A58(b)	8p red org & brt ultra ('64)	80	70
214	A58(b)	1sh bl & yel grn	2.00	1.90
215	A58(b)	2sh ol grn & ultra ('64)	2.75	2.75
		Perf. 11½		
216	A59(a)	3sh bl & blk ('64)	3.75	3.75
		Nos. 208-216 (9)	10.82	10.36

Overprint is at bottom on Nos. 214-215, at top on Nos. 192-193.

Lignum Vitae, National Flower, and Map — A67

Designs: 1½p, Ackee, national fruit, and map. 2p, Blue Mahoe, national tree, and map, vert. 2½p, Land shells (snails). 3p, Flag over map. 4p, Murex antillarum, sea shell. 6p, Papilio homerus. 8p, Streamer (hummingbird). 9p, Gypsum industry. 1sh, Stadium and statue of runner. 1sh6p, Palisadoes International Airport. 2sh, Bauxite mining. 3sh, Blue marlin and boat. 5sh, Port Royal exploration of sunken city, map, ship and artifacts. 10sh, Coat of arms, vert. £1, Flag and Queen Elizabeth II.

Perf. 14½, 14x14½

1964, May 4 **Photo.** **Wmk. 352**
Size: 26x22mm, 22x26mm

217	A67	1p bis, vio bl & green	15	15
a.		Booklet pane of 6	35	
218	A67	1½p multicolored	15	15
219	A67	2p multicolored	15	15
a.		Booklet pane of 6	85	
220	A67	2½p multicolored	15	15
221	A67	3p emer, yel & black	15	15
a.		Booklet pane of 6	1.10	
222	A67	4p violet & buff	15	15
223	A67	6p multicolored	18	15
a.		Ultramarine omitted	30.00	
224	A67	8p multicolored	22	15
a.		Red omitted		

Perf. 14½x14, 13½x14½, 14x14½
Size: 32x26mm, 26x32mm

225	A67	9p blue & yel	25	15
226	A67	1sh yel brn & blk	30	15
a.		Yellow brown omitted	200.00	
b.		Black omitted	550.00	
227	A67	1sh6p sl, buff & bl	42	18
228	A67	2sh bl, brn red & black	65	35
229	A67	3sh grn, saph & dk bl, perf. 14½x14	1.10	65
a.		Perf. 14x14½	1.90	1.25
230	A67	5sh bl, blk & bis	1.50	85
231	A67	10sh multicolored	2.25	1.75
a.		Blue ("Jamaica" etc.) omitted	150.00	
232	A67	£1 multicolored	5.00	3.25
		Nos. 217-232 (16)	12.77	8.53

See Nos. 306-318. For overprints, see Nos. 248-251. For surcharges, see #279-291, 305.

Scout Hat, Globe, Neckerchief — A68

Scout Emblem, American Crocodile — A69

Design: 3p, Scout belt buckle.

Perf. 14½x14, 14

1964, Aug. 27 — Wmk. 352

233 A68 3p pink, black & red 15 15
234 A68 8p ultra, black & olive 20 20
235 A69 1sh ultra & gold 35 35

6th Inter-American Scout Conference, Kingston, Aug. 25-29.

Gordon House, Kingston, and Commonwealth Parliamentary Association Emblem — A70

Designs: 6p, Headquarters House, Kingston. 1sh6p, House of Assembly, Spanish Town.

1964, Nov. 16 Photo. *Perf. 14½x14*

236 A70 3p yel green & blk 15 15
237 A70 6p red & black 16 15
238 A70 1sh6p ultra & black 38 35
Set value 53

10th Commonwealth Parliamentary Conf.

Common Design Types are pictured beginning on page 176.

Eleanor Roosevelt — A71

1964, Dec. 10 — Wmk. 352

239 A71 1sh lt green, blk & red 25 22

Eleanor Roosevelt (1884-1962) on the 16th anniv. of the Universal Declaration of Human Rights.

Map of Jamaica and Girl Guide Emblem — A72

Girl Guide Emblems — A73

Perf. 14x14½, 14

1965, May 17 Photo. Wmk. 352

240 A72 3p lt blue, yel & yel grn 15 15
241 A73 1sh lt yel grn, blk & bis 30 30
Set value 36

50th anniv. of the Girl Guides of Jamaica.

Salvation Army Cap — A74

Design: 1sh6p, Flag bearer, drummer and globe, vert.

Perf. 14x14½, 14½x14

1965, Aug. 23 Photo. Wmk. 352

242 A74 3p dp blue, yel, mar & blk 15 15
243 A74 1sh6p emerald & multi 38 38
Set value 44

Centenary of the Salvation Army.

Paul Bogle, William Gordon and Morant Bay Court House A75

1965, Dec. 29 Unwmk. *Perf. 14x13*

244 A75 3p vio blue, blk & brn 15 15
245 A75 1sh6p yel green, blk & brn 35 35
246 A75 3sh pink & brown 65 65

Cent. of the Morant Bay rebellion against governor John Eyre.

ITU Emblem, Telstar, Telegraph Key and Man Blowing Horn — A76

Perf. 14x14½

1965, Dec. 29 Photo. Wmk. 352

247 A76 1sh gray, black & red 45 45

Cent. of the ITU.

Nos. 221, 223, 226-227 Overprinted: "ROYAL VISIT / MARCH 1966"

Perf. 14½, 14½x14

1966, Mar. 3 Photo. Wmk. 352

Size: 26x22mm

248 A67 3p emer, yel & black 15 15
249 A67 6p multicolored 22 20

Size: 32x26mm

250 A67 1sh yel brown & blk 38 32
251 A67 1sh6p slate, buff & blue 65 65

See note after Antigua No. 162.

Winston Churchill A77

1966, Apr. 18 *Perf. 14, 14x14½*

252 A77 6p olive green & gray 30 26
253 A77 1sh violet & sepia 56 48

Sir Winston Leonard Spencer Churchill (1874-1965), statesman and WWII leader.

Runner, Flags of Jamaica, Great Britain and Games' Emblem A78

Designs: 6p, Bicyclists and waterfall. 1sh, Stadium. 3sh, Games' Emblem.

Perf. 14½x14

1966, Aug. 4 Photo. Wmk. 352

254 A78 3p multicolored 15 15
255 A78 6p multicolored 15 15
256 A78 1sh multicolored 28 28
257 A78 3sh gold & dk vio blue 75 75
a. Souvenir sheet of 4 2.75 2.75

8th British Empire and Commonwealth Games, Aug. 4-13, 1966.

No. 257a contains 4 imperf. stamps with simulated perforations similar to Nos. 254-257. Issued Aug. 25, 1966.

Bolivar Statue, Kingston, Flags of Jamaica and Venezuela — A79

1966, Dec. 5 *Perf. 14x14½*

258 A79 8p multicolored 25 25

150th anniv. of the "Bolivar Letter," written by Simon Bolivar, while in exile in Jamaica.

Jamaican Pavilion A80

1967, Apr. 28 *Perf. 14½x14*

259 A80 6p multicolored 16 15
260 A80 1sh multicolored 28 28

EXPO '67 Intl. Exhibition, Montreal, Apr. 28-Oct. 27.

Donald Burns Sangster — A81

Perf. 13x13½

1967, Aug. 28 — Unwmk.

261 A81 3p multicolored 15 15
262 A81 1sh6p multicolored 35 35
Set value 42 42

Sir Donald Burns Sangster (1911-1967), Prime Minister.

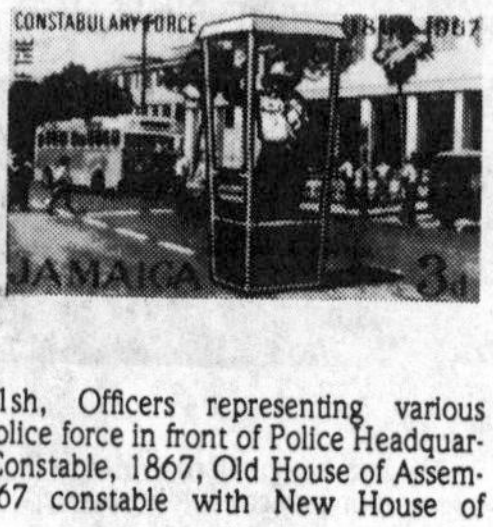

Traffic Police and Post Office A82

Designs: 1sh, Officers representing various branches of police force in front of Police Headquarters. 1sh6p, Constable, 1867, Old House of Assembly, and 1967 constable with New House of Assembly.

Perf. 13½x14

1967, Nov. 28 Photo. Wmk. 352

Size: 42x25mm

263 A82 3p red brown & multi 15 15

Size: 56½x20½mm

Perf. 13½x14½

264 A82 1sh yellow & multi 35 35

Size: 42x25mm

Perf. 13½x14

265 A82 1sh6p gray & multi 55 55

Centenary of the Constabulary Force.

A Human Rights set of three (3p, 1sh, 3sh) was prepared and announced for release on Jan. 2, 1968. The Crown Agents distributed sample sets, but the stamps were not issued. Designs show bowls of food, an abacus and praying hands. On Dec. 3, Nos. 271-273 were issued instead. Value, $75.

Wicketkeeper, Emblem of West Indies Cricket Team — A82a

Designs: No. 266, Wicketkeeper and emblem of West Indies Cricket Team. No. 267, Batsman and emblem of Marylebone Cricket Club. No. 268, Bowler and emblem of West Indies Cricket Team.

1968, Feb. 8 Photo. *Perf. 14*

266 A82a 6p multicolored 30 30
267 A82a 6p multicolored 30 30
268 A82a 6p multicolored 30 30
a. Horiz. strip of 3, #266-268 1.00

Visit of the Marylebone Cricket Club to the West Indies, Jan.-Feb. 1968.

Sir Alexander and Lady Bustamante A83

1968, May 23 *Perf. 14½*

269 A83 3p brt rose & black 15 15
270 A83 1sh olive green & black 22 22
Set value 29 29

Labor Day, May 23, 1968.

Human Rights Flame and Map of Jamaica A84

Designs: 1sh, Hands shielding Human Rights flame, vert. 3sh, Man kneeling on Map of Jamaica, and Human Rights flame.

1968, Dec. 3 Wmk. 352 *Perf. 14½*

271 A84 3p multicolored 15 15
a. Gold (flame) omitted 110.00
272 A84 1sh multicolored 22 22
273 A84 3sh multicolored 75 75
a. Gold (flame) omitted 110.00

International Human Rights Year.

ILO Emblem A85

Unwmk.

1969, May 23 Litho. *Perf. 14*

274	A85	6p black & orange yel	15	15
275	A85	3sh black & brt green	60	60

50th anniv. of the ILO.

WHO Emblem, Children and Nurse — A86

Designs: 1sh, Malaria eradication, horiz. 3sh, Student nurses.

1969, May 30 Photo. *Perf. 14*

276	A86	6p org, black & brown	15	15
277	A86	1sh blue grn, blk & brn	22	22
278	A86	3sh ultra, black & brn	60	60

WHO, 20th anniv.

Nos. 217-219, 221-223, 225-232 Surcharged with New Value and: "C-DAY 8th SEPTEMBER 1969"

1969, Sept. 8 Wmk. 352 *Perf. 14½*

Size: 26x22mm, 22x26mm

279	A67	1c on 1p multi	15	15
280	A67	2c on 2p multi	15	15
281	A67	3c on 3p multi	15	15
282	A67	4c on 4p multi	15	15
283	A67	5c on 6p multi	16	15
a.		Blue (wing dots) omitted	*40.00*	

Perf. 14½x14, 13½x14½, 14x14½

Size: 32x26mm, 26x32mm

284	A67	8c on 9p multi	25	16
285	A67	10c on 1sh multi	30	22
286	A67	15c on 1sh6p multi	42	30
287	A67	20c on 2sh multi	65	50
288	A67	30c on 3sh multi	85	65
289	A67	50c on 5sh multi	1.00	85
290	A67	$1 on 10sh multi	2.00	1.90
291	A67	$2 on £1 multi	4.75	3.50
		Nos. 279-291 (13)	10.98	8.83

Introduction of decimal currency.

The old denomination is obliterated by groups of small rectangles on the 1c and 3c, and with a square on the 2c, 4c and 8c; old denominations not obliterated on others.

Madonna and Child with St. John, by Raphael — A87

Christmas (Paintings): 2c, The Adoration of the Kings, by Vincenzo Foppa. 8c, The Adoration of the Kings, by Dosso Dossi.

1969, Oct. 25 Litho. *Perf. 13*

292	A87	2c vermilion & multi	15	15
293	A87	5c multicolored	18	18
294	A87	8c orange & multi	30	30
		Set value	54	54

First Jamaica Penny — A88

Design: 3c, First Jamaica halfpenny.

1969, Oct. 27 *Perf. 12x12½*

295	A88	3c brt pink, blk & silver	15	15
296	A88	15c emerald, blk & silver	30	30
		Set value	37	37

Centenary of the first Jamaican coinage.

George William Gordon — A89

Crucifixion, by Antonello da Messina — A90

Portraits: 3c, Sir Alexander Bustamante (1884-1977). 5c, Norman W. Manley (1893-1969). 10c, Marcus M. Garvey (1887-1940). 15c, Paul Bogle (1820-1865).

Perf. 12x12½

1970, Mar. 11 Photo. Unwmk.

297	A89	1c lt violet & multi	15	15
298	A89	3c lt blue & multi	15	15
299	A89	5c lt gray & multi	15	15
300	A89	10c pale rose & multi	25	25
301	A89	15c pale green & multi	48	48
		Set value	96	96

National heroes connected with Jamaica's independence.

1970, Mar. 23

Easter: 3c, Christ Appearing to St. Peter, by Annibale Carracci. 20c, Easter lily.

302	A90	3c pink & multi	15	15
303	A90	10c gray green & multi	30	30
304	A90	20c gray & multi	60	60

No. 219 Surcharged 2c ■

1970, July 16 Wmk. 352 *Perf. 14½*

305	A67	2c on 2p multicolored	15	15

Type of Regular Issue, 1964
Values in Cents and Dollars

Designs: 1c, Lignum vitae and map. 2c, Blue mahoe and map, vert. 3c, Flag over map. 4c, Murex antillarum, sea shell. 5c, Papilio homerus. 8c, Gypsum industry. 10c, Stadium and statue of runner. 15c, Palisadoes International Airport. 20c, Bauxite mining. 30c, Blue marlin and boat. 50c, Port Royal exploration of sunken city, map, ship and artifacts. $1, Coat of arms, vert. $2, Flag and Queen Elizabeth II.

1970 Wmk. 352 Photo. *Perf. 14½*

Size: 26x22mm, 22x26mm

306	A67	1c bister & multi	15	15
307	A67	2c gray green & multi	15	15
308	A67	3c emer, yel & black	15	15
309	A67	4c violet & buff	15	15
310	A67	5c green & multi	18	15

Perf. 14½x14, 13½x14½, 14x14½

Size: 32x26mm, 26x32mm

311	A67	8c blue & yellow	28	15
312	A67	10c yel brn & black	40	18
313	A67	15c multicolored	60	28
314	A67	20c multicolored	80	45
315	A67	30c multicolored	90	60
316	A67	50c multicolored	1.40	1.00
317	A67	$1 multicolored	2.75	1.75
318	A67	$2 multicolored	5.50	3.75
		Nos. 306-318 (13)	13.41	8.91

Issue dates: Nos. 306-312, Sept. 7; Nos. 313-318, Nov. 2.

Bright's Cable Gear on "Dacia" A91

Designs: 3c, Telegraph cable ship "Dacia." 50c, Double current Morse key, 1870, and map of Jamaica.

1970, Oct. 12 Litho. *Perf. 14½*

319	A91	3c red orange & multi	15	15
320	A91	10c blue green & multi	38	15
321	A91	50c emerald & multi	1.65	1.65

Centenary of telegraph service.

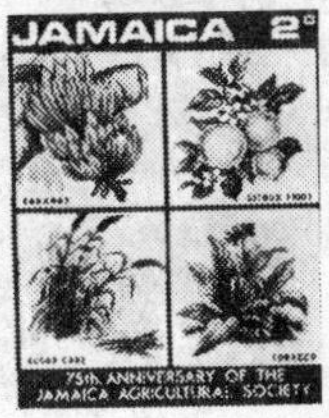

Bananas, Citrus Fruit, Sugar Cane and Tobacco — A92

1970, Nov. 2 Wmk. 352 *Perf. 14*

322	A92	2c brown & multi	15	15
323	A92	10c black & multi	38	38
		Set value	46	44

Jamaica Agricultural Society, 75th anniv.

"The Projector," 1845 — A93

Locomotives: 15c, Engine 54, 1944. 50c, Engine 102, 1967.

1970, Nov. 21 Litho. *Perf. 13½*

324	A93	3c green & multi	18	18
325	A93	15c org brown & multi	1.00	1.00
326	A93	50c multicolored	3.50	3.50

125th anniv. of the Jamaican railroad.

Kingston Cathedral — A94

Designs: 10c, 20c, like 3c. 30c, Arms of Jamaica Bishopric.

1971, Feb. 22 *Perf. 14½*

327	A94	3c lt green & multi	15	15
328	A94	10c dull orange & multi	22	22
329	A94	20c ultra & multi	45	45
330	A94	30c gray & multi	75	75

Centenary of the disestablishment of the Church of England.

Henry Morgan, Ships in Port Royal Harbor A95

Designs: 15c, Mary Read, Anne Bonny and pamphlet on their trial. 30c, 18th century merchantman surrendering to pirate schooner.

1971, May 10 Litho. Wmk. 352

331	A95	3c red brown & multi	15	15
332	A95	15c gray & multi	90	90
333	A95	30c lilac & multi	2.00	2.00

Pirates and buccaneers.

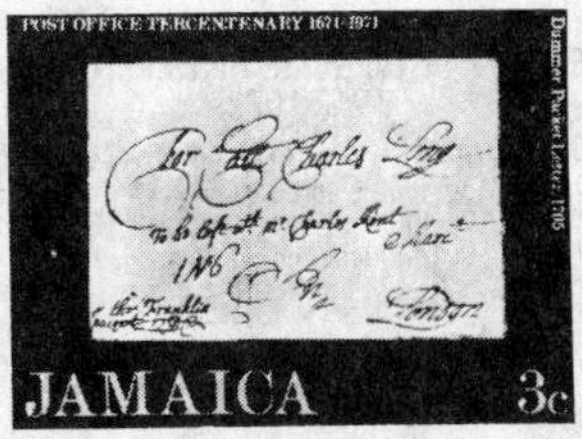

Dummer Packet Letter, 1705 — A96

Designs: 5c, Stampless cover, 1793. 8c, Post office, Kingston, 1820. 10c, Modern date cancellation on No. 312. 20c, Cover with stamps of Great Britain and Jamaica cancellations, 1859. 50c, Jamaica No. 83a, vert.

1971, Oct. 30 *Perf. 13½*

334	A96	3c dk carmine & black	15	15
335	A96	5c lt ol grn & black	20	20
336	A96	8c purple & black	30	30
337	A96	10c slate, black & brn	38	38
338	A96	20c multicolored	75	75
339	A96	50c dk gray, blk & org	1.90	1.90
		Nos. 334-339 (6)	3.68	3.68

Tercentenary of Jamaica Post Office.

Earth Station and Satellite — A97

1972, Feb. 17 *Perf. 14x13½*

340	A97	3c red & multi	15	15
341	A97	15c gray & multi	60	60
342	A97	50c multicolored	1.75	1.75

Jamaica's earth satellite station.

Bauxite Industry — A98

National Stadium — A99

Perf. 14½x14, 14x14½

1972-79 Litho. Wmk. 352

343	A98	1c Pimento, vert.	15	15
344	A98	2c Red ginger, vert.	15	15
345	A98	3c shown	15	15
346	A98	4c Kingston harbor	15	15
347	A98	5c Oil refinery	15	15
348	A98	6c Senate Building, Univ. of the West Indies	15	15

Perf. 13½

349	A99	8c shown	15	15
350	A99	9c Devon House, Hope Road	15	15
351	A99	10c Stewardess and Air Jamaica plane	15	15
352	A99	15c Old Iron Bridge, vert.	15	15
353	A99	20c College of Arts, Science & Technology	20	18
354	A99	30c Dunn's River Falls, vert.	30	26
355	A99	50c River raft	52	42
356	A99	$1 Jamaica House	1.00	90
357	A99	$2 Kings House	1.50	1.40

Perf. 14½x14

Size: 37x26½mm

358	A99	$5 Map and arms of Jamaica ('79)	3.25	3.25
		Nos. 343-358 (16)	8.27	7.91

For overprints, see Nos. 360-362, 451.

Nos. 345, 351, 355 Overprinted: "TENTH ANNIVERSARY INDEPENDENCE 1962-1972"

1972, Aug. 8 *Perf. 14½x14, 13½*

360 A98 3c multicolored 15 15
361 A99 10c multicolored 28 28
362 A99 50c multicolored 1.40 1.40

Arms of Kingston — A100

Design: 5c, 30c, Arms of Kingston, vert.

1972, Dec. 4 *Perf. 13½x14, 14x13½*

363 A100 5c pink & multi 15 15
364 A100 30c lemon & multi 75 75
365 A100 50c lt blue & multi 1.25 1.25

Centenary of Kingston as capital.

Mongoose and Map of Jamaica A101

Designs: 40c, Mongoose and rat. 60c, Mongoose and chicken.

Perf. 14x14½

1973, Apr. 9 **Litho.** **Wmk. 352**

366 A101 8c yel green & blk 22 22
367 A101 40c blue & black 1.10 1.10
368 A101 60c salmon & black 1.90 1.90
a. Souvenir sheet of 3, #366-368 4.00 4.00

Centenary of the introduction of the mongoose to Jamaica.

Euphorbia Punicea — A102

Flowers: 6c, Hylocereus triangularis. 9c, Columnea argentea. 15c, Portlandia grandiflora. 30c, Samyda pubescens. 50c, Cordia sebestena.

1973, July 9 *Perf. 14*

369 A102 1c dp green & multi 15 15
370 A102 6c vio blue & multi 22 22
371 A102 9c orange & multi 35 35
372 A102 15c brown & multi 55 55
373 A102 30c olive & multi 1.10 1.10
374 A102 50c multicolored 1.90 1.90
Nos. 369-374 (6) 4.27 4.27

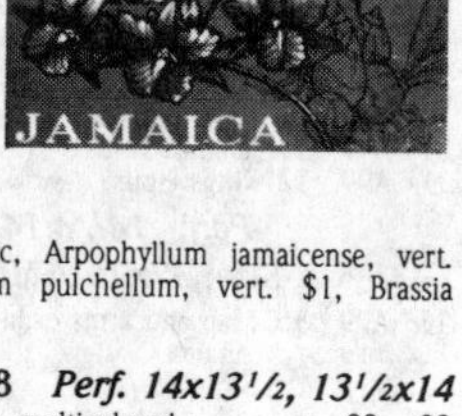

Broughtonia Sanguinea A103

Orchids: 10c, Arpophyllum jamaicense, vert. 20c, Oncidium pulchellum, vert. $1, Brassia maculata.

1973, Oct. 8 *Perf. 14x13½, 13½x14*

375 A103 5c multicolored 22 22
376 A103 10c multicolored 45 45
377 A103 20c slate & multi 90 90
378 A103 $1 ultra & multi 4.50 4.50
a. Souv. sheet of 4, #375-378, perf 12 6.25 6.25

Mailboat "Mary" (1808-1815) — A104

Designs: Mailboats.

Perf. 13½ (5c, 50c), 14½ (10c, 15c)

1974, Apr. 8 **Wmk. 352**

379 A104 5c shown 18 15
a. Perf. 14½ 7.50 1.25
380 A104 10c "Queensbury" (1814-27) 48 38
381 A104 15c "Sheldrake" (1829-34) 75 55
382 A104 50c "Thames" (1842) 2.25 1.90
a. Souv. sheet of 4, #379-382, perf 13½ 5.00 3.50

Jamaican Dancers — A105

Designs: Dancers.

1974, Aug. 1 **Litho.** *Perf. 13½*

383 A105 5c green & multi 15 15
384 A105 10c black & multi 26 26
385 A105 30c brown & multi 65 65
386 A105 50c lilac & multi 1.40 1.40
a. Souvenir sheet of 4, #383-386 3.00 3.00

National Dance Theatre.

Globe, Letter, UPU Emblem A106

1974, Oct. 9 *Perf. 14*

387 A106 5c plum & multi 15 15
388 A106 9c olive & multi 30 30
389 A106 50c multicolored 1.50 1.50

Centenary of Universal Postal Union.

Senate Building and Sir Hugh Wooding A107

Designs: 10c, 50c, Chapel and Princess Alice. 30c, like 5c.

1975, Jan. 13 **Wmk. 352**

390 A107 5c yellow & multi 15 15
391 A107 10c salmon & multi 20 20
392 A107 30c dull org & multi 55 55
393 A107 50c multicolored 1.00 1.00

University College of the West Indies, 25th anniversary.

Commonwealth Symbol — A108

Commonwealth Symbol and: 10c, Arms of Jamaica. 30c, Dove of peace. 50c, Jamaican flag.

1975, Apr. 29 **Litho.** *Perf. 13½*

394 A108 5c buff & multi 15 15
395 A108 10c rose & multi 22 22
396 A108 30c vio blue & multi 80 65
397 A108 50c multicolored 1.25 1.00

Commonwealth Heads of Government Conference, Jamaica, Apr.-May.

Graphium Marcellinus A109

Koo Koo, "Actor-boy" A110

Butterflies: 20c, Papilio thoas melonius. 25c, Papilio thersites. 30c, Papilio homerus.

1975, Aug. 25 **Litho.** *Perf. 14*

398 A109 10c lt green & multi 60 42
399 A109 20c lt green & multi 1.25 85
400 A109 25c lt green & multi 1.75 1.25
401 A109 30c lt green & multi 2.00 1.50
a. Souvenir sheet of 4, #398-401 6.00 4.50

See Nos. 423-426, 435-438.

1975, Nov. 3 **Litho.** **Wmk. 352**

Christmas: 10c, Red "set-girls." 20c, French "set-girls." 50c, Jawbone or "House John Canoe." Festival dancers drawn by I. M. Belisario in Kingston, 1837.

402 A110 8c multicolored 18 18
403 A110 10c olive & multi 24 24
404 A110 20c ultra & multi 45 45
405 A110 50c multicolored 1.25 1.25
a. Souvenir sheet of 4, #402-405, perf. 13½ 3.25 3.25

See Nos. 416-418.

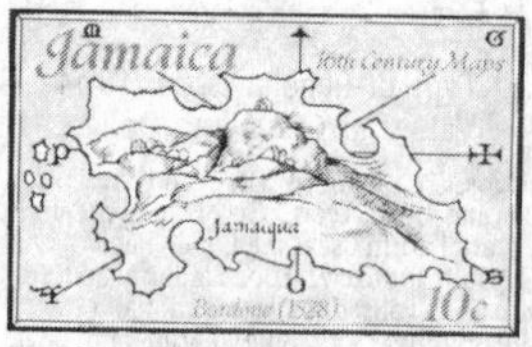

Map of Jamaica, by Benedetto Bordone, 1528 — A111

Maps of Jamaica by: 20c, Tommaso Porcacchi, 1576. 30c, Theodor DeBry, 1594. 50c, Barent Langenes, 1598.

1976, Mar. 12 *Perf. 13½x14*

406 A111 10c brown, buff & red 20 20
407 A111 20c bister & multi 42 42
408 A111 30c lt blue & multi 65 65
409 A111 50c multicolored 1.25 1.25

See Nos. 419-422.

Olympic Rings A112

1976, June 14 **Litho.** *Perf. 13½x14*

410 A112 10c black & multi 22 22
411 A112 20c blue & multi 45 45
412 A112 25c red & multi 55 55
413 A112 50c green & multi 1.10 1.10

21st Olympic Games, Montreal, Canada, July 17-Aug. 1.

Map of West Indies, Bats, Wicket and Ball A112a

Prudential Cup — A112b

1976, Aug. 9 **Unwmk.** *Perf. 14*

414 A112a 10c lt blue & multi 50 50
415 A112b 25c lilac rose & blk 1.25 1.25

World Cricket Cup, won by West Indies Team, 1975.

Christmas Type of 1975

Belisario Prints, 1837: 10c, Queen of the "set-girls." 20c, Band of Jawbone John Canoe. 50c, Koo Koo, "actor-boy."

1976, Nov. 8 **Wmk. 352** *Perf. 13½*

416 A110 10c brick red & multi 20 20
417 A110 20c bister & multi 40 40
418 A110 50c tan & multi 1.00 1.00
a. Souv. sheet of 3, #416-418, perf 14 2.50 2.50

Christmas.

Map Type of 1976

Maps of Jamaica by: 9c, Edmund Hickeringill, 1661. 10c, John Ogilby, 1671. 25c, House of Visscher, 1680. 40c, John Thornton, 1689.

1977, Feb. 28 **Litho.** *Perf. 13*

419 A111 9c lt blue & multi 20 20
420 A111 10c buff & multi 24 24
421 A111 25c multicolored 60 60
422 A111 40c multicolored 1.00 1.00

Butterfly Type of 1975

Butterflies: 10c, Eurema elathea. 20c, Dynamine egaea. 25c, Atlantea pantoni. 40c, Hypolimnas misippus.

1977, May 9 **Wmk. 352** *Perf. 13½*

423 A109 10c black & multi 60 60
424 A109 20c black & multi 1.25 1.25
425 A109 25c black & multi 1.50 1.50
426 A109 40c black & multi 2.50 2.50
a. Souvenir sheet of 4, #423-426, perf 14½ 6.25 6.25

Scout Emblem, Doctor Bird, Outline of Jamaica — A113

1977, Aug. 5 **Litho.** *Perf. 14*

427 A113 10c multicolored 22 16
428 A113 20c multicolored 35 32
429 A113 25c multicolored 52 42
430 A113 50c multicolored 1.10 85

6th Caribbean Jamboree, Hope Gardens, Kingston, Aug. 3-17.

Trumpeter A114

Designs: 10c, 3 clarinetists. 20c, 2 kettle drummers, vert. 25c, Cellist and trumpeter, vert.

1977, Dec. 19 Litho. *Perf. 14*

431 A114	9c multicolored	32	28
432 A114	10c multicolored	40	32
433 A114	20c multicolored	80	60
434 A114	25c multicolored	1.00	80
a.	Souvenir sheet of 4, #431-434	3.25	2.50

Jamaica Military Band, 50th anniversary.

Butterfly Type of 1975

Butterflies: 10c, Callophrys crethona. 20c, Siproeta stelenes. 25c, Urbanus proteus. 50c, Anaea troglodyta.

1978, Apr. 17 Litho. *Perf. 14½*

435 A109	10c black & multi	42	42
436 A109	20c black & multi	85	85
437 A109	25c black & multi	1.10	1.10
438 A109	50c black & multi	2.00	2.00
a.	Souvenir sheet of 4, #435-438	5.75	4.50

Half Figure with Canopy — A115

Norman Manley Statue — A116

Arawak Artifacts, found 1792: 20c, Standing figure. 50c, Birdman.

1978, July 10 Litho. *Perf. 13½x13*

439 A115	10c multicolored	20	20
440 A115	20c multicolored	42	42
441 A115	50c multicolored	1.10	1.10
a.	Souv. sheet of 3, #439-441, perf 14	1.75	1.75

1978, Sept. 25 Litho. Wmk. 352

Designs: 20c, Alexander Bustamante statue. 25c, Kingston coat of arms. 40c, Gordon House Chamber, House of Representatives.

442 A116	10c multicolored	15	15
443 A116	20c multicolored	42	42
444 A116	25c multicolored	32	32
445 A116	40c multicolored	52	52

24th Commonwealth Parliamentary Conf.

Salvation Army Band A117

Designs: 20c, Trumpeter. 25c, "S" and Cross entwined on pole of Army flag. 50c, William Booth and Salvation Army shield.

1978, Dec. 4 *Perf. 14*

446 A117	10c multicolored	16	16
447 A117	20c multicolored	32	32
448 A117	25c multicolored	38	38
449 A117	50c multicolored	75	75

Christmas; Salvation Army centenary.

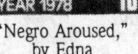

"Negro Aroused," by Edna Manley — A118

Arawak Grinding Stone, c. 400 B.C. — A119

1978, Dec. 11 *Perf. 13*

450 A118	10c multicolored	20	20

International Anti-Apartheid Year.

No. 351 Overprinted: "TENTH / ANNIVERSARY / AIR JAMAICA / 1st APRIL 1979"

1979, Apr. 2 Litho. *Perf. 13½*

451 A99	10c multicolored	20	20

1979, Apr. 23 *Perf. 14*

Arawak Artifacts (all A.D.): 10c, Stone implements, c. 500, horiz. 20c, Cooking pot, c. 300, horiz. 25c, Serving boat, c. 300, horiz. 50c, Storage jar fragment, c. 300.

452 A119	5c multicolored	15	15
453 A119	10c multicolored	15	15
454 A119	20c multicolored	22	22
455 A119	25c multicolored	28	28
456 A119	50c multicolored	55	55
	Nos. 452-456 (5)	1.35	1.35

Jamaica No. 183, Hill Statue A120

Hill Statue and Stamps of Jamaica: 20c, No. 83a. 25c, No. 5. 50c, No. 271.

1979, Aug. 13 Litho. *Perf. 14*

457 A120	10c multicolored	15	15
458 A120	20c multicolored	18	18
a.	Souvenir sheet of 1	35	35
459 A120	25c multicolored	22	22
460 A120	50c multicolored	45	45

Sir Rowland Hill (1795-1879), originator of penny postage.

Children, IYC Emblem A121

International Year of the Child: 20c, Doll, vert. 25c, "The Family." 25c, "House on the Hill." 25c, 50c are children's drawings.

1979, Oct. 1

461 A121	10c multicolored	15	15
462 A121	20c multicolored	18	18
463 A121	25c multicolored	22	22
464 A121	50c multicolored	42	42

Tennis, Montego Bay — A122

Jamaican Tody — A123

Designs: 2c, Golfing, Tryall Hanover. 4c, Horseback riding, Negril Beach. 5c, Old Waterwheel, Tryall Hanover. 6c, Fern Gully, Ocho Rios. 7c, Dunn's River Falls, Ocho Rios.

10c, Doctorbird. 12c, Yellow-billed parrot. 15c, Hummingbird. 35c, White-chinned thrush. 50c, Jamaican woodpecker. 65c, Rafting Martha Brae Trelawny. 75c, Blue marlin fishing, Port Antonio. $1, Scuba diving, Ocho Rios. $2, Sail boats, Montego Bay.

Perf. 13½

1979-80 Litho. Wmk. 352

465 A122	1c multicolored	15	15
466 A122	2c multicolored	15	15
467 A122	4c multicolored	15	15
468 A122	5c multicolored	15	15
469 A122	6c multicolored	15	15
470 A122	7c multicolored	15	15
472 A123	8c multicolored	15	15
473 A123	10c multicolored	15	15
474 A123	12c multicolored	15	15
475 A123	15c multicolored	15	15
476 A123	35c multicolored	22	22
477 A123	50c multicolored	32	32
478 A122	65c multicolored	40	40
479 A122	75c multicolored	48	48
480 A122	$1 multicolored	60	60
481 A122	$2 multicolored	1.25	1.25
	Set value	3.90	3.90

Issue dates: Nos. 465-470, Nov. 26; Nos. 472-481, May 1980.

For surcharges, see Nos. 581-582, 665-666.

Institute of Jamaica Centenary — A124

1980, Feb. 25 Litho. *Perf. 13½*

484 A124	5c shown	15	15
485 A124	15c Institute building, 1980	16	16
486 A124	35c "The Ascension" on microfilm reader, vert.	40	40
487 A124	50c Hawksbill and green turtles	52	52
488 A124	75c Jamaican owl, vert.	80	80
	Nos. 484-488 (5)	2.03	2.03

Don Quarrie, 1976 Gold Medalist, 200-Meter Race, Moscow '80 Emblem A125

1952 4x400-meter Relay Team: a, Arthur Wint. b, Leslie Laing. c, Herbert McKenley. d, George Rhoden.

1980, July 21 Litho. *Perf. 13*

489 A125	15c shown	15	15
490	Strip of 4	2.50	1.25
a.-d.	A125 35c any single	60	30

22nd Summer Olympic Games, Moscow, July 19-Aug. 3.

Parish Church, Kingston A126

1980, Nov. 24 Litho. *Perf. 14*

491 A126	15c shown	15	15
492 A126	20c Coke Memorial	16	16
493 A126	25c Church of the Redeemer	20	20
494 A126	$5 Holy Trinity Cathedral	4.00	4.00
a.	Souvenir sheet of 4, #491-494	4.50	4.50

Christmas.

Tube Sponge A127

1981, Feb. 27 Wmk. 352 *Perf. 14*

495 A127	20c Blood cup sponge, vert.	18	18
496 A127	45c shown	40	40
497 A127	60c Black coral, vert.	52	52
498 A127	75c Tire reef	65	65

See Nos. 523-527.

Indian Coney A128

Designs: b, Facing left. c, Eating. d, Family.

1981, May 25 Wmk. 352 *Perf. 14*

499	Strip of 4	1.00	1.00
a.-d.	A128 20c any single	25	25

Royal Wedding Issue

Common Design Type

1981, July 29 Litho. *Perf. 15*

500 CD331	20c White orchid	15	15
501 CD331	45c Royal coach	30	30
502 CD331	60c Couple	40	40

Perf. 13½

503 CD331	$5 St. James' Palace	3.50	3.50
a.	Souvenir sheet of 1	3.50	3.50
b.	Booklet pane of 4, perf. 14x14½	7.00	

Also issued in sheets of 5 + label, perf. 13½.

Intl. Year of the Disabled A129

1981, Sept. 14 Wmk. 352 *Perf. 13½*

504 A129	20c Blind weaver	18	18
505 A129	45c Artist	40	40
506 A129	60c Learning sign language	52	52
507 A129	1.50 Basketball players	1.25	1.25

World Food Day A130

Perf. 13x13½, 13½x13

1981, Oct. 16 Litho. Wmk. 352

508 A130	20c No. 218	18	18
509 A130	45c No. 76, vert.	40	40
510 A130	$2 No. 121	1.75	1.75
511 A130	$4 No. 125	3.50	3.50

Bob Marley (1945-1981), Reggae Musician — A131

Designs: Portraits of Bob Marley and song titles.

1981, Oct. 20 Wmk. 373 *Perf. 14½*

512 A131	1c multicolored	15	15
513 A131	2c multicolored	15	15
514 A131	3c multicolored	15	15
515 A131	15c multicolored	30	30
516 A131	20c multicolored	42	42
517 A131	60c multicolored	1.25	1.25
518 A131	$3 multicolored	6.50	6.50
	Nos. 512-518 (7)	8.92	8.92

Souvenir Sheet

519 A131	$5.25 multicolored	6.50	6.50

Christmas A132

1981, Dec. 11 Wmk. 352 *Perf. 14*

520 A132	10c Webb Memorial Baptist Church	15	15
521 A132	45c Church of God	38	38
522 A132	$5 Bryce United Church	4.00	4.00
a.	Souvenir sheet of 3, #520-522, perf. 12½x12	4.50	4.50

See Nos. 547-549.

Marine Life Type of 1981

1982, Feb. 22 Litho. *Perf. 14*

523 A127 20c Gorgonian coral, vert. 18 18
524 A127 45c Hard sponge 40 40
525 A127 60c Sea cow 52 52
526 A127 75c Plume worm 65 65
527 A127 $3 Coral-banded shrimp 2.75 2.75
Nos. 523-527 (5) 4.50 4.50

Scouting Year — A133

Princess Diana, 21st Birthday — A134

Designs: 20c, 45c, 60c, Various scouts. $2, Baden-Powell.

1982, July 12 Litho. *Perf. 13½*

528 A133 20c multicolored 18 18
529 A133 45c multicolored 38 38
530 A133 60c multicolored 48 48
531 A133 $2 multicolored 1.75 1.75
a. Souvenir sheet of 4, #528-531 3.00 3.00

1982, Sept. 1 *Perf. 14½*

532 A134 20c Lignum vitae 18 18
533 A134 45c Couple in coach 42 42
534 A134 60c Wedding portrait 55 55
a. Booklet pane of 3, #532-534 1.25
535 A134 75c Saxifraga longifolia 65 65
536 A134 $2 Diana 1.90 1.90
537 A134 $3 Viola gracilis major 2.75 2.75
a. Booklet pane of 3, #535-537 5.50
Nos. 532-537 (6) 6.45 6.45

Souvenir Sheet

538 A134 $5 Honeymoon 4.00 4.00

Nos. 535, 537 in sheets of 5.

Nos. 532-538 Overprinted: "ROYAL BABY / 21.6.82"

1982, Sept. 13

539 A134 20c multicolored 18 18
540 A134 45c multicolored 42 42
541 A134 60c multicolored 55 55
a. Booklet pane of 3, #539-541 1.25
542 A134 75c multicolored 65 65
543 A134 $2 multicolored 1.90 1.90
544 A134 $3 multicolored 2.75 2.75
a. Booklet pane of 3, #542-544 5.50
Nos. 539-544 (6) 6.45 6.45

Souvenir Sheet

545 A134 $5 multicolored 5.00 5.00

Birth of Prince William of Wales, June 21.

Lizard Cuckoo Capturing Prey — A135

Designs: b, Searching for prey. c, Calling. d, Landing. e, Flying.

1982, Oct. 25

546 Strip of 5 4.50 4.50
a.-e. A135 $1 any single 90 90

Christmas Type of 1981

Perf. 13x13½

1982, Dec. 8 Wmk. 352

547 A132 20c United Pentecostal Church 22 22
548 A132 45c Disciples of Christ Church 45 45
549 A132 75c Open Bible Church 75 75

Visit of Queen Elizabeth II — A136

1983, Feb. 14 Litho. *Perf. 14*

550 A136 $2 Queen Elizabeth II 1.90 1.90
551 A136 $3 Arms 2.75 2.75

CD334

1983, Mar. 14 Litho. Wmk. 352

552 CD334 20c Dancers 18 18
553 CD334 45c Bauxite mining 38 38
554 CD334 75c Map 65 65
555 CD334 $2 Arms, citizens 1.75 1.75

Commonwealth Day.

25th Anniv. of Intl. Maritime Org. A137

1983, Mar. 17 Litho. *Perf. 14*

556 A137 15c Cargo ship 15 15
557 A137 20c Cruise liner 18 18
558 A137 45c Container vessel 40 40
559 A137 $1 Intl. Seabed Headquarters 95 95

21st Anniv. of Independence A138

Prime Ministers Norman Washington Manley and Alexander Bustamante.

1983, July 25 Litho. *Perf. 14*

560 A138 15c blue & multi 15 15
561 A138 20c lt green & multi 20 20
562 A138 45c yellow & multi 45 45

World Communications Year — A139

1983, Oct. 18 Wmk. 352 *Perf. 14*

563 A139 20c Ship-to-shore radio 18 18
564 A139 45c Postal services 42 42
565 A139 75c Telephone communication 70 70
566 A139 $1 TV satellite 95 95

Christmas 1983 A140

Paintings: 15c, Racing at Caymanas, by Sidney McLaren. 20c, Seated Figures, by Karl Parboosingh. 75c, The Petitioner, by Henry Daley, vert. $2, Banana Plantation, by John Dunkley, vert.

1983, Dec. 12 Litho. *Perf. 13½*

567 A140 15c multicolored 15 15
568 A140 20c multicolored 15 15
569 A140 75c multicolored 42 42
570 A140 $2 multicolored 1.00 1.00

Alexander Bustamante (1884-1977), First Prime Minister
A141 A141a

1984, Feb. 24 Litho. *Perf. 14*

571 A141 20c Portrait 15 15
572 A141 20c Blenheim (birthplace) 15 15
a. Pair, #571-572 30 30

Sea Planes A142

1984, June 11 Litho. *Perf. 14*

573 A142 25c Gypsy Moth 18 18
574 A142 55c Consolidated Commodore 42 42
575 A142 $1.50 Sikorsky S-38 1.15 1.15
576 A142 $3 Sikorsky S-40 2.25 2.25

1984 Summer Olympics A143

1984, July 11

577 A143 25c Bicycling 15 15
578 A143 55c Relay race 30 30
579 A143 $1.50 Running 85 85
580 A143 $3 Women's running 1.75 1.75
a. Souvenir sheet of 4, #577-580 3.50 3.50

Nos. 469, 474 Surcharged

1984, Aug. 7 Litho. *Perf. 13½*

581 A122 5c on 6c #469 15 15
582 A123 10c on 12c #474 15 15
Set value 15 15

Early Steam Engines A144

1984, Nov. 16 Litho. *Perf. 13½*

583 A144 25c Enterprise, 1845 18 18
584 A144 55c Tank Locomotive, 1880 42 42
585 A144 $1.50 Kitson-Meyer Tank, 1904 1.15 1.15
586 A144 $3 Superheater, 1916 2.25 2.25

See Nos. 608-611.

Christmas — A145

Local sculptures: 20c, Accompong Madonna, by Namba Roy. 25c, Head, by Alvin Marriott. 55c, Moon, by Edna Manley. $1.50, All Women are Five Women, by Mallica Reynolds.

1984, Dec. 6 Wmk. 352 *Perf. 14*

587 A145 20c multicolored 15 15
588 A145 25c multicolored 18 18
589 A145 55c multicolored 42 42
590 A145 $1.50 multicolored 1.10 1.10

Jamaican Boas A146

1984, Oct. 22 Litho. *Perf. 14½*

591 A146 25c Head of boa 15 15
592 A146 55c Boa over water 35 35
593 A146 70c Boa with young 45 45
594 A146 $1 Boa on branch 75 75
a. Souvenir sheet of 4, #591-594 1.75 1.75

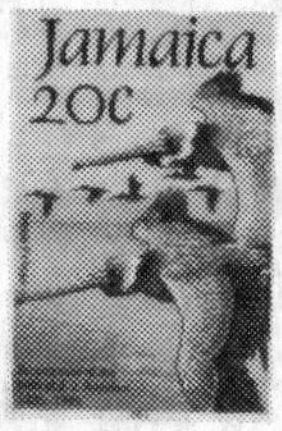

Brown Pelicans — A147

1985, Apr. 15 Wmk. 352 *Perf. 13*

595 A147 20c multicolored 15 15
596 A147 55c multicolored 22 22
597 A147 $2 multicolored 80 80
598 A147 $5 multicolored 1.90 1.90
a. Souvenir sheet of 4, #595-598 3.00 3.00

Birth bicentenary of artist and naturalist John J. Audubon (1785-1851).

Queen Mother 85th Birthday

Common Design Type

1985, June 7 Litho. *Perf. 14½x14*

599 CD336 25c Holding photograph album, 1963 15 15
600 CD336 55c With Prince Charles, Windsor Castle, 1983 22 22
601 CD336 $1.50 At Belfast University 58 58
602 CD336 $3 Holding Prince Henry 1.15 1.15

Souvenir Sheet

603 CD336 $5 Riding train 1.90 1.90

Maps of Americas and Jamaica, IYY and Jamboree Emblems A148

1985, July 30 Litho. *Perf. 14*

604 A148 25c multicolored 15 15
605 A148 55c multicolored 22 22
606 A148 70c multicolored 28 28
607 A148 $4 multicolored 1.50 1.50

Intl. Youth Year and 5th Pan-American Scouting Jamboree.

Locomotives Type of 1984

1985, Sept. 30 Size: 39x25mm

608 A144 25c Baldwin 15 15
609 A144 55c Rogers 22 22
610 A144 $1.50 Projector 60 60
611 A144 $4 Diesel 1.50 1.50

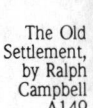

The Old Settlement, by Ralph Campbell A149

Christmas (Paintings by local artists): 55c, The Vendor, by Albert Hiue, vert. 75c, Road Menders, by Gaston Tabois. $4, Woman, Must I Not Be About My Father's Business? by Carl Abrahams, vert.

1985, Dec. 9

612 A149 20c multicolored 15 15
613 A149 55c multicolored 22 22
614 A149 75c multicolored 30 30
615 A149 $4 multicolored 1.50 1.50

Birds — A150

A151

1986, Feb. 10 Litho. *Perf. 14*

616 A150 25c Chestnut-bellied cuckoo 15 15
617 A150 55c Jamaican becard 22 22
618 A150 $1.50 White-eyed thrush 58 58
619 A150 $5 Rufous-tailed fly-catcher 2.00 2.00

Queen Elizabeth II 60th Birthday
Common Design Type

Designs: 20c, With Princess Margaret, 1939. 25c, Leaving Liverpool Street Station for Sandringham with Princes Charles and Andrew, 1962. 70c, Visiting the Montego Bay war memorial, Jamaica, 1983. $3, State visit to Luxembourg, 1976. $5, Visiting Crown Agents' offices, 1983.

1986, Apr. 21 *Perf. 14½*

620 CD337 20c scar, blk & sil 15 15
621 CD337 25c ultra & multi 15 15
622 CD337 70c green & multi 28 28
623 CD337 $3 violet & multi 1.15 1.15
624 CD337 $5 rose vio & multi 2.00 2.00
Nos. 620-624 (5) 3.73 3.73

1986, May 19

AMERIPEX '86: 25c, Bustamante Childrens Hospital. 55c, Vacation cities. $3, Norman Manley Law School. $5, Exports.

625 A151 25c multicolored 15 15
626 A151 55c multicolored 22 22
627 A151 $3 multicolored 1.15 1.15
628 A151 $5 multicolored 2.00 2.00
a. Souvenir sheet of 4, #625-628 3.50 3.50

Royal Wedding Issue, 1986
Common Design Type

Designs: 30c, At the races. $4, Andrew addressing the press.

Perf. 14½x14

1986, July 23 Wmk. 352

629 CD338 20c multicolored 15 15
630 CD338 $5 multicolored 1.90 1.90

Boxing Champions — A152

Champions: 45c, Richard "Shrimpy" Clarke, 1986 Commonwealth flyweight. 70c, Michael McCallum, 1984 WBA junior middleweight. $2, Trevor Berbick, 1986 WBC heavyweight. $4, Clarke, McCallum and Berbick.

1986, Oct. 27 Litho. *Perf. 14*

631 A152 45c multicolored 18 18
632 A152 70c multicolored 28 28
633 A152 $2 multicolored 78 78
634 A152 $4 multicolored 1.50 1.50

Flowers A153

1986, Dec. 1 *Perf. 14*

635 A153 20c Heliconia wagneriana, vert. 15 15
636 A153 25c Heliconia psittacorum 15 15
637 A153 55c Heliconia rostrata, vert. 22 22
638 A153 $5 Strelitzia reginae 2.00 2.00

Christmas. See Nos. 675-678, 706-709.

Shells — A154

1987, Feb. 23 Litho. *Perf. 15*

639 A154 35c Crown cone 15 15
640 A154 75c Measled cowrie 30 30
641 A154 $1 Trumpet triton 40 40
642 A154 $5 Rooster-tail conch 2.00 2.00

Prime Ministers A155

Natl. Coat of Arms A156

Designs: 1c-9c, Norman Washington Manley. 10c-90c, Sir Alexander Bustamante.

1987-91 *Perf. 12½x13*

643 A155 1c dull red 15 15
644 A155 2c rose pink 15 15
645 A155 3c light olive 15 15
646 A155 4c dull green 15 15
647 A155 5c slate blue 15 15
648 A155 6c ultramarine 15 15
649 A155 7c dull magenta 15 15
650 A155 8c red lilac 15 15
651 A155 9c brown olive 15 15
652 A155 10c deep rose 15 15
653 A155 20c bright orange 15 15
654 A155 30c emerald 15 15
655 A155 40c lt blue green 15 15
656 A155 50c gray olive 18 18
657 A155 60c light ultra 22 22
658 A155 70c pale violet 26 26
659 A155 80c violet 30 30
660 A155 90c light brown 32 32
661 A156 $1 dull brn & buff 35 35
662 A156 $2 orange 75 75
663 A156 $5 gray olive & greenish buff 1.75 1.75
664 A156 $10 royal blue & pale blue 3.50 3.50

Perf. 13x13½

664A A156 $25 vio & pale vio 4.75 4.75
664B A156 $50 lilac & pale lilac 9.50 9.50
Nos. 643-664 (22) 9.58 9.58

Issue dates: $25, $50, Oct. 9, 1991. Others, May 18, 1987.

Nos. 647, 653 reissued inscribed "1988," Nos. 655-656 "1991." Nos. 653, 655-656, 660-661 "1992." Nos. 652-653, 656, 660-661 "1993."

Nos. 477-478 Surcharged

1986, Nov. 3 *Perf. 13½*

665 A123 5c on 50c multicolored 15 15
666 A122 10c on 65c multicolored 15 15
Set value 15 15

A157

A158

Wmk. 352

1987, July 27 Litho. *Perf. 14*

667 A157 55c Flag, sunset 20 20
668 A157 70c Flag, horiz. 25 25

Natl. Independence, 25th anniv.

1987, Aug. 17

669 A158 25c Portrait 15 15
670 A158 25c Statue 15 15
a. Pair, #669-670 20 20
Set value 20 20

Marcus Mosiah Garvey (1887-1940), natl. hero. No. 670a has a continuous design.

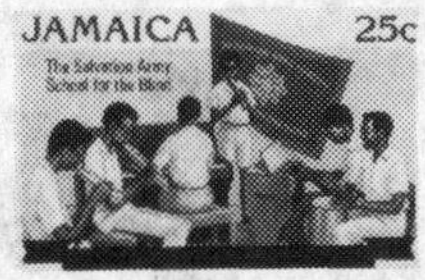

Salvation Army in Jamaica, Cent. — A159

Designs: 25c, School for the Blind. 55c, Col. Mary Booth, Bramwell-Booth Memorial Hall. $3, "War Chariot," 1929. $5, Arrival of col. Abram Davey on the S.S. Alene, 1887.

1987, Oct. 8 *Perf. 13*

671 A159 25c multicolored 15 15
672 A159 55c multicolored 22 22
673 A159 $3 multicolored 1.20 1.20
674 A159 $5 multicolored 2.00 2.00
a. Souvenir sheet of 4, #671-674 3.55 3.55

Flower Type of 1986

1987, Nov. 30 Litho. *Perf. 14½*

675 A153 20c Hibiscus hybrid 15 15
676 A153 25c Hibiscus elatus 15 15
677 A153 $4 Hibiscus cannabinus 1.50 1.50
678 A153 $5 Hibiscus rosa sinensis 1.85 1.85

Christmas. Nos. 675-678 vert.

Birds — A160

Designs: No. 679, Chestnut-bellied cuckoo, black-billed parrot, Jamaican euphonia. No. 680, Jamaican white-eyed vireo, rufous-throated solitaire, yellow-crowned elaenia. No. 681, Snowy plover, little blue heron, great white heron. No. 682, Common stilt, snowy egret, black-crowned night heron.

1988, Jan. 22 Litho. *Perf. 14*

679 A160 45c multicolored 18 18
680 A160 45c multicolored 18 18
681 A160 $5 multicolored 1.85 1.85
682 A160 $5 multicolored 1.85 1.85

Stamps of the same denomination printed se-tenant in continuous designs.

Marine Mammals A161

1988, Apr. 14 Litho. *Perf. 14*

683 A161 20c Blue whales 15 15
684 A161 25c Gervais's whales 15 15
685 A161 55c Killer whales 20 20
686 A161 $5 Common dolphins 1.80 1.80

Cricket A162

Bat, wicket posts, ball, 18th cent. belt buckle and batsmen: 25c, Jackie Hendriks. 55c, George Headley. $2, Michael Holding. $3, R.K. Nunes. $4, Allan Rae.

1988, June 6 Litho. *Perf. 14*

687 A162 25c multicolored 15 15
688 A162 55c multicolored 20 20
689 A162 $2 multicolored 75 75
690 A162 $3 multicolored 1.10 1.10
691 A162 $4 multicolored 1.45 1.45
Nos. 687-691 (5) 3.65 3.65

Intl. Red Cross and Red Crescent Organizations, 125th Annivs. — A163

Anniversary emblem, Jamaica Red Cross emblem and: 55c, Ambulances. $5, Jean-Henri Dunant, 1828-1910, treating the wounded after the Battle of Solferino, 1859.

1988, Aug. 8 Litho. *Perf. 14½*

692 A163 55c multicolored 20 20
693 A163 $5 multicolored 1.85 1.85

1988 Summer Olympics, Seoul A164

1988, Aug. 24 Wmk. 352 *Perf. 14*

694 A164 25c Boxing 15 15
695 A164 45c Cycling 18 18
696 A164 $4 Women's running 1.50 1.50
697 A164 $5 Hurdling 1.90 1.90
a. Souvenir sheet of 4, #694-697 3.75 3.75

No. 697a sold for $9.90. For surcharges, see Nos. B4-B7.

Natl. Olympic Bobsled Team A165

1988, Nov. 4 Litho. *Perf. 14*

698 A165 25c Team members 15 15
699 A165 25c Two-man bobsled 15 15
a. Pair, #698-699 25 25
700 A165 $5 Team members, diff. 1.85 1.85
701 A165 $5 Four-man bobsled 1.85 1.85
a. Pair, #700-701 3.75 3.75

Nos. 699a, 701a have continuous designs.

Labor Year — A166

Perf. 14½x14

1988, Nov. 24 **Wmk. 352**

702 A166 25c Medicine, fire fighting 15 15
703 A166 55c Handicrafts 20 20
704 A166 $3 Garment industry 1.10 1.10
705 A166 $5 Fishing 1.85 1.85

Flower Type of 1986

1988, Dec. 15

706 A153 25c Euphorbia pulcherrima, vert. 15 15
707 A153 55c Spathodea campanulata 20 20
708 A153 $3 Hylocereus triangularis, vert. 1.10 1.10
709 A153 $4 Broughtonia sanguinea 1.50 1.50

Christmas.

Methodist Church in Jamaica, Bicent. A167

Designs: 25c, Old York Castle School. 45c, Parade Chapel, Kingston, and Rev. Thomas Coke. $5, Fr. Hugh Sherlock and St. John's Church.

1989, Jan. 19 *Perf. 13½*

710 A167 25c multicolored 15 15
711 A167 45c multicolored 18 18
712 A167 $5 multicolored 1.85 1.85

Indigenous Moths — A168

Wmk. 352

1989, Aug. 30 **Litho.** *Perf. 14*

713 A168 25c *Syntomidopsis variegata* 15 15
714 A168 55c *Himantoides undataperkinsi* 20 20
715 A168 $3 *Hypercompe nigriplaga* 1.10 1.10
716 A168 $5 *Sthenognatha toddi* 1.80 1.80

See Nos. 725-728, 752-755. For surcharges and overprints see Nos. 729-732, 756-759.

A169

A171

Discovery of America, 500th Anniv. (in 1992): 25c, Arawak spear fisherman. 70c, Smoking tobacco. $5, Ferdinand and Isabella inspecting caravels. $10, Columbus studying chart.

1989, Dec. 22 *Perf. 13½*

717 A169 25c multicolored 15 15
718 A169 70c multicolored 26 26
719 A169 $5 multicolored 1.85 1.85
720 A169 $10 multicolored 3.65 3.65
a. Souvenir sheet of 4, #717-720, perf. 12½ 5.90 5.90

No. 720a exists imperf.

Wmk. 352

1990, June 28 **Litho.** *Perf. 14*

721 A171 45c multicolored 15 15
722 A171 55c multi, diff. 16 16
723 A171 $5 multi, diff. 1.50 1.50

Girl Guides of Jamaica, 75th anniv.

Indigenous Moths Type of 1989

Wmk. 352

1990, Sept. 12 **Litho.** *Perf. 14*

725 A168 25c Eunomia rubripunctata 15 15
726 A168 55c Perigonia jamaicensis 16 16
727 A168 $4 Uraga haemorrhoa 1.15 1.15
728 A168 $5 Empyreuma pugione 1.50 1.50

Nos. 725-728 Ovptd. in Black

1990, Sept. 12

729 A168 25c No. 725 15 15
730 A168 55c No. 726 16 16
731 A168 $4 No. 727 1.15 1.15
732 A168 $5 No. 728 1.50 1.50

Expo '90, International Garden and Greenery Exposition, Osaka, Japan.

Intl. Literacy Year A172

Wmk. 352

1990, Oct. 10 **Litho.** *Perf. 14*

733 A172 55c shown 16 16
734 A172 $5 Mathematics class 1.50 1.50

Christmas — A173

Children's art.

Perf. 13½x14

1990, Dec. 7 **Litho.** **Wmk. 352**

735 A173 20c To the market 15 15
736 A173 25c Untitled (houses) 15 15
737 A173 55c Jack and Jill 16 16
738 A173 70c Untitled (market) 20 20
739 A173 $1.50 Lonely (beach) 45 45
740 A173 $5 Market woman, vert. 1.45 1.45
Nos. 735-740 (6) 2.56 2.56

See Nos. 760-763.

Discovery of America, 500th Anniv. (in 1992) — A174

Maps of Columbus' voyages.

1990, Dec. 19 *Perf. 14*

741 A174 25c First, 1492 15 15
742 A174 45c Second, 1493 15 15
743 A174 $5 Third, 1498 1.45 1.45
744 A174 $10 Fourth, 1502 2.90 2.90

Souvenir Sheet

745 Sheet of 4 4.50 4.50
a. A174 25c Cuba, Jamaica 15 15
b. A174 45c Hispaniola, Puerto Rico 15 15
c. A174 $5 Central America 1.45 1.45
d. A174 $10 Venezuela 2.90 2.90

See Nos. 764-767.

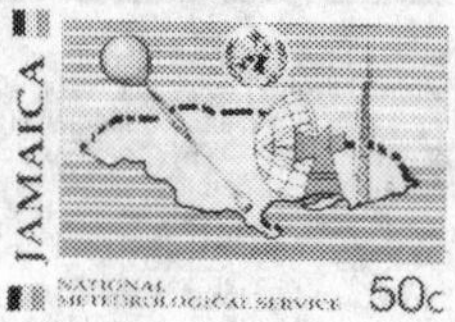

Natl. Meteorological Service — A175

1991, May 20 **Litho.** **Wmk. 352**

746 A175 50c multicolored 15 15
747 A175 $10 multicolored 1.90 1.90

11th World Meteorological Congress.

Intl. Council of Nurses Council of Natl. Representatives, Jamaica — A176

Perf. 13½

1991, June 24 **Litho.** **Wmk. 352**

748 A176 50c Mary Seacole 15 15
749 A176 $1.10 Mary Seacole House 28 28

Souvenir Sheet

750 A176 $8 Hospital at Scutari 1.95 1.95

Cyclura Collei (Jamaican Iguana) — A177

Designs: a, Head pointed to UR. b, Facing right. c, Climbing rock. d, Facing left. e, Head pointed to UL.

Wmk. 352

1991, July 29 **Litho.** *Perf. 13*

751 A177 $1.10 Strip of 5, #a.-e. 1.40 1.40

Natural History Soc. of Jamaica, 50th anniv.

Moths Type of 1989

1991, Aug. 12 *Perf. 14*

752 A168 50c Urania sloanus 15 15
753 A168 $1.10 Phoenicoprocta jamaicensis 20 20
754 A168 $1.40 Horama grotei 25 25
755 A168 $8 Amplypterus gannascus 1.50 1.50

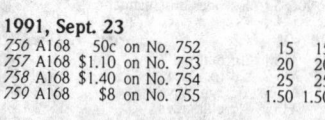

Nos. 752-755 Overprinted

1991, Sept. 23

756 A168 50c on No. 752 15 15
757 A168 $1.10 on No. 753 20 20
758 A168 $1.40 on No. 754 25 25
759 A168 $8 on No. 755 1.50 1.50

Children's Christmas Art Type

Children's drawings.

1991, Nov. 27 *Perf. 14x15*

760 A173 50c Doctor bird 15 15
761 A173 $1.10 Road scene 20 20
762 A173 $5 House, people 90 90
763 A173 $10 Cows grazing 1.80 1.80

Christmas.

Discovery of America Type of 1990

Designs: 50c, Explorers did not land at Santa Gloria because of hostile Indians. $1.10, Fierce dog used to subdue the Indians. $1.40, Indians brought gifts of fruit. $25, Columbus describes Jamaica with crumpled paper.

1991, Dec. 16 *Perf. 13½x14*

764 A174 50c multicolored 15 15
765 A174 $1.10 multicolored 15 15
766 A174 $1.40 multicolored 15 15
767 A174 $25 multicolored 2.50 2.50
a. Souvenir sheet of 4, #764-767 3.00 3.00

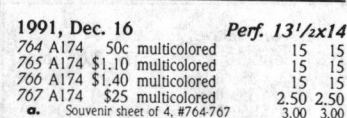

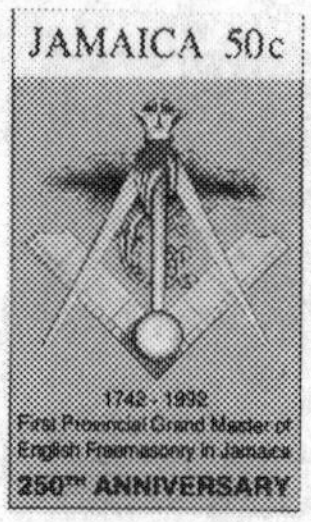

First Provincial Grand Master of English Freemasonry in Jamaica, 250th Anniv. — A178

Masonic symbols: 50c, Square and compass. $1.10, Stained glass window. $1.40, Square and compass on Bible. $25, Seeing eye.

1992, May 1 *Perf. 13½*

768 A178 50c multicolored 15 15
769 A178 $1.10 multicolored 15 15
770 A178 $1.40 multicolored 15 15
771 A178 $25 multicolored 2.50 2.50
a. Souvenir sheet of 4, #768-771 2.75 2.75

Destruction of Port Royal by Earthquake, 300th Anniv. A179

Scenes of destruction: 50c, Ship in harbor. $1.10, Homes, church. $1.40, Homes toppling. $5, Port Royal from contemporary broadsheet. $25, Fissure in street.

1992, June 7 *Perf. 14x13½*

772 A179 50c multicolored 15 15
773 A179 $1.10 multicolored 15 15
774 A179 $1.40 multicolored 15 15
775 A179 $25 multicolored 2.50 2.50

Souvenir Sheet

Perf. 13x12

776 A179 $5 multicolored 45 45

No. 776 inscribed on reverse.

Independence, 30th Anniv. — A180

1992, Aug. 6 *Perf. 13½*

777 A180 50c black & multi 15 15
778 A180 $1.10 green & multi 15 15
779 A180 $25 yellow & multi 2.25 2.25

Credit Union Movement in Jamaica, 50th Anniv. — A181

1992, Aug. 24 *Perf. 14x15*

780 A181 50c Emblem 15 15
781 A181 $1.40 Emblem, O'Hare Hall 15 15
Set value 17 17

Pottery — A182

Designs: 50c, "Rainbow" vase, by Cecil Baugh O.D. $1.10, "Yabba Pot," by Louisa Jones (MaLou) O.D. $1.40, "Sculptured Vase," by Gene Pearson. $25, "Lidded Form," by Norma Rodney Harrack.

1993, Apr. 26 *Perf. 13 1/2*

782 A182	50c	multicolored	15	15
783 A182	$1.10	multicolored	15	15
784 A182	$1.40	multicolored	15	15
785 A182	$25	multicolored	2.25	2.25

Girls' Brigade, Cent. A183

1993, Aug. 9 *Perf. 14x13 1/2*

786 A183	50c	Parade	15	15
787 A183	$1.10	Brigade members	15	15
		Set value	18	18

Jamaica Combined Cadet Force, 50th Anniv. A184

Designs: 50c, Tank, cadet, vert. $1.10, Airplane, female cadet. $1.40, Ships, female cadet, vert. $3, Cap badge, cadet.

1993, Nov. 8 *Perf. 14*

788 A184	50c	multicolored	15	15
789 A184	$1.10	multicolored	15	15
790 A184	$1.40	multicolored	15	15
791 A184	$3	multicolored	28	28
		Set value	48	48

Golf Courses A185

Designs: 50c, $1.10, Constant Spring. $1.40, $2, Half Moon. $3, $10, Jamaica Jamaica. $25, Tryall, vert.

1993-94 Litho. Wmk. 352 *Perf. 14*

792 A185	50c	yellow & multi	15	15
793 A185	$1.10	blue & multi	15	15
794 A185	$1.40	brn org & multi	15	15
795 A185	$2	lilac & multi	15	15
796 A185	$3	dark blue & multi	20	20
797 A185	$10	tan & multi	65	65
		Set value	1.20	1.20

Souvenir Sheets

798 A185	$25	green & multi	1.65	1.65
799 A185	$25	#798 inscribed with Hong Kong '94 emblem	1.65	1.65

Issue dates: Nos. 792-797, Dec. 21, 1993. No. 798, Dec. 16, 1993. No. 799, Feb. 18, 1994.

Norman Washington Manley, Birth Cent. — A186

1994, Jan. 12 *Perf. 14x15*

800 A186	$25	Portrait	1.65	1.65
801 A186	$50	Portrait, diff.	3.50	3.50
a.		Pair, #800-801	5.25	5.25

Royal Visit — A187

Designs: $1.10, Jamaican, United Kingdom flags. $1.40, Royal yacht Britannia. $25, Queen Elizabeth II. $50, Prince Philip, Queen.

1994, Mar. 1 *Perf. 14*

802 A187	$1.10	multicolored	15	15
803 A187	$1.40	multicolored	15	15
804 A187	$25	multicolored	1.65	1.65
805 A187	$50	multicolored	3.50	3.50

Air Jamaica, 25th Anniv. — A188

Wmk. 352

1994, Apr. 26 Litho. *Perf. 14*

806 A188	50c	Douglas DC9	15	15
807 A188	$1.10	Douglas DC8	15	15
808 A188	$5	Boeing 727	30	30
809 A188	$50	Airbus A300	3.00	3.00

Giant Swallowtail — A189

Various views of the butterfly.

Perf. 14x13 1/2

1994, Aug. 18 Litho. Wmk. 352

810 A189	50c	multicolored	15	15
811 A189	$1.10	multicolored	15	15
812 A189	$10	multicolored	60	60
813 A189	$25	multicolored	1.60	1.60

Souvenir Sheet

814 189	$50	multicolored	3.25	3.25

A190

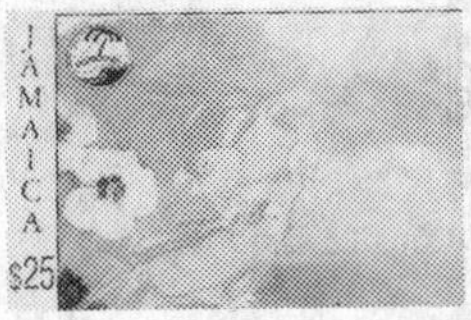

Tourism A191

Designs: 50c, Royal Botanical Gardens, by Sidney McClaren. $1.10, Blue Mountains, coffee beans, leaves. $5, Woman in hammock, waterfalls.

Tourist poster: No. 818a, Flowers, birds (c). b, Diver (d). c, Vegetation, coastline (a, d). d, Guide, tourists on raft.

Wmk. 352

1994, Sept. 7 Litho. *Perf. 14*

815 A190	50c	multicolored	15	15
816 A190	$1.10	multicolored	15	15
817 A190	$5	multicolored	30	30
		Set value	30	30

Souvenir Sheet

818 A191	$25	Sheet of 4, #a.-d.	6.00	6.00

Caribbean Tourism Conf. (#818).

SEMI-POSTAL STAMPS

Native Girl — SP1

Native Boy — SP2

Native Boy and Girl — SP3

1923, Nov. 1 Engr. *Perf. 12*

B1 SP1	1/2p	green & black	2.00	*4.00*
B2 SP2	1p	car & black	4.00	*9.00*
B3 SP3	2 1/2p	blue & black	11.00	*22.50*

Each stamp was sold for 1/2p over face value. The surtax benefited the Child Saving League of Jamaica.

Catalogue values for unused stamps in this section, from this point to the end of the section, are for Never Hinged items.

Nos. 694-697 Surcharged "HURRICANE GILBERT RELIEF FUND" and New Value in Black

Wmk. 352

1988, Nov. 11 Litho. *Perf. 14*

B4	A164	25c +25c multi	18	18
B5	A164	45c +45c multi	32	32
B6	A164	$4 +$4 multi	2.90	2.90
B7	A164	$5 +$5 multi	3.60	3.60

Red Surcharge

B4a	A164	25c + 25c	18	18
B5a	A164	45c + 45c	32	32
B6a	A164	$4 + $4	2.90	2.90
B7a	A164	$5 + $5	3.60	3.60

WAR TAX STAMPS

Regular Issues of 1906-19 Overprinted **WAR STAMP.**

1916 Wmk. 3 *Perf. 14*

MR1	A14 1/2p green		15	15
a.	Without period		11.00	*15.00*
b.	Double overprint		125.00	125.00
c.	Inverted overprint		70.00	70.00
d.	As "c," without period		350.00	
MR2	A17 3p violet, *yel*		5.50	8.25
a.	Without period		21.00	30.00

Surface-colored Paper

MR3	A17 3p violet, *yel*		1.40	1.50

Regular Issues of 1906-18 Overprinted **WAR STAMP.**

MR4	A14 1/2p green		18	15
a.	Without period		11.00	11.00
b.	Pair, one without ovpt.		475.00	375.00
c.	"R" inserted by hand		300.00	210.00
d.	"WAR" only		125.00	
MR5	A17 1 1/2p orange		16	15
a.	Without period		6.75	6.50
b.	"TAMP"		57.50	57.50
c.	"S" inserted by hand		225.00	
d.	"R" omitted		400.00	350.00
e.	"R" inserted by hand		250.00	200.00
MR6	A17 3p violet, *yel*		38	40
a.	Without period		17.00	18.00
b.	"TAMP"		225.00	140.00
c.	"S" inserted by hand		150.00	140.00
d.	Inverted overprint		300.00	175.00
e.	As "a," inverted			
	Set value, #MR4-MR6			56

Regular Issues of 1906-19 Overprinted **WAR STAMP.**

1917, Mar.

MR7	A14 1/2p green		15	15
a.	Without period		7.50	6.00
b.	Overprinted on back instead of face		90.00	
c.	Inverted overprint		13.00	10.00
MR8	A17 1 1/2p orange		15	15
a.	Without period		7.00	5.25
b.	Double overprint		90.00	90.00
c.	Inverted overprint		90.00	90.00
d.	As "a," inverted			
MR9	A17 3p violet, *yel*		22	22
a.	Without period		13.00	12.00
b.	Vertical overprint		275.00	275.00
c.	Inverted overprint		150.00	
d.	As "a," inverted			
	Set value		40	35

There are many minor varieties of Nos. MR1-MR9.

Regular Issues of 1906-19 Overprinted in Red **WAR STAMP**

1919, Oct. 4

MR10	A14 1/2p green		15	15
MR11	A17 3p violet, *yel*		22	18
	Set value		30	22

OFFICIAL STAMPS

No. 16 Overprinted in Black **OFFICIAL**

Type I - Word 15 to 16mm long.
Type II - Word 17 to 17 1/2mm long.

1890 Wmk. 2 *Perf. 14*

O1	A7 1/2p green (II)		6.00	1.00
a.	Type I		22.50	25.00
b.	Inverted overprint (II)		75.00	80.00
c.	Double overprint (II)		80.00	90.00
d.	Dbl. ovpt., one invtd. (II)		375.00	375.00
e.	Dbl. ovpt., one vert. (II)		1,100.	
f.	Double overprint (I)		400.00	

Missing "O," "L" or one or both "I's" known.

No. 16 and Type of 1889 Overprinted **OFFICIAL**

1890-91

O2	A7	1/2p green	95	15
O3	A10	1p carmine rose	1.25	15
O4	A10	2p slate	1.75	50

Watermarks

Wmk. 45- Pineapple

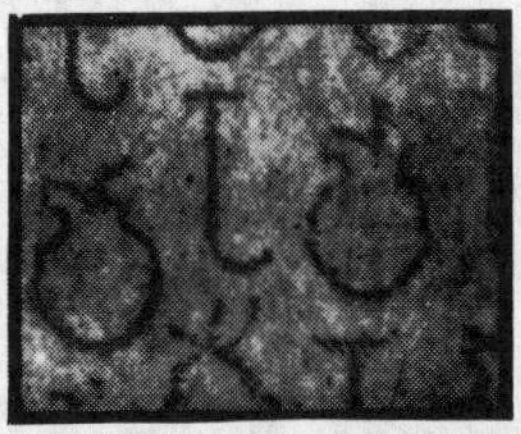
Wmk. 352- J and Pineapple, Multiple

LEEWARD ISLANDS

LOCATION — A group of islands in the West Indies, southeast of Puerto Rico
GOVT. — Former British Colony
AREA — 423 sq. mi.
POP. — 108,847 (1946)
CAPITAL — St. John

While stamps inscribed "Leeward Islands" were in use, 1890-1956, the colony consisted of the presidencies (now colonies) of Antigua, Montserrat, St. Christopher (St. Kitts) with Nevis and Anguilla, the British Virgin Islands and Dominica (which became a separate colony in 1940).

Each presidency issued its own stamps, using them along with the Leeward Islands general issues. The Leeward Islands federation was abolished in 1956.

12 Pence = 1 Shilling
20 Shillings = 1 Pound
100 Cents = 1 Dollar

Catalogue values for unused stamps in this country are for Never Hinged items, beginning with Scott 116.

Queen Victoria — A1

1890 Typo. Wmk. 2 *Perf. 14*

No.	Type	Description	Unused	Used
1	A1	½p lilac & green	30	18
2	A1	1p lilac & car	45	15
3	A1	2½p lilac & ultra	2.75	30
4	A1	4p lilac & org	3.50	*5.00*
5	A1	6p lilac & brown	3.50	*4.00*
6	A1	7p lilac & slate	2.75	*7.50*
7	A1	1sh green & car	16.00	*17.50*
8	A1	5sh green & ultra	105.00	*135.00*
		Nos. 1-8 (8)	134.25	*169.63*

Denomination of Nos. 7-8 are in color on plain tablet: "ONE SHILLING" or "FIVE SHILLINGS."
For overprints and surcharges see Nos. 9-19.

Jubilee Issue

Regular Issue of 1890 Handstamp Overprinted

1897, July 22

No.	Type	Description	Unused	Used
9	A1	½p lilac & green	5.00	*12.50*
10	A1	1p lilac & car	5.00	*11.50*
11	A1	2½p lilac & ultra	5.50	11.00
12	A1	4p lilac & org	13.00	20.00
13	A1	6p lilac & brown	22.50	30.00
14	A1	7p lilac & slate	22.50	30.00
15	A1	1sh green & car	100.00	140.00
16	A1	5sh green & ultra	375.00	550.00
		Nos. 9-16 (8)	548.50	805.00

60th year of Queen Victoria's reign.
Excellent counterfeits of Nos. 9-16 exist.
All values exist with double overprint.

Stamps of 1890 Surcharged in Black or Red:

One
Penny
b

One Penny
c

1902, Aug.

No.	Type	Description	Unused	Used
17	A1(b)	1p on 4p lilac & org	1.00	1.90
a.		Tall narrow "O" in "One"	15.00	20.00
18	A1(b)	1p on 6p lilac & brn	1.00	1.90
a.		Tall narrow "O" in "One"	21.00	30.00
19	A1(c)	1p on 7p lilac & sl	1.25	2.50

King Edward VII — A4

Numerals of ¼p, 2p, 3p and 2sh6p of type A4 are in color on plain tablet. The 1sh and 5sh denominations are expressed as "ONE SHILLING" and "FIVE SHILLINGS" on plain tablet.

1902

No.	Type	Description	Unused	Used
20	A4	½p violet & green	45	40
21	A4	1p vio & car rose	45	18
22	A4	2p violet & bister	2.00	3.00
23	A4	2½p violet & ultra	4.50	1.25
24	A4	3p violet & black	2.00	3.50
25	A4	6p violet & brown	1.65	*6.00*
26	A4	1sh grn & car rose	6.00	*7.50*
27	A4	2sh6p green & blk	22.50	*40.00*
28	A4	5sh green & ultra	27.50	*50.00*
		Nos. 20-28 (9)	67.05	*111.83*

1905-11 Wmk. 3

Chalky Paper

No.	Type	Description	Unused	Used
29	A4	½p vio & grn ('06)	90	*1.40*
30	A4	1p vio & car rose	2.25	35
31	A4	2p vio & bis ('08)	3.50	*7.00*
32	A4	2½p vio & ultra	21.00	21.00
33	A4	3p violet & black	3.75	7.00
34	A4	3p violet, *yel* ('10)	2.25	3.25
35	A4	6p vio & brn ('08)	17.50	27.50
36	A4	6p violet & red violet ('11)	2.50	3.25
37	A4	1sh grn & car rose ('08)	25.00	37.50
38	A4	1sh blk, *grn* ('11)	5.25	*8.75*
39	A4	2sh6p blk & red, *blue* ('11)	27.50	*50.00*
40	A4	5sh grn & red, *yel* ('11)	40.00	*60.00*
		Nos. 29-40 (12)	151.40	*227.00*

Nos. 29 and 33 are also on ordinary paper.

1907-11

Ordinary Paper

No.	Type	Description	Unused	Used
41	A4	¼p brown ('09)	15	*25*
42	A4	½p green	50	50
43	A4	1p carmine	1.00	15
44	A4	2p gray ('11)	1.25	*5.00*
45	A4	2½p ultramarine	1.65	2.25
		Nos. 41-45 (5)	4.55	8.15

King George V
A5 A6

Dies I and II, type A5, described at back of volume.

The ½p, 1p, 2½p and 6p denominations of type A5 show the numeral on horizontally-lined tablet. The 1sh and 5sh denominations are expressed as "ONE SHILLING" and "FIVE SHILLINGS" on plain tablet.

Die I

1912

Ordinary Paper

No.	Type	Description	Unused	Used
46	A5	¼p brown	15	15
47	A5	½p green	35	15
48	A5	1p scarlet	32	15
a.		1p carmine	45	15
49	A5	2p gray	2.10	2.00
50	A5	2½p ultramarine	1.25	*2.50*

1912-22

Chalky Paper

No.	Type	Description	Unused	Used
51	A5	3p violet, *yel*	50	1.00
52	A5	4p blk & red, *yel* (Die II) ('22)	75	*4.00*
53	A5	6p vio & red vio	1.25	*3.75*
54	A5	1sh blk, *bl grn,* ol back	1.25	*3.50*
a.		1sh black, *green*	3.50	3.00
55	A5	2sh vio & ultra, *bl* (Die II) ('22)	3.50	*6.50*
56	A5	2sh6p black & red, *blue* ('14)	8.75	17.50
57	A5	5sh green & red, *yellow* ('14)	7.50	*16.00*
		Nos. 46-57 (12)	27.67	*57.20*

1914

Surface-colored Paper

No.	Type	Description	Unused	Used
58	A5	3p violet, *yel*	35.00	*35.00*
59	A5	1sh black, *green*	30.00	*35.00*
60	A5	5sh green & red, *yel*	30.00	*37.50*

Die II

1921-32 Wmk. 4

Ordinary Paper

No.	Type	Description	Unused	Used
61	A5	¼p dk brn ('22)	15	15
a.		¼p dark brown (I) ('32)	15	20
62	A5	½p green	15	15
a.		½p green (I) ('32)	75	*4.00*
63	A5	1p carmine	25	15
a.		1p rose red (I) ('32)	80	80
64	A5	1p dp vio ('22)	38	15
65	A5	1½p rose red ('26)	85	15
66	A5	1½p red brn ('29)	42	15
a.		1½p red brown (I) ('32)	1.50	*2.50*
68	A5	2p gray ('22)	85	50
69	A5	2½p orange ('23)	5.00	*12.50*
70	A5	2½p ultra ('27)	42	32
a.		Die I ('32)	3.00	3.00
71	A5	3p ultra ('23)	5.00	*11.00*

Chalky Paper

No.	Type	Description	Unused	Used
72	A5	3p violet, *yel*	*55*	*1.25*
73	A5	4p black & red, *yel* ('23)	1.00	3.75
74	A5	5p vio & olive grn ('22)	38	*1.25*
75	A5	6p vio & red vio ('23)	3.75	7.50
a.		Die I ('32)	6.25	*10.00*
76	A5	1sh blk, *emerald* ('23)	1.25	3.75
a.		1sh black, *green* (I) ('32)	17.50	*22.50*
77	A5	2sh vio & ultra, *bl* ('22)	5.00	7.50
78	A5	2sh6p blk & red, *bl* ('23)	6.25	10.00
79	A5	3sh green & vio	6.25	*12.00*
80	A5	4sh black & scar	8.75	*20.00*
81	A5	5sh grn & red, *yel*	25.00	*30.00*
82	A6	10sh red & grn, *emer* ('28)	47.50	*50.00*

Wmk. 3

No.	Type	Description	Unused	Used
83	A6	£1 black & vio, *red* ('28)	175.00	*190.00*
		Nos. 61-66,68-83 (22)	294.15	*362.22*

Silver Jubilee Issue
Common Design Type
Perf. 11x12

1935, May 6 Engr. Wmk. 4

No.	Type	Description	Unused	Used
96	CD301	1p car & dk blue	32	32
97	CD301	1½p blk & ultra	80	80
98	CD301	2½p ultra & brn	1.40	1.40
99	CD301	1sh brn vio & ind	4.00	4.00

Coronation Issue
Common Design Type

1937, May 12 *Perf. 13½x14*

No.	Type	Description	Unused	Used
100	CD302	1p carmine	16	16
101	CD302	1½p brown	20	20
102	CD302	2½p bright ultra	32	32

Common Design Types are pictured beginning on page 176.

King George VI
A7 A8

1938-51 Typo. *Perf. 14*

No.	Type	Description	Unused	Used
103	A7	¼p brown	15	15
104	A7	½p green	15	15
105	A7	1p scarlet	15	15
a.		1p carmine ('42)	22	34
106	A7	1½p red brown	15	15
107	A7	2p gray	15	15
108	A7	2½p ultramarine	15	15
109	A7	3p dl org ('42)	18	15
a.		3p brown orange	3.50	90
110	A7	6p vio & red vio	25	25
111	A7	1sh blk, *emerald*	70	48
112	A7	2sh vio & ultra, *bl*	1.65	1.10
113	A7	5sh grn & red, *yel*	5.50	6.50
114	A8	10sh red & grn, *emer*	22.50	17.50

Two dies were used for the 1p, differing in thickness of shading line at base of "1."

Wmk. 3 *Perf. 13*

No.	Type	Description	Unused	Used
115	A8	£1 blk & vio, *scar* ('51)	12.50	15.00
a.		£1 black & brown purple, *red,* perf. 14	150.00	150.00
b.		£1 black & purple, *carmine,* perf. 14 ('41)	27.50	20.00
c.		£1 black & brown purple, *salmon,* perf. 14 ('43)	15.00	17.50
d.		Wmkd. sideways (as #115, perf. 13)	*2,000.*	
		Nos. 103-115 (13)	44.18	41.88

Issue dates: £1, Dec. 13, 1951, others, Nov. 25, 1938.
See Nos. 120-125.

Catalogue values for unused stamps in this section, from this point to the end of the section, are for Never Hinged items.

Peace Issue
Common Design Type
Perf. 13½x14

1946, Nov. 1 Wmk. 4 Engr.

No.	Type	Description	Unused	Used
116	CD303	1½p brown	15	15
117	CD303	3p deep orange	15	15
		Set value	25	25

Silver Wedding Issue
Common Design Types

1949, Jan. 2 Photo. *Perf. 14x14½*

No.	Type	Description	Unused	Used
118	CD304	2½p bright ultra	15	15

Perf. 11½x11
Engr.; Name Typographed

No.	Type	Description	Unused	Used
119	CD305	5sh green	5.75	5.75

George VI Type of 1938

1949, July 1 Typo. *Perf. 13½x14*

No.	Type	Description	Unused	Used
120	A7	½p gray	15	15
121	A7	1p green	15	15
122	A7	1½p orange & black	15	15
123	A7	2p crimson rose	24	15
124	A7	2½p black & plum	24	15
125	A7	3p ultramarine	24	15
		Nos. 120-125 (6)	1.17	
		Set value		65

UPU Issue
Common Design Types
Engr.; Name Typo. on 3p and 6p

1949, Oct. 10 *Perf. 13½, 11x11½*

No.	Type	Description	Unused	Used
126	CD306	2½p slate	40	40
127	CD307	3p indigo	60	60
128	CD308	6p red lilac	1.25	1.25
129	CD309	1sh blue green	1.50	1.50

University Issue
Common Design Types
Perf. 14x14½

1951, Feb. 16 Engr. Wmk. 4

No.	Type	Description	Unused	Used
130	CD310	3c gray black & org	30	30
131	CD311	12c lilac & rose car	95	95

Coronation Issue
Common Design Type

1953, June 2 *Perf. 13½x13*

No.	Type	Description	Unused	Used
132	CD312	3c dk green & black	25	25

Queen Elizabeth II
A9 A10

1954, Feb. 22 Typo. *Perf. 14*

No.	Type	Description	Unused	Used
133	A9	½c brown	15	15
134	A9	1c gray	15	15
135	A9	2c green	15	15
136	A9	3c orange & blk	15	15
137	A9	4c rose red	16	16
138	A9	5c blk & claret	18	18
139	A9	6c orange	22	22
140	A9	8c deep ultra	25	25
141	A9	12c rose vio & mag	38	38
142	A9	24c black & green	60	60
143	A9	48c rose vio & ultra	1.25	1.25
144	A9	60c brown & green	1.65	1.65
145	A9	$1.20 yel grn & rose red	3.25	3.25

Perf. 13

No.	Type	Description	Unused	Used
146	A10	$2.40 red & blue grn	5.00	*8.00*
147	A10	$4.80 black & claret	9.50	*15.00*
		Nos. 133-147 (15)	23.04	*31.54*

MONTSERRAT

LOCATION — West Indies southeast of Puerto Rico
GOVT. — British Crown Colony
AREA — 39 sq. mi.
POP. — 12,074 (1980)
CAPITAL — Plymouth

Montserrat was one of the four presidencies of the former Leeward Islands colony until it became a colony itself in 1956.

Montserrat stamps were discontinued in 1890 and resumed in 1903. In the interim, stamps of Leeward Islands were used. In 1903-56, stamps of Montserrat and Leeward Islands were used concurrently.

12 Pence = 1 Shilling
20 Shillings = 1 Pound
100 Cents = 1 Dollar (1951)

Catalogue values for unused stamps in this country are for Never Hinged items, beginning with Scott 104 in the regular postage section, Scott B1 in the semi-postal section, Scott O45 in the officials section.

Watermark

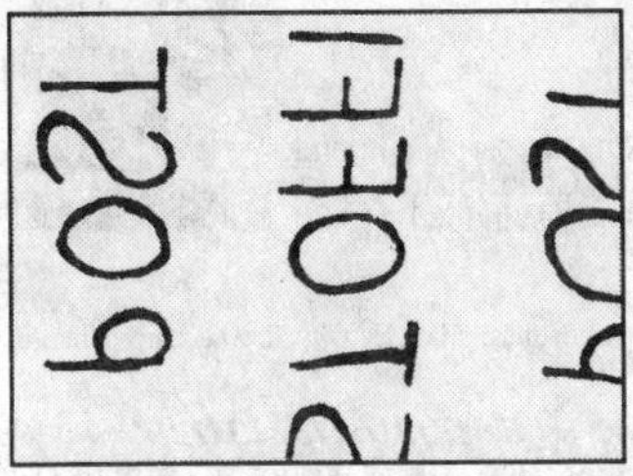

Wmk. 380- "POST OFFICE"

Stamps of Antigua Overprinted in Black

a MONTSERRAT

1876 Engr. Wmk. 1 *Perf. 14*
1 A1 1p red 15.00 15.00
a. Vert. or diag. half used as ½p on cover 1,500.
c. "S" inverted 1,500. 1,500.
2 A1 6p green 40.00 35.00
a. Vertical half used as 3p on cover
b. Vertical third used as 2p on cover
c. "S" inverted 1,750. 1,750.
d. 6p blue green 1,200.
e. As "d," "S" inverted

Nos. 1c, 2c are valued for copies with perfs touching frameline.

Some experts consider Nos. 2d, 2e to be from a trial printing.

Queen Victoria — A2

1880 Typo.
3 A2 2½p red brown 200.00 125.00
4 A2 4p blue 110.00 42.50

Antigua No. 18 Overprinted type "a" and Type of 1880

1884-85 Wmk. 2
5 A2 ½p green 2.00 4.00

Engr.
6 A1 1p rose red 6.00 12.50
a. Vertical half used as ½p on cover 2,000.
b. "S" inverted 1,000. 1,000.

Typo.
7 A2 2½p red brown 200.00 90.00
8 A2 2½p ultra ('85) 10.00 12.00
9 A2 4p blue 2,750. 250.00
10 A2 4p red lilac ('85) 4.00 *6.00*

Antigua No. 20 Overprinted type "a"

1884 Engr. *Perf. 12*
11 A1 1p red 65.00 40.00
a. "S" inverted 2,250. 2,000.
b. Vert. half used as ½p on cover 1,500.

Symbol of the Colony — A3

King Edward VII — A4

1903 Wmk. 2 Typo. *Perf. 14*
12 A3 ½p gray green 90 1.25
13 A3 1p car & black 90 30
14 A3 2p brown & black 4.25 5.00
15 A3 2½p ultra & black 1.40 1.25
16 A3 3p dk vio & brn orange 5.25 6.00
17 A3 6p ol grn & vio 7.00 9.00
18 A3 1sh vio & gray grn 9.50 12.50
19 A3 2sh brn org & gray green 14.00 20.00
20 A3 2sh6p blk & gray grn 25.00 *35.00*

Wmk. 1
21 A4 5sh car & black 110.00 *150.00*
Nos. 12-21 (10) 178.20 240.30

1904-08 Wmk. 3

Chalky Paper
22 A3 ½p grn & gray grn 90 1.10
23 A3 1p car & blk ('08) 9.00 9.00
24 A3 2p brown & black 90 1.50
25 A3 2½p ultra & blk ('06) 2.00 3.00
26 A3 3p dk vio & brn orange 1.40 1.65
27 A3 6p ol grn & vio 3.00 *4.50*
28 A3 1sh violet & gray grn ('08) 4.50 6.00
29 A3 2sh brn org & gray grn ('08) 24.00 30.00
30 A3 2sh6p blk & gray grn ('08) 26.00 30.00
31 A4 5sh car & blk ('07) 90.00 *110.00*
Nos. 22-31 (10) 161.70 *196.75*

The ½, 2, 3 and 6p are also on ordinary paper.

1908-13

Ordinary Paper
31A A3 ½p deep green 40 30
32 A3 1p carmine 50 20
33 A3 2p gray 2.50 *4.25*
34 A3 2½p ultramarine 2.50 4.25

Chalky Paper
35 A3 3p vio, *yellow* 1.65 7.00
36 A3 6p red vio & gray vio 4.50 10.00
37 A3 1sh blk, *green* 6.00 10.00
38 A3 2sh bl & vio, *bl* 17.50 30.00
39 A3 2sh 6p car & blk, *blue* 27.50 40.00
40 A4 5sh grn & scar, *yel* 60.00 80.00

Surface-colored Paper
41 A3 3p vio, *yel* ('13) 3.75 12.50
Nos. 31A-41 (11) 126.80 198.50

King George V
A5 A6

1913

Chalky Paper
42 A5 5sh green & scar, *yel* 75.00 90.00

1916-22 Wmk. 3 *Perf. 14*

Ordinary Paper
43 A6 ½p green 50 65
44 A6 1p scarlet 45 60
45 A6 2p gray 1.75 *5.00*
46 A6 2½p ultramarine 3.00 *6.00*

Chalky Paper
47 A6 3p violet, *yel* 75 *2.00*
48 A6 4p blk & red, *yel* ('22) 4.50 *9.00*
49 A6 6p dl vio & red violet 2.50 *6.00*
50 A6 1sh blk, *bl grn,* ol back 3.00 *8.00*
51 A6 2sh vio & ultra, *bl* 9.00 16.00
52 A6 2sh 6p blk & red, *bl* 11.50 20.00
53 A6 5sh grn & red, *yel* 22.50 40.00
Nos. 43-53 (11) 59.45 *113.25*

For overprints, see Nos. MR1-MR3.

1922-29 Wmk. 4

Ordinary Paper
54 A6 ¼p brown 40 55
55 A6 ½p green ('23) 18 18
56 A6 1p dp violet ('23) 65 25
57 A6 1p carmine ('29) 1.10 1.00
58 A6 1½p orange 2.75 *5.50*
59 A6 1½p rose red ('23) 45 *1.10*
60 A6 1½p fawn ('29) 1.10 35
61 A6 2p gray 65 *1.10*
62 A6 2½p ultramarine 3.50 1.10
63 A6 2½p orange ('23) 2.25 *4.50*
64 A6 3p ultra ('23) 65 *2.00*

Chalky Paper
65 A6 3p vio, *yel* ('26) 1.65 2.50
66 A6 4p black & red, *yel* ('23) 1.40 *2.75*
67 A6 5p dull vio & ol grn 3.50 *7.00*
68 A6 6p dull vio & red vio ('23) 1.50 *3.00*
69 A6 1sh blk, *emer* ('23) 2.50 *3.00*
70 A6 2sh vio & ultra, *bl* 3.75 *7.00*
71 A6 2sh 6p blk & red, *bl* ('23) 10.50 16.00
72 A6 3sh green & vio 10.50 16.00
73 A6 4sh black & scar 10.50 16.00
74 A6 5sh grn & red, *yel* ('23) 17.00 26.00
Nos. 54-74 (21) 76.48 *116.88*

Tercentenary Issue

New Plymouth and Harbor A7

1932, Apr. 18 Engr.
75 A7 ½p green 70 75
76 A7 1p red 70 75
77 A7 1½p orange brown 1.75 2.00
78 A7 2p gray 2.00 2.25
79 A7 2½p ultra 2.00 2.25
80 A7 3p orange 4.00 4.00
81 A7 6p violet 6.50 7.75
82 A7 1sh olive green 11.50 14.00
83 A7 2sh6p lilac rose 47.50 57.50
84 A7 5sh dark brown 92.50 110.00
Nos. 75-84 (10) 169.15 201.25
Set, never hinged 275.00

300th anniv. of the colonization of Montserrat.

Silver Jubilee Issue

Common Design Type

1935, May 6 *Perf. 11x12*
85 CD301 1p car & dk blue 1.00 75
86 CD301 1½p gray blk & ultra 90 *1.50*
87 CD301 2½p ultra & brn 3.50 *3.00*
88 CD301 1sh brn vio & ind 5.00 *10.00*
Set, never hinged 22.50

Coronation Issue

Common Design Type

1937, May 12 *Perf. 13½x14*
89 CD302 1p carmine 15 20
90 CD302 1½p brown 15 25
91 CD302 2½p bright ultra 25 40
Set, never hinged 90

Carr's Bay — A8

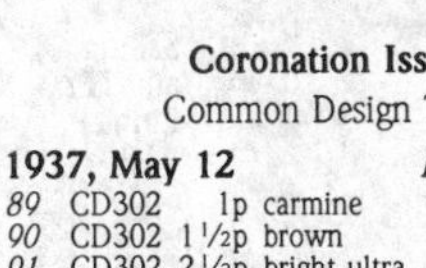

Sea Island Cotton — A9

Botanic Station — A10

1941-48 *Perf. 14*
92 A8 ½p dk grn ('42) 15 15
93 A9 1p car ('42) 15 15
94 A8 1½p rose vio ('42) 15 15
95 A10 2p red orange 28 22
96 A9 2½p brt ultra ('43) 28 24
97 A8 3p brown ('42) 35 28
98 A10 6p dull vio ('42) 35 22
99 A8 1sh brn lake ('42) 70 55
100 A10 2sh6p slate bl ('43) 2.75 2.50
101 A8 5sh car rose ('42) 3.00 3.00

Perf. 12
102 A10 10sh blue ('48) 7.00 12.50
103 A8 £1 black ('48) 10.50 17.50
Nos. 92-103 (12) 25.66 37.46
Set, never hinged 47.50

1938, Aug. 2 *Perf. 13*
92a A8 ½p 15 15
93a A8 1p 15 15
94a A8 1½p 2.00 1.65
95a A10 2p 1.65 1.65
96a A9 2½p 32 40
97a A8 3p 40 50
98a A10 6p 35 40
99a A8 1sh 2.00 2.00
100a A10 2sh6p 2.00 2.00
101a A8 5sh 5.00 *10.00*
Nos. 92a-101a (10) 14.02 *18.90*
Set, never hinged 30.00

Catalogue values for unused stamps in this section, from this point to the end of the section, are for Never Hinged items.

Peace Issue

Common Design Type

1946, Nov. 1 Engr. *Perf. 13½x14*
104 CD303 1½p deep magenta 15 15
105 CD303 3p brown 20 18
Set value 30 26

Silver Wedding Issue

Common Design Types

1949, Jan. 3 Photo. *Perf. 14x14½*
106 CD304 2½p brt ultra 16 16

Engraved; Name Typographed

Perf. 11½x11
107 CD305 5sh rose carmine 6.75 *10.00*

UPU Issue

Common Design Types

Engr.; Name Typo. on 3p and 6p

Perf. 13½, 11x11½

1949, Oct. 10 Wmk. 4
108 CD306 2½p ultramarine 40 40
109 CD307 3p chocolate 55 55
110 CD308 6p lilac 85 85
111 CD309 1sh rose violet 1.25 1.25

University Issue

Common Design Types

1951, Feb. 16 Engr. *Perf. 14x14½*
112 CD310 3c rose lil & gray blk 25 25
113 CD311 12c violet & black 75 75

Government House — A11

Designs (portrait at right on 12c, 24c and $2.40): 2c, $1.20, Cotton field. 3c, Map of Presidency. 4c, 24c, Picking tomatoes. 5c, 12c, St. Anthony's Church. 6c, $4.80, Badge of Presidency. 8c, 60c, Cotton ginning.

Perf. 11½x11

1951, Sept. 17 Engr. Wmk. 4
114 A11 1c gray 15 15
115 A11 2c green 20 20
116 A11 3c orange brown 15 15
117 A11 4c rose carmine 15 15
118 A11 5c red violet 20 20
119 A11 6c dark brown 25 25
120 A11 8c dark blue 35 35
121 A11 12c red brn & blue 65 65
122 A11 24c emer & rose carmine 1.00 1.00
123 A11 60c rose car & gray black 2.00 2.00
124 A11 $1.20 dp bl & emer 6.00 6.00
125 A11 $2.40 dp grn & gray black 7.50 *9.00*
126 A11 $4.80 pur & gray blk 15.00 *20.00*
Nos. 114-126 (13) 33.60 *40.10*

Coronation Issue
Common Design Type

1953, June 2 *Perf. 13½x13*
127 CD312 2c dark green & black 20 20

Type of 1951 with Portrait of Queen Elizabeth II

Designs: ½c, 3c, "Map of Presidency." 6c, $4.80, "Badge of Presidency." 48c, Cotton field.

1953-57 *Perf. 11½x11*
128 A11 ½c violet ('56) 15 15
129 A11 1c gray black 15 15
130 A11 2c green 15 15
131 A11 3c orange brown 30 30
132 A11 4c rose car ('55) 15 15
133 A11 5c red vio ('55) 15 15
134 A11 6c dk brown ('55) 35 35
135 A11 8c dp ultra ('55) 15 15
136 A11 12c red brn & blue ('55) 18 18
137 A11 24c emer & rose car ('55) 35 35
138 A11 48c rose violet & olive ('57) 80 80
139 A11 60c rose car & blk ('55) 1.00 1.00
140 A11 $1.20 bl & emer ('55) 2.00 2.00
141 A11 $2.40 dp green & blk ('55) 4.00 4.00
142 A11 $4.80 pur & gray black ('55) 17.50 17.50
Nos. 128-142 (15) 27.38 27.38

See Nos. 146-149, 156.

West Indies Federation
Common Design Type
Perf. 11½x11

1958, Apr. 22 Engr. Wmk. 314
143 CD313 3c green 15 15
144 CD313 6c blue 28 28
145 CD313 12c carmine rose 48 48

Type of 1953-57

Designs as before, but inscribed: "Map of the Colony" (½c, 3c) "Badge of the Colony" (6c, $4.80).

1958 Wmk. 4 *Perf. 11½x11*
146 A11 ½c violet 15 15
147 A11 3c orange brown 15 15
148 A11 6c dark brown 20 20
149 A11 $4.80 pur & gray blk 12.00 12.00

Freedom from Hunger Issue
Common Design Type
Perf. 14x14½

1963, June 4 Photo. Wmk. 314
150 CD314 12c lilac 90 80

Red Cross Centenary Issue
Common Design Type

1963, Sept. 2 Litho. *Perf. 13*
151 CD315 4c black & red 15 15
152 CD315 12c ultra & red 85 65

Shakespeare Issue
Common Design Type

1964, Apr. 23 Photo. *Perf. 14x14½*
153 CD316 12c slate blue 35 25

Type of 1953-57
Perf. 11½x11

1964, Oct. 30 Engr. Wmk. 314
156 A11 2c green 25 20

ITU Issue
Common Design Type
Perf. 11x11½

1965, May 17 Litho. Wmk. 314
157 CD317 4c ver & lilac 18 16
158 CD317 48c emer & rose red 1.25 1.10

Pineapple — A12

Wmk. 314 Upright

1965, Aug. 16 Photo. *Perf. 15x14*
159 A12 1c shown 15 15
160 A12 2c Avacado 15 15
161 A12 3c Soursop 15 15
162 A12 4c Peppers 15 15
163 A12 5c Mango 15 15
164 A12 6c Tomatoes 15 15
165 A12 8c Guava 15 15
166 A12 10c Okra 18 18
167 A12 12c Limes 28 16
168 A12 20c Oranges 35 22
169 A12 24c Bananas 55 32
170 A12 42c Onion 1.10 80
171 A12 48c Cabbage 1.40 90
172 A12 60c Papayas 1.50 1.10
173 A12 $1.20 Pumpkin 1.75 1.50
174 A12 $2.40 Sweet potato 4.50 3.50
175 A12 $4.80 Eggplant 9.00 7.25
Nos. 159-175 (17) 21.66 16.98

For surcharges, see Nos. 193-198.

1969 Wmk. 314 Sideways
159a A12 1c 15 15
160a A12 2c 30 30
161a A12 3c 38 38
162a A12 4c 52 52
163a A12 5c 60 60
166a A12 10c 1.15 1.15
168a A12 20c 1.40 1.40
Nos. 159a-168a (7) 4.50 4.50

Intl. Cooperation Year Issue
Common Design Type

1965, Oct. 25 Litho. *Perf. 14½*
176 CD318 2c lt green & claret 15 15
177 CD318 12c lt violet & green 42 42

Churchill Memorial Issue
Common Design Type

1966, Jan. 24 Photo. *Perf. 14*
Design in Black, Gold and Carmine Rose
178 CD319 1c bright blue 15 15
179 CD319 2c green 15 15
180 CD319 24c brown 48 48
181 CD319 42c violet 90 90

Royal Visit Issue
Common Design Type
Perf. 11x12

1966, Feb. 4 Litho. Wmk. 314
182 CD320 14c violet blue 32 32
183 CD320 24c dk carmine rose 60 60

WHO Headquarters Issue
Common Design Type

1966, Sept. 20 Litho. *Perf. 14*
184 CD322 12c multicolored 16 16
185 CD322 60c multicolored 75 75

UNESCO Anniversary Issue
Common Design Type

1966, Dec. 1 Litho. *Perf. 14*
186 CD323 4c "Education" 15 15
a. Orange omitted 50.00
187 CD323 60c "Science" 55 55
188 CD323 $1.80 "Culture" 2.25 2.25

On No. 186a, the squares of the lowercase letters appear in yellow.

Sailing and ITY Emblem A13

ITY Emblem and: 15c, Waterfall, Chance Mountain, vert. 16c, Beach scene. 24c, Golfers.

1967, Dec. 29 Photo. Wmk. 314
189 A13 5c multicolored 15 15
190 A13 15c multicolored 20 20
191 A13 16c multicolored 25 25
192 A13 24c multicolored 50 50

Issued for International Tourist Year.

Nos. 167, 169, 171, 173-175 and Type Surcharged **15c**

1968, May 6 *Perf. 15x14*
193 A12 15c on 12c multi 25 25
a. Wmkd. sideways ('69) 1.00 1.00
194 A12 25c on 24c multi 40 40
a. Wmkd. sideways ('69) 1.75 1.75
195 A12 50c on 48c multi 80 80
a. Wmkd. sideways ('69) 3.50 3.50
196 A12 $1 on $1.20 multi 1.25 1.25
197 A12 $2.50 on $2.40 multi 2.75 2.75
198 A12 $5 on $4.80 multi 5.50 5.50
Nos. 193-198 (6) 10.95 10.95

The surcharge bars are slightly thinner on the "Wmkd. sideways" varieties.

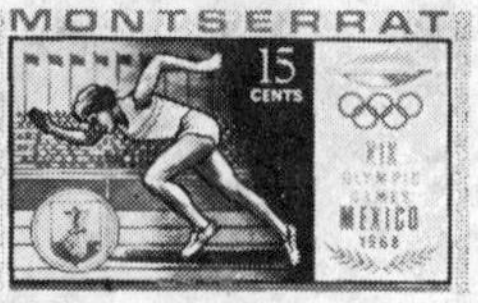

Woman Runner A14

Designs: 25c, Weight lifter. 50c, Athlete on rings. $1, Runner and Toltec sculptures, vert.

Perf. 14½x14, 14x14½

1968, July 31 Photo. Wmk. 314
199 A14 15c gold, brt grn & rose claret 15 15
200 A14 25c gold, org & blue 18 18
201 A14 50c gold, ver & green 35 35
202 A14 $1 multicolored 75 75

19th Olympic Games, Mexico City, Oct. 12-27.

Albert T. Marryshow A15

Portraits and Human Rights Flame: 5c, Alexander Hamilton. 25c, William Wilberforce. 50c, Dag Hammarskjold. $1, Rev. Martin Luther King, Jr.

1968, Dec. 2 Photo. *Perf. 14x14½*
203 A15 5c multicolored 15 15
204 A15 15c multicolored 15 15
205 A15 25c multicolored 18 18
206 A15 50c multicolored 35 35
207 A15 $1 multicolored 70 70
Nos. 203-207 (5) 1.53 1.53

International Human Rights Year.

The Two Trinities, by Murillo — A16

Map of Caribbean — A17

Christmas: 15c, 50c, The Adoration of the Magi, by Botticelli.

1968, Dec. 16 *Perf. 14½x14*
208 A16 5c red & multi 15 15
209 A16 15c dk green & multi 18 18
210 A16 25c purple & multi 28 28
211 A16 50c brown & multi 55 55

1969, May 27 Photo. *Perf. 14*

Design: 35c, 50c, "Strength in Unity," horiz.

212 A17 15c green & multi 15 15
213 A17 20c brown & multi 16 16
214 A17 35c dp carmine & multi 32 32
215 A17 50c multicolored 45 45

First anniversary of CARIFTA (Caribbean Free Trade Area).

Telephone and Map — A18

Development Projects (Map and): 25c, Book and "New Schools." 50c, Planes (air transport service). $1, Pylon and power lines.

Perf. 13½

1969, July 29 Litho. Wmk. 314
216 A18 15c multicolored 15 15
217 A18 25c multicolored 20 20
218 A18 50c multicolored 42 42
219 A18 $1 multicolored 90 90

Dolphin A19

Fish: 15c, Atlantic sailfish. 25c, Blackfin tuna and fishing boat. 40c, Spanish mackerel.

1969, Nov. 1 Photo. *Perf. 13x14*
220 A19 5c multicolored 15 15
221 A19 15c multicolored 30 30
222 A19 25c multicolored 60 60
223 A19 40c multicolored 1.00 1.00

King Caspar, Virgin and Child (Stained-glass Window) — A20

Christmas: 50c, Nativity, by Leonard Limosin, horiz.

Perf. 12½x13, 13x12½

1969, Dec. 10 Litho. Wmk. 314
224 A20 15c violet & multi 16 16
225 A20 25c red & multi 32 32
226 A20 50c orange & multi 65 65

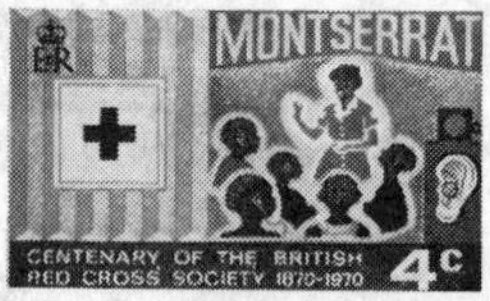

Red Cross and Distribution of Hearing Aids — A21

Red Cross and: 3c, Fund raising sale and invalid. 15c, Car bringing handicapped to work. 20c, Instruction for blind worker.

1970, Apr. 13 Litho. *Perf. 14½*
227 A21 3c multicolored 15 15
228 A21 4c multicolored 15 15
229 A21 15c multicolored 32 32
230 A21 20c multicolored 50 50

Centenary of British Red Cross Society.

Red-footed Booby A22

Birds: 2c, Killy hawk, vert. 3c, Frigate bird, vert. 4c, White egret, vert. 5c, Brown pelican, vert. 10c, Bananaquit, vert. 15c, Common ani. 20c, Tropic bird. 25c, Montserrat oriole. 50c, Greenthroated carib, vert. $1, Antillean crested hummingbird. $2.50, Little blue heron, vert. $5, Purple-throated carib. $10, Forest thrush.

Wmk. 314 Upright on Horiz. Stamps, Sideways on Vert. Stamps
Perf. 14x14½, 14½x14

1970-74 Photo.
231 A22 1c yel org & multi 15 15
232 A22 2c lt vio & multi 15 15
233 A22 3c multicolored 15 15
234 A22 4c lt grn & multi 15 15
235 A22 5c bister & multi 15 15

236	A22	10c	gray & multi	20	20
237	A22	15c	multicolored	30	30
238	A22	20c	rose brn & multi	40	40
239	A22	25c	brown & multi	50	50
240	A22	50c	lt vio & multi	1.00	1.00
241	A22	$1	multicolored	1.75	1.75
242	A22	$2.50	dl bl & multi	4.00	4.00
243	A22	$5	multicolored	8.00	8.00
243A	A22	$10	blue & multi	16.00	16.00
			Nos. 231-243A (14)	32.90	32.90

Issued: $10, Oct. 30, 1974; others July 2, 1970.
For surcharges and overprints, see Nos. 314, 317, 337-339, O1-O4.

Wmk. Sideways on Horiz. Stamps, Upright on Vert. Stamps

1972-74

231a	A22	1c	multicolored	16	15
232a	A22	2c	multicolored	25	20
233a	A22	3c	multicolored	25	20
234a	A22	4c	multicolored	35	25
235a	A22	5c	multicolored	45	28
237a	A22	15c	multicolored	1.20	75
238a	A22	20c	multicolored	1.75	1.20
239a	A22	25c	multicolored	2.50	1.50
			Nos. 231a-239a (8)	6.91	4.53

Issue dates: 1c, 2c, 3c, July 21, 1972. 5c, 15c, Mar. 8, 1973. 20c, Oct. 2, 1973. 4c, Feb. 4, 1974. 25c, May 17, 1974.

"Madonna and Child with Animals," after Dürer — A23

Christmas: 15c, $1, Adoration of the Shepherds, by Domenichino (Domenico Zampieri).

1970, Sept. 21 Litho. *Perf. 14*

244	A23	5c	lt blue & multi	15	15
245	A23	15c	red orange & multi	25	25
246	A23	20c	ol green & multi	30	30
247	A23	$1	multicolored	1.50	1.50

War Memorial, Plymouth A24

Tourist Publicity: 15c, Fort St. George and view of Plymouth. 25c, Beach at Carrs Bay. 50c, Golf Course.

1970, Nov. 30 Litho. *Perf. 14*

248	A24	5c	multicolored	15	15
249	A24	15c	multicolored	30	30
250	A24	25c	multicolored	45	45
251	A24	50c	multicolored	90	90
a.			Souvenir sheet of 4, #248-251	2.75	2.75

Girl Guide — A25

"Noli me Tangere," by Orcagna (Andrea di Cione) — A26

Girl Guides' 60th Anniv.: 15c, 25c, Brownie.

1970, Dec. 31

252	A25	10c	orange & multi	15	15
253	A25	15c	lt blue & multi	25	25
254	A25	25c	lilac & multi	42	42
255	A25	40c	multicolored	70	70

Perf. 13¹/₂x13

1971, Mar. 22 Photo. Wmk. 314

Easter: 5c, 20c, Descent from the Cross, by Jan van Hemessen.

256	A26	5c	orange brn & multi	15	15
257	A26	15c	multicolored	35	35
258	A26	20c	green & multi	45	45
259	A26	40c	blue green & multi	90	90

Distinguished Flying Cross and Medal — A27

"Nativity with Saints" (detail), by Romanino — A28

Highest Awards for Military Personnel: 20c, Military Cross and Medal. 40c, Distinguished Service Cross and Medal. $1, Victoria Cross.

Perf. 14¹/₂x14

1971, July 8 Litho. Wmk. 314

260	A27	10c	gray, vio & silver	15	15
261	A27	20c	green & multi	24	24
262	A27	40c	lt bl, dk bl & sil	48	48
263	A27	$1	red, dk brn & gold	1.25	1.25

50th anniversary of the British Commonwealth Ex-services League.

1971, Sept. 16 *Perf. 14x13¹/₂*

Christmas (Paintings): 15c, $1, Angels' Choir, by Simon Marmion.

264	A28	5c	brown & multi	15	15
265	A28	15c	emerald & multi	30	30
266	A28	20c	ultra & multi	42	42
267	A28	$1	red & multi	2.25	2.25

Piper Apache, First Landing at Olveston Airfield — A29

Designs: 10c, Beech Twin Bonanza. 15c, De Havilland Heron. 20c, Britten Norman Islander. 40c, De Havilland Twin Otter. 75c, Hawker Siddeley 748 and stewardesses.

1971, Dec. 16 *Perf. 13¹/₂x14*

268	A29	5c	multicolored	16	16
269	A29	10c	multicolored	32	32
270	A29	15c	multicolored	45	45
271	A29	20c	multicolored	65	65
272	A29	40c	multicolored	1.25	1.25
273	A29	75c	multicolored	2.00	2.00
a.			Souvenir sheet of 6, #268-273	19.00	19.00
			Nos. 268-273 (6)	4.83	4.83

14th anniversary of Leeward Islands Air Transport (LIAT).

Chapel of Christ in Gethsemane, Coventry Cathedral — A30

Easter: 10c, 75c, The Agony in the Garden, by Giovanni Bellini.

1972, Mar. 9 Litho. *Perf. 13¹/₂x13*

274	A30	5c	red & multi	15	15
275	A30	10c	blue & multi	20	20
276	A30	20c	emerald & multi	40	40
277	A30	75c	lilac & multi	2.00	2.00

Iguana A31

Designs: 15c, Spotted ameiva (lizard), vert. 20c, Frog ("mountain chicken"), vert. $1, Redfoot tortoises.

1972, June 8 Litho. *Perf. 14¹/₂*

278	A31	15c	lilac rose & multi	45	45
279	A31	20c	black & multi	55	55
280	A31	40c	blue & multi	1.10	1.10
281	A31	$1	green & multi	2.25	2.25

Madonna of the Chair, by Raphael — A32

Christmas (Paintings): 35c, Virgin and Child with Cherubs, by Bernardino Fungai. 50c, Magnificat Madonna, by Botticelli. $1, Virgin and Child with St. John and Angel, by Botticelli.

1972, Oct. 18 *Perf. 13¹/₂*

282	A32	10c	violet & multi	18	18
283	A32	35c	brt red & multi	55	55
284	A32	50c	red brown & multi	90	90
285	A32	$1	olive & multi	1.90	1.90

Silver Wedding Issue, 1972

Common Design Type

Design: Queen Elizabeth II, Prince Philip, tomatoes, papayas, limes.

Perf. 14x14¹/₂

1972, Nov. 20 Photo. Wmk. 314

286	CD324	35c	car rose & multi	35	35
287	CD324	$1	ultra & multi	1.10	1.10

Passionflower A33

Designs: 35c, Passiflora vitifolia. 75c, Passiflora amabilis. $1, Passiflora alata caerulea.

1973, Apr. 9 Litho. *Perf. 14x13¹/₂*

288	A33	20c	purple & multi	52	52
289	A33	35c	multicolored	85	85
290	A33	75c	brt blue & multi	1.25	1.25
291	A33	$1	multicolored	2.25	2.25

Easter. Black backprinting gives story of passionflower.

Montserrat Monastery, Spain — A34

Designs: 35c, Columbus aboard ship sighting Montserrat. 60c, Columbus' ship off Montserrat. $1, Arms and map of Montserrat and neighboring islands.

1973, July 16 Litho. *Perf. 13¹/₂x14*

292	A34	10c	multicolored	60	60
293	A34	35c	multicolored	1.40	1.40
294	A34	60c	multicolored	2.25	2.25
295	A34	$1	multicolored	3.50	3.50
a.			Souvenir sheet of 4, #292-295	27.50	27.50

480th anniversary of the discovery of Montserrat by Columbus.

Virgin and Child, Studio of David A35

Masqueraders A36

Christmas (Paintings): 35c, Holy Family with St. John, by Jacob Jordaens. 50c, Virgin and Child, by Bellini. 90c, Virgin and Child by Carlo Dolci.

1973, Oct. 15 Litho. *Perf. 14x13¹/₂*

296	A35	20c	blue & multi	32	32
297	A35	35c	ol bister & multi	55	55
298	A35	50c	brt green & multi	1.25	1.25
299	A35	90c	brt rose & multi	2.50	2.50

Princess Anne's Wedding Issue

Common Design Type

1973, Nov. 14 *Perf. 14*

300	CD325	35c	brt green & multi	22	22
301	CD325	$1	multicolored	65	65

1974, Apr. 8

302	A36	20c	Steel band, horiz.	28	28
303	A36	35c	shown	60	60
304	A36	60c	Girl weaving	90	90
305	A36	$1	University Center, horiz.	1.40	1.40
a.			Souvenir sheet of 4, #302-305	11.00	11.00

University of the West Indies, 25th anniv.
For surcharge see No. 316.

Hands Holding Letters, UPU Emblem A37

Designs: 2c, 5c, $1, Hands and figures from UPU Monument, Bern; UPU emblem. 3c, 50c, like 1c.

1974, July 3 Litho. *Perf. 14*

306	A37	1c	violet & multi	15	15
307	A37	2c	red & black	15	15
308	A37	3c	olive & multi	15	15
309	A37	5c	orange & black	15	15
310	A37	50c	brown & multi	55	55
311	A37	$1	grnsh blue & black	1.10	1.10
			Set value	1.85	1.85

Centenary of Universal Postal Union.
For surcharges, see Nos. 315-318.

Churchill, Parliament, Big Ben — A38

Churchill and Blenheim Palace — A39

Perf. 13x13½

1974, Nov. 30 **Unwmk.**

312	A38	35c ocher & multi	22	22
313	A39	70c brt green & multi	60	60
a.		Souvenir sheet of 2, #312-313	1.10	1.10

Sir Winston Churchill (1874-1965).

Nos. 241, 304, 310-311 Surcharged with New Value and Two Bars

Perf. 14x14½, 14

Photo., Litho.

1974, Oct. 2 **Wmk. 314**

314	A22	2c on $1 multi	22	22
315	A37	5c on 50c multi	1.10	1.10
316	A36	10c on 60c multi	3.00	3.00
317	A22	20c on $1 multi	1.00	1.00
a.		One bar in surcharge	2.25	2.25
318	A37	35c on $1 multi	2.25	2.25
		Nos. 314-318 (5)	7.57	7.57

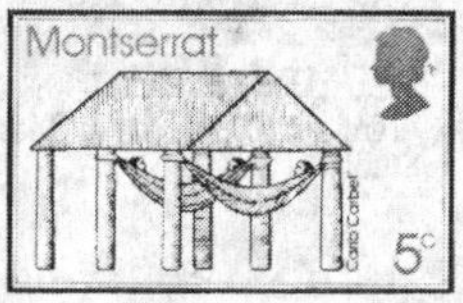

Carib Carbet (House) — A40

Carib Artifacts: 20c, Necklace (caracoli). 35c, Club. 70c, Canoe.

Wmk. 314

1975, Mar. 3 **Litho.** ***Perf. 14***

319	A40	5c dk red, ocher & blk	15	15
320	A40	20c black, ocher & dk red	20	20
321	A40	35c black, dk red & ocher	35	35
322	A40	70c ocher, dk red & blk	65	65
a.		Souvenir booklet	3.00	

No. 322a contains 2 self-adhesive panes printed on peelable paper backing with bicolored advertising on back. One pane of 6 contains 3 each similar to Nos. 320-321; the other pane of 4 contains one each similar to Nos. 319-322. Stamps are imperf. x roulette. Panes have commemorative marginal inscription.

One Bitt — A41

Old Local Coinage (1785-1801): 10c, Eighth of a dollar. 35c, Quarter dollars. $2, One dollar.

1975, Sept. 1 **Litho.** ***Perf. 14***

323	A41	5c ultra, silver & blk	15	15
324	A41	10c brown org, sil & blk	15	15
325	A41	35c green, silver & blk	38	38
326	A41	$2 brt rose, sil & blk	1.75	1.75
a.		Souvenir sheet of 4, #323-326	3.00	3.00

Explanation and description of coinage printed in black on back of souvenir sheet.

Montserrat Nos. 1 and 2 — A42

Designs: 10c, Post Office, Montserrat, and #1a (bisect) with AO8 cancel. 40c, Cover with #1a, 1b. 55c, G.B. #27 with AO8 cancel, and #2. 70c, 2 #1, 1 #1a with AO8 cancels. $1.10, Packet "Antelope" and #2.

1976, Jan. 5 ***Perf. 13½***

327	A42	5c multicolored	15	15
328	A42	10c multicolored	15	15
329	A42	40c multicolored	50	50
330	A42	55c multicolored	65	65
331	A42	70c multicolored	85	85
332	A42	$1.10 multicolored	1.25	1.25
a.		Souvenir sheet of 6, #327-332	4.00	4.00
		Nos. 327-332 (6)	3.55	3.55

Centenary of Montserrat's postage stamps.

Trinity, by Orcagna — A43

Paintings by Orcagna (Andrea di Cione): 40c, Resurrection. 55c, Ascension. $1.10, Pentecost.

Perf. 14x13½

1976, Apr. 5 **Litho.** **Wmk. 373**

333	A43	15c multicolored	15	15
334	A43	40c multicolored	28	28
335	A43	55c multicolored	32	32
336	A43	$1.10 multicolored	65	65
a.		Souvenir sheet of 4	2.00	2.00

Easter 1976. Nos. 333-336 were prepared, but not issued in 1975. Stamps are surcharged with new values; date "1975" obliterated with heavy bar. No. 336a contains one each of Nos. 333-336; "1975" in margin obliterated with heavy bar.

Nos. 235-236, 233 Surcharged 2¢ ═

Perf. 14½x14

1976, Apr. 12 **Photo.** **Wmk. 314**

337	A22	2c on 5c multi	15	15
338	A22	30c on 10c multi	65	65
339	A22	45c on 3c multi	1.10	1.10

For overprints, see Nos. O3-O4.

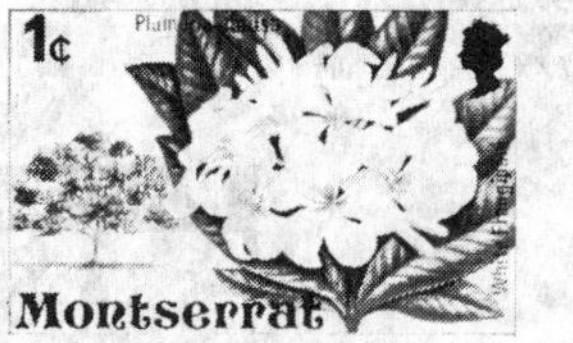

White Frangipani — A44

Designs: Flowering trees of Montserrat.

Perf. 13½x14

1976, July 5 **Litho.** **Wmk. 373**

340	A44	1c shown	15	15
341	A44	2c Cannonball tree	15	15
342	A44	3c Lignum vitae	15	15
343	A44	5c Malay apple	15	15
344	A44	10c Jacaranda	15	15
345	A44	15c Orchid tree	15	15
346	A44	20c Manjak	15	15
347	A44	25c Tamarind	16	16
348	A44	40c Flame of the Forest	24	24
349	A44	55c Pink cassia	35	35
350	A44	70c Long John	45	45
351	A44	$1 Saman	60	60
352	A44	$2.50 Immortelle	1.50	1.50
353	A44	$5 Yellow poui	3.00	3.00
354	A44	$10 Flamboyant	6.25	6.25
		Nos. 340-354 (15)	13.60	13.60

For surcharges and overprints, see Nos. 374-376, 420, 435-440, O10-O44.

Mary and Joseph on Road to Bethlehem — A45

Christmas (Map of Montserrat and): 20c, Shepherds. 55c, Virgin and Child. $1.10, Three Kings.

1976, Oct. 4 ***Perf. 14½***

355	A45	15c vio blue & multi	16	16
356	A45	20c green & multi	18	18
357	A45	55c lilac & multi	42	42
358	A45	$1.10 multicolored	90	90
a.		Souvenir sheet of 4, #355-358	2.50	2.50

Hudson River Review of Opsail 76
A46 A47

Designs: 40c, Raleigh. 75c, HMS Druid (Raleigh attacking Druid, 1776).

1976, Dec. 13 **Litho.** ***Perf. 13***

359	A46	15c multicolored	18	18
a.		Pair, #359, 362	1.50	1.50
360	A46	40c multicolored	42	42
361	A47	75c multicolored	80	80
a.		Pair, #360-361	1.25	1.25
362	A47	$1.25 multicolored	1.25	1.25
a.		Souvenir sheet of 4, #359-362, perf. 14x13½	3.00	3.00

American Bicentennial. Nos. 359a and 361a each have continuous designs.

Queen Arriving for 1966 Visit, Yacht Britannia — A48

Designs: 45c, Firing of cannons at Tower of London. $1, The crowning.

1977, Feb. 7

363	A48	30c multicolored	32	32
364	A48	45c multicolored	48	48
365	A48	$1 multicolored	1.25	1.25

25th anniv. of the reign of Queen Elizabeth II.
#363-365 were issued also in booklet panes of 4.

Epiphyllum Hookeri A49

Flowers of the Night: 15c, Ipomoea alba, vert. 55c, Cereus hexagonus. $1.50, Cestrum nocturnum, vert.

1977, June 1 **Litho.** ***Perf. 14***

366	A49	15c multicolored	15	15
367	A49	40c multicolored	38	38
368	A49	55c multicolored	52	52
369	A49	$1.50 multicolored	1.50	1.50
a.		Souvenir sheet of 4, #366-369	3.50	3.50

Princess Anne at Ground-breaking Ceremony, Glendon Hospital — A50

Designs: 40c, New deep-water jetty, Plymouth. 55c, Glendon Hospital. $1.50, Freighter unloading at new jetty.

1977, Oct. 3 **Wmk. 373** ***Perf. 14½***

370	A50	20c multicolored	15	15
371	A50	40c multicolored	22	22
372	A50	55c multicolored	32	32
373	A50	$1.50 multicolored	85	85
a.		Souvenir sheet of 4, #370-373	2.75	2.75

Development.

Nos. 349-350, 352 Surcharged with New Value and Bars and Overprinted: "SILVER JUBILEE 1977 / ROYAL VISIT / TO THE CARIBBEAN"

1977, Oct. **Litho.** ***Perf. 13½x14***

374	A44	$1 on 55c multi	75	75
375	A44	$1 on 70c multi	75	75
376	A44	$1 on $2.50 multi	75	75

Caribbean visit of Queen Elizabeth II. Surcharge has bars of differing thickness and length. No. 374 has two settings.

"Silent Night, Holy Night" — A51

Christmas Carols and Map of Montserrat: 40c, "We Three Kings of Orient Are." 55c, "I Saw Three Ships Come Sailing In." $2, "Hark the Herald Angels Sing."

1977, Nov. 14 **Litho.** ***Perf. 14½***

377	A51	5c blue & multi	15	15
378	A51	40c bister & multi	20	20
379	A51	55c lt blue & multi	28	28
380	A51	$2 rose & multi	1.00	1.00
a.		Souvenir sheet of 4, #377-380	2.00	2.00

Four-eye Butterflyfish A52

Fish: 40c, French angelfish. 55c, Blue tang. $1.50, Queen triggerfish.

1978, Feb. 27 **Wmk. 373** ***Perf. 14***

381	A52	30c multicolored	30	30
382	A52	40c multicolored	40	40
383	A52	55c multicolored	55	55
384	A52	$1.50 multicolored	1.50	1.50
a.		Souvenir sheet of 4, #381-384	3.50	3.50

Elizabeth II and St. Paul's, London — A53

Designs: 55c, Chichester Cathedral. $1, Lincoln Cathedral. $2.50, Llandaff Cathedral, Cardiff.

1978, June 2 ***Perf. 13½***

385	A53	40c multicolored	16	16
386	A53	55c multicolored	24	24
387	A53	$1 multicolored	40	40
388	A53	$2.50 multicolored	1.00	1.00
a.		Souvenir sheet of 4, #385-388	2.75	2.75

25th anniversary of coronation of Elizabeth II, Defender of the Faith. Nos. 385-388 printed in sheets of 10 stamps and 2 labels.
#385-388 were also issued in booklet panes of 2.

Alpinia — A54

Private, 1796 — A55

Flowering Plants: 55c, Allamanda cathartica. $1, Blue tree petrea. $2, Amaryllis.

1978, Sept. 18 Litho. *Perf. 13½x13*

389 A54	40c multicolored		26	26
390 A54	55c multicolored		38	38
391 A54	$1 multicolored		70	70
392 A54	$2 multicolored		1.40	1.40

1978, Nov. 20 Litho. *Perf. 14½*

Uniforms: 40c, Corporal, 1831. 55c, Sergeant, 1837. $1.50, Officer, 1784.

393 A55	30c multicolored	22	22
394 A55	40c multicolored	28	28
395 A55	55c multicolored	40	40
396 A55	$1.50 multicolored	1.10	1.10
a.	Souvenir sheet of 4, #393-396	2.25	2.25

See Nos. 401-404.

Cub Scouts A56

Boy Scouts: 55c, Signaling. $1.25, Cooking, vert. $2, Flag folding ceremony, vert.

1979, Apr. 2 Litho. *Perf. 14*

397 A56	40c multicolored	26	26
398 A56	55c multicolored	35	35
399 A56	$1.25 multicolored	80	80
400 A56	$2 multicolored	1.25	1.25
a.	Souvenir sheet of 4, #397-400	3.00	3.00

50th anniversary of Scouting in Montserrat.

Uniform Type of 1978

Uniforms: 30c, Private, 1783. 40c, Private, 1819. 55c, Officer, 1819. $2.50, Highlander officer, 1830.

1979, July 4 Wmk. 373 *Perf. 14*

401 A55	30c multicolored	18	18
402 A55	40c multicolored	24	24
403 A55	55c multicolored	32	32
404 A55	$2.50 multicolored	1.50	1.50
a.	Souvenir sheet of 4, #401-404	2.50	2.50

IYC Emblem, Learning to Walk A56a

1979, Sept. 17 Litho. *Perf. 13½x14*

405 A56a	$2 brown org & black	85	85
a.	Souvenir sheet	2.00	2.00

International Year of the Child.

Hill, Penny Black, Montserrat No. 1 — A57

Designs: 55c, UPU Emblem, charter. $1, UPU Emblem, cover. $2, Hill, Post Office regulations.

1979, Oct. 1 *Perf. 14*

406 A57	40c multicolored	16	16
407 A57	55c multicolored	22	22
408 A57	$1 multicolored	42	42
409 A57	$2 multicolored	85	85
a.	Souvenir sheet of 4, #406-409	4.25	4.25

Sir Rowland Hill (1795-1879), originator of penny postage; UPU membership, centenary.

Tree Lizard A58

1980, Feb. 4 Litho. *Perf. 14*

410 A58	40c Tree frog	26	26
411 A58	55c shown	38	38
412 A58	$1 Crapaud	70	70
413 A58	$2 Wood slave	1.40	1.40

Marquis of Salisbury, 1817; Postmarks, 1838, London 1980 Emblem A59

London 1980 Emblem, Ships or Planes, Stamps of Montserrat: 55c, H.S. 748, No. 349. No. 416, La Plata, 1901, type A4. No. 417, Lady Hawkins, 1929, No. 84. No. 418, Avon, 1843, Gt Britain No. 3. No. 419, Aeronca, No. 140.

1980, Apr. 14 Litho. *Perf. 14½*

414 A59	40c multicolored	22	22
415 A59	55c multicolored	30	30
416 A59	$1.20 multicolored	65	65
417 A59	$1.20 multicolored	65	65
418 A59	$1.20 multicolored	65	65
419 A59	$1.20 multicolored	65	65
a.	Souvenir sheet of 6, #414-419	3.50	3.50
	Nos. 414-419 (6)	3.12	3.12

London 1980 Intl. Stamp Exhib., May 6-14.
For surcharges see Nos. 736-740.

No. 352 Overprinted: 75th Anniversary of / Rotary International

1980, July 7 Litho. *Perf. 13½x14*

420 A44	$2.50 multicolored	1.25	1.25

Discus Thrower, Stadium, Olympic Rings — A60

Olympic Rings and Flags of Host Countries: 40c, Greece, 1896; France, 1900; US, 1904. 55c, Great Britain, 1908; Sweden, 1912; Belgium, 1920. 70c, France, 1924; Netherlands, 1928; US, 1932. $1, Germany, 1936; Great Britain, 1948; Finland, 1952. $1.50, Australia, 1956; Italy, 1960; Japan, 1964. $2, Mexico, 1968,; Fed. Rep. of Germany, 1972; Canada, 1976.

1980, July 7 Litho. *Perf. 14*

421 A60	40c multicolored	18	18
422 A60	55c multicolored	24	24
423 A60	70c multicolored	30	30
424 A60	$1 multicolored	48	48
425 A60	$1.50 multicolored	70	70
426 A60	$2 multicolored	95	95
427 A60	$2.50 multicolored	1.25	1.25
a.	Souv. sheet of 7, #421-427 + 2 labels	4.25	
	Nos. 421-427 (7)	4.10	4.10

22nd Summer Olympic Games, Moscow, July 19-Aug. 3.

Lady Nelson, 1928 A61

1980 Litho. *Perf. 14*

428 A61	40c shown	20	20
429 A61	55c Chignecto, 1913	28	28
430 A61	$1 Solent, 1878	52	52
431 A61	$2 Dee, 1841	1.10	1.10

Plume Worm — A62

1980 Litho. *Perf. 14*

432 A62	40c shown	45	45
433 A62	55c Sea fans	60	60
434 A62	$2 Coral, sponges	2.25	2.25

Nos. 340, 342, 345, 348 Surcharged

1980, Sept. 30 Litho. *Perf. 14*

435 A44	5c on 3c (#342)	15	15
436 A44	35c on 1c (#340)	16	16
437 A44	35c on 3c (#342)	16	16
438 A44	35c on 15c (#345)	16	16
439 A44	55c on 40c (#348)	28	28
440 A44	$5 on 40c (#348)	2.50	2.50
	Nos. 435-440 (6)	3.41	3.41

Zebra Butterfly — A63

Spadefish — A64

1981, Feb. 2 Wmk. 373

441 A63	50c shown	38	38
442 A63	65c Tropical checkered skipper	48	48
443 A63	$1.50 Large orange sulphur	1.10	1.10
444 A63	$2.50 Monarch	2.00	2.00

Perf. 13½

1981, Mar. 20 Litho. Wmk. 373

445 A64	5c shown	15	15
446 A64	10c Hogfish	15	15
447 A64	15c Creole wrasse	15	15
448 A64	20c Yellow damselfish	15	15
449 A64	25c Sergeant major	15	15
450 A64	35c Clown wrasse	22	18
451 A64	45c Schoolmaster	28	22
452 A64	55c Striped parrotfish	35	28
453 A64	65c Bigeye	40	32
454 A64	75c French grunt	45	38
455 A64	$1 Rock beauty	60	50
456 A64	$2 Blue chromis	1.25	1.00
457 A64	$3 Fairy basslet, blueheads	1.90	1.50
458 A64	$5 Cherubfish	3.00	2.50
459 A64	$7.50 Longspine squirrelfish	4.50	3.75
460 A64	$10 Longsnout butterflyfish	6.00	5.00
	Nos. 445-460 (16)	19.70	16.38

For surcharges and overprints see Nos. 507-508, 511-512, 515, O45-O55, O95-O97.

Inscribed 1983

1983 Wmk. 380

445a A64	5c	15	15
446a A64	10c	15	15
449a A64	25c	16	16
450a A64	35c	24	24
454a A64	75c	50	50
455a A64	$1	65	65
458a A64	$5	3.25	3.25
460a A64	$10	6.50	6.50
	Nos. 445a-460a (8)	11.60	11.60

Fort St. George (National Trust) — A65

1981, May 18 Wmk. 373 *Perf. 13½*

461 A65	50c shown	28	28
462 A65	65c Bird Sanctuary, Fox's Bay	38	38
463 A65	$1.50 The Museum	90	90
464 A65	$2.50 Bransby Point Battery	1.50	1.50

Prince Charles, Lady Diana, Royal Yacht Charlotte A66

Prince Charles and Lady Diana — A67

Illustration A67 is greatly reduced.

Wmk. 380

1981, July 13 Litho. *Perf. 14*

465 A66	90c shown	60	60
a.	Booklet pane of 4, perf. 12	3.00	
466 A67	90c shown	60	60
467 A66	$3 Portsmouth	2.00	2.00
468 A67	$3 like #466	2.00	2.00
a.	Booklet pane of 2, perf. 12	5.00	
469 A66	$4 Britannia	2.75	2.75
470 A67	$4 like #466	2.75	2.75
	Nos. 465-470 (6)	10.70	10.70

Royal wedding. Each denomination issued in sheets of 7 (6 type A66, 1 type A67).
For surcharges and overprints, see Nos. 509-510, 513-514, 578-579, O56-O61.

Souvenir Sheet

1981, Dec. *Perf. 12*

471 A67	$5 multicolored	2.75	2.75

50th Anniv. of Airmail Service A68

1981, Aug. 31 Wmk. 373 *Perf. 14*

472 A68	50c Seaplane, Dorsetshire	32	32
473 A68	65c Beechcraft Twin Bonanza	40	40
474 A68	$1.50 DeHaviland Dragon Rapide	90	90
475 A68	$2.50 Hawker Siddeley Avro 748	1.50	1.50

Methodist Church, Bethel — A69

Christmas (Churches): 65c, St. George's Anglican, Harris. $1.50, St. Peter's Anglican, St. Peter's. $2.50, St. Patrick's Roman Catholic, Plymouth.

1981, Nov. 16 Litho. *Perf. 14*

476 A69	50c multicolored	32	32
477 A69	65c multicolored	40	40
478 A69	$1.50 multicolored	90	90
479 A69	$2.50 multicolored	1.50	1.50
a.	Souvenir sheet of 4, #476-479	3.50	3.50

Wild Flowers First Discovered on Montserrat A70

1982, Jan. 18 Litho. Perf. 14½

480	A70	50c	Rondeletia buxifolia, vert.	35	35
481	A70	65c	Heliotropium ternatum	45	45
482	A70	$1.50	Picramnia pentandra, vert.	1.00	1.00
483	A70	$2.50	Diospyros revoluta	1.75	1.75

350th Anniv. of Settlement of Montserrat by Sir Thomas Warner — A70a

Jubilee Type of 1932.

Perf. 14½

1982, Apr. 17 Litho. Wmk. 373

483A	A70a	40c	green	22	22
483B	A70a	55c	red	35	35
483C	A70a	65c	brown	38	38
483D	A70a	75c	gray	42	42
483E	A70a	85c	ultra	48	48
483F	A70a	95c	orange	55	55
483G	A70a	$1	purple	60	60
483H	A70a	$1.50	olive	85	85
483I	A70a	$2	car rose	1.10	1.10
483J	A70a	$2.50	sepia	1.50	1.50
			Nos. 483A-483J (10)	6.45	6.45

21st Birthday of Princess Diana, July 1 — A70b

1982, June Wmk. 380 Perf. 14

484	A70b	75c	Catherine of Aragon, 1501	40	40
485	A70b	$1	Aragon arms	52	52
486	A70b	$5	Diana	2.75	2.75

For surcharges and overprints, see Nos. 574, O62-O64.

Scouting Year — A71

1982, Sept. 13 Litho. Perf. 14

487	A71	$1.50	Scout	95	95
488	A71	$2.50	Baden-Powell	1.50	1.50

Christmas A72

1982, Nov. 18 Wmk. 373 Perf. 14

489	A72	35c	Annunciation	22	22
490	A72	75c	Shepherds' vision	45	45
491	A72	$1.50	Virgin and Child	85	85
492	A72	$2.50	Flight into Egypt	1.50	1.50

Dragonflies — A73

1983, Jan. 19 Litho. Perf. 13½x14

493	A73	50c	Lepthemis vesiculosa	28	28
494	A73	65c	Orthemis ferruginea	38	38
495	A73	$1.50	Triacanthagyna trifida	90	90
496	A73	$2.50	Erythrodiplax umbrata	1.40	1.40

Blue-headed Hummingbird — A74

1983, May 24 Wmk. 373 Perf. 14

497	A74	35c	shown	32	32
498	A74	75c	Green-throated carib	70	70
499	A74	$2	Antillean crested hummingbird	1.90	1.90
500	A74	$3	Purple-throated carib	2.75	2.75

The $12 and $30 stamps showing the Montserrat emblem were primarily for revenue purposes.

Manned Flight Bicentenary A76

Designs: 35c, Montgolfiere, 1783, vert. 75c, De Havilland Twin Otter 310, 1981. $1.50, Lockheed Vega's around the world flight, 1933. $2, British R34 airship transatlantic flight, 1919.

1983, Sept. 19 Litho. Perf. 14

503	A76	35c	multicolored	24	24
504	A76	75c	multicolored	52	52
505	A76	$1.50	multicolored	1.00	1.00
506	A76	$2	multicolored	1.40	1.40
a.			Souvenir sheet of 4, #503-506	3.25	3.25

For surcharges, see Nos. 573, 577.

Nos. 449, 446, 467-468, 453-454, 469-470, 456 Surcharged

Wmk. 373 (A64), 380

1983, Aug. 15 Litho. Perf. 13½x14

507	A64	40c	on 25c multi	45	45
508	A64	70c	on 10c multi	75	75
509	A66	70c	on $3 multi	75	75
510	A67	70c	on $3 multi	75	75
511	A64	90c	on 65c multi	1.00	1.00
512	A64	$1.15	on 75c multi	1.25	1.25
513	A66	$1.15	on $4 multi	1.25	1.25
514	A67	$1.15	on $4 multi	1.25	1.25
515	A64	$1.50	on $2 multi	1.75	1.75
			Nos. 507-515 (9)	9.20	9.20

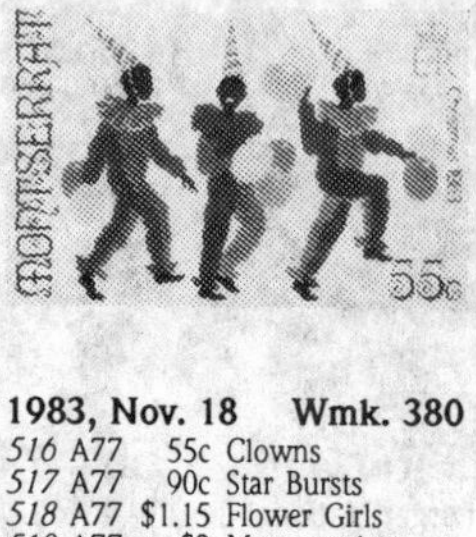

Christmas Carnival 1983 A77

1983, Nov. 18 Wmk. 380 Perf. 14

516	A77	55c	Clowns	30	30
517	A77	90c	Star Bursts	48	48
518	A77	$1.15	Flower Girls	65	65
519	A77	$2	Masqueraders	1.10	1.10

See Nos. 547-550.

Nos. 503-506 were overprinted "INAUGURAL FLIGHT Monserrat - Nevis - St. Kitts." These exist on souvenir covers with first day cancel of Dec. 15, 1983. No announcement of this set was made nor were mint copies generally available.

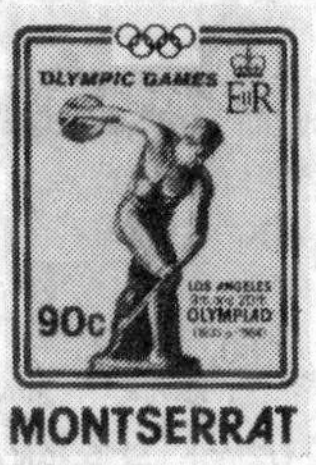

1984 Summer Olympics — A78

1984, Mar. 6 Litho. Perf. 14

520	A78	90c	Discobolus	42	42
521	A78	$1	Torch	45	45
522	A78	$1.15	Stadium	55	55
523	A78	$2.50	Flags	1.10	1.10
a.			Souvenir sheet of 4, #520-523	3.00	3.00

Cattle Egret — A79

1984, May 11

524	A79	5c	shown	15	15
525	A79	10c	Carib grackles	15	15
526	A79	15c	Common gallinule	15	15
527	A79	20c	Brown boobys	15	15
528	A79	25c	Black-whiskered vireos	16	16
529	A79	40c	Scaly-breasted thrashers	25	25
530	A79	55c	Laughing gulls	38	38
531	A79	70c	Glossy ibis	45	45
532	A79	90c	Green heron	65	65
533	A79	$1	Belted kingfisher	68	68
534	A79	$1.15	Bananaquits	80	80
535	A79	$3	Sparrow hawks	2.20	2.20
536	A79	$5	Forest thrush	3.50	3.50
537	A79	$7.50	Black-crowned night heron	5.25	5.25
538	A79	$10	Bridled quail doves	6.75	6.75
			Nos. 524-538 (15)	21.67	21.67

For surcharges, see Nos. 651-655, 663-666. For overprints, see Nos. O65-O78.

Packet Boats A80

1984, July 9 Wmk. 380 Perf. 14

539	A80	55c	Tagus, 1907	35	35
540	A80	90c	Cobequid, 1913	65	65
541	A80	$1.15	Lady Drake, 1942	75	75
542	A80	$2	Factor, 1948	1.40	1.40
a.			Souvenir sheet of 4, #539-542	3.25	3.25

Marine Life — A81

1984, Sept. Wmk. 380 Perf. 14

543	A81	90c	Top shell & hermit crab	65	65
544	A81	$1.15	Rough file shell	80	80
545	A81	$1.50	True tulip snail	1.10	1.10
546	A81	$2.50	West Indian fighting conch	2.00	2.00

Christmas Carnival Type of 1983

1984, Nov. 12

547	A77	55c	Bull Man	32	32
548	A77	$1.15	Masquerader Captain	70	70
549	A77	$1.50	Carnival Queen contestant	95	95
550	A77	$2.30	Contestant, diff.	1.50	1.50

National Emblems — A82

1985, Feb. 8 Litho. Perf. 14

551	A82	$1.15	Mango	90	90
552	A82	$1.50	Lobster Claw	1.20	1.20
553	A82	$3	Montserrat Oriole	2.50	2.50

Indigenous Orchids — A83

Queen Mother, 85th Birthday — A84

1985, May 9 Wmk. 380 Perf. 14

554	A83	90c	Oncidium urophyllum	70	70
555	A83	$1.15	Epidendrum difforme	95	95
556	A83	$1.50	Epidendrum ciliare	1.25	1.25
557	A83	$2.50	Brassavola cucullata	2.00	2.00
a.			Souvenir sheet of 4, #554-557	5.00	5.00

1985, Aug. 7 Unwmk. Perf. 12½

Portraits.

558	A84	55c	Facing right	32	32
559	A84	55c	Facing forward	32	32
560	A84	90c	Facing right, diff.	55	55
561	A84	90c	Facing left	55	55
562	A84	$1.15	Facing right, diff.	70	70
563	A84	$1.15	Glancing right	70	70
564	A84	$1.50	Facing right, diff.	90	90
565	A84	$1.50	Facing left, diff.	90	90
			Nos. 558-565 (8)	4.94	4.94

Souvenir Sheets

566		Sheet of 2	2.75	2.75
a.	A84	$2 Facing right, diff.	1.25	1.25
b.	A84	$2 Facing forward, diff.	1.25	1.25

1986, Jan. 10

567		Sheet of 2	4.25	4.25
a.	A84	$3.50 like #564	2.00	2.00
b.	A84	$3.50 like #565	2.00	2.00
568		Sheet of 2	6.75	6.75
a.	A84	$6 like #558	3.50	3.50
b.	A84	$6 like #559	3.50	3.50

Stamps of the same denomination printed se-tenant. For surcharges, see Nos. 575-576.

Cotton Industry A85

1985, Sept. 23 Unwmk. Perf. 15

569	A85	90c	Cotton plants	55	55
570	A85	$1	Carding	65	65
571	A85	$1.15	Automated loom	70	70
572	A85	$2.50	Hand loom	1.60	1.60
a.			Souvenir sheet of 4, #569-572	3.50	3.50

Nos. 504, 485, 562-563, 505, 469-470 Ovptd. or Surcharged "CARIBBEAN ROYAL VISIT 1985" in 2 or 3 Lines

Perf. 14, 12½ ($1.15)

Wmk. as Before

1985, Nov. 14 **Litho.**

573	A76	75c	multicolored	3.00	3.00
574	A64	$1	multicolored	4.25	4.25
575	A84	$1.15	multicolored	4.75	4.75
576	A84	$1.15	multicolored	4.75	4.75
577	A76	$1.50	multicolored	6.00	6.00
578	A66	$1.60	on $4 multi	3.00	3.00
579	A67	$1.60	on $4 multi	10.00	10.00
			Nos. 573-579 (7)	35.75	35.75

Nos. 575-576 printed se-tenant. Nos. 578-579 issued in sheets of 7 (6 type A66, 1 type A67). No. 579 surcharged but not overprinted.

Audubon Birth Bicentenary — A86

Illustrations of North American bird species by John J. Audubon.

1985, Nov. 29 **Unwmk.** ***Perf. 12½***

580	A86	15c	Black-throated blue warbler	15	15
581	A86	15c	Palm warbler	15	15
582	A86	30c	Bobolink	24	24
583	A86	30c	Lark sparrow	24	24
584	A86	55c	Chipping sparrow	40	40
585	A86	55c	Northern oriole	40	40
586	A86	$2.50	American goldfinch	1.85	1.85
587	A86	$2.50	Blue grosbeak	1.85	1.85
			Nos. 580-587 (8)	5.28	5.28

Stamps of the same denomination printed se-tenant.

Christmas A87

1985, Dec. 2 **Wmk. 380** ***Perf. 15***

588	A87	70c	Angel of the Lord	48	48
589	A87	$1.15	Three wise men	80	80
590	A87	$1.50	Caroling, Plymouth War Memorial	1.00	1.00
591	A87	$2.30	Our Lady of Montserrat	1.65	1.65

Girl Guides, 50th Anniv. — A88

1986, Apr. 11

592	A88	20c	Lord Baden-Powell	18	18
593	A88	20c	Guide saluting	18	18
594	A88	75c	Lady Baden-Powell	60	60
595	A88	75c	Guide cutting hair	60	60
596	A88	90c	Lord and Lady Baden-Powell	70	70
597	A88	90c	Guides in public service	70	70
598	A88	$1.15	Troop inspection, 1936	85	85
599	A88	$1.15	Guides saluting	85	85
			Nos. 592-599 (8)	4.66	4.66

Stamps of same denomination printed se-tenant.

Queen Elizabeth II, 60th Birthday — A89

Various portraits.

1986, Apr. 11 **Unwmk.** ***Perf. 12½***

600	A89	10c	multicolored	15	15
601	A89	$1.50	multicolored	1.00	1.00
602	A89	$3	multicolored	2.00	2.00
603	A89	$6	multi, vert.	4.00	4.00

Souvenir Sheet

604	A89	$8	multicolored	6.00	6.00

Halley's Comet — A90

Designs: 35c, Bayeux Tapestry (detail), 1066 sighting. 50c, Adoration of the Magi, by Giotto. 70c, Edmond Halley, trajectory diagram, 1531 sighting. $1, Sightings, 1066 and 1910. $1.15, Sighting, 1910. $1.50, Giotto space probe, comet, diagram. $2.30, US Space Telescope, comet. $4, Computer picture of photograph, 1910.

1986, May 9 ***Perf. 14***

605	A90	35c	multicolored	22	22
606	A90	50c	multicolored	35	35
607	A90	70c	multicolored	45	45
608	A90	$1	multicolored	65	65
609	A90	$1.15	multicolored	80	80
610	A90	$1.50	multicolored	1.00	1.00
611	A90	$2.30	multicolored	1.65	1.65
612	A90	$4	multicolored	2.75	2.75
			Nos. 605-612 (8)	7.87	7.87

See Nos. 625-626.

Wedding of Prince Andrew and Sarah Ferguson — A91

Design: No. 613, Andrew, vert. No. 614, Sarah, vert. No. 615, Andrew wearing cowboy hat. No. 616, Sarah wearing fur hat.

Perf. 12½x13, 13x12½

1986, July 23 **Litho.**

613	A91	70c	multicolored	40	40
614	A91	70c	multicolored	40	40
615	A91	$2	multicolored	1.10	1.10
616	A91	$2	multicolored	1.10	1.10

Stamps of the same denomination printed se-tenant.

For overprints, see Nos. 628-631.

Clipper Ships — A92

1986, Aug. 29 ***Perf. 14***

617	A92	90c	Antelope, 1793	68	68
618	A92	$1.15	Montagu, 1840	85	85
619	A92	$1.50	Little Catherine, 1813	1.10	1.10
620	A92	$2.30	Hinchingbrook, 1813	1.70	1.70
a.			Souvenir sheet of 4, #617-620	4.35	4.35

Communications — A93

Designs: 70c, Radio Montserrat, near Dagenham. $1.15, Radio Gem ZGM-FM 94, Plymouth. $1.50, Radio Antilles, O'Garro's, $2.30, Cable & Wireless telegraph office, Plymouth.

1986, Sept. 29 **Wmk. 380** ***Perf. 14***

621	A93	70c	multicolored	52	52
622	A93	$1.15	multicolored	85	85
623	A93	$1.50	multicolored	1.10	1.10
624	A93	$2.30	multicolored	1.70	1.70

Halley's Comet Type of 1986 Souvenir Sheets

1986, Oct. 10 **Unwmk.** ***Perf. 14***

625		Sheet of 4	4.25	4.25
a.	A90	40c like #605	24	24
b.	A90	$1.75 like #606	1.00	1.00
c.	A90	$2 like #607	1.25	1.25
d.	A90	$3 like #608	1.75	1.75
626		Sheet of 4	4.25	4.25
a.	A90	55c like #609	32	32
b.	A90	60c like #610	35	35
c.	A90	80c like #611	48	48
d.	A90	$5 like #612	3.00	3.00

For overprints, see Nos. 656-657.

Souvenir Sheet

Wedding of Prince Andrew and Sarah Ferguson — A94

1986, Oct. 15 ***Perf. 13x12½***

627	A94	$10	multicolored	6.00	6.00

Nos. 613-616 Ovptd. in Silver: "Congratulations to T.R.H. The Duke & Duchess of York"

Perf. 12½x13, 13x12½

1986, Nov. 14 **Litho.**

628	A91	70c	No. 613	52	52
629	A91	70c	No. 614	52	52
630	A91	$2	No. 615	1.50	1.50
631	A91	$2	No. 616	1.50	1.50

Stamps of the same denomination exist printed tete-beche and se-tenant.

Christmas — A95

1986, Dec. 12 **Unwmk.** ***Perf. 14***

632	A95	70c	Christmas rose	55	55
633	A95	$1.15	Candle flower	90	90
634	A95	$1.50	Christmas tree kalanchoe	1.20	1.20
635	A95	$2.30	Snow on the mountain	1.85	1.85
a.			Souvenir sheet of 4, #632-635, perf. 12x12½	4.50	4.50

Souvenir Sheets

Statue of Liberty, Cent. — A96

1986, Nov. 18 **Litho.** ***Perf. 14***

636	A96	$3	Statue, pedestal	2.00	2.00
637	A96	$4.50	Head	2.75	2.75
638	A96	$5	Statue, NYC	3.25	3.25

Sailing A97

1986, Dec. 10 ***Perf. 15***

639	A97	70c	shown	55	55
640	A97	$1.15	Golf	90	90
641	A97	$1.50	Plymouth Public Market	1.20	1.20
642	A97	$2.30	Air Studios	1.85	1.85

Sharks A98

1987, Feb. 2 **Wmk. 380** ***Perf. 14***

643	A98	40c	Tiger	32	32
644	A98	90c	Lemon	72	72
645	A98	$1.15	White	90	90
646	A98	$3.50	Whale	2.75	2.75
a.			Souvenir sheet of 4, #643-646, perf. 12½x12	4.00	4.00

Butterflies — A99

1987, Aug. 10 **Wmk. 380** ***Perf. 14***

647	A99	90c	Straight-line sulpher	70	70
648	A99	$1.15	Red rim	90	90
649	A99	$1.50	Hammock skipper	1.20	1.20
650	A99	$2.50	Mimic	2.00	2.00

Nos. 531, 527, 525, 532 and 535 Surcharged

1987, Apr. 6

651	A79	5c	on 70c multi	15	15
652	A79	$1	on 20c multi	80	80
653	A79	$1.15	on 10c multi	90	90
654	A79	$1.50	on 90c multi	1.20	1.20
655	A79	$2.30	on $3 multi	1.85	1.85
			Nos. 651-655 (5)	4.90	4.90

Nos. 625-626 Ovptd. for CAPEX '87 in Red and Black Souvenir Sheets

1987, June 13 **Unwmk.**

656	Sheet of 4, #a.-d.	4.50	4.50
657	Sheet of 4, #a.-d.	4.50	4.50

Orchids A100

1987, Nov. 13 Unwmk. *Perf. 14*

658	A100	90c	Oncidium variegatum, vert.	68	68
659	A100	$1.15	Vanilla planifolia	85	85
660	A100	$1.50	Gongora quinquenervis, vert.	1.15	1.15
661	A100	$3.50	Brassavola nodosa	2.60	2.60

Souvenir Sheet

662	A100	$5	Oncidium lanceanum	3.75	3.75

Christmas.

Nos. 525, 528-529 and 532 Surcharged "40th Wedding Anniversary / HM Queen Elizabeth II / HRH Duke of Edinburgh / November 1987." and New Value

Wmk. 380

1987, Nov. 20 Litho. *Perf. 14*

663	A79	5c	on 90c No. 532	68	68
664	A79	$1.15	on 10c No. 525	85	85
665	A79	$2.30	on 25c No. 528	1.85	1.85
666	A79	$5	on 40c No. 529	3.75	3.75

Exists spelled "Edingburgh."

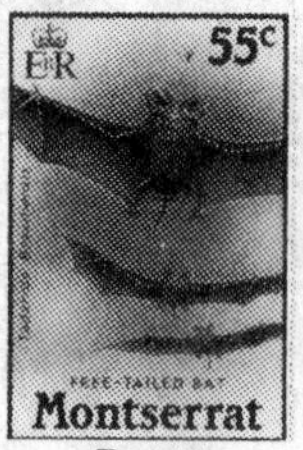

Tropical Bats — A101

Marine Birds — A102

1988, Feb. 8 Wmk. 380 *Perf. 14*

667	A101	55c	Free-tailed bat	38	38
668	A101	90c	Fruit bat	68	68
669	A101	$1.15	Fisherman bat	85	85
670	A101	$2.30	Fruit bat, diff.	1.70	1.70

Souvenir Sheet

671	A101	$2.50	Funnel-eared bat	1.90	1.90

1988, Apr. 2 Unwmk.

672	A102	90c	Magnificent frigatebird	70	70
673	A102	$1.15	Caribbean elaenia	90	90
674	A102	$1.50	Glossy ibis	1.20	1.20
675	A102	$3.50	Purple-throated carib	2.75	2.75

Souvenir Sheet

676	A102	$5	Brown pelican	4.00	4.00

Easter.

1988 Summer Olympics, Seoul — A103

Eastern architecture and events: 90c, Women's discus. $1.15, High jump. $3.50, Women's 200-meter and Seoul university building. $5, Single scull rowing, pagoda.

Unwmk.

1988, July 29 Litho. *Perf. 14*

677	A103	90c	multicolored	60	60
678	A103	$1.15	multicolored	70	70
679	A103	$3.50	multicolored	2.25	2.25

Souvenir Sheet

680	A103	$5	multicolored	3.50	3.50

Sea Shells A104

1988, Aug. 30

681	A104	5c	Golden tulip	15	15
682	A104	10c	Little knobby scallop	15	15
683	A104	15c	Sozoni's cone	15	15
684	A104	20c	Globular coral shell	15	15
685	A104	25c	Sundial	16	16
686	A104	40c	King helmet	25	25
687	A104	55c	Channeled turban	38	38
688	A104	70c	True tulip shell	45	45
689	A104	90c	Music volute	60	60
690	A104	$1	Flame auger	65	65
691	A104	$1.15	Rooster-tail conch	80	80
692	A104	$1.50	Queen conch	1.00	1.00
693	A104	$3	Teramachi's slit shell	2.00	2.00
694	A104	$5	Florida crown conch	3.25	3.25
695	A104	$7.50	Beau's murex	5.00	5.00
696	A104	$10	Triton's trumpet	6.75	6.75
			Nos. 681-696 (16)	21.89	21.89

For surcharges see Nos. 698-701, 767-770. For overprints see Nos. O79-O94.

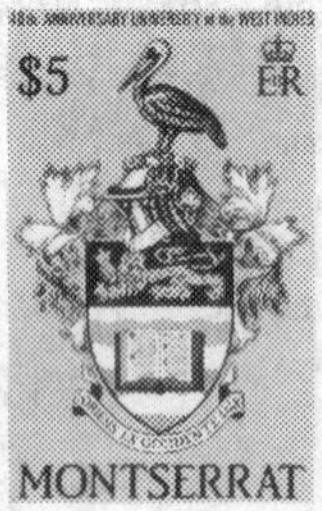

University of the West Indies, 40th Anniv. — A105

1988, Oct. 4 Litho. *Perf. 14*

697	A105	$5	multicolored	3.75	3.75

Nos. 687, 690, 693 and 694 Surcharged

HRH PRINCESS
ALEXANDRA'S VISIT
NOVEMBER 1988

40¢

Unwmk.

1988, Nov. 4 Litho. *Perf. 14*

698	A104	40c	on 55c No. 687	30	30
699	A104	90c	on $1 No. 690	68	68
700	A104	$1.15	on $3 No. 693	88	88
701	A104	$1.50	on $5 No. 694	1.15	1.15

Intl. Red Cross, 125th Anniv. A106

1988, Dec. 16

702	A106	$3.50	multicolored	2.65	2.65

Christmas — A107

Birds.

1988, Nov. 28 *Perf. 14x13½*

703	A107	90c	Spotted sandpiper	68	68
704	A107	$1.15	Ruddy turnstone	85	85
705	A107	$3.50	Red-footed booby	2.60	2.60

Souvenir Sheet

Perf. 13½x14

706	A107	$5	Aububon's shearwater	3.75	3.75

Uniforms — A108

1989, Feb. 24 Litho. *Perf. 14*

707	A108	90c	Drum major	68	68
708	A108	$1.15	Fatigue clothing	85	85
709	A108	$1.50	Khaki uniform	1.15	1.15
710	A108	$3.50	Dress uniform	2.65	2.65

Souvenir Sheet

711	A108	$5	Cadet (girl), woman	3.75	3.75

Defense Force, 75th anniv.

Easter Lilies A109

1989, Mar. 21 Litho. *Perf. 14*

712	A109	90c	Amazon	68	68
713	A109	$1.15	Salmon blood, vert.	85	85
714	A109	$1.50	Amaryllis, vert.	1.15	1.15
715	A109	$3.50	Amaryllis, diff., vert.	2.65	2.65

Souvenir Sheet

716	A109	$5	Resurrection, vert.	3.75	3.75

Ships Built in Montserrat — A110

Designs: 90c, Schooner *Morning Prince,* 1942-1948. $1.15, Cargo boat *Western Sun.* $1.50, Cargo boat *Kim G* under construction. $3.50, Cargo and passenger boat MV *Romaris.*

1989, June 30 Litho. *Perf. 13½x14*

717	A110	90c	multicolored	68	68
718	A110	$1.15	multicolored	85	85
719	A110	$1.50	multicolored	1.15	1.15
720	A110	$3.50	multicolored	2.65	2.65

See Nos. B1-B2 for surcharges.

Making of the Film *The Wizard of Oz,* 50th Anniv. A111

1989, Sept. 22 Litho. *Perf. 14*

721	A111	90c	Scarecrow	68	68
722	A111	$1.15	Cowardly Lion	85	85
723	A111	$1.50	Tin Man	1.15	1.15
724	A111	$3.50	Dorothy	2.65	2.65

Souvenir Sheet

725	A111	$5	shown	3.75	3.75

Nos. 721-724 vert.

1st Moon Landing, 20th Anniv. — A112

Designs: $1.15, Armstrong on ladder, descending from lunar module. $1.50, *Eagle,* astronaut on lunar surface. $3.50, Recovery of command module after splashdown. $5, Astronaut on the Moon, vert.

Perf. 13½x14, 14x13½

1989, Dec. 19 Litho.

726	A112	90c	shown	68	68
727	A112	$1.15	multicolored	85	85
728	A112	$1.50	multicolored	1.15	1.15
729	A112	$3.50	multicolored	2.65	2.65

Souvenir Sheet

730	A112	$5	multicolored	3.75	3.75

For overprints see Nos. 847-850.

World War II Battle Ships A113

1990, Feb. 12 Litho. *Perf. 14*

731	A113	70c	I.J.N. *Yamato*	52	52
732	A113	$1.15	USS *Arizona*	88	88
733	A113	$1.50	K.M. *Bismarck* on fire	1.15	1.15
734	A113	$3.50	HMS *Hood*	2.60	2.60

Souvenir Sheet

735	A113	$5	K.M. *Bismarck,* map	3.75	3.75

Nos. 414-418 Surcharged in Bright Rose Lilac

70¢

1990, May 3 *Perf. 14½*

736	A59	70c	on 40c #414	52	52
737	A59	90c	on 55c #415	68	68
738	A59	$1	on $1.20 #416	75	75
739	A59	$1.15	on $1.20 #417	88	88
740	A59	$1.50	on $1.20 #418	1.15	1.15
			Nos. 736-740 (5)	3.98	3.98

Stamp World London '90.

Penny Black, 150th Anniv. A114

Designs: 90c, Montserrat #5, General P.O. $1.15, Montserrat #1, postal workers sorting mail, vert. $1.50, Great Britain #1, man and woman mailing letters, vert. $3.50, Great Britain #2, mailman delivering to residence. $5, Chateau Barrack cover of 1836, Great Britain #1, landscape.

1990, June 1 *Perf. 13½x14, 14x13½*

741	A114	90c	shown	68	68
742	A114	$1.15	multicolored	88	88
743	A114	$1.50	multicolored	1.15	1.15
744	A114	$3.50	multicolored	2.60	2.60

Souvenir Sheet

745	A114	$5	multicolored	3.75	3.75

Stained-glass Windows — A115

1990, Apr. 12 Litho. *Perf. 14x15*

746 Strip of 3 4.65 4.65
a. A115 $1.15 *The Empty Tomb* 88 88
b. A115 $1.50 *The Ascension* 1.15 1.15
c. A115 $3.50 *Risen Christ with Disciples* 2.60 2.60

Souvenir Sheet

747 A115 $5 *The Crucifixion* 3.75 3.75

World Cup Soccer Championships, Italy — A116

Designs: 90c, Montserrat vs. Antigua. $1.15, US vs. Trinidad. $1.50, Montserrat team. $3.50, West Germany vs. Wales. $5, World Cup trophy.

1990, July 8 Litho. *Perf. 14*

748 A116 90c multicolored 68 68
749 A116 $1.15 multicolored 88 88
750 A116 $1.50 multicolored 1.15 1.15
751 A116 $3.50 multicolored 2.60 2.60

Souvenir Sheet

752 A116 $5 multicolored 3.75 3.75

Spinner Dolphin A117

1990, Sept. 25 Litho. *Perf. 14*

753 A117 90c shown 68 68
754 A117 $1.15 Common dolphin 88 88
755 A117 $1.50 Striped dolphin 1.15 1.15
756 A117 $3.50 Atlantic spotted dolphin 2.60 2.60

Souvenir Sheet

757 A117 $5 Atlantic white-sided dolphin 3.90 3.90

Fish A118

1991, Feb. 7 Litho. *Perf. 14*

758 A118 90c Spotted goatfish 68 68
759 A118 $1.15 Cushion starfish 88 88
760 A118 $1.50 Rock beuaty 1.15 1.15
761 A118 $3.50 French grunt 2.60 2.60

Souvenir Sheet

762 A118 $5 Trunkfish 3.90 3.90

For surcharges and overprints see Nos. O98-O99, O104, O107.

Birds A119

1991, Apr. 17 Litho. *Perf. 14*

763 A119 90c Duck 68 68
764 A119 $1.15 Hen, chicks 88 88
765 A119 $1.50 Rooster 1.15 1.15
766 A119 $3.50 Helmeted guinea fowl 2.60 2.60

For surcharges and overprints see Nos. O100, O102, O105, O108.

Nos. 684-685, 692, 695 Surcharged

1991 Litho. *Perf. 14*

767 A104 5c on 20c #684 15 15
768 A104 5c on 25c #685 15 15
769 A104 $1.15 on $1.50 #692 78 78
770 A104 $1.15 on $7.50 #695 78 78
Set value 1.60 1.60

Mushrooms — A120

Lilies — A121

1991, June 13 Litho. *Perf. 14*

771 A120 90c Panaeolus antillarum 60 60
772 A120 $1.15 Cantharellus cinnabarinus 75 75
773 A120 $1.50 Gymnopilus chrysopellus 1.00 1.00
774 A120 $2 Psilocybe cubensis 1.35 1.35
775 A120 $3.50 Leptonia caeruleocapitata 2.35 2.35
Nos. 771-775 (5) 6.05 6.05

1991, Aug. 8

776 A121 90c Red water lily 60 60
777 A121 $1.15 Shell ginger 75 75
778 A121 $1.50 Early day lily 1.00 1.00
779 A121 $3.50 Anthurium 2.35 2.35

For surcharges and overprints see Nos. O101, O103, O106, O109.

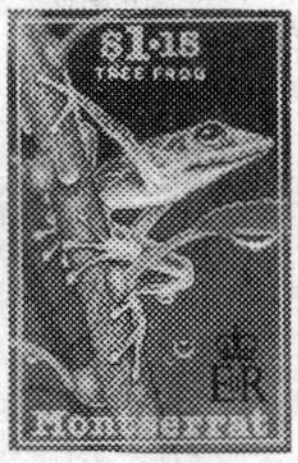

Frogs and Toads — A122

1991, Oct. 9 Litho. *Perf. 14*

780 A122 $1.15 Tree frog 75 75
781 A122 $2 Crapaud toad 1.35 1.35
782 A122 $3.50 Mountain chicken 2.35 2.35

Souvenir Sheet

Perf. 14¹/₂x14

783 A122 $5 Sheet of 1 3.50 3.50

No. 783 contains one 81x48mm stamp that incorporates designs of Nos. 780-782.

Cats A123

1991, Dec. 5

784 A123 90c Black British shorthair 60 60
785 A123 $1.15 Seal point siamese 75 75
786 A123 $1.50 Silver tabby persian 1.00 1.00
787 A123 $2.50 Birman temple cat 1.65 1.65
788 A123 $3.50 Egyptian mau 2.35 2.35
Nos. 784-788 (5) 6.35 6.35

Miniature Sheet

Discovery of America, 500th Anniv. — A124

Desings: a, $1.50, Navigating instruments. b, $1.50, Coat of arms, Columbus. c, $1.50, Columbus, Bahamian natives. d, $1.50, Queen Isabella, Columbus with petition. e, $1.50, Exotic birds. f, $1.50, Exotic plants. g, $3.00, Santa Maria, Nina and Pinta.

1992, Jan. 16 Litho. *Perf. 14*

789 A124 Sheet of 7, #a.-g. 9.15 9.15

No. 789g is 85x28mm. See No. 829.

Dinosaurs A125

1992, Aug. 1 Litho. *Perf. 14*

790 A125 $1 Tyrannosaurus 75 75
791 A125 $1.15 Diplodocus 85 85
792 A125 $1.50 Apatosaurus 1.10 1.70
793 A125 $3.45 Dimetrodon 2.50 2.50

Souvenir Sheet

794 A125 $4.60 Owen with bone, vert. 3.40 3.40

Sir Richard Owen, cent. of death.

1992 Summer Olympics, Barcelona — A126

1992, Apr. 10

795 A126 $1 Torch bearer 75 75
796 A126 $1.15 Flags 85 85
797 A126 $2.30 Olympic flame, map 1.70 1.70
798 A126 $3.60 Various events 2.75 2.75

Montserrat Oriole — A127

1992, June 30 Litho. *Perf. 13¹/₂x14*

799 A127 $1 Male 65 65
800 A127 $1.15 Male, female 75 75
801 A127 $1.50 Female feeding chicks 1.00 1.00
802 A127 $3.60 Map, male 2.40 2.40

Insects A128

1992, Aug. 20 Litho. *Perf. 15x14*

803 A128 5c Grasshopper 15 15
804 A128 10c Field cricket 15 15
805 A128 15c Dragonfly 15 15
806 A128 20c Red skimmer 15 15
807 A128 25c Pond skater 18 18
808 A128 40c Leaf weevil 30 30
809 A128 55c Leaf cutter ants 40 40
810 A128 70c Paper wasp 52 52
811 A128 90c Bee fly 68 68
812 A128 $1 Lacewing 75 75
813 A128 $1.15 Orange-barred sulphur 85 85
814 A128 $1.50 Painted lady 1.15 1.15
815 A128 $3 Bella moth 2.25 2.25
816 A128 $5 Plume moth 3.75 3.75
817 A128 $7.50 White peacock 5.50 5.50
818 A128 $10 Postman 7.50 7.50
Nos. 803-818 (16) 24.43 24.43

For overprints see Nos. O110-O125.

Christmas — A129

Designs: $1.15, Adoration of the Magi. $4.60, Angel appearing before shepherds.

1992, Nov. 26 Litho. *Perf. 13¹/₂x14*

819 A129 $1.15 multicolored 85 85
820 A129 $4.60 multicolored 3.50 3.50

Coins and Bank Notes — A130

Designs: $1, One-dollar coin, twenty-dollar notes. $1.15, Ten-cent, twenty-five cent coins, ten-dollar notes. $1.50, Five-cent coin, five-dollar notes. $3.60, One-cent, two-cent coins, one-dollar notes.

1993, Feb. 10 *Perf. 14x13¹/₂*

821 A130 $1 multicolored 70 70
822 A130 $1.15 multicolored 85 85
823 A130 $1.50 multicolored 1.05 1.05
824 A130 $3.60 multicolored 2.40 2.40

Discovery of America, 500th Anniv. (in 1992) — A131

1993, Mar. 10 Litho. *Perf. 14*

825 A131 $1 Coming ashore 80 80
826 A131 $2 Natives, ships 1.60 1.60

Organization of East Caribbean States.

Coronation of Queen Elizabeth II, 40th Anniv. — A132

Designs: $1.15, Queen, M.H. Bramble. $4.60, Queen riding in Gold State Coach.

1993, June 2 *Perf. 13½x14*

827 A132	$1.15 multicolored		88	88
828 A132	$4.60 multicolored		3.50	3.50

Columbus Type of 1992 with Added Text

IRISH CATHOLICS FROM ST. KITTS AND VIRGINIA SETTLED ON ISLAND BETWEEN 1628-1634

Designs: a, $1.15, like No. 789a. b, $1.15, like No. 789b. c, $1.15, like No. 789c. d, $1.50, like No. 789d. e, $1.50, like No. 789e. f, $1.50, like No. 789f. g, $3.45, like No. 789g.

1993, Sept. 7 **Litho.** *Perf. 14*

829 A124 Sheet of 7, #a.-g. 8.75 8.75

Nos. 829a-829g each have different added text.

Royal Air Force, 75th Anniv.
Common Design Type

Designs: 15c, Boeing Sentry, 1993. 55c, Vickers Valiant, 1962. $1.15, Handley Page Hastings, 1958. $3, 1943 Lockheed Ventura, 1943.

No. 834a, Felixstowe F5, 1921. b, Armstrong Whitworth Atlas, 1934. c, Fairey Gordon, 1935. d, Boulton Paul Overstrand, 1936.

Wmk. 373

1993, Nov. 17 **Litho.** *Perf. 14*

830 CD350	15c multicolored	15	15
831 CD350	55c multicolored	40	40
832 CD350	$1.15 multicolored	85	85
833 CD350	$3 multicolored	2.25	2.25

Souvenir Sheet

834 CD350 $1.50 Sheet of 4, #a.-d. 4.50 4.50

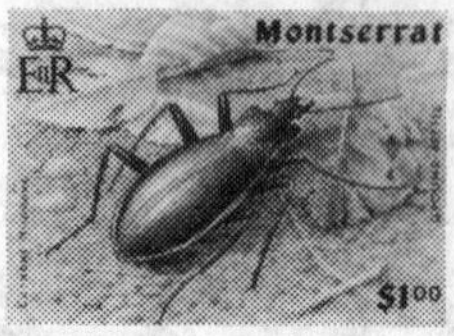

Beetles
A133

Perf. 15x14

1994, Jan. 21 **Litho.** **Unwmk.**

835 A133	$1 Ground beetle	75	75
836 A133	$1.15 Click beetle	90	90
837 A133	$1.50 Harlequin beetle	1.10	1.10
838 A133	$3.45 Leaf beetle	2.50	2.50

Souvenir Sheet

839 A133 $4.50 Scarab beetle 3.50 3.50

Hibiscus Flowers and Fruits — A134

Designs: 90c, Cotton. $1.15, Sorrel. $1.50, Okra. $3.50, Hibiscus rosa sinensis.

1994, Mar. 22 **Litho.** *Perf. 14x13½*

840 A134	90c multicolored	70	70
841 A134	$1.15 multicolored	90	90
842 A134	$1.50 multicolored	1.10	1.10
843 A134	$3.50 multicolored	2.75	2.75

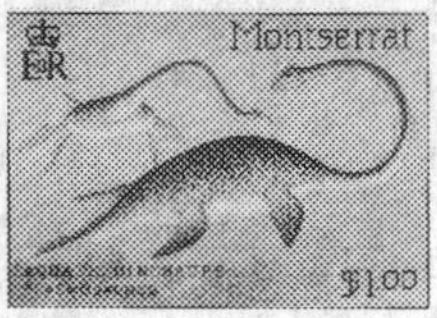

Aquatic Dinosaurs
A135

Designs: a, $1, Elasmosaurus. b, $1.15, Plesiosaurus. c, $1.50, Nothosaurus. d, $3.45, Mosasaurus.

1994, May 6 **Litho.** *Perf. 15x14*

844 A135 Strip of 4, #a.-d. 5.50 5.50

1994 World Cup Soccer Championships, US — A136

Designs: a, 90c, Montserrat youth soccer. b, $1, 1990 World Cup, US vs. England. c, $1.15, Rose Bowl Stadium, Pasadena, Calif., US. d, $3.45, German team, 1990 World Cup Winners.

1994, May 20 *Perf. 14*

845 A136 Vert. strip of 4, #a.-d. 5.00 5.00

A number has been reserved for a souvenir sheet with this set.

No. 845 printed in sheets of 2 strips + 4 labels.

Nos. 726-729 Ovptd. in Red with "Space Anniversaries" and:

40c, "Yuri Gagarin / First man in space / April 12, 1961." $1.15, "First Joint US / Soviet Mission / July 15, 1975." $1.50, "25th Anniversary / First Moon Landing / Apollo XI-July 20, 1994." $2.30, "Columbia / First Space Shuttle / April 12, 1981."

1994 **Litho.** *Perf. 13½x14*

847 A112	40c on 90c multi	30	30
848 A112	$1.15 multi	90	90
849 A112	$1.50 multi	1.10	1.10
850 A112	$2.30 on $3.50 multi	1.75	1.75
	Nos. 847-850 (4)	4.05	4.05

Obliterator on Nos. 847, 850 is black.

SEMI-POSTAL STAMPS

Catalogue values for unused stamps in this section, from this point to the end of the section, are for Never Hinged items.

Nos. 719-720 Surcharged

Hurricane Hugo Relief Surcharge $2.50

1989, Oct. 20 **Litho.** *Perf. 13½x14*

B1 A110	$1.50 +$2.50 multi	3.00	3.00
B2 A110	$3.50 +$2.50 multi	4.50	4.50

Surcharge for hurricane relief.

WAR TAX STAMPS

No. 43 Overprinted in Red or Black WAR STAMP

1917-18 **Wmk. 3** *Perf. 14*

MR1 A6	½p green (R)	15	15
MR2 A6	½p green ('18)	15	15

Type of Regular Issue of 1919 Overprinted WAR STAMP

1918

MR3 A6 1½p orange & black 25 25

Denomination on No. MR3 in black on white ground. Two dots under "d."

OFFICIAL STAMPS

Nos. O1-O44 used on Post Office and Philatelic Bureau mail. Not sold to public, used or unused.

Nos. 235-236, 338-339 Overprinted O.H.M.S.

Perf. 12½x14

1976, Apr. 12 **Photo.** **Wmk. 314**

O1 A22	5c multicolored	2.85
O2 A22	10c multicolored	4.00
O3 A22	30c on 10c multi	8.00
O4 A22	45c on 3c multi	10.00

Nos. 243-243A, also received this overprint.

Nos. 343-347, 349-351, 353 Overprinted

O.H.M.S.

Perf. 13½x14

1976, Oct. 1 **Litho.** **Wmk. 373**

O10 A44	5c multicolored	15
O11 A44	10c multicolored	15
O12 A44	15c multicolored	15
O13 A44	20c multicolored	15
O14 A44	25c multicolored	18
O15 A44	55c multicolored	40
O16 A44	70c multicolored	50
O17 A44	$1 multicolored	70
O18 A44	$5 multicolored	3.50
O19 A44	$10 multicolored	7.00
	Nos. O10-O19 (10)	12.88

Nos. 343-347, 349-351, 353-354 Overprinted O.H.M.S.

1980, Sept. 30 *Perf. 14*

O20 A44	5c multicolored	15
O21 A44	10c multicolored	15
O22 A44	15c multicolored	15
O23 A44	20c multicolored	15
O24 A44	25c multicolored	15
O25 A44	55c multicolored	35
O26 A44	70c multicolored	45
O27 A44	$1 multicolored	65
O28 A44	$5 multicolored	3.25
O29 A44	$10 multicolored	6.50
	Nos. O20-O29 (10)	11.95

Nos. 341-351, 353-354 Overprinted or Surcharged O.H.M.S.

1980, Sept. 30 **Litho.** *Perf. 14*

O30 A44	5c multicolored	15
O31 A44	5c on 3c multi	15
O32 A44	10c multicolored	15
O33 A44	15c multicolored	15
O34 A44	20c multicolored	16
O35 A44	25c multicolored	20
O36 A44	30c on 15c multi	25
O37 A44	35c on 2c multi	42
O38 A44	40c multicolored	32
O39 A44	55c multicolored	45
O40 A44	70c multicolored	60
O41 A44	$1 multicolored	80
O42 A44	$2.50 on 40c multi	2.00
O43 A44	$5 multicolored	4.00
O44 A44	$10 multicolored	8.00
	Nos. O30-O44 (15)	17.80

Catalogue values for unused stamps in this section, from this point to the end of the section, are for Never Hinged items.

Fish Issue of 1981 Nos. 445-449, 451, 453, 455, 457-458, 460 Overprinted O.H.M.S.

1981, Mar. 20 **Litho.** *Perf. 13½*

O45 A64	5c multicolored	15	15
O46 A64	10c multicolored	15	15
O47 A64	15c multicolored	15	15
O48 A64	20c multicolored	16	16
O49 A64	25c multicolored	20	20
O50 A64	45c multicolored	35	35
O51 A64	65c multicolored	50	50
O52 A64	$1 multicolored	75	75
O53 A64	$3 multicolored	2.25	2.25
O54 A64	$5 multicolored	3.75	3.75
O55 A64	$10 multicolored	7.50	7.50
	Nos. O45-O55 (11)	15.91	15.91

Nos. 465-470 Surcharged O.H.M.S. 45c

1982, Nov. 17 **Litho.** *Perf. 14*

O56 A66	45c on 90c (#465)	30	30
O57 A67	45c on 90c (#466)	30	30
O58 A66	75c on $3 (#467)	50	50
O59 A67	75c on $3 (#468)	50	50
O60 A66	$1 on $4 (#469)	65	65
O61 A67	$1 on $4 (#470)	65	65
	Nos. O56-O61 (6)	2.90	2.90

70¢

Princess Diana Issue, Nos. 484-486 Overprinted or Surcharged

O.H.M.S.

1983, Oct. 19 **Litho.** *Perf. 14*

O62 A64	70c on 75c (#484)	50	50
O63 A64	$1 (#485)	70	70
O64 A64	$1.50 on $5 (#486)	1.00	1.00

Nos. 524-536, 538 Overprinted O H M S

1985, Apr. 12 **Wmk. 380** *Perf. 14*

O65 A79	5c multicolored	15	15
O66 A79	10c multicolored	15	15
O67 A79	15c multicolored	15	15
O68 A79	20c multicolored	15	15
O69 A79	25c multicolored	18	18
O70 A79	40c multicolored	28	28
O71 A79	55c multicolored	35	35
O72 A79	70c multicolored	48	48
O73 A79	90c multicolored	60	60
O74 A79	$1 multicolored	70	70
O75 A79	$1.15 multicolored	75	75
O76 A79	$3 multicolored	2.00	2.00
O77 A79	$5 multicolored	3.50	3.50
O78 A79	$10 multicolored	6.75	6.75
	Nos. O65-O78 (14)	16.19	16.19

Nos. 681-694 and 696 Overprinted O H M S

Unwmk.

1989, May 9 **Litho.** *Perf. 14*

O79 A104	5c multicolored	15	15
O80 A104	10c multicolored	15	15
O81 A104	15c multicolored	15	15
O82 A104	20c multicolored	15	15
O83 A104	25c multicolored	18	18
O84 A104	40c multicolored	30	30
O85 A104	55c multicolored	42	42
O86 A104	70c multicolored	52	52
O87 A104	90c multicolored	68	68
O88 A104	$1 multicolored	75	75
O89 A104	$1.15 multicolored	88	88
O90 A104	$1.50 multicolored	1.15	1.15
O91 A104	$3 multicolored	2.25	2.25
O92 A104	$5 multicolored	3.75	3.75
O94 A104	$10 multicolored	7.50	7.50
	Nos. O79-O94 (15)	18.98	18.98

70¢

Nos. 446, 454a and 456 Surcharged

OHMS

1989 Wmk. 373 *Perf. 13½*
O95 A64 70c on 10c multi 52 52
O96 A64 $1.15 on 75c multi 88 88
O97 A64 $1.50 on $2 multi 1.15 1.15

Nos. 758-761, 763-766, 776-779 Surcharged or Overprinted "OHMS"

1992 Litho. *Perf. 14*
O98 A118 70c on 90c #758 1.40 1.40
O99 A118 70c on $3.50 #761 1.40 1.40
O100 A119 70c on 90c #763 1.40 1.40
O101 A121 70c on 90c #776 1.40 1.40
O102 A119 $1 on $3.50 #766 2.00 2.00
O103 A121 $1 on $3.50 #779 2.00 2.00
O104 A118 $1.15 on #759 2.30 2.30
O105 A119 $1.15 on #764 2.30 2.30
O106 A121 $1.15 on #777 2.30 2.30
O107 A118 $1.50 on #760 3.00 3.00
O108 A119 $1.50 on #765 3.00 3.00
O109 A121 $1.50 on #778 3.00 3.00
Nos. O98-O109 (12) 25.50 25.50

Nos. 803-816, 818 Ovptd. "OHMS" in Red

1993, Apr. 14 Litho. *Perf. 15x14*
O110 A128 5c multicolored 15 15
O111 A128 10c multicolored 15 15
O112 A128 15c multicolored 15 15
O113 A128 20c multicolored 15 15
O114 A128 25c multicolored 18 18
O115 A128 40c multicolored 30 30
O116 A128 55c multicolored 42 42
O117 A128 70c multicolored 52 52
O118 A128 90c multicolored 68 68
O119 A128 $1 multicolored 75 75
O120 A128 $1.15 multicolored 85 85
O121 A128 $1.50 multicolored 1.15 1.15
O122 A128 $3 multicolored 2.25 2.25
O123 A128 $5 multicolored 3.75 3.75
O125 A128 $10 multicolored 7.50 7.50
Nos. O110-O125 (15) 18.95 18.95

A number has been reserved for an additional value in this set.

NEVIS

LOCATION — West Indies, southeast of Puerto Rico
GOVT. — A former presidency of the Leeward Islands Colony (British)
AREA — 50 sq. mi.
POP. — 9,800 (1990)
CAPITAL — Charlestown

Nevis stamps were discontinued in 1890 and replaced by those of the Leeward Islands. From 1903 to 1956 stamps of St. Kitts-Nevis and Leeward Islands were used concurrently. From 1956 to 1980 stamps of St. Kitts-Nevis were used. While still a part of St. Kitts-Nevis, Nevis started issuing stamps in 1980.

See Leeward Islands and St. Kitts-Nevis.

12 Pence = 1 Shilling
100 Cents = 1 Dollar

Catalogue values for unused stamps in this country are for Never Hinged items, beginning with Scott 100 in the regular postage section and Scott O1 in the officials section.

Medicinal Spring
A1 A2

A3 A4

1861 Unwmk. Engr. *Perf. 13*
Bluish Wove Paper
1 A1 1p lake rose 250.00 100.00
2 A2 4p dull rose 875.00 275.00
3 A3 6p gray 500.00 275.00
4 A4 1sh green 1,000. 250.00

Grayish Wove Paper
5 A1 1p lake rose 15.00 15.00
6 A2 4p dull rose 67.50 55.00
7 A3 6p lilac gray 45.00 30.00
8 A4 1sh green 125.00 32.50

1867 White Wove Paper *Perf. 15*
9 A1 1p red 15.00 11.50
10 A2 4p orange 70.00 16.00
11 A4 1sh yel green 800.00 100.00
12 A4 1sh blue green 145.00 27.50

Laid Paper
13 A4 1sh yel green *16,500.* 3,250.
Manuscript cancel 900.00

No. 13 values are for copies with design cut into on one or two sides.

1876 Litho.
Wove Paper
14 A1 1p rose 8.25 9.00
14A A1 1p red 8.25 9.00
b. 1p vermilion 8.25 9.00
c. Imperf., pair 360.00
d. Half used as ½p on cover 900.00
15 A2 4p orange 165.00 20.00
a. Imperf.
b. Vert. pair, imperf. between *2,500.*
16 A3 6p olive gray 175.00 175.00
17 A4 1sh gray green 27.50 45.00
a. 1sh dark green 27.50 55.00
b. Horiz. strip of 3, perf. all around & imperf. btwn. *3,750.*

Perf. 11½
18 A1 1p vermilion 19.00 25.00
a. Horiz. pair, imperf. btwn.
b. Half used as ½p on cover 1,000.
c. Imperf., pair 195.00

Queen Victoria — A5

1879-80 Typo. Wmk. 1 *Perf. 14*
19 A5 1p violet ('80) 20.00 15.00
a. Diagonal half used as ½p on cover 475.00
20 A5 2½p red brown 82.50 65.00

1882-90 Wmk. Crown and CA (2)
21 A5 ½p green ('83) 2.00 2.50
22 A5 1p violet 47.50 21.00
a. Half used as ½p on cover 400.00
23 A5 1p rose ('84) 1.90 1.90
24 A5 2½p red brown 75.00 35.00
25 A5 2½p ultra ('84) 3.00 3.00
26 A5 4p blue 200.00 35.00
27 A5 4p gray ('84) 5.50 3.50
28 A5 6p green ('83) 250.00 *275.00*
29 A5 6p brown org ('86) 15.00 20.00
30 A5 1sh violet ('90) 42.50 62.50

Half of No. 22 Surcharged in Black or Violet

NEVIS. ½d

1883
31 A5 ½p on half of 1p *1,000.* 30.00
a. Double surcharge 450.00
32 A5 ½p on half of 1p (V) *1,250.* 30.00
a. Double surcharge 450.00

Surcharge reads up or down.

Catalogue values for unused stamps in this section, from this point to the end of the section, are for Never Hinged items.

St. Kitts-Nevis Nos. 357-369 Ovptd.

Perf. 14½x14
1980, June 23 Litho. Wmk. 373
100 A61 5c multicolored 15 15
101 A61 10c multicolored 15 15
102 A61 12c multicolored 15 15
103 A61 15c multicolored 15 15
104 A61 25c multicolored 15 15
105 A61 30c multicolored 16 16
106 A61 40c multicolored 22 22
107 A61 45c multicolored 25 25
108 A61 50c multicolored 28 28
109 A61 55c multicolored 30 30
110 A61 $1 multicolored 55 55
111 A61 $5 multicolored 2.75 2.75
112 A61 $10 multicolored 5.50 5.50
Nos. 100-112 (13) 10.76 10.76

The bars cover "St. Christopher" and "Anguilla."

The 25c and $1 also come on unwatermarked paper.

80th Birthday of Queen Mother Elizabeth — A6

1980, Sept. 4 *Perf. 14*
113 A6 $2 multicolored 1.00 1.00

Ships and Boats A6a

1980, Oct. 8
114 A6a 5c Nevis lighter 15 15
115 A6a 30c Local fishing boat 16 16
116 A6a 55c *Caona* 30 30

Size: 38x52mm
117 A6a $3 Windjammer's S.V. *Polynesia* 1.65 1.65
a. Perf. 12½x12 1.65 1.65
b. Booklet pane of 3 #117a 5.00

No. 117b separated into three parts by roulettes running vert. through the margin surrounding the stamps. See No. 538 for ovpt.

Christmas A7
Landmarks A8

1980, Nov. 20 *Perf. 14*
118 A7 5c Mother and child 15 15
119 A7 30c Heralding angel 18 18
120 A7 $2.50 Three kings 1.50 1.50

1981, Feb. 5
121 A8 5c Charlestown Pier 15 15
122 A8 10c Court House & Library 15 15
123 A9 15c New River Mill 15 15
124 A9 20c Nelson Museum 15 15
125 A9 25c St. James' Parish Church 15 15
126 A9 30c Nevis Lane 16 16
127 A9 40c Zetland Plantation 22 22
128 A9 45c Nisbet Plantation 25 25
129 A9 50c Pinney's Beach 28 28
130 A9 55c Eva Wilkin's Studio 30 30
131 A9 $1 Nevis at dawn 55 55
132 A9 $2.50 Ft. Charles ruins 1.40 1.40
133 A9 $5 Old Bath House 2.75 2.75
134 A9 $10 Nisbet's Beach 5.50 5.50
Nos. 121-134 (14) 12.16 12.16

Nos. 121-134 exist inscribed "Questa 1982," issued June 9, 1982. Same values.

See Nos. 169-181 for surcharges.

Prince Charles, Lady Diana, Royal Yacht Charlotte A9a

Prince Charles and Lady Diana — A9b

Illustration A9b is greatly reduced.

1981, June 23 Wmk. 373 *Perf. 14*
135 A9a 55c Couple, *Royal Caroline* 28 28
a. Bklt. pane of 4, perf. 12, unwmkd. 1.10 1.10
136 A9b 55c Couple 28 28
137 A9a $2 Couple, *Royal Sovereign* 95 95
138 A9b $2 like No. 136 95 95
a. Bklt. pane of 2, perf. 12, unwmkd. 2.00 2.00
139 A9a $5 Couple, HMY *Britannia* 2.25 2.25
140 A9b $5 like No. 136 2.25 2.25
Nos. 135-140 (6) 6.96 6.96

Souvenir Sheet

1981, Dec. 14 *Perf. 12*
141 A9b $4.50 like No. 136 4.00 4.00

Stamps of the same denomination issued in sheets of 7 (6 type A9a and 1 type A9b).

For surcharges see Nos. 453-454.

Butterflies — A10

1982, Feb. 16 *Perf. 14*
142 A10 5c Zebra 15 15
143 A10 30c Malachite 20 20
144 A10 55c Southern dagger tail 38 38
145 A10 $2 Large orange sulphur 1.40 1.40

For overprint see No. 452.

1983, June 8
146 A10 30c Tropical chequered skipper 22 22
147 A10 55c Caribbean buckeye, vert. 40 40
148 A10 $1.10 Common long-tailed skipper, vert. 80 80
149 A10 $2 Mimic 1.50 1.50

21st Birthday of Princess Diana, July 1 — A11

1982, June 22 *Perf. 13½x14*
150 A11 30c Caroline of Brunswick 18 18
151 A11 55c Brunswick arms 35 35
152 A11 $5 Diana 3.00 3.00

For surcharge see No. 449.

Nos. 150-152 Overprinted "ROYAL BABY"

1982, July 12
153 A11 30c multicolored 18 18
154 A11 55c multicolored 35 35
155 A11 $5 multicolored 3.00 3.00

Birth of Prince William of Wales, June 21.

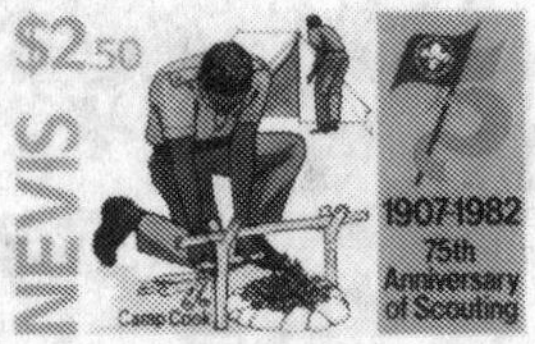

Scouting, 75th Anniv. — A12

1982, Aug. 18

156 A12 5c Cycling 15 15
157 A12 30c Running 22 22
158 A12 $2.50 Building campfire 1.90 1.90

For overprints see Nos. 447, 455.

Christmas — A13

Illustrations by youths. Nos. 159-160 vert.

Perf. 13½x14, 14x13½

1982, Oct. 20

159 A13 15c Eugene Seabrookes 15 15
160 A13 30c Kharenzabeth Glasgow 18 18
161 A13 $1.50 David Grant 90 90
162 A13 $2.50 Leonard Huggins 1.50 1.50

Coral — A14

1983, Jan. 12 ***Perf. 14***

163 A14 15c Tube sponge 15 15
164 A14 30c Stinging coral 20 20
165 A14 55c Flower coral 40 40
166 A14 $3 Sea rod, red fire sponge 2.25 2.25
a. Souvenir sheet of 4, #163-166 3.00 3.00

For overprints see Nos. 446, 448.

Commonwealth Day — A15

1983, Mar. 14

167 A15 55c HMS *Boreas* off Nevis 32 32
168 A15 $2 Lord Nelson, *Boreas* 1.25 1.25

Nos. 121 and 123-134 Ovptd.

INDEPENDENCE 1983	INDEPENDENCE 1983
No. 169	No. 170-181

1983, Sept. 23

169 A8 5c multicolored 15 15
a. Overprint larger with serifed letters
170 A9 15c multicolored 15 15
171 A9 20c multicolored 15 15
172 A9 25c multicolored 15 15
173 A9 30c multicolored 18 18
174 A9 40c multicolored 25 25
175 A9 45c multicolored 28 28
176 A9 50c multicolored 30 30
177 A9 55c multicolored 32 32
178 A9 $1 multicolored 60 60
179 A9 $2.50 multicolored 1.50 1.50
180 A9 $5 multicolored 3.00 3.00
181 A9 $10 multicolored 6.00 6.00
Nos. 169-181 (13) 13.03 13.03

Nos. 169 has 1982 inscription, 170-181 have 1983 inscription. Nos. 169a, 170-174, 177-181 exist without date inscription.

1st Manned Flight, Bicent. A16

Designs: 10c, Montgolfier Balloon, 1783, vert. 45c, Lindbergh's Sikorsky S-38 carrying mail, 1929. 50c, Beechcraft Twin Bonanza. $2.50, Sea Harrier, 1st operational V/STOL fighter.

1983, Sept. 28 **Wmk. 380**

182 A16 10c multicolored 15 15
183 A16 45c multicolored 28 28
184 A16 50c multicolored 32 32
185 A16 $2.50 multicolored 1.50 1.50
a. Souvenir sheet of 4, #182-185 2.25 2.25

Christmas A17

1983, Nov. 7

186 A17 5c Nativity 15 15
187 A17 30c Shepherds, flock 20 20
188 A17 55c Angels 35 35
189 A17 $3 Youths 2.00 2.00
a. Souvenir sheet of 4, #186-189 2.75 2.75

Leaders of the World

Large quantities of some Leaders of the World issues were sold at a fraction of face value when the printer was liquidated.

A18

A19

Leaders of the World: Locomotives.

1983-86 Litho. Unwmk. *Perf. 12½*

Pairs, Types A18-A19

190 1c 1882 Class Wee Bogie, UK 15 15
191 5c 1968 JNR Class EF81, Japan 15 15
192 5c 1878 Snowdon Ranger, UK 15 15
193 10c 1927 P.O. Class 5500, France 15 15
194 15c 1859 Connor Single Class 15 15
195 30c 1904 Large Belpaire Passenger, UK 20 20
196 30c 1829 Stourbridge Lion, US 20 20
197 45c 1934 Cock O' The North 30 30
198 55c 1945 County of Oxford, GB 35 35
199 60c 1940 SNCF Class 240P, France 40 40
200 60c 1851 Comet, UK 40 40
201 60c 1904 County Class, UK 40 40
202 60c 1926 JNR Class 7000, Japan 40 40
203 75c 1877 Nord L'Outrance, France 50 50
204 75c 1919 CM St.P&P Bipolar, US 50 50
205 75c 1897 Palatinate Railway Class P3, Germany 50 50
206 90c 1908 Class 8H, UK 60 60
207 $1 1927 King George V 70 70
208 $1 1951 Britannia 70 70
209 $1 1924 Pendennis Castle 70 70
210 $1 1960 Evening Star 70 70
211 $1 1934 Stanier Class 5, GB 70 70
212 $1 1946 Winston Churchill Battle of Britain 70 70
213 $1 1935 Mallard A4 70 70
214 $1 1899 Q.R. Class PB-15, Australia 70 70
215 $1 1836 C&St.L Dorchester, Canada 70 70
216 $1.50 1953 U.P. Gas Turbine, US 1.00 1.00
217 $1.50 1969 U.P. Centennial Class, US 1.00 1.00
218 $2 1866 No. 23 Class A, UK 1.25 1.25
219 $2 1955 NY, NH & HR FL9, US 1.25 1.25
220 $2 1837 B&O Lafayette, US 1.25 1.25
221 $2.50 1964 JNR Shin-Kansen, Japan 2.25 2.25
222 $2.50 1928 DRG Class 64, Germany 2.25 2.25
223 $3 1882 D&RGR Class C-16, US 2.25 2.25
Nos. 190-223 (34) 24.30 24.30

Issued: #190, 200, 205, 218, Apr. 26, 1985; #191, 193, 199, 221, Oct. 29, 1984; #192, 195, 201, 203, 214, 222, July 26, 1985; #194, 197, 202, 204, 215, 217, 220, 223, Oct. 1, 1986; #196, 203, 216, 219, Jan. 30, 1986; #198, 206-213, Nov. 10, 1983.

See Nos. 285-322.

British Monarchs, Scenes from History
A20 A21

1984

258 A20 5c Boer War 15 15
259 A21 5c Queen Victoria 15 15
260 A20 5c Signing of the Magna Carta 15 15
261 A21 5c King John 15 15
262 A20 50c Victoria, diff. 18 18
263 A21 50c Osborne House 18 18
264 A20 55c John, diff. 20 20
265 A21 55c Newark Castle, Nottinghamshire 20 20
266 A20 60c Battle of Dettingen 22 22
267 A21 60c King George II 22 22
268 A20 75c George II, diff. 28 28
269 A21 75c Bank of England, 1732 28 28
270 A20 $1 George II's coat of arms 38 38
271 A21 $1 George II, diff. 38 38
272 A20 $2 John's coat of arms 75 75
273 A21 $2 John, diff. 75 75
274 A20 $3 Victoria's coat of arms 1.25 1.25
275 A21 $3 Victoria, diff. 1.25 1.25
Nos. 258-275 (18) 7.12 7.12

Issue dates: Nos. 258-259, 262-263, 266-271 and 274-275, Apr. 11; others, Nov. 20.

Nos. 258-259, 260-261 and stamps of the same denomination printed se-tenant in continuous designs.

Tourism A22

1984, May 16 Wmk. 380 *Perf. 14*

276 A22 55c Golden Rock Inn 50 50
277 A22 55c Rest Haven Inn 50 50
278 A22 55c Cliffdwellers Hotel 50 50
279 A22 55c Pinney's Beach Hotel 50 50

1985, Feb. 12

280 A22 $1.20 Croney's Old Manor Hotel 80 80
281 A22 $1.20 Montpelier Plantation Inn 80 80
282 A22 $1.20 Nisbet's Plantation Inn 80 80
283 A22 $1.20 Zetland Plantation Inn 80 80

A $15 stamp picturing the seal of the colony was issued June 8, 1984. While issued for revenue purposes it was valid for postal use.

Leaders of the World Type of 1983

Classic cars.

1984-86 Unwmk. *Perf. 12½*

Pairs, Types A18-A19

285 1c 1932 Cadillac V16 Fleetwood Convertible, US 15 15
286 1c 1935 Delahaye Type 35 Cabriolet, France 15 15
287 5c 1916 Packard Twin Six Touring Car, US 15 15
288 5c 1929 Lagonda Speed Model Touring Car, GB 15 15
289 5c 1958 Ferrari Testarossa, Italy 15 15
290 10c 1934 Voisin Aerodyne, France 15 15
291 10c 1912 Sunbeam Coupe De L'Auto, GB 15 15
292 10c 1936 Adler Trumpf, Germany 15 15
293 15c 1886 Daimler 2-Cylinder, Germany 15 15
294 15c 1930 Riley Brooklands Nine, UK 15 15
295 30c 1967 Jaguar E-Type 4.2 Liter, GB 20 20
296 35c 1970 Porsche 911 S Targa, Germany 25 25
297 35c 1948 Cisitalia Pinnifarina Coupe, Italy 25 25
298 45c 1885 Benz Three-wheeler, Germany 30 30
299 45c 1966 Alfa Romeo GTA, Italy 30 30
300 50c 1947 Volkswagen Beetle, Germany 35 35
301 50c 1963 Buick Riviera 35 35
302 55c 1947 MG TC, GB 40 40
303 60c 1960 Cooper Climax, UK 40 40
304 60c 1957 Maserati Tipo 250F, Italy 40 40
305 60c 1913 Pierce Arrow Type 66, US 40 40
306 75c 1904 Ford 999, US 50 50
307 75c 1980 Porsche 928S, Germany 50 50
308 75c 1910 Oldsmobile Limited, US 50 50
309 $1 1951 Jaguar C-Type, UK 65 65
310 $1 1928 Willys-Knight 66A, US 65 65
311 $1.15 1933 MG K3 Magnette, GB 75 75
312 $1.50 1937 Lincoln Zephyr, US 1.00 1.00
313 $1.50 1937 ERA 1.5 l B Type, UK 1.00 1.00
314 $1.75 1953 Studebaker Starliner, US 1.15 1.15
315 $2 1926 Pontiac 2-door, US 1.35 1.35
316 $2.50 1966 Cobra Roadster 289, US 1.75 1.75
317 $2.50 1930 MG M-Type Midget, UK 1.75 1.75
318 $3 1966 Aston Martin DB6 Hardtop, GB 2.00 2.00
319 $3 1932 Pierce Arrow V12, US 2.00 2.00
320 $3 1971 Rolls Royce Corniche, UK 2.00 2.00
321 $3 1953 Chevrolet Corvette, US 2.00 2.00
322 $3 1919 Cunningham V-8, US 2.00 2.00
Nos. 285-322 (38) 26.65 26.65

Issued: #285, 287, 293, 296, 298, 302, 316, 318, July 25, 1984; #286, 289-290, 301, 303, 306, 317, 320, Feb. 20, 1985; #288, 295, 300, 319, Oct. 23, 1984; #291, 297, 307, 311-312, 315, Oct. 4, 1985; #292, 303, 308-309, 313, 321, Jan. 30, 1986; #294, 299, 305, 310, 314, 322, Aug. 15, 1986.

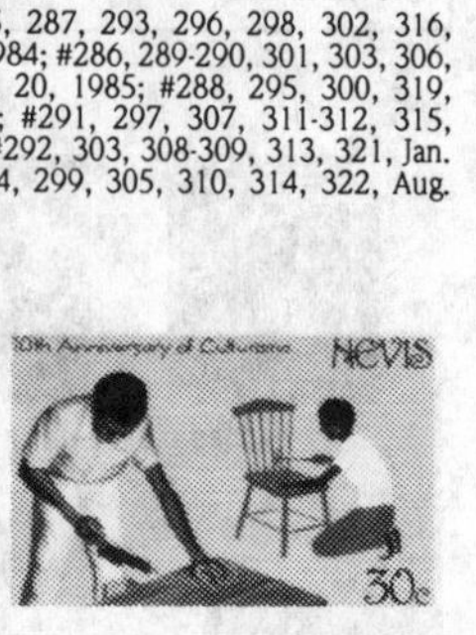

Culturama Carnival, 10th Anniv. A24

Wmk. 380

1984, Aug. 1 Litho. *Perf. 14*

361 A24 30c Carpentry 18 18
362 A24 55c Weaving mats and baskets 32 32
363 A24 $1 Ceramics 60 60
364 A24 $3 Carnival queen, folk dancers 1.75 1.75

Flowers — A25

1984, Aug. 8

365 A25 5c Yellow bell 15 15
366 A25 10c Plumbago 15 15
367 A25 15c Flamboyant 15 15
368 A25 20c Eyelash orchid 15 15
369 A25 30c Bougainvillea 16 16
370 A25 40c Hibiscus 20 20
371 A25 50c Night-blooming cereus 28 28
372 A25 55c Yellow mahoe 30 30
373 A25 60c Spider lily 32 32
374 A25 75c Scarlet cordia 40 40
375 A25 $1 Shell ginger 55 55
376 A25 $3 Blue petrea 1.65 1.65
377 A25 $5 Coral hibiscus 2.75 2.75
378 A25 $10 Passion flower 5.50 5.50
Nos. 365-378 (14) 12.71 12.71

Nos. 368 and 370 were reissued on July 23, 1986 with date inscription. Values for those two stamps are for the 1986 printing.

Independence of St. Kitts and Nevis, 1st Anniv. — A26

1984, Sept. 18

379 A26 15c Picking cotton 15 15
380 A26 55c Hamilton House 32 32
381 A26 $1.10 Self-sufficiency in food production 65 65
382 A26 $3 Pinney's Beach 1.75 1.75

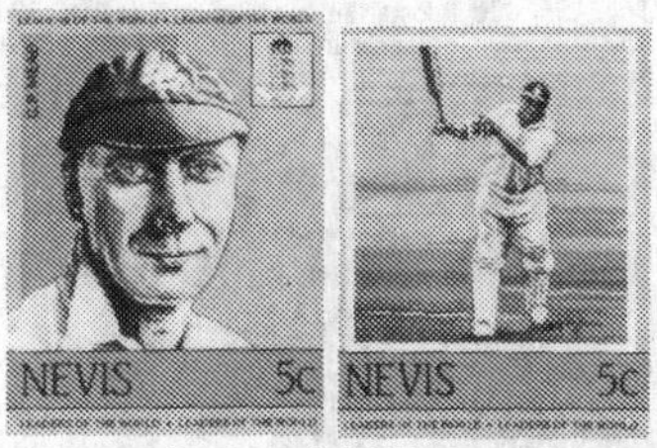
Leaders of the World
A27 A28

Cricket players and team emblems (Type A27) and match scenes (Type A28).

1984 Unwmk. *Perf. 12½*

383 A27 5c C.P. Mead, England 15 15
384 A28 5c Mead, diff. 15 15
385 A27 5c J.D. Love, Yorkshire 15 15
386 A28 5c Love, diff. 15 15
387 A27 15c S.J. Dennis, Yorkshire 15 15
388 A28 15c Dennis, diff. 15 15
389 A28 25c J.B. Statham, England 15 15
390 A27 25c Statham, diff. 15 15
391 A28 55c Sir Learie Constantine, West Indies 22 22
392 A27 55c Constantine, diff. 22 22
393 A28 55c B.W. Luckhurst, Kent 22 22
394 A27 55c Luckhurst, diff. 22 22
395 A28 $2.50 Sir Leonard Hutton, England 1.00 1.00
396 A27 $2.50 Hutton, diff. 1.00 1.00
397 A27 $2.50 B.L. D'Oliveira, England 1.00 1.00
398 A28 $2.50 D'Oliveira, diff. 1.00 1.00
Nos. 383-398 (16) 6.08 6.08

Issue dates: Nos. 383-384, 389-392 and 395-396, Oct. 23; others, Nov. 20.
Stamps picturing the same athlete are printed se-tenant in continuous designs.

Christmas
A29

Musicians from local bands: 15c, Flutist and drummer of the Honeybees Band. 40c, Guitar and barhow players of the Canary Birds Band. 60c, Shell All Stars steel band. $3, Choir, organist, St. John's Church, Fig Tree.

1984, Nov. 2 Wmk. 380 *Perf. 14*

399 A29 15c multicolored 15 15
400 A29 40c multicolored 25 25
401 A29 60c multicolored 38 38
402 A29 $3 multicolored 1.90 1.90

Birds
A30

1985, Mar. 19

403 A30 20c Broad-winged hawk 15 15
404 A30 40c Red-tailed hawk 28 28
405 A30 60c Little blue heron 42 42
406 A30 $3 Great white heron 2.00 2.00

Leaders of the World — A31

Birds.

1985 Unwmk. *Perf. 12½*

407 A31 1c Painted bunting 15 15
408 A31 1c Golden-crowned kinglet 15 15
409 A31 5c Eastern bluebird 15 15
410 A31 5c Northern cardinal 15 15
411 A31 40c Common flicker 15 15
412 A31 40c Western tanager 15 15
413 A31 55c Belted kingfisher 20 20
414 A31 55c Mangrove cuckoo 20 20
415 A31 60c Yellow warbler 22 22
416 A31 60c Cerulean warbler 22 22
417 A31 60c Sage thrasher 22 22
418 A31 60c Evening grosbeak 22 22

419 A31 $2 Burrowing owl 1.25 1.25
420 A31 $2 Long-eared owl 1.25 1.25
421 A31 $2.50 Blackburnian warbler 1.50 1.50
422 A31 $2.50 Northern oriole 1.50 1.50
Nos. 407-422 (16) 7.68 7.68

Birth bicent. of ornithologist John J. Audubon.
Issue dates: Nos. 407-408, 411-412, 417-418 and 421-422, June 3; others, Mar. 25. Nos. 415-416, 417-418 and stamps of the same denomination printed se-tenant in continuous designs.

Girl Guides, 75th Anniv. — A32

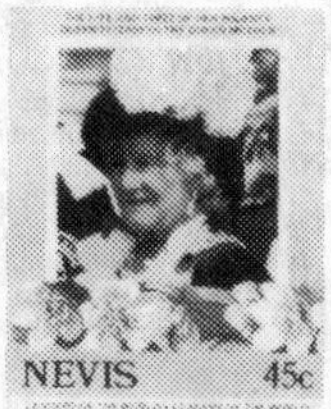
Queen Mother Elizabeth — A33

1985, June 17 Wmk. 380 *Perf. 14*

423 A32 15c Troop, horiz. 15 15
424 A32 60c Uniforms, 1910, 1985 40 40
425 A32 $1 Lord and Lady Baden-Powell 65 65
426 A32 $3 Princess Margaret 2.00 2.00

1985, July 31 Unwmk. *Perf. 12½*

427 A33 45c Black hat, white plume 30 30
428 A33 45c Blue hat, pink feathers 30 30
429 A33 75c Blue hat 52 52
430 A33 75c Tiara 52 52
431 A33 $1.20 Violet & blue hat 85 85
432 A33 $1.20 Blue hat 85 85
433 A33 $1.50 Light blue hat 1.00 1.00
434 A33 $1.50 Black hat 1.00 1.00
Nos. 427-434 (8) 5.34 5.34

Souvenir Sheets

435 Sheet of 2 3.00 3.00
a. A33 $2 As a child, c. 1910 1.50 1.50
b. A33 $2 Queen consort, c. 1945 1.50 1.50

1985, Dec. 27

436 Sheet of 2 3.00 3.00
a. A33 $3.50 similar to No. 427 1.40 1.40
b. A33 $3.50 similar to No. 428 1.40 1.40
437 Sheet of 2 5.00 5.00
a. A33 $6 like No. 433 2.50 2.50
b. A33 $6 like No. 434 2.50 2.50

Stamps of the same denomination printed se-tenant in continuous designs.
For overprints see Nos. 450-451.

Great Western Railway, 150th Anniv.
A34 A35

Railway engineers (Type A34) and their achievements (Type A35). Stamps of the same denomination printed se-tenant in continuous designs.

1985, Aug. 31

438 A34 25c Isambard Brunel 15 15
439 A35 25c Royal Albert Bridge, 1859 15 15
440 A34 50c William Dean 28 28
441 A35 50c *Lord of the Isles*, 1895 28 28
442 A35 $1 *Lode Star*, 1907 55 55
443 A34 $1 G.J. Churchward 55 55
444 A35 $2.50 Pendennis Castle Class, 1924 1.50 1.50
445 A34 $2.50 C.B. Collett 1.50 1.50
Nos. 438-445 (8) 4.96 4.96

Nos. 163, 157, 164, 151, 427-428, 144, 139-140 and 158 Ovptd. or Surcharged "CARIBBEAN ROYAL VISIT 1985" in 2 or 3 Lines

Perf. 14, 12½ (45c)

1985, Oct. 23 Wmk. as Before

446 A14 15c No. 163 15 15
447 A12 30c No. 157 30 30
448 A14 30c No. 164 30 30
449 A11 40c on 55c No. 151 40 40
450 A33 45c No. 427 45 45
451 A33 45c No. 428 45 45
452 A10 55c No. 144 55 55
453 A9a $1.50 on $5 No. 139 1.50 1.50
454 A9b $1.50 on $5 No. 140 1.50 1.50
455 A12 $2.50 No. 158 2.50 2.50
Nos. 446-455 (10) 8.10 8.10

#450-451 printed se-tenant. #453-454 issued in sheets of 7 (6 type A9a, 1 type A9b).

Christmas
A36

Anglican, Roman Catholic and Methodist churches.

1985, Nov. 5 Wmk. 380 *Perf. 15*

456 A36 10c St. Paul's, Charlestown 15 15
457 A36 40c St. Theresa, Charlestown 28 28
458 A36 60c Methodist Church, Gingerland 42 42
459 A36 $3 St. Thomas, Lowland 2.00 2.00

Spitfire Fighter Plane, 50th Anniv. — A37

1986, Mar. 24 Unwmk. *Perf. 12½*

460 A37 $1 Prototype K.5054, 1936 60 60
461 A37 $2.50 Mk.1A, 1940 1.50 1.50
462 A37 $3 Mk.XII, 1944 1.75 1.75
463 A37 $4 Mk.XXIV, 1948 2.50 2.50

Souvenir Sheet

464 A37 $6 Seafire Mk.III 4.00 4.00

Discovery of America, 500th Anniv. (in 1992) — A38

1986, Apr. 11

465 A38 75c American Indian 42 42
466 A38 75c Columbus trading with Indians 42 42
467 A38 $1.75 Columbus's coat of arms 1.00 1.00
468 A38 $1.75 Breadfruit 1.00 1.00
469 A38 $2.50 Galleons 1.50 1.50
470 A38 $2.50 Columbus 1.50 1.50
Nos. 465-470 (6) 5.84 5.84

Souvenir Sheet

471 A38 $6 Columbus, diff. 3.50 3.50

Stamps of the same denomination printed se-tenant in continuous designs picturing various maps of Columbus's voyages.

Queen Elizabeth II, 60th Birthday — A39

Various portraits. Illustration reduced.

1986, Apr. 21

472 A39 5c multicolored 15 15
473 A39 75c multicolored 55 55
474 A39 $2 multicolored 1.50 1.50
475 A39 $8 multi, vert. 6.00 6.00

Souvenir Sheet

476 A39 $10 multicolored 7.50 7.50

1986 World Cup Soccer Championships, Mexico — A40

Perf. 15, 12½ (75c, $1, $1.75, $6)

1986, May 16

Size of 75c, $1, $1.75, $6: 56x35½mm

477 A40 1c Character trademark 15 15
478 A40 2c Brazilian player 15 15
479 A40 5c Danish player 15 15
480 A40 10c Brazilian, diff. 15 15
481 A40 20c Denmark vs. Spain 15 15
482 A40 30c Paraguay vs. Chile 20 20

483 A40 60c Italy vs. W. Germany 42 42
484 A40 75c Danish team 50 50
485 A40 $1 Paraguayan team 70 70

486 A40 $1.75 Brazilian team 1.25 1.25
487 A40 $3 Italy vs. England 2.00 2.00
488 A40 $6 Italian team 4.00 4.00
Nos. 477-488 (12) 9.82 9.82

Souvenir Sheets

Perf. 12½

489 A40 $1.50 like $1.75 1.25 1.25
490 A40 $2 like $6 1.50 1.50

Perf. 15

491 A40 $2 like 20c 1.50 1.50
492 A40 $2.50 like 60c 2.00 2.00
493 A40 $4 like 30c 3.00 3.00

Nos. 478-483 and 487 vert.

Local Industry A41

1986, July 18 Wmk. 380 *Perf. 14*

494 A41 15c Textile 15 15
495 A41 40c Carpentry 25 25
496 A41 $1.20 Agriculture 75 75
497 A41 $3 Fishing 1.90 1.90

A42

Wedding of Prince Andrew and Sarah Ferguson — A43

1986, July 23 Unwmk. *Perf. 12½*

498 A42 60c Andrew, vert. 35 35
499 A42 60c Sarah, vert. 35 35
500 A42 $2 Andrew at the races 1.10 1.10
501 A42 $2 Andrew in Africa 1.10 1.10

Souvenir Sheet

502 A43 $10 Couple on Balcony 4.75 4.75

Stamps of the same denomination printed se-tenant in pairs existing in vert. and horiz. format.
See Nos. 521-524 for overprints.

Coral — A44

1986, Sept. 8 Wmk. 380 *Perf. 15*

503 A44 15c Gorgonia 15 15
504 A44 60c Fire coral 38 38
505 A44 $2 Elkhorn coral 1.25 1.25
506 A44 $3 Feather star 1.90 1.90

A45

Statue of Liberty, Cent. — A46

1986, Oct. 28 Unwmk. *Perf. 14*

507 A45 15c Statue, World Trade Center 15 15
508 A45 25c Statue, tall ship 15 15
509 A45 40c Under renovation (front) 25 25
510 A45 60c Renovation (side) 38 38
511 A45 75c Statue, Operation Sail 50 50
512 A45 $1 Tall ship, horiz. 65 65
513 A45 $1.50 Renovation (arm, head) 95 95
514 A45 $2 Ship flying Liberty flag 1.25 1.25
515 A45 $2.50 Statue, Manhattan 1.50 1.50
516 A45 $3 Workers on scaffold 1.90 1.90
Nos. 507-516 (10) 7.68 7.68

Souvenir Sheets

517 A46 $3.50 Statue at dusk 2.25 2.25
518 A46 $4 Head 2.50 2.50
519 A46 $4.50 Torch struck by lightning 2.75 2.75
520 A46 $5 Torch, blazing sun 3.00 3.00

Nos. 498-501 Ovptd. "Congratulations to T.R.H. The Duke & Duchess of York"

1986, Nov. 17 *Perf. 12½*

521 A42 60c No. 498 28 28
522 A42 60c No. 499 28 28
523 A42 $2 No. 500 1.00 1.00
524 A42 $2 No. 501 1.00 1.00

Stamps of the same denomination printed se-tenant in pairs existing in horiz. and vert. format.

Sports A47

1986, Nov. 21 *Perf. 14*

525 A47 10c Sailing 15 15
526 A47 25c Netball 20 20
527 A47 $2 Cricket 1.50 1.50
528 A47 $3 Basketball 2.25 2.25

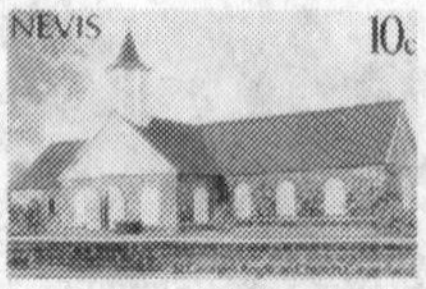

Christmas A48

Churches: 10c, St. George's Anglican Church, Gingerland. 40c, Methodist Church, Fountain. $1, Charlestown Methodist Church. $5, Wesleyan Holiness Church, Brown Hill.

1986, Dec. 8

529 A48 10c multicolored 15 15
530 A48 40c multicolored 30 30
531 A48 $1 multicolored 75 75
532 A48 $5 multicolored 3.75 3.75

US Constitution A49

Christening of the Hamilton, 1788 A50

US Constitution, bicent. and 230th anniv. of the birth of Alexander Hamilton: 40c, Alexander Hamilton, Hamilton House. 60c, Hamilton. $2, George Washington and members of the 1st presidential cabinet.

1987, Jan. 11

533 A49 15c shown 15 15
534 A49 40c multicolored 30 30
535 A49 60c multicolored 45 45
536 A49 $2 multicolored 1.50 1.50

Souvenir Sheet

537 A50 $5 shown 3.75 3.75

No. 117 Overprinted

America's Cup
1987 Winners
'Stars & Stripes'

1987, Feb. 20 Wmk. 373

538 A6a $3 multicolored 2.25 2.25

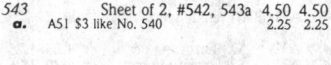

Wedding of Capt. Horatio Nelson and Frances Nisbet, Bicent. A51

1987, Mar. 11 Wmk. 380

539 A51 15c Fig Tree Church 15 15
540 A51 60c Frances Nisbet 45 45
541 A51 $1 HMS *Boreas* 75 75
542 A51 $3 Capt. Nelson 2.25 2.25

Souvenir Sheet

543 Sheet of 2, #542, 543a 4.50 4.50
a. A51 $3 like No. 540 2.25 2.25

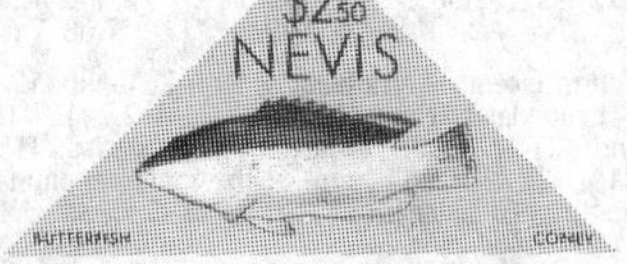

Coney Butterfish — A52

1987, July 22 Unwmk. *Perf. 15*

544 A52 60c Queen angelfish 45 45
545 A52 60c Blue angelfish 45 45
546 A52 $1 Blue thum 75 75
547 A52 $1 Red thum 75 75
548 A52 $1.50 Red hind 1.15 1.15
549 A52 $1.50 Rock hind 1.15 1.15
550 A52 $2.50 shown 1.90 1.90
551 A52 $2.50 Coney butterfish, diff. 1.90 1.90
Nos. 544-551 (8) 8.50 8.50

Stamps of the same denomination printed se-tenant.

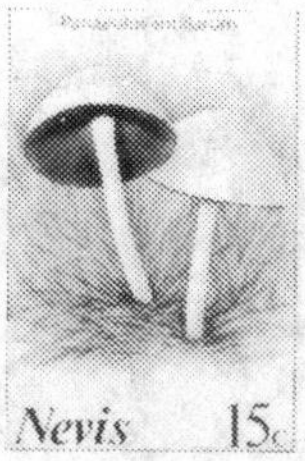

Mushrooms — A53

1987, Oct. 16 Wmk. 384 *Perf. 14*

552 A53 15c *Panaeolus antillarum* 15 15
553 A53 50c *Pycnoporus sanguineus* 38 38
554 A53 $2 *Gymnopilus chrysopellus* 1.50 1.50
555 A53 $3 *Cantharellus cinnabarinus* 2.25 2.25

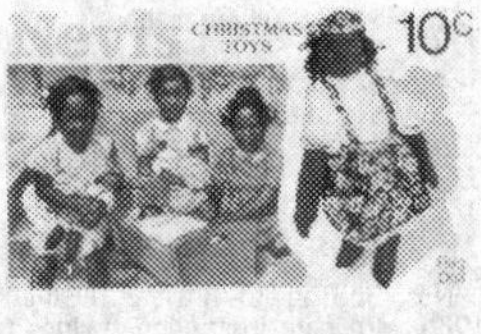

Christmas A54

1987, Dec. 4 *Perf. 14½*

556 A54 10c Rag doll 15 15
557 A54 40c Coconut boat 30 30
558 A54 $1.20 Sandbox cart 90 90
559 A54 $5 Two-wheeled cart 3.75 3.75

Sea Shells — A55

1988, Feb. 15

560 A55 15c Hawk-wing conch 15 15
561 A55 40c Roostertail conch 30 30
562 A55 60c Emperor helmet 45 45
563 A55 $2 Queen conch 1.50 1.50
564 A55 $3 King helmet 2.25 2.25
Nos. 560-564 (5) 4.65 4.65

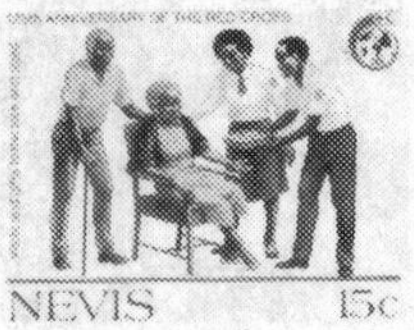

Intl. Red Cross and Red Crescent Organizations, 125th Annivs. A56

Activities: 15c, Visiting the sick and the elderly. 40c, First aid training. 60c, Wheelchairs for the disabled. $5, Disaster relief.

1988, June 20

565 A56 15c multicolored 15 15
566 A56 40c multicolored 30 30
567 A56 60c multicolored 45 45
568 A56 $5 multicolored 3.75 3.75

A57

A58

1988, Aug. 26 *Perf. 14*

569 Strip of 4 4.75 4.75
a. A57 10c Runner at starting block 15 15
b. A57 $1.20 Leaving block 90 90

c. A57 $2 Full stride 1.50 1.50
d. A57 $3 Crossing finish line 2.25 2.25
e. Souvenir sheet of 4, #569a-569d 4.75 4.75

1988 Summer Olympics, Seoul. Printed se-tenant in a continuous design. Stamps in No. 569e are 23 1/2x36 1/2.

1988, Sept. 19 Wmk. 373 *Perf. 14 1/2*

570 A58 $5 multicolored 3.75 3.75

Independence, 5th anniv.

Lloyds of London
Common Design Type

Designs: 15c, Act of Parliament incorporating Lloyds, 1871. 60c, *Cunard Countess* in Nevis Harbor, horiz. $2.50, Space shuttle, deployment of satellite in space, horiz. $3, *Viking Princess* on fire in the Caribbean, 1966.

1988, Oct. 31 Wmk. 384 *Perf. 14*

571 CD341 15c multicolored 15 15
572 CD341 60c multicolored 45 45
573 CD341 $2.50 multicolored 1.50 1.50
574 CD341 $3 multicolored 2.25 2.25

Christmas Flowers — A59

1988, Nov. 7 *Perf. 14 1/2*

575 A59 15c Poinsettia 15 15
576 A59 40c Tiger claws 30 30
577 A59 60c Sorrel flower 45 45
578 A59 $1 Christmas candle 75 75
579 A59 $5 Snow bush 3.75 3.75
Nos. 575-579 (5) 5.40 5.40

Battle of Frigate Bay, 1782 — A60

Exhibition emblem and maps. Nos. 580a-580c printed se-tenant in a continuous design. (Illustration reduced.)

1989, Apr. 17 *Perf. 14*

580 A60 Strip of 3 2.80 2.80
a. 50c multicolored 38 38
b. $1.20 multicolored 90 90
c. $2 multicolored 1.50 1.50

Size: 34x47mm

Perf. 14x13 1/2

581 A60 $3 Map of Nevis, 1764 2.25 2.25

French revolution bicent., PHILEXFRANCE '89.

Nocturnal Insects and Frogs — A61

1989, May 15

582 A61 10c Cicada 15 15
583 A61 40c Grasshopper 30 30
584 A61 60c Cricket 45 45
585 A61 $5 Tree frog 3.75 3.75
a. Souvenir sheet of 4, #582-585 4.60 4.60

Moon Landing, 20th Anniv.
Common Design Type

Apollo 12: 15c, Vehicle Assembly Building, Kennedy Space Center. 40c, Crew members Charles Conrad Jr., Richard Gordon and Alan Bean. $2, Mission emblem. $3, Moon operation in the Sun's glare. $6, Buzz Aldrin deploying passive seismic experiment package on the lunar surface, Apollo 11 mission.

1989, July 20 *Perf. 14x13 1/2*

Size of Nos. 587-588: 29x29mm

586 CD342 15c multicolored 15 15
587 CD342 40c multicolored 30 30
588 CD342 $2 multicolored 1.50 1.50
589 CD342 $3 multicolored 2.25 2.25

Souvenir Sheet

590 CD342 $6 multicolored 4.50 4.50

Queen Conchs *(Strombus gigas)* — A62

1990, Jan. 31

591 A62 10c shown 15 15
592 A62 40c Conch, diff 30 30
593 A62 60c Conch, diff 45 45
594 A62 $1 Conch, diff 75 75

Souvenir Sheet

595 A62 $5 Fish and coral 3.75 3.75

World Wildlife Fund.

Wyon Portrait of Victoria — A63

Perf. 14x15

1990, May 3 Litho. Unwmk.

596 A63 15c shown 15 15
597 A63 40c Engine-turned background 30 30
598 A63 60c Heath's engraving 45 45
599 A63 $4 Inscriptions added 3.00 3.00

Souvenir Sheet

600 A63 $5 Completed design 3.75 3.75

Penny Black, 150th anniv. No. 600 for Stamp World London '90.

A64

1990, May 3 *Perf. 13 1/2*

601 A64 15c brown 15 15
602 A64 40c deep green 30 30
603 A64 60c violet 45 45
604 A64 $4 bright ultra 3.00 3.00

Souvenir Sheet

605 A64 $5 gray, lake & buff 3.75 3.75

Penny Black 150th anniversary and commemoration of the Thurn & Taxis postal service.

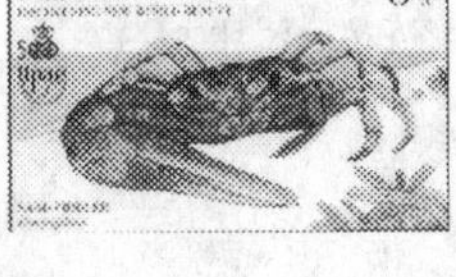

Crabs A65

Designs include UPAE and discovery of America anniversary emblems.

1990, June 25 Litho. *Perf. 14*

606 A65 5c Sand fiddler 15 15
607 A65 15c Great land crab 15 15
608 A65 20c Blue crab 15 15
609 A65 40c Stone crab 30 30
610 A65 60c Mountain crab 45 45
611 A65 $2 Sargassum crab 1.50 1.50
612 A65 $3 Yellow box crab 2.25 2.25
613 A65 $4 Spiny spider crab 3.00 3.00
Nos. 606-613 (8) 7.95 7.95

Souvenir Sheets

614 A65 $5 Wharf crab 3.75 3.75
615 A65 $5 Sally lightfoot 3.75 3.75

Queen Mother 90th Birthday
A66 A67

1990, July 5

616 A66 $2 shown 1.50 1.50
617 A67 $2 shown 1.50 1.50
618 A66 $2 Queen Consort, diff. 1.50 1.50
a. Strip of 3, #616-618 4.50 4.50

Souvenir Sheet

619 A67 $6 Coronation Portrait, diff. 4.75 4.75

Nos. 616-618 printed in sheet of 9.

A68

A69

Players from participating countries.

1990, Oct. 1 Litho. *Perf. 14*

620 A68 10c Cameroun 15 15
621 A68 25c Czechoslovakia 18 18
622 A68 $2.50 England 1.90 1.90
623 A68 $5 West Germany 3.75 3.75

Souvenir Sheets

624 A68 $5 Spain 3.75 3.75
625 A68 $5 Argentina 3.75 3.75

World Cup Soccer Championships, Italy.

Unwmk.

1990, Nov. 19 Litho. *Perf. 14*

Christmas (Orchids): 10c, Cattleya deckeri. 15c, Epidendrum ciliare. 20c, Epidendrum fragrans. 40c, Epidendrum ibaguense. 60c, Epidendrum latifolium. $1.20, Maxillaria conferta. $2, Epidendrum strobiliferum. $3, Brassavola cucullata. $5, Rodriguezia lanceolata.

626 A69 10c multicolored 15 15
627 A69 15c multicolored 15 15
628 A69 20c multicolored 15 15
629 A69 40c multicolored 30 30
630 A69 60c multicolored 45 45
631 A69 $1.20 multicolored 90 90
632 A69 $2 multicolored 1.50 1.50
633 A69 $3 multicolored 2.25 2.25
Nos. 626-633 (8) 5.85 5.85

Souvenir Sheet

634 A69 $5 multicolored 3.75 3.75

Peter Paul Rubens (1577-1640), Painter — A70

Details from The Feast of Achelous: 10c, Pitchers. 40c, Woman at table. 60c, Two women. $4, Achelous feasting. $5, Complete painting, horiz.

1991, Jan. 14 Litho. *Perf. 13 1/2*

635 A70 10c multicolored 15 15
636 A70 40c multicolored 30 30
637 A70 60c multicolored 45 45
638 A70 $4 multicolored 3.00 3.00

Souvenir Sheet

639 A70 $5 multicolored 3.75 3.75

Butterflies A71

1991-92 *Perf. 14*

640 A71 5c Gulf fritillary 15 15
641 A71 10c Orion 15 15
642 A71 15c Dagger wing 15 15
643 A71 20c Red anartia 15 15
644 A71 25c Caribbean buckeye 18 18
645 A71 40c Zebra 30 30
646 A71 50c Southern dagger tail 38 38
647 A71 60c Silver spot 45 45
648 A71 75c Doris 55 55
648A A71 80c like #647 60 60
649 A71 $1 Mimic 75 75
650 A71 $3 Monarch 2.25 2.25
651 A71 $5 Small blue grecian 3.75 3.75
652 A71 $10 Tiger 7.50 7.50
653 A71 $20 Flambeau 15.00 15.00
Nos. 640-653 (15) 32.31 32.31

Issue dates: #648A, 1992. Others, Mar. 1, 1991. Nos. 640-646, 648-653 exist dated 1992. Nos. 640-641, 644, 646, 648A exist dated 1994.

For overprints see Nos. O41-O54.

Space Exploration-Discovery Voyages — A72

1991, Apr. 22 Litho. *Perf. 14*

654 A72 15c Viking Mars lander 15 15
655 A72 40c Apollo 11 lift-off 30 30
656 A72 60c Skylab 45 45
657 A72 75c Salyut 6 55 55
658 A72 $1 Voyager 1 75 75
659 A72 $2 Venera 7 1.50 1.50
660 A72 $4 Gemini 4 3.00 3.00
661 A72 $5 Luna 3 3.75 3.75
Nos. 654-661 (8) 10.45 10.45

Souvenir Sheet

662 A72 $6 Sailing ship, vert. 4.50 4.50
663 A72 $6 Columbus' landfall 4.50 4.50

Discovery of America, 500th anniv. (in 1992) (No. 663).

Miniature Sheet

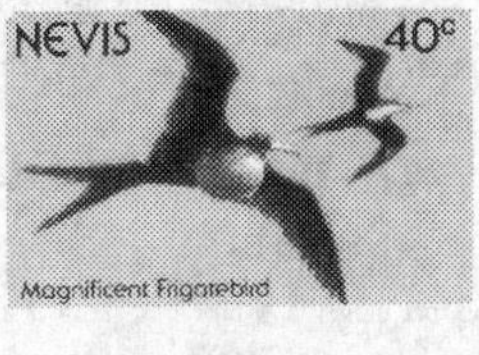

Birds A73

Designs: a, Magnificent frigatebird. b, Roseate tern. c, Red-tailed hawk. d, Zenaida dove. e, Bananaquit. f, American kestrel. g, Grey kingbird. h, Prothonotary warbler. i, Blue-hooded euphonia. j, Antillean crested hummingbird. k, White-tailed tropicbird. l, Yellow-bellied sapsucker. m, Green-throated carib. n, Purple-throated carib. o, Black-bellied tree duck. p, Ringed kingfisher. q, Burrowing owl. r, Ruddy turnstone. s, Great white heron. t, Yellow-crowned night heron.

1991, May 28

664 A73 40c Sheet of 20, #a.-t. 6.00 6.00

Souvenir Sheet

665 A73 $6 Great egret 4.50 4.50

Royal Family Birthday, Anniversary

Common Design Type

1991, July 5 Litho. *Perf. 14*

666	CD347	10c multicolored	15	15
667	CD347	15c multicolored	15	15
668	CD347	40c multicolored	30	30
669	CD347	50c multicolored	38	38
670	CD347	$1 multicolored	75	75
671	CD347	$2 multicolored	1.50	1.50
672	CD347	$4 multicolored	3.00	3.00
673	CD347	$5 multicolored	3.75	3.75
		Nos. 666-673 (8)	9.98	9.98

Souvenir Sheets

674	CD347	$5 Elizabeth, Philip	3.75	3.75
675	CD347	$5 Charles, Diana & family	3.75	3.75

10c, 50c, $1, Nos. 673, 675, Charles and Diana, 10th Wedding Anniv. Others, Queen Elizabeth II 65th birthday.

Japanese Trains A74

Locomotives: 10c, C62 Steam, vert. 15c, C56 Steam. 40c, Streamlined C55, steam. 60c, Class 1400 Steam. $1, Class 485 bonnet type rail diesel car, vert. $2, C61 Steam, vert. $3, Class 485 express train. $4, Class 7000 electric train. No. 684, D51 Steam. No. 685, Hikari bullet train.

1991, Aug. 12

676	A74	10c multicolored	15	15
677	A74	15c multicolored	15	15
678	A74	40c multicolored	30	30
679	A74	60c multicolored	45	45
680	A74	$1 multicolored	75	75
681	A74	$2 multicolored	1.50	1.50
682	A74	$3 multicolored	2.25	2.25
683	A74	$4 multicolored	3.00	3.00
		Nos. 676-683 (8)	8.55	8.55

Souvenir Sheets

684	A74	$5 multicolored	3.75	3.75
685	A74	$5 multicolored	3.75	3.75

Phila Nippon '91.

Christmas A75

Paintings by Albrecht Durer: 10c, Mary Being Crowned by an Angel. 40c, Mary with the Pear. 60c, Mary in a Halo. $3, Mary with the Crown of Stars and Scepter. No. 690, The Holy Family. No. 691, Mary at the Yard Gate.

1991, Dec. 20 Litho. *Perf. 13½*

686	A75	10c yel green & blk	15	15
687	A75	40c org brown & blk	30	30
688	A75	60c blue & black	45	45
689	A75	$3 brt magenta & blk	2.25	2.25

Souvenir Sheets

690	A75	$6 black	4.50	4.50
691	A75	$6 black	4.50	4.50

A76

A77

Mushrooms: 15c, Marasmius haematocephalus. 40c, Psilocybe cubensis. 60c, Hygrocybe acutoconica. 75c, Hygrocybe occidentalis. $1, Boletellus cubensis. $2, Gymnopilus chrysopellus. $4, Cantharellus cinnabarinus. $5, Chlorophyllum molybdites. No. 700, Our Lady of the Snows (8 mushrooms). No. 701, Our Lady of the Snows (4 mushrooms), diff.

1991, Dec. 20 Litho. *Perf. 14*

692	A76	15c multicolored	15	15
693	A76	40c multicolored	30	30
694	A76	60c multicolored	45	45
695	A76	75c multicolored	55	55
696	A76	$1 multicolored	75	75
697	A76	$2 multicolored	1.50	1.50
698	A76	$4 multicolored	3.00	3.00
699	A76	$5 multicolored	3.75	3.75
		Nos. 692-699 (8)	10.45	10.45

Souvenir Sheet

700	A76	$6 multicolored	4.50	4.50
701	A76	$6 multicolored	4.50	4.50

Queen Elizabeth II's Accession to the Throne, 40th Anniv.

Common Design Type

1992, Feb. 26 Litho. *Perf. 14*

702	CD348	10c multicolored	15	15
703	CD348	40c multicolored	30	30
704	CD348	$1 multicolored	75	75
705	CD348	$5 multicolored	3.75	3.75

Souvenir Sheets

706	CD348	$6 Queen, people on beach	4.50	4.50
707	CD348	$6 Queen, seashell	4.50	4.50

1992, May 7 Litho. *Perf. 14*

Gold medalists: 20c, Monique Knol, France, cycling. 25c, Roger Kingdom, US, 110-meter hurdles. 50c, Yugoslavia, water polo. 80c, Anja Fichtel, West Germany, foil. $1, Said Aouita, Morocco, 5000-meters. $1.50, Yuri Sedykh, USSR, hammer throw. $3, Yelena Shushunova, USSR, gymnastics. $5, Vladimir Artemov, USSR, gymnastics. No. 716, Florence Griffith-Joyner, US, 100-meter dash. No. 717, Naim Suleymanoglu, Turkey, weight lifting.

708	A77	20c multicolored	15	15
709	A77	25c multicolored	18	18
710	A77	50c multicolored	38	38
711	A77	80c multicolored	60	60
712	A77	$1 multicolored	75	75
713	A77	$1.50 multicolored	1.15	1.15
714	A77	$3 multicolored	2.25	2.25
715	A77	$5 multicolored	3.75	3.75
		Nos. 708-715 (8)	9.21	9.21

Souvenir Sheets

716	A77	$6 multicolored	4.50	4.50
717	A77	$6 multicolored	4.50	4.50

1992 Summer Olympics, Barcelona. All athletes except those on $1 and $1.50 won gold medals in 1988. No. 715 incorrectly spelled "Valimir."

Spanish Art — A78

Designs: 20c, Landscape, by Mariano Fortuny, vert. 25c, Dona Juana la Loca, by Francisco Pradilla Ortiz. 50c, Idyl, by Fortuny, vert. 80c, Old Man in the Sun, by Fortuny, vert. $1, $2, The Painter's Children in the Japanese Salon (different details), vert., by Fortuny. $3, Still Life (Sea Bream and Oranges), by Luis Eugenio Melendez. $5, Still Life (Box of Sweets, Pastry, and Other Objects), by Melendez, vert. No. 726, Moroccans by Fortuny. No. 727, Bullfight, by Fortuny.

Perf. 13x13½, 13½x13

1992, June 1 Litho.

718	A78	20c multicolored	15	15
719	A78	25c multicolored	18	18
720	A78	50c multicolored	38	38
721	A78	80c multicolored	60	60
722	A78	$1 multicolored	75	75
723	A78	$2 multicolored	1.50	1.50
724	A78	$3 multicolored	2.25	2.25
725	A78	$5 multicolored	3.70	3.70
		Nos. 718-725 (8)	9.51	9.51

Size: 120x95mm

Imperf

726	A78	$6 multicolored	4.50	4.50
727	A78	$6 multicolored	4.50	4.50

Granada '92.

A79

A80

1992, July 6 *Perf. 14*

728	A79	20c Early compass	15	15
729	A79	50c Manatee	38	38
730	A79	80c Green turtle	60	60
731	A79	$1.50 Santa Maria	1.15	1.15
732	A79	$3 Queen Isabella	2.30	2.30
733	A79	$5 Pineapple	3.80	3.80
		Nos. 728-733 (6)	8.38	8.38

Souvenir Sheets

734	A79	$6 Storm petrel, horiz.	4.50	4.50
735	A79	$6 Pepper, horiz.	4.50	4.50

Discovery of America, 500th anniv. World Columbian Stamp Expo '92, Chicago.

1992, Aug. 24 *Perf. 14½*

736	A80	$1 Coming ashore	75	75
737	A80	$2 Natives, ships	1.50	1.50

Discovery of America, 500th anniv. Organization of East Caribbean States.

Wolfgang Amadeus Mozart, Bicent. of Death (in 1991) — A81

1992, Oct. Litho. *Perf. 14*

738	A81	$3 multicolored	2.25	2.25

Souvenir Sheet

739	A81	$6 Don Giovanni	4.50	4.50

Mickey's Portrait Gallery — A82

1992, Nov. 9 Litho. *Perf. 13½x14*

740	A82	10c Minnie Mouse, 1930	15	15
741	A82	15c Mickey Mouse	15	15
742	A82	40c Donald Duck	30	30
743	A82	80c Mickey Mouse, 1930	60	60
744	A82	$1 Daisy Duck	75	75
745	A82	$2 Pluto	1.50	1.50
746	A82	$4 Goofy	3.00	3.00
747	A82	$5 Goofy, 1932	3.75	3.75
		Nos. 740-747 (8)	10.20	10.20

Souvenir Sheet

Perf. 14x13½

748	A82	$6 Plane Crazy	4.50	4.50
749	A82	$6 Mickey, Home Sweet Home, horiz.	4.50	4.50

Christmas A83

Details or entire paintings: 20c, The Virgin and Child Between Two Saints, by Giovanni Bellini. 40c, The Virgin and Child Surrounded by Four Angels, by Master of the Castello Nativity. 50c, Virgin and Child Surrounded by Angels with St. Frediano and St. Augustine, by Fra Filippo Lippi. 80c, The Virgin and Child Between St. Peter and St. Sebastian, by Giovanni Bellini. $1, The Virgin and Child with St. Julian and St. Nicholas of Myra, by Lorenzo Di Credi. $2, Saint Bernardino and a Female Saint Presenting a Donor to Virgin and Child, by Francesco Bissolo. $4, Madonna and Child with Four Cherubs, Ascribed to Barthel Bruyn. $5, The Virgin and Child, by Quentin Metsys. No. 758, The Virgin and Child Surrounded by Two Angels, by Perugino. No. 759, Madonna and Child with the Infant St. John and Archangel Gabriel, by Sandro Botticelli.

1992, Nov. 16 Litho. *Perf. 13½x14*

750	A83	20c multicolored	15	15
751	A83	40c multicolored	30	30
752	A83	50c multicolored	38	38
753	A83	80c multicolored	60	60
754	A83	$1 multicolored	75	75
755	A83	$2 multicolored	1.50	1.50
756	A83	$4 multicolored	2.25	2.25
757	A83	$5 multicolored	3.75	3.75
		Nos. 750-757 (8)	9.68	9.68

Souvenir Sheet

758	A83	$6 multicolored	4.50	4.50
759	A83	$6 multicolored	4.50	4.50

Empire State Building, New York City — A84

1992, Oct. 28 Litho. *Perf. 14*

760	A84	$6 multicolored	4.50	4.50

Postage Stamp Mega Event '92, New York City.

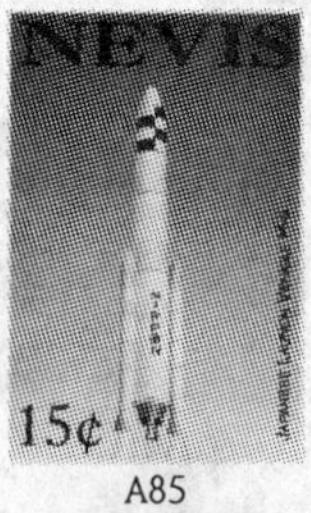

A85

A89

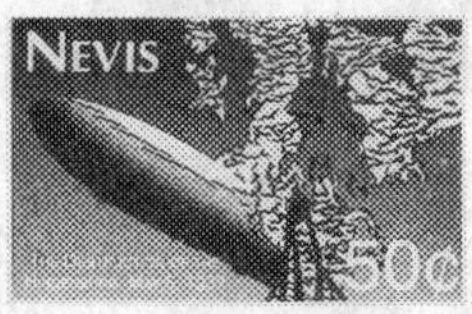

A86

A87

A88

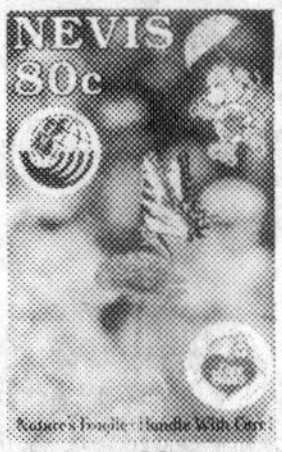

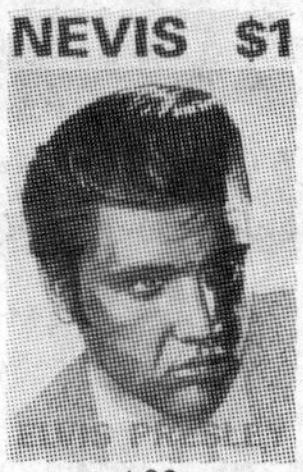

A90 A93

A91

Anniversaries and Events — A92

Designs: 15c, Japanese launch vehicle H-2. 50c, Hindenburg on fire, 1937. 75c, Charles de Gaulle, Konrad Adenauer. No. 764, Horatio Nelson Museum, Nevis. No. 765, Red Cross emblem, Nevis. No. 766, America's Cup yacht Resolute, 1920, vert. No. 767, St. Thomas Anglican Church. No. 768, Care Bear, butterfly and flower. No. 770, Blue whale. No. 771, WHO, ICN, FAO emblems, graph showing population growth. vert. No. 772, Lion, Lion's Intl. emblem. No. 773, John F. Kennedy, Adenauer. No. 774, Lebaudy, first flying machine with mechanical engine. No. 775, Soviet Energia launch vehicle SL-17.

Elvis Presley: No. 776a, Portrait. b, With guitar. c, With microphone.

Details or entire paintings, by Georges de La Tour: No. 777a, The Cheater (left). b, The Cheater (center). c, The Cheater (right). d, St. Joseph, the Carpenter. e, Saint Thomas. f, Adoration of the Shepherds (left). g, Adoration of the Shepherds (right). h, La Madeleine a La Veilleuse.

No. 778, Care Bear, palm tree, vert. No. 779, Manned manuerving unit in space. No. 780, Count Zeppelin taking off from Goppingen for Friedrichshafen. No. 781, Adenauer. No. 782, America's Cup yacht. No. 783, The Angel Departing from the Family of Tobias, by Rembrandt.

1993 Litho. *Perf. 14*

761	A85	15c	multicolored	15	15
762	A86	50c	multicolored	38	38
763	A87	75c	multicolored	58	58
764	A88	80c	multicolored	60	60
765	A88	80c	multicolored	60	60
766	A89	80c	multicolored	60	60
767	A88	80c	multicolored	58	58
768	A90	80c	multicolored	60	60
770	A88	$1	multicolored	75	75
771	A91	$3	multicolored	2.25	2.25
772	A85	$3	multicolored	2.25	2.25
773	A87	$5	multicolored	3.75	3.75
774	A86	$5	multicolored	3.75	3.75
775	A85	$5	multicolored	3.75	3.75

Perf. 14

776	A92	$1	Strip of 3, #a.-c.	2.25	2.25
			Nos. 761-776 (15)	22.84	22.84

Miniature Sheet

Perf. 12

777	A93	$1	Sheet of 8, #a.-h. + label	6.00	6.00

Souvenir Sheets

Perf. 14

778	A90	$2	multicolored	1.50	1.50
779	A85	$6	multicolored	4.50	4.50
780	A86	$6	multicolored	4.50	4.50
781	A87	$6	multicolored	4.50	4.50
782	A89	$6	multicolored	4.50	4.50

Perf. 14½

783	A92	$6	multicolored	4.50	4.50

Intl. Space Year (#761, 775, 779). Count Zeppelin, 75th anniv. of death (#762, 774, 780). Konrad Adenauer, 25th anniv. of death (#763, 773, 781). Anglican Church in Nevis, 150th anniv. Opening of Horatio Nelson Museum (#764). Nevis and St. Kitts Red Cross, 50th anniv. (#765). America's Cup yacht race (#766, 782). (#767). Lions Intl., 75th anniv. (#772). Earth Summit, Rio de Janeiro (#768, 770, 778). Intl. Conference on Nutrition, Rome (#771). Elvis Presley, 15th death anniv. (in 1992) (#776). Louvre Art Museum, bicent. (#777, 783).

Nos. 779-781 have continuous designs.

No. 783 contains one 55x89mm stamp.

Issue dates: No. 767, Mar. Others, Jan. 14.

Tropical Flowers — A94

1993, Mar. 26 Litho. *Perf. 14*

784	A94	10c	Frangipani	15	15
785	A94	25c	Bougainvillea	18	18
786	A94	50c	Allamanda	38	38
787	A94	80c	Anthurium	60	60
788	A94	$1	Ixora	75	75
789	A94	$2	Hibiscus	1.50	1.50
790	A94	$4	Shrimp plant	2.95	2.95
791	A94	$5	Coral vine	3.70	3.70
			Nos. 784-791 (8)	10.21	10.21

Souvenir Sheets

792	A94	$6	Lantana	4.50	4.50
793	A94	$6	Petrea	4.50	4.50

Butterflies A95

1993, May 17 Litho. *Perf. 14*

794	A95	10c	Antillean blue	15	15
795	A95	25c	Cuban crescentspot	18	18
796	A95	50c	Ruddy daggerwing	38	38
797	A95	80c	Little yellow	60	60
798	A95	$1	Atala	75	75
799	A95	$1.50	Orange-barred giant sulphur	1.15	1.15
800	A95	$4	Tropic queen	3.00	3.00
801	A95	$5	Malachite	3.75	3.75
			Nos. 794-801 (8)	9.96	9.96

Souvenir Sheets

802	A95	$6	Polydamas swallowtail	4.50	4.50
a.			Ovptd. in sheet margin	4.50	4.50
803	A95	$6	West Indian Buckeye	4.50	4.50
a.			Ovptd. in sheet margin	4.50	4.50

Location of Hong Kong '94 emblem on Nos. 802a-803a varies.

Nos. 802a, 802b issued Feb. 18, 1994.

Miniature Sheet

Coronation of Queen Elizabeth II, 40th Anniv. — A96

Designs: a, 10c, Official coronation photograph. b, 80c, Queen, wearing Imperial Crown of State. c, $2, Queen, sitting on throne during ceremony. d, $4, Prince Charles kissing mother's hand.

$6, Portrait, "Riding on Worcran in the Great Park at Windsor," by Susan Crawford, 1977.

1993, June 2 Litho. *Perf. 13½x14*

804	A96	Sheet, 2 each #a.-d.	10.50	10.50

Souvenir Sheet

Perf. 14

805	A96	$6	multicolored	4.50	4.50

No. 805 contains one 28x42mm stamp.

Independence of St. Kitts and Nevis, 10th Anniv. — A97

Designs: 25c, Natl. flag, anthem. 80c, Brown pelican, map of St. Kitts and Nevis.

1993, Sept. 19 Litho. *Perf. 13½*

807	A97	25c	multicolored	18	18
808	A97	80c	multicolored	60	60

1994 World Cup Soccer Championships, US — A98

Soccer players: 10c, Garaba, Hungary; Platini, France. 25c, Maradona, Argentina; Bergomi, Italy. 50c, Fernandez, France; Rats, Russia. 80c, Munoz, Spain. $1, Elkjaer, Denmark; Goicoechea, Spain. $2, Coelho, Brazil; Tigana, France. $3, Troglio, Argentina; Alejnikov, Russia. No. 816, $5, Karas, Poland; Costa, Brazil.

No. 817, Belloumi, Algeria. No. 818, Steven, England, vert.

1993, Nov. 9 Litho. *Perf. 14*

809-816	A98	Set of 8	10.00	10.00

Souvenir Sheets

817-818	A98	$5 each	3.75	3.75

Christmas A99

Works by Albrecht Durer: 20c, Annunciation of Mary. 40c, The Nativity. 50c, Holy Family on a Grassy Bank. 80c, The Presentation of Christ in the Temple. $1, Virgin in Glory on the Crescent. $1.60, The Nativity, diff. $3, Madonna and Child. $5, The Presentation of Christ in the Temple (detail).

No. 827, Mary with Child and the Long-Tailed Monkey, by Durer. No. 828, The Rest on the Flight into Egypt, by Fragonard, horiz.

1993, Nov. 30 *Perf. 13*

819-826	A99	Set of 8	10.00	10.00

Souvenir Sheets

827-828	A99	$6 each	4.50	4.50

Tuff Mickey — A100

Disney's Mickey Mouse playing: 10c, Basketball. 50c, Volleyball. $1, Soccer. $5, Boxing.

No. 837, $6, Tug-of-war. No. 838, Ringing carnival bell with hammer, vert.

Disney's Minnie Mouse: 25c, Welcome to my island, vert. 80c, Sunny and snappy, vert. $1.50, Happy hoopin', vert. $4, Jumping for joy, vert.

Perf. 14x13½, 13½x14

1994, Mar. 15 Litho.

829	A100	10c	multicolored	15	15
830	A100	25c	multicolored	18	18
831	A100	50c	multicolored	38	38
832	A100	80c	multicolored	60	60
833	A100	$1	multicolored	75	75
834	A100	$1.50	multicolored	1.10	1.10
835	A100	$4	multicolored	3.00	3.00
836	A100	$5	multicolored	3.75	3.75
			Nos. 829-836 (8)	9.91	9.91

Souvenir Sheets

837	A100	$6	multicolored	4.50	4.50
838	A100	$6	multicolored	4.50	4.50

Hummel Figurines — A101

Designs: 5c, Umbrella Girl. 25c, For Father. 50c, Apple Tree Girl. 80c, March Winds. $1, Have the Sun in Your Heart. $1.60, Blue Belle. $2, Winter Fun. $5, Apple Tree Boy.

1994, Apr. 6 Litho. *Perf. 14*

839-846	A101	Set of 8	8.50	8.50
845a		Souv. sheet of 4, #839, 843-845	3.50	3.50
846a		Souv. sheet of 4, 1 each #840-842, 846	5.00	5.00

Beekeeping A102

Designs: 50c, Beekeeper cutting wild nest of bees. 80c, Group of beekeepers, 1987. $1.60, Decapping frames of honey. $3, Queen bee rearing.

$6, Queen bee, worker bees, woman extracting honey.

1994, June 13 Litho. *Perf. 14*

847-850	A102	Set of 4	4.50	4.50

Souvenir Sheet

851	A102	$6	multicolored	4.50	4.50

Miniature Sheet

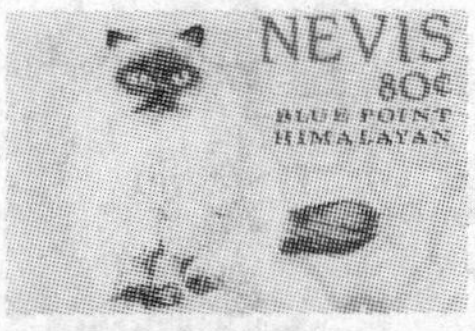

Cats A103

Designs: a, Blue point Himalayan. b, Black & white Persian. c, Cream Persian. d, Red Persian. e, Persian. f, Persian black smoke. g, Chocolate smoke Persian. h, Black Persian.

No. 853, Brown tabby Persian. No. 854, Silver tabby Persian.

1994, July 20

852 A103 80c Sheet of 8, #a.-h.	4.75	4.75

Souvenir Sheets

853-854 A103 $6 each	4.50	4.50

Marine Life A104

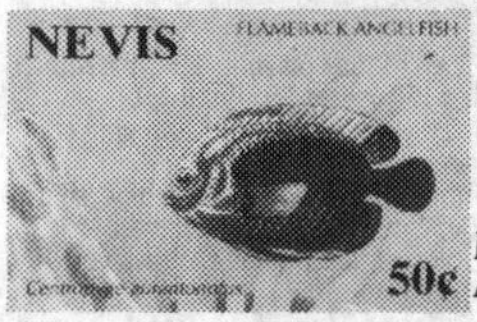

Marine Life A104a

Designs: 10c, Striped burrfish. 25c, Black coral, white & yellow, vert. 40c, Black coral, white & red, vert. 50c, Black coral, yellow & green, vert. 80c, Black coral, spiral-shaped, vert. $1, Blue-striped grunt. $1.60, Blue angelfish. $3, Cocoa damselfish.

No. 864a, Flameback angelfish. b, Reef bass. c, Honey gregory. d, Saddle squirrelfish. e, Cobalt chromis. f, Cleaner goby. g, Slendertail cardinalfish. h, Royal gramma.

No. 865, Sailfish, vert. No. 866, Blue marlin.

1994, July 25 Litho. *Perf. 14*

856-863 A104	Set of 8	5.75	5.75
860a	Strip of 4, #857-860	1.50	1.50
860b	Min. sheet, 3 each #857-860	4.50	4.50

Miniature Sheet of 8

864 A104a 50c #a.-h.	3.00	3.00
i. Ovptd. in sheet margin	3.00	3.00

Souvenir Sheets

865-866 A104a $6 each	4.50	4.50

Nos. 857-860, World Wildlife Fund.

Issued: No. 864i, 8/16/94. Nos. 860b, 864-866, 7/25/94. No. 864i overprinted in sheet margin with PHILAKOREA '94 emblem.

Local Architecture — A105

Designs: 25c, Residence, Barnes Ghaut Village. 50c, House above grocery store, Newcastle. $1, Treasury Building, Charlestown. $5, House above supermarket, Charlestown. $6, Apartment houses.

1994, Aug. 22

867-870 A105 Set of 4	5.00	5.00

Souvenir Sheet

871 A105 $6 multicolored	4.50	4.50

Order of the Caribbean Community — A106

First award recipients: 25c, William Demas, economist, Trinidad and Tobago. 50c, Sir Shridath Ramphal, statesman, Guyana. $1, Derek Walcott, writer, Nobel Laureate, St. Lucia.

1994, Sept. 1

872-874 A106 Set of 3	1.25	1.25

Miniature Sheet of 8

PHILAKOREA '94 — A107

Folding screen, longevity symbols embroidered on silk, Late Choson Dynasty: a, #1. b, #2. c, #3. d, #4. e, #5. f, #6. g, #7. h, #8.

1994 Litho. *Perf. 14*

875 A107 50c #a.-h.	3.00	3.00

OFFICIAL STAMPS

Catalogue values for unused stamps in this section are for Never Hinged items.

Nos. 103-112 Ovptd. "OFFICIAL"

Perf. 14½x14

1980, July 30 Litho. Wmk. 373

O1	A61	15c multicolored	15	15
O2	A61	25c multicolored	15	15
O3	A61	30c multicolored	15	15
O4	A61	40c multicolored	18	18
O5	A61	45c multicolored	22	22
O6	A61	50c multicolored	22	22
O7	A61	55c multicolored	25	25
O8	A61	$1 multicolored	45	45
O9	A61	$5 multicolored	2.25	2.25
O10	A61	$10 multicolored	4.50	4.50
		Nos. O1-O10 (10)	8.52	8.52

Inverted or double overprints exist on some denominations.

Nos. 123-134 Ovptd. "OFFICIAL"

1981, Mar. *Perf. 14*

O11	A9	15c multicolored	15	15
O12	A9	20c multicolored	15	15
O13	A9	25c multicolored	15	15
O14	A9	30c multicolored	15	15
O15	A9	40c multicolored	15	15
O16	A9	45c multicolored	16	16
O17	A9	50c multicolored	18	18
O18	A9	55c multicolored	20	20
O19	A9	$1 multicolored	35	35
O20	A9	$2.50 multicolored	90	90
O21	A9	$5 multicolored	1.90	1.90
O22	A9	$10 multicolored	3.75	3.75
		Nos. O11-O22 (12)	8.19	8.19

Nos. 135-140 Ovptd. or Surcharged "OFFICIAL" in Blue or Black

1983, Feb. 2

O23	A66	45c on $2 #137	32	32
O24	A67	45c on $2 #138	32	32
O25	A66	55c #135	40	40
O26	A67	55c #136	40	40
O27	A66	$1.10 on $5 #139 (Bk)	80	80
O28	A67	$1.10 on $5 #140 (Bk)	80	80
		Nos. O23-O28 (6)	3.04	3.04

Inverted or double overprints exist on some denominations.

Nos. 367-378 Ovptd. "OFFICIAL"

1985, Jan. 2 Wmk. 380

O29	A25	15c multicolored	15	15
O30	A25	20c multicolored	15	15
O31	A25	30c multicolored	16	16
O32	A25	40c multicolored	22	22
O33	A25	50c multicolored	28	28
O34	A25	55c multicolored	30	30
O35	A25	60c multicolored	32	32
O36	A25	75c multicolored	42	42
O37	A25	$1 multicolored	55	55
O38	A25	$3 multicolored	1.65	1.65
O39	A25	$5 multicolored	2.75	2.75
O40	A25	$10 multicolored	5.50	5.50
		Nos. O29-O40 (12)	12.45	12.45

Nos. 640-646, 648-653 Ovptd. "OFFICIAL"

1993 Litho. *Perf. 14*

O41	A71	5c multicolored	15	15
O42	A71	10c multicolored	15	15
O43	A71	15c multicolored	15	15
O44	A71	20c multicolored	15	15
O45	A71	25c multicolored	18	18
O46	A71	40c multicolored	30	30
O47	A71	50c multicolored	38	38
O48	A71	75c multicolored	55	55
O49	A71	80c multicolored	60	60
O50	A71	$1 multicolored	75	75
O51	A71	$3 multicolored	2.25	2.25
O52	A71	$5 multicolored	3.75	3.75
O53	A71	$10 multicolored	7.50	7.50
O54	A71	$20 multicolored	15.00	15.00
		Nos. O41-O54 (14)	31.86	31.86

Dated "1992."

NEW BRUNSWICK

LOCATION — Eastern Canada, bordering on the Bay of Fundy and the Gulf of St. Lawrence.
GOVT. — Former British Province
AREA — 27,985 sq. mi.
POP. — 285,594 (1871)
CAPITAL — Fredericton

At one time a part of Nova Scotia, New Brunswick became a separate province in 1784. Upon joining the Canadian Confederation in 1867 its postage stamps were superseded by those of Canada.

12 Pence = 1 Shilling
100 Cents = 1 Dollar (1860)

Values of New Brunswick Nos. 1-4 vary according to condition. Quotations are for fine copies. Very fine to superb specimens sell at much higher prices, and inferior or poor copies sell at reduced prices, depending on the condition of the individual specimen.

Crown of Great Britain and Heraldic Flowers of the United Kingdom — A1

1851 Unwmk. Engr. *Imperf.*

Blue Paper

1	A1	3p red	1,350.	165.00
a.		3p dark red	1,500.	190.00
b.		Half used as 1½p on cover		*3,500.*
2	A1	6p olive yellow	3,000.	325.00
a.		6p orange yellow	3,000.	350.00
b.		Half used as 3p on cover		*2,750.*
c.		Quarter used as 1½p on cover		*25,000.*
3	A1	1sh brt red violet	11,000.	2,250.
a.		Half used as 6p on cover		
b.		Quarter used as 3p on cover		
4	A1	1sh dull violet	11,500.	3,250.
a.		Half used as 6p on cover		*20,000.*
b.		Quarter used as 3p on cover		*20,000.*

The reprints are on stout white paper. The 3p is printed in orange and the 6p and 1sh in violet black. Value about $100 per set of 3.

Charles Connell — A2

1860 *Perf. 12*

5	A2	5c brown	*3,250.*	

No. 5 was prepared for use but not issued.

Locomotive A3

Victoria A4

A5

A6

Steam and Sailing Ship — A7

Edward VII as Prince of Wales — A8

1860-63 White Paper *Perf. 12*

6	A3	1c red lilac	8.50	8.50
a.		1c brown violet	16.00	14.00
b.		Horiz. pair, imperf. vert.	350.00	
7	A4	2c orange ('63)	4.00	4.00
a.		Vertical pair, imperf. horiz.	400.00	
8	A5	5c yellow green	3.50	3.50
a.		5c blue green	3.50	3.50
b.		5c olive green	50.00	11.00
9	A6	10c vermilion	17.50	15.00
a.		Half used as 5c on cover		600.00
10	A7	12½c blue	20.00	19.00
11	A8	17c black	19.00	18.00

NEWFOUNDLAND

LOCATION — Island in the Atlantic Ocean off the coast of Canada, and Labrador, a part of the mainland
GOVT. — Former British Dominion
AREA — 42,734 sq. mi.
POP. — 321,177 (1945)
CAPITAL — St. John's

Newfoundland was a self-governing Dominion of the British Empire from 1855 to 1933, when it became a Crown Colony. In 1949 it united with Canada.

Values of early Newfoundland stamps vary according to condition. Quotations for Nos. 1-23 are for fine copies. Very fine to superb specimens sell at much higher prices, and inferior or poor copies sell at reduced prices, depending on the condition of the individual specimen.

12 Pence = 1 Shilling
100 Cents = 1 Dollar (1866)

Watermark

Wmk. 224-Coat of Arms

Crown of Great Britain and Heraldic Flowers of the United Kingdom — A1

Rose, Thistle and Shamrock — A3

A2

A4

A5

A6

A7

A8

1857 Unwmk. Engr. *Imperf.*

Thick Porous Wove Paper with Mesh

1	A1	1p brown violet	50.00	*90.00*
2	A2	2p scarlet ver	9,000.	2,750.
3	A3	3p green	250.00	250.00
4	A4	4p scarlet ver	3,750.	1,200.
a.		Half used as 2p on cover		*15,000.*
5	A1	5p brown violet	210.00	250.00
6	A5	6p scarlet ver	8,500.	2,250.
7	A6	6½p scarlet ver	1,500.	*1,650.*
8	A7	8p scarlet ver	190.00	*200.00*
a.		Half used as 4p on cover		3,750.
9	A8	1sh scarlet ver	9,500.	3,500.
a.		Half used as 6p on cover		*13,500.*

1860

Thin to Thick Wove Paper, No Mesh

11	A2	2p orange	175.00	*100.00*
11A	A3	3p green	37.50	80.00
12	A4	4p orange	1,100.	600.00
b.		Half used as 2p on cover		*10,750.*
12A	A1	5p vio brown	55.00	*100.00*
13	A5	6p orange	1,400.	325.00
15	A8	1sh orange	16,500.	3,000.
b.		Half used as 6p on cover		*13,500.*

A 6½p orange exists as a souvenir item.

1861-62

15A	A1	1p vio brown	90.00	*150.00*
16	A1	1p reddish brown	2,500.	
17	A2	2p rose	75.00	*175.00*
18	A4	4p rose	30.00	*70.00*
a.		Half used as 2p on cover		
19	A1	5p reddish brown	30.00	60.00
a.		5p orange brown	30.00	*60.00*
20	A5	6p rose	10.00	*45.00*
a.		Half used as 3p on cover		*5,000.*
21	A6	6½p rose	40.00	*80.00*
22	A7	8p rose	35.00	*105.00*
23	A8	1sh rose	20.00	*105.00*
a.		Half used as 6p on cover		*12,000.*

Some sheets of Nos. 11-23 are known with the papermaker's watermark "STACEY WISE 1858" in large capitals.

No. 16 was prepared but not issued.

False cancellations are found on Nos. 1, 3, 5, 8, 11, 11A, 12A and 17-23.

Forgeries exist of most or all of Nos. 1-23.

Codfish — A9

Harp Seal — A10

Prince Albert — A11

Victoria — A12

Fishing Ship — A13

Victoria — A14

1865-94 ***Perf. 12***

Thin Yellowish Paper (Except No. 29)

24	A9	2c green	37.50	18.00
a.		White paper	25.00	12.50
b.		Half used as 1c on cover		*3,750.*
25	A10	5c brown	275.00	175.00
a.		Half used as 2c on cover		
26	A10	5c black ('68)	150.00	65.00
27	A11	10c black	150.00	50.00
a.		White paper	80.00	22.50
b.		Half used as 5c on cover		*4,000.*
28	A12	12c pale red brn	165.00	110.00
a.		White paper	20.00	19.00
b.		Half used as 6c on cover		*2,250.*
29	A12	12c brn, *white* ('94)	17.50	15.00
30	A13	13c orange	45.00	37.50
31	A14	24c blue	15.00	13.00

See Nos. 38, 40.

Edward VII as Prince of Wales A15

Queen Victoria A16

1868-94

32	A15	1c violet	17.50	17.50
32A	A15	1c brown lilac (re-engr. '71)	24.00	24.00
33	A16	3c ver ('70)	110.00	75.00
34	A16	3c blue ('73)	150.00	12.00
35	A16	6c dull rose ('70)	6.50	6.50
36	A16	6c car lake ('94)	9.50	9.50

In the re-engraved 1c the top of the letters "N" and "F" are about ½mm from the ribbon with "ONE CENT." In No. 32 they are fully 1mm away. There are many small differences in the engraving.

1876-79 ***Rouletted***

37	A15	1c brn lilac ('77)	35.00	14.00
38	A9	2c green ('79)	47.50	22.50
39	A16	3c blue ('77)	125.00	5.50
40	A10	5c blue	100.00	5.50

A17

A19

A18

A20

1880-96 ***Perf. 12***

41	A17	1c violet brown	6.50	5.75
42	A17	1c gray brown	6.50	5.75
43	A17	1c brown ('96)	20.00	20.00
44	A17	1c deep green ('87)	4.50	2.00
a.		1c gray green	6.50	2.75
45	A17	1c green ('97)	4.50	2.00
46	A19	2c yellow green	10.00	8.00
47	A19	2c green ('96)	20.00	12.00
48	A19	2c red org ('87)	8.00	4.00
a.		Imperf., pair	140.00	
49	A18	3c blue	13.00	3.00
51	A18	3c umber brn ('87)	9.00	2.75
52	A18	3c vio brown ('96)	30.00	30.00
53	A20	5c pale blue	150.00	6.00
54	A20	5c dark blue ('87)	65.00	4.50
55	A20	5c bright bl ('94)	10.00	3.00

Newfoundland Dog — A21

Schooner — A22

1887-96

56	A21	½c rose red	4.00	3.00
57	A21	½c orange red ('96)	17.50	17.50
58	A21	½c black ('94)	3.50	3.00
59	A22	10c black	30.00	24.00

Queen Victoria — A23

1890

60	A23	3c slate	4.75	50
a.		3c gray lilac	6.50	50
b.		3c brown lilac	10.00	50
c.		3c lilac	6.50	50
d.		3c slate violet	12.00	65
e.		Vert. pair, imperf. horiz.	400.00	

For surcharges, see Nos. 75-77.

Victoria A24

Cabot (John?) A25

Cape Bonavista — A26

Caribou Hunting — A27

Mining — A28

Logging — A29

Fishing — A30

Cabot's Ship "Matthew" — A31

Willow Ptarmigan A32

Seals A33

Salmon Fishing — A34

Colony Seal — A35

Iceberg off St. John's A36

Henry VII A37

1897, June 24

61	A24	1c deep green	1.40	90
62	A25	2c carmine lake	1.75	90
63	A26	3c ultramarine	2.75	90
64	A27	4c olive green	3.50	1.75
65	A28	5c violet	4.00	1.75
66	A29	6c red brown	3.75	2.00
67	A30	8c red orange	6.25	3.00
68	A31	10c black brown	7.25	3.00
69	A32	12c dark blue	8.00	3.50
70	A33	15c scarlet	8.75	3.25
71	A34	24c gray violet	9.50	4.50
72	A35	30c slate	20.00	12.00
73	A36	35c red	40.00	24.00
74	A37	60c black	6.50	3.50
		Nos. 61-74 (14)	123.40	64.95

400th anniv. of John Cabot's discovery of Newfoundland; 60th year of Victoria's reign. The ship on the 10c was previously used by the American Bank Note Co. as the "Flagship of Columbus" on US No. 232. The portrait on the 2c, intended to be of John Cabot, is said to be a Holbein painting of his son, Sebastian.

For surcharges and overprints, see Nos. 127-130, C2-C4.

No. 60a Surcharged with Bars and

ONE CENT No. 75 **ONE CENT** No. 76 **ONE CENT** No. 77

1897, Oct.

75	A23	1c on 3c gray lilac	10.50	8.50
76	A23	1c on 3c gray lilac	70.00	62.50
77	A23	1c on 3c gray lilac	350.00	325.00

Nos. 75-77 exist with red surcharge and with double surcharge, one in red and one in black, but are not known to have been issued.

Edward VIII as a Child — A38

Victoria — A39

Edward VII as Prince of Wales — A40

Queen Alexandra as Princess of Wales — A41

Queen Mary as Duchess of York — A42

George V as Duke of York — A43

1897-1901 **Engr.**

78	A38	½c olive green	1.25	1.40
79	A39	1c carmine rose	1.75	1.80
80	A39	1c yel grn ('98)	1.00	15
a.		1c deep green	1.40	15
b.		Vert. pair, imperf. horiz.	140.00	
81	A40	2c orange	2.00	2.25
82	A40	2c ver ('98)	3.75	32
83	A41	3c orange ('98)	6.25	32
a.		Vert. pair, imperf. horiz.	275.00	
84	A42	4c violet ('01)	9.00	2.25
85	A43	5c blue ('99)	10.00	1.55
		Nos. 78-85 (8)	35.00	10.04

Imperf., Pairs

78a	A38	½c	200.00
82a	A40	2c	160.00
83b	A41	3c	160.00
84a	A42	4c	225.00

Map of Newfoundland — A44

1908, Sept.

86	A44	2c rose carmine	10.50	90

Guy Issue

James I — A45

Arms of the London and Bristol Co. — A46

John Guy — A47

Lord Bacon — A50

Guy's Ship, the "Endeavour" A48

View of Cupids A49

View of Mosquito — A51

Logging Camp — A52

Edward VII — A54

George V — A55

Paper Mills — A53

SIX CENT TYPES
I- "Z" of "COLONIZATION" reversed.
II- "Z" of normal.

1910, Aug. 15 **Litho.** ***Perf. 12***

87	A45	1c deep green, perf. 12x11	80	55
a.		Perf. 12	1.65	1.10
b.		Perf. 12x14	1.40	80
c.		Horiz. pair, imperf. btwn.	200.00	
e.		Vert. pair, imperf. btwn.	240.00	
88	A46	2c carmine	3.00	50
a.		Perf. 12x14	3.25	35
b.		As "a," horiz. pair, imperf. between	275.00	
c.		Perf. 12x11½	100.00	75.00
89	A47	3c brown olive	5.00	5.00
90	A48	4c dl violet	7.50	5.00
91	A49	5c ultramarine, perf. 14x12	5.50	1.65
a.		Perf. 12	7.50	2.50
92	A50	6c cl, type I	35.00	27.50
92A	A50	6c cl, type II	11.00	11.00
b.		Imperf., pair	240.00	
93	A51	8c pale brown	20.00	20.00
94	A52	9c olive green	20.00	20.00
95	A53	10c vio black	20.00	20.00
96	A54	12c lilac brown	20.00	20.00
a.		Imperf., pair	360.00	
97	A55	15c gray black	25.00	25.00
		Nos. 87-97 (12)	172.80	156.20

Tercentenary of the Colonization of Newfoundland.

On No. 87 printing flaws such as "NFW" and "JANES" exist.

1911 **Engr.** ***Perf. 14***

98	A50	6c brown vio	10.00	9.00
99	A51	8c bister brn	25.00	22.50
100	A52	9c olive grn	20.00	19.00
101	A53	10c violet blk	35.00	35.00
102	A54	12c red brown	30.00	30.00
103	A55	15c slate grn	30.00	30.00
b.		Horiz. pair, imperf. btwn.		
		Nos. 98-103 (6)	150.00	145.50

Imperf., Pairs

98a	A50	6c	275.00
99a	A51	8c	160.00
100a	A52	9c	275.00
101a	A53	10c	275.00
103a	A55	15c	275.00

Royal Family Issue

Queen Mary — A56

George V — A57

Prince of Wales (Edward VIII) — A58

Prince Albert (George VI) — A59

Princess Mary — A60

Prince Henry — A61

Prince George — A62

Prince John — A63

Queen Alexandra — A64

Duke of Connaught — A65

Seal of Colony — A66

1911, June 19 ***Perf. 13½x14, 14***

104	A56	1c yellow grn	1.10	15
105	A57	2c carmine	1.25	15
106	A58	3c red brown	12.00	12.00
107	A59	4c violet	10.50	7.75
108	A60	5c ultra	4.50	85
109	A61	6c black	10.00	10.00
110	A62	8c blue (paper colored through)	30.00	30.00
a.		8c peacock blue	32.50	32.50
111	A63	9c bl violet	12.00	12.00
112	A64	10c dark green	16.00	16.00
113	A65	12c plum	16.00	16.00
114	A66	15c magenta	16.00	16.00
		Nos. 104-114 (11)	129.35	120.90

Coronation of King George V.

Imperf., Pairs

104a	A56	1c	275.00
105a	A57	2c	275.00
108a	A60	5c	200.00
113a	A65	12c	225.00
114a	A66	15c	47.50

Trail of the Caribou Issue

Caribou
A67 A68

1919, Jan. 2 *Perf. 14*

115	A67	1c green	65	15
116	A68	2c scarlet	85	28
117	A67	3c red brown	1.00	15
118	A67	4c violet	1.50	65
119	A68	5c ultramarine	1.75	65
120	A67	6c gray	9.00	7.75
121	A68	8c magenta	6.50	5.75
122	A67	10c dark green	4.25	1.75
123	A68	12c orange	16.00	14.00
124	A67	15c dark blue	15.00	15.00
125	A67	24c bister	15.00	15.00
126	A67	36c olive green	12.50	12.50
		Nos. 115-126 (12)	84.00	73.63

Services of the Newfoundland contingent in WWI.

Each denomination of type A67 is inscribed with the name of a different action in which Newfoundland troops took part.

Exist imperf., value per pair, $175.

For overprint and surcharge see Nos. C1, C5.

No. 72 Surcharged in Black

TWO
CENTS

1920 *Perf. 12*

127	A35	2c on 30c slate	3.50	3.50
a.		Inverted surcharge	275.00	

Nos. 70 and 73 Surcharged in Black

THREE
CENTS

THREE CENTS
Type I - Bars 10½mm apart.
Type II - Bars 13½mm apart.

128	A33	3c on 15c scar (I)	135.00	135.00
a.		Inverted surcharge	*1,000.*	
129	A33	3c on 15c scar (II)	6.00	6.00
130	A36	3c on 35c red	6.00	6.00
a.		Lower bar omitted	100.00	100.00
b.		Inverted surcharge		
c.		"THREE" omitted	*400.00*	

Twin Hills, Tor's Cove — A70

South West Arm, Trinity — A71

War Memorial, St. John's — A72

Humber River — A73

Coast of Trinity — A74

Upper Steadies, Humber River — A75

Quidi Vidi, near St. John's — A76

Caribou Crossing Lake — A77

Humber River Canyon — A78

Shell Bird Island — A79

Mt. Moriah, Bay of Islands — A80

Humber River near Little Rapids — A81

Placentia, from Mt. Pleasant — A82

Topsail Falls near St. John's — A83

1923-24 Engr. *Perf. 14, 13½ x 14*

131	A70	1c gray green	90	15
a.		Booklet pane of 8	240.00	240.00
132	A71	2c carmine	90	15
a.		Booklet pane of 8	100.00	100.00
133	A72	3c brown	1.40	15
134	A73	4c brn violet	1.65	1.10
135	A74	5c ultramarine	1.90	1.25
136	A75	6c gray black	2.50	2.50
137	A76	8c dull violet	1.90	1.75
138	A77	9c slate green	12.00	12.00
139	A78	10c dark violet	2.25	1.25
140	A79	11c olive green	4.00	4.00
141	A80	12c lake	3.75	3.75
142	A81	15c deep blue	4.50	4.25
143	A82	20c red brn ('24)	4.25	3.50
144	A83	24c blk brn ('24)	21.00	21.00
		Nos. 131-144 (14)	62.90	56.80

For surcharge see No. 160.

Imperf., Pairs

131b	A70	1c	140.00
132b	A71	2c	140.00
134a	A73	4c	140.00
135a	A74	5c	140.00
136a	A75	6c	140.00
137a	A76	8c	140.00
138a	A77	9c	140.00
139a	A78	10c	140.00
140a	A79	11c	140.00
141a	A80	12c	140.00
142a	A81	15c	130.00

Map of Newfoundland A84

Steamship "Caribou" A85

Queen Mary, George V — A86

Prince of Wales — A87

Express Train — A88

Newfoundland Hotel, St. John's — A89

Heart's Content — A90

Cabot Tower, St. John's — A91

War Memorial, St. John's — A92

GPO, St. John's — A93

First Nonstop Transatlantic Flight, 1919 — A94

Colonial Building, St. John's — A95

Grand Falls, Labrador — A96

Perf. 14, 13½x13, 13x13½

1928, Jan. 3

145	A84	1c deep green	75	40
146	A85	2c deep carmine	1.10	35
a.		Imperf., pair	175.00	
147	A86	3c brown	1.25	28
148	A87	4c lilac rose	1.65	1.10
149	A88	5c slate green	3.00	2.00
150	A89	6c ultramarine	2.00	1.90
151	A90	8c lt red brown	3.00	2.50
152	A91	9c myrtle green	3.50	3.25
153	A92	10c dark violet	3.50	2.75
154	A93	12c brn carmine	2.50	2.00
155	A91	14c red brown	3.50	2.75
156	A94	15c dark blue	4.75	3.50
157	A95	20c gray black	4.75	2.50
158	A93	28c gray green	12.00	12.00
159	A96	30c olive brown	5.50	3.50
		Nos. 145-159 (15)	52.75	40.78

See Nos. 163-182.

No. 136 Surcharged in Red or Black

THREE
CENTS

Type I - 5mm between "CENTS" and bar.
Type II- 3mm between "CENTS" and bar.

1929 *Perf. 14x13½*

160	A75	3c on 6c gray black (II) (R)	1.90	1.90
a.		Inverted surcharge (II)	500.00	

The stamps with black surcharge, type I and II, were 1st or trial printings, and were not issued. There were 50 copies of each.

Types of 1928 Issue Re-engraved

1c - On No. 145 the lines of the engraving are thinner and the impression is clearer than on No. 163. On the former "C. BAULD" is above "C. NORMAN." On the latter these words are transposed.

2c - On the 1928 stamp the "D" of "NEWFOUNDLAND" is 1mm from the scroll at the right; the flag at the stern is lower than the top of the boat davit. On the 1929 stamp the "D" is ½mm from the scroll and the flag rises above the davits.

3c - On the 1928 stamp the pearls at the top of the crown, the jewels of the tiara and the pillars flanking the portraits are all unshaded. On the reengraved stamp there are small curved lines inside the pearls, the jewels of the tiara are in solid color, and the pillars have vertical shading lines. On the 1928 stamps the tablets with "THREE" and "CENTS" have a background of crossed lines (vertical and horizontal). On the 1929 stamp the background is of horizontal lines only.

4c - On the 1928 stamp the figures "4" have shading of horizontal and diagonal crossed lines. There are six circles at each side of the portrait.

On the 1929 stamp the "4s" have shading of horizontal lines only. There are five roses at each side of the portrait.

5c - The crossbars of the telegraph pole touch the frame at the left on the 1929 stamp but just clear it on the 1928 stamp. In the 1928 issue the foliate ornaments beside and below the figures "5" end in small scrolls and a small spur. These spurs are omitted on the 1929 stamp.

6c - On the re-engraved stamp the columns at right and left of the picture have heavy wavy outlines on the inner sides. There is no period after "JOHNS." The numerals in the lower corners are 1½mm wide instead of 1¼mm.

8c - The impression of the 1928 stamp is clear, that of 1931 is slightly blurred. The 1928 stamp has three horizontal lines above "EIGHT CENTS" and four berries on the laurel branch at the right side. On the 1931 stamp there are two horizontal lines and three berries.

10c - On the re-engraved stamp there is no period after "ST. JOHN'S." The letters of "TEN CENTS" are slightly larger and the numerals "10" slightly smaller than in 1928. Inside the "0" of "10" at the right there are two vertical lines instead of three. The clouds are fainter in 1929 and the cross upheld by the figure on the monument is more distinct. On the 1928 stamp the torch at the left side terminates in a single tongue of flame. On the 1929-30 stamp it terminates in two tongues.

15c - On the 1928 stamp the "N" of "NEWFOUNDLAND" is 1½mm. from the left frame, the "L" of "LEAVING" is under the first "A" of "AIRPLANE" and the apostrophe in "JOHN'S" breaks the first line above it.

On the 1929 stamp the "N" of "NEWFOUNDLAND" is 1mm from the left frame, the "L" of "LEAVING" is below the "T" of "FIRST" and the apostrophe in "JOHN'S" does not touch the line above it.

20c - On the 1928 stamp the points of the "W" of "NEWFOUNDLAND" are truncated. The "O" is wide and nearly round. The columns that form the sides of the frame have a shading of evenly spaced horizontal lines at their inner sides.

On the 1929-31 stamp the points of the "W" form sharp angles. The "O" is narrow and has a small opening. Many lines have been added to the shading on the inner sides of the columns, making it almost solid.

30c - 1928 stamp. Size: 19¼x24½mm. At the outer side of the right column there are three strong and two faint vertical lines. Faint period after "FALLS."

1931 stamp. Size: 19x25mm. At the outer side of the right column there are two strong vertical lines and a fragment of the lower end of a faint one. Clear period after "FALLS." A great many of the small lines of the design have been deepened making the whole stamp appear darker.

1929-31 Unwmk. *Perf. 13½ to 14*

163	A84	1c green	80	25
a.		Double impression	*300.00*	
b.		Imperf. horiz.	145.00	
164	A85	2c deep carmine	80	15
165	A86	3c dp red brown	95	15
166	A87	4c magenta	1.40	60
167	A88	5c slate green	2.00	60
168	A89	6c ultramarine	5.50	4.00
169	A92	10c dark violet	2.75	85
170	A94	15c deep blue ('30)	16.00	14.00
171	A95	20c gray blk ('31)	27.50	11.50
		Nos. 163-171 (9)	57.70	32.10

Imperf., Pairs

163c	A84	1c	110.00
164a	A85	2c	100.00
165a	A86	3c	100.00
166a	A87	4c	100.00

As the watermark 224 does not show on every stamp in the sheet, pairs are found one with and one without watermark. This applies to all stamps with watermark 224.

Types of 1928 Issue
Perf. 13½ to 14

1931 Re-engraved Wmk. 224

172	A84	1c green	1.00	50
a.		Horiz. pair, imperf. btwn.	360.00	
173	A85	2c red	1.50	60
174	A86	3c red brown	1.50	50
175	A87	4c rose	2.00	75
176	A88	5c grnsh gray	5.00	3.50
177	A89	6c ultramarine	10.00	8.25
178	A90	8c lt red brn	10.00	8.25
179	A92	10c dk violet	6.25	3.75
180	A94	15c deep blue	20.00	15.00
181	A95	20c gray black	16.00	4.50
182	A96	30c olive brown	15.00	12.50
		Nos. 172-182 (11)	88.25	58.10
		Set, never hinged	140.00	

Codfish — A97

George V — A98

Queen Mary — A99

Prince of Wales — A100

A101

Princess Elizabeth A102

Salmon Leaping Falls — A103

Newfoundland Dog — A104

Harp Seal Pup — A105

Cape Race — A106

Sealing Fleet — A107

Fishing Fleet Leaving for "The Banks" — A108

FIVE CENT
Die I - Antlers even, or equal in height.
Die II - Antler under "T" higher.

1932-37 Engr. *Perf. 13½, 14*

183	A97	1c green	75	18
a.		Booklet pane of 4, perf. 13	57.50	
184	A97	1c gray black	15	15
a.		Bklt. pane of 4, perf. 13½	40.00	
b.		Booklet pane of 4, perf. 14	47.50	
185	A98	2c rose	75	15
a.		Booklet pane of 4, perf. 13	32.50	
186	A98	2c green	60	15
a.		Bklt. pane of 4, perf. 13½	18.00	
b.		Booklet pane of 4, perf. 14	24.00	
d.		Horiz. pair, imperf. btwn.	160.00	
187	A99	3c orange brn	60	15
a.		Bklt. pane of 4, perf. 13½	40.00	
b.		Booklet pane of 4, perf. 14	47.50	
c.		Booklet pane of 4, perf. 13	57.50	
188	A100	4c deep violet	2.50	85
189	A100	4c rose lake	30	15
190	A101	5c vio brn, perf. 13½ (Die I)	3.75	50
191	A101	5c dp vio, perf. 13½ (Die II)	50	15
a.		5c dp vio, perf. 13½ (Die I)	6.00	60
c.		Horiz. pair, imperf. btwn. (I)	160.00	
192	A102	6c dull blue	5.00	5.00
193	A103	10c olive black	60	40
194	A104	14c int black	1.40	1.10
195	A105	15c magenta	1.40	1.10
196	A106	20c gray green	1.40	45
197	A107	25c gray	1.50	1.00
198	A108	30c ultra	16.00	14.00
199	A108	48c red brn ('37)	5.00	2.50
		Nos. 183-199 (17)	42.20	27.98
		Set, never hinged	65.00	

Two dies were used for 2c green, one for 2c rose.

See Nos. 253-266.

Imperf., Pairs

183b	A97	1c	72.50
184c	A97	1c	32.50
186c	A98	2c	32.50
187d	A99	3c	57.50
189a	A100	4c	47.50
190a	A101	5c	100.00
191b	A101	5c	40.00
192a	A102	6c	100.00
193a	A103	10c	65.00
196a	A106	20c	100.00
197a	A107	25c	100.00
198a	A108	30c	325.00
199a	A108	48c	80.00

Queen Elizabeth when Duchess of York — A109

Corner Brook Paper Mills — A110

Loading Iron Ore at Bell Island — A111

1932

208	A109	7c red brown	70	70
a.		Horiz. pair, imperf. between	350.00	
209	A110	8c orange red	70	55
a.		Imperf., pair	80.00	
210	A111	24c light blue	1.65	1.65
a.		Imperf., pair	100.00	
		Set, never hinged	4.25	

See Nos. 259, 264.

No. C9 Overprinted Bars and

L. & S. Post.

1933, Feb. 9 Wmk. 224 *Perf. 14*

211	AP6	15c brown	6.00	4.75
		Never hinged	7.50	
a.		Pair, one without overprint	1,250.	
b.		Overprint reading up	800.00	

"L. & S." stands for "Land and Sea."

Sir Humphrey Gilbert Issue

Sir Humphrey Gilbert A112

Compton Castle, Home of the Gilbert Family A113

Gilbert Coat of Arms — A114

Eton College — A115

Token from Queen Elizabeth I A116

Sir Humphrey Receiving Royal Patents for Colonization A117

Sir Humphrey's Ships Leaving Plymouth, 1583 — A118

The Ships Arriving at St. John's — A119

Annexation of Newfoundland, Aug. 5, 1583 — A120

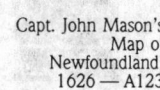

Coat of Arms of England A121

Sir Humphrey on the Deck of the "Squirrel" A122

Capt. John Mason's Map of Newfoundland, 1626 — A123

Queen Elizabeth I A124

Gilbert Statue at Truro A125

Perf. 13½, 14

1933, Aug. 3 Wmk. 224 Engr.

212	A112	1c gray black	50	38
213	A113	2c green	60	38
214	A114	3c yellow brn	85	60
215	A115	4c carmine	85	25
216	A116	5c dull violet	1.10	60
217	A117	7c blue	6.00	6.00
218	A118	8c orange red	3.50	3.50
219	A119	9c ultramarine	4.00	4.00
220	A120	10c red brown	4.00	3.00
221	A121	14c black	8.25	8.00
222	A122	15c claret	7.50	7.50
223	A123	20c deep green	5.00	4.00
224	A124	24c vio brown	9.00	9.00
225	A125	32c gray	9.00	9.00
		Nos. 212-225 (14)	60.15	56.21
		Set, never hinged	110.00	

350th anniv. of annexation of Newfoundland to England, Aug. 5, 1583, by authority of Letters Patent issued by Queen Elizabeth I to Sir Humphrey Gilbert.

Imperf., Pairs

212a	A112	1c	32.50
213a	A113	2c	32.50
214a	A114	3c	125.00
215a	A115	4c	35.00
216a	A116	5c	100.00
219a	A119	9c	100.00
220a	A120	10c	110.00
224a	A124	24c	110.00

Silver Jubilee Issue

Common Design Type

1935, May 6 Wmk. 4 *Perf. 11x12*

226	CD301	4c bright rose	75	45
227	CD301	5c violet	75	60
228	CD301	7c dark blue	1.75	1.75
229	CD301	24c olive green	4.50	4.50
		Set, never hinged	10.00	

Coronation Issue

Common Design Type

1937, May 12 *Perf. 11x11½*

230	CD302	2c deep green	35	35
231	CD302	4c carmine rose	35	25
232	CD302	5c dark violet	60	60
		Set, never hinged	1.75	

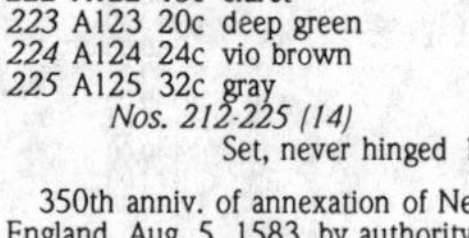
Codfish A126

Map of Newfoundland — A127

Caribou A128

Corner Brook Paper Mills A129

Salmon A130

Newfoundland Dog — A131

Harp Seal Pup — A132

Cape Race A133

Loading Iron Ore at Bell Island A134

Sealing Fleet A135

Fishing Fleet Leaving for "The Banks" A136

Two dies of the 3c
Die I - Fine impression.
Die II - Coarse impression.

Perf. 13, 13½, 14

1937, May 12 Wmk. 224

233	A126	1c gray black	25	15
234	A127	3c org brn, die I	1.00	38
a.		Die II	75	25
b.		Vert. or horiz. pair, imperf. btwn. (II)	200.00	
235	A128	7c blue	1.10	85
236	A129	8c orange red	1.10	85
a.		Imperf., pair	140.00	
237	A130	10c olive gray	2.00	1.65
a.		Double impression		
238	A131	14c black	1.50	1.50
239	A132	15c rose lake	1.75	1.50
a.		Vert. pair, imperf. between	160.00	
240	A133	20c green	1.40	1.10
241	A134	24c turq blue	1.90	1.75
a.		Vert. pair, imperf. between	250.00	
242	A135	25c gray	1.90	1.65
243	A136	48c dark violet	2.00	1.90
		Nos. 233-243 (11)	15.90	13.28
		Set, never hinged	25.00	

Princess Elizabeth — A139

Designs: 2c, King George VI. 3c, Queen Elizabeth. 7c, Queen Mother Mary.

1938, May 12 *Perf. 13½*

245 A139 2c green	1.40	15
246 A139 3c dark carmine	1.40	20
247 A139 4c light blue	1.40	15
248 A139 7c dark ultra	1.10	75
Set, never hinged	7.00	

See Nos. 254-256, 258, 269.

George VI and Queen Elizabeth A141

1939, June 17 **Unwmk.**

249 A141 5c violet blue	55	55
Never hinged	65	

Visit of King George and Queen Elizabeth.

No. 249 Surcharged in Brown or Red

2

CENTS

1939, Nov. 20

250 A141 2c on 5c vio blue (Br)	60	60
251 A141 4c on 5c vio blue (R)	50	50
Set, never hinged	1.40	

There are many varieties of broken letters and figures in the settings of the surcharges.

Sir Wilfred Grenfell and "Strathcona II" A142

1941, Dec. 1 **Engr.** *Perf. 12*

252 A142 5c dull blue	22	20
Never hinged	25	

Grenfell Mission, 50th anniv.

Types of 1931-38

1941-44 **Wmk. 224** *Perf. 12½*

253 A97 1c dark gray	15	15
254 A139 2c deep green	15	15
255 A139 3c rose carmine	18	15
256 A139 4c blue	35	15
257 A101 5c violet (Die I)	35	15
258 A139 7c vio blue ('42)	55	55
259 A110 8c red	42	35
260 A103 10c brownish blk	42	30
261 A104 14c black	80	65
262 A105 15c pale rose vio	85	75
263 A106 20c green	75	60
264 A111 24c deep blue	1.00	85
265 A107 25c slate	1.00	85
266 A108 48c red brown ('44)	1.50	1.00
Nos. 253-266 (14)	8.47	6.65
Set, never hinged	14.00	

Nos. 254 and 255 are re-engraved.

Memorial University College — A143

1943, Jan. 2 **Unwmk.** **Engr.** *Perf. 12*

267 A143 30c carmine	80	75
Never hinged	1.10	

No. 267 Surcharged in Black

TWO CENTS

1946, Mar. 23

268 A143 2c on 30c carmine	18	18
Never hinged	25	

Princess Elizabeth A144

Deck of the Matthew A145

Perf. 12½

1947, Apr. 21 **Wmk. 224** **Engr.**

269 A144 4c light blue	20	15
Never hinged	25	

Princess Elizabeth's 21st birthday.

1947, June 23

270 A145 5c rose violet	20	15
Never hinged	25	
a. Horiz. pair, imperf. between		

Cabot's arrival off Cape Bonavista, 450th anniv.

AIR POST STAMPS

No. 117 Overprinted in Black

FIRST TRANS-ATLANTIC AIR POST, April, 1919.

1919, Apr. 12 **Unwmk.** *Perf. 14*

C1 A67 3c red brown	*14,000.*	*8,000.*

No. 70 Surcharged in Black

Trans-Atlantic AIR POST, 1919. ONE DOLLAR.

1919, June 9 *Perf. 12*

C2 A33 $1 on 15c scarlet	90.00	90.00
a. Without comma after "Post"	125.00	110.00
b. As "a," without period after "1919"	250.00	250.00

No. 73 Overprinted in Black

AIR MAIL to Halifax, N.S. 1921

1921, Nov. 7

C3 A36 35c red	82.50	82.50
a. With period after "1921"	95.00	95.00
b. Inverted overprint	*2,750.*	
c. As "a," inverted	*2,800.*	

No. C3 was printed in sheets of twenty-five, containing varieties of wide and narrow space between "AIR" and "MAIL," date shifted to right, and with and without period after date.

No. 74 Overprinted in Red

Air Mail DE PINEDO 1927

1927, May 21

C4 A37 60c black	*25,000.*	*6,250.*

No. 126 Surcharged in Black

Trans-Atlantic AIR MAIL By B. M. "Columbia" September 1930 Fifty Cents

1930, Sept. 25 *Perf. 14*

C5 A67 50c on 36c ol grn	*4,000.*	*4,000.*

Dog Sled and Airplane — AP6

First Transatlantic Mail Airplane and Packet Ship — AP7

Routes of Historic Transatlantic Flights — AP8

1931, Jan. 2 **Engr.** **Unwmk.**

C6 AP6 15c brown	7.00	7.00
a. Horiz. or vert. pair, imperf. btwn.	500.00	
C7 AP7 50c green	12.00	12.00
a. Horiz. or vert. pair, imperf. btwn.	500.00	500.00
C8 AP8 $1 blue	40.00	40.00
a. Horiz. or vert. pair, imperf. btwn.	500.00	

1931 **Wmk. 224**

C9 AP6 15c brown	4.50	4.50
a. Horiz. pair, imperf. btwn.	450.00	
b. Vert. pair, imperf. btwn.	600.00	
c. Imperf., pair		
C10 AP7 50c green	18.00	18.00
a. Horiz. or vert. pair, imperf. between	400.00	
b. Imperf. vert., pair	400.00	
C11 AP8 $1 blue	52.50	47.50
a. Vert. pair, imperf. btwn.	450.00	
b. Imperf. vert., pair		
c. Horiz. pair, imperf. btwn.	450.00	
d. Vert. pair, imperf. horiz.	325.00	

As the watermark 224 does not show on every stamp in the sheet, pairs are found one with and one without watermark.

For overprint, see No. 211. For surcharge, see No. C12.

No. C11 Surcharged in Red

TRANS-ATLANTIC WEST TO EAST Per Dornier DO-X May, 1932. One Dollar and Fifty Cents

1932, May 19

C12 AP8 $1.50 on $1 blue	175.00	175.00
a. Inverted surcharge	*7,500.*	

A stamp of this design was produced in the US in 1932 by a private company under contract with Newfoundland authorities. The government canceled the contract and the stamp was not valid for prepayment of postage.

"Put to Flight" — AP9

"Land of Heart's Delight" AP10

"Spotting the Herd" — AP11

"News from Home" — AP12

"Labrador, The Land of Gold" — AP13

1933, June 9 **Engr.** *Perf. 11½, 14*

C13 AP9 5c lt brown	6.00	6.00
b. Horiz. pair, imperf. btwn.		
C14 AP10 10c yellow	7.50	7.50
C15 AP11 30c blue	16.00	16.00
C16 AP12 60c green	27.50	27.50
C17 AP13 75c bister	27.50	27.50
Nos. C13-C17 (5)	84.50	84.50
Set, never hinged	120.00	

Imperf., Pairs

C13a	AP9	5c	150.00
C14a	AP10	10c	100.00
C15a	AP11	30c	350.00
C16a	AP12	60c	400.00
C17a	AP13	75c	275.00

No. C17 Surcharged in Black

1933 GEN. BALBO FLIGHT. $4.50

1933, July 24 *Perf. 14*

C18 AP13 $4.50 on 75c bister	250.00	250.00
Never hinged	375.00	

Return flight from Chicago to Rome of the squadron of Italian seaplanes under the command of Gen. Italo Balbo.

The inverted surcharge was not regularly issued. The $4.50 on No. C14, 10c yellow, is a proof.

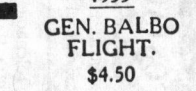

View of St. John's — AP14

1943, June 1 **Unwmk.** *Perf. 12*

C19 AP14 7c bright ultra	30	24
Never hinged	38	

POSTAGE DUE STAMPS

D1

Perf. 10-10½, Compound

1939-49	Litho.	Unwmk.	
J1	D1 1c yellow green	2.00	2.00
a.	Perf. 11 ('49)	2.75	2.75
J2	D1 2c vermilion	2.00	2.00
a.	Perf. 11x9 ('46)	2.75	2.75
J3	D1 3c ultramarine	2.50	2.50
a.	Perf. 11x9 ('49)	3.25	3.25
J4	D1 4c yellow orange	3.50	3.00
a.	Perf. 11x9 ('49)	4.50	4.50
J5	D1 5c pale brown	1.75	1.75
J6	D1 10c dark violet	1.75	1.75
	Nos. J1-J6 (6)	13.50	13.00
	Set, never hinged	20.00	

1949	Wmk. 224	*Perf. 11*	
J7	D1 10c dark violet	6.00	6.00
	Never hinged	8.50	
a.	Vert. pair, imperf. btwn.	175.00	

NOVA SCOTIA

LOCATION — Eastern coast of Canada between the Gulf of St. Lawrence and the Atlantic Ocean
GOVT. — A former British Crown Colony
AREA — 21,428 sq. mi.
POP. — 386,500 (1871)
CAPITAL — Halifax

Nova Scotia joined the Canadian Confederation in 1867 and is now a province of the Dominion. Postage stamps of Canada are used.

12 Pence = 1 Shilling
100 Cents = 1 Dollar (1860)

> Values of Nova Scotia stamps vary according to condition. Quotations for Nos. 1-7 are for fine four margin copies. Very fine to superb specimens sell at much higher prices, and inferior or poor copies sell at reduced prices, depending on the condition of the individual specimen.

Queen Victoria — A1

Crown of Great Britain and Heraldic Flowers of the Empire — A2

1851-53	Unwmk. Engr.	*Imperf.*	
	Blue Paper		
1	A1 1p red brown ('53)	1,250.	275.
a.	Half used as ½p on cover		
2	A2 3p blue	400.	75.
a.	Half used as 1½p on cover		*2,500.*
3	A2 3p dark blue	550.	75.
a.	Half used as 1½p on cover		*3,500.*
4	A2 6p yellow green	2,500.	200.
a.	Half used as 3p on cover		*3,500.*
5	A2 6p dark green	6,000.	450.
a.	Half used as 3p on cover		*3,500.*
6	A2 1sh reddish violet	13,000.	2,000.
a.	Half used as 6p on cover		*30,000.*
7	A2 1sh dull violet	14,000.	2,750.

Reprints are on thin hard white paper. 1p in brown, 3p in blue, 6p dark green, 1sh violet black. Value about $300 per set.

No. 6 was reproduced by the collotype process in a souvenir sheet distributed at the London International Stamp Exhibition 1950.

Queen Victoria — A3

A5

A6

1860-63		*Perf. 12*	
	White or Yellowish Paper		
8	A3 1c black	3.00	2.75
a.	White paper	3.00	2.75
b.	Half used as ½c on cover		*5,000.*
c.	Horiz. pair, imperf. vert.	125.00	
9	A3 2c lilac	3.25	3.00
a.	Yellowish paper	3.25	3.00
b.	Half used as 1c on cover		*2,500.*
10	A3 5c blue	175.00	3.00
a.	Yellowish paper	225.00	3.50
b.	Half used as 2½c on cover		
11	A5 8½c green	2.75	*6.00*
a.	White paper	2.75	*6.00*
12	A5 10c vermilion	3.50	3.50
a.	Yellowish paper	3.25	3.25
b.	Half used as 5c on cover		*2,000.*
13	A6 12½c black	12.00	11.50
a.	White paper	12.00	11.50
	Nos. 8-13 (6)	199.50	29.75

The stamps of Nova Scotia were replaced by those of Canada.

PRINCE EDWARD ISLAND

LOCATION — In the Gulf of St. Lawrence, opposite the provinces of New Brunswick and Nova Scotia
GOVT. — A former British Crown Colony
AREA — 2,184 sq. mi.
POP. — 92,000 (estimated)
CAPITAL — Charlottetown

Originally annexed to Nova Scotia, Prince Edward Island was a separate colony from 1769 to 1873, when it became a part of the Canadian Confederation. Postage stamps of Canada are now used.

12 Pence = 1 Shilling
100 Cents = 1 Dollar (1872)

A1

A2

Queen Victoria — A3

1861, Jan. 1	Unwmk. Typo.	*Perf. 9*	
1	A1 2p dull rose	275.00	100.00
a.	2p deep rose	275.00	100.00
b.	Rouletted		*2,000.*
c.	Horiz. pair, imperf. between	*4,000.*	
d.	Diagonal half used as 1p on cover		*1,500.*
2	A2 3p blue	500.00	225.00
a.	Diagonal half used as 1½p on cover		
b.	Double impression	1,500.	
3	A3 6p yellow green	800.00	350.00

A4

A5

Perf. 11, 11½, 12 and Compound

1862-65			
	White or Yellowish Paper		
4	A4 1p yellow orange	12.00	12.00
a.	1p brown orange	12.00	12.00
b.	Imperf., pair	150.00	
c.	Half used as ½p on cover		*750.00*
5	A1 2p rose	3.50	3.50
a.	Yellowish paper	3.50	3.50
b.	Imperf., pair	75.00	
c.	Horiz. pair, imperf. vert.	125.00	
d.	Vert. pair, imperf. horiz.	125.00	
e.	Diagonal half used as 1p on cover		*1,500.*
f.	"TWC" for "TWO"	24.00	15.00
6	A2 3p blue	5.75	4.75
a.	Yellowish paper	6.50	4.75
b.	Imperf., pair	90.00	
c.	Vert. pair, imperf. horiz.	150.00	
d.	Diagonal half used as 1½p on cover		200.00
7	A3 6p yellow green	30.00	30.00
a.	6p blue green	30.00	30.00
b.	Imperf.		
c.	Diagonal half used as 3p on cover		
8	A5 9p violet	21.00	21.00
a.	Imperf., pair	200.00	200.00
b.	Horiz. pair, imperf. vert.	200.00	
c.	Diagonal half used as 4½p on cover		*1,500.*

Queen Victoria
A6 A7

1868			
9	A6 4p black	4.75	9.50
a.	Yellowish paper	7.50	10.50
b.	Horiz. pair, imperf. vert.	75.00	
c.	Diagonal half used as 2p on cover		*1,000.*
d.	Imperf., pair	60.00	
e.	Horiz. pair, imperf. between	75.00	

1870, June 1	Engr.	*Perf. 12*	
10	A7 4½p brown	18.00	*22.50*

A8

A9

A10

A11

A12

A13

1872, Jan. 1	Typo.	*Perf. 12, 12½*	
11	A8 1c brown orange	3.00	3.00
a.	Imperf., pair	75.00	
12	A9 2c ultra	6.00	12.00
a.	Imperf., pair	125.00	
b.	Diagonal half used as 1c on cover		
13	A10 3c rose	12.00	7.75
a.	Imperf., pair	125.00	
b.	Diagonal half used as 1½c on cover		
c.	Horiz. or vert. pair, imperf. between	175.00	
14	A11 4c green	3.00	*9.00*
a.	Imperf., pair	100.00	
15	A12 6c black	3.00	*9.00*
a.	Horiz. pair, imperf. btwn.	100.00	
b.	Half used as 3c on cover		*600.00*
16	A13 12c violet	3.00	*12.00*
a.	Imperf., pair	100.00	
b.	Half used as 6c on cover		
	Nos. 11-16 (6)	30.00	*52.75*

ST. CHRISTOPHER

LOCATION — Island in the West Indies, southeast of Puerto Rico
GOVT. — A Presidency of the former Leeward Islands Colony
AREA — 68 sq. mi.
POP. — 18,578 (estimated)
CAPITAL — Basseterre

Stamps of St. Christopher were discontinued in 1890 and replaced by those of Leeward Islands. For later issues, inscribed "St. Kitts-Nevis" or "St. Christopher-Nevis-Anguilla," see St. Kitts-Nevis.

12 Pence = 1 Shilling

Queen Victoria — A1

Wmk. Crown and C C (1)

1870, Apr. 1	Typo.	*Perf. 12½*	
1	A1 1p dull rose	47.50	35.00
2	A1 1p lilac rose	16.00	16.00
3	A1 6p green	82.50	13.00

1875-79		*Perf. 14*	
4	A1 1p lilac rose	55.00	12.00
b.	Diagonal half used as ½p on cover		1,050.
5	A1 2½p red brown ('79)	150.00	130.00
6	A1 4p blue ('79)	125.00	15.00
7	A1 6p green	22.50	6.75
a.	Horiz. pair, imperf. vert.		

For surcharges, see Nos. 18-20.

1882-90	Wmk. Crown and C A (2)		
8	A1 ½p green	50	50
9	A1 1p rose	38	50
a.	Half used as ½p on cover		
10	A1 1p lilac rose	450.00	70.00
a.	Diagonal half used as ½p on cover		
11	A1 2½p red brown	225.00	65.00
12	A1 2½p ultra ('84)	2.00	2.50
13	A1 4p blue	350.00	37.50

14 A1 4p gray ('84) 1.00 1.25
15 A1 6p olive brn ('90) 65.00 *325.00*
16 A1 1sh violet ('87) 65.00 65.00

For surcharges, see Nos. 17, 21-23.

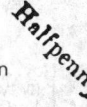

No. 9 Bisected and Handstamp Surcharged in Black

Halfpenny

1885, Mar.
17 A1 ½p on half of 1p 16.00 22.50
c. Unsevered pair 110.00 120.00

The handstamped surcharge exists inverted, double, vertical, unsevered pair, one without surcharge, etc.

No. 7 Surcharged in Black:

ONE PENNY.
Nos. 18, 21

FOUR PENCE
No. 19

4d.
No. 20

1885-86 **Wmk. 1**
18 A1 1p on 6p green ('86) 14.00 25.00
a. Inverted surcharge 6,250.
19 A1 4p on 6p green 37.50 *47.50*
a. Period after "PENCE" 57.50 60.00
b. Double surcharge 1,750.
20 A1 4p on 6p green ('86) 45.00 60.00
a. Without period after "d" 210.00 250.00
b. Double surcharge 1,400. 1,500.

No. 18 with double surcharge is known only with revenue cancellation.

Nos. 8 and 12 Surcharged in Black Like No. 18 or:

ONE PENNY.
No. 22

ONE PENNY.
No. 23

1887-88 **Wmk. 2**
21 A1 1p on ½p green 19.00 27.50
22 A1 1p on 2½p ('88) 35.00 50.00
a. Inverted surcharge *7,000.* *4,500.*
23 A1 1p on 2½p ('88) *10,000.* *10,000.*

Nos. 22-23 may have been printed using the same type. The bar on No. 22 is done by hand. No. 23 probably is a sheet that was missed when the bars were added.

ST. KITTS

LOCATION — West Indies southeast of Puerto Rico
GOVT. — With Nevis, Associated State in British Commonwealth
AREA — 65 sq. mi.
POP. — 35,104 (1980)
CAPITAL — Basseterre

See St. Christopher for stamps used in St. Kitts until 1890. From 1890 until 1903, stamps of the Leeward Islands were used. From 1903 until 1956, stamps of St. Kitts-Nevis and Leeward Islands were used concurrently. See St. Kitts-Nevis for stamps used through June 22, 1980, after which St. Kitts and Nevis pursued separate postal administrations.

100 Cents = 1 Dollar

Catalogue values for all unused stamps in this country are for Never Hinged items.

Watermark

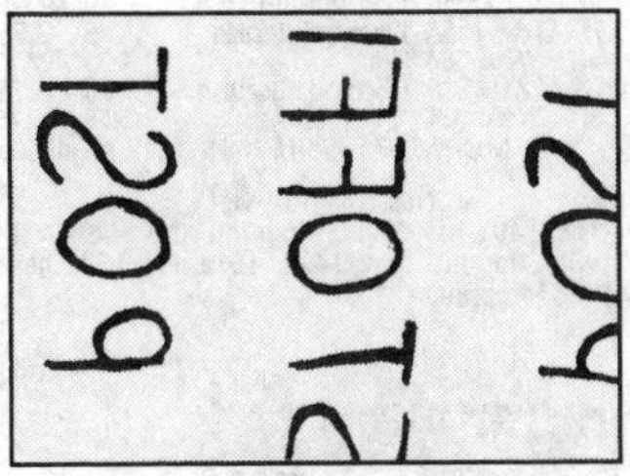

Wmk. 380- "POST OFFICE"

St. Kitts-Nevis Nos. 357-369 Ovptd.

St. Kitts

Perf. 14½x14
1980, June 23 **Litho.** **Wmk. 373**
25 A61 5c multicolored 15 15
26 A61 10c multicolored 15 15
27 A61 12c multicolored 15 15
28 A61 15c multicolored 15 15
29 A61 25c multicolored 20 20
30 A61 30c multicolored 22 22
31 A61 40c multicolored 30 30
32 A61 45c multicolored 35 35
33 A61 50c multicolored 38 38
34 A61 55c multicolored 42 42
35 A61 $1 multicolored 75 75
36 A61 $5 multicolored 3.75 3.75
37 A61 $10 multicolored 7.50 7.50
Nos. 25-37 (13) 14.47 14.47

All but 12c, 45c, 50c, exist unwatermarked. Same values.

Ships — A2

1980, Aug. 8 *Perf. 13½*
38 A2 4c HMS *Vanguard*, 1762 15 15
39 A2 10c HMS *Boreas*, 1787 15 15
40 A2 30c HMS *Druid*, 1827 18 18
41 A2 55c HMS *Winchester*, 1831 35 35
42 A2 $1.50 *Philosopher*, 1857 95 95
43 A2 $2 S.S. *Contractor*, 1930 1.25 1.25
Nos. 38-43 (6) 3.03 3.03

Nos. 38-43 not issued without overprint.

Queen Mother, 80th Birthday — A3

1980, Sept. 4 *Perf. 14*
44 A3 $2 multicolored 1.00 1.00

Christmas A4

1980, Nov. 10 *Perf. 14½*
45 A4 5c Magi following star 15 15
46 A4 15c Shepherds, star 15 15
47 A4 30c Bethlehem, star 16 16
48 A4 $4 Adoration of the Magi 2.25 2.25

Birds — A5

Military Uniforms — A6

1981 **Wmk. 373** *Perf. 13½x14*
49 A5 1c Frigatebird 15 15
50 A5 4c Rusty-tailed flycatcher 15 15
51 A5 5c Purple-throated carib 15 15
52 A5 6c Burrowing owl 15 15
53 A5 8c Purple martin 15 15
54 A5 10c Yellow-crowned night heron 15 15

Perf. 14
Size: 38x25mm
55 A5 15c Bananaquit 15 15
56 A5 20c Scaly-breasted thrasher 15 15
57 A5 25c Grey kingbird 16 16
58 A5 30c Green-throated carib 18 18
59 A5 40c Ruddy turnstone 24 24
60 A5 45c Black-faced grassquit 28 28
61 A5 50c Cattle egret 30 30
62 A5 55c Brown pelican 32 32
63 A5 $1 Lesser Antillean bullfinch 60 60
64 A5 $2.50 Zenaida dove 1.50 1.50
65 A5 $5 Sparrow hawk 3.00 3.00
66 A5 $10 Antillean crested hummingbird 6.00 6.00
Nos. 49-66 (18) 13.78 13.78

Issue dates: Nos. 51, 54-66, Feb. 5. Others, May 30. Also exist with "1982" imprint.
For overprints, see Nos. 112-122.

1981-83 *Perf. 14½*

Foot Regiments: 5c, Battalion Company sergeant, 3rd Regiment, c. 1801. 15c, Light Company private, 15th Regiment, c. 1814. No. 69, Battalion Company officer, 45th Regiment, 1796-7. No. 70, Officer, 15th Regiment, c. 1780. No. 71, Officer, 9th Regiment, 1790. No. 72, Light Company officer, 5th Regiment, c. 1822. No. 73, Grenadier, 38th Regiment, 1751. No. 74, Battalion Company officer, 11th Regiment, c. 1804.

67 A6 5c multi 15 15
68 A6 15c multi ('83) 15 15
69 A6 30c multi 18 18
70 A6 30c multi ('83) 18 18
71 A6 55c multi 35 35
72 A6 55c multi ('83) 35 35
73 A6 $2.50 multi 1.50 1.50
74 A6 $2.50 multi ('83) 1.50 1.50
Nos. 67-74 (8) 4.36 4.36

Issue dates: 5c, Nos. 69, 71 and 73, Mar. 5, 1981. Others, May 25, 1983.

Prince Charles, Lady Diana, Royal Yacht Charlotte A6a

Prince Charles and Lady Diana — A6b

Illustration A6b is greatly reduced.

1981, June 23 *Perf. 14*
75 A6a 55c Saudadoes 38 38
76 A6b 55c Couple 38 38
a. Bklt. pane of 4, perf. 12½x12, unwmkd. 2.00
77 A6a $2.50 The Royal George 1.65 1.65
78 A6b $2.50 like 55c 1.65 1.65
a. Bklt. pane of 2, perf. 12½x12, unwmkd. 4.00
79 A6a $4 HMY Britannia 2.75 2.75
80 A6b $4 like 55c 2.75 2.75
Nos. 75-80 (6) 9.56 9.56

Souvenir Sheet
1981, Dec. 14 *Perf. 12½x12*
81 A6b $5 like 55c 6.00 6.00

Wedding of Prince Charles and Lady Diana Spencer. Nos. 76a, 78a issued Nov. 19, 1981.

Natl. Girl Guide Movement, 50th Anniv. — A7

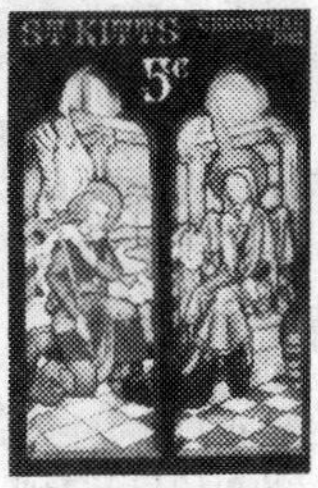

Christmas — A8

Designs: 5c, Miriam Pickard, 1st Guide commissioner. 30c, Lady Baden-Powell's visit, 1964. 55c, Visit of Princess Alice, 1960. $2, Thinking-Day Parade, 1980s.

1981, Sept. 21
82 A7 5c multicolored 15 15
83 A7 30c multicolored 18 18
84 A7 55c multicolored 35 35
85 A7 $2 multicolored 1.25 1.25

1981, Nov. 30

Stained-glass windows.

86 A8 5c Annunciation 15 15
87 A8 30c Nativity, baptism 18 18
88 A8 55c Last supper, crucifixion 35 35
89 A8 $3 Appearance before Apostles, ascension to heaven 1.90 1.90

Brimstone Hill Seige, Bicent. A9

1982, Mar. 15
90 A9 15c Adm. Samuel Hood 15 15
91 A9 55c Marquis de Bouille 48 48

Souvenir Sheet
92 A9 $5 Battle scene 3.25 3.25

No. 92 has multicolored margin picturing battle scene. Size: 96x71mm.

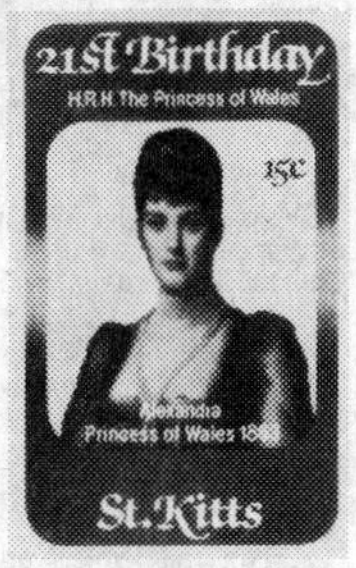

21st Birthday of Princess Diana, July 1 — A10

Designs: 15c, Alexandra of Denmark, Princess of Wales, 1863. 55c, Paternal arms of Alexandra. $6, Diana.

1982, June 22 *Perf. 13½x14*
93 A10 15c multicolored 15 15
94 A10 55c multicolored 32 32
95 A10 $6 multicolored 3.50 3.50

Nos. 93-95 Ovptd. ROYAL BABY

1982, July 12
96 A10 15c multicolored 15 15
97 A10 55c multicolored 32 32
98 A10 $6 multicolored 3.50 3.50

Birth of Prince William of Wales.

Scouting, 75th Anniv. — A11

Merit badges.

1982, Aug. 18 *Perf. 14x13½*

99	A11	5c	Nature	15	15
100	A11	55c	Rescue	35	35
101	A11	$2	First aid	1.25	1.25

Christmas — A12

Children's drawings.

1982, Oct. 20

102	A12	5c	shown	15	15
103	A12	55c	Nativity	32	32
104	A12	$1.10	Three Kings	65	65
105	A12	$3	Annunciation	1.75	1.75

Commonwealth Day
Common Design Type

Designs: 55c, Cruise ship Stella Oceanis docked. $2, RMS Queen Elizabeth 2 anchored in harbor off St. Kitts.

1983, Mar. 14 *Perf. 14*

106	CD334	55c	multicolored	35	35
107	CC334	$2	multicolored	1.25	1.25

Boys' Brigade, Cent. — A14

Designs: 10c, Sir William Smith, founder. 45c, Brigade members outside Sandy Point Methodist Church. 50c, Drummers. $3, Badge.

1983, July 27

108	A14	10c	multicolored	15	15
109	A14	45c	multicolored	30	30
110	A14	50c	multicolored	32	32
111	A14	$3	multicolored	1.90	1.90

Nos. 51, 55-59 and 62-66 Ovptd.

INDEPENDENCE 1983
a

INDEPENDENCE 1983
b

1983, Sept. 19

112	A5(a)	5c	multicolored	15	15
a.			Local overprint	8.25	4.25
113	A5(b)	15c	multicolored	15	15
114	A5(b)	20c	multicolored	15	15
115	A5(b)	25c	multicolored	16	16
116	A5(b)	30c	multicolored	18	18
117	A5(b)	40c	multicolored	25	25
118	A5(b)	55c	multicolored	35	35
119	A5(b)	$1	multicolored	60	60
120	A5(b)	$2.50	multicolored	1.65	1.65
121	A5(b)	$5	multicolored	3.00	3.00
122	A5(b)	$10	multicolored	6.25	6.25
			Nos. 112-122 (11)	12.89	12.89

Nos. 113-122 have "1982" imprint. Nos. 113, 116, 118-122 exist without imprint. No. 112 is without imprint. No. 112 with imprint is twice the value.

No. 112a has serifed letters and reads down on imprinted stamp. Exists reading up and without imprint.

Manned Flight Bicent. A15

Designs: 10c, *Montgolfiere*, 1783, vert. 45c, Sikorsky *Russian Knight*, 1913. 50c, Lockheed TriStar. $2.50, Bell XS-1, 1947.

1983, Sept. 28 **Wmk. 380**

123	A15	10c	multicolored	15	15
124	A15	45c	multicolored	30	30
125	A15	50c	multicolored	32	32
126	A15	$2.50	multicolored	1.65	1.65
a.			Souvenir sheet of 4, Nos. 123-126	2.40	2.40

1st Flight of a 4-engine aircraft, May 1913 (45c); 1st manned supersonic aircraft, 1947 ($2.50).

Christmas A16

1983, Nov. 7

127	A16	15c	shown	15	15
128	A16	30c	Shepherds	22	22
129	A16	55c	Mary, Joseph	42	42
130	A16	$2	Nativity	1.50	1.50
a.			Souvenir sheet of 4, #127-130	2.30	2.30

Batik Art A17

1984-85

131	A17	15c	Country bus	15	15
132	A17	40c	Donkey cart	20	20
133	A17	45c	Parrot, vert.	24	24
134	A17	50c	Man under palm tree, vert.	25	25
135	A17	60c	Rum shop, cyclist	30	30
136	A17	$1.50	Fruit seller, vert.	80	80
137	A17	$3	Butterflies, vert.	1.50	1.50
138	A17	$3	S.V. Polynesia	1.50	1.50
			Nos. 131-138 (8)	4.94	4.94

Issue dates: 15c, 40c, 60c, No. 138, Feb. 6, 1985. Others, Jan. 30, 1984.

Marine Life — A18

1984, July 4

139	A18	5c	Cushion star	15	15
140	A18	10c	Rough file shell	15	15
a.			Wmk. 384 ('86)	15	15
141	A18	15c	Red-lined cleaning shrimp	15	15
142	A18	20c	Bristleworm	15	15
143	A18	25c	Flamingo tongue	15	15
144	A18	30c	Christmas tree worm	16	16
145	A18	40c	Pink-tipped anemone	22	22
146	A18	50c	Smallmouth grunt	28	28
147	A18	60c	Glasseye snapper	35	35
a.			Wmk. 384 ('88)	35	35
148	A18	75c	Reef squirrelfish	42	42
149	A18	$1	Sea fans, flamefish	55	55
150	A18	$2.50	Reef butter-flyfish	1.40	1.40
151	A18	$5	Black soldierfish	2.75	2.75
a.			Wmk. 384 ('88)	2.75	2.75
152	A18	$10	Cocoa damselfish	5.75	5.75
a.			Wmk. 384 ('88)	5.75	5.75
			Nos. 139-152 (14)	12.63	12.63

Nos. 149-152 vert.

No. 140a has "1986" imprint; also exists with "1988" imprint. Nos. 147a, 151a and 152a have "1988" imprint.

4-H in St. Kitts, 25th Anniv. A19

1984, Aug. 15

153	A19	30c	Agriculture	20	20
154	A19	55c	Animal husbandry	38	38
155	A19	$1.10	Pledge, flag, youths	75	75
156	A19	$3	Parade	2.00	2.00

1st Anniv. of Independence — A20

Designs: 15c, Construction of Royal St. Kitts Hotel. 30c, Folk dancers. $1.10, O Land of Beauty, vert. $3, Sea, palm trees, map, vert.

1984, Sept. 18

157	A20	15c	multicolored	15	15
158	A20	30c	multicolored	20	20
159	A20	$1.10	multicolored	80	80
160	A20	$3	multicolored	2.25	2.25

Christmas A21

1984, Nov. 1

161	A21	15c	Opening gifts	15	15
162	A21	60c	Caroling	42	42
163	A21	$1	Nativity	70	70
164	A21	$2	Leaving church	1.40	1.40

Ships A22

1985, Mar. 27 *Perf. 13½x14*

165	A22	40c	Tropic Jade	28	28
166	A22	$1.20	Atlantic Clipper	85	85
167	A22	$2	M.V. Cunard Countess	1.40	1.40
168	A22	$2	Mandalay	1.40	1.40

Mt. Olive Masonic Lodge, 150th Anniv. — A23

Christmas — A24

Designs: 15c, James Derrick Cardin (1871-1954). 75c, Lodge banner. $1.20, Compass, Bible, square, horiz. $3, Charter, 1835.

1985, Nov. 9 *Perf. 15*

169	A23	15c	multicolored	15	15
170	A23	75c	multicolored	55	55
171	A23	$1.20	multicolored	90	90
172	A23	$3	multicolored	2.25	2.25

1985, Nov. 27 **Unwmk.**

173	A24	10c	Map of St. Kitts	15	15
174	A24	40c	Golden Hind	30	30
175	A24	60c	Sir Francis Drake	45	45
176	A24	$3	Drake's shield of arms	2.25	2.25

Visit of Sir Francis Drake to St. Kitts, 400th anniv.

Queen Elizabeth II, 60th Birthday — A25

Designs: 10c, With Prince Philip. 20c, Walking with government officials. 40c, Riding horse in parade. $3, Portrait.

1986, July 9 *Perf. 14*

177	A25	10c	multicolored	15	15
178	A25	20c	multicolored	15	15
179	A25	40c	multicolored	30	30
180	A25	$3	multicolored	2.25	2.25

For overprints, see Nos. 185-188.

Royal Wedding Issue, 1986
Common Design Type

Designs: 15c, Prince Andrew and Sarah Ferguson, formal engagement announcement. $2.50, Prince Andrew in military dress uniform.

Perf. 14½x14

1986, July 23 **Wmk. 384**

181	CD338	15c	multicolored	15	15
182	CD338	$2.50	multicolored	1.85	1.85

Agriculture Exhibition — A26

Children's drawings: 15c, Family farm, by Kevin Tatem, age 14. $1.20, Striving for growth, by Alister Williams, age 19.

1986, Sept. 18 *Perf. 13½x14*

183	A26	15c	multicolored	15	15
184	A26	$1.20	multicolored	90	90

Nos. 177-180 Ovptd. "40th ANNIVERSARY / U.N. WEEK 19-26 OCT." in Gold

1986, Oct. 22 **Unwmk.** *Perf. 14*

185	A25	10c	multicolored	15	15
186	A25	20c	multicolored	15	15
187	A25	40c	multicolored	30	30
188	A25	$3	multicolored	2.25	2.25

World Wildlife Fund — A27

Various green monkeys, Cercopithecus aethiops sabaeus.

1986, Dec. 1
189 A27 15c multi 15 15
190 A27 20c multi, diff. 16 16
191 A27 60c multi, diff. 48 48
192 A27 $1 multi, diff. 80 80

Auguste Bartholdi — A28

Statue of Liberty, Cent. — A29

Perf. 14x14½, 14½x14
1986, Dec. 17
193 A28 40c shown 32 32
194 A28 60c Torch, head, 1876-78 48 48
195 A28 $1.50 Warship Isere, France 1.20 1.20
196 A28 $3 Delivering statue, 1884 2.40 2.40

Souvenir Sheet
197 A29 $3.50 Head 2.75 2.75

Nos. 194-195 horiz.

British and French Uniforms — A30

Sugar Cane Industry — A31

Designs: No. 198, Officer, East Norfolk Regiment, 1792. No. 199, Officer, De Neustrie Regiment, 1779. No. 200, Sergeant, Third Foot the Buffs, 1801. No. 201, Artillery officer, 1812. No. 202, Private, Light Company, 5th Foot Regiment, 1778. No. 203, Grenadier, Line Infantry, 1796.

1987, Feb. 25 ***Perf. 14½***
198 A30 15c multicolored 15 15
199 A30 15c multicolored 15 15
200 A30 40c multicolored 30 30
201 A30 40c multicolored 30 30
202 A30 $2 multicolored 1.50 1.50
203 A30 $2 multicolored 1.50 1.50
a. Souvenir sheet of 6, #198-203 4.00 4.00
Nos. 198-203 (6) 3.90 3.90

1987, Apr. 15 ***Perf. 14***

Designs: No. 204a, Warehouse. b, Barns. c, Steam emitted by processing plant. d, Processing plant. e, Field hands.
No. 205a, Locomotive. b, Locomotive and tender. c, Open cars. d, Empty and loaded cars, tractor. e, Loading sugar cane.

204 Strip of 5 60 60
a.-e. A31 15c any single 15 15
205 Strip of 5 3.00 3.00
a.-e. A31 75c any single 60 60

Visiting Aircraft A32

Perf. 14x14½
1987, June 24 **Wmk. 373**
206 A32 40c L-1011-500 Tri-Star 30 30
207 A32 60c BAe Super 748 45 45
208 A32 $1.20 DHC-6 Twin Otter 90 90
209 A32 $3 Aerospatiale ATR-42 2.25 2.25

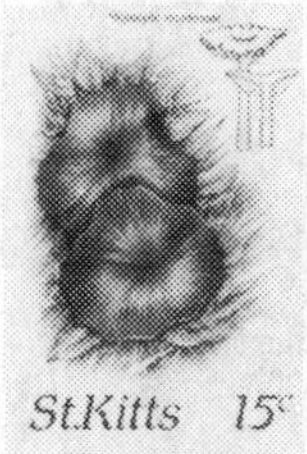

Fungi — A33

Carnival Clowns — A34

1987, Aug. 26 **Wmk. 384** ***Perf. 14***
210 A33 15c Hygrocybe occidentalis 15 15
211 A33 40c Marasmius haematocephalus 30 30
212 A33 $1.20 Psilocybe cubensis 90 90
213 A33 $2 Hygrocybe acutoconica 1.50 1.50
214 A33 $3 Boletellus cubensis 2.25 2.25
Nos. 210-214 (5) 5.10 5.10

1987, Oct. 28 ***Perf. 14½***
215 A34 15c multi 15 15
216 A34 40c multi, diff. 30 30
217 A34 $1 multi, diff. 75 75
218 A34 $3 multi, diff. 2.25 2.25

Christmas 1987. See Nos. 235-238.

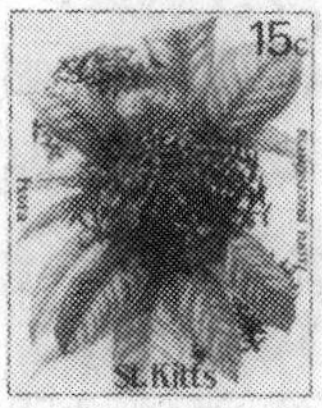

Flowers — A35

1988, Jan. 20
219 A35 15c Ixora 15 15
220 A35 40c Shrimp plant 30 30
221 A35 $1 Poinsettia 75 75
222 A35 $3 Honolulu rose 2.25 2.25

Tourism A36

1988, Apr. 20 **Wmk. 373**
223 A36 60c Ft. Thomas Hotel 45 45
224 A36 60c Fairview Inn 45 45
225 A36 60c Frigate Bay Beach Hotel 45 45
226 A36 60c Ocean Terrace Inn 45 45
227 A36 $3 The Golden Lemon 2.25 2.25
228 A36 $3 Royal St. Kitts Casino and Jack Tar Village 2.25 2.25
229 A36 $3 Rawlins Plantation Hotel and Restaurant 2.25 2.25
Nos. 223-229 (7) 8.55 8.55

See Nos. 239-244.

Leeward Islands Cricket Tournament, 75th Anniv. — A37

Independence, 5th Anniv. — A38

Designs: 40c, Leeward Islands Cricket Assoc. emblem, ball and wicket. $3, Cricket match at Warner Park.

1988, July 13 ***Perf. 13x13½***
230 A37 40c multicolored 30 30
231 A37 $3 multicolored 2.25 2.25

1988, Sept. 19 **Wmk. 384** ***Perf. 14½***

Designs: 15c, Natl. flag. 60c, Natl. coat of arms. $5, Princess Margaret presenting the Nevis Constitution Order to Prime Minister Simmonds, Sept. 19, 1983.

232 A38 15c shown 15 15
233 A38 60c multicolored 45 45

Souvenir Sheet
234 A38 $5 multicolored 3.75 3.75

Christmas Type of 1987

Carnival clowns.

1988, Nov. 2 **Wmk. 373**
235 A34 15c multi 15 15
236 A34 40c multi, diff. 30 30
237 A34 80c multi, diff. 60 60
238 A34 $3 multi, diff. 2.25 2.25

Tourism Type of 1988
Wmk. 384
1989, Jan. 25 **Litho.** ***Perf. 14***
239 A36 20c Old Colonial House 15 15
240 A36 20c Georgian House 15 15
241 A36 $1 Romney Manor 75 75
242 A36 $1 Lavington Great House 75 75
243 A36 $2 Treasury Building 1.50 1.50
244 A36 $2 Government House 1.50 1.50
Nos. 239-244 (6) 4.80 4.80

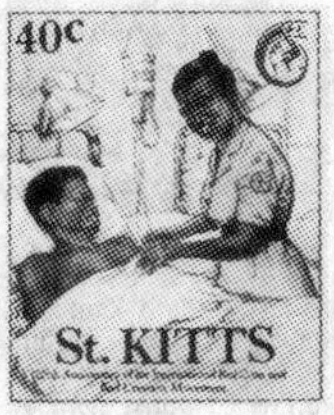

Intl. Red Cross and Red Crescent Organizations, 125th Annivs. (in 1988) — A39

Perf. 14x14½
1989, May 8 **Litho.** **Wmk. 384**
245 A39 40c shown 30 30
246 A39 $1 Ambulance 75 75
247 A39 $3 Anniv. emblem 2.25 2.25

Moon Landing, 20th Anniv.
Common Design Type

Apollo 13: 10c, Lunar rover at Taurus-Littrow landing site. 20c, Fred W. Haise Jr., John L. Swigert Jr., and James A. Lovell Jr. $1, Mission emblem. $2, Splashdown in the South Pacific. $5, Buzz Aldrin disembarking from the lunar module, Apollo 11 mission.

1989, July 20 ***Perf. 14***
Size of Nos. 249-250: 29x29mm
248 CD342 10c multicolored 15 15
249 CD342 20c multicolored 15 15
250 CD342 $1 multicolored 75 75
251 CD342 $2 multicolored 1.50 1.50

Souvenir Sheet
252 CD342 $5 multicolored 3.75 3.75

Souvenir Sheet

Conflict on the Champ-de-Mars — A40

1989, July 7
253 A40 $5 multicolored 3.75 3.75

PHILEXFRANCE '89, French revolution bicent.

Outline Map of St. Kitts — A41

1989 ***Perf. 15x14***
255 A41 10c purple & blk 15 15
256 A41 15c red & blk 15 15
257 A41 20c org brn & blk 15 15
259 A41 40c bister & blk 30 30
261 A41 60c blue & blk 45 45
265 A41 $1 green & blk 75 75
Nos. 255-265 (6) 1.95 1.95

This is an expanding set. Numbers will change if neccessary.

Discovery of America, 500th Anniv. (in 1992) A42

Designs: 15c, Galleon passing St. Kitts during Columbus's 2nd voyage, 1493. 80c, Coat of arms and map of 4th voyage. $1, Navigational instruments, c. 1500. $5, Exploration of Cuba and Hispaniola during Columbus's 2nd voyage, 1493-1496.

1989, Nov. 8 **Wmk. 384** ***Perf. 14***
269 A42 15c multicolored 15 15
270 A42 80c multicolored 60 60
271 A42 $1 multicolored 75 75
272 A42 $5 multicolored 3.75 3.75

World Stamp Expo '89 — A43

Exhibition emblem, flags and: 15c, Poinciana tree. 40c, Ft. George Citadel, Brimstone Hill. $1, Light Company private, 5th Foot Regiment, 1778. $3, St. George's Anglican Church.

1989, Nov. 17 **Wmk. 373**
273 A43 15c multicolored 15 15
274 A43 40c multicolored 30 30
275 A43 $1 multicolored 75 75
276 A43 $3 multicolored 2.25 2.25

Butterflies A45

Designs: 15c, Junonia evarete. 40c, Anartia jatrophae. 60c, Heliconius charitonius. $3, Biblis hyperia.

Perf. 13½
1990, June 6 **Litho.** **Wmk. 373**
277 A45 15c multicolored 15 15
278 A45 40c multicolored 30 30
279 A45 60c multicolored 45 45
280 A45 $3 multicolored 2.25 2.25

Nos. 277-280 with EXPO '90 Emblem Added to Design

1990, June 6
281 A45 15c multicolored 15 15
282 A45 40c multicolored 30 30
283 A45 60c multicolored 45 45
284 A45 $3 multicolored 2.25 2.25

Expo '90, International Garden and Greenery Exposition, Osaka, Japan.

Cannon on Brimstone Hill, 300th Anniv. A46

Designs: 15c, 40c, View of Brimstone Hill. 60c, Fort Charles under bombardment. $3, Men firing cannon.

1990 June 30 Wmk. 384 *Perf. 14*

285	A46	15c multicolored	15	15
286	A46	40c multicolored	30	30
287	A46	60c multicolored	45	45
288		Pair	2.75	2.75
a.		A46 60c multicolored	45	45
b.		A46 $3 multicolored	2.25	2.25

Nos. 288a-288b share a continuous design.

Souvenir Sheet

Battle of Britain, 50th Anniv. — A47

1990, Sept. 15

289		Sheet of 2	4.50	4.50
a.-b.		A47 $3 any single	2.25	2.25

Ships A48

1990, Oct. 10 Wmk. 373

294	A48	10c Romney	15	15
295	A48	15c Baralt	15	15
296	A48	20c Wear	15	15
297	A48	25c Sunmount	18	18
298	A48	40c Inanda	30	30
299	A48	50c Alcoa Partner	36	36
300	A48	60c Dominica	45	45
301	A48	80c CGM Provence	60	60
302	A48	$1 Director	72	72
303	A48	$1.20 Typical barque, 1860-1880	90	90
304	A48	$2 Chignecto	1.50	1.50
305	A48	$3 Berbice	2.25	2.25
306	A48	$5 Vamos	3.75	3.75
307	A48	$10 Federal Maple	7.25	7.25
		Nos. 294-307 (14)	18.71	18.71

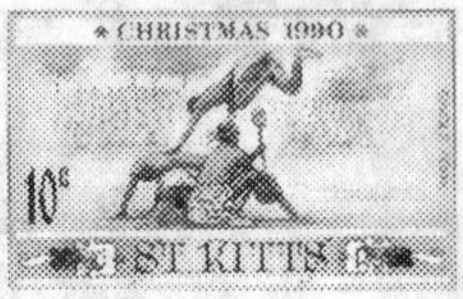

Christmas A49

Traditional games.

1990, Nov. 14 *Perf. 14*

308	A49	10c Single fork	15	15
309	A49	15c Boulder breaking	15	15
310	A49	40c Double fork	30	30
311	A49	$3 Run up	2.25	2.25

Flowers — A50

Natl. Census — A51

Perf. 14x13¹/₂, 13¹/₂x14

1991, May 8 Litho. Wmk. 373

312	A50	10c White periwinkle, horiz.	15	15
313	A50	40c Pink oleander, horiz.	30	30
314	A50	60c Pink periwinkle	45	45
315	A50	$2 White oleander	1.45	1.45

1991, May 13 Wmk. 384 *Perf. 14*

316	A51	15c multicolored	15	15
317	A51	$2.40 multicolored	1.80	1.80

Elizabeth & Philip, Birthdays

Common Design Types

Perf. 14¹/₂

1991, June 17 Litho. Wmk. 384

318	CD346	$1.20 multicolored	82	82
319	CD345	$1.80 multicolored	1.25	1.25
a.		Pair, #318-319 + label	2.07	2.07

Fish — A52

1991, Aug. 28 Wmk. 373 *Perf. 14*

320	A52	10c Nassau grouper	15	15
321	A52	60c Hogfish	45	45
322	A52	$1 Red hind	72	72
323	A52	$3 Porkfish	2.15	2.15

University of the West Indies A53

Designs: 15c, Chancellor Sir Shridath Ramphal, School of Continuing Studies, St. Kitts. 50c, Administration Bldg., Cave Hill Campus, Barbados. $1, Engineering Bldg., St. Augustine Campus, Trinidad & Tobago. $3, Ramphal, Mona Campus, Jamaica.

1991, Sept. 25 Wmk. 384

324	A53	15c multicolored	15	15
325	A53	50c multicolored	36	36
326	A53	$1 multicolored	72	72
327	A53	$3 multicolored	2.15	2.15

Christmas A54

Various scenes of traditional play, "The Bull."

1991, Nov. 6 Wmk. 373

328	A54	10c multicolored	15	15
329	A54	15c multicolored	15	15
330	A54	60c multicolored	45	45
331	A54	$3 multicolored	2.15	2.15

Queen Elizabeth II's Accession to the Throne, 40th Anniv.

Common Design Type

1992, Feb. 6 Wmk. 384

332	CD349	10c multicolored	15	15
333	CD349	40c multicolored	28	28
334	CD349	60c multicolored	42	42
335	CD349	$1 multicolored	70	70

Wmk. 373

336	CD349	$3 multicolored	2.05	2.05
		Nos. 332-336 (5)	3.60	3.60

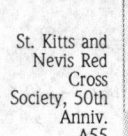

St. Kitts and Nevis Red Cross Society, 50th Anniv. A55

Designs: 10c, Map of St. Kitts and Nevis. 20c, St. Kitts and Nevis flag. 50c, Red Cross House, St. Kitts. $2.40, Jean-Henri Dunant, founder of Red Cross.

Perf. 13¹/₂x14

1992, May 8 Litho. Wmk. 373

337	A55	10c multicolored	15	15
338	A55	20c multicolored	15	15
339	A55	50c multicolored	35	35
340	A55	$2.40 multicolored	1.70	1.70

Discovery of America, 500th Anniv. — A56

1992, July 6 *Perf. 13*

341	A56	$1 Coming ashore	70	70
342	A56	$2 Natives, ships	1.40	1.40

Organization of East Caribbean States.

A57

Christmas — A58

Designs: 25c, Fountain, Independence Square. 50c, Berkeley Memorial drinking fountain and clock. 80c, Sir Thomas Warner's tomb. $2, War Memorial.

1992, Aug. 19 *Perf. 12¹/₂x13*

343	A57	25c multicolored	18	18
344	A57	50c multicolored	35	35
345	A57	80c multicolored	58	58
346	A57	$2 multicolored	1.40	1.40

Stained glass windows: 20c, Mary and Joseph. 25c, Shepherds. 80c, Three Wise Men. $3, Mary, Joseph and Christ Child.

1992, Oct. 28 Wmk. 384 *Perf. 14¹/₂*

347	A58	20c multicolored	15	15
348	A58	25c multicolored	18	18
349	A58	80c multicolored	56	56
350	A58	$3 multicolored	2.25	2.25

Royal Air Force, 75th Anniv.

Common Design Type

Designs: 25c, Short Singapore III. 50c, Bristol Beaufort. 80c, Westland Whirlwind. $1.60, English Electric Canberra.

No. 355a, Handley Page 0/400. b, Fairey Long Range Monoplane. c, Vickers Wellesley. d, Sepecat Jaguar.

Wmk. 373

1993, Apr. 1 Litho. *Perf. 14*

351	CD350	25c multicolored	18	18
352	CD350	50c multicolored	38	38
353	CD350	80c multicolored	60	60
354	CD350	$1.60 multicolored	1.20	1.20

Miniature Sheet

355	CD350	$2 Sheet of 4, #a.-d.	6.00	6.00

Diocese of the Northeastern Caribbean and Aruba, 150th Anniv. — A59

Coronation of Queen Elizabeth II, 40th Anniv. — A60

Designs: 25c, Diocesan Conference, Basseterre, horiz. 50c, Cathedral of St. John the Divine. 80c, Diocesan coat of arms and motto, horiz. $2, First Bishop, Right Reverend Daniel G. Davis.

Perf. 13¹/₂x14, 14x13¹/₂

1993, May 21 Litho. Wmk. 384

356	A59	25c multicolored	18	18
357	A59	50c multicolored	35	35
358	A59	80c multicolored	55	55
359	A59	$2 multicolored	1.40	1.40

1993, June 2 *Perf. 14¹/₂x14*

Royal regalia and stamps of St. Kitts-Nevis: 10c, Eagle-shaped ampulla, #119. 25c, Anointing spoon, #334. 80c, Tassels, #333. $2, Staff of Scepter with the Cross, #354a-354c.

360	A60	10c multicolored	15	15
361	A60	25c multicolored	18	18
362	A60	80c multicolored	55	55
363	A60	$2 multicolored	1.40	1.40

Girls' Brigade Intl., Cent. A61

1993, July 1 *Perf. 13¹/₂x14*

364	A61	80c Flags	55	55
365	A61	$3 Badge, coat of arms	2.10	2.10

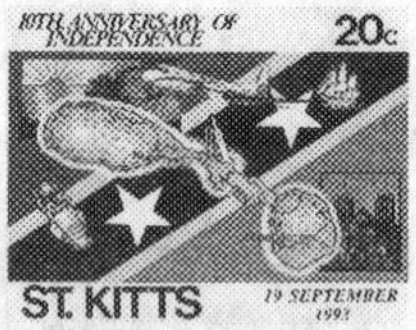

Independence, 10th Anniv. — A62

Designs: 20c, Flag, map of St. Kitts and Nevis, plane, ship and island scenes. 80c, Natl. arms, independence emblem. $3, Natl. arms, map.

Wmk. 373

1993, Sept. 10 Litho. *Perf. 14*

366	A62	20c multicolored	15	15
367	A62	80c multicolored	55	55
368	A62	$3 multicolored	2.00	2.00

Christmas — A63

A64

Perf. 13¹/₂x14

1993, Nov. 16 Litho. Wmk. 373

369	A63	25c Roselle	16	16
370	A63	50c Poinsettia	32	32
371	A63	$1.60 Snow on the Mountain	1.00	1.00

Wmk. 384

1994, Feb. 18 Litho. *Perf. 14*

Prehistoric Aquatic Reptiles: a, Mesosaurus. b, Placodus. c, Liopleurodon. d, Hydrotherosaurus. e, Caretta.

372	A64	$1.20 Strip of 5, #a.-e.	4.50	4.50
373	A64	$1.20 #372 ovptd. with Hong Kong '94 emblem	4.50	4.50

15-Cent Minimum Value
The minimum value for a single stamp is 15 cents. This value reflects the costs of handling inexpensive stamps.

Souvenir Sheet

Treasury Building, Cent. — A65

Perf. 13½

1994, Mar. 21 Litho. Wmk. 373

374	A65	$10	multicolored	7.50	7.50

Order of the Caribbean Community — A66

First award recipients: Nos. 375a, 376a, Sir Shridath Ramphal, statesman, Guyana. Nos. 375b, 376b, Emblem of the Order. Nos. 375c, 376c, Derek Walcott, writer, St. Lucia. Nos. 375d, 376d, William Demas, economist, Trinidad and Tobago.

Wmk. 373

1994, July 13 Litho. *Perf. 14*

375	A66	10c	Strip of 5, #a, c, d, 2 #b.	38	38
376	A66	$1	Strip of 5, #a, c, d, 2 #b.	3.75	3.75

CARICOM, 20th anniv. (#375b, 376b).

OFFICIAL STAMPS

Nos. 28-37 Ovptd. "OFFICIAL"

Perf. 14½x14

1980, June 23 Litho. Wmk. 373

O1	A61	15c	multicolored	15	15
O2	A61	25c	multicolored	15	15
O3	A61	30c	multicolored	16	16
O4	A61	40c	multicolored	24	24
O5	A61	45c	multicolored	26	26
O6	A61	50c	multicolored	30	30
O7	A61	55c	multicolored	32	32
O8	A61	$1	multicolored	60	60
O9	A61	$5	multicolored	3.00	3.00
O10	A61	$10	multicolored	5.75	5.75
			Nos. O1-O10 (10)	10.93	10.93

Unwmk.

O2a	A61	25c	16	16
O3a	A61	30c	18	18
O4a	A61	40c	32.50	32.50
O7a	A61	55c	35	35
O8a	A61	$1	65	65
O9a	A61	$5	3.25	3.25
O10a	A61	$10	6.00	6.00
		Nos. O2a-O10a (7)	43.09	43.09

Nos. 55-66 Ovptd. "OFFICIAL"

1981, Feb. 5 *Perf. 14*

O11	A5	15c	multicolored	15	15
O12	A5	20c	multicolored	15	15
O13	A5	25c	multicolored	18	18
O14	A5	30c	multicolored	18	18
O15	A5	40c	multicolored	26	26
O16	A5	45c	multicolored	30	30
O17	A5	50c	multicolored	32	32
O18	A5	55c	multicolored	35	35
O19	A5	$1	multicolored	65	65
O20	A5	$2.50	multicolored	1.65	1.65
O21	A5	$5	multicolored	3.25	3.25
O22	A5	$10	multicolored	6.50	6.50
			Nos. O11-O22 (12)	13.94	13.94

Nos. 75-80 Ovptd. or Surcharged "OFFICIAL" in Ultra or Black

1983, Feb. 2

O23	A66	45c on $2.50 No. 77	42	42
O24	A67	45c on $2.50 No. 78	42	42
O25	A66	55c No. 75	50	50
O26	A67	55c No. 76	50	50
O27	A66	$1.10 on $4 No. 79 (B)	1.00	1.00
O28	A67	$1.10 on $4 No. 80 (B)	1.00	1.00
		Nos. O23-O28 (6)	3.84	3.84

Nos. 141-152 Ovptd. "OFFICIAL"

1984, July 4 Wmk. 380

O29	A18	15c	multicolored	15	15
O30	A18	20c	multicolored	15	15
O31	A18	25c	multicolored	15	15
O32	A18	30c	multicolored	16	16
O33	A18	40c	multicolored	22	22
O34	A18	50c	multicolored	28	28
O35	A18	60c	multicolored	35	35
O36	A18	75c	multicolored	42	42
O37	A18	$1	multicolored	60	60
O38	A18	$2.50	multicolored	1.50	1.50
O39	A18	$5	multicolored	3.00	3.00
O40	A18	$10	multicolored	5.75	5.75
			Nos. O29-O40 (12)	12.73	12.73

ST. KITTS-NEVIS

(St. Christopher-Nevis-Anguilla)

LOCATION — West Indies southeast of Puerto Rico

GOVT. — Associated State in British Commonwealth

AREA — 153 sq. mi.

POP. — 48,000, excluding Anguilla (est. 1976)

CAPITAL — Basseterre, St. Kitts

St. Kitts-Nevis was one of the presidencies of the former Leeward Islands colony until it became a colony itself in 1956. In 1967 Britain granted internal self-government.

See "St. Christopher" for stamps used in St. Kitts before 1890. From 1890 until 1903, stamps of the Leeward Islands were used. From 1903 until 1956, stamps of St. Kitts-Nevis and Leeward Islands were used concurrently.

Starting in 1967, issues of Anguilla are listed under that heading. Starting in 1980 stamps inscribed St. Kitts or Nevis are listed under those headings.

12 Pence = 1 Shilling
20 Shillings = 1 Pound
100 Cents = 1 Dollar (1951)

Catalogue values for unused stamps in this country are for Never Hinged items, beginning with Scott 91 in the regular postage section and Scott O1 in the officials section.

Columbus Looking for Land — A1

Medicinal Spring — A2

Wmk. Crown and C A (2)

1903 Typo. *Perf. 14*

1	A1	½p	green & violet	2.75	2.00
2	A2	1p	carmine & black	3.25	40
3	A1	2p	brown & violet	5.00	*12.00*
4	A1	2½p	ultra & black	10.00	3.25
5	A2	3p	orange & green	6.00	8.25
6	A1	6p	red violet & blk	4.00	4.00
7	A1	1sh	orange & green	6.50	*10.00*
8	A2	2sh	black & green	8.25	10.00
9	A1	2sh6p	violet & blk	13.00	*22.50*
10	A2	5sh	ol grn & gray vio	30.00	*42.50*
			Nos. 1-10 (10)	88.75	*114.90*

1905-18 Wmk. 3

11	A1	½p	green & violet	5.50	4.25
12	A1	½p	green	32	28
13	A2	1p	carmine & blk	3.25	1.10
14	A2	1p	carmine	32	28
15	A1	2p	brown & violet	90	1.25
16	A1	2½p	ultra & blk	16.00	7.00
17	A1	2½p	ultra	52	52
18	A2	3p	orange & green	1.40	*2.50*
19	A1	6p	red vio & gray blk ('08)	2.00	*7.75*
a.			6p purple & gray ('08)	4.25	*7.75*
20	A1	1sh	org & grn ('09)	4.25	*14.00*
21	A2	5sh	ol grn & gray vio ('18)	24.00	*52.50*
			Nos. 11-21 (11)	58.46	*91.43*

Nos. 13, 19a and 21 are on chalky paper only and Nos. 15, 18 and 20 are on both ordinary and chalky paper.

For stamp and type overprinted see #MR1-MR2.

King George V — A3

A4

1920-22

Ordinary Paper

24	A3	½p	green	90	1.10
25	A4	1p	carmine	1.10	55
26	A3	1½p	orange	70	70
27	A4	2p	gray	3.00	*4.25*
28	A3	2½p	ultramarine	1.40	*3.00*

Chalky Paper

29	A4	3p	vio & dull vio, *yel*	1.65	*4.25*
30	A3	6p	red vio & dull vio	2.00	*5.25*
31	A4	1sh	blk, *gray grn*	2.25	*6.00*
32	A3	2sh	ultra & dull vio, *blue*	9.00	*18.00*
33	A4	2sh 6p	red & blk, *blue*	9.00	*20.00*
34	A3	5sh	red & grn, *yel*	10.00	*32.50*
35	A4	10sh	red & grn, *grn*	27.50	*55.00*
36	A3	£1	blk & vio, *red* ('22)	180.00	*300.00*
			Nos. 24-36 (13)	248.50	*450.60*

1921-29 Wmk. 4

Ordinary Paper

37	A3	½p	green	22	30
38	A4	1p	rose red	28	30
39	A4	1p	dp violet ('22)	90	90
40	A3	1½p	rose red ('25)	1.75	*3.00*
41	A3	1½p	fawn ('28)	35	75
42	A4	2p	gray	1.40	1.75
43	A3	2½p	ultra ('22)	45	60
44	A3	2½p	brown ('22)	90	*3.00*

Chalky Paper

45	A4	3p	ultra ('22)	1.50	*3.25*
46	A4	3p	vio & dull vio, *yel*	60	*1.75*
47	A3	6p	red vio & dull vio ('24)	1.75	*3.00*
48	A4	1sh	black, *grn* ('29)	3.00	*5.50*
49	A3	2sh	ultra & vio, *bl* ('22)	4.25	*11.00*
50	A4	2sh6p	red & blk, *bl* ('27)	9.00	*18.00*
51	A3	5sh	red & grn, *yel* ('29)	17.00	*35.00*
			Nos. 37-51 (15)	43.35	*88.10*

No. 43 exists on ordinary and chalky paper.

Caravel in Old Road Bay — A5

1923 Wmk. 4

52	A5	½p	green & blk	1.25	*2.50*
53	A5	1p	violet & blk	1.40	1.90
54	A5	1½p	carmine & blk	2.50	*3.75*
55	A5	2p	dk gray & blk	2.50	*2.75*
56	A5	2½p	brown & blk	3.75	*5.75*
57	A5	3p	ultra & blk	3.75	*5.75*
58	A5	6p	red vio & blk	5.00	*10.00*
59	A5	1sh	ol grn & blk	8.00	*16.00*
60	A5	2sh	ultra & blk, *bl*	22.50	*45.00*
61	A5	2sh6p	red & blk, *blue*	40.00	*62.50*
62	A5	10sh	red & blk, *emer*	190.00	*325.00*
			Nos. 52-62 (11)	280.65	*480.90*

Wmk. 3

63	A5	5sh	red & blk, *yel*	87.50	*175.00*
64	A5	£1	vio & blk, *red*	1,000.	*1,500.*

Tercentenary of the founding of the colony of St. Kitts (or St. Christopher).

Silver Jubilee Issue

Common Design Type

Inscribed "St. Christopher and Nevis"

Perf. 11x12

1935, May 6 Engr. Wmk. 4

72	CD301	1p	car & dk blue	35	35
73	CD301	1½p	gray blk & ultra	50	50
74	CD301	2½p	ultra & brown	1.25	1.25
75	CD301	1sh	brn vio & ind	4.00	4.00

Coronation Issue

Common Design Type

Inscribed "St. Christopher and Nevis"

1937, May 12 *Perf. 13½x14*

76	CD302	1p	carmine	18	18
77	CD302	1½p	brown	18	18
78	CD302	2½p	bright ultra	38	38
			Set, never hinged	1.25	

George VI A6

Medicinal Spring A7

Columbus Looking for Land — A8

Map Showing Anguilla A9

Perf. 13½x14 (A6, A9), 14 (A7, A8)

1938-48 Typo.

79	A6	½p	green	15	15
80	A6	1p	carmine	15	15
81	A6	1½p	orange	15	15
82	A7	2p	gray & car	16	16
83	A6	2½p	ultra	28	28
84	A7	3p	car & pale lilac	35	35
85	A8	6p	rose lil & dull grn	1.40	1.10
86	A7	1sh	green & gray blk	90	90
87	A7	2sh6p	car & gray blk	3.00	2.50
88	A8	5sh	car & dull grn	3.00	3.00

Typo., Center Litho.

Chalky Paper

89	A9	10sh	brt ultra & blk	13.00	*21.00*
90	A9	£1	brown & blk	18.00	*22.50*
			Nos. 79-90 (12)	40.54	*52.24*
			Set, never hinged	60.00	

Issue dates: ½p, 1p, 1½p, 2½p, Aug. 15, 1938. 2p, 1941. 3p, 6p, 2sh, 5sh, 1942. 1sh, 1943. 10sh, £1, Sept. 1, 1948.

For types overprinted see Nos. 99-104.

1938, Aug. 15 *Perf. 13x11½*

82a	A7	2p	7.25	3.50
84a	A7	3p	1.40	1.40
85a	A8	6p	1.40	1.40
86a	A7	1sh	2.75	2.25
87a	A7	2sh6p	9.25	9.25
88a	A8	5sh	35.00	*22.50*
		Nos. 82a-88a (6)	57.05	*40.30*

Catalogue values for unused stamps in this section, from this point to the end of the section, are for Never Hinged items.

Peace Issue

Common Design Type

Inscribed "St. Kitts-Nevis"

1946, Nov. 1 Engr. *Perf. 13½x14*

91	CD303	1½p	deep orange	15	15
92	CD303	3p	carmine	15	15
			Set value	25	25

Silver Wedding Issue

Common Design Types

Inscribed: "St. Kitts-Nevis"

1949, Jan. 3 Photo. *Perf. 14x14½*

93	CD304	2½p	bright ultra	16	16

Engraved; Name Typographed

Perf. 11½x11

94	CD305	5sh	rose carmine	4.50	*5.00*

UPU Issue

Common Design Types
Inscribed: "St. Kitt's-Nevis"

Engr.; Name Typo. on 3p, 6p

1949, Oct. 10 *Perf. 13½, 11x11½*

95	CD306	2½p ultra	18	18
96	CD307	3p deep carmine	35	35
97	CD308	6p red lilac	90	90
98	CD309	1sh blue green	1.50	1.50

Types of 1938 Overprinted in Black or Carmine:

ANGUILLA ANGUILLA

TERCENTENARY 1650-1950 On A6 TERCENTENARY 1650—1950 On A7-A8

Perf. 13½x14, 13x12½

1950, Nov. 10 **Wmk. 4**

99	A6	1p carmine	15	15
100	A6	1½p orange	15	15
a.		Wmk. 4a (error)	600.00	
101	A6	2½p ultra	15	15
102	A7	3p car & pale lilac	15	15
103	A8	6p rose lil & dl grn	25	25
104	A7	1sh grn & gray blk (C)	42	42
		Nos. 99-104 (6)	1.27	1.27

300th anniv. of the settlement of Anguilla.

University Issue

Common Design Types
Inscribed: "St. Kitts-Nevis"

Perf. 14x14½

1951, Feb. 16 **Engr.** **Wmk. 4**

105	CD310	3c org yel & gray blk	18	18
106	CD311	12c red violet & aqua	52	52

St. Christopher-Nevis-Anguilla

Bath House and Spa, Nevis — A10

Map — A11

Designs: 2c, Warner Park, St. Kitts. 4c, Brimstone Hill, St. Kitts. 5c, Nevis. 6c, Pinney's Beach, Nevis. 12c, Sir Thomas Warner's Tomb. 24c, Old Road Bay, St. Kitts. 48c, Picking Cotton. 60c, Treasury, St. Kitts. $1.20, Salt Pond, Anguilla. $4.80, Sugar Mill, St. Kitts.

1952, June 14 *Perf. 12½*

107	A10	1c ocher & dp grn	15	15
108	A10	2c emerald	15	15
109	A11	3c purple & red	18	18
110	A10	4c red	22	22
111	A10	5c gray & ultra	32	32
112	A10	6c deep ultra	38	38
113	A11	12c redsh brn & dp blue	60	60
114	A10	24c car & gray blk	90	70
115	A10	48c vio brn & ol bister	2.50	2.50
116	A10	60c dp green & ocher	2.50	2.50
117	A10	$1.20 dp ultra & dp green	6.00	6.00
118	A10	$4.80 car & emer	14.00	14.00
		Nos. 107-118 (12)	27.90	27.70

Coronation Issue

Common Design Type

1953, June 2 *Perf. 13½x13*

119	CD312	2c brt green & blk	18	15

Types of 1952 with Portrait of Queen Elizabeth II.

Design: ½c, Salt Pond, Anguilla. 8c, Sombrero Lighthouse. $2.40, Map of Anguilla and Dependencies.

1954-57 **Engr.** *Perf. 12½*

120	A10	½c gray olive ('56)	15	15
121	A10	1c ocher & dp grn	15	15
a.		Horiz. pair, imperf. vert.		
122	A10	2c emerald	15	15
123	A11	3c purple & red	15	15
124	A10	4c red	15	15
125	A10	5c gray & ultra	15	15
126	A10	6c deep ultra	28	22
127	A11	8c dark gray ('57)	45	22
128	A11	12c redsh brn & dp blue	28	22
129	A10	24c carmine & blk	52	45
130	A10	48c brn & ol bister	1.25	1.25
131	A10	60c dp grn & ocher	1.75	1.65
132	A10	$1.20 dp ultra & dp green	3.75	2.75
133	A10	$2.40 red org & blk ('57)	6.75	4.25
134	A10	$4.80 carmine & emer	13.00	11.00
		Nos. 120-134 (15)	28.93	22.91

Issue dates: 24c-$1.20, $4.80, Dec. 1, 1954. ½c, July 3, 1956. 8c, $2.40, Feb. 1, 1957. Others, Mar. 1, 1954.

Alexander Hamilton and Nevis Scene — A12

1957, Jan. 11 *Perf. 12½*

135	A12	24c dp ultra & yellow grn	38	38

Bicent. of the birth of Alexander Hamilton.

West Indies Federation

Common Design Type

Perf. 11½x11

1958, Apr. 22 **Engr.** **Wmk. 314**

136	CD313	3c green	15	15
137	CD313	6c blue	25	25
138	CD313	12c carmine rose	50	50

Federation of the West Indies, Apr. 22, 1958.

Stamp of Nevis, 1861 — A13

Designs (Stamps of Nevis, 1861 issue): 8c, 4p stamp. 12c, 6p stamp. 24c, 1sh stamp.

1961, July 15 *Perf. 14*

139	A13	2c green & brown	15	15
140	A13	8c blue & pale brown	22	22
141	A13	12c carmine & gray	32	32
142	A13	24c orange & green	70	70

Centenary of the first stamps of Nevis.

Red Cross Centenary Issue

Common Design Type

1963, Sept. 2 **Litho.** *Perf. 13*

143	CD315	3c black & red	18	18
144	CD315	12c ultra & red	1.40	1.40

New Lighthouse, Sombrero — A14

Loading Sugar Cane, St. Kitts — A15

Designs: 2c, Pall Mall Square, Basseterre. 3c, Gateway, Brimstone Hill Fort, St. Kitts. 4c, Nelson's Spring, Nevis. 5c, Grammar School, St. Kitts. 6c, Mt. Misery Crater, St. Kitts. 10c, Hibiscus. 15c, Sea Island cotton, Nevis. 20c, Boat building, Anguilla. 25c, White-crowned pigeon. 50c, St. George's Church tower, Basseterre. 60c, Alexander Hamilton. $1, Map of St. Kitts-Nevis. $2.50, Map of Anguilla. $5, Arms of St. Christopher-Nevis-Anguilla.

1963, Nov. 20 **Photo.** *Perf. 14*

145	A14	½c blue & dk brn	15	15
146	A15	1c multicolored	15	15
147	A14	2c multicolored	15	15
a.		Yellow omitted	150.00	
148	A14	3c multicolored	15	15
149	A15	4c multicolored	15	15
150	A15	5c multicolored	15	15
151	A15	6c multicolored	15	15
152	A15	10c multicolored	22	22
153	A14	15c multicolored	30	30
154	A15	20c multicolored	40	40
155	A14	25c multicolored	52	52
156	A15	50c multicolored	1.10	1.10
157	A14	60c multicolored	1.25	1.25
158	A14	$1 multicolored	2.25	2.25
159	A15	$2.50 multicolored	4.00	4.00
160	A14	$5 multicolored	7.00	7.00
		Nos. 145-160 (16)	18.09	18.09

For overprints, see Nos. 161-162.

1967-69 **Wmk. 314 Sideways**

145a	A14	½c ('69)	15	15
147b	A14	2c	15	15
148a	A14	3c ('68)	18	18
153a	A14	15c ('68)	42	42
155a	A14	25c ('68)	1.50	75
158a	A14	$1 ('68)	4.50	4.50
		Nos. 145a-158a (6)	6.90	6.15

Nos. 148 and 155 Overprinted: "ARTS / FESTIVAL / ST. KITTS / 1964"

1964, Sept. 14

161	A14	3c multicolored	15	15
162	A14	25c multicolored	30	30

ITU Issue

Common Design Type

Perf. 11x11½

1965, May 17 **Litho.** **Wmk. 314**

163	CD317	2c bister & rose red	15	15
164	CD317	50c grnsh blue & olive	95	95

Intl. Cooperation Year Issue

Common Design Type

1965, Oct. 25 *Perf. 14½*

165	CD318	2c blue grn & claret	15	15
166	CD318	25c lt violet & green	70	70

Churchill Memorial Issue

Common Design Type

1966, Jan. 24 **Photo.** *Perf. 14*

Design in Black, Gold and Carmine Rose

167	CD319	½c bright blue	15	15
168	CD319	3c green	15	15
169	CD319	15c brown	55	55
170	CD319	25c violet	1.00	1.00

Royal Visit Issue

Common Design Type

1966, Feb. 14 **Litho.** *Perf. 11x12*

171	CD320	3c violet blue	15	15
172	CD320	25c dk carmine rose	70	70

World Cup Soccer Issue

Common Design Type

1966, July 1 **Litho.** *Perf. 14*

173	CD321	6c multicolored	15	15
174	CD321	25c multicolored	50	50

Festival Emblem With Dolphins — A16

Unwmk.

1966, Aug. 15 **Photo.** *Perf. 14*

175	A16	3c gold, grn, yel & blk	15	15
176	A16	25c silver, grn, yel & blk	42	42
		Set value	48	48

Arts Festival of 1966.

WHO Headquarters Issue

Common Design Type

1966, Sept. 20 **Litho.** *Perf. 14*

177	CD322	3c multicolored	15	15
178	CD322	40c multicolored	70	70

UNESCO Anniversary Issue

Common Design Type

1966, Dec. 1 **Litho.** *Perf. 14*

179	CD323	3c "Education"	15	15
180	CD323	6c "Science"	18	18
181	CD323	40c "Culture"	1.10	1.10

Independent State

Government Headquarters, Basseterre — A17

Designs: 10c, Flag and map of Anguilla, St. Christopher and Nevis. 25c, Coat of Arms.

Perf. 14½

1967, July 1 **Wmk. 314** **Photo.**

182	A17	3c multicolored	15	15
183	A17	10c multicolored	15	15
184	A17	25c multicolored	38	38
		Set value	58	58

Achievement of independence, Feb. 27, 1967.

Charles Wesley, Cross and Palm — A18

Designs: 3c, John Wesley. 40c, Thomas Coke.

1967, Dec. 1 **Litho.** *Perf. 13x13½*

185	A18	3c dp lilac, dp car & blk	15	15
186	A18	25c ultra, grnsh blue & blk	28	28
187	A18	40c ocher, yellow & blk	55	55

Issued to commemorate the attainment of autonomy by the Methodist Church in the Caribbean and the Americas, and to commemorate the opening of headquarters near St. John's, Antigua, May 1967.

Cargo Ship and Plane A19

Perf. 13½x13

1968, July 30 **Litho.** **Wmk. 314**

188	A19	25c multicolored	26	26
189	A19	50c brt blue & multi	55	55

Issued to publicize the organization of the Caribbean Free Trade Area, CARIFTA.

Martin Luther King, Jr. — A20

Mystical Nativity, by Botticelli — A21

Perf. 12x12½

1968, Sept. 30 Litho. Wmk. 314

190	A20	50c multicolored	48	48

Dr. Martin Luther King, Jr. (1929-68), American civil rights leader.

Perf. 14½x14

1968, Nov. 27 Photo. Wmk. 314

Christmas (Paintings): 25c, 50c, The Adoration of the Magi, by Rubens.

191	A21	12c brt violet & multi	15	15
192	A21	25c multicolored	25	25
193	A21	40c gray & multi	45	45
194	A21	50c crimson & multi	55	55

Snook A22

Fish: 12c, Needlefish (gar). 40c, Horse-eye jack. 50c, Red snapper. The 6c is mis-inscribed "tarpon."

Perf. 14x14½

1969, Feb. 25 Photo. Wmk. 314

195	A22	6c brt green & multi	15	15
196	A22	12c blue & multi	18	18
197	A22	40c gray blue & multi	60	60
198	A22	50c multicolored	75	75

Arms of Sir Thomas Warner and Map of Islands — A23

Designs: 25c, Warner's tomb in St. Kitts. 40c, Warner's commission from Charles I.

1969, Sept. 1 Litho. *Perf. 13½*

199	A23	20c multicolored	24	24
200	A23	25c multicolored	30	30
201	A23	40c multicolored	60	60

Issued in memory of Sir Thomas Warner, first Governor of St. Kitts-Nevis, Barbados and Montserrat.

Adoration of the Kings, by Jan Mostaert — A24

Christmas (Painting): 40c, 50c, Adoration of the Kings, by Geertgen tot Sint Jans.

1969, Nov. 17 *Perf. 13½*

202	A24	10c olive & multi	15	15
203	A24	25c violet & multi	28	28
204	A24	40c yellow grn & multi	52	52
205	A24	50c maroon & multi	65	65

Pirates Burying Treasure, Frigate Bay — A25

Caravels, 16th Century A26

Designs: 1c, English two-decker, 1650. 2c, Flags of England, Spain, France, Holland and Portugal. 3c, Hilt of 17th cent. rapier. 5c, Henry Morgan and fire boats. 6c, The pirate L'Ollonois and a carrack (pirate vessel). 10c, Smugglers' ship. 15c, Spanish 17th cent. piece of eight and map of Caribbean. 20c, Garrison and ship cannon and map of Spanish Main. 25c, Humphrey Cole's astrolabe, 1574. 50c, Flintlock pistol and map of Spanish Main. 60c, Dutch Flute (ship). $1, Capt. Bartholomew Roberts and document with death sentence for his crew. $2.50, Railing piece (small cannon), 17th cent. and map of Spanish Main. $5, Francis Drake, John Hawkins and ships. $10, Edward Teach (Blackbeard) and his capture.

Wmk. 314 Upright (A25), Sideways (A26)

1970, Feb. 1 Litho. *Perf. 14*

206	A25	½c multicolored	15	15
207	A25	1c multicolored	15	15
208	A25	2c multicolored	15	15
209	A25	3c multicolored	15	15
210	A26	4c multicolored	15	15
211	A26	5c multicolored	15	15
212	A26	6c multicolored	15	15
213	A26	10c multicolored	22	22
214	A25	15c *Hispanianum*	50	50
215	A25	15c *Hispaniarum*	38	38
216	A26	20c multicolored	38	38
217	A25	25c multicolored	42	42
218	A26	50c multicolored	85	85
219	A25	60c multicolored	2.00	1.00
220	A25	$1 multicolored	2.50	1.65
221	A26	$2.50 multicolored	3.75	3.25
222	A26	$5 multicolored	7.50	6.75
		Nos. 206-222 (17)	19.55	16.45

Coin inscription was misspelled on No. 214, corrected on No. 215 (issued Sept. 8).

Wmk. 314 Sideways (A25), Upright (A26)

1973-74

206a	A25	½c multicolored	15	15
208a	A25	2c multicolored	15	15
209a	A25	3c multicolored	15	15
211a	A26	5c multicolored	18	18
212a	A26	6c multicolored	25	25
213a	A26	10c multicolored	38	38
215a	A25	15c multicolored	45	45
216a	A26	20c multicolored	75	75
217a	A25	25c multicolored	52	52
218a	A26	50c multicolored	1.25	1.25
220a	A25	$1 multicolored	2.00	2.00
222A	A26	$10 multi ('74)	17.50	17.50
		Nos. 206a-220a,222A (12)	23.73	23.73

Issue dates: $10, Nov. 16, others, Sept. 12.

1975-77 Wmk. 373

207b	A25	1c multi ('77)	15	15
209b	A25	3c multi ('76)	15	15
210b	A26	4c multi ('76)	15	15
211b	A26	5c multicolored	15	15
212b	A26	6c multicolored	15	15
213b	A26	10c multi ('76)	16	15
215b	A25	15c multi ('76)	25	22
216b	A26	20c multicolored	22	16
219b	A25	60c multi ('76)	1.00	1.00
220b	A25	$1 multi ('77)	2.00	1.50
		Nos. 207b-220b (10)	4.38	3.78

Pip Meeting Convict, from "Great Expectations" — A27

Designs: 20c, Miss Havisham from "Great Expectations." 25c, Dickens' birthplace, Portsmouth, vert. 40c, Charles Dickens, vert.

Perf. 13x13½, 13½x13

1970, May 1 Litho. Wmk. 314

223	A27	4c gold, Prus blue & brn	15	15
224	A27	20c gold, claret & brn	32	32
225	A27	25c gold, olive & brn	42	42
226	A27	40c dk blue, gold & brn	75	75

Charles Dickens (1812-70), English novelist.

Local Steel Band A28

Designs: 25c, Local string band. 40c, "A Midsummer Night's Dream," 1963 performance.

1970, Aug. 1 *Perf. 13½*

227	A28	20c multicolored	28	28
228	A28	25c multicolored	38	38
229	A28	40c multicolored	60	60

Issued to publicize the 1970 Arts Festival.

St. Christopher No. 1 and St. Kitts Post Office, 1970 — A29

Designs: 20c, 25c, St. Christopher Nos. 1 and 3. 50c, St. Christopher No. 3 and St. Kitts postmark, Sept. 2, 1871.

Perf. 14½

1970, Sept. 14 Litho. Wmk. 314

230	A29	½c green & rose	15	15
231	A29	20c vio blue, rose & grn	40	40
232	A29	25c brown, rose & grn	55	55
233	A29	50c black, grn & dk red	1.90	1.90

Centenary of stamps of St. Christopher.

Holy Family, by Anthony van Dyck — A30

Christmas: 3c, 40c, Adoration of the Shepherds, by Frans Floris.

1970, Nov. 16 *Perf. 14*

234	A30	3c multicolored	15	15
235	A30	20c ocher & multi	30	30
236	A30	25c dull red & multi	40	40
237	A30	40c green & multi	60	60

Monkey Fiddle A31

Flowers: 20c, Mountain violets. 30c, Morning glory. 50c, Fringed epidendrum.

1971, Mar. 1 Litho. *Perf. 14*

238	A31	½c multicolored	15	15
239	A31	20c multicolored	30	30
240	A31	30c multicolored	48	48
241	A31	50c multicolored	85	85

Chateau de Poincy, St. Kitts — A32

Designs: 20c, Royal poinciana. 50c, De Poincy's coat of arms, vert.

1971, June 1 Litho. Wmk. 314

242	A32	20c green & multi	30	30
243	A32	30c dull yellow & multi	45	45
244	A32	50c brown & multi	90	90

Philippe de Longvilliers de Poincy became first governor of French possessions in the Antilles in 1639.

East Yorks A33

Designs: 20c, Royal Artillery. 30c, French Infantry. 50c, Royal Scots.

1971, Sept. 1 *Perf. 14*

245	A33	½c black & multi	15	15
246	A33	20c black & multi	48	42
247	A33	30c black & multi	80	65
248	A33	50c black & multi	1.25	1.10

Siege of Brimstone Hill, 1782.

Common Design Types are pictured beginning on page 176.

Crucifixion, by Quentin Massys — A34

Perf. 14x13½

1972, Apr. 1 Litho. Wmk. 314

249	A34	4c brick red & multi	15	15
250	A34	20c gray green & multi	48	48
251	A34	30c dull blue & multi	70	70
252	A34	40c lt brown & multi	95	95

Easter 1972.

Madonna and Child, by Bergognone — A35

Paintings: 20c, Adoration of the Kings, by Jacopo da Bassano, horiz. 25c, Adoration of the Shepherds, by Il Domenichino. 40c, Madonna and Child, by Fiorenzo di Lorenzo.

1972, Oct. 2 *Perf. 13½x14, 14x13½*

253	A35	3c gray green & multi	15	15
254	A35	20c deep plum & multi	38	38
255	A35	25c sepia & multi	45	45
256	A35	40c red & multi	70	70

Christmas 1972.

Silver Wedding Issue, 1972

Common Design Type

Design: Queen Elizabeth II, Prince Philip and pelicans.

1972, Nov. 20 Photo. *Perf. 14x14½*

257	CD324	20c carmine rose & multi	35	35
258	CD324	25c ultra & multi	48	48

Warner Landing at St. Kitts — A36

Designs: 25c, Settlers growing tobacco. 40c, Building fort at "Old Road." $2.50, Warner's ship off St. Kitts, Jan. 28, 1623.

1973, Jan. 28 Litho. *Perf. 14x13½*

259 A36	4c	pink & multi	15	15
260 A36	25c	brown & multi	55	55
261 A36	40c	blue & multi	90	90
262 A36	$2.50	multicolored	3.75	3.75

350th anniversary of the landing of Sir Thomas Warner at St. Kitts.

For overprints, see Nos. 266-269.

The Last Supper, by Juan de Juanes A37

Easter (The Last Supper, by): 4c, Titian, vert. 25c, ascribed to Roberti, vert.

Perf. 14x13½, 13½x14

1973, Apr. 16 Photo. Wmk. 314

263 A37	4c	blue black & multi	15	15
264 A37	25c	multicolored	52	52
265 A37	$2.50	purple & multi	3.25	3.25

Nos. 259-262 Overprinted:

VISIT OF
H. R. H. THE PRINCE OF WALES 1973

1973, May 31 Litho. *Perf. 14x13½*

266 A36	4c	pink & multi	15	15
267 A36	25c	brown & multi	24	24
268 A36	40c	blue & multi	38	38
269 A36	$2.50	multicolored	2.75	2.75

Visit of Prince Charles, May 1973.

Harbor Scene and St. Kitts-Nevis No. 3 — A38

Designs: 25c, Sugar mill and No. 2. 40c, Unloading of boat and No. 1. $2.50, Rock carvings and No. 5.

1973, Oct. 1 Litho. *Perf. 13½x14*

270 A38	4c	salmon & multi	15	15
271 A38	25c	lt blue & multi	60	60
272 A38	40c	multicolored	1.10	1.10
273 A38	$2.50	multicolored	3.75	3.75
a.		Souvenir sheet of 4, #270-273	8.75	8.75

70th anniv. of 1st St. Kitts-Nevis stamps.

Princess Anne's Wedding Issue

Common Design Type

1973, Nov. 14 *Perf. 14*

274 CD325	25c	brt green & multi	22	22
275 CD325	40c	citron & multi	40	40

Virgin and Child, by Murillo — A39

Christ Carrying Cross, by Sebastiano del Piombo — A40

Christmas (Paintings): 40c, Holy Family, by Anton Raphael Mengs. 60c, Holy Family, by Sassoferrato. $1, Holy Family, by Filippino Lippi, horiz.

1973, Dec. 1 Litho. *Perf. 14x13½*

276 A39	4c	brt blue & multi	15	15
277 A39	40c	orange & multi	50	50
278 A39	60c	multicolored	80	80
279 A39	$1	multicolored	1.40	1.40

1974, Apr. 8 *Perf. 13*

Easter: 25c, Crucifixion, by Goya. 40c, Trinity, by Diego Ribera. $2.50, Burial of Christ, by Fra Bartolomeo, horiz.

280 A40	4c	olive & multi	15	15
281 A40	25c	lt blue & multi	30	30
282 A40	40c	purple & multi	48	48
283 A40	$2.50	gray & multi	3.00	3.00

University Center, St. Kitts, Chancellor Hugh Wooding — A41

1974, June 1 *Perf. 13½*

284 A41	10c	blue & multi	15	15
285 A41	$1	pink & multi	1.25	1.25
a.		Souvenir sheet of 2, #284-285	1.90	1.90

University of the West Indies, 25th anniv.

Nurse Explaining Family Planning — A42

Designs: 4c, Globe and hands reaching up, vert. 40c, Family, vert. $2.50, WPY emblem and scale balancing embryo and world.

Wmk. 314

1974, Aug. 5 Litho. *Perf. 14*

286 A42	4c	blk, blue & brn	15	15
287 A42	25c	multicolored	26	26
288 A42	40c	multicolored	42	42
289 A42	$2.50	lilac & multi	2.50	2.50

Family planning and World Population Week, Aug. 4-10.

Churchill as Lieutenant, 21st Lancers — A43

Knight of the Garter — A44

Designs: 25c, Churchill as Prime Minister. 60c, Churchill Statue, Parliament Square, London.

1974, Nov. 30

290 A43	4c	dull violet & multi	15	15
291 A43	25c	yellow & multi	30	30
292 A44	40c	lt blue & multi	42	42
293 A44	60c	lt blue & multi	65	65
a.		Souvenir sheet of 4, #290-293	1.50	1.50

Sir Winston Churchill (1874-1965).

Souvenir Sheets

Boeing 747 over St. Kitts-Nevis — A45

1974, Dec. 16 *Perf. 14x13½*

294 A45	40c	multicolored	60	60
295 A45	45c	multicolored	70	70

Opening of Golden Rock Intl. Airport.

The Last Supper, by Doré — A46

Easter: 25c, Jesus mocked. 40c, Jesus falling beneath the Cross. $1, Raising the Cross. Designs based on Bible illustrations by Paul Gustave Doré (1833-1883).

1975, Mar. 24 *Perf. 14½*

296 A46	4c	ultra & multi	15	15
297 A46	25c	lt blue & multi	30	30
298 A46	40c	bister & multi	45	45
299 A46	$1	salmon pink & multi	1.10	1.10

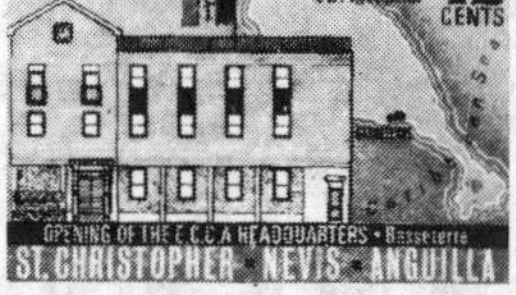

ECCA Headquarters, Basseterre, and Map of St. Kitts — A47

Designs: 25c, Specimen of $1 note, issued by ECCA. 40c, St. Kitts half dollar, 1801, and $4 coin, 1875. 45c, Nevis "9 dogs" coin, 1801, and 2c, 5c, coins, 1975.

Perf. 13½x14

1975, June 2 Wmk. 373

300 A47	12c	orange & multi	16	16
301 A47	25c	olive & multi	32	32
302 A47	40c	vermilion & multi	50	50
303 A47	45c	brt blue & multi	55	55

East Caribbean Currency Authority Headquarters, Basseterre, opening.

Evangeline Booth, Salvation Army — A48

Colfer Swinging Club — A49

Designs (IWY Emblem and): 25c, Sylvia Pankhurst, suffragette. 40c, Marie Curie, scientist. $2.50, Lady Annie Allen, teacher.

Perf. 14x14½

1975, Sept. 15 Litho. Wmk. 314

304 A48	4c	orange brn & blk	15	15
305 A48	25c	lilac pur & blk	32	32
306 A48	40c	blue, vio bl & blk	52	52
307 A48	$2.50	yellow brn & blk	3.25	3.25

International Women's Year 1975.

1975, Nov. 1 *Perf. 14*

308 A49	4c	rose red & blk	15	15
309 A49	25c	yellow & blk	30	30
310 A49	40c	emerald & blk	45	45
311 A49	$1	blue & blk	1.10	1.10

Opening of Frigate Bay Golf Course.

St. Paul, by Sacchi Pier Francesco — A50

Christmas (Paintings, details): 40c, St. James, by Bonifazio di Pitati. 45c, St. John, by Pier Francesco Mola. $1, Virgin Mary, by Raphael.

Wmk. 373

1975, Dec. 1 Litho. *Perf. 14*

312 A50	25c	ultra & multi	25	25
313 A50	40c	multicolored	45	45
314 A50	45c	red brown & multi	52	52
315 A50	$1	gold & multi	1.10	1.10

Virgin Mary — A51

The Last Supper — A52

Stained Glass Windows: No. 317, Christ on the Cross. No. 318, St. John. 40c, The Last Supper (different). $1, Baptism of Christ.

Perf. 14x13½

1976, Apr. 14 Litho. Wmk. 373

316	A51	4c black & multi	15	15
317	A51	4c black & multi	15	15
318	A51	4c black & multi	15	15
a.		Triptych, #316-318	16	16

Perf. 14½

319	A52	25c black & multi	26	26
320	A52	40c black & multi	40	40
321	A52	$1 black & multi	1.00	1.00
		Set value	1.80	1.80

Easter 1976. No. 318a has continuous design.

Map of West Indies, Bats, Wicket and Ball — A52a

Prudential Cup — A52b

Unwmk.

1976, July 8 Litho. *Perf. 14*

322	A52a	12c lt blue & multi	52	45
323	A52b	40c lilac rose & blk	1.65	1.25
a.		Souvenir sheet of 2, #322-323	4.00	4.00

World Cricket Cup, won by West Indies Team, 1975.

Crispus Attucks and Boston Massacre — A53

Designs: 40c, Alexander Hamilton and Battle of Yorktown. 45c, Thomas Jefferson and Declaration of Independence. $1, George Washington and Crossing of the Delaware.

1976, July 26 Litho. Wmk. 373

324	A53	20c gray & multi	18	18
325	A53	40c gray & multi	32	32
326	A53	45c gray & multi	35	35
327	A53	$1 gray & multi	1.00	75

American Bicentennial.

Nativity, Sforza Book of Hours — A54

Queen Planting Tree, 1966 Visit — A55

Christmas (Paintings): 40c, Virgin and Child, by Bernardino Pintoricchio. 45c, Our Lady of Good Children, by Ford Maddox Brown. $1, Christ Child, by Margaret W. Tarrant.

1976, Nov. 1 *Perf. 14*

328	A54	20c purple & multi	18	18
329	A54	40c dk blue & multi	40	40
330	A54	45c multicolored	42	42
331	A54	$1 multicolored	90	90

1977, Feb. 7 Litho. *Perf. 14x13½*

Designs: 55c, The scepter. $1.50, Bishops paying homage to the Queen.

332	A55	50c multicolored	35	35
333	A55	55c multicolored	40	40
334	A55	$1.50 multicolored	1.10	1.10

25th anniv. of the reign of Elizabeth II.

Christ on the Cross, by Niccolo di Liberatore — A56

Easter: 30c, Resurrection (Imitator of Mantegna). 50c, Resurrection, by Ugolino, horiz. $1, Christ Rising from Tomb, by Gaudenzio.

Wmk. 373

1977, Apr. 1 Litho. *Perf. 14*

335	A56	25c yellow & multi	20	20
336	A56	30c deep blue & multi	24	24
337	A56	50c olive green & multi	40	40
338	A56	$1 red & multi	80	80

Estridge Mission A57

Designs: 20c, Mission emblem. 40c, Basseterre Mission.

1977, June 27 Litho. *Perf. 12½*

339	A57	4c blue & black	15	15
340	A57	20c multicolored	22	22
341	A57	40c orange yel & blk	42	42
		Set value	69	69

Bicentenary of Moravian Mission.

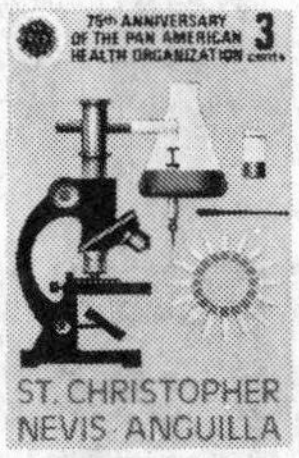

Microscope, Flask, Syringe — A58

Designs: 12c, Blood, fat and nerve cells. 20c, Symbol of community participation. $1, Inoculation.

1977, Oct. 11 Litho. *Perf. 14*

342	A58	3c multicolored	15	15
343	A58	12c multicolored	15	15
344	A58	20c multicolored	16	16
345	A58	$1 multicolored	85	85

Pan American Health Organization, 75th anniversary (PAHO).

Three Kings — A59

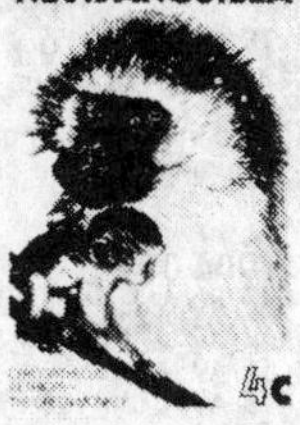

Green Monkey and Young — A60

Christmas, Stained-glass Windows, Chartres Cathedral: 4c, Nativity, West Window. 40c, Virgin and Child. $1, Virgin and Child, Rose Window.

1977, Nov. 15 Wmk. 373

346	A59	4c multicolored	15	15
347	A59	6c multicolored	15	15
348	A59	40c multicolored	30	30
349	A59	$1 multicolored	75	75

Perf. 14½

1978, Apr. 15 Litho. Wmk. 373

Green Monkeys: 5c, $1.50, Mother and young sitting on branch. 55c, like 4c.

350	A60	4c multicolored	15	15
351	A60	5c multicolored	15	15
352	A60	55c multicolored	45	38
353	A60	$1.50 multicolored	1.25	1.00

Elizabeth II Coronation Anniversary Issue

Common Design Types

Souvenir Sheet

Unwmk.

1978, Apr. 21 Litho. *Perf. 15*

354		Sheet of 6	5.00	5.00
a.		CD326 $1 Falcon of Edward III	75	75
b.		CD327 $1 Elizabeth II	75	75
c.		CD328 $1 Pelican	75	75

No. 354 contains 2 se-tenant strips of Nos. 354a-354c, separated by horizontal gutter with commemorative and descriptive inscriptions and showing central part of coronation procession with coach.

Tomatoes A61

Designs: 2c, Defense Force band. 5c, Radio and TV station. 10c, Technical College. 12c, TV assembly plant. 15c, Sugar cane harvest. 25c, Craft Center. 30c, Cruise ship. 40c, Sea crab and lobster. 45c, Royal St. Kitts Hotel and golf course. 50c, Pinneys Beach, Nevis. 55c, New Runway at Golden Rock. $1, Cotton pickers. $5, Brewery. $10, Pineapples and peanuts.

Perf. 14½x14

1978, Sept. 8 Wmk. 373

355	A61	1c multicolored	15	15
356	A61	2c multicolored	15	15
357	A61	5c multicolored	15	15
358	A61	10c multicolored	15	15
359	A61	12c multicolored	15	15
360	A61	15c multicolored	15	15
361	A61	25c multicolored	15	15
362	A61	30c multicolored	18	18
363	A61	40c multicolored	22	22
364	A61	45c multicolored	25	25
365	A61	50c multicolored	28	28
366	A61	55c multicolored	32	32
367	A61	$1 multicolored	55	55
368	A61	$5 multicolored	2.75	2.75
369	A61	$10 multicolored	5.75	5.75
		Nos. 355-369 (15)	11.35	11.35

For overprints, see Nevis 100-112, O1-O10.

Investiture — A62

King Bringing Gift — A63

Designs: 10c, Map reading. 25c, Pitching tent. 40c, Cooking. 50c, First aid. 55c, Rev. W. A. Beckett, founder of Scouting in St. Kitts.

Perf. 13½

1978, Oct. 9 Litho. Wmk. 373

370	A62	5c multicolored	15	15
371	A62	10c multicolored	15	15
372	A62	25c multicolored	25	25
373	A62	40c multicolored	45	45
374	A62	50c multicolored	52	52
375	A62	55c multicolored	55	55
		Nos. 370-375 (6)	2.07	2.07

50th anniversary of St. Kitts-Nevis Scouting.

1978, Dec. 1 *Perf. 14x13½*

Christmas: 15c, 30c, King bringing gift (diff.). $2.25, Three Kings paying homage to Infant Jesus.

376	A63	5c multicolored	15	15
377	A63	15c multicolored	15	15
378	A63	30c multicolored	28	28
379	A63	$2.25 multicolored	2.00	2.00

Canna Coccinea — A64

Flowers: 30c, Heliconia bihai. 55c, Ruellia tuberosa. $1.50, Gesneria ventricosa.

1979, Mar. 19 *Perf. 14*

380	A64	5c multicolored	15	15
381	A64	30c multicolored	28	25
382	A64	55c multicolored	52	42
383	A64	$1.50 multicolored	1.40	1.10

See Nos. 393-396.

Rowland Hill and St. Christopher No. 1 — A65

Rowland Hill and: 15c, St. Kitts-Nevis No. 233. 50c, Great Britain No. 4. $2.50, St. Kitts-Nevis No. 64.

Perf. 14½

1979, July 2 Litho. Wmk. 373

384	A65	5c multicolored	15	15
385	A65	15c multicolored	15	15
386	A65	50c multicolored	32	32
387	A65	$2.50 multicolored	1.50	1.50

Sir Rowland Hill (1795-1879), originator of penny postage.

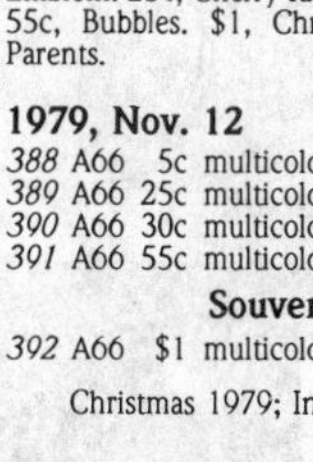

The Woodman's Daughter, by Millais — A66

Paintings by John Everett Millais and IYC Emblem: 25c, Cherry Ripe. 30c, The Rescue, horiz. 55c, Bubbles. $1, Christ in the House of His Parents.

1979, Nov. 12 Litho. *Perf. 14*

388	A66	5c multicolored	15	15
389	A66	25c multicolored	28	28
390	A66	30c multicolored	32	32
391	A66	55c multicolored	60	60

Souvenir Sheet

392	A66	$1 multicolored	1.10	1.10

Christmas 1979; Intl. Year of the Child.

Flower Type of 1979

Flowers: 4c, Clerodendrum aculeatum. 55c, Inga laurina. $1.50, Epidendrum difforme. $2, Salvia serontina.

1980, Feb. 4 Litho. *Perf. 14*

393 A64 4c multicolored	15	15
394 A64 55c multicolored	40	40
395 A64 $1.50 multicolored	1.10	1.10
396 A64 $2 multicolored	1.50	1.50

Nevis Lagoon, London 1980 Emblem A67

1980, May 6 Litho. *Perf. 13½*

397 A67 5c shown	15	15
398 A67 30c Fig Tree Church, vert.	20	20
399 A67 55c Nisbet Plantation	35	35
400 A67 $3 Lord Nelson, by Fuger, vert.	1.90	1.90

Souvenir Sheet

401 A67 75c Nelson Falling, by D. Dighton	90	65

London 80 Intl. Phil. Exhib., May 6-14; Lord Nelson, (1758-1805), 175th death anniv.

WAR TAX STAMPS

No. 12 Overprinted **WAR TAX**

1916 Wmk. 3 *Perf. 14*

MR1 A1 ½p green	15	15

Type of 1905-18 Issue Overprinted **WAR STAMP**

1918

MR2 A1 1½p orange	15	15

OFFICIAL STAMPS

> **Catalogue values for unused stamps in this section are for Never Hinged items.**

Nos. 359, 361, 363-369 Overprinted: OFFICIAL

Perf. 14½x14

1980 Litho. Wmk. 373

O1 A61 12c multicolored	15	15
O2 A61 25c multicolored	16	16
O3 A61 40c multicolored	26	26
O4 A61 45c multicolored	30	30
O5 A61 50c multicolored	32	32
O6 A61 55c multicolored	35	35
O7 A61 $1 multicolored	65	65
O8 A61 $5 multicolored	3.25	3.25
O9 A61 $10 multicolored	6.75	6.75
Nos. O1-O9 (9)	12.19	12.19

ST. LUCIA

LOCATION — Island in the West Indies, one of the Windward group
GOVT. — Independent state in British Commonwealth
AREA — 240 sq. mi.
POP. — 126,800 (est. 1984)
CAPITAL — Castries

The British colony of St. Lucia became an associated state March 1, 1967, and independent in 1979.

12 Pence = 1 Shilling
100 Cents = 1 Dollar (1949)

> **Values for Nos. 1-26 are for copies with perfs. cutting into the design.**

> **Catalogue values for unused stamps in this country are for Never Hinged items, beginning with Scott 127 in the regular postage section, Scott C1 in the air post section, Scott J3 in the postage due section, and Scott O1 in the officials section.**

Watermark

Wmk. 5- Small Star

Queen Victoria — A1

Perf. 14 to 16

1860, Dec. 18 Engr. Wmk. 5

1 A1 (1p) rose red	95.00	75.00
a. Double impression		
2 A1 (4p) deep blue	325.00	250.00
3 A1 (6p) green	425.00	300.00

For types overprinted see #15, 17, 19-26.

1863 Wmk. 1 *Perf. 12½*

4 A1 (1p) lake	37.50	42.50
a. Imperf., pair	4,250.	
5 A1 (4p) slate blue	140.00	120.00
a. Imperf., pair	4,500.	
6 A1 (6p) emerald	190.00	150.00

1864

7 A1 (1p) deep black	11.00	11.00
b. Imperf., pair	1,000.	
8 A1 (4p) yellow	100.00	50.00
a. (4p) olive yellow	250.00	65.00
9 A1 (6p) violet	55.00	30.00
a. (6p) lilac	175.00	42.50
b. Imperf., pair	2,000.	
10 A1 (1sh) red orange	200.00	42.50
a. (1sh) orange	200.00	42.50
b. Imperf., pair	2,250.	

Perf. 14

11 A1 (1p) deep black	15.00	15.00
12 A1 (4p) yellow	65.00	25.00
13 A1 (6p) pale lilac	52.50	25.00
a. (6p) deep lilac	55.00	32.50
14 A1 (1sh) orange	150.00	30.00

Type of 1860 Surcharged in Black or Red:

HALFPENNY — a
2½ PENCE — b

1881

15 A1(a) ½p green	30.00	30.00
17 A1(b) 2½p scarlet	17.50	15.00

1883-84 Wmk. Crown and CA (2)

19 A1(a) ½p green	12.50	14.00
20 A1(a) 1p black (R)	12.50	14.00
a. Half used as ½p on cover		*2,000.*
21 A1(a) 4p yellow	200.00	27.50
22 A1(a) 6p violet	32.50	32.50
23 A1(a) 1sh orange	225.00	150.00

1884 *Perf. 12*

24 A1(a) 4p yellow	350.00	32.50

Half penny

1885 Wmk. 1 *Perf. 12½*

25 A1 ½p emerald	60.	
26 A1 6p slate blue	1,600.	

Nos. 25 and 26 were prepared for use but not issued.

A5

Die B

For explanation of dies A and B see back of this section of the Catalogue.

1883-98 Typo. Wmk. 2 *Perf. 14*

27 A5 ½p green ('91)	50	28
a. Die A ('83)	2.75	2.25
28 A5 1p rose (die A) ('83)	19.00	16.00
29 A5 1p lilac ('91)	1.00	40
a. Die A ('86)	2.75	2.75
b. Die A, imperf., pair	700.00	
30 A5 2p ultra & brn org ('98)	1.50	1.50
31 A5 2½p ultra ('91)	1.50	60
a. Die A ('83)	12.50	2.25
32 A5 3p lilac & grn ('91)	2.75	2.75
a. Die A ('86)	30.00	16.00
33 A5 4p brown ('93)	2.50	2.50
a. Die A ('85)	12.50	3.50
b. Die A, imperf., pair	1,050.	
34 A5 6p vio (die A) ('85)	275.00	275.00
a. Imperf., pair	1,800.	
35 A5 6p lil & bl ('86)	8.50	10.50
a. Die A ('91)	2.50	2.50
36 A5 1sh brn org (die A) ('85)	400.00	135.00
37 A5 1sh lilac & red ('91)	2.50	*7.50*
a. Die A ('86)	42.50	30.00
38 A5 5sh lilac & org ('91)	18.00	*40.00*
39 A5 10sh lilac & blk ('91)	45.00	*55.00*
Nos. 27-39 (13)	777.75	547.03

Nos. 32, 32a, 35a and 33a Surcharged in Black:

ONE HALF PENNY — No. 40
½d — No. 41
ONE PENNY — No. 42

1892

40 A5 ½p on 3p lil & grn	32.50	25.00
a. Die A	50.00	50.00
b. Dbl. surch., die B	900.00	850.00
c. Invtd. surch., die B	2,000.	750.00
d. Triple surch., one on back	*1,800.*	*1,650.*
41 A5 ½p on half of 6p lilac & blue	14.00	10.50
a. Slanting serif	180.00	180.00
c. Without the bar of "½"	180.00	160.00
d. "2" of "½" omitted	400.00	400.00
e. Surcharged sideways	425.00	
f. Double surcharge	500.00	500.00
42 A5 1p on 4p brown	5.00	5.50
b. Double surcharge	165.00	
c. Inverted surcharge	1,050.	550.00

No. 40 is found with wide or narrow "O" in "ONE," and large or small "A" in "HALF."

Edward VII A9

The Pitons A10

Numerals of 3p, 6p, 1sh and 5sh of type A9 are in color on plain tablet.

1902-03 Typo.

43 A9 ½p violet & green	60	40
44 A9 1p violet & car rose	1.60	65
46 A9 2½p violet & ultra	4.50	4.50
47 A9 3p violet & yellow	4.50	5.00
48 A9 1sh green & black	7.50	7.00
Nos. 43-48 (5)	18.70	17.55

Wmk. 1 sideways

1902, Dec. 16 Engr.

49 A10 2p brown & green	3.75	3.75

Fourth centenary of the discovery of the island by Columbus.

1904-05 Typo. Wmk. 3

50 A9 ½p violet & green	60	40
51 A9 1p violet & car rose	1.00	25
52 A9 2½p violet & ultra	3.00	1.50
53 A9 3p violet & yellow	5.00	2.75
54 A9 6p vio & dp vio ('05)	3.25	3.25
55 A9 1sh green & blk ('05)	13.00	15.00
56 A9 5sh green & car ('05)	25.00	32.50
Nos. 50-56 (7)	50.85	55.65

#50, 51, 52, 54 are on both ordinary and chalky paper. #55 is on chalky paper only.

1907-10

57 A9 ½p green	75	24
58 A9 1p carmine	2.00	24
59 A9 2½p ultra	1.50	1.25

Chalky Paper

60 A9 3p violet, *yel* ('09)	3.25	3.25
61 A9 6p violet & red violet	4.25	4.50
a. 6p violet & dull vio ('10)	7.50	*10.50*
62 A9 1sh black, *grn* ('09)	6.50	7.25
63 A9 5sh green & red, *yel*	30.00	*40.00*
Nos. 57-63 (7)	48.25	*56.73*

King George V
A11 A12

Numerals of 3p, 6p, 1sh and 5sh of type A11 are in color on plain tablet.

For description of dies I and II see back of this section of the Catalogue.

Die I

1912-19

Ordinary Paper

64 A11 ½p deep green	32	32
65 A11 1p scarlet	55	40
a. 1p carmine	55	22
66 A12 2p gray ('13)	2.00	4.25
67 A11 2½p ultra	1.25	90

Chalky Paper

Numeral on White Tablet

68 A11 3p violet, *yel*	70	1.00
a. Die II	3.75	7.25
69 A11 6p vio & red vio	2.25	*6.00*
70 A11 1sh black, *green*	4.25	6.75
a. 1sh black, *bl grn,* ol back	3.50	5.00
71 A11 1sh fawn	3.00	6.00
72 A11 5sh green & red, *yel*	25.00	*50.00*
Nos. 64-72 (9)	39.32	*75.62*

A13

A14

1913-14

Chalky Paper

73 A13 4p scar & blk, *yel*	2.50	*4.50*
74 A14 2sh6p black & red, *bl*	14.00	*20.00*

Surface-colored Paper

75 A13 4p scarlet & blk, *yel*	90	*1.75*

Die II

1921-24 Wmk. 4

Ordinary Paper

76 A11 ½p green	38	16
77 A11 1p carmine	2.25	*4.75*
78 A11 1p dk brn ('22)	40	35
79 A13 1½p rose red ('22)	1.25	85
80 A12 2p gray	35	35
81 A11 2½p ultra	65	*1.25*
82 A11 2½p orange ('24)	4.75	*7.50*
83 A11 3p ultra ('22)	1.10	*2.00*

Chalky Paper

84 A11 3p violet, *yel*	65	*1.75*
85 A13 4p scar & blk, *yel* ('24)	65	*1.25*
86 A11 6p vio & red vio	1.10	*3.50*
87 A11 1sh fawn	1.50	*4.00*
88 A14 2sh6p blk & red, *bl* ('24)	9.50	*15.00*
89 A11 5sh grn & red, *yel*	18.50	*32.50*
Nos. 76-89 (14)	43.03	*75.21*

Silver Jubilee Issue

Common Design Type

1935, May 6 Engr. *Perf. 13½x14*

91 CD301 ½p green & blk	15	15
92 CD301 2p gray blk & ultra	42	42
93 CD301 2½p blue & brn	1.00	1.00
94 CD301 1sh brt vio & indigo	3.00	3.00

Port Castries A15

Columbus Square, Castries A16

Ventine Falls A17

Soldiers' Monument A19

Fort Rodney, Pigeon Island — A18

Government House — A20

Seal of the Colony — A21

1936, Mar. 1 *Perf. 14*

Center in Black

95	A15	½p light green	15	15
a.		Perf. 13x12	35	28
96	A16	1p dark brown	16	15
a.		Perf. 13x12	1.75	1.40
97	A17	1½p carmine	22	18
a.		Perf. 12x13	10.00	2.75
98	A15	2p gray	48	45
99	A16	2½p blue	48	40
100	A17	3p dull green	60	60
101	A15	4p brown	60	60
102	A16	6p orange	90	85
103	A18	1sh light blue, perf. 13x12	1.40	1.25
104	A19	2sh6p ultra	8.75	8.50
105	A20	5sh violet	13.00	*16.00*
106	A21	10sh carmine rose, perf. 13x12	52.50	47.50
		Nos. 95-106 (12)	79.24	76.63

Nos. 95a, 96a and 97a are coils.
Issue date: Nos. 95a, 96a, Apr. 8.

Coronation Issue
Common Design Type

1937, May 12 *Perf. 11x11½*

107	CD302	1p dark purple	15	15
108	CD302	1½p dark carmine	18	18
109	CD302	2½p deep ultra	18	18

King George VI A22

Columbus Square, Castries A23

Government House — A24

The Pitons — A25

Loading Bananas — A26

Arms of the Colony — A27

Perf. 12½ (#111, 1½, 2½, 3, 3½, 8p, 3sh, 5sh, £1), 12 (2sh, 10sh)

1938-48

110	A22	½p green, perf. 14½x14	15	15
a.		Perf. 12½ ('43)	15	15
111	A22	1p deep violet	82	15
a.		Perf. 14½x14	1.00	40
112	A22	1p red, Perf. 14½x14 ('47)	32	24
a.		Perf. 12½	24	20
113	A22	1½p carmine ('43)	15	15
a.		Perf. 14½x14	20	16
114	A22	2p gray, Perf. 14½x14	15	15
a.		Perf. 12½ ('43)	16	16
115	A22	2½p ultra ('43)	15	15
a.		Perf. 14½x14	16	15
116	A22	2½p violet ('47)	15	15
117	A22	3p red orange ('43)	32	24
a.		Perf. 14½x14	20	20
118	A22	3½p brt ultra ('47)	20	20
119	A23	6p mag, perf. 13½	50	50
a.		Perf. 12 ('48)	1.50	1.10
120	A22	8p choc ('46)	42	42
121	A24	1sh lt brn, perf. 13½	50	50
a.		Perf. 12 ('48)	1.50	1.10
122	A25	2sh red vio & sl bl	1.30	1.30
123	A22	3sh brt red vio ('46)	3.25	3.25
124	A26	5sh rose vio & blk	2.25	2.25
125	A27	10sh black, *yel*	3.75	3.75
126	A22	£1 sepia ('46)	8.50	8.50
		Nos. 110-126 (17)	22.88	22.05

See Nos. 135-148.

Catalogue values for unused stamps in this section, from this point to the end of the section, are for Never Hinged items.

Peace Issue
Common Design Type
Perf. 13½x14

1946, Oct. 8 **Wmk. 4** **Engr.**

127	CD303	1p lilac	15	15
128	CD303	3½p deep blue	45	45

Silver Wedding Issue
Common Design Types

1948, Nov. 26 **Photo.** *Perf. 14x14½*

129	CD304	1p scarlet	15	15

Engraved; Name Typographed
Perf. 11½x11

130	CD305	£1 violet brown	21.00	32.50

UPU Issue
Common Design Types
Engr.; Name Typo. on 6c, 12c.
Perf. 13½, 11x11½

1949, Oct. 10 **Wmk. 4**

131	CD306	5c violet	15	15
132	CD307	6c deep orange	18	18
133	CD308	12c red lilac	40	40
134	CD309	24c blue green	65	65

Types of 1938
Values in Cents and Dollars

1949, Oct. 1 **Engr.** *Perf. 12½*

135	A22	1c green	18	15
a.		Perf. 14	75	75
136	A22	2c rose lilac	24	15
a.		Perf. 14½x14	2.00	2.00
137	A22	3c red	32	22
138	A22	4c gray	32	22
a.		Perf. 14½x14		*2,500.*
139	A22	5c violet	40	24
140	A22	6c red orange	40	24
141	A22	7c ultra	50	30
142	A22	12c rose lake	85	75
a.		Perf. 14½x14 ('50)	500.00	275.00
143	A22	16c brown	75	65

Perf. 11½

144	A27	24c Prus blue	95	80
145	A27	48c olive green	2.50	2.50
146	A27	$1.20 purple	3.25	3.25
147	A27	$2.40 blue green	8.00	8.00
148	A27	$4.80 dark car rose	17.00	17.00
		Nos. 135-148 (14)	35.66	34.47

Nos. 144 to 148 are of a type similar to A27, but with the denomination in the top corners and "St. Lucia" at the bottom.
For overprints, see Nos. 152-155.

University Issue
Common Design Types
Perf. 14x14½

1951, Feb. 16 **Wmk. 4**

149	CD310	3c red & gray black	16	16
150	CD311	12c brown carmine & blk	45	45

Phoenix Rising from Burning Buildings — A28

Perf. 13½x13

1951, June 19 **Engr. & Typo.**

151	A28	12c deep blue & carmine	42	42

Reconstruction of Castries.

Nos. 136, 138, 139 and 142 Overprinted in Black

N 1
E 9
W 5
1
CONSTITUTION

1951, Sept. 25 *Perf. 12½*

152	A22	2c rose lilac	15	15
153	A22	4c gray	20	20
154	A22	5c violet	24	24
155	A22	12c rose lilac	40	40

Adoption of a new constitution for the Windward Islands, 1951.

Coronation Issue
Common Design Type

1953, June 2 **Engr.** *Perf. 13½x13*

156	CD312	3c carmine & black	18	18

Queen Elizabeth II A29

Arms of St. Lucia A30

1953-54 **Engr.** *Perf. 14½x14*

157	A29	1c green	15	15
158	A29	2c rose lilac	15	15
159	A29	3c red	15	15
160	A29	4c gray	15	15
161	A29	5c violet	15	15
162	A29	6c orange	15	15
163	A29	8c rose lake	18	18
164	A29	10c ultra	22	20
165	A29	15c brown	30	25

Perf. 11x11½

166	A30	25c Prus blue	55	50
167	A30	50c brown olive	1.25	1.00
168	A30	$1 blue green	2.75	2.50
169	A30	$2.50 dark car rose	7.25	5.75
		Nos. 157-169 (13)	13.40	11.28

Issue dates: 2c, Oct. 28. 4c, Jan. 7, 1954. 1c, 5c, Apr. 1, 1954. Others, Sept. 2, 1954.

West Indies Federation
Common Design Type
Perf. 11½x11

1958, Apr. 22 **Wmk. 314**

170	CD313	3c green	15	15
171	CD313	6c blue	20	20
172	CD313	12c carmine rose	40	40

16th Century Ship and Pitons — A31

St. Lucia Stamp of 1860 — A32

1960, Jan. 1 *Perf. 12½x13*

173	A31	8c carmine rose	24	24
174	A31	10c orange	32	32
175	A31	25c dark blue	70	70

Granting of new constitution.

1960, Dec. 18 **Engr.** *Perf. 13½*

176	A32	5c ultra & red brown	32	32
177	A32	16c yel grn & blue blk	65	65
178	A32	25c carmine & green	90	90

Centenary of St. Lucia's first postage stamps.

Freedom from Hunger Issue
Common Design Type

1963, June 4 **Photo.** *Perf. 14x14½*

179	CD314	25c green	70	70

Red Cross Centenary Issue
Common Design Type
Wmk. 314

1963, Sept. 2 **Litho.** *Perf. 13*

180	CD315	4c black & red	15	15
181	CD315	25c ultra & red	1.00	1.00

A33

A34

Fishing Boats, Soufrière Bay — A35

Designs: 15c, Pigeon Island. 25c, Reduit Beach. 35c, Castries Harbor. 50c, The Pitons. $1, Vigie Beach, vert. $2.50, Queen Elizabeth II, close-up.

Perf. 14½

1964, Mar. 1 **Wmk. 314** **Photo.**

182	A33	1c dark car rose	15	15
183	A33	2c violet	15	15
184	A33	4c brt blue green	15	15
185	A33	5c slate blue	15	15
186	A33	6c brown	15	15
187	A34	8c lt blue & multi	15	15
188	A34	10c multicolored	16	16
189	A35	12c multicolored	18	18
190	A35	15c blue & ocher	22	22
a.		Wmkd. sideways ('68)	20	20
191	A35	25c multicolored	38	38
192	A35	35c dk blue & buff	65	52
193	A35	50c brt blue, blk & yel	90	85
194	A35	$1 multicolored	2.00	1.65
195	A34	$2.50 multicolored	4.00	3.50
		Nos. 182-195 (14)	9.39	8.36

For overprints, see Nos. 215-225.

Shakespeare Issue
Common Design Type

1964, Apr. 23 *Perf. 14x14½*

196	CD316	10c bright green	38	38

ITU Issue
Common Design Type
Perf. 11x11½

1965, May 17 **Litho.** **Wmk. 314**

197	CD317	2c red lilac & brt pink	15	15
198	CD317	50c lilac & yel grn	1.75	1.75

Intl. Cooperation Year Issue
Common Design Type

1965, Oct. 25 Wmk. 314 *Perf. 14½*

199 CD318	1c blue grn & claret	15	15
200 CD318	25c lt violet & grn	50	50

Churchill Memorial Issue
Common Design Type

1966, Jan. 24 Photo. *Perf. 14*

Design in Black, Gold and Carmine Rose

201 CD319	4c bright blue	15	15
202 CD319	6c green	15	15
203 CD319	25c brown	40	40
204 CD319	35c violet	60	60

Royal Visit Issue
Common Design Type

1966, Feb. 4 Litho. *Perf. 11x12*

205 CD320	4c violet blue	15	15
206 CD320	25c dk carmine rose	75	75

World Cup Soccer Issue
Common Design Type

1966, July 1 Litho. *Perf. 14*

207 CD321	4c multicolored	15	15
208 CD321	25c multicolored	45	45

WHO Headquarters Issue
Common Design Type

1966, Sept. 20 Litho. *Perf. 14*

209 CD322	4c multicolored	15	15
210 CD322	25c multicolored	45	45
	Set value	50	50

Common Design Types are pictured beginning on page 176.

UNESCO Anniversary Issue
Common Design Type

1966, Dec. 1 Litho. *Perf. 14*

211 CD323	4c "Education"	15	15
212 CD323	12c "Science"	30	30
213 CD323	25c "Culture"	70	70

Associated State
Nos. 183, 185-194 Overprinted in Red: "STATEHOOD / 1st MARCH 1967"

Perf. 14½

1967, Mar. 1 Photo. Wmk. 314

215 A33	2c violet	15	15
216 A33	5c slate blue	15	15
217 A33	6c brown	15	15
218 A34	8c lt blue & multi	22	18
219 A34	10c multicolored	25	22
220 A35	12c multicolored	32	28
221 A35	15c blue & ocher	65	35
222 A35	25c multicolored	85	50
223 A35	35c dk blue & buff	1.25	65
224 A35	50c multicolored	1.25	85
225 A35	$1 multicolored	2.75	2.25
	Nos. 215-225 (11)	7.99	5.73

The 1c and $2.50, similarly overprinted, were not sold to the public at the post office but were acknowledged belatedly (May 10) by the government and declared valid. The 1c, 6c and $2.50 overprints exist in black as well as red. No. 213 also exists with this overprint in blue and in black.

Madonna and Child with St. John, by Raphael — A36

Cricket Batsman and Gov. Frederick Clarke — A37

1967, Oct. 16 Wmk. 314 *Perf. 14½*

227 A36	4c black, gold & multi	15	15
228 A36	25c multicolored	35	35

Christmas 1967.

Perf. 14½x14

1968, Mar. 8 Photo. Wmk. 314

229 A37	10c multicolored	15	15
230 A37	35c multicolored	55	55

Visit of the Marylebone Cricket Club to the West Indies, Jan.-Feb. 1968.

"Noli me Tangere," by Titian — A38

Martin Luther King, Jr. — A39

Easter: 10c, 25c, The Crucifixion, by Raphael.

1968, Mar. 25 *Perf. 14½*

231 A38	10c multicolored	15	15
232 A38	15c multicolored	15	15
233 A38	25c multicolored	20	20
234 A38	35c multicolored	28	28

Perf. 13½x14

1968, July 4 Photo. Wmk. 314

235 A39	25c dp blue, blk & brn	25	25
236 A39	35c violet, blk & brn	35	35

Dr. Martin Luther King, Jr. (1929-68), American civil rights leader.

Virgin and Child in Glory, by Murillo — A40

Christmas: 10c, 35c, Virgin and Child, by Bartolomé E. Murillo.

Perf. 14½x14

1968, Oct. 17 Photo. Wmk. 314

237 A40	5c dark blue & multi	15	15
238 A40	10c multicolored	18	18
239 A40	25c red brown & multi	35	35
240 A40	35c deep blue & multi	52	52

Purple-throated Carib — A41

Birds: 15c, 35c, St. Lucia parrot.

1969, Jan. 10 Litho. *Perf. 14½*

241 A41	10c multicolored	34	34
242 A41	15c multicolored	38	38
243 A41	25c multicolored	75	75
244 A41	35c multicolored	1.10	1.10

Ecce Homo, by Guido Reni — A42

Painting: 15c, 35c, The Resurrection, by Il Sodoma (Giovanni Antonio de Bazzi).

Perf. 14½x14

1969, Mar. 20 Photo. Wmk. 314

245 A42	10c purple & multi	15	15
246 A42	15c green & multi	16	16
247 A42	25c black & multi	28	28
248 A42	35c ocher & multi	48	48

Easter 1969.

Map of Caribbean A43

Design: 25c, 35c, Clasped hands and arrows with names of CARIFTA members.

1969, May 29 Wmk. 314 *Perf. 14*

249 A43	5c violet blue & multi	15	15
250 A43	10c deep plum & multi	15	15
251 A43	25c ultra & multi	28	28
252 A43	35c green & multi	38	38
	Set value	80	80

First anniversary of CARIFTA (Caribbean Free Trade Area).

Silhouettes of Napoleon and Josephine A44

Perf. 14½x13

1969, Sept. 22 Photo. Unwmk.

Gold Inscription; Gray and Brown Medallions

253 A44	15c dull blue	15	15
254 A44	25c deep claret	25	25
255 A44	35c deep green	38	38
256 A44	50c yellow brown	60	60

Napoleon Bonaparte, 200th birth anniv.

Madonna and Child, by Paul Delaroche — A45

Christmas: 10c, 35c, Holy Family, by Rubens.

Perf. 14½x14

1969, Oct. 27 Photo. Wmk. 314

Center Multicolored

257 A45	5c deep rose lilac & gold	15	15
258 A45	10c Prus blue & gold	15	15
259 A45	25c maroon & gold	28	28
260 A45	35c dp yellow grn & gold	45	45
	Set value	86	86

House of Assembly A46

St. Lucia stamps can be mounted in the Scott British Windward Islands album.

Queen Elizabeth II, by A. C. Davidson-Houston A47

Designs: 2c, Roman Catholic Cathedral. 4c, Castries Boulevard. 5c, Castries Harbor. 6c, Sulphur springs. 10c, Vigie Airport. 12c, Reduit beach. 15c, Pigeon Island. 25c, The Pitons and sailboat. 35c, Marigot Bay. 50c, Diamond Waterfall. $1, St. Lucia flag and motto. $2.50, Coat of arms. $10, Map of St. Lucia.

Wmk. 314 Sideways, Upright (#271-274)

1970-73 Litho. *Perf. 14½*

261	A46	1c multicolored	15	15
262	A46	2c multicolored	15	15
a.		Wmk. upright	55	55
263	A46	4c multicolored	15	15
a.		Wmk. upright	1.00	1.00
264	A46	5c multicolored	15	15
265	A46	6c multicolored	15	15
266	A46	10c multicolored	18	18
267	A46	12c multicolored	18	18
268	A46	15c multicolored	22	22
269	A46	25c multicolored	28	28
270	A46	35c multicolored	35	35
271	A47	50c multicolored	52	52
272	A47	$1 multicolored	1.00	90
273	A47	$2.50 multicolored	2.25	2.00
274	A47	$5 multicolored	4.75	3.75
274A	A47	$10 multicolored	9.00	9.00
		Nos. 261-274A (15)	19.48	18.13

Issue dates: Nos. 261-274, Feb. 1, 1970; No. 274A, Dec. 3, 1973. Nos. 262a, 263a, Mar. 15, 1974.

1975, July 28 Wmk. 373

263b	A46	4c multicolored	38	38
264a	A46	5c multicolored	48	48
266a	A46	10c multicolored	95	95
268a	A46	15c multicolored	1.50	1.50

The Three Marys at the Tomb, by Hogarth — A48

Designs: 25c, The Sealing of the Tomb. $1, The Ascension. The designs are from the altarpiece painted by William Hogarth for the Church of St. Mary Redcliffe in Bristol, 1755-56.

Roulette 8½xPerf. 12½

1970, Mar. 7 Litho. Wmk. 314

Size: 27x54mm

275 A48	25c dark brown & multi	48	48
276 A48	35c dark brown & multi	65	65

Size: 38x54mm

277 A48	$1 dark brown & multi	1.90	1.90
a.	Triptych (#275-277)	3.25	3.25

Easter 1970.

Nos. 275-277 printed se-tenant in sheets of 30 (10 triptychs) with the center $1 stamp 10mm raised compared to the flanking 25c and 35c stamps.

Charles Dickens and Characters from his Works — A49

1970, June 8 Wmk. 314 *Perf. 14*

278	A49	1c	brown & multi	15	15
279	A49	25c	Prus blue & multi	32	32
280	A49	35c	brown red & multi	40	40
281	A49	50c	red lilac & multi	60	60

Charles Dickens (1812-70), English novelist.

Nurse Holding Red Cross Emblem A50

Design: 15c, 35c, British, St. Lucia and Red Cross flags.

Perf. 14½x14

1970, Aug. 18 Litho. Wmk. 314

282	A50	10c	multicolored	15	15
283	A50	15c	multicolored	18	18
284	A50	25c	buff & multi	28	28
285	A50	35c	multicolored	42	42

Centenary of British Red Cross Society.

Madonna with the Lilies, by Luca della Robbia — A51

Lithographed and Embossed

1970, Nov. 16 Unwmk. *Perf. 11*

286	A51	5c	dark blue & multi	15	15
287	A51	10c	violet blue & multi	16	16
288	A51	35c	carmine lake & multi	55	55
289	A51	40c	deep green & multi	70	70

Christmas 1970.

Christ on the Cross, by Rubens — A52

Easter: 15c, 40c, Descent from the Cross, by Peter Paul Rubens.

Perf. 14x13½

1971, Mar. 29 Litho. Wmk. 314

290	A52	10c	dull green & multi	15	15
291	A52	15c	dull red & multi	15	15
292	A52	35c	brt blue & multi	36	36
293	A52	40c	multicolored	48	48

Moule à Chique Lighthouse A53

Design: 25c, Beane Field Airport.

1971, Apr. 30 *Perf. 14½x14*

294	A53	5c	olive & multi	15	15
295	A53	25c	bister & multi	50	50

Opening of Beane Field Airport.

View of Morne Fortune (Old Days) — A54

Designs show for each denomination an old print and a contemporary photograph of the same view. 10c, Castries City. 25c, Pigeon Island. 50c, View from Government House. Plain frame around contemporary views.

Perf. 13½x14

1971, Aug. 10 Litho. Wmk. 314

296	A54	5c	yellow & multi	15	15
297	A54	5c	lt blue & multi	15	15
298	A54	10c	yellow & multi	15	15
299	A54	10c	lt blue & multi	15	15
300	A54	25c	yellow & multi	30	30
301	A54	25c	lt blue & multi	30	30
302	A54	50c	yellow & multi	60	60
303	A54	50c	lt blue & multi	60	60
			Nos. 296-303 (8)	2.40	2.40

Stamps of the same denomination are printed se-tenant in sheets of 30.

Virgin and Child, by Verrocchio — A55

Virgin and Child painted by: 10c, Paolo Moranda. 35c, Giovanni Battista Cima. 40c, Andrea del Verrocchio.

1971, Oct. 15 *Perf. 14*

304	A55	5c	green & multi	15	15
305	A55	10c	brown & multi	15	15
306	A55	35c	ultra & multi	50	50
307	A55	40c	red & multi	65	65

Christmas 1971.

St. Lucia, School of Dolci, and Arms A56

1971, Dec. 13 *Perf. 14x14½*

308	A56	5c	gray & multi	15	15
309	A56	10c	lt green & multi	18	18
310	A56	25c	tan & multi	45	45
311	A56	50c	lt blue & multi	90	90

National Day.

Lamentation, by Carracci A57

Easter: 25c, 50c, Angels Weeping over Body of Jesus, by Guercino.

1972, Feb. 15 Wmk. 314

312	A57	10c	lt violet & multi	15	15
313	A57	25c	ocher & multi	42	42
314	A57	35c	ultra & multi	50	50
315	A57	50c	lt green & multi	85	85

Teachers' College and Science Building A58

Designs: 15c, University Center and coat of arms. 25c, Secondary School. 35c, Technical College.

1972, Apr. 18 Litho. *Perf. 14*

316	A58	5c	multicolored	15	15
317	A58	15c	multicolored	16	16
318	A58	25c	multicolored	28	28
319	A58	35c	multicolored	40	40

Opening of Morne Educational Complex.

Steam Conveyance Co. Stamp and Map of St. Lucia — A59

Designs: 10c, Castries Harbor and 3c stamp. 35c, Soufriere Volcano and 1c stamp. 50c, One cent, 3c, 6c stamps.

1972, June 22 *Perf. 14½*

320	A59	5c	yellow & multi	15	15
321	A59	10c	violet blue & multi	15	15
322	A59	35c	car rose & multi	44	44
323	A59	50c	emerald & multi	1.00	90

Centenary of St. Lucia Steam Conveyance Co. Ltd. postal service.

Holy Family, by Sebastiano Ricci A60

1972, Oct. 18 *Perf. 14½x14*

324	A60	5c	dk brown & multi	15	15
325	A60	10c	green & multi	16	16
326	A60	35c	carmine & multi	60	60
327	A60	40c	dk blue & multi	80	80

Christmas 1972.

Silver Wedding Issue, 1972

Common Design Type

Design: Queen Elizabeth II, Prince Philip, St. Lucia coat of arms and St. Lucia parrot.

1972, Nov. Photo. *Perf. 14x14½*

328	CD324	15c	car rose & multi	20	20
329	CD324	35c	olive & multi	42	42

Weekday Headdress A61

Arms of St. Lucia A62

Women's Headdresses: 10c, For church wear. 25c, Unmarried girl. 50c, Formal occasions.

1973, Feb. 1 Wmk. 314 *Perf. 13*

330	A61	5c	multicolored	15	15
331	A61	10c	dark gray & multi	18	18
332	A61	25c	multicolored	45	45
333	A61	50c	slate blue & multi	90	90

Coil Stamps

1973, Apr. 19 Litho. *Perf. 14½x14*

334	A62	5c	gray olive	30	30
a.			Watermark sideways ('76)	15	15
335	A62	10c	blue	45	45
a.			Watermark sideways ('76)	15	15
336	A62	25c	claret	45	45

H.M.S. St. Lucia A63

Designs: Old Sailing ships.

1973, May 24 Litho. *Perf. 13½x14*

337	A63	15c	shown	20	20
338	A63	35c	"Prince of Wales"	52	52
339	A63	50c	"Oliph Blossom"	70	70
340	A63	$1	"Rose"	1.40	1.40
a.			Souv. sheet of 4, #337-340, perf. 15	4.25	4.25

Banana Plantation and Flower A64

Designs: 15c, Aerial spraying. 35c, Washing and packing bananas. 50c, Loading.

1973, July 26 Litho. *Perf. 14*

341	A64	5c	multicolored	15	15
342	A64	15c	multicolored	30	20
343	A64	35c	multicolored	70	55
344	A64	50c	multicolored	1.10	1.00

Banana industry.

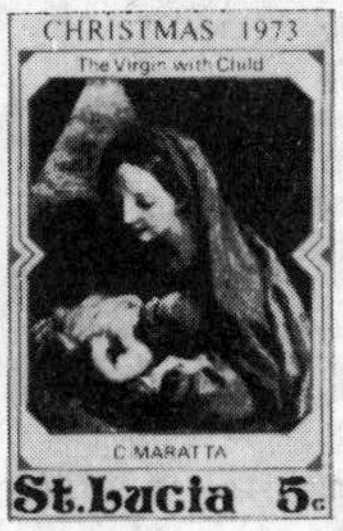

Madonna and Child, by Carlo Maratta — A65

Christmas (Paintings): 15c, Virgin in the Meadow, by Raphael. 35c, Holy Family, by Angelo Bronzino. 50c, Madonna of the Pear, by Durer.

1973, Oct. 17 Litho. *Perf. 14x13½*

345	A65	5c	citron & multi	15	15
346	A65	15c	ultra & multi	18	18
347	A65	35c	dp green & multi	48	48
348	A65	50c	red & multi	80	80

Princess Anne's Wedding Issue

Common Design Type

1973, Nov. 14 Wmk. 314 *Perf. 14*

349	CD325	40c	gray green & multi	28	28
350	CD325	50c	lilac & multi	38	38

The Betrayal of Christ, by Ugolino A66

Easter (Paintings by Ugolino, 14th Cent.): 35c, The Way to Calvary. 80c, Descent from the Cross. $1, Resurrection.

1974, Apr. 1 *Perf. 13½x13*

351	A66	5c	ocher & multi	15	15
352	A66	35c	ocher & multi	30	30
353	A66	80c	ocher & multi	70	70
354	A66	$1	ocher & multi	80	80
a.			Souvenir sheet of 4, #351-354	2.75	2.75

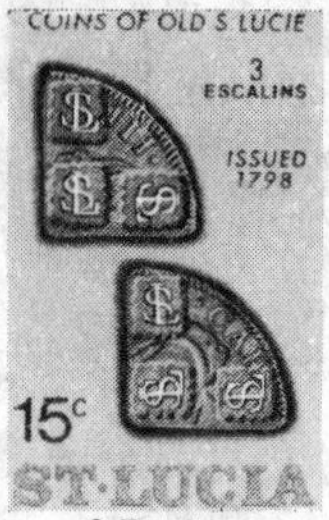

3 Escalins, 1798 — A67

Baron de Laborie, 1784 — A68

Pieces of Eight: 35c, 6 escalins, 1798. 40c, 2 livres 5 sols, 1813. $1, 6 livres 15 sols, 1813.

1974, May 20 *Perf. 13½*

355	A67	15c lt olive & multi	16	16
356	A67	35c multicolored	35	35
357	A67	40c green & multi	40	40
358	A67	$1 brown & multi	95	95
a.		Souvenir sheet of 4, #355-358	2.50	2.50

Coins of Old St. Lucia.

Perf. 14½

1974, Aug. 29 Litho. Wmk. 314

Portraits: 35c, Sir John Moore, Lieutenant Governor, 1796-97. 80c, Major General Sir Dudley St. Leger Hill, 1834-37. $1, Sir Frederick Joseph Clarke, 1967-71.

359	A68	5c ocher & multi	15	15
360	A68	35c brt blue & multi	38	38
361	A68	80c violet & multi	85	85
362	A68	$1 multicolored	1.00	1.00
a.		Souvenir sheet of 4, #359-362	2.75	2.75

Past Governors of St. Lucia.

Virgin and Child, by Verrocchio — A69

Christmas (Virgin and Child): 35c, by Andrea della Robbia. 80c, by Luca della Robbia. $1, by Antonio Rossellino.

1974, Nov. 13 Wmk. 314 *Perf. 13½*

363	A69	5c gray & multi	15	15
364	A69	35c pink & multi	28	28
365	A69	80c brown & multi	60	60
366	A69	$1 olive & multi	75	75
a.		Souvenir sheet of 4, #363-366	2.25	2.25

Churchill and Gen. Montgomery — A70

Design: $1, Churchill and Pres. Truman.

1974, Nov. 30 *Perf. 14*

367	A70	5c multicolored	15	15
368	A70	$1 multicolored	75	75

Sir Winston Churchill (1874-1965).

Crucifixion, by Van der Weyden — A71

Easter: 35c, "Noli me Tangere," by Julio Romano. 80c, Crucifixion, by Fernando Gallego. $1, "Noli me Tangere," by Correggio.

Perf. 14x13½

1975, Mar. 27 Wmk. 314

369	A71	5c brown & multi	15	15
370	A71	35c ultra & multi	32	32
371	A71	80c red brown & multi	70	70
372	A71	$1 green & multi	80	80

Nativity — A72

Adoration of the Kings — A73

Designs: No. 375, Virgin and Child. No. 376, Adoration of the Shepherds. 40c, Nativity. $1, Virgin and Child with Sts. Catherine of Alexandria and Siena.

Perf. 14½

1975, Dec. Litho. Wmk. 314

373	A72	5c lilac rose & multi	15	15
374	A73	10c yellow & multi	15	15
375	A73	10c yellow & multi	15	15
376	A73	10c yellow & multi	15	15
a.		Strip of 3, #374-376	40	40
377	A72	40c yellow & multi	40	40
378	A72	$1 blue & multi	1.00	1.00
a.		Souv. sheet of 3, #373, 377-378	2.00	2.00
		Nos. 373-378 (6)	2.00	2.00

Christmas 1975.

"Hanna," First US Warship A74

Revolutionary Era Ships: 1c, "Prince of Orange," British packet. 2c, "Edward," British sloop. 5c, "Millern," British merchantman. 15c, "Surprise," Continental Navy lugger. 35c, "Serapis," British warship. 50c, "Randolph," first Continental Navy frigate. $1, Frigate "Alliance."

Perf. 14½

1976, Jan. 26 Litho. Unwmk.

379	A74	½c multicolored	15	15
380	A74	1c multicolored	15	15
381	A74	2c multicolored	15	15
382	A74	5c multicolored	15	15
383	A74	15c multicolored	32	16
384	A74	35c multicolored	85	40
385	A74	50c multicolored	1.10	60
386	A74	$1 multicolored	2.75	1.25
a.		Souv. sheet of 4, #383-386, perf. 13	4.75	3.00
		Nos. 379-386 (8)	5.62	3.01

American Bicentennial.

Laughing Gull — A75

Birds: 2c, Little blue heron. 4c, Belted kingfisher. 5c, St. Lucia parrot. 6c, St. Lucia oriole. 8c, Brown trembler. 10c, American kestrel. 12c, Red-billed tropic bird. 15c, Common gallinule. 25c, Brown noddy. 35c, Sooty tern. 50c, Osprey. $1, White-breasted thrasher. $2.50, St. Lucia black finch. $5, Rednecked pigeon. $10, Caribbean elaenia.

Wmk. 314 (1c); 373 (others)

1976, May 7 Litho. *Perf. 14½*

387	A75	1c gray & multi	15	15
388	A75	2c gray & multi	15	15
389	A75	4c gray & multi	15	15
390	A75	5c gray & multi	15	15
391	A75	6c gray & multi	15	15
392	A75	8c gray & multi	15	15
393	A75	10c gray & multi	15	15
394	A75	12c gray & multi	15	15
395	A75	15c gray & multi	16	15
396	A75	25c gray & multi	25	22
397	A75	35c gray & multi	32	28
398	A75	50c gray & multi	48	42
399	A75	$1 gray & multi	1.00	85
400	A75	$2.50 gray & multi	2.50	2.25
401	A75	$5 gray & multi	5.00	4.25
402	A75	$10 gray & multi	10.00	8.50
		Nos. 387-402 (16)	20.91	18.12

Map of West Indies, Bats, Wicket and Ball — A75a

Prudential Cup — A75b

1976, July 19 Unwmk. *Perf. 14*

403	A75a	50c lt blue & multi	1.00	1.00
404	A75b	$1 lilac rose & black	2.00	2.00
a.		Souvenir sheet of 2, #403-404	3.25	3.25

World Cricket Cup, won by West Indies Team, 1975.

Arms of H.M.S. Ceres — A76

Madonna and Child, by Murillo — A77

Coats of Arms of Royal Naval Ships: 20c, Pelican. 40c, Ganges. $2, Ariadne.

1976, Sept. 6 Wmk. 373 *Perf. 14½*

405	A76	10c gold & multi	15	15
406	A76	20c gold & multi	20	20
407	A76	40c gold & multi	40	40
408	A76	$2 gold & multi	1.75	1.75

1976, Nov. 15 Litho. *Perf. 14½*

Paintings: 20c, Virgin and Child, by Lorenzo Costa. 50c, Madonna and Child, by Adriaea Isenbrandt. $2, Madonna and Child with St. John, by Murillo. $2.50, Like 10c.

409	A77	10c multicolored	15	15
410	A77	20c multicolored	28	28
411	A77	50c multicolored	60	60
412	A77	$2 multicolored	2.25	2.25

Souvenir Sheet

413	A77	$2.50 multicolored	3.00	3.00

Christmas.

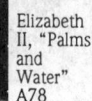

Elizabeth II, "Palms and Water" A78

Perf. 14½

1977, Feb. 7 Litho. Wmk. 373

414	A78	10c multicolored	15	15
415	A78	20c multicolored	15	15
416	A78	40c multicolored	30	30
417	A78	$2 multicolored	1.40	1.40

Souvenir Sheet

418	A78	$2.50 multicolored	1.75	1.75

25th anniv. of the reign of Elizabeth II.

Scouts of Tapion School — A79

Nativity, by Giotto — A80

Designs: 1c, Sea Scouts, St. Mary's College. 2c, Scout giving oath. 10c, Tapion School Cub Scouts. 20c, Venture Scout, Soufrière. 50c, Scout from Gros Islet Division. $1, $2.50, Boat drill, St. Mary's College.

1977, Oct. 17 Unwmk. *Perf. 15*

419	A79	½c multicolored	15	15
420	A79	1c multicolored	15	15
421	A79	2c multicolored	15	15
422	A79	10c multicolored	15	15
423	A79	20c multicolored	20	20
424	A79	50c multicolored	50	50
425	A79	$1 multicolored	1.00	1.00
		Set value	1.90	1.90

Souvenir Sheet

426	A79	$2.50 multicolored	2.00	2.00

6th Caribbean Boy Scout Jamboree, Kingston, Jamaica, Aug. 5-14.

1977, Oct. 31 Litho. *Perf. 14*

Christmas (Virgin and Child by): 1c, Fra Angelico. 2c, El Greco. 20c, Caravaggio. 50c, Velazquez. $1, Tiepolo. $2.50, Adoration of the Kings, by Tiepolo.

427	A80	½c multicolored	15	15
428	A80	1c multicolored	15	15
429	A80	2c multicolored	15	15
430	A80	20c multicolored	15	15
431	A80	50c multicolored	35	35
432	A80	$1 multicolored	70	70
433	A80	$2.50 multicolored	1.75	1.75
		Nos. 427-433 (7)	3.40	3.40

Suzanne Fourment in Velvet Hat, by Rubens — A81

Rubens Paintings: 35c, Rape of the Sabine Women (detail). 50c, Ludovicus Nonnius, portrait. $2.50, Minerva Protecting Pax from Mars (detail).

Perf. 14x14½

1977, Nov. 28 Litho. Wmk. 373

434	A81	10c multicolored	15	15
435	A81	35c multicolored	15	15
436	A81	50c multicolored	48	48
437	A81	$2.50 multicolored	2.25	2.25
a.		Souv. sheet of 4, #434-437, perf. 15	3.25	3.25

Peter Paul Rubens (1577-1640).

Yeoman of the Guard and Life Guard A82

Dress Uniforms: 20c, Groom and postilion. 50c, Footman and coachman. $3, State trumpeter and herald. $5, Master of the Queen's House and Gentleman at Arms.

Unwmk.

1978, June 2 **Litho.** *Perf. 14*

438 A82 15c multicolored 15 15
439 A82 20c multicolored 15 15
440 A82 50c multicolored 32 32
441 A82 $3 multicolored 2.00 2.00

Souvenir Sheet

442 A82 $5 multicolored 3.00 3.00

25th anniv. of coronation of Elizabeth II.

Nos. 438-441 exist in miniature sheets of 3 plus label, perf. 12.

Queen Angelfish A83

Tropical Fish: 20c, Four-eyed butterflyfish. 50c, French angelfish. $2, Yellowtail damselfish. $2.50, Rock beauty.

1978, June 19 **Litho.** *Perf. 14½*

443 A83 10c multicolored 15 15
444 A83 20c multicolored 15 15
445 A83 50c multicolored 45 45
446 A83 $2 multicolored 1.75 1.75

Souvenir Sheet

447 A83 $2.50 multicolored 2.50 2.50

French Grenadier, Map of Battle A84

Designs: 30c, British Grenadier and Bellin map of St. Lucia, 1762. 50c, British fleet opposing French landing and map of coast from Gros Islet to Cul-de-Sac. $2.50, Light infantrymen and Gen. James Grant.

1978, Nov. 15 **Litho.** *Perf. 14*

448 A84 10c multicolored 15 15
449 A84 30c multicolored 24 24
450 A84 50c multicolored 40 40
451 A84 $2.50 multicolored 2.00 2.00

Bicent. of Battle of St. Lucia (Cul-de-Sac).

Annunciation A85

Christmas: 55c, 80c, Adoration of the Kings.

Perf. 14x14½

1978, Dec. 4 **Wmk. 373**

452 A85 30c multicolored 22 22
453 A85 50c multicolored 35 35
454 A85 55c multicolored 40 40
455 A85 80c multicolored 55 55

Independent State

Hewanorra Airport — A86

Independence: 30c, New coat of arms. 50c, Government house and Allen Lewis, first Governor General. $2, Map of St. Lucia, French, St. Lucia and British flags.

1979, Feb. 22 **Litho.** *Perf. 14*

456 A86 10c multicolored 15 15
457 A86 30c multicolored 20 20
458 A86 50c multicolored 32 32
459 A86 $2 multicolored 1.25 1.25
a. Souvenir sheet of 4, #456-459 2.00 2.00

Paul VI and John Paul I A87

Pope Paul VI and: 30c, Pres. Anwar Sadat of Egypt. 50c, Secretary General U Thant and UN emblem. 55c, Prime Minister Golda Meir of Israel. $2, Martin Luther King, Jr.

1979, May 7 **Litho.** *Perf. 14*

460 A87 10c multicolored 15 15
461 A87 30c multicolored 25 25
462 A87 50c multicolored 42 42
463 A87 55c multicolored 45 45
464 A87 $2 multicolored 1.75 1.75
Nos. 460-464 (5) 3.02 3.02

In memory of Popes Paul VI and John Paul I.

Jersey Cows A88

Agricultural Diversification: 35c, Fruits and vegetables. 50c, Waterfall (water conservation). $3, Coconuts, copra industry.

1979, July 2 **Litho.** *Perf. 14*

465 A88 10c multicolored 15 15
466 A88 35c multicolored 30 30
467 A88 50c multicolored 42 42
468 A88 $3 multicolored 2.50 2.50

Lindbergh's Route over St. Lucia, Puerto Rico-Paramaribo — A89

1979, Nov. **Litho.** *Perf. 14*

469 A89 10c Lindbergh, hydroplane 15 15
470 A89 30c shown 24 24
471 A89 50c Landing at La Toc 40 40
472 A89 $2 Flight covers 1.65 1.65

Lindbergh's inaugural airmail flight (US-Guyana) via St. Lucia, 50th anniversary.

Prince of Saxony, by Cranach the Elder — A90

IYC (Emblem and): 50c, Infanta Margarita, by Velazquez. $2, Girl Playing Badminton, by Jean Baptiste Chardin. $2.50, Mary and Francis Wilcox, by Stock. $5, Two Children, by Pablo Picasso.

1979, Dec. 6 **Litho.** *Perf. 14*

473 A90 10c multicolored 15 15
474 A90 50c multicolored 40 40
475 A90 $2 multicolored 1.65 1.65
476 A90 $2.50 multicolored 2.00 2.00

Souvenir Sheet

477 A90 $5 multicolored 3.50 3.50

A91

A92

Maltese Cross Cancels and: 10c, Penny Post notice, 1839. 50c, Hill's original stamp design. $2, St. Lucia #1. $2.50, Penny Black. $5, Hill portrait.

1979, Dec. 10

478 A91 10c multicolored 15 15
479 A91 50c multicolored 32 32
480 A91 $2 multicolored 1.25 1.25
481 A91 $2.50 multicolored 1.50 1.50

Souvenir Sheet

482 A91 $5 multicolored 3.00 3.00

Sir Rowland Hill (1793-1879), originator of penny postage.

Nos. 478-481 also issued in sheets of 5 plus label, perf. 12x12½.

1980, Jan. 14

IYC Emblem, Virgin and Child Paintings by: 10c, Virgin and Child, by Bernardino Fungi, IYC emblem. 50c, Carlo Dolci. $2, Titian. $2.50, Giovanni Bellini.

483 A92 10c multicolored 15 15
484 A92 50c multicolored 40 40
485 A92 $2 multicolored 1.65 1.65
486 A92 $2.50 multicolored 2.00 2.00
a. Souvenir sheet of 4, #483-486 4.50 4.50

Christmas 1979; Intl. Year of the Child.

St. Lucia Conveyance Co. Ltd. Stamp, 1873 — A92a

London 1980 Emblem and Covers: 30c, "Assistance" 1p postmark, 1879. 50c, Postage due handstamp, 1929. $2, Postmarks on 1844 cover.

Wmk. 373

1980, May 6 **Litho.** *Perf. 14*

487 A92a 10c multicolored 15 15
488 A92a 30c multicolored 20 20
489 A92a 50c multicolored 35 35
490 A92a $2 multicolored 1.40 1.40
a. Souvenir sheet of 4, #487-490 2.50 2.50

London 1980 Intl. Stamp Exhib., May 6-14.

Intl. Year of the Child — A93

Space scenes. 1c, 4c, 5c, 10c, $2, $2.50 horiz.

1980, May 29 **Litho.** *Perf. 11*

491 A93 ½c Mickey on rocket 15 15
492 A93 1c Donald Duck spacewalking 15 15
493 A93 2c Minnie Mouse on moon 15 15
494 A93 3c Goofy hitch hiking 15 15
495 A93 4c Goofy on moon 15 15
496 A93 5c Pluto digging on moon 15 15
497 A93 10c Donald Duck, space creature 15 15
498 A93 $2 Donald Duck paddling satellite 2.00 2.00
499 A93 $2.50 Mickey Mouse in lunar rover 2.50 2.50
Nos. 491-499 (9) 5.55 5.55

Souvenir Sheet

500 A93 $5 Goofy on moon 4.00 4.00

Queen Mother Elizabeth, 80th Birthday A94

1980, Aug. 4 **Litho.** *Perf. 14*

501 A94 10c multicolored 15 15
502 A94 $2.50 multicolored 1.75 1.75

Souvenir Sheet

Perf. 12½x12

503 A94 $3 multicolored 2.00 2.00

HS-748 on Runway, St. Lucia Airport, Hewanorra A95

Perf. 14½

1980, Aug. 11 **Litho.** **Wmk. 373**

504 A95 5c shown 15 15
505 A95 10c DC-10, St. Lucia Airport 15 15
506 A95 15c Bus, Castries 15 15
507 A95 20c Refrigerator ship 15 15
508 A95 25c Islander plane 18 18
509 A95 30c Pilot boat 22 22
510 A95 50c Boeing 727 38 38
511 A95 75c Cruise ship 55 55
512 A95 $1 Lockheed Tristar, Piton Mountains 75 75
513 A95 $2 Cargo ship 1.50 1.50
514 A95 $5 Boeing 707 3.75 3.75
515 A95 $10 Queen Elizabeth 2 7.25 7.25
Nos. 504-515 (12) 15.18 15.18

For surcharges, see Nos. 531-533.

1984, May 15 **Wmk. 380**

507a A95 20c 15 15
508a A95 25c 18 18
509a A95 30c 22 22
512a A95 $1 75 75
513a A95 $2 1.50 1.50
515a A95 $10 7.25 7.25
Nos. 507a-515a (6) 10.05 10.05

Shot Put, Moscow '80 Emblem — A96

1980, Sept. 22 **Litho.** *Perf. 14*

516 A96 10c shown 15 15
517 A96 50c Swimming 25 25
518 A96 $2 Gymnastics 1.10 1.10
519 A96 $2.50 Weight lifting 1.40 1.40

Souvenir Sheet

520 A96 $5 Passing the torch 2.75 2.75

22nd Summer Olympic Games, Moscow, July 19-Aug. 3.

A97

A98

1980, Sept. 30 *Perf. 14*

521 A97 10c Palms, coast at dusk 15 15
522 A97 50c Rocky shore 25 25
523 A97 $2 Sand beach 1.10 1.10

524 A97 $2.50 Pitons at sunset 1.40 1.40

Souvenir Sheet

525 A97 $5 Two-master 2.75 2.75

Rotary International, 75th Anniversary.

1980, Oct. 23 Litho. *Perf. 14*

Nobel Prize Winners: 10c, Sir Arthur Lewis, Economics. 50c, Martin Luther King, Jr., peace, 1964. $2, Ralph Bunche, peace, 1950. $2.50, Albert Schweitzer, peace, 1952. $5, Albert Einstein, physics, 1921.

526 A98 10c multicolored 15 15
527 A98 50c multicolored 32 32
528 A98 $2 multicolored 1.25 1.25
529 A98 $2.50 multicolored 1.65 1.65

Souvenir Sheet

530 A98 $5 multicolored 3.25 3.25

Nos. 506-507, 510 Surcharged:

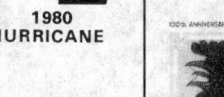

1980
HURRICANE

$1.50 RELIEF

1980, Nov. 3 Litho. *Perf. 14¹/₂*

531 A95 $1.50 on 15c multi 1.50 1.50
532 A95 $1.50 on 20c multi 1.50 1.50
533 A95 $1.50 on 50c multi 1.50 1.50

Nativity, by Battista — A99

Angel and Citizens of St. Lucia — A100

Christmas: 30c, Adoration of the Kings, by Bruegel the Elder. $2, Adoration of the Shepherds, by Murillo.

1980, Dec. 1 *Perf. 14*

534 A99 10c multicolored 15 15
535 A99 30c multicolored 22 22
536 A99 $2 multicolored 1.50 1.50

Souvenir Sheet

537 Sheet of 3 2.00 2.00
a. A100 $1 any single 65 65

Agouti — A101

1981, Jan. 19 Litho. *Perf. 14*

538 A101 10c shown 15 15
539 A101 50c St. Lucia parrot 38 38
540 A101 $2 Purple-throated carib 1.50 1.50
541 A101 $2.50 Fiddler crab 1.90 1.90

Souvenir Sheet

542 A101 $5 Monarch butterfly 4.00 4.00

Royal Wedding Issue
Common Design Type

1981, June 16 Litho. *Perf. 14*

543 CD331 25c Couple 16 16
544 CD331 50c Clarence House 32 32
545 CD331 $4 Charles 2.50 2.50

Souvenir Sheet

546 CD331 $5 Glass coach 4.50 4.50

Nos. 543-545 also printed in sheets of 5 plus label, perf. 12, in changed colors.

549 CD331 Booklet 8.75 8.75
a. Pane of 1, $5, Couple 3.50 3.50
b. Pane of 6 (3x50c, Diana, 3x$2, Charles) 5.25 5.25

A102

A103

Picasso Birth Centenary: 30c, The Cock. 50c, Man with Ice Cream. 55c, Woman Dressing her Hair. $3, Seated Woman. $5, Night Fishing at Antibes.

1981, May Litho. *Perf. 14*

550 A102 30c multicolored 20 20
551 A102 50c multicolored 35 35
552 A102 55c multicolored 38 38
553 A102 $3 multicolored 2.00 2.00

Souvenir Sheet

554 A102 $5 multicolored 4.00 4.00

Perf. 14¹/₂

1981, Sept. 28 Litho. Wmk. 373

555 A103 10c Industry 15 15
556 A103 35c Community service 35 35
557 A103 50c Hikers 50 50
558 A103 $2.50 Duke of Edinburgh 2.50 2.50

Duke of Edinburgh's Awards, 25th anniv.

Intl. Year of the Disabled A104

1981, Oct. 30 Litho. *Perf. 14*

559 A104 10c Louis Braille 15 15
560 A104 50c Sarah Bernhardt 32 32
561 A104 $2 Joseph Pulitzer 1.25 1.25
562 A104 $2.50 Henri de Toulouse-Lautrec 1.65 1.65

Souvenir Sheet

563 A104 $5 Franklin D. Roosevelt 3.50 3.50

A105

A107

A106

Christmas: Adoration of the King Paintings.

1981, Dec. 15

564 A105 10c Sfoza 15 15
565 A105 30c Orcanga 22 22
566 A105 $1.50 Gerard 1.10 1.10
567 A105 $2.50 Foppa 1.90 1.90

1981, Dec. 29 Unwmk.

568 A106 10c No. 1 15 15
569 A106 30c No. 251 34 34
570 A106 50c No. 459 55 55
571 A106 $2 UPU, St. Lucia flags 2.25 2.25

Souvenir Sheets

572 A106 $5 GPO, Castries 5.50 5.50

First anniv. of UPU membership.

Unwmk.

1981, Dec. 11 Litho. *Perf. 14*

1980s Decade for Women (Paintings of Women by Women): 10c, Fanny Travis Cochran, by Cecilia Beaux. 50c, Women with Dove, by Marie Laurencin. $2, Portrait of a Young Pupil of David. $2.50, Self-portrait, by Rosalba Carriera. $5, Self-portrait, by Elisabeth Vigee-Le Brun.

573 A107 10c multicolored 15 15
574 A107 50c multicolored 35 35
575 A107 $2 multicolored 1.50 1.50
576 A107 $2.50 multicolored 1.75 1.75

Souvenir Sheet

577 A107 $5 multicolored 3.50 3.50

1982 World Cup Soccer A108

Designs: Various soccer players.

1982, Feb. 15 Litho. *Perf. 14¹/₂*

578 A108 10c multicolored 15 15
579 A108 50c multicolored 38 38
580 A108 $2 multicolored 1.50 1.50
581 A108 $2.50 multicolored 1.90 1.90

Souvenir Sheet

582 A108 $5 multicolored 2.75 3.75

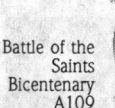

Battle of the Saints Bicentenary A109

Wmk. 373

1982, Apr. 13 Litho. *Perf. 14*

583 A109 10c Pigeon Isld. 15 15
584 A109 35c Battle 28 28
585 A109 50c Admirals Rodney, DeGrasse 38 38
586 A109 $2.50 Map 1.90 1.90
a. Souvenir sheet of 4, #583-586 3.00 3.00

Scouting Year — A110

Christmas 1982 — A111

1982, Aug. 4 Litho. *Perf. 14*

587 A110 10c Map reading 15 15
588 A110 50c First aid 40 40
589 A110 $1.50 Camping 1.25 1.25
590 A110 $2.50 Campfire sing 2.00 2.00

Princess Diana Issue
Common Design Type

Perf. 14¹/₂x14

1982, Sept. 1 Unwmk.

591 CD332 50c Leeds Castle 35 35
592 CD332 $2 Diana 1.40 1.40
593 CD332 $4 Wedding 2.75 2.75

Souvenir Sheet

594 CD332 $5 Diana, diff. 3.50 3.50

Wmk. 373

1982, Nov. 10 Litho. *Perf. 14*

Paintings: 10c, Adoration of the Kings, by Brueghel the Elder. 30c, Nativity, by Lorenzo Costa. 50c, Virgin and Child, Fra Filippo Lippi. 80c, Adoration of the Shepherds, by Nicolas Poussin.

595 A111 10c multicolored 15 15
596 A111 30c multicolored 22 22
597 A111 50c multicolored 38 38
598 A111 80c multicolored 60 60

Commonwealth Day
Common Design Type

1983, Mar. 14 Litho.

599 CD334 10c Twin Peaks 15 15
600 CD334 30c Beach 28 28
601 CD334 50c Banana harvester 45 45
602 CD334 $2 Flag 1.75 1.75

Crown Agents Sesquicentennial A112

Perf. 14¹/₂

1983, Apr. 1 Litho. Wmk. 373

603 A112 10c Headquarters, London 15 15
604 A112 15c Road construction 15 15
605 A112 50c Map 42 42
606 A112 $2 First stamp 1.65 1.65

World Communications Year — A113

Unwmk.

1983, July 12 Litho. *Perf. 15*

607 A113 10c Shipboard intercommunication 15 15
608 A113 50c Air-to-air 45 45
609 A113 $1.50 Satellite 1.40 1.40
610 A113 $2.50 Computer communications 2.25 2.25

Souvenir Sheet

611 A113 $5 Weather satellite 4.25 4.25

Coral Reef Fish A114

1983, Aug. 23

612 A114 10c Longspine squirrelfish 15 15
613 A114 50c Banded butter-flyfish 48 48
614 A114 $1.50 Blackbar soldierfish 1.40 1.40
615 A114 $2.50 Yellowtail snappers 2.25 2.25

Souvenir Sheet

616 A114 $5 Red hind 4.50 4.50

For overprint, see No. 800.

Locomotives A115

Perf. 12½

1983, Oct. 13 Litho. Unwmk.

617 A115 35c Princess Coronation 22 22
618 A115 35c Princess Coronation, diff. 22 22
619 A115 35c Duke of Sutherland 22 22
620 A115 35c Duke of Sutherland, diff. 22 22
621 A115 50c Leeds United 30 30
622 A115 50c Leeds United, diff. 30 30
623 A115 50c Lord Nelson 30 30
624 A115 50c Lord Nelson, diff. 30 30
625 A115 $1 Bodmin 60 60
626 A115 $1 Bodmin, diff. 60 60
627 A115 $1 Eton 60 60
628 A115 $1 Eton, diff. 60 60
629 A115 $2 Flying Scotsman 1.25 1.25
630 A115 $2 Flying Scotsman, diff. 1.25 1.25
631 A115 $2 Stephenson's Rocket 1.25 1.25
632 A115 $2 Stephenson's Rocket, diff. 1.25 1.25
Nos. 617-632 (16) 9.48 9.48

Stamps of same denominations printed in se-tenant pairs.
See Nos. 653-660, 674-701, 711-726, 739-746, 774-781, 807-822, 850-861.

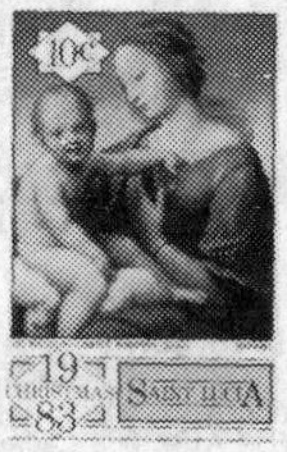

Virgin and Child Paintings by Raphael — A115a

Wmk. 373

1983, Oct. 24 Litho. *Perf. 14*

632A A115a 10c Niccolini-Cowper Madonna 15 15
632B A115a 30c Holy Family with a Palm Tree 18 18
632C A115a 50c Sistine Madonna 32 32
632D A115a $5 Alba Madonna 3.00 3.00

Christmas.

Battle of Waterloo, A116; King George III, A117

Perf. 12½

1984, Mar. 13 Litho. Unwmk.

633 A116 5c shown 15 15
634 A117 5c shown 15 15
635 A116 10c George III, diff. 15 15
636 A117 10c Kew Palace 15 15
637 A116 35c Arms of Elizabeth I 18 18
638 A117 35c Elizabeth I 18 18
639 A116 60c Arms of George III 30 30
640 A117 60c George III, diff. 30 30
641 A116 $1 Elizabeth I, diff. 50 50
642 A117 $1 Hatfield Palace 50 50
643 A116 $2.50 Spanish Armada 1.25 1.25
644 A117 $2.50 Elizabeth, I, diff. 1.25 1.25
Nos. 633-644 (12) 5.06 5.06

Stamps of same denomination se-tenant in continuous design.

Colonial Building, Late 19th Cent. A118

Local Architecture. 10c, vert.

Perf. 14x13½, 13½x14

1984, Apr. 6 Wmk. 380

645 A118 10c Buildings, mid-19th cent. 15 15
646 A118 45c shown 35 35
647 A118 65c Wooden chattel, early 20th cent. 50 50
648 A118 $2.50 Treasury, 1906 1.90 1.90

For overprints, see Nos. 796, 801.

Logwood Tree and Blossom — A119

Perf. 13½x14, 14x13½

1984, June 12 Wmk. 380

649 A119 10c shown 15 15
650 A119 45c Calabash 35 35
651 A119 65c Gommier, vert. 50 50
652 A119 $2.50 Rain tree 1.90 1.90

For overprint, see No. 802.

Locomotive Type of 1983

Cars (side and front views). Stamps of same denomination se-tenant.

Perf. 12½

1984, June 25 Litho. Unwmk.

653 A115 5c Bugatti 57SC, 1939 15 15
654 A115 5c Side 15 15
655 A115 10c Chevrolet Bel Air, 1957 15 15
656 A115 10c Side 15 15
657 A115 $1 Alfa Romeo, 1930 65 65
658 A115 $1 Side 65 65
659 A115 $2.50 Duesenberg, 1932 1.50 1.50
660 A115 $2.50 Side 1.50 1.50
Nos. 653-660 (8) 4.90 4.90

Endangered Reptiles A120

Wmk. 380

1984, Aug. 8 Litho. *Perf. 14*

661 A120 10c Pygmy gecko 15 15
662 A120 45c Maria Isld. ground lizard 35 35
663 A120 65c Green iguana 50 50
664 A120 $2.50 Couresse snake 1.90 1.90

For overprint, see No. 797.

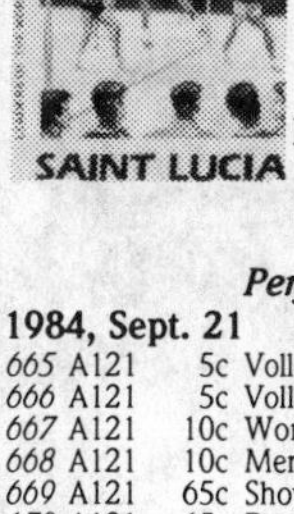

Leaders of the World, 1984 Olympics — A121

Perf. 12½

1984, Sept. 21 Litho. Unwmk.

665 A121 5c Volleyball 15 15
666 A121 5c Volleyball, diff. 15 15
667 A121 10c Women's hurdles 15 15
668 A121 10c Men's hurdles 15 15
669 A121 65c Showjumping 40 40
670 A121 65c Dressage 40 40
671 A121 $2.50 Women's gymnastics 1.50 1.50
672 A121 $2.50 Men's gymnastics 1.50 1.50
Nos. 665-672 (8) 4.40 4.40

Stamps of same denomination se-tenant horiz.

Locomotive Type of 1983

1984, Sept. 21 Litho. *Perf. 12½*

674 A115 1c TAW 2-6-2T, 1897 15 15
675 A115 1c Side view only 15 15
676 A115 15c Crocodile 1-C.C.-1, 1920 15 15
677 A115 15c Side view only 15 15
678 A115 50c The Countess 0.6.0T, 1903 28 28
679 A115 50c Side view only 28 28
680 A115 75c Class GE6/6C.C., 1921 42 42
681 A115 75c Side view only 42 42
682 A115 $1 Class P8, 4.6.0, 1906 55 55
683 A115 $1 Side view only 55 55
684 A115 $2 Der Alder 2.2.2., 1835 1.10 1.10
685 A115 $2 Side view only 1.10 1.10
Nos. 674-685 (12) 5.30 5.30

Stamps of same denomination printed se-tenant vert.

Locomotive Type of 1983

Designs: Automobiles

1984, Dec. 19 Litho. *Perf. 12½*

686 A115 10c Panhard and Levassor, 1889 15 15
687 A115 10c Side view only 15 15
688 A115 30c N.S.U. RO-80 Saloon, 1968 18 18
689 A115 30c Side view only 18 18
690 A115 55c Abarth, Balbero, 1958 32 32
691 A115 55c Side view only 32 32
692 A115 65c TRV Vixen 2500M, 1972 38 38
693 A115 65c Side view only 38 38
694 A115 75c Ford Mustang Convertible, 1965 45 45
695 A115 75c Side view only 45 45
696 A115 $1 Ford Model T, 1914 60 60
697 A115 $1 Side view only 60 60
698 A115 $2 Aston Martin DB3S, 1954 1.25 1.25
699 A115 $2 Side view only 1.25 1.25
700 A115 $3 Chrysler Imperial CG, 1931 1.75 1.75
701 A115 $3 Side view only 1.75 1.75
Nos. 686-701 (16) 10.16 10.16

Stamps of same denomination printed se-tenant vert.

Christmas — A122

Abolition of Slavery, 150th Anniv. — A123

Wmk. 380

1984, Oct. 31 Litho. *Perf. 14*

702 A122 10c Wine glass 15 15
703 A122 35c Altar 28 28
704 A122 65c Creche 55 55
705 A122 $3 Holy family, abstract 2.50 2.50
a. Souv. sheet of 4, #702-705 3.50 3.50

1984, Dec. 12 Litho. *Perf. 14*

Engraving details, Natl. Archives, Castries: 10c, Preparing manioc. 35c, Working with cassava flour. 55c, Cooking, twisting and drying tobacco. $5, Tobacco production, diff.

706 A123 10c bright buff & blk 15 15
707 A123 35c bright buff & blk 25 25
708 A123 55c bright buff & blk 40 40
709 A123 $5 bright buff & blk 3.50 3.50

Souvenir Sheet

710 Sheet of 4 5.00 5.00
a. A123 10c like No. 706 15 15
b. A123 35c like No. 707 25 25
c. A123 55c like No. 708 40 40
d. A123 $5 like No. 709 3.50 3.50

#710a-710d se-tenant in continuous design.

Locomotives Type of 1983

1985, Feb. 4 Unwmk. *Perf. 12½*

711 A115 5c J.N.R. Class C-53, 1928, Japan 15 15
712 A115 5c C-53, diff. 15 15
713 A115 15c Heavy L, 1885, India 15 15
714 A115 15c Heavy L, diff. 15 15
715 A115 35c QGR Class B18¼, 1926, Australia 25 25
716 A115 35c QGR, diff. 25 25
717 A115 60c Owain Glyndwr, 1923, U.K. 40 40
718 A115 60c Glyndwr, diff. 40 40
719 A115 75c Lion, 1838, U.K. 52 52
720 A115 75c Lion, diff. 52 52
721 A115 $1 Coal Engine, 1873, U.K. 70 70
722 A115 $1 Coal Engine, diff. 70 70
723 A115 $2 No. 2238 Class Q6, 1921, U.K. 1.25 1.25
724 A115 $2 Q6, diff. 1.25 1.25
725 A115 $2.50 Class H, 1920, U.K. 1.65 1.65
726 A115 $2.50 Class H, diff. 1.65 1.65
Nos. 711-726 (16) 10.14 10.14

Stamps of same denomination printed se-tenant.

Girl Guides, 75th Anniv. — A124

Butterflies — A125

1985, Feb. 21 Wmk. 380 *Perf. 14*

727 A124 10c multicolored 15 15
728 A124 35c multicolored 30 30
729 A124 65c multicolored 60 60
730 A124 $3 multicolored 2.75 2.75

For overprint, see No. 795.

1985, Feb. 28 Unwmk. *Perf. 12½*

731 A125 15c Clossiana selene 15 15
732 A125 15c Inachis io 15 15
733 A125 40c Philaethria werneckei 30 30
734 A125 40c Catagramma sorana 30 30
735 A125 60c Kallima inachus 40 40
736 A125 60c Hypanartia paullus 40 40
737 A125 $2.25 Morpho rhetenor helena 1.50 1.50
738 A125 $2.25 Ornithoptera meridionalis 1.50 1.50
Nos. 731-738 (8) 4.70 4.70

Stamps of same denomination printed se-tenant.

Locomotive Type of 1983

Designs: Automobiles

1985, Mar. 29

739 A115 15c 1940 Hudson Eight, USA 15 15
740 A115 15c Hudson, diff. 15 15
741 A115 50c 1937 KdF, Germany 35 35
742 A115 50c KdF, diff. 35 35
743 A115 $1 1925 Kissel Goldbug, USA 70 70
744 A115 $1 Goldbug, diff. 70 70
745 A115 $1.50 1973 Ferrari 246GTS, Italy 95 95
746 A115 $1.50 Ferrari, diff. 95 95
Nos. 739-746 (8) 4.30 4.30

Stamps of same denomination printed se-tenant.

Military Uniforms — A126

Designs: 5c, Grenadier, 70th Foot Reg., c. 1775. 10c, Grenadier Co. Officer, 14th Foot Reg., 1780. 20c, Battalion Co. Officer, 46th Foot Reg., 1781. 25c, Officer, Royal Artillery Reg., c. 1782. 30c,

Officer, Royal Engineers Corps., 1782. 35c, Battalion Co. Officer, 54th Foot Reg., 1782. 45c, Grenadier Co. Private, 14th Foot Reg., 1782. 50c, Gunner, Royal Artillery Reg., 1796. 65c, Battalion Co. Private, 85th Foot Reg., c. 1796. 75c, Battalion Co. Private, 76th Foot Reg., 1796. 90c, Battalion Co. Private, 81st Foot Reg., c. 1796. $1, Sergeant, 74th (Highland) Foot Reg., 1796. $2.50, Private, Light Co., 93rd Foot Reg., 1803. $5, Battalion Co. Private, 1st West India Reg., 1803. $15, Officer, Royal Artillery Reg., 1850.

1985, May 7 Wmk. 380 *Perf. 15*

747 A126 5c multicolored 15 15
748 A126 10c multicolored 15 15
749 A126 20c multicolored 18 18
750 A126 25c multicolored 20 20
a. Wmk. 384 ('88) 25 25
751 A126 30c multicolored 25 25
752 A126 35c multicolored 28 28
753 A126 45c multicolored 35 35
754 A126 50c multicolored 40 40
755 A126 65c multicolored 55 55
756 A126 75c multicolored 65 65
757 A126 90c multicolored 75 75
758 A126 $1 multicolored 80 80
759 A126 $2.50 multicolored 2.00 2.00
760 A126 $5 multicolored 4.00 4.00
761 A126 $15 multicolored 10.50 10.50
Nos. 747-761 (15) 21.21 21.21

Nos. 749-750 reissued inscribed 1986, Nos. 747-750, 1989.
See Nos. 876-879.

1987 Unwmk.

747a A126 5c 15 15
748a A126 10c 15 15
751a A126 30c 25 25
753a A126 45c 35 35
754a A126 50c 40 40
759a A126 $2.50 2.00 2.00
760a A126 $5 4.00 4.00
Nos. 747a-760a (7) 7.30 7.30

Issue dates: Nos. 747a-748a, Feb. 24. Nos. 751a-760a, Mar. 16. Dated 1986.

World War II Aircraft A127

1985, May 30 Unwmk. *Perf. 12½*

762 A127 5c Messerschmitt 109-E 15 15
763 A127 5c 109-E, diff. 15 15
764 A127 55c Avro 683 Lancaster Mark I Bomber 38 38
765 A127 55c Mark I, diff. 38 38
766 A127 60c North American P.51-D Mustang 40 40
767 A127 60c Mustang, diff. 40 40
768 A127 $2 Supermarine Spitfire Mark II 1.25 1.25
769 A127 $2 Mark II, diff. 1.25 1.25
Nos. 762-769 (8) 4.36 4.36

Stamps of the same denomination printed se-tenant.

Nature Reserves A128

Birds in habitats: 10c, Frigate bird, Frigate Island Sanctuary. 35c, Mangrove cuckoo, Savannes Bay, Scorpion Island. 65c, Yellow sandpiper, Maria Island. $3, Audubon's shearwater, Lapins Island.

1985, June 20 Wmk. 380 *Perf. 15*

770 A128 10c multicolored 15 15
771 A128 35c multicolored 30 30
772 A128 65c multicolored 55 55
773 A128 $3 multicolored 2.75 2.75

Locomotives Type of 1983

1985, June 26 Unwmk. *Perf. 12½*

774 A115 10c No. 28 Tender engine, 1897, U.K. 15 15
775 A115 10c No. 28, diff. 15 15
776 A115 30c No. 1621 Class M, 1893, U.K. 20 20
777 A115 30c No. 1621, diff. 20 20
778 A115 75c Class Dunalastair, 1896, U.K. 48 48
779 A115 75c Dunalastair, diff. 48 48
780 A115 $2.50 Big Bertha No. 2290, 1919, U.K. 1.50 1.50
781 A115 $2.50 Bertha, diff. 1.50 1.50
Nos. 774-781 (8) 4.66 4.66

Stamps of same denomination printed se-tenant.

Queen Mother, 85th Birthday — A129

Intl. Youth Year — A130

Abstracts, by Lyndon Samuel — A131

1985, Aug. 16

782 A129 40c Facing right 30 30
783 A129 40c Facing left 30 30
784 A129 75c Facing right, diff. 55 55
785 A129 75c Facing left, diff. 55 55
786 A129 $1.10 Facing right, diff. 80 80
787 A129 $1.10 Facing front 80 80
788 A129 $1.75 Facing front, diff. 1.10 1.10
789 A129 $1.75 Facing left, diff. 1.10 1.10
Nos. 782-789 (8) 5.50 5.50

Souvenir Sheets

790 Sheet of 2 2.50 2.50
a.-b. A129 $2 any single 1.25 1.25
790C Sheet of 2 4.50 4.50
e. A129 $3 like No. 782 2.25 2.25
f. A129 $3 like No. 783 2.25 2.25
790D Sheet of 2 9.00 9.00
g. A129 $6 like No. 786 4.50 4.50
h. A129 $6 like No. 787 4.50 4.50

Stamps of same denomination printed se-tenant.
For overprints, see Nos. 798-799.

1985, Sept. 5 Wmk. 380 *Perf. 15*

Illustrations by local artists: 10c, Youth playing banjo, by Wayne Whitfield. 45c, Riding tricycle, by Mark D. Maragh. 75c, Youth against landscape, by Bartholemew Eugene. $3.50, Abstract, by Lyndon Samuel.

791 A130 10c multicolored 15 15
792 A130 45c multicolored 42 42
793 A130 75c multicolored 75 75
794 A130 $3.50 multicolored 3.00 3.00

Souvenir Sheet

794A A131 $5 multicolored 4.00 4.00

Intl. Youth Year.

Stamps of 1983-5 Ovptd. "CARIBBEAN ROYAL VISIT 1985" in Two or Three Lines

Wmk. as Before

1985, Nov. *Perfs. as Before*

795 A124 35c No. 728 90 90
796 A118 65c No. 647 1.75 1.75
797 A120 65c No. 663 1.75 1.75
798 A129 $1.10 No. 786 3.00 3.00
799 A129 $1.10 No. 787 3.00 3.00
800 A114 $2.50 No. 615 6.50 6.50
801 A118 $2.50 No. 648 6.50 6.50
802 A119 $2.50 No. 652 6.50 6.50
Nos. 795-802 (8) 29.90 29.90

Masquerade Figures — A132

Madonna and Child, by Dunstan St. Omer A133

Unwmk.

1985, Dec. 23 Litho. *Perf. 15*

803 A132 10c Papa Jab 15 15
804 A132 45c Paille Bananne 35 35
805 A132 65c Cheval Bois 48 48

Miniature Sheet

806 A133 $4 multi 3.00 3.00

Christmas 1985.

Locomotives Type of 1983

Designs: Nos. 807-808, 1983 MWCR Rack Loco Tip Top, US. Nos. 809-810, 1975 BR Class 87 Stephenson Bo-Bo, UK. Nos. 811-812, 1901 Class D No. 737, UK. Nos. 813-814, 1922 No. 13 2-Co-2, UK. Nos. 815-816, 1954 BR Class EM2 Electra Co-Co, UK. Nos. 817-818, 1922 City of Newcastle, UK. Nos. 819-820, 1930 DRG Von Kruckenberg, Propeller-driven Rail Car, Germany. Nos. 821-822, 1893 JNR No. 860, Japan.

1986, Jan. 17 *Perf. 12½x13*

807 A115 5c multi 15 15
808 A115 5c multi, diff. 15 15
809 A115 15c multi 15 15
810 A115 15c multi, diff. 15 15
811 A115 30c multi 18 18
812 A115 30c multi, diff. 18 18
813 A115 60c multi 35 35
814 A115 60c multi, diff. 35 35
815 A115 75c multi 42 42
816 A115 75c multi, diff. 42 42
817 A115 $1 multi 60 60
818 A115 $1 multi, diff. 60 60
819 A115 $2.25 multi 1.40 1.40
820 A115 $2.25 multi, diff. 1.40 1.40
821 A115 $3 multi 1.75 1.75
822 A115 $3 multi, diff. 1.75 1.75
Nos. 807-822 (16) 10.00 10.00

Stamps of the same denomination printed se-tenant.

Miniature Sheets

Cook-out — A134

Designs: No. 823b, Scout sign. No. 824a, Wicker basket, weavings. No. 824b, Lady Olave Baden-Powell, Girl Guides founder.

1986, Mar. 3 Litho. *Perf. 13x12½*

823 Sheet of 2 5.50 5.50
a.-b. A134 $4 any single 2.75 2.75
824 Sheet of 2 8.00 8.00
a.-b. A134 $6 any single 4.00 4.00

Scouting anniv., Girl Guides 75th anniv. Exist with plain or decorative border.

A135

Queen Elizabeth II, 60th Birthday — A136

Various photographs.

Perf. 13x12½, 12½x13, 14x15 (A136)

1986

825 A135 5c Pink hat 15 15
826 A136 10c Visiting Marian Home 15 15
827 A136 45c Mindoo Phillip Park speech 30 30
828 A136 50c Opening Leon Hess School 34 34
829 A135 $1 Princess Elizabeth 65 65
830 A135 $3.50 Blue hat 2.25 2.25
831 A136 $5 Government House 3.25 3.25
832 A135 $6 Canberra, 1982, vert. 3.75 3.75
Nos. 825-832 (8) 10.84 10.84

Souvenir Sheets

833 A136 $7 HMY Britannia, Castries Harbor 4.50 4.50
834 A135 $8 Straw hat 5.25 5.25

Issue dates: Nos. 825, 829-830, 832, Apr. 21. Nos. 826-828, 831, 833, June 14.

State Visit of Pope John Paul II A137

1986, July 7 *Perf. 14x15, 15x14*

835 A137 55c Kissing the ground 42 42
836 A137 60c St. Joseph's Convent 45 45
837 A137 80c Cathedral, Castries 60 60

Souvenir Sheet

838 A137 $6 Pope 4.45 4.45

Nos. 837-838 vert.

Wedding of Prince Andrew and Sarah Ferguson — A138

1986, July 23 *Perf. 12½*

839 A138 80c Sarah, vert. 60 60
840 A138 80c Andrew, vert. 60 60
841 A138 $2 Couple 1.50 1.50
842 A138 $2 Andrew, Nancy Reagan 1.50 1.50

Stamps of the same denomination printed se-tenant. #841-842 show Westminster Abbey in LR.

US Peace Corps in St. Lucia, 25th Anniv. A139

1986, Sept. 25 Litho. *Perf. 14*

843 A139 80c Technical instruction 60 60
844 A139 $2 Pres. Kennedy, vert. 1.50 1.50
845 A139 $3.50 Natl. crests, corps emblem 2.60 2.60

Wedding of Prince Andrew and Sarah Ferguson — A140

1986, Oct. 15 *Perf. 15*

846 A140 50c Andrew 38 38
847 A140 80c Sarah 60 60
848 A140 $1 At altar 75 75
849 A140 $3 In open carriage 2.25 2.25

Souvenir Sheet

849A A140 $7 Andrew, Sarah 5.25 5.25

Locomotives Type of 1983

Designs: Automobiles

1986, Oct. 23 Litho. *Perf. 12½x13*

850 A115 20c 1969 AMC AMX, US 15 15
851 A115 20c AMX, diff. 15 15
852 A115 50c 1912 Russo-Baltique, Russia 30 30
853 A115 50c Russo-Baltique, diff. 30 30
854 A115 60c 1932 Lincoln KB, US 35 35
855 A115 60c KB, diff. 35 35
856 A115 $1 1933 Rolls Royce Phantom II Continental, UK 60 60
857 A115 $1 Phantom II, diff. 60 60
858 A115 $1.50 1939 Buick Century, US 90 90
859 A115 $1.50 Century, diff. 90 90
860 A115 $3 1957 Chrysler 300 C, US 1.75 1.75
861 A115 $3 300 C, diff. 1.75 1.75
Nos. 850-861 (12) 8.10 8.10

Stamps of the same denomination printed se-tenant.

Chak-Chak Band A141

1986, Nov. 7 *Perf. 15*

862 A141 15c shown 15 15
863 A141 45c Folk dancing 35 35
864 A141 80c Steel band 60 60
865 A141 $5 Limbo dancer 3.75 3.75

Souvenir Sheet

866 A141 $10 Gros Islet 7.50 7.50

Christmas A142

Churches: 10c, St. Ann Catholic, Mon Repos. 40c, St. Joseph the Worker Catholic, Gros Islet. 80c, Holy Trinity Anglican, Castries. $4, Our Lady of the Assumption Catholic, Soufriere, vert. $7, St. Lucy Catholic, Micoud.

1986, Nov.

867 A142 10c multicolored 15 15
868 A142 40c multicolored 30 30
869 A142 80c multicolored 60 60
870 A142 $4 multicolored 3.00 3.00

Souvenir Sheet

871 A142 $7 multicolored 5.25 5.25

Map of St. Lucia — A143

Perf. 14x14½

1987, Feb. 24 Litho. Wmk. 373

872 A143 5c beige & blk 15 15
  a. Wmk. 384 ('89) 15 15
873 A143 10c pale yel grn & blk 15 15
  a. Wmk. 384 ('89) 15 15
874 A143 45c orange & blk 34 34
875 A143 50c pale violet & blk 38 38
Set value 85 85

#872-873 exist inscribed 1988, #875 1989. Issued: #872a, 873a, Apr. 12. See #937.

Uniforms Type of 1985

Designs: 15c, Battalion company private, 2nd West India Regiment, 1803. 60c, Battalion company officer, 5th Regiment of Foot, 1778. 80c, Battalion company officer, 27th (or Inniskilling) Regiment of Foot, c. 1780. $20, Grenadier company private, 46th Regiment of Foot, 1778.

1987, Mar. 16 Unwmk. *Perf. 15*

876 A126 15c multicolored 15 15
877 A126 60c multicolored 42 42
878 A126 80c multicolored 55 55
879 A126 $20 multicolored 13.75 13.75

Dated 1986.

1988 Wmk. 384

876a A126 15c 15 15
877a A126 60c 42 42
878a A126 80c 55 55

Statue of Liberty, Cent.
A144 A145

1987, Apr. 29 Wmk. 373 *Perf. 14½*

880 A144 15c Statue, flags 15 15
881 A144 80c Statue, ship 60 60
882 A144 $1 Statue, Concorde jet 75 75
883 A144 $5 Statue, flying boat 3.75 3.75

Souvenir Sheet

884 A145 $6 Statue, New York City 4.50 4.50

Maps, Surveying Instruments — A147

Wmk. 384

1987, Aug. 31 Litho. *Perf. 14*

888 A147 15c 1775 15 15
889 A147 60c 1814 45 45
890 A147 $1 1888 75 75
891 A147 $2.50 1987 1.90 1.90

First cadastral survey of St. Lucia.

Victoria Hospital, Cent. — A148

Perf. 14½

1987, Nov. 4 Litho. Wmk. 384

892 A148 $1 Ambulance, nurse, 1987 75 75
893 A148 $1 Nurse, hammock, 1913 75 75
894 A148 $2 Hospital, 1987 1.50 1.50
895 A148 $2 Hospital, 1887 1.50 1.50

Souvenir Sheet

896 A148 $4.50 Main gate, 1987 3.35 3.35

Stamps of the same denomination printed se-tenant.

Christmas A149

Paintings (details) by unidentified artists.

1987, Nov. 30

897 A149 15c The Holy Family 15 15
898 A149 50c Adoration of the Shepherds 38 38
899 A149 60c Adoration of the Magi 45 45
900 A149 90c Madonna and Child 68 68

Souvenir Sheet

901 A149 $6 Holy Family 4.50 4.50

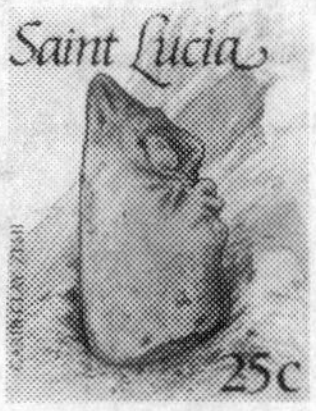

World Wildlife Fund — A150 American Indian Artifacts — A151

Amazonian parrots, Amazona versicolor.

Wmk. 384

1987, Dec. 18 Litho. *Perf. 14*

902 A150 15c multi 15 15
903 A150 35c multi, diff. 25 25
904 A150 50c multi, diff. 38 38
905 A150 $1 multi, diff. 75 75

Perf. 14½

1988, Feb. 12 Litho. Wmk. 384

906 A151 25c Carib clay zemi 18 18
907 A151 30c Troumassee cylinder 22 22
908 A151 80c Three-pointer stone 60 60
909 A151 $3.50 Dauphine petroglyph 2.60 2.60

St. Lucia Cooperative Bank, 50th Anniv. A152

Perf. 15x14

1988, Apr. 29 Litho. Wmk. 373

910 A152 10c Coins, banknotes 15 15
911 A152 45c Branch in Castries 35 35
912 A152 60c like 45c 45 45
913 A152 80c Branch in Vieux Fort 60 60

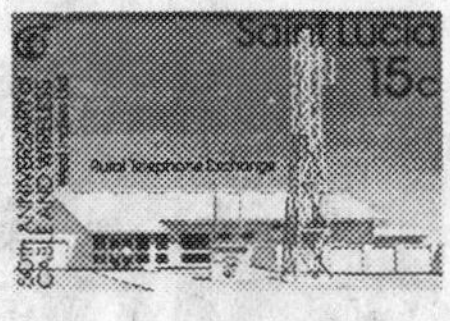

Cable and Wireless in St. Lucia, 50th Anniv. A153

Designs: 15c, Rural telephone exchange. 25c, Antique and modern telephones. 80c, St. Lucia Teleport (satellite dish). $2.50, Map of Eastern Caribbean microwave communications system.

Wmk. 384

1988, June 10 Litho. *Perf. 14*

914 A153 15c multicolored 15 15
915 A153 25c multicolored 18 18
916 A153 80c multicolored 60 60
917 A153 $2.50 multicolored 1.90 1.90

Cent. of the Methodist Church in St. Lucia A154

Perf. 14½

1988, Aug. 15 Litho. Wmk. 384

918 A154 15c Altar, window 15 15
919 A154 80c Chancel 60 60
920 A154 $3.50 Exterior 2.60 2.60

Tourism — A155

Lagoon and: 10c, Tourists, gourmet meal. 30c, Beverage, tourists. 80c, Tropical fruit. $2.50, Fish and chef. $5.50, Market.
Illustration reduced.

Perf. 14x13½

1988, Sept. 15 Litho. Wmk. 384

921 A155 Strip of 4 2.75 2.75
  a. 10c multicolored 15 15
  b. 30c multicolored 22 22
  c. 80c multicolored 60 60
  d. $2.50 multicolored 1.85 1.85

Souvenir Sheet

922 A155 $5.50 multicolored 4.00 4.00

Lloyds of London, 300th Anniv.

Common Design Type

Designs: 10c, San Francisco earthquake, 1906. 60c, Castries Harbor, horiz. 80c, *Lady Nelson,* sunk off Castries Harbor, 1942, horiz. $2.50, Castries on fire, 1948.

Wmk. 373

1988, Oct. 17 Litho. *Perf. 14*

923 CD341 10c multicolored 15 15
924 CD341 60c multicolored 45 45
925 CD341 80c multicolored 60 60
926 CD341 $2.50 multicolored 1.85 1.85

A156 A157

Christmas: Flowers.

Perf. 14½x14

1988, Nov. 22 Litho. Wmk. 384

927 A156 15c Snow on the mountain 15 15
928 A156 45c Christmas candle 35 35
929 A156 60c Balisier 45 45
930 A156 80c Poinsettia 60 60

Souvenir Sheet

931 A156 $5.50 Flower arrangement 4.00 4.00

Perf. 13½x13

1989, Feb. 22 Wmk. 373

Natl. Independence, 10th Anniv.: 15c, Princess Alexandra presenting constitution to Prime Minister Compton. 80c, Sulfur springs geothermal well. $1, Sir Arthur Lewis Community College. $2.50,

Pointe Seraphine tax-free shopping center. $5, Emblem.

932	A157	15c	Nationhood	15	15
933	A157	80c	Development	60	60
934	A157	$1	Education	75	75
935	A157	$2.50	Progress	1.90	1.90

Souvenir Sheet

936	A157	$5	With Confidence We Progress	3.75	3.75

Map Type of 1987

Perf. 14x14½

1989, Mar. 17 Litho. Wmk. 373

937	A143	$1	scarlet & black	75	75

Indigenous Mushrooms — A158

Perf. 14½x14

1989, May 22 Litho. Wmk. 384

938	A158	15c	Gerronema citrinum	15	15
939	A158	25c	Lepiota spiculata	18	18
940	A158	50c	Calocybe cyanocephala	38	38
941	A158	$5	Russula puiggarii	3.75	3.75

PHILEXFRANCE '89, French Revolution Bicent. — A159

Views of St. Lucia and text: 10c, Independence day announcement, vert. 60c, French revolutionary flag at Morne Fortune, 1791. $1, "Men are born and live free and equal in rights," vert. $3.50, Captain La Crosse's arrival at Gros Islet, 1792.

Wmk. 373

1989, July 14 Litho. *Perf. 14*

942	A159	10c	multicolored	15	15
943	A159	60c	multicolored	45	45
944	A159	$1	multicolored	75	75
945	A159	$3.50	multicolored	2.60	2.60

Intl. Red Cross, 125th Anniv. A160

1989, Oct. 10 Wmk. 384 *Perf. 14½*

946	A160	50c	Natl. headquarters	38	38
947	A160	80c	Seminar in Castries, 1987	60	60
948	A160	$1	Ambulance	75	75

Christmas Lanterns Shaped Like Buildings A161

1989, Nov. 17 *Perf. 14x14½*

949	A161	10c	multi	15	15
950	A161	50c	multi, diff.	38	38
951	A161	90c	multi, diff.	68	68
952	A161	$1	multi, diff.	75	75

Trees In Danger of Extinction — A162

1990 Wmk. 384 *Perf. 14*

953	A162	10c	Chinna	15	15
954	A162	15c	Latanier	15	15
955	A162	20c	Gwi gwi	15	15
956	A162	25c	L'encens	18	18
957	A162	50c	Bois lele	38	38
958	A162	80c	Bois d'amande	60	60
959	A162	95c	Mahot piman grand bois	70	70
960	A162	$1	Balata	75	75
961	A162	$1.50	Pencil cedar	1.10	1.10
962	A162	$2.50	Bois cendre	1.75	1.75
963	A162	$5	Lowye cannelle	3.75	3.75
964	A162	$25	Chalantier grand bois	18.50	18.50
			Nos. 953-964 (12)	28.16	28.16

Issue dates: 20c, 25c, 50c, $25, Feb. 21; 10c, 15c, 80c, $1.50, Apr. 12; 95c, $1, $2.50, $5, June 25.

For overprint see Nos. 971, O28-O39.

1992-94 Wmk. 373 *Perf. 14*

953a	A162	10c		15	15
954a	A162	15c		15	15
956a	A162	25c ('94)		18	18
957a	A162	50c		38	38

Nos. 953a, 957a exist dated "1993," Nos. 953a, 954a, 957a dated "1994."

Centenary of St. Mary's College, Intl. Literacy Year A163

Designs: 30c, Father Tapon, original building. 45c, Rev. Brother Collins, current building. 75c, Students in literacy class. $2, Door to knowledge, children.

1990, June 6 Wmk. 373

965	A163	30c	multicolored	22	22
966	A163	45c	multicolored	34	34
967	A163	75c	multicolored	55	55
968	A163	$2	multicolored	1.50	1.50

Queen Mother, 90th Birthday

Common Design Types

1990, Aug. 3 Wmk. 384 *Perf. 14x15*

969	CD343	50c	Coronation, 1937	38	38

Perf. 14½

970	CD344	$5	Arriving at theater, 1949	3.75	3.75

No. 963 Overprinted

1990, Aug. 13 *Perf. 14*

971	A162	$5	multicolored	3.75	3.75

Intl. Garden and Greenery Exposition, Osaka, Japan.

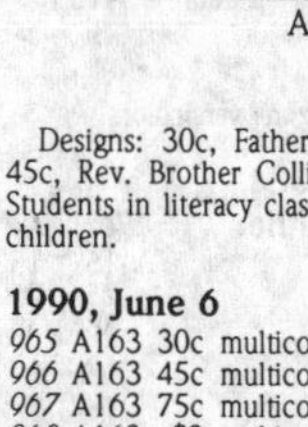

Christmas — A164

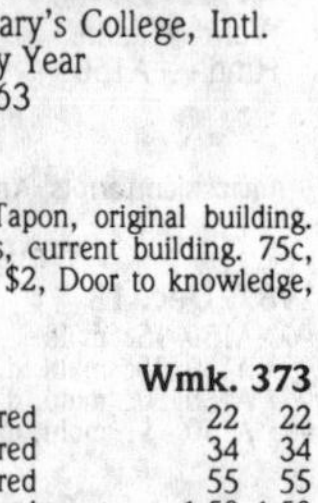

Butterflies — A166

Boats A165

Paintings: 10c, Adoration of the Magi by Rubens. 30c, Adoration of the Shepherds by Murillo. 80c, Adoration of the Magi by Rubens, diff. $5, Adoration of the Shepherds by Champaigne.

1990, Dec. 3 *Perf. 14*

972	A164	10c	multicolored	15	15
973	A164	30c	multicolored	24	24
974	A164	80c	multicolored	64	64
975	A164	$5	multicolored	3.75	3.75

1991, Mar. 27 Wmk. 373 *Perf. 14½*

Various boats.

976	A165	50c	multicolored	40	40
977	A165	80c	multicolored	65	65
978	A165	$1	multicolored	80	80
979	A165	$2.50	multicolored	2.00	2.00

Souvenir Sheet

980	A165	$5	multicolored	3.75	3.75

Wmk. 373

1991, Aug. 15 Litho. *Perf. 14*

981	A166	60c	Polydamas swallow-tail	48	48
982	A166	80c	St. Christopher's hairstreak	65	65
983	A166	$1	St. Lucia mestra	80	80
984	A166	$2.50	Godman's hairstreak	2.00	2.00

Christmas A167

Perf. 14x14½

1991, Nov. 20 Litho. Wmk. 384

985	A167	10c	Jacmel Church	15	15
986	A167	15c	Red Madonna, vert.	15	15
987	A167	80c	Monchy Church	55	55
988	A167	$5	Blue Madonna, vert.	3.45	3.45

Atlantic Rally for Cruisers A168

Designs: 60c, Cruisers crossing Atlantic, map. 80c, Cruisers tacking.

1991, Dec. 10 Wmk. 384 *Perf. 14*

989	A168	60c	multicolored	42	42
990	A168	80c	multicolored	55	55

Discovery of America, 500th Anniv. — A169

Wmk. 373

1992, July 6 Litho. *Perf. 13*

991	A169	$1	Coming ashore	68	68
992	A169	$2	Natives, ships	1.40	1.40

Organization of East Caribbean States.

Contact with New World A170

1992, Aug. 4 *Perf. 13½*

993	A170	15c	Amerindians	15	15
994	A170	40c	Juan de la Cosa, 1499	28	28
995	A170	50c	Columbus, 1502	35	35
996	A170	$5	Gimie, Dec. 13th	3.45	3.45

Christmas A171

Paintings: 10c, Virgin and Child, by Delaroche. 15c, The Holy Family, by Rubens. 60c, Virgin and Child, by Luini. 80c, Virgin and Child, by Sassoferrato.

Perf. 14½

1992, Nov. 9 Litho. Wmk. 373

997	A171	10c	multicolored	15	15
998	A171	15c	multicolored	15	15
999	A171	60c	multicolored	42	42
1000	A171	80c	multicolored	55	55

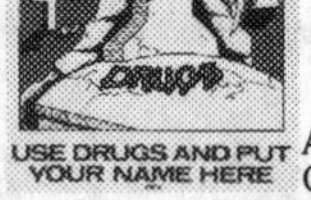

Anti-Drugs Campaign — A172

Perf. 13½x14

1993, Feb. 1 Litho. Wmk. 373

1001	A172	$5	multicolored	2.80	2.80

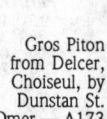

Gros Piton from Delcer, Choiseul, by Dunstan St. Omer — A173

Paintings: 75c, Reduit Bay, by Derek Walcott. $5, Woman and Child at River, by Nancy Cole Auguste.

1993, Nov. 1 Wmk. 373 *Perf. 13*

1002	A173	20c	multicolored	15	15
1003	A173	75c	multicolored	42	42
1004	A173	$5	multicolored	2.75	2.75

Christmas A174

Details of paintings: 15c, The Madonna of the Rosary, by Murillo. 60c, The Madonna and Child, by Van Dyck. 95c, The Annunciation, by Champaigne.

1993, Dec. 6 *Perf. 14*

1005	A174	15c	multicolored	15	15
1006	A174	60c	multicolored	45	45
1007	A174	95c	multicolored	70	70

Abolition of Slavery on St. Lucia, Bicent. — A175

1994, July 25 *Perf. 13*
1008 A175 20c multicolored 15 15

Souvenir Sheet

1009 A175 $5 multicolored 3.75 3.75

AIR POST STAMP

Catalogue values for unused stamps in this section are for Never Hinged items.

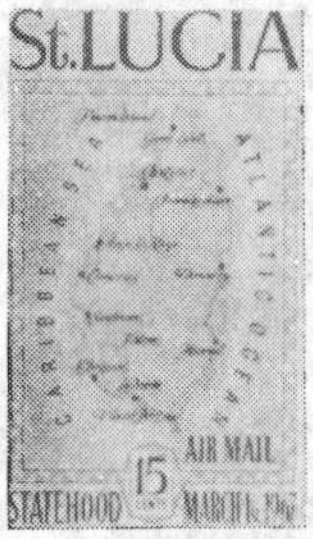

Map of St. Lucia — AP1

Perf. 14½x14
1967, Mar. 1 Photo. Unwmk.
C1 AP1 15c blue 30 30

St. Lucia's independence.
Exists imperf. and also in souvenir sheet.

POSTAGE DUE STAMPS

D1

D2

Type I - "No." 3mm wide (shown).
Type II - "No." 4mm wide.

Rough Perf. 12
1931 Unwmk. Typeset
J1 D1 1p blk, *gray bl*, type I 4.00 3.50
a. Type II 7.50 8.00
J2 D1 2p blk, *yel*, type I 5.00 6.00
a. Type II 15.00 16.00
b. Vertical pair, imperf. btwn. *4,000.*

The serial numbers are handstamped. Type II has round "o" and period. Type I has tall "o" and square period.

Catalogue values for unused stamps in this section, from this point to the end of the section, are for Never Hinged items.

1933-47 Typo. Wmk. 4 *Perf. 14*
J3 D2 1p black 1.50 *3.00*
J4 D2 2p black 3.00 *5.00*
J5 D2 4p black ('47) 2.50 *6.25*
J6 D2 8p black ('47) 3.00 *7.50*

Issue date: June 28, 1947.

Values in Cents

1949, Oct. 1
J7 D2 2c black 25 25
J8 D2 4c black 50 50
J9 D2 8c black 1.00 1.00
J10 D2 16c black 1.75 1.75

Wmk. 4a (error)

J7a D2 2c 30.00
J8a D2 4c 35.00
J9a D2 8c 67.50
J10a D2 16c 82.50

1965, Mar. 9 Wmk. 314
J11 D2 2c black 1.00 *3.00*
J12 D2 4c black 1.25 *5.00*

In the 2c center the "c" is heavier and the period bigger.
Nos. J9-J12 exist with overprint "Statehood/1st Mar. '67" in red.

Arms of St. Lucia — D3

1981, Aug. 4 Litho. Wmk. 373
J13 D3 5c red brown 15 15
J14 D3 15c green 15 15
J15 D3 25c deep orange 15 15
J16 D3 $1 dark blue 55 55
Set value 82 82

1990 Wmk. 384 *Perf. 15x14*
J17 D3 5c red brown 15 15
J18 D3 15c green 15 15
J19 D3 25c deep orange 18 18
J20 D3 $1 dark blue 75 75
Set value 1.05 1.05

WAR TAX STAMPS

No. 65 Overprinted **WAR TAX**

1916 Wmk. 3 *Perf. 14*
MR1 A11 1p scarlet 3.50 5.00
a. Double overprint 400.00 *450.00*
b. 1p carmine 27.50 30.00

Overprinted **WAR TAX**

MR2 A11 1p scarlet 20 20

OFFICIAL STAMPS

Catalogue values for unused stamps in this section are for Never Hinged items.

Nos. 504-515 Overprinted "OFFICIAL"
Perf. 14½
1983, Oct. 13 Litho. Wmk. 373
O1 A95 5c multicolored 15 15
O2 A95 10c multicolored 15 15
O3 A95 15c multicolored 15 15
O4 A95 20c multicolored 15 15
O5 A95 25c multicolored 20 20
O6 A95 30c multicolored 25 25
O7 A95 50c multicolored 40 40
O8 A95 75c multicolored 60 60
O9 A95 $1 multicolored 75 75
O10 A95 $2 multicolored 1.50 1.50
O11 A95 $5 multicolored 3.75 3.75
O12 A95 $10 multicolored 7.50 7.50
Nos. O1-O12 (12) 15.55 15.55

Nos. 747-761 Ovptd. "OFFICIAL"
1985, May 7 Litho. *Perf. 15*
O13 A126 5c multicolored 15 15
O14 A126 10c multicolored 15 15
O15 A126 20c multicolored 15 15
O16 A126 25c multicolored 15 15
O17 A126 30c multicolored 18 18
O18 A126 35c multicolored 20 20
O19 A126 45c multicolored 28 28
O20 A126 50c multicolored 30 30
O21 A126 65c multicolored 40 40
O22 A126 75c multicolored 45 45
O23 A126 90c multicolored 55 55
O24 A126 $1 multicolored 60 60
O25 A126 $2.50 multicolored 1.50 1.50
O26 A126 $5 multicolored 3.00 3.00
O27 A126 $15 multicolored 7.50 7.50
Nos. O13-O27 (15) 15.56 15.56

Nos. 953-964 Ovptd. "OFFICIAL"
1990, Feb. 21 Wmk. 384 *Perf. 14*
O28 A162 10c multicolored 15 15
O29 A162 15c multicolored 15 15
O30 A162 20c multicolored 15 15
O31 A162 25c multicolored 18 18
O32 A162 50c multicolored 38 38
O33 A162 80c multicolored 60 60
O34 A162 95c multicolored 70 70
O35 A162 $1 multicolored 75 75
O36 A162 $1.50 multicolored 1.10 1.10
O37 A162 $2.50 multicolored 1.75 1.75
O38 A162 $5 multicolored 3.75 3.75
O39 A162 $25 multicolored 18.50 18.50
Nos. O28-O39 (12) 28.16 28.16

Issued: 20c, 25c, 50c, $25, Feb. 21. 10c, 15c, 80c, $1.50, Apr. 12. 95c, $1, $2.50, $5, June 25.

ST. VINCENT

LOCATION — Island in the West Indies
GOVT. — Independent state in the British Commonwealth
AREA — 150 sq. mi.
POP. — 123,000 (est. 1984)
CAPITAL — Kingstown

The British colony of St. Vincent became an associated state in 1969 and independent in 1979.

12 Pence = 1 Shilling
20 Shillings = 1 Pound
100 Cents = 1 Dollar (1949)

Catalogue values for unused stamps in this country are for Never Hinged items, beginning with Scott 152 in the regular postage section, Scott B1 in the semi-postal section, and Scott O1 in the officials section.

Values for type A1, Nos. 1/39, are for copies with perfs. cutting into the design, Nos. 40/60 for perfs. touching the design.

Watermark

Wmk. 5- Small Star

Queen Victoria — A1

Clean-Cut Perf. 14 to 16
1861 Engr. Unwmk.
1 A1 1p rose *8,000.* 500.00
a. Imperf., pair 375.00
1B A1 6p yellow green *9,000.* 300.00

1862-66 *Rough Perf. 14 to 16*
2 A1 1p rose 22.50 11.00
a. Horiz. pair, imperf. vert. 450.00
3 A1 6p dark green 65.00 13.00
a. Imperf., pair 600.00
b. Horiz. pair, imperf. between 1,500.
4 A1 1sh slate ('66) 275.00 140.00

1863-69 *Perf. 11 to 13*
5 A1 1p rose 22.50 13.00
6 A1 4p blue ('66) 325.00 100.00
a. Horiz. pair, imperf. vert.
7 A1 4p orange ('69) 250.00 150.00
8 A1 6p deep green 250.00 60.00
8A A1 1sh slate ('66) *3,000.* 1,500.
9 A1 1sh indigo ('69) 300.00 85.00
10 A1 1sh brown ('69) 400.00 140.00

Perf. 11 to 13x14 to 16
11 A1 1p rose *4,000.* 1,500.
12 A1 1sh slate 225.00 110.00

Rough Perf. 14 to 16
1871-78 Wmk. 5
13 A1 1p black 20.00 12.50
a. Vert. pair, imperf. btwn. *6,000.*
14 A1 6p dk blue green 300.00 75.00

Clean-Cut Perf. 14 to 16
14A A1 1p black 27.50 11.00
14B A1 6p blue green 600.00 35.00
c. 6p dull blue green 600.00 35.00
15 A1 6p pale yel green ('78) 500.00 35.00
15A A1 1sh vermilion ('77) *15,000.*

For surcharge, see No. 30.

Perf. 11 to 13
16 A1 4p dark blue ('77) 400.00 100.00
17 A1 1sh deep rose ('72) 600.00 115.00
18 A1 1sh claret ('75) 600.00 200.00

Perf. 11 to 13x14 to 16
20 A1 1p black 50.00 9.00
a. Horiz. pair, imperf. btwn. *4,000.*
21 A1 6p pale yel grn ('77) 450.00 50.00
22 A1 1sh lilac rose ('72) 6,000. 300.00
23 A1 1sh vermilion ('77) 850.00 110.00
a. Horiz. pair, imperf. vert.

See Nos. 25-28A, 36-39, 42-53. For surcharges see Nos. 30, 32-33, 40, 55-60.

Victoria A2

Seal of Colony A3

1880-81 *Perf. 11 to 13*
24 A2 ½p orange ('81) 5.00 3.50
25 A1 1p gray green 95.00 6.50
26 A1 1p drab ('81) 775.00 13.00
27 A1 4p ultra ('81) 1,200. 62.50
a. Horiz. pair, imperf. btwn.
28 A1 6p yellow green 450.00 45.00
28A A1 1sh vermilion 700.00 45.00
29 A3 5sh rose 850.00 850.00

See Nos. 35, 41, 54, 598. For surcharges see Nos. 31-33.

No. 14B Bisected and Surcharged in Red **d. 1**

1880, May *Perf. 14 to 16*
30 A1 1p on half of 6p 450.00 300.00
a. Unsevered pair 1,250. 900.00

No. 28 Bisected and Surcharged in Red **d ½**

1881, Sept. 1
31 A1 ½p on half of 6p yel grn ('81) 130.00 130.00
a. Unsevered pair 600.00 550.00
b. "1" with straight top 900.00
c. Without fraction bar, pair, #31, 31c 4,500. *5,500.*

Nos. 28 and 28A Surcharged in Black:

ONE PENNY — c

4d — d

1881, Nov. *Perf. 11 to 13*
32 A1(c) 1p on 6p yel green 500. 300.
33 A1(d) 4p on 1sh vermilion 1,250. 800.

1883-84 Wmk. 2 *Perf. 12*

35	A2	½p green ('84)	25.00	20.00
36	A1	4p ultra	275.00	12.50
37	A1	4p dull blue ('84)	1,250.	300.00
38	A1	6p yellow grn	250.00	200.00
39	A1	1sh orange ver	37.50	30.00
a.		Imperf., pair		

The ½p orange, 1p rose red, 1p milky blue and 5sh carmine lake were never placed in use. Some authorities believe them to be color trials.

Nos. 35-60 may be found watermarked with single straight line. This is from the frame which encloses each group of 60 watermark designs.

Type of A1 Surcharged in Black

2½ PENCE

e

1883 *Perf. 14*

40	A1	2½p on 1p lake	6.25	1.75

1883-97

41	A2	½p green ('85)	50	50
42	A1	1p drab	25.00	2.75
43	A1	1p rose red ('85)	75	35
44	A1	1p pink ('86)	14.00	4.00
45	A1	2½p brt blue ('97)	1.25	2.50
46	A1	4p ultra	350.00	20.00
47	A1	4p red brown ('85)	900.00	20.00
48	A1	4p lake brown ('86)	15.00	2.50
a.		4p purple brown	15.00	2.50
49	A1	4p yellow ('93)	1.00	3.50
a.		4p olive yellow	350.00	350.00
50	A1	5p gray brown ('97)	5.00	10.00
a.		5p black brown	5.00	10.00
51	A1	6p violet ('88)	100.00	125.00
52	A1	6p red violet ('91)	1.25	3.50
53	A1	1sh org ver ('91)	5.00	7.50
54	A3	5sh car lake ('88)	17.50	20.00
a.		5sh brown lake	22.50	25.00

No. 40 Resurcharged in Black

1d

1885, Mar.

55	A1	1p on 2½p on 1p lake	7.50	8.00

Copies with 3-bar cancel are proofs.

Stamps of Type A1 Surcharged in Black or Violet:

2½d. — g

5 PENCE — h

FIVE PENCE — j

1890-91

56	A1(e)	2½p on 1p brt blue	50	35
a.		2½p on 1p milky blue	7.00	3.00
b.		2½p on 1p gray blue	7.00	1.75
57	A1(g)	2½p on 4p vio brn ('90)	90.00	90.00
a.		Without fraction bar	250.00	275.00

1892-93

58	A1(h)	5p on 4p lake brn (V)	9.00	12.00
59	A1(j)	5p on 6p dp lake ('93)	1.00	1.40
a.		5p on 6p carmine lake	7.00	10.00
b.		Double surcharge		5,000.

1897

60	A1(j)	3p on 1p lilac	5.00	7.50

Victoria A13

Edward VII A14

Numerals of 1sh and 5sh, type A13, and of 2p, 1sh, 5sh and £1, type A14, are in color on plain tablet.

1898 Typo. *Perf. 14*

62	A13	½p lilac & grn	85	55
63	A13	1p lilac & car rose	2.25	38
64	A13	2½p lilac & ultra	3.50	1.75
65	A13	3p lilac & ol grn	2.25	4.25
66	A13	4p lilac & org	2.25	5.25
67	A13	5p lilac & blk	4.25	7.00
68	A13	6p lilac & brn	11.00	17.50
69	A13	1sh grn & car rose	14.00	26.00
70	A13	5sh green & ultra	50.00	80.00
		Nos. 62-70 (9)	90.35	142.68

1902

71	A14	½p violet & green	65	60
72	A14	1p violet & car rose	1.25	20
73	A14	2p violet & black	2.25	2.75
74	A14	2½p violet & ultra	5.00	3.50
75	A14	3p violet & ol grn	5.00	2.75
76	A14	6p violet & brn	9.00	15.00
77	A14	1sh grn & car rose	13.00	22.00
78	A14	2sh green & violet	25.00	35.00
79	A14	5sh green & ultra	37.50	52.50
		Nos. 71-79 (9)	98.65	134.30

1904-11 Wmk. 3

Chalky Paper

82	A14	½p vio & grn	1.00	40
83	A14	1p vio & car rose	4.00	35
84	A14	2½p vio & ultra	6.25	12.00
85	A14	6p vio & brn	10.00	15.00
86	A14	1sh grn & car rose	7.50	12.00
87	A14	2sh vio & bl, *bl*	21.00	32.50
88	A14	5sh grn & red, *yel*	21.00	40.00
89	A14	£1 vio & blk, *red*	325.00	350.00
		Nos. 82-88 (7)	70.75	112.25

Nos. 82, 83 and 86 also exist on ordinary paper.

Issue dates: 1p, 1904, ½p, 6p, 1905, 2½p, 1906, 1sh, 1908, 2sh, 5sh, 1909, £1, July 22, 1911.

"Peace and Justice"
A15 A16

1907 Engr.

Ordinary Paper

90	A15	½p yellow green	60	75
91	A15	1p carmine	1.50	62
92	A15	2p orange	1.25	3.25
93	A15	2½p ultra	4.25	7.50
94	A15	3p dark violet	4.25	11.00
		Nos. 90-94 (5)	11.85	23.12

1909

Without Dot under "d"

95	A16	1p carmine	1.25	35
96	A16	6p red violet	7.00	17.50
97	A16	1sh black, *green*	3.50	6.00

1909-11

With Dot under "d"

98	A16	½p yellow grn ('10)	20	25
99	A16	1p carmine	40	16
100	A16	2p gray ('11)	1.50	3.00
101	A16	2½p ultra	1.25	1.90
102	A16	3p violet, *yel*	65	1.90
103	A16	6p red violet	2.25	6.00
		Nos. 98-103 (6)	6.25	13.21

King George V — A17

1913-14 *Perf. 14*

104	A17	½p gray green	20	20
105	A17	1p carmine	20	15
106	A17	2p gray	1.25	1.50
107	A17	2½p ultra	50	50
108	A17	3p violet, *yellow*	1.00	2.50
109	A17	4p red, *yellow*	65	1.50
110	A17	5p olive green	2.00	6.50
111	A17	6p claret	1.25	2.50
112	A17	1sh black, *green*	1.50	2.50
113	A17	1sh bister ('14)	2.50	5.00
114	A16	2sh vio & ultra	7.00	15.00
115	A16	5sh dk grn & car	15.00	25.00
116	A16	£1 black & vio	80.00	125.00
		Nos. 104-116 (13)	113.05	187.85

Issue dates: 5p, Nov. 7, No. 113, May 1, 1914, others, Jan. 1, 1913.

For overprints, see Nos. MR1-MR2.

No. 112 Surcharged in Carmine

ONE PENNY.

1915

117	A17	1p on 1sh black, *grn*	2.00	2.75
a.		"PENNY" & bar double	900.00	
b.		Without period	14.00	
c.		"ONE" omitted	900.00	
d.		"ONE" double	900.00	

Space between surcharge lines varies from 8 to 10mm.

1921-32 Wmk. 4

118	A17	½p green	15	15
119	A17	1p rose red	15	15
120	A17	1½p yel brn ('32)	80	18
121	A17	2p gray	22	18
122	A17	2½p ultra ('26)	55	45
123	A17	3p ultra	2.25	4.50
124	A17	3p vio, *yel* ('27)	45	1.40
125	A17	4p red, *yel* ('30)	1.50	4.50
126	A17	5p olive green	45	2.25
127	A17	6p claret ('27)	55	2.25
128	A17	1sh bister	1.00	2.75
129	A16	2sh brn vio & ultra	4.50	7.50
130	A16	5sh dk grn & car	11.25	22.50
131	A16	£1 blk & vio ('28)	90.00	150.00
		Nos. 118-131 (14)	113.82	198.76

Silver Jubilee Issue

Common Design Type

1935, May 6 *Perf. 11x12*

134	CD301	1p car & dk blue	25	25
135	CD301	1½p gray blk & ultra	25	25
136	CD301	2½p ultra & brn	75	75
137	CD301	1sh brown vio & ind	2.25	2.25

Coronation Issue

Common Design Type

1937, May 12 *Perf. 11x11½*

138	CD302	1p dark purple	15	15
139	CD302	1½p dark carmine	16	16
140	CD302	2½p deep ultra	40	40

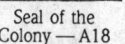

Seal of the Colony — A18

Young's Island and Fort Duvernette — A19

Kingstown and Fort Charlotte — A20

Villa Beach — A21

Victoria Park, Kingstown — A22

1938-47 Wmk. 4 *Perf. 12*

141	A18	½p green & brt bl	15	15
142	A19	1p claret & blue	15	15
143	A20	1½p scar & lt grn	15	15
144	A18	2p black & green	15	15
145	A21	2½p pck bl & ind	15	15
145A	A22	2½p choc & grn ('47)	20	20
146	A18	3p dk vio & org	15	15
146A	A21	3½p dp bl grn & ind ('47)	60	50
147	A18	6p claret & blk	25	25
148	A22	1sh green & vio	45	45
149	A18	2sh dk vio & brt blue	85	85
149A	A18	2sh6p dp bl & org brn ('47)	1.75	1.75
150	A18	5sh dk grn & car	4.00	2.50
150A	A18	10sh choc & dp vio ('47)	5.00	9.00
151	A18	£1 black & vio	10.00	12.00
		Nos. 141-151 (15)	24.00	28.40

Issue date: Mar. 11, 1938.

See Nos. 156-169, 180-184.

Catalogue values for unused stamps in this section, from this point to the end of the section, are for Never Hinged items.

Peace Issue

Common Design Type

1946, Oct. 15 Engr. *Perf. 13½x14*

152	CD303	1½p carmine	20	20
153	CD303	3½p deep blue	30	30

Silver Wedding Issue

Common Design Types

1948, Nov. 30 Photo. *Perf. 14x14½*

154	CD304	1½p scarlet	15	15

Engraved; Name Typographed

Perf. 11½x11

155	CD305	£1 red violet	21.00	22.50

Types of 1938

1949, Mar. 26 Engr. *Perf. 12*

156	A18	1c grn & brt bl	15	15
157	A19	2c claret & bl	15	15
158	A20	3c scar & lt grn	32	24
159	A18	4c gray blk & grn	15	15
160	A22	5c choc & grn	16	15
161	A18	6c dk vio & org	16	15
162	A21	7c pck blue & ind	52	35
163	A18	12c claret & blk	48	32
164	A22	24c green & vio	80	80
165	A18	48c dk vio & brt bl	1.60	1.60
166	A18	60c dp bl & org brn	1.75	1.75
167	A18	$1.20 dk grn & car	4.75	4.75
168	A18	$2.40 choc & dp vio	6.00	6.00
169	A18	$4.80 gray blk & vio	10.00	10.00
		Nos. 156-169 (14)	26.99	26.56

For overprints, see Nos. 176-179.

UPU Issue

Common Design Types

Engr.; Name Typo. on 6c, 12c

Perf. 13½, 11x11½

1949, Oct. 10 Wmk. 4

170	CD306	5c blue	20	20
171	CD307	6c dp rose violet	22	22
172	CD308	12c red lilac	52	52
173	CD309	24c blue green	1.10	1.10

University Issue

Common Design Types

1951, Feb. 16 Engr. *Perf. 14x14½*

174	CD310	3c red & blue green	22	22
175	CD311	12c rose lilac & blk	70	70

Nos. 158-160 and 163 Overprinted in Black

NEW CONSTITUTION 1951

1951, Sept. 21 *Perf. 12*

176	A20	3c scarlet & lt grn	16	16
177	A18	4c gray blk & grn	16	16
178	A22	5c chocolate & grn	16	16
179	A18	12c claret & blk	28	28

Adoption of a new constitution for the Windward Islands, 1951.

Type of 1938-47

1952

180	A18	1c gray black & green	15	15
181	A18	3c dk violet & orange	15	15
182	A18	4c green & brt blue	15	15
183	A20	6c scarlet & dp green	16	16
184	A21	10c peacock blue & indigo	28	28
		Nos. 180-184 (5)	89	89

Coronation Issue

Common Design Type

1953, June 2 *Perf. 13½x13*

185	CD312	4c dk green & blk	70	70

Elizabeth II — A23

Seal of Colony — A24

Perf. 13x14

1955, Sept. 16 Wmk. 4 Engr.

186	A23	1c orange	15	15
187	A23	2c violet blue	15	15
188	A23	3c gray	15	15
189	A23	4c dk red brown	15	15
190	A23	5c scarlet	18	15
191	A23	10c purple	28	24
192	A23	15c deep blue	28	24
193	A23	20c green	45	38
194	A23	25c brown black	90	65

Perf. 14

195	A24	50c chocolate	1.65	1.25
196	A24	$1 dull green	4.75	3.75
197	A24	$2.50 deep blue	16.00	9.50
		Nos. 186-197 (12)	25.09	16.76

West Indies Federation

Common Design Type

Perf. 11½x11

1958, Apr. 22 Wmk. 314

198	CD313	3c green	30	28
199	CD313	6c blue	50	50
200	CD313	12c carmine rose	1.00	1.00

Freedom from Hunger Issue

Common Design Type

1963, June 4 Photo. *Perf. 14x14½*

201	CD314	8c lilac	2.00	1.40

Red Cross Centenary Issue

Common Design Type

1963, Sept. 2 Litho. *Perf. 13*

202	CD315	4c black & red	85	42
203	CD315	8c ultra & red	1.65	1.25

Types of 1955

Perf. 13x14

1964-65 Wmk. 314 Engr.

205	A23	1c orange	15	15
206	A23	2c violet blue	25	25
207	A23	3c gray	80	60
208	A23	5c scarlet	48	45
209	A23	10c purple	65	48
a.		Perf. 12½	32	22
210	A23	15c deep blue	1.25	90
a.		Perf. 12½	75	50
211	A23	20c green	1.00	80
a.		Perf. 12½	16.00	6.50
212	A23	25c brown black	1.90	1.50
a.		Perf. 12½	1.90	1.40

Perf. 14

213	A24	50c chocolate ('65)	7.75	6.00
a.		Perf. 12½	3.25	3.00
		Nos. 205-213 (9)	14.23	11.13

Scout Emblem and Merit Badges — A25

1964, Nov. 23 Litho. *Perf. 14*

216	A25	1c dk brn & brt yel grn	15	15
217	A25	4c dk red brn & brt blue	15	15
218	A25	20c dk violet & orange	35	22
219	A25	50c green & red	90	90

Boy Scouts of St. Vincent, 50th anniv.

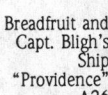

Breadfruit and Capt. Bligh's Ship "Providence" A26

Designs: 1c, Tropical fruit. 25c, Doric temple and pond, vert. 40c, Blooming talipot palm and Doric temple, vert.

Perf. 14½x13½, 13½x14½

1965, Mar. 23 Photo. Wmk. 314

220	A26	1c dk green & multi	15	15
221	A26	4c lt & dk brn grn & yel	16	15
222	A26	25c blue, grn & bister	52	35
223	A26	40c dk blue & multi	90	52

Bicentenary of the Botanic Gardens.

ITU Issue

Common Design Type

1965, May 17 Litho. *Perf. 11x11½*

224	CD317	4c blue & yellow grn	30	15
225	CD317	48c yellow & orange	3.25	2.25

Boat Building, Bequia A27

Woman Carrying Bananas — A28

Designs: 2c, Friendship Beach, Bequia. 3c, Terminal building. 5c, Crater Lake. 6c, Rock carvings, Carib Stone. 8c, Arrowroot. 10c, Owia saltpond. 12c, Ship at deep water wharf. 20c, Sea Island cotton. 25c, Map of St. Vincent and neighboring islands. 50c, Breadfruit. $1, Baleine Falls. $2.50, St. Vincent parrot. $5, Coat of arms.

Perf. 14x13½, 13½x14

1965-67 Photo. Wmk. 314

226	A27	1c multi (BEOUIA)	15	15
226A	A27	1c multi (BEQUIA) ('67)	16	16
227	A27	2c lt ultra, grn, yel & red	15	15
228	A27	3c red, yel & brn	15	15
229	A28	4c brown, ultra & yel	70	50
a.		Wmkd. sideways	50	35
230	A27	5c pur, bl, yel & grn	15	15
231	A28	6c sl grn, yel & gray	16	15
232	A28	8c pur, yel & grn	24	20
233	A27	10c org brn, yel & bluish grn	28	24
234	A27	12c grnsh bl, yel & pink	32	32
235	A28	20c brt yel, grn, pur & brn	40	35
236	A28	25c ultra, grn & vio blue	50	45
237	A28	50c grn, yel & bl	1.00	80
238	A28	$1 vio bl, lt grn & dk sl grn	2.75	2.00
239	A28	$2.50 pale lilac & multi	7.00	5.50
240	A28	$5 dull vio blue & multi	14.00	10.00
		Nos. 226-240 (16)	28.11	21.27

Issue dates: No. 226A, Aug. 8, 1967, others, Aug. 16, 1965.

For overprint, see No. 270.

Churchill Memorial Issue

Common Design Type

1966, Jan. 24 *Perf. 14*

Design in Black, Gold and Carmine Rose

241	CD319	1c bright blue	15	15
242	CD319	4c green	32	32
243	CD319	20c brown	1.90	1.25
244	CD319	40c violet	4.25	2.75

Royal Visit Issue

Common Design Type

1966, Feb. 4 Litho. *Perf. 11x12*

Portrait in Black

245	CD320	4c violet blue	50	35
246	CD320	25c dk carmine rose	5.50	3.50

WHO Headquarters Issue

Common Design Type

1966, Sept. 20 Litho. *Perf. 14*

247	CD322	4c multicolored	30	20
248	CD322	25c multicolored	2.25	1.50

UNESCO Anniversary Issue

Common Design Type

1966, Dec. 1 Litho. *Perf. 14*

249	CD323	4c "Education"	25	20
250	CD323	8c "Science"	52	42
251	CD323	25c "Culture"	3.25	2.00

View of Mt. Coke Area A29

Designs: 8c, Kingstown Methodist Church. 25c, First license to perform marriage, May 15, 1867. 35c, Arms of Conference of the Methodist Church in the Caribbean and the Americas.

Perf. 14x14½

1967, Dec. 1 Photo. Wmk. 314

252	A29	2c multicolored	15	15
253	A29	8c multicolored	15	15
254	A29	25c multicolored	50	30
255	A29	35c multicolored	60	40

Attainment of autonomy by the Methodist Church in the Caribbean and the Americas, and opening of headquarters near St. John's, Antigua, May 1967.

For overprints, see Nos. 268-269, 271.

Caribbean Meteorological Institute, Barbados — A30

Perf. 14x14½

1968, June 28 Photo. Wmk. 314

256	A30	4c cerise & multi	15	15
257	A30	25c vermilion & multi	30	20
258	A30	35c violet blue & multi	42	30

Issued for World Meteorological Day.

Martin Luther King, Jr. and Cotton Pickers A31

Perf. 13½x13

1968, Aug. 28 Litho. Wmk. 314

259	A31	5c violet & multi	15	15
260	A31	25c gray & multi	28	25
261	A31	35c brown red & multi	35	28

Dr. Martin Luther King, Jr. (1929-68), American civil rights leader.

Scales of Justice and Human Rights Flame — A32

Carnival Costume — A33

Design: 3c, Speaker addressing demonstrators, horiz.

Perf. 13x14, 14x13

1968, Nov. 1 Photo. Unwmk.

262	A32	3c orange & multi	15	15
263	A32	35c grnsh blue & vio blue	50	35
		Set value	56	40

International Human Rights Year.

1969, Feb. 17 Litho. *Perf. 14½*

Designs: 5c, Sketch of a steel bandsman. 8c, Revelers, horiz. 25c, Queen of Bands and attendants.

264	A33	1c multicolored	15	15
265	A33	5c red & dark brown	15	15
266	A33	8c multicolored	18	15
267	A33	25c multicolored	55	35
		Set value		60

St. Vincent Carnival celebration, Feb. 17.

Nos. 252-253, 236 and 255 Overprinted: "METHODIST / CONFERENCE / MAY / 1969"

Perf. 14x14½, 13½x14

1969, May 14 Photo. Wmk. 314

268	A29	2c multicolored	15	15
269	A29	8c multicolored	24	15
270	A28	25c multicolored	42	32
271	A29	35c multicolored	8.50	8.50

1st Caribbean Methodist Conf. held outside Antigua.

"Strength in Unity" A34

Designs: 5c, 25c, Map of the Caribbean, vert.

Perf. 13½x13, 13x13½

1969, July 1 Litho.

272	A34	2c orange, yel & blk	15	15
273	A34	5c lilac & multi	15	15
274	A34	8c emerald, yel & blk	22	18
275	A34	25c blue & multi	90	50
		Set value		82

1st anniv. of CARIFTA (Caribbean Free Trade Area.)

Flag and Arms of St. Vincent — A35

Designs: 10c, Uprising of 1795. 50c, Government House.

Perf. 14x14½

1969, Oct. 27 Photo. Wmk. 314

276	A35	4c deep ultra & multi	15	15
277	A35	10c olive & multi	20	18
278	A35	50c orange, gray & blk	75	60

Green Heron A36

Birds: ½c, House wren, vert. 2c, Bullfinches. 3c, St. Vincent parrots. 4c, St. Vincent solitaire, vert. 5c, Scalynecked pigeon, vert. 6c, Bananaquits. 8c, Purple-throated Carib. 10c, Mangrove cuckoo, vert. 12c, Black hawk, vert. 20c, Bare-eyed thrush. 25c, Hooded tanager. 50c, Blue-hooded euphonia. $1, Barn owl, vert. $2.50, Yellow-bellied elaenia, vert. $5, Ruddy quail-dove.

Wmk. 314 Upright on ½c, 4c, 5c, 10c, 12c, 50c, $5, Sideways on Others

1970, Jan. 12 Photo. *Perf. 14*

279	A36	½c multicolored	15	15
280	A36	1c multicolored	15	15
281	A36	2c multicolored	15	15
282	A36	3c multicolored	15	15
283	A36	4c multicolored	20	15
284	A36	5c multicolored	1.25	65
285	A36	6c multicolored	38	38
286	A36	8c multicolored	38	28
287	A36	10c multicolored	45	35
288	A36	12c multicolored	55	42
289	A36	20c multicolored	80	50
290	A36	25c multicolored	80	50
291	A36	50c multicolored	1.25	80
292	A36	$1 multicolored	3.25	1.65
293	A36	$2.50 multicolored	6.50	4.00
294	A36	$5 multicolored	16.00	10.00
		Nos. 279-294 (16)	32.41	20.28

See #379-381. For surcharges see #364-366.

Wmk. 314 Upright on 2c, 3c, 6c, 20c, Sideways on Others

1973

281a	A36	2c multicolored	25	15
282a	A36	3c multicolored	40	20
283a	A36	4c multicolored	52	28

284a	A36	5c multicolored		80	40
285a	A36	6c multicolored		80	45
287a	A36	10c multicolored		80	45
288a	A36	12c multicolored		1.40	65
289a	A36	20c multicolored		2.00	1.00
		Nos. 281a-289a (8)		6.97	3.58

DHC6 Twin Otter A37

20th anniv. of regular air services: 8c, Grumman Goose amphibian. 10c, Hawker Siddeley 748. 25c, Douglas DC-3.

Perf. 14x13

1970, Mar. 13 Litho. Wmk. 314

295	A37	5c lt blue & multi	16	15
296	A37	8c lt green & multi	32	25
297	A37	10c pink & multi	55	35
298	A37	25c yellow & multi	1.50	1.10

Nurse and Children A38

Red Cross and: 5c, First aid. 12c, Volunteers. 25c, Blood transfusion.

1970, June 1 Photo. *Perf. 14*

299	A38	3c blue & multi	15	15
300	A38	5c yellow & multi	15	15
301	A38	12c lt green & multi	30	22
302	A38	25c pale salmon & multi	60	55
		Set value		91

Centenary of British Red Cross Society.

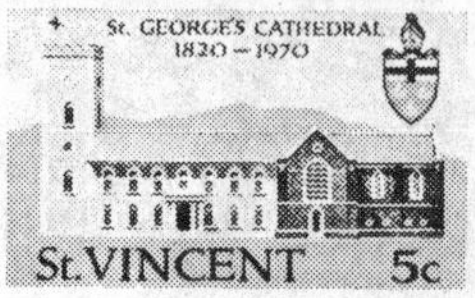

St. George's Cathedral A39

Designs: ½c, 50c, Angel and Two Marys at the Tomb, stained glass window, vert. 25c, St. George's Cathedral, front view, vert. 35c, Interior with altar.

Perf. 14x14½, 14½x14

1970, Sept. 7 Litho. Wmk. 314

303	A39	½c multicolored	15	15
304	A39	5c multicolored	15	15
305	A39	25c multicolored	32	22
306	A39	35c multicolored	45	32
307	A39	50c multicolored	60	45
		Set value	1.45	1.05

St. George's Anglican Cathedral, 150th anniv.

Virgin and Child, by Giovanni Bellini — A40

Christmas: 25c, 50c, Adoration of the Shepherds, by Louis Le Nain, horiz.

1970, Nov. 23 Litho. Wmk. 314

308	A40	8c brt violet & multi	15	15
309	A40	25c crimson & multi	28	24
310	A40	35c yellow grn & multi	45	28
311	A40	50c sapphire & multi	75	55

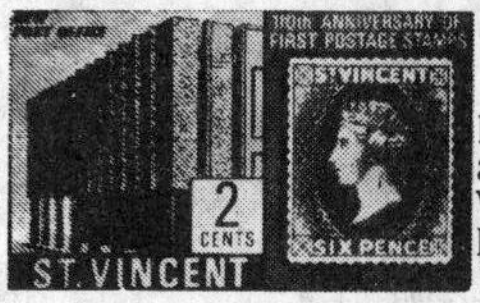

Post Office and St. Vincent No. 1B — A41

New Post Office and: 4c, $1, St. Vincent No. 1. 25c, as 2c.

1971, Mar. 29 *Perf. 14½x14*

312	A41	2c violet & multi	15	15
313	A41	4c olive & multi	15	15
314	A41	25c brown org & multi	48	32
315	A41	$1 lt green & multi	1.75	1.40

110th anniv. of 1st stamps of St. Vincent.

National Trust Emblem, Fish and Birds — A42

Designs: 30c, 45c, Cannon at Ft. Charlotte.

Perf. 13½x14

1971, Aug. 4 Litho. Wmk. 314

316	A42	12c emerald & multi	25	18
317	A42	30c lt blue & multi	55	50
318	A42	40c brt pink & multi	90	60
319	A42	45c black & multi	1.10	80

Publicity for the National Trust (for conservation of wild life and historic buildings).

Holy Family with Angels (detail), by Pietro da Cortona A43

Christmas: 5c, 25c, Madonna Appearing to St. Anthony, by Domenico Tiepolo, vert.

1971, Oct. 6 *Perf. 14x14½, 14½x14*

320	A43	5c rose & multi	15	15
321	A43	10c lt green & multi	18	15
322	A43	25c lt blue & multi	40	28
323	A43	$1 yellow & multi	1.50	1.25

Careening — A44

Designs: 5c, 20c, Seine fishermen. 6c, 50c, Map of Grenadines. 15c, as 1c.

1971, Nov. 25 *Perf. 14x13½*

324	A44	1c dp vermilion & multi	15	15
325	A44	5c blue & multi	15	15
326	A44	6c yellow grn & multi	20	15
327	A44	15c orange brn & multi	50	38
328	A44	20c yellow & multi	60	45
329	A44	50c blue, blk & plum	1.50	1.25
a.		Souvenir sheet of 6, #324-329	11.00	9.25
		Nos. 324-329 (6)	3.10	2.53

The Grenadines of St. Vincent tourist issue.

Grenadier Company Private, 1764 — A45

Designs: 30c, Battalion Company officer, 1772. 50c, Grenadier Company private, 1772.

1972, Feb. 14 *Perf. 14x13½*

330	A45	12c gray violet & multi	90	70
331	A45	30c gray blue & multi	2.25	1.75
332	A45	50c dark gray & multi	4.00	3.25

Breadnut — A46

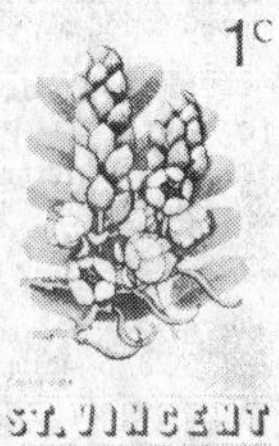

Flowers of St. Vincent — A47

1972, May 16 Litho. *Perf. 14x13½*

333	A46	3c shown	15	15
334	A46	5c Papaya	25	20
335	A46	12c Rose apples	90	60
336	A46	25c Mangoes	2.50	1.65

1972, July 31 Litho. *Perf. 13½x13*

337	A47	1c Candlestick Cassia	15	15
338	A47	30c Lobster claw	70	60
339	A47	40c White trumpet	80	70
340	A47	$1 Flowers, Soufriere tree	2.25	1.50

Sir Charles Brisbane, Arms of St. Vincent — A48

Designs: 30c, Sailing ship "Arethusa." $1, Sailing ship "Blake."

1972, Sept. 29 Wmk. 314 *Perf. 13½*

341	A48	20c yellow, brn & gold	60	45
342	A48	30c lilac & multi	65	60
343	A48	$1 multicolored	2.50	1.90
a.		Souvenir sheet of 3, #341-343	7.50	3.25

Bicentenary of the birth of Sir Charles Brisbane, naval hero, governor of St. Vincent.

Silver Wedding Issue, 1972

Common Design Type

Design: Queen Elizabeth II, Prince Philip, arrowroot plant, breadfruit foliage and fruit.

1972, Nov. 20 Photo. *Perf. 14x14½*

344	CD324	30c rose brown & multi	32	22
345	CD324	$1 multicolored	90	55

Columbus Sighting St. Vincent — A49

Designs: 12c, Caribs watching Columbus' ships. 30c, Christopher Columbus. 50c, Santa Maria.

1973, Jan. 18 Litho. *Perf. 13*

346	A49	5c multicolored	30	25
347	A49	12c multicolored	65	55
348	A49	30c multicolored	2.25	1.25
349	A49	50c multicolored	4.50	2.25

475th anniversary of Columbus's Third Voyage to the West Indies.

The Last Supper — A50

Perf. 14x13½

1973, Apr. 19 Litho. Wmk. 314

350	A50	15c red & multi	15	15
351	A50	60c red & multi	60	50
352	A50	$1 red & multi	1.25	1.00
a.		Strip of 3, #350-352	2.25	2.00

Easter.

William Wilberforce and Slave Auction Poster — A51

Designs: 40c, Slaves working on sugar plantation. 50c, Wilberforce and medal commemorating first anniversary of abolition of slavery.

1973, July 11 *Perf. 14x13½*

353	A51	30c multicolored	42	32
354	A51	40c multicolored	50	45
355	A51	50c multicolored	85	55

140th anniv. of the death of William Wilberforce (1759-1833), member of British Parliament who fought for abolition of slavery.

Families — A52

Design: 40c, Families and "IPPF."

1973, Oct. 3 *Perf. 14½*

356	A52	12c multicolored	30	20
357	A52	40c multicolored	1.00	75

Intl. Planned Parenthood Assoc., 21st anniv.

Princess Anne's Wedding Issue

Common Design Type

1973, Nov. 14 *Perf. 14*

358	CD325	50c slate & multi	75	50
359	CD325	70c gray green & multi	1.00	70

Administration Buildings, Mona University — A53

Designs: 10c, University Center, Kingstown. 30c, Mona University, aerial view. $1, Coat of arms of University of West Indies.

Perf. 14½x14, 14x14½

1973, Dec. 13

360	A53	5c multicolored	15	15
361	A53	10c multicolored	16	15
362	A53	30c multicolored	40	30
363	A53	$1 multicolored	95	60

University of the West Indies, 25th anniv.

Nos. 291, 286 and 292 Surcharged

40c

1973, Dec. 15 Photo. *Perf. 14*

364	A36	30c on 50c multi	40	40
365	A36	40c on 8c multi	52	52
366	A36	$10 on $1 multi	16.00	12.00

The position of the surcharge and shape of obliterating bars differs on each denomination.

Descent from the Cross — A54

Easter: 30c, Descent from the Cross. 40c, Pietà. $1, Resurrection. Designs are from sculptures in Victoria and Albert Museum, London, and Provincial Museum, Valladolid (40c).

1974, Apr. 10 Litho. *Perf. 13½x13*

367	A54	5c multicolored	15	15
368	A54	30c multicolored	25	18
369	A54	40c multicolored	30	22
370	A54	$1 multicolored	65	45

"Istra" A55

1974, June 28 *Perf. 14½*

371	A55	15c shown	20	15
372	A55	20c "Oceanic"	26	20
373	A55	30c "Alexander Pushkin"	42	32
374	A55	$1 "Europa"	1.25	75
a.		Souvenir sheet of 4, #371-374	2.50	1.90

Cruise ships visiting Kingstown.

Arrows Circling UPU Emblem A56

UPU, cent.: 12c, Post horn and globe. 60c, Target over map of islands, hand canceler. 90c, Goode's map projection.

1974, July 25 *Perf. 14½*

375	A56	5c violet & multi	15	15
376	A56	12c ocher, green & blue	15	15
377	A56	60c blue green & multi	42	35
378	A56	90c red & multi	65	52

Bird Type of 1970

Birds: 30c, Royal tern. 40c, Brown pelican, vert. $10, Magnificent frigate bird, vert.

Wmk. 314 Sideways on 40c, $10, Upright on 30c

1974, Aug. 29 Litho. *Perf. 14½*

379	A36	30c multicolored	70	55
380	A36	40c multicolored	1.10	80
381	A36	$10 multicolored	22.50	14.00

Scout Emblem and Badges — A57

Churchill as Prime Minister — A58

Perf. 13½x14

1974, Oct. 9 Wmk. 314

385	A57	10c lilac & multi	15	15
386	A57	25c bister & multi	35	32
387	A57	45c gray & multi	60	45
388	A57	$1 multicolored	1.25	90

St. Vincent Boy Scouts, 60th anniversary.

1974, Nov. 28 *Perf. 14½x14*

Designs (Churchill as): 35c, Lord Warden of the Cinque Ports. 45c, First Lord of the Admiralty. $1, Royal Air Force officer.

389	A58	25c multicolored	24	16
390	A58	35c multicolored	30	20
391	A58	45c multicolored	40	25
392	A58	$1 multicolored	80	60

Sir Winston Churchill (1874-1965), birth centenary. Sheets of 30 in 2 panes of 15 with inscribed gutter between.

Shepherds — A59

St. Joseph, Ass and Ox — A60

1974, Dec. 5 *Perf. 12x12½*

393	A59	3c like 8c	15	15
394	A59	3c Virgin, Child and Star	15	15
395	A60	3c like 45c	15	15
396	A60	3c Three Kings	15	15
397	A59	8c shown	16	15
398	A59	35c like No. 394	35	25
399	A60	45c shown	42	35
400	A60	$1 like No. 396	1.10	70
		Set value	2.25	1.55

Christmas. Nos. 393-396 printed se-tenant in a continuous picture.

Giant Mask and Dancers A61

Designs: 15c, Pineapple dancers. 25c, Giant bouquet. 35c, Girl dancers. 45c, Butterfly dancers. $1.25, Sun and moon dancers and float.

Wmk. 314

1975, Feb. 7 Litho. *Perf. 14*

401	A61	1c multicolored	15	15
a.		Bklt. pane of 2 + label	50	
b.		Bklt. pane of 3 (#401, 403, 405)	1.25	
402	A61	15c multicolored	16	15
a.		Bklt. pane of 3 (#402, 404, 406)	3.00	
403	A61	25c multicolored	20	16
404	A61	35c multicolored	30	18
405	A61	45c multicolored	38	22
406	A61	$1.25 multicolored	1.00	65
a.		Souvenir sheet of 6, #401-406	2.50	1.65
		Nos. 401-406 (6)	2.19	1.51

Kingstown carnival 1975.

French Angelfish A62

Designs: Fish and whales.

Two types of $2.50:
I - Line to fish's mouth.
II - Line removed (1976).

Wmk. 373

1975, Apr. 10 Litho. *Perf. 14*

407	A62	1c shown	15	15
408	A62	2c Spotfin butter-fly-fish	15	15
409	A62	3c Horse-eyed jack	15	15
410	A62	4c Mackerel	15	15
411	A62	5c French grunts	15	15
412	A62	6c Spotted goatfish	15	15
413	A62	8c Ballyhoos	15	15
414	A62	10c Sperm whale	15	15
415	A62	12c Humpback whale	16	15
416	A62	15c Cowfish	35	25
417	A62	20c Queen angelfish	32	24
418	A62	25c Princess parrotfish	35	25
419	A62	35c Red hind	60	35
420	A62	45c Atlantic flying fish	60	45
421	A62	50c Porkfish	70	60
422	A62	$1 Queen triggerfish	1.50	1.10
423	A62	$2.50 Sailfish, type I	3.25	2.25
a.		Type II	5.75	3.25
424	A62	$5 Dolphinfish	7.25	4.50
425	A62	$10 Blue marlin	13.00	9.25
		Nos. 407-425 (19)	29.28	20.59

The 4c, 10c, 20c, $1, were reissued with "1976" below design; 1c, 2c, 3c, 5c, 6c, 8c, 12c, 50c, $10, with "1977" below design; 10c with "1978" below design.

See Nos. 472-474. For surcharges, see Nos. 463-464. For overprints, see Nos. 499-500, 502-503, 572-581, 584-586.

Cutting Bananas — A63

Banana industry: 35c, La Croix packing station. 45c, Women cleaning and packing bananas. 70c, Freighter loading bananas.

1975, June 26 Wmk. 314 *Perf. 14*

426	A63	25c blue & multi	25	20
427	A63	35c blue & multi	35	28
428	A63	45c carmine & multi	45	35
429	A63	70c carmine & multi	75	65

Snorkel Diving A64

Designs: 20c, Aquaduct Golf Course. 35c, Steel band at Mariner's Inn. 45c, Sunbathing at Young Island. $1.25, Yachting marina.

Perf. 13½

1975, July 31 Litho. Wmk. 373

430	A64	15c multicolored	15	15
431	A64	20c multicolored	25	15
432	A64	35c multicolored	40	25
433	A64	45c multicolored	50	30
434	A64	$1.25 multicolored	1.25	70
		Nos. 430-434 (5)	2.55	1.55

Tourist publicity.

Presidents Washington, John Adams, Jefferson and Madison — A65

U.S. Presidents: 1c, Monroe, John Quincy Adams, Jackson, Van Buren. 1½c, Wm. Harrison, Tyler, Polk, Taylor. 5c, Fillmore, Pierce, Buchanan, Lincoln. 10c, Johnson, Grant, Hayes, Garfield. 25c, Arthur, Cleveland, Benjamin Harrison, McKinley. 35c, Theodore Roosevelt, Taft, Wilson, Harding. 45c, Coolidge, Hoover, Franklin D. Roosevelt, Truman. $1, Eisenhower, Kennedy, Lyndon B. Johnson, Nixon. $2, Ford and White House.

1975, Sept. 11 Unwmk. *Perf. 14½*

435	A65	½c violet & blk	15	15
436	A65	1c green & black	15	15
437	A65	1½c rose lilac & blk	15	15
438	A65	5c yellow grn & blk	15	15
439	A65	10c ultra & blk	15	15
440	A65	25c ocher & blk	22	22
441	A65	35c brt blue & blk	30	25
442	A65	45c carmine & blk	32	30
443	A65	$1 orange & blk	75	60
444	A65	$2 lt olive & blk	1.50	1.10
a.		Souvenir sheet of 10, #435-444 + 2 labels	7.00	6.50
		Set value	3.30	2.65

Bicentenary of American Independence. Issued in sheets of 10 stamps and 2 labels picturing the White House, Capitol, Mt. Vernon, etc.

A66

Nativity — A67

Designs: No. 445, 8c, Star of Bethlehem. No. 446, 45c, Shepherds. No. 447, $1, Kings. No. 448, 35c, Nativity.

Wmk. 314

1975, Dec. 4 Litho. *Perf. 14*

445	A66	3c deep rose & blk	15	15
446	A66	3c deep rose & blk	15	15
447	A66	3c deep rose & blk	15	15
448	A67	3c deep rose & blk	15	15
449	A66	8c blue & blk	15	15
450	A67	8c blue & blk	15	15
451	A66	35c yellow & blk	25	22
452	A67	35c yellow & blk	25	22
453	A66	45c yel grn & blk	38	28
454	A67	45c yel grn & blk	38	28
455	A66	$1 violet & blk	75	65
456	A67	$1 violet & blk	75	65
		Set value	3.00	2.60

Christmas. Stamps of same denomination printed se-tenant.

Carnival Costumes — A68

Designs: 2c, Humpty-Dumpty people. 5c, Smiling faces (masks). 35c, Dragon worshippers. 45c, Duck costume. $1.25, Bumble bee dance.

Perf. 13x13½

1976, Feb. 19 Litho. Wmk. 373

457	A68	1c carmine & multi	15	15
a.		Booklet pane of 2	20	

458	A68	2c black & multi	15	15
a.		Bklt. pane of 3, #458-460	60	
459	A68	5c lt blue & multi	15	15
460	A68	35c lt blue & multi	35	30
a.		Bklt. pane of 3, #460-462	2.25	
461	A68	45c black & multi	42	35
462	A68	$1.25 carmine & multi	1.10	85
		Set value	1.95	1.55
		Nos. 457-462 (6)	2.32	1.95

Kingstown carnival 1976. No. 457a contains one each of Nos. 457-458 with inscribed gutter between.

Nos. 409 and 421 Surcharged with New Value and Bar

1976, Apr. 8 Wmk. 314 *Perf. 14*

463	A62	70c on 3c multi	75	75
464	A62	90c on 50c multi	1.00	1.00

Yellow Hibiscus and Blue-headed Hummingbird A69

Designs: 10c, Single pink hibiscus and crested hummingbird. 35c, Single white hibiscus and purple-throated carib. 45c, Common red hibiscus and blue-headed hummingbird. $1.25, Single peach hibiscus and green-throated carib.

1976, May 20 Litho. Wmk. 373

465	A69	5c multicolored	32	25
466	A69	10c multicolored	65	48
467	A69	35c multicolored	2.00	1.50
468	A69	45c multicolored	3.25	2.50
469	A69	$1.25 multicolored	10.00	6.00
		Nos. 465-469 (5)	16.22	10.73

Map of West Indies, Bats, Wicket and Ball — A69a

Prudential Cup — A69b

1976, Sept. 16 Unwmk. *Perf. 14*

470	A69a	15c lt blue & multi	45	30
471	A69b	45c lilac rose & blk	1.40	85

World Cricket Cup, won by West Indies Team, 1975.

Fish Type of 1975

1976, Oct. 14 Wmk. 373 *Perf. 14*

472	A62	15c Skipjack	15	15
473	A62	70c Albacore	65	65
474	A62	90c Pompano	75	75

The 15c was reissued with "1977" below design.
For overprints, see Nos. 501, 582-583.

St. Mary's R.C. Church, Kingstown A70

Christmas: 45c, Anglican Church, Georgetown. 50c, Methodist Church, Georgetown. $1.25, St. George's Anglican Cathedral, Kingstown.

1976, Nov. 18 Litho. *Perf. 14*

475	A70	35c multicolored	28	28
476	A70	45c multicolored	35	35
477	A70	50c multicolored	42	42
478	A70	$1.25 multicolored	1.10	1.10

Barrancoid Pot-stand, c. 450 A.D. — A71

Designs (National Trust Emblem and): 45c, National Museum. 70c, Carib stone head, c. 1510. $1, Ciboney petroglyph, c. 4000 B.C.

1976, Dec. 16 *Perf. 13½*

479	A71	5c multicolored	15	15
480	A71	45c multicolored	32	32
481	A71	70c multicolored	50	50
482	A71	$1 multicolored	75	75

Carib Indian art and establishment of National Museum in Botanical Gardens, Kingstown.

Kings William I, William II, Henry I, Stephen A72

Kings and Queens of England: 1c, Henry II, Richard I, John, Henry III. 1½c, Edward I, II, III, Richard II. 2c, Henry IV, V, VI, Edward IV. 5c, Edward V, Richard III, Henry VII, VIII. 10c, Edward VI, Lady Jane Grey, Mary I, Elizabeth I. 25c, James I, Charles I, II, James II. 35c, William III, Mary II, Anne, George I. 45c, George II, III, IV. 75c, William IV, Victoria, Edward VII. $1, George V, Edward VIII, George VI. $2, Elizabeth II, coronation.

Perf. 13½

1977, Feb. 7 Litho. Wmk. 373

483	A72	½c multicolored	15	15
a.		Bklt. pane of 4, #483-486	15.00	
484	A72	1c multicolored	15	15
485	A72	1½c multicolored	15	15
486	A72	2c multicolored	15	15
487	A72	5c multicolored	15	15
a.		Bklt. pane of 4, #487-490	15.00	
488	A72	10c multicolored	15	15
489	A72	25c multicolored	18	16
490	A72	35c multicolored	25	20
491	A72	45c multicolored	35	28
a.		Bklt. pane of 4, #491-494	17.50	
492	A72	75c multicolored	45	35
493	A72	$1 multicolored	60	45
494	A72	$2 multicolored	1.10	90
a.		Souv. sheet of 12, #483-494, perf. 14½x14	3.50	3.50
		Set value	3.15	2.60

25th anniv. of the reign of Elizabeth II.
Nos. 483a, 487a and 491a are unwmkd.
See No. 508.

Bishop Alfred P. Berkeley, Bishop's Miters — A73

Designs: 15c, Grant of Arms to Bishopric, 1951, and names of former Bishops. 45c, Coat of arms and map of Diocese. $1.25, Interior of St. George's Anglican Cathedral and Bishop G. C. M. Woodroffe.

Perf. 13½

1977, May 12 Litho. Wmk. 373

495	A73	15c multicolored	15	15
496	A73	35c multicolored	26	22
497	A73	45c multicolored	35	32
498	A73	$1.25 multicolored	1.00	80

Diocese of the Windward Islands, centenary.

Nos. 411, 414, 472, 417, 422 Overprinted in Black or Red: "CARNIVAL 1977/ JUNE 25TH - JULY 5TH"

1977, June 2 Litho. *Perf. 14*

499	A62	5c multi	15	15
500	A62	10c multi (R)	15	15
501	A62	15c multi (R)	20	15
502	A62	20c multi (R)	38	26
503	A62	$1 multi	1.65	1.50
		Nos. 499-503 (5)	2.53	2.21

St. Vincent Carnival, June 25-July 5.
5c, 15c dated "1977," 10c, 20c, $1 dated "1976."

Girl Guide and Emblem — A74

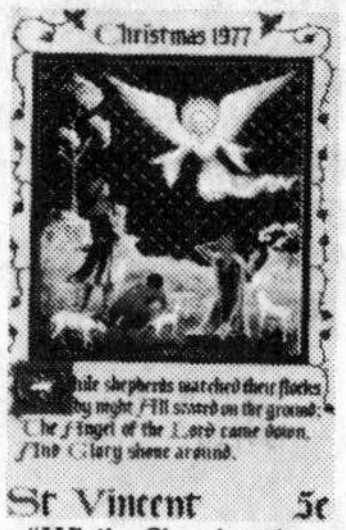

"While Shepherds Watched" — A75

Designs: 15c, Early Guide's uniform, Ranger, Brownie and Guide. 20c, Guide uniforms, 1917 and 1977. $2, Lady Baden-Powell, World Chief Guide, 1930-1977.

Perf. 13½

1977, Sept. 1 Litho. Wmk. 373

504	A74	5c multicolored	15	15
505	A74	15c multicolored	15	15
506	A74	20c multicolored	15	15
507	A74	$2 multicolored	1.25	1.00
		Set value		1.20

St. Vincent Girl Guides, 50th anniversary.

No. 494 with Additional Inscription: "CARIBBEAN / VISIT 1977"

1977, Oct. 27

508	A72	$2 multicolored	1.25	1.25

Caribbean visit of Queen Elizabeth II.

1977, Nov. Litho. *Perf. 13x11*

Christmas: 10c, "Fear not" said He. 15c, David's Town. 25c, The Heavenly Babe. 50c, Thus Spake and Seraph. $1.25, All Glory be to God.

509	A75	5c buff & multi	15	15
510	A75	10c buff & multi	15	15
511	A75	15c buff & multi	15	15
512	A75	25c buff & multi	15	15
513	A75	50c buff & multi	32	26
514	A75	$1.25 buff & multi	80	65
a.		Souvenir sheet of 6, #509-514, perf. 13½	1.75	1.60
		Set value	1.50	1.25

Map of St. Vincent — A76

Perf. 14½x14

1977-78 Litho. Wmk. 373

515	A76	20c dk blue & lt blue ('78)	20	15
516	A76	40c salmon & blk	40	30
517	A76	40c car, sal & ocher ('78)	40	30

Issued: No. 516 Nov. 30, Nos. 515, 517, Jan. 31.
For types surcharged see Nos. B1-B4.

Painted Lady and Bougainvillea — A77

Butterflies and Bougainvillea: 25c, Silver spot. 40c, Red anartia. 50c, Mimic. $1.25, Giant hairstreak.

1978, Apr. 6 Litho. *Perf. 14*

523	A77	5c multicolored	15	15
524	A77	25c multicolored	20	18
525	A77	40c multicolored	30	28
526	A77	50c multicolored	40	35
527	A77	$1.25 multicolored	1.00	90
		Nos. 523-527 (5)	2.05	1.86

Westminster Abbey — A78

Cathedral: 50c, Gloucester. $1.25, Durham. $2.50, Exeter.

Perf. 13x13½

1978, June 2 Litho. Wmk. 373

528	A78	40c multicolored	18	15
529	A78	50c multicolored	20	18
530	A78	$1.25 multicolored	52	45
531	A78	$2.50 multicolored	1.10	90
a.		Souvenir sheet of 4, #528-531, perf. 13½x14	2.00	2.00

25th anniv. of coronation of Queen Elizabeth II. Nos. 528-531 issued in sheets of 10.
#528-531 also exist in booklet panes of two.

Rotary Emblem A79

Designs: 50c, Lions International emblem. $1, Jaycees emblem.

Perf. 14½

1978, July 13 Litho. Wmk. 373

532	A79	40c brown & multi	25	25
533	A79	50c dk green & multi	30	30
534	A79	$1 crimson & multi	60	60

Service clubs aiding in development of St. Vincent.

Flags of Ontario and St. Vincent, Teacher A80

Design: 40c, Flags of St. Vincent and Ontario, teacher pointing to board, vert.

1978, Sept. 7 Litho. *Perf. 14*

535	A80	40c multicolored	25	20
536	A80	$2 multicolored	1.10	1.00

School to School Project between children of Ontario, Canada, and St. Vincent, 10th anniversary.

Arnos Vale Airport A81

Designs: 40c, Wilbur Wright landing Flyer I. 50c, Flyer I airborne. $1.25, Orville Wright and Flyer I.

1978, Oct. 19 *Perf. 14½*

537	A81	10c multicolored	15	15
538	A81	40c multicolored	25	25
539	A81	50c multicolored	30	30
540	A81	$1.25 multicolored	75	75

75th anniversary of 1st powered flight.
For overprint, see No. 568.

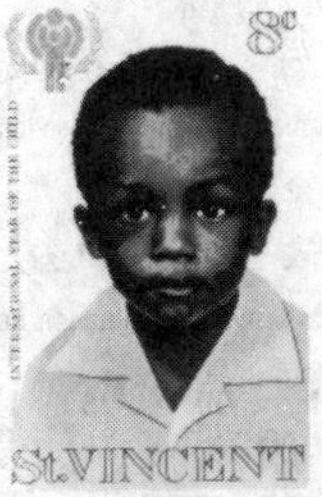

Vincentian Boy, IYC Emblem — A82

Children and IYC Emblem: 20c, Girl. 50c, Boy. $2, Girl and boy.

1979, Feb. 14 Litho. *Perf. 14x13½*

541	A82	8c multicolored	15	15
542	A82	20c multicolored	16	15
543	A82	50c multicolored	38	22
544	A82	$2 multicolored	1.65	80

International Year of the Child.

Rowland Hill — A83

Designs: 50c, Great Britain Nos. 1-2. $3, St. Vincent Nos. 1-1B.

1979, May 31 Litho. *Perf. 14*

545	A83	40c multicolored	16	16
546	A83	50c multicolored	20	20
547	A83	$3 multicolored	1.25	1.25
a.		Souvenir sheet of 6	3.50	3.50

Sir Rowland Hill (1795-1879), originator of penny postage.

No. 547a contains Nos. 545-547 and Nos. 560, 561 and 565.

Buccament Cancellations, Map of St. Vincent — A84

Designs: Cancellations and location of village.

1979, Sept. 1 Litho. *Perf. 14*

548	A84	1c shown	15	15
549	A84	2c Sion Hill	15	15
550	A84	3c Cumberland	15	15
551	A84	4c Questelles	15	15
552	A84	5c Layou	15	15
553	A84	6c New Ground	15	15
554	A84	8c Mesopotamia	15	15
555	A84	10c Troumaca	15	15
556	A84	12c Arnos Vale	15	15
557	A84	15c Stubbs	15	15
558	A84	20c Orange Hill	15	15
559	A84	25c Calliaqua	15	15
560	A84	40c Edinboro	22	22
561	A84	50c Colonarie	28	28
562	A84	80c Babou St. Vincent	48	48
563	A84	$1 Chateaubelair	60	60
564	A84	$2 Kingstown	1.25	1.25
565	A84	$3 Barrouallie	1.75	1.75
566	A84	$5 Georgestown	3.00	3.00
567	A84	$10 Kingstown	5.75	5.75
		Nos. 548-567 (20)	15.13	15.13

See No. 547a, The 5c, 10c, 25c reissued inscribed 1982.

Singles of Nos. 562-564 from No. 601a are inscribed 1980.

No. 537 Overprinted in Red: "ST. VINCENT AND THE GRENADINES AIR SERVICE 1979"

1979, Aug. 6 Litho. *Perf. 14½*

568	A81	10c multicolored	15	15

St. Vincent and Grenadines air service inauguration.

Independent State

St. Vincent Flag, Ixora Coccinea A85

Designs: 50c, House of Assembly, ixora stricta. 80c, Prime Minister R. Milton Cato.

1979, Oct. 27 *Perf. 12½x12*

569	A85	20c multicolored	15	15
570	A85	50c multicolored	25	25
571	A85	80c multicolored	40	40

Independence of St. Vincent Nos. 569-571 each printed se-tenant with label inscribed "Peace and Justice."

Nos. 407, 410-416, 418, 421, 473-474, 422-423, 425 Overprinted in Black: "INDEPENDENCE 1979"

1979, Oct. 27 Litho. *Perf. 14½*

572	A62	1c multicolored	15	15
573	A62	4c multicolored	15	15
574	A62	5c multicolored	15	15
575	A62	6c multicolored	15	15
576	A62	8c multicolored	15	15
577	A62	10c multicolored	15	15
578	A62	12c multicolored	15	15
579	A62	15c multicolored	15	15
580	A62	25c multicolored	15	15
581	A62	50c multicolored	30	30
582	A62	70c multicolored	45	45
583	A62	90c multicolored	55	55
584	A62	$1 multicolored	60	60
585	A62	$2.50 multicolored	1.50	1.50
586	A62	$10 multicolored	5.50	5.50
		Nos. 572-586 (15)	10.25	10.25

Silent Night Text, Virgin and Child A86

Silent Night Text and: 20c, Infant Jesus and angels. 25c, Shepherds. 40c, Angel. 50c, Angels holding Jesus. $2, Nativity.

1979, Nov. 1 *Perf. 13½x14*

587	A86	10c multicolored	15	15
588	A86	20c multicolored	15	15
589	A86	25c multicolored	15	15
590	A86	40c multicolored	22	22
591	A86	50c multicolored	30	30
592	A86	$2 multicolored	1.10	1.10
a.		Souvenir sheet of 6, #587-592	2.00	2.00
		Nos. 587-592 (6)	2.07	2.07

Christmas.

Oleander and Wasp — A87

Oleander and Insects: 10c, Beetle. 25c, Praying mantis. 50c, Green guava beetle. $2, Citrus weevil.

1979, Dec. 13 Litho. *Perf. 14*

593	A87	5c multicolored	15	15
594	A87	10c multicolored	15	15
595	A87	25c multicolored	15	15
596	A87	50c multicolored	32	32
597	A87	$2 multicolored	1.25	1.25
		Nos. 593-597 (5)	2.02	2.02

Type of 1880
Souvenir Sheet

1980, Feb. 28 Litho. *Perf. 14x13½*

598		Sheet of 3	2.25	2.25
a.		A3 50c brown	32	32
b.		A3 $1 dark green	60	60
c.		A3 $2 dark blue	1.25	1.25

Coat of arms stamps centenary; London 1980 Intl. Stamp Exhibition, May 6-14.

London '80 Intl. Stamp Exhibition, May 6-14 — A88

Wmk. 373

1980, Apr. 24 Litho. *Perf. 14*

599	A88	80c Queen Elizabeth II	42	42
600	A88	$1 GB #297, SV #190	50	50
601	A88	$2 Unissued stamp, 1971	1.10	1.10
a.		Souv. sheet of 6, #562-564, 599-601	7.75	7.75

Steel Band A89

1980, June 12 Litho. *Perf. 14*

602	A89	20c shown	15	15
603	A89	20c Drummers, dancers	15	15

Kingstown Carnival, July 7-8. Nos. 602-603 se-tenant.

Soccer, Olympic Rings — A90

1980, Aug. 7 *Perf. 13½*

604	A90	10c shown	15	15
605	A90	60c Bicycling	28	28
606	A90	80c Women's basketball	40	40
607	A90	$2.50 Boxing	1.25	1.25

Sport for all.

For surcharges, see Nos. B5-B8.

Agouti — A91

1980, Oct. 2 Litho. *Perf. 14x14½*

608	A91	25c shown	15	15
609	A91	50c Giant toad	26	26
610	A91	$2 Mongoose	1.10	1.10

Map of North Atlantic showing St. Vincent — A92

Maps showing St. Vincent: 10c, World. $1, Caribbean. $2, St. Vincent, sail boats, plane.

1980, Dec. 4 Litho. *Perf. 13½x14*

611	A92	10c multicolored	15	15
612	A92	50c multicolored	25	25
613	A92	$1 multicolored	48	48
614	A92	$2 multicolored	1.00	1.00
a.		Souv. sheet of 1, perf. 14	1.00	1.00

Ville de Paris in Battle of the Saints, 1782 — A93

Wmk. 373

1981, Feb. 19 Litho. *Perf. 14*

615	A93	50c shown	35	35
616	A93	60c Ramillies lost in storm, 1782	40	40
617	A93	$1.50 Providence, 1793	1.00	1.00
618	A93	$2 Mail Packet Dee, 1840	1.40	1.40

Arrowroot Cultivation A94

Wmk. 373

1981, May 21 Litho. *Perf. 14*

619	A94	25c Arrowroot processing	15	15
620	A94	25c shown	15	15
621	A94	50c Banana packing plant	24	24
622	A94	50c Banana cultivation	24	24
623	A94	60c Copra drying frames	28	28
624	A94	60c Coconut plantation	28	28
625	A94	$1 Cocoa beans	45	45
626	A94	$1 Cocoa cultivation	45	45
		Nos. 619-626 (8)	2.24	2.24

Stamps of same denomination se-tenant.

Prince Charles, Lady Diana, Royal Yacht Charlotte A94a

Prince Charles and Lady Diana — A94b

Illustration A94b is reduced.

Wmk. 380

1981, July 13 Litho. *Perf. 14*

627	A94a	60c Couple, Isabella	35	35
a.		Bklt. pane of 4, perf. 12	1.40	
628	A94b	60c Couple	35	35
629	A94a	$2.50 Alberta	1.40	1.40
630	A94b	$2.50 like #628	1.40	1.40
a.		Bklt. pane of 4, perf. 12	5.75	
631	A94a	$4 Britannia	2.50	2.50
632	A94b	$4 like #628	2.50	2.50
		Nos. 627-632 (6)	8.50	8.50

Royal wedding. Each denomination issued in sheets of 7 (6 type A94a, 1 type A94b).

For surcharges, see Nos. 891-892.

Souvenir Sheet

1981 Litho. *Perf. 12*

632A	A95b	$5 Couple	3.00	3.00

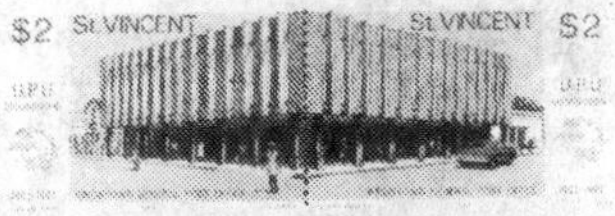

Kingstown General Post Office
A95 A96

Wmk. 373

1981, Sept. 1 Litho. *Perf. 14*

633	A95	$2 multicolored	1.25	1.25
634	A96	$2 multicolored	1.25	1.25

UPU membership centenary.

First Anniv. of UN Membership A96a

Wmk. 373

1981, Sept. 1 **Litho.** ***Perf. 14***

634A A96a $1.50 Flags 65 65
634B A96a $2.50 Prime Minister Cato 1.10 1.10

"The People that Walked in Darkness . . ." — A97

1981, Nov. 19 **Litho.** ***Perf. 12***

635 A97 50c shown 22 22
636 A97 60c Angel 28 28
637 A97 $1 "My soul . . ." 45 45
638 A97 $2 Flight into Egypt 90 90
a. Souvenir sheet of 4, #635-638 1.90 1.90

Christmas. For surcharge, see No. 674.

Re-introduction of Sugar Industry, First Anniv. — A98

1982, Apr. 5 **Litho.** ***Perf. 14***

639 A98 50c Boilers 35 35
640 A98 60c Drying plant 40 40
641 A98 $1.50 Gearwheels 1.00 1.00
642 A98 $2 Loading sugar cane 1.40 1.40

50th Anniv. of Airmail Service A99

1982, July 29 **Litho.** ***Perf. 14***

643 A99 50c DH Moth, 1932 35 35
644 A99 60c Grumman Goose, 1952 40 40
645 A99 $1.50 Hawker-Siddeley 748, 1968 1.00 1.00
646 A99 $2 Britten-Norman Islander, 1982 1.40 1.40

21st Birthday of Princess Diana, July 1 — A99a

Wmk. 380

1982, June **Litho.** ***Perf. 14***

647 A99a 50c Augusta of Saxe, 1736 35 35
648 A99a 60c Saxe arms 40 40
649 A99a $6 Diana 4.00 4.00

For overprints, see Nos. 652-654.

Scouting Year — A100

1982, July 15 **Wmk. 373**

650 A100 $1.50 Emblem 1.00 1.00
651 A100 $2.50 "75" 1.75 1.75

For overprints, see Nos. 890, 893.

Nos. 647-649 Overprinted: "ROYAL BABY"

1982, July **Wmk. 380**

652 A99a 50c multicolored 32 32
653 A99a 60c multicolored 35 35
654 A99a $6 multicolored 3.50 3.50

Birth of Prince William of Wales, June 21.

Carnival A101

1982, June 10 **Litho.** ***Perf. 13½***

655 A101 50c Butterfly float 32 32
656 A101 60c Angel dancer, vert. 35 35
657 A101 $1.50 Winged dancer, vert. 90 90
658 A101 $2 Eagle float 1.25 1.25

Cruise Ships A103

Wmk. 373

1982, Dec. 29 **Litho.** ***Perf. 14***

662 A103 45c Geestport 30 30
663 A103 60c Stella Oceanis 40 40
664 A103 $1.50 Victoria 1.00 1.00
665 A103 $2 QE 2 1.40 1.40

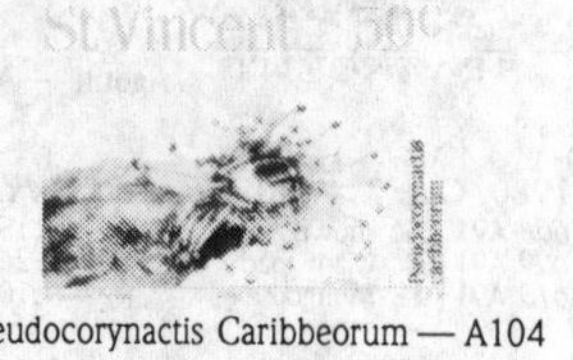

Pseudocorynactis Caribbeorum — A104

Sea Horses and Anemones. 60c, $1.50, $2 vert.

1983, Jan. 12 **Wmk. 373** ***Perf. 12***

666 A104 50c shown 35 35
667 A104 60c Actinoporus elegans 40 40
668 A104 $1.50 Arachnanthus nocturnus 1.00 1.00
669 A104 $2 Hippocampus reidi 1.40 1.40

For overprint, see No. 886.

Commonwealth Day — CD334

Wmk. 373

1983, Mar. 14 **Litho.** ***Perf. 14***

670 CD334 45c Map 30 30
671 CD334 60c Flag 40 40
672 CD334 $1.50 Prime Minister Cato 1.00 1.00
673 CD334 $2 Banana industry 1.40 1.40

No. 635 Surcharged

Wmk. 373

1983, Apr. 26 **Litho.** ***Perf. 12***

674 A97 45c on 50c multi 45 45

A104a

A105

Wmk. 373

1983, July 6 **Litho.** ***Perf. 12***

675 A104a 45c Handshake 32 32
676 A104a 60c Emblem 45 45
677 A104a $1 Map 70 70
678 A104a $2 Flags 1.40 1.40

10th anniv. of Chaguaramas (Caribbean Free Trade Assoc.)

Perf. 12x11½

1983, Oct. 6 **Litho.** **Wmk. 373**

679 A105 45c Founder William A. Smith 30 30
680 A105 60c Boy, officer 40 40
681 A105 $1.50 Emblem 1.00 1.00
682 A105 $2 Community service 1.40 1.40

Boys' Brigade centenary. For overprint, see No. 887.

Christmas A106

1983, Nov. 15 **Litho.** ***Perf. 12***

683 A106 10c Shepherds at Watch 15 15
684 A106 50c The Angel of the Lord 40 40
685 A106 $1.50 A Glorious Light 1.15 1.15
686 A106 $2.40 At the Manger 2.00 2.00
a. Souvenir sheet of 4, #683-686 3.75 3.75

Classic Cars — A107

1983, Nov. 9 **Litho.** ***Perf. 12½***

687 A107 10c Ford Model T 15 15
688 A107 10c Ford Model T, diff. 15 15
689 A107 60c Supercharged Cord 26 26
690 A107 60c Supercharged Cord, diff. 26 26
691 A107 $1.50 Mercedes-Benz 70 70
692 A107 $1.50 Mercedes-Benz, diff. 70 70
693 A107 $1.50 Citroen Open Tourer 70 70
694 A107 $1.50 Citroen Open Tourer, diff. 70 70
695 A107 $2 Ferrari Boxer 95 95
696 A107 $2 Ferrari Boxer, diff. 95 95
697 A107 $2 Rolls-Royce Phantom 95 95
698 A107 $2 Rolls-Royce Phantom, diff. 95 95
Nos. 687-698 (12) 7.42 7.42

Stamps of same denomination printed in se-tenant pairs.

1983, Dec. 8 **Litho.** ***Perf. 12½x13***

Locomotives. Stamps of same denomination se-tenant.

699 A107 10c King Henry VIII 15 15
700 A107 10c King Henry VIII, diff. 15 15
701 A107 10c Royal Scots Greys 15 15
702 A107 10c Royal Scots Greys, diff. 15 15
703 A107 25c Hagley Hall 15 15
704 A107 25c Hagley Hall, diff. 15 15
705 A107 50c Sir Lancelot 20 20
706 A107 50c Sir Lancelot, diff. 20 20
707 A107 60c B12 Class 24 24
708 A107 60c B12 Class, diff. 24 24
709 A107 75c No. 1000 Deeley Compound 32 32
710 A107 75c No. 1000, diff. 32 32
711 A107 $2.50 Cheshire 1.00 1.00
712 A107 $2.50 Cheshire, diff. 1.00 1.00
713 A107 $3 Bulleid Austerity 1.25 1.25
714 A107 $3 Austerity, diff. 1.25 1.25
Nos. 699-714 (16) 6.92 6.92

See Nos. 747-760A, 773-782, 815-828A, 906-917.

Fort Duvernette A108

Perf. 14x14½

1984, Feb. 13 **Litho.** **Wmk. 380**

715 A108 35c View 26 26
716 A108 45c Wall, flag 34 34
717 A108 $1 Canon 72 72
718 A108 $3 Map 2.30 2.30

Flowering Trees — A109

Perf. 13½x14

1984, Apr. 2 **Litho.** **Wmk. 373**

719 A109 5c White frangipani 15 15
720 A109 10c Genip 15 15
721 A109 15c Immortelle 15 15
722 A109 20c Pink poui 15 15
723 A109 25c Buttercup 18 18
724 A109 35c Sandbox 26 26
725 A109 45c Locust 34 34
726 A109 60c Colville's glory 45 45
727 A109 75c Lignum vitae 55 55
728 A109 $1 Golden shower 72 72
729 A109 $5 Angelin 3.60 3.60
730 A109 $10 Roucou 7.25 7.25
Nos. 719-730 (12) 13.95 13.95

World War I Battle Scene, A110 — King George V, A111

1984, Apr. 25 **Litho.** ***Perf. 13x12½***

731 A110 1c shown 15 15
732 A111 1c shown 15 15
733 A110 5c Battle of Bannockburn 15 15
734 A111 5c Edward II 15 15
735 A110 60c George V, diff. 45 45
736 A111 60c York Cottage, Sandringham 45 45
737 A110 75c Edward II, diff. 60 60
738 A111 75c Berkeley Castle 60 60
739 A110 $1 Arms of Edward II 75 75

740 A111 $1 Edward II, diff. 75 75
741 A110 $4 Arms of George V 2.75 2.75
742 A111 $4 George V, diff. 2.75 2.75
Nos. 731-742 (12) 9.70 9.70

Stamps of same denomination se-tenant in continuous design.

Carnival A112

Wmk. 380

1984, June 25 Litho. *Perf. 14*

743 A112 35c Musical fantasy 26 26
744 A112 45c African woman 34 34
745 A112 $1 Market woman 75 75
746 A112 $3 Carib hieroglyph 2.25 2.25

Car Type of 1983

Locomotives (front and side views). Stamps of same denomination se-tenant.

1984, July 27 Litho. *Perf. 12½*

747 A107 1c Liberation Class 141R, 1945 15 15
748 A107 1c Side 15 15
749 A107 2c Dreadnought Class 50, 1967 15 15
750 A107 2c Side 15 15
751 A107 3c No. 242A1, 1946 15 15
752 A107 3c Side 15 15
753 A107 50c Dean Goods, 1883 26 26
754 A107 50c Side 26 26
755 A107 75c Hetton Colliery, 1822 32 32
756 A107 75c Side 32 32
757 A107 $1 Penydarren, 1804 52 52
758 A107 $1 Side 52 52
759 A107 $2 Novelty, 1829 95 95
759A A107 $2 Side 95 95
760 A107 $3 Class 44, 1925 1.65 1.65
760A A107 $3 Side 1.65 1.65
Nos. 747-760A (16) 8.30 8.30

Slavery Abolition Sesquicentennial — A113

1984, Aug. 1 Litho. *Perf. 14*

761 A113 35c Hoeing 26 26
762 A113 45c Gathering sugar cane 34 34
763 A113 $1 Cutting sugar cane 75 75
764 A113 $3 Abolitionist William Wilberforce 2.25 2.25

1984 Summer Olympics — A114

Military Uniforms — A115

1984, Aug. 30 Unwmk. *Perf. 12½*

765 A114 1c Judo 15 15
766 A114 1c Weight lifting 15 15
767 A114 3c Bicycling (facing left) 15 15
768 A114 3c Bicycling (facing right) 15 15
769 A114 60c Swimming (back stroke) 30 30
770 A114 60c Breast stroke 30 30
771 A114 $3 Running (start) 1.50 1.50
772 A114 $3 Running (finish) 1.50 1.50
Nos. 765-772 (8) 4.20 4.20

Stamps of same denomination se-tenant.

Car Type of 1983

1984, Oct. 22 Litho. *Perf. 12½*

773 A107 5c Austin-Healey Sprite, 1958 15 15
774 A107 5c Side 15 15
775 A107 20c Maserati, 1971 15 15
776 A107 20c Side 15 15
777 A107 55c Pontiac GTO, 1964 24 24
778 A107 55c Side 24 24
779 A107 $1.50 Jaguar, 1957 65 65
780 A107 $1.50 Side 65 65
781 A107 $2.50 Ferrari, 1970 1.10 1.10
782 A107 $2.50 Side 1.10 1.10
Nos. 773-782 (10) 4.58 4.58

Stamps of same denomination se-tenant.

1984, Nov. 12 Wmk. 380 *Perf. 14*

783 A115 45c Grenadier, 1773 32 32
784 A115 60c Grenadier, 1775 45 45
785 A115 $1.50 Grenadier, 1768 1.15 1.15
786 A115 $2 Battalion Co. Officer, 1780 1.50 1.50

Locomotives Type of 1985

1984, Nov. 21 Litho. *Perf. 12½x13*

787 A120 5c 1954 R.R. Class 20, Zimbabwe 15 15
788 A120 5c Class 20, diff. 15 15
789 A120 40c 1928 Southern Maid, U.K. 22 22
790 A120 40c Southern Maid, diff. 22 22
791 A120 75c 1911 Prince of Wales, U.K. 42 42
792 A120 75c Prince of Wales, diff. 42 42
793 A120 $2.50 1935 D.R.G. Class 05, Germany 1.40 1.40
794 A120 $2.50 Class 05, diff. 1.40 1.40
Nos. 787-794 (8) 4.38 4.38

Stamps of the same denomination printed se-tenant.

Cricket Players — A116

1985, Jan. 7 Litho. *Perf. 12½*

795 A116 5c N.S. Taylor, portrait 15 15
796 A116 5c Taylor at wicket 15 15
797 A116 35c T.W. Graveney with bat 20 20
798 A116 35c Graveney, portrait 20 20
799 A116 50c R.G.D. Willis at wicket 30 30
800 A116 50c Willis, portrait 30 30
801 A116 $3 S.D. Fletcher at wicket 1.75 1.75
802 A116 $3 Fletcher, portrait 1.75 1.75
Nos. 795-802 (8) 4.80 4.80

Orchids — A117

Audubon Birth Bicent. — A118

1985, Jan. 31 Litho. *Perf. 14*

803 A117 35c Epidendrum ciliare 26 26
804 A117 45c Ionopsis utricularioides 34 34
805 A117 $1 Epidendrum secundum 75 75
806 A117 $3 Oncidium altissimum 2.25 2.25

1985, Feb. 7 Litho. *Perf. 12½*

Illustrations of North American bird species by artist/naturalist John J. Audubon.

807 A118 15c Brown pelican 15 15
808 A118 15c Green heron 15 15
809 A118 40c Pileated woodpecker 25 25
810 A118 40c Common flicker 25 25
811 A118 60c Painted bunting 35 35
812 A118 60c White-winged crossbill 35 35
813 A118 $2.25 Red-shouldered hawk 1.40 1.40
814 A118 $2.25 Crested caracara 1.40 1.40
Nos. 807-814 (8) 4.30 4.30

Stamps of the same denomination printed se-tenant.

Car Type of 1983

1985

815 A107 1c 1937 Lancia Aprilia, Italy 15 15
816 A107 1c Aprilia, diff. 15 15
817 A107 25c 1922 Essex Coach, US 15 15
818 A107 25c Essex, diff. 15 15
819 A107 55c 1973 Pontiac Firebird Trans Am, US 24 24
820 A107 55c Trans Am, diff. 24 24
821 A107 60c 1950 Nash Rambler, US 28 28
822 A107 60c Nash, diff. 28 28
823 A107 $1 1961 Ferrari Tipo 156, Italy 48 48
824 A107 $1 Ferrari, diff. 48 48
825 A107 $1.50 1967 Eagle-Weslake Type 58, US 70 70
826 A107 $1.50 Eagle, diff. 70 70
827 A107 $2 1953 Cunningham C-5R, US 1.00 1.00
828 A107 $2 C-5R, diff. 1.00 1.00
Nos. 815-828 (14) 6.00 6.00

Souvenir Sheet

828A Sheet of 4 10.00 10.00
b. A107 $4 1967 Eagle-Weslake Type 58, US 2.25 2.25
c. A107 $4 Eagle-Weslake, diff. 2.25 2.25
d. A107 $5 1961 Ferrari Tipo 156, Italy 2.75 2.75
e. A107 $5 Tipo, diff. 2.75 2.75

Stamps of the same denomination printed se-tenant. Issue dates: 1c, 55c, $2, Mar. 11. 25c, 60c, $1, $1.50, June 7.

Herbs and Spices — A119

1985, Apr. 22 *Perf. 14*

829 A119 25c Pepper 20 20
830 A119 35c Sweet marjoram 28 28
831 A119 $1 Nutmeg 75 75
832 A119 $3 Ginger 2.25 2.25

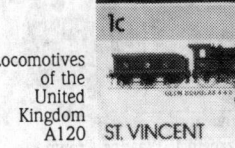

Locomotives of the United Kingdom A120

1985, Apr. 26 *Perf. 12½*

833 A120 1c 1913 Glen Douglas 15 15
834 A120 1c Front 15 15
835 A120 10c 1872 Fenchurch Terrier 15 15
836 A120 10c Rear 15 15
837 A120 40c 1870 No. 1 Stirling Single 18 18
838 A120 40c Front 18 18
839 A120 60c 1866 No. 158A 28 28
840 A120 60c Front 28 28
841 A120 $1 1893 No. 103 Class Jones Goods 45 45
842 A120 $1 Front 45 45
843 A120 $2.50 1908 Great Bear 1.25 1.25
844 A120 $2.50 Front 1.25 1.25
Nos. 833-844 (12) 4.92 4.92

Stamps of the same denomination printed se-tenant. See #787-794, 849-860, 960-967.

Traditional Instruments A121

1985, May 16 *Perf. 15*

845 A121 25c Bamboo flute 20 20
846 A121 35c Quatro 28 28
847 A121 $1 Bamboo base, vert. 75 75
848 A121 $2 Goat-skin drum, vert. 1.50 1.50
a. Sheet of 4, #845-848 2.75 2.75

Locomotives Type of 1985

1985, June 27 *Perf. 12½*

849 A120 5c 1874 Loch, U.K. 15 15
850 A120 5c Front 15 15
851 A120 30c 1919 Class 47XX, U.K. 16 16
852 A120 30c Front 16 16
853 A120 60c 1876 P.L.M. Class 121, France 30 30
854 A120 60c Front 30 30
855 A120 75c 1927 D.R.G. Class 24, Germany 35 35
856 A120 75c Front 35 35
857 A120 $1 1889 No. 1008, U.K. 50 50
858 A120 $1 Front 50 50
859 A120 $2.50 1926 S.R. Class PS-4, USA 1.25 1.25
860 A120 $2.50 Front 1.25 1.25
Nos. 849-860 (12) 5.42 5.42

Stamps of the same denomination printed se-tenant.

A122

A123

Queen Mother, 85th birthday: Photographs.

1985, Aug. 9

861 A122 35c Facing right 16 16
862 A122 35c Facing left 16 16
863 A122 85c Facing right, diff. 38 38
864 A122 85c Facing left, diff. 38 38
865 A122 $1.20 Facing right, diff. 55 55
866 A122 $1.20 Facing left, diff. 55 55
867 A122 $1.60 Facing front 75 75
868 A122 $1.60 Facing left, diff. 75 75
Nos. 861-868 (8) 3.68 3.68

Souvenir Sheet

869 Sheet of 2 2.50 2.50
a. A122 $2.10 Facing right, diff. 1.25 1.25
b. A122 $2.10 Facing front, diff. 1.25 1.25

Stamps of the same denomination printed se-tenant.
For overprints, see Nos. 888-889.

1985, Dec. 19 Litho. *Perf. 12½*

869C Sheet of 2 3.75 3.75
e. A122 $3.50 like #863 1.75 1.75
f. A122 $3.50 like #864 1.75 1.75
869D Sheet of 2 6.25 6.25
g. A122 $6 like #861 3.25 3.25
h. A122 $6 like #862 3.25 3.25

1985, Aug. 16

Photographs of Elvis Presley (1935-1977), American entertainer.

870 A123 10c In concert 15 15
871 A123 10c Facing front 15 15
872 A123 60c In concert, diff. 35 35
873 A123 60c Facing left 35 35
874 A123 $1 In concert, diff. 60 60
875 A123 $1 Facing front, diff. 60 60
876 A123 $5 Wearing leather jacket 3.00 3.00
877 A123 $5 Facing left, diff. 3.00 3.00
Nos. 870-877 (8) 8.20 8.20

Souvenir Sheets

878 Sheet of 4 72 72
a. A123 30c like #870 18 18
b. A123 30c like #871 18 18
879 Sheet of 4 1.20 1.20
a. A123 50c like #872 30 30
b. A123 50c like #873 30 30
880 Sheet of 4 3.50 3.50
a. A123 $1.50 like #874 85 85
b. A123 $1.50 like #875 85 85
881 Sheet of 4 10.00 10.00
a. A123 $4.50 like #876 2.50 2.50
b. A123 $4.50 like #877 2.50 2.50

Nos. 878-881 contain two of each stamp.
Stamps of the same denomination printed se-tenant.
Two $4 "stamps" were not issued.
For other Presley souvenir sheet see No. 1567.
For overprints, see Nos. 1005-1016.

Flour Milling
A124

1985, Oct. 17 Wmk. 373 *Perf. 15*

882	A124	20c	Conveyor from elevators	15	15
883	A124	30c	Roller mills	22	22
884	A124	75c	Office	55	55
885	A124	$3	Bran finishers	2.25	2.25

Nos. 667, 680, 863-864, 650, 631-632, 651 Ovptd. "CARIBBEAN / ROYAL VISIT / -1985-" or Surcharged with 3 Black Bars and New Value in Black

1985, Oct. 27 *Perfs. as Before*

886	A104	60c	multicolored	*1.25*	*1.25*
887	A105	60c	multicolored	*1.25*	*1.25*
888	A122	85c	multicolored	*2.00*	*2.00*
889	A122	85c	multicolored	*2.00*	*2.00*
890	A100	$1.50	multicolored	*3.50*	*3.50*
891	A94a	$1.60	on $4	*3.75*	*3.75*
892	A94b	$1.60	on $4	*3.75*	*3.75*
893	A100	$2.50	multicolored	*5.75*	*5.75*
			Nos. 886-893 (8)	*23.25*	*23.25*

Michael Jackson (b. 1960), American Entertainer — A125

Photographs.

1985, Dec. 2 *Perf. 12½*

894	A125	60c	Portrait	28	28
895	A125	60c	On stage	28	28
896	A125	$1	Singing	52	52
897	A125	$1	Portrait, diff.	52	52
898	A125	$2	Black jacket	1.00	1.00
899	A125	$2	Red jacket	1.00	1.00
900	A125	$5	Portrait, diff.	2.75	2.75
901	A125	$5	Wearing white glove	2.75	2.75
			Nos. 894-901 (8)	9.10	9.10

Stamps of same denomination printed se-tenant.

Souvenir Sheets
Perf. 13x12½

902	Sheet of 4, 2 each	90	90
d.-e.	A125 45c like #894-895	20	20
902A	Sheet of 4, 2 each	1.90	1.90
f.-g.	A125 90c like #896-897	45	45
902B	Sheet of 4, 2 each	3.00	3.00
h.-i.	A125 $1.50 like #898-899	70	70
902C	Sheet of 4, 2 each	8.25	8.25
j.-k.	A125 $4 like #900-901	2.00	2.00

Christmas
A126

Children's drawings: 25c, Serenade, 75c, Poinsettia. $2.50, Jesus, Our Master.

1985, Dec. 9 Wmk. 373 *Perf. 14*

903	A126	25c	multicolored	18	18
904	A126	75c	multicolored	55	55
905	A126	$2.50	multicolored	1.90	1.90

Car Type of 1983

1986, Jan. 27 *Perf. 12½*

906	A107	30c	1916 Cadillac Type 53, US	18	18
907	A107	30c	Cadillac, diff.	18	18
908	A107	45c	1939 Triumph Dolomite, UK	28	28
909	A107	45c	Dolomite, diff.	28	28
910	A107	60c	1972 Panther J-72, UK	35	35
911	A107	60c	Panther, diff.	35	35
912	A107	90c	1967 Ferrari 275 GTB/4, Italy	55	55
913	A107	90c	Ferrari, diff.	55	55
914	A107	$1.50	1953 Packard Caribbean, US	90	90
915	A107	$1.50	Packard, diff.	90	90
916	A107	$2.50	1931 Bugatti Type 41 Royale, France	1.50	1.50
917	A107	$2.50	Royale, diff.	1.50	1.50
			Nos. 906-917 (12)	7.52	7.52

Stamps of same denomination printed se-tenant.

Halley's Comet
A127

Wmk. 380

1986, Apr. 14 Litho. *Perf. 15*

918	A127	45c	shown	35	35
919	A127	60c	Edmond Halley	45	45
920	A127	75c	Newton's reflector telescope	55	55
921	A127	$3	Local astronomer	2.25	2.25
a.			Souvenir sheet of 4, #918-921	3.60	3.60

Souvenir Sheets

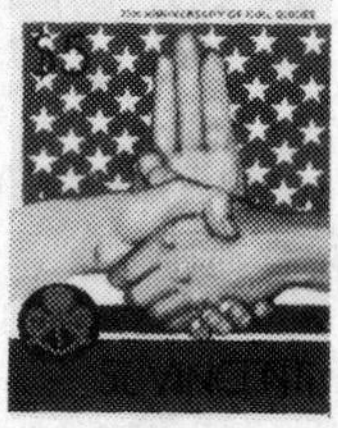

Scouting Movement, 75th Anniv. — A127a

American flag and Girl Guides or Boy Scouts emblem and: No. 922b, Scout sign, handshake. No. 922c, Paintbrushes and pallet. No. 922d, Knots. No. 922e, Lord Baden-Powell.

1986, Feb. 25 Litho. *Perf. 13x12½*

922	Sheet of 2	4.50	4.50
b.-c.	A127a $5 any single	2.25	2.25
922A	Sheet of 2	5.50	5.50
d.-e.	A127a $6 any single	2.75	2.75

"Capex '87" overprints on this issue were not authorized.

Elizabeth II Wearing Crown Jewels — A128

Elizabeth II at Victoria Park
A129

Various portraits.

1986, Apr. 21 Wmk. 373 *Perf. 12½*

923	A128	10c	multicolored	15	15
924	A128	90c	multicolored	55	55
925	A128	$2.50	multicolored	1.50	1.50
926	A128	$8	multi, vert.	5.00	5.00

Souvenir Sheet

927	A128	$10	multicolored	6.25	6.25

Perf. 15x14

1986, June 14 Wmk. 373

Designs: No. 928, with Prime Minister Mitchell. No. 929, Arriving at Port Elizabeth. No. 930, at Independence Day Parade.

928	A129	45c	multicolored	35	35
929	A129	60c	multicolored	45	45
930	A129	75c	multicolored	55	55
931	A129	$2.50	multicolored	1.90	1.90

Souvenir Sheet

932	A129	$3	multicolored	2.25	2.25

Queen Elizabeth II, 60th birthday.

Discovery of America, 500th Anniv. (1992) — A130

1986, Jan. 23 Litho. *Perf. 12½*

933	A130	60c	Fleet	45	45
934	A130	60c	Columbus	45	45
935	A130	$1.50	At Spanish Court	1.10	1.10
936	A130	$1.50	Ferdinand, Isabella	1.10	1.10
937	A130	$2.75	Fruit, Santa Maria	2.05	2.05
938	A130	$2.75	Fruit	2.05	2.05
			Nos. 933-938 (6)	7.20	7.20

Souvenir Sheet

939	A130	$6	Columbus, diff.	4.50	4.50

Stamps of same denomination printed se-tenant in continuous designs.

1986 World Cup Soccer Championships, Mexico — A131

1986, May 7 Litho. *Perf. 15*

940	A131	1c	Emblem	15	15
941	A131	2c	Mexico	15	15
942	A131	5c	Mexico, diff.	15	15
943	A131	5c	Hungary vs. Scotland	15	15
944	A131	10c	Spain vs. Scotland	15	15
945	A131	30c	England vs. USSR	18	18
946	A131	45c	Spain vs. France	28	28
947	A131	$1	England vs. Italy	60	60

Perf. 13½
Size: 56x36mm

948	A131	75c	Mexico	42	42
949	A131	$2	Scotland	1.25	1.25
950	A131	$4	Spain	2.50	2.50
951	A131	$5	England	3.00	3.00
			Nos. 940-951 (12)	8.98	8.98

1986, July 7 Souvenir Sheets

952	A131	$1.50	like #950	65	65
952A	A131	$1.50	like #941	65	65
953	A131	$2.25	like #949	95	95
954	A131	$2.50	like #948	1.00	1.00
954A	A131	$3	like #946	1.10	1.10
955	A131	$5.50	like #951	2.50	2.50

Nos. 941-944, 946, 947, vert.

Wedding of Prince Andrew and Sarah Ferguson
A132

A132a

Perf. 12½x13, 13x12½

1986, July 23 Litho.

956	A132	60c	Andrew	35	35
957	A132	60c	Sarah	35	35
958	A132	$2	Andrew, horiz.	1.25	1.25
959	A132	$2	Andrew, Nancy Reagan, horiz.	1.25	1.25

Stamps of the same denomination printed se-tenant.

For overprints, see Nos. 976-979.

A number of unissued items, imperfs., part perfs., missing color varieties, etc., were made available when the Format International inventory was liquidated.

1986, Nov. Litho. *Perf. 13x12½*

959A	A132a	$10	In coach	6.00	6.00

Locomotives Type of 1985

Designs: Nos. 960-961, 1926 JNR ABT Rack & Adhesion Class ED41 BZZB, Japan. Nos. 962-963, 1883 Chicago RR Exposition, The Judge, 1A Type, US. Nos. 964-965, 1973 BM & LPRR E60C Co-Co, US. Nos. 966-967, 1972 GM (EMD) SD40-2 Co-Co, US.

1986, July *Perf. 12½x13*

960	A120	30c	multi	18	18
961	A120	30c	multi, diff.	18	18
962	A120	50c	multi	30	30
963	A120	50c	multi, diff.	30	30
964	A120	$1	multi	60	60
965	A120	$1	multi, diff.	60	60
966	A120	$3	multi	1.75	1.75
967	A120	$3	multi, diff.	1.75	1.75
			Nos. 960-967 (8)	5.66	5.66

Stamps of the same denomination printed se-tenant.

Trees — A133

1986, Sept. *Perf. 14*

968	A133	10c	Acrocomia aculeata	15	15
969	A133	60c	Pithecellobium saman	45	45
970	A133	75c	Tabebuia pallida	55	55
971	A133	$3	Andira inermis	2.25	2.25

Anniversaries
A134

1986, Sept. 30

972	A134	45c	Cadet Force emblem, vert.	35	35
973	A134	60c	Grimble Building, GHS	45	45
974	A134	$1.50	GHS class	1.10	1.10
975	A134	$2	Cadets in formation	1.50	1.50

St. Vincent Cadet Force, 50th anniv., and Girls' High School, 75th anniv.

Nos. 956-959 Overprint. "Congratulations to T.R.H. The Duke & Duchess of York" in Silver

Perf. 12½x13, 13x12½

1986, Oct. **Litho.**

976 A132	60c	No. 956	45	45
977 A132	60c	No. 957	45	45
978 A132	$2	No. 958	1.50	1.50
979 A132	$2	No. 959	1.50	1.50

Stamps of the same denomination exist printed tete-beche and se-tenant.

The Legend of King Arthur — A134a

1986, Nov. 3 *Perf. 14*

980	A134a	30c	King Arthur	18	18
980A	A134a	45c	Merlin raises Arthur	28	28
980B	A134a	60c	Arthur pulls Excalibur from stone	38	38
980C	A134a	75c	Camelot	45	45
980D	A134a	$1	Lady of the Lake	60	60
980E	A134a	$1.50	Knights of the Round Table	90	90
980F	A134a	$2	Holy Grail	1.20	1.20
980G	A134a	$5	Sir Lancelot	3.00	3.00
			Nos. 980-980G (8)	6.99	6.99

Statue of Liberty, Cent. — A134b

Statue of Liberty, Cent. — A135

Various views of the statue.

1986, Nov. 26 **Litho.** *Perf. 14*

980H	A134b	15c	multicolored	15	15
980I	A134b	25c	multicolored	16	16
980J	A134b	40c	multicolored	25	25
980K	A134b	55c	multicolored	35	35
980L	A134b	75c	multicolored	50	50
980M	A134b	90c	multicolored	60	60
980N	A134b	$1.75	multicolored	1.10	1.10
980O	A134b	$2	multicolored	1.25	1.25
980P	A134b	$2.50	multicolored	1.65	1.65
980Q	A134b	$3	multicolored	1.90	1.90
			Nos. 980H-980Q (10)	7.91	7.91

Souvenir Sheets

981	A135	$3.50	multicolored	2.25	2.25
982	A135	$4	multicolored	2.50	2.50
983	A135	$5	multicolored	3.00	3.00

Fresh-water Fishing A136

1986, Dec. 10 *Perf. 15*

984 A136	75c	Tri tri fishing	58	58
985 A136	75c	Tri tri	58	58
986 A136	$1.50	Crayfishing	1.10	1.10
987 A136	$1.50	Crayfish	1.10	1.10

Stamps of the same denomination printed se-tenant.

1987 Wimbledon Tennis Championships A137

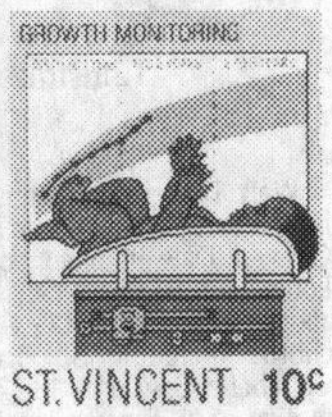

Natl. Child Survival Campaign A138

1987, June 22 *Perf. 13x12½*

988 A137	40c	Hana Mandlikova	24	24
989 A137	60c	Yannick Noah	35	35
990 A137	80c	Ivan Lendl	48	48
991 A137	$1	Chris Evert Lloyd	60	60
992 A137	$1.25	Steffi Graf	75	75
993 A137	$1.50	John McEnroe	95	95
994 A137	$1.75	Martina Navratilova	1.10	1.10
995 A137	$2	Boris Becker	1.25	1.25
		Nos. 988-995 (8)	5.72	5.72

Souvenir Sheet

996		Sheet of 2	3.50	3.50
a.	A137 $2.25 like $2		1.75	1.75
b.	A137 $2.25 like $1.75		1.75	1.75

1987, June 10 *Perf. 14x14½*

997 A138	10c	Growth monitoring	15	15
998 A138	50c	Oral rehydration therapy	38	38
999 A138	75c	Breast-feeding	58	58
1000 A138	$1	Universal immunization	75	75

For overprints, see Nos. 1040-1043.

Carnival, 10th Anniv. — A139

Designs: 20c, Queen of the Bands, Miss Prima Donna 1986. 45c, Donna Young, Miss Carival 1985. 55c, M. Haydock, Miss. St. Vincent and the Grenadines 1986.

1987, June 29 *Perf. 12½x13*

1001 A139	20c	multicolored	15	15
1002 A139	45c	multicolored	35	35
1003 A139	55c	multicolored	42	42
1004 A139	$3.70	multicolored	2.75	2.75

Nos. 870-881 Overprinted "THE KING OF ROCK AND ROLL LIVES FOREVER . AUGUST 16TH" and "1977-1987" (Nos. 1005-1012) or "TENTH ANNIVERSARY" (Nos. 1013-1016)

1987, Aug. 26 **Litho.** *Perf. 12½*

1005 A123	10c	like No. 870	15	15
1006 A123	10c	like No. 871	15	15
1007 A123	60c	like No. 872	40	40
1008 A123	60c	like No. 873	40	40
1009 A123	$1	like No. 874	65	65
1010 A123	$1	like No. 875	65	65
1011 A123	$5	like No. 876	3.25	3.25
1012 A123	$5	like No. 877	3.25	3.25
		Nos. 1005-1012 (8)	8.90	8.90

Souvenir Sheets

1013	Sheet of 4	90	90
a.	A123 30c like No. 870	22	22
b.	A123 30c like No. 871	22	22
1014	Sheet of 4	1.50	1.50
a.	A123 50c like No. 872	35	35
b.	A123 50c like No. 873	35	35
1015	Sheet of 4	4.50	4.50
a.	A123 $1.50 like No. 874	1.10	1.10
b.	A123 $1.50 like No. 875	1.10	1.10
1016	Sheet of 4	13.00	13.00
a.	A123 $4.50 like No. 876	3.25	3.25
b.	A123 $4.50 like No. 877	3.25	3.25

Stamps of the same denomination printed se-tenant. Nos. 1013-1016 contain two of each stamp.

Portrait of Queen Victoria, 1841, by R. Thorburn A140

Portraits and photographs: 75c, Elizabeth and Charles, 1948. $1, Coronation, 1953. $2.50, Duke of Edinburgh, 1948. $5, Elizabeth, c. 1980. $6, Elizabeth and Charles, 1948, diff.

1987, Nov. 20 **Litho.** *Perf. 12½x13*

1017 A140	15c	multicolored	15	15
1018 A140	75c	multicolored	45	45
1019 A140	$1	multicolored	60	60
1020 A140	$2.50	multicolored	1.50	1.50
1021 A140	$5	multicolored	3.00	3.00
		Nos. 1017-1021 (5)	5.70	5.70

Souvenir Sheet

1022 A140	$6	multicolored	4.50	4.50

Sesquicentennial of Queen Victoria's accession to the throne, wedding of Queen Elizabeth II and Prince Philip, 40th anniv.

Nos. 997-1000 Ovptd. "WORLD POPULATION / 5 BILLION / 11TH JULY 1987"

1987, July 11 **Litho.** *Perf. 14x14½*

1040 A138	10c	on No. 997	15	15
1041 A138	50c	on No. 998	38	38
1042 A138	75c	on No. 999	58	58
1043 A138	$1	on No. 1000	75	75

Automobile Centenary — A143

Automotive pioneers and vehicles: $1, $3, Carl Benz (1844-1929) and the Velocipede, patented 1886. $2, No. 1049, Enzo Ferrari (b. 1898) and 1966 Ferrari Dino 206SP. $4, $6, Charles Rolls (1877-1910), Sir Henry Royce (1863-1933) and 1907 Rolls Royce Silver Ghost. No. 1047, $8, Henry Ford (1863-1947) and Model T Ford.

1987, Dec. 4 *Perf. 13x12½*

1044 A143	$1	multicolored	60	60
1045 A143	$2	multicolored	1.10	1.10
1046 A143	$4	multicolored	2.25	2.25
1047 A143	$5	multicolored	3.00	3.00

Souvenir Sheets

1048 A143	$3	like No. 1044	2.25	2.25
1049 A143	$5	like No. 1045	3.75	3.75
1050 A143	$6	like No. 1046	4.50	4.50
1051 A143	$8	like No. 1047	6.00	6.00

Soccer Teams — A144

1987, Dec. 4

1052 A144	$2	Derby County	1.10	1.10
1053 A144	$2	Leeds United	1.10	1.10
1054 A144	$2	Tottenham Hotspur	1.10	1.10
1055 A144	$2	Manchester United	1.10	1.10
1056 A144	$2	Everton	1.10	1.10
1057 A144	$2	Liverpool	1.10	1.10
1058 A144	$2	Portsmouth	1.10	1.10
1059 A144	$2	Arsenal	1.10	1.10
		Nos. 1052-1059 (8)	8.80	8.80

A145 A146

A Christmas Carol, by Charles Dickens (1812-1870) — A147

Portrait of Dickens as left page of book and various scenes from novels as right page of book.

1987, Dec. 17 *Perf. 14x14½*

1060 A145	6c	multicolored	15	15
1061 A146	6c	Mr. Fezziwig's Ball	15	15
1062 A145	25c	multicolored	20	20
1063 A146	25c	Ghost of Christmases to Come	20	20
1064 A145	50c	multicolored	38	38
1065 A146	50c	The Cratchits	38	38
1066 A145	75c	multicolored	55	55
1067 A146	75c	Carolers	55	55
		Nos. 1060-1067 (8)	2.56	2.56

Souvenir Sheet

1068 A147	$5	Reading book to children	3.75	3.75

Stamps of the same denomination printed se-tenant in continuous designs.

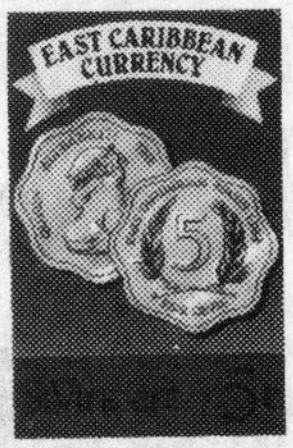

Eastern Caribbean Currency — A148

Various Eastern Caribbean coins (Nos. 1069-1081) and banknotes (Nos. 1082-1086) in denominations equaling that of the stamp on which they are pictured.

1987-89 **Litho.** *Perf. 15*

1069	A148	5c	multicolored	15	15
1070	A148	6c	multicolored	15	15
1071	A148	10c	multicolored	15	15
1072	A148	12c	multicolored	15	15
1073	A148	15c	multicolored	15	15
1074	A148	20c	multicolored	15	15
1075	A148	25c	multicolored	20	20
1076	A148	30c	multicolored	24	24
1077	A148	35c	multicolored	28	28
1078	A148	45c	multicolored	35	35
1079	A148	50c	multicolored	38	38
1080	A148	65c	multicolored	50	50
1081	A148	75c	multicolored	58	58
1082	A148	$1	multi, horiz.	75	75
1083	A148	$2	multi, horiz.	1.50	1.50
1084	A148	$3	multi, horiz.	2.25	2.25
1085	A148	$5	multi, horiz.	3.75	3.75
1086	A148	$10	multi, horiz.	7.50	7.50
1086A	A148	$20	multi, horiz.	15.00	15.00
			Nos. 1069-1086A (19)	34.18	34.18

Issue dates: $20, Nov. 7, 1989. Others, Dec. 11.

1991 *Perf. 12*

1071a	A148	10c	15	15
1073a	A148	15c	15	15
1074a	A148	20c	15	15
1075a	A148	25c	18	18
1078a	A148	45c	32	32

1079a	A148	50c	35	35
1080a	A148	65c	45	45
1081a	A148	75c	55	55
1082a	A148	$1	70	70
1083a	A148	$2	1.40	1.40
1085a	A148	$5	3.50	3.50
	Nos. 1071a-1085a (11)		7.90	7.90

1991 ***Perf. 16***

1071b	A148	10c	15	15
1073b	A148	15c	15	15
1074b	A148	20c	15	15
1075b	A148	25c	18	18
1078b	A148	45c	32	32
1079b	A148	50c	35	35
1080b	A148	65c	44	45
1081b	A148	75c	55	55
1082b	A148	$1	70	70
1083b	A148	$2	1.40	1.40
1085b	A148	$5	3.50	3.50
	Nos. 1071b-1085b (11)		7.89	7.90

US Constitution Bicentennial A149

Christopher Columbus's fleet: 15c, Santa Maria. 75c, Nina and Pinta. $1, Hour glass, compass. $1.50, Columbus planting flag of Spain on American soil. $3, Arawak natives. $4, Parrot, hummingbird, corn, pineapple, eggs. $5, $6, Columbus, Spanish royal coat of arms and caravel.

1988, Jan. 11 ***Perf. 14½x14***

1087	A149	15c	multicolored	15	15
1088	A149	75c	multicolored	58	58
1089	A149	$1	multicolored	75	75
1090	A149	$1.50	multicolored	1.15	1.15
1091	A149	$3	multicolored	2.25	2.25
1092	A149	$4	multicolored	3.00	3.00
	Nos. 1087-1092 (6)			7.88	7.88

Souvenir Sheets

Perf. 14x14½, 14½x14

1093	A149	$5	multicolored	3.75	3.75
1093A	A149	$6	multicolored	4.50	4.50

US Constitution, bicent.; 500th anniv. of the discovery of America (in 1992).

Brown Pelican — A150

1988, Feb. 15 ***Perf. 14***

1094	A150	45c multicolored	35	35

See No. 1298.

A151

Tourism — A152

1988, Feb. 22 **Litho.** ***Perf. 15***

1095	A151	10c Windsurfing, diff., vert.	15	15
1096	A151	45c Scuba diving, vert.	35	35
1097	A151	65c shown	50	50
1098	A151	$5 Chartered ship	3.75	3.75

Souvenir Sheet

Perf. 13x12½

1099	A152	$10 shown	7.50	7.50

A153

Destruction of the Spanish Armada by the English, 400th Anniv. — A154

16th cent. ships and artifacts: 15c, Nuestra Senora del Rosario, Spanish Chivalric Cross. 75c, Ark Royal, Armada medal. $1.50, English fleet, 16th cent. navigational instrument. $2, Dismasted galleon, cannon balls. $3.50, English fireships among the Armada, firebomb. $5, Revenge, Drake's drum. $8, Shoreline sentries awaiting the outcome of the battle.

1988, July 29 **Litho.** ***Perf. 12½***

1100	A153	15c	multicolored	15	15
1101	A153	75c	multicolored	58	58
1102	A153	$1.50	multicolored	1.15	1.15
1103	A153	$2	multicolored	1.50	1.50
1104	A153	$3.50	multicolored	2.60	2.60
1105	A153	$5	multicolored	3.75	3.75
	Nos. 1100-1105 (6)			9.73	9.73

Souvenir Sheet

1106	A154	$8 multicolored	6.00	6.00

Cricket Players A156

1988, July 29 **Litho.** ***Perf. 14½x14***

1108	A156	15c	D.K. Lillee	15	15
1109	A156	50c	G.A. Gooch	38	38
1110	A156	75c	R.N. Kapil Dev	58	58
1111	A156	$1	S.M. Gavaskar	75	75
1112	A156	$1.50	M.W. Gatting	1.15	1.15
1113	A156	$2.50	Imran Khan	1.90	1.90
1114	A156	$3	I.T. Botham	2.25	2.25
1115	A156	$4	I.V.A. Richards	3.00	3.00
	Nos. 1108-1115 (8)			10.16	10.16

A souvenir sheet containing a $2 stamp like No. 1115 and a $3.50 stamp like No. 1114 was not issued by the post office.

1988 Summer Olympics, Seoul A158

1988, Dec. 7 **Litho.** ***Perf. 14***

1116	A158	10c	Running	15	15
1117	A158	50c	Long jump, vert.	38	38
1118	A158	$1	Triple jump	75	75
1119	A158	$5	Boxing, vert.	3.75	3.75

Souvenir Sheet

1120	A158	$10	Torch	7.50	7.50

1st Participation of St. Vincent athletes in the Olympics.

For overprints see Nos. 1346-1351.

Christmas — A159

Walt Disney characters: 1c, Minnie Mouse in freight car. 2c, Morty and Ferdy in open rail car. 3c, Chip 'n Dale in open boxcar. 4c, Huey, Dewey, Louie and reindeer. 5c, Donald and Daisy Duck aboard dining car. 10c, Gramma Duck conducting chorus including Scrooge McDuck, Goofy and Clarabelle Cow. No. 1127, Mickey Mouse in locomotive. $6, Santa Claus in caboose. No. 1129, Mickey, Minnie Mouse and nephews in train station, vert. No. 1130, Characters riding carousel, vert.

Perf. 14x13½, 13½x14

1988, Dec. 23 **Litho.**

1121	A159	1c multicolored	15	15
1122	A159	2c multicolored	15	15
1123	A159	3c multicolored	15	15
1124	A159	4c multicolored	15	15
1125	A159	5c multicolored	15	15
1126	A159	10c multicolored	15	15
1127	A159	$5 multicolored	3.75	3.75
1128	A159	$6 multicolored	4.50	4.50
	Nos. 1121-1128 (8)		9.15	9.15

Souvenir Sheets

1129	A159	$5 multicolored	3.75	3.75
1130	A159	$5 multicolored	3.75	3.75

Babe Ruth (1895-1948), American Baseball Star — A160

1988, Dec. 7 **Litho.** ***Perf. 14***

1131	A160	$2 multicolored	1.50	1.50

India '89, Jan. 20-29, New Delhi — A161

Exhibition emblem and Walt Disney characters: 1c, Mickey Mouse as snake charmer, Minnie Mouse as dancer. 2c, Goofy tossing rings at a chowsingha antelope. 3c, Mickey, Minnie, blue peacock. 5c, Goofy and Mickey as miners, Briolette diamond. 10c, Goofy as count presenting Orloff Diamond to Catherine the Great of Russia (Clarabelle Cow). 25c, Regent Diamond and Donald Duck as Napoleon (portrait) in the Louvre. $4, Minnie as Queen Victoria, Mickey as King Albert, crown bearing the Kohinoor Diamond. $5, Mickey and Goofy on safari. No. 1140, Mickey as Nehru, riding an elephant. No. 1141, Mickey as postman delivering Hope Diamond to the Smithsonian Institute.

1989, Feb. 7 **Litho.** ***Perf. 14***

1132	A161	1c multicolored	15	15
1133	A161	2c multicolored	15	15
1134	A161	3c multicolored	15	15
1135	A161	5c multicolored	15	15
1136	A161	10c multicolored	15	15
1137	A161	25c multicolored	20	20
1138	A161	$4 multicolored	3.00	3.00
1139	A161	$5 multicolored	3.75	3.75
	Nos. 1132-1139 (8)		7.70	7.70

Souvenir Sheets

1140	A161	$6 multicolored	4.50	4.50
1141	A161	$6 multicolored	4.50	4.50

Entertainers of the Jazz and Big Band Eras A162

Designs: 10c, Harry James (1916-83). 15c, Sidney Bechet (1897-1959). 25c, Benny Goodman (1909-86). 35c, Django Reinhardt (1910-53). 50c, Lester Young (1909-59). 90c, Gene Krupa (1909-73). $3, Louis Armstrong (1900-71). $4, Duke Ellington (1899-1974). No. 1150, Charlie Parker, Jr. (1920-55). No. 1151, Billie Holiday (1915-59).

1989, Apr. 3 **Litho.** ***Perf. 14***

1142	A162	10c multicolored	15	15
1143	A162	15c multicolored	15	15
1144	A162	25c multicolored	18	18
1145	A162	35c multicolored	26	26
1146	A162	50c multicolored	38	38
1147	A162	90c multicolored	68	68
1148	A162	$3 multicolored	2.25	2.25
1149	A162	$4 multicolored	3.00	3.00
	Nos. 1142-1149 (8)		7.05	7.05

Souvenir Sheets

1150	A162	$5 multicolored	3.75	3.75
1151	A162	$5 multicolored	3.75	3.75

Holiday misspelled "Holliday" on No. 1151.

Miniature Sheet

Noah's Ark — A163

Designs: a, Clouds, 2 birds at right. b, Rainbow, 4 clouds. c, Ark. d, Rainbow, 3 clouds. e, Clouds, 2 birds at left. f, African elephant facing right. g, Elephant facing forward. h, Leaves on tree branch. i, Kangaroos. j, Hummingbird facing left, flower. k, Lions. l, White-tailed deer. m, Koala at right. n, Koala at left. o, Hummingbird facing right, flower. p, Flower, toucan facing left. q, Toucan facing right. r, Camels. s, Giraffes. t, Sheep. u, Ladybugs. v, Butterfly (UR). w, Butterfly (LL). x, Snakes. y, Dragonflies.

1989, Apr. 10 ***Perf. 14***

1152	A163	Sheet of 25	7.50	7.50
a.-y.		40c any single	30	30

Easter — A164

Paintings by Titian: 5c, Baptism of Christ. 30c, Temptation of Christ. 45c, Ecce Homo. 65c, Noli Me Tangere. 75c, Christ Carrying the Cross. $1, Christ Crowned with Thorns. $4, Lamentation Over Christ. $5, The Entombment. No. 1161, Pieta. No. 1162, The Deposition.

1989, Apr. 17 ***Perf. 13½x14***

1153	A164	5c multicolored	15	15
1154	A164	30c multicolored	22	22
1155	A164	45c multicolored	35	35
1156	A164	65c multicolored	48	48
1157	A164	75c multicolored	56	56
1158	A164	$1 multicolored	75	75

1159 A164 $4 multicolored 3.00 3.00
1160 A164 $5 multicolored 3.75 3.75
Nos. 1153-1160 (8) 9.26 9.26

Souvenir Sheets

1161 A164 $6 multicolored 4.50 4.50
1162 A164 $6 multicolored 4.50 4.50

Telstar II and Cooperation in Space — A165

Designs: 15c, Recovery of astronaut L. Gordon Cooper, Mercury 9/Faith 7 mission. 35c, Satellite transmission of Martin Luther King's civil rights march address, 1963. 40c, U.S. shuttle STS-7, first use of Canadarm, deployment and recovery of a W. German free-flying experiment platform. 50c, Satellite transmission of the 1964 Olympics, Innsbruck (speed skater). 60c, Vladimir Remek of Czechoslovakia, 1st non-Soviet cosmonaut, 1978. $1, CNES Hermes space plane, France, ESA emblem and Columbus space station. $3, Satellite transmission of Pope John XXIII (1881-1963) blessing crowd at the Vatican. $4, Ulf Merbold, W. Germany, 1st non-American astronaut, 1983. No. 1171, Launch of Telstar II, May 7, 1963. No. 1172, 1975 Apollo-Soyuz mission members shaking hands.

1989, Apr. 26 Litho. *Perf. 14*

1163 A165 15c multicolored 15 15
1164 A165 35c multicolored 28 28
1165 A165 40c multicolored 30 30
1166 A165 50c multicolored 38 38
1167 A165 60c multicolored 45 45
1168 A165 $1 multicolored 75 75
1169 A165 $3 multicolored 2.25 2.25
1170 A165 $4 multicolored 3.00 3.00
Nos. 1163-1170 (8) 7.56 7.56

Souvenir Sheets

1171 A165 $5 multicolored 3.75 3.75
1172 A165 $5 multicolored 3.75 3.75

Cruise Ships A166

1989, Apr. 21 Litho. *Perf. 14*

1173 A166 10c Ile de France 15 15
1174 A166 40c Liberte 30 30
1175 A166 50c Mauretania 38 38
1176 A166 75c France 55 55
1177 A166 $1 Aquitania 75 75
1178 A166 $2 United States 1.50 1.50
1179 A166 $3 Olympic 2.25 2.25
1180 A166 $4 Queen Elizabeth 3.00 3.00
Nos. 1173-1180 (8) 8.88 8.88

Souvenir Sheets

1181 A166 $6 Queen Mary 4.50 4.50
1182 A166 $6 QE 2 4.50 4.50

Nos. 1181-1182 contain 84x28mm stamps.
For overprints see Nos. 1352-1361.

Souvenir Sheet

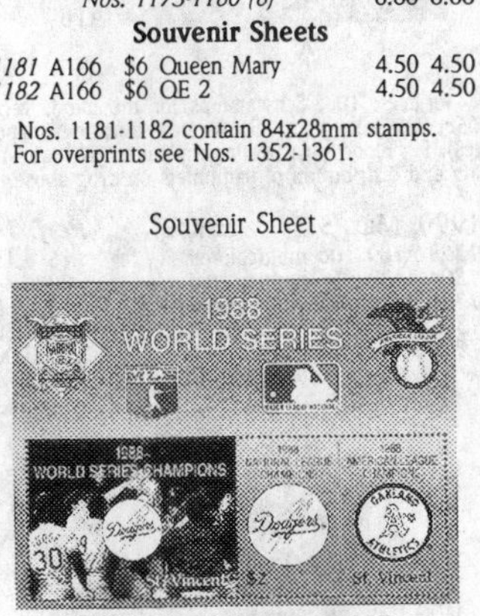

1988 World Series — A167

Designs: a, Dodgers emblem and players celebrating victory. b, Emblems of the Dodgers and the Oakland Athletics.

1989, May 3 Litho. *Perf. 14x13½*

1183 Sheet of 2 3.00 3.00
a.-b. A167 $2 any single 1.50 1.50

World Wildlife Fund, St. Vincent Parrots A168

Indigenous Birds — A169

1989, Apr. 5 *Perf. 14*

1184 A168 10c Parrot's head 15 15
1185 A168 20c Parrot's wing span 15 15
1186 A169 25c Mistletoe bird 18 18
1187 A168 40c Parrot feeding, vert. 30 30
1188 A168 70c Parrot on rock, vert. 52 52
1189 A169 75c Crab hawk 58 58
1190 A169 $2 Coucou 1.50 1.50
1191 A169 $3 Prince bird 2.25 2.25
Nos. 1184-1191 (8) 5.63 5.63

Souvenir Sheets

1192 A169 $5 Doctor bird 3.75 3.75
1193 A169 $5 Soufrieres, vert. 3.75 3.75

Fan Paintings — A170

By Hiroshige unless otherwise stated: 10c, Autumn Flowers in Front of the Full Moon. 40c, Hibiscus. 50c, Iris. 75c, Morning Glories. $1, Dancing Swallows. $2, Sparrow and Bamboo. $3, Yellow Bird and Cotton Rose. $4, Judos Chrysanthemums in a deep ravine in China. No. 1202, Rural Cottages in Spring, by Sotatsu. No. 1203, The Six Immortal Poets Portrayed as Cats, by Kuniyoshi.

1989, July 6 Litho. *Perf. 14x13½*

1194 A170 10c multicolored 15 15
1195 A170 40c multicolored 30 30
1196 A170 50c multicolored 38 38
1197 A170 75c multicolored 58 58
1198 A170 $1 multicolored 75 75
1199 A170 $2 multicolored 1.50 1.50
1200 A170 $3 multicolored 2.25 2.25
1201 A170 $4 multicolored 3.00 3.00
Nos. 1194-1201 (8) 8.91 8.91

Souvenir Sheets

1202 A170 $6 multicolored 4.50 4.50
1203 A170 $6 multicolored 4.50 4.50

Hirohito (1901-89) and enthronement of Akihito as emperor of Japan.

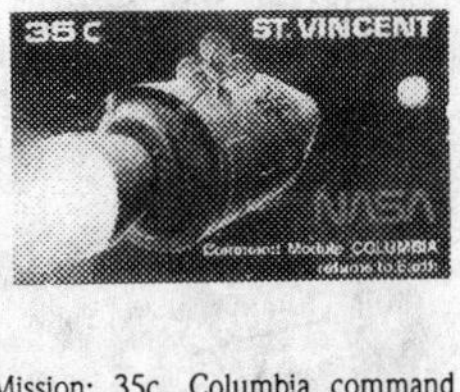

First Moon Landing, 20th Anniv. A171

Apollo 11 Mission: 35c, Columbia command module. 75c, Lunar module Eagle landing. $1, Rocket launch. No. 1207a, Buzz Aldrin conducting solar wind experiments. No. 1207b, Lunar module on plain. No. 1207c, Earthrise. No. 1207d, Neil Armstrong. No. 1208, Separation of lunar and command modules. No. 1209a, Command module. No. 1209b, Lunar module. $6, Armstrong preparing to take man's 1st step onto the Moon.

1989, Sept. 11 *Perf. 14*

1204 A171 35c multicolored 28 28
1205 A171 75c multicolored 58 58
1206 A171 $1 multicolored 75 75
1207 Strip of 4 6.00 6.00
a.-d. A171 $2 any single 1.50 1.50
1208 A171 $3 multicolored 2.25 2.25
Nos. 1204-1208 (5) 9.86 9.86

Souvenir Sheets

1209 Sheet of 2 4.50 4.50
a.-b. A171 $3 any single 2.25 2.25
1210 A171 $6 multicolored 4.50 4.50

No. 1207 has continuous design.

Players Elected to the Baseball Hall of Fame — A172

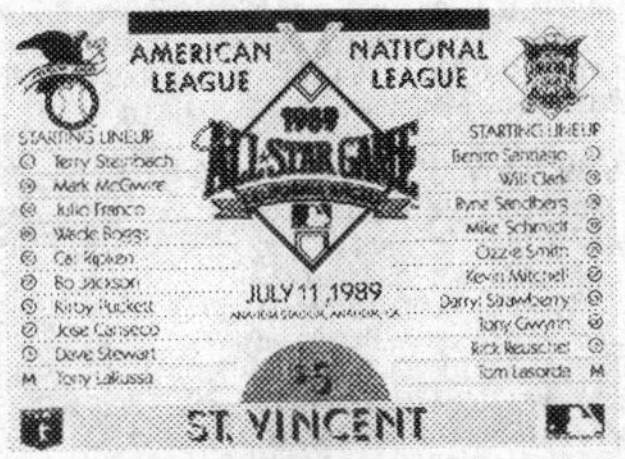

1989 All-Star Game, July 11, Anaheim, California — A173

Rookies and Team Emblems A174

Rookies of the Year, Most Valuable Players and Cy Young Award Winners A175

1989, July 23 Litho. *Perf. 14*

1211 A172 $2 Cobb, 1936 1.50 1.50
1212 A172 $2 Mays, 1979 1.50 1.50
1213 A172 $2 Musial, 1969 1.50 1.50
1214 A172 $2 Bench, 1989 1.50 1.50
1215 A172 $2 Banks, 1977 1.50 1.50
1216 A172 $2 Schoendienst, 1989 1.50 1.50
1217 A172 $2 Gehrig, 1939 1.50 1.50
1218 A172 $2 Robinson, 1962 1.50 1.50
1219 A172 $2 Feller, 1962 1.50 1.50
1220 A172 $2 Williams, 1966 1.50 1.50
1221 A172 $2 Yastrzemski, 1989 1.50 1.50
1222 A172 $2 Kaline, 1980 1.50 1.50
Nos. 1211-1222 (12) 18.00 18.00

"Yastrzemski" is misspelled on No. 1221.

Size: 116x82mm

Imperf

1223 A173 $5 multicolored 3.75 3.75

Miniature Sheets

No. 1224: a, Dante Bichette, 1989. b, Carl Yastrzemski, 1961. c, Randy Johnson, 1989. d, Jerome Walton, 1989. e, Ramon Martinez, 1989. f, Ken Hill, 1989. g, Tom McCarthy, 1989. h, Gaylord Perry, 1963. i, John Smoltz, 1989.

No. 1225: a, Bob Milacki, 1989. b, Babe Ruth, 1915. c, Jim Abbott, 1989. d, Gary Sheffield, 1989. e, Gregg Jeffries, 1989. f, Kevin Brown, 1989. g, Cris Carpenter, 1989. h, Johnny Bench, 1968. i, Ken Griffey Jr., 1989.

No. 1226: a, Chris Sabo, 1988 Natl. League Rookie of the Year. b, Walt Weiss, 1988 American League Rookie of the Year. c, Willie Mays, 1951 Rookie of the Year. d, Kirk Gibson, 1988 Natl. League Most Valuable Player. e, Ted Williams, Most Valuable Player of 1946 and 1949. f, Jose Canseco, 1988 American League Most Valuable Player. g, Gaylord Perry, Cy Young winner for 1972 and 1978. h, Orel Hershiser, 1988 National League Cy Young winner. i, Frank Viola, 1988 American League Cy Young winner.

Perf. 13½

1224 Sheet of 9 4.00 4.00
a.-i. A174 60c any single 44 44
1225 Sheet of 9 4.00 4.00
a.-i. A174 60c any single 44 44
1226 Sheet of 9 4.00 4.00
a.-i. A175 60c any single 44 44

For surcharges see Nos. B9-B11.

French Revolution Bicent., PHILEXFRANCE '89 — A176

French governors and ships.

1989, July 7 Litho. *Perf. 13½x14*

1227 A176 30c Goelette 22 22
1228 A176 55c Corvette 42 42
1229 A176 75c Fregate 36 58 58
1230 A176 $1 Vaisseau 74 75 75
1231 A176 $3 Ville de Paris 2.25 2.25
Nos. 1227-1231 (5) 4.22 4.22

Souvenir Sheet

1232 A176 $6 Map 4.50 4.50

Miniature Sheet

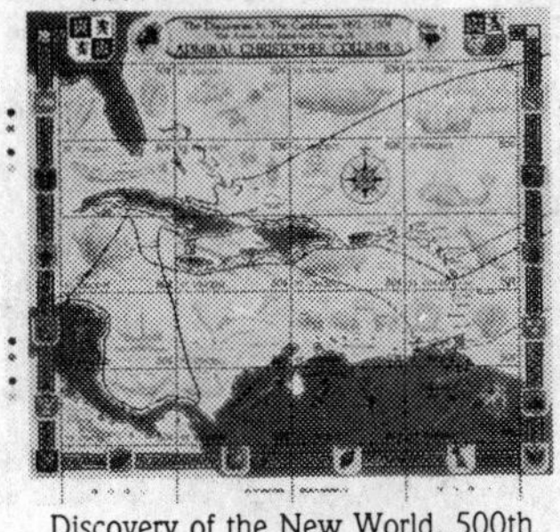
Discovery of the New World, 500th Anniv. (in 1992) — A177

Designs: a, Map of Florida, queen conch and West Indian purpura. b, Caribbean reef fish. c, Sperm whale. d, Columbus's fleet. e, Cuba, Isle of Pines, remora. f, The Bahamas, Turks & Caicos Isls., Columbus raising Spanish flag. g, Navigational instruments. h, Sea monster. i, Kemp's Ridley turtle, Cayman Isls. j, Jamaica, parts of Cuba and Hispaniola, magnificent frigatebird. k, Caribbean manatee, Hispaniola, Puerto Rico, Virgin Isls. l, Caribbean Monk seal, Anguilla and Caribbean isls. m, Mayan chief, galleon, dugout canoe. n, Masked boobies. o, Venezuelan village on pilings and the Netherlands Antilles. p, Atlantic wing oyster, lion's paw scallop, St. Vincent, Grenada, Trinidad & Tobago, Barbados. q, Panama, great hammerhead and mako sharks. r, Brown pelican, Colombia, Hyacinthine macaw. s, Venezuela, Indian bow and spear hunters. t, Capuchin and squirrel monkeys.

1989, Aug. 31 *Perf. 14*

1233 A177 Sheet of 20 9.50 9.50
a.-t. 50c any single 47 47

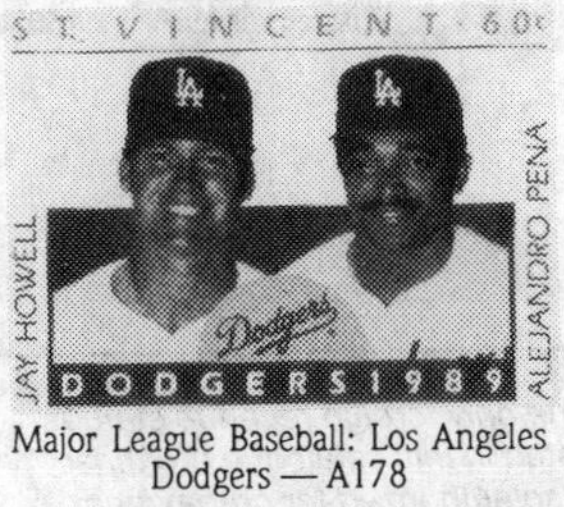

Major League Baseball: Los Angeles Dodgers — A178

No. 1234: a, Jay Howell, Alejandro Pena. b, Mike Davis, Kirk Gibson. c, Fernando Valenzuela,

John Shelby. d, Jeff Hamilton, Franklin Stubbs. e, Dodger Stadium. f, Ray Searage, John Tudor. g, Mike Sharperson, Mickey Hatcher. h, Coaches Amalfitano, Cresse, Ferguson, Hines, Mota, Perranoski, Russell. i, John Wetteland, Ramon Martinez.

No. 1235: a, Tim Belcher, Tim Crews. b, Orel Hershiser, Mike Morgan. c, Mike Scioscia, Rick Dempsey. d, Dave Anderson, Alfredo Griffin. e, Team emblem. f, Kal Daniels, Mike Marshall. g, Eddie Murray, Willie Randolph. h, Manager Tom Lasorda, Jose Gonzalez. i, Lenny Harris, Chris Gwynn, Billy Bean.

1989, Sept. 23 **Perf. 12½**

1234	Sheet of 9	4.00	4.00
a.-i.	A178 60c any single	44	44
1235	Sheet of 9	4.00	4.00
a.-i.	A178 60c any single	44	44

See Nos. 1344-1345.

1990 World Cup Soccer Championships, Italy — A179

1989, Oct. 16 **Litho.** **Perf. 14**

1236	A179	10c	shown	15	15
1237	A179	55c	Youth soccer teams	42	42
1238	A179	$1	Natl. team	75	75
1239	A179	$5	Trophy winners	3.75	3.75

Souvenir Sheets

1240	A179	$6	Youth soccer team	4.50	4.50
1241	A179	$6	Natl. team, diff.	4.50	4.50

Fauna and Flora A180

1989, Nov. 1

1242	A180	65c	St. Vincent parrot	50	50
1243	A180	75c	Whistling warbler	58	58
1244	A180	$5	Black snake	3.75	3.75

Souvenir Sheet

1245	A180	$6	Volcano plant, vert.	4.50	4.50

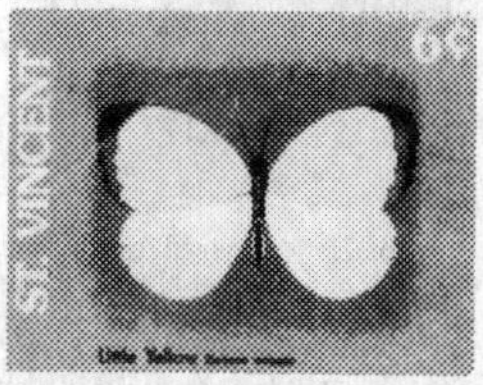

Butterflies A181

Perf. 14x14½, 14½x14

1989, Oct. 16

1246	A181	6c	Little yellow	15	15
1247	A181	10c	Orion	15	15
1248	A181	15c	American painted lady	15	15
1249	A181	75c	Cassius blue	58	58
1250	A181	$1	Polydamus swallowtail	75	75
1251	A181	$2	Guaraguao skipper	1.50	1.50
1252	A181	$3	The Queen	2.25	2.25
1253	A181	$5	Royal blue	3.75	3.75
			Nos. 1246-1253 (8)	9.28	9.28

Souvenir Sheets

1254	A181	$6	Monarch	4.50	4.50
1255	A181	$6	Lesser whirlabout, barred sulphur	4.50	4.50

The only foreign revenue stamps listed in this catalogue are those also authorized for prepayment of postage.

Exhibition Emblem, Disney Characters and US Natl. Monuments A182

Designs: 1c, Seagull Monument, UT. 2c, Lincoln Memorial, Washington, DC. 3c, Crazy Horse Memorial, SD. 4c, Uncle Sam Wilson, Troy, NY. 5c, Benjamin Franklin Natl. Memorial, Philadelphia, PA. 10c, Statue of George Washington, Federal Hall, NY. $3, John F. Kennedy's birthplace, Brookline, MA. $6, George Washington's home, Mount Vernon, VA. No. 1264, Mt. Rushmore, SD. No. 1265, Stone Mountain, GA.

1989, Nov. 17 **Perf. 13½x14**

1256	A182	1c	multicolored	15	15
1257	A182	2c	multicolored	15	15
1258	A182	3c	multicolored	15	15
1259	A182	4c	multicolored	15	15
1260	A182	5c	multicolored	15	15
1261	A182	10c	multicolored	15	15
1262	A182	$3	multicolored	2.25	2.25
1263	A182	$6	multicolored	4.50	4.50
			Nos. 1256-1263 (8)	7.65	7.65

Souvenir Sheets

1264	A182	$5	multicolored	3.75	3.75
1265	A182	$5	multicolored	3.75	3.75

World Stamp Expo '89.

Souvenir Sheet

The Washington Monument, Washington, DC — A183

1989, Nov. 17 **Litho.** **Perf. 14**

1266	A183	$5	multicolored	3.75	3.75

World Stamp Expo '89.

Miniature Sheets

Major League Baseball — A184

Players, owners and commissioner.

No. 1267: a, Early Wynn. b, Cecil Cooper. c, Joe DiMaggio. d, Kevin Mitchell. e, Tom Browning. f, Bobby Witt. g, Tim Wallach. h, Bob Gibson. i, Steve Garvey.

No. 1268: a, Rick Sutcliffe. b, A. Bartlett Giamatti, commissioner. c, Cory Snyder. d, Rollie Fingers. e, Willie Hernandez. f, Sandy Koufax. g, Carl Yastrzemski. h, Ron Darling. i, Gerald Perry.

No. 1269: a, Mike Marshall. b, Tom Seaver. c, Bob Milacki. d, Dave Smith. e, Robin Roberts. f, Kent Hrbek. g, Bill Veeck, owner. h, Carmelo Martinez. i, Rogers Hornsby.

No. 1270: a, Barry Bonds. b, Jim Palmer. c, Lou Boudreau. d, Ernie Whitt. e, Jose Canseco. f, Ken Griffey, Jr. g, Johnny Vander Meer. h, Kevin Seitzer. i, Dave Dravecky.

No. 1271: a, Glenn Davis. b, Nolan Ryan. c, Hank Greenberg. d, Richie Allen. e, Dave Righetti. f, Jim Abbott. g, Harold Reynolds. h, Dennis Martinez. i, Rod Carew.

No. 1272: a, Joe Morgan. b, Tony Fernandez. c, Ozzie Guillen. d, Mike Greenwell. e, Bobby Valentine. f, Doug DeCinces. g, Mickey Cochrane. h, Willie McGee. i, Von Hayes.

No. 1273: a, Frank White. b, Brook Jacoby. c, Boog Powell. d, Will Clark. e, Ray Kroc, owner. f, Fred McGriff. g, Willie Stargell. h, John Smoltz. i, B. J. Surhoff.

No. 1274: a, Keith Hernandez. b, Eddie Mathews. c, Tom Paciorek. d, Alan Trammell. e, Greg Maddux. f, Ruben Sierra. g, Tony Oliva. h, Chris Bosio. i, Orel Hershiser.

No. 1275: a, Casey Stengel. b, Jim Rice. c, Reggie Jackson. d, Jerome Walton. e, Bob Knepper. f, Andres Galarraga. g, Christy Mathewson. h, Willie Wilson. i, Ralph Kiner.

1989, Nov. 30 **Perf. 12½**

1267	Sheet of 9	2.00	2.00
a.-i.	A184 30c any single	22	22
1268	Sheet of 9	2.00	2.00
a.-i.	A184 30c any single	22	22
1269	Sheet of 9	2.00	2.00
a.-i.	A184 30c any single	22	22
1270	Sheet of 9	2.00	2.00
a.-i.	A184 30c any single	22	22
1271	Sheet of 9	2.00	2.00
a.-i.	A184 30c any single	22	22
1272	Sheet of 9	2.00	2.00
a.-i.	A184 30c any single	22	22
1273	Sheet of 9	2.00	2.00
a.-i.	A184 30c any single	22	22
1274	Sheet of 9	2.00	2.00
a.-i.	A184 30c any single	22	22
1275	Sheet of 9	2.00	2.00
a.-i.	A184 30c any single	22	22

No. 1268 is incorrectly inscribed "Finger." Cochrane is misspelled "Cochpane" on No. 1272g.

See No. 1277.

Miniature Sheet

Achievements of Nolan Ryan, American Baseball Player — A185

Portrait and inscriptions: a, 383 League-leading strikeouts, 1973. b, No hitter, Kansas City Royals, May 15, 1973. c, No hitter, Detroit Tigers, July 15, 1973. d, No hitter, Minnesota Twins, Sept. 28, 1974. e, No hitter, Baltimore Orioles, June 1, 1975. f, No hitter, Los Angeles Dodgers, Sept. 26, 1981. g, Won 100+ games in both leagues. h, Struck out 200+ batters in 13 seasons. i, 5000th Strikeout, Aug. 22, 1989, Arlington, Texas.

1989, Nov. 30 **Litho.** **Perf. 12½**

1276	Sheet of 9	13.50	13.50
a.-i.	A185 $2 any single	1.50	1.50

For overprints see Nos. 1336-1337.

1989, Nov. 30 **Litho.** **Perf. 12½**

1277	A184	30c Mike Greenwell, Boston Red Sox	22	22

No. 1277 issued in sheets of 9.

Coat of Arms, No. 570 — A186

Boy Scouts and Girl Guides — A187

1989, Dec. 20 **Perf. 14**

1278	A186	65c	multicolored	50	50

Souvenir Sheet

1279	A186	$10	multicolored	7.50	7.50

Independence, 10th anniv.

1989, Dec. 20 **Perf. 14**

Lord or Lady Baden-Powell and various scouts or girl guides.

1280	A187	35c	Boy's modern uniform	28	28
1281	A187	35c	Guide, ranger, brownie	28	28
1282	A187	55c	Boy's old uniform	42	42
1283	A187	55c	Mrs. Jackson	42	42
1284	A187	$2	75th anniv. emblem	1.50	1.50
1285	A187	$2	Mrs. Russell	1.50	1.50
			Nos. 1280-1285 (6)	4.40	4.40

Souvenir Sheets

1286	A187	$5	Canoeing, merit badges	3.75	3.75
1287	A187	$5	Flag-raising, Camp Yourumei, 1985	3.75	3.75

Christmas — A188

Paintings by Da Vinci and Botticelli: 10c, The Adoration of the Magi (holy family), by Botticelli. 25c, The Adoration of the Magi (witnesses). 30c, The Madonna of the Magnificat, by Botticelli. 40c, The Virgin and Child with St. Anne and St. John the Baptist, by Da Vinci. 55c, The Annunciation (angel), by Da Vinci. 75c, The Annunciation (Madonna). No. 1294, Madonna of the Carnation, by Da Vinci. $6, The Annunciation, by Botticelli. No. 1296, The Virgin of the Rocks, by Da Vinci. No. 1297, The Adoration of the Magi, by Botticelli.

1989, Dec. 20 **Perf. 14**

1288	A188	10c	multicolored	15	15
1289	A188	25c	multicolored	18	18
1290	A188	30c	multicolored	22	22
1291	A188	40c	multicolored	30	30
1292	A188	55c	multicolored	42	42
1293	A188	75c	multicolored	58	58
1294	A188	$5	multicolored	3.75	3.75
1295	A188	$6	multicolored	4.50	4.50
			Nos. 1288-1295 (8)	10.10	10.10

Souvenir Sheets

1296	A188	$5	multicolored	3.75	3.75
1297	A188	$5	multicolored	3.75	3.75

Bird Type of 1988

1989, July 31 **Litho.** **Perf. 15x14**

1298	A150	55c	St. Vincent parrot	42	42

Lions Intl. of St. Vincent, 25th Anniv. (in 1989) A189

Services: 10c, Scholarships for the blind, vert. 65c, Free textbooks. 75c, Health education (diabetes). $2, Blood sugar testing machines. $4, Publishing and distribution of pamphlets on drug abuse.

1990, Mar. 5 **Litho.** **Perf. 14**

1303	A189	10c	multicolored	15	15
1304	A189	65c	multicolored	48	48
1305	A189	75c	multicolored	58	58
1306	A189	$2	multicolored	1.50	1.50
1307	A189	$4	multicolored	3.00	3.00
			Nos. 1303-1307 (5)	5.71	5.71

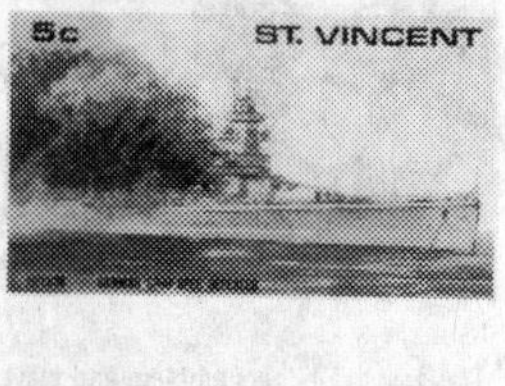

World War II A190

Historic events: 5c, Defeat of the Graf Spee, Dec. 13-17, 1939. 10c, Charles De Gaulle calls the French Resistance to arms, June 18, 1940. 15c, The British drive the Italian army out of Egypt, Dec. 15, 1940. 25c, US destroyer Reuben James torpedoed off Iceland, Oct. 31, 1941. 30c, MacArthur becomes allied supreme commander of the southwest Pacific, Apr. 18, 1942. 40c, US forces attack Corregidor, Feb. 16, 1945. 55c, HMS King George V engages the Bismarck, May 27, 1941. 75c, U.S. fleet enters Tokyo Harbor, Aug. 27, 1945. $5, Russian takeover of Berlin completed, May 2, 1945. No. 1317, Battle of the Philippine Sea, June 18, 1944. No. 1318, Battle of the Java Sea, Feb. 28, 1942.

1990, Apr. 2 *Perf. 14x13½*

1308 A190 5c multicolored 15 15
1309 A190 10c multicolored 15 15
1310 A190 15c multicolored 15 15
1311 A190 25c multicolored 18 18
1312 A190 30c multicolored 22 22
1313 A190 40c multicolored 30 30
1314 A190 55c multicolored 42 42
1315 A190 75c multicolored 58 58
1316 A190 $5 multicolored 3.75 3.75
1317 A190 $6 multicolored 4.50 4.50
Nos. 1308-1317 (10) 10.40 10.40

Souvenir Sheet

1318 A190 $6 multicolored 4.50 4.50

Penny Black, 150th Anniv. — A191

Great Britain No. 1 (various plate positions).

1990, May 3 **Litho.** *Perf. 14x15*

1319 A191 $2 "NK" 1.50 1.50
1320 A191 $4 "AB" 3.00 3.00

Souvenir Sheet

1321 A191 $6 Simulated #1, "SV" 4.50 4.50

Stamp World London '90 — A192

Walt Disney characters in British military uniforms: 5c, Donald Duck as 18th cent. Admiral. 10c, Huey as Bugler, 68th Light Infantry, 1854. 15c, Minnie Mouse as Drummer, 1st Irish Guards, 1900. 25c, Goofy as Lance Corporal, Seaforth Highlanders, 1944. $1, Mickey Mouse as officer, 58th Regiment, 1879, 1881. $2, Donald Duck as officer, Royal Engineers, 1813. $4, Mickey Mouse as Drum Major, 1914. $5, Goofy as Pipe Sergeant, 1918. No. 1330, Scrooge as Company Clerk and Goofy as King's Lifeguard of Foot. No. 1331, Mickey Mouse as British Grenadier.

1990, May **Litho.** *Perf. 13½x14*

1322 A192 5c multicolored 15 15
1323 A192 10c multicolored 15 15
1324 A192 15c multicolored 15 15
1325 A192 25c multicolored 18 18
1326 A192 $1 multicolored 75 75
1327 A192 $2 multicolored 1.50 1.50
1328 A192 $4 multicolored 3.00 3.00
1329 A192 $5 multicolored 3.75 3.75
Nos. 1322-1329 (8) 9.63 9.63

Souvenir Sheets

1330 A192 $6 multicolored 4.50 4.50
1331 A192 $6 multicolored 4.50 4.50

Queen Mother 90th Birthday
A193 A194

1990, July 5 *Perf. 14*

1332 A193 $2 shown 1.55 1.55
1333 A193 $2 Queen Mother signing book 1.55 1.55
1334 A194 $2 shown 1.55 1.55

Souvenir Sheet

1335 A194 $6 Like No. 1334 4.75 4.75

No. 1276 Overprinted Miniature Sheets

a **Sixth No-Hitter**
11 June 90
Oakland Athletics

b **300th Win**
Milwaukee Brewers
July 31, 1990

1990, July 23 **Litho.** *Perf. 12½*

Sheets of 9

1336 A185(a) $2 #1336a-1336i 13.50 13.50
1337 A185(b) $2 #1337a-1337i 13.50 13.50

World Cup Soccer Championships, Italy — A195

Players from participating countries.

1990, Sept. 24 **Litho.** *Perf. 14*

1338 A195 10c Argentina 15 15
1339 A195 75c Colombia 55 55
1340 A195 $1 Uruguay 75 75
1341 A195 $5 Belgium 3.75 3.75

Souvenir Sheets

1342 A195 $6 Brazil 4.50 4.50
1343 A195 $6 West Germany 4.50 4.50

Dodger Baseball Type of 1989

No. 1344: a, Hubie Brooks, Orel Hershiser. b, Manager Tom Lasorda, Tim Crews. c, Fernando Valenzuela, Eddie Murray. d, Kal Daniels, Jose Gonzalez. e, Dodger centennial emblem. f, Chris Gwynn, Jeff Hamilton. g, Kirk Gibson, Rick Dempsey. h, Jim Gott, Alfredo Griffin. i, Coaches, Ron Perranoski, Bill Russell, Joe Ferguson, Joe Amalfitano, Mark Cresse, Ben Hines, Manny Mota.

No. 1345: a, Mickey Hatcher, Jay Howell. b, Juan Samuel, Mike Scioscia. c, Lenny Harris, Mike Hartley. d, Ramon Martinez, Mike Morgan. e, Dodger Stadium. f, Stan Javier, Don Aase. g, Ray Searage, Mike Sharperson. h, Tim Belcher, Pat Perry. i, Dave Walsh, Jose Vizcaino, Jim Neidlinger, Jose Offerman, Carlos Hernandez.

Hyphen-hole roulette 7

1990, Sept. 21

1344 Sheet of 9 4.00 4.00
a.-i. A178 60c any single 44 44
1345 Sheet of 9 4.00 4.00
a.-i. A178 60c any single 44 44

Nos. 1116-1120 Ovptd. or Similarly — **JOE DELOACH U.S.A.** — **STEVE LEWIS U.S.A.** — **PAUL ERANG KENYA**

1990, Oct. 18 *Perf. 14*

1346 A158 10c shown 15 15
1347 A158 50c "CARL / LEWIS / U.S.A." 38 38
1348 A158 $1 "HRISTO / MARKOV / BULGARIA" 75 75
1349 A158 $5 "HENRY / MASKE / E. GERMANY" 3.75 3.75

Souvenir Sheets

1350 A158 $10 USSR, US medals 7.50 7.50
1351 A158 $10 South Korea, Spain medals 7.50 7.50

Overprint on No. 1350 reads "FINAL MEDAL STANDINGS / USSR / GOLD 55 / SILVER 31 / BRONZE 46 and USA / GOLD 36 / SILVER 31 / BRONZE 27."

Overprint on No. 1351 reads "FINAL MEDAL STANDINGS / S. KOREA / GOLD 12 / SILVER 10 / BRONZE 11 and SPAIN / GOLD 1 / SILVER 1 / BRONZE 2."

Nos. 1173-1182 Overprinted

1990, Oct. 18 **Litho.** *Perf. 14*

1352 A166 10c *Ile de France* 15 15
1353 A166 40c *Liberte* 30 30
1354 A166 50c *Mauretania* 38 38
1355 A166 75c *France* 55 55
1356 A166 $1 *Aquitania* 75 75
1357 A166 $2 *United States* 1.50 1.50
1358 A166 $3 *Olympic* 2.25 2.25
1359 A166 $4 *Queen Elizabeth* 3.00 3.00
Nos. 1352-1359 (8) 8.88 8.88

Souvenir Sheets

1360 A166 $6 *Queen Mary* 4.50 4.50
1361 A166 $6 *QE 2* 4.50 4.50

Overprint on #1360-1361 is 12mm in diameter.

Orchids — A196

Designs: 10c, Dendrophylax funalis, Dimeranda emarginata. 15c, Epidendrum elongatum. 45c, Comparettia falcata. 60c, Brassia maculata. $1, Encyclia cochleata, Encyclia cordigera. $2, Cyrtopodium punctatum. $4, Cattelya labiata. $5, Bletia purpurea. No. 1370, Ionopsis utricularioides. No. 1371, Vanilla planifolia.

1990, Nov. 23

1362 A196 10c multicolored 15 15
1363 A196 15c multicolored 15 15
1364 A196 45c multicolored 35 35
1365 A196 60c multicolored 45 45
1366 A196 $1 multicolored 75 75
1367 A196 $2 multicolored 1.50 1.50
1368 A196 $4 multicolored 3.00 3.00
1369 A196 $5 multicolored 3.75 3.75
Nos. 1362-1369 (8) 10.10 10.10

Souvenir Sheets

1370 A196 $6 multicolored 4.50 4.50
1371 A196 $6 multicolored 4.50 4.50

Christmas A197

Details from paintings by Rubens: 10c, Miraculous Draught of Fishes. 45c, $2, Crowning of Holy Katherine. 50c, St. Ives of Treguier. 65c, Allegory of Eternity. $1, $4, St. Bavo Receives Monastic Habit of Ghent. $5, Communion of St. Francis. No. 1380, St. Ives of Treguier (entire). No. 1381, Allegory of Eternity. No. 1382, St. Bavo Receives Monastic Habit of Ghent. No. 1383, The Miraculous Draft of Fishes.

1990, Dec. 3 **Litho.** *Perf. 14*

1372 A197 10c multicolored 15 15
1373 A197 45c multicolored 35 35
1374 A197 50c multicolored 38 38
1375 A197 65c multicolored 48 48
1376 A197 $1 multicolored 75 75
1377 A197 $2 multicolored 1.50 1.50
1378 A197 $4 multicolored 3.00 3.00
1379 A197 $5 multicolored 3.75 3.75
Nos. 1372-1379 (8) 10.36 10.36

Souvenir Sheets

1380 A197 $6 multicolored 4.50 4.50
1381 A197 $6 multicolored 4.50 4.50
1382 A197 $6 multi, horiz. 4.50 4.50
1383 A197 $6 multi, horiz. 4.50 4.50

Miniature Sheet

Intl. Literacy Year A198

Canterbury Tales: a, Geoffrey Chaucer (1342-1400), author. b, "When April with his showers sweet..." c, "When Zephyr also has,..." d. "And many little birds make melody..." e, "And palmers to go seeking out strange strands..." f, Quill pen, open book. g, Bluebird in tree. h, Trees, rider's head with white hair. i, Banner on staff. j, Town. k, Rider's head, diff. l, Blackbird in tree. m, Old monk. n, Horse, rider. o, Nun, monk carrying banner. p, Monks. q, White horse, rider. r, Black horse, rider. s, Squirrel. t, Rooster. u, Chickens. v, Rabbit. w, Butterfly. x, Mouse.

1990, Dec. 12 *Perf. 13½*

1384 Sheet of 24 7.20 7.20
a.-x. A198 40c any single 30 30

Vincent Van Gogh (1853-1890), Painter A198a

Self-Portraits.

1990, Dec. 17 **Litho.** *Perf. 13*

1385 A198a 1c 1889 15 15
1386 A198a 5c 1886 15 15
1387 A198a 10c 1888, with hat & pipe 15 15
1388 A198a 15c 1888, painting 15 15
a. Strip of 4, #1385-1388 30 30
1389 A198a 20c 1887 15 15
1390 A198a 45c 1889, diff. 35 35
1391 A198a $5 1889, with bandaged ear 3.75 3.75
1392 A198a $6 1887, with straw hat 4.50 4.50
a. Strip of 4, #1389-1392 8.75 8.75
Nos. 1385-1392 (8) 9.35 9.35

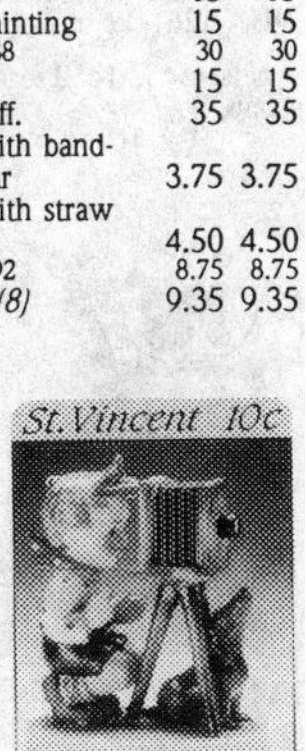

Hummel Figurines — A199 M.J. Hummel

1990, Dec. 30 **Litho.** *Perf. 14*

1393 A199 10c Photographer 15 15
1394 A199 15c Boy with ladder & rope 15 15
1395 A199 40c Pharmacist 30 30
1396 A199 60c Boy answering telephone 45 45
1396A A199 $1 Bootmaker 75 75

1396B	A199	$2 Artist	1.50	1.50
1397	A199	$4 Waiter	3.00	3.00
a.		Sheet of 4, 15c, 40c, $2, $4	5.00	5.00
1398	A199	$5 Mailman	3.75	3.75
a.		Sheet of 4, 10c, 60c, $1, $5	5.00	5.00
		Nos. 1393-1398 (8)	10.05	10.05

Souvenir Sheets

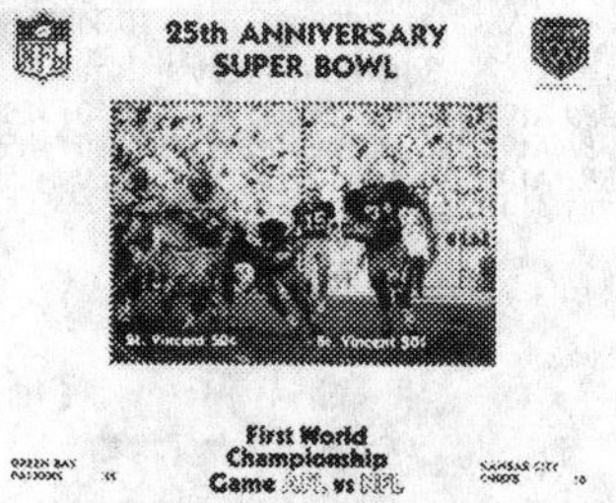

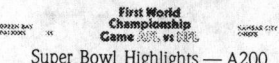

Super Bowl Highlights — A200

Designs: Nos. 1400-1424, 1425-1449, Super Bowl I (1967) through Super Bowl XXV (1991). Nos. 1425-1449 picture Super Bowl Program Covers. Nos. 1443, 1449 horiz.

1991, Jan. 15 Litho. *Perf. 13½x14*

1400-1424	A200	Set of 25	18.00	18.00

Nos. 1400-1423 contain two 50c stamps printed with continuous design showing game highlights. No. 1424 contains three 50c stamps showing AFC and NFC team helmets and the Vince Lombardi Trophy.

Size: 99x125mm

Imperf

1425-1449	A200	$2 Set of 25	37.50	37.50

Miniature Sheets

Discovery of America, 500th Anniv. (in 1992) A201

No. 1450: a, 1c, US #230. b, 2c, US #231. c, 3c, US #232. d, 4c, US #233. e, $10, Sailing ship, parrot. f, 5c, US #234. g, 6c, US #235. h, 8c, US #236. i, 10c, US #237.

No. 1451: a, 15c, US #238. b, 30c, US #239. c, 50c, US #240. d, $1, US #241. e, $10, Compass rose, sailing ship. f, $2, US #242. g, $3, US #243. h, $4, US #244. i, $5, US #245.

No. 1452, Bow of sailing ship. No. 1453, Ship's figurehead.

1991, Mar. 18 Litho. *Perf. 14*

Sheets of 9

1450	A201	#1450a-1450i	7.35	7.35
1451	A201	#1451a-1451i	18.00	18.00

Souvenir Sheets

1452	A201	$6 multicolored	4.50	4.50
1453	A201	$6 multicolored	4.50	4.50

Nos. 1452-1453 each contain one 38x31mm stamp.

Jetsons, The Movie — A202

Hanna-Barbera characters: 5c, Cosmo Spacely, vert. 20c, Elroy, Judy, Astro, Jane & George Jetson, vert. 45c, Judy, Apollo Blue, vert. 50c, Mr. Spacely, George, vert. 60c, George, sprocket factory. $1, Apollo Blue, Judy, Elroy and Grungees. $2, Jane and George in Grungee cavern. $4, George, Elroy, Jane and Little Grungee, vert. $5, Jetsons leaving for Earth, vert. No. 1463, Jetsons in sprocket factory. No. 1464, Jetsons traveling to Orbiting Ore Asteroid.

1991, Mar. 25 Litho. *Perf. 13½*

1454	A202	5c multicolored	15	15
1455	A202	20c multicolored	15	15
1456	A202	45c multicolored	35	35
1457	A202	50c multicolored	38	38
1458	A202	60c multicolored	45	45
1459	A202	$1 multicolored	75	75
1460	A202	$2 multicolored	1.50	1.50
1461	A202	$4 multicolored	3.00	3.00
1462	A202	$5 multicolored	3.75	3.75
		Nos. 1454-1462 (9)	10.48	10.48

Souvenir Sheets

1463	A202	$6 multicolored	4.50	4.50
1464	A202	$6 multicolored	4.50	4.50

The Flintstones Enjoy Sports — A203

1991, Mar. 25

1465	A203	10c Boxing	15	15
1466	A203	15c Soccer	15	15
1467	A203	45c Rowing	35	35
1468	A203	55c Dinosaur riding	42	42
1469	A203	$1 Basketball	75	75
1470	A203	$2 Wrestling	1.50	1.50
1471	A203	$4 Tennis	3.00	3.00
1472	A203	$5 Cycling	3.75	3.75
		Nos. 1465-1472 (8)	10.07	10.07

Souvenir Sheets

1473	A203	$6 Baseball, batting	4.50	4.50
1474	A203	$6 Baseball, sliding home	4.50	4.50

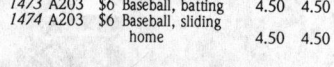

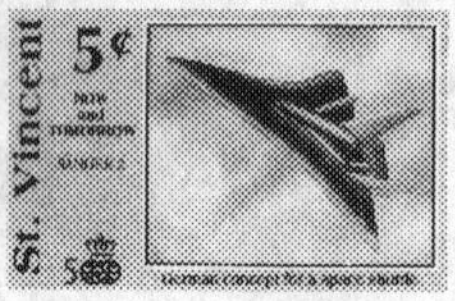

Voyages of Discovery A204

Designs: 5c, Sanger 2. 10c, Magellan probe, 1990. 25c, Buran space shuttle. 75c, American space station. $1, Mars mission, 21st century. $2, Hubble space telescope, 1990. $4, Sailship to Mars. $5, Craf satellite, 2000. No. 1483, Sailing ship, island hopping. No. 1484, Sailing ship returning home.

1991, May 13

1475	A204	5c multicolored	15	15
1476	A204	10c multicolored	15	15
1477	A204	25c multicolored	18	18
1478	A204	75c multicolored	55	55
1479	A204	$1 multicolored	75	75
1480	A204	$2 multicolored	1.50	1.50
1481	A204	$4 multicolored	3.00	3.00
1482	A204	$5 multicolored	3.75	3.75
		Nos. 1475-1482 (8)	10.03	10.03

Souvenir Sheets

1483	A204	$6 multicolored	4.50	4.50
1484	A204	$6 multicolored	4.50	4.50

Discovery of America, 500th anniv. (in 1992).

Royal Family Birthday, Anniversary

Common Design Type

1991, July Litho. *Perf. 14*

1485	CD347	5c multicolored	15	15
1486	CD347	20c multicolored	15	15
1487	CD347	25c multicolored	18	18
1488	CD347	60c multicolored	45	45
1489	CD347	$1 multicolored	75	75
1490	CD347	$2 multicolored	1.50	1.50
1491	CD347	$4 multicolored	3.00	3.00
1492	CD347	$5 multicolored	3.75	3.75
		Nos. 1485-1492 (8)	9.93	9.93

Souvenir Sheets

1493	CD347	$5 Elizabeth, Philip	3.75	3.75
1494	CD347	$5 Charles, Diana, sons	3.75	3.75

20c, 25c, $1, Nos. 1492, 1494, Charles and Diana, 10th wedding anniversary. Others, Queen Elizabeth II, 65th birthday.

Miniature Sheets

Japanese Trains A205

Designs: No. 1495a, D51 steam locomotive. b, 9600 steam locomotive. c, Chrysanthemum emblem. d, Passenger coach. e, C57 steam locomotive. f, Oil tank car. g, C53 steam locomotive. h, First steam locomotive. i, C11 steam locomotive.

No. 1496a, Class 181 electric train. b, EH-10 electric locomotive. c, Special Express emblem. d, Sendai City Class 1 trolley. e, Class 485 electric train. f, Sendai City trolley street cleaner. g, Hakari bullet train. h, ED-11 electric locomotive. i, EF-66 electric locomotive.

No. 1497, C55 steam locomotive, vert. No. 1498, Series 400 electric train. No. 1499, C62 steam locomotive, vert. No. 1500, Super Hitachi electric train, vert.

1991, Aug. 12 Litho. *Perf. 14x13½*

1495	A205	75c Sheet of 9, #a.-i.	5.00	5.00
1496	A205	$1 Sheet of 9, #a.-i.	6.75	6.75

Souvenir Sheets

Perf. 13x13½

1497	A205	$6 multicolored	4.50	4.50
1498	A205	$6 multicolored	4.50	4.50
1499	A205	$6 multicolored	4.50	4.50
1500	A205	$6 multicolored	4.50	4.50

Phila Nippon '91. Nos. 1497-1500 each contain 27x44mm or 44x27mm stamps.

Miniature Sheets

Entertainers — A206

Nos. 1501a-1501i, Various portraits of Madonna.

Italian entertainers: No. 1502a, Marcello Mastroianni. b, Sophia Loren. c, Mario Lanza (1921-59). d, Federico Fellini. e, Arturo Toscanini (1867-1957). f, Anna Magnani (1908-73). g, Giancarlo Giannini. h, Gina Lollobrigida. i, Enrico Caruso (1873-1921).

Nos. 1503a-1503i, Various portraits of John Lennon.

1991, Aug. 22 *Perf. 13*

1501	A206	$1 Sheet of 9, #a.-i.	6.75	6.75
1502	A206	$1 Sheet of 9, #a.-i.	6.75	6.75
1503	A206	$1 +2c, Sheet of 9, #a.-i.	6.90	6.90

Souvenir Sheets

Perf. 12x13

1504	A206	$6 Madonna	4.50	4.50

Perf. 13

1505	A206	$6 Luciano Pavarotti, horiz.	4.50	4.50

No. 1503 is semi-postal with surtax going to the Spirit Foundation.

No. 1504 contains one 28x42mm stamp. Compare with No. 1566. See Nos. 1642-1643, 1729, 2055.

Intl. Literacy Year — A207

Walt Disney characters in "The Prince and the Pauper": 5c, Pauper pals. 10c, Princely boredom. 15c, The valet. 25c, Look alikes. 60c, Trading places. 75c, How to be a prince. 80c, Food for the populace. $1, Captain's plot. $2, Doomed in the dungeon. $3, Looking for a way out. $4, A Goofy jailbreak. $5, Long live the real prince. No. 1518, Crowning the wrong guy. No. 1519, Mickey meets the captain of the guard. No. 1520, Real prince arrives. No. 1521, Seize the guard.

1991, Nov. 18 *Perf. 14x13½*

1506	A207	5c multicolored	15	15
1507	A207	10c multicolored	15	15
1508	A207	15c multicolored	15	15
1509	A207	25c multicolored	18	18
1510	A207	60c multicolored	45	45
1511	A207	75c multicolored	55	55
1512	A207	80c multicolored	60	60
1513	A207	$1 multicolored	75	75
1514	A207	$2 multicolored	1.50	1.50
1515	A207	$3 multicolored	2.25	2.25
1516	A207	$4 multicolored	3.00	3.00
1517	A207	$5 multicolored	3.75	3.75
		Nos. 1506-1517 (12)	13.48	13.48

Souvenir Sheets

1518	A207	$6 multicolored	4.50	4.50
1519	A207	$6 multicolored	4.50	4.50
1520	A207	$6 multicolored	4.50	4.50
1521	A207	$6 multicolored	4.50	4.50

1991, Nov. 18

Walt Disney's "The Rescuers Down Under": 5c, Miss Bianca, Heroine. 10c, Bernard, Shy Hero. 15c, Maitre d'Francois. 25c, Wilbur, the Albatross. 60c, Jake, the Aussie kangaroo mouse. 75c, Bernard, Bianca and Jake in the outback. 80c, Bianca and Bernard. $1, Marahute, the magnificent rare eagle. $2, Cody and Marahute. $3, McLeach and his pet Goanna, Joanna. $4, Frank, the frill-necked lizard. $5, Endangered animals: Red Kangaroo, Krebbs Koala, and Polly Platypus. No. 1534, Cody with the rescuers. No. 1535, Delegates of Intl. Rescue Aid Society. No. 1536, Wilbur's painful touchdown "down under." No. 1537, Wilbur transports Miss Bianca and Bernard to Australia.

1522	A207	5c multicolored	15	15
1523	A207	10c multicolored	15	15
1524	A207	15c multicolored	15	15
1525	A207	25c multicolored	18	18
1526	A207	60c multicolored	45	45
1527	A207	75c multicolored	55	55
1528	A207	80c multicolored	60	60
1529	A207	$1 multicolored	75	75
1530	A207	$2 multicolored	1.50	1.50
1531	A207	$3 multicolored	2.25	2.25
1532	A207	$4 multicolored	3.00	3.00
1533	A207	$5 multicolored	3.75	3.75
		Nos. 1522-1533 (12)	13.48	13.48

Souvenir Sheets

1534	A207	$6 multicolored	4.50	4.50
1535	A207	$6 multicolored	4.50	4.50
1536	A207	$6 multicolored	4.50	4.50
1537	A207	$6 multicolored	4.50	4.50

Brandenburg Gate, Bicent. — A209

Designs: 50c, Demonstrator with sign. 75c, Soldiers at Berlin Wall. 90c, German flag, shadows on wall. $1, Pres. Gorbachev and Pres. Bush shaking hands. $4, Coat of Arms of Berlin.

1991, Nov. 18 Litho. *Perf. 14*

1538	A209	50c multicolored	38	38
1539	A209	75c multicolored	55	55
1540	A209	90c multicolored	70	70
1541	A209	$1 multicolored	75	75

Souvenir Sheet

1542	A209	$4 multicolored	3.00	3.00

Wolfgang Amadeus Mozart, Death Bicent. A210

Designs: $1, Scene from "Marriage of Figaro." $3, Scene from "The Clemency of Titus." $4, Portrait of Mozart, vert.

1991, Nov. 18

1543	A210	$1 multicolored	75	75

1544	A210	$3 multicolored	2.25	2.25

Souvenir Sheet

1545	A210	$4 multicolored	3.00	3.00

17th World Scout Jamboree, Korea — A211

Designs: 65c, Adventure tales around camp fire, vert. $1.50, British defenses at Mafeking, 1900, Cape of Good Hope #179. $3.50, Scouts scuba diving, queen angelfish.

1991, Nov. 18 Litho. *Perf. 14*

1546	A211	65c multicolored	48	48
1547	A211	$1.50 multicolored	1.15	1.15
1548	A211	$3.50 multicolored	2.65	2.65

Souvenir Sheet

1549	A211	$5 multicolored	3.75	3.75

Charles de Gaulle, Birth Cent. A212

De Gaulle and: 10c, Free French Forces, 1944. 45c, Churchill, 1944. 75c, Liberation of Paris, 1944.

1991, Nov. 18 Litho. *Perf. 14*

1550	A212	10c multicolored	15	15
1551	A212	45c multicolored	35	35
1552	A212	75c multicolored	55	55

Souvenir Sheet

1553	A212	$5 Portrait	3.75	3.75

Anniversaries and Events — A213

Designs: No. 1554, Woman, flag, map. No. 1555, Steam locomotive. $1.65, Otto Lilienthal, glider in flight. No. 1557, Gottfried Wilhelm Liebniz, mathematician. No. 1558, Street warfare.

1991, Nov. 18

1554	A213	$1.50 multicolored	1.15	1.15
1555	A213	$1.50 multicolored	1.15	1.15
1556	A213	$1.65 multicolored	1.25	1.25
1557	A213	$2 multicolored	1.50	1.50
1558	A213	$2 multicolored	1.50	1.50
		Nos. 1554-1558 (5)	6.55	6.55

Swiss Confedration, 700th anniv. (#1554). Trans-Siberian Railway, 100th anniv. (#1555). First glider flight, cent. (#1556). City of Hanover, 750th anniv. (#1557). Fall of Kiev, Sept. 19, 1941 (#1558).

Miniature Sheet

Heroes of Pearl Harbor A214

Congressional Medal of Honor recipients: a, Myrvyn S. Bennion. b, George H. Cannon. c, John W. Finn. d, Francis C. Flaherty. e, Samuel G. Fuqua. f, Edwin J. Hill. g, Herbert C. Jones. h, Isaac C. Kidd. i, Jackson C. Pharris. j, Thomas J. Reeves. k, Donald K. Ross. l, Robert R. Scott. m, Franklin Van Valkenburgh. n, James R. Ward. o, Cassin Young.

1991, Nov. 18 *Perf. 14½x15*

1559	A214	$1 Sheet of 15, #a.-o.	11.25	11.25

Miniature Sheets

Famous People — A215

Golfers: No. 1560a, Player. b, Faldo. c, Ballesteros. d, Hogan. e, Nicklaus. f, Norman. g, Olazabal. h, Bobby Jones.

Statesmen and historical events: No. 1561a, Hans-Dietrich Genscher, German Foreign Minister, winged victory symbol. b, Destruction of Berlin Wall. c, Charles de Gaulle delivering radio appeal, Winston Churchill, de Gaulle. d, Dwight D. Eisenhower, de Gaulle, Normandy invasion. e, Brandenburg Gate. f, German Chancellor Helmut Kohl, mayors of East, West Berlin. g, De Gaulle and Konrad Adenauer. h, George Washington and Lafayette, De Gaulle and John F. Kennedy.

Chess masters: No. 1562a, Francois Andre Danican Philidor. b, Adolph Anderssen. c, Wilhelm Steinitz. d, Alexander Alekhine. e, Boris Spassky. f, Bobby Fischer. g, Anatoly Karpov. h, Garri Kasparov.

Nobel Prize winners: No. 1563a, Einstein, physics. b, Roentgen, physics. c, William Shockley, physics. d, Charles Townes, physics. e, Lev Landau, physics. f, Marconi, physics. g, Willard Libby, chemistry. h, Ernest Lawrence, physics.

Entertainers: No. 1564a, Michael Jackson. b, Madonna. c, Elvis Presley. d, David Bowie. e, Prince. f, Frank Sinatra. g, George Michael. h, Mick Jagger.

No. 1565, Roosevelt, de Gaulle, Churchill at Morocco Conf., 1943. No. 1566, Madonna. No. 1567, Elvis Presley.

1991, Nov. 25 Litho. *Perf. 14½*

1560	A215	$1 Sheet of 8, #a.-h.	6.00	6.00
1561	A215	$1 Sheet of 8, #a.-h.	6.00	6.00
1562	A215	$1 Sheet of 8, #a.-h.	6.00	6.00
1563	A215	$1 Sheet of 8, #a.-h.	6.00	6.00
1564	A215	$2 Sheet of 8, #a.-h.	12.00	12.00

Souvenir Sheets

Perf. 14

1565	A215	$6 multicolored	4.50	4.50
1566	A215	$6 multicolored	4.50	4.50
1567	A215	$6 multicolored	4.50	4.50

Nos. 1565-1567 each contain one 27x43mm stamp.

See Nos. 1642-1643, 1729-1730 for more Elvis Presley stamps.

Walt Disney Christmas Cards — A216

Designs and year of issue: 10c, Goofy, Mickey and Pluto decorating Christmas tree, 1982. 45c, Mickey, reindeer, 1980. 55c, Christmas tree ornament, 1970. 75c, Baby duck holding 1944 sign, 1943. $1.50, Characters papering globe with greetings, 1941. $2, Lady and the Tramp beside Christmas tree, 1986. $4, Donald, Goofy, Mickey and Pluto reciting "Night Before Christmas," 1977. $5, Mickey in doorway of Snow White's Castle, 1965. No. 1576, People from around the world, 1966. No. 1577, Mickey in balloon basket with people of different countries, 1966.

1991, Dec. 23 *Perf. 13½x14*

1568	A216	10c multicolored	15	15
1569	A216	45c multicolored	35	35
1570	A216	55c multicolored	42	42
1571	A216	75c multicolored	55	55
1572	A216	$1.50 multicolored	1.15	1.15
1573	A216	$2 multicolored	1.50	1.50
1574	A216	$4 multicolored	3.00	3.00
1575	A216	$5 multicolored	3.75	3.75
		Nos. 1568-1575 (8)	10.87	10.87

Souvenir Sheets

1576	A216	$6 multicolored	4.50	4.50
1577	A216	$6 multicolored	4.50	4.50

Environmental Preservation — A217

1992, Jan. Litho. *Perf. 14*

1578	A217	10c Kings Hill	15	15
1579	A217	55c Tree planting	42	42
1580	A217	75c Botanical Gardens	58	58
1581	A217	$2 Kings Hill Project	1.50	1.50

Queen Elizabeth II's Accession to the Throne, 40th Anniv.

Common Design Type

1992, Feb. 6

1582	CD348	10c multicolored	15	15
1583	CD348	20c multicolored	15	15
1584	CD348	$1 multicolored	75	75
1585	CD348	$5 multicolored	3.75	3.75

Souvenir Sheets

1586	CD348	$6 Queen, beach	4.50	4.50
1587	CD348	$6 Queen, harbor	4.50	4.50

Queen Elizabeth II's Acession to the Throne, 40th Anniv. A217a

Designs: No. 1587A, Queen Elizabeth II. No. 1587B, King George VI.

1993, Mar. 2 Embossed *Perf. 12*

Without Gum

1587A	A217a	$5 gold		
1587B	A217a	$5 gold		

1992 Winter Olympics, Albertville — A218

1992 Summer Olympics, Barcelona — A219

1992, Apr. 21 Litho. *Perf. 14*

1588	A218	10c Women's luge, horiz.	15	15
1589	A218	15c Women's figure skating	15	15
1590	A218	25c Two-man bob-sled, horiz.	18	18
1591	A218	30c Mogul skiing	24	24
1592	A218	45c Nordic combined, horiz.	35	35
1593	A218	55c Ski jump, horiz.	42	42
1594	A218	75c Giant slalom, horiz.	58	58
1595	A218	$1.50 Women's slalom	1.15	1.15
1596	A218	$5 Ice hockey, horiz.	3.75	3.75
1597	A218	$8 Biathlon	6.00	6.00
		Nos. 1588-1597 (10)	12.97	12.97

Souvenir Sheets

1598	A218	$6 Downhill skiing	4.50	4.50
1599	A218	$6 Speed skating	4.50	4.50

1992, Apr. 21

Designs: 10c, Women's synchronized swimming duet, horiz. 15c, High jump. 25c, Small-bore rifle, horiz. 30c, 200-meter run. 45c, Judo. 55c. 200-meter freestyle swimming, horiz. 75c, Javelin. $1.50, Pursuit cycling. $5, Boxing. $8, Women's basketball. No. 1610, Tennis. No. 1611, Board sailing.

1600	A219	10c multicolored	15	15
1601	A219	15c multicolored	15	15
1602	A219	25c multicolored	18	18
1603	A219	30c multicolored	22	22
1604	A219	45c multicolored	35	35
1605	A219	55c multicolored	42	42
1606	A219	75c multicolored	55	55
1607	A219	$1.50 multicolored	1.15	1.15
1608	A219	$5 multicolored	3.75	3.75
1609	A219	$8 multicolored	6.00	6.00
		Nos. 1600-1609 (10)	12.92	12.92

Souvenir Sheets

1610	A219	$15 multicolored	11.25	11.25
1611	A219	$15 multicolored	11.25	11.25

World Columbian Stamp Expo '92, Chicago — A220

Walt Disney characters visiting Chicago area landmarks: 10c, Mickey, Pluto at Picasso Sulpture. 50c, Mickey, Donald admiring Frank Lloyd Wright's Robie House. $1, Gus Gander at Calder Sculpture in Sears Tower. $5, Pluto in Buckingham Memorial Fountain. No. 1616, Mickey painting Minnie at Chicago Art Institute, vert.

1992, Apr. Litho. *Perf. 14x13½*

1612	A220	10c multicolored	15	15
1613	A220	50c multicolored	38	38
1614	A220	$1 multicolored	75	75
1615	A220	$5 multicolored	3.75	3.75

Souvenir Sheet

Perf. 13½x14

1616	A220	$6 multicolored	4.50	4.50

Nos. 1617-1621 have not been used.

Granada '92 — A221

Walt Disney characters from "The Three Little Pigs" in Spanish military uniforms: 15c, Big Bad Wolf as General of Spanish Moors. 40c, Pig as Captain of Spanish infantry. $2, Pig in Spanish armor, c. 1580. $4, Pig as Spaniard of rank, c. 1550. $6, Little Pig resisting wolf from castle built of stone.

1992, Apr. 28 *Perf. 13½x14*

1622	A221	15c multicolored	15	15
1623	A221	40c multicolored	30	30
1624	A221	$2 multicolored	1.50	1.50
1625	A221	$4 multicolored	3.00	3.00

Souvenir Sheet

1626	A221	$6 multicolored	4.25	4.25

Nos. 1627-1631 have not been used.

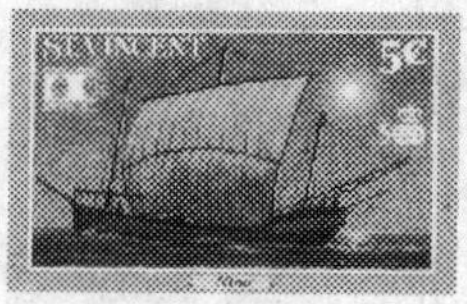

Discovery of America, 500th Anniv.
A222

1992, May 22 *Perf. 14*

1632	A222	5c Nina	15	15
1633	A222	10c Pinta	15	15
1634	A222	45c Santa Maria	35	35
1635	A222	55c Leaving Palos, Spain	42	42
1636	A222	$4 Columbus, vert.	3.00	3.00
1637	A222	$5 Columbus' arms, vert.	3.75	3.75
		Nos. 1632-1637 (6)	7.82	7.82

Souvenir Sheet

1638	A222	$6 Map, vert.	4.50	4.50
1639	A222	$6 Sailing ship, vert.	4.50	4.50

World Columbian Stamp Expo '92, Chicago. Nos. 1638-1639 contain one 42x57mm stamp.

Bonnie Blair, US Olympic Speed Skating Champion — A223

Designs: No. 1641a, Skating around corner. b, Portrait holding skates. c, On straightaway.

1992, May 25 *Perf. 13½*

1640	A223	$3 multicolored	2.25	2.25

Souvenir Sheet

1641	A223	$2 Sheet of 3, #a.-c.	4.50	4.50

World Columbian Stamp Expo '92. No. 1641b is 48x60mm.

Entertainers Type of 1991
Miniature Sheet

Various portraits of Elvis Presley.

1992, May 25 *Perf. 13½x14*

1642	A206	$1 Sheet of 9, #a.-i.	6.75	6.75

Souvenir Sheet
Perf. 14

1643	A206	$6 multicolored	4.50	4.50

No. 1643 contains one 28x43mm stamp.
See Nos. 1729-1730.

Hummingbirds
A224

1992, June 15 *Perf. 14*

1644	A224	5c Rufous-breasted hermit	15	15
1645	A224	15c Hispaniolan emerald	15	15
1646	A224	45c Green-throated carib	35	35
1647	A224	55c Jamaican mango	42	42
1648	A224	65c Vervain	50	50
1649	A224	75c Purple-throated carib	58	58
1650	A224	90c Green mango	70	70
1651	A224	$1 Bee	78	78
1652	A224	$2 Cuban emerald	1.55	1.55
1653	A224	$3 Puerto Rican emerald	2.30	2.30
1654	A224	$4 Antillean mango	3.00	3.00
1655	A224	$5 Streamertail	3.75	3.75
		Nos. 1644-1655 (12)	14.23	14.23

Souvenir Sheets

1656	A224	$6 Antillean crested	4.50	4.50
1657	A224	$6 Bahama woodstar	4.50	4.50
1658	A224	$6 Blue-headed	4.50	4.50

Genoa '92 Intl. Philatelic Exhibition.

Butterflies
A225

Designs: 5c, Dull astraptes, vert. 10c, White peacock. 35c, Tropic queen, vert. 45c, Polydamas swallowtail, vert. 55c, West Indian buckeye. 65c, Long-tailed skipper, vert. 75c, Tropical checkered skipper. $1, Crimson-banded black, vert. $2, Barred sulphur, vert. $3, Cassius blue. $4, Florida duskywing. $5, Malachite, vert. No. 1671, Cloudless giant sulphur, vert. No. 1672, Julia. No. 1673, Zebra longwing.

1992, June 15 **Litho.** *Perf. 14*

1659	A225	5c multicolored	15	15
1660	A225	10c multicolored	15	15
1661	A225	35c multicolored	28	28
1662	A225	45c multicolored	35	35
1663	A225	55c multicolored	42	42
1664	A225	65c multicolored	48	48
1665	A225	75c multicolored	58	58
1666	A225	$1 multicolored	75	75
1667	A225	$2 multicolored	1.50	1.50
1668	A225	$3 multicolored	2.25	2.25
1669	A225	$4 multicolored	3.00	3.00
1670	A225	$5 multicolored	3.75	3.75
		Nos. 1659-1670 (12)	13.66	13.66

Souvenir Sheets

1671	A225	$6 multicolored	4.50	4.50
1672	A225	$6 multicolored	4.50	4.50
1673	A225	$6 multicolored	4.50	4.50

Genoa '92.

A226

A227

Medicinal Plants: No. 1674a, Coral vine. b, Cocoplum. c, Angel's trumpet. d, Lime. e, White ginger. f, Pussley. g, Sea grape. h, Indian mulberry. i, Plantain. j, Lignum vitae. k, Periwinkle. l, Guava.

1992, July 22 **Litho.** *Perf. 14*
Miniature Sheet

1674	A226	75c Sheet of 12, #a.-l.	6.75	6.75

Souvenir Sheets

1675	A226	$6 Aloe	4.50	4.50
1676	A226	$6 Clove tree	4.50	4.50
1677	A226	$6 Wild sage	4.50	4.50

1992, July 2 **Litho.** *Perf. 14*

Mushrooms: 10c, Collybia subpruinosa. 15c, Gerronema citrinum. 20c, Amanita antillana. 45c, Dermoloma atrobrunneum. 50c, Inopilus maculosus. 65c, Pulveroboletus brachyspermus. 75c, Mycena violacella. $1, Xerocomus brasiliensis. $2, Amanita ingrata. $3, Leptonia caeruleocaptata. $4, Limacella myochroa. $5, Inopilus magnificus. No. 1690, Limacella guttata. No. 1691, Amanita agglutinata. No. 1692, Trogia buccinalis.

1678	A227	10c multicolored	15	15
1679	A227	15c multicolored	15	15
1680	A227	20c multicolored	15	15
1681	A227	45c multicolored	35	35
1682	A227	50c multicolored	38	38
1683	A227	65c multicolored	48	48
1684	A227	75c multicolored	58	58
1685	A227	$1 multicolored	75	75
1686	A227	$2 multicolored	1.50	1.50
1687	A227	$3 multicolored	2.25	2.25
1688	A227	$4 multicolored	3.00	3.00
1689	A227	$5 multicolored	3.75	3.75
		Nos. 1678-1689 (12)	13.49	13.49

Souvenir Sheets

1690	A227	$6 multicolored	4.50	4.50
1691	A227	$6 multicolored	4.50	4.50
1692	A227	$6 multicolored	4.50	4.50

Baseball Players — A228

Designs: #1693, Ty Cobb. #1694, Dizzy Dean. #1695, Bob Feller. #1696, Whitey Ford. #1697, Lou Gehrig. #1698, Rogers Hornsby. #1699, Mel Ott. #1700, Satchel Paige. #1701, Babe Ruth. #1702, Casey Stengel. #1703, Honus Wagner. #1704, Cy Young.

1992, Aug. 5 **Litho.** *Imperf.*
Self-Adhesive
Size: 64x89mm

1693-1704	A228	$4 Set of 12	36.00	

Nos. 1693-1704 printed on thin card and distributed in boxed sets. To affix stamps, backing containing player's statistics must be removed.

A229

A230

1992 Winter Olympic Gold Medalists, Albertville: No. 1705a, Alberto Tomba, Italy, giant slalom. b, Fabrice Guy, France, Nordic combined. c, Patrick Ortlieb, Austria, men's downhill. d, Vegard Ulvang, Norway, cross country. e, Edgar Grospiron, France, freestyle Mogul skiing. f, Kjetil-Andre Aamodt, Norway, super giant slalom. g, Viktor Petrenko, Russia, men's figure skating.

No. 1706a, Kristi Yamaguchi, US, women's figure skating. b, Pernilla Wiberg, Sweden, women's giant slalom. c, Lyubov Yegorova, Unified Team, women's 10-kilometer cross country. d, Josef Polig, Italy, combined Alpine skiing. e, Finn Christian-Jagge, Norway, slalom. f, Kerrin Lee-Gartner, Canada, women's downhill. g, Steffania Belmondo, Italy, women's 30-kilometer cross country.

No. 1707, Alberto Tomba, diff. No. 1708, Kristi Yamaguchi, diff.

1992, Aug. 10 **Litho.** *Perf. 14*
Sheets of 7

1705	A229	$1 #a.-g. + label	5.25	5.25
1706	A229	$1 #a.-g. + label	5.25	5.25

Souvenir Sheets

1707	A229	$6 multicolored	4.50	4.50
1708	A229	$6 multicolored	4.50	4.50

1992 **Litho.** *Perf. 14½*

1709	A230	$1 Coming ashore	75	75
1710	A230	$2 Natives, ships	1.50	1.50

Discovery of America, 500th anniv. Organization of East Caribbean States.

Miniature Sheet

Opening of Euro Disney — A231

Walt Disney movies: #1711a, Pinocchio. b, Alice in Wonderland. c, Bambi. d, Cinderella. e, Snow White and the Seven Dwarfs. f, Peter Pan.

1992 **Litho.** *Perf. 13*

1711	A231	$1 Sheet of 6, #a.-f.	4.50	4.50

Souvenir Sheet
Perf. 12½

1712	A231	$5 Mickey Mouse	3.75	3.75

Christmas
A232

Details or entire paintings of The Nativity by: 10c, Hospitality Refused to the Virgin Mary and Joseph, by Jan Metsys. 40c, Albrecht Durer. 45c, The Nativity, by Geertgen Tot Sint Jans. 50c, The Nativity, by Tintoretto. 55c, Follower of Jan Joest Calcar. 65c, Workshop of Fra Angelico. 75c, Master of the Louvre Nativity. $1, Filippino Lippi. $2, Petrus Christus. $3, Edward Burne-Jones. $4, Giotto. $5, The Birth of Christ, by Domenico Ghirlandaio. No. 1725, Nativity, by Jean Fouquet. No. 1726, Sandro Botticelli. No. 1727, Gerard Horenbout.

1992, Nov. **Litho.** *Perf. 13½x14*

1713	A232	10c multicolored	15	15
1714	A232	40c multicolored	30	30
1715	A232	45c multicolored	35	35
1716	A232	50c multicolored	38	38
1717	A232	55c multicolored	42	42
1718	A232	65c multicolored	48	48
1719	A232	75c multicolored	58	58
1720	A232	$1 multicolored	75	75
1721	A232	$2 multicolored	1.50	1.50
1722	A232	$3 multicolored	2.25	2.25
1723	A232	$4 multicolored	3.00	3.00
1724	A232	$5 multicolored	3.75	3.75
		Nos. 1714-1724 (11)	13.76	13.76

Souvenir Sheets

1725	A232	$6 multicolored	4.50	4.50
1726	A232	$6 multicolored	4.50	4.50
1727	A232	$6 multicolored	4.50	4.50

Souvenir Sheet

Jacob Javits Convention Center, NYC — A233

1992, Oct. 28 **Litho.** *Perf. 14*

1728	A233	$6 multicolored	4.50	4.50

Postage Stamp Mega Event '92, NYC.

No. 1642 Inscribed Vertically "15th Anniversary"

Nos. 1564, 1567 Inscribed or Ovptd. "15th Anniversary" and "Elvis Presley's Death / August 16, 1977" in Margin

1992, Dec. 15 ***Perf. 13½x14***

1729 A206 $1 Sheet of 9, #a.-i. 6.75 6.75

Perf. 14½

1729J A215 $2 Sheet of 8, #k.-r. 12.00 12.00

Perf. 14

1730 A215 $6 multicolored 4.50 4.50

Baseball Players — A234

Members of Baseball Hall Fame — A235

1992, Nov. 9 **Litho.** ***Perf. 14***

1731 A234 $5 Howard Johnson 3.75 3.75
1732 A234 $5 Don Mattingly 3.75 3.75

1992 Summer Olympics, Barcelona.

1992, Dec. 21

Player, year inducted: No. 1733, Roberto Clemente, 1973. No. 1734, Hank Aaron, 1982. No. 1735, Tom Seaver, 1992.

1733 A235 $2 multicolored 1.50 1.50
1734 A235 $2 multicolored 1.50 1.50
1735 A235 $2 multicolored 1.50 1.50

Fishing Industry A236

1992, Nov.

1736 A236 5c Fishing with rods 15 15
1737 A236 10c Inside fishing complex 15 15
1738 A236 50c Landing the catch 38 38
1739 A236 $5 Fishing with nets 3.75 3.75

Uniting the Windward Islands A237

Children's paintings: 10c, Island coastline. 40c, Four people standing on islands. 45c, Four people standing on beach.

1992, Nov. **Litho.** ***Perf. 14***

1740 A237 10c multicolored 15 15
1741 A237 40c multicolored 30 30
1742 A237 45c multicolored 35 35

Miniature Sheets

US Olympic Basketball "Dream Team" — A238

Designs: No. 1744a, Scottie Pippen. b, Earvin "Magic" Johnson. c, Larry Bird. d, Christian Laettner. e, Karl Malone. f, David Robinson.

No. 1745a, Michael Jordan. b, Charles Barkley. c, John Stockton. d, Chris Mullin. e, Clyde Drexler. f, Patrick Ewing.

1992, Dec. 22 **Litho.** ***Perf. 14***

1744 A238 $2 Sheet of 6, #a.-f. 9.00 9.00
1745 A238 $2 Sheet of 6, #a.-f. 9.00 9.00

1992 Summer Olympics, Barcelona.

A239

A240

A241

A242

Anniversaries and Events: 10c, Globe and UN emblem. 45c, Zeppelin Viktoria Luise over Kiel Regatta, 1912, vert. 65c, Food products. No. 1749, America's Cup Trophy and Bill Koch, skipper of America 3. No. 1750, Konrad Adenauer, German flag. No. 1751, Adenauer, diff. No. 1752, Snow leopard. $1.50, Caribbean manatee. $2, Humpback whale. No. 1755, Adenauer, John F. Kennedy. No. 1756, Lions Intl. emblem, patient having eye exam. No. 1757, Space shuttle Discovery, vert. No. 1758, Adenauer, Pope John XXIII. $5, Michael Schumacher, race car. $6, Count Zeppelin's first airship over Lake Constance, 1900. No. 1761, Gondola of Graf Zeppelin. No. 1762, Formula I race car. No. 1763, Sailing ship, steam packet. No. 1764, Adenauer at podium. No. 1765, Woolly spider monkey. No. 1765A, People waving to plane during Berlin airlift.

1992-93 **Litho.** ***Perf. 14***

1746 A239 10c multicolored 15 15
1747 A239 45c multicolored 35 35
1748 A242 65c multicolored 48 48
1749 A239 75c multicolored 58 58
1750 A239 75c multicolored 58 58
1751 A239 $1 multicolored 75 75
1752 A239 $1 multicolored 75 75
1753 A239 $1.50 multicolored 1.15 1.15
1754 A239 $2 multicolored 1.50 1.50
1755 A239 $3 multicolored 2.25 2.25
1756 A239 $3 multicolored 2.25 2.25
1757 A239 $4 multicolored 3.00 3.00
1758 A239 $4 multicolored 3.00 3.00
1759 A240 $5 multicolored 3.75 3.75
1760 A239 $6 multicolored 4.50 4.50
Nos. 1746-1760 (15) 25.04 25.04

Souvenir Sheets

1761 A239 $6 multicolored 4.50 4.50
1762 A240 $6 multicolored 4.50 4.50
1763 A241 $6 multicolored 4.50 4.50
1764 A239 $6 multicolored 4.50 4.50
1765 A239 $6 multicolored 4.50 4.50
1765A A239 $6 multicolored 4.50 4.50

UN Intl. Space Year (#1746, 1757). Count Zeppelin, 75th anniv. of death (#1747, 1760-1761). Intl. Conference on Nutrition, Rome (#1748). America's Cup yacht race (#1749). Konrad Adenauer, 25th death anniv. (#1750-1751, 1755, 1758, 1764). Earth Summit, Rio de Janeiro (#1752-1754, 1765). Lions Intl., 75th anniv. (#1756). Belgian Grand Prix (#1759, 1762). Discovery of America, 500th anniv. (#1763). Konrad Adenauer, 75th death anniv. (#1765A).

Issue dates: Nos. 1747, 1759-1762, Dec. No. 1763, Oct. 28. Nos. 1746, 1749, 1750-1751, 1755-1758, 1764, Dec. Nos. 1752-1754, 1765, Dec. 15. No. 1765A, June 30, 1993.

A243

A244

Care Bears Promote Conservation: 75c, Bear, stork. $2, Bear riding in hot air balloon, horiz.

1992, Dec. **Litho.** ***Perf. 14***

1766 A243 75c multicolored 58 58

Souvenir Sheet

1767 A243 $2 multicolored 1.50 1.50

1993 **Litho.** ***Perf. 14***

Elvis Presley (1935-1977): b, Portrait. c, With guitar. d, With microphone.

1767A A244 $1 Strip of 3, #b.-d. 2.25 2.25

Walt Disney's Beauty and the Beast — A245

Designs: 2c, Gaston. 3c, Belle and her father, Maurice. 5c, Lumiere, Mrs. Potts and Cogsworth. 10c, Philippe. 15c, Beast and Lumiere. 20c, Lumiere and Feather Duster.

No. 1774a, Belle and Gaston. b, Maurice. c, The Beast. d, Mrs. Potts. e, Belle and the Enchanted Vase. f, Belle discovers an Enchanted Rose. g, Belle with wounded Beast. h, Belle. i, Household objects alarmed.

No. 1774k, Belle and Chip. l, Lumiere. m, Cogsworth. n, Armoire. o, Belle and Beast. p, Feather Duster. q, Footstool. r, Belle. All vert.

No. 1775, Belle reading, vert. No. 1776, Lumiere, diff., vert. No. 1776A, Lumiere, Mrs. Potts. No. 1776B, Belle, lake and castle, vert. No. 1776C, The Beast, vert.

Perf. 14x13½, 13½x14

1992, Dec. 15 **Litho.**

1768 A245 2c multicolored 15 15
1769 A245 3c multicolored 15 15
1770 A245 5c multicolored 15 15
1771 A245 10c multicolored 15 15
1772 A245 15c multicolored 15 15
1773 A245 20c multicolored 15 15
Set Value 42 42

Miniature Sheets

1774 A245 60c Sheet of 9, #a.-i. 4.00 4.00
1774J A245 60c Sheet of 8, #k.-r. 4.00 4.00

Souvenir Sheets

1775 A245 $6 multicolored 4.50 4.50
1776 A245 $6 multicolored 4.50 4.50
1776A A245 $6 multicolored 4.50 4.50
1776B A245 $6 multicolored 4.50 4.50
1776C A245 $6 multicolored 4.50 4.50

Louvre Museum, Bicent. A246

Details or entire paintings by Jean-Auguste-Dominique Ingres: No. 1777a, Louis-Francois Bertin. b, The Apotheosis of Homer. c, Joan of Arc. d, The Composer Cherubini with the Muse of Lyric Poetry. e, Mlle Caroline Riviere. f, Oedipus Answers the Sphinx's Riddle. g, Madame Marcotte. h, Mademoiselle Caroline Riviere.

Details or entire paintings by Jean Louis Andre Theodore Gericault (1791-1824): No. 1778a, The Woman with Gambling Mania. b, Head of a White Horse. c, Wounded Cuirassier. d, An Officer of the Cavalry. e, The Vendean. f, The Raft of the Medusa. g-h, The Horse Market (left, right).

Details or entire paintings by Nicolas Poussin (1594-1665): No. 1779a-1779b, The Arcadian Shepherds (left, right). c, Ecstasy of Paul. d-e, The Inspiration of the Poet (left, right). f-g, St. John Baptizing (left, right). h, The Miracle of St. Francis Xavier.

Details or entire paintings by Eustache Le Sueur (1616-1655): No. 1780a-1780b, Melpomene, Erato & Polyhymnia (left, right). By Poussin: c, Christ and Woman Taken in Adultery. d, Spring. e, Autumn. f-h, The Plague of Asdod (left, center, right).

No. 1781a, The Beggars, by Pieter Brueghel, the Elder (1520-1569). b, The Luncheon, by Francois Boucher (1703-1770). c, Louis Guene, Royal Violinist, by Francois Dumont (1751-1831). d, The Virgin of Chancellor Rolin, by Jan Van Eyck. e, Conversation in the Park, by Thomas Gainsborough. f, Lady Alston, by Gainsborough. g, Mariana Waldstein, by Francisco de Goya. h, Ferdinand Guillemardet, by Goya.

No. 1782, The Grand Odalisque, horiz. No. 1783, The Dressing Room of Esther, by Theodore Chasseriau (1819-1856). No. 1784, Liberty Guiding the People, by Eugene Delecroix (1798-1863), horiz.

1993, Apr. 19 ***Perf. 12x12½***

Sheets of 8

1777 A246 $1 #a.-h. + label 6.00 6.00
1778 A246 $1 #a.-h. + label 6.00 6.00
1779 A246 $1 #a.-h. + label 6.00 6.00
1780 A246 $1 #a.-h. + label 6.00 6.00
1781 A246 $1 #a.-h. + label 6.00 6.00

Souvenir Sheet

Perf. 14½

1782 A246 $6 multicolored 4.50 4.50
1783 A246 $6 multicolored 4.50 4.50
1784 A246 $6 multicolored 4.50 4.50

UN Intl. Space Year (#1746, 1757). Count Zeppelin, 75th anniv. of death (#1747, 1760-1761). Intl. Conference on Nutrition, Rome (#1748). America's Cup yacht race (#1749). Konrad Adenauer, 25th death anniv. (#1750-1751, 1755, 1758, 1764). Earth Summit, Rio de Janeiro (#1752-1754, 1765). Lions Intl., 75th anniv. (#1756). Belgian Grand Prix (#1759, 1762). Discovery of America, 500th anniv. (#1763). Konrad Adenauer, 75th death anniv. (#1765A). Nos. 1783-1784 each contain a 55x88mm or 88x55mm stamp.

Paintings on Nos. 1777d and 1777h were switched.

Numbers have been reserved for two additional souvenir sheets in this set.

Miniature Sheets

A247

A247a

Scenes from Disney Animated Films A247b

Symphony Hour (1942): No. 1787a, Maestro Mickey. b, Goofy plays a mean horn. c, On first bass with Clara Cluck. d, Stringing along with Clarabelle. e, Donald on drums. f, Clarabelle all fiddled out. g, Donald drumming up trouble. h, Goofy's sour notes. i, Mickey's moment.

No. 1794, Bird's-eye-view of Goofy. No. 1795, Mickey and Macaroni enjoying applause.

The Small One: No. 1791k, Morning comes in Nazareth. l, Good morning, small one. m, Too old to keep. n, Heatbroken. o, Nazareth markplace. p, Auction mockery. q, Off the auction block. r, Lonely and dejected. s, Happy and useful again.

No. 1804, Hard Work in Nazareth. No. 1805, Finding a buyer in Nazareth.

The Three Little Pigs (1933): No. 1792a, Fifer Pig building house of straw. b, Fiddler Pig building house of sticks. c, Practical Pig building house of bricks. d, The Big Bad Wolf. e, Wolf scaring two lazy pigs. f, Wolf blowing down staw house. g, Wolf in sheep's clothing. h, Wolf blowing down twig house. i, Wolf huffs and puffs at brick house.

No. 1806, Animator's sketch of little pig and brick house. No. 1807, Little pigs playing and singing at piano, vert.

How to Play Football (1944): No. 1792k, Cheerleaders. l, Here comes the team. m, In the huddle. n, Who's got the ball? o, Who, me coach? p, Halftime pep talk. q, Another down, and out. r, Only a little injury. s, Up and at 'em.

No. 1807A, Goofy demonstrating how to score touchdown. No. 1807B, Goofy shouting "Hooray for the team," vert.

Rescue Rangers: No. 1793a, Special agents. b, Chip 'n Dale, ready for action. c, Chip 'n Dale on stakeout. d, Gadget in gear. e, Gadget and Monterey Jack rescue Zipper. f, Zipper confers with Monterey Jack. g, Zipper zaps fat cat. h, Team work. i, Innovative Gadget.

No. 1807C, Gadget at controls of Ranger plane, vert. No. 1807D, Dale, vert.

Darkwing Duck: No. 1793k, Darkwing Duck. l, Launchpad McQuack. m, Gosalyn. n, Honker Muddlefoot. o, Tank Muddlefoot. p, Herb & Binkie Muddlefoot. q, Drake Mallard, aka Darkwing Duck. r, Darkwing Duck logo.

No. 1807E, Quarterjack. No. 1807F, Darkwing Duck and Launchpad to the rescue in Ratcatcher.

Clock Cleaners (1937): No. 1788a, Goofy gets in gear. b, Donald on the mainspring. c, Donald in the works. d, Mickey's fine-feathered friend. e, Stork with bundle of joy. f, Father Time. g, Goofy, Mickey leaping upward. h, Donald, Goofy, Mickey out of gear. i, Donald, Goofy, Mickey with headaches.

No. 1796, On the edge of Goofyness. No. 1797, Gonged-out Goofy.

The Art of Skiing (1941): No. 1789a, The ultimate back scratcher. b, Striking a pose. c, And we're off. d, Divided he stands. e, A real twister. f, Hangin' in there. g, Over the hill. h, At the peak of his form. i, Up a tree.

No. 1798, Film poster for Art of Skiing with Goofy slaloming down mountain. No. 1799, Goofy home in bed at last.

Orphan's Benefit (1941): No. 1790a, Mickey introduces Donald. b, Donald recites "Little Boy Blue." c, Orphan mischief. d, Clara Cluck, singing sensation. e, Goofy's debut with Clarabelle. f, Encore for Clara and Mickey. g, A Bronx cheer. h, Donald blows his stack. i, Donald's final bow.

No. 1800, Caveman ballet. No. 1801, Mickey tickles the ivories.

Thru the Mirror (1936): No. 1791a, Mickey steps thru the looking glass. b, Mickey finds a tasty treat. c, Mickey's nutty effect. d, Hats off to Mickey. e, What a card, Mickey. f, Mickey dancing with the Queen Hearts. g, A real two-faced opponent. h, Mickey with a pen mightier than a sword. i, Mickey awake at last.

No. 1802, Mickey's true reflection. No. 1803, Mickey hopping home.

Perf. 14x13¹/₂, 13¹/₂x14

1992, Dec. 15 — Litho.

1787	A247	60c	Sheet of 9, #a.-i.	4.00	4.00
1788	A247	60c	Sheet of 9, #a.-i.	4.00	4.00
1789	A247	60c	Sheet of 9, #a.-i.	4.00	4.00
1790	A247	60c	Sheet of 9, #a.-i.	4.00	4.00
1791	A247	60c	Sheet of 9, #a.-i.	4.00	4.00
1791J	A247a	60c	Sheet of 9, #k.-s.	4.00	4.00
1792	A247	60c	Sheet of 9, #a.-i.	4.00	4.00
1792J	A247a	60c	Sheet of 9, #k.-s.	4.00	4.00
1793	A247a	60c	Sheet of 9, #a.-i.	4.00	4.00
1793J	A247b	60c	Sheet of 8, #k.-r.	3.60	3.60

Souvenir Sheets

1794	A247	$6	multicolored	4.50	4.50
1795	A247	$6	multicolored	4.50	4.50
1796	A247	$6	multicolored	4.50	4.50
1797	A247	$6	multicolored	4.50	4.50
1798	A247	$6	multicolored	4.50	4.50
1799	A247	$6	multicolored	4.50	4.50
1800	A247	$6	multicolored	4.50	4.50
1801	A247	$6	multicolored	4.50	4.50
1802	A247	$6	multicolored	4.50	4.50
1803	A247	$6	multicolored	4.50	4.50
1804	A247a	$6	multicolored	4.50	4.50
1805	A247a	$6	multicolored	4.50	4.50
1806	A247	$6	multicolored	4.50	4.50
1807	A247	$6	multicolored	4.50	4.50
1807A	A247	$6	multicolored	4.50	4.50
1807B	A247	$6	multicolored	4.50	4.50
1807C	A247a	$6	multicolored	4.50	4.50
1807D	A247a	$6	multicolored	4.50	4.50
1807E	A247b	$6	multicolored	4.50	4.50
1807F	A247b	$6	multicolored	4.50	4.50

Fish
A248

1993, Apr. 1 — Litho. — *Perf. 14*

1808	A248	5c	Sergeant major	15	15
1809	A248	10c	Rainbow parrotfish	15	15
1810	A248	55c	Hogfish	42	42
1811	A248	75c	Porkfish	58	58
1812	A248	$1	Spotfin butterflyfish	75	75
1813	A248	$2	Trunkfish	1.50	1.50
1814	A248	$4	Queen triggerfish	3.00	3.00
1815	A248	$5	Queen angelfish	3.75	3.75
			Nos. 1808-1815 (8)	10.30	10.30

Souvenir Sheets

1816	A248	$6	Bigeye, vert.	4.50	4.50
1817	A248	$6	Smallmouth grunt, vert.	4.50	4.50

Birds — A249

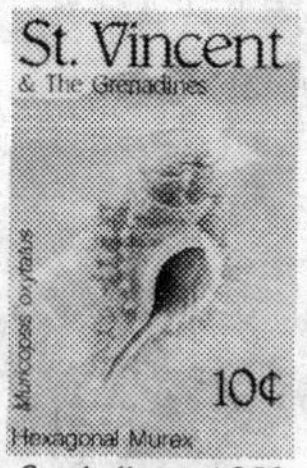

Seashells — A250

Designs: 10c, Brown pelican. 25c, Red-necked grebe, horiz. 45c, Belted kingfisher, horiz. 55c, Yellow-bellied sapsucker. $1, Great blue heron. $2, Crab hawk, horiz. $4, Yellow warbler. $5, Northern oriole, horiz. No. 1826, White ibises, map, horiz. No. 1827, Blue-winged teal, map, horiz.

1993, Apr. 1 — Litho. — *Perf. 14*

1818	A249	10c	multicolored	15	15
1819	A249	25c	multicolored	18	18
1820	A249	45c	multicolored	35	35
1821	A249	55c	multicolored	42	42
1822	A249	$1	multicolored	75	75
1823	A249	$2	multicolored	1.50	1.50
1824	A249	$4	multicolored	3.00	3.00
1825	A249	$5	multicolored	3.75	3.75
			Nos. 1818-1825 (8)	10.10	10.10

Souvenir Sheets

1826	A249	$6	multicolored	4.50	4.50
1827	A249	$6	multicolored	4.50	4.50

1993, May 24 — Litho. — *Perf. 14*

1828	A250	10c	Hexagonal murex	15	15
1829	A250	15c	Caribbean vase	15	15
1830	A250	30c	Measled cowrie	22	22
1831	A250	45c	Dyson's keyhole limpet	35	35
1832	A250	50c	Atlantic hairy triton	38	38
1833	A250	65c	Orange-banded marginella	48	48
1834	A250	75c	Bleeding tooth	55	55
1835	A250	$1	Pink conch	75	75
1836	A250	$2	Hawk-wing conch	1.50	1.50
1837	A250	$3	Music volute	2.25	2.25
1838	A250	$4	Alphabet cone	3.00	3.00
1839	A250	$5	Antillean cone	3.75	3.75
			Nos. 1828-1839 (12)	13.53	13.53

Souvenir Sheets

1840	A250	$6	Flame auger, horiz.	4.50	4.50
1841	A250	$6	Netted olive, horiz.	4.50	4.50
1842	A250	$6	Wide-mouthed purpura, horiz.	4.50	4.50

Miniature Sheet

Yujiro Ishihara, Actor — A251

Various portraits: No. 1843a, $1. b, 55c. c, $1. d, 55c. e, 55c. f, 55c. g, $1. h, 55c. i, $1.

No. 1844a, 55c. b, $1. c, $2. d, $2.

No. 1845a, 55c. b, $2, c, $1. d, $2.

No. 1846a, 55c. b, $2. c, $4.

No. 1847a, 55c. b, $4. c, $4.

1993, May 24 — Litho. — *Perf. 13¹/₂x14*

1843	A251	Sheet of 9, #a.-i.	5.25	5.25

Souvenir Sheets

1844	A251	Sheet of 4, #a.-d.	4.25	4.25

Stamp Size: 32x41mm

Perf. 14¹/₂

1845	A251	Sheet of 4, #a.-d.	4.25	4.25

Stamp Size: 60x41mm

Perf. 14x14¹/₂

1846	A251	Sheet of 3, #a.-c.	5.00	5.00
1847	A251	Sheet of 3, #a.-c.	6.50	6.50

Automobiles — A252

Designs: $1, 1932 Ford V8, 1915 Ford Model T, Henry Ford's first car. $2, Benz 540K, 1928 Benz Stuttgart, 1908 Benz Racer. $3, 1911 Blitzen Benz, 1905 Benz Tourenwagen, 1894 Benz. $4, 1935 Ford, 1903 Ford A Runabout, 1913 Ford Model T Tourer. No. 1852, Karl Benz. No. 1853, Henry Ford.

1993, May — Litho. — *Perf. 14*

1848	A252	$1	multicolored	75	75
1849	A252	$2	multicolored	1.50	1.50
1850	A252	$3	multicolored	2.25	2.25
1851	A252	$4	multicolored	3.00	3.00

Souvenir Sheets

1852	A252	$6	multicolored	4.50	4.50
1853	A252	$6	multicolored	4.50	4.50

First Ford motor, cent. (#1848, 1851, 1853). First Benz motor car, cent. (#1849-1850, 1852).

Miniature Sheet

Coronation of Queen Elizabeth II, 40th Anniv. — A253

Designs: a, 45c, Official coronation photograph. b, 65c, Opening Parliament, 1980s. c, $2, Coronation ceremony, 1953. d, $4, Queen with her dog, 1970s.

No. 1855, Portrait of Queen as a child.

1993, June 2 — Litho. — *Perf. 13¹/₂x14*

1854	A253	Sheet, 2 each #a.-d.	11.00	11.00

Souvenir Sheet

Perf. 14

1855	A253	$6	multicolored	4.50	4.50

No. 1855 contains one 28x42mm stamp.

Moths — A254

1993, June 14 — Litho. — *Perf. 14*

1856	A254	10c	Erynnyis ello	15	15
1857	A254	50c	Aellopos tantalus	38	38
1858	A254	65c	Erynnyis alope	48	48
1859	A254	75c	Manduca rustica	55	55
1860	A254	$1	Xylophanes pluto	75	75
1861	A254	$2	Hyles lineata	1.50	1.50
1862	A254	$4	Pseudosphinx tetrio	3.00	3.00
1863	A254	$5	Protambulyx strigilis	3.75	3.75
			Nos. 1856-1863 (8)	10.56	10.56

Souvenir Sheets

1864	A254	$6	Xylophanes tersa	4.50	4.50
1864A	A254	$6	Utetheisa ornatrix	4.50	4.50

A255

A256

Aviation Anniversaries — A257

Designs: 50c, Supermarine Spitfire. No. 1866, Graf Zeppelin over Egypt, 1931, Hugo Eckener. No. 1867, Jean Pierre Blanchard, balloon, George Washington. No. 1868, De Havilland Mosquito. No. 1869, Eckener, Graf Zeppelin over New York, 1928. $3, Eckener, Graf Zeppelin over Tokyo, 1929. $4, Philadelphia's Walnut State Prison, balloon lifting off. No. 1872, Hawker Hurricane. No. 1873, Hugo Eckener, vert. No. 1874, Blanchard's Balloon, vert.

1993, June — Litho. — *Perf. 14*

1865	A255	50c	multicolored	38	38
1866	A256	$1	multicolored	75	75
1867	A257	$1	multicolored	75	75
1868	A255	$2	multicolored	1.50	1.50
1869	A256	$2	multicolored	1.50	1.50
1870	A256	$3	multicolored	2.25	2.25
1871	A257	$4	multicolored	3.00	3.00
			Nos. 1865-1871 (7)	10.13	10.13

Souvenir Sheets

1872	A255	$6	multicolored	4.50	4.50
1873	A256	$6	multicolored	4.50	4.50
1874	A257	$6	multicolored	4.50	4.50

Royal Air Force, 75th anniv. (#1865, 1868, 1872). Dr. Hugo Eckener, 125th anniv. of birth (#1866, 1869-1870, 1873). First US balloon flight, bicent. (#1867, 1871). Tokyo spelled incorrectly on No. 1870.

Wedding of Japan's Crown Prince Naruhito and Masako Owada A258

Cameo portraits of couple and: 65c, Princess. $5, Prince in ritual Shinto priest's dress. No. 1877, Princess, photographers, vert.

1993, June 30 — Litho. — *Perf. 14*

1875	A258	65c	multicolored	48	48
1876	A258	$5	multicolored	3.75	3.75

Souvenir Sheet

1877	A258	$6	multicolored	4.50	4.50

1994 Winter Olympics, Lillehammer, Norway — A259

Designs: 45c, Marc Girardelli, silver medalist, giant slalom, 1992. $5, Paul Accola, downhill, 1992. $6, Thommy Moe, downhill, 1992.

1993, June 30 Litho. *Perf. 14*

1878	A259	45c multicolored	35	35
1879	A259	$5 multicolored	3.75	3.75

Souvenir Sheet

1880	A259	$6 multicolored	4.50	4.50

Picasso (1881-1973) — A260

Paintings: 45c, Massacre in Korea, 1951. $1, Family of Saltimbanques, 1905. $4, La Joie de Vivre, 1946. $6, Woman Eating a Melon and Boy Writing, 1965, vert.

1993, June 30

1881	A260	45c multicolored	35	35
1882	A260	$1 multicolored	75	75
1883	A260	$4 multicolored	3.00	3.00

Souvenir Sheet

1884	A260	$6 multicolored	4.50	4.50

Willy Brandt (1913-1992), German Chancellor — A261

Designs: 45c, Brandt, Richard Nixon, 1971. $5, Brandt, Robert Kennedy, 1967. $6, Brandt at signing of "Common Declaration," 1973.

1993, June 30

1885	A261	45c multicolored	35	35
1886	A261	$5 multicolored	3.75	3.75

Souvenir Sheet

1887	A261	$6 multicolored	4.50	4.50

A262

A263

Copernicus (1473-1543): 45c, Astronomical instrument. $4, Space shuttle lift-off. $6, Copernicus.

1993, June 30

1888	A262	45c multicolored	35	35
1889	A262	$4 multicolored	3.00	3.00

Souvenir Sheet

1890	A262	$6 multicolored	4.50	4.50

1993, June 30

European Royalty: 45c, Johannes, Gloria Thurn & Taxis. 65c, Thurn & Taxis family, horiz. $1, Princess Stephanie of Monaco. $2, Gloria Thurn & Taxis.

1891	A263	45c multicolored	35	35
1892	A263	65c multicolored	48	48
1893	A263	$1 multicolored	75	75
1894	A263	$2 multicolored	1.50	1.50

Inauguration of Pres. William J. Clinton — A264

Designs: $5, Bill Clinton, children. $6, Clinton wearing cowboy hat, vert.

1993, June 30

1895	A264	$5 multicolored	3.75	3.75

Souvenir Sheet

1896	A264	$6 multicolored	4.50	4.50

Polska '93 — A265

Designs: No. 1897, Bogusz Church, Gozlin. No. 1898a, $1, Deux Tetes (Man), by S.I. Witkiewicz, 1920, vert. No. 1898b, $3, Deux Tetes (Woman), vert. No. 1899, Dancing, by Wladyslaw Roguski, vert.

1993, June 30

1897	A265	$6 multicolored	4.50	4.50
1898	A265	Pair, #a.-b.	3.00	3.00

Souvenir Sheet

1899	A265	$6 multicolored	4.50	4.50

1994 World Cup Soccer Qualifying A266

St. Vincent vs: 5c, Mexico. 10c, Honduras. 65c, Costa Rica. $5, St. Vincent goalkeeper.

1993, Sept. 2

1900-1903	A266	Set of 4	4.25	4.25

Cooperation with Japan — A267

Designs: 10c, Fish delivery van. 50c, Fish aggregation device, vert. 75c, Trawler. $5, Fish complex.

1993, Sept. 2

1904-1907	A267	Set of 4	4.75	4.75

Pope John Paul II's Visit to Denver, CO A268

Design: $6, Pope, Denver skyline, diff.

1993, Aug. 13

1908	A268	$1 multicolored	75	75

Souvenir Sheet

1909	A268	$6 multicolored	4.50	4.50

No. 1908 issued in sheets of 9.

Miniature Sheet

Corvette, 40th Anniv. — A269

Corvettes: a, 1953. b, 1993, c, 1958, d, 1960. e, "40," Corvette emblem (no car). f, 1961. g, 1963. h, 1968, i, 1973. j, 1975. k, 1982. l, 1984.

1993, Aug. 13 *Perf. 14x13½*

1910	A269	$1 Sheet of 12, #a.-l.	9.00	9.00

Taipei '93 A270

Designs: 5c, Yellow Crane Mansion, Wuchang. 10c, Front gate, Chung Cheng Ceremonial Arch, Taiwan. 20c, Marble Peifang, Ming 13 Tombs, Beijing. 45c, Jinxing Den, Beijing. 55c, Forbidden City, Beijing. 75c, Tachih, the Martyr's Shrine, Taiwan. No. 1917, Praying Hall, Xinjiang, Gaochang. No. 1918, Chih Kan Tower, Taiwan. $2, Taihu Lake, Jiangsu. $4, Chengde, Hebei, Pula Si. No. 1921, Kaohsiung, Cheng Ching Lake, Taiwan. No. 1922, Great Wall.

Chinese paintings: No. 1923a, Street in Macao, China, by George Chinnery. b, Pair of Birds on Cherry Branch. c, Yellow Dragon Cave, by Patrick Procktor. d, Great Wall of China, by William Simpson. e, Dutch Folly Fort Off Conton, by Chinnery. f, Forbidden City, by Procktor.

Chinese silk paintings: No. 1924a, Rhododendron. b, Irises and bees. c, Easter lily. d, Poinsettia. e, Peach and cherry blossoms. f, Weeping cherry and yellow bird.

Chinese kites: No. 1925a, Dragon and tiger fighting. b, Two immortals. c, Five boys playing round a general. d, Zheng Chenggong. e, Nezha stirs up the sea. f, Immortal maiden He.

No. 1926, Giant Buddha, Longmen Caves, Luoyang, Hunan. No. 1927, Guardian and Celestial King, Longmen Caves, Hunan, vert. No. 1928, Giant Buddha, Yungang Caves, Datong, Shanxi, vert.

1993, Aug. 16 Litho. *Perf. 14x13½*

1911	A270	5c multicolored	15	15
1912	A270	10c multicolored	15	15
1913	A270	20c multicolored	15	15
1914	A270	45c multicolored	35	35
1915	A270	55c multicolored	42	42
1916	A270	75c multicolored	55	55
1917	A270	$1 multicolored	75	75
1918	A270	$1 multicolored	75	75
1919	A270	$2 multicolored	1.50	1.50
1920	A270	$4 multicolored	3.00	3.00
1921	A270	$5 multicolored	3.75	3.75
1922	A270	$5 multicolored	3.75	3.75
		Nos. 1911-1922 (12)	15.27	15.27

Miniature Sheets

1923	A270	$1.50 Sheet of 6, #a.-f.	6.75	6.75
1924	A270	$1.50 Sheet of 6, #a.-f.	6.75	6.75
1925	A270	$1.50 Sheet of 6, #a.-f.	6.75	6.75

Souvenir Sheets

1926	A270	$6 multicolored	4.50	4.50

Perf. 13½x14

1927	A270	$6 multicolored	4.50	4.50
1928	A270	$6 multicolored	4.50	4.50

No. 1925e issued missing "St." in country name. Some sheets of No. 1925 may have been withdrawn from sale after discovery of error.

With Bangkok '93 Emblem

Designs: 5c, Phra Nakhon Khiri (Rama V's Palace), vert. 10c, Grand Palace, Bangkok. 20c, Rama IX Park, Bangkok. 45c, Phra Prang Sam Yot, Lop Buri. 55c, Dusit Maha Prasad, vert. 75c, Phimai Khmer architecture, Pak Tong Chai. No. 1935, Burmese style Chedi, Mae Hong Son. No. 1936, Antechamber, Central Prang, Prasat Hin Phimai. $2, Brick chedi on laterite base, Si Thep, vert. $4, Isan's Phanom Rung, Korat, vert. No. 1939, Phu Khau Thong, the Golden Mount, Bangkok. No. 1940, Islands, Ang Thong.

Thai Buddha sculpture: No. 1941a, Interior of Wat Hua Kuang Lampang, vert. b, Wat Yai Suwannaram, vert. c, Phra Buddha Sihing, City Hall Chapel, vert. d, Wat Ko Keo Suttharam, vert. e, U Thong B image, Wat Ratburana crypt, vert. f, Sri Sakyamuni Wat Suthat, vert.

No. 1942a-1942f: Various details from Mural at Buddhaisawan Chapel.

Thai painting: No. 1943a, Untitled, by Arunothai Somsakul. b, Mural at Wat Rajapradit. c, Mural at Wat Phumin (detail). d, Serenity, by Surasit Souakong. e, Scenes of early Bangkok mural (detail). f, Ramayana.

No. 1944, Roof detail of Dusit Mahaprasad, vert. No. 1945, Standing Buddha, Hua Hin, vert. No. 1946, Masked dance.

Perf. 13½x14, 14x13½

1993, Aug. 16 Litho.

1929	A270	5c multicolored	15	15
1930	A270	10c multicolored	15	15
1931	A270	20c multicolored	15	15
1932	A270	45c multicolored	35	35
1933	A270	55c multicolored	42	42
1934	A270	75c multicolored	55	55
1935	A270	$1 multicolored	75	75
1936	A270	$1 multicolored	75	75
1937	A270	$2 multicolored	1.50	1.50
1938	A270	$4 multicolored	3.00	3.00
1939	A270	$5 multicolored	3.75	3.75
1940	A270	$5 multicolored	3.75	3.75
		Nos. 1929-1940 (12)	15.27	15.27

Miniature Sheets

1941	A270	$1.50 Sheet of 6, #a.-f.	6.75	6.75
1942	A270	$1.50 Sheet of 6, #a.-f.	6.75	6.75
1943	A270	$1.50 Sheet of 6, #a.-f.	6.75	6.75

Souvenir Sheets

1944	A270	$6 multicolored	4.50	4.50
1945	A270	$6 multicolored	4.50	4.50
1946	A270	$6 multicolored	4.50	4.50

With Indopex '93 Emblem

Indopex '93 emblem with designs: 5c, Local landmark, Gedung site, 1920. 10c, Masjid Jamik Mosque, Sumenep. 20c, Bromo Caldera, seen from Penanjakan. 45c, Kudus Mosque, Java. 55c, Kampung Naga. 75c, Lower level of Borobudur. No. 1953, Dieng Temple, Dieng Plateau. No. 1954, Temple 1, Gedung Songo group, Semarang. $2, Istana Bogor, 1856. $4, Taman Sari complex, Yogyakarta. No. 1957, Landscape near Mt. Sumbing, Central Java. No. 1958, King Adityawarman's Palace, Batusangar.

Paintings: No. 1959a, Female Coolies, by Djoko Pekik. b, Family Outing, by Sudjana Kerton. c, My Family, by Pekik. d, Javanese Dancers, by Arthur Melville. e, Leisure Time, by Kerton. f, In the Garden of Eden, by Agus Djaja.

No. 1960a, Tayubon, by Pekik. b, Three Dancers, by Nyoman Gunarsa. c, Nursing Neighbor's Baby, by Hendra Gunawan. d, Imagining within a Dialogue, by Sagito. e, Three Balinese Mask Dancers, by Anton H. f, Three Prostitutes, by Gunawan.

Masks: No. 1961a, Hanuman. b, Subali/Sugnwa. c, Kumbakarna. d, Sangut. e, Jatayu. f, Rawana.

No. 1962, Relief of Sudamala story, Mt. Lawu. No. 1963, Plaque, 9th Cent., Banyumas, Central Java. No. 1964, Panel from Ramayana reliefs, vert.

1993, Aug. 16 Litho. *Perf. 14x13½*

1947	A270	5c multicolored	15	15
1948	A270	10c multicolored	15	15
1949	A270	20c multicolored	15	15
1950	A270	45c multicolored	35	35
1951	A270	55c multicolored	42	42
1952	A270	75c multicolored	55	55
1953	A270	$1 multicolored	75	75
1954	A270	$1 multicolored	75	75
1955	A270	$2 multicolored	1.50	1.50
1956	A270	$4 multicolored	3.00	3.00
1957	A270	$5 multicolored	3.75	3.75
1958	A270	$5 multicolored	3.75	3.75
		Nos. 1947-1958 (12)	15.27	15.27

Minature Sheets

1959	A270	$1.50 Sheet of 6, #a.-f.	6.75	6.75
1960	A270	$1.50 Sheet of 6, #a.-f.	6.75	6.75
1961	A270	$1.50 Sheet of 6, #a.-f.	6.75	6.75

Souvenir Sheets

1962	A270	$6 multicolored	4.50	4.50
1963	A270	$6 multicolored	4.50	4.50

Perf. 13½x14

1964	A270	$6 multicolored	4.50	4.50

Reggie Jackson, Selection to Baseball Hall of Fame — A271

1993, Oct. 4 *Perf. 14*

1965 A271 $2 multicolored		1.50	1.50

Christmas A272

Details or entire woodcut, The Adoration of the Magi, by Durer: 10c, 35c, 40c, $5.

Details or entire paintings by Rubens: 50c, Holy Family with Saint Francis. 55c, 65c, Adoration of the Shepherds. $1, Holy Family.

No. 1974, The Adoration of the Magi, by Durer, horiz. No. 1975, Holy Family with St. Elizabeth & St. John, by Rubens.

Perf. 13½x14, 14x13½

1993, Nov. 18

1966-1973 A272 Set of 8	7.00	7.00

Souvenir Sheets

1974-1975 A272 $6 each	4.50	4.50

Miniature Sheet

Legends of Country Music A273

Various portraits of: a, f, l, Roy Acuff. b, g, j, Patsy Cline. c, h, i, Jim Reeves. d, e, k, Hank Williams, Sr.

1994, Jan. 17 Litho. *Perf. 13½x14*

1976 A273 $1 Sheet of 12, #a.-l.	9.00	9.00

Mickey's Portrait Gallery A274

Mickey Mouse as: 5c, Aviator. 10c, Foreign Legionnaire. 15c, Frontiersman. 20c, Best Pals, Mickey, Goofy, Donald. 35c, Horace, Clarabelle. 50c, Minnie, Frankie, Figuro. 75c, Donald, Pluto today. 80c, Party boy Mickey. 85c, Best Friends, Minnie, Daisy. 95c, Mickey's Girl, Minnie. $1, Cool forties Mickey. $1.50, Mickey, "Howdy!", 1950. $2, Totally Mickey. $3, Minnie, Mickey. $4, Congratulations Mickey, birthday cake. $5, Uncle Sam.

No. 1993, Donald Duck, early photo of Mickey, horiz. No. 1994, Minnie disco dancing, horiz. No. 1995, Mickey photographing nephews, horiz. No. 1996, Pluto, Mickey looking at wall of photos.

1994, May 5 Litho. *Perf. 13½x14*

1977 A274	5c	multicolored	15	15
1978 A274	10c	multicolored	15	15
1979 A274	15c	multicolored	15	15
1980 A274	20c	multicolored	15	15
1981 A274	35c	multicolored	25	25
1982 A274	50c	multicolored	38	38
1983 A274	75c	multicolored	55	55
1984 A274	80c	multicolored	60	60
1985 A274	85c	multicolored	65	65
1986 A274	95c	multicolored	70	70
1987 A274	$1	multicolored	75	75
1988 A274	$1.50	multicolored	1.10	1.10
1989 A274	$2	multicolored	1.50	1.50
1990 A274	$3	multicolored	2.25	2.25
1991 A274	$4	multicolored	3.00	3.00
1992 A274	$5	multicolored	3.75	3.75
		Nos. 1977-1992 (16)	16.08	16.08

Souvenir Sheets

Perf. 14x13½

1993 A274	$6	multicolored	4.50	4.50
1994 A274	$6	multicolored	4.50	4.50
1995 A274	$6	multicolored	4.50	4.50
1996 A274	$6	multicolored	4.50	4.50

Breadfruit A275

Intl. Year of the Family A276

1994, Jan. Litho. *Perf. 13½x14*

1997 A275	10c	Planting	15	15
1998 A275	45c	Captain Bligh, plant	35	35
1999 A275	65c	Fruit sliced	50	50
2000 A275	$5	Fruit on branch	3.75	3.75

1994, Jan. *Perf. 14x13½, 13½x14*

2001 A276	10c	Outing	15	15
2002 A276	50c	Praying in church	38	38
2003 A276	65c	Working in garden	50	50
2004 A276	75c	Jogging	55	55
2005 A276	$1	Portrait	75	75
2006 A276	$2	Running on beach	1.50	1.50
		Nos. 2001-2006 (6)	3.83	3.83

Nos. 2001-2004, 2006 are horiz.

Library Service, Cent. A277

1994, Jan. *Perf. 14x13½*

2007 A277	5c	Mobile library	15	15
2008 A277	10c	Old public library	15	15
2009 A277	$1	Family education	75	75
2010 A277	$1	Younger, older men	75	75

Barbra Streisand, 1993 MGM Grand Garden Concert — A278

1994, Jan.

2011 A278 $2 multicolored	1.50	1.50

Issued in sheets of 9.

A279

A280

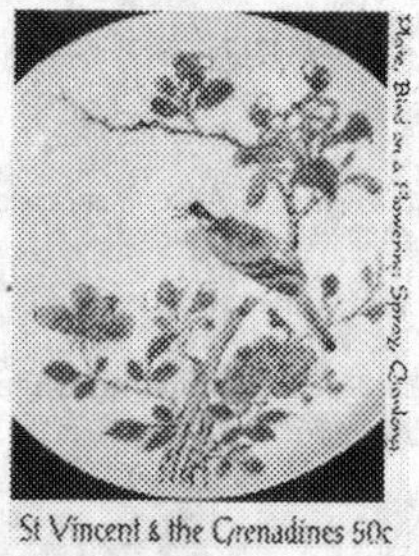

Hong Kong '94 — A281

Hong Kong '94 — A282

Stamps, 19th cent. painting of Hong Kong Harbor: No. 2012, Hong Kong #626, ship under sail. No. 2013, Ship at anchor, #1548.

Porcelain ware, Qing Dynasty: No. 2014a, Bowl with bamboo & sparrows. b, Bowl with flowers of four seasons. c, Bowl with lotus pool & dragon. d, Bowl with landscape. e, Shar-Pei puppies in bowl (not antiquity). f, Covered bowl with dragon & pearls.

Chinese dragon boat races: No. 2015a, Dragon boats. b, Tapestry of dragon races. c, Dragon race. d, Dragon boats, diff. e, Chinese crested dog. f, Dragon boats, 4 banners above boats.

Chinese junks: No. 2016a, Junk, Hong Kong Island. b, Junk with white sails in harbor. c, Junk with inscription on stern, Hong Kong Island. d, Junk KLN B/G. e, Chow dog, junk. f, Junk with red, white sails, Hong Kong Island.

Chinese seed stitch purses: No. 2017a, Vases, fruit on pink purse. b, Peonies, butterflies. c, Vase, fruit on dark blue purse. d, Vases, fruit on light blue purse. e, Fu-dog. f, Flowers.

Chineses pottery: No. 2018a, Plate, bird on flowering spray, Qianlong. b, Large dish, Kangxi. c, Egshell plate, cocks on rocky ground, Yongzheng. d, Gladen dish decorated with Qilin curicorn, Yuan. e, Porcelain pug dog. f, Dish with Dutch ship, Uryburg, Qianlong.

Ceramic figures, Qing Dynasty, vert: No. 2018h, Waterdropper. i, Two women playing chess. j, Liu-Hai. k, Laughing twins. l, Seated hound. m, Louhan (Ma Ming).

No. 2019: Dr. Sun Yat-sen. No. 2020: Chiang Kai-shek.

Dinosaurs: No. 2021a, Triceratops. b, Unidentified, vert. c, Apatosaurus (d). d, Stegosaurus, vert.

1994, Feb. 18 *Perf. 14*

2012	A279	40c multicolored	30	30
2013	A279	40c multicolored	30	30
a.		Pair, #2012-2013	60	60

Miniature Sheets

2014	A280	40c Sheet of 6, #a.-f.	1.90	1.90
2015	A280	40c Sheet of 6, #a.-f.	1.90	1.90
2016	A280	45c Sheet of 6, #a.-f.	2.00	2.00
2017	A280	45c Sheet of 6, #a.-f.	2.00	2.00
2018	A281	50c Sheet of 6, #a.-f.	2.25	2.25

Perf. 13

2018G	A280	50c Sheet of 6, #h.-m.	2.25	2.25

Souvenir Sheets

2019	A281	$2 multicolored	1.50	1.50
2020	A281	$2 multicolored	1.50	1.50
2021	A282	$1.50 Sheet of 4, #a.-d.	4.50	4.50

Nos. 2012-2013 issued in sheets of 5 pairs. No. 2013a is a continuous design.

Portions of the design on No. 2021 have been applied by a thermographic process producing a shiny, raised effect.

New Year 1994 (Year of the Dog) (#2014e, 2015e, 2016e, 2017e, 2018e, 2018 l). Hong Kong '94 (#2018G, 2021).

Miniature Sheet

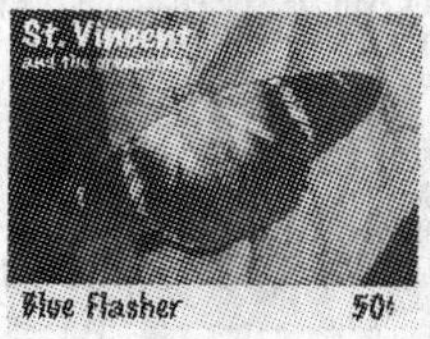

Hong Kong '94 — A283

Butterflies: a, Blue flasher. b, Tiger swallowtail. c, Lustrous copper. d, Tailed copper. e, Blue copper. f, Ruddy copper. g, Viceroy. h, California sister. i, Mourning cloak. j, Red passion flower. k, Small flambeau. l, Blue wave. m, Chiricahua metalmark. n, Monarch. o, Anise swallowtail. p, Buckeye.

1994, Feb. 18 Litho. *Perf. 14½*

2022 A283 50c Sheet of 16, #a.-p.	6.00	6.00

A284

A285

Players: No. 2023, Causio. No. 2024, Tardelli. No. 2025, Rossi. No. 2026, Bettega. No. 2027, Platini, Baggio. No. 2028, Cabrini. No. 2029, Scirea. No. 2030, Furino. No. 2031, Kohler. No. 2032, Zoff. No. 2033, Gentile.

$6, Three European Cups won by team, horiz.

1994, Mar. 22 Litho. *Perf. 14*

2023-2033 A284 $1 Set of 11	8.25	8.25

Souvenir Sheet

2034 A284 $6 multicolored	4.50	4.50

Juventus football (soccer) club of Turin.

1994, Apr. 6 Litho. *Perf. 14*

Orchids: 10c, Epidendrum ibaguense. 25c, Ionopsis utricularioides. 50c, Brassavola cucullata. 65c, Enclyclia cochleata. $1, Liparis nervosa. $2, Vanilla phaeantha. $4, Elleanthus cephalotus. $5, Isochilus linearis.

No. 2043, Rodriguezia lanceolata. No. 2044, Eulophia alta.

2035-2042 A285 Set of 8	10.00	10.00

Souvenir Sheets

2043-2044 A285 $6 each	4.50	4.50

A286

Dinosaurs — A287

Designs: No. 2045a, Protoavis (e). b, Pteranodon. c, Quetzalcoatlus (b). d, Lesothosaurus (a, c, e-h). e, Hetrodontosaurus. f, Archaeopteryx (b, e). g, Cearadactylus (f). h, Anchisaurus.

No. 2046a, Dimorphodon (e). b, Camarasaurus (e, f). c, Spinosaurus (b). d, Allosaurus (a-c, e-h). e, Rhamphorhynchus (a). f, Pteranodon (b). g, Eudimorphodon (c). h, Ornithomimus.

No. 2047a, Dimorphodon (b). b, Pterodactylus (a). c, Rhamphorhynchus (b). d, Pteranodon. e, Gallimimus. f, Setgosaurus. g, Acanthopholis. h, Trachodon (g). i, Thecodonti (j). j, Ankylosaurus (i). k, Compsognathus. l, Protoceratops.

No. 2048a, Hesperonis. b, Mesosaurus. c, Plesiosaurus. d, Squalicorax (a). e, Tylosaurus (d, g). f, Plesiosoar. g, Stenopterygius ichthyosaurus (j). h, Stenosaurus (f). i, Eurhinosaurus longirostris (e, f, h, l). j, Cryptocleidus oxoniensis. k, Caturus (h, i, j, l). l, Protostega (k).

No. 2049a, Quetzalcoatlus. b, Diplodocus (a). c, Spinosaurus (f, g). d, Apatosaurus (c). e, Ornitholestes. f, Lesothosaurus (e). g, Trachodon. h, Protoavis. i, Oviraptor. j, Coelophysis (i). k, Ornitholestes (j). l, Archaeopteryx.

No. 2050, horiz: a, Albertosaurus. b, Chasmosaurus (c). c, Brachiosaurus. d, Coelophysis (e). e, Deinonychus (d). f, Anatosaurus. g, Iguanodon. h, Baryonyx. i, Steneosaurus. j, Nanotyrannus. k, Camptosaurus (j). l, Camarasaurus.

No. 2051, Tyrannosaurus rex. No. 2052: Triceratops, horiz. No. 2053, Pteranodon, diplodocus carnegii, horiz. No. 2054, Styracosaurus.

1994, Apr. 20 Litho. *Perf. 14*

2045 A286 75c Sheet of 8, #a.-h.	4.50	4.50
2046 A286 75c Sheet of 8, #a.-h.	4.50	4.50

Miniature Sheets of 12

2047-2050 A287 75c #a.-l, each	6.75	6.75

Souvenir Sheets

2051 A286 $6 multi	4.50	4.50
2052-2054 A287 $6 each	4.50	4.50

No. 2048 is horiz.

Entertainers Type of 1991
Miniature Sheet

Various portraits of Marilyn Monroe.

1994, May 16 *Perf. 13½*

2055 A206 $1 Sheet of 9, #a.-i.	6.75	6.75

1994 World Cup Soccer Championships, US — A288

Team photos: No. 2056, Colombia. No. 2057, Romania. No. 2058, Switzerland. No. 2059, US. No. 2060, Brazil. No. 2061, Cameroon. No. 2062, Russia. No. 2063, Sweden. No. 2064, Bolivia. No. 2065, Germany. No. 2066, South Korea. No. 2067, Spain. No. 2068, Argentina. No. 2069, Bulgaria. No. 2070, Greece. No. 2071, Nigeria. No. 2072, Ireland. No. 2073, Italy. No. 2074, Mexico. No. 2075, Norway. No. 2076, Belgium. No. 2077, Holland. No. 2078, Morocco. No. 2079, Saudi Arabia.

1994 *Perf. 13½*

2056-2079 A288 50c Set of 24	9.00	9.00

Miniature Sheets of 9

First Manned Moon Landing, 25th Anniv. A289

Famous men, aviation & space scenes: No. 2080a, Fred L. Whipple, Halley's Comet. b, Robert G. Gilruth, Gemini 12. c, George E. Mueller, Ed White walking in space during Gemini 4. d, Charles A. Berry, Johnsville Centrifuge. e, Christopher C. Kraft, Jr., Apollo 4 re-entry. f, James A. Van Allen, Explorer I, Van Allen Radiation Belts. g, Robert H. Goddard, Goddard Liquid Fuel Rocket, 1926. h, James E. Webb, Spirit of '76 flight. i, Rocco A. Patrone, Apollo 8 coming home.

No. 2081: a, Walter R. Dornberger, missile launch, 1942. b, Alexander Lippisch, Wolfgang Spate's ME-163B. c, Kurt H. Debus, A4b Launch, 1945. d, Hermann Oberth, Oberth's Spaceship, 1923. e, Hanna Reitsch, Reichenberg (type 2) Piloted Bomb. f, Ernst Stuhlinger, Explorer I, 2nd stage ignition. g, Werner von Braun, Rocket Powered He112. h, Arthur Rudolph, Rudolph Rocket Motor, 1934. i, Willy Ley, Rocket Airplane, Greenwood Lake NY.

No. 2082, Hogler N. Toftoy. No. 2083, Eberhardt Rees.

1994, July 12 *Perf. 14*

2080-2081 A289 $1 #a.-i, each	6.75	6.75

Souvenir Sheets

2082-2083 A289 $6 each	4.50	4.50

Nos. 2082-2083 each contain one 50x38mm stamp.

D-Day, 50th Anniv. A290

Designs: 40c, Supply armada. $5, Beached cargo ship unloads supplies.

$6, Liberty ship.

1994, July 19 Litho. *Perf. 14*

2084 A290 40c multicolored	30	30
2085 A290 $5 multicolored	3.75	3.75

Souvenir Sheet

2086 A290 $6 multicolored	4.50	4.50

New Year 1994 (Year of the Dog) — A291

Designs: 10c, Yorkshire terrier. 25c, Yorkshire terrier, diff. 50c, Golden retriever. 65c, Bernese mountain dog. $1, Vorstehhund. $2, Tibetan terrier. $4, West highland terrier. $5, Shih tzu.

No. 2095a, Pomeranian. b, English springer spaniel. c, Bearded collie. d, Irish wolfhound. e, Pekingese. f, Irish setter. g, Old English sheepdog. h, Basset hound. i, Cavalier King Charles spaniel. j, Kleiner munsterlander. k, Shetland sheepdog. l, Dachshund.

No. 2093, Afghan hound. No. 2094, German shepherd.

1994, July 21

2087-2094 A291 Set of 8	10.00	10.00

Miniature Sheet of 12

2095 A291 50c #a.-l.	4.50	4.50

Souvenir Sheets

2096-2097 A291 $6 each	4.50	4.50

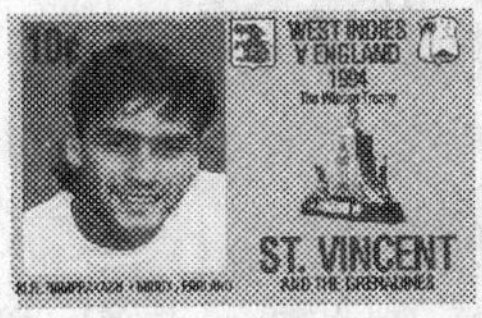

English Touring Cricket, Cent. A292

Designs: 10c, M.R. Ramprakash, England. 30c, P.V. Simmons, W. Indies. $2, Sir. G. St. A. Sobers, W. Indies, vert.

$3, Firsh English team, 1895.

1994, July 25

2098-2100 A292 Set of 3	1.90	1.90

Souvenir Sheet

2101 A293 $3 multicolored	2.25	2.25

A293

Intl. Olympic Committee, Cent. — A294

Designs: 45c, Peter Frennel, German Democratic Republic, 20k walk, 1972. 50c, Kijung Son, Japan, marathon, 1936. 75c, Jesse Owens, US, 100-, 200-meters, 1936. $1, Greg Louganis, US, diving, 1984, 1988.

$6, Katja Seizinger, Germany, Picabo Street, US, Isolde Kastner, Italy, women's downhill, 1994.

1994, July 25

2102-2105 A293 Set of 4	2.00	2.00

Souvenir Sheet

2106 A294 $6 multicolored	4.50	4.50

PHILAKOREA '94
A295 A296

Designs: 10c, Oryon Waterfall. 45c, Outside P'yongyang Indoor Sports Stadium, horiz. 65c, Pombong, Ch'onhwadae. 75c, Uisangdae, Naksansa. $1, Buddha of the Sokkuram Grotto, Kyangju, horiz. $2, Moksogwon, horiz.

Nos. 2113a-2113h, Various letter pictures, eight panel screen, 18th cent. Choson Dynasty.

Letter pictures, 19th cent. Choson Dynasty: No. 2114a, Fish. No. 2114b, Birds. Nos. 2114c-2114d, 2114h, Various bookshelf pictures. Nos. 2114e-2114g, Various designs from six-panel screen.

No. 2115, Hunting scene, embroidery on silk, Choson Dynasty, horiz. No. 2116, Chongdong Mirukbul.

1994, July 25 *Perf. 14*

2107-2112 A295 Set of 6	3.75	3.75

Miniature Sheets of 8
Perf. 13½

2113-2114 A296 50c #a.-h.	3.00	3.00

Souvenir Sheets
Perf. 14

2115-2116 A295 $4 each	3.00	3.00

Miniature Sheet of 9

Star Trek, The Next Generation, 7th Anniv. — A297

Designs: No. 2117a, Capt. Picard. b, Cmdr. Riker. c, Lt. Cmdr. Data. d, Lt. Worf. e, Cast members. f, Dr. Crusher. g, Lt. Yar, Lt. Worf. h, Q. i, Counselor Troi.

$10, Cast members, horiz.

1994 Litho. *Perf. 14x13½*

2117 A297 $2 #a.-i.	14.00	14.00

Souvenir Sheet
Perf. 14x14½

2118 A297 $10 multicolored	5.75	5.75

No. 2117e exists in sheets of 9. No. 2118 contains one 60x40mm stamp.

Intl. Year of the Family A298

1994 *Perf. 14*

2119 A298 75c multicolored	55	55

Order of the Caribbean Community — A299

First award recipients: $1, Sir Shridath Ramphal, statesman, Guyana, vert. $2, Derek Walcott, writer, St. Lucia, vert. $5, William Demas, economist, Trinidad and Tobago.

1994, Sept. 1

2120-2122 A299 Set of 3	6.00	6.00

Miniature Sheets of 6 or 12

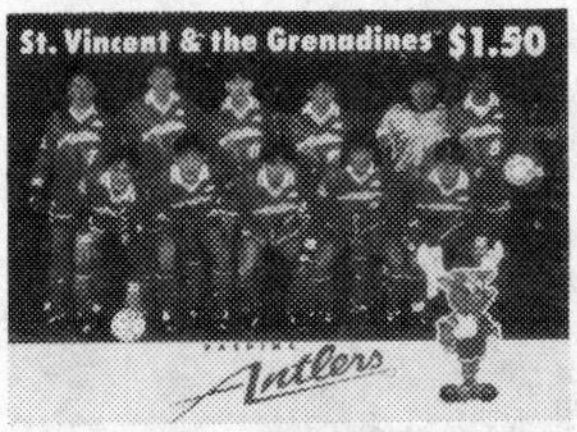

Japanese Soccer — A300

Team photos: No. 2123a, Kahsima Antlers. b, JEF United. c, Red Diamonds. d, Verdy Yomiuri. e, Nissan FC Yokohama Marinos. f, AS Flugels. g, Bellmare. h, Shimizu S-pulse. i, Jubilo Iwata. j, Nogoya Grampus Eight. k, Panasonic Gamba Osaka. l, Sanfrecce Hiroshima FC.

Jubilo Iwata, action scenes: Nos. 2124a, c-d, 55c. b, e, $1.50. f, $3, Team picture.

Red Diamonds, action scenes: Nos. 2125a, c-d, 55c. b, e, $1.50. f, $3, Team pictue.

Nissan FC Yokohama Marinos, action scenes: Nos. 2126a, c-d, 55c. b, e, $1.50. f, $3, Team picture.

Verdy Yomiuri, action scenes: Nos. 2127a, c-d, 55c. b, e, $1.50. f, $3, Team picture.

Nagoya Grampus eight, action scenes: Nos. 2128a, c-d, 55c. b, e, $1.50. f, $3, Team picture.

Kashima Antlers, action scenes: Nos. 2129a, c-d, 55c. b, e, $1.50. f, $3, Team picture.

JEF United, action scenes: Nos. 2130a, c-d, 55c. b, e, $1.50. f, $3, Team picture.

AS Flugels, action scenes: Nos. 2131a, c-d, 55c. b, e, $1.50. f, $3, Team picture.

Bellmare, action scenes: Noa. 2132a, c-d, 55c. b, e, $1.50. f, $3, Team picture.

Sanfrecce Hiroshima FC, action scenes: Nos. 2133a, c-d, 55c. b, e, $1.50. f, $3, Team picture.

Shimizu S-pulse, action scenes: Nos. 2134a, c-d, 55c. b, e, $1.50. f, $3, Team picture.

Panasonic Gamba Isajam, action scenes: Nos. 2135a, c-d, 55c. b, e, $1.50. f, $3, Team picture.

League All-Stars: No. 2136a, $1.50, League emblem. b, 55c, Shigetatsu Matsunaga. c, 55c, Masami Ihara. d, $1.50, Takumi Horiike. e, 55c, Shunzoh Ohno. f, 55c, Luiz Carlos Pereira. g, 55c, Tetsuji Hashiratani. h, 55c, Carlos Alberto Souza Dos Santos. i, $1.50, Rui Ramos. j, 55c, Yasuto Honda. k, 55c, Kazuyoshi Miura. l, $1.50, Ramon Angel Diaz.

1994 *Perf. 14x13½*

2123 A300 #a.-l.	7.75	7.75
2124-2135 A300 #a.-f., each	5.75	5.75

Perf. 13½x14

2136 A300 #a.-l., vert.	7.75	7.75

SEMI-POSTAL STAMPS

Catalogue values for unused stamps in this section are for Never Hinged items.

Map Type of 1977-78 Overprinted: "SOUFRIERE / RELIEF / FUND 1979"

and New Values, "10c+5c" etc.

Litho. and Typo.

1979 Wmk. 373 *Perf. 14½x14*

B1	A76 10c + 5c multi	15	15
B2	A76 50c + 25c multi	35	35
B3	A76 $1 + 50c multi	70	70
B4	A76 $2 + $1 multi	1.40	1.40

The surtax was for victims of the eruption of Mt. Soufrière.

Nos. 604-607 Surcharged: "HURRICANE / RELIEF / 50c"

1980, Aug. 7 Litho. *Perf. 13½*

B5	A90 10c + 50c multi	30	30
B6	A90 60c + 50c multi	52	52
B7	A90 80c + 50c multi	65	65
B8	A90 $2.50 + 50c multi	1.50	1.50

Surtax was for victims of Hurricane Allen.

Nos. 1224-1226 Surcharged "CALIF EARTHQUAKE RELIEF" on 1 or 2 Lines and "+10c"

1989, Nov. 17 Litho. *Perf. 13½x14*

B9	Sheet of 9	4.50	4.50
a.-i.	A174 60c +10c #1224a-1224i	50	50
B10	Sheet of 9	4.50	4.50
a.-i.	A174 60c +10c #1225a-1225i	50	50
B11	Sheet of 9	4.50	4.50
a.-i.	A175 60c +10c #1226a-1226i	50	50

WAR TAX STAMPS

No. 105 Overprinted **WAR STAMP.**

Type I - Words 2 to 2½mm apart.
Type II - Words 1½mm apart.
Type III - Words 3½mm apart.

1916 Wmk. 3 *Perf. 14*

MR1	A17 1p car, type III	1.50	1.50
a.	Double ovpt., type III	175.00	200.00
b.	1p carmine, type I	1.75	1.75
c.	Comma after "STAMP", type I	7.50	10.00
d.	Double overprint, type I	150.00	150.00
e.	1p carmine, type II	80.00	80.00

Overprinted **WAR STAMP**

MR2	A17 1p carmine	25	25

OFFICIAL STAMPS

Catalogue values for unused stamps in this section are for Never Hinged items.

Nos. 627-632 Ovptd. "OFFICIAL"

1982, Nov. Litho. *Perf. 14*

O1	A66 60c Couple, Isabella	30	30
O2	A67 60c Couple	30	30
O3	A66 $2.50 Couple, Alberta	1.25	1.25
O4	A67 $2.50 Couple	1.25	1.25
O5	A66 $4 Couple, Britannia	2.00	2.00
O6	A67 $4 Couple	2.00	2.00
	Nos. O1-O6 (6)	7.10	7.10

ST. VINCENT GRENADINES

LOCATION — Group of islands south of St. Vincent
CAPITAL — None

St. Vincent's portion of the Grenadines includes Bequia, Canouan, Mustique, Union and a number of smaller islands.

Catalogue values for unused stamps in this area are for Never Hinged items.

All stamps are a type of St. Vincent unless otherwise noted or illustrated.

See St. Vincent Nos. 324-329a for six stamps and a souvenir sheet issued in 1971 inscribed "The Grenadines of St. Vincent."

Princess Annes's Wedding Issue
Common Design Type

1973, Nov. 14 Litho. *Perf. 14*

1	CD325 25c green & multi	25	25
2	CD325 $1 orange brn & multi	1.00	1.00

Bird Type of 1970 and St. Vincent Nos. 281a-285a, 287a-289a Overprinted

GRENADINES OF (a) **GRENADINES OF** (b)

1974 Photo. Wmk. 314 *Perf. 14*

3	A36(a)	1c multicolored	15	15
4	A36(a)	2c multicolored	15	15
5	A36(b)	2c multicolored	60	60
6	A36(a)	3c multicolored	15	15
7	A36(b)	3c multicolored	90	90
8	A36(a)	4c multicolored	15	15
9	A36(a)	5c multicolored	15	15
10	A36(a)	6c multicolored	15	15
11	A36(a)	8c multicolored	18	18
12	A36(a)	10c multicolored	20	20
13	A36(a)	12c multicolored	25	25
14	A36(a)	20c multicolored	50	50
15	A36(a)	25c multicolored	55	55
16	A36(a)	50c multicolored	1.10	1.10
17	A36(a)	$1 multicolored	2.25	2.25
18	A36(a)	$2.50 multicolored	4.50	4.50
19	A36(a)	$5 multicolored	12.00	12.00
		Nos. 3-19 (17)	23.93	23.93

Nos. 8-9, 12-13, 17-18 vert.
Issue dates: #5, 7, June 7. Others, Apr. 24.

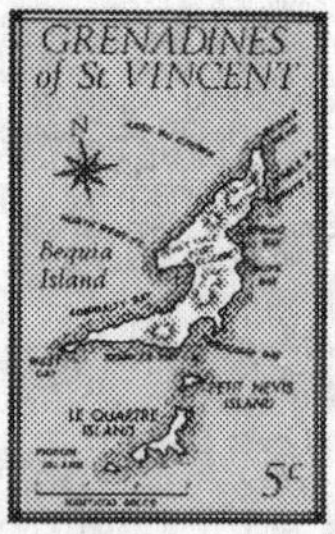

Maps of Islands — G1

Perf. 13x12½

1974, May 9 Litho. Wmk. 314

20	G1 5c Bequia	15	15
21	G1 15c Prune	15	15
22	G1 20c Mayreau	20	20
23	G1 30c Mustique	30	30
24	G1 40c Union	40	40
24A	G1 $1 Canouan	1.00	1.00
	Nos. 20-24A (6)	2.20	2.20

No. 20 has no inscription at bottom. No. 84 is dated "1976."
See Nos. 84-111.

UPU Type of 1974

2c, Arrows circling UPU emblem. 15c, Post horn, globe. 40c, Target over map of islands, hand canceler. $1, Goode's map projection.

1974, July 25 Litho. *Perf. 14½*

25	A56 2c multicolored	15	15
26	A56 15c multicolored	15	15
27	A56 40c multicolored	40	40
28	A56 $1 multicolored	1.00	1.00

Bequia Island G2

Designs: 5c, Boat building. 30c, Careening at Port Elizabeth. 35c, Admiralty Bay. $1, Fishing Boat Race.

1974

29	G2 5c multicolored	16	16
30	G2 30c multicolored	1.00	1.00
31	G2 35c multicolored	1.25	1.25
32	G2 $1 multicolored	3.50	3.50

Shells — G3

Designs: 1c, Atlantic thorny oyster. 2c, Zigzag scallop. 3c, Reticulated helmet. 4c, Music volute. 5c, Amber pen shell. 6c, Angular triton. 8c, Flame helmet. 10c, Caribbean olive. 12c, Common sundial. 15c, Glory of the atlantic cone. 20c, Flame auger. 25c King venus. 35c. Long-spined star-shell. 45c, Speckled tellin. 50c, Rooster tail conch. $1, Green star-shell. $2.50, Incomparable cone. $5, Rough file clam. $10, Measled cowrie.

1974-77 Wmk. 373

33	G3	1c multicolored	15	15
34	G3	2c multicolored	15	15
35	G3	3c multicolored	15	15
36	G3	4c multicolored	15	15
37	G3	5c multicolored	15	15
38	G3	6c multicolored	15	15
39	G3	8c multicolored	15	15
40	G3	10c multicolored	15	15
41	G3	12c multicolored	16	16
42	G3	15c multicolored	20	20
43	G3	20c multicolored	28	28
44	G3	25c multicolored	35	35
45	G3	35c multicolored	50	50
46	G3	45c multicolored	65	65
47	G3	50c multicolored	70	70
48	G3	$1 multicolored	1.40	1.40
49	G3	$2.50 multicolored	3.50	3.50
50	G3	$5 multicolored	7.00	7.00
51	G3	$10 multicolored	14.00	14.00
		Nos. 33-51 (19)	29.94	29.94

Issue dates: Nos. 33-50, Nov. 27, 1974. No. 51, July 12, 1976.
Nos. 36-40, 43, 45, 47-48, exist dated "1976." #40, 42-45, 49-50 exist dated "1977."

Churchill Type

Designs (Churchill as): 5c, Prime Minister. 40c, Lord Warden of the Cinque Ports. 50c, First Lord of the Admiralty. $1, Royal Air Force officer.

1974, Nov. 28

52	A58 5c multicolored	15	15
53	A58 40c multicolored	30	30
54	A58 50c multicolored	35	35
55	A58 $1 multicolored	75	75

Mustique Island G4

1975, Feb. 27 Wmk. 373

56	G4 5c Cotton House	15	15
57	G4 35c Blue Waters, Endeavour	28	28
58	G4 45c Endeavour Bay	35	35
59	G4 $1 Gelliceaux Bay	80	80

Butterflies G5

1975, May 15 *Perf. 14*

60	G5 3c Soldier martinique	15	15
61	G5 5c Silver-spotted flambeau	18	18
62	G5 35c Gold rim	1.25	1.25
63	G5 45c Bright blue, Donkey's eye	1.65	1.65
64	G5 $1 Biscuit	3.50	3.50
	Nos. 60-64 (5)	6.73	6.73

Views of Petit St. Vincent G6

1975, July 24 *Perf. 14½*

65	G6 5c Resort pavilion	15	15
66	G6 35c Harbor	50	50
67	G6 45c Jetty	65	65
68	G6 $1 Sailing in coral lagoon	1.40	1.40

Christmas G7

Island churches: 5c, Ecumenical Church, Mustique. 25c, Catholic Church, Union. 50c, Catholic Church, Bequia. $1, Anglican Church, Bequia.

1975, Nov. 20 Wmk. 314

69	G7 5c multicolored	15	15
70	G7 25c multicolored	20	20
71	G7 50c multicolored	40	40
72	G7 $1 multicolored	85	85

Union Island G8

1976, Feb. 26 Wmk. 373 *Perf. 13½*

73	G8 5c Sunset	15	15
74	G8 35c Customs and post office	35	35
75	G8 45c Anglican Church	45	45
76	G8 $1 Mail boat	1.00	1.00

Staghorn Coral G9

1976, May 13 *Perf. 14½*

77	G9 5c shown	15	15
78	G9 35c Elkhorn coral	50	50
79	G9 45c Pillar coral	60	60
80	G9 $1 Brain coral	1.40	1.40

US Bicentennial Coins — G10

1976, July 15 *Perf. 13½*

81	G10 25c Washington quarter	28	28
82	G10 50c Kennedy half dollar	55	55
83	G10 $1 Eisenhower dollar	1.10	1.10

St. Vincent Grenadines Map Type of 1974
Bequia Island

1976, Sept. 23 Litho. *Perf. 14*

84	G1 5c grn, brt grn & blk	15	15
85	G1 10c multicolored	15	15
a.	Bklt. pane of 3 (2 #84, 85)	18	18
86	G1 35c multicolored	28	28
a.	Bklt. pane of 3 (2 #85, 86)	45	45
87	G1 45c multicolored	35	35
a.	Bklt. pane of 3 (#84, 85, 87)	48	48
b.	Bklt. pane of 3 (2 #86, 87)	90	90
	Set value	75	75

For previous 5c see No. 20.

Canouan Island

1976, Sept. 23

88 G1	5c multicolored	15	15
89 G1	10c multicolored	15	15
a.	Bklt. pane of 3 (2 #88, 89)	18	18
90 G1	35c multicolored	28	28
a.	Bklt. pane of 3 (2 #89, 90)	45	45
91 G1	45c multicolored	35	35
a.	Bklt. pane of 3 (#88-89, 91)	48	48
b.	Bklt. pane of 3 (2 #90, 91)	90	90
	Set value	75	75

Mayreau Island

1976, Sept. 23

92 G1	5c multicolored	15	15
93 G1	10c multicolored	15	15
a.	Bklt. pane of 3 (2 #92, 93)	18	18
94 G1	35c multicolored	28	28
a.	Bklt. pane of 3 (2 #93, 94)	45	45
95 G1	45c multicolored	35	35
a.	Bklt. pane of 3 (#92-93, 95)	48	48
b.	Bklt. pane of 3 (2 #94, 95)	90	90
	Set value	75	75

Mustique Island

1976, Sept. 23

96 G1	5c multicolored	15	15
97 G1	10c multicolored	15	15
a.	Bklt. pane of 3 (2 #96, 97)	18	18
98 G1	35c multicolored	28	28
a.	Bklt. pane of 3 (2 #97, 98)	45	45
99 G1	45c multicolored	35	35
a.	Bklt. pane of 3 (#96-97, 99)	48	48
b.	Bklt. pane of 3 (2 #98, 99)	90	90
	Set value	75	75

Petit St. Vincent

1976, Sept. 23

100 G1	5c multicolored	15	15
101 G1	10c multicolored	15	15
a.	Bklt. pane of 3 (2 #100, 101)	18	18
102 G1	35c multicolored	28	28
a.	Bklt. pane of 3 (2 #101, 102)	45	45
103 G1	45c multicolored	35	35
a.	Bklt. pane of 3 (#100-101, 103)	48	48
b.	Bklt. pane of 3 (2 #102, 103)	90	90
	Set value	75	75

Prune Island

1976, Sept. 23

104 G1	5c multicolored	15	15
105 G1	10c multicolored	15	15
a.	Bklt. pane of 3 (2 #104, 105)	18	18
106 G1	35c multicolored	28	28
a.	Bklt. pane of 3 (2 #105, 106)	45	45
107 G1	45c multicolored	35	35
a.	Bklt. pane of 3 (#104-105, 107)	48	48
b.	Bklt. pane of 3 (2 #106, 107)	90	90
	Set value	75	75

Union Island

1976, Sept. 23

108 G1	5c multicolored	15	15
109 G1	10c multicolored	15	15
a.	Bklt. pane of 3 (2 #108, 109)	18	18
110 G1	35c multicolored	28	28
a.	Bklt. pane of 3 (2 #109, 110)	45	45
111 G1	45c multicolored	35	35
a.	Bklt. pane of 3 (#108-109, 111)	48	48
b.	Bklt. pane of 3 (2 #110, 111)	90	90
	Set value	75	75

Mayreau Island G11

Designs: 5c, Station Hill school, post office. 35c, Church at Old Wall. 45c, Cruiser at anchor, La Souciere. $1, Saline Bay.

1976, Dec. 2 *Perf. 14½*

112 G11	5c multicolored	15	15
113 G11	35c multicolored	25	25
114 G11	45c multicolored	35	35
115 G11	$1 multicolored	75	75

Queen Elizabeth II, Silver Jubilee G12

Coins: 25c, Coronation Crown. 50c, Silver Wedding Crown. $1, Silver Jubilee Crown.

1977, Mar. 3

116 G12	25c multicolored	30	30
117 G12	50c multicolored	65	65
118 G12	$1 multicolored	1.25	1.25

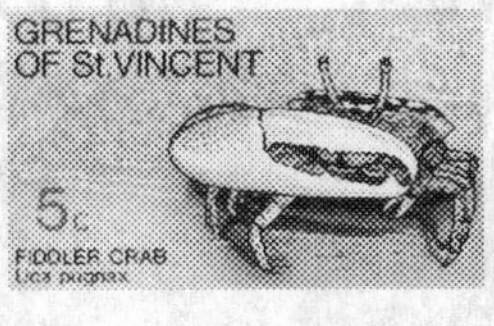

Fiddler Crab G13

1977, May 19

119 G13	5c shown	15	15
120 G13	35c Ghost crab	35	35
121 G13	50c Blue crab	50	50
122 G13	$1.25 Spiny lobster	1.25	1.25

Prune Island G14

1977, Aug. 25

123 G14	5c Snorkel diving	15	15
124 G14	35c Palm Island Resort	28	28
125 G14	45c Casuarina Beach	35	35
126 G14	$1 Palm Island Beach Club	80	80

Map Type of 1977 Overprinted

SILVER JUBILEE 1952-1977

ROYAL VISIT MUSTIQUE

30TH OCTOBER, 1977

Perf. 14½x14

1977, Oct. 31 **Wmk. 314**

127 A76	40c multicolored (R)	28	28
128 A76	$2 multicolored (B)	1.40	1.40

Canouan Island G15

1977, Dec. 8 **Wmk. 373** *Perf. 14½*

129 G15	5c Clinic, Charlestown	15	15
130 G15	35c Town jetty, Charlestown	32	32
131 G15	45c Mailboat, Charlestown	40	40
132 G15	$1 Grand Bay	90	90

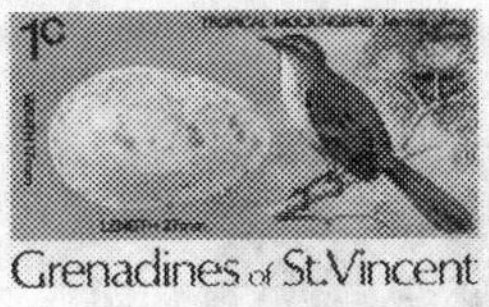

Birds and Eggs G16

1978, May 11 *Perf. 13x12*

133 G16	1c Tropical Mockingbird	15	15
134 G16	2c Mangrove cuckoo	15	15
135 G16	3c Osprey	15	15
136 G16	4c Smooth bellied ani	15	15
137 G16	5c House wren	15	15
138 G16	6c Bananaquit	15	15
139 G16	8c Carib grackle	15	15
140 G16	10c Yellow bellied elaenia	15	15
141 G16	12c Collared plover	15	15
142 G16	15c Cattle egret	15	15
143 G16	20c Red footed booby	15	15
144 G16	25c Red-billed tropic bird	18	18
145 G16	40c Royal tern	28	28
146 G16	50c Rusty tailed flycatcher	35	35
147 G16	80c Purple gallinule	55	55
148 G16	$1 Broad winged hawk	70	70
149 G16	$2 Common ground dove	1.40	1.40
150 G16	$3 Laughing gull	2.00	2.00
151 G16	$5 Brown noddy	3.50	3.50
152 G16	$10 Grey kingbird	7.25	7.25
	Nos. 133-152 (20)	17.86	17.86

Nos. 139, 143, 149 exist imprinted "1979." Nos. 137-138, 140, 142, 144 exist imprinted "1980."

Nos. 147-148 imprinted "1979" are from No. 175a. Nos. 145-146, 150 imprinted "1980" are from No. 189a.

For surcharge see No. 266.

Elizabeth II Coronation Anniv. Type

Cathedrals.

1978, June 2 *Perf. 13½*

153 A78	5c Worcester	15	15
154 A78	40c Coventry	30	30
155 A78	$1 Winchester	75	75
156 A78	$3 Chester	2.25	2.25
a.	Souv. sheet of 4, #153-156, perf. 14	3.45	3.45

Turtles G17

1978, July 20 *Perf. 14*

157 G17	5c Green turtle	15	15
158 G17	40c Hawksbill turtle	30	30
159 G17	50c Leatherback turtle	40	40
160 G17	$1.25 Loggerhead turtle	1.00	1.00

Christmas G18

Christmas scenes and verses from the carol "We Three Kings of Orient Are".

1978, Nov. 2

161 G18	5c Three kings following star	15	15
162 G18	10c Gold	15	15
163 G18	25c Frankincense	15	15
164 G18	50c Myrrh	30	30
165 G18	$2 With infant Jesus	1.25	1.25
a.	Souvenir sheet of 5 + label, #161-165	2.25	2.25
	Nos. 161-165 (5)	2.00	2.00

Sailing Yachts — G19

1979

166 G19	5c multicolored	15	15
167 G19	40c multi, diff.	35	35
168 G19	50c multi, diff.	45	45
169 G19	$2 multi, diff.	1.90	1.90

Wildlife Type of 1980

1979, Mar. 8 *Perf. 14½*

170 A91	20c Green iguana	15	15
171 A91	40c Manicou	25	25
172 A91	$2 Red-legged tortoise	1.40	1.40

Sir Rowland Hill Type of 1979

Designs: 80c, Sir Rowland Hill. $1, Great Britain Types A1 and A5 with "A10" (Kingstown, St. Vincent) cancel. $2, St. Vincent #41 & 43 with Bequia cancel.

1979, May 21 *Perf. 13x12*

173 A83	80c multicolored	48	48
174 A83	$1 multicolored	75	75
175 A83	$2 multicolored	1.25	1.25
a.	Souvenir sheet of 6, #173-175, 147-149	5.25	5.25

IYC Type of 1979

Children and IYC emblem: 6c, Boy. 40c, Girl. $1, Boy, diff. $3, Girl and boy.

1979, Oct. 24 *Perf. 14x13½*

176 A82	6c multicolored	15	15
177 A82	40c multicolored	22	22
178 A82	$1 multitolored	1.10	1.10
179 A82	$3 multicolored	1.75	1.75

Independence Type of 1979

Designs: 5c, National flag, Ixora salici-folia. 40c, House of Assembly, Ixora odorata. $1, Prime Minister R. Milton Cato, Ixora jayanica.

1979, Oct. 27 *Perf. 12½x12*

180 A85	5c multicolored	15	15
181 A85	40c multicolored	30	30
182 A85	$1 multicolored	80	80

Printed se-tenant with label inscribed "Independence of St. Vincent and the Grenadines."

False Killer Whale G20

1979, Jan. 25 *Perf. 14*

183 G20	10c shown	15	15
184 G20	50c Spinner dolphin	45	45
185 G20	90c Bottle nosed dolphin	75	75
186 G20	$2 Blackfish	1.75	1.75

London '80 Type

1980, Apr. 24 *Perf. 13x12*

187 A88	40c Queen Elizabeth II	25	25
188 A88	50c St. Vincent #227	32	32
189 A88	$3 #1-2	1.90	1.90
a.	Souvenir sheet of 6, #187-189, 145-146, 150	5.25	5.25

Olympics Type of 1980

1980, Aug. 7 *Perf. 13½*

190 A90	25c Running	18	18
191 A90	50c Sailing	35	35
192 A90	$1 Long jump	70	70
193 A90	$2 Swimming	1.40	1.40

Christmas — G21

Scenes and verse from the carol "De Borning Day."

1980, Nov. 13 *Perf. 14*

194 G21	5c multicolored	15	15
195 G21	50c multicolored	40	40
196 G21	60c multicolored	50	50
197 G21	$1 multicolored	80	80
198 G21	$2 multicolored	1.65	1.65
a.	Souvenir sheet of 5 + label, #194-198	3.00	3.00

Bequia Island G22

1980, Nov. 13 *Perf. 14½*

199 G22	50c P.O., Port Elizabeth	32	32
200 G22	60c Moonhole	40	40
201 G22	$1.50 Fishing boats, Admiralty Bay	1.00	1.00
202 G22	$2 Friendship Rose at jetty	1.25	1.25

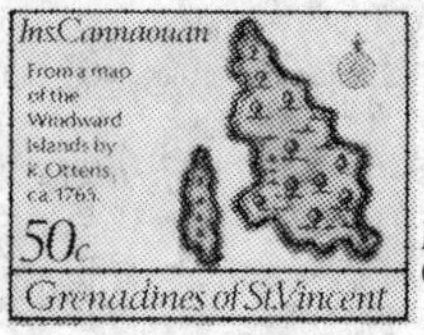

Map by R. Ottens, c. 1765 — G23

Maps: Nos. 204, 206 by J. Parsons, 1861. No. 208, by T. Jefferys, 1763.

1981, Apr. 2 *Perf. 14*

203 G23 50c Ins. Cannaouan 30 30
204 G23 50c Cannouan Island 30 30
a. Pair, #203-204 60 60
205 G23 60c Ins. Moustiques 40 40
206 G23 60c Mustique Island 40 40
a. Pair, #205-206 80 80
207 G23 $2 Ins. Bequia 1.25 1.25
208 G23 $2 Bequia Island 1.25 1.25
a. Pair, #207-208 2.50 2.50

Royal Wedding Types

1981, July 17 **Wmk. 380**

209 A94a 50c Couple, the Mary 38 38
a. Booklet pane of 4, perf. 12 1.50 1.50
210 A94b 50c Couple 38 38
211 A94a $3 Couple, the Alexandra 2.25 2.25
212 A94b $3 like #210 2.25 2.25
a. Booklet pane of 2, perf. 12 5.00 5.00
213 A94a $3.50 Couple, the Britannia 2.75 2.75
214 A94b $3.50 like #210 2.75 2.75
Nos. 209-214 (6) 10.76 10.76

Each denomination issued in sheets of 7 (6 type A94a, 1 type A94b).
For surcharges see Nos. 507-508.

Souvenir Sheet

1981 *Perf. 12*

215 A94b $5 like #210 3.50 3.50

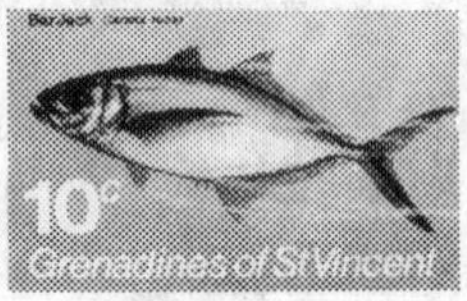

Bar Jack G25

1981, Oct. 9 **Wmk. 373** *Perf. 14*

218 G25 10c shown 15 15
219 G25 50c Tarpon 40 40
220 G25 60c Cobia 50 50
221 G25 $2 Blue marlin 1.75 1.75

Ships G26

1982, Jan. 28 *Perf. 14x13½*

222 G26 1c Experiment 15 15
223 G26 3c Lady Nelson 15 15
224 G26 5c Daisy 15 15
225 G26 6c Carib canoe 15 15
226 G26 10c Hairoun Star 15 15
227 G26 15c Jupiter 15 15
228 G26 20c Christina 15 15
229 G26 25c Orinoco 16 16
230 G26 30c Lively 20 20
231 G26 50c Alabama 30 30
232 G26 60c Denmark 40 40
233 G26 75c Santa Maria 50 50
234 G26 $1 Baffin 70 70
235 G26 $2 QE 2 1.40 1.40
236 G26 $3 Britannia 2.00 2.00
237 G26 $5 Geestar 3.50 3.50
238 G26 $10 Grenadines Star 6.75 6.75
Nos. 222-238 (17) 16.96 16.96

For overprint see No. 509.

G27

G29

1982, Apr. 5 *Perf. 14*

239 G27 10c Prickly pear fruit 15 15
240 G27 50c Flower buds 40 40
241 G27 $1 Flower 75 75
242 G27 $2 Cactus 1.65 1.65

Princess Diana Type of Kiribati

1982, July 1 **Wmk. 380** *Perf. 14*

243 A99a 50c Anne Neville 35 35
244 A99a 60c Arms of Anne Neville 40 40
245 A99a $6 Diana, Princess of Wales 4.25 4.25

For overprints see Nos. 248-262.

1982, July 1 **Wmk. 373** *Perf. 14½*

246 G29 $1.50 Old, new uniforms 1.00 1.00
247 G29 $2.50 Lord Baden-Powell 1.75 1.75

75th anniversary of Boy Scouts.

Nos. 243-245 Ovptd. "ROYAL BABY / BEQUIA"

1982, July 19 **Wmk. 380** *Perf. 14*

248 A99a 50c multicolored 35 35
249 A99a 60c multicolored 40 40
250 A99a $6 multicolored 4.25 4.25

"ROYAL BABY / CANOUAN"

1982, July 19

251 A99a 50c multicolored 35 35
252 A99a 60c multicolored 40 40
253 A99a $6 multicolored 4.25 4.25

"ROYAL BABY / MAYREAU"

1982, July 19

254 A99a 50c multicolored 35 35
255 A99a 60c multicolored 40 40
256 A99a $6 multicolored 4.25 4.25

"ROYAL BABY / MUSTIQUE"

1982, July 19

257 A99a 50c multicolored 35 35
258 A99a 60c multicolored 40 40
259 A99a $6 multicolored 4.25 4.25

"ROYAL BABY / UNION"

1982, July 19

260 A99a 50c multicolored 35 35
261 A99a 60c multicolored 40 40
262 A99a $6 multicolored 4.25 4.25

Christmas Type of 1981

1982, Nov. 18 *Perf. 13½*

263 A97 10c Mary and Joseph at inn 15 15
264 A97 $1.50 Animals of stable 1.00 1.00
265 A97 $2.50 Nativity 1.75 1.75
a. Souvenir sheet of 3, #263-265 3.00 3.00

No. 146 Surcharged

45¢

1983, Apr. 26 **Wmk. 373** *Perf. 13x12*

266 G16 45c on 50c multicolored 38 38

Union Island G30

1983, May 12 *Perf. 13½*

267 G30 50c Power Station, Clifton 35 35
268 G30 60c Sunrise, Clifton Harbor 42 42
269 G30 $1.50 School, Ashton 1.00 1.00
270 G30 $2 Frigate Rock, Conch Shell Beach 1.40 1.40

Treaty of Versailles, Bicent. — G31

1983, Sept. 15 *Perf. 14½x14*

271 G31 45c British warship 30 30
272 G31 60c American warship 42 42
273 G31 $1.50 US troops, flag 1.00 1.00
274 G31 $2 British troops in battle 1.40 1.40

200 Years of Manned Flight G32

Designs: 45c, Montgolfier balloon 1783, vert. 60c, Ayres Turbo-thrush Commander. $1.50, Lebaudy "1" dirigible. $2, Space shuttle Columbia.

1983, Sept. 15 *Perf. 14*

275 G32 45c multicolored 30 30
276 G32 60c multicolored 42 42
277 G32 $1.50 multicolored 1.00 1.00
278 G32 $2 multicolored 1.40 1.40
a. Souvenir sheet of 4, #275-278 3.25 3.25

British Monarch Types of 1984

1983, Oct. 25 **Unwmk.** *Perf. 12½*

279 A110 60c Arms of Henry VIII 22 22
280 A111 60c Henry VIII 22 22
281 A110 60c Arms of James I 22 22
282 A111 60c James I 22 22
283 A110 75c Henry VIII 30 30
284 A111 75c Hampton Court 30 30
285 A110 75c James I 30 30
286 A111 75c Edinburgh Castle 30 30
287 A110 $2.50 Mary Rose 95 95
288 A111 $2.50 Henry VIII, Portsmouth harbor 95 95
289 A110 $2.50 Gunpowder Plot 95 95
290 A111 $2.50 James I & Gunpowder Plot 95 95
Nos. 279-290 (12) 5.88 5.88

Stamps of same denomination se-tenant.

Old Coinage — G33

1983, Dec. 1 **Wmk. 373** *Perf. 14*

291 G33 20c Quarter and half dollar, 1797 15 15
292 G33 45c Nine bitts, 1811-14 30 30
293 G33 75c Six and twelve bitts, 1811-14 50 50
294 G33 $3 Sixty six shillings, 1798 1.90 1.90

Locomotives Type of 1985

1984-87 **Litho.** **Unwmk.** *Perf. 12½*

Pairs, Type A120

295 1c 1948 Class C62, Japan 15 15
296 1c 1898 P.L.M. Grosse C, France 15 15
297 5c 1892 Class D13, US 15 15
298 5c 1903 Class V, UK 15 15
299 10c 1980 Class 253, UK 15 15
300 10c 1968 Class 581, Japan 15 15
301 10c 1874 1001 Class, UK 15 15
302 10c 1977 Class 142, East Germany 15 15
303 15c 1899 T-9 Class, UK 15 15
304 15c 1932 Class C12, Japan 15 15
305 15c 1897 Class T15, Germany 15 15
306 20c 1808 Catch-me-who-can, UK 15 15
307 35c 1900 Claud Hamilton Class, UK 25 25
308 35c 1948 Class E10, Japan 25 25
309 35c 1937 Coronation Class, UK 25 25
310 40c 1936 Class 231, Algeria 28 28
311 40c 1927 Class 4P, UK 28 28
312 40c 1979 Class 120, West Germany 28 28
313 45c 1941 Class J, US 32 32
314 45c 1900 Class 13, UK 32 32
315 50c 1913 Slieve Gullion Class S, UK 35 35
316 50c 1929 Class A3, UK 35 35
317 50c 1954 Class X, Australia 35 35
318 60c 1895 Class D16, US 45 45
319 60c 1904 J. B. Earle, UK 45 45
320 60c 1879 Halesworth, UK 45 45
321 60c 1930 Class V1, UK 45 45
322 60c 1986 Class 59, UK 45 45
323 70c 1935 Class E18, Germany 55 55
324 75c 1923 Class D50, Japan 60 60
325 75c 1859 Problem Class, UK 60 60
326 75c 1958 Class 40, UK 60 60
327 75c 1875 Class A, US 60 60
328 $1 1907 Star Class, British 85 85
329 $1 1898 Lyn, UK 85 85
330 $1 1961 Western Class, UK 85 85
331 $1 1958 Warship Class 42, UK 85 85
332 $1 1831 Samson Type, US 85 85
333 $1.20 1854 Hayes, US 90 90
334 $1.25 1902 Class P-69, US 95 95
335 $1.50 1865 Talyllyn, UK 1.25 1.25
336 $1.50 1899 Drummond's Bug, UK 1.25 1.25
337 $1.50 1913 Class 60-3 Shay, US 1.25 1.25
338 $1.50 1938 Class H1-d, Canada 1.25 1.25
339 $2 1890 Class 2120, Japan 1.60 1.60
340 $2 1951 Clan Class, UK 1.60 1.60
341 $2 1934 Pioneer Zephyr, US 1.60 1.60
342 $2.50 1948 Blue Peter, UK 2.00 2.00
343 $2.50 1874 Class Beattie Well Tank, UK 2.00 2.00
344 $3 1906 Cardean, UK 2.25 2.25
345 $3 1840 Fire Fly, UK 2.25 2.25
a. Souvenir sheet of 4, #324, 345
346 $3 1884 Class 1800, Japan 2.25 2.25
Nos. 295-346 (104) 38.54 38.54

Issued: #297, 299, 303, 307, 313, 318, 328, 342, 3/15/84; #295, 298, 296, 308, 319, 329, 335, 344, 10/9/84; #296, 304, 324, 345, 1/31/85; #300, 310, 315, 343, 5/17/85; #309, 323, 333, 339, 9/16/85; #305, 314, 320, 325, 330, 336, 340, 346, 3/14/86; #301, 311, 316, 321, 326, 331, 334, 337, 5/5/87; #302, 312, 3317, 322, 327, 332, 338, 341, 8/26/87.

Spotted Eagle Ray — G34

Wmk. 380

1984, Apr. 26 **Litho.** *Perf. 14*

399 G34 45c shown 30 30
400 G34 60c Queen trigger fish 40 40
401 G34 $1.50 White spotted file fish 1.00 1.00
402 G34 $2 Schoolmaster 1.40 1.40

For overprint see No. 504.

Cricket Players Type of 1985

1984-85 **Unwmk.** *Perf. 12½*

Pairs, Type A116

403 1c R. A. Woolmer, portrait 15 15
404 3c K. S. Ranjitsinhji, portrait 15 15
405 5c W. R. Hammond, in action 15 15
406 5c S. F. Barnes, portrait 15 15
407 30c D. L. Underwood, in action 15 15
408 30c R. Peel, in action 15 15
409 55c M. D. Moxon, in action 20 20
410 60c W. G. Grace, portrait 22 22
411 60c L. Potter, portrait 22 22
412 $1 E. A. E. Baptiste, portrait 40 40
413 $1 H. Larwood, in action 40 40
414 $2 A. P. E. Knott, portrait 80 80
415 $2 Yorkshire & Kent county cricket clubs 80 80

416 $2.50 Sir John Berry Hobbs, portrait 1.00 1.00
417 $3 L. E. G. Ames, in action 1.10 1.10
Nos. 403-417 (30) 12.08 12.08

Size of stamps in No. 415: 58x38mm.
Issued: #403, 407, 410, 412, 414, 417, 8/16/84; #406, 408, 413, 416, 11/2/84; #409, 411, 415, 2/22/85.

Canouan Island G35

1984, Sept. 3 Wmk. 380
433 G35 35c Junior secondary school
434 G35 45c Police station 30 30
435 G35 $1 Post office 70 70
436 G35 $3 Anglican church 2.00 2.00

Night-blooming Flowers — G36

1984, Oct. 15
437 G36 35c Lady of the night 24 24
438 G36 45c Four o'clock 30 30
439 G36 75c Mother-in-law's tongue 50 50
440 G36 $3 Queen of the night 2.00 2.00

Car Type of 1983

1984-86 Unwmk. *Perf. 12½*
Pairs, Type A107
441 5c 1959 Facel Vega, France 15 15
442 5c 1903 Winton, Britain 15 15
443 15c 1914 Mercedes-Benz, Germany 15 15
444 25c 1936 BMW, Germany 15 15
445 45c 1954 Rolls Royce, Britain 18 18
446 50c 1934 Frazer Nash, Britain 20 20
447 60c 1931 Invicta, Britain 22 22
448 60c 1974 Lamborghini, Italy 22 22
449 $1 1959 Daimler, Britain 38 38
450 $1 1932 Marmon, US 38 38
451 $1.50 1966 Brabham Repco, Britain 60 60
452 $1.75 1968 Lotus Ford 70 70
453 $3 1949 Buick, US 1.25 1.25
454 $3 1927 Delage, France 1.25 1.25
Nos. 441-454 (28) 11.96 11.96

Issued: #441, 444, 446, 457, 11/28/84; #442, 447, 449, 452, 4/9/85; #443, 445, 448, 450, 452, 454, 2/20/86.
Stamps issued 2/20/86 not inscribed "Leaders of the World."

Christmas Type of 1983
Perf. 14½

1984, Dec. 3 Litho. Wmk. 380
469 A106 20c Three wise men, star 15 15
470 A106 45c Journeying to Bethlehem 28 28
471 A106 $3 Presenting gifts 1.90 1.90
a. Souvenir sheet of 3, #469-471 2.30 2.30

Shellfish G37

1985, Feb. 11 *Perf. 14*
472 G37 25c Caribbean king crab 17 17
473 G37 60c Queen conch 40 40
474 G37 $1 White sea urchin 70 70
475 G37 $3 West Indian top shell 2.00 2.00

Flowers — G38

1985, Mar. 13 Unwmk. *Perf. 12½*
476 G38 5c Cypripedium calceolus 15 15
477 G38 5c Gentiana asclepiadea 15 15
478 G38 55c Clianthus formosus 18 18
479 G38 55c Celmisia coriacea 18 18
480 G38 60c Erythronium americanum 22 22
481 G38 60c Laelia anceps 22 22
482 G38 $2 Leucadendron discolor 80 80
483 G38 $2 Meconopsis horridula 80 80
Nos. 476-483 (8) 2.70 2.70

Stamps of same denomination printed se-tenant.

Water Sports G39

1985, May 9 Wmk. 380 *Perf. 14*
484 G39 35c Windsurfing 24 24
485 G39 45c Water skiing 30 30
486 G39 75c Scuba diving 50 50
487 G39 $3 Deep sea fishing 2.00 2.00

Tourism.

Fruits and Blossoms G40

1985, June 24 *Perf. 15*
488 G40 30c Passion fruit 18 18
489 G40 75c Guava 50 50
490 G40 $1 Sapodilla 70 70
491 G40 $2 Mango 1.40 1.40
a. Souvenir sheet of 4, #488-491, perf. 14½x15 2.75 2.75

For overprint see No. 503.

Queen Mother Type of 1985

1985, July 31 Unwmk. *Perf. 12½*
492 A122 40c Facing right 20 20
493 A122 40c Facing forward 20 20
494 A122 75c Facing right, diff. 38 38
495 A122 75c Facing left, diff. 38 38
496 A122 $1.10 Facing right, diff. 55 55
497 A122 $1.10 Facing forward, diff. 55 55
498 A122 $1.75 Facing right, diff. 90 90
499 A122 $1.75 Facing left, diff. 90 90
Nos. 492-499 (8) 4.06 4.06

Souvenir Sheet
500 Sheet of 2 1.65 1.65
a. A122 $2 As girl facing forward 80 80
b. A122 $2 Facing left 80 80

Stamps of same denomination printed se-tenant.
Souvenir sheets containing two $4 or two $5 stamps exist.

Nos. 213-214, 236, 399, 488, and 496-497 Overprinted or Surcharged "CARIBBEAN ROYAL VISIT 1985" in 1, 2 or 3 Lines

1985, Oct. 27 *Perfs., Wmks. as Before*
503 G40 30c On #488 15 15
504 G37 45c On #399 25 25
505 A122 $1.10 On #496 60 60
506 A122 $1.10 On #497 60 60
507 A94a $1.50 On $3.50, #213 85 85
508 A94b $1.50 On $3.50, #214 85 85
509 G26 $3 On #236 1.65 1.65
Nos. 503-509 (7) 4.95 4.95

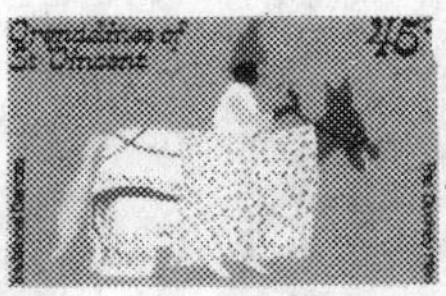

Traditional Dances G41

1985, Dec. 16 Unwmk. *Perf. 15*
510 G41 45c Donkey man 28 28
511 G41 75c Cake dance, vert. 45 45
512 G41 $1 Bois-bois man, vert. 70 70
513 G41 $2 Maypole dance 1.40 1.40

Queen Elizabeth II 60th Birthday Type

Designs: 5c, Elizabeth II. $1, At Princess Anne's christening. $4, As Princess. $6, In Canberra, 1982. $8, Elizabeth II with crown.

1986, Apr. 21 *Perf. 12½*
514 A128 5c multicolored 15 15
515 A128 $1 multicolored 40 40
516 A128 $4 multicolored 1.65 1.65
517 A128 $6 multi, vert. 2.50 2.50

Souvenir Sheet
518 A128 $8 multicolored 3.25 3.25

Handicrafts — G41a

Wmk. 380
1986, Apr. 22 Litho. *Perf. 15*
519 G41a 10c Dolls 15 15
520 G41a 60c Basketwork 35 35
521 G41a $1 Scrimshaw 60 60
522 G41a $3 Model boat 1.90 1.90

World Cup Soccer Championship, Mexico — G42

Perf. 12½, 15 (#525-528)
1986, May 7 Unwmk.
523 G42 1c Uruguayan team 15 15
524 G42 10c Polish team 15 15
525 G42 45c Bulgarian player 18 18
526 G42 75c Iraqi player 30 30
527 G42 $1.50 S. Korean player 60 60
528 G42 $2 N. Ireland player 80 80
529 G42 $4 Portuguese team 1.65 1.65
530 G42 $5 Canadian team 1.90 1.90
Nos. 523-530 (8) 5.73 5.73

Souvenir Sheets
531 G42 $1 like #529 40 40
532 G42 $3 like #523 1.25 1.25

Size: Nos. 525-528, 25x40mm.

Fungi — G43

Wmk. 380
1986, May 23 Litho. *Perf. 14*
533 G43 45c Marasmius pallescens 30 30
534 G43 60c Leucocoprinus fragilissimus 40 40
535 G43 75c Hygrocybe occidentalis 50 50
536 G43 $3 Xerocomus hypoxanthus 2.00 2.00

Royal Wedding Type of 1986

1986 Unwmk. *Perf. 12½*
537 A132 60c Sarah, Diana 22 22
538 A132 60c Andrew 22 22
539 A132 $2 Anne, Andrew, Charles, Margaret, horiz. 80 80
540 A132 $2 Sarah, Andrew, horiz. 80 80

Souvenir Sheet
541 A132a $8 Andrew, Sarah, in coach 3.25 3.25

Issue dates: Nos. 537-540, July 18. No. 541, Oct. 15.
Stamps of same denomination printed se-tenant.

Nos. 537-540 Ovptd. in Silver "Congratulations to TRH The Duke & Duchess of York" in 3 Lines

1986, Oct. 15
542 A132 60c on #530 22 22
543 A132 60c on #531 22 22
544 A132 $2 on #532 80 80
545 A132 $2 on #533 80 80

Dragonflies G44

1986, Nov. 19 *Perf. 15*
546 G44 45c Brachymesia furcata 30 30
547 G44 60c Lepthemis vesiculosa 40 40
548 G44 75c Perithemis domitta 50 50
549 G44 $2.50 Tramea abdominalis, vert. 1.65 1.65

Statue of Liberty Type
Souvenir Sheets

Each stamp shows different views of Statue of Liberty and a different US president in the margin.

1986, Nov. 26 *Perf. 14*
550 A135 $1.50 multicolored 60 60
551 A135 $1.75 multicolored 70 70
552 A135 $2 multicolored 80 80
553 A135 $2.50 multicolored 1.00 1.00
554 A135 $3 multicolored 1.10 1.10
555 A135 $3.50 multicolored 1.40 1.40
556 A135 $5 multicolored 1.90 1.90
557 A135 $6 multicolored 2.25 2.25
558 A135 $8 multicolored 3.25 3.25
Nos. 550-558 (9) 13.00 13.00

Birds of Prey — G45

Christmas — G46

1986, Nov. 26 Litho.
560 G45 10c Sparrow hawk 15 15
561 G45 45c Black hawk 28 28
562 G45 60c Duck hawk 35 35
563 G45 $4 Fish hawk 2.50 2.50

1986, Nov. 26
564 G46 45c Santa playing drums 28 28
565 G46 60c Santa wind surfing 32 32
566 G46 $1.25 Santa water skiing 80 80
567 G46 $2 Santa limbo dancing 1.25 1.25
a. Souvenir sheet of 4, #564-567 2.75 2.75

Queen Elizabeth II, 40th Wedding Anniv. Type of 1987

1987, Oct. 15 *Perf. 12½*
568 A140 15c Elizabeth, Charles 15 15
569 A140 45c Victoria, Albert 18 18
570 A140 $1.50 Elizabeth, Philip 60 60

571	A140	$3 Elizabeth, Philip, diff.	1.25	1.25
572	A140	$4 Elizabeth, portrait	1.65	1.65
		Nos. 568-572 (5)	3.83	3.83

Souvenir Sheet

573	A140	$6 Elizabeth as Princess	2.50	2.50

Victoria's accession to the throne, 150th anniv.

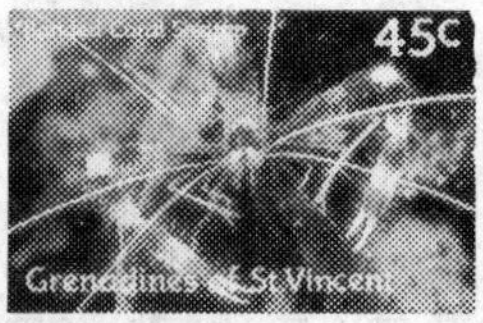

Marine Life G48

1987, Dec. 17 *Perf. 15*

574	G48	45c Banded coral shrimp	28	28
575	G48	50c Arrow crab, flamingo tongue	32	32
576	G48	65c Cardinal fish	40	40
577	G48	$5 Moray eel	3.25	3.25

Souvenir Sheet

578	G48	$5 Puffer fish	3.25	3.25

America's Cup Yachts — G49

1988, Mar. 31 *Perf. 12½*

579	G49	50c Australia IV	32	32
580	G49	65c Crusader II	40	40
581	G49	75c New Zealand K27	48	48
582	G49	$2 Italia	1.25	1.25
583	G49	$4 White Crusader	2.50	2.50
584	G49	$5 Stars and Stripes	3.25	3.25
		Nos. 579-584 (6)	8.20	8.20

Souvenir Sheet

585	G49	$1 Champosa V	60	60

Bequia Regatta G50

1988, Mar. 31 *Perf. 15*

586	G50	5c Seine boats	15	15
587	G50	50c Friendship Rose	32	32
588	G50	75c Fishing boats	48	48
589	G50	$3.50 Yacht racing	2.25	2.25

Souvenir Sheet

Perf. 12½

590	G50	$8 Port Elizabeth	5.25	5.25

Tourism — G51

Aircraft of Mustique Airways, Genadine Tours.

1988, May 26 *Perf. 14x13½*

591	G51	15c multicolored	15	15
592	G51	65c multi, diff.	40	40
593	G51	75c multi, diff.	48	48
594	G51	$5 multi, diff.	3.25	3.25

Souvenir Sheet

595	G51	$10 Waterfall, vert.	6.50	6.50

No. 595 contains one 35x56mm stamp.

Great Explorers G52

Designs: 15c, Vitus Bering and the St. Peter. 75c, Bering and pancake ice. $1, David Livingstone and the Ma-Robert. $2, Livingstone meeting Henry M. Stanley. $3, John Speke (1827-1864) and Sir Richard Burton (1821-1890) welcomed at Tabori. $3.50, Speke, Burton at Lake Victoria. $4, Crewman of Christopher Columbus spotting land. $4.50, Columbus, exchange of gifts. $5, Sextant. $6, Columbus' ship landing in Bahamas, 1492.

1988, July 29 *Perf. 14*

596	G52	15c multicolored	15	15
597	G52	75c multicolored	48	48
598	G52	$1 multicolored	60	60
599	G52	$2 multicolored	1.25	1.25
600	G52	$3 multicolored	1.90	1.90
601	G52	$3.50 multicolored	2.25	2.25
602	G52	$4 multicolored	2.50	2.50
603	G52	$4.50 multicolored	2.75	2.75
		Nos. 596-603 (8)	11.88	11.88

Souvenir Sheets

604	G52	$5 multicolored	3.50	3.50
605	G52	$6 multicolored	4.00	4.00

Nos. 602-603, 605 picture 500th anniversary discovery of America emblem.

A number of unissued items, imperfs., part perfs., missing color varieties, etc., were made available when the Format International inventory was liquidated.

Cricketers — G53

1988, July 29 *Perf. 15*

606	G53	20c A. I. Razvi	15	15
607	G53	45c R. J. Hadlee	28	28
608	G53	75c M. D. Crowe	48	48
609	G53	$1.25 C. H. Lloyd	80	80
610	G53	$1.50 A. R. Boarder	95	95
611	G53	$2 M. D. Marshall	1.25	1.25
612	G53	$2.50 G. A. Hick	1.50	1.50
613	G53	$3.50 C. G. Greenidge, horiz.	2.25	2.25
		Nos. 606-613 (8)	7.66	7.66

A $3 souvenir sheet in the design of the $2 stamp was not a postal issue according to the St. Vincent P.O.

Tennis Type of 1987

1988, July 29 *Perf. 12½*

614	A137	15c Pam Shriver, horiz.	15	15
615	A137	50c Kevin Curran	32	32
616	A137	75c Wendy Turnbull	48	48
617	A137	$1 Evonne Cawley	65	65
618	A137	$1.50 Ilie Nastase, horiz.	95	95
619	A137	$2 Billie Jean King	1.25	1.25
620	A137	$3 Bjorn Borg	1.90	1.90
621	A137	$3.50 Virginia Wade	2.25	2.25
		Nos. 614-621 (8)	7.95	7.95

Souvenir Sheet

622		Sheet of 2	3.00	3.00
a.		A137 $2.25 Stefan Edberg	1.50	1.50
b.		A137 $2.25 Steffi Graf	1.50	1.50

No. 616 inscribed "Turnball" in error.

India '89, International Stamp Exhibition, New Dehli — G54

Disney characters and sites in India.

1989, Feb. 7 *Perf. 14x13½*

623	G54	1c Fatehpur Sikri	15	15
624	G54	2c Palace on Wheels	15	15
625	G54	3c Old fort, Delhi	15	15
626	G54	5c Pinjore Gardens	15	15
627	G54	10c Taj Mahal	15	15
628	G54	25c Chandni Chowk	16	16
629	G54	$4 Agra Fort, Jaipur	2.50	2.50
630	G54	$5 Gandhi Memorial	3.50	3.50
		Nos. 623-630 (8)	6.91	6.91

Souvenir Sheets

631	G54	$6 Qutab Minar, vert.	4.00	4.00
632	G54	$6 Palace of the Winds	4.00	4.00

Japanese Art Type

Paintings: 5c, The View at Yotsuya, by Hokusai. 30c, Landscape at Ochanomizu, by Hokuju. 45c, Itabashi, by Eisen. 65c, Early Summer Rain, by Kunisada. 75c, High Noon at Kasumigaseki, by Kuniyoshi. $1, The Yoshiwara Embankment by Moonlight, by Kuniyoshi. $4, The Bridge of Boats at Sano, by Hokusai. $5, Lingering Snow on Mount Hira, by Kunitora. No. 641, Colossus of Rhodes, by Kunitora. No. 642, Shinobazu Pond, by Kokan.

1989, July 6 *Perf. 14x13½*

633	A170	5c multicolored	15	15
634	A170	30c multicolored	22	22
635	A170	45c multicolored	35	35
636	A170	65c multicolored	50	50
637	A170	75c multicolored	58	58
638	A170	$1 multicolored	75	75
639	A170	$4 multicolored	3.00	3.00
640	A170	$5 multicolored	3.75	3.75
		Nos. 633-640 (8)	9.30	9.30

Souvenir Sheets

641	A170	$6 multicolored	4.50	4.50
642	A170	$6 multicolored	4.50	4.50

Miniature Sheet

1990 World Cup Soccer Championships, Italy — G55

Soccer players and landmarks: a, Mt. Vesuvius. b, The Colosseum. c, Venice. d, Roman Forum. e, Leaning Tower of Pisa. f, Florence. g, The Vatican. h, The Pantheon.

1989, July 10 *Perf. 14*

643		Sheet of 8	9.00	9.00
a.-h.		G55 $1.50 any single	1.10	1.10

Discovery of America 500th Anniv. Type of Antigua & Barbuda

UPAE emblem and American Indians: 25c, Smoking tobacco. 75c, Rolling tobacco. $1, Body painting. No. 647a, Starting campfire. No. 647b, Woman drinking from bowl. No. 647c, Woman frying grain or corn patties. No. 647d, Adult resting in hammock using stone mortar and pestle. $4, Smoothing wood. No. 649, Chief. No. 650, Fishing with bow and arrow.

1989, Oct. 2 **Litho.** *Perf. 14*

644	A196	25c multicolored	18	18
645	A196	75c multicolored	58	58
646	A196	$1 multicolored	75	75
647		Strip of 4	4.50	4.50
a.-d.		A196 $1.50 any single	1.10	1.10
648	A196	$4 multicolored	3.00	3.00
		Nos. 644-648 (5)	9.01	9.01

Souvenir Sheets

649	A196	$6 multicolored	4.50	4.50
650	A196	$6 multicolored	4.50	4.50

No. 647 has continuous design.

1st Moon Landing Type

Designs: 5c *Columbia* command module. 40c, Neil Armstrong saluting flag on the Moon. 55c, Command module over Moon. 65c, *Eagle* liftoff from Moon. 70c, *Eagle* on the Moon. $1, Command module re-entering Earth's atmosphere. $3, Apollo 11 mission emblem. $5, Armstrong and Buzz Aldrin walking on the Moon. No. 659, Apollo 11 launch, vert. No. 660, Splashdown.

1989, Oct. 2 *Perf. 14*

651	A171	5c multicolored	15	15
652	A171	40c multicolored	30	30
653	A171	55c multicolored	42	42
654	A171	65c multicolored	50	50
655	A171	70c multicolored	52	52
656	A171	$1 multicolored	75	75
657	A171	$3 multicolored	2.25	2.25
658	A171	$5 multicolored	3.75	3.75
		Nos. 651-658 (8)	8.64	8.64

Souvenir Sheets

659	A171	$6 multi, vert.	4.50	4.50
660	A171	$6 multicolored	4.50	4.50

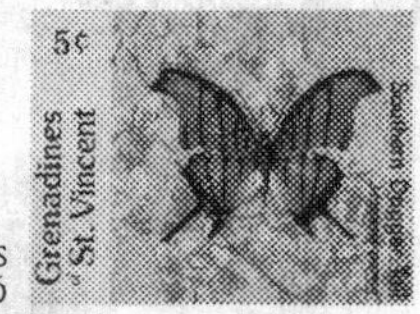

Butterflies G56

1989, Oct. 16 **Litho.** *Perf. 14x14½*

661	G56	5c Southern dagger tail	15	15
662	G56	30c Androgeus swallowtail	22	22
663	G56	45c Clench's hairstreak	35	35
664	G56	65c Buckeye	48	48
665	G56	75c Venezuelan sulphur	58	58
666	G56	$1 Mimic	75	75
667	G56	$4 Common longtail skipper	3.00	3.00
668	G56	$5 Carribean buckeye	3.75	3.75
		Nos. 661-668 (8)	9.28	9.28

Souvenir Sheets

669	G56	$6 Flambeau	4.50	4.50
670	G56	$6 Queen, large orange sulphur, Ramsden's giant white	4.50	4.50

Flora — G57

1989, Nov. 1 **Litho.** *Perf. 14*

671	G57	80c Solanum urens	60	60
672	G57	$1.25 Passiflora andersonii	95	95
673	G57	$1.65 Miconia andersonii	1.25	1.25
674	G57	$1.85 Pitcairnia sulphurea	1.40	1.40

Christmas — G58

Walt Disney characters and classic automobiles.

Perf. 14x13½, 13½x14

1989, Dec. 20

675	G58	5c 1907 Rolls-Royce	15	15
676	G58	10c 1897 Stanley Steamer	15	15
677	G58	15c 1904 Darracq Genevieve	15	15
678	G58	45c 1914 Detroit Electric Coupe	35	35
679	G58	55c 1896 Ford	42	42
680	G58	$2 1904 REO Runabout	1.50	1.50
681	G58	$3 1899 Winton Mail Truck	2.25	2.25
682	G58	$5 1893 Duryea Car	3.75	3.75
		Nos. 675-682 (8)	8.72	8.72

Souvenir Sheets

683 G58 $6 1912 Pope-Hartford 4.50 4.50
684 G58 $6 1908 Buick Model 10 4.50 4.50

Nos. 683-684 vert.

Battles of World War II
G59

Designs: 10c, 1st Battle of Narvik, Apr. 10, 1940. 15c, Allies land at Anzio, Jan. 22, 1944. 20c, Battle of Midway, June 4, 1942. 45c, Allies launch offensive on Gustav Line, May 11, 1944. 55c, Allies take over zones in Berlin, July 3, 1945. 65c, Battle of the Atlantic, Mar. 1-20, 1943. 90c, Allies launch final phase of North African Campaign, Apr. 22, 1943. $3, US forces land on Guam, July 21, 1944. $5, US 7th Army meets the 3rd Army across the Rhine, Mar. 26, 1945. No. 694, Battle of Leyte Gulf, Oct. 23, 1944. No. 695, The Dambusters Raid, May 16, 1943.

1990, Apr. 2 Litho. *Perf. 14*

685 G59 10c multicolored 15 15
686 G59 15c multicolored 15 15
687 G59 20c multicolored 15 15
688 G59 45c multicolored 35 35
689 G59 55c multicolored 42 42
690 G59 65c multicolored 50 50
691 G59 90c multicolored 68 68
692 G59 $3 multicolored 2.25 2.25
693 G59 $5 multicolored 3.75 3.75
694 G59 $6 multicolored 4.50 4.50
Nos. 685-694 (10) 12.90 12.90

Souvenir Sheet

695 G59 $6 multicolored 4.50 4.50

Penny Black, 150th Anniv. — G60

Designs: $1, Stamp World London '90 emblem. $5, Negative image of the Penny Black. $6, Penny Black with non-existent letters.

1990, May 3 *Perf. 14x15*

696 G60 $1 pale rose & blk 75 75
697 G60 $5 pale violet & blk 3.50 3.50

Souvenir Sheet

698 G60 $6 dull blue & blk 4.50 4.50

Stamp World London '90.

Disney Characters Portraying Shakespearian Roles — G61

Designs: 20c, Goofy as Marc Antony in "Julius Caesar." 30c, Clarabelle Cow as nurse in "Romeo and Juliet." 45c, Pete as Falstaff in "Henry IV." 50c, Minnie Mouse as Portia in "The Merchant of Venice." $1, Donald Duck holding head of Yorick in "Hamlet." $2, Daisy Duck as Ophelia in "Hamlet." $4, Donald and Daisy Duck as Benedick and Beatrice in "Much Ado About Nothing." $5, Minnie Mouse and Donald Duck as Katherine and Petruchio in "The Taming of the Shrew." No. 707, Mickey and Minnie Mouse portraying Romeo and Juliet. No. 708, Clarabelle Cow as Titania in "A Midsummer Night's Dream."

1990, May *Perf. 14x13½*

699 G61 20c multicolored 15 15
700 G61 30c multicolored 22 22
701 G61 45c multicolored 34 34
702 G61 50c multicolored 38 38
703 G61 $1 multicolored 75 75
704 G61 $2 multicolored 1.50 1.50
705 G61 $4 multicolored 3.00 3.00
706 G61 $5 multicolored 3.75 3.75
Nos. 699-706 (8) 10.09 10.09

Souvenir Sheets

707 G61 $6 multicolored 4.50 4.50
708 G61 $6 multicolored 4.50 4.50

World Cup Soccer Championships, Italy — G62

World Cup Trophy and players from participating countries.

1990, Sept. 24 Litho. *Perf. 14*

709 G62 25c Scotland 18 18
710 G62 50c Egypt 38 38
711 G62 $2 Austria 1.50 1.50
712 G62 $4 United States 3.00 3.00

Souvenir Sheets

713 G62 $6 Holland 4.50 4.50
714 G62 $6 England 4.50 4.50

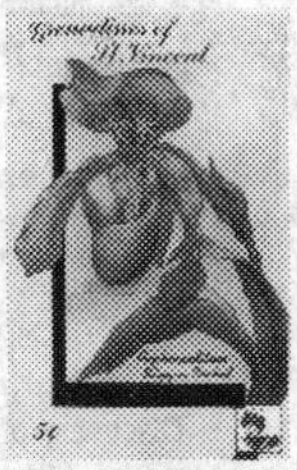

Orchids — G63

Designs: 5c, Paphiopedilum. 25c, Dendrobium phalaenopsis, Cymbidium. 30c, Miltonia candida. 50c, Epidendrum ibaguense, Cymbidium Elliot Rogers. $1, Rossioglassum grande. $2, Phalaenopsis Elisa Chang Lou, Masdevallia coccinea. $4, Cypripedium accale, Cypripedium calceolus. $5, Orchis spectabilis. No. 723, Epidendrum ibaguense, Phalaenopsis. No. 724, Dendrobium anosmum.

1990, Nov. 23 Litho. *Perf. 14*

715 G63 5c multicolored 15 15
716 G63 25c multicolored 18 18
717 G63 30c multicolored 22 22
718 G63 50c multicolored 38 38
719 G63 $1 multicolored 75 75
720 G63 $2 multicolored 1.50 1.50
721 G63 $4 multicolored 3.00 3.00
722 G63 $5 multicolored 3.75 3.75
Nos. 715-722 (8) 9.93 9.93

Souvenir Sheets

723 G63 $6 multicolored 4.50 4.50
724 G63 $6 multicolored 4.50 4.50

Expo '90, Intl. Garden and Greenery Exposition, Osaka, Japan.

Birds
G64

1990, Nov. 26

725 G64 5c Common ground dove 15 15
726 G64 25c Purple martin 18 18
727 G64 45c Painted bunting 35 35
728 G64 55c Blue-hooded euphonia 42 42
729 G64 75c Blue-gray tanager 55 55
730 G64 $1 Red-eyed vireo 75 75
731 G64 $2 Palm chat 1.50 1.50
732 G64 $3 North American jacana 2.25 2.25
733 G64 $4 Green-throated carib 3.00 3.00
734 G64 $5 St. Vincent parrot 3.75 3.75
Nos. 725-734 (10) 12.90 12.90

Souvenir Sheets

735 Sheet of 2 4.50 4.50
a. G64 $3 Bananaquit 2.25 2.25
b. G64 $3 Magnificent frigatebird 2.25 2.25
736 G64 $6 Red-legged honeycreeper 4.50 4.50

newblock=y

Queen Mother 90th Birthday Type

Photographs: Nos. 737a-737i, From 1900-1929. Nos. 738a-738i, From 1930-1959. Nos. 739a-739i, From 1960-1989. Nos. 740-748, Enlarged photographs used for Nos. 737-739.

1991, Feb. 14 Litho. *Perf. 14*

Miniature Sheets of 9, #a.-i.

737 A193 $2 blue & multi 13.50 13.50
738 A193 $2 pink & multi 13.50 13.50
739 A193 $2 green & multi 13.50 13.50

Souvenir Sheets

740 A193 $5 like #737a 3.75 3.75
741 A193 $5 like #737f 3.75 3.75
742 A193 $5 like #737h 3.75 3.75
743 A193 $5 like #738b 3.75 3.75
744 A193 $5 like #738f 3.75 3.75
745 A193 $5 like #738g 3.75 3.75
746 A193 $5 like #739b 3.75 3.75
747 A193 $5 like #739d 3.75 3.75
748 A193 $5 like #739h 3.75 3.75

Paintings by Vincent Van Gogh — G65

Designs: 5c, View of Arles with Irises in the Foreground. 10c, View of Saintes-Maries, vert. 15c, An Old Woman of Arles, vert. 20c, Orchard in Blossom, Bordered by Cypresses. 25c, Three White Cottages in Saintes-Maries. 35c, Boats at Saintes-Maries-De-La-Mer. 40c, Interior of a Restaurant in Arles. 45c, Peasant Woman, vert. 55c, Self-Portrait, Sept. 1888, vert. 60c, A Pork Butcher's Shop Seen From a Window, vert. 75c, The Night Cafe in Arles. $1, Portrait of Milliet, Second Lieutenant of the Zouaves, vert. $2, The Cafe Terrace on the Place Du Forum Arles, at Night, vert. $3, The Zouave, vert. $4, Two Lovers (Fragment), vert. No. 764, Still Life: Blue Enamel Coffeepot, Earthenware and Fruit. No. 765, Street in Saintes-Maries. No. 766, A Lane Near Arles. No. 767, Harvest at La Crau, with Montmajour in the Background. No. 768, The Sower.

1991, June 10 Litho. *Perf. 13½*

749 G65 5c multicolored 15 15
750 G65 10c multicolored 15 15
751 G65 15c multicolored 15 15
752 G65 20c multicolored 15 15
753 G65 25c multicolored 18 18
754 G65 35c multicolored 28 28
755 G65 40c multicolored 30 30
756 G65 45c multicolored 35 35
757 G65 55c multicolored 42 42
758 G65 60c multicolored 45 45
759 G65 75c multicolored 58 58
760 G65 $1 multicolored 75 75
761 G65 $2 multicolored 1.50 1.50
762 G65 $3 multicolored 2.25 2.25
763 G65 $4 multicolored 3.00 3.00
764 G65 $5 multicolored 3.75 3.75
Nos. 749-764 (16) 14.41 14.41

Size: 102x76mm

Imperf

765 G65 $5 multicolored 3.75 3.75
766 G65 $5 multicolored 3.75 3.75
767 G65 $6 multicolored 4.50 4.50
768 G65 $6 multicolored 4.50 4.50

Royal Family Birthday, Anniversary

Common Design Type

1991, July 5 Litho. *Perf. 14*

769 CD347 10c multicolored 15 15
770 CD347 15c multicolored 15 15
771 CD347 40c multicolored 30 30
772 CD347 50c multicolored 38 38
773 CD347 $1 multicolored 75 75
774 CD347 $2 multicolored 1.50 1.50
775 CD347 $4 multicolored 3.00 3.00
776 CD347 $5 multicolored 3.75 3.75
Nos. 769-776 (8) 9.98 9.98

Souvenir Sheets

777 CD347 $5 Henry, William, Charles, Diana 3.75 3.75
778 CD347 $5 Elizabeth, Andrew, Philip 3.75 3.75

10c, 50c, $1, Nos. 776-777, Charles and Diana, 10th wedding anniversary. Others, Queen Elizabeth II, 65th birthday.

Phila Nippon '91 — G66

Japanese locomotives: 10c, First Japanese steam. 25c, First American steam locomotive in Japan. 35c, Class 8620 steam. 50c, C53 steam. $1, DD-51 diesel. $2, RF 22327 electric. $4, EF-55 electric. $5, EF-58 electric. No. 787, Class 9600 steam, vert. No. 788, Class 4100 steam, vert. No. 789, C57 steam, vert. No. 790, C62 steam, vert.

1991, Aug. 12 Litho. *Perf. 14x13½*

779 G66 10c red, green & black 15 15
780 G66 25c red, green & black 18 18
781 G66 35c red, green & black 26 26
782 G66 50c red, green & black 38 38
783 G66 $1 red, green & black 75 75
784 G66 $2 red, green & black 1.50 1.50
785 G66 $4 red, green & black 3.00 3.00
786 G66 $5 red, green & black 3.75 3.75
Nos. 779-786 (8) 9.97 9.97

Souvenir Sheets

Perf. 12x13

787 G66 $6 red, black & green 4.50 4.50
788 G66 $6 red, black & green 4.50 4.50
789 G66 $6 red, black & green 4.50 4.50
790 G66 $6 red, black & green 4.50 4.50

Brandenburg Gate Type

Designs: 45c, Brandenburg Gate and Soviet Pres. Mikhail Gorbachev. 65c, Sign. 80c, Statue, soldier escaping through barbed wire. No. 794, Berlin police insignia. No. 795, Berlin coat of arms.

1991, Nov. 18 Litho. *Perf. 14*

791 A209 45c multicolored 35 35
792 A209 65c multicolored 48 48
793 A209 80c multicolored 60 60

Souvenir Sheets

794 A209 $5 multicolored 3.75 3.75
795 A209 $5 multicolored 3.75 3.75

Wolfgang Amadeus Mozart Type

Portrait of Mozart and: $1, Scene from "Abduction from the Seraglio." $3, Dresden, 1749. No. 799, Portrait, vert. No. 800, Bust, vert.

1991, Nov. 18 Litho. *Perf. 14*

797 A210 $1 multicolored 75 75
798 A210 $3 multicolored 2.25 2.25

Souvenir Sheets

799 A210 $5 multicolored 3.75 3.75
800 A210 $5 multicolored 3.75 3.75

Boy Scout Type

Designs: $2, Scout delivering mail and Czechoslovakian (local) scout stamp. $4, Cog train, Boy Scouts on Mt. Snowdon, Wales, vert. Nos. 803-804, Emblem of World Scout Jamboree, Korea.

1991, Nov. 18 Litho. *Perf. 14*

801 A211 $2 multicolored 1.50 1.50
802 A211 $4 multicolored 3.00 3.00

Souvenir Sheets

803 A211 $5 tan & multi 3.75 3.75
804 A211 $5 violet blue & multi 3.75 3.75

Lord Robert Baden-Powell, 50th death anniv. and 17th World Scout Jamboree, Korea.

De Gaulle Type

Designs: 60c, De Gaulle in Djibouti, 1959. No. 807, In military uniform, vert. No. 808, Portrait as President.

1991, Nov. 18 Litho. *Perf. 14*

806 A212 60c 45 45

Souvenir Sheets

807 A212 $5 multicolored 3.75 3.75
808 A212 $5 multicolored 3.75 3.75

A number has been reserved for additional value in this set.

Anniversaries and Events Type of 1991

Designs: $1.50, Otto Lilienthal, aviation pioneer. No. 810, Train in winter, vert. No. 811, Trans-Siberian Express Sign. No. 812, Man and woman celebrating. No. 813, Woman and man wearing hats. No. 814, Georg Ludwig Friedrich Laves, architect of Hofheater, Hanover. No. 815, Locomotive, Trans-Siberian Railway, vert. No. 816, Cantonal arms of Appenzell and Thurgau. No. 817, Hanover, 750th anniv.

1991, Nov. 18 Litho. *Perf. 14*

809 A213	$1.50	multicolored	1.15	1.15
810 A213	$1.75	multicolored	1.30	1.30
811 A213	$1.75	multicolored	1.30	1.30
812 A213	$2	multicolored	1.50	1.50
813 A213	$2	multicolored	1.50	1.50
814 A213	$2	multicolored	1.50	1.50
		Nos. 809-814 (6)	8.25	8.25

Souvenir Sheets

815 A213	$5	multicolored	3.75	3.75
816 A213	$5	multicolored	3.75	3.75
817 A213	$5	multicolored	3.75	3.75

First glider flight, cent. (#809). Trans-Siberian Railway, cent. (#810-811, 815). Swiss Confederation, 700th anniv. (#812-813, 816). City of Hanover, 750th anniv. (#814, 817). No. 815 contains one 42x58mm stamp.

Miniature Sheet

Pearl Harbor Type of 1991

Designs: a, Japanese submarines and aircraft leave Truk to attack Pearl Harbor. b, Japanese flagship, Akagi. c, Nakajima B5N2 Kate, attack leader. d, Torpedo bombers attack battleship row. e, Ford Island Naval Air Station. f, Doris Miller earns Navy Cross. g, USS West Virginia and USS Tennessee ablaze. h, USS Arizona destroyed. i, USS New Orleans. j, Pres. Roosevelt declares war.

1991, Nov. 18 *Perf. 14¹/₂x15*

818 A214	$1	Sheet of 10, #a.-j.	7.50	7.50

Disney Christmas Card Type

Card design and year of issue: 10c, Mickey in sleigh pulled by Pluto, 1974. 55c, Donald, Pluto, and Mickey watching marching band, 1961. 65c, Greeting with stars, 1942. 75c, Mickey, Donald watch Merlin create a snowman, 1963. $1.50, Mickey placing wreath on door, 1958. $2, Mickey as Santa beside fireplace, 1957. $4, Mickey manipulating "Pinnochio" for friends. $5, Prince Charming and Cinderella dancing beside Christmas tree, 1987. No. 827, Snow White, 1957, vert. No. 828, Santa riding World War II bomber, 1942, vert.

Perf. 14x13¹/₂,13¹/₂x14

1991, Nov. 18

819 A216	10c	multicolored	15	15
820 A216	55c	multicolored	42	42
821 A216	65c	multicolored	48	48
822 A216	75c	multicolored	58	58
823 A216	$1.50	multicolored	1.15	1.15
824 A216	$2	multicolored	1.50	1.50
825 A216	$4	multicolored	3.00	3.00
826 A216	$5	multicolored	3.75	3.75
		Nos. 819-826 (8)	11.03	11.03

Souvenir Sheets

827 A216	$6	multicolored	4.50	4.50
828 A216	$6	multicolored	4.50	4.50

Nos. 819-826 are horiz.

Queen Elizabeth II's Accession to the Throne, 40th Anniv.

Common Design Type

1992, Feb. 6 Litho. *Perf. 14*

829 CD348	15c	multicolored	15	15
830 CD348	45c	multicolored	35	35
831 CD348	$2	multicolored	1.50	1.50
832 CD348	$4	multicolored	3.00	3.00

Souvenir Sheets

833 CD348	$6	Queen at left, beach	4.50	4.50
834 CD348	$6	Queen at right, building	4.50	4.50

World Columbian Stamp Expo Type

Walt Disney characters as famous Chicagoans: 10c, Mickey as Walt Disney walking past birthplace. 50c, Donald Duck and nephews sleeping in George Pullman's railway cars. $1, Daisy Duck as Jane Addams in front of Hull House. $5, Mickey as Carl Sandburg. No. 839, Grandma McDuck as Mrs. O'Leary with her cow, vert.

1992, Apr. Litho. *Perf. 14x13¹/₂*

835 A220	10c	multicolored	15	15
836 A220	50c	multicolored	38	38
837 A220	$1	multicolored	75	75
838 A220	$5	multicolored	3.75	3.75

Souvenir Sheet

Perf. 13¹/₂x14

839 A220	$6	multicolored	4.50	4.50

Nos. 840-844 have not been used.

Granada '92 Type

Walt Disney characters as Spanish explorers in New World: 15c, Aztec King Goofy giving treasure to Big Pete as Hernando Cortes. 40c, Mickey as Hernando de Soto discovering Mississippi River. $2, Goofy as Vasco Nunez de Balboa discovering Pacific Ocean. $4, Donald Duck as Francisco Coronado discovering Rio Grande. $6, Mickey as Ponce de Leon discovering Fountain of Youth.

1992, Apr. *Perf. 14x13¹/₂*

845 A221	15c	multicolored	15	15
846 A221	40c	multicolored	30	30
847 A221	$2	multicolored	1.50	1.50
848 A221	$4	multicolored	3.00	3.00

Souvenir Sheet

Perf. 13¹/₂x14

849 A221	$6	multicolored	4.50	4.50

Nos. 850-854 have not been used.

Discovery of America, 500th Anniv. Type

Designs: 10c, King Ferdinand and Queen Isabella. 45c, Santa Maria and Nina in Acul Bay, Haiti. 55c, Santa Maria, vert. $2, Columbus' fleet departing Canary Islands, vert. $4, Sinking of Santa Maria off Hispanola. $5, Nina and Pinta returning to Spain. No. 861, Columbus' fleet during night storm. No. 862, Columbus landing on San Salvador.

1992, May 22 Litho. *Perf. 14*

855 A222	10c	multicolored	15	15
856 A222	45c	multicolored	35	35
857 A222	55c	multicolored	42	42
858 A222	$2	multicolored	1.50	1.50
859 A222	$4	multicolored	3.00	3.00
860 A222	$5	multicolored	3.75	3.75
		Nos. 855-860 (6)	9.17	9.17

Souvenir Sheets

861 A222	$6	multicolored	4.50	4.50
862 A222	$6	multicolored	4.50	4.50

World Columbian Stamp Expo '92, Chicago.
Nos. 863-866 have not been used.

Mushrooms — G67

Designs: 10c, Entoloma bakeri. 15c, Hydropus paraensis. 20c, Leucopaxillus gracillimus. 45c, Hygrotrama dennisianum. $1, Lentinus bertieri. $2, Dennisiomyces griseus. $3, Xerulina asprata. $5, Lepiota spiculata. No. 879, Pluteus crysophlebius. No. 881, Amanita lilloi.

1992, July 2

867 G67	10c	multicolored	15	15
868 G67	15c	multicolored	15	15
869 G67	20c	multicolored	15	15
870 G67	45c	multicolored	35	35
874 G67	$1	multicolored	75	75
875 G67	$2	multicolored	1.40	1.40
876 G67	$3	multicolored	2.25	2.25
878 G67	$5	multicolored	3.75	3.75
		Nos. 867-878 (8)	8.95	8.95

Souvenir Sheets

879 G67	$6	multicolored	4.50	4.50
881 G67	$6	multicolored	4.50	4.50

Numbers have reserved for additional values in this set.

Mushroom Type of 1992

Designs: 50c, Leucoagaricus hortensis. 65c, Pyrrhoglossum pyrrhum. 75c, Amanita craeoderma. $4, Hygrocybe acutoconica. No. 880, Lepiota volvatua.

1992, July 2 Litho. *Perf. 14*

871 G67	50c	multicolored	38	38
872 G67	65c	multicolored	48	48
873 G67	75c	multicolored	58	58
877 G67	$4	multicolored	3.00	3.00

Souvenir Sheet

880 G67	$6	multicolored	4.50	4.50

Butterfly Type of 1992

Designs: 15c, Nymphalidae paulogramma 20c, Heliconius cydno. 30c, Ithomiidae eutresis hypereia. 45c, Eurytides Columbus koll, vert. 55c, Papilio ascolius. 75c, Anaea pasibula. 80c, Heliconius doris. $1, Nymphalidae persisama pitheas. $2, Nymphalidae batesia hypochlora. $3, Heliconius erato. $4, Elzunia cassandrina. $5, Ithomiidae sais. No. 894, Pieridae dismorphia orise. No. 895, Nymphalidae podotricha. No. 896, Oleria tigilla.

1992, June 15 Litho. *Perf. 14*

882 A225	15c	multicolored	15	15
883 A225	20c	multicolored	15	15
884 A225	30c	multicolored	22	22
885 A225	45c	multicolored	35	35
886 A225	55c	multicolored	42	42
887 A225	75c	multicolored	58	58
888 A225	80c	multicolored	60	60
889 A225	$1	multicolored	75	75
890 A225	$2	multicolored	1.50	1.50
891 A225	$3	multicolored	2.25	2.25
892 A225	$4	multicolored	3.00	3.00
893 A225	$5	multicolored	3.75	3.75
		Nos. 882-893 (12)	13.72	13.72

Souvenir Sheets

894 A225	$6	multicolored	4.50	4.50
895 A225	$6	multicolored	4.50	4.50
896 A225	$6	multicolored	4.50	4.50

Genoa '92.

Hummingbirds Type of 1992

Designs: 5c, Antillean crested, female, horiz. 10c, Blue-tailed emerald, female. 35c, Antillean mango, male, horiz. 45c, Antillean mango, female, horiz. 55c, Green-throated carib, horiz. 65c, Green violet-ear. 75c, Blue-tailed emerald, male, horiz. $1, Purple throated carib. $2, Copper-rumped, horiz. $3, Rufous-breasted hermit. $4, Antillean crested, male. $5, Green breasted mango, male. No. 909, Blue-tailed emerald. No. 910, Antillean mango, diff. No. 911, Antillean crested, male, diff.

1992, July 7 Litho. *Perf. 14*

897 A224	5c	multicolored	15	15
898 A224	10c	multicolored	15	15
899 A224	35c	multicolored	28	28
900 A224	45c	multicolored	35	35
901 A224	55c	multicolored	42	42
902 A224	65c	multicolored	48	48
903 A224	75c	multicolored	58	58
904 A224	$1	multicolored	75	75
905 A224	$2	multicolored	1.50	1.50
906 A224	$3	multicolored	2.25	2.25
907 A224	$4	multicolored	3.00	3.00
908 A224	$5	multicolored	4.00	4.00
		Nos. 897-908 (12)	13.91	13.91

Souvenir Sheets

909 A224	$6	multicolored	4.50	4.50
910 A224	$6	multicolored	4.50	4.50
911 A224	$6	multicolored	4.50	4.50

Genoa '92.

Discovery of America Type

1992 Litho. *Perf. 14¹/₂*

912 A230	$1	Coming ashore	75	75
913 A230	$2	Natives, ships	1.50	1.50

Organization of East Caribbean States.

Summer Olympics Type of 1992

Designs: 10c, Volleyball, vert. 15c, Men's floor exercise. 25c, Cross-country skiing, vert. 30c, 110-meter hurdles. 45c, 120-meter ski jump. 55c, Women's 4x100-meter relay, vert. 75c, Triple jump, vert. 80c, Mogul skiing, vert. $1, 100-meter butterfly. $2, Tornado class yachting. $3, Decathlon. $5, Equestrian jumping. No. 926, Ice hockey. No. 927, Single luge. No. 928, Soccer.

1992, Apr. 21 Litho. *Perf. 14*

914 A219	10c	multicolored	15	15
915 A219	15c	multicolored	15	15
916 A218	25c	multicolored	18	18
917 A219	30c	multicolored	22	22
918 A218	45c	multicolored	35	35
919 A219	55c	multicolored	42	42
920 A219	75c	multicolored	58	58
921 A218	80c	multicolored	60	60
922 A219	$1	multicolored	75	75
923 A219	$2	multicolored	1.50	1.50
924 A219	$3	multicolored	2.25	2.25
925 A219	$5	multicolored	3.75	3.75
		Nos. 914-925 (12)	10.90	10.90

Souvenir Sheets

926 A218	$6	multicolored	4.50	4.50
927 A218	$6	multicolored	4.50	4.50
928 A219	$6	multicolored	4.50	4.50

Christmas Art Type of 1992

Details or entire paintings: 10c, Our Lady with St. Roch and St. Anthony of Padua, by Giorgione. 40c, St. Anthony of Padua, by Master of the Embroidered Leaf. 45c, Madonna and Child in a Landscape, by Orazio Gentileschi. 50c, Madonna and Child with St. Anne, by Leonardo da Vinci. 55c, The Holy Family, by Giuseppe Maria Crespi. 65c, Madonna and Child, by Andrea Del Sarto. 75c, Madonna and Child with Sts. Lawrence and Julian, by Gentile da Fabriano. $1, Virgin and Child, by School of Parma. $2, Madonna with the Iris in the style of Durer. $3, Virgin and Child with St. Jerome and St. Dominic, by Filippino Lippi. $4, Rapolano Madonna, by Ambrogio Lorenzetti. $5, The Virgin and Child with Angels in a Garden with a Rose Hedge, by Stefano da Verona. No. 941, Virgin and Child with St. John the Baptist, by Botticelli. No. 942, Madonna and Child with St. Anne, by Leonardo da Vinci. No. 943, Madonna and Child with Grapes, by Lucas Cranach the Elder.

1992, Nov. Litho. *Perf. 13¹/₂x14*

929 A232	10c	multicolored	15	15
930 A232	40c	multicolored	30	30
931 A232	45c	multicolored	35	35
932 A232	50c	multicolored	38	38
933 A232	55c	multicolored	42	42
934 A232	65c	multicolored	48	48
935 A232	75c	multicolored	58	58
936 A232	$1	multicolored	75	75
937 A232	$2	multicolored	1.50	1.50
938 A232	$3	multicolored	2.25	2.25
939 A232	$4	multicolored	3.00	3.00
940 A232	$5	multicolored	3.75	3.75
		Nos. 929-940 (12)	13.91	13.91

Souvenir Sheets

941 A232	$6	multicolored	4.50	4.50
942 A232	$6	multicolored	4.50	4.50
943 A232	$6	multicolored	4.50	4.50

Anniversaries and Events — G68

Designs: 10c, Nina in the harbor of Baracoa. No. 948, Columbus' fleet at sea. No. 949, America 3, US and Il Moro, Italy. No. 945, Zeppelin LZ3, 1907. No. 946, Blind man with guide dog, vert. No. 947, Guide dog. No. 950, German flag, natl. arms, Konrad Adenauer. No. 951, Hands breaking bread, vert. $2, Mars, Voyager 2. $3, Berlin airlift, Adenauer. No. 954, Wolfgang Amadeus Mozart, Constanze, vert. No. 955, Adenauer, Cologne after World War II. No. 956, Zeppelin LZ 37 shot down over England, World War I. $5, Buildings in Germany, Adenauer. No. 958, Scene from "Don Giovanni," vert. No. 959, Columbus looking through telescope. No. 960, Count Ferdinand von Zeppelin, facing right. No. 960A, Count Ferdinand von Zeppelin, facing left. No. 961, Mars Observer. No. 962, Adenauer with hand on face, vert. No. 963, Adenauer, diff.

1992, Dec. *Perf. 14*

944 G68	10c	multicolored	15	15
945 G68	75c	multicolored	58	58
946 G68	75c	multicolored	58	58
947 G68	75c	multicolored	58	58
948 G68	$1	multicolored	75	75
949 G68	$1	multicolored	75	75
950 G68	$1	multicolored	75	75
951 G68	$1	multicolored	75	75
952 G68	$2	multicolored	1.50	1.50
953 G68	$3	multicolored	2.25	2.25
954 G68	$4	multicolored	3.00	3.00
955 G68	$4	multicolored	3.00	3.00
956 G68	$4	multicolored	3.00	3.00
957 G68	$5	multicolored	3.75	3.75
		Nos. 944-957 (14)	21.39	21.39

Souvenir Sheets

958-963 G68	$6	each	4.50	4.50

Discovery of America, 500th anniv. (#944, 948, 959). Count Zeppelin, 75th death anniv. (#945, 956, 960-960A). Lions Intl., 75th anniv. (#946-947). Konrad Adenauer, 25th death anniv. (#950, 953, 955, 957, 962-963).America's Cup yacht race (#949). Intl. Conference on Nutrition, Rome (#951). Intl. Space Year (#952, 961). Wolfgang Amadeus Mozart, bicent. of death (in 1991) (#954, 958).

Issued: Nos. 945, 956, 960-960A, Dec. 15. Others, Dec.

Miniature Sheets

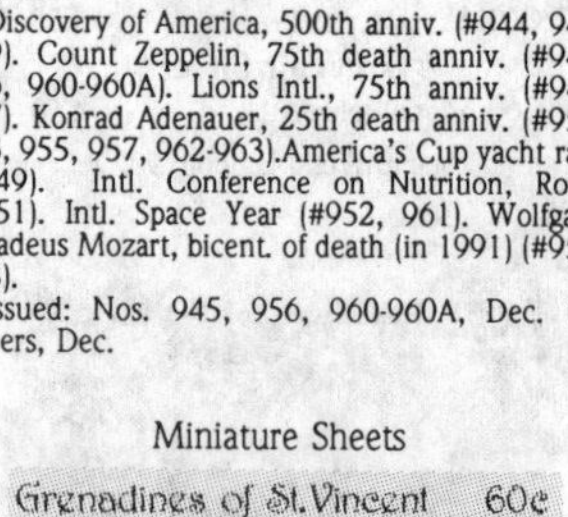

Walt Disney's Tales of Uncle Scrooge — G69

Goldilocks (Daisy Duck) and the Three Bears: No. 964a, Comes upon the house. b, Finds three bowls of soup. c, Finds three chairs. d, Ventures upstairs. e, Tries Papa Bear's bed. f, Falls asleep in Baby Bear's bed. g, The Three Bears return home. h, Baby Bear finds Goldilocks in his bed. i, Goldilocks awakens.

No. 970, The Three Bears in the forest, vert. No. 971, Goldilocks runs home.

The Princess (Minnie Mouse) and the Pea: No. 965a, Prince Mickey in search of a bride. b, Princess Minnie caught in a storm. c, Queen Clarbelle meets the princess. d, Royal family entertains Princess Minnie. e, Queen places a pea on the mattress. f, Mattresses upon mattresses. g, Princess Minnie at her bed-chamber. h, Princess Minnie very tired the next morning. i, A true princess for a real prince.

No. 972, Prince Mickey's useless search for a true princess. No. 973, Mickey's royal family lived happily ever after.

Little Red Riding Hood (Minnie Mouse): No. 966a, Off to Grandmother's. b, Stopping for flowers. c, Followed by the wolf. d, Frightened by the wolf. e, Wolf charges into Grandmother's house. f, Little Red Riding Hood at Grandmother's door. g, "What big teeth you have." h, Calling woodsman for help. i, Woodsman to the rescue.

No. 974, Little Riding Hood on the way to Grandmother's, vert. No. 975, A happy ending.

Hop O'-My-Thumb (Mickey, Minnie, family): No. 967a, Poor woodcutter without food for his children. b, Pebbles to find way back. c, Sadly leaving children's forest. d, Surveying from tree top. e, Ogress sends boys to bed. f, Ogre and his magic seven-league boots. g, Ogre chasing boys. h, Taking the magic seven-league boots. i, Running to Royal Palace.

No. 976, Boy of woodcutter with bag over shoulder. No. 977, Woodcutter's family reunited.

Pied Piper of Hamelin (Donald, Mickey and friends): No. 968a, Mayor (Donald) offers reward. b, Piper Mickey accepts the challenge. c, Piper leads rats to the river. d, Piper promises revenge. Children follow Piper outside village gates. f, Mayor and townspeople watch from above. g, Children follow Piper through countryside. h, Children pass through the cavern. i, All closed off from Hamelin, except for one.

No. 978, Pied Piper leading rats past town square. No. 979, Piper Mickey encouraging children in land of sweets, vert.

Puss in Boots (Goofy, Donald and friends): No. 969a, Gift for the king. b, Puss brings Marquis of Carabas to bathe in river. c, Puss calls for king's help. d, King introduces his daughter (Daisy Duck). e, Puss and reapers. f, Puss received by the Ogre. g, Ogre changed into a lion. h, Ogre changed into a mouse. i, Puss shows off Marquis' castle.

No. 980, Miller's estate, Donald with cat, Puss, donkey. No. 981, Marriage of Marquis of Carabis to daughter of the king, vert.

Perf. 14x13½, 13½x14

1992, Dec. 15 Litho.

964	G69	60c Sheet of 9, #a.-i.	4.25	4.25
965	G69	60c Sheet of 9, #a.-i.	4.25	4.25
966	G69	60c Sheet of 9, #a.-i.	4.25	4.25
967	G69	60c Sheet of 9, #a.-i.	4.25	4.25
968	G69	60c Sheet of 9, #a.-i.	4.25	4.25
969	G69	60c Sheet of 9, #a.-i.	4.25	4.25

Souvenir Sheets

Perf. 13½x14, 14x13½

970-981	G69	$6 each	4.50	4.50

Disney Animated Films Type
Miniature Sheets

Duck Tales (Donald Duck and family): No. 982a, Scrooge McDuck, Launchpad. b, Scrooge reads treasure map. c, Collie Baba's treasure revealed. d, Webby finds magic lamp. e, Genie and new masters. f, Webby gets her wish. g, Scrooge McDuck, Genie. h, Retrieving the magic lamp. i, Villain Merlock, Genie.

No. 984, Webby's tea party, vert. No. 985, Treasure of the lost lamp, vert.

Darkwing Duck: No. 983a, Darkwing Duck. b, Tuskerninni. c, Megavolt. d, Bushroot. e, Steelbeak. f, Eggman. g, Agent Gryzlikoff. h, Director J. Gander Hooter.

No. 985A, Gosalyn. No. 985B, Honker, horiz.

Perf. 14x13½, 13½x14

1992, Dec. 15 Litho.

982	A247a	60c Sheet of 9, #a.-i.	4.00	4.00
983	A247b	60c Sheet of 8, #a.-h.	3.60	3.60

Souvenir Sheets

984	A247a	$6 multicolored	4.50	4.50
985	A247a	$6 multicolored	4.50	4.50
985A	A247b	$6 multicolored	4.50	4.50
985B	A247b	$6 multicolored	4.50	4.50

Miniature Sheets

G71

Disney Animated Films — G72

The Great Mouse Detective: No. 986a, Olivia and Flaversham. b, Olivia's mechanical mouse. c, Ratigan's evil scheme. d, Ratigan and Mechanical Mouse Queen. e, Fidget pens ransom note. f, Basil studies clues. g, Fidget holds Olivia captive. h, Ratigan in disguise. i, Basil and Dr. Dawson, crime stoppers.

Oliver & Company: No. 987a, Dodger. b, Oliver. c, Dodger and Oliver. d, Oliver introduced to the Company. e, Oliver meets Fagin. f, Fagin's bedtime story hour. g, Oliver sleeping with Dodger. h, Fagin's trike. i, Georgette and Tito.

The Legend of Sleepy Hollow: No. 988a, Ichabod Crane comes to town. b, Ichabod meets Katrina Van Tassel. c, Schoolmaster Ichabod Crane. d, Ichabod and rival, Brom Bones. e, Ichabod and Katrina at Halloween dance. f, Ichabod is scared of ghosts. g, Ichabod in Sleepy Hollow. h, Ichabod and his horse. i, Meeting the Headless Horseman.

No. 989, Detective Basil holding pipe. No. 990, Detective Basil holding magnifying glass. No. 991, Oliver. No. 992, Oliver and kittens. No. 993, Ichabod Crane, children praying, vert. No. 994, Headless Horseman.

Perf. 14x13½, 13½x14

1992, Dec. 15 Litho.

986	G71	60c Sheet of 9, #a.-i.	4.00	4.00
987	G71	60c Sheet of 9, #a.-i.	4.00	4.00
988	G72	60c Sheet of 9, #a.-i.	4.00	4.00

Souvenir Sheets

989-994	G71	$6 each	4.50	4.50

Elvis Presley Type of 1993

Designs: a, Portrait. b, With guitar. c, With microphone.

1993 Litho. *Perf. 14*

1001	A244	$1 Strip of 3, #a.-c.	2.25	2.25

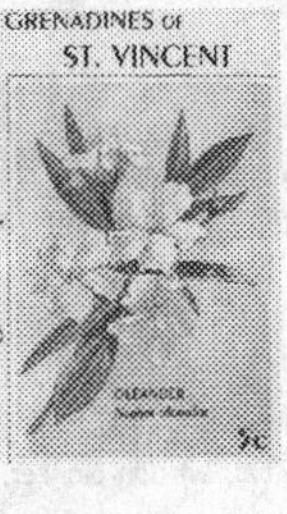

Medicinal Plants — G73

Designs: 5c, Oleander. 10c, Beach morning glory. 30c, Calabash. 45c, Porita tree. 55c, Cashew. 75c, Prickly pear. $1, Shell ginger. $1.50, Avocado. $2, Mango. $3, Blood flower. $4, Sugar apple. $5, Barbados lily.

1994, May 20 Litho. *Perf. 13½x13*

1002-1013	G73	Set of 12	14.00	14.00

SEMI-POSTAL STAMPS

Nos. 190-193 Surcharged

HURRICANE
RELIEF
50¢

1980, Aug. 7 Litho. *Perf. 13½*

B1	A90	25c + 50c Running	50	50
B2	A90	50c + 50c Sailing	70	70
B3	A90	$1 + 50c Long jump	1.00	1.00
B4	A90	$2 + 50c Swimming	1.75	1.75

OFFICIAL STAMPS

Nos. 209-214 Ovptd. "OFFICIAL"

1982, Oct. 11

O1	A66	50c on No. 209	35	35
O2	A67	50c on No. 210	35	35
O3	A66	$3 on No. 211	2.00	2.00
O4	A67	$3 on No. 212	2.00	2.00
O5	A66	$3.50 on No. 213	2.50	2.50
O6	A67	$3.50 on No. 214	2.50	2.50

BEQUIA

All stamps are types of St. Vincent ("A" illustration letter), St. Vincent Grenadines ("G" illustration letter) or Bequia ("B" illustration letter).

"Island" issues are listed separately beginning in 1984. See St. Vincent Grenadines Nos. 84-111, 248-262 for earlier issues.

Locomotive Type of 1985

1984-87 Litho. Unwmk. *Perf. 12½*
Pairs, Type A120

1	1c	1942 Challenger Class, US	15	15
2	1c	1908 S3/6, Germany	15	15
3	5c	1944 2900 Class, US	15	15
4	5c	1903 Jersey Lily, UK	15	15
5	10c	1882 Gladstone Class, UK	15	15
6	10c	1909 Thundersley, UK	15	15
7	15c	1860 Ser Class 118, UK	15	15
8	25c	1893 No. 999 NY Central & Hudson River, US	20	20
9	25c	1921 Class G2, UK	20	20
10	25c	1902 Jr. Class 6400, Japan	20	20
11	25c	1877 Class G3, Germany	20	20
12	35c	1945 Niagara Class, US	28	28
13	35c	1938 Manor Class, UK	28	28
14	40c	1880 Class D VI, Germany	32	32
15	45c	1914 K4 Class, US	35	35
16	50c	1960 Class U25B, US	40	40
17	55c	1921 Stephenson, UK	42	42
18	55c	1909 Class H4, US	42	42
19	60c	1922 Baltic, UK	48	48
20	60c	1903 J.R. 4500, Japan	48	48
21	60c	1915 Class LS	48	48
22	75c	1841 Borsig, Germany	60	60
23	75c	1943 Royal Scot, UK	60	60
24	75c	1961 Krauss-Maffei, US	60	60
25	$1	1928 River IRT, UK	80	80
26	$1	1890 Electric, UK	80	80
27	$1	1934 A.E.C., UK	80	80
28	$1.50	1929 No. 10000, UK	1.25	1.25
29	$2	1904 City Class, UK	1.60	1.60
30	$2	1901 No. 737, UK	1.60	1.60
31	$2	1847 Cornwall, UK	1.60	1.60
32	$2.50	1938 Duke Dog Class, UK	2.00	2.00
33	$2.50	1881 Ella, UK	2.00	2.00
34	$3	1910 George V Class, UK	2.40	2.40
		Nos. 1-34 (68)	23.01	23.01

Issued: #1, 3, 5, 8, 12, 15, 28-29, 2/22/84; #2, 4, 6, 13, 22, 25, 32, 34, 11/26/84; #9, 17, 19, 30, 2/1/85; #10, 18, 20, 23, 26, 33, 8/14/85; #7, 11, 14, 16, 21, 24, 27, 31, 11/16/87.

Stamps issued 11/16/87 are not inscribed "Leaders of the World."

St. Vincent Grenadines Nos. 222-238
Ovptd. "BEQUIA"

Perf. 14x13½

1984, Aug. 23 Wmk. 373

69	G26	1c on No. 222	15	15
70	G26	3c on No. 223	15	15
71	G26	5c on No. 224	15	15
72	G26	6c on No. 225	15	15
73	G26	10c on No. 226	15	15
74	G26	15c on No. 227	15	15
75	G26	20c on No. 228	15	15
76	G26	25c on No. 229	15	15
77	G26	30c on No. 230	20	20
78	G26	50c on No. 231	32	32
79	G26	60c on No. 232	40	40
80	G26	75c on No. 233	48	48
81	G26	$1 on No. 234	65	65
82	G26	$2 on No. 235	1.25	1.25
83	G26	$3 on No. 236	2.00	2.00
84	G26	$5 on No. 237	3.25	3.25
85	G26	$10 on No. 238	6.75	6.75
		Nos. 69-85 (17)	16.50	16.50

Car Type of 1983

1984-87 Unwmk. *Perf. 12½*
Pairs, Type A107

86	5c	1953 Cadillac, US	15	15
87	5c	1932 Fiat, Italy	15	15
88	5c	1968 Excalibur, US	15	15
89	5c	1952 Hudson, US	15	15
90	10c	1924 Leyand, UK	15	15
91	20c	1911 Marmon, US	15	15
92	20c	1950 Alfa Romeo, Italy	15	15
93	20c	1968 Ford Escort, UK	15	15
94	20c	1939 Maserati 8 CTF, Italy	15	15
95	25c	1963 Ford, UK	18	18
96	25c	1958 Vanwall, UK	18	18
97	25c	1910 Stanley, US	18	18
98	35c	1948 Ford Wagon, US	25	25
99	40c	1936 Auto Union, Germany	32	32
100	45c	1907 Chadwick, US	35	35
101	50c	1924 Lanchester, UK	40	40
102	50c	1957 Austin-Healy, UK	40	40
103	60c	1935 Brewster-Ford, US	48	48
104	60c	1942 Willys Jeep, US	48	48
104	65c	1929 Isotta, Italy	50	50
106	75c	1940 Lincoln, US	60	60
107	75c	1964 Bluebird II, UK	60	60
108	75c	1948 Moore-Offenhauser, US	60	60
109	75c	1936 Ford, UK	60	60
110	80c	1936 Mercedes Benz, Germany	65	65
111	90c	1928 Mercedes Benz SSK, Germany	72	72
112	$1	1907 Rolls Royce, UK	75	75
113	$1	1955 Citroen, France	75	75
114	$1	1936 Fiat, Italy	75	75
115	$1	1922 Dusenberg, US	75	75
116	$1	1957 Pontiac Bonneville, US	75	75
117	$1.25	1916 Hudson Super Six, US	1.00	1.00
118	$1.25	1977 Coyote Ford, US	1.00	1.00
119	$1.50	1960 Porsche, Germany	1.25	1.25
120	$1.50	1970 Plymouth, US	1.25	1.25
121	$1.75	1933 Stutz, US	1.35	1.35
122	$2	1910 Benz-Blitzen, Germany	1.60	1.60
123	$2	1933 Napier Railton, UK	1.60	1.60
124	$2.50	1978 BMW, Germany	2.00	2.00
125	$3	1912 Hispano Suiza, Spain	2.40	2.40
126	$3	1954 Mercedes Benz, Germany	2.40	2.40
127	$3	1927 Stutz Black Hawk, US	2.40	2.40
		Nos. 86-127 (84)	31.74	31.74

Issued: #86, 99, 112, 119, 9/14; #87, 90-91, 95, 106, 113, 124-125, 12/19; #88, 96, 101, 114, 117, 122, 6/25/85; #92, 100, 120, 123, 9/26/85. #97, 102, 105, 107, 115, 126, 1/29/86; #93, 103, 108, 111, 116, 127, 12/23/86. #89, 94, 98, 104, 109-110, 118, 121, 7/22/87.

Beginning on Sept. 26, 1985, this issue is not inscribed "Leaders of the World."

1984 Summer Olympics — B1

Dogs — B2

1984, Sept. 14 *Perf. 12½*

170	B1	1c Men's gymnastics	15	15
171	B1	1c Women's gymnastics	15	15
172	B1	10c Men's javelin	15	15
173	B1	10c Women's javelin	15	15
174	B1	60c Women's basketball	24	24
175	B1	60c Men's basketball	24	24
176	B1	$3 Women's long jump	1.10	1.10
177	B1	$3 Men's long jump	1.10	1.10
		Nos. 170-177 (8)	3.28	3.28

Stamps of same denomination printed se-tenant.

1985, Mar. 14 *Perf. 12½*

178	B2	25c Hungarian Kuvasz	15	15
179	B2	25c Afghan	15	15
180	B2	35c Whippet	15	15
181	B2	35c Bloodhound	15	15
182	B2	55c Cavalier King Charles Spaniel	22	22
183	B2	55c German Shepherd	22	22
184	B2	$2 Pekinese	80	80
185	B2	$2 Golden Retriever	80	80
		Nos. 178-185 (8)	2.64	2.64

Stamps of same denomination printed se-tenant.

World War II Warships B3

1985, Apr. 29 *Perf. 12½*
186 B3 15c HMS Hood 15 15
187 B3 15c as #186, diff. 15 15
188 B3 50c HMS Duke of York 22 22
189 B3 50c as #188, diff. 22 22
190 B3 $1 KM Admiral Graf Spee 38 38
191 B3 $1 as #190, diff. 38 38
192 B3 $1.50 USS Nevada 55 55
193 B3 $1.50 as #192, diff. 55 55
Nos. 186-193 (8) 2.60 2.60

Stamps of same denomination printed se-tenant.

St. Vincent Grenadines Flower Type

1985, May 31 *Perf. 12½*
194 G38 10c Primula veris 15 15
195 G38 10c Pulsatilla vulgaris 15 15
196 G38 20c Lapageria rosea 15 15
197 G38 20c Romneya coulteri 15 15
198 G38 70c Anigozanthos manglesii 25 25
199 G38 70c Metrosideros collina 25 25
200 G38 $2.50 Protea laurifolia 90 90
201 G38 $2.50 Thunbergia grandiflora 90 90
Nos. 194-201 (8) 2.90 2.90

Stamps of same denomination printed se-tenant.

Queen Mother Type of 1985

Various Portraits of Queen Mother

1985, Aug. 29 *Perf. 12½*
202 A122 20c Blue hat 15 15
203 A122 20c Violet hat 15 15
204 A122 65c Blue hat, diff. 25 25
205 A122 65c Tiara 25 25
206 A122 $1.35 Blue hat, diff. 52 52
207 A122 $1.35 White hat 52 52
208 A122 $1.80 Blue hat, diff. 70 70
209 A122 $1.80 Pink hat 70 70
Nos. 202-209 (8) 3.24 3.24

Souvenir Sheets
210 Sheet of 2 1.65 1.65
a. A122 $2.05 Hat 80 80
b. A122 $2.05 Tiara 80 80
211 Sheet of 2 2.75 2.75
a. A122 $3.50 like #204 1.25 1.25
b. A122 $3.50 like #205 1.25 1.25
212 Sheet of 2 4.75 4.75
a. A122 $6 like #202 2.25 2.25
b. A122 $6 like #203 2.25 2.25

Stamps of same denomination printed se-tenant.

Queen Elizabeth II Type of 1986

Various portraits.

1986, Apr. 21
213 A128 5c multi 15 15
214 A128 75c multi 30 30
215 A128 $2 multi 80 80
216 A128 $8 multi, vert. 3.25 3.25

Souvenir Sheet
217 A128 $10 multi 4.00 4.00

B4

World Cup Soccer Championships, Mexico, 1986 — B5

1986 July 3 *Perf. 12½, 15 (B5)*
218 B4 1c South Korean team 15 15
219 B4 2c Iraqi team 15 15
220 B4 5c Algerian team 15 15
221 B4 10c Bulgaria vs. France 15 15
222 B5 45c Belgium 22 22
223 B4 60c Danish team 28 28
224 B4 75c Italy vs. W. Germany 35 35
225 B4 $1.50 USSR vs. England 65 65
226 B5 $1.50 Italy, 1982 champions 65 65
227 B5 $2 W. Germany 95 95
228 B5 $3.50 N. Ireland 1.65 1.65
229 B4 $6 England 2.75 2.75
Nos. 218-229 (12) 8.10 8.10

Souvenir Sheets
230 B4 $1 like No. 219 45 45
231 B4 $1.75 like No. 221 85 85

Royal Wedding Type of 1986

Perf. 12½x13, 13x12½

1986, July 15
232 A132 60c Andrew 24 24
233 A132 60c Andrew in helicopter 24 24
234 A132 $2 Andrew in crowd 75 75
235 A132 $2 Andrew, Sarah 75 75

Souvenir Sheet
236 A132a $8 Andrew, Sarah in coach 3.25 3.25

Nos. 234-235 horiz.

Railway Engineers and Locomotives — B6

Designs: $1, Sir Daniel Gooch, Fire Fly Class, 1840. $2.50, Sir Nigel Gresley, A4 Class, 1938. $3, Sir William Stanier, Coronation Class, 1937. $4, Oliver V. S. Bulleid, Battle of Britain Class, 1946.

1986, Sept. 30 *Perf. 13x12½*
237 B6 $1 multicolored 48 48
238 B6 $2.50 multicolored 1.25 1.25
239 B6 $3 multicolored 1.40 1.40
240 B6 $4 multicolored 1.90 1.90

Nos. 232-235 Ovptd. "Congratulations to TRH The Duke & Duchess of York" in 3 Lines

1986 *Perf. 12½x13, 13x12½*
241 A132 60c on No. 232 22 22
242 A132 60c on No. 233 22 22
243 A132 $2 on No. 234 75 75
244 A132 $2 on No. 235 75 75

Royalty Portrait Type

Portraits and photographs: 15c, Queen Victoria, 1841. 75c, Elizabeth, Charles, 1948. $1, Coronation, 1953. $2.50, Duke of Edinburgh, 1948. $5, Elizabeth c. 1980. $6, Elizabeth, Charles, 1948, diff.

1987, Oct. 15 *Perf. 12½x13*
245 A140 15c multicolored 15 15
246 A140 75c multicolored 35 35
247 A140 $1 multicolored 48 48
248 A140 $2.50 multicolored 1.25 1.25
249 A140 $5 multicolored 2.50 2.50
Nos. 245-249 (5) 4.73 4.73

Souvenir Sheet
250 A140 $6 multicolored 3.00 3.00

Great Explorers Type of St. Vincent Grenadines

Designs: 15c, Gokstad, ship of Leif Eriksson (c. 1000). 50c, Eriksson and bearing dial. $1.75, The Mathew, ship of John Cabot. $2, Cabot, quadrant. $2.50, The Trinidad, ship of Ferdinand Magellan. $3, Arms, portrait of Christopher Columbus. $3.50, Columbus' ship Santa Maria. $4, Magellan, globe. $5, Anchor, long boat, ship.

1988, July 11 **Litho.** *Perf. 14*
251 G52 15c multicolored 15 15
252 G52 50c multicolored 35 35
253 G52 $1.75 multicolored 90 90
254 G52 $2.00 multicolored 1.40 1.40
255 G52 $2.50 multicolored 1.75 1.75
256 G52 $3.00 multicolored 2.00 2.00
257 G52 $3.50 multicolored 2.50 2.50
258 G52 $4.00 multicolored 2.75 2.75
Nos. 251-258 (8) 11.80 11.80

Souvenir Sheet
259 G52 $5.00 multicolored 3.50 3.50

Tennis Type of 1987

1988, July 29 *Perf. 13x13½*
260 A137 15c Anders Jarryd 15 15
261 A137 45c Anne Hobbs 25 25
262 A137 80c Jimmy Connors 50 50
263 A137 $1.25 Carling Bassett 75 75
264 A137 $1.75 Stefan Edberg, horiz. 1.00 1.00
265 A137 $2.00 Gabriela Sabatini, horiz. 1.20 1.20
266 A137 $2.50 Mats Wilander 1.50 1.50
267 A137 $3.00 Pat Cash 1.80 1.80
Nos. 260-267 (8) 7.15 7.15

No. 263 inscribed "Carlene Basset" instead of "Carling Bassett."

French Revolution Bicentennial B7

Designs: 1c, Grandma Duck as French peasant woman. 2c, Donald and Daisy celebrating liberty. 3c, Minnie as Marie Antoinette. 4c, Clarabelle and patriotic chair. 5c, Goofy in Republican citizen's costume. 10c, Mickey and Donald planting liberty tree. No. 274, Horace taking Tennis Court Oath. $6, Grand Master Mason McDuck. No. 276, Dancing the Carmagnole. No. 277, Philosophers at Cafe La Procope.

1989, July 7 *Perf. 13½x14*
268 B7 1c multicolored 15 15
269 B7 2c multicolored 15 15
270 B7 3c multicolored 15 15
271 B7 4c multicolored 15 15
272 B7 5c multicolored 15 15
273 B7 10c multicolored 15 15
274 B7 $5 multicolored 3.00 3.00
275 B7 $6 multicolored 3.50 3.50
Nos. 268-275 (8) 7.40 7.40

Souvenir Sheets
276 B7 $5 multicolored 3.00 3.00
277 B7 $5 multicolored 3.00 3.00

Anniversaries and Events Type

Design: $5, Otto Lilienthal, aviation pioneer.

1991, Nov. 18 **Litho.** *Perf. 14*
278 A213 $5 multicolored 3.75 3.75

Numbers have been reserved for additional values in this set.

Japanese Attack on Pearl Harbor, 50th Anniv. B8

Designs: 50c, Kate from second-wave over Hickam Field. $1, B17 sights Zeros in Pearl Harbor attack. $5, Firefighters rescue sailors from blazing USS Tennessee.

1991, Nov. 18
287 B8 50c multicolored 38 38
288 B8 $1 multicolored 75 75

Souvenir Sheet
289 B8 $5 multicolored 3.75 3.75

Wolfgang Amadeus Mozart, Death Bicentennial B9

Mozart and: 10c, Piccolo. 75c, Piano. $4, Violotta.

No. 293, Mozart's last composition, Lacrimosa from the Requiem Mass. No. 294, Bronze of Mozart by Adrien-Etienne Gaudez, vert. No. 295, Score of opening of the "Paris" symphony, K297.

1991 **Litho.** *Perf. 14*
290 B9 10c multicolored 15 15
291 B9 75c multicolored 58 58
292 B9 $4 multicolored 3.00 3.00

Souvenir Sheets
293 B9 $6 multicolored 4.50 4.50
294 B9 $6 multicolored 4.50 4.50
295 B9 $6 multicolored 4.50 4.50

Nos. 293-295 each contain one 57x42mm or 42x57mm stamp.

Boy Scout Type

Designs: 50c, Lord Baden-Powell and killick hitch knot. $1, Baden-Powell and clove hitch knot. $2, Drawing of Boy Scout by Baden-Powell, vert. $3, American First Class Scout badge, vert. $6, Baden-Powell and Lark's head knot.

1991
296 A211 50c multicolored 38 38
297 A211 $1 multicolored 75 75
298 A211 $2 multicolored 1.50 1.50
299 A211 $3 multicolored 2.25 2.25

Souvenir Sheet
300 A211 $6 multicolored 4.50 4.50

UNION ISLANDS

All stamps are types of St. Vincent ("A" illustration letter), St. Vincent Grenadines ("G" illustration letter) or Union ("U" illustration letter).

"Island" issues are listed separately beginning in 1984. See St. Vincent Grenadines Nos. 84-111, 248-262 for earlier issues.

British Monarch Type of 1984

Perf. 12½

1984, Mar. 29 **Litho.** **Unwmk.**
1 A110 1c Battle of Hastings 15 15
2 A111 1c William the Conqueror 15 15
3 A110 5c William the Conqueror, diff. 15 15
4 A111 5c Abbaye Aux Dames 15 15
5 A110 10c Skirmish at Dunbar 15 15
6 A111 10c Charles II 15 15
7 A110 20c Arms of Willian the Conqueror 15 15
8 A111 20c William the Conqueror, diff. 15 15
9 A111 60c Charles II 22 22
10 A110 60c St. James Palace 22 22
11 A110 $3 Arms of Charles II 1.10 1.10
12 A111 $3 Charles II, Great Fire of London 1.10 1.10
Set value 3.00 3.00

Stamps of same denomination printed se-tenant.

Locomotives Type of 1985

1984-87 *Perf. 12½*

Pairs, Type A120
13 5c 1813 Puffing Billy, UK 15 15
14 5c 1911 Class 9N, UK 15 15
15 5c 1882 Class Skye Bogie, UK 15 15
16 10c 1912 Class G8, Germany 15 15
17 15c 1954 Class 65.10, Germany 15 15
18 15c 1900 Castle Class, UK 15 15
19 15c 1887 Spinner Class 25, UK 15 15
20 15c 1951 Fell #10100, UK 15 15
21 20c 1942 Class 42, Germany 15 15
22 20c 1951 Class 5MT, UK 15 15
23 25c 1929 P.O. Rebuilt Class 3500, France 18 18
24 25c 1886 Class 123, UK 18 18
25 30c 1976 Class 56, UK 22 22
26 30c 1897 Class G5, US 22 22
27 40c 1947 9400 Class, UK 30 30
28 45c 1888 Sir Theodore, UK 35 35
29 45c 1929 Class Z, UK 35 35
30 45c 1896 Atlantic City RR, US 35 35
31 50c 1906 45xx Class, UK 38 38
32 50c 1912 Class D15, UK 38 38
33 50c 1938 Class U4-b, Canada 38 38
34 60c 1812 Prince Regent, UK 45 45

35 60c 1920 Butler Henderson, UK 45 45
36 60c 1889 Elidir, UK 45 45
37 60c 1934 7200 Class, UK 45 45
38 60c 1911 Class Z, UK 45 45
39 75c 1938 Class C, Australia 58 58
40 75c 1879 Sir Haydn, UK 58 58
41 75c 1850 Aberdeen No. 26, UK 58 58
42 75c 1883 Class Y14, UK 58 58
43 75c 1915 River Class, UK 58 58
44 $1 1936 D51 Class, Japan 75 75
45 $1 1837 L&B Bury, UK 75 75
46 $1 1903 Class 900, US 75 75
47 $1 1904 Class H-20, US 75 75
48 $1 1905 Class L, UK 75 75
49 $1.50 1952 Class 4, UK 1.10 1.10
50 $1.50 1837 Campbell's 8-Wheeler, US 1.10 1.10
51 $1.50 1934 Class GG1, US 1.10 1.10
52 $2 1924 Class 01, Germany 1.50 1.50
53 $2 1920 Gordon Highlander, UK 1.50 1.50
54 $2 1969 Metroliner Railcar, US 1.50 1.50
55 $2 1951 Class GP7, US 1.50 1.50
56 $2.50 1873 Hardwicke Precedent Class, UK 1.75 1.75
57 $2.50 1899 Highflyer Class, UK 1.75 1.75
58 $3 1925 Class U1, UK 2.25 2.25
59 $3 1880 Class 7100, Japan 2.25 2.25
60 $3 1972 Gas Turbine Prototype, France 2.25 2.25
Nos. 13-60 (96) 37.50 37.50

Issued: #13, 34, 44, 52, 8/9/84; #14, 16, 21, 23, 39, 45, 56, 58, 12/18/84; #15, 31, 35, 53, 3/25/85; #17, 25, 28, 36, 40, 49, 57, 59, 1/31/86; #18, 29, 37, 41, 46, 50, 54, 60, 12/23/86; #19, 24, 27, 32, 38, 42, 47, 55, 9/87; #20, 22, 26, 308, 33, 43, 48, 51, 12/4/87.

Beginning on Jan. 31, 1986, this issue is not inscribed "Leaders of the World."

St. Vincent Grenadines Nos. 222-238 Overprinted "UNION ISLAND"

Perf. 14x13½

1984, Aug. 23 **Wmk. 373**

109 G26 1c on No. 222 15 15
110 G26 3c on No. 223 15 15
111 G26 5c on No. 224 15 15
112 G26 6c on No. 225 15 15
113 G26 10c on No. 226 15 15
114 G26 15c on No. 227 15 15
115 G26 20c on No. 228 15 15
116 G26 25c on No. 229 16 16
117 G26 30c on No. 230 20 20
118 G26 50c on No. 231 35 35
119 G26 60c on No. 232 40 40
120 G26 75c on No. 233 45 45
121 G26 $1 on No. 234 70 70
122 G26 $2 on No. 235 1.40 1.40
123 G26 $3 on No. 236 2.00 2.00
124 G26 $5 on No. 237 3.40 3.40
125 G26 $10 on No. 238 6.50 6.50
Nos. 109-125 (17) 16.61 16.61

Cricket Players Type of 1985

1984, Nov. **Unwmk.** *Perf. 12½*

Pairs, Type A116

126 1c S. N. Hartley 15 15
127 10c G. W. Johnson 15 15
128 15c R. M. Ellison 15 15
129 55c C. S. Cowdrey 40 40
130 60c K. Sharp 48 48
131 75c M. C. Cowdrey, in action 60 60
132 $1.50 G. R. Dilley, in action 1.25 1.25
133 $3 R. Illingworth, in action 2.25 2.25
Nos. 126-133 (16) 5.78 5.78

Classic Car Type of 1983

1985-86 *Perf. 12½*

142 1c 1963 Lancia, Italy 15 15
143 5c 1895 Duryea, US 15 15
144 10c 1970 Datsun, Japan 15 15
145 10c 1962 BRM, UK 15 15
146 50c 1927 Amilcar, France 35 35
147 55c 1929 Duesenberg, US 40 40
148 60c 1913 Peugeot, France 48 48
149 60c 1938 Lagonda, UK 48 48
150 60c 1924 Fiat, Italy 48 48
151 75c 1957 Alfa Romeo, Italy 60 60
152 75c 1957 Panhard, France 60 60
153 75c 1954 Porsche, Germany 60 60
154 90c 1904 Darraco, France 70 70
155 $1 1927 Daimler, UK 85 85
156 $1 1949 Oldsmobile, US 85 85
157 $1 1934 Chrysler, US 85 85
158 $1.50 1965 MG, UK 1.25 1.25
159 $1.50 1922 Fiat, Italy 1.25 1.25
160 $1.50 1934 Bugatti, France 1.25 1.25
161 $2 1963 Watson/Meyer-Drake, US 1.60 1.60
162 $2.50 1917 Locomobile, US 2.00 2.00
163 $3 1928 Ford, US 2.50 2.50
Nos. 142-163 (44) 18.12 18.12

Issued: #142, 146, 151, 162, 1/4/85; #143, 148, 155, 158, 5/20/85; #144, 147, 149, 152, 154, 156, 159, 161, 7/15/85; #145, 150, 153, 157, 160, 163, 7/30/86.

Beginning on 7/30/86, this issue is not inscribed "Leaders of the World."

Birds — U1

Butterflies — U2

1985, Feb. *Perf. 12½*

186 U1 15c Hooded warbler 15 15
187 U1 15c Carolina wren 15 15
188 U1 50c Song sparrow 20 20
189 U1 50c Black-headed grosbeak 20 20
190 U1 $1 Scarlet tanager 40 40
191 U1 $1 Lazuli bunting 40 40
192 U1 $1.50 Sharp-shinned hawk 60 60
193 U1 $1.50 Merlin 60 60
Nos. 186-193 (8) 2.70 2.70

Stamps of same denomination printed se-tenant.

1985, Apr. 15

194 U2 15c Cynthia cardui 15 15
195 U2 15c Zerynthia rumina 15 15
196 U2 25c Byblia ilithyia 15 15
197 U2 25c Papilio machaon 15 15
198 U2 75c Carterocephalus palaemon 30 30
199 U2 75c Acraea anacreon 30 30
200 U2 $2 Anartia amathea 80 80
201 U2 $2 Salamis temora 80 80
Nos. 194-201 (8) 2.80 2.80

Stamps of same denomination printed se-tenant.

Queen Mother Type of 1985

Various portraits of Queen Mother honoring 85th birthday.

1985, Aug. 19

202 A122 55c Mortarboard 18 18
203 A122 55c Blue hat 18 18
204 A122 70c Turquoise hat 24 24
205 A122 70c Blue hat, diff. 24 24
206 A122 $1.05 Without hat 35 35
207 A122 $1.05 White hat 35 35
208 A122 $1.70 White hat, violet feathers 65 65
209 A122 $1.70 Blue hat, diff. 65 65
Nos. 202-209 (8) 2.84 2.84

Souvenir Sheets

210 Sheet of 2 1.50 1.50
a. A122 $1.95 Crown 75 75
b. A122 $1.95 Hat, diff. 75 75
211 Sheet of 2 1.65 1.65
a. A122 $2.25 Like No. 208 80 80
b. A122 $2.25 Like No. 209 80 80
212 Sheet of 2 5.00 5.00
a. A122 $7 Like No. 206 2.50 2.50
b. A122 $7 Like No. 207 2.50 2.50

Stamps of same denomination printed se-tenant.

Elizabeth II 60th Birthday Type of 1986

Designs: 10c, Wearing scarf. 60c, Riding clothes. $2, Wearing crown and jewels. $8, In Canberra, vert. $10, Holding flowers.

1986, Apr. 21

213 A128 10c multicolored 15 15
214 A128 60c multicolored 24 24
215 A128 $2 multicolored 75 75
216 A128 $8 multicolored 3.25 3.25

Souvenir Sheet

217 A128 $10 multicolored 4.00 4.00

U3

World Cup Soccer Championships, Mexico — U4

Perf. 12½ (U3), 15 (U4)

1986, May 7

218 U3 1c Moroccan team 15 15
219 U3 10c Argentinian team 15 15
220 U4 30c Algerian player 15 15
221 U3 75c Hungarian team 32 32
222 U3 $1 Russian team 45 45
223 U4 $2.50 Belgian player 1.10 1.10
224 U4 $3 French player 1.25 1.25
225 U4 $6 W. German player 2.50 2.50
Nos. 218-225 (8) 6.07 6.07

Souvenir Sheets

226 U3 $1.85 like No. 222 85 85
227 U3 $2 like No. 219 85 85

Souvenir sheets contain one 60x40mm stamp.

Prince Andrew Royal Wedding Type

Perf. 12½x13, 13x12½

1986, July 15

228 A132 60c Andrew with cap 24 24
229 A132 60c Andrew, diff. 24 24
230 A132 $2 Sarah Ferguson 75 75
231 A132 $2 Sarah, Andrew 75 75

Nos. 228-231 Overprinted in Silver "CONGRATULATIONS TO T.R.H. THE DUKE & DUCHESS OF YORK" in 3 Lines

1986, Oct.

232 A132 60c on No. 228 24 24
233 A132 60c on No. 229 24 24
234 A132 $2 on No. 230 75 75
235 A132 $2 on No. 231 75 75

Queen Elizabeth II Wedding Anniv. Type of St. Vincent Grenadines

1987, Oct. 15 *Perf. 12½*

236 G47 15c like No. 568 15 15
237 G47 45c like No. 569 22 22
238 G47 $1.50 like No. 570 70 70
239 G47 $3 like No. 571 1.40 1.40
240 G47 $4 like No. 572 1.75 1.75
Nos. 236-240 (5) 4.22 4.22

U5

Disney characters in various French vehicles: 1c, 1893 Peugeot. 2c, 1890-91Panhard-Levassor. 3c, 1910 Renault. 4c, 1919 Citroen. 5c, 1878 La Mancelle. 10c, 1891 De Dion Bouton Quadricycle. $5, 1896 Leon Bollee Trike. No. 248, 1911 Brasier Coupe. No. 249, French road race. No. 250, 1769, Cugnot's artillery tractor.

1989, July 7 *Perf. 14x13½*

241 U5 1c multicolored 15 15
242 U5 2c multicolored 15 15
243 U5 3c multicolored 15 15
244 U5 4c multicolored 15 15
245 U5 5c multicolored 15 15
246 U5 10c multicolored 15 15
247 U5 $5 multicolored 3.75 3.75
248 U5 $6 multicolored 4.50 4.50
249 U5 $6 multicolored 4.50 4.50
250 U5 $6 multicolored 4.50 4.50
Nos. 241-250 (10) 18.15 18.15

PHILEXFRANCE '89.

SOUTH GEORGIA

LOCATION — Island in South Atlantic Ocean, 1,100 mi. east of Tierra del Fuego
GOVT. — Dependency of Falkland Islands
AREA — 1,450 sq. mi.
POP. — 22 (1975)
CAPITAL — Grytviken Harbor (chief town)

South Georgia remained a dependency of the Falkland Islands in 1962 when three other dependencies became Antarctic Territory, a separate colony. In 1985 South Georgia and the South Sandwich Islands became a separate colony. See Falkland Islands Dependencies Nos. 3L1-3L8.

12 Pence = 1 Shilling
20 Shillings = 1 Pound
100 Pence = 1 Pound (1971)

Catalogue values for all unused stamps in this country are for Never Hinged items.

Reindeer A1

Sperm Whale — A2

Designs: 1p, South Sandwich Islands map. 2½p, Penguins. 3p, Fur seals. 4p, Finback whale and ship. 5½p, Elephant seals. 6p, Sooty albatross. 9p, Whaling ship. 1sh, Leopard seal. 2sh, Shackleton's cross. 2sh6p, Wandering albatross. 5sh, Elephant and fur seals. 10sh, Plankton and krill (shrimp). £1, Blue whale.

Wmk. 314 Upright

1963, July 10 **Engr.** *Perf. 15*

1 A1 ½p dull red 24 24
a. Perf. 14x15 ('67) 1.40 *2.00*
b. Watermark sideways ('70) 1.40 *3.75*
2 A2 1p violet blue 20 18
3 A2 2p blue green 28 20
4 A1 2½p black 42 32
5 A2 3p olive 48 32
6 A1 4p green 55 40
7 A1 5½p dull violet 60 60
8 A2 6p orange 60 60
9 A1 9p blue 1.10 90
10 A1 1sh lilac 1.25 1.10
11 A1 2sh cit & lt blue 5.75 4.75
12 A1 2sh6p blue 5.75 5.75
13 A1 5sh ocher 12.00 12.00
14 A2 10sh rose claret 27.50 25.00
15 A1 £1 ultra 85.00 70.00

1969, Dec. 1

Design: £1, King penguins.

16 A2 £1 slate green 15.00 *24.00*
Nos. 1-16 (16) 156.72 146.36

Stamps and Type of 1963 Surcharged with New Value (Decimal Currency) and 3 Bars

Wmk. 314 Upright; Sideways on ½p

1971, Feb. 15 *Perf. 15*

17 A1 ½p on ½p dull red 60 75
a. Wmk. upright ('73) 75 75
18 A2 1p on 1p vio blue 70 90
a. Wmk. sideways ('76) 2.25 2.75
19 A1 1½p on 5½p dull vio 55 70
20 A2 2p on 2p blue grn 45 55
21 A1 2½p on 2½p black 55 70
22 A2 3p on 3p olive 60 75
23 A1 4p on 4p green 70 90
24 A2 5p on 6p orange 1.00 1.25
25 A1 6p on 9p blue 42 52
26 A1 7½p on 1sh lilac 1.75 2.00
27 A1 10p on 2sh cit & lt bl 10.50 7.50
28 A1 15p on 2sh6p blue 14.00 13.00
29 A1 25p on 5sh ocher 10.50 7.50
30 A2 50p on 10sh rose cl 32.50 32.50
a. Wmk. sideways ('76) 32.50 32.50
Nos. 17-30 (14) 74.82 69.52

Two types of surcharge are found on ½p, 1p, 1½p and 50p.

1977 **Wmk. 373**

17b A1 ½p on ½p dull red 25 25
18b A2 1p on 1p vio blue 70 70
19b A1 1½p on 5½p dl vio 1.10 1.10

21b	A1	2½p	on 2½p black	1.25	1.25
22b	A2	3p	on 3p olive	1.25	1.25
23b	A1	4p	on 4p green	3.50	3.50
24b	A2	5p	on 6p orange	2.00	2.00
26b	A1	7½p	on 1sh lilac	7.00	7.00
27b	A1	10p	on 2sh cit & lt bl	7.00	7.00
28b	A1	15p	on 2sh6p blue	7.00	7.00
29b	A1	25p	on 5sh ocher	7.00	7.00
30b	A2	50p	on 10sh lil rose ('79)	14.00	14.00
			Nos. 17b-30b (12)	52.05	52.05

Ernest Shackleton and "Quest" A3

Designs: 1½p, "Endurance" in ice of Weddell Sea. 5p, Launching of sailboat "James Caird." 10p, Route of "James Caird" to South Georgia.

1972, Jan. 5 Litho. *Perf. 13½*

31	A3	1½p	vio bl, blk & yel	55	55
32	A3	5p	bl grn, blk & yel	1.00	1.00
33	A3	10p	lt blue & blk	2.00	2.00
34	A3	20p	multicolored	4.00	4.00

Sir Ernest Shackleton (1874-1922), explorer of Antarctica.

Silver Wedding Issue, 1972

Common Design Type

Design: Queen Elizabeth II, Prince Philip, elephant seal and king penguins.

1972, Nov. 20 Photo. *Perf. 14x14½*

35	CD324	5p	slate grn & multi	95	95
36	CD324	10p	violet & multi	1.90	1.90

Princess Anne's Wedding Issue

Common Design Type

1973, Dec. 1 Litho. *Perf. 14*

37	CD325	5p	citron & multi	38	38
38	CD325	15p	slate & multi	1.10	1.10

Churchill, Parliament and Big Ben — A4

Design: 25p, Churchill and battleship.

1974, Dec. 14 Litho. *Perf. 14½*

39	A4	15p	vio blue & multi	1.50	1.50
40	A4	25p	orange & multi	2.25	2.25
a.			Souvenir sheet of 2, #39-40	6.75	6.75

Sir Winston Churchill (1874-1965).

Capt. James Cook — A5

Cook's "Possession" — A6

Design: 16p, Possession Bay.

1975, Apr. 26 Wmk. 314

41	A5	2p	multicolored	1.50	1.00
42	A6	8p	multicolored	2.50	2.00
43	A6	16p	multicolored	4.00	3.75

Bicentenary of Capt. Cook's discovery of South Georgia.

"Discovery" and Biological Laboratory — A7

Designs: 8p, "William Scoresby" and Nansen-Pettersson water sampling bottles. 11p, "Discovery II" and plankton net. 25p, Biological station and krill (shrimp).

Wmk. 373

1976, Dec. 21 Litho. *Perf. 14*

44	A7	2p	multicolored	48	40
45	A7	8p	multicolored	1.25	95
46	A7	11p	multicolored	1.50	1.50
47	A7	25p	multicolored	3.75	3.75

25th anniversary of the biological investigations of the "Discovery."

Queen with Regalia and Westminster Abbey — A8

Designs: 6p, Prince Philip visiting Shackleton Memorial, 1957. 33p, Queen in procession after coronation.

1977, Feb. 7 *Perf. 13½x14*

48	A8	6p	multicolored	35	35
49	A8	11p	multicolored	60	60
50	A8	33p	multicolored	1.75	1.75

25th anniv. of the reign of Elizabeth II.

Elizabeth II Coronation Anniversary Issue

Common Design Types

Souvenir Sheet

Unwmk.

1978, June 2 Litho. *Perf. 15*

51		Sheet of 6	4.50	*6.50*
a.	CD326	25p Panther of Henry VI	75	75
b.	CD327	25p Elizabeth II	75	75
c.	CD328	25p Fur seal	75	75

No. 51 contains 2 se-tenant strips of Nos. 51a-51c, separated by horizontal gutter with commemorative and descriptive inscriptions and showing central part of coronation procession with coach.

Resolution A9

Cook's voyages: 6p, Map of South Georgia and South Sandwich Islands with Cook's route. 11p, King penguin, drawing by Forster. 25p, Cook after Flaxman/Wedgwood medallion.

1979, Feb. 14 Litho. *Perf. 11*

52	A9	3p	multicolored	60	60
53	A9	6p	multicolored	80	80
54	A9	11p	multicolored	1.50	1.25

Lithographed; Embossed

55	A9	25p	multicolored	1.90	1.50

SOUTH GEORGIA and SOUTH SANDWICH ISLANDS

Queen Elizabeth II 60th Birthday

Common Design Type

Designs: 10p, With King George and Queen Mary at christening of Prince Charles, 1948. 24p, Engagement of Prince Charles and Lady Diana, Buckingham Palace Music Room, 1981. 29p, Order of the British Empire, service at St. Paul's Cathedral, London, 1974. 45p, Banquet for Canadian Prime Minister Trudeau during the 1976 Olympics. 58p, Visiting Crown Agents' offices, 1983.

1986, Apr. 21 Wmk. 384 *Perf. 14½*

101	CD337	10p	multicolored	25	25
102	CD337	24p	multicolored	60	60
103	CD337	29p	multicolored	75	75
104	CD337	45p	multicolored	1.10	1.10
105	CD337	58p	multicolored	1.50	1.50
			Nos. 101-105 (5)	4.20	4.20

Common Design Types are pictured beginning on page 176.

Wedding of Prince Andrew and Sarah Ferguson — A12

1986, Nov. 10 Litho. *Perf. 14½*

106	A12	17p	Couple at Ascot	50	50
107	A12	22p	Wedding	65	65
108	A12	29p	Andrew, helicopter	85	85

Birds A13

1987, Apr. 24 Litho. Wmk. 384

109	A13	1p	Dominican gull	15	15
110	A13	2p	Blue-eyed cormorant	15	15
111	A13	3p	Wattled sheathbill	15	15
112	A13	4p	Brown skua	15	15
113	A13	5p	Cape pigeon	18	18
114	A13	6p	South Georgia diving petrel	20	20
115	A13	7p	South Georgia pipit	24	24
116	A13	8p	South Georgia pintail	28	28
117	A13	9p	Fairy prion	30	30
118	A13	10p	Chinstrap penguin	35	35
119	A13	20p	Macaroni penguin	68	68
120	A13	25p	Light-mantled sooty albatross	85	85
121	A13	50p	Southern giant petrel	1.75	1.75
122	A13	£1	Wandering albatross	3.50	3.50
123	A13	£3	King penguin	10.25	10.25
			Nos. 109-123 (15)	19.18	19.18

3, 4, 7, 8, 20, 25, 50p and £3 vert.

Intl. Geophysical Year, 30th Anniv. — A14

1987, Dec. 5 Litho. *Perf. 14½*

124	A14	24p	shown	82	82
125	A14	29p	Grytviken Whaling Station	98	98
126	A14	58p	Glaciologist	1.95	1.95

Sea Shells — A15

1988, Feb. 26 Wmk. 384 *Perf. 14½*

127	A15	10p	Gaimardia trapesina	38	38
128	A15	24p	Margarella tropidophoroides	88	88
129	A15	29p	Trophon scotianus	1.05	1.05
130	A15	58p	Chlanidota densesculpta	2.10	2.10

Lloyds of London, 300th Anniv.

Common Design Type

Designs: 10p, Queen Mother at the official opening of the Lloyds Building, Lime Street, 1957. 24p, Lindblad Explorer, horiz. 29p, Leith Harbor whaling station, horiz. 58p, Whale oil tanker Horatio on fire.

1988, Sept. 17 *Perf. 14*

131	CD341	10p	multicolored	35	35
132	CD341	24p	multicolored	80	80
133	CD341	29p	multicolored	98	98
134	CD341	58p	multicolored	1.95	1.95

Glacier Formations A16

1989, July 31

135	A16	10p	Glacier headwall	35	35
136	A16	24p	Accumulation area	85	85
137	A16	29p	Ablation area	1.05	1.05
138	A16	58p	Calving front	2.05	2.05

Combined Services Expedition, 1964-65 A17

1989, Nov. 28 *Perf. 14x14½*

139	A17	10p	"Last ordeal" of the trek	32	32
140	A17	24p	Survey of Royal Bay	78	78
141	A17	29p	HMS *Protector*	95	95
142	A17	58p	1st Ascent of Mt. Paget	1.85	1.85

Queen Mother, 90th Birthday

Common Design Types

Designs: 26p, Queen Mother. £1, King, Queen & Air Raid Wardens, 1940

Perf. 14x15

1990, Sept. 15 Wmk. 384

143	CD343	26p	multicolored	88	88

Perf. 14½

144	CD344	£1	blue & black	3.40	3.40

Shipwrecks — A18

Wmk. 384

1990, Dec. 22 Litho. *Perf. 14*

145	A18	12p	Brutus	45	45
146	A18	26p	Bayard	1.00	1.00
147	A18	31p	Karrakatta	1.20	1.20
148	A18	62p	Louise	2.40	2.40

Elizabeth & Philip, Birthdays

Common Design Types

1991, July 2 *Perf. 14½*

149	CD345	31p	multicolored	1.00	1.00
150	CD346	31p	multicolored	1.00	1.00
a.			Pair, #149-150 + label	2.00	2.00

Elephant Seals — A19

1991, Nov. 2 Wmk. 373 *Perf. 14*

151 A19 12p Two bulls 38 38
152 A19 26p One bull 85 85
153 A19 29p Using sand as sun-screen 95 95
154 A19 31p Bull, close up 1.00 1.00
155 A19 34p Harem on beach 1.10 1.10
156 A19 62p Cow and pup 2.00 2.00
Nos. 151-156 (6) 6.28 6.28

Queen Elizabeth II's Accession to the Throne, 40th Anniv.

Common Design Type

1992, Feb. 6

157 CD349 7p multicolored 25 25
158 CD349 14p multicolored 45 45
159 CD349 29p multicolored 90 90
160 CD349 34p multicolored 1.10 1.10
161 CD349 68p multicolored 2.20 2.20
Nos. 157-161 (5) 4.90 4.90

South Georgia Teal
A20

1992, Mar. 22 Wmk. 384

162 A20 2p Adult, young 15 15
163 A20 6p Adult, nest of eggs 20 20
164 A20 12p Four swimming 40 40
165 A20 20p Adult, two chicks 65 65

World Wildlife Fund.

South Georgia Whaling Museum
A21

Designs: 15p, Abandoned factory, Grytviken. 31p, Whaler's lighter, bones. 36p, King Edward Cove. 72p, Museum Building.

Perf. 13 1/2

1993, June 29 Litho. Wmk. 373

166-169 A21 Set of 4 4.50 4.50

Macaroni Penguins
A22

Designs: 16p, Swimming underwater. 34p, Part of rookery. 39p, Two juveniles. 78p, Two adults.

Perf. 14x14 1/2

1993, Dec. 10 Litho. Wmk. 373

170-173 A22 Set of 4 4.75 4.75

Ovptd. with Hong Kong '94 Emblem

1994, Feb. 18

174-177 A22 Set of 4 4.75 4.75

Whales and Dolphins
A23

Designs: 1p, Hourglass dolphin. 2p, Southern right whale dolphin. 5p, Long-finned pilot whale. 8p, Southern bottlenose whale. 9p, Killer whale. 10p, Minke whale. 20p, Sei whale. 25p, Humpback whale. 50p, Southern right whale. £1, Sperm whale. £3, Fin whale. £5, Blue whale.

Wmk. 373

1994, Jan. 24 Litho. *Perf. 14*

178 A23 1p multicolored 15 15
179 A23 2p multicolored 15 15
180 A23 5p multicolored 15 15
181 A23 8p multicolored 22 22
182 A23 9p multicolored 25 25
183 A23 10p multicolored 28 28
184 A23 20p multicolored 55 55
185 A23 25p multicolored 70 70
186 A23 50p multicolored 1.40 1.40
187 A23 £1 multicolored 2.75 2.75
188 A23 £3 multicolored 8.25 8.25
189 A23 £5 multicolored 14.00 14.00
Nos. 178-189 (12) 28.85 28.85

Native Wildlife
A24

Wmk. 384

1994, Sept. 28 Litho. *Perf. 14*

190 A24 17p Bull elephant seals 52 52
191 A24 35p Fur seal, vert. 1.10 1.10
192 A24 40p Gray-headed albatrosses 1.25 1.25
193 A24 65p King penguins, vert. 2.00 2.00
Nos. 190-193 (4) 4.87 4.87

SEMI-POSTAL STAMPS

Liberation of South Georgia, 10th Anniv. — SP1

Designs: 14p+6p, King Edward Point, Winter 1982. 29p+11p, Queen Elizabeth 2 in Cumberland Bay. 34p+16p, Royal Marines on South Sandwich Islands. 68p+32p, HMS Endurance and Wasp Helicopter.

Wmk. 384

1992, June 20 Litho. *Perf. 14*

B1 SP1 14p +6p multicolored 65 65
B2 SP1 29p +11p multicolored 1.30 1.30
B3 SP1 34p +16p multicolored 1.65 1.65
B4 SP1 68p +32p multicolored 3.25 3.25
a. Souvenir sheet of 4, #B1-B4 6.85 6.85

Surtax for Soldiers', Sailors' and Airmen's Families Association.

TOBAGO

LOCATION — An island in the West Indies lying off the Venezuelan coast north of Trinidad
GOVT. — A former British Colony
AREA — 116 sq. mi.
POP. — 25,358
CAPITAL — Scarborough (Port Louis)

In 1889 Tobago, then an independent colony, was united with Trinidad under the name of Colony of Trinidad and Tobago. It became a ward of that colony January 1, 1899.

12 Pence = 1 Shilling
20 Shillings = 1 Pound

Queen Victoria
A1 A2

Wmk. Crown and C C (1)

1879 Typo. *Perf. 14*

1 A1 1p rose 20.00 16.00
2 A1 3p blue 24.00 20.00
3 A1 6p orange 17.50 16.00
4 A1 1sh green 275.00 50.00
a. Half used as 6p on cover
5 A1 5sh slate 475.00 625.00
6 A1 £1 violet *4,250.*

Stamps of the above set with revenue cancellations sell for a small fraction of the price of postally used copies.

Stamps of Type A1, watermarked Crown and C A, are revenue stamps.

1880

Manuscript Surcharge

7 A1 1p on half of 6p org *4,500.* *800.*

1880

8 A2 1/2p brown violet 13.50 20.00
9 A2 1p red brown 32.50 16.00
a. Half used as 1/2p on cover 1,650.
10 A2 4p yellow green 150.00 22.50
a. Half used as 2p on cover 1,650.
11 A2 6p bister brown 250.00 100.00
12 A2 1sh bister 32.50 18.00
a. Imperf.

No. 11 Surcharged in Black — **2½ PENCE**

1883

13 A2 2 1/2p on 6p bister brn 10.00 7.50
a. Double surcharge 3,000. 1,350.

1882-96 Wmk. Crown and C A (2)

14 A2 1/2p brown vio ('83) 1.90 *9.75*
15 A2 1/2p dull green ('86) 22 28
16 A2 1p red brown ('82) 2.00 1.90
a. Diagonal half used as 1/2p on cover
17 A2 1p rose ('86) 28 28
18 A2 2 1/2p ultra ('83) 1.10 80
19 A2 4p yel grn ('84) 150.00 55.00
20 A2 4p gray ('85) 55 80
a. Imperf., pair 1,800.
21 A2 6p bis brn ('84) 400.00 250.00
a. Imperf.
22 A2 6p brn org ('86) 1.10 2.25
23 A2 1sh olive bis ('94) 2.00 3.75
24 A2 1sh brn org ('96) 7.50

Stamps of 1882-96 Surcharged in Black:

½ PENNY — Nos. 25-29
2½ PENCE — No. 30

1886-92

25 A2 1/2p on 2 1/2p ultra 1.40 *4.25*
a. Inverted surcharge
b. Pair, one without surcharge 8,000.
c. Space between "1/2" and "PENNY" 3mm 12.00 *14.00*
d. Double surcharge 1,250. 875.00
26 A2 1/2p on 4p gray 9.50 *14.00*
a. Space between "1/2" and "PENNY" 3mm
b. Double surcharge 1,650.
27 A2 1/2p on 6p bis brn 1.50 *3.50*
a. Inverted surcharge 1,400.
b. Space between "1/2" and "PENNY" 3mm 22.50 *30.00*
c. Double surcharge 1,500.
28 A2 1/2p on 6p brn org 45.00 55.00
a. Space between "1/2" and "PENNY" 3mm 200.00 *250.00*
b. Double surcharge 1,750.
29 A2 1p on 2 1/2 ultra 7.50 5.50
a. Space between "1" and "PENNY" 4mm 60.00 *60.00*
b. Half used as 1/2p on cover *1,650.*
30 A2 2 1/2p on 4p gray 4.50 *5.00*
a. Double surcharge 1,650.

Revenue Stamp Type A1 Surcharged in Black — **½d POSTAGE**

1896

31 A1 1/2p on 4p lilac & rose 8.75 12.50
a. Space between "1/2" and "d" 1 1/2 to 2 1/2mm 15.00 17.50

Tobago stamps were replaced by those of Trinidad or Trinidad and Tobago.

TRINIDAD

LOCATION — West Indies, off the Venezuelan coast
GOVT. — British Colony which became part of the Colony of Trinidad and Tobago in 1889
AREA — 1,864 sq. mi.
POP. — 387,000
CAPITAL — Port of Spain

12 Pence = 1 Shilling
20 Shillings = 1 Pound

In 1847 David Bryce, owner of the "Lady McLeod," issued a blue, lithographed, imperf. stamp to prepay his 5-cent rate for carrying letters on his sail-equipped steamer between Port of Spain and San Fernando, another Trinidad port. The stamp pictures the "Lady McLeod" above the monogram "LMcL," expressing no denomination. Value, used (pen canceled), $10,000.

"Britannia"
A1 A2

1851-53 Unwmk. Engr. *Imperf.*

Blued Paper

1 A1 (1p) brick red ('53) 140.00 45.00
a. (1p) brown red ('53) 300.00 40.00
2 A1 (1p) purple brown 6.00 *30.00*
3 A1 (1p) blue 6.00 *30.00*
a. (1p) deep blue 10.00 *30.00*
4 A1 (1p) gray 25.00 25.00
a. (1p) gray brown 13.00 *18.00*

1854-57

White Paper

6 A1 (1p) brown red ('57) 1,500. 40.00
7 A1 (1p) gray 15.00 *40.00*
8 A1 (1p) black violet 9.00 *20.00*

See Nos. 14, 18, 22, 27, 33, 39, 43, 45, 48, 58. For surcharges see Nos. 62-64.

1852 Litho.

Yellowish Paper

9 A2 (1p) blue *11,500.* 1,750.
a. (1p) deep blue *11,500.* 1,500.
b. White paper 1,400.

1853

Bluish Paper

10 A2 (1p) blue *8,000.* 2,400.

Same, Lines of Background More or Less Worn

1855-60

Thin Paper

11 A2 (1p) slate blue *5,500.* 400.00
12 A2 (1p) blue 275.00
a. (1p) greenish blue 400.00
13 A2 (1p) rose 11.00 *450.00*
a. (1p) dull red 11.00 *450.00*

A3

1859 Engr. *Imperf.*

White Paper

14 A1 (1p) dull rose 600.00 50.00
15 A3 4p gray lilac 30.00 *150.00*
a. 4p dull lilac *425.00*
16 A3 6p green 325.00
17 A3 1sh slate blue 40.00 *175.00*

Pin-perf. 12 1/2

18 A1 (1p) dl rose red 750.00 35.00
a. (1p) lake 750.00 35.00
19 A3 4p brown lilac *10,000.* 700.00
20 A3 6p deep green 2,250. 200.00
21 A3 1sh black violet *5,000.* 400.00

Pin-perf. 14

22 A1 (1p) rose red 95.00 21.00
a. (1p) carmine 210.00 21.00

23 A3 4p brown lilac 85.00 *100.00*
a. 4p violet 110.00
b. 4p dull violet 900.00 110.00
24 A3 6p deep green 350.00 75.00
25 A3 6p yellow green 65.00 65.00
a. Vert. pair, imperf. between *4,250.*
26 A3 1sh black violet *12,000.* *500.00*

Nos. 18-26 with full perforations on all sides sell at higher prices.

1860 ***Clean-cut Perf. 14 to 15 1/2***
27 A1 (1p) dull rose 100.00 30.00
a. (1p) lake 100.00 30.00
b. Horiz. pair, imperf. vert. *3,000.*
29 A3 4p violet brown 100.00 45.00
a. 4p dull violet 300.00
30 A3 6p deep green 225.00 160.00
31 A3 6p yellow green 175.00 110.00
32 A3 1sh black violet

1861 ***Rough Perf. 14 to 16 1/2***
33 A1 (1p) dull rose 82.50 11.00
34 A3 4p gray lilac 550.00 27.50
35 A3 4p brown lilac 175.00 27.50
a. 4p dull violet 575.00 27.50
36 A3 6p green 350.00 35.00
a. 6p blue green 700.00 35.00
37 A3 1sh indigo 1,000. 130.00
a. 1sh purplish blue 1,250. 200.00

1863 ***Perf. 11 1/2 to 12***
Thick Paper
39 A1 (1p) carmine 50.00 11.00
a. Perf. 11 1/2-12x11 *500.00*
40 A3 4p dull violet 65.00 20.00
41 A3 6p dp blue green *700.00* 20.00
a. Perf. 11 1/2-12x11 *4,500.*
42 A3 1sh indigo 1,000. 70.00

Perf. 12 1/2
43 A1 (1p) lake 16.00 11.00

Perf. 13
45 A1 (1p) lake 22.00 11.00
46 A3 6p emerald 300.00 32.50
47 A3 1sh brt violet 4,000. 225.00

1864-72 **Wmk. 1** ***Perf. 12 1/2***
48 A1 (1p) red 11.00 1.10
a. (1p) lake 17.00 1.90
b. (1p) rose 2.00 1.10
c. (1p) carmine 17.00 1.10
d. Imperf., pair *800.00* *800.00*
49 A3 4p brt violet 45.00 5.50
a. 4p pale violet 90.00 6.00
b. Imperf. *600.00*
50 A3 4p lilac 25.00 5.50
a. 4p gray lilac
51 A3 4p gray ('72) 60.00 2.75
52 A3 6p blue green 50.00 3.00
a. 6p emerald 35.00 8.25
53 A3 6p yellow grn 35.00 2.25
a. 6p dp grn 350.00 8.25
b. Imperf., pair *800.00*
54 A3 1sh purple 40.00 3.75
a. 1sh lilac 40.00 3.75
b. 1sh violet 90.00 3.75
c. 1sh red lilac 125.00 3.75
d. Imperf. *750.00*
55 A3 1sh orange yel ('72) 75.00 1.65

See Nos. 59-61A, 65. For surcharge see No. 67.

Queen Victoria — A4

1869-94 **Typo.** ***Perf. 12 1/2***
56 A4 5sh dull lake 55.00 37.50
a. Imperf., pair *1,250.*

Perf. 14
57 A4 5sh claret ('94) 12.00 20.00

For overprint see No. O7.

1876 **Engr.** ***Perf. 14***
58 A1 (1p) carmine 3.00 55
a. (1p) red 30.00 70
b. (1p) lake 3.00 55
c. Half used as 1/2p on cover 600.00
59 A3 4p gray 35.00 1.65
60 A3 6p yellow green 35.00 1.10
a. 6p deep green 35.00 1.10
61 A3 1sh orange yel 32.50 2.75

Perf. 14x12 1/2
61A A3 6p yellow green *3,250.*

Type A1 Surcharged in Black **HALFPENNY**

1879 **Wmk. 1** ***Perf. 14***
62 A1 1/2p lilac 3.00 3.00

Same Surcharge
1882 **Wmk. Crown and C A (2)**
63 A1 1/2p lilac *250.00* 42.50
64 A1 1p carmine 7.00 50
a. Half used as 1/2p on cover 400.00

Type of 1859
1882 **Wmk. 2**
65 A3 4p gray 75.00 3.00

No. 60 Surcharged by pen and ink in Black or Red

1882 **Wmk. 1**
67 A3 1p on 6p green (R) 3.00 1.50
a. Half used as 1/2p on cover 400.00
b. Black surcharge *1,900.*

Counterfeits of No. 67b are plentiful. Various handwriting exists on both 60 and 60a.

A7

A8

A9

1883-84 **Typo.** **Wmk. 2**
68 A7 1/2p green 30 15
69 A7 1p rose 1.00 15
a. Half used as 1/2p on cover 200.00
70 A7 2 1/2p ultra 2.00 15
a. 2 1/2p blue 2.00 25
71 A7 4p slate 2.50 40
72 A7 6p olive brn ('84) 1.40 1.10
73 A7 1sh orange brn ('84) 4.00 1.75
Nos. 68-73 (6) 11.20 3.70

For overprints see Nos. O1-O6.

1896-1904 ***Perf. 14***
ONE PENNY:
Type I - Round "O" in "ONE."
Type II - Oval "O" in "ONE."

74 A8 1/2p lilac & green 15 15
75 A8 1/2p gray grn ('02) 15 15
76 A8 1p lil & car, type I 45 15
77 A8 1p lil & car, type II ('00) 225.00 2.75
78 A8 1p blk, *red*, type II ('01) 22 15
a. Value omitted *12,000.*
79 A8 2 1/2p lilac & ultra 75 30
80 A8 2 1/2p vio & bl, *bl* ('02) 3.25 75
81 A8 4p lilac & orange 1.50 1.50
82 A8 4p grn & ultra, *buff* ('02) 1.25 1.25
83 A8 5p lilac & violet 2.50 2.50
84 A8 6p lilac & black 2.50 2.25
85 A8 1sh grn & org brn 3.75 4.00
86 A8 1sh blk & bl, *yel* ('04) 3.75 3.00

Wmk. C A over Crown (46)
87 A9 5sh green & org 22.50 25.00
88 A9 5sh lil & red vio ('02) 18.00 22.50
89 A9 10sh grn & ultra 110.00 130.00
90 A9 £1 grn & car 95.00 110.00
Nos. 74-90 (17) 490.72 306.40

No. 82 also exists on chalky paper. Nos. 88 and 90 exist on both ordinary and chalky paper.
Circular "Registrar General" cancels are revenue usage and of minimal value.
See Nos. 92-104.

Trinidad and Tobago stamps can be mounted in the Scott British East Caribbean album.

Landing of Columbus — A10

1898 **Engr.** **Wmk. 1**
91 A10 2p gray vio & yel brn 1.25 60

400th anniv. of the discovery of the island of Trinidad by Columbus, July 31, 1498.

1904-09 **Wmk. 3**
Chalky Paper
92 A8 1/2p gray green 35 22
93 A8 1p blk, *red*, type II 35 15
94 A8 2 1/2p vio & bl, *bl* 12.50 75
95 A8 4p blk & car, *yel* ('06) 65 95
96 A8 6p lilac & blk ('05) 3.75 3.00
97 A8 6p vio & dp vio ('06) 1.40 1.40
98 A8 1sh blk & bl, *yel* 3.25 2.00
99 A8 1sh vio & bl, *yel* 2.75 3.25
100 A8 1sh blk, *grn* ('06) 95 65
101 A9 5sh lil & red vio ('07) 27.50 37.50
102 A9 £1 grn & car ('07) 125.00 165.00
Nos. 92-102 (11) 178.45 214.87

The 1/2p and 1p also exist on ordinary paper.
For overprints see Nos. O8-O9.

1906-07
103 A8 1p carmine ('07) 65 15
104 A8 2 1/2p ultramarine 42 15
Set value 24

A11

A12

1909
Ordinary Paper
105 A11 1/2p gray green 15 15
106 A12 1p carmine 15 15
107 A11 2 1/2p ultramarine 1.50 1.00

For overprint see No. O10.

POSTAGE DUE STAMPS

D1

Wmk. Crown and C A (2)
1885, Jan. 1 **Typo.** ***Perf. 14***
J1 D1 1/2p black 24.00 11.50
J2 D1 1p black 1.25 15
J3 D1 2p black 7.50 22
J4 D1 3p black 15.00 25
J5 D1 4p black 12.00 4.25
J6 D1 5p black 14.00 55
J7 D1 6p black 22.50 5.00
J8 D1 8p black 24.00 5.75
J9 D1 1sh black 30.00 9.00
Nos. J1-J9 (9) 150.25 36.67

1906-07 **Wmk. 3**
J10 D1 1p black 2.00 15
J11 D1 2p black 2.50 15
J12 D1 3p black 2.75 20
J13 D1 4p black 3.75 3.25
J14 D1 5p black 4.50 3.75
J15 D1 6p black 7.00 6.25
J16 D1 8p black 10.50 11.00
J17 D1 1sh black 17.50 15.00
Nos. J10-J17 (8) 50.50 39.75

See Trinidad and Tobago Nos. J1-J16.

OFFICIAL STAMPS

Postage Stamps of 1869-84 Overprinted in Black **O S**

1893-94 **Wmk. 2** ***Perf. 14***
O1 A7 1/2p green 22.50 *30.00*
O2 A7 1p rose 32.50 *40.00*
O3 A7 2 1/2p ultra 32.50 *40.00*
O4 A7 4p slate 35.00 *42.50*
O5 A7 6p olive brown 40.00 *47.50*
O6 A7 1sh orange brown 50.00 *55.00*

Wmk. Crown and C C (1)
Perf. 12 1/2
O7 A4 5sh dull lake 82.50 *165.00*
Nos. O1-O7 (7) 295.00 *420.00*

Nos. 92 and 103 Overprinted **OFFICIAL**

1909-10 **Wmk. 3** ***Perf. 14***
O8 A8 1/2p gray green 60 85
O9 A8 1p carmine 20 32
a. Double overprint 315.00
b. Inverted overprint 165.00
c. Vertical overprint 50.00

Same Overprint on No. 105
1910
O10 A11 1/2p gray green 20 25

Stamps of Trinidad have been superseded by those inscribed "Trinidad and Tobago."

TRINIDAD AND TOBAGO

LOCATION — West Indies off the coast of Venezuela
GOVT. — Republic
AREA — 1,980 sq. mi.
POP. — 1,160,000 (est. 1984)
CAPITAL — Port-of-Spain

The two British colonies of Trinidad and Tobago were united from 1889 until 1899, when Tobago became a ward of the united colony. From 1899 until 1913 postage stamps of Trinidad were used. The two islands became a state in August 1962, and the independent Republic of Trinidad and Tobago on August 1, 1976.

12 Pence = 1 Shilling
20 Shillings = 1 Pound
100 Cents = 1 Dollar (1935)

Catalogue values for unused stamps in this country are for Never Hinged items, beginning with Scott 62 in the regular postage section and Scott J9 in the postage due section.

"Britannia"
A1 A2

1913 **Typo.** **Wmk. 3** ***Perf. 14***
Ordinary Paper
1 A1 1/2p green 15 15
2 A1 1p scarlet 35 15
a. 1p carmine 15 15
4 A1 2 1/2p ultra 1.65 28

Chalky Paper
5 A1 4p scar & blk, *yel* 1.00 85
6 A1 6p red vio & dull vio 2.25 1.75
7 A1 1sh black, *green* 1.75 1.75
a. 1sh black, *emerald* 1.40 1.40
b. 1sh black, *bl grn, ol back* 1.65 1.65
Nos. 1-2,4-7 (6) 7.15 4.93

1914

Surface-colored Paper

8 A1 4p scar & blk, *yel* 3.50 *5.50*
9 A1 1sh black, *green* 1.10 1.65

Chalky Paper

10 A2 5sh dull vio & red vio 21.00 *35.00*
11 A2 £1 green & car 110.00 *165.00*

1921-22 Wmk. 4

Ordinary Paper

12 A1 ½p green 48 15
13 A1 1p scarlet 15 15
14 A1 1p brown ('22) 18 15
15 A1 2p gray ('22) 1.90 38
16 A1 2½p ultra 52 80
17 A1 3p ultra ('22) 1.50 1.40

Chalky Paper

18 A1 6p red vio & dull vio 1.10 95
19 A2 5sh dull vio & red vio 25.00 *37.50*
20 A2 £1 green & car 80.00 *140.00*
Nos. 12-20 (9) 110.83 *181.48*

For overprints see #B2-B3, MR1-MR13, O1-O5.

"Britannia" and King George V — A3

1922-28

Ordinary Paper

21 A3 ½p green 15 15
22 A3 1p brown 15 15
23 A3 1½p rose red 18 15
24 A3 2p gray 22 18
25 A3 3p ultra 75 32

Chalky Paper

26 A3 4p red & blk, *yel* ('28) 2.50 65
27 A3 6p red vio & dl vio 5.00 *10.00*
28 A3 6p red & grn, *emer* ('24) 1.25 75
29 A3 1sh blk, *emer* ('25) 1.25 1.00
30 A3 5sh vio & dull vio 18.00 *25.00*
31 A3 £1 rose & green 90.00 *140.00*

Wmk. Multiple Crown and C A (3)

Chalky Paper

32 A3 4p red & blk, *yel* 60 60
33 A3 1sh blk, *emerald* 3.00 3.25
Nos. 21-33 (13) 123.05 *182.20*

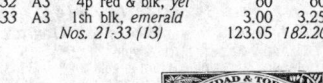

First Boca — A4

Designs: 2c, Agricultural College. 3c, Mt. Irvine Bay, Tobago. 6c, Discovery of Lake Asphalt. 8c, Queen's Park, Savannah. 12c, Town Hall, San Fernando. 24c, Government House. 48c, Memorial Park. 72c, Blue Basin.

1935-37 Engr. Wmk. 4 *Perf. 12*

34 A4 1c emer & bl, perf. 12½ ('36) 15 15
a. Perf. 12 50 15
35 A4 2c lt brn & ultra, perf. 12½ ('36) 18 15
a. Perf. 12 70 15
36 A4 3c red & black 15 15
a. Perf. 12½ ('36) 18 15
37 A4 6c bl & brn, perf. 12½ ('37) 32 20
a. Perf. 12 35 20
38 A4 8c red org & yel grn 52 60
39 A4 12c dk violet & blk 52 35
a. Perf. 12½ ('37) 95 75
40 A4 24c ol grn & blk 1.00 55
a. Perf. 12½ ('37) 1.75 1.50
41 A4 48c slate green 15 4.50
42 A4 72c mag & sl grn 12.50 13.00
Nos. 34-42 (9) 20.59 19.65

Silver Jubilee Issue

Common Design Type

1935, May 6 *Perf. 11x12*

43 CD301 2c black & ultra 15 15
44 CD301 3c car & blue 20 20
45 CD301 6c ultra & brn 42 42
46 CD301 24c brn vio & ind 1.75 1.75

Coronation Issue

Common Design Type

1937, May 12 *Perf. 13½x14*

47 CD302 1c deep green 15 15
48 CD302 2c yellow brown 15 15
49 CD302 8c deep orange 24 24

First Boca — A13

Agricultural College — A14

Mt. Irvine Bay, Tobago — A15

Memorial Park — A16

General Post Office and Treasury A17

Discovery of Lake Asphalt — A18

Queen's Park, Savannah A19

Town Hall, San Fernando A20

Government House — A21

Blue Basin A22

George VI A23

Perf. 11½x11

1938-41 Wmk. 4 Engr.

50 A13 1c emer & blue 15 15
51 A14 2c lt brn & ultra 15 15
52 A15 3c dk car & blk 4.50 30
52A A15 3c vio brn & bl grn ('41) 15 15
53 A16 4c brown 2.50 85
53A A16 4c red ('41) 20 15
54 A17 5c mag ('41) 15 15
55 A18 6c brt bl & sep 15 15
56 A19 8c red org & yel grn 15 15
57 A20 12c dk vio & blk 45 15
58 A21 24c dk ol grn & blk 30 15
59 A22 60c mag & sl grn 75 42

Perf. 12

60 A23 $1.20 dk grn ('40) 1.75 60
61 A23 $4.80 rose pink ('40) 11.00 4.50
Nos. 50-61 (14) 22.35 8.02

Watermark sideways on Nos. 50-59.

Catalogue values for unused stamps in this section, from this point to the end of the section, are for Never Hinged items.

Peace Issue

Common Design Type

Perf. 13½x14

1946, Oct. 1 Engr. Wmk. 4

62 CD303 3c brown 18 18
63 CD303 6c deep blue 25 25

Silver Wedding Issue

Common Design Types

1948, Nov. 22 Photo. *Perf. 14x14½*

64 CD304 3c red brown 20 20

Engr. *Perf. 11½x11*

65 CD305 $4.80 rose car 17.00 *25.00*

UPU Issue

Common Design Types

Engr.; Name Typo. on 6c, 12c

Perf. 13½, 11x11½

1949, Oct. 10 Wmk. 4

66 CD306 5c red violet 16 16
67 CD307 6c indigo 26 20
68 CD308 12c rose violet 55 45
69 CD309 24c olive 1.00 80

University Issue

Common Design Types

Inscribed: "Trinidad"

1951, Feb. 16 Engr. *Perf. 14x14½*

70 CD310 3c chocolate & grn 25 18
71 CD311 12c purple & blk 70 55

First Boca — A25

Elizabeth II — A26

Designs: 2c, Agricultural College. 3c, Mt. Irvin Bay, Tobago. 4c, Memorial Park. 5c, General Post Office and Treasury. 6c, Discovery of Lake Asphalt. 8c, Queens Park, Savannah. 12c, Town Hall, San Fernando. 24c, Government House. 60c, Blue Basin.

1953, Apr. 20 *Perf. 11½x11*

72 A25 1c yel grn & dp blue 15 15
73 A25 2c org brn & sl blue 15 15
74 A25 3c vio brn & blue grn 15 15
75 A25 4c red 15 15
76 A25 5c magenta 15 15
77 A25 6c blue & brown 20 15
78 A25 8c red org & dp green 20 15
79 A25 12c dk violet & blk 25 15
80 A25 24c dk ol grn & blk 52 18
81 A25 60c rose car & grnsh blk 90 35

Perf. 11½

82 A26 $1.20 dark green 2.25 1.50
a. Perf. 12 2.25 1.50
83 A26 $4.80 rose pink 9.25 6.25
a. Perf. 12 9.25 6.25
Nos. 72-83 (12) 14.32 9.48

For surcharge see No. 85.

Common Design Types are pictured beginning on page 176.

Coronation Issue

Common Design Type

1953, June 3 *Perf. 13½x13*

84 CD312 3c dark green & blk 15 15

No. 73 Surcharged "ONE CENT"

Perf. 11½x11

1956, Dec. 20 Wmk. 4

85 A25 1c on 2c org brn & sl blue 70 70

West Indies Federation

Common Design Type

Perf. 11½x11

1958, Apr. 22 Engr. Wmk. 314

86 CD313 5c green 15 15
87 CD313 6c blue 15 15
88 CD313 12c carmine rose 28 28
Set value 40

Cipriani Memorial, Port-of-Spain A27

Queen's Hall, Port-of-Spain A28

Designs: 5c, Whitehall. 6c, Treasury Building. 8c, Governor General's House. 10c, General Hospital, San Fernando. 12c, Oil refinery. 15c, Crest of colony. 25c, Scarlet ibis. 35c, Lake Asphalt (Pitch). 50c, Jinnah Memorial Mosque. 60c, Anthurium lilies. $1.20, Copper-rumped hummingbird and hibiscus. $4.80, Map.

Perf. 13½x14, 14x13½

1960, Sept. 24 Photo. Wmk. 314

Size: 22½x25mm, 25x22½mm

89 A27 1c dark gray & buff 15 15
a. Wmkd. sideways ('66) 15 15
90 A28 2c ultra 15 15
91 A28 5c dark blue 15 15
92 A28 6c lt red brown 15 15
93 A28 8c yellow green 15 15
94 A28 10c light purple 15 15
95 A28 12c bright red 16 15
96 A28 15c orange 48 18
97 A28 25c dk blue & crimson 38 15
98 A28 35c green & black 55 18
99 A28 50c blue, yel & olive 65 24
100 A27 60c multicolored 85 32
a. Perf. 14 ('65) 160.00 24.00

Size: 48x25mm

101 A28 $1.20 multicolored 2.75 1.00
102 A28 $4.80 lt bl & lt yel grn 6.00 4.00
Nos. 89-102 (14) 12.72 7.12

See #116. For overprints see #123-124, 126.

Scouts and Map of Trinidad and Tobago — A29

1961, Apr. 4 *Perf. 13½x14*

103 A29 8c multicolored 20 20
104 A29 25c multicolored 42 42

2nd Caribbean Scout Jamboree, Valsayn Park, Trinidad, Apr. 4-14.

Independent State

Underwater Scene from Painting by Carlisle Chang — A30

Designs: 8c, Elizabeth II and new Terminal Building, Piarco Airport. 25c, Elizabeth II and Hilton Hotel. 35c, Map and greater bird of paradise. 60c, Map and scarlet ibis.

1962, Aug. 31 Photo. *Perf. 14½*

105 A30 5c blue green 15 15
106 A30 8c slate 15 15
107 A30 25c purple 24 24
108 A30 35c emer, yel, brn & blk 28 28
109 A30 60c ultra, black & ver 45 45
Nos. 105-109 (5) 1.27 1.27

Issued to mark Trinidad and Tobago's independence, Aug. 31, 1962.

Freedom from Hunger Issue

Protein Food — A31

1963, June 1 *Perf. 14x13½*

110 A31 5c henna brown 15 15
111 A31 8c citron 15 15
112 A31 25c violet blue 40 40
Set value 60

See note in Common Design section.

Girl Guide Emblem A32

Perf. 14½x14

1964, Sept. 15 **Wmk. 314**

113 A32 6c red, dk blue & yel 15 15
114 A32 25c brt blue, dk bl & yel 30 30
115 A32 35c lt green, dk bl & yel 45 45

50th anniv. of the Trinidad and Tobago Girl Guide Association.

Arms of Independent State — A33

1964, Sept. 15 *Perf. 14x13½*

116 A33 15c orange 60 40

For overprint see No. 125.

ICY Emblem A34

Unwmk.

1965, Nov. 15 **Litho.** *Perf. 12*

Granite Paper

117 A34 35c dull yel, red brn & grn 35 35

International Cooperation Year, 1965.

Eleanor Roosevelt — A35

Perf. 13½x14

1965, Dec. 10 **Wmk. 314**

118 A35 25c vio blue, red & blk 22 22

Issued to honor Eleanor Roosevelt and to publicize the Eleanor Roosevelt Memorial Foundation.

"Redhouse," Parliament Building — A36

Designs: 8c, Map of Trinidad and Tobago, royal yacht "Britannia" and arms of State. 25c, Flag and map. 35c, Flag, Trinity Hills, General Post Office, sugar cane, coconut palms and derricks.

1966, Feb. 8 **Photo.** **Wmk. 314**

119 A36 5c ultra, red, blk & grn 16 16
120 A36 8c ultra, sil, blk & yel brn 24 24
121 A36 25c red, blk & emerald 70 70
122 A36 35c ultra, red, blk & grn 1.00 1.00

Visit of Elizabeth II and Prince Philip.

Nos. 93, 94, 116 and 100 Overprinted: "FIFTH YEAR OF / INDEPENDENCE / 31st AUGUST 1967"

Perf. 14x13½, 13½x14

1967, Aug. 31 **Photo.** **Wmk. 314**

123 A28 8c yellow green 15 15
124 A28 10c lt purple 15 15
125 A33 15c orange 20 20
126 A27 60c multicolored 80 80

On 60c, the overprint is arranged in 5 lines.

Carnival Symbols — A37

Designs: 10c, Calypso King, vert. 15c, Steel band. 25c, Chinese masks. 35c, Carnival King, vert. 60c, Carnival Queen, vert.

Unwmk.

1968, Feb. 16 **Litho.** *Perf. 12*

127 A37 5c pink & multi 15 15
128 A37 10c vio blue & multi 15 15
129 A37 15c multicolored 15 15
130 A37 25c multicolored 15 15
131 A37 35c dk purple & multi 18 18
132 A37 60c brown ol & multi 35 35
Set value 85 85

Issued to publicize the Trinidad Carnival.

WHO Emblem and Eye Examination A38

Dancing Children and Human Rights Flame A39

Wmk. 314

1968, May 7 **Photo.** *Perf. 14*

133 A38 5c rose red, gold & blk 15 15
134 A38 25c orange, gold & blk 32 32
135 A38 35c brt blue, gold & blk 40 40

1968, Aug. 5 *Perf. 14*

136 A39 5c carmine, yel & blk 15 15
137 A39 10c brt blue, yel, & blk 15 15
138 A39 25c yel grn, yel & blk 26 26
Set value 46 46

International Human Rights Year.

Bicycling and Map A40

Designs (Olympic Rings, Map of Trinidad and Tobago and): 15c, Weight lifting. 25c, Relay race. 35c, Running. $1.20, Map of Mexico and flags of Mexico and Trinidad and Tobago.

Photo.; Gold Impressed (except $1.20)

1968, Oct. 12 *Perf. 14*

139 A40 5c violet, gold & multi 15 15
140 A40 15c red, gold & multi 15 15
141 A40 25c orange, gold & multi 15 15
142 A40 35c brt grn, gold & multi 26 18
143 A40 $1.20 blue, gold & multi 1.00 1.00
Nos. 139-143 (5) 1.71 1.63

19th Olympic Games, Mexico City, Oct. 12-27.

Cacao A41

Designs: 3c, Sugar refinery. 5c, Redtailed chachalaca. 6c, Oil refinery. 8c, Fertilizer plant. 10c, Green hermit (hummingbird) vert. 12c, Citrus fruit, vert. 15c, Coat of arms, vert. 20c, 25c, Flag and map of islands, vert. 30c, Wild poinsettia, vert. 40c, Scarlet ibis. 50c, Maracas Bay. $1, Blooming tabebuia (tree) vert. $2.50, Fishermen hauling in net. $5, Red House, Port-of-Spain.

Photo.; Silver or Gold Impressed

1969, Apr. 1 **Wmk. 314** *Perf. 14*

144 A41 1c silver & multi 15 15
145 A41 3c gold & multi 15 15
a. Wmk. upright ('74) 50 50
146 A41 5c gold & multi 15 15
a. Wmk. upright ('73) 7.50 4.00
147 A41 6c gold & multi 15 15
a. Wmk. upright ('74) 30 25
148 A41 8c silver & multi 15 15
149 A41 10c gold & multi 15 15
b. Wmk. 373 ('76) 30 25
150 A41 12c silver & multi 15 15
151 A41 15c silver & multi 15 15
152 A41 20c gold & multi 20 15
153 A41 25c silver & multi 25 15
154 A41 30c silver & multi 30 18
155 A41 40c gold & multi 40 25
156 A41 50c silver & multi 50 30
157 A41 $1 gold & multi 1.00 75
158 A41 $2.50 gold & multi 3.00 2.50
159 A41 $5 gold & multi 6.00 5.00
Nos. 144-159 (16) 12.85 10.48

For overprint see No. 187.

Capt. A. A. Cipriani, ILO Emblem and Gate — A42

ILO, 50th Anniv.: 15c, Industrial Court's & ILO emblems, & Woodford Square gate.

Unwmk.

1969, May 1 **Photo.** *Perf. 12*

160 A42 6c dp car, gold & blk 15 15
161 A42 15c brt blue, gold & blk 20 20
Set value 28 28

Union Jack and Flags of CARIFTA Members A43

Designs: 6c, Cornucopia, vert. 30c, Map of Caribbean, vert. 40c, Jet plane and "Strength through Unity" emblem.

1969, Aug. 1 *Perf. 14x13½, 13½x14*

162 A43 6c lilac, gold & multi 15 15
163 A43 10c multicolored 15 15
164 A43 30c red, emer, blk & gold 40 40
165 A43 40c blue, blk, grn & gold 52 52

Caribbean Free Trade Area (CARIFTA).

Moon Landing and Earth A44

Designs: 40c, Lunar landing module and astronauts on moon, vert. $1, Astronauts Aldrin at control panel, and Armstrong collecting rocks.

1969, Sept. 1 **Litho.** *Perf. 14*

166 A44 6c multicolored 15 15
167 A44 40c multicolored 50 50
168 A44 $1 multicolored 1.25 1.25

See note after US No. C76.

Maces of Senate and House of Representatives A45

Designs: 10c, Chamber of Parliament. 15c, View of Kennedy Complex, University of the West Indies at St. Augustine. 40c, Cannon and view of Scarborough from Fort King George.

Perf. 14x13½

1969, Oct. 23 **Photo.** **Wmk. 314**

169 A45 10c multicolored 15 15
170 A45 15c multicolored 20 20
171 A45 30c lt blue & multi 38 38
172 A45 40c multicolored 50 50

15th Conf. of the Commonwealth Parliamentary Assoc., Port-of-Spain, Oct. 4-19.

Congress Emblem and Landscape A46

Carnival King as "Man in the Moon" A47

Designs: 6c, Congress emblem (steel drum and bird). 30c, Palms, landscape and emblem, horiz.

Perf. 14x13½, 13½x14

1969, Nov. 2 **Litho.** **Unwmk.**

173 A46 6c red, black & gold 15 15
174 A46 30c lt blue, plum & gold 35 35
175 A46 40c ultra, black & gold 45 45

24th Cong. of the Intl. Junior Chamber of Commerce.

1970, Feb. 2 **Wmk. 314** *Perf. 14*

Designs: 6c, Carnival Queen as "City Beneath the Sea." 15c, Bambara god (antelope) from the Band of the Year. 30c, Pheasant Queen (Chanticleer) of Malaya. 40c, Steel Band of the Year with 1969 Calypso and Road March Kings, horiz.

176 A47 5c dk brown & multi 15 15
177 A47 6c dk blue & multi 15 15
178 A47 15c violet bl & multi 15 15
179 A47 30c dk green & multi 28 28
180 A47 40c green & multi 38 38
Set value 90 90

Issued to publicize the Trinidad Carnival.

Mahatma Gandhi and Indian Flag — A48

Design: 10c, Gandhi monument, vert.

Unwmk.

1970, Mar. 2 **Photo.** *Perf. 12*

181 A48 10c ultra & multi 32 22
182 A48 30c crimson & multi 90 70

Mohandas K. Gandhi (1869-1948), leader in India's fight for independence.

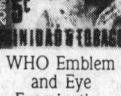

"Culture, Science, Arts and Technology" A49

UN, 25th Anniv.: 10c, Children of various races, map of Trinidad and Tobago and "UNICEF." 20c, Noah's ark, rainbow, dove and UN emblem.

1970, June 26 Photo. *Perf. 13½*

183 A49	5c multicolored	15	15
184 A49	10c multicolored	15	15
185 A49	20c multicolored	30	30

UPU Headquarters, Bern — A50

1970, June 26 Unwmk. *Perf. 12*

186 A50	30c ultra & multi	38	38

Opening of new UPU Headquarters in Bern.

No. 146 Overprinted: "NATIONAL / COMMERCIAL / BANK / ESTABLISHED / 1.7.70"

Photo.; Gold Embossed

1970, July 1 Wmk. 314 *Perf. 14*

187 A41	5c gold & multi	15	15

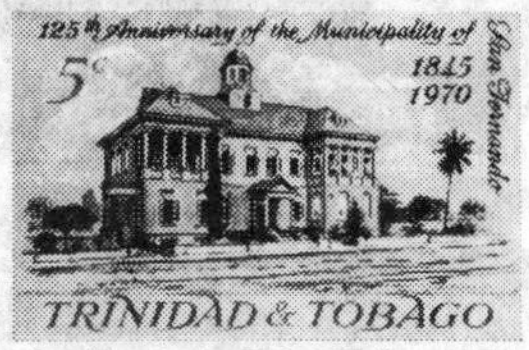

San Fernando Town Hall — A51

Designs: 3c, East Indian Immigrants, 1820, after painting by Cazabon, vert. 40c, Ships in San Fernando Harbor, 1860, after painting by Michel J. Cazabon.

Perf. 14x13½, 13½x14

1970, Nov. Litho. Wmk. 314

188 A51	3c bister & multi	15	15
189 A51	5c lemon & multi	15	15
190 A51	40c lemon & multi	60	50
	Set value	75	62

Municipality of San Fernando, 125th anniv.

Madonna and Child, by Titian — A52

Paintings: 3c, Adoration of the Shepherds, School of Saville. 30c, Adoration of the Shepherds, by Louis Le Nain. 40c, Virgin and Child with St. John and Angel, by Morando. $1, Adoration of the Magi, by Paolo Veronese.

Perf. 13½

1970, Dec. 8 Unwmk. Litho.

191 A52	3c dull org & multi	15	15
a.	Booklet pane of 2	15	
192 A52	5c brt pink & multi	15	15
a.	Booklet pane of 2	22	
193 A52	30c lt utra & multi	28	28
a.	Booklet pane of 2	70	
194 A52	40c yellow grn & multi	40	40
a.	Booklet pane of 2	90	
b.	Souvenir sheet of 4, #191-194	2.00	2.00
195 A52	$1 pale lilac & multi	1.00	1.00
	Nos. 191-195 (5)	1.98	1.98

Brocket Deer — A53

Perf. 14x13½

1971, Aug. 9 Litho. Wmk. 314

196 A53	3c shown	18	15
197 A53	5c Collared peccary	25	15
198 A53	6c Paca	35	22
199 A53	30c Agouti	1.75	1.10
200 A53	40c Ocelot	2.25	1.40
	Nos. 196-200 (5)	4.78	3.02

Capt. A. A. Cipriani A54

Virgin and Child with St. John, by Bartolommeo A55

Design: 30c, Chaconia medal (for distinction in social field).

1971, Aug. 31 *Perf. 14*

201 A54	5c multicolored	15	15
202 A54	30c multicolored	38	38
	Set value		43

9th anniversary of independence. Capt. Arthur Andrew Cipriani (died 1945) was mayor of Port of Spain and member of First Executive Council.

1971, Oct. 25 Litho. *Perf. 14x14½*

Christmas: 5c, Local creche. 10c, Virgin and Child with Sts. Jerome and Dominic, by Filippino Lippi. 15c, Virgin and Child with St. Anne, by Gerolamo dai Libri.

203 A55	3c yellow & multi	15	15
204 A55	5c dull blue & multi	15	15
205 A55	10c red & multi	26	26
206 A55	15c orange & multi	42	42
	Set value	85	83

Satellite Earth Station, Matura A56

Dish Antenna A57

Design: 40c, Satellite over earth (Africa).

1971, Nov. 18 *Perf. 14*

207 A56	10c ultra & multi	15	15
208 A57	30c green & multi	42	42
209 A57	40c black & multi	55	55
a.	Souvenir sheet of 3	1.65	1.65

Opening of Satellite Earth Station at Matura. No. 209a contains 3 imperf. stamps with simulated perforations similar to Nos. 207-209.

Morpho Hybrid A58

Butterflies: 5c, Purple mort bleu. 6c, Jaune d'abricot. 10c, Purple king shoemaker. 20c, Southern white pape. 30c, Little jaune.

1972, Feb. 18 Photo. Wmk. 314

210 A58	3c olive & multi	20	15
211 A58	5c ocher & multi	32	18
212 A58	6c yellow & multi	40	22
213 A58	10c yel grn & multi	80	35
214 A58	20c lilac & multi	1.65	75
215 A58	30c dull grn & multi	2.50	1.10
	Nos. 210-215 (6)	5.87	2.75

S.S. Lady McLeod and Stamp A59

Designs (Lady McLeod Stamp and): 10c, Map of Trinidad and Tobago. 30c, Commemorative inscription.

1972, Apr. 12 Litho. *Perf. 14½x14*

216 A59	5c blue & multi	15	15
217 A59	10c blue & multi	18	18
218 A59	30c blue & multi	55	55
a.	Souvenir sheet of 3, #216-218	1.65	1.65

125th anniv. of the Lady McLeodstamp.

Trinity Cross — A60

Medals: 10c, Chaconia medal. 20c, Hummingbird medal. 30c, Medal of Merit.

1972, Aug. 28 Photo. *Perf. 13½x13*

219 A60	5c blue & multi	15	15
220 A60	10c multicolored	15	15
221 A60	20c yellow grn & multi	28	28
222 A60	30c brt rose & multi	42	42
a.	Souvenir sheet of 4, #219-222	1.25	1.25

10th anniversary of independence. See Nos. 235-238.

Olympic Rings, Relay Race Medal, 1964 A61

Designs (Olympic Rings and): 20c, Bronze medal, 200-meters, 1964. 30c, Bronze medals, weight lifting, 1952. 40c, Silver medal, 400-meters, 1964. 50c, Silver medal, weight lifting, 1948.

1972, Sept. 7 Litho. *Perf. 14*

223 A61	10c yellow & multi	15	15
224 A61	20c multicolored	30	30
225 A61	30c lilac & multi	40	40
226 A61	40c lt blue & multi	52	52
227 A61	50c orange & multi	60	60
a.	Souvenir sheet of 5, #223-227 + label	2.00	2.00
	Nos. 223-227 (5)	1.97	1.97

20th Olympic Games, Munich, Aug. 26-Sept. 11.

Holy Family, by Titian — A62

Christmas: 3c, Adoration of the Kings, by Dosso Dossi. 30c, Like 5c.

1972, Nov. 9 Photo. Wmk. 314

228 A62	3c blue & multi	15	15
229 A62	5c rose lilac & multi	15	15
230 A62	30c lt green & multi	62	62
a.	Souvenir sheet of 3, #228-230	1.50	1.50

ECLA Headquarters, Santiago, Chile — A63

Designs: 20c, INTERPOL emblem. 30c, WHO emblem. 40c, University of West Indies Administration Building.

1973, Aug. 15 Litho. Wmk. 314

231 A63	10c orange & multi	15	15
232 A63	20c multicolored	24	24
233 A63	30c ultra & multi	40	40
234 A63	40c lilac & multi	52	52
a.	Souvenir sheet of 4, #231-234	1.50	1.50

Economic Commission for Latin America, 25th anniv. (10c); Intl. Criminal Police Organization, 50th anniv. (20c); Intl. Meteorological cooperation, cent. (30c); Admission of 1st students to the University of West Indies, 25th anniv. (40c).

Medal Type of 1972 Redrawn

Medals: 10c, Trinity Cross. 20c, Medal of Merit. 30c, Chaconia medal. 40c, Hummingbird medal.

1973, Aug. 30 Photo. *Perf. 14½x14*

235 A60	10c dark green & multi	15	15
236 A60	20c dark brown & multi	25	25
237 A60	30c dark blue & multi	42	42
238 A60	40c deep violet & multi	52	52
a.	Souvenir sheet of 4, #235-238, perf. 14	1.65	1.65

11th anniv. of independence. "Trinidad and Tobago" in one line on #235-238.

General Post Office, Port of Spain A64

Design: 40c, Conference Hall and flags, Chagaramas.

1973, Oct. 8 Photo. *Perf. 14*

239 A64	30c multicolored	40	40
240 A64	40c multicolored	52	52
a.	Souvenir sheet of 2, #239-240	1.10	1.10

2nd Commonwealth Conf. of Postal Administrations, Trinidad, Oct. 8-20. On #240a the perforations extend through margin and divide map.

Virgin and Child, by Murillo — A65

1973, Oct. 22 *Perf. 14½x14*

241 A65	5c pink & multi	15	15
242 A65	$1 lt blue & multi	1.25	1.25
a.	Souv. sheet of 2, #241-242, perf. 14	1.65	1.65

Christmas 1973.

Post Office and UPU Emblem — A66

UPU, Cent.: 50c, Map of Islands, UPU emblem, means of transportation.

1974, Nov. 18 Photo. ***Perf. 13½x14***

243 A66 40c brt purple & multi 50 50
244 A66 50c blue gray & multi 65 65
a. Souvenir sheet of 2, #243-244 21.00 21.00

Humming Bird I, Transatlantic Crossing, 1960 — A67

Design: 50c, Globe, Humming Bird II, Harold and Kwailan La Borde.

1974, Dec. 2 ***Perf. 14½***

245 A67 40c multicolored 52 52
246 A67 50c multicolored 70 70
a. Souvenir sheet of 2, #245-246 3.00 3.00

First anniversary of the voyage around the world by Harold and Kwailan La Borde aboard Humming Bird II, 1969-1973.

"Equality" and IWY Emblem A68

1975, June 23 Litho. Wmk. 314

247 A68 15c multicolored 28 28
248 A68 30c multicolored 55 55

International Women's Year 1975.

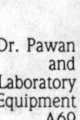

Dr. Pawan and Laboratory Equipment A69

Design: 25c, Vampire bat, microscope, syringe, bat's head.

Perf. 14x14½

1975, Sept. 23 Photo. Wmk. 373

249 A69 25c yellow & multi 40 40
250 A69 30c lt blue & multi 48 48

Isolation of rabies virus by Dr. Joseph Lennox Pawan (1887-1957).

Boeing 707, BWIA Emblem, Air Routes A70

Designs: 30c, Boeing 707 on ground. 40c, Boeing 707 in the air.

Perf. 14½

1975, Nov. 27 Litho. Wmk. 373

251 A70 20c dark blue & multi 25 25
252 A70 30c deep ultra & multi 35 35
253 A70 40c dull green & multi 50 50
a. Souvenir sheet of 3, #251-253 1.25 1.25

British West Indian Airways, 35th anniv.

Land of the Hummingbird Costume — A71

Carnival 1976: $1, Carib Prince riding pink ibis. Designs show prize-winning costumes from 1974 carnival.

1976, Jan. 12 Photo. ***Perf. 14½***

254 A71 30c multicolored 25 25
255 A71 $1 multicolored 80 80
a. Souvenir sheet of 2, #254-255 1.10 1.10

Angostura Building, Port of Spain A72

Designs (Exposition Medals, obverse and reverse): 35c, New Orleans, 1885-86. 45c, Sydney, 1879. 50c, Brussels, 1897.

1976, July 14 Litho. ***Perf. 13***

256 A72 5c bister & multi 15 15
257 A72 35c yellow grn & multi 35 35
258 A72 45c blue & multi 42 42
259 A72 50c violet & multi 52 52
a. Souvenir sheet of 4, #256-259, perf. 14 1.50 1.50

Sesquicentennial of the manufacture of Angostura Bitters.

Map of West Indies, Bats, Wicket and Ball — A72a

Prudential Cup — A72b

1976, Oct. 4 Unwmk. ***Perf. 14***

260 A72a 35c lt blue & multi 55 55
261 A72b 45c lilac rose & blk 75 75
a. Souvenir sheet of 2, #260-261 2.00 2.00

World Cricket Cup, won by West Indies Team, 1975.

Columbus Sailing through the Bocas, by A. Camps-Campins — A73

Paintings: 10c, View, by Jean Michael Cazabon. 20c, Landscape, by Cazabon. 35c, Los Gallos Point, by Cazabon. 45c, Corbeaux Town, by Cazabon.

1976, Nov. 1 Litho. Wmk. 373

262 A73 5c ocher & multi 15 15
263 A73 10c lilac & multi 15 15
264 A73 20c green & multi 15 15
265 A73 35c red orange & multi 20 20
266 A73 45c blue & multi 25 25
a. Souvenir sheet of 5, #262-266 80 80
Set value 68 68

For overprints see Nos. 325, 327.

Hasely Crawford and Gold Medal A74

1977, Jan. 4 Litho. ***Perf. 12½***

267 A74 25c multicolored 52 45
a. Souvenir sheet of 1 60 50

Hasely Crawford, winner of 100-meter dash at Montreal Olympic Games.

Sikorsky S-38 (Lindbergh's Plane) A75

Designs: 35c, Charles Lindbergh delivering first airmail to Port of Spain, 1927. 45c, Boeing 707, British West Indies Airways. 50c, Boeing 747, British Airways.

1977, Apr. Wmk. 373 ***Perf. 13***

268 A75 20c lt blue & multi 30 30
269 A75 35c lt blue & multi 48 48
270 A75 45c lt blue & multi 60 60
271 A75 50c lt blue & multi 1.10 75
a. Souvenir sheet of 4, #268-271, perf. 14 3.00 3.00

50th anniv. of airmail to Trinidad and Tobago.

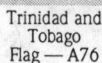

Trinidad and Tobago Flag — A76

White Poinsettia — A77

Designs: 35c, Coat of arms. 45c, Government House.

1977, July 26 Litho. ***Perf. 13½x13***

272 A76 20c yellow & multi 22 22
273 A76 35c red & multi 38 38
274 A76 45c lt blue & multi 45 45
a. Souvenir sheet of 3, #272-274, perf. 14 1.25 1.25

Inauguration of the Republic, Aug. 1, 1976.

1977, Oct. 11 Litho. ***Perf. 14½***

Christmas: 45c, 50c, Red poinsettia.

275 A77 10c multicolored 15 15
276 A77 35c multicolored 30 30
277 A77 45c multicolored 40 40
278 A77 50c multicolored 42 42
a. Souvenir sheet of 4, #275-278 1.40 1.40

Robinson Crusoe Hotel, Tobago A78

Designs: 15c, Turtle Beach Hotel, Tobago. 25c, Mount Irvine Hotel, Tobago. 70c, Mount Irvine beach, Tobago. $5, Holiday Inn, Trinidad.

Wmk. 373

1978, Jan. 17 Litho. ***Perf. 14***

279 A78 6c multicolored 15 15
280 A78 15c multicolored 15 15
281 A78 25c multicolored 16 16
282 A78 70c multicolored 45 45
283 A78 $5 multicolored 3.25 3.25
a. Souvenir sheet of 5, #279-283 4.50 4.50
Nos. 279-283 (5) 4.16 4.16

For overprint see No. 326.

Paphinia Cristata A79

Orchids: 30c, Caularthron bicornutum. 40c, Miltassia. 50c, Oncidium ampliatum. $2.50, Oncidium papilio.

1978, June 7 Wmk. 373 ***Perf. 14***

284 A79 12c multicolored 15 15
285 A79 30c multicolored 24 24
286 A79 40c multicolored 32 32
287 A79 50c multicolored 40 40
288 A79 $2.50 multicolored 2.00 2.00
a. Souvenir sheet of 5, #284-288 3.50 3.50
Nos. 284-288 (5) 3.11 3.11

Miss Universe and Trophy — A80

Designs: 35c, Portrait with crown. 45c, Miss Universe in evening dress.

1978, Aug. 2 Litho. ***Perf. 14½***

289 A80 10c multicolored 15 15
290 A80 35c multicolored 30 30
291 A80 45c multicolored 35 35
a. Souvenir sheet of 3, #289-291 1.00 1.00

Janelle (Penny) Commissiong, Miss Universe, 1977.

Tayra A81

1978, Nov. 7 ***Perf. 13½x14***

292 A81 15c shown 18 15
293 A81 25c Ocelot 28 24
294 A81 40c Porcupine 45 38
295 A81 70c Yellow anteater 95 65
a. Souvenir sheet of 4, #292-295 2.00 2.00

"Burst of Beauty" — A82

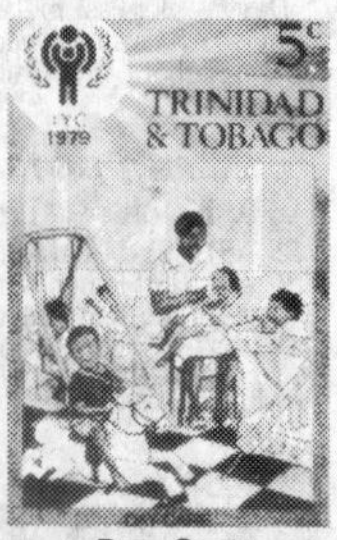

Day Care Center — A83

Costumes: 10c, Rain worshipper. 35c, Zodiac. 45c, Praying mantis. 50c, Eye of the hurricane. $1, Steel orchestra.

1979, Feb. 1 Litho. ***Perf. 13½***

296 A82 5c multicolored 15 15
297 A82 10c multicolored 15 15
298 A82 35c multicolored 24 24
299 A82 45c multicolored 30 30
300 A82 50c multicolored 35 35
301 A82 $1 multicolored 65 65
Nos. 296-301 (6) 1.84 1.84

Unwmk.

1979, June 5 Litho. ***Perf. 13***

IYC Emblem and: 10c, School lunch program. 35c, Dental care. 45c, Nursery school. 50c, Free school bus. $1, Medical care.

302 A83 5c multicolored 15 15
303 A83 10c multicolored 15 15
304 A83 35c multicolored 22 22
305 A83 45c multicolored 28 28
306 A83 50c multicolored 32 32
307 A83 $1 multicolored 65 65
a. Souvenir sheet of 6, #302-307 1.90 1.90
Nos. 302-307 (6) 1.77 1.77

International Year of the Child.

Geothermal Exploration A84

Designs: 35c, Hydrogeology. 45c, Petroleum exploration. 70c, Preservation of the environment.

1979, July 3 Wmk. 373

308 A84	10c multicolored		15	15
309 A84	35c multicolored		28	28
310 A84	45c multicolored		35	35
311 A84	70c multicolored		55	55
a.	Souvenir sheet of 4, #308-311		1.50	1.50

4th Latin American Geological Cong., July 7-15.

Map of Tobago and Tobago No. 1 A85

Designs: 15c, Tobago Nos. 2 & 7. 35c, Tobago Nos. 28 & 11. 45c, Tobago Nos. 25 & 4. 70c, Great Britain No. 28 used in Scarborough and Tobago No. 5. $1, General Post Office, Scarborough and Tobago No. 6.

Perf. 13½x14

1979, Aug. 1 Litho. Wmk. 373

312 A85	10c multicolored	15	15
313 A85	15c multicolored	15	15
314 A85	35c multicolored	22	22
315 A85	45c multicolored	28	28
316 A85	70c multicolored	45	45
317 A85	$1 multicolored	65	65
a.	Souvenir sheet of 6, #312-317	1.90	1.90
	Nos. 312-317 (6)	1.90	1.90

Centenary of Tobago's postage stamps.

Rowland Hill, Trinidad and Tobago No. 109 A86

Hill and: 45c, Trinidad and Tobago #273. $1, Trinidad #62, Tobago #10.

1979, Oct. 4 *Perf. 13*

318 A86	25c multicolored	15	15
319 A86	45c multicolored	28	28
320 A86	$1 multicolored	60	60
a.	Souvenir sheet of 3, #318-320	1.25	1.25

Sir Rowland Hill (1795-1879), originator of penny postage.

Poui Tree A87

Designs: 10c, Court House. 50c, Royal Train locomotive. $1.50, Bacchante freighter.

Perf. 14½

1980, Jan. 21 Litho. Wmk. 373

321 A87	5c multicolored	15	15
322 A87	10c multicolored	15	15
323 A87	50c multicolored	45	45
324 A87	$1.50 multicolored	1.40	1.40
a.	Souvenir sheet of 4, #321-324	2.00	2.00

Princes Town centenary.

Nos. 262, 279, 263 Overprinted in 3 or 5 Lines:
"1844-1980 POPULATION CENSUS 12th MAY 1980"

1980, Apr. 8 Litho. *Perf. 14*

325 A73	5c multicolored	15	15
326 A78	6c multicolored	15	15
327 A73	10c multicolored	15	15
	Set value	20	20

Scarlet Ibis Hen and Nest — A88

Scarlet Ibis: b, Nest and eggs. c, Chick in nest. d, Male. e, Male and female.

Perf. 14½

1980, May 6 Litho. Wmk. 373

328	Strip of 5, multi	2.50	2.50
a.-e.	A88 single stamp	50	50

Bronze and Silver Medals, 1948, 1952 — A89

Wmk. 373

1980, July 22 Litho. *Perf. 14*

329 A89	10c shown	15	15
330 A89	15c Hasely Crawford, 1976 gold medal	15	15
331 A89	70c 1964 silver, bronze medals	65	65

Souvenir Sheet

332 A89	$2.50 Moscow '80 emblem, vert.	1.65	1.65

22nd Summer Olympic Games, Moscow, July 19-Aug. 3.

Charcoal Production A90

Wmk. 373

1980, Sept. 8 Litho. *Perf. 14*

333 A90	10c shown	15	15
334 A90	55c Logging	32	32
335 A90	70c Teak plantation	40	40
336 A90	$2.50 Watershed management	1.50	1.50
a.	Souvenir sheet of 4, #333-336	3.00	3.00

11th Commonwealth Forestry Conference.

Elizabeth Bourne, Judiciary and Isabella Tesbier, Government — A91

Decade for Women: No. 338, Beryl McBurnie, dance and culture; Audrey Jeffers, social work. No. 339, Dr. Stella Abidh, public health; Louise Horne, nutrition.

1980, Sept. 29

337 A91	$1 multicolored	70	70
338 A91	$1 multicolored	70	70
339 A91	$1 multicolored	70	70

Stadium and Netball League Emblem A92

1980, Oct. 21

340 A92	70c multicolored	55	55

1979 World Netball Tournament, Port-of-Spain.

Athlete, Man in Wheelchair, IYD Emblem A93

Perf. 14½

1981, Apr. 6 Litho. Wmk. 373

341 A93	10c shown	15	15
342 A93	70c Amputee with crutch	38	38
343 A93	$1.50 Blind people	85	85
344 A93	$2 IYD emblem	1.10	1.10

International Year of the Disabled.

Marine Preservation A94

1981, July 7 Litho. *Perf. 13x13½*

345 A94	10c Land	15	15
346 A94	55c shown	42	42
347 A94	$3 Sky	2.50	2.50
a.	Souvenir sheet of 3, #345-347	3.00	3.00

World Food Day — A95

1981, Oct. 16 Litho. *Perf. 14½x14*

348 A95	10c Produce	15	15
349 A95	15c Rice threshing, mill	15	15
350 A95	45c Bigeye	30	30
351 A95	55c Cow, pig, goats	38	38
352 A95	$1.50 Poultry	1.00	1.00
353 A95	$2 Smallmouth grunt	1.40	1.40
a.	Souvenir sheet of 6, #348-353	3.50	3.50
	Nos. 348-353 (6)	3.38	3.38

President Awards — A96

1981, Nov. 30 *Perf. 14*

354 A96	10c First aid	15	15
355 A96	70c Motor mechanics	50	50
356 A96	$1 Hiking	70	70
357 A96	$2 President giving award	1.40	1.40

Commonwealth Pharmaceutical Conference — A97

1982, Feb. 12 Litho. *Perf. 14½x14*

358 A97	10c Pharmacist	15	15
359 A97	$1 Pluchea symphitfolia	85	85
360 A97	$2 Nopalea cochenilifera	1.65	1.65

Scouting Year — A98

25th Anniv. of Tourist Board — A99

1982, June 28 Litho. *Perf. 14*

361 A98	15c Production	15	15
362 A98	55c Tolerance	45	45
363 A98	$5 Discipline	4.00	4.00

Perf. 13½x14

1982, Oct. 18 Litho. Wmk. 373

364 A99	55c Charlotteville	45	45
365 A99	$1 Boating	85	85
366 A99	$3 Fort George	2.50	2.50

Pa Pa Bois — A100

Designs: Various folklore characters.

1982, Nov. 8

367 A100	10c multicolored	15	15
368 A100	15c multicolored	15	15
369 A100	65c multicolored	55	55
370 A100	$5 multicolored	4.25	4.25
a.	Souvenir sheet of 4, #367-370	5.50	5.50

Canefarmers' Centenary — A101

1982, Dec. 13 Litho. *Perf. 14*

371 A101	30c Harvest	42	42
372 A101	70c Loading bullock cart	95	95
373 A101	$1.50 Field	2.00	2.00
a.	Souvenir sheet of 3, #371-373, perf. 14½	5.50	5.50

20th Anniv. of Independence — A102

1982, Dec. 28 *Perf. 13½x14*

374 A102	10c Natl. Stadium	15	15
375 A102	35c Caroni Arena Water Treatment Plant	26	26
376 A102	50c Mount Hope Maternity Hospital	38	38
377 A102	$2 Natl. Insurance Board Mall, Tobago	1.50	1.50

Commonwealth Day — A103

1983, Mar. 14 *Perf. 14*
378 A103 10c Flags 15 15
379 A103 55c Satellite view 42 42
380 A103 $1 Oil industry, vert. 75 75
381 A103 $2 Maps, vert. 1.50 1.50

10th Anniv. of CARICOM A104

1983, July 11 **Litho.** *Perf. 14*
382 A104 35c Jet, map 65 65

World Communications Year — A105

1983, Aug. 5 *Perf. 14½*
383 A105 15c Operator 15 15
384 A105 55c Scarborough PO, Tobago 45 45
385 A105 $1 Textel Building 80 80
386 A105 $3 Morne Bleu Receiving Station 2.50 2.50

Commonwealth Finance Ministers Conference — A106

Wmk. 373
1983, Sept. 19 **Litho.** *Perf. 14*
387 A106 $2 multicolored 1.50 1.50

World Food Day — A107

1983, Oct. 17 *Perf. 14x13½*
388 A107 10c Kingfish 15 15
389 A107 55c Flying fish 40 40
390 A107 70c Queen conch 52 52
391 A107 $4 Red shrimp 3.00 3.00

Flowers — A108

1983, Dec. 14 **Wmk. 373** *Perf. 14*
392 A108 5c Bois pois 15 15
393 A108 10c Maraval Lily 15 15
394 A108 15c Star grass 15 15
395 A108 20c Bois caco 15 15
396 A108 25c Strangling fig 18 18
397 A108 30c Cassia moschata 20 20
398 A108 50c Chalice flower 35 35
399 A108 65c Black stick 45 45
400 A108 80c Columnea scandens 55 55
401 A108 95c Cats Claws 65 65
402 A108 $1 Bois l'agli 70 70

Size: 38½x26mm

403 A108 $1.50 Eustoma exeltatum 1.00 1.00
404 A108 $2 Chaconia, horiz. 1.40 1.40
405 A108 $2.50 Chysothemis pulchella, horiz. 1.75 1.75
406 A108 $5 Centratherum punctatum, horiz. 3.50 3.50
407 A108 $10 Savanna flower, horiz. 6.75 6.75
Nos. 392-407 (16) 18.08 18.08

"1984" imprint: #392, 393, 394, 396.
"1989:" #392.

1985-89 **Wmk. 384**
392a A108 5c 15 15
393a A108 10c 15 15
395a A108 20c ('89) 15 15
396a A108 25c ('89) 15 15
397a A108 30c ('87) 16 16
399a A108 65c ('87) 35 35
400a A108 80c ('87) 45 45
401a A108 95c 65 65
402a A108 $1 70 70
403a A108 $1.50 ('87) 80 80
404a A108 $2 ('87) 1.10 1.10
405a A108 $2.50 ('89) 1.40 1.40
406a A108 $5 3.25 3.25
407a A108 $10 6.75 6.75
Nos. 392a-407a (14) 16.21 16.21

"1985" imprint: #392a, 393a, 401a, 402a, 406a, 407a.
"1987:" #393a, 397a, 399a, 400a, 403a, 404a.
"1988:" #395a, 406a, 407a.
"1989:" #393a, 397a, 399a, 402a, 403a, 404a, 406a.

Castles on Chess Board A109

1984 Summer Olympics A110

World Chess Fedn., 60th Anniv.: Various chess pieces.

Wmk. 373
1984, Sept. 12 **Litho.** *Perf. 14*
408 A109 50c multicolored 35 35
409 A109 70c multicolored 48 48
410 A109 $1.50 multicolored 1.00 1.00
411 A109 $2 multicolored 1.40 1.40

1984, Sept. 21 *Perf. 14x14½*
412 A110 15c Swimming 15 15
413 A110 55c Running 42 42
414 A110 $1.50 Yachting 1.10 1.10
415 A110 $4 Bicycling 3.00 3.00
a. Souvenir sheet of 4, #412-415 5.00 5.00

St. Mary's Children's Home, 125th Anniv. A111

1984, Nov. 13 **Litho.** *Perf. 13½*
416 A111 10c Children's band 15 15
417 A111 70c St. Mary's Home 65 65
418 A111 $3 Group scene 3.00 3.00

Christmas 1984 — A112

1984, Nov. **Litho.** *Perf. 14*
419 A112 10c Parang Band 15 15
420 A112 30c Musical notes, Poinsettia 25 25
421 A112 $1 Bandola, Cuatro, Bandolin 85 85
422 A112 $3 Fiddle, Guitar, Double Bass 2.50 2.50

Emancipation, 150th Anniv. — A113

1984, Oct. 22 **Litho.** *Perf. 13½x13*
423 A113 35c Slave ship 35 35
424 A113 55c Map, Slave Triangle 55 55
425 A113 $1 Book by Eric Williams 1.00 1.00
426 A113 $2 Toussaint L'Ouverture 2.00 2.00
a. Souvenir sheet of 4, #423-426 4.00 4.00

Labor Day — A114

Labor leaders: No. 427, A.A. Cipriani and T.U.B. Butler. No. 428, A. Cola Rienzi and C.T.W.E. Worrell. No. 429, C.P. Alexander and Q. O'Connor.

Wmk. 373
1985, June 17 **Litho.** *Perf. 14*
427 A114 55c dull rose & blk 50 50
428 A114 55c brt green & blk 50 50
429 A114 55c lt orange & blk 50 50

Ships — A115

Perf. 14½
1985, Aug 20 **Litho.** **Wmk. 373**
430 A115 30c Lady Nelson 22 22
431 A115 95c Lady Drake 75 75
432 A115 $1.50 Federal Palm 1.10 1.10
433 A115 $2 Federal Maple 1.50 1.50

UN Decade for Women A116

Women in the arts, public service and education: No. 434, Sybill Atteck, Marjorie Padmore. No. 435, May Cherrie, Evelyn Tracey. No. 436, Jessica Smith-Phillips, Irene Omilta McShine.

1985, Oct. 30 **Wmk. 384** *Perf. 14*
434 A116 $1.50 multicolored 1.10 1.10
435 A116 $1.50 multicolored 1.10 1.10
436 A116 $1.50 multicolored 1.10 1.10

Intl. Youth Year — A117

Anniversaries and events: 10c, Natl. Cadet Force, 75th anniv. 65c, Girl Guides, 75th anniv.

1985, Nov. 27 *Perf. 14x14½*
437 A117 10c Cadet emblem 15 15
438 A117 65c Badges, anniv. emblem 48 48
439 A117 95c shown 70 70

A118

A119

Sisters of St. Joseph de Cluny in Trinidad, 150th Anniv.: 10c, Sister Anne-Marie Javouhey, founder. 65c, St. Joseph's Convent, Port-of-Spain. 95c, Statue of Sr. Anne-Marie.

Perf. 14x14½
1986, Mar. 19 **Litho.** **Wmk. 384**
440 A118 10c multicolored 15 15
441 A118 65c multicolored 45 45
442 A118 95c multicolored 70 70

Perf. 14½
1986, Apr. 21 **Litho.** **Wmk. 384**
443 A119 10c At the Cenotaph 15 15
444 A119 15c Aboard HMY Britannia 15 15
445 A119 30c With Pres. Clarke 15 15
446 A119 $5 Receiving bouquet 2.50 2.50

Queen Elizabeth II, 60th birthday.

Locomotives, AMERIPEX '86 — A120

Perf. 14½x14
1986, May 26 **Wmk. 373**
447 A120 65c Arma tank locomotive 32 32
448 A120 95c Canadian-built No. 22 55 55
449 A120 $1.10 Tender engine 60 60
450 A120 $1.50 Saddle tank 85 85
a. Souvenir sheet of 4, #447-450 2.50 2.50

Boy Scouts, 75th Anniv. — A121

1986, July 21 **Wmk. 384** *Perf. 14*
451 A121 $1.70 Campsite 1.00 1.00
452 A121 $2 Uniforms, 1911, 1986 1.20 1.20

Dr. Eric Williams (1911-1981), First Prime Minister — A122

Wmk. 373
1986, Sept. 25 **Litho.** *Perf. 14*
453 A122 10c Graduating college, 1935 15 15
454 A122 30c Wearing red tie 18 18
a. Black tie 18 18
455 A122 95c Pro-Chancellor of UWI 58 58
456 A122 $5 Williams, prime minister's residence 3.00 3.00
a. Souvenir sheet of 4, #453-456 4.00 4.00

Nos. 453-454 vert.

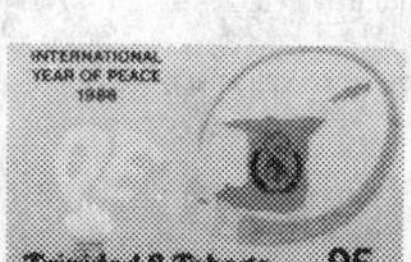

Intl. Peace Year — A123

1986, Oct. 30 **Wmk. 384**

457 A123 95c shown 58 58
458 A123 $3 Dove 2.40 2.40

Giselle LaRonde, Miss World 1986 — A124

Wmk. 384

1987, July 27 **Litho.** ***Perf. 14***

459 A124 10c Wearing folk costume 15 15
460 A124 30c Bathing suit 16 16
461 A124 95c Crown 50 50
462 A124 $1.65 Crown and sash 85 85

Republic Bank, 150th Anniv. A125

Designs: 10c, Colonial Bank, Port of Spain. 65c, Cocoa plantation. 95c, Oil fields. $1.10, Tramcar, Belmont Tramway Co.

Wmk. 373

1987, Dec. 21 **Litho.** ***Perf. 14***

463 A125 10c buff, red brn & blk 15 15
464 A125 65c buff, red brn & blk 32 32
465 A125 95c buff, red brn & blk 50 50
466 A125 $1.10 buff, red brn & blk 58 58

Defense Force, 25th Anniv. — A126

Various army, coast guard and navy uniforms.

Wmk. 384

1988, Feb. 29 **Litho.** ***Perf. 14***

467 A126 10c Army 15 15
468 A126 30c Army (women) 18 18
469 A126 $1.10 Navy, army, coast guard 60 60
470 A126 $1.50 Navy 82 82

Cricket A127

Bat, wicket posts, ball, 18th cent. belt buckle and batters: 30c, George John. 65c, Learie Constantine. 95c, Sonny Ramadhin. $1.50, Gerry Gomez. $2.50, Jeffrey Stollmeyer.

Wmk. 373

1988, June 6 **Litho.** ***Perf. 14***

471 A127 30c multicolored 16 16
472 A127 65c multicolored 35 35
473 A127 95c multicolored 52 52
474 A127 $1.50 multicolored 85 85
475 A127 $2.50 multicolored 1.40 1.40
Nos. 471-475 (5) 3.28 3.28

Oilfield Workers' Trade Union, 50th Anniv. — A128

50, Star, oil well and: 10c, Uriah Buzz Butler, labor leader. 30c, Adrian C. Rienzi, pres. from 1937-42. 65c, John Rojas, pres. from 1943-62. $5, George Weekes, pres. from 1962-87.

Perf. 14½

1988, July 11 **Litho.** **Wmk. 384**

476 A128 10c dk car, dp org & gold 15 15
477 A128 30c multicolored 18 18
478 A128 65c dp green, dp org & gold 38 38
479 A128 $5 brt ultra, dp org & gold 2.75 2.75

Borough of Arima, Cent. — A129

Designs: 20c, Mary Werges, Santa Rosa Church. 30c, Gov. W. Robinson, royal charter. $1.10, Mayor C.P. Lopez greeting Gov. Robinson at train station. $1.50, Mayor J.F. Wallen, centennial emblem.

Perf. 14½

1988, Aug. 22 **Litho.** **Wmk. 384**

480 A129 20c multicolored 15 15
481 A129 30c multicolored 18 18
482 A129 $1.10 multicolored 62 62
483 A129 $1.50 multicolored 85 85

Lloyds of London, 300th Anniv.

Common Design Type

Designs: 30c, Queen Mother at the "Topping Out" ceremony of new Lloyds's building, 1984. $1.10, BWIA Tristar 500, horiz. $1.55, ISCOTT iron and steel mill, horiz. $2, *Atlantic Empress* on fire off Tobago.

1988, Nov. 21 **Litho.** ***Perf. 14***

484 CD341 30c multicolored 15 15
485 CD341 $1.10 multicolored 52 52
486 CD341 $1.55 multicolored 75 75
487 CD341 $2 multicolored 95 95

Unification of the Islands, Cent. — A130

Torch and: 40c, Natl. arms, 1889, and 1p Type A1. $1, Badge from Tobago flag and Tobago No. 31. $1.50, Badge from Trinidad flag and Trinidad No. 71. $2.25, Natl. arms, 1989, and No. 274.

Perf. 14½

1989, Mar. 20 **Litho.** **Wmk. 384**

488 A130 40c multicolored 20 20
489 A130 $1 multicolored 48 48
490 A130 $1.50 multicolored 70 70
491 A130 $2.25 multicolored 1.05 1.05

Rare Species A131

Designs: a, *Pipile pipile.* b, *Phyllodytes auratus.* c, *Cebus albifrons trinitatis.* d, *Tamandua tetradactyla.* e, *Lutra longicaudis.* Printed se-tenant in a continuous design.

Perf. 14x14½

1989, July 31 **Wmk. 373**

492 Strip of 5 2.40 2.40
a.-e. A131 $1 any single 48 48

A132

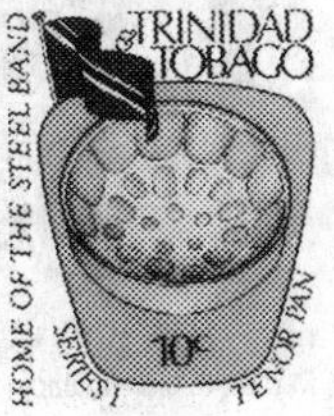

A133

1989, Oct. 2 ***Perf. 14½***

493 A132 10c Men using walking sticks 15 15
494 A132 40c City Hall 20 20
495 A132 $1 Guides and leader 48 48
496 A132 $2.25 Volunteers, anniv. emblem 1.10 1.10

Blind Welfare, 75th anniv. (10c), Port-of-Spain City Hall, 75th anniv. (40c), Girl Guides, 75th anniv. ($1), and Red Cross, 50th anniv. ($2.25).

Perf. 14½x14

1989, Nov. 30 **Wmk. 384**

Drum instruments played in a steel band.

497 A133 10c Tenor 15 15
498 A133 40c Guitar 20 20
499 A133 $1 Cello 48 48
500 A133 $2.25 Bass 1.10 1.10

Mushrooms A134

1990, May 3 ***Perf. 14x13½***

501 A134 10c *Xeromphalina tenuipes* 15 15
502 A134 40c *Dictyophora indusiata* 20 20
503 A134 $1 *Leucocoprinus birnbaumii* 50 50
504 A134 $2.25 *Crinipellis perniciosa* 1.10 1.10

Stamp World London '90.

Scarlet Ibis A135

1990, Sept. 7 ***Perf. 14***

505 A135 40c Immature bird 20 20
506 A135 80c Mating display 40 40
507 A135 $1 Adult male 48 48
508 A135 $2.25 Adult, egg & young 1.05 1.05

World Wildlife Fund.

Yellow Oriole — A136

1990, Dec. 17 **Litho.** **Wmk. 384**

509 A136 20c shown 15 15
510 A136 25c Green rumped parrotlet 15 15
511 A136 40c Fork-tailed flycatcher 20 20
512 A136 50c Copper rumped hummingbird 24 24
513 A136 $1 Bananaquit 48 48
514 A136 $2 Semp 95 95
515 A136 $2.25 Channel-billed toucan 1.05 1.05
516 A136 $2.50 Bay headed tanager 1.20 1.20
517 A136 $5 Green honeycreeper 2.40 2.40
518 A136 $10 Cattle egret 4.80 4.80
519 A136 $20 Golden olive woodpecker 9.60 9.60
520 A136 $50 Peregrine falcon 23.50 23.50
Nos. 509-520 (12) 44.72 44.72

For overprints see Nos. 565-568.

University of the West Indies — A137

Chancellors and Campus Buildings: 40c, HRH Princess Alice, Administration Building. 80c, Sir Hugh Wooding, Main Library. $1, Sir Allen Lewis, Faculty of Engineering. $2.25, Sir Shridath Ramphal, Faculty of Medical Studies.

Perf. 13½x14

1990, Oct. 15 **Litho.** **Wmk. 373**

521 A137 40c multicolored 20 20
522 A137 80c multicolored 40 40
523 A137 $1 multicolored 50 50
524 A137 $2.25 multicolored 1.10 1.10

Britsh West Indies Airways, 50th Anniv. A138

Airplanes: 40c, Lockheed Lodestar. 80c, Vickers Viking 1A. $1, Vickers Viscount 702. $2.25, Boeing 707. $5, Lockheed TriStar 500.

1990, Nov. 27 ***Perf. 14***

525 A138 40c multicolored 20 20
526 A138 80c multicolored 40 40
527 A138 $1 multicolored 50 50
528 A138 $2.25 multicolored 1.10 1.10

Souvenir Sheet

529 A138 $5 multicolored 2.50 2.50

Ferns — A139

1991, July 1 ***Perf. 13½***

530 A139 40c Lygodium volubile 20 20
531 A139 80c Blechnum occidentale 40 40
532 A139 $1 Gleichenia bifida 50 50
533 A139 $2.25 Polypodium lycopodiodes 1.10 1.10

Trinidad & Tobago in World War II — A140

Designs: 40c, Firing practice by Trinidad & Tobago regiment. 80c, Fairey Barracuda surprises U-boat. $1, Avro Lancaster returns from bombing raid. $2.25, River class frigate on convoy duty. No. 538a, Supermarine Spitfire. b, Vickers Wellington.

Perf. 13½x14

1991, Dec. 7 Litho. Wmk. 384

534 A140	40c	multicolored	20	20
535 A140	80c	multicolored	40	40
536 A140	$1	multicolored	50	50
537 A140	$2.25	multicolored	1.10	1.10

Souvenir Sheet

538 A140	$2.50	Sheet of 2, #a.-b.	2.50	2.50

H. E. Rapsey — A141

Inca Clathrata Quesneli — A142

Holy Name Convent — A143

Religions of Trinidad and Tobago — A145

1992, Mar. 30 Wmk. 373 *Perf. 14*

539 A141	40c	multicolored	20	20
540 A142	80c	multicolored	40	40
541 A143	$1	multicolored	50	50

No. 539, Building and Loan Association, cent. No. 540, Trinidad & Tobago Field Naturalists' Club. No. 541, Holy Name Convent, cent.

1992, Apr. 21 Litho. *Perf. 14*

Designs: No. 544, Baptist, baptism by immersion. No. 545, Muslim, minaret. No. 546, Hindu, Brahman..the source of all. No. 547, Christianity, cross. No. 548, Baha'i, slogan.

544 A145	40c	multicolored	20	20
545 A145	40c	multicolored	20	20
546 A145	40c	multicolored	20	20
547 A145	40c	multicolored	20	20
548 A145	40c	multicolored	20	20
		Nos. 544-548 (5)	1.00	1.00

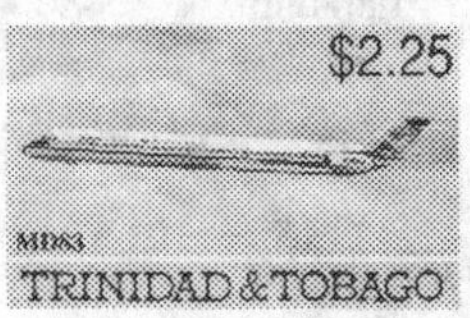

BWIA Aircraft A146

Wmk. 373

1992, Aug. 6 Litho. *Perf. 14*

549 A146	$2.25	MD83	1.15	1.15
550 A146	$2.25	L1011	1.15	1.15

Natl. Museum and Art Gallery, Cent. A147

Perf. 14½

1992, Dec. 7 Litho. Wmk. 384

551 A147	$1	multicolored	50	50

The Scott International album provides spaces for an extensive representative collection of the world's postage stamps.

Christmas — A148

1992, Dec. 21

552 A148	40c	multicolored	20	20

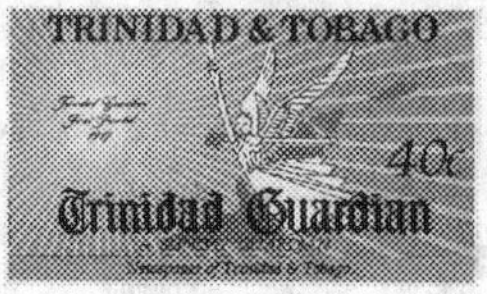

Trinidad Guardian, 75th Anniv. A149

1992, Dec. 23

553 A149	40c	multicolored	20	20

Philatelic Society of Trinidad & Tobago, 50th Anniv. A150

1992, Dec. 30

554 A150	$2.25	multicolored	1.15	1.15

CARICOM (Caribbean Economic Community), 20th Anniv. — A151

Map of CARICOM nations, portraits of West Indian men: 50c, $1.50, $2.75, $3, Derek Walcott, Sir Shridath Ramphal, William Demas.

$6, Order of the Caribbean Community. Illustration reduced.

Perf. 13x13½

1994, Jan. 31 Litho. Wmk. 373

555 A151	50c	pink & multi	18	18
556 A151	$1.50	green & multi	52	52
557 A151	$2.75	gray & multi	95	95
558 A151	$3	violet & multi	1.00	1.00

Souvenir Sheet

Perf. 13½x13

559 A151	$6	multicolored	2.00	2.00

No. 559 contains one 34x56mm stamp.

Drum Instruments Played in a Steel Band — A152

1994, Feb. 11 *Perf. 14x15*

560 A152	50c	Quadrophonic pan	18	18
561 A152	$1	Tenor base pan	35	35
562 A152	$2.25	Six pan	80	80
563 A152	$2.50	Rocket pan	90	90

Alwyn Roberts, Calypso Singer — A153

1994, Feb. 11 *Perf. 14*

564 A153	50c	multicolored	18	18

Nos. 510-511, 514, 518 Ovptd. with Hong Kong '94 Exhibition Emblem

Wmk. 384

1994, Feb. 18 Litho. *Perf. 14*

565 A136	25c	multicolored	15	15
566 A136	40c	multicolored	15	15
567 A136	$2	multicolored	70	70
568 A136	$10	multicolored	3.50	3.50

Hotels & Lodges — A154

Designs: No. 569, Trinidad Hilton. No. 570, Sandy Point Village, Tobago. No. 571, Asa Wright Nature Center and Lodge. No. 572, ML's Bed and Breakfast.

Wmk. 373

1994, Aug. 10 Litho. *Perf. 14*

569 A154	$3	multicolored	1.10	1.10
570 A154	$3	multicolored	1.10	1.10
571 A154	$3	multicolored	1.10	1.10
572 A154	$3	multicolored	1.10	1.10

Snakes A155

Designs: 50c, Boa constrictor. $1.25, Horse whip or vine snake. $2.50, Bushmaster. $3, Large coral snake.

Wmk. 373

1994, Sept. 19 Litho. *Perf. 14*

573 A155	50c	multicolored	18	18
574 A155	$1.25	multicolored	45	45
575 A155	$2.50	multicolored	90	90
576 A155	$3	multicolored	1.10	1.10
		Nos. 573-576 (4)	2.63	2.63

SEMI-POSTAL STAMPS

Emblem of Red Cross — SP1

Perf. 11, 12

1914, Sept. 18 Typo. Unwmk.

B1 SP1	½p	red (on cover)	325.00

This seal was allowed to pay ½p postage on one day, Sept. 18, 1914, with the funds going to the Red Cross. Value unused, $12.50.

No. 2 Overprinted in Red (Cross) and Black (Date):

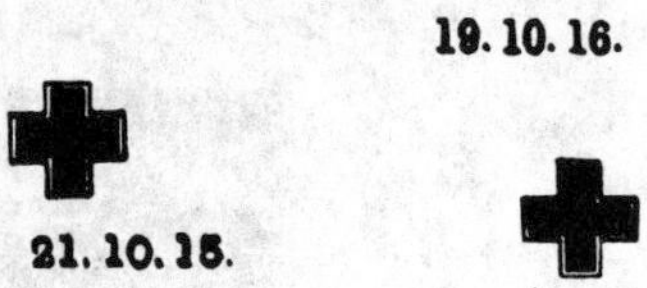

a b

1915, Oct. 21 Wmk. 3 *Perf. 14*

B2 A1 (a)	1p	scarlet	25	25

1916, Oct. 19

B3 A1 (b)	1p	scarlet	15	15
a.		Date omitted		

POSTAGE DUE STAMPS

D1

D2

1923-45 Typo. Wmk. 4 *Perf. 14*

J1	D1	1p	black	38	48
J2	D1	2p	black	60	60
J3	D1	3p	black ('25)	75	65
J4	D1	4p	black ('29)	2.25	2.25
J5	D1	5p	black ('45)	14.00	1.90
J6	D1	6p	black ('45)	19.00	19.00
J7	D1	8p	black ('45)	24.00	24.00
J8	D1	1sh	black ('45)	47.50	47.50
			Nos. J1-J8 (8)	108.48	96.38

Catalogue values for unused stamps in this section, from this point to the end of the section, are for Never Hinged items.

Denominations in Cents

1947, Sept. 1

J9	D1	2c	black	22	22
J10	D1	4c	black	60	60
J11	D1	6c	black	1.10	1.10
J12	D1	8c	black	1.50	*1.65*
J13	D1	10c	black	1.50	*1.65*
J14	D1	12c	black	1.65	*2.75*
J15	D1	16c	black	1.65	*3.25*
J16	D1	24c	black	3.75	*8.50*
			Nos. J9-J16 (8)	11.97	*19.72*

Nos. J9-J16 also exist on chalky paper.

Wmk. 4a (error)

J9a	D1	2c	35.00
J11a	D1	6c	60.00
J14a	D1	12c	87.50

1970 Unwmk. Litho. *Perf. 14x13½*

Size: 18x23mm

J17	D2	2c	green	15	15
J18	D2	4c	carmine rose	20	20
J19	D2	6c	brown	15	15
J20	D2	8c	lt violet	15	15
J21	D2	10c	brick red	15	15
J22	D2	12c	dull orange	40	40
J23	D2	16c	brt yellow grn	16	16
J24	D2	24c	gray	24	24
J25	D2	50c	blue	50	50
J26	D2	60c	olive green	60	60
			Nos. J17-J26 (10)	2.70	2.70

Perf. 13½x14

1976-77 Litho. Unwmk.

Size: 17x21mm

J27	D2	2c	green	15	15
J28	D2	4c	carmine rose	20	20
J29	D2	6c	brown	28	28
J30	D2	8c	lt violet	40	40
J31	D2	10c	brick red	48	48
J32	D2	12c	dull orange	58	58
			Nos. J27-J32 (6)	2.09	2.09

Issue dates: 4c, 12c, Apr. 1, 1976. 2c, 6c, 8c, 10, 1977.

The letters in the top label on Nos. J27-J32 are larger with D's and O's more squarish than the oval letters on Nos. J17-J26. "Postage Due" is 13mm long and is composed of finer letters than on Nos. J17-J26, which have a 14mm inscription.

WAR TAX STAMPS

Nos. 1-2 Overprinted **WAR TAX**

1917 Wmk. 3 *Perf. 14*

MR1 A1 1p scarlet 18 18
a. Invtd. overprint 200.00 *200.00*

Overprinted **WAR TAX**

MR2 A1 ½p green 15 15
a. Overprinted on face and back 350.00
b. Pair, one without overprint 250.00
MR3 A1 1p scarlet 15 15
a. Pair, one without overprint 250.00
b. Double overprint 125.00
Set value 24 24

Overprinted **WAR TAX**

MR4 A1 ½p green 22 22
MR5 A1 1p scarlet 15 15

Overprinted **WAR TAX**

MR6 A1 ½p green 15 15
MR7 A1 1p scarlet 15 15
Set value 24 24

Overprinted **WAR TAX**

MR8 A1 ½p green 15 15
MR9 A1 1p searlet 17.50 21.00

Overprinted **WAR TAX**

MR10 A1 1p scarlet 15 15
a. Inverted overprint 100.00 *100.00*

Overprinted **WAR TAX**

MR11 A1 1p scarlet 15 15
a. Double overprint 200.00 *200.00*
b. Inverted overprint 100.00 *100.00*

Overprinted **War Tax**

1918

MR12 A1 ½p green 15 15
MR13 A1 1p scarlet 15 15
a. Double overprint 120.00 *120.00*

The War Tax Stamps show considerable variations in the colors, thickness of the paper, distinctness of the watermark, and the gum. Counterfeits exist of the errors of Nos. MR1-MR13.

OFFICIAL STAMPS

Regular Issue of 1913 Overprinted **OFFICIAL**

1913 Wmk. 3 *Perf. 14*

O1 A1 ½p green 32 40

Same Overprinted **OFFICIAL**

1914

O2 A1 ½p green 2.75 3.00

Same Overprinted **OFFICIAL.**

1916

O3 A1 ½p green 1.00 1.00
a. Double overprint 22.50

Same Overprint without Period

1917

O4 A1 ½p green 60 60

Same Overprinted **OFFICIAL**

1917, Aug. 22

O5 A1 ½p green 20 20

The official stamps are found in several shades of green and on paper of varying thickness.

TURKS AND CAICOS ISLANDS

LOCATION — A group of islands in the West Indies, at the southern extremity of the Bahamas
GOVT. — British colony; a dependency of Jamaica until 1959
AREA — 192 sq. mi.
POP. — 7,436 (1980)
CAPITAL — Grand Turk

12 Pence = 1 Shilling
20 Shillings = 1 Pound
100 Cents = 1 US Dollar (1969)

Catalogue values for unused stamps in this country are for Never Hinged items, beginning with Scott 90.

Dependency's Badge
A6 A7

1900-04 Engr. Wmk. 2 *Perf. 14*

1 A6 ½p green 1.65 *2.00*
2 A6 1p rose 1.50 1.65
3 A6 2p black brown 45 60
4 A6 2½p gray blue ('04) 65 70
a. 2½p blue ('00) 6.50 7.00
5 A6 4p orange 85 *1.50*
6 A6 6p violet 1.50 *3.00*
7 A6 1sh purple brn 1.50 *3.00*

Wmk. 1

8 A7 2sh violet 40.00 *60.00*
9 A7 3sh brown lake 45.00 *65.00*
Nos. 1-9 (9) 93.10 *137.45*

1905-08 Wmk. 3

10 A6 ½p green 42 42
11 A6 1p carmine 7.25 1.65
12 A6 3p violet, *yel* ('08) 2.50 *5.00*

King Edward VII — A8

1909, Sept. 2 *Perf. 14*

13 A8 ½p yellow green 15 15
14 A8 1p carmine 18 20
15 A8 2p gray 2.50 3.50
16 A8 2½p ultra 1.40 2.00
17 A8 3p violet, *yel* 60 1.50
18 A8 4p red, *yel* 3.50 *5.25*
19 A8 6p violet 4.50 6.00
20 A8 1sh black, *green* 3.75 *6.50*
21 A8 2sh red, *grn* 17.50 *32.50*
22 A8 3sh black, *red* 19.00 *35.00*
Nos. 13-22 (10) 53.08 *92.60*

Turk's-Head Cactus A9 — George V A10

1910-11 Wmk. 3

23 A9 ¼p claret 15 15
24 A9 ¼p red ('11) 15 15
Set value 16 22

See Nos. 36, 44.

1913-16

25 A10 ½p yellow green 32 45
26 A10 1p carmine 42 45
27 A10 2p gray 95 1.25
28 A10 2½p ultra 1.40 1.10
29 A10 3p violet, *yel* 60 1.25
30 A10 4p scarlet, *yel* 1.25 2.00
31 A10 5p olive grn ('16) 2.75 4.00
32 A10 6p dull violet 2.00 2.75
33 A10 1sh orange 1.40 2.75
34 A10 2sh red, *bl grn* 5.50 8.00
a. 2sh red, *grnsh white* ('19) 17.50 *32.50*
b. 2sh red, *emerald* ('21) 6.25 8.50
35 A10 3sh black, *red* 11.00 16.00
Nos. 25-35 (11) 27.59 40.00

Issue dates: 5p, May 18, 1916, others, Apr. 1, 1913.
For overprints see Nos. MR1-MR13.

1921, Apr. 23 Wmk. 4

36 A9 ¼p red 40 *55*
37 A10 ½p green 55 50
38 A10 1p scarlet 55 50
39 A10 2p gray 80 1.00
40 A10 2½p ultra 2.00 1.10
41 A10 5p olive green 3.50 *5.75*
42 A10 6p dull violet 5.25 *8.25*
43 A10 1sh brown orange 11.00 *16.00*
Nos. 36-43 (8) 24.05 *33.65*

A11 A12

Inscribed "Postage"

1922-26

44 A9 ¼p gray black ('26) 15 15
45 A11 ½p green 20 25
46 A11 1p brown 75 90
47 A11 1½p rose red ('25) 75 90
48 A11 2p gray 60 85
49 A11 2½p violet, *yel* 30 35
50 A11 3p ultra 75 1.00
51 A11 4p red, *yel* 1.25 1.65
52 A11 5p yellow grn 1.25 1.65
53 A11 6p dull violet 1.65 2.00
54 A11 1sh orange 1.75 2.25
55 A11 2sh red, *green* 4.25 5.75

Wmk. 3

56 A11 2sh red, *green* ('25) 7.50 11.50
57 A11 3sh black, *red* ('25) 4.25 6.50
Nos. 44-57 (14) 25.40 35.70

Issue dates: Nos. 47, 56-57, Nov. 24. No. 44, Oct. 11. Others, Nov. 20.

Inscribed "Postage and Revenue"

1928, Mar. 1 Wmk. 4

60 A12 ½p green 15 15
61 A12 1p brown 15 15
62 A12 1½p red 38 26
63 A12 2p dk gray 95 26
64 A12 2½p vio, *yel* 40 *70*
65 A12 3p ultra 48 *1.00*
66 A12 6p brown vio 1.25 *2.50*
67 A12 1sh brown org 1.65 *3.75*
68 A12 2sh red, *grn* 5.25 *14.00*
69 A12 5sh green, *yel* 15.00 *50.00*
70 A12 10sh violet, *bl* 37.50 *80.00*
Nos. 60-70 (11) 63.16 *152.77*

Silver Jubilee Issue
Common Design Type

1935, May 6 *Perf. 11x12*

71 CD301 ½p green & blk 35 30
72 CD301 3p ultra & brn 85 65
73 CD301 6p ol grn & lt bl 1.50 1.25
74 CD301 1sh brn vio & ind 4.00 3.75

Coronation Issue
Common Design Type

1937, May 12 *Perf. 13½x14*

75 CD302 ½p deep green 15 15
76 CD302 2p gray 15 15
77 CD302 3p brt ultra 20 20
Set value 40 40

Raking Salt — A13 Salt Industry — A14

1938-45 Wmk. 4 *Perf. 12½*

78 A13 ¼p black 15 15
79 A13 ½p green 15 15
80 A13 1p brown 15 15
81 A13 1½p carmine 15 15
82 A13 2p gray 15 15
83 A13 2½p orange 15 15
84 A13 3p ultra 15 15
85 A13 6p rose violet 4.75 1.90
85A A13 6p blk brn ('45) 26 35
86 A13 1sh bister 95 1.50
86A A13 1sh dk ol grn ('45) 55 75
87 A14 2sh rose car 95 1.50
88 A14 5sh green 3.00 4.50
89 A14 10sh dp violet 4.25 5.50
Nos. 78-89 (14) 15.76 17.05

Catalogue values for unused stamps in this section, from this point to the end of the section, are for Never Hinged items.

Peace Issue
Common Design Type

1946, Nov. 4 Engr. *Perf. 13½x14*

90 CD303 2p gray black 18 15
91 CD303 3p deep blue 25 15
Set value 25

Silver Wedding Issue
Common Design Types

1948, Sept. 13 Photo. *Perf. 14x14½*

92 CD304 1p red brown 16 15

Perf. 11½x11
Engr.; Name Typo.

93 CD305 10sh purple 7.50 *10.00*

Dependency's Badge — A17

Flag and Merchant Ship — A18

Map of the Islands — A19

Victoria and George VI A20

1948, Dec. 14 Engr. *Perf. 12½*

94 A17 ½p green 15 15
95 A17 2p carmine 22 25
96 A18 3p deep blue 42 45
97 A19 6p violet 70 75
98 A20 2sh ultra & blk 1.10 *1.40*
99 A20 5sh blue grn & blk 2.75 *4.75*
100 A20 10sh chocolate & blk 4.25 *6.75*
Nos. 94-100 (7) 9.59 *14.50*

Cent. of political separation from the Bahamas.

UPU Issue
Common Design Types
Engr.; Name Typo. on 3p, 6p
Perf. 13½, 11x11½

1949, Oct. 10 **Wmk. 4**

101	CD306	2½p	red orange	15	15
102	CD307	3p	indigo	25	25
103	CD308	6p	chocolate	50	50
104	CD309	1sh	olive	1.00	1.00

Common Design Types are pictured beginning on page 176.

Loading Bulk Salt — A21

Dependency's Badge — A22

Designs: 1p, Salt Cay. 1½p, Caicos mail. 2p, Grand Turk. 2½p, Sponge diving. 3p, South Creek. 4p, Map. 6p, Grand Turk Light. 1sh, Government House. 1sh6p, Cockburn Harbor. 2sh, Government offices. 5sh, Salt Loading.

1950, Aug. 2 **Engr.** ***Perf. 12½***

105	A21	½p	deep green	28	15
106	A21	1p	chocolate	35	15
107	A21	1½p	carmine	45	18
108	A21	2p	red orange	45	18
109	A21	2½p	olive green	60	25
110	A21	3p	ultra	60	25
111	A21	4p	rose car & blk	90	38
112	A21	6p	ultra & blk	1.00	40
113	A21	1sh	bl gray & blk	1.10	48
114	A21	1sh6p	red & blk	2.25	1.00
115	A21	2sh	ultra & emer	3.00	1.10
116	A21	5sh	black & ultra	5.00	3.00
117	A22	10sh	purple & blk	15.00	*8.25*
			Nos. 105-117 (13)	30.98	*15.77*

Coronation Issue
Common Design Type

1953, June 2 ***Perf. 13½x13***

118	CD312	2p	red orange & blk	30	24

M. S. Kirksons A23

Design: 8p, Flamingos in flight.

1955, Feb. 1 **Wmk. 4** ***Perf. 12½***

119	A23	5p	emerald & blk	65	52
120	A23	8p	yellow brn & blk	90	70

Queen Elizabeth II — A24

Bonefish A25

Pelican and Salinas — A26

Designs: 2p, Red grouper. 2½p, Spiny lobster. 3p, Albacore. 4p, Muttonfish snapper. 5p, Permit. 6p, Conch. 8p, Flamingos. 1sh, Spanish mackerel. 1sh6p, Salt Cay. 2sh, Caicos sloop. 5sh, Cable office. 10sh, Dependency's badge.

Perf. 13½x14 (1p), 13½x13

1957-60 **Engr.** **Wmk. 314**

121	A24	1p	lil rose & dk bl	15	15
122	A25	1½p	orange & slate	15	15
123	A25	2p	ol & brn red	15	15
124	A25	2½p	brt grn & car	15	15
125	A25	3p	purple & blue	15	15
126	A25	4p	blk & dp rose	18	18
127	A25	5p	brown & grn	22	22
128	A25	6p	ultra & car	30	30
129	A25	8p	black & ver	42	42
130	A25	1sh	blk & dk blue	60	60
131	A25	1sh6p	vio bl & dk brn	1.25	1.25
132	A25	2sh	lt brn & vio bl	1.75	1.75
133	A25	5sh	brt car & blk	3.25	3.25

Perf. 14

134	A26	10sh	purple & blk	7.50	7.50

Perf. 14x14½
Photo.

135	A26	£1	dk red & brn	20.00	20.00
			Nos. 121-135 (15)	36.22	36.22

Issued: £1, Nov. 1, 1960, others, Nov. 25, 1957.

Map of Islands A27

Perf. 13½x14

1959, July 4 **Wmk. 4** **Photo.**

136	A27	6p	ol grn & salmon	22	25
137	A27	8p	violet & salmon	28	30

Granting of a new constitution.

Freedom from Hunger Issue
Common Design Type
Perf. 14x14½

1963, June 4 **Wmk. 314**

138	CD314	8p	carmine rose	50	50

Red Cross Centenary Issue
Common Design Type

1963, Sept. 2 **Litho.** ***Perf. 13***

139	CD315	2p	black & red	15	15
140	CD315	8p	ultra & red	85	85

Shakespeare Issue
Common Design Type

1964, Apr. 23 **Photo.** ***Perf. 14x14½***

141	CD316	8p	green	30	30

ITU Issue
Common Design Type
Perf. 11x11½

1965, May 17 **Litho.** **Wmk. 314**

142	CD317	1p	ver & brown	15	15
143	CD317	2sh	emer & lt blue	85	85

Intl. Cooperation Year Issue
Common Design Type

1965, Oct. 25 **Wmk. 314** ***Perf. 14½***

144	CD318	1p	blue grn & claret	15	15
145	CD318	8p	lt violet & green	60	60

Churchill Memorial Issue
Common Design Type

1966, Jan. 24 **Photo.** ***Perf. 14***
Design in Black, Gold and Carmine Rose

146	CD319	1p	bright blue	15	15
147	CD319	2p	green	15	15
148	CD319	8p	brown	45	45
a.			Gold impression double	*200.00*	
149	CD319	1sh6p	violet	1.00	1.00

Royal Visit Issue
Common Design Type

1966, Feb. 4 **Litho.** ***Perf. 11x12***
Portraits in Black

150	CD320	8p	violet blue	55	55
151	CD320	1sh6p	dk car rose	1.10	1.10

Andrew Symmers Landing with Union Jack A28

Designs: 8p, Andrew Symmers, his signature, Royal Warrant and Union Jack. 1sh6p, New coat of arms, Royal Cypher and St. Edward's crown.

Perf. 13½

1966, Oct. 1 **Unwmk.** **Photo.**

152	A28	1p	dk blue & dp org	15	15
153	A28	8p	dk blue, dl yel & car	26	30
154	A28	1sh6p	multicolored	48	55

200th anniv. of the landing of Andrew Symmers, British agent, establishing the ties with Great Britain.

UNESCO Anniversary Issue
Common Design Type
Wmk. 314

1966, Dec. 1 **Litho.** ***Perf. 14***

155	CD323	1p	"Education"	15	15
156	CD323	8p	"Science"	38	38
157	CD323	1sh6p	"Culture"	75	75

Turk's-head Cactus — A29

Boat Building A30

Designs: 2p, Donkey cart. 3p, Sisal industry. 4p, Conch industry. 6p, Salt industry. 8p, Skin diving. 1sh, Fishing. 1sh6p, Water skiing. 2sh, Crawfish industry. 3sh, Map of Islands. 5sh, Fishing industry. 10sh, Coat of arms. £1, Queen Elizabeth II.

Perf. 14½x14, 14x14½

1967, Feb. 1 **Photo.** **Wmk. 314**

158	A29	1p	violet, red & yel	15	15
159	A30	1½p	choc & org yel	15	15
160	A29	2p	gray, yel & sl	15	15
161	A29	3p	green & dk brn	15	15
162	A30	4p	grnsh bl, blk & pink	15	15
163	A29	6p	blue & dk brn	15	15
164	A29	8p	aqua, dk bl & yel	18	18
165	A30	1sh	grnsh bl & red brn	30	30
166	A29	1sh6p	brt grnsh bl, yel & brn	48	48
167	A30	2sh	multicolored	60	60
168	A30	3sh	grnsh bl & mar	85	85
169	A30	5sh	sky bl, dk bl & yel	1.50	1.50
170	A30	10sh	multicolored	3.00	3.00
171	A29	£1	dk car rose, sil & dk bl	6.00	6.00
			Nos. 158-171 (14)	13.81	13.81

See Nos. 181, 217-230. For surcharges see Nos. 182-195.

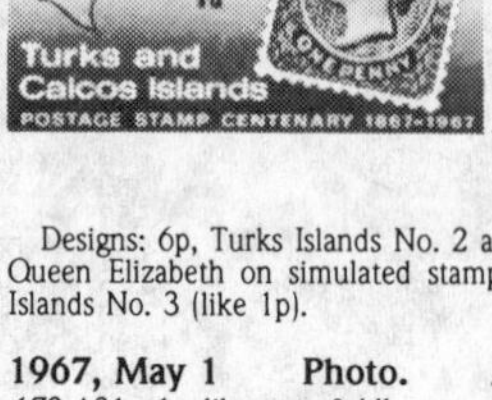
Turks Islands No. 1 A31

Designs: 6p, Turks Islands No. 2 and portrait of Queen Elizabeth on simulated stamp. 1sh, Turks Islands No. 3 (like 1p).

1967, May 1 **Photo.** ***Perf. 14½***

172	A31	1p	lilac rose & blk	15	15
173	A31	6p	gray & black	22	22
174	A31	1sh	Prus blue & blk	42	42

Centenary of Turks Islands stamps.

Human Rights Flame A32

1968, Apr. 1 ***Perf. 14x14½***

175	A32	1p	lt green & multi	15	15
176	A32	8p	lt blue & multi	22	22
177	A32	1sh6p	multicolored	42	42

International Human Rights Year.

Martin Luther King, Jr. and Protest March of 1968 A33

1968, Oct. 1 **Photo.** **Wmk. 314**

178	A33	2p	dk blue, dk & lt brn	15	15
179	A33	8p	dk car rose, dk & lt brn	20	20
180	A33	1sh6p	dp vio, dk & lt brn	42	42

Martin Luther King, Jr. (1929-68), American civil rights leader.

Nos. 158-171 Surcharged

4c

Designs as before and: ¼c, Coat of arms like 10sh.

Perf. 14x14½, 14½x14

1969, Sept. 8 **Photo.** **Wmk. 314**

181	A30	¼c	lt gray & multi	15	15
182	A29	1c	on 1p multi	15	15
183	A29	2c	on 2p multi	15	15
184	A29	3c	on 3p multi	15	15
185	A30	4c	on 4p multi	15	15
186	A29	5c	on 6p multi	15	15
187	A29	7c	on 8p multi	15	15
188	A30	8c	on 1½p multi	15	15
189	A30	10c	on 1sh multi	22	22
190	A29	15c	on 1sh6p multi	35	35
191	A30	20c	on 2sh multi	48	48
192	A30	30c	on 3sh multi	55	55
193	A30	50c	on 5sh multi	90	90
194	A30	$1	on 10sh multi	2.25	2.25
195	A29	$2	on £1 multi	9.50	9.50
			Nos. 181-195 (15)	15.45	15.45

The surcharge is differently arranged on each denomination to fit the design; the old denomination is obliterated with a rectangle on the 8c and 15c.

See Nos. 217-230.

1969 **Wmk. 314 Sideways**

182a	A29	1c	on 1p	15	15
183a	A29	2c	on 2p	15	15
184a	A29	3c	on 3p	15	15
186a	A29	5c	on 6p	18	18
187a	A29	7c	on 8p	27	27
190a	A29	15c	on 1sh6p	70	70
195a	A29	$2	on £1	7.25	7.25
			Nos. 182a-195a (7)	8.85	8.85

Nativity with John the Baptist — A34

Designs from the Book of Hours of Eleanora, Duchess of Tuscany: 3c, 30c, Flight into Egypt.

Perf. 13x12½

1969, Oct. 20 **Litho.** **Wmk. 314**

196	A34	1c	plum & multi	15	15
197	A34	3c	dk blue & multi	15	15
198	A34	15c	olive & multi	30	30
199	A34	30c	yellow brn & multi	55	55

Christmas.

Coat of Arms — A35

1970, Feb. 2 Litho. *Perf. 13x12½*

200	A35	7c brown & multi	15	15
201	A35	35c violet blue & multi	75	75

New Constitution, inaugurated June 16, 1969.
See No. 769.

Christ Bearing the Cross, by Dürer — A36

Albrecht Dürer Engravings: 7c, Christ on the Cross. 50c, The Lamentation for Christ.

Perf. 13½x14

1970, Mar. 17 Engr. Wmk. 314

202	A36	5c dp blue & blk	15	15
203	A36	7c vermilion & blk	18	18
204	A36	50c dk brown & multi	1.10	1.10

Easter.

Dickens and "Oliver Twist" Scene A37

Charles Dickens and Scene from: 3c, "A Christmas Carol." 15c, "Pickwick Papers." 30c, "The Old Curiosity Shop."

Perf. 13½x13

1970, June 17 Litho. & Engr.

205	A37	1c yel, red brn & blk	15	15
206	A37	3c sal pink, sl & blk	15	15
207	A37	15c salmon, bl & blk	40	40
208	A37	30c lt blue, ol & blk	85	85

Charles Dickens (1812-70), English novelist.

Red Cross Ambulance, 1870 — A38

Design: 5c, 30c, Red Cross ambulance, 1970.

1970, Aug. 4 Litho. *Perf. 13½x14*

209	A38	1c orange & multi	15	15
210	A38	5c ocher & multi	16	15
211	A38	15c brt pink & multi	52	32
212	A38	30c multicolored	1.00	60

Centenary of British Red Cross Society.

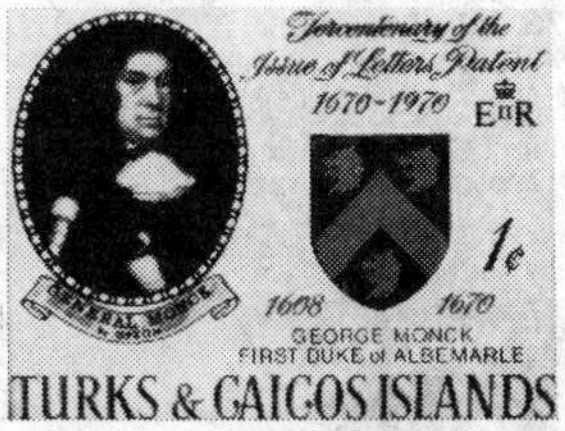

Gen. George Monck, Duke of Albemarle, and his Coat of Arms — A39

Designs: 8c, 35c, Coats of arms of Charles II and Queen Elizabeth II.

1970, Dec. 1 Litho. *Perf. 12½x13½*

213	A39	1c multicolored	15	15
214	A39	8c multicolored	28	25
215	A39	10c multicolored	35	30
216	A39	35c multicolored	1.25	95

Tercentenary of the issue of Letters Patent to the Six Lords Proprietors.

Types of 1967
Values in Cents and Dollars

Designs: 1c, Turk's-head cactus. 2c, Donkey cart. 3c, Sisal industry. 4c, Conch industry. 5c, Salt industry. 7c, Skin diving. 8c, Boat building. 10c, Fishing. 15c, Water skiing. 20c, Crawfish industry. 30c, Map of Islands. 50c, Fishing industry. $1, Arms of Colony. $2, Queen Elizabeth II.

Perf. 14x14½, 14½x14

1971, Feb. 2 Photo. Wmk. 314

217	A29	1c violet, red & yel	15	15
218	A29	2c gray, yel & slate	15	15
219	A29	3c green & dk brown	15	15
220	A30	4c grnsh bl, blk & pink	15	15
221	A29	5c blue & dk brown	15	15
222	A29	7c aqua, dk bl & yel	18	18
223	A30	8c choc & org yel	22	22
224	A30	10c grnsh bl & red brn	28	28
225	A29	15c brt grnsh bl, yel & brn	45	45
226	A30	20c multicolored	65	65
227	A30	30c grnsh bl & mar	1.00	1.00
228	A30	50c sky bl, dk bl & yel	1.50	1.50
229	A30	$1 blue & multi	3.00	3.00
230	A29	$2 dk car rose, sil & dk blue	6.00	6.00
		Nos. 217-230 (14)	14.03	14.03

The ¼c, released with this set is a shade of No. 181, the background being a greenish, slightly darker gray.

Queen Conch and Emblem A40

Tourist publicity (Sun, Sea and Sand Emblem and): 1c, Seahorse, vert. 15c, American oyster catcher. 30c, Blue Marlin.

Perf. 14½x14, 14x14½

1971, May 2 Litho. Wmk. 314

232	A40	1c multicolored	15	15
233	A40	3c multicolored	15	15
234	A40	15c multicolored	52	52
235	A40	30c multicolored	1.00	1.00

Pirate Sloop A41

Designs: 3c, Pirates burying treasure. 15c, Marooned pirate. 30c, Buccaneers.

1971, July 17 *Perf. 14½x14*

236	A41	2c multicolored	15	15
237	A41	3c multicolored	15	15
238	A41	15c multicolored	60	60
239	A41	30c multicolored	1.10	1.10

Adoration of the Virgin and Child, from Wilton Diptych, French School, c. 1395
A42 A43

1971, Oct. 12 Litho. *Perf. 14x13½*

240	A42	2c dull brn & multi	15	15
241	A43	2c dull brn & multi	15	15
242	A42	8c green & multi	22	24
243	A43	8c green & multi	22	24
244	A42	15c dk blue gray & multi	50	45
245	A43	15c dk blue gray & multi	50	45
		Nos. 240-245 (6)	1.74	1.68

Christmas.

Rocket Launch, Cape Canaveral A44

Designs: 10c, Space capsule in orbit around earth. 15c, Map of Turks and Caicos Islands and splashdown. 20c, Distinguished Service Medal, vert.

1972, Feb. 21 *Perf. 13½*

246	A44	5c lt blue & blk	16	15
247	A44	10c multicolored	35	30
248	A44	15c lt green & multi	52	45
249	A44	20c blue & multi	70	60

First orbital flight by US astronaut Lt. Col. John H. Glenn, Jr., and splashdown off Turks and Caicos Islands, 10th anniversary.

The Three Crosses, by Rembrandt — A45

Details from Etchings by Rembrandt: 2c, Christ Before Pilate, vert. 30c, Descent from the Cross, vert.

Perf. 14x13½, 13½x14

1972, Mar. 17

250	A45	2c lilac & black	15	15
251	A45	15c pink & black	40	40
252	A45	30c yellow & black	85	85

Easter.

Richard Grenville and "Revenge" — A46

Discoverers and explorers of the Americas: ¼c, Christopher Columbus, Niña, Pinta and Santa Maria, vert. 10c, Capt. John Smith and three-master, vert. 30c, Juan Ponce de León and three-master.

1972, July 4

253	A46	¼c multicolored	15	15
254	A46	8c multicolored	60	20
255	A46	10c multicolored	75	25
256	A46	30c multicolored	2.00	75

Silver Wedding Issue, 1972
Common Design Type

Design: Queen Elizabeth II, Prince Philip, turk's-head cactus and spiny lobster.

Perf. 14x14½

1972, Nov. 20 Photo. Wmk. 314

257	CD324	10c ultra & multi	28	28
258	CD324	20c multicolored	52	52

Treasure Hunting, c. 1700 — A47

Designs: 5c, Replica of silver bank medallion, 1687, obverse. 10c, Same, reverse. 30c, Scuba diver, 1973.

Perf. 14x14½

1973, Jan. 18 Litho. Wmk. 314

259	A47	3c Prus blue & multi	15	15
260	A47	5c plum, silver & blk	18	18
261	A47	10c brt rose, silver & blk	35	35
262	A47	30c violet blue & multi	1.10	1.10
a.		Souvenir sheet of 4, #259-262	2.75	2.75

Treasure hunting.

Arms of Jamaica, Turks and Caicos Islands — A48

1973, Apr. 16 Litho. *Perf. 13½x14*

263	A48	15c buff & multi	38	35
264	A48	35c lt green & multi	80	80

Centenary of annexation to Jamaica.

Sooty Tern — A49

Birds: 1c, Magnificent frigate bird. 2c, Noddy tern. 3c, Blue gray gnatcatcher. 4c, Little blue heron. 5c, Catbird. 7c, Black-whiskered vireo. 8c, Osprey. 10c, Flamingo. 15c, Brown pelican. 20c, Parula warbler. 30c, Northern mockingbird. 50c, Ruby-throated hummingbird. $1, Bahama bananaquit. $2, Cedar waxwing. $5, Painted bunting.

Wmk. 314 Sideways

1973, Aug. 1 Litho. *Perf. 14*

265	A49	¼c yellow & multi	15	15
266	A49	1c pink & multi	15	15
267	A49	2c orange & multi	15	15
268	A49	3c lilac rose & multi	30	30
269	A49	4c lt blue & multi	15	15
270	A49	5c lt green & multi	22	22
271	A49	7c salmon & multi	25	25
272	A49	8c blue & multi	30	30
273	A49	10c brt blue & multi	38	38
274	A49	15c tan & multi	55	55
275	A49	20c brt yel & multi	1.50	1.50
276	A49	30c yellow & multi	1.25	1.25
277	A49	50c yellow & multi	2.00	2.00
278	A49	$1 blue & multi	4.25	4.25
279	A49	$2 gray & multi	8.50	8.50
		Nos. 265-279 (15)	20.10	20.10

1974-75 Wmk. 314 Upright

266a	A49	1c pink & multi ('75)	25	25
267a	A49	2c orange & multi	50	50
268a	A49	3c lil rose & multi ('75)	75	75
275a	A49	20c brt yel & multi ('75)	2.50	2.50

1976-77 Wmk. 373

265a	A49	1/4c yellow & multi ('77)	15	15
266b	A49	1c pink & multi ('77)	15	15
267b	A49	2c orange & multi ('77)	15	15
268b	A49	3c lilac rose & multi	15	15
269a	A49	4c lt bl & multi ('77)	15	15
270a	A49	5c lt grn & multi ('77)	15	15
273a	A49	10c brt bl & multi ('77)	22	22
274a	A49	15c tan & multi ('77)	35	35
275b	A49	20c brt yel & multi	45	45
276a	A49	30c yel & multi ('77)	65	65
277a	A49	50c yel & multi ('77)	1.10	1.10
278a	A49	$1 blue & multi ('77)	2.25	2.25
279b	A49	$2 gray & multi ('77)	4.50	4.50
279A	A49	$5 yel grn & multi	11.50	11.50
		Nos. 265a-279A (14)	21.92	21.92

Bermuda Sloop — A50

Old Sailing Ships: 5c, HMS Blanche. 8c, US privateer Grand Turk and packet Hinchinbrooke. 10c, HMS Endymion. 15c, RMS Medina. 20c, HMS Daring.

1973, July 19 Litho. *Perf. 13½*

280 A50	2c multicolored	15	15
281 A50	5c multicolored	18	18
282 A50	8c multicolored	30	30
283 A50	10c multicolored	40	40
284 A50	15c multicolored	60	60
285 A50	20c multicolored	85	85
a.	Souvenir sheet of 6, #280-285	3.50	3.50
	Nos. 280-285 (6)	2.48	2.48

Princess Anne's Wedding Issue

Common Design Type

1973, Nov. 14 Wmk. 314 *Perf. 14*

286 CD325	12c blue grn & multi	26	26
287 CD325	18c slate & multi	40	40

Lucayan Stool A51

Designs: Lucayan artifacts.

1974, July 17 Litho. *Perf. 14½*

288 A51	6c shown	15	15
289 A51	10c Broken wood bowl	22	18
290 A51	12c Greenstone axe	28	22
291 A51	18c Wood bowl	40	34
292 A51	35c Animal head, fragment of stool	80	65
a.	Souvenir sheet of 5, #288-292	3.50	3.50
	Nos. 288-292 (5)	1.85	1.54

Carvings made by Lucayan Indians, first inhabitants of the islands.

Grand Turk G.P.O. A52

UPU Emblem and: 12c, Map of Turks and Caicos Islands and local mail sloop. 18c, "United Service" (globe and "UPU"). 55c, Design symbolic of the Islands joining the UPU in 1881.

1974, Oct. 9 Wmk. 314 *Perf. 14*

293 A52	4c yellow & multi	15	15
294 A52	12c blue & multi	28	25
295 A52	18c violet & multi	40	38
296 A52	55c lt blue & multi	1.25	1.10

Centenary of Universal Postal Union.

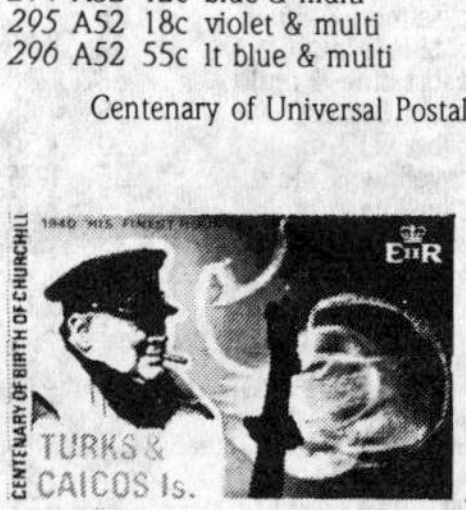

"His Finest Hour" A53

Design: 12c, Churchill and Franklin D. Roosevelt.

1974, Nov. 30 Wmk. 373

297 A53	12c multicolored	32	32
298 A53	18c multicolored	48	48
a.	Souvenir sheet of 2, #297-298	80	80

Sir Winston Churchill (1874-1965).

Spanish Captain, c. 1492 — A54

Old Windmill, Salt Cay — A55

Uniforms: 20c, Officer, Royal Artillery, 1783. 25c, Officer, 67th Foot, 1798. 35c, Private, First West India Regiment, 1833.

1975, Mar. 26 Wmk. 314 *Perf. 14½*

299 A54	5c blue & multi	15	15
300 A54	20c blue & multi	55	50
301 A54	25c blue & multi	65	60
302 A54	35c blue & multi	95	85
a.	Souvenir sheet of 4, #299-302	3.00	3.75

1975, Oct. 16 Litho. Wmk. 373

Salt industry: 10c, Pink salt pans, horiz. 20c, Salt raking at Salt Cay, horiz. 25c, Unprocessed salt ready for shipment.

303 A55	6c violet & multi	16	15
304 A55	10c lt brown & multi	26	20
305 A55	20c red & multi	52	38
306 A55	25c magenta & multi	70	45

Star Coral A56

1975, Dec. 4 Litho. Wmk. 373

307 A56	6c shown	20	15
308 A56	10c Elkhorn coral	32	25
309 A56	20c Brain coral	65	50
310 A56	25c Staghorn coral	85	60

Schooner — A57

American Bicentennial: 20c, Ship of the line. 25c, Frigate Grand Turk. 55c, Ketch.

1976, May 28 *Perf. 14x13½*

311 A57	6c orange & multi	30	15
312 A57	20c violet blue & multi	90	28
313 A57	25c brown & multi	1.00	35
314 A57	55c multicolored	1.75	80
a.	Souvenir sheet of 4, #311-314	4.25	5.25

Turks and Caicos Islands No. 151 A58

Design: 25c, Turks and Caicos Islands No. 150.

1976, July 14 Wmk. 373 *Perf. 14½*

315 A58	20c carmine & multi	60	45
316 A58	25c violet blue & multi	70	60

Visit of Queen Elizabeth II and Prince Philip to the Caribbean, 10th anniversary.

Virgin and Child, by Carlo Dolci — A59

Christmas: 10c, Virgin and Child with St. John, by Botticelli. 20c, Adoration of the Kings, from Retable by the Master of Paradise. 25c, Adoration of the Kings, illuminated page, French, 15th century.

1976, Nov. 10 Litho. *Perf. 14x13½*

317 A59	6c multicolored	15	15
318 A59	10c orange & multi	16	16
319 A59	20c red lilac & multi	35	35
320 A59	25c multicolored	42	42

Queen with Regalia — A60

Designs: 6c, Queen presenting Order of British Empire to E. T. Wood, Grand Turk, 1966. 55c, Royal family on balcony of Buckingham Palace. $5, Portrait of Queen from photograph taken during her 1966 visit to Grand Turk.

1977 Litho. *Perf. 14x13½*

321 A60	6c multicolored	15	15
322 A60	25c multicolored	42	48
323 A60	55c multicolored	95	95

Souvenir Sheet

Perf. 14

324 A60	$5 multicolored	5.00	4.00

25th anniv. of the reign of Elizabeth II.

Nos. 322 and 323 were also issued in booklet panes of 2.

Issue dates: #321-323, Feb. 7. #324, Dec. 6.

Friendship 7 Capsule A61

Designs: 3c, Lunar rover, vert. 6c, Tracking Station on Grand Turk. 20c, Moon landing craft, vert. 25c, Col. Glenn's rocket leaving launching pad, vert. 50c, Telstar 1 satellite.

Perf. 13½

1977, June 20 Litho. Wmk. 373

325 A61	1c multicolored	15	15
326 A61	3c multicolored	15	15
327 A61	6c multicolored	15	15
328 A61	20c multicolored	38	35
329 A61	25c multicolored	45	42
330 A61	50c multicolored	95	85
	Nos. 325-330 (6)	2.23	2.07

US Tracking Station on Grand Turk, 25th anniversary.

Adoration of the Kings, 1634 by Rubens — A63

Rubens Paintings: 1/4c, Flight into Egypt. 1c, Adoration of the Kings, 1624. 6c, Madonna with Garland. 20c, $1, Virgin and Child Adored by Angels. $2, Adoration of the Kings, 1618.

1977, Dec. 23

331 A63	1/4c multicolored	15	15
332 A63	1/2c multicolored	15	15
333 A63	1c multicolored	15	15
334 A63	6c multicolored	15	15
335 A63	20c multicolored	26	20
336 A63	$2 multicolored	2.50	2.50
	Nos. 331-336 (6)	3.36	3.30

Souvenir Sheet

337 A63	$1 multicolored	1.90	1.90

Christmas and 400th birth anniversary of Peter Paul Rubens (1577-1640).

Map of Turks Island Passage A64

Designs: 20c, Grand Turk lighthouse and sailboat (LUG cargo vessel). 25c, Deepsea fishing yacht. 55c, S.S. Jamaica Planter.

Wmk. 373, Unwmkd.

1978, Feb. 2 Litho. *Perf. 13½*

338 A64	6c multicolored	15	15
339 A64	20c multicolored	40	35
340 A64	25c multicolored	50	45
341 A64	55c multicolored	1.10	1.10
a.	Souv. sheet of 4, #338-341, unwmkd.	2.50	3.00

Turks Island Passage, a major Caribbean shipping route.

No. 341a exists watermarked.

Queen Victoria in Coronation Regalia — A65

British Monarchs in Coronation Regalia: 10c, Edward VII. 25c, George V. $2, George VI. $2.50, Elizabeth II.

1978, June 2 Litho. *Perf. 14*

342 A65	6c multicolored	15	15
343 A65	10c multicolored	15	15
344 A65	25c multicolored	40	30
345 A65	$2 multicolored	3.25	2.50

Souvenir Sheet

346 A65	$2.50 multicolored	3.75	2.75

25th anniversary of coronation of Queen Elizabeth II. Nos. 342-345 also issued in sheets of 3 plus label, perf. 12.

Wilbur Wright and Flyer 3 A66

Aviation Progress: 6c, Cessna 337 and Wright brothers. 10c, Southeast Airlines' Electra and Orville Wright. 15c, C47 cargo plane on South Caicos runway. 35c, Norman-Britten Islander at

Grand Turk airport. $1, Orville Wright and Flyer, 1902. $2, Wilbur Wright and Flyer.

1978, June 29 Litho. *Perf. 14½*

347 A66	1c	multicolored	15	15
348 A66	6c	multicolored	15	15
349 A66	10c	multicolored	15	15
350 A66	15c	multicolored	25	20
351 A66	35c	multicolored	1.50	50
352 A66	$2	multicolored	3.25	2.50
		Nos. 347-352 (6)	5.45	3.65

Souvenir Sheet

353 A66	$1	multicolored	2.00	1.50

Queen Elizabeth II — A67

Designs: 15c, Ampulla and anointing spoon. 25c, St. Edward's crown.

Imperf. x Roulette 5

1978, July 24 Litho.

Self-adhesive

354	Souvenir booklet	6.00	
a.	A67 Bklt. pane of 3, 15c, 25c, $2	3.50	
b.	A67 Bklt. pane, 3 each, 15c, 25c	2.25	

25th anniv. of coronation of Queen Elizabeth II. #354 contains #354a-354b printed on peelable paper backing with music and text of hymns.

Hurdling A68

1978, Aug. 3 Litho. *Perf. 15*

355 A68	6c	shown	15	15
356 A68	20c	Weight lifting	32	28
357 A68	55c	Boxing	90	75
358 A68	$2	Bicycling	3.25	2.75

Souvenir Sheet

359 A68	$1	Sprinting	2.75	2.50

11th Commonwealth Games, Edmonton, Canada, Aug. 3-12.

Fish — A69

1978-79 Litho. *Perf. 14*

360 A69	1c	Indigo hamlet	15	15
361 A69	2c	Tobacco fish	15	15
362 A69	3c	Passing Jack	15	15
363 A69	4c	Porkfish	15	15
364 A69	5c	Spanish grunt	15	15
365 A69	7c	Yellowtail snapper	15	15
366 A69	8c	Foureye butterflyfish	15	15
367 A69	10c	Yellow fin grouper	16	16
368 A69	15c	Beau Gregory	25	25
369 A69	20c	Queen angelfish	35	35
370 A69	30c	Hogfish	50	50
371 A69	50c	Fairy Basslet	85	85
372 A69	$1	Clown wrasse	1.65	1.65
373 A69	$2	Stoplight parrotfish	3.50	3.50
374 A69	$5	Queen triggerfish	8.50	8.50
		Nos. 360-374 (15)	16.81	16.81

Issue dates: 1c, 3c, 5c, 10c, 15c, 20c, Nov. 17, 1978; others Feb. 6, 1979.

Nos. 368-369, 372-374 exist dated 1983.

1981, Dec. 15 *Perf. 12½x12*

360a	A69	1c	15	15
364a	A69	5c	15	15
367a	A69	10c	16	16
369a	A69	20c	35	35
371a	A69	50c	85	85
372a	A69	$1	1.65	1.65
373a	A69	$2	3.50	3.50
374a	A69	$5	8.50	8.50
		Nos. 360a-374a (8)	15.31	15.31

Virgin with the Goldfinch, by Dürer — A70

Dürer Paintings: 20c, Virgin and Child with St. Anne. 35c, Nativity, horiz. $1, Adoration of the Kings, horiz. $2, Praying Hands.

1978, Dec. 11 Litho. *Perf. 14*

375 A70	6c	multicolored	15	15
376 A70	20c	multicolored	28	24
377 A70	35c	multicolored	50	42
378 A70	$2	multicolored	2.75	2.50

Souvenir Sheet

379 A70	$1	multicolored	1.25	1.25

Christmas and 450th death anniversary of Albrecht Dürer (1471-1528), German painter.

Ospreys A71

Endangered Species: 20c, Green turtle. 25c, Queen conch. 55c, Rough-toothed dolphin. $1, Humpback whale. $2, Iguana.

1979, May 17 Litho. *Perf. 14*

380 A71	6c	multicolored	18	18
381 A71	20c	multicolored	40	28
382 A71	25c	multicolored	48	35
383 A71	55c	multicolored	1.10	75
384 A71	$1	multicolored	2.00	1.40
		Nos. 380-384 (5)	4.16	2.96

Souvenir Sheet

385 A71	$2	multicolored	3.75	2.50

The Beloved, by Dante Gabriel Rossetti A72

Paintings and IYC Emblem: 25c, Tahitian Girl, by Paul Gauguin. 55c, Calmady Children, by Sir Thomas Lawrence. $1, Mother and Daughter (detail), by Gauguin. $2, Marchesa Elena Grimaldi, by Van Dyck.

1979, July 2 Litho. *Perf. 14*

386 A72	6c	multicolored	15	15
387 A72	25c	multicolored	42	30
388 A72	55c	multicolored	95	65
389 A72	$1	multicolored	1.65	1.75

Souvenir Sheet

390 A72	$2	multicolored	3.50	3.00

International Year of the Child.

Stampless Cover and "Medina" A73

Designs: 20c, Map of Islands and Rowland Hill. 45c, Stamped envelope and "Orinoco." 75c, Paddlewheeler "Shannon" and letter. $1, Royal Packet "Trent," map of Islands. $2, New and old seals.

1979, Aug. 27 Litho. *Perf. 14*

391 A73	6c	multicolored	15	15
392 A73	20c	multicolored	35	24
393 A73	45c	multicolored	75	55
394 A73	75c	multicolored	1.25	90
395 A73	$1	multicolored	1.65	1.25

Perf. 12

396 A73	$2	multicolored ('80)	3.50	3.50
a.		Souv. sheet of 1, perf. 14 ('79)	3.50	3.50
		Nos. 391-396 (6)	7.65	6.59

Nos. 391-395 were issued in sheets of 40, and in sheets of 5 stamps plus label, in changed colors, perf. 12.

No. 396 issued May 6, 1980 in sheet of 5 plus label picturing signal flags and map.

No. 396a overprinted: "BRASILIANA 79"

Souvenir Sheet

1979, Sept. 10 Litho. *Perf. 14*

397 A73	$2	multicolored	3.75	3.75

Brasiliana 79 Intl. Philatelic Exhibition, Rio de Janeiro, Sept. 15-23.

Cuneiform Script — A74

Designs: 5c, Egyptian papyrus; Chinese writing. 15c, Greek runner; Roman post horse; Roman ship. 25c, Pigeon post; railway post; steamship postal packet. 40c, Balloon post; first airmail plane; supersonic airmail jet. $1, Original stamp press (3 designs each of 5c, 15c, 25c, 40).

Imperf. x Roulette 5, Imperf. ($1)

1979, Sept. 27 Litho.

Self-adhesive

398	Souvenir booklet	*6.60*	
a.	A74 Bklt. pane of 1 ($1)		
b.	A74 Bklt. pane, 3 each 5c, 15c		
c.	A74 Bklt. pane, 3 each 25c, 40c		

Sir Rowland Hill (1795-1879), originator of penny postage. No. 398 contains 3 booklet panes on peelable paper backing with descriptions of stamp designs.

International Year of the Child — A74a

Designs: Aquatic scenes.

1979, Nov. 2 Litho. *Perf. 11*

399 A74a	¼c	Pluto and starfish	15	15
400 A74a	½c	Minnie Mouse	15	15
401 A74a	1c	Mickey Mouse skin-diving	15	15
402 A74a	2c	Goofy riding turtle	15	15
403 A74a	3c	Donald and dolphin	15	15
404 A74a	4c	Mickey Mouse and fish	15	15
405 A74a	5c	Goofy surfing	15	15
406 A74a	25c	Pluto and lobster	60	25
407 A74a	$1	Daisy Duck water-skiing	2.50	1.00
		Set value	3.50	1.50

Souvenir Sheet

Perf. 13½x14

408 A74a	$1.50	Goofy	3.25	1.50

St. Nicholas, Icon, 17th Century — A75

Icons or Illuminations: 3c, Emperor Otto II, 10th century. 6c, St. John, Book of Lindisfarne. 15c, Christ and angels. 20c, Christ attended by angels, Book of Kells, 9th century. 25c, St. John the Evangelist. 65c, Christ enthroned, 17th century. $1, St. John, 8th century. $2, St. Matthew, Book of Lindisfarne.

1979, Nov. 26

409 A75	1c	multicolored	15	15
410 A75	3c	multicolored	15	15
411 A75	6c	multicolored	15	15
412 A75	15c	multicolored	25	20
413 A75	20c	multicolored	35	25
414 A75	25c	multicolored	42	32
415 A75	65c	multicolored	1.10	85
416 A75	$1	multicolored	1.65	1.25
		Nos. 409-416 (8)	4.22	3.32

Souvenir Sheet

417 A75	$2	multicolored	3.50	2.50

Christina's World, by Andrew Wyeth — A76

Art Treasures: 10c, Ivory leopards, Benin, 19th century. 20c, The Kiss, by Gustav Klimt, vert. 25c, Portrait of a Lady, by Rogier van der Weyden, vert. 80c, Sumerian bull's head harp, 2600 B.C., vert. $1, The Wave, by Hokusai. $2, Holy Family, by Rembrandt, vert.

1979, Dec. 19 Litho. *Perf. 13½*

418 A76	6c	multicolored	15	15
419 A76	10c	multicolored	16	15
420 A76	20c	multicolored	35	25
421 A76	25c	multicolored	42	32
422 A76	80c	multicolored	1.40	1.10
423 A76	$1	multicolored	1.65	1.25
		Nos. 418-423 (6)	4.13	3.22

Souvenir Sheet

424 A76	$2	multicolored	3.50	2.50

Pied-billed Grebe A77

1980, Feb. 20 Litho. *Perf. 14*

425 A77	20c	shown	40	28
426 A77	25c	Ovenbirds	50	35
427 A77	35c	Marsh hawks	70	50
428 A77	55c	Yellow-bellied sapsucker	1.10	70
429 A77	$1	Blue-winged teals	1.90	1.40
		Nos. 425-429 (5)	4.60	3.23

Souvenir Sheet

430 A77	$2	Glossy ibis	4.00	3.75

Stamp Under Magnifier, Perforation Gauge, London 1980 Emblem — A78

1980, May 6 Litho. *Perf. 14x14½*

431 A78	25c	shown	42	42
432 A78	40c	Stamp in tongs, gauge	70	70

Souvenir Sheet

433 A78	$2	Exhibition Hall	3.50	2.50

London 1980 International Stamp Exhibition, May 6-14.

Trumpet Triton — A79

1980, June 26 Litho. *Perf. 14*

434	A79	15c	shown	25	25
435	A79	20c	Measled cowry	35	35
436	A79	30c	True tulip	50	50
437	A79	45c	Lion's paw	75	75
438	A79	55c	Sunrise tellin	95	95
439	A79	70c	Grown cone	1.25	1.25
			Nos. 434-439 (6)	4.05	4.05

Queen Mother Elizabeth, 80th Birthday — A80

1980, Aug. 4 Litho. *Perf. 14*

440	A80	80c	multicolored	2.25	2.50

Souvenir Sheet

Perf. 12

441	A80	$1.50	multicolored	2.50	2.50

Pinocchio — A81

Christmas: Scenes from Walt Disney's Pinocchio.

1980, Sept. 25 *Perf. 11*

442	A81	1/4c	multicolored	15	15
443	A81	1/2c	multicolored	15	15
444	A81	1c	multicolored	15	15
445	A81	2c	multicolored	15	15
446	A81	3c	multicolored	15	15
447	A81	4c	multicolored	15	15
448	A81	5c	multicolored	15	15
449	A81	75c	multicolored	1.50	1.50
450	A81	$1	multicolored	2.00	2.00
			Nos. 442-450 (9)	4.55	4.55

Souvenir Sheet

451	A81	$2	multi, vert.	4.00	4.00

Medical Examination, Lions — A82

1980, Oct. 8 Litho. *Perf. 14*

452	A82	10c	shown	16	16
453	A82	15c	Scholarships, Kiwanis	25	25
454	A82	45c	Education, Soroptimists	75	75
455	A82	$1	Lobster boat, Rotary	1.65	1.65

Souvenir Sheet

456	A82	$2	Funds for schools, Rotary	4.00	4.00

Lions, Rotary, Kiwanis and Soroptimists service organizations; 75th anniv. of Rotary Intl.

Martin Luther King, Jr. (1929-68) — A83

Human Rights Leaders: 30c, John F. Kennedy. 45c, Roberto Clemente (1934-72), baseball player. 70c, Frank Worrel (1927-67), cricket player. $1, Harriet Tubman (1823-1913), born slave, helped others escape to freedom. $2, Marcus Garvey (1887-1940), Jamaican black nationalist leader.

1980, Dec. 22 Litho. *Perf. 14*

457	A83	20c	multicolored	35	35
458	A83	30c	multicolored	50	50
459	A83	45c	multicolored	75	75
460	A83	70c	multicolored	1.25	1.25
461	A83	$1	multicolored	1.65	1.65
			Nos. 457-461 (5)	4.50	4.50

Souvenir Sheet

462	A83	$2	multicolored	3.75	3.75

Racing Yachts A84

Designs: Racing yachts.

1981, Jan. 29 Litho. *Perf. 14*

463	A84	6c	multicolored	15	15
464	A84	15c	multicolored	25	25
465	A84	35c	multicolored	60	60
466	A84	$1	multicolored	1.65	1.65

Souvenir Sheet

467	A84	$2	multicolored	4.00	4.00

South Caicos Regatta. No. 467 contains one 28x42mm stamp.

Pluto Listening to Sea Shell — A85

1981, Feb. 16 *Perf. 13 1/2x14*

468	A85	10c	shown	25	25
469	A85	75c	Pluto on raft, dolphin	1.90	1.90

Souvenir Sheet

470	A85	$1.50	Pluto	3.00	3.00

50th anniversary of Walt Disney's Pluto.

Night Queen Cactus — A86

1981, Feb. 10 *Perf. 14*

471	A86	25c	shown	45	45
472	A86	35c	Ripsaw cactus	65	65
473	A86	55c	Royal strawberry cactus	1.00	1.00
474	A86	80c	Caicos cactus	1.50	1.50

Souvenir Sheet

475	A86	$2	Turks head cactus	4.00	4.00

Donald Duck and Louie with Easter Egg — A87

Easter: Various Disney characters with Easter eggs.

1981, Mar. 20 Litho. *Perf. 11*

476	A87	10c	multicolored	25	25
477	A87	25c	multicolored	65	65
478	A87	60c	multicolored	1.65	1.65
479	A87	80c	multicolored	2.00	2.00

Souvenir Sheet

480	A87	$4	multicolored	8.00	8.00

Woman with Fan, 1909 — A88

1981, May 28 Litho. *Perf. 14*

481	A88	20c	shown	35	35
482	A88	45c	Woman with Pears, 1909	80	80
483	A88	80c	The Accordionist, 1911	1.50	1.50
484	A88	$1	The Aficionado, 1912	1.50	1.50

Souvenir Sheet

485	A88	$2	Girl with a Mandolin, 1910	4.00	4.00

Pablo Picasso (1881-1973).

Royal Wedding Issue

Common Design Type and

A88a

1981, June 23 Litho. *Perf. 14*

486	CD331	35c	Couple	60	60
487	CD331	65c	Kensington Palace	1.10	1.10
488	CD331	90c	Charles	1.50	1.50

Souvenir Sheet

489	CD331	$2	Glass coach	3.50	3.50

Self-adhesive

Imperf. x Roulette 5 (20c, $1), Imperf. ($2)

1981, July 7

490		Booklet	14.00
a.	A88a	Pane of 6 (3x20c, Lady Diana, 3x$1, Charles)	9.00
b.	A88a	Pane of 1, $2, Couple	5.00

Nos. 486-488 also printed in sheets of 5 plus label, perf. 12, in changed colors.

Underwater Marine Biology Observation A89

1981, Aug. 21 Litho. *Perf. 14*

491	A89	15c	shown	28	28
492	A89	40c	Underwater photography	70	70
493	A89	75c	Diving for wreckage	1.40	1.40
494	A89	$1	Diver, dolphins	1.75	1.75

Souvenir Sheet

495	A89	$2	Diving flag	4.00	4.00

Br'er Rabbit Barricading his Door — A90

Christmas: Scenes from Walt Disney's Uncle Remus.

1981, Nov. 2 Litho. *Perf. 14x13 1/2*

496	A90	1/4c	multicolored	15	15
497	A90	1/2c	multicolored	15	15
498	A90	1c	multicolored	15	15
499	A90	2c	multicolored	15	15
500	A90	3c	multicolored	15	15
501	A90	4c	multicolored	15	15
502	A90	5c	multicolored	15	15
503	A90	75c	multicolored	1.50	1.50
504	A90	$1	multicolored	2.00	2.00
			Nos. 496-504 (9)	4.55	4.55

Souvenir Sheet

505	A90	$2	multicolored	4.75	4.75

Flags of Turks and Caicos Islands A91

Maps of Various Islands: a, Grand Turk. b, Salt Cay. c, South Caicos. d, East Caicos. e, Middle Caicos. f, North Caicos. g, Caicos Cays. h, Providenciales. i, West Caicos.

1981, Dec. 1 *Perf. 14*

506		Strip of 10	3.50	3.50
a.-j.	A91	20c any single	35	35

Caribbean Buckeyes — A92

Scouting Year — A93

1982, Jan. 21 Litho. *Perf. 14*

507	A92	20c	shown	40	40
508	A92	35c	Clench's hairstreaks	70	70
509	A92	65c	Gulf fritillarys	1.30	1.30
510	A92	$1	Bush sulphurs	2.00	2.00

Souvenir Sheet

511	A92	$2	Turk Isld. leaf butterfly	4.00	4.00

1982, Feb. 17 Litho. *Perf. 14*

512	A93	40c	Flag ceremony	65	65
513	A93	50c	Building raft	80	80
514	A93	75c	Cricket match	1.25	1.25
515	A93	$1	Nature study	1.50	1.50

Souvenir Sheet

516	A93	$2	Baden-Powell, salute	3.50	3.50

1982 World Cup Soccer — A94

Designs: Various soccer players.

1982, Apr. 30 Litho. *Perf. 14*

517	A94	10c	multicolored	18	18
518	A94	25c	multicolored	45	45
519	A94	45c	multicolored	80	80

520 A94 $1 multicolored 1.75 1.75

Souvenir Sheet

521 A94 $2 multi, horiz. 3.50 3.50

#517-520 issued in sheets of 5 + label.

Phillis Wheatley (1753-1784), Poet, and Washington Crossing Delaware
A95

Washington's 250th Birth Anniv. and F.D. Roosevelt's Birth Centenary: 35c, Washington, Benjamin Banneker (1731-1806), astronomer and mathematician, map. 65c, FDR, George Washington Carver (1864-1943). 80c, FDR with stamp collection. $2, FDR examining Washington stamp.

1982, May 3 Litho. *Perf. 14*

522 A95 20c multicolored 40 40
523 A95 35c multicolored 70 70
524 A95 65c multicolored 1.30 1.30
525 A95 80c multicolored 1.60 1.60

Souvenir Sheet

526 A95 $2 multicolored 4.00 4.00

Second Thoughts, by Norman Rockwell — A96

1982, June 23 Litho. *Perf. 14x13½*

527 A96 8c shown 15 15
528 A96 15c The Proper Gratuity 28 28
529 A96 20c Before the Shot 35 35
530 A96 25c The Three Umpires 45 45

Princess Diana Issue

Common Design Type

1982 Litho. *Perf. 14½x14*

530A CD332 8c Sandringham 15 15
530B CD332 35c Wedding 55 55
530C CD332 $1.10 Diana 1.75 1.75

1982, July 1 *Perf. 14½x14*

531 CD332 55c Sandringham 1.00 1.00
532 CD332 70c Wedding 1.00 1.00
533 CD332 $1 Diana 1.75 1.75

Also issued in sheetlets of 5 + label.

Souvenir Sheet

534 CD332 $2 Diana, diff. 4.00 4.00

Skymaster over Caicos Cays
A97

1982, Aug. 26 Litho. *Perf. 14*

535 A97 8c shown 15 15
536 A97 15c Jetstar, Grand Turk 28 28
537 A97 65c Helicopter, South Caicos 1.10 1.10
538 A97 $1.10 Seaplane, Providenciales 2.00 2.00

Souvenir Sheet

539 A97 $2 Boeing 727 4.00 4.00

Christmas — A98

Christmas: Scenes from Walt Disney's Mickey's Christmas Carol.

1982, Dec. 1 Litho. *Perf. 13½*

540 A98 1c multicolored 15 15
541 A98 1c multicolored 15 15
542 A98 2c multicolored 15 15
543 A98 2c multicolored 15 15
544 A98 3c multicolored 15 15
545 A98 3c multicolored 15 15
546 A98 4c multicolored 15 15
547 A98 65c multicolored 1.40 1.40
548 A98 $1.10 multicolored 2.75 2.75
Nos. 540-548 (9) 5.20 5.20

Souvenir Sheet

549 A98 $2 multicolored 4.50 4.50

Trams and Locomotives — A99

1983, Jan. 18 Litho. *Perf. 14*

550 A99 15c West Caicos trolley tram 25 25
551 A99 55c West Caicos steam locomotive 95 95
552 A99 90c Mule-drawn tram, East Caicos 1.50 1.50
553 A99 $1.60 Sisal locomotive, East Caicos 2.75 2.75

Souvenir Sheet

554 A99 $2.50 Steam engine 4.50 4.50

CD334

1983, Mar. 14

555 CD334 1c Woman crossing guard 15 15
556 CD334 8c Wind and solar energy sources 15 15
557 CD334 65c Sailing 1.10 1.10
558 CD334 $1 Cricket game 1.75 1.75
a. Block of 4, #555-558 3.00 3.00

Commonwealth Day.

Easter — A100

Crucifixion, by Raphael. $2.50 shows entire painting.

1983, Apr. 7 Litho. *Perf. 14*

559 A100 35c Mary Magdalene, St. John 60 60
560 A100 50c Mary 90 90
561 A100 95c Angel looking to heaven 1.65 1.65
562 A100 $1.10 Angel looking to earth 2.00 2.00

Souvenir Sheet

563 A100 $2.50 multicolored 5.00 5.00

Piked Whale
A101

1983 Litho. *Perf. 14*

564 A101 50c shown 1.00 1.00
565 A101 65c Right whale 1.30 1.30
566 A101 70c Killer whale 1.40 1.40
567 A101 95c Sperm whale 1.90 1.90
568 A101 $1.10 Gooseback whale 2.20 2.20
569 A101 $2 Blue whale 4.00 4.00
570 A101 $2.20 Humpback whale 4.40 4.40
571 A101 $3 Longfin pilot whale 6.00 6.00
Nos. 564-571 (8) 22.20 22.20

Souvenir Sheet

572 A101 $3 Fin whale 6.00 6.00

Issue dates: 50c, $2.20, No. 571, May 16; 70c, 95c, $2, June 13; others July 11. Issued in sheets of four.

For overprints see Nos. 637-639.

Manned Flight Bicentenary — A102

1983, Aug. 30 Litho. *Perf. 14*

573 A102 25c 1st hydrogen balloon, 1783 50 50
574 A102 35c Friendship 7, 1962 70 70
575 A102 70c Montgolfiere, 1783 1.40 1.40
576 A102 95c Columbia space shuttle 1.90 1.90

Souvenir Sheet

577 A102 $2 Montgolfiere, Columbia 4.00 4.00

Ships
A103

1985 Litho. *Perf. 12½x12*

578 A103 4c Dug-out canoe 15 15
579 A103 5c Santa Maria 15 15
580 A103 8c Spanish treasure galleons 15 15
581 A103 10c Bermuda sloop 15 15
582 A103 20c Privateer Grand Turk 30 30
583 A103 25c Nelson's Frigate Boreas 35 35
584 A103 30c Warship Endymion 48 48
585 A103 35c Bark Caesar 60 60
586 A103 50c Schooner Grapeshot 75 75
587 A103 65c Invincible 1.10 1.10
588 A103 95c Magicienne 1.50 1.50
589 A103 $1.10 Durban 1.75 1.75
590 A103 $2 Sentinel 3.00 3.00
591 A103 $3 Minerva 4.75 4.75
592 A103 $5 Caicos sloop 7.00 7.00
Nos. 578-592 (15) 22.18 22.18

Issue dates: 4c, 8c, 10c, 30c, 65c, $1.10, $5, Mar. 5c, 20c, 25c, 35c, 50c, 95c, $2, Aug. 12. $3, Dec.

1983-84 *Perf. 14*

578a A103 4c 15 15
579a A103 5c 15 15
580a A103 8c 15 15
581a A103 10c 18 18
582a A103 20c 38 38
583a A103 25c 48 48
584a A103 30c 55 55
585a A103 35c 65 65
586a A103 50c 95 95
587a A103 65c 1.25 1.25
588a A103 95c 1.75 1.75
589a A103 $1.10 2.00 2.00
590a A103 $2 3.75 3.75
591a A103 $3 5.75 5.75
592a A103 $5 9.50 9.50
Nos. 578a-592a (15) 27.64 27.64

Issue dates: 10c, 30c, 65c, $1.10-$3, Oct. 5. 8c, 25c, 50c, 95c, Dec. 16. 4c, 5c, 20c, 35c, $5, Jan. 9, 1984.

For overprints see Nos. 744-746.

Christmas
A104

Designs: Scenes from Walt Disney's Oh Christmas Tree.

1983, Nov. *Perf. 11*

593 A104 1c Fifer Pig 15 15
594 A104 1c Fiddler Pig 15 15
595 A104 2c Practical Pig 15 15
596 A104 2c Pluto 15 15
597 A104 3c Goofy 15 15
598 A104 3c Mickey Mouse 15 15
599 A104 35c Gyro Gearloose 70 70
600 A104 50c Ludwig Von Drake 1.00 1.00
601 A104 $1.10 Huey, Dewey and Louie 2.20 2.20
Nos. 593-601 (9) 4.80 4.80

Souvenir Sheet

Perf. 13½

602 A104 $2.50 Around the tree 5.50 5.50

John F. Kennedy (1917-1963), 20th Death Anniv. — A105

1983, Dec. 22 Litho. *Perf. 14*

603 A105 20c multicolored 40 40
604 A105 $1 multicolored 2.00 2.00

Classic Cars
A106

1984, Mar. 15 Litho. *Perf. 14*

605 A106 4c Cadillac V-16, 1933 15 15
606 A106 8c Rolls Royce Phantom III, 1937 16 16
607 A106 10c Saab 99, 1969 20 20
608 A106 25c Maserati Bora, 1973 48 48
609 A106 40c Datsun 260Z, 1970 80 80
610 A106 55c Porsche 917, 1971 1.10 1.10
611 A106 80c Lincoln Continental, 1939 1.65 1.65
612 A106 $1 Triumph TR3A, 1957 2.00 2.00
Nos. 605-612 (8) 6.54 6.54

Souvenir Sheet

613 A106 $2 Daimler, 1886 4.00 4.00

125th anniv. of first commercially productive oil well, Drake's Rig, Titusville, Pa. Nos. 605-612 se-tenant with labels showing flags and auto museum names. No. 613 for 150th birth anniv. of Gotlieb Daimler, inventor of high-speed internal combustion engine.

Easter — A107 CORREGGIO 15c

450th death anniv. of Antonio Allegri Correggio (Various cameo portraits of Correggio, paintings): 15c, Rest on the Flight to Egypt with St. Francis. 40c, St. Luke and St. Ambrose. 60c, Diana and her Chariot. 95c, Deposition of Christ. $2, Nativity with St. Elizabeth and the Infant St. John.

1984, Apr. 9

614 A107	15c multicolored		30	30
615 A107	40c multicolored		80	80
616 A107	60c multicolored		1.20	1.20
617 A107	95c multicolored		1.90	1.90

Souvenir Sheet

618 A107	$2 multi, horiz.	4.00	4.00

1984 Los Angeles Olympics — A108

Various Disney characters participating in Olympic sports.

1984, Feb. 21 Litho. *Perf. 14*

619 A108	1c 500-meter	15	15
620 A108	1c Diving	15	15
621 A108	2c Single kayak	15	15
622 A108	2c 1000-meter kayak	15	15
623 A108	3c Highboard diving	15	15
624 A108	3c Kayak slalom	15	15
625 A108	25c Freestyle swimming	50	50
626 A108	75c Water polo	1.50	1.50
627 A108	$1 Yachting	2.00	2.00
	Nos. 619-627 (9)	4.90	4.90

Souvenir Sheet

628 A108	$2 Platform diving	4.75	4.75

1984, Apr. *Perf. 12½x12*

Same Designs

619a	A108	1c	15	15
620a	A108	1c	15	15
621a	A108	2c	15	15
622a	A108	2c	15	15
623a	A108	3c	15	15
624a	A108	3c	15	15
625a	A108	25c	50	50
626a	A108	75c	1.50	1.50
627a	A108	$1	2.00	2.00
	Nos. 619a-627a (9)		4.90	4.90

Souvenir Sheet

628a	A108	$2	4.75	4.75

Nos. 619a-628a inscribed with Olympic rings emblem. Printed in sheets of 5.

Sir Arthur Conan Doyle (1859-1930) — A109

Scenes from the Adventures of Sherlock Holmes.

1984, July 16 Litho. *Perf. 14*

629 A109	25c Second Stain	50	50
630 A109	45c Final Problem	90	90
631 A109	70c Empty House	1.40	1.40
632 A109	85c Greek Interpreter	1.75	1.75

Souvenir Sheet

633 A109	$2 Doyle, vert.	4.00	4.00

Nos. 567-568, 572 Overprinted with UPU Emblem and: "19TH UPU CONGRESS / HAMBURG, WEST GERMANY./ 1874-1984"

1984 Litho. *Perf. 14*

637 A101	95c multicolored	1.90	1.90
638 A101	$1.10 multicolored	2.20	2.20

Souvenir Sheet

639 A101	$3 multicolored	5.50	5.50

AUSIPEX '84 A110

Darwin, Ship, Map of Australia, Fauna.

1984, Aug. 22 *Perf. 14x13½*

640 A110	5c Clown fish	15	15
641 A110	35c Monitor lizard	70	70
642 A110	50c Rainbow lorikeets	1.00	1.00
643 A110	$1.10 Koalas	2.25	2.25

Souvenir Sheet

644 A110	$2 Grey kangaroo	4.00	4.00

Christmas — A111

Scenes from Walt Disney's The Toy Tinkers.

1984 Litho. *Perf. 14*

645 A111	20c multicolored	45	45
646 A111	35c multicolored	75	75
647 A111	50c multicolored	1.10	1.10
648 A111	75c multicolored	1.65	1.65
649 A111	$1.10 multicolored	2.50	2.50
	Nos. 645-649 (5)	6.45	6.45

Souvenir Sheet

650 A111	$2 multicolored	4.50	4.50

No. 648 issued in sheets of 8. Issue dates: 75c, Nov. 26, others, Oct. 8.

Audubon Birth Bicentenary — A112

Cameo portrait of Audubon, signature and illustrations from Birds of North America.

1985, Jan. 28 Litho. *Perf. 14*

651 A112	25c Dendroica magnoliae	45	45
652 A112	45c Asio flammeus	80	80
653 A112	70c Zenaida macroura	1.25	1.25
654 A112	85c Progne subis	1.50	1.50

Souvenir Sheet

655 A112	$2 Haematopus ostralegus	4.00	4.00

Intl. Civil Aviation Org., 40th Anniv. A113

Pioneers & inventions: 8c, Leonardo da Vinci, 15th century glider wing. 25c, Sir Alliott Verdon Roe, 1949 C. 102 Jet. 65c, Robert H. Goddard, first liquid fuel rocket launch, 1926. $1, Igor Sikorsky, 1939 Sikorsky VS300. $2, Aviator Amelia Earhart, 1937 Lockheed 10E Electra.

1985, Feb. 21

656 A113	8c multicolored	16	16
657 A113	25c multicolored	50	50
658 A113	65c multicolored	1.30	1.30
659 A113	$1 multicolored	2.00	2.00

Souvenir Sheet

660 A113	$2 multicolored	4.00	4.00

Arrival of the Statue of Liberty in New York, Cent. A114

Designs: 20c, Flags of US, France, Franklin, Lafayette. 30c, Designer Frederic A. Bartholdi, engineer Gustave Eiffel, Statue, Eiffel Tower. 65c, Isere, arriving in New York with Statue, 1885. $1.10, Fund raisers Louis Agassiz, H. W. Longfellow, Charles Sumner, Joseph Pulitzer. $2, Dedication day, Oct. 28, 1886.

1985, Mar. 28

661 A114	20c multicolored	38	38
662 A114	30c multicolored	55	55
663 A114	65c multicolored	1.25	1.25
664 A114	$1.10 multicolored	2.25	2.25

Souvenir Sheet

665 A114	$2 multicolored	4.25	4.25

Royal Navy A115

Designs: 20c, Sir Edward Hawke, Royal George. 30c, Lord Nelson, H.M.S. Victory. 65c, Adm. Sir George Cockburn, H.M.S. Albion. 95c, Adm. Sir David Beatty, H.M.S. Indefatigable. $2, 18th century naval gunner, cannons.

1985, Apr. 17

666 A115	20c multicolored	38	38
667 A115	30c multicolored	55	55
668 A115	65c multicolored	1.25	1.25
669 A115	95c multicolored	1.90	1.90

Souvenir Sheet

670 A115	$2 multicolored	4.25	4.25

Intl. Youth Year A116

Anniversaries: 25c, Return of Halley's Comet, 1986. 35c, Mark Twain (1835-1910), Mississippi river boat. 50c, Jakob Grimm (1785-1863), Hansel & Gretel, vert. 95c, Grimm, Rumpelstiltskin, vert. $2, Twain, Grimm, portraits.

1985, May 17

671 A116	25c multicolored	48	48
672 A116	35c multicolored	65	65
673 A116	50c multicolored	95	95
674 A116	95c multicolored	1.90	1.90

Souvenir Sheet

675 A116	$2 multicolored	4.25	4.25

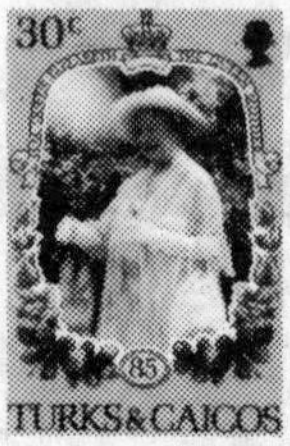

Queen Mother, 85th Birthday — A117

Designs: 30c, Queen Mother outside Clarence House, vert. 50c, Visiting Biggin Hill Airfield by helicopter. $1.10, 80th birthday portrait, vert. $2, With Prince Charles at the 1968 Garter Ceremony, Windsor Castle, vert.

1985, July 15

676 A117	30c multicolored	65	65
677 A117	50c multicolored	1.00	1.00
678 A117	$1.10 multicolored	2.25	2.25

Souvenir Sheet

679 A117	$2 multicolored	4.00	4.00

George Frideric Handel — A118

Johann Sebastian Bach — A119

Handel or Bach and: 4c, King George II, Zadok the Priest music, 1727. 10c, Queen Caroline, Funeral Anthem, 1737. 15c, Bassoon, Invention No. 3 in D Major. 40c, Natural horn, Invention No. 3 in D Major. 50c, King George I, Water Music, 1714. 60c, Viola d'amore, Invention No. 3 . . . 95c, Clavichord, Invention No. 3 . . . $1.10, Queen Anne, Or la Tromba from Rinaldo. No. 688, Handel, portrait. No. 689, Bach, portrait.

1985, July 17 *Perf. 15*

680 A118	4c multicolored	15	15
681 A118	10c multicolored	20	20
682 A119	15c multicolored	28	28
683 A119	40c multicolored	80	80
684 A118	50c multicolored	1.00	1.00
685 A119	60c multicolored	1.25	1.25
686 A119	95c multicolored	1.75	1.75
687 A118	$1.10 multicolored	2.25	2.25
	Nos. 680-687 (8)	7.68	7.68

Souvenir Sheets

688 A118	$2 multicolored	4.00	4.00
689 A119	$2 multicolored	4.00	4.00

Motorcycle Centenary A120

Flag of US, UK, Fed. Rep. of Germany or Japan and: 8c, 1915 dual cylinder Harley-Davidson. 25c, 1950 Thunderbird Triumph. 55c, 1985 BMW K100RS. $1.20, 1985 Honda 1100 Shadow. $2, 1885 Daimler Single Track, vert.

1985, Sept. 4 *Perf. 14*

690 A120	8c multicolored	16	16
691 A120	25c multicolored	52	52
692 A120	55c multicolored	1.10	1.10
693 A120	$1.20 multicolored	2.50	2.50

Souvenir Sheet

694 A120	$2 multicolored	4.25	4.25

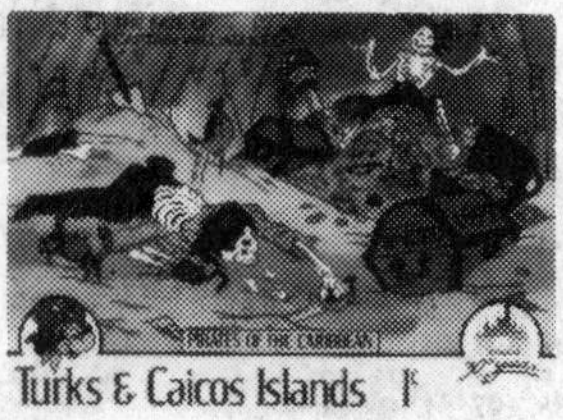

Pirates of the Caribbean — A121

Disneyland, 30th Anniv.: No. 695, Fate of Capt. Kidd. No. 696, Pirates imprisoned. No. 697, Bartholomew Roberts, church-going pirate. No. 698, Buccaneers in battle. No. 699, Bride auction. No. 700, Plunder. No. 701, Singing pirates. No. 702, Blackbeard. No. 703, Henry Morgan. No. 704, Mary Read, Anne Bonney.

1985, Oct. 4 Litho. *Perf. 14*

695 A121	1c multicolored	15	15
696 A121	1c multicolored	15	15
697 A121	2c multicolored	15	15
698 A121	2c multicolored	15	15

699 A121 3c multicolored 15 15
700 A121 3c multicolored 15 15
701 A121 35c multicolored 70 70
702 A121 75c multicolored 1.50 1.50
703 A121 $1.10 multicolored 2.20 2.20
Nos. 695-703 (9) 5.30 5.30

Souvenir Sheet

704 A121 $2.50 multicolored 5.00 5.00

Girl Guides, 75th Anniv. A122

Uniforms of Turks and Caicos and: 10c, Papua New Guinea and China brownies. 40c, Surinam and Korea brownies. 70c, Australia and Canada girl guides. 80c, West Germany and Israel girl guides.

1985, Nov. 4

705 A122 10c multicolored 20 20
706 A122 40c multicolored 80 80
707 A122 70c multicolored 1.40 1.40
708 A122 80c multicolored 1.60 1.60

Souvenir Sheet

709 A122 $2 Anniv. emblem 4.00 4.00

Grand Turk Chapter, 35th anniv.

World Wildlife Fund A123

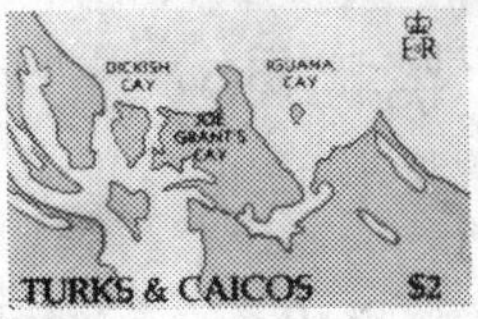

Map of the Islands A124

Turks & Caicos ground iguanas.

1986, Nov. 20 *Perf. 14*

710 A123 8c multicolored 16 16
711 A123 10c multicolored 20 20
712 A123 20c multicolored 40 40
713 A123 35c multicolored 70 70

Souvenir Sheet

714 A124 $2 multicolored 4.00 4.00

A125

Christmas — A126

Wedding pictures.

1986, Dec. 19 **Litho.** *Perf. 14*

715 A125 35c Couple 70 70
716 A125 65c Sarah in coach 1.30 1.30
717 A125 $1.10 Couple, close-up 2.20 2.20

Souvenir Sheet

718 A125 $2 In Westminster Abbey 4.00 4.00

Wedding of Prince Andrew and Sarah Ferguson.

1987, Dec. 9 **Litho.** *Perf. 14*

Illuminations by miniaturist Giorgio Giulio Clovio (1498-1578) from the Farnese Book of Hours: 35c, Prophecy of the Birth of Christ to King Achaz. 50c, The Annunciation. 65c, The Circumcision. 95c, Adoration of the Kings. $2, The Nativty.

719 A126 35c multicolored 70 70
720 A126 50c multicolored 1.00 1.00
721 A126 65c multicolored 1.30 1.30
722 A126 95c multicolored 1.90 1.90

Souvenir Sheet

723 A126 $2 multicolored 4.00 4.00

Accession of Queen Victoria to the Throne of England, 150th Anniv. A127

Ships and memorials: 8c, HMS Victoria, Victoria Cross. 35c, SS Victoria, coin. 55c, Victoria & Albert I, Great Britain No. 1. 95c, Victoria & Albert II, Victoria Public Library, Turks & Caicos. $2, Bark Victoria.

1987, Dec. 24

724 A127 8c multicolored 16 16
725 A127 35c multicolored 70 70
726 A127 55c multicolored 1.10 1.10
727 A127 95c multicolored 1.90 1.90

Souvenir Sheet

728 A127 $2 multicolored 4.00 4.00

US Constitution Bicentennial A128

Designs: 10c, NJ state flag. 35c, Freedom of Worship, vert. 65c, US Supreme Court, vert. 80c, John Adams, vert. $2, George Mason, vert.

1987, Dec. 31

729 A128 10c multicolored 15 15
730 A128 35c multicolored 50 50
731 A128 65c multicolored 1.40 1.40
732 A128 80c multicolored 2.00 2.00

Souvenir Sheet

733 A128 $2 multicolored 4.00 4.00

Discovery of America, 500th Anniv. (in 1992) A129

Emblem and: 4c, Caravel, first sighting of land, Oct. 12, 1492. 25c, Columbus meets with Indians, Oct. 14. 70c, Fleet anchored in harbor, Oct. 15. $1, Landing, Oct. 16. $2, Nina, Pinta and Santa Maria.

1988, Jan. 20

734 A129 4c multicolored 15 15
735 A129 25c multicolored 50 50
736 A129 70c multicolored 1.40 1.40
737 A129 $1 multicolored 2.00 2.00

Souvenir Sheet

738 A129 $2 multicolored 4.00 4.00

Sea Scouts Salute Jamboree and Australia A130

Australia Bicent.: 8c, Arawak artifact, scouts exploring cave on Middle Caicos, vert. 35c, Santa Maria, scouts rowing to Hawks Nest. 65c, Scouts diving to explore a sunken Spanish galleon, vert. 95c, Plantation worker cutting sisal, scouts exploring plantation ruins. $2, Splashdown of Friendship 7, piloted by John Glenn, Feb. 20, 1962, vert.

1988, Feb. 12 **Litho.** *Perf. 14*

739 A130 8c multicolored 16 16
740 A130 35c shown 70 70
741 A130 65c multicolored 1.30 1.30
742 A130 95c multicolored 1.90 1.90

Souvenir Sheet

743 A130 $2 multicolored 4.00 4.00

Nos. 581, 583 and 590 Ovptd. "40th WEDDING ANNIVERSARY / H.M. QUEEN ELIZABETH II / H.R.H. THE DUKE OF EDINBURGH"

1988, Mar. 14 **Litho.** *Perf. 14*

744 A103 10c multicolored 20 20
745 A103 25c multicolored 50 50
746 A103 $2 multicolored 4.00 4.00

A131

A132

1988, Aug. 29 **Litho.**

747 A131 8c Soccer 16 16
748 A131 30c Yachting 60 60
749 A131 70c Cycling 1.40 1.40
750 A131 $1 Running 2.00 2.00

Souvenir Sheet

751 A131 $2 Swimming 4.00 4.00

1988 Summer Olympics, Seoul.

1988, Sept. 5 **Litho.**

Billfish Tournament: 8c, Passenger jet, fishing boat and fisherman reeling-in giant swordfish. 10c, Photographing prize catch. 70c, Fishing boat, lighthouse. $1, Blue marlin. $2, Sailfish.

752 A132 8c multicolored 16 16
753 A132 10c multicolored 20 20
754 A132 70c multicolored 1.40 1.40
755 A132 $1 multicolored 2.00 2.00

Souvenir Sheet

756 A132 $2 multicolored 4.00 4.00

Christmas A133

Paintings by Titian: 15c, Madonna and Child with St. Catherine and the Infant John the Baptist, c. 1530. 25c, Madonna with a Rabbit, c. 1526. 35c, Virgin and Child with Sts. Stephen, Jerome and Mauritius, c. 1520. 40c, The Gypsy Madonna, c. 1510. 50c, The Holy Family and a Shepherd, c. 1510. 65c, Madonna and Child, c. 1510. $3, Madonna and Child with St. John the Baptist and St. Catherine, c. 1530. No. 764, Adoration of the Magi, c. 1560. No. 765, The Annunciation, c. 1560.

1988, Oct. 24 **Litho.**

757 A133 15c multicolored 30 30
758 A133 25c multicolored 50 50
759 A133 35c multicolored 70 70
760 A133 40c multicolored 80 80
761 A133 50c multicolored 1.00 1.00
762 A133 65c multicolored 1.30 1.30
763 A133 $3 multicolored 6.00 6.00
Nos. 757-763 (7) 10.60 10.60

Souvenir Sheets

764 A133 $2 multicolored 4.00 4.00
765 A133 $2 multicolored 4.00 4.00

Visit of Princess Alexandra, 1st Cousin of Queen Elizabeth II A134

Various portraits and: 70c, Government House. $1.40, Map. $2, Flora, vert.

1988, Nov. 14 **Litho.** *Perf. 14*

766 A134 70c multicolored 1.40 1.40
767 A134 $1.40 multicolored 2.80 2.80

Souvenir Sheet

768 A134 $2 multicolored 4.00 4.00

Arms Type of 1970 Without Inscription

Perf. 14½x15

1988, Dec. 15 **Litho.** **Unwmk.**

769 A35 $10 multicolored 20.00 20.00

Pre-Columbian Societies and Their Customs — A135

UPAE and discovery of America anniv. emblems and: 10c, Hollowing-out tree to make a canoe, vert. 50c, Body painting and statue. 65c, Three islanders with body paint. $1, Canoeing, vert. $2, Petroglyph.

1989, May 15 **Litho.** *Perf. 14*

770 A135 10c multicolored 20 20
771 A135 50c multicolored 1.00 1.00
772 A135 65c multicolored 1.30 1.30
773 A135 $1 multicolored 2.00 2.00

Souvenir Sheet

774 A135 $2 multicolored 4.00 4.00

Discovery of America 500th anniv. (in 1992).

Souvenir Sheet

Lincoln Memorial, Washington, D.C. — A136

1989, Nov. 17 **Litho.** *Perf. 14*

775 A136 $1.50 multicolored 3.00 3.00

World Stamp Expo '89.

Miniature Sheets

American Presidential Office, 200th Anniv. — A137

US presidents, historic events and monuments.

No. 776: a, Jackson, early train. b, Van Buren, origins of baseball and Moses Fleetwood Walker, 1st black to play professional baseball. c, Harrison, Harrison's "Keep the Ball Rollin'" slogan and parade. d, Tyler, annexation of Texas, 1845. e, Polk, 1st US postage stamps (#2), 1847, and discovery of gold in California, 1849. f, Taylor, Mexican-American War, 1847.

No. 777: a, Hayes, end of Civil War reconstruction. b, Garfield, Garfield leading Union soldiers in the Battle of Shiloh. c, Arthur, opening of the Brooklyn Bridge, 1883. d, Cleveland, Columbian Exposition, 1893 (US #245). e, Benjamin Harrison, Pan-American Union building, map. f, McKinley, Spanish-American War (Rough Riders Monument, by Solon Borglum).

No. 778: a, Hoover, 1933 Olympic Games, Los Angeles and Lake Placid (American sprinter Ralph Metcalf and Norwegian figure skater Sonja Henie). b, Franklin Delano Roosevelt, Roosevelt's support of the March of Dimes (dime, 1946). c, 150th anniv. of inauguration of Washington, New York World's Fair, 1939. d, Truman, founding of the U.N., 1945. e, Eisenhower, invasion of Normandy, 1944. f, Kennedy, Apollo 11 mission, 1969.

1989, Nov. 19 *Perf. 14*

776	Sheet of 6	6.00	6.00
a.-f.	A137 50c any single	1.00	1.00
777	Sheet of 6	6.00	6.00
a.-f.	A137 50c any single	1.00	1.00
778	Sheet of 6	6.00	6.00
a.-f.	A137 50c any single	1.00	1.00

Fraser is incorrectly spelled "Frazer" on No. 778c.

Christmas — A138

Religious paintings by Giovanni Bellini: 15c, Madonna and Child. 25c, The Madonna of the Shrubs. 35c, The Virgin and Child. 40c, The Virgin and Child with a Greek Inscription. 50c, The Madonna of the Meadow. 65c, The Madonna of the Pear. 70c, The Virgin and Child, diff. $1, Madonna and Child, diff. No. 787, The Madonna with John the Baptist and Another Saint. No. 788, The Virgin and Child Enthroned.

1989, Dec. 18

779	A138	15c	multicolored	30	30
780	A138	25c	multicolored	50	50
781	A138	35c	multicolored	70	70
782	A138	40c	multicolored	80	80
783	A138	50c	multicolored	1.00	1.00
784	A138	65c	multicolored	1.30	1.30
785	A138	70c	multicolored	1.40	1.40
786	A138	$1	multicolored	4.00	4.00
			Nos. 779-786 (8)	10.00	10.00

Souvenir Sheets

787	A138	$2	multicolored	4.00	4.00
788	A138	$2	multicolored	4.00	4.00

Souvenir Sheet

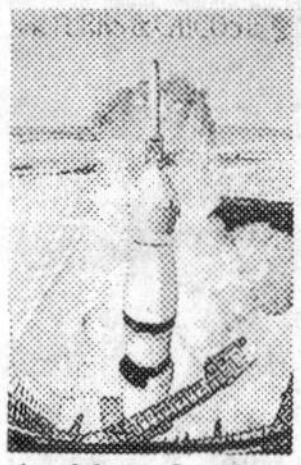

1st Moon Landing, 20th Anniv. — A139

Flowers — A140

Designs: a, Liftoff. b, Eagle lunar module on Moon's surface. c, Aldrin obtaining soil samples. d, Neil Armstrong walking on Moon. e, Columbia and Eagle in space.

1990, Jan. 8

789	Sheet of 5	5.00	5.00
a.-e.	A139 50c any single	1.00	1.00

1990, Jan. 11 **Litho.** *Perf. 14*

790	A140	8c	*Zephyranthes rosea*	16	16
791	A140	10c	*Sophora tomentosa*	20	20
792	A140	15c	*Coccoloba uvifera*	30	30
793	A140	20c	*Encyclia gracilis*	40	40
794	A140	25c	*Tillandsia streptophylla*	50	50
795	A140	30c	*Maurandella antirrhiniflora*	60	60
796	A140	35c	*Tillandsia balbisiana*	70	70
797	A140	50c	*Encyclia rufa*	1.00	1.00
798	A140	65c	*Aechmea lingulata*	1.30	1.30
799	A140	80c	*Asclepias curassavica*	1.60	1.60
800	A140	$1	*Caesalpinia bahamensis*	2.00	2.00
801	A140	$1.10	*Capparis cynophallophora*	2.20	2.20
802	A140	$1.25	*Stachytarpheta jamaicensis*	2.50	2.50
803	A140	$2	*Cassia biflora*	4.00	4.00
804	A140	$5	*Clusia rosea*	10.00	10.00
805	A140	$10	*Opuntia bahamana*	20.00	20.00
			Nos. 790-805 (16)	47.46	47.46

1994 *Perf. 12*

790a	A140	8c	16	16
791a	A140	10c	20	20
792a	A140	15c	30	30
793a	A140	20c	40	40
794a	A140	25c	50	50
795a	A140	30c	60	60
796a	A140	35c	70	70
797a	A140	50c	1.00	1.00
798a	A140	65c	1.25	1.25
799a	A140	80c	1.60	1.60
800a	A140	$1	2.00	2.00
801a	A140	$1.10	2.25	2.25
802a	A140	$1.25	2.50	2.50
803a	A140	$2	4.00	4.00
		Nos. 790a-803a (14)	17.46	17.46

Birds A141

1990, Feb. 19

806	A141	10c	Yellow-billed cuckoo	20	20
807	A141	15c	White-tailed tropic bird	30	30
808	A141	20c	Kirtland's warbler	40	40
809	A141	30c	Yellow-crowned night heron	60	60
810	A141	50c	West Indian tree duck	1.00	1.00
811	A141	80c	Yellow-bellied sapsucker	1.60	1.60
812	A141	$1	American kestrel	2.00	2.00
813	A141	$1.40	Mockingbird	2.80	2.80
			Nos. 806-813 (8)	8.90	8.90

Souvenir Sheets

814	A141	$2	Osprey	4.00	4.00
815	A141	$2	Yellow warbler	4.00	4.00

Fish A142

1990, Feb. 12 **Litho.** *Perf. 14*

816	A142	8c	Queen parrotfish	16	16
817	A142	10c	Queen triggerfish	20	20
818	A142	25c	Sergeant major	50	50
819	A142	40c	Spotted goatfish	80	80
820	A142	50c	Neon goby	1.00	1.00
821	A142	75c	Nassau grouper	1.50	1.50
822	A142	80c	Jawfish	1.60	1.60
823	A142	$1	Blue tang	2.00	2.00
			Nos. 816-823 (8)	7.76	7.76

Souvenir Sheets

824	A142	$2	Butter hamlet	4.00	4.00
825	A142	$2	Queen angelfish	4.00	4.00

Butterflies A143

1990, Mar. 19

826	A143	15c	White peacock	30	30
827	A143	25c	Cloudless sulphur	50	50
828	A143	35c	Mexican fritillary	70	70
829	A143	40c	Fiery skipper	80	80
830	A143	50c	Chamberlain's sulphur	1.00	1.00
831	A143	60c	Pygmy blue	1.20	1.20
832	A143	90c	Dusky swallowtail	1.80	1.80
833	A143	$1	Antillean dagger wing	2.00	2.00
			Nos. 826-833 (8)	8.30	8.30

Souvenir Sheets

834	A143	$2	Thomas's blue	4.00	4.00
835	A143	$2	9 Queen species	4.00	4.00

Nos. 826, 831 and 833 vert.

America Issue A144

Fish, UPAE and discovery of America 500th anniv. emblems.

1990, Apr. 2

836	A144	10c	Rock beauty	20	20
837	A144	15c	Coney	30	30
838	A144	25c	Red hind	50	50
839	A144	50c	Banded butter-flyfish	1.00	1.00
840	A144	60c	French angelfish	1.20	1.20
841	A144	75c	Blackbar soldierfish	1.50	1.50
842	A144	90c	Stoplight parrotfish	1.80	1.80
843	A144	$1	French grunt	2.00	2.00
			Nos. 836-843 (8)	8.50	8.50

Souvenir Sheets

844	A144	$2	Gray angelfish	4.00	4.00
845	A144	$2	Blue chromis	4.00	4.00

Penny Black, 150th Anniv. — A145

British Pillar Boxes — A146

Designs: 25c, 1p essay in blue, without letters. 35c, Letter Box #1, 1855. 50c, Penfold Box, 1866. 75c, Great Britain #3, essay. $1, 2p blue essay. $1.25, Air mail box, 1935. No. 852, Great Britain #1. No. 853, K type box, 1979.

1990, May 3 **Litho.** *Perf. 14*

846	A145	25c	bluish blk	50	50
847	A146	35c	gray & pale brn	70	70
848	A146	50c	gray & dk blue	1.00	1.00
849	A145	75c	red brown	1.50	1.50
850	A145	$1	dk blue	2.00	2.00
851	A146	$1.25	gray & blue	2.50	2.50
			Nos. 846-851 (6)	8.20	8.20

Souvenir Sheets

852	A145	$2	black	4.00	4.00
853	A146	$2	blk & red brn	4.00	4.00

Stamp World London '90.

Queen Mother, 90th Birthday — A147

1990, Aug. 20 **Litho.** *Perf. 14*

854	A147	10c	multicolored	20	20
855	A147	25c	multi, diff.	50	50
856	A147	75c	multi, diff.	1.50	1.50
857	A147	$1.25	multi, diff.	2.50	2.50

Souvenir Sheet

858	A147	$2	multi, diff.	4.00	4.00

Birds A148

1990, Sept. 24 **Litho.** *Perf. 14*

859	A148	8c	Stripe-headed tanager, vert.	16	16
860	A148	10c	Black-whiskered vireo	20	20
861	A148	25c	Blue-grey gnatcatcher	50	50
862	A148	40c	Lesser scaup	80	80
863	A148	50c	White-cheeked pintail	1.00	1.00
864	A148	75c	Common stilt	1.50	1.50
865	A148	80c	Common oystercatcher, vert.	1.60	1.60
866	A148	$1	Tricolored heron	2.00	2.00
			Nos. 859-866 (8)	7.76	7.76

Souvenir Sheets

867	A148	$2	Bahama woodstar	4.00	4.00
868	A148	$2	American coot	4.00	4.00

Christmas A149

Different details from paintings by Rubens: 10c, 50c, 75c, No. 876, Triumph of Christ over Sin and Death. 35c, 45c, 65c, $1.25, No. 877, St. Theresa Praying for the Souls in Purgatory. Nos. 876-877 show entire painting.

1990, Dec. 17 **Litho.** *Perf. 14*

869	A149	10c	multicolored	20	20
870	A149	35c	multicolored	70	70
871	A149	45c	multicolored	90	90
872	A149	50c	multicolored	1.00	1.00
873	A149	65c	multicolored	1.30	1.30
874	A149	75c	multicolored	1.50	1.50
875	A149	$1.25	multicolored	2.50	2.50
			Nos. 869-875 (7)	8.10	8.10

Souvenir Sheets

876	A149	$2	multicolored	4.00	4.00
877	A149	$2	multicolored	4.00	4.00

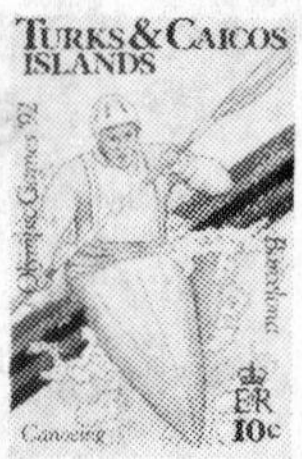

1992 Summer Olympics, Barcelona — A150

1991, Jan. 17

878	A150	10c	Kayaking	20	20
879	A150	25c	Track	50	50
880	A150	75c	Pole vault	1.50	1.50
881	A150	$1.25	Javelin	2.50	2.50

Souvenir Sheet

882	A150	$2	Baseball	4.00	4.00

No. 878 inscribed Canoeing.

Voyages of Discovery A151

Designs: 5c, Henry Hudson, 1611. 10c, Roald Amundsen (airship), 1926. 15c, Amundsen (ship), 1906. 50c, USS Nautilus, 1958. 75c, Robert Scott, 1911. $1, Richard Byrd, Floyd Bennett, 1926. $1.25, Lincoln Ellsworth, 1935. $1.50, Cook, 1772-75. No. 891, The Nina. No. 892, The search for land.

1991, Apr. 15 **Litho.** *Perf. 14*

883	A151	5c	multicolored	15	15
884	A151	10c	multicolored	20	20
885	A151	15c	multicolored	30	30
886	A151	50c	multicolored	1.00	1.00
887	A151	75c	multicolored	1.50	1.50
888	A151	$1	multicolored	2.00	2.00
889	A151	$1.25	multicolored	2.50	2.50
890	A151	$1.50	multicolored	3.00	3.00
			Nos. 883-890 (8)	10.65	10.65

Souvenir Sheets

891	A151	$2	multicolored	4.00	4.00
892	A151	$2	multicolored	4.00	4.00

Discovery of America, 500th anniv. (in 1992).

Butterflies — A152

1991, May 13 — Litho. — *Perf. 14*

893	A152	5c White peacock	15	15
894	A152	25c Orion	50	50
895	A152	35c Gulf fritillary	70	70
896	A152	45c Caribbean buckeye	90	90
897	A152	55c Flambeau	1.10	1.10
898	A152	65c Malachite	1.30	1.30
899	A152	70c Florida white	1.40	1.40
900	A152	$1 Great southern white	2.00	2.00
		Nos. 893-900 (8)	8.05	8.05

Souvenir Sheets

901	A152	$2 Giant hairstreak	4.00	4.00
902	A152	$2 Orange-barred sulphur	4.00	4.00

Extinct Animals A153

1991, June 3

903	A153	5c Protohydrochoerus	15	15
904	A153	10c Phororhacos	20	20
905	A153	15c Prothylacynus	30	30
906	A153	50c Borhyaena	1.00	1.00
907	A153	75c Smilodon	1.50	1.50
908	A153	$1 Thoatherium	2.00	2.00
909	A153	$1.25 Cuvieronius	2.50	2.50
910	A153	$1.50 Toxodon	3.00	3.00
		Nos. 903-910 (8)	10.65	10.65

Souvenir Sheets

911	A153	$2 Mesosaurus	4.00	4.00
912	A153	$2 Astrapotherium	4.00	4.00

Royal Family Birthday, Anniversary

Common Design Type

1991 — Litho. — *Perf. 14*

913	CD347	10c multicolored	20	20
914	CD347	25c multicolored	50	50
915	CD347	35c multicolored	70	70
916	CD347	45c multicolored	90	90
917	CD347	50c multicolored	1.00	1.00
918	CD347	65c multicolored	1.30	1.30
919	CD347	80c multicolored	1.60	1.60
920	CD347	$1 multicolored	2.00	2.00
		Nos. 913-920 (8)	8.20	8.20

Souvenir Sheets

921	CD347	$2 Elizabeth, Philip	4.00	4.00
922	CD347	$2 Diana, sons, Charles	4.00	4.00

10c, 45c, 50c, $1, No. 922, Charles and Diana, 10th wedding anniv., issued: July 29. Others, Queen Elizabeth II, 65th birthday, issued: June 8.

For overprints see Nos. 1020-1022.

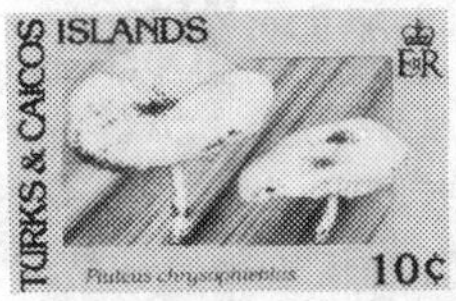

Mushrooms A154

Designs: 10c, Pluteus chrysophlebius. 15c, Leucopaxillus gracillimus. 20c, Marasmius haematocephalus. 35c, Collybia subpruinosa. 50c, Marasmius atrorubens, vert. 65c, Leucocoprinus birnbaumii, vert. $1.10, Trogia cantharelloides, vert. $1.25, Boletellus cubensis, vert. No. 931, Gerronema citrinum. No. 932, Pyrrhoglossum pyrrhum, vert.

1991, June 24 — Litho. — *Perf. 14*

923	A154	10c multicolored	20	20
924	A154	15c multicolored	30	30
925	A154	20c multicolored	40	40
926	A154	35c multicolored	70	70
927	A154	50c multicolored	1.00	1.00
928	A154	65c multicolored	1.30	1.30
929	A154	$1.10 multicolored	2.20	2.20
930	A154	$1.25 multicolored	2.50	2.50
		Nos. 923-930 (8)	8.60	8.60

Miniature Sheets

931	A154	$2 multicolored	4.00	4.00
932	A154	$2 multicolored	4.00	4.00

Paintings by Vincent Van Gogh — A155

Paintings: 15c, Weaver Facing Left, with Spinning Wheel. 25c, Head of a Young Peasant with Pipe, vert. 35c, The Old Cemetery Tower at Nuenen, vert. 45c, Cottage at Nightfall. 50c, Still Life with Open Bible. 65c, Lane at the Jardin du Luxembourg. 80c, The Pont du Carrousel and the Louvre. $1, Vase with Poppies, Cornflowers, Peonies and Chrysanthemums, vert. No. 941, Entrance to the Public Park. No. 942, Plowed Field.

1991, Aug. 26 — *Perf. 13*

933	A155	15c multicolored	30	30
934	A155	25c multicolored	50	50
935	A155	35c multicolored	70	70
936	A155	45c multicolored	90	90
937	A155	50c multicolored	1.00	1.00
938	A155	65c multicolored	1.30	1.30
939	A155	80c multicolored	1.60	1.60
940	A155	$1 multicolored	2.00	2.00
		Nos. 933-940 (8)	8.30	8.30

Size: 107x80mm

Imperf

941	A155	$2 multicolored	4.00	4.00
942	A155	$2 multicolored	4.00	4.00

Phila Nippon '91 — A156

Japanese steam locomotives.

1991, Nov. 4 — Litho. — *Perf. 14*

943	A156	8c Series 8550	16	16
944	A156	10c C 57	20	20
945	A156	45c Series 4110	90	90
946	A156	50c C 55	1.00	1.00
947	A156	65c Series 6250	1.30	1.30
948	A156	80c E 10	1.60	1.60
949	A156	$1 Series 4500	2.00	2.00
950	A156	$1.25 C 11	2.50	2.50
		Nos. 943-950 (8)	9.66	9.66

Souvenir Sheets

951	A156	$2 C 62	4.00	4.00
952	A156	$2 C 58	4.00	4.00

Christmas A157

Details or entire paintings by Gerard David: 8c, Adoration of the Shepherds. 15c, Virgin and Child Enthroned with Two Angels. 35c, The Annunciation (outside wings). 45c, The Rest on the Flight into Egypt. 50c, The Rest on the Flight into Egypt, diff. 65c, Virgin and Child with Angels. 80c, The Adoration of the Shepherds, diff. $1.25, The Perussis Altarpiece. No. 961, The Adoration of the Kings. No. 962, The Nativity.

1991, Dec. 23 — *Perf. 12*

953	A157	8c multicolored	16	16
954	A157	15c multicolored	30	30
955	A157	35c multicolored	70	70
956	A157	45c multicolored	90	90
957	A157	50c multicolored	1.00	1.00
958	A157	65c multicolored	1.30	1.30
959	A157	80c multicolored	1.60	1.60
960	A157	$1.25 multicolored	2.50	2.50
		Nos. 953-960 (8)	8.46	8.46

Souvenir Sheets

Perf. 14½

961	A157	$2 multicolored	4.00	4.00
962	A157	$2 multicolored	4.00	4.00

Boy Scouts A160

Designs: No. 968, Member of Boy Scout Service Corps at New York World's Fair, 1964-65. No. 969, Lord Robert Baden-Powell, vert. $2, Silver Buffalo Award.

1991 — Litho. — *Perf. 14*

968	A160	$1 multicolored	2.00	2.00
969	A160	$1 multicolored	2.00	2.00

Souvenir Sheet

970	A160	$2 multicolored	4.00	4.00

17th World Scout Jamboree, Korea.

Anniversaries and Events — A161

Designs: 25c, Astronaut releasing communications satellite. 50c, Tree with dead side, healthy side. 65c, Emblems, globe, food products. 80c, Fish in polluted, clean water. $1, Runners, Lions Intl. emblem. $1.25, Orbiting quarantine facility modules. No. 977, Planned orbital transfer vehicle for Mars. No. 977A, Industrial pollution, clean beach.

1992-93 — Litho. — *Perf. 14*

971	A161	25c multicolored	50	50
972	A161	50c multicolored	1.00	1.00
973	A161	65c multicolored	1.30	1.30
974	A161	80c multicolored	1.60	1.60
975	A161	$1 multicolored	2.00	2.00
976	A161	$1.25 multicolored	2.50	2.50
		Nos. 971-976 (6)	8.90	8.90

Souvenir Sheets

977	A161	$2 multicolored	4.00	4.00
977A	A161	$2 multicolored	4.00	4.00

Intl. Space Year (#971, 976-977). Earth Summit, Rio de Janeiro (#972, 974, 977A). Intl. Conference on Nutrition, Rome (#973). Lions Intl., 75th anniv. (#975).

Issued: Nos. 972, 974, 977A, Jan. 1993; others, Dec. 1992.

Queen Elizabeth II's Accession to the Throne, 40th Anniv.

Common Design Type

1992, Feb. 6 — Litho. — *Perf. 14*

978	CD348	10c multicolored	20	20
979	CD348	20c multicolored	40	40
980	CD348	25c multicolored	50	50
981	CD348	35c multicolored	70	70
982	CD348	50c multicolored	1.00	1.00
983	CD348	65c multicolored	1.30	1.30
984	CD348	80c multicolored	1.60	1.60
985	CD348	$1.10 multicolored	2.20	2.20
		Nos. 978-985 (8)	7.90	7.90

Souvenir Sheets

986	CD348	$2 Queen at left, boat dock	4.00	4.00
987	CD348	$2 Queen at right, shoreline	4.00	4.00

Spanish Art — A162

Paintings: 8c, St. Monica, by Luis Tristan. 20c, 45c, The Vision of Ezekiel: The Resurrection of the Flesh (different details) by Francisco Collantes. 50c, The Martyrdom of St. Philip, by Jose de Ribera. 65c, St. John the Evangelist, by Juan Ribalta. 80c, Archimedes by Jose de Ribera. $1, St. John the Baptist in the Desert by de Ribera. $1.25, The Martyrdom of St. Philip (detail), by de Ribera. No. 992, The Baptism of Christ by Juan Fernandez Navarrete. No. 997, Battle between Christians and Moors at El Sotillo, by Francisco de Zurbaran.

1992 — Litho. — *Perf. 13*

988	A162	8c multicolored	16	16
989	A162	20c multicolored	40	40
990	A162	45c multicolored	90	90
991	A162	50c multicolored	1.00	1.00
992	A162	65c multicolored	1.30	1.30
993	A162	80c multicolored	1.60	1.60
994	A162	$1 multicolored	2.00	2.00
995	A162	$1.25 multicolored	2.50	2.50
		Nos. 988-995 (8)	9.86	9.86

Size: 95x120mm

Imperf

996	A162	$2 multicolored	4.00	4.00
997	A162	$2 multicolored	4.00	4.00

Granada '92.

Discovery of America, 500th Anniv. A163

Commemorative coins, scenes of first voyage: 10c, Nina, ship. 15c, Pinta, ship. 20c, Santa Maria, Columbus' second coat of arms. 25c, Fleet at sea, ships. 30c, Landfall, sailing ship. 35c, Setting sail, Columbus departing. 50c, Columbus sighting New World, Columbus. 65c, Columbus exploring Caribbean, ship. 80c, Claiming land for Spain, Columbus, priest and cross. $1.10, Columbus exchanging gifts with native, Columbus, native.

No. 1008, Coins like #998-1000. No. 1009, Coins like #1004, 1006-1007.

1992, Oct. — Litho. — *Perf. 14*

998	A163	10c multicolored	20	20
999	A164	15c multicolored	30	30
1000	A164	20c multicolored	40	40
1001	A164	25c multicolored	50	50
1002	A164	30c multicolored	60	60
1003	A164	35c multicolored	70	70
1004	A164	50c multicolored	1.00	1.00
1005	A164	65c multicolored	1.30	1.30
1006	A164	80c multicolored	1.60	1.60
1007	A164	$1.10 multicolored	2.20	2.20
		Nos. 998-1007 (10)	8.80	8.80

Souvenir Sheets

1008	A164	$2 multicolored	4.00	4.00
1009	A164	$2 multicolored	4.00	4.00

Christmas A164

Details or entire paintings by Simon Bening: 8c, Nativity. 15c, Circumcision. 35c, Flight to Egypt. 50c, Massacre of the Innocents.

By Dirk Bouts: 65c, The Annunciation. 80c, The Visitation. $1.10, The Adoration of the Angels. $1.25, The Adoration of the Wise Men. No. 1018, The Virgin and Child. No. 1019, The Virgin Seated with the Child.

1992, Nov. — Litho. — *Perf. 13½x14*

1010	A164	8c multicolored	16	16
1011	A164	15c multicolored	30	30
1012	A164	35c multicolored	70	70
1013	A164	50c multicolored	1.00	1.00
1014	A164	65c multicolored	1.30	1.30
1015	A164	80c multicolored	1.60	1.60
1016	A164	$1.10 multicolored	2.20	2.20
1017	A164	$1.25 multicolored	2.50	2.50
		Nos. 1010-1017 (8)	9.76	9.76

Souvenir Sheets

1018	A164	$2 multicolored	4.00	4.00
1019	A164	$2 multicolored	4.00	4.00

Nos. 915, 918, & 921 Ovptd. in Red or Black — Royal Visit HRH Duke of Edinburgh 20th March 1993

1993, Mar. 20 Litho. *Perf. 14*

1020 CD347 35c on #915		70	70
1021 CD347 65c on #918		1.30	1.30

Souvenir Sheet

1022 CD347 $2 on #921 (Bk) 4.00 4.00

Miniature Sheet

Coronation of Queen Elizabeth II, 40th Anniv. — A165

Designs: a, 15c, Chalice and paten from royal collection. b, 50c, Official coronation photograph. c, $1, Coronation ceremony. d, $1.25, Queen, Prince Philip.
$2, New Portrait.

1993, June 2 Litho. *Perf. 13½x14*

1023 A165 Sheet, 2 each #a.-d. 10.00 10.00

Souvenir Sheet

Perf. 14

1024 A165 $2 multicolored 4.00 4.00

No. 1024 contains one 28x42mm stamp.

Christmas A166

Details or entire woodcut, Mary, Queen of the Angels, by Durer: 8c, 20c, 35c, $1.25.
Details or entire paintings by Raphael: 50c, $1, Virgin and Child with St. John the Baptist. 65c, The Canagiani Holy Family. 80c, The Holy Family with the Lamb.
No. 1033, Mary, Queen of the Angels, by Durer. No. 1034, The Canagiani Holy Family, diff., by Raphael.

Perf. 13½x14, 14x13½

1993, Dec. Litho.

1025-1032 A166 Set of 8 9.50 9.50

Souvenir Sheets

1033-1034 A166 $2 each 4.00 4.00

Dinosaurs A167

Designs: 8c, Omphalosaurus. 15c, Coelophysis. 20c, No. 1043, Triceratops. 35c, No. 1044, Dilophosaurus. 50c, Pterodactylus. 65c, Elasmosaurus. 80c, Stegosaurus. $1.25, Euoplocephalus.

1993, Nov. 15 Litho. *Perf. 14*

1035-1042 A167 Set of 8 8.00 8.00

Souvenir Sheets

1043-1044 A167 $2 each 4.00 4.00

Birds A168

Designs: 10c, Killdeer. 15c, Yellow-crowned night heron, vert. 35c, Northern mockingbird. 50c, Eastern kingbird, vert. 65c, Magnolia warbler. 80c, Cedar waxwing, vert. $1.10, Ruby-throated hummingbird. $1.25, Painted bunting, vert. No. 1053, American kestrel. No. 1054, Ruddy duck.

1993, Dec.

1045 A168	10c multicolored		20	20
1046 A168	15c multicolored		30	30
1047 A168	35c multicolored		70	70
1048 A168	50c multicolored		1.00	1.00
1049 A168	65c multicolored		1.40	1.40
1050 A168	80c multicolored		1.65	1.65
1051 A168	$1.10 multicolored		2.25	2.25
1052 A168	$1.25 multicolored		2.50	2.50
	Nos. 1045-1052 (8)		10.00	10.00

Souvenir Sheets

1053 A168	$2 multicolored	4.00	4.00
1054 A168	$2 multicolored	4.00	4.00

Fish A169

Designs: 10c, Bluehead wrasse. 20c, Honeycomb cowfish. 25c, Glasseye snapper. 35c, Spotted drum. 50c, Jolthead porgy. 65, Smallmouth grunt. 80c, Peppermint bass. $1.10, Indigo hamlet.
No. 1063, Bonnethead shark. No. 1064, Sharpnose shark.

1993, Dec. 15

1055-1062 A169 Set of 8 8.00 8.00

Souvenir Sheets

1063-1064 A169 $2 each 4.00 4.00

1994 World Cup Soccer Championships, US — A170

Designs: 8c, Segio Goycoechea, Argentina. 10c, Bado Illgner, Germany. 50c, Nico Claesen, Belgium. 65c, West German team. 80c, Cameroun team. $1, Santin, Francescoli, Uruguay; Cuciuffo, Argentina. $1.10, Sanchez, Mexico.
No. 1072, Imre Garaba, Hungary, vert. No. 1073, Pontiac Silverdome.

1994, Sept. 26 Litho. *Perf. 14*

1065-1071 A170 Set of 7 8.50 8.50

Souvenir Sheets

1072-1073 A170 $2 each 4.00 4.00

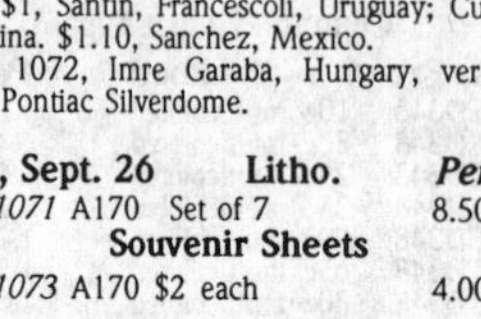

Mushrooms — A171

Designs: 5c, Xerocomus guadelupae, vert. 10c, Volvariella volvacea, vert. 35c, Hygrocybe atrosquamosa. 50c, Pleurotus ostreatus. 65c, Marasmius pallescens. 80c, Coprinus plicatilis, vert. $1.10, Bolbitius vitellinus. $1.50, Pyroglossum lilaceipes, vert.
No. 1082, Lentinus edodes. No. 1083, Russula cremeolilacina, vert.

1994, Oct. 10

1074-1081 A171 Set of 8 8.25 8.25

Souvenir Sheets

1082-1083 A171 $2 each 4.00 4.00

WAR TAX STAMPS

Regular Issue of 1913-16 Overprinted — WAR TAX

1917 Wmk. 3 *Perf. 14*

Black Overprint at Bottom of Stamp

MR1 A10 1p carmine		18	30
a. Double overprint		150.00	
b. "TAX" omitted			
c. Pair, one without ovpt.			
MR2 A10 3p violet, *yel*		32	38
a. Double overprint		90.00	

Black Overprint at Top or Middle of Stamp

1917

MR3 A10 1p carmine	15	15
a. Inverted overprint	25.00	
b. Double overprint	32.50	16.00
c. Pair, one without overprint	200.00	
MR4 A10 3p violet, *yel*	60	85
a. Double overprint	17.50	
b. Dbl. ovpt., one inverted	37.50	

Same Overprint in Violet or Red

1918-19

MR5 A10 1p car (V) ('19)	25	25
a. Double overprint	14.00	
b. "WAR" omitted	100.00	
MR6 A10 3p violet, *yel* (R)	3.50	3.50
a. Double overprint	50.00	

Regular Issue of 1913-16 Overprinted in Black — WAR TAX

1918

MR7 A10 1p carmine	20	20
MR8 A10 3p violet, *yel*	50	50

Same Overprint in Red

1919

MR9 A10 3p violet, *yel* 25 25

Regular Issue of 1913-16 Overprinted in Black — WAR TAX

MR10 A10 1p carmine	15	15
a. Double overprint	100.00	100.00
MR11 A10 3p violet, *yel*	32	32

Regular Issue of 1913-16 Overprinted — WAR TAX

MR12 A10 1p carmine	15	15
a. Double overprint	*100.00*	
MR13 A10 3p violet, *yel*	38	38

CAICOS

Catalogue values for all unused stamps in this country are for Never Hinged items.

Turks & Caicos Nos. 360, 364, 366, 369, 371-373 Ovptd. with Black Bar and "CAICOS ISLANDS"

Unwmk.

1981, July 24 Litho. *Perf. 14*

1	A69	1c	Indigo hamlet	15	15
2	A69	5c	Spanish grunt	15	15
3	A69	8c	Foureye butterflyfish	15	15
4	A69	20c	Queen angelfish	38	38
5	A69	50c	Fairy basslet	95	95
6	A69	$1	Clown wrasse	1.90	1.90
7	A69	$2	Stoplight parrotfish	3.75	3.75
			Nos. 1-7 (7)	7.43	7.43

Royal Wedding Issue

Common Design Type

Turks & Caicos Nos. 486-489 Ovptd. with Black Bar and "Caicos Islands"

1981, July 24

8 CD331	35c	Charles & Diana	85	85
9 CD331	65c	Kensington Palace	1.65	1.65
10 CD331	90c	Prince Charles	2.25	2.25

Souvenir Sheet

11 CD331 $2 Glass coach 17.50 17.50

Roulette x Imperf. (#12a), Imperf. (#12b)

1981, Oct. 29

Self-Adhesive

12 Souvenir booklet	27.50	
a. A88a Pane, 3 each 20c, Diana, $1, Charles)	15.00	
b. A88a Pane of 1 $2, Couple	10.00	

Nos. 8-11 exist with overprint in all capital letters, value about five times above. Nos. 8-10, in both overprint types, also exist in sheets of 5 plus label in changed colors, perf. 12.

Diver with Lobster and Conch Shell — C1

1983-84 *Perf. 14*

13 C1	8c	shown	16	16
14 C1	10c	Hawksbill turtle	20	20
15 C1	20c	Stone idol, Arawak Indians	40	40
16 C1	35c	Sloop construction	70	70
17 C1	50c	Marine biology	1.00	1.00
18 C1	95c	707 Jetliner	1.90	1.90
19 C1	$1.10	15th cent. Spanish ship	2.25	2.25
20 C1	$2	British soldier, Fort St. George	4.00	4.00
21 C1	$3	Pirates Anne Bonny, Calico Jack	6.00	6.00
		Nos. 13-21 (9)	16.61	16.61

Issue dates: #13-19, June 6, 1983. #20-21, May 18, 1984.
For overprints see Nos. 47-49.

Christmas Type of Turks and Caicos

Walt Disney characters in Santa Claus is Coming to Town.

1983, Nov. 7 *Perf. 11*

22 A104	1c	Chip 'n Dale	15	15
23 A104	1c	Goofy & Patch	15	15
24 A104	2c	Morty, Ferdie & Pluto	15	15
25 A104	2c	Morty	15	15
26 A104	3c	Donald, Huey, Dewey and Louie	15	15
27 A104	3c	Goofy & Louie	15	15
28 A104	50c	Uncle Scrooge	1.25	1.25
29 A104	70c	Mickey Mouse & Ferdie	1.75	1.75
30 A104	$1.10	Pinocchio, Jiminy Cricket and Figaro	2.50	2.50
		Nos. 22-30 (9)	6.40	6.40

Souvenir Sheet

Perf. 13½x14

31 A104 $2 Morty & Ferdie, fireplace 6.00 6.00

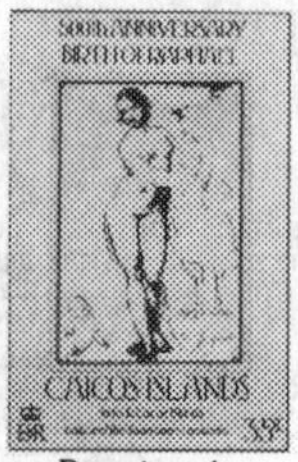

Drawings by Raphael — C2

1984 Summer Olympics, Los Angeles — C3

Designs: 35c, Leda and the Swan. 50c, Study of Apollo for Parnassus. 95c, Study of two figures for The Battle of Ostia. $1.10, Study for the Madonna of the Goldfinch. $2.50, The Garvagh Madonna.

1983, Dec. 15 *Perf. 14*

32 C2	35c multicolored	70	70
33 C2	50c multicolored	1.00	1.00
34 C2	95c multicolored	1.90	1.90

35 C2 $1.10 multicolored 2.25 2.25

Souvenir Sheet

36 C2 $2.50 multicolored 5.00 5.00

500th birth anniv. of Raphael.

1984, Mar. 1

37 C3 4c High jump 15 15
38 C3 25c Archery 50 50
39 C3 65c Cycling 1.25 1.25
40 C3 $1.10 Soccer 2.25 2.25

Souvenir Sheet

41 C3 $2 Show jumping, horiz. 4.00 4.00

Easter — C4

Walt Disney characters: 35c, Horace Horsecollar, Clarabelle Cow. 45c, Mickey, Minnie & Chip. 75c, Gyro Gearloose, Chip 'n Dale. 85c, Mickey, Chip 'n Dale. $2.20, Donald sailing with nephews.

1984, Apr. 15 *Perf. 14x13½*

42 C4 35c multicolored 70 70
43 C4 45c multicolored 90 90
44 C4 75c multicolored 1.50 1.50
45 C4 85c multicolored 1.75 1.75

Souvenir Sheet

46 C4 $2.20 mulitcolored 4.75 4.75

Nos. 18-19 Ovptd. with emblem and "Universal Postal Union 1874-1984"

1984, June 19 *Perf. 14*

47 C1 95c multicolored 1.90 1.90
48 C1 $1.10 multicolored 2.25 2.25

No. 20 Ovptd. "AUSIPEX 1984"

1984, Aug. 22

49 C1 $2 multicolored 4.00 4.00

Columbus' First Landfall — C5

1984, Sept. 21

50 C5 10c Sighting manatees 20 20
51 C5 70c Fleet 1.40 1.40
52 C5 $1 West Indies landing 2.00 2.00

Souvenir Sheet

53 C5 $2 Fleet, map 4.00 4.00

Columbus' first landing, 492nd anniv.

Christmas C6

Walt Disney characters: 20c, Santa Claus, Donald and Mickey. 35c, Donald at refrigerator. 50c, Donald, Micky riding toy train. 75c, Donald carrying presents. $1.10, Huey, Louie, Dewey and Donald singing carols. $2, Donald as Christmas tree.

Perf. 13½x14, 12x12½ (75c)

1984, Nov. 26

54 C6 20c multicolored 48 48
55 C6 35c multicolored 85 85
56 C6 50c multicolored 1.25 1.25
57 C6 75c multicolored 1.75 1.75
58 C6 $1.10 multicolored 2.75 2.75

Souvenir Sheet

Perf. 13½x14

59 C6 $2 multicolored 4.50 4.50

No. 57 printed in sheets of 8.

Audubon Birth Bicentenary — C7

1985, Feb. 12 *Perf. 14*

60 C7 20c Thick-billed vireo 40 40
61 C7 35c Black-faced grassquit 70 70
62 C7 50c Pearly-eyed thrasher 1.00 1.00
63 C7 $1 Greater Antillean bullfinch 2.00 2.00

Souvenir Sheet

64 C7 $2 Stripe-headed tanagers 4.00 4.00

No. 64 exists imperf.

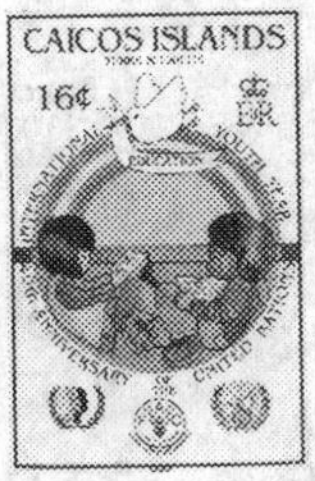

Intl. Youth Year — C8

1985, May 8

65 C8 16c Education 32 32
66 C8 35c Health 70 70
67 C8 70c Love 1.40 1.40
68 C8 90c Peace 1.75 1.75

Souvenir Sheet

69 C8 $2 Peace dove, child 4.00 4.00

UN 40th anniv.

Intl. Civil Aviation Org., 40th Anniv. C9

1985, May 26

70 C9 35c DC-3 70 70
71 C9 75c Convair 440 1.50 1.50
72 C9 90c TCNA Islander 1.75 1.75

Souvenir Sheet

73 C9 $2.20 Hang glider 4.50 4.50

Queen Mother, 85th Birthday Type of Turks & Caicos

1985, July 7

74 A117 35c Wearing green hat 70 70
75 A117 65c With Princess Anne, horiz. 1.25 1.25
76 A117 95c Wearing white hat 1.90 1.90

Souvenir Sheet

77 A117 $2 Inspecting guardsmen 4.00 4.00

Mark Twain, 150th Birth Anniv. — C10

Walt Disney characters in Tom Sawyer, Detective (Intl. Youth Year): 8c, Mickey and Goofy as Tom and Huck reading reward poster. 35c, Meeting Jake Dunlap. 95c, Spying on Jubiter Dunlap. $1.10, With Pluto finding body. No. 86, Unmasking Jubiter Dunlap.

Walt Disney characters portraying Six Soldiers of Fortune (The Brothers Grimm, Bicent.): 16c, Donald receiving his meager pay. 25c, Donald meets Horace Horsecollar as strong man. 65c, Donald meets Mickey the marksman. $1.35, Goofy wins footrace against Princess Daisy. No. 87, Soldiers with sack of gold.

1985, Dec. 5 *Perf. 14x13½*

78 C10 8c multicolored 15 15
79 C10 16c multicolored 32 32
80 C10 25c multicolored 50 50
81 C10 35c multicolored 70 70
82 C10 65c multicolored 1.25 1.25
83 C10 95c multicolored 1.90 1.90
84 C10 $1.10 multicolored 2.25 2.25
85 C10 $1.35 multicolored 2.75 2.75
Nos. 78-85 (8) 9.82 9.82

Souvenir Sheet

86 C10 $2 multicolored 4.50 4.50
87 C10 $2 multicolored 4.50 4.50

Stamps are no longer being produced for Caicos.

TURKS ISLANDS

LOCATION — West Indies, at the southern extremity of the Bahamas
GOVT. — Former dependency of Jamaica
AREA — 616 sq. mi.
POP. — 2,000 (approx.)
CAPITAL — Grand Turk

In 1848 the Turks Islands together with the Caicos group, lying to the northwest, were made a British colony. In 1873 the Colony became a dependency under the government of Jamaica although separate stamp issues were continued. Postage stamps inscribed Turks and Caicos Islands have been used since 1900.

12 Pence = 1 Shilling

Values for Nos. 1-42 are for stamps with rough perfs running through the design.

Watermark

Wmk. 5- Small Star

Queen Victoria — A1

Perf. 11½ to 13

1867 **Unwmk.** **Engr.**

1 A1 1p rose 22.50 30.00
2 A1 6p gray black 32.50 32.50
3 A1 1sh slate blue 32.50 32.50

Perf. 11 to 13x14 to 15

1873-79 **Wmk. 5**

4 A1 1p dull red 20.00 20.00
a. Horiz. pair, imperf. btwn. *7,500.*
b. Perf. 11-12 1,000.
5 A1 1p rose red ('79) 30.00 30.00
6 A1 1sh violet *4,250. 2,250.*

Stamps offered as No. 6 are often copies from which the surcharge has been removed.

Stamps of 1867-79 Surcharged in Black:

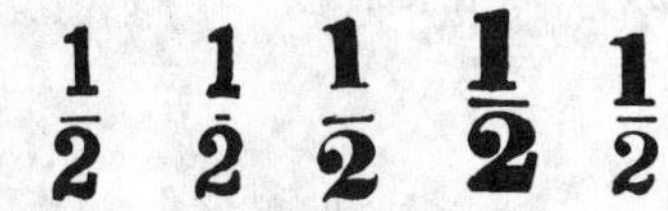

a b c d e

12 settings of the ½p, 9 of 2½p, and 6 of 4p.

1881 **Unwmk.** *Perf. 11 to 13*

7 (a) ½p on 6p gray blk 40.00 40.00
7A (b) ½p on 6p gray blk 27.50
8 (b) ½p on 1sh slate bl 35.00 42.50
a. Double surcharge *3,000.*
8B (c) ½p on 1sh slate bl *12,500.*
c. Without fraction bar

Perf. 11 to 13x14 to 15

Wmk. 5

9 (a) ½p on 1p dull red 21.00 21.00
a. Double surcharge
10 (b) ½p on 1p dull red 27.50 27.50
11 (c) ½p on 1p dull red 18.00 18.00
a. Double surcharge *2,000.*
12 (d) ½p on 1p dull red 90.00
a. Without fraction bar 775.00
b. Double surcharge
13 (e) ½p on 1p dull red 300.00
14 (a) ½p on 1sh violet 100.00 100.00
a. Double surcharge 850.00
15 (b) ½p on 1sh violet 175.00 175.00
a. Without fraction bar 450.00
16 (c) ½p on 1sh violet 80.00 80.00

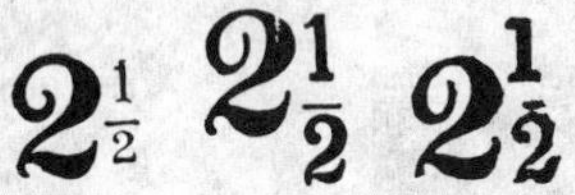

f g h

Perf. 11 to 13

Unwmk.

17 (f) 2½p on 6p gray blk *6,000.*
18 (g) 2½p on 6p gray blk 350. 350.
a. Horiz. pair, imperf. between
b. Double surcharge *4,500.*
19 (h) 2½p on 6p gray blk 150. 150.

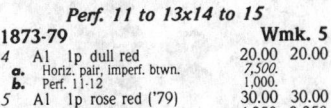

i j

Perf. 11 to 13x14 to 15

Wmk. 5

20 (i) 2½p on 1sh violet 1,100.
21 (h) 2½p on 1sh violet 575. 575.
22 (j) 2½p on 1sh violet *4,500.*

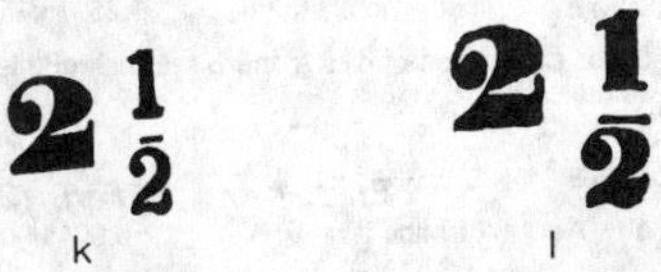

k l

m n

Perf. 11 to 13

Unwmk.

24 (k) 2½p on 6p gray blk *8,500.*
25 (k) 2½p on 1sh slate bl *8,500.*
26 (l) 2½p on 1sh slate bl 600.
27 (m) 2½p on 1sh slate bl 1,200.
a. Without fraction bar 3,750.
28 (n) 2½p on 1sh slate bl 6,500.

2½
o

Perf. 11 to 13x14 to 15
Wmk. 5

29 (l) 2½p on 1p dull red 300.
30 (o) 2½p on 1p dull red 500.
31 (l) 2½p on 1sh violet 450.
a. Double surcharge of "½" 3,500.
32 (o) 2½p on 1sh violet 800.
b. Double surcharge of "½" *5,750.*

4 4 4
p q r

Perf. 11 to 13
Unwmk.

33 (p) 4p on 6p gray black 45.00 45.00
34 (q) 4p on 6p gray black 350.00 350.00
35 (r) 4p on 6p gray black 275.00 275.00

Copies of No. 33 with top of "4" painted in are sometimes offered as No. 35.

Perf. 11 to 13x14 to 15
Wmk. 5

36 (r) 4p on 1p dull red 375. 375.
a. Inverted surcharge 3,000.
37 (p) 4p on 1p dull red 375. 375.
a. Inverted surcharge 3,000.
38 (p) 4p on 1sh violet 300. 300.
39 (q) 4p on 1sh violet *1,000.*

Wmk. Crown and C C (1)
1881 Engr. *Perf. 14*

40 A1 1p brown red 16.00 16.00
a. Diagonal half used as ½p on cover
41 A1 6p olive brown 57.50 45.00
42 A1 1sh slate green 75.00 62.50

A2

A3

1881 **Typo.**
43 A2 4p ultramarine 45.00 22.50

1882-95 Engr. Wmk. 2
44 A1 1p orange brn ('83) 10.50 12.00
a. Half used as ½p on cover 1,500.
45 A1 1p car lake ('89) 60 85
46 A1 6p yellow brn ('89) 2.00 3.00
47 A1 1sh black brn ('87) 1.50 3.00
a. 1sh deep brown 1.75 4.00

Typo.
Die A

48 A2 ½p dull green ('85) 2.00 3.50
a. ½p blue green ('82) 5.50 6.00
49 A2 2½p red brown ('82) 7.25 8.00
50 A2 4p gray ('84) 4.00 2.25
a. Half used as 2p on cover 1,200.

Die B

51 A2 ½p gray green ('94) 30 30
52 A2 2½p ultra ('93) 70 70
53 A2 4p dk vio & bl ('95) 1.25 3.75

For explanation of dies A and B see back of this volume.

1887 Engr. *Perf. 12*
54 A1 1p carmine lake 5.00 5.00

No. 49 Surcharged in Black **One Penny**

1889
55 A2 1p on 2½p red brown 3.50 4.00
a. Double surcharge
b. Double surcharge, one inverted

No. 50 Surcharged in Black **1d. / 2**

Two types of surcharge:
Type I - Upper bar continuous across sheet.
Type II - Upper bar breaks between stamps.

1893
56 A2 ½p on 4p gray (I) 90.00 90.00
a. Type II 180.00 105.00

This surcharge exists in five settings.

1894 **Typo.**
57 A3 5p olive grn & carmine 1.50 3.75
a. Diagonal half used as 2½p on cover 3,000.

VIRGIN ISLANDS

LOCATION — West Indies, southeast of Puerto Rico
GOVT. — British colony
AREA — 59 sq. mi.
POP. — 12,034 (1980)
CAPITAL — Road Town

The British Virgin Islands constituted one of the presidencies of the former Leeward Islands colony until it became a colony itself in 1956. For many years stamps of Leeward Islands were used concurrently.

The Virgin Islands group is divided between Great Britain and the United States. See Danish West Indies.

12 Pence = 1 Shilling
20 Shillings = 1 Pound
100 Cents = 1 Dollar (1951)
100 Cents = 1 US Dollar (1962)

Catalogue values for unused stamps in this country are for Never Hinged items, beginning with Scott 88 in the regular postage section and Scott O1 in the officials section.

Virgin and Lamps
A1

St. Ursula
A2

A3

A4

1866 Litho. Unwmk. *Perf. 12*
Toned or White Paper

1 A1 1p green 35.00 *40.00*
a. Toned paper 35.00 *40.00*
c. Perf. 15x12, toned paper 5,000. *6,000.*
2 A3 6p rose 47.50 67.50
a. Large "V" in "VIRGIN" 575.00 *600.00*
b. White paper 65.00 *80.00*
c. As "a," white paper 400.00 *500.00*

Copies offered as No. 1c frequently have forged perfs.

1867-70 *Perf. 15*
3 A1 1p blue grn ('70) 50.00 57.50
4 A1 1p yel grn ('68) 62.50 67.50
a. Toned paper 80.00 65.00
5 A2 4p lake, *buff* 27.50 45.00
a. 4p lake, *rose* 27.50 45.00
6 A3 6p rose 500.00 *500.00*
a. Toned paper ('68) 325.00 *375.00*

7 A4 1sh rose & blk 140.00 175.00
a. Toned paper 140.00 200.00
b. Double lined frame 140.00 175.00
c. As "b," bluish paper 165.00 200.00

Colored Margins

8 A4 1sh rose & blk 30.00 30.00
a. White paper 30.00 30.00
b. Bluish paper 825.00 1,000.
c. Central figure omitted *75,000.*

Copies of No. 8c have perfs. trimmed on one or two sides.

1878 Wmk. 1 *Perf. 14*
9 A1 1p green 55.00 60.00

See #16-17, 19-20. For surcharge see #18.

Queen Victoria — A5

1880 **Typo.**
10 A5 1p green 27.50 37.50
11 A5 2½p red brown 45.00 55.00

1883-84 **Wmk. 2**
12 A5 ½p yellow 60.00 *67.50*
13 A5 ½p green 2.25 5.75
a. Imperf., pair 1,750.
14 A5 1p rose 9.25 11.00
15 A5 2½p ultra ('84) 2.75 4.25

No. 13a probably is a plate proof.

1887 **Litho.**
16 A2 4p brick red 26.00 30.00
a. 4p brown red 32.50 30.00
17 A3 6p violet 13.00 22.50

No. 8 Surcharged in Violet **4D**

1888 Unwmk. *Perf. 15*
18 A4 4p on 1sh dp rose & blk 77.50 80.00
a. Double surcharge *10,000.*
b. Inverted surcharge *45,000.*

1889 Wmk. 2 *Perf. 14*
19 A1 1p carmine 1.40 1.65
20 A4 1sh brown 42.50 57.50
a. 1sh black brown 55.00 70.00

St. Ursula with Sheaf of Lilies
A7

Edward VII
A8

1899 **Engr.**
21 A7 ½p yellow grn 55 32
a. "PFNNY" 55.00 75.00
b. "F" without cross bar 55.00 82.50
c. Horiz. pair, imperf. between *10,000.*
22 A7 1p red 1.50 1.25
23 A7 2½p ultra 8.00 6.50
24 A7 4p chocolate 6.00 8.50
a. "PENCF" 1,750. 1,750.
25 A7 6p dark violet 3.50 4.00
26 A7 7p slate green 5.50 8.00
27 A7 1sh ocher 13.00 *16.00*
28 A7 5sh dark blue 42.50 *55.00*
Nos. 21-28 (8) 80.55 *99.57*

1904 Typo. Wmk. 3
29 A8 ½p violet & bl grn 42 55
30 A8 1p violet & scar 65 95
31 A8 2p violet & bis 5.50 4.25
32 A8 2½p violet & ultra 1.50 2.50
33 A8 3p violet & blk 2.00 *3.50*
34 A8 6p violet & brn 3.75 *5.50*
35 A8 1sh green & scar 4.00 *7.00*
36 A8 2sh6p green & blk 20.00 35.00
37 A8 5sh green & ultra 32.50 55.00
Nos. 29-37 (9) 70.32 114.25

Numerals of 2p, 3p, 1sh and 2sh6p of type A8 are in color on plain tablet.

George V
A9

Colony Seal
A10

Die I

For description of dies I and II see back of this volume.

1913
Ordinary Paper

38 A9 ½p green 52 50
39 A9 1p scarlet 2.25 1.65
a. 1p carmine 4.00 4.25
40 A9 2p gray 1.90 1.90
41 A9 2½p ultra 2.50 2.25

Chalky Paper

42 A9 3p vio, *yel* 1.65 1.50
43 A9 6p dl vio & red vio 2.50 2.00
44 A9 1sh blk, *green* 3.50 *4.25*
45 A9 2sh6p blk & red, *bl* 24.00 *22.50*
46 A9 5sh grn & red, *yel* 37.50 *42.50*
Nos. 38-46 (9) 76.32 *79.05*

Numerals of 2p, 3p, 1sh and 2sh6p of type A9 are in color on plain tablet.

1921 **Wmk. 4**
Die II

47 A9 ½p green 60 65
48 A9 1p carmine 1.10 1.20

For overprints see Nos. MR1-MR2.

1922 **Wmk. 3**
49 A10 3p violet, *yel* 1.10 1.00
50 A10 1sh black, *emerald* 85 1.00
51 A10 2sh6p blk & red, *bl* 4.25 *4.50*
52 A10 5sh grn & red, *yel* 25.00 *27.50*

1922-28 **Wmk. 4**
53 A10 ½p green 18 24
54 A10 1p rose red 28 35
55 A10 1p violet ('27) 55 1.10
56 A10 1½p rose red ('27) 1.00 1.10
57 A10 1½p fawn ('28) 2.25 2.00
58 A10 2p gray 65 1.40
59 A10 2½p ultra 1.25 2.25
60 A10 2½p orange ('23) 2.75 2.75
61 A10 3p dl vio, *yel* ('28) 1.00 1.90
62 A10 5p dl lil & ol grn 6.50 *11.00*
63 A10 6p dl vio & red vio 85 1.50
a. 6p brown lilac & red violet 85 1.10
64 A10 1sh blk, *emer* ('28) 2.25 2.75
65 A10 2sh6p blk & red, *bl* ('28) 14.00 14.00
66 A10 5sh grn & red, *yel* ('23) 16.00 *20.00*
Nos. 53-66 (14) 49.51 *62.34*

The ½, 1, 2 and 2½p are on ordinary paper, the others on chalky.

Silver Jubilee Issue
Common Design Type

1935, May 6 Engr. *Perf. 11x12*
69 CD301 1p car & dk blue 16 20
70 CD301 1½p black & ultra 20 28
71 CD301 2½p ultra & brn 55 70
72 CD301 1sh brn vio & ind 2.75 3.25
Set, never hinged 7.50

Coronation Issue
Common Design Type

1937, May 12 *Perf. 11x11½*
73 CD302 1p dark carmine 15 15
74 CD302 1½p brown 15 15
75 CD302 2½p deep ultra 35 35
Set, never hinged 90

King George VI and Seal of the Colony — A11

1938-47 Photo. *Perf. 14*
76 A11 ½p green 15 15
77 A11 1p scarlet 15 15
78 A11 1½p red brown 15 15
79 A11 2p gray 15 15
80 A11 2½p ultra 15 15
81 A11 3p orange 18 16
82 A11 6p deep violet 32 30
83 A11 1sh olive bister 50 45
84 A11 2sh6p sepia 2.50 *3.50*

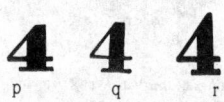

85	A11	5sh rose lake	3.75	4.50
86	A11	10sh brt blue ('47)	7.75	9.75
87	A11	£1 gray blk ('47)	12.00	16.00
		Nos. 76-87 (12)	27.75	35.41
		Set, never hinged	40.00	

Catalogue values for unused stamps in this section, from this point to the end of the section, are for Never Hinged items.

Peace Issue
Common Design Type

Perf. 13½x14

1946, Nov. 1 Engr. Wmk. 4

88	CD303	1½p red brown	15	15
89	CD303	3p orange	16	16
		Set value	26	26

Silver Wedding Issue
Common Design Types

1949, Jan. 3 Photo. *Perf. 14x14½*

90	CD304	2½p brt ultra	38	38

Engr.; Name Typo.

Perf. 11½x11

91	CD305	£1 gray black	13.00	13.00

UPU Issue
Common Design Types

Engr.; Name Typo. on Nos. 93 & 94

1949, Oct. 10 *Perf. 13½, 11x11½*

92	CD306	2½p ultra	35	35
93	CD307	3p deep orange	42	42
94	CD308	6p red lilac	80	75
95	CD309	1sh olive	2.25	1.40

University Issue
Common Design Types

1951 Engr. *Perf. 14x14½*

96	CD310	3c red brn & gray blk	25	25
97	CD311	12c purple & black	85	85

Map of the Islands — A12

1951, Apr. 2 Wmk. 4 *Perf. 14½x14*

98	A12	6c red orange	25	25
99	A12	12c purple	35	35
100	A12	24c olive grn	55	55
101	A12	$1.20 carmine	2.25	2.25

Restoration of the Legislative Council, 1950.

Sombrero Lighthouse A13

Map of Jost van Dyke A14

Designs: 3c, Sheep. 4c, Map, Anegada. 5c, Cattle. 8c, Map, Virgin Gorda. 12c, Map, Tortola. 24c, Badge of the Presidency. 60c, Dead Man's Chest. $1.20, Sir Francis Drake Channel. $2.40, Road Town. $4.80, Map, Virgin Islands.

Perf. 12½x13, 13x12½

1952, Apr. 15

102	A13	1c gray black	22	22
103	A14	2c deep green	55	35
104	A14	3c choc & gray blk	28	28
105	A14	4c red	45	45
106	A14	5c gray blk & rose lake	90	80
107	A14	8c ultra	55	55
108	A14	12c purple	1.00	1.00
109	A13	24c dk brown	1.10	1.10
110	A14	60c blue & ol grn	1.75	1.75
111	A14	$1.20 ultra & blk	4.00	4.00
112	A14	$2.40 hn brn & dk grn	7.25	7.25
113	A14	$4.80 rose car & bl	14.00	14.00
		Nos. 102-113 (12)	32.05	31.75

Coronation Issue
Common Design Type

1953, June 2 *Perf. 13½x14*

114	CD312	2c dk green & blk	25	25

Map of Tortola — A15

Brown Pelican A16

Designs: 1c, Virgin Islands sloop. 2c, Nelthrop Red Poll bull. 3c, Road Harbor. 4c, Mountain travel. 5c, St. Ursula. 8c, Beach scene. 12c, Boat launching. 24c, White Cedar tree. 60c, Skipjack tuna. $1.20, Treasury Square. $4.80, Magnificent frigatebird.

Perf. 13x12½

1956, Nov. 1 Engr. Wmk. 4

115	A15	½c claret & blk	15	15
116	A15	1c dk bl & grnsh bl	15	15
117	A15	2c black & ver	15	15
118	A15	3c olive & brt bl	15	15
119	A15	4c blue grn & brn	15	15
120	A15	5c gray	18	18
121	A15	8c dp ultra & org	25	25
122	A15	12c car & brt ultra	35	35
123	A15	24c dull red & grn	75	75
124	A15	60c yel org & dk bl	2.50	2.50
125	A15	$1.20 car & yel grn	3.50	3.50

Perf. 12x11½

126	A16	$2.40 vio brn & dl yel	11.00	11.00
127	A16	$4.80 grnsh bl & dk brn	24.00	24.00
		Nos. 115-127 (13)	43.28	43.28

Types of 1956 Surcharged ≡ 2¢

Perf. 13x12½

1962, Dec. 10 Wmk. 314

128	A15	1c on ½c	15	15
129	A15	2c on 1c	15	15
130	A15	3c on 2c	15	15
131	A15	4c on 3c	15	15
132	A15	5c on 4c	15	15
133	A15	8c on 8c	22	22
134	A15	10c on 12c	30	30
135	A15	12c on 24c	38	38
136	A15	25c on 60c	80	80
137	A15	70c on $1.20	2.00	2.00

Perf. 12x11½

138	A16	$1.40 on $2.40	4.75	4.75
139	A16	$2.80 on $4.80	9.25	9.25
		Nos. 128-139 (12)	18.45	18.45

Freedom from Hunger Issue
Common Design Type

1963, June 4 Photo. *Perf. 14x14½*

140	CD314	25c lilac	52	52

Red Cross Centenary Issue
Common Design Type

Wmk. 314

1963, Sept. 2 Litho. *Perf. 13*

141	CD315	2c black & red	15	15
142	CD315	25c ultra & red	90	90

Shakespeare Issue
Common Design Type

1964, Apr. 23 Photo. *Perf. 14x14½*

143	CD316	10c ultramarine	24	24

Bonito — A17

Map of Tortola Island — A18

Designs: 2c, Seaplane at Soper's Hole. 3c, Brown pelican. 4c, Dead Man's Chest (mountain). 5c, Road Harbor. 6c, Fallen Jerusalem Island. 8c, The Baths, Virgin Gorda. 10c, Map of Virgin Islands. 12c, Ferry service, Tortola—St. Thomas. 15c, The Towers. 25c, Plane at Beef Island Airfield. $1, Virgin Gorda Island. $1.40, Yachts, Tortola. $2.80, Badge.

Perf. 13x12½

1964, Nov. 2 Engr. Wmk. 314

144	A17	1c gray ol & dk bl	15	15
145	A17	2c rose red & ol	15	15
146	A17	3c grnsh bl & sep	15	15
147	A17	4c carmine & blk	15	15
148	A17	5c green & blk	18	18
149	A17	6c orange & blk	22	22
150	A17	8c pink & blk	32	32
151	A17	10c lt violet & mar	38	38
152	A17	12c vio bl & Prus grn	45	45
153	A17	15c gray & yel grn	55	55
154	A17	25c purple & yel grn	85	85

Perf. 13x13½

Size: 27x30½mm

155	A18	70c bister brn & blk	2.75	2.75
156	A18	$1 red brn & yel grn	3.75	3.75
157	A18	$1.40 pink & blue	5.25	5.25

Perf. 11½x12

Size: 27x37mm

158	A18	$2.80 rose lilac & blk	10.00	10.00
		Nos. 144-158 (15)	25.30	25.30

For surcharges see Nos. 173-175. For overprints see Nos. 190-191.

ITU Issue
Common Design Type

Perf. 11x11½

1965, May 17 Litho. Wmk. 314

159	CD317	4c yellow & bl grn	15	15
160	CD317	25c blue & org yel	80	80

Intl. Cooperation Year Issue
Common Design Type

1965, Oct. 25 Wmk. 314 *Perf. 14½*

161	CD318	1c blue grn & cl	15	15
162	CD318	25c lt violet & grn	65	65

Churchill Memorial Issue
Common Design Type

1966, Jan. 24 Photo. *Perf. 14*

Design in Black, Gold and Carmine Rose

163	CD319	1c brt blue	15	15
164	CD319	2c green	15	15
165	CD319	10c brown	40	40
166	CD319	25c violet	1.00	1.00

Royal Visit Issue
Common Design Type

1966, Feb. 22 Litho. *Perf. 11x12*

167	CD320	4c violet blue	15	15
168	CD320	70c dk car rose	2.25	2.25

Stamps of 1866 — A19

Designs: 5c, R.M.S. Atrato, 1866. 25c, Beechcraft mail plane on Beef Island Airfield and 6p stamp (No. 2). 60c, Landing mail at Road Town, 1866, and 1p stamp (No. 1).

Perf. 12½x13

1966, Apr. 25 Wmk. 314

169	A19	5c grn, yel, red & blk	15	15
170	A19	10c yel, grn, red, blk & rose	20	20
171	A19	25c lt grn, bl, red, blk & rose	50	50
172	A19	60c bl, red, blk, & grn	1.00	1.00

Centenary of Virgin Islands postage stamps.

Nos. 155, 157-158 Surcharged with New Value and Two Bars

Perf. 13x12½, 11½x12

1966, Sept. 15 Engr. Wmk. 314

173	A18	50c on 70c	1.90	1.90
174	A18	$1.50 on $1.40	4.25	4.25
175	A18	$3 on $2.80	8.75	8.75

UNESCO Anniversary Issue
Common Design Type

1966, Dec. 1 Litho. *Perf. 14*

176	CD323	2c "Education"	15	15
177	CD323	12c "Science"	25	25
178	CD323	60c "Culture"	1.00	1.00

Map and Seal of Virgin Islands A20

Perf. 14½

1967, Apr. 18 Photo. Wmk. 314

179	A20	2c gold, grn & org	15	15
180	A20	10c gold, rose red, grn & org	15	15
181	A20	25c gold, red brn, grn & org	28	28
182	A20	$1 gold, bl, grn & org	1.10	1.10

Introduction of new constitution.

Common Design Types are pictured beginning on page 176.

Map of Virgin Islands, Bermuda and C.S. Mercury A21

Designs: 10c, Communications center, Chalwell, Virgin Islands. 50c, Cable ship Mercury.

1967, Sept. 14 Wmk. 314 *Perf. 14½*

183	A21	4c green & multi	15	15
184	A21	10c dp plum & multi	15	15
185	A21	50c bister & multi	80	80

Completion of the Bermuda-Tortola, Virgin Islands, telephone link.

Blue Marlin A22

Designs: 10c, Sergeant fish (cobia). 25c, Peto fish (Wahoo). 40c, Fishing boat, map of Virgin Islands and fishing records.

Perf. 12½x12

1968, Jan. 2 Photo. Wmk. 314

186	A22	2c multicolored	15	15
187	A22	10c multicolored	25	25
188	A22	25c multicolored	48	48
189	A22	40c multicolored	80	80

Game fishing in Virgin Islands waters.

Nos. 151 and 154 Overprinted: "1968 / INTERNATIONAL / YEAR FOR / HUMAN RIGHTS"

1968, July 1 Engr. ***Perf. 13x12½***

190	A17	10c lt vio & mar	20	20
191	A17	25c pur & green	52	52

Martin Luther King, Bible and Sword A23

1968, Oct. 15 Litho. ***Perf. 14***

192	A23	4c dl org, vio & blk	15	15
193	A23	25c dl org, gray grn & blk	50	50

Martin Luther King, Jr. (1929-68), American civil rights leader.

DHC-6 Twin Otter A24

Designs: 10c, Hawker Siddeley 748. 25c, Hawker Siddeley Heron. $1, Badge from cap of Royal Engineers.

1968, Dec. 16 Unwmk. ***Perf. 14***

194	A24	2c brn red & multi	15	15
195	A24	10c grnsh bl, blk & red	16	16
196	A24	25c ultra, lt bl, org & blk	42	42
197	A24	$1 green & multi	1.65	1.65

Opening of enlarged Beef Island Airport.

Long John Silver and Jim Hawkins — A25

Tourist and Rock Grouper — A26

Scenes from Treasure Island: 10c, Jim's escape from the pirates, horiz. 40c, The fight with Israel Hands. $1, Treasure trove, horiz.

Perf. 13½x13, 13x13½

1969, Mar. 18 Photo. Wmk. 314

198	A25	4c dp car & multi	15	15
199	A25	10c multicolored	22	22
200	A25	40c ultra & multi	65	65
201	A25	$1 black & multi	2.00	2.00

Robert Louis Stevenson (1850-94). The Virgin Islands were used as the setting for "Treasure Island."

1969, Oct. 20 Litho. ***Perf. 12½***

Tourist Publicity: 10c, Yachts in Road Harbor, Tortola, horiz. 20c, Tourists on beach in Virgin Gorda National Park, horiz. $1, Pipe organ cactus and woman tourist.

202	A26	2c multicolored	15	15
203	A26	10c multicolored	18	18
204	A26	20c multicolored	35	35
205	A26	$1 multicolored	1.75	1.75

Carib Canoe A27

Ships: 1c, Santa Maria. 2c, H.M.S. Elizabeth Bonaventure. 3c, Dutch buccaneer, 1660. 4c, Thetis (1827 merchant ship). 5c, Henry Morgan's ship. 6c, Frigate Boreas. 8c, Schooner L'Eclair, 1804. 10c, H.M.S. Formidable. 12c, H.M.S. Nymph burning. 15c, Packet Windsor Castle fighting French privateer. 25c, Frigate Astrea, 1808. 50c, H.M.S. Rhone. $1, Tortola sloop. $2, H.M.S. Frobisher. $3, Booker Line Viking (cargo ship). $5, Hydrofoil Sun Arrow.

Wmk. 314 Sideways

1970, Feb. 16 ***Perf. 14½***

206	A27	½c brn & ocher	15	15
207	A27	1c bl, lt grn & vio	15	15
208	A27	2c red brn, org & gray	15	15
209	A27	3c ver, bl & brn	15	15
210	A27	4c brn, bl & vio bl	15	15
211	A27	5c grn, pink & blk	15	15
212	A27	6c lil, grn & blk	16	16
213	A27	8c lt ol, yel & brn	24	24
214	A27	10c ocher, bl & brn	28	28
215	A27	12c sep, yel & dp cl	35	35
216	A27	15c org, grnsh bl & brn	42	42
217	A27	25c bl, grnsh gray & pur	60	60
218	A27	50c rose car, lt grn & brn	1.25	1.25
219	A27	$1 brn, sal pink & dk grn	2.50	2.50
220	A27	$2 gray & yel	5.00	5.00
221	A27	$3 brn, ol bis & dk bl	7.75	7.75
222	A27	$5 lil & gray	12.50	12.50
		Nos. 206-222 (17)	31.95	31.95

For overprints see Nos. 235-236.

1973, Oct. 17 Wmk. 314 Upright

206a	A27	½c	15	15
209a	A27	3c	45	45
210a	A27	4c	75	75
211a	A27	5c	75	75
214a	A27	10c	1.50	1.50
215a	A27	12c	1.75	1.75
		Nos. 206a-215a (6)	5.35	5.35

Wmk. 314 Sideways

1974, Nov. 11 ***Perf. 13½***

207a	A27	1c	15	15
214b	A27	10c	20	20
215b	A27	12c	24	24
216a	A27	15c	30	30

"A Tale of Two Cities," by Dickens A28

Charles Dickens: 10c, "Oliver Twist." 25c, "Great Expectations."

1970, May 4 Litho. ***Perf. 14½***

223	A28	5c blk, gray & pink	15	15
224	A28	10c blk, pale yel grn & blue	40	40
225	A28	25c blk, yel & lt yel grn	1.00	1.00

Hospital Visitor A29

Designs: 10c, Girl Scouts receiving first aid training at lake side. 25c, Red Cross and Virgin Islands coat of arms.

1970, Aug. 10 Wmk. 314 ***Perf. 14***

226	A29	4c multicolored	15	15
227	A29	10c multicolored	30	30
228	A29	25c multicolored	75	75

Centenary of British Red Cross.

Mary Read — A30

Pirates: 10c, George Lowther. 30c, Edward Teach (Blackbeard). 60c, Henry Morgan.

1970, Nov. 16 Wmk. 314 ***Perf. 14***

229	A30	½c dp rose & multi	15	15
230	A30	10c blue grn & multi	32	32
231	A30	30c ultra & multi	1.00	1.00
232	A30	60c multicolored	2.00	2.00

Children Spelling out "UNICEF" A31

1971, Dec. 13

233	A31	15c tan & multi	40	40
234	A31	30c lt blue & multi	80	80

25th anniv. of UNICEF.

Nos. 210 and 217 Dated "1972" and Overprinted: "VISIT OF / H.R.H. / THE / PRINCESS MARGARET"

1972, Mar. 7 ***Perf. 14½***

235	A27	4c multicolored	15	15
236	A27	25c multicolored	42	42
		Set value	50	50

Seaman, 1800 — A32

Designs: 10c, Boatswain, 1787-1807. 30c, Captain, 1795-1812. 60c, Admiral in full dress uniform, 1787-1795.

1972, Mar. 17 ***Perf. 14x13½***

237	A32	½c yellow & multi	15	15
238	A32	10c brt pink & multi	40	40
239	A32	30c orange & multi	1.10	1.10
240	A32	60c blue & multi	2.50	2.50

INTERPEX, 14th Intl. Stamp Exhib., NYC, Mar. 17-19.

Silver Wedding Issue, 1972

Common Design Type

Design: Queen Elizabeth II, Prince Philip, sailfish and "Sir Winston Churchill" yacht.

1972, Nov. 24 Photo. ***Perf. 14x14½***

241	CD324	15c ultra & multi	40	40
242	CD324	25c Prus blue & multi	60	60

Allison Tuna A33

1972, Dec. 12 Litho. ***Perf. 13½x14***

243	A33	½c Wahoo	15	15
244	A33	½c Blue marlin	15	15
245	A33	15c shown	42	42
246	A33	25c White marlin	65	65
247	A33	50c Sailfish	1.10	1.10
248	A33	$1 Dolphin	2.50	2.50
	a.	Souvenir sheet of 6, #243-248	7.50	7.50
		Nos. 243-248 (6)	4.97	4.97

Game fish. Nos. 243-244 printed checkerwise in sheets of 25.

Lettsom House and Medal A34

Themes from Quaker History: ½c, Dr. John Coakley Lettsom, vert. 15c, Dr. William Thornton, vert. 30c, US Capitol, Washington, DC, and Dr. Thornton who designed it. $1, Library Hall, Philadelphia, and William Penn.

1973, Mar. 9 Litho. ***Perf. 13½***

249	A34	½c rose & multi	15	15
250	A34	10c multicolored	20	20
251	A34	15c multicolored	30	30
252	A34	30c ultra & multi	60	60
253	A34	$1 multicolored	1.90	1.90
		Nos. 249-253 (5)	3.15	3.15

INTERPEX, 15th Intl. Phil. Exhib., NYC, Mar. 9-11.

Hummingbirds on 1c Coin — A35

Coins and Beach Scenes: 5c, Zenaida doves. 10c, Kingfisher. 25c, Mangrove cuckoos. 50c, Brown pelicans. $1, Magnificent frigate birds.

1973, June 30 Wmk. 314 ***Perf. 14½***

254	A35	1c orange & multi	15	15
255	A35	5c lt blue & multi	15	15
256	A35	10c pale ultra & multi	18	18
257	A35	25c yellow & multi	40	40
258	A35	50c lt violet & multi	75	75
259	A35	$1 ultra & multi	2.25	2.25
		Nos. 254-259 (6)	3.88	3.88

New Virgin Islands coinage.

Princess Anne's Wedding Issue

Common Design Type

1973, Nov. 16 Wmk. 314 ***Perf. 14***

260	CD325	5c citron & multi	15	15
261	CD325	50c bl grn & multi	80	80

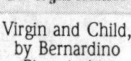

Virgin and Child, by Bernardino Pintoricchio A36

Arms of French Minesweeper Canopus A37

Christmas (Paintings of the Virgin and Child by): 3c, Lorenzo Credi. 25c, Carlo Crivelli. 50c, Bernardino Luini.

1973, Dec. 7 ***Perf. 14x14½***

262	A36	½c lt green & multi	15	15
263	A36	3c rose & multi	15	15
264	A36	25c ocher & multi	48	48
265	A36	50c lt blue & multi	95	95

1974, Mar. 22 Wmk. 314 *Perf. 14*

266 A37	5c	shown	15	15
267 A37	18c	USS Saginaw	38	38
268 A37	25c	HMS Rothesay	50	50
269 A37	50c	HMCS Ottawa	1.00	1.00
a.		Souvenir sheet of 4, #266-269	3.00	3.00

INTERPEX Phil. Exhib., NYC, Mar. 22-24.

Famous Explorers — A38

1974, Aug. 19 *Perf. 14½*

270 A38	5c	Columbus	15	15
271 A38	10c	Sir Walter Raleigh	25	25
272 A38	25c	Sir Martin Frobisher	65	65
273 A38	40c	Sir Francis Drake	1.10	1.10
a.		Souvenir sheet of 4, #270-273	2.25	2.25

Sea Shells A39

1974, Sept. 30 *Perf. 13x13½*

274 A39	5c	Trumpet triton	24	24
275 A39	18c	West Indian murex	80	80
276 A39	25c	Bleeding tooth	1.10	1.10
277 A39	75c	Virgin Island latirus	3.50	3.50
a.		Souvenir sheet of 4, #274-277	7.50	7.50

St. Mary, Aldermanbury, London, — A40

Design: 50c, St. Mary, Fulton, Missouri.

1974, Nov. 30 Wmk. 373 *Perf. 14*

278 A40	10c	multicolored	16	16
279 A40	50c	multicolored	85	85
a.		Souvenir sheet of 2, #278-279	1.40	1.40

Sir Winston Churchill (1874-1965).

Figurehead from "Boreas" — A41

Figureheads: 18c, The Golden Hind. 40c, Crowned lion from the "Superb." 85c, Warrior, from the "Formidable."

Perf. 13½x13

1975, Mar. 14 Wmk. 314

280 A41	5c	multicolored	15	15
281 A41	18c	multicolored	40	40
282 A41	40c	multicolored	85	85
283 A41	85c	multicolored	1.65	1.65
a.		Souv. sheet of 4, #280-283, perf. 14	4.50	4.50

INTERPEX, 17th Phil. Exhib., NYC, Mar. 14-16.

Rock Beauty A42

Designs: Fish.

1975 Wmk. 373 *Perf. 14*

284 A42	½c	shown	15	15
285 A42	1c	Squirrelfish	15	15
286 A42	3c	Queen triggerfish	15	15
287 A42	5c	Blue angelfish	15	15
288 A42	8c	Stoplight parrotfish	16	16
289 A42	10c	Queen angelfish	22	22
290 A42	12c	Nassau grouper	25	25
291 A42	13c	Blue tang	25	25
292 A42	15c	Sergeant major	30	30
293 A42	18c	Jewfish	38	38
294 A42	20c	Bluehead wrasse	42	42
295 A42	25c	Gray angelfish	55	55
296 A42	60c	Glasseye snapper	1.25	1.25
297 A42	$1	Blue chromis	2.00	2.00
298 A42	$2.50	French angelfish	5.25	5.25
299 A42	$3	Queen parrotfish	6.25	6.25
300 A42	$5	Four-eye butterflyfish	10.50	10.50
		Nos. 284-300 (17)	28.38	28.38

Issue dates: $5, Aug. 15. Others, June 16.

½c, 5c, 8c, 10c, 12c, 13c, 15c, 20c reissued dated "1977."

St. Georges Parish School A43

Designs: 25c, Legislative Council Building. 40c, Mace and gavel of Legislative Council. 75c, Scroll with dates of historical events.

1975, Nov. 27 Litho. Wmk. 373

301 A43	5c	ultra & multi	15	15
302 A43	25c	green & multi	50	50
303 A43	40c	ocher & multi	80	80
304 A43	75c	ultra & multi	1.50	1.50

Restoration of Legislative Council, 25th anniv.

Copper Mine Point A44

Historic Sites: 18c, Dr. Thornton's Ruin, Pleasant Valley. 50c, Callwood distillery. 75c, The Dungeon.

1976, Mar. 12 Litho. *Perf. 14½*

305 A44	5c	red & multi	15	15
306 A44	18c	red & multi	35	35
307 A44	50c	red & multi	1.00	1.00
308 A44	75c	red & multi	1.50	1.50

Massachusetts Brig Hazard — A45

Designs: 22c, American Privateer Spy. 40c, Continental Navy Frigate Raleigh. 75c, Frigate Alliance and HMS Trepasy.

1976, May 29 Wmk. 373 *Perf. 14*

309 A45	8c	multicolored	28	20
310 A45	22c	multicolored	70	52
311 A45	40c	multicolored	1.40	1.00
312 A45	75c	multicolored	2.50	1.75
a.		Souvenir sheet of 4, #309-312	7.00	7.00

American Bicentennial.

Government House, Tortola A46

Designs: 15c, Government House, St. Croix, vert. 30c, Flags of US and British Virgin Islands, vert. 75c, Arms of British and US Virgin Islands.

1976, Oct. 29 Litho. *Perf. 14*

313 A46	8c	green & multi	15	15
314 A46	15c	green & multi	22	22
315 A46	30c	green & multi	45	45
316 A46	75c	green & multi	1.10	1.10

US and British Virgin Islands Friendship Day, 5th anniversary.

Holy Bible — A47

Designs: 8c, Queen visiting Agricultural Station, Tortola, 1966. 60c, Presentation of Holy Bible.

1977, Feb. 7 *Perf. 14x13½*

317 A47	8c	silver & multi	15	15
318 A47	30c	silver & multi	60	60
319 A47	60c	silver & multi	1.10	1.10

25th anniv. of the reign of Elizabeth II.

For overprints see Nos. 324-326.

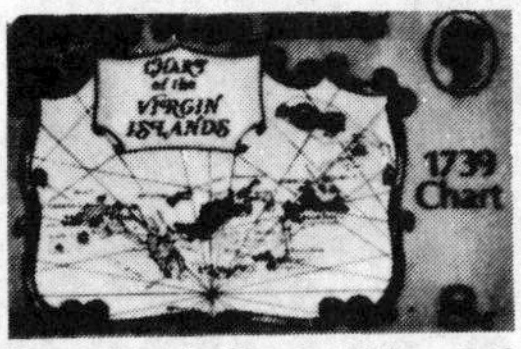

Virgin Islands Chart, 1739 — A48

18th Century Maps of Virgin Islands: 22c, 1758. 30c, 1775. 75c, 1779.

1977, June 12 Wmk. 373 *Perf. 13½*

320 A48	8c	multicolored	22	20
321 A48	22c	multicolored	55	48
322 A48	30c	multicolored	70	60
323 A48	75c	multicolored	1.65	1.50

Type of 1977 Inscribed: "ROYAL VISIT"

Designs: 5c, Queen visiting Agricultural Station, Tortola, 1966. 25c, Holy Bible. 50c, Presentation of Holy Bible.

1977, Oct. 26 Litho. *Perf. 14x13½*

324 A47	5c	yel brn & multi	15	15
325 A47	25c	dk blue & multi	40	40
326 A47	50c	purple & multi	80	80

Caribbean visit of Queen Elizabeth II.

Divers Checking Equipment — A49

Tourist publicity: 5c, Cup coral inside bow of "Rhone." 8c, Sponge growing on superstructure of "Rhone." 22c, Sponge and cup coral. 30c, Scuba diver searching for sponges in cave. 75c, Marine life.

1977, Dec. 15 Wmk. 373 *Perf. 13½*

327 A49	½c	multicolored	15	15
328 A49	5c	multicolored	15	15
329 A49	8c	multicolored	20	20
330 A49	22c	multicolored	52	52
331 A49	30c	multicolored	70	70
332 A49	75c	multicolored	1.75	1.75
		Nos. 327-332 (6)	3.47	3.47

Corals A50

1978, Feb. 10 *Perf. 14*

333 A50	8c	Fire	25	25
334 A50	15c	Staghorn	45	45
335 A50	40c	Brain	1.10	1.10
336 A50	75c	Elkhorn	2.00	2.00

Elizabeth II Coronation Anniversary Issue

Common Design Types

Souvenir Sheet

1978, June 2 Unwmk. *Perf. 15*

337	Sheet of 6	4.75	4.75
a.	CD326 50c Falcon of the Plantagenets	75	75
b.	CD327 50c Elizabeth II	75	75
c.	CD328 50c Iguana	75	75

No. 337 contains 2 se-tenant strips of Nos. 337a-337c, separated by horizontal gutter.

Lignum Vitae A51

Flowering Trees: 22c, Ginger thomas. 40c, Dog almond. 75c, White cedar.

1978, Sept. 4 Litho. *Perf. 13x13½*

338 A51	8c	multicolored	20	20
339 A51	22c	multicolored	52	52
340 A51	40c	multicolored	90	90
341 A51	75c	multicolored	2.00	2.00
a.		Souvenir sheet of 4, #338-341	3.75	3.75

Eurema Lisa — A52

Butterflies: 22c, Dione vanillae. 30c, Heliconius charitonius. 75c, Hemiargus hanno.

1978, Dec. 4 Wmk. 373 *Perf. 14*

342 A52	5c	multicolored	22	18
343 A52	22c	multicolored	80	65
a.		Sheet of 9, 6 #342, 3 #343	4.50	4.50
344 A52	30c	multicolored	1.00	90
345 A52	75c	multicolored	2.25	2.25

Spiny Lobsters A53

Conservation: 15c, Iguana, vert. 22c, Hawksbill turtle. 75c, Black coral, vert.

1979, Feb. 10 Litho.

346 A53	5c	multicolored	15	15
347 A53	15c	multicolored	50	35
348 A53	22c	multicolored	70	55
349 A53	75c	multicolored	2.00	1.75
a.		Souvenir sheet of 4, #346-349	3.50	3.50

Strawberry Cactus — A54

West Indies Girl and Church — A55

Native Cacti: 5c, Snowy cactus. 13c, Barrel cactus. 22c, Tree cactus. 30c, Prickly pear. 75c, Dildo cactus.

1979, May 7 Wmk. 373 *Perf. 14*

350 A54 ½c multicolored 15 15
351 A54 5c multicolored 15 15
352 A54 13c multicolored 28 28
353 A54 22c multicolored 50 50
354 A54 30c multicolored 65 65
355 A54 75c multicolored 1.65 1.65
Nos. 350-355 (6) 3.38 3.38

1979, July 9 *Perf. 14x14½*

Children and IYC Emblem: 10c, African boy and dancers. 13c, Asian girl and children playing. $1, European girl and bicycle.

356 A55 5c multicolored 15 15
357 A55 10c multicolored 16 16
358 A55 13c multicolored 20 20
359 A55 $1 multicolored 1.50 1.50
a. Souvenir sheet of 4, #356-359 2.25 2.25

International Year of the Child.

No. 118 — A56

Pencil Urchin — A57

Rowland Hill's Signature and: 13c, Virgin Islands No. 11, horiz. 75c, Unissued Great Britain 2sh stamp, 1910, horiz. $1, Virgin Islands No. 8c.

1979, Oct. 1 Photo. *Perf. 13½*

360 A56 5c multicolored 15 15
361 A56 13c multicolored 24 24
362 A56 75c multicolored 1.40 1.40

Souvenir Sheet

363 A56 $1 multicolored 1.75 1.75

Sir Rowland Hill (1795-1879), originator of penny postage.

For overprints see Nos. 389-390.

1979-80 Litho. *Perf. 14*

364 A57 ½c Calcified algae 15 15
365 A57 1c Purple-tipped sea anemone 15 15
366 A57 3c Starfish 15 15
367 A57 5c shown 15 15
368 A57 8c Triton's trumpet 15 15
369 A57 10c Christmas tree worms 18 18
370 A57 13c Flamingo tongue snails 22 *22*
371 A57 15c Spider crab 28 28
372 A57 18c Sea squirts 32 *32*
373 A57 20c Tree tulip 35 35
374 A57 25c Rooster tail conch 45 45
375 A57 30c Fighting conch 55 55
376 A57 60c Mangrove crab 1.10 *1.10*
377 A57 $1 Coral polyps 1.75 1.75
378 A57 $2.50 Peppermint shrimp 4.50 4.50
379 A57 $3 West Indian murex 5.25 5.25
380 A57 $5 Carpet anemone 9.00 9.00
Nos. 364-380 (17) 24.70 24.70

Issue dates: 5c, 8c, 10c, 15c, 20c, 25c, $2.50, $3, Dec. 17. Others, Apr. 1, 1980.

Nos. 367-368, 370-371, 373, 375 reissued inscribed 1982.

For overprints see Nos. O1-O15.

Rotary Athletic Meet, Tortola, Emblem A58

1980, Mar. 3 Litho. *Perf. 13½x14*

381 A58 8c shown 15 15
382 A58 22c Paul P. Harris 35 35
383 A58 60c Mount Sage National Park 1.00 1.00
384 A58 $1 Anniversary emblem 1.50 1.50
a. Souvenir sheet of 4, #381-384 3.25 3.25

Rotary International, 75th anniv.

Brown Booby, London 1980 Emblem A59

1980, May 6 Wmk. 373 *Perf. 14*

385 A59 20c shown 35 35
386 A59 25c Magnificent frigatebird 45 45
387 A59 50c White-tailed tropic bird 90 90
388 A59 75c Brown pelican 1.40 1.40
a. Souvenir sheet of 4, #385-388 3.50 3.50

London 80 Intl. Stamp Exhib., May 6-14.

Nos. 361-362 Overprinted:
"CARIBBEAN
COMMONWEALTH
PARLIAMENTARY
ASSOCIATION
MEETING
TORTOLA 11-19 JULY 1980"

1980, July 7 Photo. *Perf. 13½*

389 A56 13c multicolored 24 24
390 A56 75c multicolored 1.40 1.40

Sir Francis Drake — A60

1980, Sept. 26 Litho. *Perf. 14½*

391 A60 8c shown 15 15
392 A60 15c Queen Elizabeth I 24 24
393 A60 30c Drake knighted 48 48
394 A60 75c Golden Hinde 1.25 1.25
a. Souvenir sheet of 4, #391-394 2.25 2.25

400th anniv. of circumnavigation of the world.

Jost Van Dyke A61

1980, Dec. 1 Wmk. 373 *Perf. 14*

395 A61 2c shown 15 15
396 A61 5c Peter Island 15 15
397 A61 13c Virgin Gorda 22 22
398 A61 22c Anegada 38 38
399 A61 30c Norman Island 50 50
400 A61 $1 Tortola 1.65 1.65
a. Souvenir sheet of 1 2.00 2.00
Nos. 395-400 (6) 3.05 3.05

Dancing Lady — A62

1981, Mar. 3 Litho. *Perf. 11*

401 A62 5c shown 15 15
402 A62 20c Love in the mist 35 35
403 A62 22c Red pineapple 38 38
404 A62 75c Dutchman's pipe 1.25 1.25
405 A62 $1 Maiden apple 1.65 1.65
Nos. 401-405 (5) 3.78 3.78

Royal Wedding Issue
Common Design Type

1981, July 22 Litho. *Perf. 14*

406 CD331 10c Bouquet 16 16
407 CD331 35c Charles, Queen Mother 60 60
408 CD331 $1.25 Couple 2.00 2.00

#406-408 each se-tenant with decorative label.

Duke of Edinburgh's Awards, 25th Anniv. — A63

1981, Sept. 16 Wmk. 373 *Perf. 14*

409 A63 10c Stamp collecting 16 16
410 A63 15c Running 25 25
411 A63 50c Camping 85 85
412 A63 $1 Duke of Edinburgh 1.65 1.65

Intl. Year of the Disabled A64

1981, Oct. 19 Litho. *Perf. 14*

413 A64 15c Children 30 30
414 A64 20c Fort Charlotte Children's Center 40 40
415 A64 30c Playing music 60 60
416 A64 $1 Center, diff. 2.00 2.00

A65

A66

Virgin and Child (Christmas): Details from Adoration of the Shepherds, by Rubens. 50c, horiz.

1981, Nov. 30 Litho. *Perf. 14*

417 A65 5c multicolored 15 15
418 A65 15c multicolored 24 24
419 A65 30c multicolored 48 48
420 A65 $1 multicolored 2.00 2.00

Souvenir Sheet

421 A65 50c multicolored 1.00 1.00

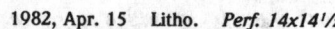

1982, Apr. 15 Litho. *Perf. 14x14½*

Hummingbirds on local flora.

422 A66 15c Green-throated carib, erythrina 35 35
423 A66 30c Same, bougainvillea 70 70
424 A66 35c Antillean crested hummingbird, granadilla passiflora 80 80
425 A66 $1.25 Same, hibiscus 2.75 2.75

10th Anniv. of Lions Club of Tortola A67

1982, May 3 *Perf. 13½x14*

426 A67 10c Helping disabled 18 18
427 A67 20c Headquarters 35 35
428 A67 30c Map 50 50
429 A67 $1.50 Emblem 2.50 2.50
a. Souvenir sheet of 4, #426-429 3.75 3.75

Princess Diana Issue
Common Design Type

1982, July 1 Litho. *Perf. 14*

430 CD333 10c Arms 16 16
431 CD333 35c Diana 55 55
432 CD333 50c Wedding 80 80
433 CD333 $1.50 Portrait 2.50 2.50

10th Anniv. of Air BVI (Natl. Airline) A68

1982, Sept. 10 Wmk. 373 *Perf. 14*

434 A68 10c Douglas DC-3 20 20
435 A68 15c Britten-Norman Islander 30 30
436 A68 60c Hawker-Siddeley 1.20 1.20
437 A68 75c Planes 1.50 1.50

Scouting Year A69

1982, Nov. 18

438 A69 8c Emblem, Flag raising 16 16
439 A69 20c Cub scout, nature study 40 40
440 A69 50c Kayak, sea scout 1.00 1.00
441 A69 $1 Camp Brownsea Is., Baden-Powell 2.00 2.00

Commonwealth Day — A70

1983, Mar. 14 *Perf. 13½x14*

442 A70 10c Legislature in session 16 16
443 A70 30c Wind surfing 52 52
444 A70 35c Globe 60 60
445 A70 75c Flags 1.25 1.25

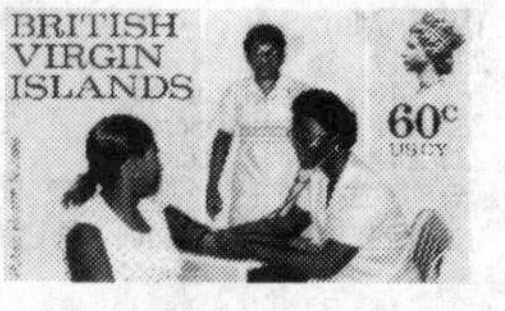

Nursing Week A71

1983, May 9 Litho. *Perf. 14½*

446 A71 10c Florence Nightingale (1820-1910), vert. 18 18
447 A71 30c Nurse, assistant, vert. 55 55
448 A71 60c Public health 1.10 1.10
449 A71 75c Peebles Hospital 1.40 1.40

Boat Building A72

1983, July 25 *Perf. 14*

450 A72 15c First stage 30 30
451 A72 25c 2nd stage 50 50
452 A72 50c Launching 1.00 1.00
453 A72 $1 First voyage 1.90 1.90
a. Souvenir sheet of 4, #450-453 4.75 4.75

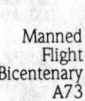

Manned Flight Bicentenary A73

1983, Sept. 15 Wmk. 373 *Perf. 14*

454 A73 10c Grumman Goose 16 16
455 A73 30c De Havilland Heron 50 50
456 A73 60c EMB Bandeirante 1.00 1.00
457 A73 $1.25 Hawker-Siddeley 748 2.00 2.00

Christmas — A74

Raphael Paintings.

1983, Nov. 7 Litho. *Perf. 14½*

458 A74 8c Madonna & Child with Infant Baptist 15 15
459 A74 15c La Belle Jardiniere 28 28
460 A74 50c Madonna del Granduca 95 95
461 A74 $1 Terranuova Madonna 1.90 1.90
a. Souvenir sheet of 4, #458-461 3.50 3.50

World Chess Federation, 60th Anniv. A75

1984, Feb. 20 Litho. *Perf. 14*

462 A75 10c Local tournament 30 30
463 A75 35c Chess pieces, vert. 1.00 1.00
464 A75 75c 1980 Olympiad, Winning board, vert. 2.25 2.25
465 A75 $1 Gold medal 3.25 3.25

Lloyd's List Issue

Common Design Type

1984, Apr. 16 Litho. *Perf. 14½x14*

466 CD335 15c Port Purcell, Tortola 30 30
467 CD335 25c Boeing 747 50 50
468 CD335 50c Shipwreck of RMS Rhone 1.00 1.00
469 CD335 $1 Booker Viking 2.00 2.00

Souvenir Sheet

UPU Congress A76

1984, May 16 Wmk. 373 *Perf. 14*

470 A76 $1 Emblem, jet, mailboat 2.00 2.00

1984 Summer Olympics A77

1984, July 3

471 A77 15c Runners 35 35
472 A77 15c Runner 35 35
473 A77 20c Wind surfers 48 48
474 A77 20c Wind surfer 48 48
475 A77 30c Yachts 70 70
476 A77 30c Yacht 70 70
Nos. 471-476 (6) 3.06 3.06

Souvenir Sheet

477 A77 $1 Torch bearer, vert. 2.00 2.00

Stamps of same demonination se-tenant.

Festival (Slavery Abolition Sesquicentennial) A78

Designs: No. 478: a, Steel band. b, Calypso dancers. c, Dancers (men). d, Woman in traditional dress. e, Parade float.

No. 479 (Sail color of boat(s) in foreground): a, Green & white. b, Red & white, white, purple & white. c, white, yellow & white, blue & white. d, Yellow, red & white. e, Purple & white, white.

Nos. 478 and 479 each in continuous design.

1984, Aug. 14 *Perf. 13½x14*

478 Strip of 5, Parade 95 95
a.-e. A78 10c, any single 18 18
479 Strip of 5, Regatta 2.75 2.75
a.-e. A78 30c, any single 55 55

Local Boats A79

1984, Nov. 15 Wmk. 373 *Perf. 13*

480 A79 10c Sloop 25 25
481 A79 35c Fishing boat 80 80
482 A79 60c Schooner 1.50 1.50
483 A79 75c Cargo boat 1.75 1.75
a. Souvenir sheet of 4, #480-483 3.75 3.75

New Coinage A80

1985, Jan. 15 Litho. *Perf. 14½*

484 A80 1c Hawksbill Turtle 15 15
485 A80 5c Bonito 15 15
486 A80 10c Great Barricuda 20 20
487 A80 25c Blue Marlin 50 50
488 A80 50c Dolphin 1.00 1.00
489 A80 $1 Spotfin Butterfly Fish 2.00 2.00
a. Miniature sheet of 6, #484-489 4.00 4.00
Nos. 484-489 (6) 4.00 4.00

Birds — A81

1985, July 3 Wmk. 373 *Perf. 14*

490 A81 1c Boatswain bird 15 15
491 A81 2c Night gaulin 15 15
492 A81 5c Rain bird 15 15
493 A81 8c Mockingbird 18 18
494 A81 10c Chinchary 25 25
495 A81 12c Wild pigeon 28 28
496 A81 15c Bittlin 35 35
497 A81 18c Blach witch 40 *40*
498 A81 20c Pond shakey 45 45
499 A81 25c Killy-killy 55 55
500 A81 30c Thrushie 70 70
501 A81 35c Marmi dove 80 *80*
502 A81 40c Little gaulin 95 *95*
503 A81 50c Ground dove 1.10 1.10
504 A81 60c Blue gaulin 1.40 1.40
505 A81 $1 Pimleco 2.25 2.25
506 A81 $2 White booby 4.75 4.75
507 A81 $3 Cow bird 6.75 6.75
508 A81 $5 Turtle dove 11.50 11.50
Nos. 490-508 (19) 33.11 33.11

For overprints see Nos. O16-O34.

1987, Oct. 28 Wmk. 384

494a A81 10c 30 30
496a A81 15c 45 45
498a A81 20c 60 60
499a A81 25c 75 75
501a A81 35c 1.05 1.05
505a A81 $1 3.00 3.00
507a A81 $3 9.00 9.00
Nos. 494a-507a (7) 15.15 15.15

Queen Mother, 85th Birthday — A82

Audubon Birth Bicent. — A83

Portraits.

1985, Aug. 26 Litho. *Perf. 12½*

509 A82 10c Facing right 20 20
510 A82 10c Facing left 20 20
511 A82 25c Facing right 50 50
512 A82 25c Facing left 50 50
513 A82 50c Facing right 1.00 1.00
514 A82 50c Facing forward 1.00 1.00
515 A82 75c Facing right 1.50 1.50
516 A82 75c Facing forward 1.50 1.50
Nos. 509-516 (8) 6.40 6.40

Souvenir Sheets

1985-86 Litho. *Perf. 13x12½*

517 Sheet of 2 4.00 4.00
a.-b. A82 $1 dull grn & multi 2.00 2.00
518 Sheet of 2 4.00 4.00
a.-b. A82 $1 orange & multi 2.00 2.00
519 Sheet of 2 10.00 10.00
a.-b. A82 $2.50 dl yel & multi 5.00 5.00

Issue dates: No. 517, Dec. 18. Nos. 518-519, Feb. 18, 1986.

For overprints see Nos. 528-531.

1985, Dec. 17 *Perf. 15*

520 A83 5c Seaside sparrow 15 15
521 A83 30c Passenger pigeon 60 60
522 A83 50c Yellow-breasted chat 1.00 1.00
523 A83 $1 American kestrel 2.00 2.00

Cruise Ships — A84

1986, Jan. 27

524 A84 35c Flying Cloud 65 65
525 A84 50c Newport Clipper 95 95
526 A84 75c Cunard Countess 1.40 1.40
527 A84 $1 Sea Goddess 1.90 1.90

Nos. 511-512, 515-516 Ovptd. "MIAMI / B.V.I. / INAUGURAL FLIGHT"

1986, Apr. 17 Litho. *Perf. 12½*

528 A82 25c on No. 511 50 50
529 A82 25c on No. 512 50 50
530 A82 75c on No. 515 1.50 1.50
531 A82 75c on No. 516 1.50 1.50

Queen Elizabeth II, 60th Birthday — A85

Perf. 13x12½, 12½x13

1986, Apr. 21 Litho.

532 A85 12c Portrait, 1958 22 22
533 A85 35c Maundy service 65 65
534 A85 $1.50 Contemporary photograph 2.75 2.75
535 A85 $2 Canberra, 1982, vert. 3.75 3.75

Souvenir Sheet

536 A85 $3 Contemporary photograph, diff. 6.00 6.00

Wedding of Prince Andrew and Sarah Ferguson — A86

1986, July 23 *Perf. 12½*

537 A86 35c Couple, vert. 70 70
538 A86 35c Sarah, vert. 70 70
539 A86 $1 Andrew 2.00 2.00
540 A86 $1 Sarah, diff. 2.00 2.00

Stamps of the same denomination exist se-tenant.

Nos. 537-540 Overprinted "Congratulations to T.R.H. The Duke & Duchess of York" were not issued.

Traditional Rum Production A87

1986, July 30 *Perf. 14*

541 A87 12c Harvesting sugar cane 32 32
542 A87 40c Grinding 1.10 1.10
543 A87 60c Distillery 1.65 1.65
544 A87 $1 Transport 2.75 2.75

Souvenir Sheet

545 A87 $2 Up Spirits ceremony, 19th cent. 5.50 5.50

Souvenir Sheet

Wedding of Prince Andrew and Sarah Ferguson — A88

1986, Oct. 15 Litho. *Perf. 13x12½*

546 A88 $4 multicolored 8.00 7.00

Cable-Laying Ships — A89

1986, Oct. 15 Wmk. 380 *Perf. 12½*

547	A89	35c Sentinel	70	70
548	A89	35c Retriever	70	70
549	A89	60c Cable Enterprise	1.20	1.20
550	A89	60c Mercury	1.20	1.20
551	A89	75c Recorder	1.50	1.50
552	A89	75c Pacific Guardian	1.50	1.50
553	A89	$1 Great Eastern	2.00	2.00
554	A89	$1 Cable Venture	2.00	2.00
		Nos. 547-554 (8)	10.80	10.80

Souvenir Sheets

555		Sheet of 2	1.60	1.60
a.-b.	A89	40c, like #547-548	80	80
556		Sheet of 2	2.00	2.00
a.-b.	A89	50c, like #549-550	1.00	1.00
557		Sheet of 2	3.25	3.25
a.-b.	A89	80c, like #551-552	1.60	1.60
558		Sheet of 2	6.00	6.00
a.-b.	A89	$1.50, like #553-554	3.00	3.00

Cable and wireless in the islands, 20th anniv. Stamps of the same denomination printed se-tenant.

Souvenir Sheets

Statue of Liberty, Cent. — A90

Various views of the statue.

1986, Dec. 15 Litho. *Perf. 14*

559	A90	50c multicolored	95	95
560	A90	75c multicolored	1.65	1.65
561	A90	90c multicolored	1.75	1.75
562	A90	$1 multicolored	2.00	2.00
563	A90	$1.25 multicolored	2.50	2.50
564	A90	$1.50 multicolored	3.00	3.00
565	A90	$1.75 multicolored	3.50	3.50
566	A90	$2 multicolored	3.75	3.75
567	A90	$2.50 multicolored	5.00	5.00
		Nos. 559-567 (9)	24.10	24.10

A91

Shipwrecks A92

1987, Apr. 15 *Perf. 14*

572	A91	12c Spanish galleon, 18th cent.	35	35
573	A91	35c HMS Astrea, 1808	1.00	1.00
574	A91	75c RMS Rhone, 1867	2.00	2.00
575	A91	$1.50 SS Rocus, 1929	4.25	4.25

Souvenir Sheet

576	A92	$2.50 Brig Volvart, 1918	7.00	7.00

Virgin Islands stamps can be mounted in the Scott British Leeward Islands album.

Natl. Flags, Outline Maps — A93

Botanical Gardens — A94

1987, May 28

577	A93	10c Montserrat	20	20
578	A93	15c Grenada	28	28
579	A93	20c Dominica	38	38
580	A93	25c St. Kitts-Nevis	48	48
581	A93	35c St. Vincent and Grenadines	65	65
582	A93	50c Virgin Isls.	95	95
583	A93	75c Antigua & Barbuda	1.40	1.40
584	A93	$1 St. Lucia	1.90	1.90
		Nos. 577-584 (8)	6.24	6.24

11th Meeting of the Organization of Eastern Caribbean States.

1987, Aug. 12 Wmk. 384

585	A94	12c Spider lily	24	24
586	A94	35c Barrel cactus	70	70
587	A94	$1 Wild plantain	2.00	2.00
588	A94	$1.50 Little butterfly orchid	3.00	3.00

Souvenir Sheet

589	A94	$2.50 White cedar	5.00	5.00

Postal Service Bicent. A95

Designs: 10c, 18th Cent. packet, #7 canceled "A13." 20c, Map of the islands, #22 canceled "A91." 35c, Tortola Post Office and Customs House, and #5 canceled "Tortola De 20 61." $1.50, Mail plane and #154 canceled "Road town No 2 64 Tortola W.I." $2.50, Late 19th cent. steam packet and #10 canceled "A Tortola Ap 12 70."

1987, Dec. 17 Litho. *Perf. 14½*

590	A95	10c multicolored	28	28
591	A95	20c multicolored	55	55
592	A95	35c multicolored	1.00	1.00
593	A95	$1.50 multicolored	4.25	4.25

Souvenir Sheet

594	A95	$2.50 multicolored	5.00	5.00

Paintings by Titian — A96

Designs: 10c, Salome, 1512. 12c, Man with the Glove, c. 1520-1522. 20c, Fabrizio Salvaresio, 1558. 25c, Daughter of Roberto Strozzi, 1542. 40c, Pope Julius II. 50c, Bishop Ludovico Beccadelli, 1552. 60c, Philip II. $1, Empress Isabella of Portugal, 1548. No. 603, Emperor Charles V at Muhlberg, 1548. No. 604, Pope Paul III and His Grandsons, 1546.

Perf. 13½x14

1988, Aug. 11 Unwmk.

595	A96	10c multicolored	20	20
596	A96	12c multicolored	24	24
597	A96	20c multicolored	40	40
598	A96	25c multicolored	50	50
599	A96	40c multicolored	80	80
600	A96	50c multicolored	1.00	1.00
601	A96	60c multicolored	1.20	1.20
602	A96	$1 multicolored	2.00	2.00
		Nos. 595-602 (8)	6.34	6.34

Souvenir Sheet

603	A96	$2 multicolored	4.00	4.00
604	A96	$2 multicolored	4.00	4.00

1st Annual Open Chess Tournament A97

Designs: 35c, Pawn and Transporter aircraft over Sir Francis Drake Channel. $1, King and Jose Raul Capablanca (1888-1942), Cuban chess master and world champion from 1921 to 1927. $2, Match scene.

1988, Aug. 25 Unwmk. *Perf. 14*

605	A97	35c multicolored	70	70
606	A97	$1 multicolored	2.00	2.00

Souvenir Sheet

607	A97	$2 multicolored	4.00	4.00

1988 Summer Olympics, Seoul A98

1988, Sept. 8

608	A98	12c Hurdling	24	24
609	A98	20c Windsurfing	40	40
610	A98	75c Basketball	1.50	1.50
611	A98	$1 Tennis	2.00	2.00

Souvenir Sheet

612	A98	$2 Running	4.00	4.00

Intl. Red Cross, 125th Anniv. A99

Safety warnings and steps in administering cardiopulmonary resuscitation (CPR): 12c, "Don't swim alone." 30c, "No swimming during electrical storms." 60c, "Don't eat before swimming." $1, "Proper equipment for boating." No. 617a, Turn victim on back. No. 617b, Position victim's chin so breathing passages are not blocked. No. 617c, Mouth-to-mouth resuscitation. No. 617d, Chest compressions. Nos. 617a-617d vert.

1988, Sept. 26

613	A99	12c multicolored	24	24
614	A99	30c multicolored	60	60
615	A99	60c multicolored	1.20	1.20
616	A99	$1 multicolored	2.00	2.00

Souvenir Sheet

617		Sheet of 4	4.00	4.00
a.-d.	A99	50c any single	1.00	1.00

#617a-617d has a continuous design.

Visit of Princess Alexandra — A100

World Wildlife Fund — A101

Various photographs of the princess.

1988, Nov. 9 Litho. *Perf. 14*

618	A100	40c shown	80	80
619	A100	$1.50 multi, diff.	3.00	3.00

Souvenir Sheet

620	A100	$2 multi, diff.	4.00	4.00

1988, Nov. 15

Brown pelicans, *Pelecanus Occidentalis.*

621	A101	10c Pelican in flight	20	20
622	A101	12c Perched	24	24
623	A101	15c Close-up of head	30	30
624	A101	35c Swallowing fish	70	70

Reptiles, Marine Mammals and Birds A102

Designs: 20c, Anegada rock iguana. 40c, Virgin gorda dwarf gecko. 60c, Hawksbill turtle. $1, Humpback whale. No. 629, Northern shoveler, American widgeon and ring-necked ducks. No. 630, Trunk turtle.

1988, Nov. 15

625	A102	20c multicolored	40	40
626	A102	40c multicolored	80	80
627	A102	60c multicolored	1.20	1.20
628	A102	$1 multicolored	2.00	2.00

Souvenir Sheets

629	A102	$2 multicolored	4.00	4.00
630	A102	$2 multicolored	4.00	4.00

Spring Regatta A103

Various yachts.

1989, Apr. 7 Litho. *Perf. 14*

631	A103	12c multi, diff., vert.	24	24
632	A103	40c shown	80	80
633	A103	75c multi, diff., vert.	1.50	1.50
634	A103	$1 multi, diff.	2.00	2.00

Souvenir Sheet

635	A103	$2 multi, diff., vert.	4.00	4.00

Pre-Columbian Societies and Their Customs — A104

1989, May 18

636	A104	10c Hammock	20	20
637	A104	20c Making a fire	40	40
638	A104	25c Carvers	50	50
639	A104	$1.50 Arawak family	3.00	3.00

Souvenir Sheet

640	A104	$2 Ritual	4.00	4.00

Discovery of America 500th anniv. (in 1992).

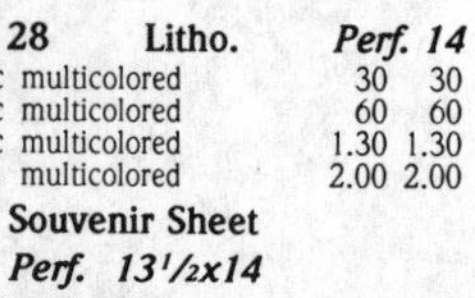

1st Moon Landing, 20th Anniv. A105

Highlights of the Apollo 11 mission: 15c, Lunar surface, mission emblem. 30c, Buzz Aldrin conducting solar wind experiment. 65c, Raising American flag. $1, Recovery of crew after splashdown. $2, Portrait of crew.

1989, Sept. 28 Litho. *Perf. 14*

641	A105	15c multicolored	30	30
642	A105	30c multicolored	60	60
643	A105	65c multicolored	1.30	1.30
644	A105	$1 multicolored	2.00	2.00

Souvenir Sheet

Perf. 13½x14

645	A105	$2 multicolored	4.00	4.00

No. 645 contains one 37x46mm stamp.

Methodist Church, 200th Anniv. A106

Designs: 12c, Black Harry, Nathaniel Gilbert preaching. 25c, Book symbolizing role of the church in education. 35c, East End Methodist Church, 1810. $1.25, John Wesley, modern youth choir. $2, Thomas Coke.

1989, Oct. 24 *Perf. 14*

646 A106 12c multicolored 24 24
647 A106 25c multicolored 50 50
648 A106 35c multicolored 70 70
649 A106 $1.25 multicolored 2.50 2.50

Souvenir Sheet

650 A106 $2 multicolored 4.00 4.00

1990 World Cup Soccer Championships, Italy — A107

Various athletes.

1989, Nov. 6

651 A107 5c shown 15 15
652 A107 10c multi, diff. 20 20
653 A107 20c multi, diff. 40 40
654 A107 $1.75 multi, diff. 3.50 3.50

Souvenir Sheet

655 A107 $2 Natl. team 4.00 4.00

Princess Alexandra, Sunset House A108

Royal Yacht Britiannia — A109

Designs: b, Princess Margaret, Government House. c, Hon. Angus Ogilvy, Little Dix Bay Hotel. d, Princess Diana and her children, Necker Island Resort.

1990, May 3 **Litho.** *Perf. 14*

656 Min. sheet of 4 4.00 4.00
a.-d. A108 50c any single 1.00 1.00

Souvenir Sheet

657 A109 $2 multicolored 4.00 4.00

Stamp World London '90.

Audubon's Shearwater A110

1990, May 15

658 A110 5c shown 15 15
659 A110 12c Red-necked pigeon 24 24
660 A110 20c Common gallinule 40 40
661 A110 25c Green heron 50 50
662 A110 40c Yellow warbler 80 80
663 A110 60c Smooth-billed ani 1.20 1.20
664 A110 $1 Antillean crested hummingbird 2.00 2.00
665 A110 $1.25 Black-faced grassquit 2.50 2.50
Nos. 658-665 (8) 7.79 7.79

Souvenir Sheets

666 A110 $2 Egg of royal tern 4.00 4.00
667 A110 $2 Egg of red-billed tropicbird 4.00 4.00

Blue Tang A111

1990, June 18

668 A111 10c shown 20 20
669 A111 35c Glasseye 70 70
670 A111 50c Slippery Dick 1.00 1.00
671 A111 $1 Porkfish 2.00 2.00

Souvenir Sheet

672 A111 $2 Yellowtail snapper 4.00 4.00

A112

A113

1990, Aug. 30 **Litho.** *Perf. 14*

673 A112 12c multicolored 24 24
674 A112 25c multi, diff. 50 50
675 A112 60c multi, diff. 1.25 1.25
676 A112 $1 multi, diff. 2.00 2.00

Souvenir Sheet

677 A112 $2 multi, diff. 4.00 4.00

Queen Mother, 90th birthday.

1990, Dec. 10 **Litho.** *Perf. 14*

Various soccer players.

678 A113 12c multicolored 24 24
679 A113 20c multi, diff. 40 40
680 A113 50c multi, diff. 1.00 1.00
681 A113 $1.25 multi, diff. 2.50 2.50

Souvenir Sheet

682 A113 $2 multi, diff. 4.00 4.00

World Cup Soccer Championships, Italy.

1992 Summer Olympics, Barcelona A114

1990, Dec. 20 **Litho.** *Perf. 14*

683 A114 12c Judo 24 24
684 A114 40c Yachting 80 80
685 A114 60c Hurdles 1.20 1.20
686 A114 $1 Show jumping 2.00 2.00

Souvenir Sheet

687 A114 $2 Windsurfing 4.00 4.00

Copper Mine Ruins A115

1991, Mar. 1 **Litho.** *Perf. 14*

688 A115 10c Cyanthea arborea, vert. 20 20
689 A115 25c shown 50 50
690 A115 35c Mt. Healthy windmill ruin, vert. 70 70
691 A115 $2 Baths, Virgin Gorda 4.00 4.00

National Park Trust.

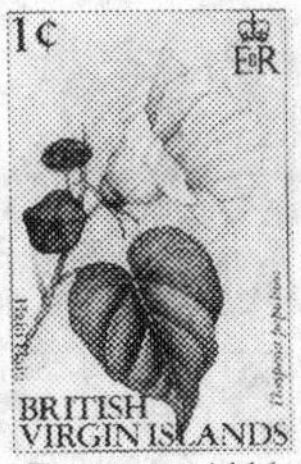

Flowers — A116

Butterflies — A117

1991, May 1 **Litho.** *Perf. 14*

692 A116 1c Haiti Haiti 15 15
693 A116 2c Lobster claw 15 15
694 A116 5c Frangipani 15 15
695 A116 10c Autograph tree 20 20
696 A116 12c Yellow allamanda 24 24
697 A116 15c Lantana 30 30
698 A116 20c Jerusalem thorn 40 40
699 A116 25c Turk's cap 50 50
700 A116 30c Swamp immortelle 60 60
701 A116 35c White cedar 70 70
702 A116 40c Mahoe tree 80 80
703 A116 45c Pinguin 90 90
704 A116 50c Christmas orchid 1.00 1.00
705 A116 70c Lignum vitae 1.40 1.40
706 A116 $1 African tulip tree 2.00 2.00
707 A116 $2 Beach morning glory 4.00 4.00
708 A116 $3 Organ pipe cactus 6.00 6.00
709 A116 $5 Tall ground orchid 10.00 10.00
710 A116 $10 Ground orchid 20.00 20.00
Nos. 692-710 (19) 49.49 49.49

Issue dates: $10, May 1992. Others, May 1, 1991.

For overprints see Nos. O37-O51.

1991, June 28 **Litho.** *Perf. 14*

711 A117 5c Cloudless sulphur 15 15
712 A117 10c Flambeau 20 20
713 A117 15c Caribbean buckeye 30 30
714 A117 20c Gulf fritillary 40 40
715 A117 25c Polydamus swallowtail 50 50
716 A117 30c Little sulphur 60 60
717 A117 35c Zebra 70 70
718 A117 $1.50 Malachite 3.00 3.00
Nos. 711-718 (8) 5.85 5.85

Souvenir Sheets

719 A117 $2 Monarch, horiz. 4.00 4.00
720 A117 $2 Red rim, horiz. 4.00 4.00

Voyages of Discovery A118

Ships of explorers: 12c, Ferdinand Magellan, 1519-1521. 50c, Rene-Robert de la Salle, 1682. 75c, John Cabot, 1497-1498. $1, Jacques Cartier, 1534. $2, Columbus' ship, 1493 woodcut, vert.

1991, Sept. 20 **Litho.** *Perf. 14*

721 A118 12c multicolored 24 24
722 A118 50c multicolored 1.00 1.00
723 A118 75c multicolored 1.50 1.50
724 A118 $1 multicolored 2.00 2.00

Souvenir Sheet

725 A118 $2 multicolored 4.00 4.00

Vincent Van Gogh (1853-1890), Painter — A119

Paintings: 15c, Cottage with Decrepit Barn and Stooping Woman. 30c, Paul Gauguin's Armchair, vert. 75c, Breton Women. $1, Vase with Red Gladioli, vert. $2, The Dance Hall in Arles (detail).

1991, Nov. 1 *Perf. 13*

726 A119 15c multicolored 30 30
727 A119 30c multicolored 60 60
728 A119 75c multicolored 1.50 1.50
729 A119 $1 multicolored 2.00 2.00

Souvenir Sheet

730 A119 $2 multicolored 4.00 4.00

Christmas A120

Entire paintings or details by Quinten Massys: 15c, The Virgin and Child Enthroned. 30c, The Virgin and Child Enthroned, diff. 60c, The Adoration of the Magi. $1, Virgin in Adoration. No. 735, The Virgin Standing with Angels. No. 736, The Adoration of the Magi.

1991, Dec. 12 **Litho.** *Perf. 12*

731 A120 15c multicolored 30 30
732 A120 30c multicolored 60 60
733 A120 60c multicolored 1.20 1.20
734 A120 $1 multicolored 2.00 2.00

Souvenir Sheets

Perf. 14½

735 A120 $2 multicolored 4.00 4.00
736 A120 $2 multicolored 4.00 4.00

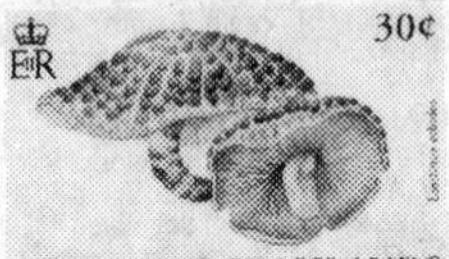

Mushrooms A121

1992, Jan. 15 *Perf. 14*

737 A121 12c Agaricus bisporus, vert. 24 24
738 A121 30c Lentinus edodes 60 60
739 A121 45c Hyrocybe acutoconica, vert. 90 90
740 A121 $1 Gymnopilus chrysopellus 2.00 2.00

Souvenir Sheet

741 A121 $2 Pleurotus ostreatus 4.00 4.00

Queen Elizabeth II's Accession to the Throne, 40th Anniv.

Common Design Type

1992, Feb. 6 **Litho.** *Perf. 14*

742 CD348 12c multicolored 24 24
743 CD348 45c multicolored 90 90
744 CD348 60c multicolored 1.20 1.20
745 CD348 $1 multicolored 2.00 2.00

Souvenir Sheet

746 CD348 $2 multicolored 4.00 4.00

Discovery of America, 500th Anniv. A122

Designs: 10c, Queen Isabella, vert. 15c, Columbus' fleet. 20c, Columbus' second coat of arms, vert. 30c, Landing Monument on Watling Island, Columbus' signature. 45c, Columbus, vert. 50c, Flag of Ferdinand & Isabella, Columbus landing on Watling Island. 70c, Convent at La Rabida, vert. $1.50, Replica of Santa Maria at New York World's Fair, 1964-65. No. 755, Columbus' second fleet. No. 756, Map.

1992, May 26 **Litho.** *Perf. 14*

747 A122 10c multicolored 20 20
748 A122 15c multicolored 30 30
749 A122 20c multicolored 40 40
750 A122 30c multicolored 60 60

751	A122	45c multicolored	90	90
752	A122	50c multicolored	1.00	1.00
753	A122	70c multicolored	1.40	1.40
754	A122	$1.50 multicolored	3.00	3.00
		Nos. 747-754 (8)	7.80	7.80

Souvenir Sheet

755	A122	$2 multicolored	4.00	4.00
756	A122	$2 multicolored	4.00	4.00

1992 Summer Olympics, Barcelona — A123

1992, Aug. **Litho.** ***Perf. 14***

757	A123	15c Basketball	30	30
758	A123	30c Tennis	60	60
759	A123	60c Volleyball	1.20	1.20
760	A123	$1 Soccer	2.00	2.00

Souvenir Sheet

761	A123	$2 Olympic flame	4.00	4.00

Ministerial Government, 25th Anniv. — A124

Designs: 12c, Social progress and development. 15c, Map of Virgin Islands. 45c, Administration complex. $1.30, International finance.

1993, Apr. **Litho.** ***Perf. 14***

762	A124	12c multicolored	24	24
763	A124	15c multicolored	30	30
764	A124	45c multicolored	90	90
765	A124	$1.30 multicolored	2.60	2.60

Tourism A125

Designs: 15c, Swimming from anchored yacht. 30c, Sailboat, vert. 60c, Scuba diver in pink wet-suit. $1, Snorkelers, anchored boat, vert. No. 770a, Trimaran, vert. No. 770b, Scuba diver, vert.

1993, Apr. **Litho.** ***Perf. 14***

766	A125	15c multicolored	30	30
767	A125	30c multicolored	60	60
768	A125	60c multicolored	1.20	1.20
769	A125	$1 multicolored	2.00	2.00

Souvenir Sheet

770	A125	$1 Sheet of 2, #a.-b.	4.00	4.00

Coronation of Queen Elizabeth II, 40th Anniv. A126

Designs: No. 771a, 12c, Official coronation photograph. b, 45c, Dove atop Rod of Equity and Mercy. c, 60c, Royal family. d, $1, Recent color photo.

1993, June 2 **Litho.** ***Perf. 13½x14***

771	A126	Sheet, 2 each #a.-d.	8.75	8.75

A souvenir sheet containing a $2 stamp was not an authorized issue.

Discovery of Virgin Islands, 500th Anniv. A127

Designs: 3c, Ferdinand and Isabella supporting Columbus. 12c, Departure of Columbus. 15c, Departure of second voyage. 25c, Arms, flag of British Virgin Islands. 30c, Columbus, Santa Maria. 45c, Columbus' second fleet at sea. 60c, Rowing ashore. $1, Landing of Columbus. No. 781, Natives watching ships. No. 782, Columbus, two ships of his fleet.

1993, Sept. 24 **Litho.** ***Perf. 14***

773	A127	3c multicolored	15	15
774	A127	12c multicolored	25	25
775	A127	15c multicolored	30	30
776	A127	25c multicolored	50	50
777	A127	30c multicolored	60	60
778	A127	45c multicolored	90	90
779	A127	60c multicolored	1.25	1.25
780	A127	$1 multicolored	2.00	2.00
		Nos. 773-780 (8)	5.95	5.95

Souvenir Sheets

781	A127	$2 multicolored	4.00	4.00
782	A127	$2 multicolored	4.00	4.00

Secondary Education and Library Services, 50th Anniv. A128

Designs: 5c, Historical documents. 10c, Sporting activities. 15c, Stanley W. Nibbs, educator, vert. 20c, Bookmobile. 30c, Norwell E. Harrigan, educator, vert. 35c, Public library's annual summer program. 70c, Text. $1, High school.

Perf. 14x13½, 13½x14

1993, Dec. **Litho.**

783	A128	5c multicolored	15	15
784	A128	10c multicolored	18	18
785	A128	15c multicolored	28	28
786	A128	20c multicolored	38	38
787	A128	30c multicolored	55	55
788	A128	35c multicolored	65	65
789	A128	70c multicolored	1.25	1.25
790	A128	$1 multicolored	1.90	1.90
		Nos. 783-790 (8)	5.34	5.34

Anegada Ground Iguana — A129

Designs: 5c, Crawling right. 10c, Head up to right. 15c, View from behind. 45c, Head up to left. $2, Head.

1994, Jan. **Litho.** ***Perf. 14***

791	A129	5c multicolored	15	15
792	A129	10c multicolored	18	18
793	A129	15c multicolored	28	28
794	A129	45c multicolored	85	85

Souvenir Sheet

795	A129	$2 multicolored	3.75	3.75

World Wildlife Fund.

Rotary Club of Virgin Islands, 25th Anniv. A130

Designs: 15c, Disaster relief airlift. 45c, Kids, Sea "Kats." 50c, Donated hospital equipment. 90c, Paul P. Harris (1868-1947), founder of Rotary Intl.

1994, June 3 **Litho.** ***Perf. 14***

796	A130	15c multicolored	28	28
797	A130	45c multicolored	85	85
798	A130	50c multicolored	95	95
799	A130	90c multicolored	1.65	1.65

Miniature Sheet of 6

First Manned Moon Landing, 25th Anniv. A131

Designs: No. 800a, Anniversary emblem. b, Lunar landing training vehicle. c, Apollo 11 lift-off, July 16, 1969. d, Lunar module Eagle in flight. e, Moon landing site approached by Eagle. f, 1st step on Moon, July 20, 1969.

No. 801, Mission patch, crew signatures.

1994, Sept. 30 **Litho.** ***Perf. 14***

800	A131	50c #a.-f.	6.00	6.00

Souvenir Sheet

801	A131	$2 multicolored	4.00	4.00

WAR TAX STAMPS

Regular Issue of 1913 Overprinted **WAR STAMP**

1916-17 **Wmk. 3** ***Perf. 14***

Die I

MR1	A9	1p scarlet	25	25
a.		1p carmine	1.00	1.00
MR2	A9	3p violet, *yellow*	1.00	1.00

OFFICIAL STAMPS

Catalogue values for unused stamps in this section are for Never Hinged items.

Nos. 365-368, 370-380 Overprinted "OFFICIAL" in Silver

1985, July **Litho.** ***Perf. 14***

O1	A57	1c multi	15	15
O2	A57	3c multi	15	15
O3	A57	5c multi	15	15
O4	A57	8c multi	16	16
O5	A57	13c multi	25	25
O6	A57	15c multi	30	30
O7	A57	18c multi	35	35
O8	A57	20c multi	40	40
O9	A57	25c multi	50	50
O10	A57	30c multi	60	60
O11	A57	60c multi	1.00	1.00
O12	A57	$1 multi	1.75	1.75
O13	A57	$2.50 multi	4.50	4.50
O14	A57	$3 multi	5.25	5.25
O15	A57	$5 multi	9.00	9.00
		Nos. O1-O15 (15)	24.51	24.51

Nos. 490-508 Ovptd. "OFFICIAL"

1986 **Litho.** ***Perf. 14***

O16	A81	1c multicolored	15	15
O17	A81	2c multicolored	15	15
O18	A81	5c multicolored	15	15
O19	A81	8c multicolored	16	16
O20	A81	10c multicolored	20	20
O21	A81	12c multicolored	24	24
O22	A81	15c multicolored	30	30
O23	A81	18c multicolored	36	36
O24	A81	20c multicolored	40	40
O25	A81	25c multicolored	50	50
O26	A81	30c multicolored	60	60
O27	A81	35c multicolored	70	70
O28	A81	40c multicolored	80	80
O29	A81	50c multicolored	90	90
O30	A81	60c multicolored	1.00	1.00
O31	A81	$1 multicolored	1.75	1.75
O32	A81	$2 multicolored	3.50	3.50
O33	A81	$3 multicolored	5.25	5.25
O34	A81	$5 multicolored	9.00	9.00
		Nos. O16-O34 (19)	26.11	26.11

Issue dates: 1c, 5c, 10c, 15c, 20c, 25c, 30c, 35c and $5, July 3. Others, Jan. 28.

Nos. 694-695, 698, 701-706, 708 Ovptd. "OFFICIAL"

1991, Sept. **Litho.** ***Perf. 14***

O37	A116	5c multicolored	15	*15*
O38	A116	10c multicolored	20	*20*
O41	A116	20c multicolored	40	*40*
O44	A116	35c multicolored	70	*70*
O45	A116	40c multicolored	80	*80*
O46	A116	45c multicolored	90	*90*
O47	A116	50c multicolored	1.00	*1.00*
O48	A116	70c multicolored	1.40	*1.40*
O49	A116	$1 multicolored	2.00	*2.00*
O51	A116	$3 multicolored	6.00	*6.00*
		Nos. O37-O51 (10)	13.55	*13.55*

Used values are for c-t-o copies.

Nos. O37-O38, O41, O44-O49, O51 were not available to the general public unused until mid-1992.

This set probably was never used in the Virgin Islands.

Nos. 694-695, 698, 700-706, 708 Ovptd. "OFFICIAL"

1992 **Litho.** ***Perf. 14***

O55	A116	5c multicolored	15	15
O56	A116	10c multicolored	20	20
O59	A116	20c multicolored	*40*	*40*
O61	A116	30c multicolored	*60*	*60*
O62	A116	35c multicolored	70	70
O63	A116	40c multicolored	80	80
O64	A116	45c multicolored	90	90
O65	A116	50c multicolored	1.00	1.00
O66	A116	70c multicolored	1.40	1.40
O67	A116	$1 multicolored	2.00	2.00
O69	A116	$3 multicolored	6.00	6.00
		Nos. O55-O69 (11)	14.15	14.15

Ovpt. on Nos. O55-O56, O59, O61-O67, O69 is 15½mm long. Ovpt. on Nos. O37-O51 is 19mm long.

Dies of British Colonial Stamps Referred to in the Catalogue

DIE A

DIE B

DIE A:
1. The lines in the groundwork vary in thickness and are not uniformly straight.
2. The seventh and eighth lines from the top, in the groundwork, converge where they meet the head.
3. There is a small dash in the upper part of the second jewel in the band of the crown.
4. The vertical color line in front of the throat stops at the sixth line of shading on the neck.

DIE B:
1. The lines in the groundwork are all thin and straight.
2. All the lines of the background are parallel.
3. There is no dash in the upper part of the second jewel in the band of the crown.
4. The vertical color line in front of the throat stops at the eighth line of shading on the neck.

DIE I

DIE II

DIE I:
1. The base of the crown is well below the level of the inner white line around the vignette.
2. The labels inscribed "POSTAGE" and "REVENUE" are cut square at the top.
3. There is a white "bud" on the outer side of the main stem of the curved ornaments in each lower corner.
4. The second (thick) line below the country name has the ends next to the crown cut diagonally.

DIE Ia.
1 as die II.
2 and 3 as die I.

DIE Ib.
1 and 3 as die II.
2 as die I.

DIE II:
1. The base of the crown is aligned with the underside of the white line around the vignette.
2. The labels curve inward at the top inner corners.
3. The "bud" has been removed from the outer curve of the ornaments in each corner.
4. The second line below the country name has the ends next to the crown cut vertically.

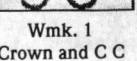

Wmk. 1
Crown and C C

Wmk. 2
Crown and C A

Wmk. 3
Multiple Crown and C A

Wmk. 4
Multiple Crown and Script C A

Wmk. 4a

Wmk. 314
St. Edward's Crown and C A Multiple

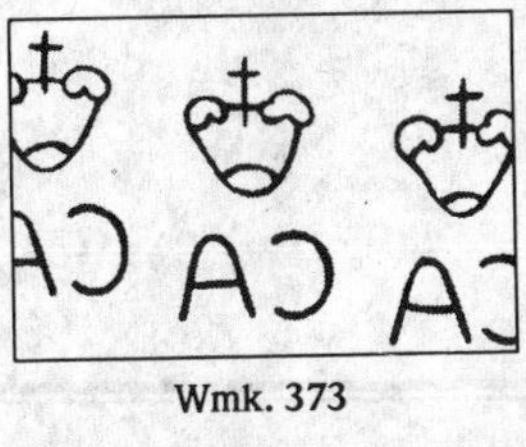
Wmk. 373

Wmk. 384

British Colonial and Crown Agents Watermarks

Watermarks 1 to 4, 314, 373, and 384, common to many British territories, are illustrated here to avoid duplication.

The letters "CC" of Wmk. 1 identify the paper as having been made for the use of the Crown Colonies, while the letters "CA" of the others stand for "Crown Agents." Both Wmks. 1 and 2 were used on stamps printed by De La Rue & Co.

Wmk. 3 was adopted in 1904; Wmk. 4 in 1921; Wmk. 314 in 1957; Wmk. 373 in 1974; and Wmk. 384 in 1985.

In Wmk. 4a, a non-matching crown of the general St. Edwards type (bulging on both sides at top) was substituted for one of the Wmk. 4 crowns which fell off the dandy roll. The non-matching crown occurs in 1950-52 printings in a horizontal row of crowns on certain regular stamps of Johore and Seychelles, and on various postage due stamps of Barbados, Basutoland, British Guiana, Gold Coast, Grenada, Northern Rhodesia, St. Lucia, Swaziland and Trinidad and Tobago. A variation of Wmk. 4a, with the non-matching crown in a horizontal row of crown-CA-crown, occurs on regular stamps of Bahamas, St. Kitts-Nevis and Singapore.

Wmk. 314 was intentionally used sideways, starting in 1966. When a stamp was issued with Wmk. 314 both upright and sideways, the sideways varieties usually are listed also – with minor numbers. In many of the later issues, Wmk. 314 is slightly visible.

Wmk. 373 is usually only faintly visible.

Numerical Index of Vol. 1 Watermark Illustrations

Watermark	Country
1, 2, 3, 4, 4a, 314, 373, 384	British Colonies
1a,1b	Ceylon
5	Antigua
	Natal
	St. Lucia
	St. Vincent
	Turks Islands
5-6	Barbados
	Grenada
	Queensland
6	Ceylon
	New Zealand
	St. Helena
	South Australia
	Tasmania
	Victoria
7	Grenada
	South Australia
8-11	Australia
12-13	Australia
	New South Wales
	Queensland
13	Papua New Guinea
	Tasmania
	Victoria
	Western Australia
14	Bechuanaland
15-16	Cape of Good Hope
17	Fiji
18-24	Great Britain
25-31	Great Britain
29	Bechuanaland
32-35	Great Britain
33	Palestine
36-39	India
40	India
41	Cochin

Watermark	Country
42	Hyderabad
43	Cochin
	Travancore
44	Ireland
45	Jamaica
46	Labuan
47	Johore
	Maldive Islands
	Papua New Guinea
	Sarawak
	South Africa
	Zanzibar
48	Mesopotamia
49-52	Tasmania
49-50	Victoria
49-58	New South Wales
55	Australia
59-63	New Zealand
61	Aitutaki
	Niue
61-62	Cook Islands
62	Samoa
	Tonga
64	New Zealand
65-70	Queensland
70	New South Wales
	South Australia
	Tasmania
	Victoria
	Western Australia
71	Johore
	Sarawak
	Sudan
	Zanzibar
72-73	South Australia
74	Papua New Guinea
	South Australia

Watermark	Country
74	Western Australia
75	Victoria
75-78	Tasmania
79	Tonga
80, 80a, 81	Victoria
82, 83	Western Australia
111-114	Danish West Indies
125	Cameroons
	Togo
138-139	Ionian Islands
139	Victoria
161	Bushire
177	South Africa
179	Sudan
190-191	United States
	Philippines
196	India
199	New South Wales
201	South Africa
203	Australia
211	Hyderabad
214	Sudan
219	Great Britain
224	Newfoundland
228	Australia
	Papua New Guinea
231	Sarawak
233	Maldive Islands
250-251	Great Britain
253	Cook Islands
	New Zealand
	Niue
	Samoa
254	Burma
257	Burma
	Philippines

Watermark	Country
259	Great Britain
262	Ireland
274	Bahawalpur
290	Ceylon
294	Cochin
298	Great Britain
308	Great Britain
309	United Nations
314	British Colonies
322	Great Britain
324	India
325	Ghana
330	South Africa
335	Nigeria
336	Sierra Leone
338	Malaya (Selangor)
344	Cyprus
345	Sudan
348	South Africa
351	Pakistan
352	Jamaica
354	Malta
355	Samoa
357	Malawi
359	South Africa
360	India
362	Lesotho
364	Guyana
366	Singapore
373	British Colonies
378	Malaysia
379	Nigeria
380	Kiribati
384	British Colonies
387	Papua New Guinea
388	Malaysia

1996 Vol. 1A Number Changes

Number in 1995 Catalogue	Number in 1996 Catalogue
United States	
564b	deleted
2521b	deleted
2594	2593
2594B	2594
2604-2608	2602-2606
2608A-2608B	2607-2608
O53a	deleted
Cuba	
223	223a
223a	223
Palau	
137-138	134-135
140-145A	136-142
Ryukyu Islands	
56a	deleted
Dominica	
419a	419A
Leeward Islands	
17b	deleted
111a	deleted

Number in 1995 Catalogue	Number in 1996 Catalogue
Nevis	
190-257	190-223
285-360	285-322
Newfoundland	
87d, 87f	footnoted
St. Vincent Grenadines	
295-398	295-346
403-432	403-417
441-468	441-454
Bequia	
1-68	1-34
86-169	86-127
Union Islands	
13-108	13-60
126-141	126-133
142-185	142-163
Virgin Islands	
21d	deleted
772	footnoted

INDEX

SCOTT®

ANNUAL

BEST OF THE PHILATELIC PRESS

WITH A SPECIAL SALUTE TO WORLD WAR II

Editor, Stuart Morrissey ❖ Associate Editor, Sarah Stuck

Dear Catalogue User:

We selected the following articles as representing the best philatelic writing over the last few years. In reviewing many, many newspapers, magazines and journals it occurred to us that much of the best stuff was World War II related. So we decided to use it as a theme, although some of what follows has no connection with the war.

In each case, we have been given permission by the writers to reprint their material. Every article also acknowledges the publication in which the article originally appeared.

I hope you have as much pleasure reading this as we did putting it together.

Stuart Morrissey

Stuart Morrissey
Vice President and Publisher

Morchella elata
REPUBLICA DA
Guinè Bissau
9 00 P
POLSKA 8 zł
НР БЪЛГАРИЯ поща
32 cm
1986 ПОЧТА СССР 5
DDR
Europaische
40 cm
НР БЪЛГАРИЯ поща
Russula vesca
4 Ft
Párducgalóca
Amanita pantherina
MAGYAR POSTA
Lao
1985
POSTES
0,50 k
42 ст
БЪЛГАРИЯ BULGARIA
ДИПЛЕНКА
GYROMITRA ESCULENTA
Lao
1985
POSTES
POLSKA 10 50 zł

The good, the bad and the beautiful: Mushrooms on Stamps

by Barbara L. Anderson

To the careful observer, a walk through the woods on a fine spring morning, or an early autumn trek across a meadow reveals the fascinating world of the fleshy fungi. Mushrooms can be found year round in the woods, fields, and your own front lawn Colorful, variable in form and shrouded in mystery, mushrooms occupy a unique place in the plant world. A member of the lowest plant group called Thallophytes, they thrive on dead and dying plant or animal matter. Fungi serve a valuable function in the chain of life, breaking down decaying materials and returning them to the earth and air to feed living organisms.

Of the approximately 300,000 species of worldwide fungi, about 250 have been pictured on stamps. A handful of varieties are depicted repeatedly however and a nice topical collection can be built around one or two genera.

Mushrooms have been consumed for food and used for medicinal purposes since ancient times. The fermentation reactions of various fungi gave mankind the tools to make beer, alcohol, wine and vinegar. The yeast fungi provided the world with leavened bread. Folklore and superstitution have always surrounded the mushroom family and fungi were standard equipment for witches, sorcerors and other mystics.

Fungus plant diseases such as mildews, rusts and smuts have cost millions of dollars in crop and property damage. The greatest famine in history occurred in Ireland in 1846 when a mildew destroyed the potato crop. Ireland recognized the Great Famine of 1845-50 on a 1982 issue (Scott 519). Conversely, a lowly blue-green mold, Penicillium notatum gave the world penicillin, one of the great discoveries of modern medicine. Penicillin mold appears on a 1967 Great Britain stamp, a one-shilling value in a set honoring British discoveries (Scott 519).

A diverse kingdom about which much remains unknown and undiscovered, mushrooms can be appreciated solely for their uniqueness of shape and their rainbow-range of colors. Appearing full blown literally overnight enhances their magic. The explanation for their sudden appearance is relatively simple. When a ripe spore or reproductive body drops onto a spot where moisture and decaying matter are present, a network of fine white threads develops. This network called mycelium remains underground, spreading and developing into miniature mushrooms. When conditions are ripe and adequate warmth and moisture reach the budding fungi, they expand in minutes, rising above the ground as fully grown organisms. As the spores ripen in the gills on the underside of the cap, they are carried off in the wind and the mushroom wilts and dies.

To the careful observer, a walk through the woods or a trek across a meadow reveals the fascinating world of mushrooms.

The most often asked question about mushrooms has to be "Is it poisonous or can I eat it?" Good question and not one to be answered lightly.

Many false legends surround fungi edibility but most are without foundation. Rules for identification should be followed carefully; the chances of accidental poisoning are probably negligible. Better however to be safe than sorry.

Edible mushrooms have long been considered one of the most succulent of foods. Delicate in flavor and compatible with a broad variety of dishes, the imaginative cook enjoys incorporating mushrooms into salads, vegetable dishes, and entrees. Served alone they can be sauteed, stuffed or rolled into a mushroom tart. Let's start with the "good."

Agaricus campestris, the species from which the supermarket variety was developed, is the world's most famous mushroom. Commonly called Pasture Mushroom, the genus includes many edible species and is relatively easy to identify. Agaricus grows in the open, often appearing overnight on lawns, golf course, and meadows during summer and fall. Hungary issued a beautiful edible mushroom series in 1984 and depicts A. campestris on the 2-forint value (Scott 2876). The species also shows up on stamps from Burkina Faso (Scott 746), and Yugoslavia (Scott 1619). A. bisporous is highlighted on a 1974 4-value set from the Republic of China, issued in honor of the 9th International Congress on Cultivation of Edible Fungi.

The first warm and wet May morning in the Midwest brings out eager souls searching the woods and ravines for Morels. The gray-brown conical caps force their way

Mushrooms can be found year round. Of the 300,000 species, about 250 have been pictured on stamps. Shown are Sweden Scott 1259-1264, Canada Scott 1245-1248 and Hungary Scott 2873-2879.

through the decaying leaves of the forest floor just as the early spring wild flowers burst forth. Morchella esculenta is unexcelled in flavor and best enjoyed all by itself. Frequently found thriving under elm trees, orchards, and burnt-over ground, they may appear several years in a row, then disappear for a time. All Morels are edible, native throughout the U.S. and appearing at varying times as the spring rains move east.

M. esculenta rears its intriguing head on the previously cited Hungarian 1984 series (Scott 2875) and again on a 1989 Canadian block of four (Scott 1246). Other Morchella species make an appearance on stamps from Guinea-Bissau (Scott 635b), France (Scott 2052), Romania (Scott 1231), and Denmark (Scott 624).

Picked at their peak, the Puffballs are prime edibles. The Calvatia species develop into a large, globular shape which tapers down to a narrow base. Lycoperdon species are smaller and often grow in dense clusters. As long as the interior is a solid and clean white mass, Puffballs are eminently edible. They grow on lawns, in fields and woodlots, appearing throughout the growing season. They are most abundant in autumn and their round smooth surface feels like kid gloves. Before you think someone left their bowling ball out on the lawn, look carefully, it may be a giant Puffball. The unique and delicious Puffball is not a popular subject on stamps, but a 1980 set from Poland includes an example of Langermannia gigantea, a synonym for Calvatia gigantea. This particular set features an interesting variety of some of the more bizarre forms of fungi (Scott 2397-2402).

You must rise very early in the morning to capture the quickly fading Coprinus species. Commonly called Inky Caps or Shaggy Manes, this large genus contains several savory treasures. However, in a process called autodigestion, most varieties liquify into an inky black mess by the time you get them home. Coprinus comatus, one of the Shaggy Manes often called Lawyer's Wig, is a favorite of connoisseurs and appears on numerous postal issues. Found in early spring and late fall, they prefer cool moist weather and decaying or buried wood.

The jaunty little Shaggy Mane is forever preserved on a 1981 Australian postal issue (Scott 807). A 1987 Bulgarian mushroom set (Scott 3232-3237) not only depicts a colorful array of mushrooms but shows cross sections for each one. C. comatus appears on the 32-centime value (Scott 3235). This same species shows up again on stamps from Laos (Scott 629), Niger (Scott 719), and Romania (Scott 1230).

The Sulphur Shelf mushrooms or Polypores are the tough woody fungi seen growing conspicuously on trees. Many species are too rugged for good eating, but several types are delicious when young. P. umbellatus, P. sulphureus, P. ovinus, and P. frondosus are all edible but rarely depicted on stamps. The U.S. Trust Territory of Palau issued a mushroom block of four in 1989 which includes Polyporous (Scott 208-211). The botanical designations for this set are not well defined however. Excellent in sauces, the Chanterelles are one of the most famous groups of edible fungi. Cantharellus cibarius is easily recognized by its bright yellow funnel-shaped cap. Appearing in summer and fall, C. cibarius prefers forested areas, usually in association with conifers and hardwoods.

Drawing again from the exquisite 1984 Hungarian edible mushroom set (Scott 2873-2879), we see C. cibarius on the 3-forint value (Scott 2878). The golden yellow cap also appears on a 1989 Norwegian booklet pair (Scott 888b-888c), an older triangle set from Poland (Scott 846), and a 1958 series from Romania (Scott 1234).

The king of the "bad" is unquestionably the deadly Amanita. Responsible for most mushroom fatalities, the genus includes the most poisonous mushrooms in the world. Some European species are considered edible but North American varieties are to be avoided under any circumstances.

Amanita muscaria is a highly popular subject for stamps with its colorful cap of red, orange or yellow. Found growing under hardwoods and conifers, it thrives from summer to fall. A. muscaria is depicted in all its scarlet glory on numerous postals including Hungary (Scott 3048), the familiar 1959 Polish triangle set (Scott 848), an attractive Russian set of 1986 (Scott 5455) and an outstanding series from Laos (Scott 627). Other frequently illustrated Amanita species include A. phalloides or Death Cap, which sports a greenish cap, and A. pantherina, reputed to have hallucinogenic properties. Examples of A. phalloides are nicely rendered on a 1989 Czech stamp (Scott 2759), a Hungarian issue of 1986 (Scott 3046) and a monster postal from Bulgaria (Scott 3597).

A. pantherina, a really most attractive plant, is displayed on the 1991 Bulgarian set (Scott 3599) and another handsome 1986. Hungarian set (Scott 3050). Look but don't eat!

Occasionally confused with the highly favored Morel species, the Gyromitra genus is another gem to avoid. Consumed with relish in Europe and the Pacific Northwest, Gyromitra is too chancy and best avoided. Certain species contain a deadly toxin called monomethylhydrazine (MMH) which is used in rocket fuels. The caps of the Morel species have pits and ridges whereas the Gyromitras are folded into brain-like convolutions. The difference in their relative appearance is obvious when comparing another monster stamp from Bulgaria (Scott 3601) and a DDR issue of 1974 (Scott 1537) included in a set of poisonous European mushrooms (Scott 1533-1540).

The Inocybes or "Little Brown Mushrooms" should also be bypassed for the dinner table. They are a difficult genera to identify and many are toxic. They like wooded areas, growing on the soil surface or thoroughly decayed wood. Most Inocybes have little pointed caps with a knob in the center. Depending on the species, they appear from spring through winter. Inocybe species are occasionally included in mushroom sets, specifically that nice 1986 Hungarian set (Scott 3047) and the DDR series of poisonous varieties (Scott 1538).

The Russula genus varies widely in edibility and color. Red, orange, yellow, purple, green, black and white are all represented. Requiring a lengthy stewing time, Russula species should be eaten with caution. The flavor deteriorates quickly but their gorgeous colors give great pleasure without the discomfort or danger. The 1987 Bulgarian set which shows cross section drawings features R. vesca (Scott 3236). An exemplary 1988 series from Monaco shows R. olivacae on a 7-franc value (Scott 1630). Plump and green R. virescens is featured on the 5-franc value of a 1987 French set (Scott 2053). This particular set (Scott 2050-2053) not only displays colorful illustrations of fully developed mushrooms, but also indicates a cross section and a fruiting body. Another example from a Guinea-Bissau set of 1985 shows R. virescens (Scott 635e).

The Coral fungi are usually classified as Clavaria, Ramaria, or Sparassis and like their marine counterparts, come in an astonishing variety of colors and shapes. Club-shaped, fingerlike, branched, bunched and ruffled, the Clavarias adorn conifer forests from July until frost. Most are deliciously edible, others are bitter or tough. Of the wide variety of mushrooms illustrated on stamps, the Coral fungi have been sorely neglected. A few examples exist; the lovely 1989 Canadian block includes Clavulinopsis fusiformis (Scott 1247), and the 1980 Polish series pictures Sparassis crispa on the 8-zloty value (Scott 2401).

A 1978 Swedish booklet of 6 deserves special mention. Engraved by Czeslaw Slania, the mushroom issue commemorated the death centenary of Elias Fries (1794-1878), a world famous botanist. The continuous design illustrates six different edible species including Ramaria botrytis, one of the Coral fungi.

Picky eaters and those with sensitive stomachs should and probably will avoid even the tastiest edible mushrooms of the wild. But the fabulous fungi of field and forest (sorry) can be enjoyed visually throughout the year. Coming upon a bright yellow mushroom during an autumn woodland stroll, when skies are gray and trees are bare, is the highpoint of anyone's day. The thrill of discovery is like no other, and when winter winds blow and a walk in the woods sounds unpleasant, let your fingers do the walking through your stamp album. Only a bare handful of the mushroom species depicted on worldwide stamps have been discussed here. Pick up a mushroom field guide and with your album in the other hand, explore the incredible world of these lovely members of the plant kingdom. ❖

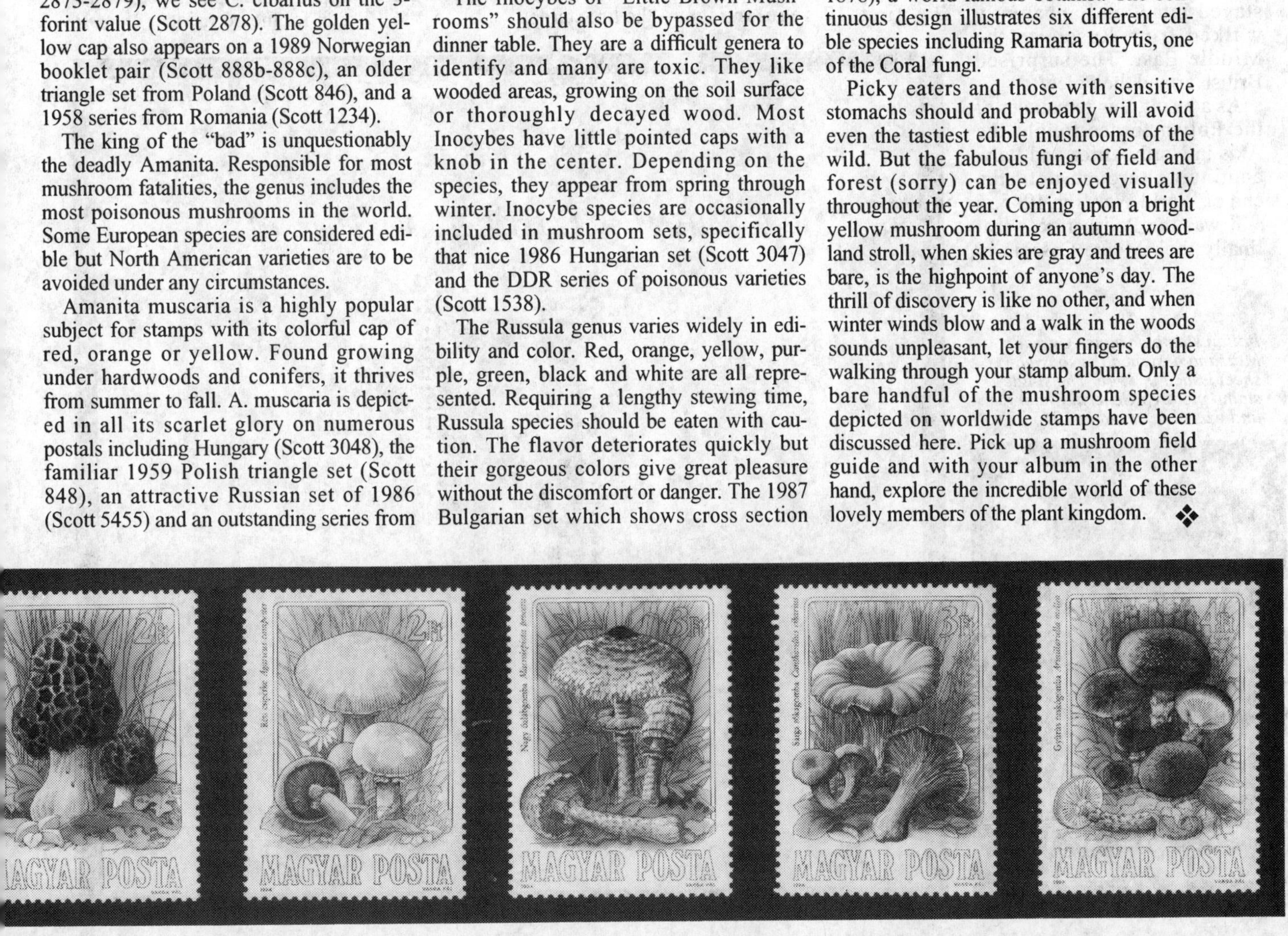

Polish Stamps Produced in Italy

by Robert E. Lana

Why were Polish stamps designed by an Italian, printed by Italians and issued and used in Italy? The answer to this question lies embedded within the chaos intrinsic to any far-reaching war.

When the Germans over-ran Poland in 1939, a large contingent of the Polish army retreated into Russia. The Russians, suspicious of the Poles' willingness to fight alongside them, given the long-standing animosity between the two countries, disarmed them.

Remarkably, the Polish army stayed intact and apparently walked from Russia to the Middle East. The surprised British armed the Poles.

As a result, this remainder of the Polish forces fought the Axis in North Africa and Italy, continuing through until the end of World War II in 1945.

It was the Polish forces that finally took Monte Cassino in southern Italy during one of the most famous battles of WWII.

Four months after the war ended, Polish troops were still on occupation duty in Italy and the Middle East. On Dec. 30, 1945, Gen. Anders, commander of the Polish forces, entered into an agreement with the Italian post office to produce stamps for use by members of the Polish corps.

Soldiers, of course, were allowed to send cards and letters free, but there was a need for stamps to pay postage for the mailing of packages and registered letters.

In 1946, 29 regular stamps, three airmail stamps and five souvenir sheets were issued. The first 17 regular-issue stamps were denominated in Polish groszy and zlotys, with 100 groszy equaling 1 zloty. The remaining 12 regular stamps were denominated in Italian lire.

The first two airmail stamps, and the first two souvenir sheets were issued in Polish denominations. The other airmail stamp and the last three sheetlets were in Italian lire.

The stamps were valid for use in 30 post offices established in Italy and the Middle East.

Interestingly, Italian citizens were free to use the stamps denominated in lire. Only Polish troops stationed in Barl in the heel of Italy could use the lire stamps.

The Polish stamps were valid even for registered letters and packages sent through the Italian civil post office. However, Polish stamps canceled with Italian postmarks are exceedingly rare.

Perhaps the most attractive of these 1946 issues were those stamps designed by Italy's premier stamp artist, Corrado Mezzana. The illustration depicts both a Mezzana designed souvenir sheet and a stamp from the first issue.

In 1954, several of these stamps were overprinted in London by the Polish government in exile to commemorate the victory at Monte Cassino. The Italian government approved a special cancellation for the occasion. ❖

Italian stamp designer Corrado Mezzana designed the souvenir sheet issued in 1946. The single stamp pictures General Anders and was also issued in 1946.

Railway strike has two-wheeled solution

by Dick Richardson

A strike by the American Rail way Union in 1894 created the opportunity for a new, although short-lived, local postage stamp. These stamps, known as Bicycle Mail locals, are listed on page 269 of the Scott *1994 Specialized Catalogue of United States Stamps*.

On the morning of July 7, 1894, a Fresno Calif. man started off on his bicycle on the first leg of a 210-mile journey to transport mail between Fresno and San Francisco. Thus began the Fresno and San Francisco Bicycle Mail route. Less than two weeks later, the railroad strike was over and the bicycle mail service was officially ended, although stamps from the post were sold and used philatelically for many more months.

Although the bicycle post service was not in existence very long, the stamps created (Scott 12L1 and 12L2) generated their share of notoriety, with envelopes being printed and even counterfeit reproductions of the stamp created. And, at one time, Scott called the stamp an advertising stunt and dropped its listing for a year.

The story began May 11, 1894, when workers of the Pullman Company in Chicago called a strike over wage reductions. The American Railway Union came to the aid of the strikers and ordered a boycott of all Pullman cars on June 26. The railroads refused to operate any trains that had Pullman cars assigned to them, and rail traffic came to a halt in the San Joaquin Valley of California, leaving the towns isolated from San Francisco.

Lowell B. Cooper, in this book *The Fresno and San Francisco Bicycle Mail of 1894*, states that the idea for a bicycle mail service was suggested to Arthur C. Banta, owner of the Victor Cyclery shop in Fresno, possibly on July 1 by a John C. Nourse, who worked at a local grocery store.

With the seed planted, Banta then set about organizing the mail route, printing flyers and recruiting riders. Banta represented the Overman Wheel Co. agency in Fresno and made arrangements for mail deliveries and pickups at the Overman agencies in San Jose and San Francisco. Mail could also be picked up and delivered at other points along the route, and arrangements were made for mail delivery to two towns south of Fresno, Fowler and Selma. These towns are noted on the accompanying map.

On July 6, the other principal involved in the bicycle mail operation, Eugene Donze, a Fresno engraver, proposed to Banta that a stamp be made, and he returned to his office that evening to make the die. Also on July 6, the Fresno postmaster may have become aware of the pending mail service and, although it was initially thought that the delivery of mail would violate postal regulations, it was determined that no law would be broken since the riders would only carry mail to the nearest post office that could deliver the mail. Banta charged 25¢ for his stamp, or 30¢ for an envelope and stamp. In addition to the bicycle stamp, all envelopes also had to be franked with appropriate U.S. postage.

At 4:30 a.m. on July 7, the first rider took off with 15 letters. Ten more were picked up along the way.

With new riders taking over at selected stops, the mail was relayed to San Jose, where the McFarland brothers, who also had a bicycle route, finished delivering the initial mail to San Francisco. On subsequent days, the Fresno riders went to San Francisco. Besides carrying mail and packages from Fresno and intermediate points to San Francisco, the cyclists also brought letters and goods back with them.

When the first mail left Fresno, it did

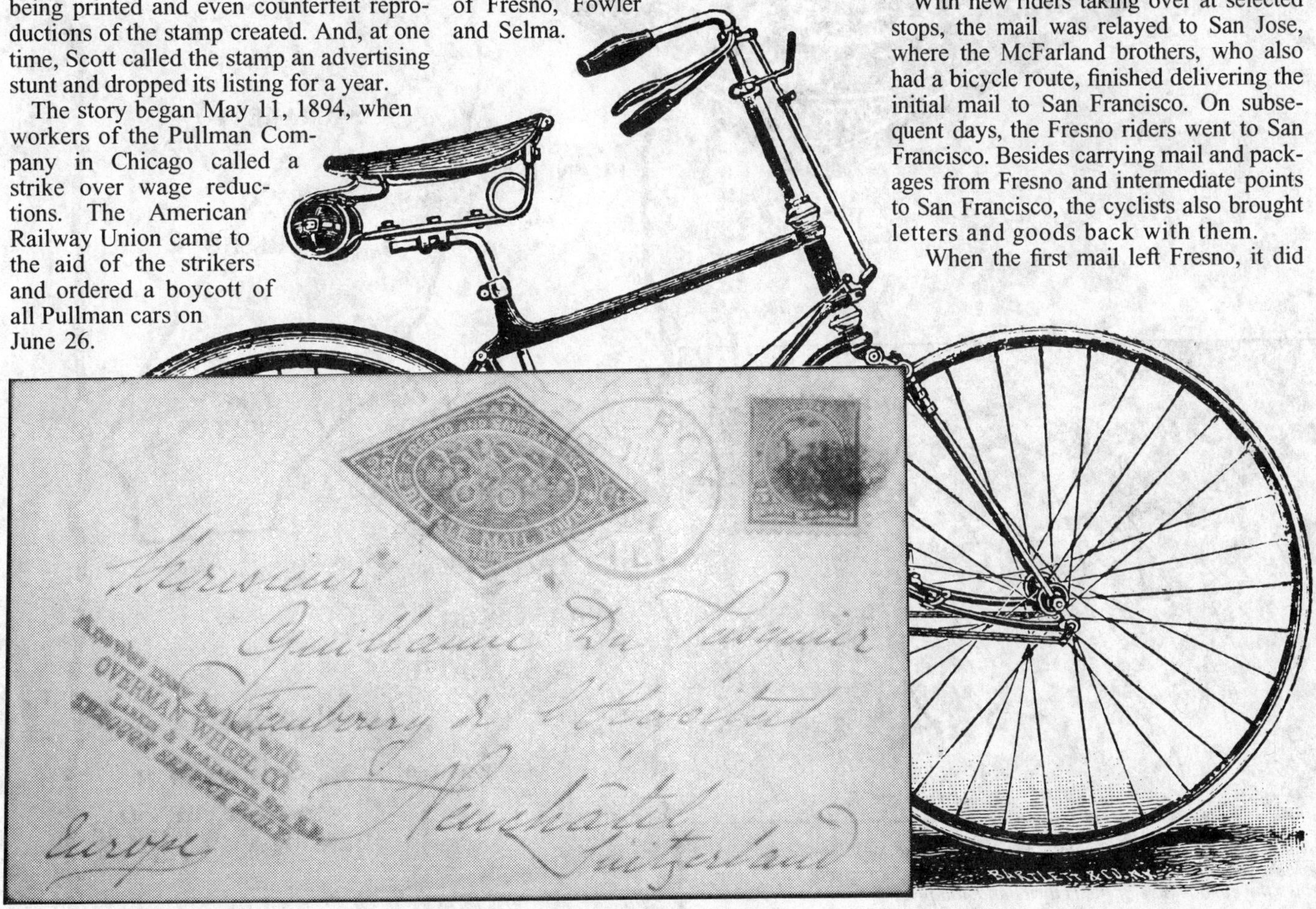

Stamp designs created by Eugene Donze for the bicycle post. Die I shows the misspelling of San Francisco. Die I recut features the correction and the addition of Donze's initials (below). Die II, created later, was never officially used (lower left). The defaced original die is shown at far left.

This cover, postmarked July 11, 1894, bears a copy of the first printing of Bicycle Mail stamps that feature a misspelling of San Francisco. The cover also shows the earliest use of the return handstamp.

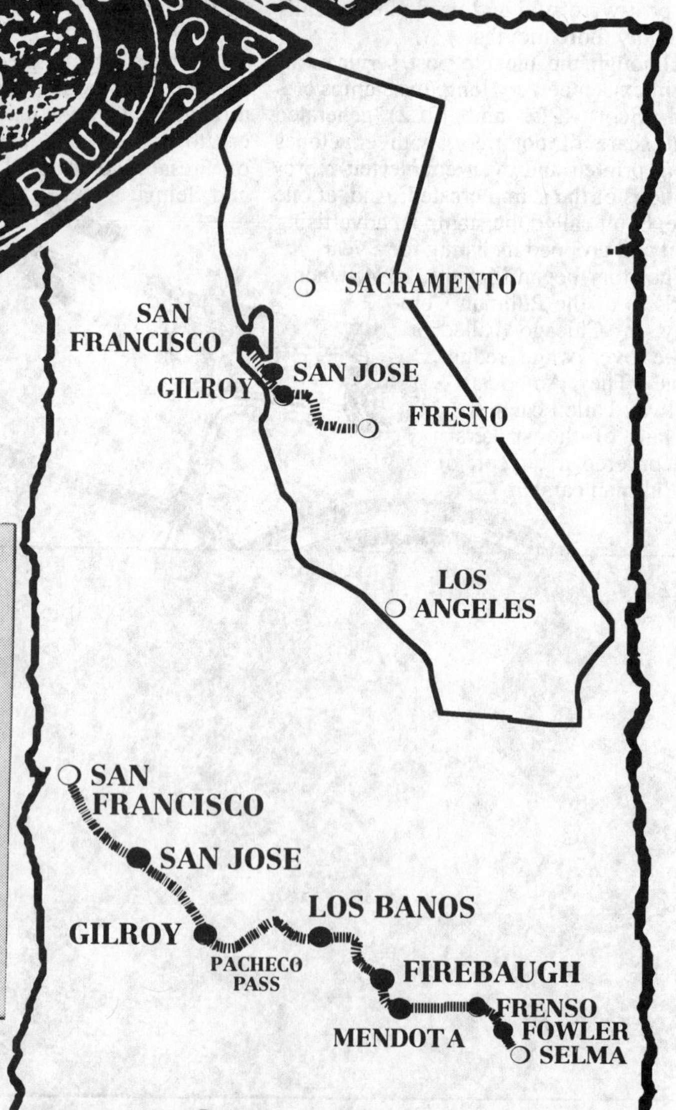

At left is the original 1894 bicycle hand stamp used on strike mail. At right is the pictorial cancel to be used on re-enactment covers and as a Frespex show cancel.

Hundred-year-old handstamp updated

The Fresno Philatelic Society of Fresno, Calif., will celebrate the 100th anniversary of the Fresno and San Francisco Bicycle Mail Route at Frespex 94, to be held March 12 and 13 at the Fresno District Fairgrounds.

Members of the Fresno Cycling Club will carry cacheted envelopes from Fresno to San Francisco on March 11 and return to Fresno the following day. The cachet will show the map of the original 1894 route.

A special cancel showing a bicycle similar to one depicted on the original rubber handstamp used on mail that was sent from Fresno during the railway strike will also be used. Cacheted covers also can be purchased for the show dates of March 12 and 13. Reprints of minisheets of a block of six Bicycle Mail stamps will be available in two colors (blue and orange) imperforate and perforate. The original stamp was green.

The stamp show also will feature exhibits of some of the 1894 Bicycle Mail.

To order cachets or stamp reprints, write to the Fresno Philatelic Society, Box 5694, Fresno, CA 93755.

not have the bicycle stamp. The first lot of 816 stamps was delivered that day after the first mail had left. It was quickly discovered by a local stamp collector that San Francisco was misspelled as “San Fransisco” on the stamps, and Donze had to touch up the first “s” in Fransisco to make it look like a “c.” About 1,000 stamps from the retouched die were printed.

According to Cooper, the original stamp was never used, “because the earliest known use of any bicycle stamp was a product of this retouched die, carried on the 5 a.m. Sunday mail run.” At least one cover, however, is known with the misspelling. Cover No. 42, dated July 11, 1894 (from the July 10 run), bears a copy of the original printing. It is also the first recorded use of the return handstamp.

On July 15, 1894, federal troops ended the railway strike and regular mail service began to take place, although it was some time before all was once again normal. The last official bicycle mail left Fresno July 16, 1894, and arrived in San Francisco on July 18. On July 17 and 19, some additional mail was sent from Fresno to San Francisco for philatelic purposes.

During the life of the bicycle mail route, about 1,800 stamps and 250 envelopes were printed, but nowhere near this many were actually used. Author Cooper believes that “in addition to the 380 non-philatelic covers carried over the post, there were perhaps two hundred philatelic covers. This gives us about 580 total covers carried of which perhaps 150 exist today (1982). Of the surviving covers about 80 percent are philatelic.”

> *“On July 7, 1894, a Fresno Calif. man started off on his bicycle on the first leg of a 210-mile journey. Thus began the Fresno and San Francisco Bicycle Mail route.”*

Despite the fact that the bicycle mail route was no longer in service, the stamp story did not yet end.

Approximately 2,000 more stamps and 150 envelopes were printed for philatelic purposes shortly after the mail service was discontinued. Donze received requests for stamps and Banta mailed advertising flyers and ran magazine ads during 1894, offering stamps and franked envelopes for sale.

In August of 1894, Donze engraved a new die, which he defaced with one horizontal line and five vertical ones, claiming that the original die had thus been destroyed. Stationery using this defaced die was printed for Donze and Banta. But it was quickly discovered that this was a counterfeit and Donze was forced to produce the real die, which was defaced with one horizontal line and one vertical line.

In 1935, Banta, who then lived in San Francisco, organized a memorial rerun of the bicycle mail. He made electrotypes from the original defaced die and had about 2,000 stamps printed for the May 1 re-enactment.

Then, in 1936, the listing of the Bicycle Mail Route stamps was dropped from the 1937 edition of the Scott *Specialized Catalogue of United States Stamps* because the stamps were considered an advertising stunt. Banta wrote a six-page letter to Scott Stamp and Coin Co. in which he defended the legitimacy of his stamp. The listing was restored for the 1938 catalogue and has remained since.

The complete story of the bicycle mail can be read in Cooper’s book, published in 1982 by Leonard H. Hartmann. ❖

Hooray for Hollywood

BY BARBARA L. ANDERSON

When I was 12 years old in 1946, I was at the peak of my youthful philatelic activities. Like most youngsters, my purchases consisted primarily of penny approvals. I never went to a stamp show, nor did I join a club. Growing up in Chicago, I certainly had ample opportunity for both; however, my parents had no interest in stamps and encouraged me in other endeavors. Lacking an enthusiastic mentor I collected and enjoyed pretty much in a vacuum but still managed to collect some treasures.

Favorites from that period include a group of ten covers (seven of which are illustrated here) addressed to film stars, dated June, July, or August of 1946. Mailed to various film studios in California, including Warner Brothers in Burbank, Columbia Pictures in Hollywood, and Metro-Goldwyn-Mayer in Culver City, the covers originated in different areas of Great Britain. How did they come onto the philatelic market? Perhaps some forward-thinking secretary retrieved them from the stars' wastebaskets! I have no recollection of where or how I obtained them.

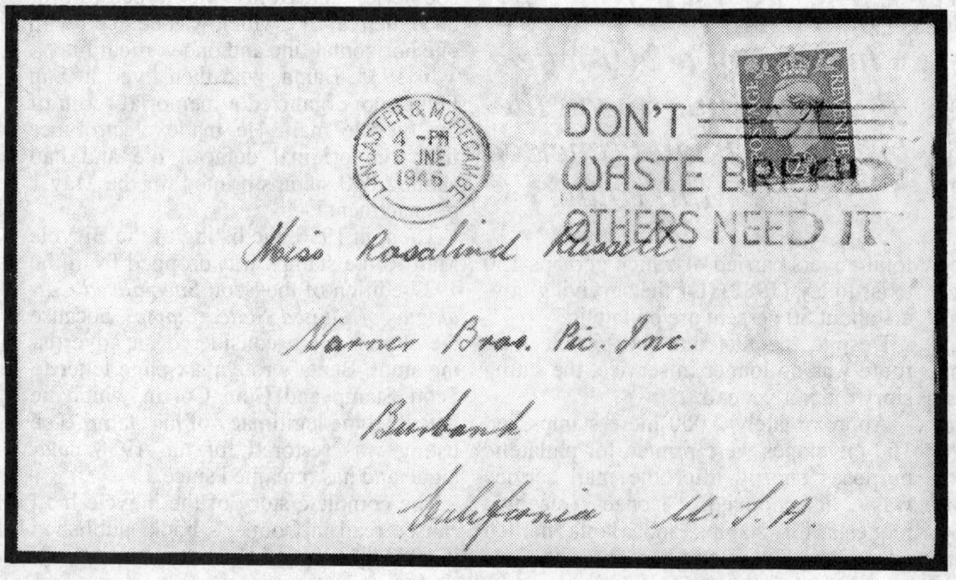

The first cover, illustrated in Figure 1, is addressed to Rosalind Russell, the delightful dark-haired actress best known for her portrayal of Auntie Mame. How I miss her madcap comedic talent! That year Russell made the film *Sister Kenny*, a drastic departure from her customary wry and cynical characterizations. Perhaps the writer had a personal interest in Sister Kenny's unorthodox but successful treatment for polio.

I love the cover's marking, "DON'T/WASTE BREAD/ OTHERS NEED IT." Britain was recovering from World War II at that point, and shortages were surely a fact of life. The same cancel appears on two other covers, dated June 13 and 15. Perhaps this cancel was used during the month of June throughout the whole country.

The June 6 Russell cover carries Scott No. 239, the 2 1/2-pence King George V1 definitive from the 1937-39 series. The postmark is from Lancaster and Morecambe -- towns in northern England on Morecambe Bay in the Irish Sea.

Glenn Ford failed to pick up the letter shown in Figure 2, as indicated by a red handstamp "UNCALLED FOR AT/METRO-GOLDWYN-MAYER." Ford's film, Gilda, was released in 1946 and undoubtedly generated an enormous amount of fan mail. This cover, dated London, June 13, 1946, bears the BREAD cancellation. The British Peace set of two values had been issued June 11 and the writer used the new 2 1/2-pence value (Scott No. 264) for his letter to Ford.

Ford's costar in *Gilda*, Rita

Figure 2
A cover addressed to Glenn Ford.

Figure 3
A cover addressed to Rita Hayworth

Figure 4
A cover addressed to Irene Dunne.

Figure 5 A cover addressed to Willard Parker.

Figure 6 A cover addressed to Larry Parks.

Figure 7 A cover addressed to Janet Blair.

Hayworth -- the sensuous pin-up girl of the 1940's -- received the fan letter illustrated in Figure 3. Surely this is only one of thousands! The cover was postmarked in Bath, Somerset, on June 25, 1946, and it bears the 2 1/2-pence Peace issue. Do you remember her seductive rendition of "Put the Blame on Mame?" And that black dress. Wow!

Figure 4 is addressed to Irene Dunne, one of the superstars of the 30s and 40s. The cover was mailed from Glasgow on June 18. No BREAD cancellation appears, which might lead us to suspect the cancel was not used in Scotland. However, the cover in Figure 5, addressed to Willard Parker Esq., carried the BREAD cancel and is postmarked Edinburgh (June 15, 1946). Willard Parker, a tall wavy-haired leading man married to actress Virginia Fields, played Cole Younger in *Young Jesse James* and starred in action films like *Apache Drums.*

A cover addressed to Larry Parks at Columbia Pictures is shown in Figure 6. Remember him? After he appeared in *Jolson Sings Again* in 1949, moviegoers really never heard from Parks again. The cover is stamped with the King George VI definitive and postmarked June 13 in Finsbury Park, N.4, most likely a postal station in London.

Janet Blair, perhaps best remembered for the *Fuller Brush films*, received a letter from Burnley & Nelson, located in Lancashire (Figure 7). Besides the movies, Blair performed on the stage. I saw her play Nellie Forbush in *South Pacific* many years ago in Chicago. The cover was postmarked August 6, 1946, and features the 2 1/2-pence Peace issue.

I have always enjoyed these covers, but I have found the real fun of such treasures is in sharing them with others. ❖

Lincoln's background fades with time - *and acid*

by Wayne L. Youngblood

Every once in awhile an item so bizarre turns up that a story about it practically writes itself. In this case it is an item that turned up in the Jan. 25-26, 1994, Lowell S. Newman & Co. sale No. 11. The item, lot 615, was photographed and described as follows:

"90¢ 'Albino' 1869 Pictorial Issue (122), Only the vignette and a trace of cancel left on a stamp 'treated' to a lavoric acid bath, with a 1974 note by Perry Fuller telling of the event; sadly it is o/w sound and apparently once a very nice stamp cataloging $1150.00, unusual (to say the least)." Adding to the tale is the fact the stamp fetched only $16 (plus the 10 percent buyer's fee). This is only slightly more than one percent of the stamp's current value.

At one time the stamp, the high value of the 1869 series, was a gorgeous example. Each corner of the 90¢ stamp has a neat corner perforation, and the design was very well centered, with large margins on three sides. The cancel, a carved cork marking, was unobtrusively placed in the lower-right corner and there is a strongly embossed, well-centered grill on the back side of the stamp. A neat vertical layout line runs the length of the right side. There were virtually no defects on the stamp, and by all standards, this example of Scott 122 was a premium copy.

The stamp now has no carmine background. It is nothing more than a strongly engraved proof-like vignette of Abraham Lincoln, with a lightly embossed frame line design visible only under the proper lighting. Other than the missing color, the stamp is undamaged and is still rather attractive. How did this once nice-looking stamp meet its fate?

A close examination of the poor stamp provided me with a lead. A small, very faint manuscript "X" cancel can be seen on Lincoln's forehead. This no doubt was found to be offensive to one owner of the stamp and probably was the reason for the so-called cleaning treatment.

As mentioned in the lot description, a note of explanation by Perry Fuller was included. Fuller was a fairly well-known stamp dealer during the middle decades of this century. The rather self-explanatory note, dated June 15, 1974, tells the sad tale of the stamp's demise. It is reproduced as follows:

"Mr. James E. Hughes (Hughes Towing Co. of Philadelphia, Penn.) bought this stamp from me. Because it was dirty, Mr. Hughes wanted it cleaned. We put it in a bath of Lavoric Acid. I didn't want to do this but Mr. Hughes insisted. Since it was just about lunch-time, we went to lunch. When we came back, the stamp was bleached out all except the head. I've had this for some time but thought you'ld (sic) like it for your collection. At the time of cleaning, the stamp belonged to Mr. Hughes; he didn't want it after the bleaching out of the carmine design."

Now, I'm not a chemist, but it seems to me that exposing your stamps to acid is not a particularly good idea. I was not able to find any information about lavoric acid, but did stumble upon a listing for lauric acid, which may be what the stamp was exposed to. Lauric acid is crystalline fatty acid that is commonly found in soaps and cleaning compounds. Therein may lie the explanation why only the carmine color was bleached out.

Early carmine-colored inks used to print postage stamps were derived from carminic acid, the by-product of dried cochineal bugs. These insects are native to Mexico and Central America. It takes 70,000 of these bugs to create a single pound of cochineal, from which the pigmentation is created. The chemical composition of the ink can vary as greatly as the bugs themselves or the types of cactus they fed upon. Given the organic base of the carmine ink, it is easy to see why lauric acid could dissolve the ink color without harming the basic stamp. At any rate, the treatment was totally successful in removing the carmine color. This should be a lesson in exposing our stamps to substances considered safe for most purposes.

I suspect that the history of this stamp goes back further than its treatment. As nice of an example as it was, the stamp probably was previously offered at auction, although I have not been able to locate it. At any rate, this unusual collector-created albino freak adds a new dimension to a collection and is certainly a conversation piece. ❖

This stamp is not a proof. The carmine background of the stamp was inadvertently bleached out by a collector who wanted the stamp cleaned. Carmine-colored ink of the 19th century was derived from the cochineal bug, shown below.

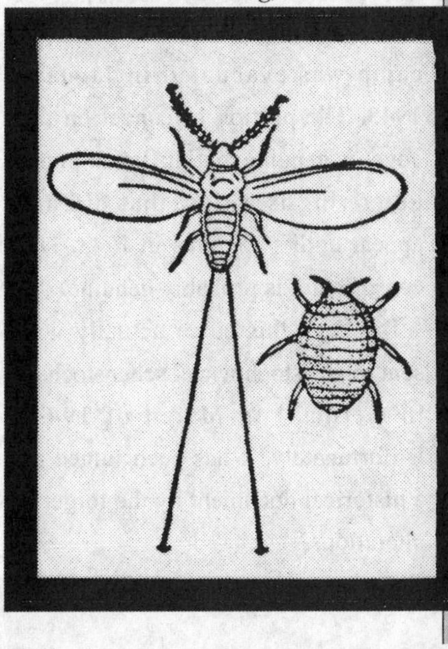

A FORGED LETTER FROM HELL

BY KEN LAWRENCE

In 1988, a professor in Czestochowa sent me the illustrated cover, a Concentration Camp Auschwitz prisoner's letter-sheet, for which he desired "in trade" a $20 bill, wrapped in carbon paper. That was a bargain price, so I paid as requested. It wasn't until four years afterward, when I was mounting my exhibit for display, that I realized the cover had been faked, though several clues should have alerted me earlier.

The stamp itself is wrong. Correct postage was twelve pfennigs, and the rules printed at the left state that each inmate may receive, along with two postcards or letters per month, five German stamps of twelve-pfennig denomination. Still, a 15-pfennig stamp was close enough that I paid no attention to the discrepancy. For most collecting purposes, slightly overpaid covers are not unusual.

Close inspection of the cancel reveals that the portion on the stamp does not align perfectly with the portion on the letter-sheet, but it's a very good match. Comparison with a genuine Auschwitz cover reveals that the letters of OBERSCHLES (Upper Silesia) on the stamp are not in the correct position for a genuine Auschwitz postmark. Proof that the cover has been altered is the date. The stamp is postmarked March 20, 1940, but the Auschwitz concentration camp wasn't built until May of that year.

Often prisoner covers are found without postage stamps affixed, sometimes because the stamps were removed by censors searching for hidden messages, and many of those covers appear on the collector market "enhanced" by the addition of stamps that were not originally connected with the covers to increase their visual appeal for collectors.

Most such covers can be restored to their original condition by removing the stamps, but that won't work with my cover. In this case, the forger not only added the alien stamp, but also altered the contents to agree with it by making the date of the letter March 17, 1940. (Censorship accounts for the delay between the dates of writing and posting on concentration camp prisoners' mail.) Also, something has been erased next to the censor's K.L. Auschwitz handstamp at the top.

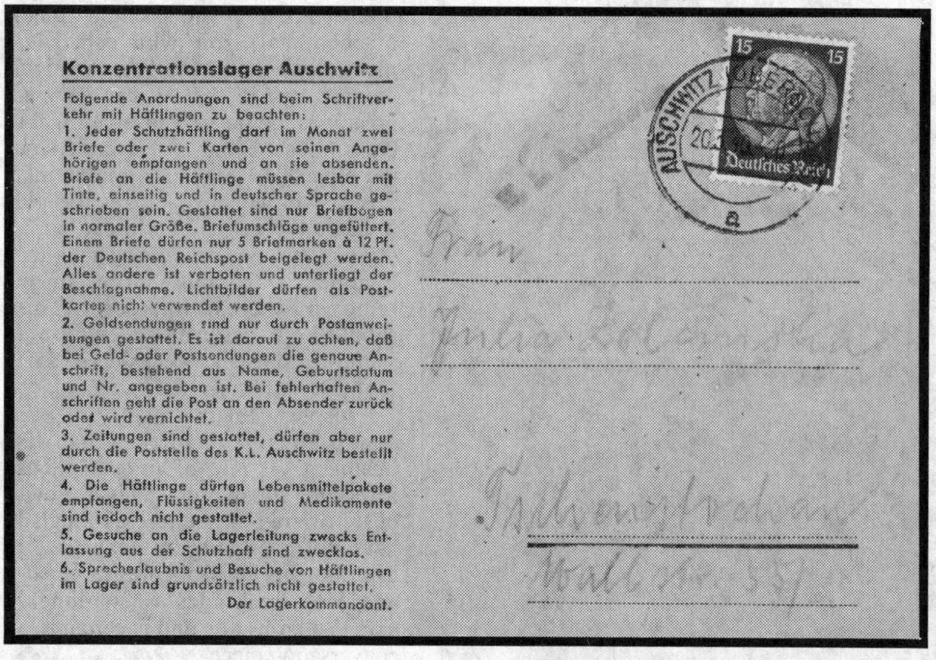

Once I had detected the faked elements, comparison with unaltered Auschwitz covers revealed this cover's likely history. The lettersheet is genuine, but of a type that was used from late 1943 until the camp was evacuated in January 1945. The portion of cancel on the cover is genuine, but the break in the outer ring is a flaw that did not appear until some time in 1943. The censor mark is probably genuine.

I believe this cover actually was sent to Czestochowa (Tschenstochau in German) in March of 1944. Unfortunately, it has been ruined as a historical document by the forger's alterations. ❖

Autographs leave mark on collection

by Judith Monteverdi

The three leather-bound volumes are worn and fraying with time. Started some 90 years ago by a young woman named Rae Ehrenberg, a visual walk through history was created through years of collecting. What began as a collection of envelopes, letters and documents bearing autographs of famous figures in American history became a living collection, interwoven with Ehrenberg's enthusiasm for stamp collecting. She assembled a philatelic autograph collection of persons whose portraits have appeared on stamps, those of persons who have designed stamps and autographs of individuals who had the Franking privilege.

In April 1972, Rae Ehrenberg presented her collection of philatelic-related autographs to The Association of South Jersey Stamp Clubs, Inc., which was sponsoring its 36th Sojex show, a three-day national-level exhibit and bourse at the Dennis hotel in Atlantic City. She had established herself as well known among collectors several decades before. An award receiver many times for her other numerous collections, both here and abroad, Ehrenberg had not previously entered a stamp exhibit that encompassed another field of collecting; in this case renowned autographs. Ehrenberg received a bronze award at Sojex 72 for her philatelic autograph collection.

Upon her death, Ehrenberg left behind some very important collections that were later sold. Not sold was her autograph collection. It was left to me, her granddaughter. Today, I sit and turn the pages of these volumes in awe of the life and times of those who, with quill pen in hand, put their stroke to paper a century ago. One item in the collection is particularly interesting to me. It is a small card that was written and signed by our 18th president, Ulysses S. Grant, dated Jan. 6, 1876, to the Secretary of State, Mr. Hamilton Fish. The note urged "immediate attention" to some "important business." Grant has been featured on numerous United States stamps, beginning with Scott 223, issued in 1890. A longer letter, addressed to the Honorable Edward Pierrepont, Attorney General in 1877, was signed by Rutherford B. Hayes, our 19th president. Hayes wrote of the great reception the English had for Gen. Grant, and how this reception pleased our country. He continued by mentioning railroad riots that kept everyone "busy," and that so far national troops had not had to fire a single shot. "The army", Hayes stated, remains too small for the emergency." Today we read of these men in history books, several steps away from their personal thoughts. Hayes first appeared on a U.S. stamp in 1922, on the 11¢ value of the 1922 series, Scott 563.

With each page of my grandmother's collection there is a movement through time.

In 1881, from the Western Union Telegraph Company, is a written and signed telegram from James A. Garfield, while president elect, stating that he could not be present at the "bar meeting." A century-old telegram such as this is so different from the teletype messages of today. Only a few months later, Garfield was shot, on July 2, 1881. He died 2½ months later, on Sept. 19, 1881. The first stamp bearing his likeness, Scott 205, was released April 10, 1882.

Another page in the album reveals a 5-by 7-inch card with a 3¢ violet U.S. postage stamp and the signatures of President Woodrow Wilson and Postmaster General Albert Burleson, stating that the affixed 3¢ Victory Stamp (Scott 537) is stamp No. 2 of the first sheet printed. This was a souvenir created to be presented to a dignitary of the day. It was given to a stamp collector by Burleson in 1927 (please see sidebar story).

In 1891, Susan B. Anthony was the leader of the Womens' Suffrage Movement. Anthony was not an attractive woman, possessing the appearance of a spinster with her wire-rimmed glasses, her graying hair held securely off her shoulders in a bun and her dark-colored dresses

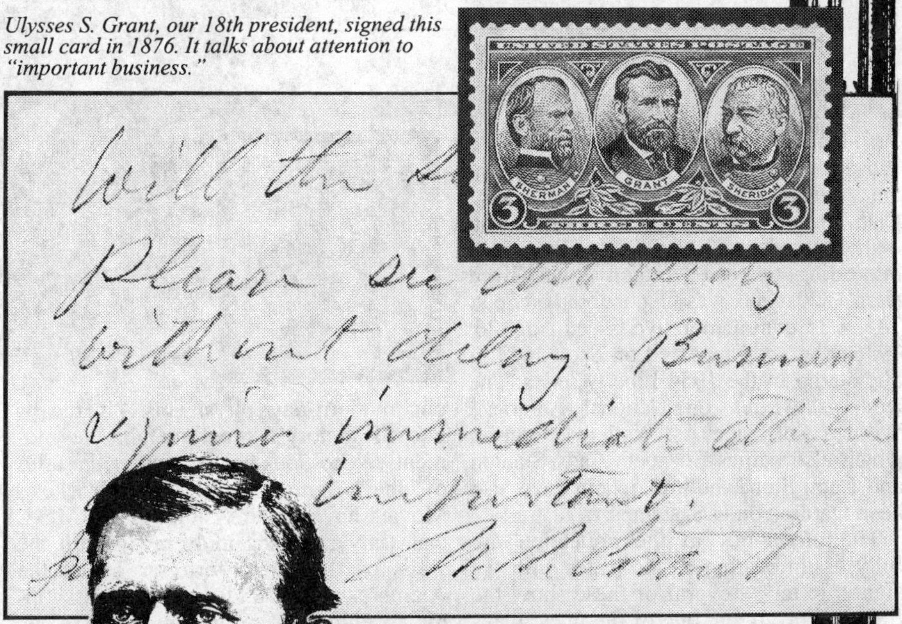

Ulysses S. Grant, our 18th president, signed this small card in 1876. It talks about attention to "important business."

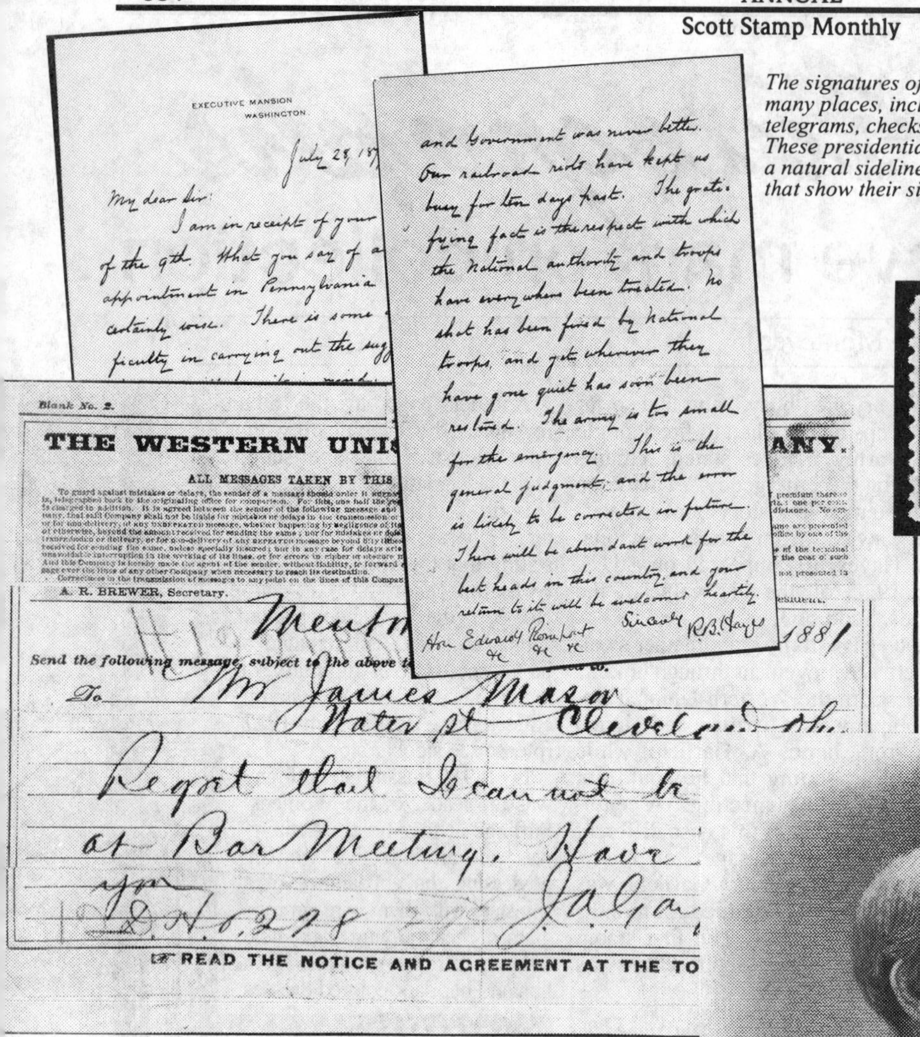
EXECUTIVE MANSION
WASHINGTON
July 23, 18
My dear Sir:
I am in receipt of your ... of the 9th. What you say of a ... appointment in Pennsylvania ... certainly wise. There is some ... ficulty in carrying out the sug...

and Government was never better. Our railroad riots have kept us busy for ten days past. The gratifying fact is the respect with which the National authority and troops have everywhere been treated. No shot has been fired by National troops, and yet wherever they have gone quiet has soon been restored. The army is too small for the emergency. This is the general judgment, and the error is likely to be corrected in future. There will be abundant work for the best heads in this country and your return to it will be welcomed heartily.
Sincerely
R.B. Hayes

Blank No. 2.
THE WESTERN UNI... ANY.
ALL MESSAGES TAKEN BY THIS
A. R. BREWER, Secretary.
Send the following message, subject to the above t...
1881
To Mr James Mason
Water St Cleveland Oh...
Regret that I can not b...
at Bar Meeting. Have ...
you
J. A. Ga...
READ THE NOTICE AND AGREEMENT AT THE TO...

The signatures of our presidents can be found in many places, including free franks, letters, telegrams, checks and other documents. These presidential autographs are a natural sideline to the stamps that show their signers.

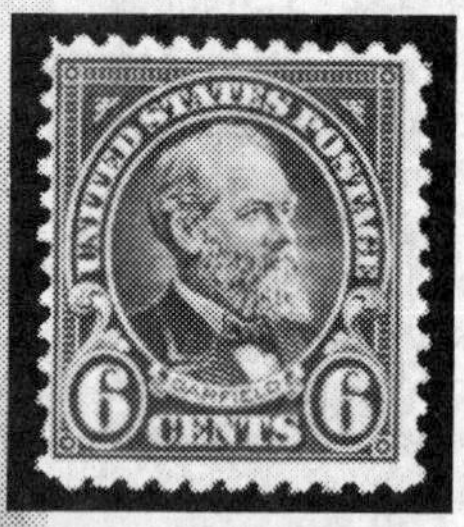

buttoned high at the neck with a simple brooch. However, reading one of her letters to "My dear Helen Potter," I note that this stern-looking woman touches on kindness and a gentle manner. This exemplifies that the strongest of leaders have a soft side to lend. These words, of a woman who set so many precedents for women of today, are interesting to read. Anthony, who lived from 1820-1906, was first honored on Scott 784, a 3¢ commemorative issued Aug. 26, 1936. She later appeared on Scott 1051, a 50¢ stamp in the 1954 Liberty series. The letter is written on National American Woman Sufferage Association letterhead, which also names Elizabeth Cady Stanton and Lucy Stone, both of whom have also been featured on U.S. stamps.

The envelopes in the collection are fully as interesting as the pages with the signed letters. Several of these show the franking privilege, one of the finest ways for stamp collectors to obtain autographs. This privilege was given to presidents, their widows and other political notables. A free frank is simply a signature in the upper right-hand corner of the envelope, indicating free postage. My favorite is an undated envelope franked by Sam Houston. Houston, who lived from 1793-1863, was known in history as a hero in the battle of the Alamo. Although Houston's signature appears as indecipherable as our modern-day physicians', it recalls one of history's most memorable moments. Who does not remember the tales of the Alamo and Davey Crockett? Movies have made visions of the Mexican army storming and crawling up the walls of this great fortress. Today the Alamo's walls stand amongst the shopping centers of San Antonio, Texas. Holding the envelope, I see Sam Houston as somewhat of a "gentlemen's cowboy," standing erect with his broad rimmed hat, long black waist coat, knee-high leather boots and proudly holding his rifle. This is how he appears on Scott 1242, a 1962 commemorative honoring him. Houston was also pictured on Scott 776, a 1936 3¢ commemorative marking the Alamo. Both Crockett and the Alamo have also been featured on stamps.

Another free-franked cover in the collection is dated March 28, 1856. The cover is addressed to William C. Baldwin, and was signed by James Buchanan, our 15th president. Buchanon has appeared on two U.S. stamps; Scott 820, a 15¢ stamp from the 1938 Presidential series, and 2217F from the 1986 Ameripex souvenir sheets.

Two other envelopes in the collection that feature the franking privilege are those of two famous first ladies; Edith Roosevelt, widow of Theodore Roosevelt, and Eleanor Roosevelt, widow of Franklin D. Roosevelt. The collection possesses two envelopes bearing Eleanor's name. One features an original autograph of Eleanor Roosevelt, and the other a rubber-stamped image. Call it technology, the need for expediency or the freedom of

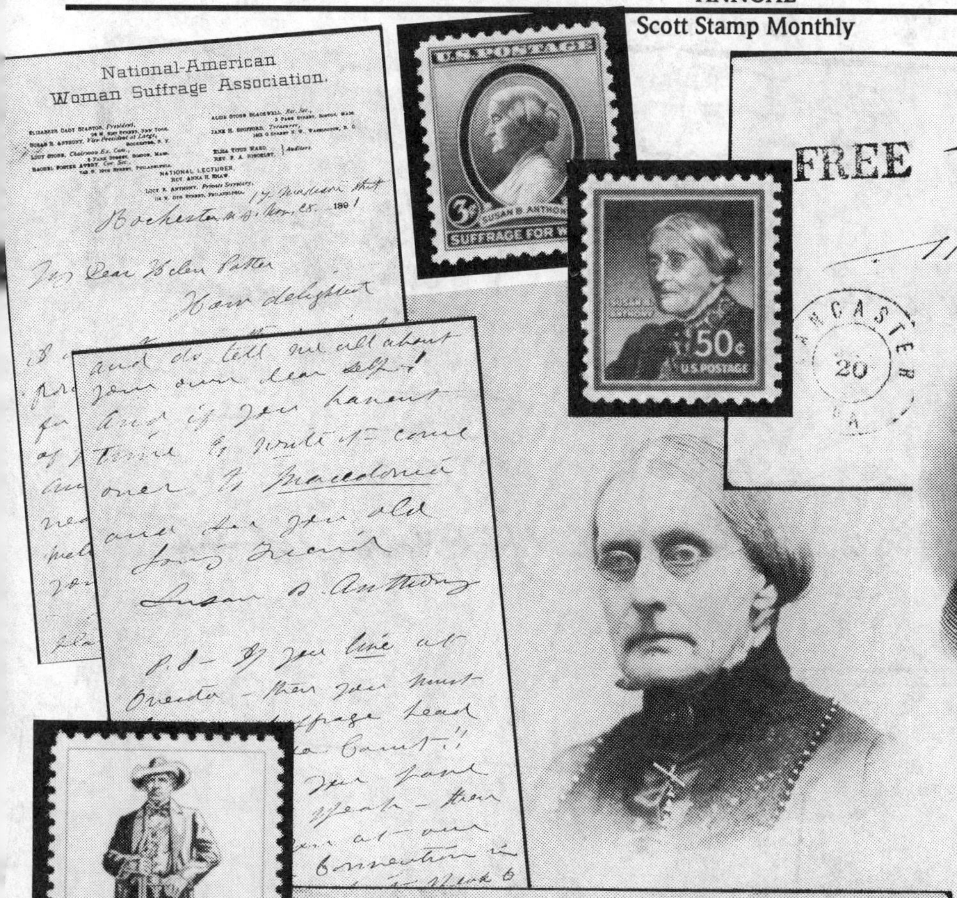

Free franks, such as the James Buchanan signature above, are not limited to presidents. Presidential widows and politicians have also been allowed the priviledge. At left is a Sam Houston free frank from his political years. Above left is an interesting letter signed by suffragette Susan B. Anthony.

wrist, the rubber stamp was in use during Eleanor Roosevelt's time. Although Edith Roosevelt has never appeared on a U.S. stamp, Eleanor has. She was featured first on a 5¢ commemorative, Scott 1236, and again on a 20¢ stamp, Scott 2105.

Moving on we find an autographed check, made payable to the "Lyons Furniture Agency" in the sum of $15, penned by our 30th president, Calvin Coolidge, who coined the phrase, "If you don't say anything, you won't be called on to repeat it!" Although the signature predates his time in the White House, it is a nice item nonetheless. By his own count, Coolidge shook hands with 1,900 White House visitors in a 34-minute period of time!

On June 14, 1939, my grandmother received a letter from Albert Einstein, which is kept within the pages of this collection. Although the letter is typewritten, it is signed in ink and written on Mr. Einstein's personal embossed stationery. I cannot re-read his words enough. Although we relate to Einstein as a great scientist of this century, he also was a great humanitarian who devoted a great deal of his life to the plight of the Jewish people. He speaks in the letter as follows: "The power of resistance which has enabled the Jewish people to survive for thousands of years has been based to a large extent on traditions of mutual helpfulness. In these years of affliction our readiness to help one another is being put to an especially severe test. May we stand this test as well as did our fathers before us." Einstein congratulates my grandmother in his letter for her "splendid work on behalf of the refugees during Dedication Week." Despite the monetary value of this letter, I personally hold the words I see and read as a great value to my family's heritage. Einstein has been featured on two U.S. stamps. He was first shown on the 8¢ Prominent Americans series stamp, Scott 1285, and again on a 15¢ commemorative from 1978, Scott 1774, which honored the centennial of his birth.

In May 1960, I was finishing my first year in junior high. Our United States senator, John F. Kennedy, was running for president. Although I was too young to vote, I still can recall all the excitement this young man generated. Three years later I would stand with the nation and cry over his assassination. The letter in my grandmother's collection, typewritten and short, is on Kennedy's campaign stationery, bearing his photograph and stating, "U.S. Senator, John F. Kennedy for President." Written to a now-defunct company, the letter ends, "With Every Good Wish, I am Sincerely, Jack Kennedy," his signature in ink. Again, monetary value is no issue for me. I lived through the excitement and the tragic end of John F. Kennedy. The possession of this signed letter is history that I saw unfold. Kennedy has been featured on

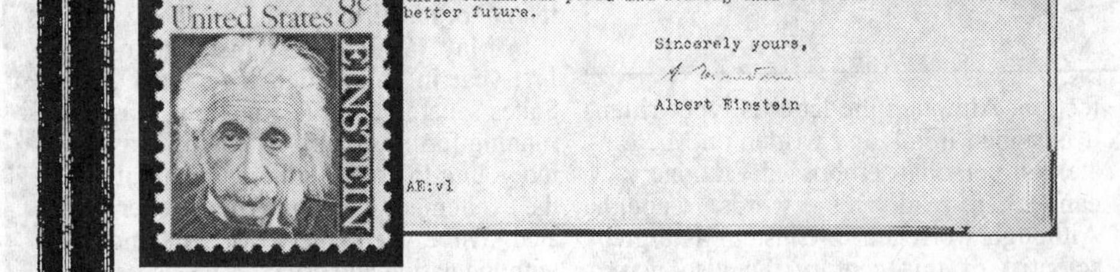

Mr. Berthold Ehrenberg,
Simon Danenberg & Co.,
150, William St.,
New York, N. Y.

My dear Mr. Ehrenberg:

May I offer my sincere congrat[...] you on the splendid work you have undert[...] behalf of the refugees during Dedication[...]

The power of resistance which h[...] the Jewish people to survive for thousan[...] years has been based to a large extent o[...] tions of mutual helpfulness. In these years of affliction our readiness to help one another is being put to an especially severe test. May we stand this test as well as did our fathers before us.

We have no other means of self-defense than our solidarity and our knowledge that the cause for which we are suffering is a momentous and sacred cause.

It must be a source of deep gratificatio[n] to you to be making so important a contribution toward rescuing our persecuted fellow-Jews from their calamitous peril and leading them toward a better future.

Sincerely yours,

Albert Einstein

AE:vl

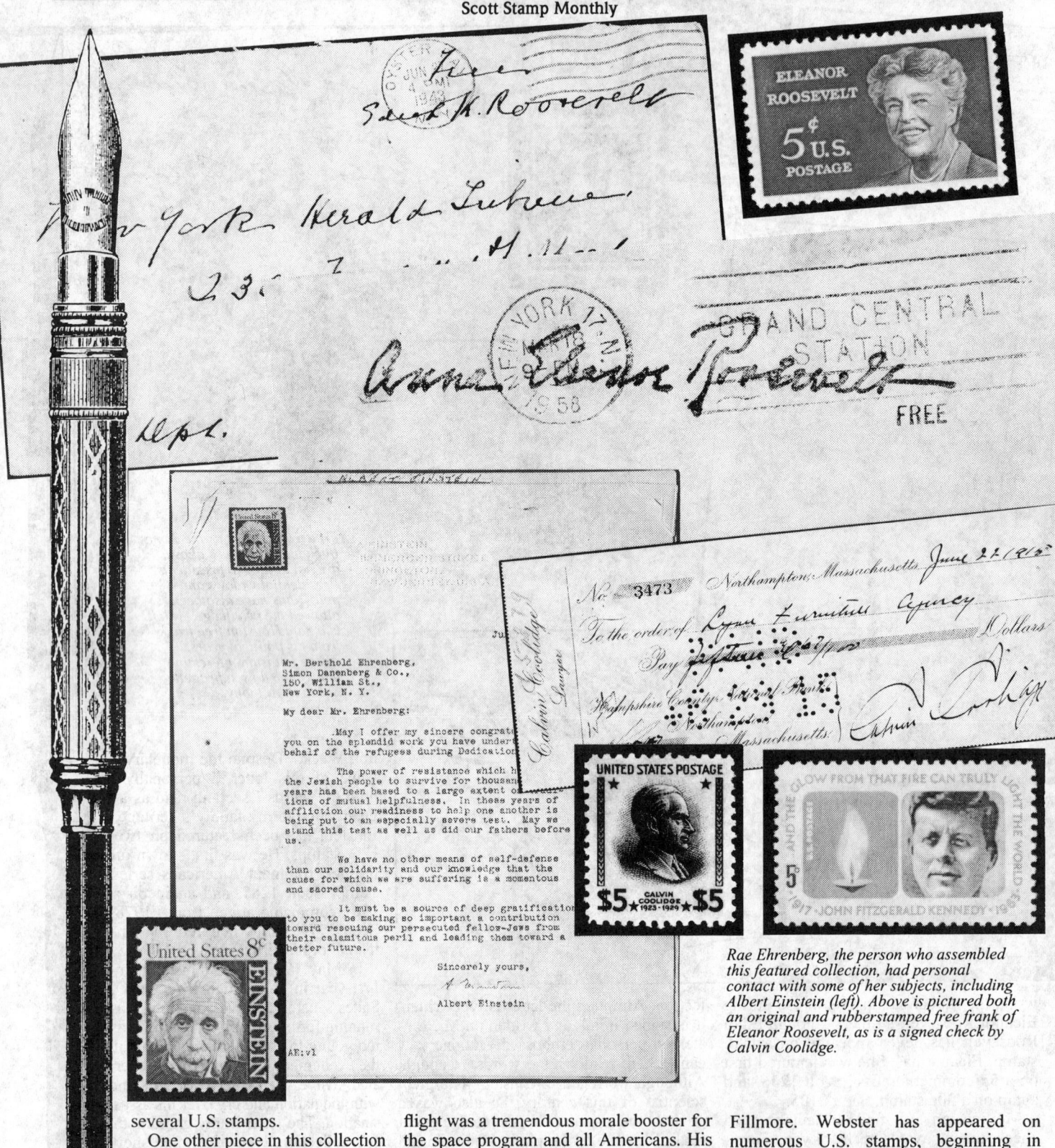

Rae Ehrenberg, the person who assembled this featured collection, had personal contact with some of her subjects, including Albert Einstein (left). Above is pictured both an original and rubberstamped free frank of Eleanor Roosevelt, as is a signed check by Calvin Coolidge.

several U.S. stamps.

One other piece in this collection to which I relate is a letter from Lt. Col. John H. Glenn, Jr. He wrote to my grandmother thanking her for her interest of the flight of the Friendship 7 spacecraft. He states, "Each flight is a stepping stone in our ever expanding manned space flight research program." I remember Feb. 20, 1962, as Project Mercury lifted from its launch pad in Cape Canaveral. I remember the earlier flights of Alan Shepard and Gus Grissom, but John Glenn, Jr., making his first orbital flight was a tremendous morale booster for the space program and all Americans. His letter included an autographed first-day cover," an envelope with the first-day canceled Project Mercury stamp affixed. Since Glenn is still living, he has not been featured on a U.S. stamp, but the autographed cover is significant because of his relationship to the U.S. space program.

Additional highlight items from my grandmother's collection include a free-franked letter from Daniel Webster, Secretary of State under Presidents William Henry Harrison, John Tyler and Millard Fillmore. Webster has appeared on numerous U.S. stamps, beginning in 1870, with a 15c bank note issue, Scott 141. He most recently appeared in 1969 on a 6¢ commemorative, Scott 1380.

A letter datelined June 11, 1884, from the executive mansion is signed by our 21st President, Chester A. Arthur. An autographed calling card is also enclosed with the letter. Arthur has appeared on two U.S. stamps, including Scott 826 and 2218c.

Another political figure, Cordell Hull, Secretary of State under Franklin D.

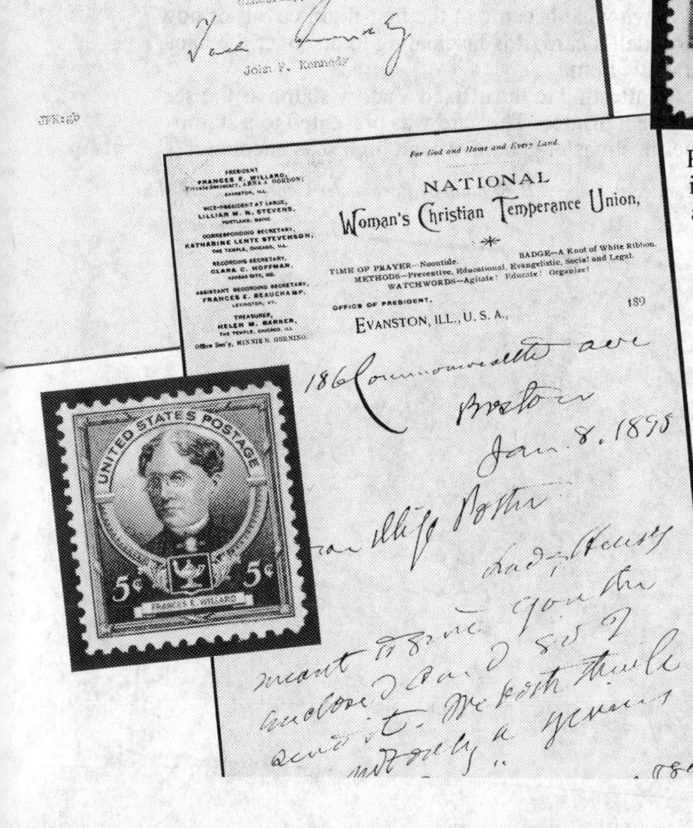

Other U.S. stamp subjects, including John F. Kennedy, Cordell Hull, Chester A. Arthur, Daniel Webster and Francis Willard are featured in the Ehrenberg autograph collection.

Roosevelt, is represented in the collection. It is an autographed thank you letter for Christmas greetings. Hull appeared on a 5¢ commemorative in 1963, Scott 1235.

Two more individuals whose autographs appear in the collection are featured in the 1940 Famous Americans series. Francis E. Willard was pictured on Scott 872. She was leader of the National Women's Christian Temperance Union for a number of years. A personal letter written on NWCTU stationery and signed by Willard is contained in the collection.

Finally, Jane Addams, a social worker who established Chicago's Hull House Community Center, is represented on Scott 878, and on a 15¢ postal card marking the centennial of the establishment of Hull House, Scott UX134. Addams' signature appears on a 1913 letter written on Hull House stationery.

One cannot tire from examining a collection of this sort. Through the years I have frequently pulled these books from their shelf and have leafed gently through their pages. Carefully photocopying their contents, my children have used many of these letters and documents for their school history reports. I have thought many times of giving the collection a facelift with new pages and bindings, but I feel that in the "making better" I would lose touch with the authenticity of its age. A letter from Robert Todd Lincoln, Secretary of War, regarding an AWOL soldier of the "late war" would lose character if placed upon a page within a newly bought

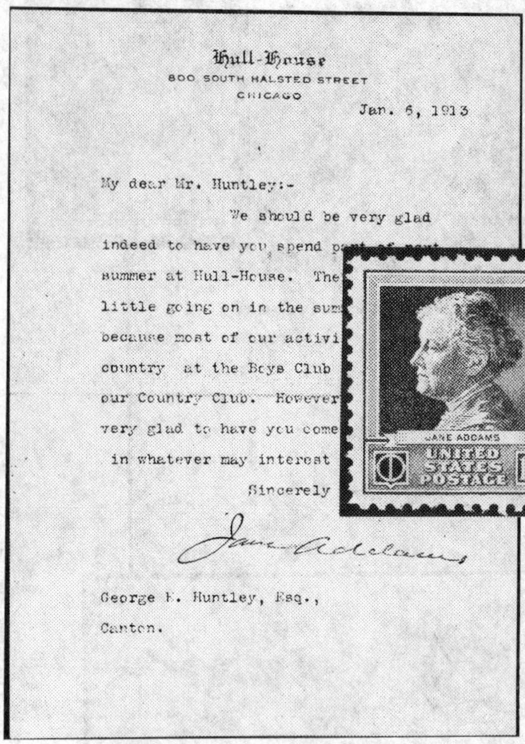
Hull-House
800 South Halsted Street
Chicago

Jan. 6, 1913

My dear Mr. Huntley:-

We should be very glad indeed to have you spend p... summer at Hull-House. The... little going on in the sum... because most of our activi... country at the Boys Club ... our Country Club. However ... very glad to have you come ... in whatever may interest ...

Sincerely

George F. Huntley, Esq.,
Canton.

Jane Addams, founder of Chicago's Hull House, signed the illustrated letter. Both Addams and Hull House have been featured on U.S. issues.

binder. It is better to be kept dust free, upon a shelf, and savor the visual imagery of times long since gone, but not forgotten.

If you are interested in collecting autographs and manuscripts, you may wish to join the Manuscript Society. Founded in 1948 as the National Society of Autograph collectors, the Manuscript Society now includes more than 1,400 collectors worldwide. The group publishes a quarterly journal and newsletters. Annual membership is $25. For more information, please write to The Manuscript Society, David R. Smith, Director, 350 N. Niagra St., Burbank, CA 91505. ❖

VICTORY BY SEA

by Wayne L. Youngblood

One of the items contained in the Rae Ehrenberg autograph collection has an interesting story behind it. It is a 5-by 7-inch card with a copy of Scott 537, the 3¢ Victory stamp, attached. The undated card simply states, "I hereby certify that the Three-cent Victory stamp affixed to this card is stamp No. 2 of the first sheet printed." The signatures of President Woodrow Wilson and Postmaster General Albert Burleson appear above the statement, and Third Assistant Postmaster General A.M. Dockery's autograph is found below. This type of item was created by various postmasters general as souvenirs to be given to dignitaries.

In the case of the illustrated card, it was presented by Burleson in 1927 to a sea captain. The original story regarding the card appeared as a letter in the Nov. 28, 1927, issue of Mekeel's Weekly Stamp News. The sea captain, A.B. Randall, was a stamp collector and member of the American Philatelic Society (Member No. 6635). It was he who wrote the letter.

At the time of his encounter with Burleson, Randall was captain of the Atlantic, a transatlantic liner owned by the United States Lines. Randall noted that Burleson was to be a passenger on a trip to Plymouth, England, and thought to bring a May 15, 1918, first-flight cover bearing the 24¢ airmail stamp, Scott C3. The cover had been personally signed and addressed by Burleson to Ralph Pulitzer of the New York World. The cover had subsequently been given to Randall by an official of the newspaper.

Once aboard ship, Randall took the opportunity to invite Burleson, his wife and daughter to his cabin, whereupon he mentioned the introduction of airmail and showed the cover, asking if Burleson remembered it. A pleased, but startled, Burleson exclaimed, "Where did you get this and why?" Randall then told Burleson he was a collector and had been one since he was a small boy. The two gentlemen continued to visit about stamps and other postal matters.

Before leaving Randall's ship, Burleson asked for the cover. He then wrote the following on the back: "Again, after nine years I write on this envelope, this time in appreciation of a delightful voyage on the S.S. Republic under the command of my friend Captain A.B. Randall. May 1927 A.S. Burleson."

Upon Burleson's return to his home in Austin, Texas, he sent Randall the illustrated card. He and Randall had other visits on subsequent trips.

Although it is not known what became of the first-flight cover, or how Ehrenberg obtained Randall's card, it is fascinating to discover the background behind this specific item.

The autographed card attesting to the affixed Victory stamp as the second one from the first sheet printed. The card was presented to a stamp collector by the former postmaster general after a high seas encounter.

Shown here is the card presented to Capt. A.B. Randall by Postmaster General A.S. Burleson.

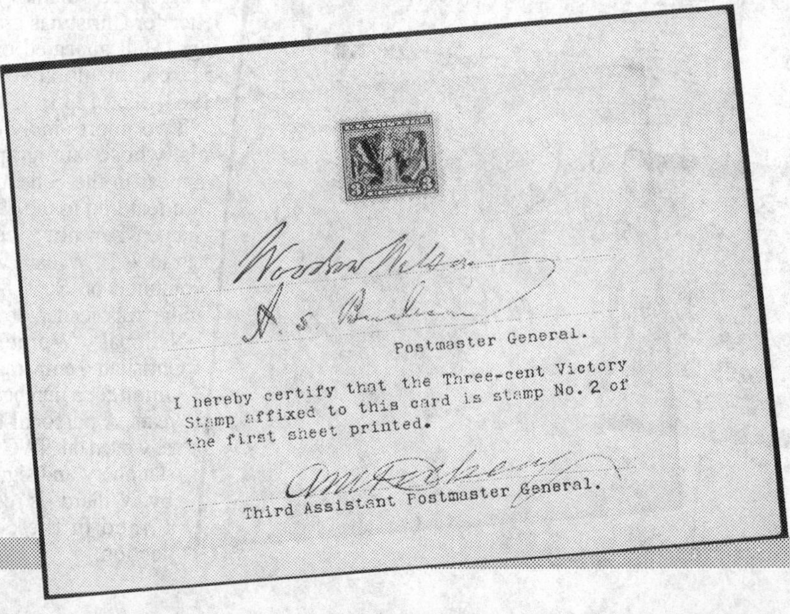
Postmaster General.

I hereby certify that the Three-cent Victory Stamp affixed to this card is stamp No. 2 of the first sheet printed.

Third Assistant Postmaster General.

CILHI SEARCH AND RECOVERY
MISSION TO LOCATE THE
REMAINS OF THE MISSING 22
MEN OF THE GOETTGE PATROL
LOST NEAR THE MATANIKAU RIVER,
GUADALCANAL ON 12 AUG 1942.
Paul A Bethke
PAUL A. BETHKE
CPT, QM
TEAM LEADER
SOLOMON ISLANDS 60c
Mangrove Kingfisher
GEORGE COSENTINI
10826 SAGEBERRY
HOUSTON, TX 77089
U.S.A

Nearly forty-five years to the day after Lt. Col. Frank Goettge's patrol was ambushed on Guadalcanal, the remains of those killed were located. This cover sent by the commander of the recovery team commemorates the discovery.

Cover Recalls Deadly Ambush of Marine Patrol on Guadalcanal

BY GEORGE COSENTINI

On August 7, 1942, the United States' First Marine Division landed on Guadalcanal, a key stepping stone on the road to defeating the forces of Japan. The going was particularly rough for the first few days. The Marines had a toehold around what would become Henderson Field, but they were trying to determine where the strength of the Japanese defenders was located.

Patrol reports indicated that most of the enemy troops were positioned between Kokumbona and the Matanikau river. After much discussion with the Commanding General, Lt. Col. Frank Goettge, the Division intelligence officer, decided to organize another patrol, one that he would lead himself. The Commanding General agreed only with reluctance, Goettge would have made a prize prisoner for the Japanese.

Goettge assembled a twenty-five man patrol that included a surgeon and a Lt. Cory, who was fluent in Japanese. The patrol planned to land on the west side of the Matanikau, avoid contact with the Japanese and get into the hills on reconnaissance, then return to the Marine's perimeter.

The exact reason that the mission turned into a tragedy probably never will be known. Perhaps unfamiliarity with the terrain led the patrol to land at the wrong location - where the Japanese were waiting. The Japanese let the patrol come ashore, then cut down its members in an action that lasted no more than five minutres.

There were 3 survivors. Sgt. C.C. Arndt returned to the perimeter early the next morning with first news of the patrol's fate. A Cpl. Spaulding and Sgt. F.L. Few later made their way back to the Marines' lines.

Relief patrols were sent out but no trace was found of Goettge's patrol.

The patrol had gone out on August 12, 1942. Almost 45 years later to the day - on August 8, 1987 - a team from the Central Identification Laboratory - Hawaii (CILHI), led by Capt. Paul Bethke, finally discovered the remains of the ill-fated group of brave Marines. The mission of CILHI, which is located at Fort Shafter, Hawaii, is to find and identify remains from World War II and the Vietnam War.

The cover mailed from the Solomon Islands on August 8 commemorates the success of a CILHI team in locating the remains of the Goettge patrol.

I am grateful to Paul not only for sending me the cover but especially for the great work he and his team do under extremely difficult circumstances. America in in debt to them all. ❖

Acknowledgements

A tip of the Marine cap to Ted Bahry, the ultimate Marine, who provided some information on this action. Useful information is also found in two books, Pearl Harbor to Guadalcanal (In the five volume History of the U.S. Marine Corps operations in World War II) by Lt. Col. Frank O. Hough, Maj. Verle E. Ludwig and Henry I. Shaw, Jr. (c. 1955) and The Battle for Guadalcanal, by Samuel B. Griffith II (1979). A brief description of this patrol can be found in The U.S. Army in World War II - Chronology 1941 - 1945

The Author

George Cosentini, a frequent contributor to the AP, is a hazardous materials specialist. He collects covers from World War II to the present from all the military services and says his main interest is APOs.

WHEN U.S. STAMPS WENT TO WAR

by George Amick

The death of President Franklin D. Roosevelt, the surrender of the Third Reich and the suicide of Adolf Hitler, the atomic bombing of Hiroshima and Nagasaki and the surrender of Japan all came in a span of a little over four months in 1945.

Victory constituted a fantastic release for Americans, as it was for all the Allied nations. For half a decade, the war had dominated U.S. life, affecting all activity, public and private.

And, like other things, U.S. postage stamps of the period reflected this national single-mindedness. One of the common questions during that time was "Don't you know there's a war on?" Look at your stamp album pages for these years: You knew there was a war, all right.

The first clue is that there were far fewer issues than normal, as the country's stamp-collecting president turned his attention to more important matters, and the Bureau of Engraving and Printing kept its presses busy producing war bonds and war savings stamps and motor vehicle use tax stamps and ration coupons.

In 1940, the last full year of peace for America, 44 new U.S. postage stamps appeared. During the next five years - the war years - there was a total of only 35.

And never before or since has the subject matter of U.S. commemoratives been so narrowly focused for so long a time. The great majority of those 35 stamps had war-related themes.

This sometimes involved some reaching by postal officials. The 1944 stamp commemorating the 100th anniversary of Morse's telegraph (Scott 924) was described by Postmaster General Frank C. Walker as "in recognition of the contribution which electrical communications have made to the war effort."

The stamp issued a few months later for the 50th anniversary of motion pictures (Scott 926) pictured an audience of servicemen on a South Pacific island watching a film projected on a screen hung between palm trees.

Though new issues were cut back, the reduction wasn't as drastic as some had feared after the attack on Pearl Harbor December 7, 1941. The New York Times reported the following week that "no new postal paper except stamps actually needed is looked for during the duration of the conflict." That didn't happen, to stamp collectors' relief.

But even before Pearl Harbor, U.S. stamps were influenced by the war, which had begun in Asia in 1937 with the Japanese invasion of China and in Europe in 1939 with the German drive into Poland.

President Roosevelt had authorized the Post Office Department to prepare a stamp or souvenir sheet for May 1940 to mark the 100th anniversary of the first postage stamp, Great Britain's Penny Black. The betting was that the sheet would reproduce early U.S. stamps, probably the 5¢ and 10¢ 1847s (Scott 1-2).

But in April the State Department advised the White House and Post Office Department that to postally recognize one of the belligerent nations while the U.S. was striving to remain neutral might be misconstrued. FDR agreed, and the proposed issue was scrapped.

As time went by, the U.S. tilted more toward the Allies, and some of its actions, such as Lend-Lease and the swap of 50 over-age destroyers to the British for naval and air bases, would have made a simple stamp issue for the Penny Black's centennial seem mild indeed.

After the Axis powers conquered France in June 1940, swept over most of Western Europe and began heavy bombing of British cities, the U.S. got serious about its own rearmament. Congress, in response to FDR's plea, appropriated $13 billion to beef up the armed forces, authorized extensive controls over industrial production and enacted the first peacetime draft.

FDR and others concluded that a set of stamps to promote the National Defense program would be just the thing, following the precedent of the stamp he had authorized in 1933 to drum up support for the National Recovery Act (Scott 732).

So on October 16, 1940 - the day young men were required to register for the draft - the Post Office Department issued 1, 2 and 3¢ stamps in the regular size (Scott 899-901), bearing the slogan "For Defense" and picturing the Statue of Liberty, an antiaircraft gun and the "torch of enlightenment," respectively. These were designed from pencil sketches by FDR himself.

The stamps aroused no great excitement in the U.S., and were so common that dealers and collectors discarded used copies, but the British, oddly enough, loved them. One British dealer reportedly sold them for a dime a set. And British stamp publications cited them as examples of what their country should be doing in the way of propaganda.

"Is it too much to hope," asked Stamp Collecting, "that now that America has shown the way the postoffice panjandrums may be stirred into activity with a realization of both the psychological and financial possibilities of an issue of British war stamps?" Answer: Yes, it was. Britain never did issue any stamps with war themes during World War II. Meanwhile, the war was prompting other developments, some of them oddball. One national women's organization began collecting canceled stamps to be sent to Great Britain for dye extraction to pay for children's hospital beds. This effort fizzled out after chemical experts disclosed that it would take one million stamps to produce one pound of pigment worth about $5, while the cost of extraction would be several times that amount. used stamps in bulk would be of far more interest (and value) to collectors, of course, and so people saving stamps for pigment salvage were urged instead to donate them to hospitals for stamp-collecting therapy for war victims.

A new type of U.S. cover - with "free" written across the upper right corner - was born March 27, 1942, when

National Defense Stamps Were Designed by Franklin D. Roosevelt (U.S. Scott 899-901)

American servicemen were excused from thereafter having to stamp their letters. As a result, Post Office studies showed, average mailings by GIs increased from three a week to more than 4.5; by June 1944 the average was up to six. (Rep. David Ward of Maryland introduced a bill directing that a special free stamp be printed for this purpose, and FDR himself liked the idea and had a design for such a stamp created, but nobody could figure out just what practical use it would be, and the subject was dropped.)

After the U.S. entered the war, the Post Office was deluged with requests that it replace the Defense stamps with something more timely. The first to be supplanted was the first-class-rate stamp, the 3¢. in its place the department adapted a striking design prepared by Mark O'Dea of the Maritime Commission for a poster promoting "ships for victory" - an eagle, its wings outstretched in a V for victory, surrounded by 13 stars. The ship slogan was replaced by "Win the War," and a bundle of arrows was placed in the eagle's talons.

The stamp (Scott 905), issued July 4, 1942, would become the most familiar of all postage stamps during the war years, with 20.6 billion printed - the largest number

ever for a commemorative. A year or more after the war ended in 1945, many post offices continued to have them in stock. Its familiarity tended to cause people to overlook the simple effectiveness of its design, which New York artist Leon Helguera later would list among his ten favorite stamp designs of all time.

Helguera was one of a group of artists who in 1942-43 took part in an extraordinary volunteer effort to provide the U.S. with first-rate designs for war propaganda stamps. The project, which originated in the American Institute of Graphic Arts and the Society of Illustrators and was chaired by Paul F. Bernadier, generated dozens of sketches for proposed stamps, showing servicemen, planes, ships, tanks, war production, allegorical symbols and so on.

Only two stamps actually resulted from the committee's efforts, but these, like the Win the War, were very attractive. One, by Helguera, pictured a pyramid of upraised swords fronted by an olive branch and carried the slogan "Nations United for Victory" (Scott 907); the design, Helguera said, flashed into his mind one morning while he was shaving. It replaced the Defense 2¢. The other (Scott 908), a 1¢, featured the famous "Four Freedoms" which FDR had defined in his 1941 State of the Union address. The Bureau of Engraving and Printing adapted the design from a bas-relief in plaster prepared by sculptor Paul Manship, the only stamp designer ever to choose such a medium for his message.

The volunteer committee also was briefly the victim of a bureaucratic communications gap. In mid-1942 it was told by the Office of Facts and Figures, an agency created to marshal public support for the war effort, that the Post Office planned to release a stamp honoring Nazi-conquered Czechoslovakia; the stamp would pay special tribute to the memory of Lidice, the village that was razed and whose men were executed in retaliation for the assassination of Reinhard Heydrich, chief of the German Security Police. The Office asked the artists to prepare drawings for the stamp which it would then lay before FDR for his choice.

The committee prepared 61 drawings and announced it would turn over any payment to war relief. But then came the bad news from Assistant Postmaster General Ramsey S. Black, who said the department "does not have a Lidice stamp under consideration" and hadn't authorized any design work by "private artists and outside agencies."

The episode had a happy postscript, though, in what turned out to be the most remarkable stamp set of the war - a set that would have been outstanding at any time but which, under wartime conditions, was dazzling. This was the Overrun Countries issue of 1943-44 (Scott 909-21).

The artists' committee met early in 1943 with postal officials who told them the president had authorized a series of stamps to honor not only Czechoslovakia but also eight other occupied countries in Europe, and to hold out the hope of eventual liberation for them.

Never before had more than two colors been used on a U.S. stamp, but these stamps would feature the flags of the nations in full colors. Because the Bureau of Engraving and Printing had neither the time nor the equipment to do the job, it would be farmed out to the American Bank Note Company of New York at 54 cents per 1,000 stamps - considerably higher than the cost to the Bureau of producing single-color stamps. This would mark the first time the U.S. had gone to a private stamp printer since American Bank Note produced the Columbian Exposition commemoratives (Scott 230-45) in 1893.

The artists made several suggestions that were adopted: that the stamps be commemorative size, that the outside borders be a dark shade to set off the flags properly, and that they all be 5-centers, corresponding to the overseas first-class rate. There was some discussion over whether the phoenix, symbol of rebirth, should be used in the design, because the Japanese often had depicted a phoenix on their stamps. However, the border design finally chosen did feature the bird, as well as a female figure breaking the chains of oppression.

The original nine countries listed for honor were Poland, Czechoslovakia, Norway, Luxembourg, the Netherlands, Belgium, France, Greece and Yugoslavia. Later Albania

The Iwo Jima Stamp Was Banned on Mail to Japanese P.O.W. Camps (U.S. Scott 929)

and Austria were added - though a few people complained that Austria didn't belong, asserting that the country really hadn't been overrun and in fact had welcomed annexation to Germany in 1938.

For some reason Denmark, which the Nazis had occupied in the spring of 1940, was overlooked, until Danish-born A. E. Pade of Denver, Colorado, a well-known stamp dealer, launched a campaign among Danish-Americans to convince the Post Office that it was discriminating against their homeland. Though the Danes hardly constituted a major voting bloc, their message got through and on June 28 the Post Office announced that Denmark's flag would grace a 12th and final stamp of the series.

The 12 were issued over a six-month period, with the first day of sale of each in Washington. In addition, the Polonus Philatelic Society successfully lobbied to have Chicago share first-day ceremonies for the Poland stamp, the first of the series.

With a steel-blue frame and flags in one to three colors, the stamps were beautiful and became highly popular. However, students of printing details were frustrated by the private contractor's refusal to disclose any information about production except to say that the frame designs were engraved and the flags and country names done by offset. For this reason the Scott Catalogue editors declined to list the "irregularities, flaws, blemishes and 'errors' which are numerous to this issue." The flag stamps, unlike any previous U.S. commemoratives, carried no plate numbers, but each pane bore the name of the appropriate country in the top right selvage, creating name blocks rather than plate number blocks for collectors.

In April 1944 the Post Office announced that two countries occupied by the Japanese also would be honored - the Philippines and Korea. (Two years earlier, China had been honored on the fifth anniversary of its struggle against the Japanese with a 5¢ commemorative, Scott 906, picturing two national heroes, America's Lincoln and China's Sun Yat-sen.) Though the implication was that both the new stamps would be of the Overrun Countries type, only the Korea turned out to be. It gave the series the only variety recognized by Scott, the so-called "Korpa error," not a true error but a minor printing flaw on the 26th stamp in each pane.

The stamp for the Philippines - at that time a U.S. commonwealth - was a 3¢ purple (Scott 925) showing the island of Corregidor in Manila Bay, where U.S. and Filipino defenders made their last stand in 1942. Collectors were disappointed that it wasn't another in the flag series, and nicknamed it the "pork chop stamp" because of the resemblance of the island, as shown, to a chop in a frying pan.

From early in the war there had been calls for a series of stamps honoring the armed forces, and in January 1945 Sen. Joseph C. O'Mahoney of Wyoming, a former assistant postmaster general, wrote a long appeal to Postmaster General Walker urging this kind of "graceful and deserved tribute to our servicemen." The catalyst for the series, though, turned out to be the publication the following month of the most famous photograph of the war, and one of the most famous of all time - Joe Rosenthal's shot for the Associated Press of U.S. Marines raising the flag on Iwo Jima's Mount Suribachi. The dramatic picture excited Americans, and Sen. O'Mahoney quickly fired off another letter to Walker asking that it be used on a stamp honoring the Marines. He also called for the use of another AP photo, of U.S. soldiers crossing the Rhine at Remagen, on a stamp for the Army.

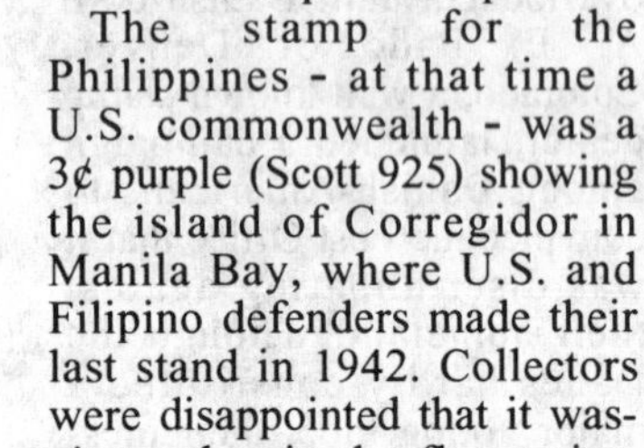

The Army Issue Was To Have Shown the Remagen Bridge (U.S. Scott 934)

FDR, only a few days before his death, OK'd the idea of Iwo Jima and Remagen stamps. On June 7 Walker announced that the Iwo Jima stamp for the Marines would be issued, and a few days later added that similar postal recognition would be given the Army, navy, Coast Guard and Merchant Marine.

Until virtually the eve of the announcement, officials had publicly worried that the Rosenthal photo wouldn't work if reduced to postage stamp size. Their fears were groundless. The Iwo Jima stamp (Scott 929), vertically oriented and printed in Marine green, was handsome with the picture dominating.

Many commented that this stamp broke precedent by showing living persons - although, in fact, live people had been depicted on several earlier commemoratives, from the 2¢ Trans-Mississippi (Scott 286) to the 2¢ Arbor Day (Scott 717). Others worried about showing a large unfurled American flag that would be defaced by post-office cancelers. (Obviously, that particular concern has long since faded away.)

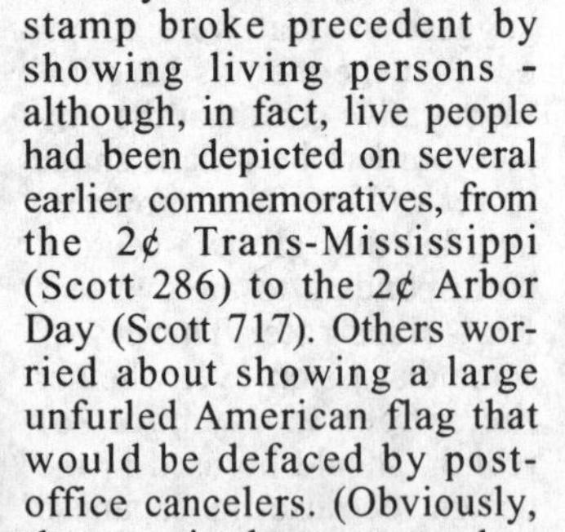

Sailors in Summer Whites at Corpus Christi, Texas (U.S. Scott 935)

An odd footnote: The Post Office officially barred use of the Iwo Jima stamp on mail to prisoners of war held by the Japanese. It explained that the stamp might offend the enemy and lead to confiscation of the mail. This problem didn't arise with the remaining Armed Forces stamps, however; they didn't make their appearance until after the war ended on August 14, 1945.

The Army stamp (Scott 934) didn't show the Remagen bridge after all, but used another AP photo of a great parade of U.S. soldiers through Paris after its liberation. In order to include in the honor the Air Force - which then was a branch of the Army - the War Department added to the photo six bombers flying overhead; unaccountably, it chose B-29s, which never saw service in the European theater.

The Navy stamp (Scott 935) pictured a group shot of smiling sailors in summer whites at the Corpus Christi, Texas, Naval Air Station. The Coast Guard commemorative (Scott 936) showed a drawing of an invasion barge heading for the beach, and the Merchant Marine stamp (Scott 939) depicted a Liberty Ship unloading cargo.

The death of FDR as the European war was rushing to a close led to a series of memorial stamps (Scott 930-35) picturing the four-term president. It also led to a last-minute scramble to change the design of the 5¢ stamp to be issued April 25, less than two weeks later, to mark the conference opening in San Francisco that day to permanently organize the United Nations.

FDR himself had selected a simple design for the stamp featuring the words "Toward United Nations," the date, and an olive branch. Descriptive details were announced by the Post Office April 12, only hours before the president died. The next day postal officials huddled to decide whether and how to alter the design, and Bureau artists prepared a sketch that reduced the size of the lettering and added a profile picture of FDR. Time was too short, though, for a complete new engraving, and the final decision was to place quotation marks around the wording on the original die and add the name "Franklin D. Roosevelt" in small letters (Scott 928). Some 1.2 million stamps were sold on the first day, April 25, in San Francisco, breaking all records for a 5¢ stamp.

The U.S. had marked the end of World War I with a commemorative (Scott 537) back in the days when commemoratives were few and far between, and it was universally assumed that peace this time also would lead to a stamp, perhaps a series. The Post Office let it be known shortly after V-J Day that it was planning something along this line, and asked for design suggestions. Leon Helguera of the artists' committee, for one, responded with several sketches featuring a dove of peace and a tolling Liberty Bell.

Perhaps it was the long delay in executing peace treaties with the ex-enemies, caused by disputes between the western Allies and the Soviet Union. Perhaps it was the swift onset of the Cold War with the Soviets. Perhaps it was the absence of a stamp collector in the White House to give the necessary push. Whatever the reason, the victory stamp never was issued.

The closest thing to it was a little 3¢ commemorative issued in 1946 to honor veterans (Scott 940), illustrating the gold lapel pin which the vets had dubbed the "ruptured duck." It was an oddly inconclusive conclusion to the story of the U.S. stamps of World War II. ❖

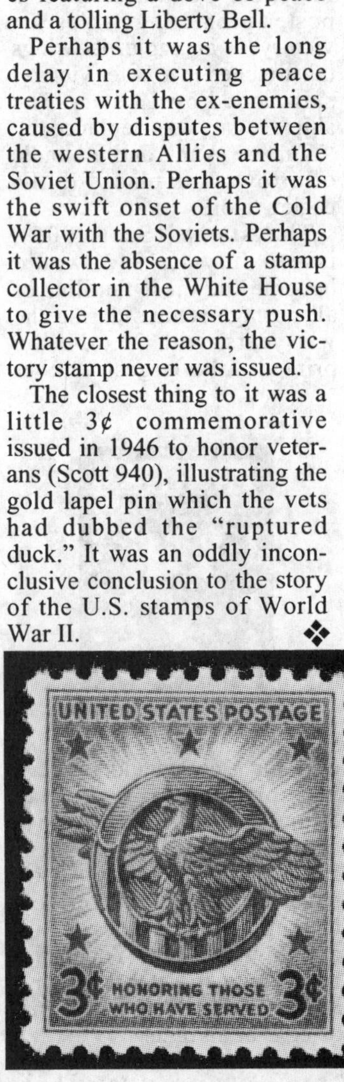

WWII PATRIOTICS WITH HUMOROUS IMAGES

by Allison W. Cusick

Military life has always been a fertile field for comedians and cartoonists. During World War II artists lightened the burdens of soldiers and civilians with humorous images of life in the Armed Services.

In an earlier article I looked at harsh, even vicious, patriotic cachet cartoons which demonized the enemy. The cachets in this installment represent a gentler aspect. Previous segments of this series appeared in Linn's, March 14, April 11, June 13 and Sept. 12, 1994.

The old jokes of military life are rehashed in a colorful group of cartoons printed by American Art Service. More than a dozen cachets by this maker are known. The multicolored designs are printed on either blue or tan envelopes.

The cachet in Figure 1 is a good example of this series. The company cook whips the tired soldiers towards a new record in potato-peeling. Other designs include a sailor painting the names of his sweethearts on the prow of his ship and a soldier dumping a woman unceremoniously from his lap in order to salute a passing officer.

American Art Service cachets are signed below the cachet with the name and a 1942 copyright notice. They frequently are found on nonphilatelic mail, though the illustrated example is philatelic. I suspect these patriotics were sold largely to the general public and were not of philatelic origin. Can anyone provide information on these attractive patriotics?

A delightful series of military cartoons are signed "East Coast Lefty." These casually-drawn cachets emphasis the humorous aspects of naval service.

The cachet in Figure 2 depicts a naval guard walking the dock while carrying an umbrella. The blue, thermographed cachet is signed at lower right.

"East Coast Lefty" was Walter Lupton of Pico, California. Lupton was a prolific artist who designed cachets for several makers of naval covers from the late 1930s through the 1940s. Most of Lupton's designs are signed with his nickname or the initials "ECL." Many dozens of Lupton's cachets are known. Unfortunately, I've found no personal information on the man.

The illustrated cover (Figure 2) was produced by Walter G. Crosby of nearby San Pedro, California. Crosby was just one of the cover dealers for whom Lupton designed cachets. We looked at Crosby's career in two previous columns in Linn's, 10 May 1993 and 10 May 1994.

Now the big question. Why was "East Coast Lefty" in California? Can anyone enlighten us?

The cachet in Figure 3 is a refreshing remainder that it was possible during the war to caricature the enemy without descending to virulence.

Lee H. Cornell of Wichita, Kansas created three cachets based upon the Kicking Mule of U.S. fancy cancel fame. Here's one of them (Figure 3).

The U.S. mule kicks Hitler and his cohorts into a flying triangle. The figures are drawn in a spirit of fun. They lack the vicious aspects usually encountered in such portraits.

Cornell's designs are signed at the bottom of the cachet and dated 1943. Cornell printed 5,000 of the cachets in Figure 3. They were sold at 25¢ for thirty-five envelopes or $1 per 100 including postage!

Dale Myers featured Cornell and his cachets in the May 1994 issue of *The American Philatelist.*

Cornell, I'm happy to say, is alive and well today at 90.

Is good humor a key to longevity? ❖

Figure 2

Figure 3

Figure 1
The humor of military life is featured in a series of cachets by American Art Service. The cook urges soliders to set a potato-peeling record in this example.

Figure 2
Many enjoyable cartoons of naval service were drawn by Walter Lupton, known as "East Coast Lefty". Walter Crosby printed this envelope showing a guard walking the docks with an umbrella.

Figure 3
The Axis leaders were caricatured in a humorous fashion by Lee Cornell. His designs lack the viciousness often found in images of the enemy.

My favorite stamps and memories

by Donald J. Landis

We simply don't see the same image in the mirror today as we saw years ago. That earlier, and possibly better, image is gone forever and now can only be found in photographs. To see yourself as you were decades ago, the family photo album must be dragged out.

It is possible that we as philatelists have it better, since we can ignore the changes in ourselves and concentrate on stamps that now cover a period of more than 150 years, so we pull out the albums or stockbooks. Stamps do not change in appearance unless it is due to an uncommon deterioration of paper or gum. Therefore, most stamps in our albums look just like they were the first day we saw them. The postage stamp, much like a musical piece heard many times can bring us back to the time we first saw it. This could be the reason so many collectors leave collecting after youth to get on with their careers, only to return to the hobby at a later age when memories become more important.

I have, for some years, kept a memory packet in my wallet for this reason. Having given up smoking and coffee, my memory packet provides relief after stressful periods. I can pull it out and relive my novice stamp collector period that started in the late 1940s. Having made quite a few of these filled glassines, I would like to share my memories of various issues and illustrate a few of my favorites.

How did the young collector, more than 40 years ago, get introduced to his hereafter lifelong interest? From the age of 10 I was a collector of airplane cards and bullets. Many readers of today will think that the latter interest was a bit weird, but that time was but a few years after America's World War II victory, and many dwellings had small artillery projectiles as home decorations. In 1948, a friend had a big box of almost unsorted stamps, which he traded me for my bullets. Thus I was introduced to the world of philately.

I was already nearsighted at that age, and my parents were needlessly worried that this new hobby would further damage my eyesight. On first forbidding me the new avocation – I offered my parents the possibility of returning to ammunition collecting, some of which were live rounds. They quickly relented and my life as a philatelist began. That box of stamps was a good mixture, and I can still clearly remember going through it. Quite a few items in my memory packet were found in that mixture.

United States issues were the most common, but of great interest to me. There are so many issues from our homeland on which I could focus. Scott 807 and 905 were not included in the box, but were plentiful elsewhere. These 3¢ Jefferson and Win the War stamps were regular postage in my young years, along with the 1 1/2¢ Martha Washington for unsealed greeting cards and circulars.

In those days the album that I had omitted many of the early issues, as the first page alone went up to, and included, the 1890 series Scott 219-229. Yet that first page was so important to young collectors, since some of the oldies were represented. On it, my early favorite was – and still is – the 2¢ Blackjack, Scott 73. As kids we had a very limited budget and the $1.50 that this issue as used then cost placed it at the top of my acquisitive power at that time.

Many other U.S. favorites come to mind, such as the 1940 Famous American series of 35 stamps. In 1951, I received as a Christmas gift the 21 used 1¢ to 3¢ stamps from the set and it seemed to me at the time as a fine gift. I now have mint 5¢ and 10¢ stamps of this issue in my stock book.

Sometimes, I wish there was a machine with which the higher values now in my possession could have been added to my stamp album at that time. Then, the Presidentials of 1938 were still available at face value in all post offices, and many of us purchased sheets of the 1/2¢ Franklin, Scott 803, the only sheet we could afford. Scott 974, the 1948 3¢ Juliette Gordon Low, was another favorite of mine. I can remember the boxes of chocolate malt ball cookies that the Girl Scouts sold at the time. My sister was a scout, and any of her unsold boxes were purchased by father and consumed by us. The taste of those cookies returns

upon seeing the Low stamp.

Scott C38, the 5¢ New York Jubilee issue of 1948, was then snapped up by collectors and, like the Famous Americans, experienced an incredible increase in catalogue value for only a year or two. This probably encouraged youngsters like myself to invest our modest incomes in 3¢ mint sheets, which we later sold for somewhat less than face value.

Another of my favorites is Scott 1015, the 1952 3¢ Newspaper Boy issue. At that time I was a paper boy and appreciated the honor of my early profession honored philatelically, even before my father's much more important teaching profession, which was recognized in 1957.

Great Britain stamps were a common foreign stamp supply for the mid-century American collector. Queen Victoria adhesives dating from 1855-1900 were found in most mixtures. Scott 89, issued in 1881, was often found in these, along with low-value Edwardian issues. Many of these stamps bore town location and cancellation dates that were ignored by young collectors and are now sought after by bull's-eye cancel collectors. My British memory piece is the 25th wedding anniversary issue of King George VI and Queen Elizabeth, Scott 267. The bright blue adhesive was very attractive then and remains so. A coincidence that I could not have appreciated at the time about Queen Victoria and Queen Elizabeth (Queen Mother) is that both survived their husbands by 40 years or more.

Brazil had many issues often seen by 1950s collectors. With more than 500 issues of regulars and airmails by that time, the country was well represented in mixtures. We didn't see the early bull's-eye stamps from this land. Instead, there were the exciting Santos Dumont (Scott C24) and other aviators airmails. The aviation theme excited us all. Dumont's earlier powered dirigibles led us to read about other pioneers, including the Montgolfier brothers, Langley, Wright brothers and others.

Space was barely heard of, but there was mention of the WAC Corporal (V-2) bumper (staged) rocket launchings in *Popular Science* and *Boy's Life* of 1948-52. Who would have then thought of a manned moon landing occurring only two decades later? Probably not even the producers of *Destination Moon*, a big box office motion picture then, had a clue. Perhaps the most common mixture stamps that I have enjoyed over the years are the 1933-40 Brazil Faith and Energy Allegory stamps, Scott 384-385, 435, 471 and 491. The set featured the values of a more conservative, but more energetic and forward-moving age than we see today.

Bulgaria was neither then (or now) a buzz word among young collectors. Despite this, I had my favorites, Scott Q1-Q18. I enjoy these because you don't need to understand the cyrillic alphabet to realize the stamps' purpose. These 1941-42 parcel post issues had a good 20 or more years lead on the Postal People series of the United States or other countries. My main association with the set in 1952 was that it was part of a wholesale approval set from Don Shepard who then provided wholesale stamp packets for aspiring stamp dealers. Though the glassines sent included stamps from early Iron Curtain and South American countries (and so not the greatest material), the prices were modest and he did provide an instruction pamphlet for the novice dealer.

For a time in 1950, my best friend and I worked for a local stamp dealer in Easton, Pa., classifying and sorting. He ran the business out of his large house and paid us in stamps only. Most of us sooner or later dabble with dealing as it is only a step up from trading. Many stamp dealers, like writers, work for the love of the trade and little more than cover expenses.

With almost 1000 stamps issued by 1950, China fascinated us then in an age when 80 percent of my friends also collected. Not only were the stamps plentiful, but the country was mysterious, was the site of recent conflict (Korea's stamps then were also sought for this reason) and the stamps were affordable. A "wholesale" packet of 500 mostly different small Chinese stamps then cost a dollar. Wow! what a bargain.

King Farouk stamps of Egypt were often seen in the mixtures of the 1950s. He was, even then, known to be one of the world's richest stamp collectors. Furthermore, he ascended the throne of Egypt in 1936, my birth year, and was deposed in 1952, when my collecting experience spanned only four years. Many of the early Egyptian issues from the prior century, featuring the Pyramids

Shown are some of the author's favorite stamps, each which evokes an emotional response. In some cases the design is significant to the author. In others, the stamps bring back memories.

As a child, the author found stamps intriguing, some for obvious reasons. Others, such as the Tannu Tava stamps at upper right, evoked excitement and a spirit of adventure to a young mind.

and Sphinx, were of low catalogue value and were accessible to the young collector. These, too, caught my interest.

Germany is, no doubt, one of the most attractive collecting areas for collectors of all ages. The early German State material was not often seen by the 1950s stamper, with the exception of the common values of Wurtemburg. However, we were confronted with many German stamps featuring the allegory of that land – Germania. While not as confusing as our Washington-Franklin series of roughly the same time period, there were some 50 Germania stamps of four distinct series, with different background shading, watermarks and legends.

Being a stamp collector familiar with scenes on stamps can fix a picture in your mind for a later tourist visit. Some 30 years after beginning collecting, I was toured the German city of Rudesheim, where the Germania statue featured on those stamps is located. Hindenburg 1920s and 1930s stamps were commonly seen in 1950s mixtures, but his successor, Adolf Hitler, wins the popularity contest of the juvenile collector hands down.

Hitler stamps were very common in the material received in my first stamp assortment box. There were of many values and colors of the set, and all were very inexpensive.

Then, all school children knew what an evil figure Hitler was. Just a few years earlier, *Life* magazine had featured post-execution photos of his hanged henchmen. Despite the great deal of Hitler-directed hate, most of these stamps survived and are still with us. Some 30 years later at my stamp stand on an American military base, 10-15-year-old children would snap up these items of Hitlermania at a nickel or dime apiece, though one could safely bet that none of them could define the WWII inclusive dates of 1939-45.

I never really got introduced to the stamps of Hungary until about 1951, when I became involved with Mrs. Raub's seventh grade stamp club, held at 11 a.m. every Friday. There were 30 or so students who participated. This was a far cry from the 1980s, when I was asked by a teacher to give a 45-minute session to 3rd grade students about stamps. The first year three children showed up and the second year only one came. Back in 1952, multicolored Hungarian overprints were shown and bought by us all for a penny or two per stamp. Such colors, in an age when most stamps were only one-color, were quite a novelty.

Monaco was another favorite country. There was, for example, the Roosevelt triangle that was often seen in the 1950s, but perhaps more attention was paid by young collectors to the nude female and male statues of sculptor Bosio, found on Scott 209-213. This was the strait-laced age where the only place an uncovered female bosom could be seen was in *National Geographic* magazines. There was a country that had a more shocking stamp for us, and that was Spain. The Goya nude Macha stamps all bore the uncovered duchess of Alba. We didn't know her name at the time, but the painter's name was known by all young male stamp collectors, even if we didn't know any American artists. "Goya? Yeah! He's the one who painted the naked lady." Many years later, in the Prado Museum, I was able to view this wonder and appreciate the other varied styles of Spain's greatest painter.

Stamp fantasies were common forty some years ago, including the "Melaku Selatan" ones, featuring people dancing around a globe. Many of these items have now been picked up as legitimate issues, at least by some catalogues. Finally, one of my favorite groups of stamps comes from the land of Tannu Tuva (about the location of Mongolia). These stamps were bargains and were snapped up by us kids, but not so now. These items are now eagerly sought and the prices for them have risen rapidly.

San Marino is the last stop, with its 1947 Roosevelt series (14), another appreciated multicolored issue. That same year the small land also issued a six-stamp set on the centenary of the first U.S. postage stamp.

With the exception of the first Blackjack stamp, all items mentioned in this article were then inexpensive, and most are still so today. If you miss these old friends, a dozen or more of them can be picked up for less than $20. I could come up with many more for several more articles, and I'm sure that many readers have their own favorites, each with the memories they bring. ❖

Pitcairn Scott 1-8, the first stamps of Pitcairn, depict different aspects of the "Bounty" story. Shown below is Pitcairn Scott 156, which pictures Fletcher Christian, the man commonly credited with leading the mutiny.

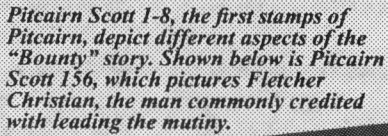

Why collect stamps about PITCAIRN?

by R. E. Bowley

Today, many stamp collectors collect stamps because of their designs. In some cases, these collectors save stamps by country. For others, the focus is a specific topic or theme (a theme tells the story of a topic).

Before I was a teen, I had the world at my fingertips through my stamps. I knew about the language, currency and a lot of geography and history of all countries at that time. As a result, I was an avid reader.

When the Nordoff and Hall romantic novels were published in the 1930s, I was ecstatic. I particularly enjoyed *Mutiny on the Bounty, Pitcairn's Island* and *Men against the Sea*. I could not get much farther from southern Ontario on this planet than the middle of the South Pacific Ocean.

Little else about Pitcairn could be found in the library available to me at the time. This tiny British colony halfway between Panama and New Zealand was relatively unknown. Nor, as I quickly found out, was there much about Norfolk Island, an Australian territory 600 miles north of New Zealand. The entire Pitcairn colony was moved to Norfolk Island in 1856. This is represented on Pitcairn 203-205 and Norfolk Island 277-279. In the 1930s, Pitcairn and Norfolk Islands were both using New Zealand stamps.

Then, glory be, in 1940 Pitcairn issued its own set of stamps, Scott 1-8. Five of these stamps from the first set related to the *Bounty* story.

In 1951, two more stamps, Scott 5A and Scott 6A, were issued, one showing the *Bounty* Bible. Would I ever hold it in my hands? On the 1-penny (Scott 2) and the 2-shilling 6-pence (Scott 8), the left side of the design contained figures, labeled in the Scott Catalogue, "Fletcher Christian with crew."

In 1967, this scene was again shown indistinctly in the upper-left of Scott 86. This image was reproduced from part of a colored engraving made in the 1790s by Robert Dodd. It shows Bligh and his followers about to be cast off from the *Bounty* in a small launch.

In 1947, Norfolk Island began its stamp issues with the famous Norfolk pine design, Scott 1-12. Its history started to unfold in its stamp designs from its discovery in 1774 by Captain James Cook, its use as a penal colony starting in 1789, to the coming of the Pitcairners in 1856. The interrelationship between these two islands was established. Would I ever get to visit one or both of them?

Following service in World War II, I completed my university degree. My aim was to work for a few years and then teach. I got married and started to raise a family. Stamps took a back seat (sound familiar?). However, I continued to keep an eye open for information about the South Seas.

In 1963, I left industry to take my industrial chemistry background into the classroom at the high school level. Before long, I realized that I had to have some sanity time each night before I went to bed. Aha! Working with stamps.

I remembered seeing an article in the *National Geographic* about Pitcairn in the 1950s. I traced it to the December 1957 issue, pages 725-89. There was a photo of the postmaster, Oscar Clark, standing with a mound of mail bags in front of his tiny frame post office.

In 1965, I wrote Clark to inquire about getting mint stamps and first-day covers. Nine months later, I received an affirmative answer. Thus started a marvelous correspondence and friendship, including an exchange of crafts similar to those pictured on Pitcairn 91-94 and 194-197. I also received the mate to the walking cane that Oscar carved for Prince Philip when he visited the island in 1971 (Scott 160).

My research into the history of the two islands now continued in depth. I found that Polynesian folklore contained a story about a chief who sailed away from Otaheite (phonetic for today's Tahiti) about 600 A.D. to found a colony on what he called "Mitakiterangi" (meaning "isolated place"), about 1,000 miles to the southeast. This explained the petroglyphs and other artifacts found on Pitcairn (Scott 119-122). Having native petroglyphs near my hometown, I wondered about their similarities. Was Thor Heyerdahl's hypothesis about the migration of mankind correct? Would I ever get to climb down a rope on Pitcairn to see those rock carvings and perhaps find the sun carved above one of the figures?

In 1976, the Pitcairn set commemorating the American Bicentennial (Scott 156-159) was released. One vertical stamp, Scott 156, showed the same figure that appeared on Scott 2 and Scott 8, this time labeled "Fletcher Christian." My searching has led me to believe that Fletcher Christian did not lead the mutiny on April 21, 1789. If this were so, then he probably would not be standing on the top of the poop deck railing with saber on shoulder, watching Bligh being cast adrift in the tiny launch.

Not until after I had had my dream come true with a trip to both Pitcairn and Norfolk Islands in 1989 did I write to that stamp's designer, Jennifer Toombs of England. She admitted in her reply that taking this one figure out of Dodd's design and labeling him Fletcher Christian was "pure assumption at the time." The Dodd engraving, which accompanies this article, is more clearly reproduced on other stamps, such as Pitcairn 321 and Norfolk 455, as well as souvenir sheets, such as Aitutaki 434 and Tonga 713.

While I was on Pitcairn, I stayed with Betty and Tom Christian, Tom being a direct descendent of Fletcher Christian. He is the senior radio operator (Pitcairn 221) at the station on Taro Ground (Pitcairn 108 and 201). Tom is convinced from hand-me-down family stories that Fletcher was not the leader of the mutiny. They travel around the tiny 1-by-1 1/2-mile volcanic island on three-wheelers now (Pitcairn 357).

One day, when we were wheeling it up to Taro Ground, Tom waved vaguely off to the bush and said, "Tis said that Fletcher was buried in there," and then shook his head. He is convinced that Fletcher was not killed in the uprising in the early 1790s and, further, that he got away from Pitcairn.

This inspired me to go to England in 1992. I have found reasonable proof that Fletcher Christian did indeed get back to England. There is evidence at Moorland Close (Pitcairn 335). There must have been a good reason for Norfolk 454 to show the Round House on the island in Lake Windermere in Cumbria, the home of Fletcher's favorite cousin Isabella Curwen. He called Mauatua, his Polynesian consort, Isabella after her. This was a natural place for him to have gone, incognito, of course.

While in England, I tracked down Fletcher's mother and maternal grandparents, about whom very little has been written. Most authors have referred to Moorland Close as the "Christian Farm" which it was not, really. It belonged to Jacob Dixon and his wife, Mary Fletcher, in the early 1700s. When they died, their daughter Ann inherited the farm. She married Charles Christian of nearby Cockermouth. One of their sons was Fletcher, named after his maternal grandmother's family. Charles died when Fletcher was four years old. The home on the farm is correctly labeled as the birthplace of Fletcher Christian on Pitcairn Scott 335.

When I returned home from Pitcairn, I

The Pitcairn and Norfolk Island stamps shown below mark the 125th anniversary of the Pitcairn residents being relocated to Norfolk Island in 1856.

Scott 321b, above, shows a fanciful version of the mutiny with Fletcher Christian leading his shipmates.

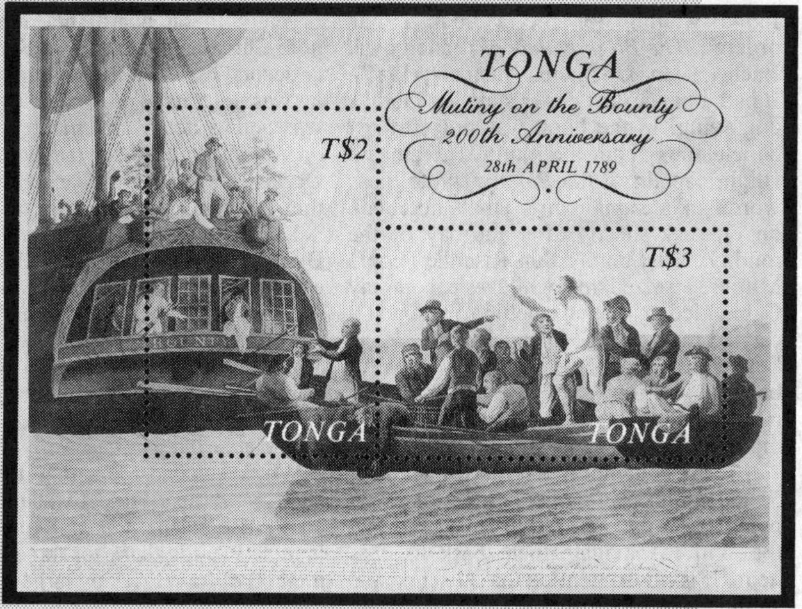

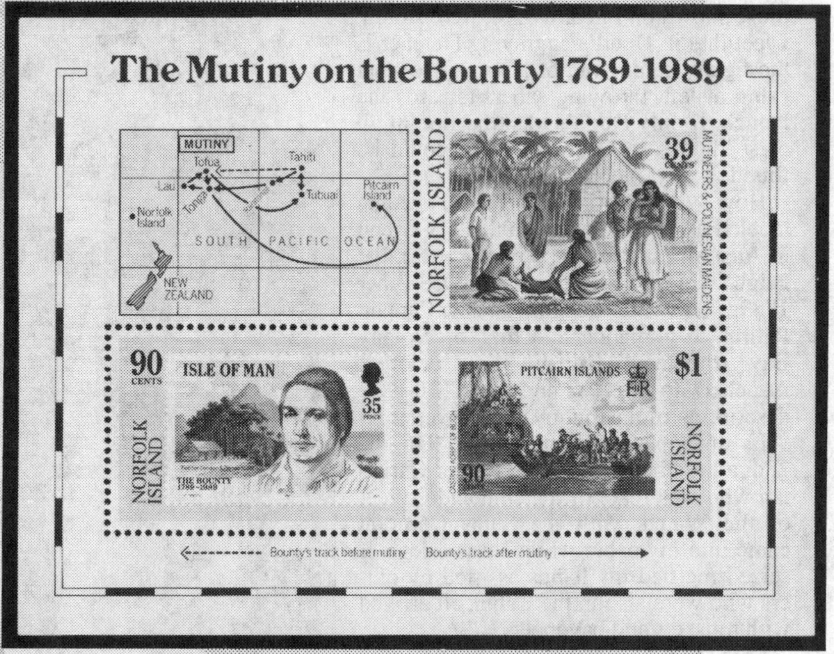

A number of different stamps, including those shown here, picture an aging Dodd print that shows Captain Bligh being set adrift. The author is convinced that Fletcher Christian did not lead the mutiny, and that the figure attributed to be him is not.

found waiting for me a book I had ordered: *The Bligh Notebook*, edited by J. Bach (Allen & Unwin, Australia, 1987). It had a paper dust cover showing Dodd's engraving. In the book was proof of my conclusions about the mutiny. Lieutenant Bligh, captain of the *Bounty*, wrote these words in a signalman's small notebook on or very shortly after the day of the mutiny: "Just before Sun Rise the People Mutinied seized me while asleep in my Cabin tied my hands behind my back - carried me on Deck in my Shirt . . ." The key word is "People." This has always been the British Navy name for "seamen." Thus the seamen apparently mutinied and there was no real leader.

It is my contention that the seamen kept Fletcher Christian on board the *Bounty*, he being the only one they trusted who had the skill to navigate them back to Otaheite. It is my contention that Fletcher was confined to the captain's cabin, where some of the breadfruit saplings, such as those shown on Pitcairn 320f, were stored. I feel that in Dodd's engraving Fletcher is the figure leaning out of a window of that cabin at left, throwing sabers towards the launch. If only Dodd's identification of all these figures in his work of art could be found.

How did Christian really become labeled as leader of the mutiny? A friend in Australia sent me a copy of a letter that Bligh wrote from Capetown in December 1789. This was to his friend Captain Phillip, Commander-in-Chief of Botany Bay (the new British penal colony). Attached to this letter was a 10-page description of the mutiny - a new version.

In this epistle, Bligh wrote: "On the 28th a little before sunrise Fletcher Christian who was mate of the ship and Officer of the Watch, with the Ships Corporal came into my cabin while I was asleep & seized me tied my hands assisted by others who were also in the Cabin, all arrived with muskets and bayonets . . ."

This fanciful version of the mutiny was illustrated on Pitcairn 321b. However, none of these figures resemble the known body or facial characteristics of Fletcher Christian (Pitcairn 322b or Isle of Man 393). After much research, I found that the composite artist's impression of Christian was made by Larry Learworth in 1972 for Richard Hough, author of *Captain Bligh & Mr. Christian*.

Bligh had survived the 3,600-mile journey across the wild Pacific from Tofua to Timor (map of route, French Polynesia C119; details Fiji 234, 295 and 606) in 40 days, with 18 others in the little launch. This has been hailed a miracle of navigation, attributed to Bligh. Balderdash! All he had to do was head dead west and he could not miss Australia. It was a miracle of survival and seamanship, the latter probably provided by the first mate, William Elphinstone and the master, John Fryer, both on board the launch. Please note Christian was taken on Sept. 7, 1787, as second mate. At the time of the mutiny, he was not "mate" as written by Bligh. He was acting lieutenant, made so by Bligh on March 2, 1788, in the South Atlantic Ocean on the way to Cape Horn - which they could not get around (Pitcairn 320c).

For the first time, then, at Capetown, Bligh revealed his strategy. He had now established a scapegoat on whom to put the blame when he faced his inevitable court martial. He embellished this story after he got back to England with what I now believe was a forged log of his entire voyage. I could go on about this but will not belabor the point.

What was most exciting for me as a super retirement project was to be accepted by the Island Council of Pitcairn to land and reside there for three weeks. My method of travel was by large planes from Toronto to Dallas to Tahiti, and then 1,000 miles to Mangareva in the small inter-island plane (French Polynesia C175). From there I sailed in a small 39-foot yawl with an Australian skipper and his girlfriend, who had landed status on Pitcairn, along with two young Americans from New York.

We had just lost sight of Mangareva on our 300-mile sailing journey to Pitcairn, when a violent storm hit us. It was probably the tail-end of hurricane Gilbert. It had devastated parts of Florida and Mexico and then headed west into the Pacific in a most unusual way. After a very short lesson in navigation, I had two four-hour watches alone on deck at the helm in pitch dark while the others were ill below. The waves were higher than the length of the boat and rain and sleet pelted me. With gale-force winds, it was a real challenge to keep the boat, with its tiny motor, on

These two sets of stamps, Scott 91-94 and 194-197, show crafts native to the Pitcairn residents. These crafts are the source of great pride.

Scott 176a, a souvenir sheet, celebrates Pitcairn's annual "Bounty Day." Each year a replica of the ship is created and burned to mark the anniversary of settling the islands.

Above is a charred copy of Scott 297, one of thousands of Pitcairn stamps burned by Pitcairn Officials during the author's visit.

course. I had never before been on a boat of any size on an ocean. It was a terrifying experience for two days and three nights. Just a year later, this same yawl drifted ashore on Pitcairn and broke up - the wood of the hull was quite rotten. Someone had been watching over me.

When I reached Pitcairn, I was welcomed by my friends. Unfortunately, Oscar Clark had died in 1981, but Tom Christian and others took on correspondence with me. So, as in a small village, I was well known already when I made my request to visit. During the three weeks of my visit, I was accepted as a member of the island community, not as a visitor. I took part in all kinds of island activities, such as climbing 500 feet down the face of the cliff heading to the petroglyphs (Pitcairn 119). I did find the outline of the sun in the rock. It was filled with lichen. It would have to be scraped out and then the groove painted as the others had been so they could be photographed easily. It was also a favorite place down there to fish from the rocks. There was another scary climb up to Fletcher's Cave (Pitcairn 105 and 200), still used as a place for contemplation. These are things the islanders did with ease. It taxed my 67-year-old muscles.

As a very great privilege, I was allowed to hold the *Bounty* Bible (Pitcairn 5A and 108) in my hands. It is stored in a locked box in the Seventh Day Adventist church (Pitcairn 170).

I watched Jacob Warren carve a gannet (Pitcairn 196) for me. Betty Christian and Jacob's wife, Mavis, both painted hattie leaves (Pitcairn 229b) for me. Betty's mother, Millie, made a tall pandanus basket in five colors (Pitcairn 230a) for my wife, who was back home. Betty's father, Warren, carved a model of the famous Pitcairn wheelbarrow (Pitcairn 195) from the miro wood that is unique to the Pitcairn group. Ben Christian made a vase (Pitcairn 93) from miro with his special design. Tom's sister, Thelma, carved a two-and-a-half-foot shark (with real shark's teeth inserted) from the darker tao wood. Her husband, Len Brown, the best craftsman on the island, and their daughter Clarice made a model of the *Bounty* (Pitcairn 28) for me. The hull was miro and the white sails were carved from orangewood. I also tried my hand at all these crafts. These beautiful things were carefully packed and mailed home. They arrived three months after I did.

Perhaps the most astounding activity in which I participated was the burning of off-sale Pitcairn stamps, shown on Pitcairn 171A. It is a long-standing Pitcairn tradition to publicly burn all off-sale postage stamps. The postmaster at the time was Brian Young. He knew of my collecting interests and held up the burn until I got there. This included the remains of the definitive set showing Fish (Pitcairn 231-243), which had been replaced by Visiting Ships (Scott 298-309); the $3 souvenir sheet for the Australian bicentennial (Pitcairn 297); and others. On Sept. 30, I assisted in burning $131,334.05 face value of Pitcairn stamps, souvenir sheets and covers, a number etched in my memory. I wept unashamedly throughout the three-hour exercise. The following day, I examined the remains dumped from the bottoms of the three barrels and found some charred bits that I carefully packaged up and mailed home.

I returned to Tahiti by sail (a boring trip on flat seas), and then flew on to New Zealand and Norfolk Island. There I continued my research for 10 days before returning home.

So, this is where stamp collecting can lead you. You may not have the same opportunities for research, intrigue and enjoyment, but you can certainly find your own ground for growth. ❖

R.E. Bowley, a collector since age 9, left industry in 1963 to begin a 22-year teaching career. As part of his education goals, Bowley kept a stamp on display in his laboratory at all times. This was meant to spur students on to become more inquisitive. He was given one local and two national awards for innovative teaching.

Is it a souvenir sheet,

by William W. Cummings

If there is any one thing that can be said about philately it is that the terminology leaves a great deal to be desired. Many terms we use are not only confusing, but technically incorrect as well. We probably all tell our spouses that we will pick up a sheet of stamps at the post office. Of course we know that the only true sheets of stamps that exist, of stamps printed during the past 50 years, reside in official archives. We are, philatelically, going to purchase a pane of stamps. We also know better than to ask the postal clerk for a pane. Yet, we refer freely to souvenir sheets, which frequently are nothing more than panes cut from sheets. Therefore many of these items technically should be referred to as souvenir panes. Or should they?

Few areas of philately have so many terms that have such imprecise definitions as that of those funny little panes. The terms are many: souvenir sheet, miniature sheet, sheetlet, small sheets, and others. Choosing a term to describe a particular item is where the problem arises.

The American Stamp Collector's Dictionary (Konwiser, 1949) cited R. A. Barry of the Souvenir Issues Association as specifying that a souvenir sheet had to be issued for a philatelic or special event or purpose. Similar sheets issued solely for the convenience of the printer or the post office, or for any other reason, were miniature sheets. He limited the number of stamps in the sheets to a maximum of 25.

That was fine in 1940. At that time the United States had one, the International Philatelic Exhibition (White Plains) souvenir sheet. Great Britain and Canada had none; and France and Germany, being somewhat more prolific, had 3 and 11, respectively. By contrast, the *Scott Stamp Monthly* issues for February and March 1993 listed an awesome total of 142 new souvenir sheet listings for the world. But these listing can be confusing. Consider the following.

Is the World Wildlife Fund commemorating a special event or purpose in the original sense? Or are the items miniature sheets? Sheetlets can be easy to describe, at least to some members of the hobby. They are sheets (panes?) of stamps issued with fewer stamps than the normal printing. A stamp printed in sheets of 100 might have a later printing in sheets of 25. The latter sheet would be a sheetlet. At least, as long as it isn't a souvenir sheet like the White Plains item. How does one describe a sheet such as Palau Scott 218? It contains 25 different stamps. Is it a souvenir sheet honoring a special event - the Apollo 11 mission? Is it a miniature sheet because of the number of stamps? Or has the proliferation of these types of items made traditional descriptions obsolete?

Perhaps the time has come for the Scott catalogues to simplify the listings and stop trying to categorize a bewildering array of similar items.

Are they souvenir sheets?

Our definition of souvenir and miniature sheets has specified that there must be one or more stamps that can be removed and used for postage. Barry, too, referred to the selvage. Once again, modern merchandising and production methods have created some unusual problems.

Egypt was one of the first to start blurring the distinction between stamps and souvenir sheets. The 1975 Revolution 23rd Anniversary stamp, Scott 986, was but an omen of what was to come. Issued in sheets of 6, the stamp design measured an awesome 71 millimeters by 80mm. The stamp size was

miniature sheet, or sheetlet?

3 inches by 3 1/4 inches! The 1976 24th anniversary edition completed the transition. The 110m stamp, Scott 1012, was issued imperf and is the same size as Scott 986. Again, this is nothing but a big stamp.

Newer items, such as Gabon 592 and Lebanon 508, improve on the concept by including the vignettes of issued stamps. Postally they must be used intact, since the vignettes have no postal value. These, too, are just large stamps, rather than souvenir sheets.

No matter how precise one tries to make definitions, there are always some items that end up on the fence. Mexico, Scott 1357, shows a "stamp," perforations and all. Here the catch is that the perfs are printed, not punched. This one has been classified as a stamp.

No country has stranger almost-souvenir-sheet items than Albania. Here, all sense of philatelic order has been cast to the winds. The 1975 Michelangelo stamp, Scott 1660, has nice printed perfs around the picture, but the denomination and country name are outside of that area. The 1976 Innsbruck Olympic Games stamp, Scott 1725, has one big picture, but two vertical rows of perfs set off the skaters. This theme has continued in various forms. The 1977 Mio paintings set includes a 2.05 lek stamp that has perforations separating the denomination and country from the rest of the stamp. Quite spectacular is the 1986 World Cup Soccer stamp. Here there are vertical and horizontal perforations, but they create a soccer ball/globe label, with the country name on the top label and denomination on the left label. These, too, have been classified as stamps, not souvenir sheets.

As editors, we are aware that any mail delivery can contain an item that will challenge traditional definitions. Actually, we look forward to the latest items. After all, who, 20 years ago, would have expected to see stamps with interchangeable vignettes? And from Canada, no less! Change definitely is the name of this game. ❖

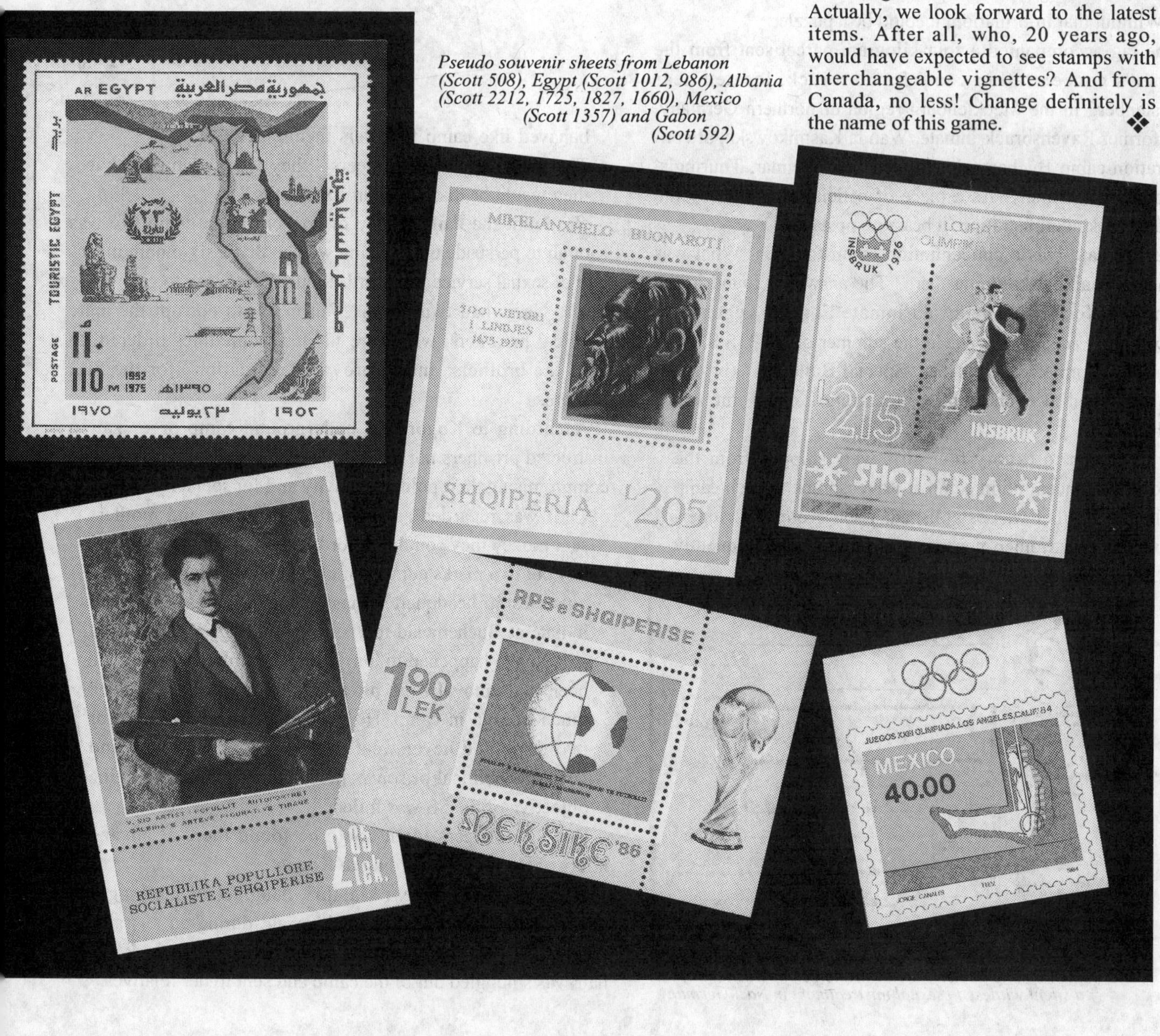

Pseudo souvenir sheets from Lebanon (Scott 508), Egypt (Scott 1012, 986), Albania (Scott 2212, 1725, 1827, 1660), Mexico (Scott 1357) and Gabon (Scott 592)

Sexual Slavery in the Concentration Camps

BY KEN LAWRENCE

One of the most notorious Nazi concentration camps was Buchenwald, located on a mountaintop just six miles from Weimar, the traditional home of German culture since the Middle Ages.

All mail from German concentration camps is disquieting, because it reminds us of the Nazi regime's cruelty. It seems that no matter what degree of barbarism occurred, postal and philatelic evidence has survived to tell the story.

The Parcel tag shown here is a drab document, with no stamps to enhance its visual appeal, but it illustrates one aspect of concentration camp life reported in a former inmate's memoir. Without that information, it could be a puzzler.

The tag accompanied a four-kilogram parcel sent from the women's concentration camp Ravensbruck, located near Fuerstenberg in the Mecklenburg region of northern Germany, to a former Ravensbruck inmate, Wanda Kasmikowska, at concentration camp Buchenwald, located near Weimar, Thuringia, in southern Germany. As a piece of official mail sent by the Ravensbruck administration, it bears no postage.

Buchenwald was a concentration camp for men. What was Wanda Kasmikowska doing there? The answer is found in the memoir of former Buchenwald inmate Eugene Kogon, *The Theory and Practice of Hell*. In the summer of 1943, S.S. chief Heinrich Himmler ordered that "Special Buildings" (brothels) be established at each men's concentration camp, including Buchenwald.

> "Eighteen to twenty-four girls were shipped from the women's concentration camp at Ravensbruck to each camp where a brothel was established. Each group was supervised by two women non-coms of the SS, who frequently behaved like camp followers themselves.
>
> The girls were all volunteers - they were promised that they would be discharged in six months."

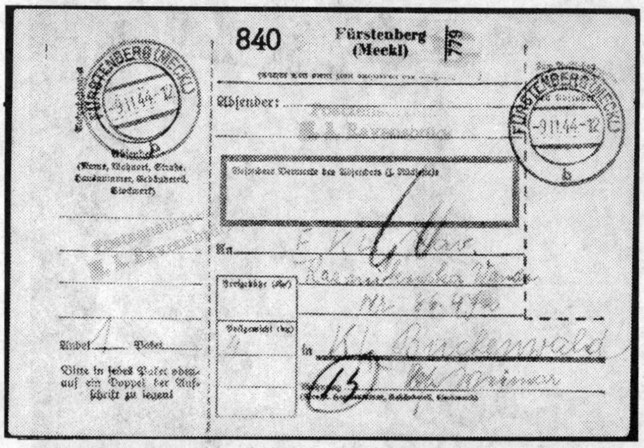

840 Fürstenberg (Meckl) 779

Absender:

Name, Wohnort, Straße, Hausnummer, Gebäudeteil, Stockwerk

An

Bitte in jedes Paket oben auf ein Doppel der Aufschrift zu legen!

in Kl. Buchenwald

This parcel card from women's concentration camp Ravensbrück to a woman inmate at men's concentration camp Buchenwald is a silent witness to sexual mistreatment in Nazi Germany.

No doubt the daily reality of concentration camp life was enough to persuade those young women that a six-month indenture of sexual service was worth enduring as a way to get out.

The Nazis had two purposes in mind: to corrupt the male political prisoners, who were invited, sometimes ordered, to visit the brothels, and to provide "recreation" for the S.S. officers.

According to Kogon, the underground camp organization instructed prisoners not to patronize the brothels, both to avoid compromising their political activity and for social reasons.

> "It was regarded as shameful that wives and mothers sent money they could ill afford, only to have the prisoners pay out two marks admission to the brothel. But at the very outset camp headquarters has compelled the senior camp inmate at Buchenwald to visit the building. The least that could have happened to him if he had refused would have been his removal from office, which might have created much trouble in camp. He yielded, after holding out for two days, and never went back a second time. By and large, all political prisoners hewed to this line, so that the objective of the SS was foiled."[

But S.S. officers often could be found there at advanced hours of the night, according to Kogon.

He wrote that Princess Mafalda, daughter of the king and queen of Italy who died at Buchenwald during an air raid on August 24, 1944, had been one of the sex slaves. A lock of her hair was smuggled out of the camp and sent to her relatives.❖

PAGE ZERO

BY DOUGLAS N. CLARK AND NANCY B. ZIELINSKI CLARK

We always have found it fun to look inside someone else's album. So when we came across a Scott *American Album*, 1949 edition, among the philatelic effects of Nancy's father, the late Gardner Brown, we decided to take a closer look.

Brown had been a rather prominent collector of France, but he kept his lifelong U.S. collection, some of which he had inherited from his father. The collection had passed on from the album we found. The only stamps that remained were on page zero.

Page zero represents the front of the book. In this case it contained a group of stamps for which the collector just could not find spaces. These stamps must have been hated by the album's owner; after all it is no fun to put twelve stamps on a page where not one of them belongs. While the previous owner walked away from them, their page zero status drew our attention more than U.S. regular issue stamps would.

Just as the "back of the book" usually refers to special delivery stamps, postage dues, officials, revenues, and so forth, page zero is generally reserved for stamps that came before the regular issues, in this case, U.S. postmaster provisionals. The stamps occupying our page zero are something else. First, none of them are *actual* U.S. postmaster provisionals. Second, all of these stamps are more valuable used than mint (and all but one are mint). And third, all but one are fakes.

Most of the stamps on the page are carriers and locals -- stamps issued by private companies that provided city delivery in competition with the postal service, in the 1840s and 1850s. When their activity became illegal under the act that established the Post Office monopoly, some of the companies discovered that stamp collectors coveted their stamps. They flooded the market with reprints and facsimilies. This and the fact that the usual laws against counterfeiting do not apply to carriers and locals, account for the low esteem in which these adhesives were held by the users of U.S. postage stamp albums. (By "usual laws," we mean those statutes that allow the T-men to enter the premises and confiscate counterfeit U.S. postage stamps and revenues. It is, of course, also illegal to deal in counterfeit carriers and locals if they are represented as genuine.) Genuine carriers and locals, genuinely used on cover are, by the way, valuable and desirable.

Of the three remaining stamps on our page zero that are not carriers or locals, two are counterfeit Confederate postmaster provisionals. The two counterfeit Confederates are crude examples, and, although they are not marked facsimile, they cannot have been intended to fool anyone. This type of counterfeit probably was produced to help young and beginning collectors fill spaces in their albums.

The last stamp -- the only used stamp on the page, and the only genuine one -- is a Nashville, Tennessee, Confederate 5¢ postmaster provisional similar to the Knoxville (one of the fakes). Although damaged, it is a rare and desirable stamp.

Even the cancel on the genuine Nashville provisional is unusual and tells a story about the stamp. What is visible is "...XPRESS Co.../...G 14." This is enough to identify the marking as the Nashville ADAMS EXPRESS COMPANY oval, and the date as August 14, 1861.

On June 1, 1861, the U.S. Post Office Department had cut off the mail lines joining the North with the Confederate post offices. The Adams Express Company initiated a private express service between Nashville and Louisville, Kentucky, under which letters of Confederate origin could be deposited in a Union post office. The United States put a stop to the service on August 26, 1861.

The Nashville postmaster provisional, on its original cover, would have been tied, together with a U.S. adhesive (probably a perforated 3¢ 1857 issue), by the Adams Express Co. oval. In years past, someone had soaked the stamps off cover, placing the common 3¢ stamp in an album, and consigning the Nashville postmaster provisional to page zero. A glance at most any catalogue will reveal that the value of a Nashville provisional on cover with an express company marking is worth about ten times as much as a used single.

It is no surprise that most of the stamps relegated to page zero of this album are *not* philatelic treasures. After all, the album owners, as far as we know, were not philatelically ignorant. But it is worth keeping in mind that just about any philatelic source is likely to produce an item that tells a worthwhile story.

More information about carriers and locals can be found in

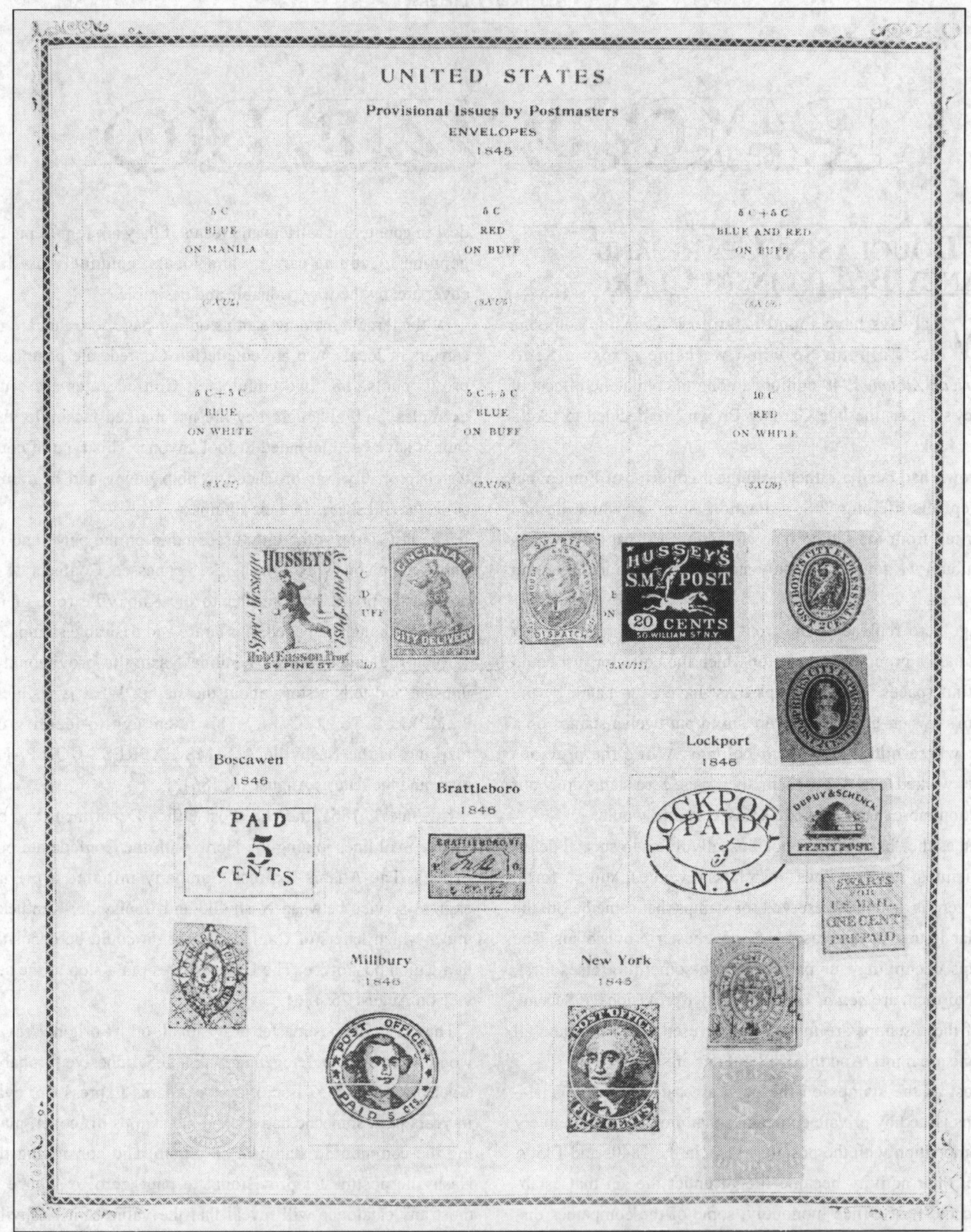

This page zero from a 1949 edition of Scott's American Album includes eleven fakes -- locals, carriers, Confederate postmaster provisionals -- and one genuine item, a Nashville, Tennessee, Confederate 5¢ postmaster provisional.

the article "Local Stamps," by Herman Hearst, Jr. in the *Forty-Third American Philatelic Congress Book*, published by the Congress in 1977. *The New Dietz Confederate States Catalog and Handbook*, published by Bogg & Laurence Publishing Company, Inc., in 1986, tells about Confederate postmaster provisionals, expresses and Confederate postal service. ❖

The Authors

Douglas N. Clark and Nancy B. Zielinski Clark are collectors of U.S. postal history, specializing in Massachusetts, Maine, railroad and ship mail. Both are frequent exhibitors and judges, while she recently was elected to the APS Board of Directors.

Germany's military post issues of 1942-44

by Fred W. Baumann

Between the airmails and Official stamps in the Scott catalog"s back-of-the-book listings for Germany are four adhesives that had an important role to play during World War II.

Like the United States and most other Western nations, Germany offered free military mail service ("Feldpost") to members of its armed forces in time of war.

But unlike the United States, which fought WWII on a truly global basis, Germany had a direct overland route to most of the territory it occupied during the conflict. Mail between troops and their families back in Germany was chiefly carried by truck or train.

That changed after Hitler invaded the Soviet Union in 1941. German troops swiftly advanced hundreds upon hundreds of miles into a hostile land that had only the most rudimentary roads. What few rail lines there were had to be converted mile by mile to accommodate the different gauge of the German trains. And all routes were constantly menaced by partisans. Delayed movement of mail to the Eastern Front threatened the already minimal morale of German soldiers serving there. To meet that problem, in April 1942, the German military postal service began to operate an airmail service.

Because of the limited space available on German military transport planes, stamps were issued to ration airmail service fairly among the soldiers. Each received four stamps each month - two for use on his mail home, the other two for use by the recipients there on letters sent back to him.

Figure 1 shows the perforated version of the stamp. It aptly depicts Germany's aerial workhorse, the Junkers Ju-52 transport, which carried most military airmail (and nearly everything else the Germans transported by air).

Though established to serve the forces on the Eastern Front, military airmail service later was extended to Greece, the Aegean Islands, the Baltic and Norway.

There is no denomination on the stamp, of course, because the service was free. This adhesive was affixed to a letter in order to show that the sender was entitled to use military airmail service.

The stamp was printed in sheets of 100 perforated 13 1/2 (Scott MC1) and later issued in a rouletted version as well (Scott MC1a). Both are quite common, unused or used.

In an excellent study of German military airmail service begun in the Germany Philatelic Society's January 1987 *German Postal Specialist*, military mail specialist Gianluigi Soldati also illustrates a far scarcer and rather good forgery of the perforated stamp produced by British Intelligence in panes of 20 printed four by five.

According to Soldati, the forgery "was intended for franking propaganda material to be sent through the Feldpost system from Norway to Germany." Germany's Michel catalog describes this so-called propaganda forgery as perf 12, and values it at 100 deutschemarks - about 400 times the Scott catalog value of a genuine, unused stamp!

Figure 2 shows the later, rouletted version (Scott MQ1a) of a red brown stamp issued July 10, 1942 (Scott MQ1), for use on parcels in Germany's military postal service, with the Nazi eagle and swastika emblem. Its "ZULASSUNGS-MARKE/ DEUTSCHE FELDPOST" inscription translates as "Permit stamp/German military mail."These stamps served to ration parcel post service just as the earlier permit stamps rationed airmail, in order to make the most of the limited transportation capacity that was available for non-essential material. According to *Billig's Philatelic Handbook,* one (and later two) of the Figure 2 stamps were made available to personnel in qualifying units each month, to be sent home to their families.

Although small packets up to 250 grams could be sent in regular mail, larger parcels required both postage and the use of these parcel post permit stamps. The rate was one permit stamp and 20 pfennigs for parcels from 250g to 1 kilogram, and two permit stamps and 40pf for parcels of 1kg to 2kg.

A much smaller stamp in this design (Scott MQ2), printed in bright green, was issued Oct. 20, 1944, for use on Christmas gift parcels to the front weighing up to 1kg.

Figure 3 shows a 40pf Hitler Head stamp overprinted "FELDPOST/2kg." the last German regular military post issue of the war (Scott MQ3). Released just 35 days after the 1944 Christmas military parcel post stamps, the Figure 4 stamp indicates how rapidly Germany was deteriorating as the end of 1944 (and the Third Reich) grew near. The Figure 3 stamps were issued specifically to facilitate shipment of up to "2 kg" of winter clothing from German families to their sons, brothers and fathers in the military.

Though the two 1944 military parcel post issues (Scott MQ2-3) catalog $1.65 unused in Scott, they are valuable postally used, and downright rare on piece or wrapper.

Unfortunately, most of the canceled copies of these stamps that exist have fraudulent, backdated or favor cancels. If they haven't been authenticated by a competent expert, you should regard all of them as fake. Always insist on expertizing them before you buy. That caveat applies even more rigorously to the many still scarcer Michel-listed "INSELPOST" provisional overprints that were added to some of these stamps for temporary service in far-flung German-occupied regions. ❖

Figure 1.

Figure 3.

Figure 2.

Figure 1. Germany's military airmail permit stamp.

Figure 2. This 1942 military parcel permit stamp is a type made available to military personnel.

Figure 3. This 40 pfennig Hitler Head was overprinted "FELDPOST/2kg" in November 1944 for use on parcels of winter clothing sent to German soldiers.

The spotlight is on the stamp that got away

by Ken Lawrence

On May 11, 1909, the United States Post Office Department issued a 6¢ orange George Washington coil stamp with double-line watermark and gauge 12 vertical perforations. No one purchased any of these stamps when they were placed on sale, first in New York and later in Washington, D.C. All 6¢ coil stamps were then withdrawn from sale and destroyed. Not a single copy survived in anyone's stamp collection. Figure 1 shows how a strip of these stamps appeared.

For two weeks, the 6¢ coils were advertised on the front pages of the two main philatelic newspapers published at the time, *Mekeel's Weekly Stamp News* and *Redfield's Stamp Weekly*, yet none were sold. The dealer who had placed the ads, Edward Stern, withdrew the ads and apologized to collectors for having made the offer.

Naturally, a stamp that doesn't exist has no Scott catalogue number, but if someone had purchased and kept even one example, the stamp would probably be U.S. Scott 355A, positioned between the 5¢ and 10¢ side-wound coil stamps of 1909.

The destruction of a stamp issue for lack of interest could only have occurred at a time when coil stamps were in their infancy. Procedures for ordering coils from the Bureau of Engraving and Printing were informal in 1909, which made it relatively easy for almost anyone to order a new stamp. In this case, the order was initiated by a New York stamp dealer. But, in 1909, few stamp collectors or dealers really understood the significance of coil stamps. Even the terminology applied to coils was confusing. Thus, when the new 6¢ stamps were delivered, they weren't what Stern thought he had ordered, so he refused to buy them.

For the full story, let's begin at the beginning

The first U.S. coil stamps were privately manufactured in 1906 and 1907 from 400-subject imperforate sheets of 1¢ green Benjamin Franklin (Scott 314) and 2¢ carmine George Washington (Scott 320) stamps from the series of 1902 and 1903. After privately perforated coils had proven they had merit, they were followed by government-produced coils manufactured at the BEP.

The first government coils were issued in 1908. They included vertical and horizontal versions of the 1¢ Franklin (Scott 316 and 318) and 2¢ Washington (Scott 321 and 322), plus a vertical-format 5¢ blue Abraham Lincoln coil (Scott 317). All were from the same 1902-03 series designs. Vertical-format coils were perforated horizontally, and horizontal-format coils were perforated vertically, with the same gauge 12 perforations used on sheet and booklet stamps at that time. All U.S. postage stamps at that time had double-line watermarks.

Since U.S. coil stamps were perforated in just one dimension, with two parallel non-perforated straight edges, the philatelic press called them "part perforates." The term was ambiguous, because it also applied to sheet stamps that had been perforated in one direction but left imperforate in the other.

Then, as today, most collectors shunned stamps with straight edges. In 1908, all but a very few collectors regarded coil stamps as just ordinary stamps with two straight edges, and thus not desirable. That is one reason why nearly all early U.S. coil stamps are scarce and expensive today.

Collectors finally began to take interest in coil stamps near the end of 1910, when the USPOD ordered changes in the perforations applied to Bureau-manufactured coils. Because gauge 8 1/2 perforations were a new variety, available only on coil stamps, coils were regarded in a new light.

The first Bureau coils were made the same way as private coils; imperforate sheets were pasted together side-to-side or end-to-end. Perforations were applied in one direction, and the sheets were slit into single-subject ribbons in the other direction. The strips were then wound on cores into 500- and 1,000-stamp coils, with paper leader strips at the head and tail. BEP also manufactured imperforate coils, similarly slit but not perforated. They are listed in the "Imperforate Coils" section of the *Scott Specialized Catalogue of United States Stamps* (page 266 of the 1995 edition).

At first, all coil stamps were made for use in mechanical stamp vending or affixing machines. Manufacturers who needed stamps for their equipment could order imperforate sheets and make them into coils, or they could order government coils processed at the BEP in one of four formats; imperforate or perforated, wound vertically or horizontally.

Later in 1908, when the Washington-Franklin designs (also known as the Third Bureau Issue) replaced the designs of the 1902-03 series (the Second Bureau Issue), the same rules applied. Manufacturers or owners of stamp vending or affixing machines could order these stamps in 400-subject imperforate sheets, or in 500- or 1,000-stamp vertical or horizontal coils, with or without perforations.

Most postal clerks refused to sell coils or imperforate sheets to anyone other than these mailers. Eventually, some stamp dealers found ways to obtain them, either from friendly postal employees or from employees of firms authorized to use the stamps. Post offices were not authorized to sell partial imperforate sheets or partial coils. A premium of 6¢ was charged for each 500-stamp coil, in addition to the face value of the stamps.

In 1914, the USPOD relaxed these rules and, for the first time, permitted sales of smaller quantities of coil stamps directly to collectors. These were sold only by the Washington, D.C., post office to mail-order customers. This was the forerunner of today's Philatelic Fulfillment Service Center. By then coils had achieved a high degree of popularity with collectors, and sufficient quantities of most have survived.

Now, let's return to 1909, when government coil stamps were barely one year old

A New York stamp dealer, Edward Stern of the Economist Stamp Co., ordered a coil of 500 6¢ stamps from his local post office. On May 7, 1909, the New York postmaster forwarded Stern's order to Washington. The Bureau prepared one 500-stamp coil in the 6¢ denomination and shipped it to the New York post office.

Meanwhile, Stern had placed ads in the May 15, 1909, issue of *Mekeel's*, and in the following week's issue of *Redfield's*, offering pairs for sale at 18¢ postpaid, strips of three for 26¢ and larger strips for 8c per stamp, plus 2¢ postage. Figure 2 shows Stern's *Mekeel's* ad.

One indication that Stern had no understanding of coils was the omission of listings for premium position items, such as guide-line or paste-up pairs. From the beginning of their specialty, the handful of early coil collectors preferred to collect line pairs because they provided proof that the stamps came from coils, rather than perforated sheets, which were severed along the guide lines into 100-stamp panes. That was the origin of coil line pair collecting.

The 6¢ coil would have included paste-ups at 20-stamp intervals, and guide lines halfway between each paste-up, creating

Figure 1:
This photographic reconstruction shows how the 6¢ orange George Washington coil stamps of 1909 appeared. Although the stamps were placed on sale at two post offices, no one bought them, so all copies were destroyed.

approximately 25 of each item. One or two of the paste-ups would have included a plate number below, and several would have included other marginal markings.

When Stern went to pick up his coil, it wasn't what he had expected, so he refused to purchase it. In a letter apologizing to his customers, he explained: "When we ordered these from the postmaster, we thought they were going to deliver them imperforate between, but instead they can only be perforated at sides and imperforate at top and bottom in strips which, of course, have no philatelic value or interest whatsoever, as any perforated all-around stamps can be cut or trimmed off and have the same appearance as these."

Mekeel's editor publicly scolded the Economist Stamp Co. for advertising stamps it didn't have in stock. "We cannot refrain from calling the attention of our advertisers to the impracticability of advertising wares upon the mere pros-pect of stocking the same. We have had similar occurrences before and feel that this plain word must be spoken."

After Stern declined to purchase the coil he had ordered, the New York postmaster returned it to Washington. There it was placed in stock and offered for sale to at least one stamp dealer named Nevin, who also turned it down.

Nevin, however, notified well-known New York dealer J. M. Bartels of the coil's existence. On his next visit to Washington a short time later, Bartels brought along $30, hoping to purchase the roll of 6¢ stamps. Unfortunately for Bartels, the coil had been turned in for destruction a week earlier. In the classic book *United States Postage Stamps of the Twentieth Century*, Max Johl wrote, "Thus by one week philatelists were saved from having to worry about getting what would have been one of the outstanding rarities of the twentieth century."

Nevertheless, collectors worried for some time about the stamp and its possible existence. Over the next dozen years, several collectors claimed to have examples of the 6¢ coil. Each time, the report was published, only to be refuted by the experts. These included J. M. Bartels, who knew the facts from first-hand experience, and Philip H. Ward Jr., the principal scholar of coil stamps.

In a 1920 monograph titled "Coil Stamps of the United States," Ward wrote, "Several of these 6¢ stamps have turned up here of late but they are all undoubtedly trimmed specimens. I saw a very fine pair with wide margins that had been purchased some years back from a small dealer and had remained in the hands of its present owner since that time. The present owner is a man of the highest integrity, but it was trimmed before it reached him, for a close examination by glass showed traces of three perforation holes as well as a scissor cut."

A report in *Mekeel's* three years earlier had built up hopes, only to see them dashed. New issues columnist Percy McGraw Mann had published this teaser in the July 28, 1917 issue: "Mr. C. A. Price submits a more interesting 6¢ stamp current type and states: 'Herewith find a current issue 6¢ coil perforated stamp which I have never seen catalogued . . . It was used by the state in sending out auto tags.'"

Mann was skeptical, but he sent an inquiry to BEP. A week later he followed up with his own examination of the stamp. "Last week we had occasion to mention a 6¢ stamp submitted by Mr. Price, for which he entered a claim that it was a coil stamp that he had never seen before. The specimen submitted was imperforate top and bottom and perforated 10 at the sides. It was also precanceled 'Charleston, W. Va.' We remarked that we had doubts as to its being a coil stamp. We now wish to prove that our doubts were correct. In the first place, the specimen appeared to be cut with a knife or scissors at the bottom, the cut not being overly perfect as it would be if cut by a coiling machine, while the top was rough on the edge. Also, we have not had the experience of seeing a coil stamp with a printed precancel."

If Mann had quit there, the rumor would have been scotched quickly, but he went on to quote from the letter he had received from BEP director Joseph E. Ralph. Ralph's letter listed all coil stamps that had been manufactured by the Bureau, including the single 500-stamp 6¢ coil of 1909. For Mann this was news, since he wasn't aware of the roll's fate.

"The last paragraph of Mr. Ralph's letter startled us," Mann continued. "It discloses the fact that the 6¢ stamp of the 1908 issue, watermarked outline Roman capitals, perforated 12 vertically, imperforate horizontally, was issued in coil form. It will become Scott's No. 328b. Whether any of this coil of 500 6¢ stamps will be located by stamp collectors, we cannot at present state, nor whether it is secretly known by some collector or dealer who has not given the information to the philatelic public. However, we should think it should be one of the philatelic rarities of the United States."

Finally, in the Aug. 18, 1917, issue of *Mekeel's*, Mann put the story to rest by quoting Bartels' first-hand account of the 6¢ coil, and by noting that Ward and others had supplied corroborating information.

Another claim was more difficult to squelch, and persisted at least until 1921, perhaps later.

Rev. G. E. Richter reported an example of the 6¢ coil on a cover postmarked Jan. 21, 1915, from Hartford, Conn. The sender was Silas Chapman Jr., a millionaire philanthropist and prominent stamp collector. Richter showed the cover to Eustace B. Power of Stanley Gibbons Inc., a leading philatelic author and expert on U.S. stamps. Power pronounced the stamp genuine.

Richter wrote to *Mekeel's*, "Mr. Power, whose standing as an authority on U.S. issues of the 20th century is well known, has examined the stamp which is under discussion, and after careful inspection, with microscope, dividers, millimeter scale, and comparison with the other denominations of that issue, declared it apparently O.K. and was willing to back his opinion with real money, which he offered me on the spot. Mr. Ward's statement that the stamp is not the requisite height does not seem to be borne out by Mr. Power's measurements or my own - and I have gone over it again most carefully."

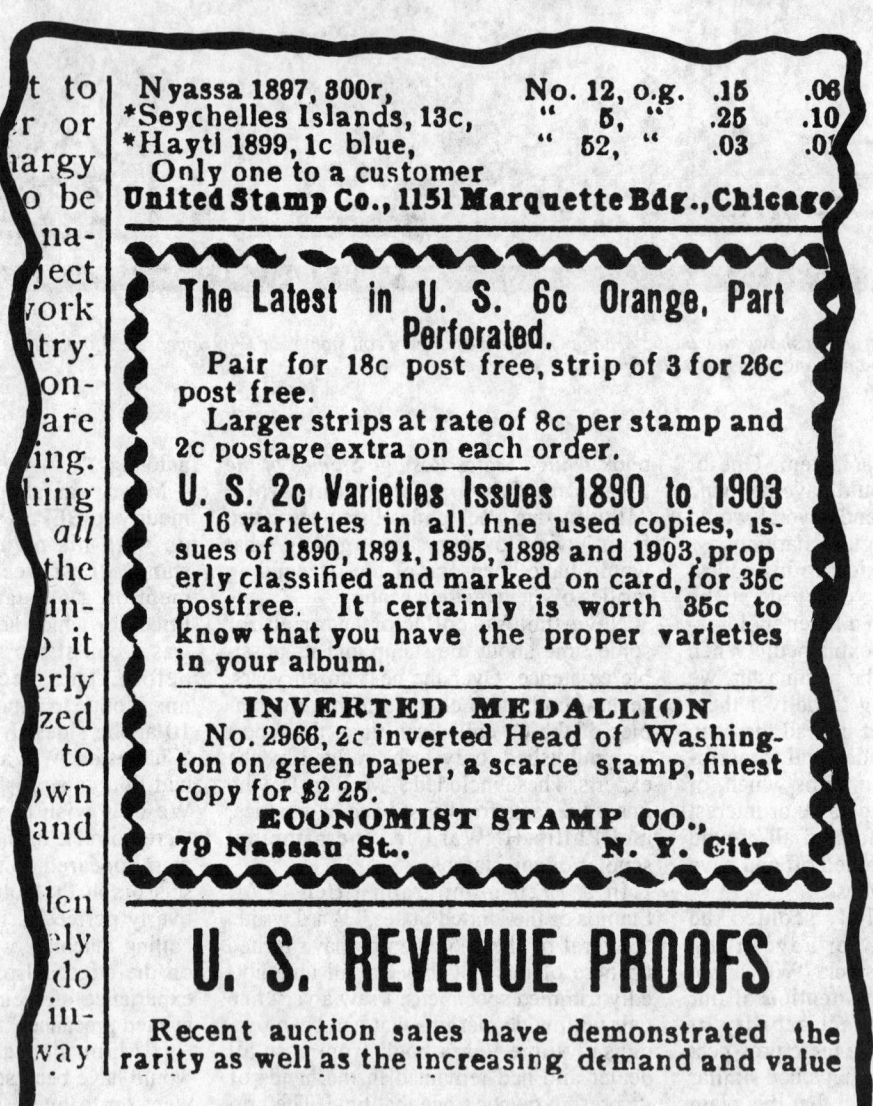

Figure 2: This advertisement in the May 15, 1909, issue of "Mekeel's Weekly Stamp News" offered "6-cent Orange, Part Perforated" (coil) stamps for sale. Economist Stamp Co. withdrew the offer two weeks later, after refusing to purchase the stamps from the New York post office.

Richter should have taken Power's money and run.

Ward replied, "Where U.S. coils are concerned I do not bow to the opinion of Mr. Power nor anyone else, for I believe I have given more study to coils than any other student and to date my article upon the subject is the only ever published covering the entire ground. It may be of interest to mention that Mr. Power's excellent book on 20th Century included both the 3¢ perf. 12 double line watermark coil and the 1¢ with every other row of perfs. missing, and as a result of my studies these were later deleted. I just mentioned this to show that none of us can be right all the time.

"I still maintain that the 6¢ coil does not exist and I further claim that no authority has any ground for passing upon a single specimen in the face of all the evidence against it."

On a trip to Washington D.C., in 1921, Richter persuaded USPOD and BEP officials to search their records for proof that the coil had been destroyed. By then, 12 years after the fact, the destruction order itself was long gone and the employee who had destroyed the stamps could not be located. Like so many philatelic dreamers, Richter therefore concluded that the stamp on his cover "must remain a mystery."

Ward would have none of that. As a sophisticated stamp collector, Chapman would have remembered owning such a stamp if it had been a genuine coil, but he did not. Ward closed out the debate with this:

"I have had the pleasure of examining this cover and it is positively my opinion that the stamp is nothing more than a trimmed variety. The owner of the cover has had some little correspondence with the Post Office Department and if they should attempt to make another search of their files they will simply be able to confirm the information that I obtained from them as well as from the Bureau and that is that one coil was made and one was destroyed. It will take more evidence than that which has been produced to prove that such a variety exists."

Since 1921, no one has offered a serious challenge to Ward's conclusion, so the 6¢ coil of 1909 survives only as a footnote reference in scholarly monographs - the stamp that got away. ❖

Scouting for the elusive Boy Scout collectible

by Wayne L. Youngblood

Most every topical collector eventually runs into an extremely appropriate item for his collection that is not immediately apparent as such. This is precisely the case with an item that has existed for a number of years, but is not widely recognized as an important Boy Scout topical item.

Back in the early 1960s, the Government Post Office of Great Britain occasionally sent souvenir items to those who subscribed to the Philatelic Bulletin. For a cost of 25 pence, subscribers could get the latest information on British stamps directly from the post office and, at least for awhile, some rather nice stamp-related collectibles. Among those items distributed to collectors by GPO were then-current stamps bearing the printed word "cancelled," aerograms with additional government printing and a very elusive item that should belong in many Boy Scout topical collections. As was previously mentioned, the Boy Scout connection in this case is not immediately obvious.

According to several sources, the September/October 1964 Philatelic Bulletin contained two free items for collectors. Both were versions of the British photogravure-printed four-line text only "For Testing Purposes Only" labels. The legend was contained in an oval in the center of the design and was considered the successor to the plain green British test item fondly referred to as the "Poached Egg."

One test label was a single definitive-sized test coil. The other was a red pair that was perforated all around but imperf between.

The British used test labels at that time for many of the same manufacturing purposes as the United States, but had an extensive postal vending machine system in place long before the United States. As a result, as early as the 1930s test labels were needed by technicians to test stamp-vending machines. As the post office became more mechanized, the need for test labels in connection with stamp affixing machines and other equipment also grew, leading to several types and varieties of British test labels.

Included with the gift test labels to GPO subscribers was a note that explained that test labels were very seldom seen by the public and that the publishers felt readers would like to see examples of the labels then in use. This portion of the note referred to the previously mentioned single label.

What's the connection to Scouting at this point? It seems as though the red imperf-between test labels were created for a very specific purpose a few years earlier.

Included with the note about the single test label was a notation that the red label was a specimen of a special label created to test certain stamp-affixing machines used in connection with the 1957 World Scout Jamboree issue, Scott 334-336. These machines were being tested to automatically apply the Scout stamps to official first-day covers. The test labels had to be the same size as the Scouting commemoratives. This explains the double-size imperf-between labels.

To identify the imperf-between test labels as Scout-related items, the GPO printed them in the same red color as the 2-penny scarlet stamp, Scott 334, creating a truly unusual yet significant Boy Scout collectible that is not apparent to the casual observer.

It is not known how many of the Scout test labels were produced or distributed, but they are not often seen. When these items are found, however, they are likely to sell for only a few dollars if their significance is unrecognized. ❖

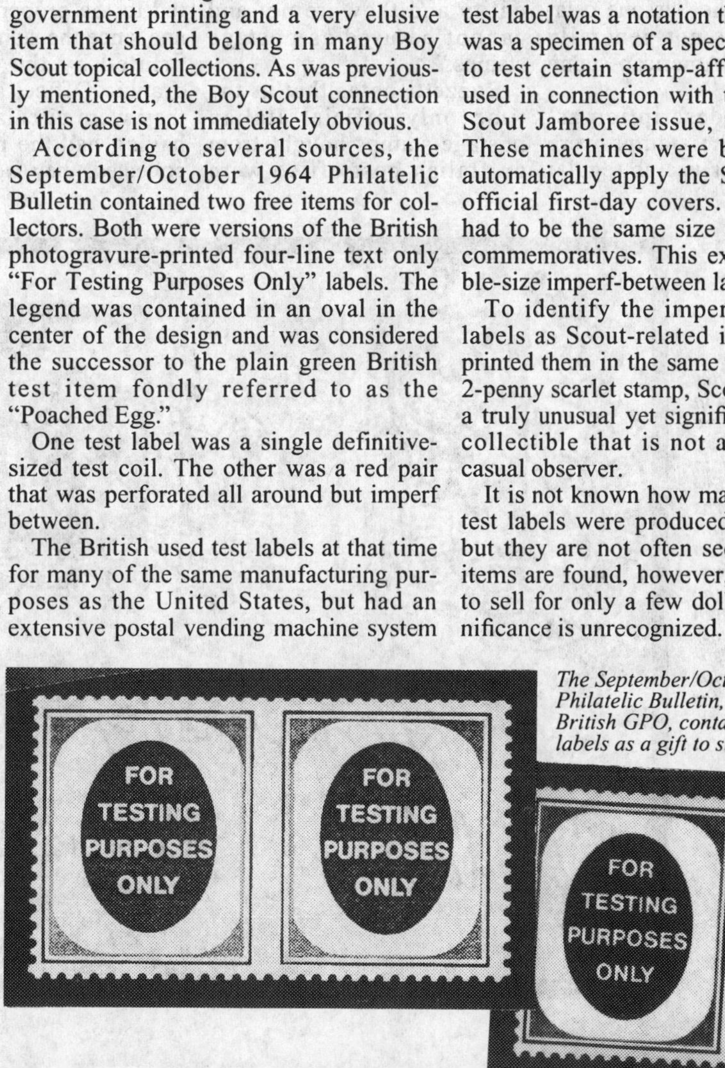

The September/October 1964 Philatelic Bulletin, created by the British GPO, contained two test labels as a gift to subscribers. One of these is a highly desirable Boy Scout-related collectible.

UPDATING POLISH CORPS STAMP USAGE

by Robert E. Lana

Having written an article on the stamps of the Polish Corps in Italy during World War II, (Linn's, June 8, 1992, page 33), I was particularly interested in a comment made recently by Luciano Buzzetti, in a Posta Militare, the newsletter of the Association of Collectors of Italian Military Post.

Buzzetti is one of the world's top experts on Italian military post, so his opinion is to be heeded. The article I wrote for Linn's described the reasons why the stamps were printed and their use by Polish forces. The information essentially comes from the Sassone catalog, which is not generally accessible to American stamp collectors.

Sassone's description assumes that the stamps were sanctioned for use as regular postage. Buzzetti's interpretation is somewhat different.

He states (in Italian): "In all these years I have maintained that the vignettes printed for the Polish Corps in 1946 were not postage stamps."

Buzzetti's conviction was born when he encountered issues of the journal Italia Filatelica printed in Rome shortly after the end of World War II. In one of the issues a notice by the Italian Federation of Stamp Dealers stated, "The Allied Commission has officially declared that the stamps printed with the words "Poczta Osiedii Polskich W Italii" and with the value in lire, were not issued by any officially recognized postal entity and they are not and cannot be used as postage stamps."

Buzzetti notes that at the time only official Italian postage stamps bought from an Italian post office were valid for franking mail. According to contemporary regulations, charity labels could not be applied on the addressed side of the envelope of a letter or package going through the mail system.

Another document reported in the same article states: "The Provincial Office of the Post Office of Bari assures that it has not given any authorization to allow a special postal service to function in the foreign community camped at Trani and Barletta."

The term "foreign community" used here clearly meant the Polish forces.

In addition, the Italian post office declared that since the stamp design was not submitted to the proper authorities, and since the stamps were not printed by the State Poligraphic Office, and because they were circulated without having had the proper taxes collected, they were not valid for postage.

Buzzetti concludes that not only were the stamps never valid for postage, but that this was never the intent of the allied or Polish military commands. Buzzetti then quotes a passage, written in English, from Ryszard Wagner's *History of the Polish Army Postal Service-Middle East and Italy 1940-1948*

"Labels issued by the War Relief Services-National Catholic Welfare Conference in December 1945 for the above settlements, as well as other postal emissions that appeared later, were of private origin and as such not accepted for postal or semi-postal purposes by the Polish Field Post Office."

Buzzetti notes that the Sassone and other catalogs list these labels as legitimate stamps, but do so incorrectly since the stamps never received postal authorization. ❖

An airmail letter from Barletta in Apuglia, where Polish troops were stationed, to Rome. The five Polish Corps stamps were canceled by an Italian-type canceler used by the Corps. Although the letter probably reached its destination, the stamps were not valid for postage.

This Merritt cover, dated December 7, 1941, 7 a.m., was submitted to the Philatelic Foundation, and, in April 1991, received a certificate with the notation, "and we are of the opinion that it is a genuine usage."

BY ROBERT G. METCALF

Wow! was my reaction upon seeing this Pearl Harbor cover. The stamp dealer displaying it at a Chicago stamp show was equally enthusiastic and not quite ready to part company with it. But that incredible postmark - "December 7/ 7 AM/1941/Honolulu, Hawaii/N. Air Sta. Pearl Harbor" - had me hooked. After many follow-up letters and phone calls, the dealer finally agreed to sell, and the cover became a cherished possession in my collection.

Since 1991 marked the fifty-year anniversary of the attack, I felt compelled to learn more about this cover, the man who had sent it, the woman who had received it, and the circumstances of this letter posted just before the attack.

Specific information about the Pearl Harbor attack was found in Gordon W. Prange's *December 7, 1941 - The Day the Japanese Attacked Pearl Harbor*. At precisely 0753, the famous code words "Tora, Tora, Tora" [Tiger, Tiger, Tiger] were sent back to Tokyo signaling the attack had begun.

Obviously from 0753 on, no mail would have been canceled. The 7 a.m. time line in the Merritt cover postmark logically would have recorded the last mail canceling from the Pearl Harbor area for several days. With all the excitement and confusion, mail no doubt would have been very low on a list of naval priorities.

The dealer could not supply any information on the cover and indicated he knew nothing of the cover's provenance. This fact did not surprise me, as many dealers protect and keep sources confidential - a key trait necessary for success in the trade.

Nevertheless, my interest could not be thwarted, and the chase for information and leads about this intriguing cover had begun.

Finding the Man Behind the Cover

My initial interest was in the man who had sent the cover, Lieutenant Commander L.M. Merritt. Over a period of months, the National Personnel Records Center (military personnel records) informed me by letter that no information could be obtained without an individual's number. All records were indexed by serial number; the individual's name was of no help.

Since I had hit a dead end with the records center, I turned to researching the addressee. A call to Columbus, Ohio, telephone information produced a phone number for Agnes Merritt at 654 Wilson Avenue. Imagine my excitement when I realized the addressee was still at the same place after almost fifty years.

My initial call resulted in just what I had hoped for - a first-hand account from the wife of Lieutenant Commander Lester M. Merritt, the originator of my cover.

Mrs. Merritt is a very charming and intelligent alumna (Phi Beta Kappa) of Hunter College. As a retired school teacher, she is no stranger to research, and she graciously answered my questions. Her most memorable remark during our introductory phone call was "You philatelists never cease to amaze me."

She was very generous with information about her husband, who had died in 1958.

Lester Merritt graduated as a ceramic engineer from Ohio State University in 1918. He entered Officers Training School during World War I and received a commission as an ensign, the rank he held to the end of that war. After World War I, Commander Merritt remained in the naval reserve until he was recalled into active service in August 1941 and stationed at Pearl Harbor.

He distinguished himself as Officer-in-Charge of Carrier and Aircraft Tender Maintenance from September 1942 to September 1946, receiving the Bronze Star with the following citation:

"For meritorious service in connection with operations against the enemy while a member of the Staff of Commander Service Force, U.S. Pacific Fleet from September 1942 to September 1946 and serving as Officer-in-Charge of Carrier and Aircraft Tender Maintenance. During this period of unprecedented expansion, he displayed a high degree of ingenuity and resourcefulness in skillfully organizing this section and in undertaking with success and expedition the many and difficult maintenance and improvement problems which continually arose in carriers of the Pacific Fleet. His sound knowledge and application of engineering principles and industrial processes enabled carriers of the Fleet to operate for extended periods in the forward areas without major overhaul and his good judgment and careful planning of availability periods for the vessels under his cognizance resulted in their expeditious overhaul with minimum periods of absence from the battle line. His calm assurance in advising operating commanders of future performance of their units made it possible for them to place their operations with minimum regard to mechanical attrition. His high degree of leadership and cooperation, untiring effort and unswerving devotion to duty were outstanding, and his services and conduct throughout were in keeping with highest traditions of the United States Naval Service."

When quizzed about mail from her husband, Mrs. Merritt stated she received mail from her husband regularly until the December 7 attack, and then almost two weeks passed before she got any letters. She did not specifically remember receiving the December 7, 1941, cover (illustrated), but provided an interesting account of her husband's experience. He was stationed on Ford Island at the time.

"He apparently was shaving when the attack came," said Mrs. Merritt, "and his reaction was, 'Why do they need to practice on Sunday?' The men never dreamed of an attack but just thought there was a practice stint."

Since Commander Merritt was shaving at the time of the attack - 8 a.m., according to published accounts - the cover would have had to have been deposited for mail on the previous Saturday evening.

This photo of Commander Merritt was taken in 1941, while he was stationed in Honolulu. According to Mrs. Merritt, it was the only one she had of her husband taken during the war.

Our talk also revealed that Commander Merritt was an ardent philatelist who was very active in the Columbus, Ohio, philatelic organization. Upon his death in 1958, his extensive stamp and envelope collection had passed to his only son. This undoubtedly was the source of my cover, but just one part of my philatelic puzzle.

A Collector Assist

For information about the mail system at Pearl Harbor, I turned to a fellow member of the St. Louis APS Life Chapter No. 4, Captain Robert W. Murch (USNR Retired). He has a collection of World War II naval mail and is the author of "Pearl Harbor Memorabilia - Of the 101 Naval Vessels Present Only Six Lacked Postal Facilities" (Linn's Stamp News, December 6, 1971).

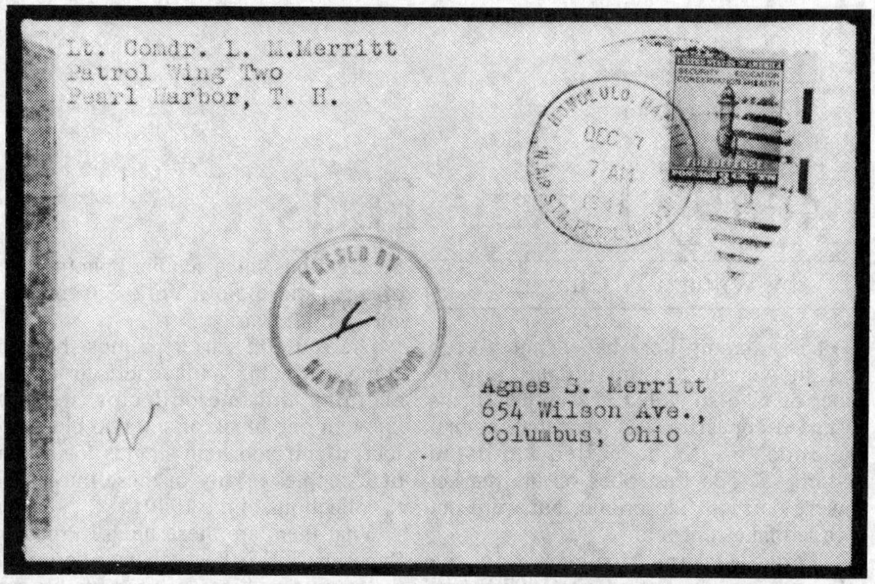

Two December 7, 1941, Pearl Harbor covers from Commander Merritt are known to exist. The one on the title page of this article belongs to the author; the other, shown here, belongs to dealer Stan Bednarczyk.

Murch not only had data on ship cancels but also was able to supply information on the postmarks from an April 1970 listing from the Universal Ship Cancellation Society's Log.

Five years after the Linn's thirtieth anniversary of Pearl Harbor article, Murch reported, "Only six postal cancellations have been reported with the date December 7, 1941, from the Pearl Harbor area: Pennsylvania, a battleship; Raleigh, a light cruiser; Shaw, a destroyer; Hulbert, a seaplane tender; Schley, a destroyer; and "Honolulu, Hawaii hand cancel from the Navy Yard, Pearl Harbor." Covers also existed from the battleship Nevada, dated December 6, 1941, salvaged from the ship's post office early in 1942. Back-dated "fake" covers also exist from the battleship Tennessee, with a "7:30 am 7 December, 1941, T-6 hand cancel."

Another clipping from Murch, written by Ward Speaker, discussed a Pearl Harbor cover with a cancel similar to my Merritt cover (Western Stamp Collector, December 1975). Unlike the Merrit cover, his cover's postmark did not carry a time indicator line. Comparison of the two postmarks shows similarities, but the lines, Navy Yard and N. Air Sta., suggest two separate postal facilities. The censor markings also are slightly different in print spacing and type style.

Speaker also notes that his cover was not received until around December 15, 1941, which confirms Mrs. Merritt's memory that almost two weeks passed before the resumption of Pearl Harbor mail from Commander Merritt.

A Researcher Assist

My next contact was with one of phialtely's most prolific writers, Richard Graham, also of Columbus, Ohio. Graham was not only an acquaintance of Lester Merritt but was also aware of the existence of my December 7, 1941, cover and believed that other Pearl Harbor covers from Commander Merritt might exist. No one to Graham's recollection had fully researched the question.

The End of the Trail

While attending another midwest stamp show, I met stamp dealer Stan Bednarczyk, also of Columbus, Ohio. Much to my surprise, I discovered he knew I had the Merritt cover and had one just like it.

A close comparison of the two covers shows slight differences - for instance, the "Lt. Comdr." rank follows the name on my cover and precedes the name on the one belonging to Bednarczyk. Both covers show very careful attention to opening and remain in pristine condition.

Both covers were in Lester Merritt's stamp collection, which was sold by Merritt's son to another Columbus stamp dealer. Stan's cover was purchased directly from the Columbus dealer, and my cover went to another party before it was sold to the dealer from whom I had purchased it.

According to Bednarczyk, these two covers were the only ones postmarked December 7, 1941, in Lester Merritt's collection. Other covers sent to relatives and fellow Columbus collectors may exist, but none have been reported or documented.

The two known Merritt covers are authentic and could have been canceled after the attack, with back dating of the time and date. An argument also could be made for two letters to the same individual, each deposited for mail at different times prior to 7 a.m. on Sunday, where both were processed with the same dating. The addressor blocks are different and mail processing and handling in all probability was not given much attention during the period immediately after 0753.

As Murch wrote, censorship was started immediately on December 7 and remained in effect until September 1945. Both covers would have been affected by the censorship period.

One point is certain. Commander Lester M. Merritt, as an advanced collector of naval covers, realized the importance and meaning of the postmark "December 7/ 7 AM/1941/Honolulu, Hawaii/N. Air Sta. Pearl Harbor." His legacy lives on in these covers, which have been preserved for other philatelists to enjoy.

❖

Robert G. Metcalf, a contractor from Mt. Vernon, Illinois, is a postal history collector who enjoys research, writing, and philatelic exhibiting. He is a frequent speaker at the Webster Groves [Missouri] stamp club and was recipient of the Jere Hess Barr award from the American Philatelic Congress in 1989.

Really Private Perfs

by William W. Cummings

It is amazing how bad pennies keep showing up. In this instance a number of fake so-called private perf items started appearing last year that, at first glance, might be called "unlisted stamps." The first ones on the market were correctly described, but were not called fakes outright.

Those stamps turned up in the Superior Galleries Summer 1993 Stamp Auction, held June 28-30. Lots 598 and 599 were a block of six Scott 500 (used on piece), and an unused block of four Scott 525. These were described as having cut-out, or hand-made, perfs. The blocks still sold for $198 and $231, respectively. We thought little of them until the Jan. 15, 1994, Weiss Philatelics auction catalog arrived. There, lot 2090 was a pair of Scott 409 and a block of four Scott 531. These were described as having an unknown roulette presumed to be very rare. The Scott United States editor notified the auction house that the items were fakes and they were offered as such on the floor of the auction. Even so, the lot sold for $220, a price very close to the Superior realizations. In the same auction, lot 1504 contained five used values of the 1895 issue with the same unknown roulette. That lot sold for $110.

The matter probably would have dropped there, but I happened to glance through some back issues of the *New York Precancel News* and saw what looked like another of these "private roulettes" on a New York City local precancel of the Washington-Franklin period. That copy is owned by Arnold Selengut, president of the Precancel Stamp Society. He exhibited the stamp with an article written by John Boker, Jr. The article probably appeared in a *Precancel Optimist* published sometime in the 1940s. A theory for the existence of the stamp, attributed to Herman "Pat" Herst, Jr. by Boker in the article, was that a bank held a number of imperf sheets as collateral that became its property when the bank foreclosed. The bank, as the story goes, had the stamps rouletted so that they could be used on mail. The bank could have been holding imperf sheets for a Schermack user. In recent correspondence, Herst has disclaimed any association with the report. Selengut has since acquired photocopies of three more New York City precancels with the variety.

The roulette variety almost has become common. With reports from two auctions and one collector, we now know of one block of six, two blocks of four, a pair and nine singles for a total of 25 copies. Many of these trace back to collections of the 1940s.

What then, are these items? Probably Superior said it best when it described the stamps as "rare perfs made by cutting out every other perf (author unknown)." And that is just what they are. I examined the Selengut copy with a 20-power glass, and the rounding at the base of the remaining perfs was obvious, once I knew what to look for. The remaining perf teeth perfectly match a perf 11 stamp. We are illustrating the Selengut copy here, with an enlargement of the perf area. This should help remove any lingering doubt as to their status. Also illustrated is a made-to-order coil pair done for this article, in 8 minutes or so, using a sharp blade.

Not every "private perf" is listed in the Scott Vending and Affixing Machine Perforations section of the United States Specialized. When an unlisted item is offered, one must remember that in most cases it is being offered as is. This one isn't.

These unusual hyphen-hole perfs are fake.

And one that is

United States and vending and affixing machine perforation stamp collectors occasionally run across a rather odd item that does not fit into the normal scheme of things. This is a perf 14 vertical coil that has a rubber-stamped New York, N.Y., precancel. The basic precanceled imperforate stamp was created for use in Schermack machines. This stamp is entirely different than the previously mentioned item. This one is genuine. It is a private coil that was used by the Boy Scouts of America Executive Council in 1922. This stamp was listed at least as early as the 1928 edition of the Rotnem precancel catalogue. The catalogue value was $5. The 1930 edition was published by the Hoover Brothers and the value was then raised to $20. Both were very high values for that time.

Does anyone have any information as to why this stamp should not be listed in the *United States Specialized*? It is a commercial item that seems to have better credentials than some of the stamps currently listed. My assumption is that while these stamps were coils created for use by the Schermack machines, some were sold to the Boys Scouts, who had them perfed. Since the organization did not have a "vending and affixing machine," the stamps were affixed by hand. This made them private perfs, outside the scope of that section of the Specialized Catalogue. In any case, this would make a knockout item for a Boy Scout topical collection. ❖

Anyone interested in finding out more about precancels can contact James Hirstein, PSS Secretary, Box 4072, Missoula, MT 59806.

TANKS and other WEAPONS

by George Griffenhagen

Following World War I, most military strategists believed that a fast-moving cavalry would always triumph over the lumbering tank; this belief was founded on the trench-warfare experience of World War I when the tank only had to traverse cratered terrain and had to sustain massed machine-gun fire. However, there were those who predicted the mechanized nature of future warfare; their view proved far more accurate since the tank dominated military tactics in virtually every ground operation of World War II. The design of tanks progressed more rapidly during 1939-1945 than it did in the previous 30 years.Blitzkrieg ("lightning war") was a term which described the successes of the German Army led by tanks, commencing with the invasion of Poland in September, 1939, and followed in April-June, 1940, by the conquest of Denmark, Norway, Holland, Belgium, Luxembourg and France.

The earliest German tanks, with open tops and no turrets, were described by the Nazis as "agriculture tractors" to disguise their true purpose. By 1939, the Germans had built more powerful tanks including the Panzer II and Panzer (called Panzerkampfwagen or PzKw for short); Panzer III were used extensively in most of the World War II campaigns. The Germans also took over the production facilities of the Czechoslovak LT-39 tank which the Germans redesignated Panzer-38.

However, the principal weapons of the German armored divisions eventually became the Tiger (Panzer VI) and the Panther (Panzer V). At the time of its introduction in August 1942, the Tiger was the world's most powerful tank, and the Tiger took a heavy toll of the comparatively vulnerable Allied tanks during the early campaigns in North Africa. The Panther, which was first produced in 1943, featured a long, sloping frontal plate (copied from the Russian T-34 tank) that was hard to penetrate.

After the Tiger entered service, the Germans commenced production in December 1943 of a massive new tank - the Tiger II or Konistiger, also known as the "Tiger Royal" and the "King Tiger." But only 484 Tiger II were ever produced, and they only saw service on the Eastern Front after May 1944, and in the Battle of the Bulge in December 1944.

The Red Army possessed more tanks than any other power in 1940. They tested their weapons first in Manchuria and then in Finland, but their T-26 and BT-7 were no match for the German guns, and they suffered enormous losses. This all changed when new Russian tank designs were introduced. The KV heavy tank (named after Soviet Marshal Klimenti Voroshilov) made its appearance in 1940. But it was the T-34 medium tank that proved to be the Soviet's finest weapon. Its diesel engine reduced the risk of fire; its broad treads facilitated deployment in mud and snow; and the steel turret, cast all in one piece, was highly resistant to penetration by German anti-tank weapons.

The Germans upgraded their Tiger tanks with 88 mm guns to counteract the 76 mm weapons carried by the tough Russian T-34 tanks; the Russians responded by upgrading the firepower of their KVs and T-34s. The July 1943 battle of Kursk was the largest tank battle in history with

Panzer IV (above left) and Sturmgeschutz II (above right) (Germany Scott B228 & B264)

Panzer VI Tigers Invade Russia But Tigers First Appeared in 1942 (Marshall Islands Scott 282)

Panther Tamed in Normandy (Maldives Scott 1433)

The T-34 Was Russia's Finest Tank (Russia Scott 5219)

Russian Tanks Turn Tide at Kursk Largest Tank Battle in History (Russia Scott 6132)

Italian M 13/40s Routed at Beda Fomm (Marshall Islands Scott 275)

First British Tank-Borne Flamethrower (Grenada Scott 378)

British Crusader I inNorth Africa (Grenada Scott 1830)

Ha-Go Tanks Attack Bataan (Japan Scott B6)

Free French Used Shermans (French Polynesia Scott C14)

Sherman Rolls Off Assembly Line (U.S.A. Scott 2559e)

M-4 Sherman in Battle of the Bulge (Grenada-Grenadines Scott 1171)

2,800 German tanks confronting 3,600 Soviet tanks.

The JS-II (named for Josef Stalin) was a heavy tank fitted with huge 122 mm guns; these super-tanks were first used in battle at the end of 1944, and they were first revealed to western observers in the Berlin Victory Parade of September 1945.

When the war broke out, the British relied on the Infantry Mark II (which became known as the Matilda), and the Infantry Mark (which was known as the Valentine because the design was introduced on St. Valentine's Day, 1938); but virtually all British tanks were lost during the Dunkirk evacuation. With less than 100 tanks left in the United Kingdom, Vauxhall Motors Ltd. undertook a "crash" program to design and build replacements. By June 1941, the Infantry Mark IV (known as the Churchill) was operational and joined the Crusader Mark I cruiser tank in North Africa. The British subsequently developed a series of tanks including the Centaur, the Cromwell and the Challenger, all of which saw their first action during or after the invasion of Normandy. The British Comet was not deployed until after the Rhine crossing in 1945.

The Italians employed the Carro Armato L6 light reconnaissance tank and the Carro Armato M 13/40 medium tank. While these tanks were adequate for colonial policing, they proved to be useless for the mechanized warfare of World War II. The frontal armor of the Carro Armato was outclassed by the British weapons in North Africa, and the Italians were routed at Beda Fomm.

The French used a variety of tanks including the Renault of various designs, and the heavier Hotchkiss; but these tanks were lightly armed and so lightly armored they were no match for the German panzers when they invaded France in 1940. The best French tank was the Char-B, but it was poorly used by the French against the invading Germans; those tanks that survived were used by the Germans for training and as mountings for self-propelled guns.

The Japanese employed tanks almost exclusively for infantry support, and they built very few heavy tanks. The Ha-Go light infantry tank was designed by Mitsubishi in 1935, while the Chi-Ha medium tank, introduced in 1937, was the most widely used Japanese tank of World War II. In an attempt to improve its firepower, the Japanese added a 75 mm field gun to the turret of the Chi-Ha, but it remained inferior to the U.S. Sherman against which it was matched. In 1944, the Japanese commenced development of a heavier Chi-Ri tank, but only a prototype had been completed when World War II ended.

The United States was ill-prepared for armored warfare when World War II commenced. The M-2-A-4 light tank, armed with a 37 mm gun, was the best in the U.S. Army. The efficiency of the vast American automobile industry was harnessed to produce the M-3 Grant medium tank which saw its first action in North Africa, and its counterpart the M-3 Stuar, also called "Honey" by the British who used them in North Africa, and by the Australians who used them for jungle warfare in the Pacific.

As soon as the Grant design was finalized in March 1941, work commenced on a new tank armed with a 75 mm gun mounted in a fully traversable turret. The resulting M-4 Sherman medium tank was first used operationally at El Alamein in 1942, and the Sherman became the mainstay of Allied offensive operations for the rest of the war. The M-24 Chaffee light tank was introduced in July 1944, but few saw action during World War II. The Canadians produced the Ram which was widely used for training purposes; but the Ram never saw battle-action since the Canadians used the Sherman. The U.S. also supplied the Free French Army with over 1,000 M-3 Grants and M-4 Shermans for their participation in the liberation of France.

The Germans led the world in half-track design - vehicles with wheels in the front and tracks at the back; these half-tracks were used as armored personnel carriers in support of their panzer divisions. The Germans also employed armored scouting cars which were pioneered by Mercedes-Benz; the heaviest was the Puma which entered service in 1943. The U.S. was the other major manufacturer of half-tracks using vehicles produced by White, Autocar, Diamond T, and International Harvester. The Japanese employed various types of armored cars, while the Soviets depended on the four-wheeled BA-64, and the British relied on the small, fully-tracked Bren Carrier which was used extensively in North Africa.

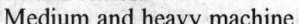

U.S. Marines Firing Machine Gun (Maldive Islands Scott 1431)

2-1/2 Ton GMC Hauls Howitzer (U.S.A. Scott 2559a)

From the *M-1* to the *V-2*

The rifle was the standard weapon of the World War II infantryman. The German Army's standard rifle was the Manser Kar 98which was more accurate than the British Lee-Enfield rifle. Both the Russian Mosin-Nagant and the Japanese Ariska were rugged and reliable weapons, while the Garand or M-1semi-automatic rifle was standard issue to the U.S. foot soldier. Even though the M-1 was not universally available when the United States entered the war, it eventually proved that the semi-automatic rifle was a viable weapon in the hands of the infantryman.

A new, shoulder-fired weapon introduced during World War II was the German Panzerchreck, the British PIAT, and the American Bazooka (named because of its resemblance to a musical instrument improvised by a popular radio comedian). These launchers fired a hollow-charge shell which was rendered molten by the detonation of its casing, and for the first time in history a foot soldier had a weapon specifically designed to penetrate armor.

One of the most effective weapons of World War II was the flame-thrower. The Germans developed the Einstossflamenwerfer 46 for use against the Russian ROKS-3. The Japanese used two types of flame-throwers for clearing the Far East jungles, while the British used the Marsden Portable Flame Thrower. The Americans introduced their Portable Flame Thrower M1 in January 1943 at Guadalcanal, and found it most effective against the Japanese in heavily foliated areas. Flame-throwers were also added to the armament of specially-designed tanks by both the Axis and Allies.

Medium and heavy machine

German Mortar Crew (Germany Scott B261)

German Grenade Assault (Germany Scott B223)

German Heavy Artillery (Germany Scott B224)

German Anti-Aircraft Unit (Germany Scott B225)

Medium and heavy machine guns were employed by all armies. The British used the Vickers, while the Americans employed the Browning. The Japanese machine gun was the Taisho based on the French Hotchkiss, while the Russians used the Goryunov adopted from the earlier Maxim. The Germans perfected the MG-34 and the MG-42, both belt-fed, mounted on tripods, and precursors of today's general purpose machine guns.

The mortar provided high-angle fire support for the infantry, and was employed by all armies during World War II. The mainstay for the German Army was the Schwerer Grantwerfer, capable of launching a 7.7 pound bomb up to 2,600 yards. A short-barreled version for airborne use, called the Stummeelwerfer, was also employed by the Germans. The British mortars were all descendants of the World War I Strokes, while the U.S. mortar was a derivative of the 81 mm Brandt. The U.S. Chemical Warfare Service's 4.2-inch rifled mortar was extensively used, and was a great favorite with the Marines.

The two main artillery weapons used for direct support of ground forces in World War II were the field gun and the howitzer. The former fired a high-velocity shell some 15,000 yards, while the short-barreled howitzer lobbed a weightier, high-explosive projectile at shorter ranges. The light 105 mm howitzer was favored because of its mobility. The use of a wide variety of field guns on the Eastern Front was especially notable. While the Russians produced 85 mm and 100 mm versions of its field guns, their operations against the Germans were supported by anything and everything that was available and would fire.

Howitzers and field guns were also built on the framework of tanks, called self-propelled guns. Among the many self-propelled guns used by the Germans was the Brummbar ("grizzly bear") with an assault howitzer on a Tiger chassis. Inspired by the Germans, the Russians placed considerable emphasis on self-propelled guns including the SU-100 with a 100 mm gun built on a T-34 chassis. The American M-7 Howitzer Motor Carriage was armed with a 105 mm howitzer; in British service it was known as the Priest.

The Germans devoted considerable effort to produce long-range artillery, including 280 mm K-5 railway guns which fired 560-pound projectiles. Several of these weapons were employed with devastating effect on the Anzio beachhead in 1944. One of these railway guns, dubbed "Anzio Annie" by the American troops, was later salvaged and is now on display at the U.S. Ordinance Museum in Aberdeen, Maryland. The Americans countered with the 155mm Long Tom and the 240 mm howitzer. But it was the American 8-inch howitzer that was finally able to silence German artillery deep in enemy territory. Even dedicated tanker General George Patton admitted that the war "was largely won by the artillery."

The heaviest of the German railway guns was the 800 mm Gustav which was built by the Krupp works. It was the largest gun in the world, firing five ton shells. It had to be partly dismantled for rail travel, and 4,120 men were needed to assemble, operate, maintain, and guard Gustav. Its only recorded appearance in action was at the siege of Sevastopole in 1942, and briefly outside of Warsaw in 1944.

The Germans devoted much energy to the development of anti-aircraft (Flak) guns; in fact, it was their Flak-88 which led to the wide use of the multi-purpose "88." Both the British and the Soviets employed versions of the mobile Bofors which had been developed in the 1930s by the Swedish armaments industry. All sides used barrage balloons to channel aircraft into corridors of fire, and searchlights were employed to pick out individual targets at night. But it was the development of radar that made anti-aircraft an effective weapon. Its use was pioneered by the British whose Chain Home Defense System was installed across southern England just before the war.

While rocket development commenced in Germany in the 1920s, the first multiple rocket projector to reach combat service was the Soviet Katyusha which was used against the Germans; it fired a bank of 15 warheads some 6,500 yards. The Germans countered with the Nebelwerfer, a six-barrelled weapon with the somewhat longer range. The success of these weapons prompted both armies to develop larger and more powerful versions, although German rocket development concentrated on the V-1, and V-2 missiles. The V-1 flying "buzz" bomb with a one-ton warhead was launched from fixed ramps and traveled at about 350 miles per hour to a target at a maximum range of 150 miles. The V-2 (or A-) rocket was capable of supersonic speed, often flying at an altitude of over 50 miles.

World War II introduced mechanized warfare as some had predicted in the 1930s, but much of that equipment has been antiquated by even deadlier weapons of destruction. Hopefully mankind will abide by the advice offered by the man who is credited with the famous quotation, "Praise the Lord and pass the ammunition." Howell Forgy revised his quote in 1944 with these words:

"When enough people really praise the Lord, it will no longer be necessary to pass the ammunition."

The organization of a World War II thematic collection by types of weapons offers an intriguing approach. ❖

Germany Railway Artillery (Germany Scott B267)

Nebelwerfer Rocket Launcher (Germany Scott B268)

References

Eddy Bauer, The History of World War II(Galahad Books, New York, 1966).

Fred W. Baumann, "Stamps Show the Evolution of Tanks," Linn's Collector's Guide to Topical (Special Supplement to Linn's Stamp News, May 14, 1990).

Lida Mayo, United States Army in World War II: The Ordnance Department on Beachhead and Battlefront (Office of the Chief of Military History, U.S. Army, Washington, DC, 1968).

Janusz Piekalkiewicz, Tank War 1939-1945 (Blanford Press, Great Britain, 1986). Originally published as Krieg der Panzer 1939-1945 (Sudwest Verlag, Munich, Germany, 1981).

Elizabeth-Anne Wheal, Stephen Pope, and James Taylor, A Dictionary of the Second World War (Peter Bedrick Books, New York, 1990).

Peter Young, World Almanac of World War II (Pharos Books, New York, 1981).

Peter Young, editor, Illustrated Encyclopedia of World War II. Eighteen volumes, based on original text of Eddy Bauer, profusely illustrated (Marshall Cavendish, New York, 1972).

B.T. White, Tanks and Other Armoured Fighting Vehicles of World War II (Exeter Books, New York, 1983).

Bridge tricks uncovered by cover

by Peter Martin

The illustrated cover appears innocent enough but, like many postal items, it has a fascinating story behind it.

On its surface, the cover would appear to be an ordinary 1965 registered letter sent from a Rio de Janeiro, Brazil, hotel to Ralph Swimer in London, England, but appearances can be very deceiving. This cover was part of a chain of events that rocked the British bridge establishment and made headlines around the world.

Ralph Swimer was the non-playing captain of the British bridge team entered in the 1965 World Championship held in Buenos Aries, Argentina. The championship involved teams from Great Britain, the United States, Italy and Argentina.

During the championship, several American players noted that Terence Reese and Boris Shapiro, Britain's greatest bridge partnership, were cheating by using illegal finger signals. They reported their suspicions to World Bridge Federation officials who, along with Swimer, observed the pair during subsequent play. The bridge officials held an inquiry and found the pair guilty. The British team conceded the matches it had already played and finished the tournament with its remaining players.

On May 23, the final day of the event, Shapiro called Swimer aside, confessed and asked him what to do. Shapiro said he was considering suicide and pleaded with him not to tell anybody.

Swimer wrote a four-page letter about the meeting with the last paragraph stating, "I'm writing these words while it is all fresh in my mind. I hope not ever to repeat them and am posting to London in case anything should happen to me before arriving home."

Swimer enclosed the pages inside an envelope from the Leme Palace Hotel that he marked "Personal. Only open after death." That envelope he placed inside the one illustrated.

Both author and letter arrived safely so Swimer put it away.

When everyone returned to England, the popular Reese and Shapiro were brought before a British tribunal, The Foster Inquiry. After 15 months the court found the pair not guilty on the basis of "reasonable doubt."

Through some maneuvering by defense attorneys, the letter was not brought into evidence at the tribunal. It was not until two years later that the letter was opened in connection with a libel action.

Despite the finding by the Foster Inquiry, Reese and Shapiro never again participated in bridge at the international level.

Alan Truscott, the *New York Times* bridge columnist, in his book *The Great Bridge Scandal, The Full Story of the Most Famous Cheating Case in Card Playing History*, published by Yarborough Press in 1969, lays out brilliantly the case against Reese and Shapiro.

The case put forth by Reese is contained in *Story of an Accusation* printed by Simon and Schuster in 1966.

Thus, this unassuming, but documented, cover enters into international bridge championship history as a major player. ❖

This common-looking registered cover from Brazil contained information that rocked the international bridge community.

King Carl XIV John – Marshal of France and the Throne of Sweden

by David C. Akin

When a childless and senile Charles XIII replaced Gustavus IV on the Swedish throne, following a coup d'etat in 1809, the search for a successor began. Within the group of people searching for an appropriate crown prince, a small faction believed that a suitable successor to Charles XIII could be found within Napoleon's family or the French marshalate. The man ultimately selected was Jean Baptiste Bernadotte, Prince of Ponte Corvo, Marshal of France.

Born Jan. 26, 1763, in Pau, Jean was the youngest of Henri Bernadotte's five children. Following his father's death in 1780, Bernadotte enlisted in the Royal Maritime Regiment. At the age of 25, with only eight years of service, he was promoted to the rank of company sergeant major. After reaching the highest enlisted rank possible in February 1790, that of regimental sergeant major, Bernadotte was promoted to lieutenant in November 1791, and transferred to the 36th Infantry Regiment. This promotion would not have been possible prior to the start of the revolution, which saw the abolition of regulations prohibiting anyone not of the nobility from becoming an officer.

Going into action at Ruzlheim for the first time in May 1793, Bernadotte learned that he was capable of leading men in combat. By his words and actions, he was able to rally his troops and prevent a break in the French lines. His skills would be severely tested during 1794, the most significant year of his career.

Bernadotte began the year as a captain. He advanced to the field rank of battalion commander in February and was named colonel

The descendents of Jean Baptiste Bernadotte, King Charles XIV John, continue to occupy the throne of Sweden. Most of them have appeared on postage stamps.

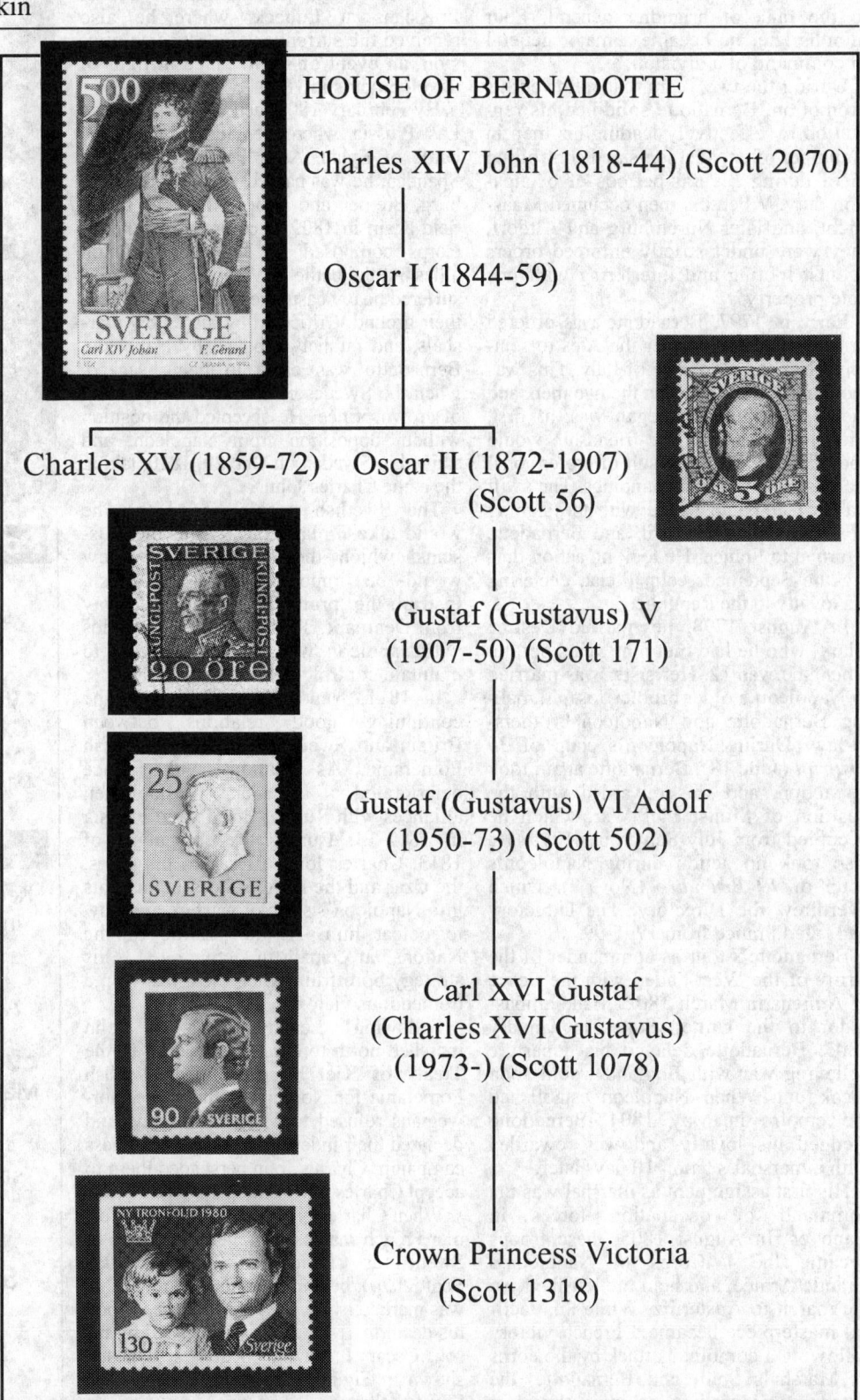

HOUSE OF BERNADOTTE

Charles XIV John (1818-44) (Scott 2070)

Oscar I (1844-59)

Charles XV (1859-72)

Oscar II (1872-1907) (Scott 56)

Gustaf (Gustavus) V (1907-50) (Scott 171)

Gustaf (Gustavus) VI Adolf (1950-73) (Scott 502)

Carl XVI Gustaf (Charles XVI Gustavus) (1973-) (Scott 1078)

Crown Princess Victoria (Scott 1318)

in command of the 71st Demi-Brigade in April. As with many units involved in the French Revolutionary War, the morale of the 71st ebbed and flowed with the tide of battle. On a number of occasions, Bernadotte was forced to rally his men to prevent a disorderly retreat. For his actions leading his troops against Austrian forces at the battle of Fleurus on June 26, Bernadotte was elevated on the field to the rank of brigadier general. Four months later he became a major general in command of a division.

During the two years that followed his promotion, Bernadotte solidified his reputation by effectively leading his men in a number of engagements and controlling them during several periods of occupation duty. When his men occupied Maastricht, and later Nuremburg and Altdorf, they were under strictly enforced orders against looting and interfering with private property.

Early in 1797, Bernadotte was ordered to lead his division over the Alps to reinforce Napoleon's Army of Italy. This was the first meeting between the two men, and the relationship that began was, at first, friendly. Unhappily, the friendship would soon deteriorate as a result of professional jealousy and misunderstandings. The swift Italian Campaign ended with the signing of an armistice in April, and Bernadotte returned to France. He took no action during the September coup d'etat, declaring his loyalty to the Republic.

In August 1798, he married Desiree Clary, who he had met nine years before, when she was 12. Her sister was married to Napoleon's older brother Joseph, making Bernadotte and Napoleon brothers-in-law. During Napoleon's coup of *30 Prairial* (June 18), Bernadotte again took no action, and was rewarded with the position of Minister of War, which he occupied from July-September 1799. He also took no action during Napoleon's coup of *19 Brumaire* (Nov. 9), which overthrew the Directory. The Directory had ruled France from 1795-99.

Bernadotte's tour as commander of the Army of the West ended with the Peace of Amiens in March 1802. Made ambassador to the United States in January 1803, Bernadotte delayed his departure believing war with England would soon break out. When Napoleon established the empire in May 1804, Bernadotte pledged his loyalty and was rewarded with a marshal's baton 10 days later.

His first assignment as marshal was the command of occupation forces in Hanover. In August 1805, these troops became the I Corps of Napoleon's Grande Armee, and held the left flank on the march to Austerlitz. While this tactical masterpiece became a French victory following a combined attack by the corps of Marshals Soult and Bernadotte, the latter was accused of lacking enthusiasm during the pursuit phase of the battle.

In June 1806, Bernadotte was created Prince of Ponte-Corvo, the second of the marshals to receive a title. By September, Napoleon had his army on the move toward Jena-Auerstadt where a great battle took place in October. Bernadotte's corps was late arriving at the scene, and marched to the sound of the guns. During the pursuit phase his men trapped the last Prussians at Lubeck, where he also received the surrender of a Swedish division, an event of significance in light of developments in 1809.

By February 1807, action had shifted to East Prussia, where Bernadotte missed the battle of Eylau. After being wounded at Spanden, he was named governor of Hamburg, Bremen and Lubeck. He took to the field again in 1809 in command of the IX Corps composed of Napoleon's Saxon allies. At the battle of Wagram, the Saxons suffered heavy casualties and failed to hold their ground. Criticized by his fellow marshals, and publicly rebuked by Napoleon, Bernadotte was close to being sacked, when the Swedes offered him the position of crown prince. He accepted the position without opposition from Napoleon, and arrived in Sweden on Oct. 20, 1810, taking the name Charles John.

The Swedish people hoped that he would take Finland back from the Russians, which the crown prince knew would be impossible to accomplish. Instead, he proposed to take Norway from Denmark. This put Sweden at odds with Napoleon, who needed the Danes to maintain control of the Baltic Sea.

In 1811, Napoleon responded to the continuing good relations between Britain and Sweden by seizing Swedish Pomerania. As relations with France deteriorated, Sweden established alliances with Russia, Britain and Prussia in 1812-13. During the campaigns of 1813, Charles John offered to his allies, the Czar and the King of Prussia, insights into Napoleon's style of warfare and how to defeat him. At the "Battle of the Nations" at Leipzig in October 1813, his strategy bore fruit, when the allies won a tremendous victory.

Following Leipzig, Charles John marched north to defeat the Danes. In the Treaty of Kiel he exchanged Swedish Pomerania for Norway. Initially, the Norwegians refused to accept the treaty, and declared their independence. In a bloodless campaign, Charles John persuaded them to accept Charles XIII as king.

When Charles XIII died in 1818, the former French marshal assumed the throne of Sweden as Charles XIV John (Sweden Scott 2070), beginning a 26-year reign that was marked by peace and prosperity. Upon his death in 1844, he was succeeded by his son Oscar I, having begun a dynasty, shown in Figure 1, that still occupies the Swedish throne. ❖

A.L. "Mick" Michael, Martin Sellinger Robert A. Siegel

The Boys
Left to right: Martin Sellinger, Julius Stolow, Mick Michael and Bob Siegel

The Girls
Left to right: Miriam Siegel, Ann Stolow, Enid Michael and Harriet Sellinger

Loving memories of a passing era

by Martin Sellinger

The passing of legendary stamp auctioneer Robert Siegel on Dec. 3, 1993, brought to mind, in no uncertain terms, that we are seeing the closing of an era of great philatelic personalities. Siegel was one of a full generation of philatelic greats that is now passing.

My thoughts and memories of Bob start about 1950 when I was a fledgling in a new (actually very old) office at 116 Nassau Street. There is no need to explain how awed I was to be in the Stamp Center Building with neighbors who were in the highest echelons of commercial philately. I wouldn't presume to call any of them friends yet.

Then, from casual association, and the fact that in 1955 by chance I bought a house in White Plains that was around the corner from the Siegel residence, we became friends. Among the many friends I made through Bob was "Mick" Michael, who did wonders in building Stanley Gibbons, and Ryohei Ishikawa, the renowned collector and builder of famous collections. Speaking of Ishikawa, I must remark that he was the greatest and warmest host that I have ever encountered. We visited him in Tokyo during the 1970s. Aside from entertaining us at his home and his restaurant in the Ginza, Ishikawa invited us, along with his close friends, to the opening of Maxim's of Tokyo for a fabulous and very memorable Christmas dinner.

There is one favorite memory I have of Bob that I must share with you. Once, I was staying at my usual London Hilton and watching the evening news on the BBC. Lo and behold, there was, on the news, the New York Auction House of Robert Siegel, auctioning off at a new record-breaking price the famous British Guiana Scott 13, the unique and most valuable stamp in the world. At that moment there was a loud knock at the door. I answered it and, as if by magic, there stood Robert Siegel in the flesh. At the close of his sale, he had taken the next plane to London for rest, relaxation and business, which is where he found me.

And then there was the time spent with Bob and his wife in the Caribbean. Actually, that was the best vacation I have ever had. My wife Harriet and I took a 10-day island-hopping jaunt with the three most wonderful couples. The group included Ann and Julius Stolow, who we were extremely fond of; Enid and Mick Michael; and Miriam and Bob Siegel. The trip took place during March 1968, and no one in the world ever got along better, more warmly or had a better time than we did. We made a pact, the boys of course, that anyone who would talk stamps during the trip would be penalized and fined; it happened so many times after only a half hour that we finally gave up and never looked back. Any time there was even the slightest delay during the trip, one of us took cards out to play Gin Rummy - on a table, bench or box - it didn't matter.

The annual rarity sales of Robert A. Siegel Auction Galleries have been important events, and the 30th Anniversary sale on Nov. 20, 1993, was no exception. This, and the Margaret Woodson Fisher sale which ended Nov. 22, were the last sales that Bob attended in person, but I am sure he will be looking on when the future great sales take place under the expert guidance of Scott Trepel, the firm's president.

Bob Siegel will be sorely missed by all of us who knew him, but he will be long, long remembered. ❖

Burma's close shave with the Japanese

by Raymond Lamont-Brown

Britain declared war on Japan Dec. 8, 1941, and Burma was invaded from Thailand by the Japanese some hours later. Already, a special coded order, "Climb Mt. Nitkita," had been transmitted by Japan's naval headquarters to the carrier force moving toward Hawaii. The order meant the execution of an attack on Pearl Harbor. In Tokyo, premier Hideki Tojo unleashed the Japanese dogs of war in the Pacific and, as a consequence, a whole new range of postal systems were to be implemented in southeast Asia under Japanese occupation.

By May 1, 1942, with the fall of Mandalay, the inadequately equipped British defending forces of the 17th Indian Division and the 1st Burma Division were pushed out of Burma by Lt. Gen. Shojiro Iida's XVth Army. The British retreat was the longest in the history of British warfare.

Burma now became a part of the Japanese "Co-prosperity sphere" for occupied territory under 32 "governors of districts" with Imperial Nipponese Army officers as "Peace Commissioners."

On Aug. 1, 1942, Tokyo ordered the setting up of a Central Executive Committee under the socialist politician-collaborator, Dr. Ba Maw, as puppet Chief Administrator.

Working under the commander in chief of the Japanese Army in Burma, Ba Maw oversaw the economic rape of Burma for the Japanese. Burma was given a phony independence in 1943, with Ba Maw as Prime Minister. Burma was forced to declare war on Britain and the United States.

As the Japanese military machine began to garrison southeast Asia countries, the mainland Japanese government ordered the issue of a considerable number of occupation stamps. These are usually divided into four categories. Overprinted or defaced issues of the respective countries; Japanese empire regular issues used unmarked; Japanese empire regular issues overprinted; and new issues, but predominantly the latter. There was also a separate issue for the Shan States, found in the eastern part of Burma, bordering China, the French protectorate of Laos and Thailand. Closely related to the Thais, the Shan remain the largest ethnic minority in Burma.

These Japanese occupation stamps of Burma, Scott 2N38-2N40, were released August 1, 1943. Note the crude letterpress printing style that distinguishes them. Like many similar issues, these stamps are scarcer properly used than mint.

In all, Burma was to have five new issues, and the Shan States one, but it can be noted that Burma did have a circulation of Japanese mainland stamps of 1937 issues with anna and rupee (16 anna equalled 1 rupee) overprints during 1942. The 2-sen Japanese "First Shows Series" stamp of 1937 showing the War God Nogi (General Count Maresuke Nogi, 1849-1912), was issued in Japan to celebrate the Fall of Singapore, March 17, 1942, to Lt. Gen. Tomoyuki Yamashita, and circulated in Burma in 1942.

To put in motion a fast postal rehabilitation of Burma, emergency steps were taken June 1, 1942, with the issue of watermarked business paper showing the handstamp han (seal) of Shizuo Yano. Yano was the chairman of the Postal Administration Reconstruction Committee, and the "chairman's stamp" took the place of the Burmese 1 anna. Perforated, the stamp showed the seal in vermilion, on paper watermarked with "ABSORBO DUPLICATOR," and the outline of an elephant in a part of the cut sheet.

It should be remembered that during the period up to June 1, 1942, the postage stamps of Burma for 1937 (India type), 1938 and 1939 were overprinted with peacock designs, and the Yon Thon (official use) peacock overprint for 1939, were used both by the Burmese and Japanese for awhile.

The next issue came in two phases, which can be separately identified by monetary changes. The two first definitive stamps were issued June 10 and Oct. 15, respectively in 1942. The 1-anna scarlet shows a farmer plowing a rice field with two oxen; the watermark reads "ELEPHANT BRAND," with the outline of a trumpeting elephant. The 1-anna scarlet was overprinted 5¢ in black to form the October 1942 issue. Both (as they were the same stamp issue) are lithographed on vertically laid paper and are perforated 11 by 12, with calligraphy in Japanese.

To suit the change in the monetary system for Burma, the Japanese post office, issued March 15-17, 1943, a set of eight lithographed stamps with the same picture and calligraphy as the 1-anna stamp, but on a white wove paper and unwatermarked. The denominations were now typographed: 1¢, orange; 2¢, yellow; 3¢, blue; 5¢, carmine; 10¢, violet brown; 15¢, red violet; 20¢, dull purple; and 30¢, blue green.

These stamps, from the October 1, 1943, definitive set, (Scott 2N41-2N50) were printed by letterpress, but are much more skillfully done than their predecessors.

By Feb. 15, 1943, the Japanese produced a 5¢ scarlet "Burma State Crest" issue, with Burmese calligraphy. On Aug. 1, 1943, the occupying powers issued a set of three stamps for Burma to mark the declaration of independence under the puppet government of Ba Maw. The 1¢ orange shows a Burmese worker carving the word "independence" in national script; 2¢ blue depicts a cheering peasant with Burmese flag; and the 5¢ rose exhibits a Burmese boy marching with a national flag. These were typographed on white paper and were unwatermarked.

Far and away the largest issue was the 10-stamp "revised stamps" of Oct. 1, 1943, which included 1¢ deep salmon; 2¢ yellow green; and 3¢ violet, which shows a Burmese girl with water jar on her head and a palm tree. These stamps contain both Japanese and Burmese print. The 5¢ rose, 10¢ blue, 15¢ vermilion, 20¢ yellow green and 30¢ brown stamps show an elephant with rider, carrying a log. These stamps feature dual-language calligraphy. The 1r vermilion and 2r violet show a Watchtow-

This cover shows a 5¢ Burma definitive, Scott 2N44, which was used domestically. The stamp was applied over a stamped envelope. Cover courtesy of Yasukazu Furuuchi.

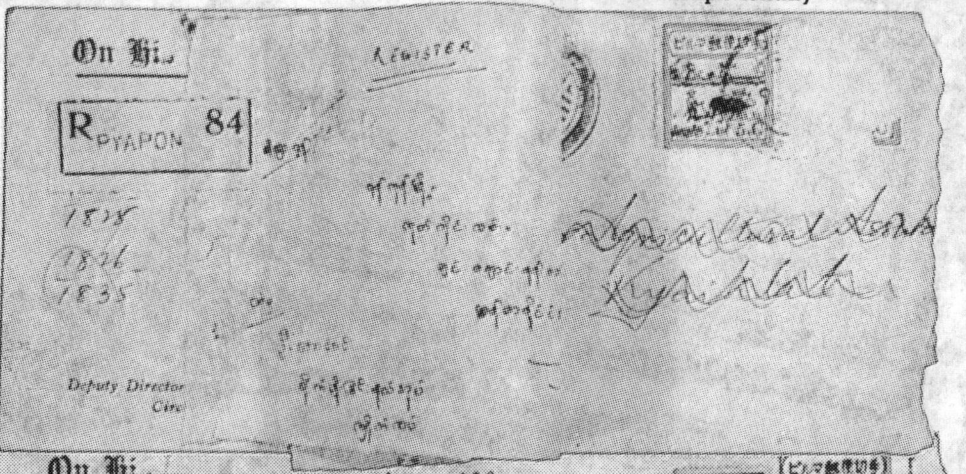

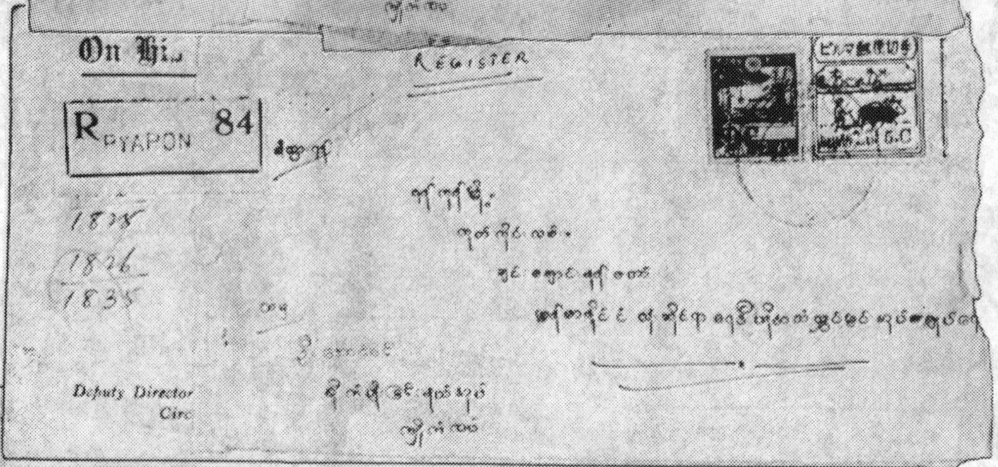

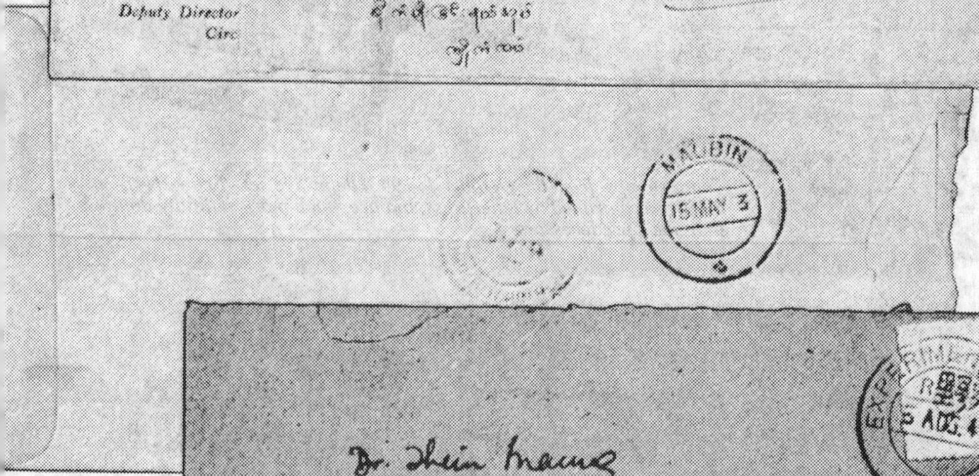

er at Mandalay Palace. These, too, have dual-language calligraphy.

On Oct. 1, 1943, the Japanese occupying authorities issued their stamps for the Shan States. This was a necessary move, as the Shan States had united into a federation in 1922 and had enjoyed a long tradition of quasi-independence. This group was racially quite distinct from the Burmese.

The Japanese ceded certain of the Shan States to Thailand in the year of their special Shan stamp issues. The stamps were to appear in two forms, with the following as the basic issue: The 1¢ brown, 2¢ yellow green, 3¢ violet, and 5¢ ultramarine show a covered native ox cart. The stamps feature dual language, but with Dai Nippon Teikoku Yubin (Imperial Japanese War Post). The 10¢ blue, 20¢ red and 30¢ brown show a Shan woman with turban. These stamps also feature dual language and calligraphy.

These stamps were perforated and lithographed on unwatermarked white paper, and were the basis of a second print (using the same plates) of an issue Nov. 1, 1944; an imprint in black for "Burmese State," and value was added just under the Imperial Post calligraphy. The full 1943 set was reissued.

By the time the Shan States had received their first issue of occupation stamps, the Japanese High Command in Burma had been reorganized. The Japanese XV Army now fell to the command of Lt. Gen. Renya Mutaguchi who now began the Japanese evacuation of Burma. The Japanese surrendered to the Allies Aug. 14, 1945, and the Japanese forces capitulated Sept. 12 of the same year, but not before leaving these fascinating issues behind. ❖

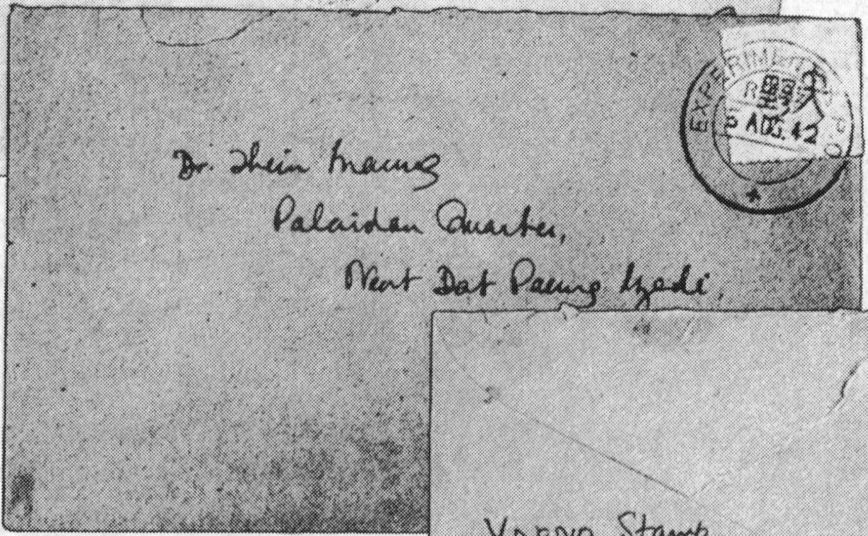

The top three illustrations show different views of the same cover. The original use of the cover (top) shows use of the 5¢ farmer stamp. A slip of paper was affixed over the cover and the envelope was reused, this time as a registered piece of mail (above center). Two markings appear on the cover's reverse (above). Scott 2N1, the personal seal of Shizuo Yano, the Japanese official in charge of the Posts and Telegraph Dept., was used on this 1942 cover from the Rangoon Experimental Post Office. Such covers are rare. Both covers are possessed by Masayoshi Tsuchiya.

Missent to Enemy Country

BY FREDERICK A. BROFOS

The "stampless cover" illustrated on this page, upon closer examination, proved to have a most unusual story behind it.

Evidently the Norwegian post office did not provide a handstamp reading the equivalent of "Missent to enemy country" because such a bizarre occurrence was not expected to happen. Nevertheless, just such a regrettable incident did take place in the early part of World War II, when Great Britain and Germany were the main belligerents and Norway was still neutral.

If more than one letter had gone astray, such as a whole mail sack, the case undoubtedly would have gained international attention through newspaper reports. A diplomatic protest from Germany would have been likely, and heads might have rolled at the Oslo Post Office.

One assumes, though, that only one letter was involved. It had been sent on December 8, 1939, from Nesbyen, Norway, destined for Hamburg, Germany. Somehow, it was misdirected to England where the letter was confiscated. In addition, the British censor removed and retained the 30-ore postage stamp, perhaps to look for a secret message. The empty envelope then was resealed with the usual label, reading "P.C. 66 OPENED BY CENSOR 44," and returned to Norway.

This put the Norwegian postal authorities in an embarrassing position. The matter seems to have been investigated both by the Oslo Post Office (case 828/1940) and the Norwegian Postal Administration (case 440/1940). Eventually, a letter of apology was sent to the German postal authorities, along with the empty envelope. The latter was forwarded by the Germans to the original addressee in Hamburg, accompanied by their own explanatory letter. The translation follows.

Hamburg 36, March 2, 1940

The President of the Reichs Postal Administration
I B 2 1021-4/1 Zens 273
To Mr. Karl Hennig
Hamburg 19
Winterhuderquai 16
1 Letter Envelope

The Norwegian Postal Administration has informed the Reichs Minister of Posts that the letter belonging to the accompanying envelope was opened by the British censor, probably through carelessness of its [Norway's] officials in misdirecting it to England and thus letting it fall into the hands of the British censor. They have expressed to the Reichs Minister of Posts their deepest regrets for this unpleasant event and have informed us that preventive measures have been taken to avert, as much as possible, any similar occurrences.

By Order (illegible signature)

This typewritten letter, on paper watermarked *Behörden Eigentum* [official property] includes in the heading *Zens 273*, obviously an abbreviation for *Zensur*. Presumably the Reichs Postal Minister passed the case on down the line to be answered by the German Censor Office at Hamburg. That office had been organized in February 1940 to examine mail between Norway, Denmark, and the Reich.

In 1928, the original sender of the letter, Ditlef Frantzen, one-time postmaster of the small town of Nesbyen, founded TUBFRIM, an enterprise to combat tuberculosis by selling donated stamps. The addressee, Karl Hennig was a German stamp wholesaler, who probably was a large purchaser of Norwegian stamp mixtures.

The Author

Frederick A. Brofos, of Warner, New Hampshire, collects the stamps and postal history of Norway. He is now retired from the telecommunications industry. ❖

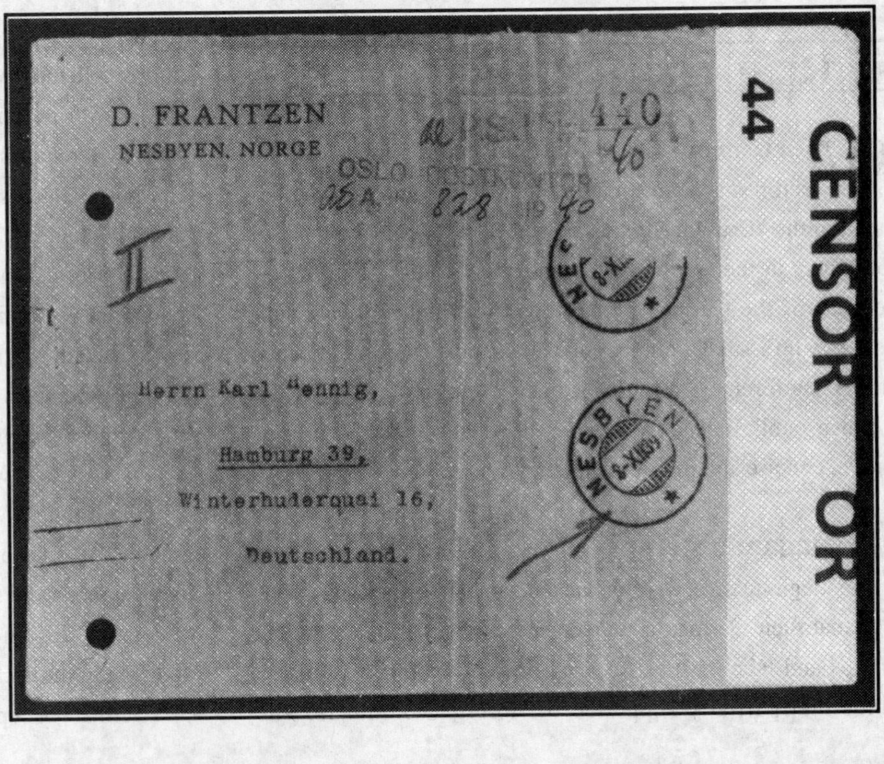

As the war progressed in Russia, the Germans emphasized heroic military combat scenes that gave volunteers a feeling of glory, as depicted on this Dutch post card showing volunteers in a German assault tank.

Legion Propaganda in the Third Reich

BY RENE CHAVEZ

When Germany invaded the Soviet Union in June 1941, Europeans from occupied and neutral countries participated in the "Crusade Against Bolshevism." The enlistment of foreigners in the German armed forces was successful in part because of the German propaganda units and pro-Nazi supporters who issued a number of stamps, post cards and posters eulogizing foreign volunteer legions.

Much public interest was aroused by those colorful, imaginative, concise and provocative items.

Propaganda stamps

The Legionnaires were given the same free-franking privilege that their German comrades had; however, special legion stamps and labels were issued by private committees to raise funds that partially supported the foreign volunteers. The stamps fell into two general classifications: legion labels, printed with no postal value and used as such on field post (usually purchased by volunteers and family members), and semi-postal stamps, produced in the country that formed the particular legion. These stamps did have postal value. The term semi-postal indicates a stamp with two values on it. The first number is the actual cost of postage, while the second is a surtax, used in this instance to support the volunteers.

Family members or collectors often arranged for complete sets of these labels or semi-postal stamps to be affixed to envelopes, which were then canceled to order at Waffen-SS recruiting offices. Most of the legion covers that were mailed through the field post system were examined and censored. These stamps were sold by pro-Nazi sponsors and at local post offices. The legion stamps are listed in Michel Deutschland catalogue in the section *"Deutsche Besetzungsausgaben 1939-45"* (German Occupation issues 1939-45).

Figure 1

Figure 2

The propaganda aspects of the legion stamps, postcards or posters often portray foreign volunteers as Teutonic Knights. For example, one cover with a set of four Flemish Legion stamps shows medieval Flemish Knights (figure 1).

Stamps with valid postal values were issued in Norway and the Netherlands. These stamps represented legionnaires as patriots fighting for a unified Europe against communism. The cover in figure 2 illustrates a stamp of a Norwegian Legionnaire giving orders. On his left arm is an emblem showing "the cross of Saint Olaf," the symbol used by members of the Quisling (Nazi) party. In the background of the Legionnaire stamp are both the Norwegian and Finnish flags. The propaganda value was to encourage members of the Quisling Party to enlist in the Finnish forces; however, most volunteers ended up joining the German Waffen-SS. The cover was mailed by a volunteer and censored by German military authorities, with a blue *"Geprüft Feldpostprüfstelle"* (Inspected Field Post Examiners Office).

Legion propaganda labels commemorated special military events. A pair of Danish Legion labels was issued to commemorate the memorial service of a fallen leader. The Danish commander Count Christian F. von Schalburg, who was killed in action on the Eastern Front was one such officer commemorated (figure 3). The vertical se-tenant pairs were sold in blocks of ten by pro-Nazi Danish groups in early 1943.

The Danish government even approved a military burial ceremony honoring the Danish commander. In addition a Norwegian Legion Label was issued to commemorate the participation of Norwegian volunteers in the 1940 Russo-Finnish war (figure 4). The French Vichy government sent out a token

Figure 3

Figure 1
Flemish legion cover with a set of four labels. Each field post stamp had a surtax of fifty francs for the benefit of family members. An SS roller cancel was applied.

Figure 2
A first day cover mailed to a Norwegian volunteer. The semi-postal stamp was issued to benefit legionnaires and their family.

Figure 3
The se-tenant pair commemorates the Danish commander Count Christian F. von Schalburg. The upper label bears the denomination of "50" and the Danish inscription "Ved Ofre Skabtes Danmarks AEre" (Our sacrifice created Denmark's honor). The lower label has no denomination but same inscription with one of the shields bearing the SS runes.

Figure 4
This Norwegian cover was mailed to the foreign trade office for South Bavaria at Munich. Below is a Norwegian legion label showing a steel helmet in the center with flags of Norway and Finland on either side. This label commemorates the 1939-40 Russo-Finnish Winter War. The cover shows a circular Berlin transit censor marking (Ab).

Figure 5
A complete set of five legion labels, issued in 1942, honors the French Volunteers of the Legion Against Bolshevism in Russia. Each field post stamp had a surtax of one franc. Note the label showing French legionnaires saluting Napoleon's grenadiers.

expeditionary volunteer force of legionnaires to the Russian Front. In honor of the event, the Vichy government in 1942 issued a set of five stamps honoring the Legion of Volunteer French Against Bolshevism on the 130th anniversary of the "Battle of Borodino" during Napoleon's drive towards Moscow (figure 5). This set illustrates how the legionnaires and the French Grand Army's grenadiers were similar.

Besides honoring legionnaires, pro-Nazi party groups issued other charity labels such as Christmas Seals indicating that to some extent Nazi party members were of Christian faith compared to the atheistic communist. Three Christmas labels with stylized Swastikas from the "DNSP" (Danish National Socialist Party) are shown in figure 6. In addition, stamps, postal cancels with propaganda inscriptions honoring volunteer legions were used in occupied countries. Illustrated in figure 7 is a French cover from Cannes with a machine cancellation celebrating the anniversary of the French Volunteer Legion. The Norwegian cover in figure 8 has a cancel "NORSK FRONT," honoring Norwegian volunteers on the Eastern Front.

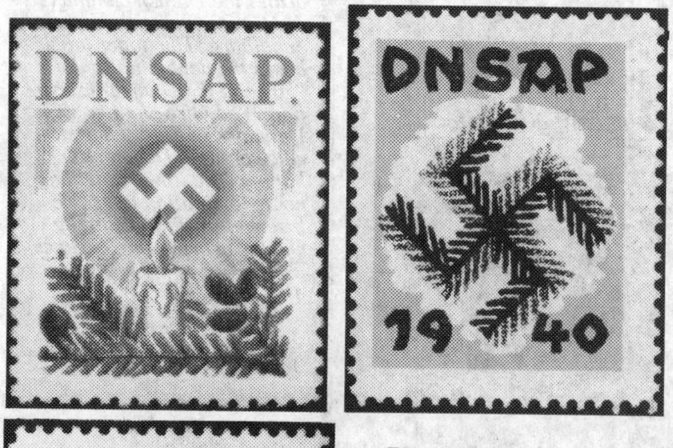

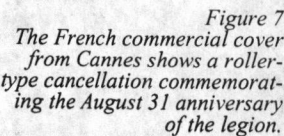

Figure 6
Three Danish Nazi party Christmas labels with stylized swastikas.

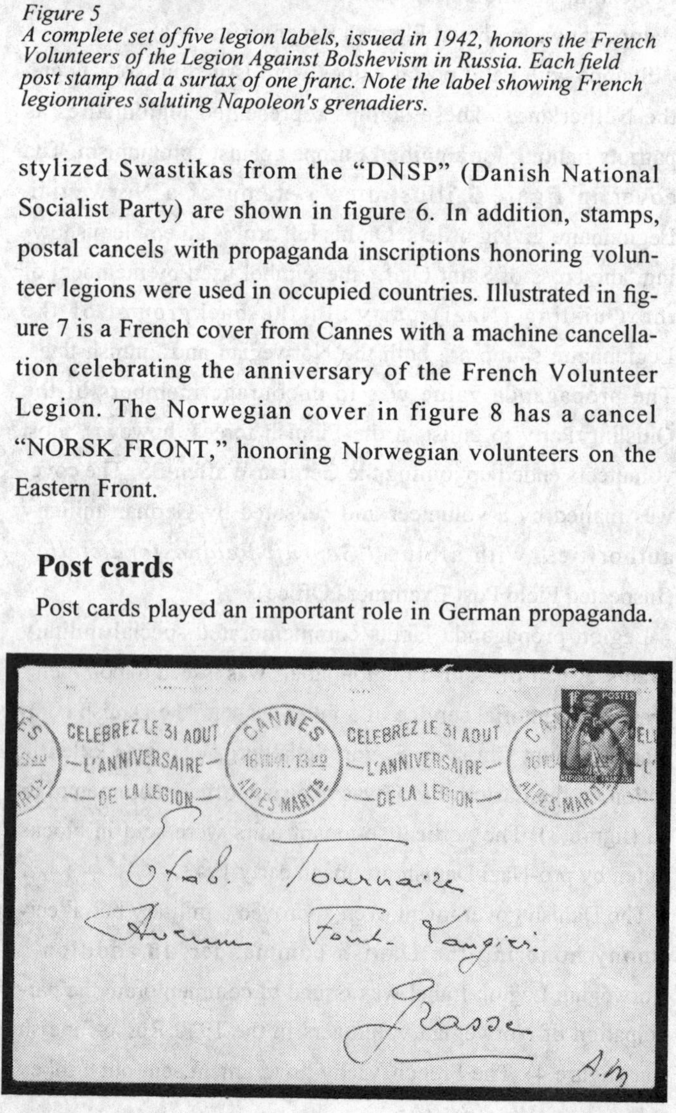

Figure 7
The French commercial cover from Cannes shows a roller-type cancellation commemorating the August 31 anniversary of the legion.

Post cards

Post cards played an important role in German propaganda.

Figure 8
This Norwegian cover from Oslo illustrates a stylized roller cancel of a shield heart and the words "NORSK FRONT." Even at this late date, April 1945, many Norwegians still were fighting in Berlin.

Germans and pro-Nazi groups prepared and issued several postcards honoring volunteers. During the initial stages of war against Russia, the German forces were powerful. Many foreigners were impressed with the German military might. This gave the German propaganda machine an opportunity to encourage enlistment of foreign volunteers either through post cards or posters. For example, the recruiting post cards in figure 9 is a black and white photo of a Flemish nurse and soldier with the inscription "JOIN THE WAFFEN-SS AND GERMAN RED CROSS." Another recruiting post card figure 10 shows a medieval Walloon knight mounted on a horse and a German Tiger tank below. As the war progressed in Russia, the Germans emphasized heroic military combat scenes that gave volunteers a feeling of glory.

Posters

The Third Reich's propaganda included recruiting posters with invitations to foreigners to join the Waffen-SS for the "European Crusade Against Bolshevism." The SS, which originally represented purely "Aryan" members, now consisted of non-Aryan Europeans who wanted to preserve "civilization" against communism.

Endnote: In the pre-war years, the SS was a small Praetorian Guard. It became the Waffen (armed) SS in November 1939. In the course of the war it grew to include more that 600,000 troops in combat units, recruiting centers, death camps, and reserve forces. The Waffen SS turned into a multinational mass army that, by war's end, contained a minority of German troops. ❖

Figure 9
A Flemish recruiting post card shows a black and white picture of a nurse and soldier. Many foreigners joined the Waffen-SS, and women, the German army red cross unit.

Figure 10
A Walloon Waffen-SS recruiting post card. In the summer of 1943 a Walloon Assault Brigade was formed. Later converted into the 28th SS Panzer-Grenadier Division.

George Frederick Cumming Smillie, Engraver

by David C. Akin

In today's world of high-speed stamp production, the craft of the engraver has almost been overshadowed by computer-generated images printed by offset lithography or gravure. Many philatelists, this writer included, consider engraved postage stamps to be more visually attractive than those produced by other methods.

One of the United States' most gifted and prolific engravers was G.F.C. Smillie, who worked at the Bureau of Engraving and Printing (BEP) as chief engraver from 1894-1922. Born in New York, Nov. 22, 1854, Smillie, who liked to be called Fred, came from a distinguished family of engravers. In addition to training at Cooper Union and the National Academy of Design in New York, Smillie studied with his uncle James Smillie and with Alfred Jones, who was superintendent of the picture department at American Bank Note Co.

Fred Smillie's career began in 1871, when he went to work at the American Bank Note Co. (ABNC). His first security engraving, *The Reapers,* was completed the following year.

In April 1887, Smillie went to the Canadian Bank Note Co., where he worked until March 1888. After a short stint with the Homer Lee Bank Note Co., Smillie went first to the Hamilton Bank Note Co. and then the Western Bank Note Co. In 1894, he joined the BEP at a salary of $6,000 per year. He returned to ABNC in 1922, where he worked until his death in January 1924.

Smillie specialized in the production of engraved pictures and portraits. His work appeared on U.S. and foreign postage stamps, stock certificates, corporate bonds, foreign currency, and U.S. bonds and currency. Among the portraits he created for foreign postage stamps are Dom Pedro (Brazil Scott 71), Columbus (Chile Scott 28) and King Alfonso XII (Spain Scott 331 and 340). These were all produced during Smillie's tenure at ABNC. While he worked at the BEP, he created the portraits of Jose Rizal, William McKinley, Miguel Lopez de Legaspi, Adm. William T. Sampson and Benjamin Franklin that were

Shown below are some of the U.S. stamp designs engraved by G.F.C. Smillie.

Below: U.S. Scott 287 and 294

U.S. Scott 314

Below: U.S. Scott 302 and 303

U.S. Scott 327

Below: U.S. Scott 305 and 306

Below: U.S. Scott 310 and 324

used on the Philippines definitive issue of 1906 (Scott 241-242, 244, 247 and 250).

As chief engraver at the BEP, Smillie undertook the production of portraits and pictures that appeared on both U.S. stamps and currency. He engraved the portraits of Franklin, Washington, Jackson, Lincoln, Grant, Sherman, Clay and Madison that were used on the first Bureau Issue of 1894 (Scott 246-250, 253-255, 257, 259 and 262). Smillie also worked on the 1902-03 definitive series, creating the portraits of Franklin, George Washington, Jackson, Grant, Garfield, Martha Washington, Jefferson, Madison and Marshall (Scott 100-303, 305-306, 310 and 312-313).

Fred also engraved the vignettes on some of America's most attractive and popular commemorative stamps. Marquette on the Mississippi, Indian Hunting Buffalo, and the Western Mining Prospector from the Trans-Mississippi issue of 1898 (Scott 285, 287 and 291) were his first commemoratives. These were followed by the *City of Alpena* on Scott 294, the portraits of Jefferson, Monroe and McKinley and the map of the Louisiana Purchase on Scott 325-327. Pocahontas (Scott 330) from the Jamestown Issue and the *Mayflower,* the Landing of the Pilgrims and Signing of the Compact (Scott 548-550) from the Pilgrim Tercentenary Issue round out Smillie's work on U.S. commemoratives.

In a number of cases, Smillie used the same artistic concept for different purposes. One of the most prominent is the Landing of the Pilgrims engraving, which appeared on Scott 549, and on the reverse of the Series 1915 $5 Federal Reserve

In addition to numerous U.S. stamp designs, G.F.C. Smillie engraved quite a few foreign stamps. Examples of U.S. and foreign stamps are shown below: Chile Scott 28, Brazil Scott 71, Philippines Scott 242 and 250, Spain Scott 331, and U.S. Scott 548-550.

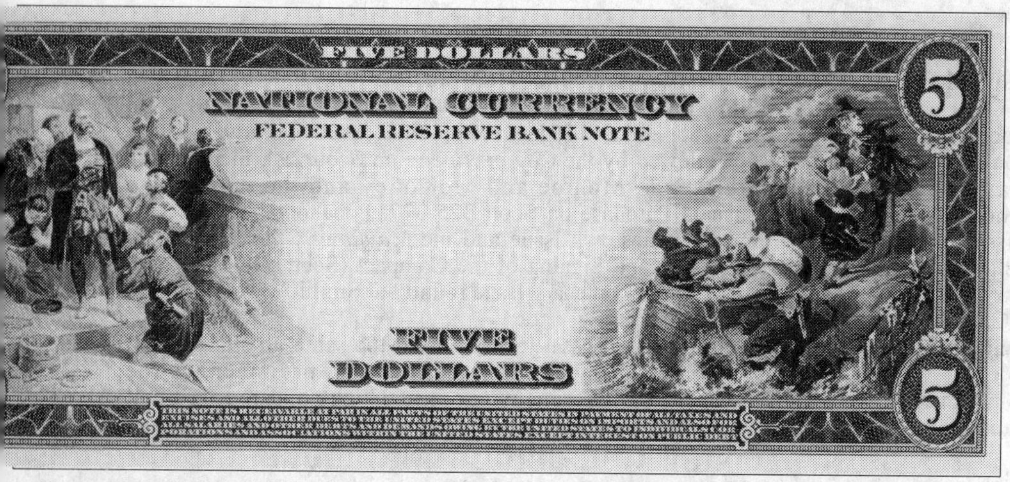

Shown on numismatic souvenir card Scott 62, the reverse of the series 1915 $5 Federal Reserve Bank Note, contains Smillie's "Landing of the Pilgrims." The same scene, reduced in size and slightly modified, appears on Scott 549, above.

Smillie was also an accomplished bank note engraver, as evidenced by his designs at left and below left.

Note. The large size of early 20th-century U.S. banknotes provided engravers with the opportunity to create some extraordinary works of art.

Four other BEP numismatic souvenir cards illustrate Smillie's talents. The $1, $2 and $5 Silver Certificates of the 1896 Series, often called the Educational Series, are considered by many currency collectors to be the most attractive U.S. currency ever produced. The obverse of the $2 Silver Certificate is titled *Science Presenting Steam and Electricity to Commerce and Manufacture* and is shown on Scott 5. Smillie, who engraved the figures from an original design by Edwin H. Blashfield, also created the obverse illustration for the $5 Silver Certificate, which was titled *Electricity Presenting Light to the World.*

In 1914 Smillie engraved a portrait of Grover Cleveland that was later placed on the Series 1923 $20 Federal Reserve Note. While the series was never used, collectors can appreciate the portrait and the obverse of the note on a souvenir card issued by the BEP in January 1994 (Scott 70). Another "Unfinished Masterpiece," according to the BEP, is the Series 1899 $10 Silver Certificate that carries the image of the battleship *Massachusetts* and portraits of Stephen Decatur and William Bainbridge. The portraits were created by Smillie prior to 1901. The silver certificate that was never issued appears on a March 1994 souvenir card for the American Numismatic Association convention (Scott 71).

The vignette on the Series 1914 $100 Federal Reserve Note is illustrated on Scott 68. The design features Agriculture, Prosperity, America, Peace and Commerce and was engraved from an original drawing by Kenyon Cox. Unlike many notes that are filled with intricate designs, this note has a lot of open white space, allowing the viewer to appreciate the subtle beauty of the engraving. ❖

AIRCRAFT OF WORLD WAR II

by Kenneth Wood

World War II was the first major war, the course of which was decisively influenced by airpower. There has been much heated discussion over the years concerning how the decisions of commanders affected the outcome of the war, and to what extent bombing led to the defeat of Germany.

While the massive Allied build-up of airpower and the production of some magnificent aircraft types played an important role, there is no doubt that the Germans, despite the flood of propaganda about the much-vaunted Luftwaffe, were ill-prepared for a long war and never did develop any strategic capability. This contributed greatly to the German loss. Virtually all the German aircraft were designed for use in support of ground forces during a violent but brief attack on a selected enemy, as depicted on a German 1943 semi-postal

(Scott B226). The ignominious collapse of France created a very false picture of German airpower, particularly with regard to that weapon of terror, the *Junkers 87* (also called *Stuka* derived from the German generic name for a dive bomber). It was soon found that, against a determined opponent, the *Junkers 87* was very much a paper tiger, and was shot from the sky by the dozen over southern England.

The world's first strategic air battle began over southern England during the long, hot summer of 1940. The lower right airplane depicted on the Marshall Islands block of four (Scott 261-264) is the *Junkers 87* dive bomber which was soon withdrawn. The aircraft in the lower left is the *Messerschmidtt Bf 109* which was an excellent aircraft, but it had a short range so could remain over England only a few minutes before the low-fuel warning light came on. This made it difficult to properly protect the bombers and restricted the main air battles to southern England, mainly over the counties of Kent and Sussex.

Had Germany possessed large, long-range bombers supported by fighters capable of taking them to their targets and used them efficiently, it is very possible that the Battle of Britain would have been won by Germany, resulting in invasion and defeat for Britain in 1940. Given the unsuitable equipment and inept commanders, it is to the great credit of the German pilots that they came so close to winning the battle, which was primarily intended to sweep the Royal Air Force from the sky and gain air superiority prior to an invasion attempt.

There is no question that the British pilots had three great advantages during the Battle of Britain: extreme motivation, the *Spitfire*, and outstanding ground control utilizing their radar network. The British also had the advantage of fighting over their own territory so that every pilot shot down stood a good chance of surviving and fighting again, whereas every German brought down was lost for the war.

Britain was fortunate in having two of the best fighter aircraft of their day, both privately developed - the *Supermarine Spitfire* and the *Hawker Hurricane*. The beautiful *Spitfire* was marginally better than the *Messerschmitt Bf 109*, while the *Hurricane*, though not as good, was deadly against the bombers and shot down more aircraft than did the *Spitfire*.

Britain's main problem was a shortage of trained pilots and as these were lost, they were replaced by pilots with only a few hours of experience flying a modern fighter aircraft and no combat experience at all. Many did not survive their first flight against the enemy. Had the Germans pressed their attacks on Royal Air Force fighter stations instead of switching

Spitfire attacking Stuka
(Scott's Catalog Notwithstanding)
(Great Britain Scott 434)

to other targets, it is likely that the battle would have gone differently.

After the evacuation from Dunkirk, British ground forces were in no condition to repel any attack that managed to gain a foothold on Britain's coast. So all depended on the Royal Air Force. Lord Dowding, who commanded the British Fighter Command during the battle and was responsible for the organization of the radar network, was the man who really won the battle. His reward was to be fired as soon as it was over. This was one of Churchill's few shabby acts and one that is hard to understand. It can only be attributed to Dowding's rather abrasive personality. His nickname was "Stuffy" and he is said to have been a difficult man with whom to work. Nevertheless,

(Marshall Islands Scott 261-264)

Supermarine Spitfire (Bermuda Scott 649)

Hawker Hurricane (Canada Scott 876)

B-17 Flying Fortress (Sierra Leone Scott 1177)

North American P-51 Mustang (St. Lucia Scott 766)

if it could be said that one man won World War II, that man was Dowding.

Although the Battle of Britain was a turning point in the war, this was not immediately obvious at the time, and Britain continued to fight on alone with little light in view at the end of the tunnel. The small size and outdated equipment of the British ground forces and the far-flung responsibilities of the Royal Navy meant that only airpower could carry the fight to the enemy.

In 1940, the Royal Air Force bombers consisted of the medium, twin-engine aircraft typified by the *Vickers Wellington* and the *Handley Page Hampden*. These were no more efficient than were German bombers.

The next step was the creation of a strong force of large, four-engine bombers under the command of Sir Arthur Harris , and these were soon in action over Germany. Fortunately, work on this force of strategic bombers had started several years earlier. The best and most widely used was the *Avro Lancaster*. It was derived, almost as an afterthought, from the unsuccessful *Manchester*, when it was decided to replace its two engines with four Merlins, creating one of the world's best bombers.

Apart from night bombing, about all the Royal Air Force could do was to mount so-called "intruder" operations, and for this came the *Bristol Beaufighter*. Rugged and hard-hitting, it was called "Whispering Death" by the recipients of its attentions. Both as a ground attack airplane and as a night fighter, it was a fine aircraft.

Another aircraft of this period that was to gain fame as a precision bomber and target marker was the *De Havilland Mosquito*. It was built of wood and was so fast that it required no defensive armament. It soon became legendary for such pinpoint exploits as breaching prison walls to release resistance fighters captured by the Germans.

With the entry of the United States into the war, the build-up of Allied airpower began in earnest. While the RAF bombed at night, the U.S. built up a large force of four-engine bombers that soon began to make massive raids by day. Then the skies of southern England reverberated with the beat of thousands of engines as the *B-17 Flying Fortress* and *B-24 Liberators* heading across the Channel. The writer has vivid memories of watching hundreds of these large aircraft in the skies at one time, and feeling thankful that he was not on the receiving end.

As the invasion of occupied Europe approached, the bombers began to pound road and rail communications in France in order to prevent the Germans from bringing forces to repel the landings. By this time, the Germans had been virtually driven from the sky over northwestern France. The Normandy D-Day landings faced much less opposition than would have been the case had roads, bridges, and rail routes remained intact.

Three very different American aircraft contributed to the success of the Allies during this period. One of these was the *Douglas DC-*, known in military circles as the *C-47* and as the *Dakot* by the British; they were used in large numbers as a transport and glider tug.

The *Lockheed P-38 Lightning* was an excellent twin-engine fighter, and the *North American P-51 Mustang* is considered by many to have been one of the best fighter aircraft of all time when powered with the Rolls Royce Merlin engine. With long-range fuel tanks, it was able to escort U.S. day bombers all the way to their targets, and was responsible for saving the daylight bombing offensive at a time when it was in danger of being cancelled because of losses to German fighters.

Meanwhile in the Pacific war, the long struggle to defeat the Japanese air force was making progress. The Japanese were using aircraft such as the *Mitsubishi A6M Zero-Sen* fighter, the *Aichi D3* dive bomber, and the *Mitsubishi Kitai-21* heavy bomber. The early stages of the Pacific conflict were marked by battles between aircraft from opposing carrier forces as they attempted to sink the other's ships. One such example of this is depicted on Marshall Islands stamps (Scott 313 and 315) illustrating two Japanese *Nakajima B5N2* torpedo planes (Allied code name Kate and two U.S. *Douglas Dauntless* dive bombers attacking enemy ships in the Battle of Midway. Other U.S. aircraft frequently used in the Pacific included the *Gruman F6F Hellcat* and the *Chance Vought F4U-1 Corsair*.

Eventually, island bases were established from which the bombing of Japan itself by a large force of *B-29* bombers was begun. The *B-29* was a development of the *B-17 Flying Fortress*, and was

Avro Lancaster Strategic Bomber (Belize Scott 1006)

De Havilland Mosquito Bomber (Belize Scott 1005)

Douglas DC-3 "Dakota" (British Indian Ocean Territory Scott 136)

Japanese Nakajima "Kate" (Marshall Islands Scott 315)

Messerschmitt 262 Jet
(Antigua & Barbuda Scott 1178)

Boeing B-29 "Enola Gay"
(Sierra Leone Scott 1181)

known as the *Super Fortress*. It was never used in Europe despite the claim that it is the aircraft depicted on the U.S. Army issue marking the liberation of Paris (U.S.A., Scott 934).

In Europe, following the liberation of France and most of the Low Countries, Allied air superiority was almost complete, and the Germans were finally coming to realize that they needed some new aircraft types in large numbers and very quickly if they were to combat the masses of bombers that were laying waste to Germany by day and night. The results were such advanced airplanes as the rocket-propelled *Messerschmitt 163B Komet*, and the world's first operational jet fighter, the *Messerschmitt 262*

Had the latter aircraft been put into service in quantity earlier, it could well have turned the war in the air against the Allies. Fortunately, Hitler's foolish demand that it be redesigned as a bomber had delayed the program and when it finally saw service, it was too late to have any impact on the outcome of the war.

The British *Gloster Meteor* was the only Allied jet aircraft to see World War II service. It never met the *Messerschmitt 262* in combat and it is doubtful if it could have matched its performance.

British Gloster Meteor
(Ascension Island Scott 558)

Finally, Germany was beaten and soon after, a *B-29* named "Enola Gay" Dropped the first of two atomic bombs that brought the war against Japan to an end. A comparison of the *B-29* which ended the war, with the obsolescent Bristol Blenheim and *Fairey Battle* bombers with which Britain had entered the war in 1939 illustrates the progress in military aviation made during the war years.

The *Blenheim IV* carried 1,300 pounds of bombs at 198 miles per hour. It had a range of 1,460 miles, while the *Fairey Battle* carried 1,000 pounds of bombs for 1,000 miles at 210 miles per hour. In contrast, the *B-29* could carry 20,000 pounds of bombs at 300 miles per hour, and had a range of 6,500 miles.

Another example of wartime progress was the *Spitfire*, one of the very few types of aircraft to remain in production during the entire war. The *Spitfire Mark* I of 1939 had a top speed of 362 miles per hour, a ceiling of 31,000 feet, and a range of 395 miles. It was armed with eight machine guns. The *Supermarine Spiteful F-16*, a 1945 descendent of the *Spitfire*, could fly at 475 miles per hour, had a ceiling of 43,000 feet, and a range of 1,315 miles with drop tanks. It was armed with four 20 mm cannons and had a gear for underwing rockets or two 1,000 pound bombs. No other World War II aircraft type was as greatly developed as was the beautiful *Spitfire*.

The story of World War II aviation could go on and on, but space precludes more than this brief overview. There are many more stamps picturing the aircraft that played a role in the conflict. Their collection can provide a fascinating insight into the history of those turbulent years. ❖

About the Author:
Kenneth A. Wood, 1979 ATA Distinguished Topical Philatelist, and Stamp Collector editor 1968-1980, is a native of Hastings, England. He later lived at Tunbridge Wells in Kent where he had a front-row seat for the Battle of Britain. He joined the Air Training Corps in 1938 with the intention of becoming an RAF fighter pilot, an ambition thwarted by poor eyesight. He is author of several books on philately and the long-running "Philately in Flight" series that has appeared in Stamp Collector since 1983. His address is 2430 Tudor Way, Albany, OR 97321-5661.

Bibliography

Cajus Bekker, The Lufftwaffe Diaries, Doubleday, New York, 1968.

Gene Gurney, Great Air Battles, Franklin Watts, New York, 1963.

Lloyd S. Jones, U.S. Bombers, 1928 to 1980s, Aero Publishers, Fallbrook, CA 1980.

Kenneth Munson, Fighters Between the Wars 1919-1939, Blandford, Great Britain, 1970.

David Mondey, British Aircraft of World War II, Hamlyn, Great Britain, 1982.

Roger Parkinson, Summer 1940: The Battle of Britain, David McKay, New York, 1977.

James F. Sunderman, World War II in the Air, Franklin Watts, New York, 1963.

HPO covers: a pleasant detour

by Thomas LaMarre

Are you looking for an inexpensive but challenging specialty? Consider collecting highway post office covers. Although the highway post office service had a relatively short life, it generated hundreds of collectible postmarks and cachets.

As early as 1899, the United States Post Office Department began using motor trucks to carry mail. The government assured the public, "Each is equipped so that a mule may be hitched to it, should it refuse to run."

The development of more reliable trucks, as well as improved highways, enabled the USPOD to inaugurate star routes. These were closed-pouch truck routes over which mail was transported to small post offices off the beaten path.

The idea of processing mail in moving vehicles on highways was a logical progression. However, it took many years to implement. The impetus was the dismantling of the railway mail service that began during the 1930s.

Rural communities had depended on the railway mail service since the Civil War. To make up for the loss of the service, the highway post office system was launched.

The movement for an HPO system originated in the Stockton, Calif., area in 1925. Changes in railway schedules there disrupted mail service. Although in some instances highway routes were much shorter than rail routes — and could have resulted in faster deliveries — the USPOD initially opposed the establishment of a highway post office system. Railway mail workers endorsed the concept anyway.

In 1927, James F. Cooper presented the idea of an HPO system to the Sacramento branch of the railway post office. It was then submitted to the Eighth Division convention in San Francisco, and was approved at the Railway Mail Association's national convention.

A presidential veto killed highway post office legislation, but its supporters refused to give up. A new bill was drafted and, on July 11, 1940, President Franklin D. Roosevelt signed it into law. Ironically, the USPOD took full credit for the idea.

The HPO system was designed to be a distribution network capable of sustaining rapid pick-up, sorting and dispatch of mail to key points between two terminal cities.

Mail that was processed aboard HPO buses was transferred along the route

Figure 1: L.W. Staehle prepared this cacheted cover (franked with Scott 894) for the opening of the second HPO route.

Figure 2: Early HPO cancellations had short killer bars, as on this Staehle cover franked with Scott 901.

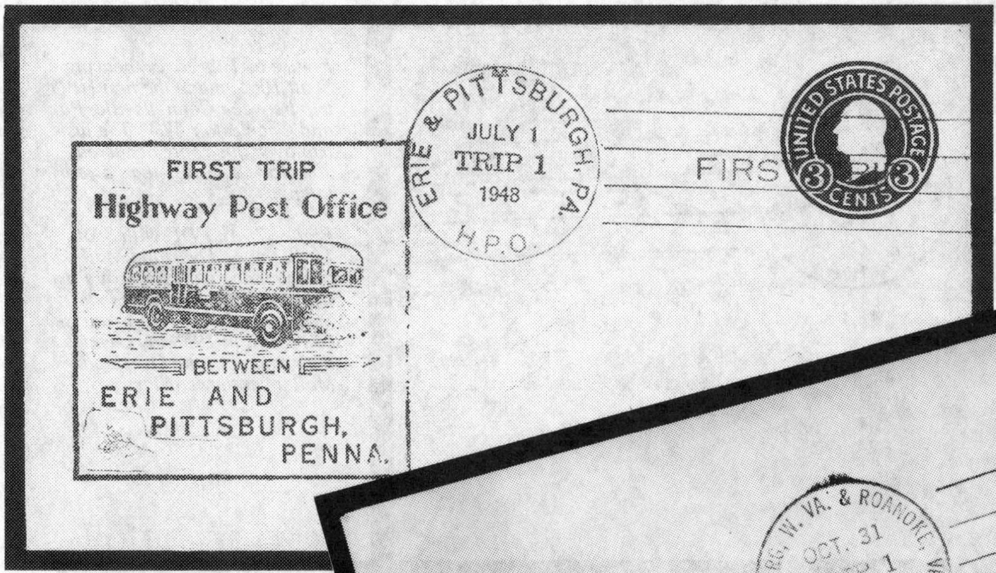

Figure 3: Rubber-stamped first-trip cachets, such as this one, were applied at the terminal.

Figure 4: HPO service was established between Martinsburg, W.V., and Roanke, Va., in 1953, celebrated by this cover with Scott 1023.

Figure 5: Franked with Scott 1029, this 1954 first-trip cover is typical of the inexpensive HPO covers that are available.

to connecting star routes, mail trains and post offices in rural communities.

HPO No. 1 was a hastily modified White passenger bus with a "pancake" type engine. It went into service Feb. 10, 1941, covering a 184-mile route between Washington, D.C., and Harrisonburg, Va. HPO No. 1 has been restored and now rests in the collection of the National Postal Museum.

The selection of the first HPO route involved more than politics. Because the route had a wide range of terrain (from flat to hilly), and served both urban and rural areas, the Washington-Harrisonburg route was considered the perfect testing ground.

The HPO system attracted philatelists' attention from the start. Collectors who prized first-day and first-flight covers discovered a new collecting specialty: first-trip highway post office covers.

Metal handstamps were used to postmark regular mail on the buses, but bumpy roads often made it a challenging task. To ensure clear impressions on philatelic mail, first-trip postmarks and cachets were rubber-stamped at the terminals. Collectors' covers were then loaded into the bus and carried to the other terminal.

Some HPO postmarks are more difficult to find on regular mail than on philatelic covers.

The highway post office system grew slowly in its early years. On May 3, 1941, service was established between South Bend and Indianapolis, Ind. Figure 1 shows a cover prepared by L.W. Staehle of New York City to mark the event. It has a "TRIP 2" HPO postmark, and a green and gold cachet depicting the state capitol, a highway post office bus and an Overland Mail stagecoach. Trip 2 denotes the return leg of the HPO run.

I recently paid $6 for the cover, which is franked with Scott 894, commemorating the 80th anniversary of the Pony Express. Although the HPO system was more closely based on the railway mail service than the Pony Express, many cacheted HPO covers depict a Pony Express rider.

On Aug. 4. 1941, a highway post office route was inaugurated between San Francisco and Pacific Grove, Calif. The cover pictured in Figure 2 is another Staehle creation, valued at about $4. Like the Fig-

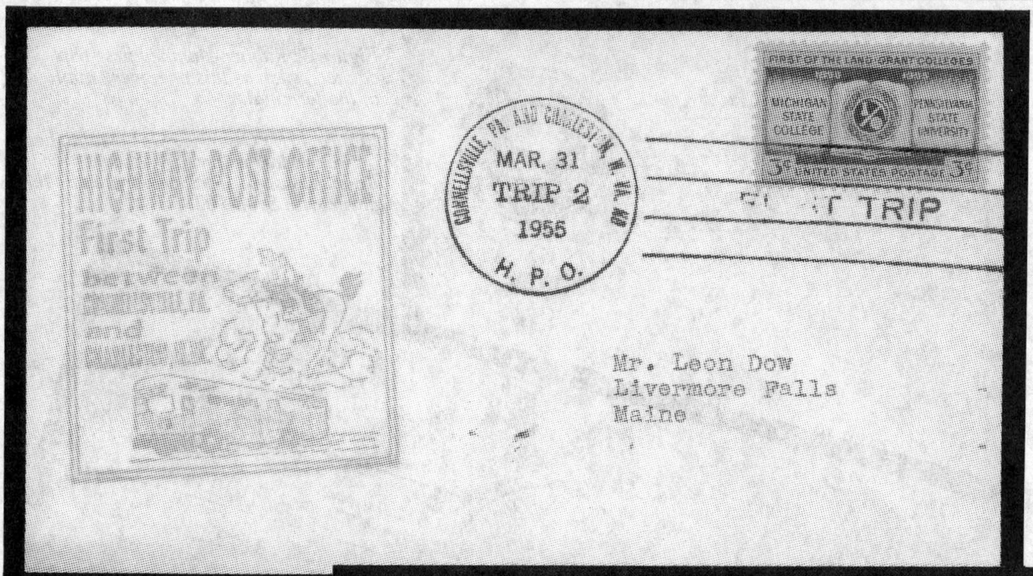

Figure 6: This cover, bearing Scott 1065, made the first HPO trip between Connellsville, Pa., and Charleston, W.V. The last trip over this route occurred Jan. 15, 1956, less than a year later.

Figure 7: An FDC with Scott 1120, the 4¢ Overland Mail commemorative. Highway Post Office No. 1 was driven from St. Louis, Mo., to San Francisco, Calif., in 1958 to re-enact the running of the Overland Mail a century earlier.

ure 1 example, this cover sports a green and gold cachet, only this time it pictures the Golden Gate Bridge, a streamlined HPO bus and the USPOD seal.

Plans to expand the highway post office service were put on hold during World War II. However, by 1948 there were 16 HPO routes in operation, including one between Erie and Pittsburgh, Pa. The cover shown in Figure 3 has a black rubber-stamped cachet and long killer bars in the "FIRST TRIP" cancellation to accommodate blocks of stamps.

Expansion of the HPO service slowed in 1951, when only three new routes were added. But 31 routes were inaugurated in 1952, and more followed in 1953. Among them was a route between Martinsburg, W.V., and Roanoke, Va. Figure 4 shows a first-trip cover with a simple red cachet. Priced at only 40¢, this cover turned up at a recent show.

At the peak of the HPO service in the 1950s, nearly 200 routes were in operation. The Figure 5 cover commemorates the inauguration of the route between La Crosse, Wis., and Cedar Rapids, Iowa, in 1954. It has a blue-green cachet, June 16 postmark and June 17 backstamp (a postmark applied to the back of a cover at the receiving office).

Some HPO routes had short lives. For example, on March 31, 1955, a route was established between Connellsville, Pa., and Charleston, W.V. First-trip covers, such as the one shown in Figure 6, received a bright green cachet depicting a Pony Express rider and bus. But less than 10 months later, on Jan. 15, 1956, the route was discontinued.

Most HPO trucks and buses were government-owned. The rest, including railway post office buses owned by railroads, served contract routes. Railway post office bus route covers have the same markings as railway mail, but with the word "TRIP" and a numeral in the postmark. In January 1956, all RPO bus routes became highway post office routes.

In 1958, a 4¢ stamp, Scott 1120, was released for the centennial of the Overland Mail Service. A first-day cover of that stamp is shown in Figure 7. Highway Post Office No. 1 was driven from St. Louis to San Francisco, stopping at various places, to re-enact the running of the Overland Mail a century earlier. A complete set of covers postmarked on each leg of the trip is valued at $40-$50.

A drastic change in the way mail was handled during the 1960s helped kill HPO service. As the number of post offices decreased, greater quantities of mail were handled at concentration points. Large, urban post offices were at the heart of the plan. They distributed mail to sectional centers, identified by the first three digits of the ZIP code system that was introduced in 1962.

Increased mechanization and automation also helped eliminate the highway post office system, which dwindled during the 1960s. The service was finally discontinued in 1972.

Highway Post Office No. 1 was decommissioned around 1960. However, a postal worker in the department's Bureau of Transport hid it in various post office garages to prevent it from being scrapped or sold.

The General Services Administration eventually found the bus, and a firm that sold Underwood typewriters acquired it for use as a mobile showroom. When the bus had outlived its usefulness, it was eventually sold to a vehicle collector who parked it in a field in La Plata, Md.

In 1968, the United Federation of Postal Clerks acquired the bus and donated it to the Smithsonian Institution. It recently received a complete restoration, and was driven on a re-enactment run in 1991, the 50th anniversary of the service. This was a fitting tribute to the service that brought us so many collectible covers. ❖

Mute cancels tell no tales

by Rev. Leonard Tann

The cover that is shown in Figure 1 (stamped side) was mailed in Riga, Russia, in September, 1914. It bears a total of 14 kopeks postage, paid with the then-current Romanoff Jubilee stamps of 1913. The four stamps are canceled by a "square-with-cross" postmark. The cancel gives no location or dated information. The outbreak of World War I a month earlier panicked the Russian Imperial authorities, and orders went out to all areas adjacent to the "war zone" to stop using ordinary postmarks with location names and dates. These markings were to be substituted with mute or dumb cancels. The theory was to defeat espionage, and to prevent useful information being communicated to the enemy. This was because considerable sections of the population in the affected areas were German, of German origin or were sympathetic to the enemy and possibly hostile to Russia.

Throughout the area these dumb postmarks were introduced. Some were target cancels, bull's-eyes, crosses, star-bursts and others. In small post offices the canceling devices were made of wood or cork cut-outs, while bigger post offices -- like Riga -- used metal or rubber handstamps. The regulations also stipulated that letters or cards should not bear the name and address of the sender or, as was the custom, the name and location of the firm or business.

Figure 2 shows the other side of the Figure 1 cover. Not only does it improperly bear the name and address of the sender in the upper left corner (A.E. Shmidt, Riga, PO Box No. 600), but the post office disobeyed its own regulations by letting it pass. There is a dull red rectangle of the Registration handstamp; large "Z" (Zakaznoye, meaning registered); "RIGA CENTRAL" and number. This has been partly obliterated by the mauve handstamp struck over it, which reads "Registered."

The cover is addressed to Abo, located in the then-Russian-ruled Grand Duchy of Finland. It was opened by censors at Helsingfors (Helsinki), resealed with a red wax seal and the censor sealing label in 3 languages -- Russian, Finnish and Swedish. The cover arrived at Abo, as witnessed by the receipt postmark at the upper left in Figure 1.

Imperial Russia collapsed in war and revolution in 1917. By late 1918, the Baltic Provinces of Czarist Russia were independent Latvia, Lithuania and Estonia, with Riga the capital then -- as it is again -- of independent Latvia.

The cover stands as a nearly 80-year-old mute testimony to the postal clerks of Riga. ❖

Figure 1
The boxed postal markings with crosses on these stamps were applied in 1914 as mute, or dumb, markings by postal clerks at Riga, to avoid giving out potential information to the enemy.

Figure 2
The address side of the Figure 1 cover shows how postal clerks at Riga disobeyed their own wartime regulations. The cover bears a return address.

Razor blade helps develop sharp wit

by Wayne L. Youngblood

What does a philatelic editor do for fun? Although I can't answer that question for other editors, I can share with you one of my own more enjoyable pursuits; cut and paste, or razor-blade, rarities. Rather than collecting them, I create these invaluable items.

As a young child, I once saw an example of the nude 1934 3¢ United States Mother's Day commemorative - a rare variety that remains uncatalogued to this day! The stamp, shown in Figure 1, was created by cutting and superimposing Spain Scott 397 (from the 1930 Goya set) over the U.S. stamp (Scott 737-738). Since the ink color was nearly identical and the image size close enough to be carefully trimmed, the resulting stamp was highly impressive. It left an indelible imprint on me that continued to work on my subconscious mind throughout my adolescence and young adulthood.

Figure 1

Years later, while involved with an extremely lengthy telephone call, my hands started working as if they had a mind of their own, slowly trimming and refining a stamp that fit well with another stamp design to create an instant rarity. After showing my creation around to the delight of some of my friends, I began working on other items, searching for unusual twists of one sort or another. I even made up stories as to how these previously unknown varieties were accidentally created during printing and processing.

Figure 2

Figure 3

After a couple of years of dabbling with my razor blade, both my skill level and collection had grown to the point of having a filled stock page. It was suggested that I begin exhibiting these choice items, so I began working on a story line and flow to fill a one-frame exhibit. I

Figure 4

Figure 5

Figure 6

Figure 7

also attempted to provide material that was missing from some of the more notable exhibits of the time to build a frame of reference for the viewer.

My exhibit, titled "Die II: Adventures in Stamp Design," came out of the chute at World Columbian Stamp Expo in May 1992, and has been touring various shows since then. It combines my love of mixing various stamp designs with a large portion of blarney to create what I feel is one of the most fun exhibits on the circuit. The following is a summary of the exhibit - a brief history of U.S. stamps through the miracle of blarney. Please keep in mind that my descriptions of the stamps is nonsense, intended to weave a semi-believable humorous story.

The fabricated focus of the exhibit was to show a number of scarce and, in many cases, previously unreported design proposals, errors and plate varieties.

Shown at left in Figure 2 is the original proposed design for the 1992 29¢ World Columbian Stamp Expo commemorative, which was released Jan. 24 of the year. The design was later changed to the version shown at right when it was discovered that the U.S. Postal Service had pictured the wrong penguins.

Figure 8

The U.S. 1869 pictorial series is sometimes referred to as the first U.S. commemorative series. Little is known of the origins of the idea of commemoration of people and events on stamps, but the U.S. Post Office Department conducted several early design experiments with that idea in mind.

The triple-rate overseas cover shown in Figure 3 (improperly franked with 25¢, rather than 45¢) was posted May 18, 1869. It bears the unique 10¢ Eagle and King commemorative issue.

As a side note, the undeliverable letter (for reasons marked) was returned to sender.

Although scarcer than most early com-

Figure 9

Figure 10

Figure 11

memorative experiments, Columbus-related design proposals do exist.

The 1893 Columbian series, printed by

Figure 12

Figure 13

Figure 14

Figure 15

Figure 16

Figure 17

the American Bank Note Co., was originally intended to be a small-sized definitive issue. Shown in Figure 4 is the only known surviving essay of the proposed series. As is often the case, this 8¢ value is used. Other examples of Columbian definitive proposals have been located used on cover.

The 1893 cover shown in Figure 5 bears the original intended design of the 2¢ value at left. The cover was rejected, assessed postage due (with revised 2¢ Columbian added) and sent on its way. Note that the issued version of the 2¢ Columbian borrowed its design from the rejected design shown in Figure 4.

The 2¢ value of the 1893 Columbians was not the only one to have design modifications made. Several different vignettes were tried for the 1¢ value before the final one was selected. One such experiment is shown in Figure 6.

Most troublesome in the 1893 series was the 4¢ value. The design was approved, plates were made and stamps were printed before it was discovered the design had historical inaccuracies. A used example of that rarity is shown in Figure 7.

Shortly after the USPOD Philatelic Agency was created in the early 1920s, the final U.S. Columbus error was created. The 5¢ 1922 stamp was created to mark the 430th anniversary of the landing of Columbus, and a design was worked up. It was later rejected in favor of the Theodore Roosevelt stamp that was released. During the transfer process, however, one position in the sheet was rocked in with the Columbus portrait and a few sheets were inadvertently sold. The block shown in Figure 8 bears an example of the single Columbus cliche (position 46). The block was coincidentally precanceled in Columbus, Ohio.

Long considered to be perhaps the most boring U.S. stamp series, the Washington-Franklins had a more exciting beginning than the final product would seem to indicate. The pressing demands of World War I necessitated halting plans for many of the more creative proposed designs in the series. One early version, shown in Figure 9, featured a koala bear as part of an animal learning theme. The 2¢ value was to feature two pandas, and so on.

One of the early proponents of creative stamp design was a young man by the name of Mac Sennett. He proposed a 5¢ design showing one of his Keystone Kops. Deemed to be too commercial, the design was changed to feature a now-unidentified statesman. This design, too, was dropped, with the final version picturing an old favorite: George Washington. All three are shown in Figure 10.

The Washington-Franklins are not without major varieties. Shown in Figure 11, connected to a normal stamp, is the scarce doubled-Washington, created when the siderographer failed to completely remove a bad impression when he was creating the printing plate.

When the USPOD began considering designs for the 1922 definitive series, an inadvertent stamp design served as the source of further inspiration. After the vignette of a single 1/2¢ Nathan Hale stamp was inverted, USPOD realized the potential for utilizing separate portraits and frames. The original 1 1/2¢ value of the series honored the late Bill Harding, founder of the Harding Glass mine in northern New Mexico. The general public felt he was too obscure, so the portrait of Warren G. Harding was dropped into the existing frame with Bill Harding's last name, thereby saving engraving time. The Harding stamps are shown in Figure 12.

One of the scarcest issues of the 20th century is the stamp shown in Figure 13. After the 1935 Michigan Centenary stamp was released, Detroit residents clamored for another commemorative to meet the then-current 33¢ airmail rate for mailing automotive steering wheels to England (where they were then installed on the wrong side). As a result of this demand, USPOD issued a very small quantity of the 33¢ stamps. Since there were few collectors involved with the 1930s automobile industry, very few 33¢ Michigan stamps exist and none are known on cover.

Another scarce issue is shown in Figure 14. The 10¢ Alexander Graham Bell stamp was originally produced as it is shown at left. However, postal patrons, unhappy with Bell's sallowed appearance, requested a change in design, resulting in the more familiar version shown at right. Due to the unpopularity of the original stamp, very few were saved.

Two more 1940s-era stamps drew considerable criticism and were later changed.

The 1942 Kentucky Statehood Centennial issue, shown in Figure 15, originally was designed to show the juxtaposition of pioneer and modern times. Critics of the design, which showed Daniel Boone overlooking a modern city, forced a design change. The building and street were eliminated and replaced by a river, trees and an additional figure. Note the similarity in shape between the original street and river.

The 1948 Poultry Centennial issue was the source of much change and embarrassment to the USPOD. In fact, a well-documented and researched exhibit exists for this stamp. However, missing from the exhibit are the two unique design essays shown in Figure 16.

During the 1960s, much innovation and technological change took place. As a result numerous intentional and non-intentional varieties occurred. One of the most well known of these in both respects is the 1962 Dag Hammarskjold issue.

After the discovery of a few inverts of the yellow color, USPOD had millions printed to destroy their value. One pane of another major error on this issue was discovered at the time, but has remained hidden for more than 30 years. Shown in Figure 17, for the first time, is the notable Double Dag variety.

Figure 18

Finally, most collectors think that the first U.S. Disney stamp was released in 1968, two years after Walt Disney's 1966 death. However, the 1966 FIPEX souvenir sheet shown in Figure 18, dispels this myth. The design, showing Mickey delivering a letter on roller skates, was planned as a tribute to Disney. Realizing the stamp could not be issued as planned when Disney died, postal officials simply removed Mickey from the design, leaving the large, unprinted gap. The original press run was destroyed, leaving this single existing example.

I continue to add new discoveries to this rare and desirable collection as time goes by. Where else can such finds be made? ❖

War and Remembrance

by Peter McCarthy

Hastily prepared and ill-equipped, Canada's troops in World War II Hong Kong were thrown into the theatre of war not long before the colony fell. Their valiant efforts were given little recognition. As Prisoners of War, the correspondence they were allowed was meagre, but the letters they wrote and received are a small testament to human spirit and endurance.

Sgt. J.E.D. Smith 5th from left centre row.

War is not a subject that is easily celebrated. For all its seeming glory, it is undeniably cruel and tragic. However, at this particular time we are in the midst of commemorating one of the most tragic events to have taken place in recent time - World War II.

In the 50 years since the beginning and end of that great conflict, much has been written about the so-called "highlights." From the dark days of the Battle of the Atlantic to victory at sea; Dunkirk, the Battle of Britain and the heroes it produced; the African campaign as well as from the American viewpoint, Pearl Harbour and the victorious battles in the Pacific, culminating with the Allied effort of D-Day.

Canada contributed more than its share of men, women and materials to the cause. However, there's one particular area where a great contribution was made and very little was ever heard of or written about - The Battle of Hong Kong. Lieutenant John E.D. (Jake) Smith was one Canadian who contributed to the war effort there. His diary, and a wealth of P.O.W. postal history, are all that remains of his time there.

Canada, being a British colony, was reluctantly committed to assist in the Pacific when called upon. Two regiments were provided, The Winnipeg Grenadiers and The Royal Rifles of Canada. The Grenadiers, as would be expected, were made up of men from the western provinces, while The Royal Rifles were recruited from the cities and towns of Quebec and the Maritime provinces. Lieutenant Smith was a communications officer with No. 1 Platoon, Royal Rifles.

Both regiments were poorly trained and ill-equipped for the task they were given. The Rifles received much of their training in Huntingdon, Quebec, and spent most of their time performing barracks duty in Botsford, Newfoundland. The Grenadiers did much of the same in the sun and heat of Bermuda.

The regiments were mustered and sent from British Columbia aboard the transport ship Awatea and H.M.C.S. Prince Robert, arriving in Hong Kong on Nov. 16, 1941. Much of their equipment had been left behind and eventually ended up in Australia. The garrison however, had been bolstered.

The Japanese attacked Hong Kong on December 8, one day after Pearl Harbour. The poorly trained and ill-equipped garrison soldiers were no match for the crack Japanese troops that outnumbered the British and Canadians by a large margin.

It has been said that many of the troops were unfamiliar with the weapons they had to handle. But as Lieutenant John Smith (who was promoted from Sergeant after leaving Canada) pointed out at the beginning of his personal journal, No. 1 Platoon was a regimental signal platoon and not a rifle platoon and as such carried arms for self protection only. The platoon had trained as signalers. These men were forced into combat situations out of sheer necessity.

For the Japanese, this was to be a short campaign. No more than a few days. As it turned out, the battle was long and furious, with the Allies under constant shell fire.

Again from Jake Smith's diary of December 18: "I was unable to sleep, the shelling was the heaviest so far during the war but our wires remained intact." On December 19 he wrote: "At daylight all hell broke loose."

December 25 was a Christmas the men who served in Hong Kong will always remember. It dawned with the enemy having broken through the lines and the Allies in complete disarray. The governor surrendered to the Japanese late that day and it was confirmed on the following day, December 26.

If the Allies thought they had been through hell to that point, it is only because they had no idea what lay ahead. The former barracks of Sham Shui Po, Argyle Street, Fort Stanley and North Point to name a few, were now turned into P.O.W. camps. Rape, torture and murder were the order of the day.

Eventually, many of the P.O.W.s were sent to camps in Japan, where they were forced to work at shipyards and in coal mines under inhumane conditions. Many were to die of various diseases, malnutrition and/or beatings.

Escape was virtually impossible. The prisoners were grouped in fives and were told that if one escaped the remaining four would be shot. If five escaped, 25 would be shot. The risk was too great to attempt escape.

With the fall of Hong Kong there were, naturally, great concerns from home as to the welfare of loved ones. It was a long time before word came through, despite strenuous efforts by both the government and the Red Cross. The Japanese were in no hurry to negotiate and allow P.O.W. correspondence. The Department of National Defence's greatest concern of course, was to establish a positive condition of each individual and also to establish the

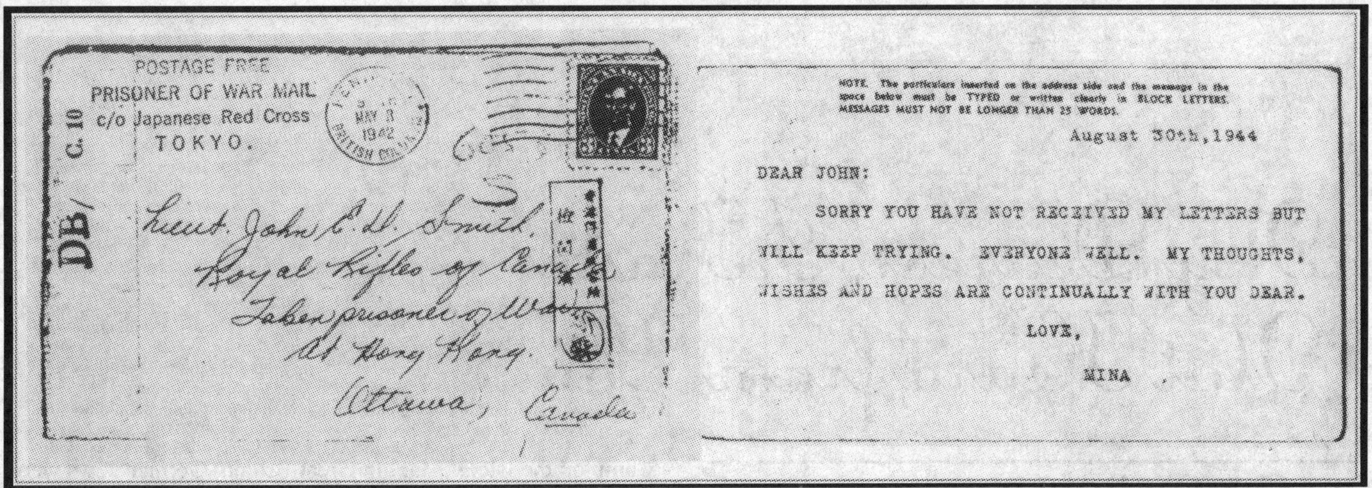

location of each survivor. That in itself was no mean task.

In some cases, relatives didn't find out the fate of their loved ones until the following August. Although letters and parcels were sent, they were not getting through. Instructions and information were sent to next of kin as the directive, dated Oct. 31, 1942 (addressed to William Lester whose son, Wilbert, a rifleman, was a P.O.W. in Japan) points out. Contrary to the department's belief, very few Red Cross parcels ever reached the P.O.W.s.

As can be seen by the letters addressed to Lieutenant John Smith in the latter part of 1942, instructions as to the manner a letter was to be addressed were explicitly adhered to and yet, they were only received on a sporadic basis in 1944. The dates of receipt are recorded in pencil by Lieutenant Smith in the same orderly fashion that he displayed while writing his war journal in the days before the fall of Hong Kong.

Much of that is explained by a further directive sent to next of kin dated Feb. 22, 1944, whereby Japanese authorities finally granted permission for P.O.W.s to receive letters as per their specifications. One of those was to limit letters to 25 words. At the time it still wasn't clear if heading date and closing were included in the limitations. It was clearly stated that non-conformity with regulations would result in mail not being delivered.

Special cards were printed to help letter writers follow instructions, thereby insuring the receipt of a loved one's message. Everything of course, was subject to Canadian and Japanese censors.

It is interesting to note that although Prisoner Of War mail was postage free, in some cases relatives affixed first class and air mail rate postage.

With the dropping of the Atom bomb on Hiroshima on August 6, and on Nagasaki August 9, 1945, the Japanese agreed to surrender. The three and a half years of incarceration in sub-human conditions left their mark on each and every soul that came home. They were far different people from those that landed in Hong Kong in November of 1941.

On arrival in Canada, more problems awaited the former P.O.W.s in the form of government bureaucracy. It was thought these men could just take up where they left off before enlistment. Such was not the case. There were tropical diseases, fevers and above all, the psychological effects of a war-time spent as a prisoner to be dealt with. The government wasn't very sympathetic or understanding. Even pay for their time as P.O.W.s was debated. There was no glory in Hong Kong.

The formation of the Hong Kong Veterans Association and their fight on behalf of the men brought forth some results. Recognition of their efforts was slow in coming and it wasn't until 1993 that the Hong Kong veterans finally received the Defense of Great Britain medal, 53 years after the fact.

There is relatively little postal history available that relates to this small valiant group who defied a mighty army and to some degree stalled the Japanese march through the Pacific. In trying to ignore their bitter memories, most of the veterans of the Hong Kong campaign destroyed reminders of their days as P.O.W.s, even though that part of their lives will never be totally forgotten.

Lieutenant John Smith passed away a few years ago after a lengthy career as a brakeman on the railroad, but before doing so, left what correspondence he had to his good friend Louis Tremblay.

There are very few survivors of the Battle of Hong Kong left today, but Wilbert Lester and Eddie Campbellton, residents of Richmond, PQ, are seen daily walking to the post office.

They'll also be seen together on November 11 as they turn out for Remembrance Day ceremonies, even though their day of remembrance will always be December 25. ❖

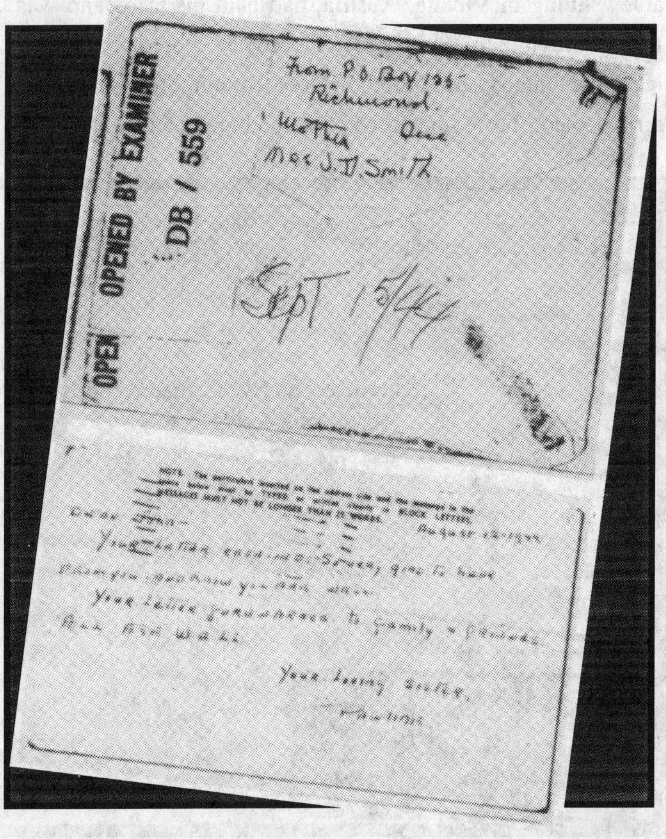

John E.D. Smith dated the back of the letters he received from family. Meanwhile, back home, his loved ones lapped-up any news they got from the P.O.W. and forwarded it on to friends. The 25-word limit was a constant reminder of the limitations imposed upon them.

My Dearest, I Have Not Heard from You

BY GUSTAV POHLIG

I discovered a sad story through a grouping of correspondence, consisting of two documents, a post card, and six letters - all unopened. I opened them, hoping for some information, but found only a few lines expressing the longing of the writer for his wife. Every letter ended with the same words: I have not heard from you for a year (or two). While the letters themselves provided very little information, the outsides of the envelopes told a tragic story.

According to a tax office document (Figure 1), the husband, a Jew living in Vienna, Austria, had paid his taxes and was free to emigrate in March 1939. The covers suggest that he did leave the country, emigrating to Great Britain. Shortly after his arrival there, however, he was interned and sent to Mooragh Camp on the Isle of Man. In Great Britain, German Jews were treated as Germans, and that meant internment.

On June 18, 1940, in a letter to a relative in New York, he writes: "Did you hear anything from my wife in Vienna? I am anxious to get any news." The letter could not be delivered and was returned to the Mooragh Camp. In the meantime, the writer, who had survived the sinking of the *Arandora Star* in the Irish Sea, had been sent to Australia on board the horror ship *Dunera* and was interned at Hay Camp. The letter followed him there (Figure 2).

A post card from his wife, sent in August of 1940 from Vienna, did not reach him at Mooragh Camp either and was forwarded to Australia as well (Figure 3). The return address shows the ominous Sara which Jewish women were forced to use. She writes: "I hope to see you soon in America. I have the affidavit, and I wrote for the ship's tickets." How happy the husband must have been.

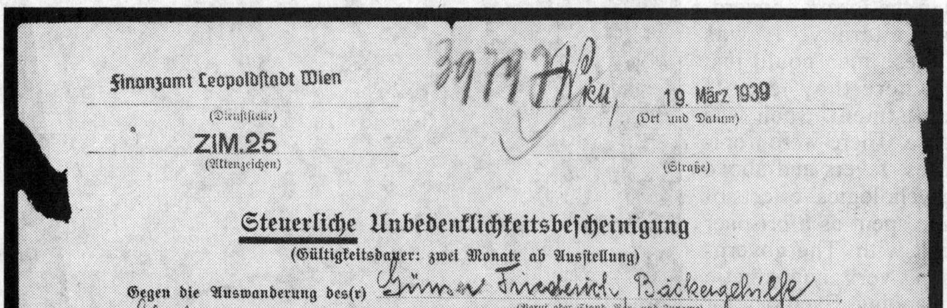
Finanzamt Leopoldstadt Wien — Wien, 19. März 1939
(Dienststelle) (Ort und Datum)
ZIM.25
(Aktenzeichen) (Straße)

Steuerliche Unbedenklichkeitsbescheinigung
(Gültigkeitsdauer: zwei Monate ab Ausstellung)

Gegen die Auswanderung des(r) Gunser Friedrich Bäckergehilfe
(Beruf oder Stand, Vor- und Zuname)
2. Glockeng. 30a/1, geboren am 25.2.1906 in
(Wohnung)
und seiner Ehefrau ……, geborene ……, geboren am
in ……, und seiner Kinder …… geboren am
……, geboren am ……, geboren am
habe ich keine Bedenken.
Devisenstelle Wien
(Unterschrift)

Figure 1.
An affidavit from a tax office, valid for two months after the date of issue, indicates that all taxes for Friedrich Gunser had been paid, and, as far as the office was concerned, there was no objection to his emigration.

The next letter from Australia to Vienna, written in November of 1940 - "I have not received any letters from you" - came back with the notice Abgereist ohne Angabe der Adresse/parti, sans laisser d'adresse [moved without forwarding address] (Figure 4). Presumably the wife had been sent to a concentration camp.

One letter from the father of the internee, written in October of 1941 and showing the name Israel for Jewish men, was received in Australia. This suggests that the family in Austria knew of the transfer to that country (Figure 5).

In the next letter, written in January 1943, our friend bemoans the fact that he had heard nothing from his

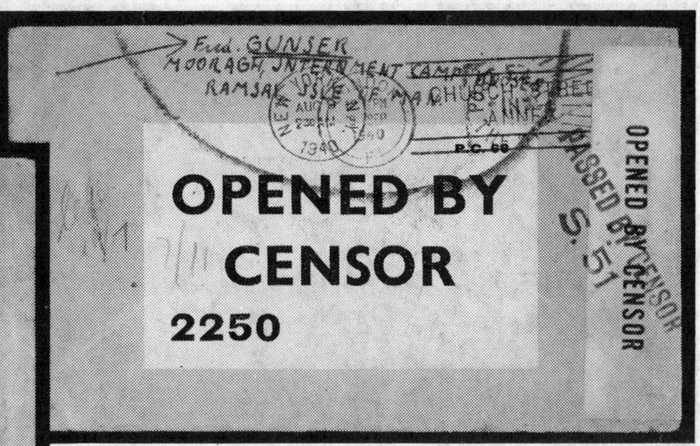

Figure 2.
The letter was opened by the Australian and British censors. It went by way of New York and London to Australia.

Figure 3.
A post card from Vienna bears a machine inspection stamp "Censored by OKW" (in Frankfurt) and a British Civil Censor octagonal handstamp.

Every letter ended with the same words: I have not heard from you for a year (or two).

Figure 4.
The front of the cover bears a diamond-shaped censor marking from Melbourne, Australia, and an "Ab" Berlin hand transit stamp. The back of the cover is marked "Opened by Censor 3" in Melbourne.

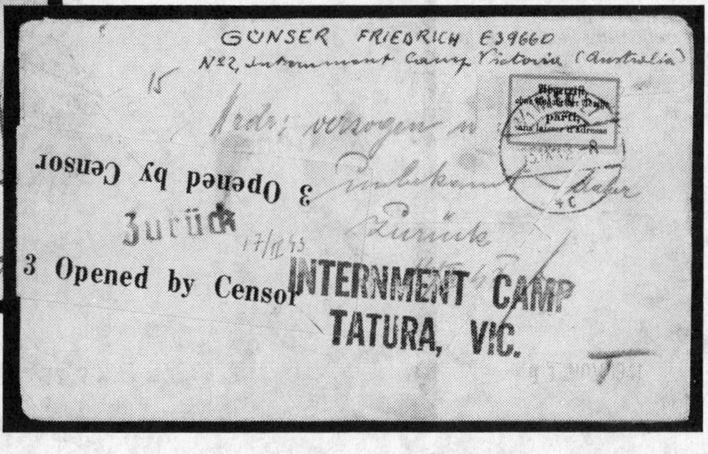

Figure 5.
The cover shows an Egyptian censor mark in circle on the front. The cover was backstamped in Cairo but not opened in Egypt; it also was censored in Melbourne, Australia.

wife for more than a year. The handwritten notice on the back of the envelope says: Empf. Judin, ausgesiedelt [Recipient a Jew, resettled (deported)]. The letter was returned to the writer (Figure 6).

Another letter from February 1943 reads: "I have not heard from you since December 1941." It also bears a handwritten notice in German which translates as "Resettled! (Deported) Is a Jew." The letter was sent back to Tatura Camp, where the writer was living now (Figures 7 and 8).

The last letter written in April 1943 says, "I hope you had a nice Easter and Heinrich is a good boy in school." Again, the ominous notice appears on the reverse: Recipient resettled, Jewess (Figures 9 and 10). The letter was returned to Australia, but the writer had left for Israel in the meantime. It was sent on to Israel, but it was not opened either. By now, the man must have known that he would never see his wife again. ❖

References

Collas, Phil. The Postal History of Internees and POWs in Australia During WWII.The Royal Philatelic Society of Victoria, 1982.

Patkin, Benzion. The Dunera Internees. Cassel, Australia, 1979

Whitney, I.T. Isle of Man, Stamps and Postal History. B.P.H. Publications Ltd., 1981.

The Author

Gustav Pohlig is a retired schoolteacher who specializes in POW covers and stationery. He has written other POW stories for the *American Philatelist.*

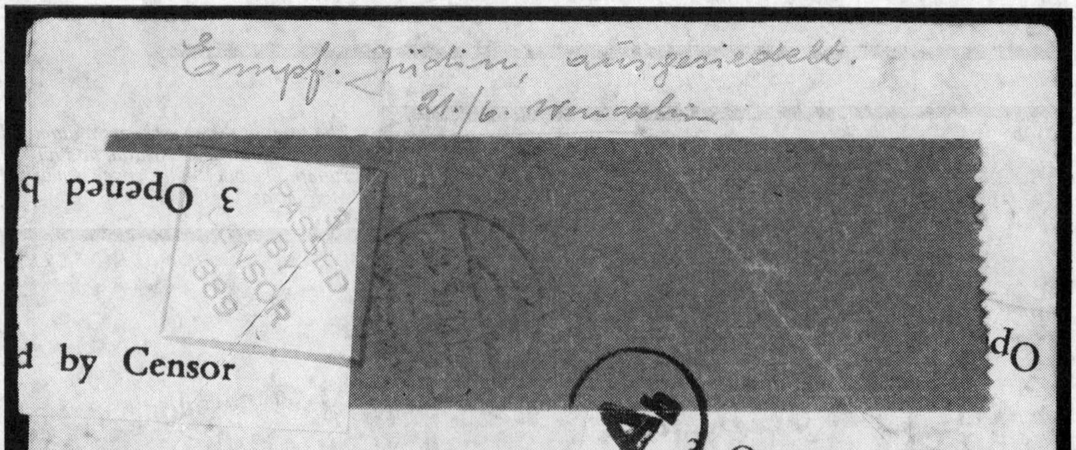

Figure 6.
Markings on the back of this cover include a "PASSED BY CENSOR"; a Berlin transit stamp (Ab), where it was opened and sealed with neutral closing tape; and a manuscript note, indicating that the recipient was resettled.

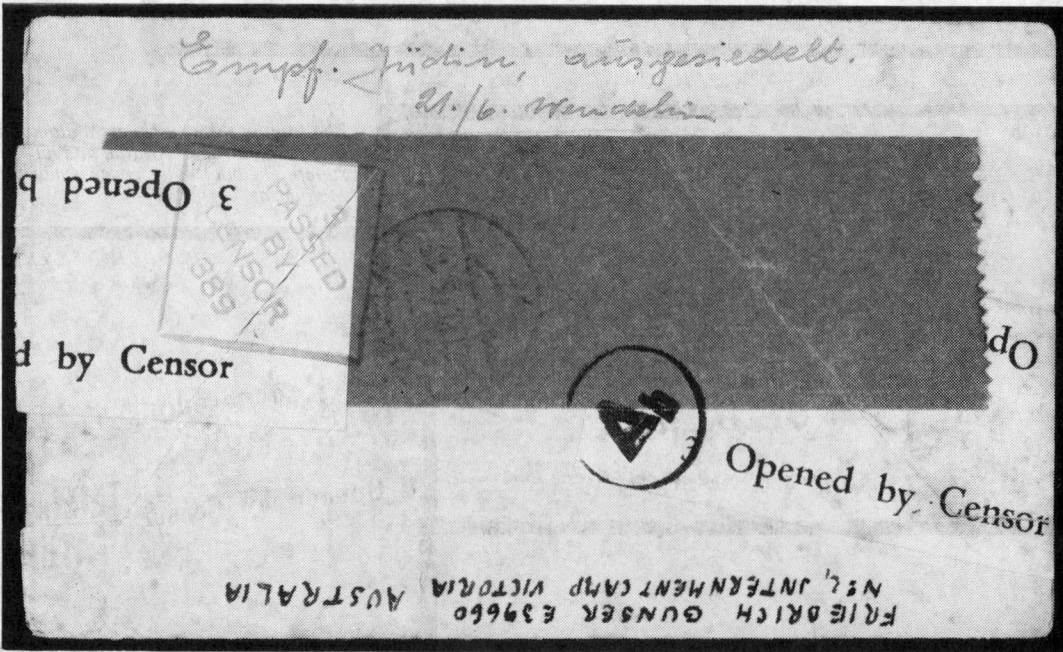

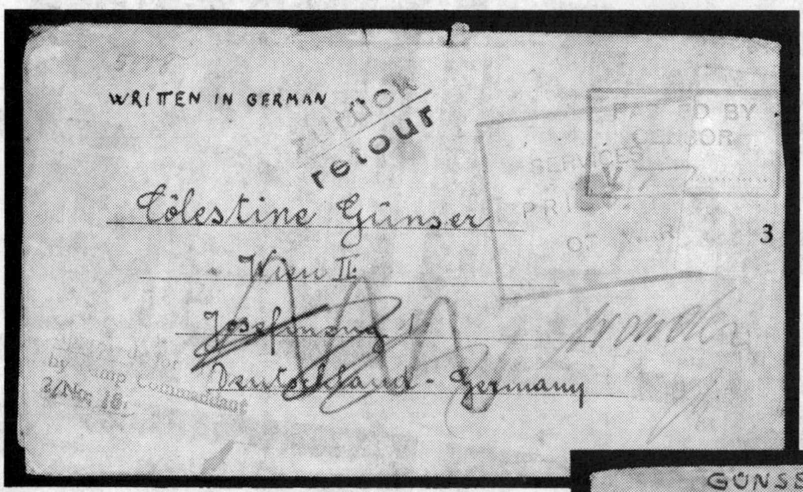

Figure 7.
This cover was returned to Gunser with several censor markings and an "Approved for by Camp Commandant 2/No.18."

Figure 8.
The back of the cover (Figure 7) bears closing labels from Berlin and Melbourne.

Figure 9.
The last cover in the series was canceled in Melbourne on April 27, 1943.

Figure 10.
The back of the cover (Figure 9) was canceled on July 27, 1943, in Vienna.

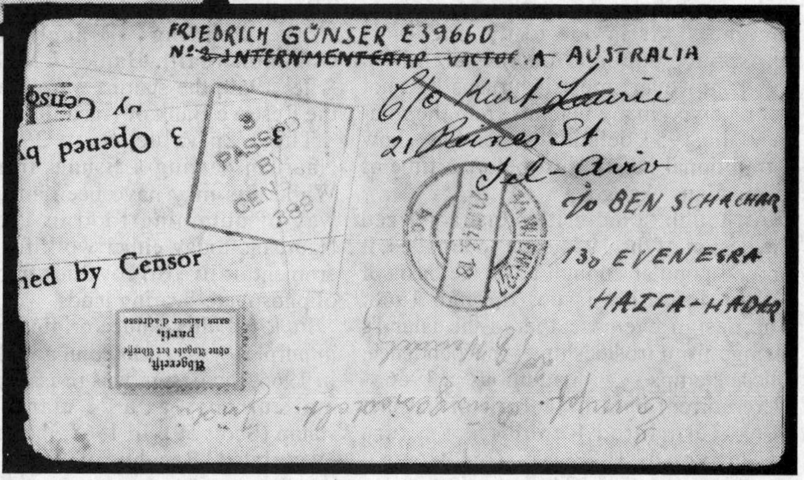

The simple daily life of Nauru, a once-poor Pacific island, was depicted on a 1954 series of pictorial definitives. These stamps, issued in various forms, were in use through the 1960's, after the island became wealthy.

Nauru: the 1954 definitives

by Steve Pendleton

On Feb. 6, 1954, the Central Pacific island of Nauru issued a nine-stamp pictorial definitive set, Scott 39-47. These stamps, picturing scenes of island life, were the first issued for that island since 1947. For the first time in its history, Nauru finally had a set of stamps that pictured its way of life in a variety of ways.

Nauru today is known as one of the richest countries on earth in per capita income. This is due to the once-vast phosphate deposits on the island. In 1954, however, most Nauruans had not yet received many benefits from the mining. The 1954 definitives therefore show a traditional Nauru, just before a time of tremendous change.

Although some critics characterized the design of the 1954 set as outmoded, it proved popular enough to be the basis of Nauru definitive issues through 1968. The design even weathered the island's change from trusteeship to independence. These stamps -- with additions in 1966 -- were current until the release of the first non-overprinted Republic of Nauru definitives of 1973. This represents a total run of 19 years. In fact, six of the designs of the original set were used at least three times, four of those with an additional printing. Another design was used as the basis of design for two aerograms. For outmoded stamp designs, someone must have liked them.

The 1954 stamps were first produced while the island was under Australian administration, the Aussies having taken it from the Germans in World War I. Thus the first printings were done by the Note Printing Branch of the Commonwealth Bank of Melbourne. After 1960, the stamps were prepared by the Reserve Bank of Australia.

The 1/2p value, Scott 39, shows a Nauruan casting a fishnet from shore. While this may have been an important way of obtaining food in 1954, most Nauruans today either work for the government or live off royalties from the use of phosphate-bearing lands.

In 1961, this value (originally printed in purple) was reprinted in a violet shade. In 1966, the design was re-issued in decimal currency as a 2¢ claret-colored stamp (Scott 59). In 1968, the stamp was overprinted "Republic of Nauru" in black and became Scott 73.

Scott 40, the 1p, shows one of the most beautiful spots on Nauru, Anibare Bay. Lying on the east side of the island, it is considered to have the best beach.

This green stamp was reprinted twice -- as an emerald-green shade in 1961, and as a deep green color in 1965. In 1966, the design was used in the new currency as a 1¢ value, Scott 58. This time the stamp was blue. It was given a red "Republic" overprint in 1968, becoming Scott 72.

A 3 1/2p value, Scott 41, was next in the series. This stamp shows the British Phosphate Corporation vessel *Trienza* next to the huge cantilever by which the phosphate is delivered to the ships. Such an arrangement is necessary because of the deep drop-off from the shore; it is impossible for a pier to be built.

In 1958, Scott 41, issued as a red stamp, was reprinted in a vermilion shade. In 1966, the design became a 3¢ value in the decimal set, with a color change to green (Scott 60). In 1968, the stamp received a black "Republic" overprint and became Scott 74.

The 4p value, Scott 42, shows a frigate

Nauru stamps of the 1954, designs come in three series: Scott 39-47, old currency; Scott 58-71, in cents and dollars; and Scott 72-85, 1969 Republic overprints. Versions of these issues are shown here on both first-day and commercial covers.

bird, one of the most spectacular birds of the South Pacific. In 1958, the stamp was reprinted in a deep blue shade. In 1966, it became a 10¢ value in the decimal series, with a color change to dark red, Scott 65. The stamp then became Scott 79 in the 1968 "Republic" overprint series.

A Nauruan canoe decorates the 6p value, Scott 43. While canoes are still seen around Nauru, they are not sailed by the Nauruans. The islanders are much too busy with their outboards. The 6p stamp is one of only three designs from this set that was not reissued or reprinted in some way.

A small hut-like building called the Domaneab is shown on the 9p value, Scott 44. This stamp design also was not repeated in any form.

In 1954, when the stamps were released, the Domaneab was the meeting place of the only government in which Nauruans were allowed to participate, the Nauru Local Government Councils. Today's Domaneab is located in Uaboe district. Today Nauru is a parliamentary democracy; its government buildings are located in several districts.

The 1sh value, Scott 45, shows an idyllic South Seas scene of palm trees by the shore. A cloudy sunset serves as an appropriate backdrop to the scene.

The 1sh value is perhaps the most popular of the 1954 series. It was reissued as a 5¢ dark blue decimal value in 1966, Scott 62. It was also overprinted in orange in 1968, transforming it into Scott 76. In addition, this same design was used for two Nauru aerograms.

In 1970, a 10¢ "short" envelope aerogram was issued. In 1971, a similar design but longer envelope was released. It, too, was a 10¢ value. Since these items are postal stationery, they are not found in Scott.

One of the few remaining livable areas in Nauru's interior is shown on the 2sh6p value, Scott 46. No other stamps in later series carry this design. Scott 46 shows Buada lagoon, a small stretch of water in the district of that name. Many Nauruans live along its shores. Today, the interior of Nauru is covered by worked-out phosphate fields, which have a desolate moon-like appearance.

The high value in the set, the 5sh, Scott 47, depicts a map of the island. One of the amazing things shown by the map is the number of districts (13) in an eight-square-mile island. Before the arrival of Europeans, these districts were clan boundaries and were the source of much argument. Some clans had only a few hundred acres of land.

In 1966, the map design became a claret-colored $1 value stamp, Scott 71. In 1968 the "Republic" overprint was applied in black, creating Scott 85.

Most of these stamps were used on mail and, unlike some sets, catalogue higher mint than used. Trying to find these stamps used on cover, however, is a real challenge.

There are several reasons for this. First, since Nauru is such a tiny country (one sports-minded visitor claimed to have run completely around it before breakfast), there is not much call for local letter writing. All mail has to be picked up at the post office.

Second, the population of Nauru in 1954 was only 3,517. Of this, about 1,800 are natives. About 1,700 people from other islands and from Europe were on the island to mine the phosphate. By 1966, the total population had risen to more than 6,000, still a small number. At independence, Nauru had the second smallest population of any sovereign nation in the world.

For those who did write from Nauru, one unusual destination was popular; a sports betting company in Australia. It would seem that betting is a major pastime on Nauru. There is another thing you can bet on. Seeing the 1954 Nauru set in your album will give you an unforgettable picture of what a South Sea isle was once like. ❖

Philatelic soul brother

by Les Winick

Have you ever wondered if your double existed somewhere on this Earth – a person who acts like you, thinks like you, but in another body? There are a group of people who feel that everyone has a double somewhere. Personally, I never felt that way until I met my double.

I am a topical stamp collector and my specialty is space and rockets. I started collecting space after the launch of Sputnik I in 1957 and have kept it up since then. About twenty years ago, a stamp collector friend in California sent me a German language article on collecting rocket mail. The friend wanted to know if it was a German translation of something that I had previously written.

The article covered an area in which I had done some research about the V-I rocket, but I had never written anything on the subject. I tracked down the author through the magazine and we started corresponding. The collector's name was Alfred Klein and he lives in Budingen, a suburb of Frankfurt, Germany.

The two friends discovered each other. We both collected and specialized in the same segments of philately. Both were born in the same year and same month. They both had the exact same type of English Tudor home, each with an indoor swimming pool. (How many indoor pools are there in Germany or the U.S.?)

Winick and Klein both sold curtains and draperies for a living, both had a son who opened a retail store devoted to textiles in the very same month and year. Klein only speaks and writes German, Winick only English. Friends translate their letters for them.

Alfred was president of the German Space Philatelic Group and Les was president of the U.S. Space Topics Study Group. Klein was a founder of the local Budingen Stamp Club and Winick did the same thing for the Park Forest (Illinois) Stamp Club. Both had served their countries during World War II.

Author Les Winick, left, with Philatelic soul brother Alfred Klein.

We arranged to meet in London during the 1980 International Stamp Exhibition. During the four days we spent together, I knew exactly what he wanted to do, where he wanted to go, and even what he was going to order in a restaurant. One waitress who spoke German and English told us later that we had both separately offered her a job in our homes translating our letters.

It was a very peculiar feeling that is difficult to describe, walking beside someone, watching and knowing what window he will stop at, which way he will turn at a corner, and even when he is ready to go into a pub for a beer. We were even ready for naps at the same time each day.

At an International Astro Exhibition in Switzerland, Klein displayed an exhibit of rocket mail material from the 1920s and 1930s. Winick's exhibit started with the Cuba rocket mail experiment of 1939. If you placed the two exhibits together, they would have formed one cohesive logical display. Yet neither of us knew what the other was going to exhibit. Each of us won a gold medal at this FIP exhibition.

One night in Switzerland, I went to a banquet and Klein went to a different affair. After the banquet, I told my wife that I wanted to find my friend. I knew that he had driven to Switzerland from Germany and was in a trailer park near the exhibition site. Since it was 1 a.m., my wife thought that I was crazy, but went along to humor me.

I drove my rented car into a trailer park, made a left-hand turn and stopped at the first trailer with lights on. Naturally, it was Alfred's. They were waiting for us, with chilled wine and four glasses on the table.

Over the years, we have literally traded thousands of dollars worth of space philatelic material with no type of accounting system. When one finds something that he thinks the other can use in his collection, off it goes. The question of money or value has never come up and we are both satisfied with our trades.

Although we address each other as *Lieber Bruder* (Dear Brother), we have been able to find only one major difference in our lifestyles, thoughts and hobbies over the many years that we have known each other. Alfred Klein is presently married to his third *frau*, Les Winick has been married for 47 years to the same person. ❖

HOW STAMPS DESTROYED ADOLPH HITLER'S WISH

by Michele M. Patrick

The opening of the U.S. Holocaust Memorial Museum in Washington D.C. was one of the defining events of 1993; already, nearly three quarters of a million people have toured the exhibits. To commemorate the Memorial's inauguration, the U.S. postal service issued a postal card which featured a drawing of the Museum (Illustration 1). The building's stark design and dour colors echo the grimness and bleakness of the Nazi concentration camps.

The issuing of a postal item is fitting, because the ultimate goal of the Museum is to ensure that the world never forgets the Holocaust. Similarly, one of the chief functions of postage stamps is to commemorate the past, whether it be people, ideas or events. By doing so, stamps help preserve history and ensure that we never forget.

By ensuring that the world "never forgets," the postage stamps of Czechoslovakia, and now the Czech Republic, have prevented a sinister goal of Adolph Hitler from becoming a reality. This goal is commemorated in a small section of the Holocaust Museum, a section devoted to the story of Lidice. In 1942, Hitler declared that the little village of Lidice, near Prague in the then "Reich Protectorate of Bohemia and Moravia," was to be erased from the map and, more importantly, from human memory - as though it had never existed.

Hitler's order was in revenge for the killing of the so called "blond beast," Rheinhard Heydrich. Heydrich, Himmler's chief lieutenant, is usually credited with being the chief architect of the Holocaust. He organized and chaired the Wannsee Conference, a meeting of 15 senior SS men held in Berlin in January 1942. There, Heydrich outlined and ironed out the administrative aspects of what he termed, "the coming Final Solution of the Jewish problem." Much of what is documented in the Holocaust Museum is Heydrich's handiwork.

In September 1941, Heydrich had been sent to Prague as "Reich Protector." He was to liquidate all resistance and to ensure that Czech industries, among the largest and most modern in the world at that time, provided a continuous supply for the Nazi war machine.

In the spring of 1942, two Czech commandos were flown from England, into occupied Czechoslovakia, to assassinate Heydrich. They waited for him on the road to his office in Hradcany Castle and ambushed his car. When their guns jammed, the commandos hurled a bomb at Heydrich's car; the Reich Protector died on June 4, 1942. (Illustration 2, the death mask of Rheinhard Heydrich).

Hitler ordered savage reprisals; among them, he chose the village of Lidice - a few stories suggest by sticking a pin in a map of Bohemia and Moravia - to be wiped off the face of the earth. On June 10, 1942 Gestapo and SS troops arrived in Lidice and shot all 172 male inhabitants above the age of 15. The 195 women were sent to Ravensbruk concentration camp. Seven babies out of 90 children were judged sufficiently Aryan to be sent to German homes; none ever returned. The remainder were placed in German "educational institutions." But the Nazi barbarism did not end here. Every living person who had been born in the village, but who had moved, was traced and executed.

All buildings were burned to the ground and their foundations dynamited. Gardens and trees were uprooted. Even the stream which ran through the town was diverted from its natural course. All that remained was a barren field with patches of asphalt. [A film of the entire operation was made for Hitler.] All references to Lidice were also removed from road signs, maps, etc.

Illustration 2

Although the Nazis committed worse atrocities elsewhere, the calculated nature of the reprisal and the ruthless precision with which it was carried out was unparalleled. It was also the only instance where Hitler declared that a place would no longer exist in the present - or the past.

With the destruction of the Third Reich, a memorial garden, with roses donated from around the world, was planted at Lidice. A museum, which shows the film intended for Hitler, was established. A new village of "Lidice" was also founded very nearby, and a few survivors of the tragedy did return. Moreover, towns around the world, from the U.S. to Scotland, renamed themselves "Lidice."

Yet, the Czechoslovak, and now the Czech, government has undertaken one measure which, more than

Illustration 1

Illustration 3

Illustration 4

Illustration 5

Illustration 6

Illustration 7

any other, ensures that Hitler's sinister wish remains unfulfilled. Every five years, on the anniversary of the massacre, the Czech postal service issues Lidice commemoratives. Beginning in 1947, most of the stamps have featured symbols of grief and resurrection or, evoking the memorial garden, a simple rose. For example, the 1957 issues combine both of these themes. One stamp depicts the face of a woman, half in the light and half shrouded in the darkness of grief (Illustration 3). The other commemorative bears a fully blossoming pink rose (Illustration 4).

One of the 1962 Lidice stamps shows a smiling young girl, with pink roses in her hair. Behind the girl, there stands a figure of a grieving woman in black (Illustration 5). Again employing the rose motif, the 1967 issue depicts a single red rose bud (Illustration 6).

More abstract in nature than the previous designs, the 1972 stamp features a hand reaching upward from among stylized ruins (Illustration 7). This last stamp beautifully illustrates the theme of resurrection.

It is through its "philatelic act of remembrance" that the Czech government proclaims to the world that it will never forget Lidice. Consequently, thanks to the power of the simple postage stamp, Hitler's wish to "erase the memory of Lidice" remains unfulfilled. As the motto of the U.S. Holocaust Memorial Museum proclaims, "For the dead, and the living, we must bear witness..." ❖

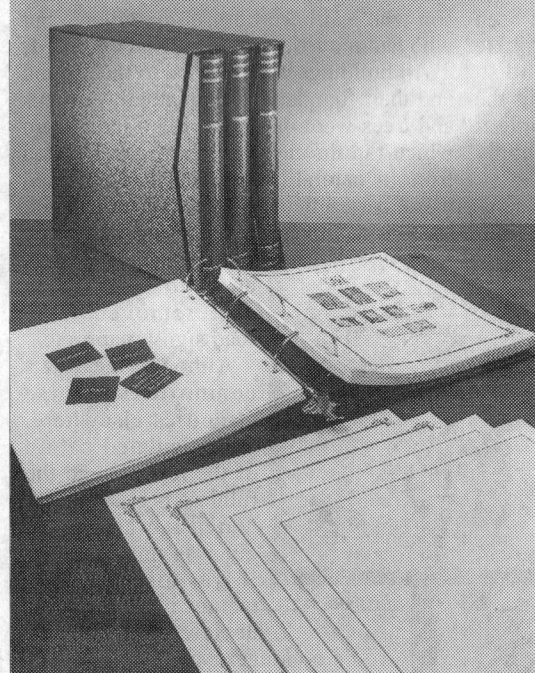

GE college bowl postal card

by Charles Fricke

An unusual United States postal stationery item was created by a television show sometime during the early 1960s. Although not a legitimate variety, the card and the story behind it are quite interesting.

The *GE College Bowl* was televised from Jan. 4, 1959 to June 16, 1963 on CBS, then from Sept. 22, 1963 to June 14, 1970 on NBC. This information appeared in two books on television programming.

The *GE College Bowl* program consisted of two four-member teams from America's colleges and universities, challenging each other to answer rapid-fire questions posed by Allen Ludden (1959-62) or Robert Earle (1962-70) as arbiters. The popular Sunday night television program offered the same type of competition as did the *Quiz Kids* program of the radio era.

Sometime during the early years of the show, at one point in the program, a 1¢ U.S. postal card with an address was flashed on the screen. According to Frank B. Stratton of Lakeland, Fla., Allan Thatcher, a Florida stamp dealer, noticed the show's use of the 1¢ postal card when the postal card rate was 3¢ at that time.

The 1¢ rate had been raised to 2¢ Jan. 1, 1952, and then to 3¢ Aug. 1, 1958.

When Allen Thatcher contacted the show's director about the goof, the problem was immediately corrected. The producers took a 1¢ Jefferson postal card and, with artist's handiwork, changed it to show a "3" where there previously was a "1." They then deleted that portion of the stamp design showing the words "ONE CENT," and scrambled the name "JEFFERSON" in the bottom panel. In addition, a hand-inked simulated machine cancel using dotted lines was included. The card, as it then appeared, is shown in Figure 1.

For use on the TV screen, show producers reproduced the modified "3¢" postal card (black and white reproduction) and then added the address to which a 3¢ postal card was to be sent. That final copy, shown in Figure 2, was then used on the program.

As a show of appreciation to Thatcher for his calling attention to the goof, the show's producers sent him the original "1¢" modified to "3¢" Jefferson postal card, as well as a copy of the final "3¢" postal card reproduction with the address as used on the program.

One might wonder how the producers of a trivia contest show could have goofed by using the 1¢ postal card when the rate was 3¢, but after 30 years we'll probably never know. One thing we do know is that the card is probably unique in its use, application and type.

My thanks go to Frank B. Stratton for the background history on this unusual card. My thanks also to Geraldine Duclow, head of the theater collection, Logan Square branch of the Free Library of Philadelphia.

THIS SIDE OF CARD IS FOR ADDRESS
THIS SIDE OF CARD IS FOR ADDRESS
College Bowl Contest
Box 4734
Chicago, Illinois

Figure 1: This 1¢ Jefferson postal card was modified to 3¢ to correct a television depiction goof.

Figure 2: The final 3¢ postal card was reproduced, and the address as used on the program was added.

'Cornflakes' Number Now Known

BY DR. WERNER M. BOHNE

Although more than forty years have passed since the end of World War II, definitive information on some aspects of "Operation Cornflakes" has never been made public. One of the most vexing missing links has been full statistical data on some details of this fascinating Allied propaganda operation.

A major problem is that much of the material was tucked away in participants' private archives, including those of Gen. William "Wild Bill" Donovan, head of the Office of Strategic Services (OSS), which undertook "Cornflakes" in the waning days of the war. With the deaths and/or retirements of these individuals, some files are now coming to light, as estates and other collections are sold or donated to libraries.

Some recently released documents contain numbers that collectors and researchers long have sought. Among them are two original production reports that spell out the numbers of propaganda items produced and distributed by the Morale Operation of the OSS in the Mediterranean Theater of Operations during the final weeks of the war. Included are the actual numbers of "stamps" produced by the OSS for "Cornflakes" and other operations, along with specific information on all of the propaganda materials produced in Italy: leaflets, an Italian newspaper, a "Hitler-mark," French leaflets, Russian leaflets, instructions for partisans, and the like.

A grand total of more than 30 million propaganda items was produced by the end of the war, including 726,550 facsimile German postage stamps. The total distribution of the stamps reached 516,118, much of it unrelated to the "Cornflakes" drops. Stamps also were passed to several countries for propaganda and espionage purposes. Despite these large numbers, the survival rate was small and the stamps are now fairly scarce; individual items command high prices at auction.

It should be mentioned that the American propaganda effort had a second philatelic component. The OSS also produced Hitler-head stamps with a skull showing through the Fuhrer's portrait. This was meant to indicate that Hitler represented the death of Germany. These stamps were intended entirely for propaganda and were widely distributed throughout Europe.

The OSS report listing the "Hitler heads" is believed to refer to these death-head stamps. The figures show that 1,138,500 were printed, with 329,000 shipped to Bari; 73,500 to Brindisi; 106,650 to North Italy; 519,400 to Algiers; and 18,350 to France. Another 31,000 were given "special" distribution. Some presumably were among the "Cornflakes" fake air-drop mail, along with the OSS-published German-language propaganda newspaper *Das Neue Deutschland* and anti-Nazi stickers.

"Cornflakes" was one of those elaborate - and expensive - operations that are the delight of bureaucracies. The idea was to introduce Allied propaganda into the German mail system to undermine German morale on the home front, create fear of defeat, and destroy confidence in the leadership of Adolf Hitler.

Efforts to distribute anti-German propaganda inside the Third Reich had been frustrated by lack of a viable underground, and by the close control the government held over communications. Even distribution of *Das Neue Deutschland*

The Author

Dr. Werner M. Bohne, a collector since 1932 and a philatelic writer since 1945, has served the hobby in many ways. He is accredited as an international judge by both the APS and the Germany Philatelic Society; he is a long-standing member of several expertization committees; he is a past president and a current director of the GPS, and of several other philatelic organizations in the United States and abroad. He also is the president of the Commission on Expertization and Forgery Prevention of the Federation Internationale de Philatelie. Dr. Bohne is the author of the GPS Reference Manual of Forgeries, now in its eighth volume.

Figure 1.
The Stabilimento Aristide Staderini in Rome, where stamps, leaflets, and other propaganda items were printed for the OSS. From "The Story of Cornflakes, Pig Iron and Sheet Iron."

(The New Germany) inside Germany and to the Fuhrer's military units was extremely difficult. Air drops of the newspaper and other propaganda materials enjoyed some success, but far from enough to meet expectations.

As stated in "The Story of Cornflakes, Pig Iron and Sheet Iron," the report prepared by the 2677th Headquarters Detachment of the OSS in the Mediterranean Theater of Operations (MEDTO), several plans were discussed for moving propaganda materials into Germany more effectively. Most were discarded for practical reasons.

Libich, who was in charge of "Cornflakes," began a detailed study of the German postal system. Copies of postal regulations, letters, mail sacks, and postage stamps had to be obtained - and they had to be current. Former German mail clerks interned in what the report calls "POW cages" were interviewed, and their information was cross-checked with that from other sources.

Postage stamps resembling the current Hitler-portrait series of 1941 had to be produced to frank the phony mail.

One proposal, for example, considered infiltrating mail trains moving from Switzerland into Germany. However, the neutral stance of Switzerland made such an operation impossible.

Air drops of leaflets over Hungary actually were tried but, again, without meaningful results. Much of the material fell into open country.

The plan finally adopted - "Cornflakes" - was offered by Jan Libich. His idea was to drop mail sacks filled with propaganda materials in the vicinity of bombed rail mail cars. It was hoped that the Germans would consider these part of the legitimate mail shipment and, thus, would return the phony mail sacks to the German postal system, which, in turn, would forward them in the usual manner.

Putting the plan into effect turned out to be a much greater task than its proponents had anticipated. A massive amount of research and preparation was necessary before the operation could be mounted. And, as the OSS report concedes, every detail "had to be perfect in every respect" to avoid detection.

Das Neue Deutschland

„Die Zukunft gehört jenen, die sich auf sie vorbereiten!"

Erscheint halbmonatlich — Süddeutsche Ausgabe — 15. Oktober 1944

DER WEG INS NICHTS

Immer wieder hören wir in den letzten Wochen „beruhigende" Erklärungen verschiedener Regierungsmitglieder, dass wir noch über genügend Vorräte an Rohmaterialien verfügen, um den Krieg fortsetzen zu können. Aber auf wie lange? Da sich Deutschland heute in der Lage einer belagerten Festung befindet, der jede Zufuhr abgeschnitten ist, vermindern sich die vorhandenen Roh-

Himmler greift nach dem Marschallsstab

Die Wehrmacht in Fesseln

Es ist uns gelungen, Einsicht in die neuen Verordnungen zu nehmen, die Himmler die ... masenahmen umfassen unter vielen anderen auch die folgenden Punkte: ... Ernennung eines neuen Befehlshabers das Kommando auszuüben.

SONDERNUMMER

Das Neue Deutschland

„Die Zukunft gehört jenen, die sich auf sie vorbereiten!"

Erscheint halbmonatlich — Süddeutsche Ausgabe — 26. Juli 1944

Für Euren Schutz!

Anweisungen zur Sicherung der Bewegung und ihrer Mitglieder:

1) Wenn es auch dem Neuen Deutschland gelungen ist, Mitglieder der Bewegung in der Gestapo, in der Partei selber, und in vermeintlich nationalsozialistisch gesinnten Kreisen der Wehrmacht, unterzubringen, so sind trotzdem derartige Personen unter gar keinen Umständen von andern Mitgliedern ins Vertrauen zu ziehen.

2) Niemals sind Fernsprecher oder Telegramme für Benachrichtigungen zwischen Mitgliedern zu verwenden.

Hitler im Sterben?

Die Wahrheit über die Vorfälle des. 20. Juli

Inmitten der jetzigen politischen Krise. ist es von grösster Wichtigkeit, einwandfrei den Grad der Verletzungen festzustellen, welche Hitler bei dem Anschlag auf sein Leben erlitten hat, und zu ermitteln, inwieweit ihn diese, jetzt und in Zukunft, an der Ausübung der Reichsgeschäfte verhindern werden.

einen Augenblick Goebbels' Fassung der Vorgänge des 20. Juli Glauben schenken, jenem Märchen, das da schlankweg behauptet, Herr Hitler hätte kaum mehr als leichte Verbrennungen durch eine Bombe erlitten, welche in nur 2 Meter Entfernung von ihm explodierte und zumindest dreizehn andere Personen, die sich in demselben Raum befanden, entweder tötete oder zumindest

Figure 2.
Two issues of Das Neue Deutschland dated July 26, 1944, and October 15, 1944, report the bomb attack on Hitler of July 20, 1944.

Figure 3.
Sgt. Nick Los, winner of the Legion of Merit for work behind the lines in Greece, slides a "Nazi" mail bag into a bomb. From "The Story of Cornflakes, Pig Iron and Sheet Iron."

Figure 4.
Bombs are stuffed with mail, ready to go. From "The Story of Cornflakes, Pig Iron and Sheet Iron."

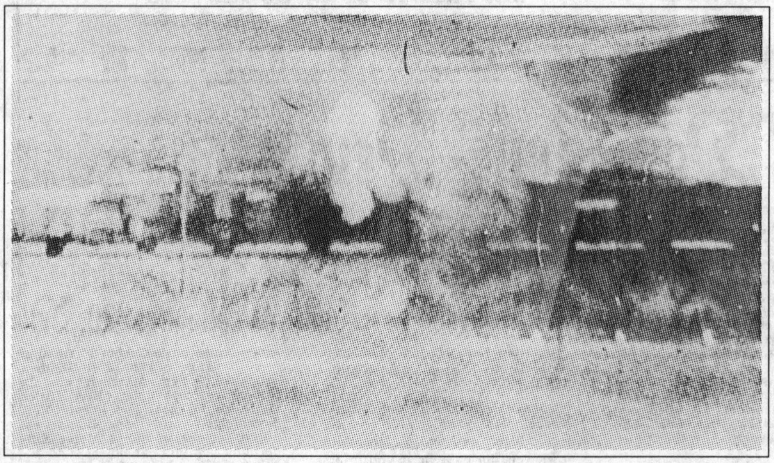

Figure 5.
A U.S. Army Air Forces picture of an acutal "Cornflakes" operation. The photo is clipped from a 16mm newsreel of a train run in Austria. The plane has raked the locomotive with machine gun fire and steam pours from the engine. Another pilot drops a "Cornflakes" bomb directly on a box car.

Counterfeit German 6-pfennig and 12-pfennig stamps - the basic postal rates for post cards and letters - were produced at the OSS printing facility in Rome. Large numbers of mail sacks were manufactured, and proper systems of packing and labeling were developed.

An immediate complication occurred in August 1944, when the German postal system changed its cancellation style. These new cancels had to be researched and correctly imitated, and it took "weeks of search" to get the job done.

"Cornflakes" would work only if authentic-looking mail were stuffed into the mail sacks, so real names and addresses of people living inside Germany were needed. Telephone directories of major cities listed some two million suitable addresses, but these then had to be handwritten on envelopes - typing would have been a giveaway. A staff was organized and soon was producing in excess of 15,000 hand-addressed envelopes a week.

While envelope preparation was proceeding, operational work also was progressing, under the guidance of Lt. Jack Daniels, at Bari in occupied Italy. A fighter group of the U.S. Army Air Forces was detailed for the bombing and mail-dropping runs. Practice quickly revealed that customary air tactics had to be modified considerably for the attacks on mail-carrying trains and the dropping of fake mail sacks. The air effort was focused on Austria, just across the border.

Suddenly, the huge task of addressing mail came to a standstill. All completed work had to be discarded and new procedures adopted. Beset by ruinous bombing and shortages, the German postal system had imposed limits on the mail: In the future, only business correspondence would be forwarded! The kind of private mail being produced by "Cornflakes" would no longer be accepted by the German postal authorities. Now samples of business envelopes had to be reproduced and addressed.

As a result of these delays, the first mail drop did not occur until February 5, 1945. The pilots reported one destroyed locomotive and twelve rail cars left burning. Eight fake mail bags were dropped on target, two hit a tree a mile away, six others were returned to base.

Altogether, twelve mail flights were made, the last on March 31, with very poor results. Damage to the train could not be assessed and, of sixteen "Cornflakes," only eight actually were dropped on the target. Two could not be released because of mechanical failure, four were returned to base because the pilot failed to set the dropping system's arming switch, and one bag was simply reported "lost."

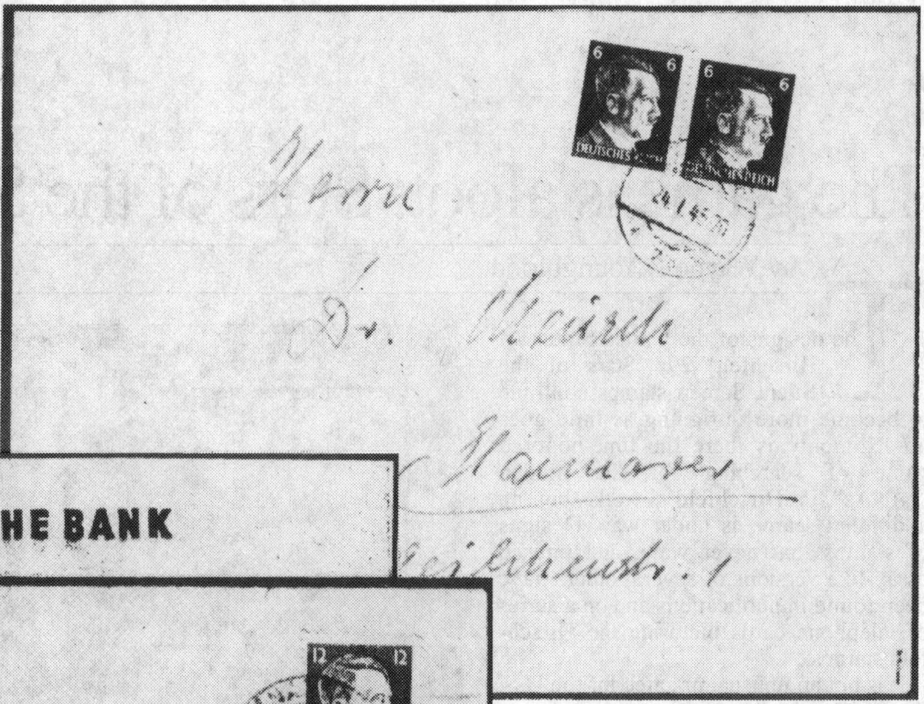

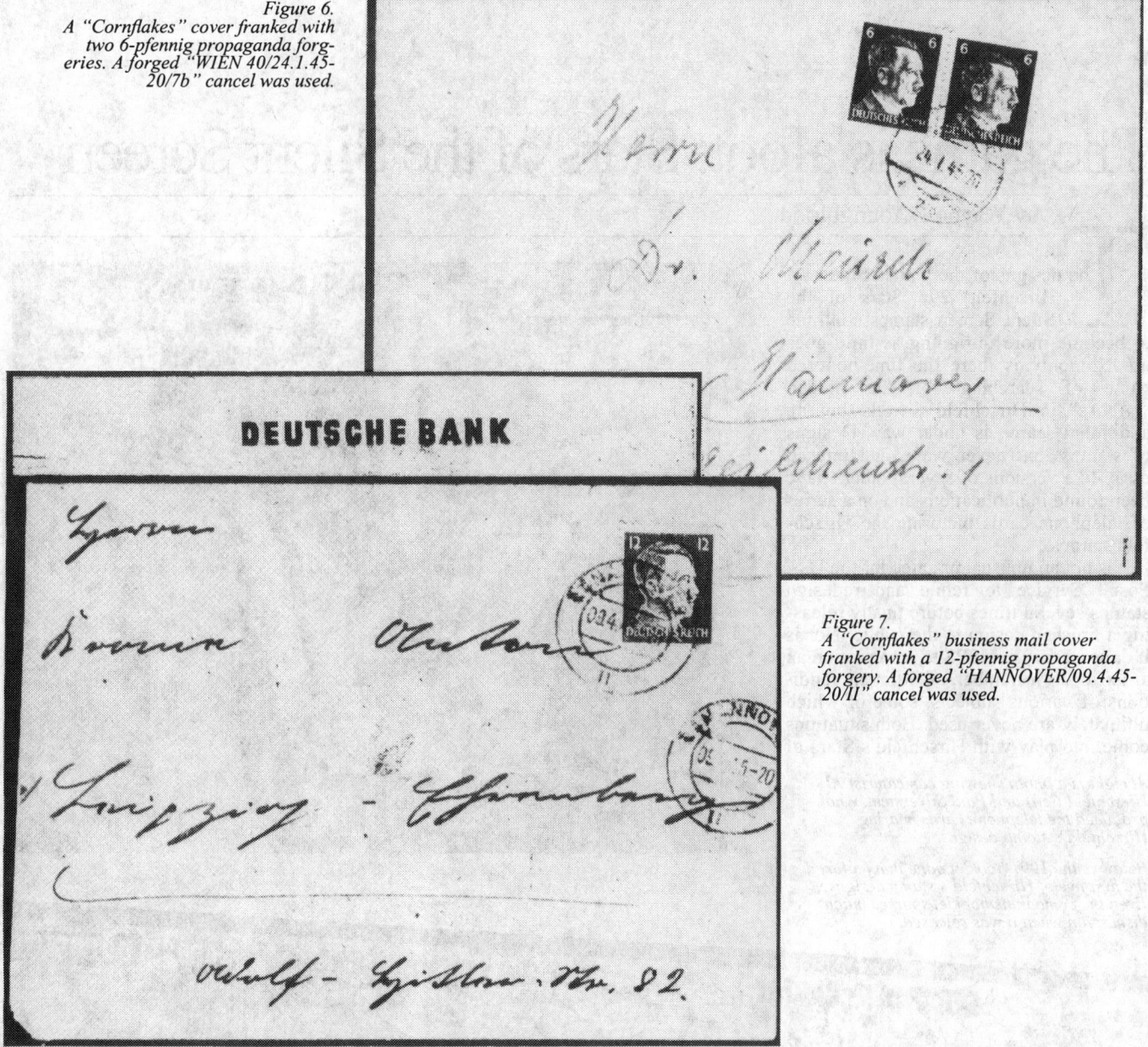

Figure 6.
A "Cornflakes" cover franked with two 6-pfennig propaganda forgeries. A forged "WIEN 40/24.1.45-20/7b" cancel was used.

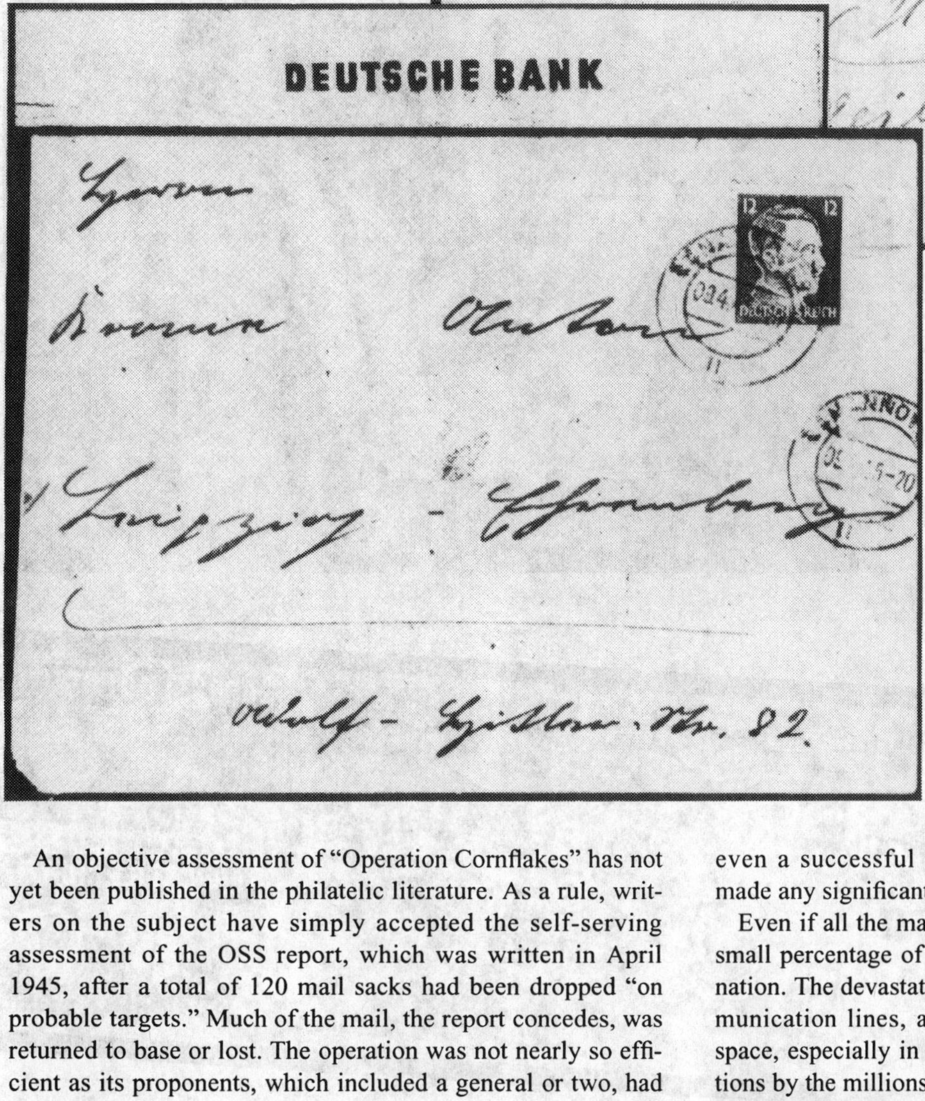

Figure 7.
A "Cornflakes" business mail cover franked with a 12-pfennig propaganda forgery. A forged "HANNOVER/09.4.45-20/II" cancel was used.

An objective assessment of "Operation Cornflakes" has not yet been published in the philatelic literature. As a rule, writers on the subject have simply accepted the self-serving assessment of the OSS report, which was written in April 1945, after a total of 120 mail sacks had been dropped "on probable targets." Much of the mail, the report concedes, was returned to base or lost. The operation was not nearly so efficient as its proponents, which included a general or two, had anticipated.

In addition, the rapid progress of American forces under Gen. George S. Patton had just about eliminated suitable targets by the end of March.

In fact, the operation was too long delayed to be even moderately effective. Even if the change in German postal regulations had not occurred, the timing was poor. By the time the plan was sufficiently organized and supplied, Germany was already in a state of dissolution. The military and civilian collapse of the Third Reich was so rapid and so complete that even a successful propaganda campaign could not have made any significant difference in the outcome of the war.

Even if all the mail had been dropped successfully, only a small percentage of it could possibly have reached its destination. The devastating Allied bombings had destroyed communication lines, along with much of the German living space, especially in cities. People were moving to new locations by the millions. In such populous cities as Berlin, many addresses no longer existed. Mail addressed according to old telephone directories would, therefore, have been futile, as well as suspect.

It seems obvious that, even if all of the operational goals of "Cornflakes" had been achieved, it would have made no significant contribution to the war. By the time the first "Cornflakes" bags fell near Amstetten, Austria, the military outcome was already inevitable. The huge "Operation Cornflakes" effort - including the loss of a pilot and the dedication of precious resources - produced no comparable benefits. ❖

The game is afoot: Stars of the Silent Screen

by Wayne L. Youngblood

The designs of the United States Al Hirschfeld 29¢ Stars of the Silent Screen stamps continue to become more intriguing as time goes on. Not only is there the time-honored game of searching for the hidden "NINAs" in Hirschfeld's work, but an additional search is under way. Designs of stamps that never were, and unused essay-like versions of several others have been found in publications and on a series of telephone cards picturing the Hirschfeld stamps.

It is not an unusual practice for the U.S. Postal Service to refine and redesign stamps several times before finally releasing a finished design to the public. Nor is it unusual for the USPS to commission an artist to do a number of different renditions of various subjects, some of which ultimately are never used. Both situations come into play with Hirschfeld's Stars of

At right is a photo showing caricaturist Al Hirschfeld (left) and Paul Silverstein, who produced the telephone cards bearing Hirschfeld's stamp designs.

Below is the 1991 booklet pane that featured the first five of Hirschfeld's stamp designs. Even the comedians booklet spurred much discussion when it was released.

the Silent Screen stamps, complicated by the fact that USPS apparently inadvertently released illustrations of unused versions of the stamps to several sources. This includes unused and changed designs, as well as artwork that was reworked prior to the stamps' release. But, before going into detail, every good story has its beginning, and that is the best place to start with this one, too.

The November 1981 issue of *Stamp World*, a short-lived monthly philatelic magazine published by Amos Press, carried an interview regarding U.S. stamp design. One of the individuals interviewed was Howard Paine, art director for *National Geographic* magazine and newly appointed design coordinator for the USPS' Citizens' Stamp Advisory Committee.

Commenting on what he'd like to see in the future, Paine stated he would like to try some adventurous things in stamp design. "I'd like to see some of the great caricaturists design stamps," Paine said "Al Hirschfeld could do theater people."

By the late 1980s, Paine's wish came true. The USPS began negotiations with Hirschfeld to design commemorative stamps depicting popular entertainers of the past. Hirschfeld, in turn, designed pro-

At left is an early mock-up of the Stars of the Silent Screen block. The Mary Pickford and Pola Negri stamps were later replaced by Lon Chaney and John Gilbert. Even those designs that remain differ from the final version.

posals for 25 different U.S. stamps. Early on, Hirschfeld was told by USPS he could not hide his distinctive "NINA" in any of his caricatures, since USPS did not allow secret marks (Nina is Hirschfeld's daughter). Sometime later, with Postmaster General Anthony Frank's intervention, USPS allowed Hirschfeld to hide the name in the caricatures, since it is such an integral part of his distinctive style. This is why "NINA" can't be found in every design, and why a number of completed designs were reworked to include the name.

The first five of Hirschfeld's designs were accounted for when the 29¢ Comedians stamps were released Aug. 29, 1991. Those stamps, released in booklet format (Scott 2562-2566), pictured Laurel and Hardy, Edgar Bergen and Charlie McCarthy, Jack Benny, Fanny Brice, and Abbott and Costello. Early reports of what comedians would be pictured also included Charlie Chaplin, Buster Keaton and Harold Lloyd. It was thought that Chaplin and Keaton were dropped from the final list because of their questionable political status. After all, despite Brice's popularity, Chaplin is unarguably a more notable figure in comedy history.

Since Chaplin, Keaton and Lloyd have now been recognized on U.S. stamps, and as part of the Hirschfeld series in particular, the reason for the last-minute cut may have been more closely related to an early USPS attempt at being so-called politically correct to balance the heavily male-weighted Comedians issue with a recognized comedienne.

On April 27, the Stars of the Silent Screen stamps were released. The format was a bit unusual, with two mini-panes of 20 stamps appearing in each 40-stamp pane. This means that each pane of 40 can be saved complete, separated into two mini panes with a tab at top, or broken down into four blocks of 10, two with plate numbers and two with the Stars of the Silent Screen tab at top. Scott 2828a was assigned for the se-tenant block of 10 stamps.

With the release of these stamps, another 10 of Hirschfeld's designs were accounted for, bringing the known total to 15 of the original 25. Individual Scott numbers for the Silent Screen Stars stamps include 2819 (Rudolph Valentino), 2820 (Clara Bow), 2821 (Charlie Chaplin), 2822 (Lon Chaney), 2823 (John Gilbert), 2824 (Zasu Pitts), 2825 (Harold Lloyd), 2826 (Keystone Cops), 2827 (Theda Bara) and 2828 (Buster Keaton).

But more designs were to come. The April 1994 issue of *cronaca filatelica*, a glossy stamp magazine published in Italy, featured a USPS publicity photo of a block of 10 Silent Screen Stars stamps that doesn't match the actual issue. The article accompanying the illustration prominently featured the two Italian stars in the block: Rudolph Valentino and Pola Negri. Pola Negri? Where did she come from? Further inspection revealed a Mary Pickford design as well. Lon Chaney and John Gilbert did not appear in this version, designs of other stamps were changed and the arrangement of the block was slightly different.

With the addition of these two new designs, confirmed to *Scott Stamp Monthly* by USPS as part of the original 25, our tally now grows to 17. Added to this is a Hirschfeld caricature for a Bing Crosby stamp that won't be issued. The image of this stamp was released to MeKeel's after the design was killed. Crosby will be depicted a bit more realistically later this year in the Legends of American Music series. Our count of known Hirschfeld designs now grows to 18, leaving to the imagination the subjects of seven more stamps that may be released at a future date.

Why were the Pickford and Negri stamps cut from the 1994 issue? Robin Minard, a spokeswoman for the USPS told *Scott Stamp Monthly* that no agreement could be reached with the Pickford family about licensing rights. This doesn't mean a Mary Pickford stamp will never be released. A stamp bearing her likeness could eventually be released if an agreement is reached.

In the case of the Pola Negri stamp, the problem is simple. "She's not dead enough," Minard quipped, meaning that Negri, who died in 1987, is still ineligible by the CSAC 10-year rule, which states that individuals must be dead at least 10 years

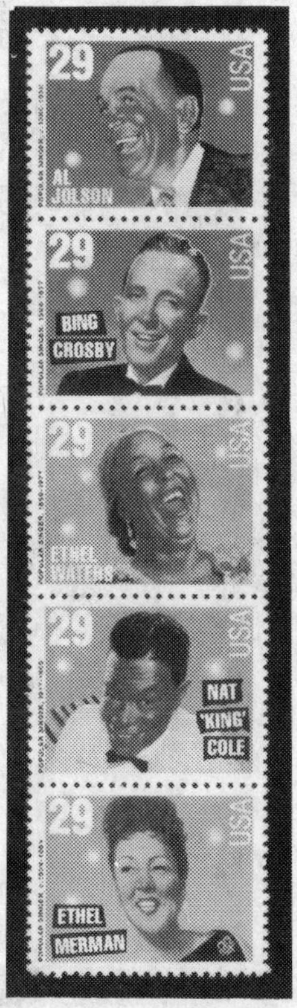

Shown above is the Hirschfeld Bing Crosby stamp design that will not be used. At right is a booklet pane containing the Crosby stamp as it will appear later this year.

before being pictured on a postage stamp. Only presidents are exempt from this rule. This may also be the case with others in the Hirschfeld series.

Further muddying the design waters of this issue are the different versions of at least seven of the 10 Stars of the Silent Screen stamps that were released. This artwork, which includes rearranged design elements and reworked drawings, appeared both in the previously mentioned *cronaca filatelica* article and on a line of U.S. telephone cards that picture the 10 stamps.

Paul Silverstein, president of Global Telecommunication Solutions (GTS), pointed out a difference between the final stamp and his version of the Rudolph Valentino stamp, but had no idea how significantly different his cards are from the final stamps. They essentially are reproductions of essays.

GTS produces a line of telephone cards bearing the designs of postage stamps. As the hobby of moneycard collecting continues to pick up speed in this country, GTS leads the pack for bridging the gap between moneycard and stamp collecting, two hobbies that are very closely related in many ways. These cards, good for 16 minutes of domestic telephone time, cost $10 apiece (about 59¢ per minute), a comparable rate to AT&T prepaid card rates. In most cases, total production of GTS stamp telephone cards is between 1,000 and 3,000. This is as opposed to 150 million or more for a standard commemorative stamp. In addition to creating the basic stamp cards, GTS created first-day covers for the Hirschfeld set. The company's own telephone cards were windowed in and used as the cachet. Hirschfeld then autographed 250 sets of FDCs.

As a USPS licensee, Silverstein focuses primarily on producing cards with designs of new stamp issues. As previously mentioned, some of his firm's most recent cards featured the Stars of the Silent Screen stamps, which, as the Margo Feiden Gallery (who represents Hirschfeld) told *Scott Stamp Monthly*, highly impressed Hirschfeld. These cards included the old versions of the Hirschfeld artwork.

The older designs and their differences from the stamps, as depicted on GTS telephone cards and by *cronaca filatelica*, are as follows:

Rudolph Valentino. The design of this stamp has been reworked and design ele-

Shown above is the Stars of the Silent Screen block as it actually appears. Bordering these pages are the telephone card designs that differ from the final version. Differences are described in the text.

ments have been moved. The garment on Valentino's right shoulder was reworked and changed to include what appears to be a "NINA." In addition, the name and value tablets have been moved. The denomination now obscures most of the reworked garment, and Valentino's name now reads up the left side.

Clara Bow. The design has been

reworked and design elements have been moved on this stamp as well. The scarf around Bow's neck has been redrawn on the finished stamp to include "NINA," and the word "Bow" has been moved to the far left of the design. The value tablet no longer intrudes as far into Bow's hat.

Charlie Chaplin. All design elements on this stamp are virtually the same as the early artwork, except that the "P" in Chaplin has been tilted in the final version.

Lon Chaney. No significant design changes could be found on this stamp.

John Gilbert. No significant design changes could be found on this stamp.

Zasu Pitts. Although the name and value tablets are in the same position as the early artwork, the design has been reworked to include "NINA." The name now appears in the garment on her right shoulder. It previously had been missing.

Harold Lloyd. The basic drawing of Lloyd appears to be the same, but the name and value tablets have been changed from the earlier artwork. Lloyd's name now reads upward at left, and the denomination has been moved to the lower-right corner.

Keystone Cops. Most of the design elements on this stamp appear to be unchanged. However, the original version showed a fifth Keystone Cop, partially visible behind the value tablet. This figure was removed from the final version.

Theda Bara. The basic design remains unchanged from the earlier version, but the hair draping over her right shoulder has been reworked to include the word "NINA."

Buster Keaton. No significant design changes could be found on this stamp.

At one time, prior to the release of the Stars of the Silent Screen Stamps, the spelling of Keystone Cops was hotly debated. It has since been confirmed by USPS, Margo Feiden Gallery and others that either the "C" or "K" spelling of "Cops" is acceptable, so there is no actual design error on either the stamps or telephone cards.

As with all telephone cards, the GTS stamp cards can be collected mint or used. Each card's personal identification number, or PIN, is revealed by scratching a small panel off the back of the card. The presence of this panel determines a mint card. As telephone calls are made, credit is automatically subtracted from the card's value, leaving the basic card available as a used collectible.

If you wish to contact GTS, please write to GTS, 342 Madison Ave., Suite 1034, New York, NY 10017, or call 1-800-929-4301.

The game will continue. As yet, we don't know who the other seven subjects of Hirschfeld's original 25 are, or when the stamps depicting them will be released. Including the Pickford and Negri stamp designs, nine more are possible, since only the Crosby design has been positively axed. One thing is sure: When these new designs do appear, collectors will no doubt rush to spot the "NINAs," and to compare the new stamps with early artwork. ❖

Unruly Indeed, *a book review*

by Stuart Morrissey

> And now, just what all stampdom has been waiting for: a new book written by a psychoanalyst that explains why we have the urge to collect.
>
> *Collecting: An Unruly Passion Psychological Perspectives*
>
> *by Dr. Werner Muensterberger*

Unruly indeed. Consider the following, according to Dr. Muensterberger:

◆ **As children we found support by cuddling a magical object, such as a teddy bear**. We were emotionally fragile youngsters.

◆ **We are control freaks**. We desire manageable companions. It's my way or the highway. And, our desire for completeness is developed out of a desire to control.

◆ **Collectors have a chronic longing for objects rather than people**. Our stamps offer assurance against the despair and loneliness that is a result of our childhood experiences.

◆ **Collecting is a means of undoing the strains and stresses of early life and achieving the promise of goodness. Our acquisitions help us cope with inner feelings of uncertainty.**

◆ **Our need for experts and certificates of authenticity is associated with a latent need for parental approval**. We are adult children looking for the blessing of an authority figure who will provide guidance and help eliminate conflicts. Experts assist us in diminishing guilt feelings that rise from self indulgence.

We are lucky that Dr. Muensterberger never attended a stamp show as part of his field work. Who knows what he may have concluded upon observing the swarms of vinyl briefcases girded by the standard two-inch metal bands around the middle, crumpled shirts with bulging pockets filled by wantlists and the sea of sweaters that button down the front?

Next, you find yourself on Dr. Muensterberger's overstuffed green couch, and the psychoanalyst is firing at close range. The first shot grazes you and the second bounces off the fat wantlist that rests in your shirt pocket directly over your heart. Then, Dr. Muensterberger rises from his chrome and leather Bauhaus-style chair and starts firing point blank. He manages to squeeze off a few direct hits.

◆ **Collectors have an unrelenting need, even hunger, for acquisitions.** There is no saturation point. A few hours after an enjoyable acquisition, the hunger returns. We cannot understand our consuming habit.

◆ **Nothing can express the inner experience of a collector when contemplating or acquiring a new object.**

◆ **Previous ownership or provenance is like a borrowed lineage or genealogy.**

◆ **A collector's possessions not only serve gratification needs, but also function for retaliatory purposes.**

Let's face it. Most collectors who enjoy the social aspect of the hobby love to duel in a friendly game of one-upmanship. Remember that imperforate plate number coil strip you purchased last month and how much fun it was to wave it in front of your buddy who also collects PNCs? Dr. Muensterberger is on to something here.

The line about experts is also fun, but I'd be careful the next time you buy or sell Canal Zone, Scott 2, with violet handstamped overprint. You may also want to exercise some care in what you tell your friend about his local cover that used to be owned by Count Ferrary.

The author takes time to track the collecting obsession back to ancient history. He asserts that the Romans, with their culture of war and conquest, loved battle for the sake of booty - especially art, which was systematically shipped back to Rome for re-sale to collectors. Even Caesar had people on the lookout for pieces to add to his cameo collection.

Several "psychobiographies" attempt to illustrate the author's theories. We are

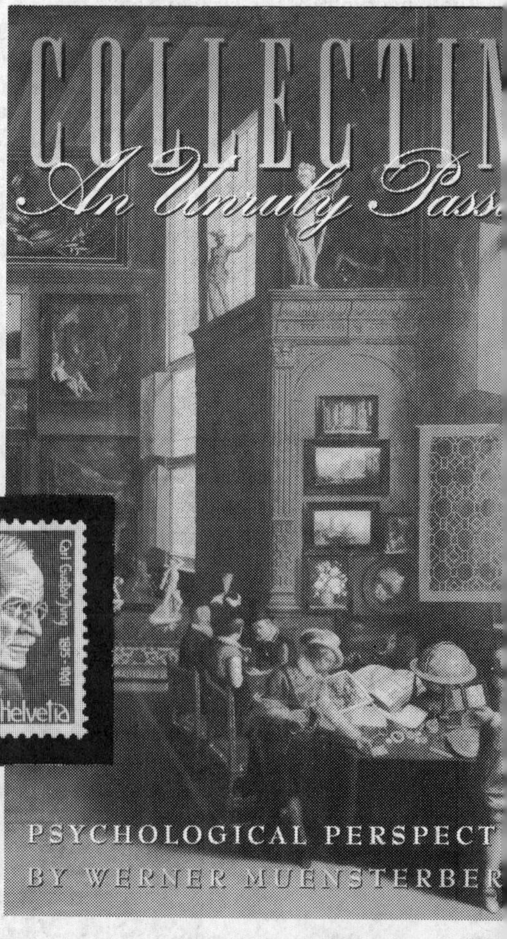

introduced to Balzac, the 19th-century French novelist, a hopeless collector of nearly anything and everything. Balzac is broke and his personal relationships doomed as a result of his exploits as a collector. The man was out-of-control.

Next we meet Hans Kraus, a famous British antiquarian book and manuscript collector/dealer. Apparently Kraus also has some problems balancing his collecting passion with the other elements of his life. He referred to his collection as "a mistress of another kind, softer and more exciting" than the real thing. Perhaps he realized that no matter how his passion for books messed up his life they were still relatively safe, as compared to taking on a mistress.

The author relates his experiences with a collecting friend that he refers to as Martin G. This individual loves to chase oriental antiques. We accompany Martin G. on his business trips to Hong Kong, where his main interest is treasure hunting among antique dealers. He gets so carried away at times that he promises himself to never make another acquisition. Yet, this obsessive friend, like a compulsive gambler who pledges he will never enter another casino, cannot make the leap of faith. Although Dr. Muensterberger refers to Martin G. as his friend, I wonder if it's not someone he seeks to revenge.

The problem with the psychobiographies, and most of the other theories in this book, is their similarity to Sigmund Freud's famous works. The concepts spring forth from the study of people who have serious problems. It's obvious that most stamp collectors have balanced lives, which, among other things, their hobby reinforces.

There are some folks who have taken collecting to excess. Maybe you even know a few. Friends tell me of one man who is a very successful stock broker who lives a bare bones lifestyle so he can compete at auction for U.S. rarities.

So what's the bottom line? Buy this book. You just can't find this much entertainment for your dollar anywhere else.

An Unruly Passion delivers like a serious movie that contains nonstop, unintentional laughter. It treats collecting with the same reverence as the routine about the boy who so eloquently describes all of the ink blobs in the Rorschach test and, upon leaving the psychologists office says, "hey doc, do you know where I can buy any of those dirty pictures?"

Victoria's Secret

INTERVIEW WITH DR. MUENSTERBERGER

◆ ***When were you first drawn to study collectors?*** I have been aware of them for many years.

◆ ***What fascinates you most about collectors?*** Irrelevant. Some people look for objects in shops, others seek artifacts in caves.

◆ ***Do you see any real differences between types of collectors? For example, are there any real differences between stamp collectors, coin collectors and people who accumulate teddy bears?*** Often there is an evolution. Someone begins collecting stamps and later collects porcelain. The important point is that someone has the inclination to collect.

◆ ***Have you ever collected anything?*** I have a big library, although I don't collect books. I am interested in Art History (Dr. Muensterberger also holds a Ph.D. in Art History), but I don't collect art either. However, I do believe I may be disposed to collecting.

◆ ***Do you have any hobbies or recreational pursuits?*** I own several dogs. I am a dog lover.

◆ ***I noticed you have a dog sitting beside you in the photo on the back flap of the book dust jacket.*** Yes, for a very important reason.

◆ ***And what was the reason?*** Victoria helped me write the book.

◆ ***Helped you write the book?*** Yes. As a matter of fact, I often recommend to my patients who are in psychoanalysis to get a dog.

◆ ***In your book you suggest that objects collectors own and seek are often a substitute for people. Can a dog or pet also be a substitute for people?*** Yes, indeed.

◆ ***Have you ever recommended to one of your patients to collect anything?*** Never. ❖

WOMEN BEHIND BARBED WIRE

BY GUSTAV POHLIG

Many civilians, women and children among them, were interned during World War II by the Axis Powers as well as the Allies. Some were members of the Templers, a religious group of Germans who had migrated to Palestine 130 years ago and who were taken to Australia in 1941 to live with their children in Tatura, a family camp. These children never saw a house, a car, a horse, or a cow before the age of 6. A family had only a small living area, and privacy was almost non-existent. Nisei families interned in the United States endured a similar fate.

Women, however, were not always kept in family camps. In many cases they were separated from their husbands for years, living in separate camps together with single women. The following covers are examples of mail written to or by women imprisoned during World War II.

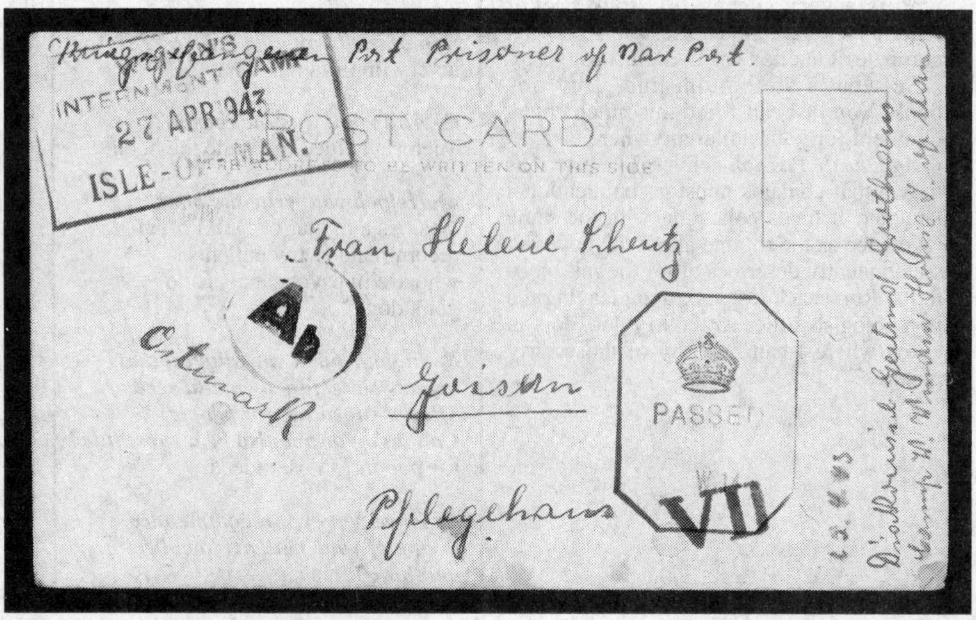

This post card was written in 1943 by a deaconess interned in Windsor House, Isle of Man, to a friend in Austria. She expresses hope that she will be discharged soon, as older deaconesses had been released already.

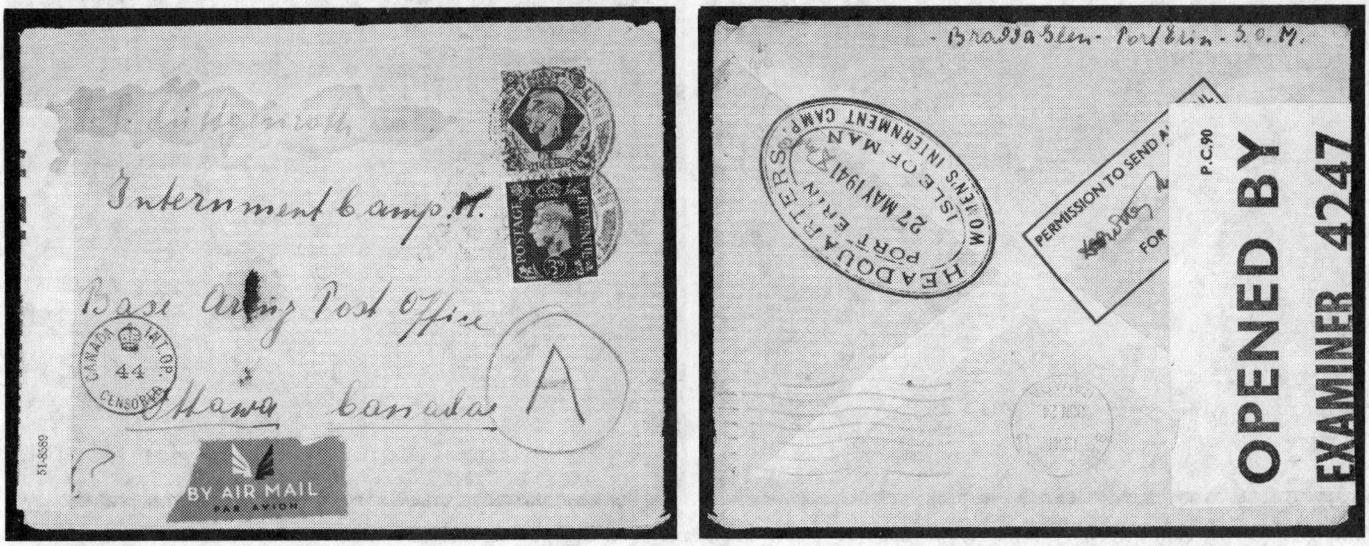

An envelope from an inmate of the women's camp in Port Erin, Isle of Man, to an internee in Camp A (Farnham) in Canada which held internees from October 1940 to July 1941. It shows a clear headquarter's stamp and a boxed permission to send air mail. The stamps paid for the air mail service.

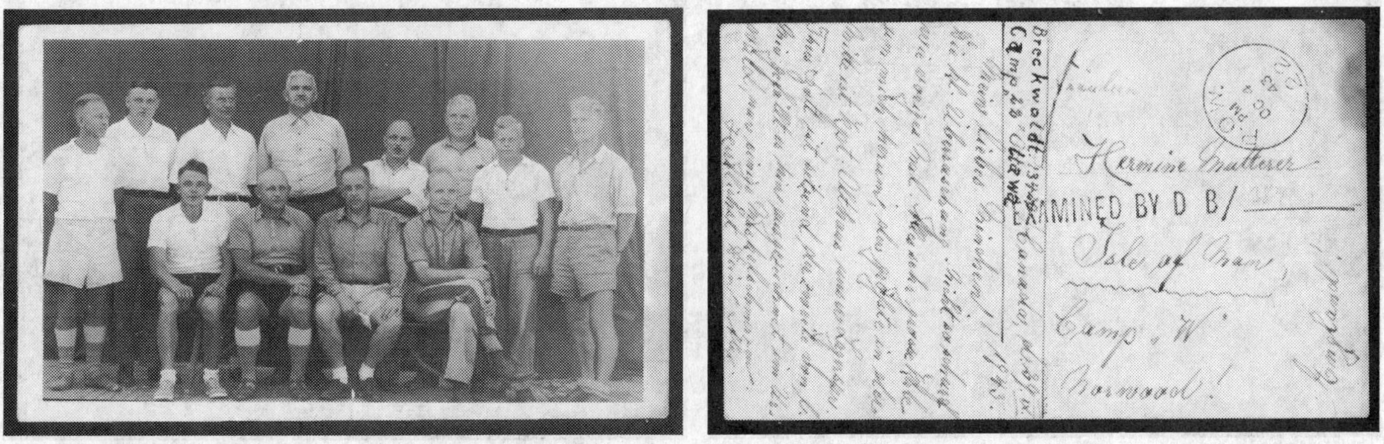

A photo card sent by a prisoner of war in Camp 22 (Mimico) in Canada to a woman in Camp W, Isle of Man. The photo shows the camp leader, Captain Olthaus, with men who probably were former members of the German merchant marine.

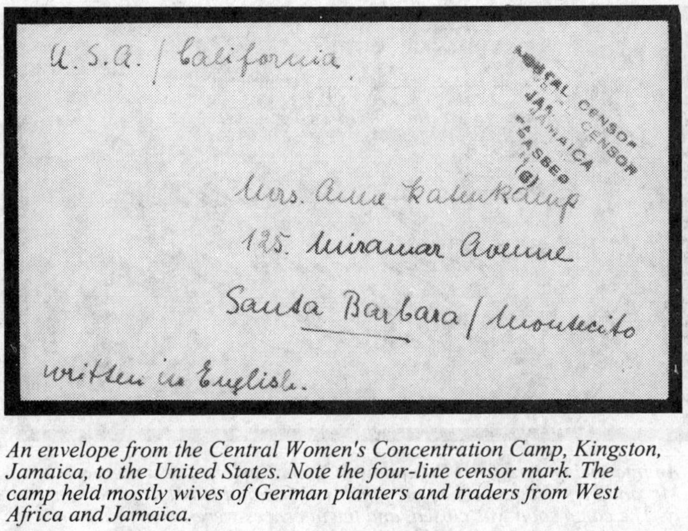

An envelope from the Central Women's Concentration Camp, Kingston, Jamaica, to the United States. Note the four-line censor mark. The camp held mostly wives of German planters and traders from West Africa and Jamaica.

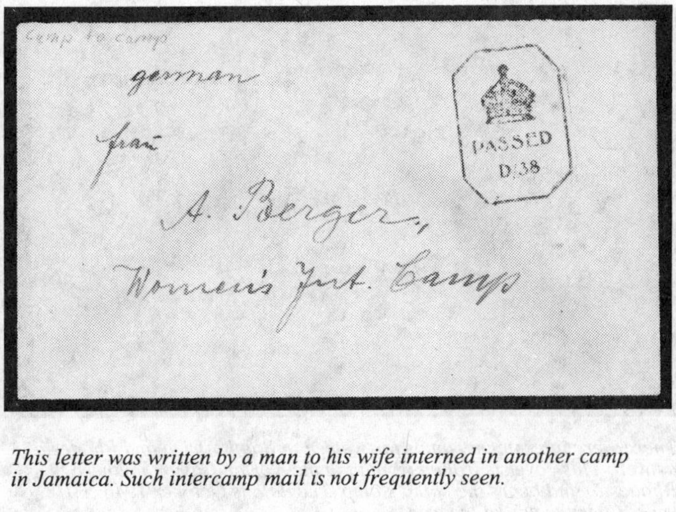

This letter was written by a man to his wife interned in another camp in Jamaica. Such intercamp mail is not frequently seen.

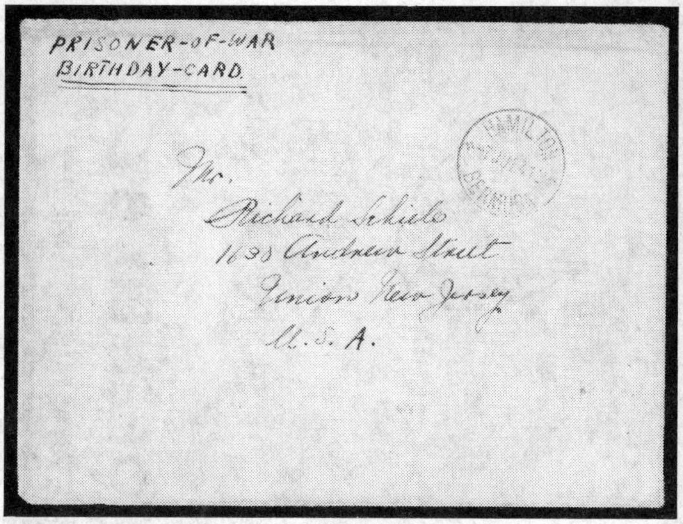

Although the writer calls herself a prisoner of war, she was actually in internee in St. George's Barracks, Bermuda.

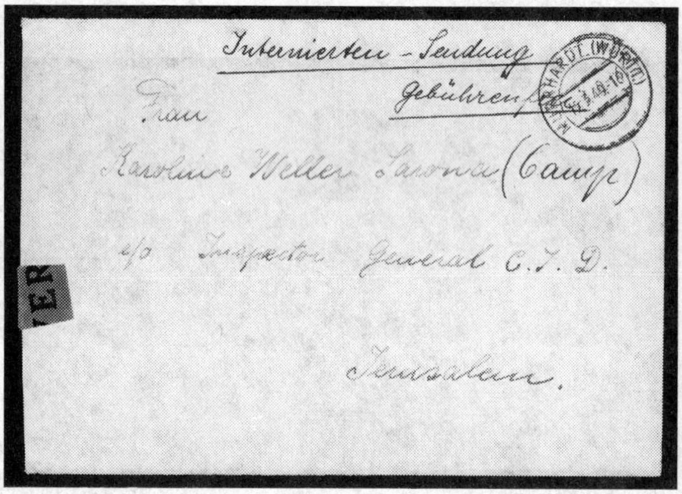

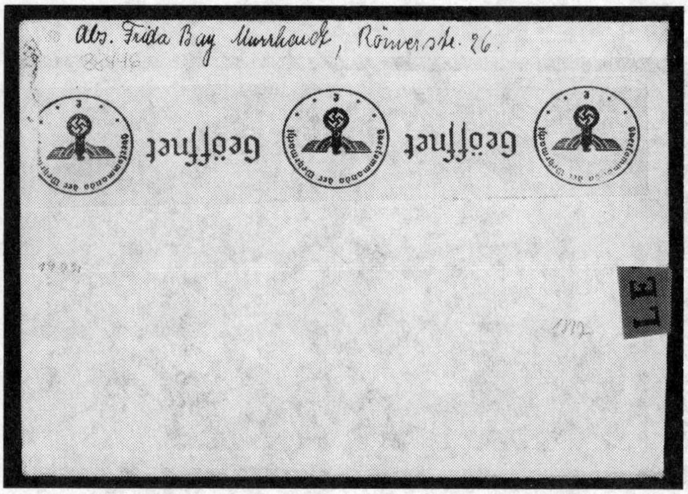

This envelope is addressed to a Templer in Sarona, Palestine. In the beginning of the war, the German settlements in Palestine were surrounded by barbed wire and so became internment camps. In August 1941, Templers were taken to Australia. The envelope shows the German censor tape.

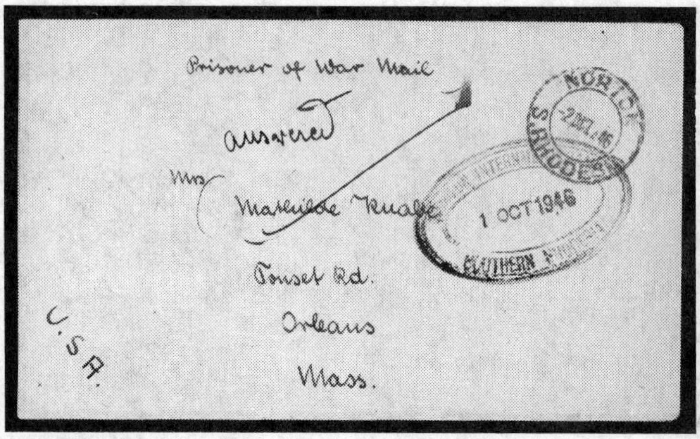

There were internment camps for women in South Africa and Rhodesia as well. This cover is from a woman in the Norton Camp, Southern Rhodesia, and bears the camp stamp. The date is October 1946, 1 1/2 years after the end of the war.

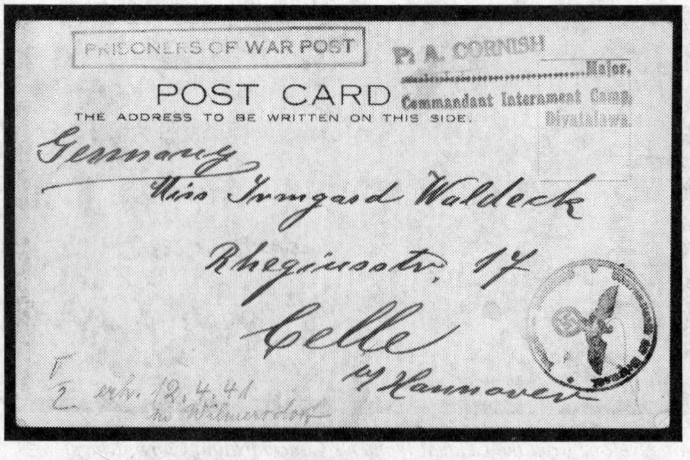

An interesting card from Diyatalawa Camp, Ceylon. The writers were Mr. and Mrs. Hagenbeck of the famous circus and Hamburg zoo family. The camp soon was closed, and the internees were taken first to Hazirabagh and then in 1942 to the family camp Satara in India.

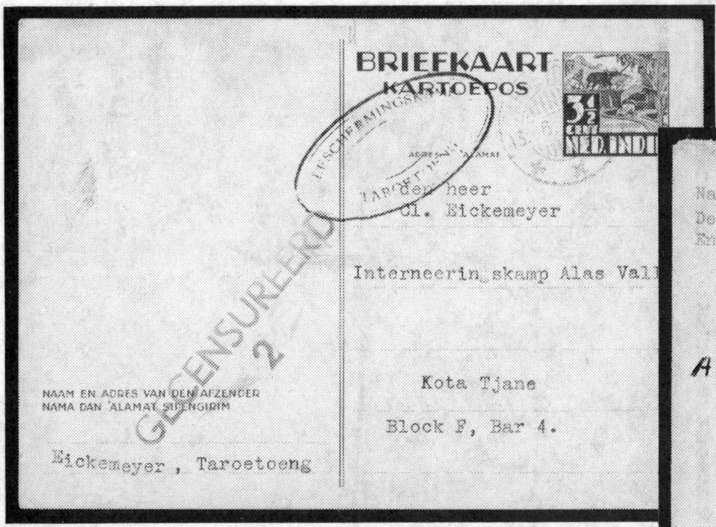

An example of a card from the Netherlands East Indies written by a wife to her husband interned in another camp. The interned Germans were taken to India in January of 1942. One of the three transport ships was sunk near Sumatra and 500 men died.

The United States interned Germans, Italians, and Nisei Americans. Fort Stanton was opened early in the war. The crew of the German liner Columbus was interned there. This cover bears a stamp which was not necessary, as internee mail was postage free. It is addressed to an organization that supplied prisoners of war and internees with sundries, cigarettes, and clothing. Some internees opted to become American citizens and eventually left the camp.

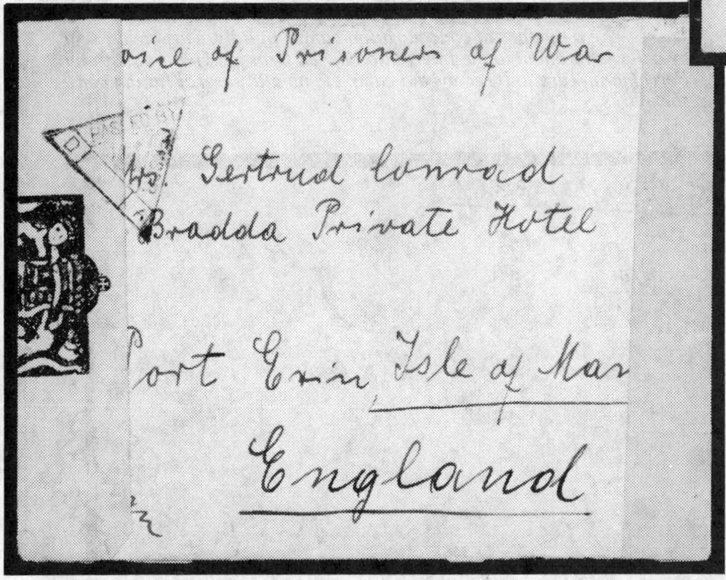

An envelope from a woman interned at the Yercaud Camp in India to a woman in one of the hotels in Port Erin, Isle of Man, which had been converted to house women internees. Yercaud was closed in 1942, and the inmates were sent to Purahandar and Satara. The triangular censor mark and the censor tape were applied in India.

Among the interned Jews were, of course, many women. This cover is from an inmate of Camp de Gurs in Southern France to a woman in the United States who helped numerous Jews. It was censored at the camp and received a censor tape applied in Bermuda. The fate of the sender is not known; many Jews from this camp were sent to German concentration camps, where they perished.

Cernauti in Romania was the seat of a concentration camp for Jews. While regular mail was postage free, the registration fee had to be paid by affixing a stamp. A censor mark is on the back of the cover, while the front bears a five-digit number applied by the International Red Cross.

There were a number of concentration camps in Italy. This cover, sent by a Jewish woman to the International Red Cross in Geneva, is from Ferramonti-Tarsia. It received a camp stamp and several Italian censor marks.

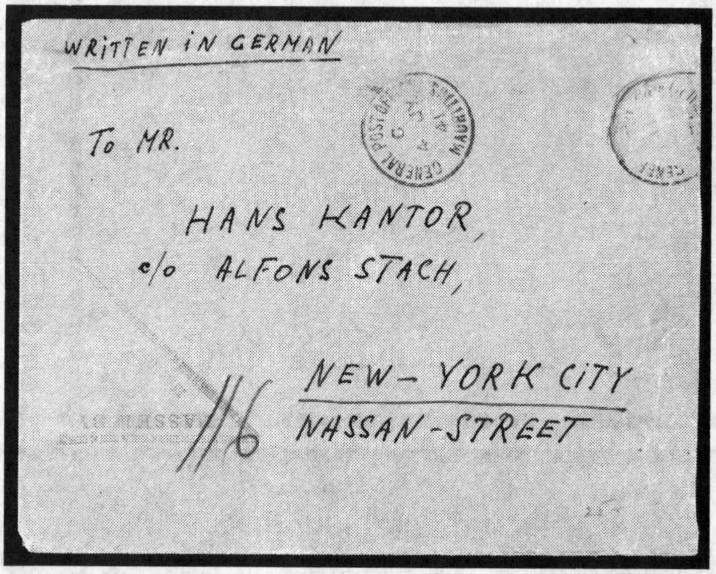

After the oil industry and powerful Arab interests prevented the landing in Palestine of ships carrying Jewish refugees from Europe, some were transported to Mauritius. There they desperately tried to migrate to other countries - mainly to North and South America, but they were not welcomed by governments there, either. This cover, showing a faint triangular Mauritius censor mark, was written by a Jewish woman to a Nassau Street address. At that time, Nassau Street was the center of the philatelic market in the United States.

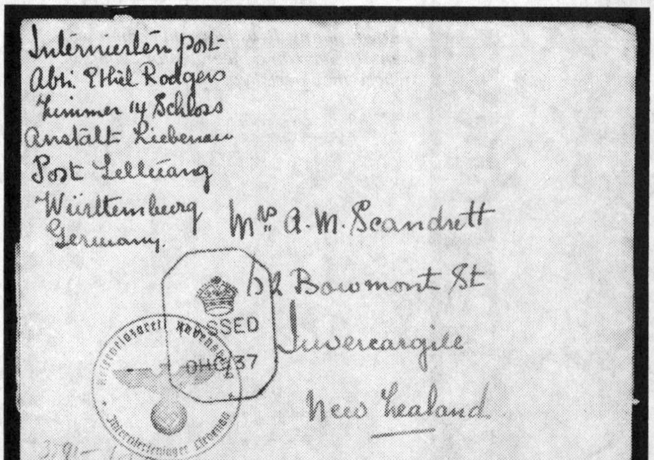

Some women from the British Empire were interned at the Liebenau castle, a former Catholic rest home in Southern Germany. The cover shows the round Liebenau stamp and the Bombay, India, censor mark. The Frankfurt censor tape (Riemer E-52) and the stamp (Riemer-3a) are on the back.

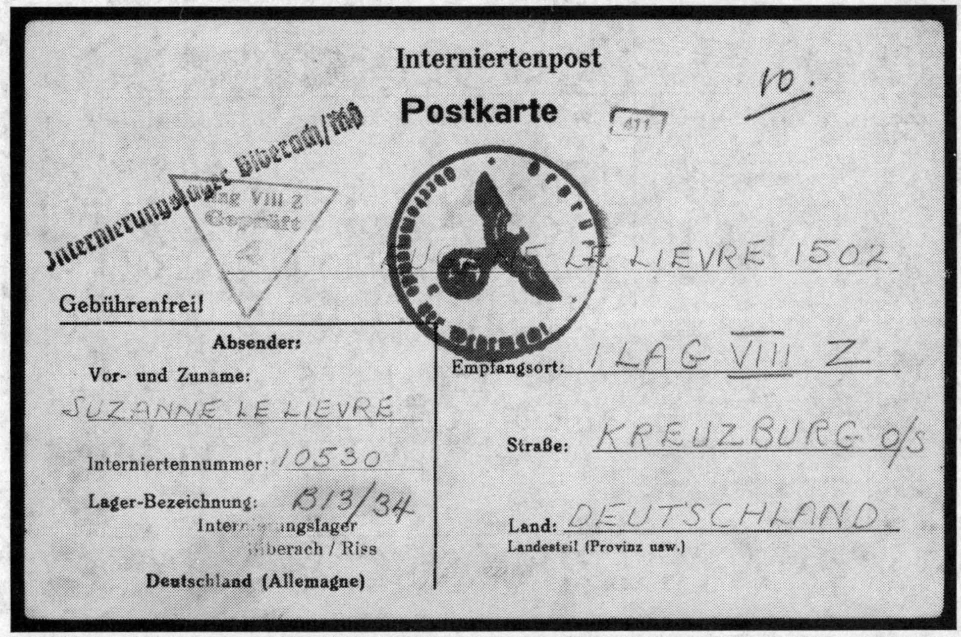

These covers are examples of intercamp mail, written by husbands to their wives or vice versa. Many inhabitants of the Channel Islands were sent to German internment camps after the occupation by the German army. Men and women were sometimes in separate camps - here in Compiegne, France, and Laufen, Biberach and Kreuzburg in Germany. Eventually, many families were reunited in Wurzach and Biberach in November 1942.

The card from Biberach to Kreuzburg shows the censor marks of both camps and the Frankfurt censor office. The card from Laufen to Compiegne bears the ILLag VII (Laufen) censor mark, while the letter from Compiegne to Laufen was censored in both camps.

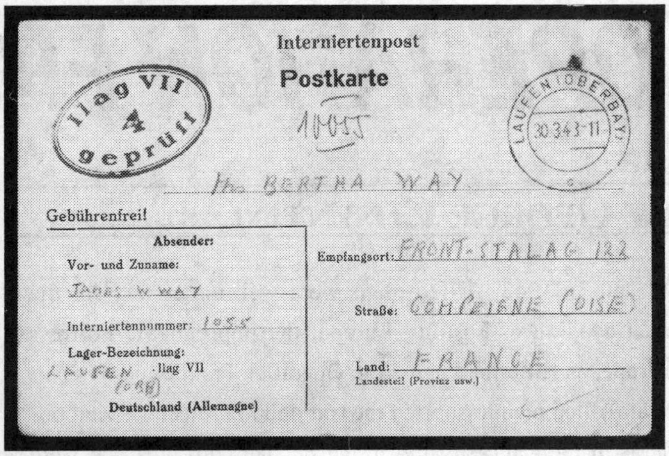

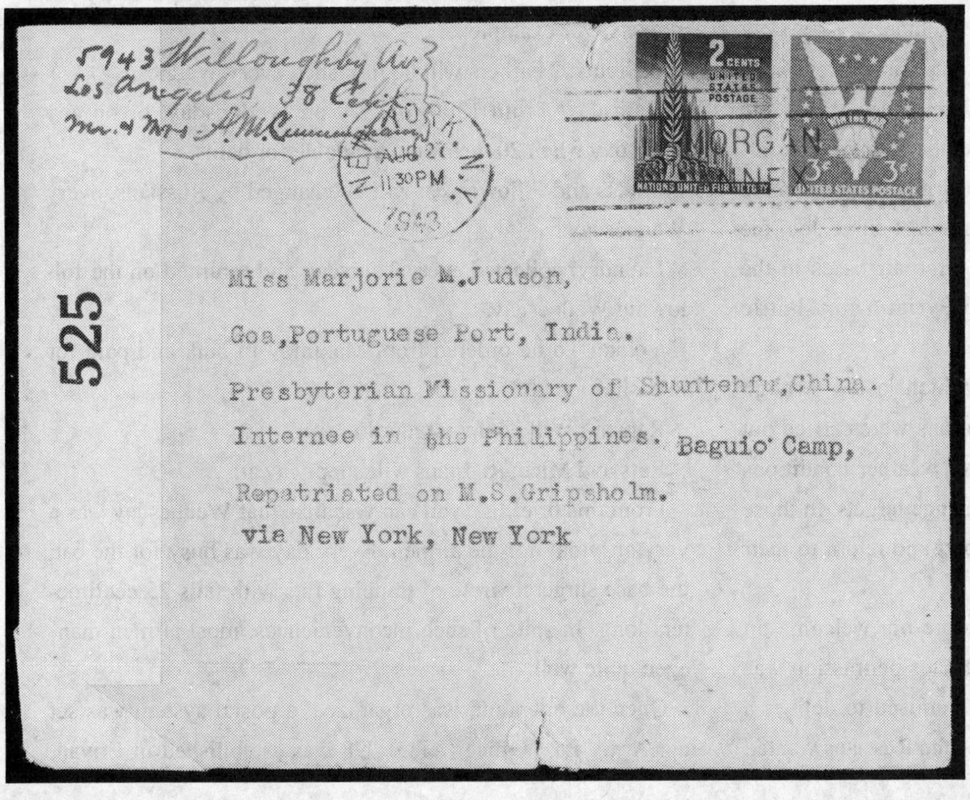

Women who were members of allied nations were interned by the Japanese. This cover is addressed to a missionary in China, interned in the Philippines and then evacuated on board the Swedish liner Gripsholm via Goa, Portuguese India.

The Author

Gustav Pohlig is a retired schoolteacher who specializes in POW covers and stationery. He has written other POW articles for the AP.

❖

For the Christmas Holidays of 1943, a card was printed in the Middle East, extolling the friendship between American and Russian soldiers. The card, which also gives a capsule description of the land, was posted at Ahwaz, Iran (APO 680) and cancelled in Teheran (APO 523)

OPERATION FRANTIC JOE

BY GEORGE COSENTINI

Late in 1943, Allied plans were well under way for the invasion of Festung Europa, the impregnable Fortress Europe, as Hitler had named it. Operation Frantic Joe was part of an Allied plan to shorten the war and to protect the vital oilfields in the Caucasus and in the Persian Gulf area that were being eyed hungrily by the German war machine.

Frantic Joe 1, the official name of the mission, later shortened to "Frantic," began June 2, 1944, with planes of the 15th Air Force taking off from Foggia, in Southern Italy. The targets to be bombed were in Romania, too far for the bombers to make their runs and return. Under Operation Frantic Joe, the B-17s, with their fighter escorts, used three air bases in the Soviet Union, Poltava, Mirgorod and Pyriatin for shuttle bombing runs.

"Frantic" included seven missions, which lasted through mid-September 1944. A few small scale runs were carried out at the request of the Russians when poor weather conditions prevented good bombing runs over long range targets. In those few instances the U.S. planes would depart and return to their temporary bases in the USSR.

Although foreign troops historically were not welcome on Russian soil, an exception was made. Perhaps permission was granted because the U.S. Military had promised to deliver a copy of the Norden bombsight, something the Russians wanted very badly.

No one knows what went on unofficially. Officially, under the "Frantic" arrangement, the Soviet Union limited the Allied air field support to approximately 1,000 men. When the first contingent of U.S. airmen arrived on site, they found airfields that had to be rebuilt, repaired or improvised. They also found a volume of restrictive rules and regulations imposed by the Soviets. For example:

Haircuts: 2 barbers will be furnished every Wednesday

Bath day: From 1300 to 1800 on Wednesday, or on any other day when 20 men were available for baths.

Sheets and Pillowcases: will be changed by Russians, every Wednesday.

Laundry: collected every Thursday and returned on the following Wednesday.

Vodka: To be ordered from Maximov in bulk and paid for in cash

Repairs: Will do upon request.

Rats and Mice: Russians will supply a cat....

From this brief list, you can visualize that Wednesday was a very busy day for the airmen. Every day was busy for the cat; the base surgeon wrote of trapping rats with tails 25 centimeters long. In spite of such inconveniences, most airmen managed quite well.

Once the operation was organized, a postal system was set up. Army Post Office (APO) 798 was estabilished in Erivan,

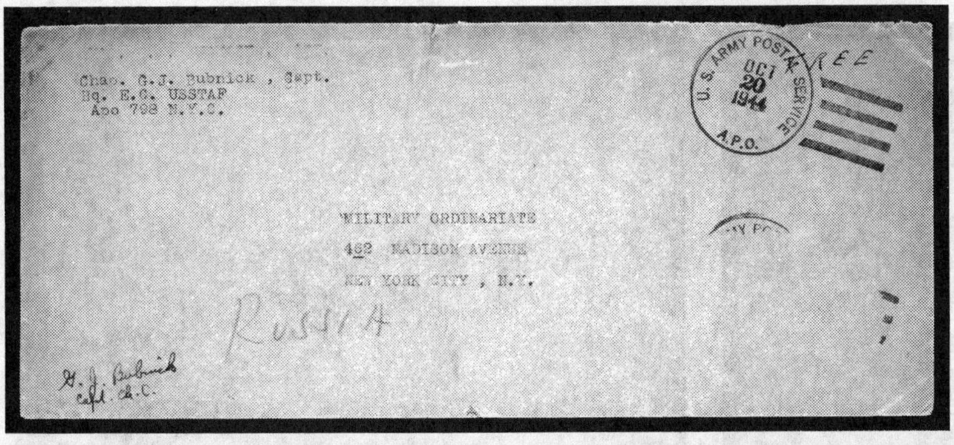

From the headquarters of the Eastern Command, U.S. Strategic Tactical Air Force Capt. G. J. Bubnick, Chaplain Corps, probably stayed behind with a skeleton crew of approximately 200 men assigned to the task of dismantling the bases. This is an example of the APO 798 cancel with the number removed from the circular date stamp.

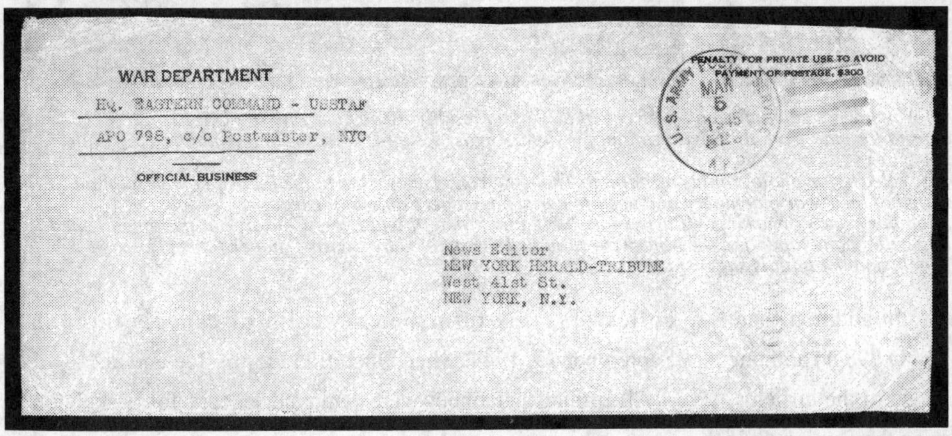

Another cover from the Eastern Command, U.S. Strategic Tactical Air Force, APO 798 (Erivan, USSR), bears a cancel from APO 523, Teheran, Iran, the headquarters of the Persian Gulf Command -- one of the many available routes for mail and supplies.

Posted and canceled at APO 824, Abadan, Iran, this cover is from an employee of the Douglas Aircraft Company. This location was a stepping stone for planes that were sent to the Soviet Union under their own power, rather than being shipped in crates.

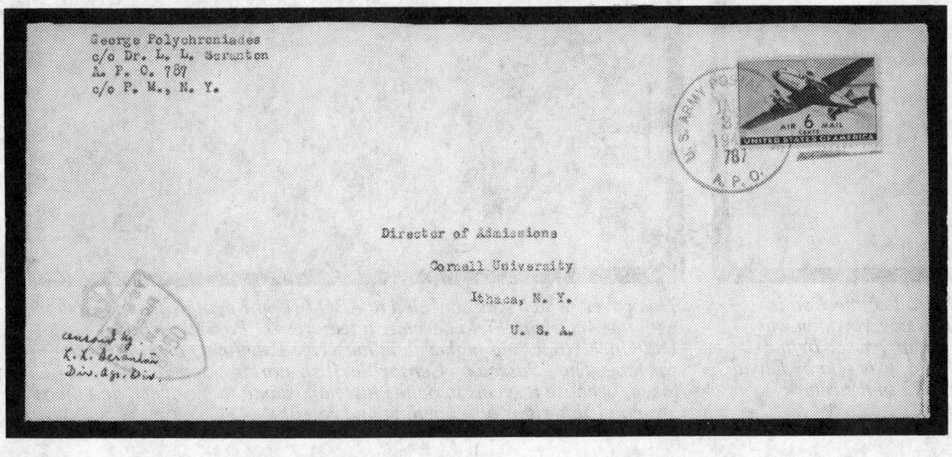

Although posted at an American APO, 787 in Cairo, Egypt, this cover bears no U.S. Censor marks. It was examined by L.L. Scranton, Director, Adjutant General Division, and validated with a British censor marking.

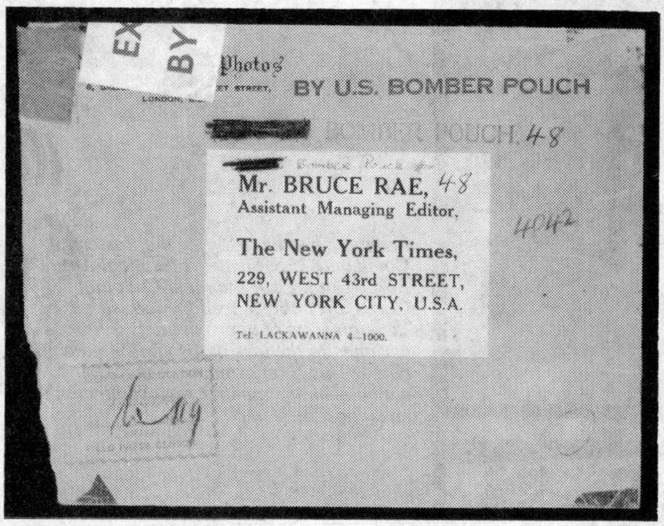

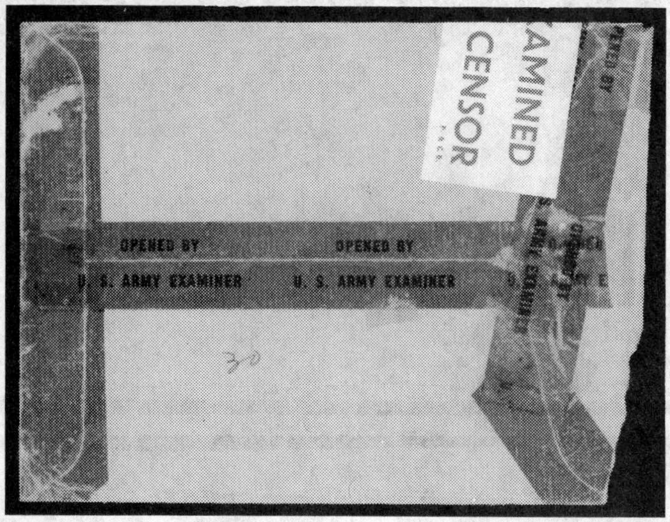

Military mail could take different routes, many of which were camouflaged by APOs, like 798, not readily associated with the USSR. Although this particular cover probably was not used for mail from the Soviet Union, the date, August 7, 1944, places it in the middle of Frantic 5, which lasted from August 6 to 8, 1944.
It is possible that this cover was used to mail press releases or photographs, or both, to The New York Times. Due to the lack of commercial and passenger aircraft, some of the bombers were gutted of their war machinery and used to carry passengers and vital cargo.
Featured on this cover are the scarce "By U.S. Bomber Pouch" marking; "Passed for Publication/Shaef/Field Press Censor," at the time located in London; "Opened by U.S. Examiner" resealing cellophane tape; and the otherwise standard "Examined by Censor" paper tape. The tape's color is unusual, orange instead of the normal black, and the initials suggest it is British.

USSR, during the first week in April 1944. In addition there were 2 detached offices, one at Mirgorod (APO 798-1) and one at Pyriatin (APO 798-2). Erivan was not close to the airfields, but it was close to the supply lines connecting the Persian Gulf Command in Teheran, Iran, and the locations in the Soviet Union to which the supplies were being sent.

I know of two types of cancels from APO 798: one has the APO number in the circular datestamp with a four bar killer, at times called a Flag cancel. Another type has no APO number. Theoretically all APO numbers were to be removed for security reasons. In due time, however, the numbers reappeared. For collectors, this furnished a wealth of cancels through September 19, 1944, when Operation Frantic Joe ended.

All ground personnel were removed, except for a skeleton crew, which remained behind to dismantle the facilities and ship the parts back to U.S. bases.

The Author

George Cosentini, a frequent contributor to the AP, is a hazardous materials specialist. He collects covers from Word War II to the present from all military services and says his main interest is APOs.

Another item of interest coming out of the USSR-Iran connection is double censoring by U.S. and British censors. This cover, which was canceled at APO 616 in Egypt, from a bomber group, passed by the U.S. Army Examiner and also by RAF Censor No. 8, was sent by David Westheimer of "Von Ryan Express" fame. APO 1222 in the return address was at the time in Ramat David, Palestine.

This cover, which was canceled at APO 616 in Egypt, is from a writer with the American Field Service. It features a "Passed by Base Examiner" (one step higher than the Army Examiner) and paper censor tape. The "Passed by Censor" British marking appears to be token, because it seems to be the last handstamp to be struck and there are no visible signs of reopening and resealing.

The complexity and the cooperation needed to handle the mails in and around the Persian Gulf Command area are illustrated by this cover. Canceled with APO 523 in Teheran, Iran, this cover features a variety of censor markings and standard U.S. resealing tape. Civilian mail, such as this, usually bypassed the lowest level of censorship, the Army Examiner, and went directly to the Base Officer. It was then opened and resealed by examiners of the "Anglo-Soviet-Persian" commission. My best guess is that this type of mail was censored both by the military and by the civilians. If anyone has any information on this commission, I would be very interested in receiving it.

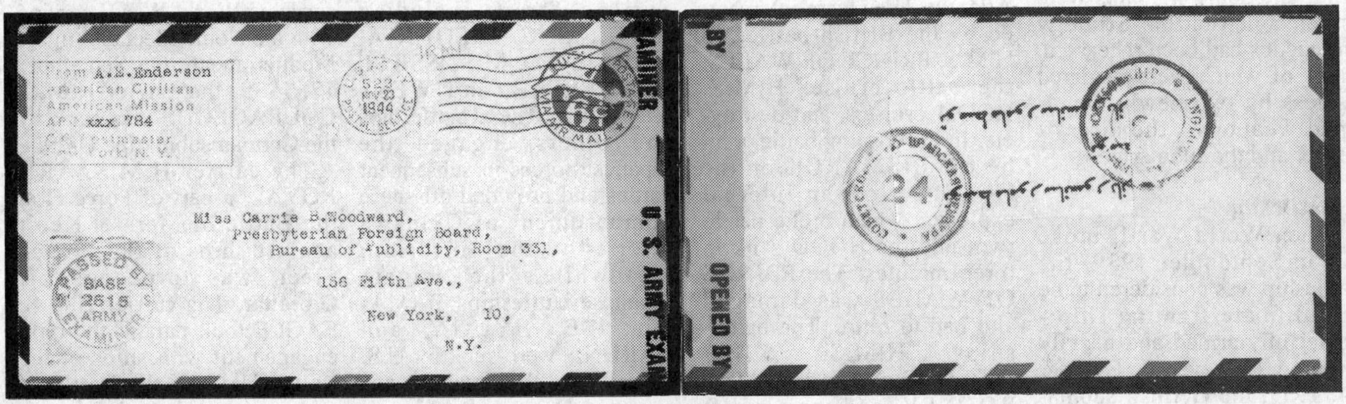

The message on the back of this cover, "Opened by the Censorship Agent," appears in Persian and in Russian. An equivalent message appears on the taped end of the cover.

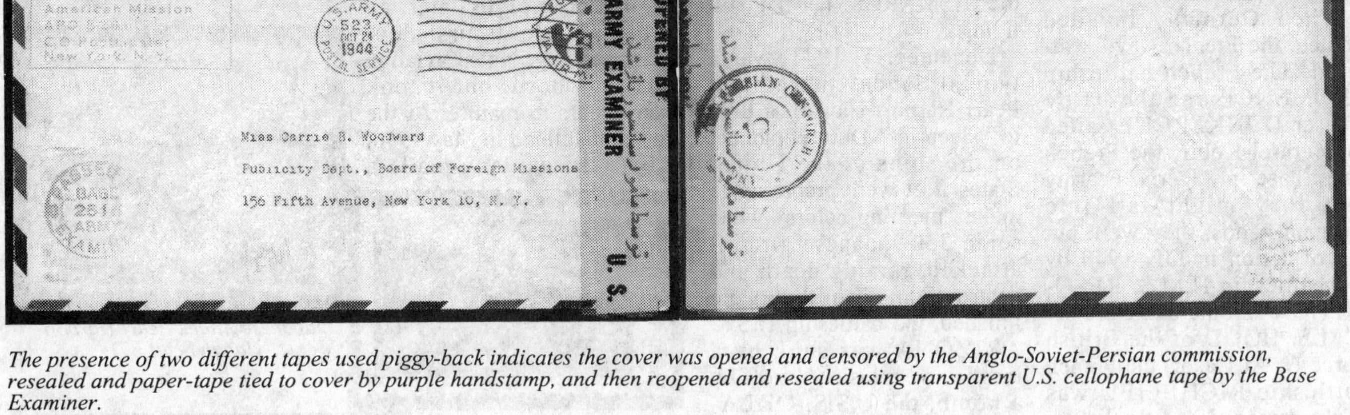

The presence of two different tapes used piggy-back indicates the cover was opened and censored by the Anglo-Soviet-Persian commission, resealed and paper-tape tied to cover by purple handstamp, and then reopened and resealed using transparent U.S. cellophane tape by the Base Examiner.

Acknowledgements.

While assembling the covers and researching the facts for this article, I had the good fortune to be in touch with several former U.S. Airmen who took part in Operation Frantic Joe. From them I received informations, clippings, copies and encouragement. My heartfelt thanks goes to Professor Peter Chelkowski, who kindly furnished the translation of the Persian handstamps and censor tapes. A tip of the hat also to the Historical Branch of the Air Force, which provided a roll of 16 mm film that contained most of the information for which I was looking. ❖

WARSHIPS OF WORLD WAR II

by William Coffey

At the outbreak of World War II, the navies of the world powers - France, Germany, Great Britain, Italy, Japan, and the United States - were at the peak of their power. Old warships had been modernized, many new ships had been built, and some warships were under construction. Strategy and tactics had been rehearsed, many of which were rendered useless by two newly developed weapons - the aircraft carrier and the submarine.

Battleships

When World War II broke out in September 1939, the battleship was considered to be the ultimate fighting ship - powerfully armed and heavily armored. However, on October 14, 1939, the German submarine (U-47) slipped through the mine field protecting the entrance to Scapa Flow, anchorage of the British Home Fleet in the Orkney Islands, and sank the battleship H.M.S. ROYAL OAK.

When Germany invaded France, the French Navy scattered. The French battleship PROVENCE and the battle cruiser DUNKERQUE sailed to Mers-el-Kebir, the French naval base in Algeria. Fearing that they might fall into German hands, they were put out of action in July 1940 by the battleship H.M.S. RESOLUTION and the battle cruiser H.M.S. HOOD of the British Force H. At Dakar, the French battleship RICHELIEU was badly damaged and the battleship LORRAINE was put out of action.

The British battleship WARSPITE engaged a number of Italian warships protecting a convoy. After a brief exchange of gunfire, the Italian ships fled to Taranto, the main base of the Italian navy's battlefleet. In the November 1940 Battle of Taranto, the Italian battleship CONTE DI CAVOUR was sunk.

The German battleship BISMARCK sailed from Gotenhaven in May 1941 accompanied by the cruiser PRINZ EUGIN, intending to join the German commerce raiders in the western Atlantic. They were intercepted by the British battleship H.M.S. PRINCE OF WALES, the battle cruiser H.M.S. HOOD, cruisers, and destroyers. In the ensuing battle, a hit by the BISMARCK on the HOOD set off an internal explosion which broke her in two, and the HOOD sank in three minutes. The PRINCE OF WALES was damaged and had to retire. The battleships H.M.S. KING GEORGE V and H.M.S. RODNEY, and the aircraft carrier H.M.S. ILLUSTRIOUS joined the fray; together they reduced the BISMARCK to a floating hulk. Torpedoes from the cruiser H.M.S. DORSETSHIRE finally sank the BISMARCK, her flag still flying.

December 7, 1941, was a typical Sunday morning at Pearl Harbor, Hawaii, a time to "sleep-in." Duty personnel on the ships of the United States fleet were preparing to make "morning colors" when some 350 Japanese aircraft attacked, raining death and destruction. When they were finished, the battleship U.S.S. ARIZONA was sunk by a magazine explosion set off by a bomb; the U.S.S. OKLAHOMA had capsized; and the U.S.S. WEST VIRGINIA and the U.S.S. CALIFORNIA were sitting upright on the bottom seriously damaged. The battleships U.S.S. MARYLAND, U.S.S. PENNSYLVANIA, and U.S.S. TENNESSEE were damaged, but were able to steam to the West Coast for repairs. The U.S.S. NEVADA was able to get under way, but was again heavily bombed and had to be beached.

Four new battleships, completed in 1941, took part in the early years of the Battle of the Pacific. The old battleships damaged at Pearl Harbor returned for the Battle of Surigao Strait, including the U.S.S. CALIFORNIA, MARYLAND, MISSISSIPPI, TENNESSEE, and WEST VIRGINIA. These battleships and others engaged the Japanese forces in subsequent battles and provided off-shore bombardment of Okinawa prior to the invasion. Meanwhile, the mighty Japanese battleships YAMATO, ISE, HYUGA, and HARUNA were sunk by U.S. aircraft, and the Japanese surrender was signed on board the battleship U.S.S. MISSOURI in Tokyo Bay.

The Aircraft Carrier

The first airplane took off from a ship in November 1910; two months later, an airplane made its first shipboard landing. Naval aviation was thus born, but it took many years to mature. At the Battle of Jutland in May 1916, a British seaplane made a reconnaissance flight, the first use of aircraft in a naval battle. Naval aviation grew up in the years between the wars, and matured during World War II.

At the outbreak of World War II, Great Britain had seven carriers, France had one, and Germany none. One of the British carriers, H.M.S. FURIOUS, had operated successfully in World War I, and she survived World War II serving with the Home Fleet and in the Mediterranean. On September 17, 1939, the carrier H.M.S. COURAGEOUS was sunk by the German submarine U-29.

The carrier H.M.S. ARK ROYAL, a part of Force H at the Battle of Mers-el Kebir against ships of the French Fleet, was torpedoed off Gibraltar. The carrier H.M.S. EAGLE took part in the only engagement with ships of the Italian Navy at the Battle of Calabria, while aircraft of H.M.S. ILLUSTRIOUS attacked Italian airfields on the island of Rhodes. H.M.S. INDOMITABLE went aground in the China Sea depriving Force Z of air cover;

Japanese Attack Pearl Harbor
(Japan Scott B7)

British Battleship
ROYAL OAK
(Marshall Islands Scott 240)

"Battleship Row"
in Pearl Harbor
(U.S.A. Scott 2559i)

U.S. Battleship MARYLAND (Kiribati Scott 612e)

U.S. Aircraft Carrier LEXINGTON (Marshall Islands Scott 309)

British Battlecruiser HOOD (Marshall Islands Scott 279)

U.S. Cruiser INDIANAPOLIS (Kiribati Scott 611c)

she later served in the Mediterranean.

The importance of the aircraft carrier as a combat ship was proved by the Japanese in the surprise attack on Pearl Harbor. Five Japanese carriers, including AKAGI and HIRYU, launched some 350 bomber, torpedo, and fighter planes 275 miles from Hawaii. Fortunately, the aircraft carriers U.S.S. LEXINGTON, U.S.S. SARATOGA, and U.S.S. WASP were not at Pearl Harbor. Suddenly the age-old primary strategy of "control of the sea" became "control of the air." In the Mediterranean the battle for control of the air was fought between enemy land-based and Allied carrier-based aircraft. On many occasions in the Pacific theater, it was a battle between carrier-based airplanes on both sides.

Task Groups in the Pacific were formed around aircraft carriers. The U.S.S. ENTERPRISE group attacked Kwajelein in the Marshall Islands, while the U.S.S. YORKTOWN group hit the Gilbert Islands. Rabaul was raided by the LEXINGTON and YORKTOWN, and other Japanese-held islands were also raided. On April 18, 1942, U.S.S. HORNET launched sixteen B-25 bombing planes on a daring bombing raid of Tokyo, Yokohama, Kobe, and Nagoya. The results were primarily psychological on both sides.

The Battle of Coral Sea was the world's first carrier air battle. A Japanese invasion force, including the carrier SHOHO, headed for Port Moresby, New Guinea, was intercepted by U.S. forces led by the U.S.S. YORKTOWN and the U.S.S. LEXINGTON. The opposing carriers never saw each other, and aircraft action ranged over a distance of 300 miles. The carrier SHOHO was sunk, another was damaged, and the Japanese invasion force was recalled. But the U.S. lost the LEXINGTON and two other ships.

The Battle of Midway was the turning point of the Pacific war. Almost the entire Japanese fleet set out to invade Midway Island, but a U.S. force, including three carriers, awaited them. In the ensuing air battle, the Japanese carriers AKAGI and HIRYU and the U.S.S. YORKTOWN were sunk. The Japanese invasion ships turned back.

So, the pattern of many Pacific island invasions - too numerous to detail here - included a Carrier Task Force Group to maintain control of the air. In the final thrust, the Carrier Fleet, now Admiral Halsey's Third Fleet, sank the new Japanese carrier AMAGI, and the Japanese battleships ISE, HYUGA, and HARUNA. The once mighty battleship had been superseded by the aircraft carrier.

The Cruiser

Like the battleship, the cruiser was a large, fast, powerful ship at the outbreak of World War II. While some cruisers served as the eyes of the fleet, many others were the spearhead of attacks on enemy ships.

The first engagement of warships in World War II occurred in the South Atlantic where the German ADMIRAL GRAF SPEE was preying upon commercial shipping. The GRAF SPEE was built within the World War I tonnage limits of a heavy cruiser, but she was so heavily armed that she was called a "pocket battleship." On December 13, 1939, the British heavy cruiser H.M.S. EXETER, the light cruiser H.M.S. AJAX, and the New Zealand cruiser ACHILLES intercepted the GRAF SPEE off the River Plate. All ships suffered severe damage in the engagement, and the GRAF SPEE ran for the neutral port of Montevideo to make repairs, she sailed down the river and was scuttled by her crew in the estuary rather than face the large British fleet she erroneously thought was awaiting.

When the Italian fleet, including the heavy cruisers TRENTO and TRIESTE, sortied to intercept a convoy, they were met by British ships including the light cruiser H.M.A.S. PERTH (ex-H.M.S. AMPHION) in the Battle of Matapan. The heavy cruiser H.M.A.S. CANBERRA helped sink the German ship COBURG, but she was in turn sunk in the Battle of Savo Island.

In the sinking of the BISMARCK, the heavy cruisers H.M.S. SUFFOLK and H.M.S. NORFOLK shadowed the BISMARCK until engagement; the cruiser H.M.S. SHEFFIELD took part, and the H.M.S. DORSETSHIRE sank the BISMARCK with torpedoes. The Russian cruiser CHERVONAYA UKRAINA was sunk by an aerial bomb at Sevastopole.

In the Pacific theater, the heavy cruiser U.S.S. ST. LOUIS was the first ship to get under way after the attack on Pearl Harbor. She downed three Japanese airplanes, sank a Japanese midget submarine, and took part in the Battle of Kula Bay against eight Japanese destroyers.

The light cruiser U.S.S. NEW ORLEANS took part in the Battle of Tassafaronga, and the heavy cruiser U.S.S. QUINCY was sunk in the Battle of Savo Islands. The heavy cruiser U.S.S. INDIANAPOLIS delivered the atom bomb to Tinian Island in the Marianas, and four days later while enroute to Leyte, she was torpedoed and sunk. The oldest ship at Pearl Harbor, the de-commissioned U.S.S. BALTIMORE, built in 1888, was not damaged.

During the Allied campaign in Norway, the French cruiser EMILE BERTIN, which had joined the Axis forces, was bombed. The Australian cruiser H.M.S. AUSTRALIA participated in the operation at Dakar, and took part in the Battle of Coral Sea and many landings in the Pacific. She survived five "kamikaze" attacks, and the war.

The last old-fashioned naval battle occurred in March 1943 off the Komandorski Islands when a Japanese convoy escorted by four cruisers and four destroyers headed for the Aleutians was intercepted by an American force of two cruisers and four destroyers. The two battle lines fired at each other until they ran out of ammunition; the cruiser U.S.S. SALT LAKE CITY, a U.S. destroyer, and a Japanese cruiser were damaged. The Japanese force turned back, and this was the last such battle.

In August 1942, the heavy cruiser U.S.S. AUGUSTA carried President Franklin D. Roosevelt to a meeting with British Prime Minister Winston Churchill in Placentia Bay, Newfoundland.

The Destroyer

The destroyer at the beginning of World War II had come a long way from the first torpedo boat built to launch the

Japanese Destroyer ARASHIO (Marshall Islands Scott 331)

U.S. Patrol Boat PT-109 (Guyana Scott 2708b)

first torpedo. Initially called "torpedo boat destroyer," the name was shortened to "destroyer." The invention of the steam turbine gave the destroyer a speed of up to 45 knots. Armed with torpedo tubes, two 5-inch guns, and depth charges, the destroyer was the principle defense against U-boats. Some were fitted as mine-layers, and others were employed as high-speed troop transports.

In the first month of World War II (September 1939), the British destroyers H.M.S. FIREDRAKE, H.M.S. FOXHOUND, and H.M.S. FAULKNOR sank the German submarine U-39 off the Hebrides; this was Germany's first U-boat loss.

The Canadian destroyer H.M.C.S. SAGUENAY took part in a joint Canadian-British convoy escort operation, the beginning of the battle of the Atlantic. Germany's initial strategy was the interdiction of food supplies and war materials to Great Britain. Convoys were escorted by destroyers, frigates, sloops, and corvettes; in the Mediterranean, heavier ships were also used. The first U.S. ship to be lost in World War II was the destroyer U.S.S. REUBEN JAMES while escorting a convoy.

Many destroyers took part in the Norway invasion. The Norwegian destroyer SLEIPNER was bombed, but captured two ships. H.M.S. COSSACK was hit by enemy shellfire and set afire; she was beached on enemy-held ground, the fire was extinguished, and she was subsequently rescued to take part in the sinking of the BISMARCK.

Other destroyers taking part in the Norway invasion were the Polish BLYSKAWICA, H.M.S. FORESTER, H.M.S. GREYHOUND, H.M.S. HESPERUS, the sloop H.M.S. AUCKLAND (which was later sunk off Torbruk) and H.M.S. PELICAN.

During the evacuation of troops at Dunkirk when 338,226 troops were removed in eight days under heavy aerial attack, H.M.S. GALLANT and H.M.S. GREYHOUND were put out of action; the Polish BLYSKAWICA took the GREYHOUND in tow. H.M.S. ACTIVE and H.M.S. FOXHOUND took part in the Battle of Mers-el-Kebir, while the French sloop SAVORGNAN DE BRAZZA was captured by the British and turned over to the Free French forces.

In September 1940, President Roosevelt loaned Great Britain 50 destroyers (4-stackers) and ten Coast Guard cutters on a Lend-Lease Agreement in exchange for a 99-year lease on certain British military bases. These ships were placed in convoy escort service, and included the destroyers H.M.S. GEORGETOWN (ex-U.S.S. MADDOX), H.M.S. BUSTON (ex-U.S.S EDWARDS), H.M.S. ROCKINGHAM (ex-U.S.S. SWASEY), and H.M.S. BANIFF (ex-Coast Guard cutter U.S.C.G. SARANAC).

Of the destroyers at Pearl Harbor on December 7, 1941, the U.S.S. CASSIN and the U.S.S. DOWNS were hit and blew up. The U.S.S. SHAW was badly damaged but later repaired, and the U.S.S. WARD destroyed one of the Japanese midget submarines.

Submarines

In World War I, there was a question of the morality of using the submarine against merchant ships, and Germany discontinued the practice. However, in World War II, there were no such compunctions. German U-boats (a shortened term for unterseeboot) were highly successful against Allied convoys until a sufficient number of escort craft and aircraft could be placed in service. These eventually overcame the threat of U-boats against convoys. Nevertheless, the submarine was always a deadly menace to surface ships, and were often more efficient than gunfire.On September 17, 1939, the captured Polish submarine ORZEL, navigating instruments and charts having been confiscated by the Germans, made a dash for freedom and succeeded in joining the British Fleet. She subsequently torpedoed a German troop transport off Norway, and sank a German mine layer, but was reported lost in June 1940.

German submarine U-47 sank the British battleship H.M.S. ROYAL OAK at Scapa Flow, and U-30 mistook the passenger ship ATHENIA as a troop transport ship and sank her without warning with a great loss of life. The destroyer U.S.S. REUBEN JAMES was sunk by U-552 or U-562 (accounts differ). The design of the Marshall Islands stamp (Scott 286) is in error since the U-boat was on the surface when she fired the torpedo that sank the REUBEN JAMES.

When the French surrendered to the Germans, the submarine SURCOUF, then the largest in the world, fled to Great Britain. She took part in the expedition to secure St. Pierre and Miquelon Islands for the Free French, but was lost in 1942. The Turkish submarine SAKARYA, as the U.S.S. BOARFISH, made four patrols in the South Pacific from December 1944 to August 1945.

It has been said that if the Germans had had more submarines they might have won World War II. Unquestionably the loss of lives and materials to submarines is appalling.

Amphibious Vessels

The landing of invasion troops on an enemy-held beach was not new, but it was brought to a high degree of efficiency during World War II. Several specially-designed watercraft were developed and put into service.

The attack transport (APA), such as the ARTHUR H. MIDDLETON, was the largest of the amphibious craft. She transported invasion troops, landing craft (LCVP) carried the troops to the beach. Another large ship was the Landing Ship Tank (LST) which carried tanks and trucks; her bow was driven hard on the beach and the vehicles were driven through the bow doors and over a ramp onto the beach.

The DUKW was about the size of a LCVP, and had four wheels so that it could be driven onto the beach as a land vehicle. Amphibious warfare was costly in lives, but it was the only way to retake enemy-held territory.

Miscellaneous Craft

The Motor Torpedo Boats are represented by PT-41 and PT-109. The latter became famous when she attacked Japanese destroyers of the "Tokyo Express." Commanded by Lt. John F. Kennedy (later to become U.S. President), PT-109 was rammed

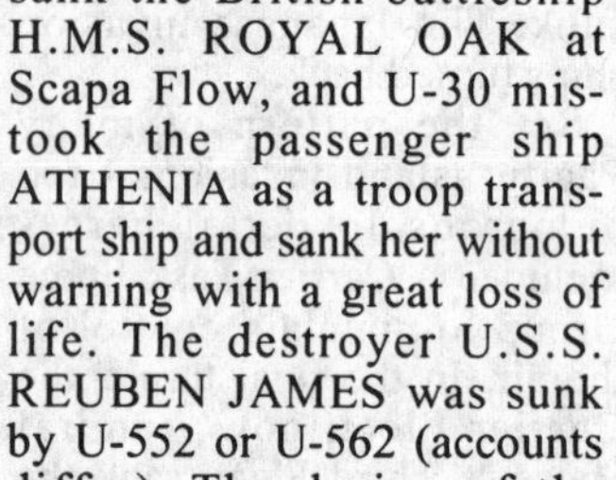

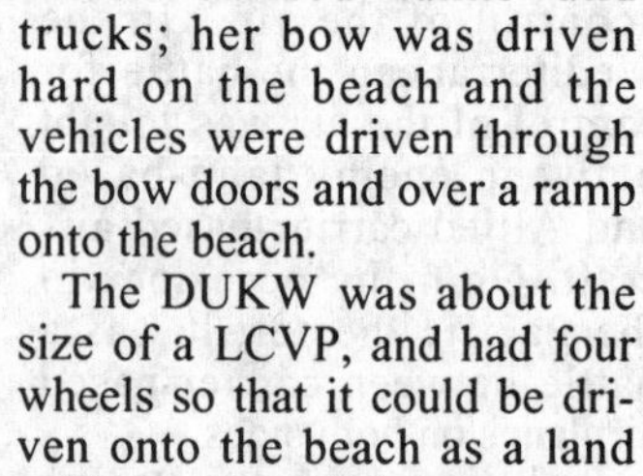

U-Boat and Submarine Officer (Germany Scott B218 & B260)

German U-Boat in the Atlantic (Guyana Scott 2708h)

U.S. DUKW Lands in Sicily (U.S. Scott 2765e)

and cut in two by the Japanese destroyer AMAGIRI. PT-41, under the command of John D. Bukeley, USN, evacuated General Douglas MacArthur, Mrs. MacArthur, Philippine president Quezon, his wife, and many others from Corregidor when the Japanese invaded the Philippines.

The numerous non-combatant support ships of the U.S. Navy are known as the Fleet Auxiliaries or "The Train;" many are depicted on stamps. The seaplane tender U.S.S. AVOCET (AVP 4), built as a mine-sweeper in 1918, survived the attack on Pearl Harbor. The old repair ship U.S.S. VESTAL, once the collier ERIE, was tied up alongside U.S.S. ARIZONA; VESTAL was hit by two bombs and was beached. The oiler U.S.S. NEOSHO was not hit at Pearl Harbor, and got under way only to be sunk at the Battle of Coral Sea.

Many troop ships are depicted on stamps. The British LADY OF MAN, MANX MAID, and the New Zealand DOMINION MONARCH were converted passenger ships. The troopships H.M.S. STRATHAIRD and H.M.S. BATORY (also ex-passenger ships) evacuated troops at Dunkirk.

As we bring this to a close, we realize that many warships and auxiliary craft have not been mentioned. Many more warships will probably be depicted on stamps issued in the coming year for the 50th anniversary of the invasion of Normandy.

Much research remains to be done in this field. Those having personal information on ships or naval actions should communicate with the editor of Watercraft Philately, Robert Tessier, P.O. Box 23092, Washington, DC 20026; he is authoring a serialized chronological account of naval actions and the ships involved in World War II. Information on joining the ATA Ships on Stamp Unit may be obtained from Unit Secretary Robert P. Stuckert, 2750 Highway 21 East, Point Lick, KY 40461.

Many conclusions can be drawn from World War II. While the battleship was useful on numerous occasions because of its firepower, it eventually became apparent that the battleship was obsolete. Airplanes from carriers engaged the enemy several hundred miles away far more effectively than direct ship firepower. Witness the destruction at Pearl Harbor by the Japanese aircraft from carriers, the Battle of Coral Sea, and the Battle of Midway. The old concept of naval warfare changed greatly. Considering the astronomical losses on both sides, the ultimate conclusion is that it must never happen again. ❖

U.S. Landing Craft Infantry (LCI) (Maldive Islands Scott 1440)

References

Wallace B. Black and Jean F. Blashfield, Battle of the Atlantic, Crestwood House, New York, 1991.

Peter Bolton, Collect Ships on Stamps, Stanley Gibbons Publications, London, England, 1993.

James C. Fahey, The Ships and Aircraft of the U.S. Fleet, Annapolis, Maryland (War Edition 1941, 8th Edition 1966).

Ernest A. McKay, Undersea Terror: U-Boat Wolf Packs in World War II, Julian Messner, New York, 1962.

Samuel Eliot Morison, The Two-Ocean War: A Short History of the United States Navy in the Second World War, Little Brown and Company, Boston, 1963.

Helmet Pemsel, A History of War at Sea, Annapolis, Maryland, 1978.

Jack Sweetman, American Naval History: An Illustrated Chronology, Annapolis, Maryland, 1984.

Robert L. Tessier, "Naval Events of World War II," Watercraft Philately, March-April 1991 to the present.

About the Author:

William A. Coffey, a retired commander of the U.S. Naval Reserves, was on active duty at the Naval Training Station in Norfolk, Virginia, when the Japanese attacked Pearl Harbor. He served briefly as beachmaster on the attack transport U.S.S. McCRACKEN (APA 198), and spent the final year of the war as personnel officer on the staff of the Amphibious Administration Command on Guam. He is author of the five volume Historical Sketches of Watercraft on Stamps. His mailing address is 3613 Kanawha Avenue, S.E., Charleston WV 25304.

World War II Germany: Hitler's proving ground for propaganda stamps

by Brian Baur

Shortly after his ascension to the Chancellorship of Germany in 1933, Adolf Hitler had a set of 31 definitive stamps produced featuring the profile of President Paul von Hindenburg (Scott 415-431).

Taken from a set of seven stamps issued in 1932 (Scott 391-397), and a 1933 set of 14 (Scott 400-414), to honor von Hindenburg on his 85th birthday, the new set was an omen. Watermarked into the paper the stamps were printed on was the soon to be universal symbol of hate, the swastika.

Hitler quickly discovered the potential power of the postage stamp not only to persuade, but to illicit sympathy, pride, unification of thought and, most importantly, fear.

In 1934, Hitler began to showcase the intentions of the Third Reich via the postage stamp. On June 30 he had a set of four stamps issued in remembrance of the lost colonies of Germany, Scott 432-435. He followed this up with two stamps released August 26 to mark the Saar plebiscite, Scott 444-445, which called for an immediate return of the Saar to Germany. The 6pf stamp depicts an allegory titled "Saar belongs to Germany."

The Third Reich celebrated the return of the Saar Jan. 16, 1935, with a set of four stamps that portrayed a Mother representing allegorical Germania, hugging a child representing the returning Saar, Scott 448-451. As with most stamps of the period these, too, were printed on swastika-watermarked paper.

In these pre-war years, Hitler also used the postage stamp to acclimate his people to his ideologies and methods. In 1935 he released sets honoring German war heroes, Scott 452-453; The Hitler Youth Movement, Scott 463-464; The 1935 Nazi Congress at Nuremberg, Scott 465-466; and a set commemorating the 12th anniversary of the first Munich Beer Hall Putsch of November 1923, Scott 467-468. These stamps showed a Nazi soldier and swastika flag.

The next year saw the release of a set of two stamps commemorating the 1936 Nazi Congress, which featured a crowd of German citizens giving the new straight-arm Nazi salute to a huge white swastika, Scott 479-480. This was followed by a set of two stamps honoring the "Reich Air Protection League," Scott 481-483.

The year 1937 also saw the first postal portrayal of Hitler himself, who chose to have released April 13, a semi-postal souvenir sheet of four perforate 6pf stamps depicting him, Scott B102, to commemorate his 48th birthday. The sheet was re-released a little more than a week later in imperforate form for the German International Philatelic Exhibition, Scott B104. The surtax on the semi-postals were ostensibly earmarked for Hitler's "National Culture fund."

Hitler evidently became enamored with honoring himself on his birthday, and did so regularly on semi-postals until the 1944 stamp, Scott B271, which was the last German face-different wartime stamp featuring Hitler. It marked his 55th birthday.

The year 1938 was a busy propaganda year for German stamps. It opened Jan. 28 with a set of two semi-postals commemorating the fifth anniversary of the assumption of power by the Nazis (Scott B116-B117).

April 1938 was a month of celebration in Germany. The obligatory Hitler birthday stamp, Scott B118, was released, as was a set of two stamps that featured an identical design, but with different perforation and design sizes. The stamps, Scott 484-485, which show a German and Austrian youth marching united under the Nazi flag, celebrated the annexation of Austria.

Aside from the Sept. 1 release of the 1938 version of the annual Nazi Congress semi-postal, which featured a portrait of the Fuhrer (Scott B120), Germany also celebrated the long-awaited return of the Sudetenland to the Reich with a set of two stamps featuring a Sudeten couple, Scott 132-133. The couple, carrying tools, is shown walking back into Germany.

German dictator Adolf Hitler was the first of a number of dictators to discover the value and power of postage stamps as propaganda tools. The stamps in the following pages are all referred to in the text. Most are obvious propaganda, some are not. The Hindenberg profile stamp, below right, was from Hitler's first propaganda set. It is printed on swastika-watermarked paper.

These two stamps, Germany 444 and 449, are typical examples of Hitler propaganda. The stamp at left, released before the Saar was returned to Germany, translates to "Saar belongs to Germany." The stamp at right shows the happy reunion of Mother Gemania and the Saar child. The grim reality of the reunion was no cause for celebration.

As 1939 opened and the German War Machine geared up for its blitzkrieg of worldwide terror, Hitler's annual birthday semi-postal was issued April 13 (Scott B137), followed by a single semi-postal featuring the Fuhrer and honoring the "Day of National Labor," Scott B140.

The last pre-war stamp was also a semi-postal, Scott B147, issued Aug. 25, 1939, to commemorate the annual Nazi Congress that tied up any loose ends in regard to what was to take place in September.

After the invasion of Poland in the beginning of September 1939, Germany celebrated the unification of Danzig with the Reich with a set of two stamps depicting St. Mary's church and the Krantor building in Danzig, Scott 492-493. The stamps were released Sept. 18, 1939.

In July 1940, a set of two semi-postals, Scott B174-B175, commemorated the return of Eupen-Malmedy to the Reich. The stamps featured views of those areas.

On Jan. 30, 1941, Germany marked, with a single semi-postal stamp, the agreements made between Hitler and Italy's Benito Mussolini which culminated in the Rome-Berlin Axis. That issue, Scott B189, portrays both the Fuhrer and Duce, and their respective fascist symbols. Italy also marked the occasion by releasing its own set of 6 stamps of the two Hitler-facing-Mussolini designs, Scott 413-418.

As the war escalated in Europe during 1941, Hitler ordered a new series of regular postage stamps produced in various denominations, all featuring his profile, Scott 506-527 and 529. He also, of course, continued his annual birthday semi-postals, Scott B190, and took the opportunity to boast of his annexation of Styria and Carinthia with a set of four semi-postals released Sept. 29, 1941, Scott B194-B197.

Aside from the stamps glorifying his existence and subjugation of other lands, Hitler commemorated, in August 1942, his hold over his own people with the single stamp honoring his Storm Troopers, Scott 528.

As the tide of the war began to turn in favor of the Allies, the semi-postal stamps of Germany began to show the traces of panic that must have been evident in Berlin at that time.

Hitler began Jan. 26, 1943, by commemorating the 10th anniversary of the Nazi rise to power, with a single stamp depicting the Brandenburg Gate and the swastika, Scott B216. Incidentally, another semi-postal released the same day, Scott B217, was issued specifically for use in obtaining philatelic cancels. These cancels were another form of propaganda.

On March 12, a series of 12 stamps was released, depicting German military might in the forms of paratroopers, submarines, grenade assaults, tanks, motorized marksmen and heavy artillery, Scott B218-B229.

As the bad news from the various fronts came back to Berlin in 1943, Hitler began to scour the country for younger and younger soldiers to wage his war and express undying allegiance to him. He commemorated this blind obedience with a single March 26, 1943, semi-postal stamp, Scott B230, showing two children and the Nazi flag on the "Day of Youth Obligation," when all children were required to swear an oath of allegiance to Hitler.

For his 54th birthday in April 1943, Hitler honored himself with a series of six semi-postal stamps (Scott B231-B236) featuring his profile instead of the usual one stamp.

On June 26, 1943, the Fuhrer had a set of four semi-postals, Scott B237-B240, issued showing the importance of the "Reich Labor Service Corpsmen" in the war effort. In an effort to keep his people working, the stamps depicted various laborers toiling for the final victory.

By the end of 1943 and the beginning of 1944, Hitler was back to commemorating the old days, beginning with a single stamp marking the 20th anniversary of the 1923 putsch, Scott B250. The stamp, released Nov. 5, 1943, featured a Nazi crusader and the legend "And Despite All, You Were Victorious." On Jan. 29, 1944, a single stamp commemorating the 11th year of Nazi power in Germany was released, Scott B252.

In February 1945, with the Red Army closing in on Berlin, a last-ditch stamp depicting the "People's Army" of Prussia and their proclamation to fight and repel the Russians was issued, Scott B291.

April of 1945 was absent its usual Hitler birthday tribute, but the 12th anniversary of the Nazi assumption of power was remembered with a set of two stamps depicting a Storm Trooper and an Elite Storm Trooper, Scott B292-B293. These two stamps were on sale for only a very short time, as the Allies marched into Berlin to end the terror.

Although Hitler considered Benito Mussolini to be the father of fascism in the 1930s and 1940s, it was Hitler who discovered how to effectively use the postage stamp for the purpose of showcasing himself and his exploits, as well as controlling the thinking of his own people. The stamps also served the purpose of instilling fear in the people of other nations. Since many of the stamps were semi-postals, they also served the useful function of raising additional money.

These days, unfortunately, it is a common sight to see dictators' faces and their vainglorious exploits plastered on the postage of the lands they subjugate. This is just one more stubborn legacy of Adolf Hitler that persists. ❖

WORLD WAR II ANNIVERSARY SHEETLETS

by Daniel Keren

One of the most popular topical stamps in recent years has been a series of sheetlets commemorating the 50th Anniversary of various aspects of the Second World War. These postage stamps have been issued by the United States Postal Service, Palau (a U.S. administered U.N. Trust Territory in the Western Pacific) and a number of small British Commonwealth nations.

Most American stamp collectors are quite familiar with the five-year program initiated in 1991 by the United States Postal Service. Each year until 1995, which will commemorate the 50th anniversary of the American-led Allied victories over Germany and Japan, the United States will release a sheetlet of ten stamps with a central border portion with an additional decorative design.

In stamp collector polls both the 1991 and 1992 issues were voted the "Most Significant" issues of the year. In addition, the 1991 sheetlet was also voted most attractive U.S. stamp issue of that year.

What appears to be happening is that these stamp issues are cutting across generational borders. There are many tens of thousands of WWII veterans who are still alive, healthy and they are purchasing these stamps as mementos of their younger years when they went through hell to preserve liberty and freedom from the threat of the Axis Powers.

Also, the children of those Americans who went to war, the so-called Baby Boomers have come into their own professionally and they too are fascinated by all the television documentary programs and books that are coming out now to recall America's participation in the war. It is interesting to note that France and Great Britain have not issued significant stamp issues for the 50th Anniversary of the Second World War. The War was a turning point in their national histories, one which saw the rapid decline of their once mighty colonial empires.

Even the grandchildren of those who fought in the Second World War are interested in the 50th Anniversary stamps being issued by the United States and other nations.

The Inter-Governmental Philatelic Cooperation of New York, which represents a number of foreign postal administrations around the world, decided to suggest to a number of countries they work with the concept of issuing similar sheetlets of postage stamps to mark the 50th Anniversary of America's participation in World War II.

Nine nations opted to take part in the first installment of the IGPC orchestrated 50th Anniversary of World War II Stamp Collection. Those stamps focused on 1991 being the 50th Anniversary of the historic Japanese sneak attack on Pearl Harbor, an event which forced America into the global war and was to be a major turning point in 20th Century history.

Among the British Commonwealth nations that along with Palau issued World War II Anniversary sheetlets in 1991 were Antigua and Barbuda ("Wreckage of the U.S.S. Arizona"), Guyana ("Target: Pearl Harbor"), Maldives ("American Leaders of the Pacific Theater"), St. Vincent ("Congressional Medal of Honor Recipients of Pearl Harbor"), St. Vincent Grenadines ("Position of U.S. Ships on Dec.7th"), Sierra Leone ("Aerial Attack on Pearl Harbor"), Tanzania ("British Role in the Pacific Theatre of War"), and Uganda ("From Pearl Harbor to Midway"). Palau's sheetlet also detailed "The Pacific Theatre of War".

What was probably most interesting in that program was that the Turks and Caicos Islands was originally supposed to issue the sheetlet on The British Role in the Pacific Theatre that was eventually issued by Tanzania. However, the Turks and Caicos is a British crown colony and as such, their stamp program must be approved by the British Foreign Office in London.

The British Foreign Office flat-out refused to present the stamp designs to Her Majesty, Queen Elizabeth II for her approval. They felt for sure that the Queen would object to such stamps showing such British defeats as the fall of Malaya, Hong Kong, Singapore and the sinking of a couple of important British naval ships. Tanzania, an independent

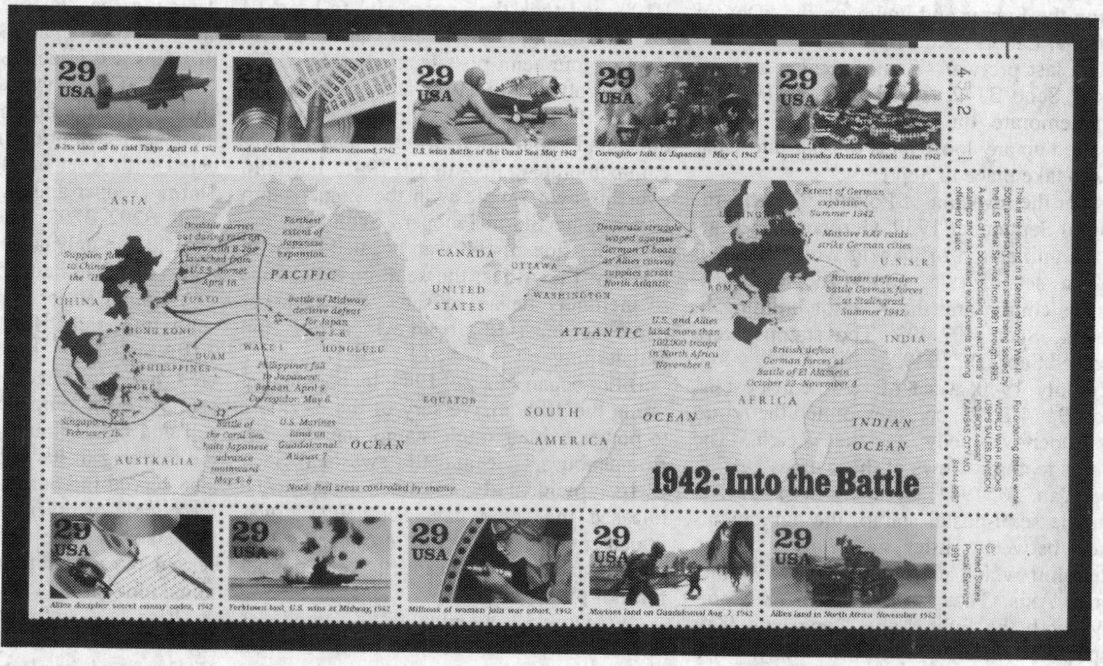

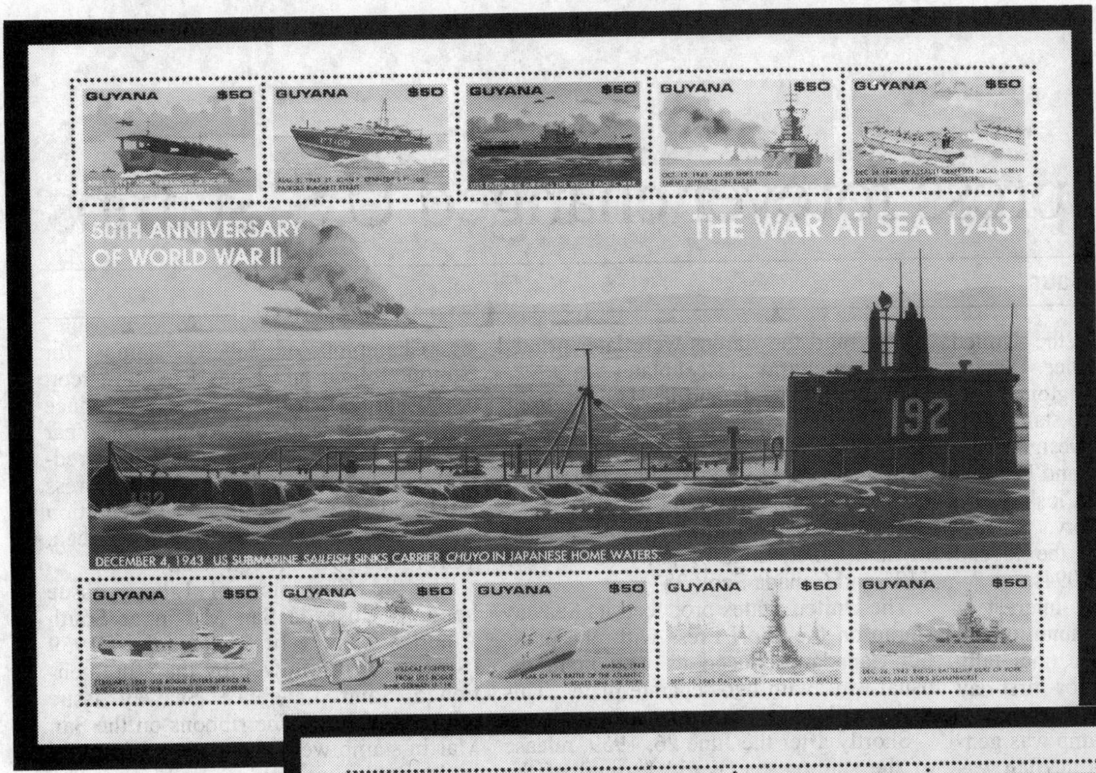

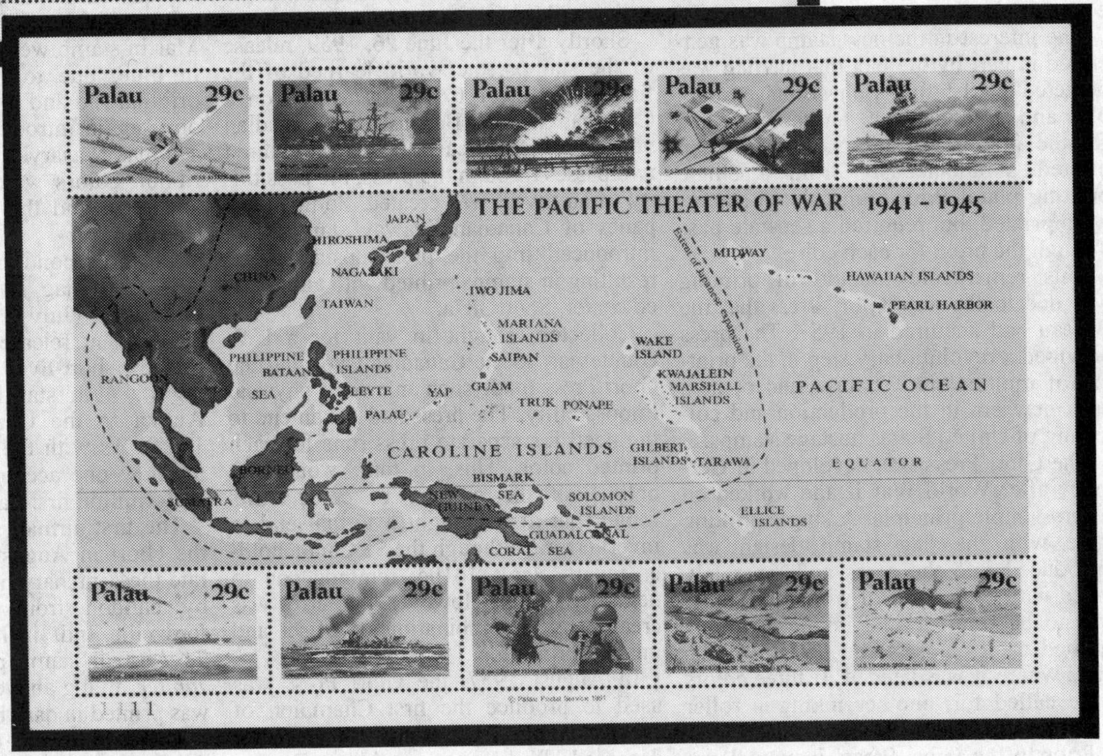

nation that did not need to get the Queen's permission, was offered the issue and decided to join the Omnibus. Sales for the entire Nine-Nation Pearl Harbor Stamp Collection has proven to be quite strong.

In 1992, just five nations joined the U.S. in issuing World War II Anniversary sheetlets. They were Niuafo'ou ("Newspaper Headlines of World War II"), Palau ("Aviation Powers of the Pacific Theater"), Gambia ("From Pearl Harbor to Midway"), Solomon Islands ("50th Anniversary/ Battle of Guadalcanal") & Tonga ("The Pacific Theater").

In 1993, only two countries joined the U.S.A. in issuing 50th Anniversary sheetlets - Guyana and Palau. Guyana issued two sheetlets for the year 1943. One recalled major Air battles and the second highlighted important sea engagements in both the Pacific and Atlantic. Palau's third sheetlet is titled "The Turning Tide in the Pacific" and notes America's taking command of the fight against Japan.

In 1994, more nations issued anniversary sheetlets insofar as the important 50th Anniversary of the D-Day Invasion of Normandy was celebrated. And, of course, 1995 will recall the final months of Allied victories against the Axis Powers, culminating in the surrender of Japan aboard the U.S.S. Missouri in Tokyo Bay. Excitement for stamps honoring those American victories will no doubt reflect back on the entire program. Now is the time for the collector to fill the empty spaces in their topical albums before some of these sheetlets become difficult to find.

The Giori press forever changed U.S. stamps

by Brian C. Baur

On July 4, 1957, the United States Post Office Department in Washington, D.C., released a 4¢ commemorative stamp featuring the American flag. Designed by veteran Bureau of Engraving and Printing stamp designer Victor S. McCloskey, Jr., the stamp featured Old Glory, proudly unfurled in the breeze, and the legend "Long May It Wave" (Scott 1094).

The stamp prompted great interest in both the stamp collecting community and the general public. When the final tally was in, 523,879 requests for first-day covers had been serviced.

The interest in the new stamp was generated in part by the fact that the flag was depicted in the full, rich colors of dark blue and deep carmine. These colors had for the first time on U.S. stamps, been printed simultaneously from a single printing plate! Prior multicolored stamps were printed, but required a separate pass through the press for each color.

This remarkable method of printing was due to the new Giori Press that the Bureau had acquired in 1957. The press provided a revolutionary step in the printing of multicolored stamps, and opened up a new era in the production and collecting of United States postage stamps.

The Giori Press was developed in Germany after World War II and worked on a very simple principle. A single printing plate with the flag stamp design was introduced into the press and separately inked with each color of which the stamp was to be printed. The inking-in rollers applied each color to the portion of the plate where it was needed. If three colors were called for, another inking-in roller could be added to the setup.

Prior to the Giori Press' inaugural run in 1957, the largest multicolor set of U.S. stamps was the Overrun Nations series of 1943-44 (Scott 909-921). Bi-colored stamps had been produced as singles, and as part of the Washington-Franklin, 1922 series and 1938 Presidential series. Each required two passes through the press. To produce these overrun nations stamps, a combination of lithography and steel engraving had to be used. Since the presses at the Bureau of Engraving and Printing were not equipped to handle the printing, the job was contracted out to the American Bank Note Co. of New York. There the flags were first printed by lithography and the frames were later printed from line-engraved steel plates.

In 1959, Canada and the United States jointly issued a stamp to mark the opening of the Saint Lawrence Seaway. Both nations were to issue stamps in red and dark blue colors, utilizing the same basic design of maple leaf and eagle enclosed in intertwined rings of unity (U.S. Scott 1131 and Canada Scott 387).

The United States produced its Seaway stamp on the Giori Press with one plate, but Canada produced its version in the usual way, with two separate plates. This action had major consequences.

Shortly after the June 26, 1959, release of the stamps, the world learned of the first major error to be discovered on a Canadian stamp. Because the Canadian version of the Seaway Stamp required two passes through the press, the possibility of an invert was created. Some of the panes of Canadian Seaway stamp were introduced into the press upside down, resulting in stamps printed with an inverted center, Scott 387a.

Collectors sought in vain for a U.S. counterpart to the Canadian error, but the Giori Press made such an error a physical impossibility. The press had put an end to the need for separate press runs for each printed color. This, in turn, would not only limit the number of color shifts found, but also brought a virtual end to invert errors, although the $1 Candleholder invert, Scott 1610c, reminds one to never say never. However, that error was created by a combination of offset and intaglio printing.

In August 1957, the Giori Press was used to produce the first Champion of Liberty stamp honoring the recently deceased Philippine president Ramon Magsaysay (Scott 1096). For the first time the new press printed in three colors, carmine, ultramarine and ocher. The same colors and process would be used in producing the 8¢ values for the entire Champions of Liberty series, Scott 1111, 1118, 1125, 1137, 1148, 1160, 1166, 1169 and 1175.

The last Giori printing of 1957 occurred in November, when the Bureau produced a 3¢ Wildlife Conservation stamp depicting whooping cranes in blue, ocher and green, Scott 1098.

During 1958, the Giori was only called upon on four occasions. Aside from the 8¢ Champion of Liberty stamps for Simon Bolivar and Lajos Kossuth (Scott 1111 and 1118), it was used to produce the 3¢ International Geophysical Year issue in May, printed in black and red-orange (Scott 1107). In October, the press produced the 4¢ Forest Conservation issue, depicting a forest scene in green, yellow and brown (Scott 1122).

The 8¢ Champion of Liberty issue honoring Jose de San Martin of South America was the first Giori job of 1959 (Scott 1126), followed by the aforementioned Saint Lawrence Seaway issue released in June. The ribbons on the San Martin stamp were changed to print only in blue, due to inking problems. The original red and blue ribbon colors were once again introduced in 1960, with the Thomas Masaryk issue, Scott 1148. The ribbon colors were reversed (now blue and red), and the bottom ribbons were shortened.

On the second anniversary of the first American Flag stamp produced on the Giori Press (July 4, 1959), the Post Office Department released a stamp portraying the new short-lived American Flag boasting its 49th star for the admission of Alaska to the Union on Jan. 3 (Scott 1132). As with the first Giori flag issue, the new one accounted for more than a half- million first-day covers.

The first airmail stamp was printed on the Giori in August 1959 to commemorate the centenary of the carrying of mail by balloon from Lafayette to Crawfordsville, Ind., in 1859 (Scott C54). The 7¢ Airmail stamp portrayed the balloon *Jupiter,* flying above a cheering crowd. It was printed in dark blue and red.

There followed, on August 26th, the third conservation stamp produced on the Giori press. The 4¢ Soil Conservation issue, Scott 1133, depicted a panoramic farm scene printed in blue, green and ocher.

Another Giori airmail stamp soon followed. This 10¢ issue, printed in violet blue and bright red, commemorated the 1959 Pan American Games in Chicago, Ill. It was released on Aug. 27th, 1959, the opening day of the games (Scott C56).

In September, the 8¢ Champion of Liberty issue for Ernst Reuter was released in its usual color scheme of carmine, ultramarine and ocher (Scott 1137).

Figure 1: The 48-Star Flag of 1957, Scott 1094, was the first U.S. stamp produced on the Giori press.

Figure 2: The 8¢ Magsaysay Champion of Liberty issue, Scott 1096, was the first three-color stamp produced on the new press.

Figure 3: The Giori press' first Conservation stamp, Scott 1098, commemorated wildlife.

Figure 4: Giori press' bold reproduction of Michelangelo's Creation of Adam for the International Geophysical Year, Scott 1107, utilized orange and black.

The final Giori Press stamp for 1959 was the 15¢ Statue of Liberty airmail, released Nov. 20 and printed in black and orange (Scott C58). This stamp was later reprinted with a different frame line (Scott C63).

The Giori press revolutionized multicolor intaglio stamp printing and was the workhorse of that process for 10 years. In 1968, the Huck multicolor press was put into operation at the Bureau. This new press was capable of printing stamps in as many as nine colors.

This, in turn, was followed in 1971 by the Andreotti multicolor gravure press. It utilized the photogravure system in which a stamp design is photographed through a fine screen that breaks the design up into minute dots. The dots are etched into the plate and the depressions hold the ink, which is lifted out by the paper when pressed against the plate.

The Giori press continued to produce stamps as well while these others were put to work. The Giori press was finally taken out of service and scrapped, but it won't be forgotten. It is the Giori press we remember for introducing single-press-run multicolor printing of stamps in the United States. ❖

Figure 5: Forests were the theme of the second U.S. Conservation stamp, Scott 1122.

Figure 6: The U.S. version of the 1959 Saint Lawrence Seaway stamp, Scott 1131. Unlike the Canadian version, a color invert was physically impossible on the Giori press.

Figure 7: The new 1959 49-star American Flag, Scott 1132, with Alaska's star added.

Figure 8: Soil Conservation commemorative of 1959, Scott 1133.

Figure 9: The first of the smaller-sized champions of Liberty issue (1958), which pictured Simon Bolivar, featured red and blue ribbons (left). When the 1959 San Martin stamp (center) was released, the ribbons were altered to print only in blue. This was due to inking problems. By 1960, when the Thomas Masaryk stamp was released, bi-colored ribbons were back. The colors were reversed (blue and red) with the bottom ribbon shortened.

German POW's Years in Australian Camp Are Recalled

Figure 1.
No. 13 POW Group, Murchison.
Gustav Pohlig is seated in the front row, far right.

A Time to Remember

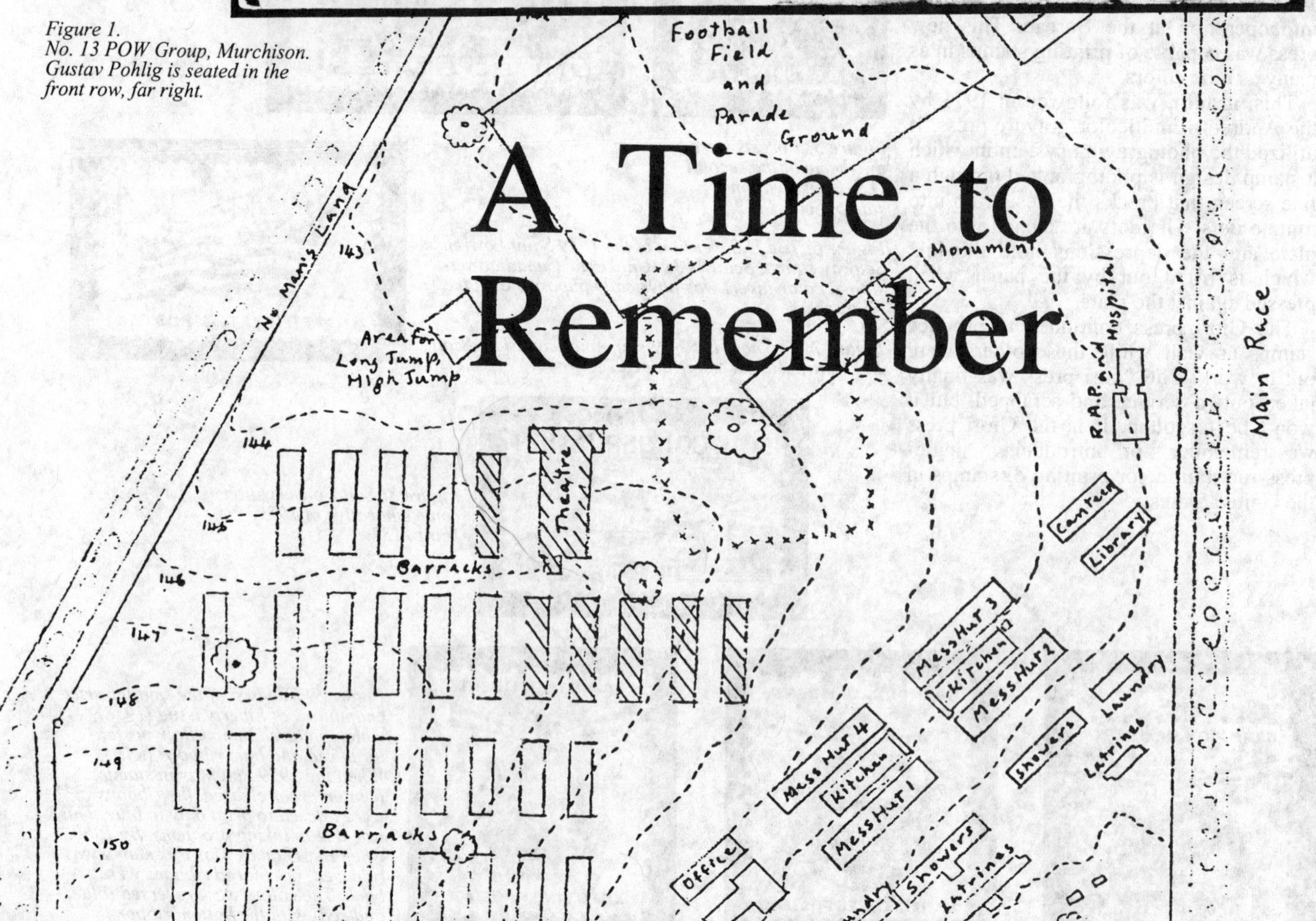

BY ROBERT G. METCALF

On November 8, 1987, a solemn figure stood in silence inside a now unused jail that once had held him prisoner. More than forty years earlier, he had been confined there for three days.

On the concrete walls of the cells, the marks made by prisoners counting the days of their confinement are still visible. The walls are thick, there are no windows; in the summer heat of southeastern Australia, this place must have been a hellhole. Today, the jail is the only building that survives of No. 13 Prisoner of War Group, Murchison, Victoria, Australia.

The jail once stood behind barbed wire. A jail within a jail. A jail that played an important part in the life of Gustav Pohlig, prisoner No. 41669, who spent five and a half years in No. 13 POW Group, Murchison.

Young Gustav grew up in Darmstadt, Germany. He left school early to help support the family, working as a nurseryman. That job was to prove significant during his internment at Murchison.

In 1938, he was called up for service in the German army. He took part in the campaign in France, then marched all the way back to Germany in the fall of 1940. In March 1941, he was sent to Naples, then to Tripoli, in North Africa. From there, his unit rode on motorcycles toward Tobruk, where Rommel was waiting. Before they reached the port, however, they were ordered to bypass Tobruk and to continue on to Capuzzo and Sollum in the northwestern corner of Egypt.

German forces, Gustav Pohlig among them, seized both places and advanced toward Halfaya Pass, about twenty miles inside Egypt. The only road from the coastal plains to the high plateau wound through the pass, and it was of extreme importance for both the British and the German armies. Gustav's outfit, far in front of the main lines, had little in the way of supplies.

On May 15, 1941, their position was over-run by British troops, and Gustav was taken prisoner. He was sent first to Mersa Matruh in Egypt, where Greek guards provided little information about his eventual destination. From there he was moved to a camp on the Suez Canal, where he had the opportunity to notify the Red Cross of his capture. This information, relayed through the Vatican to his family in Germany, didn't reach his mother until August.

In the meantime, much to their surprise, Gustav and 935 other ranks, along with forty-seven officers, were put aboard the *Queen Elizabeth* and set sail, still not knowing their destination. Many hoped it would be South Africa. When they learned they were bound for Australia, they were amazed - the farthest corner of the earth from Europe!

On August 23, 1941, the prisoners disembarked at Sydney harbor, all of them uncertain, the surroundings strange. From there, they traveled by train to Hammond Siding (Victoria), where the officers were separated from the other ranks. While the officers were transported by truck to an impressive-looking building at Dhurringile, the other ranks were marched some three miles west of the town of Murchison to an area of bare fields, occasional trees, and a barbed wire-fenced perimeter. This was to become No. 13 POW Group, Murchison.

Until barracks were built, the prisoners were housed in tents. Eventually, the camp would have

Figure 2.
Gustav Pohlig indicates the grove of eucalyptus trees he planted some forty-five years earlier.

Figure 3.
Gustav, seated at right, in one of the many female roles he played as a member of the theater group.

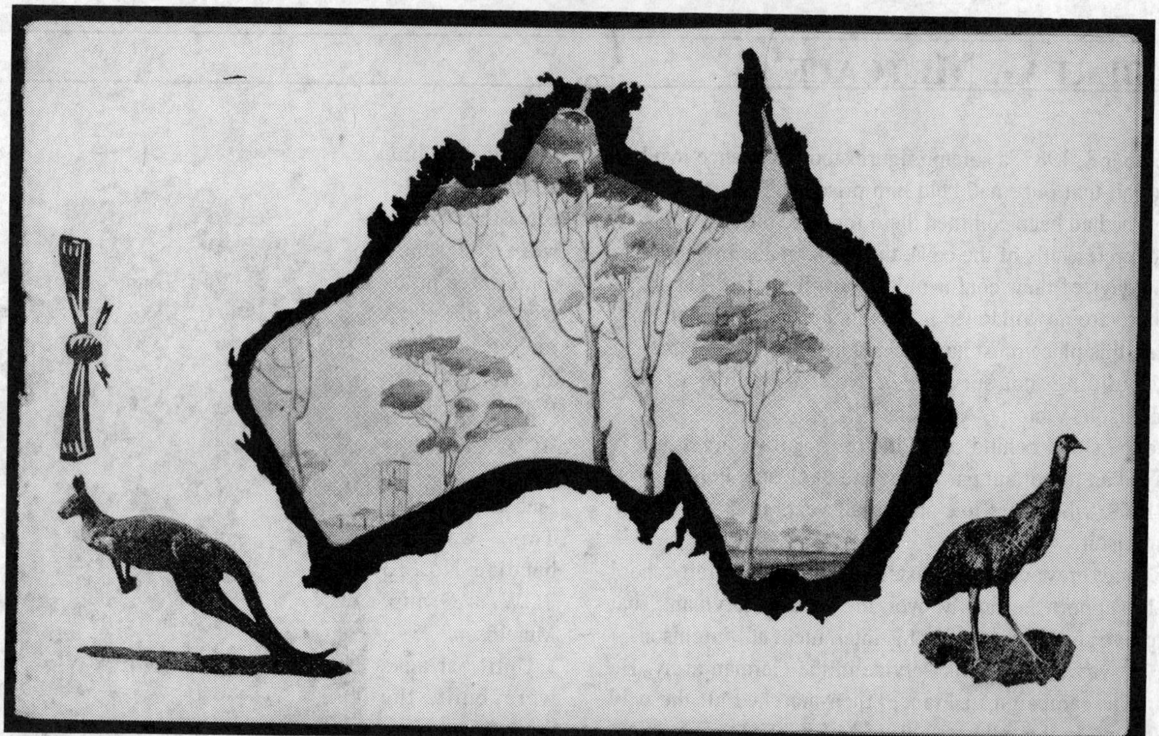

Figure 4.
On his first Christmas in captivity, in 1941, Gustav sent this card to his aunt. It was the first of a series provided by the YMCA.

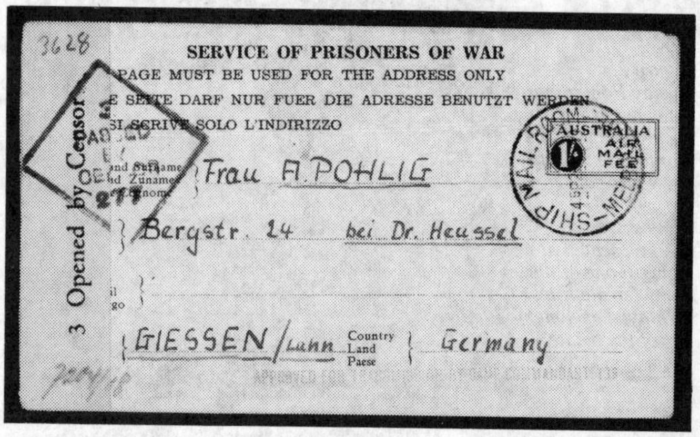

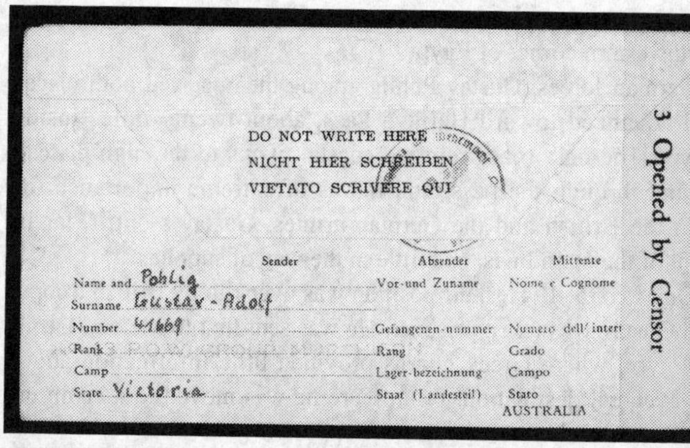

Figure 5.
Gustav sent this letter to his mother, unaware that she had been killed two weeks earlier in an air raid. It was censored by both Australia and Germany.

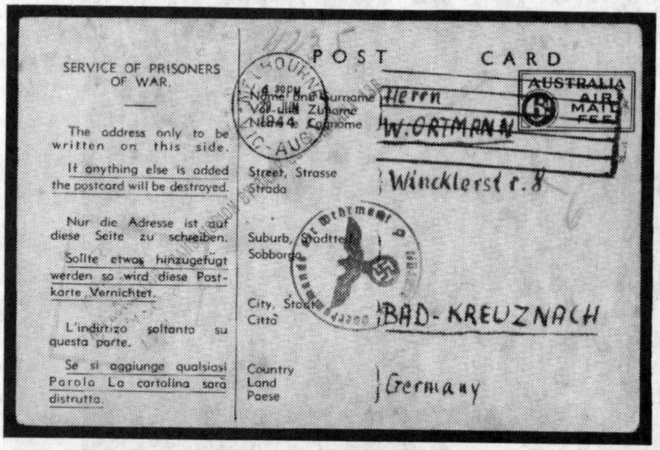

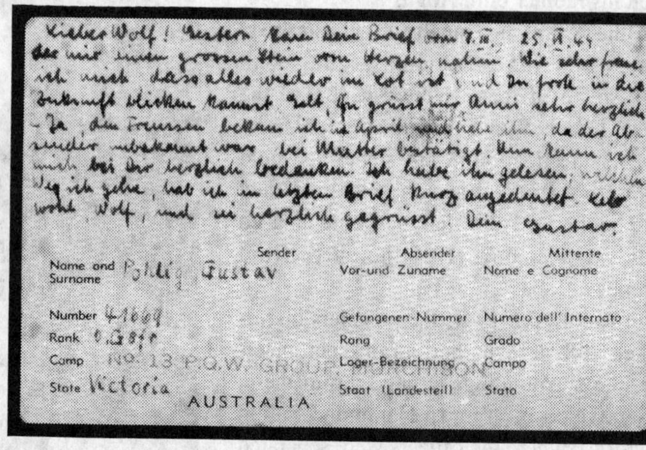

Figure 6.
A post card sent to an army friend of Gustav's, at his home address. These air mail cards (and 1/- lettersheets) were in use from December 1943.
The German censor mark, in red, was applied in Berlin.

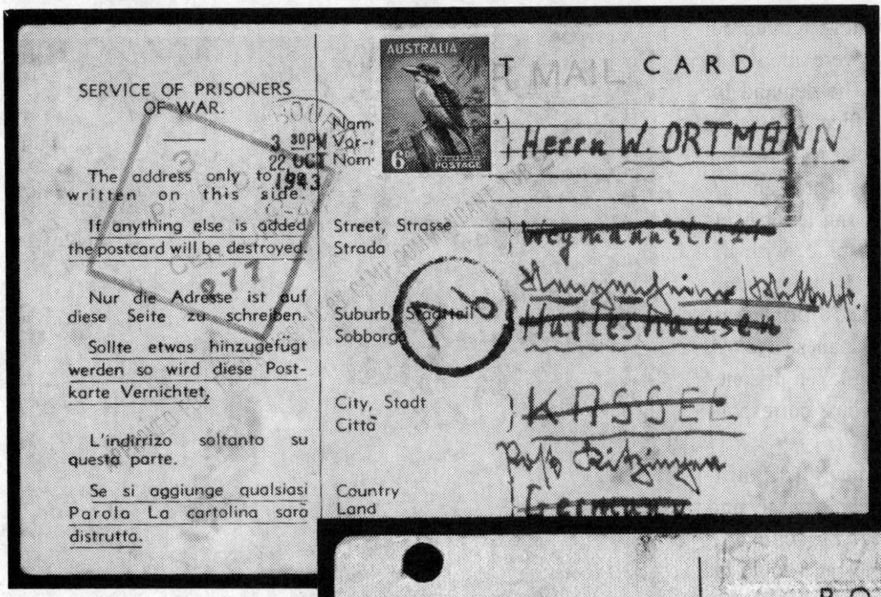

Figure 7.
This air mail card had to be re-directed; the addressee's home had been destroyed in a bombing raid. The card bears both Australian and German censor markings.

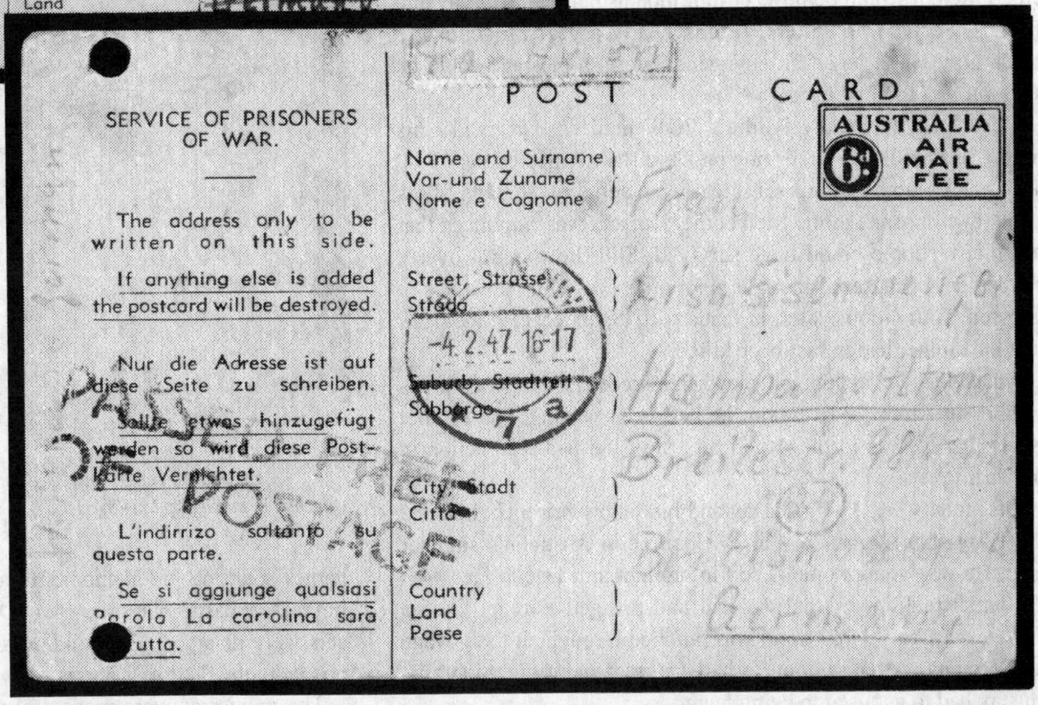

Figure 8.
This card was written by a friend of Gustav's aboard the **Orontes** *after its departure from Melbourne on January 1, 1947. It probably was given to a guard at Freemantle, who forwarded it through military channels.*

four compounds, A,B,C, and D; each could house 1,000 prisoners. The German POWs were sure their stay in Australia would be short; they were convinced Germany would win the war quickly.

Gustav was assigned to compound 13D, where all types of activities soon were organized, including schooling and a theater group in which he was very active. He played many of the female roles for the theater group.

As might be expected in a POW camp, tunneling also was organized as soon as the first barracks were built. But the tunnels eventually were detected. In that part of Australia, the soil at tunneling depth is a rather chalky white, and the prisoners had a hard time disposing of it. Flower beds were laid out between the huts, and at night the whitish soil was carried out, put on the flower beds, and covered with the darker topsoil. All looked rosy in the garden.

When the rainy season came, however, fate lent a hand. The rains washed away the topsoil, exposing the white earth and leading to the discovery of the tunnels. Because of this, the prisoners of camp 13 D were moved to 13 B, which was on a hill in an otherwise flat area. There prisoner No. 41699 stayed until his release in 1947.

Gustav found life in camp 13 B to be beneficial. During the years of his internment, he was able to study hard, thanks to books sent to the camp by the Red Cross, by German-speaking residents of Melbourne, and from Germany itself. By the end of the war, the camp library had some 15,000 books. Sports were also important to the prisoners, both for exercise and for morale, and the YMCA provided most of their equipment.

A Mr. Moodie bought seeds for the prisoners to grow vegetables and flowers, and on other occasions he brought records. In 1942, Gustav was able to put his experience as a nurseryman to use as he planted eucalyptus trees in and around the mess-hall area and the theater barracks. Trees also were planted along the way from the camp entrance to the hospital.

During World War II, Australia ultimately became responsible for 25,720 internees and prisoners of war, most of them German, Italian, and Japanese servicemen. Handling their mail posed many problems, primarily because of the distances involved.

According to the Geneva Convention, surface mail was carried free of postal charges, but items sent air mail or by registered post had to be pre-paid by means of postage stamps. These the prisoners could buy with their monthly wages, which varied according to their rank and the duties they performed around the camp. Toward the end of the war, POWs also were permitted to work outside the camps, in Australia's fields, forests, and quarries.

To ease the burden on Australia's postal administration and to provide some uniformity, lettersheets were distributed to the POWs. Further, all personnel within the camps had an allowance allocation of out-bound mail. From approximately November 1942, non-commissioned officers and other ranks were allowed to send two letters and four post cards per month. The demand for air mail postage was so great that the camp post office always had to have fairly large quantities of 6d and 1/-stamps on hand: The air mail rate to Germany and Italy was 6d for post cards and 1/- for the lettersheets. In 1943, imprinted post cards and lettersheets were issued, the 6d and 1/- values appearing in blue, with the words "Australia Air Mail Fee."

As a matter of interest to the postal historian, a 5d printed air mail lettersheet also was issued, for use by the Japanese POWs. But few, if any, were used. To the Japanese, being taken prisoner was a worse fate than dying on the battlefield. Thus, correspondence was not encouraged.

The journey of Gustav's mail to and from Germany was difficult. Often, it would be three or four months before his family and friends received his letters. It took nearly a year for replies to reach him. However, if an emergency arose, a message could be sent through the Red Cross.

Very little of Gustav Pohlig's POW mail has survived - his mother was killed in an air raid on Darmstadt in September 1944. Two weeks after the raid, Gustav saw an aerial photograph of his hometown in ruins in the Melbourne *Sun*, and was convinced that not many people could have survived. Still, he was not overly concerned, because he thought his mother was with her sister in Giessen. Four months later, in January 1945, he received the news that his mother had in fact been killed.

Gustav had yet another shock when he received a letter from his brother in America, to whom he had been writing. His brother wrote that he was in the American army, and had seen action in the Pacific!

On January 21, 1947, Gustav and his fellow prisoners boarded the P&O ship *Orontes* at Port Melbourne in Australia's summer heat. He was going home. The trip brought him face to face with the harsh realities of the war that had ravaged Europe. On the *Orontes,* a British ship, food was rationed throughout the voyage to Germany. After five and a half years of plenty in Australia, Gustav had to get used to being hungry.

He arrived in Germany in March, where it was fifteen degrees Celsius in Cuxhaven. From there he was taken to Dachau, the former concentration camp, then the discharge center for the American Zone in Europe.

Although many of the German POWs had wanted to stay in Australia - they had no homes to return to - the Geneva Convention stated that all prisoners had to be repatriated. Eventually, some of the former POWs returned to settle in Australia.

Gustav Pohlig went back to college, his schooling in No. 13 POW Group, Murchison, having been recognized by the authorities in Germany. When he graduated, he became a teacher. In 1954, he emigrated to the United States, where he taught for twenty-five years. Today, he lives in upstate New York.

Gustav had always wanted to return to Murchison, which had played such an important part in his life. But he was apprehensive about what memories would flow back.

During his 1987 visit, he saw for the first time the German cemetery at Tatura where some of his fellow soldiers are buried. He was moved as he read the memorial stones set in the lawn, the names sparking his memory. He also saw for the first time the impressive castle-like structure at Dhurringile where German officers were detained. The building today is used as a low-security prison by the State of Victoria.

The memories were made real when Gustav stood under the now-impressive eucalyptus trees he had planted more than forty years earlier. And as he walked the grounds, he was startled that parts of the flower gardens still were visible. He was amazed and yet relieved that his work had survivied the war and stood the test of time. The monuments of No. 13 POW Group, Murchison, made his return a time to remember. ❖

Figure 9.
Gustav Pohlig and Barbara Winter on the grounds of No. 13 POW Group, Murchison, during their 1987 visit.

References
1. Collas, P., The Postal History of Internees and Prisoners of War in Australia During World War II (The Royal Philatelic Society of Victoria: 1982).
2. Winter, Barbara, Stalag Australia (Angus of Robertson: 1982).

The Author

George Speirs, an APS member in Australia, is a keen student of the postal history of the Gilbert & Ellice Islands Colony, and wrote about them for the AP in October 1981. His story of a South African prisoner of war was published in the AP in January 1984.

What Have Catalogue Values Done For You Lately?

by Stuart Morrissey
Vice President/Publisher

Unless you've been away from our hobby for awhile or working so hard you haven't noticed, there was a major change in the method of determining Scott values a few years ago. We now use retail values. A retail value is defined as what a collector can expect to pay for a particular stamp in the condition of fine to very fine. Whether you are a new issues junkie, the classics-only type or one of the hardy who still collects worldwide, you need to be familiar with how catalogue values work.

In the old days Scott used what we refer to as "reference" values. Stamps were discounted, often deeply, from Scott Catalogue values. The discounts ranged from 20 to 80 percent of catalogue value, although there were a few areas, like U.S. Match and medicine revenues or Canal Zone, where you sometimes had to pay well over catalogue. There was no consistency for the various discounts from country to country or even within a specific country from period to period.

There were plenty of folks who liked the discount game. When you paid $25 for a stamp that catalogued $60 it felt good. You could bid at auction or mail sales at even greater discounts from catalogue value and often win the desired lot.

Then something really strange happened. The 1989 Scott Catalogue was released with many distinctly lower values. At the time most collectors and all dealers were convinced that values were on the upswing. Suddenly it became very noisy around the office.

How could such a development have occurred?

The publisher at the time was very far removed from the day-to-day activity of valuing stamps. He hadn't a clue about what happened until it was too late. Without announcement and for no apparent reason values were all of a sudden lowered. The phones started ringing and the dealer voices were so loud and angry I was convinced that the receiver at our end was about to melt.

What really happened was that prior to the 1989 catalogue a totally different system was in place for determining values. Bill Salomon, Bert Taub, George Holschauer, and Irving Koslow, long established dealers, provided input and the Scott editors reviewed and ultimately finalized the values. The dealer consultants were paid for this service.

Then it all changed. Scott decided to hire its own value analysts. The 1989 catalogue was the first edition that was solely the work of the in-house value editors. In that edition there was an attempt to balance the discounts between countries. A number of values were reduced for the highly discounted countries.

Some dealers were convinced that it was all an insidious plot to sell more catalogues. There were rumors that the 1989 catalogue was a desperate move designed to save Scott from financial ruin.

Although Scott was financially sound, the company was in a serious dilemma. For the next edition the catalogue had to either return to the unbalanced value structure of the past or use values that reflected real world stamp prices. The middle ground that the 1989 catalogue occupied was clearly unacceptable.

In its search for direction, Scott ran several ads showing Canada's beautiful engraved stamp that depicts the schooner *Bluenose*, Scott 158. The ads asked collectors what approach Scott should use to value this stamp. Collectors overwhelmingly indicated that they wanted values that reflected real world prices and not a value from which to discount.

In addition, Scott pulled out an extensive marketing research project conducted by McGraw Hill in 1987. McGraw Hill is a very large publishing company based in New York that has a well-respected group that performs marketing research work. The study, which took a look at many aspects of Scott customers, confirmed that many collectors were looking for real world values.

Scott made the decision to continue the use of retail values. A team of us traveled to stamp shows across the country to inform and explain. We spoke from the podium to large groups, discussed the situation with dealers across bourse tables and conversed with all types of collectors.

The introduction to the catalogue was completely revised and rewritten. Pictures of stamps were added so everyone would know what we meant when we stated fine to very fine condition. Thousands of extra introductions were reprinted and distributed to whomever was interested or wished to inform their customers.

From the beginning about 95% of collectors favored the new direction based on countless letters, phone calls and stamp show conversations. However, I would estimate that about 10% or less of dealers liked the idea. Auctioneers were seething as they feared that auction lots were doomed to command lower realizations.

Now, after six retail editions, most of the smoke has faded. Dealers and collectors feel comfortable using the current catalogue, although there are still a few notable holdouts who still go by the 1988 catalogue. It's weird to see the 1988 edition used, as many stamps now have a retail value that is higher than the reference values contained in the 1988 book.

If we could turn back the hands of time I would not have changed the system. Blasphemous? Perhaps. I just don't believe that the extreme disruption created by the change was healthy. But, hold on before you quote me out of context.

Now that the change has taken place I'm glad it happened. Of course I had little control as I became publisher after these events took place. However, I believe that we now have a vastly better valuing system.

What catalogue values should do for you is give you an idea about how much you would have to pay for an item on your wantlist.

You should not have to understand a maze of discounts, although some discounting and negotiation can always be expected. And Scott can do a lot for everyone by sticking to its current value system for the future stability of our great hobby. ❖

Time to Change the Legends

BY GARY B. WEISS

At first glance, the over-sized cover illustrated in Figure 1 is quite unattractive. The paper is brown and the cover itself is worn and somewhat shabby. In fact, it was "Received in Bad Condition/ at San Francisco, Calif./Damaged in Transit," and the intervening years have not improved its appearance.

One stamp - probably a second 8-cent value - is missing from the cover, and the other stamps are defective. When this item was sold at auction by Harmers of New York on June 25, 1986, the catalogue description for lot No. 420 noted this damage to the stamps, and there was almost no competition in the bidding for it.

Nevertheless, this cover represents a great bargain, not in terms of monetary value, but in terms of the new information it yields about the hand-stamped Philippines "VICTORY" overprints - information that necessitates changes in the legends surrounding these stamps.

The popularity of the hand-stamped "VICTORY" overprinted issues of the Philippine Islands can be attributed to many factors. Some collectors enjoy them for their rarity - even the most common of these stamps were issued in quantities of less than 25,000 - while others are impressed by the high prices some of them command. I like the crude nature of the issue. The most common attraction of these stamp, however, is the history that is intertwined with their issuance, and the legends surrounding them.

The hand-stamped "VICTORY" overprints were prepared during World War II, only nineteen days after American troops had landed in Leyte. They were prepared so that current stamps could be distinguished from the bulk of the pre-war issues that still were in enemy hands in other parts of the islands.

The rubber stamp used for these overprints was hand-carved and applied individually to whatever stamps were available. During its first day of use, it broke in two and was pinned back together. Thus, there are two distinct varieties of the overprint: Type 1 is the overprint before damage, and Type 2 is the overprint made with the repaired hand-stamp. The latter shows a defect in the letter "T," and the letters "VIC" do not line up properly with "TORY."

According to Murphree,[1] stamps were overprinted whenever enough had accumulated. This procedure accounts for the four different dates of issue - November 8, December 3, December 14, and December 28, 1944. Different stamps were "liberated" at different times, thus accounting for the different first days of issue. Careful records supposedly were kept of the quantities issued, as well as of the dates of issue.

According to the Scott Specialized Catalogue, ten overprinted stamps (Scott Nos. 464-65, 471-74, 477, 479-81) were issued on November 8, 1944. Although not mentioned in Scott, No. E9 also is known to have been issued on November 8. Scott lists the date of issue of Scott Nos. 469 and 476 as December 14. All of these issues on first day cover are considered rare, and Ritzer and Kaufman[2] commented that they had never seen or heard of the 12-cent blue (Scott No. 476) on first day cover.

Figure 1 shows a cover franked with Scott Nos. 469 and 476, as well as Nos. 465, 471-72, 480-81, and E9 - all with Type 2 overprints - and canceled on the first day of use of any "VICTORY" overprints, November 8, 1944.

Obviously, one possibility is that this cover is fraudulent. In fact, Williams[3] has suggested that the date of issue of the various stamps may be important in determining a forgery. However, this cover has been signed by George B. Sloane and examined by a number of other experts, including the American Philatelic Expertizing Service, and was issued certificate No. 59764 as genuine in all respects.

Thus, this cover seems to prove that the first day of Scott No. 469 and No. 476 was actually November 8, and that the issue dates of these two stamps in the catalogues must now be changed. The dates of issue of the other "VICTORY" overprints, while probably truly first days, must also be suspect and may be only the earliest known dates of use.

It is also generally accepted that the overprints were applied

Figure 1
This faulty cover is valuable to collectors of the "VICTORY" overprints for the new information it provides, as well as for its status as the only recorded first day cover of the rare Scott No. 476.

to the stamps prior to their usage. Evidence to support this includes the existence of unused stamps, as well as the existence of covers franked with both Type 1 and Type 2 overprints.

The 20-cent stamp on this cover (Figure 2) is remarkable in that both the "VICTORY" overprint and the cancellation tie the stamp to the cover. The "Y" of the overprint can be seen to be applied to both the stamp and the envelope. Therefore, in this case, the overprint must have been applied to the stamp after the stamp was affixed to the envelope. It should be noted that this stamp is smaller than the other stamps on the cover, and the overprint is almost the same width as the stamp.

It is possible that, after the stamps were applied to the first day covers, it was noted that this particular 20-cent stamp lacked the overprint. Errors are known of the "VICTORY" overprint in which one stamp of a pair or larger multiple lacks the overprint. If this was the case, the error was corrected by overprinting the stamp after it was on the cover and before the cover was sent through the mails.

Another possibility - the explanation I favor - is that many of the "VICTORY" overprints were applied to stamps already on first day covers. If more than one person was involved in preparing the stamps and covers, someone would have had to stand idly by until overprinting was accomplished on adequate numbers of stamps to affix to the covers. Perhaps this second person began to affix unoverprinted stamps to covers while awaiting the overprinted stamps. Later, he would have passed his pile of franked envelopes to the person doing the overprinting.

Evidence in favor of this theory is the presence of three partial, offset, "VICTORY" overprints on the reverse of this cover. These appear to have been transferred from the stamps of another cover. The transfer could have taken place at the time of preparation, while the ink was still wet. Or it may have occurred many years later, if the covers were stored improperly.

Still other explanations may be possible. In any case, this cover proves that at least one - and, therefore, possibly more - of the "VICTORY" overprints was applied after the stamp was affixed to a cover.

Thus, this cover really was a great bargain. It demonstrates two new findings related to the "VICTORY" overprints: when some of the stamps were issued, and how at least some of them were overprinted. ❖

References
**1. Murphree, Idul L. "Philippines: The 1944-45 Provisional Victory Issue," The Collectors Club Philatelist, 1954: Vol. 33, No. 3, pp 119-130.*
**2. Ritzer, Steve, and Lewis Kaufman. "Philippine Islands First Day Covers (American Dominion) - Part V," First Days, March 1972: Vol 17, pp. 20-22.*
**3. Williams, R.C. "Forgeries in the Victory Handstamps," Philippine Philatelic News, September 1986: Vol. 8, pp 11-13.*

**Available from the American Philatelic Research Library, P.O. Box 8338, State College, PA 16803.*

The Author
Dr. Gary B. Weiss collects the stamps and postal history of the U.S. possessions, especially Canal Zone, the Ryukyu Islands, and the Philippines. He is the Ryukyu section editor of the American Air Mail Catalogue and editor of the Canal Zone Philatelist.

Figure 2
Both the cancellation and the "Y" of the "VICTORY" overprint clearly tie the stamp to the cover

Stamps charted Third Reich's ambitions

Figure 1. One of four 1934 stamps depicting leaders of various German colonies, which were stripped from Germany after World War I.

by Fred W. Baumann

Japan's surprise attack on Pearl Harbor 52 years ago last December came as a monstrous shock to most Americans. It was the decisive event that propelled the United States irrevocably into World War II.

By contrast, Germany's preparations for its war of conquest in Europe - a war that had begun more than two years before - were telegraphed long before the first shots were ever fired.

Few astute collectors of German stamps from the immediate prewar period can have had any doubts about the sincerity of Hitler's desire to conquer the continent. No one needs help to recognize dive bombers, torpedo boats and storm troopers on wartime German stamps. More interesting and only slightly less dramatic than Germany's WWII stamps are the ones that preceded them.

Many prewar Third Reich commemoratives celebrate German technical or military know-how (Scott 452-53, 459-62, 469-72, 481-83). Others pay melodramatic homage to the Nazi Party and its auxiliaries (Scott 442-43, 454-55, 463-68, 479-80, 490-91).

But the most alarming prewar stamps stated Germany's claim to increasingly large swathes of real estate, beginning with those parts of the kaiser's realm that had been amputated under the Versailles Treaty.

The harsh terms of the treaty that followed WWI paved the way for Hitler's rise to power, thus sowing the seeds of WWII. In the hands of his brilliant propagandists, Versailles became a symbol of the injustice that the rest of Europe had visited upon an undeserving Germany - an iniquity, the Nazis claimed, that had to be overturned and avenged.

Among the humiliations of Versailles was that it stripped Germany of its hard-won colonial territories. As if to rub salt in the wound, these losses were recalled in a four-stamp set issued in June 1934 (Scott Scott 432-35), depicting various German colonial leaders.

Figure 1 shows the 12-pfennig value depicting Karl Peters, the 19th-century explorer who founded the Society for German Colonization in 1884, established the German East Africa Company and advanced the creation of the German East African Protectorate of Tanganyika.

After Versailles, the lion's share of Tanganyika went to Great Britain under a League of Nations mandate, with lesser bits for Belgium and Portugal. Germany was forced out of Africa - an insult to German pride that still rankled, as those who designed these stamps were certainly well aware.

Two months later, a pair of German stamps (Scott 444-45), including the stamp on the left in Figure 2, heralded the coming referendum that would decide the fate of the Saar, an important coal and steelmaking region on the western German border with France.

After WWI, the mines of the Saar became French property, as the Versailles Treaty put it, in "compensation for the damage to the north of France and as part payment toward the total reparation." The Saar itself fell under the authority of the League of Nations for 15 years until the 1935 plebiscite, in which the Nazis campaigned stridently for the return of the region to Germany.On Jan. 13, 1935, successful propaganda and strong anti-French resentment combined to produce a landslide in which more than 90 percent voted to rejoin Germany. On Jan. 16, Germany issued a set of four stamps with identical designs in celebration (Scott 448-51). One of the stamps is shown on the right in Figure 2. Its design depicts Saar as a girl returning to the smiling, cheerful embrace of Mother Germany. Lest postal patrons prove too simpleminded to grasp the schmaltzy symbolism, an inscription at the top of the stamp translates as, "The Saar sweeps home!"

Figure 2. German stamps issued before the 1935 plebiscite to decide the fate of Saar (left) and three days after its people voted overwhelmingly to return to Germany

Hitler next turned his attention towards Austria, where the homegrown Nazi Party and its sympathizers gave his ambitions for anschluss, or union with Germany, a formidable edge.Well aware that his predecessor had been murdered and that potential allies in France and Britain were more interested in appeasing than confronting Hitler, Austrian Chancellor Kurt von Schuschnigg resisted anschluss until he was finally forced from power in March 1938. German troops accompanied by Hitler arrived in Austria to a cheering reception the following day.

Less than a month later, an April 10 plebiscite in the two countries - now dubbed "greater Germany" - recorded a vote of more than 99 percent in favor of union. Two days before the polls opened, stamps bearing identical designs - one printed in Berlin (484), the other in Vienna (485) - had already been issued to celebrate the preordained outcome. Figure 3 shows the Viennese version of the stamp denominated "6rpf" (for "reichspfennig" - these may be the only postage stamps to display values in this way). Two men - Germany and Austria - bear

Figure 3. Issued two days before the plebiscite it commemorates, this stamp celebrates the achievement of Hitler's ambition of combining his nation with Austria to form "greater Germany."

the swastika flag, under the familiar Nazi slogan of "One people! One empire! One leader!"

The last of Hitler's prewar conquests was Czechoslovakia, where a strong German minority concentrated in various enclaves in the Sudeten region bordering Germany had been agitating for independence for years. In fact, after the Austrian anschluss Hitler planned on a military offensive to seize western Czechoslovakia, but French and British appeasement again delivered a far cheaper victory.

Czechoslovakia's fate was sealed by the Munich agreement signed Sept. 20, 1938, ceding to Germany all parts of the Sudetenland with a German-speaking majority. In the two months that followed, a pro-German independent Slovakian state was established. Other slices of Czech territory were thrown to Hungary and Poland. The western remnant of what had been Czechoslovakia, now dubbed Bohemia and Moravia, became a so-called German protectorate, which guaranteed Hitler direct control of the important heavy industry there.

Figure 4 shows one of two semipostals (Scott B132-33) issued Dec. 2, 1938, on which a Sudeten miner and his wife admire the newest corner of the "greater Germany." Four encyclopedias failed to shed any light on the date inscribed on the stamp. The German-language Michel catalog, however, describes the stamp as having been issued for "the plebiscite in Sudetenland on 4 December 1938." That makes this another stamp like the one in Figure 3, issued to applaud the results of a vote that hadn't yet taken place.

The plebiscite presumably asked if the Sudetenland should become part of Germany - a matter Hitler was willing to settle to his satisfaction, one way or another. The trappings of democratic choice again had been adroitly manipulated to dress up a fateful decision taken not by a nation, but by a dictator and his cronies. ❖

Figure 4. A Sudeten German husband and wife appear on this 1938 semipostal issued after the annexation of the Sudetenland and dismemberment of Czechoslovakia.

Index and Identifier

All page numbers shown are those in this Volume 1A.

Postage stamps that do not have English words on them are shown in the Identifier which begins on page 654.

Illustrated Identifier

This section pictures stamps or parts of stamp designs that will help identify postage stamps that do not have English words on them.

Many of the symbols that identify stamps of countries are shown here as well as typical examples of their stamps.

See the Index and Identifier on the previous pages for stamps with inscriptions such as "sen," "posta," "Baja Porto," "Helvetia," "K.S.A.", etc.

Linn's Stamp Identifier is now available. The 144 pages include more 2,000 inscriptions and over 500 large stamp illustrations. Available from Linn's Stamp News, P.O. Box 29, Sidney, OH 45365.

HEADS, PICTURES AND NUMERALS

GREAT BRITAIN

Great Britain stamps never show the country name, but, except for postage dues, show a picture of the reigning monarch.

Victoria

Edward VII

George V

Edward VIII

George VI

Elizabeth II

Silhouette (sometimes facing right, generally at the top of stamp)

The silhouette indicates this is a British stamp. It is not a U.S. stamp.

VICTORIA

Queen Victoria

INDIA

Other stamps of India show this portrait of Queen Victoria and the words "Service" and "Annas."

AUSTRIA

YUGOSLAVIA

(Also BOSNIA & HERZEGOVINA if imperf.)

BOSNIA & HERZEGOVINA

Denominations also appear in top corners instead of bottom corners.

HUNGARY

Another stamp has posthorn facing left

BRAZIL

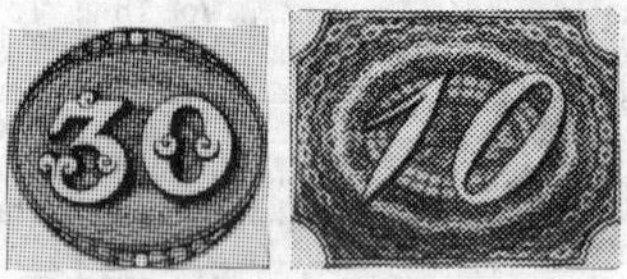

AUSTRALIA

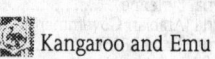

Kangaroo and Emu

NEW ZEALAND

GERMANY

Mecklenburg-Vorpommern

SWITZERLAND

ORIENTAL INSCRIPTIONS

CHINA

Any stamp with this one character is from China (Imperial, Republic or People's Republic).

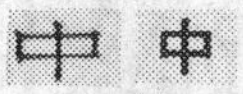

Some Chinese stamps show the Sun

Most stamps of Republic of China show this series of characters.

Stamps with the China character and this character are from People's Republic of China.

Calligraphic form of People's Republic of China

Chinese stamps without China character

REPUBLIC OF CHINA

PEOPLE'S REPUBLIC OF CHINA

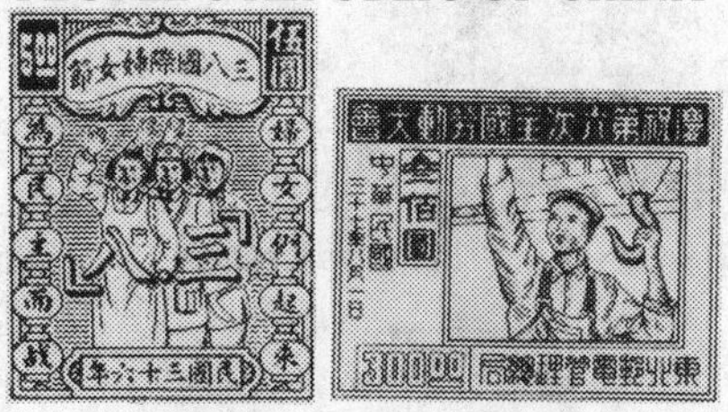

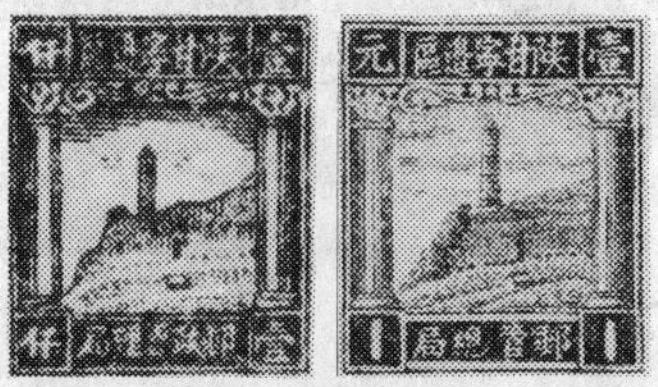

Mao Tse-tung

MANCHUKUO

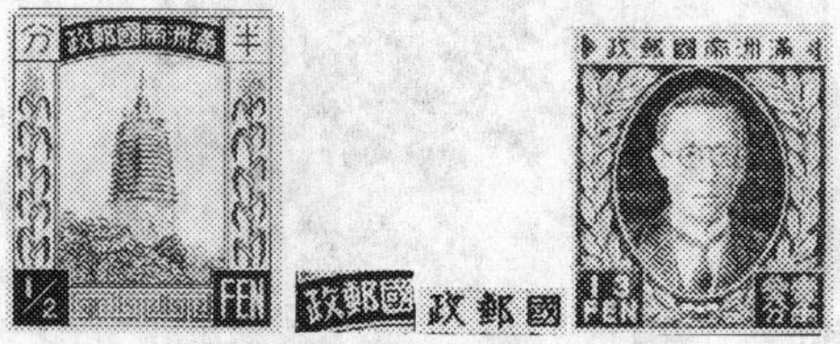

Temple

The first 3 characters are common to many Manchukuo stamps.

Emperor Pu-Yi

The last 3 characters are common to other Manchukuo stamps

Orchid Crest

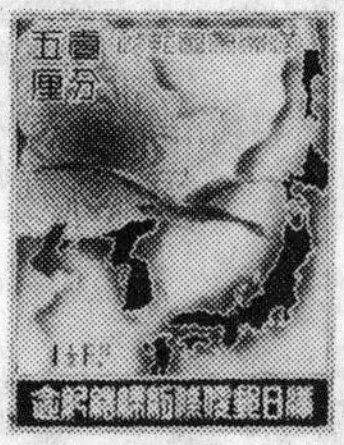

Manchukuo stamp without these elements

JAPAN

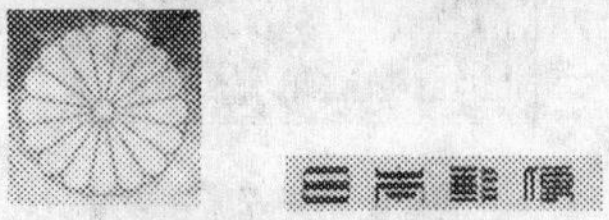

Chrysanthemum Crest Country Name

Japanese stamps without these elements

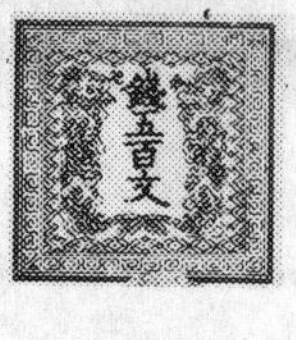

RYUKYU ISLANDS

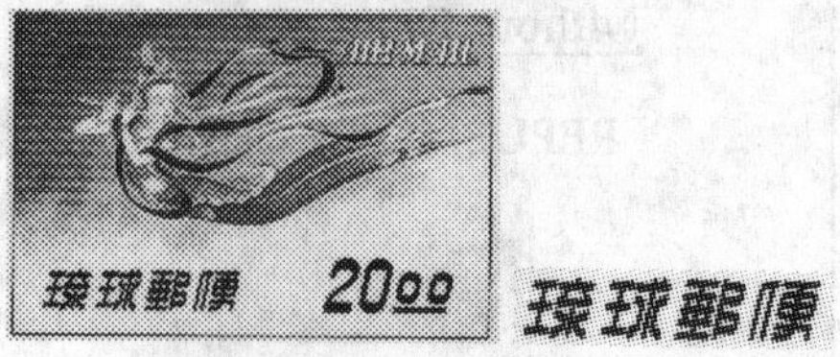

Country Name

PHILIPPINES (Japanese Occupation)

Country Name

NORTH BORNEO (Japanese Occupation)

Indicates Japanese Occupation

Country Name

MALAYA (Japanese Occupation)

Indicates Japanese Occupation

Country Name

BURMA (Japanese Occupation)

Indicates Japanese Occupation

Country Name

Other Burma Japanese Occupation stamps without these elements

Burmese Script

KOREA

These two characters, in any order, are common to stamps from the Republic of Korea (South Korea) or the unlisted stamps of the People's Democratic Republic of Korea (North Korea)

This series of four characters can be found on the stamps of both Koreas.

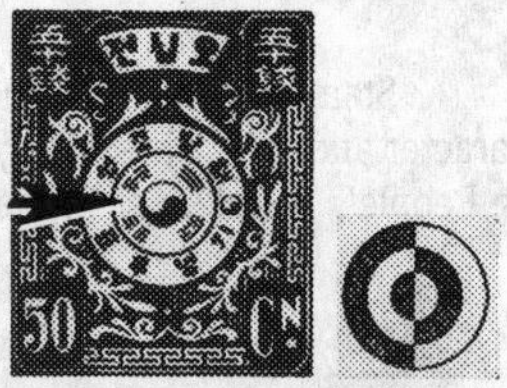

Yin Yang appears on some stamps

Indicates Republic of Korea (South Korea)

THAILAND

Country Name

King Prajadhipok and Chao P'ya Chakri

CENTRAL AND EASTERN ASIAN INSCRIPTIONS

INDIA - FEUDATORY STATES

Alwar

Bhor

Bundi

Similar stamps come with different designs in corners and differently drawn daggers (at center of circle)

Faridkot

Hyderabad

Similar stamps exist with straight line frame around stamp, and also with different central design which is inscribed "Postage" or "Post & Receipt."

Indore

Jammu & Kashmir

Jhalawar

Nowanuggur

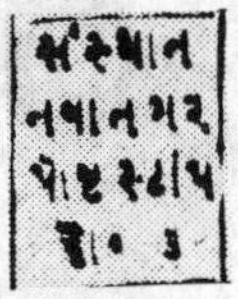

Rajpeepla

Soruth

BANGLADESH

NEPAL

Similar stamps are smaller, have squares in upper corners and have five or nine characters in central bottom panel

TANNU TUVA

ISRAEL

GEORGIA

ARMENIA

The four characters are found somewhere on pictorial stamps. On some stamps only the middle two are found.

ARABIC INSCRIPTIONS

AFGHANISTAN

Many early Afghanistan stamps show Tiger's head, many of these have ornaments protruding from outer ring, others show inscriptions in black

Arabic Script

Mosque Gate & Crossed Cannons

BAHRAIN

EGYPT

IRAN

Country Name

Note Crown

Lion with Sword

JORDAN

LEBANON

Similar types have denominations at top and slightly different design

LIBYA

Country Name in various styles

Other Libya stamps show Eagle and Shield (head facing either direction) or Red, White and Black Shield (with or without eagle in center).

SAUDI ARABIA

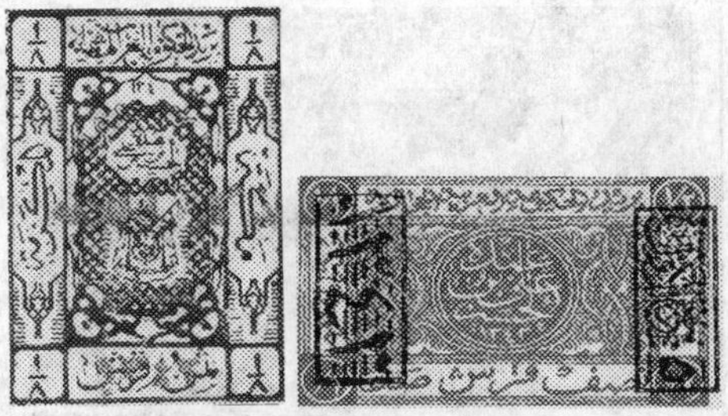

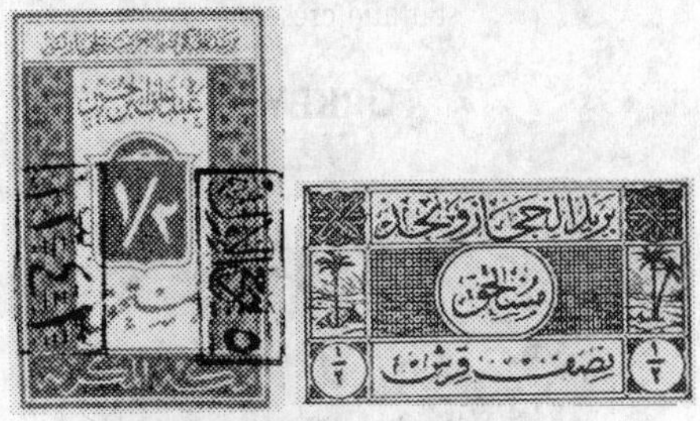

Note Tughra (Central design)

Palm Tree and Swords

SYRIA

THRACE

YEMEN

PAKISTAN - Bahawalpur

Country Name in top panel, star and crescent

TURKEY

Star & Crescent

Tughra (similar tughras can be found on stamps of Afghanistan and Saudi Arabia)

Mohammed V

Mustafa Kemal

Plane, Star and Crescent

TURKEY IN ASIA

Other Turkey in Asia pictorials show star & crescent

GREEK INSCRIPTIONS

GREECE

Country Name in various styles (Some Crete stamps overprinted with the Greece country name are listed in Crete.)

Lepta

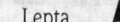

ΔΡΑΧΜΗ	ΔΡΑΧΜΑΙ	ΛΕΠΤΟΝ
Drachma	Drachmas	Lepton

Abbreviated Country Name ΕΛΛ

Other forms of Country Name

No country name

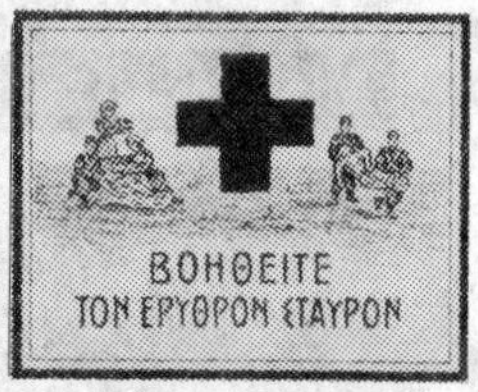

CRETE

Country Name

These words are on other stamps

Grosion

Crete stamps with a surcharge that have the year "1922" are listed under Greece.

EPIRUS

Country Name

IONIAN ISLANDS

CYRILLIC INSCRIPTIONS

RUSSIA

Postage Stamp

Imperial Eagle

Postage in various styles

Abbreviation for Kopeck 

 Abbreviation for Ruble

 Russia

Abbreviation for Russian Soviet Federated Socialist Republic

Abbreviation for Union of Soviet Socialist Republics

RUSSIA - Army of the North

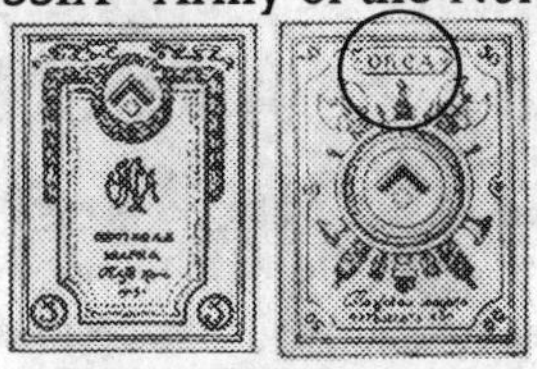

"OKCA"

RUSSIA - Wenden

RUSSIAN OFFICES IN THE TURKISH EMPIRE

These letters appear on other stamps of the Russian offices.

The unoverprinted version of this stamp and a similar stamp were overprinted by various countries (see below).

ARMENIA

FAR EASTERN REPUBLIC

Country Name

SOUTH RUSSIA

Country Name

FINLAND

Circles and Dots on stamps similar to Imperial Russia issues

BATUM

Forms of Country Name

TRANSCAUCASIAN FEDERATED REPUBLICS

Abbreviation for Country Name

KAZAKHSTAN

Country Name

KYRGYZSTAN

КЫРГЫЗСТАН

Counrty Name

ROMANIA

TADJIKISTAN

Counrty Name & Abbreviation

UKRAINE

Country Name in various forms

The trident appears on many stamps, usually as an overprint.

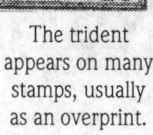

Abbreviation for Ukrainian Soviet Socialist Republic

WESTERN UKRAINE

Abbreviation for Country Name

AZERBAIJAN

Country Name

Azerbaijan Soviet Socialist Republic

MONTENEGRO

Country Name in various forms

Abbreviation for country name

No country name (A similar Montenegro stamp without country name has same vignette.)

SERBIA

Country Name in various forms

Abbreviation for country name

YUGOSLAVIA

Showing country name

No Country Name

MACEDONIA

Country Name

BULGARIA

Country Name

Postage

Stotinka

Abbreviation for Stotinki

Stotinki (plural)

Country Name in various forms and styles

Н Р България

No country name

Abbreviation for Lev, leva

MONGOLIA

Country name in one word

Tugrik in Cyrillic

Country name in two words

Mung in Cyrillic

Mung in Mongolian

Tugrik in Mongolian

Arms

No Country Name

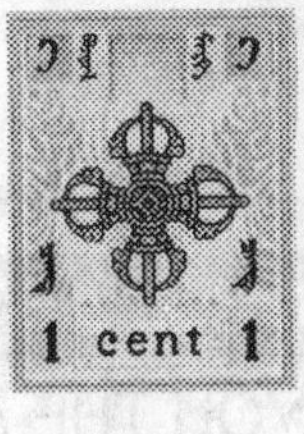

INDEX TO ADVERTISERS – 1996 VOLUME 1A

READER SERVICE CARD ADVERTISER'S INDEX

The following is a listing of the advertisers in this Volume 1A who offer Scott readers the convenience of using the Reader Service Card to request information on the products or services shown below. The Reader Service Card, along with instructions on completion and mailing, is located in the back of this catalogue. If the card is missing, write numbers on a postcard or letter, include your name, address, city, state and zip and mail to: Scott Publishing Co. Reader Service Dept. 96-S, P.O. Box 828, Sidney, OH 45365 U.S.A.

Reader Service Number

12 ARON R. HALBERSTAM PHILATELISTS, LTD.
P.O. Box 150168, Van Brunt Station
Brooklyn, NY 11215-0168
ELUSIVE BRITISH COMMONWEALTH - FREE LIST.
(See our advertisement on pages 247, 263, 321 and the Yellow Pages.)

Reader Service Number

99 SCOTT STAMP MONTHLY MAGAZINE
P.O. Box 828, Sidney, OH 45365
Circle #99 and we will bill you $17.95 for a 1-year (12 issues) subscription (U.S. only)

100 SCOTT MOUNTS
P.O. Box 828, Sidney, OH 45365
FREE Sample Package.

1996 Volume 1A

DEALER DIRECTORY YELLOW PAGE LISTINGS

This section of your Scott Catalogue contains advertisements to help you conveniently find what you need, when you need it...!

Accessories

H & S ROGG
P.O. Box 1076
Port Richey, FL 34673-1076
813-848-7697

FREEWAY STAMP SUPPLIES
635 S. Raymond Ave.
Suite D
Fullerton, CA 92631
714-447-8100 or 800-447-8105
714-447-8100 FAX

Albums & Accessories

THE KEEPING ROOM
P.O. Box 257
Trumbull, CT 06611-0257
203-372-8436

Antarctic Territories

BOMBAY PHILATELIC CO., INC.
P.O. Box 7719
Delray Beach, FL 33484-7719
407-499-7990
407-499-7553 FAX

Accessories

Accessories

Appraisals

APX
P.O. Box 952
Yakima, WA 98907
509-452-9517

BIRMINGHAM COIN AND JEWELRY
1287 S. Woodward
Birmingham, MI 48009
810-642-1234
810-642-4207 FAX

RANDY SCHOLL STAMP COMPANY
Southampton Square
7460 Jager Court
Cincinnati, OH 45230-4344
513-624-6800
513-624-6440 FAX

THE STAMP SHOP
614 Massachusetts Ave.
Indianapolis, IN 46204
317-631-0631

UNIQUE ESTATE APPRAISALS
1937 NE Broadway
Portland, OR 97232
503-287-4200

Approvals - British Commonwealth

49ER STAMP CO.
P.O. Box 416
Lebanon, NH 03766

Approvals - Disney

STUART KATZ
P.O. Box 656 SM
Middleton, MA 01949
508-777-2327

Approvals - Personalized

THE KEEPING ROOM
P.O. Box 257
Trumbull, CT 06611-0257
203-372-8436

Approvals - Topicals

STUART KATZ
P.O. Box 656 SM
Middleton, MA 01949
508-777-2327

Approvals - United States

STUART KATZ
P.O. Box 656 SM
Middleton, MA 01949
508-777-2327

Approvals - Worldwide

49ER STAMP CO.
P.O. Box 416
Lebanon, NH 03766

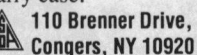

TAKE A 20% DISCOUNT ON EVERY PRICE ON THIS PAGE

SCOTT NATIONAL/SPECIALTY SERIES

Sold **pages only** by grouping and section. **Binder, Labels sold separately.**

NATIONAL SERIES

U S National Singles		Comm. Plate Blocks		**SPECIALTY SERIES** Canada	
1845-1934	**29.95**	1901-1940	**29.95**	1851-1952	**29.95**
1935-1976	**29.95**	1940-1959	**29.95**	1953-1978	**29.95**
1977-1993	**29.95**	1959-1968	**29.95**	1979-1992	**34.95**
Postal Stationery		1969-1973	**24.95**	Great Britain	
1853-1992	**59.95**	1973-1980	**29.95**	1840-1992	**89.95**
Post Cards		1980-1988	**39.95**	Binders	
1873-1981	**41.95**	1989-1992	**29.95**	2-Post	**35.00**
1982-1992	**34.95**	Reg. Pl. Blks 1918-91	**49.90**	3 Ring	**25.00**

All Other Country (Regional) Pages Available

MINKUS COUNTRY PAGES

Sold **pages only** by grouping and section. **Binder, Labels, sold separately.**

UNITED STATES 3-RING PAGES

Commem. Sin. to 92	**60.00**	1919-1937	**20.00**	1971-1978	**34.25**
Regular Sin. to 92	**45.00**	1938-1950	**20.00**	1979-1983	**27.00**
Plate Blocks		1951-1960	**20.00**	1984-1987	**27.00**
1919-1992	**189.00**	1961-1970	**27.00**	1988-1991	**27.00**

REGIONAL—COUNTRY 2-POST PAGES

Brit Possession	**135.00**	St. Vincent Grenadines	**69.00** / **35.00**	France 1849-1992	**95.00**
Brit. Asia II		All, 9 Vols.	**375.00**	Germany	
Trucial States	**99.00**	Br Carib. II		1849-1992	**75.00**
Hong Kong	**29.00**	Bahamas	**29.00**	Berlin	**25.00**
Kuwait, Bah.	**39.00**	Barbados	**29.00**	D.D.R.	**79.00**
Malaysia	**49.00**	Cayman	**29.00**	All, 3 Vols	**155.00**
Qatar	**29.00**	Jamaica	**29.00**	Hungary	
Singapore	**29.00**	Montserrat	**29.00**	1871-1992	**135.00**
Others	**79.00**	Nevis	**29.00**	Mexico	
All, 7 Vols.	**299.99**	St. Kitts	**29.00**	1856-1992	**65.00**
Br Carib. I		St. Lucia	**29.00**	Russia	
Anguilla	**35.00**	Trinidad	**29.00**	Old States	**49.00**
Antigua	**69.00**	Turks & Cai.	**29.00**	1857-1961	**69.00**
Barbuda	**59.00**	Virgin Is.	**29.00**	1962-1992	**105.00**
Dominica	**69.00**	All, 11 Vols.	**275.00**	All, 3 Vols.	**175.00**
Grenada	**99.00**	China		Binders:	
Grenadines.	**69.00**	Taiwan 1879-1992	**75.00**	3 Ring	**18.50**
Redonda	**25.00**	PRC 1949-1992	**79.00**	2-Post	**22.50**

All Other Country (Regional) Pages Available

LIGHTHOUSE HINGELESS COUNTRY ALBUMS

Hingless albums includes Perfect Binder with country name

UNITED STATES ALBUMS		**CANADA ALBUMS**	
Vol. 1 1847-1964	**$349.00**	Vol. 1 1851-1971	**$239.00**
Vol. 2 1965-1985	**299.00**	Vol. 2 1972-1993	**339.00**
Vol. 3 1986-1993	**239.00**		
Vol. 1-3 As a Set in 3 Binders 1847-1993	**695.00**	**ISRAEL TABS ALBUMS**	
UNITED NATIONS ALBUMS		Vol. 1 1948-1969	**297.00**
Vol. 1 New York	**266.00**	Vol. 2 1970-1989	**349.00**
Vol. 2 Geneva, Vienna	**229.00**	Vol. 3 1990-1993	**116.00**

All Other Country (Regional) Pages Available

WE ALSO CARRY (AND SELL AT DISCOUNT)
WHITE ACE - HARRIS - LINDNER - SAFE - KABE - HAWID - ELBE - G&K
PLUS ALL COIN SUPPLIES

SHOWGARD MOUNTS

Available with black or clear backs

STRIPS 215mm long: Sizes 20, 22, 24, 25, 27, 28, 30, 31, 33, 36, 39, 41, 44, 48, 50, 52, 57, 61 — **$5.50** per pkg.

STRIPS 240mm long: Sizes 63, 66, 68, 74, 80, 82, 84, 89, 100, 120 — **$6.25** per pkg.

STRIPS 264mm long: Sizes 70, 91, 105, 107 — **$8.75** per pkg.

PRECUT SIZES FOR SINGLES: Sizes C, CV, J, JV, AH, E, EH, T, U, N, KV, — **$2.50** per pkg.

PRECUT SIZES FOR BLOCKS: Sizes 57/65, 106/55, 105/67, 127/70, 67/25, 140/89, 165/94 — **$4.25** per pkg.

SHOWGARD MOUNT ORDERS OVER $100 NET DEDUCT 10% ADDITIONAL DISCOUNT

G&K DUAL POCKET COVER ALBUMS

Museum quality, 100% archival top loading PolyPro film pages. Available with crystal-clear pages to permit viewing of covers from both sides, -or- with a center of textured black PolyPro film for mounting covers on both sides (black background). Deluxe 2″ padded binders heavy-duty double-D ring allows pages to lie perfectly flat. Capacity 200 covers. Page size: 8¼x9″ Pocket size: 7⅛x4¼″. Colors: Black, Blue, Brown, Wine Red, Grey.

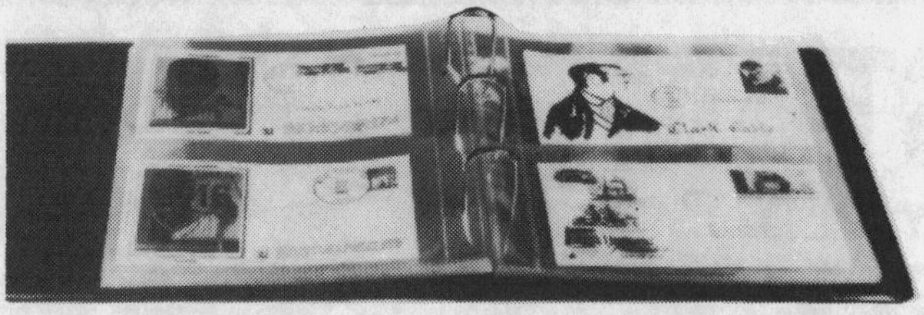

Album with 34 crystal-clear pages, holds 136 covers **GK-136A $15.95**
Album with 34 black background pages, holds 136 covers **GK-136AM 17.25**

EUROPEAN SIZE

Crystal-clear only, Page size: 8⅞x11″ Pocket size: 8¼x5⅛″
Album with 34 pages **GK-136E $16.95**

G&K DELUXE SHEET ALBUM

Museum quality 3-layered, archival page, with a sheet of textured jet black PolyPro film between 2 layers of crystal-clear PolyPro film. A vertical seal prevents sheets drifting towards the rings. Deluxe padded double D-ring binders allow the pages to lie perfectly flat. Colors: Blue, Brown, Black, Wine Red.

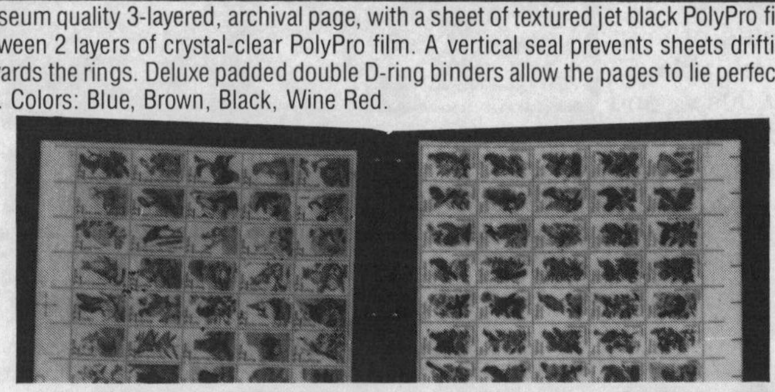

Album with 50 2-sided pages, holds 100 full sheets **GK-200A $29.50**

--- IT'S HERE ---

The ALL-NEW 1995 SUBWAY STAMP SHOP DISCOUNT CATALOG

80 pages of Stamps, Packets, Albums, Accessories and Reference Books at **Discount Prices.**

$1.00 postage appreciated

TO PLACE AN ORDER
CALL TOLL FREE 1-800-221-9960

• Charge it to your **VISA** or **Mastercard** -$20 min. • All orders normally shipped within 2 business days

• Customer Service: (814) 946-1000
• 24 hour Fax (814) 946-9997

SHIPPING CHARGES

Orders up to $20: **Add $2**, Orders over $20: **Add 10%**, Orders over $250: **Add 5%**
ORDERS SHIPPED BY FED EX: East Cost Thru **MN - IA - MO - AR - LA - East NE - KS - OK**
Orders up to $50: **Add $8**, Orders up to $100 : **Add $10**, Orders over $100: **Add 10%**
ORDERS SHIPPED BY FED EX: All states West of Above - **CALL for rates**
ORDERS SHIPPED TO CANADA (By Post Office) **Twice the U.S. Shipping Rate**
ORDERS SHIPPED TO CANADA BY FED EX: 10 lbs-$26, 20 lbs-$35, 50 lbs-$49, 100 lbs-$69
PA Residents: **Add Sales Tax**
Other countries: Write for exact mail and FED-EX shipping rates.
We Pay all Brokerage fees on Canadian/Foreign orders shipped by FED-EX.
Actual duty and taxes are the responsibility of the customer.

SUBWAY STAMP SHOP, INC.
2121 BEALE AVENUE, DEPT. S
ALTOONA, PA 16601

Approvals - United States

Free Color Catalog Saves You 30-60% on Scarce U.S. Stamps

Mystic's *New* catalog saves you money on scarce and desirable U.S. stamps. Expanded to 100 pages, the catalog shows thousands of U.S. and foreign stamps in full color. Loaded with wonderful stamp offers, it's yours FREE!

Oversize pictures illustrate differences on early U.S. stamps. Fascinating history, valuable collecting tips. Send for your catalog today and receive special stamp collector's information and pricelists along with other interesting offers on approval. Everything you need to know to enjoy this great hobby!

☑ **YES!** Send me Mystic's new FREE 100-page color catalog of Hard to Find United States Stamps
Mystic Stamp Company
Dept. E235, Camden, NY 13316

Name ____________________

Address ____________________

City/State/Zip ____________________

Mystic Stamp Company
America's Leading Stamp Dealer

Approvals - Worldwide

M & H DAVISON
Box 510 - T
South Sutton, NII 03273-0510

WEST NISSOURI STAMP CO.
P.O. Box 4641-A
London, Ontario N5W 5L7
CANADA
519-432-0080 or 519-432-0286

Auction House

B TRADING CO.
114 Quail Street
Albany, NY 12206
518-465-3497 TELEPHONE & FAX

REGENCY PHILATELIC AUCTIONS, LTD.
LeChateau Village #106
10411 Clayton Road
St. Louis, MO 63131
800-782-0066
314-997-2231 FAX

Approvals - Worldwide

FOR YOUR COLLECTING PLEASURE WRITE TO...
The Rideout Stamp Family - Manson, Wilma, Ronald

For over 30 years we have been mailing fine selections of General World and Topical groups Postpaid both ways on approval. Our vast stock and experience Guaranteed to please you. You may ask for any special groups you would like to inspect and with your first selection we have a nice set of stamps which we will include as a thank you for trying our service. You may cancel at anytime. You have up to 30 days to inspect the approvals without a reminder being sent. We aim to please you. Try us soon. I, Manson Rideout, am a 30+ years APS (life) member, also long time ATA.

MANSON RIDEOUT PHILATELIST LTD.
P.O. Box 1009, Houlton, Maine 04730
Or in Canada RR #1, Upper Woodstock, N.B., Canada E0J 1Z0

Approvals - United States

55 MINT U.S. STAMPS

only $4.95

OVER HALF-A-CENTURY OLD!

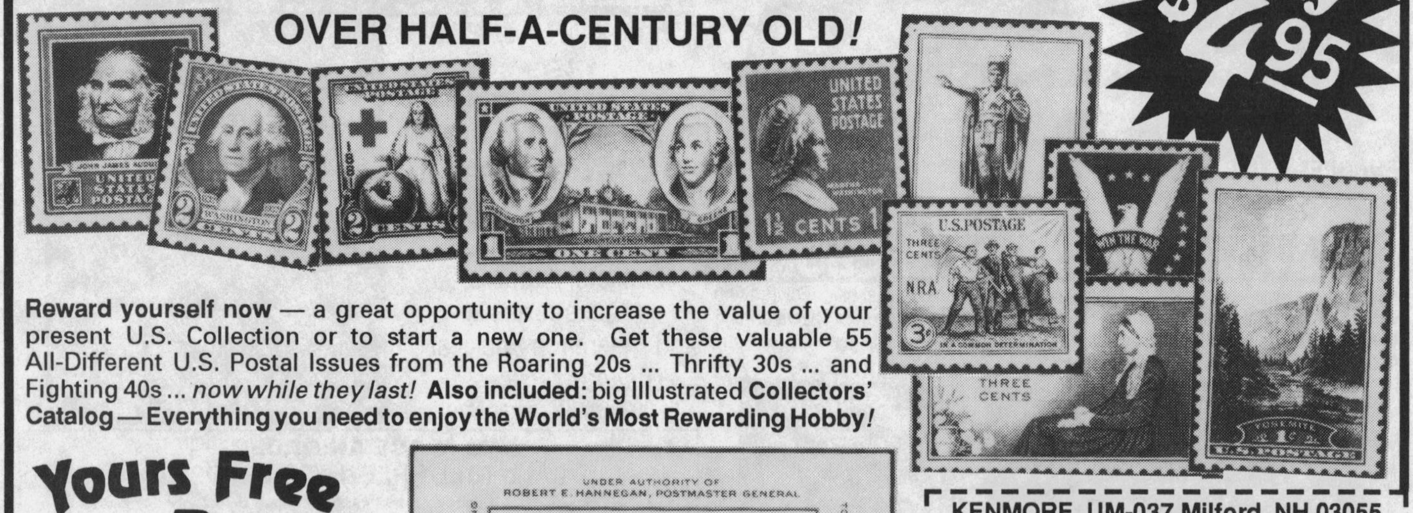

Reward yourself now — a great opportunity to increase the value of your present U.S. Collection or to start a new one. Get these valuable 55 All-Different U.S. Postal Issues from the Roaring 20s ... Thrifty 30s ... and Fighting 40s ... *now while they last!* **Also included**: big Illustrated **Collectors' Catalog — Everything you need to enjoy the World's Most Rewarding Hobby**!

Yours Free as a Bonus!
Valuable
First
U.S. Postage Issues
of 1847
COMMEMORATIVE SHEET!

Actual Size Is Much Larger!

KENMORE, UM-037 Milford, NH 03055
90-DAY MONEY BACK GUARANTEE IF NOT DELIGHTED!

YES! Enclosed is $4.95. Send me your valuable Half-Century-Old 55 Mint U.S. Collection ***Plus my Free Bonus*** at once! I agree to receive other Mint U.S. Issues on 10-Day Free Examination from your Shop-at-Home Stamps-On-Approval Service from which I may buy any or none, return balance, cancel Service anytime.

Name ____________________

Address ____________________

City, State, Zip ____________________

Approvals - Worldwide

1,000 STAMPS $2.95

GUARANTEED WORTH OVER $30 AT INTERNATIONAL CATALOG PRICES!

Save These Valuable Postage Stamps NOW While They Last!

Reward yourself now — a great opportunity to increase the value of your present collection or to start a new one. You get 1,000 all-different postage stamps from over 55 countries *Plus Big Illustrated Collectors' Catalog* — **Everything to Enjoy the World's Most Rewarding Hobby!** ***GREAT FAMILY FUN!***

YOURS FREE! **''FINDER'S GUIDE TO RARE AND VALUABLE POSTAGE STAMPS!''** This fascinating illustrated booklet will enable you to tell at a glance **how to recognize rare stamps — stamps once considered relatively common and now worth up to hundreds and thousands of dollars each!**

Also, selections of other sensational stamps from our 10-Day Free Examination Shop-At-Home Approval Service. Buy any or none — return balance — cancel Service anytime. Send $2.95 NOW!

90-DAY MONEY-BACK GUARANTEE IF NOT DELIGHTED!

KENMORE, Milford OP-119, N.H. 03055

Auctions

CEE-JAY STAMP AUCTIONS, INC.
P.O. Box 321
Waldorf, MD 20604
301-843-2022
301-705-7255 FAX

CHARLES G. FIRBY AUCTIONS
6695 Highland Road, Suite #106
Waterford, MI 48327
810-666-5333
810-666-5020 FAX

HARMER-SCHAU AUCTION GALLERIES INC.
617A Second Street
Petaluma, CA 94952
707-778-6454
707-763-6772 FAX

LAKESIDE PHILATELIC AUCTIONS
3935 Lakeside Rd. Ste. 7A
Comp. 4 RR# 2
Penticton, BC V2A 6J7
CANADA

SAM HOUSTON PHILATELICS
13310 Westheimer #150
Houston, TX 77077
713-493-6386
713-496-1445 FAX

STAMP CENTER/DUTCH COUNTRY AUCTIONS
4115 Concord Pike
Wilmington, DE 19803
302-478-8740
302-478-8779 FAX

★ PUBLIC AUCTIONS ★

5 to 6 sales a year and each contains about 2000 lots cataloging between $50-$10,000 Scott. Each sale covers the entire world and includes at least 150 collections, dealer's stocks or accumulations.

CATALOG FREE UPON REQUEST!

Cee-Jay Stamp Auctions, Inc.
P.O. Box 321
Waldorf, Maryland 20604
Phone (301)843-2022 • FAX (301)705-7255

Auctions

STAMP KING / RICHARD E. DREWS AUCTIONS
7139 W. Higgins Road
Chicago, IL 60656
312-775-2100
312-792-9116 FAX

Automatic Album Update Service

DELAWARE VALLEY STAMP CO.
69 Strasburg Road
Atglen, PA 19310
610-593-6684

Auctions - Public

SUBURBAN STAMP INC.
176 Worthington Street
Springfield, MA 01103
413-785-5348
413-746-3788 FAX

Baseball Cards

JAMES REEVES
P.O. Box 219SP
Huntingdon, PA 16652
814-643-5497 TELEPHONE & FAX

Auctions

ALAN BLAIR PUBLIC AUCTIONS

1. REGULARLY SCHEDULED AUCTIONS
2. WIDE VARIETY OF MATERIAL
3. MOST LOTS $10 to $200 VALUE
4. WRITE FOR CONSIGNMENT INFORMATION

5407 LAKESIDE AVENUE
RICHMOND, VA 23228
Ph. 804-266-3071 • Fax 804-264-6140

Qualified Auctioneer

Schiff Auctions

Buyers, Auctioneers & Appraisers of U.S. & Worldwide Stamps & Covers

We have been catering to the individual buyer and seller since 1947. Let us put our expertise to work for you when selling your stamps, covers or your collection. Whether consigning to public auction or selling outright, call us first. Contact us before sending stamps. Be sure to include your address and telephone number.

CATALOG SUBSCRIPTIONS	N. AMERICA	OVERSEAS
1 Year with Realizations	$10.00	$18.00
1 Year Catalog Only	$7.50	$15.00
1 Catalog with Realizations	$1.50	$2.50
1 Catalog Only	$1.00	$1.50

JACQUES C. SCHIFF, JR., INC.
195 Main St., Ridgefield Park, NJ 07660 USA
Telephone 201-641-5566 from NYC 662-2777
FAX 201-641-5705

OFFICIAL AUCTIONEERS:
AMERIPEX 1986.
WORLD STAMP EXPO 1989.
WORLD COLUMBIAN STAMP EXPO 1992.
YEARLY: COMPEX-CHICAGO.

QUALIFIED AUCTIONEER

Booklets – British Commonwealth

• BOOKLETS •

I SELL: BRITISH COMMONWEALTH | CANADA & G.B. ARE SPECIALTIES!

All B.C. Countries, Inc. RARE items. Write or phone for FREE LIST.

I BUY: Collections, Accumulations, Scarce & Rare Individual Items. Mail or fax details or phone.

SANDY McMULLEN (W.A. McMULLEN Ltd.)
P.O. Box 638, Station F, Toronto, M4Y 2N6 Canada
Ph. 416-221-4337, fax 416-221-4337 Member CSDA

Booklets – United States

★ NEED MODERN ERA U.S.?? ★

S & B RENOLL FEATURES:
LARGE/SMALL HOLE COILS; PANES with PARTIAL PLATE #'S; MARGIN BARS; HOLES/NO HOLES; WET/DRY PRINTING; PLATE BLOCKS & SINGLES with DRY/WET GUM; as well as AIRS.

For AMERICA'S **BEST BUY** SEND A 52¢ STAMP... receive our NEW ILLUSTRATED 1995 PRICE LIST. DISCOUNT SCHEDULE ($ave up to **20% OFF LIST PRICE**) & a discount coupon GOOD on FIRST ORDER -

S & B RENOLL
BOX 225A, HANOVER, PA 17331-0225
"Business Established 1899"

★ SATISFACTION GUARANTEED - ALWAYS!! ★

British Commonwealth

BOMBAY PHILATELIC CO., INC.
P.O. Box 7719
Delray Beach, FL 33484-7719
407-499-7990
407-499-7553 FAX

CENTURY STAMP CO., LTD.
1715 Lakeshore Road West
Mississauga, Ontario L5J 1J4
CANADA
905-822-5464 TELEPHONE & FAX

EDWARD J. MCKIM
1373 Isabelle
Memphis, TN 38122

INTERSTAMP
312 S. Cedros Avenue Suite 326
Solana Beach, CA 92075
619-755-2259
619-755-9113 FAX

J.S.C. - SC
Box 28484
Philadelphia, PA 19149
215-743-0207 TELEPHONE & FAX

LAKESIDE PHILATELICS
3935 Lakeside Rd. Ste. 7a
Comp. 4 RR# 2
Penticton, BC V2A-6J7
CANADA

British Commonwealth

MARLIN LARSON
217 Country Garden Lane
San Marcos, CA 92069
619-744-1435
619-744-5119 FAX

McMILLAN & WIFE
2740 Sarver Lane
San Marcos, CA 92069
619-744-1435
619-744-5119 FAX

REGENCY STAMPS, LTD.
Le Chateau Village #106
10411 Clayton Road
St. Louis, MO 63131
800-782-0066
314-997-2231 FAX

THE BRITISH COMMONWEALTH
O•F N•A•T•I•O•N•S

We are active buyers and sellers of stamps and postal history of all areas of pre-1960 British Commonwealth, including individual items, collections or estates.

Want lists from all reigns are accepted with references.

"VISIT OUR BOOTH AT MOST MAJOR SHOWS"

L. W. Martin, Jr.
CROWN COLONY STAMPS
P.O. Box 1198
BELLAIRE, TEXAS 77401
PH. (713) 781-6563 • FAX (713) 789-9998

British Commonwealth

BRITISH COMMONWEALTH

WE ARE SPECIALISTS IN THE REIGN OF KING GEORGE VI

We have large Stocks of Varieties, Shades & perforations, also Multiples including Plate and Imprint Blocks - NH, LH and FU Condition.
WANT LISTS (Scott or SG Numbers) Welcome.
Fast Reliable Service. Dollar cheques accepted.
Write and let us know what you collect from this fascinating period.

MURRAY PAYNE LIMITED

Stuart Babbington and Dickon Pollard
P.O. Box 1135, Axbridge, Somerset, BS26 2EW, United Kingdom
Phone +44-1934-732511 • Fax +44-1934-733498

For Elusive Items of Pre-1960 BRITISH COMMONWEALTH

Aron R. Halberstam Philatelists Ltd.
P.O. Box 150168, Van Brunt Station, Brooklyn, NY 11215-0168
TOLL FREE 1-800-343-1303
Phone 718-788-3978 • FAX 718-965-3099

Send for our Free monthly lists or Send us your want lists

VISA and MasterCard accepted on all orders

We are also eager buyers of... collections and accumulations of British Commonwealth as well as Worldwide.

• Circle No. 12 on Reader Service Card •

BRITISH EMPIRE
EXCLUSIVELY

WANT LISTS INVITED FROM SERIOUS COLLECTORS OF THE **BRITISH EMPIRE.**
EMPHASIS ON PRE-1935. REFERENCES PLEASE.

WE ARE BUYERS OF BETTER BRITISH COMMONWEALTH STAMPS, POSTAL HISTORY AND SPECIALIST MATERIAL.

Victoria Stamp Company

Established 1962
PHOEBE A. MacGILLIVARY
P.O. BOX 745, RIDGEWOOD, NJ 07451
PHONE 201-652-7283 • FAX 201-612-0024

TOP PRICES PAID for
COMMONWEALTH & GREAT BRITAIN

COLLECTIONS, SINGLE ITEMS, SETS MINT & USED URGENTLY REQUIRED
Please Write, Call or Fax Us With What You Have to Offer!

NICK CARTER

8031 Wadsworth Blvd., #B4-164, Arvada, CO 80003
Phone/Fax (303) 425-5852
Willing To Travel To See Collections

Canada

AMERICAN COIN & STAMP EXCHANGE
330 So. Gallatin Road
Madison, TN 37115
615-865-8791

CENTURY STAMP CO., LTD.
1715 Lakeshore Road West
Mississauga, Ontario L5J 1J4
CANADA
905-822-5464 TELEPHONE & FAX

J.S.C. - SC
Box 28484
Philadelphia, PA 19149
215-743-0207 TELEPHONE & FAX

MEKEEL'S WEEKLY STAMP NEWS
Box 5050-sy
White Plains, NY 10602
800-MEKEEL-1
914-997-7261 FAX

HAROLD B. GORDON

- **Lovely group of 1859's for the specialist**
- **BNA covers from stampless onward**
- **Appraisers for insurance, estates**
- **Auction Agents**

We offer a clean attractive stock of B.N.A. stamps & postal history.

Whether you buy or sell, our service is personal and professional.

5507 Elgin Avenue
Montreal, Que. H4V 2G7
(514) 486-1028
CSDA, APS, RPSC, BNAPS.

Canada - Duck Stamps

METROPOLITAN STAMP CO. of CHICAGO, INC.
P.O. Box 1133
Chicago, IL 60690-1133
815-439-0142
815-439-0143 FAX

SAM HOUSTON DUCK CO.
P.O. Box 820087
Houston, TX 77282
713-493-6386 or 800-231-5926
713-496-1445 FAX

Canal Zone

BROOKSIDE STAMPS
P.O. Box 412
Worthington, OH 43085
614-436-0524

Classic U.S. Stamps & Covers

THE STAMP SHOP
614 Massachusetts Ave.
Indianapolis, IN 46204
317-631-0631

Computer Software

Collections

BOMBAY PHILATELIC CO., INC.
P.O. Box 7719
Delray Beach, FL 33484-7719
407-499-7990
407-499-7553 FAX

HUNT & CO.
1512 W. 35th St. Cutoff
Suite 300
Austin, TX 78731
512-458-5687 or 800-458-5745
512-458-6531 FAX

SHARI'S STAMPS
104-3 Old Highway 40 #130
O'Fallon, MO 63366
800-382-3597

Conservation Stamps

SAM HOUSTON DUCK CO.
P.O. Box 820087
Houston, TX 77282
713-493-6386 or 800-231-5926
713-496-1445 FAX

Covers

HILLTOP STAMP SERVICE
P.O. Box 626
Wooster, OH 44691
216-262-5378

Custom Collection Builders

HUNT & CO.
1512 W. 35th St. Cutoff
Suite 300
Austin, TX 78731
512-458-5687 or 800-458-5745
512-458-6531 FAX

Discount Supplies

VERUS DISCOUNT STAMP CO.
P.O. Box 187
West Chicago, IL 60186
708-896-8938

Duck Stamps

HUNT & CO.
1512 W. 35th St. Cutoff
Suite 300
Austin, TX 78731
512-458-5687 or 800-458-5745
512-458-6531 FAX

Duck Stamps

SAM HOUSTON DUCK CO.
P.O. Box 820087
Houston, TX 77282
713-493-6386 or 800-231-5926
713-496-1445 FAX

TRENTON STAMP & COIN CO.
1804 RT. 33
Trenton, NJ 08690
800-446-8664
609-587-8664 FAX

Errors, Freaks & Oddities

SAM HOUSTON PHILATELICS
13310 Westheimer #150
Houston, TX 77077
713-493-6386
713-496-1445 FAX

Errors - Major

SUBURBAN STAMP INC.
176 Worthington Street
Springfield, MA 01103
413-785-5348
413-746-3788 FAX

Falkland Islands

J.S.C. - SC
Box 28484
Philadelphia, PA 19149
215-743-0207 TELEPHONE & FAX

Inverted Centers - World

MARTIN SELLINGER
Box 47
White Plains, NY 10602
914-948-4246
914-682-7384 FAX

Literature

MEKEEL'S WEEKLY STAMP NEWS
Box 5050-sy
White Plains, NY 10602
800-MEKEEL-1
914-997-7261 FAX

Mail Bid Sales

Lots & Collections

RANDY SCHOLL STAMP COMPANY
Southampton Square
7460 Jager Court
Cincinnati, OH 45230-4344
513-624-6800
513-624-6440 FAX

Mail Bid Sales

CONNEXUS
P.O. Box 453
Guilford, CT 06437
203-453-4298
203-458-2220 FAX

QUEST INTERNATIONAL
P.O. Box 139A,
Thames Ditton,
Surrey, KT7 OER,
UNITED KINGDOM
44-181-398-7740
44-181-398-4661 FAX

Mail Order

B & D HOBBIES
P.O. Box 4
Gladstone, OR 97027
503-656-3149

BOB BECK
Box 3209 Harbourtown Station
Hilton Head Island, SC 29928
803-671-3241

Mail Order

HUNT & CO.
1512 W. 35th St. Cutoff
Suite 300
Austin, TX 78731
512-458-5687 or 800-458-5745
512-458-6531 FAX

LOG HOUSE PHILATELIST
Box 267 Harju Road
Grand Marais, MI 49839

SHARI'S STAMPS
104-3 Old Highway 40 #130
O'Fallon, MO 63366
800-382-3597

Mail Sales

DALE ENTERPRISES INC.
P.O. Box 539
Emmaus, PA 18049
610-433-3303
610-965-6089 FAX

Marine Conservation Stamps & Prints

METROPOLITAN STAMP CO. of CHICAGO, INC.
P.O. Box 1133
Chicago, IL 60690-1133
815-439-0142
815-439-0143 FAX

Newfoundland

New Issues - Retail

New Issues

DAVIDSON'S STAMP SERVICE
P.O. Box 20502
Indianapolis, IN 46220
317-255-9408

New Issues - Retail

BOMBAY PHILATELIC CO., INC.
P.O. Box 7719
Delray Beach, FL 33484-7719
407-499-7990
407-499-7553 FAX

HERRICK STAMP CO.
P.O. Box 219
Lawrence, NY 11559
516-569-3959
516-569-7093 FAX

New Issues - Wholesale

BOMBAY PHILATELIC CO., INC.
P.O. Box 7719
Delray Beach, FL 33484-7719
407-499-7990
407-499-7553 FAX

Philatelic Societies

AMERICAN PHILATELIC SOCIETY
Dept TZ P.O. Box 8000
State College, PA 16803
814-237-3803
814-237-6128 FAX

Postcards

AURORA BOREALIS STAMP & SUPPLY
2273 S. 65th Street
Milwaukee, WI 53219
800-362-1010
414-543-0340 FAX

Price Lists

J.S.C. - SC
Box 28484
Philadelphia, PA 19149
215-743-0207 TELEPHONE & FAX

Price List- Marine Conservation Stamps & Prints

METROPOLITAN STAMP CO. of CHICAGO, INC.
P.O. Box 1133
Chicago, IL 60690-1133
815-439-0142
815-439-0143 FAX

Price List - U.S. Federal / Foreign Ducks

METROPOLITAN STAMP CO. of CHICAGO, INC.
P.O. Box 1133
Chicago, IL 60690-1133
815-439-0142
815-439-0143 FAX

Proofs & Essays

SUBURBAN STAMP INC.
176 Worthington Street
Springfield, MA 01103
413-785-5348
413-746-3788 FAX

Publications / Collector

GLOBAL STAMP NEWS
P.O. Box 97
Sidney, OH 45365-0097
513-492-3183
513-492-6514 FAX

MEKEEL'S WEEKLY STAMP NEWS
Box 5050-sy
White Plains, NY 10602
800-MEKEEL-1
914-997-7261 FAX

Romania

GEORGE ARGHIR
Detunata 17-27 PO BOX 521
RO-3400 Cluj-Napoca 9
ROMANIA
+40-64-194410 TELEPHONE/FAX

Safes - Stamps

KINGSBERY MANUFACTURING CORP.
715 West Zavala Street
Crystal City, TX 78839
800-445-0763

Special Offers

Stamp Accessories

BROOKLYN GALLERY COIN & STAMP
8725 4th Avenue
Brooklyn, NY 11209
718-745-5701
718-745-2775 FAX

Stamp Shows

BEACH PHILATELICS
P.O. Box 150
Virginia Beach, VA 23458-0150
804-425-8566 TELEPHONE & FAX

CONNECTICUT STAMP SHOWS
Box 5050-sy
White Plains, NY 10602
800-MEKEEL-1
914-997-7261 FAX

HIGHTSTOWN SECOND SATURDAY BOURSE
Monmouth St.(RTE.633) opposite
Ramada Inn
Exit 8 New Jersey Turnpike
Hightstown, NJ 08520

STAMP STORES

Arizona

AMERICAN STAMP & COIN CO.
7225 N. Oracle Rd.
Suite #102
Tucson, AZ 85704
520-297-3456

B.J.'S STAMPS / BARBARA J. JOHNSON
6342 W. Bell Road
Glendale, AZ 85308
602-878-2080
602-412-3456 FAX

California

ASHTREE STAMP & COIN
2410 N. Blackstone
Fresno, CA 93703
209-227-7167

BROSIUS STAMP & COIN
2105 Main Street
Santa Monica, CA 90405
310-396-7480

FISCHER - WOLK PHILATELICS
24771 "G" Alicia Parkway
Laguna Hills, CA 92653
714-837-2932

HERB'S STAMP CENTER
11748 Washington Place
West Los Angeles, CA 90066
310-397-3883

California

KENRICH CO.
9418-A Las Tunas Drive
Temple City, CA 91780
818-286-3888
818-286-6035 FAX

NATICK STAMPS & HOBBIES
405 S. Myrtle Avenue
Monrovia, CA 91016
818-305-7333
818-305-7335 FAX

STANLEY M. PILLER
3351 Grand Ave.
Oakland, CA 94610
510-465-8290
510-465-7121 FAX

THE STAMP GALLERY
1515 Locust Street
Walnut Creek, CA 94596
510-944-9111

Colorado

ACKLEY'S ROCKS & STAMPS
3230 N. Stone Ave.
Colorado Springs, CO 80907
719-633-1153

SHOWCASE STAMPS
3865 Wadsworth Blvd.
Wheat Ridge, CO 80033
303-425-9252
303-425-7410 FAX

Connecticut

J&B STAMPS & COLLECTIBLES
41 Colony Street
Meriden, CT 06451
203-235-7634

MILLER'S STAMP SHOP
41 New London Turnpike
Uncasville, CT 06382
203-848-0468 TELEPHONE & FAX

Washington, D.C.

WOODWARD & LOTHROP STAMP DEPT.
11th & G St. NW
Washington, DC 20013
202-879-8028

Florida

BEACH STAMP & COIN
971 E. Eau Gallie Blvd.
and Highway A1A Suite G
Melbourne Beach, FL 32937
407-777-1666

Florida

ARLINGTON STAMP & COIN CO.
1350 University Blvd.,North
Jacksonville, FL 32211-5226
904-743-1776

HAUSER'S COIN & STAMP
3425 S. Florida Ave.
Lakeland, FL 33803
813-647-2052
813-644-5738 FAX

HUGO'S STAMP EMPORIUM
P.O. Box 5527
Lake Worth, FL 33466
407-966-7517

INTERCONTINENTAL/RICARDO DEL CAMPO
7379 Coral Way
Miami, FL 33155-1402
305-264-4983
305-262-2919 FAX

JACK'S COINS & STAMPS
801 Northlake Blvd.
North Palm Beach, FL 33408
407-844-7710

JERRY SIEGEL/STAMPS FOR COLLECTORS
1920 E. Hallandale Beach Blvd.
Suite 507
Hallandale, FL 33009
305-457-0422 TELEPHONE & FAX

NEW ENGLAND STAMP
4987 Tamiami Trail East
Village Falls Professional Ctr
Naples, Fl 33962
813-732-8000
813-732-7701 FAX

ST. JOHN'S STAMP SHOP
2 Aviles Street
St. Augustine, FL 32084
904-829-9673

SARASOTA STAMP DEPOT
1564 Main Street
Sarasota, FL 34236
813-365-5415

THE STAMP PLACE
576 First Avenue North
St. Petersburg, FL 33701
813-894-4082

WINTER PARK STAMP SHOP
199 E. Welbourne Ave.
Suite 201
Winter Park, FL 32789
800-845-1819
407-628-0091 FAX

STAMP STORES

STAMP STORES

Georgia

Georgia

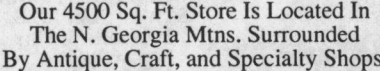

STAMPS UNLIMITED OF GEORGIA
133 Carnegie Way
Room 250
Atlanta, GA 30303
404-688-9161

Illinois

THE COLLECTORS DEN / L.V. FISCHER
P.O. Box 88148
Carol Stream, IL 60188-0148
708-545-9930 TELEPHONE & FAX

H.C. STAMP & COIN CO.
10 Crystal Lake Plaza
Crystal Lake, IL 60014
815-459-3940

MARSHALL FIELD'S STAMP DEPT.
111 N. State Street
Chicago, IL 60602
312-781-4237

STAMP KING / RICHARD E. DREWS AUCTIONS
7139 W. Higgins Road
Chicago, IL 60656
312-775-2100
312-792-9116 FAX

Indiana

J & J COINS & STAMPS
7019 Calumet Avenue
Hammond, IN 46324
219-932-5818

KNIGHT STAMP & COIN COMPANY
301 Main Street
Hobart, IN 46342
800-634-2646

THE STAMP SHOP
614 Massachusetts Ave.
Indianapolis, IN 46204
317-631-0631

VILLAGE STAMP AND COIN
40 E. Cedar
Zionsville, IN 46077
317-873-6762

Kentucky

COLLECTORS STAMPS LTD.
4012 DuPont Circle #313
Louisville, KY 40207
502-897-9045

TREASURE ISLAND COINS & STAMPS
232 W. Broadway
Louisville, KY 40202
502-583-1222

Louisiana

LIVINGSTON STAMP & RARE BOOK CO.
13595 Henry Drive
Denham Springs, LA 70726
504-665-7815

Maryland

BALTIMORE COIN & STAMP EXCHANGE INC.
10194 Baltimore National Pike
Unit 104
Ellicott City, MD 21042
410-418-8282
410-418-4813 FAX

BULLDOG STAMP CO.
4641 Montgomery Ave.
Bethesda, MD 20814
301-654-1138

DELMARVA STAMPS & COLLECTIBLES
23 Salisbury Mall
Civic Avenue
Salisbury, MD 21801
410-742-7077

STAMP & COIN WORLD
511-A Delaware Avenue
Towson, MD 21286
410-828-4465 or 800-452-4560

Massachusetts

BATTLE GREEN STAMP COMPANY
4 Muzzey Street
Lexington, MA 02173
617-862-2330

FALMOUTH STAMP & COIN
11 Town Hall Square
Falmouth, MA 02540
508-548-7075 or 800-341-3701

Massachusetts

J & N FORTIER
484 Main Street
Worcester, MA 01608
508-757-3657

KAPPY'S COINS & STAMPS
534 Washington St.
Norwood, MA 02062
617-762-5552
617-762-3292 FAX

ARLINGTON WARREN COLLECTIBLES
89 Warren St.
Arlington, MA 02174
617-641-1640
617-641-0870 FAX

Michigan

AMERICA'S STAMP STOP
23333 Orchard Lake Rd.
Farmington, MI 48334
810-474-4460

BIRMINGHAM COIN AND JEWELRY
1287 S. Woodward
Birmingham, MI 48009
810-642-1234
810-642-4207 FAX

MEL COON STAMPS
3833 Twelve Mile
Berkley, MI 48072
810-398-6085
810-398-4549 FAX

LIBERTY COINS & STAMPS
300 Frandor Avenue
Lansing, MI 48912
517-351-4720

THE MOUSE AND SUCH
696 N. Mill Street
Plymouth, MI 48170
313-454-1515

Minnesota

CROSSROADS STAMP SHOP
2211 West 54th Street
Minneapolis, MN 55419-1515
612-928-0119

Missouri

KNIGHT'S COINS & STAMPS
323 South Ave.
Springfield, MO 65806
417-862-3018

REGENCY STAMPS, LTD.
Le Chateau Village #106
10411 Clayton Road
St. Louis, MO 63131
800-782-0066
314-997-2231 FAX

Nebraska

TUVA ENTERPRISES
209 So. 72nd Street
Omaha, NE 68114
402-397-9937

New Hampshire

BRUNELLE STAMPS & COINS
25 East Broadway
Derry, NH 03038
603-432-2658
603-437-7279 FAX

New Jersey

A.D.A STAMP CO., INC.
910 Boyd Street
Toms River, NJ 08753
908-240-1131
908-240-2620 FAX

BERGEN STAMPS & COLLECTABLES
717 American Legion Dr.
Teaneck, NJ 07666
201-836-8987

CHARLES STAMP SHOP
47 Old Post Road
Edison, NJ 08817
908-985-1071
908-819-0549 FAX

COLONIAL COINS & STAMPS
1865 Rt. #35
Wall Township, NJ 07719
908-449-4549

FAIRIDGE STAMP INC.
447 Broadway
Westwood, NJ 07675
201-666-8869

RON RITZER STAMPS & COLLECTIBLES
Millburn Mall
2933 Vauxhall Road
Union, NJ 07088
908-687-0007 TELEPHONE & FAX

TRENTON STAMP & COIN CO.
1804 RT. 33
Trenton, NJ 08690
800-446-8664
609-587-8664 FAX

New York

B.B.C. STAMP & COIN INC.
185 East Main St.
P.O. Box 2141
Setauket, NY 11733-0715
516-751-5662

JOHN'S COINS, CARDS & STAMPS INC.
36 West 34th Street
2nd Floor
New York, NY 10001
212-244-2646

LINCOLN COIN & STAMP
33 West Tupper Street
Buffalo, NY 14202
716-856-1884

SUBURBAN STAMPS, COINS AND COLLECTIBLES
120 Kreischer Road
North Syracuse, NY 13212
315-452-0593

VILLAGE STAMPS & COINS
22 Oriskany Blvd.
Yorkville Plaza
Yorkville, NY 13495
315-736-1007 or 800-490-1007

Ohio

CROWN & EAGLE
5303 N. High Street
Columbus, OH 43214
614-436-2042

J L F STAMP STORE
3041 E. Waterloo Road
Akron, OH 44312
216-628-8343

STAMP STORES

Ohio

LAZARUS STAMP DEPT.
141 S. High St.
5th Floor
Columbus, OH 43215
614-463-3214

THE LINK STAMP CO.
3461 E. Livingston Ave.
Columbus, OH 43227
614-237-4125 or 800-546-5726

NEWARK STAMP COMPANY
49 North Fourth Street
Newark, OH 43055
614-349-7900

RANDY SCHOLL STAMP COMPANY
Southampton Square
7460 Jager Court
Cincinnati, OH 45230-4344
513-624-6800
513-624-6440 FAX

Oregon

AL'S STAMP & COIN
2132 West 6th
Eugene, OR 97402
503-343-0091

D'S TOYS & HOBBIES
3312 N. Highway 97
Bend, OR 97701
503-389-1330

UNIQUE ESTATE APPRAISALS
1937 NE Broadway
Portland, OR 97232
503-287-4200

Pennsylvania

KAUFMANN'S STAMP DEPT.
400 Fifth Ave.
Pittsburgh, PA 15219
412-232-2598

LARRY LEE STAMPS
322 S. Front Street
Wormleysburg, PA 17043
717-763-7605

PENNSYLVANIA STAMP CO.
229 Sixth Street
McKeesport, PA 15132
800-545-6604

PHILLY STAMP & COIN CO. INC.
1804 Chestnut Street
Philadelphia, PA 19103
215-563-7341
215-563-7382 FAX

WORLD OF STAMPS & COINS
Route 611
Fountain Court Mall
Bartonsville, PA 18321
717-343-0259

Rhode Island

PODRAT COIN EXCHANGE INC.
769 Hope Street
Providence, RI 02906
401-861-7640
401-272-3032 FAX

South Carolina

THE STAMP OUTLET
Oakbrook Center #9
Summerville, SC 29484
803-873-4655

Tennessee

HERRON HILL, INC.
5007 Black Road
Suite 140
Memphis, TN 38117-4505
901-683-9644

Texas

ALAMO HEIGHTS STAMP SHOP
1201 Austin Hwy
Suite 128
San Antonio, TX 78209
210-826-4328

ARTEX STAMPS FOR COLLECTORS
3216 W. Park Row
Suite M
Arlington, TX 76013
817-265-8645

AUSTIN STAMP & COIN
13107 F M 969
Austin, TX 78724
512-276-7793

DALLAS STAMP GALLERY
1002 North Central Expressway
Suite 501
Richardson, TX 75080
800-759-9109
214-669-4742 FAX

HUNT & CO.
1512 W. 35th St. Cutoff
Suite 300
Austin, TX 78731
512-458-5687 or 800-458-5745
512-458-6531 FAX

METROPLEX STAMP CO.
11811 Preston Road At
Forest Lane
Dallas, TX 75230
214-490-1330

SAM HOUSTON PHILATELICS
13310 Westheimer #150
Houston, TX 77077
713-493-6386
713-496-1445 FAX

Utah

HIGHLAND STAMP SHOP
4835 S. Highland Dr. #1346
Salt Lake City, UT 84117
801-272-1141

Virginia

CENTURY STAMPS & COINS
6436 Brandon Ave.
Springfield, VA 22150
703-569-0739

KENNEDY'S STAMPS & COINS
7059 Brookfield Plaza
Springfield, VA 22150
703-569-7300

LATHEROW & CO. INC.
5054 Lee Highway
Arlington, VA 22207
703-538-2727

PRINCE WILLIAM STAMP & COIN CO.
14011-H St. Germain Dr.
Centreville, VA 22020
703-830-4669

Washington

HIDDEN TREASURES INC.
9960 Silverdale Way
Silverdale, WA 98383
360-692-1999

PEOPLE'S STAMP SERVICE
4132 F. Street
West Bremerton, WA 98312
360-377-1210

RAINIER PHILATELIC INC.
15405 First Avenue South
Burien, WA 98148
206-248-2367

TACOMA MALL BLVD. COIN & STAMP
5225 Tacoma Mall Blvd. E-101
Tacoma, WA 98409
206-472-9632

THE STAMP & COIN PLACE
1310 Commercial
Bellingham, WA 98225
360-676-8720
360-647-6947 FAX

THE STAMP GALLERY
10335 Main Street
Bellevue, WA 98004
206-455-3781 TELEPHONE & FAX

Wisconsin

AURORA BOREALIS STAMP & SUPPLY
2273 S. 65th Street
Milwaukee, WI 53219
800-362-1010
414-543-0340 FAX

HERITAGE STAMPS
11400 W. Bluemound Rd.
Milwaukee, WI 53226
800-231-6080
414-369-0741 FAX

JIM LUKES' STAMP & COIN
815 Jay Street
P.O. Box 1780
Manitowoc, WI 54221
414-682-2324

Supplies

FREEWAY STAMP SUPPLIES
635 S. Raymond Ave.
Suite D
Fullerton, CA 92631
714-447-8100 or 800-447-8105
714-447-8100 FAX

Supplies & Accessories

BEACH PHILATELICS
P.O. Box 150
Virginia Beach, VA 23458-0150
804-425-8566 TELEPHONE & FAX

GLOBAL STAMP & COIN
460 Ridge Street
Lewiston, NY 14092
800-368-4328
715-754-8513 FAX

Supplies - Mail Order

GOPHER SUPPLY CO.
2499 Rice St. Suite 132
Roseville, MN 55113
612-486-8007
612-486-8441 FAX

Supplies - Mail Order

STAMPCRAFT
P.O. Box 2425
Santa Clara, CA 95055
800-245-5389
408-241-4440 FAX

Supplies - Protective Sleeves

HOBBY HOUSE DISTRIBUTING
P.O. Box 18025
Indianapolis, IN 46218
317-547-1372

Supplies - Stamps & Coins

GOLD COAST COIN & STAMP SUPPLIES
1007 NE 43rd Street
Ft. Lauderdale, FL 33334
305-565-4688
305-565-4689 FAX

M.A. STORCK CO.
652 Congress Street
Portland, ME 04104
800-734-7271

Supplies - U.S. Stamps

CALUMET STAMPS
P.O. Box 83
Griffith, IN 46319
219-924-4836

Topicals

CHARLES P. SCHWARTZ
P.O. Box 165
Mora, MN 55051
612-679-4705

Topicals - Columbus

MR. COLUMBUS
Box 1492
Frankenmuth, MI 48734

Topicals - Miscellaneous

AKSARBEN TOPICALS
P.O. Box 2033
Council Bluffs, IA 51502-2033
712-322-9061

BOMBAY PHILATELIC CO., INC.
P.O. Box 7719
Delray Beach, FL 33484-7719
407-499-7990
407-499-7553 FAX

MEKEEL'S WEEKLY STAMP NEWS
Box 5050-sy
White Plains, NY 10602
800-MEKEEL-1
914-997-7261 FAX

MINI - ARTS
Estherville, IA 51334
712-362-4710

United Nations

BEACH PHILATELICS
P.O. Box 150
Virginia Beach, VA 23458-0150
804-425-8566 TELEPHONE & FAX

United States

AMERICAN COIN & STAMP EXCHANGE
330 So. Gallatin Road
Madison, TN 37115
615-865-8791

BEACH PHILATELICS
P.O. Box 150
Virginia Beach, VA 23458-0150
804-425-8566 TELEPHONE & FAX

DALE ENTERPRISES INC.
P.O. Box 539
Emmaus, PA 18049
610-433-3303
610-965-6089 FAX

HUNT & CO.
1512 W. 35th St. Cutoff
Suite 300
Austin, TX 78731
512-458-5687 or 800-458-5745
512-458-6531 FAX

MEKEEL'S WEEKLY STAMP NEWS
Box 5050-sy
White Plains, NY 10602
800-MEKEEL-1
914-997-7261 FAX

GARY POSNER, INC.
6340 Avenue N. Suite 121
Brooklyn, NY 11234
800-323-4279
718-241-2801 FAX

United States

REGENCY STAMPS LTD.
Le Chateau Village #106
10411 Clayton Road
St. Louis, Mo 63131
800-782-0066
314-997-2231 FAX

DAVID TOMERAASEN
P.O. Box 178100
San Diego, CA 92177-8100
619-276-1288
619-274-1200 FAX

United States - Booklet Panes

DALE ENTERPRISES INC.
P.O. Box 539
Emmaus, PA 18049
610-433-3303
610-965-6089 FAX

United States - Classics

GARY POSNER, INC.
6340 Avenue N. Suite 121
Brooklyn, NY 11234
800-323-4279
718-241-2801 FAX

United States - Classics / Modern

SUBURBAN STAMP INC.
176 Worthington Street
Springfield, MA 01103
413-785-5348
413-746-3788 FAX

United States - Duck Stamps

HUNT & CO.
1512 W. 35th St. Cutoff
Suite 300
Austin, TX 78731
512-458-5687 or 800-458-5745
512-458-6531 FAX

SAM HOUSTON DUCK CO.
P.O. Box 820087
Houston, TX 77282
713-493-6386 or 800-231-5926
713-496-1445 FAX

United States - EFOS

GARY POSNER, INC.
6340 Avenue N. Suite 121
Brooklyn, NY 11234
800-323-4279
718-241-2801 FAX

United States - Federal Ducks

METROPOLITAN STAMP CO. of CHICAGO, INC.
P.O. Box 1133
Chicago, IL 60690-1133
815-439-0142
815-439-0143 FAX

United States - Mint

HUNT & CO.
1512 W. 35th St. Cutoff
Suite 300
Austin, TX 78731
512-458-5687 or 800-458-5745
512-458-6531 FAX

United States - Plate Blocks

BEACH PHILATELICS
P.O. Box 150
Virginia Beach, VA 23458-0150
804-425-8566 TELEPHONE & FAX

GARY POSNER, INC.
6340 Avenue N. Suite 121
Brooklyn, NY 11234
800-323-4279
718-241-2801 FAX

United States - Rare Stamps

GARY POSNER, INC.
6340 Avenue N. Suite 121
Brooklyn, NY 11234
800-323-4279
718-241-2801 FAX

United States - Singles: Classic & Modern

AL SOTH
P.O. Box 22081
Milwaukie, OR 97269
503-794-0956

United States - State Duck Stamps

SAM HOUSTON DUCK CO.
P.O. Box 820087
Houston, TX 77282
713-493-6386 or 800-231-5926
713-496-1445 FAX

United States - Transportation Coils

DALE ENTERPRISES INC.
P.O. Box 539
Emmaus, PA 18049
610-433-3303
610-965-6089 FAX

United States - Used

BICK INTERNATIONAL
P.O. Box 854
Van Nuys, CA 91408
818-997-6496
818-988-4337 FAX

United States - Used Custom Packets

BICK INTERNATIONAL
P.O. Box 854
Van Nuys, CA 91408
818-997-6496
818-988-4337 FAX

United States - Want Lists

GARY POSNER, INC.
6340 Avenue N. Suite 121
Brooklyn, NY 11234
800-323-4279
718-241-2801 FAX

Want Lists

BOMBAY PHILATELIC CO., INC.
P.O. Box 7719
Delray Beach, FL 33484-7719
407-499-7990
407-499-7553 FAX

HUNT & CO.
1512 W. 35th St. Cutoff
Suite 300
Austin, TX 78731
512-458-5687 or 800-458-5745
512-458-6531 FAX

Want Lists - Worldwide

ST. JOHN'S STAMP SHOP
2 Aviles Street
St. Augustine, FL 32084
904-829-9673

Wanted - Estates

TOWN & COUNTRY STAMPS LTD.
P.O. Box 13542-S
St. Louis, MO 63138
314-869-7063
314-869-7851 FAX

Wanted - U.S.

GARY POSNER, INC.
6340 Avenue N. Suite 121
Brooklyn, NY 11234
800-323-4279
718-241-2801 FAX

Wholesale - Accessories

SCOTT - EDELMAN SUPPLY CO.
1111 E. Truslow Avenue
Fullerton, CA 92631
714-680-6188
714-680-0962 FAX

Wholesale - British Commonwealth

LAKESIDE PHILATELICS
3935 Lakeside Rd. Ste. 7A
Comp. 4 RR# 2
Penticton, BC V2A 6J7
CANADA

Wholesale - Canada

LAKESIDE PHILATELICS
3935 Lakeside Rd. Ste. 7A
Comp. 4 RR# 2
Penticton, BC V2A 6J7
CANADA

Wholesale Collections

A.D.A STAMP CO., INC.
910 Boyd Street
Toms River, NJ 08753
908-240-1131
908-240-2620 FAX

Wholesale Philatelic & Numismatic Accessories

ECONOMICAL WHOLESALE CO.
6 King Philip Road
Worcester, MA 01606
508-853-3127

Wholesale Philatelic & Numismatic Accessories

HARRY EDELMAN
111-37 Lefferts Blvd.
P.O.Box 20140
So. Ozone Park, NY 11420
718-641-2710
718-641-0737 FAX

M. C. CLAYTON
290 East Grand Avenue
S. San Francisco, CA 94080
415-873-7577
415-873-7573 FAX

GLASCOCK, INC.
P.O. Box 18888
San Antonio, TX 78218
210-655-2498
210-655-2585 FAX

GOLD COAST COIN & STAMP SUPPLIES
1007 NE 43rd Street
Ft. Lauderdale, FL 33334
305-565-4688
305-565-4689 FAX

CHARLES R. HEISLER INC.
500 Oak Grove Drive
Lancaster, PA 17601
800-784-6886
717-299-2366 FAX

LEDO SUPPLY CO.
P.O. Box 1749
Sandpoint, ID 83864
800-257-8331

M.A. STORCK CO.
652 Congress Street
Portland, ME 04104
800-734-7271

NORTHERN ILLINOIS COIN & STAMP INC.
122 S. Grove Ave.
Elgin, IL 60120
708-695-0110
708-695-1154 FAX

POLLARD COIN & STAMP SUPPLY CO., INC.
5220 E. 23rd Street
Indianapolis, IN 46218
317-547-1306
317-547-1311 FAX

SCOTT WESTERN
5670 Schaefer Ave. No. L
Chino, CA 91710
909-590-5030
909-465-6368 FAX

Wholesale Supplies

DOUBLE J. STAMPS
P.O. Box 1127
Arlington Heights, IL 60006
708-843-8700
708-843-2878 FAX

JOHN VAN ALSTYNE STAMPS & SUPPLIES
1787 Tribute Rd. Suite J
Sacramento, CA 95815
916-565-0600
916-565-0539 FAX

Wholesale - U.S.

GARY POSNER, INC.
6340 Avenue N. Suite 121
Brooklyn, NY 11234
800-323-4279
718-241-2801 FAX

World War II

MEKEEL'S
Box 5050-sy
White Plains, NY 10602
800-MEKEEL-1
914-997-7261 FAX

Worldwide

ROBERT E. BARKER
P.O. Box 888063
Dunwoody, GA 30356
800-833-0217
404-671-8918 FAX

BLUE WATER STAMPS
P.O. Box 20074
Lambton Mall Postal Outlet
Sarnia, Ontario N7S 6J3
CANADA
519-869-8787

MEL COON STAMPS
3833 Twelve Mile
Berkley, MI 48072
810-398-6085
810-398-4549 FAX

HERITAGE STAMPS
11400 W. Bluemound Rd.
Milwaukee, WI 53226
800-231-6080
414-369-0741 FAX

THE STAMP SHOP
614 Massachusetts Ave.
Indianapolis, IN 46204
317-631-0631

Worldwide

Worldwide

Worldwide - Price Lists

HALL'S STAMPS (ITEX)
P.O. Box 8095
Spokane, WA 99203
509-536-9378 TELEPHONE & FAX

Worldwide - Year Sets

BOMBAY PHILATELIC CO., INC.
P.O. Box 7719
Delray Beach, FL 33484-7719
407-499-7990
407-499-7553 FAX

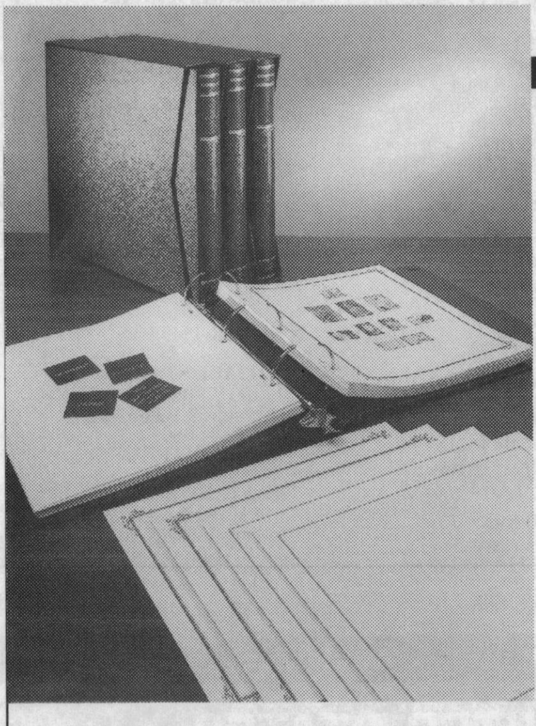

For information about membership in America's national philatelic society send attached card or contact

American Philatelic Society
P.O. Box 8000, Dept. Z
State College, PA 16803
(814) 237-3803

AMERICAN PHILATELIC SOCIETY

Founded 1886: In our 2nd century of service to collectors

Find out about the benefits of membership in America's national stamp society. Send this postpaid card for a descriptive brochure of the many APS services.

Z-96

* Monthly Magazine
* Sales Circuits
* Philatelic Library
* Stamp Insurance
* Correspondence Courses
* Seminars
* Local Stamp Clubs
* Specialty Societies
* Expertizing Service
* And Much More

PLEASE PRINT:

Name: ______________________

Address: ______________________

____

Send $1.00 with this card to receive a sample copy of The American Philatelist

Linn's Stamp News

911 Vandemark Rd.
P.O. Box 29
Sidney, OH 45365-9918

Mail this card to receive our special subscription offer.

Linn's Stamp News the world's largest weekly stamp newspaper and marketplace. Indispensable reading and entertainment with the stamps you want and the news you need. Try us and see why we're number one.

26 issues only $19.95

Name______________________

Address______________________

City______________________

State, Zip______________________

( ) Bill me later

4MFG7

Linn's Stamp News P.O. Box 29 Sidney, OH 45365

SCOTT
Serving collectors since 1863

Reader Service Card

A Free Service for our Readers

If the Reader Service Card has been used, see the Reader Service Card Advertiser's Index facing the Dealer Directory "Yellow Pages" Section

SCOTT
Serving collectors since 1863

Reader Service Card

A Free Service for our Readers

Circle #91 for information about *Scott Stamp Monthly* magazine and Catalogue Update.

Circle #99 to subscribe to *Scott Stamp Monthly* magazine and catalogue update. We will bill you $17.95 for a 1-year (12 issues) subscription (U.S. only).

Use this convenient postcard for more facts on the products or services described or advertised in this issue.

1	11	21	31	41	51	61	71	81	91
2	12	22	32	42	52	62	72	82	92
3	13	23	33	43	53	63	73	83	93
4	14	24	34	44	54	64	74	84	94
5	15	25	35	45	55	65	75	85	95
6	16	26	36	46	56	66	76	86	96
7	17	27	37	47	57	67	77	87	97
8	18	28	38	48	58	68	78	88	98
9	19	29	39	49	59	69	79	89	99
10	20	30	40	50	60	70	80	90	100

Caution: incomplete or illegible inquiries will not be processed, (please print)

Name ______________________

Address ______________________ ☐ Office ☐ Residence

City ______________________ State ____________ Zip ____________

R01A6

Country Date